ABOUT T...

This map ...
Encyclopa...
third of th...
Based in t...
Torres Strait Islander Studies, the proje...
years (1988–94) to complete. The map attempts, using all the published resources available at the time, to represent all the language or tribal or nation groups of the indigenous people of Australia. The references used, and some brief information about each group, are included in the Encyclopaedia.

The regions were analysed by using the watershed basins as a template and then superimposing all the groups on that base and determining where such factors as culture, language and trade indicated the relationships between groups to be.

DISCLAIMER NOTICE

This map indicates only the general location of larger groupings of people, which may include smaller groups such as clans, dialects or individual languages in a group. Boundaries are not intended to be exact. The views expressed in this publication are those of the author and not those of the Australian Institute of Aboriginal and Torres Strait Islander Studies. For more detailed information about the groups of people in a particular region, contact the relevant land councils.

Not suitable for use in Native Title and other Land Claims

ACKNOWLEDGEMENT

Names and regions as used by Dr D. R. Horton in his book *The Encyclopaedia of Aboriginal Australia* published in 1994 by Aboriginal Studies Press for the Australian Institute of Aboriginal and Torres Strait Islander Studies (PO Box 553 Canberra, ACT 2601).

THE OXFORD
COMPANION TO
AUSTRALIAN
HISTORY

THE OXFORD COMPANION TO AUSTRALIAN HISTORY

EDITED BY
GRAEME DAVISON
JOHN HIRST
STUART MACINTYRE

WITH THE ASSISTANCE OF
HELEN DOYLE
KIM TORNEY

OXFORD
UNIVERSITY PRESS

OXFORD
UNIVERSITY PRESS

253 Normanby Road, South Melbourne, Australia

Oxford University Press is a department of the University of Oxford.
It furthers the University's objective of excellence in research, scholarship,
and education by publishing worldwide in

Oxford New York

Athens Auckland Bangkok Bogotá Buenos Aires Cape Town
Chennai Dar es Salaam Delhi Florence Hong Kong Istanbul
Karachi Kolkata Kuala Lumpur Madrid Melbourne Mexico City
Mumbai Nairobi Paris Port Moresby São Paulo Shanghai Singapore
Taipei Tokyo Toronto Warsaw

with associated companies in Berlin Ibadan

OXFORD is a trade mark of Oxford University Press
in the UK and certain other countries

National Library of Australia
Cataloguing-in-Publication data:

The Oxford companion to Australian history.

Rev. ed.

Includes index.

ISBN 0 19 551503 X

1. Australia—History—Encyclopedias. I. Davison, Graeme, 1940- .
II. Macintyre, Stuart, 1947- . III. Hirst, J. B. (John Bradley), 1942- .
IV. Doyle, Helen, 1967- . V. Torney, Kim.

994.003

Edited by Janet Mackenzie
Indexed by Kim Torney
Text and cover designed by Steve Randles
Maps of Australia and Aboriginal Australia by Jane Lawson, LANDINFO
Melbourne and Sydney maps and state maps by Joseph Lucia
Typeset by Desktop Concepts Pty Ltd, Melbourne
Printed by McPherson's Printing Group

PREFACE

This *Companion* offers a comprehensive, authoritative and lively guide to Australian history. It covers all periods and aspects of Australian history. It rests on the most recent and significant scholarship. And it is written, as far as possible, in clear, vivid, non-technical language. We hope that it will become the book of first reference for academic and general historians, students of Australian history, journalists and politicians, and readers here and overseas.

It draws on a large body of specialist scholarship, including work done by historians inside and outside the academy, as well as by other researchers and writers. Thirty years ago a keen student could claim a reading knowledge of almost all the significant writing on Australian history; but the volume of new work has so grown in range and specialisation that even professional historians can hope to remain in command of only a fraction of what is published. The *Companion* aims to make the fruit of this work available to a general readership in a form that summarises its findings and points the way towards a more detailed understanding of the topic. Some of this work is available in books, journals, and other forms of publication, but much of it is specialised and not easily accessible. The *Companion* draws also on key reference works such as the *Australian Dictionary of Biography*, the *Australian National Dictionary*, *Australians: A Historical Dictionary*, and other publications listed in the entry for **reference works**; but complements these as a systematic guide to Australian history.

The *Companion* consists of entries varying in length from 100 to 2000 words on a wide range of subjects: events, persons, topics, themes, catchphrases, and allusions. The significance of the subject has been a fundamental criterion for selection of the entries and determination of their length, but at a time when the understanding of Australian history is keenly contested, this criterion is itself open to challenge. The new understandings of Australia's past conveyed by feminist and Aboriginal scholarship, for example, call for different emphases from the older treatments that stressed national events and the achievement of notable public figures. Our approach has been to assess significance according to the changing balance of historical scholarship. Thus the reader will find an explanation of the **Ripon Regulations** and other such staple fare of colonial history; but there is also recognition of **Aboriginal resistance** leaders and **femininity** as important areas of recent attention.

The *Companion* aims to show how Australia's history has been interpreted as well as how it has been made. There are major entries on branches of history, such as **environmental history** and **religious history**, which offer both a survey of the field and a commentary on the changing approaches and methods of those who have worked in it. Other entries on institutions, individuals, and aspects of Australian life also identify and comment on the way their subjects have been understood and assessed. This dimension of historical recording and commentary extends beyond academic study to take in popular writing, fiction, art, public display, film, and television, and these forms are also considered where appropriate.

In the *Australian Dictionary of Biography*, Australians already have at their disposal one of the world's outstanding biographical dictionaries. By including biographical entries in the *Companion* we have sought not to duplicate it but to select those individuals who because of their influence, representative character, or claim upon the attention of historians have assumed special significance in Australian history. Thus while all prime ministers and most governors prior to the introduction of representative government are included, only a selection of colonial and state premiers and religious and business leaders have entries. The *Companion* departs from the convention of biographical dictionaries that provide systematic details of parentage, education, appointments and offices, marriage and descendants. We have instead selected the most important aspect of each subject's career for discussion and evaluation. Similarly, we have listed honours and distinctions only when these are relevant to the entry.

The *Companion* pays particular attention to the interpreters of Australia history. It includes entries on a large number of writers and scholars, past and present, who have contributed to the understanding of the subject. Most, but by no means all, are historians: the principle for inclusion of novelists, dramatists, poets, artists, film-makers, and other cultural creators has been their role in shaping historical consciousness. The entries for living historians are generally confined to those who have completed their professional careers, though a few exceptions are made for younger historians who have exerted a particular influence.

The editorial group has written a significant proportion of the longer entries and the great bulk of the shorter ones. In commissioning entries we have invited leading scholars in the field, but—in conformity with the principle that the entry should assess the published work on that subject—have generally sought to ensure that contributors write on subjects in which their own work is not central. An effort was made to include contributors from different parts of the country, and to achieve some gender balance: the inability of some to accept our invitation to contribute has modified, but we hope not compromised, this intention.

Since the first publication of the *Companion* in 1998 we have been pleased to receive many appreciative comments from readers and reviewers. It is clear that the book is already fulfilling our hope of bringing the fruit of recent Australian historical scholarship to a wide audience of journalists, museum professionals, teachers, and general readers. Our correspondents have also offered criticisms, corrections, and suggestions for new entries. In due course, we hope to produce a new and expanded edition incorporating many of these suggestions as well as our own new thinking. In the meantime, this revised edition enables us to make a number of additions designed to bring the *Companion* up to date and to correct a small number of errors in the first printing. We have expanded some entries, such as those on John Howard and Olympic Games, to take account of significant events since 1998. We have revised the references to include important new publications. And in some instances, such as entries on Aboriginal topics, we have taken account of new developments in historiography. Among the many who have assisted us in this revision, we wish to make special mention of Kim Torney, for whom *The Oxford Companion to Australian History* has become almost a constant companion.

Graeme Davison
John Hirst
Stuart Macintyre
May 2001

ACKNOWLEDGMENTS

A *Companion* should be companionable, and this one testifies to the generosity and good nature of a large number of people who were prepared to share their expertise in and appreciation of Australian history.

The project was made possible by a large grant from the Australian Research Council. It commenced with assistance from La Trobe, Melbourne and Monash Universities, and throughout its preparation benefited from the support of our colleagues. The secretariat at the University of Melbourne was supported by Lynne Wrout, Martine Walsh, and other administrative staff of the history department, while Rosemary Johnston facilitated our work at Monash.

At Oxford University Press we were assisted by Felicity Edge and Geraldine Corridon. Our publisher Peter Rose was as patient as a production schedule allows, and unfailingly encouraging. Janet Mackenzie's editorial skills were greatly appreciated.

Many scholars offered advice, made suggestions, and answered queries. We give particular thanks to Bain Attwood, the late John Barrett, Jan Bassett, Warren Bebbington, Geoffrey Bolton, Tim Bonyhady, Barbara Caine, Joy Damousi, Brian Fletcher, Stephen Garton, Jenny Gregory, Patricia Grimshaw, Beverley Kingston, Noeleen Kyle, Marilyn Lake, Peter McGregor, Campbell Macknight, Andrew Markus, David Merrett, Bruce Moore, Michael Piggott, Marian Quartly, John Rickard, Sue Rickard, Jill Roe, Michael Roe, Tim Rowse, Peter Spearritt, Jennifer Stock, John Thompson, James Walter, and Patrick Wolfe. John Ritchie, the general editor of the *Australian Dictionary of Biography*, kindly allowed us to draw on the riches of that indispensable reference work. Reference staff at the National Library of Australia and the state and university libraries provided bibliographical guidance.

Mandy Paul provided a very helpful evaluation of reference works in the early stages of our planning. Damien Cash wrote a number of entries at short notice on a wide range of subjects, and turned gaps into strengths. Michael Adcock, Doug Scobie, and James Bennett assisted with the verification of references.

Our overriding obligation is to Kim Torney and Helen Doyle. Both were employed as research assistants, but they quickly assumed much greater responsibilities than that role suggests. They established the secretariat, set up the database, conducted correspondence, smoothed difficulties, undertook research, and drafted a large number of short entries. At times when the attention of the three editors wavered, they maintained the momentum of the *Companion*. Its completion is testimony to their skill, efficiency, and goodwill.

Graeme Davison
John Hirst
Stuart Macintyre

HOW TO USE THE COMPANION

Entries are arranged in alphabetical order.

A word in bold within the text (e.g. 'Ned **Kelly** was eventually hanged') indicates a cross-reference to another relevant headword. An item appears in bold only at its first appearance in an individual entry; if the reference is merely incidental, it has not been marked. Within entries covering notable families, such as the Boyds and the Sutherlands, the names of individual family members not given separate entries of their own appear in capitals.

In some cases, the word in bold differs slightly from the headword. For example, the term '**Communist** Party of Australia' appears thus in some entries while the actual headword is **Communism**; '**Constitutional crisis**' appears thus although the headword of the relevant entry is **Constitutional crises**. These variations are made for reasons of euphony and only where the actual headword will be found in correct alphabetical order.

In biographical entries where the subject has a pseudonym, the headword uses the name by which the subject is best known. Thus the entry for Joseph **Furphy** appears under that headword and not that of his nom-de-plume, Tom Collins; but the entry for A.H. Davis appears under Steele **Rudd**, and Nellie **Melba** appears thus rather than under her natal name, Helen Porter Mitchell.

'See also' at the end of an entry indicates that there is another substantial entry with a bearing on the subject.

The subject index at the back of the book is intended to reinforce the system of cross-references and to make it easier for readers to identify entries of kindred interest.

The authors of all longer entries are identified. A number of short entries were written in-house and involved substantial collaboration; accordingly they are identified by the initials of the member of the editorial team who drafted the entry:

DC Damien Cash
GD Graeme Davison
HD Helen Doyle
JH John Hirst
SM Stuart Macintyre
PR Peter Rose
KT Kim Torney

The *Companion* guides the reader to the relevant literature. The method of citation is kept as spare as possible. A book is usually identified by author, short title, and date of publication; sometimes one of the first two items is omitted, but the details are sufficient to find an item through an author or title entry in a library catalogue. Journal articles are usually identified by the name of the journal and the year in which it was published. Unpublished theses are identified by title, institution, and date of completion, and the cumulative guide to higher degree theses that enables them to be located is included in the entry on **reference works**. Films are dated by the year of release.

Maps are to be found at the end of the book, preceding the index.

CONVERSIONS

Area

1 acre = 0.4 ha
1 square yard = 0.8 m^2
1 square mile = 2.6 km^2

Currency

£1 was equal to 20 shillings (s.), and 1 shilling was equal to 12 pence (d.). When Australia changed to decimal currency in 1966, $2 was equal to £1.
1 guinea = £1 1s.

Length

1 inch = 25 mm
1 foot = 30 cm
1 yard = 0.9 m
1 mile = 1.6 km

Mass

1 ounce = 28 g
1 pound = 454 g
1 stone = 6 kg

Volume

1 bushel = 36.4 L
1 pint = 568 mL
1 gallon = 4.6 L

ABBREVIATIONS

ABC	Australian Broadcasting Corporation	CBE	Companion of the Order of the British Empire
AC	Companion of the Order of Australia		
ACH	*Australian Cultural History*	CLF	Commonwealth Literary Fund
ACT	Australian Capital Territory	CMG	Companion of the Order of St Michael and St George
ACTU	Australian Council of Trade Unions		
ADB	*Australian Dictionary of Biography*	CSIRO	Commonwealth Scientific Industrial and Research Organisation
AEHR	*Australian Economic History Review*		
AFL	Australian Football League	DBE	Dame of the Order of the British Empire
AFS	*Australian Feminist Studies*		
AHA	Australian Historical Association	DLP	Democratic Labor Party
AHS	*Australian Historical Studies* (1988–); formerly *HSANZ, HS*	DSO	Distinguised Service Order
		ed./eds	edited by
AJPH	*Australian Journal of Politics and History*	et al.	and others
AIF	Australian Imperial Force	FAW	Fellowship of Australian Writers
ALP	Australian Labor Party	FRGS	Fellow of the Royal Geographical Society
AM	Member of the Order of Australia	FRS	Fellow of the Royal Society
ANA	Australian Natives Association	HMAS	His/Her Majesty's Australian Ship
AND	*Australian National Dictionary*	HMCS	His/Her Majesty's Colonial Ship
ANZAAS	Australia and New Zealand Association for the Advancement of Science	HMS	His/Her Majesty's Ship
		HSANZ	*Historical Studies: Australia and New Zealand* (1940–April 1967), later *HS*
ANZAC	Australia and New Zealand Army Corps		
ANZUS	Australia, New Zealand, and the United States	*HS*	*Historical Studies* (October 1967–88); later *AHS*
AO	Officer of the Order of Australia	*HRA*	*Historical Records of Australia*
APAIS	Australian Public Affairs Information Service	*JAPH*	*Journal of Politics and History*
		JAS	*Journal of Australian Studies*
ARL	Australian Rugby League	*JRAHS*	*Journal of the Royal Australian Historical Society*
ASEAN	Association of South-East Asian Nations		
ASIO	Australian Security Intelligence Organisation	*JRHSQ*	*Journal of the Historical Society of Queensland*
ATSIC	Aboriginal and Torres Strait Islander Commission	KBE	Knight Commander of the Order of the British Empire
AWU	Australian Workers Union	KC	King's Counsel
BA	Bachelor of Arts	*LH*	*Labour History*
BBC	British Broadcasting Commission	LLB	Bachelor of Laws
BEM	British Empire Medal	MA	Master of Arts
BHP	Broken Hill Proprietary Company Limited	MBE	Member of the Order of the British Empire
BSc	Bachelor of Science	MC	Military Cross
CAE	College of Advanced Education	*MHJ*	*Melbourne Historical Journal*

MHR	Member of the House of Representatives	RAN	Royal Australian Navy
MLA	Member of the Legislative Assembly	Rev.	Reverend
MLC	Member of the Legislative Council	RFC	Royal Flying Corps
MP	Member of Parliament	RHSV	Royal Historical Society of Victoria
NATO	North Atlantic Treaty Organisation	RN	Royal Navy
NSW	New South Wales	RSL	Returned and Services League
NT	Northern Territory	SA	South Australia
NZ	New Zealand	SBS	Special Broadcasting Service
OAM	Medal of the Order of Australia	SEATO	South-East Asia Treaty Organisation
OBE	Officer of the Order of the British Empire	SP	starting price
OM	Order of Merit (Britain)	TAFE	Technical and Further Education
PhD	Doctor of Philosophy	UAP	United Australia Party
PNG	Papua New Guinea	UK	United Kingdom
POW	prisoner of war	UN	United Nations
PPRAHS	*Papers and Proceedings of the Royal Australian Historical Society*	USA	United States of Amercia
		VC	Victoria Cross
PPTHRA	*Papers and Proceedings of the Tasmanian Historical Research Association*	VHJ	*Victorian Historical Journal* (1975–)
		VHM	*Victorian Historical Magazine* (1911–74)
QC	Queen's Counsel	WA	Western Australia
Qld	Queensland	WAAAF	Women's Auxiliary Australian Air Force
RAAF	Royal Australian Air Force	WEA	Workers Educational Association
RAF	Royal Air Force	WRAAC	Women's Royal Australian Army Corps
RAHS	Royal Australian Historical Society	YMCA	Young Men's Christian Association
		YWCA	Young Women's Christian Association

DIRECTORY OF CONTRIBUTORS

ABBOTT, M.J.
  Melbourne
ADAIR, Daryl
  Department of Human Movement Studies
  University of Queensland
AITKEN, Richard
  Melbourne
AITKIN, Don
  University of Canberra
ALEXANDER, Alison
  School of History and Classics
  University of Tasmania
ALLEN, Jim
  Archaeology and Natural History
  Research School of Pacific and Asian Studies
  Australian National University
ALOMES, Stephen
  Moss Point
  NSW
ASHTON, Paul
  Department of Writing, Social, and Cultural Studies
  University of Technology, Sydney
ASTBURY, Leigh
  School of Literary, Visual and Performance Studies
  Monash University, Vic.
ATKINSON, Alan
  Department of History
  University of New England, NSW
ATTWOOD, Bain
  School of Historical Studies
  Monash University, Vic.
BANNON, J.C.
  Adelaide
BARNES, John
  English Program
  La Trobe University, Vic.
† BASSETT, Jan
BAVIN-MIZZI, Jill
  School of Social Studies
  Murdoch University, WA

BEAUMONT, Joan
  Faculty of Arts
  Deakin University, Vic.
BEBBINGTON, Warren
  Faculty of Music
  University of Melbourne
BENNETT, Michael
  Department of History and Classics
  University of Tasmania
BERTRAND, Ina
  Cinema Program
  La Trobe University, Vic.
BINNS, Georgina
  Main Library
  Monash University, Vic.
BIRD, Delys
  Faculty of Arts
  University of Western Australia
BLAINEY, Geoffrey
  Melbourne
BLOND, Philip
  Perth
BOLTON, Geoffrey
  Murdoch University, WA
BONGIORNO, Frank
  School of Classics, History and Religion
  University of New England, NSW
BONYHADY, Tim
  Centre for Cross-Cultural Research
  Australian National University
† BOURKE, Paul
BOURNE, Warren
  Department of Music Studies
  University of Adelaide
BRETT, Judith
  Anthropology and Sociology
  La Trobe University, Vic.
BRIDGE, Carl
  Sir Robert Menzies Centre for Australian Studies
  London, England

BRITAIN, Ian
School of Historical Studies
Monash University, Vic.

BROOME, Richard
Department of History
La Trobe University, Vic.

BROWN, Nicholas
Department of Foreign Affairs and Trade

BROWN, Patricia M.
Perth

BURGMANN, Verity
Department of Political Science
University of Melbourne

BURNESS, Peter
Australian War Memorial
Canberra

CAREY, Hilary M.
Department of History
University of Newcastle, NSW

CARMENT, David
Faculty of Arts
Northern Territory University

CARROLL, John
Anthropology and Sociology
La Trobe University, Vic.

CASH, Damien
Melbourne

CASTLES, Francis G.
Department of Social Policy
University of Edinburgh

CASTLES, Ian
Academy of the Social Sciences
Canberra

CATHCART, Michael
The Australian Centre
University of Melbourne

CHETKOVICH, Jean
Perth

COCHRANE, Peter
Department of History
University of Sydney

CONNOLLY, Chris
Department of History
University of Canterbury
Christchurch, NZ

CONNORS, Jane
ABC Radio
Sydney

COPER, Michael
Faculty of Law
Australian National University

CORNELL, Christine
Sydney

COSTAR, Brian
School of Public Policy
Monash University, Vic.

COWEN, Zelman
Melbourne

CROSSTHWAITE, Jim
Department of Natural Resources and Environment,
Vic.

CUNNINGHAM, Stuart
School of Media and Journalism
Queensland University of Technology

CURTHOYS, Ann
Department of History
Australian National University

DAMOUSI, Joy
Department of History
University of Melbourne

DARE, R.G.
Department of History
University of Adelaide

DARGAVEL, John
Urban Research Program
Research School of Social Sciences
Australian National University

DARIAN-SMITH, Kate
The Australian Centre
University of Melbourne

DAVIDSON, Dianne
Perth

DAVIDSON, Jim
Asian and International Studies
Victoria University of Technology

DAVIES, Susanne
School of Law and Legal Studies
La Trobe University, Vic.

DE GARIS, Brian
History Program
Murdoch University, WA

DEERY, Phillip
Asian and International Studies
Victoria University of Technology

† DENHOLM, David
DENHOLM, Zita
Wagga Wagga, NSW

DENING, Greg
Melbourne

DENOON, Donald
Research School of Pacific and Asian Studies
Australian National University

DINGLE, Tony
Department of Economics
Monash University, Vic.

DUNSTAN, Keith
Melbourne

Contributors

ELY, Richard
  School of History and Classics
  University of Tasmania
EMY, Hugh
  Melbourne
EVALINE, Joan
  Department of Organisational and Labour Studies
  University of Western Australia
EVANS, Nicholas
  Department of Linguistics and Applied Linguistics
  University of Melbourne
FAHEY, Charles
  School of Arts and Education
  La Trobe University, Bendigo, Vic.
FERRES, Kay
  Faculty of Humanities
  Griffith University, Qld
FERRIER, Carole
  Department of English
  University of Queensland
FEWSTER, Kevin
  Powerhouse Museum
  Sydney
FINLAYSON, Brian
  School of Anthropology, Geography and Environmental Studies
  University of Melbourne
FINNANE, Antonia
  Department of History
  University of Melbourne
FINNANE, Mark
  School of Humanities
  Griffith University, Qld
FITZPATRICK, David
  Department of Modern History
  Trinity College
  University of Dublin, Ireland
FITZPATRICK, Peter
  Centre for Drama and Theatre Studies
  Monash University, Vic.
FLETCHER, Brian H.
  Department of History
  University of Sydney
FORT, Carol
  Department of History
  University of Adelaide
FOSTER, Leonie
  Melbourne
FOX, Charlie
  Department of History
  University of Western Australia
FOX, Paul
  Philatelic Archives
  Australia Post

FRANCES, Raelene
  School of History
  University of New South Wales
FRASER, Morag
  Eureka Street Magazine
  Melbourne
FREESTONE, Robert
  Planning and Urban Development Program
  University of New South Wales
FRENCH, Maurice
  Faculty of Arts
  University of Southern Queensland
FROST, Alan
  Department of History
  La Trobe University, Vic.
FROST, Lionel
  Department of Economics and Finance
  La Trobe University, Vic.
FROST, Lucy
  School of English
  University of Tasmania
FROST, Warwick
  Department of Management
  Monash University, Vic.
GALBALLY, Ann
  Department of Fine Arts
  University of Melbourne
GALLIGAN, Brian
  Department of Political Science
  University of Melbourne
GAMMAGE, Bill
  Humanities Research Centre
  Australian National University
GANTER, Regina
  Faculty of Humanities
  Griffith University, Qld
GARDEN, Don
  Department of History
  University of Melbourne
GARTON, Stephen
  Department of History
  University of Sydney
GAUNTLETT, Stathis
  Hellenic Program
  La Trobe University, Vic.
GILLESPIE, Jim
  Politics Discipline
  School of History, Philosophy and Politics
  Macquarie University, NSW
GILLIES, Malcolm
  Faculty of Performing Arts
  University of Adelaide

GOODALL, Heather
  Department of Writing, Social and Cultural Studies
  Faculty of Humanities and Social Sciences
  University of Technology, Sydney
GOODMAN, David
  Department of History
  University of Melbourne
GOOT, Murray
  Politics Discipline
  School of History, Philosophy and Politics
  Macquarie University, NSW
GOVOR, Elena
  Research School of Social Sciences
  Australian National University
GRAHAM-TAYLOR, Sue
  Perth
GREGORY, Jenny
  Centre for Western Australian History
  University of Western Australia
GREY, Jeffrey
  University College
  University of New South Wales
  Australian Defence Force Academy
  Canberra
GRIFFITHS, Tom
  History Program
  Research School of Social Sciences
  Australian National University
GRIMSHAW, Patricia
  Department of History
  University of Melbourne
HAESE, Richard
  Department of Art History
  La Trobe University, Vic.
HAINS, Brigid
  School of Historical Studies
  Monash University, Vic.
HAMANN, Conrad
  School of Literary, Visual and Performance Studies
  Monash University, Vic.
HAMILTON, Paula
  Department of Writing, Social and Cultural Studies
  University of Technology, Sydney
HAMILTON, Annette
  School of Behavioural Sciences
  Macquarie University, NSW
HANCOCK, Ian
  Australian Dictionary of Biography
  Australian National University
HARRISS, Ian
  School of Business Studies
  Charles Sturt University, NSW
HARTLEY, Richard
  Perth

HAY, Roy
  School of Australian and International Studies
  Deakin University, Vic.
HAZLEHURST, Cameron
  Mapleton, Qld
HENNING, Graydon
  Department of Economic History
  University of New England, NSW
HICKS, Neville
  Department of Community Medicine
  University of Adelaide
HOLLOWAY, Ian
  Faculty of Law
  Australian National University
HOLMES, John
  Department of History
  University of Queensland
HOLMES, Katie
  Department of History
  La Trobe University, Vic.
HOLTON, Sandra
  Department of History
  University of Adelaide
HOLTON, Graham
  Melbourne
HOOTON, Joy
  Canberra
HORNE, Donald
  Sydney
HORNE, Julia
  University Archives
  University of New South Wales
HORNER, David
  Strategic and Defence Studies Centre
  Research School of Pacific and Asian Studies
  Australian National University
HUDSON, Wayne
  Faculty of Humanities
  Griffith University, Qld
HUGO, David
  Queensland
HYSLOP, Anthea
  Department of History
  Australian National University
INGLESON, John
  Office of Deputy Vice-Chancellor
  University of New South Wales
INGLIS, Ken
  Australian Dictionary of Biography
  Australian National University
IRVING, Helen
  Faculty of Law
  University of Sydney
IRVING, Terry
  Department of Government
  University of Sydney

Contributors

JENKINS, John
  Philosophy Program
  La Trobe University, Vic.
JOHNSON, Lesley
  University of Technology, Sydney
JOHNSTON, W. Ross
  Department of History
  University of Queensland
JOHNSTON, Allan
  School of Social Inquiry
  Deakin University, Vic.
JONES, Barry
  Parliament House
  Canberra
JONES, Philip
  Department of Anthropology
  South Australian Museum
JUPP, James
  Centre for Immigration and Multicultural Studies
  Research School of Social Sciences
  Australian National University
KARSKENS, Grace
  Department of History
  University of Sydney
KEATING, Chris
  Department of Writing, Social and Cultural Studies
  University of Technology, Sydney
KENNEDY, Brian
  Melbourne
KERCHER, Bruce
  School of Law
  Macquarie University, NSW
KINGSTON, Beverley
  School of History
  University of New South Wales
KIRKBY, Diane
  Department of History
  La Trobe University, Vic.
KNOX, Bruce
  School of Historical Studies
  Monash University, Vic.
KWAN, Elizabeth
  Canberra
KYLE, Noeline J.
  Cultural and Policy Studies
  Queensland University of Technology
LACK, John
  Department of History
  University of Melbourne
LAKE, Marilyn
  Department of History
  La Trobe University, Vic.

LAYMAN, Lenore
  School of Social Inquiry
  Murdoch University, WA
LEE, Jenny
  Melbourne
LEGGE, John
  School of Historical Studies
  Monash University, Vic.
LINN, Rob
  Adelaide
† LIVINGSTON, Kevin
LLOYD, Brian E.
  Melbourne
LOGAN, William S.
  Faculty of Arts
  Deakin University, Vic.
LOVE, Peter
  School of Social and Behavioural Science
  Swinburne University of Technology, Vic.
LOVE, Harold
  School of Literary, Visual and Performance Studies
  Monash University, Vic.
LYONS, Mark
  School of Management
  University of Technology, Sydney
MACKERRAS, Colin
  Faculty of Asian and International Studies
  Griffith University, Qld
MACKINNON, Alison
  Institute for Social Research
  University of South Australia
MACKNIGHT, Campbell
  School of History and Classics
  University of Tasmania
MADDOCK, Rodney
  Business Council of Australia
  Melbourne
MAGAREY, Susan
  Research Centre for Women's Studies
  University of Adelaide
MAHER, Laurence
  Melbourne
MANNE, Robert
  Politics
  La Trobe University, Vic.
MARKUS, Andrew
  School of Historical Studies
  Monash University, Vic.
MARSDEN, Susan
  Canberra

MARTIN, A.W.
  Canberra
MASSAM, Katharine
  Uniting Church Theological Hall
  University of Melbourne
MATTHEWS, Brian
  Europe–Australia Institute
  Victoria University of Technology
MAYNE, Alan
  Department of History
  University of Melbourne
McCALMAN, Janet
  Department of History and Philosophy of Science
  University of Melbourne
McCARTHY, Wendy
  Sydney
McCARTY, John
  Melbourne
McCLELLAND, Peter
  Perth
McCONVILLE, Chris
  Faculty of Arts
  Sunshine Coast University, Qld
McDONALD, Peter
  Division of Demography and Sociology
  Research School of Social Sciences
  Australian National University
McGRATH, Ann
  School of History
  University of New South Wales
McKENNA, Mark
  School of Humanities
  Australian National University
McKERNAN, Michael
  Canberra
McLACHLAN, Noel
  Melbourne
MEANEY, Neville
  Department of History
  University of Sydney
MEIN SMITH, Philippa
  History Department
  University of Canterbury
  Christchurch, NZ
MENGHETTI, Diane
  School of History
  James Cook University of North Queensland
MERRETT, David
  Department of Management
  University of Melbourne
MERRITT, John
  Bungendore, NSW

MITCHELL, Bruce A.
  Walcha, NSW
MOORE, Bruce
  Australian National Dictionary Centre
  Australian National University
MOORE, Clive
  Department of History
  University of Queensland
MORAN, Albert
  Faculty of Humanities
  Griffith University, Qld
MORPHY, Howard
  Centre for Cross-Cultural Research
  Australian National University
MORRISON, Elizabeth
  Melbourne
MORTON, Richard
  Melbourne
MUECKE, Stephen
  Faculty of Humanities
  University of Technology, Sydney
MURPHY, John
  Department of Social Sciences and Social Work
  RMIT University, Vic.
NELSON, Elizabeth
  Department of History
  University of Melbourne
NELSON, Hank
  Research School of Pacific and Asian Studies
  Australian National University
NIALL, Brenda
  School of Literary, Visual and Performance Studies
  Monash University, Vic.
OLIVER, Bobbie
  Research Institute for Cultural Heritage
  Curtin University of Technology, WA
OLSSEN, Erik
  History Department
  University of Otago
  Dunedin, NZ
OSBORNE, Graeme
  Communication and Education
  University of Canberra
OXLEY, Deborah
  Department of Economics
  University of New South Wales
PEARCE, Sharyn
  School of Humanities
  Queensland University of Technology
PEEL, Mark
  School of Historical Studies
  Monash University, Vic.

Contributors

PENNEY, Jan
 Central Goldfields Regional Library
 Bendigo
PESMAN, Ros
 College of Humanities and Social Sciences
 University of Sydney
PHILLIPS, Jock
 Historical Branch
 Department of Internal Affairs
 Wellington, NZ
PHILLIPS, Walter
 Melbourne
PIERCE, Peter
 Department of English
 James Cook University of North Queensland
PIGGIN, Stuart
 Robert Menzies College
 Macquarie University, NSW
PLOWMAN, David
 Graduate School of Management
 University of Western Australia
POWELL, Alan
 Southeast Asian and Australian Studies
 Faculty of Arts
 Northern Territory University
POWELL, J.M.
 School of Geography and Environmental Science
 Monash University, Vic.
POWELL, Graeme
 Manuscript Librarian
 National Library of Australia
 Canberra
POYNTER, John
 The Australian Centre
 University of Melbourne
PREST, W.R.
 Department of History
 University of Adelaide
QUARTLY, Marian
 School of Historical Studies
 Monash University, Vic.
QUINLAN, Michael
 School of Industrial Relations and Organisational
 Behaviour
 University of New South Wales
RASMUSSEN, Carolyn
 Department of History
 University of Melbourne
READ, Peter
 Humanities Research Centre
 Australian National University
REYNOLDS, Robert
 Department of History
 University of Sydney

RICHARDS, Eric
 Department of History
 Flinders University of South Australia
RICKARD, John
 School of Historical Studies
 Monash University, Vic.
RIDDETT, Lyn
 ACT
ROBIN, Libby
 Centre for Resource and Environmental Studies
 Australian National University
ROCHE, Michael
 Department of Geography
 Massey University
 Palmerston North, NZ
ROE, Jill
 Department of Modern History
 Macquarie University, NSW
ROE, Michael
 School of History and Classics
 University of Tasmania
ROPER, Michael
 Department of Sociology
 University of Essex
 Colchester, England
ROWSE, Tim
 Centre for Aboriginal Economic Policy Research
 Australian National University
RUBINSTEIN, William D.
 Department of History
 University of Wales
 Aberystwyth
 Dyfed, Wales
RUSSELL, Penny
 Department of History
 University of Sydney
RUTLAND, Suzanne
 Department of Semitic Studies
 University of Sydney
RYAN, Lyndall
 Australian Studies
 University of Newcastle (Central Coast)
SAEED, Abdullah
 Melbourne Institute of Asian Languages and Societies
 University of Melbourne
SAYERS, Andrew
 National Portrait Gallery
 Canberra
SCATES, Bruce
 School of History
 University of New South Wales
SCHEDVIN, Boris
 University of Melbourne

SCHREUDER, Deryck
  University of Western Australia
SCOBIE, Doug
  Department of History
  University of Melbourne
SCURFIELD, Judith
  Map Library
  State Library of Victoria
SEDDON, George
  Department of English
  University of Western Australia
SELLECK, Richard
  Faculty of Education
  Monash University, Vic.
† SERLE, Geoffrey
SHAW, A.G.L.
  Melbourne
SHERIDAN, Tom
  Department of Economics
  University of Adelaide
SHERLOCK, Peter
  Department of History
  University of Melbourne
SHERRATT, Tim
  Canberra
SIMMS, Marian
  Department of Political Science
  Australian National University
SINCLAIR, W.A.
  Department of Economics
  Monash University, Vic.
SKENE, Judy
  Perth
SMART, Judith
  School of Social Science and Planning
  RMIT University, Vic.
SMITH, Barry
  History Program
  Research School of Social Sciences
  Australian National University
SNOOKS, Graeme
  Economics Program
  Research School of Social Sciences
  Australian National University
SPEARRITT, Peter
  School of Political and Social Inquiry
  Monash University, Vic.
SPONGBERG, Mary
  School of History, Philosophy and Politics
  Macquarie University, NSW
STANFORD, Rohati
  Graduate School of Management
  University of Western Australia
STANNAGE, Tom
  Division of Humanities

John Curtin University, Perth
STARKE, Maree
  Perth
STELL, Marion
  Office of PVC
  James Cook University of North Queensland
STRAUSS, Jennifer
  School of Literary, Visual and Performance Studies
  Monash University, Vic.
SWAIN, Shurlee
  Department of Humanities
  Australian Catholic University
  Ballarat, Vic.
TAKSA, Lucy
  School of Industrial Relations
  University of New South Wales
† TEMPLETON, Jacqueline
THEOBALD, Marjorie
  Department of Education Policy and Management
  University of Melbourne
THOMAS, Julian
  Key Centre for Cultural Studies
  Griffith University, Qld
THOMAS, Nicholas
  Department of Anthropology
  Goldsmith's College
  University of London
THOMPSON, John
  Canberra
THOMSON, Alistair
  Centre for Continuing Education
  Sussex University, England
THOMSON, Helen
  School of Literary, Visual and Performance Studies
  Monash University, Vic.
TOBIN, Greg
  Faculty of Social Sciences
  Flinders University of South Australia
TONKINSON, Myrna
  Department of Anthropology
  University of Western Australia
TONKINSON, Robert
  Department of Anthropology
  University of Western Australia
TOOLE, Kellie
  Department of History
  University of Adelaide
TORNEY-PARLICKI, Prue
  Department of History
  University of Melbourne
TRACE, Keith
  Department of Economics
  Monash University, Vic.

Contributors

TRINCA, Mathew
Department of History
University of Western Australia

TRUMBLE, Angus
Art Gallery of South Australia

TUCAK, Layla
Perth

TULLOCH, John
School of Journalism, Media and Cultural Studies
Cardiff University

TURNER, Graeme
Department of English
University of Queensland

TYLER, Deborah
Department of Urban and Social Policy
Victoria University of Technology

VAMPLEW, Wray
School of Arts and Humanities
De Montfort University
Leicester, England

VICZIANY, Marika
National Centre for South-Asian Studies
Melbourne

WALKER, David
School of Australian and International Studies
Deakin University, Vic.

WALLACE-CRABBE, Chris
The Australian Centre
University of Melbourne

WALTER, James
Griffith University, Qld

WARDEN, James
Aboriginal Medical Services Alliance Northern Territory
Darwin

WASHINGTON, Paul
School of Social Sciences and Liberal Studies
Charles Sturt University, NSW

WATERHOUSE, Richard
Department of History
University of Sydney

WATERSON, Duncan
Department of Modern History
Macquarie University, NSW

WHITE, Richard
Department of History
University of Sydney

WHYTE, Jean
Melbourne

WILCOX, Craig
Sydney

WILSON, Sandra
Department of Asian Studies
Murdoch University, WA

WINTER, Jay
Pembroke College
Cambridge University, England

WOODBURN, Susan
Department of Community Medicine
University of Adelaide

WOTHERSPOON, Garry
School of Economics and Political Science
University of Sydney

YULE, Jane
Melbourne

A

ABC, see **Australian Broadcasting Corporation**

Aboriginal and Torres Strait Islander organisations

have emerged from the indigenous adaptation to colonisation and from efforts to govern indigenous Australians more effectively and equitably.

Though there were episodes of collective action by Aborigines—from armed resistance to petitions—in the nineteenth century, the Australian Aboriginal Progressive Association was the first visible indigenous organisation, emerging in 1924. Similar bodies—the Australian Aborigines' League, the Aborigines Progressive Association—soon followed in the 1930s. Political grievance was not their only stimulus. During World War II, Aboriginal preacher Doug Nicholls founded the Churches of Christ Aboriginal Mission in Fitzroy (Vic.), to evangelise and to provide welfare services.

Governments did not encourage indigenous Australians to form associations until the 1950s. Once committed to assimilation policy, however, they began to favour indigenous participation in voluntary associations whose concerns ranged from assisting church and government welfare efforts, to political campaigns to change discriminatory laws and policies. Governments were comfortable when helped by such bodies, but uneasy when criticised. Assimilationists wanted indigenous Australians to learn to participate in the '**Australian way of life**', but they did not want these organisations to become vehicles for the assertion of Aboriginal or Torres Strait Islander rights and identity, as the inter-war organisations had done. In the 1950s and 1960s, relationships were sometimes tense between governments and such organisations as the Coolbaroo League (and its successor, the Aboriginal Advancement Council (WA)), several state-based 'Aborigines Advancement Leagues', the Federal Council for the Advancement of Aborigines and Torres Strait Islanders (FCAATSI), and the Foundation for Aboriginal Affairs. In Queensland, the government favoured

OPAL (the One People of Australia League) as an 'apolitical' alternative to the more assertive FCAATSI.

By the late 1960s, two axes of difference had emerged among the organisations flourishing under 'assimilation'. Was their aim 'welfare' or 'politics'? That distinction was impossible to make when FCAATSI—with its many 'welfare' affiliates—lobbied on policy issues. And were 'political' organisations asserting the civil rights of blacks and whites (and led by both), or were they championing unextinguished indigenous identities (and made up only of indigenous Australians)? FCAATSI was wracked by the latter issue in the early 1970s.

As assimilation gave way to 'self-determination' policy in the early 1970s, governments began to fund the proliferation of indigenous organisations. Officials had come to believe that indigenous communal traditions—if reformed as associations and councils—were more likely to enhance than to hinder the government of a nation that they now conceived of in plural terms. By 1996, over 5000 Aboriginal and Torres Strait Islander organisations had been incorporated under the Aboriginal Councils and Associations Act 1976. They fall into three broad groups.

One group is *land-holding* organisations. Since 1966 Australian governments have vested title over old reserves and other lands in specially designed 'trusts' and other bodies corporate.

Representative organisations make up the second group. The National Aboriginal Consultative Committee (1973–77) and the National Aboriginal Conference (1977–85) were elected, advisory assemblies. In 1989, the Hawke government replaced the Conference and the appointed Aboriginal Development Commission with the Aboriginal and Torres Strait Islander Commission (ATSIC). ATSIC is led by elected Regional Councils and national Commissioners, both enjoying executive powers over just under half of the Commonwealth programs for indigenous Australians. As well, land rights laws have typically created representative regional bodies—such as

1

the Northern and Central Land Councils of the Northern Territory—to service the land-owning trusts. The administration of the Native Title Act 1993 has added 25 Native Title Representative Bodies to this crowded landscape.

Finally, there are *service delivery* organisations—publicly subsidised, indigenous-controlled, local and regional organisations that administer sport, housing, schools, legal, medical, and municipal services, and the production and sale of art. Their leading personnel are also prominent within the regional councils of ATSIC and the representative organs of land-rights and native-title regimes.

Indigenous Australia has become highly 'organised' since 1970, raising difficult issues concerning these bodies' culturally hybrid processes and long-term political objectives. Too often basic issues of 'self-determination' have been conveyed to the public as if they were merely problems—technical and moral—in the financial acquittal of public subsidies.

TIM ROWSE

Aboriginal art is among the oldest in the world. Work produced today is quite similar to that produced over 20 000 years ago as bark paintings, rock paintings and engravings, and body painting. Yet there has also been considerable change. Contact with outsiders at various times in **Aboriginal history** has usually given rise to artistic response and formal changes. The northern coast was the point of contact for **Macassan** traders and others. Torres Strait Islanders have artistic traditions that are more like those of New Guinea than Australia. The most radical changes occurred after European **invasion**, and more recently there have been new departures in style, materials, and distribution as a result of high levels of organisation and promotion of Aboriginal art. Howard Morphy's *Aboriginal Art* (1998) is an authoritative survey.

Explorers and anthropologists tended to discount the value of Aboriginal art. Objects were seen as having utilitarian or ceremonial value, and were collected for ethnographic significance, or as souvenirs of the primitive. When George **Grey** discovered Wandjina figures in the Kimberley in 1837, he assumed these cave paintings were too sophisticated to have been created by local people. There is still dispute about the origin of another quite different style of rock painting, the Bradshaw figures, from the same area.

Anthropologists have argued that artistic expression was not traditionally professionalised in Aboriginal Australia, and that artistic activities were inseparable from the rest of the culture. The kinds of designs produced for body marking (in ochres, blood, feathers, charcoal) or for painting on bark (especially the well-known 'cross-hatched' designs of Arnhem Land) or on ceremonial grounds (Central Australia) were chosen for reasons of tribe, totem, clan, individual birth-site or a particular site along a 'dreaming' track, relating the design to mythic or legendary narratives. While certain objects might be traded or exchanged as gifts in the traditional economies, there was no accumulation of objects for their artistic merit, as in a gallery. Certain wooden and stone sacred objects would be kept in secret storage for ceremonial purposes. Other objects of artistic significance, like head-dresses, ornaments, or ground paintings, might not be preserved after a particular ceremony or performance was over.

From early in post-contact history, Aboriginal people in missions and other settlements were encouraged to paint in a more Western way. Andrew Sayers in *Aboriginal Artists of the Nineteenth Century* (1994) examines the work of Aboriginal painters, such as Tommy McRae and William **Barak** in Victoria in the 1860s. Many communities were encouraged to find a cheap art or craft to sell to visitors, such as painted boomerangs, carved emu eggs, boab nuts, and shells and toas.

In the 1950s Albert **Namatjira**, an Arrernte man, emerged as a significant figure in mainstream Australian landscape painting. Borrowing in style and technique from the watercolours of Hans **Heysen** and Harold Herbert, and under the patronage of Rex Battarbee, Namatjira worked in watercolours on board or canvas. His paintings were composed as landscape scenes with ranges, gorges, and gum trees; the traditional associations of the sites he painted was overlooked. Namatjira became famous as much as a figure of **assimilation** as an artist, assimilation being the government cultural policy for Aboriginal people at the time. The paintings were thus a formal demonstration that an Aboriginal person could master a Western medium.

In the late 1950s and early 1960s there was a growing interest in Aboriginal art, which was most often thought about as Arnhem Land bark paintings. Major collectors were Stuart Scougall, Tony Tuckson (Art Gallery of New South Wales), and the anthropologists Ronald and Catherine **Berndt**. In this period Yirawala became known as the 'Picasso of Arnhem Land', as the Australian art world, including painters such as Fairweather, Tuckson, and Drysdale, became well aware of Aboriginal art. It was also exhibited internationally and exported.

In the early 1970s there was a renaissance in Aboriginal arts generally, supported by government initiatives as well as by a growing climate of acceptance and positive revaluation of Aboriginal peoples and their cultures. This tended to have the effect of reformulating art as a more commercial practice, independent of ceremony. In the visual arts the most significant advances took the form of the regeneration and adaptation of traditional forms for painting in Western media for Western markets. In 1971 a schoolteacher at Papunya in Central Australia, Geoffrey Bardon, encouraged the local people to develop and sell their paintings.

The style, known popularly as 'dot painting', became an international artistic success and spread to other communities (Yuendumu, Balgo, Haast's Bluff, Turkey Creek, Utopia). It now encompasses batik and fabric, printing, carving, weaving, and pottery. The best of these artists have improvised personal styles based on tribal traditions, but allowing innovation and great personal expression—Clifford Possum Tjapaltjarri, Mick Namerari Tjapaltjarri, Kwementyay Kngwarreye, Rover Thomas, Ginger Riley. International success of Aboriginal art was spurred on by the important exhibition and book *Dreamings* (1988); 'Aratjara' (touring

Europe in 1994); and representations at the Venice Biennale in 1990 and 1997.

Meanwhile more urbanised Aboriginal people were doing important work in styles which made intellectual reference to traditional forms (Lin Onus, Leah King Smith, Fiona Foley, Trevor Nickolls), worked in a naive style (Ian Abdullah) or engaged European traditions with postmodernist appropriation techniques (Gordon Bennett, Tracey Moffatt, Destiny Deacon). Issues of intellectual property and copyright have emerged in debates about collective versus individual ownership of traditional designs, for instance the mosaic created by Central Australian artist Michael Jagamara Nelson for the forecourt of the new Australian Parliament House in Canberra in 1988. Aboriginal art has increasingly been appropriated, sometimes without acknowledgment or reward, for commercial or promotional purposes. Some of this work has spilled over into the design and decorative arts, resulting in the creation of fashion, interior decoration, logos, and even the decoration of Qantas aeroplanes as a uniquely Australian marketing feature.

Aboriginal art has been the most significant development in the history of Australian art since 1970. The influences have been profound: as a source of money and recognition for Aboriginal communities; as a catalyst for understanding of Aboriginal culture on the part of non-Aboriginal people, facilitating political processes concerned with land rights and reconciliation; and in achieving international recognition for Aboriginal peoples, their art, and their cultures.

STEPHEN MUECKE

Aboriginal cultural ownership attributes custodianship to present-day Aborigines of the sacred objects, lands, and knowledge of their **heritage**. This rationale underpins sacred site and native title legislation, but has been more often used to argue for the recovery and reburial of Aboriginal skeletal remains previously held in archaeological and museum collections. The reburial of skeletal remains has sparked heated debate over the respective merits of scientific and cultural claims. For example, the planned reburial of the Kow Swamp remains in 1990, by limiting further scientific analysis of the material, met with strong criticism from archaeologists. The **Lake Mungo** case, however, was acclaimed for its cooperative compromise in 1992: the remains of Lake Mungo Woman were reburied traditionally, but a key to the burial box was made available to both the archaeologists and Aborigines with cultural ownership claims, thus establishing joint access rights. Debate between scientists and Aboriginal owners over access to such remains was generated in the 1990s when archaeologists from La Trobe University were ordered to return artefacts excavated in Tasmania, which they claimed to be of international archaeological significance. Prominent prehistorian John **Mulvaney** has criticised the denial to future generations of the opportunity to undertake scientific study of material which, he argues, is of 'universal value'. Nevertheless, claims for Aboriginal cultural ownership have proved increasingly powerful.

HD

Aboriginal history refers to the history of indigenous (Aboriginal and Torres Strait Islander) peoples in Australia, and is frequently used as a shorthand for one aspect of that history, their interactions with non-Aboriginal peoples. In the former, broader, sense, there is still relatively little writing; though **Aboriginal narratives**, together with work on **Aboriginal art**, **Aboriginal languages**, **Aboriginal myths and legends**, the **Dreamtime**, and **archaeology**, make valuable contributions to the development of a broad and long historical understanding.

In the latter, more restricted sense, Aboriginal history has developed since the late 1960s from a neglected to a highly significant and well-known field within Australian historiography. Historians have a complex past of their own on Aboriginal history issues: on the one hand, they are largely responsible for a **pioneer** legend which for many decades erased Aboriginal experience from Australian history; and on the other, more recently they have been in the forefront of attempts to develop greater public awareness of a destructive colonial past. Debates within and around the field have usually focused less on empirical detail than on evaluative and ethical issues, and the relation of this history to the responsibilities of non-Aboriginal Australians in the present.

Nineteenth-century histories varied widely in their attitude to Aboriginal people and cultures, sometimes sympathetic, more often crudely racist, regarding them as 'savages' and 'low on the scale of humanity'. Yet they often also exhibited awareness of a history of frontier conflict, and worried over its moral implications. Henry **Melville** spent many pages in *The History of Van Diemen's Land* (1835) on depredations, murders, and conflict. John **West's** *History of Tasmania* (1852) provided detailed and sympathetic accounts of the indigenous people and the frontier conflict. Three decades later, G.W. **Rusden's** *History of Australia* (1883) also pointed to the prevalence of slaughter, which 'can be denied by none who know the course of Australian history'.

Yet over the next eight or nine decades, such denial was extensive. The 'slaughter' written about by Melville, West, and Rusden gradually faded from public consciousness and written histories. Aboriginal existence itself almost disappeared from the national historical narrative.

The revival of interest occurred in the 1930s and led to the publication of three specialist studies: Edmund Foxcroft's *Australian Native Policy* (1941); Paul **Hasluck's** *Black Australians* (1942), and the journalist Clive Turnbull's *Black War* (1948). Yet these had little impact on most historians: the general histories of the 1950s, produced to meet the growth in university and other study of Australian history, had even less Aboriginal material than their predecessors.

Those who crossed disciplinary boundaries were the first to resurrect historical knowledge of Aboriginal–European relations; archaeologist John **Mulvaney's** two-part article 'The Australian Aborigines' (*HSANZ*, 1958), and art historian Bernard **Smith's** now-classic *European Vision and the South Pacific 1768–1850* (1960) both traced European understanding of Aboriginal people. William **Stanner's** 1968 Boyer lectures broadcast by the Australian Broadcasting

Corporation identified historians as contributing to 'the great Australian silence' on Australia's violent colonial past. Trained in a North American tradition of ethno-history little practised in Australia, Diane Barwick brought a mixture of anthropological and documentary research methods to the fledgling field: her essays on the history of Aboriginal experience on missions and reserves quickly became an intellectual landmark. Most influential of all was Charles **Rowley**, whose three volumes—*The Destruction of Aboriginal Society* (1970), *Outcasts in White Australia* (1970), and *The Remote Aborigines* (1971)—put Aboriginal history on a new footing. Exhibiting a strong emphasis on policy issues, drawing attention to social and economic effects of dispossession, discriminatory government policies, and institutionalised racism, this work helped provide a sound chronological and analytical structure for the histories which followed.

A younger generation of historians began to enter the field. Peter Corris was among the first with *Aborigines and Europeans in Western Victoria* (1968); Bob Reece published his MA thesis on the clashes over Aboriginal policy between settlers and the **Colonial Office**, peaking in the **Myall Creek massacre** and trials, as *Aborigines and Colonists* (1974). Influenced by **New Left** critiques of racism, many of the new histories had a Marxist emphasis on the destructiveness of capitalism in a colonial context, and its drive to exploit both land and labour, as well as an interest in trying to explain the presence and persistence of racial ideology. One notable example was Raymond Evans, Kay Saunders, and Kathryn Cronin, *Exclusion, Exploitation and Extermination: Race Relations in Colonial Queensland* (1975).

The journal *Aboriginal History* was initiated at the Australian National University in 1977, with Diane Barwick as its first editor, and over the following 20 years supported the growth of scholarship in the field. Influential early essays included Lyndall Ryan on Aboriginal people of Bass Strait (1977); Jeremy Beckett on George Dutton, an Aboriginal drover (1978); and Peter Read on the dispersal policy and child removal in NSW (1983). It was to be many years before other historical journals carried significant Aboriginal content: *AHS* regularly carried material from the late 1980s, and both the *JAS* and *LH* produced their first special issues on Aboriginal history in 1992 and 1996 respectively.

The new scholarship was synthesised in Richard Broome's *Aboriginal Australians* (1982), a survey history much used in university teaching which sold more than 25 000 copies, with a revised edition appearing in 1994. While signalling a desire to stress Aboriginal initiative and resistance, the text, like the scholarship on which it was based, tends to emphasise a story of dispossession, racial domination, exploitation, and the destructive processes of colonisation.

Historians in the 1980s began to place greater emphasis on indigenous people's perceptions, understandings, and active responses to colonisation. Henry **Reynolds** in *The Other Side of the Frontier* (1981) read colonial sources against the grain to explore Aboriginal responses to European invasion. Noel Loos used oral histories in north Qld to help

provide the perspective of the colonised, and to counterbalance the European perspective of the written sources, in *Invasion and Resistance* (1982). Lyndall Ryan's *The Aboriginal Tasmanians* (1981) emphasised the destruction of people and culture in Tasmania, as well as the ways in which Tasmanian Aboriginal women sought alliances with European whalers in order to survive. Ann McGrath in '*Born in the Cattle*' (1987) used **oral history** alongside conventional written sources to argue—somewhat controversially—that, despite many oppressive features, the cattle industry enabled Aborigines to find a way to stay on their own country and look after it.

'*Born in the Cattle*' also brought the new **women's history** and Aboriginal history together, giving a gendered analysis of Aboriginal labour, and focusing also on the sexual dynamics of race relations on the cattle stations. Though originating in a similar intellectual climate, women's history and **gender relations** history had at first been quite distinct from Aboriginal history. The founding Australian feminist histories of 1975 paid scant attention to race and ethnicity, or to the power relations and differences between white and Aboriginal women. In the 1990s, influenced by developments within feminist theory internationally, and a heightened attention to Aboriginal demands at home, questions of race and gender came closer together.

Theoretical developments also affected the field. Marxist approaches continued to have an influence, especially in studies of Aboriginal employment, such as Dawn May, *Aboriginal Labour and the Cattle Industry* (1994). Bain Attwood's work registered something of a shift from Marxist to post-structuralist approaches from the late 1980s: *The Making of the Aborigines* (1989) was written in the tradition of E.P. Thompson, with its notion of a group or class of people being 'made' by their historical experiences. Aboriginal people were also 'made', their identifiability as a single people the product of the onslaught by the missionaries and similar 'agents of European "civilisation"' who sought to change Aboriginal consciousness, their 'minds and hearts', thus 'making them anew'. In the collection *Power, Knowledge and Aborigines* (1992), Attwood's introduction applied the insights of Foucault and Said to Aboriginal history, with an emphasis on the ways European Australians 'know' 'Aborigines', and produce historically and culturally specific discourses of their own.

Aboriginal accounts of the colonial past are increasingly heard. Aboriginal people stress in public debate their prior occupation, direct experience of invasion and racism, and struggles for survival. This counter-history is told especially through Aboriginal narratives—autobiographies, life stories, biographies, oral histories—reaching maximum public impact and apotheosis in the **Stolen Generations** report, published as *Bringing Them Home* (1997). The best-known internationally of these narratives is one of the earliest, Sally **Morgan's** *My Place* (1987). Closer to the aims and methods of professional historians was *Auntie Rita* (1994), told in both the autobiographical voice of a Murri woman, Rita Huggins, and the part-autobiographical, part-analytical voice of her daughter, Jackie, an academically trained historian and writer.

The proliferation and power of Aboriginal narratives placed non-Aboriginal historians in a new situation. Some worked collaboratively with Aboriginal authors in the production of written texts based on transcribed oral history interviews, such as Peter Read, *Down There With Me on the Cowra Mission* (1984); Margaret Somerville with Patsy Cohen in *Ingelba and the Five Black Matriarchs* (1990), and with Marie Dundas, May Mead, Janet Robinson, and Maureen Sulter in *The Sun Dancin'* (1994); and Deborah Bird Rose in *Hidden Histories* (1991).

Others continued to produce histories of Aboriginal–European interactions, using a variety of sources. Some began to search for instances of colonists' interest in and respect for Aboriginal culture, and of humanitarian and political action. Reynolds in *Frontier* (1987), *The Law of the Land* (1987), and *This Whispering in Our Hearts* (1998) emphasised the influence of the humanitarians on colonial policy in relation to Aboriginal land rights in the 1830s and 1840s, while Mulvaney's *Encounters in Place* (1989) evoked the complexity and variety of Aboriginal–European interactions historically. The political activism of the period before and after World War II began to acquire a history: Jack Horner, *Vote Ferguson for Aboriginal Freedom: A Biography* (1974), Peter Read, *Charles Perkins: A Biography* (1990), and Heather Goodall, *Invasion to Embassy* (1996), all stress the long-standing and sometimes mixed-race character of pro-Aboriginal political struggle. Tom Griffiths, *Hunters and Collectors* (1996), explored the complexity and ambiguity of colonists' story-telling about the colonial past, through written histories, historic sites, and museums.

Aboriginal history entered public consciousness to an even greater extent with the **Mabo** decision and native title legislation in 1992–93, and the subsequent **Wik** decision and the Stolen Generations report in 1997. Reynolds's work was important both in supplying historical information and argument for the legal case for recognition of native title, and in providing histories which were accessibly written and available to a large public, while Ann McGrath's collection, *Contested Ground* (1995), brought to a wide audience the historical research undertaken by the History Project of the Royal Commission into Aboriginal Deaths in Custody. In this heightened political atmosphere, fundamental conflicts emerged. Support for Pauline Hanson's One Nation Party brought to light a popular backlash against histories, dubbed '**black armband history**' by Geoffrey **Blainey**, which emphasised the devastating effects of the invasion, dispossession, segregation, exploitation, institutionalisation, and child removal policies of the past. Prime Minister **Howard** in October 1996 said that he sympathised fundamentally with Australians who are insulted when they are told that we have a racist, bigoted past.

Public debate on Aboriginal issues has continued to stimulate new historical questions and research. The centenary of Federation drew historical and public attention to the exclusion of Aboriginal people from political rights in the Constitution. The notion of 'Stolen Generations' came under closer scrutiny from government and right-wing critics, while historians devoted increased attention to the history of child removal and government policies more broadly—for example, Anna Haebich, *Broken Circles* (2000), and Tim Rowse, *Obliged to Be Difficult* (2000). Public and historical debate over the relevance of the term '**genocide**' to Aboriginal history intensified, along with suggestions that historians such as Reynolds had overestimated the loss of life through frontier massacres (see, for example, Keith Windschuttle in *Quadrant*, 2000).

In their increased attention to Aboriginal history, however, it seemed that historians paid a high price, losing their earlier ability to provide apparently unifying national narratives. Popular understandings of the place of Aboriginal history in Australian history remain unsettled and deeply divided.

ANN CURTHOYS

Aboriginal land rights traditionally arose for men and women both from inheritance and from fulfilment of their particular obligations. Land was the structuring principle of much remembered cultural knowledge, allowing the mapping of kinship relations, historical knowledge, great song cycles and dramas, and religious and environmental knowledge.

Despite initial British ignorance of indigenous land relationships, Aboriginal people made their responses to the invasion clear: they tried to negotiate with the newcomers, but expressed anger when resources were destroyed and when the settlers assumed they had exclusive possession of land and water. In many areas, indigenous owners were forced into armed resistance to defend their access to vital economic and cultural resources. The doctrine of **terra nullius** notwithstanding, the British learnt very quickly that Aboriginal people held strong affinities to particular areas of land, and much early colonial writing records this growing recognition.

There was wide publicity in the 1830s and 1840s over high Aboriginal death tolls during intense fighting over the growing encroachment of white squatters onto grasslands in Tasmania, Victoria, and NSW. Work by Henry **Reynolds** has revealed the growing concern of the British government with these clashes. The officials pressured the Australian colonial governments to recognise indigenous property rights in land, to guarantee continuing Aboriginal access to land for traditional purposes, and to compensate indigenous owners for permanently alienated land. This pressure was partially effective, leading to the setting aside of some reserves in the continent's south-east, and to guaranteed Aboriginal access to pastoral leases; these reservations continue to exist in pastoral leases in SA, WA, and the NT. The directives from London for the recognition of native property rights were resented in the colonies, and in many cases either ignored or undermined. Gradually, as celebratory national histories were written during the late nineteenth and early twentieth centuries, acknowledgment of Aboriginal affiliation to land and accounts of British recognition of native title disappeared, until Stephen **Roberts's** *The Squatting Age in Australia 1835–1847* could be published in 1935 with no mention of Aborigines at all.

Aboriginal land rights

Aboriginal people had not abandoned their land. Even under intense pressure of frontier violence, they tended to move around their traditional country, seeking safe refuge, rather than moving into the territory of neighbouring peoples. When the worst of the fighting ended, some Aborigines were drawn into the European rural economy. Frequently, on sheep and cattle stations, they could live on their own country, visit sites and care for them at the same time as they mustered stock or undertook droving treks. Both indigenous and European economies and cultures coexisted in these circumstances for many decades—until the late 1930s in north-western NSW, and until the present in central, western and northern Australia. This coexistence was not necessarily recognised by pastoralists or whites generally, who often failed to acknowledge publicly or even to see that the people they perceived as impoverished Aboriginal camp residents were at the same time attentive traditional land custodians and skilled stockworkers. These patterns have been explored by Ann McGrath, '*Born in the Cattle*' (1987); Dawn May, *Aboriginal Labour and the Cattle Industry* (1994); Heather Goodall, *Invasion to Embassy* (1996); and Anna Haebich, *For Their Own Good* (1998).

Coexistence of indigenous and capitalist economies was more difficult on intensely cultivated land in agricultural areas, and Aboriginal people often moved during the later nineteenth century to secure a safe residential or farming area within their traditional country. Sometimes the camp-sites they chose were recognised by a permissive occupancy and on other occasions Aboriginal families were able to save enough to purchase a selection. Frequently, Aboriginal groups appealed to a local authority—a priest, a policeman, or a politician—to help them gain land in inalienable free-hold, which they could farm in peace and pass on to their descendants. In NSW, Victoria, and SA such appeals resulted in the government acting piecemeal on the old pattern of reserving Crown land 'for the use of Aborigines' and to set aside many reserves on Aboriginal request.

In NSW these lands made up over half of the Crown lands reserved for Aborigines by 1910—around 15 000 acres out of 30 000 acres. These independent farming or residential reserves existed alongside many other reserves created to contain or control Aboriginal residence, but the government and the Aboriginal residents had very different perceptions of the independent reserves. The government saw itself as engineering an abandonment of traditional culture, whereas the Aboriginal farmers saw themselves as simultaneously successful farmers and responsible upholders of traditions. The very success of the farms led to their loss in the 1920s under pressure of closer settlement and soldier settlement programs. This generated Aboriginal political movements like the Australian Aboriginal Progressive Association in NSW (1924–27), which had as its major demands the restoration of all the revoked reserves, enough additional land for all Aboriginal families in regions they regarded as home, and the protection of all Aboriginal children from removal by the state.

Pressure mounted on Aboriginal and Torres Strait Islander peoples after World War II, as all state governments acted more aggressively to erode indigenous land and to resocialise its owners by **assimilation**. Aboriginal political actions, such as the **Pilbara walkoff** in WA in 1946, were often interpreted by white opponents and supporters alike as aimed at achieving pay and work conditions equal to white workers, but in fact the Aboriginal participants often made land one of their goals. Explicit demands for land escalated during the early 1960s in NSW as more reserves were revoked. The Lake Tyers community in Victoria rallied to save its land from revocation. In 1963 the Yolngu at Yirrkala, NT, protested at the incursion onto their land by bauxite miners by sending a symbolic bark petition to Canberra, and in 1966 the **Gurindji** people struck for decent wages and for restoration of their control over their land. The issue of land and land rights was taken up with increasing enthusiasm by non-Aboriginal Australians, in parallel with their deeper awareness of cultural reassertion in decolonisation movements around the world. Often, however, land rights was seen as an issue generated by 'traditional' living people, without recognition that Aborigines of the south-east, in NSW and Victoria, had been focusing their political activities on land for nearly 200 years.

Aboriginal hopes were raised after the strong demonstration of goodwill in the 1967 referendum, and the formal handing back of Lake Tyers in 1970, but they were then bitterly disappointed by the Blackburn decision in 1971 rejecting Yirrkala demands taken to court three years earlier. Aborigines were even more deeply angered by the federal government's refusal on Australia Day 1972 to recognise any Aboriginal rights to land. This led south-eastern Aboriginal people to undertake what became a major symbolic demonstration. On the lawns of Parliament House they set up the powerfully evocative **Tent Embassy**—a fragile canvas and plastic shelter for people who had been made outsiders in their own country.

The Tent Embassy and the changing climate of public opinion allowed the acknowledgment of Aboriginal rights to land by the federal Labor government in 1972, resulting in the Land Rights Act in 1976. The legislation applied to the NT and ACT only, and was very restricted. Only people who could demonstrate the most strictly defined 'traditional ownership' could be claimants, although ironically the very process of hearing NT land claims has demonstrated how incomplete previous understandings of traditional land-holding had been. Under the act, reserves became 'Aboriginal freehold' without claim and Aborigines could claim only vacant Crown land and pastoral properties whose leases they held. There was no acknowledgment of historical affiliation, or of claims on the basis of economic need, but a land fund had been established earlier to purchase some land for those whose traditional country had been alienated under pastoral leases. The Aboriginal struggle to win recognition of their rights to land and the land claim hearings themselves have led to a greatly enhanced understanding of traditional relationships to land, as well as creating an extensive record of Aboriginal memories of invasion and colonisation in the NT, described in Nancy

Williams, *The Yolngu and Their Land* (1986), and Deborah Bird Rose, *Dingo Makes Us Human* (1992).

The NT Land Rights Act was followed by piecemeal legislation in various states. In SA unconditional freehold was granted to the remote Pitjantjatjara people in 1981, and in 1984 the Maralinga Tjaruta were handed over, although little was offered to people closer to Adelaide. In Qld the government avoided the issue altogether by secretly abolishing all Aboriginal reserves overnight, in March 1982, and reclassifying these areas as 'local government areas'. In NSW the Land Rights Act (1983) acknowledged the limitations of the claim process when so little land remained 'vacant Crown land'. It set up an innovative land fund which was resourced for a limited time by a percentage of the state's land tax. The federal Labor Party had promised national legislation to override disparate state laws, but when in power it retreated in 1985 under intense pressure from the mining industry and the Labor government of WA—a state with a conservative population and a huge proportion of its inland still designated as 'vacant Crown land'.

In 1992 the High Court of Australia acknowledged in the **Mabo** decision that native title did exist at the time of the British invasion and that it had continued to exist in the Torres Strait. It did not define native title—the court said that this remains to be defined by Aboriginal people. The federal government's response was the Native Title Act (1993), which acknowledged that native title had existed on all Australian land, and that it could continue to exist in circumstances where the Crown had not acted inconsistently by alienating the land. While the law severely limited the criteria for successful claims before the Native Title Tribunal, Aborigines have nevertheless explored the potential of the new law, resulting in the first mainland judgment acknowledging native title at Crescent Head, NSW, in 1996. The Native Title Act also established an Indigenous Land Corporation to purchase land in areas unavailable for claim. The High Court in the 1996 **Wik** judgment decided that native title can continue to exist, in limited form, on and under pastoral lease, but debate continued as to the Liberal–National government's attempt to reduce the rights found by the court.

Despite the limitations of land rights and native title legislation, Aboriginal people have continued to pursue many avenues to regain some security of access and custodial control over their land. Some claims have been won under state and federal land rights legislation, and some land has been purchased. Negotiation has begun in many areas to achieve regional agreements guaranteeing Aboriginal access to pastoral land, and such an agreement was reached at Cape York. Native title also applies to the sea, a neglected aspect of considerable significance. Aboriginal ownership of national parks with lease-back to the state has become widely practised, allowing Aboriginal participation in developing innovative management, interpretation, and conservation plans. Finally, Aborigines have utilised state and federal heritage and national parks legislation, which, although often hotly contested, offers some protection for significant Aboriginal places on public and private land, such as gravesites, carved and painted work, carved trees, and artwork.

HEATHER GOODALL

Aboriginal languages numbered about 250 at the time of European incursion into Australia; further division into politically recognised dialect differences gives some 600 distinct linguistic varieties. This makes Aboriginal Australia one of the most diverse areas of the world linguistically, and in some districts an 80-kilometre journey will pass through the territories of three languages less closely related than English, Russian, and Hindi. Multilingualism was the norm—indeed, a necessity—given the tradition in many areas of marrying outside one's language group. To the extent that 'tribes' can be identified, this is primarily on the basis of language.

All Australian languages are ultimately related, with the single exception of Miriam Mer, the language of the eastern Torres Strait, which is related to Papuan languages of the Fly River family. Australian languages are remarkably similar in their sound systems, but their grammars exhibit a great deal of variation. Over much of Australia the grammars resemble Latin or Ancient Greek in their use of case suffixes to show grammatical functions, freeing words to occur in any order. On the other hand, many languages of Arnhem Land are 'polysynthetic', allowing a whole sentence to be expressed with a single complex word. Useful surveys are R.M.W. Dixon, *The Languages of Australia* (1980); Colin Yallop, *Australian Aboriginal Languages* (1982); and *The Macquarie Book of Aboriginal Words* (1994).

Through genocide, discrimination, and policies of linguistic assimilation, many Australian languages are no longer spoken, or spoken only by a few old people. This loss is continuing, despite changes since the 1980s in public attitudes, the popularity of Aboriginal-language bands like Yothu Yindi, the introduction of bilingual education in many communities, and federal recognition of Aboriginal language rights through the 1991 White Paper, which outlined a national policy on language and literacy. Yet Australian languages are one of our most important sources for understanding the continent's human past.

First, they are an important vehicle for **oral history**, whether of recent history (see, for example, the memoirs of tracker Nyibayarri, translated from Gooniyandi by Bill McGregor, 1995) or of events before the coming of Europeans. Dixon, in a survey of Aboriginal legends ('Origin Legends and Linguistic Relationships', *Oceania*, 1996), concludes that many have a factual basis. Some are corroborated by geology, such as legends concerning the flooding of Port Phillip Bay about 10 000 years ago and volcanic eruptions in the Atherton Tableland at least 13 000 years ago. Others, concerning the directions of ancestral settlement, are corroborated by reconstructions made through comparative linguistics: in the Cairns rainforest region, the Yidiny people tell of ancestors coming from the north, while their southerly Dyirbal-speaking neighbours tell of founding beings coming from the south; in each case this is in line with the linguistic evidence.

Second, the identification of borrowed words allows us to trace the direction and nature of cultural contacts. Analysis of the hundreds of loan words from Macassarese and Malay in languages of the Arnhem Land coast allows us to infer the relative chronology of two stages of **Macassan** contact with regard to local developments in material culture and social organisation. A brilliant piece of linguistic detective work by Patrick McConvell (*Oceania*, 1985) tracked down the origins of the widespread system of dividing societies into eight 'skins' or 'subsections', which regulates kinship and marriage across much of northern Australia. By seeing what sound changes the terms undergo in particular languages, and what further affixes they accumulate, we can map out the paths by which the system diffused across much of northern Australia, and assign rough dates to its arrival on the Arnhem coast by interleaving the 'phonological stratification' of the subsection terms with the treatment of Macassan loan words.

Third, by applying the comparative method, we can develop a family tree showing the relationships among Australian languages. Results so far suggest a surprisingly uneven distribution of diversity across the continent: of the 20 or so families, 19 are wedged into the Kimberley and the Top End, while the remaining family—called Pama-Nyungan after the words for 'person' in the extreme north-east and south-west—covers the remaining seven-eighths of the continent. Controversy continues about how this is to be interpreted. Was there a major expansion of Pama-Nyungan speakers, probably around five millennia ago, at the expense of other languages previously spoken in the area? This correlates with a number of significant changes in the archaeological record of the same period. Or is it an effect of the order in which different parts of the continent were settled? A number of papers discussing this and related problems are collected in McConvell and Evans (eds), *Archaeology and Linguistics: Aboriginal Australia in Global Perspective* (1997). (See also **Languages**.)

NICHOLAS EVANS

Aboriginal missions were on a smaller scale than in other areas of British settlement and were generally deemed a failure by contemporaries. Historical accounts have since highlighted Aborigines' rejection of Christianity, authoritarian missionary policies, insufficient governmental support, and settler opposition, and emphasised the destructive impact of missions upon indigenous culture.

In the 1990s, scholarship suggests this interpretation overlooked the role missionaries played in the survival and regeneration of Aborigines. In seeking to 'Christianise and civilise', missionaries certainly believed it necessary to destroy traditional culture. Yet these dedicated men and women were exceptional in regarding Aborigines as fellow human beings capable of 'uplift', and at best their missions alleviated the suffering of fringe-dwellers and saved communities from extermination by protecting Aborigines from the worst ravages of colonisation. By sustaining a thin strand of humanitarianism in Australia they also provided a political framework for several generations of leaders, including William **Cooper**.

The most successful missions were those in which Aborigines were agents in their foundation and management, the missionaries learned and respected Aboriginal cultural practices and the authority of the traditional landowners, and relationships developed in which the imperatives of Aboriginal kinship and religion coexisted with those of white paternalism and Christianity.

BAIN ATTWOOD

Aboriginal myths and legends refer to Aboriginal religious or creation beliefs which together are now more commonly understood as the **Dreamtime**. In relating the journeys and sagas of ancestral-spirit beings, these narratives provide explanations about the beginnings of life, the creation of humans, animals, and landscape features, and the development of customs and social organisation. Creation beliefs are recorded in oral memory, through stories and dance, and in story-paintings. They are generally specific to particular localities, although some themes, such as the Rainbow Serpent, reappear in various forms.

European fascination with these narratives led to their inclusion in some nineteenth-century works on Aboriginal culture and in the collections of amateur collectors, such as Katie Langloh **Parker** in the 1890s. Anthropologists continued to gather these as stories in the twentieth century, which resulted in several published collections, including those by A.P. **Elkin** and A.W. Reed. Popular collections, such as those produced by C.P. **Mountford** and illustrated by Ainslee Roberts, were simplified versions of creation stories; many were appropriated as children's stories. The naming of such collections as 'myths and legends' also tended to undermine their spiritual significance. Mythology also enters into Aboriginal contact history—a point made by Peter Sutton in Ian Keen (ed.), *Being Black* (1988), and Kenneth Maddock in Jeremy Beckett (ed.), *Past and Present* (1988).

HD

Aboriginal narratives *Narrative* means both the story-telling styles in which a sequence of events may be presented, and the form of artistic expression distinct from, say, analysis or exposition. Among Aboriginal narratives we can identify, first, the traditional, expressed in Aboriginal languages; second, those expressed in Aboriginal English, some quite close in their format to traditional narrative; and third, contemporary forms, encompassing novels, history, plays, etc., which may be expressed in general or Aboriginal English.

The themes of traditional narratives, expressed in local languages, include topical events and journeys of **Dreamtime** ancestors. One well-established form, the song cycle, can describe the heroic journeys of ancestral figures as they created the world. Some of these have been translated, such as Ronald **Berndt's** *Djanggawul* (1952), and T.G.H. **Strehlow's** *Songs of Central Australia* (1971). Other traditional styles are homiletic in character, or recount adventures and incidents which occurred several generations ago. A recent translated example is R.M. Dixon's *Little Eva at*

Moonlight Creek (1994), which refers to sighting an aeroplane during World War II:

> With wings placed,
> One on top of the other,
> The biplanes travel northwards.
> One in front of the other.
> The propellors are turning.
> On the camouflaged planes,
> The planes have wings,
> They have armpits.

The themes of stories which involve pastoralists or explorers often depict Aborigines bringing retribution on themselves, engaging in fair fights, killing other Aborigines, losing heroically, or acknowledging the worth of certain whites. Sometimes the stories incorporate European figures like Ned **Kelly**, John McDouall **Stuart**, or Captain **Cook** who, acquiring semi-mythic status, act in the same way as Dreaming figures.

During the 1980s and 1990s narratives were recounted in Aboriginal English, and transcribed and published by non-Aborigines. Most of these are concerned with recent history or **autobiography**. Grace and Harold Koch's *Kaytetye Country* (1993) and Jay and Peter Read's *Long Time Olden Time* (1991) are of recent events, but others, like Elsie Jones's *The Story of the Falling Star* (1989), are Dreaming stories. They continue older styles of narrative such as dramatisation, repetition, and direct speech. This is an extract from *Kaytetye Country*: 'And they, they, they takem and takem inside and lettem camp with them. Next morning they sendem back. Longa that old man. And the—little bit, he took some, some salt meat and ah, nickie-nickie tobacco and some little bit tea and sugar.'

Many narratives have also been written in more conventional language and forms by Aboriginal authors. Fictional or non-fictional narratives from the 1960s and 1970s, such as the plays of Jack **Davis**, frequently present Aborigines as victims of discrimination and injustice. Novels and short stories of the 1980s by Archie Weller and Mudrooroo Narrogin (Colin Johnson) present Aborigines as less homogeneous, more internally divided, and to some extent responsible for their own lives. In this extract Archie Weller, in the short story 'Violet Crumble', refers to the disunited Aboriginal community as well as the environment: Sam, the surfer, says, '"My mob used to hang round me like flies ... One day I had a big brawl and told them all to clear off. I shifted over east for a few years and haven't looked back since."' But there are always the jagged rocks waiting for him below the surface, below the waves he rides so well. So he can smash into them and they will tear his beautiful black body apart.

Much modern literature has a self-conscious political stance, because authors saw their work affecting the political struggle. The hidden influence of Aboriginal spirituality in everyday life has been taken up by, for instance, the Murri (Queensland Aboriginal) novelist Sam Watson, *The Kadaitcha Sung* (1990).

Autobiographical narrative or life history, often produced with the cooperation of a non-Aboriginal co-writer, has eclipsed fiction in the last decade. Of these, the best-known is Sally **Morgan's** *My Place* (1987). The same search for an Aboriginal identity was pursued in many accounts by children who had been physically separated from their parents (Barbara Cummings, *Take This Child*, 1990; Coral Edwards and Peter Read, *The Lost Children*, 1989), while narratives by women who had not been removed, including Evelyn Crawford's *Over My Tracks* (1993), revealed a wide range of experience and emotion which made Aboriginal lives more comprehensible to non-Aborigines. Aboriginal historians writing in the formal Western mode chose narrative forms, generally adopting the theme of victim and resistance. The few examples of the genre, though important at the time of publication, are now rather dated.

Developments late in the century were an increase in accounts of urban life (three books by Ruby Langford), discussions as to the extent to which Aboriginal writers wish to be treated as indigenous rather than Australian or world writers, and a questioning of the **Aboriginality** of certain authors writing as Aborigines. Aboriginal narrative, distinctly different in form, theme, and presentation, has now joined the literary conversation of Australia. Its own views of life and history, while in some senses within the world's indigenous literatures, are also an essential part of the Australian literary mainstream.

PETER READ

Aboriginal nomenclature presents problems for the historians of Australia's indigenous people. Most commonly, the terms *Aboriginals*, *Aborigines* and *Aboriginal people* have been used. The *AND* gives printed uses of *Aboriginal* and *Aborigine* since the late 1820s. (The same source tells that the term *native*, used by Captain **Cook** in his 1770 journal, remained in use as recently as 1960—in the *Northern Territory News*—before the *Bulletin* corralled it in inverted commas in 1963.)

Alec Chisholm's 1958 edition of the *Australian Encyclopaedia* gave *aboriginal* as the singular of *aborigines*. The Commonwealth government's *Style Manual* (3rd edn, 1978) preferred *Aboriginal* for the singular noun and the adjective, but accepted as the plural form of the noun both *Aboriginals* and *Aborigines*. Clearly, in the passage of 20 years, the political mobilisations of indigenous Australians earned them an upper-case 'A'. Since the people of the **Torres Strait** began, in the early 1970s, to articulate their distinct claims as an indigenous people, there has been good reason to refer to *Aborigines and Torres Strait Islanders* (sometimes abbreviated to *ATSIS* in bureaucratic communications).

The fifth edition of the *Style Manual* (1994) retained *Aboriginal* as the singular noun, and *Aborigines* or *Aboriginal peoples* as the plural—and precluded *Aborigine*. In the *Encyclopedia of Aboriginal Australia* (1994) there is no entry on *Aborigines*, but the opening entry (by Marcia Langton) is headed *Aboriginal* and refers to the *Aboriginal person*, to *Aborigines*, and to *Aboriginal people*. If this is the latest approved usage, then evidently *Aboriginal* and *Aboriginals* as nouns have been set aside, and the adjectival form *Aboriginal* has come to be coupled with nouns which underline personhood and (very important in the language of international law) 'peoplehood'.

Ethnographic writing has long contrived collective names for indigenous people which are more specific to regions and to languages. Lorimer Fison and Alfred **Howitt** in 1880 published *Kamilaroi and Kurnai*, thus using terms from indigenous speech to name two 'tribes' whose ancient domains, it was thought, could be defined by lines on a map. In similar vein, Baldwin **Spencer** and F.J. Gillen called their 1927 book about the people of the MacDonnell Ranges, Central Australia, *The Arunta*. Habits of naming changed. Spencer referred to 'the Melville and Bathurst Islanders' in his *Native Tribes of the Northern Territory of Australia* (1914), but these people had been renamed *the Tiwi* by 1930, their ethnographer (C.W.M. Hart) glossing the Islanders' word as 'we, the only people'.

Such localised names from indigenous languages have sometimes been given prominence through political mobilisation. When the people of the NT's Victoria River region claimed land in 1966, they were referred to (and sometimes referred to themselves) as *the Gurindji*, a term which had first surfaced in ethnographic scholarship in 1900.

The term *koori* was noted in 1834 to mean 'man, mankind' in some languages of south-east Australia. Indigenous Australians from the continent's south-eastern corner have made *koori* their preferred term for themselves. In 1985, the Koori historian James Miller wrote in *Koori: A Will to Win—The Heroic Resistance, Survival and Triumph of Black Australia* that 'the word *Aboriginal* is a Latin-derived English word which was originally used to refer to any native people of any part of the world … [it] did not give my people a separate identity'; he noted the term's colonial provenance and racist associations.

Notwithstanding Miller's objections, historians who need to refer to indigenous Australians as a statistical category or as a national constituency with a politicised ethnic identity are likely to find *Aboriginal people*, *Aborigines and Torres Strait Islanders*, or *Indigenous Australians/indigenous Australians* more appropriate. (Editors currently differ over whether to put the first letter of 'Indigenous' in upper case.) Terms such as *Koori* (NSW, Victoria and Tasmania), *Yolngu* (NT), *Wiradjuri* (NSW), *Guugu-Yalanji* (Qld), *Tiwi* (NT), *Anangu* (Central Australia), *Yapa* (NT), *Murri* (Qld), *Kaurna* (SA) and *Nyoongah* (southern WA) have found use in recent regional histories of Australian colonialism. To name your 'people', first define your place.

TIM ROWSE

Aboriginal protection was constantly debated, as the moving frontier created new groups of dispossessed Aborigines. Could they be 'civilised' through contact with whites, or did they need to be protected by being segregated from the worst aspects of colonial society? Humanitarians increasingly believed that Aborigines should be moved onto Aboriginal reserves, which would function as asylums caring for 'a dying race' or as reformatories where paternal superintendents could 'raise' able-bodied Aborigines, particularly the young, by inculcating the virtues of hard work, thrift and sobriety. Many Aborigines also called for protection, but hoped reserves would provide them with an opportunity to sustain their communities and enjoy relative economic and cultural independence. Growing respectability and a deepening racism in colonial society also caused many whites to demand protection from Aboriginal fringe-dwellers; they looked upon reserves as camps where disorderly Aborigines could be concentrated, and cheap labour and sexual partners could be drawn or dumped according to the needs of white men.

Between the late nineteenth century and the 1930s, many Aborigines were 'protected' by special acts of parliament. Victoria had enacted legislation in 1869 and 1886, and the earlier act and a Queensland one of 1897 provided a model for other acts—WA (1905), NSW (1909), SA (1910) and the NT (1911)—whereby governments assumed legal responsibility for Aborigines and established special bureaucracies (generally called 'Protection Boards'). These were empowered to control Aborigines' affairs by prescribing their place of residence, determining conditions of employment, and assuming the care and custody of children. At the same time, discriminatory federal legislation also denied Aborigines basic rights and entitlements enjoyed by other Australians. By the 1930s the administration of these acts was the subject of much criticism by Aboriginal organisations and welfare groups, especially in Melbourne and Sydney, but the 'protective' regime remained until 1957–66, during which time the various states progressively repealed much or all of their discriminatory legislation.

When **Aboriginal history** began to be written in the late 1960s, attention was paid to the introduction of 'protectionist' legislation and the confinement of Aborigines to the poorly resourced reserves. Historians argued that successive generations were stripped of their traditional culture and became decultured outcasts, and emphasised Aborigines' loss of autonomy as they became dependent upon paternalistic overseers. These historians overlooked the possibility that protection might have saved the lives of many Aborigines and the fact that in some instances reserves met their aspirations, however briefly. This critique led scholars, such as Charles D. **Rowley**, to recommend policies of similar logic to the programs of dispersal or **assimilation** which have been variously implemented by governments—an example of what Peter Read has called 'a thirty-year oscillation between enthusiasm and disillusionment' in Aboriginal policy and practice. The despair and hopelessness which life 'under the act' could cause, and Aborigines' resentment towards what they often called the 'Destruction Board' (especially over the removal of their children, now often referred to as the **Stolen Generations**), is evident in Aboriginal accounts given by Kevin **Gilbert** and others.

In the 1980s another generation of historians examined the protection legislation, paying closer attention to how the acts actually worked in practice. Andrew Markus showed there was considerable regional variation in their impact; Aborigines in eastern states were the most affected, but even there those living on supervised reserves at any one time never numbered more than 40 per cent of the Aboriginal population. Other studies suggested that few administrators ever succeeded in regulating the lives of all Aborigines under their control, because they were hindered by government reluctance to provide the necessary personnel and money, or were foiled by local white communities and Aborigines themselves.

Read, Anna Haebich, Heather Goodall, and anthropologist Barry Morris also countered Rowley's thesis of 'fatal impact' by emphasising cultural adaptability and continuity among reserve communities: Aborigines had retained some elements of traditional cultural knowledge and practices in the form of religious belief, close relations with land, and extensive kinship bonds which prized reciprocity, sharing and egalitarianism rather than individual achievement or material gain. They also argued that Aborigines had chosen to withdraw from white society and maintain a distinctive group identity.

Other historians have offered a different perspective on this phenomenon by suggesting that Aborigines' experience on reserves under protectionist legislation provided the basis for a new social identity, an Aboriginal consciousness which transcended the traditional differentiation between Aboriginal clans on the basis of specific kin, geographical, linguistic, and other local affiliations. As a NSW community leader Shirley Smith (**MumShirl**) once commented: 'I'll tell you. An Aboriginal is anyone that knows what it was like down on Erambie mission, West Cowra, thirty year ago.'

Aboriginal protection, often criticised as an example of racism, can also be seen, paradoxically, to have provided Aborigines with the means of nurturing a distinctive culture and identity.

BAIN ATTWOOD

Aboriginal resistance has different meanings. Until the 1970s within Western historiography—and in popular, as distinct from academic, understandings to the present—resistance has been defined physically. Recognition has been accorded particularly to armed resistance to superior force, designed to defend and assert the rights of subordinate groups. In the Australian context the judgment generally reached was that Aboriginal people had not effectively 'resisted' the coming of the British as they had not organised themselves for warfare: the notion that this country was 'settled' rather than 'invaded' was thus widespread.

While accepting the premises of this conceptual framework, from the late 1960s onwards historians critically examined its evidential basis and in most cases found untenable the notion of Aboriginal passivity and peaceful occupation. Work published in the 1970s and 1980s documented the long and bloody record of conflict in many parts of the continent. In the course of this research the deeds of Aboriginal groups and individuals who engaged in guerrilla and other forms of armed resistance were highlighted. The locale and timing of violent conflict were established, along with details of the actions of tribal groups and individuals. A pantheon of warrior heroes—patriots, defenders of the country—included Pemulwuy (of Eora descent), **Mosquito** (Kuring-gai), Windradyne (Wiradjuri), Mannalargenna (Paredarerme or Pyemmairrener), Walyer (Tommeginne), **Yagan** (Wajuk), Calyute (Pinjarup), Jandamarra (Punuba), Nemarluk (Kamor). Brief biographical sketches are to be found in David Horton (ed.), *Encyclopaedia of Aboriginal Australia* (1994); examples of more substantial works are Eric Willmot's novel, *Pemulwuy: The Rainbow Warrior* (1987), and Howard Pederson and Banjo Woorunmurra's *Jandamarra and the Bunuba Resistance* (1995).

While attention continues to be directed to the process of violent conflict which accompanied dispossession, more diverse understandings of resistance have developed during the 1980s and 1990s. In part this is the result of a willingness to listen to Aboriginal testimony, but also of a fundamental shift in conceptualisation of power, no longer seen exclusively in terms of material force in which one side has total control and the other has all its options foreclosed—a situation described as a zero-sum game. Historians are now concerned with resistance in active and passive forms, organised and impromptu, group and individual, male and female, political, economic, and cultural.

Henry **Reynolds's** work heralded the changed approach in Australian historiography, particularly *The Other Side of the Frontier* (1981). In contrast with Eurocentric assumptions which informed research to the 1980s, Reynolds sought to ground analysis in Aboriginal understandings; his re-reading of documentary sources, informed by anthropological knowledge and his personal experience and contacts, allowed him to explore the complexity of Aboriginal responses. He sought to establish what Aboriginal people 'saw' when they first confronted the British and how they attempted actively to shape relations.

In addition to re-examining basic assumptions, recent work has shifted attention from what had become the richly researched field of frontier conflict to Aboriginal responses following disruption to their traditional patterns of life: to pastoral properties and fringe camps; institutions such as children's homes, missions, reserves, and prisons; and to major centres of population, where from the 1920s onwards political organisations were formed to assert claims for equality and land and to maintain and transmit culture.

Intergroup relations are oriented by a people's sense of self. It has been argued that in their reluctance to change aspects of their worldview, Aboriginal people stand at the extreme end of the continuum of peoples brought into contact with European civilisation. Generation after generation they have denied the premise of the invaders, that Aboriginal sovereignty was extinguished and land, the basis of life, now belonged to others. The sense of distinctiveness and self-worth, evident in celebrations of survival, has continued to form the basis of resistance. Resistance is thus manifested in the separation that existed, and continues to exist, in place of residence and in the scorning of imported religions, of European systems of education, and of the culture of materialism and consumerism. Individual resistance extends in its positive manifestations to various forms of communal activity, in its negative to self-destructive behaviour such as acts of self-mutilation, risk-taking, and suicide in prisons. Paul Wilson's *Black Death White Hands* (1982) presents a powerful discussion of conditions of life on Queensland reserves.

Such an understanding is not without elements of romanticism. There was no pan-Aboriginal identity in the nineteenth century—indeed, it did not emerge until well into the twentieth—and responses varied on an individual and group basis. Some willingly 'came in', accommodating their lives to the new world, and groups of men enlisted in police and paramilitary forces on the side of the colonisers against other Aboriginal peoples. Some remained on the fringes not so much because of the resilience of their culture as because of limited options in a racist society. In such a perspective, the idea of 'resistance' as a major category for analysis of the contact experience is challenged. A younger generation of historians, to some extent arriving at conclusions previously held only by their conservative predecessors, have argued that to reach a balanced understanding as much attention needs to be devoted to accommodation and cooperation as to resistance.

Recent approaches, particularly those of the 1990s, reflect postmodern theorisation, which brings into question attempts to provide a unified approach to history. Master narratives such as national histories are replaced by a range of different accounts and voices, categories of analysis are interrogated and fractured, the tentative nature of knowledge emphasised. The work of Henry Reynolds (and that of others less distinguished) has come under criticism for its universalist approach, bipolar categorisation, insensitivity to gender, and uncomplicated morality. One aspect of analysis is the critique of 'essentialism', for example the idea that there is an abiding 'Aboriginal' value system. Attention is directed to the multiplicity of factors shaping identity, on uncovering the complex patterns of Aboriginal lives.

The new approach has yielded more theorisation than practice, although some important book-length studies have appeared, including Ann McGrath's *Born in the Cattle* (1987) and Peggy Brock's *Outback Ghettos* (1993). Major commentators on the writing of Aboriginal history include Bob Reece, Ann Curthoys, Bain Attwood, Tim Rowse, and Peter Read. A range of different approaches is evident in research in the 1990s, which is of much greater diversity than the historiography of earlier decades. Bain Attwood in *The Making of the Aborigines* (1989) emphasises a constantly unfolding process of identity formation, in contrast to Heather Goodall's *Invasion to Embassy* (1996), which sees constancy in the struggle for land.

A considerable body of **oral history** has been published presenting the individual stories of Aboriginal people, particularly from parts of Australia 'remote' to white Australians, the north and interior. These accounts relate the skills, including magic, with which white intruders were managed and contact maintained with the land. The leading scholar in the field, Bruce Shaw, has collected and edited five volumes of recollections since his much-acclaimed *My Country of the Pelican Dreaming* (1981). Such publications raise the crucial issue of the capacity of European historiography to encompass traditional (a term not easily defined) Aboriginal understandings of 'resistance'. As Lenore Coltheart has argued (in Jeremy Beckett, ed., *Past and Present*, 1988), historical 'writing about Aborigines is, necessarily, the imposition of an alien explanatory framework on Aboriginal experience and understanding', a perspective most forcefully developed in Tony Swain's *A Place for Strangers* (1993).

ANDREW MARKUS

Aboriginality derives from the word *aborigine*, meaning 'from the beginning'. In Australia, this word was eventually capitalised to refer specifically and collectively to the continent's indigenous inhabitants (except for **Torres Strait Islanders**). Aboriginality has several meanings, notably the official, imposed meanings that have changed over time, and the meanings infused into the term by those on whom it was imposed, which are also developing and changing. In the past, official definitions had a strong emphasis on biological characteristics. In the 1970s, this approach was abandoned in favour of Aboriginal self-identification and community acceptance. In the discourse of both Aboriginal and other Australians, however, a biological component of Aboriginality is often expressed or implied.

Prior to the British **invasion**, all Aboriginal societies had economies based on hunting and gathering, and were characterised by strong territorial anchorages and complex social, organisational, and religious institutions. Across the continent there were marked continuities in physical characteristics and cultural features, and many linkages based on relations of kinship, affinity, exchange, and religion. However, individual and group identities were defined largely in local terms, and there was thus no notion of a collective pan-Aboriginal identity. Instead, much finer distinctions between groups and categories of people were made, largely on the basis of cultural and linguistic differences.

The British set the indigenous people clearly apart from themselves and designated them collectively as a category of very different—and markedly inferior—beings. They judged the indigenes in terms of negatives (no houses, herds, agriculture, chiefs, churches, and so on), and deemed their nomadic lifestyle shiftless and parasitic. In unregulated frontier situations, many colonists equated them with vermin, to be driven off the land or exterminated. For the indigenous inhabitants, the disastrous aftermath of the invasion—dispossession, marginalisation, and exclusion—established the conditions for an ethnogenesis grounded in shared experience of racism, subjugation and deprivation. Today, Aboriginality conveys meanings involving pan-Australian connections as well as local and personal identity.

Although organised Aboriginal protests about injustices and calls for collective action date from the 1920s, it was not until the 1960s that pan-Aboriginal sentiment began to take on national political significance. The impetus for this was provided by urban-based Aborigines, those most knowledgeable of, and enmeshed within, the dominant society, and whose political strategies frequently included appeals couched in collective, pan-Aboriginal terms. For many Aborigines in the remote interior and northern parts of Australia, local identities remain primary, but there is now greater awareness of shared Aboriginal concerns and increasing political collaboration across regional and cultural boundaries. With the expansion of political consciousness and action among Aboriginal people, several important developments have occurred: notably, the progressive dismantling of restrictive legislation, and the advent of government policies encouraging Aboriginal participation in the management of their affairs and aimed at improving the poor socio-economic conditions in which many Aborigines live. Slogans such as 'cultural revival is survival' characterise major efforts among Aboriginal people to foster a positively defined and distinctive Aboriginality; others, such as 'White Australia has a Black history', indicate the continuing invocation of Aborigines' shared, historical oppression in their struggle for social justice.

Land rights have for decades been an important rallying cry and symbolic focus for the pan-Aboriginal movement. The historic **Mabo** decision of Australia's High Court in 1992 affirmed the existence of native title to land. Although there has been considerable opposition to this decision by many Australians, particularly powerful vested interests, and the practical benefits of title may accrue only to a minority of the Aboriginal population, Mabo is of great symbolic significance. It specifies—and therefore legitimises—Aboriginal culture in the form of 'laws and customs' as the key determinant of native title. This provides a powerful and timely reinforcement of Aboriginality.

The concept of Aboriginality is not uniform, and Aboriginal and non-Aboriginal perceptions of it vary enormously. The power of Aboriginality as a symbol and locus of ethnic identity may relate to its very diffuseness. Few scholars have attempted to state the constituents of Aboriginality, though Jeremy Beckett (ed.), *Past and Present: The Construction of Aboriginality* (1988), is one attempt. Popular images and representations of Aboriginality are often negative, or at least ambivalent. Powerful contradictory representations coexist: for example, the idealised 'noble savage' that is used to promote tourism in the NT versus frequent references to drunken, welfare-dependent Aboriginal people. Against these stereotypes, Aboriginal people articulate positive images of continuity with their ancestral past and contemporary vitality and authenticity in the face of persistent oppression and denial of rights. What they stress most often is their 'blood' tie to the original inhabitants of Australia and values that they consider distinctively Aboriginal.

The federal government policy of reconciliation between Aborigines and other Australians, pursued from the 1980s, aims to foster acceptance and inclusion of Aboriginal people, and acknowledgment of their status as prior owners of the continent. In a parallel manner, there appears to be a moving away from Aboriginality predominantly defined and expressed by Aboriginal people in a rhetoric of resistance, towards a more culture-centred emphasis—one that may be more easily accommodated in a self-described multicultural society—on Aboriginal commonalities, continuity, and cultural survival, and on full participation, in these terms, in the totality of Australian life.

MYRNA AND BOB TONKINSON

Aborigines believe that they have lived in their land from the beginning of time, or that their distant ancestors came from over the sea. The oldest ground-edge axes in the world, dating from some 20 000 years ago, have been found in Arnhem Land. Scientists testing old occupation sites by thermoluminescence have suggested an Aboriginal presence of up to 60 000 years. The upper limit, on the basis of generally accepted scientific knowledge, indicates an Aboriginal occupation of not more than 100 000 years. Population estimates at 1788 vary between 200 000 and 1.25 million.

Aborigines for many centuries had probably organised themselves socially in extended familes of hunter-gatherers in every part of the country from rainforests to deserts. (**Torres Strait Islanders** have a separate status and are considered in a separate entry.) They recognised themselves, and were recognised by their neighbours, as having specific rights and responsibilities towards specific country. Certain areas were used for gathering food, others were relevant to cultural and spiritual life. Valued goods such as greenstone were traded through complex cultural exchange rituals extending over many hundreds of kilometres.

Aboriginal life, except for the exchange cycles, was locally self-sufficient in tools, weapons, and foodstuffs. In some parts of the country, periodic burning, or **fire-stick farming**, ensured ideal conditions for human movement and pasture for large animals hunted by men. Women caught small animals and, to judge by post-1788 traditional society, were responsible for most gathering and food preparation. Hunting, gathering, and preparation, highly skilled and organised, left Aboriginals with generous leisure time for the highly complex religious, social, and spiritual life which has fascinated European scholars for more than two centuries. Through many millennia Aboriginals evolved complex cultural and religious relationships with the country in which they lived, mythologies involving both its creation by spiritual beings, and their continuing spiritual presence within it (see **Dreamtime**). Responsibility to country was a two-way relationship between the land itself and its human guardians, who through renewal and other ceremonies protected the well-being of the land and the spirit ancestors.

The invading British, despite some ineffectual ethical and philosophical concern, showed little respect for Aboriginal culture or lifeways. They adopted the de facto policy that became known as *terra nullius*, which assumed that for legal purposes the indigenous inhabitants had no claim to the country. Diseases endemic in Europe, such as typhoid and influenza, became major causes of morbidity and death. **Massacres** and malnutrition also accounted for a very substantial reduction in the initial population. In many areas of Australia the gene pool was drastically reduced, as well as the absolute numbers of people. Among the people of the Victoria River Downs region (NT) in 1880 were some 1500 Karangpuru speakers. A century later it was found that the few survivors of the group were all descended from the same individual.

Much of the post-1788 Aboriginal history is encompassed in the question: to what extent have Aborigines wanted to be, and been allowed to be, outside the mainstream culture of Australia? Governor **Phillip** was directed to enjoin the Sydney Aboriginals to 'live in amity and kindness' with the British, which perhaps implied a parallel rather than an incorporated identity; but in 1814 Governor **Macquarie** began a school for Aboriginal children, designed to educate and socialise them into British cultural norms. Within a generation the British had charted an inclusionist course for Aboriginals, which has waxed more than it has waned. Missionary endeavours in the nineteenth century followed the policy of attracting or forcing Aboriginals into the dominant British-Australian culture and population. Education at mission stations imparted not only Christian but cultural and behavioural precepts—habits of indoor discipline for children. On the pastoral stations in the north and west, cultural incorporation was reinforced by physical punishment for pastoral workers who absconded.

Aboriginal reaction to crude assimilationist policies was mixed. Perhaps most followed the line of least resistance by waiting to see what would happen, while some chose to cooperate with the British as mission helpers. Others remained uncooperative as long as they were able, and Aboriginals in many parts of Australia told stories of individuals who remained to die in the bush. Other groups, especially in southern Australia, literally occupied the middle ground. They lived, from time to time, in camps of extended families just outside the stations or missions, neither wholly accepting nor wholly rejecting the British, until moved on by health officials or police. Some made their own hideaways with their extended families; others of mixed descent lived as though they were white.

By 1890 state administrations were beginning to take over what remained of mission station education, reinforcing conformity to the ethics of work and education. This more formal entry of the state into Aboriginal administration directed policy toward the controlled incorporation of most Aborigines into the body politic. Children, later known as the **Stolen Generations**, were removed from their parents in greater numbers, and British-style education was more rigorously undertaken in special institutions. Confronted by the obvious desire of many Aboriginal families to remain on the large government stations, Victoria was the first to forcibly separate younger self-identifying Aboriginals with an apparent preponderance of British genes (in practice, those who looked fairly 'white') and drive them from its stations into the community. The older and darker people were to die on the reserves in obscurity; those expelled were expected to produce progeny no longer recognisably Aboriginal within a couple of generations. Other states followed Victoria's lead, until by 1912 every state in the

Commonwealth (except Tasmania, which denied it had any remaining Aboriginals) had its own legislation; this defined certain people as Aboriginals, refused to recognise others, established institutions for children forcibly removed, maintained stations for the elderly and dark-skinned, and ejected the others. Qld and WA followed a different policy of trucking Aboriginals, sometimes over a thousand kilometres, to large reserves which they were not permitted to leave; education within these reserves, however, remained strictly oriented to the production of an industrial and rural working class in culture, attainments, expectations and education. Aboriginals living in remote areas continued to follow traditional hunting and gathering lifestyles.

The years between the two world wars brought two significant developments. The first was the formal association of southern Aboriginals for political purposes. By the late 1930s leaders from the larger reserves, especially Cummeragunja (Victoria), had met the prime minister, sent a petition to the British king, and published a newspaper. Because of the harsh conditions of the period 1925–35, they saw the eventual closure of the reserves and the achievement of equal citizens' rights as a desirable aim. There was probably more ambiguity in these aims than now appears: the tone of the Aboriginals was militant; they intended to remain one recognisable people, and they were deeply conscious of the injustices visited upon them. The second development was sponsored by the state and Commonwealth governments, which at a meeting in 1937, partly in answer to the strident tone of the southern Aboriginal leaders, adopted the policy of **assimilation** for almost all Aboriginals. New programs were initiated to close reserves and move the residents into towns.

The desire among Aboriginals for continuing close association with each other was challenged after World War II, not only by assimilationist governments intent on saving money by closing reserves, but also by well-meaning whites who believed that, while Aboriginals should be released from the repressive conditions and legislation in which they were held, the struggle should not be purely an indigenous one. The Aborigines also pressed for equality and the end of discrimination, but it was not until the late 1960s that individuals like Kath Walker (**Oodgeroo Noonuccal**) and Charles **Perkins**, travelling overseas, observed the special place given to other indigenous peoples rather than the merely equal place to which most Aboriginals still aspired. Assimilation, so trenchantly pursued by governments until the mid-1960s, began to crumble in the face of Aboriginal demands. The call by the **Tent Embassy** (1972) for **Aboriginal land rights**, based on prior occupation, indicated the extent to which the leadership was demanding a separate and special, rather than simply equal, place within the nation. In a climate of reassessment, Aboriginal demands were to some extent met by the **Whitlam** and **Fraser** federal governments, which created the National Aboriginal Advisory Council (1973), the NT Land Rights Act (1976), and the Aboriginal Development Commission (1980), and funded separate Aboriginal legal and medical services in the states. Aboriginal self-managed organisations such as housing cooperatives and homeland (**outstation**) movements flourished. Though Aborigines were blamed for the perceived shortcomings of their independent or separatist initiatives, the underlying reason for the dismemberment of bodies like the Aboriginal Development Commission and the creation of the Aboriginal and Torres Strait Islander Commission under tight legislative control (1988) was the changing bipartisan political climate now demanding the return of Aborigines into the larger Australian economy and polity.

The High Court in 1992 brought down the famous **Mabo** judgment, which recognised native title. Prime Minister **Keating** followed the judgment with the Native Title Act (1993), which established an opportunity for Aboriginals, in somewhat restricted circumstances, to claim native title within areas such as national parks and unalienated Crown land. The High Court's subsequent **Wik** judgment (1996), that pastoral leases did not necessarily extinguish native title, caused Aboriginals and their supporters to rejoice, but aroused consternation among members of the federal Coalition and some state governments.

In 1997, the most extreme conservative position was a return to assimilation, whereby Aboriginals would remain entirely without special privilege within the Commonwealth. The most extreme indigenous position was that of the Aboriginal Provisional Government, which looked towards an almost-independent Aboriginal state. More moderate Aboriginal leaders, like Marcia Langton, Patrick and Mick Dodson, and Noel Pearson, insisted on the conceptual separateness of Aborigines within the nation, including the right to control their own community, national organisations, and land base.

The self-identifying Aboriginal population is close today to 300 000, some 1.5 per cent of the total Australian population. Aborigines continue to suffer from a high arrest rate, high infant mortality, and life-expectancy at least 15 years below the Australian average. Only 20 languages were still being actively transmitted to children from more than 500 in 1788.

PETER READ

Aborigines Advancement League, see **Aboriginal and Torres Strait Islander organisations**

Acclimatisation societies were established in several Australian colonies in the mid-nineteenth century to colonise the indigenous Australian environment with exotic flora and fauna. Advocates of acclimatisation believed themselves deprived of 'useful' birds, animals and plants, and regarded the native flora and fauna as ugly. Accordingly, they sought to create an 'improved' natural environment—ideally, one that was comparable with 'home'. By setting free introduced species—traditional targets for hunting, such as rabbits, deer and foxes, and 'singing' birds, such as sparrows, thrushes and blackbirds—they could imitate familiar (European) modes of sport and forms of pleasure. Above all, they could obtain visual reassurance. The societies also built captive collections of exotic species in **zoological gardens**. Growing appreciation of indigenous flora and fauna in the

1890s, which coincided with a burst of popular nationalistic sentiment, led to a measure of protection of Australian plants and animals through the reservation of public lands as state and national parks. In his study of **pests** in Australia, *They All Ran Wild* (1969), Eric **Rolls** claimed 'there was never a body of eminent men so foolishly, so vigorously, and so disastrously wrong' as the members of acclimatisation societies.

HD

Accord, in full the Prices and Incomes Accord, was an agreement between the **trade unions** and the Labor governments of the 1980s. Its purpose was to prevent a wage explosion such as had undermined the **Whitlam** Labor government in 1974. Negotiated between the **ACTU** and federal Labor during 1982, the Accord was formally adopted by a special union conference in early 1983.

The unions agreed to limit wage increases in return for increases in the social wage and job-creation measures. A series of further Accord agreements covering wages, taxes, and superannuation were struck over the following years. While the Accord lasted formally until the Labor government fell in 1996, its utility was exhausted much earlier. Its history is traced in Gwynneth Singleton, *The Accord and the Australian Labor Movement* (1990).

SM

ACTU is the Australian Council of Trade Unions (called the Australasian Council of Trade Unions until 1947), the national peak organisation of the Australian union movement. The ACTU was formed in May 1927 at an All-Australian Trade Union Congress in Melbourne. It emerged from the wreckage of various unsuccessful efforts to form a national **trade union** organisation stretching back to the late 1880s, including the ill-fated **One Big Union**. The attacks of employers and anti-Labor governments on trade unions during World War I and the 1920s provided unions with a powerful motive to cooperate in self-defence.

The state trades and labour councils were to be the ACTU's branches, although individual unions also affiliated. Most historians have seen the formation of the ACTU as a compromise between the objectives of moderate and militant unionism. On the one hand, it built on existing union structures and largely accepted the principle of compulsory **arbitration**; on the other, it was formally committed to **socialism** and industrial unionism in preference to craft unions.

One of the barriers to the progress of the ACTU during the first 40 years of its existence was the large and powerful **Australian Workers Union**, which held aloof from the council until 1967. In the early years, it accused the ACTU of being a 'red' organisation, and itself aspired to be the one big union of Australian workers. Nevertheless, from the fall of the **Bruce** government in 1929, the council gradually came to be recognised by governments of all colours as the principal national voice of the Australian unions. Relations between the ACTU and the Labor governments of J.H. **Scullin**, John **Curtin** and J.B. **Chifley** were not always harmonious, but the ACTU lobbied them with some success and played a significant role in shaping the arbitration system. Relations with non-Labor governments of the 1930s and early 1940s were less friendly, although even these gradually came to recognise the ACTU as the national voice of the union movement. The coalition governments of the 1950s and 1960s actively sought the cooperation of the ACTU to promote full employment and economic growth, objectives shared by the council under its president Albert **Monk**.

R.M. Martin (in *Australian Quarterly*, 1958, and *Journal of Industrial Relations*, 1962) suggested that the ACTU was largely ineffective in its efforts to influence union behaviour or governments until the 1950s because of a want of finance and a lack of authority over its affiliates. This interpretation was contested by Graham Dunkley, who showed that between 1927 and the 1950s the ACTU played a significant role in several major interstate disputes, lobbied governments, and organised **basic wage** cases in the Arbitration Court.

While there were strong militant influences in the ACTU from the outset, Communist Party influence in the ACTU reached a peak at the end of World War II. Thereafter, the **Australian Labor Party**'s anti-communist Industrial Groups were able to exercise greater control over the ACTU's affairs, their influence reaching its zenith in the early 1950s. The aggressive tactics and successes of the Groupers, however, provoked resistance from within the union movement and the ALP, and precipitated their decline. The growth of left-wing influence in the ACTU culminated in the election of R.J. **Hawke** as president in 1969. While many of the legislative initiatives of the **Whitlam** Labor government pleased the ACTU, the growth of inflation led to conflicts over wage restraint, and there was personal rivalry between Whitlam and Hawke. The anti-Labor **Fraser** government also clashed with the ACTU over wages policy and industrial legislation.

The ACTU was a party to a series of **Accords** with the Hawke and **Keating** Labor governments. Initially, this required the ACTU to accept wage restraint in order to reduce unemployment and inflation, and promote economic growth. In return, the government agreed to introduce tax cuts, improvements in social security and other policies favoured by the unions. The ACTU also sought to modernise the union movement with amalgamations and an increasing emphasis on services to members. The considerable influence of the ACTU in this period did not stem a decline of union coverage.

The ACTU has featured prominently in many histories of unions, socialism and the ALP. However, Jim Hagan's *The History of the ACTU* (1981) is the only detailed published account. Hagan traces the struggles between advocates of **labourism** and socialism in the ACTU over policy, ideology and industrial strategy up to 1980, and places these conflicts in the context of broader changes in the Australian economy, **industrial relations** system, and international and domestic politics. Graham Dunkley's doctoral thesis 'The ACTU, 1927–1950' (Monash University, 1974) was a detailed pioneering study of the organisation's first two decades. Frank Farrell's *International Socialism and Australian Labour* (1981) examines the ACTU's relationship to international socialism and union militancy in the 1920s. A large collection of the ACTU's records is located in the Noel Butlin Archives Centre at the Australian National University.

FRANK BONGIORNO

Adam-Smith, Patricia Jean 'Patsy' (1924–   ), popular freelance historian, grew up in isolated Victorian country towns. Her experiences as the daughter of a railway worker and postmistress–stationkeeper formed the basis for her first book, the vivid, autobiographical *Hear the Train Blow* (1964, 1984). *Goodbye Girlie* (1994) records her experiences during World War II and after. Adam-Smith's fascination with the 'ordinary—extraordinary—women and men of our land' found further expression in *The Anzacs* (1978), *Outback Heroes* (1981), *The Shearers* (1982), *Australian Women at War* (1984), and *Prisoners of War* (1992). The popular success of her work is in large part due to the simpler past she evokes and the stoic, heroic nature of the people who inhabit it.

KT

Adams, Francis William Lauderdale (1862–93) lived in Australia for less than six years but wrote prolifically and passionately about Australian society. An English radical who came to Australia because he suffered from tuberculosis, he wrote for the *Boomerang*, the **Brisbane Courier**, and the **Bulletin**. Adams is best known for his social observation. In *The Australians* (1893) he concluded that Australia was 'the best place in the world … for the rank and file', and the bushman the 'one unique national type yet produced in Australia'. His poems collected in the *Songs of the Army of the Night* (1888) were bitterly critical of capitalism and imperialism, and predicted the triumph of democracy in Australia.

KT

Adams, George, see **Tattersalls**

Adelaide, the capital city of **South Australia**, is situated on what its Anglo-Indian founder, the Surveyor-General William **Light**, described in 1836 as 'an immense plain of level and advantageous ground' between the Mount Lofty Ranges and the eastern shore of St Vincent Gulf. Adelaide has dominated its rural hinterland to an extent unsurpassed by any other Australian capital. SA has always had even fewer sizeable provincial urban centres, and a proportionately larger capital city, than other colonies and states. The urban imbalance that produced this unique one-town state, or city-state, was, as Anthony Denholm claims (in Anna Rutherford, ed., *Populous Places*, 1992), 'neither planned nor desired' by the would-be systematic colonisers of SA.

The city that Light laid out and named after the German consort of King William IV is still a distinct urban entity. Light's innovative plan called for both the main city grid and

North Adelaide, its extension across the Torrens River, to be surrounded by a belt of reserved parklands which separate the city proper from the suburbs beyond. While piecemeal alienation of these parklands for official, cultural, and recreational purposes has continued to the present day, their value as open space is now more widely recognised by South Australians, as it has long been by foreign visitors and generations of town-planners. The Fabian socialist Sidney Webb characterised Adelaide at the end of the nineteenth century as 'wisely planned and full of amenity', resembling a small German provincial capital, 'with its parks and gardens, its little court society, its absence of conspicuous industrialism, and its general air of laying itself out to enjoy quietly a comfortable life' (A.G. **Austin**, ed., *The Webbs' Australian Diary 1898*, 1965).

Settlement within the city proceeded in a halting, uneven fashion. By 1860, half of Adelaide's total population lived outside Light's city limits, for numerous suburban villages had sprung up after 1840 at the expense of the city proper (especially its underdeveloped southern wards), where land prices never lost their speculative premium acquired in the colony's earliest years. This unusually rapid suburbanisation was caused by a combination of differential land costs, high real wages for labour (generating realistic aspirations to mass home-ownership), and effective public transport, not (as in Europe) mere pressure of population. The resultant sprawl of detached, single-family dwellings with spacious backyards made metropolitan Adelaide an extreme example of the low-density Australasian urban centre, as distinct from older European and American 'walking' cities. By the late nineteenth century Adelaide's most thickly settled areas housed only one-eighth as many people as the equivalent regions in Sydney.

These comparative perspectives distinguish the work of Denholm; Pamela Statham (ed.), *The Origins of Australia's Capital Cities* (1989); and Lionel Frost, *The New Urban Frontier* (1991). The more conventional urban biographies, or chronicles, commence with the town clerk Thomas Worsnop's 'attempt to elucidate the origin and progress of this City', emphasising its role as 'birthplace of Municipal Government, not only in Australia, but in the whole British Colonial Empire' (1878). Sequels include J.J. Pascoe's celebratory *History of Adelaide and Vicinity with a General Sketch of the Province of South Australia* (1901), and a trio of more recent works commissioned by Adelaide City Council: Derek Whitelock's popular *Adelaide 1836–1976: A History of Difference* (1977); the well-documented historical introduction to *Heritage of the City of Adelaide* (1990); and Peter Morton's lively *After Light: A History of the City of Adelaide and its Council 1878–1928* (1996). Whitelock's subtitle points to a characteristic preoccupation with Adelaide's distinctiveness (or lack thereof), whether in endorsing or contesting conventional stereotypes—the city of churches, or pubs, or culture, or Light, the most staid or hypocritical of cities, Garden, Festival, or Queen City, overblown country town, or Athens of the South. The attention such labels command may be an index of provincial insecurity, waxing and waning with the city-state's fluctuating economic fortunes.

The short history of Australia's first planned city has not followed a smoothly predictable trajectory. It is marked by wild swings of expansion and contraction, optimism and pessimism, from the bankruptcy of the late 1830s to the minerals boom of the 1840s, through the depressions of the 1880s–90s and 1930s, industrial expansion before and after World War II, and the savage recessions of the mid-1970s and early 1990s. Yet Adelaide's demographic and economic growth rates were already slowing by the end of the nineteenth century. So the intensive industrialisation associated with Sir Thomas **Playford's** quarter-century premiership, a process perceptively sketched by Hugh **Stretton** in *Ideas for Australian Cities* (1970), may have merely postponed an inevitable decline in relative economic and political clout. Nor could Don **Dunstan's** effective campaign to project Adelaide as an epicentre of cultural and social enlightenment prevent the city falling behind both Brisbane and Perth in the capital-city population stakes.

Despite pioneering efforts by Professor G.C. **Henderson** to establish a research school of local history at the University of Adelaide during the first decades of the twentieth century, modern historical scholarship on SA is relatively thin. Despite some notable recent work—including an exemplary 1973 study of Adelaide's interaction with the rest of SA by J.B. Hirst, perceptive accounts by Michael Williams of the making of the South Australian townscape, and Mark Peel's analysis of good and hard times in the satellite town of Elizabeth (1995)—the history of Adelaide, both city and metropolis, remains largely unwritten.

WILFRID PREST

Advertiser, a **newspaper**, was founded in Adelaide on 12 July 1858 by Congregational minister John Henry Barrow. The *South Australian Advertiser*, as it was known until 1899, was progressive in tone and liberal in its political sympathies. Its first issue proclaimed its independence, liberalism, and catholic sentiment. In 1863 the proprietors launched the country's first penny paper, the *Express*. The *Advertiser's* firm protectionist stance was at odds with the conservative *Register*—a situation that echoed the *Age–Argus* opposition in Melbourne. Rivalry between the *Advertiser* and the *Register* was fierce, and the two went to great lengths in competition for lead stories. The paper's single most enduring figure was J.L. (Langdon) **Bonython**, who started as a junior reporter on the *Advertiser* in 1864, aged 16, became a part-owner in 1879, and sole proprietor and editor in 1893; a son and grandson continued the family's long association with the paper. In 1929, under the chairmanship of Lloyd Dumas, the company was transferred to Advertiser Newspapers Limited, a subsidiary of the Herald & Weekly Times Ltd. In 1931 it merged with the *Register*, in effect becoming the state's sole morning newspaper. The *Express* and *South Australian Chronicle* ceased publication in 1951 and 1975 respectively. Rupert **Murdoch** acquired the paper when his News

Corporation gained control of the Herald & Weekly Times, and in 1997 he turned it into a tabloid.

HD

Advertising has always been a form of communication designed to influence consumers' behaviour. Its form, organisation, methods and content have all changed. Print forms have always been important, and at the end of the twentieth century accounted for nearly 50 per cent of total advertising expenditure. Print has ranged from the simple bill poster to catalogues, circulars, sales notices, price lists, 'junk mail', and most significantly, newspapers: these were cheap to produce and were widely disseminated. With the introduction of colour printing came the influential lifestyle magazines, plus coloured labels and wrappers which assisted in 'brand naming', for example, the colourful bird of Rosella Soup.

By the 1920s, radio offered an alternative to print. In 1923, retailers Farmer & Company launched 2FC, the first commercial radio station, followed by Grace Brothers (2GB) and others. Advertisements were placed within programs and radio plays—the 'soaps', which took their name from the products which supported them. From around the same time, cinema provided another forum for advertising, but it was the little cinema in the box, the **television**—introduced to Australia in 1956—which promised a visual entry into every household. A multiplicity of products clamoured for the attention of the viewing public. The 1990s saw a new revolution—on the Internet.

In part, the increasing complexity of advertising resulted from the emergence of an advertising industry. It began in the late nineteenth century with the 'admen' who bought and sold newspaper space, and designed advertisements. Then, from 1905, select firms began to employ their own advertising managers. Soon after, other firms sought the services of the new independent advertising agencies. The industry established its first journal, *The Reason Why*, in 1908, and by 1918 held the first Australasian Conference on Advertising. Once established, the industry grew rapidly, frequently boosted by developments in radio and television. At the end of the century, the Australian industry comprised more than 500 dedicated agencies plus an incalculable number of in-house departments, and about $3.5 billion is spent annually on advertising in the major media. The industry has tended to be male-dominated, foreign-owned, subjected to limited (and currently dwindling) regulation, and is entrenched: no company can safely take a unilateral stand sacrificing advertising without jeopardising market share.

Over the course of the twentieth century, advertising became a business equipped with a range of techniques. Mirroring international developments, retailers and marketeers acted cooperatively to establish clever marketing strategies: Mother's Day in 1918; 'Spring shopping week' in 1925; and Father's Day in 1929. The growth of a national market saw advertising funded less by retailers and more by manufacturers, with the concomitant rise of brand names. 'Scientific selling' emerged, with its focus on sales techniques, store layout, stock management, merchandising, window displays, and customer management. Modern psychology became influential, divining 'unconscious' desires and instincts. As identified by Gail Reekie in *Temptations: Sex, Selling and the Department Store* (1993), 'dramatic selling' was to be used on women who were believed to respond emotionally, and more reasoned selling was employed to appeal to the logic men were supposed to possess. From the 1950s, market research became a key component in developing advertising strategies. However, even the growth of market research failed to break down gendered expectations among advertising industry professionals. Gail Reekie observed that 'a persistent tension existed in market-research literature between men's desire to manage female consumer behaviour and women's apparent refusal to cooperate or respond as advertisers wished'. According to Beverley Kingston in *Basket, Bag and Trolley: A History of Shopping in Australia* (1994), research disaggregated the male-breadwinner family: target groups with their own special interests and needs were identified. In the 1990s advertisers identify both mass markets and 'niche' markets, adding women, children, gays, generation-Xers, 'dinks' (couples with 'double income no kids'), and other acronyms to their list. Advertising now constitutes only one element in a broader marketing strategy, which typically includes product design, packaging, pricing, and distribution methods. More on the techniques used in advertising can be gleaned from the *Journal of Advertising History*.

Advertising played an active part in the drama of consumer desire. Creating a consumer culture meant going beyond satisfying needs, to creating wants. Ann Stephen wrote in 'Selling Soap: Domestic Work and Consumerism', *LH* (1991), that it was 'constructions based on fear and loss that instilled the desire for consumption'. Purchase offered the promise of success. In the example of soap in the 1920s, a clever concoction of eugenics, white supremacy, health reform, and body beautiful movements were employed, and each '"beauty secret" for white skin … unleashed fears of being undesirable, unfeminine, dirty and not white'. Advertising utilised ideas about femininity, and also national interests. As the century progressed, and the context changed, so too did advertising messages. In 'Female Desires: The Meaning of World War II', *AHS* (1990), Marilyn Lake identified a shift in depictions of women, as maternity gave way to sex appeal and youth as the new aspirations. Throughout the century, masculinity was also redefined many times, from an aristocratic form, to muscular, to the ocker, and beyond. Partly this reflected changing target audiences, but also changing definitions of what it meant to be a man. Australian images still rely heavily—and effectively—on rural symbolism, be it in selling beer or four-wheel-drive vehicles to the urban market. Recent research views advertising as a site of cultural production, both monitoring and influencing our development. Advertisements can thus be usefully read for what they say about gender, other social relations, and 'Australian character'.

Deborah Oxley

Age, a Melbourne **newspaper** founded by John and Henry Cooke, was first published on 17 October 1854, and soon acquired by the Syme family. David **Syme** continued as proprietor following the death of his brother Ebenezer in 1860, and established a paper of unrivalled influence in Melbourne. Unequivocally liberal, the *Age* supported free selection, free and secular state education, tariff protection, and control of factories. At the time of Federation, it was the country's leading broadsheet and outsold its rival, the conservative Melbourne *Argus*, by five to one. Syme's sons continued the paper after his death in 1908. The *Age* operated as a public company from 1945. Ranald McDonald, managing editor and descendant of the Symes, and Graham Perkin, a notable liberal editor, presided over the newspaper's revival in the 1960s and 1970s. In 1983 the *Age* was taken over by the **Fairfax** group. A commemorative publication, *The Age: 125th Anniversary*, appeared in 1979.

HD

Agents-General, see **British–Australian relations**

Agricultural shows were held in Australia by agricultural societies from the 1820s, imitating counterparts in Britain and Europe. They were primarily a means of promoting new agricultural technology, both by educating local farmers, and encouraging and rewarding innovation. Prizes were awarded to farming equipment and produce—a farming implement's commercial success often relied on the prizes won at local shows. An earlier agricultural contest, the ploughing match, tested both the ploughman's skill and the plough's efficiency. The Van Diemen's Land and NSW Agricultural Societies both held their first show in 1822, but shows did not become major events until the advent of government support in the later nineteenth century. Some discussion of their development and the associated agricultural societies is given in Geoff Raby's *Making Rural Australia* (1996) and in Brian Fletcher's *The Grand Parade* (1988). Shows also introduced competitions in bush skills, such as wood-chopping, boxing, shearing, and horse-riding; and in domestic arts, such as baking, preserving, and needlework. In the twentieth century, the parade became a highlight and producers introduced complimentary sample bags, or show bags, of their goods. As well as demonstrating agricultural improvements, the shows offered a variety of sideshow entertainment, from so-called freak shows to travelling boxing troupes, and, later, motorised rides for children. By the interwar period most states held a public Show Day holiday. Agricultural shows were a rich medium for a range of popular folk activities that are largely neglected by historians.

HD

Agriculture has never been the occupation of the great bulk of the people. In Europe and North America rural societies growing their own food were gradually transformed as agriculture was commercialised, industry developed, and towns grew. This was not the pattern of development in Australia. It became a rich society through a commercial **pastoralism** which supported large port cities; agriculture played a subordinate part. In the second century of European settlement agriculture became an important sector of the economy but in a commercialised and mechanised form, employing few people and exporting most of its products overseas.

When nearly all the good lands were used for sheep and **cattle**, agriculture was located in the coastal areas. The chief crops were **wheat** and maize. Some maize was eaten by very poor farmers, but it was generally a fodder crop for **horses**. In eastern Australia in the pastoral age not enough wheat was grown to supply local needs. Tasmania and then SA were the granaries for the east. In SA from the 1840s agriculture was mechanised with the invention of the **stripper**. Here, unlike in the east, the coastal lands were suited to wheat. Because the coastline of SA is indented, as wheat-growing expanded northwards the farms were still close to the sea and hence transport costs were low. As Tasmania lost out in wheat to SA, it concentrated on potatoes, oats, and later fruit, which it supplied to the mainland.

The modern wheat belt in the east, which runs behind the Great Dividing Range from southern Qld to northern Victoria, gradually took shape from the 1870s when railways first reached these lands. Victoria surpassed SA in wheat in the 1890s, and NSW became the premier wheat state in the 1910s. The distinction between agriculture and pastoralism began to disappear. Wheat farmers rested their land by grazing it with sheep; large pastoral properties were let out to wheat farmers or acquired by the state under **closer settlement** schemes and subdivided for farmers. In most of the wheat belt farmers concentrate on cropping, sheep, or cattle, according to what brings the best return. Beyond the wheat belt there is a much larger area of land which is only suitable for grazing.

As grain growing moved inland, **dairying**, horticulture, and hay-making became the chief industries in the coastal lands. The coastal **sugar** plantations in Qld, first developed in the 1860s, were transformed in the early twentieth century into family farms of the usual sort as central mills were formed for processing the cane, the **Pacific Island labourers** were repatriated, and government protection and subsidies covered the costs of white harvesting labour.

Agriculture generally flourished in Australia when farms were large, labour needs low, and access to distant markets good. Farming was primarily a way of making money. For a long time official policy and expert opinion wanted a different agriculture: smaller farms, more intense and varied cultivation, more self-sufficiency. It is often thought that the Australian environment made such an agriculture impossible. However, where the land has been farmed by **German** or **Italian** peasants, something more like a peasant agriculture has emerged, which suggests that cultural factors have been important in the shaping of Australian agriculture. In England at the time of Australian colonisation agriculture was the most commercialised in Europe; in Ireland peasant agriculture was degraded and impoverished. Neither provided a model for the sort of farming that was officially favoured, which was inspired by a nostalgia for the English yeoman farmer who had virtually disappeared in England. Moreover, many of Australia's farmers did not have an agricultural background of any sort. Frequently farmers came from pastoral work or the goldfields; if they did not succeed on the land, they moved on to the cities. In a highly mobile society, agriculture would be pursued only so long as its rewards matched what could be obtained elsewhere.

From the late nineteenth century **irrigation** was hailed as a means of overcoming the vagaries of Australia's **climate** and making small-scale agriculture possible. In a few areas it did allow small orchards and dairy farms to develop. Its most spectacular effect has been since the 1960s when it has allowed the rapid expansion of the new industries of rice and cotton, on large properties worked mechanically.

Since World War II there has been a remarkable increase in the productivity of agriculture. Sown pastures have been used more extensively, mechanisation has been carried further, more effective fertilisers have been discovered, and the rabbit **pest** was almost eliminated in the 1950s. Still, farmers' costs have increased more rapidly than their returns so that income levels have been maintained only by a further reduction in the number of farms, from 200 000 in 1950 to 125 000 in 1990. In this period the area under agriculture in WA grew rapidly so that it became the largest wheat-producing state.

Since World War I there have been numerous government marketing schemes for agricultural produce which have averaged returns or increased them by maintaining higher domestic prices. These were part of the policy of **protection** all round which compensated farmers for the higher costs imposed by tariffs. In the 1980s a new body, the National Farmers Federation, was in the forefront of the attack on tariffs. The triumph of economic rationalism has also meant the dismantling of the marketing schemes. The family farm, which is still the Australian ideal, has become directly exposed to the vagaries of the world market.

From 1987 the National Farmers Federation produced a biennial reference book, *Australian Agriculture*, which gives an account of each industry and a history of agriculture.

JOHN HIRST

AIF, or Australian Imperial Forces, so-named by William Throsby **Bridges**, inspector-general of the Commonwealth Military Force, was formed in August 1914 at the outbreak of war with Germany. The AIF, with the NZ forces, attained something of a mythic status after its display of bravery in the 1915 **Gallipoli** campaign, and acquired the name 'Anzacs'. After the war, official war historian C.E.W. **Bean** completed the multi-volume *Official History of Australia in the War of 1914–1918* (1921–42), and numerous battalion histories appeared. Lloyd **Robson's** *The First AIF: A History of its Recruitment* (1970) re-examines the enlistment process. The Second AIF was formed at the outbreak of **World War II**; its history can be found in the 22-volume official history edited by Gavin **Long**. (See also **Digger**, **World War I**, **World War II**.)

HD

Alcheringa, see Dreamtime

Alcohol was unknown to the Aborigines, but since 1788 almost all immigrants have come from cultures in which the use of alcohol had long been widespread and deeply embedded. Early arrivals soon discovered that neither their drinking habits nor their accustomed methods of drink production transferred easily to the infant settlement. Russel **Ward** in *The Australian Legend* (1958) claimed that early colonists took to the bottle with such enthusiasm that 'no people on the face of the earth ever absorbed more alcohol per head of population'. He argued that the 'typical' Australian, the (male) embodiment of the **Australian Legend**, developed into a heavy drinker. Yet, as later studies have shown (A.E. Dingle in *HS*, 1980), alcohol consumption was high by international standards only for brief periods when populations were dominated by male adults, as was the case during the early convict years and the gold rushes. For most of the nineteenth century colonists drank less alcohol than their relatives in Britain, and consumed it in different forms. Spending on drink usually competed not only with the demands of family, house, and home for a share of the family wage, but also with the propaganda of a **temperance** movement which preached the evils of alcohol. Drink consumption fluctuated markedly with changed economic conditions, falling to low levels during **depressions**.

By the 1820s people in NSW were drinking on average four times as much rum and other spirits as they would have done had they remained in Britain. This was possible because spirits were easily imported, or distilled locally, and could be carried long distances without deteriorating. Brewing a palatable beer or importing one in good condition proved much more difficult, so that only one-third as much beer was being consumed as in England and Wales. Spirit drinking subsequently declined to levels comparable to those prevailing in Britain, and tastes shifted towards brandy and whisky, the latter reputedly becoming fashionable as a result of Queen Victoria's well-known liking for it. During the second half of the nineteenth century, beer consumption rose at the expense of spirits, and local brews took a larger share of the market from imports; country towns of any size each supported a brewery. Nevertheless, it was not until the early years of the twentieth century, when new methods of fermentation and new yeast strains were married with refrigerated storage, that a stable, palatable, and distinctive Australian lager-style beer emerged. By this time technologies of large-scale production, combined with lower transport costs as the railway network spread across the continent, favoured big producers in the capital cities and the country breweries closed down. As output rose, the number of independent producers shrank to a handful. Keith Dunstan has written a history of brewing (1987).

Wine production posed fewer difficulties, especially in suitable locations in NSW, Victoria, and SA. Here viable wine-producing regions became established, often drawing heavily on the expertise of Swiss, French, German, and Italian migrants. The heady expansion of the Victorian wine industry followed by its savage contraction in the last decade of the nineteenth century is the subject of David Dunstan's *Better than Pommard! A History of Wine in Victoria* (1994). Per capita consumption levels that fluctuated around four to seven litres were tiny in comparison with France or Italy, but were two to three times higher than in Britain. By the end of the century there were significant variations in both the amounts and types of drink consumed in each colony, with Western Australians flushed with gold heading the list, and Tasmanians the most abstemious.

Levels of drink consumption changed considerably during the twentieth century. They reached a low point during the Depression of the 1930s, when only 34 litres of beer, three-quarters of a litre of spirits, and a little over a litre and half of wine were consumed. Subsequent recovery has varied between drinks. Spirits remain far less popular than in the nineteenth century. Beer consumption, in contrast, increased fourfold to the early 1970s. Since then it has been in gradual decline because of health and drink-driving campaigns. Brewers have attempted to win back drinkers with low-alcohol beers. They also market Australian beers aggressively overseas. Wine consumption remained below nineteenth-century levels until the late 1960s, but then tripled by the early 1980s to reach 21 litres per head. This too has subsequently fallen back somewhat, but the wine industry transformed itself during these years as people increasingly consumed their alcohol with food. While boutique wineries have greatly increased, the bulk of production is controlled by a handful of companies. The industry has become so technologically sophisticated that it exports its expertise as well as its greatly improved wines. More than one-third of production in the expanding industry is currently being exported. (See also **Pubs**.)

TONY DINGLE

Alexander, Frederick (1899–1996) was head of the Department of History at the University of Western Australia from its development as a separate department in 1931 until his retirement in 1966. His *Campus at Crawley* (1963) is a history of the university. The interest in international affairs that he formed as an undergraduate at the University of Melbourne was reinforced by his involvement with the League of Nations Union. His first book, *From Paris to Locarno and After* (1928), examined its development. Alexander spoke to the general community through a fortnightly column on world affairs in the *West Australian* among other extra-curricular activities. During a speech published in a special tribute volume of *Studies in Western Australian History* (1988), he described his growing sense through the 1930s of the lack of informed understanding about contemporary America. This culminated in a year's study tour from which he produced *Australia and the United States* (1941). Alexander pursued this interest in *Moving Frontiers: An American Theme and its Application to Australian History* (1947). His involvement with education outside the university included

the directorship of Adult Education and long-term chairmanship of the Library Board of Western Australia; his influence was recognised with the naming, in 1986, of the new state library as the Alexander Library. Alexander published his memoirs, *On Campus and Off*, in 1987.

KT

Alexander, Samuel (1859–1938), philosopher, won renown with the publication in 1920 of his work on speculative metaphysics, *Space, Time and Deity*. Alexander had enjoyed a brilliant academic career at the University of Melbourne, culminating in a scholarship to Oxford. He later became the first professing Jew to hold a fellowship at Oxford and was appointed professor of philosophy at the University of Manchester in 1893. Although he never returned to Australia, Alexander remained influential in Australian universities, serving on the advisory committees which recommended appointments to the chair of philosophy at the University of Melbourne in 1911 and 1935. His influence was also felt at the University of Sydney through John **Anderson**, whose arguments drew heavily upon Alexander's. A supporter of feminism and Zionism, Alexander was the first Australian awarded the Order of Merit. A theatre at Monash University bears his name.

KT

Aliens is a category which has been accorded a number of meanings through the course of Australian history. In popular usage it has been an elastic term employed to designate outsiders. In the new nation settled predominantly from Great Britain and Ireland, *alien* has differentiated not the native-born from immigrants, but those of the 'motherland' and their descendants from Europeans (particularly southern and eastern) and Asians. The acceptance of aliens as full members of the Australian community, even after long years of residence and naturalisation—or, in some cases, Australian birth—has been challenged and at times denied, particularly during crises occasioned by war or high unemployment.

In law, *alien* designated 'a person who is not a British subject' or Irish citizen, in the absence of a specific status of Australian citizen, until 1949. To 1946 a female British subject who married an alien was deemed an alien. The status of Australian citizen was introduced under the Nationality and Citizenship Act (1948), but the link between Australian citizenship and British status was retained until 1984.

Australian governments have regulated the admission and deportation, naturalisation, and condition of residence of aliens. In the twentieth century the Commonwealth of Australia, acting under powers contained in Section 51 (xix) and (xxvi) of the Constitution, assumed the major responsibility, although legislation enacted by some states was significant in limiting ownership of land and occupational freedom. Some legislation was directed specifically at a sub-group of aliens, defined on the basis of ascribed race.

ANDREW MARKUS

ALP, see Australian Labor Party

American–Australian relations have been crucial in modern Australian history. Although the USA, with its immense population, wealth, vitality, and national self-awareness has dominated the relationship, Australia has adapted these American influences to its British tradition and immigrant experience.

The histories of America and Australia are both similar and different. Those similarities and differences partly account for the character of the relationship, the mutual expectations, and the extent of shared intimacy. Both countries were once British colonies which pushed indigenous peoples out of their path, settled new lands, and created prosperous, progressive societies which embraced egalitarian democracy and mythologised their 'frontiers'. But while America rebelled against Britain, turned its back on the corrupt Old World of Europe, and defined itself as a new nation in a 'new world', Australia neither disowned its British origins nor adopted a clear national identity, instead accepting a modified version of the Old World class and fatalist attitudes. Whereas the USA, it is said, was founded by Puritans, Australia was founded by convicts.

The timing and nature of the two colonising processes have also made a difference. The American colonies of the seventeenth and eighteenth centuries belonged to a pre-modern world, and in their fertile, well-watered lands they established the national type of the self-sufficient, individualistic, yeoman farmer. By contrast, Australia, with its dry and inhospitable interior, favoured large grazing properties, and the nineteenth-century colonists coming from a modernising Britain took more readily to urban life, and looked to the collective state for support and security. The attempts of American historians to conceptualise these relationships between processes of immigration and settlement, such as Frederick Jackson Turner's **frontier** thesis and Louis Hartz's **fragment thesis**, have also influenced Australian historical writing.

The shadow of the American Revolution loomed large in Australian history. The penal colony of NSW was established after the victorious Americans refused to allow Britain to continue to send felons to their country. As Noel McLachlan (*HS*, 1977) shows, the Australian colonists in their struggle for self-rule sometimes invoked the American example in order to warn the imperial government against blocking their wishes. In debating their colonial constitutions in the 1850s, the politicians and press looked to the American Republic and the reforms of Jacksonian democracy. Alexis de Tocqueville's *Democracy in America* (1835) was cited both for and against the American model. But, despite these references to the USA, all the colonies adopted forms of government based on the Westminster system. The excitement and unrest caused on the Victorian and NSW goldfields, which had attracted more than 5000 Americans, provoked widespread fears of social disruption on the pattern of California and caused colonists to idealise their British constitutional inheritance. The British constitution, suitably adapted to colonial conditions, protected 'rational liberty' and 'ordered progress' from the excesses of American 'mobocracy', 'vigilantism', and 'lynch law'. The American presence is described by E. Daniel Potts and Annette Potts in *Young America and Australian Gold: America and the Gold Rush of the 1850s* (1974), while David Goodman, *Gold Seeking: Victoria and California in the 1850s* (1994), explores the cultural comparisons.

In the latter half of the nineteenth century the colonies adopted democratic practices, such as universal manhood suffrage, which had been pioneered in America. Yet the American precedents merely gave additional authority to an English Chartist program. Indeed, as Lionel Fredman showed in *The Australian Ballot: The Story of American Reform* (1968), Australia, pursuing that program, gave the secret ballot to America. Likewise the separation of **church and state**, the exclusive funding of a public school system, the Selection Acts for the breaking up of large land holdings, and the women's suffrage movement, while drawing support from American parallels, were primarily the result of a British liberal tradition working itself out in Australian circumstances. American social visionaries, such as Henry George in his *Progress and Poverty* (1879), were a source of inspiration for the early labour movement, but they had no lasting effect on Australian reform. America's 'bourgeois' Progressives, as Michael **Roe** showed in *Nine Australian Progressives* (1984), with their call for moral purity and national efficiency, had a greater impact, especially on education, child welfare, health, eugenics, municipal government, and factory management.

America's most significant contribution to Australian political life was as a model for Federation. The architects of the Commonwealth Constitution followed the American one in its overall structure, in its division of powers between the federation and the states, and in its two houses of parliament, the House of Representatives and the Senate—the first representing the people and the second the states. Yet the Commonwealth Constitution was formally an act of the British parliament and contained no Bill of Rights. American observers often could not help but think that the newer nation was somewhat retarded and lacking in 'national soul'.

From the early years of the twentieth century, with Japan's victory over Russia and Germany's challenge to *Pax Britannica*, Australians turned to the USA to underwrite their security in the Pacific, looking to their fellow 'Anglo-Saxons' across the Pacific for help in defending 'White Australia' against the 'Yellow Peril'. Thus they sought both to persuade the USA to extend the umbrella of its Monroe Doctrine to the South Pacific and to establish their own 'Australian Monroe Doctrine' for the same area. These efforts proved fruitless, however, until Japan attacked Pearl Harbor in December 1941 and America used Australia as a base from which to fight the Pacific War. Almost one million American service personnel, including about 100 000 African-Americans, passed through Australia on the way to the battle-front. Their impact is the subject of E. Daniel Potts and Annette Potts, *Yanks Down Under 1941–1945* (1985). At first they were universally welcomed as saviours.

Women saw the well-paid GIs as embodiments of Hollywood glamour and romance; of the 12 000 who married Yanks, about 10 000 migrated to the USA. But as the war receded from Australia's shores, resentments and doubts arose. Was the American presence a reassurance against Asian enemies or a danger to national independence? Roger Bell, *Unequal Allies: Australian–American Relations and the Pacific War* (1977), explores the issue.

During the Cold War (1950–72) the American relationship was central to Australian strategy and politics. Following the Chinese revolution, America extended its containment alliance system from Europe to Asia, and Australia through **ANZUS** and **SEATO** became a loyal, if minor, partner in that system. It fought under American leadership in Korea and Vietnam. Australia, troubled by the rise of national movements and Communist insurgencies in its 'near north', sought the protection of what Prime Minister **Menzies** in 1962 hailed as a 'great and powerful friend'. Norman Harper, in *A Great and Powerful Friend* (1987), made this the theme of his study of Australian–American relations. As Britain withdrew from east of Suez, Australia became ever more dependent on the American alliance. It standardised its military organisation and equipment with that of the USA, achieved close cooperation in intelligence activities—including assisting the CIA to destabilise the Allende Marxist regime in Chile—and agreed to the USA setting up bases on Australian soil which could be used to launch its Polaris missiles, and to receive signals from its early-warning satellite system.

America had an increasing impact on what Australians—following the American example—called their way of life. The USA overtook Britain as the major supplier of investment capital. American corporations acquired a preeminent position in the three most dynamic and profitable postwar industries—automobiles, petro-chemicals, and mining—and American-controlled transnational companies absorbed local firms. America also replaced Britain as the chief source of imports; by 1970 it was providing about one-quarter of the total. Since Australia's major exports, its agricultural and mining products, had to compete with America's own, Australia had a chronic deficit in its trade with the USA, which grew from approximately $A50 million in 1950 to $A500 million in 1970.

American popular culture spread through the land. In the suburbs, Australians overwhelmingly took to American-style household conveniences and gadgetry. American cheap fast-food chains, such as Kentucky Fried Chicken and McDonald's, both responded to and altered family eating habits. From the 1920s, Hollywood films had great influence; in the television era, American movies and music came to dominate mass entertainment, and pop and rock stars gained cult followings. However it must be asked—as Phillip and Roger Bell do in *Implicated: The United States in Australia* (1993)—whether these styles are peculiarly American or simply a manifestation of the modern, in which America often played the leading part.

From the 1960s, America also influenced high culture. For the first time Australian universities taught and researched American history and literature. Americans, in poetry and art, were the avant-garde. The **Whitlam** Labor government, which was somewhat critical of America's Cold War policies and of America's role in Australia's economy, purchased Jackson Pollock's *Blue Poles*, an outstanding example of American abstract painting, for the Australian National Gallery at a cost of A$1 million. Neville Meaney, 'The United States', in W.J. Hudson (ed.), *Australia in World Affairs 1971–75* (1980), considers these developments.

Since the 1970s, with America's defeat in Vietnam, its withdrawal from the Asian mainland, and the end of the Cold War, American–Australian relations have lost some of their intimacy and intensity. However, the alliance was revitalised in new form when the USA supported Australia diplomatically and materially so that it could take the commanding role in the UN intervention in **East Timor**.

NEVILLE MEANEY

Anderson, John (1893–1962) was Australia's most important philosopher in the first half of the twentieth century. He was born in Lanarkshire, Scotland, the son of a socialist, anti-clerical schoolmaster. Educated at the University of Glasgow, where he won many prizes and distinctions, he soon reacted against the dominant school of Absolute Idealism and began to develop his own distinctive brand of realism, under the influence of Samuel **Alexander**.

After appointments in Cardiff, Glasgow, and Edinburgh, he came to the Challis chair of philosophy at the University of Sydney in 1927 and held it until his retirement in 1958. The doctrinaire Scots empiricist would become as Australian as a magpie. He worked out his realist system of logic, metaphysics, ethics, and aesthetics, and fathered a vigorous local school characterised by inquiry, independence, and a deep commitment to philosophy as a way of life. Anderson's central doctrine was that 'there is only one way of being'—that of ordinary things and complex activities in space and time; and he opposed all forms of relativism, subjectivism, and religion. He derived his propositional view of reality and his 'pluralism without ultimates' from classical sources and his own extended critical reflections on Alexander, Hegel, and Marx, particularly the latter. Anderson's was a this-worldly philosophy, and is well summed up in a favourite Heraclitean fragment: 'This world, which is the same for all, no one of gods or men has made; but it was ever, is now, and ever shall be an ever-living fire, with measures kindling, and measures going out'.

Anderson was a formidable public figure, a stinging gadfly to the bourgeoisie, and fierce controversialist who, over decades, outraged most of Sydney's clergy and conventionally minded citizenry. From an early Marxist phase, he espoused and applied 'freethought' and criticism in everything, championing Sigmund Freud and James Joyce; and he opposed all forms of censorship and mind control—except perhaps, as one student wit observed, his own. Anderson encouraged discipleship, and the bonds between him and his students were intense and complex. Several, including A.J. 'Sandy' Anderson, D.M. Armstrong, A.J. Baker, Eugene

Kamenka, J.L. Mackie, P.H. Partridge, and J.A. Passmore, were to become prominent philosophers in their own right and the chief guardians of his reputation.

Published collections of Anderson's writings appeared in *Studies in Empirical Philosophy* (1962), *Education and Inquiry* (1980), and *Art and Reality* (1982). A.J. Baker provides a dense exposition of the general philosophy in *Australian Realism* (1986) and of the social and political philosophy in *Anderson's Social Philosophy* (1979). But he is an Andersonian, a close disciple, and not a historian. Biographical essays by former students include P.H. Partridge's in *The Australian Highway* (1958), W.M. O'Neil's entry in the *ADB* and J.A. Passmore's entry in the *Encyclopedia of Philosophy*. But Eugene Kamenka's affectionate portrait in Leonie **Kramer** et al. (eds), *The Greats* (1986), sums him up best: 'Anderson was without question Australia's most original and creative philosopher … He exuded and attracted ability, sharpness of mind, penetration, theoretical force.' Brian Kennedy's biography, *A Passion to Oppose* (1995), is the first serious attempt to look at the life as a whole, locating Anderson and his circle firmly in their Scottish and Australian contexts, and drawing on newly available personal papers to illuminate the conflicts of his private, as well as his public, life. Anderson still has much to impart about universities and the intellectual life; his calls to unfettered inquiry, criticism, and the Socratic way of life are both perennial and timely.

BRIAN KENNEDY

Anderson, Maybanke Susannah (1845–1927) was a feminist reformer with a keen interest in education, who arrived in Sydney in 1855. She trained as a teacher, then married and bore seven children. When her husband deserted the family in 1885, Anderson (then Wolstenholme) established a school for young ladies, Maybanke College, in the family home. She was a foundation member of the Womanhood Suffrage League of New South Wales, belonged to the Women's Literary Society, and helped establish the Kindergarten Union. Anderson also edited a fortnightly paper, the *Woman's Voice*, from 1894 to 1895, when financial and health problems forced its closure. Her many interests are discussed in Jan Roberts's sympathetic biography (1993). After her marriage in 1899 to Francis Anderson, professor of philosophy at the University of Sydney, she continued her active interest in the welfare of women and children; this included organising the Women Evening Students Association. Anderson wrote many articles and books, the best-known being *Mother Lore* (1919). A longtime member of the **National Council of Women**, Anderson worked to win the right for women to be municipal councillors. Later in life, she developed an interest in local history and wrote about Hunter's Hill and Pittwater.

KT

Angas family was a founding dynasty of SA. Indeed, the title of an early biography of GEORGE FIFE ANGAS (1789–1879) by Edwin Hodder (1891) cast him as the 'father and founder of South Australia'. A successful English businessman, George Angas did not live in SA until 1851. Prior to that, his involvement had been as a founding member of the **South Australian Company**, which he used to fulfil his vision of 'a place for refuge for pious dissenters of Great Britain'. He arranged for groups of settlers to sail to the colony, including persecuted German **Lutherans** and supported the struggling colony before a British parliamentary committee in 1841. Douglas **Pike**'s *Paradise of Dissent* (1957) gives a detailed account of this period. When he did migrate, following his second son, JOHN HOWARD (1823–1904), he settled at Angaston, the town named after him. He served as a member of the colony's Legislative Assembly until 1866 and remained an active philanthropist until his death. His eldest son, GEORGE FRENCH (1822–86), rejected business for art. His travels around Australia resulted in *Savage Life and Scenes in Australia and New Zealand* (1847), *Views of the Gold Regions of Australia* (1851), and *Australia, a Popular Account* (1855). He was secretary to the Australian Museum 1853–60, and later he returned permanently to England. John Tregenza has written his biography (1980).

KT

Anglican Church took this name in 1981 to signify that it is an independent constituent member of the worldwide Anglican Communion. It was previously called the Church of England in Australia. Because of habits of thought acquired in its long history as an established church, its theological emphasis on the incarnation, and its claim until recently to have the largest nominal adherence of any Christian denomination in Australia, Anglicanism has contended that Christianity should be the foundation of civil society. The role of the churches, Anglicanism contends, is either to build a Christian nation or keep it Christian. This understanding explains many of the Anglican Church's struggles in the course of Australian history.

The Anglican Church has experienced a very gradual erosion of its majority status in the population. Nominal Anglicans were 53 per cent of the Australian population in 1851, 44 per cent in 1921, and in 1986 only 24 per cent, which was second to the Roman **Catholics**. The numerical and assumed superiority of the Church of England and its establishmentarian ethos have given a peculiarly Anglican atmosphere to Australian Protestantism, making it very different in character from, for example, American Protestantism. The long Anglican hegemony also helps to explain why revival has not been as conspicuous a part of Australian religious experience as it is in America. Revivalism flourishes in areas where there are few institutionalised restraints on emotionalism. In Australia institutionalised parish Anglicanism has been ubiquitous.

Throughout the nineteenth century the Church of England was forced to adjust to non-establishment status and accept its role as another denomination in a secular state. It had to develop the machinery of synodical self-government. It lost its monopoly over **education**. Along with those of other churches its theological formularies were excluded from the curricula of **universities**. And it had to adjust first to too little state support; then (from 1836 with the **Church**

Acts) to the ignominy of receiving state aid on the same basis as other Christian denominations; eventually, a generation later, to the abolition of state aid and the necessity of becoming just another voluntary organisation.

The Church of England in Australia developed diocesan, provincial, and general synods for the self-government of the Church. Today there are 24 dioceses grouped into five provinces. Because it was felt that the Church of England was still not free to fashion its own destiny, further constitutional reform preoccupied the church for the next half-century. The 1962 constitution freed the church to determine for itself its faith, worship and discipline, and the next quarter of a century was marked by growth in its central administration. In 1978 the first full-time secretary of General Synod was appointed, and liturgical reform also found expression in that year in the production of *An Australian Prayer Book*. These developments do not signal a radical break with the past, however. The church's beliefs are still enshrined in the *Book of Common Prayer* of 1662, especially in the catechism and 39 articles of that book, and the diocese is still the sovereign unit of government.

Diocesan sovereignty is the product both of the chronic suspicion of episcopal power which has been endemic among many Anglican lay people in Australian history and of the determination, particularly in the evangelical Diocese of Sydney, to prevent one diocese from imposing its preferred brand of churchmanship (Anglo-Catholic, evangelical or liberal) on another. Sydney's celebrated penchant for isolation in the twentieth century was preceded in the nineteenth century by Melbourne's determined isolationism under its first bishop, the evangelical Charles Perry. The determination is an evangelical quality. So too is the lack of interest in a national Australian church. Evangelicals have not proved unambiguous advocates of national unity and have given to Australian Anglicanism most of any countercultural determination it has expressed, including the stout refusal to ordain women to the priesthood.

The Anglican Church has not fared well historiographically. Preoccupied with legal, structural and party matters, its historians have not reflected extensively on its spirituality, scholarship, theological education, missions, and evangelism. There have been important biographies of bishops (especially George Shaw on **Broughton**, A. de Q. Robin on Perry, and Peter Hempenstall on **Burgmann**) and histories of dioceses (for example, A.P. **Elkin** on Newcastle, Clyde on the Riverina, Judd and Cable on Sydney, and Porter on Melbourne). David Hilliard has written a history of the Province of South Australia. Analyses of Anglican identity are rare, although the second secretary of General Synod, Bruce Kaye, wrote *A Church without Walls: Being Anglican in Australia* (1995), which owes much to the author's study of Richard Hooker, the seventeenth-century architect of Anglican polity, and to the recent studies on Anglicanism written by Sykes and J.E. Booty. Numerous biographies of evangelical Anglican clergy and missionaries have been written by Marcus Loane and Keith Cole. Loane has also written important studies on Archbishop Mowll and Moore Theological College. Specialised

histories have covered the involvement of the Church of England in the education debates of the nineteenth century, and of the relations between **church and state** (especially the histories of Ross Border, *Church and State in Australia*, 1962, and John Davies, *Australian Anglicans and Their Constitution*, 1993). The Anglo-Catholic tradition in Australia has been explored by John Moses, Brian Parker, Colin Holden, and David Hilliard. The extensive and always authoritative research of Ken Cable, the most learned historian of Australian Anglicanism, must be gleaned from his numerous articles and from his card file on Australian Anglican clergymen.

STUART PIGGIN

Anglo-Australian, in its early usage, referred to Australians of English birth or descent, or to things or organisations of English origin, loyalties, or sentiment. In the late nineteenth century the word identified a particular social set closely oriented to things and happenings of English interest; this type is perhaps best exemplified fictionally in the characters of Martin **Boyd's** Langton quartet. The term also applied to ex-colonists who had returned to London but maintained interests in Australia.

More broadly the term denotes the Australian Anglophile—or one with a strong attachment to things British, such as S.M. **Bruce**, Herbert **Brookes**, or Robert **Menzies**. This description, however, is generally a retrospective one; contemporaries described such persons as imperialists or members of the Round Table. (See also **British–Australian relations**.)

HD

Angry Penguins was a quarterly arts journal founded at the University of Adelaide in 1940 by poet Max Harris, the title taken from a line in his poem, 'Mithridatum of Despair'. It sought to provide space for Australian expressions of modernism, particularly surrealism, symbolism and expressionism, and attracted a group of radical writers, artists, and intellectuals—among them John Reed, Sidney **Nolan**, Albert Tucker, and Geoffrey **Dutton**, who together became known as the Angry Penguins. Reed joined Harris as co-editor, and production moved to Melbourne.

Two poets, James **McAuley** and Harold Stewart, invented an Australian poet named Ern Malley, and created a posthumous collection of his poetry, which they submitted to the journal. They claimed their motive was to determine through 'serious experiment' whether the moderns could detect its meaningless nature. Harris, unaware of the trickery, praised the poems and published them in the Autumn 1944 issue of *Angry Penguins*. The poems' exposure as a hoax—known as the 'Ern Malley Affair'—and Harris's conviction for publishing obscene material, humiliated Harris and the Angry Penguins. This sparked a long-running debate between conservative and avant-garde champions about the merits of modernism. Michael Heyward's *The Ern Malley Affair* (1993) discusses the journal, the hoax, and its aftermath.

HD

Ansett, Reginald Myles (1909–81) developed his extensive transport business from the modest beginnings of a car passenger service between Ballarat and Maryborough, Victoria. He entered the **aviation** industry in 1935 with a service from Melbourne to Hamilton, and by the late 1940s had established Ansett Transport Industries. His 1957 purchase of the Australian National Airlines (later Ansett Airlines) made him a major figure in the developing industry, as the only private owner in a national duopoly. Ansett was a staunch advocate of private enterprise, and encouraged Ansett Airlines to diversify widely into tourism, manufacturing and television. Tough with both his family and employees, he once dismissed air hostesses as 'a bunch of old boilers'.

KT

Anstey, Francis George 'Frank' (1865–1940) was the principal left-wing figure in the federal Labor caucus of the 1920s. He was born into a poor London family that moved frequently, allowing him little formal education. Anstey stowed away at the age of 11, jumped ship in Sydney and spent 10 years as a seaman. He eventually moved to Melbourne in the early 1890s. Anstey became a well-known advocate for labour and served as local member for East Bourke (later Brunswick) 1902–10, then moved into federal parliament as member for Bourke. During his time in East Bourke he became a mentor to John **Curtin**. Anstey represented the populist Labor tradition; he advocated public ownership, attacked bankers and financiers, and supported the creation of the Commonwealth Bank. His antagonism to financial monopolies, with its anti-Semitic overtones—apparent in his books, *The Kingdom of Shylock* (1915), and *Money Power* (1921)—is discussed by Peter Love in *Labour and the Money Power* (1984). Anstey wrote for the radical *Tocsin* and *Labor Call* and campaigned against **conscription** in the 1916 and 1917 referendums. His account of the Russian Revolution, *Red Europe* (1919), was written after a lengthy tour of Europe. Anstey became minister for health and repatriation in the **Scullin** government of 1929–31, until he was dropped for criticising the government's financial policies. His memoirs, edited by Peter Cook (*HS*, 1979), provide a trenchant account of this period. Anstey retired, disillusioned, in 1934.

KT

Antarctica and Australia were joined in the supercontinent **Gondwana** until 95 million years ago. They are thus geological cousins as well as neighbours, and this has encouraged Australia's close involvement with the frozen continent since the mid-nineteenth century. These natural and historical connections are frequently invoked to support Australia's bold claim to the Australian Antarctic Territory, which constitutes about 42 per cent of the continent.

In 1772–75 **Cook** circumnavigated the Antarctic region without sighting land, and surmised that any great land-mass veiled by the stormy Southern Ocean would be frozen and inhospitable. However, speculation about the possibility of another Terra Incognita in the southern hemisphere contin-

ued to fuel imperial curiosity. Australia was a staging-post for the next wave of Antarctic exploration. American, British, and French expeditions all sailed from Australian ports on their way to survey the Antarctic coast in the early 1840s. Alongside this well-documented imperial history lies a more shadowy past: the voyages of sealers and whalers from many nations, particularly to the sub-Antarctic islands.

During the 1880s politicians and members of Melbourne's learned societies, including von **Mueller** and Gavan **Duffy**, campaigned energetically but unsuccessfully for an Australian Antarctic expedition (Lynette Cole, *Proposals for the First Australian Antarctic Expedition*, 1990). At the time no-one had ever wintered on the continent, and very few landings had been made. Antarctic exploration promised Australians both intellectual and economic rewards, but most importantly it was a fresh field of imperial endeavour, and an opportunity for colonial science to prove its mettle. Antarctica was to be colonised by knowledge rather than settlement.

It was not until 1911 that an Australasian Antarctic Expedition was mounted, due largely to the forceful personality of its leader, Douglas **Mawson**. It was an ambitious undertaking costing over £40 000 (much of it state and Commonwealth funds). The overarching goal of the expedition was scientific investigation, and it was infused with Mawson's progressive values: the idealisation of scientific expertise; technological innovation; and utilitarian conservation. Frank **Hurley's** photography and Mawson's book failed to pay off the expedition's debts, but endure as evocative historical sources. Mawson's status as an icon of Australian character is currently undergoing a revival, stimulated by the republication in 1996 of his *The Home of the Blizzard* (1915). This popular enthusiasm for the heroic virtues of an individual explorer–scientist is in contrast to the current dominant paradigm of academic history, which stresses social and cultural interpretation, and downplays the role of the 'great individual'.

Mawson's most significant contribution to Antarctic political history was made on his lesser-known expeditions in 1929–31. These were state-sponsored for explicitly political aims, in the light of increasing international interest in Antarctic resources, especially by whaling nations and the USA. Oceanography, marine biology, and the mapping of the coastline were the major priorities, and it was during these voyages that Mawson proclaimed British possession of the continent and surrounding seas between 45 degrees and 160 degrees east. This proclamation was the basis for the gazetting and acceptance of the Australian Antarctic Territory in 1933.

In the period after World War II Australia's Antarctic endeavour was 'big science': highly centralised and controlled by government. Phillip **Law** was the dynamo behind the establishment of Australia's first permanent continental base in 1954. His administration of the Australian National Antarctic Research Expeditions (ANARE) between 1949 and 1966 was marked by a focus on logistics, management, and the development of a network of Antarctic bases.

Antarctica's contemporary political landscape was largely shaped in the late 1950s. Massive expeditions by the USA in the immediate postwar period were powerful demonstrations of military logistics and technology. Despite increasing Cold War tensions over the status of Antarctica, international scientific collaboration was promoted by the International Geophysical Year (1957–58). The Antarctic Treaty was drawn up in 1959 and came into effect in 1961. It set aside all territorial claims; promoted the reservation of the continent for peaceful, especially scientific, purposes; and prohibited military bases and nuclear activity.

Although Australia was a prominent founding signatory of the Antarctic Treaty, it continues to promote its territorial claim in Antarctica, and to use history as one of the prime justifications of that claim. In 1990 Australia and France defied the other treaty states by refusing to ratify a proposed Minerals Convention: Antarctica had became an international focus for wilderness preservation.

The ambiguous political status of the continent is echoed in the varying symbolic values it has carried for Australia: from colony's colony to rich whaling ground and, more recently, environmental *cause célèbre*. Antarctic politics and law have been extensively analysed: Peter Beck, *The International Politics of Antarctica* (1986), and Gillian Triggs, *International Law and Australian Sovereignty in Antarctica* (1986). Historical scholarship is weaker, and Robert Swan's *Australia in the Antarctic* is best supplemented with Stephen Murray-Smith's *Sitting on Penguins* (1988). Tim Bowden's commissioned history of ANARE is a significant contribution to the field.

BRIGID HAINS

Anti-transportation was a national protest movement directed against the **transportation** of convicts to Tasmania and its resumption in a new guise in the mainland. Tasmania received all Australian-bound convicts from 1840, when transportation to the mainland was abolished. From 1847 organised opposition to this huge influx began. On the mainland the opposition was to the British government's scheme of sending 'exiles', offenders supposedly reformed by imprisonment, who were to be free on arrival. The anti-transportationists refused to regard them as other than convicts. In 1848 and 1849 protests in Melbourne at the arrival of exiles led Superintendent **La Trobe** to divert ships to Geelong and Sydney. The arrival of one of these ships, the *Hashemy*, in Sydney occasioned a huge protest meeting. In 1851 the anti-transportation league in Launceston, Tasmania, coordinated an Australasian Anti-Transportation League which had support in Adelaide, Melbourne, Sydney, and Canterbury, NZ. The league adopted a **flag**, the Union Jack with the **Southern Cross**.

The movement drew up petitions to the queen and appointed agents to lobby in London. It saw itself as producing a moral regeneration, washing away the convict stain which had so damaged the reputation of the colonies and the colonists. Although it was resolutely loyal and lawful in its methods, its dignified protests indicated that the colonists were being pushed beyond endurance. The **Colonial Office** heeded the protests in 1852 and abandoned transportation to eastern Australia for good (it commenced to

WA in 1850). John **West**, who led the Launceston movement, made anti-transportation the glorious finale to his *History of Tasmania* (1852, 1971), an account which should be balanced by A.G.L. **Shaw**, *Convicts and the Colonies* (1966).

JH

Antiquarianism is an approach to the study of the past that values the collection and preservation of historical documents and objects for their antiquity alone, but has been criticised for its lack of interpretative analysis. German philosopher Friedrich Nietzsche argued in 1874 in *The Use and Abuse of History* that its application to the study of history ultimately led to uncritical nostalgia. J.A. **La Nauze** (in *HSANZ*, 1959) identified amateur historians as antiquarian, and professional historians as non-antiquarian, scholarly and superior. The collections of genealogists, local historical societies, and nineteenth-century museums were accordingly ignored by professional historians as being of little importance. Graeme Davison, however, noted the boom of heritage and nostalgia in Australia in the 1980s (*AHS*, 1988), and welcomed the rise of a new, more critical form of antiquarianism. Similarly, Tom Griffiths, in *Hunters and Collectors: The Antiquarian Imagination in Australia* (1996), has reassessed the role of amateurs in the making of Australian history, emphasising the significance of amateurs' collections and collecting to the development of popular understandings of the past.

HD

ANZAAS, see **Australian and New Zealand Association for the Advancement of Science**

Anzac was devised in 1915, reputedly by a New Zealand signaller, as a telegraphic code name for the Australian and New Zealand Army Corps, and adopted by General **Birdwood**. In April of that year he selected and named 'Anzac Cove' as the landing site on the **Gallipoli** Peninsula; the battle at Gallipoli subsequently became known as the Anzac campaign. The word quickly gained popular appeal. In 1916 the first anniversary of the Gallipoli landing was named **Anzac Day**, and war correspondent C.E.W. **Bean** entitled his collection of war anecdotes *The Anzac Book* (1916). *Anzac* soon came to mean any Australian or New Zealand soldier, regardless of whether he had fought at Gallipoli or not. As well as implying fortitude and bravery, the word signified a physical type—tall, bronzed, and fit. After the war it was used to describe an ex-soldier, but in **World War II**, when the forces of the two countries operated more independently, it was less common. The Anzac biscuit, using oats and golden syrup, was an improvement on the jaw-breaking wartime Anzac wafer issued by the army, and remains popular. The word is protected by law from commercial use. (See also **Anzac Legend**.)

HD

Anzac Day—25 April—is widely regarded as Australia's national day, yet like most commemorative occasions it has had a contested history. Within a few weeks of the landing at **Gallipoli** by members of the Australian and New Zealand

Army Corps (**Anzac**) on 25 April 1915, journalists, military publicists and the soldiers themselves were proclaiming the landing as an event of national significance, a 'baptism of fire' through which the soldiers of the two new nations had proved their military manhood. In 1916 Australian servicemen in France commemorated the event within their units, while in Australia there was a ground swell of support—linked to recruiting and actively promoted by the State War Councils—to mark the anniversary. The Anglican Canon Garland of the Queensland Anzac Day Commemoration Committee developed many of the practices that were adopted around the country, and on that first anniversary church services in the morning were followed by public meetings in the evening at which one minute of silence was observed. The state Commemorative Committees and the newly formed Returned Soldiers' and Sailors' Imperial League of Australia (see **Returned and Services League**) concurred that it was necessary 'to educate the people to strictly observe Anzac Day', and that schoolchildren in particular should appreciate 'the imperishable tradition' of the landing. Yet in the immediate postwar years there was a decline in public support for a celebratory national pageant; many of the bereaved preferred more personal forms of mourning or simple commemorative church services, and some veterans were wearied by the war and did not wish to remember or commemorate it.

A number of factors affected a transformation in attitude and practice by the end of the decade. From the mid-1920s there was widespread interest in 'spirit soldiers', as bereaved parents or wives sought to communicate with the war dead. The publication of soldiers' memoirs suggests that veterans now wanted—or needed—to articulate and derive positive meaning from their war experiences. Many ex-servicemen contrasted wartime comradeship with the social divisiveness and hardship of postwar civilian society, and relished a day of national esteem which also served to justify **repatriation** demands. The RSL, which had previously organised services and marches for returned men on Anzac Day, became more vociferous in its calls for public commemoration of 'the Diggers' day'.

There followed several years of intense argument about the form and meaning of Anzac Day commemoration. There was disagreement between ex-servicemen and the churches, and between Catholic and Protestant leaders, over the religious and secular content of the day. Organisations representing bereaved families wanted Anzac Day to be primarily a citizens' tribute to the dead, while ex-servicemen favoured a day which also promoted the needs of returned men. There was dissent about the extent to which the day should emphasise mourning or celebration, with organised labour in particular opposed to militaristic celebration of war. Employers and workers argued about whether or not 25 April should be a public industrial holiday, and about who should pay for loss of income and earnings; church leaders and women's temperance organisations wanted a day which would be 'closed' for public houses, gambling and horse-racing, and echoed the fears of public authorities about the intemperate dangers of carnival and the more **larrikin** features of the Digger reputation. The outcome of these debates and the particular forms

of Anzac Day varied from state to state, but by 1927 legislation which institutionalised 25 April as Australia's national public holiday had been passed in every state. Certain features gradually became standard practice in country towns and city centres throughout Australia: the Dawn Service, with a march by ex-servicemen and women, followed by a commemorative ceremony later in the morning; unit reunions are held in the afternoon and evening.

Participation at Anzac Day marches and ceremonies was boosted by the call to arms in World War II and a new cohort of veterans. However, by the 1960s Anzac Day was identified by some critics as a boozy veterans' reunion that had little relevance for other Australians. Alan **Seymour's** controversial play *The One Day of the Year* (1962), articulated and crystallised this concern. During the **Vietnam War**, Anzac Day came under attack from anti-war protesters, and afterwards from peace activists and feminists. Aboriginal activists argued that the event ignored the first Australians who had fought and died to defend their land against invasion.

Despite these setbacks and criticisms, there was an extraordinary resurgence of participation and interest in Anzac Day in the last quarter of the twentieth century. In part this was influenced by a more general blossoming of an Australian nationalism, guided by political leaders but rooted in popular cultural representations of Australian history and, more specifically, Australian **military history**. Key events—such as the 50th and 75th anniversaries of 1965 and 1990, and the 'Australia Remembers' campaign of 1995—were important catalysts for media and public attention, as were the declining numbers of 'original' Anzacs. Yet clearly Anzac Day is a successful national event because of its resonance for a wide variety of Australians. It has offered veterans a valued opportunity to remember dead friends and meet up with old mates, and a way to make positive sense of a troubling or painful experience. For many Australians who have lost friends and relatives in overseas wars, Anzac Day provides an occasion for personal remembrance and a public affirmation about the meaning and purpose of that loss.

Given the significance of Anzac Day, it is surprising that it does not have its own published history. Ken **Inglis** has written many influential articles about Anzac commemoration, now collected in John Lack (ed.), *Anzac Remembered* (1998). Marilyn Lake's chapter on 'The Power of Anzac' in Michael McKernan and Margaret Browne (eds), *Australia: Two Centuries of War and Peace* (1988), and Alistair Thomson's *Anzac Memories* (1994) explore the contested history and meanings of the event. For the history and significance of Anzac Day in NZ, see Jock Phillips et al. (eds), *The Great Adventure: New Zealand Soldiers Describe the First World War* (1988).

ALISTAIR THOMSON

Anzac Legend tells of the disastrous Allied landing at **Gallipoli** in 1915 and the role of Australian and NZ soldiers in the campaign on the Turkish peninsula between April 1915 and January 1916. It is a legend because it converted military defeat into moral victory. The outcome of the operation mattered not; of much greater significance was the conduct of those who tried to realise unattainable objectives. As with the British evacuation from Dunkirk in 1940, a moment of heroism was plucked out of an hour of disaster; that moment has been relived ever since.

The descriptions of the first landing, especially that of the English journalist Ellis Ashmead-Bartlett, were rapturously received in Australia. Australian soldiers had been put to the most severe test and had triumphantly survived. Australia as a nation had stepped onto the world stage. The sense of taking part in history was shared during the campaign itself by many of the men who landed at Gallipoli. Within a month of the landing, on **Empire Day**, the story of the great event in which they had taken part was already being told. The Australian war correspondent, C.E.W. **Bean**, collected stories from the soldiers and on the spot shaped them into *The Anzac Book* (1916). In 1916 Australian troops marked the first anniversary of the landing. Two years later, they did so in a way which deepened and reinforced the legend. On 24 April 1918, Australian troops at **Villers–Bretonneux**, about 10 kilometres from Amiens on the Somme front in France, stopped the German advance, their last major offensive of the war. There the tide turned, and the Anzacs had been there to turn it. **Anzac Day** in 1918 produced the decisive victory that had eluded Australian and NZ troops at Gallipoli three years before.

This triumphalism extended retrospectively to the original landing. True, the Turks had not been dislodged from the high ground above the beaches at Gallipoli in 1915. But the failure of the military operation as a whole, or of individual encounters in it, was—the legend held—not the responsibility of the Anzacs. To many of them, Gallipoli was a British disaster ennobled, if not effaced, by the dignity and pride of the men from Australia and NZ who had been there.

Success or failure on the field of battle, though, was not at the heart of the legend. Like other warrior legends, it organised tales about the past war in order to control comportment and galvanise action in the future. The men of Anzac thereby became iconic figures. They symbolised not only the strength of character of the men who took part in the landing, but also their living legacy. The way they lived and died presented a high ideal describing the way we should face life and death; most of us will never attain that ideal, but the fact that it is there is of lasting significance.

One such narrative, based on truth but embroidered with details highlighting the message, is the tale of **Simpson and his donkey**. This English-born stretcher bearer, killed on 18 May 1915, came to symbolise courage, individual initiative, sacrifice, tenderness. Who he was became what he had done. These were the bywords of the Anzac Legend, built up out of stories of tenacity, defiance, stoicism and suffering.

Legends surround family history, and the exploits of those who landed at Anzac Cove were recorded in family stories shared by the nation. An example is the case of Padre T.P. Bennett. He landed at Gallipoli on 2 September, and lived the life of a chaplain: arranging burial ceremonies, writing to families, holding services in the Anglican rites, visiting the men under shellfire and sniping. Sharing the hardships, he won the affection of the men. His commanding officer, Colonel Crouch, wrote a poem about him in October 1915. It was sent back to Bennett's home and

published in the local paper in Warrnambool, Victoria. Its simple verse was ideal for legend-making:

THE PADRE
Who is the friend of all the corps
From Melbourne pier to Anzac shore
And tries to serve us more and more!
The padre!

Eight more stanzas made the same heart-felt point, taken up by the family, shared by the town from which he came, a brick in the edifice of the Anzac Legend in the making. Bennett survived the evacuation from Gallipoli in December 1915, and continued to comfort the men and the families of those who had been killed. He knew they were half a world away, and gave them whatever information he had, as tragic as it was, about what had happened to their loved ones. 'War is about mothers searching for their sons amid that vast carnage', Bennett later told his son. 'They were persistent and terrible and tragic.'

The Anzac Legend did not demonise the Turks against whom Allied soldiers and sailors fought. On the contrary, hostility to Germany and the German soldiers remained much stronger than any lingering animosity to 'Johnny Turk'. The very name describes a modicum of respect; it even suggests affection of the kind reciprocated in the Turkish memorial on Anzac Avenue near the **Australian War Memorial**. The Turkish monument has an inscription based on the words of the Turkish officer commanding the defenders at Gallipoli. Mustafa Kemal, later known as Ataturk, asked the mothers of the men who had come from afar and who had died in Gallipoli to rest in the knowledge that their sons had been taken into the families of their former enemies, now friends and companions in remembrance.

The Anzac Legend is part of nation-building through story-telling. It is commemorated on Anzac Day and in **war memorials**. It is also a central part of family life and an element in the transmission of family memories. The narratives, both national and familial, dealt with sacred themes: loyalty, endurance, sacrifice, love, death, redemption through the lessons taken by the living from the lives of the dead. The story also helped families mourn, in suggesting some redemptive element in the sacrifice of so many lives in so distant a part of the world. These messages were configured in public ceremony and in private gatherings. In both, family history met History and fused the particular with the general.

So many stories of Anzac men circulated among families that they became part of the cultural landscape. Organisations dedicated to looking after the orphans of the war, like **Legacy**, were carriers of these memories. More informal gatherings did the same.

Later generations heard war stories of grandfathers and great-uncles among the Anzacs so frequently that it is not at all surprising that well into the 1980s and 1990s there was a broad readership for books, films, television programs and events surrounding the Anzacs. Visits to the Australian War Memorial and pilgrimages to war cemeteries in Europe and to Gallipoli itself expressed this multi-generational language of collective memory. In the late 1990s, there is little evidence that these carriers of the Anzac Legend, who live it out with their feet, are fading away.

Like most legends, the story of the Anzacs obscures as much about the war and its aftermath as it illuminates. In later years, working-class veterans told less ennobling tales about their war. Mateship was sacred, but not always extended to officers. Some were angry about postwar troubles, and how little help they got from the society they had ostensibly fought to defend and preserve. The individual memories of soldiers and their relationship to the Legend are explored in Alistair Thomson's *Anzac Memories* (1994).

The Anzac Legend has no place for women in it, and ignores Aborigines too. Whether or not it is a support for sexism or racism is debatable, but it is certainly a stylised history of white European masculinity *in extremis*. The pre-eminent historian of the legend is Ken **Inglis**. See 'The Australians at Gallipoli', *HS* (1970), and 'Men, Women and War Memorials: Anzac Australia', *Daedalus* (1987).

JAY WINTER

ANZUS Treaty is a regional defence agreement between Australia, NZ, and the USA. It was negotiated in 1951 in response to common fears of communist expansion in South-East Asia, and Australian and New Zealand disquiet over the terms of the peace treaty the USA had concluded with Japan. By means of the ANZUS treaty the Australian government sought to gain the protection of a powerful ally and ensure that it would form part of the US strategic orbit. Most historians of Australian foreign policy followed the account given by the minister for external affairs, Percy **Spender**, in *Exercises in Diplomacy* (1969), which suggests that Australia skilfully extracted the agreement from a reluctant USA; later revisionist interpretations suggest that the treaty served the Cold War global strategy of the USA. While the three signatories affirmed their desire 'to declare publicly and formally their sense of unity, so that no potential aggressor could be under the illusion that any one of them would stand alone in the Pacific area', the treaty did not bind the USA to unconditional military support of its allies and its ambiguities have never been put to the test. Despite the suspension of NZ from the treaty in 1986 over its opposition to visiting nuclear vessels, the Australian government demonstrated continuing attachment.

SM

Arabanoo, alias Manly (c.1761–89), the first Aboriginal hostage of the British at Port Jackson, resided at the governor's house and in an adjacent hut from December 1788 until his death in May 1789. Because the Eora people avoided the settlement, Governor **Phillip** decided it was necessary to train an intermediary to demonstrate 'the many advantages they would enjoy by mixing with us'. A group of Kuringgai-speakers at Manly Cove, clan territory of the Kayimai, was thus enticed to engage with the British seamen, who then seized two of their men. One escaped, but Arabanoo was secured by a rope around his neck, put in a boat, and imprisoned in a convict hut. On a harbour trip,

he made a desperate attempt to return to his people by jumping overboard fully clothed.

Historians' opinions reflect the ambivalence of contemporaries towards the captive. He has been portrayed, variously, as a cross between 'a saint and a regimental mascot' (M. Barnard Eldershaw, *Phillip of Australia*, 1939); an outsider shunned by his own people (Isabel McBryde, *Guests of the Governor*, 1989); and a proud man who refused to collaborate with the British and was unimpressed by their social organisation (Jan Kociumbas, *Possessions: The Oxford History of Australia, vol. 2*, 1992). Contemporary British commentators wondered whether his mastery of English was impeded by his ability or their poor tutoring. They compared him with the next captive, the extrovert **Bennelong**. According to Phillip, however, by March 1789, Arabanoo was 'perfectly satisfied with his situation' so he was released from all restraints. Captain Watkin **Tench** dubiously concluded that Arabanoo was consequently the 'only native' who 'attached to us from choice', and preferred the 'comforts of a civilized system' to a 'precarious subsistence among wilds and precipices'. In fact, Arabanoo was neither saint, resistance fighter, genius, nor converted imperialist, but in his attempts to negotiate two worlds he exhibited impressive adaptability and courage.

Arabanoo's initial reluctance to reveal his name earned him the alias Manly. His usual appearance was transformed by a close haircut, a shaved beard, scrubbed skin, and English clothing. He warmed to friendly treatment by his captors, enjoyed their gifts of fish, duck, and pork, but declined bread, salt meat, and liquor. He dined at a side table of the governor's, and sometimes at his table. He became a keen student of British etiquette and developed good relations with key figures among the ruling elite, especially Governor Phillip, whom he accompanied on boat trips. Despite his circumstances, his independence of mind enabled him to maintain a strong sense of dignity. If insulted, he retaliated swiftly and turned mockery against its instigator.

When an old Aboriginal man and his child were brought up to Sydney Cove in April 1789, both suffering from smallpox, Arabanoo tended them with dedication. Others soon arrived, but only two children survived. Arabanoo caught the disease and died within six days.

Arabanoo led Governor Phillip to reassess the debased 'savage' image imparted by earlier British visitors. In time, it was thought he would have been an effective 'conciliator' between the different peoples. Phillip attended his funeral and arranged for him to be buried in his private garden. As **Hunter** commented: 'Every person in the settlement was concerned for the loss of this man.'

ANN MCGRATH

Arbitration was a distinctive Australasian device for the resolution of industrial conflict and the regulation of employment. Created in the aftermath of the **strikes** and lockouts of the 1890s to contain **industrial relations** within a quasi-judicial framework, it both ameliorated and institutionalised class conflict. While frequently challenged, it proved a remarkably durable device for most of the twentieth century—one that shaped the political economy according to the national ethos of the **fair go**.

There were international precedents for applying the principle of conciliation and arbitration to industrial disputes, and some attempts to do so in Australia before 1890. Australia and NZ were unique in their adoption of a more rigorous system of compulsory arbitration by state tribunals with the power to compel participation and enforce determinations. The first such scheme was enacted in NZ in 1894, but followed a model devised by the South Australian premier, C.C. **Kingston**, in 1890. WA created its arbitration court in 1900, NSW in 1901, and the Commonwealth in 1904. Qld followed, while Victoria and Tasmania, and initially SA, opted for a system of **wages boards** of a less judicial character.

The genesis of arbitration is disputed. Unions, which were greatly weakened by the **Maritime Strike** and subsequent depression, generally supported its introduction. Employers generally opposed it. Hence the **Australian Labor Party** quickly included industrial arbitration on its federal platform, and made its establishment a condition of support in the early Commonwealth parliaments. Labor publicists, such as W.M. **Hughes** and W.G. **Spence**, hailed it as a vindication of the just entitlements of workers. But arbitration of interstate industrial disputes was included as a Commonwealth power as the result of the efforts of Kingston, H.B. **Higgins** and other middle-class liberal reformers, who sought to restore social harmony and avoid the damaging consequences of protracted industrial conflict. The origins and early impact of arbitration are discussed in Stuart Macintyre and Richard Mitchell (eds), *Foundations of Arbitration* (1989).

Higgins, who became the second president of the Commonwealth Arbitration Court, conceived his jurisdiction as 'a new province for law and order'. He was assisted in this by the Commonwealth's adoption of the **new protection**, whereby local employers received tariff advantages provided they paid their employees a 'fair and reasonable wage'. Higgins's determination of this wage in the Harvester Case of 1907 led eventually to a national system of wage regulation. By means of court registration of unions and employer associations, and the issue of common awards across whole industries, the initial purpose of dispute settlement broadened into a comprehensive regulation of employment conditions. The process was resisted by employers, who successfully appealed to the High Court to restrict the ambit of Higgins's court, and by militant workers, who chafed against its dampening effect on direct action. The **Engineers' case** of 1921 removed the first obstacle, and the success of **trade union** officials in using arbitration to entrench their organisational authority overcame the second.

By the 1920s, then, the overwhelming majority of Australian workers were covered by federal and state awards, which prescribed their wages, hours, and conditions of employment according to an amalgam of ethical and economic principles. Unions sometimes challenged adverse awards and defied the prohibition of strikes, and the **Bruce**–Page government strengthened the Commonwealth

court's penal powers against such action. The principal challenge came at the end of the decade, when the Bruce–Page government determined to withdraw from industrial arbitration (except in the maritime industry) as part of its endeavour to reduce wage levels. The decisive defeat of the government on this issue in the national election of 1929 demonstrated public support for arbitration. Union support was shaken by the Commonwealth Arbitration Court's 10 per cent reduction of the basic wage in 1931 and subsequent reluctance to restore the cut, but typically even the most militant unions used their increased bargaining power as the economy recovered later in the decade to secure new awards.

The dual role of the Commonwealth Court of Conciliation and Arbitration as a dispute-settling tribunal and a regulator of wages strained its independence. The government shaped its activities through appointments to the court and frequent amendments to its procedures. At the end of World War II the **Chifley** government used the court to delay wage increases and reduction of hours, and in 1953 the court ceased its practice of making automatic quarterly adjustments to the basic wage. Stronger unions responded by demanding higher margins for skill and above-award payments, which strained the court's authority. In response to a 1955 High Court decision that the court could not combine arbitral and judicial functions, an Industrial Court was separated from the Conciliation and Arbitration Commission, but the emphasis on legalism and precedent did not diminish. Through the efforts of the ACTU industrial advocate, R.J. **Hawke**, the unions made major gains in national wage cases during the 1960s and early 1970s.

Arbitration came under challenge during the 1980s with the deregulation of the economy and the dismantling of the arrangements that had allowed public agencies to prescribe wages and conditions of work. The challenge was led by the Business Council and promoted by the H.R. Nicholls Society, formed in 1986 by New Right critics of the 'industrial relations club'. While the Hawke government resisted the calls to deregulate the labour market, it undermined the authority of the Conciliation and Arbitration Commission by expecting it to give effect to wage agreements worked out with union representatives under the **Accord**. Subsequently the federal Labor government replaced that tribunal with a new Industrial Relations Commission, and allowed for enterprise agreements to be struck in conjunction with industry-wide awards.

The **Howard** government went further in its encouragement of enterprise agreements and individual employment contracts in preference to awards, which it confined to a much narrower range of conditions. Employers and employees were encouraged to bargain directly, and more disputes ended in the courts. Conservative state governments assisted the diminution of arbitration by abandoning or circumscribing their own tribunals. If the opening decades of the twentieth century saw the spread of arbitration and wage fixation to cover the great majority of Australian wage-earners, the last decade witnessed a substantial retreat.

Archaeology

Arbitration has generated a very large body of commentary spanning economic history, labour and business history, industrial relations, and labour law. The report of the Committee of Review of Australian Industrial Relations, chaired by Keith Hancock (1985), provides a substantial defence of its efficacy. A full history of its rise and fall, supporters and opponents, remains to be written.

STUART MACINTYRE

Archaeology studies the material remains of human actions. It encompasses a wide range of past material culture, from discarded food scraps to shipwrecks, architecture, and jettisoned technology. Its time depth is constrained only by the limits of hominid history itself. Documentary historians are comfortable with some of this evidence—Mayan inscriptions or tombstones are, at one level at least, merely specialised documents—and they happily embrace landscape studies which might elucidate battle strategies or pinpoint the specific locations of historical sites such as the first Government House in Sydney or the **Eureka Stockade** in Ballarat. The work of amateur historians in the nineteenth century was commonly pursued alongside that of natural historians, a relationship examined by Tom Griffiths, *Hunters and Collectors* (1996). During the twentieth century, however, the academic discipline of history severed those connections, and the discipline of archaeology developed later and at a remove from it.

Some historians continued to use archaeological evidence—J.L. O'Brien's analysis of domestic architecture in Melbourne and Keith **Hancock's** discovery of the Monaro landscape are two among many. Equally, the discordance of Aboriginal histories which commonly dismiss the first 99.5 per cent of Aboriginal settlement in a brief prologue in favour of the documented last 200 years, has occasionally been balanced by books such as Geoffrey **Blainey's** *Triumph of the Nomads* (1975); Blainey drew particularly on the archaeological work of John **Mulvaney**.

The reluctance of historians to embrace archaeological evidence reflects in equal part the concerted shift of archaeology in the second half of this century towards a plethora of scientific techniques, where archaeologists work increasingly in partnership with a range of natural and pure scientists to produce histories which are frequently narrow in scope, often arcane in subject matter, and commonly too technically complex for the non-specialist historian to do anything other than to take the conclusions at face value. An obvious example of this is the use of various radiometric dating techniques to identify when the first Aboriginal settlers arrived in Australia. The most common of these techniques, radiocarbon dating, applied across the islands of Tasmania, Australia, and New Guinea (which formed a single continent up until about 10 000 years ago), suggests that people first arrived in this continent about 40 000 years ago. An alternative radiometric technique, luminescence dating, now suggests an arrival date of at least 60 000 years ago, with some claims more than double this. Deciding among these competing claims involves complicated archaeological and scientific debates, which raise methodological considerations of peripheral interest to historians seeking facts from archaeological data.

Since the 1950s this schism—one foot on the historical shore, the other on the departing archaeological science vessel—has been a source of continued debate among archaeologists. In Australia some have continued to provide a seamless narrative, from the Aborigines who lived through the last Ice Age, some 20 000 years ago, to those described by nineteenth-century explorers; others, increasingly in recent times, have emphasised that the data available to us from the deep past allow us only to construct knowledge of past human behaviours of an archaeological rather than historical or anthropological kind: 'the reconstruction of a historical or social picture of prehistoric cultures, written in historical narrative, is a valid but incidental and dangerous aspect of archaeology', proclaimed the British archaeologist Graeme Clarke in 1969.

Notwithstanding the theoretical and methodological debates, prehistoric archaeology in Australia has made significant contributions to community awareness of Aboriginal history during the last 30 years. In that time the known antiquity of Aboriginal settlement has quadrupled, even on the most conservative estimates; views that initial colonising events were rare and accidental have been tempered by the accumulating body of data from Australia, New Guinea, and island South-East Asia. We now have a clearer understanding of the achievement of settling a previously empty continent and the adaptations made to new landscapes and their flora and fauna—these were people who arrived as tropical coastal dwellers, but by c.30 000 years ago had occupied environments as diverse as the central deserts and the periglacial uplands of Tasmania. We have new views on the technological skills of these original colonisers, and the great antiquity of their art, personal adornment, and spirituality reflected in burial practices.

Closer associations have occurred between historians and historical archaeologists—those who study the material remains of European settlement in Australia—although at nowhere near the levels which early proponents of this area of archaeology might have hoped. In Australia and elsewhere historical archaeology has suffered a crisis of identity; whether it qualifies as a legitimate academic discipline remains uncertain. After an initial flurry of projects in this field in the 1960s, academic archaeology departments were generally slow to adopt historical archaeology, which lacked any strong theoretical basis or clear claims to the generation of new historical knowledge. Historical archaeology continued as a minor component in some academic departments, seen mainly as a supplement to documentary history. Its major manifestation remained, during the 1970s and 1980s, within the developing cultural heritage industry. Current interest in historical archaeology in universities appears to be increasing and, with the diversification of subjects now studied by documentary historians, opportunities for cross-disciplinary research should increase. Subjects such as colonisation, migration, mining, convictism, and the development of pastoralism and agriculture all seem to provide opportunities for specialist investigations using archaeological techniques and approaches.

With several important exceptions, marine archaeology (mainly underwater **shipwrecks**) in Australia has mirrored the experience of historical archaeology, with research in this area being mainly the prerogative of cultural heritage development and management. In WA, some decades of quality research on Dutch and British wrecks has provided a good intellectual basis for the development of this subject elsewhere, such as James Cook University in Townsville, whose underwater archaeologists are currently collaborating with the Queensland Museum on the excavation of HMS *Pandora*, which sank in Torres Strait in 1791. Shipwrecks provide important time capsules for archaeology: in the Australian context, for example, they allow detailed study of well-preserved samples of goods being imported into and exported from the colonial settlements, as well as direct data for **maritime history**. Other unexpected opportunities also arise: in the case of the *Pandora*, along with the normal shipboard materials recovered has been an extensive collection of rare Polynesian artefacts, made all the more valuable by the *terminus ante quem* provided by the date of the shipwreck.

General coverage of Australian archaeology is given in Josephine Flood, *Archaeology of the Dreamtime* (1983, 1995), and Harry Lourandos, *Continent of Hunter-Gatherers* (1977).

JIM ALLEN

Archer, William Henry (1825–1909) established official statistics in Victoria and was the founder of Fabianism in Australia. He trained in London as an actuary before migrating to Melbourne in 1852, and in the following year took charge of the new system of compulsory civil registration of births, deaths, and marriages. As assistant registrar-general, Archer supervised the production of both annual and retrospective series of data, while in his privately published *Facts and Figures* he popularised statistics as 'a store of useful information, and an affirmation of the multitudinous benefits of progress'. He followed overseas developments closely and fostered greater uniformity in statistical practice in the Australian colonies. Archer's career in the Victorian civil service was handicapped by his prominence as a Catholic layman, and he was a victim of premier Berry's mass dismissal on **Black Wednesday** in 1878. Subsequent business ventures and a parliamentary candidature were unsuccessful. Sale of property allowed him to pursue scientific and linguistic studies, painting, and sculpture. In *Australia's First Fabians* (1993), Race Mathews observes that Archer was emblematic of the improving, idealistic, anxious class of administrators who created the Fabian Society, which he joined in 1890. Margot Beever's MA thesis at the University of Melbourne (1971) explores his public career and intellectual interests.

SM

Archibald, Jules François (1856–1919) journalist, was a co-founder, long-time editor, and part-owner of the *Bulletin* magazine. He gave the paper its distinctive racy style; he discovered and nurtured its most talented writers;

and he articulated, though he did not invent, its distinctive brand of **radical nationalism**.

The son of a country policeman, Archibald grew up in Warrnambool, Victoria, where he was apprenticed in the printery of the local paper and conceived an ambition to be a journalist. He subsequently worked on newspapers in Melbourne. Living on the fringes of Melbourne bohemia, he absorbed a love of French literature and exchanged his baptismal name, John Feltham, for the more exotic Jules François. In 1878, after losing a job in the Victorian civic service, he travelled in Qld, working for a time as a miner on the Palmer River goldfields—his only personal experience of frontier life.

He drifted back to Sydney where, in partnership with John Haynes and William McLeod, he founded a new weekly paper, the *Bulletin*. The first issue, which appeared in January 1880, carried Archibald's impassioned account of the hanging of the Wantabadgery bushrangers. No sooner was the paper launched, however, than it ran into trouble. An action for libel was brought against the paper for its exposé of the lewd shenanigans of St Patrick's Day revellers at Clontarf. In the upshot Archibald and his colleagues were imprisoned for debt, but W.H. Traill, the author of the offending piece, emerged as the dominant partner in the paper. In 1883 Archibald's health broke down and he travelled to London, hoping perhaps to make his fortune on Fleet Street. He failed, but continued to supply the *Bulletin* with articles reflecting his intense engagement with London society and his admiration of the 'new journalism'. He returned to Australia in 1885 on the same vessel as Tom **Roberts**. Traill sold out in 1886 and, for the next 20 years—the peak of its influence—the *Bulletin* was Archibald's paper.

In 1885 he married Rosa Frankenstein, who had followed him out from London. The marriage was unhappy and childless; and he had little other life, private or public, outside the *Bulletin*. Because he followed his own principle of journalistic anonymity, it is hard to isolate his contribution from those of his lieutenants, especially A.G. **Stephens** and James Edmond, and the paper's manager, William McLeod. The paper's distinctive brand of iconoclastic, racist, republican nationalism chimed with elements of his personality, but the paper was not simply a mouthpiece for his own views. Sylvia Lawson's *The Archibald Paradox* (1983) probes the paradoxical nature of his influence: 'the working of editorial magic in which, necessarily, the magician disappeared in smoke'. He was a talented, and ruthless, sub-editor. 'The pencil, when blue, is mightier and more cruel than the sword', he declared.

The *Bulletin* was his crown and his cross; restless apart from it, its demands gradually wore him down and in 1902, exhausted and depressed, he handed it over to Edmond. Even then he could not rest and was soon at work on a new venture, a monthly magazine named the *Lone Hand*. (The name, which recalls the solitary prospector of his mining days, had been Archibald's suggested title for the *Bulletin*.) Before the first issue appeared, his mental equilibrium gave way and, at the instigation of McLeod and with the consent of his wife, he was certified and consigned to Callan Park Asylum where he remained, intermittently, until 1910. His reminiscences of the 'The Genesis of the Bulletin', which appeared in the first issue of the *Lone Hand* in 1907, were composed from notes written in Callan Park.

He made a complete recovery, but in 1914 sold his interest in the *Bulletin*. His will, made in 1916, included two famous and characteristic bequests—a public fountain to be designed by a French sculptor, and a prize for Australian portraiture; but the largest share of his £90 000 fortune was devoted to the 'relief of distressed Australian journalists'.

GRAEME DAVISON

Archibald Prize, funded by a legacy left by J.F. **Archibald** and valued at $10 000, is Australia's most prestigious prize for portraiture and has been awarded annually by the Art Gallery of New South Wales since 1921. Archibald's prescriptive conditions for the prize—that it be a portrait in oil or watercolour, 'preferably of some man or woman distinguished in Arts, Letters, Science, or Politics'—have often made it contentious. William Dobell's winning portrait of Joshua Smith in 1943 sparked controversy between traditionalists and modernists. Two entrants unsuccessfully took court action against the judges' decision, arguing that the prize had been awarded to a caricature and not, as specified, to a portrait. Multiple winners of the Archibald include John **Longstaff**, William Dargie, Clifton Pugh, and Brett Whiteley.

HD

Architectural history in Australia began, not with the formal studies of academic historians, but with contemporary evaluations of the traditions at the disposal of local architects. In his contemporary review *Sydney in 1848*, the artist Joseph Fowles argued that Sydney had an architectural culture comparable with buildings in London and the great provincial cities of England and Scotland, a claim later repeated by Alexander **Sutherland** for Melbourne in the 1880s. In the wake of Fowles, Australia's historical and critical imagination fed offshore on the *Ecclesiologist*, the British *Builder*, and other European and American sources.

Critical writing in the new building journals of the 1880s infused these broad historical overviews with national sentiment, Gothic Revivalism, and influences from the Arts and Crafts movement. John **Sulman**, 'An Australian Style' in *Australasian Builder* (1887), and E. Wilson Dobbs, *Rise and Growth of Australasian Architecture* (1891), addressed the value of earlier Australian architecture, particularly of the convict era, scrutinised recent tendencies, and urged a distinctively Australian architecture. They saw **national identity** reflecting natural maturity in culture and sought to identify authentic traditions and genres. They established a model for decades of later architectural history and criticism.

By 1900 the influence of the Gothic Revival and critics such as Ruskin was declining, but the values of the Arts and Crafts movement still dominated criticism. An international tendency toward classical and Renaissance forms in larger buildings was accepted tacitly in architectural debate, and many architects reacted against earlier, highly personal

criticism by John Horbury Hunt and his contemporaries by avoiding debate and speculation. This critical silence preserved Australia's 1890s historiography in amber. Old Colonial architecture remained the focus of exploration. James Barnet, Frank Walker, and others proclaimed **Greenway** the leading Colonial architect, and George Sydney Jones linked early Colonial design to a visibly twentieth-century, flat-roofed, open-planned architecture. Hardy **Wilson** argued that Colonial Georgian was a touchstone of Australian architecture, and he struggled to revive its forms and link it to Asian architecture in an aesthetic and spiritual unity. By 1925 designs of Greenway, John Verge, Edmund Blackett, William **Wardell**, and Horbury Hunt were being set for measured drawings in the technical schools and university ateliers. All were discussed in John Sulman's general history for the *Australian Cyclopaedia* (1929), and John D. Moore reworked this coverage for the London *Architectural Review* in 1949.

Australians in the 1930s conceived modern architecture as an extension of valid Colonial Georgian principles. Raymond McGrath, *Twentieth Century Houses* (1934), a British text which influenced Australian architects, argued that international Modern architecture was a rebirth of Georgian and Empire taste and of values in Western culture generally. George Beiers's *Houses of Australia: A Survey of Domestic Architecture* (1948) amplified this view. Robin **Boyd** gradually abandoned his youthful architectural socialism to define modern architecture around values of good taste, visual order, and cultural maturity. His caricatures of Victorian and **Federation architecture** echo earlier attacks by his novelist uncle, Martin (1923). He followed Sulman's vision of Australian architectural history as a Georgian Eden succeeded by a mechanical sequence of stylistic decline, but forecast a new era as Modern architecture combined distinctiveness and maturity, and brought Australia and international modernism into harmony.

In *Victorian Modern* (1947), *Australia's Home* (1952), and *The Australian Ugliness* (1960), Boyd popularised 1890s arguments on evolution and national maturity and introduced new protagonists such as Harry Seidler, Roy Grounds, and Walter Burley **Griffin**. He developed two of Hardy Wilson's ideas: that the house was the crucial arena of architectural history in Australia, and that suburbia, pictured in beguiling sketches and vignettes, was the realm of inertia. Boyd awed Australian architects with written sound and fury, and is still gospel for many after half a century. J.M. **Freeland's** *Architecture in Australia* (1968) applied similar views to a general history of Australian public and domestic architecture. He covered more ground but was more partisan than Boyd, privileging, above all, a pure, resolved architecture—buildings beyond the strivings of historical debate and contention.

Freeland's views came under criticism (Boyd's were largely immune) and most architectural history appearing in Australia took Boyd–Freeland constructs as a starting point. Morton Herman's research, independent of Boyd's, concentrated scholarly attention on *The Early Australian Architects and Their Work* (1954), delineating the Colonial Eden with detailed documentation. Philip Cox and Clive Lucas in *Australian Colonial Architecture* (1978) traversed the same territory, though with more tolerance towards the Regency, and particularly John Verge. Though maintaining the progressive degeneration arguments of Freeland, Boyd, and their predecessors on the later nineteenth century, these younger architects had a clearer sense of Old Colonial's ideological loading. Their analysis of overseas sources was more detailed and specific, and they explored, even if they did not resolve, the spectre of provincialism as a characteristic in Australian Colonial culture. Boyd had seen provincialism as one of the banes of Australian architecture. James Broadbent's *The Golden Decade*, with Clive Lucas (1978), and *The Australian Colonial House* (1997) gave provincialism a new centrality as a defining, if still somewhat negative, characteristic of Australian architecture. A distant metropolis was increasingly assumed in Australia's architectural histories, both as a source and a yardstick of transgressions. But was this metropolis necessarily as cohesive (or as British) as Australian architect–historians seemed to see it?

Biography provided an ideal framework for an interpretation in which a few heroic individuals struggled against conservative opponents and Australian apathy. Promising studies of Walter Burley Griffin by James Birrell (1964) and Donald Johnson (1977) dwelt more on Griffin's perceived tribulations than on his architecture. Their subject emerges as an oddly correct exemplar of overseas practice, distinctive only in being American rather than British. Joern Utzon and the **Sydney Opera House** yield similarly frustrating stories, in which Utzon's architecture, and his neglected urbanism, are buried under a welter of tall-poppy lamentations, neither refutable nor provable. Retrospectives by and about Harry Seidler claim for their hero a mantle of metropolitan authenticity (Europe via the USA and Brazil) and reassert the dynamic of architect–visionary fighting a cultural reaction and inertia found, apparently, only in suburban Australia. In these accounts Europe and USA become utopias of uninterrupted and universally accepted classicism, refinement, modernism, and maturity. They mostly omit architectural comparisons with such disreputable, but once potent, influences as Third Reich reactions, Beaux-arts classicism, British dislike of the foreign, and Italian critical insecurity, and they pass over any career difficulties their heroes had in Europe or the USA. The Griffin biographies never mention that Wright and Sullivan were on skid row in America, and that the Chicago and Prairie Schools had collapsed.

This view presented Australia's architectural future as either a *mature* immersion in resolved overseas forms or a complete renunciation of foreign inheritance. The logical outcome of the latter was the critical ascendancy of Glenn Murcutt, who combined an endearing use of untutored-looking materials, a detailed rethink of homestead pavilion and verandah, and architectural allusions to Hardy Wilson, Aboriginal bark shelters, tents, supposedly guileless machine forms, and the long houses of New Guinea and the Malay–Indonesian tradition. As subject and springboard Murcutt has dominated Philip Drew's viewpoint on Australian architecture and general culture since the publication of Drew's *Leaves of Iron* (1985). Murcutt is seen overseas as what the metropolis wants Australian architecture to be.

Ideologically, he is at the centre of Australia's historical mainstream. Jennifer Taylor's account of broad directions in Sydney, *An Australian Identity* (1972), and her more general *Australian Architecture Since 1960* (1986, 1995) maintain the tradition of viewing the house as the arena of change, particularly in her development of Boyd's observations on the Sydney School as a coherent and innovative movement. But she notes its difficulties in shifting to any urban level and adopts a more pluralistic approach to stylistic influences.

Meanwhile, there has been a rise in history that challenges the dominant narrative of Australian architecture. The **heritage** movement stimulated a new appreciation of styles previously regarded as barren, and fostered the emergence of a new generation of architect–historians with a strong interest in conservation, such as David Saunders, George Tibbits, and Miles Lewis, and of humanities-trained historians, such as Joan and James Kerr. Lewis's *Victorian Primitive* (1977) and *Victorian Churches* (1989) prompted a more open-minded scrutiny of Victorian architecture and a challenge to the moral and pedagogical primacy of the Colonial Georgian and Regency. Bernard **Smith** (in his critique of Freeland in *HS*, 1969), and *The Architectural Character of Glebe, Sydney* (1973) led a historical revaluation of the Federation period. Peter Cuffley, another non-architect, examined the 'forbidden' realm of average suburban architecture in his volumes on Australian houses of the 1920s and 1930s (1991), and the 1940s and 1950s (1993). Social historians have largely made the running in charting the postwar vernacular, as for example in Graeme Davison et al. (eds), *The Cream Brick Frontier* (1995). The planning historian Robert Freestone reinterpreted the Australian influence of the Garden City in *Model Communities* (1989). The Griffin retrospectives of 1988, where Marion Mahony's role was reassessed by Australians, exhibited some of the newer directions of Australian architectural history represented in the work of Philip Goad, Conrad Hamann, Harriet Edquist, Winsome Callister, and Peter and Helen Proudfoot. The range of work emerging through heritage practice and legislation now forces architects to face historical issues from all periods in Australian design and hence, increasingly, to revise the now-besieged standard histories of Australian architecture.

CONRAD HAMANN

Architecture in Australia was shaped through an interaction between imported, especially European and American, styles and traditions, and local influences, including landscape, climate, materials, and national ideals.

The first European settlers found only bark shelters in Aboriginal communities, although permanent stone structures have been discovered more recently in western Victoria. Unable to work stone or brick, convict workmen resorted to local materials and vernacular building techniques, such as sticks and clay (wattle and daub), rushes, thatch, and split hardwood slabs. These, and other basic materials such as adobe or pisé (rammed earth), persisted in vernacular building into the early twentieth century, when buildings in the Victorian Mallee were still being built from tree roots. By the 1790s, though, brick and stone were being used more frequently. Soldiers and their families adapted the encircling verandas of India and the West Indies to Australian houses such as Elizabeth Farm (1794) and to public buildings such as Sydney's Old Mint and Rum Hospital (1809). Climate modified this style: Queensland houses rose off the ground on stumps to escape termites, and shrouded the verandahs in gossamer screens, while Victoria's homesteads shed the encircling verandas for double gables and return verandahs that let more sun in.

A more self-conscious **profession** of architecture emerged only gradually, initially through the influence of army engineers, such as George Barney, and speculative builders such as Francis **Greenway** and John Verge, some of whom, such as James Blackburn, James Barnet and William **Wardell**, also had some civil engineering or surveying experience. Articled training became more common in the later nineteenth century, often in the large new government architects' offices, whose prominence and influence was distinctive in Australia till the 1980s, when free-market ideology closed them. Technical colleges (from 1890) and the universities (from 1920) offered more formal training, combining studio and formal courses in a form still largely current.

Greenway, Verge, William Archer and other early architects were essentially Regency in outlook and formal usage, though Greenway was tied by limited building resources to a bare-bricked, simplified combination of forms that came to be seen as an Australian counterpart of English Georgian. All gravitated to the contemporary English interest in Greek temple fronts, the picturesque, and the romantic use of mediaeval forms. Verge was the most elegant and cautious of them; others were cruder in their detail but more original. In Tasmania Blackburn went the furthest, introducing the first conspicuously Renaissance revival bank (1844), the first Gothic church (1840) and the first houses in the round-arched Italian manner.

These three elements—Renaissance, Gothic, and Italianate—became the basis of the Victorian style characteristic of the colonies' burgeoning towns and cities after 1850. Traditionally these styles have been seen as mutually exclusive but recent research argues that they shared common compositional and urbanistic concerns. Victorian architecture was distinguished by the fusion of diverse components and types (arcades, towers, return verandas, indented or sculpted facades) and an eclectic mixture of Gothic, mixed Renaissance, antique and even Baroque references. Britain's Gothic Revivalists were inspired by a romantic and ethical mission to revive a truly Christian architecture. Three of its most intense practitioners, Augustus Pugin, John Pearson, and William Butterfield, left works here, but their local disciples, such as Edmund Blacket and William Wardell, though similarly skilled, were willing to work in non-Gothic modes when required. They were engaged in a forward-looking mission to construct cities which would have ethics, visual richness and urban sensitivity. The real exception was Horbury **Hunt**, whose vigorous churches and cathedrals in NSW, informed by the sculpture and colour of High Victorian Gothic, took a more individual course.

Hunt's design prefigured the new mixture of imagery, ethics and regional expression now known collectively as Federation. Its hallmarks were a turning away from symmetrical facades, a search for natural and direct expression in form and planning, and an emphasis on distinctive Australian identity. Similar movements arose in Europe and USA, but the combination of verandahs, hipped roofing, and expressed movement—most fully developed in detached houses with a strong visual relationship to the street, such as those of Beverley Ussher and Alfred Dunn—gave Australian Federation its distinctiveness and strength. The Federation 'agreement' lasted till c. 1914, but cooled visibly after 1900 and gradually split into distinct movements. These included a more specific revival by Hardy **Wilson** and others of early Colonial architecture as the basis for an authentically Australian architecture, and a more conscious Mediterranean emphasis exhibited, for example, in the design by Rodney Alsop and Conrad Sayce of the new University of Western Australia.

American cultural influence was already pronounced in Australian architecture long before World War II. Department stores, cinemas, factories and service stations all took cues from American sources, although they were usually grafted onto earlier styles. The 'Californian Bungalow' was a condensed Federation house, differing only in its servantless scale and the adoption of a contained frontality. 'Spanish Mission' was as much a populist version of the Mediterranean mode as a stylistic import. Art Deco, however, was used more specifically here, as an extension of structural emphasis rather than as the ornamental surfacing that it provided in France or the US. Tall buildings, particularly those with asymmetrically placed corner towers, recognised the grid pattern of Australian cities in a way that their symmetrically stacked US counterparts did not.

The same individuality marked Australia's reception of more experimental forms of modernism. Several architects in the late Federation period had developed open-planned, sometimes flat-roofed, houses and institutional buildings stripped of most ornament; these drew out a range of arts and crafts movement and Federation ideas. The **Griffins'** synthesis of modern materials and engineering technique was similarly based in nineteenth-century struggles to find a place for nature in city forms. The **Canberra** plan of 1912 and their Capitol Cinema of 1921–24 were variations on this theme, fusing urbanism and nature in a single unfolding fabric of rock crystal forms. The Functional architecture of the early 1930s onward was less an emulation of Walter Gropius or Le Corbusier than a broad fusion of American, British, Scandinavian, Finnish, Dutch, and German expressionist influences. These were put together on Australian terms by a range of architects, from the heroic hospitals of Arthur Stephenson through to the complex pluralism of Frederick Romberg's apartment buildings. Harry Seidler's breathtaking refinement of detail and visual purism, when it appeared after World War II, was aided by a new interpretation of modern architecture as belonging to 'modern masters' and their inheritance. By this time though, the 'accomplished form' was paramount and earlier links with urbanism and regional reference were under challenge.

Seidler had to struggle with this problem as much as anyone, and in large-scale building a long period of streamlined corporate productivism prevailed before the emergence of a new monumentalist concern, seen first in buildings such as Joern Utzon's **Sydney Opera House** of 1956–73 and the sinew of Melbourne's Olympic Pool of 1955–56. It hit with full force in Canberra's monumental program in the 1970s: Aldo Giurgola's Parliament House, Colin Madigan's High Court and Gallery, and John Andrews's Cameron offices and college buildings. They all affirmed 'Australia' in vast and pugilistic concrete. Where this monumental push went from there was less certain. The activism on which Australia's architectural modernism was predicated never focused for long on the possibility of a new social order. Taste, not social criticism, remained the rallying cry. Australia's everyday suburbs were cast as villains, despoiled by exploitation, vulgarity, and speculative building. Yet the typical postwar suburban house, reviled constantly in architectural circles, was actually an extension of the hipped-roof Colonial Revival houses of Hardy Wilson and his pursuit of good taste.

It can be seen in middle-class houses of the early 1930s and became part of the building mainstream in A.V. **Jennings's** Victorian exhibition estates.

An alternative to both the suburbs and the lost cities came from a regionalist modern architecture first expressed in Roy Grounds's and Harry Rembert's houses and public buildings of the 1930s and 1940s. Referring to the tradition of the homestead and celebrating the play of an Australian light and texture, this work guided a series of successors, from Alastair Knox in the late 1940s through to architects connected with the Sydney School in the period 1956–64, and some Melbourne architects of the 1970s. Since 1980 Glenn Murcutt and some of his contemporaries have continued to reaffirm the focus of Australian cultural authenticity in the bush or the Australian landscape. The difficulty was to adapt this view to the demands of the predominantly urban or suburban lives of the great majority of Australians. Murcutt and Melbourne architects such as Graeme Gunn or Peter Crone were unobtrusively skilful at working outside the pastoral idyll, but the initiative here has been connected principally with Maggie Edmond and Peter Corrigan, and their pursuit of an Australian urbanism that is both critical of prevailing Australia and yet based visually in the grain of Australian urban circumstance. This has ranged from houses through churches and small public buildings up to major work for universities and colleges. It recalls the comprehensiveness of Federation architecture, and has stimulated rich and varied work by younger Australian architects since.

CONRAD HAMANN

Archives are collections of records of public and private organisations that provide an indispensable resource for research into Australian history. While the maintenance of records has long been a function of government and administration, the origins of modern archives are usually attrib-

uted to a French revolutionary decree of 1794, which opened the records to public scrutiny as part of the attack on privilege and the affirmation of public accountability. Similarly, the origins of history as a scientific discipline are associated with systematic archival research practices that developed in the first half of the nineteenth century. Professional archivists thus developed a dual function, acting both as functionaries in a bureaucratic process of records management and as auxiliaries of the historical profession among the user groups in the preservation and organisation of source materials.

Many of the records created by colonial administration of the Australian colonies found their way to London and thence to the British Public Record Office. Some were subsequently transcribed by Australian researchers such as James **Bonwick** and J.F. Watson, and published in the *Historical Records of Australia* and other such works. The **Australian Joint Copying Project** continued and extended this work in microform. Phyllis Mander-Jones's guide to *Manuscripts in the British Isles Relating to Australia, New Zealand and the Pacific* (1972) is supplemented by the handbooks of the project.

Most local public records were held and abandoned by agencies of the colonial governments as part of the administrative process. A small portion were collected by state **libraries** from the late nineteenth century as part of their manuscript collections. Some state libraries created separate archives departments in the first half of the twentieth century, and some acquired custodial powers. It was not until 1920 that the first autonomous state archives was created, in SA, at the instigation of G.C. **Henderson**, who as professor of history at the University of Adelaide had emphasised the scholarly and imperial significance of archives. NSW and Victoria did not create their state public record offices until well after World War II, and the century ended with all state and territory governments having established archives, though the ACT's arrangements are minimal and lack statutory backing.

The realisation of a national archives was also protracted. When Ernest **Scott** and G.A. **Wood** reviewed the *Historical Records of Australia* in 1926, they recommended the creation of a Commonwealth archives, but a 1927 bill lapsed. Until 1942 the Commonwealth Parliamentary Library was the archival repository for a limited range of Commonwealth records. In that year John **Curtin** appointed a War Archives Committee to determine procedures for the preservation of war records. The **Australian War Memorial** became the archival authority for all Commonwealth records concerned with defence, and the Commonwealth National Library (as it then was) assumed responsibility for all other records with the appointment in 1944 of an Archives Officer. Upon the constitution of the National Library of Australia in 1961, the Commonwealth Archives Office was established as an autonomous authority and in 1974 reconstituted as the Australian Archives. This history is explored in Sue McKemmish and Michael Piggott (eds), *The Records Continuum* (1994).

The Australian Archives (renamed the National Archives of Australia in 1998) is based in Canberra and has regional offices in all the state capitals and in Darwin. The Archives Act of 1983 empowers it to prevent destruction of records, and operates in conjunction with the Freedom of Information Act to provide a statutory right of access to Commonwealth records, except for those that are exempted by a process of classification. Most records over 30 years old are thus available, though the restrictions imposed by the reluctance of security organisations to allow access remain contentious. Changes in public administration have weakened the quality of government records, resource constraints strain the custodial capacity of the National Archives, and the shift from paper to electronic records presents its custodians with sharp challenges. Archives are governed by provenance and function, rather than subject, and their use requires an understanding of changing administrative structures. Computerised finding aids allow a search of National Archives records in any of its offices; although they currently list only a fraction of the entire holdings, there are plans to extend them and the National Archives has produced a number of subject guides (see<http://www.naa.gov.au>).

The Australian War Memorial remains the principal repository of Australian military records, and under the creative leadership of its deputy director, Michael McKernan, fostered the revival of military history during the 1980s. His history of the memorial, *Here Is Their Spirit* (1991) covers its archival activities. The National Film and Sound Archives (now Screen Sound Australia) was created in 1984 from the holdings of the National Library. The Australian Institute of Aboriginal and Torres Strait Islander Studies has stimulated research into Aboriginal history.

A large number of non-government organisations—businesses, churches, schools, universities—maintain their own archives with varying conditions of access. The archives of **BHP**, Westpac, the **Catholic** and **Anglican** Churches, and the **Australian Broadcasting Corporation** are noteworthy. Other such organisations deposit their records in the National Library, state libraries or university archives. The records of the federal **Australian Labor Party** and **Liberal Party** are in the National Library of Australia. The Noel Butlin Archives Centre at the Australian National University contains the records of the **ACTU**, many national unions, pastoral companies, and various other bodies. The University of Melbourne Archives contains the records of major banks and mining companies, the Victorian branches of most trade unions, and assorted radical movements. A number of regionally based universities, particularly in NSW, also operate collecting archives. Most of these have published guides to their collections, and some provide entries on holdings to the on-line *Register of Australian Archives and Manuscripts*.

Many company records were gathered, deposited and preserved on the initiative of the Business Archives Council, which flourished in the 1960s and 1970s. During the 1980s and 1990s the Australian Science and Technology Heritage Centre at the University of Melbourne performed a similar role for scientists and scientific organisations.

The archives profession emerged among public servants, librarians and historians. Training now occurs through courses in librarianship and information management, and the Australian Society of Archivists maintains a lively forum on practical and conceptual issues through conferences and its journal, *Archives and Manuscripts*. Its manual, *Keeping Archives* (1987, 1993), offers insight into archival practices. The contribution of historians to such discussion has declined. They were influential in laying the foundations of archives, and still serve on governing and advisory bodies. They are frequent users and infrequent teachers of archivally based undergraduate subjects. Their failure to engage more closely in debate on funding for archives such as the Noel Butlin Archives centre and archival issues at a time when modern managers are so careless of institutional memory is unfortunate.

STUART MACINTYRE

Argus, named after a mythological Greek creature with 100 eyes, was a Melbourne **newspaper** founded by William Kerr in 1846. Kerr, who had previously worked on J.P. **Fawkner's** *Advertiser*, sold out to Edward Wilson and J.S. Johnston in 1848, but remained editor. From June 1849 the paper appeared daily, and a weekend supplement, the *Australasian*, appeared from 1864. In the 1850s the *Argus* generally set a democratic, liberal, and reformist position. It advocated separation and anti-transportation, vilified Governor **La Trobe**, and coined the cry, 'Unlock the Lands!', but was equivocal in its treatment of **Eureka** (*HSANZ*, 1954) and expressed anti-labour views. George **Higinbotham** served as editor 1856–59. Higinbotham's support of full manhood suffrage in 1856 prompted a series of letters to the editor from Wilson, the proprietor, who questioned the rapid pace of reform. The *Herald* provided some competition, but overwhelmingly the *Argus* outsold its rivals combined. William Howitt described it in 1855 as 'the *Times* of the colony'.

From the 1860s the paper became aligned with the conservatives in Victorian politics, and it was overtaken in circulation and influence by the *Age* long before the end of the century. After World War II it changed to a tabloid and was acquired by a British press chain. It ceased publication in 1957. There is a published index for the years 1846–59, 1860–69, and 1910–49; the compilation of an index for the other years is a continuing project.

HD

Art history in Australia is essentially a twentieth-century invention. In the nineteenth century statements about the history of Australian art were limited and sporadic. Their tone was generally anticipatory rather than retrospective. John Lhotsky's summary of the visual arts in his *Australia, in its Historical Evolution* (1839) is typical; while admitting the youth of Australian culture, Lhotsky measured the rapid advancement of taste by the quality of imported artworks. Lhotsky mentioned several artists at work in the colonies but dismissed most of their works, concluding, regretfully, that 'Australian sky and nature awaits, and merits real artists to portray it'.

In September 1888 the leading Melbourne art critic James Smith attempted to sum up the brief history of art in Victoria

(*Argus*, 11 September 1888). He dated the beginning of art in the colony to the 1850s. Smith anticipated a number of the enduring ideas in Australian art history, namely that the early colonists were too preoccupied with survival and making money to have time or interest in the visual arts; that Australia's early artists were 'natives of Europe who brought the technical methods, the traditions, the manner of looking at nature and the experience they acquired there'; and that landscape is the genre in which Australian art will find its greatest and most distinctive expression.

In 1906 the Melbourne journalist William Moore included in his *Studio Sketches* a 'plain unvarnished account' of 'The Beginning of Art in Victoria'. Moore's interest in the history of Australian art led him to collect a large and invaluable body of data which he published as the first thorough study of Australian art history—his two-volume *Story of Australian Art* (1934). Moore's book was avowedly written as an interesting story, and he rarely interrupted the mix of biography and anecdote to examine a work of art in detail. Its value lies in the information which he obtained not only from his contemporaries but also from their nineteenth-century predecessors. He drew, for example, on the compilation of colonial artists' biographies made by the bibliophile and collector Sir William Dixson, which were published between 1919 and 1923 in *JRAHS*.

Moore's pioneering study, and much of the writing in the journal *Art in Australia* (1916–42), established the view that the key date in the foundation of an 'Australian school' of painting was the return to Australia of Tom **Roberts** in 1885 and the subsequent formation of the **Heidelberg School**. This has been the most pervasive and least challenged notion in Australian art history. When Bernard **Smith** wrote *Place, Taste and Tradition* (1945), he too stated that the Heidelberg painters 'were the first to achieve valid artistic solutions to the difficulties presented by the Australian landscape'. Smith's *Australian Painting* (1962) continued to treat 1885 as a seminal date—Chapter 4 of the book is entitled 'Genesis 1885–1914'. The importance and the enduring public regard for the Heidelberg School was confirmed in 1985 with the National Gallery of Victoria's immensely popular exhibition, *Golden Summers*.

Place, Taste and Tradition, a robust and vigorous account on Marxist principles, can justly be considered to be the first attempt to write a history of Australian art from a historical, rather than a narrative or anecdotal, position. Smith's thesis was that Australian art can best be understood as the modification of a European tradition by local forces. The book established Bernard Smith as Australia's foremost art historian, a position which was strengthened by the appearance of *European Vision and the South Pacific* (1960) and *Australian Painting* (1962). Both these books sought to show how the art of this region interacted with a broader European cultural ideology. In his introduction to the latter volume, Smith stated that 'while it may be said that Australian art is a European art flourishing in the South East Asian world … the physical environment of the country and, later, the social character and composition of a new

nation have influenced the course which art has taken in Australia'.

A great deal of art history since the publication of *Australian Painting* has accepted the basic shape Smith gave to the story of art in Australia. Robert **Hughes's** *The Art of Australia* (1970) did not offer a strikingly different cast of characters than those with which Smith had peopled his art historical drama; however Hughes did tell the story with an engaging, often highly amusing tone, as he did in his series of 10 films made for television, *Landscape with Figures* (1975).

The orthodoxy of Smith's *Australian Painting* remained unassailed until the late 1970s, when a greater awareness of the complexities of Australian colonial art began to show that it was possible to see Australian nineteenth-century art in a new light. Academic study of Australian art was a late development. The first Australian chair of fine art had been endowed by Keith **Murdoch** at the University of Melbourne in 1937, but another 30 years passed before the Power Institute of Fine Arts was established, again through private patronage, at the University of Sydney. Much knowledge of Australian art resided in dealer galleries, art museums and exhibitions, rather than books or academic discourse. Two of the most significant art dealers, Joseph Brown in Melbourne and Frank McDonald in Sydney, both researched, unearthed and promoted under-appreciated colonial art. State art galleries in Sydney, Melbourne and Hobart, and later Adelaide and the National Gallery of Australia, began to purchase the works of colonial artists with newly rehabilitated reputations. From the late 1960s Daniel Thomas, curator of Australian art at the Art Gallery of New South Wales, began experiments with historically appropriate 'Salon' style displays at that institution; later at the National Gallery of Australia he attempted to show through all-inclusive displays that the history of Australian art should not be seen simply as a history of painting, but as a history including the decorative arts, drawings, prints, photographs, and design. Most art museums in Australia subsequently embraced the inclusive display philosophy.

In his catalogue essay for the exhibition *Australian Art in the 1870s* (Art Gallery of New South Wales, 1976), Thomas argued that 'Australian art before the 1880s has not received the attention it deserves'. In the last 25 years that neglect has been repaired with several monographs on colonial artists and, more importantly, original and stimulating research on Australian colonial art. Areas of art history subjected to renewed scrutiny include landscape painting in Tim Bonyhady's *Images in Opposition* (1985); patronage in *The Artist and the Patron* (1988); and the role of women artists in various works by Joan Kerr. Kerr's monumental *Dictionary of Australian Artists … to 1870* (1992), while not a history, does justify its claim to have expanded the view of the richness of Australian colonial art by highlighting the variety of colonial art forms, many of them the preserve of amateur and dilettante.

In twentieth-century art history there has likewise been an explosion of publishing over the last two decades. Much of this has concentrated on the periods between the world wars and immediately after World War II. The most influential and original works have included Humphrey **McQueen's** *The Black Swan of Trespass* (1979); Richard Haese's study of 1940s art, *Rebels and Precursors* (1981); Mary Eagle's *Australian Modern Painting* (1990); and Christopher Heathcote's *A Quiet Revolution* (1995), a study of Melbourne art 1946–68 which takes issue with Bernard Smith's version on a number of counts. Ian Burn's study of the elsewhere denigrated post-Heidelberg landscape tradition, *National Life and Landscape* (1990), is best understood in the context of the overall project of this artist/art historian to understand Australian modernism, stimulatingly elucidated in his book of essays *Dialogue: Writings in Art History* (1991).

The most interesting questions in the 1980s and 1990s emerged from the study of **Aboriginal art**. While Aboriginal art has long been interpreted from anthropological and ethnographic viewpoints, traditional techniques of art historical inquiry have, until recently, been used infrequently. Many of the questions raised in the catalogue of the exhibition *Dreamings: The Art of Aboriginal Australia* (1988) and in Howard Morphy's thematically organised *Aboriginal Art* (1998) bear directly on the question of an art history of Aboriginal art. In *Aboriginal Artists of the Nineteenth Century* (1994), Andrew Sayers attempted to look at artists using art historical methods, as had various writers on the history of the watercolour painters of Central Australia and on the painters of the Western Desert. The crucial role of art in historical and contemporary politics is a major theme of *The Oxford Companion to Aboriginal Art and Culture* (2000) and the subject of several essays included there.

ANDREW SAYERS

Arthur, George

Arthur, George (1784–1854), lieutenant-governor of **Van Diemen's Land** from 1824 to 1836, was an efficient, hard-working army officer and a zealous Evangelical. Under his control, the colony developed from a small, haphazard settlement plagued by **bushrangers** to a prosperous, well-ordered community, but the governor was condemned then and since for his autocratic rule.

He eradicated bushrangers and brought order to the convicts. Believing that reform was possible and that convicts' fates should be determined by their actions, he set up grades of servitude, from virtually free ticket-of-leave holders, through those assigned to work for settlers, to those in government work and, for repeat offenders, **penal settlements**. Good behaviour led to ascent through the grades; bad behaviour, descent. Arthur established a model penal settlement at **Port Arthur**, trained young convicts in trades, and appointed police magistrates throughout the island so convicts were all under direct supervision. Arthur's system was criticised as harsh, but for its time it was fair and humane; it ran competently and often did result in reformation. His Black Books, which recorded the career of every convict, still survive—a wonderful resource for historians.

As European settlement spread, clashes with the Aborigines developed into the **Black War**. Arthur sympathised with both Aborigines and Europeans, and determined to move the Aborigines to a separate settlement. After the expensive Black Line failed, G.A. **Robinson** brought in the remaining 200 Aborigines, who were settled on Flinders Island.

Arthur had virtually sole power; he was advised by only a nominated Legislative Council. Despite his organisational skills, criticism of him grew. Difficulty with incompetent and corrupt subordinate officials resulted in dismissals and resentment, and to promotion of his two efficient nephews, which led to claims of nepotism. He was unsympathetic to calls for trial by jury and for a representative assembly, and tried to stifle the press. Local landowners resented his police magistrates taking some of their influence. His inflexible manner was disliked and he was criticised for corruption, though apparently he made his large fortune honestly. The anti-Arthur press flourished, but others praised his competent rule and the 'wholesome tone and moral restraint' he bestowed. John **West** concluded that he was entitled to more than respectful remembrance, a verdict with which biographers agreed: M.C.I. Levy, *Governor George Arthur: A Colonial Benevolent Despot* (1953), and A.G.L. **Shaw**, *Sir George Arthur, Bart, 1784–1854* (1980). However, some local works portrayed him as autocratic, and W.D. Forsyth in *Governor Arthur's Convict System* (1935) was also critical. The British government showed its approval of Arthur's rule by making him lieutenant-governor of Upper Canada, then governor of the Presidency of Bombay.

ALISON ALEXANDER

Ash Wednesday, 16 February 1983 (named because the day fell on Ash Wednesday of the Christian calendar), was the worst day of bushfires in Victoria and SA since **Black Friday**, 1939. The fires were exacerbated by extreme temperatures and drought. Among the worst-affected areas were Aireys Inlet, Anglesea, Cockatoo, Mount Macedon, Upper Beaconsfield, Belgrave, and Warburton in Victoria, and the Adelaide Hills and Clare Valley in SA. A total of 71 lives were lost, 2300 houses destroyed, and 350 000 hectares of land burned. Valuable artistic property of musician Percy Jones and opera singer Joan Hammond was also lost. (See also **Disasters**.)

HD

Ashes, the name of the Australia–England **cricket** Test series, derives from a notice placed in the London *Sporting Times* on 2 September 1882 after England's first defeat on home soil in the ninth Test against Australia: 'In Affectionate Remembrance of English Cricket Which Died at the Oval on 29th August, 1882. Deeply lamented by a large circle of sorrowing friends and acquaintances. R.I.P. N.B.—The body will be cremated and the ashes taken to Australia'. During the subsequent 1882–83 Test series in Australia, the captain of the winning English eleven, the Hon. Ivo Bligh, declared his mission was to recover the Ashes for England. A group of Melbourne women reputedly presented him with a wooden urn containing the ashes of the bails or stump, which has since been kept at Lord's Cricket Ground. Australia–England Test series have subsequently been played for 'The Ashes of Cricket'. While there is some controversy about where the

Ashes were first presented, the prevailing view is that it was at a match held at W.J.T. **Clarke's** Rupertswood property, near Sunbury, Victoria. A commemorative match was held at Rupertswood in 1995.

HD

ASIO, see **Australian Security Intelligence Organisation**

Askin, Robert (Robin William) (1909–81) was an influential Liberal politician, and premier of NSW from 1965 until his retirement in 1975. He became member for Collaroy in 1950; by 1959 he was Liberal Party leader. Six years later he ousted a Labor government through cultivation of its traditional supporters. The association of the Askin government with corruption and organised crime is documented by Geoffrey Reading, *High Climbers: Askin and Others* (1989), and David Hickie, *The Prince and the Premier* (1985). A shrewd and tough politician, Askin vigorously defended states' rights, and is best remembered for his reported comment that police should 'Run over the bastards', when the car of the visiting US President, Lyndon B. Johnson, was held up in the street by anti-Vietnam War protesters. Robin became Robert in 1971 and, a year later, he was knighted.

KT

Assassinations have been remarkably uncommon in Australia. Few in public office have been deliberately killed. Perhaps the only clear assassination was the fatal shooting of John Newman, the state Labor member for Cabramatta, NSW, in 1994. Less certain is the mysterious disappearance in 1977 of NSW Liberal politician and anti-drug campaigner, Donald MacKay. Others to have died violently in public office include Justice David Opas of the Family Court in 1980; the Turkish Consul-General, Sarik Ariyak, and his bodyguard, Engin Sever, in 1980; and the Greek Consul-General, Constantine Giannaris, in 1981.

Attempted assassinations are more common. Catholic priest Father Geoghegan was shot at in the street in 1846, and later claimed that three attempts had been made on his life. Henry O'Farrell caused a sensation in 1868 when he shot at and injured the visiting Duke of Edinburgh in 1868. He was subsequently arrested and sentenced to death. His brother Peter O'Farrell shot at the archbishop of Melbourne, J.A. Goold, in 1882. The editor of the Melbourne *Age* was shot at by an angry former colleague in the 1880s, but also survived.

Targets of suspected assassins in the twentieth century include the federal leader of the Australian Labor Party, Arthur **Calwell**, in 1966 (Peter Kocan, his assailant, was later sentenced to life imprisonment), and Prince Charles, who was fired at with a starting gun in 1994 by a student activist who was attempting to raise public awareness of Cambodian detainees in Australia. A letter bomb addressed to the Queensland premier in 1975 injured two office staff. The infrequency of assassination in Australia suggests a relative lack of intensity of political and religious feeling, and probably stems more from the existence of other avenues of debate, and the effects of a

parliamentary rather than presidential system of government, than from the ineptitude of would-be assassins.

HD

Assignment system was the allocation of **convicts** to private employers. It was begun by the officers of the **New South Wales Corps**, who controlled the colony after Governor **Phillip's** departure. They took convicts from government farms and assigned them to their own. At first the convicts were still fed and clothed at public expense, but the British government objected to this and insisted that masters maintain their convict servants. The amount of food and clothing to be supplied was set by regulation, and convicts had the right to complain to the magistrates if the ration was not provided. The standard convict punishment of flogging could be imposed only by the magistrate. The government retained the right to withdraw convicts from masters who ill-treated them. Assignment greatly reduced the cost of the convict system, but the British critics of transportation objected to punishment and reformation being left to private masters whose chief concern was their own profit. The 1838 Molesworth committee condemned assignment as slavery and the government moved quickly to abolish it. **Transportation** continued to Tasmania, with the convicts being kept in the government's hands (see **probation system**), and worked in gangs under paid overseers. This produced its own abuses, and British officials soon wished they had not so precipitately abandoned assignment.

JH

Assimilation has been the aim of government policy towards Aborigines for much of the nineteenth and twentieth centuries, and was the declared objective from the 1950s until the 1970s. The term itself was taken from **immigration** policy, and attests to the common logic of a population policy shaped in turn by notions of race, ethnicity, and culture.

While the early colonial period was marked by dispossession and repression, there were both official and philanthropic efforts to convert the Aborigines to Christianity, to reconstitute their way of life and draw them into the European economy. The failure of these assimilationist endeavours brought recourse to **Aboriginal protection**, so that in the second half of the nineteenth century reserves separated Aborigines from the outside world, in the belief that they were incapable of adapting to it and in anticipation of their imminent demise. In practice many Aborigines remained outside the reserves, or moved between them and more autonomous arrangements. In response, the colonial and state governments drew a sharper distinction between the Aborigines on the reserves, and those typically of mixed descent who were removed from the reserves and expected to be absorbed into Australian society. That policy, first adopted in Victoria in 1886 and followed elsewhere by 1912, was racially discriminatory, but differed from other countries' treatment of indigenous people in its narrow definition of racial authenticity.

In 1937 a meeting of federal and state representatives declared that the destiny of the mixed-race population was to be absorbed into the white population. It led after World War II to the goal of assimilation, defined at another federal and state gathering in 1951 in the statement that 'all persons of Aboriginal blood or mixed blood in Australia will live like white Australians do'. In the course of its adoption, assimilation shifted from a genetic to a cultural policy. In 1937 it was still thought that 'full-bloods' were dying out, so that the only foreseeable future for half-castes was to intermarry with the white population; by 1951 the emphasis was on training all indigenous Australians to adopt the Australian way of life. Assimilation was served both by the removal of discriminatory laws and the intensification of discriminatory practices designed to break down separate Aboriginal identity; its most tragic aspect was the forcible removal of the **Stolen Generations** of Aboriginal children from their parents. As cultural identity became more important, the contradictions of the policy became intolerable and it was replaced by self-determination. It is not easy to fix the date of its abandonment. A speech by Prime Minister William **McMahon** in 1971 signalled it was no longer government policy, but not all public servants noticed the change. Only after Gordon Bryant became minister for Aboriginal affairs in the **Whitlam** government, at the end of 1972, did the Commonwealth finally relinquish its assimilation objective.

Assimilation was also an objective of immigration policy, especially after World War II. The discouragement of difference softened in the 1960s to the more liberal objective of integration, which in turn yielded in the 1970s to **multiculturalism**.

SM

Astley, William ('Price Warung')

Astley, William ('Price Warung') (1855–1911) achieved popular recognition for his grim stories about convict days, which appeared frequently in the *Bulletin* of the early 1890s, and were published in book form as *Tales of the Convict System* in 1892. Astley came to Australia from England as a young child and grew up in Melbourne. He claimed that his interest in convicts was aroused in his youth by meeting a man who had served as medical officer in penal stations during the 1840s. This led to a long study of information about the convict times, using a wide range of sources—written, oral, and physical—during his 15-year stint as an itinerant journalist. Astley's insistence that his stories, set in centres of secondary punishment, were 'essentially historical' was accepted by both contemporary and many later commentators. Barry Andrews examines Astley's working methods in a preface to the reprint of *Tales of the Convict System* (1975), which he edited, and his biographical study, *Price Warung (William Astley)* (1976). The depiction of the convicts as the 'scapegoats of English society', brutalised by gaolers and an oppressive system, reinforced the nationalist, anti-imperialist mood of the late 1880s and early 1890s. Astley left the *Bulletin* in 1893 to become editor of the *Australian Workman*; in 1896 he was organising secretary of the Bathurst People's Federal Convention and later helped

to publicise the 'yes' campaign at the federal referendum. Ill-health and drug addiction marked the rest of his life.

KT

Astronomy is the scientific study of the universe, its contents and phenomena. Aborigines were keen observers of the sun, moon, and stars, and knowledge of the heavens was an important part of their spiritual beliefs. Astronomy was vital to eighteenth- and nineteenth-century European navigation, and the charting of eastern Australia by James **Cook** in 1770 was incidental to an astronomical expedition to observe the transit of Venus at Tahiti. Early Australian observatories were established at Dawes Point, NSW (1788), Parramatta, NSW (1821), and Williamstown, Victoria (1853). The Great Melbourne Telescope, built by Thomas Grubb of Dublin, was the largest in the world from 1868 to 1908. In the late nineteenth century, southern-hemisphere astronomy was pioneered by John Tebbutt, Francis Abbott, James Oddie, Walter Gale, and other amateurs. Tebbutt discovered the great comets of 1861 and 1881, and was commemorated on the first Australian $100 note in 1984. Modern Australian astronomy rose from Canberra's Mount Stromlo Observatory (1910) to its zenith in the Anglo-Australian Telescope at Siding Spring, NSW (1974), which in 1978 made the first optical recording of a neutron star and in 1987 observed the eruption of SN1987A, the first supernova visible to the naked eye since 1604. Radio astronomy, in which Australia is an international leader, was pioneered by the **CSIRO** through the Parkes radiotelescope (1961), Mills Cross radiotelescope (1965), Culgoora radioheliograph (1967), and Australia Telescope (1990) in western NSW. Australian radio astronomers assisted Apollo moon missions and were first to identify the existence of radio galaxies, and numerous pulsars and quasars. A comprehensive, non-technical history is Raymond Haynes et al., *Explorers of the Southern Sky* (1996).

DC

Atomic testing was undertaken in Australia between 1952 and 1963 by the British government. The Australian government readily supplied test sites and logistical support, in the mistaken expectation that greater access to nuclear technology would result. Twelve full-scale nuclear devices were exploded in Australia at three sites: the Monte Bello Islands, off the north-western Australian coast (1952, 1956), Emu Field, SA (1953), and **Maralinga**, SA (1956–58), with radioactively dirty 'minor' trials continuing at Maralinga until 1963.

Opposition to the testing program grew throughout the 1950s with increased awareness of the dangers of radioactive fallout. Fears of atomic pollution heightened in the 1970s, when the French began atmospheric testing of nuclear weapons in the Pacific. Lingering concern over health effects led eventually to the establishment of a royal commission into the British tests in 1984. The commission examined safety precautions, and the 'black mist' that had reportedly engulfed Aboriginal communities. It also questioned the role of Australian scientific observers, particularly the physicist

Ernest Titterton. After a long political and legal struggle, the clean-up proceeded and the land was returned to its owners, but some parts will never be safe for long-term occupation. Robert Milliken's *No Conceivable Injury* (1986) provides a readable account of the royal commission and its background, while Lorna Arnold's official history of the tests, *A Very Special Relationship* (1987), plays down the health effects.

TIM SHERRATT

ATSIC, see **Aboriginal and Torres Strait Islander organisations**

Aussie is a colloquial diminutive that emerged during World War I to describe Australia (the country) or an Australian person, the latter implying a native-born, non-Aboriginal Australian. Prefixes such as *true blue*, *dinki-di*, and *dinkum* further emphasised this characterisation. In wartime, *Aussie* was used affectionately to describe a happy-go-lucky, non-complaining, stoic Australian character. Australian soldiers in France began publishing a magazine of the same name in 1918, and this was subsequently produced in Sydney until 1931. The popular song, 'Is he an Aussie is he?', further popularised the term in the 1940s.

In the 1960s and 1970s, however, *Aussie* became an increasingly pejorative term, which alluded to a lack of sophistication and even crudity as depicted, for example, in the ocker humour of Barry 'Bazza' McKenzie and Paul Hogan. An element of self-promotion and pride in this plainly vulgar Australian—albeit parodied—was evident in *Oz* magazine, founded in Sydney in 1963, then published in London 1966–73. Following large-scale European immigration to Australia in the years following World War II, *Aussie* was used to differentiate between 'old' Australians and the new arrivals and their children.

HD

Austerica is a word coined by the architect Robin **Boyd** in *The Australian Ugliness* (1960) to signify the slavish imitation by Australians in the period after World War II of American styles, especially the cheapest and nastiest forms of mass-production. Deriving the word from an amalgam of *Australian* and *American*, Boyd also meant it to carry echoes of *austerity*, or cheapness, and *hysterical*, suggesting the manic enthusiasm of its adherents. 'Austerica's chief industry', Boyd wrote, 'is the imitation of the froth on the top of the American soda-fountain drink. Its religion is glamour and its devotees are psychologically displaced persons who picture heaven as the pool terrace of a Las Vegas hotel.' Boyd himself was not anti-American—he had recently visited the USA, where he developed an admiration for the work of American architects, including Walter Gropius, with whom he kept up a friendly correspondence. His ire was reserved for the exaggerated and superficial aspects of American style, such as neon-lit motels, drive-ins, cars with fins, and stove-pipe trousers. The word *Austerica* enjoyed a brief vogue, mainly among the readers of *Meanjin*, *Nation*, and other intellectuals of the left, who overlooked Boyd's patrician superiority, and

widened the word's application to include Australian tutelage to American economic imperialism and foreign policy. In 1967 Geoffrey **Serle**, later Boyd's biographer, conjured up the frightening prospect of 'Austerica Unlimited'. But the word never really caught on—perhaps because people knew when they were being patronised, and because there were too many reasons to like the new American-derived consumer products to be fussy about their style or origin.

GD

Austin, Albert Gordon (1918–90), **educational historian**, was born in Melbourne, and educated at Coburg and Melbourne High Schools, Melbourne Teachers' College and the University of Melbourne. He served in the AIF at Tobruk, Alamein, Lae and Finschhafen, being awarded a Military Cross at the first battle of Alamein in 1942. Having taught with distinction in high schools, Austin was appointed in 1956 as lecturer and in 1966 as professor and dean of the Faculty of Education, University of Melbourne. He retired in 1978, partly because of illness contracted during war service.

Austin's first book, *George William Rusden and National Education in Australia 1849–1862* (1958), is still the best study of this neglected figure. *Australian Education 1788–1900* (1961) established Austin as the leading historian of Australian education. Austin's analysis of the evolution of public schooling and relations of **church and state** displayed rigorous scholarship (often lacking in previous writings on educational history), urbanity, stylistic elegance, a national perspective and, at a time when the state aid debate was bitter, detachment. His *Select Documents in Australian Education* (1963) made available some of the scattered sources he had used.

Administrative demands and ill-health restricted Austin's research opportunities. Nevertheless he scrupulously edited *The Webbs' Australian Diary 1898* (1965), wrote the lively school text, *The Australian School* (1966), and, with R.J.W. Selleck, produced *The Australian Government School 1830–1914* (1975). Margaret **Sutherland** set his poem, 'Tobruk', to music (c. 1969).

R.J.W. SELLECK

Australasia, literally 'southern Asia', is a geographic term first used by French explorers in the mid-seventeenth century. Although occasionally used in the nineteenth century to include the south-eastern lands of Asia, and more often including New Guinea, NZ and other surrounding islands, the term 'Australasia' was also used to refer solely to the Australian continent. This latter meaning was intended by W.C. **Wentworth** in a poem entitled 'Australasia', which he submitted, unsuccessfully, for the chancellor's gold medal at Cambridge in 1823. 'Australasia' gained popularity in the late nineteenth and early twentieth centuries as a term that principally embraced Australia and NZ—but declined thereafter. Its use survives in the names of various organisations, including trade unions. The term's linking of NZ with Australia, which suggested that the two countries shared common interests and a common destiny, was endured unhappily by New Zealanders, who saw the term as a threat to their separate identity. By the mid-twentieth century, 'Australasia' encompassed a wider territory that included the Asian continent, but this use has since been superseded by the term 'Asia–Pacific region'. (See also **New Zealand–Australian relations**.)

HD

Australia Council was established by the **Gorton** government in 1968, largely through the initiative of H.C. **Coombs**, as a means of developing the performing arts in Australia. It took over the responsibilities of earlier bodies that assisted literature, music, and art. Jean Battersby served as the first director. In promoting the development of performing arts, the council funded the building and establishment of state theatre and art complexes in capital cities during the 1970s and 1980s. The council operates through the Aboriginal and Torres Islander Arts Board, the Literature Fund, the Performing Arts Board, and the Community Cultural Development Board. Opera Australia is funded separately.

The allocation of grants and fellowships has sparked major divisions within the arts community. Several critics, led by poet Les **Murray**, attacked the Australia Council in 1994 for favouring particular writers; others criticised the council for allegedly subsidising an excessive quantity of Australian fiction, much of which failed to sell. The former director, Tom Shapcott, reviews the council's record of promotion and assistance in *The Literature Board: A Brief History* (1988).

HD

Australia Day, formerly known as First Landing Day, Anniversary Day, and Foundation Day, commemorates 26 January 1788, when Captain Arthur **Phillip** raised the Union Jack and declared the foundation of the Colony of NSW. Anniversary Day was celebrated in early colonial NSW and marked by a regatta from 1837. The other colonies were reluctant to recognise it, preferring to observe their respective **foundation** days, but were prompted by the **Australian Natives Association** to accept it in 1888. National awareness of the day was impeded when Catholics renamed **Empire Day** as Australia Day in 1911, and the Red Cross adopted the same name for its fund-raising day in 1915. The lack of a common name caused further confusion; it was ANA Day in Victoria until 1931, and Anniversary Day in NSW until 1932. Official sesquicentennial celebrations marked 26 January 1938, but Aboriginal people protested with a Day of Mourning to mark the beginning of the invasion of their people. The Commonwealth created an Australia Day Council in 1946 to raise public awareness of the day. The Australian of the Year award, inaugurated in 1960, and the recipients of Australian honours, are announced on the day. The 1988 Bicentennial celebrations, which culminated in an extravagant display of fireworks and tall ships on Sydney Harbour, were condemned by pro-Aboriginal groups, who launched the Treaty 88 Campaign and rallied behind slogans such as 'white Australia has a black history' and '40 000 years doesn't make a bicentennial'. The Australia Day Council has subsequently scouted alternatives to 26 January for Australia Day because of this sensitivity. K.S.

Inglis outlined the background to, and development of, the day in *HSANZ* (1967).

HD

Australia Felix, which translates from the Latin as *happy* or *fortunate southern land*, was the name given to the fertile lands of south-west Victoria by Major Thomas **Mitchell** on his overland journey from the Murray River to Portland Bay in 1836, in search of suitable pastures. The term became popular in contemporary historical and literary works, including George Henry Haydon, *Five Years' Experience in Australia Felix* (1846); William Westgarth, *Australia Felix, or a Historical and Descriptive Account of the Settlement of Port Phillip, New South Wales* (1848); the *Australia Felix Monthly Magazine*, published in Geelong (1848–49); and Isabella Bishops, *Australia Felix: Impressions of Victoria* (1877). Henry Handel **Richardson** gave the title *Australia Felix* (1917) to the first novel in her trilogy, *The Fortunes of Richard Mahony*, and in 1970, historical geographer J.M. Powell published *The Public Lands of Australia Felix: Settlement and Land Appraisal in Victoria 1834–1891*.

HD

Australia First Movement was a right-wing nationalist organisation that emerged during the years of World War II; it was formed in Sydney in 1941. Its fiercely xenophobic promotion of Australian literature and art—free from deference to British culture—was a preoccupation of one of its leading figures, P.R. **Stephensen**. But the movement's main platform was opposition to Australia's involvement in the war. It supported the defence of Australia at the expense of the Allies' coordinated war effort. The arrests of four people in WA charged with conspiring with the Japanese led to the arrest and detention in 1942 of 16 members of the Australia First Movement in Sydney and to the suppression of the movement. Most of the detainees were released later that year; the last was released in August 1945. B.W. Muirden wrote an account of the movement in *The Puzzled Patriots* (1968).

HD

'Australia for the Australians', the motto adopted by radical nationalists in the late nineteenth century, was first coined by the banker George Meudell, in an article in the *Melbourne Review* in 1882. Meudell, a leader of the radical wing of the **Australian Natives Association**, argued that, under the benign influence of the Australian environment, the native-born would create a democracy purer and more perfect than their immigrant parents. His views did not win general support, even within the association, which, however, later adopted the phrase as a motto. In 1888, with the colonies in uproar over the unwelcome arrival of Chinese immigrants, the radical weekly, the Sydney **Bulletin**, lifted the phrase to its masthead. 'By the term Australian', it explained, 'we mean not merely those who have been born in Australia … [but] all white men who come to these shores with a clean record.' 'No nigger, no Chinaman, no lascar, no kanaka, no purveyor of cheap coloured labour is an Australian.' Aborigines, according to the *Bulletin*, were pitiable but not

'Australians'. With the official adoption of the **White Australia** policy, the phrase received new inflection—in 1908 the *Bulletin* changed its masthead to 'Australia for the White Man'. It remained unchanged until 1960, when Donald **Horne**, in his first act as editor, removed it.

GD

Australia (the name) is an adaptation of *terra australis incognita*, a Latin term meaning 'the unknown south land'. Ancient geographers, such as Ptolemy, had long suspected its existence. In 1606 the Spanish navigator Fernandez de Quiros glimpsed the continent which he piously named Terra Australis del Espiritu Santo. James **Cook** recognised the precedence of the Spaniards and Dutch navigators but believed de Quiros's discovery lay to the north-west of the coast he named New South Wales. The application of the anglicised version, *Australia*, to the whole continent belonged to its circumnavigator, Matthew **Flinders** in 1805. 'It is necessary … to geographical propriety that the whole body of land should be designated under the one general name', he argued, and that it was 'best to refer back to the original Terra Australis, or Australia' as 'being descriptive of its situation' and 'having antiquity to recommend it'. Governor **Macquarie** used the name in official correspondence and in 1817 proposed its official adoption. Later applied to the new colonies in the southern and western portions of the continent, it quickly became common usage. Henry **Parkes** even proposed to rename NSW *Australia* in the late 1880s, but it was the natural and uncontested title for the Federation of 1901.

GD

'Australia Unlimited' was the title of a book published by the writer and publicist E.J. **Brady**, in 1918. It provided a description, with lavish photographic illustration, of the country's natural resources. Everywhere Brady travelled, he found 'Wonder, Beauty, Unequalled Resource'. The collocation turned upside down the limited-liability provisions of company law to suggest that there were no limits to the productive potential of Australia. Furthermore, Brady argued that the lesson of the recent World War I was that Australia must become 'the richest and most powerful, as she is now the freest and most prosperous, nation of the world'. Brady's phrase found resonance in the immigration and **development** schemes of the 1920s, as embodied in Prime Minister S.M. **Bruce's** parallel slogan of 'Men, Money and Markets', though Brady's vision extended further into the **Dead Heart** of the continent, which he said was more properly called the 'Red Heart, destined one day to pulsate with life'.

SM

Australian is a national **newspaper** which was founded by Rupert **Murdoch** in 1964. William **Wentworth** and Robert Wardell had used the same title for an earlier paper, which was first published in 1824 and ran until 1848. Proclaiming itself 'independent' and 'free', this radical organ represented the free press by criticising the position of the **exclusives** and advocating political reforms.

Murdoch's *Australian* set new standards of national reportage under the editorship of Maxwell Newton in the 1960s. It developed a more conservative tone after 1975 but subsequently moved upmarket, with considerable coverage of the arts. Under the editorship of Paul Kelly after 1984, the paper further developed its emphasis on national issues. A monthly supplement, *The Australian's Review of Books*, was launched in 1996.

HD

Australian Aborigines' League, see **Aboriginal and Torres Strait Islander organisations**; **Cooper, William**

Australian and New Zealand Association for the Advancement of Science (ANZAAS) has for more than a century held biennial congresses for the discussion and dissemination of knowledge in a wide range of scientific disciplines. Following the model of the British Association, an Australasian Association of colonial scientific societies was formed in 1884 on the suggestion of Archibald **Liversidge**; it adopted the present title in 1930.

History was grouped with geography as a section of ANZAAS at its thirteenth meeting in Sydney, in 1911, when G.C. **Henderson** proposed in his presidential paper on 'Colonial Historical Research' that history should become a research-based scientific discipline. The geographers subsequently withdrew to leave Section E of ANZAAS to the historians. In the absence of any national society of their own, ANZAAS gatherings subsequently became the principal forum of the academic historical profession; leading academics such as R.M. **Crawford** and J.A. **La Nauze** used the presidential addresses to the history section to survey the discipline. At the Adelaide congress of ANZAAS in 1980 the historians voted to withdraw, and have since organised their own biennial conference under the auspices of the Australian Historical Association. ANZAAS declined, until in 1997 it determined to cease operation.

SM

Australian Army existed in permanent form only from 1948 with the formation of the Australian Regiment, which became 'Royal' in the following year. Previously there had been permanent specialist forces such as engineers and artillery, but no infantry. The forces sent to the two world wars were specially raised and operated under the name Australian Imperial Force (**AIF**). The infantry available for the **defence** of Australia were the part-time soldiers of the Citizen Military Forces (**CMF**), now known as the Reserves. The Army's history is now treated in volume 1 of *The Australian Centenary History of Defence* (2001).

JH

Australian ballot, see **Elections**

Australian Broadcasting Corporation, formerly the Australian Broadcasting Company (1928–32) and the

Australian Broadcasting Commission (1932–83), has been Australia's major public broadcaster for more than 70 years.

From the first, radio was seen as a nationalising force. In 1918 the Marconi Company sent the first direct **radio** transmission to Australia from Wales, and barely a year later Ernest Fisk, the founder of AWA (Amalgamated Wireless Australasia), gave the first Australian demonstration of the wireless by broadcasting 'God Save the King' to a meeting of the Royal Society of New South Wales from his office in Sydney, a few blocks away. In 1928 the Commonwealth government announced that it would establish a national broadcasting service, the Australian Broadcasting Company, in Sydney. The Australian Broadcasting Commission Act was passed in 1932 to take over the national network set up by the Australian Broadcasting Company. Like the British Broadcasting Corporation on which it was modelled, the ABC was established as an independent corporation, governed by a board of commissioners, and financed by licence fees; unlike the BBC, however, its technical services were once provided by the postmaster-general. Being Australian once meant being facsimiles of the best of British, and the ABC emulated the style of the BBC's founding director, John Reith. It endorsed the philosophy that broadcasting was a civilising activity: for many years, ABC radio news-readers wore evening dress.

In adopting the BBC model, the creators of the ABC assumed that the national broadcaster would have two primary objectives: the creation of a well-informed public by broadcasting accurate, wide-ranging, non-partisan information, and the cultivation of excellence in content, scope, and technique. It would not aim for popularity for its own sake but would offer programs that educated, enlightened, and entertained. The character of the organisation was strongly influenced by its early leaders. Charles Moses, an English-born, powerfully built, ex-car salesman with a BBC accent, was catapulted from talks director to general manager of the infant organisation in 1935 and stayed until 1964. Richard Boyer, farmer, ex-serviceman and Methodist, was chairman of the commission from 1945 to 1961: he is the subject of a valuable biography by Geoffrey **Bolton**. Although never close personally, they exemplified the blend of high and middle-brow culture, the sense of national mission, and the moral seriousness which defined the ABC. The nickname 'Aunty', adopted in the 1960s on the model of the BBC, captured both the suggestion of staidness, and the deep affection, which the organisation inspired in its listeners.

The ABC developed radio into an art form. In the early years all programs went to air live because there was no means of recording program material. Over 50 per cent of broadcasting time was devoted to music and by 1937 the ABC employed 319 musicians full-time. It placed the state symphony orchestras on a more professional footing, but also gave regular air-time, and employment, to dance bands and singers, such as the choristers of the long-running 'Village Glee Club'. Spoken-word programs included news, education, and drama. The first Australian Drama Week was held

in 1936, with Australian plays being broadcast every night for a week. The radio serial 'Blue Hills' by Gwen **Meredith**, a regular feature of 'The Country Hour', brought a popular blend of bush humour and homespun wisdom to millions of listeners in the city as well as the bush.

From the beginning, the ABC's civilising mission gave it a special responsibility for the education of the nation's youth. 'The Argonauts', a radio club for children, enrolled its listeners as fellow adventurers with the heroes of Homer's *Odyssey*, and awarded them honours ('Dragon's Tooth', 'Golden Fleece', etc.) for contributing poems, drawings and answers to quiz questions. The writer Ruth **Park**, creator of the serial 'The Muddle-Headed Wombat', and pianist Linley Evans, 'Mr Melody Man', were among regular 'personalities'. Ida Elizabeth Jenkins, *Good Rowing!* (1982), gathers reminiscences of former Argonauts. By 1953 over 80 per cent of all Australian schools regularly utilised ABC Schools Broadcasts on such subjects as music, nature study, and health as an integral part of their weekly curriculum.

The government of Australia was challenged by the new development of **television**. Ben **Chifley**, the prime minister, agreed to introduce television in 1949, but six months later lost office. Chifley believed the job of television, even more than that of radio, was to deliver entertainment to tired workers. **Menzies**, the new prime minister, was quoted as saying to a visitor from the BBC: 'I hope this thing will not come to Australia within my term of office.' Like Churchill, he thought television was a peep-show, and he delayed its arrival for as long as he could. There was no great clamour for television. Newspapers and commercial operators were apprehensive about the competition, but it was the ABC which pressed ahead, convinced of the value of television. From the beginning, while it had responsibility for a national service, it had to compete with commercial television interests. It therefore had to define a role in the broadcasting industry. For the most part it has taken the high moral ground and has been a creative innovator and tastemaster.

It is as a gatherer, interpreter, and disseminator of news that the ABC has had its most important influence on Australian life. It provides the largest national independent news-gathering agency, managing a global and Australia-wide communications network. Through Radio Australia—now severed from the ABC—it created an overseas radio and television service which achieved high recognition in Asia and the Pacific region. Its television current affairs programs, 'Four Corners' and 'This Day Tonight', were pioneers of investigative reporting and a national training-ground for television journalists.

As Ken **Inglis** shows in his magisterial official history, *This is the ABC* (1983), issues of political 'balance', 'independence', and 'accountability' have been contested throughout the organisation's history. Conservatives have complained of left-wing bias and 'permissiveness' in program content. Its defenders, such as Aunty's Nieces and Nephews, have warned against hostile board appointments, political interference in program management, and budget cuts. A committee of inquiry appointed by the **Fraser** government recommended the transformation of the commission into a board.

Under the **Howard** government these conflicts became acute. The ABC was now expected to compete with the commercial networks for ratings yet maintain its traditional public-service obligations, and to meet the challenge of new media, such as the Internet, yet reduce its dependence on government funding. The appointment in 1999 of Jonathan Shier, an expatriate commercial television executive, as managing director, and the sackings and resignations that followed, signalled the government's determination to effect a radical change in the culture of the national broadcaster. According to one alarmed staff member, Quentin Dempster, the ABC was engaged in a *Death Struggle* (2000).

WENDY MCCARTHY

Australian Capital Territory, see **Canberra**

Australian Church, see **Strong, Charles**

Australian Council of Trade Unions, see **ACTU**

Australian Democrats is a minor political party whose platform sits somewhere between those of the **Liberal Party** and the **Australian Labor Party**. Don Chipp formed the party in 1977, with members of the Australia Party and the New Liberal Movement, following his resignation from the Liberal Party. General disaffection with the two-party system made the new party an attractive alternative; two candidates, including Chipp, won seats in the Senate at the elections that year. The Democrats continued to poll well in subsequent federal elections, generally winning at least 10 per cent of the vote; they also won seats at state elections, proving particularly popular in SA. They held the balance of power in the Senate for most of the 1980s and until 1996; in 1990 they held a total of eight seats in the Senate. The Democrats developed a far more consultative and participatory politics than the main parties and, while they have sided with both Labor and Liberal over different issues, they have moved to the left on a range of issues that motivate their progressive middle-class membership. Don Chipp was succeeded by Janine Haines as party leader in 1986, Janet Powell in 1990, and John Coulter in 1991. Cheryl Kernot was elected leader in 1993 but resigned her membership of the party in 1997 in order to join the Labor Party. She was succeeded as leader by Meg Lees, who was replaced by Natasha Stott Despoja in 2001.

HD

Australian Financial Review is a financial **newspaper** published by the **Fairfax** press in Sydney since 1951. It was established as a weekly but converted to a bi-weekly in 1961 and a daily in 1963. The *Australian Financial Times*, published by **Packer's** Consolidated Press, was a brief competitor, running for less than 12 months in 1961–62.

Although it was a specialist business paper, the *Financial Review* developed a wider readership as a result of its substantial neutral coverage of politics and informed criticism of government economic policy in the 1960s and 1970s. In 1997 it introduced a weekend supplement.

HD

Australian Flying Corps, see **Royal Australian Air Force**

Australian Imperial Force, see **AIF**

Australian Inland Mission was established by the Presbyterian Church in 1912, following a plan proposed by Reverend John **Flynn**, the mission's first superintendent, as a means of serving people living in isolated, outlying areas of central and northern Australia. Flynn is the subject of Ion **Idriess's** *Flynn of the Inland* (1932) and Max Griffiths's *The Silent Heart* (1993); he was succeeded in 1951 by Fred McKay. Operating under the motto 'for Christ and the continent', the mission's objective was the provision of four main needs: spiritual care, health care, literature, and education. Under Flynn's leadership, the mission established the Aerial Medical Service in 1928 at Cloncurry, Qld, which was made possible by the pedal wireless set that Alf Traeger had first trialled in 1926. This service was reconstituted as the Flying Doctor Service in 1939, with a royal charter added in 1954. Ernestine **Hill** wrote an account of the service, *Flying Doctor Calling* (1947). The radio network established for the Flying Doctor Service was also used by the School of the Air to assist correspondence lessons for schoolchildren in isolated parts of Australia. Other services provided by the mission are nursing homes, a children's hostel in Adelaide, and an old-timers' settlement in Alice Springs.

HD

Australian Institute of International Affairs, an unofficial body concerned to promote the study of international relations, was formed in 1933 by the amalgamation of the several branches of the Royal Institute of International Affairs in Sydney (1924), Melbourne (1925), and Brisbane (1932). The Royal Institute itself had resulted from informal discussions among members of delegations to the Paris Peace Conference in 1919. J.G. **Latham**, F.W. **Eggleston**, and R.R. **Garran** had taken part in the discussions; they joined the British Institute when it was formed in 1921, and were active in establishing Australian branches.

After 1933 branches of the institute were established in all states. These formed vigorous discussion societies, meeting regularly to hear informed speakers, to discuss aspects of international affairs and, by means of study groups, to conduct research. The federal organisation administered, in the 1950s, 1960s, and 1970s, lectures by distinguished overseas visitors such as Bertrand Russell, Julian Huxley, William O. Douglas, and Paul Manglapus. Known as the Dyason

Lectures, they were funded initially by E.C. **Dyason**, a Melbourne businessman. The institute has directed major research projects, resulting in a wide range of specialist and general publications, including a regular series of volumes on 'Australia in World Affairs'. It holds regular national conferences and publishes the *Australian Journal of International Affairs*. Through its meetings, publications, and conferences the institute over the years has helped to shape Australian attitudes to the outside.

JOHN LEGGE

Australian Joint Copying Project began in October 1945 when the Commonwealth National Library and the Public Library of New South Wales agreed to share the costs of microfilming historical records in the UK relating to Australia and the Pacific. The project was intended to carry on the work begun by James **Bonwick** and continued by J.F. **Watson** in making unique sources accessible to historians and other researchers working in Australia.

For most of its life the project was managed by one or two full-time staff based in the Australian High Commission in London. Filming commenced at the Public Record Office in August 1948 and continued without a break for 45 years. A total of 10 419 reels were produced. About two-thirds comprise British official records, most notably those of the **Colonial Office**, ranging in date from 1740 to about 1955. The remaining reels contain copies of private records of Australian, NZ and Pacific interest located in hundreds of repositories throughout Britain and Ireland. They include holdings of national and university libraries, county record offices, museums, learned societies, religious archives, and businesses, as well as papers of private individuals and families.

The project came to an end in June 1993, mainly on account of funding difficulties. Complete or substantial sets of the film are held in eight libraries and archives in Australia and NZ, and several other libraries hold selected reels. The National Library has published a series of handbooks describing the records that were filmed, while Phyllis Mander-Jones, *Manuscripts in the British Isles Relating to Australia, New Zealand and the Pacific* (1972) provides details of the principal repositories.

GRAEME POWELL

Australian Labor Party (ALP) is the oldest political party in Australia. Its origins lie in the formation of electoral organisations by trade unionists and socialists from the late 1880s. The defeat of the unions in the **strikes and lockouts** of the early 1890s stimulated the turn to parliamentary action, and the new party achieved greatest initial success in NSW (where it won 35 seats in the 1891 elections) and Qld. These early labour parties went by various names in the different colonies: the Labour Electoral League in NSW, the Australian Labour Federation in Qld, the United Labor Party in SA, the Progressive Political League in Victoria. They came together in 1900 to form the federal Labor Party; spelling varied between Labor and Labour until 1912 when the former term was established.

The party's organisation has remained federal in character. Each state constituted a branch, made up of affiliated unions and individual members organised in local branches. Policy was determined by the annual state conference; it was binding on the parliamentary representatives, who were expected to sign a pledge to support it. The parliamentary party constituted the **caucus**, which elected the party leader and determined parliamentary policy. The cohesion and strength of this new political force were quickly evident. Before 1914 Labor had held office in all the states, albeit briefly in some, and constituted a majority government in the Commonwealth. Its formation and growth are surveyed by D.J. Murphy (ed.), *Labor in Politics* (1975), while Ray Markey and Frank Bongiorno provide more analytical accounts of the party's social and ideological composition in NSW and Victoria.

The policy and tactics of the Australian Labor Party were less clear. Initially it put forward a limited platform of objectives, chiefly concerned with security of employment, regulation of wages and working conditions, and old-age pensions, along with progressive taxation and the extension of democracy. A strong nationalist element was immediately apparent in strong support for a **White Australia** policy and national defence—emphasised by the national appellation, which distinguished the Australian Labor Party from most overseas counterparts. Again initially, the state and federal parliamentary parties were prepared to offer other parties 'support in return for concessions', as the NSW parliamentary leader George **Black** declared in 1891. But Labor's speedy success hastened the **Fusion** of the non-Labor parties, thereby closing off such opportunities, and in any case the Australian Labor Party came to insist on complete independence.

George Black also declared in 1891 that the new party had not come into politics to make and unmake ministries but 'to make and unmake social conditions'. The Australian Labor Party presented itself as the political arm of the organised working class, a social movement with a historic mission to eradicate privilege and inequality. Its language and ritual emphasised this regenerative purpose; in works such as *Australia's Awakening* (1909) by the former shearers'-leader-turned-senator, W.G. **Spence**, and *The Case for Labor* (1910) by W.M. **Hughes**, it emphasised a millenarian destiny. Socialists sought to turn the strong anti-capitalist ethos of the Australian Labor Party into a clear commitment, but were unable to overcome electoral pragmatism. The nearest they came to success was at the 1921 federal conference, which qualified the objective of 'nationalisation of banking and all principal industries' with the declaration that the party proposed collective ownership 'for the purpose of preventing exploitation, and to whatever extent may be necessary for that purpose'. Bede **Nairn**, *Civilising Capitalism* (1973), discounts the influence of socialism in the Australian Labor Party; Bruce O'Meagher (ed.), *The Socialist Objective* (1983), suggests its significance.

The early Labor Party withstood frequent criticism and defection. Leaders chafed at party control of policy. Doctrinaire socialists and industrial unionists condemned the moderation and gradualism of Labor in office. Attempts by Labor ministries to flout party policy, or by conference and the executive to enforce it, led to resignations and expulsions, most dramatically during World War I when the Labor Prime Minister W.M. Hughes and NSW Premier W.A. **Holman** abandoned the Australian Labor Party in the **split** over **conscription**. These episodes in turn fuelled a mythology of solidarity and excoriation of the Labor 'rat'. That a party of striking moderation by the standards of international social democracy could generate enduring tribal loyalty is partly explained by its distinctive structure. The affiliated trade unions benefited from the patronage it bestowed, and in turn sustained it throughout the tensions between the industrial and political wings.

This relationship also accounts for Labor's mixed fortunes in the interwar years. The federal Australian Labor Party was weakened by the wartime split, and did not regain government until 1929. Its failure to protect living standards from the effects of **Depression** brought further splits, both from the left and the right wings, and it remained in opposition from 1932 until 1941. But state Labor parties enjoyed significant terms of office in NSW, SA, Tasmania, and Victoria, dominated Western Australian politics, and in Qld held government for all but the Depression years. At the state level Labor was able to exploit the significant political rewards of development projects and public utilities. These arrangements entrenched powerful cliques that used their control of membership and parliamentary pre-selection to circumvent the party's democratic rules. V.G. **Childe**, *How Labour Governs* (1923), was an early diagnosis of this problem.

Labor factionalism also had a **sectarian** aspect. **Irish** Catholics were always prominent in the Australian Labor Party, more so after the split of 1917. Their suspicion of socialism and antagonism to communism was exacerbated by the anti-fascist popular front of the 1930s. The growing influence in the Australian Labor Party of the **Movement** and the industrial Groups gave these alignments a sharp ideological edge.

John **Curtin** led the federal Australian Labor Party to unprecedented success during World War II. Succeeding a series of weak and indecisive conservative ministries, he overcame the resistance of his party to conscription and provided a strong, progressive national leadership. Labor's plans for **postwar reconstruction** extended the power of the Commonwealth and the ambit of the public sector to secure economic growth, full employment, and increased social welfare provision, and to promote egalitarian values. Labor held office until 1949, when it succumbed to the new **Liberal Party** and its Country Party coalition partner.

There followed the longest period out of national office the Australian Labor Party had experienced. Its difficulties in the Cold War climate, which led to a further split in 1954 with the defection of the anti-communist wing, were exacerbated by economic and social change that eroded the party's electoral base and political platform. By the end of the 1960s the Australian Labor Party was out of office in all seven Australian parliaments, and D.W. Rawson wondered if

it was doomed to *Labor in Vain?* (1966). A new generation of reformers, drawn largely from the professions, advanced policies to reform the party structure and broaden the party's electoral support beyond its traditional trade union base. They achieved greatest success in SA, where Don **Dunstan** held office 1967–68 and 1970–79; NSW, where Neville **Wran** was premier 1976–86; and nationally in Gough **Whitlam's** accession to the federal leadership in 1967. Whitlam mobilised middle-class support for an ambitious program of public provision, and his hectic term of government 1972–75 marks the high-water mark of social democracy in Australia.

Following his **Dismissal**, the downturn of the economy, and the retreat from public provision, the Australian Labor Party placed primary emphasis on issues of economic management. At the centre of the program with which it won the federal election of 1983, it placed the **Accord**, an agreement with the unions to hold down wages in order to restore employment. State Labor governments followed the **Hawke** federal government during the 1980s in deregulating the finance sector, dismantling industrial protection and emphasising market efficiency. While unions enjoyed a privileged status, the Labor Party relied increasingly on the support of a coalition of social movements, the **Greens**, the feminists, and Aboriginal and welfare organisations, whose demands it sought to reconcile with business interests. By the end of the decade this uneasy arrangement broke down, with spectacular failures of state finances in SA, Victoria, and WA. When it was swept from government in 1996, the Party seemed exhausted. Membership had declined—partly because its leaders determined policy with little regard to its rules and platform, partly because party branches and conferences were dominated by tightly controlled factions, and partly because political energy was channelled into social movements. Andrew Scott, *Fading Loyalties* (1991), analyses the changing membership of the Australian Labor Party. Yet in 1998 the ALP won back many of the seats it had lost in the Commonwealth parliament, and by 2001 it held office in five of the six states. Its electoral resilience surpasses the capacity to renew policy and purpose.

L.F. Crisp provides the standard account of the structure and policies of *The Australian Federal Labor Party 1901–1951* (1955), and Ross McMullin's commissioned centenary history, *The Light on the Hill* (1991), is an evocative account of its leading figures, while John Faulkner and Stuart Macintyre (eds), *True Believers* (2001), marks the centenary of the federal caucus. There are state histories of the Australian Labor Party in NSW by Graham Freudenberg, and Jim Hagan and Ken Turner; in Qld by Ross Fitzgerald and Harold Thornton; and in Tasmania by Richard Davis. Jim Moss, *Sound of Trumpets* (1985), is a broader history of the labour movement in SA. The left and the right continue to dispute possession of the Australian Labor Party in their respective claims to be the 'true believers', faithful to Labor traditions. The Lloyd Ross forum in NSW follows Bede Nairn in celebrating the triumph of pragmatism as *Civilising*

Capitalism; Stuart Macintyre in 'Who Are the True Believers?' (*LH*, 1996) traces the continuity of a more radical purpose.

STUART MACINTYRE

Australian Legend is a term popularised by Russel **Ward's** influential work of the same name, published in 1958, which 'attempts to trace the historical origins and development of the Australian legend or national *mystique*'. In doing so, Ward codified the so-called 'typical Australian': 'a practical man, rough and ready in his manners and quick to decry any appearance of affectation in others …'. He identified the emergence of these character traits among the **convicts** and, later, among bush people and other itinerant workers. He asserted that the nature of their work and the masculine world they inhabited reinforced particular social behaviour and traditions, and encouraged the egalitarian, democratic, and nationalistic beliefs that found wider expression during the nation-building enthusiasm of the 1890s. Strong criticism from feminist historians and other critics drew attention to the partiality of the legend. Miriam **Dixson**, for example, points to the absence of women in both his character description and historical analysis. **Aborigines** and other non-European Australians are subsidiary to Ward's analysis. A significant text nonetheless, *The Australian Legend* has been used exhaustively in teaching Australian history, particularly in delineating different understandings of the Australian character. A special issue of *HS* (1978) discussed Ward's thesis.

HD

Australian Medical Association is Australia's leading medical practitioners' organisation. It was formed in Canberra in 1961, succeeding the Australian branches of the British Medical Association (BMA), which originated in 1832 to support medical science and its professional reputation and interests. Autonomous branches were established in SA in 1879, Victoria and NSW in 1880, Qld in 1894, WA in 1898, and Tasmania in 1911. The inaugural federal meeting, held in Melbourne in May 1912, led to publication of the first *Medical Journal of Australia* in 1914. While earlier medical organisations were essentially learned societies and patronage networks, the BMA became a vehicle for more militant medical professionals. The BMA's successful opposition to national insurance in the 1930s is discussed by James Gillespie, *The Price of Health* (1991), and its defeat of what it called 'socialised medicine' in the mid-1940s is described by L.F. Crisp, *Ben Chifley* (1960). Literature dealing with the history of the BMA and AMA is surveyed in Bryan Gandevia et al. (eds), *An Annotated Bibliography of the History of Medicine and Health in Australia* (1984). Recent AMA activities have included political lobbying, publications, congresses, public liaison, and maintenance of professional and ethical standards. The AMA's conservatism partly explains a significant relative decline in membership since 1962, although its image was polished between 1993 and 1995 under the presidency of Brendan Nelson, a young Tasmanian doctor with a diamond earring, who began a federal political career in 1996. (See also **Professions**.)

DC

Australian Natives Association was a **benefit society** formed in Melbourne in 1871, with membership restricted to men born in Australia. It depicted itself as a national organisation since it ignored old-world ethnic divisions and avoided the ritual and secrecy of the established friendly societies, which were offshoots of British associations. Its membership grew rapidly in the 1880s, particularly in the goldfields towns as the first Australian-born generation came of age in these migrant communities. As well as providing the standard sickness, medical, and funeral benefits, the association was concerned with mutual improvement and civic responsibility.

In the 1880s it committed itself to **Federation** and was the chief supporter of the Victorian government's attempt to secure inter-colonial cooperation to counter German and French activities in the Pacific. It promoted the celebration of 26 January as the national holiday. In the 1890s it sponsored the formation of **federation leagues** and its members played an important part in the 'yes' campaigns at the referendums. As a national organisation, it encouraged the formation of branches in the other colonies, with only limited success. In Victoria it was deeply rooted in local communities and became a nursery of politicians. A distinguished account of its history and influence is provided by Marian Aveling (Quartly), 'A History of the Australian Natives Association 1871–1900' (PhD thesis, Monash University, 1970). In the twentieth century it continued to grow, but gradually its nationalist concerns became less central and relevant, and it ended its days as one of several private health funds. It amalgamated with Manchester Unity in 1993 to form Australian Unity.

JH

Australian Patriotic Association was formed in Sydney in 1835 by **emancipists** and liberals to demand full civil and political rights for the colonists. They wanted removal of restrictions on the operation of juries and replacement of the nominated Legislative Council by an elected Assembly. Their key concern was that no bars should be placed on ex-convicts as jurors, electors, and representatives, which was what the **exclusive** free settlers wished. W.C. **Wentworth** was the leading figure in the association, still a fiery advocate, but moving away from his early radicalism. The association was controlled by its most substantial subscribers and was content with the English restrictions on voting rights. It employed an English MP to lobby on its behalf. He did not give complete satisfaction because, faced with the extreme caution of the British government about constitutional change in NSW, he was prepared to accept less than the association demanded. The British government avoided a decision on the rival claims of emancipists and exclusives by continuing the existing constitutional arrangements from year to year. When the government introduced an elective element into the Legislative Council in 1842, no bar was placed on the participation of ex-convicts. By this time, with the end of **transportation**, the division between exclusives and emancipists was losing its significance. The work of the association is described in A.C.V. **Melbourne**, *Early Constitutional Development in Australia* (1934, 1963).

JH

Australian Rules football is the most popular and significant of the sporting codes created in this country. It was first played on the parklands of inner Melbourne in the 1850s and its origins are keenly disputed. At the time, several of the leading English public schools had their own forms of football; that of Rugby was codified in written rules in 1845 and quickly imitated. In 1858 T.W. **Wills**, the secretary of the Melbourne Cricket Club and a former Rugby pupil, suggested that cricketers should keep fit in winter by playing football, and in July of that year sides from Melbourne Grammar School and Scotch College played in a game umpired by Wills.

In the following year Wills helped draft the rules of what became known as Australian Rules, whose distinctive features were an oval ball, the absence of an offside rule, and provision for handling the ball. This genealogy has been disputed by those who argue for more popular, or even indigenous, origins. Football was played in various forms before its codification: some have suggested that diggers on the Victorian goldfields played an early version of Gaelic football; some have suggested that Aborigines had their own game. The issue is considered by Geoffrey **Blainey**, *A Game of Our Own* (1990), and A. Mancini and G.M. Hibbins, *Running with the Ball* (1987).

The first clubs, Melbourne and Geelong, were formed in 1858 and 1859, and a regular competition was formalised by the Victorian Football Association in 1877. It flourished as a commercial spectator sport, benefiting from the relative affluence and leisure enjoyed by the colonists, the public transport system, and press coverage. It exemplified qualities that Australians regarded as distinctive: vigour and skill, teamwork and individual prowess, the open spaces of an arena larger than for any other football code, the inclusive nature of a game played by all classes and supported by women as well as men. The principal clubs were suburban, but drew players from local and rural competitions. Although player payments could be substantial, an amateur ethos prevailed. Tasmania, SA and later WA adopted the game as the principal winter sport, but **Rugby** was preferred in NSW and Qld.

The Victorian Football League (VFL) broke away from the earlier Association in 1897. In 1907 the Australian Football Council was formed, to standardise rules and conduct interstate matches, but for most of the century the competitions based in the state capitals remained paramount. With increasing attendances—one in 10 Melburnians watched one of the six League games of a Saturday afternoon in the 1920s—and larger gates, administrators were preoccupied with regulating the recruitment, transfer, and payment of players. Football retained tenacious local loyalties, overlaid by denominational and social rivalries, mediated by the search for success and corresponding reward. The advent of television coverage and commercial sponsorship exacerbated these pressures, and the dominant VFL increasingly drained the resources of the interstate leagues. In response to commercial imperatives, the federal structure of the VFL yielded to corporate organisation. The chief executives transferred South Melbourne to Sydney, and

created new clubs in Brisbane, Adelaide, and Perth to establish the national competition of the Australian Football League. Experiments with private ownership proved unsuccessful, and the membership of the sixteen AFL clubs now exceeds 400 000. The need to increase player payments, if only to compete with the salaries offered by other sports with international coverage, was offset by recruitment regulations and salary caps designed to maintain an even competition. In this respect, football as a business resists the logic of monopoly capitalism.

Australian Rules football has generated a large literature of club histories, ghosted player memoirs, chronicles, and compilations. It has entered into fiction, verse, and cinema, and captured the imagination of artists such as **Streeton** and Noel Counihan. Ian **Turner** was the first historian to take football seriously as a form of popular culture, and with Leonie Sandercock wrote the history *Up Where, Cazaly?* (1981). Robert Pascoe, *The Winter Game* (1995), gives the greatest attention to the game's interstate growth, while Richard Stremski, *Kill for Collingwood* (1986), and John Lack et al., *Unleashed* (1996), suggest the possibilities of the club history. But even Turner's annual Ron Barassi Memorial Lecture retained a note of parody. The same qualities are apparent in Jack Hibberd and Garrie Hutchinson, *The Barrackers' Bible* (1983), as well as in the widely imitated group of urban professionals who began on community radio as the Coodabeen Champions. A mixture of passion, nostalgia, and masculine bawdy infuses the cult of youthful athleticism.

STUART MACINTYRE

Australian Security Intelligence Organisation (ASIO) was established in 1949 to gather security intelligence, evaluate its significance, and advise government. ASIO's publication, *ASIO Now* (1996), defines security intelligence as 'information on certain types of activity which might harm Australia ... acts of foreign interference, espionage, sabotage, politically motivated violence, the promotion of communal violence, and attacks on Australia's defence system'. Before ASIO was set up, security intelligence was gathered by military authorities, including the Defence Department and the Navy, and from 1919 by the Investigation Branch of the federal attorney-general's department. Soviet espionage activities were highlighted in 1946 by the defection of Igor Gouzenko, a cipher clerk in the Soviet embassy in Canada. Gouzenko's revelations, US unease, and British government pressure encouraged Ben **Chifley's** Labor Government to create ASIO, which was subsequently moulded by Brigadier Sir Charles Spry, its director-general from 1950 to 1970. The **Petrov Affair** in 1954 established ASIO's reputation, but left-wing critics increasingly suspected links between ASIO and conservative politics. In March 1973 the Labor attorney-general, Lionel **Murphy**, used Commonwealth police to launch an inept early-morning raid on ASIO's Canberra and Melbourne offices. Various conspiracy theories and allegations of unlawful ASIO methods were eventually disproved by Mr Justice Hope, who conducted royal commissions into Australian intelligence in 1974–77 and 1983–84. Hope was nevertheless critical of

ASIO's administration, and his recommendations were adopted in legislation in 1979 and 1986. ASIO's identification of KGB spy Valeriy Ivanov was a triumph in 1983, but the post-Cold War era has seen ASIO search for a new role. Sensational and unreliable information surrounds ASIO's history. Two recent works from differing perspectives are Harvey Barnett, *Tale of the Scorpion* (1988), and David McKnight, *Australia's Spies and Their Secrets* (1994).

DC

Australian War Memorial, prominently situated on Anzac Avenue, in alignment with Capital Hill, Canberra, is a tribute to the Australian men and women who died at war. C.E.W. **Bean's** vision for the building, which was to be 'at once museum, archive and shrine', was made possible through official policy of the First **AIF** that each soldier be issued with a camera and diary. Designed by Emil Sodersten and John Crust and officially opened in 1941, this neo-classical shrine comprises a series of galleries, each of which commemorates a particular theatre of war and displays official war records and memorabilia, dioramas of battles, war trophies, soldiers' personal belongings, and other relics of war. In its central cloisters the names of all the Australians who died at war are inscribed on the walls. Though it was erected initially to remember those who died in **World War I**, the memorials and displays for **World War II**, and subsequent wars in **Korea**, **Malaya**, and **Vietnam**, were later incorporated. The memorial continues to acquire and preserve historic records relating to Australia's **military history** and is an important centre for Australian war studies. Much of the material exhibited focuses on strategy and technology, and reinforces traditional war imagery. It does not recognise the Aborigines and settlers who died as a result of inter-racial warfare during the period of first contact. In 1993, the Unknown Soldier was reburied at the Memorial, to mark the 75th anniversary of the end of World War I. Michael McKernan's history of the memorial, entitled *Here Is Their Spirit*, appeared in 1991.

HD

Australian Way of Life, a phrase denoting social beliefs and customs uniquely or distinctively Australian, gained currency from the late 1940s. George Caiger's *The Australian Way of Life* (1953) signalled its arrival as a subject of serious analysis. The phrase was derived from the 'American Way of Life' and reflected a shift from British models of **national identity**, which had emphasised a common biological and political lineage, to American ones, which emphasised common democratic beliefs and values. As such, argues Richard White in *Inventing Australia* (1981), it answered several emergent needs: assuring newcomers of non-British origin that they could become Australians too; reinforcing links to Cold War allies and resistance against non-democratic, especially communist, enemies; and grounding national sentiment in the seemingly homogeneous culture of a suburban, consumerist society. Its rhetorical value was always more obvious than its content. 'What is this way of life?' a

puzzled journalist inquired. 'No one tells me what this is! Yet always they tell me I must adopt it!'

GD

Australian Women's National League was an influential women's conservative political organisation in the early twentieth century. Formed in 1904 in Victoria, by 1914 it had attracted 52 000 members on a populist platform of anti-socialism, support for monarchy, and promotion of women's particular interests. The league's influence derived from its grassroots electioneering role, and astute and formidable presidents, including Lady Janet **Clarke**, Agnes 'Eva' Hughes, and Elizabeth 'May' Couchman. It actively promoted like-minded organisations (those in Tasmania and WA subsequently adopted its name) while attempting to suppress liberal rivals; the 1912 fracas with the women's section of the pro-**Deakin** People's Liberal Party was a notable example of the latter.

The league reflected the view that women's social and political interests necessitated organisational autonomy from 'men's groups'; although, until a policy change in 1927, women should not directly enter parliament to protect their interests but instead encourage 'suitable men' to act on their behalf.

By the early 1940s the league was ready to integrate into mainstream conservative politics; Couchman was an important backer of R.G. **Menzies's** efforts to form a new organisation to succeed the moribund **United Australia Party**. The league merged with the Victorian division of the **Liberal Party** in 1945, having first (and uniquely) secured equal representation for women within its administrative structure.

DOUG SCOBIE

Australian Women's Weekly was launched in Sydney in 1933 by publishers Frank **Packer** and E.G. **Theodore**. Immediately successful, it sold 120 000 copies of its first issue and was subsequently introduced in the other states. Following the departure of founding editor George Warnecke in 1939, the *Weekly* has employed only women editors, including the long-standing Alice Jackson. Aimed at the wife and mother, the *Weekly* gave high priority to the virtues of domesticity; provided advice on fashion and beauty; and presented a range of articles related to domestic economy, including recipes, household hints, and needlework. It also included regular short and serialised fiction, reviews, poetry, and cartoons. The *Weekly*'s support for the Women's **Land Army** during World War II offered brief relief from its promotion of otherwise traditional views on women's roles and responsibilities. In the 1950s its columns reflected the popular resurgence of domesticity and traditional values, to which it added regular coverage of the British royal family. This element has continued, but has become increasingly diluted with Hollywood celebrities. The magazine converted to a monthly publication in 1982 but retained its original title. The *Weekly* is a rich and little-tapped source in the study of gender and **women's history**. An indexing project, funded by the Australian Research Council, is in progress in SA.

HD

Australian Workers Union was for nearly a century the largest Australian trade union. Formed in 1894, it incorporated pastoral, rural, mining, construction, and other workers, assisted by sympathetic state Labor governments and skilful use of **arbitration**. The union's initial support for socialism and industrial militancy, commemorated in its founding secretary W.G. **Spence's** *Australia's Awakening* (1909), soon yielded to a xenophobic populism. The AWU played an important role in the formation of the **Australian Labor Party** and exerted great influence in Labor governments in Qld, WA, and NSW during the early part of this century, shaping their policies to advance its own interests. It blocked attempts to establish a rival **One Big Union** of Australian workers at the end of World War I, and refused to affiliate to the **ACTU** until 1967. Condemned by its critics as 'Australia's Worst Union', it suffered debilitating internal disputes after World War II and declined with the contraction of its occupational base to a membership of 100 000 in the 1980s. In 1993 it amalgamated with a conglomerate of metal and manufacturing unions to form the AWU–FIME (Federation of Industrial, Manufacturing and Engineering Employees). A commissioned history by Mark Hearn and Harry Knowles, *One Big Union*, appeared in 1996.

SM

Australiana refers to a range of collectable documents and objects relating to Australia, particularly those with significance to Australian history. The term was first applied to documentary materials, such as explorers' log books and maps; diaries of prominent early settlers; and early published works, such as those collected by David Scott **Mitchell** or, later, those published by George **Robertson** or in the *Bulletin*. Mitchell's prized collection provided the basis for the Mitchell Library collection. Australiana later incorporated items which were peculiarly Australian in origin, such as the makeshift furniture of the Depression era, or which depicted symbols characteristic of Australia, particularly flora and fauna, or Aboriginal motifs. The self-conscious national identity that developed in the 1890s, and found expression in the Federation and Art Nouveau styles, gave natural motifs greater prominence in Australian furniture and home décor. Images of kangaroos, emus, and lyrebirds appeared on mass-produced kitchen chairs, and kookaburras depicted in lead-lighting decorated the front doors of many homes. Similar images appeared on biscuit tins, tea caddies, and ashtrays. Now considerably broader in definition, the term embraces general Australian ephemera.

HD

Autobiography has only recently attracted the attention of historians as a genre. Rather than assessing the claims of autobiography as a form of history, they preferred eclectically to draw upon autobiographical writing as a convenient primary source, often using it to add an experiential leavening to sober narratives based on more orthodox, documentary material.

The *Memoirs* of the thrice-transported convict, James Hardy **Vaux** (1819), said to be the first full-length autobiography written in Australia, is representative of a picaresque genre, the authenticity of which has sometimes been an issue. Manning **Clark** thought Alexander **Harris's** *Settlers and Convicts* (1847, originally published under the pseudonym 'An Emigrant Mechanic') appeared 'to contain as much fiction as fact'. On the other hand, fictional narratives such as Henry **Savery's** *Quintus Servinton* (1830), claimed to be the first Australian novel, and James Tucker's *Ralph Rashleigh* (written in the 1840s but not published until 1929), have also been interpreted as autobiographical texts. Later in the century the memoir of the old colonist came into vogue. Titles such as *Recollections of Squatting in Victoria* (1883) by E.M. **Curr**, and *Pages from the Journal of a Queensland Squatter* (1901) by Oscar de Satge, aptly describe narratives more concerned with recapturing the pioneering experience than with personal reflection.

The memoir, as a record of events witnessed and people met, is sometimes distinguished from autobiography proper, with its concern with the self. The Romantic elevation of the individual encouraged introspection, and it is understandable that novelists should be drawn to this more demanding form of autobiography. The experience of childhood, in particular, commanded attention. So Henry Handel **Richardson's** latter-day account of her childhood, *Myself When Young* (1948), can be compared with her much earlier novel, *The Getting of Wisdom* (1910), and Miles **Franklin's** 'factual' *Childhood at Brindabella* (1963) with the 'fictional' *My Brilliant Career* (1901).

The true flowering of Australian autobiography occurred after World War II against a background of a heightening interest in Australian history and literature. The publication of Hal **Porter's** beautifully crafted *The Watcher on the Cast-Iron Balcony* in 1963 is often seen as a defining moment in the emergence of the modern genre. It carried the subtitle, *An Australian Autobiography*, and reflected, not only a quest for the mother whose death frames the narrative, but a need to recover, in historical detail, the world in which he grew up. Likewise, Donald **Horne** described his own first volume of autobiography, *The Education of Young Donald* (1967), as an exercise in 'sociography', locating his childhood in a social history which historians themselves had failed to provide. Patrick Morgan's article 'Keeping it in the Family' (*Overland*, 1974) was an early attempt at a historical interpretation of the autobiographies of Porter and Horne, along with Graeme McInnes's *The Road to Gundagai* (1965) and George **Johnston's** novel *My Brother Jack* (1964). He pointed to the impact of World War I on a generation of fathers, and saw in the interwar experience of the four families signs of a middle class in decline.

Porter and Horne went on to write further volumes of autobiography, and other writers to have written extensively in this mode include expatriates Jack **Lindsay**, with the three-volume *Life Rarely Tells* (1958–62) and Clive James, in his *Unreliable Memoirs* (1980). Nor have historians been immune from the autobiographical virus. G.V. **Portus** and W.K. **Hancock** might be seen as having set the ball rolling with *Happy Highways* (1953), *Country and Calling* (1954), and

Professing History (1976), but other practitioners include Fred **Alexander**, Manning **Clark**, Kathleen **Fitzpatrick**, Bernard **Smith**, Russel **Ward**, and Alan Frost.

The popularity of autobiography with the reading public is best demonstrated by two extraordinary publishing successes—A.B. **Facey's** monumental but matter-of-fact saga of an Australian Everyman, *A Fortunate Life* (1981), and Sally **Morgan's** quest for her Aboriginal identity, *My Place* (1987). The growing interest in **genealogy** and family history has stimulated the appetite for autobiography, while **oral history** has provided opportunities for the telling of life stories. This has perhaps been particularly relevant to the integration of women into history, contrasting examples being Rhonda Wilson's collection of working-class women's lives, *Good Talk* (1985), and the autobiographical essays of professional women brought together in Patricia Grimshaw and Lynne Strahan (eds), *The Half-Open Door* (1982).

The expanding market for autobiography has encouraged diversification. So the self-justifying political memoir, from Henry **Parkes's** *Fifty Years in the Making of Australian History* (1892) down to *The Hawke Memoirs* (1994), can be clearly distinguished from the lightweight, often ghosted personal story offered by the sports hero. Sally Morgan's *My Place* can be placed in the context of other autobiographical quests for identity, which might be seen as constituting a sub-genre, such as Robert Dessaix's poignant search for the mother who gave him up for adoption, *A Mother's Disgrace* (1994), or Germaine **Greer's** querulous pursuit of her father, *Daddy, We Hardly Knew You* (1989). Sometimes, as in Andrew Reimer's *Inside Outside* (1992) or Arnold Zable's *Jewels and Ashes* (1991), the quest for identity takes the writer backwards from Australia to a half-remembered, or unvisited, parental homeland. Such works are often biographical as much as they are autobiographical (or the other way around), as is also the case with another sub-genre, the AIDS memoir. John Foster's telling of the story of his Cuban lover, Juan, *Take Me to Paris Johnny* (1993), must also reveal something of 'Johnny'. Perhaps such works also demand a greater emotional self-exposure than has been customary in Australian autobiography: was it significant that so many writers seemed more comfortable in writing about family and childhood than in exploring their adult experience?

Morgan's *My Place* also relates to another burgeoning sub-genre, the Aboriginal life story. Often the result of collaborative oral histories, these autobiographies are less concerned with exploring the self or with recovering the lost Eden of childhood than with recording the story of oppression and reclaiming the history of a family or a people. In their political and personalised affirmation of Aboriginality, they challenge and detach themselves from the European historical narrative.

The postmodern cult of subjectivity has encouraged many historians and biographers to declare their presence in the narrative, introducing an autobiographical element. In works as diverse as Greg Dening's *Performances* (1996), Mark Peel's *Good Times, Hard Times* (1995), and Brian Matthews's

Louisa (1987), the author becomes, to a greater or lesser extent, a participant.

There has also been an upsurge of critical writing about Australian autobiography, among the most notable being Richard Coe, *When the Grass Was Taller* (1984); John Colmer, *Australian Autobiography* (1989); and Joy Hooton, *Stories of Herself When Young* (1990). It has now become so fashionable to all but obliterate the distinction between autobiography and fiction that in *Artful Histories* (1996) David McCooey feels obliged to defend the historical nature of autobiography. He sees a paradox, however: while autobiography is concerned with the self, it is also anti-individualistic, in that its practice is 'conversational', an exchange between writer and reader about what life was like.

The modern blurring of the boundaries between autobiography and fiction interestingly recalls the similar ambiguities of the convict memoirs. Historians will continue to assess autobiographies critically for their value as evidence, even while appraising, with greater sophistication, the art and artifice of autobiography as a genre. It is of the nature of autobiography that the story is unfinished: the narrative is a sentence which lacks the full stop of death. The autobiography has a purpose or agenda, even if, in the case of oral life histories, a collaborative one. But autobiography remains too rich a source for human experience to be overlooked by historians, and some of the methodological problems it poses—for example, the role of memory in the construction of history—dramatise contemporary preoccupations of the discipline.

JOHN RICKARD

Aviation was pursued in Australia before the Wright brothers' 1903 flight, though the best-known of Australia's aeronautical pioneers, Lawrence **Hargrave**, never achieved true flight. Three persons claim the honour of having made the first powered flight in Australia: Colin Defries flew 400 metres in a straight line in December 1909, but did not turn or otherwise control his aeroplane; Fred Custance demonstrated such control while flying a Blériot monoplane for more than five minutes in March 1910; while a day later the illusionist Houdini (Fred Weiss) successfully flew a Voisin biplane at Diggers Rest, Victoria.

Rapid progress in aviation technology during and immediately after World War I made long-distance flight possible. In 1919 brothers Ross and Keith **Smith** flew from London to Australia in 27 days 20 hours. In 1928 Bert **Hinkler** completed the first solo flight between England and Australia in a record 16 days, while Charles **Kingsford Smith** and Charles Ulm made the first trans-Pacific crossing the same year. Australian pilots played a role in pioneer aviation out of all proportion to the nation's size and international standing, and were hailed as explorers of a new frontier.

The earliest scheduled domestic air services were subsidised mail runs linking outback communities, beginning in December 1921 with Major Norman Brearley's Western Australian Airways Geraldton–Derby service. **Qantas**, established in 1920, operated a Charleville–Cloncurry (Qld) service in 1922, which later extended to Brisbane. This era of under-powered aeroplanes, unfinished trips, and forced landings is lovingly portrayed by John Gunn in *The Defeat of Distance: Qantas 1919–39* (1985). Australia's capital cities were not linked by air until the early 1930s. Australian National Airways (ANA), operated by Kingsford Smith and Ulm, commenced a regular, unsubsidised Brisbane–Sydney service in January 1930, and added Sydney–Melbourne in June. However, ANA failed in mid-1931, a victim of the Depression and a loss of public confidence due to the crash of its Avro X *Southern Cloud*. Commercially viable airlines developed in the mid-1930s. A new ANA, formed in 1936 by the merger of Holyman Airways and Adelaide Airways, operated from Hobart through Melbourne and Adelaide to Perth. R.M. **Ansett** began operating Hamilton–Melbourne services in February 1936. By 1939 Ansett Airlines was operating a route network of 3000 kilometres, including Melbourne–Sydney via Narrandera, Melbourne–Adelaide via Mildura, and Adelaide–Broken Hill–Mildura–Sydney.

Regular international services did not commence until 1934, when Qantas joined with Imperial Airways to provide flights to London via Singapore. From July 1938 the route was operated by the luxurious Empire flying boats. The service was suspended during World War II.

In 1945 the Labor government attempted to nationalise the airline industry, but was frustrated by the High Court. So the government-owned airline, Trans Australia Airlines (TAA), competed with both ANA and Ansett until 1957, when Ansett's takeover of ANA created a duopoly. From 1951 until the late 1980s Australian domestic aviation developed under the plethora of legislation collectively referred to as the two-airline policy, under which scheduled airline services between designated trunk ports were provided exclusively by TAA and Ansett. While the Commonwealth could not legally prevent other airlines from offering interstate services, it had power of approval over aircraft imports. At its height, the policy regulated competition so closely that the airlines appeared to be Tweedledum and Tweedledee. Stanley Brogden, *Australia's Two-Airline Policy* (1968), remains the best reference to the complex legislation underlying the duopoly.

International aviation was also tightly regulated. The Chicago Convention of 1944 recognised the complete and exclusive sovereignty of states over their airspace. Under Australian policy, Qantas, now government-owned, was the sole carrier designated on international routes. Christopher Findlay subjects international aviation policy to close, critical scrutiny in *The Flying Kangaroo: An Endangered Species?* (1985). By the 1980s, in both the international and domestic spheres, the costs of regulation—low levels of economic efficiency and relatively unresponsive fare regimes—were widely recognised.

The 1990s were an era of deregulation and globalisation. Economic regulation of interstate aviation ended in October 1990. Compass Airlines immediately entered the market, but its challenge was short-lived. The Ansett–Qantas duopoly was again challenged in 2000, with the entry of discount carriers Impulse and Virgin. Competition has improved airline efficiency, the real cost of flying has fallen, and the range of fares available has widened. Internationally, Qantas is no longer Australia's sole designated carrier; Ansett—now owned by Air New Zealand and Singapore Airlines—having the right to offer services to Japan and South-East Asia. To be competitive in the 1990s, airlines must offer services across several continents. To do so, airlines are entering into strategic alliances, such as the One World Alliance, which includes British Airways and Qantas. Globalisation may yet abolish the distinction between domestic and international aviation, changing yet again the face of Australian aviation.

KEITH TRACE

Ayers Rock, see **Uluru**

B

Backhouse, James (1794–1869), Quaker missionary, arrived in Hobart from England in 1832. Initially concerned for the welfare of convicts, he also visited many of the Aboriginal settlements during his three years in Van Diemen's Land. He was encouraged by Lieutenant-Governor **Arthur** to make detailed reports on conditions in the penal and Aboriginal establishments, and, with the support of Governor **Bourke**, did the same during his 1835–37 stay in NSW. These reports were sent to the Society of Friends in London and the Colonial Office and were influential in reforms of the penal system. He was a keen botanist and sent an extensive collection of Australian vegetation and manuscripts of his botanical observations to Kew Gardens. The genus *Backhousia* was later named for him. His *Narrative of a Visit to the Australian Colonies* (1843) provides a detailed account of the situation of convicts and Aborigines. His sister Sarah Backhouse wrote a memoir (1870).

KT

Baillieu family for 100 years was Australia's largest and most successful family grouping in mining, finance, pastoralism, and real estate. The Australian family was founded by JAMES GEORGE BAILLIEU (1832–97), an English seaman of Belgian descent, who jumped ship at Port Phillip Heads and swam ashore to Queenscliff in 1853. There he prospered as a boatman, lighthouse-keeper, and publican, but it was his children led by the second son, WILLIAM LAWRENCE (1859–1936), who elevated the family into wealth and power. Like all the Baillieus, 'W.L.' towered both physically and mentally over his peers. He made the right friends and, despite no personal capital, had risen to the front rank of the land-boomers by 1887. His losses were as large as those of his friends, but in a secret composition in 1892 he paid just sixpence in the pound, only to recover so quickly that he was known to be very rich indeed by 1900.

He began again in real estate, but, fascinated by mining and its financing, soon invested in black coal and gold, then moved to mining interests in four states. He was at the centre of Australian mining for the rest of his life. His brothers EDWARD LLOYD (1867–1939), known as 'Prince', and RICHARD PERCY CLIVE (1874–1941) founded the family sharebroking company in 1892, and three younger brothers in turn began business careers linked by strong family loyalty but not dynastic tyranny. Characteristically, they later named a family company Mutual Trust. In 1897 W.L. travelled to England to raise further capital, and the family began an association with British business and high society that continues to this day.

In 1910 W.L. built headquarters for the family's interests in Collins Street, Melbourne. **Collins House**, the headquarters of more than 50 companies serviced by a common secretariat, became for 60 years the symbol of Australian capitalism—reviled by the left, sniped at by the jealous. The disgraces of 1892 were not readily forgiven in Melbourne society, but by the time W.L. died in 1936, the family had eclipsed its rivals. It sent its sons to Oxford and Cambridge; W.L.'s son CLIVE LATHAM (1889–1967), after a distinguished business career in the UK, was rewarded in 1953 by being made Baron Baillieu, the first Australian hereditary peer with sons to succeed him. Marriage to members of other distinguished and wealthy Australian families added to the family's talent and influence. W.L.'s niece MERLYN (1900–82) married Sidney **Myer**. W.L. as a politician was an independent, later a Liberal, and W.S. **Robinson** came to regard him as 'the greatest of all men who set out to develop Australia'. The family was philanthropic; a large bequest to the University of Melbourne created its Baillieu Library.

The most incisive account of the family is J.R. Poynter's entry in the *ADB*. Useful works are Geoffrey **Blainey**, *The Rush That Never Ended* (1963), Michael **Cannon**, *The Land Boomers* (1967), and W.S. Robinson's fine memoir, *If I Remember Rightly* (1967), but this subject still awaits its historians.

JANET MCCALMAN

Baines, Sarah Jane 'Jennie' (1866–1951) has become an increasingly represented figure in the women's movement. Born in Birmingham, she began work in a factory at 11, and later joined the Independent Labour Party and the temperance movement. A mother of five by 1899, Baines became an organiser in the women's suffrage movement of the Pankhursts. Frequently imprisoned, she went on several hunger-strikes. Adopting a pseudonym, she fled to Melbourne with her family in 1913. Soon she was working for the **Women's Political Association** and supported Vida **Goldstein's** candidature for the federal electorate of Kooyong (Victoria). Baines also joined the Victorian Socialist Party and was co-founder of the Women's Peace Army. She went on a hunger-strike when gaoled for refusing to pay a fine imposed for displaying a red flag during World War I. A special Federal Cabinet meeting released her and she continued to work in the labour movement.

KT

Baker, Mary Ann (1834–1905) became notorious as the companion of the bushranger Captain Thunderbolt (Fred Ward). Born to an Aboriginal mother and convict shepherd father in NSW, she seems to have met Ward when he was working as a stockman in the 1840s. Baker was most probably the Aboriginal woman supposed to have helped him escape from Cockatoo Island after his 1856 conviction for horse-stealing. She accompanied the **bushranging** Thunderbolt during the 1860s and bore him at least three children. When she and the children were captured in 1866, her intelligence and literacy were noted. Details of her later life are sketchy; it seems that she returned to her parents at Stroud and later married a stationhand at Mudgee.

KT

Baker, Sidney John (1912–76) pioneered the study of Australian idiom and its relationship to the national culture. Born in NZ, he moved to Sydney in 1935 where he worked as a journalist. His *Popular Dictionary of Australian Slang* (1941) was soon followed by what has remained his major work, *The Australian Language*, published in 1945, revised in 1966, and with a 1953 supplement, *Australia Speaks*. Although he suffered from multiple sclerosis, Baker researched and wrote prolifically. As well as contributing to encyclopedias and dictionaries, he wrote *Australian Pronunciation* (1947), *The Drum: Australian Character and Slang* (1959), and a study of Matthew **Flinders**, *My Own Destroyer* (1962).

KT

Bandler, Faith (Ida Lessing) (1920–) came into prominence as an Aboriginal activist in 1956 when, with Pearl **Gibbs**, she founded the Aboriginal Australian Fellowship (see **Aboriginal and Torres Strait Islander organisations**), whose lobbying for citizenship rights culminated in the successful 1967 federal **referendum**. She was born in Murwillumbah, NSW; her father was a New Hebrides Islander who had been blackbirded to work on the Queensland canefields. Bandler told his story in *Wacvie* (1977) and *Marani in Australia* (1980, with Len Fox). She remained active in the Aboriginal rights campaign as a left-wing member of the executive of the Federal Council for the Advancement of Aboriginal and Torres Strait Islanders, a personal account of which she wrote in 1989. She has also edited a history of the Aboriginal Australian Fellowship, *The Time Was Ripe* (1983, with Fox). Bandler refused the MBE offered her in 1976, but accepted an OAM in 1984.

KT

Banfield, Edmund James (1852–1923) was a journalist who achieved international recognition for his writings about life on Dunk Island, off the coast of far north Qld. Born in England, he came with his family to Victoria in 1854 and they settled in Ararat, where his father began the *Ararat Advertiser*. Banfield became a reporter but by 1897 poor health forced him to leave the *Townsville Daily Bulletin*, and he moved to Dunk Island. His health improved greatly and he began making notes of natural history and philosophical observations about life on the island. These formed the basis for *Confessions of a Beachcomber* (1908), which was universally praised for its charm and detailed observations of nature. The romantic appeal of his life is evoked by Michael Noonan's biography, *A Different Drummer* (1983).

KT

Banks and banking have been an integral part of the Australian economy since early in the nineteenth century. However, their influence has been altered over time by developments elsewhere in the financial system and as a result of regulation by governments. The 1890s bank crashes have dominated extensive literature on this subject. That dramatic episode serves as the great divide in periodisation between the 'free banking' era of the nineteenth century and the subsequent imposition of a comprehensive set of controls over banks, which lasted until deregulation in the 1980s. Subsequent scholarship has indicated that a revisionist interpretation of various aspects of the history of Australian banks and banking might be in order.

S.J. **Butlin's** magisterial *Foundations of the Australian Monetary System 1788–1851* (1953) describes the slow growth of banking on Australian soil. This delay was primarily due to a shortage of currency that was not rectified until the 1820s. The importance of the establishment of the Bank of New South Wales in 1817 and a handful of other indigenous banks shortly afterwards should not be overestimated. These institutions possessed very limited financial resources. Their business was still overshadowed by private arrangements between individuals, and the **commissariat** was to hold sway in foreign exchange dealings until the 1830s.

Australian banking was transformed in scale and scope by the arrival of a number of British banks in the 1830s. These linked the expanding pastoral economies of Australia with Britain by transferring capital, handling trade bills, and dealing in currency markets. They transformed domestic banking in several ways. Their capital resources far outstripped those of the domestic banks, most of which they acquired, and their managers were better trained. They opened branches, offered interest on deposits, and opted for a Scottish system of lending on cash credits, or overdrafts, rather than bill discounting. The parameters of Australian banking were set from the 1830s until the diversification of these 'trading banks' into savings bank and finance company subsidiaries in the 1950s and 1960s.

The success of these pioneering British banks brought forth another influx of British competitors in the 1850s and, more importantly, swelled the ranks of indigenous banks later in the century. These new Australian banks were, as D.T. Merrett argued in 'Paradise Lost: British Banks in Australia' (in Geoffrey Jones, ed., *Banks as Multinationals*, 1990), little more than clones of their British competitors. Gradually the increasing numbers of local banks eroded the earlier dominance of the British banks, so that they held roughly 70 per cent of bank assets in Australia before the end of the century.

The British connection was overshadowed in another respect. The pioneering British overseas banks came under the oversight of the Treasury through its administration of the Colonial Bank Regulations of 1840 and 1846, which imposed some prudential standards designed to protect the interests of depositors. The amount of notes a bank could issue was limited to a ratio of its capital, and restraints were placed on the banks' lending books to direct them away from illiquid and speculative lending. However, the newly independent colonies replaced the British Treasury as bank regulator from the early 1860s. All came to adopt a *laissez-faire* attitude that was to have important ramifications later.

The 1880s brought a spectacular growth of bank lending. Buoyed by a strong inflow of British capital, and with nearly 40 per cent of deposits raised in Britain, banks were able to satisfy the demands of both government and private customers. The number of banks rose, and all competed vigorously for new business. Furthermore, other financial institutions emerged that competed with the banks at the margins of their territory. Insurance companies, pastoral companies, building societies, and land mortgage companies helped the rising tide of lending during the 1870s and 1880s.

The drying up of British capital inflow after the Baring crisis of 1890 spelt the end of the over-extended financial system. As asset prices fell and borrowers defaulted, the lending institutions came under pressure. The fringe financiers fell first. Eventually, the banks too began to experience financial losses, falling share prices, and panicking depositors. Thirteen of Australia's 22 banks closed their doors in early 1893. All but two reopened within the year. However, all the survivors had been forced to reconstruct. Their creditors agreed to extend the term of their now locked-up deposits, and in some cases to accept preference shares in lieu of deposits. On the other hand, the shareholders agreed to put up fresh capital to keep the banks in business, while the accumulated loses wiped out their earlier investments.

This event irrevocably changed the public esteem enjoyed by banks. They were no longer seen as reliable custodians and vehicles of 'development'; instead, they had become untrustworthy institutions that had lost the people's money. Peter Love, *Labour and the Money Power* (1984), showed how radicals and populists seized on these events to demonise the bankers as agents of 'money power'. Many other historians, including Michael **Cannon**, *Land Boom and Bust* (1972), have exposed some of the shady practices followed by a number of banks. However, Merrett has argued in *AEHR* (1989) and *VHJ* (1993) that many of the criticisms of their collective cupidity have been greatly exaggerated.

The behaviour of private trading banks over the next half-century underwent a significant change. The many histories of individual banks—S.J. **Butlin**, *Australia and New Zealand Bank* (1961); G.N. **Blainey**, *Gold and Paper: A History of the National Bank of Australasia* (1958); R.F. Holder, *Bank of New South Wales* (1970); R.J. Wood, *The Commercial Bank of Australia* (1990)—chronicle how they became very conservative in their lending, and much less competitive than they had been in the decades leading up to the crash. Governments became more actively involved in banking affairs. Surprisingly, no government introduced any important legislative reform of banking in the aftermath of the crash. The more significant response by the public sector was in the provision of banking services on its own account. Depositors flocked to the guaranteed state savings banks after the crash. State governments applied these funds to their own capital issues and to lending for farms and housing through credit fonciers. The Commonwealth government took over the issue of bank notes in 1910 as a revenue measure. It then followed the states by establishing its own bank, the Commonwealth Bank of Australia, in 1912, which competed for both trading and savings bank business.

The new federal government bank was driven forward by two quite distinct impulses. First, its business grew rapidly relative to the private banks. It captured government accounts when the public sector was expanding. The Commonwealth's savings bank deposit base increased quickly, an expansion accelerated by its absorption of a number of state savings banks. Second, a wider set of forces directed that this bank become a central bank. Little of substance was achieved before the outbreak of World War II, despite the suggestions of the Bank of England in the 1920s, and first steps towards policy formation taken in the **Depression** of the 1930s. This latter role was to thoroughly politicise banking and the role of the Commonwealth Bank in particular.

The onset of World War II brought a decisive end to the agonising about the appropriate role for the Commonwealth Bank that followed the report of the royal commission on money and banking in 1937. Australian banking was an instrument of public policy despite the banks' successful campaign against the Labor government's nationalisation proposal in 1947. The Commonwealth Bank, reconstituted after the separation of the **Reserve Bank of Australia** in 1959, was answerable to the government of the day, while the private banks were subject to the oversight and direction of the Reserve Bank. The principal aim of these regulations was to manage the economy, and not to prevent a recurrence of an 1890s-style crash. Boris

Schedvin's official history of the Reserve Bank, *In Reserve* (1992), argues that the policy weapons handed to the bank were a legacy of the unique circumstances of the war, and demonstrates their increasing ineffectiveness in achieving macroeconomic fine-tuning. The lengthy process of deregulation during the 1960s and 1970s owed far more to disaffected regulators than to any pressure brought to bear on governments by banks and other financial institutions.

The sweeping away of the last vestiges of regulation in the early 1980s by the **Hawke–Keating** government prompted another period of turbulence in Australian banking history, not least of which was the privatisation of the Commonwealth Bank. For the first time in more than a century there were a number of highly publicised bank failures, including several state-owned banks. This instability reflected a radically changed environment in which Australian financial markets were once again linked to those of the rest of the world by a floating exchange rate, new foreign banks, and communication technology that allowed instantaneous transfer of funds. These same technologies refashioned banking away from a reliance on branches to automatic teller machines and credit cards. Consumer dissatisfaction grew as banks, whose revenue base was squeezed by non-bank providers of banking services, attempted to charge fees for services once provided free to one set of customers but paid for by higher charges on others. Governments responded in the time-honoured way by setting up more inquiries. The central bank belatedly concerned itself with ensuring the safety of the system by imposing stringent prudential regulations roughly 100 years after the need for them was manifestly apparent.

DAVID MERRETT

Banks, Joseph (1743–1820) was the botanist who sailed with **Cook** on his first voyage of discovery. He was born into a wealthy, landed English family. By inheritance and good management, he added to his patrimony throughout his life but, uncommonly, he used his wealth in the pursuit of his scientific and cultural interests.

At Oxford University he developed a passion for botany, but finding no-one who could instruct him adequately, he hired a tutor who taught him the new Linnaean precepts. In 1766 he spent some months collecting on the shores of Newfoundland and Labrador. Then, in 1768, he joined Cook on the *Endeavour*. He took with him a party of scientists and artists, including the Swedish naturalist Daniel Solander. The voyage lasted three years, and began a massive expansion of knowledge, geographical, scientific, and ethnographic. As well as observing the transit of Venus at Tahiti, Cook charted the coasts of both the large islands of NZ and of eastern Australia. Banks and Solander made very extensive collections—indeed, a mutual acquaintance told Linnaeus that the pair returned to England 'laden with the greatest treasure of Natural History that ever was brought into any country at one time by two persons'. And, whatever their inadequacies in the light of later understandings, Cook's and Banks's descriptions marked the beginning of modern knowledge of Tahitian, Maori, and Aboriginal culture.

In 1778 Banks became president of the Royal Society, a position he retained until his death. As Dawson Turner's massive calendar *The Banks Letters* (1958 and supplements) amply demonstrates, in this capacity he conducted a vast correspondence on a multitude of subjects with the learned of Europe and North America. For decades, he advised the king and a succession of governments on such subjects as fen-drainage, sheep-breeding, agriculture, coinage, hemp cultivation and manufacture, exploration, and colonisation. He sent a succession of young men to the ends of the earth to collect exotic or useful plants, insects, and animals, which he then distributed to other areas. The famous Royal Botanic Gardens at Kew, of which Banks was effectively director, became a central point in this exchange, while the botanical gardens at Jamaica and St Vincent, St Helena, Calcutta, and Sydney were lesser sources. Banks's role was similar to that of a modern scientific commission; but he played it largely single-handed, and without payment.

As **natural history** began to diverge into the modern scientific disciplines, Banks tended to take conservative positions. Nonetheless—as John Gascoigne in *Joseph Banks and the English Enlightenment* (1994) and various of the authors in *Sir Joseph Banks: A Global Perspective* (1994) indicate—he continued to encourage scientific endeavour, actively fostering, for example, the development of geology. Instrumental in the British government's 1786 decision to colonise NSW, Banks remained interested in the Australian continent until his death. During his lifetime, Europeans discovered more about the world than in any previous period; and in 1780, Captain James King, Cook's companion on the third circumnavigation, neatly identified Banks's role in this when he described him as 'the common center of we discoverers'. The best biography is Harold Carter, *Sir Joseph Banks* (1988).

ALAN FROST

Baptist Church was a Nonconformist denomination established in Britain in the early seventeenth century, with particular strength in Wales and northern England. Baptist missionary societies, intent on converting 'heathen' populations, sent missionaries to the Asia–Pacific region in the early 1800s. The first recorded Baptist service was held in Sydney in 1831. Baptists, divided into sects which included the more Calvinistic Particular Baptists and Strict Baptists, comprised the smallest of the major Protestant denominational groups in Australia. Strongly **evangelical**, the Baptist philosophy centred on the Christian rite of baptism, recognising spiritual cleansing or rebirth through full immersion as essential for the salvation of repenting 'sinners'. Baptists established missions to Aborigines and the urban poor. Their first missionary society was formed in Adelaide in 1864, and the Home Mission Board continued work with Aborigines in Central Australia. The Church also built schools and theological colleges. Despite some state differences, Baptists generally ranked slightly lower in social status than **Methodists** and **Congregationalists**. J.D. Bollen has written *Australian Baptists: A Religious Minority* (1975).

HD

Barak, William (1824–1903) became known and respected as a spokesman on Aboriginal affairs and was given the title of the 'last king of the Yarra Yarra tribe'. Barak (or Beruk) was from the Woiworung people of the Kulin nation. As a boy, he witnessed the signing of **Batman's** 'treaty'; after some schooling at Langhorne's mission, he served in Dana's **Native Police** Corps, where he was given the name William. Barak moved to Coranderrk reserve in 1863, and remained there as leader until his death. Although Barak was never fully initiated, anthropologists, notably A.W. **Howitt**, drew upon Barak's extensive knowledge of Aboriginal life. Increasingly recognised for his corroboree paintings, Barak is one of the central artists in Andrew Sayers's *Aboriginal Artists of the Nineteenth Century* (1994). A memorial to him, erected in Healesville by the **Australian Natives Association** (1934), now stands in the Coranderrk Cemetery.

KT

Bark petition, see **Aboriginal land rights**; **Yunupingu, Galarrwuy and Mandawuy**

Barnard, Marjorie Faith (1897–1987), history and fiction writer, wrote under both her own name and as 'M. Barnard Eldershaw', in collaboration with Flora Eldershaw (1897–1956), whom she met studying history at the University of Sydney. After graduating with first-class honours, Barnard was offered a scholarship to Oxford but her father insisted she decline. She became a librarian, then resigned in 1935 to write full-time. Four collaborative novels had been published by 1937, two of which were set in nineteenth-century Sydney: *A House Is Built* (1929), joint winner of the *Bulletin's* novel competition, and *Green Memory* (1931). The partnership also produced several histories, *Phillip of Australia* (1938), *The Life and Times of Captain John Piper* (1939), and *My Australia* (1939). The 1947 publication of the futuristic novel *Tomorrow and Tomorrow and Tomorrow*, the uncensored version of which only appeared in 1983, was their last joint work. Barnard continued to write prolifically. She produced two major histories, *Macquarie's World* (1941) and *A History of Australia* (1962), and other minor works that included two books on Sydney (1947, 1956), and studies of Francis **Greenway** (1961) and Lachlan **Macquarie** (1964). In 1967 she published the first substantial study of Miles **Franklin**. She won the Patrick White Literary Award in 1983 and received an honorary DLitt from the University of Sydney in 1986. Some of her correspondence appears in Carol Ferrier, A*s Good as a Yarn with You* (1992); Maryanne Dever's *Plaque with Laurels* (1995) considers the work of M. Barnard Eldershaw.

KT

Barnett, (Frederick) Oswald (1883–1972) was the most influential anti-slum campaigner of the 1930s and an architect of housing policy in Victoria and the Commonwealth in the early 1940s.

From his working-class Methodist childhood Barnett acquired firm commitments to self-improvement—he became a successful accountant—and the Social Gospel. In the late 1920s, as an anti-smoking campaigner, he visited the homes of children in the back-slums of Melbourne and was appalled by what he saw. His first impulse—to rescue the 'neglected' children from their 'unfit' parents—led to the foundation of the Methodist Babies Home. But he also sought to abolish the **slums** themselves. His tract, *The Unsuspected Slums* (1933), became a best-seller. Barnett was a brilliant publicist and organiser, and forged a powerful anti-slum alliance of church, political, press, and industrial forces which culminated in the appointment of the 1937 Slum Abolition Board. He wrote the report recommending the establishment of the Victorian Housing Commission and later served as its vice-chairman. His brief venture into the federal sphere, as a member of the Commonwealth Housing Commission, was less successful. Barnett's militant brand of Christian Socialism made him suspect during the Cold War, when he was obliged to resign from the Housing Commission.

Barnett recalled his life in an unpublished memoir, 'I Remember' (1965: Victorian Housing Ministry Library), and in an interview with E.W. Russell appended to the latter's *The Slum Abolition Movement in Victoria 1933–37* (1972). The fullest account of his career is in Renate Howe (ed.), *New Houses for Old* (1988), although there are also illuminating glimpses, through the eyes of his children, in Janet McCalman's *Journeyings* (1993).

GD

Barrett, James William (1862–1945), ophthalmologist, progressive, committee-man, graduated in medicine from the University of Melbourne in the early 1880s and then went to London for specialist studies in ophthalmology. He returned to private practice in Melbourne in 1887. Barrett became a lecturer in the school of medicine and was later elected to the university council where he took an active role in curricular and administrative reforms. His interest in progressive social reform proved boundless; it encompassed vocational training, workers' education, slum removal, nursing, town-planning, child health (including kindergartens), the YMCA, and national parks. Many of these aspects are examined by Michael **Roe** in *Nine Australian Progressives* (1984). The establishment of the **Bush Nursing Association** in 1910, with his sister Edith, is perhaps the most tangible of Barrett's achievements. He wrote two books about the medical corps, *The Australian Army Medical Corps in Egypt* (1918) and *A Vision of the Possible* (1919), after his own, often stormy, wartime experiences. Rebuffed in 1920 in his attempt to enter parliament, Barrett turned to the university, and became chancellor in 1935; he was elected president of the British Medical Association in the same year. Barrett was regarded by many progressives as their chief obstacle and, in 1939, was dumped by the council. *The Twin Ideals* (1918), a collection of his papers, gives the best indication of his preoccupations.

KT

Barrington, George (?1755–1804) was a renowned London pickpocket to whom was incorrectly attributed the authorship of many books about his experiences in NSW, as well as the famous prologue describing convicts:

True patriots all; for be it understood,
We left our country for our country's good.

Born in Ireland, Barrington's manners and eloquence allowed him to ply his trade in London society. They also helped him to avoid the consequences until 1790, when he was convicted of theft and sentenced to seven years' transportation. Barrington's good behaviour soon earned him a conditional pardon, which was made absolute in 1796 when he was appointed chief constable at Parramatta. He continued in this role until 1800, when deteriorating mental health forced his resignation.

KT

Barry, John Vincent (1903–69) was an eminent lawyer, and later a Victorian Supreme Court judge, whose interest in criminology and convict history resulted in two biographies, *Alexander Maconochie of Norfolk Island* (1958) and *The Life and Death of John Price* (1964). Barry helped found the Australian Council for Civil Liberties and establish the Victorian Parole Board. Opposed to **capital punishment**, he led Australian delegations to the two United Nations Congresses for the Prevention of Crime and Treatment of Offenders.

KT

Barry, Redmond (1813–80) was an impecunious Anglo-Irish lawyer who arrived in Melbourne in 1839 and, according to **Garryowen**, 'identified himself with every stage of its wonderful progress' until his death. Barry's enthusiastic involvement with the cultural and social development of the community is related in Ann Galbally's 1995 biography, *Redmond Barry: An Anglo-Irish Australian*. He was a founder of the Melbourne Mechanics Institute; president of the Melbourne Club; and a driving force in the development of the Melbourne Public Library, in front of which his statue now stands, and the University of Melbourne, of which he was the first chancellor. A prominent supporter of the movement for separation from NSW, he was Victoria's first solicitor-general before his appointment as judge of the Supreme Court in 1852. Considered a severe judge, he is best remembered for presiding over the trials of several of the **Eureka** rebels in 1855 and that of Ned **Kelly** in 1880. Barry's death shortly after Kelly's execution appeared an eerie fulfilment of the outlaw's promise to meet him in the beyond. Although he never married, his long relationship with a Mrs Louisa Barrow produced four children, all of whom bore his name. Although criticised by the Anglican bishop, the relationship did not seem to harm Barry socially or professionally—he was awarded a knighthood in 1877.

KT

Barton, Edmund (1849–1920), first prime minister of the Commonwealth of Australia and a key figure in the **Federation** movement, represented the interests and the spirit of the Australian-born and -educated younger generation. As prime minister he superintended the establishment of the machinery for federal government, before handing over to **Deakin** in 1903 and joining **Griffith** and **O'Con-**nor on the bench of the first High Court. There, for a further 17 years, he quietly pursued his ideas of a federal system of government for Australia. He died suddenly while on holiday in the Blue Mountains in 1920.

Born in Glebe, NSW, Barton developed a reputation, sketched in Deakin's critical portrait in *The Federal Story* (1944) as one of the 'Men of 1891', for indolence and self-indulgence, with too great a love of the good life. Handsome, with a liberal and generous intellect and a genial and affectionate nature, 'Toby' Barton was one of those to whom life seemed kind, though he also suffered sleepless nights with his 'blue devils'. At the University of Sydney he carried off prizes, graduated with first-class honours in classics, and played cricket with enthusiasm. While studying law, he visited Newcastle to play cricket and met Jeanie Ross. 'How I love that girl', he wrote in the diary he kept at the time; they were married at the end of 1877. Two years later, he won his first seat in the NSW lower house.

For the next 20 years he juggled a career in politics with the need to earn an adequate income through the law. A note in his surviving papers in the National Library of Australia shows him in 1886 calculating whether he could afford to give up the £1500 he earned annually as speaker of the Legislative Assembly. No orator, and conservative by instinct, he was unsuited to the factional politics of NSW. He was a protectionist; he briefly held office under Dibbs 1891–93, and then devoted himself to the federal movement. The idea of 'a nation for a continent, and a continent for a nation', as he put it at a meeting in Ashfield, provided scope for his real talent as a constitutional lawyer, and the various drafts of the **Constitution** owed much to his work. He was leader of the 1897–98 Federal Convention. By 1900 it was unthinkable to Deakin and his federal movement colleagues that anyone else should be entrusted with the establishment of the machinery of the first Commonwealth government. He led a moderate protectionist government. Not until he collapsed in his office in August 1903 was he permitted to leave politics for the High Court, though even there he worried. 'Will it be easy to make Griffith laugh?' he asked Deakin.

John Reynolds's *Edmund Barton* (1948), the first of the modern biographies of the federal fathers, challenged the image of indolent Toby Barton, and Geoffrey **Bolton**'s more recent biography (2000) strengthens the argument that his subject was 'the only man for the job' of leading Australia to nationhood. The question asked by the advertising campaign of the Council for the Centenary of Federation—'What sort of a country is it that does not know the name of its first prime minister?'—might well underestimate Barton's growing esteem.

BEVERLEY KINGSTON

Barton, George Burnett (1836–1901), the older brother of Edmund, was described by the *Bulletin* after his death as 'the first purely literary man produced by New South Wales'. His tendency to disputation was evident early when his studies at the University of Sydney were curtailed by a public dispute with the principal over courses. He went to London and was admitted to the Bar, but eventually returned to NSW as a journalist. In 1864 he became editor of the *Sydney Punch*. He briefly held a government appointment but lost it after admitting to his authorship of a piece ridiculing the government. He was appointed reader in English literature at the University of Sydney in 1865, then three years later went to NZ as editor of the *Otago Daily Times*. Barton returned to the law after prosecution for libel by the government, and by the 1880s was back in Sydney. In 1887 he was appointed to bring out a new edition of the *Official History of New South Wales*, which he parleyed into agreement that he should produce a 15-volume *History of New South Wales from the Records*. Typically, Barton and the government fell out over the project, and he left after completing only the first volume, *Governor Phillip, 1783–89* (1889). G.B. was involved in the Federation movement and wrote a 'Historical Sketch of Australian Federation' for inclusion in the 1891 *Yearbook of Australia*.

KT

Barwick, Garfield Edward John (1903–97), conservative politician and eminent lawyer, is remembered and reviled by many Australians for his advice to the governor-general, John **Kerr**, supporting the 1975 **Dismissal** of Gough **Whitlam** as prime minister. He offers a detailed rationale for this advice in *Sir John Did His Duty* (1983). The child of a poor Methodist family, Barwick was a scholarship boy whose sense of being an outsider is examined in David Marr's critical biography, *Barwick* (1980; 1992). He was admitted to the NSW Bar in 1927, and ability and hard work soon resulted in a thriving law practice. He became a KC in 1941, by which time he had shed his youthful Methodist and Labor principles to become a lawyer of the establishment, successfully opposing the **Chifley** government's attempts at nationalisation, acting for the **Menzies** government in its attempt to ban the Communist Party of Australia and for **ASIO** during the **Petrov** royal commission. A fervent royalist, he received recognition in 1953 with a knighthood. Menzies persuaded him to enter federal politics in 1958. As attorney-general he initiated Australia's first national divorce laws, the 1959 Matrimonial Causes Act, and controversial legislation allowing greater powers to security organisations. As minister for external affairs (1962–64), Barwick oversaw the beginning of Australia's involvement in Vietnam. He left politics in 1964 to become chief justice of the **High Court**, a position he held until his retirement in 1981. His most tangible legacy from this period is the monumental High Court building in Canberra. Barwick's autobiography, *A Radical Tory*, appeared in 1995.

KT

Basic wage is the name given to minimum wage awards determined by Commonwealth and state tribunals from the early twentieth century under the **arbitration** system. In his Harvester judgment of 1907, H.B. **Higgins**, the president of the Commonwealth Arbitration Court, laid down a minimum wage; based on the cost of living, it applied to all adult males working under Commonwealth awards, and he subse-

quently used the Commonwealth statistician's price index to adjust it. A lesser minimum was similarly calculated for female workers. From 1913 the adjustments for the cost of living were applied automatically, and state tribunals subsequently adopted the practice for wage-earners working under state awards. The basic wage was for unskilled workers, and additional payments were specified for occupational skills. Higgins first used the term *basic wage* in 1911, and it quickly became a common usage expressive of Australian expectations.

The basic wage was cut by 10 per cent in 1931, and only partially restored when the **Depression** eased as the court modified the needs basis of the basic wage by the principle of industry's capacity to pay. Automatic cost-of-living adjustments ceased in 1953. In 1967 the court ended its practice of determining a separate basic wage with additional margins for skill in favour of a total wage, and henceforth the term was abandoned. (See also **Social laboratory**.)

SM

Bass, George (1771–?1803), an English naval surgeon with a passion for **exploration**, is best known for confirming that Tasmania was separated from mainland Australia by the strait that now bears his name. Bass made his discovery during two voyages: to Western Port Bay on the south-east coast of the mainland in 1797–98, and then, with Matthew **Flinders**, circumnavigating Tasmania in 1798–99. Earlier, they had explored the south coast of NSW in the tiny *Tom Thumb*. Bass returned to England in 1800, married, and became a trader. In 1803 he sailed to Chile; nothing more is known of his fate.

KT

Bassett, Flora Marjorie 'Marnie' (1889–1980), historian, was born at the University of Melbourne, where her father, David Masson, was professor of chemistry. Privately educated and trained as a secretary, she showed a strong interest in history and attended Ernest **Scott's** lectures. With Scott's encouragement, she wrote an article about the foundation of the university for the *University Review* (June 1913). Wartime work in England interrupted her subsequent research. She eventually returned, married, and settled to domestic life, but once her children had grown, she returned to history. Her study of Philip Gidley **King's** wife, Anna, *The Governor's Wife* (1940), pioneered women's history; this was followed in 1954 by *The Hentys*, a study of the pioneering family at Portland, generally regarded as her most important work. Other books include *Realms and Islands* (1962), *Behind the Picture* (1966), and *Letters from New Guinea, 1921* (1969). She was awarded the honorary degree of DLitt by Monash and Melbourne universities, and was a foundation fellow of the Australian Academy of the Humanities.

KT

***Batavia*, wreck of the**, took place on the night of 4 June 1629 on the reefs of islands in the Indian Ocean, about 30 kilometres off the western coast of Australia. The *Batavia* was a Dutch ship, contracted under the East India Company for the spice trade, and named after the Indonesian trading port to which it was sailing. Following the wreck, Captain Francisco Pelsaert led a party that proceeded by boat to Batavia for assistance, leaving his crew of men, women and children as castaways. A group of the survivors mutinied, forcing the others to submit to their control or be punished. When Pelsaert returned, the leaders of the mutiny were captured and executed. Recovered in the 1970s, the wreck underwent restoration and preservation before being displayed at the Western Australian Maritime Museum. Henrietta Drake-Brockman's account, *Voyage to Disaster* (1963), was followed by Hugh Edwards's *Islands of Angry Ghosts* (1966). Palsaert's own account of the voyage, first published as *Ongeluckige Voyagie, Van't Schip Batavia, Nae de Oost-Indien* in 1647, appeared in English translation in the *Western Mail* in 1897 and was republished in 1994. A fictionalised account by Rupert Gerritsen, *And Their Ghosts May Be Heard*, appeared the same year. (See also **Exploration by sea**.)

HD

Bate, Weston (1925–) led the movement of academically trained historians into the writing of **local history** in the early 1960s. His *History of Brighton* (1962, revised 1983) was written as a University of Melbourne master's thesis while Bate was a teacher at Melbourne Grammar School; it utilised a wide range of local sources—some, like rate-books, seldom used before—to build up a richly textured social map of an evolving suburban community. Local history, Bate remarked, was like an iceberg of which only the top one-tenth of the research appeared in the text. He rejoined the history department of the University of Melbourne in the mid-1960s and began his major work, a history of Ballarat, published in two volumes, *Lucky City* (1978) and *Life After Gold* (1993). The central chapters of his first volume, on the Eureka rebellion, illustrate his approach—a detailed reconstruction of the economic and spatial settings leads to a vigorous narrative of the event itself. Like his predecessor, W.B. Withers, Bate celebrates the locals' conviction that 'Ballarat was the true Australia.' As foundation professor of Australian studies at Deakin University from 1973, and later as president of the Royal Historical Society of Victoria, he promoted the teaching of Australian urban and regional history, and fostered links between the universities and local historical societies and museums. His detailed reconstruction of Ballarat's Main Street in the gold era became the inspiration for one of the main features of Sovereign Hill, Australia's most successful **pioneer settlement**.

GD

Bates, Daisy May (1859–1951), strait-laced do-gooder, pioneer anthropologist, true friend to the Aborigines, or eccentric recluse? At different times Daisy Bates has been described in all these terms. In a long and often difficult life, she covered up many aspects of her past.

Born Catholic Daisy O'Dwyer in County Tipperary, she later claimed descent from a high-born Protestant family.

After working as a governess in England she mysteriously set off alone for Townsville in north Qld at the age of 24, where she became a governess on an outback station in 1883. There she met a young stockman, known as Edwin Murrant, and they married in 1884. She claimed to be 21; he was 19. Careful research has shown beyond doubt that he was Harry 'The Breaker' **Morant**. Although they never divorced, Daisy later married John (Jack) Bates at Nowra in 1885. She again gave her age as 21 and described herself as 'spinster'. She gave birth to a son, Arnold, in 1896, but abandoned the family and returned to England. Not long after, her husband bought a station in the remote north-west of WA, and she returned to join him, intrigued by English newspaper accounts about Aboriginal slavery in that state. Travelling through the district accompanied by local Aboriginal people, she began writing about their lives and customs. She abandoned Arnold and Jack again, and moved to Perth, after being commissioned by the government in 1904 to research and write about the **Aboriginal languages** of the state.

In 1910 she joined the expedition of A.R. Radcliffe-Browne (then simply A.R. Brown, a young English anthropologist) to the north-west of WA. Their uneasy partnership dissolved quickly, leaving her with much bitter feeling; she believed he never acknowledged her substantial contributions to his work, and accused him of plagiarism. This charge has never been proved, but certainly she assisted his research in many ways that he never acknowledged in his published writings. She had been preparing a three-volume work of her own, and the state government agreed to publish it. This agreement was overturned when a new Labor government was elected, and her employment was terminated.

In 1914 she gave a paper at the Australian meeting of the British Association for the Advancement of Science. At this stage she saw herself primarily as an anthropologist and expert on Aboriginal life and customs, a view which was certainly shared by some eminent scientists of the day. In 1920, aged 61, she moved to Ooldea, SA, on the transcontinental railway line, where she set up a large tent near the Aboriginal camp. Desert dwellers from the remote north and west had arrived in increasing numbers, attracted to this remote outpost by novel experiences and new sources of food. She continued to live there, with brief interruptions, for the next 25 years, and it was during this period that her image as an eccentric was established. She made much of her intimacy with her Aboriginal companions; their name for her, Kabbarli, is given hallowed significance, but in fact it is a kinship term used as a mark of respect. Like them, she had no income, but managed to make some money by writing scandalous and shocking pieces for the newspapers, asserting, for instance, that Aboriginal mothers ate their newborn babies and that a large number of people of German origin in SA were spies. She was an ardent monarchist and took every opportunity to meet members of the British royal family, including the Duke of York (later George V) in 1901 and the Duke of Gloucester in 1934. In that year she was awarded the Order of the Commander of the British Empire.

During her later years she continued to write articles about her life with the Aborigines, and these were subsequently published as *The Passing of the Aborigines* in 1938. The book sold well in Australia, Britain, and the USA. Nevertheless she remained very poor, and camped alone by the River Murray about 150 kilometres from Adelaide, preparing the voluminous notes and papers she presented finally to the Parliamentary Library in Canberra in 1941. Her last years were difficult and lonely. She had no family and few acquaintances, and suffered from poor sight caused by years in the desert. At the age of 81 she returned to live on the railway near Ooldea, hoping to recover her relationship with the local Aborigines. But times had changed and finally the Commonwealth government provided her with a small pension until her death in 1951 at the age of 91.

Daisy Bates remains an enigma. She seems to have been from the first a woman who could not accept the normal social constraints and expectations of her culture and time. She obviously longed to be accepted as a scientist and founder–anthropologist by a peer group of male scholars. Yet her attitudes remained fixed in a nineteenth-century mould, and there is little evidence of a broad-ranging intellect or genuine scientific passion for her field of study. She lived in close association with Aboriginal people for most of her life, but never questioned the justice of their dispossession nor the notion that they were necessarily 'a dying race'. Her writings today, although studded with fascinating observation, are not taken seriously in the way that others of her time still are, for example, the works of Baldwin **Spencer**.

Although neglected and ignored during her later years, Daisy Bates became of increasing interest to a new generation concerned with placing both women and indigenous people into an emerging national consciousness. Elizabeth Salter published a popular account in 1971, *Daisy Bates: The Great White Queen of the Never Never*, while Ernestine **Hill's** memoir gives a subjective account, in which Daisy Bates appears as a kind of missionary activist whose sole interest was the welfare of those she thought of as a dying race. Isobel White defended Bates's contributions to Aboriginal studies in 'Mrs Bates and Mr Brown: An Examination of Rodney Needham's Allegations' *Oceania* (1981); her editing of and introduction to Bates's *The Native Tribes of Western Australia*, finally published in 1985, brings to fruition 12 years of close research into Bates's writings and is a monumental study, consolidating and clarifying much rambling and repetitious material. It is striking now to realise how little Daisy Bates was able to analyse the contradictions of the colonial frontier, even as she could see every day what was happening to 'her' Aborigines. She hovers, a puzzling figure, at the junction between a nineteenth- and a twentieth-century consciousness. Sidney **Nolan** painted her, but his painting was not widely reproduced. Maie **Casey** wrote the libretto for the opera *The Young Kabbarli*, which was the first Australian opera recorded in Australia. With music composed by Margaret **Sutherland**, it was first performed at the Theatre Royal in Hobart in 1965. There seems to have been only two subsequent performances, in Adelaide and

Melbourne, in 1972. Julia Blackburn published a fictional account, *Daisy Bates in the Desert*, in 1994. Daisy Bates is too puzzling a figure to be comfortably located within the pantheon of 'great Australians', to be an icon or image for any period of Australian history.

ANNETTE HAMILTON

Batman, John (1801–39) is regarded, with John Pascoe **Fawkner**, as the founder of Melbourne. Born in NSW of a convict father, he became a farmer in Van Diemen's Land, where he achieved notoriety for capturing the bushranger Matthew **Brady**. He also took part in the infamous Black Line in the campaign to capture the Tasmanian Aborigines. Attracted by the lure of unexplored land, Batman helped form the **Port Phillip Association**, sailing as its agent to the mainland in 1835. He explored the lower reaches of the Yarra River and supposedly chose the site for Melbourne with the comment, later widely quoted, that 'this will be the place for a village'. Some scholars doubt that he reached the present site of Melbourne. Batman attempted to validate his claim to large tracts of land by entering into a sale treaty with local chiefs, which Alastair Campbell discusses critically in *John Batman and the Aborigines* (1987). In the four years that were left before syphilis killed him, he attempted to establish the security of his claim in Port Phillip based on the validity of the treaty and his own position as first settler, a role also sought by Fawkner. Initially forgotten, a glorified Batman was returned to the public memory by James **Bonwick** in his 1856 history of the settlement. By the 1934–35 Melbourne centenary celebrations he was regarded as worthy of commemoration. The publication in 1979 of a biography by C.P. Billot began the process of reassessment.

KT

Battle of Brisbane was a large-scale riot that took place in Brisbane on 26 November 1942. While the brawling was essentially between the Australian soldiers and the US servicemen who were stationed in Brisbane during **World War II**, the violence is believed to have been provoked by the US military police's harassment of an American. The ensuing fighting, which involved many Australian soldiers, resulted in the death of one, and serious injuries to several Australian and American soldiers. Peter A. Thomson and Robert Macklin produced a study (2000).

HD

Battye, James Sykes (1871–1954) was head of the Victoria Public Library in Perth from 1894, and of the library, museum, and art gallery of WA from 1912 until his death. He was also a founder of the Western Australian Historical Society. He was educated and trained in Melbourne, and submitted *Western Australia: A History* (1924) to the University of Melbourne for award of a doctorate of letters. He built the public library collection to more than 100 000 volumes by World War I, but it languished between the wars and was castigated in the Munn–Pitt report on Australian **libraries** in 1935. Battye was early in appreciation of the value of government records, which he began to acquire in 1903, but this activity also lost momentum; the state archives were not established until 1945. The state history collection of the State Library of Western Australia is named after him.

His own research resulted in the *Cyclopedia of Western Australia* (1912–13), a *History of the North West of Australia* (1915), and the 1924 state history, which was produced with public assistance. It is assessed by Geoffrey **Bolton** in C.T. Stannage (ed.), *New History of Western Australia* (1981), as a form of monumental history in which constitutional and political advances guide WA's development.

SM

Baudin, (Thomas) Nicolas (1754–1803), French sailor, cartographer and naturalist, led an expedition from France in 1800 to complete the French cartographic survey of the Australian coast and undertake scientific investigations. The two ships, *Le Naturaliste* and *Le Géographe*, arrived on the west coast in 1801 and eventually made their way in early 1802 to **Van Diemen's Land**. Baudin travelled to Sydney, where he received a generally friendly reception, tempered by suspicion as to French motives for the expedition. The assessment by Matthew **Flinders** of Baudin's work as 'rather below mediocrity' helped to form the critical judgment that held sway for over a century. Baudin sent *Le Naturaliste* back to France with the expedition results, and bought a schooner to continue with the survey. He and Louis Freycinet travelled along the south coast and stopped at King Island, exacerbating fears of French colonisation plans. They travelled up the west coast to Timor, then to Mauritius, where Baudin died. When Freycinet published his complete atlas in 1812, he virtually ignored Baudin's part in the work, condemning him to obscurity. A re-evaluation of his role, begun by Ernest **Scott** in *Terre Napoléon* (1910), continued with Christine Cornell's translation of his journal in 1974. Frank Horner's *The French Reconnaissance* (1987) is a detailed examination of the 1801–03 expedition.

KT

Baxter, Annie Maria, see **Dawbin (Baxter), Annie Maria**

Baynton, Barbara Jane (1857–1929) is best known for stories written during the 1890s and collected as *Bush Studies* (1902). A child of the pioneer endeavour, wife of a poor selector, she wrote short stories that would be valued 100 years later as a female counter to Henry **Lawson's**; yet she denied the past which impelled her fiction, and wanted to be counted a grand dame in the drawing-rooms of Europe, with a title and a place in the aristocracy.

Baynton disguised her origins, creating a romantic fantasy to explain why she grew up in out-of-the-way parts of NSW. Her grandson and first biographer, Henry Gullet (whose 'Memoir' was published in *Bush Studies*, 1965), believed that she was the daughter of Penelope Ewert, a bride sailing to Australia who fell in love with the dashing Captain Kilpatrick. When the ship reached Sydney, the lovers eloped, retreating to the bush, where they ensured that the children born were imbued with cultivated manners and tastes. More probably, Baynton's parents were a carpenter and his wife, whose home in the Scone district she escaped by becoming a governess and in 1880 marrying a selector, Alexander Frater. Seven years later, when Frater ran off with one of his wife's relatives, Barbara took her three children to Sydney, where she was said to have sold Bibles door-to-door before divorcing Frater in 1890, and the next day marrying a wealthy 70-year-old retired doctor, Thomas Baynton.

From this moment, Barbara Baynton was on her way to becoming a fashionable woman and a writer. Five poems published by the *Bulletin* between 1897 and 1902 are derivative in language and highly emotional, with the poet as woman sundered from homeland and mother grieving for a dead child. Her fiction, in contrast, is stamped with a distinctive voice, achieved when an accumulation of detail promising authenticity conjures up nightmarish terror, grim humour, and an altogether bleak vision of life among the battlers. None of the pleasantries or piety associated with middle-class femininity plays any part in her austere portrayal of the bush as a place where hardship breeds cruelty without heroism. The *Bulletin* accepted the single Baynton story published in Australia during her lifetime only after editing it down to a bush anecdote.

Baynton, determined to publish, sailed with her manuscript to England; there through a chance meeting with the critic and publisher's reader, Edward Garnett, *Bush Studies* was published by Duckworth & Co. in 1902, to be followed by a novel, *Human Toll* (1907), and a second short story collection, *Cobbers* (1917). After Dr Baynton's death in 1904, she lived mainly in London, and became well-known as a collector of antiques. In 1921 she married Lord Headley, an engineer thought to have converted to Islam while building a bridge over the Ganges; they soon separated. As Lady Headley, Barbara Baynton may have achieved her social ambitions, but it is as the woman who refused the received version of the Australian bush that she is remembered. A biography by Penne Hackforth-Jones was published in 1989.

LUCY FROST

Bean, Charles Edwin Woodrow (1879–1968) was a journalist and historian who did more than any other individual to create and maintain the **Anzac Legend**.

He was a patriotic native-born Australian with a deep attachment to the British Empire. His father was an Englishman, and he was educated at a private school in England and at Oxford University. Though trained for the law, he soon took up journalism on his return to Australia. From 1908 he was reporter, special correspondent, and leader-writer on the *Sydney Morning Herald*. Some of his articles from these years formed the basis of *On the Wool Track* (1910), a heartfelt idealisation of Anglo-Saxon men toughened by the bush. On the outbreak of war, he narrowly won the election conducted by the journalists' union to determine who should be Australia's official war correspondent. He accompanied the Australian

Imperial Force (**AIF**) throughout the war and was always close to the fighting. While at **Gallipoli**, he collected pieces written by soldiers and carefully edited them to create *The Anzac Book* (1916), which K.S. **Inglis** calls 'the Anzacs' school magazine'.

He drew up the proposal for *The Official History of Australia in the War of 1914–1918* (1921–42) and was appointed editor. Bean succeeded in making the 12-volume series a monument to the men of the First AIF. His own six volumes, on Gallipoli and the Western Front, form the core of the work. They provided a detailed narrative, written in a lively, plain style, based on the activities of front-line soldiers, and so established a new mode of **military history**. Bean argued that the war tested the Australian national character; that Australian soldiers demonstrated superior virtues, which stemmed mainly from their bush background; and that 'on the 25th of April, 1915 … the consciousness of Australian nationhood was born'. As L.L. **Robson** showed in *HS* (1973), Bean over-emphasised the rural origins and democratic nature of the First AIF.

Bean supported the founding and development of the **Australian War Memorial**, an institution whose composite nature—memorial, museum, and archives—owes much to his vision for it; his contribution is discussed in Michael McKernan's *Here Is Their Spirit: A History of the Australian War Memorial 1917–1990* (1991). During World War II, Bean helped to create the Commonwealth Archives, and published *The Old A.I.F. and the New* (1940) and *War Aims of a Plain Australian* (1943).

The official history sold well, was highly regarded by the official war historians of other countries, and earned Bean literary honours; but during his lifetime it was largely ignored by Australian historians and literary critics, with the notable exceptions of H.M. **Green** in his *A History of Australian Literature*, vol. 1 (1961), and K.S. **Inglis** in his essay in *Meanjin* (1965). After Bean's death, interest increased, partly because of Inglis's Macrossan Lecture of 1969, published as *C.E.W. Bean, Australian Historian* (1970). Kevin Fewster selected and annotated *Gallipoli Correspondent: The Frontline Diary of C.E.W. Bean* (1983) and Denis Winter selected *Making the Legend: The War Writings of C.E.W. Bean* (1992). Dudley McCarthy wrote a limited biography entitled *Gallipoli to the Somme: The Story of C.E.W. Bean* (1983).

JAN BASSETT

Beaurepaire, Francis Joseph Edmund 'Frank'

(1891–1956) was a swimmer who won numerous local and international titles, held 15 world records, and swam in three **Olympic Games** at which he won six medals, but never a gold. Graham Lomas captures the competitive nature of the man in his biography, *The Will to Win* (1960). In 1922 Beaurepaire co-founded in Melbourne the Beaurepaire Tyre Service; over the following years a number of other profitable companies were formed using the Olympic trade name. Beaurepaire was active in community affairs: he helped found and support the extensive *Herald* Learn-to-Swim campaign; he was lord mayor 1940–42, and a conservative member of the Legislative Council for 10 years. He

donated money to the University of Melbourne to establish a sports centre, now known as the Beaurepaire Centre. Possibly his greatest gift to the community was his leadership of the bid that won the 1956 Olympic Games for Melbourne. He died suddenly, several months before the games.

KT

Becker, Ludwig

(1808–61) was the artist and naturalist on the ill-fated 1860 Victorian Exploration Expedition to the Gulf of Carpentaria led by Robert O'Hara **Burke**; during this expedition Becker succumbed to scurvy and dysentery at Bulloo, south of Coopers Creek. Born in Germany, Becker arrived in Van Diemen's Land in 1850: he spent two years there pursuing his scientific interests, supporting himself by painting miniatures. He then worked on the Bendigo goldfields for two years before settling in Melbourne, where he immersed himself in intellectual and artistic activities, including work for Ferdinand von **Mueller**. Although Becker lacked proper equipment and Burke's support, he managed to send back full reports and complete many sketches, meteorological observations, and notes on the Aborigines. These are held in the La Trobe Collection at the State Library of Victoria, and have been reproduced by Marjorie Tipping in *Ludwig Becker* (1979). In her *Dictionary of Australian Artists* (1992), Joan Kerr claims that his work was 'the most significant product' of the expedition.

KT

Bedford, (George) Randolph

(1868–1941) was an ardent republican nationalist and Labor supporter who wrote regularly in the *Bulletin* and the *Lone Hand*. After working on several newspapers, including the Adelaide *Advertiser* and the Melbourne *Age*, he founded the *Clarion*, a journal that combined his passions for mining and literature. Several of the **Lindsays** wrote for the *Clarion*; Norman supposedly used Bedford's flamboyant moustache and wide hat for the character of Bunyip Bluegum in *The Magic Pudding* (1918). Even though a member of the Qld Legislative Council (1917–22) and the Legislative Assembly (1923–41), Bedford was a prolific writer, producing many short stories, plays, travel pieces, and novels. The autobiographical *Naught to Thirty-Three* (1944) is considered his most important work. In the preface to the 1976 edition, Geoffrey **Blainey** claimed the book as an expression of 'the most articulate and influential phase of Australian nationalism'.

KT

Benefit societies

were working-class fraternities based on a British model, formed in most Australian cities and towns from the mid-nineteenth century. Many were also friendly societies. The main societies in Australia included the **Australian Natives Association**, Buffaloes, Druids, Foresters, Free Gardeners, Freemasons, Hibernians, Oddfellows, Protestant Alliance, Rechabites, and Sons of Temperance. Their meetings followed the ceremony of lodge procedures, and their elaborate banners and regalia were displayed at civic processions, such as those celebrating the **Eight-Hour Day**.

Tea meetings, balls, and dramatic and sporting events were held regularly. The societies attracted many workers, for whom a sole wage was a precarious means of support. In the absence of government pensions, the accumulation of members' contributions established a valuable fund, out of which benefits were paid. Those financially disadvantaged by the sickness or death of the male breadwinner were the main recipients. In the case of a member's death, the society usually bore the funeral costs and often provided continuing support to widows. The chief benefit was medical care provided by doctors who entered into contracts with the societies. With the notable exception of Geoffrey **Blainey's** *Odd Fellows* (1991), benefit societies have been largely ignored by historians. Today they operate as private life and health insurance societies, and provide a range of financial services.

HD

Benevolent asylums were charitable institutions modelled on the poor houses of Britain that provided care to the poor and the destitute. The first benevolent asylum was established in Sydney 'for the poor blind, aged and infirm' in 1820 through the endeavours of a private charitable society, the Benevolent Society of New South Wales, which was founded in 1813 with the support of Governor **Macquarie** and financial support from the government. A benevolent asylum opened in Melbourne in 1851 for the aged and incurable who were too poor to afford a private hospital. Although initially operating with private funds, within a decade the Melbourne asylum relied heavily on public money. Similar government-supported institutions were established in major cities and provincial towns in many of the colonies. They were gradually subsumed into the public hospital system and superseded by the introduction of **social welfare** entitlements.

HD

Bennelong (c.1764–1813), one of two Aborigines captured in November 1789 on the order of Governor **Phillip**, was an early victim of the disruption caused to Aboriginal life by European settlement. Phillip hoped to learn about customs and language from Bennelong and Colbee, and possibly to use them as emissaries to other Aborigines. Both soon escaped, but not before Bennelong's open, inquiring attitude had caused him to sample European life and learn some English. The spearing of Phillip in September 1790, which Bennelong saw, re-established his contact with the settlement as he came to inquire after Phillip's health. He became the governor's favourite of Phillip, and dined frequently at Government House. Phillip had a hut built for him on what became Bennelong Point, now the site of the **Sydney Opera House**. The writings of **Hunter**, **Collins** and **Tench** present him as an engaging, intelligent character. In 1792 Bennelong and another adventurous young man, Yemmerrawanyea, sailed with Phillip to England. Yemmerrawanyea died in 1794; Bennelong, in poor health, returned to Australia in 1795 to find his second wife gone and himself belonging to neither white nor

Aboriginal society. His descent into alcoholism was rapid. He died as the result of a tribal fight.

KT

Bennett, Samuel (1815–78), Cornish-born newspaperman and historian, came to Australia in 1841 as a printer for the *Sydney Morning Herald*. He moved to the *Empire* as co-owner in 1859, and it was here that he published, in weekly parts, what was intended to be a full history of Australia. He was forced by work pressures to curtail his history, published in 1865 as *The History of Australian Discovery and Colonisation*, which has been described as a 'significant early history of Australian exploration'. Bennett continued to expand his holdings. He opened Sydney's first evening newspaper, the *Evening News*, and the widely read weekly, the *Australian Town and Country Journal*, which is a valuable source of information about colonial society.

KT

Bent, Thomas (1839–1909), politician and land speculator, became famous in Victoria as a local booster and logroller. He began work as a market gardener, then became rate-collector for Brighton, a position that he used to win support for his political ambitions. He served as MLA for Brighton, from 1871 to 1894, and again from 1900 to 1909, always ensuring that the residents were looked after. Bent's extensive land speculation is documented in Michael **Cannon's** *The Land Boomers* (1966), and in Margaret Glass's biography, *Tommy Bent* (1993), which also examines the dichotomous public attitudes. Honoured by many, mainly Brighton residents, as a good man, he was reviled by others, including much of the press, as a scoundrel intent upon promoting his own interests. Typically, Bent would purchase large tracts of land, use his influence to ensure that a railway line went through that area, then subdivide the land and sell for a large profit. His 1881 appointment to the position of minister for railways was particularly apt; his behaviour gave rise to the famous tag 'Bent by name, bent by nature'. Bent's term as premier of Victoria from 1904 coincided with the belated recovery from **depression** which enabled him to relax the crippling public parsimony. But he became increasingly eccentric, bursting into song or verse during parliamentary sittings and falling asleep at public meetings. In December 1908 his government fell to a vote of no confidence. Rather than resign, Bent called an election. He died soon after and received a state funeral; the people of Brighton donated the money to erect a statue in his honour.

KT

Bernays, Charles Arrowsmith (1862–1940) inherited a fluency in the rules of parliamentary practice from his father, Lewis Adolphus, clerk of the Queensland Legislative Assembly, 1860–1908. After serving an apprenticeship as Hansard reporter and sergeant-at-arms, Charles was clerk of the assembly from 1920 (and of the parliament after 1922)—until his retirement in 1932. His knowledge and experience of parliamentary behaviour are brought together in *The*

Condensed Rulings of the Speakers of the Legislative Assembly of Queensland (1924).

A second major interest was **political history**. No effective work had yet appeared covering Qld's political developments during the colonial period. In 1918 Bernays gave a 98-page overview on the state's political history to the Historical Society of Queensland. Out of this arose his magisterial *Queensland Politics During Sixty (1859–1919) Years* (1919). Looking somewhat dated now, the work is still a useful compendium on the colonial parliament—replete with summations of the parliamentary sessions, limited analysis of legislation on topics such as land, and chatty glimpses into the behaviour of many politicians. In 1931 his sequel followed, *Queensland—Our Seventh Political Decade, 1920–1930*. The same format was adopted; while shading his political inclinations, Bernays expressed a certain satisfaction with the Moore conservative government elected in 1929—as evidenced, for example, in his criticisms of Labor's state enterprises. His *Roll of the Queensland Parliament 1860–1926* (1926) is an early biographical register of politicians.

W. ROSS JOHNSTON

Berndt, Catherine Helen (1918–94) and **Ronald Murray** (1916–90), husband and wife, were influential in the development of Australian anthropology. They met at the University of Sydney, where they studied under A.P. **Elkin**. They worked in PNG as well as Arnhem Land, southeastern SA, and the Western Desert. The Berndts conducted their fieldwork as a team—Catherine worked with the women, Ronald with the men—and published widely, both jointly and separately. Yet their academic careers illustrated the handicaps imposed on women. Ronald was foundation professor of anthropology at the University of Western Australia 1963–81, while Catherine held part-time appointments. She wrote some influential articles in the early 1960s that criticised **assimilationist** government practices, and was a prominent commentator on women's place in Aboriginal society. Both were interested in sexuality, and wrote graphically on the subject. Among their major works are *The World of the First Australians* (1964), *The Aboriginal Australians: The First Pioneers* (1978, 1982), and *Australian Aboriginal Art: A Visual Perspective* (1982). They campaigned for improved Aboriginal welfare and were early members of the Australian Institute for Aboriginal Studies and the Aboriginal Arts Board. In 'Paternalism's Changing Reputation' (*Mankind* 1988), Tim Rowse discusses their criticism of Aboriginal administration formulated in the 1940s, but only published in 1987 as *End of an Era*. A collection of essays, *Going it Alone? Prospects for Aboriginal Autonomy* (1990), was produced in their honour. Their final joint publication, *A World that Was* (1993), is an extensive study of the Yaraldi people of the Lower Murray area in SA, and was the fulfilment of a promise made to these people during the original research in the early 1940s. The extensive collection of Aboriginal artworks and artefacts that they donated to the University of Western Australia is housed there in the Berndt Museum.

KT

Berry Blight was a period of economic depression in the Colony of Victoria, triggered by **Black Wednesday**, 9 January 1878: in response to the Legislative Council's refusal to pass a Supply Bill providing permanent payment to members, the premier, Graham **Berry**, advised the Victorian governor, Sir George **Bowen**, to sack about 300 public servants.

Berry was an English immigrant active in Victorian politics from the 1850s who came into office as the leader of a liberal reform movement. His motive was to punish the senior public servants considered sympathetic to the conservatives. A parliamentary deadlock ensued, which caused reduced confidence in the Victorian economy, the transferral of much Victorian capital to NSW, and a sharp fall in Victorian property values. Social commentator Richard **Twopeny** regarded the blight as 'a reaction against the selfish and inconsiderate policy of the squatters when they were in power'. The ministry finally agreed to a compromise in March 1878, and while most of the public servants were reinstated the following month, several notable ones were not, including William **Wardell** and W.H. **Archer**.

HD

Berry, Graham, see **Berry Blight**

BHP, known in full as the Broken Hill Proprietary Co. Ltd, was formed in 1885 at Broken Hill, NSW, to mine silver, lead and zinc ores, and was registered in Melbourne. It quickly expanded into SA, where it took up **mining** leases at Iron Knob, near Port Augusta, and constructed a port at Whyalla. In 1915 BHP opened the country's first major steelworks. This facilitated the further mining of iron ore, along with other base metals, thus stimulating the growth of the Australian metal mining industry and industrial development in general. Efficient operations and the exploitation of high-quality mineral reserves ensured BHP's growth. It established steelworks at Port Kembla in 1933, and flourished under tariff protection and the astute leadership of Essington **Lewis**. During the mineral boom of the late 1960s, BHP—by then dubbed 'The Big Australian'—began off-shore drilling for oil and natural gas. Subsequent diversification and foreign ventures were not always successful. In 1997 BHP closed its Newcastle steelworks, and in 2001 decided to abandon steel-making altogether when it merged with the London-based mining company Billiton.

HD

Bicentennial History Project was proposed in 1977 by Ken **Inglis** of the Australian National University, as a gift by the historical profession to the nation for the 1988 Australian Bicentenary. It consisted of five reference volumes—a historical atlas; historical dictionary; guide to sources; chronology and gazetteer; and volume of historical statistics—and five so-called 'slice' volumes surveying Australian society and culture in the years 1788, 1838, 1888, 1938, and 1939–88. Inglis likened the 'slices' to literary versions of a living history museum: these vivid, closely textured panoramas of the country at particular arbitrarily chosen moments would appeal to a wide readership and inspire historians, working in collaboration, to challenge received narrative versions of the Australian past. Each volume had its own slant: *1788* was largely devoted to pre-1788 Aboriginal society; *1838* took an 'ethnographic' approach to early colonial society; *1888* was influenced by the French *Annales* school's synthesis of environmental, social, and cultural history; *1938* used oral history to tap contemporary memory; *1939–1988* investigated trends in the recent past. Working groups published bulletins of research-in-progress: two of these, *The Push from the Bush* (1838) and *Australia 1888*, became significant outlets for new research. The project fostered new approaches and collaborations among younger historians. The volumes were published as a package, *Australians: A Historical Library*, in 1987–88 by Fairfax, Syme & Weldon, and some 13 000 were sold. Graeme Davison offers a defence of the slice approach in *New Zealand Journal of History* (1982) and Oliver MacDonagh reviews the project's history in *Australians: The Guide and Index* (1987).

GD

Big Brother Movement

Big Brother Movement, founded in 1924 by Sir Richard Linton, arranged for the emigration of 14–19-year-old British and Irish boys to Victoria, NSW and SA, and their subsequent employment and foster-care. Promoted through the New Settlers League of Australia, the movement operated on the premise that younger immigrants were more adaptable than older ones, and would meet demands for farm labour while preserving **White Australia**. Each boy was issued with an Australian Big Brother, or moral guardian, who was responsible for meeting him on arrival, accompanying him to his place of employment, and writing to and visiting him regularly. Little Brothers were expected to work hard, save money, correspond regularly with both their parents and their Big Brothers, abstain from alcohol until aged 21, and lead moral lives. Despite some later accusations of child exploitation, the movement attracted thousands of boys and was generally regarded as successful. The movement abandoned its British migration program in 1982, and instead established a scholarship program for young Australians studying in the UK. A glowing view of the movement's success was presented in its magazine, *The New Australian*.

HD

Bigge, John Thomas

Bigge, John Thomas (1780–1843) was the author of several influential, if sometimes inaccurate, reports on the conditions in the colony of NSW. The inquiry he headed was established because of concerns in the **Colonial Office** that **Macquarie's** administration had changed the penal regime to such an extent that **transportation** was no longer an effective deterrent to crime. Bigge, who had served as chief justice of Trinidad, was appointed as commissioner in 1819 and produced three detailed reports during 1822–23, each of which dealt with different aspects of the colony—its general state, the judiciary, and agriculture and trade. Governor Macquarie, who clashed with the younger man, reacted unfavourably to the findings that his treatment of **emancipists** and **convicts** was too lenient, and his program of public works too expensive. Some long-term results of the reports were the separation of Van Diemen's Land and NSW, legal reforms, the establishment of a Legislative Council in NSW, and increased encouragement of the pastoral industry. John Ritchie discussed both the man and his reports in *Punishment and Profit* (1970).

KT

Biographical dictionaries begin with *Men of the Time in Australia, Victorian Series*, published in Melbourne in 1878 by McCarron, Bird & Co. J. Henniker **Heaton**, English journalist and postal reformer, published *Australian Dictionary of Dates and Men of the Time* in Sydney and London in 1879. The longest entry is for T.S. **Mort** (eight columns), followed by W.C. **Wentworth** (seven). Many long-forgotten figures, and some New Zealanders, are included.

David **Blair**, the Irish-born Victorian journalist and parliamentarian, produced a grandiose *Cyclopædia of Australasia, or, Dictionary of Facts* in 1881. In a long, boastful preface Blair wrote the 'value of the present volume to any Australian boy vastly outweighs' the Greek and Roman historians. He shamelessly plagiarised Heaton without acknowledgment: hundreds of paragraphs are mere transcriptions. There is a substantial original entry on the **Kelly** gang.

Philip **Mennell**, the *Age* journalist, returned to England in 1883, revisiting Australia in 1891, 1895, and 1900. His *Dictionary of Australasian Biography* was published in 1892 in London. There were 2000 entries in 542 pages, covering the period 1855–92.

Fred **Johns**, born in Michigan, was a journalist for the Adelaide *Register* and chief Hansard reporter in the South Australian parliament from 1914 until his death. *Johns's Notable Australians*, subtitled *Who They Are and What They Do, Brief Biographies of Men and Women of the Commonwealth*, was published in Melbourne in 1906. There are about 1500 entries on living subjects, densely packed into 189 pages, with a seven-page addenda briefly recording those who had died since 1901. He acknowledged the work of Mennell, Blair, Heaton, the British *Who's Who*, and *Debrett's Peerage, Baronetage and Knightage*. The 1908 edition (published in Adelaide) was called *Johns's Notable Australians and Who is Who in Australasia*. Fred Johns's *Annual* followed in 1912, 1913, and 1914. *Who's Who in the Commonwealth of Australia* appeared in 1922, and after a five-year gap *Who's Who in Australia 1927–28*, all published by himself. *An Australian Biographical Dictionary*, Johns's last work, completed by his daughter Mildred Hockney, was published in Melbourne in 1934.

Who's Who in Australia was acquired by the Herald & Weekly Times Ltd on Fred Johns's death, and appeared under the editorship of Errol Knox in 1933–34, 1935, and 1938. The style was different, with shorter but more numerous entries. Until 1988 it usually appeared every three years. Michael Wilkinson's company Information Australia then bought *Who's Who in Australia*. Revised extensively, currently running to 1720 pages, it has been published annually since 1991. The 1997 edition is counted as the 33rd.

The first edition of *The Australian Encyclopædia* edited by A.W. **Jose** and H.J. Carter, was published in two volumes in 1925–26. Biographical entries were particularly strong. The sixth edition of *Australian Encyclopædia* (1996) expanded the biographical emphasis of the fourth (1983) and fifth (1988) editions.

Percival Serle (1871–1951), an accountant and independent scholar in Melbourne, wrote *Dictionary of Australian Biography*, published in two volumes in 1949 by Angus & Robertson. The work comprised, in Serle's words, '1030 biographies of Australians, or men [sic] who were closely connected with Australia and died before 1942'. Forty-two women were included. The average length of entry was 640 words. Serle's was a notable achievement, marked by balance and judgment.

The *Australian Dictionary of Biography* was conceived by the historian Keith **Hancock** when he was founding director of the Research School of Social Sciences at the Australian National University. Initially he hoped that Manning **Clark** and M.H. **Ellis** would collaborate in its development, but that unlikely partnership broke down in acrimony, described by Ann **Moyal** in *Breakfast with Beaverbrook* (1995). The first volume appeared in 1966 under the general editorship of Douglas **Pike**.

The first 12 volumes took Australia's biographical record to 1939, in 7211 entries written by 2500 contributors. Four further volumes will treat subjects who flourished after 1939 and who died in the years 1940–80. Pike was general editor for volumes 1 to 5, Bede **Nairn** for volume 6, Nairn and Geoffrey **Serle** (son of Percival, mentioned above) for volumes 7 to 10, Serle for volume 11, and John Ritchie for volumes 12 to 15. Fifteen volumes had appeared by 2000 and the *ADB* is generally regarded as Australia's greatest scholarly achievement in the humanities. As the *ADB* has evolved, entries have generally expanded. In the first two volumes entries more than 10 columns long were rare, even for subjects of the greatest importance. They are now far more frequent.

In addition to a range of older compilations of colonial notables, there are more recent biographical dictionaries for the NT, Tasmania, and WA. Gentry, pastoralists, politicians, and occupational groups are among topical compilations, and a biographical dictionary of the labour movement is being prepared. In 1988 Heather Radi (ed.), *200 Australian Women*, appeared.

Notable Australians, subtitled *The Pictorial Who's Who*, was published in 1978 by Paul Hamlyn as a competitor to *Who's Who in Australia*. Despite the valuable set of photographs and superior setting, it did not survive. *Debrett's Handbook of Australia* has an impressive format, with many photographs of royalty and of decorations, useful both for display and for reference. There is some editorial material, rather nostalgic in tone, on etiquette, protocol, and 'good form', including helpful advice on how to deal with stone fruit at formal dinners. There are thousands of biographical entries. The alphabetical order is sometimes shaky, suggesting some computer problems. First published in 1982 (as *Debrett's Handbook of Australia and New Zealand*), it appeared in a fifth edition in 1991.

Who's Who of Australian Women was published by Methuen Australia (1982), compiled by Andrea Lofthouse, based on research by Vivienne Smith (1939–78). There are 1425 entries, including valuable commentaries by many of the subjects. *The People Who Made Australia Great* covered the lives of 200 subjects, most drawn from the *ADB*; published by Collins Australia (1988), it was part of the commemoration of the Bicentenary of European settlement.

Reed Reference Publishing, Melbourne, has published four biographical works, including *Monash Biographical Dictionary of 20th Century Australia* (1994), a useful compilation of 2200 entries on persons living and dead, in 568 pages. For deceased subjects, it draws heavily on the *ADB*; for the living, *Who's Who in Australia* and newspaper and magazine articles. Entries include convicted murderers (usually excluded from *Who's Who*) and many show-business people. The same publisher has also produced *Contemporary Australians 1995–96* (1995) and *Contemporary Australian Women 1996/97* (1996), edited by Nicolas Brasch. The latter has more than 2000 entries, including contact details, and is a working rather than an analytical tool. *A Sense of Purpose: Great Australian Women of the 20th Century* (1996) is an expanded reworking of 545 entries from the *Monash Biographical Dictionary*, many illustrated.

BARRY JONES

Biography, the writing of a life, is an activity practised by historians in company with other academic, professional and amateur writers. It is a popular and deceptively simple genre that spans the filial memoir and the critical study, and ranges from the formal record to the imaginative re-creation that spills into fiction.

The first Australian biographies took the form of published memorials to the eminent and noteworthy, as an extended, more considered, and permanent version of the obituary. The conventions of such works had already been established: typically, they took the form of a life and times of the subject, frequently incorporated correspondence and public statements, and were freely embellished with reminiscences by family and friends. Nineteenth-century examples include William Woolls, *A Short Account of the Labours of the Rev. Samuel Marsden* (1844), and E.E. Morris, *A Memoir of George Higinbotham* (1895). There was also the more commercial type of biography that capitalised on public notoriety or sensation. Thus Thomas Wells published an account of *Michael Howe, the Last and Worst of the Bushrangers* in 1818, while John Morgan related *The Life and Adventures of William Buckley* in 1852.

Literary biography developed quickly. In 1866 G.B. **Barton** published *The Poets and Prose Writers of New South Wales*; the death of Marcus **Clarke** was marked by *The Marcus Clarke Memorial Volume* (1884) and in the same year E.A.

Martin published *The Life and Speeches* of Daniel **Deniehy**. Adam Lindsay **Gordon's** life was recorded by J.H. Ross in *The Laureate of the Centaurs* (1888). Biography at this time was principally a branch of literature, though historians such as James **Bonwick** also exploited it. The appearance between 1879 and 1892 of the **biographical dictionaries** of J.H. **Heaton**, David **Blair**, and Philip **Mennell** met a growing interest in biography as a public record.

The first generation of academic historians employed biography as a key device in their creation of a national history. For G.A. **Wood**, Ernest **Scott**, and G.C. **Henderson**, biography humanised an otherwise austere discipline. In their teaching of British and European history they dwelt on heroic figures who surmounted circumstances to enlarge freedom and foster progress; such exemplary individuals provided inspirational models of conduct, just as the villains of the past warned of the consequences of ignoble action. In their **school histories** of Australia these historians found local equivalents in the explorers, governors, and statesmen who guided the colonies to nationhood. Henderson's *Sir George Grey* (1907), Scott's life of **Flinders** (1914), and Wood's *Voyage of the 'Endeavour'* (1925) initiated a style of exhortatory biography that was continued by G.V. **Portus** in *Fifty Famous Australians* (c.1958), by Vance **Palmer** in *National Portraits* (1940), and then from the 1950s in the series of short lives written by leading Australian historians for Oxford University Press.

At the hands of writers such as Frank **Clune**, Ernestine **Hill**, and Ion **Idriess**, biography remained a lucrative form of writing on popular and colourful subjects during the first half of the twentieth century, but the market for more serious work was still restricted. In 1920 Ernest Scott rejected Walter **Murdoch's** invitation to collaborate on the life of Alfred **Deakin** because he believed it would yield no more than £100 for two years' work (S. Macintyre, *A History for a Nation*, 1994). Murdoch had himself been commissioned by Deakin's son-in-law, Herbert **Brookes**, to write the biography, and this arrangement still provided the impulse for much biographical activity. Frequently it dictated the contents—as in Ambrose Pratt's 1908 biography of David **Syme**—or brought intractable dispute. C.E. Sayers's commissioned life of Keith **Murdoch** was set aside, and other biographers have suffered the same fate. Alternatively, the biographer was motivated by family duty, friendship, or affinity for the subject. Nettie **Palmer's** life of her uncle H.B. **Higgins** (1931) was a distinguished example. H.V. **Evatt** used the life of William **Holman** to explore the predicament of an *Australian Labour Leader* (1940), and Lloyd Ross took *William Lane and the Australian Labour Movement* (1935) to trace the socialist alternative. Miles **Franklin** and Kate Baker paid tribute to *Joseph Furphy* (1944).

The major biographies were produced at this time by writers and freelance scholars seeking to define binding national traditions. George **Mackaness** wrote lives of **Banks** (1936), **Phillip** (1937), and **Bligh** (1931) as prescient founders; M.H. **Ellis** used **Macquarie** (1947), **Greenway** (1949), and **Macarthur** (1955) to uphold private enterprise

and condemn state interference; Marjorie **Barnard** and Flora Eldershaw created a more liberal Phillip (1938). All these works were based on archival research and relentless in their narrative format. The academics, meanwhile, chose less notable figures to pursue their chosen themes: thus Edward **Shann's** use of the **Bussell family** in *Cattle Chosen* (1926) to illuminate land settlement, or W.D. Forsyth's Gothic rendition of *Governor Arthur's Convict System* (1935).

Professional historians turned more frequently to biography as the academic enterprise took root in the 1950s and 1960s. Explorers, governors, politicians, religious leaders, generals, scientists, and intellectuals lent themselves to studies with naturally defined boundaries, allowed the elaboration of interpretive themes and the testing of hypotheses through the detailed case study. While choice of subject was constrained by the availability of personal papers, there was now far greater stress on contextualisation. The more distinguished—which included Kathleen **Fitzpatrick**, *John Franklin* (1949), and Margaret **Kiddle**, *Caroline Chisholm* (1950)—evoked personality and milieu. The most distinguished was John **La Nauze's** two-volume life of Alfred Deakin (1965). Meanwhile the establishment of the *Australian Dictionary of Biography* at the Australian National University gave further impetus to the pursuit.

Yet it was La Nauze who most forcefully articulated the profession's mistrust of biography. He insisted that it was an inappropriate subject for postgraduate study, that the novice historian was too immature to comprehend a completed life. Those of a more positivist mode found the sheer singularity of biography a defect, while others persuaded of structural historical causation (such as **Marxist historians** and followers of the *Annales* school) repudiated its exaggeration of human agency.

Some biographers responded to these strictures with a greater concern for the psychological dimension. At the University of Melbourne the political scientist Alan Davies was already exploring what became known as the psychosocial approach to life history; his students included such accomplished biographers as Judith Brett, Graham Little, and James Walter, who helped found the Institute for Modern Biography at Griffith University in 1977. Overseas, such work as Erik Erikson's *Young Man Luther* (1958) produced the school of psychohistory. Allan **Martin** was the first Australian historian to apply these insights to major biography, in *Henry Parkes* (1980). Walter had already produced a study of a living subject, Gough **Whitlam**, in 1980; John Rickard's life of H.B. Higgins (1984) also shows their influence, as does Brett's study of *Robert Menzies' Forgotten People* (1992). The best survey of this approach to biography is that of James Walter in Ian Donaldson et al. (eds), *Shaping Lives* (1992).

Intellectual biography emerged also as a way of mediating structure and agency. Thus Don Watson took Brian **Fitzpatrick** (1978) as both a product of Melbourne's secular meliorist tradition and a contributor to libertarian **radical nationalism**. Subsequent studies, such as that of Warren Osmond on Frederic **Eggleston's** holistic social science (1985), Geoffrey **Serle** on Robin **Boyd's** modernism (1995), and Peter Beilharz on Bernard **Smith's** post-colonialism (1997), have made a significant contribution to the **history of ideas**.

There were further innovations in the 1980s. In place of the older assumption of a life, finished, complete, and independent of its narrator, new works were more reflexive and experimental. They fractured the narrative, inserted themselves and other authorial voices into the text, blurred the boundaries between then and now, fact and fiction. The notable Australian examples were literary biographies, such as Brian Matthews's life of Louisa **Lawson** (1987), or biographies in a literary mode, such Drusilla Modjeska's *Poppy* (1990). Other notable examples include Sylvia Lawson, *The Archibald Paradox* (1983), which recreated the 'great print circus' of the early *Bulletin* and reflected on how it had been misremembered. John Rickard in *A Family Romance: The Deakins at Home* (1996) is among the few historians to follow these leads.

The popular appeal of biography is probably greater than ever; indeed, the written life serves almost as the printed equivalent of that other index to celebrity, the portrait entered for the **Archibald Prize**. The politician, the businessman, the sports champion, the artist—there are few notable living Australians who lack a book celebrating their achievements, while the literary pantheon of former notables is constantly enlarged. The changing patterns of biographical commemoration serve as an index of changed values: John Hetherington's impressive life of Field Marshal **Blamey** (1973) and Geoffrey Serle's outstanding *John Monash* (1982) are now outweighed by the redactions of Edward (Weary) **Dunlop**.

Historians have largely dropped their suspicion of the genre. They grasp biography as one of the commercially viable means of publication; they use it to vivify their monographs and illustrate their general works. Feminist biography has both extended and qualified the understanding of the women's movement in Australia. Accounts of lives lived partly in Australia and partly elsewhere, such as Diane Kirkby's study of the labour organiser Alice **Henry** (1991) and Jim Davidson's of the musical publisher Louise Hanson-Dyer (1994), have recovered lost connections. While prosopography, or collective biography, has not been widely practised, its possibilities are suggested by Mollie Gillen, *The Founders of Australia* (1989) and Janet McCalman, *Journeyings: The Biography of a Middle-Class Generation 1920–1990* (1993). Those who regard biography as a mere ancillary of their discipline underestimate it.

STUART MACINTYRE

Birdwood, William Riddell (1865–1951) was appointed commander-in-chief of the Australian and NZ forces in Europe in November 1914, and led them through the **Gallipoli** campaign and in France. He was involved in the development of the **Anzac** acronym and identified with it so closely that he adopted it as part of his title when he became a baronet. It was Birdwood who gave the name Anzac Cove to the first landing site at Gallipoli; he and his

staff were responsible for the planning of the Anzac landing. However, and in spite of his being British, he remained popular with the troops for his willingness to visit the front line. As administrative and operational commander of the **AIF**, Birdwood appointed Australians to command positions whenever possible and kept the Australian government informed on matters relating to the corps. His 1920 tour of Australia was triumphant and, after he retired from the Indian Army, he dearly hoped to be appointed as Australia's governor-general. This was denied him by the **Scullin** government's appointment of the first Australian-born governor-general, Isaac **Isaacs**.

KT

Bjelke-Petersen, Johannes 'Joh' (1911–) was an idiosyncratic premier of Qld who held office from 1968 to 1987, although he never attracted more than 39 per cent of votes. Astute appeals to a deeply conservative rural Qld, promotion of a xenophobic attitude towards the rest of Australia, and a gerrymander, all contributed to his survival. These matters are examined in detail by Hugh Lunn in *Johannes Bjelke-Petersen: A Political Biography* (1978, 1984). Born of devout Danish-Lutheran parents who had struggled to establish the farm he worked, Bjelke-Petersen entered the Queensland parliament in 1947 as a Country (later **National**) Party member. He was a strenuous champion of development, so that the unions, socialists, and Aborigines seeking land rights all incurred his wrath at some time. His controversial appointment of a non-Labor candidate to fill a casual Senate vacancy in 1975 allowed the opposition to block supply, which resulted in the **Dismissal** of the **Whitlam** government. His reign ended in 1987 with the failure of his attempt to move into federal politics, the 'Joh for Canberra' campaign, which destabilised the federal Liberal–National coalition. Later that year he resigned as premier and National Party leader after increasingly insistent allegations of corruption were levelled at his administration. Charges were laid against him, but were eventually dropped. His loyal wife, Florence, known as Flo, was a senator 1981–93; she was known for her pumpkin scones, he for his bizarre use of language. One of his most famous phrases forms the title of his memoirs, *Don't You Worry About That!* (1990).

KT

Black-armband history, a phrase coined by Geoffrey **Blainey** in his Latham Lecture (*Quadrant*, 1993), signified a pessimistic reading of Australian history which, he contended, had gained undue acceptance. Earlier generations had been raised on an optimistic 'three cheers' view of history; the 'black armband view of history' represented the 'swing of the pendulum ... to an opposite extreme that is ... decidedly jaundiced'. Blainey placed much of the blame for the spread of the 'gloomy' view of Australia's past on the histories of Manning **Clark** and the 'guilt industry' encouraged by influential bodies outside the historical profession, such as the **Australian Broadcasting Corporation**, the **Australian Labor Party**, educational institutions, and the **High Court**. Black-armband history purportedly placed too much emphasis on the dispossession of Aboriginal Australians, environmental destruction, racism, and sexism. Although Blainey was the first to coin the phrase, he was not the first to apply the words 'black armband' in the context of Australian history. In the Aboriginal protest movement, as early as 1970, and most notably in 1988, the wearing of black armbands was a symbol of the historical dispossession of Aboriginal peoples.

History became a strong theme in the rhetoric of Prime Minister Paul **Keating**, whose Redfern Speech on Aboriginal reconciliation ('We took the traditional lands and smashed the traditional way of life') mourned the misdeeds of past Australians. After the election of the coalition government in March 1996, Prime Minister John **Howard** rejected the black-armband view of Australian history, asserting that 'the balance sheet of Australian history is a generous and benign one'. Howard's attacks on black-armband history served as a strategic political device by appealing to Australian patriotism.

MARK McKENNA

Black Friday, 13 January 1939, was a day of catastrophic **bushfires** in Victoria and one of Australia's worst natural **disasters**. Fires had burned since December 1938, intensified by severe drought and high temperatures. They became increasingly uncontrollable during the week leading up to 13 January, finally merging with great ferocity and disastrous results. The fires centred on the forest towns north-east of Melbourne, where the town of Noojee and the Matlock Forest were ravaged, but also sprang up randomly across the state. A total of 71 Victorians lost their lives—a record number matched on **Ash Wednesday** in 1983. Property and stock damage was extensive, and 1000 homes were destroyed. The Victorian government established a royal commission, *To Inquire into the Causes of and Measures Taken to Prevent the Bush Fires of January 1939*. Judge L.B. Stretton, father of the historian Hugh, conducted the inquiry and wrote the report, arguably the most distinguished piece of writing in the history of Australian parliamentary inquiries. The fire is described by Stephen Pyne, *Burning Bush: A Fire History of Australia* (1991), and Tom Griffiths, *Secrets of the Forest* (1992).

HD

Black, George Mure (1854–1936), socialist and republican, was an early leader of the **Australian Labor Party** in NSW. An emigrant from Scotland, he worked during the 1880s as a sub-editor of the *Bulletin*, spoke at the Domain, debated at the School of Arts and, with William **Holman** and Billy **Hughes**, was an early member of the Australian Socialist League. As one of the 35 Labor members elected to the NSW parliament in 1891, he proposed that caucus be bound by majority decisions and stated Labor's parliamentary strategy of 'support in return for concessions': 'we have not come into this House to make and unmake ministries. We have come here to make and unmake social conditions.'

Black's erratic domestic life and increasing reluctance to accept party discipline handicapped his political career, and

he lost his parliamentary seat in 1898. He returned to journalism, remained active in the Labor Party, and was returned to parliament 1910–17. With Holman, he was expelled from the Labor Party for his support of **conscription**. Black's *History of the NSW Labor Party* (1910) was an early exercise in the triumphal mode of **labour history**.

SM

Black Thursday, 6 February 1851, was a day of devastating **bushfires** in Victoria. Many lives were lost, homes and livestock were destroyed, and clouds of smoke reached as far as northern Tasmania. Occurring only a month after the colony's separation celebrations, it came as a blow to the celebratory optimism. For C.M.H. **Clark**, the fires represented the threatening forces of nature to which European Australians would always be vulnerable. Artist William **Strutt**, who toured the affected districts in the fire's aftermath, combined his sketches to create the large oil-painting, *Black Thursday* (1851), now displayed in the State Library of Victoria, which vividly captured the expressions of terror of people and animals fleeing the fire. William Westgarth, in *Personal Recollections of Early Melbourne and Victoria* (1888), provides one of the best contemporary accounts of the fire.

HD

Black trackers were Aborigines employed by some colonial police forces to assist in the search for criminals hiding in, or people lost in, the bush. Their skills and potential usefulness were officially recognised as early as 1825, when the NSW Legislative Council recommended to Governor **Brisbane** that 'one or two natives' be attached to small groups of soldiers to search for bushrangers. Governor **Darling** took up the idea with a general order in March 1826 that 'intelligent natives' be attached to police groups. Trackers had already been used to hunt for bushrangers and escaped convicts in NSW and Tasmania. The best-known of these was probably **Mosquito**, who helped capture Michael **Howe**. Another major role for the trackers was in **bush searches**, where they were instrumental in saving many lives, or at least finding bodies. Qld maintained the largest number of trackers after the disbandment of the **native police** and the other colonies often called on them for help; Victoria employed several Queensland men in the pursuit of the **Kelly** gang. Newspaper reports of the trackers' work dwelt on the uncanniness of their skills, and linked it to their 'savage simplicity'; intelligence and years of diligent training were discounted. The numbers of trackers declined from the turn of the century, due to increasing urbanisation, tracker dogs, and new technology. Only Qld still has a tracker contingent. Max Jones's *Tracks* (1992) includes anecdotes of his use of black trackers in SA, and Gary Presland relates their experiences in Victoria (1998).

KT

Black War, fought between Aborigines and Europeans in **Van Diemen's Land** during the 1820s, led to the near destruction of the Tasmanian **Aborigines**. Despite the effective guerrilla-style attacks, ultimately it was the Europeans, in greater numbers and armed with muskets, who inflicted more fatalities. The battles culminated in the Black Line of 1829–30, a human chain stretching across the south-eastern corner of the island, designed to capture the remaining Tasmanians. It was a costly failure; only one man and a boy were caught. Governor George **Arthur** subsequently commissioned G.A. **Robinson** to locate and make contact with the remaining Aborigines and to transfer them to Wybalenna on Flinders Island. Early histories such as John **West's** *History of Tasmania* (1852) and James **Bonwick's** *The Last of the Tasmanians; Or, the Black War of Van Diemen's Land* (1870) dealt extensively with the Black War; then there was a long silence. In the twentieth century, it was re-examined by Clive Turnbull in *Black War: The Extermination of the Tasmanian Aborigines* (1948) and Henry **Reynolds** in *Fate of a Free People* (1995).

HD

Black Wednesday, 9 January 1878, was a day of **constitutional crisis** for the Victorian parliament. A deadlock had emerged between the two houses in 1877, when the Legislative Council rejected a proposed Appropriation Bill which included a measure for continuing the payment of members of the Legislative Assembly. While the Assembly supported the measure, the Council only allowed temporary payment measures and thus refused to pass the bill. Deprived of revenue, the Berry government, in a decree published on 9 January 1878, dismissed some 300 senior public servants, including judges, police magistrates, and Crown prosecutors. The incident triggered a period of economic recession, known as the **Berry Blight**. Payment of members was finally secured in March 1878, and most of those dismissed were reinstated the following month. Alfred **Deakin** wrote a personal account, *The Crisis in Victorian Politics 1879–1881* (1957).

HD

Blackbirding, see **Pacific Island labourers**

Blackburn, Maurice McCrae (1880–1944) and **Doris Amelia** (1889–1970) were married in 1914 to form a partnership that was political and philosophical, as well as personal. Maurice specialised in trade union law and civil liberty cases through the law firm he founded in 1922, Maurice Blackburn & Co. He was already a member of the Victorian Socialist Party and **Australian Labor Party**. Elected as member for Essendon in 1914, he lost the seat in 1917, mainly due to his anti-war stand, which Doris shared. She had moved from an early involvement with the **Women's Political Association** into the broader issues of civil rights and the peace movement. Both campaigned vigorously during the 1916–17 anti-conscription campaign. In spite of the demands of a young family, Doris served as president of the Women's International League for Peace and Freedom, and supported the Free Kindergarten Movement and the Citizens Education Fellowship. Maurice won the federal seat of Bourke in 1934 and held it until 1943, despite

conflict with the ALP which resulted in his being twice expelled from the party—over his participation in the left-wing Movement Against War and Fascism in 1936, and in the Australia–Soviet Friendship League in 1941. His opposition to conscription in 1942 confirmed his heroic status as a man of unbending principle. Carolyn Rasmussen's doctoral thesis, 'Defending the Bad Against the Worse' (University of Melbourne, 1984), is the principal source. Doris accepted a more prominent political role after Maurice's death, in 1946 winning Bourke as an Independent Labor member. After her 1949 defeat she worked for various voluntary organisations and helped establish the Aboriginal Advancement League. (See **Aboriginal and Torres Strait Islander Organisations**.)

KT

Blainey, Geoffrey Norman (1930–) is the most prolific, wide-ranging, inventive, and—in the 1980s and 1990s—most controversial of Australia's living historians.

Blainey grew up in country Victoria, moving house each three or four years as his father, a Methodist clergyman, ministered at Mortlake, Leongatha, Geelong, and Ballarat. 'I learned without knowing it, history from the towns I lived in when young', he later recalled. Several distinguished Australian historians, including Keith **Hancock** and Manning **Clark**, were sons of the vicarage; but small-town Methodism—a religion of the lower middle and working class—may have instilled an outlook more intellectually independent and socially insecure than theirs. After World War II the family moved to Melbourne, where Blainey was educated at Wesley College and the University of Melbourne. Clark, under whom he studied Australian history, remembered him as a shy boy, wise beyond his years, sitting attentively at the back of the class. He did not follow the traditional path of bright graduates, from a History Department tutorship to an Oxbridge scholarship; he left instead for the west coast of Tasmania to undertake a commission arranged by Max **Crawford** to write the history of the Mount Lyell Mining Company. Over the next decade as a freelance historian he would write half a dozen books, including histories of both his *almae matris*, Wesley College and the University of Melbourne, of a bank, an industrial company, and several mining companies. He was probably the first academically trained Australian historian to earn a living by his pen. Many features of his later work reflect this unorthodox apprenticeship: his respect for the lore of practical men; his keen interest in landscape and technology; his businesslike approach to writing; his ability to communicate vividly, and without scholarly paraphernalia, to a wide readership; and his robust independence of outlook. He became, as Robert Pascoe observed in *The Manufacture of Australian History* (1978), the 'lone prospector' of Australian history.

In 1961 Blainey returned to the University of Melbourne as senior lecturer, later professor, of economic history. *The Rush That Never Ended* (1963), a general history of Australian mining, harvested the research of the previous decade, some of which, like his commissioned history of ICIANZ, the company chiefs had declined to publish. It also marked a shift from the vigorous narrative style of *The Peaks of Lyell* (1954) and *Mines in the Spinifex* (1960) to a more analytical and revisionist approach. From the chronology of mineral finds he edged towards a general 'theory of mineral discovery'. The **Eureka** rebellion, he argued in a celebrated chapter, was not a workers' insurrection, as the Left had traditionally argued, but a tax revolt by small capitalists, pushed by the harsh logistics of deep-lead mining to the end of their financial tether. Blainey's was materialist history in a heroic vein, a story of economic progress in which little men—prospectors, engineers, small shareholders—as well as great capitalists sought to master the forces of nature.

Blainey's next, and most famous, book, *The Tyranny of Distance* (1966), began as a history of transport in Australia, but in the process of writing, he began to view his subject from a fresh angle, not as the study of mobility, but of what prevented it. 'The idea of distance', he decided, 'may be as revealing as say Frederick Jackson Turner's "frontier theory" is in probing the history of the United States.' Distance might not explain why things happened, but it forced a search for new explanations: why Australia was settled, how its towns and cities grew, even why its society was so peaceful, masculine, and egalitarian. NSW, he argued, was not settled just as a prison but as way-station and supply base on the sea-lanes of empire. (See **Settlement**.)

The Tyranny of Distance illustrates Blainey's characteristic approach to history: the overturning—sometimes even the inversion—of conventional wisdom, his broad synoptic view of events, his attraction to homely analogies and mechanistic explanations. 'One of my difficulties', he later admitted, 'is that I'm half a determinist.' Sometimes, his critics suspected, the determinism derived from his fondness for powerful metaphors as much as a logic embedded in the events themselves. Was distance really a 'tyrant'? John Hirst asked (*HS*, 1975), pointing to the strong evidence, even within Blainey's own book, of its opposite: mobility.

Blainey's geographical and chronological range increased with his explanatory ambitions. *The Causes of War* (1973) scanned two and half centuries in search of the laws of human conflict. What needed to be explained, he argued, was not the outbreak of war but the outbreak of peace. He sceptically reviewed the influence of culprits and scapegoats, power balances and economic rivalries in the generation of hostilities. In *The Great See-Saw* (1988) he charted the long swings of optimism and pessimism in Western society since 1750.

By the mid-1970s Blainey had become a national figure. In 1977 he was appointed to the Ernest Scott chair of history. He made a television series, *The Blainey View* (1982); chaired the Literary Board of the Australia Council and the Australia–China Council; was a commissioner of the Australian Heritage Commission; and, with his friend, the prehistorian John **Mulvaney**, served on a committee of inquiry into Australian museums. *Triumph of the Nomads* (1975), his pioneering 'history of ancient Australia', was a

daring synthesis of the work of Mulvaney and his fellow archaeologists which also reflected continuing themes in Blainey's writing. The Aborigines of ancient Australia 'triumphed' through mastery of their environment; just as the Europeans in turn triumphed by virtue of technological superiority over them: 'People who could not boil water were confronted by the nation which had recently contrived the steam engine.'

Blainey had always marched to a different drum from his left-leaning academic colleagues. Since his days as a freelance historian, he had maintained close relations with the Melbourne business community, especially the mining industry. In 1966 he had visited the Soviet Union, but his book *Across a Red World* (1968) described a bleaker, more rigid society than Manning Clark had found a decade earlier. Blainey's travels only reinforced his deep, but increasingly troubled, sense of Australian patriotism.

In March 1984, in an address to the Warrnambool Rotary Club, Blainey called for the level of Asian immigration to be cut. Always provocative, Blainey's challenge to the bipartisan policy of non-discriminatory **immigration** provoked a fire-storm of condemnation. His younger colleagues were angry and appalled, his older friends bewildered and dismayed. 'Always a loner, never a team player', Manning Clark concluded sadly. Blainey himself seemed surprised by the uproar. Historical realism, he claimed, had carried him to this 'unpalatable' conclusion. Under attack, he dug in, hardening his stance. *All for Australia* (1984) argued that immigration policy was being designed in a 'secret room' by a cabal of politicians and public servants without the knowledge of parliament and people.

Because of this controversy, Blainey's relations with colleagues at the University of Melbourne grew strained; in 1988 he resigned his chair and became, once again, a freelance historian and commentator. He wrote histories of Pacific Dunlop and Alcoa, contributed a regular column to the Murdoch press, and delivered philippics against the **Keating** government, the Aboriginal Land Rights movement, the High Court, and his fellow historians. In his Latham Lecture (*Quadrant*, 1993) Blainey called for a truer 'balance sheet of our history'. His generation had been reared on the 'three cheers' view of history. But recent historians had succumbed to the **black-armband** view—a gloomy perspective on Australia's past which dulled national pride and slowed economic progress. Blainey's homely metaphors—balance sheets, pendulums, seesaws—were suggestive of his self-image as a lone voice of reason in an Australia sliding towards disaster. In *A Shorter History of Australia* (1994), he revisited many old themes—distance, technology, sport—but his voice was now more urgent, his political judgments more sharply partisan.

By the century's turn this book could be seen as a rehearsal for possibly his most ambitious work, *A Short History of the World* (2000). In 600 pages he reviews four million years of human history, with characteristic emphasis on technology, geography, and geopolitics, and a new alertness to the influence of the great world religions.

Blainey is among the most widely admired Australian historians, but his work has been slow to receive sustained critical attention. His contributions to John Moses (ed.), *Historical Disciplines and Culture in Australia* (1979), and R.M. Crawford et al., *Making History* (1985), are illuminating personal statements. Critical studies by Kathy Laster (*Meanjin*, 1984), Andrew Markus and Merle Ricklefs (eds), *Surrender Australia?* (1985), and Humphrey McQueen, *Suspect History* (1997), concentrate on the public controversialist; Geoffrey Bolton et al. (eds), *Geoffrey Blainey and Australian History* (2002), the product of a 70th birthday conference, is a more comprehensive assessment.

GRAEME DAVISON

Blair, David (1820–99) is best known for his journalism, but a peripatetic working life also included surveying, gold prospecting, and politics. Born in Ireland, he came to NSW in 1850 and trained as a Presbyterian minister under J.D. **Lang**. Blair lived briefly on the Turon goldfield, then returned to Sydney to work on the *Empire* with Henry **Parkes**. By 1852 he was in Victoria as a sub-editor of the *Argus*. A strong supporter of the **Eureka** miners, Blair quit the *Argus* and joined the *Age*. He was a man of causes, among them the Land Reform League, which took him into the House of Assembly in 1856 as member for Talbot. He pursued his reform interests as a member of various commissions, including those involving penal reform and education. An obituary in the *Age* described Blair as having 'wielded a very vigorous pen', but his style of journalism was ill-suited to the reading public of the 1880s. A mark of his self-confidence was the high assessment he made of his two major works, the *History of Australasia* (1879) and *Cyclopaedia of Australasia* (1881), which he regarded as gifts to the people.

KT

Blair, Harold (1924–76) used his celebrity as an Aboriginal operatic singer to promote Aboriginal welfare. Born on Cherbourg reserve in Qld, Blair was separated from his mother and raised at Purga mission, where he received a limited education. Encouraged to continue singing by Marjorie Lawrence, he entered a radio talent quest in 1945 and won acclaim. The public donated generously to form the Harold Blair Trust, which enabled him to enter the Melbourne (later Melba Memorial) Conservatorium of Music. Shortly after his marriage in 1949 to a fellow student, Blair went to the USA for further study. He returned to Australia in 1951 for an arduous series of touring concerts with the **Australian Broadcasting Commission**, which reputedly damaged his voice. He became involved with the Moral Rearmament movement and, increasingly, with Aboriginal advancement. Blair began the Aboriginal Children's Project which provided holidays for Aboriginal children. The problems of his later years, which included artistic decline and the breakdown of his marriage, were highlighted in a television documentary, *Harold* (1994). This contrasted with the previously accepted, sanitised version of his life as portrayed by Kenneth Harrison in *Dark Man, White World* (1975).

KT

Blamey, Thomas Albert (1884–1951) was commander-in-chief of the Australian Military Forces 1942–45, and one of Australia's most outstanding and controversial soldiers.

Born at Wagga Wagga, NSW, Blamey worked as a schoolteacher before determining on a military career. He served with distinction at **Gallipoli**, and by 1918 was senior staff officer to Sir John **Monash**, the commander of the Australian Corps in France. Monash praised his 'infinite capacity for taking pains'; but Monash's predecessor, General **Birdwood**, thought that while Blamey was 'an exceedingly able little man', he was 'by no means a pleasing personality'.

In 1925 Blamey was appointed chief commissioner of the Victoria Police. He was conservative in outlook and authoritarian in approach, and was also perhaps head of the secret right-wing White Army. Loyal to his friends, he could be ruthless with enemies. His tenure as commissioner was marred by scandal in 1925 when a man with Blamey's police badge was found in a brothel, and in 1936 his career appeared to be in ruins when he was forced to resign after lying to protect one of his senior police officers.

As commander of the Second **AIF**, Blamey served in the Middle East from mid-1940 until early 1942. He seemed unable to avoid controversy, whether over the exaggerated rumours of his drinking and womanising, or the more serious claims that he was 'physically and mentally broken' in the Greek campaign. Yet he fought the British generals to keep the Australian force together, and successfully demanded the withdrawal of the Australians from the besieged town of Tobruk.

In March 1942 Blamey became commander-in-chief of the Australian Military Forces and Commander Allied Land Forces under General Douglas MacArthur. It was an immense and complicated task as the army soon expanded to half a million, and Prime Minister John **Curtin** preferred to accept advice from the American general. At the height of the fighting on the **Kokoda Track**, Curtin ordered Blamey to New Guinea, where he sacked the Australian commander, Lieutenant-General Rowell—as described critically by Rowell in his 1974 autobiography, and more sympathetically by John Hetherington in *Blamey: Controversial Soldier* (1973). Blamey's critics accused him of relieving or isolating possible rivals, such as Generals Bennett, Lavarack, Robertson, and Rowell. However, Blamey was convinced that he was best equipped to fight for Australia's interests against the Americans'. No other Australian commander had Blamey's political acumen, force of personality, or grasp of wider issues, and years after his death many surviving senior officers continued to praise his military record.

In his biography, Hetherington concentrates on Blamey's personality rather than his conduct as a commander. While not ignoring Blamey's faults, Hetherington gives a favourable account, as does Blamey's wartime aide, Norman Carlyon, in *I Remember Blamey* (1980). Peter Charlton, in *The Unnecessary War* (1983), accuses Blamey of ordering the mopping-up campaigns of 1945 for his own aggrandisement. The official histories, especially those by Gavin **Long**, Dudley McCarthy, and David Dexter, provide sound analyses of Blamey's performance, and David Horner, in books on the command crisis of 1942 and Australian strategic decision-making during the war, seeks to provide a balanced assessment.

DAVID HORNER

Blaxland, Gregory (1778–1853) joined with William Lawson (1774–1850) and W.C. **Wentworth** in 1813 in an expedition to cross the Blue Mountains. Blaxland came to NSW from England in 1806 and established a farm; it was his desire to acquire larger tracts of grazing land that made him an explorer. Several years after the expedition he presented himself as leader, and has since been regarded as the originator of the plan of following the ridges as a means of crossing this barrier. The 1813 expedition is generally held to be the first crossing of the range, although this has since been questioned by Chris Cunningham, *The Blue Mountains Rediscovered* (1996). Blaxland's frequently anthologised account of the expedition was published in 1823. Joanna Armour Richards produced a detailed documentary account of the expedition, including material from the journals of all three men, *Blaxland–Lawson–Wentworth, 1813* (1979).

KT

Bligh, William (1754–1817) was an English naval officer, governor of NSW, and central character in one of the young colony's greatest crises. He sailed with Captain James **Cook** on the 1776 voyage and then served in the navy and merchant service. Notoriety came with his 1787 appointment to command HMS *Bounty* on an expedition to collect breadfruit plants from Tahiti. The crew mutinied soon after leaving Tahiti, casting Bligh and 18 of the crew adrift in a small boat with little food and water. Bligh's superb navigation and strong leadership got them safely across the 6000 kilometres to Timor in six weeks. The subsequent court martial acquitted him of undue harshness in command, but the legend remained; it is examined in the numerous accounts of the incident, including George **Mackaness's** *The Life of Vice-Admiral William Bligh* (1931, 1951). Paul Brunton produced *Awake Bold Bligh* (1989), an edited version of Bligh's letters describing the mutiny. The imaginative appeal of the incident is testified to by many novels, plays, poems, and films. Greg Dening's *Mr Bligh's Bad Language* (1992) is a sophisticated exploration of the mutiny and its representations.

Bligh was appointed governor of NSW in 1805 with support from Joseph **Banks** and, immediately upon his arrival in 1806, he began to deal vigorously with the abuses in the liquor trade, the currency system, and the use of convicts. This brought him into conflict with the **New South Wales Corps**, especially John **Macarthur**, who had profited from the existing system. Bligh's attempt in 1808 to have Macarthur arrested led to the military revolt known as the **Rum Rebellion**, in which the corps commander, Major George **Johnston**, placed Bligh under arrest. He remained there until early 1809 when he agreed to return to England but, once aboard the ship, directed it to Hobart. He returned briefly to Sydney in 1810 upon the arrival of the new governor, Lachlan **Macquarie**, and then to London. After a trial, Johnston was cashiered and the charges against

Bligh rejected. The nature of a man who can inspire such dramas has proved a powerful attraction for all sorts of writers. H.V. **Evatt** argued for Bligh in his *Rum Rebellion* (1938) and strongly contested M.H. **Ellis's** sympathetic treatment of Macarthur's role in the revolt. This favouring of Bligh over Macarthur and the NSW Corps is supported by Mark Hearn and Ross Fitzgerald in *Bligh, Macarthur and the Rum Rebellion* (1988), which also examines the historical disputes over the incident. A long radio serial about Bligh by Rex Rienets, *Stormy Petrel*, became a series on Australian television. John Ritchie's detailed introduction to the proceedings of Johnston's court martial, *A Charge of Mutiny* (1988), illuminates the characters and background to the revolt.

KT

Boake, Barcroft Henry Thomas (1866–92), poet, is best known for his grim evocation of outback Australia, epitomised by 'Where the Dead Men Lie' (1891), which depicts a greedy absentee landlord profiting from the hardship of the people who work in the 'wastes of the Never Never'. Boake grew up in Sydney but preferred the bush, where he worked variously as surveyor, drover, and boundary rider. Influenced by the life and death of Adam Lindsay **Gordon**, Boake published his poems in the **Bulletin** 1890–91. On a visit to Sydney, he became depressed and disappeared; he was eventually found, hanging from his own stockwhip. A.G. **Stephens** published a collection of Boake's poems in 1897, and Clement Semmler wrote a biography, *Barcroft Boake: Poet of the Stockwhip* (1965).

KT

Board, Peter (1858–1945) was the first director of **education** in NSW (1905–22) and one of the architects of the Australian government school system. He attended Fort Street Public School and was among the first evening students at the University of Sydney, obtaining his BA (1889) and MA (1891). He became headmaster of MacDonaldtown Public School in 1884 and an inspector in 1893, serving in the districts of Lismore, Albury, and Newcastle. Like his Victorian contemporary Frank Tate, Board was influenced by progressive educational ideas in North America and Europe: his reports on primary education (1903) and American educational systems (1909), written after overseas study tours, influenced reforms in such matters as rural education, state high schools, and kindergartens. Board saw schools as an engine of national development and promoted the teaching of history as a foundation of civic education. His firm defence of the principle of free education led to his resignation as director in 1922 in protest against the reintroduction of fees in high schools. He continued to be active in educational matters, chairing committees of inquiry in WA and Tasmania. A.R. Crane and W.G. Walker wrote a biography in 1957, and Board's papers are in the Mitchell Library, Sydney.

NOELINE J. KYLE

Boat people, a term first used in the 1970s, refers to the Vietnamese refugees who fled their country by sea, many of whom arrived in Australia. After the fall of Saigon in 1975, and the reunification of North and South Vietnam under a communist government, thousands of Vietnamese were displaced or subjected to political persecution. They endured disease and shortages of food and water at sea, and many boat people witnessed the murder of family members by pirates. The first boat people arrived in **Darwin** in 1976. The unfamiliar sight of these flimsy crowded vessels shocked Australian audiences and awakened old fears of the yellow hordes. The Vietnamese were followed in the late 1980s and early 1990s by refugees from war-torn Kampuchea (Cambodia) and parts of China. In the 1990s people arriving from the Middle East by sea were met with greater hostility and were more likely to be called 'illegal immigrants'. Nancy Viviani, *The Long Journey* (1984), examines government policy and the experience of the boat people.

HD

Bodyline is the name given to a cricketing tactic, a Test series, and a crisis in **British–Australian relations**. The touring English side of 1932–33 devised what it called 'fast leg theory' to restrict the scoring opportunities of the Australian side, and especially Don **Bradman**, who had scored a record 974 runs in the previous Test series in England. By directing their bowling to the leg stump, and supporting it with a net of close fieldsmen, they forced the batsman to take short-pitched balls on the body. The tactic, practised with particular effectiveness by the fast bowler Harold Larwood, enabled the English to win the series by four matches to one. Its employment caused mounting antagonism towards the English side, and especially the captain Douglas Jardine, whose aloof condescension exacerbated local feeling. At a time when the imperial relationship was strained by the financial consequences of the **Depression**, and especially the insistence by the Bank of England on Australian debt reduction, bodyline became an imperial controversy. The Australian Board of Control protested to the Marylebone Cricket Club, and the issue was discussed by both the Australian and British governments. Reminiscences by players have been followed by numerous historical studies, and an Australian television series.

SM

Boer War (Anglo-South African War), 1899–1902, was fought between British forces and the Boer republics over control of southern Africa. It was a cruel and bitter war in which the British Army suffered some early defeats before it could bring its might to bear on the small irregular Boer forces. In June 1900 British troops entered the Boer capital Pretoria, and victory seemed to be theirs. However, the Boers conducted a guerrilla war to which the British eventually responded by denying shelter and assistance to the enemy bands, erecting blockhouses, operating mounted columns, and moving civilians into concentration camps.

Australians were keen to participate in the war to uphold British might and demonstrate their loyalty to the empire that was their own protector. The first troops despatched

from Australia were drawn from each of the colonies' existing volunteer and militia forces, with a small regular component. These were men with some degree of training, some of whom took part in the early important battles of the war. As the enemy was highly mobile and the fighting was conducted over great distances, the British Army requested Australia to supply mounted troops. Special Bushmen's Contingents were raised from civilians who could shoot and ride. About half the Australians sent to the war served in these units, which were particularly valued for their resourcefulness and scouting ability. The despatch of troops became a Commonwealth responsibility following Federation, and in 1902 eight battalions of Australian Commonwealth Horse were sent. Only four arrived in time to see active service.

Sixteen thousand Australians served in colonial and Commonwealth units in South Africa; 606 of these were killed or died of illness, disease, or wounds. For the first time Australian women went to war as nurses, and one died. More than 700 men were wounded; casualty figures are not recorded for the thousands who served in South African irregular or imperial units. Six Australians were awarded the Victoria Cross.

Although some of the Australian units numbered about 1000 men, their contribution was often lost among the larger British formations, and it is difficult to identify actions in which Australians featured most prominently. At the Elands River depot in the Transvaal, a mixed force of about 300 Australians (mostly from NSW and Qld), together with 200 Rhodesians, were besieged by the Boers. From 4 August 1900, they defiantly held out for 13 days until finally relieved. Their action was widely publicised as an example of Australian courage and resolve.

After 1900 public enthusiasm for the war waned in Australia. Opposition to the war increased among radicals and in the Australian Labor Party, though it was not as strong as in Britain itself. Anti-imperial sentiment was fuelled by disgust at the methods employed by the British, and some questioned how Australia's interests could be served by its involvement. Colonial loyalists were enraged at these 'pro-Boers'. Because of their opposition to the war, Henry **Higgins** lost his seat in the Victorian parliament and Professor Arnold **Wood** only just escaped being dismissed from his chair of history at the University of Sydney. Volunteers continued to come forward to serve in South Africa, but some of the soldiers at the front were losing enthusiasm. With the major battles fought and the Boers' capitals captured, the war moved into a shabby guerrilla phase that required troops to destroy homes and crops, and displace civilians.

There were disasters and controversy too. On 12 June 1901, 350 men of the 5th Victorian Mounted Rifles were attacked by the Boers while camped in the evening at Wilmansrust in Eastern Transvaal. The Australians were routed, suffering 18 dead and over 40 wounded. Three Victorians, who had been enraged by accusations of cowardice, were convicted for inciting mutiny and sentenced to imprisonment. Two Australians serving in a South African irregular unit, Lieutenants H.H. 'Breaker' **Morant** and P. Handcock, were executed in 1902 for killing a Boer prisoner.

The early stages of the war were well covered by Australian journalists. Banjo **Paterson's** reports, republished as *From the Front* (2000), praised the Australian bushman as a natural soldier. Several contemporary books about the war appeared; among these *Tommy Cornstalk* (1902) is notable for its treatment of the war from a soldier's perspective. Although no Australian official history of the war was published, *The Official Records of the Australian Military Contingents to the War in South Africa* (n.d.), intended as a statistical register and reference, and valuable for its rolls of names of those who served, appeared a decade after the war. There was no serious study of the war until 75 years later, when R.L. Wallace, *The Australians at the Boer War* (1976), and L.M. Field, *The Forgotten War* (1979), were published.

The war was quickly overshadowed by the immensity of the two world wars. It is commemorated in a few striking **war memorials**, such as those in Brisbane, Adelaide, and Ballarat, and smaller monuments in many country towns and in some street names. Controversy about the Morant and Handcock executions was revived by the successful film *Breaker Morant*, released in 1980.

PETER BURNESS

Boiling down was the process of melting down the carcasses of stock, mainly sheep, reducing them to fat which could then be converted into tallow. Introduced into the colonies with the development of large-scale sheep farming, boiling-down works proliferated in the early 1840s, when economic downturn resulted in lower prices for **wool**.

HD

'Boldrewood, Rolf' (Thomas Alexander Browne) (1826–1915) became famous as the author of *Robbery Under Arms*, a novel about **bushranging**. Initially serialised in the *Sydney Mail* (1882–83), it was the 1889 revised edition that attracted international as well as national recognition. Browne came from England with his family as a young child. When the family fortunes fell in the 1840s, he became a successful farmer in western Victoria, only to fail himself in the 1860s. He was police magistrate and goldfields commissioner at Gulgong in the early 1870s, and spent the next 20 years filling that position in several NSW towns. His best writing is drawn from experience gained during these years. The unmistakably Australian voice of the narrator of *Robbery Under Arms* and the historical basis of many of the incidents and characters give the novel an immediate, authentic appeal. Its dramatic quality was quickly recognised; it has formed the basis for a play, several films and numerous radio serialisations. Many of his other, less successful, novels are romantic in the style of his favourite author, Sir Walter Scott, from whose work he also took his pseudonym. After retirement Browne returned to Melbourne, about which he had earlier written an evocative collection of short pieces, *Old Melbourne Memories* (1884). A collection of his work,

Rolf Boldrewood, edited by Robert Brissenden, appeared in 1979; Paul de Serville's appeared in 2000.

KT

Bolte, Henry Edward (1908–90), long-serving premier of Victoria, came to power by chance and held it against all expectations. A farmer, he entered the Victorian parliament in 1947 and was appointed deputy leader of the then Liberal and Country Party in 1951, although Arthur Rylah received more votes, because of a convention that either the leader or deputy should come from the country. Following the 1953 death of the leader of the opposition in a plane crash on his way to the coronation of Queen Elizabeth, Bolte defeated Rylah for the leadership. Peter Blazey, in his affectionate *Bolte: A Political Biography* (1972, 1990), claims that this was widely regarded as a stop-gap appointment. With the Australian Labor Party **Split**, the Cain Labor government fell. Bolte became premier and treasurer, remaining in office until his 1972 retirement. Described variously as larrikin or populist, he cannily exploited the image of a no-nonsense man of the people which was the basis of his success. This was often manifested in memorable one-liners—of striking teachers, 'I don't have a doorstep low enough for them to sit on', and of striking railworkers, 'They can march up and down till they're bloody well footsore!' He divided the community with his refusal in 1967 to commute the death sentence for Ronald Ryan. Although he extended shopping hours, introduced compulsory seatbelt legislation, and ended the **six o'clock swill**, Bolte preferred economic to social reforms. He led many delegations overseas to promote Victoria and to seek investment for its development. Bolte died of lung cancer, defiantly smoking to the end while quipping that 'The last smoke I have will be in the crematorium.'

KT

Bolton, Geoffrey Curgenven (1931–) is a much-travelled and versatile historian. Born and educated in Western Australia, he was a postgraduate student at Oxford, and has held academic posts in Canberra, Melbourne, Brisbane, and London; he has also occupied chairs of history in three Western Australian universities. From his research at Oxford came a study of the Irish Act of Union. At the Australian National University he pioneered regional history with his study of north Qld, *A Thousand Miles Away* (1963). While at Monash he wrote the biography of *Dick Boyer* (1967)—and in 1992 he delivered the Boyer lectures. His return to a chair of history at the University of Western Australia brought *A Fine Country to Starve In* (1972), at once the first social history of the **Depression** and an argument for the distinctively pragmatic localism of his native state. Younger radicals sometimes bracket Bolton with Paul **Hasluck** as exponents of the 'gentry school of history' which glosses over WA's inequalities and insular intolerance. Both came from modestly respectable families (Bolton has described his in *Daphne Street*, 1996), and both found ready opportunity and acceptance; yet neither was uncritical of complacent localism.

Bolton's eschewal of extremism is also apparent in his general history of Australia after World War II for *The Oxford History of Australia*, of which he was general editor. This volume, subtitled 'The Middle Way', appeared in 1990. His biography of Edmund Barton (2000) extols the same preference for moderation. Yet in both his career and his writing he has been a pioneer. As the foundation professor of history at Murdoch University from 1979 to 1989, he initiated the teaching of **environmental history**, from which came *Spoils and Spoilers* (1981). From 1982 to 1985 he was also the first professor of Australian studies at what is now the Sir Robert Menzies Centre in London, revisiting interests he had earlier expressed in his study of *Britain's Legacy Overseas* (1973).

SM

Bonner, Neville Thomas (1922–99) attracted attention as the first Aboriginal member of federal parliament. A poverty-stricken childhood, described by Angela Burger in her sympathetic biography (1979), included little formal education. He worked as a labourer and carpenter; he also held a supervisory position at the Aboriginal settlement on Palm Island, Qld. In 1971 the **Liberal Party** selected him to fill a casual vacancy in the Senate for Qld. From 1963 to 1973 Bonner was president of the One People of Australia League (OPAL); the Senate gave him a larger forum to develop his advocacy for Aboriginal rights and the environment, although he was criticised by some for accepting the 'white' system. His outspoken criticism of the Queensland National–Liberal Party government eventually cost him preselection; his attempt to win as an independent in 1983 failed.

KT

Bonwick, James (1817–1906) wrote prolifically on colonial history and was a pioneer **archivist**. The son of a carpenter, he became a schoolteacher while still in his teens and in 1840 married Esther Beddow, the daughter of a Baptist clergyman; the Nonconformist emphasis on temperance, moral reform, and social improvement shaped his subsequent career. Husband and wife were selected in 1841 to conduct the new government school in Hobart. Bonwick later established his own schools in Tasmania, SA and finally Victoria, but never with lasting application or success.

Bonwick's first writings were school texts in geography and history. During the 1850s, between educational ventures, he published literary magazines and wrote on the *Discovery and Settlement of Port Phillip* (1856). Later works included *John Batman* (1867); *Daily Life and Origin of the Tasmanians* (1870); and *The Last of the Tasmanians* (1870). He had first become interested in 'writing the narrative of the now departed people' on an 1842 visit to the Aboriginal settlement on Flinders Island. In this and other work Bonwick emphasised the Arcadian virtue of the Aboriginal material and moral culture, but never questioned the inevitability of its supersession by European civilisation; the indigenous people represented a primitive antiquity incapable of adaptation. As he put it, 'they knew no past, they wanted no future'.

While working in England as an immigration agent for the Queensland government during the 1870s, Bonwick began research on documentary records of the British colonisation of Australia. *The First Twenty Years of Australia* (1882) and *Port Phillip Settlement* (1883) embodied the results. In 1883 he persuaded the Queensland government to commission him to transcribe archival material, a scheme already undertaken by the Canadians. Bonwick later performed similar work for the SA, Tasmanian, and NSW governments as well as the Melbourne Public Library. Many of his transcripts were used in the *Historical Records of New South Wales* (1892–1901) and the *Historical Records of Australia* (1914–26). He published *An Octogenarian's Reminiscences* the year before his death in England. Untrained in history, his work infused the nineteenth-century faith in the authority of the fact with a conviction of the providential benefits of progress.

SM

Bonython family became prominent in SA initially through the efforts of (JOHN) LANGDON BONYTHON (1848–1939), who arrived in Adelaide from London as a child. At the age of 16 he became a journalist with the Adelaide *Advertiser*, earning enough from mining speculation by 1879 to buy a share in the paper, and becoming sole proprietor in 1893. His long editorship of the paper (1884–1923) and his huge personal wealth made him an influential figure in SA. He supported small business over large landowners and was a liberal progressive in his politics. He was also a generous public benefactor, and helped establish the Commonwealth Literary Fund, which he chaired for more than 20 years. His son (JOHN) LAVINGTON (1875–1960) was also involved in the newspaper world and edited the *Saturday Express*. (HUGH RESKYMER) 'KYM' (1920–), son of John Lavington, is known for his involvement with jazz music and as a director of art galleries. His writing includes *Modern Australian Painting, 1950–1975* (1976) and an autobiography, *Ladies' Legs and Lemonade* (1979).

KT

Books are the principal tools of historians both for storing information and for disseminating their work to the reading public. The book trade developed rapidly in a colonial society marked by high rates of literacy and respect for the authority of the printed word: the clergyman on the **First Fleet** brought more than 4000 books and pamphlets. While local book production was soon established, the nineteenth-century trade was dominated by the import of books from Britain by local booksellers. Wallace Kirsop has explored the patterns of the nineteenth-century trade in *Books for Colonial Readers* (1994).

By the end of the century local publishers such as Angus & Robertson had created extensive lists of Australian fiction and non-fiction, but the book industry continued to be dominated by British publishing houses, which held copyright throughout the Empire long after the Dominions achieved independence. Although some established local operations, these Australian agencies concentrated on the promotion and sale of the British list or of colonial editions of works published in Britain. This dominance weakened after World War II with the emergence of new local publishers, which benefited from government assistance and growing demand for Australian titles, and more recently from the entry of US-based multinational publishers. The rapid growth in secondary and tertiary education fostered the expansion of the publishing industry so that the annual list of *Australian Books in Print* grew from 52 pages when it first appeared in 1956, to 1350 pages in 1996; about 10 000 new books are published annually. There is a general survey of *The Book in Australia*, edited by D.H. Borchardt and Wallace Kirsop (1988), while a large-scale project is preparing a multi-volume *History of the Book in Australia*.

The close relationship between journalism and the writing of history in the colonial period fostered local publication. Henry **Melville**, the editor of a Hobart newspaper, was imprisoned for his criticism of the administration of Lieutenant-Governor **Arthur**. While in prison he wrote *The History of the Island of Van Diemen's Land*, and then printed it; the work was published anonymously in 1835 but smuggled on board a ship and republished in London. John **West** was both a **Congregational** minister and newspaper editor; his *History of Tasmania* (1852) was published in Launceston. But J.D. **Lang** and most other early historians published their principal works in Britain, where their arguments for political change were ultimately directed. G.W. **Rusden's** ambitious *History of Australia* (1883), on the other hand, was jointly published in London, Melbourne, and Sydney. Early **school histories**, such as those of James **Bonwick**, Alexander **Sutherland**, and A.W. **Jose**, were locally published; Ernest **Scott**, however, wrote his *Short History* (1916) for Oxford University Press.

The first academic historians generally published in London, Cambridge, or Oxford. Scott, a shrewd negotiator, placed two of his exploration histories with Angus & Robertson, and another text with the local office of Macmillan, but went to J.M. Dent with his two-volume anthology of exploration history and edited the principal interwar survey of Australian history for Cambridge University Press. Dent published G.C. **Henderson's** 1907 biography of George Grey. Edward **Shann's** two major histories were published by the university presses of Oxford and Cambridge, and Keith **Hancock** wrote *Australia* (1930) for a series commissioned by the London firm of Ernest Benn. Stephen **Roberts** published his early studies of land settlement and his later school texts locally, but took the best-selling *House That Hitler Built* (1937) to Methuen in London. The reasons for this pattern were partly commercial— British publication usually brought larger sales—and partly the desire for prestige and wider academic recognition.

In the period between the two world wars Angus & Robertson continued to publish a wide range of popular history and **biography**, and such major series as **Bean's** official war history. The Australian branch of Macmillan became an important scholarly publisher, challenged only by Melbourne University Press after this first Australian academic publisher was established in 1922. It remained a small

operation until after World War II, when the expansion of university education allowed first Gwyn James and then Peter Ryan to build it into a major scholarly publishing house. James and Ryan were both historians, and history was at the forefront of their lists. James arranged for Melbourne University Press to produce the *Australian Dictionary of Biography* and persuaded a reluctant press board to accept Manning **Clark's** *History*; Ryan published the first works of Geoffrey **Blainey**, established a lasting partnership with Geoffrey **Serle** and developed a particular strength in biography. Other universities established their own presses after World War II, and these provided an outlet for historical research on state and regional themes during the 1960s and 1970s, but perhaps failed to take full advantage of the growing opportunities. From the 1980s the commercial climate for monographs with limited print-runs was far less favourable. Some, such as the University of Queensland Press, sought survival in fiction and more popular titles; some, such as Sydney University Press and the Australian National University Press, succumbed; others, such as New South Wales University Press, have only recently re-entered the risky field of monograph publication; while others still, such as the University of Western Australia Press, struggle on.

The fundamental difficulty for these university presses is that, while they need profits from high-volume titles to offset the meagre returns from specialist ones, the authors are inclined to offer them only manuscripts of limited appeal and take their more popular works elsewhere. The principal postwar textbooks were published by the commercial presses—Gordon **Greenwood**, *Australia: A Social and Political History* (1955), by Angus & Robertson, which also published Manning Clark's two volumes of *Select Documents* (1950, 1955); Frank **Crowley**, *A New History of Australia* (1974), by Heinemann; the short histories of Clark, **Crawford**, **Shaw** and Russel **Ward** by Mentor, Hutchinson, Faber, and Ure Smith; and John Rickard, *Australia: A Cultural History* (1988), by Longman Cheshire. The Australian branches of the British publishing firms were better equipped to exploit the expanded educational market and the growing general interest in Australian history. Cassell commissioned a series of documentary extracts and commentary on major themes. Nelson published Crowley's collections of documents. Macmillan secured some of Geoffrey Blainey's most popular works. Thames and Hudson produced John Mulvaney's *The Prehistory of Australia* (1969). Penguin Books took a chance with the young Humphrey **McQueen** and Anne **Summers**, and secured large sales of *A New Britannia* (1970) and *Damned Whores and God's Police* (1975), while David Denholm, *The Colonial Australians* (1979), demonstrated new possibilities of pictorial history. Penguin also popularised such foundational works as Bill Gammage, *The Broken Years* (1975, but first published by the Australian National University Press in 1974), and Henry **Reynolds**, *The Other Side of the Frontier* (1982, but first published by James Cook University in 1981).

The two leading English university presses remained important publishers of history. Oxford University Press achieved notable success with Russel Ward, *The Australian Legend* (1958), and its subsequent four-volume *Oxford History of Australia*. Cambridge University Press commissioned a major series of works from the 1980s, but declining sales forced its abandonment in 1996.

A new market appeared as the burgeoning antiquarian book trade pushed up the price of older works. Macmillan, Penguin Books, and Heinemann all launched reprint series during the 1970s. The State Library of South Australia embarked on a program of facsimile publication that was initially highly successful. Most reprint series were short-lived because the antiquarian market was still thin, and demand concentrated on particular fields such as exploration history and women's fiction.

New Australian publishers were perhaps quicker to sense the potential of original writing. Sun Books, established in 1965 by former staff of Penguin Books, published Blainey's *The Tyranny of Distance* in 1966. The partnership of Sylvia Hale and John Iremonger in Sydney fostered the expansion of **labour history**; Iremonger subsequently joined Allen & Unwin and commissioned a durable series of surveys of 'The Australian Experience'. Hilary McPhee and Diana Gribble supported **women's history** and also published the four-volume *People's History of Australia*, edited by Verity Burgmann and Jenny Lee (1988). Ian Templeman at the Fremantle Arts Centre Press followed the best-selling autobiography of Albert **Facey**, *A Fortunate Life* (1981), with an even more widely read exploration of Aboriginal identity, Sally **Morgan**, *My Place* (1987). The most ambitious attempt of the historical profession to reach a wider audience, with the **Bicentennial History Project**, was published by Kevin Weldon in conjunction with the **Fairfax** newspaper company. Some 13 000 sets of the 10-volume series were sold.

Throughout the 1960s and 1970s a growing stream of postgraduate theses in Australian history found their way into print and onto reading lists. Edited collections of essays were assembled on topical subjects to fill out the curriculum. During the 1980s the enthusiasm of publishers faltered as sales waned. Australian authors had to compete with the best of overseas history writing in the most open English-language market in the world. Australian readers remained interested in **Aboriginal history**, the **First Fleet**, and **convict** history (beloved of antiquarians and especially popular in Sydney), the **gold rushes** (especially popular in Melbourne). the turn of the century (with its **Federation** and nationalist resonances), World Wars I and II, the **Vietnam War**, and **Whitlam**; but between these peaks lay troughs of neglect relieved only by outcrops of explorers and pioneers (with regional significance). An increasing number of new books were the product of **commissioned history**, heavily subsidised for promotional purposes that determined their subjects and treatment.

There is anxious discussion of the reasons and the remedy. The contraction of history teaching, the fragmentation of the curriculum, the recourse to the photocopier, and the inability of the book to hold the attention of students habituated to other sources of information and entertainment are all cited as contributory factors, but the narrow and esoteric character of the doctoral thesis is perhaps most often blamed. The imperative to publish is maintained by the academic system of appointment, promotion, and reward; the need to be read has no corresponding inducement apart from the pressures of the market. Historians are urged to write more accessibly on larger, more significant subjects, yet the growing recourse to in-house, desk-top, or electronic publication allows the advice to be disregarded. In the mid-1990s there were more than 500 doctoral candidates pursuing historical research, and little likelihood that more than a handful of the completed theses would find their way into print, even in revised form. It is a situation that afflicts the profession and impoverishes the appreciation of Australian history.

The history of Australian book publishing is served by various biographies and company histories. The Bibliographical Society of Australia and New Zealand produces a bulletin, and among its other publications, Wallace Kirsop's *Books for Colonial Readers* (1995) is noteworthy. The History of the Book in Australia project is preparing a three-volume history; volume 2, edited by John Arnold and Martyn Lyons, is shortly to appear.

STUART MACINTYRE

Boote, Henry Ernest (1865–1949) arrived in Brisbane from Liverpool in 1889 to work as a compositor. Proudly working-class and self-educated, he quickly became involved with the developing labour movement. He edited several Queensland labour newspapers—the *Bundaberg Guardian* (1894–96), noted for its opposition to the use of Kanaka labour, the *Gympie Truth* (1896–1902), and the Brisbane *Worker* (1902–11)—before moving to Sydney to write for the *Australian Worker*. As editor (1914–43) he became friend and confidant of many leading Labor figures, including **Scullin**, **Fisher**, **Curtin** and **Evatt**, and had considerable influence over policy. During the 1916 **conscription** debate he was an effective promoter of the 'No' case. It was largely his agitation that brought about the 1920 royal commission which freed 10 of the gaoled members of the **Industrial Workers of the World**. A prolific writer, Boote wrote essays, some of which are collected in *A Fool's Talk* (1915), verse, satire, political pamphlets, and novels, including *The Human Ladder* (1920).

KT

Booth, Mary (1869–1956), educated in Sydney, qualified in medicine at Edinburgh University in 1899. By the time of her return to Sydney she had developed a greater interest in social welfare than medicine. Booth lectured at girls' schools on hygiene and wrote on infant mortality. During World War I she established the Soldiers' Club and a fund for war widows. She also founded the Anzac Fellowship of Women, of which she was president 1921–56.

KT

Borders were well understood and observed in Aboriginal society. Stephen Davis and Victor Prescott explain in *Aborigi-*

nal Frontiers and Boundaries in Australia (1992) that clan or tribal boundaries tended to coincide with watercourses and topographic features, although, in some cases, a frontier zone rather than a line separated neighbouring tribal groups. This socio-political structure was ignored by Europeans entering the continent and, despite the work of anthropologists since the 1920s, remains incompletely understood.

The geographical pattern of indigenous borders has also assumed greater importance during the 1990s because of the acceptance of **Aboriginal land rights**.

British settlement led to the internal division of the continent into colonies. Bill Gammage considers the rationale of the 'Early Boundaries of NSW' in *HS* (1981). In the first decades of settlement there was considerable debate about whether land occupation should be permitted before a system of territorial division was implemented. In NSW 'Limits of Location' (**Nineteen Counties**) were set, and from 1831 these formed an important regional boundary. However, **squatters** moved beyond the approved settlement zone and created a new pastoral **frontier**. When NSW, Victoria, SA, and Tasmania obtained self-government in 1856, Qld in 1859, and WA in 1890, the colonies were separate political entities, each with its own legislature, administration, and relationship with Britain. The boundaries between them were officially delimited. With **Federation**, these boundaries between colonies became internal state boundaries. Support for Federation tended to be greatest among people living near the boundaries because it promised an Australian customs union and easier movement across the border.

The precursors of today's system of **local government** boundaries appeared in NSW in 1833 with the establishment of police districts designed to provide settlers with police protection. This moved away from the British idea of counties and parishes as the territorial units of local government. With the exception of SA, other colonies set up similar systems. W.S. Logan ('The Evolution and Significance of Local Government Boundaries in Victoria', *Australian Geographical Studies*, 1966) describes the Victorian case, where a set of rural 'road districts' and urban boroughs, towns, and cities were created from the 1850s which became the basis of that colony's local government hierarchy; counties and parishes were used only for the purposes of surveying land and registering land titles.

The impact of these political boundaries on the border zones they divide has varied significantly over time. During the nineteenth century, the colonial boundaries acted as a barrier to the flow of people and goods, and also divided the areas over which the various colonial governments imposed developmental policies. Customs and migration controls were imposed at the boundaries. Each colony had its own postal service as well as policies regarding the use of land, protection and development of forests, construction and maintenance of roads, fostering of agriculture and industry. Each capital city sought to establish its economic grip over its colonial territory through centralising railway, road, and telecommunications policies. Thus, for instance, the NSW–Victorian border along the **Murray River** came to mark a break in railway gauge between Sydney and Melbourne as well as a contrast between free-trade policies and protectionist policies which were to result in significantly different colonial economies and capital cities.

Under the Commonwealth **Constitution**, the colonies—now states—lost their power to control the flow of people and goods. Section 92 of the Constitution prohibits the restriction of trade and commerce between states. Customs duties now apply only to goods crossing Australia's national borders. The control of communications, currency, patents, and copyright are federal powers, as, too, are immigration, emigration, and the naturalisation of aliens. While resource development remained with the states under the Constitution, federal powers have gradually extended into this arena, provoking bitter states' rights disputes (see **Commonwealth–state relations**). The **Whitlam** government's attempt in the 1970s to establish a system of regional authorities was seen as a threat by the states and has been almost entirely dismantled. But efforts to achieve national policies continue (for example, in educational curricula and standards, and gun laws), steadily reducing the significance of state boundaries. Conventional notions of space, distance, boundary impacts, and states' rights are rendered obsolete by new technology (such as computers and the Internet) and global economic and cultural operations. The High Court upheld the Whitlam government's 1974 legislation which asserted Commonwealth control over the whole offshore area. Against this, however, in the case of WA, SA, Qld, and the NT, the states' economic interests have been extended in recent decades into uninhabited border zones, especially to exploit new mineral resources.

Being an island continent with few close neighbours, Australia has been fortunate not to have had major border conflicts leading to international or national crises. Nevertheless the 1879 realignment by the British government of Qld's boundary with **Papua New Guinea** to take in the Torres Strait Islands caused controversy. With the discovery of oil reserves in the Timor Gap, the previously unimportant international border between Indonesia and Australia required sensitive negotiation to resolve tensions. A 1989 treaty defines areas in which Indonesia and Australia have exclusive exploitation rights, and an area for joint exploration and exploitation projects.

Australia is a signatory to the United Nations Convention on the Law of the Sea, which came into force in November 1994. Already in 1990, however, Australia had extended its territorial sea to 12 nautical miles in accordance with Article 3 of the convention and, under the Maritime Legislation Amendment Act of August 1994, had proclaimed an exclusive economic zone of 200 nautical miles and adopted a definition of the Australian continental shelf in line with Article 76 of the convention. Australia's fishing rights within the exclusive economic zone are occasionally infringed by Indonesian fishing boats that stray into Australian waters and are usually impounded.

WILLIAM S. LOGAN

Botanic gardens were first laid out in Sydney (1816) and Hobart (1818), followed by Perth, Melbourne, and Adelaide. Landscaped in the picturesque English style and concerned with the acquisition, collection, pleasing display, and study of plants, these **gardens** emulated both the aesthetic style and scientific objectives of Kew Gardens, London. Both exotic and indigenous species were acclimatised, and specialised sections, such as rosaries, ferneries, borders, and cactus gardens, developed. Specimen trees were regarded as highly desirable elements. The Melbourne Botanic Gardens, laid out largely under the directorship of German botanist Ferdinand von **Mueller**, and later extended by William **Guilfoyle**, were regarded in the late nineteenth century as among the best examples of specimen gardens in the world. Botanic gardens became a popular use of public land in provincial towns, especially in mining towns, where such displays of civilisation were thought to alleviate the harsh surroundings. The importance of botanic gardens as sites of cultural heritage was little recognised until the adoption of the 1979 **Burra Charter** and growth of **heritage** conservation in the 1980s.

HD

Botany Bay, located south of Port Jackson, was named by Joseph **Banks** because of the many plant specimens he collected there in 1770. On his return to England, Banks declared its suitability as the site of a penal colony. On 18 January 1788, Captain **Phillip** and his party came ashore first at a site on Botany Bay, but, due to the lack of fresh water and the unsafe harbour, transferred to the more suitable Sydney Cove. The original choice is falsely remembered as the destination of subsequent convict ships in the folk song 'Botany Bay', and for a long time the name was used pejoratively for the colony. In the twentieth century, heavy industrial development, including the construction of a Sydney Airport runway over its northern shore, has polluted the bay. Concern for its future well-being initiated the Botany Bay Project in the 1970s, a social and economic survey of the area directed by economic historian Noel **Butlin**.

HD

Bottom-of-the-harbour scheme refers to tax-avoidance schemes used by large corporations in the 1970s and early 1980s. The practice was widespread in Sydney (hence the reference to Sydney Harbour) but was also prevalent in Melbourne. The term derives from the practice of stripping companies of their assets in order to avoid tax, and selling the remains; the company records, mostly irretrievable, were said to have disappeared to 'the bottom of the harbour'. Subsequent investigations into this spate of corporate tax avoidance implicated numerous prominent Australian business leaders.

HD

Bounty immigrants were assisted immigrants, mainly from Britain, whose passage to Australia was financed by a government bounty. This was a means of encouraging immigration, particularly of young married couples and single women, who would satisfy the demand for labour. This approach followed **Wakefield's** theory of systematic colonisation. In 1835 Governor **Bourke** proposed that the NSW government pay a bounty to private shipping agents, who met requests for labourers from private settlers or companies, for each suitable immigrant they landed. The selection, transportation and employment of immigrants otherwise rested with the agents, many of whom were criticised for the poor conditions of the ships they used and their overriding interest in profit-making. The British government abandoned this system in 1841 but subsequently introduced other forms of assisted **immigration**. R.B. **Madgwick** discusses the bounty system in *Immigration into Eastern Australia* (1937).

HD

Bourgeois hegemony was a concept popularised by **New Left** historians in the 1970s. *Bourgeois* is the adjectival form of *bourgeoisie*, which in its Marxist sense signifies the capitalist class; *hegemony* refers to the way in which that class maintains its dominance over other classes. The term was taken from the Italian communist Antonio Gramsci, who developed it in works written in prison between the wars and published in English translation from the 1960s. Gramsci argued that, in addition to its ownership of the means of production and the machinery of state power, the capitalist class controlled civil society through intellectual and cultural means.

This emphasis on ideology appealed to New Left intellectuals as they developed a radical critique of the institutions of civil society. Humphrey **McQueen's** *A New Britannia* (1970) assailed Australian nationalism and radicalism for complicity with bourgeois hegemony, while in 'Radical History and Bourgeois Hegemony', *Intervention* (1972), Stuart Macintyre accused the **Old Left** historians of perpetuating liberal illusions. The concept of bourgeois hegemony is central to the analysis by R.W. Connell and T.H. Irving of *Class Structure in Australian History* (1980). Gramsci's work has been a formative influence on subsequent cultural history, though his concern with both class conflict and class domination has been largely abandoned. (See also **Class**.)

SM

Bourke, Richard (1777–1855), an Irish landowner and British army officer, was the first liberal governor of NSW, holding office from 1831 to 1837. He supported the **emancipists'** claim for civil and political rights and for the establishment of an elected Assembly. As an instalment of reform, he pushed through the nominated Council a measure to provide civilian juries in criminal cases, with ex-convicts being eligible for jury service. This alarmed the free emigrant landowners, who attempted to discredit Bourke in England by claiming that another of his measures—a limitation on the powers of magistrates—was endangering convict discipline. The liberals and emancipists rallied to support the governor. This bitter party warfare was designed to influence the British government's decision on the colony's future constitution, a matter which it did not settle until well after Bourke's departure. His lasting legacy was his **Church Act**, which provided public funds on the same basis to Anglican, Presbyterian, and Catholic churches. His plan to replace public support for church schools by a national system of **education** met too much opposition and had to be dropped. The liberals and emancipists honoured him with a statue which stands outside the State Library in Macquarie Street, Sydney. His biography has been written by Hazel King (1971).

JH

Bowen, George Ferguson (1821–99) proceeded from an academic and literary beginning to become a striking, though hardly typical, example of the professional governor of the second half of the nineteenth century. Between 1859 and 1887 he administered governments in Australia and NZ, Mauritius, and Hong Kong. His success was equivocal.

The eldest son of a Church of Ireland clergyman, Bowen took a first in classics at Oxford. A philhellene, he obtained appointments in the Ionian Islands, including, in 1854, secretary to the Lord High Commissioner. In Corfu he enhanced his reputation as a classicist, and made a name as an author and traveller. He also acquired an Ionian wife, the Countess Diamantina Roma of Zante, and through her very political family a taste for intrigue.

During seven years as governor of Qld, his voluminous despatches and private letters helped publicise the colony (and himself: a tendency which never left him); and he handled the colony's 1866 political crisis skilfully. In the **Colonial Office** also, his 'eccentricities' were always of some concern, but he was raised to GCMG in 1862 and promoted to NZ in the last stages of the last Maori Wars. There, however, late in 1869 he earned Lord Granville's displeasure by not cooperating sufficiently in the Gladstone government's decision to withdraw all imperial troops.

Despite this, Bowen was promoted further—perhaps, in part, because his political associate in Qld, R.G.W. Herbert, was now permanent under-secretary in the Colonial Office—by being made governor of Victoria in 1873. There he placed great store on social generosity, in which Lady Bowen played a great part; and it was much to his taste that he became the first occupant of the new, grand Government House. But, returning after a year's furlough early in 1876, he faced the latest contest of the era in which 'property and intelligence' considered itself threatened by 'democracy', and suffered for his policy during the **constitutional crisis** involving the Berry ministry. Bowen believed he was bound to accept ministerial advice, almost without limit: Herbert privately assured him that would be the view of the Colonial Office under Lord Carnarvon. This displeased Legislative Council supporters in Victoria. More importantly, a new secretary of state, Sir Michael Hicks-Beach, censured Bowen; and he who had hoped to become governor of NSW was given instead Mauritius and then Hong Kong.

BRUCE KNOX

Boyd, Benjamin (?1797–1851), a colorful entrepreneur, was involved with shipping, whaling, banking, and squatting.

Born in London of a Scottish family, Boyd became a stockbroker and formed the Royal Bank of Australia in 1840. He travelled to Australia in 1842 to establish a Sydney branch. Boyd bought grazing properties and recruited **Pacific Island labourers** to solve the labour shortage. He established a whaling station at Boydtown (named after him) on Twofold Bay, NSW, which was also a port for his coastal steamships. None of these ventures prospered, and Boyd was dismissed as a director of the Royal Bank in 1847. To escape his creditors, he headed for the Californian goldfields. After his return to Australia he disappeared in the Solomon Islands, apparently murdered by natives. Marion Diamond's *Ben Boyd of Boydtown* (1988, 1995) gives a full account of his activities.

KT

Boyd family has made a remarkable contribution to the arts in Australia, in painting and pottery, sculpture, architecture, and literature. Strong family bonds and a shared belief in art as a natural activity rather than a special vocation have fostered minor as well as major talents, and it has been part of the Boyd ethos to praise creative work of every kind.

The artistic tradition began with the marriage in Melbourne in 1886 of EMMA MINNIE À BECKETT (1858–1936) to ARTHUR MERRIC BOYD (1862–1940). Boyd's father was military secretary to an early governor of Victoria. Emma Minnie was a grand-daughter of Victoria's first chief justice, Sir William à Beckett, and of John Mills, an ex-convict who made a fortune as a Melbourne brewer and publican. The Mills inheritance, which supported a generation of à Becketts in affluent leisure, enabled Arthur and Emma Minnie Boyd to develop their talents as *plein air* landscape painters on the fringe of the **Heidelberg School**, with no need to sell their work. As the family fortunes declined, the three sons of Arthur and Emma Minnie Boyd struggled towards a degree of professionalism. MERRIC (1888–1959) established a pottery at Murrumbeena; with his wife, painter DORIS GOUGH (1889–1960), and their five children, he lived there in eccentric poverty, temperamentally unable to sell his work. PENLEIGH (1890–1923), whose landscape paintings were close in style and spirit to those of his parents, won some public recognition in his short lifespan. MARTIN (1893–1972) lived most of his adult life in Britain and Italy, but his best-known novels, *The Montforts* (1928), *The Cardboard Crown* (1953), and *A Difficult Young Man* (1955), drew on his Boyd and à Beckett family history, and on his Australian background. They are, in their way, self-conscious histories of an imperilled class, the Anglo-Australian cultural elite.

In the third generation, the idea of 'the Boyds' as a collective identity emerged mainly through Merric Boyd's sons, ARTHUR (1920–99) and DAVID (1924–), who became potters and painters, and GUY (1923–88), who moved from pottery to sculpture. All three became fully professional, but by continuing the idea of art as a family activity they retained the spirit of the earlier generations. Marriages to fellow artists consolidated the family tradition. David Boyd's wife Hermia was a ceramic artist. Merric's elder daughter LUCY (1916–) worked with her husband Hatton Beck in the Murrumbeena pottery. Her sister MARY (1926–) married painter John Perceval, who also worked in the Boyd pottery. The status of the Murrumbeena Boyds was reinforced by the success of their cousin ROBIN (1919–71), Penleigh's son, as architect, writer, and social critic. A leading apostle of modernism, he attacked what he called 'the Australian Ugliness' in his book of that name (1960). Robin Boyd was also the author of the classic architectural history *Australia's Home* (1952)

In the 1960s the Boyds caught the imagination of the general public as well as the art establishment. Arthur, Guy, and David exhibited in Britain, where Arthur established a permanent base. From the late 1970s, he divided his time between Suffolk and Bundanon, the Shoalhaven property in NSW that he gave to the nation in 1993. Arthur Boyd is one of the unquestioned great names in Australian painting. For the fourth generation, many of them practising artists, the value of being a Boyd is problematical. The younger Boyds and Percevals can expect that their work will be looked at—but always in Arthur's shadow.

There are many scholarly monographs on Arthur Boyd. Franz Philipp's 1967 study stresses the European heritage, especially the Bruegel influence, and explores Boyd's religious iconography. Ursula Hoff (1986) discusses Arthur Boyd's mastery of a variety of styles, including the lyrical landscapes that invoke the work of Emma Minnie and Arthur Merric Boyd, along with Tom **Roberts** and the Heidelberg School.

In *The Art of David Boyd* (1973), Nancy Benko stresses Hermia Boyd's partnership in her husband's ceramic art. Anne Von Bertouch and Patrick Hutchings, *Guy Boyd* (1976), place Guy Boyd's sculpture in the family context. In *The Art of the Boyds* (1991), Patricia Dobrez and Peter Herbst explore the idea of a unifying attitude to culture and society in a study of all four generations. Brenda Niall's *Martin Boyd: A Life* (1988) looks at the novelist as family historian and mythmaker. In *Robin Boyd: A Life* (1995), Geoffrey **Serle** finds Robin Boyd's lasting contribution to Australian cultural life in his writings on social planning, and domestic and public architecture.

BRENDA NIALL

Boyes, George Thomas William Blamey (1787–1853), senior public servant in Van Diemen's Land, is notable for his extensive diaries, which historians have found invaluable. A reading of his *Diaries and Letters*, edited by Peter Chapman (1985), suggests a conservative, cultured, often satiric man, who expressed his dislike for 'the Mob'. Himself a capable amateur painter, interested in literature and music, Boyes was appalled by the rougher aspects of colonial life and wrote freely of these. As auditor, he was fully involved in the social life of the ruling group in Van Diemen's Land. Boyes held a number of different positions, including acting colonial secretary and commissioner for the settlement of land grant claims. He was something of an opportunist who took advantage of this posting to repair his finances. Initially unable to afford to take his family with him to Van Diemen's Land, he remained separated from them for nine years, until

his financial position improved and he overcame his concern about his children's education.

KT

Braddon Blot, see Braddon, Edward Nicholas

Braddon, Edward Nicholas (1829–1904) settled in north-western Tasmania in 1878 after a varied career in India. He turned his rundown property into a profitable concern and, in 1879, was asked to stand for the local seat, which he won. An extremely capable politician, he served as Tasmania's agent-general in London and helped float the Mount Lyell Mining Co. among other ventures. He returned to Tasmania in 1893 and became premier the following year, remaining in office for five years. His was a vigorous government which pursued an active program of public works, and he was renowned in the public service for his savage cuts, known as 'Braddon's axe'. Braddon enabled George Adams to run the national **Tattersalls** lotteries from Tasmania, which provided revenue for the state. A committed federalist, Braddon was elected as a Tasmanian delegate to the 1897–98 Federal Convention. Recognising the need to win acceptance of the Constitution by the smaller states, he introduced section 87, called the 'Braddon clause', whereby three-quarters of the revenue from customs and excise would be returned to the states. The proposal was criticised as the 'Braddon Blot' and amended before **Federation** so that the arrangement would continue for only 10 years. During the 1951 Jubilee celebrations Braddon was honoured in Tasmania as a founding father.

KT

Bradfield, John Job Crew (1867–1943) is often described as the father of the **Sydney Harbour Bridge**. As a civil engineer working for the NSW Public Works Department in 1912, he was given responsibility for the 'Sydney Harbour Bridge and City Transit' branch. In 1915 he produced a report recommending a city underground railway, a bridge crossing, and electrification of suburban rail lines. Known as the Bradfield Plan, this formed the basis for the development of Sydney's transport system. Its implementation was not without problems, usually financial, and Bradfield had to promote the scheme vigorously. Upon the eventual completion of the bridge in 1932, the approach road and bridge section was named for him. He was also involved in the construction of the Story and St Lucia bridges in **Brisbane**. An interest in water conservation led to his developing an imaginative plan, which now bears his name, for the irrigation of inland Qld via tunnels carrying water drawn from dammed rivers on the coastal side of the Great Dividing Range. Richard Raxworthy's 1989 biography is *Unreasonable Man: Life and Works of JJC Bradfield*.

KT

Bradman, Donald George (1908–2001), born in Cootamundra, NSW, but brought up in Bowral, was the most successful cricketer of all time. His Test average of 99.94 (from an aggregate of 6996) places him in a separate category from every other player. He was clinical and highly focused on quantitative success, but he did not grind his way to mammoth totals. Instead, he scored at a very rapid rate. Strangely, he had all the shots, but he was distinguished by none.

Bradman was more than a man: he remains a potent, but highly complex, symbol of a nation. His origins may have been in the bush, but his batting was referred to variously in the language of industry, technology, science, and economic calculation. **Bodyline** bowling was introduced in Australia in 1932–33 in order to curb his phenomenal success. Bradman's response was to move away to leg in order to slash the ball through the gaps in the off-side. Some argued that he was reckless; others that he displayed a lack of character.

Bradman's strained interaction with fellow players has always been a contentious issue. Shy and remote, Bradman did not easily form close friendships. Some, however, have suggested that **sectarianism** played a major part in the estrangement between Bradman, a Freemason, and his Catholic colleagues, such as Bill O'Reilly and Jack Fingleton.

In his post-playing career Bradman was a successful businessman and a **cricket** administrator. In his many years with the Australian Board of Control, Bradman wielded enormous power. The awe in which he was held allowed him to extend his influence beyond the formal limits of his office. The national fascination with Bradman did not cease with his retirement from the field of play; and it shows no sign of abating. He is the only Australian to have been knighted for services to cricket. His legendary status is now institutionalised in the Bradman Museum at Bowral and a permanent exhibition at the State Library of South Australia.

The Bradman literature is vast. By Bradman himself, there is *The Art of Cricket* (1958); and by others there are Irving Rosenwater, *Sir Donald Bradman: A Biography* (1978); and Charles Williams, *Bradman: An Australian Hero* (1996).

IAN HARRISS

Brady, Edwin James (1869–1952), poet, journalist and writer, produced only one profitable book, *Australia Unlimited* (1918). It was a study of Australia's primary industries and its title reflects his belief in the potential of the country. As a youth working as a shipping clerk in Sydney Brady developed a passion for the sea which became the subject of much of his writing. He edited the socialist *Australian Workman* for a time, and wrote for various other papers and magazines. His verse first appeared in the *Bulletin* in 1891, which put him in touch with fellow writers such as Henry **Lawson** and J.F. **Archibald**. He wrote detailed accounts of his travels. *The King's Caravan* (1911) recounts his wagon journey from Parramatta to Townsville in 1899–1900, and *River Rovers* (1911) describes a trip down the Murray River. Brady lived most of the last half of his life at the coastal town of Mallacoota, Victoria, writing, inventing, and planning. His autobiography, 'Life's Highway', was published in instalments in *Southerly* (1952–55).

KT

Brady, Matthew (1799–1826) became a **bushranger** after his escape in 1824 from the **penal settlement** at Macquarie Harbour. Transported to **Van Diemen's Land** four years earlier, he roamed the island with his gang for two years before being captured and executed. Their most spectacular feat was to hold up the Sorrell township. He replied to the large reward offered for his capture by posting his own reward for the capture of the lieutenant-governor, George **Arthur**. These exploits and the popular perception that he used violence only in self-defence held great appeal for contemporary writers, who represented Brady sympathetically, as does Richard Butler in his biographical novel, *And Wretches Hang* (1977).

KT

Bragg, William Henry (1862–1942), and his son **(William) Lawrence** (1890–1971), are the most significant scientists to have worked extensively in Australia. The technique of X-ray-crystallography which they invented jointly and led internationally, closely based on their Australian experience, has revealed the atomic structure of matter, notably of biological modules, including DNA.

William was born in England and educated at Cambridge University. Only 23 years old, he was appointed professor of mathematics and physics at the University of Adelaide (1886–1909). He carried a huge teaching load, was an accomplished sportsman, and was widely known. He married Gwendoline, the third daughter of Charles **Todd**. Their first child, Lawrence, was born and educated in Adelaide—at St Peter's College and the University of Adelaide, where his father was often his teacher. The need to enhance student practical experience and a willingness to give public demonstrations of X-rays and radios (1890s) introduced William to research, which he began in earnest in 1903. He did pioneering work on alpha-particles emitted from radioactive materials, and was elected a fellow of the Royal Society. He then investigated X-rays, suggesting they were particles, while European-based researchers thought they were wave-like.

Lawrence graduated with first-class honours in mathematics late in 1908 (aged 18); the family left for England early in 1909—William for the chair of physics at Leeds, Lawrence to undertake a Cambridge BA in natural science and subsequent research in the Cavendish Laboratory. Initially unproductive, they then collaborated to found the science of X-ray-crystallography, for which they were jointly awarded the 1915 Nobel Prize in Physics. John Jenkin, *The Bragg Family in Adelaide* (1986), recounts their Australian careers.

JOHN JENKIN

Brennan, Christopher John (1870–1932) discovered the writings of the French symbolists while studying at the University of Berlin on a travelling scholarship, following his early success as a student of classics and philosophy at the University of Sydney in the early 1890s. When he returned to Sydney in 1894 without a doctorate, he took a job at the Public Library and concentrated on writing poetry which, with the symbolist influence, was completely different from the ballads and nationalist verse of the day. The sexual aspects of his poetry, his anti-British stance during the **Boer War**, and his increasingly bohemian habits impeded his academic career. Eventually in 1909 he was appointed lecturer in modern literature; in 1920 he became associate professor in German and comparative literature. A charismatic teacher, Brennan achieved legendary status as a member of the Sydney bohemia and figures largely in Peter Fitzpatrick's study, *The Sea Coast of Bohemia* (1992). This unconventional behaviour, culminating in an open relationship with a married woman, caused his dismissal from the university in 1925; he descended into alcoholism and poverty. His main volume of poetry, usually referred to as *Poems (1913)*, appeared in 1914. Axel Clark's substantial biography, *Christopher Brennan* (1980), discusses the strong autobiographical basis for the poems, with their theme of man's search for paradise.

KT

Brick veneer is the name for a free-standing house with a timber frame and a single thickness, or veneer, of bricks. The bricks do not support the roof, which rests on the timber frame. Sometimes the bricks are applied only as a veneer; usually the timber frame rests on brick footings, or on a concrete slab, and the walls are attached to the frame with wire ties. Frame houses with brick cladding had been built in North America for a century or more, and similar structures were occasionally built in colonial Australia—the eating room at Tyntynder homestead near Swan Hill (1851) is one of several claimants to the title of 'the first brick veneer'. Its popularity dates from the mid-1930s when suburban councils permitted it as a cheaper form of construction in the formerly exclusive brick-only areas, and the term *brick veneer* first appeared in building journals. After World War II, it swiftly eclipsed all other forms of house construction, rising from about one-fifth of new Victorian houses in the early 1950s to four-fifths a decade later. The triple-fronted cream brick veneer became a symbol of the aesthetic and social conformity of the postwar suburbs, where, as Barry **Humphries's** *alter ego* Edna Everage sang, 'the cream brick veneers stay hygienic for years in Highett, the place of my dreams'.

GD

Bridges, Royal Tasman 'Roy' (1885–1952), journalist, novelist, and historian, was born in Hobart; as a wide-eyed schoolboy he became fascinated with the 'romance' of history and myth when he read Charles Hanson's *Siege of Troy and the Wanderings of Ulysses*. After obtaining a BA degree at the University of Tasmania, he worked as a newspaper journalist from 1904, mostly with the Melbourne *Age* between 1909 and the late 1920s. Bridges wrote more than 30 fictional works, including various historical novels set in early Tasmania and Port Phillip. In 1917 **BHP** commissioned him to write a **business history**, *From Silver to Steel: The Romance of the Broken Hill Proprietary* (1920), which despite some 'reconstructed' dialogue is a valuable product of extensive oral and business history. *One Hundred Years: The*

Romance of the Victorian People (1934) collated a series of historical articles commissioned by Keith **Murdoch** for Victoria's centenary. Bridges's family history, *That Yesterday Was Home* (1948), includes a brief autobiography. Minor collections of Bridges's papers are held at the National Library of Australia, the Royal Historical Society of Victoria, and the State Library of Victoria. His major collection in the University of Tasmania was catalogued by D.H. Borchardt and B. Tilley, *Studies in Australian Bibliography, No. 4* (1956).

DC

Bridges, William Throsby (1861–1915) named and commanded the First **AIF**, raised in 1914. Scottish-born and educated in England and Canada, he joined his family in NSW in 1879. His army career, which began in 1885, included service as a gunnery instructor, secondment to the British Army in the Boer War, and involvement with military intelligence, defence planning and organisation. He became an advocate for the 'imperial' approach to defence, as opposed to a specifically Australian perspective. Bridges was given the task of establishing a military college; Duntroon was opened in 1911 and he remained commandant there until his appointment in 1914 as inspector-general of the AIF. Once in Egypt, he insisted on strict discipline for the troops, determined to keep them in a single body rather than distributed among the British Army. He landed at **Gallipoli** with the 1st Division and, appalled at the confusion, called for withdrawal but was overruled. Daily visits to the front lines won him the respect and affection of his men. Bridges was shot by a sniper mid-May 1915 and died several days later. His grave, designed by Walter Burley **Griffin**, overlooks Duntroon.

KT

Brisbane is the capital of the State of **Queensland** and the third-largest city in Australia. Mi-an-jin, the bend of the Brisbane River now constituting the central business district of Brisbane, was a regular meeting spot and place of refreshment for the Aboriginal group who later became known as the Duke of York clan; across the river was the Coorparoo clan. These were two of the groups who made up the Yuggera people, who inhabited the lands around the mouth of the river.

About May 1825 Commandant Miller occupied the area with troops and convicts, establishing a permanent base for the **Moreton Bay** Penal Establishment. The move to this site, from the initial depot at Redcliffe (established September 1824), was another step in Governor **Brisbane's** implementation of the recommendations of the **Bigge** report. Brisbane Town emerged as the administrative and military base for the convict establishment until 1842; it was also developing as the economic centre for the Moreton region, with activities concentrating on the agricultural, pastoral, timber, and mining industries.

In the succeeding period of free settlement (post-1842), Brisbane's dominance of the developing northern region was under challenge by rivals, most notably Ipswich; but after the separation of the colony of Qld from NSW in December 1859 it became the capital, and its pre-eminence was assured.

W.R. Johnston's study, *Brisbane, the First Thirty Years* (1988), links Brisbane to its surrounding hinterland through surveys and land sales, while tracing the development of a European community during difficult founding years.

Brisbane boomed in the 1880s, along with the rest of Qld. Its population increased by 174 per cent during the decade, and 'socially and economically it was transformed from a town into a city'. Substantial buildings were under construction, and a small financial and industrial elite was emerging. Ronald Lawson, in *Brisbane in the 1890s* (1973), dissects Brisbane as an urban society in the decade following the boom. Applying sociological approaches to historical data, he examines the structure of social differentiation and the operation of a mature urban community.

Brisbane's stature as the metropolitan centre for Qld was held back from the 1890s, partly because Qld was developing in a more decentralised and regional fashion than the rest of mainland Australia, but also because of the **depression** of the early 1890s. The 1893 financial crash, combined with severe flooding in the Brisbane River that year, debilitated the capital's emerging financial and urban elite. Brisbane's reputation as a branch office and warehouse city became fixed, reinforced by the emphasis that successive state governments gave to rural interests. Brisbane's (and Qld's) manufacturing base remained weak throughout the twentieth century.

The city's vulnerability during World War II prevented it from participating strongly in the industrialisation taking place in Australia's south-east. Nor did it attract as many postwar immigrants. It had overtaken Adelaide by the end of the war, but fell behind in the 1950s and did not catch up again until the 1970s. In the 1950s, Brisbane was still known and loved as a big country town, its visual character defined by the looping course of the Brisbane River and wide-verandahed houses set amid oleanders and palms. The essence of being a 'Briso' (or Brisbanite), growing up in the 1940s and 1950s in that languid, sub-tropical, conservative town, is captured in David **Malouf's** *Johnno* (1976) and Hugh Lunn's *Over the Top with Jim* (1989).

Brisbane's administrative history diverged from that of other Australian capitals after the implementation in 1924–25 of the Greater Brisbane scheme, an innovation discussed by Gordon **Greenwood** and John Laverty in *Brisbane 1858–1959* (1959). Brisbane became the largest municipal area in Australia and, it was claimed, the second-largest in the world. Yet, with only a minority of Queenslanders in the capital, it could never rival the power of the state parliament.

The administration of Clem Jones modernised Brisbane. The hallmark was sewerage—'from 38 per cent to almost 96 per cent sewered in the space of a decade'. Coinciding with the development ethos of state conservative governments, by the 1970s inner Brisbane was 'rebuilt' with modern office blocks and transport systems. Brisbane's sprawl, dictated by the winding river and the meandering hills, lapped over its official boundaries (approximately 79 200 hectares) to create a conurbation that stretched from Noosa in the north to south of the state border. Despite yet another severe flood in 1974, this growing confidence was expressed in events such as the staging of the Commonwealth Games in 1982 and World Expo '88. John Cole's *Shaping a City: Greater Brisbane 1925–1985* (1984) takes a management and promotional approach to the city's history, stressing municipal achievements within a political framework.

Detailed research into Brisbane's history is carried out by members of the Brisbane History Group, whose *Papers* (1981–) cover a wide range of topics, such as Rod Fisher's studies of Frogs Hollow in 1888 (1989) or early photography (1985).

W. Ross Johnston

Brisbane Courier was one of Brisbane's major daily newspapers between 1864 and 1933. It arose out of the *Courier* and its antecedent, the *Moreton Bay Courier* (1846). Between 1882 and 1925 the *Observer* came out of the *Courier* offices as an evening edition. Rivalry between the *Courier* and the *Daily Mail* was resolved in August 1933 by their merger, under the control of Keith **Murdoch** and John **Wren**. As part of the Herald & Weekly Times chain, the *Courier-Mail* has since been acquired by Rupert Murdoch's News Corporation.

W. Ross Johnston

Brisbane Line was an imaginary line drawn by a defence strategist in 1942 that extended south-west from a point north of Brisbane, Qld, and demarcated the land which was to be defended in the event of a Japanese invasion of Australia. Recognising the limited military personnel available to defend Australia, and a conviction that the more populated areas should be given priority, the plan proposed to defend Australia's east coast, but exclude north Qld, the NT, and most of WA. For security reasons and lest it encourage fear amongst the people and hostility towards the government, the military authorities denied the existence of a Brisbane line, which was alleged in October 1942 by the Sydney Labor MHR Eddie Ward. A subsequent royal commission found that the commander-in-chief of the home forces, Sir Iven Mackay, had advised the government of such a plan in early 1942, but it was never formally approved. Paul Burns assesses *The Brisbane Line Controversy* (1998).

HD

Brisbane, Thomas Makdougall (1773–1860) was governor of NSW 1821–25, an appointment he possibly sought because of an interest in astronomy which he had pursued in an observatory at the family home in Scotland, Brisbane House. After a distinguished army career, Brisbane arrived in the colony to take over from Lachlan **Macquarie**. J.D. **Lang's** assessment of him as lazy became the accepted view, but it was under his direction that proper land surveys were undertaken, making possible the 1831 **Ripon Regulations**. Brisbane had an observatory built at Parramatta, and published an account of his observations. He donated his astronomical instruments and much of his scientific library to the colony.

KT

British–Australian Relations

British–Australian relations were at first more than *relations* because Britain's assertions of sovereignty over the eastern half of the continent in 1788, and over the rest of the country in 1824, 1829, and 1879, meant that Australia was essentially a part of Britain. Ruled by Britain, colonists drew on British political tradition to expand their freedoms. They believed that as Britons they shared a unique inheritance of liberty. From the beginning, traditionalists and reformers alike deployed the patriotic language and symbolism of Britons. Yet the colonies constantly challenged the ideas and standards of the mother country. They would be British, but in their own fashion. Australia was both an extension of British society and a departure from it. In their new circumstances colonists were able to produce a distinctive culture, more open and tolerant than the one at Home. They implemented a number of British ideals before Britain did—manhood suffrage, payment for parliamentarians, and the vote for women.

Britain retained their loyalty and affection by progressively conceding their demands for greater freedom and autonomy over a period of more than a century. This was a discreet statesmanship that fitted with free-trade imperialism and some indifference to the formal Empire. The close ties between British and Australian business elites and Anglophile attitudes among the social establishment have suggested an equation between loyalism and political conservatism, but after **transportation** ended most Australians experienced the Empire as enlightened and liberal. British culture in Australia was marked by a sense of historical continuity, by shared memories and literature, and by unifying notions of collective destiny.

In the first half of the nineteenth century Britain conceded a free press, trial by jury, advisory councils to governors which were partly elected by male property-owners, and the cessation of transportation in the eastern colonies. In the 1850s liberalisation widened with the granting of responsible self-government to most colonies, although significant limitations remained. **Governors** continued to answer to London. The colonial parliaments could not legislate on matters beyond their own borders, and veto provisions over colonial legislation applied though were rarely used. Premiers had no direct access to the British government or the Crown. Judicial powers were also restricted. The **Privy Council** in London remained the highest court of appeal, while Britons outside the UK had no appeal access to the House of Lords.

The colonies could not declare war, negotiate treaties, exchange diplomats or join associations of states; their only legitimate point of contact with the outside world was London, where they appointed agents-general to facilitate emigration, loan funds, and other government business. However, for most colonials these restrictions were experienced as valued ties. Economic interdependence, defence needs, and racial sentiment underpinned imperial loyalty and ruled out the possibility of a lasting push for full independence. That inclination was repeatedly undercut by concessions from London and the gradual inclusion of the colonies in consultation processes, such as colonial or **imperial conferences**, which began in 1887.

Yet there was still scope for tensions in the British–Australian relationship. **Tariff** protection in Victoria, strident ideas about the rights of labour, fear of the English Poor Law system, and insistence on **White Australia** suggest distinctive values in the colonies. Colonial identity was sharpened by the counterfoil of English snobbery. The savage edge to relations between Irish Catholics and Protestants tested the boundaries of Britishness for more than a century. The fiercely nationalist *Bulletin* won a mass following in the 1880s with scandalous lampooning of the British ruling class, while those who wanted to remain loyal complained about British indifference to Australian interests. While Australia hastened to the aid of Britain in World War I, a majority of states voted against **conscription**. The hardships of the Depression fuelled 'money-power' talk about British rentiers, and the **bodyline** strategy in Test cricket (1932–33) was seen by many as the same unfairness in another realm. In 1941 when Britain's poorly defended military base at Singapore fell to the Japanese, the difference between imperial and Australian interests became more obvious to many. The ambivalence about Englishness is discussed in Michael **Roe**, 'An Historical Survey of Australian Nationalism', *VHM* (1971).

But tensions were mostly circumscribed by a sense of common cause. Australian nationalists who rejected Empire were reduced in numbers as the nineteenth century neared its end and imperialist rivalries mounted. Even the *Bulletin* was compromised by race sentiment. The quintessential nationalist organisation, the **Australian Natives Association**, founded in Victoria in 1872, made the cultivation of national feeling its main concern. It was neither servile in its attitude to England nor radical in its approach to money and property, and it was passionately versed in the 'scripture' of British freedom. This was the format for widely held dual loyalties.

The self-interest and sentiment which guaranteed attachment to Britain in the nineteenth century continued into the twentieth. Federation can be regarded as a milestone in a search for distinction within the framework of Britishness, not a departure from that framework. The term **Commonwealth of Australia** was acceptable because its association with the evolution of a mystical, balanced British constitution far outweighed its republican connotations. The monarch retained the same reserve powers over federal legislation as hitherto over colonial, Australian prime ministers had no direct access to British governments—they had to go through the **Colonial Office**, Privy Council appeals survived colonial opposition, and external affairs remained in imperial hands. The new federation might have inherited forms of dependency which had marked the colonies, but symbolically it seemed to be shedding its colonial trappings.

This is why **republicanism** did not catch on and royalism was often fervent. Much of what Australian republicans sought was achieved under constitutional **monarchy**. Monarchy's survival in Britain required its 'reinvention' in the nineteenth century, a process of popularising and personalising it as never before. In Australia, colonists were all too ready to participate in this process—to believe in a British monarchy which they identified with democracy, modernisation, welfare and, most importantly, the embrace of Empire. As the colonies and the Commonwealth took on greater political responsibility, public opinion turned more to the Crown as the symbolic link with the mother country.

With the **Statute of Westminster** (1931), constitutionally the Crown became the sole link between Britain and its independent Dominions. Australia had not asked for this formal declaration, which had been sought by South Africa, Ireland, and Canada. Loyalism was strongest in Australia because its dependence on Britain for defence was greatest and because it was ethnically and sentimentally closest to Britain. Until quite recently the vast majority of Australians were of British descent and race conscious. Ninety per cent of the population was still of Anglo-Celtic ancestry in 1947 when the first government-assisted 'alien' immigrant stepped ashore. Australians shared the same language, relied on British news for knowledge of the world, and were schooled in an education system which sustained British loyalties, though Catholic schools complicated the picture. People drew on an imperial heritage for self-enhancement and race pride, contributed significantly to that heritage in two world wars, and lived out their lives in a web of institutional and personal connections which emphasised the attachment to Home. Technological change reinforced Empire sentiment, notably faster sea travel, the telegraph connection with London (1872), the advent of women's magazines in the 1880s, and radio broadcasting—King George V's first broadcast to the Empire came from the Empire Exhibition at Wembley on 23 April 1924. Identity transcended the purely national. Empire had become an imagined community, British by virtue of its white citizens who, as Alfred **Deakin** explained, 'control it, give it authority force and weight, whose character and courage sustain it in the day of battle'. The dual loyalty to Australia and Empire is classically described in W.K. **Hancock's** *Australia* (1930).

After World War II, the Empire quickly broke up. During the war the defence tie with the USA was forged and confirmed with the **ANZUS Treaty** in 1951. In 1973 Britain joined the European Economic Community, which ended imperial trade preference. About 30 per cent of imports came from the UK in the early 1960s compared with just six per cent 30 years later, while exports to the UK over the same period dropped from 20 per cent to four per cent.

In Australia the loosening of cultural ties with Britain drew momentum from large-scale programs of non-British immigration after the war, the influence of American culture, and a 'baby boom' which greatly increased the number of Australians whose forebears in Australia went back three generations or more. Dramatic shifts in self-perception were evident in an effusion of national feelings and symbols. An Australian Heritage Commission and a national system of **honours** were established in 1975. The validating function of a local film industry, television, and theatre, and of literature and art grounded in Australian experience, all showed that Britain was no longer the fountainhead. John **Kerr's** disputed use of the vice-regal prerogative, in dismissing the Labor prime minister in 1975, was a major blow to the British connection and brought the resurgence of republicanism in Australia after some 80 years of quiescence.

PETER COCHRANE

British Commonwealth, see **Commonwealth of Nations (British)**

Broadcasting, see **Radio**

Broken Hill Proprietary Ltd, see **BHP**

Brookes, Herbert Robinson (1867–1963) was a cultured, public-spirited, philanthropic, Protestant zealot, whose activities spanned a remarkable range of interests. The eldest surviving son of a wealthy and gifted family (his youngest brother, Norman, was Australia's first Wimbledon champion), Herbert trained as an engineer and achieved success as an industrialist. His first marriage in 1897 to the daughter of Charles **Strong**, the founder of the liberal Australian Church, brought personal tragedy when she died two years later. His second marriage, in 1905 to Alfred **Deakin's** daughter Ivy, brought lasting happiness and close friendship with Deakin. He was a leading supporter of Deakin's **Liberal Party**, and led the association of businessmen who financed it and its successor parties.

Brookes served the Commonwealth in a number of official capacities. He was a member of the Board of Trade and the Tariff Board during the 1920s, and from 1929 to 1930 represented Australia as commissioner-general to the USA. In the 1930s he was a foundation member of the **Australian Broadcasting Commission**. He was also an active member of the Round Table, the League of Nations Union and the English Speaking Union, guided the finance committee of the University of Melbourne and gave generously to it and other institutions. Ivy Brookes was equally involved in the League of Nations Union and was a leading member of the **National Council of Women**, the **Housewives Association**, and the board of the Women's Hospital. Together they formed the T.E. Browne Society, which met in their South Yarra residence to share literary and musical interests.

Brookes's moral gravity resembled that of Deakin and, like his father-in-law, he more than once declined a knighthood. Brookes was also an imperial loyalist, and World War I hardened loyalty into intolerance of the labour movement and Catholicism. He urged **Hughes** to intensify surveillance of radicals, feuded with **Mannix**, and financed the sectarian Protestant Federation. He is a striking exemplar of the Anglo-Australian Protestant ascendancy that ruled interwar Australia. His nephew Rohan Rivett published a biography in 1965, but the voluminous papers in the National Library invite further attention.

SM

Broughton, William Grant (1788–1853) was head of the **Anglican Church** in Australia, as archdeacon from 1829, and after 1836 as first bishop. He was a high churchman who came to NSW under the patronage of the Duke of Wellington thinking he was to head the established church. His position was almost immediately undermined by the suspension and then the abandonment of the **Church and Schools Corporation**, which was to have given the church an independent income. Then Governor **Bourke's** 1836 **Church Act**, which gave financial support to Anglicans, Presbyterians, and Catholics on the same basis, put an end to Anglican pre-eminence. Over the next 20 years Broughton fought a rearguard action in defence of his church, while at the same time he worked creatively to establish a new basis for its financial support and governance. He was determinedly anti-Catholic and cleverly used general Protestant distrust of Rome to defeat Bourke's plan for national schools. He succeeded in keeping state support for his church schools. His conservatism and high-churchmanship made him suspect in the colony, but he was respected for his devotion to his calling. G.P. Shaw wrote his biography (*Patriarch and Patriot*, 1978).

JH

Browne, T.A., see 'Boldrewood, Rolf'

Brown, (William) Jethro (1868–1930) was a jurist in the state experiments in industrial reform at the turn of the century. From humble origins in SA, he proceeded to Cambridge where he studied under the notable legal historian, F.W. Maitland. In 1893 he was appointed to a foundation lectureship, later a chair, in law and modern history at the University of Tasmania; from 1901 to 1906 he was professor of comparative and constitutional law in the University College of Wales, and from 1906 to 1913 professor of law at the University of Adelaide. *The New Democracy* (1899) extolled the imminent Commonwealth as a force for efficiency and social justice, and later writings interpreted the law as an expression of changing social needs. *The Prevention and Control of Monopolies* (1914) drew on knowledge derived from conduct of government inquiries. As president of the Industrial Court of SA from 1916, he sought to foster industrial democracy, but wartime divisions and growing class turmoil thwarted his optimism. He is one of Michael **Roe's** *Nine Australian Progressives* (1984).

SM

Bruce, Minnie Grant 'Mary' (1878–1958) wrote the enormously influential children's books known as the Billabong series. Fifteen books, written between 1910 and 1942, with estimated sales of two million copies made her one of the best-known Australian authors of her time. The novels were set on Billabong station, an unchanging, idealised re-creation of her own bush childhood at Sale, Victoria. The stories deal with classic 'bush' virtues—mateship, honesty, resourcefulness, and hard work. Bruce came to novel writing after a period as a journalist, during which she wrote for the *Leader* and the *Age*, *Lone Hand* and *Table Talk*. She wrote prolifically, including a book of Aboriginal legends, *The Stone Axe of Burkamukk* (1922). Critical studies of her have been made by Alison Alexander in the biography

Billabong's Author (1979) and Brenda Niall in her comparative study of the fictional worlds of Bruce and Ethel **Turner**, *Seven Little Billabongs* (1979).

KT

Bruce, Stanley Melbourne (1883–1967) was prime minister of Australia 1923–29, high commissioner in London 1933–45, company director, and man of imperial affairs. A product of mercantile Melbourne, he assimilated so successfully into the English upper class that his capacity and resolution as a representative of Australian interests were seriously underestimated.

From Melbourne Grammar School, Bruce proceeded to Cambridge where he rowed and read law. He fought in an English regiment during World War I, and won the Military Cross. His business acumen as the chairman of the family's trading company, Paterson, Laing and Bruce, and connections through marriage to the Victorian establishment brought election as a **Nationalist** to federal parliament in 1917; as treasurer from 1921 he was well placed to overthrow the profligate W.M. **Hughes** in 1923. As prime minister Bruce affected an imperturbable hauteur: his expensive tastes, the plus-fours and spats belied a formidable ambition and energy. Through his policy of 'Men, Money and Markets' he sought to foster national development within an imperial framework: empire migration and rural settlement were fostered by an ambitious agreement between Australia and Britain; the London money market provided capital for public infrastructure; and Australian farmers produced a greater range of commodities for the British market. While Bruce stressed the need for greater efficiency, he accepted the responsibility of government to maintain living standards through maintenance of the **basic wage**. Although he exploited industrial militancy to win general elections in 1925 and 1928, industrial relations proved his nemesis as the downturn in the international economy created growing pressure to reduce Australian wage costs. Thwarted in his efforts to secure additional federal powers to prevent strikes, he decided eventually to vacate the field; Hughes persuaded several members to cross the floor of the House of Representatives and defeat the government measure. At the ensuing election the government was defeated and Bruce lost his own seat to the secretary of the Melbourne Trades Hall Council.

Although he was returned to office along with the **United Australia Party** at the end of 1931, his hopes of regaining the leadership proved fruitless and in 1933 he accepted the high commissionership in London. After the death of **Lyons** in 1939, and again following Labor's electoral victory in 1946, Bruce sounded support for a return to Australian politics; on both occasions he found it insufficient and returned to England. His ready access to British ministers, his substantial service at the League of Nations, and his prescient grasp of the dangers to Australia in the event of a new European war made him an influential intermediary during the 1930s but, although he served in the imperial War Cabinet from 1942, Churchill restricted his involvement.

After retiring from the high commission in 1945, he was created a viscount, and he chaired the Food and Agriculture Organization of the UN. Neither the authorised biography by Cecil Edwards, *Bruce of Melbourne* (1965), nor Alfred Stirling's account of his career in London (1974) have fully rehabilitated his domestic reputation as an Anglophile reactionary, but Heather Radi in the *ADB* suggests his innovatory significance. He is likely to become better appreciated as one of the shrewdest in a line of Australian statesmen, running from **Deakin** to **Menzies**, who mediated the imperial relationship.

STUART MACINTYRE

Bryant, Mary (1765–?), a convict in the **First Fleet**, achieved notoriety for her escape to Timor in 1791 in a small boat, as part of a group of convicts that included her husband, William. One of the convicts wrote *Memorandoms* as James Martin (1937), a narrative of the voyage. They were returned to England; William died, but Mary was pardoned in 1793. Her story fascinated writers and has spawned many works, including *A First Fleet Family* (Louis Becke and Walter Jeffery, 1896); *The Strange Case of Mary Bryant* (Geoffrey Rawson, 1938); and *Spindrift* (Anthony Veitch, 1980). She figures in Thomas **Keneally's** novel, *The Playmaker* (1987), and also in the play that it inspired, *Our Country's Good* (1988) by Timberlake Wertenbaker.

KT

Buckland River riots, which took place at the Buckland River goldfields near Mount Buffalo in 1857, were the worst attacks by white diggers on **Chinese** miners in Victoria. The dominance of Chinese miners at the Buckland incensed white diggers, who believed they were 'robbing us of our gold fields'. Falling gold returns and rising unemployment aggravated racist attitudes. Xenophobic tensions erupted following a political meeting on 4 July 1857, when a mob of about 100 white miners attacked and forcibly evicted 2500 Chinese from the settlement, burning their tents, stores, and possessions. Three Chinese died of subsequent exposure, several drowned, and many others were injured. Arrests were made, but the court refused to hear any Chinese witnesses; several diggers were subsequently released. Many Chinese returned to the diggings following assurances of government protection. The riots are often cited as antecedent to the development of the **White Australia** policy.

HD

Buckley, William (1780–1856), escaped convict, was transported to Australia for receiving stolen goods, and spent a brief period at the abortive settlement at Sorrento, Victoria, before making his escape with two others in 1803. He lived with the Watourong people in the Geelong region for 32 years before giving himself up to white settlers at Indented Head in 1835. Commonly referred to as the **'wild white man'**, Buckley became something of a legend in early Melbourne. A portrait of 1886, which depicts a tall, bearded, barefoot man dressed in a possum-skin cloak, contributed towards an enduring romantic image. Colonial

authorities at **Port Phillip** recognised the value of his knowledge of Aboriginal language and culture, and employed him as an interpreter. However, Buckley found himself caught between two cultures and was increasingly uncomfortable with his role as intermediary. He moved to Hobart in 1837. While John Morgan's *The Life and Adventures of William Buckley* (1852) is thought to include some fabrication, James **Bonwick's** *The Wild White Man and the Blacks of Victoria* (1863), which drew from Bonwick's conversations with Buckley before his death, is regarded as a more reliable source. A later study is *Buckley's Hope* (1980) by Craig Robertson, and Barry Hill's epic poem, *Ghosting William Buckley*, was published in 1993.

HD

Building societies originated in England in the early nineteenth century as institutions through which working men could pool their savings and raise loans on small cottages. Liberal reformers favoured the movement, not only because it reinforced home ties, but because it encouraged thrift and endowed virtuous working men with political rights, which were then available only to property-owners. From 1847, when the first building societies legislation was passed in NSW, the societies expanded rapidly in Australia, eventually capturing an even larger fraction of the population than in Britain. The first societies were organised as 'terminating societies', in which members borrowed from the pool of savings contributed by other borrowers; by the 1880s these were outnumbered by 'permanent societies', which increasingly operated as banks, and often engaged in property speculation on their own account. Late colonial observers, such as Richard **Twopeny**, gave them much of the credit for the comparatively high rates of home-ownership among Australian working men. Historians—following Noel **Butlin**, whose *Investment in Australian Economic Development, 1861–1900* (1964) gives the best short account of their financial role—have generally concurred. This verdict has been disputed by R.V. Jackson (*LH*, 1984). As directors of building societies, men of humble origin could sometimes rise to become financial tycoons; their success was often short-lived, however, and the societies' histories, from the collapse of the Premier Building Society in 1890 to that of the Pyramid Building Society a century later, have been punctuated by financial scandals.

GD

Bulletin, a Sydney paper founded in 1880 by J.F. **Archibald** and John Haynes, became the leading national weekly in Australia, a position which, through several changes of ownership and editorial policy, it retains. In the 1880s and 1890s, it became the sponsor of a distinctive radical national literature, the 'Bulletin School'.

Controversy surrounds the paper's origins, with Archibald, Haynes, and another early part-owner, W.H. Traill, each laying claim as founder. Haynes probably conceived the paper and chose its title, modelled on the San Francisco *Bulletin*. Traill's fiery editorial denouncing a larrikin picnic at Clontarf in 1881 provoked a libel action that briefly landed Haynes and Archibald in gaol; but he later helped to rescue the paper financially and tilted its editorial stance towards secularism and **protectionism**. But it was Archibald who gave the paper its distinctive style and who, as Sylvia Lawson shows in *The Archibald Paradox* (1983), became its editorial master over the next two decades. He drew in part upon overseas models, such as *Reynolds Weekly*, the racy London paper, but added a distinctive and colloquial Australianism. The *Bulletin* became, as he intended, an 'organ of revolt' against a 'cant-ridden' society, its stance defined as much by opposition as affirmation, by ridicule rather than analysis. In 1882 Traill had secured the services of the American cartoonist Livingston **Hopkins** ('Hop'), whose deadly caricatures of bloated capitalists, monocled aristocrats, pinch-faced **wowsers**, slanty-eyed Chinese, and toffy-nosed new chums were ranged against its hero, the raw-boned handsome Australian workingman. Its policy was a distillation of 'advanced' democratic and nationalistic thinking: **republicanism**, abolition of titles, one vote per person, the direct election of ministers by parliament, secularism, land nationalisation, federation, and 'Australia for the Australians', its slogan for the preservation of a **White Australia**.

Originally the *Bulletin* had been a Sydney paper, but Archibald made it national. It was one of the few weeklies that carried reports from all the colonies, including excellent mining and financial news. By the late 1880s it had overtaken the *Town and Country Journal* as the biggest-selling weekly in Australia, its Christmas issue sometimes of 80 000 copies. Even conservative observers, affronted by its 'vulgarity', acknowledged the pervasive influence of 'the **Bushman's Bible**'. In 1886 Archibald threw its pages open to its readers: 'Every man with brains has at least one good story to tell … mail your work to the *Bulletin* which pays for accepted matter.' He encouraged his contributors to address a national readership: 'I want you to remember that Australia is a big place', he advised a new recruit, 'Banjo' **Paterson**, exhorting him to write for 'the pearler up at Thursday Island and the farmer down in Victoria'. By the mid-1890s the *Bulletin* had become the vehicle for a self-conscious school of Australian bush writing. On the inside wrappers of its distinctive crimson cover (the Red Page), its literary editor, A.G. **Stephens**, responded to readers' contributions, encouraging and refining the often raw talents of a stable that eventually included Paterson, Henry **Lawson**, Edward **Dyson**, William **Astley** and, later, Joseph **Furphy**, Miles **Franklin**, and Barbara **Baynton**.

'The *Bulletin* is a clever youth. It will become a dull old man', Archibald had predicted. In 1907 he retired as editor; under his successors, William Macleod and James Edmond, the paper drifted steadily to the Right. Some talented cartoonists, including Norman **Lindsay**, stayed on, but its role as a radical gadfly had been usurped by *Smith's Weekly*. The *Bulletin* had opposed the **Boer War** but swung round to the **conscription** side during World War I. On only one issue—White Australia—did it maintain its old fervour. Its circulation declined from about 40 000 in the late 1930s to barely 30 000 shortly before it was sold in 1961 by the Prior

family, who had run it since 1927, to the **Packer family**, who installed Donald **Horne** as editor (1961–62, 1967–72). Under Douglas **Stewart**, editor of the Red Page since 1940, the literary content of the paper was already strong. Horne changed the format, hired a new stable of cartoonists, including Bruce **Petty** and Les Tanner, and lowered the old racist motto 'Australia for the White Man' from the masthead. His successors, who included Peter Coleman and Trevor Kennedy, bolstered the paper's business coverage, reduced and eventually eliminated its literary content, and aligned it firmly on the right of politics. In 1984 its transformation from an 'organ of revolt' to a news magazine was completed when it merged with the Australian edition of the American magazine *Newsweek*.

Patricia Rolfe, a *Bulletin* journalist, wrote *The Journalistic Javelin* (1979), the only comprehensive history; but it is disjointed and uncritical. More satisfactory are Lawson, *The Archibald Paradox*; the memoirs of Archibald (*Lone Hand*, 1907); Norman **Lindsay**, *Bohemians of the Bulletin* (1965); and Douglas Stewart, *Writers of the Bulletin* (1977).

GRAEME DAVISON

Bungaree (?–1830), of the Kuring-gai people, was valued as a mediator by early governors of NSW. He accompanied **Flinders** on his 1801–02 expedition, and sailed with Philip King to the north-west coast of WA; both men praised his diplomacy in dealing with Aboriginal groups. Governor **Macquarie**, who thought highly of Bungaree, presented him with a king-plate that was inscribed 'King of the Blacks' and helped establish him on a farm. When this enterprise failed, Macquarie arranged for Bungaree to be given a boat and net for commercial fishing. Bungaree was celebrated by Europeans for his humorous imitations of them.

KT

Bunyip, a mythic, man-eating, amphibious animal which inhabits water-holes, swamps, and lakes, is enshrined in the Aboriginal and non-Aboriginal mythology of eastern Australia. The creature was described by many, including William **Buckley** in western Victoria, as a hybrid of various other animals. It was especially feared by women and children. Influenced by Aborigines' accounts of the creature, white settlers and explorers reinforced the myth with reputed sightings. Evidence that giant mammals had coexisted with Aborigines several thousand years ago provided one basis for this legend. Bunyips were blamed for the death of cattle and bullocks that became bogged in swamp-land or waterholes, their stiff bodies left to rot in the mud. Another explanation comes from the discovery of stray seals in the rivers and lakes of south-eastern Australia, which had travelled inland through the river system, and become trapped. The mystery surrounding the bunyip gave the word its wider currency. G.C. Mundy recorded in 1852 that it was 'a Sydney synonym for imposter, pretender, humbug and the like'; the following year it was used by Daniel **Deniehy** in his attack on the '**bunyip aristocracy**'.

HD

Bunyip aristocracy was a term coined by Daniel **Deniehy** in his attack on W.C. **Wentworth's** proposal for the introduction of hereditary titles in NSW. As chairman of the select committee that drafted the NSW constitution in 1853, Wentworth advocated the creation of a class of nobility who could fill positions in the NSW upper house, and thus emulate the British House of Lords. Fearing that the growing agitation for reform in Australia foretold the advance of barbarism, Wentworth felt this measure would protect 'civilisation' and the balance of the British constitution. Though a colonial peerage was supported by wealthy landowners such as James **Macarthur**, popular opposition to the clause led to its exclusion from the constitution bill. In a famous public address in Sydney on 15 August 1853, Deniehy mocked the local peerage as a 'bunyip aristocracy' and denounced it as contradictory to notions of democracy and egalitarianism. His play on the word *bunyip*, with its overtones of anachronistic absurdity, reflected the refusal by Australians to institutionalise an upper class. While most historians share Deniehy's contempt for the proposal, Ged Martin's *Bunyip Aristocracy* (1986) argues that it was a serious possibility.

HD

Bureaucracy, according to political scientist Alan Davies, is something for which Australians have a talent. This capacity is surprising, given the national reputation for casualness and anti-authoritarianism. Indeed, Sol Encel, in *Equality and Authority* (1970), argued that Australian **egalitarianism** was constantly threatened and diminished by the unusual power wielded by bureaucrats.

In the eighteenth century Britons prided themselves on not having a bureaucracy, which was seen as the instrument by which Continental monarchs kept their people in thrall. Nevertheless, just as the first European settlement in Australia was being planned, Britain began the process by which its tiny civil service was transformed into something like a modern bureaucracy. Offices ceased to be the property of those who held them; officers had to do the work themselves and not by deputy; they were paid a salary rather than being expected to live off fees and perks; and offices without any duties attached (sinecures) were abolished. Because of these changes, the Australian colonies were bequeathed by their British rulers an honest and efficient civil service.

Its history, however, followed a very different course from that of its parent. The crowning reform in Britain in the 1850s was the abolition of appointment by political patronage in favour of competitive examination. By this device the middle class secured access to a service whose political masters still came overwhelmingly from the aristocracy and gentry. In the 1850s in Australia liberal-democratic politicians, newly arrived in power, were not inclined to put any limit on their right to make appointments to the civil service. To conduct an examination would be undemocratic because it would favour those who had the advantage of education. At this time in NSW the examination to test competency of those nominated by patronage was abolished. Politicians were free to seek appointments for their constituents of all sorts, as well as for their friends and relations. The wide range of the state's activities meant there were many officers to be recruited, not only clerks, but teachers, warders, nurses, porters, and policemen. In the **faction** politics of the early decades of **democracy**, when parties were weak or non-existent, civil service patronage was one means by which ministries secured the support of individual MPs and so held their majority together. In this respect the democratic politics of nineteenth-century Australia mimicked the aristocratic politics of eighteenth-century Britain.

Governments in the faction period were usually short-lived; a ministry which lasted 12 months had done well. The quality of government suffered less from this instability than might be expected because the civil service, though appointed by patronage, had security of tenure and often at the highest levels was staffed by people of outstanding ability who were better known and more highly respected than many of their political masters: examples are Egan as under-treasurer in NSW, and Goyder as surveyor-general and **Todd** as postmaster-general in SA.

In the absence of strong **local government**, a centralised bureaucracy became the standard mode by which colonial governments ruled and serviced their citizens. The trend began when Governor **Bourke** appointed commissioners of Crown lands in the **squatting** districts. As holders of large tracts of land, the squatters thought of themselves as would-be gentry and, as such, natural rulers; Bourke and the British government thought of them as a lawless, engrossing horde who needed to be checked. Hence the creation of a professional corps of commissioners to collect tax, supervise, and discipline. Officers of the same sort, commissioners, were appointed in the 1850s to run the goldfields in NSW and Victoria. In the latter colony, rule by bureaucrat received its only check when after **Eureka** commissioners were replaced by elected mining courts and wardens. The inauguration of responsible government and liberal democracy led to no check to centralised bureaucracy; in fact it was extended to police, education, and public health. A minister for education could boast that, by looking at his watch and the official timetable, he knew what lessons were being taught in each one of his schools.

Bureaucracy took an even firmer hold on the polity from the late nineteenth century as bureaucratic forms were invoked to take issues 'out of politics' so that they would be handled equitably and scientifically.

The **Tariff** Board, created in 1921, was to end the clashing interests and special pleading endemic in the setting of tariffs by assessing submissions and making recommendations to parliament. The Grants Commission was created in 1933 to make recommendations on the distribution of Commonwealth funds to the states. By setting a normal standard of services and assessing the resources and circumstances of each of the states, the commission was to ensure that the differences between the states would mean as little as possible to the Australian citizen. No other federation has its like. The **Arbitration** Court, established in 1907, should be considered another bureaucracy of this type, though its independence was enhanced by its status as a court. But the 'law' it administered was the regulations (awards) that it had itself devised to determine wages for every level of skill and the distribution of labour in every industry.

It is this search for distributive justice by bureaucratic means that Encel saw as the paradox of egalitarianism: 'the search for equality ... breeds bureaucracy; bureaucracy breeds authority; and authority undermines the equality which bred it'. The answer to this might well be that the authority of bureaucracy is not seen as threatening; on the contrary, authority which is 'just doing its job' is preferred by a people who would not accept the social pretension of a ruling class and continues to resent politicians who have plainly sought authority.

From the late nineteenth century the civil service itself was put beyond politics. Public Service Boards in the states and the new Commonwealth now controlled recruitment, promotion, and organisation. Having held on to patronage much longer than the British, Australian politicians removed their services more completely from their own control. The Public Service Boards, committed to equitable treatment of their employees, were a clear target for the strong public service unions, whose notion of equity was that long service should be rewarded over claims to superior worth or education and that managers should have as little discretion as possible. Encel uncovers another paradox: a progressive society produced a service of unusual 'rigidity and conservatism with special emphasis on seniority'. Generally recruits entered as teenagers at the lowest level. Office boys could rise to be managers, but this good principle was perverted, as **Hancock** lamented (*Australia*, 1930), 'into a practical rule that no one shall become a manager who has not been an office boy'. The services nevertheless had to recruit trained personnel as lawyers, doctors, and engineers. Egalitarianism had to acknowledge these so-called experts, who frequently came to occupy senior administrative posts in the absence of other educated people trained for this task. An elite corps of graduates with a general education, along British lines, was fiercely resisted by the unions. Graduate recruitment had been allowed from 1933 and many graduates were recruited to cope with the tasks of World War II, but it was only in the 1960s that a clear career path was provided for them.

In the 1970s the view changed: a democratic service was not one which gave poor boys their chance; rather it should mirror the gender and ethnic composition of the wider society and be more directly accountable to it. Recruitment and promotion have been shaped to produce a representative service of this sort: its decisions have become subject to review by tribunals and ombudsman, and its deliberations to freedom of information requests. The service has also been made more directly responsible to politicians by the abolition of the Public Service Board.

These changes were designed to make the bureaucracy less bureaucratic, that is, less hermetic and independent. The bureaucratic cast of the polity has been undermined further by the abandonment of the regulation of the economy and the contraction of government activity. As government activity has become more suspect, the service has taken the protective colouring of the management ethos of the private sector. The bureaucracy itself was blamed for these changes by Michael Pusey (*Economic Rationalism in Canberra*, 1991), who found that it was dominated by economists and a belief in economic rationalism. This was to mistake effects for causes. Since the war, economists have always been prominent among the graduates, a continuation of the respect for 'experts'.

Yet with all these changes, the bureaucratic mode can still be effectively invoked. Australia has given the world a new form of bureaucrat, the femocrat, a feminist employed in the service to ensure that equal opportunity policy is followed, to give general advice on the effects of government policy on women, and to develop specific programs to assist them. This mode of securing change is in marked contrast to American feminism's concern with seeking redress and control through the courts. The Australian trust in the state is not easily overcome. As one feminist wrote: 'despite my scepticism about the so-called democratic process of government and my philosophical abhorrence of the modern capitalist state, when I want something done I look to just that arena' (Anna Yeatman, *Bureaucrats, Technocrats, Femocrats*, 1990). That approach continues to breed bureaucracy.

JOHN HIRST

Burgmann, Ernest Henry (1885–1967) was a radical Anglican clergyman who became known as the 'Red Bishop'. The church took him from his bush origins as a timbercutter in northern NSW, a milieu he evoked in his autobiographical *The Education of an Australian* (1944), to the University of Sydney. As warden of St John's College, first in Armidale and later transferred to Morpeth, near Newcastle, he connected Christianity to new intellectual currents, and emerged in the **Depression** of the 1930s as a strong social critic of capitalism. In 1934 Burgmann became bishop of Goulburn (subsequently Goulburn and Canberra) and was drawn into the left-wing peace movement. During World War II he became president of the Australia–Soviet Friendship League and a strong supporter of the Labor government; in the subsequent Cold War he was a frequent critic of the **Menzies** government's foreign and domestic policies. Peter Hempenstall's *The Meddlesome Priest* (1993) explores the interrelationship of his Christian beliefs and radical nativism.

SM

Burke, Robert O'Hara (1821–61) led the first expedition to cross the Australian continent from south to north in 1860–61. An Anglo-Irish gentleman, Burke was a soldier and member of the Irish Mounted Constabulary during the 1840s. In 1853 he joined the Victoria police and served as inspector and superintendent in various goldfield towns. His blunt leadership skills were evident during the **Buckland River riots** when he pushed his men on an 80-kilometre march in 24 hours. He had no exploration experience, but was sufficiently well-connected and persuasive to convince the Royal Society of Victoria to appoint him leader of the 'Victorian Exploring Expedition'—a title suggesting the aspirations of its Melbourne promoters, who hoped to write the newly rich colony of Victoria into **exploration history**. They were less interested in scientific or geographical knowledge than in the glory of being first across Australia. And Burke did not let them down, at the cost of seven lives, one his own.

His expedition, the first to use camels, departed Melbourne as a well-provisioned pageant in August 1860. Impatient and seeking to travel light, Burke foolishly split his party and dumped supplies at Menindee, NSW. He also left a waiting group at Coopers Creek, SA, while he took second-in-command William Wills, and John King and Charles Gray on a dash to the Gulf of Carpentaria, which they reached in February 1861 ahead of SA's J. McDouall **Stuart**. Gray died on the return journey. The others arrived starved and exhausted at Coopers Creek on 21 April 1861, dismayed to find the unrelieved waiting party had left for Menindee just hours earlier. Burke and Wills perished after Burke decided to head for Mount Hopeless in SA instead of Menindee. King survived by living with Aborigines before being rescued by A.W. **Howitt's** search party in September 1861. Four men died in waiting and relief parties. Victoria made **heroes** of Burke and Wills, but the expedition contributed little to exploration. It was a Pyrrhic victory and a subsequent royal commission condemned Burke.

The State Library of Victoria holds records of the expedition. Sources were outlined by Ian McLaren in *VHM* (1959). Kathleen **Fitzpatrick's** entry on Burke in the *ADB* is an excellent introduction which draws on an earlier article in *HSANZ* (1963). Tim Bonyhady's *Burke and Wills: From Melbourne to Myth* (1991) provides a comprehensive cultural analysis. Numerous narratives of the expedition are less reliable. Andrew Jackson's *Robert O'Hara Burke and the Australian Exploring Expedition of 1860* (1862) was apparently linked to Burke family interests and vindicated Burke. Wills's father published *A Successful Exploration Through the Interior of Australia* (1863), which praised his son's role while condemning Burke and others. An eyewitness account, Hermann Beckler's *Burke's Expedition: A Journey to Central Australia*, remained almost unknown before publication as *A Journey to Cooper's Creek* (1993). Frank **Clune's** *Dig* (1937) achieved a wide audience, but was diminished by his technique of combining contemporary evidence with invented dialogue. Alan **Moorehead's** *Cooper's Creek* (1963) is a more scholarly popular account. That it is still possible to throw new light on the story was proved by zoologist Tom Bergin: *In the Steps of Burke and Wills* (1981) showed that Burke's forced schedule caused navigational inaccuracies and precluded hunting, which might have prevented fatal dietary deficiencies.

Epic dimensions have been supplied by poets Henry **Kendall** in 'The Fate of the Explorers, Burke and Wills' (1861) and Adam Lindsay **Gordon** in 'Gone' (1867). There are plays by Colin Thiele and Bill Reed. **Films** include Fran-cis Birtles's documentary *Across Australia on the Track of Burke and Wills* (1915); the big-budget feature *Burke and Wills* (1985); and a comedy, *Wills and Burke* (1985). The story has also inspired artists Sidney **Nolan**, S.T. **Gill**, John **Longstaff**, and others. Major contemporary works were produced by William **Strutt** and Ludwig **Becker**, whose sketches were published in Marjorie Tipping (ed.), *Ludwig Becker: Artist and Naturalist with the Burke and Wills Expedition* (1979). Charles Summers's bronze statue, one of many **monument**s to the explorers, was unveiled in 1865 at the intersection of Collins and Russell Streets, Melbourne. It has been moved several times since; its restlessness seems strangely symbolic of the great city that dreamed of conquering a continent and still wonders whether it did.

DAMIEN CASH

Burnet, (Frank) Macfarlane (1899–1985) won international acclaim for his innovative research in virology and immunology. An introspective country boy, Burnet won a scholarship to Geelong College, Victoria, where he became uncomfortably aware of class and intellectual differences, and then went on to study medicine at the University of Melbourne. After completing a doctorate at London University, he pursued his developing interest in bacterial viruses at the Lister Institute. He returned to Melbourne in 1928 to become assistant director of the Walter and Eliza Hall Institute, where, with Jean **Macnamara**, he discovered that there was more than one strain of the poliomyelitis virus. He went on to investigate influenza viruses and vaccines. Appointed director of the institute in 1944 and professor of experimental medicine at the University of Melbourne, he established a Clinical Research Unit. His work on immunology won him, with Peter Medawar, the 1960 Nobel Prize in medicine. His many publications reflect both scientific and social interests. These include *Changing Patterns: An Atypical Autobiography* (1968), which contains very little personal detail, being rather an idiosyncratic account of the changes Burnet noted in biological research; *Credo and Comment: A Scientist Reflects* (1979), and a history of the Walter and Eliza Hall Institute (1971). Christopher Sexton has produced a biography, *The Seeds of Time* (1991).

KT

Burnum Burnum (1936–97), Aboriginal rights activist, was born to the Wurunjeri people at Wallaga Lake on the south coast of NSW. He was taken from his parents as a baby and was brought up in government missions and children's homes. As Harry Penrith he played first-grade **Rugby** League in the 1950s and later became active in Aboriginal rights campaigns. He helped found the Aboriginal **Tent Embassy** in 1972, and in 1976, the year he changed his name to Burnum Burnum, he organised the removal of **Truganini's** skeleton from the Tasmanian Museum and its cremation. Burnum Burnum received international recognition on **Australia Day** 1988 when he raised the Aboriginal flag on the coast of Dover, England, as part of a public attack on white celebrations of the Bicentenary. He co-presented a film entitled *Triumph of the Nomads* in 1984 with Geoffrey **Blainey**, based on Blainey's book of the same name. He became a popular children's story-teller and wrote *Burnum Burnum's Aboriginal Australia: A Traveller's Guide* (1988).

HD

Burra Charter takes its name from the town of Burra, SA, where the charter was drafted at a 1978 conference on the conservation of historical sites held under the auspices of Australia Icomos (International Council on Monuments and Sites). Based in part on the Venice Charter (1964), the Burra Charter focuses on the identification and care of the historic fabric of Australian places, to ensure that their cultural significance is preserved. Its guidelines on proper maintenance, preservation, restoration, reconstruction, and adaption of historic sites emphasise the importance of retaining this historic fabric. Since its ratification in 1988, the Burra Charter has formed the basis of policy adopted by **heritage** conservation practitioners. Members of Australia Icomos are bound by its code.

HD

Bush is the word used since the beginnings of European settlement to describe the rough, uncleared country in the Australian interior and, later, the ways of life and folk traditions of those who lived there. Since the late nineteenth century 'the bush', often written with a capital 'B', has been exalted as a source of national ideals; as such, it remains an enduring topic of debate among historians, literary critics, and other students of **national identity**.

Said to derive from the Dutch *bosch*, and to have made its way to Australia possibly by way of the USA, *bush* originally meant 'thickly forested country'. In his 1790 journal, Ralph **Clark** noted the disappearance of Aborigines into 'the bush'; vegetation thick enough to hide in. Convicts too might seek its refuge and by the 1820s 'taking to the bush' meant becoming a fugitive. **Bushranger** became the standard name for an escapee or outlaw, while the bush itself acquired associations of wildness and lawlessness that were to cling to it for more than a century. In time the word shed its literal association with thick vegetation and was applied generally to any country, open or treed, beyond the settled coast. 'Bush' and 'town' were thus defined in opposition to each other. In 1833, in one of the first of many self-conscious discussions of the term, W.H. Breton explained that 'Bush is the term commonly used for country *per se*: "he resides in the bush" implies that the person does not reside in, or very near, a town'.

Aesthetic responses to the Australian bush were strongly influenced by European Romanticism. Some early colonial painters and poets were drawn to mountain ranges, fern gullies, and harbours which they could depict, after the style of Turner or Wordsworth, as picturesque or even sublime. But others viewed the Australian bush as a grotesque inversion of the European ideal. Marcus **Clarke** compared the ethos of the Australian bush to that of Edgar Allan Poe's poetry—'Weird Melancholy'. 'That wild dreamland termed the Bush' was an accumulation of absences—songless birds, flowers with no perfume, and forests where no leaves fell. Clarke's epithets—'monotonous', 'gloomy', 'barren', 'timeless'—reverberated in the colonial imagination for more than half a century. Henry **Lawson**, for example, would later refer to 'the grand Australian bush—the nurse and tutor of eccentric minds, the home of the weird and of much that is different from things in other lands'.

For all its weirdness, contemporaries recognised the bush as the most distinctive and formative of Australian environments. From the 1830s onwards they noted the improvised simplicity of *bush beds*, *bush carpentry*, *bush fare*, and *bush tea*, as well as the warmth of *bush hospitality* and the indispensability of *bush experience*. In 1847 the self-styled 'Emigrant Mechanic' Alexander **Harris** noticed the 'habits of mutual helpfulness' which prevailed among workingmen in the bush. 'It is a universal feeling that a man ought to be able to trust his mate in anything', he observed. Anthony **Trollope** later described the code of honour, and the hard-drinking and swearing among the 'nomad tribe' of bush workers who laboured on the stations of the interior. Bush ways were seen as rougher, but more genuine, than those of the city or the Old Country. *Bushmanship* was the talent, akin to that of Aborigines, for finding one's way through the bush, relying only on natural signs; to be *bushed* was to lose one's way, perhaps figuratively as well as geographically. *Bushman*—used from the 1820s—was a term of honour, connoting mastery of a harsh environment; but *bushy* and *bushwhacker*—which gained currency late in the century—suggested awkwardness and rustic innocence.

Bush was always geographically indeterminate. There were subtle regional variations in usage. South Australians, as John Hirst noted in *Adelaide and the Country* (1973), preferred to speak of the *country* rather than the *bush*, a habit which reflected an easier relationship between the capital of that colony and its hinterland than between 'Sydney and the Bush'. Henry Lawson visualised the map of NSW and Qld divided into several sub-regions of bush—from 'up the country', through 'right up the country' to 'outback' and 'never-never'—stretching from the coastal plains to the far interior. But these were attempts to pin down terms which always eluded precise definition.

'It was I who insisted on the capital B for bush', Lawson boasted—but he was not the first to promote the bush as a basis for national ideals. Like young nationalists elsewhere, the ***Bulletin*** writers believed that national character could not be acquired, second-hand, from European parents, but must be rooted in native soil and forged through a heroic struggle with the land. The visiting English socialist Francis **Adams** acknowledged that 'the one powerful and unique national type yet produced in Australia is … the Bushman'. The shearers and stockmen of the Australian interior, he argued, were the prototype of a 'New Race'; they were not men of limited horizons and ambitions, but—thanks largely the influence of bush unionism—were progressive, ambitious, often well-read. Adams's idealism was not universally shared. In 1892 readers of the *Bulletin* witnessed a duel in doggerel between the two leading bush poets, Banjo **Paterson**, who championed the romantic view of the man on horseback, and Henry Lawson, the more sardonic view of the man with a swag. Paterson's was the more popular view among contemporaries, although Lawson and his fellow realists, who included Joseph **Furphy** and Barbara **Baynton**, may have had more enduring influence.

Among the painters of the **Heidelberg School**, the conflict between realists and romantics was more muted. Fred **McCubbin**, aesthetically closest to the realists, painted sentimental scenes of bush life—the lost child, the swagman down on his luck, the bush burial—although he usually set them in the coastal forests rather than in the bleached inland plains. His younger colleagues took a sunnier view of the bush and its inhabitants. Tom **Roberts's** 'Shearing the Rams' idealised the shearers as specimens of 'strong masculine labour'. Arthur **Streeton** dismissed Clarke's melancholy view of the bush as 'rubbish', insisting that he could feel more reverent in the bush than he could in a church. By the 1890s the bush was becoming a place of recreation, even of pantheistic worship. Businessmen, enervated by the pressures of city life, sought spiritual as well as physical refreshment in the new pastime of bushwalking. The bush spirits who inhabit the later landscapes of Streeton and Sydney Long, like the gumnut babies of May **Gibbs's** children's stories, were part of a broader movement to make the bush, in Bernard **O'Dowd's** words, 'the scroll on which we are to write/Mythologies our own'.

Contemporary statesmen, guided by ideals of national efficiency, looked to the bush as the foundation of the nation's future greatness. Even before the Great War began, the journalist Charles **Bean** had identified the features of bush life—sleeping in the open air, learning to ride and shoot, fighting bushfires—which prepared the Australian for battle. 'The bushman is the hero of the Australian boy; the arts of the bush life are his ambition … he learns something of half the arts of a soldier by the time he is ten years old.' **Anzac** vindicated his prophecy and fused Australia's bush and military traditions. When the war was over, statesmen sought to bolster rural life with **bush nursing** hospitals, bush fire brigades, and model bush schools. As the bush was gradually domesticated, the frontiers of romance were pushed further out to the mangrove swamps and spinifex country of the Far North.

The bush was an odd symbol of national life for a country always precociously urban. Was it a reality or an ideal? Was the heroic bushman a 'coming man' or a dying breed? Twentieth-century historians progressively laid bare the intellectual scaffolding of the myth. In 1939 M. Barnard Eldershaw had already recognised *bush* as a 'code-word' embodying 'a complex of ideas' larger and more diffuse than its immediate object. It became an essential building block in the efforts of the **Old Left** in the 1940s to indigenise a Marxist interpretation of Australian history. Russel **Ward's** *The Australian Legend* (1958), the most influential exploration of the national myth, acknowledged its mythical character, yet insisted that the traits popularly associated with the 'typical Australian'—mateship, anti-authoritarianism, stoicism, hard drinking, swearing—derived from the **frontier** experiences of the real bush workers. His critics have questioned both his characterisation of the typical Australian and his explanation of its origins. Graeme Davison (*HS*, 1978) and Richard White (*Inventing Australia*, 1981) looked to the distinctively urban milieu of the *Bulletin* writers—Sydney's counter-culture of cheap boarding-houses and radical politics—to explain their idealisation of the bush. 'The bush myth', Davison wrote, 'was the reflex of the urban nightmare.' Feminists have pondered the significance of the old adage, 'The bush is no place for a woman.' Was the aggressive masculinity of the bush myth a frightened response of urban intellectuals to the growth of feminising ideologies of respectability, as Marilyn Lake argued (*AHS*, 1986)? Was the bushman's mastery of the land an image of the domination he also exerted over women, as Kay Schaffer contended in *Women and the Bush* (1988)?

In the 1990s the bush, once the economic as well as symbolic core of the nation, has been marginalised. Drought, declining prices, debt, and depopulation—old adversaries acting with unprecedented savagery—have invested the word with a new sense of melancholy and resentment. It becomes the badge of the rural battlers—timber workers, mountain stockmen, and shooters—resisting the claims of Aborigines, environmentalists, and Canberra politicians to turn bush into 'native title' 'wilderness', or 'heritage'. Yet the bush myth has displayed amazing powers of endurance. When Australian novelists and poets were embracing new urban and international themes, the bush romance remained, as Graeme Turner noted in *National Fictions* (1986), the staple theme of Australian films. Elements of the old bush culture—bush bands, bush tucker, bush clothing, vernacular bush architecture—have been absorbed into the Australian and international mainstream, where they circulate and reproduce themselves independently of the environment from which they came.

GRAEME DAVISON

Bush nursing extended the principle of district nursing, already well-developed in Britain and other parts of the Empire, to the Australian bush. The movement was inaugurated in 1909 by the Countess of Dudley, the beautiful, bountiful, and soon-to-be estranged wife of the Australian governor-general. It gained support especially among **progressive** intellectuals, such as the long-serving secretary of the Victorian Association, James **Barrett**, who saw it as a means of supporting rural communities and thus combating the harmful drift of population to the city. The scheme, as originally conceived, was expected to be self-supporting but it faltered until grants from the Red Cross, state governments, and charitable trusts placed it on a more sustainable footing. In Victoria, where the movement began, bush nurses were often stationed at centres which later developed into small bush hospitals. Each centre was autonomous, although travelling superintendents employed by the state association maintained oversight of the system. The movement was strongest in Victoria, Tasmania and SA; in 1953–54 about

Bush searches

100 of the nation's 150 centres were located there. Since the 1980s pressures for centralisation and rationalisation have forced the closure of many bush hospitals. James Barrett wrote an outline history of the Victorian association in 1932; Susan Priestley's *Bush Nursing in Victoria 1910–1985: The First 75 Years* (1986) extends the story.

GD

Bush searches quickly became recognised as a characteristic feature of Australian colonial life and were frequently represented in literature that tried to be distinctively Australian. These include works by Henry **Kingsley**, *The Recollections of Geoffry Hamlyn* (1859), Marcus **Clarke**, 'Pretty Dick' (1869), Henry **Lawson**, 'The Babies in the Bush' (1901), and Tom **Collins**, *Such Is Life* (1903), all of which utilise the added pathos of lost children. This was a common, but by no means the only, cause of bush searches. The extent to which the **bush** was identified with being lost is apparent in the coining of the term 'bushed', meaning to be lost, which was noted as early as 1844.

Distinctive aspects of these searches include large-scale community involvement and the frequent use of Aboriginal **black trackers**. The first recorded use of black trackers in a bush search in WA took place near Fremantle in 1834. Migo and Mollydobbin tracked a missing five-year-old boy for more than 10 hours over very rough country. Aboriginal perseverance and joy at finding lost children is a prominent trope of popular accounts. One such story is that of the Duff children, lost for nine days in the Victorian Wimmera in 1864. Heavy rain hampered the large local contingent of volunteers; within a day of Aborigines being brought into the search they found the children, amazingly all still alive. The incident generated poems, numerous art works and stories, including the illustrated *Cooeey* (1889) by William **Strutt**, and 'Lost in the Bush', known to generations of Victorian schoolchildren from their *School Readers*.

Quite often the searches yielded no result, as in the case of 'The Three Lost Children' at Daylesford, Victoria. Three young boys wandered into dense bush in the winter of 1867 and, although the searchers eventually numbered over 700, the boys were not found. Three months later, a dog carrying a small child's skull alerted a settler to check the area thoroughly. The remains of the boys were found, the younger two actually in the hollow of a large tree. The family of two of the boys established scholarships at the local primary school which continue today, a memorial was erected in the cemetery, and 'The Three Lost Children's Memorial Reserve and Walking Track' was established in 1988. The community was indelibly marked by the incident.

Modern communications have made recent incidents a national experience. The story of 4-year-old Stephen Walls, lost in the New England Ranges of NSW in 1960, was covered closely by newspapers and television stations around the country. The search reputedly involved 5000 people, and a popular song, 'Little Boy Lost' by Johnny Ashcroft, told his story.

With the increasing popularity of bushwalking in the 1950s, a different type of bush search developed, involving professionals from various state government departments, as well as the locals. The states formed search-and-rescue units to conduct the searches. Dogs replaced trackers; radio communications aided the coordination; helicopters and small planes enabled large areas to be covered. Yet in many ways, little has changed. The body of an 8-year-old, lost in the NT in 1993, was found after a nine-day search involving police, soldiers, and volunteers on horseback and in planes. Like so many before him, he had shed much of his clothing, including shoes, and had covered a remarkable distance.

KT

Bushfires have been part of the Australian environment for millions of years, whether sparked by lightning strikes or by human action. The use of fire by Aborigines to assist their hunting of animals helped to shape both the grassland and forest environments, and large-scale, slow-burning fires continue to be part of the cycle of regeneration in vast areas of the inland and the tropical north. Colonists were quick to adopt the Aboriginal use of the fire-stick to manage the grasslands more effectively, but the introduction of large-scale cereal farming and more intensive utilisation of forest resources in the later stages of European settlement elevated bushfire to the status of a major seasonal hazard, in that it became difficult to continue the traditional use of fire for clearing native vegetation and stubble without risking damaging summer burns.

In the late nineteenth century colonial legislatures tried to reduce the incidence of man-made bushfires by regulating the use of fire in the high-risk summer months, but without a great deal of success. The introduction of railways and small steam engines to power farm machinery added to the risks presented by lightning strikes, smokers, and the occasional arsonist. Bushfire joined **drought** and **flood** as the periodic destroyers of rural tranquillity, and cut deeply into the national self-image. While the painters William **Strutt**, Eugene von **Guérard** and John **Longstaff** captured the visual drama of large-scale bushfires, Henry **Lawson** stressed fire's capacity to blight the hopes of struggling farmers.

It was not until the mid-twentieth century that technology made it possible for state fire control agencies to manage all but the most severe outbreaks in rural and forested areas. The development of **weather forecasting** assisted authorities to regulate high-risk behaviour by enforcing fire bans on specific days and publicising them through the media. Local volunteer firefighting brigades coordinated by state agencies and using better equipment were then able to contain most conventional grassland fires. Fire discipline in rural areas increased as the rural population declined, machinery replaced fire as a farm tool, and rural communities responded to campaigns to reduce fire risk.

In the late twentieth century the growth of conservation parks widened the long-running controversy about the merits of controlled burning in forests and national parks; but it has been the spread of housing into the highly volatile bushland surrounding major metropolitan centres that has made bushfire a major area of concern to a much larger proportion of the Australian population. Semi-urban populations have been far more reluctant than rural communities to modify their environment by reducing local fire loads, and the **Ash Wednesday** fires in Victoria and SA in February 1983 killed more than 70 people in both the urban hinterland and in rural areas. Yet the protracted bushfire crisis of January 1994 in NSW resulted in severe damage to property in semi-urban areas and to national parks, but comparatively few deaths. When bushfire was almost entirely a rural hazard, even those directly involved could minimise risk, and losses were mostly confined to livestock, fencing, and other farm assets. When multiple fatalities did occur, the circumstances were often unusual; in the case of the Victorian fires of 1939, most of the 71 deaths occurred in forest settlements and at sawmilling sites from which escape was extremely difficult.

Forest and grass fires continue to occur each summer in the great arc of settlement from Qld through to Tasmania and across to the south-west of WA. Periodic slow-burning fires attract little attention in vast areas of the inland during the dry season; outbreaks close to the urban centres have come to attract media attention and impact more directly on the political system. Despite its persistence, the place of bushfire in the national experience has been given more attention by fire scientists, foresters, geographers, meteorologists, health professionals, fire control agencies, government committees and journalists than by historians and social scientists. R.M. Wettenhall's study of the Hobart fires of 1967, which took 62 lives, is still the only study by a political scientist of the management of a major bushfire emergency. Manning **Clark** used a brief account of Victoria's '**Black Thursday**' bushfires of 1851 to introduce the fourth volume of his epic *History of Australia*, but most single-volume studies refer to bushfire hazards only in passing. Some fire control agencies have produced historical accounts of their operations, but the journalist W.S. Noble's *Ordeal by Fire* (1977), an account of the Victorian '**Black Friday**' fires of 1939, stands as perhaps the only narrative of a major fire event. Stephen J. Pyne's *Burning Bush: A Fire History of Australia* (1991) draws on the substantial literature generated by natural scientists, specialists in Aboriginal history, and environmentalists, to place the Australian experience within the global context of wildfire.

GREG TOBIN

Bushman's Bible was the name given to the *Bulletin*, the Sydney weekly, in tribute to its strong readership in the outback. The title, first claimed by the paper itself in 1888, was adopted more widely, thanks partly to the influence of the radical English journalist Francis **Adams**, who heard a backblocks shearer say: 'If I'd only one sixpence left I'd buy the *Bulletin* with it'.

GD

Bushranging provided Australia with its first, most enduring and best-known popular **heroes**. Bushrangers were initially runaway convicts who roamed through the **bush** and emerged from it to rob settlers and travellers on the roads. They established a mode of operation which was

continued by emigrant and native-born robbers for almost 100 years. Bushranging flourished in three periods: during the transportation of convicts to NSW and Tasmania; in Victoria during the gold rushes of the 1850s; and in NSW in the 1860s, when the bushrangers were native-born young men. The last and most famous bushranger, Ned **Kelly**, operated in Victoria in the late 1870s and was hanged at Melbourne gaol in 1880.

Bushrangers survived by being skilled in bushcraft, but the bush generally did not afford them a living. They had to rob to survive, or depend on supplies from supporters. They were a danger to society, but remained in contact with it and so constantly gave opportunity for their capture.

Only in Tasmania did bushrangers come close to self-sufficiency in the bush. In the colony's early years when food was in short supply, convicts were given dogs and guns to hunt kangaroo for their masters. Bushrangers used the skills so acquired for their own support. They lived on kangaroo flesh, dressed in kangaroo skins, and traded flesh and skins with the settlers. They still committed robberies—so regularly, indeed, that they forced settlers to abandon their farms—but they became the *de facto* rulers of the interior. They were more like colonies of runaway slaves in the Americas, and like them negotiated with the government as equals over pardons and amnesties. Michael **Howe** styled himself in these negotiations as Governor of the Ranges. Soldiers rather than police were sent to do battle against them. They posed a threat to the very survival of the colony as a British possession.

The ballads which celebrated the bushrangers and their exploits claimed that, like Robin Hood, they robbed the rich and protected the poor. The cynical view is that they robbed the rich because the rich had more to be taken, or that they lived up to the Robin Hood image only to gain support. The truth is that most bushrangers robbed indiscriminately and took no pains to disguise the fact. Since the houses of the rich were better protected, the convict bushrangers more regularly robbed small ex-convict farmers and travellers on the road. The gangs led by Frank **Gardiner** and Ben **Hall** in NSW in the 1860s were so uninterested in the image of protectors of the poor that they robbed children, seized gold-diggers' winnings, and turned their horses out to graze in a poor man's crop. It is true that two famous bushrangers did discriminate in their targets. Bold Jack **Donohue**, who operated in NSW in the 1820s, robbed only the rich, usually as travellers on the roads, and so comprehensively that he left them naked. Ned Kelly robbed only banks, and while he had access to the safe burnt the mortgages of small settlers to free them from debt. In this, as in so much else, Ned was making himself into myth.

The numerous chroniclers of bushrangers, whether they extenuated or condemned their deeds, treated them as individuals, as heroes or villains. Historians have since been concerned to understand them as a social phenomenon. In *The Australian Legend* (1958) Russel **Ward** took the solidarity of convicts as the seed-bed of the national character and saw this exemplified in the support of convicts and ex-convicts for bushrangers who had been driven to their trade by harsh masters. John McQuilton in *The Kelly Outbreak*

(1979) argued that support for Kelly in north-east Victoria was a form of social protest by selectors who were struggling to establish themselves in a world still dominated by squatters. D.J. Shiel, Ben Hall's biographer (1983), saw his society as one where certain groups remained powerless to improve their lives.

Bushrangers undoubtedly enjoyed support, but not as extensive as such explanations claim. Unwillingness to help the police indicated fear of bushrangers as well as support for them. Betrayal and informing always undercut convict solidarity, and bushrangers could rely confidently only on particular associates who might be workmates, shipmates, or fellow countrymen. The bonds among the **Irish** were particularly strong, and they were more ready to support an Irish rebel. The Irish tie also operated in the cases of the 1860s gangs in NSW and Ned Kelly, whose support networks were more kin and friends than settlers generally.

The claim for general support rests on the assumption of general discontent. But some convicts were well treated and assisted their masters to catch bushrangers; not all selectors in Kelly country were poor, and some of the disputes over water and stock were among selectors rather than between selectors and squatters; the supporters of Ben Hall and Frank Gardiner included small squatters, owners of substantial property, which is an indication of the opportunities open to ex-convict stockmen and their children.

The circumstances which encouraged bushranging might alternatively be identified as a sparsely settled countryside interspersed with tracts of wilderness, where the government's control was weak and the institutions of civil society non-existent, and where settlers were satisfied to hold onto their land, stock, and access to water and otherwise to live and let live. In convict times substantial settlers formed posses to hunt bushrangers when their crimes became serious, but later the matter was left to the police.

Temptation rather than harsh treatment or blighted prospects might explain the course of the bushranger's career. It did not necessarily require a tyrannical master for a convict to decide that a life in the bush was preferable to hard labour. The gold rushes introduced highly valuable and readily portable property into an area where there had been none, and lured many onto the roads. Cattle- and horse-stealing were endemic in the bush, from which it was only a small step to bushranging proper. Ned Kelly boasted of the number of horses he had stolen.

The social explanation has taken encouragement from the work of Eric Hobsbawm in *Primitive Rebels* (1959), a study of 'social bandits' in Southern Europe in the nineteenth and twentieth centuries. There was a remarkable similarity between these peasant rebels and bushrangers, which has encouraged Australian scholars to see them arising out of a similar level of poverty and oppression. But if rebels of similar sort emerge in peasant societies under threat of modernisation and on the frontier of settler capitalism, the conclusion might rather be that 'social bandits' can flourish in a variety of social circumstances. The recurrence and attraction of the outlaw hero is studied by Graeme Seal in

The Outlaw Legend: A Cultural Tradition in Britain, America and Australia (1996). Interpretations which question the usual form of the social explanation of bushranging can be found in two La Trobe University theses, J.A. McKinnon, 'Convict Bushrangers in NSW' (MA thesis, 1979), and D. Morrissey, 'Selectors, Squatters and Stock-thieves' (PhD thesis, 1987), and in John Hirst, *The Strange Birth of Colonial Democracy* (1988).

There is no doubt that bushrangers attracted admiration beyond the area of their operation. This first became widespread in NSW in the 1860s. The bushrangers' exploits were made known to the whole colony by telegraph and newspaper, and the bushrangers took care to make themselves newsworthy. Their police opponents were a new centralised force, composed chiefly of immigrants, which was designed to be more efficient than the local forces which it replaced. The bushrangers delighted to show how inefficient the police were. Humiliation of the police rather than robbery was often their aim. They captured police, stripped their uniforms from them, and then used them themselves as the most effective disguise. After taking the local policeman captive, the Ben Hall gang took over the town of Canowindra, and held a party in the pub. It was this boldness, flashness as it was termed at the time, which made them such appealing figures. Native-born young men showing up the **new chum** police were proto-nationalist figures. They were not the oppressed speaking for the oppressed, but exuberant, self-confident bushmen showing they were masters of the land and all its inhabitants. They had an admiring public in Sydney—to the despair of some of the respectable people, who were the more concerned because the respectable were among the admirers. If the bushrangers had robbed the rich to give to the poor, they would have been much more problematic figures.

Ned Kelly became the pre-eminent Australian hero. He imitated the Canowindra hold-up in his raid on Jerilderie, and at Glenrowan planned something which would make the whole world take notice: the ruin of the train bringing police reinforcements. When this plan was foiled, he appeared in home-made armour for his last confrontation with the police and so provided an unforgettable image of his defiance, now made into a national icon by **Nolan's** paintings.

Russel Ward took the admiration of bushrangers as confirmation of his view that the anti-authoritarian attitudes of the founding population had become part of the national character. Whatever his critics say of his thesis, they cannot deny the singular fact that this nation has no heroes who come anywhere near the bushrangers in public esteem, though they may not follow him in thinking it a sign of good health.

JOHN HIRST

Business history has not achieved the prominence in Australian historiography that it enjoys elsewhere. With a few notable exceptions, Australia's most outstanding historians have not been attracted to it and the field has been dominated by amateur historians and journalists. The majority of those who first entered the lists did so to produce commissioned histories of individual companies. Few rose above the mundane; they possessed neither the necessary skills to ask the right questions nor the capacity to analyse the data made available to them. While academic historians and economic historians became more important contributors after World War II, their writings were not strongly influenced by the new developments in the methodologies employed by their peers, particularly in the USA and Great Britain. Australian business history remained dominated by business 'biography', and, for the most part, did not place its subjects in a wider context. The failure of many 'entrepreneurial' companies following the stockmarket crash of 1987 has shifted the emphasis of contemporary writings to a search for the seeds of failure rather than success.

Business history, as distinct from collections of business records, was virtually non-existent in Australia before the end of the nineteenth century, except as a broken thread in autobiography. The centenary celebrations in 1888 and Federation in 1901 brought forth the first collections of business biography as the editors of commemorative encyclopaedias filled their multi-volume works with stories of glorious achievements won in the face of adversity. These chronicles, based on information given by the subjects who paid for the privilege of appearing, were the forerunners of more comprehensive compilations. Such publications were directed towards a new audience, the investor. The growing number of public companies provided financial reports and chairmen's addresses in compliance with the regulations of stock exchanges and company law. R.L. Nash, a financial journalist, used them to produce an irregular series entitled *The Australasian Joint Stock Companies' Year Book* between 1898 and 1914 that provides a mine of information on thousands of companies, while Alexander Jobson's *Investment Digest (of Australia and New Zealand)*, and the *Digest Year Book of Public Companies*, begun in the early 1920s, are still in print. The *Bulletin* magazine published a monthly 'Wild Cat' section from 1923 until the 1960s. Other more statistically oriented publications, notably the *Delfin Digest*, emerged in the 1960s, while an annual list of the top 1000 companies first published in 1963 has been continued to the present day by *Business Review Weekly*.

This growing body of information about individual companies, together with the publicly available data generated in the course of inquiries by the **Tariff** Board, Commonwealth **Arbitration** Court, **wages boards**, evidence before royal commissions, and other parliamentary inquiries, did little to stimulate independent scholarship about Australian companies before World War II. However, radicals, whose work was heavily influenced by British and US precedents, attacked the growth of trusts, monopolies, and foreign ownership of Australian companies. For the most part, theirs was a reaction to the emergence of 'big business'. H.L. Wilkinson's *The Trust Movement in Australia* (1914) was one of the earliest critiques. A group of

pamphleteers, including J.N. Rawlings, Len Fox, E.W. Campbell, Brian **Fitzpatrick**, Eric Aarons, and Pete Thomas—all but one of them members of the **Communist** Party—carried the story of monopoly and foreign ownership forward with great vigour from the 1930s until the 1960s. Their polemical style was complemented by the careful scholarship of E.L. Wheelwright, whose *Ownership and Control of Australian Companies* (1957) and later work with Judith Miskelly, *Anatomy of Australian Manufacturing Industry* (1967), documented the growing importance of salaried managers in controlling Australian business, and the growth of market dominance by a small number of firms. Wheelwright's pioneering work has been continued by Hylda Rolfe and Michael Lawriwsky. The political economy school at the University of Sydney has provided an institutional base for this radical tradition.

Histories of individual businesses began to appear in increasing numbers after World War I. Nearly all were privately published, brief, and little more than an uncritical memorial to their founders. Their production was usually prompted by the passing of some milestone such as the death of the founder or the anniversary of commencement. Some nuggets are to be found amongst the dross. The study by Roy **Bridges**, *From Silver to Steel: The Romance of the Broken Hill Proprietary* (1920), was the first of the many books written about Australia's most famous company. Its narrative was laced with statistics. Another work of note is George Taylor's *Making it Happen: The Rise of Sir Macpherson Robertson* (1934), which goes well beyond extolling the virtues of the owner to explain the success of his vast business enterprise. The author demonstrates the role played by technology, purchasing, marketing, good relations with workers, and organisation-building in modern manufacturing.

The character of Australian business history changed significantly in the 1950s and 1960s as professional historians began to write more substantial histories, many of which were commissioned by the country's leading companies. The standard of these works lifted the genre to a new plane. Geoffrey **Blainey's** brilliant story-telling approach to the histories of mining fields—*The Peaks of Lyell* (1954); *Mines in the Spinifex* (1960); *The Rise of Broken Hill* (1968)—together with his edited memoirs of W.S. **Robinson**, *If I Remember Rightly* (1967), his histories of a Melbourne engineering company, *Johns & Waygood Limited* (1956), and the National Bank of Australasia, *Gold and Paper* (1958), and a biography of BHP's Essington **Lewis**, *The Steel Master* (1971), stamped him as Australia's outstanding business historian. *Foundations of the Australian Monetary System 1788–1851* (1953) and *Australia and New Zealand Bank* (1961) by S.J. **Butlin** were works of the highest standard of scholarship, and served as templates for later commissioned histories of individual banks. The pastoral industry was studied by Alan Barnard, whose *The Australian Wool Market 1840–1900* (1958), *Visions and Profits: Studies in the Business Career of T.S. Mort* (1961), and the edited volume, *The Simple Fleece* (1962), illuminated a once dark landscape. Margaret Steven, *Merchant Campbell, 1769–1846* (1965), and others focused on the activities of merchants in early colonial times. More recently, Frank Broeze, *Mr Brooks and the Australian Trade* (1993), carried this story forward into mid-century.

Business history had begun to reach a far wider audience. Businessmen, librarians, and academics were drawn together to preserve records and to promote their use. A Business Archives Council of Australia was established in 1954. The support of its members was instrumental in the formation of the Labour and Business Archive (now the Noel Butlin Archives) at the Australian National University in the late 1950s and the business and labour collections of the University of Melbourne Archives in 1960. Some companies also established their own archives. From 1961 the council published *Business Archives and History*, which provided a forum for debate about the nature and use of business history, and for the first time published articles in the genre. Many of Australia's leading economic historians published the fruits of their research in this journal, and its successor, the *Australian Economic History Review*. Business history increasingly formed part of the curriculum in economic history courses taught in Australian universities.

Australian business history did not continue its momentum through the 1970s and 1980s. While the number of company histories and journal articles published continued to grow, and many were of outstanding quality, Australian business history did not follow the important conceptual advances and new techniques employed overseas, particularly those generated by the work of Alfred Chandler in the USA. Other sources of inspiration, the outstanding histories of foreign companies with subsidiaries in Australia, such as those by W.J. Reader, *Imperial Chemical Industries* (1970–75), or Charles Wilson's *The History of Unilever*, 2 vols (1954), had an insignificant impact on the approach taken by local authors. By comparison, Australian scholarship remained myopic and theoretically impoverished. It concentrated on the particular while ignoring the larger context of the private sector economy, particularly the rise of big business, and its symbiotic relations with their suppliers, customers, employees and the state. It retained a heavy emphasis on biography rather than the study of organisations.

By the end of the 1980s, the terrain had been reclaimed by journalists. It was they who chronicled the rise and demise of many of Australia's 'entrepreneurial' companies. The enormous success of Trevor Sykes's excellent books, *Two Centuries of Panic: A History of Corporate Collapses in Australia* (1988) and *The Bold Riders: Behind Australia's Corporate Collapses* (1994), suggests that a wider audience exists for works in the tradition of the American muckrakers than for the old-style romance of business success stories. The more academic studies that make up the very best of business history commissioned and published overseas are almost unknown in Australia.

DAVID MERRETT

Bussell family are among the best-known early settlers of WA, and figure prominently in discussion of the colonial family. Although they were well-educated and cultured, the death of their father, an Anglican clergyman, left them without an income. Attracted by promising reports of the **Swan** River colony, four sons, JOHN, CHARLES, VERNON, and ALFRED, sailed for WA in 1829 aboard the *Warrior*. Among the passengers was Georgiana **Molloy** and her husband, who remained friends of the family. The Bussells took up land at Augusta but did not prosper; over the following four years their crops failed, livestock disappeared, and their house burnt down. By this time, however, the boys had been joined by more of the family, who provided both physical and emotional support. The family moved in 1834 to the area which became known as Busselton, and established the property Cattle Chosen, the title of E.O.G. **Shann's** history of the family (1978). John and Alfred were both justices of the peace and members of the Legislative Council. Family members married into other well-known Western Australian families, most notably the Brockmans. Perhaps the most widely known of the Bussell family was GRACE (1860–1935), who was dubbed the 'Australian Grace Darling' for her part in the rescue of approximately 50 passengers from a sinking steamer, the *Georgette*, in December 1876.

KT

Butlin, Noel George (1921–91) made major contributions to understanding most phases of Australian economic development, before and after 1788. His seminal works were published in the early 1960s after more than a decade of intensive and innovative research, which at the time was only possible with the resources provided by the recently established Australian National University.

Australian Domestic Product, Investment and Foreign Borrowing 1861–1938/39 (1962) provided a comprehensive set of national accounts that most subsequent interpretations have taken as their point of departure. *Investment in Australian Economic Development 1861–1900* (1964) provided a sophisticated account of economic expansion in the second half of the nineteenth century based on resource exploitation and a large public sector (**state socialism**), and the subsequent economic collapse in the 1890s. The interpretation—not fully accepted by his colleagues— emphasised the Australian origins of the boom and depression, a modification of earlier writers who regarded Australia as a small dependent economy within the British imperial system.

Butlin was born at Singleton, NSW, the youngest child of a working-class family, and was educated at Maitland Boys' High School and the University of Sydney. After a period in wartime administration, he was appointed a lecturer in economics at the University of Sydney in 1946. But he was too shy to be a gifted teacher, and the years at the University of Sydney were a strain—particularly with his brother, Sydney **Butlin**, as dean of economics and professor. In 1949 he was awarded a Rockefeller Fellowship to Harvard University and returned in 1951 to an appointment at the Research School of Social Sciences at the ANU, where he remained until his death in 1991.

Butlin built a powerful and influential school of post-graduate **economic history** at the ANU. He supervised many graduate students in the disciplines of economics, economic statistics, and economic history. He was an inspiring, demanding, and even dominating supervisor. There was generally a strong emphasis on quantification and the macro economy, couched in language often inaccessible to the general historian. After his pioneering work, Butlin experienced difficulty in finding a new project to satisfy his intense creativity. He investigated the cost of motor vehicle collisions, participated in the North American debate on antebellum slavery, and in 1974 was appointed director of the Botany Bay Project, an early environmental impact assessment. It appeared that Butlin had been lost to economic history.

In the 1980s, however, Butlin mellowed noticeably and returned to economic history for a final decade of brilliant creativity. The Australian national accounting estimates were extended back to 1788 with the intention of writing a comprehensive economic history of Australia. The result was *Forming a Colonial Economy: Australia 1810–1850* (1994). Regarding 1788 as an arbitrary date for the history of an economy, he imaginatively explored the pre-contact economy in *Economics and the Dreamtime* (1993). In *Our Original Aggression* (1983) he argued that the Aboriginal population in south-eastern Australia had been decimated by two smallpox epidemics, running ahead of white settlement, and hence population estimates made at first contact were completely erroneous.

In this final phase he was increasingly open to conventional historical discourse, critical of the formalist trend in economics, and saddened by the evident decline in his discipline, which he felt powerless to prevent.

C.B. SCHEDVIN

Butlin, Sydney James (1910–77) pioneered the historical study of Australian money and **banking** according to rigorous professional standards. He was a member of the Faculty of Economics at the University of Sydney from 1934 and completed his career at the Australian National University.

In *Foundations of the Australian Monetary System 1788–1851* (1953) he produced a scholarly work of rare distinction, in part a reaction against the broad generalisations in earlier writers, such as Edward **Shann** and Brian **Fitzpatrick**, and the absence of documentation in Timothy **Coghlan's** *Labour and Industry*. He wrote a two-volume account of the World War II economy as part of the official history; volume 1 was published in 1955 and volume 2 (with C.B. Schedvin) in 1977. His commissioned history of the leading Anglo-Australian bank, *Australia and New Zealand Bank* (1961), was as much a financial history of Australia until World War II as of an individual set of banks. At the time of his death he was preparing an official history of the **Reserve Bank of Australia**, and an account of monetary and banking history 1851–1914. Both have been published with the assistance of his daughter Judith.

C.B. SCHEDVIN

C

Caire, Nicholas John (1837–1918) was one of Australia's best-known and most influential early landscape **photographers**. He arrived in SA from Guernsey with his family in 1858, and by 1867 was operating a photographic studio in Adelaide. By 1871 he was established in Bendigo, Victoria. His 1875 series, *Views of Bendigo*, was extremely successful; it emboldened him to move to Melbourne, where he produced the *Views of Victoria (General Series)*, which also sold well. The rapidly expanding railway system of the 1880s made it easier for Caire to reach the bush. It was around this time that he began the rural genre photos which reflected and reinforced the emerging nationalism of the period. The bush workers and battling settlers in his photos are heroic in their 'typical' Australianness. Caire gave up studio work to concentrate on landscape photography. He preferred lush forest areas, and worked around Gippsland, Healesville, Marysville, and Mount Buffalo, which provided the fern glades and huge trees that he favoured. His photos were used by the Victorian Railways in tourist promotions and appeared frequently in Melbourne's leading illustrated newspapers. The postcard craze of the early 1900s provided an enormous market for his scenes. Upon his death the *Bulletin* asserted that 'in his photographic way he was an explorer'.

KT

Cairns, James Ford (1914–) is an idealistic left-wing politician who came to prominence in the 1960s as a critic of Australian foreign policy and especially the **Vietnam War**. His leadership of the protest movement culminated in the **Moratorium**, which he conducted with moral passion and dignified forbearance. He had worked as a policeman before completing a PhD degree at the University of Melbourne and lecturing in economic history there. As federal Labor member for Yarra (1955–69) and later Lalor (Victoria) (1969–77), when the **Whitlam** government won power he became minister for secondary industry and over-seas trade, and then served as treasurer and deputy prime minister 1974–75.

It was in this capacity that he became embroiled in a damaging series of scandals. It began with what the media dubbed the 'Morosi Affair', after his appointment of an unlikely candidate, Junie Morosi, as his private secretary. This sparked a round of media speculation and innuendo, which the Opposition fanned. Cairns was further damaged by being a member of the Executive Council that allowed Rex Connor to seek overseas loans, thus precipitating the disastrous **loans affair**. Later he was found to have misled parliament over a letter he signed which gave a local businessman permission to seek overseas loans; as a result Cairns was dismissed from the ministry. After his retirement in 1977, Cairns became increasingly involved in alternative lifestyles. A prolific writer, he has written much on the importance of the individual, including *Human Growth* (1984), *The Untried Road* (1990), and *Towards a New Society* (1993). Hawking his books at suburban markets, he was a lone figure who somehow failed to fit into the Labor pantheon. His quixotic aspect—but not his eloquent courage—is captured in the title of Paul Ormonde's biography, *A Foolish Passionate Man* (1981).

KT

Call to Australia, known in full as the Call to Australia Citizens Movement, is a conservative political party established in 1977 by the Rev. Fred Nile. The party takes an extreme conservative position on social issues. It promotes traditional family values and Christian morality, and condemns homosexuality, pornography, and abortion. Its policies are closely tied to the Festival of Light, a religious movement founded in 1973, of which Nile is a director. Nile and his wife Elaine Nile were elected to represent the Call to Australia Party in the NSW Legislative Council in 1981 and 1988; two other members also won seats in NSW in the 1980s.

HD

Call to the Nation was issued in November 1951 by the heads of the four major Christian denominations and chief justices of most states, and appealed to 'all Australians to advance moral standards'. The call had been initiated by the chief justice of Victoria, Sir Edmund Herring, and a Catholic activist, Paul McGuire, who shared a concern about the threat of **communism** and the 'terrible deterioration of the moral fibre of our people'. Robert **Menzies**, whose referendum to outlaw the Communist Party had been defeated in September 1951, gave private support to the campaign, which distributed 1.5 million copies of the *Call*, mainly through churches, local councils, lodges, and RSL clubs. David Hilliard (*AHS*, 1997) notes that the *Call* evoked mainly token approval, although more vocal opposition came both from the Left and from some Christians.

GD

Calwell, Arthur Augustus (1896–1973) had arguably the greatest impact on postwar Australia of any politician, despite his electoral failures. As minister for **immigration** 1945–49, he persuaded a dubious Australian people of the need for an extensive policy of European immigration. As part of the promotion for this he coined the tag **New Australians**, although this is not associated with him as closely as his now infamous pun that 'two Wongs do not make a White'. In later life he admitted to having 'lived dangerously as a politician', and he was certainly a dogged adversary. He took the **Curtin** government (from whose first ministry he had been omitted) roundly to task over its 1941 and 1942 budgets, which he claimed failed to implement Labor policy. Once in the ministry with the information portfolio, his already difficult relations with newspaper proprietors deteriorated until, in April 1944, he had copies of the Sydney *Sunday Telegraph* seized for breaking **censorship** rules. When the other Sydney dailies published statements challenging censorship powers, he had them seized too. It was then that cartoonists began caricaturing him as a cockatoo. Because he had been a key figure in the Labor Party machine for many years, the **Split** which produced the **Democratic Labor Party** caused him great pain. Although a devout Catholic, he stayed with **Evatt** and the **Australian Labor Party**, thereby losing many close friends, including Archbishop **Mannix**. He became leader of the Australian Labor Party in 1960, with Gough **Whitlam** as his deputy, and narrowly lost the 1961 election. It was during the 1963 campaign that a photograph, which showed Calwell and Whitlam waiting to hear a decision of the party's federal conference, was exploited by **Menzies**, who asserted that the Australian Labor Party was run by 36 **'faceless men'**. Even an attempted **assassination** could not help Calwell win the 1966 election, during which tensions with Whitlam increased. Calwell stood aside as leader in 1967, but remained in parliament until 1972, the same year in which he published his autobiography *Be Just and Fear Not*. Colm Kiernan, a long-time family friend, published an admiring biography, *Calwell*, in 1978.

KT

Cambridge, Ada (1844–1926) produced a detailed account of her time in Australia as a country clergyman's wife and a developing writer in *Thirty Years in Australia* (1903). Before this she had published verse and contributed romantic stories to the *Australasian*, several of which were later published as novels. Her fourth novel, *A Marked Man* (1890), brought financial success. She contributed to many other journals and newspapers, and achieved recognition in England as well as Australia. A second autobiographical volume, *The Retrospect* (1912), dealt mainly with her first return trip to England in 1908. While traditionally perceived as a romantically conventional writer, Cambridge has been reassessed by feminists who have discovered her to be a radical writer who questioned marriage, sexuality, religion, and middle-class morality. Two studies reflect this reassessment: Margaret Bradstock and Louise Wakeling, *Rattling the Orthodoxies* (1991), and Audrey Tate, *Ada Cambridge* (1991).

KT

Campbell, David Watt (1915–79) returned to a family property near Canberra after serving as a pilot during World War II. Here he divided his time between poetry and farming, the one growing out of the other. His family were long-established settlers, who were comfortable both financially and in their relationship with the land. His circle of Canberra friends included Manning **Clark**. Campbell's verse, which first appeared in 1942 in the ***Bulletin***, was pastoral, lyrical, and distinctively Australian. His two volumes of largely autobiographical short stories, *Evening Under Lamplight* (1959) and *Flame and Shadow* (1976), were republished in 1987 with a foreword by David **Malouf**. Campbell also produced *The History of Australia* (1976) with the painter Keith Looby. *Poetry Australia* published a special edition dedicated to him in December 1981, and Harry Heseltine edited *A Tribute to David Campbell* (1987).

KT

Campbell, Eric (1893–1970) was a NSW solicitor who founded a paramilitary group, the New Guard, in 1931. This grew out of his military background (he served with distinction in World War I) and strong anti-communism. Like other **secret armies**, the New Guard was committed to suppressing disloyalty to the Empire and sharply criticised Jack **Lang's** Labor government. Its most notable exploit was the premature cutting of the ribbon opening the Sydney Harbour Bridge by one of its members, Francis de Groot, ahead of Premier Lang. With Lang's dismissal in 1932, the New Guard declined rapidly. Campbell embraced fascism and subsequently published his account of the New Guard in *The Rallying Point* (1965).

KT

Canadian exiles were political prisoners transported to Australia in 1839 for their involvement in a series of failed uprisings against British rule in Canada. The insurrections were led by William Lyon Mackenzie in Upper Canada (Ontario), and by Louis Joseph Papineau and Wolfred

Nelson in Lower Canada (Quebec). Lieutenant-Governor George **Arthur**, recently arrived from Van Diemen's Land, ensured the rebels were not let off lightly, and a total of 149 men were transported to Van Diemen's Land and NSW. Those from Upper Canada, mainly US citizens, were regarded as 'Yankee sympathisers' and held responsible for inciting insurrection. They were sent to Hobart and dealt a harsher punishment than the rest. Three men managed to escape the island in a fishing boat; others who tried to copy them were sent to Port Arthur. Those from Lower Canada, predominantly French-Canadians, were spared the severity of Norfolk Island due to the intercession of Bishop **Polding**, and instead served time at Longbottom Stockade on the Parramatta Road, Sydney. Many of the French-Canadians received free pardons in 1844, and the majority eventually returned to their homeland. Narratives of the experiences of a number of the exiles have been published, most recently that of François-Maurice Lepailleur (1972). Canadian historians Beverley D. Boissery and F. Murray Greenwood have discussed the incident in *HS* (1978); Boissery has also written *A Deep Sense of Wrong* (1996).

HD

Canberra, the nation's capital, embodies the conviction of its founders that the centre of government should also be a model city, reflecting the ideals of the new nation. But its location, like much else in its history, was determined by expediency as much as idealism. Since neither Sydney nor Melbourne was willing for the other to become the national capital, the founders of the Commonwealth effected a compromise: Melbourne would be the interim capital, but a site for a permanent capital would be selected by the new parliament within NSW, not less than 100 miles from Sydney. In 1902 a Capital Sites Enquiry Board had inspected several potential sites on the southern tablelands, including Yass, Goulburn, Bombala, and Dalgety. The responsible minister, King **O'Malley**, favoured an inland site with a bracing climate—'the sanatorium and nerve centre of Australia'; but, as Roger Pegrum shows in *The Bush Capital* (1983), topographical, climatic, logistic, and aesthetic considerations influenced the parliament's choice in 1909 of a stretch of eucalypt-dotted grassland along the valley of the Molonglo River, in view of the Southern Alps and within striking distance of the Sydney rail.

'I name the capital of Australia Canberra, with the accent on the *Can*', Lady Denman, wife of the governor-general, declared in 1913, confirming the Aboriginal name given to the area since the 1850s and anticipating a new history of national endeavour. Australia was following a path already trodden by the USA, and O'Malley—an American by birth—may have been influenced, in part, by a determination to learn from Washington's mistakes. The new Australian Capital Territory would be 100 times larger than the District of Columbia. By opting for a system of leasehold land tenure, O'Malley, a disciple of the land reformer Henry George, may have sought to avoid the clashes of public and private interests that had bedevilled Washington's early

history. The design of the new capital was decided through an international competition. The entries are reproduced and perceptively reviewed in John Reps, *Canberra 1912* (1997). Walter Burley **Griffin**, a 32-year-old Chicagoan, won from a field of 72. As Peter Harrison shows in *Walter Burley Griffin, Landscape Architect* (1995), Griffin's design skilfully blended elements of L'Enfant's famous plan of Washington, with its symbolic geography of monumental buildings and grand axial vistas, and the naturalistic landscape principles and 'big vision' of the American 'City Beautiful' movement. Peter Proudfoot's *The Secret Plan of Canberra* (1994) suggests, more speculatively, that Griffin's interest in theosophy was also an influence. In Australia, Griffin clashed with his public servant masters and finally resigned in protest against their parsimony and interference in 1921. The 'simple, pleasing and unpretentious buildings' favoured by his successors are exemplified by the temporary Parliament House opened in 1927, when the Commonwealth parliament at last relocated there. The principle of naming suburbs for former prime ministers and federal founders and streets for other national heroes was adopted in 1928. By 1930 a young Keith **Hancock** had already decided that Griffin's plan had failed. 'Canberra is springing up in the familiar Australian way as a kind of suburban garden parcelled into plots by a network of paths that have no obvious beginning and lead to no visible end.' It was 'a garden city in which the garden is more emphasised than the city'.

Depression and war slowed Canberra's development. By 1954 it had reached the 25 000 inhabitants of Griffin's blueprint, yet still looked sparse and unfinished—'a good sheep station spoilt', as one wit remarked. The temporary Parliament House and the National War Memorial (1934–41)—the poles of Griffin's 'land axis'—were the only buildings of any grandeur. Like other parliamentarians, Robert **Menzies** had considered Canberra a cold and comfortless place; yet, as Eric Sparke shows in *Canberra 1954–1980* (1988), long residence in the prime minister's Lodge made him the father of Canberra's postwar renaissance. In 1957 he invited the British planner Sir William Holford to review Griffin's scheme; Holford's prestige and personal influence with Menzies helped revitalise the planning enterprise. An ever-growing Commonwealth public service was gradually relocated from Melbourne, imposing its minute gradations of status and seniority upon suburbs still officially 'mixed' in social composition. By the late 1960s, as population rose towards 100 000, Canberra's planners, inspired by a blend of British Newtown and American Radburn principles, extended new tendrils of bushy automobile suburbs to the north (Belconnen) and south (Woden). The symbolic geography of Griffin's plan slowly became legible. The Australian National University (1949) and the Russell Hill defence complex (1958) established its western and eastern poles, linked via Griffin's 'water axis' when the lake named for him was filled in 1964. On its south shore, the monumental architecture of the National Library (1968), National Gallery (1982), and High Court (1980) adorned a ceremonial precinct completed when the 'new and permanent'

Parliament House designed by Mitchell, Giurgola, and Thorpe crowned Capital Hill in 1988.

Canberra became the most affluent, best-planned and best-educated city in Australia. 'There are no beggars, no street singers, no hoboes or spivs, no soup kitchens ... no slums', Kenneth **Slessor** observed in 1966. It was also the least democratic. From 1957 a benevolent autocracy, the National Capital Development Commission, planned and administered it. Citizens elected an Advisory Council but, as its members complained after a mass resignation in 1969, ministers routinely ignored their advice. Taxpayers subsidised Canberra's pleasant lifestyle through public service salaries and excellent social services (estimated at about $200 per capita above the rest of Australia in 1976), though less than other Australians often believed; the real cost to the nation was in insulating its public service rulers so effectively from the less pleasant places on which their decisions fell. With substantial government subsidies for their roads, schools, and hospitals, some Canberrans preferred tyranny to higher taxes and rejected a referendum for self-government in 1976. The **Hawke** government at last forced Canberra to be free and fiscally more self-reliant in 1987. Labor, traditionally the party of big government, held power locally until 1995, when **Keating's** public service cuts began to bite.

In the 1990s harder times created a new Canberra, more compact, more privatised, less antiseptically tidy than the old. Neo-Federation villas and neo-Georgian townhouses now squat cheek by jowl in brand-new suburbs that look more 'city' than 'garden'. The proliferation of shopping malls and restaurants has broken down the old pattern of planned neighbourhoods centred on primary schools and shopping centres. When Prime Minister **Howard** forsook the Lodge for Kirribilli House in Sydney, and further reduced the size of the public service, Canberrans knew that their easy days were over. Now numbering over 300 000, Canberra is Australia's most populous inland city. With a casino, national Rugby League Club, soaring divorce rate, flourishing mail-order pornography industry—even hoboes and a soup kitchen—it has lost the innocence of the 'bush capital' without quite becoming urbane. There are grandmothers who have lived there all their lives; yet locals still ask 'Where do you come from?', expecting the answer to be 'Sydney' or 'Melbourne'. No other Australian city is visited more religiously, admired more grudgingly, or reviled more unreasonably. Once a symbol of national ideals, it is also, for some, a symbol of national disenchantment.

GRAEME DAVISON

Canberra Times, a **newspaper**, was established by the Shakespeare family in 1926 and acquired by John **Fairfax** and Sons in 1964, when under the editorship of J. D. Pringle. It expanded its coverage and drove Rupert Murdoch's new *Australian* to Sydney in 1967. It passed at the end of the 1980s to Kerry Packer, who sold it to Kerry Stokes, who in turn sold it in 1998 to the Rural Press, Ltd. It reports local events in the national capital, and developments in politics

and the public service, but has wielded significant influence beyond the scope of a regional newspaper.

HD

Cannon, Michael Montague (1929–), journalist and historian, won acclaim for his first published work, *The Land Boomers* (1966), a trenchant account of the improprieties behind Melbourne's boom and bust in the 1880s. After working as deputy-director of Melbourne University Press (1966–69), Cannon went on to publish prolifically in Australian and Victorian history. His books present a populist view of themes of Australian history which appeals to the general reader. His three volumes—*Who's Master? Who's Man?* (1971), *Life in the Country* (1973), and *Life in the Cities* (1975), republished as *The Roaring Days* in 1998—made a significant contribution to nineteenth-century Australian **social history**; subsequent works, however, had a limited academic impact. Several works, such as *Who Killed the Koories?* (1990), were criticised for their anecdotal style and lack of critical assessment, and his editorship of seven volumes of Victoria's early official records, *Historical Records of Victoria* (1981–91), which cover the period 1836–39, was clouded in debate over the editorial practices. Later works, which include *Old Melbourne Town* (1991), *Melbourne After the Gold Rush* (1993), and *The Human Face of the Great Depression* (1996), are lavish and comprehensive, and continue his documentation of Victorian history. Cannon's journalistic background inspired the publication of a biography of John **Norton** (*That Damned Democrat*, 1981) and the memoirs of his grandfather, Monty Grover (*Hold Page One*, 1993).

HD

Cape Grim massacre, which involved the murder of at least 30 Aborigines, took place in the north-western corner of Tasmania in 1827 on pastoral land leased by the Van Diemen's Land Co. Two years after the incident, a shepherd from the area informed G.A. **Robinson** of a **massacre**. Local Aborigines told Robinson that the victims were pushed by shepherds from a steep rocky cliff, later named Suicide Cove, where they fell and perished. They believed this had been brought on as a result of Aborigines' attacking sheep owned by the Van Diemen's Land Co., but claimed that the wrong group of Aborigines had in fact been punished. While Robinson was eager to avenge the deaths of those murdered, the company's agent, Edward Curr (father of E.M. **Curr**), dismissed the story as highly exaggerated and no official investigation was undertaken. In attempting to ascertain the details of the incident while undertaking research for her *Community of Thieves* (1992), Cassandra Pybus met with opposition from the pastoral company, which continues to deny that the massacre ever took place.

HD

Capital punishment, as administered under the criminal law in Australia, has taken only one form—hanging. From the founding of Botany Bay to 1967, the punishment was administered as the ultimate penalty of the law, in great frequency during the convict era but much less so later. In spite of its declining use and now formal abolition, public opinion continues to be divided over the death penalty, with frequent calls for its reintroduction as a response to violent crimes.

During the convict era some hundreds were hanged for a range of crimes that still included offences against property which, by the later decades, no longer bore the death penalty in Britain. Capital punishment was used as a crude method of control of the large convict population. Hangings were public affairs and sometimes, as at Pinchgut Island in Sydney Harbour, the bodies were gibbeted—left on the noose after death as a sign of the consequences of crime. The most intense use of the death penalty occurred in Tasmania under Governor **Arthur**; more than 100 hangings took place over two years, 1826 and 1827, as Arthur sought to control the activities of escaped convicts who had become bushrangers (R.P. Davis, *The Tasmanian Gallows*, 1974). Sometimes the punishment aroused strong public feeling in sympathy with the condemned—large and sympathetic crowds attended the hanging of Matthew **Brady** in Hobart in 1826, as they would gather outside the Melbourne Gaol on the day Ned **Kelly** was hanged in 1880.

From the 1850s most colonies abandoned public hangings, and instead conducted them in gaols before invited witnesses, including the press. An exception was occasional exemplary public hangings of Aborigines, disproportionate numbers of whom suffered the death penalty in several colonies in the nineteenth century. Later, in 1958–59, controversy over the conviction in SA and death sentence passed on an Aboriginal man, Rupert Max Stuart, contributed to the growing success of the campaign against capital punishment (K.S. **Inglis**, *The Stuart Case*, 1961). In Victoria, the unsuccessful campaign to stop the 1967 execution of Ronald Ryan, following his conviction for the murder of a prison warder in an escape attempt, attracted such sustained public attention throughout Australia that no further executions have taken place. These cases reverberate still, being the subject of drama, such as Barry Dickins, *Remember Ronald Ryan* (1994), and a television documentary.

Most of those hanged were men, but the hanging of women, especially of those convicted of infanticide, usually incited major debate on justice and the merits of the death penalty (Michael **Cannon**, *The Woman as Murderer*, 1994). The role of the Executive Council in making the final decision on execution of the death sentence enabled public opinion and political calculation to influence this punishment to a marked degree (Carolyn Strange, ed., *Qualities of Mercy*, 1996). In particular cases, the government, governor, and judiciary all found themselves at the centre of fierce debate over the merits of hanging—such as that of Jenny Lee in 1951, the last woman executed in Victoria, or much earlier, in the sentencing to death of a number of youths in the **Mount Rennie rape** in Sydney in 1887.

The abolition of capital punishment was frequently urged in colonial politics and after. Opponents of the death penalty cited lack of evidence of its deterrent value, the danger of executing an innocent person following a wrong conviction, and the civilising tendencies of the modern age. As the number of executions declined, the intensity of the debate around each new case increased; those favouring retention insisted that rare executions sustained the message that crime would not pay. Qld was the first state to enact an abolition statute, in 1922, implementing Labor Party policy and enabled politically by the almost simultaneous abolition of the conservative Legislative Council. Frequent attempts at abolition in other states were unsuccessful until 1968 in Tasmania, after which the other states followed suit over the succeeding years. In NSW—the state where the first hanging had taken place in May 1788—no hanging took place after 1939; but it was the last to enact comprehensive abolition—in 1985. (See also **Crime and punishment**.)

MARK FINNANE

Captivity narratives refer to accounts of Europeans detained by, or residing with, non-European peoples. By the eighteenth century, the captivity (and survival) genre was commonly associated with the kidnapping of white settlers by indigenous peoples as a tactic of warfare in North America. In the nineteenth century, increasingly romantic and formulaic texts of actual and fictional white 'captivity' in various colonial locales were widely published throughout the English-speaking world, including the Australian colonies. Told from a European perspective, these articulated imperial ideologies of white racial and cultural superiority over non-white peoples. When the 'captive' was female, such narratives expressed settler anxieties about cross-racial sexual relations and miscegenation.

The attitudes of Australian settlers towards whites who lived with Aborigines were influenced by the histories of cross-racial intimacy in other colonial situations, especially in North America. Much of the racially and sexually charged imagery evoked in Australian captivity literature echoes that used in contemporary American texts. But the material circumstances and dynamics of race relations on successive Australian frontiers were vastly different from North America. Aboriginal resistance to colonisation aimed to drive Europeans away rather than take them hostage. Indigenous peoples acted as the saviours of runaway convicts, bushrangers, explorers, and castaways. The only forcible abductions in Australia were those of Aborigines by whites. Aboriginal men, women, and children were 'taken' by settlers as guides, interpreters, labourers, domestic servants, and sexual partners in colonial Australia. Government policies sanctioned the forced removal of Aboriginal children from their own society—up to the **Stolen Generations** of the twentieth century.

The majority of white 'captivity' cases recorded in Australia involve castaways. In the early colonial period, expeditions were frequently despatched to locate survivors of **shipwrecks** in Australian and Pacific waters. If a white woman was believed to have survived, the rescue was launched with additional zeal and received considerable publicity. When the *Stirling Castle* was wrecked off the

Queensland coast in 1836, an expedition from Moreton Bay eventually rescued the captain's wife, Eliza **Fraser**, and a handful of male crew members. Kay Schaffer, *In the Wake of First Contact* (1995), examines the representations of Fraser's plight.

The lesser-known Barbara Thompson was marooned off Cape York in 1844. She lived with the Kaurareg of Muralag (Prince of Wales) Island, who treated her with kindness until her 'rescue' by the survey vessel *Rattlesnake* in 1849. The *Rattlesnake's* official artist, Oswald Brierly, recorded Thompson's observations of Kaurareg culture, as reproduced in David R. Moore, *Islanders and Aborigines at Cape York* (1979).

Colonial governments recognised the value of 'captives' as cross-cultural intermediaries. The escaped convict William **Buckley**, for example, survived with the aid of Aborigines in the Port Phillip District from 1803 to 1835. Re-entering settler society, the **'wild white man'** was pardoned, and pressed into service as a government interpreter. Sailor James Morrill (Murrills) (1824–65), shipwrecked off the Great Barrier Reef in 1846, lived with Aborigines near Mount Elliott for 17 years. His knowledge of indigenous language and culture was used by settlers in their dealings with Aborigines.

During periods of intense frontier conflict, rumours that Aborigines held white captives often circulated. In the Gippsland region of Victoria in the 1840s, 'sightings' of a white woman with Aborigines stirred residents of Port Phillip to hold public meetings and fund expeditions. Gippsland settlers joined the search, and carried out massacres of local Aborigines, as examined by Don Watson in *Caledonia Australis* (1984), and Julie Carr in *The Captive White Woman* (2001). Although no such woman was located, this incident illustrates the potency of the racialised and sexualised dimensions of captivity narratives.

Hysteria about white women 'captives' endured into the twentieth century. Rumours that Aborigines had detained two white female survivors of the *Douglas Mawson*, wrecked in the Gulf of Carpentaria in 1923, resulted in official searches. A 'scientific' film, *Blonde Captive*, which concluded with a scene of a white woman living with Aborigines in WA (later proved a hoax), created a minor scandal in the early 1930s. Popular histories and journalistic accounts of frontier life regularly featured captivity tales. Ion **Idriess**, for example, retold Barbara Thompson's story in *Isles of Despair* (1947), while Charles Barrett's *White Blackfellows* (1948) strung together a series of captivity and castaway incidents. Fictional treatments of 'captivity' episodes include Patrick **White's** *A Fringe of Leaves* (1976) and David **Malouf's** *Remembering Babylon* (1993). More recently, captivity narratives have attracted a renewed attention from historians drawing upon post-colonial perspectives.

The Australian **prisoner-of-war** experience of World War I, and in particular **World War II**, generated a related strand of writing on captivity and survival. Like the traditional frontier tales, these memoirs drew upon popular racial myths of white superiority to describe the barbarity of Turkish (World War I) and Japanese (World War II) captors. Betty Jeffrey's *White Coolies* (1954) provides a good example of the perpetuation of gender, race, and sexual stereotypes in such writing.

KATE DARIAN-SMITH

Carboni, Raffaello (1817–75) arrived on the Ballarat goldfields in 1853 after a turbulent youth in Italy. He was caught up in the miners' grievances and joined the rebels in the **Eureka Stockade**. Although outside the stockade during the battle, Carboni was charged with treason. Following his acquittal, he wrote an account of the revolt, *The Eureka Stockade* (1855), which he sold at the Eureka site on the first anniversary of the battle. This was reprinted in 1942 and is regarded as a reliable, if melodramatic, account of the incident and its underlying causes. After his return to Italy, Carboni wrote a long allegorical poem, *Gilburnia*, based on his Ballarat experiences. He is the colourful subject of John Romeril's 1980 play, *Carboni*, and he also features in other Eureka literature, including Louis **Esson's** play, *The Southern Cross* (1946). Desmond O'Grady produced a biography, *Raffaello, Raffaello*, in 1985.

KT

Carey, Peter Philip (1943–   ), writer and erstwhile advertising man, now resident in the USA, averred that 'What you end up wanting to talk about is Australian history.' In several novels that is what he has done, although in playful and unexpected ways. *Illywhacker* (1985) traversed Australia's past from 1861 to the present of its 139-year-old narrator, Herbert Badgery, who turned on the national history the sceptical eye of one unconvinced of sagas of progress. *Oscar and Lucinda* (1988), for which Carey won the Booker Prize, related a strange passage from England to Australia and the frontier world there encountered by the title characters. It was also, perhaps, a parody of the journey into the wilderness in Patrick **White's** *Voss* (1957). In *The Unusual Life of Tristan Smith* (1994), Carey complexly examined post-colonial relations through the dominance of Efica by Voorstand. Efican houses designed by the renowned Belinda Burastin are 'light as thoughts, prayers, wishes that history had been otherwise'. Eficans have (like Australians?) 'the hunger of the historically dispossessed or transplanted for what they feel is the real world'. *Jack Maggs* (1997) reimagined not only Charles Dickens's *Great Expectations* (1860) and its setting in Victorian England, but notions of Australia among Britons to whom it seemed so remote and improbable a destination. Yet this place and its history is 'the real world' to which Carey's fiction returns and renews, as in his *True History of the Kelly Gang* (2000).

PETER PIERCE

Carr, Thomas Joseph (1839–1917), Irish-born Catholic archbishop, was appointed bishop of Galway in 1883 and came to Victoria as archbishop of Melbourne in 1886. He was conservative and, although mindful of appeasing the Irish view, was concerned to build a respectable and pious **Catholic** community that would integrate with the increasingly secular Australian society. In seeking priests who would fit this mould, he generally favoured the Australian-born, who had trained at Manly, over the Irish, many of whom he regarded as insufficiently 'cultured' for colonial Catholic society. Establishing a Catholic education system was his chief concern, crowned by the foundation of Newman College at the University of Melbourne in 1916. He oversaw a vast building program in Victoria, which included the completion of St Patrick's Cathedral. Carr became increasingly political with age, particularly after **Moran's** death in 1911. He remained aloof from the Labor Party while it continued to advocate secular education and, with his successor Daniel **Mannix**, refused to appease Archbishop Kelly of Sydney by signing a condemnation of the 1916 Easter Rising in Dublin. A collection of Carr's essays, *Lectures and Replies*, was published in 1907; and a biography, by T.P. Boland, appeared in 1997.

HD

Casey family spans Australian history from the convict era to the closing years of the British Empire. CORNELIUS GAVIN CASEY (1810–96) came to Tasmania from England in 1833 and served as surgeon at the penal settlement of **Port Arthur**. His success as an investor was surpassed by his son, RICHARD GARDINER (1846–1919), who worked as a jackeroo in Victoria, managed pastoral properties in NSW, and established still larger pastoral enterprises in Qld. Mining investments as well as his successful reconstruction of the **Goldsbrough** Mort pastoral company created a substantial fortune. His two elder sons, RICHARD GARDINER (1890–1976) and DERMOT (1897–1977), were educated in Melbourne and England. Both men served in World War I and both were awarded the Military Cross. Dermot Casey became an archaeologist, and was a founder of the Institute of Aboriginal and Torres Strait Islander Studies.

During the 1920s Richard Casey served as liaison officer for the Australian prime minister S.M. **Bruce** in London. He returned to Australia in 1931 to enter politics, was immediately elected to the Commonwealth parliament, and by 1935 was federal treasurer. Shyness, impatience with politics and a patrician style ultimately frustrated his ambitions. Bested by R.G. **Menzies** in the struggle for party leadership in 1939, he served briefly as Australian representative to the USA, then as British minister of state in the Middle East, and finally as governor of Bengal. His postwar re-entry into Australian politics again saw him lose to Menzies. As minister for external affairs 1951–60, he was a devout Cold Warrior and oversaw the transfer of dependence from the UK to the USA. He retired from parliament with a life peerage, and subsequently served as governor-general 1965–69. Casey published extensively and *Australian Father and Son* (1966) records the family history. His wife MAIE, née Ryan (1892–1983), from a prominent Victorian family, shared his dynastic pride and her *An Australian Story* (1962) covers four generations of Ryans. Among other literary works, she also edited *Early Melbourne Architecture* (1953). There is a biography of Richard Casey by W.J. Hudson (1986) and one of Maie by Diane Langmore (1997).

SM

Cash, Martin (1808–77) was transported from Ireland to NSW in 1827. Suspected of cattle-duffing, he fled to Van Diemen's Land in 1837, after receiving his ticket-of-leave. Two years later he was sentenced to imprisonment at **Port Arthur** for theft. He escaped and became leader of a successful **bushranging** gang. Once captured, he was sentenced to life imprisonment on **Norfolk Island**, but he was pardoned in 1856 as a reformed character. On his return to Tasmania, he was received warmly as a colourful identity. His purported biography, *The Adventures of Martin Cash* (1870), was probably written by its editor, James Lee Burke. It was the source for the escape from Port Arthur in Marcus **Clarke's** *His Natural Life* (1874). Frank **Clune** told his story in *Martin Cash* (1955).

KT

Castaways, see **Captivity narratives**

Castle Hill Rising was an armed uprising in 1804 at Castle Hill, north of Parramatta, NSW, that was inspired by the 1798 rebellion by United Irishmen at Vinegar Hill in Wexford, Ireland. Also known as 'Australia's battle of Vinegar Hill', the insurrection was later regarded as a precedent for **Eureka**. Adopting the 1798 battle cry 'Death or Liberty!', a group of mainly Irish convicts rose up against the authorities at Castle Hill government farm on 5 March 1804. The Irish resented their imprisonment at the hands of the British and the unjust treatment of convicts, and—according to one account—demanded 'a ship to take us Home'. Armed with guns and hand-made pikes and pitchforks, they planned to march on Sydney. However, an informer warned John **Macarthur**, who alerted the military. Governor **King** proclaimed martial law and the rising was suppressed. Of the insurgents, 24 were killed and some 300 arrested. The leaders were sentenced to death and the others to savage punishment. An account of the rising is provided by Bob Connell in *MHJ* (1963) and Lynette Ramsay Silver in *The Battle of Vinegar Hill: Australia's Irish Rebellion 1804* (1989).

HD

Catchpole, Margaret (1762–1819) was transported to NSW in 1801 after having been twice sentenced to death in England—first for horse-stealing and then for a daring escape from gaol. A diligent, capable worker, she became a valued member of the Richmond community. After her pardon in 1814 she worked as a midwife and ran a small store. Her letters home, held in the Mitchell Library, Sydney, give a graphic account of the contemporary life of the colony. They were used in an altered form by Richard Cobbold in his romanticised work, *The History of Margaret Catchpole* (1845).

KT

Catholic Church is the denomination of Western Christianity in communion with the Pope that traces its faith in Jesus Christ to the community formed around the apostles. Since the European Reformation of the sixteenth century, it has commonly been referred to as the Roman Catholic Church, as if defined by papal allegiance, but for Catholics themselves the adjective *Roman* was a disparaging qualifier of the church's claim to unique status as 'the one true faith'.

The Catholic Church in Australia has drawn its influences most strongly from Ireland, which in turn drew on French Catholicism, including a narrowly Jansenist strand of morality, and looked to the authority of Rome. The possibility of establishing a Catholic presence in Australia was first raised in 1630 by Cristoforo Borri, an Italian Jesuit missionary in India, and in 1681 the Roman Congregation for Evangelisation of Nations appointed the Italian Dominican, Victorio Riccio, to lead a missionary effort from the Spanish Philippines. Riccio died before plans could be acted on; a century later, when the British claimed eastern Australia and established a penal colony in NSW, there was no official recognition of Catholicism. Nevertheless about 10 per cent of the early convicts were Catholics, and a network formed among **emancipists** to pray the rosary and maintain other devotional practices. In 1798 three priests, James Dixon, James Harold, and Peter O'Neil, were transported among prisoners from the Irish rebellion. Dixon was conditionally pardoned in 1803; he worked as a chaplain with a government salary until he came under suspicion of promoting sedition in 1804. By 1810 all three had left the colony, and the Catholic community was petitioning Rome for a chaplain. A firebrand Cistercian, Jeremiah Flynn, was appointed. He lobbied the government of NSW for recognition of his status; when that was refused, he travelled to Sydney anyway. He arrived in 1817 and worked clandestinely until he was deported in 1818.

Following recommendations of the **Bigge** Commission, Australian Catholicism gained government recognition in 1820 (before Catholic emancipation in Britain). Two Catholic chaplains, John Joseph Therry and Philip Connolly, were appointed, and representation in Rome followed the foundation of an Australian hierarchy in 1833, led by English (not Irish) Benedictines, Bishop John Bede **Polding** and his Vicar-General, William Ullathorne. Polding hoped initially that Australian Catholicism would be shaped above all by Benedictine monasticism, but his vision faded before missionary realities of a scattered population and the absence of recruits. A diocesan structure filled by Irish bishops emerged with the creation of separate sees in Sydney, Hobart Town, and Adelaide in 1842, Perth in 1845, Melbourne, Port Victoria, and Maitland in 1847; these missionary dioceses were later divided further so that by 1995, when the Catholic Church formed the largest religious grouping in Australia with 24.1 per cent of the population, there were 26 Australian dioceses.

Nineteenth-century Catholicism was marked by the expansion of the number and scope of religious congregations, and early Australian bishops recruited vowed men and women to Australia from many parts of Europe (but particularly Ireland) to work in teaching, nursing, missions to Aboriginal groups, and social reform movements. Education, and especially simple catechesis for children, was the major priority of religious congregations and the church in general. The single comprehensive history remains Ronald Fogarty, *Catholic Education in Australia 1806–1950* (1959), although conflict over state aid to church schools in 1840–70 and again in the 1960s has concerned general historians of both centuries as a key instance of **sectarianism**, also reviewed by Michael Hogan, *The Sectarian Strand* (1987).

The Catholic Church in Australia has also been affected in its style and preoccupation by the two councils of the church held since 1788. The First Vatican Council (1870) defined papal infallibility, and was characterised by a profound distrust of the modernising European world. Catholicism in Australia was sharply divided from Protestantism and **liberalism**, and devotional practice was marked by increasingly anti-modernist Marian piety. John Molony, *The Roman Mould of the Australian Catholic Church* (1969), shows that Rome was the organisational centre; even the move to encourage specific Australian **nationalism** to circumvent British questioning of **Irish** Catholic loyalty to the Empire was made by bishops, notably Sydney's Cardinal **Moran**, who looked first to Rome. The Irish tradition of local bishops exercising local power has been seen rarely in Australia, and most clearly in the controversial episcopate of Melbourne's Daniel **Mannix**.

In the twentieth century **communism** replaced liberalism as the outside threat, against which Catholicism was to be a spiritual fortress. Ordinary Catholics, carried into the middle class by secondary schools, also emerged as a political force. European writing of the 1920s on 'Catholic Action' was first translated into English in *Restoring All Things* (1939), co-edited by Australian author Paul McGuire. In Australia the self-confident move to redeem the world became increasingly focused on defeating communism and its sympathisers. The ensuing campaign is narrated by Tom Truman, *Catholic Action and Politics* (1959), David Shinnick, *Journey into Justice* (1982), Gerard Henderson, *Mr Santamaria and the Bishops* (1982), and Bruce Duncan, *Crusade or Conspiracy?* (2001).

The competing strands of Catholic spirituality are examined in Katharine Massam, *Sacred Threads* (1996). On the one hand there was emphasis on the next life, and on the other concerns to take Catholic values to the public sphere; a simultaneous fear of this world and a desire to embrace it were woven through the deliberations of the Second Vatican Council (1962–66). This council affirmed episcopal 'collegiality', in contrast to the nineteenth-century vision of papal 'monarchy', and self-consciously opened the windows of the church to an ecumenical, theologically plural, and even secular, world. The most obvious outcome in Australia as elsewhere was a shift from Latin to the vernacular in the liturgy, but changes in authority were even more profound. The means of implementing collegial governance had not been defined, and the implications of Vatican II were hotly debated, while the 1968 encyclical *Humanae Vitae* rejecting artificial contraception ended an era of near-unanimous acceptance of papal authority by unquestioning priests and people.

Changes in historical writing reflect the conciliar changes. As awareness of competing traditions within Catholicism has increased, so historical work has moved from an institutional focus towards accounts of hidden voices. This trend also reflects the international movement of **religious history** towards questions of faith and belief. The strong tradition of clerical biography has expanded to include women members of religious orders, collective biography of religious foundations, and work both promoting and prompted by the beatification of Mary **MacKillop**; diocesan and parish histories, often structured around bishops and priests as key decision-makers, increasingly pay attention to a network of interests in church life. A popular genre of personal reminiscence has emphasised the particularity of Catholic experience against monolithic assumptions. Work on women's groups by Sally Kennedy, *Faith and Feminism* (1985), and Hilary M. Carey, *Truly Feminine, Truly Catholic* (1987), has shown the complexity of lay negotiations with the hierarchy and the diversity of Catholic orthodoxy. As migrant experience has moved into focus, Frank Lewins, *The Myth of the Universal Church* (1978), and Adrian Pittarello, *Soup Without Salt* (1980), have extended the non-Irish experience of church, and Patrick **O'Farrell** has explored the particularities of **Irish** culture imported to Australia.

In mainstream Australian historical writing a preoccupation with public and political life has worked to sideline discussion of **religion**, and especially the dynamics of faith and belief, except for instances when religion has explicitly intersected with the public domain. Thus, with the exception of C.M.H. **Clark's** *History of Australia* (1962–87), where Catholicism is a thematic foil for men of the Enlightenment and progress, Australian Catholicism has been explored in general history through a relatively small number of episodes. The limited treatment in general histories and the experience of Catholicism as outside mainstream assumptions of Australia first prompted compensatory Catholic histories that edged towards a separate historiography, as in Eris **O'Brien**, *The Foundation of Australia 1786–1800* (1937), James Murtagh, *Australia: The Catholic Chapter* (1946), and history textbooks for schools such as Agatha Le Breton, *The Story of Australia* (1913), and David Gabriel Purton, *The Story of the Church* (1934). Three writers have worked on the broad canvas of Catholicism as an institution in Australia, significantly all from a base in the Sydney records. Patrick O'Farrell, *The Catholic Church and Community* was first published as *The Catholic Church in Australia: A Short History* in 1968, and revised in 1977, 1985, and 1992; it established historical touchstones for the church and made key themes accessible to a wider readership, tracing the emergence of an Australian-Irish identity and a Catholicism somewhat at odds with the state. Edmund Campion added more consciously cultural history with *Rockchoppers: Growing Up Catholic in Australia* (1982) and *Australian Catholics* (1987); Naomi Turner worked extensively with oral sources in *Catholics in Australia: A Social History* (1992), and *Ways of Belonging: Stories of Australian Catholics 1910–90* (1993). The separate development of Australian Catholic historiography was first reviewed in 1958 by K.S. **Inglis** in *HSANZ*, and subsequently as part of four general reviews of Australian religious historiography in the *Journal of Religious History*: by

O'Farrell in 1976, by J.D. Bollen et al. in 1980, by Alan Gilbert in 1988, and by H.M. Carey et al. in 2001.

KATHARINE MASSAM

Cattle arrived with the First Fleet, and immediately proved their adaptability to Australian conditions by straying over 70 kilometres to the productive Cowpastures land by the Nepean River, to be rediscovered, flourishing and multiplying, seven years later. Their adaptability, toughness, and mobility have given cattle, with **horses**, a near-universal role in support of pioneer settlement, and also, unlike horses, in the ongoing **pastoral** utilisation of all suitable lands not required for 'higher' uses.

Cattle have been appropriately described as self-propelling, self-fuelling, self-reproducing four-legged machines for converting forage into proteins and energy in the form of meat, hides, milk, and other products; they have always offered the near-instant promise of a basic subsistence and a livelihood, even in harsh, relatively unproductive and remote environments. They adapted to lands too hot or too cold, too humid or too arid, too swampy or too rugged or 'vermin'-infested for sheep. Where sheep enterprises failed under the attacks of dingoes, or diseases, or the seeds of spear grasses, which quickly displaced kangaroo grasses under grazing pressure, landholders had no choice but to switch to cattle. Cattle-grazing continues to be the only recognised means for the broadacre utilisation of vast areas of modest to low potential.

On more favoured pastoral lands, however, cattle were readily displaced by sheep, because of their inability to produce a high-value, durable product, such as wool, capable of bearing costly and slow transport, storage, and tranship-ment to distant overseas markets. Thus the supply–demand equation has worked persistently against cattle. Availability of cheap pastoral lands and other low-cost inputs, coupled with very poor access to markets, has ensured an endemic problem of oversupply, with short-lived booms followed by prolonged depressions. Booms were associated with the opening of new markets. During the gold rushes, rapid population growth triggered a succession of localised booms and stimulated the practice of driving mobs to distant but briefly lucrative markets. With the introduction in 1880 of refrigeration, which gave beef access to overseas markets, the cattle industry was placed on a more secure footing, though price instability continues to be a severe structural problem.

In this context, cost minimisation, linked to an emphasis on quantity rather than quality, became the hallmark of successful cattle enterprises, a point emphasised by Rolf **Boldrewood** in *Australian Grazier's Guide* (1879, edited by J.S. Ryan 1994). Cattlemen became the archetypal **pioneers** in an unprecedented land rush of continental dimensions. They experienced success and failure on a grand scale, as eloquently portrayed in family histories, notably Mary **Durack's** *Kings in Grass Castles* (1959) and Judith **Wright's** *The Generations of Men* (1959).

In the late nineteenth century, instability and flux in the cattle industry, coupled with droughts and depressions, enabled opportunistic but purposeful growth of cattle empires, most notably that of Sidney **Kidman**. Large-scale purchases of low-cost land and cattle, during hard times, enabled Kidman to acquire chains of cattle stations in pursuit of a strategy of locational diversification. The pace of transfer of his cattle, generally southwards towards fattening pastures and markets, was readily adjusted in response to local seasonal conditions and prices.

In Australia's more remote regions, large company-owned cattle stations, sometimes grouped in chains, still exist as an effective adaptation to the burdens of remote location and lack of regional infrastructure, as well as in pursuit of locational diversification. These working stations, embracing areas as large as 16 000 square kilometres, with up to 60 000 cattle and 40 workers in the mustering season, still fit the image of the pioneering station, with names such as Anna Creek, Bulloo Downs, Carandotta, Alexandria, Brunette Downs, Victoria River Downs, and Wave Hill achieving legendary status.

During much of Australia's history, cattle have been of critical importance as 'prime movers' of overland freight, while also moving themselves on the hoof to markets. Primitive roads were traversed by bullockies and stock-routes by drovers, on journeys requiring weeks or even months. While bullock teams were displaced by rail and road early in the twentieth century, long-distance **droving** along certain inland stock-routes remained economically viable until late this century, when they were displaced by road trains.

The cattle industry continues to adapt to changes in technology and markets, becoming more competitive in favoured lands through pasture improvement, enhanced breeding, and intensive feed-lotting, while remote northern areas increasingly rely on exports of live young cattle to Asian markets.

JOHN HOLMES

Caucus originally signified a meeting of the parliamentary members of a political **faction** or party. It was given formal status in the rules of the **Australian Labor Party**, which bound all parliamentary members to vote as the caucus determined and provided for caucus election of ministers and shadow ministers. The caucus of the ALP thus exercised a stronger control over the parliamentary leadership than was the case in non-Labor parties, and overturned Cabinet decisions on such policies as **conscription** in World War I and economic policy in the **Depression** government of James **Scullin**; the latter episode forms the subject of Warren Denning's *Caucus Crisis* (1937). Its power was tempered by electoral exigency and weakened by the emergence of factions in the ALP, which now effectively determine the outcome of caucus meetings.

SM

Cawley, Evonne Fay (née Goolagong) (1951–), **tennis** player, was acclaimed a heroine and named Australian of the Year in 1971 when, aged 19, she won Wimbledon, after winning the French Open the previous year. Her small-town background and Aboriginality were emphasised by the media, which tended to represent her as a 'natural genius'; when her playing faltered, she was described as having 'gone walkabout'. After her marriage, she took her husband's name and retired from competition to have children. She returned to win Wimbledon again in 1980 and then made her home in the USA, coaching. In the early 1990s she returned to live in Australia and began to explore her Aboriginal background, something that Aboriginal activists had criticised her for not doing during her playing days. This culminated in an autobiography, *Home!* (with Phil Jarratt, 1993), written under a blend of her married name and her reclaimed surname.

KT

Cazaly, Roy (1893–1963) was an **Australian Rules** footballer well known for his spectacular high marking in the 1920s. A South Melbourne team-mate's call of 'Up there, Cazaly!' was adopted by the crowd and entered the Australian idiom as a rallying cry. It was reportedly used by soldiers in North Africa in World War II, and appears in Ray **Lawler's** *Summer of the Seventeenth Doll* (1955). In 1979 a promotional song by Mike Brady revived the phrase. Cazaly's high-flying also provided inspiration for some of Noel Counihan's paintings, one of which is reproduced on the cover of Leonie Sandercock and Ian **Turner's** *Up Where, Cazaly?* (1981).

KT

Cemeteries were based initially on village burial grounds in England, often small, overcrowded, and badly planned. Examples in NSW and Tasmania reflect this style, such as that alongside Francis **Greenway's** St Matthew's Church at Windsor, NSW. From the 1830s onwards, influenced by English architect J.C. Loudon and the garden cemetery movement, cemeteries were planned as orderly public reserves, satisfying the dual purposes of improved hygiene and moral standards, and according to a pleasing design. The layouts of Victorian cemeteries were influenced by Albert Purchas's design for the Melbourne General Cemetery (1852). They comprised an orderly arrangement of burial plots, often with the four major denominations, **Catholic**, Church of England (**Anglican**), **Presbyterian**, and **Methodist**, represented by four quadrants, and minor denominations contained in smaller compartments. Cemeteries became highly designed landscapes, replete with curved pathways, lawns, avenues, and specimen trees, subdued floral borders, and often adorned with fountains and Gothic-style shelters and chapels. The wealthy erected elaborate monuments and fenced graves from the mid-nineteenth century onwards. Possibly the most spectacular cemetery is Waverley Cemetery near Sydney, laid out on a cliff overlooking the Pacific Ocean. Increased interest in **genealogy** and **heritage** has led to greater availability of cemetery records for research and the listing of notable cemeteries on heritage registers. Useful sources are the **National Trust** of Australia (Victoria), *Cemeteries: Our Heritage* (1992) and, for SA, Robert Nicol, *At the End of the Road* (1994).

HD

Censorship was first exercised by colonial governors. Using the English common law and legislative control of printing presses, they suppressed conduct, speech, and publications which threatened public order and public decency.

As the self-governing colonies achieved political stability, concern with public order gave way to strict Victorian conceptions of morality. The colonies absorbed and put into legislative form the common law test of obscenity formulated in *R v Hicklin* (1868) under which material having a tendency to deprave and corrupt was suppressed. Thereafter, colonial censors turned their attention more closely to stamping out obscene literature. Peter Coleman, in *Obscenity, Blasphemy, Sedition* (1963), examines the seizures of and bans on works of, for example, Boccaccio, Zola, Rabelais, de Maupassant, and Balzac. Alison Carroll shows in *Moral Censorship and the Visual Arts in Australia* (1989) that these forms were subjected to similar strict moral scrutiny, and theatre was also subject to censorship. Victorian prudery and religious dogma accounted for the prosecution of purveyors of information about birth control.

On the outbreak of World War I, national censorship controls were introduced to safeguard national security. The Bolshevik Revolution and the emergence of the **Communist** Party of Australia ushered in a new age of political surveillance and censorship, examined by Frank Cain, *The Origins of Political Surveillance in Australia* (1983). In 1920, the Commonwealth parliament passed amendments to the Crimes Act 1914 and used it during the 1920s and 1930s to stop the flow of communist and fascist literature into Australia.

Federation created a dual censorship system under which the Commonwealth controlled imports of printed material and cinematographic films. Initially, the Commonwealth was sparing in its import controls. However, in 1929 it banned James Joyce's *Ulysses* (1922). Thereafter, a more vigorous regime denied Australians the right to read works by contemporary writers, including Aldous Huxley, Radclyffe Hall, George Orwell, Frank Harris, John Dos Passos, and Ernest Hemingway. Concerns about the corruption of Australian youth led to the imposition of a ban in 1938 (lifted in 1960) on the importation of American comics. Ina Bertrand considers *Film Censorship in Australia* (1978).

Brian Penton, in *Censored!* (1947), describes the confrontation between the Commonwealth and the newspapers which resulted from the rigid system of wartime censorship imposed by the National Security Act 1939. Fear of communism revived with the onset of the Cold War and brought severe restrictions on dissident left-wing speech, most notably in the sedition prosecution and imprisonment of the Communist Party general secretary, L.L. **Sharkey**, in 1949 for pro-Soviet statements. The campaign to extirpate communism peaked with the Communist Party Dissolution Act 1950, which was declared unconstitutional by the **High Court of Australia** in 1951. The **Menzies** government also introduced the D-notice, a press self-censorship system whereby newspaper editors refrained from publishing stories on prohibited subjects. The existence of this system was not publicly disclosed until 1967.

After World War II, the moral crusade continued. Its harshest manifestation was the obscenity prosecution and imprisonment of Robert Close in 1949 for his novel *Love Me Sailor* (1945). D.H. **Lawrence's** *Lady Chatterley's Lover* (1928), J.D. Salinger's *Catcher in the Rye* (1951), Vladimir Nabokov's *Lolita* (1955), Mary McCarthy's *The Group* (1963), and Philip Roth's *Portnoy's Complaint* (1969) were some of the novels prevented from entering Australia or prosecuted by state governments for obscenity. Similar controls curbed the flow of sexually explicit and experimental or politically controversial films into Australia. Additional controls were imposed on entertainment and artistic activities following the introduction of television in Sydney and Melbourne in 1956.

From the 1960s, literary and artistic censorship declined. By 1968 significant relaxation of Commonwealth controls had occurred, especially under the Liberal–Country Party customs minister, Don Chipp. This trend continued following the election of the Australian Labor Party **Whitlam** government in 1972 and the installation of Lionel **Murphy** as customs minister. The states also liberalised their policies. The heated public controversy which preceded and prompted this sea-change is explained in Geoffrey **Dutton** and Max Harris (eds), *Australia's Censorship Crisis* (1970). By the mid-1970s, the century-long Victorian concern with stemming the morally corrupting influence of prurient material had been replaced with a libertarian commitment to allow individuals to see, hear, and read what they chose.

By the late 1980s, this trend had run its course. Some feminists argued that pornography fostered violence against women. Other critics cited the need to protect the rights of vulnerable minorities. These changes led to laws against incitement to racial hatred (including the Commonwealth Racial Hatred Act, 1995) and homosexual vilification. Technological change, including the introduction of the video recorder, subscription television, and the Internet, brought argument for stricter controls over graphic depictions of violence and pornography. The controversial English holocaust historian, David Irving, was denied entry to Australia. There were campaigns for the removal of 'offensive' books from public libraries and school curricula, a development examined in Claire Williams and Ken Dillon, *Brought to Book* (1993). The recognition by the High Court in 1992 of an implied right in the Australian Constitution to freedom of political communication looked increasingly lonely.

LAURENCE W. MAHER

Census taking, the periodic collection and tabulation of information about the composition and character of the population, became a function of government from the beginning of the Australian colonies, which were settled as modern statistics were being developed. Colonial administrators, especially those influenced by Benthamite ideas, believed that in numbering a people they could better govern it. Early governors from **Phillip** onwards authorised musters of the convict population; the first comprehensive census of NSW was made by Governor **Darling** in 1828. Regular censuses on the British model were made decennially in NSW (from 1851), Victoria (1854), Qld (1861), SA

(1861), Tasmania (1861), and WA (1891). These enumerate the ages, birthplaces, marital condition, occupations, housing types and—almost uniquely in nineteenth-century societies—the religious affiliations of the population. The best description of the methods and problems of the colonial census-taker is Timothy **Coghlan's** introduction to the 1891 NSW census. Since 1911 the Census has been a responsibility of the Commonwealth Statistician. In recent years the range of data collected by the Census has been expanded to cover such matters as income and savings, automobile ownership, and travel habits. To the disappointment of genealogists and historians, Australian official statisticians, unlike their British and American counterparts, have routinely destroyed household returns after the compilation of the official reports. In 2001, however, as a Centenary of Federation gesture, householders were invited for the first time to authorise the archival retention of their returns as a gift to the national heritage. (See also **Historical statistics**.)

GD

Cerutty, Percy Wells (1895–1975) became an athletics coach in the 1950s after himself being a champion marathon runner. Unconventional in his training methods, he aroused considerable controversy in athletics circles. His belief in naturalistic training, with success dependent upon athletes training through the pain barrier, developed from his own earlier experiences of poor mental and physical health which conventional medicine had not been able to help. From his reading he developed what he called the 'Stotan creed', a blend of the Stoic and Spartan philosophies. His success with such runners as Herb Elliot made his revolutionary coaching methods influential, although his often eccentric behaviour antagonised many athletes and coaches.

KT

Chaffey, George (1848–1932) and **William Benjamin** (1856–1926) were Canadian engineers who established an **irrigation** colony in California in the 1880s. They came to Australia in 1886 after meeting Alfred **Deakin** during his visit to America to investigate irrigation methods. After some bickering with the Victorian government, the Chaffeys were granted land to develop an irrigated settlement along the **Murray River**. They formed Chaffey Bros Ltd, and established townships at Mildura and Renmark with irrigated blocks for fruit-growing. After the firm went into liquidation in 1895, George returned to the USA. William remained in Mildura where he became a revered figure. He lived to see the successful development of wine grape and dried fruit industries in the area, and founded the Mildura (later Mildara) winery.

KT

Chamberlain, Alice Lynne 'Lindy' (1948–) became the centre of an intense media and public debate after the mysterious disappearance of her baby daughter, Azaria, on a family camping trip to **Uluru** (Ayers Rock) in 1980. The body was never found, and a coroner's inquest found that the baby had been taken by a dingo, as Lindy and her husband Michael had claimed. Bizarre stories of witchcraft and wild public speculation continued, fuelled by the parents' apparent lack of emotion at the loss of their child. Even their membership of the Seventh Day Adventist Church was adduced as evidence against them. After a second inquest, the Chamberlains were tried for murder in the Darwin Supreme Court in 1982. The trial caused great controversy and division in the Australian community. Lindy was convicted of murder and sentenced to life imprisonment; Michael received a suspended sentence as an accessory. The discovery of a baby's jacket four years later led to yet another inquiry, which found serious flaws in the earlier forensic evidence. The Chamberlains were pardoned and eventually won over $1 million in compensation from the NT government. The incident was covered extensively by the media, and anything relating to the family was regarded as newsworthy. The marriage did not survive, and Lindy moved to the USA. She published the autobiographical *Through My Eyes* in 1990. John Bryson explored the story in *Evil Angels* (1985), which was later made into a feature film.

KT

Charlwood, Donald Ernest (1915–) based his first novel, *No Moon Tonight* (1956), on his own experiences of bombing raids over Germany during World War II. Two further autobiographical volumes, *Marching as to War* (1990) and *Journeys into Night* (1991), deal with his life before and during the war. An evocative novel based on his own childhood at Frankston, *All the Green Year* (1965), became a popular school text and was made into a television series. The other major focus of his writing has been the emigrant shipboard experience, various aspects of which he considered in *Wrecks and Reputations* (1977), *Settlers Under Sail* (1978), and *The Long Farewell* (1981). His postwar career in air-traffic control led to his writing a history of the profession in Australia, entitled *Take-off to Touchdown* (1967).

KT

Chauvel, Charles Edward (1897–1959) and **Elsa May** (1898–1983), were pioneers of the Australian **film industry**. They met in 1926 when Elsa played the heroine in a silent movie that Charles directed. Once married, Elsa gave up acting and collaborated with her husband in producing numerous movies, though the extent of her contribution remained largely unrecognised. Their first sound production was *In the Wake of the Bounty* (1933). The Chauvels wanted to produce films that reflected Australian history and culture. Their enormously successful portrayal of the Australian Light Horse, *Forty Thousand Horsemen* (1940), both drew upon and reinforced the myths of mateship and the Australian digger. Charles's uncle, HARRY CHAUVEL (1865–1945), was a commander of the Light Horse during World War I. The Chauvels portrayed the Australian digger again in *The Rats of Tobruk* (1944), and the hardships and heroism of early pioneers in *Sons of Matthew* (1949). *Jedda* (1955) was an attempt, albeit melodramatic, to examine race relations in Australia. They

117

completed a television series, *Australian Walkabout*, for the BBC, not long before Charles's death in 1959. Elsa wrote *My Life with Charles Chauvel* (1973); and their daughter Susanne Chauvel Carlsson produced a biography, *Charles and Elsa Chauvel: Movie Pioneers* (1983). The writer ELYNE MITCHELL (1913–) is the daughter of Harry Chauvel.

KT

Chevalier, Nicholas (1828–1902) was a Russian-born artist who arrived in Australia in late 1854. He became a prominent cartoonist for the *Melbourne Punch*, later working for the *Illustrated Australian News*. His cartoon work is discussed by Marguerite Mahood in *The Loaded Line* (1973). Also an accomplished landscape painter, he spent three months in 1862 as the official artist on Professor Neumayer's geological survey of Victoria. His painting, *The Buffalo Ranges, Victoria*, won a government competition in 1864 to commemorate the founding of the Victorian Art Gallery. He travelled extensively around Victoria, sketching, before he left for England in 1869, and is widely represented in Australian public art galleries. Melvin N. Day examines his complete career in *Nicholas Chevalier, Artist* (1981).

KT

Chidley, William James (1860–1916) developed social and sexual theories which threw him into direct conflict with the accepted moralities of the early 1900s. He believed that he had cured himself of an earlier medical crisis by vegetarianism and sexual abstinence, and propounded his belief in *The Answer* (1911). The book argued that 'our false coition makes villains of us all', and prescribed an alternative technique of sexual intercourse. The book's explicit nature, combined with the fact that Chidley sold it on the streets wearing only a short white tunic, aroused official ire. He was frequently arrested, committed several times to mental asylums, and was incarcerated at the time of his death. A Chidley Defence Committee formed in 1916 and his case was debated in the NSW parliament. The issues raised of personal freedom and official abuse of the mental health system are central to Alma de Groen's play *Chidley* (1976). Chidley sent a manuscript of his autobiography to Havelock Ellis, who thought highly of it. The full autobiography, *Confessions of William James Chidley*, edited by Sally McInerney, was finally published in 1977.

KT

Chifley, Joseph Benedict 'Ben' (1885–1951), federal leader of the Australian Labor Party and prime minister 1945–49, has legendary status in the labour movement. His patient rise from humble origins to eminence, his simple tastes and homespun manner, inspired general affection. His practical, prudent administration of **postwar reconstruction** combined national leadership with a vision of a just social order that he articulated in the phrase 'the **light on the hill**'; it remains the most powerful of all Labor catchcries.

Chifley began work in the NSW railways at the age of 15 in his birthplace of Bathurst, and advanced to locomotive driver by 1914. Dismissed and later reinstated at a lower grade for his part in the 1917 transport strike, he helped establish the Australian Federated Union of Locomotive Enginemen in 1920. He entered federal parliament in 1928 and was defeated at the end of 1931 as the **Australian Labor Party** succumbed in NSW to a schism between the federal party and the supporters of J.T. **Lang**. Much of Chifley's energy was spent during the 1930s in seeking to rebuild the federal ALP, and in 1935 he unsuccessfully challenged Lang in his state electorate of Auburn. He returned to federal parliament in 1940 and in the following year became treasurer in the **Curtin** war ministry. His experience on the federal royal commission on banking established in 1935 equipped him with a grasp of the enhanced economic role of government, and he directed the war economy with vigour. A significant expansion of social welfare provision and uniform federal income tax were among his innovations. H.C. **Coombs** was one of the able young economists whose expertise he tapped, and in *Trial Balance* (1981) Coombs testifies to Chifley's acumen.

Following Curtin's death, Chifley was elected ALP leader and prime minister by a large majority of the caucus. He proceeded with the ambitious scheme of postwar reconstruction, which included public construction, new government enterprises and large-scale immigration, but was frustrated in efforts to establish a national health scheme. The High Court's rejection in 1947 of his attempt to regulate banking led to the ill-fated decision to nationalise banks, which damaged the popularity of a government that had been re-elected in 1946. Foreign affairs were left largely to the management of H.V. **Evatt**, though Chifley placed greater emphasis on the relationship with Labour-governed Britain. Support of sterling was one reason for Chifley's curbs on consumption and labour costs, and the impatience of the unions culminated in the 1949 national coal strike, which Chifley fought 'boots and all', gaoling the miners' leaders and freezing their funds. Tom Sheridan, *Division of Labour* (1989) raises substantial criticisms of Chifley's conduct of industrial relations. The strains contributed to Labor's electoral defeat later in the year.

In opposition, Chifley was beset by growing division between right and left, and Labor was heavily defeated after a double dissolution in 1951. His death, in his room at the Hotel Kurrajong while dignitaries celebrated the fiftieth anniversary of the Commonwealth at a state ball, effaced all criticism. A volume of his speeches, *Things Worth Fighting For*, appeared in 1952; L.F. Crisp's biography in 1961. Paul **Keating's** suggestion that Chifley was, like Curtin, 'just a trier', is an aberrant judgment by an admirer of Lang. Chifley's cottage by the Bathurst railyards has been preserved, since the death of his wife, as a public museum. Its modest simplicity stands as a monument to an austere and greatly loved man.

STUART MACINTYRE

Child endowment was a government payment to mothers to assist with the expenses of children. While the principle had wide currency in the early twentieth century among industrial countries, it had particular influence in Australia where pronatalists had secured a maternity allowance in 1912 and the **basic wage** was meant to support a family. The 1920 royal commission into the Commonwealth basic wage conducted by A.B. **Piddington** recommended the introduction of child endowment as an alternative to the payment of a family basic wage to all men regardless of their family responsibilities, an approach that divided feminists from the male-dominated trade union movement. Marilyn Lake, in *LH* (1992), suggests that the early-twentieth-century campaign for child endowment drew on concepts of citizenship to pursue women's independence and challenge the paternalist state. Though the Commonwealth failed to accept Piddington's recommendation, the NSW government of J.T. **Lang** did introduce the measure in 1927.

It was adopted nationally in 1943 and provided for the payment to the mother of five shillings per week for each child under 16 other than the first, an amount that afforded some relief to large, low-income families. Though the payment was extended to the first child in 1950, inflation eroded its value. In 1976, when taxation allowances for dependent children were abolished, the payments were increased and renamed the family allowance. Subsequently the principle of universality was abandoned in favour of means-tested payments, and a distinctive familial measure has become absorbed into the common framework of **social welfare**.

SM

Childe, Vere Gordon (1892–1957) was a prehistorian and the author of the first analysis of parliamentary socialism in action, *How Labour Governs: A Study of Workers' Representation in Australia* (1923, 1964). He was the most influential of the radical intellectuals, from middle-class backgrounds, who sided with the labour movement in the early twentieth century. Between 1917 and 1921, in Sydney and Brisbane, Childe was a notable lecturer, writer, and lobbyist for peace groups, trade unions, and the Labor Party. He had hoped for an academic career, but the conservatives who controlled the universities used his pacifist and socialist ideas to deny him academic positions on three occasions. The leader of the **Australian Labor Party** in NSW, however, made Childe his personal assistant in 1919, and sent him to London to advise the government on developments in European social democracy. The fall of the government put an end to this role in 1922.

Remaining in Britain, Childe became a leading prehistorian. He was the first Abercromby professor of prehistoric archaeology in the University of Edinburgh 1927–46 and professor of prehistoric archaeology and director of the Institute of Archaeology at the University of London to 1956. In the late 1930s he became increasingly open about his interest in Marxism, and participated in several intellectual projects of the British Communist Party, which, however, he did not join. He wrote 21 books and hundreds of articles and reviews. Meanwhile, his influence on Australian labour intellectuals grew. They were challenged by the pungent and cryptic argument of *How Labour*

Governs, and attracted by Childe's demonstration that it was possible—at least in Britain—to achieve academic distinction while remaining active as a public intellectual of the left. Among historians, the publication in 1942 of *What Happened in History* (which sold 300 000 copies) influenced a generation of Marxists, in Britain and Australia, including Russel **Ward**. Childe's sudden death, soon after returning to Australia in 1957, posed questions about exile and return that were, and are, irresistible to post-colonial intellectuals.

There is an extensive literature on Childe the scholar. His seminal role in cultural-historical archaeology is assessed in David Harris (ed.), *The Archaeology of V. Gordon Childe* (1994), and in Sally Green, *Prehistorian: A Biography of V. Gordon Childe* (1981)—the most accessible for the general reader. It has to be remembered, however, that Childe was over 30 when he began his career in archaeology. It was not until 1995 that a book dealing with Childe's education and political experiences in Australia appeared: *Childe and Australia: Archaeology, Politics and Ideas*, edited by Peter Gathercole, T.H. Irving, and Gregory Melleuish. Gathercole's forthcoming biography, which aims to bring the academic and political sides of Childe together, may be sampled in his 'Childe in History', the sixth Gordon Childe Memorial Lecture, published in the *Bulletin of the Institute of Archaeology, London* (1994).

How Labour Governs, as an intervention in politics, has attracted a number of different readings, facilitated by Childe's ironic style and his failure to produce a promised second volume. Labour intellectuals who have taken the book as a point of reference for their arguments include H.V. **Evatt**, E.M. Higgins, and Graham Freudenberg. One interpretation, during the Cold War, that Childe was an ineffectual, Leftist dilettante who became disillusioned with working-class politics, is difficult to sustain in the light of Childe's other political writings and his wholehearted commitment to labour's cause throughout his life. A different slant is produced by intellectuals on the Labor Party's left and right, who welcome or reject the book as an attack on parliamentary socialism. These commentators neglect Childe's Guild Socialist strategy, in which the Labor Party would play a special role in introducing democracy into industry and the state. Remembering that Childe's intellectual and political formation occurred before the Russian Revolution, but that *How Labour Governs* appeared after it, helps to explain these readings. In the post-communist era we may expect new readings.

TERRY IRVING

Children were a subject of intense concern in colonial Australia. From the early 1820s, when Commissioner **Bigge** noted the superiority of native-born children to their convict parents, to the 1880s, Australians scrutinised the behaviour of their children for clues to the character of the coming nation. 'What shall we do with our boys?' gold-rush parents asked anxiously. ('Marry them to our girls,' one wit replied.) Boys, exemplified by the **Little Boy from Manly**, were at the forefront of national debate, but girls too were expected to play their part.

Children

The Australian child was the product of a more spacious and relaxed environment than its British or Irish parents had enjoyed, a change which was not always seen as an improvement. 'I have a holy horror of babies', confessed the English public schoolboy and newly-wed Richard **Twopeny** in 1883, '… but for general objectionableness I believe there are none to compare with the Australian baby … He has breathed the free air of Australian independence too early to have much regard for the fifth commandment.' Twopeny shared the disdain of other English visitors for the conduct and bearing of the native-born, a disdain matched by the anxiety of English mothers watching their children run free. To Australian-born commentators, on the other hand, observations of the free-spirited young Australian became celebrations of the birth of Australian **national identity**, and of the pleasing difference between the Australian child and its British parent. 'Young Australia', as Ken **Inglis** showed in Guy Featherstone (ed.), *The Colonial Child* (1981), was at the centre of intersecting debates about childhood, environment, race, and nation.

Differences between Australian-born children and their British counterparts or parents readily took on an overlay of meanings about **British–Australian relations**. Australia was often depicted as the child of Britain—an especially lusty infant who would grow up and achieve independence from its mother's apron-strings. Along the way, the growing child would cast off outmoded customs and the stifling class structure of the Old World. Traditionalists, like Twopeny, believed that the Australian child should remain grateful to its British parent, and mindful of obligations to home and imperial siblings.

Through the ages people have seen the future in the face of the child. But the connection which colonial Australians made between the welfare of their children and national destiny was shaped by a more recent history. Concerns about 'child-life' began to be raised in Britain in the mid-nineteenth century, producing a range of legislation concerned with the welfare of children, such as the regulation of child labour. In Australia these issues were framed by racist concerns about the capacity of 'British stock' to populate a country distant from Britain without undergoing environmentally induced degeneration. In 1875 Redmond **Barry** launched an inquiry to discover whether 'the race in its transplantation to Australian soil retains undiminished the vigour and fire and stamina of the strong old fire of which it is an offshoot'. He tried to find the answer by measuring the physique of young cricket players. By 1902 T.A. **Coghlan**, the NSW government statistician, had classified children into degrees of 'Australianship' as part of an official quest to make the Australian child as 'near as possible the ideal human type'. He arranged for detailed measurements to be made of each child, in order to discover whether Australian children of British origin were becoming more like those in neighbouring countries, or—more disturbingly—whether they were coming to resemble the indigenous peoples. Shortly afterwards state Education Departments introduced school medical inspections, partly in order to monitor the physical and mental fitness of the emerging 'Australian race'.

Attitudes towards children were also connected to the changing demographic structure of colonial society. Richard Twopeny had written at a moment of transition: the gold-rush generation had almost come to the end of their reproductive lives. In 1871, 42 per cent of Australians were children under the age of 14, an all-time record. These children grew up, typically, in large families, with perhaps four or five siblings, though usually without grandparents living close by. The next generation would grow up in smaller families, but lived in less crowded and more comfortable households. As Ann Larson argues in *Growing Up in Melbourne* (1994), by the 1880s parents, especially the middle class and the respectable working class, were limiting their families in order to give each child a better chance in life. These children were more likely to go to school regularly and to continue beyond the years of compulsory schooling. They were the focus of a more intense, and perhaps more kindly, parental regard. Parental ambitions for their children's prosperity and happiness may thus have reinforced the national preoccupation with the future of 'Young Australia'.

The 1870s, the decade when the post-gold-rush baby-boom peaked, was also the decade when schooling started to become compulsory—at least in law. In practice, school attendance was often still irregular and the tuition rudimentary, regimented, and sometimes resented. Yet the state school slowly became the most powerful socialising and nationalising force in the land. Henry **Lawson**, who attended a state school in the 1870s, used a reader devised for the Irish National system and adapted for colonial use. Along with thousands of others he would have read, for example, that 'The inhabitants of New Holland are among the lowest and most degraded to be found on the surface of the Earth'. Some Aboriginal parents registered their opposition to their children's compulsory attendance at schools like Ramahyuck, Victoria, where the teacher was in the habit of referring to her charges as 'horrible nasty creatures'.

By the beginning of the twentieth century, public concern gradually shifted from the excessive independence of the bush child to the unfriendly and confining environment of the city child. Naturalistic ideas of child development, such as those of Pestalozzi and Froebel, viewed the countryside as an ideal place to grow up in. City children, by contrast, inhabited a milieu that seemingly inhibited their natural development. Photographs taken by anti-slum campaigners of little boys playing cricket in inner-city lanes evoked, not their resilient childish spirit, but the hazards of street life. **Progressive** reformers created a range of new institutions—the baby health centre, the free **kindergarten**, and the municipal playground—designed to redress the ills of the city environment.

The decline of the birth-rate, which had begun in the 1890s, bottomed in the **Depression** of the 1930s: by the end of World War II children under the age of 14 were barely a quarter of the Australian population. Not until the 1950s and 1960s did the children of the postwar baby-boom shift the power balance between the generations. From the

1920s onwards, as Kerreen Reiger shows in *The Disenchantment of the Home* (1985), Australian families were encouraged to become child-centred and to concern themselves with the quality of family relationships. The quiet, obedient child was no longer straightforwardly 'good', at least according to the conceptualisations of normal children promulgated by the emerging experts of child psychology. By the 1950s the problem of environment was no longer conceived just in terms of climate and region. Children were conceived as inhabiting social, educational, emotional, and familial environments, and a lack of fit between the individual child and any of these zones was believed to produce maladjustment. Mothers became responsible for their children's emotional, psychic, and cognitive development. For this they required a knowledge of ages and stages, the assistance of psychologists, teachers, doctors, and the child's father, and to keep a watchful eye over their children. New houses were built with family rooms and a clear line of sight into the backyard, where children could amuse themselves with educational toys rather than swinging on the clothes line. For many children, though, watching **television** has become a preferred pastime. For parents this has produced a new task: how to provide a space of regulated freedom for the child consumer in a globalised market, where few of the badges of childhood are 'made in Australia'.

How have Australian children made sense of the experiences of childhood? Historians have frequently drawn on memoirs and autobiographies of remembered childhoods, along with the more fragmentary sources produced by children themselves. Gwyn Dow and June Factor (eds), *Australian Childhood* (1991), provides a valuable introduction to this literature, and Margaret Barbalet's *Far from a Low Gutter Girl* (1983) remains unusual in giving voice to institutionalised children. Brenda Niall and Ian Britain (eds), *Oxford Book of Australian Schooldays* (1997), ranges historically from 1795 to 1995, and includes the schooling of Aboriginal children. For white administrators, schools proved convenient sites for the collection and removal of children. Jan Kociumbas draws on sources produced by children in *Australian Childhood: A History* (1997), but also examines those produced by adults charged with the care of children in a range of capacities since colonisation. Kociumbas tests the claims of Australian **egalitarianism** against the lives of different groups of children, and shares the judgment of others in the related fields of **educational**, **family**, and **welfare history** who find them wanting.

DEBORAH TYLER

Chinese–Australian relations are among the most important in Australia's foreign policy. Although the fear of China has been common in Australian history, relations have been mainly cordial since 1972.

The influx of Chinese onto the goldfields from the 1850s created an initial friction in the relationship. In 1887, two Chinese commissioners visited Australia to look into the conditions of the Chinese residents, concluding that Chinese suffered discrimination in Australia. Amid a strong fear of China and mass Chinese immigration into Australia, a bitter debate involving China, Britain, and the Australian colonies led to the passage of bills in all colonies prohibiting any further entry of Chinese.

Low-level trade between China and Australia began soon after Federation, expanding to significant wheat sales in some years in the 1920s and 1930s. Australian Christian missionaries arrived in strength in the early 1920s, but an anti-Christian campaign in 1927 forced nearly 100 to depart. Numbers grew again in 1933–34, when a maximum of 188 Australian missionaries in the field in China associated themselves closely with the government of the avowedly Christian Chiang Kai-shek. Some Australian individuals achieved high influence in China. The most famous was George Ernest **Morrison** from Geelong, who was correspondent for *The Times* 1897–1912 and political adviser to Chinese presidents between 1912 and 1920. Another was W.H. Donald, who became a strong supporter and adviser of Chiang Kai-shek.

In 1934 Minister for External Affairs John **Latham** visited China, along with several other Asian countries, but he was not impressed with China's performance and recommended a 'firm' policy. Australia and the Republic of China did not establish diplomatic relations until 1941, when Frederic **Eggleston** became Australia's minister to wartime capital Chongqing. Although the two countries were allies, proposals for a treaty between them came to nothing and relations remained cool. Eggleston was pro-China, and there was some goodwill towards China in Australia. However, Australian wartime aid was parsimonious; several untoward incidents occurred, such as a strike by Chinese seamen in Perth in 1942 in which two Chinese were killed.

When the People's Republic of China was established on 1 October 1949, the **Chifley** Labor government in Australia refused to recognise it. One of Chifley's reasons was that his government was shortly to face an election. Another was reluctance to give opposition leader R.G. **Menzies** the chance to attack him for communist sympathies, especially since Menzies was already making a major issue of the threat of world **communism**. As prime minister, Menzies considered recognising the People's Republic, since Britain did so in January 1950. However, the participation by Australia and China on opposite sides in the **Korean War** (1950–53) had the effect of convincing the Australian government of China's aggressive intentions and of freezing the two countries' bilateral relations for nearly two decades. Successive coalition governments until the early 1970s based their attitude to China on fear of the downward thrust of Asian communism. At the same time, with strong support from the Country Party, wheat exports began in the early 1960s.

The Cultural Revolution, erupting in August 1966, convinced the coalition government now led by Harold **Holt** that the Chinese leadership was both aggressive and mad, and helped intensify the fear of China. It was Holt who took a step from which Menzies had shrunk: sending an embassy to Taipei and consequently formalising Australia's recognition of the Republic of China in Taiwan as the legal government of all China. In July 1971, at the invitation of Chinese Premier Zhou Enlai, Gough **Whitlam** led an **ALP** delegation to China, only to be condemned for his initiative by Prime Minister William **McMahon**. One of Whitlam's first major actions as prime minister was to recognise the People's Republic. Australia viewed the government as 'the sole legal government of China' and 'acknowledged' China's claim to Taiwan. Whitlam believed that a 'wider detente' was necessary to bring China into the mainstream of regional and world affairs and, from 31 October to 4 November 1973, made the first visit of an Australian prime minister to China.

When Malcolm **Fraser** replaced Whitlam as prime minister in November 1975, he maintained, consolidated, and even improved the positive relationship with China which his predecessor had built. Fraser's first overseas visit, in June 1976, was to Japan and China. In the latter country a severe political crisis, including the death of Communist Party chairman Mao Zedong in September, was to bring it to an entirely different political agenda based on modernisation and rising prosperity. Fraser had two main reasons for favouring good relations with China. The first was that he shared China's deep distrust of the Soviet Union, regarding it as the main threat to regional world peace. The other was economic, as Australia's export strategy complemented China's incipient modernisation. The first years of the Fraser government were remarkably free of divisive political issues. However, disagreement later emerged over Cambodia, where Vietnamese troops had overthrown the genocidal government of Pol Pot early in January 1979, replacing it with one sympathetic to Vietnam. Although both Australia and China wanted the Vietnamese troops to withdraw from Cambodia, China was eager to see Pol Pot back in power, an outcome anathema to Australia.

Fraser revisited China in August 1982, offering his counterpart Zhao Ziyang a return invitation. Although Fraser lost the March 1983 elections to the ALP, Bob **Hawke** becoming the prime minister, Zhao's visit went ahead as planned in April. It ushered in a period characterised by warm relations, both nationally and between the prime ministers of the two countries. Hawke welcomed General Secretary Hu Yaobang to Australia in April 1985 and Premier Li Peng in November 1988, and went to China in May 1986. He even spoke of a 'special relationship' between the two countries. Trade and other economic relations were high on the agenda. The Department of Trade launched the China Action Plan to expand the economic relationship soon after Zhao Ziyang's 1983 visit. Australian exports to China surpassed $1 billion for the first time in the 1984/85 financial year. Despite the generally cordial relations, the Cambodia issue remained a source of contention throughout the 1980s, although this problem was solved when Vietnam withdrew its troops in 1989 and, shortly after, China and Vietnam 'normalised' their relations.

A more serious issue arose when in June 1989 Chinese troops crushed a large-scale democratic student movement. Hawke attended a memorial service for deceased students,

while Foreign Minister Gareth Evans declared that 'business as usual' with China was 'simply not an option'. Although trade continued to increase and relations later largely recovered, Australia's concern with human rights remained a source of friction in the relationship.

Paul **Keating**, who became prime minister at the end of 1991, accelerated the push into Asia. He visited China in June 1993, to secure trade and investment deals. Shortly after the Keating visit, a series of Australia–China Trade and Investment Forums began which pushed economic relations to new heights. Other than human rights, the main divisive issue under Keating was Taiwan. Although Australia continued to recognise only one China, the People's Republic, it allowed the establishment of the semi–official Taipei Economic and Cultural Office in 1992, and trade remained healthy. In 1996, the first year of John **Howard**'s coalition government, Chinese–Australian relations suffered. Much to China's annoyance, a Howard government minister visited Taiwan in that year, and the Dalai Lama's visit to Australia included meetings with Howard and his Foreign Minister. However, early in 1997, Howard made a successful visit to China, which Chinese President Jiang Zemin returned in September 1999. The problem over illegal immigrants from China was largely solved when it reached its peak in the first half of 1999; the two governments agreed to cooperate in stopping the flow. Trade continued to grow, reaching A$10 billion in 1998–99, and was set to continue growing with China's admission to the World Trade Organisation.

There is a growing literature on Chinese–Australian relations. Among book-length studies, the earliest is Henry Albinski, *Australian Policies and Attitudes Toward China* (1965). Edmund Fung and Colin Mackerras, *From Fear to Friendship: Australia's Policies towards the People's Republic of China 1966–1982*, and Eric Andrews, *Australia and China: The Ambiguous Relationship* (both 1985), cover different periods, the second being a general history of Chinese–Australian relations from the beginnings to shortly before the date of publication. Hugh Dunn and Edmund Fung (eds), *Sino-Australian Relations* (1985), and Colin Mackerras (ed.), *Australia and China* (1996), offer general coverage of the relationship in the periods 1972–85 and 1985–95 respectively. (See also **Chinese in Australia**.)

COLIN MACKERRAS

Chinese in Australia came at an early stage of the country's colonial history. A tiny Chinese population grew rapidly after 1848 under a system of indentured labour. Indentured Chinese immigrants worked in all colonies, serving as stationhands, plantation workers, miners, on public works, and as personal servants. Most came from the southeastern provinces of Guangdong and Fujian or, in the case of those in WA, from Singapore.

From 1851 the gold rush brought many thousands more Chinese, primarily to Victoria and NSW; about 45 000 prospectors arrived in Victoria alone in 1854–58. In a sprawling survey of the Chinese in Australia, Eric **Rolls**

(1992) describes the accompanying racial tensions, which sometimes led to severe riots such as those at **Buckland River** in 1857 and **Lambing Flat**, 1860–61. These problems resulted in the first restrictions on Chinese **immigration**. The colonial governments differed on the issue. Policy varied in accordance with the proportion of Chinese in the total population—high in Victoria, low in Tasmania—and also with the need for manpower, which, as Jan Ryan shows in *Ancestors* (1995), was acute in WA.

In 1888, an inter-colonial conference resolved most of these differences by introducing severe, although not uniform, restrictions on further immigration from China. The Immigration Restriction Act of 1901 subsequently imposed a de facto bar on all non-European immigration through selective application of a **dictation test**, and the Naturalisation Act of 1903 explicitly identified non-Europeans as ineligible for Australian citizenship. Numbers of Chinese in Australia declined from 38 000 in 1880 to less than half this number 40 years later.

The shrinking Chinese population was concentrated in the eastern states and was largely urban. It included few women. The men worked as market gardeners, carpenters, laundrymen, and in small business. Robert Travers, in *Australian Mandarin* (1982), traced the life of the most famous of them, **Quong Tart**, who became a prosperous and well-respected member of Sydney society. Rolls, *Citizens* (1996), draws attention to the Sydney banana merchants Ma Ying Piu and Philip Gockchin, founders respectively of the Sincere and Wing On multinational merchant empires.

Some, including Quong Tart, took European wives. Others commuted between Australia and a family base in China. This rather fluid community, internally divided into different native-place associations, sought relations with both the host and the ancestral society. It celebrated Federation with public ceremony while actively supporting political parties in China. Saturday schools were organised for the instruction in Chinese of children who otherwise attended local state schools.

Eric Andrews, *Australia and China* (1985), and Lachlan Strahan, *Australia's China* (1996), show improvement in Australian attitudes towards China after the Japanese invasion of 1937. This did not affect immigration policy. During World War II Chinese refugees were granted asylum and many contributed to the war effort, but they were ejected with little ceremony, and occasionally much controversy, at the war's end, during Arthur **Calwell's** tenure as minister for immigration. The numbers of Chinese in Australia reached a low point of about 7000 in 1947.

The coalition government that assumed office in 1949 undertook no radical revision of policy but adopted a more flexible approach to its administration. Naturalisation of non-European residents of Australia was possible from 1956, and the Immigration Restriction Act of 1901 was replaced in 1958 with the Migration Act, which opened the door to a small number of Chinese migrants. Migration policy was further liberalised in the 1960s until the **White Australia** policy was finally abandoned.

The Chinese ethnic population of Australia grew slowly in the 1970s and then rapidly during the 1980s, due both to political developments in the region and to Australia's encouragement of skilled and business migrants. The fall of Saigon in 1975 and the Sino-Vietnamese war of 1979 brought a large number of Vietnamese refugees, of whom by 1986 more than one-third were self-professedly of Chinese ethnic origin. Migration from Hong Kong reached a peak of more than 13 000 in 1990–91 with the territory's imminent reversion to China in 1997. Finally, the Tiananmen massacre of 1989 resulted in an extension of rights of residence to around 20 000 Chinese students then in Australia, and subsequently to their family members through the family reunification agreement.

By the late twentieth century, the ethnically Chinese population of Australia was highly diverse. The 'astronaut' families from Hong Kong float between the old and new homes, often with the father earning a living in Hong Kong while the mother keeps house for student children in Melbourne or Sydney. Sang Ye's interviews with immigrants from mainland China (*The Year the Dragon Came*, 1996) reveal a rather poorer migrant community with considerable difficulties of adjustment. Third-, fourth- and fifth-generation Australians of Chinese origin, fewer in number, have little beyond ancestral place sentiments to link them to the newcomers. Divided from each other by class, language, and place of origin, the Chinese in Australia constitute many communities, which are brought together mainly by public celebrations of Chinese New Year.

ANTONIA FINNANE

Chisholm, Caroline (1808–77) was a social reformer and activist over a period of 30 years in early NSW and Victoria. She investigated problems faced by poor single women and large, poor families in migration and settlement, and pressed colonial officials and philanthropists for the will, and the resources, to improve conditions, all with remarkable effectiveness. She is one of the few women in nineteenth-century Australia to attain international recognition for **philanthropy**.

She was born in Northampton, England, the daughter of a prosperous Protestant farming family, and introduced by her mother to a sense of obligation. When she married Archibald Chisholm, an officer in the army of the East India Company, on 27 December 1830, she converted to Catholicism. She entered the marriage with the understanding that she would be free to continue her engagement in charitable activities, a promise that her spouse honoured throughout their marriage. At Madras, India, she established a live-in school for soldiers' daughters, of British and mixed Indian–British descent, with a strong emphasis on basic literacy, numeracy, and practical skills of housewifery. This apprenticeship in public assistance shaped her later strategies and goals.

In 1838 the Chisholms, with two young sons, arrived in NSW. In the first years Chisholm concentrated on improving the life chances of the numerous, often Irish, single girls and women migrants who, unable to find employment or adequate shelter, often faced a choice between **prostitution** and destitution. When taking groups of young women into her own home for domestic training and assistance in finding employment seemed irritatingly inadequate, Chisholm persuaded Governor **Gipps** to open the disused army barracks as a female refuge and canvassed well-to-do colonists for funds to keep it open. Meanwhile she established networks to place the women in **domestic service**, accompanying them herself on their trips to take up employment in the interior.

By the mid-1840s Chisholm was convinced of the need for promotion of **closer settlement** through family farms, as a solution to the needs of poor, large families. By bringing more white women to the outback, she hoped to reduce the atrocities visited upon Aboriginal women by white men on the frontiers of white settlement. She wrote to Earl **Grey**, secretary of state for the colonies, in terms that were later to become famous: 'For all the clergy you can despatch, all the school-masters you can appoint, all the churches you can build, and all the books you can export, will never do much good without what a gentleman in that Colony very appropriately called "God's Police"—wives and little children—good and virtuous women.'

The Chisholms established themselves for several years in London to further Caroline's scheme for the Family Colonisation Loan Society, which was responsible for despatching thousands of hopeful seekers of a better life southwards to the Australian colonies. Back in the colonies, this time in Melbourne, the Chisholms did all in their power to see these migrants firmly established. Increasingly Chisholm used her renown to intervene publicly on a range of issues: 'unlocking the lands' of pastoralists, the conditions of working-class work and housing, democratic government. In 1866, her health precarious, she returned with her husband to England, where she died in 1877.

British Victorians placed Caroline Chisholm beside the Quaker prison reformer Elizabeth Fry and the Anglican founder of the nursing profession Florence Nightingale in their pantheon of outstanding women. An Australian biographer, Mary Hoban, in 1973 saw her as appropriate for canonisation. Margaret **Kiddle**, her first biographer, was impressed in 1950 with Chisholm's combination of extraordinary administrative acumen and capacity for persevering, practical work, as were Keith **Hancock** and Manning **Clark** in their histories of Australia. In *Damned Whores and God's Police* (1975), Anne **Summers** took Chisholm's phrase as emblematic; she interpreted male acceptance of Chisholm in the public sphere as purchased by her accommodation with traditional policies that matched female values of domesticity and subservience. It is a view of her work that has generally prevailed.

PATRICIA GRIMSHAW

Chocolate soldier was a term coined by Irish playwright George Bernard Shaw in his play *Arms and the Man* (1898) (after Virgil's *Aeneid*). It describes an infantryman who, assuming that the preceding artillery would have already slain the enemy, went into battle with chocolates in his pack rather than bullets. Shaw's play disparages the empty heroics

of the cavalryman, who traditionally cut the more dashing figure; by escaping the battle, the infantryman perversely emerges as the true hero. Australians used the term in World War I to describe soldiers who did not fight because they had missed the battle altogether, such as the men of the 8th Infantry Brigade who arrived in Egypt after the **Gallipoli** campaign was over. A slightly altered meaning emerged during World War II, when *chocolate soldier* or *chocko* became a derogatory label for conscripted militiamen engaged only in domestic service, the reputed rationale being that, like chocolates, they would melt in the sun. Such men were also called *koalas* because they could not be shot or exported. After 1943, when the Australian Labor Party widened the area in which conscripted men could fight to include all theatres of war south of the equator, the term applied to militiamen fighting in the Pacific.

HD

Church Act, drawn up by Governor **Bourke** in 1836, was designed to provide equitable support to the three major denominations—Anglican, Catholic, and Presbyterian—and so put an end to claims for Anglican supremacy. Government funds amounting to £30 000 were set aside to provide financial assistance to these denominations. This prompted a spate of church-building and led to increased numbers of clergy.

HD

Church and Schools Corporation was designed by Archdeacon T.H. Scott in 1825 to support the clergy and schools of the Church of England. Under Scott's plan, the Church of England would take over the existing schools in the colony of NSW, and assume responsibility for a new network of infant schools, parish schools, grammar schools, and orphan schools, as well as a university. One-seventh of the colony's Crown lands was granted to fund the corporation. However, the scheme was abandoned in 1833 following financial difficulties and opposition from other denominations to the privileged role given to the Church of England. Scott's successor, William **Broughton**, subsequently attempted to resurrect the corporation's objectives with a proposal to establish two government-supported Church of England grammar schools in NSW.

HD

Church and state in England at the time of European settlement of Australia were constituted on the Erastian principle. The word *church* in relation to the Church of England referred not to a distinct, self-governed corporate entity, recognised by law as the church of the realm, but to part of the realm itself—the ecclesiastical part—whose doctrine, discipline, and governance were defined and regulated by parliament.

From the eighteenth century legal doubt existed whether the religion established in England was also legally established in colonies settled by British subjects. Despite these doubts, the British government acted initially as if religion were legally established in NSW and Van Diemen's

Land. Governor **Phillip** was required to arrange, where possible, for **Anglican** public worship. Clergymen, such as Richard **Johnson** and Robert **Knopwood**, served in proclaimed parishes of the English kind, although not in English circumstances. Archdeacon T. Scott, who arrived in 1825, presided over the recently created **Church and Schools Corporation**, endowed with one-seventh of colonial land, to maintain the clergy of the Church of England and Anglican schools. Scott was also empowered by royal Letters Patent to convene an Archdeacon's Court whose 'lawful decrees' were enforceable by the 'civil power'.

The next 40 or so years witnessed a drastic religious transformation in England and the Australian colonies. In England most civil and religious disabilities of Protestant Nonconformists and **Catholics** were removed. In the 1830s, largely in reaction to the admission of Nonconformists and Catholics into parliament—the supreme law-making body for the church—a 'high church' reaction gathered strength, rediscovering or inventing the theory that the Church of England was not a part, but a partner, of the state. In the colonies, however, the status and concept of the Church of England changed irretrievably. The Erastian view that the Church was, by law, part of the colonial civil order was, by the 1860s, decisively displaced by the idea that all churches, including the Church of England, were voluntary religious societies whose right to practise their religion and hold property was legally recognised. The best study of early relations between the Church of England and the state remains Ross Border's *Church and State in Australia 1788–1872* (1962).

The reduced status of the Church in the Australian colonies began with the suspension of the Church and Schools Corporation in 1829. The **Church Acts** in NSW and Van Diemen's Land (1836 and 1837 respectively) began a quiet revolution, granting significant financial aid to the major non-Anglican (including Catholic) churches. These acts inaugurated a kind of multiple religious establishment, stimulating debate on whether the Church of England was established in ways that other state-maintained churches were not.

The Letters Patent under which William **Broughton** was appointed Bishop of Sydney, and Francis Nixon Bishop of Tasmania, empowered them to convene Consistorial Courts to enforce the ecclesiastical law of England. Their efforts to do so were successfully resisted by governors **Bourke**, **Gipps** and **Eardley-Wilmot**, who were quietly supported in this by the **Colonial Office**. The governors won. After 1847 Letters Patent creating colonial bishoprics ceased to confer this legal power.

The Supreme Court of New South Wales ruled in 1861 that the Church of England had no precedence over other religious groups, and confirmed that English ecclesiastical law had no force in the colony. In effect, all religious associations were equally free before the law to practise their preferred religion, provided only they did not breach the general law in doing so.

A series of decisions by senior English courts from the early 1860s affirmed that appointing colonial Anglican bishops by royal Letters Patent did not have the effect of legally establishing the Church of England in that colony. An Anglican church thus created was simply a voluntary association organised on a consensual basis. By this time Anglicans in many colonies had come to the view that they could practise their religion more effectively as a voluntary association than as a remote and subordinate appendage of the English ecclesiastical establishment. By the close of the 1860s state aid to churches, including the Church of England, had been discontinued in most colonies. State aid to denominational education continued longer, but after 1880 survived only in one colony.

However, the end of a beneficial link between the churches and the state did not mean that the Erastian ideal perished. Churches and the state were separated, but not religion and the state. For about another century Australian legislatures remained supportive of Christianity in general, and, more cautiously, of Protestant-style civic puritanism. Few publicly disputed that the civil order had, or should have, an inherent religious dimension. Australia, it was often said in pulpits, parliaments, classrooms, and the press, was a Christian country. A righteous national life was called for from Protestant pulpits, modelled on God's law as stated in the Bible. Parliamentary sessions, first a few, later all, began with prayer. Public and commercial activities on Sunday were restrictively regulated by law. **Temperance** reforms, usually advocated in religio-moral terms, sometimes reached statute books, most effectively during World War I. **Education Acts** made, and still make, supportive provision for religious instruction in state schools. Blasphemy—never defined by Australian courts, but mostly assumed to refer only to vilification of Christianity—remains an offence in nearly all Australian jurisdictions, as does the use of profane language in public. In 1884 the NSW Supreme Court, in a disturbance of religious worship case, ruled that Christianity in the broadest sense was part of the common law of the colony.

The legal relation between churches, as voluntary associations, and the state has varied little in concept since the 1860s. The voluntary association model suited most civically reformist Protestants, since loyalty to their denomination did not impede militant inter-denominational and trans-denominational religio-civic agitation. It suited Catholics and High Anglicans, facilitating the building of institutional and educational ramparts against Protestantism, secularism, and worldly temptation generally. It suited exclusivist, doctrinally rigorous, worldliness-fearing groups—for instance, Brethren and Particular Baptist—for similar reasons. Non-Christians also valued collective privacies afforded by the model.

Until the 1950s and 1960s, the energy fostering the creation and maintenance of Erastian civic forms was formidable. Lay militancy was as important as clerical effort, although Anglican, **Methodist**, **Presbyterian**, **Congregational**, and **Baptist** clergy, sometimes acting through local councils of churches, mostly took the lead in public. On some issues, such as abortion and contraception, Catholics have long favoured statutory prohibition or restriction, although not in Erastian terms. Traditionally, Catholics see their church as partner of the state, not part of it.

Under Section 116 of the Commonwealth **Constitution**, the Commonwealth is prohibited from making any law for establishing any religion, or for imposing any religious observances, or for prohibiting the free exercise of any religion, and no religious test shall be required to qualify for any office or public trust under the Commonwealth. No state constitution (with the partial exception of Tasmania's) contains these prohibitions. From Federal Convention debates it is clear they were chiefly intended to keep the Commonwealth clear of communally divisive religious controversies by ensuring that religion remain a subject on which the Commonwealth could not legislate at all. However, Section 116 did not imply hostility to religion as such, or deny a religious dimension to civil life. The Constitution's preamble declared that the people of the colonies, in forming an indissoluble Commonwealth, relied on 'the Blessing of Almighty God'. For details and historical background see Richard Ely, *Unto God and Caesar* (1976). The extent to which Section 116 prevents the Commonwealth legislating on religious matters may be judged by reference to the 1981 High Court ruling (*DOGS* case) that Commonwealth laws providing financial aid to church schools did not breach Section 116 because the subject-matter of those laws was not religion, but education.

In the 1980s and 1990s legislatures and courts did not favour Protestant styles of civic virtue. Little remains of restrictive Sunday laws; in state schools the norm is even-handedness between religions, and between religion and no religion. But Erastian vestiges continue: blasphemy remains a crime. Legislative sessions begin still with prayers which are Christian in provenance and connotation. Mainstream churches declaim, still, against social and economic injustice, but mostly deploy religiously neutral ethical principles. The Erastian concept of a national covenant and destiny under God is nearly dead. Multiculturalism has made it almost unsayable.

But while religion has left the public square, churches have, institutionally, returned in force. As bodies whose purpose is advancement of religion, churches are treated as charities, qualifying for an extensive exemption from Commonwealth, state and local taxes and charges. Church schools are not only exempt from such charges but, as education providers, receive substantial financial aid from Commonwealth and states. A trickle of state aid in the early 1960s has become a large flow. About 30 per cent of school-age children attend church schools. In the 1980s and 1990s, many public welfare services were contracted out to private—often church–linked—agencies. The religious dimensions of this institutional success story defy easy interpretation. While mainstream churches flourish as corporate service-providers, church attendance declines.

The section titled 'Religion' in Jean and Richard Ely, *Halsbury's Laws of Australia*, vol. 23, states the current law relating to religion. J.S. Gregory, *Church and State* (1973), and Keith Mason, *Constancy and Change* (1990), provide a historical overview of links between religion and the law.

RICHARD ELY

Church of England, see **Anglican Church**

Churinga, or *tjuringa*, from the Arrernte language, refers in the broadest sense to an object or a practice—such as a song, story, or ceremony—which Aborigines regard as sacred. *Churinga* also refers to objects, usually made from stone or wood and decorated in totemic style with incisions or painting. They are usually placed in safe-keeping on that person's death, and can be passed on for many generations, thus representing an important link with the ancestors. Churinga have been subject to depredation and collection. (See also **Dreamtime**.)

HD

Cilento, Phyllis Dorothy (1894–1987) and **Raphael West** (1893–1985) were both doctors. After their marriage Phyllis specialised in women's and children's health, publishing widely in that field, and in nutrition and vitamin therapy. For more than 50 years she wrote an influential 'Medical Mother' column for Brisbane newspapers. Her autobiography, *Lady Cilento: My Life*, was published in 1987. Raphael specialised in tropical medicine, working in New Guinea and then as Qld's director-general of health and medical services from 1934 to 1946. As a supporter of the **White Australia** policy, he was interested in the survival of the white man in the tropics, and published a book of that title in 1925. His other publications included several works on tropical diseases, *Triumph in the Tropics: A Historical Sketch of Queensland* (with Clem Lack, 1959) and, published posthumously, *Captain Walker's Marathon* (1986). Fedora Fisher explores his interests in her 1994 biography, *Raphael Cilento*.

KT

Citizen Military Forces, see **CMF**

Citizenship means, broadly, membership of a political community. Beyond this minimal definition, however, lies much debate. For many decades before it was legally defined in Australia, the term *citizen* was widely employed to refer to non-politicians taking part in public events. It also described highly respected individuals who had made an outstanding public contribution. Thus the prominent Chinese-born businessman and philanthropist **Quong Tart**, although a member of a racial minority that the majority of Australians sought to exclude from citizenship rights, was known in the late nineteenth century as 'a citizen in the best sense of the word'.

In their campaign for the vote, women suffragists described themselves similarly, as law-abiding, tax-paying 'citizens', making a major public contribution by doing the bulk of the charitable and educational work (see Helen Irving (ed.), *A Woman's Constitution*, 1996).

By common law, all those born 'within the King's allegiance' in Britain or its colonies were subjects. Strictly, the term *citizen* was confined to members of a republic. However, ideas such as civil and political rights, associated with citizenship, still applied to subjects. Until World War I, subject status acquired by birth was inalienable. Individuals could also be naturalised as subjects, but naturalisation held only in the place where it had been granted, and had no validity elsewhere in the Empire.

From the 1880s Australian colonial law enforced this limitation on naturalised subjects. It also restricted the movement and employment of Chinese persons and the numbers entering Australia. Although in theory all British subjects were entitled to equal treatment under the law, these restrictions were also applied to Chinese subjects.

In the Federal Conventions of the 1890s, John **Quick** from Victoria moved to have a definition of *citizenship* included in the Australian **Constitution** and for the rights of citizens to have constitutional protection. However, since other Convention delegates could not agree on what citizenship meant and most did not want 'coloured' residents protected, they settled for the familiar term *subject*. Section 117 was written into the Constitution, prohibiting discrimination against 'a subject of the Queen', but only on the grounds of residence.

In the early years of the Commonwealth, despite official British disapproval, commitment to a 'white' citizenship strengthened. The Immigration Restriction Act (commonly called the **White Australia** policy) was passed in 1901. It applied until the late 1960s. Where the first Commonwealth Franchise Act of 1902 extended citizenship rights to white women, it excluded almost all 'coloured' persons, including Aborigines, who remained disenfranchised in Commonwealth elections until 1962. With World War I, British law was changed so that subjects of German origin could be deprived of 'citizenship' rights and, in some cases, lose their subject status altogether. Australia followed. The era of the inclusive, inalienable character of British subject status was over.

After 1945, the colonies—now called Dominions—could pass separate citizenship laws, and Australian women won their campaign to retain subject/citizenship status upon marriage to a non-British alien. In 1948 the **Chifley** Labor government passed the first Nationality and Citizenship Act. Citizenship Conventions for 'new Australians' were also introduced at that time. Australians were simultaneously citizens and British subjects until 1984, when citizen status became exclusive. In the same year, British nationals in Australia lost their privileged rights in respect of voting and naturalisation.

In 1967 a path-breaking **referendum**—often called the citizenship referendum—altered the Australian Constitution so that the Commonwealth could make special laws for the Aboriginal people, and could include Aboriginal natives in 'reckoning the numbers of the people of the Commonwealth.' Aboriginal Australians, already legal citizens, were now 'counted' as citizens, although as Brian Galligan and John Chesterman show in *Citizens without Rights* (1997), they still lacked rights. Social equality and equal access to power remain remote.

In the 1950s the ideas of T.H. Marshall, who argued that full citizenship required economic as well as civil and politi-

cal rights, became influential in Australia. In the 1970s developments such as equal pay for women and land rights for NT Aborigines extended notions of citizenship beyond formal political entitlements. Numerous new forms of 'citizenship' (including 'environmental', 'multicultural', and 'global') have since been identified, as discussed in Wayne Hudson and John Kane (eds), *Rethinking Australian Citizenship* (2000).

Citizenship emerged as a focus of both conservative and progressive politics in the 1990s. In 1994, the **Keating** Labor government established a Civics Expert Group to promote citizenship education. This was reaffirmed in 1997 by the **Howard** Liberal government, which launched a 'Discovering Democracy' program under the direction of the renamed Civics Education Group.

The 1990s also saw further debate about Aboriginal citizenship, and about entitlements for Australian residents without legal citizenship or with dual citizenship. Alistair Davidson has argued, in *From Subject to Citizen* (1997), that Australia still lacks a democratic citizenship. The uncertainty about whether citizenship is a legal category or an attribute of civil society will ensure that these debates continue.

HELEN IRVING

Clapp family made notable contributions to public transport. FRANCIS BOARDMAN CLAPP (1833–1920) migrated to Australia from the USA in 1853 to build the legendary coaching business, **Cobb & Co**. He subsequently formed the Melbourne Omnibus Company, which in the 1880s won the right to operate cable trams on tracks leased from a municipal trust. Clapp's operations expanded subsequently from Melbourne to other cities. HAROLD WINTHROP (1875–1952), his son, worked for his father before moving to the USA, where he held senior positions in a number of **railway** companies. As chairman of the Victorian Railway commissioners from 1920 he introduced American management methods, with particular emphasis on technological innovation, a corporate approach to industrial relations, and aggressive commercial promotion. The popularisation of orange juice, sold at a kiosk at Flinders Street Station, was one of his novelties. From 1939 to 1942 he was general manager of the aircraft construction branch of the Commonwealth government, and from 1942 to 1951 Commonwealth director-general of land transport. A forceful, self-promoting, brusque and demanding administrator with an American accent, Clapp embodied the gospel of scientific management.

SM

Clark, Andrew Inglis (1848–1907) was a federationist who helped draft the Commonwealth **Constitution**. A lawyer and parliamentarian in Tasmania, he was an advanced liberal and admirer of the USA with a strong attachment to republican ideals—there was a portrait of Mazzini in every room of his home. Prior to the Federal Convention in Sydney in 1891, to which he was a delegate, he circulated a draft constitution and served in Sydney as a member of the drafting committee with Charles **Kingston** and Samuel **Griffith**. Following the testimony of Robert **Garran** and Alfred **Deakin**, Griffith is given credit for the final draft which was adopted by the Convention and formed the basis of all subsequent efforts. Clark was not present on the Queensland government vessel which Griffith used when he made the draft, as he was ill with influenza; but Alex Castles (in Marcus Haward and James Warden (eds), *An Australian Democrat*, 1996) and John Williams (in *AJPH*, 1996) argue that Griffith relied heavily on Clark's draft, especially for the American federal model. Clark took no further part in the federal movement, though he continued to encourage it and write upon its constitutional and judicial principles. The book of essays edited by Haward and Warden provides insight into this attractive figure whose biography remains to be written.

SM

Clark, (Charles) Manning Hope (1915–91), historian, was author of the monumental *A History of Australia* (six volumes, 1962–87), a work which has been described by its admirers as 'a majestic blue gum' of Australian historical scholarship, the one which best helps Australians 'know who we are'; and by its detractors as 'gooey subjective pap' and 'history without facts'. Yet few deny that Clark is Australia's most famous historian. In its attempts to define what mattered in the Australian experience, Clark's *History* sits alongside the novels of Patrick **White** and the paintings of Sidney **Nolan** as one of the great achievements of the generation immediately following World War II.

Clark had a conventional scholarly career at Melbourne and Oxford universities, and at Canberra University College and the Australian National University, where he was professor 1949–75. But he always tried to stand 'a pace apart' from academic history. Rejecting the narrow confines of both the dominant conservative empiricism and the crude Marxism of his day, Clark worked in a much older literary tradition. He would not be a 'dryasdust', a 'measurer', a 'straitener', a 'science of history man'. He sought to be what the Ancient Greeks called an *istor*, or prophet-storyteller, a bard, a wisdom man. He borrowed freely from the Bible, the Book of Common Prayer, and the whole canon of Western and Australian literature. He particularly admired the great novelists and historians of the nineteenth century and, like his hero Fyodor Dostoevsky, wanted to 'be there when everyone suddenly understands what it has all been for'. (Both Clark and Dostoevsky suffered from epilepsy, an affliction which the ancients thought bestowed second sight.) And he also felt a special affinity with Henry **Lawson**, who, like Clark, had fought a drink problem and sided habitually with the underdog. Clark would be an antipodean Gibbon. His history would penetrate beneath mere narrative, address the great human questions of the Fall of Man, of forgiveness, of life and death, clothe them in Australian form, and show how Australian experience could 'contribute to the great conversation of humanity'.

The structure was epic, as was the theme: how Europeans had brought their religions and philosophies to Australia (Catholicism, Protestantism, and the Enlightenment); how they had tried to transplant their civilisation in an ancient continent; and how the continent had absorbed them. Like Virgil, Clark eventually settled on six books, ending his story a generation before the present so as to invest it with an appropriate degree of prescience. His heroes all failed nobly—**Macquarie** built Georgian Sydney but was subdued by his **fatal flaw** of vanity; Ned **Kelly** was a bushranger and folk champion who let 'the madness of old Ireland' get the better of him; **Burke** and Wills crossed a continent only to die lonely deaths in the bush trying to get home; **Bradman**, the greatest cricket batsman ever, succumbed to bodyline; **Menzies** governed a prosperous Australia but always felt himself an Austral-Briton; and **Whitlam** presided over a cultural awakening but was struck down politically before his time. Yet the nation grew, acquired its heroes, and endured the horrors of racial, sectarian and class conflict, war, and depression.

Clark learnt from Carlyle the power of the set-piece tableau, painting pictures of great symbolic, even apocalyptic, power: Macquarie's arrival in the *Dromedary* to clean up Sydney after the **Rum Rebellion**; the Great Victorian Bushfire of 1851; the death of **Truganini**; the **Anzac** landing; Menzies' first trip to Britain. There are also liturgical repetitions to underline the message of his parables—'Men in Black' are forever restricting the human spirit, the 'Galilean' and the 'Virgin' freeing it.

The organising themes, the triad of Catholicism, Protestantism, and the Enlightenment, were expanded in the middle volumes to include a sense of place ('the land, boys, we live in', the 'earth' which 'abideth forever'), and simplified in the later volumes to a clash between 'The Old Dead Tree' of European culture, and the 'Young Tree Green' of nationalist and nascently republican Australia, arboreal tropes borrowed from Lawson. True believers found Clark's message irresistible; others were irritated by his sloppiness with facts and his partisan politics.

Clark's father was an Anglican clergyman, who was born into the English working class and migrated to Sydney with his parents as a child; his mother was a Hope, descended from the colonial landed gentry. Among her forebears she included the Rev. Samuel **Marsden**. In his autobiographical writings Clark cleverly personalised the themes of his *History*. His father is forgiving and all for Australia; his mother straitlaced, proper, respectable, very 'English'. The young Manning, after many trials and tribulations, claims he sided with his 'life-affirming' father. Clark leaves the British provincialism of Protestant Melbourne for the bushy, frontier freedom of Canberra. He consciously wrote his own legend, and his autobiographical writings must be handled as critically as any other historical source.

In the 1940s and 1950s Clark was a conventional scholar, editing three volumes of documents for the study of Australian history, and challenging the dominant **Old Left** nationalism of historians like Brian **Fitzpatrick** and Russel **Ward**. His inaugural lecture at the Australian National University in 1954 was welcomed by the editor of the conservative magazine *Quadrant* as beginning a **counter-revolution in Australian historiography**. It questioned the facile understandings of mateship and explored the continuity of European influences, such as religion and the Enlightenment, in the Australian setting. Yet in 1960 he published a sympathetic account of his travels in the Soviet Union, *Meeting Soviet Man*. 'Soviet Man', he declared with the studied ambiguity that marked all his ideological pronouncements, deserved to be 'taken seriously'. By the 1970s Clark had thrown in his lot with the Labor side, and the pessimism of his early volumes gave way to a nationalist, republican optimism. Whitlam and **Hawke** welcomed him as a supporter. The press turned to him as 'the best guru in the business'. Clark, with the props of a big, dark brown Stetson hat, a wide belt, a goatee beard, and a Tiresias-like expression, relished the role, and in the last 15 years of his life accepted a demanding schedule of speaking engagements all over the continent. In the Bicentennial year his *History* was even turned into a musical which ran for several weeks in Melbourne.

A new generation of historians since the 1960s has found Clark's essentially literary, high political, and 'great man' biographical approach less relevant to their concerns. The common people appear in Clark's *History* as a sort of Greek chorus with little individuality beyond the odd cameo role; Aborigines and women are mostly 'victims' with little human agency; economics and culture are not seen as problematical. Since Clark's death, his work and character have been subjected to an intemperate attack by his former publisher, Peter Ryan, and the *Courier-Mail* has alleged that he was an agent of influence for the Soviet union. Humphrey **McQueen** made a spirited reply in *Suspect History* (1997). Nevertheless, Clark's place in the historical and literary pantheon is assured. Stephen Holt produced a study of Clark's long intellectual apprenticeship, *Manning Clark and Australian History 1915–63* (1982), and has since written *A Short History of Manning Clark* (1999); Michael Cathcart abridged the six volumes (1993); Carl Bridge edited *Manning Clark: Essays on His Place in History* (1994); Susan Davies edited Clark's correspondence with Kathleen **Fitzpatrick** (1996); Christopher Sexton and Brian Matthews are writing full-scale biographies.

CARL BRIDGE

Clark, Ralph (1755–94) was a marine officer who arrived at Sydney Cove with the **First Fleet**. The observations he made in his diary, covering the period 1787–92, provide rich detail about the shipboard experience and the daily life of the colony, particularly at **Norfolk Island**, where he was stationed 1790–91. Clark's diary is distinguished by its romantic self-pity. His preoccupation with the sexual licence of female convicts found expression in the phrase 'damned whores', which was used by Anne **Summers** in her *Damned Whores and God's Police* (1975). A volume containing his letters and journal, edited by Paul Fidlon and R.J. Ryan, was published in 1981. Clark is the central character in Thomas **Keneally's** novel, *The Playmaker* (1987).

KT

Clarke family has possessed great riches over four generations. Its fortunes were established by WILLIAM JOHN TURNER CLARKE (?1801–74), who, even by the standards of his age, made an extraordinary climb from humble origins in the West Country of England to a butcher's shop in Hobart and then the acquisition of great swathes of pastoral property. He became known as Big Clarke and left an estate of more than 200 000 acres freehold and £2 500 000. The eldest son, WILLIAM JOHN (1831–97), dignified the wealth with a lavish country seat, Rupertswood, in Sunbury, Victoria, and a city mansion, Cliveden, in East Melbourne, along with a parliamentary career, patronage, lavish hospitality, and a baronetcy. His second wife, JANET MARION, née Snodgrass (1851–1909), brought substantial wealth of her own and was a notable philanthropist; the hostel for women students attached to Trinity College at the University of Melbourne became Janet Clarke Hall. Her two sons inherited pastoral and parliamentary interests, while their half-brother from William's first marriage, RUPERT TURNER HAVELOCK (1865–1926), assumed the family's substantial banking and financial interests. A restless, unfulfilled man, he kept residences in Melbourne, Sydney, England, and Monte Carlo as well as Rupertswood. His son from a second marriage, RUPERT WILLIAM JOHN (1919–), became the third baronet and was chairman of the National Bank 1986–92. There is a body of Clarke family history; most useful are biographies of Big Clarke (1980) and his son Sir William (1995) by Michael Clarke, grandson of Sir William.

SM

Clarke, Marcus Andrew Hislop (1846–81), journalist and novelist, was a brilliant observer of low life in the colonial city and the author of *His Natural Life*, the most famous fictional depiction of the Australian **convict** experience.

He grew up in London, the son of a prosperous lawyer, and was educated at Cholmeley Grammar School in Highgate. His mother died when he was four, and when he was 16 his father suffered a mental and financial breakdown that cut short Clarke's prospects in England and evidently prompted relatives to arrange his emigration in 1863 to Victoria. A sickly, spoiled, sophisticated youth, with more knowledge of literature than life, Clarke may have seemed even worse-equipped for the colonies than for London. Manning **Clark**, who makes him a leading character in the fourth volume of his *History*, calls him a 'Merlin, part innocent child, part devil'. With the help of an uncle, a colonial judge, he tried working as a banker, and contemplated life as a squatter, until the £800 he had brought with him was gone and he turned at last to journalism. In 1867 he began contributing a topical column, 'The Peripatetic Philosopher', under the pseudonym 'Q' to the Melbourne **Argus**. Assuming the vantage-point of an outsider, a self-styled 'upper-Bohemian', Clarke cast an irreverent eye on the faults and foibles of a city which had always taken itself too seriously. 'He is a poor philosopher', Clarke wrote of his *alter ego*, 'whose shoes are down at heel and worn out in the soles;

... and in his innermost heart has an utter contempt for everybody, himself included.' Like his great London contemporaries Thackeray, Dickens, Jerrold, and Sala, Clarke was drawn to the everyday comedy of the streets. He wrote sketches of the fashionable crowds on 'the Block' and the sharebrokers under 'the Verandah' as well as the cabmen in Bourke Street and the larrikins outside Wright's Gin Palace. He was an admirer of the French realist Balzac, author of a great sequence of novels 'called by its author *Comédie*, but which is rather history'. Clarke himself aspired to be a contemporary historian of the colonial city, as is acknowledged by Laurie Hergenhan in his edition of Clarke's journalism, *A Colonial City* (1972), and the contributors to *The Outcasts of Melbourne* (1985).

Clarke was becoming a historian in yet another sense. In 1871 he published a book of short sketches, *Old Tales of a Young Country*, on well-known episodes and characters of Australian history, such as the settlement of Sydney, the notorious pickpocket George **Barrington**, and the **Eureka Stockade**. He had also embarked on a long novel of convict life, *His Natural Life*, the first serial chapter of which appeared in February 1870 in the *Australian Journal*. Clarke was following in the path of other great convict novels, such as Victor Hugo's *Les Misérables* (1862), and his plot, with its coincidences and revelations of mistaken identity, is more melodramatic than realistic. But the core of the book, and what makes it memorable, is Clarke's vividly realised, relentlessly sombre account of the tribulations of his hero Rufus Dawes in the hellholes of Macquarie Harbour, **Port Arthur**, and **Norfolk Island**. The book, he wrote to Charles Gavan **Duffy**, was 'an attempt to expose the infamies that attached to the old transportation system, and the episodes are merely dramatised versions of the facts'. Clarke had visited Tasmania in 1870, and he drew on the memoirs and official papers he read in the Melbourne Public Library. Some episodes are based on known historical incidents: for example, the killing of the villain Maurice Frere is based, as J.V. **Barry** showed in *The Life and Death of John Price* (1964), on the murder of the notorious convict superintendent John Price. Most scholars, however, have strongly qualified the novel's claims to historical truth. 'History as such was not Clarke's object', claimed his 1958 biographer Brian Elliott, emphasising, by contrast, his psychological insight into crime and punishment. Lloyd **Robson**, whose *The Convict Settlers of Australia* (1965) showed the convicts as hardened criminals rather than victims of the law like Dawes, made a detailed study of Clarke's use of original sources in *Australian Literary Studies* (1963), concluding that he often exaggerated or took the exception for the rule. Yet Clarke's conception of history was far from literal, and historians versed in Foucaultian notions of punishment may find more truth in his exploration of the regime's extremities.

The Australian Journal was the last of several monthly magazines which Clarke had owned or edited in the late 1860s and early 1870s. When the serial publication of *His Natural Life* ended, two and a half years after it had begun,

the patience of his proprietors, and his own finances, were exhausted. He obtained a position as sub-librarian of the Public Library, while continuing to write on theatre, politics, religion, and literature for the Melbourne reviews. His pungently expressed opinions on Australian landscape ('funereal, secret and stern'), the Coming Australian Man ('The Australians will be a fretful, clever, perverse, irritable race ...'), and the conflict between religion and science ('the faith of our fathers is passing away from us') are among the most searching of his times and live in historical literature. His own life was restless, prodigal and unfulfilled. Drink, debt, and disappointment sapped his health, and he died, leaving a wife and six children, when he was only 35.

GRAEME DAVISON

Class has been a powerful force in Australian history and a long-standing preoccupation of historians. The language of class was established by the end of the nineteenth century as a way of describing social divisions generated by industrial capitalism. Pre-industrial society had maintained by law, custom, and religion a hierarchy of birth and rank; and similarly rigid divisions were at first carried into the Australian colonies with the laws that distinguished the free settler from the convict and the assertion of privileges by the **exclusives** over the **emancipists**. But with the establishment of equality before the law, the end of transportation, the advent of democratic self-government, and spread of property-ownership, such formal barriers yielded. The fear of the levelling mob that haunted early conservatives such as James **Macarthur** and later W.C. **Wentworth** could not withstand the demands of liberals for equality of opportunity and radicals for equality of esteem. Absence of deference became a hallmark of colonial society. Yet the very triumph of these principles imparted a rancorous quality to public life, as the wealthy pastoral and professional elite fought to hold on to their advantages. The visiting English radical, Charles Dilke, observed in *Greater Britain* (1869) that 'class animosity runs much higher and drives its roots far deeper into private life in Victoria than in any other English-speaking country I have seen'.

While the dominant liberal ethos enshrined the autonomy of the individual, it also recognised sectional interests. Sectors of business, trades, and occupations all formed associations to pursue these interests, so that contemporaries spoke of the mercantile, the manufacturing or the working classes (as a descriptive term, usually in the plural) in the belief that their legitimate concerns were complementary and that they could share a mutual respect and prosperity. For Dilke and local critics, class animosity was a reprehensible prejudice, an old-world evil that had no place in the new. Henry **Lawson's** youthful socialism was aimed at the pretensions of those who violated this expectation to set themselves above others:

> But the curse o' class distinctions from our shoulders
>   shall be hurled,
> An' the influence of Kindness revolutionize the world;

There'll be higher education for the toilin' starvin'
  clown,
An' the rich an' educated shall be educated down.

The **egalitarian** rejection of class as an artificial and odious imposition was joined by the beginning of the twentieth century by the recognition of class as a guiding principle of national life. The growth of the capitalist economy increased the distance between employer and employee. From the **strikes and lockouts** of the 1890s there emerged a conviction of diametrically opposed interests between labour and capital, which were institutionalised industrially in trade unions and **employers' organisations**, politically in the formation of the **Australian Labor Party**. Class became something more than a descriptive term; now used in the singular to refer to a distinct and cohesive formation, it assumed a fundamental importance as a social condition that permeated work, leisure, family, and self-expression. John Rickard's *Class and Politics* (1976) remains the fullest and most satisfactory treatment of this transition: he concludes with the prescient observation that the solidification of a class structure turned class into 'a comfort rather than a scourge'. In particular, the institutionalisation of the male breadwinner through the **basic wage** gave class a strongly masculine connotation.

Meanwhile **Old Left** historians projected the new understanding of class backwards as the dynamic of Australia's entire post-settlement experience. 'I have taken the view', wrote Brian **Fitzpatrick** in *The Short History of the Australian Labor Movement* (1940), 'that the history of the Australian people is amongst other things the history of a struggle between the organised rich and the organised poor.' His major studies of *British Imperialism and Australia 1788–1833* (1939) and *The British Empire in Australia 1834–1939* (1941) traced that struggle through the linkages of British to local capitalism. Subsequent Old Left scholars concentrated on **labour history** with works that analysed the formation of the working class and its momentum towards the socialist destiny. Robin **Gollan's** *Radical and Working-Class Politics* (1960, 1967) applied this interpretation to the growth of the unions and the establishment of the ALP; Ian **Turner's** *Industrial Labour and Politics* (1965) treated the emergence of a more militant and revolutionary challenge from 1901 to 1921.

Fitzpatrick was a freelance socialist; Gollan, Turner, and colleagues were or had been communists. Their understanding of class was shaped by socialist doctrine, and especially by the historical materialist method of Karl Marx. **Marxism** contended that classes were constituted by the forces and relations of production; the two principal classes of industrial capitalism were the owners of the means of production, the capitalists; and those who worked for them, the working class or proletariat. The two classes were locked into an antagonistic relationship because labour was the source of value, upon which capitalists relied for their profits.

Marxism was only one strand of Australian socialism, which in turn was but one of the doctrines that shaped the labour movement. The Old Left historians themselves embedded Marxism within a radical and **populist** outlook that linked the working class with a larger tradition of popular resistance—hence Fitzpatrick's formulation of 'the organised rich' and 'the organised poor', and Russel **Ward's** delineation of *The Australian Legend* (1958) that began with convicts, bushrangers, and diggers. They were conscious also of the forces that impeded class consciousness: the sectional divisions in the labour movement, careerism, the palliative effects of industrial **arbitration** and state reform. But their inscription of the working class as the inheritors and fulfillers of the national destiny had a pervasive effect on Australian historiography.

In public discourse the language of class was weakened from the middle of the twentieth century by the consensual ideologies of family, consumption, individual freedom, and national unity. In the social sciences class analysis was challenged by theories of social stratification and pluralism. But in history that challenge was far weaker. Among the few historians to explicitly dispute the emphasis on class was Bede **Nairn**, who suggested that the object of the labour movement was *Civilising Capitalism* (1973). In his subsequent biography of Jack **Lang** (1985), he insisted that class was 'irrelevant to Australian history', but in the next sentence allowed that the compound adjectives 'working-class' and 'upper-class' provided 'intelligible descriptions relating to socio-economic conditions'.

From the 1970s, however, the **New Left** arraigned the Old Left for an insufficiently rigorous understanding of class. Humphrey **McQueen** alleged in *A New Britannia* (1970) that the popular tradition celebrated by Ward and others was vitiated by racism, militarism, and acquisitive individualism; Stuart Macintyre claimed in *Intervention* (1972) that Turner's concentration on the working class was at the expense of a holistic analysis of class relations. In a subsequent article in *HS* (1978), he criticised the assumption that class consciousness was determined by class position. Historians had searched for evidence of the outlook and actions of fractions of capital and labour that corresponded with their class position; in the absence of such corroboration they fell back on explanations of class hegemony and social control. A similarly hermetic methodology was apparent in class analysis conducted across a range of disciplines during the 1970s, including sociology, political economy, philosophy, literature, art, and education.

Much of this work found its way into R. W. Connell and T.H. Irving, *Class Structure in Australian History*, in 1980. Yet their rich synthesis quickly turned out to be the highwater mark of class-based history. There would be subsequent monographs, articles, and collections of increasing theoretical sophistication and decreasing impact. The new class history published in the 1980s rejected the crude reductionism that assumed a correspondence of class structure with class expression; it expressly repudiated the teleological faith in a determinist course of historical development. But in making the post-structuralist turn, it qualified class to the point of extinction.

Climate

In one of many review articles of *Class Structure in Australian History*, John Rickard in *HS* (1981) observed that its treatment of the middle class was especially unsatisfactory. Far from dwindling, this large, various, and still mysterious category that lay between capital and labour had become dominant. His challenge remained unanswered while class historians sought to accommodate other dimensions of inequality and forms of oppression: initially race and gender; later ethnicity, sexuality, and ecology. Earlier attempts to interpret these as ancillary effects of capitalism quickly faltered. With the rise of the new social movements, class was stripped of its privileged status. With the retreat from working-class policies and the decline of class-based political loyalties, the Australian Labor Party's earlier attachment to class was reinterpreted by Frank Bongiorno, in *The People's Party* (1996), as just one of its axes. Furthermore, the linguistic turn undermined understandings of class based exclusively on materialist criteria, so that it could no longer be seen as a monolithic category: in works such as Lyn Finch, *The Classing Gaze* (1993), class was now presented as a particular discourse of **masculinity**.

By the close of the twentieth century the arrangements that had contained and ameliorated class inequalities were largely dismantled. The abandonment of full employment as a primary goal of public policy, the decline of manual work performed in large workgroups, the retreat of the welfare state, the shrinkage of trade unions, and the shift from arbitration to individual employment contracts—all these eroded long-established working-class forms. While the gulf between rich and poor grew wider, these differences were less likely to be understood in class terms. The Labor Party retained that title, but it was a party dominated by professionals that preferred to speak of **'true believers'** rather than workers. The non-Labor parties employed their own characterisations—'the forgotten people', 'middle Australia', 'the battlers'—to mark out their social constituency.

Those who sought to maintain an awareness of class returned to more open and inclusive forms of popular experience. The series *A People's History of Australia Since 1788* (1988) was conceived by Verity Burgmann and Jenny Lee as a riposte to the Bicentennial celebrations. In four volumes more than 70 contributors offered a view from the back of the house to 'a line of washing, bulging rubbish bins, and all the evidence of living and working'. Burgmann's subsequent *Power and Protest* (1993) sought to restore a class perspective to the new social movements, and Craig McGregor reasserted the importance of *Class in Australia* (1997). While the tide is out on class, material inequality remains deeply entrenched and its effects far-reaching.

Stuart Macintyre

Climate and changing perceptions of climate have profoundly influenced the human history of Australia.

Aborigines experienced dramatic alterations of climate, of which the main change began about 17 000 years ago. At that time, New Guinea, Australia and Tasmania formed one landmass, the climate in lowland Australia was perhaps four or five degrees cooler, and the sea was at least 100 metres lower than it is today. Then global temperatures increased, vast ice sheets melted in the far northern hemisphere and in the Antarctic, and sea levels rose, severing Tasmania and finally isolating Australia. Perhaps one-seventh of the continent was drowned before the sea ceased to rise, some 6000 years ago.

European explorers of Australia's coast could only guess about the climate. In 1770 **Cook** and **Banks**, after spending short periods at Botany Bay and the mouth of the tropical Endeavour River, optimistically concluded that they were seeing the land in the dry season. In fact they were at Botany Bay during the wettest time of the year: accordingly they gravely overestimated its normal rainfall and soil fertility. Without that overestimate, eastern Australia might not have been colonised by the British in the late eighteenth century.

The interior was also viewed too optimistically. The history of inland **exploration** after the traversing of the Blue Mountains in 1813 is largely the futile search for a freshwater sea or for Australian versions of the Ganges, Nile, and Mississippi. The explorer Ernest **Giles** even in the early 1870s nursed a hope of finding 'an overland route for stock' between the arid centre and the west coast. By then it was clear that this was the world's driest continent.

The frequency of **droughts** was not predicted. In the fine farming and grazing districts of the continent's south-eastern corner, the climate, while fickle by British standards, was relatively favourable between the 1840s and the late 1880s. Then came the fiery drought which, beginning in the mid-1890s, quickly halved the number of sheep. From the 1880s to the mid-1940s, except in WA, average rainfall fell markedly. Labor and later the radical wing of the Country Party flourished in many rural electorates in this dry phase. The long conservative reign of R.G. **Menzies** as prime minister (1949–66) owed much to the coming of moister years and the blunting of rural radicalism. In March 1976 the Academy of Science in its *Report of a Committee on Climatic Change* argued that since 1945 climate has tended to be drier in the south-western corner and wetter by 10 to 20 per cent in big areas of the crucial south-east.

Immigrants from the British Isles brought strong climatic preferences which Australia thwarted. Christmas and Easter fell in the wrong seasons. The hot winds—often called brickfielders or siroccos—were feared. A slow-changing national attitude to climate was heralded around 1890 by the rising **Heidelberg School** of painters; and Arthur **Streeton** actually celebrated the 'hot trying winds and slow immense summer'. When Dorothea **Mackellar** wrote her Edwardian poem, 'I Love a Sunburnt Country', most Australians did not yet agree. They preferred green, well-watered country. Hobart was the preferred holiday destination in summer.

Australia has many climates. About 39 per cent of the land lies within the tropics, but 'Tropical Australia' has never been a widely used term. Fear that the tropics harmed Europeans' health led to high loadings by life offices and a tendency, before 1901, to employ coloured labour—Kanakas on Queensland sugar plantations, Chinese in NT gold mines, and Afghans as carriers. The economy of this huge warm region was long retarded by the reluctance of Europeans to settle there. In 1995 Townsville was its only city with more than 100 000 people.

New theories about Australia's climate, past and present, have emerged since the 1970s. The El Niño—a phase of warm water on the surface of the tropical Pacific Ocean—is now seen as a cause of Australian droughts, including that severe drought which peaked in 1982–83 and helped the first electoral victory of the **Hawke** government (1983–91). Officially it is also argued that Australia is affected by the recent phase of global warming, but statistics from recent weather satellites and from long-term temperature records in the interior seem to muddy this argument.

Books which touch on climatic influences include the pioneering *Australia: A Study of Warm Environments* by Griffith **Taylor** (1940); G.C. **Bolton**, *A Thousand Miles Away* (1963); R.L. Heathcote, *Back of Bourke* (1965); and B.R. Davidson, *The Northern Myth* (1965). Geoffrey Blainey wrote on 'Climate and Australia's History' in *MHJ* (1971). A short, simple account of climate is the CSIRO's *Weather and Climate* (1986).

GEOFFREY BLAINEY

Closer settlement was a scheme for concentrated rural settlement through government repurchase, subdivision and reallocation of large estates. Following the earlier **Selection** Acts of the 1860s, new legislation was introduced in the 1890s, first in SA and soon after in the other colonies. Superior farming land was made available through subsequent legislation in the early 1900s, which allowed for the government's compulsory repurchase of large holdings. Heavy taxes levied on large holdings also encouraged voluntary repurchase. **Soldier settlement** schemes, another form of closer settlement, were introduced after World War I, and more successfully during World War II, with the compulsory acquisition of land.

The subdivision of large holdings, which generally had been used for pastoral purposes, was made in response to the growing demand for small farms, and the need to increase agricultural production and development. This, it was argued, would attract more settlers and therefore boost population. Closer settlement also fitted the agrarian ideal of a happy yeomanry, a notion that gained popularity in the 1890s amid general disillusionment with urban life. Governments made the schemes attractive and accessible by offering easy terms for land acquisition. In some cases, immigration programs were also involved, such as **group settlement** in WA. In south-eastern Australia closer settlement often ran in tandem with **irrigation** schemes, which relied on settlers practising forms of intensive agriculture, such as cropping, fruit-growing, or **dairying**. The success of closer settlement schemes hinged on the suitability of the land, the size of the holdings, settlers' farming knowledge, and government support and supervision.

HD

Clothing, see **Fashion**

Clubs are founded for general conviviality, or for special purposes, or to combine the two. They are voluntary and self-governing, and usually have to do with leisure activities, though most large clubs have perforce become also businesses.

The eighteenth century was the great age of clubs in Britain, for all classes. Labouring and artisan families had long 'clubbed' together to share costs of illness, burials, Christmas feasts, and other conviviality, a process formalised in **friendly societies**, and in lodges claiming descent from ancient craft guilds. The Oddfellows Lodge founded in Sydney in 1836 was the first of many; Geoffrey **Blainey**, in *Odd Fellows: A History of IOOF Australia* (1991), observed that for decades lodges were more important than unions to Australian workers. Lodges controlled their membership, and many proceedings were secret, but most also provided social facilities for general benefit. In 1885 the 1300 inhabitants of the Victorian country town of Camperdown enjoyed the use of Masonic, Temperance, Oddfellows, and Good Templar Halls, and a good **Mechanics Institute**.

Gentlemen's clubs formed 'on the London principles'—which included admittance 'guarded by ballot', and provision of a building for the exclusive use of the members 'as a place of resort, or of temporary residence'—came late to the penal settlements of Sydney and Hobart, where their functions were served by officers' messes, but early in the free settlements. Of the first three founded in Australia, in 1838, the Australian (Sydney) and the Melbourne Club survive, but the South Australian soon failed and was eventually replaced by the Adelaide Club (1863). By then Hobart had the Tasmanian Club (1861) and Brisbane the Queensland (1859), which soon eclipsed the North Australian Club of Brisbane's rival, Ipswich. The Weld Club opened in Perth in 1871.

The first members of these clubs were military officers, landowners, and professional and business men. Governors, service heads, and the like might be admitted *ex officio*, and clergy at a discount, but exclusion on social, religious, or ethnic grounds was common, and in some places and periods rigorous and universal. The Melbourne Club, in particular, became a symbol of established power, real enough from about the 1860s to the 1920s, though always exaggerated. The influence of the Adelaide Club was longer-lived, though narrower, and always conservative.

Smaller clubs were founded in suburbs and provincial cities. Most were exclusive within their own localities—the Hannan's Club (Kalgoorlie, 1896) specifically excluded miners, despite its name—though a few working men's clubs were founded, for example in Norwood, Adelaide, in 1884.

Paul de Serville, in *Pounds and Pedigrees: The Upper Class in Victoria 1850–1880* (1991), one of the few studies placing clubs in a social perspective, has shown that the gentlemen's clubs were far from identical. In Sydney the Union Club was founded in 1857 to be more tolerant politically than the Tory Australian Club, and the Warrigal Club (1882, now defunct) was described by a Scottish governor-general as more relaxed than either. As the Melbourne Club became more exclusive after 1850, nine other clubs were founded in Melbourne before 1881. Most failed, but the Australian (1878) met the needs of a broadening business community; the Athenaeum (1867) sought to emphasise intellect, though haphazardly; and the Yorick (1868) admitted gentlemen 'connected or sympathetic with Literature, Art or Science'. (It later merged with the Melbourne Savage Club, founded in 1894 and surviving.) The Bohemians (1875) admitted only those willing to play cricket in summer and make music in winter and, despite determining 'that the entrance fee be nil and that the subscription not exceed the entrance fee', survived until 1931. Clubs for old boys of private schools were only nominally exclusive, while those for occupational groups ranged from the Kelvin Club for professional engineers through various business and trade associations to the once ubiquitous Commercial Travellers Association (never exclusive, though linked with the older Commercial Travellers Clubs of Sydney, Melbourne, and Brisbane). The common purpose of conviviality was shared with the non-residential 'eating and talking' clubs.

Ladies organised clubs (other than those associated with churches and philanthropies) rather later than gentlemen, the first women university graduates and their supporters prominent among the founders. The Karrakatta Club founded in Perth in 1894 had intellectual intentions, and in Sydney the Women's College was the birthplace in 1901 of the Women's Club. In Melbourne the students who formed the Princess Ida Club at the university in 1888 were later active in the unusual Austral Salon (begun 1890) and in Lady **Clarke's** Australian Women's National Club before founding the Lyceum Club in 1910. No intellectual tests were required by the Alexandra Club, which emerged from the proprietary Wattle Club in 1903; its members were as emphatically ladies as the Melbourne Club's were gentlemen. Ladies of the Macquarie and the Queen's Clubs in Sydney shared the social class (and in many cases the matrimonial bed) of members of the Australian and Union Clubs.

Sporting clubs were a nineteenth-century invention. Gentlemen organised many of the first, including the exclusive hunt clubs, the very powerful Victoria Racing Club and Australian Jockey Club, and the related **Tattersall's** clubs (Sydney, 1858; Adelaide, 1870; and elsewhere). They also founded **cricket**, real tennis, rifle-shooting, and later polo clubs. Some sports were always more respectable than others: horses than dogs, dogs than pigeons, football than boxing, and (in Australia) fly-fishing than shooting. Working men were always active in sport, and in Sydney **rugby** split on social grounds, between Union and League, as rowing almost did in Melbourne (where gentlemen oarsmen complained that working men were unfairly strong). The Royal Sydney Yacht Squadron (1862), and other yacht clubs, required craft more expensive than rowboats. Class distinctions were echoed in the line drawn between the professional sportsman and the amateur, whose demise was especially hard-fought in athletics and tennis. The lawn tennis clubs founded from the 1880s (sometimes including bowling) were often socially exclusive, though the church

clubs gave a broad access to the game; tennis was, however, one of the few sports in which men and women usually belonged to the same clubs (as they did in golf clubs, though women had inferior status as 'associates'). Bushwalking became a club recreation after it ceased to be a wearisome necessity; the intellectual Wallaby Club (1894) combined 'walking and talking'. Naturalist clubs, including those specialising in bird-watching, had for a time a strong influence on state primary education.

By the late nineteenth century Australian communities were thronged with clubs, quasi-clubs in **pubs** and church organisations, and sporting associations of all sizes. Almost all country towns had racing, **cricket**, football, bowling, and tennis clubs, and lodges of various crafts and degrees of secrecy and influence. Football, and to a lesser extent cricket, came to knit the suburbs and the country towns into associations.

As Australian society became more complex, many local clubs withered and new replaced old, the Bachelors' and Spinsters' giving way to Senior Citizens'. New inventions brought new sports and new clubs, in cycling, motoring, and flying, and the Surf Life-Saving Clubs created their own sport in the twentieth century. Ski clubs arrived in the 1920s. So did new varieties of service clubs, supplanting such nineteenth-century philanthropies as the Travellers Aid Society; Rotary was established in Sydney and Melbourne in 1921, **Legacy** formed after World War I, the Lions (Liberty, Intelligence, Our National Safety) after World War II, and Apex (founded in Geelong) during the Depression. The Inner Wheel was created for Rotary wives. The **Country Women's Association** (founded 1922) was once described as the largest club in Australia; and the politically influential **Returned and Services League** provided a network of clubs for its membership, which was rigorously exclusive though not by social class.

Immigrant communities had always nourished clubs. The Melbourne Dante Alighieri Society was one of the first in the world, and German clubs (including the Deutscher Verein and Liedertafel, and the Tanunda Club in the Barossa) were numerous before most disappeared during World War I. Mid-century waves of migration brought social clubs ranging from Calabria to Lithuania in origin, and sporting clubs whose ethnic affiliations were strong enough to make soccer games nationalist contests. Other national clubs, especially the American, are mainly for business.

Governments first regulated clubs to control insurance (the friendly societies) and liquor and gambling (long flourishing in illegal 'clubs'). In NSW, changes to liquor laws in 1946–47, and above all the legalisation of gaming machines in clubs in 1956, created a unique network of social facilities based mainly on Rugby League and RSL clubs, with the Registered Clubs Association as a representative organisation. Many became pseudo-clubs, recreational premises with no genuine membership.

Clubs have always tended to become businesses, since the friendly societies gave way to mutual funds. In motoring, the state automobile associations began as sporting clubs but quickly became service organisations and insurers. The trend has accelerated. Some formerly exclusive social clubs, their facilities in less demand, now hire them out for conferences, and have widened their membership to include virtually all comers; others, especially in Sydney, have endowed themselves by developing their valuable sites. All major spectator sports, beginning with cricket and football, have been transformed by television into big businesses, their club structure replaced by large-scale national associations, epitomised by the Australian Football League. (See **Australian Rules football**.)

Clubs have a habit of recording their histories, usually to celebrate jubilees or centenaries, though sometimes to mourn mergers or closures. Most are introspective and simply reminiscent, but important stories are told in J.R. Angel, *The Australian Club 1838–1988: The First 150 Years* (1988); Ronald McNicoll, *Number 36 Collins Street: Melbourne Club 1838–1988* (1988); Joan Gillison, *A History of the Lyceum Club Melbourne* (1975); and Paul de Serville's *The Australian Club, Melbourne* (1998). Unusually light-hearted clubs are described in Joseph Johnson, *Laughter and the Love of Friends: A Centenary History of the Melbourne Savage Club 1894–1994 and a History of the Yorick Club 1868–1966* (1994). Harold Hunt chronicled *The Story of Rotary in Australia 1921–71* (1971), and R.S. Love and V.M. Branson, *Apex: The First Twenty-Five Years* (1956). Numerous centenary histories of sporting clubs, and some of lodges, have appeared in recent decades.

JOHN POYNTER

Clune, Francis Patrick (1893–1971) began his writing career in 1933 with the autobiographical *Try Anything Once*, an account of his youthful activities which included being wounded at **Gallipoli** and a stint in vaudeville. Although he wrote other autobiographical volumes, he is best known for his colourful historical novels, biographies, and exploration stories. Although Clune differentiated between these genres, all focus on sensational characters or incidents, handle evidence loosely, and employ a journalistic style. Often working in collaboration with P.R. **Stephensen**, Clune produced more than 60 books, including a study of Frank **Gardiner**, *Dark Outlaw* (1945); *Ben Hall the Bushranger* (1947) and *Wild Colonial Boys* (1948) were more comprehensive accounts of Ben **Hall** and other **bushrangers** of his time. His empathy with the underdog is also evident in *The Kelly Hunters* (1954) and *Rascals, Ruffians and Rebels of Early Australia* (1968, 1987). He was important as a historical populariser, whose works on legendary Australian figures, such as **Burke** and Wills in *Dig* (1937) and various bushrangers, were often reprinted and serialised on radio. His 1959 book on Jimmy **Governor** inspired Thomas **Keneally's** novel, *The Chant of Jimmy Blacksmith* (1972).

KT

Clunies Ross, (William) Ian (1899–1959) combined skills as a veterinary scientist and administrator during his long service with the **CSIRO** (initially CSIR) that culminated in his chairmanship (1949–59). A son of science teacher William John Clunies Ross (1850–1914), he gradu-ated in veterinary science from the University of Sydney in 1921, and shortly after received a Walter and Eliza Hall fellowship that allowed him to study in England. It was here that he began his life's work of research into parasites. Appointed parasitologist by the CSIR in 1926, Clunies Ross displayed a keen interest in the practi.cal use of research, in particular the breeding of livestock. He chaired the International Wool Secretariat in London (1937–40) before returning to Australia to become professor of veterinary science at the University of Sydney. In 1946 he moved to Melbourne as a member of the CSIR executive, and succeeded David **Rivett** as chair after the organisation was embroiled in political controversy over national security. Clunies Ross was more cooperative with the new Liberal–Country Party government and its invigilation of left-wing scientists. He worked relentlessly to promote the status of science in Australia and was a skilful publicist, once injecting himself with the myxomatosis virus to affirm its safety for humans. His contribution to Australian science was recognised by the depiction of his image on the Australian $50 note. A biography by Marjory O'Dea appeared in 1997, and L.R. Humphreys produced a biography in 1998.

KT

CMF is an abbreviation for Citizen Military Forces, which evolved from former colonial militia units that were reorganised as Commonwealth units following the Defence Act 1903. Enlistment was voluntary until 1912, when males between 18 and 26 were required to join a militia for eight years' part-time military training in return for moderate payment. Citizen forces were precluded from overseas service, although many individuals volunteered. Australia's 105 000 militiamen in **World War I** are sometimes called the forgotten army. Compulsory training was restricted in the 1920s, abolished in 1930, then recommenced (for home service only) in October 1939. During **World War II** the militia units were at first restricted to Australian territories, including PNG; from 1943 they could be deployed as far north as the equator.

After the war a permanent army was formed for the first time, and the CMF became a support for this force. In 1949 the CMF moved to a voluntary basis. When national service training for home defence was reintroduced for 18-year-olds in 1951, overall numbers rose dramatically, but voluntary enlistments declined before reorganisation again on a voluntary footing in 1960. Numbers surged when CMF enlistment facilitated avoidance of the **conscription** ballot between 1964 and 1972. Morale remained poor. T.B. Millar's *Committee of Inquiry into the CMF* (1974) recommended a wider logistic support role—the 'One Army' or 'Total Force' concept—and a name-change to Army Reserve, adopted in 1980. Paul Dibb's *Review of Australia's Defence Capabilities* (1986) found inadequate implementation of 'Total Force'. Major organisational problems were also identified by the auditor-general in 1990. The Army Reserve now comprises 45 per cent of total army strength and over 60 per cent of Land Command, but old rivalries and prejudices persist. The regular army that scoffed at CMF 'koalas' (i.e., not to be exported or shot) or 'chockos' (**chocolate soldiers**) still struggles to fully accept those it now knows as 'weekend warriors'. (See also **Defence**.)

DC

Cobb & Co. was a coaching service founded in Victoria in 1853 by a Californian, Freeman Cobb, F. B. Clapp, and two fellow Americans. The company operated its first service from Melbourne to the Forest Creek diggings (Castlemaine), and subsequently developed a network of routes throughout Victoria. Another American, James Rutherford, bought the business in 1859. He extended the service into NSW in 1862, establishing company headquarters at Bathurst, and into Qld in 1865. Under Rutherford, the company also diversified into pastoralism, shipping, and railway construction. The English-style coaches originally used in gold-rush Victoria were inadequate for traversing long distances over poor roads and difficult terrain. In response, Cobb & Co. introduced the Concord coach, a light-framed, leather-sprung American design with narrow wheels, which was well suited to Australian conditions and made possible a reliable 'fast coach' service celebrated in Henry **Lawson's** verse, 'Through stringy-bark and blue-gum, and box and pine we go—/A hundred miles shall see tonight the lights of Cobb and Co.!' The service necessitated a series of wayside stops—one every 16 kilometres—where horses could be changed, watered, and stabled, and passengers collected and put down. Speed and reliability also won the company regular mail contracts. Cobb & Co. dominated transport in the eastern colonies until the advent of the railway, which heralded its decline. The service ceased operating in 1924. A 1967 history by K.A. Austin used Lawson's 'The Lights of Cobb and Co.' as its title.

HD

Cocky, derived from *cockatoo*, is a colloquial term for a small farmer. This use of *cockatoo* had originated in the 1840s and 1850s in reference to the impermanent nature of tenant-farming. Tenants were described as suddenly taking flight, in the manner of a flock of cockatoos, and settling elsewhere. *Cocky* was later applied to small freehold farmers, especially those who took up **selections**; they were likened to cockatoos in the way they were seen to scratch out a living on relatively arid ground. Observers noted other bird-like allusions in the habits of small farmers, such as their unexpected arrival in large numbers, and their tendency to perch on fences or at the edges of squatting runs. Squatters and graziers used the term in a derogatory fashion, mocking smallholders, and scorning what they saw as their poor, inefficient, and untidy farming practices; this view encouraged the comical portrayal of cockies in popular literature, such as Steele **Rudd's** 'Selection' stories. The word was subsequently extended to farmers as a category. Variations developed, such as *cow-cocky* to describe dairy farmers, and *boss-cocky*, which originally referred to the owner of a large station but later came to mean anyone in authority.

HD

Coffee palaces provided meals and accommodation, but served coffee as a substitute for **alcohol**. Following the British example, coffee houses and **temperance** hotels were established in Australia as early as the 1840s, some with adjoining libraries to further encourage sobriety. The larger, more elaborate 'palaces' did not appear in large numbers until the 1880s. Many coffee palaces, such as the Federal (1888) or the Grand (1886; later the Hotel Windsor), both in Melbourne, were grand establishments built to accommodate hundreds of people and serviced with the latest modern amenities. Their initial success was mainly due to the influence of the temperance movement, the adherents of which made them their meeting place, but also to the rise of the fashion of coffee-drinking in Australia. They appealed to the respectable middle classes, including women, and to working-class abstainers. Many of Melbourne's coffee palaces were built by James Munro—property tycoon, politician and temperance advocate. Following the 1890s depression, however, Munro was bankrupt and most of his coffee palaces were forced to convert into licensed hotels or close. Coffee palaces had virtually disappeared by the 1930s and 1940s, though some of the buildings were adapted for other purposes.

HD

Coghlan, Timothy Augustine (1855–1926), statistician and public servant, remains one of the most often quoted authorities in Australian **social** and **economic history**. He was elevated controversially to the post of government statistician for NSW in 1886, achieved an international reputation there, and made a notable contribution to other aspects of public administration. He ended his career as agent-general for NSW in London.

Coghlan's energy, intelligence, political sense, and journalistic skill were acknowledged in the Sydney press of his time by the tag, 'Coghlan says … '. He wrote numerous newspaper articles, some pseudonymous. His most notable works were the two series, *The Wealth and Progress of New South Wales* (1886/87–1900/01) and *A Statistical Account of the Seven Colonies of Australasia* (1890–1904), in which statistics are used to support a wide-ranging commentary; and *Labour and Industry in Australia* (1918, 1969). The latter is a massive work in four volumes of 2300 pages, of much broader scope than the title suggests; it is in fact a study of the political economy of the colonies. *Childbirth in New South Wales* (1900) and *The Decline in the Birth-Rate of New South Wales* (1903) were influential contributions to the debate about the peopling of Australia, which are discussed in Neville Hicks, *'This Sin and Scandal'* (1978).

Coghlan is widely noticed in the texts which have sustained the teaching of Australian history since the 1940s. Geoffrey **Blainey**, in *The Tyranny of Distance* (1966), invokes him on matters as diverse as the collapse of the whaling industry and the comparative efficiency of steam trains and horse teams. Demographers still praise his technical analysis. One hundred years after the first appearance of *Wealth and Progress*, the editors of the *Australians 1888* volume of the

Bicentennial History (1987) used Coghlan's works as the natural statistical 'peg' for their account.

However, Coghlan's work is not always read exegetically. Brian **Fitzpatrick** did notice that '*Labour and Industry* is undocumented' and he 'often found reason to distrust the author's judgement', but it may be more profitable to adopt a history of ideas approach to the criticism of his statistics. His collections and interpretations were opinionated, as successive governments usually wanted them to be, but they were also attuned to wider movements in political economy and statistical practice. *Labour and Industry* is marked by a relatively sympathetic account of the troubles experienced by **Aborigines** and **Chinese** in colonial Australia, and by an interest in the pursuit of democracy which would include all classes, sharing decent living standards. Both perspectives influenced his criticism of a good deal of colonial public administration.

The most systematic attempt to relate Coghlan's personal and public life to the range of his writing is Desley Deacon's *Managing Gender* (1989), which shows that he was not merely a statist. Coghlan's career took him out of working-class Redfern, through public service reform, to become an operator on the London capital market by the time he published *Labour and Industry*. Nonetheless, the mix of modernist, democratic, and liberal Catholic ideas which had moulded him remained visible in his writing at the end.

NEVILLE HICKS AND SUSAN WOODBURN

Cold War, see **Communism**

Cole, Edward William (1832–1918) became the most famous bookseller in Australia through the popularity of Cole's Book Arcade in Melbourne. This opened in 1873 and was established in its Bourke Street home in 1883. With its live monkeys, funny mirrors, and the widely recognised rainbow painted over the door, the arcade was as much an amusement parlour, where the public was encouraged to browse, as it was a bookshop. Cole himself was a humanitarian rationalist with a shrewd appreciation of the power of publicity—in 1875 he advertised for a wife. He anticipated 'the gradual transformation of vast numbers of human beings from boorish, ignorant, superstitious, unreading, unthinking creatures into respectable, rational members of society'. Cole published numerous miscellanies, including the enormously popular *Cole's Funny Picture Book*, first published in 1879, and a vast range of improving literature. The business closed in 1929. *Cole of the Book Arcade*, a pictorial biography by Cole Turnley, was published in 1974.

KT

Coles, George James (1885–1977) and **Arthur William** (1892–1982) were founders of the retail chain, G.J. Coles. The eldest of the six sons of a Victorian country storekeeper, they had observed the success of the American 'five- and ten-cent stores' and sought to apply the same formula of low prices and high volumes to Australian retailing. In 1914 they opened their first store in working-class

Collingwood. Their plans for expansion were temporarily interrupted by World War I: George and Arthur served in France, and the two middle brothers were killed there. By 1924, when they opened their first Bourke Street store under the motto 'Nothing over 2s 6d', Coles had already opened eleven other stores. The business prospered in the 1930s when hard times made customers appreciate Coles's keen prices, but the boardroom tensions between the two strong-minded elder brothers erupted publicly in 1935. George, the senior figure, emerged as victor, and from the late 1930s Arthur channelled more of his energies into politics, becoming lord mayor of Melbourne in 1938 and independent MHR for Henty from 1940. In 1941 he played a characteristically quixotic role in the political manoeuvrings surrounding the fall of the **Menzies** and **Fadden** governments. He became wartime director of rationing and one of the creators of Trans-Australian Airlines. In the postwar years George devoted more time to philanthropic activity, and management of the business passed to the two younger Coles brothers, KENNETH FRANK (1896–1985) and EDGAR BARTON (1899–1981). In 1985 G.J. Coles merged with the **Myer** Emporium to become the nation's largest retail chain and Australia's largest employer.

GD

Collier, Phillip (1873–1948), born in Victoria, moved to WA in 1904 after working as a goldminer. He held the state Legislative Assembly seat of Boulder for the Labor Party 1905–48 as a mining union representative. He became opposition leader in 1917, and twice held the combined position of premier and treasurer, 1924–30 and 1933–36. He is credited with preventing a split over **conscription** in the WA branch of the **Australian Labor Party** near the end of World War I, and with moderating the push for **secession** in the mid-1930s.

KT

Collingridge, George Alphonse (1847–1931), historian, painter, and woodcut artist, came to Australia from England in 1879 to work on the *Illustrated Sydney News*. He later worked for the *Australian Town and Country Journal* and the *Sydney Mail*. He and his brother began the first journal of Australian art in 1888. He became fascinated by the maritime **exploration** of Australia and, in *The Discovery of Australia* (1895, revised 1906 as *The First Discovery of Australia and New Guinea*), supported claims that the Portuguese charted much of the continent in the sixteenth century. Among his other works are travel stories and *Pacifika, the Antediluvian World* (1928–30), which argues that the lost civilisation of Atlantis was in the Pacific.

KT

Collins, David (1756–1810), sometimes described as the first historian of NSW, gave an optimistic account of the settlement in his two-volume *An Account of the English Colony in New South Wales* (1798, 1802), intended to counter a negative English view of the colony. His *Account* was sympathetic to the plight of the Aborigines, acknowledging the harm done them by Europeans. Collins was appointed deputy judge-advocate of the **First Fleet** and, on arrival, became responsible for the colony's legal establishment. In June 1788 he also became secretary to Governor **Phillip**. After his return to England in 1797, he was appointed to head the expedition to found a new settlement in Bass Strait, where he arrived in 1803. Marjorie Tipping's *Convicts Unbound* (1988) is an account of this expedition and settlement. The site chosen, at Sorrento in Port Phillip Bay, Victoria, was judged unsuitable, and several months later Collins moved the settlement to Van Diemen's Land, where he established **Hobart** Town. Collins died in Hobart after years of battling official neglect to ensure the survival of the settlement. C.R. Collins, *Saga of Settlement* (1956), is a sympathetic study of the years in Australia; L.L. **Robson** examines his activities more dispassionately in *A History of Tasmania*, vol. 1 (1983); and John Currey has written a biography (2000).

KT

Collins House Group was a combination of Anglo-Australian financiers with extensive interests in base-metal mining and metallurgical operations. It was established in the first decade of the twentieth century by Melbourne businessmen, principally W.L. **Baillieu**, a stockbroker, and Lionel Robinson, mining broker. Both established strong connections with the City of London, which enabled them to finance the reconstruction of the North Broken Hill and South Broken Hill mining companies, the Zinc Corporation, and the Australian Smelting Corporation. The group was consolidated during World War I, when it benefited from the Australian government's cancellation of existing contracts with German interests. On Lionel's death in 1922, his younger brother W.S. **Robinson** expanded the group's interest into manufacturing, and during World War II was an adviser to both the British and Australian governments. His memoirs, *If I Remember Rightly* (1967), were edited by Geoffrey **Blainey**. Peter Richardson analysed the early history of the Group in R.T. Appleyard and C.B. Schedvin (eds), *Australian Financiers* (1988).

SM

'Collins, Tom', see **Furphy, Joseph**

Colombo Plan, a scheme promoting cooperative economic development in South and South-East Asia, began as an initiative by Australia and Ceylon (Sri Lanka) at a 1950 meeting of Commonwealth foreign ministers in Colombo. The original signatories (Australia, Canada, Ceylon, India, NZ, Pakistan, the UK, Malaya, and North Borneo) supported 'planning prosperity together' via mutually agreed assistance from donor to recipient countries. Ostensibly, the only condition was that aid contributed to a recipient's economic and social development, but in practice political motives operated. The Colombo Plan's potential to improve regional stability, and thereby enhance Australia's security, made it a major vehicle for Australian foreign policy. By

1970 membership embraced 24 countries and aid totalled $30.5 billion, including $300 million from Australia in the form of special projects, food, expertise, equipment, and the education of 10 000 Asian students in Australia. Australia's role is discussed in Percy **Spender**, *Exercises in Diplomacy* (1969); Osmar White, *The Seed of Freedom* (1961); and L.P. Goonetilleke, *The Colombo Plan* (1971).

DC

Colonial Office, the department of the imperial government that dealt with colonial affairs, was established on 17 March 1801, when its business was transferred from the Home Office. At its head was the secretary of state, who was a cabinet minister, assisted by a parliamentary under-secretary, who was a junior minister, and after 1825 by a senior civil servant as permanent under-secretary. Cabinet interfered with its business only in times of major crisis, but managing all the colonies before they received powers of local self-government was a heavy administrative burden—the office work 'half kills you from fatigue', lamented one under-secretary.

For many years historians alleged that most of the secretaries of state were mediocre men or short-lived in office, so that power rested in the hands of the permanent under-secretaries; although a few of the former were light-weights, they included significant statesmen like Lord John Russell, Lord Stanley, the third Earl **Grey**, 'not a very convertible person', Edward Cardwell, Lord Carnarvon, Joseph Chamberlain, and others who had firm views of their own. This means that the belief that the office was run by the permanent under-secretaries is a myth, spread by self-interested lobbyists. Before it was common for historians to read departmental papers, many failed to heed sufficiently the permanent heads' frequent requests for instructions. Mr 'over-secretary' James **Stephen** never deserved that title, but he and his successors, such as Herman Merivale, Frederick Rogers, and Robert Herbert (chosen through patronage not examination, for open competition for entry was not introduced until the 1870s), were experienced administrators with a wide knowledge of precedent. They readily deferred to ministers who during most of the nineteenth century were in the habit of writing important despatches themselves, but over time they came to influence the decision-making process of the office, with their extensive minuting of incoming despatches.

Lobbyists with vested interests and humanitarians concerned about the protection of indigenous peoples were ready enough to criticise particular aspects of colonial policy, and parliament was not indifferent to colonial affairs. Though most members of parliaments, like many later writers, were not interested in the details of colonial government, which frustrated the wishes of the few who were, colonial business embraced subjects of wide interest, such as colonial trade, migration, convict transportation, slavery, native welfare, indentured labour, land policy, colonial defence, expenditure, and on these subjects parliamentary discussions were frequent and sometimes bitter.

Gradually an 'office view' became more apparent as colonial secretaries and their officials became more and more reactive rather than proactive. They favoured colonial independence in local affairs whether or not 'responsible' government had been granted, and by the 1840s had come to recognise that in a struggle with a colony, the mother country was certain to be the loser. For this reason, and because of slow communication by ship, the office was usually ready to accept the advice of colonial governors, opposing this only when it seemed to counter imperial or humanitarian interests which secretaries of state felt it their strong duty to defend.

But if the principle of self-government was accepted, there were differences over what this meant. Between about 1840 and 1860, there were some, like the so-called 'colonial reformers' and Gladstone and Grey, who insisted that imperial and local matters could be easily defined and separated, arousing colonists' opposition when the former appeared to trench on the latter. In the 1860s the most outstanding defender of this position was a Victorian, George **Higinbotham**. He insisted that the Colonial Office should never interfere in local colonial affairs, and declared that self-government was a fraud since Australia was actually ruled 'by a person named Rogers'. In fact it was not the permanent under-secretary, but the secretaries of state who were more likely to be the offenders, with Cardwell reprimanding and recalling Governor **Darling** in 1866 for supporting his ministers in the **constitutional crisis** with the Legislative Council, and Lord Carnarvon telling governors to exercise the royal prerogative of mercy independently of their ministers' advice.

Over time ministers came to accept Higinbotham's views in practice, though they continued to exercise control in matters of foreign policy, which led to disputes in the 1880s over New Guinea and the Western Pacific. After Federation, **Deakin** continued to complain about the ineptitude of the office and its indifference to colonial interests. He would have liked direct communication with the British prime minister, but it was only in 1918 that **Hughes** achieved this. The demands of World War I obliged Britain to treat the self-governing colonies more as partners than subordinates. The creation of the Dominions Office in 1921 foreshadowed the **Statute of Westminster** of 1931, which effectively removed all imperial interference with the self-governing colonies, by then called Dominions, and since World War II, virtually all the former colonies have become either self-governing or independent. With that, the work of the Colonial Office has disappeared.

F.W. **Eggleston's** 'Australia and the Empire' in the *Cambridge History of the British Empire*, vol. vii (1933) remains the best short survey of the imperial relationship with Australia; for the Empire generally, see Ronald Hyam and Ged Martin, *Reappraisals in British Imperial History* (1975). (See also **British–Australian relations**.)

A.G.L. SHAW

Commissariat was the government store in Sydney and other convict settlements which purchased and supplied goods for government use, particularly food for the convicts. It provided the first substantial market for local producers; the right to supply the store and the prices paid for goods became a political issue. The British government was always anxious to reduce commissariat expenditure and its test of good government was how many convicts were 'off the store', that is, being fed by private employers or looking after themselves. The **ticket of leave** was initially a device to reduce the number of convicts on the store. The store paid for goods in sterling in the form of bills drawn on the British Treasury, which were the colony's first stock of foreign exchange. With these bills local merchants purchased goods abroad, particularly rum, for sale in the colony. They were the basis for the amazingly rapid development of commerce and industry in the tiny early settlement. The commissariat was such a key factor in economic development that it has sometimes been described as the colony's first **staple**.

JH

Commissioned history comprises a substantial and growing body of work undertaken by historians for both public and private clients. It is one of the varieties of **public history**; but, unlike **official history**, it acquires its distinctive character through the establishment of a contract between a commissioning body and a historian who is external to that body. Commissioned history can demand diverse skills, including research, writing, production, and publication. It can also call for a working knowledge of tendering, quotation, and contract; familiarity with the printing and publishing industries; and an ability to act as intermediary between client, publisher, and the market. As well as books and reports, commissioned history can include museum exhibitions, school resources, radio and television productions, films and videos, and multimedia.

It was rare for private clients to hire historians until after World War II. Sometimes a firm would hire a retired journalist to write a boosting account of its contribution to the nation's 'wealth and progress': R.T. **Bridges**, *From Silver to Steel: The Romance of the Broken Hill Proprietary* (1920), and C.C. Faulkner, *The Commonwealth Bank of Australia* (1923), were examples of this genre.

After the war, as the numbers of history honours graduates grew, their professors were sometimes able to persuade private firms and public bodies that academically trained historians would do the job better than a journalist or a retired employee. Professor Max **Crawford** helped to arrange the commission for Ken **Inglis's** *Hospital and Community: A History of the Royal Melbourne Hospital* (1958); and helped to launch the most prolific of Australia's commissioned historians, Geoffrey **Blainey**, on his career with a history of the Mount Lyell mining company, *Peaks of Lyell* (1954), and a *Centenary History of the University of Melbourne* (1957). The subjects of commissioned history have always been shaped by its market: only large private firms and public corporations could usually afford to hire a professional historian. Mining companies, banks, manufacturers, hospitals, and local government have led the way; trade unions, schools, and charitable organisations have followed.

Blainey worked as a commissioned historian for more than a decade, producing notable books on mining history (*Mines in the Spinifex*, 1960), banking (*Gold and Paper*, 1958), and **local history** (*A History of Camberwell*, 1964) before returning to academia in the mid-1960s. Inglis became an academic but later wrote another commissioned history, *This Is the ABC* (1983). The boundaries between commissioned history and academic history have remained permeable, although the intrusion of the moonlighting academic sometimes caused resentment among other commissioned historians. Weston **Bate**, who was commissioned to write a local history of Ballarat in 1964 before he re-entered academia, wrote critically, in *HSANZ* (1963), of the tendency of some academics to treat local history as a lesser branch of their trade, something that any seasoned professional could do in his or her spare time.

Economic historians took an early lead by carving out a distinct specialism in commissioned histories of **banking** and finance. L.F. **Giblin's** *The Growth of a Central Bank* was published in 1951, Blainey's *Gold and Paper* (a history of the National Bank) in 1958 and S.J. **Butlin's** *Australia and New Zealand Bank* in 1961. Butlin died before completing a commission to write a history of the Reserve Bank and the project was completed by his former pupil C.B. Schedvin as *In Reserve* (1992). Later academic contributions to commissioned banking history include D.T. Merrett, *ANZ Bank* (1985), and Ken Spillman, *Horizons: A History of the Rural and Industries Bank of Western Australia* (1989). Most of these histories maintain high standards of scholarship and independence, but nervous boards have often preferred to confer the task of official historian on loyal insiders or retirees rather than academics or independent scholars. The results have been patchy: a mixture of bland chronicle and public relations hype. A.N. Murrell's history of the Bank of Queensland (1987), for example, aims to 'maintain studied objectivity', and to resist 'the temptation to offer points of view', but it makes dull reading. Commissioned histories of companies outside the downtown financial and mining sectors have been rare, although notable exceptions are Maurice French's pioneering study of the Toowoomba Permanent Building Society (1979); Joan Kent, *Mercantile Credits: The First Fifty Years* (1985); K. Buckley and K. Klugman, *The Australian Presence in the Pacific: Burns Philp 1914–1946* (1983); and Don Garden's 1992 history of the builder A.V. **Jennings**.

While capital has often been able to afford to hire its historians and sometimes pay them well, organised labour has more often looked to sympathetic journalists, academics, or activists to do the job gratis or for token reward. Union bosses may be no more respectful of authorial independence than captains of industry, and commissioned union histories tend to be politically correct, almost to a fault. The journalist Edgar Ross was commissioned to write *A History of the Miners' Federation of Australia* (1970), billed as 'an inspiring story of courage, militancy and expanding unity, in the face of often bitter opposi-

tion'; it is an unquestioning, **Old Left**, heroic celebration. There have been some famous brawls between unions and independent-minded historians. Brian **Fitzpatrick's** history of the Seamen's Union remained unpublished for 25 years until Rowan J. Cahill completed it in 1981. Tom Zubrycki's documentary film on the **ACTU** (partly Bicentenary funded) was rejected and suppressed by the organisation after its executive took umbrage at the film-maker's interpretation. The 1990s, however, saw a significant increase in sound, union-commissioned histories such as Bradon Ellem, *In Women's Hands? A History of Clothing Trades Unionism in Australia* (1989); Bradley Bowden, *Driving Force: The History of the Transport Workers Union of Australia 1883–1992* (1993), and Mark Hearn and Harry Knowles, *One Big Union: A History of the Australian Workers Union 1886–1994* (1996).

The growth of commissioned history has accelerated over the past two decades. Analysis of a random sample of 147 commissioned works produced between 1945 and 1996 showed that commissioned histories published in book form increased from one or two a year in the early to mid-1980s to 26 in 1988. After a post-Bicentenary hangover, the annual average since has been around 10 publications, though the sample indicated 20 works for 1996. In all, more commissioned histories (74 in the sample) were published in the period 1990–96 than in the preceding 45 years.

New social and historiographical concerns have gradually influenced both the range and approach of commissioned history. **Environmental history** has been a notable beneficiary, as public authorities have begun to recognise the historical dimensions of environmental problems and as their political masters have questioned the role of the special-purpose authorities themselves. Often, however, the commissioned historian arrives just in advance of the corporate undertaker. As the books by Tony Dingle and Carolyn Rasmussen, *Vital Connections: Melbourne and its Board of Works* (1992), and David Dunstan, *Victorian Icon: The Royal Exhibition Building, Melbourne* (1996), were being researched and published, the authorities that commissioned them were being dissolved or corporatised.

Not all commissioned histories are published in book form. **Heritage** conservation generates a substantial body of commissioned work, most of it presented as desktop-published reports in small runs. Some of this work is specialised and difficult to access, but it includes some research and writing of a high order. Depending on the brief, commissioned heritage histories can also be highly empirical and site-specific, although, as more commissioning bodies adopt the practice of commissioning environmental histories as well as site inventories, their range and sophistication grow.

Commissioned history has breathed new life into some older academic specialisms, such as urban history. Perhaps the most ambitious commissioned history project in the 1990s was the Sydney City Council's Sesquicentenary History Project which, under Shirley Fitzgerald's supervision, produced seven books and three reference booklets. The principal work is Fitzgerald's *Sydney: 1842–1992* (1992). Peter Morton's *After Light: A History of the City of Adelaide and*

Its Council 1878–1928 (1996) is another example which reinforces the important role of local government authorities in the commissioning of history. Some state governments have launched major commissioned projects, perhaps the most notable being the Victorian government's Sesquicentenary three-volume history project, *The Victorians* (1984).

Not all commissioned history sees the light of day. Sometimes the termination clauses in contracts are invoked; occasionally draconian agreements have been used as bludgeons on unwary historians; and a number of completed manuscripts have been pulped or pigeon-holed rather than published, or published in such limited numbers as to effectively suppress them. Historians undertaking commissions face several dilemmas, especially the need both to satisfy the client and to maintain professional independence. 'It is like walking a tightrope all the time', reflected Shirley Fitzgerald in *Public History Review* (1993).

Does the process of 'buying' a history entail a 'sell-out' on the historian's part? David Cantor, a US historian of medicine, argues that critical distance is necessarily and drastically shortened 'by the purse-strings and obligations of contract work'. It is inevitable, he argues, that the commissioned historian, consciously or otherwise, will adopt the purpose of the commissioning body. But maintaining critical distance is not a problem unique to commissioned history: it affects all fields of knowledge-production, including those governed by academic funding agendas and ideological fashions. Aided by sound agreements and training, and the backing of professional associations, many historians continue to produce commissioned histories of the highest standards.

PAUL ASHTON AND CHRISTOPHER KEATING

Commonwealth of Australia, the **federation** of the six former colonies, was constituted by a British act of parliament in 1900, and came into being on 1 January 1901, with a proclamation by the governor-general, Lord **Hopetoun**, at Centennial Park, Sydney. The Commonwealth was established through a **Constitution** and governed under a parliamentary system consisting of a Senate and a House of Representatives. As part of the British Empire, the Commonwealth of Australia owed allegiance to the British sovereign.

The name *Commonwealth* was keenly debated at the Federal Convention of 1897–98, as Keith **Hancock** described in *Politics in Pitcairn: And Other Essays* (1947) and John **La Nauze** elaborated in *HS* (1971). For some delegates its association with the English Civil War, and the regicide Oliver Cromwell, had republican connotations, but Alfred **Deakin** assured them it had an older lineage and meant 'the common good of the people'. Responsibilities for most government services generally remained under state control. The NT and the ACT, selected as the site of the nation's political capital, came under Commonwealth control in 1911.

HD

Commonwealth of Nations (British) is a collective term for the 50 or more nations that formerly made up the British Empire. The term *Commonwealth* was added to *Empire* in 1920 (the British Empire and Commonwealth), to acknowledge the significant contribution made to the Empire by the self-governing Dominions—Australia, Canada, South Africa, and NZ—during World War I, and their more equal status at the Paris Peace Conference of 1919 and as members of the League of Nations. When after World War II nearly all Britain's colonies became independent, there was no longer an empire. The loose association of all former colonies and Britain was now called the Commonwealth, of which the British monarch is head. Regular meetings of the Commonwealth Heads of Government (CHOGM) continue today.

HD

Commonwealth Scientific and Industrial Research Organisation, see **CSIRO**

Commonwealth–state relations cover a broad range of associations, agreements, and institutional arrangements for carrying on the complex business of governing in a federal system. The **Constitution** provides the basic skeleton of federalism by setting up the Commonwealth government and enumerating its specific powers, while guaranteeing the continued existence of the states and their jurisdiction over residual powers not allocated to the Commonwealth. While most of the Commonwealth's powers are concurrent—levying excise taxes is one of the few exclusive ones—its legislation trumps that of the states if there is a conflict. The scope of Commonwealth power thus depends on the Commonwealth's vigour in using its constitutional powers and the High Court's interpretation of their scope in cases of conflict. Since the 1920 **Engineers'** case, the High Court has used a centralising method of interpreting the Commonwealth's powers in a full and plenary way regardless of the impact on the states. As a result, the Commonwealth's powers have waxed and the residual ones of the states have waned. Nevertheless, the states retain jurisdiction over key areas of public policy, including health, education, land, and civil and criminal law.

Inter-governmental relations are further skewed in the Commonwealth's favour by **taxation** and spending arrangements which are largely extra-constitutional. The Commonwealth has monopolised income tax since 1942 through imposing a high uniform rate and leaving no tax room for the states. The **Howard** government's introduction in July 2000 of a Goods and Services Tax (GST) on most goods and services, except food, has technically increased fiscal centralism. The states were placated, however, by being given the entire proceeds of the GST, which is set at 10 per cent and cannot be altered without their unanimous consent. On the expenditure side the Commonwealth uses 'tied' grants, under the Constitution's Section 96, to support major policy programs in health, education, and roads, which otherwise would come within state jurisdiction. Such tied grants account for about half the total Commonwealth grants to the states and require elaborate inter-governmental arrangements.

Communications

The growth of central power in Australian federalism since World War II was not simply at the states' expense. The size of government has expanded, with the states increasing the scope and improving the quality of their government sectors, partly to counter the Commonwealth. Peak inter-governmental forums—the annual **Premiers' Conference** that determined grants to the states, and the associated **Loan Council** that set public borrowing limits—were dominated by the Commonwealth. Nevertheless, fiscal centralisation presupposed a high level of collusion on the part of the states, and the relatively smooth functioning of complex systems of inter-governmental relations exhibited extensive cooperation as well as coercion. This is evident in the Commonwealth Grants Commission, which applies an equalisation factor to overall grants including the GST in order to compensate smaller states for revenue and expenditure disabilities. It was also evident in the Loan Council, which set borrowing limits for governments and ensured the orderly marketing of public debt, although this function has been largely replaced by recourse to market discipline.

Beginning with agriculture in the 1920s, ministerial and officials' meetings have been institutionalised for most major policy areas, while informal contacts among officials are even more extensive. This complex tangle of Commonwealth–state relations came under critical scrutiny in the 1990s as part of Australia's response to global market pressures. Deregulation of the Australian economy was coupled with greater efficiency in government to be achieved through streamlining inter-governmental arrangements. A series of Special Premiers' Conferences initiated major reform initiatives in economic infrastructure and regulatory regimes vital for microeconomic reform. These included developing new institutions for achieving national standards in key areas, adopting mutual recognition to break down regulatory duplication in other areas, and facilitating national markets for utilities, including a national electricity grid.

The reform process has been institutionalised in the Council of Australian Governments (COAG), which meets twice yearly. COAG provides a leaders' forum for microeconomic reform issues, in addition to the annual Premiers' Conference which deals with fiscal matters. While significant achievements have been made, enthusiasm has waned for tackling less tractable inter-governmental issues such as vertical fiscal imbalance, clarifying the roles and responsibilities of the Commonwealth and state governments, and reducing tied grants.

The most significant microeconomic reform was the adoption of competition policy by all governments in 1995. By requiring that government provision of goods and services be on the same footing as private provision, competition policy undermines the states' vast public utilities, which were a feature of **state socialism** in Australia. Indeed, the new economic management, which is increasingly prevalent in the Commonwealth government as well as the states, will likely be more significant than COAG in changing the roles and responsibilities of the Common-wealth and state governments, and consequently in changing Commonwealth–state relations.

BRIAN GALLIGAN

Communications with the mother country were of supreme importance to the first colonists. News carried by sailing ships took 100 days to move between Britain and Australia. When mail steamers shortened the journey to about five weeks by the late 1850s, colonial governments were under pressure to satisfy the colonists' hunger for news 'from home' with the regular transport of mail and **newspapers**. From the early 1860s regular inter-colonial postal conferences deliberated on rival overseas mail shipping routes and services.

From the mid-1850s the Australian colonies experienced the worldwide communication revolution heralded by the telegraph—whereby coded messages could be sent over great distances using electrical signals transmitted along wires—when the Victorian government opened the first telegraph line from the centre of Melbourne to Williamstown on Port Phillip Bay in March 1854. Two years later the SA, Victorian and NSW governments agreed with their persuasive superintendents of telegraphs to extend their lines to their boundaries, thus establishing an inter-colonial telegraph network among the mainland south-eastern colonies by October 1858. When the new Qld government joined its lines in 1861, there were 110 towns and cities in eastern and southern Australia on the inter-colonial network. From the beginning the telegraph was owned and administered by government departments, in contrast to the USA, and the pre-1870 English private telegraph system.

Government departments were heavy users of the telegraph, exercising increasing control over their administrators outside metropolitan centres. In Victoria, for example, in the gold-rush decade (1854–64) between 25 per cent and 50 per cent of all telegrams transmitted each year were sent by government officials. In 1864 alone more than 250 000 telegrams were despatched in Victoria.

Equally important users and promoters of the telegraph system were the proprietors and editors of colonial newspapers and business interests, especially chambers of commerce, which were its major beneficiaries. In Australia the telegraph generally preceded the **railways** (which came to depend on the telegraph for their safe management) in forging inter-regional links between merchants and entrepreneurs.

The publicly owned Australian telegraph network was linked to the privately owned overseas submarine cable network in 1872, when SA's Charles **Todd** completed the **Overland Telegraph** Line from Port Augusta to Darwin. Instead of waiting weeks for news and trade information from abroad, Australian governments, businesses, and newspapers received news that was less than 24 hours old. The East–West Telegraph linking WA to SA in 1877 completed the continental telegraph network just five years after Australia was linked to the world cable network.

Despite the extremely high cable rates (10 shillings a word until the mid-1880s), governments and newspapers remained the major users of the combined telegraph and cable services, especially after they were offered discounted rates. Public debates continued between ministers and bureaucrats from the colonies about the need for alternative cable routes to challenge the monopoly of the private British Eastern Extension Company.

By the close of the nineteenth century, Australians had become one of the largest national users of the telegraph, as it became the main vehicle for the transmission of succinct personal messages at times of celebrations (especially weddings) and tragedies. During the 1914–18 war the reception of a telegram often conveyed news of death or injury of a family member serving overseas.

The Australian Constitution in Section 51(v) gave the federal government exclusive and comprehensive power over communication in these terms: 'postal, telegraphic, telephonic, and other like services'. K.T. Livingston argues in *The Wired Nation Continent* (1996) that this was the result of extensive inter-colonial consultation over many years about communication issues which had fostered a national approach and had assisted the movement towards federal union. National events, such as the Melbourne Cup, involved an annual clearing of the telegraph lines (from 1888 onwards) to allow for the immediate flashing of the news of the winner around Australia; and the telegraph was used to create an 'imagined community' among all Australians during the celebration of the opening of the first federal parliament in May 1901: graphic examples of what Livingston calls 'technological federalism' and 'technological nationalism'.

In October 1905 the Wireless Telegraphy Act made explicit for the first time the Commonwealth's powers over 'other like services'. This began the government's legislative and regulatory control of Australia's dual system (public–private) of **radio** broadcasting in the 1920s and **television** in the 1950s.

When the Commonwealth's new Postmaster-General's Department began administering the federalised communication services in March 1901, it took on responsibility for the existing telephone, as well as postal and telegraph services. Telephone exchanges had begun operating in the capital cities from the early 1880s. By the 1890s the first major long-distance, trunk telephone services were established between Melbourne and the largest provincial cities in Victoria (Ballarat, Geelong, and Bendigo), and in NSW between Sydney and Newcastle. The Sydney–Melbourne trunk route was opened in 1907, and the first automatic telephone exchange was successfully installed (in Geelong) in 1912. An Australia-wide trunk network was achieved in December 1930, when the first telephone conversations took place between Perth and Adelaide. However, the telegraph continued to be the main medium for the exchange of news, business information, and personal messages for most Australians until after World War II. While the telegraph showed surprising resilience, the telephone rapidly became the dominant telecommunications instrument. The **Whit-**

lam government reorganised Australian public communications through the *Telecommunications Act 1975*, establishing the Australian Telecommunications Commission (and trading arm Telecom) as a separate entity from the Australian Postal Commission (Australia Post). Both were removed from Public Service Board control and the 74-year reign of the PMG over communications was ended. Given its common carrier monopoly position, Telecom was handed a social-responsibility, as well as an industrial and commercial, brief. It was required to maintain the cross-subsidisation policies that had allowed costs in rural telephone service provision to be kept down. Household penetration grew from 73 per cent in 1977 to around 93 per cent in 1985. Telecom was also involved with broadcasting through its role in the construction and maintenance of national television transmitters and FM radio.

Technological development and convergence, deregulation and privatisation stimulated by changes in overseas regulatory patterns, and stubborn rearguard actions in support of continued public control of telecommunications (especially by rural political interests) jostled with one another in the forging of new communications systems and ownership and control regimes. The advent of a domestic satellite system (AUSSAT), which became operational in 1985–86, and which initially was publicly owned, produced a more competitive telecommunications environment. From this time, often at the urging of interested entrepreneurs, Australia's major public telecommunication assets were sold, increasingly into private corporate hands. AUSSAT was sold to Optus Communications in 1990, which in turn was to fall to the British company Cable and Wireless in 1997. The merged OTC Telecom became Telstra in 1993. Subsequently, one-third of Telstra was floated on the stock market in 1997, followed by a further 16.6 per cent in 1999. Manoeuvres continue over plans to complete the privatisation of Telstra, though, once again, rural politicians have been compelled by constituents to resist the process.

Trevor Barr comments in *newmedia.com.au* (2000) that, in the absence of any clearly articulated longer-term national communications objectives, policy is shaped instead by short-term expediencies. A pattern of grudging recognition of public interest and social responsibility, of policy driven by short-term political advantage and the interests of the more influential corporate players, and of the disposal of public assets has marked both media and telecommunications development during the last quarter century. Attempts to regulate the operation of the rapidly expanding Internet have revealed an inability to deal legislatively with this quite different kind of telecommunications. The Internet's complex mix of commercial imperatives, international online linkages, potential for juvenile access, openness to socially undesirable content and uses, and a widespread unease over the perceived need to resort to censorship have provoked critical responses from many sections of society. Nonetheless, Australia's reputation for enthusiastically embracing new communications technology has continued with the Internet, as electronic commerce has spread to retailing, business-to-business commerce, service provision, and a variety of other marketing functions, as well as registering impressive growth in home usage.

Studies in communication history constitute a new field in Australian historiography and since the 1980s have become more central to the history of Australian culture, colonialism, nationalism, federalism, and imperialism. In a seminal article, 'Communication—see Transport', in G. Osborne and W.F. Mandle (eds), *New History: Studying Australia Today* (1982), Osborne argued that communication is worthy of study in its own right. American scholars had argued this for years; as James W. Carey pointed out (*Communication as Culture*, 1989), the advent of the telegraph had differentiated communication from **transport**. Osborne's analysis of general histories published before then showed that Australian historians had failed to grasp this distinction.

There have been several important commissioned or sponsored institutional histories of Australian telecommunications in the 1980s and 1990s. The most comprehensive professional study is Ann **Moyal's** commissioned history of the national carrier, Telecom (now Telstra) and its predecessors, *Clear Across Australia: A History of Telecommunications* (1984): a *tour de force* of 200 years of Australia's postal and telecommunication services that is the standard history. Moyal's book is complemented by Edgar Harcourt, *Taming the Tyrant: The First One Hundred Years of Australia's International Telecommunications Services* (1987), and James Murray, *Calling the World: The First 100 Years of Alcatel Australia* (1995). These historical studies illustrate the enormous contribution that Australian government monopolies and private companies have made, and continue to make, to national and international telecommunications.

In *Communication Traditions in 20th-Century Australia* (1995), Graeme Osborne and Glen Lewis examine the ways Australians have argued about the nature and uses of communication in society. They focus on three broad themes: first, the strongly developmental approach between 1900 and 1920 when communication technologies and transport systems built the economic and defence infrastructure of early federated Australia; second, the role of communication in community-building and defending cultural standards between 1920 and 1940; and third, the subsequent uses of public communication—the press, movies, radio and television broadcasting—in shaping public attitudes about nation-building, community development, cultural standards, and political life.

Kevin Livingston and Graeme Osborne

Communism was a revolutionary doctrine, a political movement of considerable reach and influence, and a threat that exercised conservatives for much of the twentieth century.

The doctrine had its origins in the *Communist Manifesto*, issued by Marx and Engels in 1848, and the political movement was formed in the aftermath of the Russian Revolution of 1917. The seizure of state power by the Bolsheviks in October of that year, and their call through the Communist International for workers of all countries to follow their example, attracted considerable attention in Australia. As codified by the Bolshevik leader, V.I. Lenin, communism insisted on the need for a revolutionary overthrow of capitalism and for the dictatorship of the proletariat in the subsequent transition to socialism. Lenin placed special emphasis on the leading role of the revolutionary party, and consequently on the need to safeguard its theoretical purity and maintain a military discipline in prosecuting the class war.

The early history of the Communist Party of Australia was dogged by arguments over its relationship to these new principles. The founding conference in October 1920 broke up almost immediately into two rival claimants for recognition by Moscow. Although the successful faction received some financial assistance and derived considerable prestige from its association with the Communist International, distance, censorship, and surveillance impeded its assimilation of Leninist orthodoxy. It was not until the end of the 1920s that the party was bolshevised in accordance with the rigidly authoritarian dictates of Josef Stalin, the general secretary of the Communist Party of the Soviet Union. From then until the 1960s the Australian party was a dutiful servant of the Communist International, and the effects of this relationship are emphasised by Alastair Davidson, *The Communist Party of Australia* (1969).

European communist parties were formed out of established socialist parties as the consequence of a rift between their revolutionary and reformist wings. By contrast, the Australian party gathered together doctrinaire socialists and industrial militants who opposed the **Australian Labor Party** and its affiliated **trade unions** for their failure to adopt a socialist program. The problem for Australian communists was how to challenge the tenacious pragmatism of these powerful and complementary institutional forms. Initially the party endeavoured to influence the unions and infiltrate the ALP, but communists were driven out of the Labor Party by the mid-1920s.

From the onset of the Depression in the late 1920s, the party adopted the new Communist International tactic of intransigent opposition to all forms of reformism. While unable to shake the political dominance of the ALP, it achieved some success in organising the unemployed, and through its industrial Militant Minority Movement it established a growing influence in unions covering mining, transport, the waterfront, and metal industries. In response to the rise of fascism, the Communist International shifted in the mid-1930s to a strategy of a united front, and the party accordingly broadened its activity among progressive circles of writers, artists, and peace activists. Membership increased to nearly 4000 in the 1930s.

Shortly before the outbreak of World War II, Stalin concluded a Nazi–Soviet pact, and Australian communists were therefore instructed to regard the conflict as a struggle between two imperialist camps and to oppose the national war effort. From June 1940 to December 1942 the party was an illegal organisation, yet it continued to function and increased its influence and membership. Following the entry of the Soviet Union into the war in 1941, the party gave strong support to the war effort and reached a peak membership of more than 20 000 by the end of 1944. Buoyed by an influx of recruits from the armed services and the professions, the party emphasised its popular character by a change of name to the Australian Communist Party, and sought to fuse internationalism with an Australian radical nationalism that communist intellectuals of the period helped to define.

In 1945, therefore, the party enjoyed substantial influence within the labour movement. But relations with the federal Labor government, which sought to restrain wages as part of its program of postwar reconstruction, quickly deteriorated until by 1949 Prime Minister **Chifley** mounted a boots-and-all assault on the striking miners' union and jailed its communist officials. This crucial watershed in the fortunes of Australian communism is examined by Tom Sheridan, *Division of Labour* (1989).

The onset of the Cold War, which divided the world into two armed camps, intensified suspicion of the party, and in the same year its leader Lance **Sharkey** was jailed for stating that Australian workers would welcome Soviet forces pursuing capitalist aggressors. Australian communists lost ground in many unions to the anti-communist Industrial Groups led by B.A. **Santamaria**. While the new prime minister, R.G. **Menzies**, was unsuccessful in his 1951 referendum campaign to ban the party, his 1954 royal commission into allegations of communist espionage made by the Soviet diplomat **Petrov** reinforced an atmosphere of hostility to communism. As membership sank to 6000, the party fell back on a defensive obduracy: the opportunity for reassessment afforded by Khrushchev's speech in 1956 to the Communist Party of the Soviet Union, criticising Stalin and his crimes, was lost; a further wave of defection from the party followed. By the 1960s the party was a weak, ageing, and ossified organisation.

It experienced some regeneration when the protest movement of the 1960s, associated with the **Vietnam War** and student unrest, fractured Cold War orthodoxies. As more rigid and doctrinaire members left to form the pro-Chinese Communist Party of Australia (Marxist–Lenininst) in 1967 and the pro-Soviet Socialist Party of Australia in 1971, the party became more open in its procedures and more receptive to the liberatory projects of the **New Left** that emerged from the universities. But while the party offered organisational support to many of the new social movements of the 1970s, and recruited from their activists, its abandonment of the Leninist conception of the communist party ultimately robbed it of any distinctive presence in the new political landscape. The remaining members dissolved the party in 1991.

Communism offered its adherents an all-encompassing theory and practice, and it demanded of them an absolute commitment. Its class analysis was applied to all questions, and party members engaged in a range of activities—peace movements, international campaigns, women's groups, and anti-racist and pro-Aboriginal organisations—always under the direction of the party. While appealing to intellectuals, it was distinctively proletarian in doctrine and temper. Its educational effort, extensive publications, and considerable cultural activity all emphasised the capacity of the working class, yet this supportive and enabling life under the party was marked by a beleaguered dogmatism.

Australian communism was shaped by the hostility of its opponents. From its formation the party was under the surveillance of state security agencies; their extensive files provide the basis of Frank Cain, *The Origins of Political Surveillance* (1983), and David McKnight's *Australia's Spies and Their Secrets* (1994). The Commonwealth passed new laws to proscribe its activities, and party members were subject to repeated prosecution. The press, churches, and employers' organisations campaigned against communism, while from the 1920s to the 1950s clandestine paramilitary organisations sustained anti-communist activities. The association of the party with the Soviet Union, and its presence in the trade unions, made anti-communism a major issue of domestic Australian politics, especially in the 1920s and during the Cold War, when conservative parties used allegations of communist influence in the ALP as an electoral device.

Communism generated a substantial literature, which is listed in *Communism in Australia, A Resource Bibliography* (1994), compiled by Beverley Symons. Of particular note are the works of the **Old Left** historians who had been active in the party, notably Robin Gollan, *Revolutionaries and Reformists* (1975), and Ian Turner, *Room for Manoeuvre* (1982). In contrast to the heroic certainties of older communist writings, the collapse of the cause produced a number of more adventurous autobiographical publications that explored the intersections of the personal and the political. Roger Milliss, *Serpent's Tooth* (1984), is noteworthy, though women's voices are more prominent: Joy Damousi, *Women Come Rally* (1994), explores the gendered forms of Australian communism. Stuart Macintyre, *The Reds* (1998), is the first of a two-volume general history.

STUART MACINTYRE

Congregationalism was a Nonconformist Christian denomination that held that each local congregation was self-governing and independent of any central controlling body. Congregationalists, also known as Independents, first came to Australia and the Pacific in the 1790s with the London Missionary Society, but the first church, established in 1810, did not last long.

Congregationalism began effectively in Australia in the 1830s, with the foundation of churches in Hobart (1830), Sydney (1833), Adelaide (1837), and Melbourne (1838). Largely urban and middle class, Congregationalists were prominent in commerce, journalism, and politics, especially in South Australia. Congregational Unions formed in each colony in mid-century provided opportunities for consultation and cooperation without infringing the autonomy of each church. Intercolonial Conferences held in the 1880s led to the formation of the Congregational Union of Australia and New Zealand in 1888, which met triennially from 1904 and biennially from 1925. The Congregational Union of Australia, which replaced it in 1960, was a more effective national organisation, which entered into negotiation with the **Methodist** and **Presbyterian** Churches to form the **Uniting Church in Australia** in 1977. The doctoral theses of Lindsay Lockley (Queensland, 1966) and Hugh Jackson (Australian National University, 1978) are the principal histories.

WALTER PHILLIPS

Coniston massacre was the first of a series of **massacres** perpetrated on the Anmatyerre as well as Walbri (or Warlpiri) people in the area around Coniston, near Yuendumu, NT, in 1928. Prompted in particular by the slaying of a prospector on Coniston station that year, the police made numerous punitive expeditions. The last was led by Constable William Murray, who fired on a large group of people. While Murray admitted to killing only 31, it is more probable that between 70 and 100 Walbri people died. The brutality of the police achieved its objective of bringing the Aborigines 'into submission', and many of the Walbri community left the station. The government Resident in Central Australia justified the massacre, and the police were exonerated. Criticism by church leaders and others, however, prompted an official inquiry. An account of the massacre in the Sydney *Sunday Sun* in 1933 written by Ernestine **Hill**, who supported 'punitive police raids' to protect the safety of white people in the outback, reflected the general public approval of such treatment of Aborigines by whites.

HD

Conscription for military service and training has been a controversial issue in twentieth-century Australia.

In 1911 the federal government introduced the first compulsory training scheme for boys. Some refused to enlist or to attend drills. By 1915, 636 000 had enlisted, 34 000 had been prosecuted, and 7000 detentions had been imposed. The scheme was greatly reduced after **World War I**, and suspended by the **Scullin** Labor government in 1929. During World War I, the Labor government of W.M. **Hughes** hoped to introduce conscription for overseas service by referendum. On 28 October 1916, the proposal was rejected by a narrow majority of 71 549 Australians. The bitter campaign divided the **Australian Labor Party**. In December 1917, Australians again rejected conscription by a larger majority of 166 588.

The **United Australia Party** government reintroduced conscription at the beginning of **World War II**. The whole of the voluntary militia was called up, in two drafts of 40 000 each, to receive a month's training. Many of these men volunteered to join the **AIF**, but others remained in their militia units. A total of 224 428 men enlisted in the Citizens Military Forces (CMF), compared with 460 466 in the AIF. Not all CMF members were conscripts, however. Men who failed to enlist, to attend a medical examination, or to serve in the armed services faced a maximum penalty of six months' imprisonment with hard labour. At least 90 objectors served one or more sentences, including several women who were jailed for refusing to enrol with Manpower Services. The Department of Defence claimed that only 2791 men had applied for exemption from military service as conscientious objectors during World War II, but this figure is actually the total of applications received to the end of 1943. Initially, non-combatant service was the only type of exemption granted, but in 1943 the Senate passed amendments to the National Security Regulations, allowing objectors to perform civilian work. In a few cases, unconditional exemptions were granted.

On 19 February 1943, the controversial Defence (CMF) Bill—'the Militia Bill'—became law, whereby the conscripted CMF would serve in the South-West Pacific area if required. The act reversed long-standing Labor policy that conscripted servicemen would not fight outside Australian territory. It provoked bitter criticism from some Labor members, although John **Curtin** justified his new policy by stating that it made the whole of the Australian forces available to General MacArthur for employment in the Pacific campaign.

When the war ended, conscription ceased; it was reintroduced by the **Menzies** Liberal–Country Party government's National Service Act of 1951 whereby 18-year-old males were drafted for six months' compulsory military training. The act provided exemptions to men with certain disabilities, ministers of religious orders, theological students, and conscientious objectors. Deferment was possible for men who could prove that their studies or apprenticeships would be seriously dislocated by performing national service, and those residing in remote areas. According to official figures, by June 1958, 419 913 trainees had been registered, 209 906 had been enrolled for military service, and 3679 applications had been received for exemption on the grounds either of occupation as a minister of religion or of conscientious objection. The issue of conscripts serving overseas did not arise, as servicemen who fought in Korea, Borneo, and Malaya were all volunteers.

The national service scheme ceased in 1959. The Menzies government introduced a new compulsory military service— rather than training—scheme in 1964, whereby young men born on the birthdates chosen by ballot were called up, depending upon their fitness and educational status. Deferments were allowed. The issue of conscripts serving overseas soon became paramount. In April 1965, Menzies announced that a regular infantry battalion would be sent to **Vietnam**. The new national servicemen began military training in June 1965, and the first conscripts left Australia for military combat in Vietnam on 19 April 1966. Approximately 50 000 Australians served, and almost half of these (19 450) were conscripts. Of the 442 killed, 200 were conscripts. Among the non-fatal casualties, conscripts numbered 1279 and regular soldiers 1553. In a long and bitter campaign of opposition to the war, more than 1000 conscripts applied for exemption as conscientious objectors—including those who objected specifically to service in Vietnam rather than in all wars. National service ended in 1974; no Australians have been since conscripted for military service.

Conscription has left a considerable historical literature; L.C. Jauncey's *The Story of Conscription in Australia* (1935) is an early example. During the Vietnam War such works as Ray Forward and Bob Reece, *Conscription in Australia* (1968), and Glenn Withers, *Conscription, Necessity and Justice* (1972), were published, along with numerous works examining Australian involvement in earlier wars. J.B. Hirst, 'Australian Defence and Conscription' (*AHS*, 1993–94), offered a reassessment.

BOBBIE OLIVER

Conservation was already a concern of the first European colonists. Lieutenant-Governor Francis Grose sought to protect the purity of the Tank Stream that supplied Sydney's water in 1793. When Governor Hunter realised that settlers were threatening and wasting 'useful timber' by indiscriminately felling trees on the Hawkesbury, he prohibited the cutting of timber on any public land on its banks or tributaries. But it was not until the 1860s that the term *conservation* came into common use in Australia. Although initially used by colonists primarily in relation to **forests**, *conservation* has since widened its usage to many other aspects of the material and, later, human **environment**.

Victoria, as in many issues of environmental concern, led the way. In a 'Report on the Advisableness of Establishing State Forests', the Victorian surveyor-general Charles Ligar, the assistant commissioner for lands, Clement Hodgkinson, and the secretary for mines, Robert Brough Smyth, declared in 1865: 'It is certain that if steps be not taken to enforce a more economical use of native timber, and to conserve the forests, there will soon be a difficulty in getting timber for the uses of the miner, in any of the forests adjacent to the gold workings.' But SA was first to legislate in pursuit of these ideals. F.E.H.W. Krichauff, the instigator of SA's Forest Board Act 1875, looked forward to the board taking responsibility for forest conservation. Three years later, the board appointed Australia's first conservator of forests, John Ednie Brown.

Colonial enthusiasm for water conservation was even greater. To Alfred **Deakin**, water conservation and **irrigation** were ideals of the same order as Federation and the **New Protection**. According to the NSW parliamentarian and later federal senator, Ernest Millen, no other subjects 'not impelled by the fervour of party strife' so occupied public attention. A Victorian Water Conservancy Board was established in 1880 to investigate the question of water supply; a Water Conservation Act came into force in 1881. When the Australian colonies federated in 1901, the only explicit environmental provision included in the Australian Constitution barred the new Commonwealth from abridging the right of any state to the reasonable use of river waters for conservation or irrigation.

Other forms of conservation soon also attracted attention. In a paper to the Royal Society of New South Wales in 1882, Andrew Ross called on government to investigate the properties of native grasses so that pastoralists could 'take steps to propagate or conserve those ... valuable for grazing purposes'. The destruction of native plants and grasses as a result of overstocking aroused increasing concern, and Francis Myers, who wrote for the Melbourne *Argus* as 'Telemachus', predicted in 1887 that saltbush would soon be killed out from the Murray to the Darling, while 'another decade or two and myall and boree would be gone also; shrubs and trees would also be utterly destroyed, and half the plains barren, through the gnawing out of the very roots of the grass'. With characteristic flourish, Myers declared, 'God Almighty did not conserve Australia for the nineteenth century that it should be treated in such a fashion as that.'

These various forms of conservation had different goals, despite their common language. For example, forest conservation looked to the long term, but water conservation was directed primarily at overcoming immediate shortfalls resulting from bad seasons. More significantly, forest conservation was conceived primarily as an antidote to the profligacy of humanity, whereas water conservation sought to harness the profligacy of nature. Instead of seeing nature as a system in which everything was perfect for its purpose, advocates of water conservation saw it as ripe for manipulation and improvement. Their target was 'waste in nature', as the surveyor, Edward Sanger, titled an essay in the *Victorian Review* in 1883.

Forest, water, fauna and flora conservation were all significant in the early 1900s, but soil conservation gradually attracted attention due to widespread erosion. When Australia's first minister for conservation of any type, Captain William Dunn, was appointed in NSW in 1944, he was responsible for the state's Soil Conservation Service, its Forestry Commission and its Water Conservation and Irrigation Commission but, significantly, not **national parks**, nature reserves, or fauna and flora protection. Victoria's first minister for conservation, appointed in 1950, was responsible only for soil—a political conception of conservation which prevailed through the 1960s, as discussed by Francis Ratcliffe in *Conservation and Australia* (1968).

For most of the twentieth century, conservation was widely defined as 'wise use', following the example of the American Progressive Conservation Movement. In an essay in James Barrett's *Save Australia* (1925), the chairman of Victoria's Forests Commission, Owen Jones, declared that 'real conservation' involved 'wise, non-wasteful use in the present generation; combined with every possible means of preservation for succeeding generations'. The first enduring conservation group in Australia—the Natural Resources Conservation League of Victoria, which was incorporated in 1951—shared this philosophy. So too, initially, did Australia's most significant environmental group, the Australian Conservation Foundation, which was established in 1965 under royal patronage to 'Make every effort to ensure that the land and water of the Commonwealth and its Territories are used with wisdom and foresight and that competing demands upon them are resolved in the best long-term interests of the State and Nation'.

Yet not all conservationists—a term used from at least the mid-1920s by Myles Dunphy—have conceived conservation this way, as Dunphy's *Selected Writings* (1986) reveal. When the National Parks and Primitive Areas Council of NSW adopted 'Progress with Conservation' as its slogan in 1932, its object was preservation; it wanted significant natural areas protected from development. When Dunphy optimistically declared in 1934 that 'an Age of Wastefulness' had given way to an 'Age of Conservation', his goal was wilderness protection through the establishment of a Greater Blue Mountains National Park. In his view, the only way to conserve valuable wilderness was 'to place an embargo upon roads in relation to it'.

The conflict between these different views of conservation was acute already in the 1920s and 1930s. Owen Jones implicitly deplored the stance taken by Dunphy when he declared that, if conservation involved 'the tying-up of natural resources for indefinite withholding from use, it would rightly arouse the utmost opposition'. Dunphy, in turn, berated state foresters for their policy 'of cutting out all good trees from residual Crown lands that happen to be forested, and damn the future of such cut-over lands'. In his view there was little point in trying to educate the public to respect residual Crown land when its offical conservators had power to strip it of all its best and finest trees.

This conflict assumed unprecedented proportions in the early 1970s within the Australian Conservation Foundation, prompted by the foundation's failure to oppose the flooding of Lake Pedder by Tasmania's Hydro-Electric Commission. On one side were scientists who clung to Francis Ratcliffe's original vision of the foundation as a group of experts available to give government objective advice. In 1973 this group succeeded in throwing out the foundation's council and transforming the ACF into an activist organisation, ready to confront government on issues ranging from sand-mining on Fraser Island to the damming of the Franklin River and the logging of old-growth forests. New conservation organisations such as the Wilderness Society and Greenpeace have developed a more youthful and militant strain of environmental politics. Governments, both state and federal, responded with a range of legal and administrative devices, from surveys and inventories to environmental impact statements, designed to assist the conservation of places of special environmental quality. Tim Bonyhady has reviewed the legal dimension of conservation in *Places Worth Keeping* (1993).

For most of this period, conservation had been something of a catch-all for all forms of environmental protection. It was now extended to embrace protection of the built **heritage** as well as the natural environment, a usage given legislative force in the creation of the Australian Heritage Commission, whose mission embraced the protection of historic buildings as well as the habitats of endangered species. In *Environmental Boomerang* (1973), Len Webb explained that, because of heightened awareness of the significance of pollution during the 1960s, conservation automatically implies anti-pollution measures. He also emphasised that it no longer involved just the husbanding of particular resources. Instead it had a broader, ecological

meaning: the maintenance and management of entire natural processes. In the early 1980s the World Conservation Strategy—given local expression in the 1983 National Conservation Strategy for Australia—took this definition still further. The first hint of ecologically sustainable development was apparent as the strategy defined conservation as 'the management of human use of the biosphere so that it may yield the greatest sustainable benefit to present generations while maintaining its potential to meet the needs and aspirations of future generations'.

TIM BONYHADY

Conservatism has been attributed to many individuals, groups, and parties, but very few have claimed the name. As a strong and sustained movement, conservatism is in fact a very recent arrival in Australia. John **Howard**, who became prime minister in 1996, was the first holder of the office to describe himself as a conservative.

Conservatives have defended cultural traditions, ancient institutions, established churches and ruling elites, but Australia did not possess these. Conservative pessimism about human capacity could not find purchase while Australian society was believed to be young and new, and politics was concerned with material progress and nation-building.

Liberals and radicals in the nineteenth century and Laborites in the twentieth have routinely called their opponents conservatives as a term of opprobrium, to cast them as irrational opponents of what must be the natural law of new societies: progress. They have then been puzzled that these 'conservatives' can on occasions command the support of the majority of the population. They would have been less puzzled if they had noticed that their opponents did not call themselves conservatives or comport themselves like conservative parties in Britain and Europe.

The names which they have given themselves have been various. The opponents of free selection in NSW organised themselves as the Constitutional Party, a title which was also used by the opponents of the Victorian liberals during the fierce **constitutional crises** of the 1860s and 1870s. The first organised opposition to the Labor Party in the 1890s was the National Defence League. The parties which fused in 1909 to provide a united opposition to Labor called themselves Liberal. When **Hughes** and his followers were expelled from the Labor Party in 1916–17 they regrouped in the National Labour Party. When shortly afterwards they coalesced with the Liberals, the new group called itself Nationalist. The new non-Labor organisations which eclipsed the Nationalists in the 1930s **Depression** came together as the **United Australia Party**. When that in turn broke up during World War II, a new **Liberal Party** took its place.

The names are indicative. The parties which have contested Labor's attack on capitalism and its espousal of socialism have had no need of a conservative philosophy. They appealed to **liberalism** to preserve individual liberty, private property, and free enterprise, and argued amongst themselves how far the state should support private enterprise and the general welfare. As against Labor's appeal to class, they presented themselves as the party which would govern in the interests of all. Hence the resort to the 'national' label and to a united Australia. Nor have these parties been merely reactive. The *Nationalist* declared of its sponsor, the United Australia Party, in 1937 that it 'is not a party of diehards and conservatives but is truly progressive and democratic'.

This account of the ideology of the non-Labor parties is drawn from Peter Loveday's 'The Liberals' Image of Their Party', which appears in a collection of essays titled *Australian Conservatism* (1979), edited by Cameron Hazlehurst, who was not persuaded by its contents to abandon his title. Academics too are inclined to label opponents of Labor and the defenders of the interests it attacked as conservatives. Allan Patience berates them for this and the Liberal Party for failing to have a true conservative concern for the health of society conceived of organically in 'The Liberal Party and the Failure of Australian Conservatism', in Marian Sawer (ed.), *Australia and the New Right* (1982).

The one truly conservative political grouping had a short life. It consisted of the landed gentlemen of NSW who assumed they would constitute the government when the colony acquired self-government. They opposed liberalism and **democracy**, and were quickly swept aside by liberals and democrats when the new **Constitution** came into operation. Their outlook and the reasons for their defeat are explored in J.M. Ward, *James Macarthur, Colonial Conservative 1798–1867* (1981), and John Hirst, *The Strange Birth of Colonial Democracy* (1988). The great handicap this group faced was that it was not an established ruling class. The British government had controlled the colony for so long that, in the middle of the nineteenth century, these conservatives had to claim power, a much more difficult task than maintaining it. After their failure, many of leading lights retreated to London, becoming Australia's first and only political exiles, and constantly lamented that the colony was no longer a fit place for a gentleman. Certainly their successors in parliament and in government did not deserve that name. From that time Australian parliaments rarely attracted the wealthy or the well-educated, who were periodically condemned for their dereliction of duty. The opponents of Labor in the twentieth century did not come from an established governing elite, which was another reason why they had no need to call on conservative ideas.

Conservatism became possible when Australia was viewed not as new or naturally progressive but as part of Western civilisation, possessing the same problems and facing the same threats as Western society generally. It is sometimes said that Australia lost its innocence in World War I. Manning **Clark**, in his *Short History of Australia* (1963), records Hughes's declaration on his return from Versailles that Australia was safe and pronounces 'the age of the survivors had begun'. There is some truth in this, but the faith in newness and a separate destiny did not die. The first social movement on the right to identify Australia as debased as Europe gathered around the *Catholic Worker* (founded 1936) and in Catholic Action (founded in 1937), both under the leadership of B.A. **Santamaria**. It was

fiercely critical of modern industrial capitalism and proposed a return to rural life and peasant proprietorship. Santamaria and his circle supported Franco in the **Spanish Civil War** to protect the Church and stave off **communism**. After World War II the Cold War produced a wider conservative response. The intellectuals who were prominent in opposing communism were concerned at the threat to Australia, but only as part of a worldwide struggle. They saw communism as a threat to the whole European intellectual and cultural tradition from which all that was valuable in Australia derived. Significantly, a number of the key figures were refugees from totalitarianism in Europe. They wrote with an intensity and a biting edge which was unusual in intellectual discourse hitherto.

The anti-communist intellectuals under the leadership of Richard Krygier, a Polish refugee, organised a local branch of the International Congress for Cultural Freedom. They were later embarrassed by the revelation that this body had received funding from the Central Intelligence Agency of the USA, though the agency had not exercised any direct influence over their activities. In 1956 the local congress launched *Quadrant*, the first and still the only conservative journal of opinion. The founding editor was James **McAuley**, a recent convert to Catholicism, and famous for being one of the perpetrators of the Ern Malley hoax, designed to discredit modernism in poetry. In his fight against communism, McAuley saw liberalism as the enemy; it had encouraged a selfish individualism that had broken down traditional attachments and values and so prepared the way for communism.

The *Quadrant* circle wanted to judge Australian literature by the highest European standards and scorned the indulgence shown to local products because they were self-consciously Australian. It also rejected what it saw as the narrow nationalistic account of Australian history in which Labor and the Left were the dynamic and creative force. It sought to understand Australian history more broadly as a transplantation of European civilisation, to which many groups and institutions contributed, and for this reason it welcomed the early work of Manning Clark. Peter Coleman, one of the circle, identified the historians who were in various ways critical of the role assigned to Labor as heralding a counter-revolution in Australian historiography.

The cultural transformation of the 1960s and 1970s which affected all Western societies was almost as strong in Australia as in the USA. This worldwide libertarian fervour, for which the only parallel is the expectations raised by the French Revolution, gave a new life to the conservative thought which the revolution had brought into being. The resistance to new demands for freedom or their more extreme forms has made conservatism unexceptional in Australia. The reassertion of traditional or family values, not against the old temptations which might undermine them but against an ideology which rejects them, is a conservative project. It is this which has created in the non-Labor parties a conservative wing of which Prime Minister Howard is a part.

This revolution and its reverberations gave *Quadrant* renewed purpose following the waning of the Cold War and the collapse of communism. It attacked the abolition of censorship, the growth of child-care, progressive education, and multiculturalism and lamented the lack of purpose in the new age of ruins. Some of its regular contributors were brought together in *The New Conservatism in Australia* (1982), which was edited by Robert Manne, who became editor of the journal in 1989.

The non-Labor parties are by no means uniformly conservative: in economic policy they have been a modernising force, supporting neo-classical economics and attacking long-standing institutions which have controlled economic life. *Quadrant*, too, mixed a conservative social policy with free-market economics. Under the editorship of Manne, this contradiction was confronted and the new economic policies were criticised as dogma and socially damaging. This brought Manne and his circle closer to the old social democratic left, which developed conservative concerns in the face of a revolution from the right. The two forces combined to produce *Shutdown: The Failure of Economic Rationalism and How to Rescue Australia* (1992), edited by Manne and John Carroll. Manne's defeat by the *Quadrant* editorial board followed his adoption of less conservative social and cultural views, and led to his replacement by an upholder of free-market economics.

JOHN HIRST

Constitutional crises have occurred frequently. The judgment which **Deakin** made concerning the most serious crisis in Victoria is true of them all. In *The Crisis in Victorian Politics 1879–1881* (1957), he wrote 'the strife was political only—perhaps social too in a modified degree—but little affecting the bulk of the community which went on its way making or trying to make money and amusing itself . . . little excited by the storm raging at Parliament House or occasional public meetings'. In less orderly societies, such crises would have had social consequences; it was the peacefulness of Australian society which allowed the politicians with impunity to carry matters to the brink.

Most of the crises arose as a result of a clash between the two houses of parliament. In four colonies—Victoria, SA, Tasmania, and WA—their **constitutions** had created two elected houses (a Legislative Assembly with a broad franchise and a Legislative Council with a restricted property-franchise) and no mechanism for resolving conflict between them. In NSW and Qld, the Legislative Councils were nominated by the governor, on the advice of ministers responsible to the Assembly. In these cases, a mechanism existed for resolving deadlocks between the houses. Just as in Britain the House of Lords could be coerced by the creation of new peers or the threat of it, so these Councils could be swamped by new nominees. This method was used in NSW in 1861 to carry free **selection** and in Qld in 1922 to provide the numbers to vote for the Council's abolition. The elected upper houses, by contrast, could resist the Assemblies with impunity. They could not be dissolved; the members never faced the electorate at the one time; their elections were staggered, with only a certain proportion retiring at each election.

The upper houses were given almost the same power as the lower. At the time the constitutions were formed, the House of Lords by convention did not interfere with the annual appropriation bill (the government's budget), but this convention was not transferred into the black-letter law of the colonial constitutions. In Victoria, the Council was not to amend the appropriation bill, but it could reject it outright; in the other colonies there was no limitation on the Council's power. Generally the Councils allowed the passage of the appropriation bills, though they were far readier to interfere than the Lords. This convention, such as it was, was used by governments as a way round the Council's refusal to pass other measures. A measure distasteful to the Council was tacked onto the appropriation bill in the hope the Council would pass it rather than precipitate a crisis by depriving the government of funds. But Councils naturally rejected these 'tacks'; to have passed them would have been to yield up their powers. Usually a compromise was patched up, but on two occasions in Victoria deadlock persisted and the government adopted extraordinary measures to survive after the Council had withheld supply.

The Victorian upper house was elected on the most restrictive property franchise in the country. Arrayed against it were the gold-rush migrants, liberal and democratic, who wanted to break the squatters' hold on the land and replace the free-trade policy of squatters and merchants with **protection** for local industry. The two houses were at loggerheads from the first.

The crises occurred in 1865, when the McCulloch government tacked on a protective tariff to the appropriation bill, and in 1877, when the **Berry** government tacked on payment of members. The Council on both occasions refused to pass the appropriation bill. The governments did not yield. The McCulloch government acquired funds by short-term loans from a bank, of which the premier was a director. When the government defaulted on repayment, the bank took the government to court to obtain its money, an action which the government did not contest. By court order, then, rather than an appropriation bill, money was released from the treasury. When the Berry government was deprived of funds, it sacked civil servants, mostly from the highest ranks—county court judges, police magistrates, coroners—ostensibly because their salaries could not be paid, but it was also pleased, as its opponents alleged, to punish men unsympathetic to the liberal cause. The government obtained funds by releasing monies from the treasury on the vote of the Assembly alone. The crises were settled by the Council's agreeing to pass the tariff and payment of members as separate measures, while the Assembly submitted appropriation bills free of tacks.

The governors were fully complicit in the schemes to acquire funds without parliamentary sanction. Governor **Darling** was recalled for supporting the McCulloch government so enthusiastically; Governor **Bowen's** prospects in the service were blighted because he had signed the notices for Berry's sackings. Darling's recall made him a liberal martyr, and further crises were precipitated by the

Assembly's insistence on granting his wife a large monetary reward. The liberals objected to the **Colonial Office's** punishing a governor for following the advice of his ministers and so threatening colonial self-government. **Higinbotham**, McCulloch's attorney-general, carried in the Assembly a declaration that the governor was 'an independent Sovereign in Victoria'. Even if they had been that, the governors, according to Westminster convention, should not have sanctioned the bypassing of parliament. They did so because they had little alternative. The ministers and their measures were popular; to dismiss them and force an election would only have brought them back in greater force. With an unpopular government acting illegally or unconstitutionally, a governor has more options.

The Commonwealth Constitution was designed to avoid the problems of the colonial constitutions. There was a provision to resolve deadlocks (a **double dissolution** and a joint sitting); the Senate was not to amend appropriation bills, nor was the House to tack. The Senate was still left with the right to reject appropriation bills outright. The small states insisted on that as a guarantee against unjust treatment. No one envisaged that the upper house would use its power over supply, not to object to some provision of the appropriation bill, but simply to force a government to an election. That had not happened in colonial times. It has occurred in the states since Federation: in Tasmania in 1948, and Victoria in 1947 and 1952. In 1975 it led to the **Dismissal** of the **Whitlam** Labor government.

In 1974 the Liberal opposition threatened to use its Senate majority to cut off supply to the government. Whitlam countered by calling a double-dissolution election, which he won. In 1975, when the opposition declared it would not pass supply until the prime minister called an election, Whitlam refused. His government was now certain to lose an election, but he was within his rights to argue that responsible government, as it had been understood, did not allow a hostile Senate the right to determine when a government should face the people. Like the Victorian liberal governments in the nineteenth century, he planned to 'tough it out'. He expected the governor-general to act like the Victorian governors and support the government. This is not how Sir John **Kerr** saw his role, and he would not be a party to the government's plans to obtain money from the banks as McCulloch had done. Kerr dismissed Whitlam because of his inability to obtain supply, and commissioned the opposition leader as prime minister on condition that he call an election, which Kerr could be confident that he would win. In this Kerr was correct, but he surely underestimated how much bitterness his action would cause.

The only other instance of a vice-regal dismissal of a government was less controversial. In 1931 in the depths of the Depression, Jack **Lang**, Labor premier of NSW, announced that he would no longer pay interest to British bondholders. The Commonwealth government paid the interest, and passed a law in 1932 requiring the NSW government to reimburse it. Lang sought to circumvent this measure by instructing officials not to deposit state funds in the bank. Governor Sir Philip Game told Lang he was acting illegally and that the instruction should be withdrawn. When Lang refused, the governor dismissed him. The election which followed was won by Lang's opponents. Unlike Kerr, Game had given Lang a warning and, though the matter was not tested in the courts, the premier was prima facie acting illegally, which Whitlam had not yet done when he was dismissed, though Kerr thought he was acting unconstitutionally.

Both Lang and Whitlam accepted their dismissal and their parties fought the issue in the subsequent election. Immediately upon the 1975 dismissal, some trade unions wanted to call a general strike, but this was quickly scotched by the president of the ACTU, Bob **Hawke**. Two hundred thousand people gathered in Moore Park, Sydney, to support Lang, but this was an election rally. So these crises, like the others, remained political. It is hard to avoid the suspicion that both Lang and Whitlam almost courted dismissal and, for all that important issues were at stake in these crises, the short-term political advantage in bringing on a crisis as a means of rallying support and intensifying pressure on opponents was an element in their unfolding. It is notable that, when McCulloch sent the protective tariff to the Council as a tack, this was the first time the matter had been presented to it. Knowing the Council's opposition to protection, McCulloch was deliberatively provocative. Crises are an indication that Australian politics has been played hard; the acceptance of their resolution illustrates the authority of the rule of law.

W.G. McMinn, *A Constitutional History of Australia* (1979), deals with all the crises.

JOHN HIRST

Constitutional history refers to the study of the birth and evolution of **constitutions**. In a narrow sense, the Australian Constitution is the document which in 1901 created the institutions of national government and defined their powers. In a broader sense, a constitution is taken to include as well the formal and informal political arrangements that supplement the written text; the customs, practices, traditions, and conventions that inform and control its actual operation; and the authoritative meanings, flowing mainly from judicial pronouncement, that determine its impact in particular situations.

In England, the original focal point of interest in the history of the constitution stemmed from the Whig project to place limits on the powers of the king through the 'rediscovery' of the claimed 'ancient rights of Englishmen'. Similarly, constitutional history in the early USA consisted in the main of self-justifications for the revolution.

Constitutional history in Australia is in large part the story of the evolutionary severing of the formal legal connection of Australia with the United Kingdom, and the gradual metamorphosis of the source of legitimacy of the Constitution from Imperial edict to the implied consent of the Australian people. Australian constitutional history in the first half of the nineteenth century includes the development of colonial institutions from rule by autocratic governors to **responsible self-government**; and in the latter part of the nineteenth century, the federal movement which culminated in the creation of the **Commonwealth of Australia** on 1 January 1901. Since **Federation**, themes in constitutional history have included the shifting boundaries of **Commonwealth–state relations**; the tension between the two houses of the Commonwealth parliament that in 1975 climaxed in the dramatic revival of the so-called 'reserve powers' of the Crown, which were relied upon by Governor-General Sir John **Kerr** in his **Dismissal** of the elected prime minister, Gough **Whitlam**; and, more recently, the controversial rediscovery by the **High Court** of 'implied' constitutional rights as a partial compensation for the absence in the Constitution of an express Bill of Rights.

Australian constitutional historiography can in turn be divided into distinct phases. The early period corresponds with the Whiggishness of early English and American constitutional history. The emphasis was on the attainment of the full rights of self-government; the attainment, so to speak, by Englishmen in Australia of the rights that Englishmen enjoyed in England. The standard account for NSW and Qld is A.C.V. **Melbourne**, *Early Constitutional Development in Australia*, extended by R.B. Joyce (1963); David Neal supplements it in *The Rule of Law in a Penal Colony* (1991), while W.G. McMinn, *A Constitutional History of Australia* (1979), deals with the other colonies.

The history of Federation—the story of the federal movement and the drafting of the Australian Constitution—has been told, engagingly though sometimes self-servingly, by some of the participants (notably Alfred **Deakin**, *The Federal Story*, 1944, and B.R. **Wise**, *The Making of the Australian Commonwealth 1889–1900*, 1913), and with more detachment, yet no less authority, by the respected historian J.A. **La Nauze** (*The Making of the Australian Constitution*, 1972). Most lawyers have come to it through the contemporary classic, *Annotated Constitution of the Australian Commonwealth* (1901), by John **Quick** and R.R. **Garran**. Although now overtaken by nearly a century of case law, expounding meanings about which Quick and Garran could only speculate, their book has been reprinted a number of times and is still considered to be the constitutional lawyer's bible, at least in relation to historical intentions. Other contemporary works include Harrison Moore, *The Constitution of the Commonwealth of Australia* (1902, 1910), and A. Inglis **Clark**, *Studies in Australian Constitutional Law* (1901).

The chief feature of constitutional history here, as elsewhere in the common law world, has been the Constitution's use in an instrumental way—as a means, rather than an end. The evolution of the Constitution is seen as a rhetorical tool with which to posit political arguments in favour of future change. This is apparent in the works of Manning **Clark**, and others. The telling of the constitutional story shifted from an emphasis on the inherited aspects of the constitutional system, to an emphasis on the characteristics which should differentiate the Australian Constitution from the British one. Britain still tends to remain the main comparator, but rather than representing the ideal, it now has come to repre-

sent in the eyes of some an inhibiting influence on the development of indigenous constitutional traditions.

Constitutional history, in the sense of what the framers of the Australian Constitution intended by the words they drafted, has not always influenced its judicial interpretation. Some judges would have it so, if a precise enough 'original intent' could be found, while others have been more inclined to interpret phrases of sufficient generality widely enough to encompass changed and changing circumstances, particularly in the light of the historical difficulty of formal amendment. Still others have tended to interpret the text at face value, detached from its historical context, often with equally detached consequences. But constitutional history is today regarded as relevant and useful in constitutional litigation, at least to indicate the general nature of the problem that the framers sought to solve, if not the actual meaning of the words they chose. In recent years a historical perspective (based particularly on the Conventions that drafted the Constitution) has been influential in confining the ability of the Commonwealth to enact unilaterally a law for the incorporation of companies, and in narrowing the scope of the previously quite destructive Section 92 of the Constitution, which guarantees the freedom of interstate trade.

Yet the constitutional history used by the courts has tended to be lawyers' history rather than historians' history; this has often been artificial and incomplete, with excessive reliance on formal documents rather than on their wider context and the discussions surrounding them. In this process, the work of trained historians and political scientists has, until recently, been for the most part overlooked. The political scientists, other than Brian Galligan (*Politics of the High Court*, 1987), might have been intimidated by the perceived need to master some of the technicalities of constitutional law; and the historians have focused descriptively on constitutional outcomes rather than seeking explanations and insights in the dynamics of the judicial process. The cross-disciplinary work of Geoffrey Sawer is a shining exception to these criticisms, particularly his two-volume chronological study of the intersection between constitutional law and politics in the first half of the twentieth century, *Australian Federal Politics and Law* (1956, 1963).

In some contexts, the courts have undertaken extensive historical analysis and have shown an increasing willingness to draw upon a diversity of sources, including the work of historians, in their adjudicative process. Examples are the landmark **Mabo** and **Wik** Cases of 1992 and 1996, where significant use in the former was made of the work of the historian Henry **Reynolds**.

There was some role-reversal in the avalanche of commentary on the constitutional upheaval of 1975: the lawyers set themselves up as authorities on the political conventions of responsible government, while many political scientists and other commentators, equally dogmatically, let the passion of the moment turn them into bush lawyers. The literature on this aspect of our constitutional history must be carefully assessed according to the standpoint of the observer and the distance from the events (for an interdisciplinary retrospect, and prospect, see Michael Coper and George Williams, eds, *Power, Parliament and the People*, 1997).

It is not altogether surprising that there has been a divide between lawyers' constitutional history, with its narrow boundaries, limited sources, and specific purposes, and the constitutional history of professional historians, which has been broader, although tending to ignore the dynamics of judicial interpretation and other areas of interest to lawyers. The teaching of constitutional history in Australian law schools has declined and, even when it was taught, it concentrated on British constitutional history at the expense of the US influence on our federal arrangements and on the role of the High Court. With the turning away from the imperial model for conceiving Australian constitutional history, most of these courses fell away and, for a variety of reasons, were not replaced by any other courses in **legal history**. Since there was also a decline in the teaching of history in secondary schools, Australian law students were therefore not exposed in a systemic way to much history at all. This led to an unfortunate narrowing of perspective within the legal profession.

There are signs of a revival of interest in the teaching of legal and constitutional history in Australian law schools. Along with the movement to reintroduce the study of 'civics' in secondary schools, these developments might in time produce a better understanding of constitutional history, both in the legal profession and in the community at large, and consequently a greater contribution or feeding-in of constitutional history (and a broader conception of such history) to the development of current constitutional law and practice.

MICHAEL COPER AND IAN HOLLOWAY

Constitutions in written form provide for the governance of the states and the Commonwealth. The state constitutions date from the time the colonies achieved self-government: Victoria, 1855; NSW, 1855; SA, 1856; Tasmania, 1856; Qld, 1859; WA, 1890. The constitutions were drawn up in the colonies by the single-house legislatures, in which two-thirds of the members were elected and one-third nominated by the governor, and then sent to London for approval. The making of these constitutions was treated as ordinary law-making and there was no suggestion that the constitutions derived their authority from the people.

The constitutions provided for parliaments composed of two houses: a popularly elected Assembly and a Legislative Council. Only the SA constitution allowed at the outset for all men to vote for the Assembly; the others were amended to provide for this after they came into operation. The Councils in NSW and Qld were nominated by the governor (on the advice of ministers); in Tasmania, SA, and Victoria, the Councils were elected by property-holders; in WA, a nominated Council was soon replaced by an elected one.

Under these constitutions responsible government was established: that is, the governor and his officials appointed by the Colonial Office no longer constituted the government; the governor formed a government by choosing ministers who had the support of the popular Assembly and

were responsible to it. This is what later became known as the Westminster system and, as in Britain, it was a matter of convention rather than law that ministers had to command a majority in the Assembly and that the governor was obliged to act on their advice.

The colonial parliaments had the power to pass laws for the peace, order, and good government of their people, subject to the supervision of the imperial overlord. Any colonial law could be disallowed in London, and governors were instructed not to give their assent to laws on some subjects and to refer them to the Colonial Office. These were matters on which Britain wanted to preserve uniformity in its Empire (as in marriage and divorce), or where imperial interests were affected (as in trade and shipping).

The colonists and colonial reformers in London wanted a clear demarcation to be made between local and imperial matters, and for Britain to forgo the right to interfere in local matters, but the British government refused, arguing that the distinction was hard to draw and would itself become the object of dispute. In practice Britain interfered very little; in the nineteenth century only five colonial laws were disallowed in London.

The Assemblies and Councils were given almost equal powers in the constitutions. Only in Victoria was the Council forbidden to amend the annual appropriation bill (the government's budget), which had become accepted in Britain as a limitation on the power of the House of Lords. In SA a clash over this issue occurred in the first year of the constitution's operation, which was settled by an agreement that the Council could suggest amendments, but not make them. In no constitution was there provision for resolving deadlocks between the two houses, which meant that the colonies were sometimes plunged into **constitutional crises**. A nominated Council could be brought into line with the Assembly if the governor agreed to create new members (a swamping), but it was difficult to change the mind of an elected upper house. By the twentieth century the elected upper houses created to mimic the House of Lords exercised far more power than their lordships, whose veto was decisively challenged in 1911.

The constitutions could be altered by the parliaments themselves; the only restriction which operated, in some colonies but not all, was that constitutional amendment required the support of an absolute majority in both houses. The NSW constitution, as drawn up in the colony, provided that two-thirds majorities were required to alter the composition of the Council and the electorates of the Assembly, but the British government, knowing that these parts of the constitution were controversial, provided that the protection of a two-thirds majority could itself be removed by simple majority. The first NSW parliament did just that and so made further constitutional change relatively easy.

Unlike the colonial constitutions, the federal Constitution had a long gestation and took its authority from the people. The first draft was drawn up by a Federal Convention in Sydney in 1891. This attempt at **Federation** failed, but the 1891 draft formed the basis of the Constitution adopted by the Convention of 1897–98. This body was elected by the people, to whom its handiwork was submitted for approval at referendum. Following its acceptance in Australia, the Constitution was sent to London, where with only minor amendments it was passed into law as a British act of parliament. It came into operation on 1 January 1901. The colonies were now states in the federal Commonwealth of Australia. J.A. **La Nauze**, *The Making of the Australian Constitution* (1972), is an authoritative account.

The US constitution provided the model for the Australian. It was followed in the names of the two federal houses, the House of Representatives and the Senate, and their composition (the one representing the people and the other in equal number the states); the mode of the division of powers (specified powers to the federal parliament; the rest remaining with the states); and in the establishing of a court to interpret the Constitution.

The constitution-makers faced the difficulty of reconciling the American federal system of two equally powerful houses with the principle of responsible government in which the government is responsible to the lower house, in this case the House of Representatives. J.W. **Hackett**, a Western Australian delegate to the 1891 Convention, put the dilemma: 'either responsible government will kill federation, or federation . . . will kill responsible government'. Samuel **Griffith**, the chief draftsman in 1891, wanted to preserve the federal principle by leaving open the possibility that the Commonwealth government might be composed of ministers who were not members of parliament. Most Convention delegates favoured the responsible government system to which they were accustomed, but in deference to Griffith it was not insisted on. The 1897–98 Convention settled the matter by obliging ministers to be members of parliament.

But a government responsible to the House of Representatives could not govern if the Senate had equal power over finance. To ensure the pre-eminence of the House over the annual appropriation bill and taxation, the SA agreement on the relations between the two houses was adopted: the Senate could only suggest amendments to these measures, though it was left with the power to reject them outright, the issue at the centre of the 1975 constitutional crisis.

Conceived as the upper house, the Senate was bound to be thought of as the conservative house, even though the delegates of the small colonies insisted that this was a misconception, more especially since it was to be elected by the same people as the House of Representatives. Nevertheless, liberals and democrats, angry at the record of the Legislative Councils in defeating popular measures, were determined that the Senate be finally accountable to the lower house, a desire which most of the delegates from the two large colonies shared. Thus a Senate which persisted in rejecting a measure passed by the lower house could be dissolved along with the lower house and if, following the total reconstruction of the parliament, the disagreement persisted, it was to be resolved at a joint sitting of the two houses.

Matching the mode of its adoption, the Constitution was to be amended by proposals being put by the federal parliament to the people at **referendum**. To be successful, a proposal had to win a majority of votes overall and a majority in a majority of the states. Nearly all attempts at amendment have been rejected, the people proving to be conservative guardians of their Constitution. More substantial amendment has come from the judgments of the **High Court**.

Just as the experience in the working of the colonial constitutions influenced the Commonwealth Constitution, so it has had an influence on the states. The referendum has been widely adopted to protect key aspects of state constitutions, such as the governor and the two houses of parliament. In NSW, where the reliance on the referendum is most extensive, it protects the duration of the Assembly, compulsory voting, single-member electorates, and the number of voters in electoral districts, as well as the existence of the Legislative Council, which was made elective in 1933. In Qld a referendum is required to restore the Legislative Council, which was abolished in 1922. None of the elected Councils retains a property franchise, a belated adjustment to the principles of **democracy**. In NSW and SA the Councils are elected in the same way as the Senate, with the whole state voting as one constituency.

The state and federal constitutions were originally subordinate to the imperial parliament which gave them their authority. By the **Statute of Westminster** of 1931, the Commonwealth Constitution ceased to be subordinate; by the Australia Act of 1986 the state constitutions ceased to be so and the UK parliament abdicated all constitutional right over Australia. In this severance, care was taken to protect the sovereignty of the states and to guarantee that federal and state constitutions would be amended in the manner and form which they stipulate. The Statute of Westminster and the Australia Act, as part of the constitutions of Australia, can be amended by the Commonwealth parliament acting on the request of the states.

W.G. McMinn, *A Constitutional History of Australia* (1979), is an authoritative text.

JOHN HIRST

Convict history is carried by Australia as a beloved burden. When Russel **Ward** claimed in 1958 that the convict experience was central to our national sense of self, he described a popular legend as well as creating one. Some have tried to write the convicts out of history and memory. For most makers of Australian history, though, the convicts have served as icons carrying particular understandings of the national past.

The first historical assessment of the convict era was written by John **West**, a Congregational minister. West researched and wrote his study, *The History of Tasmania* (1852), in the heat of the campaign to end **transportation** to the eastern colonies. He blamed Britain for both the brutality of the system and the unhappy impact of its victims on colonial society. The long **anti-transportation** campaign fixed the idea of the convict 'stain'—of a damaged national birth—indelibly in both England and the colonies. Immigrant historians in the following decade avoided both the imperial and the colonial shame by imagining a past as nearly as possible convict-free.

It was left to literary men like Marcus **Clarke** and William **Astley** to return to West's themes of imperial neglect and colonial degradation. Clarke's novel *His Natural Life* (1874) explicitly condemned 'the working and results of an English system of transportation' and asserted the humanity of some at least of its victims. Astley, writing short stories as 'Price Warung' in the 1890s *Bulletin*, explored the extremes of human suffering endured on the penal settlements. Their combination of moral indignation and gruesomely authentic detail captured the imagination of several generations of Australian readers. For the first half of the twentieth century, convict experience popularly meant the appalling cruelties of the prison settlement and the lash, and the convict was likely to be an innocent victim, or at least 'more sinned against than sinning'.

In the 1930s the poet Mary **Gilmore** condemned historians for excluding the convicts from the emerging national history:

> Shame on the mouth
> That would deny
> The knotted hands
> That set us high.

Russel Ward prefaced *The Australian Legend* (1958) with this quotation, together with de Tocqueville's observation that as the child is father to the man, so the future of the nation can be found in its cradle. Ward's convicts were fathers of which the nation can be fond, if not exactly proud. He drew on the literary nationalism of the *Bulletin* school for its version of Australian manhood—laconic, pragmatic, anti-authoritarian, and loyal to mates—and found the origins of the paradigm among the suffering convicts. He also found the origins of the Australian working class. At the time, critics fastened upon the class issue; Humphrey **McQueen** in *A New Britannia* (1970) thought that the convicts' acquisitive instincts labelled them as 'lumpenproletarian or petty-bourgeois'. In later years Ward was justly accused of sexism and racism in his overly sympathetic depiction of convict attitudes, but few denied his sense of the convicts' importance in the national history.

Arguments about the convict past were put on a sounder basis with the publication of L.L. **Robson's** *The Convict Settlers of Australia* in 1965 and A.G.L. **Shaw's** *Convicts and the Colonies* in 1966. Robson's work was an early exercise in cliometrics, an elaborate quantification of the records of individual convict lives kept by their judges and gaolers; not surprisingly, it focused upon their criminality. Shaw's was an administrative study of the system of transportation within the British Empire. When it turned to Robson's question, 'Who were the convicts?', it restated his conclusions with magisterial disdain: 'All in all they were a disreputable lot.'

The studies by Shaw and Robson are still cited for their ground-breaking research, but it is Ward's characterisation of the convicts as our founding fathers which has drawn historians intent on redressing the present. Miriam **Dixson's** *The Real Matilda* (1976) traced the low status of modern Australian women to the low self-esteem engendered among convict women—'our founding mothers'—by their treatment as prisoners, wives, and lovers—'the slave of slaves'. Anne **Summers** in *Damned Whores and God's Police* (1975) pursued a similar concern over a wider canvas. Summers understood women's modern dilemma as the impossible conjunction of two equally constraining historical stereotypes: the sexually available convict whore, and the socially purifying settler's wife. Both, she argued, were promoted by the imperial state.

The search for a useful convict past drove private history as well as the academic kind. Before the 1960s in eastern Australia, and rather later in WA, a convict ancestor was a matter for shame and concealment. But members of the burgeoning genealogical societies have come to regard a convict in the family as a proud badge of Australian identity. The genealogical impulse fed back into formal history with publications such as Babette Smith, *A Cargo of Women* (1988), which presented the author's convict ancestor and her shipmates as capable, self-directed women, and Portia Robinson's several histories of convict women and their daughters, including *The Women of Botany Bay* (1988). Robinson used the evidence of large numbers of individual lives to deny the readings by Dixson and Summers, and convict women appeared as improbably good mothers and respectable citizens.

Historians of ethnicity seeking a place in Australian history also turned to the convicts. As early as 1974, *Australian Genesis* by J.S. Levi and G.F.J. Bergman celebrated the achievement of **Jewish** convicts and settlers before 1850. In the 1980s Michael Cigler edited and in some cases wrote a series of histories of ethnic groups in Australia, published by the AE Press; about half of the dozen titles discovered an ancestral figure among the convicts. The **Irish** have received the most historical attention, as befits their numbers among those transported. Like the later feminists, ethnic historians tend to stress the progress of their subjects from convict to successful settler. The triumph of the emancipist is a common theme among historians of the Irish as ideologically diverse as James Waldersee, *Catholic Society in New South Wales 1788–1860* (1974); Chris McConville, *Croppies, Celts and Catholics* (1987); and Patrick **O'Farrell**, *The Irish in Australia* (1986).

The general tendency of academic history in the 1980s was towards normalising the convict experience—making it an ordinary part of a national history. Alan Frost in *Convicts and Empire* (1980) summed up his contribution to the two decades of debate about the intentions of the founders of Australia. Frost saw the convicts as imperial agents, exported to labour in the interests of strategy and trade. John Hirst's *Convict Society and Its Enemies* (1983) argued that the myth of the convict 'stain' on Australia's birth was created by contemporary critics of transportation like John West. He understood convict society as pushed by the profit motive towards the patterns of capitalist democracy. His convicts were more useful to society as workers than as objects of penal punishment; the lash became an element in labour relations.

The normalising approach was carried furthest in *Convict Workers* (1988), a collection of essays by economic historians edited by Stephen Nicholas. Its central essays revisited the cliometric approach of Lloyd Robson, counting the occupations entered on the convict registers rather than the convictions. Nicholas concluded that 'The convicts transported to Australia were ordinary British and Irish working-class men and women', similarly skilled to and better-educated than those they left behind, and that they formed the basis of a highly efficient colonial workforce. Deborah Oxley's *Convict Maids* (1996) makes the argument specifically for convict women, as wives as well as workers. These historians work with a canvas much larger than the British Empire, understanding transportation as part of a global process of forced migration alongside indentured and contract labour and slavery.

And yet the normalisers have not touched the popular imagination. The historical best-seller of the last decade was Robert **Hughes's** *The Fatal Shore* (1987). Hughes energetically (if erratically) dismissed the rationalists. Botany Bay was no proto-capitalist workplace, it was a place of exile, privation, and death—a gulag. Hughes's central concern was to display the suffering of the convicts and the viciousness of their gaolers. He revived the moral language and the pornographic detail of the nineteenth-century reformers and novelists to create a story as compelling, and as partial, as theirs.

Alan Atkinson has been a normaliser of a different sort. He was interested in establishing the convicts' own view of their masters and their entitlements, their 'moral economy', to use the term of the English historian Edward Thompson who inspired this approach. Atkinson's 'Four Patterns of Convict Protest' (*LH*, 1979) is a finely worked study in which we hear the convicts' voices. With Marian Quartly he was the editor of *Australians 1838* (1987), a volume in the **Bicentennial History Project**, which recreated convict society as a plebeian English society transforming itself in a new land—as a birth rather than a death. In *The Europeans in Australia* (1997) he further integrates convicts into convict society.

The convict experience continues to fascinate Australian historians. More than any other, this is the subject which every generation invests with its own significance. In the 1990s this means interrogating the body—its appetites, passions, privations, and delights. *Representing Convicts* (1997), edited by Ian Duffield and James Bradley, picks up the issues of class and forced migration raised by *Convict Workers*, and adds articles on tattoos and headshaving. Joy Damousi's *Depraved and Disorderly* (1997), a new history of convict women, reads the practices imposed upon the women's bodies in order to understand the anxieties and uncertainties of colonial state and culture. It is a fertile field of inquiry.

MARIAN QUARTLY

Convicts were transported from Britain as forced labour to the American and West Indian colonies in the seventeenth and eighteenth centuries, but nineteenth-century Australia was to become the site of the first self-conscious attempt to build a society on the labour of convicted felons. More than 150 000 convicts were transported to eastern Australia between 1787 and 1852, about 25 000 of them women. **Transportation** and penal servitude—forced labour—are key terms to understanding convict life in Australia, more so than conviction and criminality.

Convicts transported to America had been sold—or, more precisely, seven years of their labour had been sold—to farmers and plantation owners. In 1775 the American War of Independence put a stop to this trade, but not to the numbers (about a thousand a year) sentenced to transportation. Transportation was an integral part of the English and Irish systems of justice. With growing poverty and no organised police force, the authorities relied on a harsh system of punishment to deter those criminals whom they could not catch. Simple larceny merited transportation for seven years; compound larceny—stealing goods worth more than a shilling, perhaps $50 in today's money—merited death by hanging. In practice, judges and juries tended to commute death sentences to transportation, swelling the numbers sent across the Atlantic and, after 1775, the numbers held in English gaols.

The common gaols of England were cramped, desperately unhealthy places, designed for the temporary detention of those awaiting sentence or punishment, and soon crowded with intended transportees. As a temporary expedient, the government legislated to use these people's labour in England; the women and infirm in houses of correction; the able-bodied men dredging the rivers and harbours, working from hulks moored midstream. When attempts failed to find new markets for the convicts and their labour overseas, the government took up the idea of establishing a convict colony, a settlement in which the Crown would employ the convicts in the imperial interest. Several sites were investigated, mostly in Africa, and the choice finally, perhaps reluctantly, fell on the most distant—in NSW.

Historians have long debated the importance of 'the convict motive' in the **foundation** of the colony at Botany Bay. Some have described a hasty decision to set up a dumping-ground for convicts. Others have discovered a considered plan to extend the Empire's interests in the East. In an early and enlightening contribution to the discussion, A.G.L. **Shaw** noted in *Convicts and the Colonies* (1966) that, while the government's principal concern was 'that of ridding England of her undesirables', the wisdom of the day assumed that 'the proper use of banishment' was to so relocate the criminal that 'his labour may be useful to the state'. (See **Settlement**.)

In the early years of the Australian convict colonies, the fate of individual convicts turned largely on their perceived usefulness in creating a new society. Governor **Phillip** founded a system of labour in which, whatever their crime, people were employed according to their skills—as brickmakers, carpenters, nurses, servants, cattlemen, shepherds, and farmers. Whole groups of people benefited from being categorised as a particular kind of worker. Thus educated convicts were set to the relatively easy work of record-keeping for the convict administration. Women convicts, less than one-third of the whole, were assumed to be most useful as wives and mothers. Marriage effectively freed a woman convict from her servitude to the state; whatever her sentence, she exchanged the authority of the governor for the authority of her husband. Marriage was thought to benefit men too, by settling **emancipists** into the role of householder, small landowner, and farmer, which was imagined for them by successive governors.

Governors such as **Bligh** and **Macquarie** in NSW, and **Davey** in Van Diemen's Land, understood their colonies as societies founded and governed in the interests of the emancipists—convicts freed by pardon or by serving their time—and their native-born children. They used the labour of male convicts still under sentence to develop the public capital of the colonies: roads, bridges, courthouses, and hospitals. Emancipists were readily granted small landholdings, and convict labour to help work them. By the late 1810s thousands of emancipists were supporting themselves and often their families—though more often by wage labour than by farming their own holdings.

English critics complained that the system was too expensive and insufficiently harsh, and hence failed to deter. Colonial critics like John **Macarthur** argued that economy and deterrence could be at once achieved by taking convict labour away from costly government works and lenient emancipist employers, and directing it to the charge of large landowners like himself. The discipline of rural labour offered, moreover, the best chance of reform. This view was adopted by Commissioner **Bigge** in his 1822–23 report, which the British government accepted. The **assignment** of convicts to private employers was expanded to become their major form of employment during the 1820s and 1830s, the period when most convicts were sent to the colonies.

Assignment came to have its critics too; it was truly said to be a 'lottery', a punishment determined not by the crime but by the conditions of the workplace, the skills of the convict, and the temperament of the employer. At the same time, it was a highly regulated system, at least in nineteenth-century terms, with the state prescribing the rights and duties of both parties. In practice, the role of the colonial administration was generally to enforce discipline in the workplace. The commonest offences bringing men before the courts were all work-related, and the commonest punishment was the lash. Behind the employer stood the magistrate and the scourger, and then the chain gangs and the penal colonies, such as **Norfolk Island**, **Moreton Bay**, and **Port Arthur**. Here men toiled in agony at senseless tasks intended only to punish and deter.

Women were anomalous within assignment. The system made it harder for women to escape into marriage, yet failed to employ them. They were officially banned from heavy outdoor labour, and with jobs as indoor servants in short supply, the government 'factories' were always crowded with unassigned women. The **female factories** were originally workplaces for weaving cloth, but soon became refuges for the unemployed and the pregnant—a common conse-

quence of assignment as a house-servant. The work discipline also sat uncomfortably upon women. They could not be lashed, and the authorities were generally reluctant to send them to the penal colonies, so the factories also became places of secondary punishment. By the 1830s, the factories and their idle, unruly inhabitants stood for some observers as visible symbols of a disordered society. Others pointed to women emancipists, mothers of a law-abiding generation, as symbols of the colonies' capacity to reform.

Who were the convicts? This has been the great dispute within **convict history**. Historians have seen them variously as innocents wronged by a harsh society, professional criminals, and ordinary members of the British working class. Certainly their society was a harsh one, but the truth is more complicated. Most of the convicts were thieves, convicted in the great cities of England; only those sentenced in Ireland were commonly convicted of rural crimes. There were few innocents among them. Men generally came before the courts several times before being transported. Women were more likely to be transported for a first offence, sometimes an offence involving **prostitution**. Men and women transported in the 1820s and the 1830s were usually convicted of more serious crimes than earlier generations.

Few of the convicts were professionals who lived only by crime. Some were familiar with the culture of the London underworld, and thieves' cant became the 'flash' language of the barracks and factories. But the great majority of convicts had been working men and women, and they brought to the colonies the full range of skills available in the British workforce. Perhaps they differed from other British workers only in their relative lack of respect for chastity and property rights.

In 1838 a committee of the British House of Commons condemned transportation as 'an unclean thing' that was creating a monstrous society. Assignment was said to be slavery, corrupting the relations between masters and servants, especially female servants. As a result of this report, transportation to NSW ceased in 1840. But the needs of the British penal system prevailed, and Van Diemen's Land was required to take more than 30 000 convicts in the 1840s. The Colony of WA willingly received some 7000 male exiles between 1850 and 1868.

The charge that transportation created abnormal societies is hard to maintain, except perhaps in the case of Tasmania, where the numbers of convicts were very large in a small population. Elsewhere, ex-convicts and their children were socially indistinguishable from the free immigrants of the 1830s and 1840s—poor men and women whose immigration was assisted by governments and employers as a substitute for convict labour. Governor Phillip had said in 1786 that he 'would not wish Convicts to lay the foundations of an Empire'—but he and his successors made a success of the experiment.

MARIAN QUARTLY

Cook, James (1728–79), Yorkshire villager and apprentice grocer, North Sea collier seaman, Royal Navy master at the battle of Quebec, Newfoundland hydrographic surveyor,

Pacific explorer, Fellow of the Royal Society, is a man of myth and anti-myth. To colonisers, he was an icon of humanistic, scientific empire. To the colonised, at least in the post-colonial period of the late twentieth century, he has come to represent the violence of empires in their encounters with native peoples.

Cook's voyages inaugurated a British sphere of influence in the Pacific. Trade, missionary enterprise, and the protection of settlers' rights were the means by which it was primarily established; only in one place—the eastern portion of what contemporaries called New Holland—did Cook claim possession. On 20 August 1770 he stood on the highest part of 'Possession Island', hoisted the British colours and, in the name of King George III, took possession of the whole eastern coast down to the 38th parallel 'by the name of New South Wales'. The only concerns he expressed were about possible claims by the Dutch against George III.

These rites of possession occurred near the end of the first of Cook's three incursions into the Pacific. The first (on the *Endeavour*, 1768–71) began as part of a global scientific experiment in measuring the size of the universe by observing the transit of Venus across the sun. It ended spectacularly with the **mapping** of the north and south islands of NZ and of the whole of the east coast of Australia. In the second voyage (in the *Resolution* and *Adventure*, 1772–75) Cook made a great circuit of the Pacific south of the equator, disposing of the notion of a Great South Land. His third voyage (in the *Resolution* and *Discovery*, 1776–79) took him north in search of a North-West Passage. He 'discovered' the Hawaiian islands instead. His death at Kealakekua on the island of Hawai'i, intertwined with mythical realities of native perceptions as it was, has become a case study in the possibility of writing a 'true' history of cross-cultural encounters; this is demonstrated in Marshall Sahlins, *How 'Natives' Think: About Captain Cook, for Example* (1995).

J.C. Beaglehole and Bernard **Smith** have been the giants of Cook scholarship, the one with his editions of the *Journals of Captain James Cook* (1955–68, 3 vols), the other with the cataloguing and reproduction of the art and charts of the voyages in Rüdiger Joppien and Bernard Smith, *The Art of Captain Cook's Voyages* (1985–87, 3 vols) and *The Charts and Coastal Views of Captain Cook's Voyages* (1988–94, 3 vols).

GREG DENING

Cook, Joseph (1860–1947) was one of two coalminers to become prime minister of Australia, and the only Methodist. From the English midlands, he emigrated to Lithgow, where he became president of the miners' lodge and helped establish the local branch of the Labor Party. Elected to the NSW parliament in 1891, he became Labor leader in 1893 but in the following year broke with the party because of his refusal to accept the pledge that bound members to accept decisions of the **caucus**. Thereafter he served in George **Reid's** free-trade liberal ministry. Cook followed Reid into federal parliament in 1901 and succeeded him as leader of the free-trade party in 1908. Following the **Fusion** with Alfred **Deakin's** protectionist

liberals he was deputy leader and, after Deakin's retirement, leader of the **Liberal Party**, which narrowly won the federal election in 1913. He held office only until a subsequent election in September 1914, but as prime minister pledged Australia's full support for Britain on the outbreak of World War I. Cook later surrendered leadership of the non-Labor party to William Morris **Hughes**, though he acted as prime minister during Hughes's long absences from Australia. Earlier working-class sympathies had long since dropped away, leaving a plodding but dogged politician whom Hughes put out to grass in 1921.

SM

Cooking, see **Food**

Coombs, Herbert Cole 'Nugget' (1906–97), Australia's most prominent postwar economist, was also 'an activist and an interferer' (his own terms) across a wide range of issues, from the development of universities to the appreciation of the arts, environmental protection, and the rights of **Aborigines**. He is seen as the reformist survivor of party-political change in government—an interpretation supported by his autobiography, *Trial Balance* (1981). The diversity of Coombs's commitments also represents a search for consensus amid the economic and technological transformations of the postwar decades.

While working as a country schoolteacher, Coombs began studying at the University of Western Australia just as the **Depression** hit. He was drawn to economics as an 'understanding of what otherwise seems chaotic'. A youthful attraction to utopian **socialism** was then tempered by an interest in central banking, the subject of his 1933 PhD thesis at the London School of Economics, and an enthusiasm for Keynesian counter-cyclical theories. After returning to Australia and school-teaching, from 1935 Coombs worked successively in the Commonwealth Bank, the Treasury, as director of rationing and of the Department of Post-War Reconstruction. Leading a new, wartime generation of academically trained public servants, Coombs spoke of government's capacity to 'influence the processes of the economic system so as actively to increase human welfare', a goal he continued to pursue in his long tenure (1949–68) as governor of the Commonwealth, later **Reserve**, **Bank**.

Coombs's reformism assumed a more pragmatic cast as anticipations of postwar depression gave way to the concern that excessive private consumption—'streets jammed with opulent chromium-studded motor vehicles'—was drawing resources away from the provision of better public and community services. Throughout the 1950s he emphasised the central bank's role in enforcing monetary discipline, working through extensive, often informal networks of consultation and advice. As Boris Schedvin noted in his 1992 history of the Reserve Bank, Coombs cultivated a 'consensual style', always carefully acknowledging 'the primacy of the elected government' in public statements.

By the early 1960s Coombs was regarded by some as 'the most powerful man in Australia'. At 160 centimetres, calmly spoken with an unmistakable Australian accent, his 'nuggety', plainly dressed figure was widely familiar. Now more confident of the responsiveness of economic policy, Coombs eased the bank's controls while pursuing with increasing publicity his commitment to social equality. His initiative in establishing the Elizabethan Theatre Trust in 1954 secured patronage for the arts on a professional model, but increasingly he favoured wider assistance. The creation of the Australian Council for the Arts (later the **Australia Council**) in 1967 owed much to his influence with Harold **Holt** and William **McMahon** as prime ministers. In 1968 he became chairman of that council and of the new Council for Aboriginal Affairs. That same year, elected chancellor of the Australian National University (which he had helped form in the 1940s), Coombs expressed sympathy with student protesters' 'moral disgust' at conformity.

It was not so much the excesses of consumerism but the repressive capacities of the Establishment which came to dominate Coombs's thinking during the 1970s. He coupled this awareness to issues of environmental degradation, population strains, and the 'proletarianising' tendency of a multinational, corporate economy. Through the Royal Commission into Australian Government Administration, which he headed 1974–76, Coombs advocated a more flexible, representative bureaucracy—principles which, paradoxically, opened the way for later practices of accountability and deregulation. Extensive contacts with Aborigines led to his insistence that they must have 'unquestioned authority' within their own communities 'to make mistakes, to resolve internal problems, to confront our society'.

As a close adviser to Gough **Whitlam**, Coombs was troubled by the events of 1974–75 and the 'bitter divisions' following the **Dismissal** of the government. Subsequently he worked at greater distance from official circles, based at the Centre for Resource and Environmental Studies at the ANU, and indicted intellectuals for their complicity with 'the system'. On scant resources, he launched the Aboriginal Treaty Committee in 1979, calling for a formal declaration binding the Commonwealth to recognise Aboriginal rights. In *The Return of Scarcity* (1990) he proposed a Common Wealth Estate, dispersing to all citizens the income raised through licences regulating access to resources. Coombs's advocacy of local self-sufficiency recalls some aspects of the regionalism he espoused in the 1940s, but with less trust in the state and a pessimism in marked contrast to earlier ideals of social reconstruction. At his death, Coombs was admired for his influence and integrity: 'a mobile sacred site', who often stung Australians' consciences. His criticisms of assimilation have been challenged by Geoffrey Partington, in *Hasluck versus Coombs* (1996), while Tim Rowse assesses his role in *Obliged to be Difficult* (2000). Rowse's longer biographical study is shortly to appear.

NICHOLAS BROWN

Cooper, William (?1861–1941) was prominent in the Aboriginal rights movement during the 1930s. Cooper was born to the Yorta Yorta people in northern Victoria, but later lived and worked at the Cummeragunja reserve on the NSW side of the Murray River. In 1937 he sent a petition to King George VI, requesting civil rights. Cooper helped lead the Day of Mourning on 26 January 1938, the sesquicentenary of British settlement of Australia, when Aborigines rallied against the injustices meted out over the 150 years of European colonisation. Andrew Markus discusses the activities of Cooper and the Australian Aborigines' League in *Blood from a Stone* (1986).

HD

Cooperative settlements are schemes to create rural communities by collective endeavour. They were first proposed in NSW in the 1820s, but not established. An early attempt at **group settlement** in Van Diemen's Land in the 1840s advocated by **Grey**, the secretary of state, failed; here the convicts under the **probation system** were to be employed in cultivating land and in return be granted small plots of their own. Strictly, these were schemes for labour colonies, and should be distinguished from the voluntary settlements, such as William **Lane's** socialist **New Australia** settlement in Paraguay.

In the 1890s, when severe economic downturn threatened workers' livelihoods, cooperative rural settlement was envisaged as a means of relieving poverty and unemployment. Qld launched the first in 1891, in the wake of a similar scheme in NZ. Such schemes for village settlements and labour colonies derived from Britain and were copied in Victoria, NSW, and Tasmania. Despite some initial success, they were soon abandoned; Stephen **Roberts** attributes the failure of village settlements to unsuitable lands, and of labour colonies to misdirected effort. In NSW one such settlement had a saying: 'one nail, one slab, one day'. SA and Tasmania set up villages for people of limited means, which faced similar difficulties. In all cases, Roberts says, a spirit of cooperation was lacking. The SA settlement at Lyrup, however, survived well into the twentieth century.

Enthusiasm for cooperatives was renewed in the 1920s and 1930s, with marginally better results. A group settlement was attempted at WA, again with little success, and also in the Gippsland region of Victoria. In the 1970s back-to-the-land hippies established cooperative settlements, some of which are still functioning.

HD

Co-operatives came to Australia from Britain in the nineteenth century as voluntary organisations that conduct business for the benefit of their members. The first Australian co-operative was registered in SA in 1864. The British co-operative movement, which had close links with the labour movement, used common ownership for mutual benefit and was principally active in retailing. Such consumers' societies were established in Australia for the provision of merchandise, housing, and credit, and many service organisations began on co-operative principles. Farmers made particular use of producer co-operatives.

The co-operative principle flourished in working-class communities in the late nineteenth century, though the

Australian Labor Party developed a preference for publicly owned enterprises. Few retail co-operatives survive, and many of the more successful service organisations have been turned into companies.

SM

Copland, Douglas Berry (1894–1971) was an economist who chaired the federal committtee formed in 1931 to advise state premiers as to means of alleviating the **Depression**. Its report formed the basis for the Premiers' Plan, first called the Copland plan. Copland offered a spirited defence of his controversial strategies in *Australia in the World Crisis, 1929–33* (1934). Earlier he had served on the committee which reviewed the Australian **tariff** policy and whose 1929 report endorsed **protection**. Born in NZ, Copland pioneered the development of economics as a profession in Australia. He taught at the University of Tasmania from 1917, and was professor of economics there from 1920 until 1924, when he took up the Sidney **Myer** chair of commerce at the University of Melbourne. He was rebuffed in a bid for the vice-chancellorship in 1938. Copland forayed into the diplomatic world as Australia's minister to China (1946–48) and high commissioner to Canada (1953–56). His administrative and diplomatic skills were recognised in his appointment as foundation vice-chancellor of the Australian National University (1948–52), and later, as first principal of the Australian Administrative Staff College (1956).

KT

Coral Sea, Battle of the, was fought between the Allied naval and air forces, and the Japanese, from 5 to 8 May 1942. The Japanese were attempting to capture Port Moresby in New Guinea and thus take control of the island. The Japanese launched a series of air raids on the American cruisers, which were returned by the US Navy, supported by two Australian carriers. The Allies proved the stronger naval force. The Americans sank the Japanese light carrier *Shoho* and continued to out-fight the enemy until the Japanese were forced to withdraw to Rabaul. The Allies' victory cemented **American–Australian** links and was critical to an ultimate victory in the Pacific. While the victory prevented the Japanese capture of New Guinea by sea, it led instead to a land-based attack. (See **Kokoda Track**.) The anniversary of the battle has been marked by ceremonies in Australia attended by US representatives.

HD

Cornstalk was a term, like *currency*, which described the Australian-born in NSW in the early nineteenth century. The word, which refers to their physical size and shape, is believed to derive from the manner in which Australian-born children were seen to shoot up rapidly like cornstalks. They were observed as tall and lean, and as having 'the appearance of poplars, shorn of their branches'. Daniel Healey wrote a satirical account, *The Cornstalk: His Habits and Habitat* (1894). With the foundation of other Australian colonies, *cornstalk* became a specific name for those born in NSW; those born in the other colonies were known variously as **sandgropers**, crow-eaters, bananalanders, cabbage-patchers and **Vandemonians**. The term was also used to a lesser extent outside Australia to identify the characteristically tall, strong Australian.

HD

Corowa Conference was held at the River Murray town of that name in 1893 to discuss **Federation**. At this time the cause was languishing as no parliament had approved the constitution drawn up in 1891. The conference was organised by the recently formed federation leagues in the Riverina, which issued a general invitation to attend. The largest group of delegates from outside the region was the members of the **Australian Natives Association** from Victoria. The Victorian premier and leader of the opposition attended; the official representation from NSW was a minister. The conference passed resolutions in favour of Federation, but it became notable for an unscheduled resolution moved by John **Quick**, which called for a new beginning in constitution-making. A convention elected by the people should draw up a constitution which would then be referred to the people at referendum for approval. This scheme with minor modifications was adopted by the premiers at the **Hobart Conference**, and by this mechanism the colonies were brought to union. Corowa takes this to be the warrant for calling itself 'the birthplace of federation'. A museum in the town is devoted to justifying the claim.

JH

Correspondence, see **Letters**

Corroboree, meaning traditional Aboriginal ceremony, is a word that derives from the Dharuk language of Port Jackson and was adopted by Europeans in the first years of white settlement. Although specific to the Sydney district, the word was subsequently adopted by whites in other colonies and came to be used, often in a derogatory fashion, as a general term for gatherings of Aborigines. Later, it became a general colloquial term for gatherings of people—white or black.

Traditional corroborees involved an assembly of large numbers of people to mark significant occasions, such as victory in battle or successful hunting, and celebrated group identity and spirituality through song, dance, and story-telling. These performances attracted curious white spectators, but their Aboriginal significance was poorly understood. Others reacted with condemnation. Colonial authorities discouraged corroborees from being held close to the towns in the belief that they were inappropriate and unchristian, and would exert a bad influence on settlers of weak morality. In 1840, for example, Governor **La Trobe** banned corroborees on Melbourne's Yarra bank on Sunday afternoons. Missionaries ensured that Christian ceremonies replaced corroborees at mission stations. With white settlement, many of the traditional functions of corroborees were eroded by dispossession and displacement. They have survived, however, and become far more prominent on public occasions.

HD

Country Party, see **National Party**

Country Women's Association (CWA) is a non-profit, non-sectarian, community-based women's organisation, established largely through the efforts of Grace Emily Munro (1879–1964). Following a conference concerned with rural women's issues, Munro co-founded the first CWA in NSW in 1922, and subsequently founded 100 branches in NSW and Qld. Other branches followed in Victoria and SA. Rallying behind their battle cry 'Forward! Ever forward!', the branches of the CWA united in 1945 'to enable Countrywomen's Associations throughout Australia to speak with one voice on all national matters, more especially concerning the welfare of countrywomen and children'. As a national body, the Australian CWA became a successful lobby group that secured several improvements to government services in rural areas, particularly those related to health care and education. In the period after World War II, the association provided an important forum for rural women, many of whom lived relatively isolated lives. A declining rural population, however, has since been matched by falling membership and waning political influence. A history of the NSW branch was written by Helen Townsend (1988); and the official papers of the association (1946–69) are held in the National Library of Australia.

HD

Court, Charles Walter Michael (1911–   ), premier, arrived in WA as the infant son of English migrants. Qualifying in accountancy, he built up a substantial practice interrupted by service as an AIF officer in World War II. A Liberal, he entered state politics as MLA for Nedlands 1953–82, serving as the very influential minister for industrial **development** and the North-West 1959–71, and premier 1974–82. During WA's massive mineral boom, he forged cooperative relationships with multinational capital, ensuring provision of infrastructure but displeasing advocates of the 'free hand' such as the iron-ore magnate Lang **Hancock**. Aboriginal resistance to mineral exploration was countered with a heavy hand at Noonkanbah in 1980. He strongly resisted encroachments of federal power, though was sometimes pragmatically flexible. Socially conservative (his state retained the death penalty and criminalised **homosexuals** until after his retirement), he was capable of flashes of magnanimity. From a youth as a skilled brass band performer he grew into a patron of the arts, especially music, endowing Perth with its concert hall and a new cultural centre of museum, library, and art gallery. In retirement he remained a dignified and vigorous elder statesman with five sons prominent in public life, including RICHARD COURT (1947–   ), premier from 1993. His memoirs, *Charles Court: The Early Years* (1995), edited by Geoffrey **Blainey** and Ronda Jamieson, cover his life until 1953.

GEOFFREY BOLTON

Cowan, Edith Dircksey (1861–1932) was Australia's first female parliamentarian, representing West Perth in the Western Australian Legislative Assembly (1921–24). While she was said to 'possess the mind of a man', Cowan's concern for social justice, passion for women's causes, and scorn for party politics belie the characterisation. When she criticised the shilling charged for perambulators on trains, she suggested the minister 'be made to parade the streets of Perth with a heavy infant on one arm and a bag of groceries on the other'. Cowan's early life on a pastoral property near Geraldton was tragic: her mother died when she was seven and her father was later hanged for shooting his second wife. Inaugural secretary of the establishment Karrakatta Club in 1894, she followed the achievement of suffrage in 1899 with two decades of distinguished community service. With sharp wit and impeccable scholarship, she championed the welfare of migrants, deserted wives and children, and the inheritance rights of mothers. Her Legal Reform Act of 1923 achieved status for women as professionals, but her comment that housewives should apply for their own industrial award earned ridicule. Among many memorials are the Kings Park clock tower, Edith Cowan University, and the federal parliamentary seat of Cowan. Her image appears on the Australian $50 note.

JOAN EVALINE

Cowper, Charles (1807–75), who came of an old landowning family in NSW, was the premier who introduced the key democratic reforms of manhood suffrage, the secret ballot, and more equal electorates, and was responsible for the successful carriage of Robertson's Land **Selection** Act. As a young man he was secretary of the **Church and Schools Corporation**, designed to secure the pre-eminence of the Anglican Church, and at his election to the Legislative Council in 1843 was a moderate conservative. By the early 1850s he was a liberal and served as president of the Australasian League for the Abolition of Transportation. As liberal premier, he set his face against a radical land law, but soon yielded to the demand for free selection. He was the manager of the liberals rather than their leader, keeping his following together by astute use of patronage. He gave no impression of believing in the reforms which he effected. His opponents claimed with some justice that he was driven by the need to keep his ministerial salary. The committed democrats were disgusted that their cause had fallen into the hands of such a juggler. Daniel **Deniehy** satirised one of Cowper's most outrageous ploys in *How I Became Attorney General of New Barataria* (1860). Alan Powell has written an aptly titled biography, *Patrician Democrat* (1977).

JH

Cowra breakout was a mass escape attempt by Japanese **prisoners-of-war** at No. 12 Prisoner of War Group, Cowra, NSW. In the early morning of 5 August 1944, 1105 prisoners set fire to their huts and stormed the barbed-wire fences. The battle killed 231 Japanese and four Australian guards, and 378 prisoners cleared the outer perimeter and roamed Cowra for up to nine days before recapture. No civilian was harmed. Dozens of Japanese committed suicide, and a common interpretation suggests the escape was related to General Tojo's 'Senjinkun' decree, which stated that death was preferable to the disgrace of captivity. Kenneth 'Seaforth' McKenzie, a corporal at Cowra, fictionalised the event in *Dead Men Rising* (1951). A Japanese novel by Teruhiko Asada, *Cowra No Bodo* (1967), was translated by Ray Cowan, *The Night of a Thousand Suicides* (1970). Hugh Clarke's pioneer historical analysis, *Break-out!* (1965), was republished as *Escape to Death* (1994). Harry Gordon's *Die Like the Carp* (1978) and *Voyage from Shame* (1994) draw on extensive interviews with survivors. Charlotte Carr-Gregg, *Japanese Prisoners of War in Revolt* (1978), sees the breakout from a social anthropologist's perspective, comparing it with a similar episode at Fetherston, NZ, and concludes that the mass suicide explanation is too simplistic. A television mini-series, *The Cowra Breakout*, was produced in 1984.

DC

Cramp, Karl Reginald (1878–1956) used his position as a secondary school inspector (1923–43) to promote and shape the study of Australian history. Beginning as a pupil teacher in NSW public schools, he won a scholarship to the University of Sydney from the the Fort Street Training School. In 1906 he became lecturer in history at the newly established Sydney Teachers College; later he accepted a senior position with the Department of Public Instruction. English by birth, Cramp promoted a view of Australia tied to England by kinship cemented in battle. His interpretation of Australia's history was evident in an unproblematic hero-worship—thus *Australian Winners of the VC* (1919) and *Great Australian Explorers* (1926). He was an officer of the *Journal and Proceedings* of the **Royal Australian Historical Society**, for which he wrote prolifically. With George **Mackaness**, he wrote the first volume of a history of the Masons in NSW in 1938, and produced a further volume in 1949. An omnipresent figure, Cramp was also a member of the Captain Cook's Landing Place Trust, the **Australian and New Zealand Association for the Advancement of Science**, and the NSW branch of the **National Trust** of Australia.

KT

Crawford, Raymond Maxwell 'Max' (1906–91), historian, played a decisive role in shaping the **Melbourne School of History**. Crawford was born in Grenfell, NSW. He went to Oxford in 1927 after graduating from the University of Sydney, studied history and associated with young liberal imperialists. Later he read Toynbee and Marx, who strongly influenced his historical outlook. Although, as he conceded, he had 'not yet published any original work', Crawford was appointed professor of history at the University of Melbourne in 1937 to succeed Ernest **Scott**. He changed the curriculum to encourage students to study the variety of human experience over time and across the globe, and to ponder the enduring drama of human will struggling to live freely within the constraints of material circumstance. He called this his synoptic view of history. He also taught students to reflect on history as an intellectual endeavour by examining what he called its theory and method. An additional honours year devoted entirely to history, added to the three-year degree in 1949, was the capstone of Crawford's school of history.

Poor health after World War II limited his output. He published *The Renaissance and Other Essays* (1945) and *Australia* (1952), and edited *Ourselves and the Pacific* (1941). His article on history as a science (*HSANZ*, 1947) earned him international recognition. Following his retirement in 1970, he published a biography of his teacher George Arnold **Wood** (1975).

ROBERT DARE

Cricket has for much of the past 200 years been the most popular Australian summer sport, a source of national sentiment, and occasionally a cause of imperial or international friction. The game was first played in the early years of settlement in NSW, according to the rules recently laid down by the Marylebone Cricket Club (MCC), which codified a game that was taken to most parts of the British Empire. Clubs were established and grounds laid out in all the colonies by the middle of the nineteenth century; the first inter-colonial game was played between NSW and Victoria in 1856. The Sheffield Shield competition, in which all states now participate, dates from the 1890s.

English teams began to tour Australia from 1861 as commercial ventures, and some of the players stayed here as coaches. The Australian T.W. **Wills**, who had played county cricket in England, coached an Aboriginal team from western Victoria that went to England in 1868 to achieve considerable success in 47 fixtures against a variety of local and composite teams. John **Mulvaney** described the venture in *Cricket Walkabout* (1967; revised with Rex Harcourt, 1988). In 1877 a combined NSW and Victoria eleven defeated the touring English eleven in what is now regarded as the first Test Match. Australia's subsequent victory over England at the London Oval, in 1882, gave rise to a death notice in the *Sporting Times* ('The body will be cremated and the ashes taken to Australia') after which the regular competition between the two countries is known. The urn in which the eponymous **Ashes** are contained has always remained at Lord's in London as the property of the MCC.

The establishment of a national team fostered the growing popularity of cricket as a game and popular spectacle, assisted by the development of international **communications** and mass media. The Englishness of cricket and the code of sporting conduct it embodied attracted colonials, while at the same time it enabled them to measure their success against the parent country. In contrast to England, cricket in Australia did not formalise the distinction between amateurs and professionals, and it was accessible to most classes: the suburban backyard and the beach made it a genuinely popular pastime here. Women took up cricket with notable enthusiasm. Australians modified the English preoccupation with graceful, free-flowing style and pastoral values by application and effort. The large scoreboards that were erected at the principal grounds emphasised results.

Cricket reached the height of its popularity between the two world wars when Don **Bradman** attained unprecedented technical mastery as a batsman. In his first tour of England in 1930, he scored an unprecedented 974 Test runs. Radio coverage of the following English tour of Australia in 1932–33 increased public interest. To restrict Bradman, the English captain Douglas Jardine instructed his bowlers to direct their attack short on or outside the leg stump. The success of this **bodyline** tactic enraged Australians, caused an official complaint from the Australian board to the MCC, and was discussed by the governments of both countries. The episode is discussed by W.F. Mandle, *Going it Alone* (1978); the 50th anniversary was marked by a television series and a plethora of publications, notably Ric Sissons and Brian Stoddart, *Cricket and Empire* (1984).

Cricket has at other times become embroiled in international relations. New Zealand long chafed at Australia's failure to support its bid for Test status, and Trevor Chappell's underarm delivery in a one-day international in 1981 brought national opprobrium. The first Australian team to visit South Africa followed hard on the heels of the **Boer War**; the refusal of that country to include non-white players led to the Australian cancellation of its 1971–72 tour of this country. For R.G. **Menzies**, cricket was a tangible link to an idealised England and a bond of the British Commonwealth; more recently, the international cricket authority is beset by tension between the 'white settler' countries and those of the Indian subcontinent.

Following Bradman's retirement in 1948, there was a decline in Australian interest in the game, which faced increasing competition from other summer sports, especially **tennis**. The success of the West Indies tour in 1960–61 assisted a revival, and national television, introduced in 1970–71, furthered it. The demands of television for greater entertainment fostered increasing emphasis on the one-day game at the expense of the more leisurely five-day Test, and in turn made revenue and player payments increasingly important. The television proprietor Kerry **Packer** pursued his demands by the organisation of a breakaway World Series Cricket for two years in the 1970s, and his subsequent agreement with the Cricket Board confirmed the emphasis on sponsorship, marketing, and promotion.

Cricket has generated a large literature. Journalists frequently produced books on particular tours or Test series; ghosted memoirs; and have turned to biography and investigative works. The game's plethora of statistics and memorabilia supports a stream of heritage publications. Among fiction writers who have turned to cricket, Dal Stivens is notable. However, Australia has produced no cricket journalism of the quality of Neville Cardus, no critical writing of the acuity of C.L.R. James. Richard Cashman is the most productive of Australian sporting historians to have explored the subject. The *Oxford Companion to Australian Cricket* (1996), edited by Cashman et al., provides an extensive coverage.

STUART MACINTYRE

Crime and punishment have been an engaging part of the history of a country whose settler origins were based on the transportation of **convicts**. Two of the colonial era's finest novels spoke of it—Marcus **Clarke**, *His Natural Life* (1874) and Rolf **Boldrewood**, *Robbery under Arms* (1888). One of the country's quintessential heroes, Ned **Kelly**, was defined by his life of crime and by his hanging after a trial at which Judge Redmond **Barry** spoke of the dangers of life in new communities, 'where the bonds of society are not so well linked together as in older countries'. Such was the fear of popular sympathy with bushrangers and colourful urban criminals that governments in the early years of cinema sought to censor the representation of crime on film.

In truth, however, crime had for a long time been declining, at least as measured by available public records, and Australia, after dispossession of most of its Aboriginal people, was not an excessively violent society. A rare Australian study of crime and response to it over time, Peter Grabosky, *Sydney in Ferment* (1977), in fact belies its title. Most crime was committed by men. If the crime were serious, they were imprisoned; a small number suffered **capital punishment**, mostly for murder. Minor offenders might be fined, a punishment which was most common of all and used also for offences against public order, including drunkenness. From the later nineteenth century alternative punishments were possible, especially for first offenders who might be placed on probation to test their capacity for reform. The corporal punishment of whipping was used extensively in the convict era, but declined after the 1850s except for an occasional sentence ordered against a juvenile delinquent or a sexual offender. Women could not be whipped, and their terms of imprisonment were typically short—mostly because they committed less serious crimes. They were much less likely to offend than men, though Judith Allen, *Sex and Secrets* (1990), has argued that women committed many more crimes than were prosecuted, mostly reproduction-related crimes such as infanticide and abortion, which it mostly suited both men and women to keep out of court.

Crime was the business of **police** and the courts, and our knowledge of its incidence depends on their capacity, past and present, to detect it and their willingness to record it. The 'dark figure' of crime is that which was committed but unrecorded because police and other agents did not know about such offences, were not informed about them, or chose to ignore them. Most murders were probably known—but other categories of offence were likely to be significantly under-reported, especially sexual and domestic assaults. Although what later became known as 'white-collar' crimes, such as fraud and embezzlement, were commonly prosecuted in the late nineteenth century, significant police attention to large-scale corporate crime is much more recent. The conviction and gaoling in the 1990s of some prominent business figures, such as Alan Bond, Laurie Connell, and George Herscu, represented a new departure in Australian history.

Within the constraints of official statistics there is some evidence that rates of violent crime declined in the later nineteenth century, as they did in most comparable

Western societies. There was certainly a sharp fall in imprisonment rates between the two world wars, and in most states the capacity of prisons well exceeded their average occupancy. After World War II, however, crimes against property increased steadily, associated in some cases with increasing opportunity—shop theft and minor stealing by juveniles, including girls, for example, were increasingly common in a society in which consumer goods were multiplying. Satyanshu Mukherjee, *Crime Trends in Twentieth-Century Australia* (1981), explores the social correlates of crime rates, while Arie Freiberg and Stuart Ross, in *Sentencing Reform and Penal Change: the Victorian Experience* (1999), analyse that state's changing sentencing patterns over 150 years.

The definition of crime varies between societies and over time. A striking example of these differences is evident in the phenomena of 'criminalisation' and its opposite, 'decriminalisation'. Thus forms of behaviour such as **gambling** have been illegal under certain conditions in Australia, as examined in John O'Hara, *A Mug's Game* (1988), while their widespread customary practice has made such laws ineffective or helped produce police corruption. A similar story has been evident in the criminalisation of drug use and trafficking, which has become a concern of policing and criminal justice, and has also fostered corruption (Al McCoy, *Drug Traffic*, 1980). The widespread impact of the policing of street drunkenness has been more recently the cause of attempts to decriminalise drunkenness, so reducing the numbers detained in police lockups and gaols. The role of the media in shaping public perceptions of crime has been critical in Australia, as elsewhere, but awaits its own historians. Meanwhile, the most substantial histories of crime and responses to it are the work of historians on early colonial NSW, especially Michael Sturma, V*ice in a Vicious Society* (1983); David Neal, *The Rule of Law in a Penal Colony* (1991); and Paula Byrne, *Criminal Law and Colonial Subject* (1993).

MARK FINNANE

Crowley, Francis Keble 'Frank' (1924–), historian, played an early and important role in the growth of Australian history after World War II. Educated at the University of Melbourne and Balliol College, Oxford, he held doctorates from both at the age of 27. At the University of Western Australia, 1952–64, he established Australia's second undergraduate course in Australian history and built up a systematically planned postgraduate school using local materials. During this period he produced *The Records of Western Australia* (1953)—an impressive one-man bibliographical feat—and *Australia's Western Third* (1960), not yet supplanted as a single-author interpretation of WA, which played down pioneer achievement in favour of later history. After a year at Adelaide, he became professor of history at the University of New South Wales 1966–86, including several years as dean of the Faculty of Arts. He edited the five-volume *Modern Australia in Documents* (1973) and *A New History of Australia* (1974), the standard reference of its time, updated by his sequel *Tough Times* (1986). For some years he also served as co-editor of the reference series of the **Bicentennial History Project**. He published the first volume of a biography of John **Forrest** in 1971, completing a second volume in retirement. Based on meticulous archival fidelity, Crowley's writings largely eschew ideology; his quest for empirical objectivity somewhat masks the crisp and sardonic spoken style which made him a stimulating lecturer and supervisor.

GEOFFREY BOLTON

CSIRO (Commonwealth Scientific and Industrial Research Organisation) was founded in the midst of **World War I** by Prime Minister **Hughes**, who was impressed by Germany's technological might and wanted to create a 'national laboratory' for Australia. An Advisory Committee representing science, government, and business was set the difficult task of reconciling this vision with the realities of federalism. After the proposal's supposed centralist overtones had been softened, legislation was finally passed in 1920. The Institute of Science and Industry was established.

Unfortunately the institute, led by G.H. Knibbs, was burdened with both an ambitious research program and a severely limited budget. While some important programs were initiated, Australia's national research effort seemed destined to fail until Prime Minister S.M. **Bruce** intervened. In 1926 he introduced legislation for a new organisation, stressing its role as a coordinator of scientific research across the states. The organisation would be guided by state-based committees, and governed by a council of scientists and industrialists. The crippled institute was replaced by the Council for Scientific and Industrial Research (CSIR). This pre-history is chronicled by George Currie and John Graham in *The Origins of CSIRO* (1966).

The management of this new organisation fell to a three-man executive. Although ultimate power was invested in the council, it was the executive that shaped the programs, the structure and the spirit of CSIR. For almost 20 years this comprised just three men—G.A. Julius, a respected businessman and engineer; A.C.D. **Rivett**, formerly professor of chemistry at the University of Melbourne; and A.E.V. Richardson, an agricultural scientist.

The new CSIR concentrated on the problems of the primary industries, still the country's main source of wealth. Divisions of Animal Health, Animal Nutrition, Economic Entomology, and Economic Botany were among the first established. However, it was a research program initiated under the institute that gave CSIR its first public victory—a South American caterpillar was found to control the rapidly spreading prickly pear. But CSIR's ambitions lay beyond problem-solving for industry. Rivett, in particular, was frustrated by the reactive, short-term nature of much of the work that CSIR was forced to undertake. Committed to the freedom of scientific inquiry, and certain of the benefits that long-term, fundamental research would bring, Rivett continually sought ways of encouraging such research within CSIR. The diversity spawned by this balancing act helped give CSIR its strength.

The **Depression** and the demands of defence self-reliance focused attention on secondary industry. In 1936 Julius led a government committee that recommended CSIR take on a number of new responsibilities associated with manufacturing. These included research in aeronautics, maintenance of basic standards of measurement, and the provision of an industrial research service. CSIR's move into the physical sciences was accelerated by **World War II**. The Division of Industrial Chemistry, established to provide the desired research service, was joined by the Lubricants and Bearings Section. A radiophysics laboratory was created in secrecy to undertake the development of radar for local use. Staff numbers quadrupled from 1939 to 1945, and by 1949 CSIR was one of the largest scientific research organisations in the world. Boris Schedvin traces the organisation's development up to 1949 in *Shaping Science and Industry* (1987).

The war changed CSIR and attitudes to science. There could now be no doubt that scientific research was valuable—indeed, perhaps it was too valuable to be left in the control of scientists! Cold War hysteria and political opportunism merged in the late 1940s as the opposition parties attacked the CSIR for its handling of secret information. Rivett, the unabashed advocate for the freedom of science, was an easy target. Under pressure, the government excised aeronautics research, and initiated an inquiry by H.C. **Coombs** and W. Dunk into CSIR. In 1949 the organisation was reconstituted, its administrative structure was overhauled, and its staffing decisions were brought under the purview of the Public Service Board. CSIR became the Commonwealth Scientific and Industrial Research Organisation. Close to retirement, Rivett could not reconcile himself to the new order, and so resigned.

Rivett's martyrdom was made more poignant by the fact that under a new chair, Ian **Clunies Ross**, CSIRO was about to enter its golden age. With strong support from the responsible minister, R.G. **Casey**, the organisation was at last able to undertake a substantial program of fundamental research. The radiophysicists turned their aerials towards the sun, becoming world leaders in the new field of radio astronomy. Industrial chemistry gained international recognition in many fields of research. The success of myxomatosis in controlling rabbit numbers brought new public prestige, and a detailed program of **wool** research was undertaken.

By the late 1960s, public enthusiasm for science had begun to cool. In government circles there was a demand for increased planning and accountability. Reviews and inquiries proliferated throughout the 1970s, culminating in the 1977 report of the Birch Committee, which, while it recommended some structural changes, was basically content with CSIRO's mix of pure and applied research.

Within 10 years the rise of economic rationalism had changed the climate once more. The government directed that CSIRO should concentrate on application-based research, closely linked to the needs of industry, and raise a proportion of its own funds. After so long, perhaps, Rivett's fears were finally realised.

TIM SHERRATT

'Culotta, Nino', see O'Grady, John Patrick

Cultural cringe, a term denoting a characteristically colonial deference towards the cultural achievements of others, was coined by the literary critic and schoolmaster A.A. **Phillips** in the nationalist quarterly *Meanjin* in 1950. 'Above our writers—and other artists—looms the intimidating mass of Anglo-Saxon culture', he wrote. 'Such a situation almost inevitably produces the characteristic Australian Cultural Cringe, appearing either as the Cringe Direct, or as the Cringe Inverted, in the attitude of the Blatant Blatherskite, the God's-own-country-and-I'm-a-better-man-than-you-are Australian bore.' The phrase quickly entered the standard vocabulary of cultural nationalism, where it appeared, alternately, as a vice recently escaped or ever threatening to reassert itself. Phillips's friend, the historian Geoffrey **Serle**, made it one of the organising ideas of his history of Australian culture, *From Deserts the Prophets Come* (1973). By 1983, with cultural chauvinism on the rise, Phillips observed a tendency for the phrase to become 'a handy missile for the smugger obscurantist provincials to fling at their larger-minded betters … It is time to accord the phrase decent burial before the smell of the corpse gets too high'. But the rogue epithet refuses to be put down.

GD

Cultural history is the study of values, rituals, beliefs, pastimes, cultural production, and cultural consumption. Traditionally cultural history concentrated on high culture—theatre, literature, painting, music, and other arts—but more recently it has expanded to encompass both popular culture and more anthropological understandings of culture as a 'whole way of life'.

From its inception, cultural history in Australia developed two distinct strands. The first was concerned with culture in the sense of 'high' culture. After World War II a number of pioneering histories of the arts in Australia were published, notably H.M. **Green's** history of Australian literature, Leslie Rees's study of Australian **drama**, the **art histories** of Bernard **Smith** and Robert **Hughes**, and Roger Covell's account of Australian **music**. These histories took the value of the arts as self-evident and sought to establish the canon of significant works in each field. Underpinning these histories was a confident nationalism. Although all recognised that Australia's cultural traditions came largely from Britain and Europe, these histories demonstrated that high culture did flourish in Australia and that these traditions had been transformed by Australians to say something significant about Australian society.

This tradition was bolstered by a significant work of synthesis. Geoffrey **Serle**, *From Deserts the Prophets Come* (1973), charted the history of 'the creative spirit' in Australia, encompassing developments in most of the arts since 1788. It remains a defining account of high culture in Australia. Since its publication numerous works have treated more specific themes and problems. There have been important studies of radical nationalist writers, such as David Walker's

Dream and Disillusion (1976), John Docker's account of the different intellectual traditions of Sydney and Melbourne (*Australian Cultural Elites*, 1974), and Humphrey **McQueen's** study of modernism in Australia (*The Black Swan of Trespass*, 1979). Others have sought to expand the canon in particular areas. There have been important efforts to uncover the contribution of women to Australian culture, most notably the work of Joan Kerr and Janine Burke on women painters, and Drusilla Modjeska's studies of Australian women writers and painters. More recently there has been an explosion of interest in Aboriginal culture, particularly painting, music, and dance. Here the aim has been to chart the complexity of indigenous cultural traditions and their continuing relevance and dynamic interaction with contemporary Australia.

The second kind of cultural history is concerned with defining a distinctive Australian ethos. The pioneering work in this field was Keith **Hancock**, *Australia* (1930), which was both an account of Australian society and economy and an effort to chart the evolution of the **'Independent Australian Briton'** as both a social type and a cultural attitude. There have been many subsequent efforts to define distinctive Australian cultural attributes. In 1958, A.A. **Phillips** painted a rather dismal picture of the national ethos in his influential article on 'the **cultural cringe**'. Here Australians were impoverished by either an overly deferential and fawning respect for all things British, to the extent that anything Australian was considered inferior; or its obverse, a strident, bellicose patriotism which proclaimed all things Australian to be beyond reproach. Both inhibited the growth of a confident and sophisticated culture. Meanwhile Russel **Ward** was writing his landmark history, *The Australian Legend* (1958). Ward sought to uncover the historical roots of Australia's egalitarian mateship ethos in the experience of the nineteenth-century bush workers. For Ward, the writers of the *Bulletin* in the 1890s, such as Henry **Lawson** and Banjo **Paterson**, were key figures in this process. Unemployment, depression, and drought brought the bush workers to the cities, and here writers learned of the worker ethos and transformed it into stories and poems of lasting significance. Some historians have disputed Ward's explanation. Graeme Davison, in particular, has argued (in *HS*, 1978) that the origin of the legend was not the experience of bush workers, but rather the alienation of urban bohemians who romanticised a mythical bush past. Most cultural historians have seen the bush legend as a significant feature of Australian culture. Richard White, *Inventing Australia* (1981), marks the culmination, and perhaps the termination, of this approach to cultural history.

Other historians interested in charting the evolution of Australian culture have worked on a more confined canvas. George Nadel, *Australia's Colonial Culture* (1957), and Michael **Roe**, *Quest for Authority in Eastern Australia 1835–1851* (1965), examined the role of liberal-minded reformers in colonial Australia who did much to shape an Australian faith in egalitarianism, democracy, the utility of state intervention, personal industry, and self-improvement.

Another important concern has been the impact of the **Anzac Legend** in shaping an Australian ethos of egalitarian mateship. Here the work of C.E.W. **Bean** and Ken **Inglis** has been influential. Some historians have seen the evolution of an Australian culture in the clash of ideas and religious beliefs or the contributions of particular **ethnic groups**. Manning **Clark's** monumental *A History of Australia* (1962–87) was initially based on an idea of Australia as the product of three great cultural traditions—the Enlightenment, Protestantism, and Catholicism. Patrick **O'Farrell** argued in *The Irish in Australia* (1986) that the Australian concern with egalitarianism and radical democracy owes much to the distinctive ethos of Irish Catholic Australians.

From the 1970s these two strands of cultural history began to be questioned. Historians of popular culture criticised an excessive emphasis on high culture, with its implicit cultural elitism, arguing that popular culture is a vibrant, dynamic, and sophisticated form of cultural expression and consumption. Social historians, sometimes inspired by the cultural Marxism of E.P. Thompson and Raymond Williams, seek to recover the culture of workers, women, ethnic minorities, and indigenous peoples. Scholars influenced by the 'linguistic turn' in the humanities and social sciences argued that culture was about the production of meaning and that all forms of human activity produced symbols, signs, and meanings open to interpretation. In Alan Atkinson's *The Europeans in Australia* (1997), Tom Griffiths's *Hunters and Collectors* (1996), and David Goodman's *Gold Seeking* (1994), cultural history overlaps with the **ethnographic history**. All these groups embrace a generous definition of culture, which now includes newspapers, radio, television, and film as well as ballet, opera, sculpture, and painting.

The collection by Peter Spearritt and David Walker, *Australian Popular Culture* (1979), was an early signal of this developing interest. It included articles on radio, film, exhibitions, popular literature, and festivals. Others, notably Richard Cashman, worked on the history of **sport** in Australia. Popular culture is now a flourishing area of research. We have numerous studies of media, **film**, **television**, sport, **exhibitions**, **music**, dance, and leisure activities, pastimes, and **entertainments**. There are also a number of useful works of synthesis, notably Ian Craven (ed.), *Australian Popular Culture* (1994); John Fiske, Bob Hodge, and Graeme Turner, *Myths of Oz* (1987); and Richard Waterhouse, *Private Pleasures, Public Leisure* (1995).

It would be a mistake, however, to see the new interest in popular culture as a radical break with earlier traditions of cultural history. One of the defining features of cultural history in Australia has been its engagement with popular and vernacular traditions. Ward's *Australian Legend* was based on an analysis of **bush** ballads, and Inglis's exploration of Anzac is also alive to its diverse currents in national celebrations, oral traditions, **school history** books, marches, and memorials. Others, such as Ian **Turner**, expanded this interest to encompass children's nursery rhymes, **Australian Rules football** and graffiti. More recently, there has been interest in comics, humour, and folktales. One of the best general histories of Australian folklore is Graham Seal's *The Hidden Culture* (1989).

A number of cultural historians have attempted to move beyond the dichotomy of high and popular culture. They see a complex overlap between the two; instead of trying to distinguish between them, they have sought to chart the history of 'states of mind', rituals and cultural practices. The inspiration for this approach has been the influence of anthropological and sociological theories of culture as a 'way of life'. This was the impetus for the annual seminar held by Barry Smith and Sam Goldberg which began in 1979 and generated the journal *Australian Cultural History*. This journal was characterised by an eclectic approach on such diverse themes as practicality, schooling, religion, festivals, tall poppyism, suburbanisation, town and country, and populism. David Walker, who assumed the editorship of the journal in 1990, continues to foster this interdisciplinary approach, with issues devoted to reading, Australian perceptions of Asia, notorious crimes, travel and tourism, bodies and ageing. This concern with a diverse range of values, beliefs, and cultural rituals is also evident in such books as John Rickard's *Australia: A Cultural History* (1988): it examines politics, social life, the environment, empire loyalism, multiculturalism, and housing as systems of meaning and belief which tell us much about how Australians live and interact. It is an approach which highlights the diversity and complexity of Australian life.

STEPHEN GARTON

Cumpston, John Howard Lidgett (1880–1954) was the foundation director-general of the Commonwealth Department of Health. Born in Melbourne, Cumpston graduated in medicine from the University of Melbourne. He entered public **health** administration and became Commonwealth director of quarantine in 1913. Cumpston led the struggle for a Commonwealth Department of Health. He persuaded the Rockefeller Foundation to offer generous funds for a national hookworm eradication campaign—subject to Australia establishing a national health department. The department was founded in 1921 and was marked by a progressive nationalism, evading constitutional limits on Commonwealth powers by occupying areas that the states were unwilling to develop. The **Depression** ended this expansion, and the department only survived because of Cumpston's bureaucratic skills. With economic recovery, he developed the National Health and Medical Research Council, ensuring that it was dominated by public health administrators. Cumpston played an ambiguous role in the Labor government's plans for postwar national health services: he opposed schemes that relied on cash benefits instead of developing preventive public health services. After retiring in 1945, he wrote numerous works on the history of **exploration**. His life and professional work are described in Milton Lewis's introduction to J.H.L. Cumpston, *Health and Disease in Australia* (1989), and he is one of Michael **Roe's** *Nine Australian Progressives* (1984).

JIM GILLESPIE

Cunningham, Allan (1791–1839), botanist and explorer, born at Wimbledon, England, was employed as curator's clerk at the Royal Gardens, Kew, between 1808 and 1814. Sir Joseph **Banks** recommended his appointment as botanical collector in 1814, and his posting to NSW in 1816. Cunningham collected specimens of 450 plant species on John **Oxley's** Lachlan River expedition in 1817, and in 1817–22 he accompanied Philip Parker King on coastal survey voyages, collecting over 700 additional species from WA, Arnhem Land, northern Qld, and Van Diemen's Land. From 1823 to 1830 he combined botany with land exploration, identifying Pandora's Pass in 1823 to enable a route from Bathurst and the Hunter River to the Liverpool Plains, which he explored in 1825; and rich, grazing country in south-eastern Qld which he named the Darling Downs in 1827. He also found Cunningham's Gap in 1828, which gave access from Moreton Bay to the downs. Between 1831 and 1836 Cunningham classified his botanical collection at Kew, where his manuscripts are retained. On his return to NSW as colonial botanist in 1837, Cunningham not surprisingly found supervising the governor's 'cabbage patch' dissatisfying. W.G. McMinn's biography, *Allan Cunningham* (1970), reveals a shy, sensitive, zealous, and fastidious man who significantly advanced Australian botany and exploration, and the study of Aboriginal languages and customs.

DC

Curr, Edward Micklethwaite (1820–89), pastoralist and writer, grew up in Tasmania. His father EDWARD CURR (1798–1850) wrote *An Account of the Colony of Van Diemen's Land* (1824) and, as an agent of the Van Diemen's Land Co., helped stave off investigations into the **Cape Grim massacre** (1827). Edward Curr moved with his family to Port Phillip, settling at St Helier's near present-day Abbotsford, and established his sons on various pastoral runs. Edward was stationed first near Heathcote and later at Tongala in northern Victoria. His major work, *Recollections of Squatting in Victoria* (1883), documents his experiences of early station life. Curr became a successful pastoralist and, as a conservative Catholic, influential in local affairs. He was honoured in Victoria as the 'father of **separation**' on account of his great promotion of that cause, and his failure to win the 1843 Port Phillip election prompted a riot between his Catholic supporters and their sectarian opponents. Through his four-volume work, *The Australian Race* (1886–87), Curr contributed significantly to contact history. He made acute observations of Aboriginal life, including traditional means of land management, such as **fire-stick farming**, and the cultural and demographic changes wrought by European settlement and pastoralism. Henry **Reynolds** claims that Curr had the widest overview of European–Aboriginal relations in nineteenth-century Australia.

HD

Currency refers to money that was minted in Australia, so called to distinguish it from the British **sterling**. Local currency was discounted against sterling, hence the extension of the term to describe the Australian-born, whom free settlers regarded as inferior. Governor **Macquarie** issued paper money in 1810, and in 1813 ordered that a large quantity of Spanish dollars, which had arrived in Sydney the previous year, be converted to local currency by pressing out the centres. The ring, known as a 'holey dollar', was used as a five-shilling piece, and the centre, known as a 'dump', was traded as 15 pence. Local banknotes and paper tokens were issued by the Bank of New South Wales and circulated from its establishment in 1817. A shortage of British currency led to reliance again on foreign Spanish dollars in 1822, but in 1826 British authorities prohibited their use as legal tender. With the wealth generated by the gold rushes and associated population growth, local branches of the Royal Mint were established in Sydney (1855), Melbourne (1872), and Perth (1899). Not until 1910 was all new Australian currency marked 'Commonwealth of Australia' and British currency progressively withdrawn. In 1966 a new decimal system introduced coins and notes that depicted Australian images while retaining the image of the British monarch.

HD

Currency lads and lasses was a term popularised in the 1820s to describe the first generation of Australian-born, mostly the children of convicts or emancipists of British or Irish descent. **Currency** referred to the paper money that **Macquarie** issued in Sydney from 1810. As this local pound was depreciated against the **sterling**, the word *currency*, as recorded by Peter Cunningham in *Two Years in New South Wales* (1827), implied inferiority. By contrast, *sterling* identified the superior class of free emigrants. The physical and behavioural characteristics of currency lads and lasses impressed contemporary observers. J.T. **Bigge** in 1820 described them as tall and slender, of fair complexion, stronger and healthier than the English-born, 'active in their habits', lively and assertive, and optimistic about the future; and observed that these qualities provided 'a remarkable exception to the moral and physical character of their parents'. Their brash assertiveness and penchant for toasting themselves reflected both pride in their currency status and loyalty to their native land, which, they claimed, gave them greater rights to land than free British-born settlers. Russel **Ward** saw their belief in **democracy** and **egalitarianism**, and disdain for authority and **new chums**, as critical to the development of the Australian character. W.C. **Wentworth** was the most celebrated currency lad; others were Daniel **Deniehy** and Hamilton **Hume**. A paper called *The Currency Lad* appeared from 1832–33, and the currency lass was the subject of Edward Geoghegan's musical comedy of 1844. They are the subject of John Molony's *The Native Born* (2000).

HD

Currey, Charles Herbert (1890–1970) was drawn to his lifelong association with researching and teaching Australian history by Professor George **Wood** at the University of Sydney. He also completed a doctorate in laws

and was admitted to the Bar, but never practised. Having only briefly taught schoolchildren, Currey was appointed lecturer in history at the Sydney Teachers College on the recommendation of Karl **Cramp**. Later he became head of the college's history department. He greatly influenced the teaching of history in NSW schools by promoting changes to the primary school syllabus and writing many booklets on historical topics. He was a prominent member of the **Royal Australian Historical Society** from 1925. Many of his publications reflect his passion for legal and constitutional history—*The Irish at Eureka* (1954), *The Transportation, Escape, and Pardoning of Mary Bryant* (1963), and *Sir Frances Forbes* (1968). He also contributed to the *ADB*. He left a bequest to the State Library of New South Wales that was used to establish a memorial fellowship.

KT

Curtin, John Joseph Ambrose (1885–1945) was leader of the federal Labor Party 1935–45 and prime minister 1941–45. His long struggle against alcoholism and self-doubt, the loneliness of wartime leadership, and eventual death in office elevated him to heroic status in Labor legend.

The eldest son of Irish-born parents whose frequent moves curtailed his formal education, he grew up in the Melbourne suburb of Brunswick. Under the influence of Frank **Anstey** and Tom **Mann**, he abandoned the Catholic faith for the doctrines and practice of the Victorian Socialist Party, a small but influential group on the left of the **Australian Labor Party**. The VSP's combination of both political and industrial activism to remake social conditions, its internationalism, and the emphasis it placed on education and socialist fellowship, were formative influences on Curtin. His fervent soap-box oratory, rhetorical literary style, and experience as secretary of the Timber Workers Union brought a growing reputation. But he was highly sensitive, easily discouraged by setbacks; and in 1915 resigned from his union post to convalesce from alcoholism. In the following year he became secretary of the trade unions' national anti-conscription organisation, but resigned after the first referendum campaign.

In 1917 he married and moved to WA to make a fresh start as editor of the **Australian Workers Union's** weekly newspaper, the *Westralian Worker*, a position he held until election to federal parliament in 1928. He accommodated himself to the moderation of that union, which exerted a strong influence over the Labor Party in WA and contributed to its tenure of office from 1924 to 1930 and from 1934 until after Curtin's death. The final volume of C.M.H. **Clark's** *History of Australia* depicts a tormented exile pacing the shoreline of the Indian Ocean; Curtin did walk regularly along the beach of Cottesloe, but found pleasure with his young family in this suburban setting, and satisfaction in the range of activities and friendships that a medium-sized and largely self-sufficient city such as interwar Perth offered him. Service on a federal inquiry into social services and as Labor delegate to the International Labour Organisation in Geneva fostered a growing interest in economic policy and foreign affairs.

His experiences in Canberra from 1928 to 1931 were more damaging. He was excluded from **Scullin's** ministry and critical of its capitulation to the financial orthodoxies of the Premiers' Plan, which he challenged in the Labor Party's federal executive. Lonely and discouraged, he resumed drinking, and lost his seat of Fremantle in the 1931 federal election. The recovery from these setbacks revealed a new strength of character. Curtin won his fight with the bottle, recaptured his parliamentary seat in 1934, and in the following year was elected federal leader. The rebuilding of the Labor Party from the divisions created in the **Depression** required both patience and a capacity to endure rebuffs and insults to which no other Labor leader has been subjected. It took until the end of the decade to persuade the Australian Labor Party to abandon its isolationist stance in foreign affairs and its aversion to rebuilding the country's defence capacity. Curtin suppressed his own sympathy for sanctions against fascist aggressors in the interests of party unity, and condemned the waterside workers who refused to load pig-iron for Japan in 1938.

For similar reasons, he resisted **Menzies's** invitation after the outbreak of **World War II** to join in an all-party national government. 'I refuse to desert the great body of Labor to prop up political parties of reaction and capitalism', he insisted. After Labor made major gains in the 1940 election, and the Menzies government fell in 1941, the defection of two independents from the shortlived **Fadden** ministry allowed Curtin to form a Labor government in October 1941. It increased its parliamentary majority in the 1943 election.

Curtin's accession to national leadership is best remembered for the statement he made at the end of that year, shortly after Japan entered the war and struck south towards Australia: 'Without any inhibitions of any kind, I make it quite clear that Australia looks to America, free of any pangs as to our traditional links or kinship with the United Kingdom.' The speech was followed almost immediately by a cable message to the British prime minister, Winston Churchill, which said that any evacuation by Britain of its naval base in Singapore would be seen by Australia as an 'inexcusable betrayal'. The words were those of his colleague **Evatt**, but it was Curtin who refused Churchill's insistent request to divert troops who were returning from North Africa to defend Australia. The supposed transfer of allegiance from the older, declining imperial power to the ascendant one oversimplifies Curtin's choice. The USA and the UK had agreed to concentrate their efforts on the defeat of Hitler. Curtin's statement hardly altered the strategic priorities of the USA, but it did signal his strong support for General Douglas MacArthur, the military leader of the USA in the South-West Pacific, who set up his headquarters in Australia in March 1942. Curtin ensured that he had command of all the Allied forces, including the Australian ones, and backed MacArthur in his disputes with the Australian military.

Even in its subordinate capacity, the Australian army was short of soldiers. At the end of 1942 Curtin announced at a special federal conference of the ALP in November 1942 that Labor must drop its long-held opposition to **conscription** for overseas military service. He also demanded new levels of sacrifice from the civilian population. Government agencies controlled the economy and exercised powers over the workforce that would have been unthinkable if sought by a non-Labor government. These measures attracted criticism that exacerbated the strains of wartime leadership. As the Japanese threat receded, and his own health declined, Curtin became more irritable, more lonely, more inclined to doubt and indecision. Paul **Hasluck's** official history contains important psychological insights into Curtin's austere persona.

Curtin was accused of betraying Labor traditions. He spoke for the nation (and customarily began his wartime broadcasts with the vocative 'Men and women of Australia'), but he understood the labour movement as embodying national ideals. 'Nothing would come to the men and women of the working class as a gift from the gods', he warned. 'Everything they gained had to be fought for.' Even in the darkest days, when Japanese forces threatened to capture Port Moresby, he began planning the **postwar reconstruction** that would end unemployment, alleviate poverty, reduce inequality, and enlarge the lives of all Australians. His premature death in July 1945 silenced the critics.

Lloyd Ross, who had worked for Curtin during the war, undertook a biography but did not complete it until 1977, and the long delay did not enlarge the perspective. David Day's more recent biography (1999) is far more revealing of its subject's family and personal life, though conventional in its treatment of Labor politics. Geoffrey **Serle's** long entry in the *ADB* and subsequent sketch, *For Australia and Labor* (1998), convey Curtin's stature. The university named after him has established a John Curtin Centre on the US presidential centre model. It has published Serle's sketch, as well as a collection of speeches and writings (1995), and a collection of correspondence (2001), both edited by David Black.

STUART MACINTYRE

Cuthbert, Betty (1938–   ) was a sprinter, who between 1956 and 1964 won four Olympic gold medals, one Commonwealth gold medal, and broke 16 world records from 60 metres to 440 yards. Cuthbert was a twin, born at Merrylands, NSW. At the age of eight she won NSW state titles for the 50 and 75 yards, and four years later, she met former Olympian June Ferguson (Maston), who became her coach. As a 17-year-old Cuthbert unofficially broke the world 220-yard record, and at 18 in the 100-metre sprint she won Australia's first gold medal of the 1956 Melbourne **Olympic Games**. She soon added two more gold medals—in the 200 metres and the four-by-100-metre relay. Dubbed 'the Golden Girl' by the *Argus* on 30 November 1956, the blue-eyed, golden-haired Cuthbert was a shy, unaffected hero. She was forced to withdraw from the Rome Olympics in 1960 because of a hamstring injury, and retired. But she grew restless after 18 months' break and, following strength training with Percy **Cerutty**, made a comeback that culminated when she ran her last, most perfect race to win the 400 metres at the 1964 Tokyo Olympics. Cuthbert's outstanding athletic career is modestly recorded in her autobiography, *Golden Girl* (1966). She has since suffered from multiple sclerosis and raised funds for research. In 1978 she was appointed the first woman trustee of the Sydney Cricket Ground. Australian sporting history has few finer images than that of 'the Golden Girl', mouth agape and long legs flying to the line.

DC

Cyclone Tracy, the worst natural **disaster** to affect an Australian city, hit **Darwin** soon after midnight on Christmas Day, 1974. The cyclone killed 65 people (including 16 at sea), destroyed over 80 per cent of domestic buildings, and left the city of 46 000 people devoid of light, power, water, communications, and sanitation. In a massive national response, 35 000 people were evacuated in five and a half days. The Darwin Reconstruction Commission was formed to manage rebuilding. Major General Alan Stretton (director-general of the Natural Disasters Organisation) supervised the relief operations, which are described in his publications, *Darwin Disaster: Cyclone Tracy* (1975), *The Furious Days* (1976), and *Soldier in a Storm* (1978). Bill Bunbury's Australian Broadcasting Corporation radio series, *I Still Don't Like High Winds* (1991), was published as *Cyclone Tracy* (1994).

DC

D

Dad and Dave were characters created by Steele **Rudd**, the pen-name of Arthur Hoey Davis, in his comic stories that appeared in the *Bulletin* from 1895. Drawing on the Davis family's experiences of life on a **selection**, the tales present the comic struggles of a father and son who were ill equipped for farming at the mythical Snake Gully in Qld's Darling Downs. The stories were collected as *On Our Selection* in 1899. A silent film entitled *On Our Selection* was screened in 1920 and was remade in 1993. While the entire Rudd family had been the original subject of his stories, 'Dad and Dave' subsequently emerged as a duo in its own right. As larrikin cockies and bush simpletons, they eked out a poor living in snake-infested, rabbit-holed country. They were dim and disorganised, and their equipment was in constant disrepair, yet despite their tribulations there was an element of nostalgic affection for rural ways. They were widely popularised in the 1930s and 1940s through three further feature films, a radio series, and Stan Cross's regular comic strip in *Smith's Weekly*. Dad and Dave came to embody a popular view of the Australian male character, which challenged the stereotype of the noble and heroic **pioneer**, and encouraged urban mockery of country folk. A television series appeared in 1972.

HD

Daily Telegraph, a Sydney (tabloid) **newspaper**, was first published on 1 July 1879, with J.M. Lynch as editor. It was established by a syndicate that included Watkin Wynne, but after 1884 was managed by the *Daily Telegraph* company. Richard **Twopeny** rated it as 'very inferior' to the *Sydney Morning Herald* in its early years, but the *Telegraph* quickly gained a higher profile and increased circulation. Its sensational world scoop in 1884 announcing the German annexation of New Guinea greatly enhanced its reputation. It supported political democracy and the NSW government's **free trade** position but maintained a firm opposition to **Federation** in the 1890s. Editors included Brian **Penton**. It was briefly known as the *Daily Pictorial* in 1930–31. Under the control of Frank **Packer**'s Consolidated Press from 1936, it adopted a tabloid conservative style, though its political sympathies varied after acquisition in 1972 by Rupert **Murdoch's** News Ltd. In 1990 the *Daily Telegraph* merged with the *Daily Mirror* to form the *Telegraph–Mirror*.

HD

Daintree, Richard (1832–78) pioneered the use of **photography** in fieldwork in his time as a field surveyor with the Victorian Geological Survey (1859–64). He came from England to the Victorian goldfields in 1852, but was unsuccessful and joined the survey in 1854 as assistant geologist. During a visit to England in 1856 he became interested in photography and, upon his return to Australia, collaborated with Antoine Fauchery (1823–61) on a photographic album *Australia*, also known as *Sun Pictures of Victoria* (1858, 1983). In 1864 he became a pastoralist in northern Qld, continuing with both photography and prospecting. Daintree worked on the government geological survey of Qld, begun in 1868. During that time he made many of the fine photographic studies that he took to London for the 1871 Exhibition of Art and Industry. He proved such an enthusiastic proponent of Qld that in 1872 he was appointed agent-general in London. Ill-health forced his resignation four years later. The Daintree River was named in his honour. G.C. **Bolton's** *Richard Daintree, a Photographic Memoir* (1965) discusses the man and his work.

KT

Dairy industry in the nineteenth century involved hand-milking pasture-fed cows. House cows were commonly kept, but most production was from family farms. Reliant on sales of perishable products, farms were close to population centres. Dairies collected milk from the farms and distributed it to consumers.

The **selection** movement following the gold rushes, along with the cream separator and refrigeration, helped make dairying a major industry. Separation provided skim milk for calves and pigs, and cream for factory processing into butter, increasingly for refrigerated export. Most factories were cooperative enterprises set up by farmers themselves. As cream could be delivered bi-weekly, expansion of dairying further away from the factory became possible. Dairying was one activity giving farmers a regular income. G.S.J. Brinsmead in the *Australia 1888* bulletin (1980) analyses the late-nineteenth-century industry.

Dairying and politics were closely intertwined from early in the twentieth century. Fluctuations in butter prices became a stimulus for political mobilisation, and the early Country Party (**National Party**) was based as much in dairying areas as in wheat areas. By the 1920s an equalisation scheme gave factories and farmers the same returns for manufactured dairy products, whether sold in Australia or overseas. **Closer settlement** schemes after World War I established many new dairy farmers, and as the **Depression** hit, other farmers moved into dairying. Dairy pastures, herd management, and milking methods were by now a major focus for state departments of agriculture. Cream was increasingly collected by motorised vehicles, and dairies were now required by law to pasteurise milk. Share-farming became important in some regions.

Again after World War II, governments actively promoted the industry. Farmers received a subsidy based on production volume. **Soldier settlement** schemes created new dairying districts. The efforts to penetrate Asian markets began. Schoolchildren received free milk daily, and restrictions were placed on margarine production. The growth of urban populations increased the demand for fresh milk, and farmers with rights to supply this market were the 'lucky cousins' to the usually more distant cream suppliers. N.T. Drane and H.R. Edwards, in *The Australian Dairy Industry* (1961), describe the postwar arrangements.

From the 1960s economists warned that these arrangements penalised consumers and were inefficient. Despite the subsidies and the persistence of small, impoverished producers, there was an increase in farm-scale, made possible by widespread mechanisation in paddock and dairy shed, pasture improvement, and increased production per cow. Adjustment programs were funded by the Commonwealth from the mid-1960s. The nadir of the industry was in the 1970s. The **Whitlam** government removed both subsidies to farmers and margarine restrictions. Prices fell and production increased as farmers battled to stay ahead. Herringbone dairy sheds freed time for other farm work and were steadily adopted. The advent of refrigerated tankers ended farm-based cream separation, but the requirement to install a refrigerated vat, and to increase hygiene standards, led many farmers to quit dairying. In all states production in marginal areas withered, and Victoria became the main source of export dairy produce, while barriers to interstate trade in fresh milk remained. Kenneth Sillcock, *Three Lifetimes of Dairying in Victoria* (1972), records the changes.

The dismantling of interstate barriers at the end of the twentieth century lowered some consumer prices. However, the main effects are on farm and factory. Lower prices for fresh milk are driving many farms, especially in NSW and Queensland, out of dairying. Capital grants from a Dairy Industry Adjustment Package, funded until 2008 from a consumer levy, are available to all dairy farmers based on recent output levels; they can be used for any purpose such as farm reinvestment, debt repayment, or to help move out of dairying. Farm-gate prices in Victoria, where most milk is used to manufacture export products, have not fallen. Deregulation has also increased competitive pressure within the processing sector, in part from new international interests. Rationalisation of farmer-owned cooperatives, which still predominate in the sector, continues.

Some very large dairy farms based on wage-labour have emerged in recent years, as occurred in the last century. However, the most efficient technology has remained within reach of family farms, some of which employ an extra labourer or share-farmer, and they still dominate the dairy scene. Pasture-fed dairy herds retain a considerable cost-advantage in Australia.

Links between farmer and consumer are now more tenuous. Purchase of fresh milk is no longer a daily occurrence—the product lasts longer and is not delivered to the door. Supermarket customers now see a vast range of dairy products, which are mostly branded, in refrigerated cabinets. Much consumption of dairy product is now hidden from view. Caseine and milk powders, once by-products difficult to dispose of, are now important ingredients in the manufacture of processed food, including most margarines. Such products are the basis for significant penetration of Asian markets.

JIM CROSTHWAITE

Dalley, William Bede (1831–88), the Sydney-born son of Irish convict parents, was admitted to the Bar in 1856 and shortly afterwards elected member for Sydney. He resigned in 1860 to tour Europe, only to return to London as immigration commissioner with Henry **Parkes**. Dalley returned to a successful career at the Bar, but is chiefly remembered for two cases he lost—the defence of bushranger Frank **Gardiner** in 1864 and that of O'Farrell's alleged shooting of the Duke of Edinburgh in 1868. In 1877 he became a QC. He returned to politics in 1870 as a member of the Legislative Council. Dalley was an outspoken critic of the Parkes government, and his support for Gardiner's release precipitated its collapse. He was twice attorney-general, 1875–80 and 1883–88, and as acting colonial secretary won popular support for offering Britain Australian troops for the **Sudan campaign**. He represented NSW at the Intercolonial Conference of December 1883, and later published *Speeches on the Proposed Federal Council for Australasia* (1884). In 1886 he became Australia's first member of the Privy Council. Dalley was esteemed by his contemporaries as a literary man. He was editor and part-owner of the *Freeman's Journal*, and also wrote for the *Sydney Morning Herald* and *Punch*. Although seriously ill, in 1887 he participated in the push for clemency in the

Mount Rennie rape case, a reflection of his long opposition to the death penalty.

KT

Dampier, William (1652–1715), an English privateer, included an account of the several months he spent in 1688 on the north-western coast of **New Holland** (Australia) in *A New Voyage Round the World* (1697). As a result, in 1699 he was given command of an English naval expedition to explore the area further. He cruised along the WA coast from Shark Bay to Roebuck Bay, detailing the journey in *A Voyage to New Holland in the Year 1699* (1703, 1709). In spite of his unfavourable view of the country and its inhabitants— 'the miserablest People in the world'—the interest generated by Dampier's accounts of his travels was an important factor in later English exploration of the Pacific. He has been the subject of several biographies, and Lesley Marchant's *An Island Unto Itself: William Dampier and New Holland* (1988) includes Dampier's various descriptions of New Holland.

KT

Darcy, (James) Leslie 'Les' (1895–1917) was a boxer from a poor family of Irish descent near Maitland, NSW. He was an apprentice blacksmith when he began fighting in 1910. At Sydney Stadium on 12 June 1915 he claimed the Australian middleweight title from Mick King and later that year he thrashed the 'Oshkosh Terror', America's Eddie McGoorty, who was a leading contender for the world middleweight crown. McGoorty's legendary left hook had downed 28 opponents before Darcy, who took it on the chin, smiled, and boxed on. Darcy defeated other highly ranked Americans and wrested the Australian heavyweight title from Harold Hardwick on 19 February 1916. A tour of the USA promised financial security and the likelihood of establishing himself beyond dispute as world middleweight champion, but Darcy rejected overtures from the bullying promoter Hugh D. McIntosh, who retaliated with a smear campaign accusing him of shirking military enlistment. On the eve of the 1916 **conscription** referendum, Darcy secretly sailed for America, only to find his fights banned and US newspapers branding him a 'deserter'. He collapsed in Memphis, Tennessee, and died on 24 May 1917—of 'a broken heart', legend says, or 'poisoned by the Yanks'—but actually from septicaemia following dental repairs. He was 21.

Darcy won 46 of 50 fights, was never knocked out, and gave nearly all his winnings to his battling mother and family. Like Ned **Kelly**, **Phar Lap**, and the **Anzac Legend**, his tragedy grew larger than life. Patrick **O'Farrell** argued in *The Irish in Australia* (1986) that Darcy legends fulfilled an Irish-Australian need for self-esteem, and that his 'popular heir' was another Irish 'fighter', Daniel **Mannix**. Two recent biographies are Ray Swanwick, *Les Darcy* (1994), and Ruth **Park** and Rafe Champion, *Home Before Dark* (1995), which expanded research by the writer D'Arcy Niland (who was named after Darcy). A devout Catholic who attended Mass daily, Darcy is buried at East Maitland under a Celtic cross

with the biblical inscription: 'Being made perfect in a short space, he fulfilled a long time.'

DC

Dark, Eleanor (1901–85), daughter of writer and Labor politician Dowell O'Reilly, had her early short stories and verse published in a number of magazines, including the *Bulletin* and the *Australian Women's Mirror*, using the pseudonym 'P.O'R'. Influenced by European writers of the 1920s and 1930s, Dark was concerned to represent inward experiences. Her novels, the first of which, *Slow Dawning*, was published in 1932, show her love for the land, a rare insight into Aboriginal culture, and an interest in feminist concerns. Her best-known novels are the historical trilogy which trace the first few decades of European settlement in Australia, *The Timeless Land* (1941), *Storm of Time* (1948), and *No Barrier* (1953). These were dramatised in 1980 by the Australian Broadcasting Corporation as a mini-series. Although not communists, Dark and her husband were members of many 'front' organisations for which they were attacked in the 1940s. One of Australia's best-selling serious authors for 20 years, Dark was increasingly neglected by the public from the 1960s, although she received official recognition—an AO in 1977, and an award from the Australian Society of Women Writers in 1978. No biography has yet been published, but some of her correspondence appears in the volume of letters between women writers edited by Carole Ferrier, *As Good as a Yarn With You* (1992), and Drusilla Modjeska examines her work and life in *Exiles at Home: Australian Women Writers 1925–45* (1981).

KT

Darling, Ralph (1775–1858), governor of NSW 1825–31, was portrayed as a harsh tyrant by emancipists and their supporters. This view tended to inform subsequent writing until reappraisals by A.G.L. **Shaw** and Brian Fletcher. Darling was a Tory and military man who had risen to major-general on personal merit. He instituted wide-ranging, sometimes unpopular, reforms, including tighter control over the civil service, the banking system, and the allocation of land and convict labour. Darling appeared an aloof figure, and his military background and political views rendered him unsympathetic to the colonists' increasing desire for greater constitutional rights. Conflict between military and civil jurisdiction was the background to the incident in 1826 which Darling's detractors seized upon to prove his tyranny. An antagonistic press—led by **Wentworth's** *Australian*—used the **Sudds–Thompson** affair to call for a more representative Legislative Assembly and trial by jury. Darling inflamed the issue by responding with measures to control the press. He left NSW in 1831, to the outspoken joy of his opponents and muted regrets of others. A parliamentary inquiry eventually exonerated him from any blame over the Sudds–Thompson affair.

KT

Darwin was established under the name Palmerston in 1870 as the administrative headquarters of the **Northern Territory**, which was then under **South Australia's** control. It was located at the end of a narrow peninsula with easy access to an extensive harbour, Port Darwin; the latter had been named in 1839 by its 'discoverers', an expedition aboard HMS *Beagle*, after an earlier member of its crew, the famous naturalist Charles Darwin. The town site afforded little scope for later suburban expansion, which would be oriented away from the sea. The **Overland Telegraph** line ensured the new town's survival. A gold rush some 200 kilometres to the south brought both people and a measure of prosperity in the 1870s and 1880s. It also brought the completion of a railway to Pine Creek in 1889 and the immigration of the first **Chinese**, who faced prejudice, but whose businesses and market gardens provided essential supplies and services. **Pearling** brought immigrants from the north, including many Japanese. A devastating cyclone on 6 January 1897 caused both damage and loss of life. By the end of the nineteenth century the Larrakia people, the first inhabitants of the site, had been forced from most of their land.

When the NT passed to the Commonwealth of Australia in 1911, Palmerston was renamed Darwin. A contemporary census counted a population of 739 adult males, 166 adult females, 125 Japanese, and 107 'others' (mainly Chinese). The Aboriginal population was not counted. There were some substantial public and commercial buildings, the most prominent of which was the Residency (later Government House). The first Commonwealth administrator, Dr John Gilruth, worked hard to develop Darwin's economy and placed great hopes in the large meatworks completed in 1917. But these were unprofitable and closed in 1920, causing widespread unemployment. Gilruth's conflicts with an increasingly militant local trade union movement culminated in the **Darwin rebellion** of December 1918. With other unpopular senior officials, he was removed by the Commonwealth in 1919. The introduction of commercial aviation facilities in Darwin in the 1920s and 1930s foreshadowed an important new role for the town; what was once described as Australia's 'back door' now became its 'front door'. During the 1930s the Commonwealth established permanent military bases in Darwin, which provided employment and much-needed civilian infrastructure. The increasingly European non-Aboriginal population reached 3653 in June 1939, excluding those in the armed services.

When the Japanese entered the war in late 1941, many non-Aboriginal civilians were hurriedly evacuated. On 19 February 1942 Japanese aircraft launched a massive **Darwin bombing** raid. Other air raids followed. Over half the buildings were destroyed. Yet there were benefits. As Canberra awakened to its military importance, the **Top End** of the NT was given a network of well-built roads and the Stuart Highway was sealed between Darwin and Alice Springs.

The rebuilding of Darwin was initially slow and messy, but Commonwealth government policies on northern development and **uranium** mining generated unprecedented growth during the 1950s, 1960s and 1970s. In 1974 the population was 46 656. Private contractors did well; increased immigration by people of various nationalities, especially **Greeks**, enriched the community. **Cyclone Tracy** hit Darwin on Christmas Eve, 1974. A mass evacuation followed: there was initial speculation that the NT capital would be relocated. Darwin was, nevertheless, rapidly rebuilt and repopulated.

The pace of development accelerated after the granting of self-government to the territory in 1978. New suburbs appeared, as did a satellite town, Palmerston. There were extensive, grandiose, and sometimes controversial, capital works. In 1991 the population was 78 401, approximately one-quarter of them **Aborigines**. Despite some innovative tropical **architecture**, the general appearance and shape of Darwin owed more to imported planning principles than local influences. The city's well-being still depended heavily on Commonwealth expenditure. Attempts to capitalise on the proximity of Asia had only limited success.

For many Australians, Darwin remains a rather strange outpost at the rim of the continent—exotic, cosmopolitan, yet sometimes raw in its social relations—although the recent growth of tourism and education bring promise of change. There is only one, now outdated, general history, the journalist Douglas Lockwood's *The Front Door: Darwin 1869–1969* (1968). David Carment's *Looking at Darwin's Past: Material Evidence of European Settlement in Tropical Australia* (1996) documents many of its historical structures and sites.

DAVID CARMENT

Darwin bombing usually refers to the first Japanese air raids of 19 February 1942. The Japanese attacked with 188 carrier-borne aircraft to prevent interference with their planned Timor landing on the following day. Darwin services commanders anticipated the raids but not the scale of them. A dismal mix of inexperience, poor interservice communications, personal antagonisms, and plain inertia left the town and massed harbour shipping without warning when the air armada struck at 9.57 a.m. Eight ships went down, a dozen others were damaged, and two more vessels were sunk at sea. Bombs destroyed Darwin's wharf and the post office, with severe loss of life. Otherwise the town escaped lightly. But at midday the Japanese struck again, at the **Royal Australian Air Force** base, with 54 Ambon-based bombers. Great damage resulted. Some RAAF men stood fast. More joined a growing exodus of civilian refugees streaming south. At least 243 lives were lost in the two raids and the complacent insularity of all Australians was severely jolted. The Darwin area suffered 62 further raids before the last on 12 November 1943. None approached the scale of the first, and none caused such material and psychological damage. Alan Powell in *The Shadow's Edge* (1988) assesses these events.

ALAN POWELL

Darwin rebellion took place on 17 December 1918 when three or four hundred men led by the **Australian**

Workers Union secretary, Harold Nelson, marched on Government House to demand that the NT Administrator, Dr John Gilruth, leave the territory and submit to investigation of his administration. Gilruth's unbending attitude to industrial issues had angered the unionists; nor was he helped by his own aloofness, too readily seen as arrogance, or by the parsimonious colonial policies of his federal masters which dashed the hopes generated among Territorians by the Commonwealth's 1911 acquisition of the NT. Gilruth stood his ground and the rebellion ended in stalemate; but continuing agitation caused the government to recall him in February 1918. Eight months later, the threat of violence forced his three closest colleagues to leave Darwin. In November 1918 the **Hughes** ministry appointed a Tasmanian judge, Norman Ewing, to investigate the Gilruth regime. Ewing accused Gilruth of improper conduct and of being temperamentally unfit to administer the NT. On the evidence, the first finding is dubious and the second well-merited. Territory political lore tends to equate the Darwin rebellion with **Eureka** and the **Rum Rebellion**. Frank Alcorta, *Darwin Rebellion* (1984), gives a partisan view of the times.

ALAN POWELL

Davey, Thomas (1758–1823) was appointed lieutenant-governor of **Van Diemen's Land** in 1812, although he did not arrive in Hobart Town until 1813. He had earlier travelled as a marine guard on the First Fleet. Governor **Macquarie** immediately conceived a poor impression of Davey, which he never abandoned. By 1814 Macquarie was recommending that he be removed, citing dissipated 'Manners and Morals' as well as his condoning the smuggling of spirits. The recommendation was finally accepted in 1816 and Davey removed; in recompense the family received land grants totalling 8000 acres. He proved unsuccessful as a settler and died, impoverished, in London.

KT

David, (Tannatt William) Edgeworth (1858–1934) was professor of geology at the University of Sydney. Born in Wales, David arrived in Sydney in 1882 to begin fieldwork as assistant geological surveyor. His successes included the discovery of the South Maitland coalfields. Appointed to the chair of geology in 1890, David was an enthusiastic and inspiring teacher whose lectures were popular with both students and public. Fieldwork was central to his wide-ranging research program: 'Go and see', he exhorted theory-laden colleagues. His efforts to obtain samples by deep bore on the coral atoll of Funafuti received international attention, providing evidence for Darwin's theory of atoll formation. Inspired by his lifelong interest in glaciation, David eagerly joined the Shackleton expedition to **Antarctica** in 1907. Though the oldest member of the team, he led the successful first ascent of Mount Erebus, and with his former student, Douglas **Mawson**, undertook a perilous journey to the South Magnetic Pole. David returned to Sydney a popular hero.

In 1915, eager to contribute to the war effort, David organised a corps of miners and engineers to travel to the Western Front and later served as chief geologist to the British Expeditionary Force. He spent his final years in an ambitious attempt to produce a comprehensive summary of the geology of Australia, publishing a detailed geological map of the continent in 1932. His daughter Mary published an affectionate and entertaining biography, *Professor David* (1937).

TIM SHERRATT

Davis, A.H., see 'Rudd, Steele'

Davis Cup, see **Tennis**

Davis, Jack Leonard (1917–2000), writer and Aboriginal activist, was born in south-western WA to the Nyoongah people. After schooling at Perth Technical School, Davis worked on cattle stations, during which time he began formulating his views about Aboriginal rights in poetry and plays. He was later active in the **Tent Embassy** of 1972. Drawing on both historical and contemporary events, Davis expresses the sadness and anger felt by Aborigines that resulted from the dispossession by white settlement. He is also concerned with cultural loss, the disjunction between Aboriginal and European ways, and the hardships of life on Aboriginal settlements. His best-known plays are *The Dreamers* (1982), *No Sugar* (1985), and *Barrungin* (1988), which have been performed as a trilogy entitled *The First Born*. His plays have been performed widely, both in Australia and overseas, and have contributed to growing understanding of the sufferings of Aborigines in white Australia. His autobiography, published in 1991, is entitled a *A Boy's Life*.

HD

Dawbin (Baxter), Annie Maria (1816–1905), indefatigable diarist, arrived in Van Diemen's Land in 1834 with her husband, Lieutenant Andrew Baxter. He left the army in 1838 to establish Yessaba station, north-west of Port Macquarie, NSW. The Baxters' relationship deteriorated irretrievably during their six years there. Annie's journal records bitterly the day she found her husband 'making a Lubra his mistress!', and she refused further conjugal relations. Tied financially to her husband, Annie joined Baxter at Yambuck, his new station near Port Fairy, Victoria. She was a vivacious and intelligent woman who moved widely in colonial society and station life. These factors give depth to the 32 surviving volumes of her journal for the years 1834–68, in spite of their essentially personal nature. Annie returned to England in 1851. On a later voyage to Australia to settle Baxter's estate after his suicide, she met her second husband. Robert Dawbin was a failure, both as farmer and husband; after an attempt to settle in NZ they returned to Melbourne in 1871 and separated. In 1873 Annie published *Memories of the Past, by a Lady in Australia*. She later bought a small farm at Yan Yean, Victoria, where she remained until her death. Lucy Frost, in *A Face in the Glass* (1992), has made the journals accessible to the general reader.

KT

Day of Mourning, see **Cooper**, **William**

De Groot, Captain, see **Secret armies**; **Sydney Harbour Bridge**

Dead heart was a common colloquialism for the arid centre of the Australian continent. At first it was applied to the saltpans of Lake Eyre, which drain the great system of (usually dry) rivers that snake through eastern and Central Australia. In the hot summer of 1901–02, J.W. Gregory, the professor of geology at the University of Melbourne, led a student expedition across the Lake Eyre basin to the northern edge of the Simpson Desert. In 1906 he published a description of the region, under the title *The Dead Heart of Australia*. The phrase coined in his title rapidly passed into common use. It summed up the popular sense of disappointment which surrounded Lake Eyre. For many, its arid expanse seemed to mock white Australians' dreams of a fertile inland.

But the term had its critics. In 1935 the naturalist H.H. Finlayson published a best-seller entitled *The Red Centre: Man and Beast in the Heart of Australia*. The book set out to convince urban Australians that the so-called 'dead heart' of the Simpson Desert was a rich centre of animal, plant and human life. The term also angered many advocates of large-scale irrigation, who denounced talk of 'dead' places and 'deserts' as unpatriotic. For these optimists, the truth was that Central Australia was a verdant garden—a garden which could be brought to life by the hydro-engineer. This view was common during the 1930s and 1940s, notably among writers associated with the magazine *Walkabout*. Frank **Clune**, for example, set out to redeem the reputation of Central Australia in *The Red Heart* (1944).

In 1950, the popular bush journalist George Farwell criticised those who described much of inland Australia using 'Gregory's term, "the dead heart", little realising that he applied it only to Lake Eyre'. Despite Farwell's admonition, the term is still principally used in this broader sense today, and was used with ironic effect by Nick Parsons in his play and subsequent film entitled *Dead Heart* (1994; 1996). However, by the early 1960s the term was falling into disuse as the imaginary centre of Australia shifted from Lake Eyre to Ayers Rock. Over the next two decades Australians learned to value the rock as **Uluru**, a place of pilgrimage. Concurrently the Australian inland came to be represented as a place of spiritual significance or as a wilderness deserving protection and respect.

MICHAEL CATHCART

Deakin, Alfred (1859–1919) was second prime minister of the new Commonwealth and a central actor in the drama of Australian **Federation**. He held office in Victoria from 1883 to 1890, and led national ministries in 1903–04, 1905–08, and 1909–10. His long political career began during the era of colonial **liberalism** and ended with the consolidation of class-based national parties, a transition he resisted but of which he was a principal architect.

Deakin was born in Melbourne, the son of improving English immigrants, and educated at Melbourne Grammar School and at the University of Melbourne, where he graduated in law. A dreamy, bookish youth with eclectic interests in high-Victorian speculative thought, he was prominent in the spiritualist movement and aspired to a literary career. Admitted to the Bar in 1877, he was taken up by David **Syme**, the owner of the *Age*, who launched him into the Victorian parliament as a supporter of the radical Berry ministry during the **constitutional crisis** that he narrated in his memoir, *The Crisis in Victorian Politics 1879–1881* (1957).

At first Deakin seemed a cuckoo in the Berry nest—what would later be called a class traitor. Tall, dark, and refined (while proud of his status as a native-born Australian, he congratulated himself on the absence of a 'provincial accent'), he upheld the virtues of reason and duty against selfishness and rancour. Yet he helped arrange the compromise in 1881 that resolved the constitutional crisis, and he served in all the coalition ministries of the 1880s. It was an augury of his instinctive preference for the middle way, establishing him as a mender and a dealer. He was never the partisan, always the practical idealist, and his enthusiasm for democracy and social reform was always tempered by a mistrust of the inchoate energies of the mob.

His liberalism sought to employ the resources of the state to encourage economic development and suppress social evils. He pioneered factory legislation and initiated a state-aided **irrigation** scheme based on his inspection of similar schemes in California and, later, India. He represented his colony at the London Imperial Conference in 1887, where he asserted the interests of the Australian colonists, and was offered a knighthood (while still only 30), which he refused.

The onset of economic depression brought this phase of his career to a close. As chief secretary in 1890 during the **maritime strike** he proclaimed his sympathy for those with 'a great deal of flesh and blood with little capital' against those with 'a little flesh and blood with much capital', but he refused to countenance the tactics of the strikers and used troops to break the picket lines. As chairman or director of many of the land companies that defaulted, he incurred heavy personal losses and rebuilt his fortune at the Bar; he refused further public office after the coalition fell at the end of 1890. His earlier confidence yielded to doubt and uncertainty. 'Selfishness and shams, cant and materialism rule us, up and down and through and through', he observed in his private journal, and 'the Liberalism of the old days, of the old colonists is a spent force; we play with its name and glorify its shadow; it is dead, it has passed'. He turned both inwards, intensifying his search for meaning in solitary prayer and visionary experience, and outwards, in the campaign for Federation.

The making of nationhood in a Commonwealth of Australia became for him a sacred duty: he served as delegate to the Conventions of 1891 and 1897–98, which drafted its constitution; as campaigner in the referendums for its adoption; and then as a representative of the colonies during the final negotiations in London with the imperial government for its enactment during 1900. His own role as the Victorian leader of the federal movement, recorded in the account he wrote of *The Federal Story* (1944), was subordinated to the leading federalists in the other colonies where the opposition was greater.

As the deputy of Edmund **Barton**, and then as prime minister himself, he guided the legislative program of the liberal protectionists as they realised the new Commonwealth. Crucial here was his doctrine of the **New Protection**, which linked tariff protection for local industry to the maintenance of Australian living standards. Deakinite liberalism set limits on the operation of the market in order to nurture a particular kind of nation-building social solidarity. It safeguarded the racial purity of the nation by the racially restrictive **White Australia** policy, and complemented the destiny of a nation of independent Australians with an active defence program.

The liberal protectionists began as the largest of the three political parties in the Commonwealth parliament, but lost ground at successive elections to the conservative Free Traders and the Labor Party. Occupying the shrinking middle ground, Deakin allowed both his opponents brief turns in office in order to assert his own primacy, and the anonymous articles on Australian politics he wrote for the London *Morning Post* 1900–10 reveal both his tactical finesse and his growing disillusionment. By 1909 the liberals were so reduced that they had to join with their Free Trade opponents. Thus Deakin is claimed as a founding father of the present-day Liberal Party, and remembered by others as the last exponent of an earlier radical liberal tradition.

The **Fusion** of 1909 failed to avert a decisive Labor victory in the 1910 federal elections; Deakin's public career ended with remorse that 'everything in Australia (and in the world) is so obviously imperfect, inchoate, confused, stained, and wickedly filled with false antagonisms, coarseness and incapacity, that the promised land of humanity still lies far out of sight'. His final years were a torment of sleeplessness, declining health, and loss of memory.

Deakin's final despair also suggests the ambiguities of public life. A man of fastidious rectitude, he was repeatedly criticised for his expediency. He was warm and vivacious, but his nickname 'Affable Alfred' belied an inner reserve. Capable of inspiring devotion among a circle of younger men, he felt the absence of real intimacy. He constantly sought to bridge what he called his 'outer' and 'inner lives'. The inner life was centred on the family, first in his parental home, where he basked in the love and admiration of his elder sister Catherine, and from 1882 in a marriage to Pattie Browne that brought three daughters. The 'sacred circle' of his wife and children afforded 'a charmed sphere of peace and hallowed happiness' against 'the most withering insurrections and invasions of one's mind, heart and spirit', the 'sources of perpetual exacerbation, bitterness and foulness from which by Heaven's mercy I have been delivered'.

His first biography (1923)—subtitled 'A Sketch'—was written by a young admirer, Walter **Murdoch**, under the supervision of Deakin's son-in-law and confidant, Herbert **Brookes**. Drawing extensively on Deakin's own private writings (now in the National Library of Australia), it is more comfortable with the literary and intellectual enthusiasms of its subject than with the politics. By contrast, the two-volume biography published by John **La Nauze** in 1965 draws on a magisterial command of the history of Australian Federation. La Nauze, who also edited Deakin's two political memoirs and a selection of the articles that Deakin contributed to the *Morning Post*, wrote in the heyday of Australian political history, and his work displays a plenitude of scholarship and felicity of expression that give it lasting value. Yet he frankly admitted his temperamental distance from the spiritual quest that so preoccupied his subject, and this has been explored by Al Gabay in *The Mystic Life of Alfred Deakin* (1992). Diane Langmore has written of the Deakin marriage in *Prime Ministers' Wives* (1992), and John Rickard has published a study of the Deakin family, entitled *A Family Romance: The Deakins at Home* (1996).

Stuart Macintyre

Decentralisation, the desire to redress the concentration of population and power in Australia's coastal cities, has been an oft-expressed, but largely unfulfilled, aspiration of reformers and politicians for more than a century. As early as the 1880s decentralisation leagues had sprung up in towns on the Victorian goldfields, with the aim of curbing the seemingly relentless drift of trade, population, and political power to the metropolis. Political economists, who regarded agriculture as the foundation of national prosperity, saw big cities as parasites, especially when, as in Australia, they became almost as populous as the countryside. In 1902 the NSW statistician Timothy **Coghlan** had observed that 'the abnormal aggregation of the population into their capital cities is a most unfortunate element in the progress of these states'. A 1918 Victorian parliamentary inquiry into 'the causes of the drift of population to the metropolis' noted the impact of mechanisation on the demand for rural labour and the decline of rural industries as well as the 'the general dullness of country life'. The remedy, some reformers believed, lay in a radical redistribution of political power away from the old colonial capitals. From the 1920s rural interests, led by the Country Party (**National Party**), were at the forefront of the movements to create a **new state** in New England and for WA to secede from the Commonwealth. At the core of their concerns was a belief in the small-scale community based on the family, neighbourhood, and church, and a fear of the dehumanising tendencies of mass industrial society. As Nicholas Brown shows in *Governing Prosperity* (1995), decentralisation drew support from a wide range of postwar intellectuals, from the Catholic Rural Movement to the members of the Communist Party. A 1949 report, *Decentralisation: Its Social and Economic Implications*, prepared for the Commonwealth Division of Regional Development, acknowledged the benefits of concentrating economic activity in cities, but pointed to the countervailing costs of rising land values, traffic congestion, poor housing and health, and other problems of 'social maladjustment'. It went on to urge the creation of 'development towns', such as Albury, NSW, which it anticipated might grow into a regional centre of 250 000. Economists divided over the costs and benefits of decentralisation: Colin Clark, head of Qld's Bureau of Industry in the early 1950s, was a powerful advocate; so was his pupil Max Neutze, whose *Economic Policy and the Size of Cities* (1965) provided the intellectual rationale for the ambitious program of decentralisation launched by the **Whitlam** government through its Department of Urban and Regional Development. By underwriting the development of regional growth centres, such as Albury–Wodonga and Monarto in SA, it sought to create urban centres large enough to acquire economic momentum yet small enough to avoid the ills of the capital cities. Middle-sized cities, it hoped, would be more socially homogeneous, as well as more efficient, than big ones. But, like other aspects of the department's program, the growth centres fell foul of opposition from conservative state governments; since 1975 no federal government has paid more than lip-service to the goal of decentralisation, although some states, such as Victoria and NSW, have given small financial incentives, such as reductions in payroll tax, for firms locating outside the capital cities. Decentralisation was a policy based on the social virtues of space; but most Australian governments, preoccupied by issues of sustainability and efficiency rather than equity or harmony, now favour policies of urban consolidation.

GRAEME DAVISON

Defence is often seen as the first duty of government, and the Department of Defence was one of the original ministries of state established at **Federation**. Defence considerations have played an important part in the development of both the Australian colonies and nation from the beginning of white settlement, and war and the military have had a profound and abiding influence in shaping key facets of the national experience and self-image.

The colony of NSW was founded by the military, and for the first half-century it was largely governed and administered by officers of the Royal Navy and the British army. The garrison was supplied initially by a party of the Royal Marines. Between 1791 and 1810 the function was fulfilled by the **New South Wales Corps**, specially raised for the purpose; after this unit was relieved following the rebellion against Governor William **Bligh**, security against threats at home and abroad was guaranteed by regiments of the British army until their final withdrawal in 1870. Officers and men of the garrison provided a technologically skilled workforce which the early colony otherwise lacked, and a wealth of administrative experience—between 1788 and 1855, 31 governors, lieutenant-governors, and administrators of the colonies of NSW, Victoria, and Tasmania were drawn from the military, from a total of 34 occupants of these posts. Officers of the Royal Engineers supervised the construction of the colonies' early buildings, surveyed their new surrounds, dredged waterways to expedite commerce and traffic, built roads, and laid the foundations of the early **railways**, telegraph systems, and the Melbourne Mint.

The garrison discharged its military functions less frequently. Although soldiers were used against **Aborigines** on occasion in the early years of settlement—especially in Tasmania—and although some early members of the mounted police were soldiers transferred for duty, in general the army played a minor role in the struggle along the frontier of settlement. The role of the military in the dispossession of Aborigines has received little treatment in the relevant literature. Before the development of police forces, the military was the sole guarantor of civil order, and soldiers were used against rebellious convicts—as at **Castle Hill** in 1804—or rebellious subjects—at **Eureka** in Ballarat in 1854—or more generally to maintain discipline among the convicts. Widely despised in civil society for their role as gaolers, from the 1840s and the end of **transportation** to NSW, the popular image of the military softened, and their remaining function became defence against external attack. The parts played by the British military in colonial life are neglected areas of study, and some of what has been written about them is misleading. Pamela Statham, *A Colonial Regiment* (1992), has shown that the NSW Corps did not recruit heavily from the prisons, as previously thought, while the old idea that Bligh's deposition constituted a *coup d'état* missed many of the intricacies in the relationship between senior officers and executive authority while on colonial service.

The British military had a direct physical impact on the development of ideas about local defence, as the remains of forts on foreshores of Australia's major ports demonstrate still. Following the withdrawal of British regiments from the colonies in 1870, local forces of volunteers were raised, supplemented gradually by small bodies of permanent colonial soldiers for safeguarding fixed defences. The Royal Navy continued to operate on the Australia Station until 1913, when it was replaced by ships of the new Australian Fleet, but the Royal Navy constituted the first line of defence for all the Dominions until the fall of Singapore in 1942. The development of the self-governing colonies and Dominions in the 40 years before 1914 was matched by the growth in ideas concerning imperial defence, after 1885 overseen by the Colonial Defence Committee (subsequently the Committee of Imperial Defence). Some in both Britain and the colonies of settlement envisaged close cooperation in defence matters between the metropolitan centre and the colonies and Dominions, and the coordination of their resources from London, and a few even dreamt of imperial federation, but Britain's need to draw on and direct the use of imperial resources was accompanied by a growing assertion of local interests, and the tension between the two was never to be reconciled to either party's satisfaction. The colonial contributions to the **Boer War** (1899–1902) seemed to confirm the idea that the colonies represented important reserves of military manpower for Empire, but the local conditions which led them to volunteer frequently undercut this notion.

It has been suggested that the needs of a common defence drove the Federation movement, and Parkes's **Tenterfield oration** of 1889 is often adduced in support. Ronald Norris, *The Emergent Commonwealth* (1975), showed that this was far less significant than previously thought, and that Parkes probably used defence as a useful rhetorical hook on which to hang issues of more immediate concern. Defence was not a popular issue in the first federal parliaments, because of the expense that it represented, nor was it accorded a high priority: the original Defence Act, presented in 1901, was thrown out and was only enacted, in much modified form, in 1903. The post-Federation army suffered from a lack of resources and confusion in administration and structure, and became the subject of intense public and parliamentary criticism; it was replaced in 1910 after Field Marshal Lord Kitchener's report recommended a system of compulsory military training. This scheme, which was more widely endorsed and accepted than some subsequent accounts would suggest, was not in place long before the outbreak of **World War I** led to its suspension.

At the Imperial Conference of 1911, the British had accepted that the Dominions would respond to a general threat to the Empire in terms consistent with their own domestic political arrangements. The outbreak of war in 1914 confirmed this, and belies John Mordike's claim (*An Army for a Nation*, 1992) that the 1911 conference represented the triumph of a pro-imperial conspiracy determined to harness Dominion resources to imperial ends. During World War I Australia exercised little effective influence on the higher decision-making processes, but British authorities extended considerable organisational, administrative, and logistic support to the First **AIF**, which enabled it to remain in the field for the duration of the war.

Early postwar enthusiasm for international disarmament led to the scuttling of HMAS *Australia* and reductions in the small permanent forces, the latter a reflection of government financial stringency, and shortage of resources devoted to the army and the **Royal Australian Air Force** was one of the central characteristics of interwar defence policy. The other key feature was an emphasis on navalism epitomised by devotion to the Singapore Strategy. The dominance of the navy in strategic policy was only gradually displaced after 1937 with belated moves to rearm, although senior army officers, in particular, had pointed to the bankruptcy of Australian strategic thinking from the early 1930s. Much of the literature on this subject draws attention to the shortcomings in British policy, but generally avoids pointing up Australian complicity and willingness to be misled over British priorities in the event of a general war, while the notion of a British 'betrayal' of Australian interests, especially during **World War II**, is belied by the evidence.

World War II represented Australia's worst defence dilemma come true: a world war conducted in several theatres simultaneously, in which Britain was unable to intervene in the Pacific in sufficient force; and 20 years of Treasury parsimony had left the country unable to defend itself unaided. The respite given between 1939 and 1941, and the experience acquired by the forces fighting in Europe in those years, were critical to the successful defence against the Japanese in 1942–43. The wartime alliance with the Americans was seen as strictly temporary, though highly beneficial, and as early as 1944 the Australian government advanced plans for a scheme of postwar defence cooperation within the Commonwealth. With its financial and manpower resources severely depleted after 1945, the British sought a renewed Australian commitment to the defence of the Middle East, but the Pacific War had demonstrated the need for a regional focus in defence issues, and key members of the **Menzies** governments in the 1950s helped to move the focus of Australian strategic thinking to the defence of the 'near north'. Regional security arrangements such as ANZAM (Australia, NZ, and Malaysia) and **SEATO** were underpinned by the tripartite security treaty, **ANZUS**, concluded with the USA and NZ in 1951.

The Cold War and the doctrine of 'forward defence' kept the Australian forces continuously engaged on active service in Asia between the **Korean War** (1950–53) and the **Vietnam War** (1962–72). A period of uncertainty followed defeat in Vietnam, to be replaced in 1987 with a modified version of the 'defence of Australia' derived from the Dibb Report. This was modified by renewed emphasis on regional engagement in defence matters with the states of the Association of South-East Asian Nations, in particular, and by small commitments alongside the Americans in the Sinai, during the Gulf War (1990–91), and in Somalia (1993). Contributions to UN peace-keeping missions became increasingly important in the 1990s—notably in Cambodia in 1992 and in **East Timor** in 1999–2000. In the late 1990s the army began basing many of its units across northern Australia, from Cape York through Darwin to Broome, making a decisive break with the focus on the defence of the south-east—the old Sydney–Melbourne axis. *The Australian Centenary History of Defence* (Peter Dennis and John Coates (eds), 2001), offers a comprehensive account.

JEFFREY GREY

Democracy, in the sense of the untrammelled rule of the people, has had its advocates in Australia, but the achievement of democracy is commonly understood as the extension to all citizens of the right in equal measure to determine the composition of the parliament.

In the early nineteenth century in Australia, as in Britain, democracy was considered a dangerous concept associated with the French Revolution and the killing of kings and aristocrats. The preservation of British liberties was held to depend on the maintenance of the threefold order of King, Lords, and Commons. To have any chance of success, the advocates of the extension of political rights concentrated on widening the franchise rather than democratising the whole political order.

This approach was evident in the Australian liberal and radical movements during the 1850s, when the colonies were drawing up and amending the **constitutions** under which they secured self-government. They were successful in advocating manhood suffrage for the Assemblies and yet they were not unwilling to accept the creation of upper houses to act as a check on the lower. They preferred an upper house elected by property-holders to one nominated by the governor, which indicates how little thought they had given to the securing of popular supremacy. It is much harder to break the resistance of an elected upper house than a nominated house, which can be altered by new creations. However, to these liberals nomination smacked of privilege and favouritism. Conservatives preferred nomination just because it would create a privileged order to play the part of the British aristocracy. So a nominated council was established in NSW where conservatives were strongest (and with the application of its constitution to Qld, in that colony as well); in the other colonies Legislative Councils were elected by those owning a certain amount of property (modest in SA; extremely high in Victoria).

Still, the Assemblies were remarkably democratic bodies. They were elected by all men, by secret ballot, in more or less equal electorates, and with no property qualification for members. Thus four of the six points demanded by the British Chartists had been realised long before any were conceded in Britain. Payment of members was not yet strongly urged since the British tradition of parliamentarians as leisured gentlemen was still valued, partly because it gave gentlemanly status to politicians who had no other claim to it. The most extreme of the Chartist points, annual parliaments, had no advocates, but lessening the term of parliaments to three years was accomplished in NSW, Victoria, and SA. Even without payment of members, the Assemblies contained men of little education and less sense of decorum, and they made Australia notorious in an Empire in which Britishness and democracy were regarded as antipathetic. The new democratic polity is examined by Geoffrey **Serle** in *The Golden Age* (1963) and by John Hirst in *The Strange Birth of Colonial Democracy* (1988).

Soon after the new constitutions came into operation, the nominated Council in NSW was made to bend to the Assembly's land policy by the creation of new councillors. In Victoria the elected Council resisted the Assembly with impunity and provoked a number of **constitutional crises**. This drew Victorian liberals into an elaboration of a democratic program. They advocated payment of members (achieved on a trial basis after a long struggle in 1870), the widening of the Council franchise, and the referendum to resolve differences between the two houses. The referendum was a Swiss device made part of the liberal program at the insistence of David **Syme** of the *Age*.

In the late 1880s and 1890s in all colonies, Liberals, radicals, and the new Labor Party made a concerted attempt to democratise the constitutions. Democracy became a principle which was now unashamedly proclaimed and difficult to deny. Upper houses were able to resist reforms to themselves, but payment of members and the abolition of plural voting were carried. (In the 1850s when manhood suffrage was introduced, the property franchise had not been abandoned, except in SA, so that men with property in a number of electorates had votes in them all.) The greatest change was the extension of votes to women, achieved first in SA (1894) and last in Victoria (1909). The democratising of the constitutions can be followed in Manning **Clark's** *Select Documents in Australian History 1851–1900* (1955), which first made clear that there were two 'bites' at democracy: that in the 1850s and that at the end of the century.

At this time the Commonwealth Constitution was being drawn up. Democrats in NSW and Victoria were opposed to equal representation of the states in the Senate, which they saw as undemocratic, given the huge discrepancies in the population of the states. They failed to dislodge this principle—Federation could not have been achieved without it—but with the support of democrats in the other states, they made gains everywhere else. The Senate, though deemed the upper house, had the same electorate as the lower house; if it persisted in opposition to a lower house measure, it could be dissolved and an election held for the total membership of the parliament. Payment of members applied to both houses, and each voter could vote only once. Constitutional alteration was to be approved by the people voting at **referendum**.

In the twentieth century, Labor governments in the states were regularly thwarted by Legislative Councils. Labor policy was to abolish them and to democratise the polity further with the initiative (by which voters could petition that a matter be put to referendum) and referendum. Labor refused to allow that an upper house was a useful check on hasty measures or on an overweening government. Not without justification, it saw upper houses as representing the vested interests opposed to its program. Against elected upper houses, Labor was as helpless as liberals and radicals had been, but once it constituted the government in NSW and Qld, it was able to recommend to the governor new members for their nominee Councils. Governors in this were not bound to follow their ministers' advice, but in Qld in 1922, a Labor government found in a lieutenant-governor, who was a former Labor minister, someone willing to swamp the Council with Labor supporters, who then voted for the Council's abolition. A similar move in NSW in 1925 failed when some of the new members reneged on their commitment to vote for abolition. A non-Labor government in 1933 altered the constitution to provide that new Councillors were to be elected by the members of both houses.

The Councils elected by a property franchise survived longer. They finally agreed to be elected by universal suffrage, not as the result of an organised campaign, but as a property franchise became so outrageous that the non-Labor parties could no longer defend it. Victoria's Council yielded first in 1950, as a result of the unusual cooperation of the Labor and Country parties. The others held out much longer—WA (1964), Tasmania (1969), SA (1974).

The last battle in the democratising of the parliament was the overcoming of the huge imbalance in the population of electorates. As city populations grew, the country became over-represented, an advantage which it was reluctant to forgo, and for which it could plead the difficulty of parliamentarians serving a sparse rural population and the economic importance of its production. At the federal level the allowable difference in population between electorates was reduced from 20 per cent to 10 per cent in 1974 and the state gerrymanders have all now been removed, except for the upper house electorates in WA.

Labor was in the forefront of these movements, except in the case of the rural imbalance in the Queensland electorates of which it was the beneficiary until the 1960s. Labor's commitment to democracy was, however, compromised by its refusal to allow Labor members of parliament any discretion in interpreting the wishes of their constituents. Members were obliged to vote according to the dictates of the Labor **caucus**. Labor understood democracy as the people voting for its program which should then be implemented without any hindrances in the parliamentary machinery. This approach forced Labor's opponents into a similar discipline, though never as tight, with the result that Australian parliamentarians do not have the appearance of being the servants of their constituents.

By the second half of the twentieth century, democracy was an unassailable ideal, a universal good, assisted to this position by two world wars proclaimed to be fought on its behalf. Civil rights and liberties, which in Australia, as in other British societies, long preceded a democratic franchise, were no longer thought of as British, but simply as democratic or an entitlement flowing from international declarations and proclamations. Yet between the wars in Australia, as elsewhere, democracy was briefly brought seriously into question: by the Right, which wanted greater efficiency and stronger leadership, and by the Left, which wanted a complete social transformation. The **secret armies** and the **Communist** Party occupied the extremes; a wider distaste is explored by Peter Loveday in 'Anti-Political Political Thought' (*LH*, 1970).

The democratising of the parliaments has not convinced everyone that democracy is established. There has been a revival of interest in the initiative and referendum, no longer coming from the Left, but from right-wing groups. Identity politics claims that a parliament can not be truly representative unless it has the due proportion of women and ethnic minorities. As the lower houses of parliament have become little more than electoral colleges for the appointment of the executive, new methods to control the executive have been sought. Democracy is now more commonly thought of as polity of checks and balances, even on the Left as radicals have become more interested in protecting, extending, and entrenching individual rights than in harnessing popular power for economic and social transformation.

JOHN HIRST

Democratic Labor Party (DLP) was an anticommunist political party formed by members of the **Australian Labor Party**. It had close associations to the Catholic lay organisation, the **Movement**. In 1955 the ALP leader H.V. **Evatt** led an attack on the right-wing Australian Labor Party members who supported the Industrial Groups, which had been established to combat the influence of **communism** within the trade unions and were backed by the Movement. The breakaway section of expelled Victorian members formed the Australian Labor Party (Non-Communist), and this was incorporated in the nationwide Democratic Labor Party (DLP) in 1957. In the same year Vince **Gair**, the Labor premier of Qld, was expelled from the party, and his Queensland Labor Party later joined the DLP. The DLP proved strongest in Victoria, where B.A. **Santamaria** and Archbishop **Mannix** were the leading figures. Its allocation of preference votes to the Liberal–Country coalition effectively kept Labor out of office at state and federal level throughout the 1950s and 1960s. Assisted by the voting system of proportional representation in the Senate, the DLP achieved five members in the Senate by 1970, including Vince Gair and Frank McManus. With its introduction of government funding of Catholic schools, however, the **Whitlam** Labor government recouped many Catholic votes from the DLP; all five DLP senators lost their seats in 1974. Other DLP voters transferred their allegiance to the Liberal Party. Despite a campaign to 'vote Mac back', the party became largely irrelevant and was disbanded in 1978.

HD

Demographic history is the quantitative study of changes in the structure of human populations. From the first European settlement until the 1830s, the **population** was counted from time to time by way of musters or **censuses**, but the purpose of these counts was bureaucratic—that is, to report upon the size and composition of the population of the penal colony. Baptisms, burials, and marriages were recorded in church registers for legal purposes, but attempts, especially by Governor **Macquarie**, to centralise these sources of information failed. Then, in the 1830s, documentation of the wealth of the nation became a central role of the growing public service sector in England and Wales. This endeavour was set within the long tradition of political economy. Official statistics became a sub-branch of political economy, and vital statistics and population lay within that sub-branch. Under the leadership of William Farr, registrar-general, legislation requiring the civil registration of births, deaths, and marriages was enacted in England and Wales in the 1830s. Similar legislation was enacted in each of the Australian colonies soon afterwards. While civil registration had its legal purposes, Farr's agenda was scientific. For example, death registrations included a statement of the cause of death. Along with this, Farr developed a classification of diseases, the forerunner of today's international classifications administered by the World Health Organisation. In the 1840s, Farr established an official life table for England and Wales. The life table methodology, essentially the likelihood of experiencing a given event in a fixed period of time, remains the central tool of almost all forms of demographic analysis. In 1840 the first modern census was taken in Britain.

Demographic history

The Australian colonies were more successful than the home country in implementing registration of vital events, probably aided by the smallness of the population. However, use of the statistics for scientific purposes awaited the arrival in the Australian colonies of members of the new generation of statisticians. The first of these was W.H. **Archer**, who became registrar-general of the Colony of Victoria in 1853. As an actuary, Archer was well qualified to promote the scientific study of population in his colony. He set the example for the official statisticians who followed. Notable among these were R.M. Johnston in Tasmania, H.H. **Hayter** in Victoria, T.A. **Coghlan** in NSW, and G.H. Knibbs, the first Commonwealth statistician. All saw their role as documenting the growth of the new nation, and population growth was recognised as a key determinant of nation-building. The epitome of the genre was Coghlan's *The Wealth and Progress of New South Wales*, published in 13 editions between 1886/87 and 1900/01. No attempt was made to count or include **Aborigines** and, if the **Chinese** were missed, this was not a concern. Still within the tradition of political economy, these statisticians saw population and vital statistics as given facts which derived from natural and economic laws. The natural law approach to demographic processes was taken to its extreme in Knibbs's *The Mathematical Theory of Population* (1917). Population facts were basic, exogenous facts which, once established, became determinants of other economic and social outcomes. Economists have continued, until today, to see population and vital statistics largely as exogenous to the systems that they have investigated.

Observation of behavioural change was not part of the political economy paradigm. Indeed, following Herbert Spencer, in the latter part of the nineteenth century, behavioural change was seen mainly in a social evolutionary perspective where the time units of change were millennia or, at the least, centuries. As a consequence, the most important change in the history of population, the shift to low and controlled fertility, became well-established before it was observed by the scientists of the time. Coghlan was the first to record the new trend; his observations published in the last years of the nineteenth century led to the setting up of the NSW Royal Commission on the Decline in the Birth Rate in 1903, a story told by Neville Hicks in '*This Sin and Scandal*' (1978). Despite this lateness of observation, Coghlan's research was the most thorough of its kind anywhere in the world, and when he participated in a Royal Statistical Society debate in 1906, he was regarded as the foremost British authority on fertility statistics. The inescapable conclusion that women were exercising considerable control over their fertility took demography into the realm of behavioural sciences, but the tools of data collection and analysis in that field remained undeveloped. The way to investigate why women behaved as they did was not to ask them but to ask doctors and clergymen. The 11 NSW royal commissioners were all men of substance. Fertility behaviour was consequently interpreted in a conservative and moralistic way, and the decline in the birth-rate was attributed to the 'selfishness of women'. While demographic processes were no longer seen simply as exogenous and natural, there was a strong sense that that was the way that they should be. Population growth was seen as fundamental to Australian nationhood.

The political economy paradigm retained its force in demography for the first half of the twentieth century. The core debate was about the optimum population of Australia and the carrying capacity of the country. W.D. Borrie describes this debate in *The European Peopling of Australasia* (1992). The protagonists were mainly economists and geographers. Economic theory, food production, water supply, and other limiting factors were all used as determinants of the nation's ultimate carrying capacity. This debate revived in the 1970s and continues today within an **environmental** framework. While men were debating the optimum population, Australian women, undeterred by their condemnation by a royal commission, continued to restrict their fertility to the extent that fertility fell to below replacement levels by the early 1930s. The concept of replacement-level fertility derived from the development of the net reproduction rate and the mathematical theory of stable populations. This was the most significant advance in demographic methodology since the life table. In the 1930s economic statisticians such as Wolstenholme and **Copland** applied this new methodology to Australia. The implication of their work was that Australia's population growth would cease at a level well below its carrying capacity and well below the levels implied for a great and secure nation. Under the banner of 'populate or perish', the postwar immigration program commenced.

The emphasis on population in **postwar reconstruction** led to the recognition of demography as an academic discipline in its own right in the Research School of Social Sciences in the newly created Australian National University. This was extended to a Department of Demography in 1952 and the appointment of W.D. Borrie as professor of demography in 1957. Long-term demographic histories or historiographies were a feature of the work of this department, notably Peter McDonald, *Marriage in Australia* (1974); Lado Ruzicka and John Caldwell, *The End of Demographic Transition in Australia* (1977); and Borrie's own *The European Peopling of Australasia* (1994). In addition, the incidence of non-British migrants in the postwar migration stream generated a range of socio-cultural studies. C.A. Price's *Southern Europeans in Australia* (1963) was a classic in this new field of demographic research. Thus, behavioural or sociological research in demography came into prominence through the study of migration rather than the study of fertility, but survey methodology and the computer have, since the 1970s, led to an expansion of studies of relationships and fertility from a behaviouralist perspective. The survey approach to demographic explanation was used for the first time in Australia in the Melbourne Fertility Survey conducted in 1971 under the leadership of J.C. Caldwell. The methodology was carried further by the Australian Institute of Family Studies, using longitudinal surveys in which the same people are interviewed across time. In behavioural studies, demographic variables are seen as consequences of economic and social processes, the obverse of the political economy approach to demography.

Beyond the size and composition of the population, there is a long tradition of study of the geographic distribution of the population and population mobility within Australia. Almost all this work has been carried out by geographers or within the framework of urban and regional economic development. **Closer settlement** of rural areas was a central theme of this work in the early part of the twentieth century, and **decentralisation** to country towns was a 1970s theme. In the 1990s, attention has shifted to urban consolidation, the concentration of population in the existing boundaries of cities as distinct from the continued expansion of **suburbs** which has marked Australian history from the first white settlement. In 1994, the study of the demography of small areas took a leap forward through the establishment by Graeme Hugo of a computerised, geographical information system.

PETER MCDONALD

Deniehy, Daniel Henry (1828–65), the son of convict parents, was the best-educated and most eloquent of the radical democrats in mid-nineteenth century NSW. His parents had prospered in the colony and were able to give their son a good education, which included a grand tour of Britain and Europe while he was still in his teens. On his return he was articled to the solicitor N.D. Stenhouse, who was at the centre of Sydney's literary community. Deniehy became famous by his speech in denunciation of William **Wentworth's** scheme to create a landed nobility for the colony's upper house. He described the would-be peers as a **'bunyip aristocracy'**. His wit and brilliance made him the darling of the popular cause. He was briefly a member of the new parliament, representing Goulburn and later Bathurst, the towns where he practised law, but he could not cooperate with the liberal democrats. He was appalled at the quality of the members elected under manhood suffrage and at the devices which the liberal leader **Cowper** employed to keep his following together, which he satirised in *How I Became Attorney General of New Barataria* (1860). He died at Bathurst, a derelict alcoholic. His speeches were collected by E.A. Martin (1884), and Cyril **Pearl** has written a biography, *Brilliant Dan Deniehy* (1972).

JH

Denison, William Thomas (1804–71) was appointed lieutenant-governor of Van Diemen's Land in 1846 to replace the disgraced **Eardley-Wilmot**. He arrived from England with strong views on the need for punishment of convicts rather than reform, and modified the existing system accordingly. He also inherited a fraught political situation, which he soon exacerbated by adjourning the Legislative Council and suspending two of his judges, actions which incurred strong public condemnation. Already unpopular for his support of **transportation** and his overbearing style, Denison became much more so when a confidential report, critical of local society, became public. He was, however, a sound practical administrator, and a keen

proponent of education. He saw the colony through the end of transportation and the Victorian gold rush. In late 1854 Denison was appointed governor of NSW and governor-general of all the colonies, and sailed for Sydney. The Crimean War prompted him to strengthen Sydney's defence against sea attack, and the fort on Pinchgut Island bears his name. He steered NSW along the complex path to **responsible government** while maintaining the primacy of the Executive Council, a cause of dispute with some of his ministers. Typically, Denison ended his term as governor-general in dispute with Cabinet over the division of power.

KT

Dennis, (Clarence Michael James) C.J. (1876–1938), poet and journalist, was the creator of the Sentimental Bloke. *The Songs of a Sentimental Bloke* (1915) was one of the most popular books ever published in Australia, and the Bloke, an affectionate version of the Australian ocker, still appeals to nostalgic readers.

Born in Auburn, SA, of Irish parents, Dennis early discovered a talent for light verse, publishing in various newspapers, including the Sydney *Bulletin*, in which some sections of *The Bloke* first appeared. The 'songs' tell the story of a **larrikin** who progresses from knocking about with the city **push** to domestic bliss on a small farm with a wife and son. Dennis 'tried to tell a common but very beautiful story in coarse language' (his own description of his work), and provided a glossary 'for the use of the thoroughly genteel'. Unlike the bush ballads of an earlier generation, however, his verse does not put a genuine vernacular to poetic uses. *The Bloke*, with comic-sentimental Hal Gye drawings of the characters as cherubs, was an instant and continuing success. Dennis followed it with *The Moods of Ginger Mick* (1916), a book in the same style cleverly exploiting **mateship** and the pathos of war, and several other volumes.

A prolific writer of newspaper verse, Dennis never advanced beyond *The Bloke*. His most enduring composition may prove to be 'The Australaise: A Marching Song', which to the tune of 'Onward Christian Soldiers' humorously exploits the Great Australian Adjective.

JOHN BARNES

Depressions are sustained periods of deflation, declining economic activity, and high **unemployment**. Australia experienced major depressions during the 1840s, 1890s, and 1930s.

Their causes are a central focus of debate in **economic history**. The main point at issue in Australia has been whether these events were primarily caused by external factors or by weaknesses in the domestic **economy**. Brian **Fitzpatrick**, in *The British Empire in Australia* (1941), blamed the depressions mainly on falling export prices and crises on the London financial market, and suggested that the depressions underlined Australia's economic dependence on Britain. This thesis was widely challenged. S.J. **Butlin's** *Foundations of the Australian Monetary System* (1953) emphasised the collapse of speculative **pastoral** development as a factor in the 1840s depression, while N.G. **Butlin's** influential *Investment in Australian Economic Development* (1964) argued that the primary cause of the 1890s depression was a 'sectoral disequilibrium' produced by heavy debts and diminishing returns in the industries that had led the 1880s boom. Similarly, C.B. Schedvin, *Australia and the Great Depression* (1970), suggested that domestic policy failures and heavy public borrowing were key factors in the 1930s Depression.

The colonies' relations with Britain changed on several fronts during the 1840s. As Philip McMichael noted in *Settlers and the Agrarian Question* (1984), the British textile industry, which had spearheaded the early phases of industrialisation, experienced a major crisis in the late 1830s. The slump depressed the price of **wool**, Australia's major export, and also spurred demands to contain expenditure on the colonies. Yet, if the pressures on public finance made a downturn almost inevitable, there were complicating factors. Principal among these, as Barrie Dyster noted in an essay in *AHS* (1993), was a surge in British investment after the wool market collapse of 1836–37. At a time when business in Britain was flat, investors were attracted to the London-based colonial **banks**, which were paying 10 per cent interest on deposits. The economic difficulties in Britain thus had contradictory effects in the colonies: while they depressed export earnings and commercial activity, they also sparked an inflow of opportunistic loan capital. The combination had disastrous consequences. It created unsound 'bubble' companies, caused a surge in imports, and was accompanied by rapid inflation.

The bubble burst in 1840 after the local banks curtailed credit, producing a wave of business failures. In 1841 wool prices dropped again and Crown land sales slumped, throwing public finances into disarray. Between 1841 and 1843, according to N.G. Butlin's estimates in *Australians: Historical Statistics* (1987), government outlays were cut by 64 per cent. This had dire social consequences, especially for the thousands of assisted immigrants who had arrived in NSW in the midst of the depression. By 1844 four of the local banks had failed, innumerable merchants and pastoralists had been bankrupted, and there was widespread destitution. The effects were felt for many years. Falling asset values wiped out much of the capital accumulated by the old mercantile and landowning elite, but the pastoral industry continued to grow, setting the stage for the squatters' economic dominance in the latter part of the century.

The prelude to the 1890s depression saw a similar conjunction of heavy British lending, deteriorating export prices, and balance-of-payments problems. Facing competition overseas from Germany and the USA, Britain fell back in the 1880s on investing in its formal empire. Almost one-quarter of all British overseas investment during that decade went to Australia. The sudden capital inflow played a key role in the disequilibrium to which N.G. Butlin has attributed the 1890s depression. Easy credit underpinned the inflation of pastoral land values, political pork-barrelling over the location of new **railways**, and the urban **land boom** that reached its climax in Melbourne during 1887–88.

In keeping with the colonial elite's clubbable business style, many lending institutions disbursed their funds through patronage networks, with few procedures to monitor clients' accounts. In Melbourne especially, land companies describing themselves as 'banks' made loans to their directors, as Michael **Cannon** revealed in *The Land Boomers* (1966). Then, in November 1890, the London money market learnt that defaults by several South American governments were jeopardising the survival of Baring Brothers, its premier finance house. The news sparked a panic, and in 1891 the governments of Victoria, SA, and Qld were unexpectedly rebuffed when they tried to raise new loans. Shortly afterwards wool prices slumped, and British depositors began to withdraw funds from the colonial banks. The scandalous revelations that followed the failure of several land 'banks' did nothing to improve public confidence, and the drain of deposits became a run. In April–May 1893, 13 of the 16 major banks suspended business, plunging commerce, industry and government into chaos.

The contraction of economic activity became precipitate from 1891. Government outlays fell by almost 40 per cent between 1891 and 1895, and gross domestic product by about 30 per cent. P.G. Macarthy has used engineering trade union records to estimate that unemployment in Victoria peaked at more than 28 per cent in 1893. Among casual workers the rate was certainly much higher. Unemployment relief was scanty, and mostly involved hard labour on public works such as swamp drainage, while private charities, overwhelmed by requests for help, rationed assistance by ruthlessly weeding out the 'undeserving' poor.

There has been some debate about how far the depression affected the working class as a whole. In an influential essay in the *AEHR* (1970), Macarthy argued that workers who remained fully employed enjoyed higher real earnings because of falling prices. Contemporary sources, however, suggest that few fell into this category. There was widespread underemployment, with many factories working three- or four-day weeks. Furthermore, as Graeme Davison noted in *The Rise and Fall of Marvellous Melbourne* (1978), wages fell far more than the 'official' union rates suggest. Among those worst affected were young people, many of whom were kept on juvenile wages well into adulthood, if they worked at all. Declining marriage- and birth-rates reflected the extent of poverty and insecurity among the young.

In the long term, the 1890s depression was a watershed in Australia's economic and political development. The recovery was based on diversification away from the industries that had led the 1880s boom. There was growth in meat production and **dairying**, and the discovery of **gold** in WA boosted export earnings and intercolonial trade. Many local manufacturers took advantage of the **trade unions'** weakness to cut labour costs and modernise production techniques, dispensing with craft skills.

The 1930s Depression was an international crisis of unprecedented magnitude, but its lineaments in Australia were disturbingly familiar to those who remembered the

1890s. There was the same conjunction of falling commodity prices, balance-of-payments deficits and heavy overseas debts to a reluctant London market. A key difference, however, was that in the 1930s the state and Commonwealth governments accounted for the bulk of the debt—about 70 per cent, as against 50 per cent in the 1890s.

London had begun to baulk at Australia's public debt in 1926, when international commodity prices dipped. In 1927 the conservative **Bruce–Page** government set up a Loan Council to control the states' borrowings, but this failed to allay London's concerns. Early in 1929 a major public loan issue was rebuffed, forcing harsh expenditure cuts and the cancellation of public works, at the cost of some 200 000 jobs. The federal government also set out to cut award wages, sparking a wave of industrial unrest; then, in October 1929, it suffered a humiliating electoral defeat over its proposal to dismantle the Commonwealth **arbitration** system.

The **Scullin** Labor government, which took office in the week of the Wall Street crash, was at a loss to deal with the emerging crisis. When international commodity prices tumbled, Scullin urged farmers to grow more wheat and offered them a guaranteed price, a promise he was unable to fulfil. The fall in export earnings compounded the problem of servicing the overseas debt. In August 1930, at the instigation of Sir Otto **Niemeyer** of the Bank of England, the states and the Commonwealth agreed to balance their budgets and desist from overseas borrowing until they had repaid their short-term external debt. A currency devaluation and a 10 per cent all-round cut in award wages followed early in 1931.

The May 1931 **Premiers' Conference** agreed on a new scheme to stabilise public finances. This Premiers' Plan rested on the principle of 'equality of sacrifice': there were to be higher taxes, most government expenditures would be cut by 20 per cent, and local bond-holders would be asked to accept a reduction in interest payments.

For all this flurry of activity, public policy did little more than follow the market down. Public expenditure cuts and private retrenchment threw thousands out of work. Trade union returns showed unemployment as peaking at 30 per cent in mid-1932. Private charities were soon swamped with requests for assistance, and from 1930 the state governments introduced 'sustenance' for the unemployed, usually funded by income-tax surcharges. Relief took the form of ration vouchers worth only a small fraction of the basic wage, and was restricted to those who had sold all their assets except their homes. Several states compelled recipients to work for sustenance, and protests by relief workers were ruthlessly suppressed.

The fortunes of the employed are harder to determine. In *Recovery from the Depression* (1988), R.G. Gregory and others argue that 'it is almost as though the depression did not exist for a large proportion of the workforce'. Deflation certainly benefited those who still had money to spend, but there is little evidence that large sections of the working class were among them. In support of his contention that there was a huge gulf between the employed and unemployed,

Gregory notes that men who described themselves as unemployed at the 1933 Census had been out of work for an average of more than two years. Yet at the same Census two-thirds of all male employees reported that they were averaging less than the **basic wage**. The **oral histories** collected by Wendy **Lowenstein** in *Weevils in the Flour* (1978) and local studies, such as Janet McCalman's *Struggletown* (1984), reinforce the impression that few were immune from the Depression's effects.

Perhaps the 1930s Depression's most enduring legacy was its effect on public policy. Dissatisfaction with the deflationary orthodoxy gave a fillip to the acceptance of Keynesian strategies and strengthened the hands of those who sought to modernise the apparatus of economic management. Memories of Depression hardships also influenced the establishment of a wide-ranging system of social welfare benefits in the 1940s. For more than a generation, Australian politicians of all parties shared a commitment to ensuring that the Depression would never happen again. Unfortunately, their successors do not appear to have the same conviction.

JENNY LEE

Devanny, Jean (1894–1962) arrived in Sydney from NZ in 1929, already a novelist of some notoriety, following the banning of *The Butcher Shop* in 1926. She joined the **Communist** Party of Australia in 1930 and soon became one of the best-known political orators on the east coast. Viewed ambivalently by the party leadership, she was recognised and celebrated as an agitator and organiser by the rank and file, particularly in north Qld which she first visited in 1934, and where she set *Sugar Heaven* (1936), one of Australia's most famous strike novels.

Left historiography has had difficulties in coming to terms with the figure of Devanny because of the challenge posed by her sexual politics—assertive in theory and in practice—inside the party and in general. 'Within the Party, Jean was invariably recalled as a brilliant agitational speaker, and as a stirrer who refused to accept hypocrisy', Jack Beasley reported in 1987. While her politics were close to K. S. **Prichard's**, her practice of them was often uncompromising; their respective careers present many fascinating contrasts.

Devanny's papers, including much unpublished material, are at James Cook University. One draft of her autobiography, *Point of Departure*, was posthumously published in 1986. Carole Ferrier has written a biography (1999).

CAROLE FERRIER

Development, the exploitation of resources to achieve economic growth and population-building, acquired heightened meaning in the second half of the nineteenth century as new colonial governments became responsible for ensuring the economic and social progress of the colonies and the prosperity of colonists. In the early years of colonisation development was a necessity for the survival of tiny British outposts, a new commodity and finance market for imperial capital, and an opportunity for colonial entrepreneurs; from the 1850s it became a central tenet in the rhetoric of elected governments. In this rhetoric resources were limitless and waiting to be utilised in the project of state and nation-building. The promise of progress was sure. Developmentalism remained effectively unchallenged within the political culture until countered by environmentalism from the 1960s.

In the period prior to the 1850s colonial authorities, running gaols or struggling free settlements, were less inclined to prescribe the directions development should take. E.O.G. **Shann's** classic text, *An Economic History of Australia* (1930), celebrated the individual colonists whose efforts fuelled early nineteenth-century development, chiefly the rise of **wool** as staple in the 1820s. In contrast, Brian **Fitzpatrick** argued that early colonial development was directed by, and for the benefit of, British capitalists. In the 1850s the influx of diggers to the eastern colonies provided a further challenge to colonial governments' capacity to manage both the rapid gold development and its aftermath as ex-diggers sought new opportunities. Gold strengthened agrarianism, the dream of prosperity, independence, and contentment in family farming, and the call for 'Homesteads for the People' grew loud. Colonial governments answered this call in their 1860s development rhetoric of 'unlocking the land'.

For 100 years governments promoted agricultural development, promising to put the small man on the land. The **Selection** Acts of the 1860s made land available for smallholders and the successful development of the **wheat** belt at the end of the nineteenth century was also heavily assisted by governments. Provision of **railways**, essential for marketing agricultural products, and the raising of British capital for lending through government agencies were the major components of this assistance. Cheap land, farming advice, and infrastructure subsidies were also offered. Noel **Butlin** labelled this extensive government intervention to promote development 'colonial socialism'.

Release of land for farming further eroded **forest** resources which had been severely depleted by unrestrained cutting from the first years of colonisation. By the turn of the century governments were juggling agricultural expansion with the demands of forestry, where the development rhetoric of limitless resources had been modified to that of 'scientific forestry': wise use, careful management, and 'forest farming'. While state governments balanced this developmental conflict differently—with the states of Qld, WA, and Tasmania showing least regard for the **conservation** of forest resources—J.M. Powell's account of *Environmental Management in Australia 1788–1914* (1976) concluded that forest exploitation retained 'popular and political support' across Australia.

Peopling the continent was a complementary developmentalist goal. How could an undeveloped continent be transformed without the people to do it? The decline in the birth-rate from the 1870s and a growing sense of external threat fuelled government **immigration** programs. In the 1920s agricultural development and assisted British migration came together in the **Bruce–Page** government's

Development and Migration Commission; it promised to be a 'national clearing house for all ideas and schemes bearing upon economic development' and it promoted Empire resettlement, bringing surplus British people for empty Australian land. Most of these migrants of the period between the two world wars were directed into **closer settlement** schemes, of which **group settlement** was one expression. These government projects aimed to develop fruit and **dairying** industries on very small, often subdivided holdings. They were mostly failures, costly in both financial and human terms. Criticisms were voiced, notably by Frederic **Eggleston** (*State Socialism in Victoria*, 1932), who condemned such methods as a massive obstacle to progress and destructive of Australians' individualism; however, government interventionism was too deeply embedded to be shifted by this ideological attack.

In the twentieth century state developmentalism was reinforced by the promotion of national development by federal governments. Nowhere was this rhetoric more evident than in continuing calls to 'develop the north'. Peopling the empty spaces of northern Australia where limitless land beckoned was seen as a national obligation, increasingly loudly chorused in the 1930s. Australia had no moral or strategic defences against those foreigners who might cast covetous eyes upon an undeveloped continent if the nation did not rise to the challenge. The choice was stark: 'populate or perish'. Both federal and state governments promoted northern development and provided assistance to improve transport and communications, to upgrade the pastoral industry, to facilitate new **mining** ventures and, the biggest pipedream of all, to establish a series of **irrigation** schemes across the north. The **Ord River Scheme** in the east Kimberley was to be the first of many great engineering projects which would result in intensive agricultural settlements peopling the 'empty north'.

By far the largest national development project initiated by the federal government was the **Snowy Mountains Hydro–Electric Scheme**, begun in 1949 as a component of **postwar reconstruction**. An ambitious public work to generate hydro-electric power and extend irrigation, the scheme was a vivid expression of the scale of developmentalist thinking in the mid-twentieth century. Its labour force of recent migrants was incorporated in developmentalist rhetoric: they became **New Australians** undertaking essential development work. **Population** building quickened in postwar years, with the federal government's assisted migration program's inclusion of continental European people as well as British. In this way workers were provided for the manufacturing development of the 1950s and 1960s.

A development lesson that governments took from the 1930s **Depression** was the necessity to diversify, to supplement agricultural development with greater industrial development. In those states without much secondary industry governments would have to take a strong lead; it could not be left to the market. The successful strategy of SA premier Thomas **Playford** and auditor-general John **Wainwright** for state-led industrialisation enticed private enterprise with offers of cheap land and power, infrastructure provision, freight and tax concessions, quiescent unions, and workers' housing. This influential initiative is treated by Kyoko Sheridan (ed.), *The State as Developer* (1986). Key Western Australian public servant Russell Dumas made similar offers to establish the Kwinana industrial complex in the early 1950s (as recorded in Lenore Layman, 'Development Ideology in Western Australia 1933–1965', *HS*, 1982). Victoria also established a Division of State Development in 1950 and its premier Henry **Bolte** fostered similar schemes.

These government development initiatives facilitated the growth of the private sector and, in many cases, the expansion of large corporations into new regions. In this way they were distinctly different from pre-1914 endeavours by state governments, chiefly Labor ministries in NSW, Qld, and WA, to foster secondary industries by setting up state trading enterprises: sawmills, brickworks, dockyards, shipping, bakeries, hotels, even fish shops. This strategy had been quickly discredited, although the public enterprises were not all sold off immediately. From the 1930s most state governments pursued industrial development by competing to lure established businesses to their shores with ever more enticing packages.

State governments, particularly those of WA and Qld, promoted and facilitated the 1960s–1970s resources boom with the same development strategies. They courted foreign investment on 'selling' missions, assisted companies to find partners, guaranteed infrastructure provision where possible, signed off development agreements quickly, and kept royalties low. A favourable climate of opinion for large-scale mining development, chiefly coal and iron ore, was created in these states and downstream processing promised. At this new apogee of **'Australia Unlimited'**, WA premier Charles **Court** insisted, 'We are only at the beginning. We are a handful of people privileged to develop a great continent.'

Yet, at the same time, the uncontested sway of developmentalism was ending. Effective challenges began as **conservationism** gained popularity and organisation. An early sign was the successful 1960s–1970s campaign to prevent mining on the Great Barrier Reef. Although few mining developments have raised such opposition, nevertheless contests began to occur regularly on issues of **Aboriginal land rights**, potential environmental damage and, in the case of **uranium**, the value and dangers of nuclear power. Agricultural expansion ended with opposition to the release of yet more marginal land, intensifying as salinity became a public issue. The proud boast of the 1960s WA government—that, during the decade, it alienated one million acres of Crown land a year to agriculture—proved a last hurrah. In 1969 a successful campaign prevented the Little Desert region of the Wimmera being opened for farming, the Victorian government giving in reluctantly to the new demands. The sway once held by hydro-electric power authorities, particularly in Tasmania, weakened; resistance to the building of the Franklin Dam marked a significant shift. Population building by mass migration ended. Instead Australia began to limit its intake severely and target it precisely.

No longer could the political rhetoric of development as an unquestionable good be heard without an alternative viewpoint being effectively put. The days of grand government development projects fettered only by the visionary capacities of politicians and public servants passed with few traces. (See also **Northern Myth**.)

LENORE LAYMAN

Diarists have traditionally come from the middle and upper classes of society—those with the skills, desire, time, and materials to write. Both men and women write diaries, although the subjects on which they write tend to reflect the different spheres in which they have moved. Men have written more about public life and paid work, while the pages of women's diaries have more generally been filled with domestic arrangements, family and friendship networks. Some diaries—perhaps most—are essentially working documents, a tool for the management of the daily life of the farm, factory, or household. But men and women have also used diaries to reflect upon their spiritual or emotional life: the journals of Alfred **Deakin** provide a notable example; he wrote little about his political life. Writers, such as Nettie **Palmer**, often used a diary to practise their craft. Some diarists wrote for the duration of a specific event, such as Robert **Menzies** during his 1941 visit to Britain or the immigrant's journey to Australia, while others wrote over a long period, irrespective of their activities. Diaries might be introspective, or written as a family, war, or political record.

Diarists have provided historians with invaluable sources in the writing of Australian history. Lieutenant Ralph **Clark** wrote in florid detail of the convict women he accompanied on the voyage to Australia; George Augustus **Robinson's** journal provides detailed accounts of his interactions with Tasmanian and Victorian Aborigines. Explorers' journals, such as those of **Sturt** and **Mitchell**, were published, sometimes in heavily edited form, and became perhaps the most widely read documents of their kind. The long-kept diary of Joseph Jenkins provides an uncommon insight into the life of a swagman during his 25-year stay in Australia (William Evans, ed., *Diary of a Welsh Swagman 1869–1894*, 1975).

Diaries offer a valuable insight into the lives of colonial women. Annie Baxter **Dawbin** wrote of life in Hobart, NSW, and Port Phillip in the 1840s and 1850s, and of the loneliness of bush life and a loveless, violent marriage. Her diary, edited by Lucy Frost as *A Face in the Glass* (1992), also reveals the contradictions of colonial life for a 'lady': expected to be a civilising influence on men in the bush, yet forced through economic necessity to work hard and endure considerable physical deprivation. The diaries of the **Bussell** sisters, Fanny and Bessie, detail their early years of settlement in southern WA and the unending nature of domestic work, even for those with servants.

The growing interest in **social history** sparked a new interest in diaries and diarists. They were used as a major source in the Bicentennial history volume on *Australians 1888*. Consideration of the motives of diarists opened up other avenues of interpretation in the 1990s. Penny Russell in *A Wish of Distinction* (1994) suggests that, for upper-class women in Melbourne in the 1860s–1880s, writing a diary was an important aspect of genteel performance. Through their diaries women were able to define for themselves (and incidentally for later readers) what it meant to be a lady. Thus the description of convict women in Ralph Clark's diary might be seen as revealing more about the prejudices and values of his sex and class than about the women themselves. Rather than providing a transparent depiction of daily life, diarists convey a great deal about the preoccupations of their society.

Well-known diarists in Australia are generally those whose social status has ensured the preservation of their writings. This is especially true for male political figures such as Richard **Casey**, who wrote chiefly of political, foreign and business affairs, while the extensive diaries of John **Monash** include more personal details. The diaries of men notable for their service to the nation are also likely to have been preserved—those, for example, of Edward 'Weary' **Dunlop** or the hundreds of World War I soldiers from whose diaries Bill Gammage drew extensively in *The Broken Years* (1974). The preservation of diaries thus reflects the cultural values of the community. The survival of other diaries has been much more haphazard. In the case of early European women settlers—Agnes **Henty**, Louise Clifton, and Anne **Drysdale**—the pioneering nature of their experiences perhaps ensured the preservation of their diaries. For those whose lives might seem less remarkable, in both the nineteenth and twentieth centuries, an astute relative or mere chance may have ensured the survival of their writings. Katie Holmes discusses the diaries of such women who wrote during the 1920s and 1930s in *Spaces in Her Day* (1995). To date, very few diaries from non-British immigrants or Aboriginal Australians have come to light.

The reasons for diary writing are diverse. In *Sailing to Australia* (1994), Andrew Hassam notes that many British emigrants wrote diaries to provide those at home with a record of their journey. They may also have written to mark their passage from the old world to the new. In the nineteenth century it was not uncommon for an emigrant or visitor to Australia to publish select years of a journal, and perhaps to have written with such an intention. For a man or woman isolated on an outback station, the diary might have served as a useful companion. Some diarists charted religious pilgrimages in their journals; others recounted the trials of domestic life; while for young women writing in the years between the world wars, romance features prominently in their daily record. The use of the diary as a journal for 'self-discovery' has more recently replaced the evangelical use of the diary for self-examination. Whether diarists were writing for themselves, family or posterity, the activity of writing was important.

KATIE HOLMES

Dibbs, George Richard (1834–1904) became a well-known figure in the Sydney shipping and trade world of the

1870s. He entered the Legislative Assembly in 1874, committed to representing local business, and a staunch advocate of state responsibility for education. For supporting assisted immigration, he was branded an enemy of labour and lost his seat in 1877. Excoriated by the unions and elements of the press for being chairman of a shipping company that used Chinese labour, Dibbs regained popular support for serving a prison sentence rather than pay a fine for slander. He was returned to parliament in 1882 and was appointed colonial treasurer. Between 1885 and 1894 he served three times as premier of protectionist ministries. Elected to represent NSW at the 1891 Federal Convention, Dibbs reluctantly accepted the inevitability of the union, but he was chiefly intent on sabotaging the plans of his rival **Parkes**, which explains his support for Sydney as the federal capital. While in London the following year promoting Australia's creditworthiness, he ignored the advice of Edmund **Barton** and his republican sympathies, and accepted a knighthood. He later proposed a plan for the unification of NSW and Victoria, and the gradual absorption of the smaller colonies. In 1894 Dibbs's government was defeated; in 1895 he lost his seat.

KT

Dictation test was a compulsory procedure introduced in 1901 through the Immigration Act as a means of controlling the entry of non-European people into Australia. Potential immigrants were given a dictation test in a European language of the examiner's choice; if they failed they were denied the right to settle in Australia. In a notorious case of 1934, the test was applied to prominent Czech communist Egon **Kisch**. He failed a test in Scottish Gaelic, as expected, but the High Court ruled that Gaelic was not a European language. In 1958 the dictation test was superseded by entry permits.

HD

Dietrich, Amalie (1821–91), born in Germany, trained as a naturalist as she and her husband collected specimens. After they separated, Dietrich was employed by J.C. Godeffroy, a rich merchant, to travel to Australia and collect for his private museum in Hamburg. She arrived in Brisbane in 1863 and travelled widely for nearly a decade collecting plant, animal, and insect specimens as well as Aboriginal artefacts, before returning to Germany. Although she corresponded with Ferdinand von **Mueller**, she appears to have had little impact on Australian scientific study. However, she was highly regarded in Germany, and several plant and animal species were named in her honour.

Almost 15 years after Dietrich's death, her daughter, C.L. Bischoff, produced a version of her life, which formed the basis for subsequent writings, *Amalie Dietrich. Ein Lieben* (1909). An abridged English translation by A.L. Geddie, *The Hard Road*, appeared in 1931. This included letters purportedly describing her years in Australia. Ray Sumner's study, *A Woman in the Wilderness* (1993), includes a detailed analysis of the letters that casts doubt on their authenticity. Sumner also relates the story that Dietrich sought to have an Aboriginal shot for his skeleton, and tells of a tanned Aboriginal skin seen in the Godeffroy museum.

KT

Digger is a colloquial term of contentious origins. It emerged in gold-rush Victoria in the early 1850s, following popular use of the terms *gold-digger* and *diggings*. The rebellions at Bendigo and Ballarat, prompting calls of 'Diggers unite!', reinforced the egalitarian associations of the word, which have endured. Others argue that the word had an earlier American heritage: that it was born on the Californian goldfields and was subsequently used during the American Civil War in the 1860s.

Digger made a significant resurgence during World War I, arguably on account of the trench-digging nature of warfare. Soldiers ascribed it to themselves and their mates as a term of pride and affection. It later developed into general usage among men as a term for each other and has become inextricably linked to the enduring sense of Australian **mateship**. Prime Minister Billy **Hughes** was styled 'the Little Digger'. There remains a friendly, knockabout **larrikinism** implicit in the term, although the expression is in decline and is now more often used by older Australians. K.S. **Inglis** discusses the word's origins in *Meanjin* (1964).

HD

Dingoes, or *Canis familiaris*, were the first domesticated animals introduced to the Australian mainland but are now generally considered indigenous. They are short-haired dogs, sandy in colour, which were brought to Australia from South-East Asia between 3000 and 4000 years ago. The native dog of Thailand bears remarkable similarities. Dingoes were originally pack animals and Australia's largest carnivores, and are believed to have caused the extinction of the thylacine and Tasmanian devil on the mainland. **Aborigines** used dingoes as hunting dogs, and valued them as companions. After the arrival of European farmers, dingoes preyed at night on unpenned stock. European settlers feared dingoes' nocturnal howling and attacks on their stock, and they came to be regarded as a **pest**. Dingo-proof fences were erected, and dingoes were poisoned in large numbers, until their numbers were considerably depleted. The bounty on dingoes was the basis of a modified hunter–gatherer economy in Central Australia between the wars. The controversy over whether dingoes attack small children became a key issue in the celebrated **Chamberlain** case.

HD

Diplomacy, see **Foreign relations**

Directories, otherwise known as almanacs, post office directories, and gazetteers, list the names and addresses of individuals and businesses, usually both alphabetically and by street or town address. Directories were published for each colony and usually appeared annually. The first Australian directory was Howe's *New South Wales Almanack and Colonial*

Remembrancer (1806); it was followed by others, including *The New South Wales Calendar and General Post Office Directory* (1832–37). Although originally produced commercially, some later became official post office publications. From the 1850s the printing firm Sands & Kenny (later Sands & Macdougall) produced directories for Sydney, Melbourne, Adelaide, and country Victoria and NSW. F.F. Baillière's directories, produced in the 1860s and 1870s, covered NSW, Victoria, Qld, SA, and Tasmania, and H. Wise & Co., operating into the twentieth century, covered NSW, Victoria, and Tasmania. Other colonies also published the South Australian directories (1839–1973), the *Western Australian Almanack* (1862–89), *Walch's Tasmanian Almanac* (1863–1978), and the *Queensland Almanac–Brisbane Directory* (1859–1927). Regional and municipal directories were also published and, later, telephone directories. Directories are useful sources for **local history** and **genealogy**; they assist in determining the spread of occupations in the trades and professions, in researching the history of buildings, and in identifying commercial activity at a particular time and place.

HD

Disability came into existence when capitalist Europe industrialised in the eighteenth and nineteenth centuries. Hitherto people with disabilities had lived and worked as members of their local communities. When production shifted from the home to the factory they became unemployable, a burden to families and communities. The state responded by institutionalising them with other problem populations: the mad, the criminal, the indigent. Conceptually, then, people with disabilities were defined by their incapacity to work. People with intellectual disabilities were also conceptualised by their incapacity to reason. Labelled *aments* (literally 'without mind'), *idiots* or *imbeciles*, they were dealt with in the same way as those who had lost their reason, by incarceration in the new nineteenth-century lunatic asylums. Their situation was similar in Australia for much of the nineteenth century. People with physical disabilities were rarely incarcerated but, because they were excluded from the labour market, their circumstances were little better.

The history of people with intellectual disabilities took various routes in Australia. Until the 1970s some governments consigned those people who came under their control to 'quiet and chronic' wards in lunatic asylums or hospitals for the insane, and forgot them. NSW and Victoria, by contrast, set up separate institutions for them. In 1887 in Victoria, the Kew Idiot Asylum (later known as Kew Cottages) was established, during a moment of therapeutic optimism, to apply the belief then current in some US and European circles, that children with intellectual disabilities could be educated. The optimism was short-lived. Overcrowding, disenchantment, and particularly **eugenics**, which constructed the so-called feeble-minded as a threat to the white race, meant that people with intellectual disabilities were segregated and institutionalised. Some families kept their children with intellectual disabilities at home, but they battled on with little or no support.

Disasters

The history of people with physical disability in the nineteenth century differs because of the widely varying conditions involved. People with epilepsy and cerebral palsy were consigned to lunatic asylums. People with sight and hearing impairment were frequently segregated in specialist schools and institutions. Others were labelled *infirm*, defined as the deserving poor, and provided for by benevolent asylums or charities. Those injured in accidents became clients of public hospitals or, if they were members, became beneficiaries of friendly societies and craft unions. Still others made their way as best they could, taking work where they could find it.

Governments took more interest in physically disabled people in the twentieth century, by legislating for pensions, workers' compensation and, later, occupational health and safety. But they responded most readily to the plight of those wounded in war. The Commonwealth government set up its Repatriation Department during World War I and the Australian Rehabilitation Council during World War II, the terms *repatriation* and *rehabilitation* confirming that physical disability, historically, has been conceptualised in terms of work.

Following World War II, parents' groups began to provide services and lobby governments for assistance. Organisations such as the Crippled Children's Societies and the Western Australian Slow Learning Children's Group emerged, to become large, bureaucratic organisations. Then, in the 1970s, new ideologies of deinstitutionalisation, normalisation (providing people with disabilities with as 'normal' a life as possible) and liberation began to inform policy and practice, removing barriers to social and physical integration. The belief that intellectual disability was an incurable medical condition was superseded by developmental and educational ideas. In the 1970s and 1980s UN resolutions and programs on disability required Australian governments to make changes to their policies. People with disabilities began to organise politically. Anti-discrimination legislation was passed, including the federal Disability Discrimination Act of 1992. As the organisation of care became more complex, universities began to offer disability studies programs. The changes since the 1960s have been astonishing.

Today, however, new problems for people with disabilities have emerged. Improved health care has enabled people with disabilities to live longer, yet governments have cut services. Public attitudes are still ambiguous. Stigma is still attached to disability, despite the fact that terms like *spastic*, *cripple*, and *mental defective* are being excluded from the lexicon. People with disabilities remain disproportionately vulnerable to abuse and crime. Scientific advances in reproductive technology and genetic engineering have provided new opportunities for latter-day eugenicists, and the congregating of people in institutions make tragedies like the fire in Kew Cottages in Melbourne in 1996 an ever-present possibility. The future of people with disabilities is still clouded.

Little has been written about the history of disability in Australia. Cliff Judge, *Civilisation and Mental Retardation* (1987), and the collection edited by Errol Cocks et al., *Under Blue Skies: The Social Construction of Intellectual Disability in Western Australia* (1996), are social histories of intellectual disability. There are no published general histories of physical disability.

CHARLIE FOX

Disasters are accidents or natural events that occasion significant loss of life or extensive property damage. Wars and deliberately inflicted loss of life, such as the **massacres** of Aboriginal people by whites or the recent phenomenon of mass shootings, such as the **Port Arthur** massacre of 28 April 1996, when 35 people died, are not normally categorised as disasters. They have many similar effects, but their human agency raises different psychological issues.

Australian disasters have been accompanied by a relatively low loss of life and a relatively high economic cost. The Brisbane flood of 1974 took five lives, but caused damage estimated at $178 million. On Christmas Day in the same year, **Cyclone Tracy** took 65 lives, and damage was estimated at $500 million as most of Darwin's buildings were flattened. The Australian continent is highly susceptible to such natural disasters as **floods**, cyclones, **bushfires** and **droughts**. The gradualness of the last has enabled the avoidance of large loss of human life, although Charles **Sturt** reported witnessing Aboriginal people dying of starvation in his 1829 journey along the dried-up bed of the Darling River. The unpredictable extremes of Australian flooding caught many early settlers by surprise. Australia's worst flood disaster was at Gundagai in NSW, when on 24–26 June 1852 between 77 and 89 persons died out of a population of 250, when the Murrumbidgee River flooded. Cyclones have caused extensive loss of life in Qld, the NT, and WA. In March 1899 a cyclone at Bathurst Bay on Cape York wrecked more than 100 pearling ships and took 307 lives. The southern states of NSW, Victoria, SA, and Tasmania are particularly prone to bushfires. On **Black Friday** in Victoria on 13 January 1939, 71 died.

In the nineteenth century the greatest loss of life from disasters, as Lloyd's Register of Shipping reveals, was occasioned by **shipwrecks**, attributable to Australia's dependence on Britain for trade and immigrants. The worst of these was the wreck of the *Cataraqui* on King Island, in August 1845, when 406 died, many of them young single women. In the twentieth century, transport disasters have been less destructive of life than in many other Western countries. The worst rail disasters have been at Granville in Sydney, 18 January 1977, when 83 died, and at Sunshine, Victoria, 20 April 1908, when 44 died and 400 were injured. The Granville disaster was researched memorably by psychiatrist Beverley Raphael. Australian airlines have an enviable safety record, which is often attributed to weather conditions more suited to flying than are often found in other parts of the world. Charter flights have not attained the same safety record as commercial flights. The two worst aviation disasters both took 29 lives—at York, WA, in 1950 and at Mackay, Qld, in 1960.

Australia's dependence on mineral wealth has resulted in many **mining** accidents. The Creswick goldmine disaster, 12 December 1882, took 22 lives, while a fire in the Mount Lyell copper mine on 12 October 1912 cost 42 lives, and is the subject of Geoffrey **Blainey's** fascinating investigation in *The Peaks of Lyell* (1954). Australian coalmine disasters reflected the worldwide trend of ever more horrific disasters towards the end of the nineteenth century and the steady improvement in the second half of the twentieth century. In the Illawarra coal field the Bulli mine disaster, 23 March 1887, took 81 lives, and the Mount Kembla mine disaster, 31 July 1902, cost 96 lives—the largest peacetime land disaster in Australia's history. The latter disaster is still commemorated annually and has been the subject of the most thorough study of any Australian disaster, *The Mount Kembla Disaster* (1992), by Stuart Piggin and Henry Lee. The Mount Mulligan (Qld) mine disaster, 19 September 1921, in which 75 died, has been studied by Peter Bell.

Disasters warrant much closer attention from historians than they have received in Australia. They are usually formative events in the history of a community and accurate indicators of the stresses in the social systems which they disrupt. They illuminate the historical process, especially the nature of change and progress for which they are frequently responsible. Coronial inquests, inquiries, court cases, and royal commissions, which frequently follow disasters, together with extensive media coverage, provide the historian with abundant evidence. Survivors tend never to forget disaster experiences, which makes **oral history** more profitable than in other areas of historical inquiry. The research of sociologists and psychologists has been especially fruitful, providing the historian with much assistance in sifting and interpreting the ample evidence, and identifying issues to study in the discrete phases: pre-disaster, impact, emergency, recovery, rehabilitation or reconstruction, and the long term. The researcher might begin with the *Australian Disaster Research Directory* (1983; 1985), published by the Australian Counter Disaster College, Macedon, Victoria, and the interpretive studies edited by Peter Hinton, *Disasters: Image and Context* (1992). The best sociological study is R.L. Wettenhall on the 1967 Tasmanian bushfires (1975).

STUART PIGGIN

Dismissal refers to the events of 11 November 1975, when the governor-general, Sir John **Kerr**, dismissed the Labor government by handing Gough **Whitlam**, without prior warning, a letter which terminated his commission as prime minister. This followed a deadlock of 27 days, beginning on 15 October, when the opposition parties in the Senate deferred supply until the prime minister agreed to call an election for the House of Representatives, which he refused to do. This **constitutional crisis** was both a bitter struggle for political power and a fundamental dispute over the meaning of the Constitution and the ground rules of the political system. Whitlam argued that the party with a majority in the lower house was entitled to govern. The opposition argued that a government required the confidence of both houses to retain office. If it lost the confidence of either and tried to stay in office, it could be dismissed by the governor-general. Sir John Kerr, supported by the chief justice, Sir Garfield **Barwick**, accepted this argument and rejected Whitlam's advice. Kerr commissioned the Liberal leader, Malcolm **Fraser**, as caretaker prime minister on his assurance that he could obtain supply and would advise a general election. The governor-general granted him a **double dissolution** of both houses, using as a pretext the 21 Labor bills previously rejected twice by the Senate. Fraser subsequently won majorities in both houses.

While the **Constitution** gave Kerr the power to act as he did, his action provoked much criticism, especially his failure to warn Whitlam that he did not agree with his advice. Kerr seemed curiously indifferent to the real novelty of the argument he endorsed and to the degree to which he, too, was privileging a partisan reading of the Constitution. One crucial issue during the crisis was whether opposition senators would stay united. Whitlam advised they would not; Fraser that they would. Sir John accepted the latter's advice, although Paul Kelly in *November 1975* (1995) provides evidence suggesting that Whitlam was right. It also strengthens the arguments that Kerr intervened too soon and that Fraser was in no position to guarantee supply. His success was largely due to luck. The book makes clear that the Dismissal came about through a major breakdown in communications and trust between Whitlam and Kerr, a situation exploited adroitly by Fraser. Whitlam denied the credibility of the reserve powers, although Kerr believed strongly in the discretion vested in his office. Whitlam denied the latter any discretion at all, referred in patronising tones to 'my Viceroy', and insisted that Kerr must act only on his advice. He did not provide the governor-general with adequate written advice or furnish sufficient explanations of his own political strategy, which, beyond an express desire to defeat the Senate, was not thought out in any detail. He did not raise with Kerr how long he felt able to support the government's position. He ignored contrary advice, including warnings that he should not take Kerr's support for granted.

Since the **loans affair**, Kerr had had doubts about the advice provided by Whitlam and misgivings about his political judgment. He did not, however, make these known to his ministers, or seriously avail himself of the right to counsel them where he saw problems with their position. Arguably, he did not deal openly and honestly with his ministers: fearful of his own dismissal, he acted deliberately to induce in them a false sense of security. He was seduced by the status of his own office and saw himself too much as a judge handing down a verdict rather than a mediator between the parties. Neither Kerr nor Whitlam played the kind of role that might reasonably have been expected of them. The causes for this lay as much in their respective egos as in political events. Neither understood what was going on in the other's mind, and neither took sufficient trouble to find out.

The Dismissal provoked a substantial polemical and interpretive literature. Michael Sexton, *Illusions of Power*

(1979), is perhaps the most effective critique, and the television series *The Dismissal* (1982) reinforced the hostile view. In hindsight it is apparent that the crisis confirmed the powers of the Senate and overturned Whitlam's view of the Constitution. Subsequent research has confirmed that Australian national government is a complex hybrid system with parity between the principles of **responsible government** and those of federalism. In the last analysis, the law of the Constitution carries greater weight than Westminster-type conventions. Whether a government does require the confidence of both houses to stay in office, as a constitutional principle, has yet to be decided. The crisis exposed several anomalies in the Constitution which also remain unresolved, such as the lack of an effective constitutional provision dealing with a prolonged dispute between the houses over supply, especially one arising from a Senate decision to defer supply indefinitely. The latter situation highlights the significance of the governor-general's discretionary powers. The Dismissal showed that the constitutional powers vested in the office have more political significance than the reserve powers of the British monarch. The office is more than the cipher Whitlam presumed it to be. Just how much more is unclear.

HUGH V. EMY

Divorce became possible in the Australian colonies when the first comprehensive divorce legislation was enacted in the years immediately following the 1857 British Matrimonial Causes Act, which applied to England and Wales and which made divorce available under secular law. By 1865 all the Australian colonies except NSW had enacted divorce legislation similar to the British 1857 Act; NSW did so in 1873. This legislation provided for legal divorce only on the ground of adultery, thus introducing the notion of fault-based divorce. The sexual double standards of the time informed one notable aspect of this legislation: women needed to prove adultery aggravated by another offence such as cruelty, bigamy, or desertion, while men needed to prove only adultery.

In the late nineteenth century there was extended debate about marriage and divorce. Hilary Golder in *Divorce in 19th Century New South Wales* (1985) points out that both sides of the debate viewed marriage as an 'essential component of social and political stability'. Advocates of equal divorce rights, and of the extension of grounds for divorce, believed that divorce would relieve the social problem (and state cost) of deserted wives by giving them greater access to remarriage. The NSW Matrimonial Causes Amendment Act of 1881 provided that adultery alone was sufficient grounds for a woman to divorce her husband; not until 1923, however, had all the states made similar amendments. In the late 1880s and 1890s, additional grounds for divorce were included in new divorce legislation in the states, such as assault, desertion, and drunkenness, and other grounds, which varied for men and women. These were still all fault-based grounds in that they relied upon the 'wrong-doing' of one of the parties.

The divorce extension bills throughout Australia coincided with the politicisation and informal coalitions of women's groups, though few female activists entered into the debate on the extension of divorce. Many in the women's movement believed that 'easy divorce' might lead to a greater abandonment of wives and children, and that economically dependent women might not be able to use the reforms the way they were designed. Divorce rates increased slowly with the new legislation. Golder has shown that male petitioners were not restricted to the wealthy, and that most female petitioners were in paid employment or small business; those without independent incomes were less likely to seek divorce.

Divorce legislation in Australia changed little from the late nineteenth century to 1975. In 1959 the Commonwealth Matrimonial Causes Act consolidated the various grounds for divorce required in the different states. The grounds for divorce were still fault-based, except for the ground of five years' separation which had initially been introduced in WA in 1945. The structure of divorce law thus remained largely unchanged. Criticism of fault-based divorce emerged in the 1950s, and after 1966 there was increasing pressure for a complete reform of divorce legislation. This came in the form of the Commonwealth Family Law Act in 1975.

The Family Law Act was important in making divorce easier and more accessible. It removed all grounds for divorce based on matrimonial fault, and instead provided that the only necessary ground for divorce was an 'irretrievable breakdown' of marriage, evidenced by a separation of one year. Spouse and child maintenance, and child custody, were also to be decided on a no-fault basis. The act did not pass without controversy and long debate. Opponents of the one-year separation ground feared that marriage would become a temporary and passing relationship dissolved at the whim of one partner.

During the twentieth century divorce rates in Australia increased greatly. At the beginning of the century just four per cent of Australian marriages ended in divorce; by the 1990s about one-third of marriages did so. This increase was gradual until 1976, when the Family Law Act came into force. The jump in divorce proceedings was partly a backlog from the previous years. Since then, divorce rates have stabilised, but they continue to increase, with proportionately more couples divorcing after fewer than 10 years of marriage. This may be attributed to the tendency for couples to decide to have children later in marriage and to the shorter duration of marriage before divorce. Hayden Brown in *The Australian Family* (1996) suggests that the reasons for the increased divorce rate are partly demographic and partly the result of new attitudes towards marriage, the **family**, and its economic maintenance. Divorce, once a cause of social stigma, is now more widely accepted; marriage, once regarded as a sacred and necessary institution, is increasingly treated as a contingent arrangement.

PATRICIA GRIMSHAW AND ELIZABETH NELSON

Dixon, Owen (1886–1972), lawyer and judge, studied classics and law at the University of Melbourne before going to the Bar in 1910. As a young barrister he assisted Leo Cussen with consolidation of the Victorian statutes. His exceptional legal knowledge and advocacy skills became widely recognised after he took silk in 1922 and appeared before both the Privy Council and the High Court of Australia. In 1926 Dixon held a short-term post as acting justice of the Supreme Court of Victoria and in 1929 he accepted appointment to the **High Court**, where he was later chief justice (1952–64). Dixon also served as Australian minister to Washington (1942–44) and as UN mediator in the 1950 Kashmir dispute between Pakistan and India. Dixon enjoyed close links with R.G. **Menzies**, his former pupil, but disliked H.V. **Evatt's** meddling style. There is a left-wing view that he was the legal servant of the Establishment, but he did not ultimately allow either his connections or professed anti-communism to influence his rejection of Menzies's attempt to outlaw the **Communist** Party in 1950–51. On the High Court, Dixon's 'strict and complete legalism' dominated proceedings and raised the court's international status. In *Sir Owen Dixon: A Celebration* (1986), Ninian Stephen noted Dixon's 'masterly' grasp of equity and common law, and his 'civilised rationality' and 'absolute independence of thought' in judgments revealing 'the voice of principle speaking out against … the sin of expediency'. Brian Galligan, *The Politics of the High Court* (1987), suggests that the Communist Party (1951) and Boilermakers (1956) cases illustrate Dixon's genius for distilling essential constitutional principles. Dixon once criticised a fellow judge for 'proceeding by steps of impeccable logic to a most unjust result'. His wit was invariably sharp, though sometimes cold or flippant. Excerpts from his public addresses were published in *Jesting Pilate* (1965).

DC

Dixon, Miriam (1930–), historian, was born in Melbourne. She studied history at the University of Melbourne and the Australian National University, and taught at the University of New England (NSW). In her early work on **labour history**, some of which she wrote as Miriam Rechter, she was aligned to the **Old Left** historians. Her major work, *The Real Matilda* (1976), examines the identity of white women in Australia using a Marxist–Freudian analysis. Dixson proposed that women's low position in Australian society, and their psychological oppression and victimisation, are the result of the social make-up of the Australian nation during its formative years. A predominance of convicts, working class, and poor Irish set a pattern for discriminatory attitudes towards women, which were more extreme among the lower, less-educated classes; the working-class Australian woman became, in Lenin's phrase, 'a slave among slaves'. In Dixson's view, this pattern continued to define male–female relations in Australia. Her other works include *Greater than Lenin? Lang and Labor 1916–1932* (1977). Dixson is a grand-niece of the economic historian Edward **Shann**.

HD

Dixson, William (1870–1952) was a collector of rare Australian books, manuscripts, and art, which he donated to the State Library of New South Wales. The Dixson Gallery opened in 1929 to house part of the collection; the library's Dixson Library, containing the entire collection, opened in 1959. The collection is described by Anne Robertson in *Treasures of the State Library of New South Wales* (1988). Dixson also established the William Dixson Foundation to fund the reproduction of rare works relating to Australia and the Pacific. The Dixson Library at the University of New England (NSW) commemorates his financial assistance during its establishment.

KT

DLP, see **Democratic Labor Party**

Dog on the tuckerbox is the name of a monument on the Hume Highway, north of Gundagai, NSW, which is a popular landmark and tourist attraction. The dog, cast in bronze by the local sculptor F. Rusconi, was erected in 1932 to commemorate the district's pioneer settlers. This site on the bank of the Five Mile Creek had been a favoured stopping place for bullocky teamsters and other travellers since the mid-nineteenth century. The sculpture was inspired by the story of a bullocky's dog that sat on the tuckerbox, a container used for storing food, and defecated in it. Although believed to be much older, the story was first published in verse form in the 1880s in the *Gundagai Times*: 'Then the dog shat on the tuckerbox / Five miles from Gundagai.' The folksong popularised by Jack Moses, 'Nine (Five) Miles from Gundagai', was a later, sanitised version.

The dog is in fact situated eight miles (13 kilometres) from Gundagai, rather than five miles, as claimed in the folksong's title—a discrepancy thought to have been caused by changes to the original road layout. The well-travelled path was the subject of several other poems and ballads, the best-known being Jack O'Hagan's popular song of 1922, 'The Road to Gundagai'.

HD

Dole bludger is an expressive pejorative term for a person who avoids employment in order to benefit from social security payments. First popularised in the 1970s, it is formed from two words of older provenance. The word *dole*, which originally meant a share or portion allotted by right, was applied to the issue of rations or ration vouchers during the **Depression** of the 1930s. A *bludger*, in English and Australia usage, is a pimp who lives off the earnings of prostitutes. The two words were combined during the mid-1970s, when the end of the **long boom** caused an increase in unemployment at the same time as the federal government led by Gough **Whitlam** had increased the provision of social security. It was popularised in the media with apocryphal stories of welfare abuse and used to justify the restriction of benefits. Its historical origins are discussed by Stuart

193

Domestic service

Macintyre in Jill Roe (ed.), *Unemployment: Are There Lessons from History?* (1985).

SM

Domestic service has usually meant the provision of household labour by paid employees rather than dependants, though in Australia a great many dependants, wives and daughters especially, have provided domestic service.

In the elaborate households of the hierarchical English society of the eighteenth and nineteenth centuries, an equally elaborate complement of domestic servants was needed to attend to the many indoor and outdoor requirements, ranging from butlers to pageboys, ladies' maids to tweenies (those who served between stairs), and including gardeners and dairymaids, stable hands and grooms. *A Girl at Government House. An English Girl's Reminiscences: 'Below Stairs' in Colonial Australia*, edited by Helen Vellacott (1982), describes service in big houses in Australia, but most households were smaller and simpler. More general servants than specialists were employed and most domestic service was women's work, though in 1891 in NSW out of 55 867 domestic servants listed in the Census, 17 659 were male and 38 208 female.

Before the development of the technology which delivered water through taps, provided heat and power through switches, and disposed of sewage through pipes, domestic work was physically demanding and often dirty. Much of it was unskilled, but indoors especially there was a real element of personal service. Servants lived as part of the household and were paid largely in kind (board and lodging); their health and morals were closely supervised. As Beverley Kingston demonstrates in *My Wife, My Daughter, and Poor Mary Ann* (1975), the domestic servant was an indispensable, but warily regarded, member of the respectable middle-class household. In the early days of settlement, convict women provided domestic service (which often involved a sexual component as well), though many householders were reluctant to have these women, whose morals and other habits they regarded as irredeemable, living in and especially taking care of children. The shortage of women in colonial society led to programs to bring immigrant women, especially poor women from Ireland, to the colonies. Irish servants were soon also deemed undesirable. Many were clearly ignorant of the niceties of living in a middle-class household, and their Catholicism was held against them.

Girls born in the colonies were the preferred servants, but they showed great reluctance to accept the deferential role in which the domestic servant was cast. Australian mistresses therefore were generally required to compromise on what they imagined to be superior English standards of domestic service. It became difficult to enforce rules about residence and dress, or the use of servant names like Jane or Mary Ann. Most Australian households kept only a general servant, or managed with the part-time help of women who came to wash, sew, or clean, or a girl who came to mind the baby; thus service in Australia was not a skilled occupation. Margaret Barbalet in *Far from a Low Gutter Girl*

(1983) gives a realistic account of the status of domestic work. Perhaps only the cook in a large household, or the governess, was considered a skilled servant and paid accordingly, though even these women were often affronted by requests to undertake general work beneath their dignity. It proved almost impossible, under the onerous provisions of the Masters and Servants Act, for domestic servants to demand minimum standards of pay or conditions, but because the demand for servants was usually greater than the supply, it was not unusual for a 'girl' to leave her job without notice, or for a mistress to make significant concessions to keep her.

By the mid-twentieth century, domestic service had largely disappeared from Australia under the assaults of the Depression, war, alternative employment opportunities for women, and improved technology, which allowed every housewife to be her own servant. Some of those servants who remained were Aboriginal girls brought from reserves or missions. Even though the work might no longer be so hard and the employer might be kindly, it was a lonely and depressing life for these women with no future beyond dependence. Glenyse Ward has written a vivid account of the real hazards in *Wandering Girl* (1987). Immigration after World War II provided a new source of domestic service: women with poor English or no access to better-paid work took on temporary or casual domestic work until they could manage something better.

Though the Australian sense of **egalitarianism** is not sympathetic to the idea of domestic service, people who will clean, look after the laundry, and mind children on a permanent or casual basis have always been needed, and as women's participation in the paid workforce has grown, so has the growth of home help. While the modern trend is for much of this work to be organised by an employment agency, or carried out by contract cleaning companies, the casual market thrives—though on what scale it is not easy to say since much of it is, as it has ever been, beyond the sight of the tax system or the census form.

BEVERLEY KINGSTON

Domino theory was a metaphor used in the 1950s and 1960s to explain the strategic importance of Indochina—the theory being that if Indochina fell to **communism**, other South-East Asian countries would progressively fall, like a row of dominoes, until the communist threat reached Australia and NZ. The 'domino principle' was popularised by US President Dwight D. Eisenhower at a Washington press conference on 7 April 1954. In *The Last Domino* (1976), Malcolm Booker showed that the essential concept was much older and had been expressed in relation to South-East Asia in 1950–51 by Australian external affairs ministers Percy **Spender** and R.G. **Casey**. The domino theory proved false when there was no sequential collapse after the 'first domino', South Vietnam, was defeated by North Vietnam in 1975: while Cambodia and Laos came under communist rule, the other countries of the region remained secure. Its significance lies in the way it captured public imagination for more than two decades and influenced Australian and US foreign policy in such areas as **ANZUS**, the **Colombo Plan**, **SEATO**, and the **Vietnam War**.

DC

Don, Charles Jardine (1828–66) was by the late 1850s a leader of the Victorian trade union movement and of the **Eight Hour Day** League and MLA for the working-class seat of Collingwood, Victoria. He was a Scottish stonemason who learned public speaking and was introduced to radical thought at a mutual improvement society. He participated in the Chartist agitation in Britain during the 1840s and became a prominent street orator. Don emigrated in 1853 and, leaving his family in Melbourne, went to the goldfield at Ballarat. On his return to Melbourne, he began a long involvement with the union movement through his work in the Stonemasons Union. Don vigorously urged the cause of the working class in the assembly, but was hampered by the need to earn a living—at one time he worked as a mason on the construction of Parliament House while serving as a member. His health suffered; he began to drink heavily, and lost his seat in 1864. A biography by Des Shiel appeared in 1996.

KT

Donkey vote refers to a phenomenon whereby the candidate in a ballot **election** whose name is first on the ballot paper wins extra votes as a result. Australian voters are legally compelled to vote, and a relatively consistent proportion, around 10 per cent, indicate their preferences in the exact order in which they appear on the ballot paper. To prevent unfair advantage to those whose names are towards the beginning of the alphabet, the order of names on Australian ballot papers was changed in 1984 from an alphabetical to a random order.

HD

Donohue, John 'Bold Jack' (?1806–30) was a **bushranger** who attracted sympathy from convicts and poor **emancipists** because of his defiance of authority. It has been argued that he is the basis for Jack Doolan in the folksong *The Wild Colonial Boy*. Certainly he was sung about—the bush song *Bold Jack Donohue* was banned from public houses as treason. John Meredith's *The Wild Colonial Boy: Bushranger Jack Donahoe 1806–1830* (1982), includes the texts of the banned ballads. Donohue (whose name appears variously as Donahue, Donoghue, Donahoo), was born in Ireland and arrived as a convict in NSW in 1825; by late 1827 he had become a bushranger. Captured, he escaped and formed a gang whose hold-up victims included Samuel **Marsden**. Donohue became the most celebrated bushranger in Australia and his fatal shooting by troopers reinforced his romantic image. He is the subject of Charles **Harpur's** play, *The Bushrangers* (1853), and John Manifold's poem, 'The Afterlife of Bold Jack Donahue'.

KT

Double dissolution is the dissolving of both houses of the federal parliament, the House of Representatives and the Senate. The election which follows completely reconstitutes the parliament. As originally conceived in the 1891 draft **constitution**, the Senate was to have a permanent existence with a proportion of its members retiring at fixed intervals, and hence never subject to dissolution as a whole. This was criticised by representatives of the large states and democrats; they did not want an overmighty second chamber and they insisted that there must be a mechanism for resolving deadlocks between the two houses. In Victoria deadlocks had twice created **constitutional crises**. To meet these objections, the Constitution as adopted provided that, if the Senate twice rejected a bill from the House of Representatives, it could be dissolved, along with the Representatives, for the verdict of the people to be taken. If after the election, the same measure was submitted by the Representatives to the Senate and again rejected, a joint sitting of both houses was to settle the matter by majority voting. There were double dissolutions in 1914, 1951, 1974, 1975, 1983, and 1987, with only one joint sitting following the 1974 election. There has been some controversy over whether a governor-general has any discretion when a prime minister requests a double dissolution. It has now been settled that if the technical requirements of the Constitution have been met, a governor-general must accept the advice to dissolve both houses. (See also **Dismissal**.)

JH

Douglas credit was a movement in the period between the two world wars, based on the ideas of Major C.H. Douglas, an English engineer who proposed a radical solution to the **Depression**. Against the deflationary economic orthodoxy that guided the policies of governments at that time, he argued that the liabilities of a national economy could be offset by the value of its assets. It would thus be possible for a national credit agency to fund public services and to distribute a 'national dividend' to all citizens. With their emphasis on a rational solution that would transform scarcity into abundance without disturbing private ownership, these proposals appealed to professional and small business owners, and when Douglas toured Australia in 1934 there were nearly 200 branches of the Douglas Social Credit movement. Douglas credit also confirmed some members of the labour movement in their suspicion of **banks**, and reinforced the populist antagonism to the 'Money Power'. However, the decision of the Douglas credit movement to contest the 1934 elections caused the Labor Party to dissociate itself (see Baiba Berzins in *LH*, 1970), and the movement fell away as the Depression lifted. Its impact in Australia was less than in Canada and NZ, where it established a substantial agrarian following.

SM

Drama has had, for reasons understandable in any post-colonial society, a particular concern with cultural self-definition. In the quest for images that might embody the distinctiveness of the emerging nation from its imperial parent, the dramatic representation of its history has, however, been a relatively minor matter. Playwrights have mostly looked to contemporary subjects; certainly their preoccupation with the complexities of the local vernacular as the principal marker of cultural difference has required an immediacy of recognition from the audience that largely precludes engagement with history. Nostalgia has largely been left to the cinema, while genuine reassessment has been scarcely a theatrical subject at all.

The principal exception comes in those plays which have located their fictional plots within the recognisably recent past. Naturalism, in reflecting a society apparently directly to itself, encourages that kind of placement almost as much as it does the representation of the here-and-now. Some of the major landmarks of social realism—like Sumner Locke Elliott's study of wartime disaffection, *Rusty Bugles* (1948), and even Ray **Lawler's** *Summer of the Seventeenth Doll* (1955), which depicts a Carlton without any trace of cultural diversity—fall into this category. Earlier treatments of the bush and outback myth, such as those staged in Melbourne by the determinedly nationalistic Pioneer Players (1922–26), seem concerned with catching a moment already passed; the Pioneers' founder, Louis **Esson**, in plays like *Dead Timber* (1911), *The Drovers* (1923), and *Mother and Son* (1923), reflects that impulse to commemoration.

There have been other exceptions, most consistently the theatrical celebration of particular events and personalities which have surfaced on those recurrent waves of nationalism. The tribulations of early settlement have been mostly ignored, and the English playwright Timberlake Wertenbaker in *Our Country's Good* (1988) has provided the most distinguished treatment of convict culture. A number of plays have dramatised **Bligh** of the *Bounty*—Doris Egerton Jones, *Governor Bligh* (1930); Brian Medlin, *Governor Bligh* (1955); George Farwell, *The House that Jack Built* (1950); and Lawler, *The Man Who Shot the Albatross* (1971)—and Alexander Buzo in *Macquarie* (1971) portrayed another of **Macarthur's** adversaries. The attempt in these plays-about-governors has been to invest the history with the vigour of large personalities and their hypothetical motives, and it has proved largely unsuccessful.

The reprobates and colourful characters adjacent to the political story have proved a richer resource, and attracted more attention from the larrikin alternative to New Wave playwrights of the early 1970s than from their mostly more prestigious forebears. In Michael Boddy and Bob Ellis, *The Legend of King O'Malley* (1970), and Barry Oakley, *The Feet of Daniel Mannix* (1971), and in later studies of more marginal eccentrics like Alma de Groen, *Chidley* (1976), and Barry Dickens, *Remember Ronald Ryan* (1993), the lives of those who did not need to be treated with respect were inflated to mythic dimensions. Jack Hibberd, conducting an explicit quest to create a 'popular theatre' at Melbourne's Pram Factory, offered celebratory stage cartoons of more obviously legendary figures in *The Les Darcy Show* (1974) and *A Toast to Melba* (1976); in *Marvellous Melbourne* (1970,

with John Romeril) he dramatised a whole cityful of rogues and heroes. History in these plays was a playground, for lively invention, political polemic and nationalist self-assertion; fidelity to the facts, or sustained analysis of them, was at best a low priority.

Among the great events, the **Eureka** story has been the major source of fascination, and frustration, for Australian playwrights. Edward Duggan, *The Democrat* (1897, retitled *The Southern Cross*, 1907); E.W. O'Sullivan, *The Eureka Rebellion* (1907); E. Coulson-Davidson, *The Forerunners* (1930); Esson, *The Southern Cross* (1927); Leslie Haylen, *Blood on the Wattle* (1948); and Kenneth Cook, *Stockade* (1971)—all have struggled to stage 'our own little rebellion'. A number of things make Eureka a tough subject: the volume and complexity of 'the documents'; the distracting flamboyance of some key players (such as **Carboni**), and the impenetrable public selves of others (such as **Lalor**); and the difficulty of representing large spectacles within the cosy frame of the proscenium arch. The major problem, perhaps, has been that of finding a dramatic focus for conflicts rooted in oppositions of class, and in the experiences and imaginations of 'the people'. The same difficulty, finally, has vitiated attempts to dramatise the story of the **Kelly** gang (Douglas **Stewart's** 1942 verse play, *Ned Kelly*, is an impressive piece, but the form underlines its remoteness from the flesh-and-bones of popular myth), and has consigned the Anzac Legend to the cinema, which seems more hospitable to anonymous heroes and private sacrifices.

The musical theatre, where the chorus can be made articulate, has provided an important stage for history as it happens to ordinary people. In the left-wing New Theatre movement, musical plays like Dick Diamond's *Reedy River* (1953) gave those people a voice; in the same tradition, Nick Enright's *On the Wallaby* (1980) offered the most convincing and moving dramatisation of **Depression** experience. *Manning Clark's History of Australia—The Musical* (1988), by Don Watson and Tim Robertson in collaboration with John Romeril, was the logical culmination of this process. It played fast and loose with its vast canvas, but as well as its critique and celebration of the forces that have made the nation, it reflected and argued the importance of the 'unrecorded, unregarded extras in the scene'. More recent musicals have celebrated Australian performers such as Peter Allen (*The Boy From Oz*, 1995) and Johnny O'Keefe (*Shout*, 1985), contesting American pop culture.

History—The Musical was unusual in its concern not only to generate myth but also to assess, through the focus on **Clark** as story-teller, the processes by which myths are constructed. The only substantial involvement in that kind of self-conscious historicising emerged in plays by Aboriginal writers. Especially in Jack **Davis's** works—*Kullark* (1979), *The Dreamers* (1982), *No Sugar* (1985), and *Barungin* (1988)—the interaction of black and white Australians has been represented in a form (part-documentary, part-fictional) that aims to understand the past humanely in order to seek a more generous present. Davis's investment in the politics of his story does not preclude a sense of its historiographical complexity.

Later Indigenous playwrights have paid particular attention to the **Stolen Generations**; both John Harding (*Up the Road*, 1997) and Jane Harrison (*Stolen*, 1998, 2000) are noteworthy. (See also **Pageants**.)

PETER FITZPATRICK

Dreamtime refers to the spiritual dimension of Aboriginal existence, linking the present to the time of world creation. The concept is complex because it refers to the existence of spiritual forces in the here-and-now as well as to a time when ancestral beings emerged from beneath the surface of the earth and formed the landscape. In the time of creation the ancestors emerged from the ground, creating features such as waterholes; where they walked, they created pathways or river beds; where they plunged digging sticks into the ground, trees grew; where they died, their bodies were transformed into hills; and where they bled, lakes were formed. Their every action had a consequence in the form of the landscape, which in turn became a mnemonic for their lives and an expression of their spiritual essence. While creating the landscape, ancestral beings left behind in certain places the human beings who were to succeed them in occupying the surface of the earth. They introduced language by naming the plants and animals associated with particular places. They also instituted the ceremonial and social practices that people were to follow. After this initial period of creation, the ancestral beings generally removed themselves from the surface of the earth. They continued, however, to be integral to human existence and to intervene in the world through spirit conception and ceremonial performance.

The ancestral beings also left behind representations— songs, dances, paintings, and sacred objects—that provided evidence of their creative acts. These evidences from the ancestral past form the substance of ceremonial performance, in which their powers are summoned up to serve human ends, or to renew the fertility and productivity of the land. The ceremonies and the sacred knowledge associated with them are often referred to by Aboriginal people as their 'law'. People use the songs and paintings to recreate the Dreamtime, and to summon up the ancestral powers for many different purposes: in order to guide the soul of a dead person to its spirit home, to introduce new generations to knowledge of the powers of the ancestral beings, or to renew the spiritual strength and identity of someone recovering from injury.

The Dreamtime is important in Aboriginal politics. The ancestral beings provide the authority for people's association with place, and ancestral law can be used to establish rights to particular areas of land. The ownership of ancestral law is closely monitored, and people can only reproduce songs, paintings, dances, and so on if they have the right to do so. This present political relevance of the Dreamtime helps to blur the distinction between past and present.

In most **Aboriginal languages** there are words that refer to this Dreamtime dimension of existence: for instance, *wangarr* in the language of the Yolngu people from Eastern Arnhem Land and *djugurrba* for the Warlbiri people from the

Central Desert. The word *Dreamtime* probably arose as a translation of the Aranda word *altyerrenge*. The first published use of the word (or a close equivalent) was in Baldwin **Spencer's** introductory volume to the reports of the Horn expedition to Central Australia (1896). In analysing his and Gillen's use of the term, Spencer (*The Arunta*, 1927) argues that Alcheringa (*altyerrenge*) comprises the word for Dream (*Altjera*) and the suffix *-inga*, signifying possession or belonging to. A literal translation might have been 'belonging to dreams' or 'of the dreams'; but, in order to differentiate the concept from everyday dreams and to signify the connection to the ancestral past, he and Gillen coined the phrase 'Dream Times'. Subsequent linguistic research has confirmed the reasonableness of their translation, and indeed it may be that the term had an independent existence in contemporary discourse between Aborigines and Europeans.

Although the translation 'Dreamtime' seems appropriate for many Central Australian societies, elsewhere it applies less well. For this reason and because the connotation of past time fails to convey the sense of the Aboriginal concept, some anthropologists have been reluctant to use the term and have used a term from an Aboriginal language instead. W.E.H. **Stanner**, who has written with great insight on the metaphysical and phenomenological aspects of the concept, preferred to use the word 'Dreaming', partly on the grounds that Aboriginal people themselves often use the word and partly because it contains no reference to time (see Stanner, *White Man Got No Dreaming*, 1979). However 'Dreamtime' has become a word of common currency in the European popular imagination and it has proved difficult to combat its spread. It quickly crossed over into imaginings of the European past as well as Aboriginal antiquity. For example, as early as 1954 Vance **Palmer** had characterised the 1890s as 'the dream-time' of Australian nationalism, while in 1983 Josephine Flood entitled her 1983 prehistory of Australia *The Archaeology of the Dreamtime*. It has become common currency both because it is salient to European conceptions of otherness and because it represents, however imprecisely, an important component of Aboriginal worldviews. Thus while some analysts, such as Patrick Wolfe (*Comparative Studies in Society and History*, 1991), have seen the use of the word 'Dreamtime' as an imposition of European concepts on Aboriginal cosmologies, others such as Howard Morphy, in Tim Bonyhady and Tom Griffiths (eds), *Prehistory to Politics* (1996), have seen it a means of allowing an Aboriginal viewpoint to enter cross-cultural discourse over land, religion, and nature in Australia.

HOWARD MORPHY

Droughts are severe shortages of water—although what is considered a drought may depend as much on socially determined levels of demand as ecologically determined supply.

Australia is the driest of all the inhabited continents; its climates vary markedly over time and space, and at any given moment large parts of the country may be short of water. Since 1788 the importation of ecologically maladapted European enterprises and modes of settlement has accentuated the occurrence of drought; while subsequent changes in the demands for rural and urban water have helped or hindered the problem, it has never gone away. The Australian experience of drought has been impressively documented in art, literature, and song, but it has yet to receive its due from history, partly because of the historians' stubborn reluctance to consult the relevant scientific and technical sources.

The most important contributions to the history of drought have been made by meteorologists, climatologists, economic historians, historical geographers, and interdisciplinary environmental historians. The first two groups have provided other workers with the essential temporal and spatial framework, as well as accessible explanations of the environmental dynamics: examples include J.C. Foley, *Droughts in Australia* (1957), and W.J. Gibbs and J.V. Maher, *Rainfall Deciles as Drought Indicators* (1967). They show that major drought episodes have clustered in the mid-1860s, 1877, 1888, 1895–1903, 1911–16, 1918–20, and variously over the periods 1926–30, 1934–44, 1944–54, 1958–68, and 1972–81; the early 1980s and 1990s were also scarred by punishing droughts over large parts of the country. Some economic historians plotted the reverberating impacts of drought on regional and national development, and each state held inquiries into the economic significance of climatic variability in general and of drought in particular. Pioneering contextual statements include S.M. Wadham and G.L. Wood, *Land Utilization in Australia* (1939 and modern revisions), and Edgars Dunsdorfs, *The Australian Wheat-Growing Industry* (1956).

During the first three decades of the twentieth century, the geographer Griffith **Taylor** argued that drought was the most stringent of the 'environmental limits' to further expansion in Australia. He was howled down and drummed out, but his successors have generally followed his line. Though it contained no original environmental insights, Keith **Hancock's** vigorous *Australia* (1930) took a similar view, and after World War II most mainstream historical accounts of settlement expansion and regional change considered the periodical impacts of drought, yet seldom progressed from description to analysis. Contemporary progress in **historical geography** went somewhat further: examples include D.W. Meinig, *On the Margins of the Good Earth* (1962); T.M. Perry, *Australia's First Frontier* (1963); R.L. Heathcote, *Back of Bourke* (1965); J.M. Powell, *The Public Lands of Australia Felix* (1970); D.N. Jeans, *An Historical Geography of New South Wales to 1901* (1972). Drought featured prominently in each of these contributions; together, they explored its ramifying impacts on land administration and settlement policy, ecological change, regional and local economies, and aspects of Australian science and technology. In the 1970s and 1980s Heathcote successfully fused a long series of Australian investigations with burgeoning international programs in 'environmental hazards' research: the bulk of this work appeared in academic journals, but some was reformulated in *The Arid Lands: Their Use and Abuse* (1983) and *Australia* (2nd edn 1994).

Australian forays into **environmental history** draw on American terminology while consolidating the foundational work of historical geographers, but the latter may still provide the best context for specialised drought narratives. Two volumes by J.M. Powell illustrate the point: *Environmental Management in Australia* (1976) and *An Historical Geography of Modern Australia* (1988, 1991); so does Michael Williams, *The Making of the South Australian Landscape* (1974). The inclusion of useful interdisciplinary essays on this theme in a collection edited by Stephen Dovers, *Australian Environmental History* (1994), is indicative of the fast-expanding historical interests of ecologists and other scientists. Jenny Keating's *The Drought Walked Through. A History of Water Shortage in Victoria* (1992) shows one way of constructing social histories of drought through assiduous consultation of newspaper files. (The several related 'water histories' cited in **floods** contain further essential contextual material.) Otherwise the field as a whole remains relatively open to enterprising historical researchers. (See also **Disasters**; **Water resources**.)

J.M. POWELL

Droving, or overlanding, involved driving mobs of cattle or sheep long distances to fresh pastures or to market saleyards. The opening up of new grazing land in the late 1830s brought drovers and overlanders from NSW to Port Phillip and SA; pastures across northern Australia were opened up in the later nineteenth century, when the massive operations of the **Duracks** and Sidney **Kidman** became legendary. Invariably a man's job, droving demanded long hours in the saddle and periods of isolation, and frequent absences from wives and children. However, in Russel **Ward's** analysis, the carefree, wandering life enjoyed by drovers and stockmen, and the rough existence they endured in the bush, engendered a particular camaraderie and **mateship** which helped forge the Australian (male) character. This romantic image is generally reinforced by innumerable folksongs, ballads, and poems—epitomised by A.B. **Paterson's** 'Clancy of the Overflow'—and by the Stockman's Hall of Fame at Longreach, Qld. By contrast, the deprivation which faced drovers and their families is summed up by Tommy, in Henry **Lawson's** story 'The Drover's Wife' (1892): 'Mother, I won't never go drovin'; blast me if I do.' Aborigines who worked as drovers and stockmen on cattle stations were largely ignored until the appearance of works such as Ann McGrath's *Born in the Cattle* (1987). (See also **Overlander**.)

HD

Drysdale, Anne (1792–1853) and **Newcomb, Caroline Elizabeth** (1812–74), squatters, are brought to life in Anne Drysdale's diary, held at the State Library of Victoria. Having farmed in her own right in Fife, Scotland, Drysdale successfully applied for a pastoral lease on her arrival at Port Phillip in 1840. The following year she settled at Boronggoop, near Geelong, with Caroline Newcomb, a former governess to John **Batman's** children, who became Drysdale's lifelong companion. Drysdale and Newcomb acquired a lease on the Bellarine Peninsula in 1843, near present-day Drysdale (named later after Anne), and secured freehold title in 1848. Drysdale's diary begins with her arrival at Port Phillip in 1840, and records her life with Newcomb at

Boronggoop and later at Coryule. It provides a rich account of station management and domestic and social activities, including rare detail of house furnishings and floor plans, and documents the uncommon case of women as successful pastoralists. Drysdale and Newcomb are the subject of John Richardson's *The Lady Squatters* (1986).

HD

Duels, a means for gentlemen to settle disputes or protect their honour, were fought in the Australian colonies until the mid-nineteenth century. John **Macarthur** was an incorrigible duellist. He was party to a duel at Plymouth in 1789, just before his departure for NSW, and the following year fought another in Sydney with Captain Nepean—the first recorded duel in Australia. In 1801 he wounded Captain William Paterson, commanding officer of the NSW Corps and Macarthur's superior, in a duel resulting from Paterson's refusal to support Macarthur's disloyalty to Governor **King**. Macarthur was subsequently arrested and despatched to England for court martial. Other notable duels included that of Robert Wardell and NSW Attorney-General Saxe Bannister in 1826. Major Thomas **Mitchell** and Stuart Donaldson fought one of the last recorded duels in 1851. Garryowen found duels were regular occurrences in early Melbourne, where participants—like Redmond **Barry** and Peter Snodgrass, who faced one another in 1840—usually belonged to gentlemen's **clubs**. Edward **Curr's** refusal to fight a duel with J.C. Riddell in 1845 divided opinion in the Melbourne press. A list of Melbourne duels was compiled by Paul de Serville for his *Port Phillip Gentlemen* (1980). Duels in the colonies were mostly regarded as a mockery of the real thing, and frequently ended in a farce. The only blood spilt in a duel at Port Phillip was reputedly the result of one of the principals accidentally shooting his own toe.

HD

Duffy, Charles Gavan (1816–1903), journalist and Victorian premier, was born in County Monaghan, Ireland. A leading figure in the nationalistic Young Ireland movement, Duffy edited the radical Dublin paper, the *Nation*, for which he was tried for sedition and later released. He subsequently served in the House of Commons (1852–55). Shortly after arriving in Melbourne, Duffy won office in the 1856 Victorian election, at which he was returned by a predominantly Irish farming constituency in south-west Victoria, and immediately abolished the lower house property qualification. His measures for land reform won him popularity with Irish immigrants. However, his 1862 legislation, dubbed Duffy's Land Act, which was an attempt to enable small landholders to secure **selections**, became notorious for failing to prevent the **squattocracy** from retaining their large pastoral holdings. Duffy was premier 1871–72 and an early advocate of Federation. Although maintaining an Irish nationalist tone in several publications, including *Why Is Ireland Poor and Discontented?* (1870), Duffy's concerns in Australia became increasingly conservative and in 1880 he returned to Europe. In his reminiscences, *My Life in Two*

Hemispheres (2 vols, 1898), he wrote triumphantly, like J.F. Hogan, of Irish achievement in colonial Australia. Cyril **Pearl** published a biography in 1979. His son FRANK GAVAN DUFFY (1852–1936) became chief justice of the High Court.

HD

Dugdale, Henrietta Augusta (1826–1918), outspoken feminist and free thinker, considered that female suffrage was the means whereby women would achieve emancipation. English-born, she came to Australia with her husband in 1852. She was president of the Victorian Women's Suffrage Society, formed in 1884, and a member of the Eclectic Society and the Australasian Secular Association. She expounded her utopian belief in a future based on sexual and class equality in *A Few Hours in a Far-Off Age* (1883), dedicated admiringly to George **Higinbotham**. Although thrice married, Dugdale was very critical of the 'most powerful of our world's monsters—the only devil—*male ignorance*'. The monarchy and Christianity also received her condemnation. As an advocate of female dress reform, a place for women in politics, birth-control, and 'applying the surgeon's knife to rapists', Dugdale aroused controversy and opposition.

KT

Duhig, James (1871–1965) was Catholic archbishop of Brisbane. Born in Ireland, he emigrated in 1885 and studied for the priesthood. Following his ordination in Rome in 1896, he worked as a curate at Ipswich, Qld. He was appointed the world's youngest bishop in 1905 and made archbishop of Brisbane in 1917. Like Daniel **Mannix** in Melbourne, Duhig was committed to large-scale building programs, and erected numerous churches, parish schools, and colleges. In contrast to Mannix, however, Duhig supported **conscription** during World War I. His geniality made him a popular leader, and he enjoyed good relations with Queensland political leaders. His long reign ended with his death in 1965. Duhig published an autobiography, *Crowded Years*, in 1947 and T.P. Boland produced a biography in 1986.

HD

Dummying was a dishonest means of securing title to land that was employed by **squatters** and selectors following the **Selection** Acts of the 1860s. By setting up false buyers or 'dummies'—usually relatives, employees, or business associates—to select land on their behalf, squatters ensured that they acquired the choicest land, especially on river frontages or lakes, and maintained their large holdings. They placed dummy huts, or flying huts as they were sometimes known, at strategic points around a property to give the appearance of activity and settlement, and so to evade the regulations of compulsory residency and improvements on selections. Selectors also used dummying as a means of overcoming limitations on the size of selection blocks.

HD

Duncan, Annie Jane (1858–1943) led a sheltered middle-class life in SA until the need to earn money during a trip to London in 1893 led her to undertake training from which she emerged qualified to be an 'inspector of public nuisances'. After working in London, she returned to Australia and was appointed a factory inspector in NSW, rising to senior inspector in 1912. She spoke and wrote graphically about the terrible conditions for many women workers in factories. Duncan came to believe that her conservatism, which made her unsympathetic to Labor industrial policies, disadvantaged her, and retired in 1918.

KT

Dunera was the name of the ship that sailed from Britain to Australia in 1940 carrying many Germans and Austrians, mainly Jewish, who were deported as enemy **aliens**. As a war precautions measure, the passengers were interned in concentration camps at Tatura, Victoria, and Hay, NSW. They included many young men of talent who made their mark in Australian intellectual and artistic life after the war. As Cyril **Pearl** has pointed out in *The Dunera Scandal* (1983), their internment was a gross injustice as the men had no political connections to German fascism. A television series on the *Dundera Boys* was screnned in 1985, and Paul Bartrop and Gabrielle Eisen edited a collection of writings on the subject.

HD

Dunkley, Louisa Margaret (1866–1927) was so incensed by her own experience of discrimination that she began a campaign to redress the unequal pay and conditions for women in the Victorian Post and Telegraph Department. Her success in achieving improvements (though still not **equal pay**) generated a deal of harassment of Dunkley and her fellow activists by department administrators. This was taken up by the press and sparked a parliamentary inquiry. In the drive for complete equality, Dunkley was one of the founding members of the Victorian Women's Post and Telegraph Association, which conducted a federal campaign and achieved its goal in 1902.

KT

Dunlop, Ernest Edward 'Weary' (1907–93), surgeon, achieved fame and heroic stature as an army medical officer among Australian **prisoners-of-war** on the Burma–Siam railway. He grew up in the Victorian northeast and studied medicine at the University of Melbourne, where his feats as rugby player and heavyweight boxer earned him the nickname 'Weary', a playful allusion to the Dunlop tyre which, according to its makers, 'never wears out'. After service in the Middle East and Greece he was posted to Java, where he was among Australian troops captured by the Japanese in 1943 and subjected to forced labour on the Burma–Siam railway. He showed extraordinary ingenuity and endurance in relieving the sufferings brought about by cholera, malaria, typhoid, tropical ulcers, and malnutrition. He stood up to the brutality of his captors, putting his own life at risk in defence of his men. Throughout this ordeal he maintained a personal diary which records, in language of Spartan simplicity, the daily struggle against disease, cruelty, hopelessness, and death. The legend

of Weary Dunlop, the 'Christ of the Burma Road', developed first among his own POW comrades, and gathered strength after the war when he served as a surgeon in South Vietnam and fostered reconciliation with his Japanese captors. He became a truly national **hero** only after publication of his war diaries in 1986 and the publication of an admiring biography by Sue Ebury in 1994, shortly after his death. Statues erected by public subscription in Melbourne and Canberra depict a tall, stooping figure in a business suit, and bear the tribute of one of his POW comrades: 'A lighthouse of sanity in a universe of madness and suffering'. Margaret Geddes has edited a collection of reminiscences, *Remembering Weary* (1996).

GD

Dunstan, Albert Arthur (1882–1950), Victorian premier 1935–45 (apart from a five-day break), was an influential figure in the formation of the Country Party (later **National Party**). Born to a farming family in north-central Victoria, Dunstan joined the Victorian Farmers Union, which later supported his successful 1920 bid for the seat of Eaglehawk. He was part of the group that formed the Country Progressive Party, which eventually metamorphosed into the United Country Party, of which he became deputy leader. In 1935, with the support of Labor, Dunstan became premier. A pragmatic politician with well-honed survival skills, he opposed all moves for electoral redistribution and ensured that Country Party constituencies were 'looked after', as evidenced by his 1936 'Recovery Budget'. Yet he maintained Labor support with adroit concessions and held the middle ground between business and the unions.

KT

Dunstan, Donald Allan (1926–) served two terms— 1967–68 and 1970–79—as Labor premier of SA at a time when the state was in the vanguard of social and political reform. As a lawyer from a comfortable background, he was initially regarded with some reservations by the industrial wing of the **Australian Labor Party**, but soon became a force in the party. Reforms by his government were frequently controversial, including the decriminalisation of **homosexuality**, commitment to Aboriginal rights, abolition of **capital punishment**, and affirmation of the right to demonstrate. Richard Yeeles examines his reforms in *Don Dunstan: The First 25 Years in Parliament* (1978). Dunstan's flouting of convention extended to his wardrobe: pink shorts in parliament were a symbol of his commitment to change. Many credit his success with paving the way for later Labor governments, both federal and state. Ill-health, exacerbated by the death of his second wife, Adele Koh, prompted his retirement from politics in 1979. He gives an account of his political life, outlining what he regarded as its successes and failures, in *Felicia* (1981).

KT

Durack family were among the earliest European **pastoralists** in the Kimberley area of WA. With their vast land holdings and wealth, and their involvement in politics, social welfare, and the arts, they were the model of an Australian family dynasty.

Two brothers from Ireland arrived in Australia with their families in the mid-1850s. After a stint in Qld, many of the family, led by PATRICK 'PATSY' DURACK (1834–98), overlanded to the Ord River region, where they established a string of properties including Argyle in the Kimberley. His son, MICHAEL PATRICK (1865–1950), who was MLA for Kimberley 1918–24, argued for a separate administration for the north-west. Patsy's grand-daughter, MARY (1913–94), chronicled this saga in *Kings in Grass Castles* (1959) and *Sons in the Saddle* (1983). Together with her sister ELIZABETH (1915–2000), who provided the illustrations, Mary produced many books for children, including *Chunuma* (1936) and *To Ride a Fine Horse* (1963). Working alone, she wrote children's books which dealt with the Aboriginal experience—*The Courteous Savage:Yagan of Swan River* (1964), *Tjakamarra, Boy Between Two Worlds* (1977)—and historical works which included *The Rock and the Sand* (1969); *To Be Heirs Forever* (1976); and *The Aborigines in Australian Literature* (1978). Her first novel, *Keep Him My Country* (1955), told of the way in which a white station-owner's relationship with an Aboriginal woman brought him a spiritual understanding of the land.

Elizabeth's admission in 1997 that she had created the persona of Aboriginal painter Eddie Burrup, and exhibited 'his' paintings with explanatory statements in Pidgin, added to the controversy over ownership of **Aboriginal art**.

KT

Dutton, Geoffrey Piers Henry (1922–) is a versatile and prolific man of letters whose output includes several notable historical works. He was born at Anlaby, SA, the property established by his pastoralist forebears in 1839, and educated in the manner traditional among landed Australian families at Geelong Grammar School and Adelaide and Oxford universities. After wartime service in the RAAF (the subject of his novel *Flying Low*, 1992) he became a publisher and editor, helping to found *Australian Book Review*, Sun Books, and the *Bulletin Literary Supplement*. As well as several books of poetry, Dutton wrote *Founder of a City* (1960), a biography of William **Light**, the surveyor of Adelaide; and *The Hero as Murderer* (1967), a life of the explorer and notorious governor of Jamaica, Edward John **Eyre**. Each is a study of Empire, in which the life of an Australian hero is placed within a wider frame. 'The settlers of [a] new country', he writes, 'have two lives; the one at home which was unexciting if not unsuccessful; the one abroad which may casually call forth genius.' His *White on Black* (1974) is a pioneering study of the Australian Aborigine in art. A rebel son of the Adelaide Establishment—he was thrown out of the Adelaide Club for his professed **republicanism**—Dutton nevertheless saw himself as sharing with his contemporaries Manning **Clark**, Patrick **White**, and Arthur **Boyd** in an 'aristocratic' tradition of Australian letters. His autobiography, *Out in the Open* (1994), is a candid confession of artistic compromises and personal betrayals.

GD

Dwyer, Catherine Winifred 'Kate' (1861–1949) developed an appreciation of the problems faced by working-class people during her stay in Broken Hill (1891–93), where her husband was a headmaster. After their return to Sydney she joined the Womanhood Suffrage League and helped found the Women's Progressive Association. Her work for women's rights took her into the Labor sphere and in 1905 she was elected to the NSW executive of the **Australian Labor Party**. She helped form the Women Workers Union, intended to prevent **sweating** of domestic and outworkers, and contributed substantially to a royal commission into living conditions in Sydney (1909), and another on labour conditions for female and juvenile workers (1911). Dwyer campaigned for the 'no' vote in the two **conscription** referendums. She was nominated to stand for a Senate election due in 1916 but demurred, and in 1925 was defeated in her attempt to win the seat of Balmain. She remained a member of the ALP all her life and held a number of honorary positions. In 1921 she became one of the first female justices of the peace in NSW.

KT

Dyason, Edward Clarence Evelyn (1886–1949) was a businessman of remarkably diverse interests. His father's mining career in Bendigo provided a basis for his own practice as a mining engineer until he set up a stockbroking company in 1921; he also held interests in a range of manufacturing companies, including Pelaco and Kraft Foods. Dyason was a founding member of the Economic Society of Australia and New Zealand, a member of the national inquiry into the Australian **tariff** in 1929, and an adviser to the federal Labor treasurer, E.G. **Theodore**, in his attempts to liberalise credit in 1931. A pacifist and internationalist, Dyason travelled widely and helped establish the **Australian Institute of International Affairs**. The historian Ernest **Scott** was his brother-in-law and a colleague in many of his public interests; his daughter DIANA 'DING' DYASON (1919–89) pioneered the history and philosophy of science as an academic activity in Australia.

SM

Dyson, Edward George 'Ted' (1865–1931), writer, and **William Henry 'Will'** (1880–1938), political cartoonist, were prominent among the radical nationalists who gathered around the *Bulletin* newspaper from the 1890s. Like their friends the **Lindsays**, they had grown up on the Victorian goldfields and later moved to Melbourne; their radicalism—aesthetic as well as political—was shaped positively by local traditions of self-help, and negatively in reaction against the moral strictures of Methodism. Ted's short stories and poems, which began to appear in the *Bulletin* from the late 1880s, draw on childhood memories, humorous and sometimes melancholy, of life in declining gold towns; they offer a distinctively Victorian variation on the themes more famously developed by **Lawson** and **Paterson**. A gritty professional, he was probably among the first Australian freelance writers to earn a good living from his pen. His younger brother Will gained his first opening as illustrator of Ted's satirical stories of factory life, *Fact'ry 'Ands* (1906). He achieved fame in his own right as cartoonist for the *Daily Herald* from 1912; his portrayal of Capital, depicted as the top-hatted Fat Man, and Labour, young and muscular, dramatised the class conflicts of the time. As cartoonist and official war artist he, as much as any of his contemporaries, shaped Australian visual images of the World War I. Like his brother's, his later career was more successful commercially than artistically. Ross McMullin's *Will Dyson* (1984) emphasises his war career. His son EDWARD AMBROSE (1908–53) was a noted cartoonist for the communist press.

GD

E

Eardley-Wilmot, John Eardley (1783–1847) was appointed lieutenant-governor of Van Diemen's Land in 1843; three of his sons accompanied him and were given public office. Wilmot inherited a colony that was virtually bankrupt. Colonists resented being required to fund a penal system which they claimed was Britain's responsibility. This culminated in a clash between Wilmot and the 'Patriotic Six'—members of the Legislative Council—who resigned their seats and made the Council inoperable. He clashed often with the Anglican Archbishop Nixon, and was rebuked frequently by Whitehall for failing to report fully. Rumours of personal misconduct provided the opportunity for Gladstone to dismiss him in 1846. He died in Van Diemen's Land, lionised as a victim of Gladstone by a press and public that had previously vilified him.

KT

Earle, Augustus (1793–1838), portrait and landscape artist, arrived in Hobart in 1824, where he painted a series of watercolours before travelling to Sydney in 1825, and was soon established as the colony's leading artist. He painted many of the Sydney **exclusives** as well as a life-size oil portrait of Governor **Brisbane**, and extended his range to lithography in 1826 with his *Views of Australia* and a portrait of **Bungaree**. His undated oil portrait of this Sydney Aborigine, held by the National Library of Australia, displays a moving awareness of his subject's innate dignity and displacement. He journeyed inland to the Blue Mountains and Bathurst, and north as far as Port Macquarie, painting the watercolours which form his major contribution to Australian art. On his return to London, Earle published his lithographic *Views in New South Wales, and Van Diemen's Land* (1830). He was an influential early topographer who provided potential settlers in Britain with visualisations of the Australian colonies.

KT

East Timor showed starkly the conflict between Australia's desire for closer relations with Asian countries and growing public pressure for human rights to be accorded priority in foreign relations. The island had been divided between Portugal and Holland until Japanese invasion in World War II, resisted by an Australian force at considerable cost to the local population. After the war, the western part of the island was incorporated into the Republic of Indonesia, but East Timor remained a Portuguese colony. In 1975 East Timor was invaded by Indonesia amid internal turmoil following the collapse of Portugal's fascist regime. Successive Australian governments attempted to modify the brutality of Indonesian rule but never placated domestic critics. East Timor became an emblem for Australian willingness to subordinate the welfare of peoples suffering under authoritarian rule to economic and political advantage. Indonesian rule finally unravelled after Suharto's fall, and the East Timorese chose independence in a 1999 plebiscite. Australia organised a United Nations force to intervene in the violent aftermath, thereby ensuring that East Timor would become independent. Whether this represented a reversal of past Australian perfidy or a disastrous new anti-Asian bellicosity remained a point of contention.

SM

Eccles, John Carew (1903–97) shared the 1963 Nobel Prize for medicine for his work on the transmission of electrical impulses in the brain. From the University of Melbourne, Eccles went to Oxford in 1925 as a Rhodes scholar. He worked in England, Australia and NZ before becoming the professor of physiology in 1951 at the John Curtin School of Medical Research at the Australian National University. Apart from the Nobel Prize, he received numerous other awards, including Australian of the Year (1963), and was president of the Australian Academy of Science (1957–61). In 1966 he resigned from the ANU in protest at compulsory retirement and took a post in the USA where he worked until he retired, aged 72, and moved to Switzerland. His writing included *Evolution of the Brain: Creation of the Self* (1989); with D.N. Robinson, *The Wonder of Being Human* (1984); and *How the Self Controls its Brain* (1993).

KT

Economic history is a distinct branch of history, perhaps better described as a sub-discipline. Its association with economics, the most analytically powerful of the social sciences, raises special methodological issues. There has been considerable debate over the degree to which economics should be brought to bear on the interpretation of the past. In the writing of Australian economic history, economics has had a strong underlying presence. Australian economic historians have tended to perceive themselves as a discrete group of scholars neighboured by economists and historians. The typical institutional arrangement has been for departments of economic history to emerge within faculties of economics or commerce. These departments were established after World War II and from 1956 were served by the journal *Business Archives and History*. Renamed the *Australian Economic History Review* in 1967, it is published by the Economic History Society of Australia and New Zealand. From the late 1980s many economic history departments closed as the result of university reorganisation and the shift in faculties of economics and commerce to more vocational studies.

Current understanding of Australian economic history owes more to the work of N.G. **Butlin** than of any other figure. His dominance dates from the publication in 1962 of his annual estimates of the gross domestic product of Australia from 1861 to the beginning of World War II and his associated interpretation of the economic history of the second half of the nineteenth century in *Investment in Australian Economic Development 1861–1900* (1964).

These works supplanted the then standard economic histories of Australia of E.O.G. **Shann**, *An Economic History of Australia* (1930), and Brian **Fitzpatrick**, *British Imperialism and Australia* (1939) and *The British Empire in Australia* (1941). Shann was an economist who placed great weight on the individual initiative of white settlers. Fitzpatrick, on the other hand, saw Australia's past as an example of imperialist exploitation. Despite their differing ideologies, they were similar in describing the nineteenth-century Australian **economy** largely in terms of the development of the **wool** industry, with an interruption for the **gold rush** of the 1850s. N.G. Butlin, drawing on his comprehensive statistical estimates, revealed an Australia in which, after the 1850s, the non-primary sector of the economy was undergoing rapid growth. In his account, the government emerged with a more explicit role as a generator of economic growth, and **urbanisation** was shown to be a hitherto neglected feature.

N.G. Butlin's new interpretation was not born out of reaction against Shann and Fitzpatrick but owed much to a clearly affirmed reverence for the earlier work of T.A.

Coghlan. The latter's *Labour and Industry in Australia* (1918) was based primarily on the official statistical estimates which he, as NSW statist, had done more than anyone else to generate. It was from Coghlan that Butlin drew the inspiration for one of the key components of his historical method, an emphasis on quantification. Butlin added to this the insights which he derived from contemporary developments in economic thought and the newly accepted concept of social accounting. There are also some similarities with the work of his brother, S.J. **Butlin**, whose writing on the history of the Australian banking system, particularly *Foundations of the Australian Monetary System* (1953), combined an emphasis on detailed financial data with reference to change in the economy as a whole.

The publication of N.G. Butlin's *magnum opus* marked the beginning of an increased intensity in research into Australian economic history. Butlin was such a dominant figure that he largely set the agenda for some time. In addition, his strong sense of Australian nationalism struck a chord with his contemporaries. With the expansion of the university system from about this time, and an associated increase in the number of specialist economic historians, came a wider spread of writing on Australian economic history.

One thrust was the extension of Butlin's methods to the interpretation of Australian economic growth in the twentieth century. The Butlin series of national economic statistics ran up to the outbreak of World War II, and Butlin and others, notably Ian McLean and Jonathan Pincus in the *Journal of Economic History* (1983), used them to draw conclusions about Australia's growth performance between the 1890s and the end of the 1930s. In Colin Forster (ed.), *Australian Economic Development in the Twentieth Century* (1970), a number of authors, of whom N.G. Butlin was one, dealt with some of the key features of economic development before and after World War II. A later work edited by Rodney Maddock and Ian McLean, *The Australian Economy in the Long Run* (1987), is geared towards economic concerns current at the time of its publication. G.D. Snooks, *Depression and Recovery in Western Australia* (1974), also adopted Butlin methodology to focus on WA between the wars and, in the process, pioneered the transfer of the now dominant Australian style to regional economic history. In addition, a major research project at the Australian National University, exploring the role of government in economic development after 1900, led to the publication of N.G. Butlin, Alan Barnard, and Jonathan Pincus, *Government and Capitalism* (1982). It is largely in the context of economic development that the major **depressions** of the 1890s and the 1930s have attracted considerable attention. There are monographs by E.A. Boehm, *Prosperity and Depression in Australia 1887–1897* (1971), and C.B. Schedvin, *Australia and the Great Depression* (1970), and a good deal of other writing.

Another challenging finding of N.G. Butlin, that urban economic activity was far more important than had previously been acknowledged by historians, received ready assent and an enduring response. C.B. Schedvin and J.W. McCarty (eds), *Urbanisation in Australia* (1974), made public some of the research results, most notably those of McCarty. E.A. Dingle and D.T. Merrett in the *AEHR* (1984–85) and Lionel Frost, *The New Urban Frontier* (1991), are others to have followed. As the implications of Butlin's work became acknowledged by historians generally, **urban history** spread beyond the confines of economic history.

Possibly the most important controversy in the wake of Butlin's work has been over the role of overseas influences on Australian economic development. One part of the debate has been concerned with the degree to which decisions by overseas investors were instrumental in determining the course of events in Australia. Another has asked whether the rate of economic growth and the changing structure of the economy in the nineteenth century were dependent on the emergence of export staples based on the exploitation of natural resources.

A noteworthy progression down a different course from the mainstream has been that of Geoffrey **Blainey**. Beginning in the 1950s, Blainey graduated from the writing of **business history** to a special interest in the **mining** industry and then to a more general body of writing on Australian history. His work differs from the dominant form of Australian economic history in being less quantitative and not overtly founded on formal economics.

Recent themes suggest that Australian economic historians are moving on to a new phase of research into economic development, probing more deeply into its implications. G.D. Snooks has addressed the questions of how to incorporate the household sector into the story of economic development and of the allowance to be made for the effects of white settlement on the natural environment in *Portrait of the Family Within the Total Economy* (1994). A broadening of concern for welfare issues is also reflected in G.D. Snooks (ed.), *Wealth and Wellbeing in Australia* (1995), and in the current research being directed by Stephen Nicholas into measures of living standards other than GDP per head. There is a partly related interest in the Aboriginal economy. Geoffrey Blainey made the first excursion into pre-1788 economic history with his *Triumph of the Nomads* (1975). N.G. Butlin brought his distinctive style to **Aboriginal history** in *Our Original Aggression* (1983) and *Economics and the Dreamtime* (1993), and further pursued the theme in a new account of the emergent colonial economy in *Forming a Colonial Economy: Australia 1810–1850* (1994). Ralph Shlomowitz's numerous journal articles on the indentured labour system and associated matters in the Queensland **sugar** industry and S. Nicholas (ed.), *Convict Workers* (1988), are further indications of a new interest in particular social groups.

Australian economic historians can be said to have made a coherent contribution to the understanding of Australian society. The most recent summation of knowledge of the period of white settlement is W.A. Sinclair, *The Process of Economic Development in Australia* (1976). R.V. Jackson, *Australian Economic Development in the Nineteenth Century* (1977), and E.A. Boehm, *Twentieth Century Economic Development in Australia* (1994), cover the two main periods, and Colin White, *Mastering Risk* (1992), brings a new perspective to bear.

W.A. SINCLAIR

Economy is a term that comes from the ancient Greek word *oikonomos* which meant 'a system of household management'. Subsequently it was used to refer to the financial management of the state, which in Europe had its origins in the medieval royal household. Since the publication of Adam Smith's *The Wealth of Nations* (1776) this term—initially in the form *political economy*—has meant the system of state–market interaction by which scarce resources are employed to generate and distribute income and wealth. Only recently has its meaning been broadened to also embrace the household sector from which its name was derived.

The Aboriginal economy evolved over a period of perhaps 60 000 years. Using simple deductive economic theory, Noel **Butlin** in *Economics and the Dreamtime* (1993) has analysed the likely structure and function of Aboriginal economy in a timeless setting. He correctly insists that this early economy included not only a system of hunting and gathering that changed slowly with technical variations in the equipment employed, but also the evolving institutional arrangements that included property rights in natural resources and ritual, marriage rules, and family and inter-family customs. It was a highly successful economic system, evidenced by its unparalleled longevity, that satisfied basic needs, provided abundant leisure time (a working week of only 35 to 40 hours), and supported a rich culture. What it could not guarantee were low rates of infant mortality or protection from societies in more competitive parts of the world.

As the economic models employed by Butlin are static rather than dynamic, he focuses on outcomes rather than processes. Although he recognises that slow economic change occurred throughout the vast era of Aboriginal occupation, he is unable to analyse it. In *Portrait of the Family* (1994) and *The Dynamic Society* (1996), Graeme Snooks analyses the dynamic process of a people motivated by a desire to survive and prosper who increase their command over unused natural resources through family multiplication and migration. In this way the Australian continent was fully occupied by at least 20 000 years ago. Thereafter Aboriginal economy was organised so as to maintain a long-term balance between population and a constantly changing natural resource environment. This was a dynamic relationship, because the attempt to maintain the status quo required an innovative response. More than 7000 years before British settlement, for example, Australia's **climate** became markedly warmer and drier, thereby reducing both the area of coastal plains as the seas rose and the productivity of inland regions. In order to maintain existing populations, kinship structures, and living standards, it became necessary to develop new skills, new tools, and new organisational forms. It takes imagination, skill, and flexibility to survive and prosper in a changing physical environment.

The British invasion and settlement from 1788 led to a rapid decline in the population of the **Aborigines** through disease and violence. The Aboriginal economy was replaced by a colonial economy. It began precariously as a prison economy separated from Britain by vast distances and, until 1815, by wars with France. The provision of social infrastructure was funded by the British taxpayer (Noel Butlin, *Forming a Colonial Economy*, 1994); human capital was supplied by the forced migration of 160 000 male and female **convicts**, mainly after 1815 (Stephen Nicholas and Peter Shergold, eds, *Convict Workers*, 1988), and the emergence of public and private financial intermediaries (S.J. **Butlin**, *Foundations of the Australian Monetary System*, 1953). Essentially, small prison settlements in NSW and Van Diemen's Land were employed to establish a 'bridgehead economy' on the Australian continent in the face of considerable local difficulties and neglect by Britain. Officials and ex-officials granted themselves land, convict labour, commissariat provisions, and bills of credit drawn on the British government, to exploit small-scale agricultural and commercial opportunities. After 1815 the situation was transformed with the resumption of forced migration and, from 1821, the official encouragement of free migration and private investment. Natural resources and British funds passed from the hands of officials to free immigrants and ex-convicts. These private entrepreneurs increasingly from the mid-1820s turned to large-scale sheep farming. In the process, a prison economy was transformed into a mixed colonial economy, in which the state provided social infrastructure and private individuals exploited natural resources to produce **wool** for export to Europe. This mixed economy was to form the basis of Australian society for the following 150 years.

Detailed national accounts of the mixed colonial economy in the second half of the nineteenth century were constructed by Noel Butlin in *Investment in Australian Economic Development* (1964). The two key relationships were between the public and private sectors, and between the rural and urban sectors. Despite the large inflow of free migrants and private capital during the 1850s gold rushes, governments continued to play a vital role in the economy throughout the nineteenth century and into the middle decades of the century that followed. During the 50 years before Federation about half of Australia's total capital formation was provided by governments, and more than half of this took the form of **railway** construction. Butlin termed this 'colonial socialism'; it is more generally known as **state socialism**. It was an early demonstration of strategic leadership to provide the infrastructure required both for a more intensive use of natural resources that had been fully exploited by 1850 and for an accelerating process of **urbanisation**.

The other key structural relationship highlighted by Noel Butlin is that between the rural and urban sectors. As earlier historical scholarship had concentrated on the rural sector, it came as a surprise that more than half of Australian capital formation in the second half of the nineteenth century took place in towns and cities. Indeed, the largest investment sector was house building, an activity that consistently eclipsed investment in the pastoral industry. This simple statistical demonstration helped promote the study of urbanisation.

During the twentieth century, many of these characteristic features continued. The economy continued to draw on overseas capital, labour, and technology to exploit natural resources. Exports remained heavily dependent upon wool, wheat, and other agricultural products, with base metal **mining**, and later **oil** and coal supplementing **gold**. But owing to a determined policy of tariff **protection**, the urban concentration of the population intensified and, until the closing decades, the secondary and service industries in which they worked were restricted to a domestic market. The two world wars also gave substantial stimulus to **manufacturing**, with the opening of **BHP's** Newcastle steelworks in 1915 laying the base for heavy industry. The **Depression** of the 1930s brought a crisis in public finance, and a retreat from public capital formation, but following World War II there was a quarter-century of uninterrupted growth and unprecedented prosperity.

This **long boom** ended with the downturn of the international economy in the oil crisis of 1974–75, and brought about a protracted readjustment to new patterns of world investment, production, and trade. Demand for established export staples such as wool and wheat contracted substantially, and price competition in other resource commodities was fierce. With the exhaustion of the potential for import replacement, the manufacturing sector contracted. **Tourism** and other service industries became increasingly important to the balance of payments, while foreign debt (now overwhelmingly private) grew rapidly from the 1980s. The established forms of financial, trade, and wage regulation whereby governments sought to mediate the relationship between the rural and urban sectors were mostly abandoned. By the 1990s even essential strategic leadership was rejected.

The total economy in which these events occurred encompasses the transactions between the private, public, and household sectors. The value of household economic activity for the past two centuries has been measured by Snooks in *Portrait of the Family*. This puts the *oikos* back in *oikonomos* and repairs centuries of neglect. Snooks's new national accounting estimates of Gross Community Income rather than Gross Domestic Product reveal that Australian economic development over the past 150 years has been dominated by three roughly equal sectors—the household, public, and private sectors. This period has experienced three long (40-year) waves of economic growth separated by depressions (in the 1890s and 1930s), and in each wave a different sector has been dominant. In the second half of the nineteenth century, the dominant sector was the household as the infrastructure of urban centres was constructed; in the fragile growth of the first half of the twentieth century, the public sector led the way as the private sector faced fluctuating international fortunes; and in the golden age of the 1950s and 1960s, the previously reluctant private sector now exploiting the new international prosperity came to the fore, continuing to the century's end.

Throughout Australian history an inverse relationship exists between the household and market (private plus public) sectors. During economic booms the market sector outstrips the household sector, whereas during depressions and recessions (such as the 1890s, the 1930s, and the early 1990s) the household economy expands to absorb those workers being shed by the market sector. During an upturn, under-employed household labour is attracted to the market sector, and market goods and services replace those produced in the household; during a downturn, unemployed market workers are taken back into the household economy, and domestic goods and services replace those produced in the market. In effect, the total economy possesses an automatic countercyclical mechanism. Future analysis of Australian economic activity, therefore, must encompass the total economy rather than some subset of it.

G.D. SNOOKS

Education borrowed its institutions from Britain, but in each colony the transplanting became a reconstruction, as British models were modified or new models developed to meet new needs. Thus, unlike their ancient British counterparts, the first Australian **universities** were state institutions, established by acts of parliament, endowed by government, and controlled by councils whose membership was often appointed by government.

The universities drew most of their students from schools run by individuals to earn a living. Throughout the nineteenth century these schools were gradually displaced by what are now known as private schools—church-supported schools, the most powerful of which assumed the name and the manner of the British public schools. By the beginning of the twentieth century governments had begun to establish secondary schools which, depending on the social and political structure of the colony (more in NSW than in Victoria, for example), provided an alternative source of students for the universities. The remaining schools owned by individuals disappeared, victims of economic difficulties and competition from government schools charging lower fees.

Unlike their brothers, middle-class women were not admitted to university until late in the nineteenth century. The girls' schools developed an 'accomplishments curriculum' which (at best) included English language and literature, history, science, and modern languages—a richer curriculum than the classics offered to boys, though not leading its students towards political and economic power. These patterns are explored by Marjorie Theobald in *Knowing Women* (1996). By the early twentieth century, changing social expectations for women forced many girls' schools to close or to begin preparing students for university.

The private schools and the government secondary schools catered for a very small proportion of the population. The larger task, the provision of the elementary education considered necessary to create a literate, numerate, and orderly citizenry, was at first performed by schools run by the churches and by individuals for profit. By the early 1850s, however, governments had concluded that these were not sufficient. Accordingly, at different paces and in cooperation with the churches, they began to fund the building and staffing of elementary schools, and established bureaucracies to supervise them. By the 1880s, wearying of the conflict between the churches and the intractability of the disputes over religious instruction, governments withdrew state aid

from church schools and religious instruction from the curriculum in government schools. A.G. **Austin**, in *Australian Education 1788–1900* (1961, 1972), describes the **'free, secular and compulsory'** acts containing these decisions which consolidated the centralisation of education: colonial education departments disciplined, appointed, and paid teachers, determined the curriculum, trained teachers (eventually in their own teachers' colleges), and employed inspectors to police the implementation of their policies.

Comparisons of Australian industrial progress in the early twentieth century with that overseas suggested that state secondary schools should produce the better-educated workforce which was needed for the industrialised, capitalist democracy that Australia wished to become. Nevertheless, these schools modelled their curriculum and pedagogy on the private secondary schools. The state's secular and coeducational schools made secondary education more accessible to girls, though their curriculum and their treatment of women teachers reflected their assumption that marriage was a woman's destiny.

The **Catholic Church** would not accept the secular education of government schools and established an alternative system, united by class and ethnicity as well as religious belief: Catholics were overwhelmingly working-class and, by national heritage, Irish. Until the 1970s, Catholic schools remained outside the state system, catering to a similar socio-economic clientele and agitating for the return of state aid. Their history is recorded by Ronald Fogarty in *Catholic Education in Australia* (1959).

The needs of goldmining, and the desire to develop manufacturing, led to the establishment in the second half of the nineteenth century of institutions which can loosely be called 'technical'—schools of mines, schools of art and design, and agricultural and working men's colleges. Various in shape, more responsive to market demands than the universities and schools, and more democratic in sensibility, these were willing to tailor their courses to the needs of employers and governments. By the late nineteenth and early twentieth centuries, aware that their secondary schools were preparing students for the professions rather than industry, governments established 'junior' technical schools (or technical departments within secondary schools) to feed the technical colleges. At about the time the Sydney Technical College was established (1878), Brisbane Technical College (1882), and Melbourne Working Men's College (1887) were developing studies which eventually made them rivals of the universities.

Australia's loosely articulated educational institutions were heavily marked by the world wars and the 1930s Depression. Yet as **postwar reconstruction** began in the 1940s, they were still recognisable as institutions created in the nineteenth and early twentieth centuries. Postwar forces, especially the migration policy which contributed to the population explosion of the late 1940s and 1950s, changed Australian education drastically. In government and Catholic schools, which were required to take all students seeking entry, huge classes crowded into inadequate rooms where they were taught by ill-prepared teachers. Postwar idealism, concern for equality of opportunity, and pressure for economic and industrial growth led to the policy of secondary education for all.

By the late 1960s the swelling enrolments brought governments and the Catholic primary and secondary schools close to collapse. This crisis led governments to return the state aid withdrawn in the nineteenth century to the Catholic schools, an option now open to them because of the ebbing of **sectarianism**. Especially after the election of the Labor Party in 1972, the federal government provided per capita funds distributed on a basis of need to all schools, Catholic, private, and government.

The enrolment crisis was accompanied by social changes which altered the nature of late-twentieth-century education. By the 1970s, schools were crowded with students from a wide range of socio-economic and ethnic backgrounds, and forced to reconsider their structures, curricula, and methods. The Vietnam War, a brief but intense period of political radicalisation, changes in sexual mores, increasingly sophisticated industrial and technological growth, the decline of institutionalised religion, the progress of the women's movement, the growth of **multiculturalism**, and the tentative recognition of Aboriginal rights, including land rights—all challenged the values of the early postwar years. Australian society was being reshaped, though improvement in the opportunities for women and working-class and migrant students was not as great as the heat of the rhetoric. Indigenous Australians were still offered an education which showed little interest in their culture and which, to judge by their low enrolments at upper secondary and university levels, was an unattractive introduction to European civilisation.

In the 1980s and 1990s the previously widespread view that a general education would best empower students to adapt quickly to new demands collapsed: employers, governments, and unions insisted on the development of intellectual and practical competencies, which were directly related to the professional and technical skills judged to be needed in the market-driven economy that Australia was striving to develop.

A major reorganisation of the structure of government schooling accompanied these demands. A process of decentralisation and devolution reduced the size of the centralised bureaucracies inherited from the nineteenth century. Self-management of schools (including management of the budget) became common, inspectorial systems were dismantled, schools were amalgamated to form larger units, principals were given more power, and the appointment of teachers and principals made with greater input from the community. While important powers were transferred to the schools, the distribution of resources, as distinct from their management once they had been distributed, remained in central hands. Moreover, close oversight of school budgets, increased standardisation of curricula and government-controlled testing programs made the leaner state and federal bureaucracies as powerful as their predecessors. Computers now did much of what the banished inspectors had done. Ideologies which had stressed forms of **citizenship** or nation-building gave way to

a romantic version of private enterprise in which government schools, like the private schools (thriving, but heavily dependent on government aid), were considered as sturdy small businesses which competed in the marketplace for pupils and resources.

The universities, technical institutes and teachers' colleges inherited from the nineteenth century survived the student flood of the 1960s and 1970s by expanding in number and by a massive influx of federal funds. A binary system developed, which (not always convincingly) distinguished universities, given a strong research responsibility, from institutes of technology and colleges of advanced education. In the 1980s the binary system was abandoned. Universities, colleges, and institutes were amalgamated and brought under direct government control in a unified national system. The number of tertiary institutions was reduced from 94 in 1978 to 38 in 1991. They were all called universities and in them, whether new or old, government economic priorities increasingly influenced general policy and aspects of teaching and research previously considered the province of academic decision-making.

The language of educational discourse changed and its preoccupation with decentralisation, competitiveness, and responsiveness to market demands may suggest a reduction of government influence on schools and universities. The reality is otherwise.

R.J.W. SELLECK

Educational history properly begins in 1958 with A.G. **Austin's** *George William Rusden and National Education in Australia*. In the decade which followed, an identifiable school of historical writing emerged from the Faculty of Education at the University of Melbourne, taking as its central concern the evolution of mass systems of public education in the nineteenth century. Among the key texts were A.G. Austin, *Australian Education 1788–1900* (1961); Gwyneth Dow, *George Higinbotham: Church and State* (1964); Denis Grundy, *'Free, Secular and Compulsory': The Education Act of 1872* (1972); J.S. Gregory, *Church and State* (1973); and R.J.W. Selleck, *Frank Tate* (1982), published after he had taken up a professorship at Monash University.

Austin's preface to *Australian Education* placed his work on the nineteenth century squarely within the educational debates of the 1950s and 1960s: 'With all its imperfections this system of public education represents a vindication of the belief that every Australian child could be given an effective elementary education.' The revival of the debate over **church–state** relationships in education the 1950s was indeed tumultuous, culminating in the unsuccessful challenge by the Defence of Government Schools organisation in the High Court. It was not coincidental that the first doctoral thesis completed in the faculty, published by Brother Ronald Fogarty as *Catholic Education in Australia 1806–1950* (1959), reflected in mirror image Austin's manifesto for state education. Fogarty's implicit thesis is that the Catholic education system, the only denominational system to survive the cessation of state aid in 1872, was his church's emphatic protest against the liberal and secular ambitions of the state. Implicit also is his conviction that justice must now be done. The emergence of academic educational history around these debates ensured that the histories of state and Catholic education would be written on either side of a divide. Since Fogarty's work, the history of Catholic education has been largely fragmented in institutional histories and biographies of key players. Helen Praetz's analytical study of Catholic education in Victoria since World War II is a notable exception. The 'Melbourne school' was informed by a belief in the importance of a system of public education based on common understandings of the purpose of education, and the efficacy of morally responsible men and women in that enterprise. As economic rationalist and market-driven ideologies were placed like a grid over public education in the 1990s, these texts may be due for a sympathetic reassessment.

By the 1970s, however, public debates over education had moved on from the state-aid question. The huge and unplanned expansion in the primary, secondary, and tertiary sectors in the 1960s strained schools to breaking-point. Interest groups, radicalised by the social movements of the times, organised around issues such as equity, untrained teachers, overcrowded classrooms, and outmoded curricula. Against this background, a younger generation of 'revisionist' historians grew restless with the preoccupations and theoretical underpinnings of their elders. They turned again to the origins of state education in the nineteenth century, but asked instead why a system which had begun with such grand aims in the past had led to inequalities in the present. Grouped mainly round Ian Davey at the University of Adelaide, who drew on North American models, the revisionists implemented an agenda for research which rejected Austin's thesis of public education as a benign project of the democratic state. Underpinned by a neo-Marxist conception of the state as the embodiment of bourgeois power and economic self-interest, their early work argued that the failure of publicly funded schooling to deliver a fairer society can be explained in part by its historical origins as a means of social control in the emerging industrial Western democracies of the nineteenth century. Gender and age relations became central to this reworked revisionist project. With Foucault, its practitioners would argue for a paradigm shift in nineteenth-century forms of governance which saw the emergence of the prison, the reformatory, the asylum, and the state school. Their work bears the stamp of an era impatient with any claims of the state to harness schools to the cause of patriotism or nation-building. Other monographs in the revisionist genre are Jean Ely, *Reality and Rhetoric: An Alternative History of Australian Education* (1978); Alison Mackinnon, *One Foot on the Ladder: Origins and Outcomes of Girls' Secondary Schooling in South Australia* (1984); Pavla Miller, *Long Division: State Schooling in South Australian Society* (1986); and David McCallum, *The Social Production of Merit: Education, Psychology and Politics in Australia 1900–1950* (1990).

It is ironic that an agenda to demolish the earlier, liberal-democratic thesis on state education deflected the attention of a generation of radical historians away from the crucial role of the independent school sector in Australia's educational history. This is explained in part by the origins of revisionism in the American context, where the private sector was negligible until federal integration policies triggered a flight of middle-class white families from the public school. In England the public schools (in the sense of Eton and Winchester) have been excoriated again and again at times of national crisis such as World War I, when the products of the system were found wanting. In Australia, by contrast, the powerful independent Protestant sector has been relatively neglected as subject of serious historiographical study. Janet McCalman's *Journeyings: The Biography of a Middle-Class Generation 1920–1990* (1993) takes as its central theme the economic and cultural meanings of attendance at independent schools for a generation of Australian men and women. As with Catholic education, however, the history of this sector is fragmented in institutional histories. Though many were written by academic historians—Kathleen **Fitzpatrick** on Presbyterian Ladies College in Melbourne (1975); Greg Dening on Xavier College (1978); Ailsa Zainuíddin on Methodist Ladies College in Melbourne (1982)—in-house history has its ground rules which cannot be transgressed. If histories of girls' schools tend to be gutsier than those of boys' schools, it is because the girls' schools, under challenge from a coeducational resurgence, have been delighted to find themselves placed within a feminist framework of analysis. The mirror image of this analysis—that boys' 'public' schools produce ruling-class masculinities—is not welcome in **commissioned histories**.

Inspired by the Second Wave of the 1970s, feminist historians began to question the male-centred meta-narratives of church and state. They shared with the revisionists a concern with inequalities in the present, and turned to the origins of women's education in the past to explain the failure of educational institutions, especially coeducational institutions, to achieve equality for Australian women. Their work evolved in several ways. It looked at the politics of women's admission to universities, the career paths of the pioneer graduates, and their involvement in the suffrage movement. It asked new questions of pioneer academic schools like PLC and Brisbane Girls' Grammar, canvassing the possibility that conservative and radical agendas may have coexisted in the same institutions. It looked again at the traditional ladies' academy, as a site of women's professional and economic autonomy and as an institution capable of responding to new demands for academic qualifications. It looked with greater sensitivity at teaching as the women's profession. Important works in this tradition are Farley Kelly, *Degrees of Liberation* (1985); Noeline Kyle, *Her Natural Destiny* (1986); Marjorie Theobald, *Knowing Women* (1996); and Alison Mackinnon, *Love and Freedom* (1997).

Teacher activism in the 1970s over issues of equity, funding and staffing both inspired and informed work on teacher unionism and labour relations in the past. Bob Bessant and Andrew Spaull, *Teachers in Conflict* (1972), Bruce Mitchell, *Teachers, Education and Politics* (1975), and Spaull and Martin

Sullivan, *A History of the Queensland Teachers Union* (1989) are notable examples. The new social history manifested itself in educational history; historians wanted to know how ordinary families and ordinary teachers responded to compulsory state education and in turn shaped its agendas. Selleck and Sullivan (eds), *Not So Eminent Victorians* (1984), and Theobald and Selleck (eds), *Family, School and State in Australian History* (1990), exemplify this approach. Other scholars, such as Paul Ramsland (*Children of the Back Lanes*, 1986) and Margaret Barbalet (*Far from a Low Gutter Girl*, 1983), asked new questions about the schooling of 'outcast' children in the past. Barry Coldrey's *The Scheme: The Christian Brothers and Child Care in Western Australia* (1993), a distressing account of brutality and sexual abuse, is in this tradition rather than mainstream history of Catholic education.

Much of the ground-breaking work in the field by newer scholars lies hidden in unpublished theses and journals such as *Melbourne Studies in Education* and *History of Education Review* which are seldom read by mainstream historians.

MARJORIE THEOBALD

Egalitarianism has commonly been believed by Australians to be a distinguishing mark of their society. Sociologists, finding abundant inequalities in class and status, have considered egalitarianism to be a myth. If Australia is notably egalitarian, why did it retain knighthoods for 50 years after Canada abandoned them, and support private schools to an extent which would outrage democratic opinion in the USA? Plainly Australians have not been thorough egalitarians, but they have been egalitarians in their own way.

The equality demanded by the founding generation of migrants was the abolition of official privilege and favouritism embodied in Britain in the aristocracy, the established church, and closed corporations. They wanted no 'class legislation', by which they meant the favouring of any economic or social group. Legislatures composed in whole or in part by Crown nominees were abhorrent. Still worse was **Wentworth's** suggestion that an Australian nobility should be formed to compose the upper house of parliament. The privileged position of the Anglican Church was soon challenged and was undercut by Governor **Bourke's Church Act**, which financed all denominations on the same basis. Once the colonists themselves had charge of this issue, they abolished state aid to churches and established perfect equality by the separation of **church and state**. The movement to unlock the lands and settle them with small farmers was, in part, a demand for the abolition of official privilege: the granting by the Crown of long leases on generous terms to the **squatters**. Only access on good terms was demanded for the small man; there was no interest at this stage in organising government assistance to keep him on the land. Nor was equality of opportunity thought to require equal opportunity in education. The universal provision by the state extended to only primary education. In so far as the state was to promote opportunity, as distinct from providing a fair field and no favours, it was by 'developing the resources of the colony'—the building of roads, bridges, railways, and ports—which was the central concern of colonial politics.

That success should be open to all, rather than depending on birth or official favour, was the new freedom which made Australia a better Britain. It was signified in the colonial success stories of poor migrants rising to great wealth or the highest position in the state. But as a better Britain rather than a new foundation, Australia still valued the British signs of success. So rich men and successful politicians became gentlemen, joined gentlemen's **clubs**, built country houses, and rode to hounds; they sent their children to private schools which aped the English public schools; their wives left cards and paid calls and constituted themselves into Ladies Benevolent Societies to distribute charity to the poor; gentlemen and ladies both sought **honours**, especially knighthoods which gave a title to man and wife. Such styles and distinctions, newly acquired by those not born to them, could not become entrenched when the forces which were to democratise Western society were already gathering strength. They have all disappeared or fallen into insignificance, except for the private schools. When equality of opportunity required that secondary education be open to all, its Australian promoters had to contend with the private schools, whose traditions, endowments, and better-prepared scholars make it difficult for government schools to become their equals or be seen to be so. The private schools have become more firmly entrenched since the 1970s because of the new government policy of funding all schools, which was introduced to appease the Catholics. The difficulty of pursuing equality of opportunity in this environment is one of the issues examined in Stuart Macintyre, *Winners and Losers: The Pursuit of Social Justice in Australian History* (1985).

What became the most distinctive form of egalitarianism in Australia was first noted as an absence of deference in working people. Terms of respect such as *sir* were still used, but with less humbleness and touching of hats. This has been ascribed to convicts' scorn for their masters, but more persuasively to the shortage of labour and the opportunity of ordinary working people to live well—'meat three times a day!' The new freedom for these people was not so much the opportunity to rise, but the release from fear of the boss, as Manning **Clark** proposed in his *Select Documents in Australian History 1851–1900* (1955). These changes in status and self-confidence have not been thoroughly examined; indeed they are difficult to monitor and trace. The effects of the colonial environment are undeniable, but it should be remembered that in Britain the ties of deference were weakening, that working people had the confidence of possessing the rights of the free-born Englishman, and were beginning to assert the dignity of labour and to organise to advance their interests.

The dignity of labour in Australia still had to contend with the disdain for manual work, but in some locations the age-old certainty that high-status people did not labour disappeared. In the pastoral interior men were divided between the homestead, the overseer's quarters and the huts, but they all laboured in the enterprise. The squatter wore working clothes and had to be able to do all that he asked of his men. He was known, with his men, as a bushman, and he wore the bushman's cabbage-tree hat. In the bush, labouring as a mark of social inferiority disappeared. On the goldfields, also, high-born and low worked with their hands. Here not only did deference break down; an equality in mode of address developed: everyone on the diggings was 'mate'. This egalitarianism of manners spread only slowly to the wider society. That relations between superior and inferior had become unusually informal in Australia was evident in the notorious reluctance of Australian soldiers in World War I to salute officers, as well as in the reluctance to tip for service. As the gold-digger, the working bushman, and the soldier became archetypal national figures, their style in dealing with their superiors received firm ideological support. Australians of all sorts now put great store on their casualness in personal interaction, which has been carried to an extreme length.

When the long period of colonial prosperity ended in the 1890s, workingmen turned to the state to preserve 'fair and reasonable' wages. They achieved this through the **Arbitration** Court and its **basic wage**, which was to be sufficient to maintain a man, his wife, and three children in reasonable comfort. This could only partially offset the inequalities of a capitalist society, but the mode of the Arbitration Court itself was unusual in giving equal status as litigants to employers and employees, as John Rickard argues in *Australia* (1988), which looks for Australian distinctiveness not in the absence of social differences but in the mode of accommodating them. This is a useful way to think of Australian egalitarianism.

The expectation of working men that the government would provide work in slack times and that the court would award a living wage affected the form the **welfare** state assumed. Welfare looked after those who could not look after themselves through work. So this egalitarian society did not develop universal, insurance-type welfare schemes.

The Arbitration Court assumed, along with union litigants, that the wives of working men should be homemakers as middle-class women were. Women in the home were not part of the public realm where the egalitarianism of manners operated among men. They were the maintainers of social distinctions about which men might affect to be indifferent. Women outside the home were treated by men not as equals, but as superiors in being accorded the respect due to ladies. These divisions and distinctions have now been broken down, but it is too early to say what their effects on social relations will be. **Feminists** encourage women to be sisters, but will they also become mates?

As Australia disowned its **White Australia** past, the racial element in egalitarianism in its formative stages has come more prominently into view. The **Chinese** were never mates. Some have queried whether such a racist society deserves the name egalitarian. Others conclude that Australia was more egalitarian because of its success in excluding Asian labour. The idealism in the White Australia policy was the creation of a society where labour would not be degraded and no impermeable social barriers would be erected. John Hirst has argued in 'Australia's Absurd History' *Overland* (1990) that the success of **multiculturalism** in Australia is due in part to the egalitarian style established in old Australia.

In modern Australia **wealth distribution** and social mobility are not markedly more egalitarian than in European societies (Peter Travers and Sue Richardson, *Living Decently: Material Well-being in Australia*, 1993). But inequalities in these matters have not yet touched the egalitarianism which Australians value most. As D.H. **Lawrence** observed in *Kangaroo* (1923), still the most insightful study of this subject, 'nobody felt *better* than anybody else, or higher; only better-off. And there is all the difference in the world between feeling *better* than your fellow man, and merely feeling *better-off*'. Lawrence was attracted to this equality and then repelled by it. He thought, as others have done, that men could treat each other as equals only because they brought so little of themselves to the encounter.

JOHN HIRST

Eggleston, Frederic William (1875–1954) was a politician, diplomat, administrator and man of affairs, distinguished by intellectual rigour. Born into a successful family of Melbourne Methodists, he was forced to enter law by the back door as an articled clerk because of the depression of the 1890s. His marriage in 1897 to Lulu Henriques fostered artistic and cultural interests. He cast off denominational Christianity under the influence of social evolutionism and ethical idealism and, like his friend John **Latham**, was drawn into the high-minded circle that surrounded Alfred **Deakin**.

In 1920 Eggleston entered state parliament and held ministerial office 1924–27 in a National–Country Party coalition government. His experience as a minister for railways who defended state enterprise from private business interests led to electoral rejection and confirmed a distaste for the expediency of conservative politics as well as the flaws of utilitarianism in public life. *State Socialism in Victoria* (1932) reflected on these lessons. From 1933 to 1941 he chaired the Commonwealth Grants Commission, and sought to devise principles that would enhance the cohesiveness, efficiency, and democratic responsiveness of the national federation.

Through Deakin he had become a member of the imperialist Round Table movement before World War I. His support for national sacrifice and military conscription was tempered by service, with his friends Latham and R.R. **Garran**, in the Australian delegation to the Peace Conference. The conduct of the prime minister, W.M. **Hughes**, fell short of his standards, but he was equally disenchanted by the British class system as well as the incapacity of British statesmen to comprehend Australian ideals. He became a leading member of the **Australian Institute of International Affairs** and the League of Nations Union, and used these forums to foster appreciation of Australia's regional situation. As a speaker, writer, and public commentator, he did much to mediate the transition from an imperial to a national foreign policy. In 1941 he became the first

Australian minister in China, and in 1944 he succeeded Owen **Dixon** as minister to the USA.

After ill-health forced his return to Australia in 1945, he advised the Department of External Affairs and played a significant role in the establishment of the Australian National University. His *Search for a Social Philosophy* (1941) and *Reflections of an Australian Liberal* (1953) were attempts to systematise a role for social science in the conduct of human affairs, and to affirm the continuing need for a positive liberalism. He had no more success in breaking down the disciplinary specialism of the professors at the ANU than in attempting to carry the Deakinite torch into the pragmatic Liberal Party of R.G. **Menzies**, for his ideas and role were better suited to an earlier, transitional period. Warren Osmond's biographical study (1985) illuminates the substantial contribution of *Frederic Eggleston: An Intellectual in Australian Politics*.

STUART MACINTYRE

Eight-hour day was a precept based on the maxim of the British socialist, Robert Owen: 'eight hours labour, eight hours rest, eight hours recreation'. It was sought by a political movement founded by stonemasons in Melbourne in the 1850s. Agitation for shorter working hours had already come from Victorian shopkeepers representing the Early Closing Association, but the first proposal for concerted action was made at a meeting of the Operative Masons Society in Collingwood in February 1856. Proponents argued that more time should be available for leisure and self-improvement. Supported by other construction workers, stonemasons working on the quadrangle of the new University of Melbourne marched to the site of Parliament House on 21 April 1856. As a result, building workers were granted an eight-hour day without a pay reduction, and stonemasons celebrated with a holiday and procession on Whit Monday, 12 May 1856. The eight-hour movement spread to country districts and other colonies, though it was enjoyed by a minority of skilled workers only and frequently had to be regained. Subsequently a public holiday variously known as Eight-Hour Day or Labour Day was celebrated in most of the colonies and the intertwined numbers '888' adorned the pediment of many union buildings. The eight-hour movement was represented in the annual Anniversary Day celebrations and processions. A fortieth anniversary publication was W.E. Murphy, *History of the Eight Hours' Movement* (1896).

HD

Elder, Thomas (1818–97) was a mining and pastoral businessman and philanthropist. Born in Scotland, Elder arrived in Adelaide in 1854 and joined the family business. After his brothers' return to Britain, Elder entered partnership with Edward Stirling, John Taylor, and Robert Barr Smith. They made their fortunes by financing the development of the Wallaroo and Moonta copper mines, discovered in 1859 and 1861. Stirling and Taylor retired, leaving the firm Elder, Smith & Co. This grew into a very large wool-selling firm. The wealthy company was ideally placed to move into capitalist pasturing, using professional management, fencing, artesian bores, and massive and diverse holdings to minimise traditional risks. It acquired leases on tens of thousands of square miles of land to become one of the world's largest wool-sellers. Elder was a member of the SA Legislative Council 1863–68 and 1871–78.

Elder used his wealth to promote knowledge and culture in SA. He provided funds and camels for a number of important exploration expeditions, including that of Ernest **Giles**. He also contributed nearly £100 000 to the University of Adelaide, funding new chairs of mathematics and natural science, and supporting teaching in music and medicine. There were liberal donations to cultural associations, and a bequest of £155 000 to churches, hospitals, and other charities. Despite corporate takeovers in the 1980s that briefly transformed it into a multinational conglomerate, Elders remains a presence in the pastoral agency business. Its founder's memory is perpetuated in the name of the Elder Conservatorium, Adelaide.

CAROL FORT

Eldershaw, M. Barnard, see Barnard, **Marjorie**

Elections in democratic polities such as Australia justify and legitimate government power. For absolutist states (monarchies and dictatorships), power is justified through divine right, aristocratic authority, manifest destiny, or other special causes. Representative democracies rely on popular will expressed through the ballot box.

Electoral systems are methods designed to choose the individuals and political parties that will govern. The design is crucial, because the three main electoral models—first-past-the-post, preferential, and proportional representation—will deliver different outcomes. In Australia the second and third models are generally used. The preferential model differs from the first-past-the-post by the redistribution of votes from unsuccessful candidates if no outright majority is achieved. Proportional representation works on the principle that the proportion of votes will equal the proportion of seats. While electoral machinery reflects opinion, it also powerfully shapes the number and style of dominant political parties.

Elections began after the establishment of Legislative Councils in the Australian colonies. The introduction of self-government from the 1850s created bicameral parliaments, with elected lower houses but nominated upper houses in two colonies. The franchise was limited initially to men of property but quickly extended; women gained the right to vote at the turn of the century. Early elections were public events, and open voting required a clear declaration of choice. The secret ballot was first adopted in Victoria in 1856, and became known internationally as the 'Australian ballot'. Nineteenth-century elections used the first-past-the-post system, and were vigorously contested, intensely public occasions that required substantial resources and organisational effort to enrol voters and bring them to the polling booths.

The Commonwealth **Constitution** provided that both houses should be popularly elected. The House of Representatives comprised successful candidates in single-member electorates allocated according to population; the Senate comprised equal numbers of elected representatives of each of the states, and its membership was fixed at half the number of the lower house. The first House of Representatives had 75 members, and there are now 148. The term of each parliament was restricted to three years; senators served a six-year term with half retiring each three years. Senate casual vacancies are filled by the parliament of the senator's state rather than through by-election.

The female franchise was secured in the Commonwealth Electoral Act (1902) because that right had been won in SA and WA prior to **Federation**. Other features of the act were the adoption of the first-past-the-post system and the establishment of the **High Court** as the court of disputed returns. The act also denied Aborigines not already on the rolls the right to vote, a right not broadly regained until 1962. In 1915 a royal commission reported on electoral fraud. It found no significant problems, and concluded that irregularities were due to the new compulsory registration of electors. One simple proposal adopted to reduce irregularities was for poll clerks to rule a line through the elector's name on the roll when he or she was issued with a ballot paper.

The federal Electoral Act of 1918 installed preferential voting, a system first introduced in Qld in 1898, and reintroduced the postal ballot. Voting became compulsory in 1924. Proportional representation was introduced for Senate elections in 1948. In 1973 the adult franchise was reduced from 21 years of age to 18 as military conscription unjustly applied to men who were not old enough to vote. The Electoral Act has been altered about 70 times since 1902 and runs to nearly 400 sections. In 1973 the Australian Electoral Office was created; in 1984 the Australian Electoral Commission became a statutory authority, with responsibility for elections, boundaries, redistributions, and maintenance of the rolls. It administers divisions which differ in size from Kalgoorlie, 2.27 million square kilometres, to Wentworth, merely 26 square kilometres. The commission also conducts polls for trade unions and the Aboriginal and Torres Strait Islander Commission.

The conduct of Australian elections has been changed by the dominance of the party system, and the increasing influence of national media, public opinion **polls**, and sophisticated campaign techniques. Public funding of parties has entrenched their control of an expensive process. The older practices of town hall meetings and pub-balcony speeches have yielded to the televised national debate between party leaders, but minority groups are enabled by the system of proportional representation to maintain a strategic presence in the Senate. The author David **Malouf** has spoken of Election Day as a genuine but unrecognised national festival of colourful, ardent, yet peaceful activity centred on an act of citizenship, sustained by cups of tea, cake stalls, and school fêtes, culminating in the excitement of the race call.

JAMES WARDEN

Elkin, Adolphus Peter (1891–1979), anthropologist, became famous as an authority on Aboriginal culture and a leading influence in changing policies from protection to **assimilation** in the second quarter of the twentieth century.

Elkin, of Jewish and German parentage, grew up in the Hunter Valley, NSW, and entered the Anglican priesthood in Newcastle. He then studied anthropology at the universities of Sydney and London, where he completed a doctoral thesis on Aboriginal ritual and belief, and carried out fieldwork in the Kimberley and SA. He held simultaneous appointments as rector at Morpeth and lecturer at the University of Sydney until 1933, when the sudden resignation of his teacher–patron, A. Radcliffe-Brown, catapulted him into the chair. By training and temperament, Elkin was a functionalist, well-versed in the intellectual and political skills of adaptation and compromise. As a believer himself, he had a deep, almost mystical, appreciation of Aboriginal spirituality. He was outspokenly critical of white prejudice, for example in his vigorous campaign against abuses of the justice system in the NT. But he was also convinced that Aborigines must ultimately assimilate to the ways of the European or perish. 'The Aborigines must adjust to us. There is no escape from that.' It was a lesson he preached indefatigably, and with unshakeable self-confidence, to newspapers, Cabinet ministers, fellow anthropologists, and community groups. His book *The Australian Aborigines: How to Understand Them* (1938 and later editions) was the bible on Aboriginal society for almost 40 years. In World War II he vigorously promoted the usefulness of social science in monitoring civilian morale. Elkin's reputation has recently declined as historical opinion swung hard against the assimilationism he upheld. Tigger Wise, *The Self-Made Anthropologist* (1985), is an unflattering portrait, which nevertheless provides materials for an alternative reading of his life.

GD

Ellery, Robert Lewis John (1827–1908), Victorian government astronomer, was born at Cranleigh, England, and came to Victoria in 1851 in search of gold. Although he had trained as a medical practitioner, his real interest was in **astronomy**, which he learned at Greenwich Observatory. While practising as a surgeon in Williamstown, he noticed navigational difficulties caused by lack of accurate time determination. His lobbying resulted in the establishment of the first Melbourne Observatory at Williamstown in 1853 and his appointment as government astronomer, a post he held until 1895. Under his direction, the observatory flourished. It moved to the Melbourne Domain in 1863 and assumed responsibilities for meteorology and tidal information, and the calibration of **surveying** and navigational instruments. A brilliant and versatile scientist, Ellery was superintendent of the Geodetic Survey of Victoria from 1858 to 1874; a founder of the Royal Society of Victoria (president 1856–84); a trustee of the Public Library; and chairman of the Alfred Hospital. In 1873 he helped organise the Victorian Torpedo and Signal Corps. Ellery was elected president of the Australasian Association for the Advancement of Science (**ANZAAS**) in 1900. He produced three star catalogues and more than 50 papers on astronomy, astrophotography, **climate**, meteorology, and chronography. His work, mainly published in the *Transactions of the Royal Society of Victoria*, included 'The Survey of Victoria' in Alexander **Sutherland**, *Victoria and Its Metropolis* (1888). Mt Ellery in East Gippsland is named after him.

DC

Elliott, Harold Edward (1878–1931) was among the most popular of the citizen-soldiers who led the First **AIF** in World War I. A noted sportsman, he interrupted university studies to enlist in the Victorian contingent that served in the **Boer War**, where he was decorated and commissioned. He left his legal firm in 1914 to command a battalion at the **Gallipoli** landing, where he was wounded. Elliott was promoted to brigadier-general when the Australians transferred to the Western Front, and consolidated a reputation for personal courage, strict discipline and impolitic concern for the interests of his troops that brought him the nickname of 'Pompey'. Lack of official recognition and thwarted ambition for higher command fostered grievances that lasted long after the war, which he pursued both in the press and the federal parliament after he was elected to the Senate as a Nationalist in 1919. His eventual promotion to major-general in the militia in 1927 came too late, and in 1931 he took his life. Ross McMullin is writing a biography. Elliott's combination of exultant bellicosity and solicitude is difficult for a later generation to comprehend. Among his contemporaries he was a hero.

SM

Ellis, Malcolm Henry (1890–1969) was a journalist and historian who participated briefly and acrimoniously in planning the *ADB*. Born in outback Qld, he achieved an education through scholarships. His journalistic talent was soon apparent, as were his conservative views. In 1926 the Sydney *Daily Telegraph* sent him to London, where he reported on the League of Nations sessions. After a period freelancing, Ellis joined the *Bulletin*, and remained a contributor until his retirement. Much of his column was devoted to warning against the spread of **communism**, a theme he developed in several books, including *The Garden Path* (1949). It was his biographies of Lachlan **Macquarie** (1947), Francis **Greenway** (1949), and John **Macarthur** (1955) that received most public recognition. The colourful writing in these detailed and partisan studies reflected his journalistic background. A doughty enemy, Ellis railed against the Australian Labor Party as riddled with communists and excoriated Manning **Clark** for what he called 'history without facts'. His penchant for argument and readiness to resign from organisations—including the **Royal Australian Historical Society**, the Australian Journalists Association, and the editorial board and national committee of the *ADB*—left him, finally, an isolated figure.

KT

Emancipists were convicts who had been granted a conditional or absolute pardon before the term of their sentence had expired. This entitled them to work for wages and to own property, thus affording many—notably Samuel Terry and James Ruse—the opportunity to establish themselves as successful settlers. Later, *emancipist* commonly referred to ex-convicts in general, without differentiating between those who had been granted pardons and those who had served their full term. Emancipists demonstrated considerable solidarity, particularly in their disdain of **exclusives**. A political group, led by W.C. **Wentworth**, campaigned for legal and political reforms in the 1820s and 1830s.

HD

Emden was a German cruiser destroyed by the first HMAS *Sydney* on 9 November 1914. Following the outbreak of **World War I**, 78 Allied ships had failed to capture the *Emden*. It was attempting to attack the wireless station at Cocos (Keeling) Island when intercepted by the *Sydney* and crippled in 95 minutes of action, which killed 134 *Emden* crew but only four from the *Sydney*. As Prime Minister Andrew **Fisher** advised parliament of the **RAN's** first blood, wild cheers greeted the interjection: 'What about our "tinpot navy" now?'

DC

Empire was a Sydney **newspaper** established by Henry **Parkes** on 28 December 1850. It began as a weekly but within a month became a daily, with the aim of 'the social and political elevation of the working classes'. As editor from 1850 to 1858, Parkes used the paper to air his radical liberal views, to attack the conservatives, and to promote responsible self-government; W.C. **Wentworth** was a favourite target.

Parkes's financial difficulties in 1858 forced him to cease operations until May 1863, when Samuel **Bennett** joined him as a co-owner, and the political writer William Wilkes was appointed as an editor. The *Empire* ceased publication in 1875 when it merged with Bennett's *Evening News*.

HD

Empire Day was initiated in 1905 to promote loyalty among the dominion countries of the British Empire. It was celebrated on 24 May, Queen Victoria's birthday, with speeches, newspaper articles, and public events. Empire Day was directed especially at schoolchildren, who gathered to receive homilies followed by a school picnic or half-holiday. Firework displays were often held at night. Its popularity peaked in the years between the two world wars, largely owing to the perceived threat posed by **communism** in Australia, but waned after the 1960s along with the Empire and attachment to its memory. Maurice French related the transition in Peter Spearritt and David Walker (eds), *Australian Popular Culture* (1979). Children in Catholic schools were generally not encouraged to celebrate Empire Day; instead they celebrated Irish links with 'home' on St Patrick's Day. In 1914 Catholics waged an unsuccessful campaign to have Empire Day renamed **Australia Day**.

HD

Employers' organisations serve two main purposes: promoting the trade interests of their members, especially by influencing government policies; and participating in the system of **industrial relations** governing the employment of labour. The Sydney Chamber of Commerce (1825) was the first formal organisation representing the common interests of Australian business. It was formed not as a response to organised labour, but to promote trading interests, and similar bodies were formed in other towns and cities thereafter. From the 1830s employers also established temporary alliances in response to special labour problems in their particular industries. Once such disputes were resolved, these associations would typically disappear until needed again. An example of such non-continuous association was the meeting of ship-owners in 1837 which successfully rejected the demands of the seamen and labourers of the port of Sydney for a wage increase. Wider employer collaboration occurred, similarly, when employers wished to meet labour problems in more than one industry.

The emergence of stronger **trade unions** and the impact of industrial legislation, especially the introduction of **arbitration**, emphasised the need for employer organisations of greater permanence. A Victorian Employers Union was formed in response to the successful strike of bootmakers in Melbourne in 1884, one of many new employers' associations. The Pastoralists Associations played a key role in coordinating employer and government action to break the **shearers' strikes** in the 1890s. With these victories, and the mass unemployment caused by the depression, the need for such activity waned.

The introduction of industrial legislation at the turn of the century gave rise to the Victorian Employers Federation (1901) as an extra-parliamentary non-Labor body, which absorbed the near-defunct Victorian Employers Union in 1903. Other groups were also resurrected for political purposes in other colonies, such as the Chamber of Manufactures of New South Wales. At first these bodies resisted the passage of arbitration legislation, which encouraged union organisation and protected weak unions from hostile employers. Employers' organisations also challenged the power of the Commonwealth tribunal in the High Court. But intransigent opposition softened when employers realised that compulsory arbitration could also act in their favour to restrain union power. Organisation enabled employers to unravel the legal complexities of arbitration and prepare cases for industrial tribunals.

Broad organisations preceded those restricted to a particular industry. Employer federations were formed in Victoria (1901), NSW (1903), Qld (1904), SA (1907), and WA (1913). In 1904 a national organisation, the Central Council of Employers of Australia, was created to coordinate at the national level the activities of the federations and to restrict the scope of the Conciliation and Arbitration Act. These state and federal organisations were weakened by divisions over **tariffs** and the emergence of Chambers of Manufactures in the states and the Associated Chambers of Manufactures of Australia at the national level.

By the 1950s the growth of the Australian economy and the increase of nation-wide enterprises increased the need for national, rather than state, employer organisations. National employer coordination across industrial boundaries required more than the Associated Chambers of Manufactures of Australia and the Australian Council of Employers Federation (which had succeeded the earlier Central Council of Employers). In 1961, the National Employers Association was established to coordinate national industry associations in policy decisions that affected national wage cases and a wide range of other matters of common interest. In 1978 its role was overtaken by the Confederation of Australian Industry, which was formed by an amalgamation of Associated Chambers of Manufactures and the Council of Employers Federation. Within the confederation there existed two separate councils. The National Employers Trade Council in Canberra determined policy with respect to trade, industry, and commerce; and the National Employers Industrial Council in Melbourne handled industrial relations matters. The latter has attempted to act as the employers' counterpart of the Australian Council of Trade Unions (**ACTU**) by promoting unity of purpose and action among employers: the National Industrial Council represents the interests of all members regarding industrial relations and labour matters, at both national and international level.

Despite this promotion of unity, the greater alignment of the confederation with manufacturing interests caused former key affiliates of the Council of Employers Federation to establish their own national confederation. The National Farmers Federation joined the Australian Federation of Employers, a New Right challenge to the confederation. Another rival to the confederation is the Business Council of Australia, which consists of the chief executives of about 500 of Australia's largest companies. Formed in 1983, the Business Council is the result of a merger between Business Round Table and the Australian Industries Development Association. The Business Council has played an important part in policy debate and has actively supported large companies at national forums. It also commissioned the influential paper, *Enterprise-based Bargaining Units: A Better Way of Working* (1989).

In 1989, the Associated Chamber of Manufactures disaffiliated from the Confederation of Australian Industry. Shortly afterwards the influential Metal Trades Industry Association also withdrew from the Confederation. This was followed by a period of reorganisation on the part of employer organisations. The Confederation merged with the Australian Chamber of Commerce to form the Australian Chamber of Commerce and Industry. The Metal Trades Industry Association merged with the Australian Chamber of Manufactures to form the Australian Industry Group. Similar mergers occurred at the state level. In addition, employer organisations sought to rationalise their operations by forming Australian Chamber Net. This has been formed by six of Australia's major Chambers of Commerce and Industry. It represents a formal coalition that provides a national membership package—a one-stop shopping net for members of state-based employer groups.

D.H. PLOWMAN AND R. STANDFORD

Employment, see **Labour history**; **Unemployment**

Energy was spoken of by colonial Australians mainly as a synonym for human effort: for example, they would speak with admiration of the 'energy and enterprise' demonstrated by settlers in clearing their land or building up a business. They relied upon human muscle-power for felling trees, ploughing paddocks, shearing sheep, sinking mines, milking cows, lifting bags of wheat, and loading cargoes onto ships. Strong men were admired, and feats of physical strength—tallies of sheep shorn, fields ploughed, trees felled—went down in the annals of rural communities. While the traditional division of labour defined men's work as physically demanding and often dirty, and women's as dexterous and usually clean, there were many women, especially in farm communities, who expended more physical energy than white-collar men. Pioneering women sometimes carried heavy pails of water from stream to kitchen, balanced on yokes across their shoulders, or pulled harrows across the land like human oxen. Until the last quarter of the nineteenth century most people worked, for up to 10 hours a day, standing up, in jobs that required considerable muscle-power. Obesity was a relatively rare problem by modern standards: it is perhaps significant that rich men were conventionally pictured as fat, while working men were usually depicted as lean and muscular.

Europeans settled Australia just as Europe itself was about to be transformed by new sources of power. But while coal and steam were beginning to revolutionise the old society, the new continued to depend mainly upon the ancient technologies of wind, water, and animal power. Early views of Sydney were dominated by the sails of the ships which had propelled the newcomers across the oceans and by the vanes of the windmills which provided the settlement with its first forms of industrial power. In Hobart and Launceston the colonists captured the waters of nearby streams to power flour mills.

Animals supplemented human muscles. **Horses** were a fast form of personal transport, as well as a mark of social status; the famous **Cobb & Co.** coaches, which began to open up inland Australia from the 1850s, were the speedsters of the inland. But until the colonies got a good system of roads, the slower but stronger and more robust bullock was a much more important source of energy for transport and **agriculture**. Only in the 1880s did horse teams displace bullock teams in transporting the Riverina wool clip. In rough or mountainous country, bullocks continued to be the main form of heavy transport until the early twentieth century. On the other hand, wherever intelligence and tractability

mattered, as in mine workings and coal pits, and in pulling harvesters and ploughs, horses were the favoured form of power. They dominated urban transport, pulling cabs, coaches, drays, and trams, until the late 1870s, when the rising costs of feed and the steaming mounds of horse manure in the streets hastened the changeover to steam power.

Sydney sat above a massive new source of energy—a great underground bed of black coal that stretched from the Hunter south to the Illawarra and west to Lithgow. Its existence was known from the 1790s, but it was not systematically exploited until the mid-nineteenth century. The first steam-engines, powering mills and small coastal vessels, had appeared in the 1830s, but the prime use of coal, from the 1840s on, was for generating coal gas to light the streets and buildings of the coastal cities. Beyond the coast and the coal-fields themselves, the main boiler fuel was the less efficient but more accessible firewood. The railway locomotive and the large steam-powered factory were the most spectacular products of the steam age. The cable-tram, the hydraulic lift, the miners' cage, and the electric light also used steam power distributed by cables, water pressure, or electric current to widely dispersed points of use.

In the mid-nineteenth century animal power rivalled steam power, and firewood rivalled coal as energy sources. In the last quarter of the nineteenth century, as the supplies of firewood shrank and the **railways** spread, colonial coal consumption more than quadrupled. By the 1930s the farm-horse was yielding to the tractor, and by the 1940s the steam locomotive was giving way to the electric or diesel train. In 1945 coal—the main source of electricity as well as a major industrial fuel—had become twice as important as wood, although wood still rivalled petrol. In the following three decades, however, both the volume and sources of the nation's energy system were revolutionised. The consumption of petroleum—chiefly as automobile fuel, although also for aviation and maritime use—more than quadrupled between 1960 and 1980. The discovery of large reserves of undersea **oil and gas**, first in Bass Strait and later on the north-west continental shelf, provided a new source of domestic fuel for heating and cooking and largely abolished the nation's dependence on imported oil. The international oil-price rise of 1974 provoked new concern about Australia's dependence on fossil fuels. Renewable energy sources, such as hydro-electricity and solar power, contributed little to an energy bill which continued to grow into the 1990s even faster than that of other high energy economies like the USA. Australia is now a major energy exporter. With no nuclear power stations of its own, it remains a major exporter of **uranium**. And while local coal consumption has plateaued, coal exports have continued to boom. In the 1990s Australia mines almost 10 times as much coal as it did in 1945, when coal was the nation's largest source of energy.

Malcolm Kennedy, *Hauling the Loads: A History of Australia's Working Horses and Bullocks* (1992), is the best account of animal power, while Joy McCann and Matthew Churchward document *Victorian Steampower* (1994).

Graeme Davison surveys Australia's late colonial energy system in *Australia 1888* (1982).

GRAEME DAVISON

Engineering emerged as a professional occupation only during the period of European settlement of Australia. Originally it was a military activity concerned with fortifications and the engines of war, but in the eighteenth century civil engineering became distinguished from military engineering, and chiefly concerned with the design and building of roads, canals, bridges, harbours, and urban utilities. Mechanical engineering became a separate branch of the profession during the first Industrial Revolution, and mining, electrical, chemical, and other subdivisions followed.

The early Australian engineers were engaged in design and construction of roads, railways, and water supplies in the colonies. Most were employed by the colonial governments on public works, though the mining industry and the growth of manufacturing industries fostered private practice. Professional engineering associations were formed in the second half of the nineteenth century, during which the number of engineers in Australia grew from 50 to 1000. Schools of Mines—for example, at Ballarat (1870), Bendigo (1873), Gawler, SA (1888), and Zeehan, Tasmania (1892)—were mainly concerned with education for mine managers, although some began to provide professional engineering courses. The University of Melbourne began teaching engineering in 1860, the University of Sydney from 1883. The earlier pupillage method of training engineers was in decline when the Institution of Engineers, Australia, formed in 1919, achieved control over qualifications.

Among the major public engineering projects undertaken during the colonial period were the Overland Telegraph, harbour, railway and irrigation works, and water supply systems, of which C.Y. **O'Connor's** pipeline to the WA goldfields, completed in 1903, was perhaps the most celebrated. Australian engineers brought significant innovation to gold and metalliferous mining. Advances in **manufacturing**, **transport**, **communications**, and electric power contributed to the growth of the primary export industries. In 1905 A.G.M. Mitchell patented the thrust bearing for improved propulsion of ships.

In the first half of the twentieth century the engineering feats that gripped the public imagination were urban and industrial. The career of John **Monash**, which spanned early experiments in ferro-concrete design and construction, military leadership of the First AIF, and then development of the brown coal industry for electric power generation, might be seen as emblematic of this transition. The Victorian Louis Brennan, who had taken his invention of the torpedo to the British War Office in 1880, continued to develop munitions during World War I. The opening of the **BHP** Newcastle steelworks in 1915 fostered heavy industry, and the managing director, Essington **Lewis**, came to embody the masterful authority of the engineer as business magnate. Above all, the construction of the **Sydney Harbour Bridge** under John **Bradfield** provided the

symbol of national development. World War II further stimulated engineering, while postwar projects such as the **Snowy Mountains Hydro–Electric Scheme** and the creation of an Australian **motor car** industry continued the heroic phase of engineering. In the latter part of the twentieth century motor transport caused road and bridge engineering, and later traffic engineering, to become major activities of civil engineers.

Throughout this period the Institution of Engineers consolidated the status of professional engineers. The institution gained a royal charter in 1938 and was able to provide the title Chartered Engineer (Australia) for experienced engineers. In 1946 it fostered the Association of Professional Engineers, Australia, to seek better pay and conditions through the industrial relations system, an objective achieved in 1961. The Association of Consulting Engineers, Australia, was formed in 1952 to cater for the interests of consulting engineers. The three bodies maintain a high level of cooperation and pursue common interests. In 1988 the institution published Brian Carroll, *The Engineers: 200 Years at Work for Australia*, to celebrate its members' contribution to national prosperity.

By then, however, substantial changes were taking place in professional engineering practice. Most engineers had been used to certainty of values and stable careers leading to management of large public sector enterprises. But by the end of the twentieth century changes in the public sector caused the majority of engineers to be employed in the private sector. Organisational change in both sectors brought a drastic reduction in opportunities for career advancement, causing many more engineers to pursue careers in engineering technology rather than management, in small rather than large enterprises, and with frequent changes in employment.

The profession has developed several adaptation strategies. The Association of Professional Engineers extended its membership to scientists and managers in 1990, and developed a major facility for management education. The Institution of Engineers extended its membership to include para-professionals, and fostered articulated educational pathways and postgraduate programs for its members. In 1998 there were 120 000 professional engineers in Australia under retirement age.

BRIAN LLOYD

Engineers' case of 1920 marked an important shift in the judicial interpretation of the Commonwealth Constitution and significantly enlarged the powers of the federal government. The High Court was asked to determine whether union members of the Amalgamated Society of Engineers working in a state-owned enterprise came within the scope of the Commonwealth's **arbitration** power. Reversing its earlier doctrine of implied immunity of state instrumentalities, the majority determined that they did. Whereas the earlier doctrine had found an implied immunity that prevented the states and the Commonwealth from interfering in each other's activities, the court now held that the Commonwealth was entitled to exercise the fullest amplitude of the powers set out in its Constitution. The decision was a triumph for R.G. **Menzies**, then a junior barrister, who appeared for the union. The immediate effect was to clarify a wide scope for federal arbitration; the long-term consequence was a further strengthening of the centripetal forces in the Australian federation.

SM

Entertainment was not high among the aims of the first European colonists. Because the first Australian colonies were intended as penal settlements, their governments were reluctant to encourage recreational and sporting activities. Yet with the convicts there inevitably came the full repertoire of pre-industrial English pastimes and institutions, including fairs, horse-racing, **cricket**, football, the public house, and the theatre.

In England public pastimes were associated with gambling, violence, and disorder, which is why the colonial authorities were reluctant to sponsor or allow them. In the end they sanctioned them as a means of providing the convicts with alternative activities to **gambling** and drinking: the irony was that in sanctioning horse-racing, in particular, the authorities in fact stimulated the very vices they hoped to contain. Meanwhile, the officers and wealthy free settlers were anxious to organise their own entertainments, as a means of both amusing and legitimising themselves as a New World gentry.

Folk football did not become as firmly entrenched in Australia as it was in England, but cricket, first played in Sydney in 1803, was encouraged by the authorities as 'elegant' and 'manly'. Perhaps the most widely followed **sport** in the period before 1850 was horse-racing. The first 'meetings' consisted simply of match races on the roads of Sydney, although the first organised program was held at Hyde Park in 1810. Racing changed its complexion as thoroughbreds replaced Arabs. In Van Diemen's Land regular race meetings were held from 1813, and turf clubs were established in the colonies of Port Phillip and South Australia soon after their foundation.

Despite efforts by the authorities to suppress them, prize and cock fights were common in the period before 1850. At first they were held in public houses, but as the attempts to eliminate them intensified, they moved to unsettled areas on the outskirts of settlement. The government's task was made more difficult by the fact that wealthy and influential colonists were among the most devoted followers of prizefighting. Although it enjoyed a golden age in the 1830s and 1840s, the riotous behaviour of spectators and the illegal tactics employed by some fighters destroyed its reputation by mid-century.

A theatre existed briefly in Sydney in the 1790s and early 1800s, its reputation tarnished by the unruliness of its audiences. Later governors refused licences to aspiring entrepreneurs until Bourke provided the Sydney merchant, Barnett Levey, with one in 1832. The opening of theatres in Hobart, Melbourne, and Adelaide contributed further towards establishing it as a critical colonial institution. These theatres focused on legitimate **drama** and **opera** but halls providing popular stage entertainments also began to appear.

In the period before 1850 many public entertainments were enjoyed by plebeians, gentry, and government officials together, but in the second half of the nineteenth century this shared public culture disappeared. In its place emerged a series of institutions representing varied and sometimes conflicting cultural values, and designed to cater to more specialised audiences. Home entertainment, symbolised by the growing sales of pianos, was one trend. The increased commercialisation of recreational and leisure activities outside the home was another. Theatre entrepreneurs like J.C. **Williamson** created national networks, sophisticated advertising techniques, and extravagant productions. The trend towards specialisation continued with legitimate, melodrama, circus, minstrel show, and vaudeville companies each targeting particular audiences. Sport was marked by the promulgation of standardised rules that were applied to the various football codes as well as to cricket; the establishment of organised competitions; the introduction of professional administrators and players; the creation of a specialised sporting press; the enclosure of grounds (so that admission could be charged), and the separation of spectators from participants by the introduction of fences. At the turn of the century new technology produced amusement parks and cinemas.

The most popular spectator sports included sculling, cricket, football, and horse-racing. The first two were important in providing Australians with a sense of pride in the progress of the colonies, measured by the success of cricketers and scullers in international competition. Horse-racing gave an enormous stimulus to gambling through the creation of pony and proprietary clubs, and the subsequent increase in the number of race meetings. **Australian Rules football** became a popular spectator sport in this era—at least in the southern colonies—and this marked a significant attempt by the colonists to develop their own entertainments rather than simply import them.

Many of these late-nineteenth-century entertainments catered particularly to men. Not only were they in the majority as spectators at sporting events, but pubs too were male gathering places. Women who visited **pubs** were assumed to be prostitutes or, in the case of young women attracted to the dance halls attached to public houses, on their way to **prostitution**. The influence of the cult of 'true womanhood' meant that women were expected to find their recreations in the domestic sphere, especially through music (as Humphrey **McQueen** reminds us, this was the golden age of the piano) and the production of handcrafts. Yet women were also commonly found in theatre audiences: matinées catered particularly to mothers and children, while evening performances at theatres attracted courting couples. Like men, women drank and gambled (at cards) but this was usually done within the confines of their own homes and often in the company of other women.

Between the wars, cricket, the various football codes, and horse-racing widened their appeal (even though state governments moved to abolish pony and proprietary racing). Greyhound and harness racing emerged as new entertainments with strong regional followings, given a particular stimulus by the introduction of the on-course totalisator and the radio broadcast of meetings.

Legitimate theatre struggled to compete against cinema and radio, the entrepreneurs seeking to cater to a specialised well-to-do audience by staging musical comedies and operettas. Vaudeville programs oscillated between revues and 'turns', but finally succumbed to 'the talkies'. Cinema attracted far larger audiences than theatre or sporting events. Most of the films shown here (85 per cent in 1940) were of American origin. 'The talkies' proved even more popular than silent films. Australians liked the Hollywood versions of 'the classics', like *David Copperfield*, but were more ambivalent about films that emphasised American themes and values. Australian-made films, which tended to focus on the bush and its characters, also found a niche in the market. Another new entertainment medium, **radio**, after a hesitant beginning also flourished, and by 1942 there were some 128 stations and over a million licence holders. Radio provided a diverse range of programs, including classical and popular music, descriptions of sporting events, lectures, and plays.

World War II ushered in a new era of domesticity as returning service personnel sought refuge from the instability created by depression and war. The arrival of **television** in 1956 contributed to this emphasis on home entertainment. Cinema audiences halved between the mid-1950s and early 1960s as Australians spent their evenings watching television programs, most of which were imported from the USA. Not until the late 1960s and the introduction of a quota system did locally made programs, led by *Homicide*, match the imported products in popularity.

The trend towards the commercialisation of Australian sport accelerated in the postwar period. Cricket and football players became full-time professionals; club and national teams relied more on corporate sponsorship and funds from the sale of television rights than on gate receipts; rules were changed to make the games faster and so more spectator-oriented. In short, Australian sport became big business.

As the baby-boomers came of age in the 1960s, they rejected their parents' penchant for domestic entertainments. They provided a market for a new genre of American (and later Australian) film that dwelt on the trials and tribulations of youth. Rock 'n' roll also served as a medium of rebellion against convention. The style of dancing and the lyrics challenged the sexual orthodoxies of the 1950s. The surfing subculture which enjoyed a sustained vogue from the 1960s, with its emphasis on hedonism and the search for the perfect wave, contradicted the digger values associated with the surf life-saving movement.

In the postwar period, too, the **wowser** restrictions on entertainment were finally lifted. The **six o'clock swill**, the bans on Sunday entertainments, and the restrictions on gambling (other than on racetracks) disappeared. By the 1990s the American influence on Australian institutions of entertainment was as predominant as ever. Indeed, the grow-

ing popularity of such sports as baseball and basketball and the advent of cable television (to which no rules requiring local content apply) suggest an increasing role. Still, the establishment of Australian film and television industries and the creation of local ballet, opera, and drama companies in the postwar period have allowed the flowering of an Australian entertainment industry and stalled the arrival of *Austerica*.

Cultural history has flourished in Australia over the past 20 years. Katharine Brisbane (ed.), *Entertaining Australia* (1991), is an important study of the history of Australian theatre; Diane Collins, *Hollywood Down Under* (1987), is a model study of the role of cinema; Richard Waterhouse, *Private Pleasures, Public Leisure: A History of Australian Popular Culture Since 1788* (1995), is an overview of changing entertainment patterns.

RICHARD WATERHOUSE

Environment influenced, and was in turn influenced by, the human history of Australia. The first generations of European settlers often regarded the continent as 'hostile', 'barren' and 'inhospitable', a foe to be defeated, tamed, or subdued. The power balance, as they saw it, was in favour of nature over humans. In this century, the balance has swung in the other direction. The geographer Griffith **Taylor** and the historian Keith **Hancock** warned of the need to respect the limits imposed by environment on humans. 'The advent of the white man with his ready-made civilisation has violently disturbed the delicate balance of nature established for centuries in the most isolated of continents', Hancock wrote in 1930. Now it is common for Australian writers to perceive the environment as 'fragile', 'threatened' or 'depleted', a victim in need of protection rather than an enemy to be overcome. William Lines, *Taming the Great South Land* (1991), is an unrelenting attack on the Europeans' rape of the Australian environment: 'The great surging, restless, avaricious megatropolis of mankind now encircles the outposts of wilderness.' A few historians, such as Geoffrey **Blainey** in *The Great Seesaw* (1988), regard such attitudes as extreme, a manifestation of the pessimism which has periodically overtaken Western societies.

Australia's environment is the product of a distinctive ecological history, brilliantly surveyed in Tim Flannery's *The Future Eaters* (1994). It is geologically older, flatter, and more weathered than other lands. It is rich in minerals but its soils are shallow and relatively infertile. Much of the continent receives little rain; it has few large rivers, and the run-off to the ocean along the east coast, where vegetation is most abundant, is not copious. Its oceans, with the exception of the waters surrounding the Great Barrier Reef, a long coral barrier which stretches 2500 kilometres along the Queensland coast, yield only modest stocks of fish. The **climate** is generally warm, with winter snow falling only on a few peaks of the southern alps. It is also extremely variable: the 'droughts and flooding rains', famous in Australian folklore, reflect the influence of ENSO (the El Niño Southern Oscillation), the cyclical weather pattern associated with the warming and cooling of air and ocean currents in the

Environment

Pacific. Eucalypts ('gum trees'), acacias ('wattles'), and sclerophyll, a family of spindly hard-leafed plants well adapted to this dry climate, are the dominant plant species. The main native fauna are marsupials, a family of mammals which rear their young in a pouch (the kangaroo is the best known), and monotremes—mammals which lay eggs, such as the platypus. **Aborigines**, who have lived in this environment for more than 60 000 years, evolved a way of life which recognised, and exploited, its distinctive characteristics. They left their own mark on the **landscape**, especially through their use of fire as a tool to stimulate the growth of native grasses, the pasture on which kangaroos, emus, and other favoured game could feed.

Since 1788 Europeans have modified this environment in several ways. Their first attempts at deriving a livelihood were to exploit its oceans: within a generation they had severely depleted the numbers of whales and seals around the southern coasts and islands. When they crossed the Great Divide it was to exploit the grasslands of the interior for pasture and, later, to extract the minerals, especially gold, which lay mainly in its foothills. Almost the first action of the newcomers was to cut down trees. In the 1840s they took possession of the grasslands of western NSW and Victoria, marvelling at the open pastures already created by the Aborigines. But by the end of the century they were hacking into the thick forests of Gippsland, New England, and northern Tasmania to clear small patches of grassland for **dairy** farms. A map of Victoria in 1869 showed most of the colony, except for the Western District and the central goldfields, still under forest cover. A century later the **forest** had been pegged back by logging, farming, and **urbanisation** to perhaps one-fifth of the state. More than half of Australia's land is still used for grazing by imported animals, especially sheep and cattle.

Mining was the most devastating of new industries, although its effects were more localised than grazing or farming. Thousands of miles of underground shafts and tunnels now honeycomb the earth under such heavily mined areas as the central goldfields of Victoria, the Hunter River coalfields, the Barrier of western NSW and the goldfields of WA. On the surface the miners' labours are marked by constructed mountains of mullock; hillsides stripped bare of trees for props and fuel; and streams diverted and often polluted by the wastes from sedimentation and flotation processing. The highly mechanised techniques employed for open-cut mining and the processing of mineral sands have left deep scars on the environment of the largely remote areas where they have been practised. In a few places, such as the country around Queenstown, Tasmania, where the sulphurised fumes from copper smelters polluted the air, mining transformed green forests into blackened deserts.

Europeans were a farming people, and they hoped to make Australia into an agricultural nation. They drew their **stump-jump ploughs** and harrows across the newly cleared paddocks of the Victorian Wimmera and South Australian Mallee, turning over the shallow soil and planting new varieties of wheat, better adapted to the dry climate. At first the yields were good, but soon, as the nitrogen was depleted, they fell. Repeated ploughing loosened the texture of the soil. Heavy rains washed it into the creeks, gouging great gullies in their banks. In drought, when crops failed and dust storms swept the plains, the precious layer of soil was lifted into the air and carried sometimes hundreds of kilometres, even across the Tasman. The soil cover over much of Australia is now badly eroded.

White Australians cherished the hope that science and engineering could tame this harsh environment. In 1897 Henry **Lawson** reproached those who painted the outback in romantic colours. Its 'awful desolation', he insisted, was not a temporary effect of **drought** but its normal condition. 'The moral', he concluded, 'is the universal one: "Let us irrigate."' Already cattlemen were erecting windmills to draw water for their stock from a great artesian basin underneath the parched inland plains of NSW and Qld. The **Chaffey** brothers had begun to capture the waters of the Murray–Darling river system to lay the foundations of a prosperous irrigated fruit and wine industry. As Ernestine **Hill** suggested in her popular 1937 book, Australians were turning *Water into Gold*. Confidence in the redemptive power of **irrigation** peaked in the postwar years when the Commonwealth government initiated the massive **Snowy Mountains** and **Ord River schemes**. This confidence was short-lived. By the 1970s scientists were beginning to question both its economic benefits and environmental sustainability. Groundwater was being used faster than it could be replenished. Irrigation raised the water table and released salts from the soil, slowly rendering it infertile: by 1997 approximately one-third of Victoria's irrigation area was salinised. Insecticides and other chemicals used to improve crop yields found their way into streams, poisoning other species and stimulating the growth of toxic blue-green algae. (See **Water resources**.)

The impact of European settlement upon the Australian environment has been both limited and concentrated by its highly urbanised character. Nineteenth-century cities often lacked underground sewerage and good waste-disposal systems, and depended on noxious industries such as wool-washing, abattoirs, and tanneries; they made heavy demands upon the surrounding environment. Sometimes these hazards accumulated to the point of endangering human health through **epidemic** disease. In the twentieth century, while the threat of pollution from organic wastes abated, pollution from industrial chemicals, automobile exhausts, and aircraft noise increased. Dan Coward, *Out of Sight: Sydney's Environmental History 1851–1981* (1988), and Tony Dingle and Carolyn Rasmussen, *Vital Connections: Melbourne and its Board of Works 1891–1991* (1991), are valuable studies of the two most populous cities.

The Australian environment has been changed as much by the exotic species which Europeans brought with them as by the Europeans themselves. Some of these imports, such as the rabbit and the fox, are regarded as **pests**; but many others—the deciduous trees which now grace city parks and suburban gardens, the hawthorn hedges and pencil pines which enclose farmers' paddocks, the trout which swim in alpine streams, and the **horses** and dogs which round up stock—have also placed pressure on native species. Since 1788 the numbers of indigenous fauna and flora have continued to fall. A 1996 report on the State of the Environment found that five per cent of higher plants, 23 per cent of mammals, nine per cent of birds, seven per cent of reptiles, 16 per cent of amphibians and nine per cent of freshwater fish were extinct, endangered, or vulnerable.

In only 200 years, humans have made vast changes to the Australian environment; how, if at all, has the environment changed them? From the beginnings of European settlement, this was a fertile topic of speculation. Perhaps a hard land would breed a hardy people, better fitted for the Darwinian struggle for existence than their European ancestors. Or perhaps its material abundance would render them slothful. Some theorists were attracted to notions of climatic determinism, believing that heat and humidity would sap Australians' intellectual powers. Others, like Sir Raphael **Cilento**, asserted with equal confidence that 'the white man can live and thrive in the Australian tropics'. Theories of environmental determinism have had a poor press in the last half of the twentieth century, but it is interesting to note the recent emergence of the idea that Australian social mores, such as the code of **mateship**, were a human counterpart of the co-adaptation which has been the keynote of its ecological history. 'Perhaps', writes Tim Flannery, 'there is something quite fundamental about such social obligations that makes them indispensable in the Australian environment.'

GRAEME DAVISON

Environmental history emerged as a conscious sub-discipline in the 1970s and 1980s, though the writing of Australian history has always been suffused with a sense of the land and its difference—the observed peculiarities of antipodean nature. Its sources are many: an emphasis by colonial and early national historians on the challenges of land settlement, a long-term investment in the study of Australian land use by historical geographers, the geographic inspiration of the French *Annales* school of history, the discovery after World War II of Australian antiquity, and the recent disciplinary definition of 'environmental history' in American scholarship.

Environmental history's distinctiveness from the postwar traditions of **historical geography** resides in its closer affiliation with environmental politics, its explicit engagement with the scientific insights and metaphors of ecology, its determination to give the non-human world some agency in the historical narrative, and a stronger self-definition as a humanities discipline. According to one Australian geographer, this last quality results in 'a greater emphasis on story-telling'. Environmental history sometimes moves audaciously across time and space and species. It can thereby challenge some of the conventions of history, by questioning the anthropocentric, nationalistic, and documentary biases of the craft.

Aesthetic evaluations of the Australian landscape and utilitarian surveys of natural resources informed the earliest European accounts of Australia. As Geoffrey **Bolton** noted in an early survey of historians as interpreters of the environment (in George Seddon and Mari Davis, eds, *Man and Landscape in Australia*, 1976), colonial historians such as J.D. **Lang**, W.C. **Wentworth** and G.W. **Rusden** wrote largely for a British audience and 'appraised the country mainly in terms of its adaptability for economic investment and primary production', thereby echoing the literary conventions and strategic pitch of many explorers. The growth of local publishing and native-born audiences, together with burgeoning nationalism in the second half of the nineteenth century, encouraged writers to look instead at the adaptability of human nature, and to assess the influence of environment on society, particularly its impact on national character and ethos. The *Bulletin* writers and **Heidelberg** painters were leaders in the celebration of an Australian pastoral tradition and, by the early twentieth century, national historians such as James Collier (*The Pastoral Age in Australasia*, 1911) and Stephen **Roberts** (*History of Australian Land Settlement*, 1924) began to map the political and legislative entrenchment of pastoralism. Thirty years later, Russel **Ward's** *The Australian Legend* (1958) continued the search for the determining influence of the outback on national character, and renewed Australian interest in Frederick Jackson Turner's American **frontier** thesis.

These historians viewed land as property, resource, or determinant, rather than as vulnerable environment, even as the ecological consequences of more than a century of European settlement became alarmingly evident. The long depression and drought of the 1890s, which forced the pastoral industry to withdraw from many marginal lands, confronted Australians with environmental limits. Historians largely ignored them, and shared the nineteenth-century settlers' attitude to the environment: that exploitation would improve it, introduced species enrich it, and civilisation subdue it. Local settlement histories continued to commemorate the taming of the land and the heroic battles of pioneers against nature, although some, such as *Land of the Lyrebird* (1920), voiced surprise and regret at the environmental cost of conquest.

W.K. **Hancock's** *Australia* (1930) offered the first integrated historical statement of the negative environmental impact of Europeans on the Australian continent. 'The invaders hated trees' was one of his memorable charges. But it was historical geographers, many of them immigrants or visitors to Australia, who pioneered a sustained, disciplinary study of environmental change and sensibilities, a more sober reckoning of the environmental consequences of European settlement. The dramatic soil erosion crisis and dust storms of the 1930s and 1940s (see Francis Ratcliffe, *Flying Fox and Drifting Sand*, 1938), and the holocaust bushfire of **Black Friday**, 1939, gave urgency to their work. T. Griffith **Taylor**, foundation head of Australia's first geography department at the University of Sydney in the 1920s, wrote and spoke controversially about environmental limits to Australian settlement and population; and Archibald Grenfell **Price** placed Australian history in the context of

European expansion and moving international frontiers of disease, animals, and plants. From the 1960s geographers produced a significant series of studies of landscape change, resource appraisal, and environmental management in Australia. The most notable were J.M. Powell, *Environmental Management in Australia* (1976) and *A Historical Geography of Modern Australia* (1988); and a succession of studies of water management: D.W. Meinig, *On the Margins of the Good Earth* (1962); Michael Williams, *The Making of the South Australian Landscape* (1974); Tom Perry, *Australia's First Frontier* (1963); and Les Heathcote, *Back of Bourke* (1965).

In the period after World War II, the archaeological discovery of Aboriginal antiquity and environmental responsibility (especially associated with the work of D.J. **Mulvaney**) revealed Australia as an ancient human landscape with a long environmental history. An ecological focus began to make Australian history seem more a history of invasions and disruptions than a smooth, political footnote to Empire. In the words of George Seddon: 'The most important fact in the environmental history of Australia is that it had a radically new technology imposed upon it, suddenly, twice.'

But historians remained less sensitive to the environment than novelists, poets, geographers, archaeologists, and scientists, except occasionally at the local level. It was a farmer of the black soil plains of NSW, Eric **Rolls**, also a poet and historian, who most successfully injected those literary and scientific environmental insights into the writing of Australia's human history, particularly in two books: *They All Ran Wild* (1969), and *A Million Wild Acres* (1981), about the Pillaga 'scrub'. Organic rather than schematic, these maverick books revealed the story-telling power of an ecological sensibility. W.K. Hancock, in his retirement, returned to the study of his native land and wrote a book with a deep regional focus that he hoped would balance the sheer ambition of his earlier *Australia*. He called the new book *Discovering Monaro: A Study of Man's Impact on his Environment* (1972), drawing on archaeological and scientific studies of the Australian Alps, as well as an intensive documentary survey, maps, fieldwork, interviews, and serious use of the historian's recommended 'strong boots' (and fly fishing tackle). The book was extremely influential because of its quality and the author's status as a doyen of the discipline. Although it focused conventionally on land-use, it anticipated the cooperative alliance of historians and ecologists that flowered most notably in the 'forest history' of the 1980s and 1990s.

Another pioneer of the new environmental history was George Seddon, a connoisseur of landscape, whose book *Sense of Place* (1972) was concerned not just with the physical patterns of the Swan River coastal plain but also with the imaginative apprehension of the land, bringing together science, history, and aesthetics. In *Searching for the Snowy* (1994), Seddon eloquently worried about how to write 'an environmental history' of a river and its catchment. Seddon and the Snowy, Hancock and the Monaro, Rolls and the Pillaga: here we can discern the beginnings of regional history with a moral and environmental edge to it. National histories by Geoffrey **Blainey** (*Triumph of the Nomads*, 1975,

and *A Land Half Won*, 1980) and Geoffrey Bolton (*Spoils and Spoilers*, 1981) also began to integrate environmental perspectives with social, political and settlement histories. Agricultural science informed the history of Australian land-use in Neil Barr and John Cary, *Greening a Brown Land* (1992). **Urban history**, which fell outside the rural, natural, and indigenous sources of much environmental history, also began to make manifest its intrinsic environmental orientation (for example, Dan Coward, *Out of Sight: Sydney's Environmental History*, 1988). Stephen Dovers (ed.), *Australian Environmental History* (1994), helped define the field.

The rise of environmental politics since the late 1960s directly stimulated historical scholarship, and gave the new environmental history an occasionally apocalyptic and moralistic tone. Ecology and history were brought closer together by environmental politics: all three found stimulus in the Darwinian revolution, Hiroshima, and the landing on the moon. The US historian Donald Worster described environmental history as 'born out of a moral purpose, with strong political commitments behind it'. Rachel Carson's *Silent Spring* (1962) found an Australian parallel in A.J. Marshall's *The Great Extermination* (1966). Roderick Nash, another American writing of 'a new teaching frontier' in 1972, viewed environmental history as a further example of 'history from below', except that 'here the exploited element would be the biota and the land itself'. Histories of conservation battles, wilderness campaigns, and national parks (such as Tim Bonyhady's *Places Worth Keeping*, 1993) had a more overt political orientation than the earlier studies of conservation policy by historical geographers. Environmental sensibilities were linked with historical consciousness and racial politics by Tom Griffiths in *Hunters and Collectors* (1996).

World history and environmental history became related scholarly fashions. Alfred W. Crosby, in *Ecological Imperialism* (1986), styled Australia as one of several 'neo-Europes' and provided a long-term environmental history to explain the dominance of European animals, plants, and germs in an alien ecosystem. Stephen J. Pyne's *Burning Bush* (1992), part of a series of books on world fire, used the theme of fire and fire-management to locate Australia in world history. Tom Griffiths and Libby Robin (eds), *Ecology and Empire* (1997), returned the imperial gaze and privileged the global periphery by looking at the comparative environmental history of settler societies through the prism of Australian history. Two notable 'apocalyptic' histories of the 1990s were William Lines, *Taming the Great South Land* (1991) and Tim Flannery, *The Future Eaters* (1994). In contrast with the earlier imperial narratives of extension and continuity, these newer environmental histories emphasised the much longer environmental rhythms of the continent with which the colonial moment sometimes unknowingly interacted.

TOM GRIFFITHS

Epidemics of acute infectious disease seem to have been rare in Aboriginal Australia before the advent of Europeans. Chronic infections and parasitic infestations were probably common; but the low density and nomadic habits of the

Aboriginal peoples are thought to have preserved them from infectious diseases of the kinds that require larger or more settled communities for their maintenance. Sherry Saggers and Dennis Gray in *Aboriginal Health and Society* (1991) examine Aboriginal health before and after white settlement. Europeans brought new diseases to this continent; yet while the first recorded epidemic, in April 1789, ravaged the Aboriginal population around Sydney, it affected the European settlers not at all, even though the disease appeared to be smallpox. Its origin remains a puzzle. Was the 'variolous matter in bottles', brought with the First Fleet for medical use, somehow released among the Aborigines? Did Macassan fishermen transmit the disease to Australia? Or was the disease not smallpox but severe chickenpox? Alan Frost investigates several hypotheses in *Botany Bay Mirages* (1994).

Later epidemics of smallpox, in south-eastern Australia in 1829–31 and in the NT during the 1860s, severely affected Aboriginal communities; but cases were few among European colonists until the Victorian outbreaks of 1857 and 1868–69, and the more general epidemic of the 1880s, which began in Sydney in May 1881. The numbers of sick were relatively small but the high mortality of smallpox excited great dread and, in Sydney, extreme hostility to the Chinese community, among whom the first cases had occurred. Almost always, smallpox could be traced to recent shipboard arrivals who had somehow eluded detection by quarantine authorities. As a result, it usually appeared in those poorer neighbourhoods adjacent to the port, which were then blamed for its spread. The 1881 epidemic inspired a series of health reforms in NSW; but, as an exotic intruder with Oriental associations, smallpox also reinforced the view that threats to Australia's welfare came from Asia.

Maritime quarantine at once fended off such threats and strengthened the colonial sense of siege. Quarantine measures were first applied in Sydney as early as 1804; but there was no consistent inspection of vessels until the Quarantine Act of 1832, prompted by the prevalence of Asiatic cholera in England and elsewhere. Before that, the length of the sea voyage to Australia and the age of those leaving Britain had together excluded the major infectious diseases of European childhood; but, with the growth of immigration, and with more children among the newcomers, such ailments as scarlet fever, whooping cough, measles, chickenpox, and mumps soon made their way to the colonies. By mid-century, the population was large enough to enable them to flourish, attaining epidemic proportions every few years, with deaths occurring mainly among children under five years. Peter Curson's *Times of Crisis* (1985) explores their incidence in colonial Sydney. Measles was especially severe in Sydney in 1867 and throughout most colonies in 1875. Scarlet fever took heavy toll in SA in 1863–64, and in 1875–77 was at its worst in all the south-eastern colonies, with a total mortality around 5000.

Other infectious diseases affected adults as well as children. Diphtheria, first observed in 1858, was most aggressive in 1860, with death-rates in Victoria and SA approaching 150 per 100 000 of population; but, after a great outbreak in the latter 1880s, its severity declined, and from 1895 treatment with diphtheria antitoxin further reduced its mortality. An earlier arrival, typhoid fever, at first called 'colonial fever' and often mistaken for either typhus or dysentery, was firmly established in the colonies by 1850, becoming a regular summer scourge. With rapid urban growth, sanitary conditions deteriorated until typhoid mortality rates in the new colonial capitals were far higher than those of older English cities. Typhoid fever also flourished in the crowded communities that sprang up on the goldfields. Like other infectious diseases, it was then considered 'miasmatic' in origin: a product of foul odours rather than of filth itself. But removal of smells entailed better hygiene and, as J.H.L. **Cumpston** demonstrated in 1927–28 (*Health and Disease in Australia*, 1989), typhoid fever's decline after 1890 owed at least as much to improved public hygiene in general as to the advent of sewerage systems.

Of all epidemic diseases, plague was still the most renowned and feared. A pandemic of bubonic plague, originating in Hong Kong in 1894, reached Sydney in January 1900. By that time, medical science was beginning to recognise the role of the rat flea in its transmission and had also developed a prophylactic vaccine. Amid public panic and a rat-extermination campaign, quarantine and cleansing measures were carried to extremes in Sydney's slums, and once again the Chinese community became the scapegoat. Peter Curson and Kevin McCracken in *Plague in Sydney* (1989) document the epidemic's impact. Over seven months, only 303 people contracted the disease in Sydney; but of those, 103 died. Brisbane, Rockhampton, and Townsville endured lesser epidemics that year, and bubonic plague haunted both NSW and Qld for a decade; elsewhere, cases were few.

Epidemic influenza had appeared first in 1820, then again in 1825, recurring every few years after that in one colony or another, until the first Australia-wide epidemic in 1860. Influenza was commonly attributed to atmospheric causes: the outbreak of 1885 was called 'fog fever'. The 'Russian' influenza of 1890–91 sent thousands to bed but few to their graves, and those few mostly infants and the elderly. By contrast, the 'Spanish' influenza pandemic of 1918–19 had a high death-rate, especially among people in the prime of life, and killed many millions around the world. Humphrey **McQueen** discusses this country's experience of it in Jill Roe (ed.), *Social Policy in Australia* (1976). Strict quarantine measures spared Australia the worst of its impact; but it was nonetheless a grim ordeal which caused some 12 500 deaths, massive economic and social disruption, and tensions between federal and state governments. Like other respiratory ailments, Spanish influenza attacked Aboriginal communities with exceptional severity. The fears that this pandemic generated were revived decades later by the 'Asian' influenza epidemic of 1957, which fortunately proved much milder. In 1968, a similar worldwide epidemic was named after Hong Kong where, 30 years later, human deaths from a new strain of bird influenza caused concern.

Equal pay

By 1957, another dread disease was all but conquered: acute anterior poliomyelitis, which might cripple for life those it did not kill. Paradoxically, it struck hardest in those societies with high living standards, where, instead of developing an early immunity to 'infantile paralysis', most children encountered the virus at school-age or later, when its effects were more likely to be serious. In Australia, epidemics of polio occurred at irregular intervals, the outbreak of 1937–39 being particularly severe in Melbourne and in Tasmania. In the absence of any cure, attention centred on the treatment of paralysis, with a prolonged dispute between medical orthodoxy, which favoured splinting to prevent deformity, and the views of a Queensland nurse, Elizabeth **Kenny**, whose more active therapy won her international fame. Philippa Martyr revisits this controversy in *AHS* (1997). Poliomyelitis remains incurable; but the introduction of the Salk 'killed' vaccine in the 1950s and of the Sabin 'live' vaccine in the 1960s made it eminently preventable.

The term *epidemic*, like *plague* before it, is often applied to diseases that are greatly feared, despite being strictly *endemic*: that is, present in the community but not attacking large numbers at one time. When pulmonary tuberculosis (TB) was a death-sentence for most sufferers, although not epidemic, it earned the name 'white plague'. By 1945, TB was in decline and often curable, but a federal eradication campaign was mounted nonetheless, to ensure its early detection and treatment. Today many speak of the 'AIDS epidemic', referring to the acquired immune deficiency syndrome caused by the human immuno-deficiency virus (HIV). AIDS is so far only endemic in Australia; but its prevalence in groups at risk, the invisibility of its latent phase, and its high fatality rate have together made it the most dreaded infectious disease of our own times.

Through widespread vaccination, epidemics of smallpox, poliomyelitis, diphtheria, whooping cough, and measles have ceased to threaten us—so much so that health authorities now warn of public apathy towards immunisation against preventable infections. Amid the emergence of alarming new diseases, bacterial as well as viral, and the waning efficacy of antibiotics, such indifference seems at once a reflection and a betrayal of medicine's achievements in the twentieth century.

ANTHEA HYSLOP

Equal pay for equal work is a catchcry synonymous with women's rights. Key historical events are outlined by Jim Hagan, *The History of the ACTU* (1981), and by Jocelynne Scutt in Kay Saunders and Raymond Evans (eds), *Gender Relations in Australia* (1992). The principle of 'equal pay for equal work' in the same industry was accepted by H.B. **Higgins** in the Fruitpickers' Case (1912), but the **Arbitration** Court also perceived 'women's occupations' differed from 'men's work' and merited lower minimum wages because working women had lesser 'needs' than working men—the 1907 **basic wage** presumed the needs of a male wage-earner to support a wife and family (regardless of whether he had either). The Theatrical Employees Case (1917) determined that single women without dependants

required a different (and lesser) living wage to men. Their hardships motivated activists such as Muriel **Heagney** and Maude O'Connell.

Women received 75 per cent of the male minimum wage after the 1949–50 *Basic Wage Inquiry*. An **ACTU** proposal for 'equal pay for work of equal value' was rejected by the Arbitration Commission in June 1969, in favour of implementing 'equal pay for equal work' by January 1972. The 25 per cent differential was not eliminated, so women in occupations with a high proportion of females (e.g., nursing) remained disadvantaged. Hagan suggests little more than 10 per cent of the female workforce had achieved parity by December 1972, when the commission broadened 'equal pay for equal work' to 'equal pay for work of equal value'. Equal minimum wage rates were approved in the May 1974 National Wage Case. But this has not ended equal pay struggles. Inadequate implementation, unequal employment opportunities, and discrimination still keep women's average earnings below men's.

Equal pay is also historically significant in the context of age and race. In 1966 the North Australian Workers Union backed a strike of Aboriginal workers seeking equal pay and other rights at Wave Hill Station, NT, which Frank **Hardy** examines in *The Unlucky Australians* (1968).

DC

Ern Malley affair, see *Angry Penguins*

Esson, (Thomas) Louis Buvelot (1878–1943) is often credited with being the first dramatist to create distinctively Australian plays. He was born in Scotland and came to Australia as a child. During his career as a freelance journalist he wrote for the **Bulletin,** *Table Talk*, and *Lone Hand*. A foundation member of the Victorian Socialist Party, he also frequently contributed to its paper, the *Socialist*. He travelled extensively 1915–21 and was impressed by the works staged at the Abbey Theatre, Dublin. Encouraged by W.B. Yeats to write from his own culture, Esson produced plays with Australian settings, such as *The Time Is Not Yet Ripe* (1912) and the *The Drovers* (1920). He also collaborated with Vance **Palmer** and others to establish the Pioneer Players in 1922, inspired by the Abbey Theatre. Peter Fitzpatrick has written on Louis and Hilda Esson in *Pioneer Players* (1995). Esson's last collection, *Dead Timber and Other Plays*, appeared in 1920. Palmer published a volume of reminiscences, including some of Esson's letters in *Louis Esson and the Australian Theatre* (1948). He is commemorated in the Louis Esson Award for Drama, which is included in the Victorian Premier's Literary Awards.

KT

Ethnic groups, other than those from the British Isles, were fewer in Australia than in other British colonial societies such as Canada and South Africa, though about the same as in NZ. British imperial policy favoured free movement within the Empire and throughout the world, but Australia was sufficiently dependent on selective **immigra-**

tion for the objective of creating a 'new Britannia' to be achieved in the nineteenth century and consolidated by the **White Australia** policy in the early twentieth.

Assisted immigration policy aimed at reproducing the 'nations' and religions of the British Isles. Arrivals were classified by their origins in England, Scotland, and Ireland (though rarely Wales), and whether they were Protestant or **Catholic**. The most identifiable ethnic group in this formative stage was **Irish**, mainly Catholics, who were seven per cent of the population in 1891. Irish political and social influence was most noticeable in NSW and Queensland. The major Catholic leaders included Irish-born Cardinal **Moran** and Archbishops **Mannix** and **Duhig**. Historians such as Patrick **O'Farrell** have argued that the Irish became 'Australian Catholics', as Cardinal Moran encouraged them to do after his arrival in Sydney in 1884. However, Irish national sentiment remained strong until the 1916 conscription referendum in which Dr Mannix took an active opposing role.

Other British elements of the colonial population were less distinctive than the Irish Catholics and identified more readily with the Protestant establishment and the UK home country. The English-born have always been the largest immigrant component since 1788 in every year and every colony or state. They did not see themselves as an 'ethnic group' and others were defined as such by not being English. This assumption lingered into the 1990s in the use of the official term *non-English-speaking background* (NESB). Scots, Cornish, and Welsh created some 'ethnic communities' in the sense of organised entities. **Scots** were most prominent in Victoria and northern NSW, the Welsh on the Ballarat goldfields and the Hunter coalfield, and the Cornish in tin- and copper-mining districts of SA and other mining centres. Irish Gaelic died out rapidly as in other countries, but Scottish Gaelic and Welsh were sustained by churches using these **languages** at least until the end of the nineteenth century and, in rare cases, beyond.

An ethnic community needs specific institutions and the possibility of regeneration to survive. Otherwise it is simply a 'group' or a statistical artefact. The **Chinese** who came in large numbers to the goldfields between the 1850s and the 1890s organised self-help and religious institutions, but they were almost exclusively male and thus had difficulty in regenerating once the restrictive White Australia policy became effective. The largest number of Chinese was recorded in 1861 at 38 298 and the largest number in any colony as 25 421 in Victoria in 1857. By 1881 the largest number was in Qld and by 1891 in NSW. Most of these lived in rural and mining areas. The number of China-born did not exceed these totals again until 1986.

Other 'ethnic groups', like the Chinese, were overwhelmingly male in the nineteenth century, including the Afghan camel drivers who arrived after 1861, the **Pacific Island** cane-cutters who reached a total of over 10 000 in 1891 (mainly in Qld), and most other Asians, including Japanese and Indonesians. They did not, therefore, create lasting ethnic communities, especially as the White Australia

policy increasingly forbade family reunion after 1901 and led to the deportation of Melanesians to their home islands. European migrants, especially from Scandinavia, Greece, and Italy, also had male majorities but were not prevented from bringing out families. These were all well established by the 1890s, and were added to by Croatian Dalmatians in WA and Lebanese in NSW. All these were widely scattered in remote areas either as rural labourers, miners, or hawkers.

German rural settlers were more evenly balanced by gender and created permanent communities, especially in SA, Qld, the Victorian Wimmera, and the NSW Riverina. Along with Scandinavians, they were officially assisted by Qld, the only important example of support for non-British immigration in the colonial period. By 1891 there were 14 924 German-born, 3072 Danish-born, and 1955 Swedish- and Norwegian-born in Qld. The German-born total for Australia in 1891 was not passed again until 1954, nor the Danish-born for the same year until 1971. German settlement was drastically reduced in response to World War I, as was the maintenance of German culture through the **Lutheran churches** and schools. All German and Austrian immigration was forbidden between 1914 and 1925.

The years between the two world wars were marked by spasmodic European immigration, especially of **Italians**, **Greeks**, Croatians, Maltese, and Jews. The **Jewish** community, which traced its origins back to the **First Fleet**, changed its character with the arrival of Polish Jews in the 1920s and of refugees from Hitler in the late 1930s. The number of Italian-born reached 26 756 in 1933, with the largest number being in north Qld.

Increased southern European immigration was caused by US restrictions from 1924, but was limited by quotas and landing charges in Australia. Concentration in north Qld prompted the critical Ferry Report of 1925 and the introduction of 'British' employment quotas by the **Australian Workers Union**. As was previously the case, most non-British immigrants worked in rural areas, with the exception of the European Jews. A majority were male but some churches, clubs, and newspapers helped sustain small ethnic communities. Non-British immigrants received no public assistance with fares or settlement, in contrast to the British.

The great expansion of ethnic groups and communities began in 1947. The Displaced Persons settlement program between 1947 and 1952 introduced large numbers of Poles, Ukrainians, Estonians, Latvians, Lithuanians, Czechs, Slovaks, Hungarians, Croatians, Slovenians, Serbians, and Russians. While some of these groups had a prewar presence, most did not. **Refugees** were initially housed in former army camps, and many were sent to construction schemes such as the **Snowy Mountains**. Most resettled in the major industrial areas, especially the western suburbs of Melbourne, Sydney, and Adelaide, and in Newcastle, Wollongong, and Geelong.

Because emigration was forbidden by the communist states these communities had difficulty in expanding their numbers and most are now elderly. Hungarians were replenished by refugees from the 1956 rising, Czechs after 1968, and Poles in the 1980s. Emigration from Yugoslavia was liberalised and a migration agreement was signed in 1971. Thus the highest numbers for the Polish- and Yugoslav-born were recorded in 1991 and those from former Yugoslavia continued to rise after that, whereas most other East European groups declined from the 1970s. This did not prevent them from handing on their culture to their Australian-born children, with the Latvian and Ukrainian communities especially successful in that regard. Of the major East European languages used at home, the 1996 Census recorded 61 023 Polish-speakers, 68 126 Macedonian-speakers, 66 702 Croatian-speakers, 25 846 Hungarian-speakers, 35 392 Serbian-speakers, and 30 042 Russian-speakers.

The postwar refugee wave was completed by 1953 and then replaced by southern Europeans, especially from Italy, Greece, and Malta. In contrast to the prewar arrangements, many of these received passage assistance although not to the same extent as the British, Dutch, and Germans who were also coming in record numbers. Official policy remained **assimilationist** until the early 1970s but this had little impact on the formation of large and well-organised southern European communities in the major cities. The largest were the Italians and Greeks, whose languages remained the most commonly used other than English into the 1990s, at 367 290 and 259 019 speakers respectively in 1996. This allowed the creation of a network of organisations and media wider than previously enjoyed by ethnic groups. The Greek Orthodox Church became the fifth-largest in Australia, with 356 690 adherents in 1991.

The number and origins of ethnic groups continued to expand, following the official adoption of a universal immigration policy in 1973, the ending of White Australia, and the advocacy of **multiculturalism**. Ninety countries have supplied at least 1000 settlers, and there is considerable ethnic variety from some of these. More than 40 languages are now regularly used by more than 2000 speakers each. There are about 200 000 Muslims, 200 000 Buddhists, and over 65 000 Hindus in Australia, each with their permanent religious buildings. The great majority of Jewish youth attend Jewish schools, which receive public assistance on the same basis as other private schools. The most rapidly growing ethnic groups are from Asia and the Middle East. These included in 1996 those born in Vietnam (151 053), China (111 009), the Philippines (92 949), Malaysia (76 255), Lebanon (70 224), India (77 551), and Hong Kong (68 430). The largest non-European group, as in the nineteenth century, are Chinese. These are from many origins and backgrounds, with 324 000 using Chinese languages at home. James Jupp, *The Australian People* (1988), is a comprehensive guide.

JAMES JUPP

Ethnic history derived from studies of immigrant groups in the University of Chicago in the 1920s. Such ethnic studies had little relevance outside North America until the arrival of large numbers of immigrants in Britain and Western Europe after 1945. Ethnic histories, in contrast, have been especially important in the Balkans and Eastern Europe, where they form part of the armoury of **nationalism**. The study of 'race', in the physical sense, was well developed from the late nineteenth century but was largely discredited by its inspiration of the ideology and practice of Nazism between the 1920s and the 1940s. After 1945, under the auspices of Unesco, the term *ethnic group* became favoured over *race*, it being widely held that theories of human behaviour based on physical inheritance were unfounded. Ethnicity was concerned with culture, **language**, **religion**, or common ancestry rather than the conventional divisions of physical anthropology, such as the 'Caucasian' or 'Mongolian' races.

Marxist historians tended to see ethnicity as a form of 'false consciousness' that would disappear under socialism. Structural functionalists and other schools of 'modernisers' similarly held that ethnic variety was characteristic of 'traditional' societies and would, likewise, wither away as societies became modernised. Many liberal historians were more concerned with individual liberties, and the institutions which guarantee them, than with **national identities** which were frequently seen as rationalised by reactionary or conservative ideas. All these views influenced Australian social scientists but are now submerged by rising ethnic consciousness in many societies.

There was little ethnic variety in Australia prior to the late 1940s. Most academic interest was on **Aborigines** rather than on **ethnic groups** arising from **immigration**. Anthropology was better developed than other social sciences in this field. Studies of non-Aboriginal ethnic groups were scarcely visible at the academic level until the 1960s and have grown slowly since then.

There were some early studies of the **White Australia** policy, such as Myra **Willard's** *History of the White Australia Policy* (1923), but academic interest waned and was not revived until the policy was close to being abandoned in the 1960s. There was little serious work on the **Chinese** population, despite considerable pamphleteering and journalism from the 1880s. Few academics had the linguistic skills to study the topic and the Chinese population was seen as likely to die out, which had almost become the case by 1945.

An overall survey of non-British immigrants was provided by the Danish scholar J.S. Lyng in his *Non-Britishers in Australia* (1927). Lyng argued that 'from the colour point of view the Australians are fast becoming a homogeneous people'. Still influenced by physical anthropology, he tried to distinguish between Nordic, Alpine, and Mediterranean stock, which he admitted was difficult. He calculated from the 1891 Census that 53 per cent of white Australians were English, 13 per cent **Scots**, 23 per cent **Irish**, and 1.5 per cent Welsh, leaving a residue of about 10 per cent who were 'non-British'. He divided others between 'yellow', 'brown', and 'black' races, adopting the then conventional view that Australia should avoid the US experience, which 'through shortsightedness sowed the seed of the colour problem'. However, he was a strong advocate of ethnic variety and allowed that 'even the coloured peoples, if capable of assimilation', might take part in a varied but 'harmonic' whole.

Apart from white non-Britishers (who were mainly **German** and Scandinavian 'Nordics' by the 1920s), the only other ethnic group to attract much scholarly attention was the Irish Catholics. J.F. Hogan's *The Irish in Australia* was published in 1888 to mark the centenary of settlement, and was, like many ethnic histories, designed to commemorate the famous and successful rather than to give a rounded picture. But little followed until the period after World War II saw such publications as J.G. Murtagh, *Australia: The Catholic Chapter* (1946, 1959), and T.J. Kiernan, *The Irish Exiles in Australia* (1954). The **Jews**, too, although also present since 1788, were described mainly in articles published by the Australian Jewish Historical Society, set up in 1938 as the first (and for a long time the only) community history society. The spate of books which made the Jews among the best-described ethnic groups had to await such publications as the biographies of Sidney **Myer** and Samuel Wynn, published in the early 1960s.

Prior to 1945 Australia was a predominantly British society, pledged to White Australia, the exclusion of all non-Europeans, and the limitation of non-British **aliens**, and convinced that the Aboriginal people would soon die out along with the remaining Chinese. There was thus little incentive to study ethnic variety and most such studies focused on religious denominations rather than other cultural aspects. This started to change dramatically in 1947 with the arrival of postwar displaced persons who had a strong commitment to maintaining their culture and preserving its records. Ukrainians set up the Shevchenko Scientific Society in 1950 and it produced a massive history of Australian Ukrainians in 1966 in Ukrainian. Similar efforts were undertaken by the Poles, who had already formed a Federal Council of Polish Associations by 1950, and by the Latvians, who set up one of the largest archives of Latvian material in the world, currently located in Adelaide. Much of their material is not in English, and L. Paszkowski's major work, *Poles in Australia and Oceania 1790–1940*, had to await an English translation until 1987. A bibliographical record of Poles and Australia, produced by Stanley Robe for the Australian Institute of Multicultural Affairs in 1986, runs to over 5000 items. An important, if sometimes uneven, contribution was made by the Australian Ethnic Heritage series, edited by Michael Cigler throughout the 1980s and covering almost 20 different groups from a historical perspective.

As the ethnic variety of Australia increased rapidly from the 1950s, community historians began to project their studies backwards into Australian history. Little of this work was done by academics, and much of it was not in English. Some of it was celebratory and some of it pursued such arcane topics as the first arrival in Australia from the appropriate background. An example of this latter approach is provided by Joseph Tuso, a young convict on the **First Fleet** almost universally claimed by the **Italian** community as the first Italian to settle in Australia. Yet subsequent study shows that Tuso was not Italian and, indeed, almost nothing is known about him. These amateur enthusiasms were most apparent during 1988. Many ethnic communities proposed to write their Bicentennial histories, but few succeeded. The gap was filled by the massive encyclopedia *The Australian People*

(1988), which was funded by the Bicentennial Authority. This remains the definitive study of more than 100 ethnic groups in Australia (including extensive sections on Aborigines and the English) and is currently under revision for the centenary of Federation in 2000.

The most promising developments in recent years have included the formation of historical societies within ethnic communities, most effectively for the Italians and Chinese. These follow in the tradition of the Jewish historical society in encouraging serious scholarship rather than individual or organisational commemoration. Some governments, most notably the German and **Greek**, have encouraged studies of local communities by sponsoring conferences and publications.

Within the universities there has been only slow progress, largely as an adjunct to language and culture-based courses. Charles **Price** at the demography department at the Australian National University pioneered the scholarly study of ethnic groups in Australia, but that department had no counterpart elsewhere. Sociologists and political scientists have failed to develop the interest commonly found in North America, although there have been keen debates about the politics of **assimilation** and **multiculturalism**, as well as the success of migrants in the labour market. Academic historians have regularly convened panels on ethnic history at their conferences. Increasing interest from the 'second generation' is also creating a number of postgraduate theses, although most of these study current community concerns rather than ethnic history. The oral history work of Barry York has focused in this area and especially on the Maltese community, which has only limited written records but has been present in Australia since the 1880s.

The enthusiasm and expertise of individual historians are gradually filling the major gaps and were particularly stimulated by the 1988 Bicentenary. Oliver MacDonagh, Patrick **O'Farrell**, and David Fitzpatrick have made major contributions to the history of Irish Australians. Hugh Gilchrist has reached 1914 in his monumental history of Greek Australians, while Rabbi John Levi, Hilary and Bill Rubinstein, and Suzanne Rutland have published extensive histories of Australian Jews. Eric **Rolls's** *Sojourners* (1992) and *Citizens* (1996) join the work of C.F. Yong, C.R. May, K. Cronin, and S.W. Wang in filling in much of the detail of nineteenth-century Chinese settlement. A number of museums are serving as focal points for scholars and for the archiving of material, including the Jewish museums of Melbourne and Sydney, the Migration Museum of Adelaide, and the Chinese Museum in Melbourne.

Many of the more than 100 distinct ethnic groups in Australia have only arrived since 1975 and are of interest to social scientists rather than to historians. Most of the Slav and East European groups have published in **languages** other than English, with the exception of Frank Kunz's studies of Hungarians. Government subsidies are not generally available for historical work, though there is a large literature on immigrant settlement which has received such funding. The main challenge for the future is to incorporate ethnic history into the mainstream of Australian history as a legitimate and important component of the national story.

JAMES JUPP

Ethnographic history emerged from a particular moment in the dialogue between history and anthropology in the 1970s and assumed new forms as the debates evolved. Prominent practitioners of ethnographic history have been based in Australia, but relatively little research in Australian history itself has so far resulted from its concerns.

Ethnographic history reacted against the bald empiricism widely prevalent within the discipline, and also against what was seen as an impoverished approach to symbol and behaviour. Particularly as it was shaped and exemplified in the work of Greg Dening—the pre-eminent Australian practitioner—it therefore had both an epistemological strand and an interpretative one, though these ought not be rigidly separated. Dening fostered a self-consciousness on the part of the historian, drawing attention to the activities of research and writing, to the site of the researcher's engagement with documents, and with the manifold uncertainties of historical inquiry. He transposed the cultural relativism of the cultural anthropologist Clifford Geertz to the domain of historical knowledge itself, suggesting that academic history ought enjoy no special privilege, and that there were many ways of engaging with the past, many stories constructed from different vantage points; different histories were produced for different occasions.

The influence of Geertz, with that of Victor Turner, loomed large in the interpretation of particular situations and events. The 'thick description' that Geertz advocated was in principle highly sensitive to nuances of gesture, habit, dress, and behaviour, and related such particularities to the wider values and ethos of particular cultures. Though there was a systematising orientation here, and a suggestion that every act and statement was richly imbued with meanings and was generated by a larger text, the approach differed from Lévi-Straussian structuralism in never embracing formalism. Binary oppositions were of interest for their expressive significance, but their identification was not an aim of analysis. This balanced approach to meaning and action arose from the influence of Turner, who was interested in performance and ritual drama. In his studies of the Marquesas (*Islands and Beaches*, 1980), the death of William Gooch (*History's Anthropology*, 1988) and, perhaps most consummately, of the Bounty mutiny (*Mr Bligh's Bad Language*, 1992), Dening adopted these terms and applied them creatively in many domains, drawing attention to the richly textured nature of activities, rituals, and communications that had otherwise been seen in instrumental terms.

Given the anthropological affiliations of this work, it is not surprising that its practitioners engaged mainly with cross-cultural situations, and those of colonial settlement, in which confusions of meaning, and the provisional nature of sociality, were most richly evident. Rhys Isaacs's work on colonial Virginia (*The Transformation of Virginia*, 1982), Inga Clendinnen's *Aztecs* (1991), and Donna Merwick's work on early

New York (*Possessing Albany*, 1990) are among the renowned products of a group of Melbourne historians broadly oriented toward this type of history. (See **Melbourne School of History**.)

It is striking, however, that this approach has had relatively little direct impact on studies of the Australian frontier. Although many scholars of Australian colonial and Aboriginal history, such as Lyndall Ryan and Henry **Reynolds**, have been broadly anthropologically informed, they have not been concerned to transpose anything like a Geertzian mode of thick description, or the epistemological questions raised by historical reflexivity, into their inquiries. The work of Dening and Isaacs was one of the formative influences on the 'Push from the Bush', the group led by Marian Aveling (Quartly) and Alan Atkinson, who wrote the Bicentennial volume *Australians 1838* (1987), and on Atkinson's subsequent *The Europeans in Australia* (1997). A more complex cultural history, and one that was concerned with theories of inscription and narration, emerged in works such as Paul Carter's *The Road to Botany Bay* (1987), but there was no direct link between this overtly postmodernist history and the 'ethnographic' endeavour.

The relative lack of engagement with 'ethnographic' approaches in Australian history may be attributed to the resistance to any sort of national history in the highly relativist, ethnographic project. National histories of both conservative and radical kinds tend to place politics at their centre, either marginalising questions of culture, or insisting on the political character of cultural beliefs. In its earlier expression, ethnographic history partook of Geertz's sharp distinction between culture on one side and society, including the political, on the other. Ideas of culture have moved beyond these unhelpful distinctions, and it is notable that, as the work of Dening and others has also shifted, there has been no dogged attachment to a paradigm or to particular theoretical axioms. The very creativity of the project of ethnographic history may be most manifest in its disappearance, as an endeavour clearly distinguished from a wider range of critically reflexive cultural histories.

NICHOLAS THOMAS

Eugenics was a scientific and social reform movement concerned with improving the racial fitness of populations. Francis Galton, author of *Hereditary Genius* (1869), and Karl Pearson, foundation professor of eugenics at London University (1911), were pioneers of this movement and their ideas found favour with many scientists, doctors, and social reformers in Britain, France, Germany, North America, and Australia. It remained influential until the 1940s. Eugenicists were part of a much broader interest in the health of populations fanned by concerns about the declining birth-rates in most Western countries in the late nineteenth and early twentieth centuries. But where some groups were interested in the quantity of population, eugenists were primarily concerned with quality.

Most eugenists argued that Western societies faced a serious population crisis from what they believed was a decline in 'race fitness'. They concluded that the birth-rate was high among the 'racially unfit', while the 'racially fit' were not reproducing themselves at the same rate. This trend, if left unchecked, would lead to societies dominated by 'morons' and destined to decline and impoverishment. To propagate this message, eugenists were instrumental in developing tests for 'racial fitness', primarily intelligence tests. Through these means they sought to identify groups they classified as 'mental defectives' or the feeble-minded, idiots, and imbeciles. Eugenicists were firm proponents of the view that 'intelligence' and other types of fitness were largely hereditary. They argued that many of the social problems afflicting modern society, such as crime, poverty, delinquency, sexual 'maladjustment', and prostitution, were the natural inclinations of the 'unfit'. They opposed social policies, such as welfare and health reforms, which they believed maintained the 'unfit' and encouraged them to reproduce.

For eugenists, the solution to many social problems lay in encouraging the 'fit' to reproduce and ensuring that the 'unfit' could not. Thus, over time, 'unfitness' could be bred out of the population, ensuring social progress and prosperity. Most eugenists supported policies for the permanent segregation of the 'unfit' in institutions to minimise their chances of reproduction. Countries such as Britain, Canada, and France, and all the states of Australia legislated for the permanent segregation of 'mental defectives' by the late 1920s. A minority supported the more radical solution of sterilisation, a policy that found favour in Germany and at least 13 states of the USA in the 1930s. A sterilisation bill passed the lower house in WA in 1929, only to be defeated in the upper house.

Historians have debated the relative influence of eugenics in Australia. The early demise of the Eugenics Society of New South Wales (1912–14) suggests that before World War I, eugenics was an insignificant movement. In the interwar years small but active groups, such as the Racial Hygiene Association and the Eugenics Society of Victoria, attest the growing influence of eugenic ideas, an argument well developed by Rob Watts (*AJPH*, 1994). Carol Bacchi argued (*HS*, 1980) that Australian social reformers before the war were vigorous environmentalists, confident that improved health and welfare services would combat most social ills. After World War I they were less sanguine about progress and more inclined to the hereditarian pessimism of eugenics. But other historians, notably Watts, Helen Bourke (*Australian and New Zealand Journal of Sociology*, 1981) and Michael **Roe** in *Nine Australian Progressives* (1984), have questioned this distinction between prewar environmentalism and postwar hereditarianism, pointing to the complex coexistence of environmentalist and hereditarian ideas in the thought of many Australian intellectuals and social reformers both before and after 1914.

This argument was further developed by Stephen Garton (*HS*, 1986, and *AHS*, 1994). He demonstrated that hereditarianism and environmentalism were not different and opposed traditions in the minds of many Australian social reformers. Rather, both traditions framed crucial social policies in such areas as education, child welfare, delinquency, imprisonment, crime prevention, and mental health. Reformers used intelligence and other tests to distinguish between curable and incurable problem populations, favouring medical treatment and social welfare for the former and permanent segregation for the latter.

By the middle of the twentieth century eugenics began to fall into disrepute. From the 1930s geneticists began to criticise the crude theories of hereditary transmission that informed eugenics. A decade latter the horror of the Holocaust was ample testimony to the extremism inherent in the movement. It faded, but left a legacy in institutionalisation for problem populations that is only now beginning to disappear. Old eugenic societies were forced to change their names and policies to something more congenial. The Racial Hygiene Association, for instance, became the Family Planning Association.

STEPHEN GARTON

Eureka flag, see **Southern Cross Flag**

Eureka Stockade, a rebellion of miners on the Ballarat goldfields in 1854, has become a symbol of democratic protest and **national identity**. In October 1854 James Scobie, a Scottish digger, seeking a late drink at Bentley's Hotel in Ballarat, died after being hit on the head with a spade. Bentley was widely suspected, but he was exonerated by local magistrates. After a subsequent protest meeting, some of the crowd rushed the hotel, and burned it down. Three men were picked from the crowd and charged with the burning of the hotel. Governor Hotham ordered Bentley's arrest (he was subsequently found guilty of manslaughter), and set up an inquiry which uncovered evidence of corruption in the administration at Ballarat. The Chartist-influenced Ballarat Reform League argued that the people at Ballarat had been provoked by maladministration and injustice, and called for manhood suffrage, the abolition of the licence tax, and the opening up of the land to small farming settlement. On 11 November a large public meeting resolved that 'it is the inalienable right of every citizen to have a voice in making the laws he is called upon to obey— that taxation without representation is tyranny'. Karl Marx was to observe: 'It is not difficult to notice that these in reality are the same reasons which led to the declaration of independence of the United States of America.'

On 16 November, Hotham set up a royal commission into the goldfields. A diggers' delegation to Hotham on 27 November 'demanded' the release of the three prisoners. Hotham took objection to the word, and refused. The delegation would not retract: 'the people ... have, in their collective capacity, used that word'. At a meeting on 29 November, the rebel **Southern Cross flag** was unfurled and licences burned; the next day, Peter **Lalor** led the rebels to Eureka where they built their stockade. Ballarat was now said to be 'in a state of open and undisguised rebellion'. At 4 a.m. on Sunday, 3 December, when most of those inside the stockade were asleep, government troops attacked—about

30 diggers were killed by the soldiers, who lost five dead and 12 seriously wounded. In early 1855, the Eureka rebels were put on trial in Melbourne. Juries refused to convict any of them—despite Judge Redmond **Barry's** warning, after a thunderstorm, that 'the eye of heaven was upon them'. The royal commission recommended sweeping changes to gold-fields administration—an end to the licence system, and the introduction of the **miner's right**, which effectively gave diggers the vote—which were soon enacted.

The first histories of Eureka were those made by contemporaries—both officially, in the parliamentary inquiries and commissions, and as private authors. Of the latter, the most remarkable is Raffaello **Carboni's** *The Eureka Stockade* (1855), which offers a vivid and eccentric history by a participant. Later nineteenth-century historians of the event include Henry Gyles **Turner**.

In the liberal version of Australian history, Eureka was a central part of the story of how the Australian people became citizens through the achievement of representative and responsible government. H.V. **Evatt** argued that 'Australian democracy was born at Eureka', and Geoffrey **Serle** in *The Golden Age* (1963) endorsed the description of Eureka as a 'fight for freedom' and a 'democratic protest against arbitrary government'. The miners at Eureka struck out against British imperial authority, swore to defend the flag of the Southern Cross as a distinctively Australian symbol, and hinted at the possibility that Australia might reluctantly need to become independent of Britain. Radical nationalist historians—such as R.S. Ross in *Eureka: Freedom's Fight of '54* (1914), Robin **Gollan** in *Radical and Working Class Politics* (1960, 1967), and to some extent Manning **Clark** in *A History of Australia* (vol. 4, 1978)—have produced more heroic versions of Eureka, seeing it as one of the first important statements of Australian **nationalism**, and as perhaps the first great event in the emergence of the labour movement. An important strand of this interpretation has stressed the **Irish** presence at Eureka—a theme in C.H. **Currey's** 1954 *The Irish at Eureka* and in John Molony's 1984 narrative account, *Eureka*. Literary writing from the 1880s tended also to reproduce a nostalgic and heroic account of Eureka.

A sceptical left tradition has looked pessimistically on Eureka and its consequences. Brian **Fitzpatrick** in *The Australian People 1788–1945* (1946) argued that the diggers' achievement of political **democracy** was 'in fact more appearance than reality', while Humphrey **McQueen** in *A New Britannia* (1970) saw the effect of gold more generally on the working classes as being to sustain the belief that 'capitalism was not without promise'. Two decades later, Jan Kociumbas (*Oxford History of Australia*, vol. 2, 1992) argued that the diggers were 'seduced' by the prospect of democracy, which was only 'destined to steep them in individual acquisitiveness'.

Conservative revisionists questioned the extent to which Eureka 'caused' the democratic reforms in Victoria which came soon after, and argued that the rebellion achieved little that would not have happened anyway. The new Victorian constitution had been sent to London in March 1854, before Eureka. So I.D. Macnaughtan (in Gordon **Greenwood**, ed., *Australia: A Social and Political History*, 1955) maintained that the 'constitutional importance of the affair' was slight' because democratic reform was already assured. A consensus seemed to emerge, however, which recognised that there was a profound change in public opinion in Victoria caused in part by Eureka, which ensured that the democratic provisions of the new constitution were rapidly extended.

The other revisionist thrust was the argument that Eureka needed to be seen, not as a founding moment of organised labour in Australia, but as the protest of independent small capitalist miners against their incipient incorporation into a mining proletariat—Eureka, argued G.V. **Portus** in the 1933 *Cambridge History of the British Empire*, was 'the last picturesque pose of an order that was passing'. R.M. **Crawford** in *Australia* (1952) argued that Eureka was a revolt 'of small capitalists against official authority'. Geoffrey **Blainey** in *The Rush That Never Ended* (1963) went further and suggested that the Eureka rebellion, in achieving reform of restrictive mining regulations and rationalisation of arbitrary authority, itself 'paved the way for the rapid and orderly growth of capitalist mining and the accumulation of large fortunes in few hands'. The 1949 Ealing film, *Eureka Stockade*, which starred Chips Rafferty, ends with the reincorporation of Peter Lalor into colonial society—we see him buying land at auction, planning to marry and settle down into a life of quiet respectability. Blainey argued that the deep mining at Ballarat brought together a more stable mining population, more likely to support the kind of organisation necessary for serious rebellion; Weston **Bate** in *Lucky City* (1978) argued that, on the contrary, the deep mines were generally peaceful, and that explanation needs to be sought even more locally in the relative poverty of the Eureka lead in the weeks before the rebellion.

The Eureka Stockade has importantly been a part of a **local history**. In the 1880s a monument commemorating both soldiers and rebels was erected on the supposed site by public subscription. William Bramwell Withers published *The History of Ballarat* in 1870. Local historians have also been concerned to establish exactly where the stockade was—Jack Harvey's 1994 *Eureka Rediscovered: In Search of the Sight of the Historic Stockade* is a recent contribution. Local controversy over the true site of the rebellion has continued in debates over the interpretation to be presented in a new museum erected nearby.

Eureka is now a significant tourist asset, as well as a national symbol. At Sovereign Hill **pioneer settlement** the Eureka story is now enacted nightly in a sound-and-light production, 'Blood on the Southern Cross'. Ballarat Art Gallery's most prized exhibit is now the tattered Southern Cross flag, which had remained hidden in a cupboard from 1895, when it was acquired, until 1973, when it was again put on display. Like the Eureka legend itself, the flag has become a symbol for diverse causes, ranging from the **Communist** Party's Eureka Youth League and the Builders Labourers Federation to the National Front and small business organisations. Chris Healy, *From the Ruins of Colonialism: History as Social Memory* (1997), examines the transformation of the memory of Eureka from local story to national legend.

DAVID GOODMAN

Evangelicalism was a religious movement that began in England in the mid-eighteenth century. Inspired by the preaching of John Wesley and George Whitefield, its central tenets were the Reformation doctrine of justification by faith alone and the atoning death of Jesus Christ. It also presupposed a religious conversion in the individual with a commitment to a life of holiness through prayer and Bible-reading, supported by fellowship with the converted. Evangelicalism embraced a Puritan morality, but it was also a singing religion, inspiring a proliferation of hymns. It united Protestants in the Religious Tract Society, the British and Foreign Bible Society, the Sunday school movement, and other societies. Evangelical Protestants sought the reformation of society as well as individuals. In the 1820s and 1830s highly placed Evangelicals in London exercised strong influence on colonial affairs, especially policies to protect **Aborigines**.

Evangelical tenets and goals informed the **religion** of most Protestants in colonial Australia from 1788, including many **Anglicans**. It provided the basis for inter-denominational cooperation in various societies and evangelistic agencies. By the end of the nineteenth century, however, evangelicalism was beginning to weaken among Australian Protestants. The conflict between science and religion, and the controversy engendered by higher criticism of the Bible, challenged the theological foundations of evangelicalism. The majority adjusted to the new scholarship, espousing a liberal Protestantism while retaining evangelical values. A minority, eventually known as Conservative Evangelicals, embraced an uncompromising biblicism or fundamentalism, combined with pre-millenarian views and the pursuit of holiness. This development is generally viewed negatively by historians, but Stuart Piggin, *Evangelical Christianity in Australia* (1996), presents a positive account of Conservative Evangelicalism. Despite this division, the legacy of evangelicalism, especially its moralism, lingered well into the twentieth century.

WALTER PHILLIPS

Evangelists, often American, have been a regular feature of Australian religious life. In the 1830s, during the Second Great Awakening, the American Charles Grandison Finney first articulated the techniques of revivalism and from the 1860s William 'California' Taylor drew large crowds to camp meetings on the Victorian goldfields. Taylor, argues Hugh Jackson (*Churches and People in Australia and New Zealand*, 1987) was a 'folk evangelist' whose methods were best adapted to small-scale Victorian and SA mining communities; but by the 1880s visiting evangelists had begun to embrace the techniques of mass evangelism—large city meetings, massed choirs, and interdenominational cooperation—developed by another American, Dwight Moody. One of Moody's lieutenants, Reuben Torrey, toured

Australia in 1902; another, J. Wilbur Chapman, assisted by the musician Charles Alexander, drew large crowds in 1909. Australian Protestantism has generally failed to produce an indigenous revivalist tradition—the Methodist Alan **Walker's** Mission to the Nation (1953–54) was a rare exception. Billy Graham, whose 1959 campaign drew a capacity crowd to the Melbourne Cricket Ground, was the last of the mass evangelists. American evangelists have taken to the television screen; but while they claim a share of Australian screen time, they have not secured a comparable local audience. Historians, perhaps unduly impressed by the American comparison, have proffered reasons for the relative weakness of revivalist religion in Australia. Did the early colonial tradition of state aid to religion stultify religious innovation? Was the British urban working class from which most Australian immigrants came already too estranged from organised religion? Stuart Piggin (in Mark Hutchinson and Edmund Campion, eds, *Re-visioning Australian Colonial Christianity*, 1994) qualifies the assumption of weakness, pointing to more than 70 revivalist episodes in Australia and arguing that they have produced measurable changes in religious and moral behaviour.

GD

Evatt, Elizabeth Andreas (1933–), lawyer, developed her strong interest in law reform while working for the English Law Commission, and continued with it after her return to Australia in 1973. She was appointed deputy president of the Conciliation and Arbitration Commission (later the Industrial Relations Commission), headed the 1974–77 Royal Commission into Human Relations, and was the first judge of the **Family Court of Australia**. Evatt was also president for six years of the Australian Law Reform Commission, and a member of the United Nations Human Rights Committee. She is from a distinguished legal family—her father, Clive, was a QC; her uncle, H.V. **Evatt**, an eminent lawyer and federal Labor leader.

KT

Evatt, Herbert Vere (1894–1965) was at different stages of his crowded life an eminent lawyer and jurist, a notable scholar and historian, and an influential international statesman. He had a long and controversial career in politics, first in **Lang's** NSW Labor government (1925–27), then as attorney-general and minister for external affairs (1941–49), and finally as Labor leader of the federal opposition (1951–60).

'The Doc', as Evatt was known, was born in Maitland, NSW, to Anglo-Irish parents. His scholastic brilliance at both Fort Street High School and Sydney University was paralleled by his meteoric rise in the judiciary: at the age of 36, and after several landmark decisions, the **Scullin** government elevated Evatt to the **High Court** in 1930. By then his passionate concern for civil liberties and justice before the law was entrenched. Ten years later Evatt exchanged a legal career for politics and by 1941 joined **Curtin's** cabinet as attorney-general and minister for external affairs. The unresolved tension in Evatt between libertarian instincts and authoritarian impulses was exemplified by his wartime repression of the **Australia First Movement** and his unbanning of the **Communist** Party. The many complexities and contradictions in Evatt's public and personal life are explored in Peter Crockett's idiosyncratic yet exhaustive psycho-biography *Evatt: A Life* (1993). Far more hagiographic is Kylie **Tennant's** *Evatt: Politics and Justice* (1970), which whitewashes Evatt's recurring character deficiencies.

Evatt's flair for distilling essentials from complexities, his adroit use of legal persuasion in the pursuit of lofty ideals, and his inexhaustible energy were all evident during the conception of the UN at San Francisco in 1945. His defining role earned international applause and this, combined with his consuming ambition, in 1948 led to Evatt's becoming the only Australian ever to chair the General Assembly. This position, which Evatt, with insufficient irony, termed 'president of the world', represented the pinnacle of his public life. It was part of his tragedy that this was recognised neither by Evatt, who expected further greatness, nor by Australians, whose concerns were more parochial. However, Evatt's decisive contributions in international affairs and his successful reconciliation of national interest with a commitment to empire are explored fully and persuasively in the most recent critical biography, *Doc Evatt* (1994), co-authored by Ken Buckley, Barbara Dale, and Wayne Reynolds.

After 1949, Evatt lost both his voice on the world stage and the fruits of political power, and his decline commenced. His intellectual mastery was not matched by his political skill. As federal leader of the **Australian Labor Party** from 1951 he presided over, and probably fuelled, its bitter divisions. The culminating **Split** of 1955 destroyed his long quest to become prime minister. But there was triumph as well as tragedy. In both the High Court and on the hustings he achieved what his many admirers regard as his 'finest hour': he thwarted **Menzies's** attempts to outlaw the Communist Party in 1950–51. On the other hand his risky and ill-judged decision to appear before the **Petrov** Royal Commission in 1954 was a significant blunder. These events are the major preoccupation of Allan Dalziel's friendly assessment, aptly titled *Evatt the Enigma* (1967).

Although re-elected as parliamentary leader of the ALP after the Split, Evatt became a shadow of his former self. In 1960 he returned to the Bar, but by then his dementia was a source of scorn or pity. When Evatt died one eulogy underlined the ambiguous response which this flawed but larger-than-life individual provoked: 'Leave him to history. It will be kinder than his present-day critics'.

PHILLIP DEERY

***Examiner* (Launceston)**, Tasmania's oldest **newspaper**, was launched by James Aikenhead as a weekly on 12 March 1842. The first unofficial editor was historian and Congregational minister, John **West**, who used the paper to promote his views on reform, notably his fierce stand against **transportation**. The *Examiner* soon became a bi-weekly and was later a tri-weekly (1853); in 1877 it became a daily. With the acquisition of the *Launceston Advertiser* in 1847, the *Examiner* became the leading newspaper of northern Tasmania. The Rolfe family has maintained a long association with the paper since 1897.

HD

Exclusives was a derogatory term applied in the 1820s and 1830s to those of high social status in NSW: the members of the Legislative Council, magistrates, clergy, landholders, merchants and other wealthy free settlers. They resisted measures that would undermine their privileges; in particular they opposed reforms that would give the **emancipists** legal and political equality. The exclusives were favoured by Governor **Darling**, but actively lobbied the British administration and parliament to protect their status. Their critics included W.C. **Wentworth**, who chided them as 'the yellow snakes of the colony'. (See also **Pure Merino**.)

HD

Exhibitions, modelled on the hugely successful Great Exhibition of the Works of Industry of All Nations (London, May–October 1851) and the Paris *Exposition Universelle* (May–November 1855), took place regularly in Australia between 1854 and 1900. These exhibitions were used to promote inter-colonial commerce, to attract international interest and investment in Australian industry and **agriculture**, and to encourage **immigration**. By their huge scale, they also provided an unprecedented, spectacular source of popular **entertainment** and an occasion for patriotic trumpet-blowing.

The separate Australian colonies were variously represented by large consignments to the biggest international exhibitions held in Europe, the USA, and elsewhere, namely the Paris *Expositions Universelles* (1855, 1867, 1878, 1889, 1900), London (1862, annually 1871–74, 1886, 1899), Dublin (1865), Vienna (1873), Philadelphia (1876), Amsterdam (1883, at which Victoria alone distributed a staggering 60 000 handbooks and statistical pamphlets), Calcutta (1883–84), New Orleans (1884–85), and Chicago (1893). The earliest Australian exhibitions (1854–76) were either previews of the merchandise assembled to represent Australia at these international forums, or else limited to inter-colonial participation. The most important of these were the Melbourne Exhibition, October–December 1854, and the Intercolonial Exhibition of Australasia, Melbourne, October 1866 – February 1867.

From 1879, and throughout the 1880s and 1890s Australian exhibitions sought to attract participants from all over the world. Of these the largest and most successful were the Sydney International Exhibition, September 1879 – April 1880 (1.1 million visitors); the Melbourne International Exhibition, October 1880 – April 1881 (1.3 million); the Adelaide Jubilee International Exhibition, June 1887 – January 1888; the Centennial International Exhibition, Melbourne, August 1888 – January 1889 (2.0 million), and the Tasmanian International Exhibition, Launceston, November 1891 – March 1892. Smaller exhibitions, each reflecting local interests and commercial aspirations, were held in Adelaide (1900), Ballarat (1878, 1895–96), Brisbane (1876), Dunedin, NZ (1865,

1889–90), Hobart (1894–95), Melbourne (1861, 1872–73, 1875, 1884), and Sydney (1870, 1873).

Organised by boards of prominent commissioners appointed by colonial governments, the exhibitions consisted of sections or 'courts' from dozens of participating colonies or nations and hundreds of private and corporate exhibitors. These constituted displays of every conceivable variety of **manufactures**, agricultural produce, mineral and natural wealth, as well as paintings, sculpture, decorative and applied arts, printing, and **photography**. This jumble of objects—an industrial *wunderkammer*—could be immense in scale and value. The printing presses of the *Argus* newspaper, for example, formed a working exhibit at Melbourne's Centennial International Exhibition (1888). Ornate temporary buildings were erected to house the largest exhibitions, to varying degrees comparable with, and sometimes modelled on, Joseph Paxton's Crystal Palace, built for the Great Exhibition (London, 1851). The Royal Exhibition Building in Melbourne (1880), the only surviving example of this important phenomenon in the development of Australian **architecture**, and one of very few in the world, is the subject of David Dunstan's comprehensive history, *Victorian Icon* (1996). Sydney's Garden Palace (1879) burned down in 1882. Others were demolished.

The cultural significance of European and American exhibitions has been studied by Patricia Mainardi, *Art and Politics of the Second Empire* (1987), and Paul Greenhalgh, *Ephemeral Vistas* (1988). But the enormous literature which accompanied each Australian exhibition has only occasionally been mined systematically: it includes huge official catalogues, commercially published guides and handbooks, prospectuses circulated by exhibitors, official reports containing the deliberations of judges, lists of gold, silver and bronze medallists in categories from mining to needlework, voluminous press coverage, sheet music and lyrics of commemorative cantatas, official invitations, tickets, menus and other ephemera; there are even novels, like Ada **Cambridge**'s *A Woman's Friendship* (serialised 1889, published 1988), which had the Melbourne Centennial International Exhibition as its backdrop. Invaluable points of access to this enormous subject are Renée Free et al. (eds), *Sydney International Exhibition 1879* (1979); Graeme Davison, 'Exhibitions', *ACH* (1982–83); and *Victoria at the Great Exhibitions 1851–1900* (a special issue of the *La Trobe Library Journal*, 1995).

A great number of exhibits at Australian exhibitions eventually found their way into the newly established public libraries, museums, and art galleries of Australian cities. Between them the State Libraries of Victoria, NSW, and SA hold most catalogues of Australian exhibitions, and catalogues of European and American exhibitions at which the Australian colonies were represented. Likewise, a great deal of early scientific research into Australian geology and botany, by Ferdinand von **Mueller**, Frederick McCoy, Alfred Selwyn, and others, was funded by the commissioners of the Victorian Exhibition (Melbourne, 1861) and first published in its catalogue. And among the earliest acquisitions of the National Galleries of Victoria, New South Wales, and South Australia

were paintings and statues sent from continental Europe to the Sydney and Melbourne exhibitions of 1879–80, 1880–81, and 1888–89. These were regarded as among the finest examples of contemporary art, and form a valuable resource for the study of **art history** and taste in colonial Australia. A valuable list of key early exhibitions of art (1837–70), as distinct from 'great' exhibitions, is given by Joan Kerr (ed.), *The Dictionary of Australian Artists* (1992).

The international exhibition was a distinctive product of the high noon of industrialism and imperialism. In the twentieth century, exhibitions remained an important means of promoting trade, but as sites of symbolic rivalry between nations they steadily lost ground to the **Olympic Games**, the World Cup, and other sporting festivals. Australia continued to send exhibits and delegations to the biggest exhibitions, such as the British Empire Exhibition at Wembley in 1924, and the international Expos at Montreal in 1967 and Osaka in 1970. In 1888 Melbourne's International Centennial Exhibition had upstaged Sydney's celebrations; but a century later Brisbane's Bicentennial Expo played second fiddle to Sydney's First Fleet re-enactment and Tallships.

ANGUS TRUMBLE

Exploration by land was, until the 1970s, one of the preoccupations of Australian popular history. History books began with **exploration by sea**, explaining how the coastline of Australia had been mapped by noble Dutch and British seafarers. This map-making was seen as laying the ground for possession. It was as though the act of 'filling in the blanks' on the map of the world actually brought the land itself into being, and therefore made it available to its 'discoverer'. In popular accounts, this process was completed by the land explorers, notably John **Oxley**, Allan **Cunningham**, Thomas **Mitchell**, Charles **Sturt**, Edward **Eyre**, John McDouall **Stuart**, Ludwig **Leichhardt**, the brothers **Forrest** (for readers in WA), and the two duos, **Hume** and Hovell, and **Burke** and Wills.

An account of the principal expeditions undertaken by each of these men was written into the grand narrative of Australian history, almost as reports of their deeds were received in the capital cities. 'The Explorer' himself filled a cultural role which set him apart from **overlanders** and **squatters**, many of whom could also claim to have been the first whites to have seen particular regions of Australia.

A major expedition typically produced two key records. The first was the explorer's published report (always called his 'journal'). The second was the map on which he fixed rivers, mountains, grass plains, deserts—and sometimes information about the tribes he had encountered. This act of mapping fitted Australia into a world grid which measured positions east or west by their distance in time from the Greenwich Observatory in England. The explorer's map and journal reinforced this annexation by the ways in which they renamed the country they described. Occasionally Aboriginal names were appropriated (for example, Murrumbidgee), but usually these names were ignored for those of British dignitaries (Sydney Cove, Victoria, King George Sound), local politicians (Ayers Rock), patrons of the expedition (Chamber's Pillar) or members of the expedition itself (Sturt named the Rufus River in honour of his companion George McLeay's red hair). Other common bases on which names were coined included the visual associations of a place (Ruined Castle Valley), its geographical characteristics (Tidal River), or its place in the story of the expedition itself (Mount Disappointment).

While most 'explorers' led officially sponsored expeditions, some (like Ludwig Leichhardt) were commissioned by private investors. Exploration was undertaken for three practical ends. The first was to discover natural assets—principally rivers, and land suitable for grazing or agriculture. The second was to survey the land on behalf of the colonial government, so that it could exercise authority over remote graziers and control the leasing or sale of land. The third was to establish corridors of communication between colonies, producers, markets, and shipping ports.

The exploration parties always consisted of a team of men. The smallest groups numbered just two or three, while the best-equipped included gentlemen, Aboriginal guides and negotiators, smiths, carpenters, shipwrights, horsemen, labourers, horses, sometimes camels or bullocks, and scores of sheep and cattle. In either case, it became customary to speak of an expedition as if it were the travail of a single man or partnership—as if the white 'explorers' were somehow alone and transcendent in the midst of their men.

The first British land explorer was Arthur **Phillip**, the founding governor of NSW. In April 1788, Phillip began to investigate the people and the countryside directly north of Sydney. It was then that he observed a spectacular line of hills on the western horizon which became known as the Blue Mountains. Over the next 24 years, a few expeditions tried to cross these mountains, but were unable to scale the sheer cliffs which stood at the head of every valley. In the summer of 1812, drought began to dry the creeks and wither the grasses around Sydney. The sheep and cattle farmers who had established runs in the surrounding districts became desperate for feed. With government backing, Gregory **Blaxland**, Lieutenant William Lawson, and the young William **Wentworth** set out in May 1813 with a team of four convicts to search for pasture beyond the mountains. Following a strategy devised by Blaxland, they hacked their way up a ridge which led them above the impassable valleys. Two and a half weeks later they were standing, exhausted and sick, on the western edge of the mountainous barrier. Before them spread the undulating grassy plains of 'the interior'. Around them they saw the smoke of Aboriginal campfires: the sight left them feeling that their battle through the scrub was being observed and reported by watchers in the trees. Nevertheless, they were able to recreate the land in their writings as though the Aborigines were not fully present. To the ears of these white adventurers, the inland was a silent place, awaiting the sounds of settlement and industry. To their eyes, it was 'pasture'—enough, thought Blaxland, to last the colony for the next 30 years.

To colonial optimists, this conquest of the Blue Mountains had set the pattern for further exploration. The silence of the land would continue to retreat, just as the Aborigines would retreat, before the advance of white settlers. Grass plains, created by the Aborigines' fire-stick farming, would realise their destiny as the pastures for European stock. Indeed, it was commonplace for explorers and settlers to describe each new grassy plain as 'a gentleman's park', as if nature had a created a patrimony which the Europeans had come, at last, to claim.

To the officials and the sheep men of Sydney, the rivers which flowed inland from the western slopes of the divide were rivers filled with much promise. Not only might they water great pastures, they might also provide waterways for shipping and prescribe a logic for the future pattern of settlement. But where did they go? What was the nature of the land that lay beyond the horizon?

By the late 1820s, there were three principal theories about the interior. One said that inland Australia was a vast desert (a theory favoured by those seafarers who noted that the offshore winds, in all Australian coastal waters, were hot and dry). A second replied that the rivers surely drained into a great lake, commonly referred to as an inland sea. A third contended that there was, yet to be discovered, a great river which drained a major portion of the continent and which had its outfall in the western or southern ocean, on some corner of the coast which had not been completely surveyed.

Sturt was the most determined believer in an inland sea. Mitchell, on the other hand, was convinced there had to be a major river. Both were to be disappointed, for the Murray River which Sturt followed to the ocean did empty directly into it and did not bisect the interior. But they took their place among the ranks of explorers who extended the maps outwards from the coastal settlements. In their searches they and their colleagues found major rivers and pastures as well as deserts, mountain ranges, and dry riverbeds.

The exploration of central Australia was mainly pursued from Adelaide. Both Sturt and Eyre were based in Adelaide when they embarked on their extraordinary encounters with the most arid regions of the continent. It was from Adelaide that John McDouall Stuart launched his attempts to cross Australia from south to north—a feat he finally accomplished in 1862. Stuart was a skilled bushman, and his achievement was no mere display. It demonstrated to the colonists that theirs might not, after all, be a nation that merely fringed a continent. Fittingly, Stuart's journey mapped out the route which was followed by Australia's first electronic message to the outside world when it clicked along the **Overland Telegraph** line in 1872.

Stuart had two rivals, Robert O'Hara Burke and William Wills. Supported by a vast retinue, they were attempting to beat Stuart across the continent. Unlike most explorers, these two leaders had no Aboriginal guides to help them, no skill in geography, cartography, or living off the land. By the following July, the two men were lying dead of hunger in arid country south of Coopers Creek. Their folly was rewarded with adulation. Their fame, even today, outweighs that of Stuart and is rivalled only by the veneration of another defeated explorer, Ludwig Leichhardt.

Historians disagree about the extent of Leichhardt's skill. The Prussian achieved mythical status after his expedition of 1848, an ill-equipped venture on which he tried to cross the continent from the Darling Downs (near Brisbane) to Perth. Leichhardt, his six companions and nearly 300 animals vanished without trace.

The deaths of these three explorers—Leichhardt, Burke, and Wills—filled the cultural void which was the inland of white Australia. By their deaths, these men enabled historians, poets, stonemasons, and propagandists to invest an alien and unhistoricised land with a white-man's dreaming—they gave white stories, a white mystery, to the cultural silence.

MICHAEL CATHCART

Exploration by sea followed from the development in Europe, by 1500, of the skills and technology needed for reliable ocean voyaging. The early Spanish and Portuguese discoveries led, in just over a century, to the first European knowledge of the Australian coast. When the Dutch followed the Portuguese to the East, their primary object was trade. They quickly sought out the sources of spice production in the Moluccas, pressing on beyond; in early 1606 the *Duyfken*, a Dutch East India Company vessel commanded by Willem Jansz, crossed from the southern coast of New Guinea to the western side of Cape York Peninsula. A crewman was killed in an affray with Aborigines and after a brief coastal survey the Dutch turned away, having found no prospect of trade.

This voyage provided the first European knowledge of the Australian continent: claims for earlier discovery, associated particularly with an outline of **Java-La-Grande** on a series of sixteenth-century charts, cannot be sustained. W.A.R. Richardson in *The Portuguese Discovery of Australia: Fact or Fiction* (1989) has accounted for these charts without involving Australia.

Later in 1606, two Spanish ships under Luis Vaez de Torres passed along the southern coast of New Guinea from the east, thus sailing through Torres Strait. Brett Hilder in *The Voyage of Torres* (1980) traces their track within sight of the Australian mainland. They had come from Peru in company with a third vessel under the overall command of Pedro Fernandez de Quiros in an expedition intended, in part, to find a southern route to the Philippines. Other motives included the extension of Spanish power and Catholic Christianity. Quiros turned back to Peru from Vanuatu, but Torres pressed on to Manila. With experience, the Spanish found that the best routes across the Pacific lay further north.

A third European contact with the continent arose from a new route across the southern Indian Ocean opened up by Dutch vessels sailing to Java. In 1616 Dirk **Hartog** on the *Eendracht* left a pewter plate to mark his visit to an island off the coast of WA near Carnarvon. Many Dutch Company ships, for whom this became a regular route, sighted the Australian coast from then on. In 1622, the English East India Company vessel, the *Trial*, following the Dutch route to the Indies, was wrecked in the Monte Bello Islands; in 1629 the Dutch Company lost a major vessel, the **Batavia**, on Houtman Abrolhos. This first phase of Dutch interest included the 1623 visit of Jan Carstensz in the *Pera* and Willem Colster in the *Arnhem* to the Gulf of Carpentaria, Pieter Nuyts's traverse in 1627 of much of the south coast of the continent and Pieter Pieterszoon's 1636 discovery of Melville Island in the north.

Both the desire for new Dutch trade and an interest in useful geographical knowledge lay behind the plan, probably devised in Batavia by Franchoys Jacobszoon Visscher and warmly supported by Governor-General Antonio van Diemen, for a major expedition in 1642. The first object of Abel Janszoon **Tasman**, together with Visscher on the *Heemskerk* and *Zeehaen*, was to sail eastwards across the Indian Ocean in high latitudes. On 24 November 1642 the west coast of **Tasmania** was sighted. Although only the southern half of the island, dutifully named **Van Diemen's Land**, was charted, by going on to discover NZ and Tonga, then returning to the Indonesian archipelago along the north coast of New Guinea, Tasman completed the circumnavigation of the Australian continent. He thus demonstrated the separation of all previous discoveries of '**New Holland**', as it was called, from a hypothetical Great South Land. In 1644 Tasman, again with Visscher, sailed along the north Australian coast from the Gulf of Carpentaria to the Pilbara. By 1650, two-thirds of the continent's coast were thus widely known not only in Europe, but also wherever Dutch charts, atlases, and globes were distributed.

J.E. Heeres, *The Part Borne by the Dutch in the Discovery of Australia 1606–1765* (1899), is still a good source for these early voyages. J.P. Sigmond and L.H. Zuiderbaan in *Dutch Discoveries of Australia* (1979) discuss archaeological work on wreck sites within a general narrative. Andrew Sharp's *The Voyages of Abel Janszoon Tasman* (1968) remains the essential work on Tasman.

Further Dutch visits arose from several motives. Three more Company vessels were wrecked on the west coast, provoking searches for survivors. In 1697 Willem de Vlamingh made a careful survey of the Swan River and, further north, replaced Hartog's plate with his own. Gunter Schilder's *Voyage to the Great South Land: Willem de Vlamingh 1696–1697* (1985) provides the original documents. The casual visit in 1688 by an English vessel, the *Cygnet* under Captain Read, to King Sound is chiefly remembered by the account of William **Dampier**, a crewman, in *A New Voyage Round the World* (1697). Dampier, as captain, returned to the Pilbara coast in 1699 on a voyage intended for discovery and described in *A Voyage to New Holland* (1703–09). A few months later at New Britain he wisely—given the state of his vessel—abandoned his plan to discover the east coast of the continent. Dampier's activities stimulated new Dutch interest, particularly Martin van Delft's voyage of 1705 to Melville Island and the Cobourg Peninsula. C.C. Macknight in *The Voyage to Marege'* (1976) suggests that this, in turn, may have been connected with the beginning of the regular visits to the area, and further east into the Gulf of Carpentaria, by **Macassan** trepang fishermen. Conversely, reports of trade products coming to Macassar and Timor from the Australian coast led to a final Dutch voyage to the Gulf of Carpentaria in 1756, again searching in vain for trading prospects.

By contrast, the voyage up the continent's east coast by the *Endeavour* under James **Cook** in 1770 was a by-product of science. Coming from observing the transit of Venus in Tahiti and retracing Tasman's track, Cook had intended to take up his survey on the Tasmanian coast where Tasman had left off, but a storm drove the *Endeavour* north so that Cook, perhaps fortunately, missed Bass Strait. Cook's vessel was only the second European ship to pass through the dangerous reefs of Torres Strait. J.C. Beaglehole has magnificently edited the relevant journals.

Though Cook's outline chart of the whole continent still had many gaps, especially in the south-east, the overall shape of the coast was clear. Other factors too mark a new stage of exploration in the late eighteenth century. Reliable chronometers, first available on Cook's second voyage, allowed more reliable determination of longitude. The establishment of the British navy's hydrographic office, along with similar arrangements in France, provided stimulus and direction as both nations sought strategic advantages in trade and military rivalry. John Dunmore in *The Expedition of the St Jean-Baptiste to the Pacific 1769–1770* (1981) shows that Jean de Surville, searching for such opportunity in the South Pacific, came within a few days' sailing of Sydney in early December 1769. Another French expedition under Marion du Fresne visited the south coast of Van Diemen's Land in 1772.

From 1788 Sydney provided a local base for all further discovery. In 1798 Matthew **Flinders** in the *Norfolk* sailed through the strait north of Van Diemen's Land and named it after his friend, George **Bass**. Returning to England, Flinders assumed command of the *Investigator* with the object of 'completing the discovery' of the whole continent. Beginning from Cape Leeuwin in WA in December 1801, he followed the coast, known only from Nuyts's 1627 voyage, to the east. Passing beyond the limits of Dutch knowledge, he discovered Spencer and St Vincent Gulfs, as well as Kangaroo Island. The outline of the entire southern coast was fixed when Flinders met the Frenchman, Nicolas **Baudin**, coming from Bass Strait in the east, in Encounter Bay. There was much detailed work remaining for Flinders as he traced the coastline first to Sydney, and then northwards to Cape York, around the Gulf of Carpentaria and to Arnhem Land, where he interviewed a Macassan captain. Though much of the coast Flinders explored was known in outline from earlier voyages, no-one contributed more to the effective charting of the continent, now named Terra Australis or Australia on his general map. The introduction to Flinders's *A Voyage to Terra Australis* (1814) contains a masterly summary of previous sea exploration.

The coastal survey of northern Australia was taken up from the point at which Flinders had had to leave off in 1803 by Phillip Parker King in a series of voyages between 1818 and 1822. The transition from exploration proper to hydrographic charting can be seen most clearly in the work of John Clements Wickham, and later John Lort Stokes, on the *Beagle* between 1837 and 1843. Many sections of the coast all around Australia were examined more closely than before and a few significant discoveries made, such as Port **Darwin** and the Victoria River. Stokes's extravagant assessment of the Plains of Promise at the base of the Gulf of Carpentaria in August 1841, as reported in his *Discoveries in Australia* (1846), shows the limits of exploration by sea. As the Dutch Company authorities remarked after Tasman's voyage of 1644, those 'who shall investigate what the lands give, must walk therein and through'.

Andrew Sharp in *The Discovery of Australia* (1963) identifies the earliest European report for each section of the Australian coast.

CAMPBELL MACKNIGHT

Exploration history began with the explorers themselves. In the drawing-rooms and learned societies of Victorian London, the explorer of Africa and the East was a celebrity. He had risked his flesh in dark and sensuous lands. He could fill museum-cases with the corpses of exotic creatures and the artefacts of savage civilisations. In his writings, he stirred Victorians with the hot breath of an imaginary pagan world, and soothed them with the assurance that it was all about to change.

The Australian explorers were bound to seem mundane by comparison. **Oxley**, **Mitchell**, **Eyre**, **Sturt**, **Cunningham**, **Stuart**, and **Forrest** were gentlemen surveyors entrusted with practical tasks. They returned from 'unknown territory' laden—not with artefacts and wondrous tales— but with maps and journals, mostly designed to promote the interests of sheep farmers and the collection of rent.

In England, these Australian map-makers did not pass completely unnoticed. Some received medals from the Royal Geographical Society. Thomas Mitchell even enjoyed a brief period of celebrity during which he was knighted. Whether Mitchell was a hero or a braggart (and he has been called both), his grandiloquence outshone his fellows. In *Three Expeditions into the Interior of Eastern Australia* (1838), Mitchell appealed to a Victorian desire for 'romance', dramatising himself as a knight whose destiny it was to lead civilised men to the rivers and parklands which awaited them in a pristine Australia. Similar imagery occurs in other explorer journals, but the greater part of them is given to recording mundane details, noting mishaps, reporting boredom and despair, and attempting to provide careful descriptions of the plants, water-resources, landforms, and Aboriginal peoples. This degree of information was valuable to officials and to settlers, but such quotidian detail made the journals unappealing as literature. They lacked 'romance'.

The nineteenth-century Australian historian Julian **Tenison-Woods** complained that most journals were so 'tediously detailed that the explorers' important and interesting journeys have been made dry and repulsive by minuteness of detail'. To Tenison-Woods, these men were Australian **heroes** whose 'feats' and deeds' had yielded a land which was 'new'. His two-volume *A History of the Discovery and Exploration of Australia* (1865) maintained a scholarly fidelity to the journals, presenting a concise account of each explorer's route and key encounters. The result was not so much nationalist romance as a catalogue of stubborn endurance.

More influential was the two-volume *The History of Australian Exploration* (1888), by the nationalist writer and bushman Ernest **Favenc**. He, too, believed that exploration embraced a major part 'of the romance of our past'. He celebrated the quality which Tenison-Woods found most vexing: the fact that exploration had advanced 'by slow degrees' as 'a stubborn conflict between the explorer and the inert forces of Nature'.

This heroic, nationalist saga has been recapitulated in hundreds of books, articles, and school-texts ever since. Introducing her anthology *Australian Explorers* (1958), the historian Kathleen **Fitzpatrick** endorsed the view of her favourite explorer Ernest **Giles**: exploration was a romance built from 'the deeds and sufferings of these noble toilers in the dim and distant field of discovery'. Bill Peach, in the book *The Explorers* (1984), based on his ABC television series, declared that the explorers were 'men of courage' who had brought to life 'the great blank' on the map of Australia.

At the heart of this romance lay three men who failed, and who paid with their lives: **Burke** and Wills, and Ludwig **Leichhardt**. Leichhardt disappeared in 1848 with his six companions in an attempt to cross the continent from east to west. Over the next century, nine major searches added to the sense that the party had met an almost supernatural fate.

Novels and poems nurtured this mythology, unencumbered by historical records. In the poem 'The Lost Leichhardt', Banjo **Paterson** depicted the explorer as 'Our one Illustrious Dead', as a dreamer who had been absorbed into the mystery of outback Australia. Ernest Favenc's *The Secret of the Australian Desert* (1896) was one of several turn-of-the-century novels which linked Leichhardt to an imaginary and mysterious zone in the heart of Australia. This tradition culminated in Patrick **White's** novel *Voss* (1957), in which a visionary (and possibly mad) explorer, based largely on Leichhardt, is transfigured and destroyed in his struggle to penetrate and know the land.

Equally fantastic was the veneration of Burke and Wills. They set out on their spectacularly expensive attempt to link Melbourne to the Gulf of Carpentaria in 1860. The venture claimed seven lives, including those of Burke and Wills themselves. Though all the evidence suggested that Burke's leadership had been incompetent, the mythmakers spoke only of heroism. The explorers' deaths had invested the Centre with a romance which was played out in their triumphal funeral and in an outpouring of art. Adam Lindsay **Gordon's** 'Gone' eulogised them as heroes who had fallen in 'battle'. William **Strutt** painted *The Burial of Burke* as a patriotic idyll. **Monuments** were built along their route, including a stately bronze statue by Charles Summers erected in the heart of Melbourne.

In this mode, even folly could be recast as a kind of Australian nobility. Alan **Moorehead's** *Cooper's Creek* (1963) found heroism in the fatal innocence of Burke and Wills. Their stoic, muddled deaths were valorised in John **Longstaff's** massive and melancholy canvas, *The Arrival of Burke, Wills and King at the Deserted Camp at Cooper's Creek* (1907). Since the 1940s, the theme has been reworked in a series of stark, enigmatic paintings by Sidney **Nolan**. The diverse representations of Burke and Wills are brilliantly analysed in Tim Bonyhady, *Burke and Wills: From Melbourne to Myth* (1991).

The image of exploration as a metaphysical quest, rather than a dangerous and lonely exercise in surveying, was heightened by the addition of Charles Sturt to this list of failed dreamers. His search for a non-existent inland sea contributed so seductive an element of transcendent folly that by 1985 the historian Marcia McEwan was claiming that 'all the explorers since the crossing of the Blue Mountains … believed in the existence of an inland sea'. They were questers all.

From the outset, this view of exploration as a saga of chivalry and sacrifice was questioned. Cynics repeated the words of Leichhardt's one-time surveyor John Mann: 'Leichhardt! He was no explorer. He'd lose himself in George Street.' In the build-up to the funeral of Burke and Wills, working-class voices demanded to know why these two alone were sanctified, while the men who had died victims to those gentlemen's incompetence were ignored.

By the 1960s, the impulse to venerate the Australian explorers had waned. Several commentators, including Bonyhady and the historian Henry **Reynolds**, speculate that this decline set in after World War I, when the story of **Anzac** gave Australians a more robust mythology of heroism and sacrifice. Richard White, *Inventing Australia* (1981), a standard text of the 1980s, did not mention a single explorer in its analysis of the formative myths of Australian culture.

Since the 1980s, post-colonial sensitivity and a newfound sympathy among academic writers for the Aboriginal struggle have led to a re-examination of the role of the explorers. In *With the White People: The Crucial Role of the Aborigines in the Exploration and Development of Australia* (1990), Henry Reynolds pointed out that the explorers were not venturing into an unknown void, but traversing territory which was occupied and managed by **Aborigines**. Furthermore, they relied on Aborigines (sometimes acting willingly, sometimes under duress) to find food and water, and to negotiate transit through Aboriginal territories. Even the more conventional stories acknowledged that Burke and Wills made a fatal error when they disdained to draw on Aboriginal knowledge.

The best-known work of this period is Paul Carter's *The Road to Botany Bay* (1987). This brilliant and vexing book teases its readers into reflecting on the rhetorical strategies which various explorers used to construct landscapes in their texts. It explores landscapes which erased Aboriginal culture from the white imagination and laid out, instead, a vacant land which was rightfully British. Similar themes are played out in Ross Gibson, *The Diminishing Paradise: Changing*

Literary Perceptions of Australia (1984); Robert Dixon, *The Course of Empire: Neo-Classical Culture in New South Wales* (1986); and Simon Ryan, *The Cartographic Eye: How Explorers Saw Australia* (1997).

Though the role of the explorers in Australian history remains a subject of contest and debate, their day as national heroes has past. It is true that the statue of Burke and Wills now dominates one of Melbourne's principal intersections; but it is difficult to avoid the impression that their presence there is merely ornamental.

Michael Cathcart

Eyre, Edward John (1815–1901), explorer, began over-landing cattle soon after his arrival in NSW in 1833. He made several trips to SA in search of new land and stock routes, in the course of which he explored the Flinders Ranges, named Lake Torrens, and explored the Eyre Peninsula, which was named after him. He began an epic journey of exploration in 1840 with the intention of finding a route from Adelaide into the north of the continent. When the country proved impassable, he decided to attempt an east–west crossing. With a small party he left Fowlers Bay in early 1841 and followed the Great Australian Bight towards settlement in WA. Hampered by lack of water and intense heat, Eyre was in a perilous situation when two of the Aborigines in his party killed his overseer and took most of the supplies. With the support of the remaining Aboriginal, Wylie, Eyre reached Albany in July 1841. His *Journals of Expeditions of Discovery* (1845) was one of the inspirations for Patrick **White's** novel *Voss* (1957). Eyre's subsequent conduct as governor-in-chief of Jamaica became notorious for authoritarian excess, and is examined by Geoffrey **Dutton** in *The Hero as Murderer* (1967); Dutton also wrote *In Search of Edward John Eyre* (1982). Edward Stokes examines the expedition to WA in *The Desert Coast* (1993).

KT

F

'Faceless men' was a term used by R.G. **Menzies** in his policy speech of 30 November 1963 to describe the federal conference of the **Australian Labor Party**: 'the famous outside body, thirty-six "faceless men" whose qualifications are unknown, who have no electoral responsibility …'. The term was reputedly coined earlier that year by journalist Alan Reid when the parliamentary leader of the ALP, Arthur **Calwell**, and his deputy, Gough **Whitlam**, were photographed outside a Canberra hotel waiting to hear a decision of the ALP federal conference. Whitlam's campaign to reform the ALP led to the parliamentary leaders becoming members of the federal conference and executive.

HD

Facey, Albert Barnett (1894–1982) published one book, *A Fortunate Life* (1981), when he was 87. It sold more copies than any other Australian book to that time. In a simple, almost primitive style Facey told the story of his life, which has a typicality that has made him into an Australian Everyman. He was born in Melbourne in the 1890s **depression**, which robbed his father of his job as a quarryman and sent him to the WA goldfields, where he died. The family dispersed and Facey was cared for by his maternal grandmother, who later took him to WA to join the family of another of her daughters. Still a boy, he worked with them on a pioneering wheat farm and at eight was sent away to earn his own living. He was a bushworker, drover, railway navvy, and tent boxer. He landed at **Gallipoli**, was wounded, and returned to take up his own land as a soldier settler. The 1930s Depression ruined him and he went to Perth where he worked on the trams and was active in the union. He found prosperity finally doing up and selling properties on Perth's outskirts. Facey took his misfortunes uncomplainingly, found pleasure easily, and judged a life of much pain and deprivation as fortunate. The book itself is a more studied work than it appears, as is evident from the various manuscript versions held at the University of Western Australia. It was made into a television series in 1986. John Hirst's *The World of Albert Facey* (1992) gives further information on Facey and his family.

JH

Factions once referred to informal parliamentary groupings that preceded the emergence of the party system, and now denotes formal divisions within the party system. The term was originally pejorative, referring to parliamentarians who put their sectional or personal interests before the public good, but such alliances of convenience provided the basis of ministerial government in the colonial legislatures during the second half of the nineteenth century. Peter Loveday and A.W. **Martin**, *Parliament, Factions and Parties* (1966), established the factional pattern of NSW politics in this period. These factions, with their unstable membership and weak ideological foundations, were supplanted at the turn of the century by parties characterised by formal membership, explicit policy, and substantial extra-parliamentary organisation. Both the Labor and non-Labor parties were susceptible to division over policy and personal ambition, but it was only in the 1970s that such divisions hardened in the Labor Party into factions, with full-time organisers who enrolled members in order to control conferences and parliamentary pre-selections. By the 1980s the factional leaders of the Right, the Left, and the Centre Left exercised a remarkable degree of influence, and in the words of one, Graham Richardson, were prepared to do *Whatever It Takes* (1994) to keep it. The factions of the Liberal Party are less developed, though endemic conflict in NSW, SA, and WA suggests a comparable vehemence.

SM

Fadden, Arthur William (1894–1973), a Country Party (**National Party**) politician, was perhaps the earthiest of prime ministers. One of 10 children of a north Queensland policeman, he moved from accountancy into local, state, and finally federal politics. In 1940 he became leader of the Country Party and in August 1941, after R.G. **Menzies** resigned as prime minister, assumed national leadership until, in October, two independent members of parliament defected and Labor took office. When the Liberal–Country Party coalition regained office in 1949, Fadden served as treasurer until 1958. Gregarious and unpretentious, his memoirs, *They Called Me Artie* (1969), project his homespun image. Arthur **Calwell's** jibe that 'for forty days and forty nights you held the destiny of Australia in the hollow of your head' conveys the rough-and-tumble style that Fadden himself practised so successfully.

SM

Fair go, a colloquialism expressing a distinctively Australian sense of justice or fair play, probably originated in the late nineteenth century as a derivation from the English expression 'a fair show'. To give a person a 'fair go' was to give them a reasonable opportunity, or to ensure that the rules of competition were fair to all. So, in the game of two-up, the ringer would cry 'Fair go!' before the spinner tossed the coins. Or if things threatened to get out of hand someone would cry 'Fair go!' or 'Fair crack of the whip!'

The popularity of the phrase may have reflected wider features of a society largely plebeian in its social origins and egalitarian in outlook. The more formal expression 'fair and reasonable' was invoked by Alfred **Deakin** as the benchmark of the program of **tariffs** and arbitrated wages he called the **New Protection**. Justice **Higgins**, in his Harvester judgment, interpreted it to guarantee 'the normal needs of an average employé regarded as a human being in a civilised country'. In his seminal *Australia* (1930), W.K. **Hancock** identified it as 'the popular refrain of Australian democracy, repeated incessantly in pleas and judicial decisions, in statutes, Parliamentary debates, trade union conferences and platform orations'. What was 'fair and reasonable', he pointed out, depended on the 'special conditions of time and place'. It was an ethical concept, 'like the medieval idea of justice', but 'joined with modern optimism, which insists that man is in control of nature, and that he can make his life tolerable if he chooses to do so'. Hancock's book itself gave further authority to the concept. Though equal chances, rather than equal shares, was the original meaning of the phrase, it was increasingly extended to support political measures designed to redress social inequality. 'Fair-goes', Donald **Horne** wrote in 1964, 'are not only for oneself, but for underdogs'. The concept might justify help to less gifted students as well as pensions for the old. 'If the outside world will allow it, it seems to be there to stay', he concluded. But the outside world was not so forbearing, and in the 1980s, as the Australian economy internationalised, Justice Higgins's 'fair and reasonable' was pilloried by free-market modernisers as a quaint survival of the 'medieval just price' while the traditional Australian fair go was challenged by a new metaphor of fairness, more attuned to an internationally competitive, sport-loving society—'the level playing-field'.

GD

Fairfax family were over five generations and nearly 150 years the owners of the *Sydney Morning Herald*. No other newspaper in the world had been so long under one family's control, and no other family in Australia had formed such an entrepreneurial dynasty. JOHN FAIRFAX (1804–77) worked on and owned newspapers in England before moving to Sydney with his wife, mother, and three children in 1838. Family pride glows through the entry by JAMES OSWALD (1933–) on his great-great-grandfather in the *ADB*: 'Fairfax built up the *Herald* from a small journal to one of the most influential and respected newspapers in the empire.' James Fairfax chronicles from inside the last 30 years of the family firm's history in *My Regards to Broadway. A Memoir* (1991). (A grey tower on Broadway, at Sydney's southern edge, was the home of the firm from 1955.)

The *Herald* was nicknamed 'Granny' as early as 1848. Gavin **Souter's** commissioned history *Company of Heralds* (1981) finds in the paper a creed common across the generations: 'Christian belief, the rule of law, family life and all the middle-class virtues'. Readers were nearly always advised to vote for conservative parties; but at the federal election of 1961, when Sir WARWICK OSWALD (1901–87) believed that a credit squeeze by the government of R.G. **Menzies** was disastrous, the opposition campaign was run from a room in the *Herald* building known as the 'Labor ward'. Whatever its editorial preference, the *Herald* was more scrupulous than most other papers in the reporting of electoral politics. Souter's free hand as historian exemplified Fairfax fair-mindedness. When a fourth-generation Fairfax, VINCENT (1909–), started as a cadet reporter in 1933, the general manager told him: 'You might think the Fairfaxes own the *Herald*, but you're wrong, because the *Herald* owns the Fairfaxes'. They contributed diversely to the culture and economy of NSW.

Sir Warwick listed his recreations as the arts, philosophy, and cattle breeding. The philosophy was unusual for a Fairfax. So was his marital history. Where father and grandfather had married, and were outlived by, daughters of prominent English-born citizens of Sydney, Sir Warwick was twice divorced and three times married. Like earlier Fairfaxes he was a devout Protestant; unlike them, he lived at a time when that commitment could be combined more or less comfortably with divorce and remarriage.

When John Fairfax & Sons became a public company in 1956, with Fairfaxes retaining nearly half the shares, its other publications included the evening *Sun*, the *Sunday Sun–Herald* and the weekly *Australian Financial Review*. Having invested already in **radio**, the firm was in at the beginning of **television** that year. The *Financial Review* went daily in 1963. An interest in the Melbourne *Age* was acquired in 1966, and full control followed in 1972. The weekly *National Times* was launched in 1971, turned into the *Times on Sunday* in 1986, and closed down in 1987. The *Herald* was always at the centre of Fairfax strategies: the ultimate purpose of all other projects was to protect 'the crown jewels'.

Souter, in 1981, chronicled an orderly triumph. His second book *Heralds and Angels* (1991, 1992) reads like dynastic fiction. Sir Warwick died early in 1987; his son by the third wife, also WARWICK (1960–   ), aged 26, bought out relatives and other shareholders at prices that he could not afford to pay after stock markets around the capitalist world crashed in October. By 1990 the receiver had moved in. The publications and enterprises of John Fairfax Ltd were lost to the family, crown jewels and all.

K.S. INGLIS

Faithfull massacre claimed the lives of eight white men, who died after being speared by Aborigines. Brothers George and William Faithfull overlanded from NSW in 1838 to secure pastoral land in the Port Phillip District. Their shepherds and stock went on ahead and camped by the Broken River, near present-day Benalla, Victoria. On 11 April, a group of about 300 of the Pangerang people attacked the shepherds with spears, as retribution for alleged attacks by the Faithfulls' party and interference with their women. Eight of the shepherds were killed in the skirmish, and many of the sheep scattered into the bush were lost. The incident encouraged overlanding parties to travel together, and hastened the provision of border police in the Port Phillip District. George and William Faithfull sold out in September 1838 but subsequently took up a pastoral run on the Ovens River, where they and the Aborigines continued to do battle. In one of several retaliations, George Faithfull boasted that his party fired 60 rounds of ammunition into a large party of Aborigines, killing men, women, and children.

HD

Family in Aboriginal society consisted of a dense range of kinship relationships and complex conventions of reciprocity, duty, and obligation in ties between blood relations and relations by marriage. The social authority of individual members within a clan—older men and women, young men and girls—mirrored to a considerable extent their standing in families. People moved from a position of little power in childhood and adolescence, to considerable power in maturity, so that older men and women largely directed decisions for the group concerning marriage and childcare, work, and group location.

The invasion of white settlers brought death and destruction to Aboriginal communities, through outright murder, introduced diseases, malnutrition, and forced relocation to missions and reserves. Aborigines themselves recount stories of subsequent family arrangements undergoing reorientation with restrictions on freedom of movement, conversion to Christianity, and exposure to Western education and social systems. Aborigines sustained a strong attachment to ties of family and kin, however, and continued to acknowledge a wide range of relationships. For those Aborigines of mixed descent whom colonial administrations successively denied the meagre material support of the reserves, family links would remain a potent source of assistance and personal identity.

Australian settlers' experiences of families owed much to their heritage in the British Isles. The **convicts** who reached Australia's shores had been forcibly separated from families, including spouses (and children in the case of male convicts); only men had the option to work their passage home on the expiry of their sentence. Convicts' formation of stable de facto relationships and marriages, encouraged by colonial administrators, nevertheless paved the way for the development of substantial families. Like the increasing number of free settlers who poured onto Aboriginal lands through the nineteenth century or clung to the coastal cities, they interpreted life through Christian cultural norms that insisted on monogamous marriage, certain ways of rearing children, and reciprocal obligations with other kin, particularly parents and siblings.

Class divisions grounded in wealth and education, alongside differences in denominational religious beliefs and ethnic backgrounds (Irish Catholics or Scottish Presbyterians, for example), and rural as opposed to urban living, shaped the experiences of settler families. There was greater fluidity in the colonies than in Britain in the ways family members interacted with each other and with the communities which rapidly developed wherever white livelihoods could be sustained. In part, this resulted from male breadwinners' greater opportunities to gain wealth and to lose it, resulting in changed material circumstances for wives and children. In part it resulted from an allied factor, that men frequently moved in search of work or, in gold strikes, of instant wealth, creating greater vulnerability for families while simultaneously lessening the strength of community ties. Much male breadwinners' work was unstable, creating uncertainties about housing, food, and clothing. Thus fractured families were far more common than stories of colonial prosperity suggested. Poverty was a constant fact of life for many families, and the need for charity for women and children left without a breadwinner was far from uncommon. By contrast, some families' experiences were dominated by wealth gained from utilising large appropriated swathes of land, or from the commercial, financial, manufacturing, and professional services that men provided in the cities.

The essays in *Families in Colonial Australia* (1985), edited by Patricia Grimshaw et al., describe in detail the economies of family life. Men were expected to support wives and children, and usually undertook the central work for the income upon which the families' living was based. The labour of other family members, however, was also crucial. Wives gave birth to large numbers of children—on average five or six live births—and were responsible for their early care and moral guidance. While their domestic labour was significant for families' standards of living, many women extended their tasks, as did their children. On the land, farmers' wives, helped by older children of both sexes, undertook considerable farm work. In towns and cities, working-class youth and sometimes wives contributed to the family income through waged work, and other unwaged but similarly valuable assistance. In middle-class households the wives' household work was lessened by the employment of working-class women, and more extended education of their children, creating a context within which greater emphasis was placed on the emotional aspects of the marriage and of the parental relationship, particularly mothering. Memories of 'the Victorian family' have dwelt upon this model of family as a sentimental entity gathered under the roof of 'home sweet home'.

Towards the end of the nineteenth century and in the first decades of the twentieth, the **demographic** transition that characterises modernising societies occurred—birthrates and death-rates both fell. Family size dropped to a little over two children per family by the 1920s, as couples practised birth control, and women sought to lighten their burdens of pregnancy and child-rearing. Meanwhile, women reformers, some organised in women-only associations, gained a public voice to urge legal changes in the family that would give wives equal avenues to sue for **divorce**, reduce husbands' control over wives' earnings and property, and make mothers equal guardians of their children. They had male supporters in legislatures to effect these changes, men who also moved to confer equal citizenship rights on white women at the federal level in 1902.

These various social transformations, as Kerreen Reiger has shown in *The Disenchantment of the Home* (1985), ushered in fresh ways of viewing marriage, sexuality, housewifery, and child-rearing. This particularly noticeable in urban areas where fortunate families inhabited suburban houses, complete with electricity, gas, running water, and sewerage, surrounded by fenced gardens, rotary clothes hoists, and car garages, and opening onto paved footpaths that led to shops, schools, and public transport. For the poor in both urban and rural Australia, families coped very differently. Trained professionals now dominated an influential discussion on families, while teachers, psychologists, doctors, ministers, magistrates, and social workers joined kin and neighbours in offering advice and, in some cases, intervening to enforce new norms. Families could be broken up in the interests of preserving normative family values.

If welfare authorities considered a white child neglected by its parents or guardians, they had the authority to remove the child into state care in an orphanage or foster home. Aboriginal children were also forcibly removed from their families, but the circumstances were tragically different in a number of ways. A child under some state jurisdictions could be declared neglected simply on the basis of being Aboriginal; children of mixed descent were more vulnerable to removal in the expectation that lighter-skinned children could be assimilated more readily into white mainstream society; the authorities who removed the children took measures to prevent their relatives from having contact with them, even from knowing their whereabouts; the underlying aim was no less than the destruction of Aboriginal culture. As late as the 1960s a society that eulogised the institution of the family as imbued by nature, God, and the state with benign qualities and crucial functions enforced the break-up of thousands of families of its colonised minority—all in the name of Aborigines' own good. The report on the national inquiry into the **Stolen Generations**, *Bringing Them Home* (1997), exposed the harsh realities of many Aboriginal families' experiences.

Many of the large number of migrants after World War II brought cultural expectations of family relationships that differed from the practices of the country which was their new home. This was particularly true for those migrants from countries where the dominant religion was other than Christian. Migration increased the diversity of families, therefore, but at the same time most families were influenced by the repercussions of the pressures for change that accompanied postmodernity.

Divorce rose steadily in frequency from the 1950s. The Commonwealth Family Law Act of 1975, which removed grounds for divorce based on matrimonial fault and allowed one year's separation as evidence of irretrievable breakdown of marriage, signalled a change in many people's willingness to continue in unhappy relationships, even where young children were involved. This was often less a flight from marriage itself than a search for more fulfilling relationships, since many divorced people remarried and created 'blended' families of children by parents' previous marriages and their new unions. In contrast with the situation before World War II, many more couples lived together without marriage, some marrying when they decided to have children, others rejecting marriage altogether. Lesbian couples and gay male couples also cohabited and reared children, extending society's views on what constituted 'family'. In the 1990s the average age of marriage increased, more women delayed first births until their thirties, and more couples remained childless than ever before.

The death of the family has been much touted. Most Australians in the 1990s, for good or ill, count ties of blood or marriage as crucial for their sense of identity, for the bonds that tie them emotionally to others, and for lines of assistance, offered or received, in life crises.

PATRICIA GRIMSHAW

Family Court of Australia was established by the Family Law Act (1975) as one of the reformist measures of the **Whitlam** government. Prior to 1959 separate state **divorce** laws produced inconsistent decisions and divorce settlements that were generally disadvantageous to women. The passage of the Matrimonial Causes Act (1959) and the Marriage Act (1961) provided uniform federal legislation, but this continued to operate through separate state courts. The advent of the Family Court in 1976 provided a federal judicial mechanism. The first chief justice, Elizabeth **Evatt**, was followed by Alistair Nicholson in 1987. The function of the court is principally to grant divorce but also to determine property, guardianship, custody, and maintenance arrangements. Where previously there were 14 possible grounds for divorce, the Family Court recognises the 'irretrievable breakdown of marriage' as the sole ground.

HD

Family history, see **Genealogy**

Family wage, see **Basic wage**

Farrer, William James (1845–1906), often called 'the father of the Australian **wheat** industry', was born of yeoman stock in the English Lakes District. Farrer excelled at mathematics as a young man and graduated from Cambridge University in 1868. He began studying medicine, but migrated to Australia in 1870 after contracting tuberculosis. He gained 'colonial experience' while tutoring at George Campbell's farm at Duntroon, NSW. The backwardness of Australian pastoral and agricultural science was observed by Farrer in his paper, *Grass, and Sheep Farming* (1873), which went largely unnoticed. He moved around NSW as a surveyor from 1875 until 1886, when he acquired a small property on the Murrumbidgee River near the present site of Canberra. Here, at the farm he named Lambrigg after his mother's birthplace, Farrer built a laboratory. On three acres he laid out wheat-breeding plots, and devoted the rest of his life to selection and cross-breeding experiments. Out of hundreds of painstaking crosses each season, Farrer produced over two dozen commercially cultivated wheats and 180 parent breeds. Contrary to popular belief, his famous Federation variety, developed from 1894 to 1901, was not especially resistant to rust fungus or bunt infection, but it escaped rust because it was an early maturing type. The Federation strain was high-yielding and so drought-resistant that it enabled a vast inland extension of the wheat belt. It was the leading wheat strain in Australia 1910–25, and its russet brown ears changed the colour of harvest landscapes from gold to bronze. The man once called a 'woolly-headed crank' by local farmers was portrayed on the Australian $2 note in 1966. Archer Russell wrote his biography, *William James Farrer* (1949).

DC

Fashion in Australia has always followed Britain and Europe. Overseas buyers, importers, travellers, and Australians going 'home' brought back the latest in taste and quality, in clothes, furnishing, and personal equipment. Fashion arrived through illustrations and articles in magazines, catalogues, and trade publications. Clever seamstresses, milliners, and tradesmen quickly reproduced the latest in sleeves, bonnets, and furnishings for their wealthy clients. Australian conditions, **climate** especially, demanded some modifications to European style. British experience in India suggested ideas for lighter clothing and shade screening. However, when fashion decreed crinolines, bustles, and fussy late-Victorian frills and flounces, Australia tried to follow.

Historians of fashion and clothing in Australia have also recorded the development of distinctively Australian modes of dress. Mostly these occurred in relation to work clothes. Cedric Flower's *Clothes in Australia: A Pictorial History 1788–1980s* (1984) first appeared in 1968 as *Duck and Cabbage Tree*, reflecting the significance of the bushman's duck or moleskin trousers, and crimea or flannel shirts, and his broad-brimmed hat made of cabbage-tree palm or, later, possum or rabbit fur probably at Sydney's Akubra hat factory. Marion Fletcher, *Costume in Australia 1788–1901* (1984), also discerned evidence of a national style of dress in the work clothes of the nineteenth century, revived for the late twentieth century in the popularity of R.M. Williams riding boots, broad-brimmed hats, and Drizabone raincoats.

Men's fashions from the late nineteenth century showed a kind of egalitarianism, though their conservatism was the despair of retailers. Women remained more sensitive to the possibilities of fashion, though still constrained by what importers made available or what dressmakers could do with ideas or sketches from abroad. Skirts came up and silhouettes were boyishly flattened in Australia as elsewhere after World War I. In the 1920s, photography and new colour-printing techniques were exploited in glossy magazines, notably *The Home*, to foster an Australian sense of style; from its outset, fashion coverage was one of the strengths of the ***Australian Women's Weekly***. Clothes copied from the movies defied depression in the 1930s, while the void created by the occupation of Paris during World War II was filled in Australia from the USA. After the war the fashion magazines and department stores combined to bring Australian women the Paris 'new look', but California and Hollywood already had a claim on swimsuits and beach pyjamas. Glamorous, mature, and sophisticated postwar Paris styles translated badly into an Australia preoccupied with postponed marriage and home-making, and in the 1950s Australian women gained a reputation for dowdiness and conservatism, though high-class milliners and dressmakers like Germaine Rocher, Lillian Whiteman (Le Louvre), Beril Jents, and Zara Holt (Magg) continued to dress the wealthy elite. June Dally-Watkins pioneered a modelling school in Sydney, and modelling became the glamour career for girls, but models went abroad to make their names and marry well, or posed in tight skirts and high heels for photographers like Max Dupain with the latest vacuum cleaner or fridge. Symptoms of change were the emergence of a teenage fashion market and Paula Stafford's effective promotion of bikinis from her Surfers Paradise store. By the 1960s fashions conveyed by television and the pop music industry were competing with *haute couture*.

Since the 1870s Melbourne Cup week has been the fashion highlight of the Australian year. The appearance at the 1965 race of English model Jean Shrimpton in a simple sleeveless dress which showed her knees, and wearing neither hat, gloves, nor stockings, signalled the revolution. Skirts went up, underwear disappeared (or was minimised by lycra), french rolls and bouffant hairstyles came down, and stocking manufacturers hastily retooled to produce pantihose. Australian women shed years, and with the aid of local designers like Norma Tullo adopted the mini-skirt. Indeed they were reluctant to abandon it, even after fashion decreed the longer midi or maxi. A worldwide trend to casual, egalitarian, or peasant-inspired clothes suited Australian designers and manufacturers. Robyn Garland's swimsuits and the Palmers' cleverly cut Jag jeans became known round the world. Linda Jackson and Jenny Kee used vivid colours and designs based on Australian landscape, flora, and fauna for Flamingo Park, reintroducing a nationalist element into Australian design, since continued by Ken Done. There was a demand for Australian imagery in corporate wardrobes commissioned from local designers. Not surprisingly, the outfits designed for Australian Olympic teams, and later for television coverage of cricket and football, have caused most discussion.

Fatal flaws

Since the 1970s, women in well-paid jobs have set new fashions for work clothes, elegant and stylish, but practical and comfortable, more informal than elsewhere, often with sandals and bare legs. The natural line of the body has replaced an exaggerated female form as the basic shape for day and work clothes, and fantasy dressing inspired by film and television has replaced evening and formal wear. The convergence of grunge with high fashion in the 1990s was an indication of the growing tension between the style sought by wealth and mass-marketing necessity. But Alexandra Joel's concluding comment on Australian fashion in *Best Dressed: 200 Years of Fashion in Australia* (1984) still applies—'although we are mindful of what London, Paris, New York and Tokyo proclaim, we no longer slavishly follow. We have our own images, our own environment. We dress to reflect it, and do so in our own way.'

BEVERLEY KINGSTON

Fatal flaws in human characters are a major theme of Manning **Clark's** six-volume *A History of Australia* (1962–87). Clark's conviction was that men and women were flawed from the outset by deficiences in their moral fibre. This notion, which he perhaps learnt from his father, an Anglican minister, was a common theme of Greek theatre, and of the German philosophers Goethe and Nietzsche. In his *History* Clark continually blames the effects of greed, pride, arrogance, desperation, 'Dionysian frenzy', or 'the madness in the blood' for the failure and ultimate downfall of many of his historical characters. He attributes the failings of **Menzies** to pride; John **Macarthur** to ambition and a quick temper; William **Bligh** to 'a deep and ungovernable rage'; and Henry **Lawson** and John **Curtin** to drink. This preoccupation reflected Clark's broader, apocalyptic vision of Australia's history, which saw human failings ultimately taking their toll, and tragedy overtaking personal ambition. Clark once remarked that 'Humpty Dumpty must have a great fall. That is what art requires.' Conscious that he overworked the device, he sought to ration it in later volumes of the *History*. Carl Bridge's collection of essays on Manning Clark (1994) discusses his approach to writing.

HD

Favenc, Ernest (1845–1908) came to Australia from England as an 18-year-old and worked on cattle stations in northern Qld. Through the 1870s he contributed fiction pieces to the *Queenslander*. In 1877 he led an expedition to determine the feasibility of a railway linking Darwin to Qld, and then worked on opening up the country from the Gulf of Carpentaria over into WA. Favenc drew upon his experiences to produce his popular *History of Australian Exploration 1788–1888* (1888), for which he received support from the NSW government. He was less successful in his ambitious but sketchy *Western Australia* (1887). His fiction included short stories set in the Pacific and Qld—*Tales of the Austral Tropics* (1893) and *My Only Murder and Other Tales* (1899)—as well as historical novels that tended towards melodrama.

The Secret of the Australian Desert (1896) is a speculative account of the fate of Ludwig **Leichhardt**, while *Marooned on Australia* (1896) is based on the wreck of the **Batavia**. A monograph by Cheryl Frost, *The Last Explorer: The Life and Work of Ernest Favenc* (1983), includes a detailed assessment of his writings.

KT

Fawkner, John Pascoe (1792–1869) rivals John **Batman** as a founder of **Melbourne**. In 1835 his schooner *Enterprize* arrived at **Port Phillip** from Launceston, Van Diemen's Land, to create, as the vessel's name suggested, a commercial settlement. Fawkner was an irrepressible bush-lawyer character who established a store and hotel on the future site of Melbourne, then settled north of the town. He produced its first **newspaper**, the *Melbourne Advertiser*, in 1838 and was reputedly worth £20 000 before 1840. Hugh Anderson in *Out of the Shadow* (1962) describes how Fawkner overcame childhood poverty, the 'stain' of a convict father, and his own criminal offences and bankruptcy in 1845 to achieve respect as a municipal councillor and member of the Victorian Legislative Council in the 1850s and 1860s. A fiery liberal in the 1830s and 1840s, Fawkner became more conservative when representing commercial interests in later years. The Melbourne suburbs Fawkner and Pascoe Vale are named after him.

The true founder of Melbourne has been the subject of a long-standing controversy. C.P. Billot, in his 1979 biography of John **Batman**, credited Batman as Melbourne's founder; but after researching Fawkner's papers in the State Library of Victoria and his diary in the National Library of Australia, he reassessed his view in Fawkner's favour in *The Life and Times of John Pascoe Fawkner* (1985). Despite Batman's alleged remark, 'this will be the place for a village', Billot concluded that Batman merely wanted a private sheep-run and that it was Fawkner, more than anyone else, who first conceived and created the village that became Melbourne. Fawkner's diary was edited by Billot and published as *Melbourne's Missing Chronicle* (1982). In 1991 the Melbourne Maritime Museum launched a project to build a full-scale replica of the *Enterprize*, and in 1997 a part of Batman Park in Flinders Street was renamed Enterprize Park in a controversial decision that continued the oldest debate in Melbourne.

DC

Federal Council of Australasia was the first formal body to join the British colonies in Australia and the South Pacific, and regarded by its Victorian founders as a preliminary to a full **Federation**. It was designed at an 1883 inter-colonial conference called to deal with the incursions of European powers into the South Pacific. One of its functions was to pressure Britain to a more active policy in the region. Other colonies were not as keen as Victoria on a federal organisation, with the result that the council was a weak body; it could legislate on matters of common concern, but it had no executive and no tax-raising power. NSW, SA, and NZ did not join; Fiji did. Henry **Parkes** had earlier proposed a similar body, but he kept NSW out of this Victorian initiative, arguing that it would delay a full Federation. When Parkes in 1889 made his call for Federation, he was received with some suspicion because of his inconsistency over a federal council. One factor which may have influenced Parkes's call was a decision of SA to join the council, which left NSW isolated. The council continued to work during the 1890s as Federation was discussed, and when the federal cause faltered was sometimes considered as an alternative route to union.

JH

Federation was the greatest political achievement in Australian history, bringing together six self-governing colonies that were under no compulsion to unite. Few people in the nation so created know or honour its origins. After 100 years the only full narrative account of the federal movement remains that produced by two participants, John **Quick** and R.R. **Garran**, as part of *The Annotated Constitution of the Australian Commonwealth* (1901). In 1972 J.A. **La Nauze** published his magisterial *The Making of the Australian Constitution*, and in 1997 Helen Irving considered the same subject from a cultural perspective in *To Constitute a Nation*. La Nauze hoped his work would assist 'the future author of a much-needed general history of the federal movement'. That author is yet to appear.

The colonies had developed separately, but in the 1880s and 1890s **inter-colonial relations** became well developed and the colonies were moving to economic and social integration. As trade between the colonies grew, the **tariffs** they levied on each other became more burdensome. Many fruitless attempts had been made to set these aside or modify them. Victoria was committed to **protection** and NSW to free trade, and neither wanted to give up its chosen policy or see its opposite become a national policy. As the smaller colonies followed Victoria into protection, NSW became more suspicious of union, especially when proposed by Victoria.

The colonial governments conferred regularly and cooperated over matters of mutual concern and interest: lighthouses, post and telegraph, immigration, defence, railways, movement of stock. There would be advantages in a national government taking charge of these matters, but the mere securing of an advantage would not compel six colonies used to their own ways and highly suspicious of each other to submit themselves to a national union. Abolition of border tariffs and the establishment of inter-colonial free trade was the great advantage of union, but that presented the greatest difficulties. Some necessity or some passion would be needed to make the nation.

At first it looked like necessity. In the early 1880s the designs of France on the New Hebrides and Germany on New Guinea alarmed Australian governments, which did not want these potential enemies of Britain gaining strongholds close to their shores. The colonies met in Sydney in 1883 to plan joint action. Victoria wanted to use the occasion to form a federal union, but NSW was opposed to union, especially with Victoria in the lead. A weak **Federal Council** was planned instead, which NSW and SA did not join. If these European powers were to be resisted it would be by Britain, and the Australian governments bent their efforts with some success into prodding Britain into action. Coordinated lobbying did not require political union.

In 1889 Sir Henry **Parkes**, premier of NSW, announced in his **Tenterfield** speech that the time was ripe for federal union. Politicians in the other colonies thought this was a stunt, designed to boost Parkes but not advance the federal cause. Parkes was told that he should bring NSW into the Federal Council; to hurry the matter was to court failure. Parkes had to hurry. He was 74 years old and determined to be the father of Federation. He had linked his call to the need for united action on defence, which had been urged by a British expert, but the core of his appeal was to **nationalism** and to the fulfilment of Australia's destiny. He expanded this theme in subsequent speeches in which he offered to set aside the dispute over trade policy and allow it be settled by the new national parliament. That was a mere trifle compared with the grandeur of giving to Australia an Australian government. Here was the passion.

The national sentiment to which Parkes appealed was not selfless. For the native-born, now in a majority, to belong to a nation was to escape the inferior status of colonial birth; this theme was first explored by Robert Birrell in *A Nation of Our Own* (1995), which examines the **Australian Natives Association**, the strongest and most persistent advocate of union. National sentiment had a rival in imperial loyalty, but that common bond was also reason for putting aside what were seen as artificial barriers and forming a British nation. As Parkes said, 'The crimson thread of kinship runs through us all.' The claim that national sentiment was weak and played little part in Federation is put by W.G. McMinn, *Nationalism and Federalism in Australia* (1994).

The strength of the sentiment for union registered its first victory when Parkes got his way. Whatever the leading politicians in the other colonies said, they could not diminish his vision. They met with him in Melbourne in 1890 and agreed to call a convention in 1891 to write a federal constitution. They also accepted his strategy of appealing to national sentiment and setting aside the vexed question of trade policy.

The colonial parliaments appointed seven delegates each to the Convention that met in Sydney with Parkes in the chair. They were amazed at their own achievement in producing under **Griffith's** hand a first draft of a **Constitution**. When this was referred to the colonies for approval, the whole movement stalled. Parkes's free-trade party in NSW was not as ready as its leader to sacrifice free trade to Federation; the new Labor Party, which held the balance of power, was not interested in Federation. Discussion in the NSW parliament was postponed and there was thus little point in the other colonies proceeding. From 1891 all the eastern colonies were preoccupied with the **depression**.

The movement revived from 1893 with the formation of **Federation leagues** along the River Murray and in Sydney and a campaign by the Australian Natives Association.

Federation architecture

Representatives from these groups met at the **Corowa Conference** in July 1893 and adopted a plan for the colonies to elect delegates to a new convention and for the constitution which it framed to be referred to the electors for approval. The plan was taken up by George **Reid**, who had replaced Parkes as the free-trade premier of NSW, and he persuaded the other premiers to support it at the **Hobart Conference** in 1895. Delegates to the 1897–98 Convention were elected from four colonies, NSW, Victoria, SA, and Tasmania; the WA delegates were elected by the parliament; Qld for the moment held aloof.

Some historians have detected a new dynamic at work in this revival. Strengthening a suggestion of Allan **Martin** in 'Economic Influences in the "New Federation Movement"' (*HSANZ*, 1953), they claim that Federation had become a necessity to cope with the adverse effects of the depression and bank failures, particularly the suspicions of the London money market. A national government would improve Australia's credit rating. Certainly federationists advanced this argument, but when the Federation League used it to solicit funds from Sydney businesses the results were very disappointing. The weakness of this motive can be read in the nature of the federal compact: the Commonwealth did not take over state debts or the state railways and was not fashioned to restructure an economy. The one attempt to please London by a *Realpolitik* union aroused no local interest. In 1894 the premier of NSW, George **Dibbs**, proposed that NSW and Victoria should form a single government, pooling their debts, lands, and railways, and allowing the other colonies to join this union later on its terms. The scheme seemed entirely misplaced since the federal movement was conceived as a means of bringing together all the colonies and making a united people. The securing of the immediate economic benefit of union, inter-colonial free trade, became less pressing from 1895 when NSW adopted a pure free-trade policy. The other colonies had the best of both worlds, protection for their own industries and free access to the large NSW market.

In 1898 the constitution drawn up by the Convention was put to the people in the four south-eastern colonies and the 'yes' case prevailed in all. However, in NSW the 'yes' vote did not reach the numbers that parliament had set for approval. The premiers met to amend the constitution to make it more acceptable to NSW. The capital was now to be in that state, though not at Sydney. The financial arrangements were altered, with the unintended consequence of facilitating Commonwealth supremacy. At a second referendum in 1899, in which Qld participated, the constitution was accepted. WA held its referendum at the last minute in 1900, after the constitution had been enacted in London. The Commonwealth was proclaimed on 1 January 1901 in Centennial Park, Sydney.

Historians have argued over why people voted as they did, and the implications of the average to low turnout at the polls. R.S. Parker argued that regional economic interest was the chief determinant of the voting, a view immediately challenged by Geoffrey **Blainey** (*HSANZ*, 1949, 1950). The other contributions to this debate can be found in S.G. Foster et al. (eds), *Federation: The Guide to Records* (1998), a bibliography of primary and secondary sources. No-one doubts that calculation of economic advantage was a factor; the quarrel is how crucial it was to the overall result. Women participated in the campaigns even in places where they did not have the vote. *A Woman's Constitution?* (1996), edited by Helen Irving, discusses gender in the federal movement.

The best-known judgment about Federation, made by Alfred **Deakin** in his lively insider's account *The Federal Story* (1944), is that it was secured by a series of miracles. He came to this view after seeing that many of the politicians' decisions that advanced the cause were taken for other or ulterior motives. But when those decisions fall the same way, there is some deeper force at work. Deakin had no doubt about what that was: 'The enthusiasm for union without which the merely selfish energy would have died down and disappeared … was the mainspring of the whole movement.'

Federation has not captured the Australian imagination. The hundredth anniversary created more awareness but not much enthusiasm. Unlike the fiftieth anniversary, it did produce a spate of books. The most comprehensive attempts to capture the movement were John Hirst, *The Sentimental Nation* (2000), and Helen Irving (ed.), *The Centenary Companion to Australian Federation* (1999). Still useful is the detailed chronicle produced by two participants, John **Quick** and R.R. **Garran**, as part of their *Annotated Constitution of the Australian Commonwealth* (1901).

JOHN HIRST

Federation architecture was a popular Australian style of domestic architecture in the period 1895–1915. Bernard **Smith** coined the term in 1969, in recognition of its coincidence with the **Federation** movement, and argued that it was more appropriate than 'Queen Anne'—the English-derived term by which the style had previously been known. Despite some state differences, the Federation style is generally characterised by red-brick construction, increased window space, return verandahs, painted timber fretwork, and decorative roofs featuring terracotta tiles, finials, gargoyles, and dragons. Nationalistic sentiment is expressed in some examples of Federation style through the decorative use of Australian flora and fauna.

HD

Federation leagues were formed in the 1890s to advocate inter-colonial **Federation**. The first leagues were established in 1892 in southern NSW, where the border duties on trade across the River Murray were particularly irksome. They were composed of shopkeepers, business people, and farmers. These leagues were responsible for calling the **Corowa Conference** on Federation in 1893. In March 1893 the annual conference of the **Australian Natives Association** resolved to sponsor the formation of leagues to attract wider support than the association, which was limited to the native-born. Natives were involved in the formation of leagues in Sydney (1893), Melbourne (1895),

Adelaide (1895), and Brisbane (1898), which brought together influential figures in politics and business. The formation of the league in Sydney, where the federation cause had languished, has been ascribed by A.W. **Martin** (*HSANZ*, 1953) to the belief in the commercial world that Federation would assist to re-establish prosperity and the country's credit rating after the **Depression** of the early 1890s. **Barton** was the guiding hand behind the league's foundation, though he took care to make it a citizens' body and to limit the role of politicians in its affairs. When the **Constitution** was submitted to referendum, short-lived federation leagues were formed in many centres to campaign for a 'yes' vote. The central league in Sydney continued after Federation to protect the union, and disbanded only after the site for the capital was settled in 1909. Its papers are held in the National Library of Australia, and its history and influence are considered by D.I. Wright in *JRHAS* (1971).

JH

Felonry, a collective term for felons, was used to describe convicts and, later, the emancipated class of convicts. The word was coined by James **Mudie** in his contentious account, *The Felonry of New South Wales*, published in 1837 and subtitled 'being a faithful picture of the real romance of life in Botany Bay, with anecdotes of Botany Bay society and a plan of Sydney'.

HD

Felton Bequest was established by the philanthropist Alfred Felton (1831–1904), who amassed a considerable fortune in the colonies, first as a carter on the goldfields and later as a wholesale druggist. He was unmarried and on his death, his will bequeathed over £2 million to establish a bequest intended to support charities and also to purchase works that would 'improve public taste' for the National Gallery of Victoria. Daryl **Lindsay** gave details of the trust and its first 50 years in *The Felton Bequest: An Historical Record 1904–59* (1963), which Ursula Hoff extended in her 1983 booklet. The bequest was the single most important factor in the pre-eminence of the National Gallery of Victoria among Australian collections of European art.

KT

Female Factory was a government institution designed to accommodate, manage, and punish women **convicts**—one was at Parramatta, NSW, the other at Cascades, Tasmania. The Female Factory served several functions. It provided a labour and marriage agency, where free settlers and government could select assigned servants and where (mostly convict or ex-convict) men could choose wives; it was a profit-making textiles factory, where women made blankets and convict clothing; and it was a lying-in hospital, where pregnant women servants returned for their confinement. By the 1830s the Parramatta Factory also served as an orphanage, where the unwanted offspring of casual liaisons or unmarried women were often abandoned. A large proportion of women at

Parramatta were free women seeking private employment. Women were assigned according to a ranking system. Those with the best records were given preference over those who had been returned as unsatisfactory—for misbehaviour, pregnancy, or other transgressions—or who were second offenders. Through its administration of secondary punishment, women were subjected to the frequently harsh processes of penal logic, culminating in solitary confinement, in the hope that they would turn out as moral and useful servants. Harsh as it was, Deborah Oxley in *Convict Maids* (1996) describes the Factory as 'a female enclave and a site of sisterly insurgence'. It offered at least a means of escape from employers who might be cruel or unjust. Annette Salt observes these women's experiences in *These Outcast Women: The Parramatta Female Factory 1821–1848* (1984).

HD

Femininity preoccupied initially those who defined themselves as the gentry in nineteenth-century Australia. Supposedly innate, this femininity was said to consist of a dedication to the 'private' domestic sphere, a self-effacing modesty, and a virtuous character.

This definition of feminine propriety played a central role in the dynamics of class formation at a time of major changes in the social order. As Penny Russell shows in *A Wish of Distinction: Colonial Gentility and Femininity* (1994), 'genteel femininity' entailed a complex and nuanced performance by women of a particular social group. A performance of restraint and control, taste and morality, was directed at ensuring the continued dominance of the colonial gentry, a group modelled on the landed aristocracy of England. By displaying their class distinctiveness, while permitting a careful enlargement of their ranks to include members of the new commercial and industrial wealthy groups, who would also be expected to display appropriate femininity, women asserted considerable power in maintaining the social order. The continually shifting, and at times contested, nature of the concept of 'genteel femininity' traced by Russell points to the way what was claimed to be natural was indeed social.

By the end of the nineteenth century, a new definition of femininity was deployed by certain social groups who were concerned to intervene in and reorganise the lives of the working class through, for instance, domestic science or domestic economy educational programs. These movements had complex origins. In part, they were an initiative of the newly formed state departments of education; in part, they were led by middle-class women philanthropists; and increasingly, in the first two decades of the twentieth century, they became a preoccupation of newly emerging professional groups. All these groups declared femininity to lie in the housewifely skills of women. They differed over whether education to train women in these skills should be directed solely at improving the life conditions of the working class or whether its purpose was also to produce domestic servants. But 'home-making', they all agreed, was an expression of the feminine instinct. The contradiction of

Femininity

'teaching femininity'—'training' that which was claimed to be instinct—was ignored.

In her exploration of the increasing intervention of 'scientific experts' in all domains of women's lives in the early decades of the twentieth century, Kerreen Reiger (*The Disenchantment of the Home: Modernizing the Australian Family 1880–1940*, 1985) draws attention to the irony that lies at the heart of conceptions of femininity. The reproductive capacities of women, for instance, became a preoccupation of a range of groups and agencies who defined mothering as both the essence of women's femininity and central to their social role. As 'mothers of the race', women were claimed to be responsible for the future health and well-being of the nation. The medicalisation of pregnancy, childbirth, and infant care sought to introduce science and technical rationality into these 'natural' processes.

In the early decades of the twentieth century, the central role of conceptions of femininity in creating and maintaining class distinctions appeared to fade, although different types of femininity continued to be promoted by various agencies, including the newly emerging popular media. But in other contexts, 'women', supposedly united by their female natures or characteristics, became a more general category in domains of knowledge and expertise being developed and elaborated about women's lives. Professional 'experts' concerned with introducing more scientific approaches to childbirth and child-rearing, for example, increasingly extended their efforts beyond working-class women.

By the 1920s and 1930s, the new institutions of popular culture were beginning to elaborate conceptions of femininity in which maternity was no longer central. The cinema and advertising, in particular, became powerful agents in defining the meaning of femininity which began to be associated with **sexuality** and, later, with age. Marilyn Lake ('Female Desires: The Meaning of World War II', in *AHS*, 1990) argues that by the 1940s femininity was increasingly defined in terms of (hetero)sexual attractiveness, a quality that was seen as a matter of youthful bodily appearance directed towards the male sexual gaze.

Femininity became once more principally a question of performance as it had been for the gentry in the nineteenth century, but now much more one of presenting or producing the body in female form with the assistance of commodities from the marketplace. Advertisements directed at women in the first two decades of the twentieth century had focused on images of refinement. But by the 1920s, they were also beginning to present a more sexualised and 'modern' image of femininity. While, no doubt, addressed to a particular audience of women, images of 'flappers' represented their femininity as a matter of a youthful, modern and active social presence. In the 1950s, images of the youthful, sexual female body were increasingly definitive of femininity. Femininity became an ideal, something to be desired by all women, but something which no longer was necessarily possessed by all women. Other images of womanhood circulated in popular cultural forms—in women's magazines, the cinema, and advertising—of women as housewives and mothers, but women were also warned that preoccupation with these roles could threaten their femininity.

While these messages have persisted, more diverse images of femininity began circulating in popular cultural forms by the late 1950s and 1960s. Magazines like the *Australian Women's Weekly* could no longer necessarily address 'women' as a whole: social definitions of teenage femininity began to speak to a newly identified group of young women who were said to have separate interests and needs. Further changes have occurred in the 1980s, in large part because of the impact of Second Wave feminism itself. In the 1960s, young womanhood was defined as essentially concerned with a feminine appearance and attracting the admiring male gaze. Intellectual pursuits were considered as threatening a girl's femininity and potential marriageability. By the late 1980s and early 1990s, success at school and going to university were clearly defined as consistent with femininity as girls began to excel at school and enter universities in increasing numbers.

Jill Julius Matthews, *Good and Mad Women: The Historical Construction of Femininity in Twentieth-Century Australia* (1984), says that to be a woman is to carry a sense of failure. The history of femininity, she says, is a history of a set of contradictory and inconsistent ideals. Australian **feminist historians** from the early 1970s have been concerned to draw attention to the historical and socially constructed character of femininity. Some, like Anne **Summers** in the 1970s, have argued that this femininity is an imposition on women's culture or authentic way of being in the world. Others, like Matthews, have been more concerned to explore the impossibilities that lie at the core of historical definitions of femininity, and the opportunities these can then create, and have created, for women to become self-defining.

The focus on femininity by many feminist historians in Australia began as a strategy to make what was seen initially as an important distinction between sex and gender. Femininity, as a historically changing and often inconsistent set of ideals of what women should be, demonstrated the historical and social character of gender. Sex was a different matter—a question of biological bodies. In recent years, the distinction between sex and gender has been questioned, and histories of sexed bodies have begun to be undertaken. Matthews, for instance, in her more recent work, has looked at physical education movements and 'health and beauty' organisations of the 1920s and 1930s, tracing a history of female bodily agency. This shift reflects a more significant change in direction in feminist theory. A focus on gender as distinct from sex was associated with the argument that femininity was an imposition which women could and should want to throw off. In the 1980s feminist theorists began to celebrate 'the difference of women' and to proclaim the value of much of 'feminine culture'. While femininity continues to be understood as historically changing, it is no longer seen simply as a social cloak to be discarded. Definitions of femininity are complex, contradictory, and changing, but nevertheless formative.

LESLEY JOHNSON

Feminism refers to a politics and mode of analysis that seeks to explain and change women's oppression by men. An identifiably feminist movement first emerged in Australia in the 1880s and 1890s, although the name itself was not used until early in the twentieth century. Nineteenth-century adherents referred rather to the Woman Movement, and defined its goals as the advancement of women and the reform of society by enshrining the ideals of love, purity, and temperance. Central to their object was ending women's condition as 'creatures of sex', so they attached great importance to reforms such as raising the age of consent, and the appointment of women to a range of public positions (as doctors, factory inspectors, police) to protect women and girls from predatory men. Recognising their lack of political power, all campaigns focused on securing women's suffrage. One well-known poster of the 1890s depicted women wielding the baton of suffrage to defeat the four serpents: gambling, seduction, whisky, and cruelty.

Much of the historiography of feminism has focused on the suffrage movement, notably Audrey Oldfield's detailed examination of the campaign, colony by colony, *Woman Suffrage in Australia* (1992). There are several biographies of prominent individuals such as Rose **Scott**, Alice **Henry**, and Catherine **Spence**. However, neither Henry, who spent most of her adult life in the USA, nor Spence, who was principally concerned with electoral reform, were leaders of the Woman Movement in Australia. Rose Scott was arguably central to the movement in NSW and claimed as a major triumph the raising of the age of consent there in 1910. There are also biographies of Maybanke **Anderson**, editor of the *Woman's Voice* in NSW, and of Vida **Goldstein**, who was a leader of the suffrage movement in Victoria. There is as yet no feminist study of Louisa **Lawson**, who in 1888 founded the *Dawn*, a journal written for women, and the Dawn Club. Lawson, together with Scott, Dora Montefiore, and Mary **Windeyer**, was a founding member of the Womanhood Suffrage League, formed in Sydney in 1891.

Much of the support for suffrage, and feminist reform generally, was organised by members of the **Woman's Christian Temperance Union**, whose branches were formed in the Australian colonies from the 1880s. While the earliest feminist historical discussions of the role of the WCTU in the history of feminism reflected some libertarian discomfort with such **'wowsers'**—it is evident, for example, in Anne **Summers**, *Damned Whores and God's Police* (1975)—writing from the 1980s showed more interest and sympathy, seeing in their campaigns against drinking and sexual licence an appropriate critique of masculine culture as deleterious to women and girls. Judith Allen's work on Rose Scott, Patricia Grimshaw's study of Bessie Harrison **Lee** in Marilyn Lake and Farley Kelly (eds), *Double Time* (1985), and Marilyn Lake, 'The Politics of Respectability', *HS* (1987), illustrate this revaluation.

The historiography of feminism in Australia encouraged the popular (American-derived) understanding that the history of feminism occurred in two waves—the 1890s and the 1970s—with a long lull in between. Recent work has begun to demonstrate the vitality and importance of post-suffrage feminism in Australia, a point first made by Kay Daniels and Mary Murnane in their documentary collection, *Uphill all the Way* (1980). The achievement of (white) women's franchise was followed by the proliferation of feminist organisations. The Women's Political Education League in NSW was succeeded by the Feminist Club, founded in 1914; in Victoria, Goldstein's **Women's Political Association** was replaced from the 1920s by the Victorian Women's Citizens Movement. The post-suffrage phase of feminism attempted to build on the promise of women's citizenship, which was often understood in sexually differentiated terms as having a maternalistic character; this meant both that its program was oriented towards providing 'protection' for the most vulnerable in the community, including mothers and infants; and that women as political subjects, whether mothers or not, were understood as sharing distinctive nurturing, welfare-oriented values. Marilyn Lake elaborates these themes in Seth Koven and Sonya Michel (eds), *Mothers of a New World* (1993).

At the same time, Australian feminists remained convinced of the degrading effects of **sexuality** for women, and thus defined the individuality promised by citizenship in terms of bodily inviolability. To ensure women's protection, they generally opposed an increased availability of contraception and advocated restrictions on alcohol and the censorship of films. Several of the organisations defined the achievement of 'an equal moral standard' as a major goal, and all gave priority to securing the economic independence of women, including married women and mothers. Preoccupied with the anomalous status of the citizen-wife, they promoted schemes for motherhood endowment and equal pay, child endowment, and proposals that women have a legal right to household savings. They won equality in custody and inheritance rights for mothers. Their definition of women's subordination as a matter of 'sex slavery'—an understanding encouraged by their work with the League of Nations following the 1926 Convention on Slavery—shaped their work in the area of Aboriginal reform. Feminists such as Edith Jones, president in the 1920s of the Victorian Women Citizens Movement; Ada Bromham, member of the WCTU and women's candidate in the 1921 WA elections; and Constance Ternente Cooke, sometime president of the South Australian Women's Non-Party Association, all became actively involved in campaigns for federal control of Aboriginal affairs, for the custody rights of Aboriginal mothers, for basic citizens' rights. They also campaigned for men to be punished more severely for sexual abuse of Aboriginal women and girls, and for women to be appointed as protectors. Bromham and Mary Bennett were among the feminist witnesses to the 1933 WA royal commission into the condition of Aborigines in that state and supported Aboriginal witnesses who also gave evidence. They were joined by Bessie **Rischbieth**, founding president of the Australian Federation of Women Voters, who was one of the first to lobby, from 1927, for federal control of Aboriginal affairs. Affiliates of the AFWV included state-based, non-party groups such as the Women's Service Guild in WA and the United Associations of Women, formed by Jessie **Street** in 1929. Their 'separatist', non-party mode of doing politics—eschewing men and men's parties—came to define the meaning of 'feminism' in the 1920s and 1930s.

The AFWV was affiliated in turn to the British Commonwealth League and the International Women's Suffrage Alliance. Australian feminists were keen internationalists, regularly attending conferences in Europe and the Pacific.

During the 1940s and 1950s, feminism, like movements for Aboriginal rights, became more assimilationist, eschewing talk of difference in favour of demands for equal access to the workforce and public life. Jessie Street, organiser of the Charter conferences in 1943 and 1946 and enthusiastic supporter of the UN, campaigned for Aboriginal and women's rights. She worked closely with Faith **Bandler** in the 1950s and campaigned for a referendum on federal control of Aboriginal affairs. Feminists also demanded women's appointment to juries; the amendment of legislation which prevented married women from working in banks and the Commonwealth public service (achieved in 1966); and the right to drink in public bars (see **pubs**), asserted amid much publicity in Qld (also in 1966). The long-standing demand for **equal pay** was conceded piecemeal, with the Commonwealth **Arbitration** Court finally acknowledging the principle in 1972. By that time a new phase of feminism, the self-styled women's liberation movement, had burst onto the political scene. When women's liberationists announced their demands to a shocked and bemused world, many of the older feminist organisations were still in existence, though no-one noticed. Bessie Rischbieth had written a book to record the work of her generation of feminists, *The March of Australian Women*, published in 1964, but the history of feminism did not become part of school and university curricula, and younger feminists remained ignorant of past struggles.

When the reformist expression of the new movement, the **Women's Electoral Lobby**, arranged for all candidates in the 1972 federal election campaign to be interviewed about their attitudes to women's rights, they considered they were making history, although they were merely perpetuating a well-established mode of feminist politics. The Women's Electoral Lobby also joined the long tradition of looking to the state to redress inequalities—by demanding maternity leave, state funding of child-care centres, and equality of access to paid work and public office. Its lasting achievements include the anti-discrimination and affirmative action legislation passed by all states and the Commonwealth government.

The women's liberation critique of existing society—often called patriarchal—went further. Drawing on the language of psychology and sociology, feminists denounced 'sex roles', 'conditioning', and their treatment as 'sex objects'. Deeming the personal to be political, they interrogated everything from the value of the family, to the allocation of housework, to the vaginal orgasm; lesbianism was redefined as a political choice, and heterosexual women might be accused of sleeping with the enemy. Representations of femininity and masculinity became major concerns, whether they were manifested in beauty contests, children's stories, advertisements, films, or in the subjects taught at universities. The proliferation of women's studies courses in universities from the 1970s signalled the importance attached to the recognition that knowledge about the world shaped the world itself, and drew attention to the many ways in which man had become the measure of all things. Women's liberation, more than the feminist movements that preceded it, affected most fields of cultural endeavour, and had creative expression in novels, films, plays, painting, and dance. Ann Curthoys explores this history in Kay Saunders and Raymond Evans (eds), *Gender Relations in Australia* (1992).

Women's liberation produced its own self-critique, first pointing to the privileged position of the usually white, middle-class, educated, heterosexual women who first dominated the movement's public image. Challenges by Aboriginal and non-Anglo women further undermined feminists' confidence that they could or should claim to speak for all women. Encouraged by post-structuralist and post-colonial argument in the universities, many came to see 'women' as an impossible category, its advocates complicit in the denial of cultural and ethnic difference and identity. Some responses to this radical undermining of feminism as a political project that represents women look forward to a post-feminist politics of alliance and coalition; others look to a rejuvenated feminism which builds on difference as a resource of strength. Meanwhile, feminist voices remind us that women are still dramatically under-represented in parliament and the professions; that women still earn much less than men and are more likely to be welfare recipients; and that women are still routinely subject to male violence. Women still dream of sweet freedom.

MARILYN LAKE

Feminist history is defined by its politics, rather than by its form or subject matter. Australian contributions have ranged from short theoretical articles to detailed research-based monographs, from focused studies of women in particular sites and contexts to broad critiques of masculine ideologies of nation. What sets feminist history apart from other historical approaches is its concern with the political aspect of gender relations. Feminist history attempts to incorporate women's experience within historical analysis, while considering the impact of such inclusion upon accepted knowledge and social understandings.

From its beginnings in the mid-1970s, the development of feminist history in Australia has followed two major trajectories: on the one hand, an increasingly confident and sophisticated academic debate about its own content, theories, and methodologies, and on the other, the production of more and more books based on detailed research. At its best, it achieves a productive engagement between the two approaches. Theoretical questioning can point the way to new sources, or to reconsiderations of the old. Recent books have been published on topics as diverse as shopping and socialism, schooling and diaries, labour and gentility, sexuality and suffrage. In turn, these new works stimulate further inquiry, and reconsiderations of methodologies and significance.

The publication of four key texts in 1975 and 1976—Beverley Kingston, *My Wife, My Daughter, and Poor Mary Ann*; Edna **Ryan** and Anne Conlon, *Gentle Invaders*; Anne **Summers**, *Damned Whores and God's Police*; and Miriam **Dixson**, *The Real Matilda*—signalled a sharp rise of interest in exploring the impact of Australia's history on its women, and women's own contribution to that history. Stimulated by, and in turn stimulating, the women's liberation movement, these books established several themes which were to be of recurring interest in the following years: women's labour, sexual and domestic, paid and unpaid; their experience as victims of patriarchal ideologies and social relations; and their place in Australia's national and **foundation** mythologies.

These authors were conscious of opening up a field in which much remained to be done. Summers and Dixson reinterpreted existing male accounts of Australian history, but broke little new ground in research. Kingston made 'lightning raids' on rich primary materials, but was chiefly concerned with providing an overview of the period from 1860 to the 1930s. The book by Ryan and Conlon, more narrowly focused on women in industrial relations, was the most firmly based on new primary research. All four highlighted the need for innovative research and the development of new conceptual models in the future. Kingston, indeed, expressed in her introduction the hope that her book would soon become a 'quaint and primitive document', superseded by the more extensive research which would follow it. That her prophecy has not been entirely fulfilled indicates the strength of this early work.

It soon became clear that concurrent developments in **labour history**, family history, and **social history** would point the way for further research. Feminist history emerged—not coincidentally—at a time when the discipline as a whole was seeking to broaden its perimeters, and to complicate the unifying narratives offered by **imperial** and nationalist histories. An emphasis on fluidity, diversity, and conflict was fostered by a new interest in sources which chronicled private life and domestic ideology, or which captured the experience of the victims, the outcasts, the neglected elements in society. Kay Daniels noted in the newly established journal *Australian Feminist Studies* in 1985 that social history offered great possibilities to historians of women, but warned that they must not lose sight of the political message of their history. The flowering of **cultural history** soon afterwards, in the late 1980s and the 1990s, similarly offered both promises and challenges. Cultural theory and post-structuralism have enhanced and enriched feminist historical writing. Yet many have warned of the danger of shifting away from women's experience. The efforts of international feminist theorists to begin to deconstruct the categories of 'women' and 'experience' themselves can be viewed as potentially liberating. But they can also be seen as potentially undermining the subject position on which feminist politics is based.

The emphasis on exploring diversity presents feminist historians with a dilemma. On the one hand, they have insisted that women's experience has been hitherto left out of history, and that its inclusion must fundamentally shift the perimeters of that history. On the other hand, their critique of universal history promotes a growing awareness that differences exist not only between women and men, but among women themselves. The challenge is to represent simultaneously both the specificity and the diversity of women's experience, to acknowledge the multiple identities even of individual women, and to recognise that 'experience', and the meanings attached to experience, are themselves the product of cultural discourses as well as material and social exchanges.

Few feminist historians would attempt all these projects simultaneously. Rather, the field as a whole is enriched by these multiple and sometimes competing endeavours that create diversity within the writing as well as the subject matter of the history. A sense of political purpose helps to define the field as a whole. As Jill Julius Matthews explained in 'Feminist History', *LH* (1986), feminist history seeks to incorporate gender 'into all historical analysis and understanding'; its political purpose is 'to challenge the practices of the historical discipline that have belittled and oppressed women, and to create practices that allow women an autonomy and space for self-definition'. Beyond that shared purpose, feminist history has 'no single coherent theory'.

In responding to these challenges, Australian feminist historians have pursued many different avenues of research. There has been a sustained interest in ideological formulations of femininity within specific historical contexts, especially with reference to the impact of the new professions of medicine, psychiatry, and social science in the early twentieth century. Concurrently, there has been much research on the labour and activism of the working-class women who were so often caught in this middle-class ideological net. The more widely publicised activity of middle-class women campaigning for suffrage and citizenship rights has received considerable attention. The complexities of female subjectivity have been explored in many different contexts, using diaries and private papers as well as public documents, to examine private life, education, family patterns, domestic management, and consumption. Much recent work also examines the complex field of female sexuality in all its aspects, from heterosexual and homosexual female desire, through the social opprobrium suffered by single mothers to the violence surrounding the sexual abuse of women.

While an awareness of class differences has been central to most, if not all, of these studies—perhaps reflecting the impact of labour history in Australia—recent years have seen the emergence of a greater interest in race. Stimulated in part by critical interventions by Aboriginal writers and historians, notably Jackie Huggins, and perhaps still more by the impact of international theories of difference, some feminist historians have dwelt increasingly on Aboriginal women's experience as a crucial element of gender relations in Australia. Others have critically examined white women's role in the perpetuation of hierarchies and stereotypes of race, and in the continuing exploitation and victimisation of Aboriginal people. In an increasingly multicultural Australia, tentative efforts have been made to explore the historical contours of women's experience of ethnicity. The result has been an erosion of the comfort with which we can point to 'feminist heroines', but a simultaneous recognition of the complexity of subjectivity and the extent to which the experience of white as well as Aboriginal women has been determined by ethnicity and race.

As the questions become more complex, the answers become more diverse and more qualified. A growing number of historians have turned to biographical studies in an attempt to come to grips with the complex motivations and shifting political and social identities of individual women. In other work, a growing interest in interdisciplinarity is apparent: the blending of literary and artistic with historical analysis in the collection by Susan Magarey et al. (eds), *Debutante Nation* (1993), is an illuminating application of this. In such books the attempt is less to provide coherent overarching answers to historical questions than to open up the range of questions that can be asked simultaneously.

Meanwhile, there is a growing feeling among feminist historians that if their work becomes too complex and specialised it runs the risk of marginalisation from the so-called mainstream of historical analysis. While many have argued that the mainstream ignores developments in feminist history at its own peril, recent years have seen some significant efforts to intervene in the more classical historical narratives of Australia. The publication of the edited collection by Kay Saunders and Ray Evans, *Gender Relations in Australia* (1992), which incorporated a broad range of historical research within a general textbook format, was a landmark. It was followed in 1994 by Patricia Grimshaw et al., *Creating a Nation*, which sought to provide an alternative narrative account of Australian history—one in which gender was a central category of historical analysis.

Such publications have generated a certain amount of controversy, not only among male historians, who question the significance of the challenge they offer to mainstream history, but among feminist historians, some of whom do not agree that it is appropriate for feminist history to intervene in the mainstream, and prefer to carve out an independent path. The questions are difficult, the answers inconclusive. Should feminist historians be interested in the 'nation', or should they ignore it as a masculinist myth designed to exclude women's concerns? Is the most powerful position for feminist history one of integration, or of continued, deliberate marginality?

PENNY RUSSELL

Fenianism was a popular term for the political activities of the Irish Republican Brotherhood, a secret society formed in Ireland in 1858 (and reformed as the Irish Republican Army in 1916), which sought to re-establish Home Rule in Ireland, by force if necessary. The Fenians gathered strength from the mid-1860s, arousing fear among loyalists that extended to Australia and the USA; in 1867 they staged an unsuccessful insurrection.

In Australia the fears of Fenianism were largely unfounded; the hysteria was the result of a fierce scare campaign mounted by anti-Irish forces. Feelings intensified in January 1868 with the arrival in WA of the convict transport *Hougoumont*, carrying 62 convicted Fenians, John Boyle O'Reilly among them. The following March, Henry James O'Farrell, who professed to be a Fenian, fired a shot at the visiting Duke of Edinburgh in Sydney. By the 1870s, the 'Fenian scare', both in Australia and Ireland, had died down. Keith Amos provides an account of the movement in *The Fenians in Australia* (1988).

HD

Ferguson, John Alexander (1881–1969) combined a distinguished legal career with a passion for bibliography. Born in NZ, he studied law at the University of Sydney, and eventually served as a judge on the NSW Industrial Commission. His marriage to the daughter of bookseller and publisher, George **Robertson**, reinforced his interest in Australian history and bibliography. From 1941 to 1969 he compiled the seven-volume *Bibliography of Australia 1784–1900*, which remains a standard reference. He also produced *A Bibliography of the New Hebrides and History of the Mission Press* (1917–43). Ferguson was twice president of the **Royal Australian Historical Society** and frequently wrote for their journal. His major collection of Australiana is in the National Library of Australia.

KT

Ferguson, William (1882–1950), whose mother was Aboriginal, worked as a shearer before he became an organiser for the **Australian Workers Union** and active in the **Australian Labor Party**. In an effort to fight the increased powers of the NSW Aborigines Protection Board, in 1937 he formed the Aborigines' Progressive Association. With William **Cooper**, he was one of the organisers of the Aboriginal Day of Mourning held on Australia Day 1938 and, with John Patten, wrote a pamphlet titled *Aborigines Claim Citizen Rights!* (1938). Ferguson served on the Aborigines Welfare Board—which replaced the old Protection Board—from 1944 to 1949. Irritated by what he saw as the lack of real progress in Aboriginal affairs, he resigned from the ALP and stood as an independent candidate in the 1949 federal election, but received only 388 votes. Jack Horner's biography, *Vote Ferguson for Aboriginal Freedom*, appeared in 1974.

KT

Field, Barron (1786–1846) left an unsuccessful English legal practice in 1817 to serve as a judge of the NSW Supreme Court. He was an active member of the local Philosophical Society, helped arrange the publication of James Hardy **Vaux's** *Memoirs* and joined with other members of the society to fix a tablet commemorating James **Cook's** landing at Botany Bay. *First Fruits of Australian Poetry* (1819) was the first book of poetry published in the colony, though this does not support Field's claim to be the first

'Austral Harmonist' of the colony. His two best-known poems, 'The Kangaroo' and 'Botany-Bay Flowers', convey some sense of the particularity of the place, but in general he disliked the 'prose-dull land' and returned to England in 1824. Critical references in his *Geographical Memoirs of New South Wales* (1825) display a consistent antipathy to the Australian environment.

KT

Field naturalists' clubs are concerned with both observing and appreciating natural history. They emerged in the 1880s, organised separately in each colony, and the titles of the older club journals reflect this: *Victorian Naturalist* (founded 1884); *Queensland Naturalist* (1908); *South Australian Naturalist* (1919); and the *Western Australian Naturalist* (1947). The exception was the *Australian Naturalist* (1906–39?), published by the NSW Naturalists Club.

The Field Naturalists Club of Victoria was the first to be established, in 1880, but others soon followed. Their origins can be traced to dissatisfaction with the popular dimensions of early colonial scientific societies modelled on the Royal Society. The Field Naturalists Society of South Australia was first established in 1883 as a 'Section' of the Royal Society of South Australia. Emerging amateur field naturalists' clubs tried to retain strong links with senior scientific figures, but asserted their own amateur and popular status. Rather than join the professionalising pull towards laboratory and experimental sciences, they continued to celebrate the joys of field science. One important difference between the early scientific societies and the later field naturalists' clubs was that women were always well represented in the ranks and offices of the latter.

National natural history organisations also existed, most notably the Royal Australian Ornithologists Union (founded 1901) and the Gould League of Bird Lovers (1909). The first of these, however, has always considered itself a 'professional' organisation, despite a mixed membership of professionals and amateurs. The Gould League is primarily directed at children. Neither had the 'rational amusement' ideology of mainstream field naturalists' clubs. The clubs offered a role for 'assistant scientists', following a tradition established through the writings of Donald Macdonald, whose 'Nature Notes and Queries' and 'Notes for Boys' newspaper columns encouraged amateur natural historians (of both genders and all ages) to 'Never accept any authority as conclusive. Try and find out for yourselves.' Club journals offered space for both descriptive records of observations and scientific notes, for appreciation as well as interpretation.

The issue of collection, especially the collection of birds' eggs, caused concern within clubs. Members found it difficult to reconcile large personal collections with concern about the preservation of species. From the 1890s, the camera gradually came to replace the gun, although the collection of bird skins and eggs was endorsed by the Ornithologists Union until the 1920s and 1930s. Tables of 'exhibits' continue today, but with a sensitivity to preservation. Members of all ages bring natural history objects to meetings, using them to discuss the wonders and puzzles of field observation. Exhibits are often collected on club excursions, another important activity recorded in the club journals. A strong sense of place was nurtured through 'botanising and birding'. Often sites scientifically explored in this way were chosen because of a perceived threat from developers.

Campaigns for the **conservation** of habitat were always the concern of field naturalists' clubs, but in the development boom after World War II, this work escalated dramatically. The Field Naturalists divided in 1952 and established the Victorian National Parks Association to undertake political lobbying, leaving the original club to concentrate on natural history observation. The Ornithologists Union was bitterly divided about whether it should act as a political lobby group, and in 1969 made a formal decision to withdraw from conservation work and concentrate on science. The conservation baton has been picked up in the 1970s and later by environmentalist and Green groups with high media profiles. In the background, the field naturalists' clubs continue to monitor conservation activities, to supply information, and to support such campaigns.

The Australian Natural History Medallion established in 1939 by the Field Naturalists is awarded annually for 'special study and for increasing knowledge and appreciation of natural history in Australia'. The original medallion depicted an Aboriginal man with a canoe tree behind him, looking out over a landscape at the Southern Cross, capturing the strong cultural dimensions of natural history. The blur between the cultural and the natural is most apparent, however, at the local level. Field naturalists formed regional clubs, mostly in the period after 1945, though the Ballarat Field Club and Science Society was established in 1882. Local groups often supported the erection of monuments commemorating historical events, and had an interest in Aboriginal history and artefacts. The work of many regional field naturalists' clubs anticipated the postwar boom in **local history** societies.

Club journals are a treasure trove of local and natural history, and the major source on club activities. Colin Finney's *Paradise Revealed* (1993) describes the emergence of field naturalists' clubs and their relationship with earlier scientific societies. Tom Griffiths's *Hunters and Collectors* (1996) analyses the Australian antiquarian imagination, to which field naturalists' clubs made a significant contribution.

LIBBY ROBIN

Film, historical has recorded important moments of Australian history for almost a century. It captured the inauguration of the Commonwealth of Australia (1901), the dedication of Canberra as the capital (1927), the Australian contribution to two world wars and other lesser conflicts, the visit of Queen Elizabeth (1954), the opening of the **Sydney Harbour Bridge** and the **Sydney Opera House**—even the **Australian Rules football** final in 1909, and every **Melbourne Cup** since 1896. It has also recorded the Australian way of life more generally: for instance, *Among the Hardwoods* (1926) depicts the now vanished skills of bullock drivers and timber cutters in the hardwood forests of Gippsland, and *School in the Mailbox* (1947) shows the correspondence school bringing education and social contact to isolated outback children.

The significance of this recording function was recognised early by both federal and state governments: official government cinematographers were appointed in the first decade of the century; the Commonwealth Cinema and Photographic Branch was formed in 1921; the Australian National Films Board was appointed in 1945, with its production unit being known as the Commonwealth Film Unit from 1956, and becoming a statutory body as Film Australia in 1972. The systematic preservation of such films happened more slowly: in 1937, a National Historical Films and Speaking Record Library was established within the National Library in Canberra, and in 1984 the National Film and Sound Archive was hived off from the library to become the repository of both the nation's films and its history on film.

Most films produced in Australia have been non-fiction, but fiction film has always attracted greater public interest, and has its own important place as historical record. Even the government film unit recognised that fiction illustrates the history of the time of its production: *Mike and Stefani* (1952), for instance, is a fictionalised documentary depicting the migrant experience after World War II. But more commercial fictions, set in the present and aiming at the popular market, can also contribute to continuing historical debates. The ambivalent relation of Australia to the mother country has been depicted in films as diverse as *It Isn't Done* (1937) and *The Adventures of Barry McKenzie* (1972). In the future, it is likely that *The Adventures of Priscilla, Queen of the Desert* (1994), *The Sum of Us* (1994), and *Head On* (1998) will be examined as evidence of a particular moment in Australian attitudes to homosexuality.

However, history as subject has also been repeatedly mined for stories: our first feature-length fiction film, *The Story of the Kelly Gang* (1906), constructs a moral tale around the well-known historical events, condemning both the violence of the **Kelly** gang and the social conditions that led to their activities. This story continues to be retold periodically on film (*Ned Kelly*, 1970) and television (*The Last Outlaw*, 1980).

A conspicuous absence in the subject matter of overtly historical feature films is politics: the depiction of government policies and actions and of political leaders has been largely indirect in films (*Kangaroo*, 1987) or left to television (*The Dismissal*, 1983; *The Petrov Affair*, 1987). However, we have had films about Aboriginal history (*Manganinnie*, 1980; *The Fringe Dwellers*, 1986); land exploration (*Burke and Wills*, 1985); convicts (*For the Term of his Natural Life*, 1927); bushrangers (*Robbery under Arms*, 1985); land settlement (*The Man from Snowy River*, 1982); the gold rushes (*Eureka Stockade*, 1949); the history of aviation (*Splendid Fellows*, 1934); shearers' strikes (*Sunday Too Far Away*, 1975); and the Depression (*Caddie*, 1976). All these films interpret the events around which they build their narrative, providing motivations, representing causes and effects, often using individual participants as pegs on which to hang a complete, and often very specific, historical perspective. One common feature has been a tendency, in Barry Jones's words, towards 'recessive heroes', the ordinary person rather than a member of the elite, survivors rather than supermen or women.

It is rare for film writers or producers to be experts on the history reconstructed in their films (an exception is Ian Jones's original research on Ned Kelly and on the light-horsemen), or to employ a professional historian as adviser (an exception was Bill Gammage's role on *Gallipoli*, 1981). On the other hand, in many cases writers have taken great pains in their research, and designers have usually been scrupulous in the reconstruction of period detail. To call historical films dishonest or inaccurate, as some historians have done, is to misunderstand the process of conversion of academic history into popular history by forming and employing myth.

For myth has been the mainstay of historical film. So, alongside the newsreels and documentaries of **World War I** are fictions, such as *A Hero of the Dardanelles* (1915), that construct the 'bronzed **Anzac**' as depicted by C.E.W. **Bean**, the official war correspondent and historian. During World War II, writer–director Charles **Chauvel** both reminded Australians of the heroism of the Anzacs in the earlier conflict (*Forty Thousand Horsemen*, 1940) and demonstrated the continuity of the tradition (*Rats of Tobruk*, 1944). For film-makers, the **Vietnam War** was a more complex matter; because support for the war was not unanimous in the Australian community, it was difficult to develop traditional heroic stories around it. As a result, the only film about the war produced while it was still in progress was basically a love story set in Canberra (*Demonstrator*, 1971), and it was not until *The Odd Angry Shot* (1979) that a serious attempt was made to depict directly the ambivalent attitudes to the war of both the soldiers at the front and the people at home.

Like *The Odd Angry Shot*, many historical stories come to the screen via a **novel** or play: they are interpretations of interpretations, and with each step away from the historical events they become more enmeshed in popular myth. Kay Schaffer (*In the Wake of First Contact*, 1995) describes this process concerning the wreck of the *Stirling Castle* and the eventual rescue of Eliza **Fraser**. Even the serious histories of this latter incident were based on incomplete and often biased sources, but the story inspired plays, poems, and novels, and by the time it was filmed (*Eliza Fraser*, 1975) any chance of separating the 'facts' from the myth had vanished. The film contributed nevertheless to the shaping of Australia's views about its **national identity**, and particularly the place within that of women and Aborigines. Greg Dening (*Mr Bligh's Bad Language*, 1992) has provided a similar analysis of the continuing fascination of film with the story of the *Bounty* mutiny.

At no time in the history of Australian film have the majority of feature films been set in the past, but there was a period in the 1970s when Australian film became particularly identified with the representation of our history. Part of the reason for this was financial: the feature film revival was largely powered by a generous system of government financial support, within which Australian history was one approved subject. For a while, nostalgia was fashionable, and this moment peaked with the local and international success of *Picnic at Hanging Rock* (1975), a stunningly beautiful and evocative period reconstruction around fictional events, which were widely interpreted as having a factual basis. This, and films like *Caddie* or *The Getting of Wisdom* (1977), became the defining films of the time. They were celebrated (David Stratton, *The Avocado Plantation*, 1990) for their willingness to treat the Australian past seriously, and particularly for the prominent role they gave to women in that story after decades of neglect. They were also criticised (Sylvia Lawson, 'Bad Taste at Hanging Rock', in John Tulloch, *Conflict and Control in the Cinema*, 1976) as nostalgic and shallow—meaninglessly 'pretty', irritatingly 'respectable'. However, stepping outside this respectability was commercially risky: *Journey Among Women* (1977), which presented in a filmically adventurous fashion the story of convict women from a feminist perspective, received far less box-office support than the more nostalgic recreations of the past.

But without box-office support, the cost of period reconstructions was always difficult to justify. *For the Term of his Natural Life* (1927), which retold Marcus **Clarke's** classic story, filmed on location at Port Arthur, using glass plates to transform the ruins of the penal colony into a convincing reconstruction, was the most expensive Australian film to date. *Eliza Fraser* also set a new budget record, which helps to explain why most producers by the 1980s preferred to spread such costs over several hours of television mini-series (*The Timeless Land*, 1980; *Women of the Sun*, 1980; *Anzacs*, 1985; *Brides of Christ*, 1991).

In the 1990s, historical films were rare, and just as likely to be farce and fantasy (*Reckless Kelly*, 1993) than respectful reconstruction (*The Sound of One Hand Clapping*, 1998, or *15 Amore*, 2000). Nevertheless, the importance of film in the representation of history continues to be just as much in the contemporary films (such as *Radiance*, 1998, or *Looking for Alibrandi*, 2000), which, as time passes, become representations of their period (the empowerment of indigenous women, and the changing place of immigrants in Australian society), as in the deliberate depiction of the past as subject.

INA BERTRAND

Film industry, according to populist accounts, had precocious achievements and then succumbed to 'media imperialism'. It produced the first long narrative film, *Soldiers of the Cross* (1900), the first modern naturalist film, *The Sentimental Bloke* (1919), and its own authentic film genre, **bushranging** films, only to be crushed by Hollywood expansionism after World War I. This interpretation is found in Eric Reade, *History and Heartburn* (1979); John Baxter, *The Australian Cinema* (1970); and Andrew Pike and Ross Cooper, *Australian Films 1900–1977* (1980). It emphasises US control of distribution and a film contract system which made the developing Australian-owned exhibition chains of the 1920s increasingly dependent on major American production companies such as Paramount. These chains controlled film production values, modes of publicity and presentation, the architectural shape of cinemas, the range of film genres, and even the availability of jobs within the industry itself—as, for example, when Australian musicians were thrown out of work by the coming of sound. Despite the brief success of Cinesound in the 1930s and 1940s (even here, Sylvia Lawson suggests, Hollywood acted as 'invisible circus master'), Australia became little more than a location for offshore American production in the 1950s and 1960s and the industry only revived during the new government-generated boom of the 1970s.

This version of Australian film history should not be entirely discounted. Many of its criticisms of the film industry were shared by film-makers themselves, as well as by many groups submitting evidence to the Royal Commission into the Motion Picture Industry (1927) and later government inquiries. But it misses crucial historical relationships between film industry, film form, and national identity. For example, John Tulloch observed in *Australian Cinema* (1982) that Raymond **Longford's** early films adopted a naturalist style to evoke, nostalgically, a working-class Australia characteristic of an earlier phase of capitalism in the film industry. Later studies of Charles **Chauvel** develop this approach further. Bill Routt, in *The Cinema of Charles Chauvel* (1982), views his assumption of a naive style as a response to the 'impossible condition of colonialism', while Stuart Cunningham, *Featuring Australia* (1991), interprets his use of melodrama as a challenge to the dominant conventions of realism and modernism. Chauvel, Cunningham suggests, continuously reworked Australian ideas of **national identity** in response to changing social, political and economic circumstances. Film unions, exhibitors, distributors, and producers also played a part in determining how popular themes such as the 'bush myth' were presented. In *The Screening of Australia* (1987), Susan Dermody and Elizabeth Jacka complicated the older interpretation of Australian film history, arguing that it was precisely in the 1970s, when the Australian film industry 'revived', that the issue of cultural imperialism became especially acute. Producers and directors who sought to express a national culture while appealing to international film markets were obliged to work within the defining conditions of a 'second cinema'. Period or genre films produced under the auspices of the Australian Film Commission in the 1970s, such as Peter Weir's *Picnic at Hanging Rock* (1975) or Bruce Beresford's *Breaker Morant* (1980), reflect how troubling a condition this could be for a post-colonial nation.

Individual producers, distributors, and exhibitors inflect key tropes of 'Australianness', like the bush myth, in different ways. Cunningham argues that the Chauvel films *Sons of Matthew* (1949) and *Jedda* (1955) are each to be seen as 'obverse constructions of nationalism': the first a 'paean of praise to Anglo-Irish nation-building', the latter 'demonstrating white civilisation's attempt to write off Aboriginal culture'. Meaghan

Morris's analysis of the tax-concession-funded *Crocodile Dundee* (1986) (in *The Pirate's Fiancée*, 1988) takes the argument about the relationship between the industry and its products a step further. Here, Morris argues, national identities are asserted via the cultural markets, tastes, and styles identified with Hollywood, but the film itself culminates, through the hero's triumphant arrival in New York, in 'local Australian control of an American space'. *Crocodile Dundee* exemplifies and symbolises the difficulty of achieving national self-definition within international cultural markets.

The more explicitly theoretical approaches which have focused on industry and form have been paralleled within the film industry itself during the last 20 years by events such as the emergence of Aboriginal and women directors. Particularly strong examples of this include Tracy Moffat's film *Night Cries, A Rural Tragedy* (1990), which 'brings Jedda back to life as if forty years have passed' and where 'none of the male characters have survived and the homestead is a ruin'; and Gillian Armstrong's *My Brilliant Career* (1979), which draws upon an Australian literary classic in order to challenge foundational settler narratives, and to confound audience expectations of its ostensible romance plot. Other films about migrants and **multiculturalism** (*Death in Brunswick*, 1991, and *The Last Days of Chez Nous*, 1992), about the **suburbs** (*Muriel's Wedding*, 1994), and about the **outback** (*The Adventures of Priscilla, Queen of the Desert*, 1994) illustrate how the film industry continues to be shaped by changing markets, producers, and varying articulations of the national culture.

JOHN TULLOCH AND PAUL WASHINGTON

Finn, Edmund ('Garryowen') (1819–98), journalist and historian, was born in Ireland and came to Australia in 1841. His job as a writer for the *Port Phillip Herald* 1845–58 allowed him to witness and record some critical events of Melbourne's founding years, including sectarian outbreaks, Victoria's separation from NSW, and elections. He was subsequently employed as clerk of papers for the Victorian Legislative Council. Encouraged by Charles Gavan **Duffy**, he compiled a series of articles, using as a resource the substantial personal archive he had kept from his own press articles about early Melbourne. These appeared in the *Sydney Morning Herald*, and were published in 1880 as *The 'Garryowen' Sketches*; his pseudonym derived from the name of a secret society in his native Tipperary. These sketches were expanded on and collected in two volumes as *The Chronicles of Early Melbourne 1835–1852* in 1888. An abridged edition was published by Margaret Weidenhofer in 1967 and a facsimile edition of the original appeared in 1976. Finn also produced *Der Eggsberiences ov Hans Schwartz ... with Humourous Interleaves* (1878).

HD

Fire-stick farming, a term coined by archaeologist Rhys Jones, in Jim Allen et al. (eds), *Sunda and Sahul* (1977), describes a highly specific, localised process of deliberate, regular and organised burning of the land that has been used by Australian Aborigines for thousands of years, and contin-

ues to be used in northern Australia, as a form of land and resource management. Aborigines controlled and modified vegetation by setting fire to the land using the sticks of smouldering wood that they carried with them. This prepared the land for, and stimulated, new growth and was also a means of staking a claim on an area of land. Firing the bush affected a region's ecology by encouraging or discouraging particular plant species, and so was a means of promoting food sources. It was also responsible for the creation of Australia's open woodlands, which provided increased visibility for hunting. As N.G. **Butlin** explains, fire-stick farming was used 'to expose or capture a harvest or to generate or re-generate pastures for grazing animals'. **Conservation** practitioners have adopted a similar system of controlled burning as a precaution against **bushfires**.

HD

First AIF, see **AIF**

First Fleet comprised 11 ships which brought the first permanent British settlers to Australia. Commanded by Arthur **Phillip** on HMS *Supply*, and led by the flagship HMS *Sirius* captained by John **Hunter**, the fleet departed from Portsmouth on 13 May 1787 and arrived at **Botany Bay** on 18 January 1788. Contrary to the favourable reports in **Cook's** journal of 1770, the bay proved unsuitable as a harbour and the fleet was relocated to Sydney Cove in Port Jackson, where Phillip raised the British flag on 26 January 1788. A total of 1023 settlers disembarked, including 751 convicts and their children (23 had died during the voyage), and 252 marines and their families. Contemporary accounts of the voyage and early settlement include *The Voyage of Governor Phillip to Botany Bay* (1789) and Watkin **Tench's** *Narrative of an Expedition to Botany Bay* (1789). John Cobley combined these accounts into *Sydney Cove* (1980) and analysed *The Crimes of the First Fleet Convicts* (1982); Victor Crittenden has compiled a comprehensive bibliography (1981). As these works and the formation of the First Fleet Association suggest, the descendants of First Fleet settlers have made an increasing cult of its foundational significance.

HD

First World War, see **World War I**

Fisher, Andrew (1862–1928) was prime minister 1908–09, 1910–13, and 1914–15. He migrated to Qld from Scotland in 1885, after working as a pit-boy in the coalmines from the age of 9. He became president of the Gympie Miners Association, MLA for Gympie (1893–96), and entered the first federal parliament as Labor member for Wide Bay. He became leader of the **Australian Labor Party** in 1907 and briefly prime minister in the following year. After winning a majority at the 1910 elections, Fisher embarked on a series of major measures, which included creation of the Commonwealth Bank, the Australian navy, a national capital, and such social reforms as maternity allowances and invalid pensions. His final period as prime minister was overshadowed by

World War I; it was during the 1914 election campaign that he made the oft-reported 'last man and last shilling' pledge of Australian support for the British Empire. The burden of keeping the Labor Party committed to the war caused him to resign in favour of Billy **Hughes**, after which he served as high commissioner in London for five years.

KT

Fitchett, William Henry (1841–1928) wrote a range of popular historical works under the pseudonym 'Vedette', which included *The New World of the South: Australia in the Making* (1913) and *The Romance of Australian History* (1913). After Fitchett came to Australia from England in 1849, he worked at a number of occupations, including that of a jackeroo, before entering the Methodist ministry in 1866. He became an influential figure in the **Methodist Church** and the wider community, serving for more than 40 years as foundation principal of the Methodist Ladies College, Melbourne, and was elected first president of the united Methodist Church in 1902. He wrote a history of the school, *Forty Years at MLC* (1921). He also wrote for the Methodist church paper, the *Spectator*, and edited the Sunday family magazine, *Southern Cross*. He was foundation president (1904–07) of the general conference of the Methodist Church of Australasia and a trustee of the Public Library, Museums, and the National Gallery of Victoria. His *Deeds That Won the Empire* (1897), a collection of a series of articles first published in the Melbourne *Argus*, went to 35 printings.

KT

Fitzpatrick, Brian Charles (1905–65), historian, civil libertarian, and political maverick, was born at Warrnambool, Victoria, of Australian parents of mixed Irish, Scottish, and Manx descent. He was educated at Moonee Ponds state and Essendon High schools, winning first-class honours in English and a scholarship to the University of Melbourne. He graduated BA Hons in 1925 and was a founder of *Farrago*, the student newspaper, and of the University Labor Club. For the next 10 years he was primarily a journalist in Sydney, Melbourne, and London.

By the mid-1930s his socialist convictions had firmed. As a founder in 1935 and soon the secretary of the Australian Council for Civil Liberties, he became its one-man-band; he was especially tender to the needs of **Jewish** and other migrants, and earned the respect and cooperation of conservatives such as Sir John **Latham** and Harold **Holt**. Yet he was also a constant lobbyist on behalf of the broad Left and, in his generation, was a rare example of an independent publicist.

One of Fitzpatrick's motives for writing history was his belief that Australians could not recognise their capacity to develop as a nation without better understanding of their background. Along with those of H.V. **Evatt**, Eris **O'Brien**, Vance **Palmer**, and Hartley **Grattan**, Fitzpatrick's writings marked a long jump forward in Australian historiography and provided basic texts for the early postwar teachers of Australian history. *British Imperialism and Australia 1783–1833* (1939) and *The British Empire in Australia* (1941,

1949), both supported by university research grants, made the first substantial attempt to apply Marxist concepts of class struggle to Australian history. A.G.L. **Shaw** described these works of economic history as 'the greatest single contribution in recent years … the result of far more research than has been usual'. Fitzpatrick's view tended to dominate until N.G. **Butlin**, in the late 1950s, provided a new intellectual framework. Fitzpatrick's quickly written *Short History of the Australian Labor Movement* (1940) was a polemical stopgap: 'the history of the Australian people is among other things the struggle between the organised rich and the organised poor'. His general history *The Australian People 1788–1945* (1946) has claims to be his most important work, but its influence lessened when several historians produced able surveys in the 1950s. *The Australian Commonwealth* (1956) was an entertaining treatment of the preoccupations of the **Old Left** and of threatened liberties. In *Meanjin* in 1963 he demolished the alleged **'counter-revolution in Australian historiography'**. As Helen Bourke commented in *LH* (1974), 'There is as much of the progressive liberal about him as there is of the committed socialist'. His commitment to Marxism was always qualified.

Fitzpatrick rightly believed that a major element in the revelation and understanding of the past was the 'historian's practical and personal experience of the world'. In spite of his qualifications and strong support, his applications for university teaching posts all failed, partly because of his political beliefs and his alcoholism. His charm, mannered courtesy, wit, and tolerance of criticism were admirable virtues.

Don Watson published a biography in 1979. Fitzpatrick married Kathleen Pitt (Kathleen **Fitzpatrick**) in 1932; they separated in 1935 and were divorced in 1939. The following year he married Dorothy (Mary) Davies, who survived him on his sudden death on 3 September 1965; their children Sheila and David are noted historians.

GEOFFREY SERLE

Fitzpatrick, Kathleen Elizabeth (1905–90), historian, was born in Omeo, Victoria, and educated in Melbourne. She studied history at the University of Melbourne, took a second degree at Oxford, and later returned to the University of Melbourne as a tutor and lecturer. She was briefly married to historian Brian **Fitzpatrick**. She was associate professor at Melbourne 1948–62 and, with R.M. **Crawford**, shaped the emphasis of the **Melbourne School of History** on the study of the past as a humanistic training. She was renowned as a lecturer for grace of delivery and care for language; Susan Davies uses Fitzpatrick's advice on lecturing to describe her pedagogy in Stuart Macintyre and Julian Thomas (eds), *The Discovery of Australian History* (1995).

In addition to teaching, Fitzpatrick was actively involved in the life of the university. She published a biography of Sir John **Franklin** (1949) and a centennial history of Presbyterian Ladies College, Melbourne (1975), and edited an influential selection of the journals of *Australian Explorers* (1958). Her evocative autobiography, *Solid Bluestone Foundations* (1983), which covers her Melbourne childhood and early adulthood, brought greatest literary success. A collection of her correspondence with Manning **Clark**, entitled *Dear Kathleen, Dear Manning*, appeared in 1996. She left a large bequest to the university library in honour of her father, H.A. Pitt. A postgraduate room in the History Department commemorates her.

HD

FitzRoy, Charles Augustus (1796–1858) was appointed governor-general of NSW to succeed George **Gipps**. His aristocratic background, easy charm and varied experience in military, political and colonial service ensured that his arrival in the colony in 1846 was welcome. He recognised the value of making concessions to the colonists where possible, and it was opportune that his term of office coincided with a relaxation of policy from London and the recognition of land claims by squatters. A carriage accident in late 1847, in which he as driver was injured and his wife killed, clouded the rest of his time in the colony. Within a year, allegations began about his improper relationships with women, and his moral character was impugned in London and NSW. This culminated in a public attack by J.D. **Lang** who, in 1854, moved a vituperative amendment to the Legislative Council's farewell address to the governor in which he included the accusation that FitzRoy's 'moral influence' had been 'deleterious and baneful'.

Although FitzRoy did not instigate any notable policies, he was involved with some momentous incidents, including debates over extended franchise and a new constitution, the growing **anti-transportation** movement, and the 1851 gold rushes. He recognised that this was a transitional period of government and that limited self-rule was imminent, and this may account for his apparent lack of initiative, for which he was criticised. His request that his term of appointment be extended was not granted, and he returned to England when William **Denison** arrived to replace him in early 1855.

KT

Fiveash, Rosa (1854–1938) received international recognition for her botanical illustrations. While still a student at the Adelaide School of Art and Design, she was invited to illustrate *The Forest Fauna of South Australia*, which appeared in parts from 1882 to 1890. She was versatile, painting a large collection of Aboriginal toas and illustrating scientific papers, but flowers were her speciality. For 30 years she illustrated the works of R.S. Rogers on the orchids of SA. It was not until 1974 that a volume appeared under her name, *Rosa Fiveash's Australian Orchids*, by Noel Lothian. Most of her work is now in the South Australian State Library and Museum.

KT

Flags have a confused history which mirrors the complexities of **national identity** in a colonial culture. Two Australian flags, with the constellation of the **Southern Cross** in the fly and the Federation Star, were adopted in 1903: one, with a red ground, for merchant ships; the other,

with a blue ground, for naval or official use. They were British ensigns with the Union Jack in the place of honour denoting sovereignty. The Union Jack remained the national flag. To underline the point, the Federation celebrations of 1901 had included the introduction of Union Jacks into state schools across Australia. It was not until 1950, when the Commonwealth government decided to give a flag to every school to mark the jubilee of Federation, that it finally designated the blue ensign as the Australian national flag.

State rivalry, especially between Victoria and NSW, undermined popular acceptance of the 1903 design. Its centrepiece, the Southern Cross constellation, was from the Victorian flag and its predecessor, the flag of the Australasian League, the **anti-transportation** body of the 1840s. The NSW flag featured St George's Cross with stars, which had also been used on the flag of the **Federation** campaign. Reluctance by the Commonwealth government to use Australian flags or to clarify their use by state and local governments and the Australian public led to bitter battles over flags, especially in the years following World War I. The Labor Party and the Catholic Church promoted the Australian flags and so marked their ambivalence about Empire. To the non-Labor parties and British loyalists generally, the Australian ensigns became disloyal and unpatriotic symbols unless accompanied by the Union Jack. They championed the introduction of **Empire Day** in schools, which consolidated the use of the Union Jack as the national flag and stimulated further disputes about flags. The colours of the Australian ensigns became a further reason discouraging their use. Red, once the colour of Empire, now represented communist power. Blue also had radical associations through the **Eureka** flag: 'a rebel flag', Henry **Lawson** had called it ('Freedom on the Wallaby', 1891), 'the bonny blue' ('As Ireland Wore the Green', 1891). The Eureka flag, unlike the flags of the anti-transportation and Federation campaigns, did not include a Union Jack.

Historians exploring issues of national identity have made only passing reference to the significance of flags in marking Australians' allegiances. Others more directly concerned with flags pursued a vexillological or antiquarian interest. Frank Cayley, in *Flag of Stars* (1966), revised as *Beneath the Southern Cross: The Story of Australia through Flags* (1980), noted but did not explain Australians' reluctance to use the Australian ensigns. The fate of the Eureka flag was the subject of Len Fox's *The Strange Story of the Eureka Flag* (1963, revised 1973, 1992). Ralph Kelly, *Australian State Flags, 1965–1904: A British Admiralty Legacy* (1989), and A.C. Burton, 'Australia's Forgotten Flag' (*Crux Australis*, 1992), continue that tradition. Elizabeth Kwan made flags a resource for **ethnic history** in arguing that Australians' changing allegiances to Britain and Australia could best be understood through arguments over flags ('The Australian flag', *AHS*, 1994).

The symbols of the Australian national flag, in particular the Union Jack, have been the centre of growing debate since the early 1980s with the emergence of Ausflag Ltd and the Australian National Flag Association. Support for a new flag (and a republic) by Paul **Keating**, the Labor prime minister, and opposition by the **Liberal** and **National Parties** gave the debate a political edge. Carol A. Foley's *The Australian Flag: Colonial Relic or Contemporary Icon?* (1996) discussed arguments for and against changing the flag. While pressure to change the flag fluctuated from the late 1960s, support for the Union Jack as part of it consistently declined. The emergence of the Australian Aboriginal Flag in 1971 (and the Torres Strait Islander Flag in 1992) and the national status accorded it in 1995 added to the controversy by raising the possibility of including its colours (black, gold, and ochre) and symbols in a new flag. Attempts by the Liberal and National Parties from 1984 to ensure that the Australian national flag can only be changed by a referendum culminated in the statement on **Anzac Day** 1996 by John **Howard**, the new coalition prime minister, that his government would 'protect our great **national symbol**, the Australian flag'. Legislation ensuring this was passed in 1998.

ELIZABETH KWAN

Fleay, David Howells (1907–93) pioneered the study and conservation of Australia's native fauna. He had completed a BSc when the Melbourne Zoo asked him to establish its new Australian section in 1934. After his dismissal three years later, he was appointed director of the Sir Colin Mackenzie (Healesville) Sanctuary, Victoria, where he carried out innovative conservation and breeding experiments that resulted in the first successful breeding of platypuses in captivity. Fleay moved to the Gold Coast, Qld, in 1952 to establish a reserve for Australian wildlife, in which he aimed to preserve endangered species. He provided the Commonwealth Serum Laboratory with snake venom, including that of the taipan, for antivenom production. He received international recognition for his work and wrote for many scientific publications as well as the *National Geographic*. He also wrote several books, including *We Breed the Platypus* (1944). Fleay donated the Queensland reserve to the state in 1982.

KT

Flinders, Matthew (1774–1814) was an English naval officer, who made the first charts of the Australian coast and promoted the name **Australia**. He joined the navy as a midshipman when he was 16, and two years later sailed with Captain **Bligh** on the expedition to carry breadfruit plants from Tahiti to the West Indies. Despite the cool relations between the two, Flinders flourished on this voyage. He gained navigational experience and began practising surveying and cartography—skills at which he later so excelled that elements of his work along the Australian coastline still appear on charts in use at the end of the twentieth century. In 1795, Flinders sailed to the young settlement of Port Jackson as master's mate in the *Reliance*. Also aboard was George **Bass**, the ship's surgeon. With this adventurous companion, he shortly embarked upon two brief expeditions in the tiny *Tom Thumb*, during which he made the first of his Australian surveys. He later charted the Furneaux Group and, again

with Bass, circumnavigated Van Diemen's Land, confirming the existence of the strait so valuable to navigation. In more surveying—north of Port Jackson—he filled in some of the cartographical gaps left by Captain **Cook**.

Back in England in 1800, Flinders obtained Sir Joseph **Banks's** support for further coastal exploration of **New South Wales** and **New Holland**. His timing was good. The French were despatching Nicolas **Baudin's** expedition to Australian waters—a scientific expedition commanded by himself would be England's answer to it. Recently promoted and newly married, Flinders set out in the *Investigator* in mid-1801.

In the course of his circumnavigation of the continent, Flinders surveyed much of its uncharted southern coast (meeting Baudin along the way) and carried out extensive examinations of the Gulf of Carpentaria and Torres Strait. On his return voyage to England in a colonial-built schooner in poor condition, he was obliged to call at the French naval base at Ile-de-France (now Mauritius). Here he fell foul of the authorities, a victim of the renewal of hostilities between England and France and his own unbending pride. Despite all evidence to the contrary, the governor, General de Caen, considered him a threat to the island's security and detained him for the next six years. Released at last in 1810, Flinders returned to England to be reunited with his wife and to write *A Voyage to Terra Australis* (1814). In this he recommended the name Australia for the continent, and it was adopted and popularised by Governor **Macquarie**.

Flinders and his many achievements have been widely and justly commemorated in Australia. Ernest **Scott's** 1914 study, *The Life of Captain Matthew Flinders, R.N.*, is typical of the sympathetic treatment that he has received from historians; in 1941, Ernestine **Hill** produced a fictional rendering of his story, *My Love Must Wait*. In 1962, however, Sidney J. **Baker**, in *My Own Destroyer*, looked critically at Flinders's character, reasoning that its weaknesses were responsible for at least some of his misfortunes. The most comprehensive account appeared in 1986: Geoffrey Ingleton's *Matthew Flinders: Navigator and Chartmaker* is a perceptive work of reference and interpretation, examining every aspect of Flinders's life and work. There are statues in Sydney, Melbourne, and Adelaide. (See also **Exploration by sea**.)

CHRISTINE CORNELL

Floods have been represented in a number of ways. Hydrographers, biologists, physical geographers, and other natural scientists see them in the context of natural ecological systems, although they recognise that humans have altered their behaviour to increase or decrease the incidence of floods. Engineers are more concerned with predicting, controlling, and exploiting their incidence, and with minimising the damage to human communities; they commonly focus on the identification of particularly significant events—the '100-year flood', the '500-year flood', and so on—to provide benchmark historical evidence for the construction of control and storage structures (principally weirs and dams). Most of the Australian literature on this topic has been produced by scientists and technocrats. Like those concerned with the social effects of flooding, they tend to obscure the natural right or duty of a watercourse to exceed periodically its usual territorial claim.

If one accepts the anthropogenic inference that a flood is essentially water out of place, then the archaeological evidence suggests that flooding has been common since pre-European times. Floods feature less prominently than drought in the accounts of explorers and pioneering pastoralists, although their journals include valuable descriptions of so-called 'wild rivers'. Several colonial governors argued unsuccessfully against the occupation of natural flood plains, and destructive floods in the capitals and provincial towns were diligently annotated in contemporary newspapers, but the interpretative record remained thin until the last quarter of the nineteenth century. The most common public responses to major flooding were strident demands for fresh legislation and dam construction; these developments often yielded important quantitative and qualitative data which were consulted by later generations of technocrats—but seldom, alas, by Australia's historians. From the early twentieth century the Commonwealth Bureau of Meteorology compiled elementary chronological guides to key environmental events, and the influential water agencies in each state occasionally produced reports on floods and flood control strategies.

Lightly touched upon in regional histories and historical geographies during the 1960s and 1970s, these themes and sources were most cogently treated within a broader coverage of water management in Michael Williams, *The Making of the South Australian Landscape* (1974). Urban historians who picked up some of the insights of urban geography largely ignored the massive effects of urbanisation on surface and underground water regimes. Tiled roofs and macadamised roads profoundly altered the patterns of run-off and guaranteed more flash floods; the increasing volumes of water in turn called for strong measures to contain them.

Since most of Australia's towns and cities occupy natural flood plains, the control, mitigation, and regulation of the floods has meant an endless coming-to-terms. Beyond the bitumen the effects of flooding have encouraged a cautious accounting. The list of debits—loss of life, homes, crop land, and stock, with disruptions to communication and transport—may be partially balanced by short and long-term benefits—replenishments of precious ground water reserves, rejuvenation of wetland habitats, boosts to infrastructure needs, such as the upgrading of warning systems, emergency services, and psychological counselling, and opportunities for community bonding, the emergence of leaders, and so on.

Problems of definition preclude the drawing-up of any exhaustive national chronology of flood events and the early colonial era is poorly served. Particularly significant years taken from the Bureau of Meteorology lists may be 1863, 1870, 1875, 1889–94, 1906, 1909, 1916–17, 1921, 1925, 1929, 1931, 1934, 1949–56, 1960s generally, the mid-1970s to the early 1980s, and the mid-1990s. Measured by their human consequences, as natural **disasters**, the most catastrophic floods include those of 1852 on the Murrumbidgee (89 lives lost); western NSW in 1890, the subject of Aby Altson's famous painting *Flood Sufferings*; Victoria in 1934 (35 lives lost) and the Hunter River in 1955 (at least 22 fatalities).

Australian geographers were pioneers in the international, interdisciplinary field of 'environmental hazard' studies during the 1960s. This work continues to provide crucial methodological and contextual leads for humanities and social science researchers, as do the painstaking accounts of river history compiled by geomorphologists and hydrologists. The spate of interdisciplinary 'environmental history' writings during the 1980s and 1990s, ushered in by Geoffrey **Bolton's** *Spoils and Spoilers* (1981), helped to generate overdue scholarly interest in the pervasive role of water in the driest of the inhabited continents. Some of these recent works extended the foundational efforts of historical geographers in earlier decades—for instance, J.M. Powell's *Environmental Management in Australia* (1976) led to his *Historical Geography of Modern Australia* (1988, 1991)—but social, regional, and economic historians were also prominent and a small number of narrowly focused historical books favouring water management necessarily concentrated, in some measure, on aspects of the flood theme. Good NSW examples include Clem Lloyd, *Either Drought or Plenty* (1988), and Dan Coward, *Out of Sight* (1988); J.M. Powell's continuing series of 'water histories' has thus far taken in Victoria, Qld, and the whole of the Murray–Darling Basin: *Watering the Garden State* (1989), *Plains of Promise, Rivers of Destiny* (1991), and *The Emergence of Bioregionalism in the Murray–Darling Basin* (1993). Each incorporates an emphasis on institutional (mainly agency) history, as does Tony Dingle and Carolyn Rasmussen, *Vital Connections* (1991).

J.M. POWELL

Florey, Howard Walter (1898–1968) was an outstandingly effective medical researcher who pioneered the development and use of antibiotics. Although popular mythology credits Alexander Fleming, it was Florey and his team who gave the world the miracle drug, penicillin.

Born and educated in Adelaide, Florey went to Oxford in 1921 as a Rhodes scholar. In 1935 he was appointed to the chair of pathology there, and energetically set about developing an interdisciplinary team to tackle fundamental questions related to disease. By 1941, he and his wife Ethel were undertaking clinical trials, demonstrating the antimicrobial properties of penicillin. Florey's achievement earned him a share of the 1945 Nobel Prize for medicine. His attachment to Australia remained strong, and in 1944 he was asked to advise on the establishment of a medical research institute in Canberra. His guidance was crucial as the proposal developed into the Australian National University. Florey did not finally accept the directorship of what became the John Curtin School of Medical Research; however, he served as chancellor from 1965. He was created Baron Florey of Adelaide and Marston in 1965. Leonard Bickel celebrated his life in *Rise Up to Life* (1972); Gwyn

Macfarlane (1979) and Trevor Williams (1984) have written more detailed biographies.

TIM SHERRATT

Flying Doctor Service, see **Australian Inland Mission**

Flynn, John (1880–1951), founder of the Flying Doctor Service, devoted his life to the cause of 'a Brighter Bush'. As a young Home Missionary he studied for the **Presbyterian** ministry while working with Melbourne's inner-city poor and Victoria's remote rural communities: these experiences ignited his lifelong zeal for the practical Christianity of the Social Gospel. In 1912 he prompted the church to create the **Australian Inland Mission**. Inspired by **progressive** ideals of efficiency and moral uplift, Flynn advocated wide-ranging reforms for the outback. He was a technological visionary, grasping the potential of wireless and aviation to bring the amenities of metropolitan life (especially health) to white communities in the bush. He dreamt of uniting the vitality of the frontier with the civilising forces of modernity, and one of his campaigns was to encourage white women to settle in remote communities. Although Flynn has been criticised for his inattention to Aboriginal welfare, the infrastructure he created would eventually serve Aboriginal communities also. Flynn became an icon of the **pioneer** legend after the publication of Ion **Idriess's** best-seller *Flynn of the Inland* (1932). A good recent biography is Max Griffiths, *The Silent Heart* (1993), but Flynn is most vividly commemorated in his practical legacy of hospitals, hostels, and the Flying Doctor Service itself.

BRIGID HAINS

Food was rarely stored or preserved in Aboriginal society. The Aborigines were early enthusiasts for fresh ingredients gathered daily. Seeds and grasses, and roots and tubers were collected and prepared for eating by soaking, pounding, or cooking. Small animals were trapped and larger ones hunted, then roasted on an open fire, or cooked in their skins. The Aborigines had no fireproof utensils, so no means of boiling water. But they trapped and speared fish in inland rivers and lagoons, and collected shellfish along the coastline. Offshore they fished with lines from canoes and took small fires with them to cook their catch at its peak of freshness. As the seasons came round, they gathered for feasts of bogong moths or bunya nuts. It seems that a balance was maintained between the size of the population and what the land could provide without stress or over-exploitation of its resources. Jennifer Isaacs, *Bush Food: Aboriginal Food and Herbal Medicine* (1987), and A.B. and J.W. Cribb, *Wild Food in Australia* (1974), provide accounts.

The early European settlers were already advanced in preservation technology with salted and dried foods, and brought with them large quantities of flour, salt meat, butter in kegs, and dried goods. They were reluctant, despite shortages in their own supplies, to use Aboriginal foods (except for fish and oysters), or unable to obtain them in sufficient quantities. The successful introduction of sheep and cattle

supplied cheap and abundant meat, a particularly attractive prospect to the working people of Britain and Ireland for whom the shortage of protein, the price of bread, and later the failure of the potato crop were of daily concern. Caroline **Chisholm** was able to promote immigration to Australia with the promise of 'meat three times a day'. Meat rather than bread became synonymous with a high standard of living, and by the last decade of the nineteenth century Australia's settlers consumed more meat per head of population than any country in the world. The history of diet and nutrition in Australia can be followed through Robin Walker and Dave Roberts, *From Scarcity to Surfeit: A History of Diet and Nutrition in New South Wales* (1988) and Barbara Santich, *What the Doctors Ordered* (1995). The search for canning and freezing technologies by which meat could also be exported to the northern hemisphere has been described by K.T.H. Farrar in *A Settlement Amply Supplied* (1980). Late-nineteenth-century affluence was also evident in the quantities of sugar consumed (in cakes and biscuits, sweets, jams, jellies and cordials, and in sweetened tea). Without Chinese market gardeners, however, there would have been little innovation or enthusiasm in vegetable-growing, though the possibilities of fruit for canning and jam-making were more widely appreciated.

By the end of the nineteenth century, the argument about whether Australia should have its own approach to food appropriate to its climate and environment had begun. In *The Art of Living in Australia* (1893), Dr Philip Muskett expounded the virtues of Australian fish, wine, fruit, vegetables, and salads. SA was by then already highly regarded for the quality of its Mediterranean-style produce. Australia's high standard of living, however, was measured officially by British standards of stodge, though away from the cities and especially in the tropical north, eating habits were of necessity more varied and adventurous than the statisticians could measure. Meanwhile, many Aborigines were now starving or ill fed, without the means to buy mutton and beef, or bread and potatoes, and denied access to their traditional hunting grounds, or malnourished on the white flour and sugar dispensed by governments and missions. Educationalists in southern cities despaired of the knowledge and cooking skills of Australian girls, so at a time when experience was producing Australian-born cooks and cookery-book writers like Mina Rawson and Hannah MacLurcan, who were not afraid of mixing and matching local ingredients with traditional British styles, cooking became a subject in schools with textbooks and teachers adopting British models.

With affluence and abundance, people could begin to think of food as a fashion item or a status symbol. By the early twentieth century, upwardly mobile Australian households had become concerned about correctness at the dinner table, using French names to describe the dishes and applying all manner of rules to both diet and the presentation of food. Michael Symons's *One Continuous Picnic* (1982) details the changing fashions in food; he is very critical especially of the role of food and cookery writers in women's magazines in feminising Australian food. Yet, except for hotel dining rooms, there were few places to experience professionally cooked food, especially for the housewife who was usually entirely responsible for budgeting, marketing, cooking, and maintaining good nutrition for her family; see Anne Gollan, *The Tradition of Australian Cooking* (1978).

A transformation of Australian ideas about food began in the middle of the twentieth century, inspired in part by immigration from Europe, in part by the mass travel of young Australians. Once more it was discovered that the Australian climate could produce a wide range of foods originating from all corners of the earth. The new multicultural population provided both skills and a demand for greater variety. Traditional European and Mediterranean ingredients and methods were married with Chinese and South-East Asian experience and flavours, and proffered with a touch of Californian style to produce an eclectic cuisine sometimes described as Pacrim. The development of transport, especially air-freight, and the spread of chains of supermarkets nationwide meant that by the late twentieth century the availability of a wide range of mass-produced, manufactured, processed, and 'fresh' foods was greater than ever. Families in Darwin and on the Derwent were likely to eat the same kind of food while they watched the same kind of television. But that diet itself was changing: the traditional heavy British-style meat and three vegetables six nights a week had often given way to a lighter stir-fry or pasta dish with a salad; the home-cooked meal was often replaced with the frozen or packaged meal; and instead of the occasional Friday night fish and chips there were more frequent meals of takeaway pizza, hamburger, or fried chicken. The full flowering of Australia's eclectic food capabilities was well illustrated in the appearance in 1996 of two major reference works, Stephanie Alexander's compendium *The Cook's Companion*, and Charmaine Solomon's *Encyclopedia of Asian Food*; the former is the epitome of Melbourne's European heritage of good taste, the latter indicates Sydney's greater adventurousness. It may be somewhat longer, however, before either volume makes an impact in Cairns or Burnie. And it is still the case that the theory of good food and sound nutrition is a distant consideration in marketing and advertising, or when a shopper is studying what is available and what the household can afford.

If there is an Australian way with food, it arises from the availability of a very wide range of good-quality ingredients which are still relatively inexpensive. There has also been a renewed interest in bush foods, which has grown with the revitalisation of Aboriginal culture and the desire to find something which is uniquely Australian for promotion to tourists. Vic Cherikoff (*Uniquely Australian: The Beginnings of an Australian Bushfood Cuisine*, 1992) illustrates the tendency. Perhaps we are also, at this late stage, being forced by dwindling resources to apply knowledge and technology to foods which we long despised. Or conservation may have made the kangaroo a more obvious source. But whether kangaroo and beetroot will be accepted as the natural successor to meat pie and tomato sauce as a national dish is still uncertain.

BEVERLEY KINGSTON

Football, see **Australian Rules football**; **Rugby**

Forbes, Francis (1784–1841) took up the post of first chief justice of NSW in 1824. In this capacity he not only headed the judiciary but was also a member of the Legislative Council and later, the Executive Council. He also had the right to prevent the governor submitting a bill to the Legislative Council, a position of great power. Forbes worked well with Governor **Brisbane** but incurred with Brisbane the emnity of some influential colonists, including Hannibal **Macarthur** and Samuel **Marsden**. He differed with Governor **Darling** over many issues, including the governor's handling of the **Sudds–Thompson affair**, his attempts to control a critical press, and his rights over assigned servants. Darling sought his removal from office, but Forbes outlasted him. After serving for a time under Governor **Bourke**, Forbes was forced by ill-health to return to England in 1836, where he worked at the Colonial Office and appeared before the Molesworth committee on **transportation**. His role in NSW is considered by C.H. Currey in *Sir Francis Forbes* (1968).

KT

Foreign relations in the twentieth century have been characterised by a tension between Australia's status as a small to middle power, and its aspiration to find security and play an active role in an often unstable regional and international environment. Concurrently there has been a recurring conflict between its 'history'—that is, the cultural and ethnic heritage of Europe—and its 'geography'—its proximity to the Asia–Pacific region. Since successive Australian governments sought to resolve these tensions within strong alliance relationships, much of Australian foreign policy in this century has been typified as a progression from 'dependence' to 'independence'.

Prior to Federation, the Australian colonies, despite their lack of international status, took an active interest in issues with a foreign affairs dimension; in particular, they maintained control over **immigration** policy in order to preserve a racially homogeneous and white population, and they sought to exclude potentially hostile European and Asian powers from the South-West Pacific, a region they regarded as Australia's 'manifest destiny' to control. Roger Thompson, *Australian Imperialism in the Pacific* (1980), traces this preoccupation. Australian colonists also contributed willingly to imperial conflicts in the Sudan (K.S. **Inglis**, *The Rehearsal*, 1985), South Africa (Chris Connolly in *HS*, 1978; L.M. Field, *The Forgotten War*, 1979) and China (B. Nicholls, *Bluejackets and Boxers*, 1986).

In the first four decades after Federation, Australia strove to pursue these objectives—as well as to maintain a favourable international trading regime—within the institutional framework of British imperial foreign policy. This reliance on the machinery and intelligence of the Foreign Office has led historians to conclude that there was, at best, a 'proto' Australian foreign policy in this period, as Peter Edwards called it in his *Prime Ministers and Diplomats* (1983).

However, Neville Meaney, *The Search for Security in the Pacific 1901–14* (1976), shows that the keen sense of Australian interests distinctive from those of Britain should not be underestimated.

World War I brought a surge of national pride in the celebration of the Anzacs' exploits and a burst of international activism under Prime Minister W.M. **Hughes**. Hughes was instrumental in modifying imperial consultative machinery and in gaining Australia representation at the Paris Peace Conference of 1919. But, for all his tweaking of the noses of the Great Powers in Paris—which has been as much admired by Australian historians as it has been ignored by others—Hughes did nothing to challenge the essentially imperial context of Australian foreign relations. In the inter-war years, while other Dominions pushed for changes in the constitutional relationship with Britain, Australian non-Labor governments affirmed their loyalty to Britain. The national identity articulated in the emerging **Anzac Legend** was appropriated by the Right, and subsumed within the wider imperial and British sense of race. The Left tended to isolationism.

World War II, with its relentless exposure of Britain's demise as a global power and its confirmation of long-held fears of a threat from the Asian north, forced a reassessment. As early as 1939 Robert **Menzies** decided to establish Australia's first independent diplomatic missions overseas. As Allan **Martin** has shown in his 1993 biography, Menzies's relationship with British Prime Minister Churchill was more troubled than is commonly assumed, but it was not until the advent of the Labor government of John **Curtin** in late 1941 that there was a manifest change of style. Australia's 'looking to America', signalled in Curtin's famous statement of December 1941, was not the turning-point that has sometimes been claimed in retrospect, but under the brilliant H.V. **Evatt**, Australian foreign policy became more self-consciously independent. Evatt sought a more prominent role in the region, though again this role was conceived as the agent of the British Commonwealth. Simultaneously he was active in multilateral forums, particularly the fledgling United Nations, establishing a Labor tradition of international activism—or 'busyness', as W.J. Hudson has called it in the 1944 volume of the official *Documents on Australian Foreign Policy 1937–49* (1988). Whatever his personal abrasiveness and mercurial inconsistency, Evatt is the darling of historians of Australian foreign policy, attracting far more scholarly attention than any other foreign affairs minister (for example, Alan Renouf, *Let Justice Be Done*, 1983; Ken Buckley et al., *Doc Evatt*, 1994; and David Day, ed., *Brave New World*, 1996).

A Liberal–Country Party coalition replaced Labor in 1949, a crucial time in international politics. The Cold War extended to Asia with the emergence of Communist China, which a year later entered the **Korean War**; the sterling area was in crisis; and the forces of decolonisation unleashed by the Japanese victories in the South-East Asian region became irresistible. Menzies remained cloyingly sentimental about the mother country and the monarchy—and instinctively

willing to manifest the old 'blind loyalty' to Britain during the **Suez Crisis** of 1956, to quote the title of W.J. Hudson's 1989 monograph. But his government accepted that the USA had a key role in economic and regional security. Drawing on its tradition of being a good ally in times of crisis, Australia sought to tie its new 'great and powerful friend' to an active role in the Asian region and to close bilateral relations—the latter through the **ANZUS Treaty** (1951) and the more controversial provision to the USA of defence facilities and privileged access for investment. Within the region, successive Liberal external affairs ministers Percy **Spender** (1951–52) and Richard **Casey** (1952–59), developed the **Colombo Plan** with the aim of resistance to **communism** in emerging independent Asian countries. This was coupled with military intervention—the policy of 'forward defence', which culminated in the Australian commitment to support the USA in the **Vietnam War**.

In the historiography of Australian foreign policy, the 1960s is commonly depicted as an intellectual and policy nadir: a 'crisis of loyalty' to use the title of Bruce Grant's 1972 book. Set against the sterility of Australian policy in Vietnam, however, there was the incremental, if cautious, dismantling of the **White Australia** policy; the deft damage control during the Confrontation between Indonesia and Malaysia; and a process of sometimes halting adjustment to a decolonising region, and the withdrawal of Britain in 1967 from East of Suez.

Coming to power in 1972 after Coalition disarray over the USA's rapprochement with China and withdrawal from Vietnam, Gough **Whitlam** gave the impression of a radical new wind in foreign relations. Recognising Communist China, shifting the balance of Australian foreign relations more towards Asia than the USA, revivifying the liberal internationalism of Evatt, acknowledging the fundamental importance to Australia of Indonesia and Japan, associating Australia with the new Association of South-East Asian Nations (ASEAN), and overtly addressing the country's international stigma of racism, Whitlam set the contours of Australian foreign relations in a manner that was to become largely bipartisan. He provided a further, perhaps the outstanding, example of a feature of Australian foreign relations often commented upon—and which formed the theme of P.G. Edwards's *Prime Ministers and Diplomats* (1983)—the dominance of prime ministers in the making of foreign policy,

The return of the conservative coalition to power (1976–83) brought with it something of a reversion to the realism of the days of Menzies and Paul **Hasluck** (external affairs minister, 1964–69). But Malcolm **Fraser's** resuscitation of the bogey of the Soviet Union, which led to exaggerated expectations of cooperation with the Chinese, did not challenge the fundamentals of the new agenda. This included international human rights issues (given an acute salience by the exodus of Vietnamese **boat people** and South African apartheid), and the growing tyranny of international economic issues. In the 1980s economic opportunities became the dominant concern of Australia's relations with the fast-developing countries of East and South-East Asia—a development reflected in the amalgamation of the Departments of Foreign Affairs and Trade in 1987. This shift was also evident in the historiography: the 1976–80 volume of the series 'Australia in World Affairs', published by the Australian Institute of International Affairs, was titled *Independence and Alliance* (1983); the volume for 1981–90, *Diplomacy in the Marketplace* (1992).

Under the governments of Bob **Hawke** (1983–91) and Paul **Keating** (1991–96) the international 'busyness' of the Evatt period resurged, particularly under the intellectual and ambitious foreign minister, Gareth Evans (1987–93), who sought to shape the foreign policy agenda, nationally and internationally, with his own books (*Australia's Foreign Relations in the World of the 1990s*, with Bruce Grant, 1991; *Cooperating for Peace*, 1993). Under Evans, Australia sought to be an 'international good citizen', playing a reforming role in UN forums and contributing to peace-keeping forces (the latter, arguably, a 1980s version of the 'expeditionary force mentality' of earlier decades). While links with the USA remained important, ANZUS was no longer the centrepiece. Engagement with Asia became a *leitmotif*. It was politically convenient to overlook the degree to which Liberal ministers such as Casey had reoriented at least the foreign-policy-making machinery towards Asia, but the Labor governments established priorities that appear irreversible: most notably, a commitment to multilateral regional bodies such as Asia Pacific Economic Cooperation (APEC), and the cultivation of close relationships with Indonesia and other ASEAN nations. Although ambivalence about 'Australia as part of Asia' remains within the community, trade imperatives and the changing ethnic composition of the Australian population will ensure that engagement with Asia remains central to foreign policy. John **Howard**, coalition prime minster from 1996, claimed that the tension between Australia's history and its geography is a thing of the past.

JOAN BEAUMONT

Forests, their use or misuse, have dominated **environmental** politics since the mid-1970s. The debates began in nineteenth-century conflicts when early **conservationists** pleaded that some forests be saved from clearing for **land settlement**. Many trees which were young then are still standing as veterans, their lives first shaped by the Aboriginal **fire-stick farming** of the land. Their evolutionary history can be traced back through changing climatic periods to the drift of continents from **Gondwanaland**. At the time of European settlement, there were seven million hectares of unique forests and 180 million hectares of woodland characterised by the ubiquitous eucalypts and marsupials. Three-quarters of the 43 million hectares now remaining are still in public possession, now divided in roughly equal parts between state forests, conservation reserves and Crown land. Most have been modified to varying degrees. The small area of tropical rainforests has such a profusion of endemic species that most of them were placed on the World Heritage list in the 1980s.

A 'case for forest conservancy' was advanced in Victoria in 1865 to counter the devastation of the goldfields forests. Similar concerns in NSW led to the gazetting of permanent reservations of forest land in 1871. Erroneous arguments that forests attracted rain were advanced and the **timber industry** needed forests to be reserved from selection. However, it was not until the 1890s when large sawmills were built chiefly with British capital in WA, and later in Tasmania, that significant areas started to be reserved. The case for conservation followed an imperial model, which called for the best forests to be 'demarcated' as permanent state forests and for a cadre of professionally trained foresters, employed in public forest services, to manage them on sustained-yield principles free from 'the evil influence of politics'. L.T. Carron in *A History of Forestry in Australia* (1985) showed how the case was urged by visiting imperial foresters 1887–1916, including the prestigious Inspector-General of Forests for India, Berthold Ribbentrop, in 1895. SA created its Woods and Forests Department in 1883 largely to establish plantations, and the other states followed between 1907 and 1920. The cause of forestry was heralded by Sir Ronald **Munro-Ferguson**, governor-general 1914–20, and advanced in Empire Forestry Conferences in which he later, as Lord Novar, played an active role. Australia's 1920 Interstate Forestry Conference set a national target of 25 million acres (10 million hectares) to be reserved as state forest, a goal not reached until 1966 due to opposition from state lands departments.

The forest services failed to manage the native forests on sustained-yield principles or prevent them from being severely overcut during the 1950s and 1960s boom. The threat of a timber shortage led them, along with some companies and individuals, to increase the area of plantations until there were over one million hectares by 1990. The **Collins House Group** built three pulp mills in 1936–41. The paper industry expanded rapidly during the boom and its demand for pulpwood enabled old trees of poor timber-quality in the native forests to be replaced with even-aged crops of fast-growing young ones. Replacement greatly increased when five large mills were started in Tasmania, NSW and WA in 1970–76 to export woodchips to Japan. A few small mills followed and within a decade five times more pulpwood was being cut each year. To the foresters' surprise, this transformation of the native forests was vehemently opposed by the rising environment movement, which asserted the need to protect the habitat of native animals in old trees and other non-timber values of the forests. A dozen public inquiries and environmental impact assessments were held 1974–90, and logging practices were improved, but the quantities of woodchips exported were repeatedly increased. As the environment movement gained strength through the 1970s, it mounted campaigns to 'save' state forests from logging by having them registered as part of the **National Estate**, or transferred to **national parks** or 'wilderness' reservations. Major blockades at Terania Creek (NSW) 1979, the Franklin River (Tasmania) 1982, the Daintree rainforest (North Qld) 1982–83, and campaigns to stop new pulp mills (Tasmania and Victoria) 1988–89 were accompanied by a great many smaller events throughout the forest regions.

John Dargavel's *Fashioning Australia's Forests* (1995) shows how the environmental conflicts were exacerbated from the mid-1970s by the inevitable reduction in the quantities of sawlogs available from the overcut native forests and by labour-shedding as the industry was restructured. Years of politically damaging disputes within and between the Commonwealth and state governments led them to agree on a *National Forest Policy Statement* in 1992, which aims to provide a comprehensive national system of reserves for environmental protection while securing resources for industry. Its successful implementation remains a hope.

Forest history is an active sub-field from several perspectives. The forest is increasingly seen as an actor in history, rather than merely scenery. Studies such as Tom Griffiths, *Secrets of the Forest* (1992), and many commissioned **heritage** studies are an important part of its public history. The Australian Forest History Society, formed in 1988, holds periodic national conferences.

JOHN DARGAVEL

Forgan Smith, William, see Smith, William Forgan

Forrest brothers represent the first generation of locally born Western Australians to rise to wealth and power. JOHN FORREST (1847–1918) was an explorer, first premier of WA, and key figure in the first two decades of federal politics; ALEXANDER (1849–1901) was an explorer and entrepreneur.

John and Alexander began as surveyors; they achieved early prominence through transcontinental expeditions in 1870 and 1874, led by John with his brother as second-in-command, which through competent bushcraft crossed Australia from west to east without the drama and privation of earlier explorers. As reward, John received a grant of 5000 acres of Crown land; his journals were published as *Explorations in Australia* (1875), and he became deputy surveyor-general and later surveyor-general of WA.

Forrest was a member of the Executive and Legislative Councils from 1883 to 1890, and this experience led to his selection as the colony's first premier in 1890, a position he retained until he entered the first federal ministry in 1901. It is from this period in his life that he is most remembered, for his forceful leadership, ambitious public works program, and indefatigable promotion of agricultural development. He was fortunate in that his premiership coincided with the **gold rushes**, which brought people and capital into the colony at a time when eastern Australia was in depression. But his policies made the most of this good fortune to create a much-needed infrastructure of railways, ports, and water supply. Though his politics were generally conservative, he was also responsible for significant reforms, including the enfranchisement of women in 1899 and the establishment of an **arbitration** court in 1900, in advance of most of Australia.

Forrest was a long-term supporter of the **Federation** movement, though critics then and later have questioned this. At the Federal Conventions he failed to get a Senate as strong as he wished, but left his mark through his decisive support for a Commonwealth arbitration power and his support also for a pension power. Most of his political supporters in the West were anti-federalists, however, whereas his urban and goldfields critics leaned the other way. After last-ditch attempts to get special concessions failed, he eventually persuaded a recalcitrant Legislative Council to allow a referendum at which he led the 'yes' campaign to success, and was then elected unopposed for the seat of Swan in the first parliament.

Dubbed the 'Emperor of the West' by George **Reid**, Forrest and his wife Margaret held court from a suite in the Grand Hotel, Melbourne, when on parliamentary duty. He did not achieve his ambition of becoming prime minister, losing by one vote to Joseph **Cook** in 1913; but he was a major force in bringing about the federal **Fusion** of 1909 and held Cabinet posts for most of the period 1901–18, including five terms as treasurer. He is the only Western Australian who can stand alongside **Barton**, **Deakin**, and company as one of the great founding figures of Australian politics; and the first Australian to be made a peer. F.K. **Crowley**, *Forrest 1847–1918*, vol. 1 (1971), tells the story only to 1891.

Where his elder brother's career developed through public service, Alexander made his way as a contract surveyor. In 1879 he discovered and explored the Kimberley region, subsequently becoming a land agent. Substantial involvement in **pastoralism** and **timber** was followed in the 1890s by investments in goldmining, urban real estate, retailing, and **newspapers** which made him a very wealthy man. A member of parliament throughout the 1890s, he never held office but was government whip, and also served two three-year terms as mayor of Perth. In the public eye he was always identified with northern pastoralism and was criticised as the initiator of an alleged 'meat ring' which, it was claimed, kept beef prices high at the expense of consumers. With hindsight, he closely resembles the Western Australian entrepreneurs of the 1980s and was similarly criticised for blurring the boundaries between politics and business. He and John were at the heart of a network of social, economic, and political power and influence which included their six brothers and an army of relatives and friends. The only biography is *Alexander Forrest: His Life and Times* (1958) by a youthful G.C. **Bolton**.

BRIAN DE GARIS

Foundations are the rock upon which communities build their history. Many traditional societies have their foundation myths—Rome, for example, has the story of Romulus and Remus—but modern settler societies like Australia have demonstrated a special interest in the seminal acts of their symbolic fathers, such as explorers, discoverers, governors, and pioneers. Beginnings were important, for in the character and conduct of a society's founders, it was believed, its destiny was also revealed. In Australia, where white settlers assumed possession of the land largely without negotiation with Aborigines, the act of foundation was also the first step in the creation of a legitimating narrative through which that conquest was ratified and celebrated.

Englishmen coming to Australia looked back on a history already rich in such founding moments—Queen Elizabeth's charter for the 'plantation' of Virginia, the Pilgrim Fathers' symbolic touching of Plymouth Rock, the Quaker Robert Penn's treaty with the Indians of Pennsylvania. The bluff sea-captains and commercial adventurers who founded the Australian colonies had no special gift for symbolism, but they knew what was expected of them. Reading proclamations, hoisting flags, firing guns, laying commemorative stones, preaching sermons, making treaties, putting names on maps—by such acts the newcomers dignified what others would come to see as an **invasion**. Later generations would commemorate them in histories, **monuments**, **paintings**, and **pageants** and sometimes, when subversion rather than celebration was their purpose, in protest and burlesque.

The European foundation of Australia may be said to have begun with Captain James **Cook's** landing at Botany Bay in 1770, or perhaps with his formal claim to the east coast and its naming as 'New South Wales' at Possession Island on 22 August. But later histories more often begin with the arrival of a fleet of convict ships (the **First Fleet**) under the command of Captain Arthur **Phillip** at Sydney Cove in 1788. The reasons behind the foundation of this, the first permanent **settlement**, are treated elsewhere in this volume. Phillip had first landed at Botany Bay on 20 January 1788, but finding the site unsuitable—the harbour was shallow and unsheltered and the supply of fresh water poor—he explored the nearby harbour of Port Jackson, 'the finest harbour in the world', and settled on a site at the mouth of a creek, which became known as the Tank Stream. At midday on 26 January the officers and marines landed, the Union Jack was hoisted on a flagpole, their majesties and the Prince of Wales were toasted in porter, and the marines fired off a round of shots, after which everyone trooped back on board the ships. Over the following week the convicts were landed and a campsite laid out, but it was not until 3 February that the chaplain, Reverend Richard **Johnson**, invoked the blessings of Providence on the new colony. 'What shall I render unto the Lord for all his benefits toward me?', he asked his captive congregation. On 6 February the women convicts at last were landed, and that night a riot of debauchery ensued. Next morning Phillip assembled the whole company and read his commission as 'Commander in Chief' of NSW.

Historians have woven different tales, with different morals, around these founding acts. In many of these, Arthur Phillip becomes the symbolic father of the nation, endowed by providence with special gifts and opportunities. 'He was the founder of a new European State in a land where civilised man had never lived before', wrote Ernest **Scott**. Julian Thomas shows in his unpublished doctoral thesis on the 1938 sesquicentenary (Australian National University, 1992) how contemporary novelists and painters enhanced the image of Phillip as 'Founder of Australia'. Those, however, like **Aborigines** or **feminists**, who contest this patriarchal vision of Australian history, often reinterpret the narrative on which

is based. Phillip, they say, was not only the carrier of European civilisation but of European diseases which would all but destroy the Aboriginal peoples; not only the father of nation but an 'imperial whoremaster' who thought of women merely as the playthings of men. Turning the foundation myth on its head, a 1988 satirical film shows a fleet of Aborigines coming ashore amid a picnic party of white Australians and laying claim to a land they name 'Barbecue-area'.

The foundation of Van Diemen's Land was attended with almost no ceremony at all. The decision to establish a southern settlement had been taken by Governor **King** in 1802 largely in order to forestall a possible French settlement and to take the overflow of convicts to NSW. An expedition under the new Lieutenant-Governor David **Collins** had first explored the entrance to Port Phillip and made a camp near present-day Sorrento (where a few headstones still mark the spot), but was deterred from making a permanent settlement by the lack of fresh water and the difficulty of navigating the entrance to the bay. Meanwhile Lieutenant John Bowen had been sent to explore the Derwent and had established a camp at Risdon Cove on 11 September 1803. After abandoning the settlement at Port Phillip, Collins sailed on to the Derwent; there he succeeded Bowen, and abandoned the exposed Risdon site in favour of a more sheltered site at the mouth of what became known as the Hobart Rivulet on 22 February 1804. The decision had been made under pressure—some of Collins's men were close to mutiny when he left Port Phillip—and the settlement was effectively established by the time Collins accompanied the Rev. Robert Knopwood ashore on 26 February. Knopwood preached a sermon about the prosperity of the new settlement and prayed God's blessing on it. The best short account is in Lloyd **Robson's** A History of Tasmania, vol. 1 (1983).

Knowing one's foundation day, like knowing one's birthday, was a proof of legitimacy. Most of the Australian colonies had grown continuously on the sites their founders first chose for them. In Qld, however, the sequence of settlement was too confused to produce such a satisfying moment of foundation. 'The connection may seem tenuous indeed between modern Brisbane and the first tiny settlement of unhappy prisoners and unenthusiastic military overseers', wrote the city's official historians apologetically in 1959. The surveyor-general of NSW, John **Oxley**, who was sent in 1823 by Governor Brisbane to found a new convict settlement, first chose a site at Redcliff on Moreton Bay; it was only three months later, in a decision apparently unmarked by ceremony, that he decided to remove it to the present site of Brisbane. What date should Queenslanders regard as their birthday? The foundation day of the abortive settlement at Redcliff? The forced move to Brisbane? The official proclamation of the penal settlement in 1826? Or even perhaps the establishment of Queensland as a separate colony in 1859?

Western Australians generally date their origins from the expedition of Captain James **Stirling**, a British naval officer, to the Swan River in 1827. Stirling was so impressed by the prospects of settlement that he persuaded the British government to mount a further expedition. Captain Charles

Fremantle arrived at the mouth of the Swan and took possession of the whole of Australia not within NSW on 2 May 1829. Stirling, who arrived later, proclaimed the foundation of the colony on 18 June and formally established its capital on 12 August. Fremantle described the event: 'On the 12th, our Party increased, and there being no stone contiguous for our purpose, to celebrate the commencement of the new town, Mrs Dance cut down a tree; fired volleys, made speeches, and gave several Cheers, named the Town Perth, according to the wishes of Sir George Murray [Secretary for the Colonies].' Unfavourable geology, it would seem, cost WA the chance of having its own Plymouth Rock, though cutting down a tree was perhaps a more fitting start to the process of colonisation. Like other founders James Stirling was invested by patriots with qualities of 'vision, tenacity and enterprise'. Historians critical of this 'gentry view' of Western Australian history, however, paint its founder in less heroic hues; Tom Stannage begins *The People of Perth* by deconstructing George Pitt-Morison's heroic 1929 history painting of the foundation, throws doubt on Stirling's choice of a site for the capital, and portrays the man himself as a 'rapacious' speculator.

Probably no Australian colony was founded with higher hopes than South Australia. From the beginning its founders, the 'systematic colonisers' of the South Australian Company, had planned a semi-rural utopia free of the stain of convictism. On 28 December 1836, a date since celebrated by South Australians as Proclamation Day, the governor of the new colony, John **Hindmarsh**, gathered together some 200 new settlers at Holdfast Bay. A witness recorded: 'The Governor's Private Secretary read the Proclamation under a huge gum tree, a flag was hoisted, a party of marines from the *Buffalo* fired a *feu-de-joie* and loud hurrahs succeeded.' The scene is memorably depicted in Charles Hill's painting of 1855; the 'Proclamation Tree', which long survived at Glenelg, became a pioneer shrine. The *South Australian Record* likened the colony's founders to such other sojourners as Noah, Moses, Aeneas, and the 'stout-hearted Britons' who built up North America. Their act of foundation was 'the bright strong line between desolate barbarism and busy civilisation'. Although the new settlement was full of promise, its commander, the autocratic and avaricious Captain Hindmarsh, proved an unsatisfactory founding father; later historians have often promoted his rival, the designer of Adelaide, Colonel William **Light**, to the role.

Such rivalries were not unusual. The colony of Port Phillip, later to become Victoria, was the only Australian colony to be founded by private enterprise. In the mid-1830s rival syndicates of pastoralists and businessmen from Van Diemen's Land, led by John **Batman** and John Pascoe **Fawkner**, sought to open up the rich country across the strait at the head of Port Phillip Bay. In June Batman sailed up the Saltwater River and negotiated a 'treaty' with the Dutigalla Aborigines for land which included the present site of Melbourne; but he did not actually set foot on that section of the Yarra until November, when Fawkner and his party had already established themselves there. Each would-be founder sought to claim some shred of legitimacy for his actions: Batman through his treaty, Fawkner by recalling his father's membership, 30 years earlier, of the ill-fated Collins expedition. Governor Richard **Bourke** promptly ruled Batman's 'treaty' invalid and Fawkner's occupation illegal. Yet Victorians, to this day, continue to debate their rival claims as founders. Descendants of John Batman, a bushman and a son of convicts, plead for the erection of a monument over his grave in the Melbourne General Cemetery, while admirers of Fawkner, mainly city businessmen, contributed funds to build a replica of his ship, the *Enterprize*.

Founding fathers may have a weaker claim on the historical imagination in the age of **Mabo** than they did half a century ago. But the need for a founder, like the need for a father, may be stronger than even grown-up nations acknowledge. Pamela Statham (ed.), *The Origins of the Australian Capital Cities* (1989), contains excellent chapters on the foundations of all the states. The best discussion of colonial birthdays and how they were celebrated is in K.S. **Inglis**, *The Australian Colonists* (1974). Joan Kerr has an illustrated essay on paintings of foundations in *Australians: A Historical Dictionary* (1987).

GRAEME DAVISON

Fragment thesis was advanced by the American historian Louis Hartz in *The Founding of New Societies: Studies in the History of the United States, Latin America, South Africa, Canada, and Australia* (1964). Hartz identified Europe's colonies of settlement as fragments of Europe, whose nature and course were determined by the ideology which prevailed when they left the mother culture. So Latin America is a feudal fragment; the USA is a liberal, bourgeois fragment, and Australia is a radical, proletarian, collectivist fragment. In the New World the fragment ideology is nationalised so that its European references are lost and it comes to be regarded as a distinctive indigenous ethos. The liberal ideology becomes 'the American way'; the radical and collectivist ideology becomes mateship. Europe remains a dynamic society with ideologies in contention and new ideologies forming, but the fragments become conservative, their development limited and controlled by their founding ideology. In the twentieth century, however, the isolated and inward-looking fragments have to face those European developments which they have hitherto escaped. A new generation knows more of the wider world and realises the fragment is not the whole universe, that it has been impoverished by its isolation.

Hartz's book consists of the statement of the thesis by him and attempts by other authors to apply it to various New World countries. The Australian section was written by Richard N. Rosecrance. The thesis received respectful attention, but it did not win assent or committed followers. Nonetheless, it has been influential. In stressing the importance of origins, it gave new authority to the long-established preoccupation with **foundations** and a new excuse for not pursuing inquiry beyond them. More usefully, it directed historians away from the local environment as the chief determinant of colonial distinctiveness and towards the culture migrants brought with them, though even those who accepted this perspective employed the totally inappropriate term 'cultural baggage', which had been coined by the environmentalists who thought cultural inheritance could be readily put down or lost.

Oddly, the history which comes closest to following a Hartzian trajectory was published before Hartz wrote: Douglas **Pike's** *Paradise of Dissent: South Australia 1829–1857* (1957). The first quarter of the book is devoted to establishing the colony's foundation ideology as it was formed in Britain—civil liberty, social opportunity, equality of all religions—and the book explores how these aims, bred in opposition, became ruling paradigms in the New World. It concludes, in Hartzian terms, that the leading colonists, having achieved their aims, became complacent and conservative.

These colonists were middle-class and their ideology was untouched by collectivism. Hartz on Australia appears to be fatally flawed because of his insistence that this was a proletarian fragment, where a working-class ethos was always strong and the middle-class weak. The Labor Party's easy success and its collectivism are linked to the founding population of convicts and working-class migrants. This view had Australian authority, but was being discredited just as Hartz wrote. Its acceptance by Hartz was one of the chief criticisms levelled against him by Allan **Martin** and Geoffrey **Bolton** in an issue of *AEHR* (1973) devoted to an assessment of the thesis. Martin, a leading exponent of middle-class hegemony post-1850, considered the free-enterprise liberals who controlled the NSW parliament would have been perfectly at home in that liberal fragment, the USA. He conceded the greater collectivist tendency in the Australian polity, but saw this too as emanating from the needs of the middle class.

It might be said in Hartz's defence that there was a fundamental shift in British culture occurring just at the time the Australian colonies were settled. Working people were making claims for inclusion in the nation; reformers of various sorts were envisaging a time when 'the poor' would become respectable citizens. This shift had its effect on the *zeitgeist* of the Australian colonies and helped to give working people a higher status and their claims more consideration than in, say, the USA. The transformation of British working-class institutions into national bodies in Australia has been examined within a Hartzian framework by John Hirst (*HS*, 1984).

Feminist historians have been newly concerned with origins. Miriam **Dixson**, in *The Real Matilda* (1976), accepted Hartz's characterisation of a proletarian fragment and traced the low standing of women in Australia to the attitudes of convicts, the casual poor, and the Irish. Patricia Grimshaw thought women's standing was much higher (for otherwise why did they so early acquire the franchise?), and attributed this to the wide acceptance of companionate marriage, a later British import (*HS*, 1979) This difference highlights a central problem in Hartz: can the European inheritance be given a single characterisation and when does the fragment 'break away'?

Hartz's book is rich and provocative, juggling ideologies and their representative exponents in metaphoric, almost metaphysical, mode, a continuing challenge to the materialist and empirical approach to Australian history.

JOHN HIRST

Franklin, John (1786–1847) and **Jane** (1791–1875) arrived in Van Diemen's Land upon his appointment as lieutenant-governor in 1837 as successor to George **Arthur**. Franklin inherited a colony full of conflicting interests and hostility to government. Lack of administrative experience and a certain naivety made Franklin vulnerable to the intrigues of colonial officials, in particular the colonial secretary, John Montagu, and the treasurer, Matthew Foster. A high-minded pair, whose relationship Penny Russell considers in *For Richer, For Poorer* (1994), the Franklins promoted the intellectual life of the colony, established a natural history museum, and improved the educational system. Lady Franklin was an indefatigable traveller who resented the traditional circumscribed life of the 'governor's lady'. She maintained an active, if unfulfilled, interest in penal reform.

The conflict with the officials came to a head in 1842, when Franklin suspended Montagu. Montagu's appeal, in which he represented Lady Franklin as interfering in government business, was upheld, and Franklin was recalled in 1843. His desperate appeals finally won him the leadership of the ill-fated 1847 expedition to discover a northwest passage to the Arctic. Kathleen **Fitzpatrick's** *Sir John Franklin in Tasmania* (1949) gives a sympathetic account of his experience. The Franklins are remembered in Tasmania by the river that bears their name.

KT

Franklin, (Stella Maria Sarah) Miles (1879– 1954) has been recognised primarily for her significant, and controversial, part as a writer in shaping cultural nationalism. Her influence and the controversy continue in the interpretation of the terms of her bequest—the Miles Franklin Award for Australian literature—which require that the successful novel portray some aspect of Australian life. Franklin's advocacy of Australian writing has been more often interpreted against current debates about radical nationalism than in terms of her own diverse social and political commitments.

She was born at Talbingo, NSW, and her first novel, the autobiographical *My Brilliant Career*, appeared in 1901. The story of a young woman's rebellion against the strictures of her life on her parents' dairy farm, her life as a pupil teacher in a bush school, and her rejection of marriage to a young squatter, the novel drew on aspects of her own life. Henry **Lawson** supplied a preface which praised the work lavishly while describing it, with a touch of condescension, as 'girl's work'. The promise of the first novel was not fulfilled until *All That Swagger* (1936) won the S.H. Prior prize. The four novels Franklin published as 'Brent of Bin Bin', and the considerable energy she expended on the secret of the pseudonym, have diverted attention from her social commentary. Her critical works include a biography of Joseph **Furphy**

(1944), written with Kate Baker, and her lectures on Australian writing, *Laughter, Not for a Cage* (1956), which promoted the works of Furphy and Brent as it sketched the contours of an 'Australian' literature. That collection and her correspondence reveal a more complex engagement with social change and politics than a narrowly conceived nationalism can accommodate.

In 1905, through affiliations with feminists Rose **Scott** and Vida **Goldstein**, Franklin went to Chicago where she worked with the Women's Trade Union League and plunged into the politics of labour reform. With Alice **Henry**, she co-edited *Life and Labour*, a journal for women workers, whose industrial and intellectual interests she addressed through her own contributions, and stories from writers like Elizabeth Robins and Charlotte Perkins Gilman. Franklin's Chicago experience, described by Verna Coleman in *Her Unknown (Brilliant) Career* (1981) and Drusilla Modjeska in *Exiles at Home* (1981), left its literary traces in *The Net of Circumstance* (1915) and *On Dearborn Street* (1981).

After the collaboration with Henry broke down, Franklin moved to London in 1915. There she established a similar labour and feminist network, working in housing and urban reform movements. She waitressed at the Women's Freedom League's Minerva Café, and worked at Margaret McMillan's school for working-class children in Deptford. Among her friends there were Margaret Hodge and Harriet Newcomb, who had run a progressive school in Sydney. Franklin's friendship with the poet Mary **Fullerton** was also established in this period. Franklin acted as an agent for Fullerton's work and Fullerton reciprocated, acting as an intermediary for 'Brent of Bin Bin'.

Franklin returned to Australia permanently in 1932. A voluminous correspondence, collected by Jill Roe in *My Congenials* (1993), records the continuation of her American and English friendships. She also found a place in Australian literary and political life. She was active in the Fellowship of Australian Writers and kept in contact with an influential circle of women writers. These exchanges are reconstructed in Carole Ferrier's *As Good as a Yarn With You* (1992). They reveal racial prejudices and an apparent sexual conservatism that should be scrutinised rather than dismissed.

Miles Franklin's reputation has largely been left to literary critics. The comment by her biographer Marjorie **Barnard** in 1967 that Franklin's writing is indivisible from her living has been the measure of critical response. Franklin's endorsement of cultural nationalism produced a backlash from modernist critics who cringed at her shrill, even mindless, radicalism; others romanticise her interest in Australia and the bush as an expression of nostalgia. Feminist critics sought to retrieve her reputation by situating her work more critically within the nationalist tradition, or within a broader tradition of women's writing. An alternative account might specify the wider contexts of Franklin's work: attending to the political affiliations and personal associations which sustained it and to her own critical understanding of the role of literature in constructing 'Australian' experience.

KAY FERRES

Fraser, Dawn Lorraine (1937–), fastest woman swimmer in the world between 1956 and 1964, was born in Sydney, the youngest of eight children in a close working-class family that was dominated by her four elder brothers. Asthma problems plagued her childhood in Balmain, but long hours swimming at Elkington Park Baths brought relief. Fraser won her first amateur championship at 14, only to be banned for more than a year because she had once swum with a professional club. Harry Gallagher began coaching her in 1952. She trained with Jon Henricks and used 'legs tied' routines to build enormous upper-body strength. Aged 19 at the 1956 Melbourne **Olympic Games**, Fraser broke the oldest world record in swimming to win the 100-metre freestyle in 1:02.0. When she won again at Rome in 1960 and Tokyo in 1964, she became the first swimmer to win the same event at three successive Olympic Games. Fraser was the first female swimmer to break the one-minute barrier in the 100-metre freestyle. She won eight Olympic medals (four gold and four silver), and six gold and two silver medals at British Empire and Commonwealth Games. She drank beer, smoked heavily, and broke 39 world swimming records. Her wild streak caused many problems with officials, culminating in 1964 at the Tokyo Olympics when police arrested her trying to 'souvenir' a flag from the Imperial Palace. Consequently, she was banned for 10 years by the Amateur Swimming Union of Australia. 'It was fun while it lasted', Fraser wrote in *Gold Medal Girl* (1965). She became a publican and represented Balmain in the NSW parliament 1988–91.

DC

Fraser, Eliza (?1798–1858) was travelling with her husband, James Fraser, captain of the *Stirling Castle*, when they were shipwrecked in May 1836 off the coast of Qld. The Frasers and several other survivors landed on the Great Sandy Island—later renamed Fraser Island—where they were held by local Badtjala people. Most of the survivors, including Captain Fraser, were killed and his wife was beaten and enslaved, according to her later account—an account marked by contradictions and unanswered questions. The **Moreton Bay** settlement was galvanised in August by news of the captivity, and a rescue party sent. *A Narrative of the Capture, Sufferings, and Miraculous Escape of Mrs. Eliza Fraser* (1837), claiming to be her own account, was published anonymously, followed by many other works. Her emergence as a mythical figure is apparent in the series of paintings by Sidney **Nolan** and in Patrick **White's** novel *A Fringe of Leaves* (1976). A film, *Eliza Fraser*, appeared in 1976. She was later taken up in studies of **captivity narratives**. Kay Schaffer, *In the Wake of First Contact* (1995), and Chris Healy, *From the Ruins of Colonialism* (1997), examine various representations of the Eliza Fraser story.

KT

Fraser, (John) Malcolm (1930–), Liberal Party leader and prime minister 1975–83, won power in controversial circumstances following the **Dismissal** of the Whitlam government, and proved to be a transitional figure—foreshadowing Thatcherite economics, but attached still to the verities of nation-building.

Scion of a wealthy pastoral family, he was educated at private schools and at Oxford University, where he read politics, philosophy, and economics. Thereafter, he took up a family property in Victoria's Western District and in 1955 became the Liberal member for this area in the federal parliament. Youth and an aloof style kept him on the backbench for 10 years. In his successive portfolios, army (1966–68), education and science (1968–69 and 1971–72), and defence (1969–71), Fraser began to develop the administrative style that was to be characteristic of his prime ministership—intense application, immense demands on his staff, advice from personal networks, canvassing of a range of opinion, then a personal decision from which he could rarely be moved.

Fraser supported John **Gorton** to succeed Harold **Holt** in 1967, but he took exception to Gorton's larrikin style and failure to consult, and resigned from Cabinet in 1971, making public his criticisms of his leader. This was the catalyst for Gorton's own downfall and replacement by William **McMahon**. When Whitlam won government in 1972, Bill Snedden took over the Liberal Party leadership. Fraser's supporters then undertook a war of attrition, toppling Snedden in March 1975.

Fraser's brinkmanship was dramatically manifest later that year when, gambling on Whitlam's declining fortunes, the opposition blocked supply bills in the Senate. Governor-General Sir John **Kerr** intervened; he dismissed Whitlam and appointed Fraser as caretaker prime minister until an election—held in December—returned a Fraser government by a huge margin. Fraser won further elections in 1977 and in 1980 before being defeated in 1983, after which he resigned from parliament.

Though a strong and aggressive leader, Fraser was criticised for his record in government, not least by his own side. The economic tide was turning against the nation-building project but, although an advocate of small government and a reduced public sector, Fraser was enough of a nationalist, and still shared enough of the instincts of ameliorative liberalism, to resist the extremes of economic rationalism. When recession hit in 1982, the harbinger of Thatcher and Reagan was said to have been insufficiently rigorous.

In 1985 Fraser was appointed by the **Hawke** government as representative on an eminent persons group investigating South African apartheid. He became active in human rights and international aid agencies. As the Liberal Party embraced deregulatory economic policies, Fraser became an increasingly lonely voice calling for balance between national needs and market demands. On a series of issues that included Aboriginal **reconciliation**, the republic, refugees, and the American alliance, he broke party ranks. In his long political afterlife, a man once regarded as an unbending Tory touched the national conscience.

Patrick Weller's *Malcolm Fraser PM* (1989) analyses the prime minister's work and ways of wielding power; this remains perhaps the best Australian study of leadership and administrative style. Graham Little, contrasting Fraser's ruthless ambition with his lonely childhood and unease at the interpersonal level, presents him as the classic 'fight or flight' leader in *Strong Leadership* (1988). Alan Renouf has surveyed Fraser's foreign policy (1986), but for a wider conspectus of the views behind policy across the spectrum, see David Kemp and Denis White (eds), *Malcolm Fraser on Australia* (1986).

JAMES WALTER

'Free, secular and compulsory' were conditions set down in Victoria's Education Act of 1872 and followed by other colonies, though their **education** systems were not so rigorously secular. They retained separate religious instruction by the denominations and instruction in common Christianity but these were as unacceptable as complete secularism to the **Catholic** hierachy, which prompted the building of a separate Catholic school system. This operated without government assistance until 1964.

HD

Free thought flourished in late-nineteenth-century radical and working-class culture throughout the English-speaking world. British-derived, with roots in the Enlightenment and the French Revolution, the movement extolled reason, science, and secular values. Like Karl Marx, freethinkers regarded religion as oppressive. They envisaged a world free of churches, especially state churches like the Church of England. Espousing such causes as freedom of the press, birth control, and anti-Sabbatarianism, the movement represented radical politics before socialism. With a vigorous presence in North America as well as Australia, its characteristic methods were the public lecture and the pamphlet. Its heroes were Thomas Paine, Charles Bradlaugh, Robert Ingersoll, and Annie Besant.

Free thought found scant encouragement in early Australia, as radical settler John Boston learned in 1795, when his pig was shot when it strayed into Sydney's 'military district'. While there was no established church, evangelical religion and repressive social legislation derived from Britain abounded. After the gold rushes, the movement made its way by immigration, evangelism, and affront. Ex-Chartist Daniel Wallwork founded the first known Secular Society, in Newcastle in 1862. Sculptor Lorando Jones became its first hero, arrested in Parramatta Park for blasphemy in 1871. In Sydney in 1887, radicals and freethinkers disrupted plans to celebrate Queen Victoria's Jubilee, and claimed a glorious victory for Democracy.

The 1880s were the heyday of organised free thought in Australia. Organisation was easier in Melbourne; it is still the only scene studied, by F.B. Smith's MA thesis (University of Melbourne, 1960) and Jill Roe in *Journal of Religious History* (1968). In 1884 Bradlaugh's protégé Joseph Symes was appointed lecturer to the Australasian Secular Association (Melbourne branch, 1882–97) with funds to start a journal, *The Liberator* (1884–1904). In stiffer Sydney, efforts to unify the movement's disparate elements failed, but, as in provincial cities from Fremantle to Charters Towers, diverse and colourful autodidacts bestrode the free-thought platforms, and a Hall of Science was opened in 1890. In the short run, free thought encouraged many colonial intellectuals, including feminist Louisa **Lawson** and her son Henry, who disliked parsons. In the long run, according to the only history of **censorship** in Australia to date—*Obscenity, Blasphemy, Sedition* (1963), by Peter Coleman—it became mainstream.

In the *Encyclopedia of Unbelief* (1985), David Tribe observes Australian free-thought organisations 'flare like comets and fade as quickly'. Free thought fragmented in the 1890s. Halls of Science bespoke success; but these 'Temples of Reason' also resembled churches. Factionalism and new prescriptions, such as socialism and theosophy, caused pandemonium (as suggested in Bruce Scates, *A New Australia*, 1997). Paradoxically, the diverse origins of colonial free thought, in spiritualism, communism, republicanism, and the like, ensured survival within the small intelligentsia in the coming century (although beyond **labour history**, few strands have been traced). Meanwhile, the colonial exuberance dissipated. Lecturer Ada Campbell disappeared in NZ in the 1880s; sex reformer William **Chidley** was incarcerated as insane in 1912; and the diminutive Wallace Nelson became editor of the *Australasian Manufacturer* during World War I.

New life came from rationalist publishing initiatives and World War I, when *Ross's Monthly* (Melbourne, 1915–24) ably upheld free-thought idealism. But postwar rationalism mostly meant aridity and masculinism. The big men behind the associations were native-born businessmen: in Sydney W.J. Miles, now better known as father of the eccentric Bea, and in Melbourne industrialist W.D. Cookes, both extreme right-wing nationalists. Miles was secretary of the Rationalist Society of NSW 1914–20 and later funded P.R. **Stephensen's** *The Publicist* (1936–42). Sydney's volatile (and sectarian) circumstances strengthened the first significant native-born lecturer, Harry Scott Bennett; but Cookes and W. Glanville 'Bill' Cook kept a tight rein in Victoria. In Perth, Thomas Walker, trance lecturer risen to Cabinet minister, sought to implement free-thought reforms. Most freethinkers found new homes, usually in left-wing politics; and there was scarcely a woman in sight.

In 1927 indigenous rationalism received a great boost. Scottish-born philosophy professor, communist-cum-libertarian John **Anderson**, was appointed to the University of Sydney. The iconoclastic Anderson's University Freethought Society lasted from 1930 to 1951, when he formed the Libertarian Society. A more liberal approach was kept alive by Public Questions Societies; 'halfway houses', such as Unitarianism; and, as civil liberties and censorship became increasingly problematic in the interwar years, by Melbourne historian Brian **Fitzpatrick**.

Rationalism was largely superseded in the early 1960s by humanist societies, which formed first in Sydney following scandal surrounding the Anglican archbishop. (In Brisbane the rationalists simply changed their name.) Meanwhile, the

Cold War reactivated the free-thought tradition. Censorship became an urgent issue; and the thaw raised 'life matters'. As the influence of the churches over such matters as abortion, divorce, and sexual preference waned, secular values seemed at last to triumph in Australia.

Is free thought outdated? In traditional form, the answer must be yes, as in the failure of the Council for Defence of Government Schools, founded 1973, to prevent state aid to church schools. But to offer a definitive answer at present would be unwise. Biography suggests that free thought is firmly embedded—over half of the entries in Ray Dahlitz's *Secular Who's Who* (1994) also appear in the prestigious *ADB*—and the watchdog role of free thought is important. As the scope of religious history widens and intellectual traditions are clarified, it seems most likely that the often unruly and briefly triumphal free-thought tradition will be acknowledged as a vital component of Australian culture.

JILL ROE

Free trade, see **Protection**

Freedom Ride, based on a similar campaign undertaken by students in the USA, was a bus trip made by a group of University of Sydney students in February 1965 to towns in northern NSW which contained large Aboriginal populations. Led by Charles **Perkins** and Jim Spigelman, the participating students, historian Ann Curthoys among them, sought to survey the living conditions of Aborigines and the extent of racial disharmony. They met a particularly hostile reception at Moree and Walgett, where they protested against particular cases of white racial discrimination: Aboriginal children denied access to the local council swimming pool and Aboriginal ex-servicemen refused entry to the local RSL club.

HD

Freeland, John Maxwell (1920–83), architectural historian, graduated in architecture after war service and worked in private practice before lecturing in **architectural history**, first at the Royal Melbourne Institute of Technology and from 1957 at the University of New South Wales. *The Australian Pub* (1966) marks an important departure in Australian architectural history, not only in its blend of social and architectural analysis but in its focus on vernacular styles—an interest he developed further in *Rude Timber Buildings in Australia* (1969). *Architecture in Australia* (1968)—the first comprehensive history of the topic—aspires to a similar approach. 'The history of the architecture of a country is, in fact, the history of that country', he writes. But the organisation of the book around period styles—Colonial, Late Colonial, High Victorian, etc.—is more orthodox, and the social analysis is necessarily brief. His last book, *The Making of a Profession* (1971), is a history of the Royal Australian Institute of Architects.

GD

Freemasons, see **Benefit societies**; **Sectarianism**

Friendly societies, see **Australian Natives Association**; **Benefit societies**

Frontier was the word used in Australia and elsewhere throughout the New World to describe the areas, often wild and untamed, beyond the settled parts of the country. The word was in common use by the 1840s, when the first wave of pastoral expansion was in progress; the place had already gained the reputation of being 'inhabited by the most lawless portion of our lawless population'. The term gained wider currency after the turn of the century through the influence of the American historian Frederick Jackson Turner; according to his 'frontier thesis', first published in an article, 'The Significance of the Frontier', in 1893, the leading characteristics of US democracy—individualism and self-reliance—were those of the small farming communities of the West. The frontier thesis chimed well with the contemporary neo-Darwinian emphasis upon human interaction with the environment as a primary force in the evolution of peoples and races.

Australians developed their own versions of the frontier myth, although the place where the national spirit was created was often known by other names—**bush**, **outback** or **Never-Never**. Henry **Lawson**, for example, drew a sketch map showing the NSW interior as regionalised by frontiers of ever-increasing aridity and hardship; from east to west the traveller passed from 'up the country' and 'right up the country' to the 'outback' and the 'never-never'. The war correspondent and historian Charles **Bean** saw the frontier environment as a nursery of military virtues: fighting bushfires was how young Australians first learned the arts of battle. By the early twentieth century, the horizon of danger and adventure was moving further north and west, from the outback to 'back o' Bourke' and 'back of beyond'. John **Flynn's** Inland Mission and Flying Doctor Service, and the travel stories of Ion **Idriess** and Ernestine **Hill**, helped to define a new frontier in the remote cattle stations of the inland and the crocodile-infested waters of the NT. In the mythology of the time the frontier was no place for women. **Post-colonial** historians have since rediscovered, largely through the accounts of contemporary frontier women like the novelist Rosa **Praed**, the hidden injuries of sex and race which that myth suppressed. By World War II the frontier had moved beyond Australia's shores. In 1951 an American writer had written a study of *Australia's Frontier in New Guinea*; in 1967 John Young edited a history of *Australia's Pacific Frontier*; and in 1989 R.M. Laws described Australia's Antarctic Territory as *The Last Frontier*.

Fred **Alexander**, in his *Moving Frontiers* (1947), and Norman **Harper** may have been the first Australian historians to draw directly on Turner's 'frontier thesis'; in 1959 an American, H.C. Allen, attempted a comparative study of the American and Australian frontiers, *Bush and Backwoods*. In 1958 Russel **Ward** published *The Australian Legend*, the most influential contemporary interpretation of Australian **national identity**. Ward took over some of the evolution-

ary language of Turner's thesis, likening the influence of the frontier to 'a kind of natural selection' and tracing the influence of environmental features—remoteness, loneliness, freedom from the conventional constraints of society—upon the outlook and *mores* of those who inhabited it. But his interest in environment was balanced by a Marxist emphasis upon the ways in which its effects were mediated by the social relations of production. He argued that the typical Australian frontiersman was not a small, individualist farmer but a shearer or drover, and that his outlook was not individualist but collectivist. The frontier was where the first national type, the bushman, appeared and it was the place where national consciousness was strongest, as evidenced by the strong support of outback districts for **Federation**.

There were ambiguities in Ward's use of the frontier idea. Was the frontier a boundary or a space? Was it fixed or constantly moving? And were the mythic qualities he associated with it real or imagined? But although Ward's interpretation has been contested, the frontier has remained a significant reference point in historical writing, as it is in Australian popular mythology. The study of *Australia's First Frontier* (1963) by geographer Tom Perry plotted the spread of settlement during the founding years of NSW. Urban historians, following the lead of another American, Richard Wade, directed attention to Australia's 'urban frontier', and later to the suburban *Cream Brick Frontier* (1995). Historians of Aboriginal–white relations, led by Henry **Reynolds**, sought to look at Australian history from *The Other Side of the Frontier* (1981), while a pioneer feminist history, Miriam **Dixson's** *The Real Matilda* (1976), viewed the frontier as a site of both male brutality and female resilience.

The frontier was always both an idea and a place. It signified both a line on the map and a geographically indeterminate boundary between the known and the unknown, the civilised and the rude, the safe and the dangerous, the ordered and the anarchic. Although faith in the geographical determinism which inspired Turner and Ward has faded, the idea of the frontier and 'the noble frontiersman' retain a strong, if largely subliminal, purchase on the imagination of a nation now overwhelmingly urban and increasingly cosmopolitan. The idea sustains a belief, deeply planted in the life of new nations, that its spiritual energies come from within, from an encounter between people and the land itself. Crocodile Dundee, the hero of Paul Hogan's 1986 film, is a pastiche of Australian and American characteristics—half Henry Lawson's sardonic bushman Mitchell, and half Davy Crockett. But his triumphant journey from the frontier to the metropolis, from Kakadu to the Big Apple, is an ironic commentary on the Turnerian conviction—common to both America and Australia—that the true man is 'a man of the wild frontier'. In the late twentieth century the frontier myth, which reads Australian history from the edge to the centre, contends with rival interpretations in which meaning flows outward from a mythic Centre, denoted by **Uluru**, to the edge, or from the far corners of the globe, into an Australian melting-pot.

GRAEME DAVISON

Fullerton, Mary Eliza (1868–1946) was an avid reader and writer from her early childhood in rural Victoria. After moving to Melbourne, she attended Charles **Strong's** Australian Church, through which she was exposed to the socialist and suffragette movements in which she became active. Fullerton wrote poems, articles and stories to support herself. She lived in England from 1922 where, with encouragement from Miles **Franklin**, she published her poetry under the pseudonym 'E'. Her childhood reminiscences, *Bark House Days* (1921), are regarded as her most significant work, though she published five other books, several under male pseudonyms.

KT

Furphy was a nickname given to a type of water and sanitary cart used in military camps during World War I. The cart was invented by John Furphy, the elder brother of Joseph **Furphy**, and was manufactured at the J. Furphy & Sons iron foundry in Shepparton, Victoria. Branded on its cast-iron ends were the company name, Furphy, and slogan:

> Good, better, best.
>   Never let it rest
> Till your good is better
>   And your better—best.

As a result of soldiers' tendency to congregate around these water-carts and gossip, the rumours that circulated through camp were dubbed 'furphies', and this use subsequently entered the Australian vernacular. *Notes and Furphies* is the newsletter of the Association for the Study of Australian Literature.

HD

Furphy, Joseph ('Tom Collins') (1843–1912) was the author of the novel *Such Is Life* (1903), which he described as: 'temper, democratic; bias, offensively Australian'. Born in Yering, Victoria, Furphy's main claim to juvenile distinction was his knowledge of Shakespeare and whole chapters of the Bible by the time he was 7. After a rudimentary formal education, the young Furphy drifted through various rural jobs and an unproductive sortie to the goldfields before 'settling down' in 1867, when he married a Frenchwoman, Leonie Germaine, whose family farm and vineyard Furphy attempted—unsuccessfully—to manage. He failed as a selector, and his move to the Riverina in 1877 to become a bullock driver was a last attempt to remain master of his fate. But the drought of 1883 ruined him and he retreated to Shepparton, Victoria, where he worked for wages in his brother's foundry. Released from the deceptive freedoms of self-employment, Furphy at last had the opportunity for a rueful contempla-tion of what he called 'the Order of Things … another name for the Will of God'. Escaping the lengthening silences of his marriage, he spent hours in his 'sanctum' writing and theorising.

Into his growing manuscript Furphy poured all his auto-didactic quirkiness, obsessions, and accumulated philosophy, though it is important not to confuse his own views with those of his self-indulgent and often deluded narrator, Tom Collins. *Such Is Life* represents a series of comic and tragic variations on the theme of free will versus a species of soft determinism. Through these variations, and by means of a narrative strategy that explicitly eschews plot and conventional contrivance, Furphy seeks to give a 'fair picture of Life, as that engaging problem' has presented itself to him. A stoic amiability and great reserves of tolerance—attitudes endorsed for Furphy by his study of the philosopher Epicte-tus—cushion the hammer blows of fate which lie beneath the discursive surfaces of Tom Collins's diary entries. But for all its philosophic jauntiness, *Such Is Life* ends ambigu-ously—with a grudging suspicion that life just might be merely 'a tale told by a vulgarian, full of slang and blanky, signifying—nothing'.

Furphy was little known in his own lifetime as a writer, and *Such Is Life* was a publishing failure. Even A.G. **Stephens**, valuing the book for its 'accurate representations', did not recognise its narrative and structural originality. But seminal essays by A.K. Thomson and A.D. **Hope** (*Meanjin Papers*, 1943, 1945) drew belated attention to the book's artistic complexity. Hope made the remarkable suggestion that 'Furphy is not merely writing an odd and original book … he is putting forward an entirely new theory of the rela-tion of literature to life and announcing a revolution in the nature of prose fiction.'

Numerous essays (by, among others, John Barnes, Brian Kiernan, Julian Croft) have since elaborated upon the radical intuitions of Hope and others to reveal the eccentric bril-liance of *Such Is Life*. John Barnes produced *The Annotated Such Is Life* in 1991. Miles **Franklin** and Kate Baker, assidu-ous keepers of the Furphy flame, bequeathed invaluable evidence for later critical work and for the authoritative biography—John Barnes, *The Order of Things* (1990).

BRIAN MATTHEWS

Fusion was the amalgamation in 1909 of Alfred **Deakin's** protectionist liberals with the free-traders to form an alliance against the minority federal Labor government. The Fusion ministry he formed was defeated in the following year, but the alliance continued and subsequently adopted the title of the **Liberal Party**. It thus marks the creation of a unified non-Labor party which, despite the subsequent emergence of the Country Party (**National Party**) has continued in various reincarnations to this day. Some historians attribute this establishment of two-party politics to the success of the Labor Party, and have suggested that it initiated a pattern of the 'party of resistance' in response to the 'party of initiative'. While Labor's organisational growth and electoral popularity undoubtedly spurred Fusion, this formulation underestimates the vitality and heterogeneity of the elements brought together by the Fusion. John Rickard, *Class and Politics: New South Wales, Victoria and the Early Commonwealth 1890–1910* (1976), provides the best account.

SM

Fuzzy-wuzzy angels was an affectionate description of the indigenous people of PNG who worked to support the Australian Army during World War II as stretcher-bearers, supply-carriers, and scouts, particularly at **Kokoda**. *Fuzzy-wuzzies* had been the soldiers' nickname for Sudanese warriors, in reference to their hair. An Australian soldier's poem in 1942 resurrected the term and appended the word *angels*, to indicate that they were life-savers. Soldiers' letters home, newspaper reports, and photos—including those by famed war cameraman, Damien Parer—established both the image and the term in the Australian consciousness.

KT

G

Gair, Vincent Clair (1902–80) joined the Australian Labor Party as a 17-year-old in Qld. He entered state parliament in 1932 and became premier in 1952. As a Catholic and anti-communist, his sympathies lay with the **Democratic Labor Party** after the Labor **Split** of the mid-1950s. He was eventually expelled from the Australian Labor Party in 1957 but formed the Queensland Labor Party and remained as premier, though his government lost in the election held later that year. After the merger of the Queensland Labor Party and the DLP, Gair became a federal senator and leader of the DLP in 1965. He remained in the Senate until 1974, when he was controversially appointed ambassador to Ireland by the **Whitlam** government, a move which was seen as an attempt by Whitlam to gain control of the Senate. Gair proved temperamentally unsuited to the diplomatic world—he ignored advice from his officials, called the British ambassador 'you old bugger', and repeated earlier criticism of Billy **Snedden**. When recalled to Australia in 1976 by the **Fraser** government, his response was to ask if that was all the thanks he got for keeping the Liberals in power. Frank Mines wrote a biography, *Gair* (1975), and Brian Costar assesses his importance in D.J. Murphy et al. (eds), *The Premiers of Queensland* (1990).

KT

Gallipoli was the site of a military campaign during **World War I** in which the first significant numbers of Australians fought and died as Australians. As part of the Australian and New Zealand Army Corps (hence the label **Anzacs**) within a British and French army under General Ian Hamilton, units of the **AIF** landed on the Gallipoli Peninsula on 25 April 1915 at a beach since called Anzac Cove. Their aim was to distract the attention of defending Turkish troops from a landing further south by British regulars. Success in the campaign was intended to open the way to Constantinople and Eastern Europe, and bring victory without further slogging away in the trenches in Western Europe. But tangled hills, plunging ravines, and determined Turkish defence kept the Australians and others from scrambling far beyond the beaches, and the campaign bogged down into the same bloody stalemate it had been designed to avoid. **Bridges**, the Australian commander, **Simpson**, a brave stretcher-bearer, and hundreds of other Australians were dead within a month. War correspondents, such as Charles **Bean**, hailed the Australians for their dash in attack and doggedness in defence, and the **Anzac Legend** was born.

Summer brought heat, flies, disease, and the collapse of sanitary arrangements. The debilitated Australians joined in attacks from 6 to 10 August devised to break out of the beachheads. Every attack failed, or yielded trivial gains. At Lone Pine, 2200 Australians died to seize a few unimportant trenches. At the Nek, 375 charged to their deaths across an area the size of a tennis court, a horror that was recreated as the climax to the popular film *Gallipoli* (1981). Withdrawal was now inevitable. Partly planned by Australian staff officer Brudenell **White**, it was neatly executed and caused few casualties. The last Australian departed on 20 December. By then, 8141 had been killed or died of wounds or disease, and more than 18 000 had been wounded.

CRAIG WILCOX

Gambling has been linked to Australian character so often that one might expect its history to be nothing more than a catalogue of new and inventive ways to bet. However, Australia's gambling history is more concerned with the increasing prohibition of existing gambling in the nineteenth and early twentieth centuries, and the relaxation of these prohibitions since then.

Australian gambling was imported from Britain and Ireland, where different social classes gambled in distinctive ways. By the later nineteenth century, aristocratic gambling in Australia was entrenched on racecourses, in clubs, and the like; working-class gambling was equally well entrenched with SP bookies and a range of lotteries. Urged by evangelical Christians and other moral entrepreneurs, colonial parliaments in the late nineteenth century passed law after law to make people moral, and anti-gambling statutes were just one part of the process. All well-established forms of working-class gambling were affected, from SP bookies to **Tattersall's** lotteries. Not that the laws made much difference to the volume of gambling. Those who wanted to do it did; police, who were given the job of enforcing the unenforceable, invariably opted for control and regulation, much as they did with other so-called social evils like prostitution and sly-grogging. Yet one form of gambling remained legal: on-course betting on the races. Many working-class gamblers commented on this blatant inconsistency.

State governments began relaxing these prohibitions in the 1930s. SA and Tasmania legalised off-course betting; other states established lotteries. In the 1950s and 1960s all states legalised off-course betting, the wraps were taken off art unions and other kinds of raffles, and NSW even legalised poker machines. Bingo and lotteries expanded through the 1970s and 1980s until by the end of the 1990s every capital city had its own casino. Governments had embraced gambling with unbridled enthusiasm. The entry of organised labour to parliaments gave gamblers a political voice. After World War II the hold of the nineteenth-century moral entrepreneurs on the nation's morality began to falter. Governments began to see the prospect of revenue from running their own forms of gambling, or from licensing others and taxing them as well. Gambling's victory was not uncontested. Politicians had to bribe the community by promising that the gambling dollar would be exploited to pay for cash-starved social services, such as hospitals. The moral entrepreneurs fought hard and long but to no avail. By the 1980s, governments concerned themselves only with trying (unsuccessfully) to stamp out illegal gambling and maximising their revenue by licensing ever widening avenues for people to gamble.

Gambling today is ubiquitous. The drab respectability of a TAB speaks eloquently of its acceptability. The first casinos now look a little middle-aged even as the newer look like vulgar ostentation, and almost everybody bets on Tattslotto. Does this mean that the old saying is true, that Australians gamble on anything, even on two flies crawling up a wall? Keith Dunstan in *Wowsers* (1968) answered yes, and attributed our passion to immigrants, by nature gamblers, and particularly to Irish immigrants whose gambling was not proscribed by the Catholic Church. Maurice Cavanaugh in Jack Pollard's *Horses and Horsemen* (1965) sought the answer in nineteenth-century poverty and the prospect of escape by a big win. Geoffrey Caldwell in Don Edgar's *Social Change in Australia* (1974) looked beyond the nineteenth century to the fatalism of Australians, our ambivalence about merit, skill, and success, and our belief in luck. Fox, in Jenny Lee and Verity Burgmann (eds), *Constructing a Culture* (1988), looked to low income, boredom, monotony, and alienation and the dreams of escape, particularly by working-class men whose sense of themselves as risk-takers was suppressed by the exigencies of their lives.

Yet there are Australians who never bet and still doubt the wisdom, and oppose the proliferation, of gambling. Gambling continues to be a political issue. Ken **Inglis**, in Geoffrey Caldwell et al. (eds), *Gambling in Australia* (1985), claims the politics is an argument essentially between Catholics and Protestants. John O'Hara in *A Mug's Game* (1988) attributes the conflict to the different values of Australian working, middle, and upper classes, and gambling's victory to the adoption by governments of working-class values. If so, it is a marriage of convenience; governments could not now abandon gambling, even if they were so disposed.

CHARLIE FOX

Garden, John Smith 'Jock' (1882–1968) mixed radical zeal and chicanery in the labour movement for three decades. He came to Australia as an evangelical preacher from the north-east coast of Scotland. Becoming secretary of the New South Wales Labor Council, he led the 'Trades Hall Reds', who sought to wrest control of the labour movement from the parliamentarians. Garden was thus crucial to the foundation of the **Communist** Party of Australia; he achieved notoriety when, as Australian delegate to the fourth congress of the Communist International in 1922, he boasted that it commanded 400 000 workers. Even after he resigned from the Communist Party in 1926, he continued to promote left-wing causes such as the affiliation of the **ACTU** to the communist Pan-Pacific Trade Union Secretariat.

In 1926 he left the Communist Party. For a time he was an ally of the NSW Labor leader J.T. **Lang** and served a term in federal parliament, but his subsequent career was dogged by scandal. Arthur Hoyle has written a non-judgmental biography (1984) of this loveable rogue, who was untrustworthy, unvindictive, generous to a fault.

SM

Gardens in Australia are overwhelmingly European in ancestry, although the quest for an appropriate Australian style is a recurring theme. With a distinctive indigenous flora and extremes of climate, comparisons with a Mediterranean ideal have often been invoked.

The first settlers, concerned with survival, cultivated vegetable gardens, orchards and vineyards. Pastoral settlement later provided a source of wealth with which to shape new landscapes and create significant homestead gardens. In towns, ornamental aspirations soon complemented utilitarian needs. The range and availability of plant stocks were largely determined by trading routes, especially ports with comparable climates, and acclimatisation of exotic plants was rapid.

The earliest published horticultural advice was contained in local almanacs and books brought from Britain. Influential among these were J.C. Loudon, *Encyclopaedia of Gardening* (1822) and *Suburban Gardener* (1838); Charles McIntosh, *The Book of the Garden* (2 vols, 1853–55); and Edward Kemp, *How to Lay Out a Garden* (1858). Horticultural journals, both British and Australian, ensured that news and ideas were quickly disseminated. From the 1850s locally published gardening books were more prevalent; these titles are listed in Victor Crittenden, *A History and Bibliography of Australian Gardening Books* (1986).

Emigration to Australia, fuelled by the gold rushes that created wealth for the colonies, profoundly stimulated **town planning** and brought an influx of gardeners and nurserymen from Britain, especially Scotland. **Botanic gardens** were established, plant and seed nurseries proliferated, horticultural societies were inaugurated, and the bases of the modern horticultural industry were established. There was a significant German influence in Australian botany and horticulture in the nineteenth century; the plant distribution networks established by Ferdinand von **Mueller** and his colleagues endowed many gardens and reserves across the colonies.

The Picturesque—making landscapes in the manner of pictures—and its various manifestations were the aim of much of Australian gardening, although the gardenesque, which overlaid this picture-making with a degree of horticultural formality and often an unobtrusive symmetry, transformed it into a popular style highlighting the art of the gardener. The naturalism of landscape designer William **Guilfoyle** and the gardenesque designs of William Sangster, his counterpart in the private sphere, were perhaps the most confident expressions of this pervasive trend.

At the end of the nineteenth century architects such as the English-trained Walter Butler and Rodney Alsop worked in the Arts and Crafts idiom, with its emphasis on craftsmanship, formality, and restrained planting, while others were still promoting Guilfoylean naturalism. Australia witnessed a rise of interest in town planning in the early twentieth century and Walter Burley **Griffin** was influential in coupling town planning and landscaping, and also in promoting the use of indigenous flora. While Australian plants had been used in landscaping from the earliest days of colonisation, the fervour surrounding the wattle (which peaked during the second decade of the new century) fostered a climate in which nationalism and nature conservation became allied to horticulture. Openings for women in horticulture were provided by the absence and loss of so many men in World War I. Edna **Walling** was the most influential voice of this generation.

Modernism in the 1930s and 1940s profoundly challenged and altered local tastes and Modernist landscaping received a boost with **postwar reconstruction**, when architects and town planners led the charge. At the suburban garden level, ideas filtered slowly; there was an increasing acceptance of courtyards, pergolas, paving, sculptural use of trees, and bold-foliaged plants. World War II focused interest in vegetable gardens, but in the postwar 1950s outdoor living was in the ascendant: Americanisms, such as the barbecue and the swimming pool, made their way into the landscaper's repertoire, as home-making began to embrace landscaping as an integral component of an affluent lifestyle.

With the formation of the Australian Institute of Landscape Architects (1968) and the introduction of tertiary courses, the landscape profession at last found a unified voice, after a long period of close alliance with the nursery and horticultural trades. The building boom of the 1960s brought new opportunities for landscaping of high-rise offices, apartments, freeways, and other accoutrements of an expansive economy.

The social forces behind the formation of the various **National Trusts** contributed to interest in conserving historic gardens and to surveys of Australia's historic gardens, largely funded by the Australian Heritage Commission (1978–80). Botanists such as Joseph Maiden had been at the forefront of historical writing, bringing the exacting standards of their discipline to the task; horticulture was without similar champions until more recent decades. Two books by Howard Tanner were seminal in raising the standard of scholarship in the field of historic gardens: *Great Gardens of Australia* (1976) and *Converting the Wilderness: The Art of Gardening in Colonial Australia* (1979), which accompanied a major touring exhibition. This interest was harnessed in 1980 by the formation of the Australian Garden History Society, whose journal caters for a wide-ranging membership.

In the 1990s, sentiments such as those expressed a century earlier were again being heard in the call for greater use of Australian flora, and specifically for the use of local plants to meet regional conditions.

RICHARD AITKEN

Gardiner, Francis (1830–?1903), bushranger, was born Francis Christie near Goulburn, NSW, to a free settler father and an Aboriginal mother. He was imprisoned at Cockatoo Island for horse-stealing but granted a ticket-of-leave. Nicknamed 'the Darkie', Gardiner subsequently gained further notoriety from robberies and duffing cattle around Yass and the goldmining districts of NSW. In 1862 he masterminded the Eugowra gold escort robbery, which he carried off with the assistance of Ben **Hall**, Johnny Gilbert, and others. Gardiner subsequently fled to Apis Creek, north of Rockhampton, Qld, where he reputedly lived a quiet, reformed life as a publican and storekeeper. He managed to elude the police until his capture in 1864 when, convicted of armed robbery and attempted murder, he was sentenced to 32 years' gaol. Gardiner's sisters and friends later circulated a petition for his release, which pleaded his reformed character and poor health, and had the support of Gardiner's defence counsel W.B. **Dalley**. After much public controversy, the NSW parliament elected to release him in 1874, on the condition that he leave the colony; the **Parkes** government ultimately lost office as a result. Gardiner subsequently lived in Hong Kong and later in San Francisco, where he reputedly died in 1903. His story is told in Frank **Clune's** *Wild Colonial Boys* (1948).

HD

Garran family both wrote and made national history. ANDREW GARRAN (1825–1901) studied for the Congregational ministry in England before migrating to Australia. After working as a journalist in Melbourne and Adelaide, he joined the *Sydney Morning Herald* in 1856 and succeeded John **West** as editor from 1873 to 1885. Parkes nominated him into the Legislative Council of NSW, and he later presided over the colony's early council of arbitration. In 1886 he edited *The Picturesque Atlas of Australasia*, a lavish three-volume descriptive account with substantial historical content.

His son ROBERT RANDOLPH (1867–1957) was admitted to the NSW Bar in 1891. During the 1890s he assisted Edmund **Barton** in the establishment of the Australasian Federation League and the organisation of the **Corowa Conference**. In *The Coming Commonwealth* (1897) he outlined the history of federalism in order to advance the cause. He was secretary to G.H. **Reid** at the 1897–98 Convention, and active in the pro-Federation campaign during the 1898 and 1899 referendums. In collaboration with John **Quick**, he published the *Annotated Constitution of Australian Commonwealth* (1901); its historical introduction and appendixes occupy 260 pages and remain the most complete single account. At the request of Alfred **Deakin** he became the Commonwealth's first public servant as secretary of the Attorney-General's Department, and in 1916 W.M. **Hughes** made him solicitor-general. He retired in 1932, though he served in subsequent official positions and remained a cultural patron in Canberra until his death. Noel Francis, *The Gifted Knight* (1983), samples Garran's verse and occasional writings. His memoirs, *Prosper the Commonwealth*, published posthumously in 1958, are an important record of national affairs.

SM

'Garryowen', see Finn, Edmund

Gawler, George (1795–1869) replaced John **Hindmarsh** as governor of SA in 1838. Like his predecessor, he was a distinguished soldier without civil experience rewarded with a colonial governorship. Gawler arrived to a colony in crisis, and declared a state of emergency. He added the power of Resident Commissioner to that of governor, ending the division of power that hindered Hindmarsh. He arranged for Charles **Sturt** to survey the remaining country lands; built a prison, customs house and harbour; and introduced a police force and government administration. By 1841 SA was a well-organised and thriving colony. Land settlement was under control and self-sufficiency a definite prospect. Gawler minimised capital expenditure where possible by exchanging land for the labour of private companies, but his work did rely heavily on government funding. For this he incurred the disapproval of the Board of Commissioners and the **Colonial Office**, and was recalled in 1841. He was replaced by George **Grey**, who disliked him, and fuelled suspicions that Gawler's extravagant spending had taken the colony near to bankruptcy. Gawler retired to a life of philanthropy and religion, and saw his reputation cleared before his death. Most officials soon accepted that his expenditure was vital, and that increases in immigration and the official pressure for the colony to become self-sufficient too quickly caused the financial problems. The town north of Adelaide was named after him.

KELLIE TOOLE

Gay history is a relatively new field of investigation, closely linked to the development of a gay rights movement. Indeed, it was the activism of gay liberationists in the early 1970s which opened up gay history as an area of study. This close relationship between gay history and gay politics has continued. Gay history does not simply reflect a homosexual past; it is perhaps more a reflection of current homosexual hopes of what it might mean to be gay.

The first texts of gay history appeared in the years immediately following Gay Liberation. Jonathan Katz compiled a documentary history of American homosexuality in his *Gay American History* (1976). In Britain, Jeffrey Weeks published his path-breaking *Coming Out* (1977). The title of this book was instructive. As a social movement, Gay Liberation had urged all homosexuals to come out. In extending this phrase to encompass the development of homosexual politics, Weeks hoped to demonstrate the 'historic process' of what was usually seen as an intensely personal achievement.

Weeks's mixture of the personal and the historical reflected a broader intellectual climate. Gay history draws on **social history** and **women's history**, as well as the work of Michel Foucault. Foucault's argument that during the nineteenth century the 'homosexual became a personage, a past … a type of life, a life form', added weight to the social constructionist approach to gay history which Weeks had already sketched out. The attention of historians now turned to the web of discursive practices which had transformed the sodomite from 'a temporary aberration' into the 'new species' of the homosexual. All of these intellectual trends deepened an interest in the creation and specific histories of homosexual identities.

Gay history in Australia has taken somewhat longer to develop. It was not until the mid-1980s that the first substantial monographs began to appear. Denise Thompson's *Flaws in the Social Fabric* (1985) reviewed the early years of the gay rights movement in Sydney and the political and cultural climate in which gay activists worked. Surprisingly little of the history of the **lesbian** and gay movement in Australia has been recorded, apart from a number of reflective chapters in broader historical and political surveys. This may change in coming years as new post-structuralist critiques revise standard accounts of gay politics.

While the gay movement has generally escaped historical appraisal, gay communities have turned to gay history in an attempt to build and reinforce a sense of gay identity. Many gay community newspapers have published articles which reclaim a purported gay Australian past. The objects of historical interest have ranged from gay governors to homosexual bushrangers. This style of history, with its concern to rehabilitate hidden gay characters and stories, has much in common with the early impulse of women's history. It does not rigorously contextualise **homosexuality**, preferring instead to outline a direct lineage that joins past and present homosexuals. Robert French's *Camping by a Billabong* (1993) best represents this approach. French describes the aim of his history as 'a simple one'. It is to record 'the lives and experiences of the ancestors of our tribe'.

Oral history is another popular and accessible medium through which historians have attempted to redress the absence of homosexual histories. Garry Wotherspoon's *Being Different* (1986) drew together the stories of nine gay men who 'grew up gay' in Australia. Wotherspoon gives a voice to men whose experiences of homosexuality would have once gone unrecorded. In *Did You Meet Any Malagas?* (1993), Dino Hodge uses oral history to depict the complex history of homosexuality in the NT. His incisive questions reveal the different ways in which homosexuality is experienced through class and race. Hodge's book aside, gay history has tended to concentrate on the gay subcultures of large cities, as in Wotherspoon's *City of the Plain* (1991). Drawing upon **urban history**, Wotherspoon depicts the startling growth of Sydney's gay subculture, from the restricted social spaces of the 1930s through to the Oxford Street of the late 1980s. A gay urban history thus becomes the backdrop for studying the evolution of twentieth-century homosexual identity.

Autobiography and **biography** have provided more intimate insights into the lives of homosexual men. Robert Dessaix's elegant memoir *A Mother's Disgrace* (1994) described the blossoming of a gay lifestyle and aesthetics, as distinct from homosexuality, around Darlinghurst and Paddington during the late 1970s. Timothy Conigrave's account of his life with his lover in *Holding the Man* (1995) takes the reader from boyish romance at Xavier College in the 1970s through to the current tragedy of HIV/AIDS. John Foster, *Take Me to Paris, Johnny* (1993), and Peter Blazey, *Screw Loose: Uncalled-for Memoirs* (1997), tell their stories. From a rigorously political perspective, Dennis Altman charts the project of creating himself as a gay man, activist, and theorist in *Defying Gravity* (1997). David Marr's magisterial study of Patrick **White**, *Patrick White: A Life* (1991), revealed White's very private mode of being homosexual and his discomfort with the public theatricality of gay politics.

In the 1990s gay history, like gay politics, has taken a 'queer' turn. This has involved a more ambitious contextualisation of sexuality as a central organising principle of Western thought and culture. Like the debates between the proponents of women's history and **feminist history**, this queer development has produced some anxiety that the original objective of gay history—finding a hidden homosexual past—will be swamped by more diffuse and theoretical concerns.

ROBERT REYNOLDS

Gender relations have remained largely invisible in historical writing until the 1980s and 1990s. It has been said that the essence of every culture can be found in its notion of relations between the sexes, and that the relationship also signifies national identity, power, morality, and anxiety about social change. In Australia, this is indeed the case. The attempt to regulate relations between women and men underlies such diverse proceedings as Commissioner **Bigge's** report of 1822–23, the 1904 report of the NSW Royal Commission into the Birth Rate and the Mortality of Infants, the Harvester Judgment of 1907, and the Wages Boards decisions of the 1940s. Whether attempting to regulate convict marriages, stem declining birth-rates, or entrench a 'family wage', these reports all draw on assumptions of an ideal set of relations between the sexes.

From colonial times until the recent past, the officially sanctioned setting for relations between men and women was that of the white, heterosexual, monogamous, and legally married couple. That couple, producing white Australian babies, was seen as an essential bulwark against the vast interiors and their spurned inhabitants, and the encroachment of the more populous non-white races to the north. Thus gender relations cannot be disentangled from **race relations**: Aboriginal marriages and gender relations have been subject to strict paternal, government control. While mainstream historical explanation has tended to treat gender relations as a given, both **women's history** and **feminist history** have challenged this view, the first insisting on inserting women's experience into the historical record, the latter making gender a central category of historical analysis. A body of literature has mapped the pervasiveness of the official ideology from and before the arrival of the First Fleet, analysed the legislation which has enshrined it in the workplace and the welfare system, and recuperated women's efforts to become citizens in their own right, free of familial dependency.

Much of this new writing views gender relations as confrontational, a continuous attempt by men to forge and retain positions of authority, and of women to challenge or share that power. The influential anthology by Kay Saunders and Raymond Evans is titled *Gender Relations in Australia: Domination and Negotiation* (1992), the sub-title capturing their view of a male-dominated society as the context in which women have attempted to negotiate a better deal. Four feminist historians (Patricia Grimshaw, Marilyn Lake, Ann McGrath and Marian Quartly) signalled their intentions in the title of their path-breaking history of Australia, *Creating a Nation* (1994), where the birth of babies (or the refusal to bear them) is considered as central to the task of nation-building as the usually acknowledged activities of politics or warfare. Susan Magarey et al. (eds), *Debutante Nation: Feminism Contests the 1890s* (1993), also points to a theme of confrontation between dominant interpretations of Australian history which ignore gender and those which make gender central. In challenging shibboleths of mainstream history, works such as these have broadened and greatly enriched current Australian historical debate.

Several historical factors have been identified as leading to a particular Australian form of gender relations. Australia's **demographic history** tells much of the story. The yawning gap between the ideal family form and the reality of gender relations was exacerbated by a vast numerical imbalance between the sexes, one that endured for the entire colonial period. The predominance of males, initially convicts of working-class origin, later isolated pastoral workers on an often-violent **frontier**, led to the valorisation in Australian mythology of a particularly aggressive form of masculinity. The notion of the romantic bushman, hard-riding, hard-drinking, and wary of family ties, placed a heavy emphasis on male comradeship or **mateship**, inscribed in the works of writers such as Henry **Lawson** and writers of the *Bulletin* school, and made into legend by historians such as Russel **Ward**. According to this legend, still alive in popular culture, the Australian male character was further forged in the crucible of World War I, particularly in the **Anzac** experience.

In an influential article (*HS*, 1986), Marilyn Lake challenged the hegemony of this interpretation of the Australian 'national' character, arguing that in the 1890s, its assumed heyday, there was a major struggle between men and women for the control of the national culture. Lake's intervention, itself contested, signals a refusal to accept a masculinist representation of Australian culture at the expense of more richly nuanced accounts. Other feminist historians have revealed that the 1890s were also a period of intense questioning of sexual morality, of marriage, of 'compulsory' **maternity**, and of middle-class women's exclusion from the labour force, all contributing to a reappraisal of gender relations; as did that supreme public challenge to male power—the demand for women's suffrage. Beside *Creating a Nation* and *Debutante Nation*, Judith Allen, *Rose Scott* (1994), and Alison Mackinnon, *Love and Freedom* (1997), are important contributions to this literature. With the achievement of the women's federal vote in 1902, and a declining birth-rate which attracted the attention of a NSW royal commission, the stage was set for an equally contested set of gender relations in the twentieth century. Women sought equal citizenship in all domains.

The centrality of the state in Australia has both entrenched a dominant pattern of gender relations and, paradoxically, in the last decades of the twentieth century has assisted in its reconfiguration. Several significant industrial and legislative decisions in the early years of the century—the Harvester Judgment of 1907, the Fruit Pickers Case of 1912, and the Maternity Allowance of 1912—enshrined the 'ideal' family type, in which the male was the breadwinner, the wife and three children dependants. State-provided education systems and structures of social welfare buttressed the ideal of the male breadwinner family, assisted by the patriarchal assumptions of health and infant welfare authorities. Infringements of the dominant ideal were harshly disciplined, although the realisation of such a family form was unattainable or undesired for significant sections of working-class, migrant, and Aboriginal families. Jill Matthews, *Good and Mad Women* (1984), Kerreen Reiger, *The Disenchantment of the Home* (1985), and Shurlee Swain and Renate Howe, *Single Mothers and their Children* (1995), explore these policies. At the same time, the state became a major employer of white middle-class women as teachers, welfare workers, nurses, and public servants. The latter group (examined by Desley Deacon, *Managing Gender*, 1989), by their presence in the public domain, and their potential for political action, were to provide many of the first women to penetrate state structures in the 1960s and 1970s and claim equal rights in employment.

Marriage bars in the public service and in the state teaching labour force, lower wages for women, and restrictive legislation enforced the boundary between women's and men's work and perpetuated the myth and the reality of women's domestic 'role'. From the nineteenth century onwards, white women had resisted that fiction. As their numbers in the paid workforce grew, their levels of education (and frustration) rose, and their confidence in themselves as sexual beings developed, women's groups in the 1960s and 1970s sought equal pay, childcare, and access to safe contraception and abortion.

Much has changed between women and men. Equal Employment Opportunity and Affirmative Action legislation, as well as equal educational opportunity have challenged the dominance of the male breadwinner family (although much of the tax transfer system still supports it). The demise of the family wage, the recent shrinkage of the size and role of the state have significant implications for the work practices of women and men. The demographic figures demonstrate that marriage and maternity are no longer the main form of self-definition for many young people. The link between **sexuality** and reproduction has been severed. While increasing numbers of women take their place in the labour market, researchers show that men are not approaching domestic labour with the same enthusiasm. A more diverse society has disrupted the monocultural view of domestic relations which dominated twentieth-century white Australia. Not surprisingly, as many of David **Williamson's** plays so accurately reflect, gender relations remain contested. And for many Aboriginal, immigrant and low-income women and men, the need to acquire some form of income security remains paramount.

At the end of the nineteenth century popular culture depicted gender relations in flux as the family economy began to give way to the consumer society. Equally challenging at the twentieth century's end is the shift towards the information society, one where workplace and home are being radically transformed. The accompanying upheavals in gender relations continue to raise challenging new questions for those negotiating them.

ALISON MACKINNON

Genealogy is the study of related families, traced from generation to generation, and researched as far back as records can be found, traditionally through the male line. Genealogy was practised widely in England in the early nineteenth century, with Burke's *Genealogical and Heraldic Dictionary of the Peerage and Baronetage of the United Kingdom* appearing in 1826. Paul de Serville argues in *Pounds and Pedigrees* (1991) that it also flourished in the colonies. 'An interest in genealogy was shared by colonists of every class and background, and its popularity suggests the desire to maintain one's links and roots, to preserve one's identity of background and inheritance as much cultural and familial.'

From the outset, Australian genealogy was as much a search for local distinction as for legal descent. *Burke's Colonial Gentry* (1891) adopted a more generous and flexible definition of gentility than its English counterpart, welcoming newly rich families with no connection to land and conniving, says de Serville, in the 'casual creation of pedigrees'. Later works, such as Alexander Henderson's *Early Pioneer Families of Victoria and Riverina* (1936) and P.C. Mowle's *Pioneer Families of Australia* (1939), were published to coincide with national anniversaries, and they selected families for inclusion, not on the basis of noble connection with English landed families, but on their status as **pioneers**, first-comers to the new land. Mowle included only the descendants of families who arrived before 1838, Henderson only the first generation of Victorian squatters. The Society of Australian Genealogists was founded in Sydney in 1932 and the Genealogical Society of Victoria in 1941. One of their first tasks was to draw up definitive lists of European first-comers, a task which was complicated, however, by the sensitivities of **convict** and free ancestry. In Australia between the world wars, reverence for the sterling virtues of one's ancestors still merged with wider beliefs about the influence of heredity and the fear of 'bad blood'. Genealogical societies were later organised in each state, most since the late 1970s. Local societies in towns and regions developed from the early 1980s and have in turn formed federal bodies in each state, sometimes, as in Qld, holding joint conferences with historical societies.

Until the 1970s genealogy was a hobby pursued by a minority of enthusiasts, often in conjunction with the study of heraldry. Since then Australian genealogy has undergone a democratic revolution. Membership of genealogical societies has increased almost tenfold and the older genealogical societies have been joined by newer societies explicitly committed to the democratic principle that 'even the lowliest of commoners has a genealogy and a family history of equal interest to all'. The Australian family history boom parallels, and even exceeds, the similar boom in Britain and the USA. In Britain, writes Raphael Samuel in *History Workshop* (1985), a new generation of researchers now 'finds as much delight in discovering plebeian origins as earlier ones did the tracing of imaginary aristocratic pedigrees'. Not surprisingly, women dominate family history research. It is women who have been socialised throughout history to shoulder the major tasks of caring for children and partners, caring for aged parents and relatives, and for managing all aspects of the home. Interest and motivation are the key factors here and women, not men, appear to have these in greater abundance for keeping and preserving the complex relationships between the families in their past. Genealogy has thrived in an age when divorce, geographical mobility, and intergenerational conflict have stretched and strained family ties. By extending generational memory, family historians seek to ground personal identity in something more enduring than the shifting and temporary affiliations of a post-industrial, postmodern society. Genealogy, more than most forms of historical research, is a group activity. 'Doing the family history' is often the prelude to a family reunion, when the scattered tribes reassemble, usually on the ancestral turf, to celebrate a vestigial sense of kinship.

Genealogists have developed a sophisticated methodology based on close analysis of official records, such as census, probate, and birth, death, and marriage records. Family papers, photographs, newspaper clippings, certificates, land records, occupational registers, school history, and family stories are also everyday fare for genealogists. They have increasingly taken the lead in archiving their local and community records—indexing local newspapers, transcribing burial records from local cemeteries, copying parish registers onto databases, publishing **local histories** and pioneer biographical registers, and acquiring material for local collections. Genealogists are no longer simply antiquarians but often museologists, archivists, and family historians. They are also prolific self-publishers, for the desk-top publishing revolution has enabled many genealogists to disseminate their work, not only in print, but in charts, CD-ROMs, and videos.

Genealogy was once a quest for social status and recognition, but in the 1990s, as its base has broadened, it has become a search for identity. 'I now have an identity, knowing exactly who I am and where I come from', one genealogist writes exultantly at the end of her quest. Family history is now shaped by the complexities of personal, ethnic, and racial identity. Feminists now challenge patriarchy by tracing their descent through the female rather than the male line. Australians of non-English-speaking backgrounds ransack the fragmented records of countries torn apart by World War II to reconstitute their pasts: Mark Baker's *The Fiftieth Gate* (1997), a Jewish-Australian historian's reconstruction of his parents' ordeal in the Holocaust, is also a heroic essay in genealogy. For the **Stolen Generations** of Aboriginal Australians separated from their roots by institutionalisation and adoption, family history has now become an important instrument of national reconciliation.

The literature of Australian family history is now vast. *Australians: A Guide to Sources* (1987) contains a useful summary of work published to that date. Noeline Kyle's works, *Tracing Family History* (1985), *We Should've Listened to Grandma* (1988), and *The Family History Writing Book* (1993), document the changing character of family history and historians. The main genealogical societies and local family history societies publish journals and newsletters, and there are a number of general guides to genealogical methods and Australian sources: Errol Lea-Scarlett, *Roots and Branches* (1979 and later editions), and Nick Vine-Hall, *Tracing Your Family History in Australia* (1985), are perhaps the best known. Nearly all state and many local libraries have their own specialist genealogical collections, which now include microfilm copies of many British archival sources. Internet and email are the newest tools of family history research: Anne Foxworthy, *Genealogy on the Internet* (1995), is a valuable introduction to relevant sources and lists of URL addresses.

NOELINE J. KYLE

Genocide is a term for the mass killing of a group of people of shared nationality, race, or cultural affiliation, first applied to Nazi Germany's attempted extermination of Jews in Europe during World War II. In the 1970s the term was increasingly used in reference to the destruction of Aboriginal communities in Australia, as a result of increased awareness of frontier killings of Aborigines by Europeans, which included providing them with flour laced with arsenic. This is most widely discussed by Henry **Reynolds**. The policy of removing Aboriginal children from their parents has also been described as genocide because its aim was to prevent the transmission of Aboriginal culture and destroy Aboriginal communities (see **Stolen Generations**). Whether the term is appropriately used is a matter of fierce contention.

HD

Gentry, and its correlates *gentleman* and *gentlewoman* are ideas with a rich history in the land from which most colonial Australians came; but the kind of hierarchical rural society from which they derived proved harder to transplant to the antipodes. Falling outside both British standards of social status and Australian standards of **egalitarianism**, the gentry was an insecurely self-defined status group with a paradoxically profound sense of its own social importance. That sense of importance has been shared by few general historians, who have tended to regard them as an insignificant social category, whose obsession with petty social snobberies was irrelevant to driving historical concerns such as **class**.

Occasionally historians have attempted to come to grips with the precise composition and significance of the gentry in the Australian colonies. G.C. **Bolton** argued in 'The Idea of a Colonial Gentry' (*HS*, 1968) that the groups which achieved social and political dominance in Australia took on the 'outward and visible signs' of the British ruling elite, not as a sign of subservience to British culture, but in an attempt to express their power through available forms and symbols. The perpetuation of social forms was thus consistent with the continual broadening of the bases from which the elite was recruited. As the point at which British standards met colonial social realities, Government House assumed a special social significance. Historians have in general agreed on this significance, but have differed on whether what was most apparent was a slavish adherence to British standards, or a comprehensive redefinition of those standards to suit the needs of the colonial situation.

Specific studies have lent complexity and particularity to historical understandings of the gentry. The early years of settlement in NSW and Van Diemen's Land witnessed a sustained effort to develop a gentry based on land ownership. The conservative values implicit in such early attempts to form a ruling class were explored by Michael **Roe** in *Quest for Authority in Eastern Australia* (1965). The hierarchical structure and complex community relationships produced at a local level were carefully analysed by Alan Atkinson in his study of *Camden* (1988)—the most sustained effort at a village community to be attempted in NSW. Paul de Serville's detailed studies of the gentry of Melbourne (*Port Phillip Gentlemen*, 1980, *Pounds and Pedigrees*, 1991, and *Rolf Boldrewood*, 2000) offer a different version of the gentry: a fragment detached from the minor British aristocracy, defending

anachronistic values and standards in a hostile democratic world. Geoffrey **Serle** (*The Rush To Be Rich*, 1971) and Michael **Cannon** (*The Long Last Summer*, 1985), imply a similarly nostalgic image of the 'old guard', plaintively and ineffectually clinging to outmoded values. In contrast, John Hirst in *Adelaide and the Country* (1973) and Dirk van Dissel in Eric Richards (ed.), *Flinders Social History of South Australia* (1986) identify an Adelaide gentry in which membership was 'open to anyone with wealth so long as they were not shopkeepers'. English values were upheld, but the lifestyle of an 'English country gentleman' was almost successfully adapted to suit the large houses dotted across the city.

A number of these historians have remarked on the extent to which the very fluidity of the gentry's social composition promoted its obsession with form. This is apparent in the jockeying for position and honours, and the jealous guarding of pedigree and title, so effectively described by John Hirst in 'Egalitarianism' (in S.L. Goldberg and F.B. Smith, eds, *Australian Cultural History*, 1986). It is apparent also in the preoccupation with building and furnishing 'great homes', which manifested itself as soon as settlers escaped the immediate financial stringencies of pioneering. Barrie Dyster in *Servant and Master* (1989) explores the labour required to build and maintain these grand houses. This obsession with form also meant the gentry placed great emphasis on social ritual, mannered exchanges, and the elaborate social edifice of calls and invitations. In the **bush**, social forms gave way to practical necessity. In contrast, the urban environment became a crucial location for defining gentility. As Penny Russell shows in *A Wish of Distinction* (1994), women were central to the preservation of social standards, devoting a significant proportion of their days to 'beating the boundaries' and, still more importantly, policing genteel behaviour.

A widened concept of 'gentility' is crucial to understanding the colonial gentry. The various historical studies of the gentry in different colonies and periods, in rural and urban contexts, suggest that the borders of the colonial gentry were always and by definition imprecise. British standards were invoked, but people who met the standards of the British gentry tended to stay in Britain. It was those who were excluded who emigrated; in their new homes they sought simultaneously to gain a high social position within a more fluid social fabric, and to crystallise that position by closing off access to others. The contradictory impulses towards inclusiveness and exclusiveness were resolved largely through a preoccupation with genteel behaviour. The code of gentility was far more pervasive and important than the influence of the group of self-styled gentry.

PENNY RUSSELL

Geography, see **Historical geography**

George, Henry, see **Single tax**

Germans in Australia have been part of Australian history from the beginning of British settlement (Governor

Phillip and Augustus Alt, the first surveyor, were sons of German fathers). Substantial immigration began in 1838 with the arrival in SA of **Lutheran** refugees (known as Old Lutherans) from religious oppression in Prussia. They settled first at Klemzig, Hahndorf, and then in the Barossa Valley. German Lutheran missionaries to the Aborigines also came to SA and Qld in the 1830s, to be followed by German Moravian missionaries in the 1850s. Until recently, accounts of German immigration focused on SA and Qld. However, large numbers of Germans emigrated to NSW and Victoria in the mid-nineteenth century, many of them bounty immigrants, as described by Patricia Cloos and Jürgen Tampke, *Greetings From the Land Where Milk and Honey Flows: The German Emigration to NSW 1838–1858* (1993), and Thomas A. Darragh and Robert N. Wuchatsch, *From Hamburg to Hobsons Bay: German Emigration to Port Phillip … 1848–51* (1999). Emigrants to Victoria included Wends (a Slavonic group). More Germans went to Victoria in the **gold rushes**, giving the colony the highest German-born population in Australia in 1861. Most Germans were Lutherans, although the Rhineland emigrants to NSW were largely Catholic and were absorbed into the Australian **Catholic Church**, where tensions between Irish and German sometimes erupted. Many Germans settled on the land, as wine-growers or farmers. In the 1860s Qld, Victoria and SA encouraged their migration with offers of land in the form of land orders or free selections. Immigration continued through the 1870s and 1880s, and declined overall in the 1890s. Yet German settlers and their descendants remained the largest non-British group of Europeans in Australia from 1850 to World War I. Qld had the highest German-born population 1881–1921.

German names stand out in nineteenth-century history: the explorer Ludwig **Leichhardt**; the botanists Ferdinand von **Mueller** and Moritz Richard Schomburgk; and many others in science, education, music, politics and law, commerce, and industry, especially wine-making. Most of these came independently of the main Lutheran emigrations, a number of refugees from the 1848 revolution. They generally settled in the cities and assimilated quickly to Australian colonial society, although they formed German clubs, orchestras and Liedertafel. Some of them, or their children, married British-Australians and sent their children to Protestant private schools. Intermarriage was relatively high among single German male working-class immigrants who came, especially to Victoria and NSW, in the second half of the century and later.

Most German immigration in the nineteenth century, however, was of families who tended to settle in farming communities, generally centred on the Lutheran church with its school. These Lutherans were pietist and puritanical, expecting the imminent apocalypse. They shunned the world and other Protestants. From the outset they were regarded as ideal settlers—devout, sober, hard-working, and an example to other colonists. Their ethnic separateness and religious exclusiveness caused no concern, although tension grew among German and British Australians after the

formation of the German Empire in 1871. The German clubs in the cities fostered the pan-Germanism encouraged by the Empire, and the German-language press promoted pride in Imperial Germany and its culture. It encouraged loyalty to Australia, rather than to Britain, and favoured Australian federation as a step towards Australian independence. The pro-German and pro-Boer stance of the press provoked anti-German feeling in the decade before World War I.

The migration of the Lutheran 'Pilgrim Fathers' is one of the dominant motifs of German history in Australia, as in the latest history of Lutheranism, E. Leske, *For Faith and Freedom* (1996). However, the role of the Lutheran churches in maintaining *Deutschtum* or Germanness, and ethnic separatism, has been exaggerated. They did help to preserve the German language through church services and in schools, but the rural German community was unaffected by the urban-based club culture and the secular German press. By the end of the century native-born German Australians were losing their familiarity with German. The most theologically conservative of the Lutheran synods, the Evangelical Lutheran Synod (later Church) of Australia, introduced English into church and school around the turn of the century. At the outbreak of World War I its president pledged unqualified loyalty to Australia and the British Empire, a gesture which, however, did not spare German Australians when hostilities commenced.

The **internment** of Germans and the broader anti-German feeling during World War I, and to a lesser extent in World War II, is the other great motif in the history of Germans in Australia. Internment has been generally seen as the unwarranted result of anti-German hysteria in the Australian community. However, Jürgen Tampke, in *Australia, Willkommen* (1990) and *Ruthless Warfare* (1998), justifies Australian government policy and asserts that victimisation of enemy aliens during the war 'has been vastly exaggerated'. The number of German nationals interned—2879, excluding 1107 captured seamen—represented about 10 per cent of German-born male resident males aged 15 and over, or about 40 per cent of German nationals. Internment was a tragic experience, but no more so than the open hostility to Germans and everything German. The teaching of German in Victorian Lutheran schools was banned, and in 1917 Lutheran schools in SA were closed. Publications in German were prohibited and German place names changed to English or Aboriginal names. Some Germans even became voluntary internees as a means of survival. After the war some 5000 Germans left Australia: 696 deported, the remainder voluntary repatriates. The Australian government banned immigration from Germany until 1925. (See **Aliens**.)

According to Gerhard Fischer, *Enemy Aliens* (1989), the wartime experience and its aftermath destroyed the German community. It certainly suffered severely; some German Australians anglicised their names and abandoned Lutheranism. But the war was not the whole cause of the dissolution of German culture in Australia. The German language was losing out to English among third- and fourth-generation German Australians before the war. Some parishes of the United Evangelical Lutheran Church (formed 1921) reinstated German services but English soon became general. The German clubs reopened in the 1920s, and the German-language press revived for a diminishing readership. When German immigration resumed, it was largely of German Jewish refugees. The German-born population in Australia declined absolutely in the interwar years.

Following the outbreak of World War II, 1115 German residents and some Australian-born Germans were interned. Among them were members of the Nazi Party or suspected sympathisers, including a few pastors of the United Lutheran Church, which Nazi German representatives in Australia had cultivated since 1933. Among the 3753 overseas Germans interned in Australia were Jewish refugees brought out on the *Dunera*. German immigration revived on a large scale from 1952 making the German-born the fourth-largest non-British group in postwar Australia, the majority settling in Victoria and NSW. The postwar German immigrants were more mixed socially and religiously than previous groups. There were more German Catholics, who (with other German-speakers) formed their own communities or congregations in the capital cities. German clubs proliferated and German-language newspapers appeared once more. The Bavarianised German culture promoted for tourism in some places, however, is far removed from the austere Protestant culture brought to Australia by the earlier German settlers. While maintaining their own culture, postwar German immigrants have integrated well into Australian society, and contributed significantly to its development.

WALTER PHILLIPS

Gibbs, (Cecilia) May (1877–1969) achieved huge success with the publication of *The Gumnut Babies* (1916), which she wrote and illustrated. The endearing bush characters that she created—the gumnut babies, Snugglepot and Cuddlepie, and Bib and Bub—immediately became part of classic Australian children's literature and psyche, as did the evil Banksia Men. Their adventures were followed in further books—*Snugglepot and Cuddlepie* (1918), *Little Ragged Blossom* (1920), and *The Complete Adventures of Snugglepot and Cuddlepie* (1940). Bib and Bub were the subject of a long-running cartoon strip in Sydney papers. Gibbs's family home in Sydney, Nutcote, was saved from destruction after her death and is managed by a trust. Her papers are held in the Mitchell Library. Maureen Walsh wrote a eulogistic biography in 1985, *May Gibbs, Mother of the Gumnuts*.

KT

Gibbs, Pearl Mary (1901–83), also known as Gambanyi, became active in the campaign for Aboriginal rights—particularly for full citizenship and fair working conditions—after she began work as a domestic servant in Sydney in 1917. Frustrated in her attempts to work through the Aborigines Protection Board, she spoke directly to politicians and reached the wider community through the radio and talks to women's groups. She was the first female representative on the NSW Aborigines Protection Board (1954–57) and also founded, with Faith **Bandler**, the Aboriginal Australian Fellowship. Her ability to establish and maintain networks proved invaluable to many pioneering Aboriginal organisations.

KT

Giblin, Lyndhurst Falkiner (1872–1951) was an unusual economist. His father, a lawyer, had been premier of Tasmania. The son studied mathematics at Cambridge, played rugby for England, and prospected in the Klondike before establishing an orchard back in Tasmania. After a term in state parliament as a Labor member and war service, he became state statistician. His membership of the national inquiry into the tariff in 1929 led to appointment to a chair of economic research at the University of Melbourne, and with D.B. **Copland** and E.C. **Dyason** he advised the Commonwealth government in its response to the **Depression**. A series of newspaper articles, 'Letters to John Smith', sought to persuade Australians to accept cheerfully reduced wages. While he professed a disdain for pure theory, Giblin anticipated some elements of the relationship between trade, national income, and employment that informed Keynesian economics. He was a founding member of the Commonwealth Grants Commission, a member of the board of the Commonwealth Bank, and a principal economic adviser during World War II. His colleague Copland edited a posthumous collection of essays on *Giblin: The Scholar and the Man* (1960).

SM

Gibson, Robert (1863–1934) became a successful businessman in Australia after migrating from Scotland in 1890. He gained national recognition for his involvement in the Repatriation Commission (1917–20) and as chairman of the royal commission on public expenditure (1918–21). His greatest impact was felt during his time as chair of the Commonwealth Bank Board, beginning in 1926, when he controlled bank policy through the **Depression**. His conservative policies won praise from some and criticism from those, notably in the Labor Party, who wanted the economy stimulated.

KT

Gilbert, Kevin (1933–93), poet and playwright, was born at Condobolin, NSW, of Wiradjuri and Kamilaroi descent. He was sentenced to life imprisonment in 1957 for killing his wife. During his 14 years in gaol, he developed his talent as a writer. In an appreciation of his life, published in *Aboriginal History* (1994), Gordon Briscoe claimed it was during this time that Gilbert 'remade himself as a Koori'. Upon his release, Gilbert continued writing and became involved in the Aboriginal rights movement. He helped establish the Aboriginal **Tent Embassy** in 1972. His best-known play is *The Cherry Pickers* (1968). He was outspoken in his views on Aboriginal politics, and published two political works, *Because* *a White Man'll Never Do It* (1973) and *Living Black* (1977). He criticised Evonne **Cawley** (Goolagong) in 1980 over what he considered to be her apparent indifference to her Aboriginality. Gilbert chaired the Treaty 88 campaign and was honoured by several awards, some of which he returned.

HD

Giles, Ernest (1835–97), explorer of Australia's central and western interior, was born at Bristol, England. His parents migrated to SA in 1848, but Giles finished his schooling at Christ's Hospital, London, then settled in Adelaide in early 1851. The family soon moved to Melbourne. Giles went to Victoria's Castlemaine goldfields before becoming a Melbourne post office clerk in 1853. Retrenched in 1855, he returned to Castlemaine as assistant clerk of petty sessions. During the early 1860s he gained exploration experience while evaluating pastoral prospects west of the Darling River in NSW. Ferdinand von **Mueller** backed Giles's 1872 horseback expedition to explore Central Australia near Lake Amadeus and Mt Olga (now Katatjuta), which he named. In 1873 Giles travelled north-west from Macumba, SA, naming Gibson's Desert in honour of Alfred Gibson, who died on the journey. He first tried camels in early 1875 when exploring for Thomas **Elder** west and north-east of Fowlers Bay, SA. Later that year he proceeded west from Beltana, SA, and reached Perth via the Great Victoria Desert. He returned in 1876, heading north from Geraldton, WA, then re-crossing Gibson's Desert to arrive at Beltana after traversing more than 8000 kilometres of some of the most inhospitable country on earth.

Giles combined superb bushcraft with a romantic, almost mystical sense of the **outback**. His *Australia Twice Traversed* (1889) reveals the literary imagination which inspired Ray Ericksen to retrace Giles's path on a personal 'journey of discovery' in 1967. Ericksen's account, *West of Centre* (1972), was followed by his full-length biography, *Ernest Giles* (1978). In Australian exploration, Giles discovered more land than perhaps any other explorer, but most of it was economically poor and he did not achieve the recognition he deserved. He died of pneumonia at Coolgardie, WA, in 1897, a lowly mines office clerk who was, as he had predicted, the 'last of the Australian explorers'.

DC

Gill, Samuel Thomas (1818–80) came from England in 1839 to Adelaide, SA, where he worked as an artist. He accompanied an expedition to Spencer Gulf in 1846 and many of the drawings he made are held by the National Gallery of South Australia. The work for which he is best known is his depiction of the Victorian goldfields. His vivid, often humorous sketches capture the detail and the mood of everyday life on the diggings, with its disappointments and excitement. He produced *Victoria Gold Diggings and Diggers as They Are* in 1853, and in 1869, on commission from the Melbourne Public Library, made 40 sketches of the early goldfields. Michael **Cannon** edited a volume containing these, *The Victorian Goldfields 1852–53: An Original Album*

(1982, 1992). Gill documented other aspects of Australian colonial life in *Sketches in Victoria* (1855–56), *Sydney Illustrated* (1856), and *The Australian Sketchbook* (1856). *Samuel Thomas Gill: Artist* (1971) is a biography by K.M. Bowden; Geoffrey **Dutton**, *S.T. Gill's Australia* (1981), and Robert Raftopoulos, *S.T. Gill's Rural Australia* (1987), concentrate on specific aspects of his work.

KT

Gilmore, Mary Jean (1865–1962), poet and journalist, was among the most revered of the first generation of nationalist writers. Dymphna Cusack declared after her death that 'She not only created the stuff of which history is made. She was history.'

Mary Cameron was born near Goulburn, NSW, the eldest child of a struggling building contractor and his wife, both of Celtic backgrounds. She became a pupil-teacher when she was 12 years old, and her experience in schools in inner-city Sydney and outback NSW placed her firmly on the side of the poor and struggling worker. Mary became a committed 'Labor woman' and was the first woman member of the Australian Workers Union, as well as a member of its executive.

In 1895 Mary joined William **Lane's** utopian settlement in Paraguay where she met and married Will Gilmore, a shearer; her only child, Billy, was born there. After three years the Gilmores returned to Australia, where Mary's 'descent into hell' at her husband's family property in Casterton, Victoria, was made bearable when she became editor of the *Worker's* Women's Page in 1908. She moved back to Sydney three years later without her husband. For the next 23 years Mary used her page to 'fish for women' and to propagate her dream of an ideal socialist order based on sex and class equality. Mary was a feminist of a distinctively domestic kind, declaring: 'Woman is the highest, holiest, most precious gift to man. Her mission and throne is the family.' The flavour of her writing was often didactic, even messianic, but she was herself so approachable, and her political opinions were so leavened with homely wisdom, that her page secured a strong following. She became an object of veneration in many working-class households and consolidated her reputation as a champion of the 'little people'.

Gilmore reluctantly relinquished her page in 1931 and for the next 30 years enjoyed an active retirement. The oldest working journalist in Australia was made a Dame of the British Empire in 1937; she was fêted and lionised, her birthdays became cause for public celebration, and she held court to visitors in her Darlinghurst flat. Following her death in 1962, she received a state funeral at St Stephen's Presbyterian Church.

Gilmore built up her literary reputation in the 1890s as a regular *Bulletin* contributor. She continued to celebrate Australian identity in prose works such as *Old Days, Old Ways* (1934), a series of vivid vignettes of pioneer life. Mary was best known in her lifetime as a poet, and her role as the conscience of the nation was enhanced by inspirational wartime poems like 'No Foe Shall Gather Our Harvest'; but her poetry now seems less durable than her prose.

No biography of Mary Gilmore was published in her lifetime, and an autobiography dictated to Dorothy Catts was never published. Thereafter, potential biographers seem to have been daunted by her status as literary giant and national icon. Yet Gilmore's many contradictions—the feminist who revered powerful men, the upholder of family values who saw her husband twice in the last 30 years of their marriage, and the reputedly humble and self-deprecating woman who was nonetheless prone to insistent bouts of self-aggrandisement (as in her claim to have fostered Henry **Lawson's** creative genius)—offer fascinating themes for a biographer with an iconoclastic bent. *Mary Gilmore: A Tribute* (1965) by Dymphna Cusack, T. Inglis Moore and Barrie Ovenden is embarrassingly eulogistic, and Sylvia Lawson's *Mary Gilmore* (1966) is also deferential. W.H. Wilde's official biography, *Courage a Grace* (1988), is meticulously researched and, although tactful, less inclined to portray her as an Australian secular saint.

SHARYN PEARCE

Gilroy, Norman Thomas (1896–1977) became Australia's first native-born Catholic cardinal in 1946, six years after his appointment as archbishop of Sydney. Gilroy entered the priesthood after his return to Australia from service as a wireless operator during World War I. Although doctrinally and socially conservative, and an outspoken anti-communist, Gilroy did not support the 1950s right-wing group, the **'Movement'**, as did Archbishop **Mannix**, and preferred to exercise influence through the major political parties rather than through the **Democratic Labor Party**. Gilroy strove to expand the Catholic education system. He retired in 1971 and Graham Williams produced his biography, *Cardinal Sir Norman Gilroy* (1971).

KT

Gipps, George (1791–1847) was appointed governor of NSW in 1837 after serving in the British Army and as a member of a commission of enquiry into unrest in Canada. The experience was a preparation for difficulties during his eight years in office in Australia (1838–46).

Initially he was widely criticised for efforts to implement the instructions of the **Colonial Office** to protect Aborigines from pastoral settlers. On learning of the **Myall Creek massacre** in 1838, he was determined to punish the murderers. After a first jury acquitted all 12 defendants, he ordered seven retried. They were found guilty and hanged.

The beginning of representative government brought Gipps into conflict with the wealthy colonists who dominated the Legislative Council elected in 1843. His attempts to force graziers to pay higher rents and his attitude towards land tenure made him even more unpopular with the squatters. He was also under pressure from the rapidly increasing number of settlers in the Port Phillip District with their demands for separation. This is discussed by Ken Buckley in 'Gipps and the Graziers of New South Wales 1841–46' (*HSANZ*, 1955–56). Gipps's revealing correspondence with Charles **La Trobe**, appointed superintendent of Port Phillip in 1839, was published in 1989, edited by A.G.L. **Shaw**.

The end to transportation in 1840 did not relieve Gipps of the problem of convicts; he was responsible for the experimental Norfolk Island settlement under Alexander **Maconochie** and expressed his support for this system, urging that it be given a fair trial. Harried by the newspapers throughout most of his administration—the *Sydney Morning Herald* described him as 'the worst Governor New South Wales ever had' just prior to his departure—he was well regarded by the Colonial Office and many of the colonists. A descendant, John Gipps, provides a detailed account of Gipps's time in NSW in *Every Inch a Governor* (1996).

KT

Glynn, Patrick McMahon (1855–1931), lawyer and politician, travelled to Victoria in 1880 after practising at the Irish Bar, in the belief that Australia offered more scope for advancement in the legal profession. After several lean years in Melbourne, he was employed to open an office in Kapunda, SA, which he purchased within a few years. From 1883 to 1891 he was editor of the *Kapunda Herald*. An advocate of land nationalisation and free trade, Glynn was elected in 1887 to the House of Assembly but lost his seat three years later. In 1888 he opened another practice in Adelaide, where he was in and out of parliament during the 1890s. Glynn was elected a SA delegate to the Federal Convention of 1897–98, where his broad understanding of constitutional law was recognised. His election to the first federal parliament as a free-trader was the beginning of a long career in national politics, during which he held several key ministries. When he was finally defeated in 1919, he was the last of the 'founding fathers' to leave the parliament. His grandson, Gerald Glynn O'Collins, produced a biography (1965), and a collection of Glynn's letters to his family written between 1874 and 1927, which comment revealingly on social and political conditions in Victoria and SA (1974).

KT

Gold rushes began near Bathurst in NSW in April 1851, thanks to energetic promotion by Edward **Hargraves**, but the centre of action shifted quickly to Victoria. Ballarat, Sandhurst (Bendigo) and Mount Alexander (Castlemaine) became rich parent goldfields. St Arnaud, Ararat, Stawell, Beechworth, Walhalla, and many other fields followed. The deposits of gold had been formed over geological time by the action of water. Streams rushing down the slopes of the Great Dividing Range deposited gold—the heaviest of all minerals and rocks—at the point where the gradient flattened out onto the plains. These alluvial deposits lay close to the surface and could be mined using simple equipment like picks and shovels, with pans and rockers to wash the gold. They attracted great rushes of men: 20 000 were at work by the end of 1851. Melbourne lost half of its men, as did SA; immigrant ships started arriving early in 1852.

The Victorian goldfields population peaked at 150 000 by the end of 1858. Over half were British immigrants, and 40 000 were **Chinese**. Van Diemen's Land contributed thousands of ex-convicts; Americans and Europeans enriched the democratic tone of the goldfields. Government policy of granting very small claims gave everyone a chance, but also led to rapid exhaustion of claims and large rushes to new fields. The great rushes ended in the early 1860s. Victoria had produced 20 million ounces of gold during the decade 1851–60, one-third of world output, and NSW two million ounces. Victoria's population had increased sevenfold from 76 000 to 540 000, 45 per cent of the Australian population of 1 200 000 in 1861. Victoria was the leading colony and Melbourne the leading city; it had larger ideas, and put the Australian colonies onto the mental map of Empire. This was Victoria's 'Golden Age'.

The diaspora of prospectors from the Victorian parent goldfields and the dynamics of **prospecting** are described by Geoffrey **Blainey** in *The Rush That Never Ended* (1963). All goldfields ever discovered in Victoria were being worked by 1861, and prospectors had begun to move north along the Great Dividing Range. Discoveries in NSW at Kiandra, Lambing Flat, Young, and Forbes in the early 1860s led to large rushes. The last of the NSW rushes, to Gulgong and Home Rule in the early 1870s, were described in the writings of the gold commissioner Rolf **Boldrewood** and of Henry **Lawson**. The frontier moved on to Qld. Gympie (1867), Charters Towers (1871), the Palmer River (1872), and Mount Morgan (1883) were the leading discoveries, but the alluvial gold deposits were now smaller and more difficult to work because of tropical conditions and high transport costs. Gympie, Charters Towers, and Mount Morgan became rich reefing fields, to make Qld the leading gold region of the world in the 1880s.

The anti-clockwise gold trail around the continent now encountered difficult desert conditions. Construction of the overland telegraph from Adelaide to Darwin led to discoveries in the 1870s, but prospectors, now fewer in number but highly skilled, had to pause until the opening up of the remote Kimberley region by cattlemen. Halls Creek was rushed in 1886. Prospectors then moved along the edge of the Great Australian Desert. Southern Cross (1888), Coolgardie (1892), and Kalgoorlie (1893) were the main fields that created the great Western Australian gold boom of the 1890s. Men rushed from the eastern colonies, now in the grip of **depression**. Surface gold gave way to rich reef mines, especially at Kalgoorlie. Prospectors enjoyed their last hurrah, selling hundreds of prospects to promoters who floated mining companies on the London Stock Exchange.

Australian gold production had averaged £12 million a year in the 1850s, but declined to a low of £4.4 million in 1886. Discovery of new goldfields and the rise of reef mining had failed to compensate the decline of Victoria. Production then revived to £14 million in 1901 and stayed at that level for a decade, with Qld and WA providing the bulk of the output. The reef mines sank far underground, and used expensive machinery and complex metallurgical processes to separate the gold from the waste rock. The age of the heroes had given way to the age of technology, the lonely prospector to the mining engineer, and independent diggers to large joint-stock companies with a wage-earning labour force.

Blainey's contribution was to show that the discoveries from Ballarat to Kalgoorlie conformed to a pattern, and were not, as historians had assumed, the result of chance discoveries from time to time. He argued that rich parent alluvial fields, such as the Victorian fields in the 1850s and Coolgardie–Kalgoorlie after 1892, grubstaked large numbers of prospectors and so quickened the rate of discovery of new deposits. Poor parent fields slowed discovery, especially on the long trek from Qld to Coolgardie. He also argued that economic depressions stimulated goldmining by lowering costs and releasing labour for prospecting. Discoveries lifted Qld, Tasmania, and WA out of regional depressions and so played a counter-cyclical role in economic development.

Historians have always agreed that the gold rushes of the 1850s were a major discontinuity in Australian history. Anthony **Trollope** (1873) wrote that 'gold upheaves everything, and its disruptions are those of an earthquake'; and E.O.G. **Shann** in *Economic History of Australia* (1930) said that they were 'revolutionary'. Anxious contemporaries, as David Goodman shows in *Gold Seeking* (1994), often feared a kind of social collapse. Yet how revolutionary was gold? Earlier historians stressed the discontinuity, which enabled them to wipe out the convict heritage, and, by linking the gold rushes with the achievement of self-government and democracy, to give the colonies a fresh start. Some later historians, especially in NSW, argued for more continuity with the past: gold simply hastened developments already under way.

There was a major discontinuity in economic development. Gold displaced wool as Australia's principal export for 20 years and held second place for the rest of the century. Gold had strong linkage effects. Pastoralists sold sheep and cattle for meat and leather to the goldfields, and used the profits to buy freehold land and build fences and homesteads. Their search for more land took them to outback Qld and the Kimberley before the gold prospectors. Agriculture expanded rapidly. Farmers sent grain, fruit, and vegetables to the goldfields, and supplied oats and wheat to feed horses pulling wagons and coaches to and from the goldfields. Melbourne's population increased fourfold in the 1850s, but its share of Victoria's population declined from 38 to 23 per cent, such was the growth of the new gold cities, led by Ballarat and Bendigo. Construction of houses, schools and churches, roads, railways, and other public works drew thousands of men into building and construction. The economic achievement was to absorb a massive population increase, but to maintain the 1851 level of real income per head at the same level, of about £30 per annum in real terms, through the decade.

G.V. **Portus**, *Studies in the Australian Constitution* (1933), decided that the most important social and political effect of gold was 'the change in the quality of the population', a perspective most fully developed in Geoffrey **Serle's** history of Victoria in the 1850s, *The Golden Age* (1963). By 1861 Victoria had a large population of vigorous young people. They were more skilled than comparable groups in Britain. There were only seven women for every 10 men, but assisted migration was favouring women and the ratio would improve to nine to 10 by 1871. The gold rushes clearly gave a strong democratic impulse to Victoria, and also to the other colonies, but historians are not sure how to describe and reconcile the bourgeois and radical democratic legacies. Immigrants led the fight for free selection and, in Victoria, for tariff protection. They became farmers and businesspeople; Peter **Lalor**, the hero of **Eureka**, became a mine owner. They and their children supplied politicians and clergymen for generations to come, and created the liberal-democratic tradition of Victorian politics. The central Victorian goldfields were the birthplace in the 1870s of the Amalgamated Miners Association, and also of the Australian Shearers Union, where W.G. **Spence** organised the local men who travelled each year to northern shearing sheds. Russel **Ward's** *Australian Legend* (1958) portrayed the gold digger as a democratic hero, who embraced the same faith in socialism and mateship already adopted by the pastoral workers, so that while 'in politics and economics the golden age was a watershed ... in the development of the Australian mystique it was not'.

After a century or more of decline and stagnation, many gold towns and villages around Australian have revived with the growth of tourism, and as people from the capital cities buy and restore houses for recreation or retirement. In *Beechworth* (1987), Tom Griffiths described the tension between old residents who cling to the old past and others who have used another version of the past to make tourism the mainstay of the town. Sovereign Hill at Ballarat, one of Australia's leading tourist attractions, tries hard to keep the balance between romance and historical truth, with the former always likely to win the day.

J.W. MCCARTY

Goldsbrough, Richard (1821–86) used experience gained in the Yorkshire wool industry to establish a business in Melbourne in 1848. By 1850 he was the leading broker in Melbourne and had established the colony's first regular wool auctions. With a range of partners, Goldsbrough extended into other branches of the industry, including pastoral properties. He opened a Sydney branch in 1882 and later amalgamated with **Mort** & Co. to form the famous rural firm, Goldsbrough, Mort & Co. Ltd. He was a crucial figure in the development of the Australian **wool** industry. A large and generous man, Goldsbrough was reputed to have once 'entertained a champagne-loaded party at the Ascot races in a coach surmounted by a large emu-emblazoned flag'. Alfred Joyce vividly portrayed their social evenings in *A Homestead History* (1942).

KT

Goldstein, Vida Jane Mary (1869–1949) was the most charismatic of the second generation of first-wave feminists. A leader, too, in the anti-war agitation of 1914–18, Goldstein thereafter gave her talents to the service of Christian Science. She attracted little notice outside feminist circles until the federal electorate of Balaclava, Victoria, was renamed Goldstein in 1984.

Vida matriculated from Melbourne's Presbyterian Ladies College in 1886. Popular, fun-loving, and athletic, but also committed to social Christianity, Vida followed Charles **Strong** from the Collins Street Presbyterian Church to the Australian Church. While working as a teacher, she assisted her mother's philanthropic activities in the slums; she also canvassed signatures for the 1891 Victorian women's suffrage petition. At 30 she was leader of the United Council for Women's Suffrage, and in 1902 represented Australian women's organisations at the International Woman Suffrage Conference in Washington DC, where she was elected secretary of the new International Woman Suffrage Committee. After forming the non-party Women's Federal Political Association (later the **Women's Political Association**), Goldstein stood for the Senate in 1903, the first Commonwealth election in which all women could vote. She was the first British Empire woman to nominate for a national parliament. Although unsuccessful, she received considerable press coverage, even if her dress and bearing attracted more notice than what she said. She contested the Senate again in 1910 and 1917 and the House of Representatives seat of Kooyong in 1913 and 1914. She also began the proudly titled *Woman Voter* in 1909—the main voice of Australia's non-party women and of feminist anti-war sentiment.

Goldstein remained committed to international suffrage, travelling to England in 1911 to assist the Pankhurst suffragettes, an experience that convinced her of the strategic value of confrontation and the need for public discussion about sexual issues. The *Woman Voter* thereafter printed articles about the 'white slave traffic', venereal diseases, and sex crimes, defying the view that these were not subjects respectable women discussed. She found the war years taxing and dispiriting. Her unambiguous anti-war stance split the Women's Federal Political Association. She was harassed at public meetings; the *Woman Voter* was censored; the association's work for unemployed women was undermined, and its delegate was expelled from the **National Council of Women** which Goldstein had helped to found. Still hopeful of salvaging some lessons from the war, she attended the Women's Peace Conference in Zurich in May 1919 and spoke of the need 'to develop the international conscience' and take up 'the sword of the spirit'. The association and the *Woman Voter* folded in her absence. Convinced now at 50 that she was out of tune with the times, emotionally exhausted, and needing to take stock, Vida turned to Christian Science counselling, becoming a reader in the Melbourne church.

The details of Goldstein's life between 1900 and 1920 are well established, and Leslie Henderson's *The Goldstein Story* (1973) gives her family background, but the scattered and sparse records of Vida's later years give rise—unfairly—to an impression of reclusiveness and forsaken political convictions. Janette Bomford's biography (1993) presents her as a typical, even conventional, first-wave feminist, motivated by middle-class ideals of home protection and a conviction of the moral superiority of women. More innovative interpretations can be found in shorter pieces by Jenny Mulraney

(*AFS*, 1988), Farley Kelly (*Double Time*, 1985) and Susan Magarey (*AHS*, 1996), who together present a convincing view of Goldstein as the quintessential modern 'new woman', whose youth, confidence, femininity, and independence threatened to destabilise masculine political power and privilege.

JUDITH SMART

Gollan, Robin Allenby (1917–) is the most important of the **Old Left** group of historians. From a dairy farm at Cambewarra Mountain, near Nowra, NSW, he proceeded by scholarship to Fort Street High in Sydney and the University of Sydney. His elder brother Bill, a teacher and leading member of the **Communist** Party, encouraged both his education and his politics. He joined the party in 1936. After war service in the RAAF, he completed an MA in history at Sydney and then a doctorate at the London School of Economics. Gollan returned to a position at the Australian National University and remained there until retirement. The doctoral thesis, a study of the emergence of the labour movement in eastern Australia, was published as *Radical and Working Class Politics* (1960, 1967). It provided a framework for the study of labour history, an activity Gollan encouraged through presidency of the Labour History Society formed in the following year, and practised with a study of the NSW coalminers in 1963. He was largely responsible for the collection of trade union records in what is now the Noel Butlin Archives Centre at the Australian National University. Along with other members of the Old Left, Gollan was accused by **New Left** critics of blurring class boundaries in an idealised progressive **nationalism**; more than most, he was able to engage his critics in measured response. Having himself benefited from the support of W.K. **Hancock** during the Cold War, he was a generous mentor of younger left scholars.

In the aftermath of Khrushchev's admission to the Soviet Communist Party of Stalin's atrocities, and the Australian party's refusal to discuss those atrocities, he left it. 'I joined the party in 1936', he has explained, 'because it seemed to me the only party in Australia fully committed to a struggle for socialism and against fascism. I left it, with regret, in 1957, because this no longer seemed to be the case.' He explored that transformation in his book *Revolutionaries and Reformists* (1975), still the most satisfactory balance sheet of Australian communism.

SM

Gondwanaland, or Gondwana, refers to the large landmass or super-continent in the Southern Ocean, formed by the compression of the earth's crust between 650 and 550 million years ago. It comprised all the southern continents—Australia, **Antarctica**, South America, and Africa—and the Indian subcontinent. The physical junction of the southern continents is evident in the shared characteristics of their birds and animals, such as flightless birds, marsupials, and lungfish. The portion that included Australia split away from the single land mass of Pangaea (Africa and South America)

about 225 million years ago; it drifted south until about 120 million years ago, when it began to break up. Australia broke away from Antarctica about 45 million years ago and commenced a northward drift, taking with it Papua New Guinea and New Zealand. These three countries became a physically isolated southern landmass when the seas rose after the last ice age, but their connecting land bridges were gradually flooded. Rising seas finally isolated Tasmania from the mainland about 20 000 years ago (and Papua New Guinea about 12 000 years ago). Reg Morrison provides a narrative account of 4 billion years of Australian **natural history** in *The Voyage of the Great Southern Ark* (1988), and Mary E. White, *The Greening of Gondwana* (1986), traces the history of its plant life.

HD

Gordon, Adam Lindsay (1833–70), poet, was born in the Azores to Scottish parents. His father was a cavalry officer who passed on his love of riding to his son. After an English education, Gordon spent a reckless youth. In 1853 his parents sent him to SA, where he married and settled in a seaside cottage, Dingley Dell, near Port McDonnell. He pursued various occupations—mounted policeman, politician, and farmer—relatively unsuccessfully, but earned a reputation for his daring feats in the saddle. After his first poem appeared in 1864, Gordon produced a steady stream of ballad-style verse, much of which is collected in *Sea Spray and Smoke Drift* (1867) and *Bush Ballads and Galloping Rhymes* (1870). By the late 1860s, a series of misfortunes left him depressed and melancholy. Failure to secure title to family lands in Scotland was the final blow. Financially destitute, he committed suicide.

Gordon's ballads enjoyed remarkable popularity, and appeared in school readers long after his death, although, with the exception of 'The Sick Stockrider'—later hailed as the beginning of a distinctly Australian ballad tradition—Gordon's poetry featured little Australian content. His popularity sprang from his simple, evocative verse, augmented by the appeal of a noble birth, romantic youth, and tragic end. In 1934 he became the only Australian memorialised in the Poets' Corner at Westminster Abbey.

HD

Gorton, John Grey (1911–) was elected to the Senate for the Liberal Party in 1949 after serving as a pilot in World War II. He held a number of minor portfolios until the unexpected death in 1967 of Harold **Holt** catapulted him into the prime ministership as a compromise candidate. He thus became the only senator to win that position, although he then moved to the lower house. He turned out not to be the unifying force his colleagues hoped for, and aroused a deal of antagonism within the party because of his idiosyncratic, informal style and strengthening of the Commonwealth at the expense of the states. A decline in government popularity, due in some part to its involvement in the **Vietnam War** and conscription, made his leadership fragile. When his defence minister, Malcolm **Fraser**, resigned in

1971 and announced he could no longer work with Gorton, William **McMahon** challenged for the leadership. In a typically quixotic gesture, Gorton cast the deciding vote against himself. He resigned from the Liberal Party in 1975 and stood, unsuccessfully, as an independent Senate candidate for the ACT. Alan Reid assesses his prime ministership in *The Gorton Experiment* (1971), and Alan Trengrove published 'an informal' biography in 1969.

KT

Gould, Elizabeth (1804–41) and **John** (1804–81) formed a famous partnership as natural historians. John, a zoologist, worked as a taxidermist with the Zoological Society of London before publishing his first volumes on birds in the early 1830s, illustrated with lithographs drawn and coloured by Elizabeth. Because of their keen interest in specimens from NSW, the Goulds travelled to Australia in 1838. During their two-year stay John travelled extensively to sketch birds and mammals, while Elizabeth made many drawings of plants and animals to help in the production of final plates for the proposed works. Part one of the first volume, the magnificent *The Birds of Australia*, was published in London in 1840; the final of the 36 parts appeared in 1848. Only 84 of the plates are attributed to Elizabeth, those which she completed before her premature death. Recognition of her contribution and skill waned in the face of her husband's increasing fame. It was the discovery in 1939 and 1964 of some of her letters from Australia—now in the Mitchell Library—that returned her to public notice. John later produced *The Mammals of Australia* (1845–63) and *Handbook to the Birds of Australia* (1865). He commemorated his wife in the name of a tropical finch, and was himself remembered by the establishment of the Gould League of Bird Lovers (now simply the Gould League). A.H. Chisholm produced *The Story of Elizabeth Gould* in 1944; John has been more extensively examined in works that include *John Gould: Birdman* (1987) by Maureen Lambourne and *The Ruling Passion of John Gould* (Isabella Tree, 1991).

KT

Governor-general is an office established by the Australian **Constitution** which describes the holder as the representative of the queen, and as exercising powers and functions assigned by her. The Constitution also vests various powers in the governor-general directly; although it is settled that most of these are exercisable on ministerial advice, there are a few cases in which a discretion is reposed in him. The best-known case is the power to dismiss a minister, which was exercised by Sir John **Kerr** in November 1975. This generated angry dispute, but no action has been taken to define in detail the circumstances in which this, or any other reserve power, may be exercised.

The first governor-generals came to Australia from Britain. Some were of aristocratic lineage; others were raised to the peerage; most had parliamentary or administrative experience. Chris Cunneen, *King's Men* (1983), evokes their milieu and recounts the issues they faced. While acting as

constitutional sovereigns in their relations with the Australian government, they were also representatives of both the Crown and the British government. Thus communication between the British and Australian prime ministers passed via the governor-general and the **Colonial Office**, until W.M. **Hughes** insisted on direct communication in 1918 during World War I. The wartime governor-general, Sir Ronald **Munro Ferguson**, had significant influence on his prime minister, W.M. Hughes, and Australian war policy.

In 1926 an Imperial Conference meeting in London resolved that a governor-general should not be subject to British direction, and that he should not be a British representative, a protector of British and imperial concerns. Henceforth UK interests were to be the concern of a British diplomatic agent styled the British High Commissioner. The conference, however, did not deal specifically with the source of power to appoint a governor-general. Up to 1930 this power had been exercised by the British government. In 1930, the Australian Prime Minister J.H. **Scullin** recommended the appointment of Sir Isaac **Isaacs**, then chief justice of the High Court of Australia, who was an Australian-born resident. The king, George V, was strongly opposed to the appointment of a 'local man', and the authority of the Australian government to advise on such an appointment was questioned. The Australian prime minister persisted, and the king reluctantly appointed Isaacs. It may now be taken as settled that the source of advice on the appointment of a governor-general is the Australian prime minister. There were five appointments after Isaacs of governor-generals who came from the UK. Since 1965, with the appointment of Lord **Casey**, all appointees have been Australian. Some have had previous political careers; others have come from judicial and academic backgrounds.

The governor-general exercises a number of governmental functions. For example he assents to legislation, and does so on ministerial advice; he receives the credentials of foreign diplomatic representatives appointed to Australia; and he presides over the Executive Council in which a wide range of governmental business is transacted. While he acts on the advice of the ministers in the Council, the governor-general may raise questions about such matters as the observance of regularity in procedures, and he may seek clarification.

The most important functions of the office are those, described as ceremonial, associated with the governor-general's public appearances, travels, and speeches. By far the greater part of my time as governor-general was spent on such activities, and particularly on the preparation and delivery of a great number and variety of speeches and addresses all over Australia. In a farewell speech in Canberra in 1982, I said that I believed that through such work, through travel, speeches, and meetings with a wide range of people, the governor-general offers encouragement and recognition to many Australians who may not be very powerful or visible in the course of everyday life, and to the efforts of individuals and groups who work constructively to improve life in the nation and the community. I agree with Sir Paul **Hasluck** when he says that Australians both expect and appreciate statements by a governor-general on matters of current concern at a level different from that of any party political controversy. I also think that it is right to say with Hasluck (*The Office of the Governor-General*, 1973) that the office of governor-general is the highest single expression in the Australian governmental structure of the idea that Australians of all parties and all walks of life belong to the same nation. Recognition of this places heavy burdens and responsibilities on the Australian who holds the office.

ZELMAN COWEN

Governor, Jimmy (1875–1901), Aboriginal **bushranger**, was born near Talbragar River, NSW. In 1898 he married Ethel Page, a 16-year-old white woman. From April 1900 the couple lived on John Mawbey's property, near Gilgandra, where Governor worked as a fencing contractor with his brother Joe, nephew Peter, and two other Aborigines, Jacky Underwood and Jacky Porter. Ethel did housework for the Mawbey family. She allegedly endured taunts from Mawbey's wife and a boarder, Helen Kerz, concerning her marriage. When Governor and Underwood confronted the women on 20 July 1900, Kerz is supposed to have said: 'You black rubbish, you want shooting for marrying a white woman.' At that, the two men went berserk, killing both women and three of the Mawbey children. Underwood was soon captured, and later hanged, but the Governor brothers escaped to the bush. For 14 weeks they ranged across north central NSW, avenging old grievances, and terrorising the area with robberies and attacks on whites; four others were murdered. Jimmy Governor was captured near Wingham in October 1900, convicted, and executed at Darlinghurst Gaol. His brother was shot dead near Singleton. In *The Life of Jimmy Governor* (1979), Brian Davies relates Governor's story and suggests he should be understood in the tradition of Aboriginal resistance. Thomas **Keneally's** novel, *The Chant of Jimmie Blacksmith* (1972), was influenced by Frank **Clune's** *Jimmy Governor* (1959), and was adapted as a successful feature film by Fred Schepisi in 1978.

DC

Governors have undergone a transformation in Australia since 1788. Captain Arthur **Phillip**, first governor of NSW, was practically the absolute ruler of the penal settlement. His successors (also naval captains until Colonel Lachlan **Macquarie's** appointment in 1810) were in a similar position, though amenable to the authority of the secretary of state. Lord Sydney and his successors were remote: 'distance', in this as in other respects (as Geoffrey **Blainey** famously argued) might be said to have played a considerable role in Australian history. But other civil officers appointed by the home government (notably the judges), and English legal and administrative customs, made themselves felt; the colony's society also imposed limits on what a governor could do. The fate of Governor William **Bligh** demonstrated this; on the other hand, Governor Macquarie is well known to have imposed his ideas on the colony. Under the Crown Colony constitution inaugurated in 1824, the gover-

nor was required to work with a Legislative as well as an Executive Council—but he remained the seat of political and administrative power until the constitutional changes of the 1850s.

Between 1820 and 1855, governors of NSW were commonly Wellingtonian officers of variable quality. Sir George **Gipps**, though a colonel of Royal Engineers, had previous civil experience in Canada. His successor, Sir Charles **FitzRoy**, was in office for the ending of **transportation** and the inauguration of constitutional changes which ended (1856) in 'responsible government'. Another engineer, Sir William **Denison**, presided over the introduction of the new system, under which the governor relinquished ordinary political and administrative functions. Soldiers who took office in the colonial Empire were now opting for an increasingly professional civil service: as early as the 1840s, Captain (later Sir) George **Grey** did this when he became governor of SA. But soldiers were increasingly in a minority. Civilian 'career governors' became usual, including Sir Henry Barkly (Victoria), Sir John Young (NSW), Sir George **Bowen** (Qld; Victoria), Sir John Manners-Sutton (Viscount Canterbury) (Victoria), and Sir Hercules Robinson (NSW)—all of whom held office during the quarter-century following 1855.

As governors became increasingly like the sovereign in relation to ministers, so their 'dignified' aspect became more obvious, and their role at 'the head of colonial society' was emphasised. But they were by no means exempt from controversy: Sir Charles Darling, for instance, was embroiled in a quasi-partisan way in the Victorian **constitutional crisis** of 1865, and the secretary of state recalled him for his conduct; Bowen in 1878 also incurred displeasure locally and in London. Irrespective of individual merits, political society in the colonies became dissatisfied with mere Colonial Service governors, their attitudes being given some impetus in 1887 when the newly appointed governor of Qld, Sir Henry Blake, was discovered to have a brother of dubious reputation in the colony. By the end of the century it had become common, though not invariable, for appointments to be made from the ranks of the aristocracy, with or without political experience. This practice continued to be fairly common in both Commonwealth and states after 1901, though there was also some reversion to the appointment of senior military officers—a preference which persists to some extent today.

In the twentieth century the role and status of governors as 'constitutional sovereigns' underwent yet more considerable changes. The appointment of all had remained with the British government, whose representatives they were. The Imperial Conference of 1926, however, decided that the **governor-generals** of Dominions would no longer represent or be answerable to that government. Recommendations for their appointment soon began to pass, in practice, into the hands of Dominion prime ministers; in 1930, James **Scullin** established the right of the Australian prime minister to advise the sovereign on the appointment of the governor-general. The flow-on to the states did not begin until after World War II; formal recommendation for the appointment of state governors indeed remained with the secretary of state until the passage of the Australia Acts in 1986.

Advice to the sovereign on appointments is now wholly localised. From the 1970s some states have recommended individuals—usually now natives of the home state—very different from the traditional. A particularly significant departure from previous practice has been the appointment of women as governors.

Partly because of this autochthonous development, the vice-regal constitutional role has become, if anything, more critical. Not that it was ever less than important, and Sir Philip Game's 1932 dismissal of J.T. **Lang** as premier of NSW showed how gubernatorial functions could involve much more than the rights set out by Walter Bagehot in his commentary on the English constitution: 'to be consulted, to advise, and to warn'. In recent years, devoid of any reference to the British state, the governors of Tasmania and Qld have had to resolve serious constitutional situations. Together with the actions of Governor-General Sir John **Kerr** in 1975, such episodes would seem to indicate the position of vice-regal representatives as independent 'heads of state' in their respective spheres. If so, the transformation from 1788 is thus completed and may be seen as part of a unique development in state formation.

The queen's active role in Australia is limited to the appointment or dismissal of her representatives on the advice of prime minister and premiers, though her sovereignty, exercised by those representatives in Commonwealth and states alike, would seem to be essential to the operation of government. But it is not unchallenged. For instance, the behaviour of some state premiers in relation to their governors—such as the forced resignation of the governor of Victoria in 1985 and the attempt in NSW in 1995 to weaken the governor's role—could be seen as encroachments upon the independence of the vice-regal office. It is a question also whether the introduction of a significant element of quasi-egalitarianism into the behaviour and environment of Government Houses, and the removal of evidently dignified practices, can benefit an office which represents Majesty.

BRUCE KNOX

Goyder's Line was drawn by the surveyor-general of SA, George Goyder, in the mid-1860s to indicate the pastoral holdings most severely affected by drought. It ran broadly east–west across the colony, with a bulge in the centre reaching to Melrose in the lower Flinders Ranges. The line came to be regarded as marking the northern boundary of the area where agriculture could be safely pursued. In the good years of the 1870s the farmers objected to this restriction and it was lifted in 1874. By the early 1880s it was clear that Goyder was right. Farms and towns were abandoned; their ruins can still be seen. So great was the subsequent authority of the line that settlement in the Murray Mallee in the early twentieth century was delayed because a portion of the country was north of the line. The line still broadly marks the northern

limit of the state's agricultural lands. D.W. Meinig, *On the Margins of the Good Earth* (1962), gives a detailed account.

JH

Grainger, (George) Percy Aldridge (1882–1961), musician, ethnologist, and 'all-round man', is Australia's best-known composer. Born in Brighton, Victoria, he undertook his higher musical education in Germany, and his professional life was based in Britain (1901–14) and then the USA (1914–61); he visited Australia periodically on concert tours. The dominating influence and constant companion of his first 40 years was his mother; her suicide in 1922 had a seismic impact on his personality. Grainger rarely attempted a distinctively American or Australian style in his music, but espoused a British 'yeoman' style, as in such folksong settings as *Country Gardens* (1918), *Lincolnshire Posy* (1937), or the folksy clog dance, *Handel in the Strand* (1911–12). He generally avoided large forms, one exception being his 'music to an imaginary ballet', *The Warriors* (1916). During 1945–60 he pioneered a rudimentary form of electronic music, 'free music'.

Occasionally, Grainger sought to express images typical of the Australian landscape or people in his music, as in his *Colonial Song* (1912), *Gumsucker's March* (1914), and Whitman-inspired *Marching Song of Democracy* (1917). His Australianness emerged more readily in the resourceful, muscular image of Nordic Australian youth, which he personally battled to preserve into his fifties, and in the vision of a non-European national music which he bequeathed to later Australian composers. Grainger wrote many rambling autobiographical essays, which remain unpublished. The Grainger Museum, erected in 1938 in accordance with his own design beside the University of Melbourne Conservatorium, is the most complete Australian archive of his musical work and a vivid disclosure of the composer's own eccentric, sometimes disturbed, personality. John Bird's *Percy Grainger* (1976) is the standard biography.

MALCOLM GILLIES

Grazier, see **Pastoralist**

Great White Fleet was the name given to a fleet of 31 US warships that toured the world between 1907 and 1909. The fleet visited Sydney in August 1908 at the invitation of Prime Minister Alfred **Deakin**, who annoyed the British government by dealing directly with the Americans. The jubilant welcome given to the Americans showed the eagerness in Australia for an alliance of the white race in the Pacific against the 'yellow peril'. The world voyage of the Great White Fleet is documented by Robert A. Hart (1965), and an account of the Australian visit is given by Ruth Megaw in *JRAHS* (1970). (See also **Defence**.)

HD

Greeks in Australia arrived in chains from 1829 onwards. Most of these transportees had been pardoned and repatriated by 1837, when the earliest known free Greek settlers landed. They inaugurated an eighty-year period of fitful and often temporary Greek immigration, admirably documented in the first volume of Hugh Gilchrist's *Australians and Greeks* (1992). By the end of the nineteenth century a committed core of long-term settlers had established Greek Orthodox communities in Melbourne (1897) and Sydney (1898), which proceeded to build churches, organise schools for Greek language and religious instruction, and coordinate philanthropic and patriotic activities. Similar pan-Hellenic organisations were soon established in other states, together with a plethora of regional brotherhoods (produced by and perpetuating chain-migration) and various special-purpose associations, which all provided scope for pursuit of the national passion for politics and the exercise of elected office outside the British–Australian mainstream, where southern Europeans were generally held in low regard.

Greece's initial neutrality in World War I led to the anti-Greek riots of Kalgoorlie and Boulder (WA) in 1916 and to the inclusion of the 2200 known Greeks in an official wartime survey of potentially hostile aliens. Yet in spite of general unpopularity and periodic official sanctions, the number of Greek-born residents of Australia quadrupled between the wars in the wake of large-scale 'ethnic cleansing' in the Balkans and Asia Minor, and imposition of even stricter immigration quotas by the USA. The standing of Greeks was enhanced by Greece's heroic defiance of the Axis forces and the commitment of 16 000 Australian soldiers to its aid in 1941, but it was the sheer numbers of Greek immigrants displaced by the depredations of enemy occupation and a protracted civil war, and encouraged by the belated extension of assisted passages to them in 1952, that seeded the social and political ascent of the Greek community.

Unlike their precursors, many postwar Greek immigrants worked in factories; self-employment in catering became increasingly difficult with the growth of chain stores and fast-food franchises. Purely secular power-struggles inevitably arose (described by S. Kourbetis, *The Dawn: The Greek-Australian Left 1915–1955*, 1992), but these were overshadowed by the conflict between the older Greek Orthodox communities and the Archdiocese (established initially as a Metropolis in 1924 by the Patriarch of Constantinople). This flared up in the late 1950s over control of assets and associated issues, and intensified throughout the years of mass migration. The process is described by M.P. Tsounis in *Greeks in English-speaking Countries* (1993). Fanned by Cold War rhetoric and a burgeoning, polarised Greek-language press, the conflict continues to this day and has periodically embroiled two Orthodox Patriarchates, a succession of Greek governments, and their diplomatic missions in Australia. It has occasionally spilled embarrassingly into the mainstream media and bemused Australian dignitaries who receive competing invitations to separate commemorations of Greek national unification.

The last sizeable wave of Greek immigrants comprised refugees from the Turkish invasion of Cyprus of 1974, by which time the Greek-born alone officially numbered 160 000 and formed the most highly urbanised (87 per cent) of ethnic minorities. Greek-Australians were also poised to promote and exploit the newly articulated doctrine of **multiculturalism**, which encouraged them to overcome the defensive introspection of their precursors, and to use their increasing affluence, entrepreneurial and professional ambition, and political influence to penetrate mainstream institutions, including the arts and sport, while remaining a flamboyantly distinct cultural group. D.F. De Stoop, *The Greeks of Melbourne* (1996), is a useful local study. Unlike prewar Greeks, who apparently adhered to what M. Koromila, *In the Traces of Odysseus* (1994), called an 'inviolable' tradition of staying out of host-country politics, they also entered both sides of mainstream politics with great gusto. Initially they filled a power vacuum caused by the Labor Party split of 1955, then created Greek-speaking branches of both major political parties, and by the 1990s supplied more than a dozen members of parliament, including ministers, at both state and federal levels.

Greece was initially slow to tap the political potential of its antipodean nationals, establishing a full diplomatic legation only in 1953. Indeed, during the civil war and the Junta years (1967–74), Greek-Australians tried to exert pressure on Greek governments via the Australian government. Since the 1980s, however, there have been attempts to harness the diaspora to advance Greek foreign policy, following the supposed success of the Greek-American lobby. The **Keating** government's tergiversations on the Macedonian question are credited to Greek-Australian lobbying, as is sustained Australian support for the Republic of Cyprus.

While Greek-Australians are now patronised as model citizens, and the second generation even make popular entertainment out of parodying their parents and themselves, there is growing concern over the future. The community is ageing and needing more Greek aged-care, and current levels of Greek immigration are lower than reverse migration. Notwithstanding the unprecedented volume of Greek language available in print and electronic media in Australia and generous provision for instruction, language attrition among second and subsequent generations is marked.

STATHIS GAUNTLETT

Green bans were industrial bans enforced by builders labourers' and workers' unions in the 1970s that prevented demolition or damage to properties of built or natural heritage significance. The first such bans were placed on the demolition of a park in Carlton in Melbourne in 1970 and on the destruction of Kellys Bush in Hunters Hill in Sydney in 1971, following agitation by residents' action groups. The term *green ban* was coined by Jack **Mundey** in 1973 to distinguish these actions from traditional union black bans. Green bans won community support in inner-city Sydney and became an effective means of preserving places such as the **Rocks** and Woolloomooloo. They also impeded construction of the Newport Power Station site in Victoria between 1971 and 1978. Cooperation between trade unions and the **National Trust** in Sydney and Melbourne enabled successful blockades on demolition work at historic properties, such as the Regent Theatres in Sydney and Melbourne. Mundey, *Green Bans and Beyond* (1981), Richard Roddewig, *Green Bans: The Birth of Australian Environmental Politics* (1978), and Meredith Burgmann and Verity Burgmann, *Green Bans, Red Union* (1998), examine their background and effectiveness.

HD

Green, Dorothy (1915–91) and her husband **Henry Mackenzie** (1881–1962) shared a commitment to Australian literature. Dorothy was a journalist and schoolteacher who later lectured in English at Monash University, the Australian National University, and the Australian Defence Force Academy. She wrote on many Australian writers—most notably on Henry Handel **Richardson** in *Ulysses Bound* (1973)—always discussing the literature within its cultural and social context, with particular concern for the human dimension and an impatience with the meretricious. A collection of her writings, *The Music of Love* (1984), contains a bibliography. She also published several volumes of poetry under her birth name, Auchterlonie.

Henry was literary critic for two Sydney newspapers before he became librarian of the Fisher Library, University of Sydney, in 1921, a position he held for 25 years. His early publication, *An Outline of Australian Literature* (1930), foreshadowed what would become his lifetime's work, *A History of Australian Literature* (1961); it provides the first full survey and is especially noteworthy for its consideration of non-fiction works, including history and biography. It was revised by Dorothy in 1984–85.

KT

Greenhide is a term of English origin which describes the untanned hide of an animal, usually of cattle, which in colonial Australia provided a ready material for making ropes, whips, bridles, and halters. The word developed an Australian colloquial meaning for inexperienced settlers who were not yet accustomed to bush life, and to those who insisted on retaining genteel formalities, such as dressing for dinner, which were generally considered inappropriate in the bush.

HD

Greens are a political group concerned with protecting the environment that has gained increasing power and importance since the 1960s. Despite their unsuccessful battle in the early 1970s to stop the damming of Lake Pedder in south-western Tasmania, environmental lobby groups have since won significant victories. A federal intervention order to stop sand-mining on Fraser Island in the early 1980s was followed in 1982–83 by the highly publicised 'Save the Franklin' campaign, which opposed damming the Franklin River in Tasmania. Environmentalists exerted sufficient influence for the **Hawke** government to ban the dam which

was in a World Heritage area, an action upheld by the High Court. This success prompted their organisation. The Tasmanian story is told by Richard Flanagan and Cassandra Pybus in *The Rest of the World Is Watching* (1990). The Greens achieved national prominence in the early 1990s with an election of two senators from WA whose support was vital to the passage of key legislation. A national political party was launched in 1994.

HD

Greenway, Francis Howard (1777–1837) was an English architect transported for forgery in 1814. He was granted a ticket-of-leave soon after he arrived in NSW and began practising his former profession. Taken up by Governor **Macquarie**, he was emancipated on completion of his first commission—the lighthouse on South Head, Sydney Harbour. His other works included the **Female Factory** at Parramatta; new Government House; the Supreme Court, Sydney; and many churches, of which St Matthew's, Windsor, is considered his finest. He followed the Georgian style of the day, though he rapidly introduced design elements that responded to specifically Australian conditions. His determination to improve the quality of colonial workmanship and to impose a businesslike system of payments incurred many enemies. Eventually he and Macquarie clashed over fees, and in 1822 he was dismissed as government architect; he returned unsuccessfully to private practice. M.H. **Ellis** thought him worthy of a biography (1949), and he was long regarded as an exemplar of the reformed convict of colonial society, even appearing on the first $10 note. A major retrospective of his work was held at **Hyde Park Barracks**, Sydney, in 1997.

KT

Greenwood, Gordon (1913–86) presided over the academic study of history in Qld for more than 30 years, and played a prominent national role in the study of international relations. From the University of Sydney, where he studied under Stephen **Roberts**, he proceeded to graduate study in London, and lecturing positions at New England and Sydney before assuming the chair of history in Qld in 1949. A distinctive feature of his appointment was the coupling of history with political science; the department's dual focus was reflected in his long editorship of the *Australian Journal of Politics and History*, which he had founded in 1950. (Separate departments of history and politics were created in 1967.) Greenwood's own interests in Australian federalism and international relations spanned the two fields. The University of Queensland department was perhaps closer in spirit to the rigorously empirical, international style of Roberts's Sydney than the more philosophical approach of **Crawford's** Melbourne; but it soon developed a vigorous character of its own, especially in the study of Queensland history. He was responsible, with Norman **Harper**, for editing the first four volumes of *Australia in World Affairs* from 1950. *Australia: A Social and Political History*, which he edited in 1955, was for many years the only general scholarly survey of Australian history; Greenwood himself wrote most of the twentieth-century chapters. He was an active member of the **Australian Institute of International Affairs**, serving as research chairman (1952–61) and national president (1961–65). In these wide-ranging activities he was known and enjoyed, in Qld and elsewhere, as a *bon viveur*.

JOHN LEGGE

Greer, Germaine (1939–   ), author of *The Female Eunuch*, celebrity feminist, journalist, director of Stump Cross Books, fellow of Newnham College, Cambridge, was born in Melbourne. She was educated at a Catholic girls' school and at the University of Melbourne, where she took out joint honours in English and French in 1959. After completing an MA at the University of Sydney, she was awarded a Commonwealth scholarship and proceeded to Cambridge, where she completed a doctoral thesis on Shakespeare in 1968.

At university Greer developed a flamboyant persona, engaged in student politics, acted in both Melbourne and Sydney University drama societies, and wrote for student newspapers *Farrago* and *Honi Soit*. Involvement in Melbourne bohemianism of Drift and the Sydney Push inspired Greer's early libertarian politics, as did her engagement with **Andersonianism** at the University of Sydney. At Cambridge she enhanced her reputation for controversy and drama, being the first woman to appear in the Cambridge Footlight Smokers. After completing her doctorate, she taught at the University of Warwick. She began to write for the radical paper *Oz*, edited by fellow-expatriate Richard Neville. As part of the Underground scene, Greer could give vent to the more outrageous side of her personality; she became a minor celebrity appearing on Granada Television's *Nice Times* program and a regular at counter-culture 'happenings'. In 1968 she was briefly married to Paul de Feu, a building worker whom she had met in a pub. He later wrote of their relationship in *Let's Hear It For the Long Legged Women* (1974).

The publication of *The Female Eunuch* in 1970 thrust Greer into the spotlight as an international celebrity of women's liberation. Experience from her days at *Oz* put her in a good position to work the media. She debated with Norman Mailer, wrote for *Playboy*, and posed naked for the pornographic journal *Suck*. Since *The Female Eunuch*, her published works have continued to express her own maverick style of feminism. Both *Sex and Destiny* (1984) and *The Change* (1991) lean towards an essentialist radical feminism in their critiques of Western medicine. Her books on women's art and literature, from *The Obstacle Race* (1979) to *Slip-shod Sibyls* (1995), conspicuously disdain to engage with recent feminist critiques of the masculinist canon.

Greer has continued to work as a journalist and independent scholar, writing mainly for prestigious British newspapers. She has appeared regularly on television and hosted her own talk show. She was director of women's studies at the University of Tulsa between 1979 and 1983. Recently she has been appointed to the governing body of her alma mater, Newnham College, Cambridge. Greer has remained determinedly controversial, often earning the ire of feminists for her idiosyncratic stance on women's issues. Although maintaining her Australian citizenship, she has lived since the 1960s as a permanent expatriate in Great Britain and Italy— a facet of her life examined in Ian Britain's *Once an Australian* (1997).

In 1989 Greer published *Daddy, We Hardly Knew You*. Although ostensibly a search for her paternal origins, much of the book is revealingly autobiographical. Attempts by others to write her biography have met with hostility and threats of litigation. Christine Wallace's *Untamed Shrew* (1997) narrates the life, but the subject herself remains elusive, an object of public fascination yet also a distant and inaccessible figure.

MARY SPONGBERG

Grey, Henry George third Earl Grey (1802–94), was a highly conscientious, opinionated, far-sighted, and, in Australia, an extremely unpopular Secretary of State for Colonies. In the Whig administration of his father, he was under-secretary for the colonies (1830–33) and was influential in the adoption of **Wakefield's** policy of selling land to sponsor free **immigration**. As June Phillip establishes in *A Great View of Things* (1971), his concern was not with reducing Britain's population but in saving Australia from what he saw as the degradation of convictism. As Secretary of State (1846–52), he took a very cautious approach to granting self-government to the Australian colonies. He wanted to encourage **local government** and use that as the basis for representative institutions, and not to grant self-government without providing for some form of federal government to prevent the colonies creating **tariff** barriers against each other. The colonists were interested in neither of these projects and Grey was denounced as an out-of-touch theorist. He provoked the **anti-transportation** movement when he attempted to get the colonies to receive 'exiles', convicts allegedly on the path to reformation after a period of imprisonment. Grey considered the colonies should be prepared to serve in this way the wider purposes of empire. A similar approach led him to deny the right of the colonists to control Crown land which he thought should be held in trust by Britain for future migrants. Thus he gave **squatters** leases and not the freehold they had been demanding and provided that Aborigines should have the right to hunt over their land, a decision invoked in the **Wik** case. Self-government and control of Crown land were conceded by his immediate successor in office. J.M. **Ward** wrote *Earl Grey and the Australian Colonies* (1958). Grey defended himself in *The Colonial Policy of Lord John Russell's Administration* (1853).

JH

Grey, George (1812–98) came to Australia after serving with the British army in Ireland. He was attracted to Australia by news of Charles **Sturt's** expeditions, and proposed to the **Colonial Office** that he lead an expedition to find a site for settlement in north-western Australia. In 1838 and 1839 Grey led two bungled expeditions—during the first he was speared by Aborigines, and on the second he was shipwrecked. His journals of these expeditions were published in 1841. Grey was appointed magistrate at King George Sound in 1839, and shortly after published a vocabulary of the dialects of the Aborigines in south-western Australia. Grey returned to England in 1840, travelling via Adelaide. Once home, he was offered and accepted the position of governor of SA and worked to ingratiate himself with the Colonial Office at the expense of George **Gawler**. In bankrupt SA, Grey imposed extreme economies which included suspending public works and reducing relief to the unemployed. Angered by his autocratic actions, crowds invaded the grounds of Government House. His efforts to educate Aboriginal children and persuade adults to work for white settlers, as proposed in his 1840 report, failed.

In 1845 he was appointed governor of NZ; again he aroused opposition, and was recalled in 1853. From 1854 to 1867 he was governor of the Cape Colony in South Africa, and in 1861 reappointed to NZ where the Colonial Office hoped his influence with the Maoris might avert war. He was again recalled in 1868, but returned in 1870 to enter parliament, and served a term as premier. Grey was a New Zealand representative at the Federal Convention in 1891, but was in decline and played little part in its work. G.C. Henderson and James Rutherford have both written biographies of this idiosyncratic proconsul.

KT

Griffin, Walter Burley (1876–1937), landscape architect, and his wife **Marion Lucy Mahony** (1871–1961), architect and delineator, were designers of **Canberra** and pioneer advocates of environmental **architecture**, often confused with modernism. Other significant work includes Newman College, Melbourne, and Castlecrag on Sydney's Middle Harbour.

A unique, possibly calculated, partnership was created by the marriage of mild-mannered Walter Griffin and the forceful Marion Mahony in 1911. Both were born and bred in Chicago, and shared a passion for progressive architecture. In 1894 Marion was the second woman to graduate in architecture from Massachusetts Institute of Technology. The following year she joined Frank Lloyd Wright's Oak Park studio, where she became the greatest delineator of her generation. Walter graduated from the University of Illinois in 1895 and later became a leading light in the emerging Prairie School. The 'decisive moment' came when Wright left for Europe (1909). Marion became entranced by Griffin—'Socrates [to her] Xantippe'. The sophisticated and superbly rendered Canberra plan was submitted shortly after their marriage.

Marion's manuscript memoir, 'The Magic of America'—a crucial source—delineates four spheres of activity for their partnership: federal, municipal, imperial, and individual. Hope of 'the federal sphere' lasted from 1913 to 1921. Walter was appointed Federal Director of Design and Construction in 1913, following his win in the competition

for the design of Canberra of the previous year; his delight in 'a democracy already in the vanguard of political progress' was to take many knocks during World War I. By 1921, he was defeated by a bureaucratic and political opposition. Remarkably, Griffin's resignation saved 'the Plan'. Canberra developed so slowly that a later generation was able to redeem key features, such as the lake named after him.

In the 1920s, the Griffins turned to 'the municipal sphere', where 'building for nature' proved equally at odds with established ways. The Greater Sydney Development Association was formed to develop model estates on Middle Harbour under Walter's supervision. Hard times and leaky roofs limited Castlecrag's appeal, but anthroposophy—a mystical philosophy developed by Rudolf Steiner—sustained their idealism. India, 'the imperial sphere', offered a last great opportunity. But Walter died unexpectedly in Lucknow in 1937. Marion was with him: 'I … told him what a wonderful life I had had with him.' It was left to her to complete the work in India—an impossible task. In 1938, she departed Sydney for Chicago, never to return.

In Australia the Griffins had been generally regarded as eccentric, Marion of 'tomahawk profile' especially. By the 1950s, when what mattered was Walter and 'the [Canberra] Plan', she was a liability. Now she is seen as an asset. To the late-twentieth-century mind, it is the partnership that intrigues.

Early studies of Walter Griffin's architecture by James Birrell (1964) and Donald Johnson (1977) accord less attention to Marion's contribution than more recent scholars. The 50th anniversary of his death in 1988 stimulated new evaluations, notably *Walter Burley Griffin, A Re-View*, as well as two plays dramatising the Griffins' ideas by Peter King. Peter Harrison's *Walter Burley Griffin, Landscape Architect* was published to coincide with an exhibition of the competition designs (1995) and the 1996 Adelaide Festival included a multi-media exhibition, 'The Ethereal Eye'. Fifty years on, the Griffins are part of the national imaginary, but a balanced assessment is still to come.

JILL ROE

Griffith, Samuel Walker (1845–1920) was premier and chief justice of Qld, a founding father of the Commonwealth, and first chief justice of the High Court. He is the most puzzling of the great nineteenth-century liberal politicians.

As liberal premier 1883–88 he supported small farmers and town workers, opposed land-grant railways, and determined to put an end to the import of **Pacific Islanders** as labourers for the sugar plantations. At the 1888 election, Griffith boldly bid for working-class support by declaring that the just distribution of wealth was the great problem of the age. Griffith lost the election, but in the next two years, he elaborated his ideas on social reform in the labour newspaper the *Boomerang*, edited by William **Lane**, and in two bills which he introduced into the parliament. Surely nothing like them has ever been proposed for the statute book of a society with a capitalist economy. The Elementary Property Law was declaratory, establishing from first principles the workers' right to a decent living and a share in capitalist profit; The Divisions of Profit Act provided the machinery for ascertaining profits and allowing workers to claim their share. This was how Griffith planned to protect liberal society from social unrest and class conflict.

The bills were never debated. Three weeks after introducing them, Griffith formed an anti-labour coalition with his erstwhile opponent, Thomas **McIlwraith**. This government ruthlessly suppressed strikes, allowed the recruitment of Pacific Island labourers to continue, and promoted land-grant railways. This volte-face was spectacular, but not the only one in Griffith's career; he already had the reputation of being happy to argue both sides of a case. His nickname was Oily Sam. And yet he was genuinely committed to his social revolution by act of parliament. On his retirement from the High Court, he repeated his ideas in newspaper articles. The corollary of his approach was draconian punishments for strikers.

His utopianism was not associated with personal otherworldliness. He was determined to win professional success, wealth, and official honours and to prove he was descendant from Welsh kings. He was born in Wales, the son of a Congregational minister, and came with his family to Australia when he was eight. He went on a scholarship to the University of Sydney and completed his legal articles in Brisbane. As his biographer Roger Joyce stresses, his politics was only ever an adjunct to the law, which he continued to practise while he was premier, paying himself large sums for doing the government's legal work. He transformed himself from premier to chief justice in 1893.

Griffith appeared cold and aloof. He published a translation of Dante which was said to be Dante with the poetry left out. Yet he developed close relations with women and was a passionate husband.

Like **Barton**, he found nobility and did his best work in the service of **Federation**. He wrote the first draft of the Constitution in 1891 and piloted it through the Convention with such mastery and tact that he won the admiration of all the delegates. As first chief justice (1903–19) he upheld a federalist interpretation of the Constitution, assuming that it preserved states' rights even in cases where its words might favour the Commonwealth. He also gave constitutional advice to governor-generals. **Munro Ferguson** considered him 'by far the most outstanding personage I have met' in Australia.

JOHN HIRST

Grimshaw, Beatrice Ethel (1870–1953), writer, was born in Ireland and became a publicity agent for shipping companies. From 1904 she produced tourist literature for governments and companies in the Pacific Islands. In 1907 the London *Times* and *Sydney Morning Herald* commissioned her to report on Papua. She lived there for the next 27 years. Grimshaw was a close friend of and unofficial publicist for the Administrator, Hubert **Murray**. She accompanied him on expeditions, managed a plantation in the Milne Bay district from 1917 to 1922, and grew tobacco with her brother near Port Moresby in the 1930s. After *The*

New New Guinea (1910), she concentrated on fiction, and produced nearly 40 novels and stories, among them *When the Red Gods Call* (1911) and *The Coral Queen* (1919). *Conn of the Coral Seas* (1922) was filmed in Hollywood as *Adorable Outcast* (1928).

Grimshaw went on world tours promoting her books, which were immensely popular in Australia, Britain, and the USA, and gave radio broadcasts about her travels in the Pacific. Her novels are generally escapist romances eloquent in their expression of the desires and anxieties of gender and race. They are also vehicles for her endorsement of imperialist policies in the Pacific, consistently representing white settlers as heroic agents of civilisation in a primitive and often hostile environment. She retired to Bathurst, NSW, in 1936. A part-autobiography, *Isles of Adventure* (1930), displays her capacity for self-dramatisation and clearly presents the ambiguities in her position as a single, independent working woman who also upheld the ideals of romantic love as the foundation for marriages that sustained British imperial values and proscribed miscegenation in the remote Empire.

SM

Group, see **Movement**

Group settlement scheme, devised by James **Mitchell**, premier of WA, was an attempt to boost production of primary commodities in WA by the settlement of immigrant farmers. The British government provided the scheme with £4 million, on the condition that a large number of British migrants be accepted, and in 1921 commenced a misleading and deceitful recruiting campaign. Although promised cleared fertile lands, lush pasture, and cattle, the migrant families who arrived at Fremantle and Albany, totalling roughly 18 000 people, were transported to tin shacks with dirt floors in virgin bushland.

Mitchell's committee had planned to settle the migrants in groups of 20 in the south-west of the state. Initially the 'Groupies' lived in a village, and then moved to cottages on selected virgin blocks, which they cleared by primitive methods. They were initially paid £3 per week, but later cleared their blocks under a contract arrangement. The scheme supplied each settler with farming implements and, later, with 10 cows, and a horse and cart. The settlers had signed to repay all wages, contract work, and costs of any kind.

When contract work ceased in 1928/29, the settler was left with no income except his cream cheque, obtained by his meagre and poorly fed cows and a few pigs. Britain requested repayment of the £4 million in the midst of the **Depression**, but the WA government could not oblige and instead sold the settlers' lands to the Agricultural Bank of Western Australia, which immediately billed the settlers for all monies owed, including interest. When settlers were unable to pay the levies, the banks seized their stock, and left them destitute. The government intervened and granted free rail passage to Perth. There, displaced people gradually became absorbed in public works and state industries. J.P. Gabbedy, *Group Settlement* (1988), is the fullest account.

PHILIP BLOND

Gubba, see **Aboriginal nomenclature**

Guérard, (Johann Joseph) Eugene von (1811–1901) came to Australia in 1852 from Austria, where his father was court painter. He spent a year on the Ballarat goldfields, where he made some sketches, and later travelled as artist on expeditions led by A.W. **Howitt** and G.B. von Neumayer, completing sketches some of which he developed into paintings. His illustrated diary of the goldfields, *An Artist on the Goldfields* (1982, 1992) was edited by Marjorie Tipping. After his work was shown in Melbourne, he received commissions from prosperous landowners and the homestead became one of his frequent subjects. He painted some of his more monumental, romantic landscapes in the mid-1860s and published a volume of lithographs, *Australian Landscapes*, in 1867 (republished in 1975 with text by Tipping). In 1870 he was appointed curator of the National Gallery of Victoria and painting master, reputedly an uninspiring one, of the Art School. Forced by ill-health to resign, he returned to England in 1882. *Eugene von Guérard 1811–1901: A German Romantic in the Antipodes* (1982) by Candice Bruce et al. is an expansive account of his life and work.

KT

Guerin, (Julia Margaret) Bella (1858–1923) became the first female graduate of an Australian university when she graduated BA from the University of Melbourne in 1883. She began teaching at a Ballarat convent school and rose to the position of lady principal of the Ballarat School of Mines university classes, before resigning in 1891 to marry. After her husband's death, she returned to teaching; she became increasingly involved in the suffrage movement, notably in the Bendigo Women's Suffrage League. This took her into the wider field of politics—as vice-president of the **Women's Political Association** 1912–14 she assisted Vida **Goldstein** in her bid for the Senate and campaigned strongly for the anti-conscription movement. She committed herself to Labor and socialism, and spoke widely on such issues as the rights of illegitimate children and the need for increased female involvement in public life. She aroused considerable ire within the Labor Party in 1918 when, as vice-president of its Women's Central Organising Committee, she criticised the relegation of Labor women to support roles, describing them as 'performing poodles and packhorses'.

KT

Guilfoyle, William Robert (1840–1912), landscape designer and botanic gardens director, came with his parents in 1849 to Sydney, where his father, Michael Guilfoyle, established a nursery business. He worked for his father and trained in botany prior to his appointment as curator of Melbourne Royal Botanic Gardens in 1873. Whereas his predecessor Ferdinand von **Mueller** had been chiefly concerned with the garden's role in scientific botanical study, Guilfoyle worked at transforming the gardens into an elaborately designed landscape that featured bold foliage and sweeping lawns, in accordance with the popular picturesque style of the period. Guilfoyle was also responsible for the design of several notable provincial **botanic gardens** in Victoria, including those at Warrnambool, Koroit, Horsham, and Hamilton, as well as many private gardens in Victoria. He published several botanical texts, including *Australian Botany* (1878) and *Australian Plants Suitable for Gardens, Parks, Timber Reserves, etc.* (1911). R.T.M. Pescott's biography of Guilfoyle, subtitled 'The master of landscaping', was published in 1974.

HD

Gullett, Henry (1837–1914) and his nephew **Henry Somer Gullett** (1878–1940) were both journalists. Henry emigrated from England in 1853. He spent several years on the goldfields and in labouring jobs, then worked on the family farm at Mount Macedon, Victoria. Gullett travelled to England in 1861, hoping to establish a literary career, but returned to Australia after two years and became a reporter on the *Argus*. He went on to edit the *Australasian* (1872–85), then became associate editor on the Sydney *Daily Telegraph* (1885–90) and the *Sydney Morning Herald*—the latter through the federal referendum period. Gullett supported his friend, Henry **Parkes**, on federation and expressed his support in the *Herald*. After retirement from journalism he was nominated to the NSW Legislative Council.

Henry Somer Gullett followed him into journalism. After time on the staff of the Sydney *Daily Telegraph*, he worked in London, where he became convinced of the importance of immigration to Australia and published a handbook, *The Opportunity in Australia* (1914). During World War I he served as official war correspondent on the Western Front and in Palestine. He wrote volume 7 of *The Official History of Australia in the War of 1914–18* (1923), dealing with the AIF in Sinai, Palestine, and Syria, described by C.E.W. **Bean** as 'the most readable' of all the volumes. Gullett's interest in immigration continued after the war and in 1920, at the invitation of Billy **Hughes**, he became director of the Australian Immigration Bureau. Disagreement with Hughes over policy led to his resignation in 1922; three years later he became the Nationalist member for Henty, Victoria, and minister in the **Lyons** and **Menzies** governments. He died in a plane accident. His son, HENRY 'JO' BAYNTON SOMER, was a member of federal parliament 1946–55.

KT

Gunn, Jeannie (1870–1961) is best known as Mrs Aeneas Gunn, author of *We of the Never-Never* (1908). This and an earlier book, *The Little Black Princess* (1905), were based on her experiences as 'the Little Missus', wife of the boss—the Maluka—of a remote cattle station in the NT. Her stay at Elsey station was cut short by her husband's death, and she returned to Melbourne. Outback life was a constant revelation to Gunn, and her writings convey this sense of wonder and enjoyment as well as admiration for the stoicism, kindness, and adaptability of the outback 'characters' she depicts. Her representation of Aborigines now appears patronising and racist; her reference to a 'nigger hunt', chilling. She does, however, also offer an impassioned defence of Aboriginal rights to their traditional land and lifestyle. *We of the Never-Never* was extremely influential in shaping urban Australia's view of the outback—more than a million copies have been sold, it was adapted for schools, and a film version appeared in 1982. Elsey station and a visit to the 'homestead' reproduced for the film now form part of the NT tourist route. *The Little Missus* (1977) is a biography by Iris Nesdale.

KT

Gurindji are an Aboriginal people of NT who campaigned successfully for land rights. Gurindji land was occupied from the mid-nineteenth century by the Wave Hill pastoral station, and later owned by the British pastoral company, Vestey Ltd. Led by elder Vincent Lingiari, the Gurindji protested against poor conditions for Aboriginal labourers at Wave Hill and for ownership of their land. By walking off the station in 1966 they drew attention to their aspirations and in 1967 they petitioned unsuccessfully for the return of their land. In 1975 Prime Minister Gough **Whitlam** granted the Gurindji people leasehold rights to an area of 3250 square kilometres; in 1986 this was converted to freehold. Frank **Hardy** promoted their case in *The Unlucky Australians* (1968). (See also **Aboriginal land rights**.)

HD

H

Hackett, (John) Winthrop (?1848–1916) was an influential newspaper owner and philanthropist. A self-described 'advanced liberal' on questions such as education and female suffrage, he was a strong defender of business interests and the rights of property. The son of a Church of Ireland clergyman, he emigrated in 1875 as a graduate in law from Trinity College, Dublin. After seven years as deputy warden of Trinity College, University of Melbourne, he arrived in WA and became part-owner (and editor by 1887) of the conservative *West Australian* newspaper. Through his position, Freemasonry connections, and personal friendship with the premier John **Forrest**, Hackett wielded great influence among the propertied elite in WA.

Wary of democracy, he helped enshrine a rural gerrymander in the Legislative Council of which he was a member 1890–1916. He was instrumental in the preservation of King's Park, the establishment of the Zoological Gardens and the Western Australian Museum, and the proposal for deep sewerage and drainage systems for Perth. He was also the central figure in the establishment of free, compulsory, secular education in WA. In 1909 he chaired the royal commission which led to the establishment of the University of Western Australia where later, as chancellor, he used his casting vote to ensure no fees were charged. On his death, the University of Western Australia and the Church of England were residual legatees of considerable bequests.

JEAN CHETKOVICH

Hale, Mathew Blagden (1811–95), Anglican prelate, left his English curacy in 1847 to accompany the newly appointed bishop of Adelaide, Augustus Short. Pursuing missionary work among the Aborigines, he established a native reserve at Poonindie, near Port Lincoln in SA. With Hale's guidance, the venture, which aimed to educate and teach farming skills to Aborigines, succeeded in becoming self-supporting within 10 years. A visit to WA motivated Hale to write *The Transportation Question* (1857), in which he proposed a reformatory rather than penal policy. As first bishop of WA in 1857, he gave special emphasis to education. He served on the Board of Education of WA, opened a boys' school, and supported the introduction of the Irish National System to government schools. Hale School is named after him. During his time as Bishop of Brisbane (1875–81), Hale battled to increase recognition of the needs of remote areas of the colony.

KT

Hall, Ben (1837–65), bushranger, was born in NSW to convict parents, and took up a pastoral run at Wheogo, south of Forbes. He was arrested for highway robbery in 1862 and was acquitted; but he returned home to find his wife and son gone. Angered by subsequent police persecution for a crime he claimed he had not committed, Hall turned to **bushranging**. He teamed up with Frank **Gardiner** and local boys, including Gilbert, Dunn, and O'Meally, and from their Weddin Mountains hideout, carried out successful robberies and duffed cattle. Hall's victims were mainly wealthy landowners. The poorer settlers in the district, many of ex-convict background, harboured the gang and were rewarded with stolen goods. Hall's reputed involvement in the notorious Eugowra gold escort robbery in 1862, a scheme orchestrated by Gardiner, increased police interest in his capture, as did his subsequent hold-up of the Faithfulls' station and raid on Bathurst in 1863. The press condemned the gang as outlaws while the police, led by Frederick Pottinger, became increasingly exasperated at being consistently outwitted by them. Hall was finally betrayed, and captured by the police, who riddled his body with bullets. Their subsequent parading of his corpse through Forbes inspired the angry ballad, 'The Streets of Forbes'. Other ballads generally portray him as a victim and romantic hero, and embody the legends of his gentlemanly conduct and chivalrous deeds. Folk historians, notably Frank **Clune** in *Ben Hall* (1947) and *Wild Colonial Boys* (1948), have reinforced this view. Hall inspired **Boldrewood's** popular novel, *Robbery Under Arms* (1888), and a television series was screened in 1975.

HD

Hall, Edward Smith (1786–1860) came to Australia from London in 1811 with the intention of farming. When this failed, he entered Sydney's commercial world and, in 1826, was a co-founder of the *Monitor*. The newspaper vehemently espoused the liberal and emancipist causes, and attacked the administration of Governor **Darling**, who responded by attempting to stifle the press. Hall was imprisoned for libel, but continued his campaign. He called for representative government, trial by jury, and freedom of the press. After he sold the *Monitor* in 1838, he edited the *Australian* until 1848, and later worked on the *Empire*. In *Sir Francis Forbes* (1968) C.H. **Currey** examines the battles between Darling and the press.

KT

Hancock, Henry Richard (1836–1919) was superintendent of the Moonta Mining Company for more than 30 years. He came to Australia from Devon in 1859, and worked in several mines before his 1864 Moonta appointment. At his suggestion, many more workers were recruited from the Victorian goldfields and from Cornwall—hence his reputation as founder of SA's 'Little Cornwall'. Hancock's enthusiasm for machinery improved conditions for the workers; he replaced hand-worked pumps and crushers with a steam engine, and introduced a railway to cart ore to the smelters. A 'benevolent despot', Hancock exercised authority over the thousands of people on the Moonta leases, as indicated by the title of Mandie Robinson's biography, *Cap'n 'ancock: Ruler of Australia's Little Cornwall* (1978). An advocate of self-help and improvement, he enforced compulsory membership of a medical club and night school for boys working at the mine. He superintended the Sunday school, encouraged sporting clubs, and established a library and reading room. He also attempted to maintain the standard of living for the miners through a minimum weekly wage. When Hancock retired, his son took over as superintendent.

KT

Hancock, Langley George (1909–92) was a WA mining magnate who described himself as a 'knockabout bushman' and who epitomised the old-style pioneering spirit. He worked with his father at Mulga Downs sheep station before becoming involved in prospecting and mining. He discovered blue asbestos at Wittenoom Gorge in 1936 and iron ore in the Hamersley Ranges in 1952. He made little out of Wittenoom, which led him thereafter to avoid financial risks. Rio Tinto mined the Hamersley iron, paying Hancock royalties on ore shipped, which funded further exploration and discovery.

Hancock was passionate about free enterprise and small government. In a country made prosperous by mining, he imagined railways across the continent, tidal power and nuclear blasts for mining and development, a deepsea port to handle huge ships—and an independent WA. He promoted his views through a wide range of pamphlets and the establishment of the *Independent* newspaper in 1969 and the *National Miner* magazine in 1974.

None of Hancock's dreams came to fruition; he became a mining magnate without a mine. This was perhaps due to his own reluctance to take risks, exacerbated by the antagonism between himself and Charles **Court**, a man with his own fervent but different vision for WA.

SUE GRAHAM-TAYLOR

Hancock, (William) Keith (1898–1988) is generally acknowledged to be the most eminent of Australian historians. His reputation rests partly on his career in this country and writings on it, partly on his achievements in Britain. He was elected a fellow of All Souls College in Oxford while still in his twenties; appointed to a chair at an English university in his thirties; commissioned to write the prestigious *Survey of British Commonwealth Affairs* before World War II and edit the 27-volume official British civil history of that war after it; served as an adviser on British colonial affairs during the 1950s, and also wrote the authoritative biography of the South African leader Jan Smuts. Upon his retirement in 1968, he had held Australian posts for just 17 years. Yet he shaped the historiography and the discipline decisively.

Hancock, the son of an Anglican clergyman, spent his childhood in rural Victoria. He studied at the University of Melbourne under Ernest **Scott**, and went to Oxford as Rhodes scholar in 1922 after two years as an assistant to Edward **Shann** at the University of Western Australia. A visit to Italy brought him under the spell of the Tuscan countryside, and a study of *Ricasoli and the Risorgimento in Tuscany* (1926) followed. In that year he took up the chair of history at the University of Adelaide, but resigned in 1933 to depart once more to England, where he would remain (despite several attempts to lure him back) until 1957. The tension between *Country and Calling*, the title of his 1954 autobiography, was apparent in the contrast between the intellectual plenitude of England and the straitened academic possibilities here, but goes further than this. It is apparent in the way he appraised his homeland in the book on *Australia* (1930), written for a British series on 'the modern world'. He acknowledged that 'My chief difficulty in writing this book has been to combine intellectual detachment with my emotional attachment to Australia'. Yet its tone was stringent—that of an urbane scholar chiding a lazy and complacent pupil.

Hancock's *Australia* was the most influential of all the short histories, before or since. Many of its phrases and aphorisms passed into common currency:

- Australia has suffered too much from the greed or ignorance of its invaders.
- Wool made Australia a solvent nation and, in the end, a free one.
- Australian democracy has come to look upon the state as a vast public utility.

- The passion for equal justice can easily sour into a grudge against those who enjoy extraordinary gifts.
- Australian idealism has put too many of its eggs into the political basket.

Its conceptualisation of the environmental constraints, the imperial–colonial relationship, the distinctive political economy, **egalitarianism**, the party system, **Commonwealth–state relations**, and the utilitarian state shaped Australian historiography for several decades (as suggested by R.W. Connell, 'Images of Australia', *Quadrant*, 1968). It was novel in its departure from narrative format in favour of thematic organisation and its orchestration of material and ideas drawn from geography, economics, and contemporary political debate. Like his mentor Shann, Hancock took a pessimistic view of the policies pursued by the Commonwealth and state governments to encourage immigration, extend agriculture, promote manufacturing industry, and underwrite living standards through foreign loans, **tariff** protection, and **state socialism**. These devices drew Australia away from its role as a pastoral producer for British industry, weakened the imperial relationship, and created unrealistic expectations that vitiated public life. He suggested that affection and anxiety were two powerful impulses to write the book. Within three years of its appearance, he withdrew from the 'fecklessness and vulgarity' of Australia between the world wars and set aside Australian history, partly because he feared he might have 'overcalled [his] hand' in it and partly because his mind was on other problems.

He pursued them through the *Survey of British Commonwealth Affairs* (1937–42), a vast but closely focused inquiry into the modern forces—race, nation, markets—working on the British Dominions and the forms of statecraft that sought to contain them. Hancock was a liberal imperialist (in 1943 he published a Penguin special, *Argument of Empire*) with a keen sense of imperial responsibilities, and in 1954 he headed a mission to Uganda in an effort to resolve a dispute between the governor and regional leaders. After his work on the war history, which included his own volume with Margaret Gowing on *The British War Economy* (1949), written while he was professor of economic history at Oxford (1944–49), he became director of the Institute of Commonwealth Studies at London University. From there he began the research for the biography of Smuts that appeared in two volumes (1962, 1968).

He brought that project with him when he returned to Australia in 1957 as director of the Research School of Social Sciences at the Australian National University. His influence on the development of this crucial research centre is discussed by Stephen Foster in *The Making of the Australian National University 1946–96* (1996). Hancock placed a premium on inquiries that cut across disciplinary boundaries and exemplified his prized qualities of attachment, justice, and span. He mistrusted narrow specialisation (thus he preferred to think of history as a 'calling' rather than a profession), resented administrative tedium, and encouraged talent. Among the successful projects he initiated was the cross-disciplinary seminar on the **wool** industry that resulted in *The Simple Fleece*, edited by Alan Barnard (1962). But another venture, the establishment of the *Australian Dictionary of Biography*, began badly with his disastrous pairing of Manning **Clark** and Malcolm **Ellis**. Ann **Moyal** relates the consequences in *Breakfast With Beaverbrook* (1995), and suggests that Hancock was unable to deal with forms of behaviour outside his own experience.

Hancock continued as head of the history department when he completed his directorship of the Research School, and remained attached to the school when he retired. In 1972 he published *Discovering Monaro*, a ground-breaking work of **environmental history** on the high country around Canberra that he loved, and in *The Battle of Black Mountain* (1974) he recorded the fight to prevent the erection of a communications tower on the mountain bordering his university. He also wrote a second volume of autobiography, *Professing History* (1976), and several subsequent collections of essays, of increasingly lapidary individuality.

Hancock fostered no school of followers, and his extensive reflections on his craft are always personal. A special issue of *HS* (1968) contains testimony from former colleagues. Tim Rowse subjected *Australia* to sustained criticism in *Australian Liberalism and National Character* (1978). Kosmas Tsokhas published a psychological study in *Round Table* (1990), and the contributors to a volume edited by Anthony Low appraise *Keith Hancock: Legacies of a Historian* (2001).

STUART MACINTYRE

Hannan, Patrick 'Paddy' (1840–1925), discoverer of the Kalgoorlie goldfield, arrived in Melbourne from Ireland in December 1862. He went to live with relatives in Ballarat, where he worked in the mines. In 1867 he left for the NZ goldfields, to begin over 40 years' work as a prospector. He took part in gold rushes in the eastern colonies, Tasmania and WA, where he arrived in 1889. He worked on the Yilgarn goldfield, and joined the rush to Coolgardie. In early June 1893, he and two companions, Tom Flanagan and Dan Shea, were following a new rush to the east, when they found gold close to another party's camp near Mount Charlotte. Remaining silent, they camped in the bush until the other group had left. Hannan's discovery of the Kalgoorlie field was never seriously challenged, although he may not have found the first gold. He was a quiet, modest, temperate, and generous man, who was careful with his money and his health, and secretive in his work, attributes which helped to make him a legend in his own time. Geoffrey **Blainey** deals with Hannan's discovery in *The Golden Mile* (1993).

RICHARD HARTLEY

Hanson, Pauline see **One Nation**.

Hardy, Francis Joseph 'Frank' (1917–94) came to national attention with the clandestine publication in 1950 of his controversial *Power Without Glory*, a semi-fictional study of millionaire John **Wren**. Hardy was acquitted of the charge of criminal libel brought by Wren's family, and gave an account of the writing of the novel and the trial in *The Hard Way* (1961). Pauline Armstrong's study of *Frank Hardy and the Making of Power Without Glory* (2000) casts doubt on the reliability of that account and the personal character of its author. He came from a large family and grew up in rural Victoria, leaving school at 13 to work in a variety of labouring jobs. Influenced by the Depression, he joined the **Communist** Party during World War II. His stories of the Depression years, *Legends from Benson's Valley* (1963), display his affinity with the bush battler. Hardy joined the army in 1942 and was sent to the NT, where he began a newspaper, *Troppo Tribune*, and later joined the staff of the army magazine *Salt*. He returned to the Territory in the 1960s and became adviser to the **Gurindji** people, whose struggle for land rights he championed in *The Unlucky Australians* (1968).

Hardy was a prolific and versatile writer. *The Four-Legged Lottery* (1958) explored the place of **gambling** in working-class life. Other novels include the slapstick *The Outcasts of Foolgarah* (1971) and *But the Dead Are Many* (1975), a complex study of Communist disillusionment and suicide. His love of the Australian idiom found expression in the tall stories of 'Billy Borker'. He appeared on radio and television as a raconteur and wrote many plays, one of which, *Mary Lives* (1992), celebrated the life of his sister, actress Mary Hardy, who died in 1985. Paul Adams, *The Stranger from Melbourne* (1999), evaluates his writing.

KT

Hargrave, Lawrence (1850–1915), aeronautical inventor, took up an engineering apprenticeship in Sydney after migrating from England in 1865. He worked in New Guinea and at the Sydney Observatory before concentrating on aeronautical research. His inventions included the box kite, gliders, and a rotary engine. In 1894 he raised himself four metres off the ground using box kites. Hargrave never applied for patents for his inventions, so never benefited financially from their later use by other aeronautical inventors. His story is told by W. Hudson Shaw and Olaf Ruhen in *Lawrence Hargrave* (1977), and in *Hargrave and Son* (1978) by Elena Grainger. More recently he has been the subject of an opera, *Lawrence Hargrave Flying Alone* (c.1988).

KT

Hargraves, Edward Hammond (1816–91) claimed to be the discoverer of gold in Australia. Born in England, Hargraves worked in Australia for about 15 years before heading for the Californian goldfields in 1849. Unsuccessful there, he returned to Australia in 1851 and began prospecting for gold in the Bathurst area of NSW where the landscape reminded him of the auriferous areas in California. His primary incentive was a large reward offered by the government for payable gold finds. After discovering a small quantity of gold at a place he named Ophir, Hargraves trained his companions, John Lister and the Tom brothers, in panning techniques and went to Sydney to establish the claim and publicise the discovery, news of which marked the begin-

ning of Australia's gold rushes. Although Hargraves received the public recognition and reward, followed later by more money and a life pension, it was in fact his companions who found the payable gold—a fact that was belatedly recognised by a select committee of the Legislative Assembly in 1890. Hargraves published *Australia and its Gold Fields* in 1855, and features in most of the works dealing with the gold rushes.

KT

Harper, Norman Denholm (1906–86) pioneered the study of American history in Australia, and Australia's relations with its Asian and Pacific neighbours. Following an early career as a teacher at Melbourne High School, he was appointed to a senior lectureship in history at the University of Melbourne in 1943 and to a personal chair in American history in 1966. *Our Pacific Neighbours* (1953) introduced generations of secondary-school students to the study of the region, while a dozen more titles, culminating in *A Great and Powerful Friend: Australian–American Relations 1900–1975* (1987), chronicled Australia's involvement in world affairs, with particular emphasis on the shift from dependence on Britain to closer alliance with the USA. Harper was a singularly effective pioneer of the study of the USA. He introduced undergraduate courses in American history, fostered the careers of younger scholars, and was a foundation member and president of the Australian and NZ American Studies Association. His own research contributed to the debate surrounding Frederick Jackson Turner's **frontier** hypothesis and the origins of American democracy.

Harper's influence extended beyond teaching and research through positions such as president of the **Australian Institute of International Affairs**, as an Australian representative at numerous international conferences, and as a member of the official delegation to the General Assembly of the UN in 1968. He was an imposing man of many parts—including a strong involvement in baseball—with an aura of worldly authority that heightened his effectiveness as a teacher.

ALLAN JOHNSTON

Harpur, Charles (1813–68), poet, was born in Windsor, NSW, and attended the district school where his father taught. He took a clerical job in Sydney, and later turned to farming and grazing. His first collection of poetry, *Thoughts: A Series of Sonnets*, appeared in 1845. Self-conscious of his native-born status and his parents' emancipist background, Harpur strove to express poetically the voice of the new country. He drew on peculiarly Australian themes, such as **bushranging**, and attempted to portray a mood and character that was Australian, thus earning him the posthumous title as the first distinctively Australian poet. His best-known work, 'The Creek at the Four Graves', used as its subject an attack by Aborigines on a settlers' campsite. 'An Aboriginal Mother's Lament' expressed his great sorrow at the **Myall Creek massacre** of 1838. He was a passionate democrat and republican who wrote verse in support of these causes. His collection of love sonnets, *Rosa* (not published until

1948), was dedicated to Mary Doyle, whom he eventually married in 1850.

Some of his later poems, with a strong philosophical strain, were altered by his editor, H.M. Martin. Michael Ackland has produced a collection of Harpur's poetry and prose (1986). The writer Rosa **Praed** was Harpur's niece.

HD

Harris, Alexander (1805–74), a self-styled 'emigrant mechanic', wrote *Settlers and Convicts* (1847), a vivid and influential account of bush life in early NSW, and a notable early Australian novel, *The Emigrant Family* (1849). The son of a Nonconformist clergyman, Harris worked as a compositor in London before he lost his faith, fell into bad company, deserted from the army, and in 1825 escaped to NSW. There, it seems, he worked as a cedar cutter and as clerk to a magistrate before establishing himself on the land, though possibly under an assumed name. Russel **Ward** drew extensively on Harris's observations of bush life to illustrate the emergence of a distinctively Australian code of **mateship**. ('It is quite surprising what exertions bushmen of new countries, especially mates, will make for one another.') Only in 1961, with the republication of his later autobiography as *The Secrets of Alexander Harris*, did further details of Harris's later life emerge. He had reconverted to evangelical Christianity and returned to England; there he briefly worked as a missioner in the London slums and began to write on both colonial and religious subjects, though with motives—religious, artistic, and pecuniary—so mixed, and a social status so ambiguous, that he could no longer be said to view Australian society, as Ward had suggested, 'quite naturally from a working man's point of view'. He later emigrated to Canada. His autobiography, a reprobate's confessions, was published in the American *Saturday Evening Post* in 1858.

GD

Harrison, Henry Colden Antill (1836–1929) is often described as 'the father of **Australian Rules football**'. He played in the first games of the code's first football club founded by his cousin, T.W. **Wills**, in 1858, and was instrumental in drafting the rules adopted by the Victorian clubs in 1866. Although Harrison retired from play in 1872, he remained involved with football, serving as vice-president of the Football Association formed in 1877, and chairing the 1905 conference which formed the Australian National Football Council. He ended a long career in the public service as registrar of the Titles Office in Melbourne. A noted runner in his youth, Harrison titled his autobiography *The Story of an Athlete* (1924).

KT

Harrison, James (?1815–93) trained in Scotland as a printer before coming to Sydney in 1837 where, within a few months, he was working as a journalist. Two years later he was working on the *Port Phillip Patriot*, owned by John Pascoe **Fawkner**, whom he assisted in founding the *Geelong Advertiser*, a paper he later bought. Harrison pioneered the development of refrigeration with his experiments in ice-making—he built a plant at Geelong and, in 1856, took out a patent on his process and machinery. He moved the plant to Melbourne, looking for a larger market for his ice, but this venture also failed. In 1862 he sold the *Advertiser* to avoid bankruptcy, although remaining as editor. He later became leader-writer of the Melbourne *Age*.

Harrison recognised the potential of refrigeration for meat exports, and won a gold medal at the 1873 Melbourne Exhibition for proving that meat kept frozen for more than three months was still edible. An experimental consignment to London of frozen meat failed, and Harrison became bankrupt. A 1982 biography by W.R. Lang declares itself in the title: *James Harrison, Pioneering Genius*.

KT

Hartigan, Patrick Joseph (1878–1952), also known by his pen name, John O'Brien, was a Catholic priest and poet. His verse is based mainly on anecdotes of the lives of Catholic Irish-Australians in his rural parish of Narrandera, NSW, where Hartigan served from 1917 to 1944. Employing a colourful narrative style, colloquial language, and a wry humour, his poems told of both the ordinary and the tragic episodes of a bush parish. His work was published in *Around the Boree Log and Other Verses* (1921), in which the popular 'Said Hanrahan' appeared, and *The Parish of St Mel's*, which was published posthumously in 1954. His nephew Frank Mecham has written a biography, *'John O'Brien' and the Boree Log* (1981).

HD

Hartog, Dirck was the first European known to have landed on Australia's west coast, though little more is known about him. Hartog, whose surname also appears as Hartoochs and Hatichs, was commander of the *Eendracht*, a Dutch East India Company ship sailing from Holland to Batavia in 1616, when he landed on the site now called Dirk Hartog Island, near Shark Bay. He left behind an inscribed pewter plate recording the landing; this was replaced in 1697 by another Dutch captain, Willem de Vlamingh, with a plate that detailed both visits.

KT

Harvester Judgment, see **Basic wage**

Hasluck, Alexandra Margaret Martin, née Darker (1908–93), daughter of an engineer, was born in Perth and educated at the University of Western Australia, an upbringing described in her autobiography *Portrait in a Mirror* (1981). In 1932 she married Paul **Hasluck**, with whom she shared an interest in Western Australian history. Alexandra Hasluck's forte was biography. Her first major work, *Portrait with Background* (1955), a study of the pioneer botanist Georgiana **Molloy**, has been complemented but not supplanted by W.J. Lines's *An All Consuming Passion* (1994). *Unwilling Emigrants* (1959), based on the letters of a transportee, William Sykes, marks an early attempt to bring the convict experience into the mainstream of historiography. *Thomas Peel of Swan River* (1965) provides a thoroughly researched study of WA's first high-flying entrepreneur. Among other works, a collection of short stories, *Of Ladies Dead* (1970), evokes the Western Australian past with an imagination not always allowed rein in the disciplined scholarship of her biographies. Following her husband's term as governor-general, she edited the correspondence of one of her predecessors, *Audrey Tennyson's Vice-Regal Days* (1978), providing an informative and lively account of the Commonwealth's formative years. She was the first and only woman appointed a Dame of the Order of Australia.

GEOFFREY BOLTON

Hasluck, Paul Meernaa Caedwalla (1905–93) was a senior cabinet minister between 1951 and 1969, profoundly influencing Australian policy in PNG and the **Vietnam War**, but perhaps was more distinguished as a historian before and after his political career.

A Western Australian, Hasluck was born of Salvation Army parents of slender means, won a scholarship to Perth Modern School, and became a reporter for the *West Australian* between 1922 and 1940. Active in the (Royal) Western Australian Historical Society from its foundations in 1926, he used his shorthand to pioneer **oral history**, and, after completing a BA part-time, undertook a master's thesis on Aboriginal–white relations in nineteenth-century WA. Published as *Black Australians* (1942), it is a pioneering work in race relations enlivened by a candour and sense of equity rare at that time in **Aboriginal history**.

From 1940 to 1947 Hasluck served as a senior officer in the Department of External Affairs, taking a leading role in Australia's first delegations to the UN, but quit in 1947 after friction with his minister, H.V. **Evatt**. A post at the University of Western Australia provided scope for completing the first of two home-front volumes for the official history of Australia in the 1939–45 war, but in 1949 his career as historian was interrupted by his election as Liberal MHR for Curtin (WA). As Minister for Territories 1951–63 he upheld **assimilation** as a policy providing Aborigines equality of opportunity with other Australians. In PNG he discouraged expatriate exploitation and gave priority to grassroots education and welfare, but needed discreet international pressure before accelerating progress towards political autonomy. In charge of foreign policy from 1964 to 1969, he tenaciously defended Australia's involvement in the **Vietnam War**. An unsuccessful candidate for party leadership in 1968, he accepted appointment as governor-general (1969–74) and proved both ceremonially and politically effective.

In political retirement, Hasluck returned to history-writing. *The Government and the People, 1942–45*, the second volume of the official history, appeared in 1970—magisterial and remarkably even-handed, like its predecessor. Several works followed, reflecting on aspects of his career. *A Time for Building* (1976) covers PNG policies during his regime. It should be read in conjunction with Ian Downs's *The*

Australian Trusteeship, Papua New Guinea (1980) and Rachel Cleland's lively memoir, *Papua New Guinea: Pathways to Independence* (1985). *Mucking About* (1977), the most overtly autobiographical work, provides an engaging and perceptive account of Perth between the wars. By endorsing the view of WA in those years as a society dominated by a consensual ethos, it engendered historiographical debate from which Hasluck remained aloof. *The Office of the Governor-General* (1973, 1979) is crisp and authoritative; some have read the 1979 version for oblique insight into the 1975 **constitutional crisis**. *Diplomatic Witness* (1980) presents, not uncritically, the creation of Australian foreign policy under Evatt. *Shades of Darkness: Aboriginal Affairs 1925–1965* (1988) provides a spirited defence of reforms during that period. The posthumous publication of *The Chance of Politics* (1997) emphasised both his literary skill and his mordant judgment of colleagues. He never published reflections on the Vietnam War, but his later writings taken together are almost Thucydidean in their scope.

Robert Porter's political biography of 1993 is balanced and well researched, but does not attempt assessment of Hasluck as historian, poet, journalist, or private citizen. A full biography will require its writer to get beyond Hasluck's somewhat formal public persona to the man who ordered that at his funeral in January 1993 four trombonists should play 'When the Saints Come Marching In'.

GEOFFREY BOLTON

Hawke, Robert James Lee 'Bob' (1929–) was prime minister from 1983 to 1991 and electorally the most successful national leader of the **Australian Labor Party** since Federation. He was born in Bordertown, SA, the son of Clem, a Congregationalist minister, and Ellie, a former schoolteacher who transmitted to Bob an unwavering belief in his special destiny. Hawke pursued this destiny in politics. As a union leader (**ACTU** president 1973–78), he yoked the movement's social and political reforms to his own image as strategist and industrial peacemaker. As president of the ALP (1973–78), he was a vocal and visible adviser to (and sometimes at odds with) the **Whitlam** government. By the late 1970s Hawke was one of Australia's best-known and most popular public figures and there was talk of drafting him into parliament. In 1979, he won ALP pre-selection (for Wills), and in 1980 he was elected to federal parliament.

On 3 February 1983, Liberal Prime Minister Malcolm **Fraser** called an election to capitalise on Labor's divisions— just as its leader **Hayden** announced his resignation. Hawke, elected the Labor leader on 8 February, dominated the election campaign, and Labor won office on 5 March 1983. With treasurer Paul **Keating**, Hawke repositioned Labor as a market-oriented, realist government, pursuing private sector deregulation, public sector reform, and economic growth. An **Accord** with the unions, containing wage claims in return for reinforcement of the social wage, underwrote Hawke's economic achievements. His government succeeded in persuading the electorate that painful economic restructuring was the price to be paid for a viable future. Hawke also managed to sustain his romance with the people long past the time when divisions within Cabinet and caucus began to undermine his leadership. A chief source of division was the intense rivalry of Keating, who had decided by the mid-1980s that Hawke was not up to the job. By 1991, through two challenges, Keating persuaded most of his colleagues to agree, and Hawke was voted out. He subsequently retired from parliament and became a business consultant.

Hawke, driven by 'destiny' and self-importance, was attentive to his audience and the public responded to his charisma. Given to emotional display, a womaniser, a hard drinker and a raffish dresser, he was forgiven everything—and made self-discipline in dress and abstinence from alcohol part of his leadership regime. A shrewd negotiator, he confused strategies (like the achievement of consensus) with principles. Believing 'if the world doesn't trust you then it can ruin you', he made 'responsible' economic reform his primary goal. A residual concern for society gave latitude to others in his ministry to defend social policy while he and Keating busied themselves with the economy.

Blanche d'Alpuget's biography of Hawke (1982) was the best of a number; it raised the problem of 'manifest destiny' and narcissism, but shared Hawke's own estimate of his importance. Subsequently, she became his second wife. Paul Kelly in *The Hawke Ascendancy* (1984) finely analysed the deposition of Hayden, and in *The End of Certainty* (rev. edn 1994) gave the most cogent account of the Hawke government's economic project. Stephen Mills's *The Hawke Years* (1993), an insider defence of the Hawke government, was useful in giving a more structured exposition than Hawke's own *Memoirs* (1994). Life inside the Hawke government, and the internal party wars of the late 1980s, were best represented in Australian Broadcasting Corporation television's five-part documentary, *Labor in Power* (1993). The intense debate of the mid-1980s over Hawke's Labor credentials was represented by Graham Maddox's *The Hawke Government and Labor Tradition* (1989) and Dean Jaensch's *The Hawke–Keating Hijack* (1989). Stan Anson published a controversial psychological analysis, *Hawke: An Emotional Life*, in 1991.

JAMES WALTER

Hawker, George Charles (1818–95) was a pioneer pastoralist of SA's mid-north, and member of the House of Assembly 1858–65 and 1875–95. He was born in England, the son of Admiral Edward Hawker, who sent George and brothers Charles and James to find profitable land in SA. Frontier violence along the River Murray convinced them to search north of Adelaide and, in December 1841, finding good water at Bungaree—on the Hutt River close to present-day Clare—they established their station homestead there.

George married Bessy Seymour in 1845 and rearrangements of the brothers' partnership and extension of their leaseholdings committed him to development of Bungaree. Community distrust of squatter-pastoralism cost Hawker his first parliamentary election, but in 1858 he was elected to the

seat of Victoria in the colony's south-east, which he used to argue the squatters' cause. Financially broken by severe drought and the revaluation of his leasehold, Hawker took his family to England in 1865. In 1875, when wool prices had improved, they returned. Hawker was returned to his old parliamentary seat and, until 1881, served as treasurer, chief secretary, and commissioner of public works. In this last role he oversaw the proclamation of Hawker, the mid-north town that was named after him. Rob Linn has written of the family and Bungaree in *Bungaree: Land, Stock and People* (1992).

His grandson, CHARLES ALLAN SEYMOUR (1894–1938), studied at Cambridge and joined the British army during World War I. Twice wounded on the Western Front, he lost an eye and was able to walk only with sticks. Hawker was elected to the House of Representatives in 1929 and became a member of the **Lyons** ministry in 1932, though he resigned later in the year over the government's failure to reduce parliamentary salaries. A forceful advocate of rural interests and a supporter of the Ottawa Agreement, he criticised the government for failure to reduce **tariffs**. He died in an aircraft crash in 1938. Lilias Needham published a biography in 1969, and his friend Keith **Hancock** believed he exemplified 'the best that an Australian can do or be'. A federal electorate is named after him.

CAROL FORT

Hayden, William George 'Bill' (1933–), politician and governor-general, entered federal parliament in 1961 as Labor member for Oxley, after working in the Qld police force. As shadow minister for health and welfare (1969–72) and minister for social security (1972–75) in the **Whitlam** government, he developed a national health scheme, Medibank, the forerunner of Medicare. Hayden became leader of the Labor Party in 1977 and narrowly lost the 1980 federal election. Pushed into resigning as leader in 1983 in favour of Bob **Hawke**, his comment that 'a drover's dog' could lead the party to victory has entered the national lexicon. He was minister for foreign affairs in the Hawke government—one of his conditions for surrendering the party leadership—until he retired from politics in 1989 to become governor-general of Australia, a decision which many found at odds with his former republicanism. More recently he became chairman of **Quadrant**. Hayden retired to his farm near Ipswich, Qld, in 1996. He published his autobiography in that year and is the subject of two earlier biographies.

KT

Hayter, Henry Heylyn (1821–95), appointed government statist for Victoria in 1874, produced 20 annual volumes of the *Victorian Year Book*, in which he made statistics accessible and interesting to the lay reader. His methods were adopted throughout Australia and recommended as a model to the House of Commons. As well as two volumes of poetry, Hayter published *Notes on the Colony of Victoria* (1875) and *A Handbook to the Colony of Victoria* (1884). (See also **Historical statistics**.)

KT

Heagney, Muriel Agnes (1885–1974), labour stalwart, trade unionist, and lifelong advocate of wage justice for women workers, is one of the neglected women of Australian history. Although she devoted her life to the cause of working women, and is often alluded to in other histories, she has never been the subject of a major study.

Born into a politically active family, her childhood years spanned the period of the great strikes and depression of the 1890s, when her father became an early member of the fledgling **Australian Workers Union**. He was active in Victorian politics, founding the Richmond branch of the **Australian Labor Party**, standing for parliament as a Labor candidate, and serving on the Richmond Council.

Muriel followed in her father's political footsteps. In 1906, at the age of 21, she became a member of the same Richmond branch of the Labor Party. In 1909 she attended the first Victorian Labor Women's Conference, and began a lifelong association when she was a delegate to the Labor Party's Women's Central Organising Committee. She became its secretary in 1913. With her father she attended the All-Australian Trades Union Congress in 1921. After his death a year later, she went overseas for two years, during which time she visited Russia, worked briefly for the International Labour Organization in Geneva, and represented the Melbourne Trades Hall Council at the British Commonwealth Labour Conference in London in 1925. On her return she became a member (1926–27) of the Victorian executive of the Labor Party and stood, unsuccessfully, for state parliament in 1933.

Muriel Heagney made a major contribution to Australian women's struggle for equality in the workplace. She had been trained as a primary school teacher but left teaching in 1915 to work as a clerk in the Department of Defence. There, as the only female clerk employed, she was paid the full male rate at a time when most women received only 54 per cent of a male wage. From then on she campaigned tirelessly to secure women **equal pay**. She appeared before the royal commission on the **basic wage** (1919–20), and on behalf of the Clothing Trades Union before the Commonwealth Conciliation and Arbitration Court (1926–27). Concerned with the plight of women in the Depression, she published her now famous study of women's employment, *Are Women Taking Men's Jobs?* in 1935, and in 1937 helped found the Council for Action for Equal Pay. This story and the conflicts of Heagney with middle-class feminists in the United Association of Women is told by Jenny Bremner in Margaret Bevege et al. (eds), *Worth Her Salt* (1982). Heagney was honorary secretary of the council until 1949. Its work through the war years is told by Penny Johnson in *LH* (1986). In 1949 Heagney argued for equal pay at the Arbitration Commission's basic wage case, and when this failed she published a critique of the system of **arbitration**, entitled *Arbitration at the Crossroads* (1954).

Her work was the subject of a chapter in Suzanne Fabian and Morag Loh (eds), *The Changemakers: Ten Significant Women* (1983). At the time of her death in 1974, obituaries recalling her achievements were published by Elizabeth Reid in *Refractory Girl* (1974) and by Elisabeth Jackson in the *La Trobe Library Journal* (1975). Heagney was featured in a travelling exhibition of the history of the Australian Labor Party by the National Library of Australia in 1991 as 'one of the great women in Australian history'.

DIANE KIRKBY

Health is a collective concept about well-being within constraints which are imposed by people's environment and genes. It shares its etymological origins with words like *hail* and *whole*. Understandings of what is health vary with place, time, and culture. As part of their ecological imperialism, European migrants brought diseases such as smallpox which devastated the health of **Aborigines**. Historians have debated the extent of depopulation (N.G. **Butlin**, *Our Original Aggression*, 1983), and have argued whether depopulation and dispossession are cause and effect, and whether more Aborigines died from disease than from violence.

Health for migrants, convict or free, improved with the passage to Australia. Better health featured in advertising campaigns as part of the lure of the **'workingman's paradise'**. Economic historians have shown that **standards of living** were high by world standards. So was health status. Australian **'cornstalks'** literally looked down on the British; the infant death-rate was lower on average than in England, on a par with Scandinavia; and Australian school-children were taller and heavier than British children. But disparities by place and class existed from the start. Major differences showed up between mortality rates in urban and rural areas. Cities were particularly dangerous places for babies and these dangers rose in the **depression** and drought of the 1890s. Infectious diseases were the biggest killers in the nineteenth century. For adults the major threat was tuberculosis and for babies it was infant diarrhoea. Diarrhoea still kills Aboriginal infants. (See **Epidemics**.)

From the 1880s there was a health transition in white Australia, as in other English-speaking countries. Birth-rates declined and so did mortality rates. (See **Demographic history**.) Parents had smaller families by the twentieth century, but could confidently expect their children to grow up and live to a healthy old age. With this transition, average life-expectancy from birth has extended by 50 per cent in 100 years, and death has shifted from infancy and youth to the elderly, forcing changes in health services.

Health institutions responded to, rather than created, demographic change, at least until the 1930s, when medicine could do something more than home care. In the nineteenth century people were much more likely to consult chemists than doctors, whose prestige, as T.S. Pensabene, *The Rise of the Medical Practitioner in Victoria* (1980), notes, belongs mainly to the twentieth century. The **professionalisation** of medicine was greatly assisted by the rise of hospitals and displacement of earlier health practices, a process described by Evan Willis, *Medical Dominance* (1983). Nursing, too, only became respectable in the twentieth century as hospitals set up training schools for young women on the Nightingale model. In the nineteenth century nursing was associated with domestic service. Until the 1880s, most hospital nurses were men. So were the patients in a male-dominated society: on the goldfields at Ballarat, for example, single labouring men entered hospital because they lacked families to care for them. Hospitals were for the care of strangers. Women and children, other than unmarried mothers or lunatics admitted to refuges and asylums, were not generally admitted to hospitals until the twentieth century, when hospitals lost their stigma of charity and became institutions providing medical care for everyone.

Such patterns were not unique to Australia. It is the politics of health care which makes Australia distinctive. Under the Commonwealth constitution, health powers remained with the states. The first exception was quarantine, that ancient cordon against 'contagion'. The Quarantine Act of 1908 affirmed the commitment of the new nation to defend and develop a white Australia, although the states disputed the extent of this Commonwealth power. The federal public health priority was epidemic infectious disease; personal health services and hospitals, like Aboriginal affairs, were a state concern.

Public health interventions moved down a logical chain from the late nineteenth century to the 1920s: from cleaning up the environment through sanitation and clean water—led by metropolitan medical officers of health and their local health departments—to clean food including milk for babies, to people and their points of contact, and so to personal health services. To begin with, the emphasis was on babies and mothers, assisted by population policy and **eugenics**, which intersected with the changing emphases in public health. The maternity allowance of 1912 was arguably the first federal health initiative for mothers and babies, because it had the health objective of promoting white babies through payment of childbirth expenses (see **welfare history**). Tensions mounted between the Commonwealth and the states as health became central to social policy in the first half of the twentieth century, the idea being that the nation's health, much advanced by two world wars, was the nation's wealth. The twentieth-century trend was to increase federal health powers *vis-à-vis* the states in order to preserve human resources.

National hygienists were irritated by the anomaly that the federal government in this 'workers' welfare state' had the power to pay invalid pensions, but not the power to decrease invalidity, which was increasingly assumed to be preventable as medical knowledge improved, a view vigorously argued by J.H.L. **Cumpston**, *Health and Disease in Australia* (1927–28, edited by M.J. Lewis 1989). The committee on causes of death and invalidity in the Commonwealth, which sat during World War I, reported to the minister for trade and customs because there was no federal health department until 1921. One of its reports highlighted infant mortality, an issue which health reformers perceived as fundamental to the problems of natural increase and national efficiency.

Intervention in health and medicine differed between states. A key difference was between Labor and non-Labor states, which in turn affected the mixed economies of welfare and health (Phillipa Mein Smith, *Mothers and King Baby*, 1997). While baby health centres everywhere sought to help mothers and save babies, they were provided and funded differently according to each state's political regime. In SA and Victoria, with more conservative governments and stronger local government, the infant welfare movement was left to the voluntary sector and so made a prominent space for the women who ran it; in Qld, dominated by Labor governments, a state scheme was funded by the Golden Casket lottery from the 1920s. In all states, politicians had to be persuaded to provide support. Eager to be seen to be doing something, politicians built hospitals. The role of hospitals in community health was changing with medical advances and technology from the care of chronically to acutely ill patients. J.A. Gillespie's *The Price of Health* (1991) illustrates how Labor governments in Qld and Tasmania were first to build public hospitals; Victoria and NSW allowed pay beds in public hospitals from the 1930s, and Qld was first to make hospital care free in 1944.

The balance of power between the state and the medical profession differed between states with and without medical schools. Birth services are an example. While urbanised Australia was early to move to birth in hospital with a doctor, medical control of birth was a *fait accompli* in the states with powerful medical schools at Sydney, Melbourne, and Adelaide. There was no official support for the midwife because states supported the professionalisation of medicine.

By World War II preventive medicine was being overtaken by curative medicine, and personal health services by cash benefits. The first federal health measure for young children, the Lady Gowrie Child Centres established in the capital cities in 1939–40, marked the end of the phase of national hygiene. Attention then moved to the demand for access to medical services, which put pressure on governments to provide a national health service that would cover visits to the general practitioner, pharmaceutical products, and hospital care. But the federal Labor government in the 1940s lacked the constitutional health power to introduce a national scheme. Australia is the only liberal democracy to have legislated to establish a national health insurance system, in 1945, only to have it thrown out by the High Court. The doctors won the first round in the contest for state medicine, first because federal power was weak, and second because the medical profession was at the height of its powers as an autonomous profession from the 1930s, and unchecked by a strong central authority. Consequently the federal government went to the people and won the extra health power it needed by referendum, but not the power to insist on 'civil conscription' of doctors, who retained the right to fee-for-service. The result, from 1950, was a subsidised fee-for-service scheme. Made universal under Labor in 1975 and again under Labor from 1984, as Medicare it retained an emphasis on equity in access to health care. The shifting arrangements are presented in Ronald Mendelsohn, *The Condition of the People* (1979), and Gillespie, *The Price of Health*.

Since the 1980s, however, the rapidly rising cost of medicine has strained provision. The process and language of medicalisation is being replaced by the language of managerialism and systematisation. Ironically, more effective medical care, coupled with the ageing of the population and the altered sickness pattern from infections to chronic illnesses, has led to soaring demand and costs in the wake of massive mortality decline in the twentieth century.

Inequalities remain, although they do not always reproduce wider patterns of inequality in predictable ways. Cross-cultural studies, such as Janice Reid and Peggy Trompf (eds), *The Health of Immigrant Australia* (1990), show that immigrants live longer on average than the Australianborn because of healthier dietary habits. While screening programs acknowledge women's special risks of breast and cervical cancer, some men's health problems go largely unrecognised. Aborigines carry the major health problems in Australia, with life expectancies on a par with Bangladesh. Except for infant mortality, disparities between Aboriginal and non-Aboriginal health have increased since the 1970s, despite greater expenditure on programs (Stephen J. Kunitz, *Disease and Social Diversity*, 1994). Until the 1960s there was little recognition that the health of Aborigines warranted special attention and, as Gordon Briscoe states in Janice Reid and Peggy Trompf (eds), *The Health of Aboriginal Australia* (1991), 'there is nothing in contemporary federal or state government policies on Aboriginal health that can prevent the return of the neglect and apathy of the past'.

PHILIPPA MEIN SMITH

Hearn, William Edward (1826–88) was one of the more successful academics brought to this country in the middle of the nineteenth century to establish university education. All the foundation professors of the universities of Sydney and Melbourne were expected to span several disciplines; Hearn was particularly versatile. A graduate of Trinity College, Dublin, he came from a chair of Greek in 1854 to take up a Melbourne appointment in history, literature, political economy, and logic, and in 1874 became the foundation dean of law. Despite the fact that his parliamentary candidacy in 1859 caused the university council to prohibit professors from political activity, as a non-professorial dean he was a leading member of the Victorian Legislative Council from 1878 until his death.

Hearn wrote three substantial books on politics, history, and economics, all of them concerned with and addressed to the larger world of British scholarship. *Plutology* (1863) attempted to shift the emphasis of classical political economy from supply to demand. *The Government of England* (1867) was a work of constitutional law. *The Aryan Household* (1878), which he considered his most important work, engaged the contemporary debate over the origins of European institutions. All of these books were ambitious, unorthodox, noteworthy, and yet ultimately uninfluential interventions from the margins. J.A. **La Nauze** devotes a substantial portion of *Political Economy in Australia* (1949) to an evaluation of Hearn as an economist.

SM

Heaton, Herbert (1890–1973) pursued a career as an economic historian in Australia from 1914 to 1925. A Yorkshireman of working-class origins and sympathy, he was recruited to work for the **Workers Educational Association**, first in Tasmania and later in SA. His WEA lectures were published as *Modern Economic History* (1921), and paid special attention to Australian experience. He was a critical supporter of the local experiments in public enterprise and industrial arbitration. Nevertheless, he aroused conservative criticism in both states, and in 1925 accepted appointment as professor of economic and political science at Queen's University, Canada; he subsequently transferred to the University of Minnesota. Heaton's *Economic History of Europe* (1936) became a standard text.

SM

Heaton, John Henniker (1848–1914), journalist and biographer, arrived in NSW in 1864 and later worked for a range of publications, including the *Australian Town and Country Journal* and the **Bulletin**. In 1879 Heaton published, at his own expense, the first attempt at an Australian biographical dictionary, *Australian Dictionary of Dates and Men of the Time*. The government printer censored the text, deleting among other passages a paragraph on the **pure merinos**. Heaton instituted legal action, and the book was eventually printed in London; it has been republished as *The Bedside Book of Colonial Doings* (1984). Heaton returned to England in 1883, and served as a Conservative member of the House of Commons 1886–1910. He maintained financial and emotional links with Australia, and was a member of a group in parliament known as the Colonial Party; the press called him the 'Member for Australia'. He campaigned successfully for cheaper postal and telegraphic rates, in the belief that the Empire could be held together by a 'penny stamp'. Having previously declined a knighthood, Heaton was made a baronet in 1912.

KT

Heffron, Robert James (1890–1978) became well known as a socialist union official in his native NZ before coming to Australia in 1919, where he worked for the Federated Clothing Trades Union in Melbourne, then the Marine Stewards Union in Sydney, and was briefly a member of the Communist Party. He became Labor MLA for Botany in 1930, and held the seat until he was elected to Maroubra in 1950. He led the 1938 Labor opposition to J.T. **Lang**, and became a minister in the **McKell** government when Lang was ousted. As minister for education (1944–60) and premier of NSW (1959–64), Heffron was a major figure in the postwar development of NSW. His political career followed the trajectory of the NSW labour movement, from initial militancy as one of the 'Trades Hall Reds' in the 1920s to studied moderation annd compromise in the maintenance of office.

KT

Heidelberg School was the dominant movement in Australian **painting** from the late 1880s. Leading figures were Frederick **McCubbin**, Tom **Roberts**, Arthur **Streeton**, and Charles Conder, who set up artists' camps at Box Hill and Heidelberg, in the hill country east of Melbourne, and around Port Phillip Bay. Influenced by the French *plein air* style, they attempted to capture a momentary effect in the Australian landscape with 'a general impression of colour'. Employing lighter brush strokes and a softer palette, they captured the light, colour and mood of the Australian bush in a new, naturalistic manner. Like their literary counterparts among the *Bulletin* writers, the Heidelberg School painters formulated a clearly independent expression of **national identity**. Despite intense criticism, exponents won some praise at their first exhibition, the '9 by 5' Impressions Exhibition (1889), and their works became fashionable. The school attracted renewed attention in the 1970s, augmented by the *Golden Summers* exhibition in 1985, but has been criticised for idealising and sentimentalising bush life. In *The Artists' Camps: 'Plein Air' Painting in Australia* (1992), Helen Topliss places the works in their suburban locations and acknowledges the role of the school's little-recognised female practitioners, such as Jane **Sutherland** and Clara Southern.

HD

Helpmann, Robert Murray (1909–86), dancer, choreographer, and actor, performed in J.C. **Williamson** musicals before joining the newly formed London ballet company, the Vic-Wells (later Sadlers' Wells) in 1933. His ensuing partnership with Margot Fonteyn became renowned. In 1937 Helpmann began his acting career as Oberon in *A Midsummer Night's Dream* with the Old Vic and returned with the company for an Australian tour in 1954. He choreographed the popular ballet film *The Red Shoes* (1948), created the innovative *The Display* (1964) for the Australian Ballet, and performed in several Australian films, including *The Mango Tree* (1977). Helpmann's abilities were widely recognised: he was joint artistic director for the Australian Ballet 1965–76, artistic director of the Adelaide Festival 1970–76, and Australian of the Year in 1966. An authorised biography by Elizabeth Salter was published in 1978.

KT

Henderson, George Cockburn (1870–1944) occupied the chair of modern history and English at the University of Adelaide from 1902 to 1924, and subsequently held posts at the University of Sydney, making forays into the Pacific to prosecute his research. The son of a NSW coalminer, he was a pupil-teacher who studied at Sydney under G.A. **Wood** and then at Wood's Oxford college, Balliol. Henderson absorbed both its high moral purpose and commitment to research-based scholarship. An address on 'Colonial History' to the Australian Association for the Advancement of Science in 1911 sounded a manifesto for the science of history. At Adelaide, Henderson taught imperial and colonial history, and arranged for a local benefactor to endow a prize for work on SA history written from the original records. His report on overseas archives led to the establishment in 1920 of the first Australian state **archives**.

Overworked, and unsuccessful in two marriages, he resigned his chair and returned to Sydney. Marjorie Casson wrote a memoir (1964). Henderson's first major work, a biography of Sir George **Grey** (1907), is his most complete; it shows a far-sighted colonial administrator at work in Australia, NZ, and South Africa. His later work was on Fijian history. His career and works are discussed by Elizabeth Kwan in Stuart Macintyre and Julian Thomas (eds), *The Discovery of Australian History* (1995).

SM

Henning, Rachel Biddulph (1826–1914) first came to Australia from England in 1854 to join her brother; homesick and appalled at the crudeness of the colony, she stayed for only two years. When she returned to Australia in 1861 she was much more positive in her response, increasingly recognising the unique beauty of the land. Her **letters** to her sisters, one in England, the other in Australia, spanning the years 1853–82, provide a marvellous insight into the migrant experience and conditions of squatting life. They first appeared in the *Bulletin* during 1951 and 1952; the book form, *The Letters of Rachel Henning* (1963), was edited by David Adams. Henning spent several years with her brother on his Qld pastoral run before marrying and moving to NSW.

KT

Henry, Alice (1857–1943), suffragist and journalist, was an associate of Vida **Goldstein** and Catherine Helen **Spence** in the 1890s, when she was writing for the Melbourne *Argus* and the *Australasian* on social issues, including labour reform. She travelled to England in 1905 to lecture on female suffrage, and then to the USA, where she settled in Chicago. Henry became secretary of the local branch of the National Women's Trade Union League of America and, with her friend Miles **Franklin**, edited the league's journal, *Life and Labor*. Her books about women and work—*The Trade Union Woman* (1915) and *Women and The Labor Movement* (1923)—were published before her reluctant return to Australia in 1933. Her memoirs, edited by Nettie **Palmer**, were published posthumously. Diane Kirkby has written a biography, *Alice Henry: The Power of Pen and Voice* (1991).

KT

Henty family is celebrated as Victoria's 'first settlers'. Sussex farmer JAMES HENTY (1800–82) settled at Swan River, WA, in 1829 but decided that locality was not suited to whaling and wool-growing, and relocated in 1832 to Van Diemen's Land, where his parents and siblings soon joined him. From there, his brother EDWARD (1810–78) led the move to Portland Bay in south-western Victoria in 1834. The Port Phillip District was then outside the prescribed 'settled district' of NSW, making settlement there illegal. Two years later, on his exploratory trip through 'Australia Felix', Major **Mitchell** was greatly surprised at the industry and domesticity he found at Portland.

The story of the Hentys has provided an enduring picture of pioneer life in Victoria, which continues to be celebrated locally. The various commemorative and celebratory events of 1934 reinforced the legend. Marnie **Bassett's** weighty account of the family was published in 1954. The family papers, held at the La Trobe and Mitchell libraries, provide valuable detail about farming, whaling, pastoralism, and domestic life in early colonial Victoria; an edited collection by Lynette Peel, *The Henty Journals* (1996), covers the period 1834–39.

HD

Herald, a Melbourne daily **newspaper**, was founded in 1839, mainly owing to the initiative of Sydney journalist George Cavenagh, and was first published in January 1840 as the *Port Phillip Herald*. It changed its name to the *Melbourne Morning Herald* in 1849, but proved unsuccessful as a daily. In 1869, under the brief ownership of David **Syme**, it was converted to an evening daily. The long-serving chair of the board, Theodore Fink (1913–42), built up the paper considerably and appointed Keith **Murdoch** as editor in 1921. Under Murdoch, who succeeded Fink as chairman, the Herald & Weekly Times Ltd emerged as the largest newspaper group in Australia. The *Herald* merged with the *Sun News–Pictorial* in 1990 to create the *Herald Sun*, but by then the group had been acquired by Keith's son, Rupert Murdoch.

HD

Herbert, (Alfred Francis) Xavier (1901–84), novelist, qualified and worked as a pharmacist before embarking on a wandering tour of northern Australia, working as pearl diver, stockman, miner, and railway fettler—experiences which informed all his future writing. During a stay in England (1930–32), Herbert completed the first draft of *Capricornia*, a long novel set in the NT. Although ready two years later, it was not published until 1938 because of the failure of the publishing company, owned by P.R. **Stephensen**. The novel received immediate public and critical acclaim, winning the sesquicentenary competition and becoming a best seller.

After war service, Herbert settled near Cairns in northern Qld. There was a long period when he published no work, which culminated in the publication of four works in four years, 1959–63. The most notable of these is *Disturbing Element* (1963), an autobiography of his youth, described by Laurie Clancy as 'entertaining but untrustworthy'. Herbert then published *Poor Fellow My Country* (1975), a massive work which, like *Capricornia*, was set in the NT and explored the relationships of Aborigines and whites with the land and with each other. The destruction of Aboriginal society and the environment by the whites, and the bigotry of the ruling society, are explored mainly through the experiences of characters of mixed Aboriginal and European descent. *Poor Fellow* won the Miles Franklin Award. Works on Herbert include a collection of his writings edited by Frances de Groen and Peter Pierce (1992), and a study by Laurie Clancy (1981).

KT

Heritage, literally, the property handed down by individuals and families from generation to generation, has acquired wider usage in its extension, first to inherited customs, beliefs, and institutions held in common by a nation or community, and, more recently to natural and 'built' landscapes, buildings and environments held in trust for future generations. Australia has a Commonwealth Heritage Commission and state Heritage Councils, charged with the responsibility of conserving such items. It is to these, rather than to individual property or common beliefs, that the word *heritage* is usually applied.

Heritage is an old idea, grounded in the experience of traditional societies, where handing down property, especially land, from father to son was the basis of the social order. Its popularity in a young, highly urbanised, democratic country like Australia may seem paradoxical. Heritage is not something handed down, but something recently invented; not a product of tradition, but of the need to create one.

If colonial Australians spoke of 'heritage' it was usually of their 'British heritage' of monarchical, parliamentary, or legal institutions. Henry **Parkes** exalted the 'crimson thread of kinship' binding Australians to Britain, a phrase which signified a link at once biological, sentimental, and symbolic. By the end of the nineteenth century Australians had also begun to recognise a debt to the previous generations of Australian **pioneers**. Ernest **Scott** would later write of Australian **nationalism** as springing from 'the splendour of our own heritage and the greatness of our possibilities', while Victorian and Queensland schoolchildren would study its unfolding in textbooks entitled *Australian Heritage*. It was in this sense that the film-maker Charles Chauvel entitled his 1935 epic tribute to the Australian pioneers 'Heritage'.

The idea that heritage might be embodied in places and buildings was slower to grow, not only because Europeans were newcomers, but because their historical sensibilities were formed by European Romanticism and an ethnocentrism that excluded Aborigines from history. In the 1830s the botanist–clergyman William Woolls sorrowfully observed that 'we cannot boast of the massive structures which have been raised by the piety of our forefathers, and which are now the sacred storehouses of our predecessors, and guardians of their bones; we cannot pride ourselves upon the triumphal arch, the high-raised battlement, the moated tower, and the mouldered grandeur of times gone by'.

The material heritage that mattered to colonial Australians was the legacy of nature rather than of history. Tim Bonyhady ('The Stuff of Heritage' in Bonyhady and Tom Griffiths, eds, *Prehistory to Politics*, 1996) has shown how early advocates of nature conservation and **national parks** sought to preserve the forests, flora, and public lands of the colonies for future generations. 'I regard the forest as a heritage given to us by nature, not for spoil or to devastate, but to be wisely used, reverently honoured and carefully maintained', declared Ferdinand von **Mueller** in 1871. Such places of natural beauty were to be passed 'as a sacred patrimony from generation to generation'. This was a conception of heritage oriented to the future rather than the past, to a sense of responsibility towards children rather than a sense of obligation to forebears. **Town planning** advocates such as John **Sulman** extended it to the conservation of public parks and harbour foreshores. In stressing the idea of heritage as a 'public trust', they anticipated one of the key elements of the later heritage movement, the use of state power to limit private development.

Painters and local antiquarians were beginning to look at the remnants of convict Australia with new eyes. In 1889, when the English artist Godfrey Rivers exhibited a painting of the Sydney **Rocks**, a critic observed that it would be 'valuable as a relic of the past, when such old houses … have been swept away to make room for modern buildings'. Like the Aborigines, whose extinction was seen as an inevitable consequence of progress, the picturesque remnants of old Sydney could be studied, photographed, and recorded—but seldom preserved. Only a few of the most notable were protected as historic sites or house museums. The Tasmanian government passed special legislation to preserve **Port Arthur**. William Charles **Wentworth's** Vaucluse House, which entered public ownership in 1913, became the first notable house-museum. William Hardy **Wilson** devoted more than 20 years to recording the buildings of early NSW and Van Diemen's Land in exquisite drawings designed, not only as a historical record, but as an incentive to modern architects to return to the classical principles of Old Colonial.

Ideas of heritage had a natural appeal to cultural and political conservatives like Hardy Wilson and the founders of the **National Trust**, the voluntary organisation founded on the model of the English National Trust after World War II. Mrs Annie Wyatt, a North Sydney housewife, had already led a campaign to prevent vandalism to the Kuring-Gai Chase, a national park to the north of Sydney, when she prompted the foundation of the NSW branch of the trust in 1947. The saving of such 'treasures' was a step towards 'the evolution of a National Soul'. In Victoria, where a branch of the trust was founded in 1956 in response to the threatened demolition of the South Yarra mansion Como, its founding members included establishment figures such as Maie **Casey** and Joan **Lindsay**, co-authors of a pioneering study of *Early Melbourne Architecture* (1953).

In keeping with its elite membership, the trust aimed to conserve only 'the best' of the past, and graded heritage sites according to A, B, and C categories. Mansions, homesteads, and symbolically important public buildings were designated A; terrace houses, flour mills, and mine workings were designated C. Like its British parent, it acted as a trustee for historic properties willed to the nation; but increasingly it relied upon wider public support to persuade owners to maintain old buildings, or governments to prevent their demolition. In the late 1960s the Builders Labourers Federation, under its leader Jack **Mundey**, placed **'green bans'** on several inner-city Sydney neighbourhoods. A campaign by young professionals to save the domed banking chamber of the Union Bank in Melbourne's Collins Street in 1973 persuaded the Hamer Liberal government to pass the Historic Buildings Act the following year, the first such legislation in Australia.

The pressure to conserve natural and historic sites in Australia fed on the heightened international awareness of environmental issues following the Club of Rome report and oil-price rise of the early 1970s. The use of the word *heritage* to describe these items was first popularised by a 1970 UNESCO report, and it seems to have made its way into Australian parlance largely through its adoption by architects, planners, and bureaucrats drawn into the international circuit of what soon became known as 'heritage professionals'. In 1973 the **Whitlam** government established a committee of inquiry into the **National Estate** under Justice Robert Hope (the term *National Estate* was borrowed from the Kennedy administration in the USA) which recommended the establishment of a statutory commission to list and conserve 'the things we want to keep'. David Yencken, first head of the new body, favoured the name 'National Estate Commission' but was overruled by Whitlam who created the Australian Heritage Commission. *The Heritage of Australia*, an illustrated inventory of the National Estate, was published in 1981. The state governments, led by NSW (1977) and SA (1978), subsequently passed Heritage Acts of their own.

Heritage is a political concept grounded in a sense of shared ownership—it is 'ours'. But there could be doubts, as Isabel McBryde and her colleagues noted in 1985, about precisely *Who Owns the Past?* In 1983, when the Commonwealth government invoked its international treaty obligations to protect the World Heritage-listed Franklin River and its Aboriginal rock shelters from the Tasmanian government's plans to construct a dam for hydro-electricity, it asserted a concept of heritage that was supra-national. Meanwhile, Aborigines themselves, whose attachment to place was ancient and intense, demanded the restoration of their heritage from the nation to the local tribe or community. New Age pilgrims, travelling to **Uluru** and Kakadu, sought to adopt that ancient heritage as their own.

Democratising heritage had widened its scope. In the 1950s North Shore matrons fought to save Georgian mansions; by the 1980s heritage consultants listed factories, mines, picture palaces, even public urinals. **Gardens**, landscapes, and **shipwrecks** were added to state and national heritage registers. 'Heritage' had become as Australian as mateship and damper—and included both. There were heritage parks, heritage trails, heritage advisers, even heritage paint-colours and heritage cuisine. From the values of the past, and the things of the past, 'heritage' often seemed to have become no more than a veneer of 'pastness'.

Historians and cultural critics pondered the significance of this heritage boom. Was it a symptom of 'future shock', a track winding nostalgically back into a comfy past? Or was it a product of the postmodern fascination with time-bending and the hyper-real? And what did it all mean for its puzzled neighbours, the historians? *A Heritage Handbook* (1991), edited by Graeme Davison and Chris McConville, reflected their dilemma: should they try to slow down the heritage bandwagon or climb aboard? To its followers, heritage offered a free ticket into a past liberated from the schoolmasterly disciplines of chronology, narrative, and moral judgment. But, the more firmly Australians clung to heritage, the more tenuous, the critics feared, was their hold on history.

GRAEME DAVISON

Heroes and heroines were once considered the soul of history. 'Great men are the inspired Texts of that divine BOOK OF REVELATION ... called History', declared the Victorian sage Thomas Carlyle in *On Heroes and Hero-Worship* (1841). The Victorian era was an age of hero-worship, when the qualities of the heroic individual set the standard of morality and patriotism. Like his educated contemporaries, Carlyle drew inspiration from the heroes of the Bible, ancient Greece and Rome, and the medieval Age of Chivalry, but he also believed that a new industrial age needed its own heroes. Australians inherited his message: they honoured the heroes of the Old World but they recognised, almost from the beginning, the need for heroes of their own.

Australia itself they first regarded as a land without monuments and without heroes. Ironically, as Manning **Clark** suggests (in Stephen Graubard, ed., *Australia: The Daedalus Symposium*, 1985), the Aborigines actually 'had heroes similar to the heroes of Greek and Roman antiquity'—ancestral spirit-beings whose deeds had shaped the land itself. But the British conquerors of Australia knew little of, and cared less for, these traditions. They brought their own heroes with them. The idols of the early Victorians were the warrior-heroes of Trafalgar and Waterloo, Lord Nelson and the Duke of Wellington. Military virtues—courage, daring, fortitude, love of country, self-sacrifice—became the measure of Australian heroism too. From the 1820s to the 1920s, British military men—Drake, Nelson, Clive of India, Gordon of Khartoum—defined a pattern which Australians adapted to their own circumstances as well as they could. The explorer, who exemplified courage and fortitude in a battle against nature rather than against men; the **bushranger**, who was brave and fearless in defiance, rather than in defence, of the nation-state; the sportsman, who showed physical prowess in defence of his country's honour, though not usually at the risk of his life—each reflected elements of this heroic ideal.

Explorers became the conventional heroes of colonial Australia, surrogates for the warriors Australia did not have. They were, Clark suggests, an unremarkable lot—required by history to fill shoes too big for their feet. Yet contemporaries did not always think them so. The explorers themselves, reared on tales of heroism, were often avid seekers after glory, conscious heirs to a tradition of heroic journeying that stretched back to *The Iliad* and *The Odyssey*. 'Ithaca itself was scarcely more longed for by Ulysses than Botany Bay by the adventurers who had traversed so many thousands of miles to take possession of it', wrote Watkin **Tench**, chronicler of the First Fleet. James **Cook**, the greatest of these British voyagers, was perhaps Australia's first real hero, and his fame rose further in the nineteenth century when his humble birth, scientific skill, and humanitarianism won

the admiration of a democratic age. The history of land **exploration**, on the other hand, was less productive of satisfactory heroes, not perhaps because their deeds were so unremarkable, but because their discoveries were so disappointing. Robert O'Hara **Burke** and William John Wills, leaders of the ill-fated Victorian expedition across Australia in 1861, became the prototype of what some historians see as a distinctively Australian tradition of heroic failure. Ken **Inglis**, whose *The Australian Colonists* (1974) contains the best discussion of colonial heroes, notes among contemporaries 'a disposition to venerate dead civic heroes as victims of fate', as though admiration for heroes was somehow detached from the success of their cause. Yet in school textbooks, commemorative cairns, and grand **history paintings**, Australians installed the explorers as the heroes of what perforce remained the grand theme of their history—the colonising destiny of the British race.

Since heroes were seen as moral exemplars, especially for the young, schoolteachers took a keen interest in the cultivation of Australian hero-worship. While urging Australian boys to model themselves on soldiers and explorers, they also sought to create role-models for Australian girlhood. Grace Darling, the lighthouse-keeper's daughter who had gone with her father to the rescue of a ship wrecked off the Northumberland coast in 1838, was a new kind of heroine—young, humbly born, brave, and physically strong. Her fame spread quickly to Australia (a Collingwood pub was named after her) where she became, in turn, the model for such Australian heroines as Grace **Bussell**, who saved lives from a ship wrecked off the WA coast, and Jane Duff, the Victorian schoolgirl who helped her younger brother survive the ordeal of being lost in the bush (see **Bush searches**). Protestants and Catholics had different childhood heroes: while Victorian state school pupils read about Clive of India or General Gordon, Catholic pupils read about Father Therry or Caroline **Chisholm**.

The fatalism which pervaded Australians' attitude towards heroic explorers showed too in popular sympathy for bushrangers and other outlaws. Such anti-authoritarian traditions, Russel **Ward** argued, were strong among the convicts, especially those from Ireland where British law was widely set at defiance. Lawlessness alone, however, has seldom won outlaws or larrikins a popular following: Ned **Kelly**, who became the most celebrated bushranger, also exhibited qualities of daring, courage, eloquence, and cheeky humour which reappeared in such later variants of the Australian anti-hero as the **larrikin** and the ocker. Some sporting heroes—Doug Walters, Merv Hughes, Dawn **Fraser**, Pat Cash—show these characteristics, as do some larrikin-politicians.

Statesmen—according to a 1997 survey by *Life* magazine—have supplied more than half of America's popular heroes; by contrast, politicians are strikingly absent from Australia's pantheon. Were its political leaders unheroic (just 'triers', as one of them recently suggested) or did its peaceful history deny them the heroic role which revolution and civil war conferred on Washington and Lincoln? Tribunes of the people—the young William Charles **Wentworth**, Peter **Lalor**, Dan **Deniehy**, Graham **Berry**, Jack **Lang**, Gough **Whitlam**, Jim **Cairns**—have enjoyed moments of high acclaim, but they have seldom become national heroes, perhaps because the institutionalised opposition of parliamentary politics denied them a universal following. Winning the passionate devotion of some entails losing the respect of others. Leaders who have been able to unite the nation in times of peril, such as John **Curtin** in 1942–43, have come closest to winning heroic stature.

Sporting heroes, by contrast, may enjoy an almost unlimited following. Australia, argues Geoffrey **Blainey** in *A Shorter History of Australia* (1995), may have been the first nation to witness 'the rise of the sporting hero'. High incomes, short working hours, a temperate climate, and abundant open space and water made Australians devotees of sport. Already by the end of the nineteenth century sportsmen such as the sculler Henry Searle, the jockey Tommy Corrigan, and the cricketer F.R. **Spofforth** were national heroes. So, in a fashion, were the great race-horses, Carbine and **Phar Lap**. In the twentieth century sporting greatness became a matter of calculation as well as sentiment: Don **Bradman**, a scientific student of the game, was perhaps the first Australian hero whose greatness was measured by a statistic: a batting average of 99.94.

For more than a century Australians worshipped military heroism without being able to prove themselves in battle. When that opportunity came, in World War I, it was in circumstances that all but destroyed the assumptions of individual valour, endurance, and self-sacrifice on which their ideals were founded. 'Thrilling Deeds of Heroism' was the headline of Ellis Ashmead-Bartlett's famous first despatch from **Gallipoli**. The Australian war historian and classical scholar Charles **Bean** also portrayed the **Anzacs** as heroes in the tradition of Marathon and Thermopylae. But his ideal of heroism was strikingly different from the romantic adventurer of prewar *Boys' Own* stories; it was the heroic qualities of the AIF as a whole, rather than the deeds of the commanders or individual soldiers, which he sought to commemorate. The word *hero* seldom appears in his pages, for Bean, like many others, recoiled from its jingoistic associations. A few Anzacs, such as Albert **Jacka** VC, won public acclaim for deeds of soldierly prowess; but the most lasting fame belonged to those like Private **Simpson**, the 'man with the Donkey', who exercised bravery by relieving suffering rather than killing Turks. How that myth was created, and the purposes it served, is the subject of the most penetrating study of Australian heroism, Peter Cochrane's *Simpson and the Donkey* (1992).

After World War I democrats became wary of hero-worship, a caution reinforced by the readiness of their opponents on both the Left and Right to embrace exaggerated and malignant versions of it. In the depths of the **Depression** a few misguided patriots may have sought to make John **Monash** into a *Führer*, or Jack **Lang** into another Lenin, but most Australians retained a healthy scepticism towards great men, an attitude which the war against Hitler and the rise of Stalin did nothing to disturb. 'The Australian people made heroes of none, and raised no idols, except perhaps an outlaw, Ned Kelly, and Carbine, a horse', concluded Brian **Fitzpatrick** in 1961. A peaceful property-owning democracy had little use for heroes, except perhaps for sporting heroes. Manning Clark, an admirer of Carlyle, put heroes at the centre of his *History of Australia* (1962–87), but, in the manner of Greek tragedy, they were all beset by **fatal flaws**. The age of heroes, it seemed, was all but over.

Yet one sign of the harder times which Australia has experienced since the 1970s has been the emergence of a new kind of hero-worship. Carlyle had hoped to inspire the businessmen of his day with ideals of benevolence and self-sacrifice. But the businessmen who became the Australian folkheroes of the 1980s and 1990s were a less chivalrous breed. They attacked old-style Australian **egalitarianism** as a **tall-poppy** syndrome that thwarted ambition and wealth-creation. In 1986 a committee headed by Leonie **Kramer** selected *The Greats*, the 50 men and women who had most shaped modern Australia. Rather than hiding its successful people, the new hero-worshippers asserted, Australia needed to promote them as the role-models for a younger generation of achievers. Ann-Maree Moodie's *Local Heroes* (1997) was a representative title in a new genre of hero-worshipping biographies dedicated to the 'celebration of success and leadership'. Susan Mitchell's best-selling *Tall Poppies* (1984) and *Tall Poppies Too* (1991) showed that women had also become high achievers. Other volumes celebrated the successes of prominent Aborigines and migrant Australians.

Yet heroism was surely something more than fame or success. When the POW doctor 'Weary' **Dunlop** died in 1994 his admirers used the opportunity to remind other Australians of this crucial moral dimension of heroism. A hero, they believed, was something more than a celebrity, a role-model, or even a national icon. Like his fellow-doctor Fred **Hollows**, Dunlop embodied many traditional qualities of the Australian hero—he was a man's man, good with his fists, plain-spoken, true to his mates—as well as some strikingly new ones—an openness to Asian influences, for example. Heroism like Dunlop's may now be rare, but heroism on a smaller scale remains an important dimension of national life. Firefighters, surf lifesavers, snow rescue teams are regularly saluted by the press as 'local', 'reluctant', or 'unsung' heroes. Invoked by sub-editors in search of a headline, these terms nevertheless reflect a traditional characteristic of the Australian hero—the willingness to put one's life at risk in defence of one's mates.

GRAEME DAVISON

Herstory is a term that emerged in the early 1970s as part of new interest in **women's history**. A play on the word *history*, it points to the gender imbalance in history-writing. It appears to have been first used in 1972, by the Women's History Research Centre at Berkeley, California, as the title of a collection of newspapers, journals, and newsletters by and about women and women's organisations that were published between 1969 and 1971. The word was subsequently used in the title of several publications in women's history. In Australia, Margaret Bettison and Anne **Summers** used *Herstory* in 1980 as the title of a publication about Australian women writers.

HD

Heysen, (Wilhelm Ernst) Hans Franz (1877–1968), artist, was born in Hamburg, Germany, and migrated with his parents to SA in 1884. The family struggled financially, and Heysen left school in 1892 to work in his father's hardware store at Norwood. On weekends he roamed the hills to sketch and paint. The Adelaide watercolourist James Ashton nurtured his artistic talent. Robert Barr Smith paid for his tuition under Harry Gill at the South Australian School of Design, and four Adelaide businessmen financed a European study tour 1899–1903, after which he established an art school in Adelaide. His Melbourne exhibition, opened by Alfred **Deakin** in August 1908, was a stunning success that brought commissions from wealthy patrons, including Nellie **Melba**, who launched his Melbourne exhibitions in 1912 and 1915. He purchased The Cedars at Hahndorf in the Adelaide Hills, and lived there until his death.

Australians came to share Heysen's vision of the majestic beauty and dignity of gum trees. He is best known for portraying the rapture of giant trunks with twisted limbs, draped in sunlight and shade. But he was not just a painter of trees. On numerous trips to the Flinders Ranges he rendered the rugged grandeur of arid, inland Australia, and influenced later artists to paint the outback. He excelled in all media, especially watercolour, and produced many fine still-lifes and portraits. His studies of the Hahndorf region form a significant artistic and historical record. Heysen won the Wynne Prize nine times between 1904 and 1932. His daughter NORA (1911–) is also an artist. Colin Thiele wrote a biography, *Heysen of Hahndorf* (1968), and introduced a selection in *Hans Heysen Masterpieces* (1977).

DC

Higgins, Henry Bournes (1851–1929) was the judge who established industrial relations as 'a new province for law and order' and the creator of the **basic wage**. He is the subject of two distinguished biographies, a filial one by his niece, Nettie **Palmer** (1931), and a more psychological study by John Rickard (1984). The sub-title of the latter, 'The Rebel as Judge', identifies an important dimension of his character.

Higgins's childhood was spent in Ireland as the son of impoverished and evangelical Wesleyans. Poor health, loneliness and constant self-examination were eased by the family's migration to Melbourne and his success in university studies. He cured his stammer, abandoned religion for an austere classical rationalism, and found companionship with contemporaries such as Alfred **Deakin** and Alexander **Sutherland**. In 1885 Higgins married Mary Alice Morrison, the sister of G.E. **Morrison**. Success at the Bar enabled him to participate in public affairs, notably as a supporter of Irish Home Rule.

He was elected to the Victorian parliament in 1884 as a liberal, and with the support of the *Age* to the Federal Convention in 1897. There, in concert with C.C. **Kingston**, he secured the inclusion of a federal power of industrial conciliation and **arbitration**, and he was also responsible for Section 116 of the Constitution, which enshrines religious freedom. He campaigned against Federation during the subsequent referendum campaign, however, on the grounds that its concessions to states compromised democratic principles; and he lost his seat in the Victorian parliament in 1900 because of his opposition to the **Boer War**.

Higgins was elected to the first federal parliament as a supporter, though not a member, of the Australian Labor Party. He served as attorney-general in the Labor ministry of 1904, but found the demands of party politics uncongenial and in 1906 accepted appointment to the High Court. In the following year he succeeded R.E. **O'Connor** as president of the Commonwealth Court of Conciliation and Arbitration, and it fell to him to interpret the meaning of the 'fair and reasonable' wage enshrined in the **New Protection** legislation. His generous interpretation in the Harvester Judgment of a needs-based wage that recognised the rights of 'a human being in a civilized community' was hailed by the unions and resisted by the employers in a series of High Court challenges. One critic, H.R. **Nicholls**, who was unsuccessfully prosecuted for contempt of court in 1911, has subsequently been apotheosised as a hero by the New Right. Yet Higgins's aversion to class conflict and insistence on the rule of law in the workplace was also challenged by a wave of industrial militancy before, during, and after World War I. He promulgated his jurisdiction at home and abroad in writings published in 1922 as *A New Province for Law and Order*.

Initially a supporter of Australian participation in World War I, Higgins became disillusioned by jingoism and social rancour. The death of his only son while on service desolated him: 'My grief has condemned me to hard labour for the rest of my life.' Growing conflict with W.M. **Hughes** over the prime minister's expedient interventions in industrial disputes caused his resignation from the Arbitration Court in 1920, though he remained on the High Court bench until his death. He argued courteously with his niece Nettie's socialism and his nephew Esmonde Higgins's communism as they wrestled with the legacy of his liberalism. He continued to read widely in Australian as well as other literature, and intended to establish a chair of Celtic at the University of Melbourne; on his death, a bequest of £20 000 went instead to the Irish Academy.

STUART MACINTYRE

High Court of Australia was created by the **Constitution** in 1901, but did not come into operation until 1903 when Samuel **Griffith** was appointed the first chief justice. Its jurisdiction was defined by the Constitution as that of a federal Supreme Court in which all cases arising under the Constitution originated. As the highest court of appeal in Australia, it also hears cases from federal and state courts.

Until 1975, some appeals could be taken further—to the **Privy Council** in England. The High Court was based in Melbourne from 1903, in Sydney from 1973, and in Canberra from 1980, where a purpose-built courthouse opened. The High Court comprises one chief justice with a maximum of seven justices. Cases on constitutional matters are heard before the full bench. Garfield **Barwick** was the longest-serving chief justice (1964–81). The first woman justice, Mary Gaudron, was appointed in 1987.

Among its more influential decisions have been the **Engineers' case** of 1921; the decision that bank nationalisation by the **Chifley** government was unconstitutional; the 1951 ruling that the **Communist** Party Dissolution Act was invalid; the 1983 decision that gave the **Hawke** government the power to prevent work on Tasmania's proposed Franklin Dam; and the 1992 **Mabo** decision. Its interpretations of the Constitution have fundamentally altered **Commonwealth–state relations**. They have been discussed by Leslie Zines, *The High Court and the Constitution* (1981), and Brian Galligan, *Politics of the High Court* (1987).

HD

Higinbotham, George (1826–92), journalist, lawyer, politician, and chief justice of Victoria, was perhaps the most controversial public figure of the 1860s. Higinbotham was an ardent democrat, committed to the self-government of the people. His ideal electorate was self-governing, both in individual restraint and collective autonomy. Conviction of his own moral righteousness gave his oratory an irresistible power. But his influence lay more in the hopes and fears that he crystallised than in programs achieved.

Higinbotham was an Irishman, trained as a reporter and a lawyer in London. He arrived in Victoria in 1854 in time to witness the democratic outcome of the **Eureka** rebellion. In *A Colonial Liberalism* (1991), Stuart Macintyre shows how as editor of the *Argus* Higinbotham welcomed the establishment of universal male suffrage, though not without fear of the 'unreasoning mob'. After election to parliament in 1861, he came to see a greater threat to rational government from what he called 'the wealthy lower orders'—the landowners and merchants dominating the Legislative Council. In 1864, as attorney-general in a reformist government, he identified another threat to the expression of the people's will in the British **Colonial Office's** interference in Victoria's domestic government. (Foreign policy was a different matter, rigidly defined as an imperial concern.) Over the next five years Higinbotham provoked a series of crises between the Victorian Legislative Assembly on the one hand, and the Legislative Council and the Colonial Office on the other, all turning on perceived challenges to the authority of the people, the Legislative Assembly, the Victorian government, and George Higinbotham. These climaxed in 1869 with Higinbotham's passage through the assembly of five resolutions defining colonial **responsible government** in terms which, if accepted in Whitehall, would probably have necessitated the **separation** of Victoria from the British Empire.

In the event, nothing came of the five resolutions, and attempts to reform the Legislative Council stalled, not least because Higinbotham would accept nothing but its absolute dissolution. Nothing came of Higinbotham's other great democratic project of the 1860s, his attempt to establish a national system of **education** on a base of common Christianity. His biographer, Gwyneth Dow, shows in *George Higinbotham: Church and State* (1964) how **sectarian** opposition from jealous church groups led him reluctantly to a position of state secularism. Higinbotham failed, too, to persuade the assembly to support women's suffrage in 1873. He resigned from political life in 1876, characterising it as 'a sort of pandemonium in which a number of lost souls are endeavouring to increase one another's torture'.

His two best-known statements were both quixotic. In speaking to his 1869 resolutions on colonial self-government, he said that the colonists were in fact governed by 'a person named Rogers'—the permanent head of the Colonial Office. During the great **Maritime Strike** of 1890, he publicly wrote to the Melbourne Trades Hall Council with a donation to the strike fund.

Higinbotham's ineffectiveness was undoubtedly due to his absolute conviction of his own political and moral correctness, his refusal to compromise. But there was value in his capacity to push an idea to its limits. His enemies were surely correct in accusing him of creating class consciousness. His friends—radical and liberal politicians, trade unionists, women suffragists, republicans—honoured him and claimed him as father to their thought and action. The heavily wigged statue of Higinbotham the judge, which still stands behind the Treasury Buildings, Melbourne, gives little sense of his capacity to define the future.

MARIAN QUARTLY

Hill, Ernestine (1899–1972) began her career of travelling and writing about the more remote areas of Australia in the early 1930s. Her work was published in newspapers and journals as well as her books. These include a history of irrigation around the Murray River, *Water Into Gold* (1937); a colourful account of the establishment of the **Australian Inland Mission** and the Flying Doctor Service, *Flying Doctor Calling* (1947); and her best-known non-fiction work, *The Territory* (1951), an affectionate view of the NT and its characters. She ventured into fiction only once with *My Love Must Wait* (1941), based on the life of Matthew **Flinders**. This sympathetic, carefully researched work achieved great popular success. She was one of the few writers of her time to earn a living from writing popular, historically based literature. In her work on Daisy **Bates**, *Kabbarli* (1973), Hill claimed to have been the main writer of Bates's *The Passing of the Aborigines* (1938). She figures in Carole Ferrier's *As Good as a Yarn With You* (1992).

KT

Hindmarsh, John (1784–1860) lobbied successfully for the first governorship of SA in 1836. His distinguished naval record was rewarded with the position although he lacked experience in civil administration. Uncertainty and public conflict marked his period in office. He was answerable to the **Colonial Office**, but the Resident Commissioner was authorised by the more powerful Board of Commissioners, which was in charge of land survey and sale. This split in power compounded the difficulties of governing a new colony. Hindmarsh was well intentioned, but his autocratic manner gave offence and exacerbated conflicts.

He had alienated many on the way to SA while captaining the *Buffalo*. He restricted the freedom of emigrants and kept changing direction, wasting valuable time and resources. The experience limited the respect he could command as governor. Hindmarsh's efforts to influence the site and plan of the first town caused much animosity. He sought initially to move the capital lower down the Torrens, then fought to relocate it to Encounter Bay. Neither site was geographically suitable. The suggestion to move the capital angered not only William **Light** and those who had surveyed the region and understood the superior nature of the original position, but also the colonists who owned land and were settling into the town. Hindmarsh was recalled in 1838 and undertook other administrations. The period in SA was the only unsuccessful phase in his career.

KELLIE TOOLE

Hinkler, Herbert John Louis 'Bert' (1892–1933) received national adulation and a prize of £2000 in 1928 when he completed the first solo flight from England to Australia. Born in Qld, Hinkler went to England in 1913 to pursue his fascination with flying and found work in the Sopwith aircraft factory. At the outbreak of World War I he joined the Royal Naval Air Service, and in 1918 he became a pilot in the Royal Flying Corps. Known as the 'lone eagle', he successfully completed the first west–east South Atlantic crossing. He died when his plane crashed in Italy on another England–Australia flight. His story is told by R.D. McKenzie in *Solo* (1962).

KT

Historic Houses Trust of New South Wales was established by the NSW state government in 1980 under their Historic Houses Act to manage two government-owned properties, Elizabeth Bay House and Vaucluse House, as house-museums. Other properties, including **Hyde Park Barracks** and Elizabeth Farm, were later transferred to the trust; as with **National Trust** properties, these are open to the public. Committed to promoting the properties' cultural and educational potential for the benefit of the public, the Historic Houses Trust is concerned with researching their histories and implementing novel interpretative strategies.

HD

Historical associations, see **Historical societies**

Historical geography until the 1960s was typically concerned with either the reconstruction of the geography of a past time or the study of geographical changes over time. There are Australian examples of both approaches, though the debates that surrounded the place of historical geography in Anglo-American geography in the 1950s and 1960s largely by-passed Australia. Since the 1960s Australian historical geographers have given sustained attention to the relationship between people and environment. In a series of local and regional studies they have explored the distinctive character of pioneering settlement and its aftermath, and measured the success and failure of land settlement in unfamiliar and difficult environments. Within Australia, as elsewhere, historical geographers were critical of the quantitative emphasis of human geography in the 1960s and 1970s. They have also shown renewed interest in the historical dimensions of their research.

J.D. Rogers's *Australasia*, a volume in the series 'Historical Geography of the British Colonies', had appeared as early as 1907, but the work of scholars, such as Archibald Grenfell **Price's** *The Foundations of Settlement in South Australia* (1924), marks a more significant departure. Price's attention to the role of individuals contrasted with the bold 'environmental determinist' interpretations of his Sydney contemporary Griffith **Taylor**, then associate professor of geography at the University of Sydney.

More than most branches of Australian scholarship, historical geography has been decisively shaped by overseas influences. In 1958 a young American geographer, Donald Meinig, visited Australia to investigate the changing social and physical limits of the SA wheat frontier. His book *On the Margins of the Good Earth* (1962) anticipated some major methodological developments in human geography in the late 1960s and 1970s. By the time it was published, the expansion of the Australian university system had brought a more permanent influx of young geographers, especially from Britain and NZ. During the next decade and a half their books and monographs augmented the efforts of Australian geographers and helped to define what became the distinctive idiom of Australian historical geography. These included T.M. Perry, *Australia's First Frontier* (1963); Les Heathcote, *Back of Bourke* (1965); J.M. Powell, *The Public Lands of Australia Felix* (1970); Dennis Jeans, *Historical Geography of New South Wales to 1901* (1972); and Michael Williams, *The Making of the South Australian Landscape* (1974). All were characterised by thorough archival work, and command of official documentary and cartographic sources. While Jeans and Williams produced books in the mould of the doyen of British historical geographers, H.C. Darby, Perry paid closer attention to applications of Turner's **frontier** thesis to Australia. Heathcote and Powell, in contrast, extended the contribution of historical geography to natural resource appraisal and land management. It was, however, in Jim Cameron's work on pre-convict settlement in WA, ultimately published as *Ambition's Fire* (1981), that the use of behavioural models in historical geography gained their fullest expression.

At first historical geographers researched largely at a local, regional, or state level. John McQuilton's analysis of the social and environmental context of the **Kelly** gang, *The Kelly Outbreak* (1979), demonstrated how historical geography could illuminate one of the most celebrated events in Australian history. Most, however, have stayed closer to traditional interests of nineteenth-century **land settlement**, pioneer society, and economy, although urban themes and problems of natural resource management have attracted increasing attention.

Historical geography has developed mainly as a subspecialism in departments of geography, and often as an extension of more contemporary preoccupations. Godfrey Linge's mammoth *Industrial Awakening* (1979) is a detailed colony-by-colony account of the origins and development of manufacturing in Australia to 1890. Peter Rimmer's studies of **railways**, and work on the hierarchy of colonial cities by Mal Logan and others, have built upon more contemporary studies of Australian transport and urbanisation.

Australia still waits for an H.C. Darby or Donald Meinig to effect a grand synthesis of its historical geography. Oskar Spate, English-born professor of geography at the Australian National University, introduced some historical themes in his general guide to *Australia, New Zealand and the Pacific* (1956 and later editions); but Les Heathcote's *Australia* (1975, 1994) was the first to draw strongly on recent historical geographical scholarship. J.M. Powell's inspired work, *A Historical Geography of Modern Australia* (1988), offered 'a broad interpretative synthesis' of twentieth-century developments, framed by the contemporary interest, first problematised by Griffith Taylor, in environmental possibilities and limits.

Historical geographers themselves have made contributions beyond their specialism, notably in the production of atlases, such as J.S. Duncan's *Atlas of Victoria* (1982), T. Griffin and M. McCaskill's *Atlas of South Australia* (1986), and Cramm and McQuilton's *Australians: An Historical Atlas* (1987), the last an ambitious collaboration between historical geographers across Australia. T.M. Perry's earlier *The Discovery of Australia* (1982) explores the emergent place of *Terra Australis* in cartographic history.

In the final stage of his career, Grenfell **Price** had turned to the place of Australia in the wider world. Influenced by US cultural geographer Carl Sauer, his book *The Western Invasion of the Pacific* (1963) portrayed Western penetration as a series of moving frontiers. Powell's *Mirrors of the New World* (1977), a comparative study of European expansion in North America and Australasia from a humanistic perspective, focuses more closely on the nature of the encounter with an unfamiliar environment. But it is Oskar Spate's magisterial three volumes, *The Pacific Since Magellan* (1979–88), that best exemplifies the aspiration of Australian historical geographers to situate their work in a wider frame.

Environmental history, broadly defined, gathered renewed momentum in the USA in the late 1980s and early 1990s, calling forth sympathetic responses among both historians and geographers in Australia. Geoffrey **Bolton** and Geoffrey **Blainey** explored themes of distance and land degradation while Powell commenced an important series of studies on environmental management, beginning, in *Environmental Management in Australia 1788–1914* (1976),

with forests and mining, and culminating in recent monographs on water resources in Qld and Victoria.

Australian historians and historical geographers have shared research interests—long-standing ones in the case of environmental history—and a measure of mutual respect. Although 'boundary riding' between disciplines has been tolerated, even encouraged on occasions, there remain significant differences of approach between historians and historical geographers. Typically, historians reviewing works of historical geography offer praise if it is 'well' written: thus Spate's *The Pacific Since Magellan*, for example, enjoyed widespread praise because of its compelling narrative thread. But they tend to draw back from any visible philosophical architecture and methodological devices, judging them as overly jargonistic.

The achievements of historical geography in Australia rest firmly on the shoulders of a small number of scholars, pursuing in sustained but hardly programmatic fashion a diversity of research interests. Gaps remain to be filled: some states are better researched than others; some topics are scarcely touched. Consequently and unsurprisingly, there are still few works of synthesis for the entire country, compared, for example, with history. The silences are significant in other ways: gender and ethnicity, a springboard for much new historical and social science scholarship since the 1980s, have made little impact beyond the realm of research undertaken for postgraduate theses.

MICHAEL ROCHE

Historical journals are serial publications that promote the study and appreciation of history. They had their origins in the nineteenth-century periodicals that published essays and reviews across a broad spectrum to a general audience of educated readers—thus in Australia both the *Melbourne Review* and the *Victorian Review*, quarterlies of the 1880s, carried articles concerned with aspects of the colonial past, while in the twentieth century journals such as *Australian Quarterly* joined historical with contemporary commentary. Specifically historical journals were established in Germany, France, Britain, and other Western European countries in the second half of the nineteenth century as history was constituted as a distinct academic discipline emphasising archival research and the systematic accumulation of knowledge. This development occurred much later in Australia, where there were no more than a score of university-based historians before World War II.

Thus the first Australian historical journals were produced by the state **historical societies**. The **Royal Australian Historical Association**, formed in 1901, published its *Journal and Proceedings* from that year (in 1965 it became the *Royal Australian Historical Society Journal*). The (Royal) Victorian Historical Society, formed in 1909, followed with its *Magazine* in 1911, which passed through changes of title and is now the *Victorian Historical Journal*. The Queensland Historical Society, formed in 1913, published its *Journal* from 1915. The Western Australian Historical Society, formed in 1926, published a *Journal and*

Proceedings from 1927; initially it was known as *Early Days*. These journals were issued to members as a printed record of the papers presented and business conducted at society meetings. The members consisted principally of well-to-do descendants of early settlers, members of the professions with antiquarian enthusiasm for the local past, and a smattering of academics. The articles concentrated on colonial **foundations**, but did provide university-based historians with an opportunity for publication (the only other outlet was the proceedings of the biennial congresses of **ANZAAS**), and a forum for promoting the study of the past. The NSW and Victorian journals still serve this function; established later, the *Papers and Proceedings: Tasmanian Historical Research Association* (1951–) and *Journal of the Historical Society of South Australia* (1974–) sustain the study of their states' history.

The first academic historical journal, *Historical Studies: Australia and New Zealand*, was established in 1940. Its founders were R.M. **Crawford**, professor of history at the University of Melbourne, and Gwyn James, whom Crawford brought to Melbourne in that year. The two men modelled their journal, which appeared twice annually with a print run of 500, on professional journals such as the British *Bulletin of the Institute of Historical Research* and the *American Historical Review*, to serve 'the growing interests and pressing problems of research'. *HSANZ* included articles, reviews, lists of manuscript accessions and research theses, and 'Notes and News' that coordinated the growing profession. It published articles on non-Australian as well as Australian subjects in a conscious endeavour to promote greater professionalism, and sought to broaden its base with interstate and New Zealand members of the editorial board (after 1949 these became correspondents). In a retrospective account of the venture in *HS* (1984), Stuart Macintyre suggests that after struggling for its first decade, *HSANZ* prospered in the 1950s, when its circulation rose to 1000, with the rapid growth of university and school history.

This environment fostered new regional journals and a growing range of specialist journals catering to the interests of historians working in the branches of the discipline. The *Journal of Pacific History* and the *New Zealand Journal of History* began in 1966 and 1967. The latter event brought a change of title for *HSANZ*; it became *Historical Studies*, and retained that title until 1988 when it assumed the national prefix, *Australian Historical Studies*. In WA, *University Studies in History and Economics* (1934–38, 1953–56) was followed by *University Studies in Western Australian History* (1956–60), *University Studies in History* (1961–70), and *Studies in Western Australian History* (1977–). At the University of Queensland, Gordon **Greenwood** initiated the *Australian Journal of Politics and History* in 1955. *Business Archives and History*, founded in 1956, became the *Australian Economic History Review* in 1962. The *Journal of Religious History* was established in Sydney in 1960, though it placed much greater emphasis on the publication of articles on non-Australian subjects than most Australian-based historical journals. The formation of the Australian Society of Labour History

brought *Labour History* in 1962, and a number of newsletters issued by its local branches (notably the Melbourne *Recorder*, 1964– ; the Sydney *Hummer*, 1983– ; and Perth's *Papers in Labour History*, 1988–). The annual *Melbourne Studies in Education* (1958–) was supplemented by the *Journal of the Australian and New Zealand History of Education Society* (1972–82), now renamed the *History Education Review* (1983–). *Aboriginal History* (1977–), *Australian Cultural History* (1981–), *Journal of the Australian War Memorial* (1982–), *Sporting Traditions* (1984–), and *Historical Records of Australian Science* (1985–) are among other specialist historical journals.

There are a number of academic journals that combine historical with non-historical articles, notably the *Journal of Industrial Relations* (1960–), the *Journal of Australian Studies* (1977–), *Australian Feminist Studies* (1985–), and some non-academic journals that bear directly on the discipline, such as the *Public History Review* (1992–) of the Professional Historians Association of New South Wales. The *Australian Historical Association Bulletin* (1974–) began as a professional newsletter but includes articles on the teaching, study, promotion, and future of history. Some journals have been established to serve a particular purpose, such as the cluster of bulletins produced by the working parties of the **Bicentennial History Project**. The one concerned with the 1838 'slice' volume, *The Push from the Bush* (1978–92), outlasted the publication of the history. The working papers and other series published by various university departments and research centres are an important analogue of the journal. Individual departments of history also support their own journals, edited and produced by postgraduate students, which are nominally annual publications but appear erratically. The *Melbourne Historical Journal*, established in 1962 and with a 25th number in 1997, is probably the most durable. There is an electronic conversation group, *H-ANZAU* <http://www.unimelb.edu.au/ infoserv/>, and an *Electronic Journal of Australian and New Zealand History* (1996–) <http://www.jcu.edu.au/aff/history/new.htm>.

The guides to articles in historical journals are grossly deficient. Trevor Hogan et al., *Index to Journal Articles on Australian History* (1976), is an incomplete retrospective listing to 1975. Victor Crittenden coordinated the production of an annual *Index to Journal Articles on Australian History* to 1988, which also lists book reviews. Some historical journals are indexed in *APAIS*, and some Australian journals are covered by international citation indexes. (See **Reference works**.)

The journal is indispensable to Australian historical scholarship. The journal article is the most common form of research publication, the principal form of institutional activity measured and rewarded by universities, and the basis of employment and promotion. Yet its logistical foundations are fragile. Most journals are published by societies of like-minded enthusiasts. Retail sales are negligible and subscriptions restricted to members and libraries; *AHS*, with a circulation of some 1200, is probably the largest. Contributors are unpaid. Editorial work is mostly voluntary, at best recognised with a slight reduction of other academic duties.

Most journals rely on direct and indirect subsidies. Some have succumbed to approaches from international publishers, which take over the task of production and distribution; but frequently they increase the subscription price, and thus pass on the cost to the academic user. Attempts by universities in the 1990s to assert intellectual property rights over academic writing are a response to this predicament that does little to ease the plight of the writer and the reader.

The academic journal also shapes the practice of history more powerfully than any other form of publication. Its reviews provide the most important form of peer evaluation. Its articles, which are submitted to the judgment of anonymous readers, establish the directions of research and the discourse of the profession. As the study of Australian history developed after World War II, the journal literature marked out its essential contours and concerns, which in turn found their way onto undergraduate reading lists and into textbooks. Hence the celebrated debates about the origins of the **convicts**, the purposes of colonial land policy, the reasons for **Federation**, and the outcome of the **conscription** debate in World War I shaped the agreed understanding of the subject. That function is no longer apparent. The insistent institutional pressure to publish has brought a proliferation of journals and a volume of articles on Australian history that no scholar is able to encompass. The growing specialisation has fragmented the literature, and the fragments are enclosed in self-referential writing. The crucial junctions once created by the historiographical survey or review article have dwindled. Historians too seldom avail themselves of the distinctive opportunities of the article as a literary form, at once more closely concentrated than the monograph and yet more flexible, lighter on its feet, and able to range more widely.

STUART MACINTYRE

Historical Records of Australia, a 33-volume set of official records, had its origins in NSW in the late nineteenth century as a result of a burgeoning patriotism and a desire to give the study of history greater credibility. In 1891 the University of Sydney appointed G.A. **Wood** to the first chair of history in Australia. Three years earlier, the government of Henry **Parkes**, in planning the centennial celebrations, funded a history of the colony based on official documents then being transcribed in London at public expense by James **Bonwick**. It was from this project that the *Historical Records of Australia* eventually emerged.

The official history soon encountered difficulties and a History Board, appointed to find a way out, recommended editing and publishing the documents before writing the history. They appeared under the title *Historical Records of New South Wales*. Progress was slow and in 1902, after only seven volumes covering the years to 1811 had appeared, the government withdrew funding. Those who favoured continuation sought support from the new federal government which, after lengthy investigation, agreed to provide funds and vest control in the Library Committee of the Commonwealth Parliament. Printing was left with the

NSW Government Printer, which had produced the earlier series. The project's headquarters remained in Sydney where the Bonwick Transcripts, which now covered the period to 1830, were housed. Frederick Watson, a former radiologist who had recently helped run the Public Library, was made editor on 8 August 1912. He was well informed on Australian history, but his lack of literary talents necessitated the appointment of G.A. Wood to assist him with the background material needed for each volume. Wood handled the prickly Watson diplomatically and established a harmonious relationship with him.

Instead of merely continuing the project begun earlier, Watson decided to cover the whole of Australia, beginning in 1788, even though this involved some duplication. The NSW government was anxious to exclude sensitive material relating to the convicts. At first Watson contemplated a reserve volume for this and other material, but later decided to ignore the request. His plan was for seven series of documents, each arranged chronologically, the first and most important comprising despatches to and from London. Then were to come administrative matters; colonies other than NSW; legal papers; documents relating to exploration and to science; and finally a curious amalgam of ecclesiastical, naval, and military sources. After locating documents, Watson began the arduous task of arranging, indexing, and proof-reading them, as well as preparing introductions and annotations. He had little assistance and worked long hours under difficult conditions. His relationship with Arthur Wadsworth, the Commonwealth parliamentary librarian, was troubled and the Mitchell librarian placed obstacles in the way of his use of the Bonwick Transcripts. In addition, he became unhappy with the arrangements for his own salary, which were renegotiated several times. Matters came to a head in 1925 when, after acrimonious dispute, his work ceased with the project unfinished. The NSW volumes stopped eight years short of responsible government in 1856. Those dealing with the remaining colonies were even less advanced, and only one volume of legal papers appeared in the other series. Despite recommendations from Wood and Professor Ernest **Scott** of the University of Melbourne, Watson was not replaced. This sorry saga has been examined by Ann Mitchell in *HS* (1982).

Nevertheless, Watson's achievement was impressive. In just over a decade, allowing for 18 months' military service, he had produced 33 substantial volumes, 26 of which dealt with the eastern third of mainland Australia. Not all the governors' despatches were located and the minutes of colonial officials became available too late. Moreover, many of the enclosures which accompanied the despatches were omitted because they were set aside for inclusion in Series II which never appeared. These omissions were made good by the **Australian Joint Copying Project**. Despite all this, Watson did make available in readily useable form a vast collection of documents hitherto unsighted and previously inaccessible. The *Records* were more detailed than those then published in other British Dominions and have remained indispensable for research on colonial Australia. They attracted considerable attention and gave a great stimulus to historical writing (which from this source meant legal, constitutional, and administrative history). Watson was an amateur historian, delighting to destroy theories with the facts from his documents, who yet contributed to the professionalism of history in Australia.

In 1997 the series relating to the history of Tasmania was continued with the publication of a new volume edited by Peter Chapman, covering the year 1828. It continued the numbering of the original *HRA* and is thus designated Series III, volume VII.

BRIAN H. FLETCHER

Historical societies affirmed a nascent sense of history among the intellectual elites of the Australian colonies at the end of the nineteenth century. An embryonic **national identity** was developing with the likelihood of Federation, and this gave the colonial past a new significance. There was also a recognition that much colonial history was under threat as the early generations of colonists passed away, and that in the absence of archives or manuscript libraries there was a need for bodies to preserve historical records and reminiscences.

Between 1883 and 1885 branches of the Royal Geographical Society of Australasia were formed in NSW, Victoria, Qld, and SA; among their aims were the collection and publication of historical records of geographical interest, as well as the memoirs of notable men. The first specifically historical society was the short-lived Historical Society of Australasia (1885–86), formed in Melbourne by a distinguished group of professional men. Its aim was the 'cultivation and advancement of the study of history, and especially as it relates to Australasian colonies, and the collection of information for the compilation of a complete and accurate History of Australasia'. Next came the Australian Historical Records Society, which operated in Ballarat from 1896 to 1906.

These were followed in the next three decades by the formation of state societies: in NSW the Australian Historical Society, 1901; the Historical Society of Victoria, 1909; the Historical Society of Queensland, 1913; and the Western Australian Historical Society, 1926. SA had false starts with the South Australian Historical Society, 1926, and the Pioneers Association of South Australia, 1935. The societies were initiated, and in their early years dominated, by male elites, often professional men, interspersed with gifted amateur historians, writers, the occasional professor of history, and the descendants of early settlers. They sought vice-regal patronage, and in due course most were granted permission to use the Royal title; NSW in 1918, Victoria in 1952, Qld in 1959, and WA in 1963. They established collections which are now of considerable historical significance, and they met to read papers which were then published in their journals. Their preoccupations were essentially **antiquarian**—with **foundations**, **exploration** and **pioneering**, **genealogy**, the erection of **monuments** and tablets, the sharing of nostalgic reminiscences, and the meticulous recording of detail. The history they recorded

was a congratulatory record of progress; undesirable or unrecognised elements such as convicts, Aborigines, working people, and women were left out. The sesquicentenary of NSW and the centenaries of most of the other states in the 1920s and 1930s further stimulated the work of the societies. In their promotion of Australian history the societies were generally well ahead of the university and school curricula.

In this period local historical societies were established in some of the older centres in NSW: Parramatta in 1913, Manly in 1923, Clarence River in 1931, and Newcastle and Richmond River in 1936. There was also a scattering of societies with special interests, such as church history and the Society of Australian Genealogists (1932).

After World War II a new wave of community and academic interest in Australian history was accompanied by a marked increase in publication. Interest was stimulated further in the 1970s and 1980s by the Bicentenary of 1788, the state sesquicentenaries, and the flood of local government bodies reaching centenaries and other milestones. These stimulated the community history movement. From the mid-1950s, but especially from the 1970s, local historical societies were established in many suburbs and towns, as were local history **museums** and a diversity of other specialist groups, such as genealogical, railway, **garden**, and **military history** societies, and **National Trust** branches.

Local historical societies usually became affiliates of the state societies, which became umbrella or peak groups that coordinated and represented the community history movement. New peak societies were also founded in the remaining states and the territories: the Tasmanian Historical Research Association in 1951, the Canberra and District Historical Society in 1953, the Historical Society of the Northern Territory in 1964, and the Historical Society of South Australia in 1974. In 1977 the Federation of Australian Historical Societies was founded to link the state societies, and to represent the views of the historical and heritage communities at the federal level. By the mid-1990s it represented some 700 societies with 40 000 members.

The increasing recourse to academic modes, disciplinary specialisation, and esoteric theory by university-based historians drew them away from the antiquarian, narrative, and empirical interests of members of state and local societies. Nevertheless, within the state societies and many local ones there has been a marked broadening of interest and inclusiveness, and an increase of professionalism in conferences, publications, and other activities. While the membership of many local societies remained small, and their meetings consisted largely of small groups of elderly residents, others were large and energetic, ran stimulating programs, and continued with record collection, and patient and meticulous recording of historical detail.

Histories of the state historical societies are few. Peter Biskup has given accounts of the nineteenth-century groups in the *Canberra Historical Journal* (1989) and of the Queensland society in its *Journal* (1988); Brian Fletcher dealt with the **Royal Australian Historical Society** in *Australian History* *and New South Wales* (1993);Tom Griffiths described the early stages of the Royal Historical Society of Victoria in *Hunters and Collectors* (1996); and Paul **Hasluck** gives a revealing account of the WA society in his *Mucking About* (1977).

The growth of Australian history as an area of academic study led to the establishment of a range of professional associations. The most important was the Australian Historical Association, which was founded in Perth in 1973. Its purpose was to inform and to coordinate the profession rather than to duplicate the functions of existing societies. To that effect it published a *Bulletin of the Australian Historical Association* rather than a journal. The AHA is essentially a professional body, but membership is open to all and it has come to include a diverse range of those interested in history—about 450 in the late 1990s. Its biennial conference has become the major event on the history calendar.

DON GARDEN

Historical statistics include both the series compiled by statisticians in the past, and those created by historians through the statistical analysis of such disaggregated data as birth certificates, probates, wage books and weather reports. The writing of Australian history has been enriched both by the exceptional quality of contemporary official statistics and by innovative statistical analysis by economic, demographic, and social historians.

From the earliest days of the penal settlement at Sydney, the reports to the British authorities of successive governors of NSW included some statistics relating to the progress of the colony. The scope of statistical reporting was extended with the initiation of the system of annual reporting by *Blue Books*, common to all of the British colonies, from 1822 onwards. The *Blue Books*, named for the colour of their covers, were essentially statistical questionnaires. The standard forms, with headings and questions, were printed in London; it was the task of a senior officer in each colony, typically its chief secretary, to obtain the required information from the various responsible departments, fill in the answers, despatch two copies in time to reach the **Colonial Office** by the due date, and retain one copy 'for the information of the Governor'.

The system became an important and accepted part of the arrangements for informing the imperial government and parliament of the finances and condition of the colonies: R.W. Horton, under-secretary at the Colonial Office, affirmed in 1827 that it had 'been approved by the most rigid economists'. An incidental outcome of the *Blue Book* system was the establishment within each colony of what was, in effect, a central statistical office. Local needs for information were well served by arrangements which required the centralised collection or assembly of vital statistics, census tabulations, trade and customs data, returns of livestock numbers, records of school attendances, government financial accounts, and other statistical material.

Soon, volumes of official 'statistical registers', which converted the information in successive *Blue Books* into time series and expanded it both in scope and detail, came to be printed in the colonies. In his best-seller, *Greater Britain: A Record of Travel in English-speaking Countries during 1866 and 1867* (1868), Charles Dilke reported that Victoria's statistics were 'the most perfect in the world'; recognised its registrar-general, W.H. **Archer**, as a 'brilliant statistician'; and named as the reason for Victoria's superiority in statistics 'the immense advantage of starting clear of all tradition, unhampered and unclogged'. The 'unusually perfect condition' of Victoria's system of statistics was again highlighted in a report (1879) of the House of Commons official statistics committee, chaired by H.C.E. Childers (who had been auditor-general of Victoria when Archer began to build the system nearly 30 years earlier). Finding British official statistics to be in a state of 'confusion amounting to chaos … [and] without order, harmony or proportion', the committee commended the evidence which it had received from Victoria's government statist, H.H. **Hayter**, and endorsed its secretary's support for the establishment of 'a new statistical department' on the Victorian model.

Hayter had pioneered an approach to statistical presentation in his *Year Book* which was so successful that these volumes came to be referred to as 'Hayter's Year Book' or simply 'Hayter'. After the appointment of T.A. **Coghlan** as government statistician of NSW in 1886, Hayter's innovative approach was extended and improved in successive editions of *The Wealth and Progress of New South Wales* and *A Statistical Account of the Seven Colonies of Australasia*: series that were the precursor of *Year Book Australia*, which is still published annually. Of even greater importance was Coghlan's achievement as a national accountant. His estimates of the national income of NSW (the first officially published estimates in the world, by a margin of 40 years) were recognised by Paul Studenski in 1958 as 'far in advance of any prepared up to that time anywhere'. His four-volume economic history, *Labour and Industry in Australia* (1918), built on a lifetime of work as an official statistician.

Within five years of Federation, the Commonwealth parliament had passed legislation 'to establish a central bureau of statistics in order that [the Commonwealth] may furnish to the world statistical returns with respect to the matters under its special jurisdiction'. For half a century the states (Tasmania excepted) maintained their own statistical bureaus, but by 1960 these had been absorbed by the Commonwealth bureau and the organisation of statistical collections in Australia had become more centralised than in other advanced countries with federal systems of government. In 1975 the enactment of the Australian Bureau of Statistics Act, giving effect to the enlightened recommendations of a committee chaired by L.F. Crisp, established a legislative model for the collection, compilation, dissemination, and analysis of official statistics which has been widely followed. By the 1990s, with increasing recognition of the importance of statistics in meeting the information needs of governments and citizens in modern democracies, the Australian Bureau of Statistics was widely regarded as among the most competent, innovative, and independent of the world's official statistics agencies.

This strong tradition of official statistics in turn influenced the application of statistics to the writing of history. Although earlier historians had utilised statistics, for example in histories of migration, Noel **Butlin's** *Investment in Australian Economic Development 1861–1900* (1964) marked a new stage in the development of historical statistics, especially in his extensive use of business and trade union records to assemble long statistical series of wages and national income. His demographer colleagues at the Australian National University, under W.D. Borrie, Charles **Price**, and Jack Caldwell, were meanwhile applying sophisticated tools of analysis to official statistics to derive estimates of fertility, inter-regional migration, and other aspects of Australia's population history unremarked by contemporaries. Lloyd **Robson's** statistical analysis of the origins of the convicts, *Convict Settlers of Australia*, was begun as a doctoral thesis in demography at the Australian National University. By the 1970s, the application of statistics to history was widely seen as one of the most promising new frontiers of historical research. Cliometrics, as it was sometimes called, inspired new statistical work, based on previously untapped sources, on such topics as family structure (Patricia Grimshaw, Ann Larson), wealth-holding (W.D. Rubinstein), social mobility (Shirley Fitzgerald), educational opportunity (Ian Davey and Pavla Miller), religious observance (Walter Phillips), home ownership (R.V. Jackson, Tony Dingle, and David Merrett), and sporting attendances and performances (Wray Vamplew). While cliometrics no longer commands the high enthusiasm that it did in the 1970s, statistics remain among the most powerful tools of Australian historical research. Wray Vamplew, *Australians: Historical Statistics* (1987), is a valuable digest that also lists more specialised sources.

IAN CASTLES

History Council of New South Wales

was formed in 1995 as a peak body of historians and history organisations. The initiative came from the NSW Ministry of the Arts. The state needed a body to coordinate the field of history, which now included **public historians** and community activists, to advise on the disbursement of historical grants, and to assist in the renovation of citizenship. Historians needed government recognition to stem the career-threatening decline in the study of history, to persuade public agencies to consult and employ historians, and to encourage community activity on **heritage** issues. While discussions began under the Liberal–National government, the council was launched by newly elected Labor premier Bob Carr, an enthusiast for traditional political and narrative approaches to history. Advised by labour historian Jim Hagan, and former Labor minister for education Rod Cavalier, Carr announced at the Thirroul Railway Institute in December 1995 a five-point plan to revive history (published in *LH*, 1996): to reinstate history as an integral component of school education; to consider requiring government inquiries to engage the services of a historian; to consider the establishment of a statutory history authority; to introduce annual history prizes; and to establish an annual history lecture. The government subsequently named a travelling scholarship after the council's first elected president, Max Kelly, who died in 1996.

TERRY IRVING

Hobart (until 1881, Hobart Town) is the capital of **Tasmania**. Centring on the Derwent estuary and surrounded by Mount Wellington and other undulations, the city's situation is outstandingly beautiful. Numerous surviving nineteenth-century buildings, some of impressive architecture, enhance a potent spirit-of-place. 'Hobart Town is like a bee-hive', went one reminiscence of the 1850s, and a compelling introversion persists.

Founded in February 1804 as a convict settlement, Hobart has had continuous, modest growth—slowest around 1870, fastest around 1830, 1885, and 1950. Less dominant than other Australian capitals because of its northern rival Launceston, it has over time increased from below to above one-third of Tasmania's population. In 1996 its population was 195 800, with suburbs stretching far either side of the Derwent River.

First defined by an act of 1838, Hobart acquired city status with creation of the Anglican see of Tasmania in 1842. An 1846 attempt at municipal government failed, but from 1852 it proceeded, with incorporation following in 1857. The first elections saw an ex-convict party rout **anti-transportation** opponents. Around 1900, reformers, outraged by pervasive disease and squalor, challenged a long-established oligarchy that believed in little but minimal rates. That thrust had some impact, and while the council has ever remained under business dominance, a liberal note has sometimes sounded.

In broader social politics, Hobart's influence traditionally went conservative; in this its dominant newspaper, the **Mercury**, was representative. This situation changed in the 1980s and 1990s, with Hobart becoming the stronghold of **Green** environmentalism. The federal seat of Denison, encompassing Hobart, has changed members more often than any other in the nation, suggesting a political culture in which issues are usually fought hard, sometimes intensely.

Convictism and its aftermath penetrated Hobart deeply. The chief work on its nineteenth-century history, P.F. Bolger's *Hobart Town* (1973), argued that if biological determinism were true, Hobart must have been and continue 'a most inferior community', but that his research proved the contrary. The claim is persuasive, yet Hobart has suffered some ugly passages of human experience, along with much hard drinking and low living. In the late 1870s the Royal Navy refused to visit, because of the virulence of venereal infection. **Tattersalls** long had its base there, and the local casino (1973) became the first in Australia with legal backing.

Servicing convicts was one early economic dynamic, and port functions another. Hobart was one of the world's great whaling bases in the 1840s, and shipbuilding flourished. Other early industry met domestic needs, most famously the Cascade brewery (1832). About 1900 the business empire of Henry Jones developed, with jam-making its centrepiece, and a half-generation later the massive Electrolytic Zinc refinery and Cadbury's confectionery works followed. The great success of the 1990s is International Catamarans, whose director Robert Clifford follows Henry Jones as local boy become tycoon. Tertiary employment has always been large and governing Tasmania a central function, albeit one provoking jealousies from elsewhere in the island.

Cultural organisations have included the Royal Society of Tasmania (1843), the Tasmanian Museum and Art Gallery (1863), the Hobart Technical College (1888), and the University of Tasmania (1891). From colonial days, intellect and creativity had some force: this tradition has continued, if sometimes romanticised. From John Glover to Lloyd Rees, artists have depicted Hobart's beauty, and the two major resident poets of recent years (James **McAuley** and Gwen Harwood) both wrote of it. Public sculpture includes work by Lyndon Dadswell, Tom Bass and, above all, Stephen Walker.

Water gives a distinctive emphasis to sport. Regattas began early, from 1837, in a structure which continues. Since 1945 the Sydney–Hobart Yacht Race has become a world cynosure. Much leisure activity has a maritime flavour. Salamanca Place, site of an outstanding craft market and multifarious activity, lies beside the harbour.

As well as Bolger's *Hobart Town*, notable studies include three of different style about different suburbs: Alison Alexander's *Glenorchy* (1986) gives a dense, detailed picture of an archetypal common-people place; *Down Wapping* (1988), by several authors, achieves history-from-below of an old working-class district, now altogether redeveloped; another cooperative work, *Taroona 1808–1986* (1988), describes beguiling bourgeoisdom. Stefan Petrow has written several articles of note and a penetrating monograph, *Sanatorium of the South: Public Health and Politics in Hobart and Launceston 1875–1914* (1995).

MICHAEL ROE

Hobart Conference was a meeting of the colonial premiers in that city in January 1895, which adopted the proposal to revive **Federation**. Earlier efforts to federate on the basis of the draft constitution devised at the Sydney Convention in 1891 had broken down because of the reluctance of the colonial parliaments to endorse it. To overcome this difficulty the unofficial **Corowa Conference** of 1893 recommended that delegates to a new convention be elected directly from the colonies, and their work be submitted directly to the people by referendum. The NSW premier George **Reid** took up this suggestion and invited the other premiers to meet at Hobart in conjunction with a meeting of the **Federal Council**. While the premier of WA rejected the scheme and his Queensland counterpart set conditions upon it, the other four colonial leaders agreed and proceeded eventually to implementation, thus initiating the new Federal Convention that opened in Adelaide in 1897. The initiative is assessed by Stuart Macintyre in *VHJ* (1994).

SM

Holden, Australia's first mass-produced **motor car**, took its name from an Adelaide saddlery, coach-building, and later auto-body building firm, founded by Henry James Holden

in 1883. The American giant General Motors, which had assembled imported cars in Australia since the 1920s, had agreed with the wartime Labor government to produce a small family car for Australian conditions. Laurence Hartnett, former managing director of General Motors in Australia and Director of War Production 1940–45, describes the gestation of the plan for an Australian people's car in his memoirs, *Big Wheels and Little Wheels* (1964). Prime Minister **Chifley** saw the first FX model off the assembly line at Fishermen's Bend in November 1948. Holden quickly came to lead the market for new cars, claiming 43 per cent of sales in 1958. A utility truck was produced from 1951 and a station wagon from 1957. Although Ford, with its Australian-made Falcon, competed strongly from the early 1960s, the Holden had successfully asserted its place as 'Australia's Own Car'. The 50th birthday of the FX Holden in 1998 was marked by an exhibition at the Powerhouse Museum, 'Cars and Culture', and a commemorative history, John Wright's *Heart of the Lion*.

GD

Hollows, Frederick Cossom (1929–93), eye surgeon, helped establish the Aboriginal Medical Service at Redfern, NSW, in 1971 and pioneered the National Trachoma and Eye Health Program in 1975. Hollows's activities in the 1970s and 1980s significantly raised public awareness of Australia's appalling neglect of Aboriginal health. His medical teams visited hundreds of outback settlements, where they identified and treated eye disease, preventing blindness in thousands of cases. Successful schemes were also established overseas, notably in Nepal and Eritrea. Hollows was a hard-swearing, pipe-smoking, rough-diamond kind of doctor, born into a working-class family at Dunedin, NZ. He originally studied to become a Church of Christ minister, but the 'piety' of Bible College oppressed him. After becoming agnostic, he switched to medicine at the University of Otago in the early 1950s. As a young man, Hollows joined the Communist Party of NZ. In 1961 he studied at London's Institute of Ophthalmology and later worked at the Royal Infirmary in Cardiff, Wales, where Archibald Cochrane introduced him to epidemiology. Because his **communism** had led to victimisation by the NZ Security and Intelligence Service, he settled in Sydney in 1965 as associate professor of ophthalmology at the University of New South Wales. It was after a lecture by Frank **Hardy** in 1968 that Hollows first investigated eye disease in Aboriginal communities. He was Australian of the Year in 1990, and received a state funeral following his death from cancer in 1993. He is buried at Bourke in outback NSW. In his autobiography (with Peter Corris), *Fred Hollows* (1991), he declared: 'having a care and concern for others is the highest of the human qualities. It distinguishes us from the animals.' The Fred Hollows Foundation continues his work.

DC

Holman, William Arthur (1871–1934), premier of NSW, won the seat of Grenfell as a Labor member in 1898, 10 years after he arrived in Australia from London. Wary of

Federation, he was more committed to establishing and expanding the Labor Party in NSW. Initially, he was a silver-tongued socialist; subsequently, he emphasised the need for a broad-based popular reform program. His term as premier (1913–20) was marked by disputes with the party organisation and his 1916 expulsion from the Labor Party for supporting **conscription**. Holman continued as leader of a National Party government until losing his seat in 1920. He made a return to politics as a federal member in 1931. H.V. **Evatt** explored the dynamics of his political evolution in *Australian Labour Leader* (1942).

KT

Holt, Harold Edward (1908–67) entered politics as a protégé of Robert **Menzies**, and fulfilled his patron's hopes when he became leader of the **Liberal Party** and prime minister of Australia in 1966. Holt was educated at Wesley College, followed by law at the University of Melbourne. He practised briefly as a solicitor before winning the seat of Fawkner as a UAP member in 1935 and held the seat until a redistribution in 1949, after which he was member for Higgins. Holt joined the first Menzies government in 1939 as minister without portfolio, before enlisting in the AIF in mid-1940, only to be recalled to Canberra after the death of three senior ministers in a plane crash. He was given the portfolio of labour and national service. Although he reluctantly supported the removal of Menzies in 1941, Holt was welcomed back into the ministry following the 1949 Liberal victory; he became minister for immigration as well as labour and national service. His rise in the party was smooth: he became deputy leader of the parliamentary Liberal Party in 1956, then treasurer in 1958. It was in the latter role that he experienced his first real political setback, when his decision to create a credit squeeze led to unemployment and a large voter backlash in the 1961 elections.

Even so, he was the obvious heir apparent at Menzies's resignation in 1966. His easing of the **White Australia** policy reflected a desire to move Australia closer to Asia, and he travelled widely in the region. As an enthusiastic believer in the need to support South Vietnam, he won a landslide victory in the 1966 election but came under increasing pressure from the growing protest movement against the **Vietnam War**. His commitment to go 'all the way with LBJ' (referring to the US president, Lyndon Baines Johnson) antagonised many Australians. Disputes within the Liberal–Country Party coalition also created pressures at this time. All these factors were discussed after Holt disappeared in rough surf at Cheviot Beach, Portsea, Victoria, in late 1967. Rumours of suicide circulated, as did a bizarre story that Holt was a Chinese spy and had been whisked away aboard a mini-submarine. The overwhelming likelihood is that he drowned. A swimming pool in his electorate was named after him and a memorial plaque placed under the waters of Cheviot Beach.

KT

Holt, Joseph (1756–1826) arrived in NSW from Ireland with his family in 1800 as an exile without trial for his part in the 1798 rebellion. In NSW he became a farm manager and worked hard; by 1809 he owned 210 acres, well-stocked with sheep and cattle. The authorities regarded him suspiciously because of their fears of an Irish uprising, though Holt vigorously denied any involvement. He was convicted for his part in the **Castle Hill rising** and transported to **Norfolk Island**. He returned to farming in 1805 and secured a free pardon in 1809, which was confirmed in 1811. A year later he sold up and returned to Ireland, though several of his children remained in NSW. His memoirs, edited by T.C. Croker, were published in 1838.

KT

Holtermann Collection is a large collection of photographic negatives that includes studio portraits, and views of Sydney and of goldfield towns. The most famous of the latter are the detailed studies of the small NSW towns of Hill End and Gulgong in 1872, reproduced in Keast Burke's *Gold and Silver* (1973). The collection takes its name from Bernhardt Holtermann (1838–85), a German gold prospector, whose success enabled him to sponsor a travelling photographer, Beaufoy Merlin, to complete a series of photographs of NSW and Victoria which were intended for overseas display to encourage **immigration**. After Merlin's death, his assistant, Charles Bayliss, continued the project; he took the famous panoramic view of 1875 Sydney, known as the 'Holtermann panorama' from the tower of Holtermann's home. The lesser-known studio portraits were the work of the photographic studio of Merlin (and Bayliss), the American and Australasian Photographic Company. Burke placed more value on the documentary photos as being innately truthful. The thousands of glass negatives which comprise this collection were kept intact by family members until Burke became aware of their existence in the early 1950s. They are now held by the Mitchell Library, Sydney.

KT

Homosexual history, see **Gay history**; **Lesbian history**

Homosexuality in the form of sodomy was strongly condemned both in law and in social attitudes by the British at the time of settlement. The legal definition of sodomy (now anal intercourse) was so wide that it included any non-reproductive sexual activity, even by heterosexuals. Such condemnatory attitudes reflected the deep and pervasive influences of both Judaeo-Christianity and English Puritanism, and set the newcomers apart from the traditional indigenous cultures in Australia. They also set them apart from many other European cultures—the Mediterranean ones, where sodomy was both a widely practised form of contraception and a male-to-male sexual act, as well as those continental states where the *Code Napoléon* eventually banished anti-sodomy laws from statute books.

In NSW, where English law was deemed to operate, the crime of sodomy was a capital offence. Such sentences were carried out in England, even as late as 1824. As new colonies were established in Australia, so they took their lead

325

from English law. Although there were hangings of sodomites in the colonies, such sentences were rare and usually given only if force was involved, or if youths were the 'victims'. Such apparently more tolerant attitudes might just as much reflect concern to retain an able-bodied workforce in places where labour was in perpetual short supply. Overall, attitudes of intolerance were deeply ingrained.

During the nineteenth century the colonial parliaments occasionally legislated to criminalise male 'homosexual' acts, as they came to be known. Lesbianism never had the same legal proscription applied to it as did male homosexuality, although convict records indicate that it was not uncommon among female prisoners. The changes created new categories of male-to-male crimes (such as indecent assault), and made even homosexual affectionate acts illegal. Later still, the laws were affected by the emergent social and medical sciences. A new genus, 'the homosexual', was first 'discovered' by Doctor Karely Benkert in 1869. The distinctive quality of this new conceptualisation was that it held a person's whole being as embodied in its **sexuality**. For much of the twentieth century, the prevailing view was that there was such a person as 'a homosexual', with a set of discrete characteristics. The medical profession, which became the arbiter of understandings of sexuality, defined homosexuality as an illness, either inherited or acquired, which could be 'cured' by anything from psycho-surgery to aversion therapy. Eventually such writers as Havelock Ellis, Sigmund Freud and, later, Alfred Kinsey overturned these views.

Since the 1960s historical research has looked at how those who identified themselves as homosexual lived in a society that deemed their behaviour illegal, sinful, or pathological. Despite controls and constraints, homosexuals managed to develop strategies to conceal both their orientation and their activities from outsiders. Subcultures soon emerged in the major cities and, even in smaller towns or on the shearers' trails, friendship networks developed: terms such as *theatrical* or *artistic* or *musical* became descriptors of those who were different. An argot was developed, which allowed those 'in the life' to communicate publicly under the very noses of society. Dress codes—from certain coloured clothes to keys in a back pocket—played their part in allowing those with homoerotic desires to find others. Constraints on women meant that lesbians had less chance of living such a gay life.

The criminal status of male homosexual acts meant that the homosexual world overlapped not only with the demimonde but also with the underworld. As a shadowy and ill-understood minority, homosexuals were often attacked by mainstream society, as for example during the Cold War, when deviance of any form was suspect and new laws relating to homosexuals were created. At this time it became a crime to incite someone to commit a 'homosexual' act. Homosexuals were deemed not only criminals, but also security risks, and treated accordingly.

This very persecution of homosexuals led in turn to the emergence of a political movement—based on a new conception of homosexuality, a 'gay' identity—that is the subject of Gary Willett, *Living Out Loud* (2000). As a result, from the early 1970s, states legislated to decriminalise male homosexual activity.

The history of homosexuality in Australia is covered by C. Johnston and R. Johnston, and Liz Ross, both in Verity Burgmann and Jenny Lee (eds), *Staining the Wattle: A People's History of Australia since 1788* (1988), and by Garry Wotherspoon in *City of the Plain* (1991). (See also **Gay history**; **Lesbian history**.)

GARRY WOTHERSPOON

Honours, conferred by the sovereign as 'the fount of honour', were formerly available to all subjects of the Crown in the form of decorations or titles (including peerages). In the first half of the nineteenth century, membership of the Most Honourable Order of the Bath was very restricted and few places were available to distribute outside England, even after an extension in 1845. Lord Stanley (later Earl of Derby) in 1844 had favoured a separate colonial Order as, among other things, a counter to American republican influences in Canada. As prime minister in 1858–59, he encouraged the idea, and obtained ready cooperation from his colonial secretary, the romantic novelist Sir Edward Bulwer Lytton: some CBs and two baronetcies were the result, together with an implied promise of regular distribution of colonial honours. Again in office in 1866–68, Derby supported a proposal to adapt the Most Distinguished Order of St Michael and St George—originally designed for services in the Mediterranean—for colonial purposes. This had been pressed by Sir John Young, governor of NSW, who was anxious to recognise eminent colonists (among whom he discerned a strong desire to receive, preferably, titles) and to forestall disaffection, at least by soothing difficult politicians. There is a contrast here to the supposed prevalence of **'egalitarianism'**, as John Hirst has noticed in his article of that title in F.B. Smith and S.L. Goldberg (eds), *Australian Cultural History* (1988). The reorganisation was achieved by December 1868. The Order ranked just after the Star of India (1860) and, in the usual three divisions, was to reward official services, and those of colonists who were 'eminently distinguished … by their Talents, Merits, Virtues, Loyalty, or Services'. Its membership, especially in the first class—Knight Grand Cross (GCMG)—was restricted.

Knight Commander (KCMG) and Commander (CMG) in St Michael and St George remained the main honours to which colonists and colonial officials could reasonably aspire for the next half-century, though simple knighthoods and a few baronetcies were also conferred. Many did so aspire, especially from Australia, and there was some apprehension that disappointments detracted from any political good done by the honours.

The new century, the increasing democratisation of politics and society, and the plethora of deserts created by World War I, led to the establishment, in 1917, of the Most Excellent Order of the British Empire. In this there were five divisions, the extra ones being Officer and Member; and specific provision was made for female recipients. A British Empire

Medal and the Imperial Service Order were also instituted. Mass distribution of honours thus became possible, for the Order of the British Empire was far less restricted than the others. Some peers also were created, the last Australian so honoured being R.G. **Casey** (life baron, 1962).

Recommendations for all honours were in the hands of the secretary of state for the colonies or, after 1931, for the Dominions. In practice, he looked for nominations from governors; their judgment, under responsible government, had been early merged with the advice of the various premiers or prime ministers. During the 1930s the Dominions secretary gradually ceased to interpose himself, except formally, between Dominion prime ministers and the sovereign; after 1945 it became more and more the case that even premiers of Australian states could nominate whom they liked. The Australian Labor Party, however, had set its face against 'imperial honours' from its beginning; the 1924 constitutional crisis in Canada led the Canadian parliament to pray the king not to confer titles on residents of Canada; the Irish Free State and Afrikaner South Africa held all such things in contempt. The divisibility of the Crown, the establishment of separate citizenships, and the increasingly direct relationship between Dominion prime ministers and the sovereign, also helped the gradual failing of an honours system common to the whole Empire/Commonwealth. Increasing independence of action, moreover, and fondness for the idea of separate nationality fed, in some circles in Australia, dissatisfaction with 'British' honours.

E.G. **Whitlam** (prime minister 1972–75) inaugurated the Order of Australia expressly to supersede all other honours for Australian purposes. Under the Liberal government, 1975–82, the older honours were restored and a knighthood was added to Companion, Officer, Member, and Medal in the Order of Australia; the AK was removed under the succeeding Labor government. The old honours continued to decline, not least because of the obvious unworthiness of some states' nominees; the Queen herself brought them to an end in 1994, though she still confers honours which emanate from her personally and not on the advice of ministers, notably the Most Noble Order of the Garter (the highest of all honours), the Royal Victorian Order, and the non-titular Order of Merit. The Order of Australia—no less a royal honour—has almost exactly replaced the Order of the British Empire and has been criticised in similar terms by republicans and those who look to an 'egalitarian' distribution of honours: but it serves their purpose of ensuring that, contrary to the previous Australian experience, not even governors, High Court judges, or senior military or civil officers shall receive titular distinctions.

BRUCE KNOX

Hope, Alec Derwent (1907–2000), poet, grew up in rural NSW and Tasmania, studied at the University of Sydney, and later read English at Oxford, before returning to Australia in 1931. He became one of Australia's most influential teachers, critics, and satirists. His poetry—regarded by

some as the single most impressive body of verse written in Australia—circulated only privately until the publication in 1955 of *The Wandering Islands*. Hope was almost 50—an elder among poetic debutants—and already a professor of English at Canberra University College, later the Australian National University. Several more collections followed, earning Hope various honorary degrees and awards, including the Robert Frost Award for Poetry. Hope's poetry was notable for its technical virtuosity and craft: he remained a proponent of 'that noble, candid speech' which he attributed to the great Irish poet in his poem 'William Butler Yeats'.

His ambivalence about the depressed Australia he rediscovered is famously captured in an early poem, 'Australia'. The poet, almost glad to leave 'the lush jungle of modern thought', with its 'chatter of cultured apes', confronts

> … a vast parasite robber-state
> Where second-hand Europeans pullulate
> Timidly on the edge of alien shores.

His poetry remained international in a way that distinguishes it from much of the poetry written in postwar Australia. His influences, his inclinations, were consistently European.

Hope's criticism was equally well known and incisive: his acerbic review of Patrick **White's** *Tree of Man* announced him as a spirited debunker of modernist tendencies in Australian writing. He also wrote a volume of limpid memoirs, *Chance Encounters* (1992). Leonie **Kramer** (1979) and Kevin Hart (1992) have written monographs on his work; Joy Hooton provided a bibliography (1979). To date there is no biography.

PR

Hopetoun Blunder was the decision of the first governor-general, Lord Hopetoun, to commission William Lyne as first Commonwealth prime minister. The first elections were yet to be held, so the governor-general had no indication of parliamentary strength to guide him. It was commonly assumed that he would choose Edmund **Barton**, who had been the leader of the 1897–98 Convention which drew up the Constitution and was leader of the federal movement in NSW, the senior colony. Barton was a protectionist. George **Reid**, the free-trade leader, was naturally opposed to Barton being chosen and told Hopetoun so. Hopetoun then decided to act neutrally in regard to federal politics by choosing Lyne, the premier of the senior colony. Lyne was a second-rate politician who had been an opponent of federation, so to the committed federalists this seemed a 'blunder'. They refused to serve under Lyne, who returned his commission and recommended that Barton be sent for. This allowed the Governor-General to choose Barton on advice. In his account of the episode John **La Nauze** accepts that it was *The Hopetoun Blunder* (1957).

JH

Hopkins, Livingston York 'Hop' (1846–1927), cartoonist with the *Bulletin* (1883–1913), was born in Ohio,

USA, the thirteenth of 14 children in a puritanical family where whistling on the Sabbath was considered wrong. After fighting in the Civil War, he studied the Dupuis Method of drawing in New York under Aug Wills, whose motto was 'Use your eyes—learn to see.' Following stints with *Scribner's Weekly* and the Toledo *Blade*, he established himself as a woodcut artist, illustrating books and selling drawings to various newspapers and magazines. He wrote and illustrated *A Comic History of the United States* (1876). In 1882 W.H. Traill lured him to the *Bulletin* in Sydney, where he eventually became co-proprietor. 'When your mind presents an idea, grip it', he would say, and his *Bulletin* cartoons, signed 'Hop', lunged at major issues: 'The Spirit of Federation—Principally Jaw' (1890) spoke for itself; 'Neutrality' (1890) satirised Henry **Parkes**, his favourite subject; 'Look Before you Leap' (1895) warned of the Privy Council; 'Shifting Camp' (1898) observed Aboriginal displacement; 'Another Sacrifice to Moloch' (1899) opposed the **Boer War**; 'Piebald Possibilities' (1902) supported **White Australia**. In 'The Roll-Call' (1885) he questioned the **Sudan Campaign** and introduced the **Little Boy from Manly** who personified impetuous NSW, and later, Australia. His 'confessions' were published in the *Lone Hand* (1913–14), and the Mitchell Library, Sydney, holds some of his notebooks. A biography written by his daughter, Dorothy J. Hopkins, *Hop of the 'Bulletin'* (1929), reveals that he died a US citizen.

DC

Hordern family built a large retailing firm in Sydney. It was established by ANTHONY HORDERN (1819–76) in the mid-1850s. His two sons, ANTHONY (1842–86) and SAMUEL (1849–1909), enlarged the business considerably, opening large modern outlets and establishing offices overseas. Anthony was convinced of the potential of WA, and formed a syndicate to build a land-grant railway there as an incentive to migration. Samuel speculated in land and bred cattle and horses. His eldest son, also SAMUEL (1876–1956), directed the firm, which by now included a mail-order business as well as importing and manufacturing branches, until it was sold in 1926. He was also keenly interested in livestock breeding and, as president of Sydney's Royal Agricultural Society, was a key figure in the development of the Royal Easter Show. The Hordern Pavilion at the Sydney Showgrounds commemorates the family. There is a family history by Lesley Hordern (1985).

KT

Horne, Donald Richmond (1921–), journalist and public intellectual, created the term **Lucky Country**, the title of one of his many books. He was the son of a schoolteacher and grew up at Muswellbrook in the Hunter Valley, NSW. *The Education of Young Donald* (1967), characteristically more 'sociography' than autobiography, is a fine delineation of his parents' fun-seeking set and the social stratification of the town. At the University of Sydney he was influenced by the libertarian philosopher John **Anderson** and became a firm anti-communist. He has moved left-wards, but his anti-communist past is still held against him by those who, as he says, prefer you to be wrong at the time and right after the event. During the 1960s he was editor of **Quadrant** and the **Bulletin**, from which he dropped the masthead slogan 'Australia for the White Man'. He was a member of the political science department at the University of New South Wales from 1973, and returned there after he chaired the Australia Council 1985–90. He wrote a blistering critique of the **Dismissal** of the Whitlam government, *Death of the Lucky Country* (1976), and was a leader in the subsequent movement for a new, **republican** constitution. In 1991 he was a foundation member of the Australian Republican Movement. His writing is pungent, witty, and abounding in ideas for invigorating the culture and the polity. His works of history are *The Australian People* (1972), *Time of Hope* (1980), and *In Search of Billy Hughes* (1979), while *The Great Museum* (1984) reflects on the place of history in the contemporary world. A second volume of autobiography, *Confessions of a New Boy* (1986), was followed by *Portrait of an Optimist* (1988), and *Into the Open* (2000).

JH

Horne, Richard Henry (1802–84) became a celebrity with the publication in 1843 of an epic poem, *Orion*, which was so successful that he was often known as 'Orion' Horne. He came to Australia from England in 1852 to escape a failing marriage and restore his fortunes on the goldfields. He held and lost a number of minor posts on the Victorian diggings and in Melbourne before his appointment as warden of a goldfield near Trentham enabled him to return to serious writing. For the 1866 Melbourne Inter-colonial Exhibition he wrote a masque, *The South Sea Sisters*, which included a poetic depiction of an Aboriginal corroboree. Horne adopted 'Hengist' as his second name in 1867, when he signed it to a cantata written to celebrate the visit of the Duke of Edinburgh. He became friendly with rising young writers, including Adam Lindsay **Gordon** and Marcus **Clarke**, and helped to establish the notion of a colonial literary coterie. With the exception of his prose work, *Australian Facts and Prospects* (1859), Horne's Australian work is unremarkable. He returned to England in 1869. He is the subject of two biographies—Cyril **Pearl**, *Always Morning* (1960), and Ann Blainey, *The Farthing Poet* (1968).

KT

Horse-racing, see **Entertainment**; **Gambling**; **Horses**

Horses have been significant in **exploration**, **transport**, **sport**, and leisure; as sources of **energy**; and in legend. Horses helped white Australians possess a continent and acquire a **national identity**.

Captain Arthur **Phillip** paid a high price for seven horses at the Cape Colony and they arrived with the First Fleet in 1788. Difficult and costly to transport by sea, horses grew by natural increase rather than importation; by 1815 there were over 2400 in NSW. From the start the bloodlines of Australian horses were strongly Arab with increasing influence from thoroughbred stallions. When **Blaxland**, **Wentworth**, and Lawson crossed the Blue Mountains, they had with them four servants and four horses. The seven men travelled 80 kilometres through the mountains; they walked most of the way, much of it three times as they cut tracks, returned to their starting-point, and brought their supplies forward; the horses were used as pack animals. The horse became more significant in the exploration of the greater distances and more open country of the interior. On his expeditions Major Thomas **Mitchell** travelled with carts or drays, and in 1836 he had a four-wheeled wagonette to carry a portable boat. Bullocks used as draught and pack animals determined the speed of expeditions. Pack and draught horses were also used, but it was the saddle horses that allowed Mitchell and others to scout ahead and to the flanks and so select the track and explore much more than the line cut by the steel tyres. The explorers' frequent journal references to their horses are testimony to their dependence on those tough, grass-fed animals.

The mounted explorer, with surprise and mobility, had an advantage in encounters with Aborigines; that advantage was exploited by settlers, and black as well as white mounted troopers. The first mounted **native police** unit was formed in the Port Phillip District in 1837; later, in Qld and SA, the mounted Aboriginal troopers gained reputations for brutality, but by then Aboriginal horsemen were more numerous and better known as stockmen and drovers. Their skills as horsemen gave Aborigines a standing that helped them tolerate harsh conditions on many stations.

When thousands of head of sheep were being shifted south into the newly opened Port Phillip District, many of the drovers were on foot. Even when **overlanders** Joseph Hawdon and Charles Bonney drove cattle from NSW to Adelaide in 1838, they had more men than saddle horses. But horses were essential for controlling cattle—the Jardine brothers in their exhausting drive from Rockhampton to Cape York in 1864 started with 42 horses—and in other epic feats of droving the horses were central. From the 1820s Clydesdale, Shire and other heavy breeds were imported, but it was not until later in the century that horse teams dominated haulage. Bullocks were cheaper, their harness was simpler and more easily repaired, and the bullocks could work hard on overnight grass feeding; but horses were stronger, faster, and superior on metal roads, especially with the improved wagons that came into use at the end of the century. Until World War II horse teams hauled most wheat and wool to the railheads. The expansion of the **wheat** industry depended on the sweat of the teams. Ploughing, reworking the fallow, sowing the crop, harvesting, and carting the wheat to the stacks at the sidings were all done with teams of six, eight, or ten horses; and the bagloader, chaffcutter, dray, gig, and the children going to school might all be dependent on horse power. Perhaps one-third of the land under crop was taken up by oats grown to feed a farm's own working horses. A high-quality team of 10 horses, worth 400–500 pounds around 1900, was a large investment for a farmer or contractor.

In country towns with a population of just a thousand there was likely to be a saddler, blacksmith, coach or implement maker, and grain and fodder merchant, all dependent on the district's horses. Within towns and suburbs goods travelling to and from railway stations, garbage (sometimes including lavatory pans), and the household deliveries of milk, bread, groceries, and vegetables were carried in horse-drawn carts, drays, and wagons. Horse trams, coaches, and cabs transported people. Hearses, fire carts, and ambulances were pulled by horses.

Much of the delivery work was done by half-draft or specially bred horses. The Cleveland Bay, one of the best harness horses, was particularly adapted for coaches. Regular horse transport ran from Sydney to the Hawkesbury from 1805, and in 1819 the first long coach service linked Hobart and Launceston. Melbourne and Sydney were joined by a coach service in the late 1830s, and from the beginning of railway construction to the completion of the Sydney–Melbourne line in 1883 the coaches filled a decreasing gap. **Cobb & Co.**, the best-known of the coaching companies, entered Australia in 1853, and its last coach ran in 1924. With each coach pulled by four horses, and the team changed every 16 kilometres, a major coach route needed several hundred horses. At their height, with coaches linking far north Qld with the Western District of Victoria, Cobb & Co. were said to be harnessing 6000 horses a day.

The total number of Australian horses increased quickly in the late nineteenth century: from 432 000 in 1860, to 1 061 000 in 1880, to 1 610 000 in 1900. Horse numbers reached a peak in 1918, when there were 2 527 000, and then declined quickly in the late 1920s, more slowly in the 1930s, and again from the end of World War II. There were 1 699 000 horses in 1940; 1 057 000 in 1950; 456 000 in 1970; 310 000 in 1990. In 1920 there had been one horse for every two people: in 1990 there was about one horse for every 50 people.

The export of Australian horses was significant beyond their commercial value because the horses carried with them a peculiar Australianness. The significant trade in remount horses to the Indian army began in the 1840s: and the term *waler*, from NSW, dates from 1846. Most horses were shipped from Melbourne, but by the 1930s when the Indian army mechanised, Qld was the main supplier. Used mainly as cavalry horses, the walers also excelled as mounts at polo, race meetings, and gymkhanas. Over 350 000 horses were sold to India alone. Australian soldiers took horses to the **Sudan** in 1885 to pull gun carriages, to the **Boer War** (where their 37 245 horses suffered a high mortality), and to **World War I** (43 000 to the Light Horse and another 92 000 to other British units). Almost no waler returned to Australia from any war.

In 1810 at the Hyde Park track in Sydney, William Wentworth won on his father's horse, Gig. Race meetings were not yet regular, and match races (for a stake and side wagers) continued as a common way to decide the merits of horses. The first race meeting at Randwick, Sydney, was in 1833 and at Saltwater (Flemington, Melbourne) in 1840, and by then race meetings were being held at various country centres. Many of the best-known races on the Australian calendar have their origins in the 1860s: the Sydney and Melbourne Cups, the AJC Derby, the Epsom Handicap, and the Doncaster. Ken **Inglis** has said that by 1870 racing was the 'most nearly national sport'.

Trotting, with its lower costs and the greater chance for a part-time trainer-driver to participate, has been more open to battlers, and small country towns unable to sustain gallops hold trotting meetings. The sport progressed with the development of the light sulky in the early twentieth century and the introduction of regular night meetings at Harold Park, Sydney, in 1949.

In equestrian events at the **Olympic Games** to 1996, Australians won five gold medals, a high success rate as they were not accustomed to the discipline imposed on horse and rider in dressage and some Olympic courses. The travelling buckjumping shows, able to attract large crowds when riders with the grace and showmanship of Lance Skuthorpe were involved, were at their height after 1900. They have been replaced by the rodeo circuit, with some riders performing both in Australia and North America.

The rapid expansion of white settlement occurred just as saddle and draught horses were becoming supreme; Australian **nationalism** flourished when the horse was still dominant but threatened by the railways, so that nostalgia as well as romance touched 'The Lights of Cobb and Co.' and 'Clancy of the Overflow'. The Australian as horseman recurs in the life and art of Adam Lindsay **Gordon**; in the name and verses of 'The Breaker' **Morant**; in Tom **Roberts's** *The Breakaway*; in George Lambert's *Across the Black Soil Plains*; and especially in the paintings of Septimus Power. The overlander is celebrated in ballad, in S.T. **Gill's** painting, and in the film of that name (1946). In the 1890s Banjo **Paterson** wrote, 'The Man from Snowy River is a household word today', and he still is. Malcolm Kennedy, *Hauling the Loads* (1992), and A.T. Yarwood, *Walers* (1989), are two of the few general books. More specialised books are numerous: Ann McGrath, *Born in the Cattle* (1987), considers Aboriginal stockmen; Jim Fitzpatrick, *The Bicycle and the Bush* (1980), compares the efficiency and prestige of bicycle and horse; and Max Agnew, *Silks and Sulkies* (1986), gives a general survey of trotting.

HANK NELSON

Hospital history, see Health

Housewives' associations arose in all Australian states during World War I and the interwar period, beginning with Victoria in 1915. The Federated Association of Australian Housewives was formed under the leadership of Eleanor Glencross in 1923. The initial inspiration came from Ivy Brookes, who, in June 1915, convened a meeting of women from a variety of political groups to establish a system of cooperative buying and marketing. The organisation did not flourish, but was revived in 1920 by women with connections to the **Woman's Christian Temperance Union** and the **Australian Women's National League**. In essence a consumer-watch organisation, the Housewives Association also provided economic benefits and cooperated with the **National Council of Women** to improve the civil status of women. Nevertheless, splits occurred along **class** lines, on the issue of **temperance**, and on account of differences in personality among the leaders. Of the substantial breakaway groups in NSW and Victoria, the most important was the communist-led New Housewives' Association, formed in NSW in 1946 and eventually subsumed in the Union of Australian Women. Its history, by Barbara Curthoys and Audrey McDonald, was published in 1996.

The membership of the Housewives Associations reached a highpoint of about 200 000 in the early 1960s, but declined thereafter as increasing numbers of married women entered the workforce. It still operates in the smaller states, but the Victorian association—which had been the first and, in the organisation's heyday, the largest—ceased operation in March 1991.

JUDITH SMART

Housing has been a basic human need, an item of conspicuous consumption, an embodiment of domestic life and, in the twentieth century, an object of public policy. Since colonial times Australians have judged their **standard of living** largely by how well they have been housed.

The houses built by the first Australian colonists were shaped by styles and ideals brought from their homelands, and by the **climate**, material resources, and living patterns of the new. The standard Australian house looked different from its English, Scottish, or Irish counterpart. It stood alone, set back from the street in its own **garden** or yard rather than jammed up against its neighbour, as though to symbolise the privacy of the household. 'It is seldom two families inhabit one dwelling, therefore every man becomes absolute master of his own house', observed James Grant, who visited Sydney in 1800. The house typically consisted of a single-storey bungalow rather than a two-storey cottage or row-house. It was often built from timber, pisé, wattle-and-daub, slab, or other local materials, rather than brick or stone, and with a hipped roof of thatch or shingle. The kitchen was often separated from the rest of the house, so as to keep heat and cooking smells, fire, and convict servants at a safe distance. Like the verandahs which often surrounded it, the Australian house had stylistic affinities with the Indian bungalow, although how that influence reached Australia is still obscure.

Australia was settled in the wake of the **Evangelical** revival which made the home, headed by a virtuous wife and husband, the symbolic centre of national life. Responding to this cult of domesticity, British architects, led by John Claudius Loudon, editor of the *Architectural Magazine*, produced a new repertoire of ideal villa, cottage, and garden designs. As James Broadbent shows in *The Australian Colonial House* (1997), these were swiftly emulated, first by the NSW **exclusives**, then by the rest of the colonial bourgeoisie. Pattern-books of the period illustrate two ideal houses, the romantic Gothic house and the Italianate villa. The second—with its single-storey, axial plan, hierarchical arrangement of rooms from respectable front to functional back, and its restrained classical decoration—became the template from which a host of Australian standard designs, both grand and humble, old and recent, are derived. In Qld it was lifted on stilts above a dark and airy under-house; in Adelaide or Hobart it was often made of sandstone, in Victoria of brick or the local bluestone. Rooms were given designated functions—bedroom, kitchen, parlour—but, as the Adelaide artisan Joseph Elliott shows in his fascinating description of *Our Home in Australia* (1860, 1984), a sitting-room in the day might become a bedroom at night, and a kitchen might double as a workshop.

In an industrial era, building houses remained one of the most traditional forms of production: even in Australian cities, most houses were built, as they had been for centuries in Europe, from local materials, by small groups of tradesmen using hand tools. In 1861 many Australians lived in temporary huts or tents, but by the 1880s, as Richard **Twopeny** noted, Australian cities were entering 'the brick and stone age'. Between 1861 and 1901 the size of the average Victorian house grew from less than three to more than five rooms. New products—plate glass, wrought iron, machine-made bricks and roof tiles, gas-powered lamps and stoves—and new construction techniques, such as prefabrication, began to change the design and production of the Australian home. Yet many houses still lacked bathrooms, and most had no waterclosets until the early twentieth century.

From the 1850s to the 1950s better housing was high among the ambitions of immigrants to Australia. Many British working-class families who craved relief from noisy neighbours and oppressive landlords found it in a jerry-built cottage in an Australian suburb. In 1873 Anthony **Trollope** observed that: 'A working man in Melbourne no doubt pays more for his house or for his lodging than he would in London; but then in Melbourne the labourer or artisan enjoys a home of a better sort than would be within the reach of his brother in London doing work of the same nature, and in regard to house-rent gets more for his money than he would do at home.' The economic historian Lionel Frost (*The New Urban Frontier*, 1991) confirmed that, while housing was generally more affordable in Australia than in Britain, it was less so in crowded harbourside Sydney than in sprawling Melbourne.

Australians preferred to own their own homes. In 1891 about 35 per cent of Sydney and 42 per cent of Melbourne householders occupied houses which they either owned or were in the process of purchasing. In rural and mining areas home-ownership was even higher. (In English towns, by contrast, the proportion of owner–occupiers was negligible, and only one or two midwestern American cities had ownership levels near the Australian levels.) Relatively high wages, cheap freehold land, a tradition of do-it-yourself improvisation, and the abundant credit available on relatively long terms through **building societies** all probably played a part. Even so, paying rent remained a central fact of life for most Australian city-dwellers, especially in inner-city neigh-

bourhoods. In Britain whole neighbourhoods could be owned by a single landlord. The typical Australian landlord owned only one or two houses, often in the same neighbourhood as his own, which he (sometimes she) let out for income, especially in old age.

Australia was a well-housed nation by international standards, but it was not a land without **slums**. From the late 1850s, when Henry **Parkes** chaired an inquiry into the condition of Sydney's working class, reformers had identified pockets of overcrowded, insanitary housing in the back streets of Sydney and Melbourne. **Epidemics** of typhoid and other contagious diseases inspired municipal campaigns to clean up Sydney's and Melbourne's slums. Perhaps 5000–10 000 houses were declared 'unfit for human habitation' in Sydney and Melbourne before World War I; but authorities were often reluctant to demolish them when their inhabitants, who depended on low-rent accommodation in the inner city, had nowhere else to go. State provision of low-cost housing was insignificant in Australia until the eve of World War II, and niggardly thereafter.

By 1945 **depression** and war had left Australia with an estimated shortfall of 350 000 houses. Thousands of families were living in sleep-outs, garages, boarding-houses, or doubling up with families or friends. Labor's plans for **post-war reconstruction** had projected a massive increase in both public and private housing. In his wartime appeals to the 'forgotten people', Robert **Menzies** had also placed 'homes material, homes human and homes spiritual' at the centre of his vision for the nation; but in power after 1949 he used public finance mainly to assist private individuals to acquire homes of their own, through subsidised home finance and grants for first home buyers, rather than providing public housing for poor families. Home-ownership, which had plateaued between the wars, soared from 53 per cent in 1947 to a peak of 71 per cent in 1966. Public housing, on the other hand, never rose above 10 per cent of the national housing stock, and in the most populous states was barely half that level.

Architects and builders, reading the lessons of the war, were convinced that new techniques of mechanisation and mass production could transform the design of the Australian house, but as Alastair Greig (*The Stuff Dreams Are Made Of*, 1995) and Seamus O'Hanlon and Tony Dingle (*AHS*, 1997) have shown, modernist design was often determined by postwar austerity rather than the preferences of home-seekers, who still looked for homes that were homely as well as efficient. Modern technology has been brought into the home in the form of new appliances—refrigerators, washing machines, micro-wave ovens, dishwashers, computers—rather than in transforming the house itself. Some important changes, such as the introduction of **brick veneer** construction, had been anticipated in the 1930s, but it was only in the 1950s and 1960s, through the influence of large project builders like A.V. **Jennings**, that house building and marketing were transformed into an integrated commercial and industrial operation. The standard Australian house grew in size, adding 'family rooms', studies, pool rooms, en suite bathrooms, parents' retreats, and other specialised living spaces to the basic core of cooking, washing, living, and sleeping quarters.

For almost two centuries Australians have equated the ideal home with the detached single-family house standing within a generous garden. In the 1880s when housing reformers sought to popularise tenements, they were rejected even by the working-class tenants for whom they were intended. In the 1920s some municipalities outlawed flats, which were then beginning to appear in Sydney, and to a lesser extent in Melbourne, because they supposedly encouraged promiscuity and fast living. Since the 1970s, however, a subtle change has occurred. Family sizes have shrunk, work-hours have lengthened, more leisure time is spent in eating and playing outside the home, and governments have begun to count the environmental cost of suburban sprawl. The ideal Australian house, for both 'double-income, no kids' and 'empty-nesters', may now be a terrace or warehouse apartment in cappuccino country rather than a new house in Kingswood country. Yet, as the Institute of Family Studies discovered in 1993, young Australian families still express a strong attachment to the traditional detached single-family Australian house.

Almost half a century after it was published, Robin **Boyd's** *Australia's Home* (1952) remains the liveliest and most perceptive study of its subject. John Archer, *Building a Nation* (1987, 1996), is attractively illustrated but anecdotal. Robert Irving, *The History and Design of the Australian House* (1985), is a valuable study of stylistic and technical aspects which may be supplemented by two regional studies: Rod Fisher and Brian Crozier, *The Queensland House* (1994), and Stefan Pikusa, *The Adelaide House* (1986).

GRAEME DAVISON

Hovell, W.H., see **Hume, Hamilton, and Hovell, William Hilton**

Howard, John Winston (1939–), prime minister of Australia since 1996, grew up in a Methodist household in suburban Sydney, the youngest of a garage proprietor's four children. He became a solicitor in 1962, advanced rapidly through the organisation of the NSW **Liberal Party**, failed in an attempt to win a state seat in 1968, but secured the federal seat of Bennelong in 1974. As minister for business and consumer affairs (1975–77) in Malcolm **Fraser's** government, he brought in amendments to the Trade Practices Act outlawing union boycotts. As treasurer, (1977–83) he came to favour financial deregulation, oppose tax evasion schemes, and support a broadly based indirect tax, but could not persuade the coalition government to implement one. In opposition, he became deputy leader to Andrew Peacock (1983–85), replaced him in 1985, lost the winnable 1987 election to Bob **Hawke** when undermined by his own side of politics, and in 1989 was the victim of an ambush that returned Peacock to the party leadership. Howard remained on the opposition front bench without, according to his biographer David Barnett (1997), abandoning belief in

himself as 'a national leader'. A survivor and pragmatist, as well as an ideologue, he waited until a desperate party turned to him again in 1995. By then, experience had toughened him, while making him more determined than ever to succeed.

Capitalising on the unpopularity of Paul **Keating**, he swept into power in 1996. In government, his approach combined economic liberalism with a formidable moral and social conservatism. He pared back and out-sourced public services, implemented labour market reform to eliminate inefficiencies and uncompetitive practices, and sought to re-create the relaxed and prosperous **Menzies** years, when family values were more firmly implanted. He was barely re-elected in 1998, when he promised to introduce a goods and services tax. Howard campaigned against an Australian republic and resisted the more advanced demands for Aboriginal **reconciliation**. Derided by his elistist critics as banal, narrow, and suburban, Howard turned ordinariness into a virtue, laid claim to represent 'the battlers', and demonstrated political courage in introducing gun-control and tax reform, and in standing up to Indonesia over **East Timor**. Effective economic management enabled the Howard government to retire the public debt inherited from Labor, to survive the Asian economic crisis, and to keep unemployment, inflation, and interest rates under control. In her assessment of Howard in *Australian Prime Ministers* (2000), Michelle Grattan has described him as 'a "conviction" politician … driven by long-held values … not a doubter or agoniser'. Those values derive from an 'old Australia' rather than a modern, multicultural one. Yet while doggedly pursuing his beliefs, Howard, the realist, is always listening to the electorate, is acutely aware of its grievances, and is willing to water down dogma in order to overcome unpopularity. Even among his supporters, however, he inspires respect rather than affection and may, therefore, have to await the passage of time before receiving due recognition for his achievements.

IAN HANCOCK

Howe, Michael (1787–1818) was characterised shortly after his death in a pamphlet by Thomas Wells as *Michael Howe, the Last and Worst of the Bushrangers of Van Diemen's Land*. Howe was a deserter from the army when he was found guilty of highway robbery and sentenced to transportation. He arrived in Van Diemen's Land in 1812 and absconded the following year to the bush, where he became leader of a gang made up of other absconders and deserters. Howe became cocky; he called himself 'Lieutenant-Governor of the Woods' and sent mocking letters to Lieutenant-Governor **Davey**. Eventually he took Governor **Sorrell's** offer of a conditional pardon in return for assisting in the capture of his ex-companions. Howe failed in this and fled back to the bush where he wrote a diary, supposedly inscribed in blood on kangaroo skin. Captured once, he escaped and survived another year before being clubbed to death. His head was taken to Hobart for exhibition. James **Bonwick** wrote a biography (1873) and Howe has been represented in works of fiction, including Nat Gould's *King of the Ranges* (1902).

KT

Hudson, William (1896–1978) became known as the 'father of the Snowy' for his role as commissioner of the **Snowy Mountains Hydro-Electric** Authority 1949–67. Born in NZ, Hudson completed his training as a civil engineer overseas, after service in World War I. He became an expert on the construction of dams and hydroelectric schemes, which led to his Australian appointment. Hudson was evangelical about the scheme, and imbued the workers with unity and purpose. He introduced revolutionary work practices intended to maintain the momentum of work; among other measures, employing a private arbitrator to deal with industrial disputes and introducing a safety campaign that included compulsory seatbelts. He was also adept at promoting the scheme to the Australian populace by presenting it as a symbol of national pride. He is remembered at Cooma, NSW, the home of the Snowy Mountain Authority, by the Sir William Hudson Memorial Centre.

KT

Hughes, Robert Studley Forrest (1938–), art critic and widely read historian, was born in Sydney into a prosperous dynasty of lawyers and politicians. Educated by the Jesuits at St Ignatius College, Riverview, he proceeded to the University of Sydney, where he studied arts and architecture, but never graduated. His ambition was to be a painter, but after he left for Europe in 1964, upon completing two books on Australian art, he decided to take up criticism full time. His book *Heaven and Hell in Western Art* (1968) brought him to the attention of the editor of *Time* in New York, where he has been employed as regular art reviewer since 1970. His reviews were republished in *Nothing if Not Critical* (1990). Other books by him on artistic themes—*The Shock of the New* (1980) and *American Visions* (1997)—have emerged from successful television series. His first series, *Landscape with Figures: The Art of Australia*, was made for Australian television in 1975. His study of the Australian penal system, *The Fatal Shore* (1987), became an international best-seller, although its rhetorical bravura alienated some more orthodox practitioners of **convict history**. He has subsequently branched out into cultural history and criticism with *Barcelona* (1992) and *Culture of Complaint* (1993). He has won more recent attention as an outspoken supporter of the Australian **republican** movement.

IAN BRITAIN

Hughes, William Morris 'Billy' (1862–1952) was prime minister of a Labor government from 1915 to 1916 and, after his expulsion from the Labor Party, of a Nationalist government until 1923. He was a founder of the **Australian Labor Party** and in Labor lore its arch betrayer, or, to use the Labor term, its greatest rat.

Though commonly thought of as a Welshman, he was born in London and retained his mother's attachment to the Church of England. He migrated to Australia when he was 22. After labouring in the Qld outback, he moved to Sydney, where he took a variety of jobs and, when down on his luck, slept in the Domain—or so he claimed. He entered the NSW parliament in 1894 as one of the 'solidarity' Labor members and in 1901 transferred to the federal parliament, of which he remained a member until his death.

Hughes's offence against his party was that as prime minister he insisted that men should be conscripted for service in the Australian forces in France, although the party organisation had given strong indications of its opposition to that policy (the party platform itself was silent on the matter). To bypass the party opposition, Hughes appealed to the electorate at large by referendum in 1916. **Conscription** was narrowly rejected after a bitter campaign in which Labor Party members fought on both sides. The breach could not be healed, and after the referendum the party split permanently. Hughes and his pro-conscription ministers remained in office with the support of the Opposition with whom they merged in 1917 to form the **Nationalist Party**. Hughes was regarded with great suspicion by many of his new followers and was removed from the prime ministership in 1923 when the new Country Party (**National Party**) refused to enter a coalition if it were led by him. He remained an influential parliamentarian almost to the end of his life. In 1929 he cooperated with the Labor Party to defeat the government of S.M. **Bruce**, who had supplanted him as prime minister, when Bruce attempted to abandon the federal **arbitration** system. He served as minister in the United Australia government led by **Lyons**. In 1941–43 he led the **United Australia Party**, from which he was expelled in 1944 for cooperating with the Labor government of John **Curtin**.

As Donald **Horne** observes (*In Search of Billy Hughes*, 1979), Hughes was not a typical Labor rat. Until the split over conscription—and indeed after it—Hughes showed no slackening in his commitment to the Labor program. As attorney-general in the prewar Labor governments he had taken the leading part in the attempts to amend the constitution so that Labor policy on trusts, monopolies, and public ownership could be implemented. He had provided the most eloquent and coherent defence of the Labor program in *The Case for Labor* (1910). After the war, as prime minister in a non-Labor government, he established the Commonwealth Oil Refineries and put to the people a referendum to give the Commonwealth power to nationalise monopolies. His commitment to public ownership and government control was one reason why the Country Party would not serve under him. Hughes said of himself that he continued to stand where he had always stood, and it was the Labor Party which had left him. During the 1920s he hoped for a reconciliation with Labor which would have made him again a Labor prime minister.

According to Labor lore, he turned to conscription because he succumbed to the blandishments of the metropolis during his visit to Britain in 1916, when he became briefly a power in British politics through his advocacy of a more ruthless conduct of the war, an attack on Germany's economic power, and the creation after the war of an economically integrated empire. His speeches were widely reported and created immense enthusiasm. Hughes was fêted in establishment circles. This, according to Labor legend, turned his head and, forgetting his party and his country, he decided to conscript Australian men for imperial purposes.

Most of the historical accounts of Hughes's decision for conscription endorse the legend by allowing at least some significance to the effect of the visit. If it had an effect, it was very different from what the legend claims. This is made clear in L.F. Fitzhardinge's authoritative two-volume biography *William Morris Hughes* (1964, 1979). Hughes went to London chiefly because he was worried about the deals which the imperial government was striking with its ally Japan over the German islands in the Pacific. While he was in Britain, he became convinced that Australia's interests would be overlooked unless Britain was put under great pressure. Hughes wanted to maintain Australia's military commitment not so much to ensure that Britain won the war but so that Australia would have a powerful voice in the settlement after it.

Hughes has been the only Australian prime minister who regarded international power politics as central before he held the office. For him, like Churchill, war was not a disappointment, but a vindication of his world view. He was chiefly responsible for persuading the Labor Party to adopt compulsory training for home defence. As early as 1897 a Labor journal criticised Hughes for possessing 'the politics of Bismarck tempered by the economics of Marx'. He was an oddity in a party opposed to war and imperialism, not so much because he supported the Empire—for when the chips were down in 1914 most of the party did so—but because he could imagine a world without the British Empire and the consequences of that absence for Australia. In his words, Australia was a nation by the grace of God and the British Empire.

Hughes's great moment was at the 1919 Versailles Peace Conference. For the first time Australia had an independent voice in a grand geopolitical settlement. Hughes was scornful of President Wilson's idealism and argued relentlessly to secure Australian control over PNG and to block Japan's proposal for a declaration of racial equality, which Hughes saw as a veiled threat to the **White Australia** policy. His belligerent, larrikin style offended the diplomats but enhanced his reputation at home. He returned to a hero's welcome.

Hughes's deep belief in struggle and conflict and his preoccupation with military might invite a psychological explanation, but none of his biographers has worked in this vein. Some of the details of the life are suggestive. Hughes was short and not robust in health. His mother died when he was seven, and he was sent away from London and his father to live with an aunt in Wales. He returned to London when he was 11 to complete his elementary education, and at 13 he became a pupil-teacher. Before he was 18 he had joined a volunteer battalion of the Royal Fusiliers.

The emphasis in Fitzhardinge's biography is on Hughes's 'public career and on his style and character as revealed in it'.

It is beautifully written, scholarly, and meticulous. The introduction to the second volume provides a vivid character sketch and presents Hughes as a tragic figure, destroying his own creations, beginning with the Labor Party.

Hughes was in many respects an unattractive figure, domineering, hateful, vituperative, and impossible to work for. And yet, as Horne writes, 'people could love him from a distance for his gameness, his smallness, his humour, even his trickiness, and his ability to appear always as nothing grander than a fellow creature, as if all men really were brothers'. Horne's book is a revealing exploration of the man in politics, of how man and politician became one, and how the politician acquired legendary status.

Hughes wrote of his own career in *Crusts and Crusades* (1947) and *Politicians and Potentates* (1950). The first gives a lively account of the early days of the Labor Party which catches better than any of the histories the human effort, the social solidarities—of place and clan as well as of class—and the intellectual excitement which launched the party and gave it its early success. The tone is gently mocking, but broadly sympathetic. It was written 30 years after his 'ratting'. Hughes never disowned his Labor past; rather he celebrated the early party to better condemn the one that expelled and vilified him.

JOHN HIRST

Hume, Fergus (1859–1932), writer, is often credited with the creation of the first detective story, *The Mystery of a Hansom Cab*, set in Melbourne and published at the height of that city's land boom, in 1886. Hume, son of an English doctor, had grown up in NZ, where he trained as a lawyer but moved to Melbourne in 1885 hoping to write for the theatre. *The Mystery of a Hansom Cab*, written in the hope of attracting the attention of theatre managers, was published by the author himself and rapidly sold out. With its lurid depictions of low life in Little Bourke Street, its variegated caste of representative urban types—the detective, the society beauty, the rake, the actress—and its melodramatic plot, it was ready-made for adaptation to the theatre; the first of several stage adaptations was presented in 1888. *Madame Midas* (1888) made similar use of dark secrets from the past on the Victorian goldfields. Stephen Knight has assessed the place of Hume in the history of crime fiction, *Continent of Mystery* (1997).

GD

Hume, Hamilton (1797–1873) and **Hovell, William Hilton** (1786–1875) travelled together in 1824 on an exploratory expedition from NSW to Corio Bay near present-day Geelong. Hume was native-born and had early established a reputation as an explorer. Hovell migrated from England in 1813 and commanded trading ships for some years before settling on land in NSW. In the course of their journey southwards the men crossed a large river which they named the Hume (later called the Murray). Their original belief that they reached Western Port Bay was corrected by

Hovell on a later trip. The explorers' favourable report on the country around Port Phillip gave significant impetus to pastoral expansion in the colony. William Bland used their journals to produce *Journey of Discovery to Port Phillip, New South Wales; By Messrs. W.H. Hovell and Hamilton Hume: in 1824 and 1825*, compiled in 1831 but not published until 1837. They quarrelled on their journey, and the acrimony flared again in 1853 when Hume considered that Hovell was claiming credit as leader of the expedition. He published *A Brief Statement of Facts* (1855), to which Hovell responded in his *Reply*. This public dispute is documented by Alan E.J. Andrews in *Hume and Hovell, 1824* (1981). Hume is commemorated by the name of the highway between Sydney and Melbourne, and the Hume Weir. His house, now a museum, is located near Yass.

KT

Humour in Australia is distinctive. Anecdote and oral legend are not the only places to look in tracing its lineaments and evolutions, though anecdote seems somehow to carry a sense of authenticity, to be somehow nearer 'ground-level'. One of the archetypal jokes belonging to Australia's splendid tradition of cartoon satire and humour, however, is hilariously and literally above ground-level: two men hang precariously from a crane line at a vertiginous height; the second man, clinging to the trousers of the first and in danger of pulling them off, is remonstrating: 'For gorsake stop laughing—this is serious!'

Back down on the ground, though, the Australian anecdote has a voice, a tone, and an irony that are thoroughly distinctive and which sometimes defy translation to other English speaking cultures:

The scene is a grassy flat with a ramshackle shed in the background overhung by tall stringybarks. A battered tractor, on the carry-all of which are stacked several huge newly cut lengths of redgum, stands alongside an equally disreputable utility truck with its tray sides down. It is obvious that the redgum 'strainer' posts have to be transferred to the ute; it is equally obvious that the two men who are leaning on the bonnet of the ute are contemplating this very problem. Eventually, one of them—the one with the bush hat, check shirt, scrubby moleskins and a perpetual cigarette pasted to his lips through the smoke of which he squints and coughs—decisively begins to give directions to the other, the better-dressed, rather 'city' looking one. Following these directions but clearly having failed to understand them, he backs the ute at a certain angle to the logs on the tractor; it is the wrong angle. He is given more directions and moves the ute to a different but patently still wrong position. With every bone and angle of his body exuding massive tolerance, the man in the moleskins issues more instructions, supplementing his words with a number of choice expletives and much waving and pointing. This time, the driver gets it right and positions the truck, after which, hopping down from the driver's cabin, he gives an embarrassed grin and says: 'Sorry Tom—there can't be many more wrong ways of doing that!' Deadpan, lips scarcely moving, voice emerging in a nasal, smoky, saturnine drawl, the man in the moleskins says: 'Well, I dunno—I reckon you would've found a few, given time.'

That true anecdote contains many of the ingredients thought to be intrinsic to Australian humour: there is corrosive though not deeply wounding irony; there is a spareness of words, a **bush** setting, a vernacular ambience. Above all, the humour is what one might describe as 'kidding': the butt of the remark is being gently but firmly set up for a modestly humiliating fall.

Of course, there is much that is out of date in this scene. White Australians are and have always been an urban people. The laconic, drawling bushman undoubtedly existed—and is still to be found—but he has been nowhere near as central to our humour as conventional wisdom would have it. Though it happens to reflect the truth of that particular encounter, the all-male cast of this anecdote is typical of bush-based humour. Steele **Rudd's** stories broke this mould, with a focus on the whole family to whose various adventures 'Mum' made significant contributions, but it was well into the twentieth century before the scenes, personnel, diction, and general atmosphere of Australian humour began to be infiltrated by, and altered in response to, the influence of women. Nevertheless, journals and diaries (for example, Georgiana **McCrae's**, in which she reveals a fine and sophisticated wit); the gentle but pointed social criticism of Catherine Helen **Spence**; the novels of Miles **Franklin**, especially *My Brilliant Career* (1901), and her conduct of her various aliases; Louisa **Lawson's** women's journal, *The Dawn*, and some of her short stories; and the attacking speeches associated with the women's movement of the turn of the century, notably those of Rose **Scott**—all these clearly revealed a great reservoir of women's satiric views of the male-dominated world they lived in and in which their predecessors had survived under even greater constraints. When the balance shifted, however, it did so decisively: some of the great comic talents in Australian writing, television, film, and theatre are women and, notwithstanding many important differences between male and female humour in Australia, irony remains central.

The dry, pared-back ironic 'kidding'—which undoubtedly was a fact of bush life as the colonies evolved—found apotheosis in the stories of Henry **Lawson**, despite Lawson's growing penchant for the grim and gloomy. His character Steelman—a bush conman—is the consummate kidder, amiable, pleasant, and, if the tables are turned, courteous and philosophical. Posing as a geologist ('Go up ... and fetch me a specimen of that slaty outcrop ... just above the coeval strata'), but discovering that he has been out-generalled and 'seen through' by the boss of a railway workers camp, Steelman remarks: 'I think we'll make a start tomorrow. There's too much humour and levity in this camp to suit a serious scientific gentleman like myself.' Joseph **Furphy's** narrator Tom Collins (in *Such Is Life*, 1903) begins his account and sets the ironic tone with the memorable announcement, 'Unemployed at last'; while innumerable balladists and cartoonists fended off life's vicissitudes with a mixture of stoicism (which breeds irony) and whimsical acceptance—

the bullockies who are the subject of the ballad 'Grass Stealers', for example, who 'wouldn't steal a penny, / But they all steal grass' and who consider that

> A man who wouldn't steal
> A bit of grass to feed his horse
> Should be flung into the Darling
> Or some other watercourse.

It is that afterthought—a sort of half-dotty intentness on completion such that an alternative river has to be provided to receive the delinquent bullocky—that imbues this observation with its ironic momentum.

In the twentieth century, C.J. **Dennis** began the shift of focus to the cities, where by far the majority of Australians had always lived, with a consequent enrichment of the content of wit and humour. The kidding element remained strong, though its edge became sharper and sharper: 'Leave our flies alone, yer Pommie bastard', shouts 'Yabba' from the Sydney hill at Douglas Jardine as he swats at the local pests in the **bodyline** cricket Tests. Lenny Lower's *Here's Luck* (1930) recorded the tribulations of a suburban battler with a mixture of slapstick and misogyny. 'Dingo Loses Appeal' reports a billboard during one of the many metamorphoses of the **Chamberlain** case.

In the 1980s and 1990s stand-up comedy has boomed in Australia, while translating successfully to rigorous international venues such as the Edinburgh Festival and unforgiving New York audiences. Contemporary Australian humour has an urban, multicultural ambience; it retains the national penchant for the ironic, while at the same time incorporating an anarchic character which is partly the legacy of global developments in humour (especially, for example, the influence of the Goons and Monty Python) but is also peculiarly suited to Australian saturnine perspectives and anti-authoritarianism. 'Why is it?' asks John Clarke in his version of a poem by someone he says is the American 'Imagist', 'William Esther Williams'—

> Why is it that every year
> On remote coastlines
> Labour leaders
> Beach themselves?
> Whole schools of them,
> Apparently healthy Labour leaders
> Thousands of miles off course and stranded,
> Spume drifting from their tragic holes

—a brilliant and above all supremely confident series of satiric juxtapositions which mercilessly savage local follies, international pretensions, and topical obsessions.

All humour is, of course, in one way or another subversive of established and perceived authorities and conventions; but it seems especially to be the case with contemporary Australian satirists and comics, such as Clarke and Jean Kittson, following in the splendidly anarchic footsteps of the early Barry **Humphries**, and in the cartoons of Michael Leunig, Bruce **Petty**, and Kaz Cooke.

BRIAN MATTHEWS

Humphries, (John) Barry (1934–), entertainer, achieved celebrity in the mid-1960s through his comic stage portrayal of Australian social types. He grew up in Camberwell, a middle-class Melbourne suburb, in a house designed by his father, a well-to-do builder, and attended private schools. At the University of Melbourne he distinguished himself as an ingenious prankster and creator of a 'Dada' exhibition, then dropped out to join the Melbourne Theatre Company. His comic monologues, based on observation of his parents' Camberwell, though with echoes of English satirical writers, were first devised for an end-of-season revue in 1955. Their characters, the indomitable vulgarian Edna Everage, her hen-pecked husband Norm, and the desiccated Sandy Stone, were, as their names suggest, representatives of a society addicted to the mediocre and the middle-brow. Humphries's satire struck a chord among intellectuals beginning to recognise the **suburbs** as the newest frontier of Australian cultural life. 'This is Barry Humphries country', remarked Craig McGregor in 1966, as he launched an attack on the 'dullness', 'conformity' and 'stupefying routine' of Australian suburbia. In 1959 Humphries left for London where his *Private Eye* comic strip, 'The Adventures of Barry McKenzie', the picaresque exploits of an Australian innocent abroad, became the foundation of an international success which has transformed his alter ego, Edna, from mousy housewife to Dame Edna, coiffed and spangled superstar. He has been the subject of studies by Peter Coleman (1990), John Lahr (1991), and Ian Britain (1997), and has written about his own life in *More Please* (1992).

GD

Hunter, John (1737–1821), Scottish sailor in the Royal Navy, was second-in-command of the **First Fleet** on its voyage to Botany Bay. Once at Port Jackson, Hunter served as a magistrate, conducted land surveys, and undertook several long trips for Governor Arthur **Phillip**, one of which resulted in his being stranded on **Norfolk Island**. A year after his return to England, he published *An Historical Journal of the Transactions at Port Jackson and Norfolk Island* (1793). Hunter was appointed to replace Phillip, taking up his position in 1795. His five years in office were marred by his struggle with the **New South Wales Corps** and John **Macarthur** for control of the colony. Upon his recall to England, Hunter published his vindication in *Governor Hunter's Remarks on the Causes of Colonial Expense of the Establishment of New South Wales* (1802). He is commemorated in the Hunter River; B.R. Blaze wrote his biography, *Great Scot* (1976). Some of his original drawings are held in the **Nan Kivell** collection in the National Library of Australia, and have been published.

KT

Hurley, James Francis 'Frank' (1885–1962), photographer and film-maker, ran a Sydney postcard business when he joined Douglas **Mawson's** Australasian Antarctic Expedition in 1911 and established his reputation with stunning still photography and a documentary film, *Home of the Blizzard* (1913). Hurley went to **Antarctica** several times.

While marooned with Ernest Shackleton in 1915, he took a sequence of still photographs that captured the ice-bound *Endurance* being gradually pulverised. He gained international recognition with an epic documentary of Shackleton's ordeal, *In the Grip of the Polar Ice* (1917). Hurley's image as a swashbuckling adventurer was enhanced by clinging to the title 'Captain', his honorary rank as official war photographer for the **AIF** in 1917–18 and 1940. His views of Ypres and Passchendaele displayed at the **Australian War Memorial** emphasise that historical assessment should balance the photographer as both observer and artist. Hurley's famous World War I photograph, *Over the Top*, was a composite that fused dramatic elements from separate scenes into one image. After joining the final leg of Keith and Ross **Smith's** England–Australia flight in 1919, he produced a lecture-film, *The Ross Smith Flight* (1920). His journeys to **Papua** in 1920–23 resulted in several documentaries and a best-selling photographic book, *Pearls and Savages* (1924). He also made some minor feature films during the 1920s and worked with Ken G. Hall as a Cinesound cameraman in the 1930s. His documentary, *Symphony in Steel* (1932), traced construction of the **Sydney Harbour Bridge**, and *A Nation Is Built*

(1937) was commissioned for Australia's 150th anniversary. In later life Hurley produced photographic books on Australian landscapes and cities. After his death, Hurley's daughter Toni collaborated with Frank Legg on a biography, *Once More on My Adventure* (1966). Julian Thomas assessed Hurley's 'showmanship' in a critical essay in *Showman* (1990), the catalogue of an exhibition of the Hurley collection in the National Library of Australia.

DC

Hyde Park Barracks, designed by convict architect Francis **Greenway**, was erected in Sydney's Hyde Park by Governor **Macquarie** in 1819, as accommodation for the **convicts** employed by the government in Sydney. The building subsequently became a home for single female immigrants (1848–86), and accommodated courts and government offices (1887–1979). A prominent feature is the large central clock that ensured strict adherence to time management during the building's convict period. Managed by the **Historic Houses Trust of New South Wales** since 1979, it has been transformed into a museum.

HD

I

Ideas, history of, sometimes refers to study of the history of ideas undertaken in Australia, sometimes to the study of intellectual history in Australia, and sometimes to the history of Australian ideas. These ambiguities are significant because Australians still seem reluctant to make strong claims for their own 'ideas' and 'intellectuals'. The term *intellectual* lacks an agreed definition and is still widely used as a term of abuse. Conservative critics of intellectuals, such as Ronald Conway and John Carroll, are taken more seriously than they would be elsewhere. When the iconoclast Frank **Knopfelmacher** attacked Australian intellectuals as uncritical admirers of foreign revolutionary regimes (*Intellectuals and Politics*, 1968), he was widely admired. A dismissive attitude to intellectuals also inspired Patrick O'Brien's *The Saviours: An Intellectual History of the Left in Australia* (1977). Similarly, the notion that Australians are passionately interested in ideas and have produced original ideas has only surfaced with difficulty in the scholarly literature, partly because it conflicts with older national stereotypes. Hence the apologetic element in the classic essays on intellectuals by Vincent Buckley in Peter Coleman (ed.), *Australian Civilization* (1962); Manning **Clark**, 'Melbourne: An Intellectual Tradition' (*MHJ*, 1962); and A.F. Davies, 'Intellectuals in Politics', in *Essays in Political Sociology* (1972). Yet Australians have shown considerable interest in ideas. They have also been surprisingly good at studying their history.

Nineteenth-century Australians concerned themselves with both classical Greek and Roman and modern Western ideas, as their newspapers and libraries show. In the twentieth century the generalist concerns of essayists, lawyers, journalists, and clergymen gave way to university-based studies. Whereas nineteenth-century intellectuals were predominantly indebted to English, Scottish, and American authors, in the twentieth century Russian, Italian, Chinese, and French texts also played a significant role. Further, intellectual history in an academic sense was widely studied in departments of history, English, French, German, politics,

and classics, and scholarly books of distinction were produced, including Bruce Mansfield's study of Erasmus (1979). At the Australian National University a History of Ideas Unit emerged from the department of philosophy, and became world famous under the directorship of Eugene Kamenka. The work done was mainly on European rather than Australian ideas, though Sam Goldberg used it as a base for the seminars that generated the journal *Australian Cultural History*. Eminent international scholars (P.H. Partridge, Robert Brown, Hiram Caton, Andrzej Walicki, Knud Haakonsen) worked in the unit, as did John Passmore after his retirement from the chair of philosophy. Passmore's work on the history of philosophy was outstanding, and *A Hundred Years of Philosophy* (1957) became the standard work in English-speaking countries. Moreover, the tradition of distinguished studies of the history of philosophy and of the interdependence between philosophy and history has continued—witness Richard Campbell's magisterial study, *Truth and Historicity* (1992).

Work on Australian intellectual history developed more slowly. Whereas the History of Ideas Unit produced work which was philosophically nuanced, Australian intellectual history has been mainly studied by those primarily interested in Australia, and in its political and cultural development, or in a specific discipline or group of disciplines. Those interested in Australia, however, have often lacked a deep interest in technical ideas, while those concerned with a discipline have not made the wider connections. As a result, Australian intellectual history is still in its infancy.

No overview of Australian intellectual history has been written, and students are forced back to H.M. **Green's** *A History of Australian Literature* (1961) even for a list of names. The fact that philosophy is left to historians of philosophy has had the consequence that major studies such as S.A. Grave's *A History of Philosophy in Australia* (1984) are not integrated into general accounts of Australian history. Much Australian intellectual history has been written in terms of political and social history, as if ideas were to be judged by their political and social effects. This skews the analysis to figures of importance in Australian political and social history, and away from those with original or technically significant ideas. There has been a related tendency to downplay conservative and religious ideas, as if Australian ideas had to conform to the mythology of Australians as a utilitarian, realistic, pragmatic people. Even Tim Rowse's pioneering assertion of the diversity and importance of Australian political ideas, *Australian Liberalism and National Character* (1978), was written under the influence of Louis Althusser, and sought to demonstrate the existence of a 'hegemonic' liberal ideology.

Attempts to assess Australian ideas as such have been few. Excellent books on the colonial period, such as George Nadel's *Australia's Colonial Culture* (1957) and Ann-Mari Jorden's *The Stenhouse Circle* (1979), did not go into intellectual substance. Two works by Michael **Roe,** *Quest for Authority in Eastern Australia 1835–1851* (1965) and *Nine Australian Progressives* (1984), were lonely exceptions. Fortunately, there are now signs that Australians are getting better at dealing with their own ideas and at specifying their social role in Australian culture. Two excellent studies, Warren Osmond's *Frederic Eggleston: An Intellectual in Australian Politics* (1985) and Stuart Macintyre's *A Colonial Liberalism* (1991), attempt to take Australian ideas seriously as well as their political context. The case for the originality of Australian political thought has been made by James Walter and Brian Head in their seminal collection, *Intellectual Movements and Australian Society* (1988), and by Geoff Stokes in *Australian Political Ideas* (1994), although a tendency to prefer ideas which shaped policy is still evident. The problem of expatriate intellectuals who had original ideas was long evaded, but the tide is turning thanks to the work of Helen Bourke; the collection, *Childe and Australia* (1995), edited by Peter Gathercole, Gregory Melleuish, and Terry Irving; and Ian Britain's *Once an Australian* (1997). There is still a tendency to neglect primary sources and unpublished manuscripts. One of the few studies heavily based on primary sources is Gregory Melleuish, *Cultural Liberalism in Australia* (1995), a book which contests older biases at many points.

Specialist studies of Australian scientific and economic thought include Rod Home (ed.), *Australian Science in the Making* (1988); the early studies of Australian economic thought by Craufurd Goodwin; and Peter Groenewegen, *A History of Australian Economic Thought* (1990). There are studies that contribute to the history of ideas by means of consideration of the history of Australian art, notably those of Bernard **Smith**, which exemplify what Peter Beilharz argues in *Imagining the Antipodes* (1997) is the most sophisticated social theory yet developed in Australia. Richard Haese's work on the impact of liberal, anarchist, and communist ideas on Australian art, *Rebels and Precursors* (1981), also provides evidence of the complexity of the Australian reception of international currents. There is also a significant literature on constitutional and jurisprudential thought.

Nevertheless, Australians still fail to lionise their intellectuals in the American manner, and often hesitate to stake out claims for their independence and originality. Individual figures, from Christopher **Brennan** to John **Anderson**, have been given book-length treatment, but it is fair to note a lack of methodological sophistication. No Australian has written about an Australian intellectual as well as Australians have written about European intellectuals, with the possible exception of Peter Beilharz's recent essays on the liberalism of H.V. **Evatt** (*AJPH*, 1993) and the syndicalism of John Anderson (*Political Theory Newsletter*, 1993). In contrast, intellectual tendencies are given sensitive treatment in cultural history. Thus David Walker studied Vance **Palmer**, Louis **Esson**, Frank Wilmot, and Frederick Sinclaire as pioneers of a national Australian culture in *Dream and Disillusion* (1976), and John Docker explored the differences between Melbourne and Sydney intellectual traditions in *Australian Cultural Elites* (1974). There are also studies such as Geoffrey **Serle's** biography of the architect and critic Robin **Boyd** (1995). John **Mulvaney** and John Calaby's biography of Baldwin **Spencer**, whose work on Aborigines did so much to shape perceptions and policy, is nicely complemented by the collection on Mulvaney as a prehistorian and public intellectual edited by Tim Bonyhady and Tom Griffiths in 1996. But more detailed and less biographical studies are needed.

Accounts of Australian receptions of Nietzsche, Marx and Engels, modernist aesthetics, or French theory, do not make up for the failure to catalogue the papers of Australian intellectuals or to assay intellectual developments in WA, Tasmania, and north Qld. It is also proving difficult to get adequate recognition of the international character of Australian intellectual interchanges. Hence there is still no adequate study of Keith **Hancock**, largely because he was an imperial as well as an Australian intellectual. Some geographically sensitive intellectual history has been written. Craig Munro's *Wild Man of Letters: The Story of P.R. Stephensen* (1984), for example, provides a fine study of one key cultural intellectual, including the Queensland background to his thought. There is also an emerging body of work on women's intellectual history. Nonetheless, the bulk of the work remains to be done. As it is done, a greater sense of Australian originality may be expected to appear.

WAYNE HUDSON

Idriess, Ion Llewellyn (1889–1979) was a prolific and remarkably successful populariser of Australian historical subjects. An itinerant bushworker and adventurer, he began contributing to the *Bulletin*'s 'Aboriginalities' column and to other periodicals. His first major success was *Lasseter's Last Ride* (1931), an account of a doomed search for gold in Central Australia. Idriess wrote several novels but his most popular works were imaginative recreations of outback pioneers, remote settlements, and Australian adventurers in the Torres Strait and Papua. He applied the same methods of novelistic romance to lives of John **Flynn** and Sidney **Kidman**, as well as **Aboriginal resistance** leaders and

Immigration

Australians at war. While claiming sympathy with Aboriginal culture, he repeatedly set his own claims of direct knowledge against the southern humanitarians who condemned official repression in northern Australia. Like other popular writers of the period between the world wars, he showed a strong element of self-promotion in his professional career, and his desire for greater literary recognition exacerbated the personal strains of an irregular domestic life. These aspects emerge strongly in the biography by Beverley Eley (1995).

SM

Immigration, whether independent, assisted, or refugee, has profoundly shaped, and continues to shape, Australian society.

The earliest European arrivals were not migrants, however, but reluctant exiles, convicts and their warders; free immigration had no place in the foundation of NSW as a place of banishment and punishment. The free persons who accompanied the convicts and stayed on, or who migrated in the 1820s and 1830s to take advantage of free land and labour, saw themselves as 'colonists' or 'settlers' extending the British Empire in the Pacific. Britain was overpopulated, and Australia had a labour shortage. Free immigrants provided this labour when transportation proved inadequate, or ceased, or was rejected on moral grounds. By 1850 there were 187 000 free migrants in Australia. Most had their passages paid from the proceeds of colonial land sales, for the distance and the expense of a voyage to Australia obliged governments to subsidise immigration. This phase of Australian immigration was first studied by R.B. **Madgwick**, *Immigration into Eastern Australia 1788–1851* (1937, 1969). The assisted passage scheme initiated in 1830 for British migrants lasted 150 years.

The gold-rush decade 1851–61 brought 622 000 migrants to the colonies, 372 000 of them unassisted and 250 000 assisted. Subsidised immigration attempted to balance the sexes and provide wage labour. For the next 40 years immigration was a roller-coaster, rising with prosperity, diving steeply in hard times. All the colonies had assisted schemes, but only Qld extended it to non-British Europeans, and then only on a limited basis. Between 1861 and 1900 there arrived a further 365 000 unassisted and 400 000 assisted migrants. Colonial censuses first recorded a majority of the population as native-born in 1871, but for another 70 years Australians persisted in regarding themselves as overseas British, and later in Keith **Hancock's** phrase, as **Independent Australian Britons**.

Colonial society was riven with ethnic snobberies and religious sectarianism. In time, social and geographical mobility, and intermarriage, gave rise to the notion that transplanted English, **Scottish**, **Irish**, and Welsh had come to form in Australia a uniquely 'British' people—united, not merely coexisting ethnic groups, as in Britain. At the time of Federation in 1901, Australia was commonly boasted of as '98 per cent British'. But the processes, real and imagined, by which this 'British' identity emerged, are only now being studied. A series of books edited by Eric Richards et al., *Visible Immigrants* (1989–   ), reports this research.

By 1901, when the immigration power passed to the federal government, the rationale for immigration, particularly for assisted immigration, had changed somewhat. Economic prosperity continued important, but development was now linked to the notion of occupying the continent to forestall invasion by the 'teeming millions' of China and Japan. British Australian nationhood had become clearly identified with the preservation of the 'racial purity' of a **White Australia**. The seasonality of the rural-based colonial Australian economy made **trade unions** favour a tight labour market, and therefore oppose state-assisted immigration; fear of cheap coloured labour led unions to demand restrictions on the **Chinese** and **Pacific Island labour** which had become such a strong feature of goldmining, sugarcane farming, and certain urban trades. Non-white immigration was virtually prohibited under the federal Immigration Restriction Act of 1901.

The obsession with White Australia, which was further entrenched by the rise of **Japan** as a military power and the fear of invasion during the Pacific War 1941–45, conditioned national immigration policy until the early 1970s, long after Australia had developed significant trading links with Asia, well after the collapse of European colonialism there, and indeed even after the official abolition of the White Australia policy in the 1960s. Australia's matching obsession was with British migration and settlement.

Governments stimulated, funded, and organised British immigration on a massive scale in the decades immediately before and after World War I to strengthen Australia in the face of rising Japanese might, to replace the manhood lost or shattered on Great War battlefields, and to develop **'Australia Unlimited'**. British authorities, fearing domestic disorder at home and military challenges abroad, cooperated enthusiastically. The story is best told by Michael **Roe**, *Australia, Britain, and Migration 1915–1940* (1995). Between 1919 and 1929, 221 000 British migrants were assisted, and a further 100 000 unassisted migrants were attracted to Australia. Of the total, 90 per cent were English or Scots. Much of this immigration was linked, fancifully as it turned out, to schemes of land settlement. Large numbers of those placed on the land failed, and farm labourers drifted to the cities. Ironically, it was the unassisted and unwanted Southern European migrants (mainly **Italians**, **Greeks**, and Maltese) who enjoyed most success. Southern European migration, a mere a trickle in the late 1890s and early 1900s, strengthened in the 1920s. Their success as small farmers, market gardeners, vignerons, wood-cutters, and contractors excited much derision and resentment across the continent. Melbourne's Professor Ernest **Scott**, startled by Jens Lyng's tribute to foreigners' contribution to the economy in *Non-Britishers in Australia* (1927, 1935), felt constrained in his preface to warn readers against overestimating foreigners' role in Australian nation-building in comparison with that of the English, Scots, and Irish. It was in the Queensland sugarcane cutting and farming that 'the Olive Peril' occasioned the strongest union, Labor Party and Labor government protest. In 1925 the federal Nationalist–Country Party coalition government amended the immigration laws to allow the imposition of quotas by nationality, race, class, or group. Hard times slowed immigration, however, and the legislation became superfluous. By the late 1930s **population** experts in Britain and Australia were warning that the declining birth-rate meant that it was unlikely that Britain could continue to supply Australia's immigration needs.

War intervened, and the Pacific War transformed Australia's immigration priorities. Japan's world power status gave the Australian cry 'populate or perish' a new resonance. Under Labor, with Arthur **Calwell** as minister for immigration, the goal became an annual population increase of two per cent—half from natural increase, the rest from migration. Because of the acute shipping shortage, the £10 assisted passage scheme for Britons bore fruit too slowly, so Australia agreed to take Displaced Persons from Europe's refugee camps, under a two-year tied labour scheme. Assistance was soon extended throughout Northern Europe and, as the economy boomed from the mid-1950s, to the Mediterranean and the Middle East. British immigration continued strong, but Australia was being Europeanised by default. All major parties agreed that high and continuing immigration was essential to the health of the economy. But as Jean Martin showed in *The Migrant Presence* (1978), the social impact of immigration, and the needs of migrants, especially of those who did not speak English, were recognised only gradually.

Australia fought another Asian war in **Vietnam** 1965–70 to frustrate communism and to cement the American alliance. The conflicts in Indo-China produced a refugee crisis in South-East Asia; in the 1970s Australia accepted considerable numbers of Vietnamese and other refugees from the region. The arrival of these **boat people** effectively buried White Australia as a policy and social reality. However, boat people from the Middle East in the 1990s were not so well received. Intense debates over immigration policy and intake in 1984–85 and 1997–98 tested community and political nerve and resolve, but the bipartisan commitment to a non-discriminatory immigration program survived.

Informed and rational debate now concerns the scale of immigration, and the optimum population Australia can sustain. Australia's population doubled 1947–81 from 7.6 million to 15 million, as expected under the two per cent goal, but this goal was abandoned in the 1970s. By 1996 the population was 18.3 million, and projections for 2031 suggested a population of 20.5 million without immigration, and 25 million with immigration at 70 000 per annum. Concerns for environmental **conservation** will ensure a continuing debate.

Historical studies of Australian immigration long reflected entrenched snobberies—the superiority of the free over the bond, of the unassisted over the assisted, of the pioneer (before self-government and before the gold rush) over the goldfields adventurer, of the English over the Irish, of the Anglo-Celt over the European, of North European ('Nordics') over Southern and Eastern European, and of Britain and European over those from Asia and the Pacific Islands. Increasingly, however, historians came to challenge these stereotypes. Social mobility, intermarriage, and ideals of natural justice and Australian fair play in time discredited national and racial pecking orders and prejudices. Racial suspicion and fashionable sympathies, however, still subtly inform some studies.

The literature on Australian immigration is large. James Jupp (ed.), *The Australian People* (1988), is the essential reference work. For an indication of the range of sources and a bibliography, see John Lack and Jacqueline Templeton, *Sources of Australian Immigration History 1901–1945* (1988), and *Bold Experiment: A Documentary History of Australian Immigration Since 1945* (1995). Geoffrey Sherington, *Australia's Immigrants 1788–1988* (2nd edn, 1990), Janis Wilton and Richard Bosworth, *Old Worlds and New Australia* (1984), and James Jupp, *Immigration* (1991), offer useful overviews. References on specific sub-groups are cited in the relevant entries.

JOHN LACK

Immigration Reform Group was formed in the late 1950s by liberal humanitarians, mainly in Melbourne, to press for reform of the **White Australia** policy. Prominent members included Kenneth Rivett, Jamie Mackie, and Anthony Clunies-Ross. In its manifesto, *Immigration: Control or Colour Bar?* (1960), the group presented humanitarian, economic, and political arguments for the introduction of immigration quotas, including quotas from Asian countries. Although its plan for quotas was not followed, the group's views were influential in the decision of Prime Minister Harold **Holt** in 1966 to formally abandon the White Australia policy. Nancy Viviani has edited a study of its influence (1992).

GD

Imperial conferences were meetings of the British government and the Dominions of the Empire, which included Australia, Canada, and NZ. They dealt with issues of **trade**, **defence**, and **foreign policy**. The first imperial conference (so called by the Dominions, though the British styled it a colonial conference) took place in 1887, when representatives of the Dominions, including Alfred **Deakin**, were in London for the Queen's Jubilee. At the second London conference, held 10 years later in 1897, on the occasion of the Diamond Jubilee, delegates agreed that meetings should be held more regularly. Subsequent conferences were held in 1902, 1907, and 1911. Imperial conferences were also called for special reasons, such as those in 1909 on defence and in 1916 on the conduct of World War I.

A discussion of constitutional arrangements at the 1926 conference led to the **Statute of Westminster**, which formalised the autonomous status of the Dominions. With the use of the term **Commonwealth of Nations** after World War II, imperial conferences became known as Commonwealth conferences (and later as Commonwealth Heads of Government Meetings, or more popularly as CHOGM), which after 1969 were held biennially. The number of participating countries increased significantly in the period after World War II, when all Britain's former colonies were represented. (See also **British–Australian relations**.)

HD

Imperial history refers directly to the history of the British Empire, especially as it affected Australia, and more generally to the imposition of European political, economic, and cultural forms on the rest of the world. In the first sense it figures in Australian historiography both as a topic in its own right and an immanent presence. It shaped the writing of colonial history and informed the emergent national consciousness. Contested by the radical nationalists from the late nineteenth century, and affirmed by the interwar historical profession, this form of imperial history fell into neglect after World War II as Australia and its historians moved towards greater national autonomy. In the second sense, which is informed by theories of **post-colonialism**, a revived awareness of imperialism's discursive effect is applied to a critical reading of colonial and national history.

Early colonial exercises in imperial history include W.C. **Wentworth**, *Statistical, Historical and Political Description of the Colony of New South Wales* (1819); John Dunmore **Lang**, *A Historical and Statistical Account of New South Wales* (1834); and James **Macarthur**, *New South Wales: Its Present State and Future Prospects* (1837). All three wrote histories to influence imperial policy and published their works in London to persuade the imperial authorities of their version of the lessons of the past. John **West's** *History of Tasmania* (1852) is at once the culmination of this form of historical literature and its point of transition, for its extended demonstration of the evils of convict transportation was published locally and aimed at a colonial audience.

With the abandonment of the convict system and the granting of self-government to all the colonies except WA in the 1850s, it was no longer necessary to address such arguments to the imperial centre. The dominant theme of the historical literature produced in the second half of the nineteenth century was the triumph of local initiative. Such colonial historiography remained imperial in its assumptions, marking the successful application of British values and energies to new circumstances, albeit with room for local innovations. The Scottish merchant William Westgarth celebrated *Half a Century of Australasian Progress* (1889), just as the NSW statistician and later agent-general in London, T.A. **Coghlan**, recorded *The Progress of Australasia in the Nineteenth Century* (1903).

This era of growth ended during the 1890s in economic depression, industrial conflict, and political reconstruction that called the imperial relationship into question. Two of its principal defenders were G.W. **Rusden**, a public servant, whose three-volume *History of Australia* (1883) was an extended critique of all departures from imperial verities; and, in similar tone, the banker H.G. **Turner** wrote a *History of the Colony of Victoria* (1904) in two volumes to lament the colonists' failure to make good their British heritage.

In opposition to this conservative imperial history there was a new temper of **radical nationalism**, associated especially with the creative writers who contributed to the popular weekly *Bulletin*. Republican and stridently anti-imperial, the radical nationalists celebrated a lineage of martyred convict rebels, egalitarian gold-diggers, bush selectors, and rural workers. The past they evoked in poems and fiction was not so much history as counter-history. Against the official record of the governors and the plutocracy, they asserted a popular memory of resistance to authority, endurance, and **mateship**.

The **nationalism** that prevailed in **Federation** and the early Commonwealth was imperial in orientation. It affirmed its colonial origins in the establishment of state **historical societies**, publication of *Historical Records of Australia*, commemoration of **exploration**, and the joining of imperial to national history in school texts. A.W. **Jose** followed *The Growth of Empire* (1897) with a short *History of Australasia* (1899); W.H. **Fitchett** complemented his hortatory *Deeds That Won the Empire* (1898) with *The Romance of Australian History* (1913). In the widely used *Short History of Australia* (1916), Ernest **Scott** sought to show his young Australia readers that 'British history is their history, with its failings to be guarded against and its glories to be emulated'.

In the universities imperial nationalism took on new momentum between the wars, with the new emphasis on history as a research-based discipline. The study of Australian history developed as an integral part of British and European imperial history. Members of the fledgling profession typically studied in England after a first Australian degree, and many were active in such imperial organisations as the Round Table and the Royal Institute for International Affairs. W.K. **Hancock's** *Australia* (1930), a mordant analysis of what **'Independent Australian Britons'** had made of their patrimony, and the Australian volume of *The Cambridge History of the British Empire* (1933), edited by Scott, mark the apogee of this era of imperial nationalism.

Its rapid decline after World War II demonstrated the overreach of imperial capacity. The forced self-reliance of Australia both during and after the war and Britain's preoccupation with post-imperial problems frayed the old ties. A new nationalism, no longer coterminous with imperialism, was served by rapid expansion of Australian historical studies in the expanded university system. There was a proliferation of postgraduate research and publication on Australian topics, filling in the details of an increasingly autochthonous national history and channelling into increasingly specialised fields. This unbroken expansion of the profession, which lasted up to the 1970s, was by no means restricted to Australian specialists: British as well as continental European, American, and Asian history all flourished. It was the older imperial dimension that dwindled.

Not all Australian historians abandoned imperial interests. J.M. **Ward** and A.G.L. **Shaw** wrote extensively on nineteenth-century imperial policy in Australia and the Pacific. Peter Burrough, *Britain and Australia 1831–1855* (1967), and J.J. Eddy, *Britain and the Australian Colonies*

1818–1831 (1969), also contributed important studies to a field that had its epicentre in the *Journal of Imperial* (later *Commonwealth and Imperial*) *History* in London. Scholars such as Michael **Roe**, in *The Quest for Authority in Eastern Australia* (1965), and K.S. **Inglis**, in *The Australian Colonists* (1974), were acutely sensitive to the interplay of what was brought and what was made. Other scholars of Australian foreign relations and defence history continued to explore the imperial–colonial relationship. The era of colonial nationalism was served by Gavin **Souter's** wide-ranging study of exchanges between *Lion and Kangaroo* (1976) in the early Commonwealth period, and Chris Cunneen in *King's Men* (1983) suggested how the early **governor-generals** had mediated the exchanges. Distinguished biographies traced the careers of statesmen—Alfred **Deakin**, W.M. **Hughes**, Robert **Menzies**, R.G. **Casey**—who mediated the transition from Empire to Commonwealth. Even so, the strength of national boundaries was unmistakable: for most historians of Australia, the Empire was of interest insofar as it bore on the evolution of the colonies towards independent nationhood, and no further. J.D.B. Miller, who extended Hancock's *Survey of Commonwealth Affairs* (1974), was exceptional in his combination of Australian and wider interests.

The shift of perspective is apparent in the work of Manning **Clark**, the most influential of the postwar national historians. The early volumes of his *History of Australia* (1962–87) told a familiar story in terms of epic tragedy, a history in which the principal actors were animated by European religious and secular faiths. By the final volumes Australia had ceased to be a marginal outpost of European civilisation; its story was now a story of discovery as the newcomers threw off their encumbering derivative culture in order to grasp the wisdom of what was distinctively Australian.

The new nationalist historiography has had to accommodate demands that it recognise the cultural identities of those written out of earlier histories. **Post-colonialism** poses a sharp challenge to a settler society because it repositions the colonists as colonisers, complicit in the imperial project of domination. Thus the British settlement of Australia is now construed as an **invasion**, and much recent writing on **Aboriginal history** seeks to listen to the voices of the invaded people. The public commemoration in 1988 of the Bicentenary of British occupation negotiated these sensitivities by turning Australian history into a journey in which all participated and by which all can live together. Much contemporary discussion of the republic, through its linkages to Aboriginal reconciliation, multiculturalism, diversity, and inclusiveness, seeks to accommodate the post-colonial challenge by exorcising the imperial past.

In its more popular usage, the republic signifies a final break with the fetters of the past, a sweeping away of the last symbols and habits of deference in order to attach loyalties more securely to the new national order. The Empire here is a powerful signifier, but conspicuously vague and imprecise, for appreciation of its history has long since fallen into neglect. If the shift from colonial nationalism to independent nationalism was accompanied by an imperial amnesia, the advent of post-colonial nationalism seems to have resulted in a double displacement of the imperial past that is only now reviving, as the reconstituted nation bends back to settle accounts with its origins.

STUART MACINTYRE

Imperial preference, see **Tariff**

'Independent Australian Britons' was a term used by Keith **Hancock** in *Australia* (1930) and much copied since to describe the complexity of Australians' attitudes to their own country and to Britain. He judged that Australians believed each word in this identification to be 'essential and exact, but laid most stress upon the last'. The term had an earlier currency. Alfred **Deakin** had used it in 1900 in a letter on Australian affairs to the London *Morning Post*. The *Daily Telegraph* in Sydney had used it in its centennial supplement, 26 January 1888.

JH

Indian–Australian relations re-emerged as a major economic and strategic concern during the 1980s and 1990s, when Australia became more involved in the Asian region. This development harkened backed to the early years of white settlement in Australia, when the southern colonies were an integral part of Asian commerce. According to Geoffrey **Blainey**, *The Tyranny of Distance* (1966), the great distance between Australia and England meant that Australia became an economic satellite of India in the late eighteenth century, with Bengal providing it with much-needed supplies of food, livestock, spirits, and other necessities. The return cargoes to Calcutta included Australian coal, timber, and **horses**. Indian rice entered the Australian diet at this stage. The early **trade** was fostered by private merchants until the 1820s when new arrangements favoured trade between England and Australia. Imports from India were gradually squeezed out, but Australian exports of horses emerged as a new link in the 1830s—the Australian towns of Lucknow (NSW and Victoria) were named after the Indian destination. By the 1890s some 3000 horses were annually shipped to India. Despite this, growing tariff protection after 1825, the English trade monopoly, and high freight costs provided serious impediments to Australia–India commerce.

While Australia–India trade floundered, Indian immigrants started to arrive in significant numbers. Many of these were retired East India Company employees. In the 1830s there was a plan to resettle Anglo-Indians at Australind in WA; in 1867, the Tasmanians amended their Immigration Act (1855) to allow Anglo-Indian settlers to acquire land. One of the best-known Anglo-Indians was Edward **Braddon**, who had helped put down the Santal tribe rebellion in Bengal and became the premier of Tasmania from 1894 to 1899. Another important category of migrants was the indentured labourers like Madhoo, who arrived from Calcutta in 1837 and became one of the first coolies to officially complain about working conditions. Labour shortages in the Australian colonies did not, however, prevent the emergence of a heated debate about Indian labour. Opponents denounced the slavery of the indenture system. Towards the end of the nineteenth century, **trade unions** added their opposition to Indian migration, and the inflow stopped with the **White Australia** policy.

A third group of Indian immigrants in Australia who date their origins from the years before the Immigration Restriction Act of 1901 were free settlers of Indian community origins, mainly Sikhs and Muslims, whose descendants live in NSW and Qld. In 1968, the Sikhs of Woolgoolga, NSW, opened the first Sikh temple in Australia—a tribute to their prosperity as banana farmers and evidence of the more stable family life which resulted from the migration of Indian women. During most of the twentieth century, the settlers were mainly men who commuted to India to see their wives and families. Until recently, only grown sons were brought to Australia to help with the farming. The status of these migrants was special—particularly after World War I, when Britain recognised the contribution which Indians had made to the war effort. During the 1920s federal legislation was amended to allow Indian residents to vote and receive pensions. State laws, however, remained discriminatory.

Since World War II and the gradual abandonment of the White Australia policy, Indian immigration to Australia has diverged sharply from past patterns: typically the new Indian arrival is well educated, literate in English, from an urban-professional background, and prefers to live in Sydney, Melbourne, or Perth. During the mid-1990s the Indians formed the third-largest migrant group, and contributed to Australian urban culture by bringing with them spice and video shops and Hindi movies, and operating hundreds of Indian restaurants.

Despite the waves of Indian migration, trade and political links during the twentieth century suffered from neglect until the 1990s. During the 1930s, Australians began to woo the markets of Asia by placing Trade Commissioners in Japan, China, and Indonesia, but not in India. The *Report of the Trade Delegation to India* (1935–36) failed to appreciate the momentous changes taking place on the subcontinent. After World War II the stagnation of Indian agriculture provided opportunities for exports, but these were stunted because of India's dependence on American food aid. When India achieved food self-sufficiency in the early 1970s, what remained of Australia's prosperous wheat shipments to India collapsed. With the re-emergence of coal and diamond exports in the 1980s, commercial relations between Australia and India resumed their much earlier importance. India's rapid industrial growth during the 1980s was assisted by the export of Australian technology, expertise, and capital—especially in mining and public utilities. Renewed commerce was fostered by the abolition of protectionist regimes, economic reform, and 'Look East' foreign policies in both countries. However, the benefits of these changes have not yet allowed India to redress its large trade deficit with Australia, although imports of automotive components, cars, and trucks are growing.

The Australia–India relationship was energised by new political will during the 1990s, with numerous trade missions between the two countries, joint naval exercises, the formation of the Australia India Council and its counterpart the India Australia Council, and renewed academic interest expressed by the Indian Ocean Centre at Curtin University of Technology, WA, and the National Centre for South Asian Studies, Melbourne. Not since the 1940s, when Australia attended a conference in New Delhi to discuss Indonesian independence, has the relationship between India and Australia been so warm. The admiration that Prime Minister Nehru and H.V. **Evatt** had for each other did not, however, translate onto a wider canvas and the period 1950–84 saw the India–Australia relationship drift into the orbit of superpower politics. The new political will reflects underlying, mutual economic interests which are of increasing importance to both India and Australia who see their future as being bound up with the Asia–Pacific.

MARIKA VICZIANY

Indonesian–Australian relations have been centrally important to Australian foreign policy since 1945. Prior to the Japanese occupation of South-East Asia in late 1941 and early 1942 and Australia's involvement in the Pacific War, Australia paid little attention to what was then a Dutch colony, the Netherlands East Indies. There was a small amount of trade in the 1920s and 1930s but, despite the efforts of a small band of trade enthusiasts in Australia, economic relations were of marginal concern to either country. Surabaya and Batavia were best known to Australians as colonial ports on the long voyage home to Britain. From the mid-1920s Dutch colonial tourist authorities began to look to Australia as a source of visitors. Brochures prepared by them, and by Australian shipping lines such as Burns Philp, stressed the exotic East on Australia's doorstep and the wonders of the temple monuments in central Java. The Netherlands East Indies was in vogue as a tourist destination for adventurous Australians in the 1930s, with Bali portrayed as a paradise found.

The Pacific War changed forever Australians' indifference towards Indonesia. The 'impregnable' British fortress in Singapore proved imaginary, as did the strength of Dutch territorial bases in Java. The European colonial presence in South-East Asia, which had provided Australians with a sense of security against a populous and largely unknown Asia, was destroyed by Japan. The Australian government began for the first time to think strategically about what post-colonial South-East Asia might look like.

Defeated by the Japanese, in 1942 the Netherlands East Indies government retreated to Brisbane, from where it planned reoccupation of its colony. One of its last acts was to bring a boat-load of political prisoners from exile in what is now Irian Jaya. The Australian government was led to believe they were criminals. Once their political status was revealed, the prisoners were released. Committed Indonesian nationalists, they worked for the Allied war effort in Brisbane, Sydney, and Melbourne, kept close contact with each other, and monitored radio messages from their homeland. On 17 August 1945 they heard a radio message from Jakarta announcing the establishment of the Republic of Indonesia. They quickly established an Indonesia support committee which lobbied the Australian government, campaigned for public support, and persuaded the trade union movement, led by the Waterside Workers Federation, to place bans on Dutch shipping, thereby frustrating Dutch efforts to reoccupy Indonesia from Australian ports.

Australia was seen by Indonesia as its strongest supporter in the four-year struggle against Dutch attempts to recolonise. The events of these four years have entered official textbooks and the popular imagination in Indonesia. Fifty years later, public figures in Indonesia still refer warmly to Australia's support of the infant republic between 1945 and 1949. It is an important legacy which has helped the two countries survive difficult times in their relationship.

The myth of Australian–Indonesian relations in the five years after 1945 is that Australia unequivocally supported the Indonesians. Certainly, there was considerable support at government as well as non-government levels, but the Australian government, while sympathetic to independent Indonesia, was at the same time uneasy about the removal of the European presence from South-East Asia. Margaret George, in *Australia and the Indonesian Revolution* (1980), convincingly argued that, far from being totally supportive of Indonesia, Australian policies were in basic accord with those of Britain and the USA and that its support was qualified.

In the 1950s and the first half of the 1960s the conservative Liberal–Country Party government in Australia struggled to understand Indonesia. There was no warmth in the political relationship, and little economic activity or cultural exchange to provide ballast to it. Nevertheless, the **Colombo Plan**, established in 1950 to provide aid to newly independent countries of Asia and Africa, brought many young Indonesians to Australia for a university education. Most returned home with a lifelong affection for Australia. In 1953 a Volunteer Graduate Scheme was established in Melbourne to send young Australian graduates to work in Indonesia for two years. Dozens of young Australians participated, many of whom on their return home became active in deepening Australian–Indonesian relations.

Reflecting Australia's growing strategic interests in Indonesia, in 1956 the Australian government funded departments of Indonesian at the universities of Melbourne and Sydney, and the Australian National University. Jamie Mackie, first at the University of Melbourne and then at Monash, Herb Feith and John Legge at Monash, and a group of ANU economists led by Heinz Arndt were key players in the development of Indonesian studies.

Postwar images of Indonesia in Australia have been predominantly negative. Through to the 1980s successive Australian governments have been concerned about Indonesia primarily for defence and strategic reasons. Australian politicians and the Australian media failed to understand an Indonesia led by Sukarno (1950–65), consistently seeing it as a threat to Australia's security because of either communist subversion or military expansionism. Negative images became stronger as Indonesia moved to recover West New Guinea from the Dutch—finally achieved in 1962—and as Sukarno led his country to confrontation with Malaysia in 1963. There was relief in Australia at the failure of the attempted coup in September 1965 and the subsequent destruction of the Indonesian Communist Party by a new military-backed government. Indonesia, nevertheless, remained high on the list of perceived threats to Australia. Opinion polls in the 1980s and 1990s consistently revealed that Australians saw Indonesia as a major threat.

The post-1965 'New Order' Indonesia government of President Suharto has been an authoritarian military-dominated government. Its suppression of internal dissent and its scant regard for Western notions of liberal democracy have been frequently criticised by non-government organisations and individuals in Australia. Its intervention in Portuguese Timor in 1974, its military invasion in December 1975, and its forced incorporation of East Timor seriously soured relations. A broad and articulate spectrum of Australian society strongly opposed the invasion and has continued to be critical of Indonesian policies in East Timor. The Indonesian government was openly irritated at Australian reporting of Timor and the criticism of Indonesia within the Labor Party as well among the broader Australian society. Its irritation with the Australian media was compounded by the Indonesian-language broadcasts of Radio Australia, which often reported stories censored in Indonesian press, radio, and television. In 1980 visas of Australian correspondents in Indonesia were not renewed, and for more than a decade there were no Australian journalists based in Indonesia.

Despite negative public opinion in the 1950s and 1960s, Australian foreign ministers, in particular Percy **Spender** and R.G. **Casey**, and Australian diplomats were successful in building on the goodwill in Indonesia towards Australia. Even during Indonesia's Confrontation with Malaysia, between 1963 and 1965, when Australian troops faced Indonesian troops in Borneo, Australia managed to sustain workable, if not close, political and military relations.

The Labor government of 1983–96 more closely oriented Australia to the Asia region, and increasingly saw strengthened relations with Indonesia as crucial to its interests in South-East Asia. It established the Australia–Indonesia Institute in 1986 with a charter to strengthen links. Indonesia also began to place greater value on its relations with Australia. Ministerial visits between the two countries became commonplace, and Prime Minister **Keating** made visits to Jakarta a priority. The efforts of both countries to create better mutual understanding culminated at the end of 1995 in the Indonesia–Australia Treaty, the first defence cooperation treaty ever entered into by Indonesia and of considerable symbolic importance in recognising Australia's involvement in the region.

In 1978 a senior Indonesian official likened Australia to the appendix of South-East Asia—its function was not properly understood, it was only taken notice of when it hurt, and nobody would miss it if it was removed. The view would be different in the late 1990s. Economic relations have strengthened considerably, through two-way trade and growing Australian investment in Indonesia; there is a large and growing tourism, again in both directions; and there are extensive cultural exchanges. By 1993 Indonesia was Australia's tenth-largest export market and most of Australia's major mining companies had established joint ventures in Indonesia. Australia has become much more engaged in the Asia region and there is a much stronger mutual understanding between Australia and Indonesia at the government-to-government level. Nevertheless, Prime Minister Paul **Keating's** remark in 1994 that 'no country is more important to Australia than Indonesia' illustrates the asymmetrical relationship between Australia and Indonesia. Indonesia remains far more important to Australia than Australia to Indonesia.

There is an extensive literature on Australia–Indonesia relations. Margaret George, *Australia and the Indonesian Revolution* (1980), and J.A.C. Mackie, *Konfrontasi* (1974), are classic works. Rupert Lockwood, *Black Armada* (1975), is a fascinating account of the Indonesian political prisoners in Australia during World War II and waterside workers' actions to delay Dutch ships leaving Australian ports in 1945 and 1946. Two interesting books providing Indonesian views of the relationship are Ratih Harjono, *The White Tribe of Asia* (1993), and Richard Chauvel (ed.), *Australia di Mata Indonesia* (1989), the latter being a collection of Indonesian press articles on Australia written between 1973 and 1988. The successive five-year volumes of *Australia in World Affairs*, published by the Australian Institute of International Affairs, include authoritative chapters on Australia–Indonesia relations.

JOHN INGLESON

Industrial relations between employers and employees have exercised an important influence on the **economy** and living standards, and have been the site of significant Australian innovation.

As in other capitalist societies, such relations assume the existence of a labour market in which sellers of labour are free to bargain with the buyer. Strictly, therefore, convicts engaged in public works or assigned to masters were outside the framework of industrial relations, though Alan Atkinson showed in *LH* (1979) that they did engage in forms of collective bargaining. On the other hand, Australia was comparatively free of laws that forbade employees from forming associations to negotiate over pay and conditions. The colonial Masters and Servants Acts did impose penalties for a wide range of offences, including refusal to work, and were frequently used against the most vulnerable (such as domestic servants); but where the demand for labour was strong, they were a less effective sanction. Adrienne Merritt's doctoral thesis, 'The Development and Application of Masters and Servants Legislation in NSW 1845–1930 (Australian National University, 1981) is the fullest treatment of this neglected subject. The piecemeal introduction of laws concerning hours of work, safety issues, and regulating the employment of women and children also shaped the framework of industrial relations.

During the nineteenth century industrial relations were conducted by a process of individual or collective bargaining conducted by **trade unions** or informal associations of workers, usually with individual employers. Formal agreements were uncommon and usually restricted to skilled trades. Elsewhere, the union presented the employer with the set of conditions, and withdrew labour if they were not accepted. By these means the unions sought to establish and maintain rates of pay and working rules, with some success in times of prosperity, much less during economic downturns. By the end of the century **employers' organisations** had been formed, and in casual occupations the capacity of the unions to conduct successful bargaining was dependent on their ability to control the labour supply. Hence the issues of the closed shop and freedom of contract lay at the heart of the **maritime** and **shearers' strikes** of the 1890s.

The **strikes and lockouts** of the 1890s brought direct state regulation of industrial relations, chiefly through compulsory **arbitration** and **wages boards**. Henceforth disputes over pay and working conditions were resolved by these arbitration courts, which had power to order a settlement. While strikes and lockouts were strictly prohibited, they continued as part of the bargaining system that accompanied arbitration. Thus unions and employers would negotiate over terms that would then be ratified in an official award, or the union would seek over-award rates and conditions through industrial action, or the employers would assert control over the workforce with dismissals. The capacity of the arbitration courts to maintain their jurisdiction was frequently tested by both sides, as well as by governments that frequently amended their powers, overrode their decisions, or created special tribunals.

Industrial relations became a specialised component of company management from early in the twentieth century. The search for greater efficiency in the workplace led to the introduction of experts to reorganise the work process and train the workforce. Australian companies introduced their own welfare schemes to reduce turnover and promote loyalty. Scientific management techniques were first adopted in large enterprises, but spread after World War II. The study of industrial relations and training of its personnel in universities accentuated the trend.

The hybrid national system of industrial relations came under challenge from the 1980s as the broader economic regulatory arrangements that sustained it were eroded. The H.R. **Nicholls** Society condemned what it called the 'industrial relations club' and called for labour-market reform that would replace industrial awards with enterprise agreements, collective bargaining with individual contracts.

The Howard government legislated accordingly, and in doing so transferred much of industrial relations out of the arbitration system and into the courts. The changed landscape saw a significant increase in the prerogatives of employers; the loss of accrued entitlements when companies were liquidated symbolised the vulnerability of employees.

The government overreached itself in 1998 when it encouraged a stevedoring company to replace union members with a new workforce trained overseas in secrecy. The ensuing contest was played out on the wharves, through the media, and in the Federal Court; the union members retained their jobs. Since then the government has been unable to secure passage through the Senate of further changes to industrial relations. The study of industrial relations has generated an extensive historical literature, of which the *Journal of Industrial Relations* provides a good coverage. (See also **Labourism**.)

STUART MACINTYRE

Industrial Workers of the World was formed at a gathering in Chicago in 1905 of socialists and industrial militants dissatisfied with existing trade unions, who sought a new organisation free of occupational and national divisions. It practised revolutionary industrial unionism and rejected attempts to reform capitalism through political action. The origins of the term used to describe its adherents, 'the Wobblies', are not known. Critics suggested the initials IWW stood for 'I Won't Work'; in fact they were indefatigable in their agitation, defiant in their refrain, 'Hallelujah, I'm a Bum'.

The IWW developed a significant presence in Australia on the eve of World War I among working-class activists impatient with the limits of industrial **arbitration** and the moderation of the **Australian Labor Party**. Wobblies were distinguished by their iconoclasm and reckless effrontery. They refused patriotism and condemned the **White Australia** policy. Their outspoken opposition to the war provided federal and state governments, mostly Labor ones, with the excuse to suppress them. Twelve leaders were framed in 1916 on a charge of seditious conspiracy as a result of their campaign of direct action against the war effort. Their objective of **One Big Union** remained influential for some years, but the Industrial Workers of the World never recovered its earlier following. The best account is Verity Burgmann, *Revolutionary Industrial Unionism* (1995).

SM

Inglis, Kenneth Stanley (1929–) is a versatile and penetrating historian of Australian public culture and national character. From early studies in medical and religious history—his Oxford doctoral thesis was published as *Churches and the Working Classes in Victorian England* (1963)—Ken Inglis turned in the early 1960s to his favourite theme, the impact of war on Australia's character and tradition. In 'The Anzac Tradition' (*Meanjin*, 1965), he called for a critical yet respectful re-examination of the writings and influence of Charles **Bean** and other makers of the **Anzac Legend**. *The Australian Colonists* (1974) traced the nineteenth-century antecedents of the legend. 'The more I learned and thought about it, the more its ceremonies, monuments, and rhetoric seemed to me to constitute in some respects a civic religion', he wrote, anticipating the approach of later ethno-historians and displaying the subtle

appreciation of how Australians speak and act that became the hallmark of his writing. In 1966 he became foundation professor of history and later vice-chancellor of the University of Papua–New Guinea, returning to Australia as a research professor at the Australian National University in 1977. He led *The Australians* (1988), a multi-volume collaborative 'slice' history of Australia which he conceived as the historical profession's Bicentennial gift to the nation. *This Is the ABC* (1983), a **commissioned history** of the national broadcaster, and *Nation* (1989) reflect Inglis's strong interest in the history of the media. *Sacred Places*, his monumental study of Anzac and its impression on national memory, appeared in 1998.

GD

Institute of Public Affairs was founded in 1943 in Melbourne by C.D. Kemp, who directed it until 1975, and wrote most of its major publication, the *IPA Review*. The 1944 document *Looking Forward*, with 50 000 copies printed, was particularly influential, playing a large role in shaping the economic and social views of R.G. **Menzies**, then formulating the philosophy for the fledgling **Liberal Party**. Kemp opposed the central planning in fashion at the time, countering with a **liberalism** that emphasised the free individual and an ethic of private enterprise, but within the context of a strong sense of social responsibility, and especially that of the business and political elites.

The IPA was revitalised in the period 1982–89 by a new director, C.D. Kemp's younger son, Rod. Raising funds from large corporations, he expanded the staff and opened interstate offices. The *Review* was upgraded in 1985 and under the editorship of Ken Baker it moved into cultural areas, articulating a mainly **conservative** analysis of education, politics, foreign policy, the law, and the writing of Australian history. It advocated an increasingly radical *laissez-faire* view of the economy, hostile to any government intervention in the market. The IPA played a key role in the growth of what came to be called 'economic rationalism' or 'neo-liberalism' and its influence over both major federal political parties; it did so much to the dismay of C.D. Kemp himself, whose views were more in the mixed-economy Keynesian mould. In the years 1991–96, under the directorship of John Hyde, the IPA became so single-minded and extreme in its economic **libertarianism** that it steadily lost both influence and financial support.

JOHN CARROLL

Inter-colonial relations had become so well developed by 1900 that **Federation** was often described as giving constitutional sanction to a union already achieved. The colonies had developed largely independent of each other and on achieving self-government had taken no interest in Britain's suggestion that they should form a political association of some sort for common purposes. Each colony faced the sea, so that the import and export of goods went through its own ports. The capital cities were the trade centres of their territories, with only Brisbane and Hobart having internal rivals. Sydney held economic sway over a large area, but the boundaries of NSW were such that its northern, western, and southern fringes were closer to other capitals. Sydney's battle to extend its influence into the Riverina soured relations with Victoria, which originally had most of the region's business.

The economic integration of the colonies began as Victorian capitalists from the 1860s invested in pastoral industry in NSW and Qld. The collapse of Qld's financial institutions in the 1860s meant that the expansion of its pastoral and sugar industries was largely financed from Melbourne, Sydney, and Adelaide. By the 1880s the financial institutions of these centres were firmly interconnected, symbolised by the merging of the two leading pastoral companies, **Goldsbrough** (Melbourne) and **Mort** (Sydney).

Before 1880 most mining had been undertaken within 300 kilometres of Sydney, Melbourne, and Adelaide, and had been financed locally. The new finds in the 1880s and 1890s were more remote—in north Qld, far western NSW, the west coast of Tasmania, and on the edge of the desert in WA. These ventures were financed from London and by Melbourne and Adelaide capital. The trade in Broken Hill mining shares in 1887–88 was the first national speculation frenzy.

By the closing decades of the century there was something approaching a national labour market. A slump or slowdown in one colony would result in migration to another. Tasmania constantly lost people to the mainland and gained some in its mining boom. Thousands migrated from other colonies into Marvellous Melbourne in the 1880s and then flowed out again to WA in the 1890s **depression.** In 1901, 10 per cent of the native-born population were resident in a colony other than that of their birth. Another indication of this movement has been developed by F.J. Mines in 'The Integration of the Australasian Colonies' (MA thesis, University of Queensland, 1968). He records for each colony the year when Britain ceased to be the chief destination of money orders and was replaced by another Australian colony. Money orders were the means by which migrants sent money to relatives they had left behind. The results are: Qld 1871, NSW 1879, SA 1879, Tasmania 1882, Victoria 1884, WA 1887.

In the 1880s national associations and conferences of trade, professional, and church bodies became standard: the Chambers of Manufactures (1887), Chambers of Commerce (1888), Association for the Advancement of Science (1888). The first inter-colonial conference of trade unions was held in 1879 and the emergence of national unions of shearers and maritime unions in the 1880s was answered by similar organisations of their employers. The 1890 **Maritime Strike** was the first to involve more than one colony.

Inter-colonial **shipping**, tied up by this strike, was a large business, with firms in Sydney, Melbourne, and Adelaide operating a national network. Ships carried the bulk of goods and people between colonies. The **railways**, joined in the 1880s except for WA, carried mail and wealthy passengers. Inter-colonial trade had become substantial by the 1880s. NSW coal, Tasmanian potatoes and fruit, Queensland sugar, and South Australian wheat found markets in other colonies. Sydney was a re-export centre for overseas imports.

Inter-colonial trade was hampered by border **tariffs**. After refusing to take British advice about union in the 1850s, the colonies quickly adopted different tariff regimes. Inter-colonial conferences of governments, which began at the same time, attempted to arrive at a common tariff or agreements of a more limited sort. There was some success. In the 1850s and 1860s SA collected duties on goods imported via the **Murray River** into NSW and Victoria, and distributed the proceeds to the governments of those colonies, which meanwhile worked assiduously to divert the river traffic overland to and from their own capitals. Until 1873 Victoria paid a lump sum to NSW to allow goods to flow into the Riverina without paying customs. The agreement broke down; customs collection resumed and continued until Federation. Efforts to settle a common tariff were fruitless and were not attempted after 1881.

On other subjects, inter-colonial conferences were very productive. Nearly all the matters given to the federal parliament by the Commonwealth **Constitution** were discussed and acted upon by these conferences, which is how they were established as of national concern. By this means the colonies organised an overseas mail service, created a national **post** and telegraph network, agreed on uniform legislation to control **Chinese** immigration, established **time** zones, and lobbied the British government on **foreign relations**. The **Federal Council**, agreed on in 1883, was so weak that it diverted little business from the *ad hoc* conferences. The success of conferences in so many spheres made the need for Federation less pressing. Only the tariff problem required a different method for its resolution.

JOHN HIRST

International relations, see Foreign relations

Internet resources are becoming a useful adjunct to the established methods of Australian history-making. During the early 1990s, historians began to recognise the benefits of online library catalogues, file transfer protocols, and electronic mail. Since the mid-1990s, the software refinements that created the World Wide Web accelerated the use of networked computer resources by historians. Heady claims have been made about the Web's potential to bring vast electronic resources to our finger tips, to transform classroom learning, and to enrich the community's curiosity in its past. In actuality, the Web has to date delivered only limited auxiliary services to history professionals and consumers in Australia. However, there are indications that it can be a valuable tool for the rigorous interpretation of Australia's past.

Historians' greatest use of the Web is as a user-friendly means of access to the distance-compressing online library catalogues that became available during the 1970s. All major Australian research libraries have useful Web home pages (easily located using the search engines on Web browsers, and through the electronic signposts described below). Archive authorities, both federal and state, have also developed Web access to their collection guides and catalogues. In the main these library and archive websites streamline, rather than radically redefine, historical research work.

The Web's 'virtual' links enable users to switch speedily between multiple information sources at spatially diverse locations. The results can be confusing. Library Web servers have responded by offering a helpful 'pointer' function to the broad and expanding range of historical collections throughout Australia (see the National Library of Australia's 'Electronic Australiana' <http://www.nla.gov.au/>, which includes the useful 'Australian History on the Internet' <http://www.nla.gov.au/oz/histsite.html>). These electronic signposts are supplemented by the Web home pages of Australian universities (a comprehensive guide to which is maintained by the Australian Vice Chancellors' Committee <http://www.avcc.edu.au/australias_unis/individual_unis/index.htm>. Australian Studies centres provide other pathways to Australian history resources (for example, the Australian Studies Centre at the University of Queensland <http://www.uq.edu.au/~enrnile/>, and Monash University's National Centre for Australian Studies, <http://www.arts.monash.edu.au/ncas/index.html>).

Taken together, this network of websites is an effective research aid for professional, amateur, and student historians. It is a useful preparation for a visit to a library or archive. Notwithstanding efforts to go one step further and create Web-accessible 'virtual' libraries, which would enable users to read actual source materials online rather than electronic catalogues to those collections, there is still nothing approaching a virtual library of Australian history.

Digitised copies of library, archive, and museum research collections are nonetheless becoming available on the Web. The State Library of NSW, for example, offers the Matthew Flinders electronic archive project <http://www.slnsw.gov.au/flinders/> and the Sir Joseph Banks Electronic Archive <http://www.slnsw.gov.au/Banks/>. Its Picman index <http://www.slnsw.gov.au/picman/welcome.htm> provides online access to the pioneering Holtermann photographic collection, taken in Hill End during the early 1870s gold rush. 'Images1', on the National Library of Australia's website <http://www.nla.gov.au/images1/> contains a searchable database of over 20 000 paintings, drawings, rare prints, objects, and photographs. Still more impressive is the State Library of Victoria's Multimedia Catalogue <http://www.slv.vic.gov.au/slv/mmcatalogue/> a Web-searchable database of some 160 000 photographs, postcards, paintings, drawings, prints and posters from the oldest visual historical collection in Australia.

Is there value in attempting to expand the Web from its basic service functions? Can it become an additional, and readily accessible, means of making and communicating Australian history? Does it significantly supplement what historians do already? These questions arose most clearly in 2001 with the spate of Web resources that commemorate Australian Federation (for an introduction, see the NLA's 'Federation Gateway', <http://www.nla.gov.au/guides/federation/>). Do these Web products justify the heavy financial outlays that were necessary to create them? Do they promote an informed awareness of the past? For example, the Australasian Legal Information Institute (a collaborative venture between the Law Faculties of UTS and UNSW) maintains an electronic 'Reconciliation and Social Justice Library', which enables Web users to access key sources such as *Bringing them Home: The Report of the National Inquiry into the Separation of Aboriginal and Torres Strait Islander Children from their Families* (April 1997) <http://www. austlii.edu.au/au/special/rsjproject/rsjlibrary/hreoc/stolen/>.

Answers to these questions are starting to emerge in the sphere of cultural tourism. State heritage agencies (for example, <http://www.heritage.nsw.gov.au/index.html>; <http://www.heritage.vic.gov.au>) now deliver useful guidelines and examples for evaluating and appreciating the significance of historic places and artefacts. The History Trust of South Australia's website <http://www.history.sa.gov.au/index.htm> is especially encouraging, with its 'SA Icons Database'—still in an early stage of development—which pursues the 'dream of … building virtual galleries around important themes in South Australia's history, incorporating collections from large and small institutions in the city and the country'. The National Trust of Australia's website <http://www.austnattrust.com.au/> enables users to search the Victorian state register of historic places online.

These hopeful trends are most evident in Australian museums. Many museum home pages function only as static promotional billboards for exhibitions and programs. The new National Museum of Australia <http://www.nma.gov.au> offers teasers that beckon us to experience the real thing. The Western Australian Maritime Museum <http://www.mm.wa.gov.au/> is more innovative, presenting 'virtual galleries' on the *Batavia* shipwreck exhibition and Dutch exploration, which provide meaningful historical interpretations without requiring viewers to visit the museum hub in Fremantle. Museum Victoria's 'Little Lonsdale Street' <http://www.mov.vic.gov.au/littlelons/index-intro.html> provides an introduction to archaeological and historical research on one of Melbourne's notorious slum neighbourhoods, which supplements artefact displays in the museum's new Australia Gallery.

The Queensland Museum also uses the Web to present recent scholarship, and in so doing extends its virtual coverage to history subjects that are not contained within its physical exhibition spaces. Thus the Museum offers a 'virtual visit' to the 1791 wreck of the frigate *Pandora* <http://www.Qmuseum.qld.gov.au/>, which maritime archaeologists have been excavating since 1983. Likewise the Public Record Office of Victoria presents 'cyber-tours' of Victorian history. For example, 'Our Nation's First Capital: Federation and the City of Melbourne, 1901–27' <http://www.prov.vic.gov.au/exhib.htm>, combines text, objects, audio, and film in order to showcase its collections and apply them to well-researched history tours of the city.

The effectiveness of all such Web initiatives, however, is vitiated by two factors: the volatility of information channels (servers may be removed, their addresses—Uniform Resource Locators or URLs—often change, and their contents may not be adequately maintained and updated) and uncertainty about how to cite Web sources in precise and enduring ways (see 'Citing Sources from the Internet' <http://www.arts.unimelb.edu.au/Dept/History/resources/citation.html>).

These drawbacks are offset by the expanded interactivity in history-making that the Web permits. Increasingly, the design of web-accessible research collections is being used to encourage the interrogation of raw data. The National Centre of Excellence at the Western Australian Maritime Museum is developing the Australian National Historic Shipwreck Database Search Facility and an experimental artefact database of Western Australian shipwreck sites <http://www.mm.wa.gov.au/Museum/toc/dbtoc.html>, and the Australian Heritage Commission <http://www.environment.gov.au/heritage> maintains a Web-searchable database of the Register of the National Estate. Electronic history forums such as H-Anzau <http://h-net2.msu.edu/~anzau> encourage debate and information-sharing, and extend the boundaries of participation; their Web-searchable archives constitute a substantial and accumulating historical resource. Peer-reviewed electronic academic journals (see the *Electronic Journal of Australian and New Zealand History* <http://www.jcu.edu.au/aff/history> and the *Australian Humanities Review* <http://www.lib.latrobe.edu.au/AHR/>) formalise this process, and are being imitated by established print journals (see especially the *Journal of Australian Studies* <http://www.api-network.com/jas/main.htm>, but also *Australian Historical Studies* <http://www.ahs.unimelb.edu.au>). Several Web-based research projects (for example 'Australia Street' <http://www.australiast.uts.edu.au/> and the 'Carlton Time Tunnel' <http://www.unimelb.edu.au/infoserv/lee/htm/home.htm>) encourage Web users to contribute ideas, family histories, and historical materials to the sites.

ALAN MAYNE

Internment of **alien**, naturalised, and Australian-born residents was defended by governments during the two world wars as a necessary security precaution. More than 4000 were detained during **World War I**, and 7000 in **World War II**. Although some may have been hostile to the Allied cause, few posed any real threat to national security. More than half those interned during World War I were recent immigrants unable to find or hold jobs in the economic recession brought on by the disruption of commodity exports. The internment camps provided the only means of sustenance available to them; hundreds are listed as voluntary internees or 'surrendered destitute'. Although governments strove to limit the extent of internment in order to contain costs, they were sometimes defeated by the strength of public hostility towards 'enemy subjects'. Partly generated by anti-enemy propaganda and

wartime anxiety, this hostility rose or fell in response to news of military failures or successes. But some of it was also a carry-over from prewar antipathy to non-British—mainly southern European—immigrants. It is no coincidence that the greatest concentrations of internees—Slavs from the WA goldfields in the first war and Italians from the north Qld sugar towns in the second—came from districts where there was already a history of racial friction.

RICHARD MORTON

Invasion is a concept with an unusual place in Australian historiography. Whereas historians now routinely characterise the British colonisation of Australia as an 'invasion', as recently as the 1970s they habitually spoke of **'settlement'**. Behind these words lies a significant reinterpretation. The critical difference is the sense of an intentional, forcible appropriation of territory, involving **Aboriginal resistance** and conflict, in distinction to the peaceful disposition of dispersed colonial rule. The new phrase implies the active involvement in Australian history of the continent's indigenous inhabitants, and a great challenge therefore to the pioneering heroics elaborated in older celebratory national and imperial histories. The idea of invasion therefore embodies an apparently recent apprehension of the national past, notwithstanding the word's currency in much earlier work, such as Keith **Hancock's** *Australia* (1930). This apprehension has far-reaching consequences: some are now apparent in political and legal arguments concerning **Aboriginal land rights**, which have drawn extensively on recent historical scholarship to document what Justices Deane and Gaudron described in the **Mabo case** as a 'conflagration of oppression and conflict'. In a historiographical context, the emphasis on Aboriginal agency has been critical to establishing a **post-colonial** conception of Australian history.

The current historiography of invasion can be traced most immediately to the work of C.D. **Rowley** and a number of talented historians in the 1970s and early 1980s, including Richard Broome, Raymond Evans, Noel Loos, Lyndall Ryan, and Henry **Reynolds**. In *Exclusion, Exploitation and Extermination* (1975), Evans wrote that the frontier was 'best envisaged as a condition of severe and usually protracted struggle, where contending parties behaved towards each other in a manner analogous to the confrontation adopted in a situation of war'. These writers' concerns were theoretically and politically diverse, although all were influenced by the methods and aspirations of the humanist social history of the 1960s, and by the rapid emergence in the 1960s of a new Aboriginal movement for land rights. No less innovative, but drawing on a different methodology with different implications, was *Our Original Aggression* (1983), by the economic historian Noel **Butlin**; it argued that the indigenous population prior to colonisation had been much larger than hitherto understood.

Among all this work, Henry Reynolds's research, first published in *The Other Side of the Frontier* (1981), is still the best-known historical mapping of frontier conflicts. Reynolds attacked the paltry treatment of Aborigines in the established literature, especially Stephen **Roberts's** extended prewar studies of land settlement. Using official records, oral tradition, and anthropological, archaeological, and linguistic research, Reynolds was able to emphasise several things: the persistence and resourcefulness of Aborigines; the cultural context of Aboriginal reactions to invasion in indigenous conceptions of exchange; and the sustained violence of the colonial encounter. These themes were extended in his later books, including *Frontier* (1987) and *Fate of a Free People* (1995).

The work of Reynolds and others was well timed: it found a growing audience as Australian history publishing flourished in the 1980s, driven by an expanding academic base, sharpened political interest, and a succession of official and unofficial publications occasioned by national and state anniversaries. Survey texts such as Richard Broome's *Aboriginal Australians* (1982) were regularly reprinted, and the new general histories, culminating in the **Bicentennial History Project**, included substantial treatment of frontier relations. Despite this academic success, the notion of invasion is still politically alive. The use of the term in **school history** was resisted in Qld and criticised elsewhere. 'Invasion Day' has become a common name for 26 January since the 1988 Bicentenary. In this context it may be an element in the **black-armband** view of Australian history which alarms conservative cultural critics.

The success of 'invasion history' has had other consequences. Recent work has moved away from an emphasis on the fact of invasion: that European settlers sought to take over a continent occupied by others is now a given rather than the focus of analysis itself. While 'contact history' was once presented as an emerging subject in itself, there is now more interest in what happened both before and after contact. Reynolds has turned his attention to European laws and attitudes relating to indigenous territories, especially the doctrines of native title and *terra nullius*. The academic field of **Aboriginal history** is more concerned with the complex and sometimes densely documented processes of Aboriginal administration, transformation, and survival. Work on the mounted **native police**, notably Marie Fels, *Good Men and True* (1988), suggested the limitations of the invasion and resistance narratives. Ann McGrath's *Born in the Cattle* (1987) was influential in drawing attention to the ways Aboriginal people were involved with putatively white rural industries. The shift is signalled most clearly in the title of Heather Goodall's study of Aboriginal politics in NSW, *Invasion to Embassy* (1996).

So if invasion history as it was in the 1970s has not ceased, it has changed into something else. Its academic and political limits may have been reached fairly early. It may also have had more in common with the old histories of settlement it replaced than was first apparent. The emphasis on the 'frontier'—whichever side it was viewed from, however violent instead of peaceful it was found to have been—made it possible to reintroduce into the new history some of the problems created by the assumptions of the old. In fact

representations of **Aboriginal resistance**, although not typical, were by no means rare in the celebrations of pioneering which dominated Australian historical culture before World War II. For that older history, the frontier was a special historical hot zone where, in the act of occupation, the nation was forged and the character of the culture determined. As long as it was content to emphasise the violence of the frontier, invasion history risked a similar etiology; one not necessarily consistent with the need to document and understand the course of indigenous experience after white colonisation. While the historiography of invasion has been critical to the litigation of native title, the legal imperatives of land claims have long depended on substantiating much more than dispossession: continuities of identity and belonging are critical to the indigenous histories produced through those processes.

JULIAN THOMAS

Invention and improvisation were called for in countless ways in the settling of a new land. Early **Aborigines**, after arriving from the Indonesian archipelago, must have made endless experiments, some of them possibly fatal. They slowly learned which plants could serve as foods or medicines and which timbers, fibres, and rocks could make effective weapons and implements. They made a chain of discoveries big and small about the habits and seasonal cycles of fauna they hunted. No research journals, no Nobel Prizes, were there to record these discoveries.

Many of the discoveries made by the British and other Europeans in Australia after 1788 followed the same pattern. A strange continent, sometimes unique, it was not easily understood, tamed, or utilised. Thus, in the era of sailing ships the discovery of the prevailing winds was essential. A major discovery came from Captain John **Hunter**, who set out in the *Sirius* in 1788 from the hunger-threatened settlement of Sydney to buy food in Cape Town and decided correctly that the quickest way was the longest way—east across the Pacific and past Cape Horn. The discovery of the power of the westerly winds was used by nearly all sailing ships linking Australia and Europe. The glamorous round-the-world yacht races of the 1990s rest on that discovery.

Likewise, the exploration of the continent was a form of invention and relied, like major advances in other fields, on the cumulative work of numerous people. The paintings of the **Heidelberg School** were also an invention, giving Australians eyes with which to see a new earth and sky.

The infant **economy** could grow only on the basis of novel solutions: the breeding of the merino and Illawarra shorthorn and sheep-dog, new strains of **wheat** and the vital subterranean clover, the Granny Smith apple and the Australorp fowl, and the slow realisation that Australia was the world's largest museum of soil deficiencies for which phosphate, zinc, and cobalt would be vital fertilisers. Unusual facets of **climate**, vegetation, and labour led to clever mechanical inventions, including the **stripper, stump-jump plough**, mallee roller, **McKay's** combine harvester, and the Trewhella-jack. Australia could only become really productive in terrain, soil, and vegetation as unique and perplexing as the mallee and the black soil plains, after it had forged its own slow agricultural revolution. This revolution, not yet over, depended as much on forgotten farmers' willingness to test and adapt new ideas as on those conceiving the ideas.

Mining, like **agriculture** and **pastoralism**, was prolific in inventions because local geology and economics threw up unique obstacles and opportunities. Australia was rich in mineral resources but ingenuity was needed to find some important fields. Thus the finding of deep gold reefs at Bendigo—its boldest mines were 1.5 kilometres deep in 1901, among the deepest in the world—came from the theorising and experiments of many individuals and investors. In the 1960s and 1970s, skilled hypothesising by geologists was vital for such finds as Kambalda nickel, Bass Strait **oil**, the iron ore at Mount Tom Price, **uranium** and copper at Olympic Dam, and Argyle diamonds.

Australia posed metallurgical riddles, and the ingenious answers—even more than in farming—were copied by mining fields abroad. Broken Hill's flotation process, developed by many experimenters including mill-hands in the period 1900–14, used a myriad of rising bubbles to separate fine-grained minerals, especially zinc. One of the four or five major innovations in the history of world metallurgy, it can be seen operating on a huge scale from the heart of Siberia to the deserts of South America. In mines, as on farms, the inventiveness came from facing unique obstacles, an inheritance of Britain's interest in technology, and a willingness to dirty one's hands or risk losing face. Even today Australian graduates in, say, China or Java cause surprise because they are willing themselves to jump into a grease pit.

There is also an international stream of innovation, in which Australia took a lesser part. This stream was dominated by the populous, educated industrial countries whose quick pace of change and new needs provided the spurs. Some Australians, before they migrated or returned to England, found a notable place in this stream: men such as Louis Brennan, a Melbourne inventor of an ingenious naval torpedo, and F.M. Alexander from north-west Tasmania who had unusual influence on techniques of breathing. Some local inventors never emigrated, achieving much while far from the mental and financial stimulus of the Old World.

They include A.G.M. Michell, inventor of the thrust bearing which made possible the huge ship; William **Sutherland**, who devised 'Sutherland's constant' in physics; Lawrence **Hargrave** and his aeronautical experiments; and the lonely versatile Ballarat inventor, Henry Sutton. Before World War I inventors within the mainstream suffered by living in Australia, especially as most were without links to the young Australian universities; those innovators who were primarily responding to unique problems in primary industries gained by living here.

In these fields with worldwide applications, Australia has succeeded most in biological research in the last 60 years. Dr Neil H. Fairley's research on malaria, so vital to troops in the New Guinea and Burma campaigns, and the **CSIRO's**

campaign against the rabbit are two practical examples. Significantly, two Nobel Prizes, by **Burnet** and **Eccles**, were won in medicine in the 1960s; and the big institutes of medical research such as Walter and Eliza Hall, Baker, and Florey have world standing.

The unfamiliar conditions that spurred inventions in new regions and industries were also a spur to innovation in organising economic life. While Australians do not see themselves as star organisers, they found distinctive organising solutions to a procession of dilemmas. NSW found a genius-like solution, the punitive gold licence, to the crisis forced upon the economy by the new **gold rush** in the autumn of 1851: unfortunately the temporary solution lasted too long and helped deliver bloodshed at **Eureka** three years later. One can also give high praise to such corporate innovations as the celebrated non-forfeiture clause in life policies devised by the baby National Mutual Life in Victoria in 1869; the birth of the no-liability mining company in Victoria in November 1871; the setting up of the statutory corporation to administer the Victorian **railways** in the 1880s; W.G. **Spence's** techniques for forming in the 1880s the huge shearers' union in terrain which at first sight seemed inimical to organising; John **Quick's** ingenious formula for federating a nation; and the birth of the Flying Doctor, aided by the devising of the Traeger pedal wireless. The list could be much longer, but it would be unbalanced if it excluded the organising follies, disasters or even inertness; among these, a high ranking might go to the failure to set up one self-governing colony in the four-tenths of the continent within the tropics, and the helplessness of bankers and politicians facing their supreme crisis in the 1890s **depression**.

The word *inventor* is applied mainly to one who transforms the material world. But inventiveness can busy itself in many ways. Just as industrial America was for long the pointer to the world's economic future, so Australia was once a pointer to coming political institutions. The first inventive phase was the setting up of political **democracies**, especially in SA, Victoria, and NSW in the 1850s, with their secret ballot, short-term parliaments, and a vote for every man. It may be objected that these were British ideas, but in politics the applying of novel ideas is usually more difficult than the conceiving of them, and is just as original. Certain Australian colonies and NZ again formed a distinctive **social laboratory** in the 1890s with votes for women, compulsory **arbitration**, the selective old-age pension, the minimum wage in certain industries, and the brief appearance in Qld of the world's first Labor government. A land with one government is less likely to provide political innovations than a land where many governments can innovate.

Since the 1850s, Australia has stood, by the standards of the time, among the more innovative and improvising lands in the world. Probably the inventiveness was busier in the period 1850 to 1920 than in the following 70 years: the pioneer period offered more opportunities, more spurs. For long it was almost a dogma that this innovative spirit was creditworthy on nearly every front, and a cause for national pride, but now the opinion is far from unanimous, for technology is less in favour and its side effects are observed with concern.

Inventions and the invention record are discussed in Robert Ingpen, *Australian Inventions and Innovations* (1982), and J.P. Wild (ed.), *From Stump-Jump Plough to Interscan* (1977). On particular industries see Geoffrey Blainey, *The Rush That Never Ended: A History of Australian Mining* (1963), and Gerald Walsh, *Pioneering Days: People and Innovations in Australia's Rural Past* (1993)

GEOFFREY BLAINEY

Irish in Australia were 'a founding people' in its colonisation. This has become a standard proposition in Australian historiography. Though they were at all times only a small part of total emigration from Ireland, Irish immigrants were a higher proportion of the Australian population than in any other Irish migrant destination. Compared with the home populations, the Irish in Australia were over-represented among both the convict and assisted immigrants of the nineteenth century, and this was a recurrent cause of anxiety in the rest of the colonial community. The Irish possessed a strength of numbers, influence, and confidence beyond their fellow Irish in North America and elsewhere. They were well represented at most levels of Australian life, but in the highest reaches the Protestant Irish possibly fared better than the **Catholics**.

About 50 000 of Australia's transported **convicts** were Irish, many of them convicted outside Ireland. They included a high proportion of women, and a leavening of political and social rebels (more than 10 per cent on the most generous definition), but most were common offenders. Non-convict Irish emigration to Australia began in the 1830s through the agency of a succession of assistance schemes. The passage to Australia was generally too expensive for the poorest and most desperate of Irish emigrants, who normally went to Britain or North America. Australia's assisted Irish immigrants were overwhelmingly rural people who came especially from the modernising parts of the economy, where rural change from tillage to pasture threatened status and prospects. They included high proportions of Catholics and extraordinarily high rates of female migration, which served to correct the sex-imbalance of the colonial populations. The heaviest inflows came after the Great Famine of the second half of the 1840s and were dominated by people from south midland counties such as Clare, Limerick, and Tipperary, and from the Ulster borders, notably Cavan, Fermanagh, and Tyrone. The Irish utilised Australian immigration schemes more effectively than other groups, and this helped to reinforce particular chains of connection, and supplied the two categories of immigrant most in demand in Australia, namely agricultural labourers and domestic servants. The Irish immigrants were more literate and skilled and probably healthier than those who remained in Ireland, but were under the general average for Australian assisted immigrants as a whole.

Though the Irish were under-represented among the unassisted majority of colonial immigrants, they included a wide selection from all Irish society. In addition to the well-known recruits from Irish workhouses and country girls seeking employment and husbands, there were minor gentry, land agents, physicians, academics, lawyers, doctors, surveyors, and ministers of the churches. Though less literate and skilled than contemporaneous immigrants, the Irish moved upwards into many spheres of colonial society, especially in the public service, the professions, and the police forces. Chris McConville offers an explanation of this success in *Croppies, Celts and Catholics* (1987).

By contrast with other immigrant societies, the Irish in Australia experienced little sense of segregation, and there were few geographical or occupational concentrations of any significance. They were under-represented in the gold and other mining regions, and were diffused widely in rural areas. The same dispersion occurred within Australian cities, where most Australian Irish lived by 1891. Their record of remittances back to Ireland was up to North American standards and their return migration rates were low. There were times when the Irish figured disproportionately in colonial society as offenders, paupers, and lunatics, and they were somewhat under-represented in colonial parliaments. The Irish in Australia did not occupy ghettoes, and Irishwomen were particularly likely to marry non-Irish husbands.

Anti-Irish feeling was often whipped up in colonial Australia, frequently in conjunction with religious **sectarianism**, but it lacked sufficient virulence to reach much beyond verbal abuse. The historical record is essentially peaceable, and inter-communal friction was barely evident. There was no simmering sense of deprivation among the Irish in Australian society, and this is said to have bred a relative indifference to Irish affairs even during the Home Rule controversies. Nevertheless, visiting Irish MPs in the 1880s and 1890s attracted great attention and Irish Australians contributed more generously to the Home Rule cause than other Irish abroad. The Irish Catholic vote, reinforced by the reaction to the Easter Rising in April 1916, was probably decisive in the defeat of the **conscription** referendum. In November 1920 Hugh Mahon became the first member to be expelled from the federal parliament. His inflammatory public remarks against British policy in Ireland caused W.M. **Hughes** to castigate him as disloyal. Most Irish Australians accepted the compromise Treaty of 1921, and thereafter interest in Irish affairs dwindled.

Irish-born Australians reached their maximum number at 228 000 in 1891. Their number was down to 44 813 by 1947 in a much bigger host population, reflecting the decline of Irish migration in the twentieth century. After Independence, people from the Republic born later than 1949 were not eligible for assistance. Irish emigrants in this period were more skilled than their predecessors, often holding tertiary qualifications. They were more mobile, earned higher incomes, and endured lower unemployment levels, than the rest of Australians. Earlier, in colonial society, the Irish had Hibernicised the Catholic Church, and helped to sustain an alternative educational system that left indelible marks on Australian life and culture. The flood of non-Irish

Catholics into Australia after 1947, and the Australianisation of the clergy, both helped to weaken those correlations.

Yet Irish Australians sustained a self-conscious identity better than most other groups. Reinforcement was provided by the strong Irish association with the Catholic Church, especially by its educational wing. Historians of Irish Australia also contributed to cultural continuity, though the earliest historical work was usually filiopietistic, and dominated by political and religious biography, to the neglect of the mass of immigrants; it especially ignored the Ulster Irish. This has been repaired by some of the most sophisticated work in modern Australian social history. The Irish as convicts were examined by Bob Reece and George Rudé, and thoroughly quantified by a team of economic and social historians led by Stephen Nicholas and Peter Shergold. David Fitzpatrick clarified the statistics on the assisted immigrants of the nineteenth century, while his *Oceans of Consolation* (1994) vividly evoked the mentalities of the Irish in Australia. Richard Reid, in James Jupp (ed.), *The Australian People* (1988), has penetrated the dense interconnections which joined particular communities in Tipperary and Clare with parts of NSW. Oliver MacDonagh's pioneer work on the Irish in Victoria developed ways of tracking the Irish over censuses by their religious affiliations. The strong association with Catholicism allows religion to serve as a tracer among the otherwise anonymous masses of colonial immigrants, and gives the Irish in Australia an archival advantage over the rest of the colonial population. Patrick **O'Farrell** has explored the Irish psyche in search of the essence of Irishness, discovering among *The Irish in Australia* (1986) special collective traits and spiritual torments in the act of expatriation. He suggests that the immigrant was critically burdened by a Gaelic culture, which had been dislocated from its homeland and stranded in an alien environment. Comparative work has been promoted by the Canadian historian Donald Akenson, providing an astringent critique of some of the clichés of Irish immigrant historiography.

A recurring and unsettled question in Australian historiography concerns the relationship between the Catholic Irish and their descendants, and the Anglo-Australian Protestant establishment. At one extreme it is claimed that the Irish were systematically disadvantaged, and excluded from the central sources of power and influence before World War II. But it is also asserted that the Irish exerted a 'galvanic' influence on Australian life and character. They were prone to undermine established hierarchies and authority, being innately 'predisposed to challenge and dissent', and thus emerged as the main carriers of a radical temper in Australian politics. Certainly those of Irish descent and Catholics had a strong identification in the Labor movement, and were clearly over-represented in the upper ranks of the Labor Party apparatus, especially in the mid-century. They were correspondingly much less prominent in the rival Liberal side of political life, even though the Liberal alliance frequently attracted a substantial Catholic vote.

One feature of the persistence of Irish identity on Australia has been the willingness of people from very mixed parentage to adopt their partial Irish origins as their essential identity. Thus, for instance, Arthur **Calwell**, at best half-Irish, was exceedingly conscious of anti-Irish and anti-Catholic currents in his own life. As minister in charge of **immigration** immediately after World War II, he was animated in part by an ingrained Anglophobia. Part of his political mission was to render Australia less English. Similarly, Archbishop **Mannix** promoted the notion of Irish Catholic solidarity and welcomed confrontation. A powerful Irish strain in Australian literature has been most prominent in the ballad tradition, the persistence of censorship, the distinctive use of the English language, and a certain nationalistic tendency. Writers such as Vincent Buckley (*Cutting Green Hay*, 1983) searched among Irish roots for poetic inspiration and a historical sense of identity.

The literature and institutions of the Irish in Australia are stronger than those of the **Scots** or other groups from the British Isles, and this is well reflected in the strength of historical work devoted to the Irish in Australia. Its main weakness is a lack of comparative criteria. Insufficient empirical research is undertaken to measure the experience of the Irish against other immigrant communities in Australia and beyond. This leads to exaggerated claims about their success and failure in the colonial milieu. The idea that Irish achievement in Australia was based on their numbers in the population is undermined by the fact that they also fared relatively well even where they constituted a small minority, as in SA. The prominence of Catholics in the population of late-twentieth-century Canberra suggests not only substantial cultural assimilation, but also a strong presence in the upper reaches of occupation, income, and influence in modern Australian society.

ERIC RICHARDS

Iron and steel form a cornerstone of Australian industry. The industry—which produces pig-iron from iron ore, converts it into steel, and rolls it into various shapes—employed 26 000 people in 1995 and produced 7.9 million tonnes of raw steel. Historically, the iron and steel industry has been Australia's most successful manufacturer, being virtually the only one to operate at international levels of competitiveness since the late 1930s. This competitiveness has enabled the industry to be Australia's only long-term exporter of manufactured goods. The Australian iron and steel industry consists of a single main steel manufacturer, **BHP**, which operates three integrated steelworks in Australia—at Newcastle, Whyalla, and Port Kembla (plus another in NZ)—and a number of finishing mills (without steel-making facilities). Besides these works, Smorgon Steel and the Commonwealth Steel Company operate mini-mills which recycle scrap steel.

A number of unsuccessful attempts were made during the nineteenth century, most importantly at Mittagong (1848–66) and Lithgow (1872–82) in NSW, to establish iron smelting works in Australia. After Federation, an additional attempt to manufacture iron and steel was made at Lithgow after 1906, but this works, which survived until 1931, was poorly located relative to raw materials and markets, lacked the finance necessary for further expansion, and operated on too small a scale to be competitive; this meant that it was dependent upon government assistance in the form of tariffs, subsidies, and rail freight concessions. Helen Hughes provides a comprehensive account in *The Australian Iron and Steel Industry 1848–1962* (1964).

The operation of a soundly based, modern and integrated steel industry dates from the opening of BHP's Newcastle steelworks in 1915. Founded in 1885, BHP operated successfully as a **mining** company before being drawn to steel manufacture by its acquisition of the rich Iron Knob and Iron Monarch ore reserves in SA in 1899, and the fear that its mine at Broken Hill would eventually be exhausted. Assisted by the cessation of imports during World War I and **tariff** protection during the 1920s, BHP expanded its output to 374 000 tons of steel in 1929. During the 1920s it pursued a policy of establishing domestic demand for the output of its steel furnaces by creating subsidiary industries and encouraging other firms to set up plants for the manufacture of metal products. Steel demand in Australia slumped during the **Depression** but recovered strongly after 1932. This recovery came largely at the expense of imports, with increased tariffs, depreciation of the Australian currency, and reduction in raw material and labour costs greatly increasing the industry's competitiveness. BHP increased its production to 1 117 000 tons of ingot steel in 1939, having in 1935 taken over the Port Kembla steelworks which had been established in 1928 by the Australian Iron and Steel Limited. This company had originally operated the Lithgow works, but succumbed to financial pressures during the Depression. By 1939 BHP was producing steel priced among the lowest in the world which enabled it to export to NZ and markets in South-East Asia.

During the period 1939 to 1970, annual Australian steel production increased from just over one million tonnes to nine million tonnes. Since the end of World War II the Australian industry has been fairly competitive internationally and, unlike most of Australian manufacturing, did not depend on tariff protection in the 1950s and 1960s. Australian steel capacity lagged behind domestic requirements until 1957, but gradually new plant was opened that enabled BHP not only to satisfy local requirements but also to export.

During the 1970s, however, the Australian market for steel stagnated, and BHP committed itself to retaining in production plant that had been constructed in the 1950s. Stagnant domestic demand meant BHP had to export more steel in order to utilise its plant fully. As countries overseas (especially Japan) began building large-scale plant that used more advanced production techniques, and raw material and labour costs rose in Australia, BHP found that it had begun to lose its competitive edge in international markets. Finally, the recession of 1982–83 caused a crisis in the Australian industry. It has since restructured itself, although both capacity and employment levels have been scaled down. While government assistance under the Steel Industry Plan from

1984 to 1988 helped to encourage this process, the industry was also assisted by a strong depreciation of the Australian currency, and the closing of smaller and older plant. BHP was able to increase its export sales during the second half of the 1980s and early 1990s, but, more importantly, has moved away from the simple export of raw steel to the export of hot and cold rolled coils, zinc, lead, and paint-coated sheets. The closure of the Newcastle smelters has resulted.

MALCOLM ABBOTT

Irrigation was first practised by early settlers who channelled river water through their adjacent farms, orchards, and market gardens. More elaborate schemes involving whole districts were proposed from the mid-nineteenth century, mainly in Victoria, NSW, and SA, and introduced as private enterprises or trusts by the 1870s and 1880s. Generally, however, these floundered under exorbitant costs. Increased government control brought greater success. Schemes developed by the **Chaffey** brothers in the late 1880s for fruit-growing along the **Murray River** at Mildura, Victoria, and at Renmark, SA, were enthusiastically supported by Alfred **Deakin**, then Victorian minister for water supply. Advocates like Deakin, who toured both the USA and India to inspect their irrigation schemes, saw the exploitation of **water resources** as providing greater security for rural settlers. An extreme view held it wasteful, even sinful, not to harness and redirect river water for more productive and 'useful' purposes. The development of the Murray River area for closer settlement through irrigation is the subject of Ernestine **Hill's** *Water into Gold* (1937).

Irrigation schemes more often succeeded in areas already served by existing towns and railways. The irrigation and closer settlement schemes of the 1880s flourished together when developed concurrently, as in Victoria's Goulburn Valley, where the higher yields that resulted from intensive agriculture justified the initial costs of constructing irrigation channels. In NSW the Murrumbidgee Irrigation Area was established in 1906. After World War II new irrigation systems were made possible by the **Snowy Mountains Hydro-Electric Scheme** and the **Ord River Scheme** in WA. The extensive canal system in parts of Australia radically altered the appearance of the landscape, and by forcing down fruit prices, irrigation also changed Australian diets. Recent research has found that irrigation schemes have had a detrimental long-term effect on the ecologies of major river systems, especially the Murray–Darling, by contributing to increased salinity, blue-green algae, and river-bed erosion. (See also **Land settlement**.)

HD

Isaacs, Isaac Alfred (1855–1948) served as Australia's first native-born governor-general from 1931 to 1936. His early youth was spent in north-eastern Victoria, where he subsequently taught before he joined the Crown Law Office, Melbourne, in 1876, and began part-time legal studies at the University of Melbourne. He graduated in 1880, went to the Bar in 1882, and developed a very successful practice. Prior to Federation, which he strongly supported, Isaacs served as member for Bogong in the Victorian Legislative Assembly and became attorney-general. He demonstrated a mastery of constitutional law at the Federal Convention of 1897–98, but his didactic style created antagonism and he was excluded from the drafting committee. After Federation, he served in the House of Representatives as the protectionist member for Indi, and was attorney-general in the **Deakin** government 1905–06. He left parliament to take a seat at the **High Court**, where he advocated the expansion of Commonwealth powers, as in the **Engineers' case**. In 1924 Isaacs became a member of the judicial committee of the Privy Council and in 1930, chief justice of Australia. Late that year he was nominated as governor-general by Prime Minister **Scullin**, in spite of opposition from King George V. One of his successors in the position, Zelman Cowen, wrote a biography, *Isaac Isaacs* (1962). With John **Monash** and Sidney **Myer**, he demonstrated the capacity of Jewish immigrants of non-British origins and modest means to achieve national success.

KT

Islam is the religion that was preached in Arabia by Muhammad in the early seventh century AD. The revelations he received are in the Qur'an which, supplemented by his own sayings and actions, are the foundational texts of Islam. After Muhammad's death, Islam spread rapidly in the Middle East and Asia in the seventh, eighth, and ninth centuries. Today, Islam is professed by one-fifth of the world's population and is concentrated in Asia and Africa. There are Muslim minorities in Europe, America, and Australia.

The first contact between Islam and the Australian continent was probably through the Muslim fishermen of Macassar. By the end of eighteenth century, **Macassans** were sailing to northern Australia from the South Celebes for several months each year, mainly in search of trepang, a delicacy of Chinese cuisine. There was contact with several Aboriginal groups in the area. However, Macassan involvement waned by the late nineteenth century with the decline in their trade, due to customs duties imposed by the SA government which then administered the NT. The next Muslims to come into contact with Australia were the Malay pearl divers, but their numbers were significantly restricted by immigration policy early in the twentieth century.

The Macassans and Malays were temporary settlers. Probably the first Muslims to settle permanently were the camel drivers who arrived between 1867 and 1910 from what is now Pakistan and Afghanistan. It was Thomas **Elder**, a sheep grazier of Scottish descent, who saw the potential of camels for carrying goods on a commercial basis, particularly in the centre of Australia. Elder managed to bring in 124 camels and 34 Afghan drivers in 1866. They were placed on his sheep station at Beltana in the Flinders Ranges. With their camel teams they transported goods to camps, stations, and mines, becoming, by the 1880s, the main mode of commercial transport in outback Australia. Afghan camel

teams were also used in desert exploration. Many small settlements developed near isolated ports and freight depots, and came to include small prayer places (mosques), where Muslims performed the essential rites. The first city mosque was built in Adelaide around 1890, with the second in Perth in 1905.

With the emergence during the 1920s of mechanised long-distance transport, the camel transport industry declined and the Afghans had to find other means of livelihood. Because the Naturalisation Act denied citizenship to many non-Europeans, some left Australia and returned home. Those remaining lived under difficult conditions. By 1921, there were some 3000 Muslims in Australia. Another wave of Muslim immigrants came from Albania in the 1920s and 1930s, and Turks, Lebanese, and Egyptians followed. From 1911 to 1957, the growth-rate of the Muslim population in Australia was very slow, but from the 1950s it rose more rapidly as immigrants arrived with a wide range of linguistic, national, and ethnic origins. According to the 1991 Census, Muslim residents in Australia nominated more than 67 different countries of birth, making them one of the most ethnically diverse religious groups in Australia. Most Muslims in Australia speak Arabic, followed by Turkish, English only, Indonesian or Malay, and Urdu. The population increase has been rapid: according to the Census, the numbers rose from 22 311 in 1971 to 147 507 in 1991. This steady rise is mainly due to **immigration**, reinforced by high marriage and fertility rates. By far the greatest number of Muslims live in Melbourne and Sydney; only a very small percentage live outside the major cities.

The Islamic community in Australia has experienced its most rapid growth in the last quarter of the twentieth century. In the immediate post-World War II period, immigrants practised Islam mainly at home. There were hardly any mosques, Islamic centres, or schools to support the religious community. This became a serious problem in the 1950s, when the pressure to assimilate to the Australian way of life was greater. In the 1960s attempts were made to establish Sunday schools, mosques, Islamic societies and associations, but significant progress in establishing large Islamic educational and social institutions dates from the 1970s. Federal governments were lobbied to gain their financial support for Islamic schools and for action against religious intolerance towards Muslims. Today, there are numerous Islamic organisations devoted to a wide range of community concerns: from youth camps to women's refuges; from the Islamic media to the teaching of Arabic in schools; from women's associations to Islamic centres. In 1995, there were 65 mosques. In short, a strong institutional framework to support the development of Islam in Australia is being built, giving Muslims a better chance of survival as a distinct and important religious group within the Australian community.

Historical writing on Islam in Australia is in its infancy. Mary Jones (ed.), *An Australian Pilgrimage* (1993), and Wafia Omar and Kirsty Allen, *The Muslims in Australia* (1996), are useful introductions. Gary Bouma, *Mosques and Muslim Settlement in Australia* (1994), is an instructive case-study.

ABDULLAH SAEED

Italians in Australia arrived in considerable numbers in the 1850s gold rushes. They travelled the outback to prospect for gold or to toil in mines or in remote bush camps, as timber-fellers or sleeper-cutters, as navvies in dam and railroad construction gangs, or as cane-cutters in north Qld. Often sojourners, they worked hard and lived roughly for a few years, to return home to small farms viable only with money earned abroad. Some made repeated migrations; others settled, in the face of ostracism and prejudice, in a range of rural occupations, especially in small-scale agriculture. In his classic *The Italian Emigration of our Times* (1924), R.F. Foerster, impressed by the sheer scale and intrepidity of their transoceanic odysseys, dubbed Italians 'proletarian globetrotters'.

In the cities, plaster figure makers of Lucca, street musicians from Viggiano and Sicilian icecream makers, Venetian restaurateurs and artisans from Udine were all noticed last century. By 1900 Sicilian islanders dominated the fruit and vegetable trade in cities, and nuclei of fishermen from Capo D'Orlando (Sicily) or from Puglia's Molfetta were settled in Fremantle and in Port Pirie. The few professionals and artists or musicians were often attached to consular circles.

While not subject to the **White Australia** policy, in British Australia Italians were 'not quite white'. Leopoldo Zunini, Italian consul in WA, complained bitterly that his countrymen were portrayed in the popular press as 'somewhere between the Chinese and blackfellows, and constantly derided as "Dagos"' (*L'Australia Attuale*, 1910); and Ossie Bonutto, a 1920s itinerant cane-cutter from Udine, observed in *A Migrant's Story* (1963), that 'in north Qld I found there was some confusion in the minds of many as to whether the Italians were a white or coloured race', a distinction commonly being drawn there between 'Italian' and 'white' gangs of cutters, especially where southerners were numerous.

An influential 1925 government inquiry into **aliens** in north Qld's cane-growing region followed an influx there. Feared by trade unionists as unfair competitors in industries under pressure, and seen as successors to the Kanakas, their spectacular success in acquiring farms was resented. The Commissioner, T.A. Ferry, faithfully relaying the racial and eugenic ideas which had informed the USA's closure of the 'Golden Door' in the early 1920s, declared northern Italians to be hard-working, law-abiding, and honest pioneers, while southerners, by contrast, were opportunistic, clannish, and unassimilable—prone to form 'alien knots'. *Non-Britishers in Australia* (1935) by Jens Lyng, which divided the white race into Nordics, Alpines, and Mediterraneans according to their physical and mental attributes, was a sophisticated encapsulation of the same assumptions. For Lyng, as for Ferry, the supposed preponderance of southerners explained Qld's turbulent and unstable political history. This distinction between northerners and southerners, encouraged by northerners, has persisted, and was satirised (and perpetu-

ated) by writer John **O'Grady** posing as a northern Italian, 'Nino Culotta', in *They're a Weird Mob* (1957).

To Australians, they were all 'Italians'. But Italy was made only in 1861. The making of Italians—citizens who identified with their new nation-state—proved more difficult. Emigrants, coming from a relatively few specific villages or towns in a very few regions—with diverse histories, traditions and dialects—have identified most closely with their own places of origin (a phenomenon known as *campanilismo*), rather than with their recently forged nation. Relying in their travels on 'invisible ties' of kin and *paesani*, their settlement, dominated by chain migration, was highly localised. The marked regional basis of Italian settlement in Australia has been one of its most striking features. This is well described in C.A. **Price's** *Southern Europeans in Australia* (1963).

Ironically, while Australians anguished over 'alien knots', Italian consular officials, briefed to prevent their nationals assimilating, laboured to obliterate stubbornly held local identifications and to nurture instead an *Italian* consciousness—to forge Italians—and, in the 1930s, to win hearts and minds for fascism. Historians are more sceptical of their success than were Australian administrators, who in 1941 sent thousands into internment.

By the 1933 Census Italians were the biggest non-British immigrant group, and they have remained so with mass postwar **immigration**. In the peak years, 1951–61, 170 000 Italians arrived, usually unassisted. While most prewar Italian migrants had now achieved independence, especially in rural Australia, most postwar arrivals sought waged work, particularly in the manufacturing and construction industries. Occupying and renovating old housing stock in major cities, they established many 'little Italies', bringing colour to depressed suburbs, and subsequently carrying their preferred house and garden styles out to second and third areas of suburban settlement.

The Italian-born (272 000 at the 1991 Census) and their children are integrated throughout society. Their history and achievements are surveyed in Stephen Castles et al., *Australia's Italians* (1992). Arguably, their most visible impact has been through their culinary styles—to which Australians have assimilated remarkably. Often, through force of present and historical circumstance, they embrace a broader Italian identification, although Richard and Michal Bosworth, *Fremantle's Italy* (1993), question whether the term 'Italian' is not a construct divorced from reality. Many 'little Italies' based on villages or towns persist, and less visible, but as enduring, are the regionally based Italian farming colonies and rural networks in all states. Yet is the twinning of towns (Fremantle with both Sicily's Capo D'Orlando and Lombardy's Sernio, for example) a tribute to the resilience of old identities or to the dedication of the manufacturers of ethnicity? Historians debate the relative strength of these various identities, yet in multicultural Australia they ebb and flow and are not mutually exclusive, and most claim an Australian identity first and foremost.

JACQUELINE TEMPLETON

J

Jacka, Albert (1893–1932) was lionised as a national hero after becoming the first Australian to win the Victoria Cross in World War I. It was awarded for 'most conspicuous bravery' at **Gallipoli** when, in the course of recapturing a section of trench, he killed five Turkish soldiers and captured two more. His name and image were used on recruiting posters, and his reported laconic comment, 'I managed to get the buggers, Sir', became part of the legend. His reputation was further enhanced when he was awarded the Military Cross in France for subsequent action in which he was seriously wounded. He was awarded a bar to the MC and, by March 1917 had risen to the rank of captain. Jacka was badly gassed at **Villers-Bretonneux**, in his last action of the war. On his return to Melbourne in 1919 with the 14th Battalion, a large crowd gathered to greet him. He started a business and later served a term as mayor of St Kilda 1930–31. His early death was partly a result of physical damage received during his war service. There is a memorial in the St Kilda botanic gardens. Ian Grant wrote his biography, *Jacka: VC* (1989).

KT

Jackey Jackey, sometimes Jacky Jacky, can be a generic or specific name. It was used to denote Aboriginality in the way that 'Paddy' denoted Irishness. The name then became attached to individuals—for example the **bushranger** William Westwood who operated in the Queanbeyan area 1837–46, probably in reference to his habit of blackening his face to escape detection. In some cases it became the name by which Europeans knew individual Aborigines.

One such is Jackey Jackey (whose Aboriginal name was Galmahra), the guide and companion to Edward Kennedy on his fatal expedition to Cape York in 1848 (see **Exploration by land**). His account of their difficult trip in which eventually only he and Kennedy continued, the attack by Aborigines, his nursing of the dying explorer and burial before fleeing from further pursuit, was related in a narrative of the expedition produced in 1849 by its botanist, William Carron. He was feted for his 'faithfulness', rewarded with an elaborate silver **king-plate** and money, and members of the public shouted him drinks for his loyalty. He became an alcoholic and died of campfire burns in 1854. Judith **Wright's** poem, 'Two Sides of a Story' (1970), is a moving and perceptive portrayal of his experience.

KT

Japanese–Australian relations have been important to Australia throughout the twentieth century, first because Japan was a threat and later because it was a major economic partner. Trade and other forms of contact have existed since the 1860s; there has been a continuous if small Japanese presence in Australia, despite the Immigration Restriction Act of 1901 and the deportation of Japanese residents in Australia after **World War II**.

Interaction between the two countries became possible in the 1850s, when Japan was opened to foreign trade after more than 200 years of extremely limited contact with the outside world, and several Australians began business ventures in Japan. Australian exports to Japan started with coal in 1865. The most important groups of Japanese to come to Australia before 1901 were workers for the **pearling** and **sugar industries**, and prostitutes. Japanese workers were prized by employers for their hard work, thriftiness, and sobriety, but also feared for these same virtues: the comparative frequency with which Japanese became business proprietors and vessel owners prompted Alfred **Deakin** to remark in 1901, 'It is not the bad qualities but the good qualities of these alien races that make them dangerous to us.'

Japan was a major target of the **White Australia** policy adopted by the new Commonwealth in 1901. A 'Yellow Peril' had been identified by the 1890s, and Japan's rapid industrialisation from the 1880s onwards and its victory over China in 1895 increased the sense of danger. The

Immigration Restriction Act closed Australia to further settlement by Japanese. At the time, there were about 3600 Japanese in Australia. By 1933, numbers had dropped to 2080.

The fear of Japan increased greatly after 1905 as a result of Japan's victory over Russia, and some Australians began seriously to anticipate a Japanese invasion. According to Neville Meaney in *The Search for Security in the Pacific 1901–14* (1976), Australian defence and foreign-policy thinking were dominated by fear of Japan from 1905 to 1945, except for a brief period in the 1920s. The introduction of compulsory military service and the establishment of an Australian navy in 1911 owed much to this fear. During World War I, however, Japan was an unwelcome ally thanks to the Anglo-Japanese Alliance of 1902. Japanese ships helped to keep sea lanes open for Australian trade, freeing Australian warships for service elsewhere, and escorted Australian ships to distant battlefields. Prime Minister **Hughes** reluctantly accepted Britain's promise to Japan of the former German islands in the Pacific north of the equator, but this made him more determined to resist Japanese demands at Versailles. He took the leading part in denying Japan's request for a racial equality clause in the peace treaty. Australian suspicion of Japan eased somewhat after Japan reluctantly agreed to naval arms limitations in 1921–22.

From the early 1930s, trade between Japan and Australia grew rapidly. In fact, this could be seen as the beginning of the pattern of bilateral trade which has continued to the present, though there were serious interruptions in the 1936 **trade diversion dispute** and during war and occupation. Between 1930/31 and 1935/36, trade with Japan increased from 7.1 to 10.3 per cent of total Australian trade, and by 1936 Japan was Australia's third-largest trading partner. The Trading with the Enemy Acts of 1939 and 1940 banned all Australian trade with Japan.

Japan and Australia were at war from December 1941 until August 1945. Early Japanese victories in Asia were swift and devastating and, especially after the **Darwin bombing**, there were for a time serious fears of a Japanese invasion. Australians and Japanese fought fiercely and with many casualties in such places as Bougainville, New Britain, the New Guinea mainland, and Borneo. About 22 000 Australians became prisoners of war, 8000 of them dying in captivity. The harsh treatment of Australian prisoners by Japanese soldiers remains one of the bitterest Australian memories of World War II.

Meanwhile, 1141 Japanese residents of Australia and its territories had been placed in **internment** camps, mostly at Loveday in SA and Tatura in Victoria, along with 3160 Japanese civilians arrested overseas. Yuriko Nagata in *Unwanted Aliens* (1996) has described the round-up of almost all those deemed to be 'Japanese', including about 100 people born in Australia, within 24 hours of Pearl Harbor. Long-standing Australian fears of Japan and deep-rooted racism, as well as the high visibility of the Japanese, doubtless account for the fact that 97 per cent of the registered aliens of Japanese descent were imprisoned, compared to 31 per cent of those of Italian and 32 per cent of those of

German descent. Japanese prisoners of war were also held in Australia, and came to the attention of the nation dramatically in the **Cowra breakout** of 1944. From February 1946 onwards, almost all Japanese-born residents of Australia were forcibly returned to Japan, and the Japanese community in Australia was virtually eliminated; by contrast, most European internees were allowed to stay.

Australia made its mark on the US-dominated occupation of Japan in several ways. It played the major role, for example, in the British Commonwealth Occupation Force, a contingent headed by an Australian with its headquarters near Hiroshima, which was responsible for keeping order in the 'British sector'. Thousands of young Australians experienced the devastation of postwar Japan at first hand through service in this force. Australia also supplied the president of the International Military Tribunal for the Far East, Sir William Flood Webb of Qld, and Australian courts-martial tried 924 Japanese soldiers for war crimes. William MacMahon Ball, a political scientist from the University of Melbourne, served as British Commonwealth representative on the Allied Council for Japan in 1946–47. Ball, and more particularly his Australian economic adviser, Eric Ward, were largely responsible for the radical program of land reform, widely considered to be the most successful of the occupation reforms. Australian officials were disappointed in the peace treaty of 1951, having unsuccessfully pushed for the inclusion of specific limitations on Japanese rearmament. Fears about Japan, however, soon gave way in the atmosphere of the Cold War to mistrust of other parts of Asia.

Limited private trade between Australia and Japan reopened in 1947. By 1951, Japan was Australia's fourth-largest customer, chiefly because of the strong Japanese demand for wool. Strict controls were placed on the import of Japanese manufactured goods at this stage. There was also a complete ban on the entry of Japanese people into Australia, in keeping with the strong anti-Japanese feeling among Australians. In August 1951, however, a few former Japanese residents were allowed to return on compassionate grounds. Woolbuyers and pearlers soon followed and, in 1952, after a long struggle, described by I.R. Carter in *Alien Blossom* (1965), the first of 600 or so Japanese 'war brides' arrived. In 1986 there were about 11 000 Japanese in Australia, but by now there were few links with the prewar Japanese community. Most strikingly, the majority of male Japanese residents are now professionals rather than labourers, as they were before the war.

Complementary economies have led Australia and Japan into a close trading relationship in the postwar period, and since 1966/67 Japan has been Australia's most important customer. The Australia–Japan Agreement on Commerce of July 1957 is generally regarded as a watershed in the bilateral relationship, though as Alan Rix has argued in *Coming to Terms: The Politics of Australia's Trade with Japan 1945–57* (1986), many mechanisms and decisions facilitating trade preceded it. In the 1960s there was rapid growth in Japan's share of Australian trade, with further expansion in the 1970s. Australia has been primarily a supplier of food and raw materials, and Japan of processed and manufactured goods. The huge volume of minerals exports from Australia has been a critical factor in the development of Japan's heavy industry, as well as in the exploitation of Australia's mineral resources. In 1976, Japan drew 47 per cent of its iron ore, 43 per cent of its coal, 64 per cent of its bauxite, and all of its alumina imports from Australia. By 1985, Australia was Japan's fifth-largest trading partner. A reduction in Japan's rapid growth rates in the 1980s and 1990s led to a corresponding slow-down in its absorption of Australian exports. Political and cultural contacts have increased. Politicians regularly exchange visits. A Basic Treaty of Friendship and Co-operation was signed in 1976. A travel boom began in the 1960s, and Japanese visitors are now a mainstay of Australian tourism. Japanese-language programs, which began at the University of Sydney in 1917, had by the early 1990s been established at virtually all Australian universities and many high schools and primary schools. Contacts among student, business, and special-interest groups in Japan and Australia exist in an astonishing variety.

SANDRA WILSON

Java-la-Grande was a continent marked on the sixteenth-century Dieppe Maps which, despite significant variation in shape and alignment, is thought to correspond to Australia. The Dieppe Maps were produced by French cartographers, but are believed to rely on Portuguese charts. One of these, the Dauphin Map (1536), erroneously names the large land mass situated south of Java proper (on the Indonesian archipelago) as 'Java-la-Grande'; it was allegedly relying on an earlier map produced by Marco Polo, who is believed to have first made the mistake. The view that Java-la-Grande was, in fact, Australia was put forward by George **Collingridge** in *The Discovery of Australia* (1895), and was later taken up by Kenneth McIntyre, *The Secret Discovery of Australia* (1977), which proposes that cartographic adjustment rectifies the distortion in the coastline. (See **Exploration by sea** for the refutation of this; see also **Mahogany Ship**.)

HD

Jennings, Albert Victor (1896–1993) pioneered mass-produced and mass-marketed housing in Australia. He grew up in Melbourne's inner suburbs and left school early to follow an apprenticeship as a dental mechanic. At 19 he had already learned his first lesson in real estate when he sold a block of land, at a tidy profit, before enlisting in the First AIF. In the 1920s he joined his brother-in-law in a real estate business and in 1933 launched his first housing estates, Hillcrest in Glenhuntly and Beaumont in Ivanhoe. During World War II Jennings turned to defence housing and other state-sponsored projects, and when peace came, he was ready to meet the huge demand for housing by applying the wartime techniques of modular construction, mass production, and prefabrication. Jennings, a decent, family-loving middle-class man, had an instinctive understanding of what his customers wanted: the typical Jennings brick veneer house was as aesthetically conventional as his firm's business

organisation was novel. From house construction Jennings turned to the design and manufacture of building components, marketing, housing finance, and urban design. At its peak about 1970 Jennings built one in 30 Australian homes, more than any of its competitors. But success did not last, and by his death in 1993, Jennings's sons had lost their patrimony and the firm had been dissolved. Don Garden has told the story in an excellent company history, *Builders to the Nation* (1992).

GD

Jewry in Australia began with the **First Fleet**. By 1820 there were, in all, a few hundred Jewish convicts, mostly male, living in NSW. The earliest form of organised Jewish life was the creation of a Jewish Burial Society in Sydney in 1817. In 1828 the first Jewish services on a regular basis were held in the home of P.J. Cohen. Most of the early free settlers were Anglo-Jewish, middle-class immigrants who transposed the English pattern of Jewish practice to Australia. In 1878 the Great Synagogue, Sydney, was consecrated; its imposing structure remains a historic feature of the Sydney landscape.

Jewish settlers arrived early in all the other Australian colonies, and congregations were established in the 1840s in Hobart, Launceston, Melbourne, and Adelaide. Victorian Jewry expanded rapidly as a result of the gold rushes from only 200 Jews in 1848 to 3000 in 1861. Jews settled in the gold-rush towns of Ballarat and Bendigo, as well as in Geelong, and synagogues were soon built in these country centres. During the nineteenth century a high proportion of Jews in NSW also lived in country areas, with communities in Goulburn, Maitland, and Grafton, and later in Newcastle and Broken Hill, but few Jews now live in non-metropolitan areas. When Qld was separated officially from NSW, a number of Jewish families left Sydney for Brisbane, in 1864 forming the nucleus of the Brisbane Hebrew Congregation which consecrated its synagogue in 1886. There were Jews in WA from its very beginning in the 1820s, but the first Jewish community was not formed until 1887 in Fremantle. This community was quickly overtaken by the Perth Hebrew Congregation, which was founded in 1892 and opened its synagogue in 1897. Synagogues were also built in the gold-rush towns of Kalgoorlie and Coolgardie in WA.

In the nineteenth century Jews participated in every facet of civic, economic, and social life of Australia. Prominent figures included Sir Saul Samuels, Sir Julian Salamons, and Sir Daniel Levey. In 1917 the NSW Legislative Assembly had to close on Yom Kippur because both the Speaker and Deputy Speaker were Jewish. Australian Jewry contributed to the war effort during both **World Wars I and II**. The outstanding Jewish soldier was General John **Monash**, while Sir Isaac **Isaacs**, a leading Jewish politician at the time of Federation, became chief justice and, in 1930, was appointed the first Australian-born governor-general. In the late 1970s Sir Zelman Cowen became the second Jewish governor-general.

Australian Jewry was augmented by small numbers of Jewish refugees fleeing the Russian pogroms at the turn of the century, including businessman Sidney **Myer**, and by Polish Jews arriving in the 1920s. But these 'foreign Jews' did not have a significant impact on the community. It was the Jewish refugees who arrived largely from Central Europe in 1938–39, escaping from Nazism, who laid the basis for dramatic changes. Between 1933 and 1954 Australian Jewry doubled in size, from 23 553 to 48 436, although Jews continued to constitute only 0.54 per cent of the total population as a result of discriminatory government policies which sought to limit the number of Jewish refugees permitted to enter Australia.

Further waves of immigrants from Hungary in the mid-1950s and from South Africa, Russia, and Israel in the 1970s and 1980s have further diversified Australian Jewry. There is a range of Jewish practice from the ultra-orthodox groups, such as Adath Yisroel and the Habad movement, to the Progressive movement; nineteen Jewish day schools catering for about 70 per cent of Jewish children in Melbourne and 50 per cent in Sydney; part-time Jewish education; old-age homes; communal fundraising; and a strong Zionist structure combined in the Zionist Federation of Australia. Australian Jewry's strong ties with Israel were seen during the various wars in the Middle East. Cultural life has also developed with the growth of B'nai Brith, a service organisation; Yiddish culture is particularly strong in Melbourne with Kadimah; the Hakoah Club in Sydney has a membership of over 11 000. All the local organisations are represented at the state level by Community Councils or Boards of Deputies, and at the federal level by the Executive Council of Australian Jewry.

Jews assimilated well in the free and open society of Australia for the duration of European settlement, with the major centres being in Sydney and Melbourne. The total number of Jews in Australia today is estimated to be between 80 000 and 100 000, the Census statistics failing to take sufficient account of what it is to be a Jew. Most postwar Jewish refugees, especially those from Eastern Europe, arrived with a stronger sense of their Jewishness than they found in the assimilated Australian Jewish community. With the acceptance of multiculturalism, Australian Jewry has sought to develop its Jewish identity in all spheres—religious, educational, cultural, and social. Intermarriage rates have declined since their peak in the 1920s and members of the community are generally more open about their Jewish identity, rejecting the earlier Anglo-Jewish approach of conformity.

Postwar Jewish migrants demonstrated rapid social mobility, with individuals such as Isi Leibler, Richard Pratt, and Rabbi Joseph Gutnick of Melbourne, and Frank Lowy and the Adler family of Sydney, playing a prominent part in business. Individual Jews and the community as a whole have contributed significantly to the larger community, with later leaders, such as Sydney D. Einfeld, Professor Julius Stone, and Professor Peter Baume, coming from its ranks, as well as entertainers such as Roy 'Mo' **Rene**. The community as a whole is predominantly middle class, with most Jews in administrative, executive, and managerial occupations. There is a high proportion of second-generation Jews in the professions.

In 1978 the published material dealing with Australian Jewry was limited and patchy. The most important works were the study by George Bergman and John Levi of the convict years and early free Jewish settlement, *Australian Genesis* (1974); Israel Getzler's study of the Australian chapter of the struggle for emancipation in the colonial period; Charles A. **Price's** demographic study of Australian Jewry, (1964); and Peter Y. Medding's *From Assimilation to Group Survival* (1968). The *Australian Jewish Historical Society Journal*, founded in 1938, is the oldest ethnic history journal. Histories of Victorian Jewry in the nineteenth century by Rabbi L.M. Goldman (1954), and of South Australian Jewry, again concentrating on the nineteenth and early twentieth century, have also been published.

Since 1985 significant works have included Hilary L. Rubinstein, *The Jews in Victoria* (1985), and her complete history of Australian Jewry entitled *Chosen* (1987); Suzanne Rutland's history, *Edge of the Diaspora* (1988, 1997); the two-volume history *The Jews in Australia* (1991), by Hilary L. Rubinstein and W.D. Rubinstein; and John Goldlust's study of the Jews in Melbourne (1993). Important specialist works dealing with specific themes include Paul Bartrop, *Australia and the Holocaust 1933–45* (1994). Cyril **Pearl** has written about the anti-Semitism of John **Norton**, owner and editor of *Truth*, and the *Dunera* story.

Suzanne Rutland

Jindyworobak movement was a nationalistic literary movement founded in 1938 by Rex Ingamells, which promoted distinctively Australian art and culture. It sought 'to free Australian art from whatever alien influences trammel it, [and] to bring it into proper contact with its material'. The Aboriginal word *jindy-worobak*, meaning 'to annex, to join', was adopted as a signal for Australian artists to unite in recognition of a shared national consciousness. Their chief means of developing this identity was to draw on Aboriginal, especially **Dreamtime**, culture, which they presented affirmatively but pessimistically, as the vestiges of a 'dying race'. Their frequent misuse and misunderstanding of Aboriginal words, however, provoked derision from more avant-garde critics. The movement published regular collections of poetry until 1953, including works by Roland Robinson, Geoffrey **Dutton**, and Judith **Wright**.

HD

Johns, Frederick (1868–1932), biographer and journalist, expanded collective **biography**, which had been pioneered by David **Blair**, J. Henniker **Heaton**, and Philip **Mennell**. Johns was born at Houghton, Michigan, USA, and educated in England. In 1884, at the age of 16, Johns joined relatives in SA. After working as a journalist with the *South Australian Register* between 1885 and 1914, he was chief of SA's Hansard staff 1914–32. He edited the *South Australian Freemason* 1920–25, and contributed to the **Bulletin**. His collective biographies appeared under various titles given in the entry for **biographical dictionaries**. The Herald & Weekly Times acquired Johns's copyright and first incorporated his biographies in E.G. Knox (ed.), *Who's Who in Australia 1933–34* (1933); this series continues today. In *Australian Biographer* (1916), Johns revealed his principles: 'system and method are everything'; 'know no politics'; 'consider the national status or merit of the subject'; 'have a passion for accuracy'; and 'ascertain the facts first hand … from the subject himself direct'. Money couldn't buy space in his works, he often said; they were biographical, not autobiographical, and featured facts, free of flattery, eulogy, and opinion.

DC

Johnson, Amy (1903–41) in 1930 made the first England–Australia flight by a woman. She was born at Hull, England, and educated at Eversleigh House and the Boulevard schools, where she was an intelligent but rebellious pupil with a talent for beating the boys at their own games. She dreamed of an advertising career, but worked as a secretary. More than anything else she wanted to marry the love of her life, a Swiss Catholic, but she was Methodist and their relationship faltered. Diverting her spirit into flying, Johnson determined that this ambition would not be taken away. Constance Babington-Smith's biography, *Amy Johnson* (1967), notes 'Johnnie' was one of only two women in the world with a ground engineer's licence in 1929. With Lord Wakefield's backing, Johnson purchased a Gipsy Moth aircraft and flew from London to Darwin over 20 days in May 1930. Her triumphant landing on **Empire Day** made world headlines. Australia adored 'the lone girl flyer', although newspaper attitudes were coloured by a media war for rights to her story. Exhaustion and illness dogged her subsequent tour, possibly contributing to an accident at Brisbane, where she overshot the runway but survived unhurt. Romanticised as the 'typist who flew solo to Australia', Johnson's legend inspired public imagination in an era when **aviation** brought Australia closer to the rest of world. In 'Amy Johnson's Triumph, Australia 1930' (*AHS*, 1988) Julian Thomas argued her flight created myths which 'variously affirmed and challenged notions of femininity, geography and history'. Johnson crashed into the Thames Estuary in January 1941 and was never seen again.

DC

Johnson, Colin (Mudrooroo), see **Aboriginal narratives**

Johnson, Richard (1753–1827) came with the **First Fleet** as Australia's first clergyman. He conducted all the clerical duties of the colony for its first six years and even had a church built at his own expense. Johnson's other interest was farming; Watkin **Tench** called him the 'best farmer in the colony'. His book, *An Address to the Inhabitants of the Colonies Established in New South Wales and Norfolk Island* (1794), was the first written for distribution in the colony. A selection of his letters, edited by George **Mackaness**, was published in 1954, and he has been the subject of several biographies, notably *Australia's First Preacher* (1898) by James **Bonwick**, and Neil K. Macintosh's comprehensive *Richard Johnson* (1978).

KT

Johnston, George Henry (1912–70) began his writing career as a journalist with the Melbourne *Argus*. He became a well-known war correspondent during World War II, about which he wrote several books. From a boyhood steeped in the **Anzac** tradition, Johnston became a pacifist. After the failure of his first marriage he married fellow journalist and writer Charmian Clift (1923–69). In the early 1950s they moved to London, then settled in Greece in 1954 so that Johnston could concentrate on his writing. It was here that he produced his best work, the largely autobiographical *My Brother Jack* (1964); it is a rich study of Melbourne between the two world wars, as seen by a figure who regards himself as an outsider in comparison with his brother, Jack, who is an archetypal Aussie battler, cheerful and non-reflective in the face of continuing adversity. Johnston completed his own story in two further novels—*Clean Straw for Nothing* (1969) describes the family's time in Greece, and the introspective *A Cartload of Clay* (1971) completes the trilogy, as the family move back to Australia. Although they never achieved the stature of the first novel, these two works develop significantly the themes of expatriatism and search for meaning in life which run through it. Clift committed suicide, and Johnston died of tuberculosis contracted in Greece. Garry Kinnane's 1986 biography is an acute study of the writer.

KT

Jones, (David) Fletcher (1895–1977), clothing manufacturer, retailer and cooperative advocate, established a highly successful staff-owned business which pioneered fractional fittings for men's trousers. The son of a poor Bendigo blacksmith, Jones had limited formal education, was afflicted with a stutter, and was severely incapacitated after service in World War I. He set up as a travelling hawker in western Victoria in 1918, eventually buying a small, badly sited shop in Liebig Street, Warrnambool, in 1924. In *Not By Myself* (1976), Jones says he was broke when he moved to central Warrnambool in 1927 to establish 'The Man's Shop', which specialised in tailoring and menswear. His 'Daily Marvel' promotions helped business boom. During World War II he acquired a government contract to manufacture covert and gabardine trousers. The fabric he called 'Coverdine' became a household word, while his emphasis on fractional fittings and 'personal fittings only' pushed 'Oxford bags' and 'sloppy Joe' trousers into the past. In 1946 he opened in Melbourne with the slogan 'Nothing but trousers', later adding 'No man is hard to fit.' Influenced by Japanese social reformer Toyohiko Kagawa, Jones introduced cooperative ownership, profit-sharing based on need, and management by consultation. From 1949 Fletcher Jones and Staff created a modern factory complex at Pleasant Hill, Warrnambool, surrounded by landscaped gardens and workers' cottages. The firm diversified into women's clothing and had shops across Australia at Jones's death in 1977. The business has since passed into private ownership.

DC

Jorgenson, Jorgen (1780–1841) was a Danish seafarer who wrote of his colourful life, including a period in Van Diemen's Land. Born in Denmark, he went to sea at 15 and was sailing in Australian waters 1801–05. He became notorious for an incident in 1809 when he assisted in the overthrow of the Danish governor of Iceland. This was the basis for his later claim to be the 'ex-king of Iceland'. He returned to Van Diemen's Land in 1826, transported for theft. After receiving his ticket-of-leave in 1827, he worked variously as an explorer, writer, farmer, and convict constable who assisted the infamous Black Line (see **Black War**). The accuracy of his 'A Shred of Autobiography', published in the *Hobart Town Almanack* (1835, 1838) and as a monograph in 1981, is questionable. His account of the Aborigines of Van Diemen's Land was published in 1991, edited by N.J.B. Plomley. *The Convict King* (1891) purports to be his life story 'retold' by James Francis Hogan. His colourful life has attracted other writers, including Marcus **Clarke** in *Old Tales of a Young Country* (1871), and Frank **Clune** and P.R. **Stephensen** in *The Viking of Van Diemen's Land* (1954).

KT

Jose, Arthur Wilberforce (1853–1934), journalist and historian, emigrated from England after suffering a breakdown while studying at Oxford. In Australia he worked initially as a bush labourer, then as a teacher, and after 1888 for the University of Sydney's extension classes. From 1899 to 1904 he was a war correspondent in South Africa, an acting professor in India, and a public lecturer in England. Jose returned to Australia as correspondent for the London *Times*.

In the 1890s he wrote verse and fiction, and his autobiographical *Romantic Nineties* (1933) is a source for Sydney's cultural milieu in that decade. His first major work, *The Growth of the Empire* (1897), was later republished in English editions as a school text, and *A Short History of Australasia* (1899) passed through 15 editions in the following 30 years. Both follow the emphases of **imperial history** in their account of settler societies working out their British inheritance. Jose was an early member of the (Royal) Australian Historical Society, and editor of the first *Australian Encyclopaedia* (1925–26). During World War I he served in naval intelligence and was commissioned in 1920 to write the naval volume of the official war history, but it was substantially revised by the series editor, C.E.W. **Bean**, before it appeared in 1928. The hallmarks of his work—careful research, a didactic tone, and vivid prose—attest to the circumstances of a scholarly imperial patriot who lived by his pen.

SM

Journals, see **Historical journals**

K

Kable, Henry (1763–1846) and **Susannah** (?1762–1825) were convicts on the **First Fleet** who instituted and won the first civil action in a NSW court in July 1788. They sued the master of their transport ship for the loss of their baggage, and were awarded £15 damages by the judge-advocate, David **Collins**. The case is discussed in David Neal, *Rule of Law in a Penal Colony* (1991). Henry became a successful trader in the colony, though never to the degree of his sometime partners, Simeon Lord and James Underwood. He was involved in a wide range of ventures, including sealing, whaling, shipbuilding, farming, and land speculation.

KT

Kanaka, see **Pacific Island labourers**

Kangaroo, see **Lawrence, D.H.**

Keating, Paul John (1944–), treasurer 1983–91 and prime minister 1991–96, was instrumental in reshaping the settled assumptions of Australian political and economic life. Keating grew up in a working-class Catholic family with strong associations with the Australian Labor Party, and self-consciously associated himself with labour history through a close friendship with the elderly Jack **Lang**.

He became treasurer in 1983 when the Keynesian economics that had provided the framework for postwar economic management had lost credibility in the Anglo-American democracies, and was being replaced by an emphasis on balanced budgets, and an expansion of the role of the market in the distribution of goods and services at the expense of the state. In that year he oversaw the deregulation of the Australia financial system with the floating of the Australian dollar, the entry of foreign banks, and the substantial weakening of controls over foreign investment. Subsequently he was an enthusiastic advocate of the privatisation of government-owned enterprises, such as the Commonwealth Bank and **Qantas**.

During the 1980s Keating became convinced that the Australian economy required substantial restructuring to shift it from its historic reliance on the export of primary commodities towards a diverse, export-oriented economy based on manufacturing and services. In the process of dismantling Australia's protective tariff barrier, many traditional blue-collar Labor supporters lost their jobs.

As prime minister, Keating embarked on a program of symbolic modernisation which would rid Australia of both the constitutional and the cultural vestiges of its colonial past. He initiated a debate about Australia's becoming a republic, and argued that Australia must orient its economy and its culture to Asia, which contained the world's fastest-growing economies. In this he expressed both a radical nationalist antipathy to Britain and a realist's assessment of Australia's vulnerability as an isolated European country in the Asia–Pacific region. He also oversaw the framing and passage of the Native Title Act (1993), the government's legislative response to the High Court's **Mabo** judgment, and attempted to make this a moment of reconciliation between Aboriginal and non-Aboriginal Australians. In this he was only partially successful.

Keating was an aggressive parliamentary performer who relished verbal combat. Much of what he did was a rejection of traditional ALP policy, in line with the NSW Right's pragmatic emphasis on the opportunities of power rather than consistency of principle. Keating himself, however, stressed his belief in the responsibility of leaders to lead, arguing that it was more important to do what was right than what was popular. He was sustained in office, and in his gruelling leadership tussle with Robert **Hawke**, by a strong inner conviction in his own capacities and the rightness of his judgments. His supporters saw in this an inspirational confidence in his vision of Australia's future; his opponents saw an arrogant imposition of unpopular policies and an indifference to the problems of ordinary people's lives while he concentrated on 'the big picture'.

The best book on the federal Labor governments (1983–96) is Paul Kelly's *The End of Certainty* (rev. edn 1994). The best biography of Keating is Michael Gordon's *Paul Keating* (1996 edn).

JUDITH BRETT

Kelly, Edward 'Ned' (1855–80), bushranger, has lived two lives. One Ned Kelly was hanged in Melbourne on 11 November 1880, aged 25. The other lives, and began supplanting the first even before he died. Two photographs show these Kellys. One, taken in 1874 from slightly above, is of Ned unshaven, with thin mouth, narrow eyes, and the pinch of poverty. It shows a man at the mercy of enemies. The other, taken the day before he died from slightly below, is of Ned bearded, strong, and resolute. It shows a young statesman.

The man hanged was probably born in January 1855, eldest son of John and Ellen Kelly, née Quinn, at Beveridge, Victoria. In 1866 his father died and the family moved to a hut near Greta in north-eastern Victoria. Ned ran with the Greta larrikins, and was first arrested aged 14, for assaulting a Chinese. He spent more time in prison than as a bushranger: eight months in 1870; three years in 1871–74; four months in 1880.

In April 1878 a policeman attempting to arrest Ned's brother DAN (1861–80) was wounded at the Kelly home; Ellen was gaoled for three years and two Kelly associates for six. With warrants against them, Ned and Dan holed up in the Wombat Ranges with Joe Byrne and Steve Hart. At Stringybark Creek on 26 October this gang ambushed and killed three of four police hunting them. That December they took to **bushranging**, robbing a homestead and a Euroa bank, and in February 1879 bailing up Jerilderie, NSW. On 26 June 1880 they murdered a police informer, Aaron Sherritt, which led them and the police to a shoot-out at Glenrowan two days later. The others died; Ned escaped but, clad in his ploughshare armour, returned and was captured for execution.

Bushranger is an Australian word. It evokes bushcraft, daring, defiance, and freedom from convention, rather than crime or evil. It touches an Australian nerve: G.T. Dick's 1992 *A Bushranging Bibliography*, not exhaustive, lists over 1200 books. Ned fits the model only in part. His offences were few. He was only a fair bushman and horseman: he knew the ranges better than the police, that was all, and when that advantage was threatened by Queensland trackers he was led to the folly at Glenrowan. Yet Dick lists almost 100 titles on him, against a dozen on Ben **Hall**, foremost of the Lachlan men, who comes next.

Ned's legend came to life because he offered more than bushranging. His love of 'Kelly country' (a phrase first recorded in February 1880) let him be Australian; his courage and strength spoke for the frontier. Aged 16 he straddled and spurred a policeman in Greta's main street; aged 19 he beat Wild Wright bare-knuckle over 20 rounds. After Stringybark Creek his actions took on a sense of destiny, revealing allegiance to two traditions about injustice: the defiance of the Lachlan men, and the wrongs of Ireland. In bailing up Jerilderie and Glenrowan he imitated Hall; in his daring and fatalism he chose both a short and merry life, and martyrdom. His Jerilderie Letter evokes resistance more than crime: it protests at injustice and hints at a republic in north-east Victoria.

His time also suited legends. The telegraph and the cable spread his story speedily; photography was cheaper; finer woodcuts put graphic images into illustrated journals, which burgeoned for the first time in the 1870s. Expanding railways carried correspondents to Kelly country, and papers and journals overnight to widening readerships made literate by the new Education Acts and able to read at night by the new hurricane lamp.

The passion and partisanship of Ned's own people permeated these devices for making strangers intimate. For 13 weeks in 1879 the *Mansfield Guardian* ran 'the book of Keli', mocking the police. An 1880 lithograph showed Ned standing statesmanlike in the Beechworth dock. In 1881 J.S. Borlase told Ned's story in 38 weekly parts, then published *Ned Kelly: The Ironclad Australian Bushranger*. That year also saw A.J. Isaacs's *Ned Kelly: The Ironclad Bushranger by One of His Captors*, and probably *The Life and Adventures of the Kelly Outlaws: The Daring Australian Bushrangers*. Even his police hunters helped raise Ned, albeit with proper distaste: Hare in 1894, Chomley in 1900, Sadlier in 1913.

By then Ned was an Australian rather than merely a Victorian legend—though Victoria is still his stronghold. 'He is at present the only national hero who has become mythical', an English visitor noted in 1898. The standard texts, George Boxall's *The Story of the Australian Bushrangers* (1899) and Charles White's *History of Australian Bushranging* (4 vols, 1900–03), condemn the man and burnish the legend. In 1906 Australia's first full-length feature film, *The Story of the Kelly Gang*, and in the 1920s *Kelly Gang Jazz* by 'Charlie Vaude' and *The Authentic Story of Ned Kelly in Pictures* (?1925), by James Kenneally kept the legend apace with new technology, while in the 1930s and 1940s Depression and war kept it at the nationalist forefront. In 1929 Kenneally relied on Tom Lloyd junior, sometimes a fifth gang member, to write *The Complete Inner History of the Kelly Gang and Their Pursuers*, a pivotal defence of Ned. In 1939 Billy Blinkhorn wrote his eloquent protest song, 'Poor Ned Kelly'; on 21 June 1942 the **Australian Broadcasting Commission** broadcast Douglas **Stewart's** play, *Ned Kelly*; in 1945–65 Sidney **Nolan** painted his Kelly series; and in 1948 Max Brown's *Australian Son* moved oral accounts squarely into the written record and made public the Jerilderie Letter. Peter Carey's *True History of the Kelly Gang* (2000) is a powerful reworking of the Kelly story from the imagined vantage point of Ned, in language inspired by the Jerilderie Letter.

Kelly books have never since quit the market: the more important include *Ned Kelly: Man and Myth*, edited by Colin Cave in 1968; John McQuilton's *The Kelly Outbreak 1878–1880: The Geographical Dimension of Social Banditry* (1979), which reviews Kelly literature and best places Ned in his social and rural context; and John Molony's *I Am Ned Kelly* (1980), the best centenary account. In 1995, Ian Jones's *Ned Kelly: A Short Life* developed ideas he first offered in 1967.

Ned has prompted poetry by David Campbell; music by Peter Dawson and George Dreyfus; films, at least 17 works of fiction and five children's books; and countless 'Kellyana' items. Ned lives in Australian minds. Everyone knows who he is. At Glenrowan he heard a Kelly ballad; people still sing and write them. Victoria's cricket team is the Bushrangers, Ned's armour is its logo. 'Good on you Ned' is a compliment, 'as game as Ned Kelly' an old saying.

BILL GAMMAGE

Kendall, Henry (1839–82) wrote lyrical nature poetry, inspired by the lush landscape of Illawarra and Clarence River districts in NSW, where he spent his childhood. His first published collection (1862) was followed by his best-known work, *Leaves from Australian Forests*, in 1869. The charm of his verse established his reputation as the leading Australian colonial poet. Poems such as 'Bellbirds' demonstrated an appreciation of Australia's natural world.

Kendall's battle with alcoholism exacerbated the problems in his family life; he related the agony of his mental breakdown in the poem 'The Shadow of 1872'. By the late 1870s, his health had improved markedly, and his career and marriage simultaneously regenerated. He won the *Sydney Morning Herald* International Exhibition poetry competition in 1879 and his collection, *Song from the Mountains*, appeared the following year. Critical works include a collection of essays edited by Russell McDougall (1992) and a biography by Michael Ackland (1995).

HD

Keneally, Thomas Michael (1935–), writer and republican, studied for the Catholic priesthood but never took orders. Instead he turned to teaching and fiction-writing. His first novel, *The Place at Whitton*, was published in 1964. Much of Keneally's fiction has a historical basis. *Blood Red Sister Rose* (1974) recounts the life of Jeanne d'Arc, and *Schindler's Ark* (1982), which won the Booker Prize and was later made into an acclaimed feature film by Steven Spielberg, tells the story of war hero Oskar Schindler. Novels with Australian settings include *Bring Larks and Heroes* (1967); *The Chant of Jimmie Blacksmith* (1972), based on the story of Jimmy **Governor**; *The Cut-Rate Kingdom* (1980), based on national politics during World War II; *The Playmaker* (1987), an account of Ralph **Clark's** efforts to direct the first theatrical performance in NSW; *A River Town* (1995), which recreates Keneally's childhood town of Kempsey, NSW, in the early 1900s; and *The Cedar Shame* (1998). Religion and notions of good and evil, and punishment and redemption, are frequent themes in his fiction. Keneally has also written a travel memoir of Ireland, *Now and in Time To Be* (1991), and *Our Republic* (1993). He is a founder and prominent member of the Australian Republican Movement.

HD

Kennett, Jeffrey Gibb (1948–) became premier of Victoria in 1992 after an unprecedented decade of **Australian Labor Party** government in the state. He was an unlikely champion of the **Liberal** revival, for his impetuosity contributed to repeated electoral defeat and four challenges to his leadership until he was overthrown in 1989. An instinctive interventionist, he was out of sympathy with the enthusiasm for economic rationalism and diminution of government that overtook the Liberal Party during the decade.

Kennett regained the party leadership in 1991 and swept the discredited Labor government from office at the 1992 election. Announcing that he was 'reopening Victoria for business', he used his strong mandate to cut expenditure on education and health, reduce and reorganise the public sector on corporate principles, privatise utilities, amalgamate local government, and marginalise trade unions. Victoria had experienced similar periods of business-oriented reform after the profligacy of earlier booms, but never with the same personal dominance and ebullience as in the 1990s. His rejection by the voters in 1999 signalled that public acceptance of such strong leadership was exhausted. Tony Parkinson's biography (2000) is aptly subtitled 'The Rise and Fall of a Political Phenomenon'. Brian Costar and Nick Economou edited a policy analysis of *The Kennett Revolution* (1999).

SM

Kenny, Elizabeth (1880–1952) developed a controversial treatment for infantile paralysis (poliomyelitis; see **epidemics**) which earned her international recognition and lifelong ridicule from established medical practitioners. Kenny received the title of 'Sister' during her army service in World War I and continued to use it, despite her lack of formal qualifications. Her skills were acquired working as a bush nurse when she first treated polio victims. She returned to home nursing after the war and in 1932, using money from an innovative stretcher that she had designed and patented, established a clinic in Townsville to treat victims of polio and cerebral palsy. Her method, outlined in *Infantile Paralysis and Cerebral Diplegia* (1937), involved applying heat and encouraging movement. This was in direct opposition to the existing immobilising treatment and was condemned by a royal commission in 1938. Phillipa Martyr re-examined the controversy in 'A Small Price to Pay for Peace' (*AHS*, 1997). Nevertheless, Kenny received great popular support; other clinics were established, and she travelled to England and the USA to explain and promote her treatments. She became a heroine in America—the first of her autobiographies, *And They Shall Walk*, was published there in 1943 and a laudatory film, *Sister Kenny*, appeared in 1946. Although her understanding of the pathology of the disease was still challenged, her treatment became widely accepted by conventional practitioners. A second autobiographical volume, *My Battle and Victory*, was published in 1955.

KT

Kent Hughes, Wilfrid Selwyn (1895–1970), athlete and warrior, made a long political career out of vigilant conservatism. A Rhodes scholar and Olympic athlete, he won the Military Cross while serving in the Light Horse during World War I, and entered Victorian politics as a vehement critic of political expediency. During the Depression he flirted with fascism as 'the spirit of the age'. A staff officer in World War II, he was captured in Singapore. His years as a **prisoner of war** resulted in *Slaves of the Samurai* (1946), but he was persuaded by the threat of communism in South-East Asia to support Japan's incorporation into the regional alliance. As a federal parliamentarian and government minister, he embarrassed **Menzies** with his bellicose enthusiasms and was dropped from the government in 1956. As chairman of the organising committee for the Melbourne Olympics in the same year, he was equally controversial. A backbencher until his death in 1970, he continued to rattle the sabre, but a newspaper correspondent observed that 'he lacks the balanced judgement, the Machiavellian capacity for intrigue, which seems essential to political success'. Frederick Howard wrote a sympathetic biography (1972).

SM

Kerr, John Robert (1914–91) was appointed governor-general of Australia in 1974 after a distinguished legal career. He overcame humble beginnings to graduate in law from the University of Sydney as winner of the university medal. After service in the AIF, he prospered as a barrister with an extensive industrial practice from good labour connections. He became a judge of the Industrial Court, where his 1969 decision to imprison union official Clarrie O'Shea for contempt of court aroused controversy.

Kerr's term as governor-general was overshadowed by his decision during the political crisis of 1975 to dismiss the **Whitlam** Labor government and commission Malcolm **Fraser** as caretaker prime minister. The ensuing furore over the **Dismissal** divided the nation and brought the role of governor-general under intense scrutiny. Kerr himself was subjected to relentless harassment whenever he appeared in public. He resigned in 1977 and lived in Europe until 1984. Kerr appeared never to understand the depth of antagonism he aroused, and presented his own view of the crisis and his role in his autobiographical *Matters for Judgement* (1978, reprinted with a new preface in 1988).

KT

Kiama ghost was a term coined following the attempted **assassination** of Prince Alfred, Duke of Edinburgh, by Henry James O'Farrell in Sydney in March 1868. Following the duke's recovery and return to England, and the execution of O'Farrell, the colonial secretary Henry **Parkes** visited Kiama, on the south coast of NSW. He claimed to have sworn evidence that the assassination had been planned and that someone with knowledge of this had since been murdered. Cynics and doubters dubbed the guilty culprit the 'Kiama Ghost', alluding to folklore about a local ghost that had allegedly haunted the area since the 1830s.

HD

Kiddle, Margaret Loch (1914–58), historian, is best known for her history of the Western District of Victoria. A graduate of the University of Melbourne, Kiddle worked as secretary to Douglas **Copland** during World War II and subsequently tutored in history at the university, where she completed an MA thesis on social reformer Caroline **Chisholm** in 1947. This work was published in 1950 and has been republished several times, most recently in 1990 with an introduction by Patricia Grimshaw. She also wrote several children's books. Kiddle's research interests in Scottish and Irish **immigration**, and early pastoral settlement, became the basis of 'her life's work'—a comprehensive social history of Victoria's Western District 1834–90, published in 1961 as *Men of Yesterday*. Despite worsening health, owing to a congenital kidney disease, her research was sustained by a curiosity about her own pioneering forebears and an affinity with the pastoral landscape they created. She relied to a large extent on letters and diaries, station records and other documents, and on the fruitful personal connections she developed with descendants of Western District pioneers. She treated gently their treatment of Aborigines, profiteering, and exploitation of the land, but avoided over-romanticisation. Her treatment of Niel Black, the central character of her book, gave an unaccustomed grandeur to local history: it was he who lamented that 'we are all men of yesterday'. She was granted a year's fellowship at the Australian National University to pursue her work, and travelled extensively in England, Scotland, and Ireland in search of additional primary material. She completed the work only weeks before her death. Her work is considered in an article by Jane Carey and Patricia Grimshaw in *Gender and History* (2001).

HD

Kidman, Sidney (1857–1935), the 'Cattle King,' owned, controlled, or had a significant interest in about 90 outback pastoral stations, covering 130 000 square miles, upon his death in 1935. Kidman was born near Adelaide and received a basic education at Norwood, SA. He ran away at 13 to Kapunda and Burra, then moved to western NSW, where he found rouseabout work and bought a bullock team to cart supplies to isolated towns. He profited from cattle-buying and droving, and opened a store at Cobar, NSW, which thrived in the mid-1870s copper boom. A £400 inheritance possibly helped him to purchase Thule and Cobbrum stations near Charleville, Qld, in 1887. Kidman progressively acquired other properties to develop a 'chain of supply' that linked stations across Australia from the tropical north to Adelaide. His strategy facilitated movement of stock away from drought-affected areas, towards better-watered land and markets offering superior prices. Kidman's thriftiness was sometimes interpreted as meanness, but while he sacked employees for trivial waste, he was generous enough to donate properties and money to charitable causes. He was knighted in 1921, the day after he gave his Kapunda residence to the SA government for a high school. In 1924–27 the federal government successfully prosecuted Kidman for unpaid land tax. Jill Bowen's *Kidman: The Forgotten King* (1987) describes him as 'the greatest pastoral landholder in modern history', and reassesses Ion **Idriess's** romanticised biography, *The Cattle King* (1936). A television film, *The Cattle King*, was produced in 1984.

DC

Kindergartens, educational centres for preschool children, were among the most durable legacies of **progressive** reformers in the closing decades of the nineteenth century. Influenced by the educational theories of Pestalozzi and Froebel, and by American 'child-savers', middle-class reformers—many of them women—saw kindergartens and playgrounds as a means of rescuing working-class children from the corrupting influence of slum housing and 'unfit' parents.

The first Melbourne kindergarten was founded in 1901 and soon the inner city was encircled by a 'cordon of kindergartens'. By 1916 Free Kindergarten Unions and Kindergarten Training Colleges had been formed in most states. The standard kindergarten regime of physical exercise, baths, good food, and rest reflected a concern with health as much as education, an emphasis that marked kindergartens off from 'day nurseries' for middle-class children. Not until World War II sent mothers back into the workforce did the Commonwealth government subsidise creches and kindergartens. From 1943 the Australian Broadcasting Corporation began a national radio program, 'Kindergarten of the Air'. State governments assisted the movement with subsidies and in 1972 the **Whitlam** government promised preschool education for 'every Australian child', an objective which still remains unattained. As women's participation in the workforce rose during the 1980s, the numbers of kindergartens grew; but in the 1990s, under the influence of user-pays doctrines, they compete with cheaper non-professionalised forms of child care. Lyndsay Gardiner's *The Free Kindergarten Union of Victoria* (1982) describes the origins of the Victorian movement, while Peter Spearritt's 'Child Care and Kindergartens in Australia, 1890–1975' in Peter Langford and Patricia Sebastian (eds), *Early Childhood Education and Care in Australia* (1979), summarises the national history.

GD

King, Philip Gidley (1758–1808) was second lieutenant on the *Sirius* in the **First Fleet**. He administered the **Norfolk Island** settlement before succeeding Governor **Hunter** at Port Jackson in 1800. During his time as governor, King sought to eliminate the rum trade, develop agriculture, extend exploration, and expand public works. His journal, first published as an appendix to Hunter's *An Historical Journal* (1793), appeared separately in 1980. His time on Norfolk Island is assessed by Victor Crittenden, *King of Norfolk Island* (1993). Two descendants, John and Jonathan King, wrote his biography (1981). Jonathan has written widely on the settlement of Australia and was the driving force behind a re-enactment of the First Fleet voyage to celebrate Australia's Bicentenary.

KT

King-plates were breastplates, generally crescent-shaped and made of brass, which were presented by early colonial authorities to Aboriginal 'chiefs', designating them as 'King' or 'Queen' of a particular 'tribe'. The practice was introduced in 1815 by Lachlan **Macquarie**, who hoped to ingratiate himself with leaders of the Aboriginal community as part of the 'civilising' process. He selected 'King' **Bungaree** of Sydney and his wife as the first recipients. Although other Aborigines did not necessarily recognise the authority of the king-plate wearers in the way envisaged by the donors, the plates did convey status as marks of white favour. Settlers also adopted this means of recognising the 'loyal service' or bravery of the Aborigines, and eventually the custom spread to most colonies. The plates, usually engraved with the name and 'tribe' of the recipient and decorated with kangaroos or emus, have since become collector's items. Possibly the most notable is the elaborate silver piece awarded to **Jackey Jackey** for his assistance to explorer Edward Kennedy. Collections are held in the Mitchell Library, Sydney, and the National Museum of Australia. *King Plates* (1993) by Jakelin Troy includes many photos of plates as well as a history of their development.

KT

Kingsford Smith, Charles Edward (1897–1935) became an Australian and international hero in 1928 when he and Charles Ulm (1898–1934) in the *Southern Cross* made the first successful USA–Australia crossing of the Pacific. Kingsford Smith had won a Military Cross for action in France while serving as a pilot with the Royal Flying Corps. After the war he worked briefly overseas as a stunt pilot before returning to Australia to fly for Western Australian Airways. He and Ulm made a record-breaking flight around Australia to raise the money for their Pacific flight. 'Smithy', as he was known, continued to set aviation records—a non-stop crossing of Australia, world circumnavigation with an equatorial crossing, first Australia-to-USA flight in a single-engine plane, fastest flight from England to Australia. On the other hand, his various business ventures, including a passenger airline, failed. He wrote several accounts of his aviation adventures—*My Flying Life* (1937); *The Old Bus* (1932); and, with Ulm, *Story of 'Southern Cross' Trans-Pacific Flight* (1928). Kingsford Smith disappeared in 1935 over the Bay of Bengal, on a trip from England to Australia. He has been the subject of a film by Ken Hall, *Smithy* (1946), and several biographies, including *A Thousand Skies* (1985) by Tasman Beattie and *Smithy* (1998) by Ian Mackersey. His contribution to Australian aviation was recognised in the name of Sydney's international airport.

KT

Kingsley, Henry (1830–76), novelist and brother of English novelist Charles Kingsley, spent several years in Victoria during the turbulent decade of the 1850s. His experiences on the goldfields and on a pastoral station in western Victoria provided material for several novels, the best-known of which is *The Recollections of Geoffry Hamlyn* (1859). This family saga set amid the romance of pastoral life has been identified as the progenitor of the colonial romance novels, notably those by Rolf **Boldrewood**. Kingsley's second major work, *The Hillyars and the Burtons* (1865), relates the adventures of two English families in Australia in the 1850s; it makes much use of actual people and events, and closely follows the press battles between the *Age* and the *Argus*. Kingsley is assessed in J.S.D. Mellick, *The Passing Guest* (1983), and in a critical study by John Barnes (1971).

HD

Kingston, Charles Cameron (1850–1908), premier of SA 1893–99, was one of the chief architects of **Federation**. A dominant political figure in his colony for more than 20 years from 1881, he polarised opinion by his aggressive style, but enjoyed considerable popularity among the people. He became premier while still bound over to keep the peace following his arrest for challenging a political opponent to a duel; while premier, he endured two attacks in the street, to both of which he responded with effective and aggressive physical counterattack. His turbulent public life was matched by rumours and scandals in his private life. Kingston was able to shrug off such problems, including opposition to his admission to the Bar on the grounds that he was not of fit character, and a later citation in a society divorce case. His marriage was not happy.

His parliamentary talent was quickly recognised and he served variously as attorney-general, chief secretary, and premier. His legislative achievement was considerable. His 1893–99 government pioneered financial and administrative reforms, created vehicles of **state socialism**, and became the first to introduce female suffrage (a cause to which he was a late but enthusiastic convert). He personally drafted the first conciliation and **arbitration** legislation for the settlement of industrial disputes. He ensured that the power over interstate industrial disputes was included in the **Constitution**, and the resulting act has been one of the most influential in Australian economic and industrial life. He was regarded as one of the best statutory draftsman in Australasia.

From 1888 he took part in every significant meeting and development on the road to Federation with the exception of the 1890 Conference—a record unequalled by anyone else in Australia. He provided a draft **Constitution** for the 1891 Convention and was a connecting thread between the colonial leaders from 1894. With George **Reid** he was instrumental in restarting the process in 1894–95 on a popular basis. He presided over the 1897–98 Convention, took part in the 'Secret' Premiers' Conference compromise that resulted in the second successful referendum of 1899, and in London with **Barton** and **Deakin** ensured that Federation was implemented in 1900. His role is discussed in L.F. Crisp, *Federation Fathers* (1990), and J.C. Bannon, *The Crucial Colony* (1994).

In the first federal cabinet Kingston was a rigorous and successful minister for trade and customs, establishing and enforcing the first general **tariff**. After he resigned from the ministry over the exclusion of seamen from the conciliation and arbitration bill, his radical credentials made him a credible candidate for prime minister in the turmoil of 1903–04, but at this point his health collapsed.

While he left no personal papers and his handwriting was virtually indecipherable even to his contemporaries, it is still strange that the first full-length biography (by Margaret Glass, 1997) was only published nearly 90 years after his death. His statue, financed by public subscription and erected in 1916, stands triumphantly in the central square of his city, clad—perhaps embarrassingly for a native son of Australia who refused imperial honours—in the impressive court dress of a privy councillor.

JOHN BANNON

Kirkpatrick, J. Simpson, see Simpson and his donkey

Kisch, Egon (1885–1948) achieved celebrity during a visit to Australia of less than six months, chiefly because of the government's failure to prevent it. He was a Czech journalist and communist who wrote prolifically on world affairs in an investigative, exhortatory style he described as 'reportage'; Ken Slater's biographical essay is in *LH* (1979). Kisch was invited to Melbourne for an anti-war congress, but the minister for the interior made a declaration of exclusion against Kisch under the Immigration Act. When the ship on which he was travelling reached Melbourne in October 1934, Kisch jumped onto the wharf, broke his leg, and was put back on board. In Sydney he was released as the result of a court application, rearrested, and given a **dictation test** in (Scottish) Gaelic. Having failed the test, he was charged with being a prohibited immigrant and sentenced to six months' imprisonment. But the High Court set the conviction aside (on the grounds that Gaelic was not a European language). Kisch spoke to large crowds as he toured Australia, most notably in the West Melbourne stadium, the use of which the peace activist Mary Wren secured from her father, John **Wren**. Further proceedings resulted finally in payment of Kisch's legal costs and voluntary departure in March 1935. The Sydney journalist Tom Fitzgerald, writing as Julian Smith, covered the Kisch affair in *On the Pacific Front* (1936), and Kisch's own *Australian Landfall* appeared in 1937. The best recent account is by L.J. Louis in *LH* (1983).

SM

Knocker is a person who disparages or finds fault, often unfairly. The term is an Americanism dating back to the late nineteenth century but, as Keith Dunstan shows in his entertaining history, *Knockers* (1972, 1992), Australia has always had a special affinity for the kind of criticism known as *knocking*. The harshness and unfamiliarity of the local landscape seemed to encourage European scorn. As early as 1699 William **Dampier** described 'God's miserablest country'. The writers R.H. **Horne**, Marcus **Clarke**, D.H. **Lawrence**, and others recoiled at the melancholy grimness of the **bush**. R.E. **Twopeny** found Australian townspeople 'uncivilised'. Melbourne knocked Sydney's bad taste. Sydney knocked Melbourne's weather. Everyone knocked **Canberra**, **new chums**, and **Pommies**, but nobody knocked **Anzac Day**, not without a fight. Dunstan argued immigration and migrant 'unsureness' or ambivalence about Australia fostered a national inferiority complex. Knockers almost prevented the Melbourne **Olympic Games** and the **Sydney Opera House**. They stooped in a **cultural cringe** that said Australian accents were not good enough for **Australian Broadcasting Corporation** announcers; that a **Holden** car was second-best; and that Australian artists, singers, writers, film-makers, winemakers, and chief executives could never be as good as the imported variety. **Egalitarianism** has also contributed to a desire to 'knock off' **tall poppies**, those who rise above the field, and to cut everyone down to equal size. Political and community leaders have achieved some success in portraying the knocker as 'un-Australian', but the habit is deeply entrenched.

DC

Knopfelmacher, Frank (1923–95), intellectual, was a member of the Jewish middle class of Central Europe, was born in Vienna but raised in Czechoslovakia between the two world wars. Following the Nazi occupation of his homeland, he fled to Palestine, before fighting in a Czech Legion of the British army against the Germans. During World War II, he lost most of his family in the Holocaust. After it, he returned to Czechoslovakia and witnessed the gradual **communist** seizure of power. These experiences—of Nazism and Stalinism—shaped his adult life.

In 1948 Knopfelmacher fled Czechoslovakia for the second time. After obtaining his doctorate in Britain, he was appointed to the Department of Psychology at the University of Melbourne. He arrived in Australia in 1955 at the height of the Cold War, during the Australian Labor Party **split**. He soon became the most influential anti-communist intellectual in Australia, closely associated at the university with the fiercely anti-communist Australian Labor Party club, and outside it with B.A. **Santamaria's** National Civic Council and James **McAuley's** *Quadrant*. Although he was a brilliant polemicist—a prolific essayist and columnist—his chief influence was as a teacher.

Knopfelmacher had one great lesson to teach—that Nazism and communism, which had both brought untold misery to those who had suffered under them, represented not rival tendencies of Right and Left, but morally equivalent evils. Knopfelmacher's lesson was not original. However, because of his razor-sharp mind, his savage tongue, his profound understanding of European culture, and his great courage, no-one in Cold War Australia taught this lesson so powerfully or with such flair. Over two decades, through his lunch-time lectures and cafeteria tutorials, he changed the lives of hundreds of undergraduates. On the Left he was deeply hated and widely feared.

Knopfelmacher's life tended to lurch from one political crisis to the next. The most serious personal struggle occurred for him in 1965 when his appointment as senior lecturer in philosophy at the University of Sydney was, in unprecedented action, overturned by the professorial board. His most serious public struggle was in the defence of the Australian military commitment to the **Vietnam War** in defence of the south against the communist north. His political preoccupation was not, however, without cost. To his

regret he produced, during his academic life, no enduring philosophical or sociological work.

Knopfelmacher retired from the University of Melbourne at the end of 1988. During the next year communist power in Europe began to collapse. He had now lost the great political cause which had filled his life. In his last years, for reasons not understood even by his close friends, Knopfelmacher's primary hostility transferred from communism to Israel and its supporters.

ROBERT MANNE

Knopwood, Robert (1763–1838) began keeping a diary when appointed chaplain to the 1803 expedition to **Port Phillip** under David **Collins**. His terse entries are evocative of colonial life from the short stay at Sorrento to the development of Tasmania over the following 35 years. As the only chaplain on the island until 1819, Knopwood knew many of the settlers. A sporting cleric, whose debts had forced him to sell the family estate, Knopwood drew mixed responses. After his death, the *True Colonist* described him as a man whose 'foibles … will be cherished'. A portrait of Knopwood in Bishopscourt, Hobart, shows him mounted on a horse, trailed by his dog, and with a bottle protruding from his back pocket. Others, including **Macquarie** and John Pascoe **Fawkner**, were more critical; one described him as an agitator, the other as an immoral drunkard. Knopwood appeared in L.L. **Robson's** *A History of Tasmania*, vol. 1 (1983) as a 'swearing, debauched, drunken infidel'; a 1992 biography by Geoffrey Stephens rejects this view. The diary itself has been made available to general readers by Mary Nicholls (1977).

KT

Knox, Edward (1819–1901) founded the Colonial Sugar Refining Co. in 1855. Born in Denmark and trained in commerce, he migrated to Australia in 1840, intending to become a pastoralist. He worked in various businesses, including the Australian Sugar Co., whose liquidation allowed the establishment of CSR. Under Knox's chairmanship the company established a number of refineries, and an extensive supply of sugar cane to dominate the Australian industry. Knox was a director of many of the companies and chairman of the Commercial Banking Company of Sydney. He was a leader in the establishment of staff provident funds and was active in the committees of many charitable organisations. He handed over management of CSR to his son EDWARD WILLIAM in 1880 but remained chairman for another 21 years.

KT

Kokoda Track was a route of strategic importance during fighting between the Australians and the Japanese in New Guinea during **World War II**. After their defeat in the Battle of the **Coral Sea** and the Battle of Midway, the Japanese endeavoured to capture Port Moresby by land, advancing south from Buna and Gona on the north coast, where they had landed in July 1942. The track, which wound through the heavily timbered Owen Stanley Ranges, provided access to the Allies' garrison at Port Moresby. As the Australians advanced north, they met heavy resistance from the Japanese, who quickly captured Kokoda, situated roughly midway between Port Moresby and Buna.

The US Marines' landing at Guadalcanal on the Solomon Islands on 7 August 1942 distracted the Japanese from the New Guinea campaign, and the Allies' subsequent landing in late August at Milne Bay in eastern Papua, just ahead of an enemy landing, further weakened the Japanese position. The battle was first fought by the inexperienced militia of the 39th Battalion; from mid-August they were assisted by the 7th Division of the AIF returned from North Africa. Heavy fighting along the track continued into September. The appalling conditions—mud, heat, disease, and dense jungle—created confusion and demoralisation on both sides.

The Japanese initially gained ground, especially with the Australians' failed counter-offensive, but in reality they were over-stretched and fast ran out of supplies. The Australians persevered, benefiting enormously from assistance from the **fuzzy-wuzzy angels**, whose local knowledge of area was critical to their success. On 25 September the Japanese were ordered to withdraw to the northern coast. The counter-attack launched by the Australians three days later resulted in their retaking Kokoda on 2 November and the eventual defeat of the Japanese at Gona and Buna.

Although Australian soldiers had used the term *track*, the Americanised 'Kokoda Trail' gradually became standard and was used by the Commonwealth Battles Nomenclature Committee in the 1950s. Enthusiasm for the name 'Kokoda Track' was revived in the 1980s, following campaigning by Australian historians, including Lloyd **Robson**. An account of the Kokoda battle is given by Peter Brune, *Those Ragged Bloody Heroes* (1991).

HD

Koori, see **Aboriginal nomenclature**

Korean War began on 25 June 1950, when communist North Korea crossed the 38th parallel to invade the southern Republic of Korea. The Korean peninsula had been politically divided since the end of World War II, when the former Japanese colony was split into an area governed under US supervision in the south, and the Soviet-backed People's Democratic Republic in the north. This division was formalised in 1948, and both US and Soviet troops withdrew by 1949. When northern forces pushed into the south the following year, the UN Security Council called for assistance from member countries—a call met principally by the USA. Troubled by fears of encroaching **communism** and keen to maintain the USA as a 'great and powerful friend', Prime Minister **Menzies** committed military support from all three Australian forces within a week.

UN forces gained an immediate advantage when they launched a surprise landing near Seoul and drove far into northern territory. North Korean forces regained ground with the aid of Chinese military, who moved in over the Chinese border and pushed the enemy southwards. Thereafter neither side could establish an advantage and a truce was called in July 1953. Of the 94 000 dead suffered by the UN forces, 359 were Australian. Australia's role in the war is examined in Robert O'Neill, *Australia in the Korean War 1950–1953*, 2 vols (1981, 1985).

HD

Kramer, Leonie Judith (1924–) is an influential conservative figure in Australian literature and culture. Educated in Melbourne and Oxford, Kramer taught at the University of New South Wales for 10 years before her appointment in 1968 as professor of Australian literature at the University of Sydney. She held that position for more than 20 years, during which time she served on a number of public bodies. These included the **Australian Broadcasting Corporation** (which she chaired 1982–83) and the Universities Council of the Commonwealth Tertiary Education Commission. She has criticised educational progressivism and defended the monarchy. The work of Henry Handel **Richardson** has been the main focus of her critical writing, and she edited the controversial *Oxford History of Australian Literature* (1981), which champions the view of Australian literature as a branch of European literature. She has increasingly become involved in business, serving as director of the ANZ Banking Group and Western Mining Corporation. In 1991 she was elected chancellor of the University of Sydney.

KT

Kyabram movement arose in the aftermath of **Federation** in demands to reduce the cost of government. It took its name from the country town in northern Victoria where the campaign originated, and tapped rural suspicion of city extravagance, but its organisers were linked to urban business groups and the movement quickly spread to the metropolitan centres. In Victoria it took the form of a National Citizens' Reform Movement, in NSW the People's Reform League. Under the slogan of 'Retrenchment and Reform', these organisations endorsed candidates for the ensuing state elections, with considerable success. Each state reduced the size of its popular lower house but did little to cut expenditure, and the movement was quickly assimilated into the non-Labor side of politics. The Kyabram movement was one of those short-lived upsurges of anti-political politics that have periodically erupted during the twentieth century. Its own historian, A.L. Nielsen, styled it *The Voice of the People* (1902); John Rickard queried this claim in *Class and Politics* (1976).

SM

L

La Nauze, John Andrew (1911–89), historian, was born in WA; he attended Perth Modern School and the University of Western Australia, where he acquired a life-long love of poetry and liberalism, and Oxford University where he studied philosophy, politics, and economics with great distinction. He returned to teach economics at the University of Adelaide in 1935 and moved to the University of Sydney in 1940. He became professor of economic history at Melbourne in 1950, and in 1955 transferred to the Ernest Scott Chair of History. He succeeded W.K. **Hancock** as professor of history at the Institute of Advanced Studies at the Australian National University (1966–76).

La Nauze was encyclopaedically learned and at various times lectured in economics, English literature, history of economics, economic history, and modern European and British history. He brought a new precision and awareness of ideas to Australian history. He pioneered research into inequality in educational opportunity in Australia, the history of political economy in Australia, and **tariffs**. His *Alfred Deakin* (1965) brought a tempered elegance to political biography, while his *Making of the Australian Constitution* (1972) is magisterial. His career spanned the mean, under-staffed 1930s to the 1950s and the overburdened, expansive later 1950s and 1960s. Throughout, he was a model of austere, dedicated scholarship.

F. B. SMITH

La Trobe, Charles Joseph (1801–75), first superintendent of **Port Phillip District** and later first lieutenant-governor of **Victoria**, was born in London and educated in Switzerland. Following his appointment as superintendent in 1839, he developed a close working relationship with Governor **Gipps**; A.G.L. **Shaw** published their correspondence in 1989. The colonists' resentment of control from Sydney often made him unpopular, though they applauded his **anti-transportation** stance. The discovery of **gold** in Victoria in 1851 taxed the administration severely, and his decision to impose monthly licence fees fermented discontent which afterwards exploded at the **Eureka Stockade**.

La Trobe was an unusual **governor**, with no military background, a man of high principles and strong cultural interests—music, art, geology, botany—who established the Melbourne Botanic Gardens and promoted public institutions. His letters and papers are held by the State Library of Victoria, in the Australiana section which bears his name. His marriage to Sophie de Montmollin is discussed by Marguerite Hancock in Penny Russell (ed.), *For Richer, For Poorer* (1994).

KT

Labor Daily was a **newspaper** of the NSW labour movement founded in Sydney in 1924 with union support, especially from the Miners Federation. The leader of the NSW Labor Party, Jack **Lang**, established control during the late 1920s and it became the official organ of his breakaway Labor Party in the 1930s until opponents supplanted him in 1938. The paper was renamed the *Daily News* and was wound up during World War II. At its peak during the Depression, when the biting cartoons of George Finney appeared, it was a potent vehicle for Lang's radical **populism**, but political control proved difficult to combine with successful journalism.

SM

Labour history is a term used to encompass historical writing on a diverse range of subjects, from **trade unions**, **strikes and lockouts**, **socialism**, and the **Australian Labor Party** to working-class culture, social life, and **work** itself. An outcome of the rise of **social history** and **cultural history** since the 1960s has been a blurring of its edges, as many labour historians have moved away from an institutional emphasis towards a concentration on the social life and identities of working people.

Most early examples of labour history came from men who were active in the labour movement. W.E. Murphy,

W.G. **Spence**, and George **Black** celebrated the achievements of labour, and sought to inspire readers with tales of its glorious struggles and practical achievements. V.G. **Childe** founded a more critical school. He argued in *How Labour Governs* (1923) that the Labor Party began as 'a band of inspired Socialists' but 'degenerated into a vast machine for capturing political power'. Brian **Fitzpatrick** celebrated the struggles of labour against capital in his *Short History of the Australian Labor Movement* (1940), but also contributed to this critical tradition when he claimed in *The Australian People 1788–1945* (1946; 1951) that Labor emphasised 'nation-building through a capitalist economic system' at the expense of socialism, and had 'enlisted industrial workers under banners attractively splashed with socialist slogans for the task of Australian nation-building for others' profit'.

As John Merritt has shown (in G. Osborne and W.F. Mandle, eds, *New History*, 1982), the expansion of the universities after World War II and the development of Australian history within them provided an immense stimulus to the study of labour history, contributing to its professionalisation and academic respectability. In the 1940s and 1950s, a group of radical historians later called the **Old Left** began to research the history of the Australian labour movement. Robin **Gollan**, Ian **Turner**, Miriam **Dixson**, Eric Fry, Noel Ebbels and Lloyd Churchward were all members of the Communist Party who brought to their work strong nationalist beliefs and a high level of political commitment. In the context of the Cold War and the ascendancy of the coalition parties in federal politics, these historians emphasised the role played by the labour movement in shaping Australian national life. Armed with the conviction that **imperial history** tended to marginalise the working class and the labour movement, they wanted to recover the experiences of the 'submerged bulk' of ordinary working people. They assumed that society was divided into classes, and that masses rather than elites were the driving force in history.

The Old Left historians produced a large and influential body of historical writing. In *Radical and Working Class Politics: A Study of Eastern Australia 1850–1910* (1960), Gollan examined the development of the labour movement in the second half of the nineteenth century, from its participation in populist alliances in colonial politics to its emergence as a powerful independent political force, while Turner explored the relationship between the industrial and political wings of the labour movement in the period after Federation in *Industrial Labour and Politics* (1965). Dixson, in a doctoral thesis and series of publications, examined the turbulent history of the socialist left in NSW in the 1920s, but Fry was less concerned with politics than with the material conditions of working-class life in his influential 1956 doctoral thesis on the urban working class in Australia in the 1880s. His work was an important contribution to **urban history** as well as labour history. All these historians were influenced by Marxist theory although, as Turner himself later recognised, it was largely the vulgar variety contained in Stalinist textbooks.

The foundation of the Australian Society for the Study of Labour History in 1961 and the first appearance of its journal *Labour History* in the following year signified labour historians' growing confidence. The Australian National University, then the home of the journal, was the main centre of research in Australian labour history from the 1950s until the 1970s, its dominance assisted by the collections in the university's Archives of Business and Labour (now the Noel Butlin Archives Centre), the presence of several able labour historians on staff, and the large number of students researching doctoral theses on labour history in the Research School of Social Sciences. Trade union histories were popular, but one of the most important contributions was P.G. Macarthy's doctoral thesis on the Harvester Judgment (1967). He examined the conditions of labour between the 1890s and early 1920s and the evolution of the concept of the **basic wage**, using the quantitative methods of **economic history** as well as the approaches and sources associated with mainstream labour history. Macarthy's work continued a lineage begun by T.A. **Coghlan** in his monumental four-volume study *Labour and Industry in Australia* (1918), and continued by Fitzpatrick in his economic histories.

By the late 1950s and 1960s, there was growing disquiet among liberal historians about an alleged 'Whiggish' tendency in labour history. Developing a critique initiated by Manning **Clark** in the 1950s, these historians, who included Allan **Martin**, claimed that the Old Left boosted the achievements of the labour movement at the expense of proper appreciation of the role of the middle class, the churches, and the non-Labor parties in Australian history. The so-called counter-revolution in Australian historiography, however, rapidly ran out of steam, and it was not until the late 1960s that the reputation of the Old Left was seriously challenged.

The attack came from a group of young Marxist historians that included Terry Irving, Humphrey **McQueen** and Stuart Macintyre, and acquired the designation '**New Left**'. In his fiercely polemical *A New Britannia* (1970), McQueen criticised the Old Left historians for their failure to take into account the strength of **racism** and militarism in the labour movement. McQueen claimed that the Labor Party had never been socialist, and was 'the highest expression of a peculiarly Australian petit-bourgeoisie'. He found little genuine socialism in the labour movement, and accused the Old Left of having romanticised the struggles of the labour movement through a nationalist lens that owed more to bourgeois **liberalism** than to Marxism. Irving claimed that the Old Left's formulation of **class** was incoherent, while for Macintyre, influenced by Althusser, the radical nationalists were empiricists and moralists who shared the methodology and assumptions of bourgeois liberal historians. What the New Left did share with the Old was a conviction that an understanding of Australian history was a crucial ingredient in the transformation of Australian society.

This period also saw the rise of new social movements in Western nations that aimed to advance the rights of oppressed groups such as women, blacks, and gays. In this context, some historians challenged labour history's preoccupation with a unionised male elite, and there was a shift from the history of institutions to the culture and social life of working people. An indication of this trend was evident in 1981 when the sub-title of the journal *Labour History* became *A Journal of Labour and Social History*. Yet, although this social history of labour became increasingly popular, labour historians continued to write about unions and the Labor Party as well as biographies of labour leaders. Moreover, the growing influence of **industrial relations** theory on labour history in the 1980s and 1990s gave new vigour to the institutional strand of labour history, and furnished it with greater theoretical sophistication. Meanwhile, renewed interest in the state, ideology, **citizenship**, and the political process began to transform the political history of labour, although commemorative and traditional narrative histories of the Australian Labor Party have continued to appear.

The rise of **women's history** in the 1970s also had a significant influence on labour history. The institutional focus of much early labour history led to the marginalisation of women, since female workers were often unorganised, and therefore easily dismissed by historians as irrelevant to studies of the labour movement. The Old Left historians were interested in the public sphere, a world of political agitation inhabited mainly by male activists and organisations in the political and industrial wings of the movement. Early attempts to recover the experiences of women in the workforce included Edna **Ryan** and Anne Conlon, *Gentle Invaders* (1975); Beverley Kingston, *My Wife, My Daughter, and Poor Mary Ann* (1975); and a special issue of the journal *Labour History* on *Women at Work* (1975).

More recently, feminist labour historians influenced by the idea of gender history have investigated the construction of sexual identity in the labour movement and its relationship to working-class identity. Indeed, it is largely through the work of feminist historians such as Marilyn Lake and Joy Damousi that post-structuralist theory has had the greatest influence on labour history in Australia. Meanwhile, Raelene Frances has combined feminism and labour process theory in *The Politics of Work: Gender and Labour in Victoria, 1880–1939* (1993), a study of the workforce in the clothing, bootmaking, and printing trades. Labour process theory seeks to interpret the evolving relations between management and workers at the point of production, and, in the hands of historians such as Frances, Kosmas Tsokhas and Peter Cochrane, has contributed powerful insights into the history of work and class relations in Australia.

Labour history is now so diffuse that it is difficult to identify any unifying feature. In *Bede Nairn and Labour History*, volume 3 (1991), Verity Burgmann argued that, despite its sensitivity to inequalities in addition to class, labour history had experienced a 'strange death', because the rise of the new social movements and the apparent decline of the labour movement as an agent of change had made labour history less fashionable than social history. In response, Raelene Frances and Bruce Scates, and Ann Curthoys have pointed to the ways in which labour history has managed to adapt itself to the challenges posed by social and cultural history. The journal *Labour History* remains an important outlet for research in Australian history, and labour history is still taught in many Australian universities, as a specialist subject as well as part of broader studies of Australian history. The biennial conference of the society remains an important forum.

FRANK BONGIORNO

Labour movement, see **Labour history**

Labourism (also Laborism) is a term that historians have used in Britain, the USA, and Australia to describe the dominant ideology of the labour movement. In the late 1960s and early 1970s **New Left** historians, following their British counterparts, used the term in order to criticise an **Australian Labor Party** which they saw as committed to the preservation of capitalism and the promotion of class cooperation. In a chapter on 'Laborism and Socialism' in the collection *The Australian New Left* (1970), Humphrey **McQueen** argued that labourism was 'the historical manifestation of an integrated, subordinate work force', an outcome of the petit-bourgeois consciousness of colonial workers. The Labor Party, which professed this ideology, was anti-socialist and pro-capitalist from the time of its formation. Another New Left historian, Stuart Macintyre, argued in *Intervention* (1977) that labourism was 'based on the industrial and political practice of the trade unions'. It involved an acceptance of capitalism and a recognition of 'the legitimacy of the capitalist state' that was 'qualified by a limited but powerful class consciousness'. For Macintyre, labourism addressed the immediate concerns of the worker, while Labor **socialism** was a product of the petit bourgeoisie rather than unionists. Similarly, in his *The History of the ACTU* (1981), Jim Hagan defined labourism as the **trade unions'** belief 'that fair dealing was available and obtainable in a capitalist society', and declared its central tenets in Australia to be a **White Australia**, **tariff protection**, compulsory **arbitration**, a strong union movement, and a Labor Party. Most workers, according to Hagan, were committed to labourism rather than socialism.

These writers generally assumed that labourism was an ideology of the organised working **class** that had as its aim the modification of market outcomes by the state, but Raymond Markey has claimed in *The Making of the Labor Party in New South Wales 1880–1900* (1988) that it 'embodied a pluralist and populist, rather than a class, view of capitalist society'. He has argued that the emergence of labourism as the dominant ideology of the NSW Labor Party by 1900 was an outcome of an alliance of professional politicians and **Australian Workers Union** leaders, groups that represented the intermediate social strata of middle-class intellectuals and small farmers. Labourism thus originated outside the urban working class, whose dominant ideology was 'social democracy'. More recently, sociologists, political scientists, and historians of welfare in Australia have suggested that labourism expressed a version of social reality that constituted 'the people' as male wage-earners, with their wives and families annexed as dependants. The aim of labourism was the development of a masculinist 'wage-earners' welfare state'.

First used by critics, the concept of labourism was subsequently taken by celebrants of the Australian labour movement's moderate pragmatism. In the publications of the Lloyd Ross forum for labour history in Sydney, the Labor right celebrates the Party's role in 'civilising capitalism'. More recently, in *LH* (1994), Terry Irving has argued that the use of 'labourism' perpetuates a narrow and unhelpful understanding of the meaning of socialism that historians use to deny Labor any part in the socialist tradition. Whether used critically or affirmatively, it implies that the labour movement was subject to an 'all-embracing' bourgeois hegemony, and therefore neglects 'the elements of resistance and denial' in the history of such movements. Moreover, Irving suggested that an examination of the ways in which the concept has been used sheds more light on an intelligentsia that regards labour as 'the key social fact' than on the ideology of the working class.

Most users of the concept of labourism have indeed underestimated the complexity of working-class political discourse and ideology, and exaggerated the extent to which the labour movement has been a participant in a colonial consensus or Australian 'middle way'. On the other hand, labourism may remain a useful term to distinguish the basic assumptions and practices of Labor in politics from those involved in other working-class political strategies, such as the participation of colonial working men in populist alliances with the middle class, syndicalism, or the principles and practices of revolutionary socialism and **communism**.

The idea that an independent Labor Party, supported by a strong trade union movement, should seek a redistribution of wealth in favour of the working class through the parliamentary system has been a tenet to which any activist working within the Labor Party has had to subscribe. It meant that socialism had to be a gradual affair because Labor sought to achieve its aims through popularly elected parliaments. Labourism, to the extent that it can be shorn of its earlier pejorative uses by New Left historians, may still be an appropriate label for this set of political attitudes. It remains a part of the vocabulary of historians of the Australian labour movement.

FRANK BONGIORNO

Lake Mungo in south-western NSW was once part of the ancient Willandra Lakes system, which, owing to rich food resources, supported a large human population until about 25 000 years ago. Lake Mungo Man, the oldest intact human skeleton found in Australia, is believed to have been buried in a grave between 28 000 and 30 000 years ago. He was uncovered in 1974 by geomorphologist Jim Bowler. His discovery provided evidence of customary funerary rites, and his thin frame and physical characteristics provided an evolutionary link with Java man, which was of crucial archaeological significance. An earlier discovery in 1969 of the remains of Lake Mungo Woman, who had been buried nearby around 26 000 years ago, raised questions over **Aboriginal cultural ownership**. Her bones had been smashed into small pieces as part of the burial ritual. Following debate between scientists and Aborigines over their respective rights to her remains, a compromise was reached: Mungo Woman was reburied in 1992 in a box that needed two keys to be unlocked. One key was given to the Mungo people; the other was entrusted to archaeologists at the Australian National University. Lake Mungo has been classified as a World Heritage Area.

HD

Lalor, Peter (1827–89), engineer, Eureka rebel and politician, was born in Ireland into a landowning Catholic family with firm nationalist convictions; his father represented an Irish constituency in the British parliament, and his brother, James Fintan Lalor, was a prominent Young Irelander. Lured by gold to Victoria in 1852, Lalor emerged as a leader of aggrieved miners at Ballarat, and led the popular protest that culminated in the **Eureka Stockade** of 1854. He lost an arm in the skirmish, but escaped capture, and in the following year was elected a member of the first Victorian parliament. Lalor was twice a minister, and served as speaker of the assembly (1880–87). He resigned from office in 1887 and died two years later.

The unveiling of a statue at Ballarat in 1892, depicting a conservative Lalor in speaker's robes, sealed his rise to respectability, but simultaneously reignited working-class resentment and feelings of betrayal. Radicals and the labour movement are inclined to link Lalor with an Irish revolutionary tradition but, as Patrick **O'Farrell** points out, 'Lalor was no democrat. His leadership at Eureka was not that of a man thrust up from below, but of a descent from above.' Lalor had supported the popular movement for land reform in the 1850s, but only to the extent that it fitted with the agrarian ideal of universal rights to a farming life. Despite an abhorrence of injustice, he set himself apart from what he called 'the despised classes'—but still declined a knighthood. A federal electorate was named after him in 1948, and a sympathetic biography by L.J. Blake appeared in 1979.

HD

Lambert, George Washington Thomas (1873–1930) became an official war artist with the AIF during World War I after a decade of working as a portrait painter in London. Born in Russia with an American father, Lambert came to Australia in 1887 and lived for a time on a NSW sheep station. He painted the heroic *Across the Black Soil Plains*, for which he won the 1899 Wynne prize. In the following year he travelled to Europe for study before settling in London. As war artist, Lambert visited Egypt, **Gallipoli** and Palestine—of the latter he commented, 'I must go on painting Palestine subjects … because they are fixed in my brain by the impressions received out there.' The Australian War Memorial holds his war paintings. Lambert returned to Australia in 1921 as an established artist. He continued to paint in the heroic mould, frequently on squatting themes, for example, *Weighing the Fleece* (1922) and *The Squatter's Daughter* (1924). Anne Gray has written extensively on Lambert, most recently in *Art and Artifice*

Lambing Flat riots

(1996), and he is discussed in Andrew Motion's family history, *The Lamberts* (1986).

KT

Lambing Flat riots or Burrangong riots, which occurred at Lambing Flat goldfield, near Young, NSW, culminated in the worst atrocities committed against the **Chinese in Australia**. Hostility towards the Chinese, which was evident from the field's discovery in March 1860, was exacerbated by a weak police presence. Diggers at Lambing Flat believed themselves disadvantaged on account of the Chinese presence, and criticised Chinese habits, particularly their apparent water wastage. They formed a Protective Miners League in early 1861 'to drive the moon-faced barbarians away'. Diggers were further incensed by the government's refusal to satisfy their demands for anti-Chinese measures. Though regularly forced off the field at Lambing Flat, the Chinese returned each time. In June 1861 several thousand white diggers violently attacked the Chinese miners, burned their tents and belongings, and severed their pigtails from their scalps. About half the Chinese population, comprising between four and five hundred men, was reportedly injured in the affray. The subsequent arrest of three men on 14 July 1861 led to an angry confrontation with police, resulting in one digger being killed and others injured. In order to appease diggers' disaffection, the NSW government passed the *Chinese Immigration Restriction and Regulation Act* later that year.

HD

Land Army was a women's wartime labour force formed to replace the labour lost when farmers and labourers enlisted for service in World War II. The first land army was a voluntary service established by the **Country Women's Association** in 1940; this was superseded in 1942 by the official Australian Women's Land Army, formed under the Australian Manpower Directorate. Women were trained and employed in a variety of rural work, including the growing of fruit, vegetables, and cotton, and in poultry and dairy production; their contribution was critical to the successful cotton and fruit harvests of 1943–44. They were paid award wages, and were employed on a full-time, part-time, or casual basis. Women involved in this work enjoyed an unusual measure of freedom and independence for the duration of the war, but this came to an abrupt end when men returned home in 1945 and the Land Army was disbanded. The Land Army is the subject of Sue Hardisty (ed.), *Thanks Girls and Goodbye!* (1990).

HD

Land boom was a recurrent phenomenon that arose as a result of the sale of Crown land or the speculative buying of freehold land. The opening up of a new settled district which boasted particularly good soil or a similar attraction usually resulted in a run on land. This was characteristic of Victoria after the gold rush, where new-found wealth encouraged great optimism about future progress, leading in the 1880s to escalating property prices and intensive subdivision.

The land boom of the 1880s drew on British funds and was encouraged by local banks and building societies. Speculators invested in freehold land, such as that bordering a proposed railway line, or subdivided large properties as future suburban housing estates. The speculation frequently involved corruption among politicans, as Michael **Cannon** revealed in *The Land Boomers* (1966). Melbourne's boom in the 1880s ended with the collapse of the banks and economic **depression**.

HD

Land rights, see **Aboriginal land rights**

Land settlement in Australia has been dictated by two major factors: the desire for land of those who wanted to farm it or graze it with stock; and the attempts by governments to provide an ordered framework for the occupation of new territory. In Britain, land was owned by those with power and prestige; in Australia, it appeared that there was a vast field of opportunity for those with and without capital.

The first official notion of land settlement was described for Governor **Phillip** in his official instructions, in which it was assumed that a self-sustaining rural economy would make its own demand for land. Grants would be made available for those who applied, and small portions would be offered to emancipated convicts; for it was felt that rural labour could help redeem fallen characters. Initially, then, settlement was linked to the feeding of the population.

As early as 1800, poor farming practice had exhausted the soil and exacerbated the effect of natural disasters; as a result, farmers needed fresh soil to produce good crops. Likewise, more land was required for stock if the sheep industry were to expand. The early progress of settlement and attitudes to the environment are dealt with in T.M. Perry, *Australia's First Frontier* (1963).

At this stage natural geographical features, such as the Blue Mountains, precluded the spread to other regions in NSW. New settlements were made for strategic reasons by Lieutenant **Collins** at **Port Phillip** and **Van Diemen's Land**. Although Collins discounted the country at Port Phillip, Van Diemen's Land was settled and land grants were made at the governor's discretion. Sharon Morgan's work, *Land Settlement in Early Tasmania* (1992), aptly describes both the progress of settlement and the settlers' vision of the landscape.

It was the land grant system, under the direct authority of governors, which would be maintained throughout Australia for another 20 years and form the only official means of broadening the base of settlement. Under Governor Lachlan **Macquarie** the system of grants reached its height. Macquarie held the view that rural areas should have towns constructed as service centres and places of government. Moreover, he believed that yeomen farmers, in the British tradition, should become the backbone of society, and policy should be framed for their benefit. Few admitted that the Australian environment was more suited to grazing than intensive English **agriculture**. Large landowners and wool, growers, like John **Macarthur**, Samuel **Marsden**, and Gregory **Blaxland**, sought to expand the territory available and it was the manoeuvring of private individuals that opened a path to new land in the west beyond the Blue Mountains.

By the end of the Macquarie era, the investigations and report of Commissioner J.T. **Bigge** were altering the way in which land settlement progressed. Bigge also supported the role of small farmers, but saw that wool could provide export earnings. He encouraged a new type of settler who would purchase land from the Crown and have a permanent stake in the country. The implementation of his report paved the way for the settlement of vast tracts of land by British-backed investment companies like the Australian Agricultural Company and the Van Diemen's Land Company, and in the division of land into counties, hundreds, and parishes. The government wanted order in the occupation of land.

Order, though, was not what wool-growers saw as the future. In the 1820s and 1830s it was common for squatters to follow in the tracks of explorers such as Thomas **Mitchell** and Charles **Sturt**, and grab the best-watered pasture they could find for their flocks and herds. One writer noted that 'dispersion', not confinement, was the natural law of settlement. It was not surprising that a theory of ordered settlement and colonisation, propounded by Edward Gibbon **Wakefield**, gained the attention of the British government. SA was settled according to his plan, which married land sales, labour, and capital as an enticement to free, respectable British settlers. At **Swan River settlement**, the attempt to use convict labour and to apportion land by grant met with a host of problems and seemed to indicate that Wakefield's ideas had merit.

In NSW, Governor George **Gipps** wanted to use other means to curb the chaotic spread of squatting and to introduce permanent settlement for graziers. He believed that 'the occupation of land should be made difficult instead of easy', and wanted to use the revenue gained from land sales to squatters for assisting **immigration**. His plans to make the squatters pay more for their land met with organised opposition. Ken Buckley examined 'Gipps and the Graziers of New South Wales' (*HSANZ*, 1955–56). One of the surprising aspects of this tussle is dealt with by Barrie Dyster in 'Support for the Squatters, 1844' (*JRAHS*, 1965).

By lobbying in London, the squatters obtained much better terms than Gipps had offered them: 14-year leases on their lands. With the influx of population in the **gold rushes**, the distribution of these sheepwalks to agricultural settlers became a vital political issue. A host of **Selection** Acts in various colonies—**Robertson's** Land Acts in NSW, Nicholson's and **Duffy's** in Victoria, and Strangways' in SA—attempted to put small farmers on the land. The acts produced varying results: good in SA; initial failure and then success in Victoria; scattered success in NSW. The **wheat** belt developed in NSW only after the Selection Act was amended and railways reached across the Dividing Range. The best account of this process is a local study by Bill Gammage, *Narrandera Shire* (1986).

From the last decades of the nineteenth century, the impact of introduced **pests**, erosion, **drought**, and other natural disasters caused governments to rethink their land policies. A more 'scientific' approach to farming was espoused, and **irrigation** schemes and **closer settlement** were championed. The schemes of the **Chaffey** brothers in Victoria and SA forced governments to look at new initiatives, despite the huge cost. J.M. Powell, *Watering the Garden State* (1989), and B.R. Davidson, *Australia Wet or Dry?* (1969), explore the impact of these concepts.

The move towards more intensive settlement continued during and after World War I. The introduction of **soldier settlement** schemes was considered essential by both public and governments. These schemes were often poorly executed and caused enormous financial loss and personal catastrophe to those involved, resulting in Samuel Wadham's statement in *Land Utilization in Australia* (1939) that the attempts by governments to create systems of intensive small-scale farming in Australia were nonsensical.

In WA, a Homestead Act (1893) was developed to place settlers on new farming land, supported by loans from the government's Agricultural Bank. Similarly, in the 1920s, **group settlements** were created with the bank's support. These were put together with groups of 20 to 30 men and their families, and included many newly arrived British immigrants. Few succeeded, and those that showed promise were unable to sustain the exigencies of the great **Depression**. These débâcles are movingly explored in Geoffrey **Bolton**, *A Fine Country to Starve In* (1972), and Bill Bunbury, *Reading Labels on Jam Tins: Living Through Difficult Times* (1993).

The Depression effectively quashed plans for new progress of land settlement, and it was only the advent of World War II which eventually brought a level of security to rural industries. The war itself spawned another soldier settlement scheme—this time much altered. The first glimpse of the changed approach of governments was seen in the SA Crown Lands Development Act, 1943, which obliged government to clear and improve land before settlers were moved in. In the early 1950s, the Australian Mutual Provident Society was given the right to pursue a similar strategy in its developments and land settlement schemes in the south-east of SA. Generally, these were successful and profitable moves and a vast improvement on earlier schemes.

By the 1960s, land settlement was no longer the preserve of government action, or of private enterprise. Urban encroachment on former rural lands and the genesis of community environmental concern were changing the pattern from land development to preservation. Throughout the 1980s and 1990s the issue of **Aboriginal land rights** further affected settlement policies. The one certainty that remains unchanged is that all settlers—farmers, graziers, horticulturists, and others—have had to battle with the environment they occupied. Nothing about land settlement has been easy. S.H. **Roberts**, *History of Australian Land Settlement* (1924, 1968), is still the only single-volume treatment of the subject.

Rob Linn

Landscape is sometimes discussed as the stage or setting on which the events of Australian history have unfolded. But this is a misleading metaphor: first, because it implies a passive role for the 'stage', and second, because it assumes that the landscape was simply 'there', waiting. But it was not like that at all. The idea of a passive landscape is a biophysical version of the doctrine of *terra nullius*, that the land was not only unowned: it was available, passively receptive, and, in a sense, already 'known'—because, after all, rivers are rivers, plains are plains, forests are forests. We also tend to impose our current knowledge of the landscape on those who were encountering it for the first time: for example, school texts show the routes of the explorers on the maps of an explored land, but for the explorers themselves, the map stopped where they pitched camp each night, as Paul Carter reminds us in *The Road to Botany Bay* (1987).

The new arrivals brought their own ways of seeing, and there has been a long, difficult, and continuing process of mutual readjustment. The European taxonomies they brought with them simply broke down in an environment which did not obey Europe's rules. In **Swan River** colony, for example, early colonists observed that their stock were dying from an unknown poison but long failed to identify the culprit, a legume named *Gastrolobium calycinum*, which contains the deadly monofluoroacetic acid. As J.M.R. Cameron showed in *Ambition's Fire* (1981), they had unconsciously carried over the European assumption that legumes were excellent pasture plants. **Drought** is also, as R.L. Heathcote observed in *Geographical Review* (1969), 'a problem of perception'. To speak of 'drought' is to say that the rainfall has failed to live up to our expectations; but the failure lies with our expectations, not with the rainfall.

A history of the Australian landscape is therefore a history of the ways in which it has been perceived, and this is recorded in diverse forms: in the work of landscape painters, poems, works of fiction; in the rhetoric of politicians; in journals and diaries; and in the books and papers of **art historians**, historical geographers, and **environmental** and **social historians**, among others. Thus 'landscape' is a cultural construct, one that changes with time and place according to the perceptions and needs of a society. Generally, however, there is enough consensus at a given time to speak and write of landscapes as if they had an objective reality 'out there'. The term has long been used in both the subjective and objective sense, and it is so used here; first, to exemplify the history of the growth of scientific understanding of the land and of its evolution; second, to exemplify the history of emotional responses to it.

The landscapes of Australia are very diverse physically, ranging from the Daintree rainforest in north Qld to the Simpson Desert of Central Australia and the intensely humanised valley of the Tamar in Tasmania. Nevertheless, the continent is sufficiently distinctive to allow a few broad generalisations. Most of it is low, flat, dry, with a highly variable rainfall. It is exceptionally fire-prone; has infertile soils; enjoys great biodiversity; and is tectonically stable. Its maximum extent lies in the latitude of the thirties, that of the world's great deserts, but there is little true desert in Australia in either sense of the word: devoid of people or devoid of vegetation. Most of it is vegetated, although sparsely, and most of it is populated, although at very low density.

The variability of the rainfall is now known to be a response to ENSO (the El Niño Southern Oscillation), and this is one of the ways in which scientific research has contributed to a better understanding of the Australian environment, which remains difficult but less unpredictably so. The low fertility of the soils, which have very low levels of phosphorus and the trace elements, is a function of the age of the landscapes, most of which have undergone countless cycles of weathering without renewal. None of the three great soil-makers have been operative in the recent history of the continent: deep alluvial soils come from high mountains and big rivers; extensive volcanism can create rich soils; continental ice-sheets are soil-making machines, grinding up the bedrock to release fresh nutrients, so effective in Europe, North America and China. Not in Australia.

Another factor contributing to low fertility has been the millennia of Aboriginal **fire-stick farming**, which entailed a constant loss of nutrients. Archaeologists are making a major contribution to our understanding of the evolution of the Australian landscapes; as Sylvia Hallam noted in *Fire and Hearth* (1975), the land 'was not as God made it. It was as the Aborigines made it.' They managed and largely created the sclerophyll woodlands with a grassy understorey, regularly described as 'park-like' by the first European settlers, and so well suited to pastoral use, with sheep replacing the kangaroo; but Aboriginal land-use played a part in promoting a fire-tolerant vegetation at the expense of fire-sensitive species. It also contributed to erosion and to the extinction of the megafauna, although the extinctions may have been due to direct hunting (as Tim Flannery argues in *The Future Eaters*, 1994), habitat modification (according to John **Mulvaney**, *The Prehistory of Australia*, 1969, 1975), climate change, or two or three in combination.

Despite massive impact on the physical landscape, the megafauna, and the vegetation, Aboriginal land-use maintained a very high level of biodiversity. This has been greatly reduced by European settlement, which has led to some of the highest extinction rates in the world, largely through modification of habitat and through the introduction of exotic plants and animals. Australia is unique in being an island continent, but this has made it extraordinarily vulnerable to **pests** imported from overseas, of which the rabbit has been the most destructive. Its depredations are described in Eric **Rolls**, *They All Ran Wild* (1969).

The botanical riches of Australia are great, and are now seen as a major resource, after many decades of ill-advised clearing, especially in salt-prone land. Yet even in cleared pastures, sown with introduced species such as subterranean clover and phalaris in the south, paspalum and lucerne in the north, there are often surviving indigenous trees, generally eucalypts. 'The eucalypts', said Otto Frankel in George Seddon and Mari Davis (eds), *Man and Landscape in Australia* (1976), 'are the epitome of the Australian landscape, expressing in its one genus, its essence and its distinctiveness. We are aware of them even—in the distant background, as on the treeless plains in the tablelands; and the impact of the riverine plains, occasioned by their treeless vastness, is grand rather than monotonous because, at the back of one's mind, there are the great trees by the river some few miles away.' The oaks of Europe and the Near East may once have played a similar role of linking diverse environments within a large continuous landmass, but they do so no longer. Only in Australia are two genera, *Eucalyptus* and *Acacia*—more familiarly, the gum tree and the wattle—able to dominate a continent. The volatile oils of the eucalypt give the haze of the blue hills. The smell of the crushed or burning leaves is immediately evocative for most Australians, and the golden wattle has symbolic force, summarising these landscapes of the sun.

The changes in emotional responses to the Australian landscape have been well documented by, for example, the historical geographer J.M. Powell in *Mirrors of the New World* (1977). Barron **Field** did not care for the gum tree; the evergreen sclerophyll leaf 'does not savour of humanity—There is no flesh and blood in it: it is not of us, and is nothing to us.' Nature in Australia seemed to him to defy 'all the the dearest allegories of human life'—a comment that shows awareness that 'landscape' is in part an allegorical construct. Nature was inverted in the Antipodes, where 'all things' were 'topsy-turvey': the swans were black, the platypus, if not a hoax, certainly a paradox. In time, we grew our own allegories. Countless schoolchildren learned to 'love a sunburnt country' along with Dorothea **Mackellar**, writing from a high-rainfall refuge in Pittwater. Several generations later, the schoolchildren have had to learn to love sunscreen lotions and floppy hats.

Painters and art historians give a clear account of the way in which visual images of the landscape have changed: they began with conventions of representation that 'Europeanised' it, then the grey-greens of the **Heidelberg School**, the 'golden summers' of **Streeton**, the 'red shift' that came with Tom **Roberts** as the painters sought subjects further from the coast, followed in time by the harsh landscapes of Sidney **Nolan**, Albert **Tucker**, Fred **Williams**, and others. But if the painters—and photographers like Richard Woldendorp—moved inland, their clients and the bulk of the population remained on the coast; unless they made a once-in-a-lifetime pilgrimage to that new-made Australian Mecca, Ayers Rock, now **Uluru**.

'In a country urbanised before a landscape was colonised, a "geography" of the land continues to be shaped as much by the imagination as by reality ... [The **bush**] was a cultural reality before *the landscape* acquired a specific form', remarks the art historian, Ian Burn, in *National Life and Landscapes* (1990). Perhaps its most characteristic form is that of the obsessively ordered, tentacular suburbia of the coastal cities ('sprawling' is inept; to sprawl is to be informal and relaxed). The coast remains central to our consciousness, because that is what 'the **outback**' and 'the inland', two distictively Australian terms, are measured from.

GEORGE SEDDON

Lane, William 'Billy' (1861–1917) was a utopian socialist who created the **New Australia** settlement in Paraguay. He was born in England and arrived in Brisbane in 1885, having spent several years in North America. In 1887 he established a radical weekly, the *Boomerang*, and from 1890 was the editor of the *Worker*, the journal of the Qld labour movement.

Lane had little direct influence on the course of the Qld **shearers' strike**, but his name is often associated with it in Labor folklore. He wrote a novel, *The Workingman's Paradise* (1892), to raise money for the imprisoned unionists. The defeat of the unions disillusioned Lane; in 1893 he took a group of Australians to Paraguay to establish a socialist colony and thus 'write the history of humanity on the rocks of the Andes'. The experiment failed as dissension quickly developed among the colonists. Lane's authoritarianism and insistence that the colonists abstain from alcohol caused much of the friction. The colony split in 1894 and Lane, who had developed a pronounced Messiah complex, led his closest followers to a new site called Cosme. He left South America in 1899 and went to live in Auckland, where he wrote for the conservative *New Zealand Herald*. He edited that newspaper from 1913 until his death in 1917.

Lane has fascinated historians, political propagandists, and creative writers. He was the subject of a sympathetic biography by Lloyd Ross published in 1935. Gavin **Souter** helped to revive interest in Lane with his book on the Australians in Paraguay, *A Peculiar People* (1968). Lane also features prominently in Vance **Palmer's** play *Hail Tomorrow!* (1947) and, more recently, in a 'documentary novel' by Michael Wilding, *The Paraguayan Experiment* (1984). Historians disagree, however, over what place to accord Lane in the history of the Australian labour movement. Some have argued that he was the most powerful figure in the Qld labour movement until 1893, and that his utopian **socialism** had a lasting impact on radical politics in that colony and even beyond its borders. Others have suggested that his influence was transitory. Lane was not an original socialist thinker, but had great influence as a publicist. His socialism was sentimental and utopian. He defined socialism as 'the desire to be mates' and has Nellie, the heroine of *The Workingman's Paradise*, illustrate the meaning of socialism by kissing a sleeping prostitute on the cheek. Some historians, such as Verity Burgmann in '*In Our Time*' (1985), have stressed Lane's desire to defuse class conflict; others, such as Michael Wilding in his edition of *The Workingman's Paradise* (1980), have emphasised the influence of Marxist ideas on his thought.

Lane's reputation declined sharply in the 1970s and 1980s as historians gave closer scrutiny to his racism, while his attitude to gender attracted the attention of feminist historians. Marilyn Lake in *LH* (1986) argued that Lane's socialism arose from an anxiety about the impact of wage labour on workers' manhood. Bruce Scates (*LH*, 1990) responded with the claim that Lane was an ardent feminist who nurtured the vision of men and women enjoying equality as 'mates'. While Lane's racism has seriously damaged his reputation, his idealism is still alluring to many Australians. He has retained a place in 'the legend of the 1890s'.

FRANK BONGIORNO

Lang, John Dunmore (1799–1878) came from Scotland to be the pioneer Presbyterian minister in NSW in

1823. He was one of the most controversial figures in colonial religious and political history. As a churchman, Lang earned more notoriety than distinction; he was imprisoned once for debt and twice for libel. He was deposed from the ministry in 1842 and for 20 years presided over his own synod. He was elected to the NSW Legislative Council in 1843 and ended his political career as a member of the Legislative Assembly in 1870. A radical democrat, Lang was also the first to argue for the formation of the Australian colonies into a federated **republic**.

Lang's influence soon extended well beyond his pulpit, where his preaching was unexceptional. In 1831 he founded the Australian College, which survived to 1854. Lang sought to counteract the emancipist influence in colonial society and made several voyages to Britain to recruit respectable Protestant immigrants. His denunciation of the alleged disproportion of Irish Catholic immigrants in *The Question of Questions!* (1841) and *Popery in Australia and the Southern Hemisphere* (1847), the latter largely directed against Caroline **Chisholm's** recruitment of single Irish Catholic women, marked him out as an exceptionally bigoted Protestant. For all this, he brought out some Scottish Catholics, among them the future parents of Mary **MacKillop**. His last big **immigration** venture was a fiasco which he blamed unjustly on the Colonial Office. It led to his imprisonment for debt in Melbourne in 1850, and for libel in Sydney in 1851.

His entry into colonial politics began in sectarian uproar. Despite his blatant anti-Catholicism, however, Catholic historians generally acknowledge that Lang's shift to a radical democratic platform won him the support of Irish Catholics. As well as campaigning for a democratic constitution on Chartist principles, Lang forecast a federated Australian republic in *The Coming Event!* (1850, 1870) and *Freedom and Independence for the Golden Lands of Australia* (1852, 1857). He founded the Australian League with limited support, to work for independence. Not a doctrinaire republican, he envisaged a friendly separation from Britain.

Throughout his life Lang was vituperative and vindictive, using platform and press, especially his own newspapers—the *Colonist* 1835–40, the *Colonial Observer* 1841–44, and the *Press* 1851—to attack his opponents and alarm his friends. Highly ambitious, he nevertheless worked for the common good, as he saw it, and not for personal gain. He was remarkably self-righteous and promoted himself as well as the colony in *An Historical and Statistical Account of New South Wales* (1834, 1837, 1852, 1875) which the *Westminster Review* declared should have been called *A History of Dr Lang to which is added a History of New South Wales*. There is a comprehensive bibliography of Lang's writings by Ian McLaren (1985). D.W.A. Baker edited his *Reminiscences* for publication in 1972, with a critical introduction. His scholarly biography, *Days of Wrath* (1985), is comprehensive and critically sympathetic, leaving the reader to discern Lang's real strengths amid his obvious weaknesses. His statue in Sydney bears his wife's ascription—'Patriot and Statesman'. Of the former there can be no doubt; the latter is more contentious.

WALTER PHILLIPS

Lang, John Thomas 'Jack' (1876–1975) was a real estate agent, suburban subdivider and mayor, who became Labor premier of NSW, serving from 1925 to 1927 and from 1930 to 1932, when he was sacked by the state governor. A dominant figure in the Australian political landscape for more than half a century, Lang combined democratic impulses with a well-orchestrated campaign against his rivals, most of whom were within his own party.

He entered parliament in 1913 as member for Granville, an outer Sydney suburb. He was treasurer 1920–22, praised by the general manager of the Bank of New South Wales for his conservative financial style. He became leader in 1923 and won a narrow victory in the May 1925 elections. He introduced a widow's pension, a Workers Compensation Act, and **child endowment**, and restored the 44-hour week, first introduced by Labor in 1921. His reputation as a reformer stems from his first period in power, which ended with his defeat in the October 1927 election.

Lang did not have strong support in the parliamentary caucus, but by an alliance with the radical union leader Jock **Garden** he had himself declared leader by the party's conference. Criticised for being the tool of communists and socialists, Lang came in fact to dominate the party, expelling communists and neutralising socialists. Labor won the October 1930 election with a promise to lead NSW out of the misery of the **Depression**. In February 1931 he presented the 'Lang Plan', which proposed the suspension of interest payments to British bond-holders. Prime Minister **Scullin** and his Treasurer **Theodore** rejected the idea, but in March Lang refused to pay the bond-holders interest, stating that it was more important to pay the dole.

Lang aroused so much fear among the middle class that a paramilitary organisation, the New Guard, was formed to protect the state from him. In January 1932 its leader Eric Campbell told his supporters that the people of NSW would not permit Mr Lang to open the new Sydney Harbour Bridge; a New Guard horseman, Captain de Groot, beat Lang to the ribbon on 19 March 1932.

When the non-Labor parties came to power in Canberra in December 1931, they paid the interest on the NSW debt and used federal power to reclaim the amount from the state. On 10 May Lang issued a circular instructing public servants to send all the money they collected to the state Treasury and not to deposit it with the banks where it could be seized by the Commonwealth. Governor Game, already under pressure to dismiss Lang, arranged to meet him on the afternoon of Friday 13 May. Just before the meeting, Game received a deputation from British companies holding mortgages in NSW, under threat of a 10 per cent capital tax proposed by Lang. Game dismissed Lang on the grounds of the allegedly illegal circular to public servants, but its legality was never tested in the courts. At the elections on 11 June 1932 Lang was swept from office, never to regain power. He retained control of the state branch of the Australian Labor Party, despite federal attempts to remove him, until the late 1930s, and his supporters constituted a separate group in the Commonwealth Parliament.

Lang became a legend in his own lifetime. Jock Garden declared him to be 'greater than Lenin'. Lang promoted his own place in history in his books, *I Remember* (1956), *The Great Bust!* (1962), and *The Turbulent Years* (1970). He became a folk hero to a generation of Australians who knew little of the Depression. Bede **Nairn** (*The 'Big Fella'*, 1986) portrays him as a bully who knew when to retreat. While Nairn admits Lang's democratic impulses and populist abilities, he cannot forgive him for disrupting the Australian Labor Party, especially his attacks on Labor prime ministers **Curtin** and **Chifley**. *Jack Lang* (1977), a series of essays edited by Heather Radi and Peter Spearritt, examines all aspects of his career and the bases of his support. In 1971 Lang was readmitted to the Labor Party on the motion of his young protégé, Paul **Keating**.

PETER SPEARRITT

Languages have always proliferated, though since 1788 English as spoken by the English themselves has been the prestige language model. When the **First Fleet** arrived in 1788 more than 250 languages were spoken by the indigenous people, along with hundreds more dialects of these languages. Those on the First Fleet were also multivoiced—convicts spoke the dialects of more than 30 counties, and others born in Ireland, the Channel Islands, Scotland, Wales, North America, the West Indies, and Madagascar contributed, in small ways, to the linguistic heritage of Australia. The **gold rushes** of the 1850s brought a new influx of voices from many countries, including China. Indeed, in the nineteenth century there were pockets of Australia where English was not the dominant language.

At the end of the twentieth century, however, the number of **Aboriginal languages** still actively spoken has been whittled down to some 50. Countervailing this attrition, the migration after World War II brought a new influx of languages into Australia. More than 100 community languages are now spoken. In addition, Kriol is firmly established in northern Australia, and various forms of Aboriginal English are spoken across Australia. Auslan is the sign language of more than 7000 Australians.

In spite of this multilingualism, English has always dominated the public domain. But which English? In addition to all the other voices of the colony, a distinctive Australian English developed in its early years. From the 1820s a clash between the native-born Australian and the British visitor or immigrant is often expressed in terms of a clash of language—**currency** versus **sterling**, *old chum* versus **new chum**. The English Miss Withering in Catherine Helen **Spence's** *Clara Morison* (1854) complains about the language of the colonials: 'I understand *English,* but I see you colonists are corrupting the language sadly. It is a pity, for the purity of their diction marks the lady and gentleman … I see I must get you to explain the unintelligible words and phrases I meet with in the Adelaide newspapers, Miss Hodges. What is a "nobbler neat", for instance?' Miss Withering's puzzlement at the term *nobbler* is understandable, since it is an Australian transfer (meaning 'a measure of alcoholic spirits') from *nobble*

in the sense 'to drug or lame (a horse)' or 'to strike (especially on the head or *nob*)'. Indeed, many of the colonial terms which puzzled the new chums were not colonial-grown, but borrowings from various British dialects. Thus, *billy* is from Aberdeen, *dinkum* from Derby and Lincolnshire, *cobber* from Suffolk, *boomer* from Warwickshire, *shivoo* from Yorkshire, and *barrack for* from Northern Ireland. The conflict between currency and sterling is not simply between Australian and British. British dialects provided terms to the emerging Australian English, and it was the mixing and levelling of British dialects in the colony which produced the distinctive Australian accent. The conflict includes an undercurrent of a social conflict between British dialects and an emerging Standard British English (the purity of diction of Miss Withering's lady and gentleman).

By the end of the nineteenth century there was a strong interest, popular as well as scholarly, in Australian English, as indicated by the anonymous *Sydney Slang Dictionary* (?1882); Karl Lentzner, *Dictionary of the Slang-English of Australia* (1892); Cornelius Crowe, *The Australian Slang Dictionary* (1895); E.E. Morris, *Austral English: A Dictionary of Australasian Words, Phrases and Usages* (1898); and Joshua Lake's dictionary of Australasian words in the Australian edition of *Webster's International Dictionary of the English Language* (1898). The *Bulletin* in the 1890s published many articles dealing with Australianisms, as well as fostering writers who used a distinctively Australian idiom. This widespread popular and scholarly interest in Australian English was in part an expression of the **radical nationalist** sentiments of the 1890s. As Australia moved towards **Federation**, one might have expected a strong assertion of linguistic independence, of the kind instituted in America by Noah Webster in his *American Dictionary of the English Language* (1828). Webster's assertion of linguistic independence followed a political War of Independence. In Australia, however, the interest in Australian English waned; the incipient linguistic war of independence ran out of steam in the major public discourses; an Australian dictionary would not appear until 1976.

Nationalistic sentiment continued into the new century, but its radicalism had lost its impetus, and it carried with it such albatrosses as the **White Australia** policy, the dictation test, and racist attitudes towards the indigenous people. Whatever the motives of later segregationist or assimilationist policies, the assumption was that the voices of Aboriginal Australia would disappear. The **immigration** policy after World War I favoured British migrants, signalling adherence to Empire and to the implicit policy of monolingualism. There had been schools which taught in community languages in the nineteenth century, but these disappeared. In this postwar climate, Australian English was not a topic of serious interest: received or standard English was the prestige form. W.H. Downing's *Digger Dialects* (1919) reminds us of the significance of war in the creation of the Australian lexicon, but there is a large gap between this work and the appearance of the first edition of Sidney **Baker's** *The Australian Language* in 1945. A.G. Mitchell's *The Pronunciation of English in Australia* (1946) was hostilely received. Thus while the lexical element and the pronunciation of Australian English have always been part of the construction of Australian identity, an odd feature of the history of the linguistic expression of this myth of identity is that in the first half of the twentieth century the lexical and pronunciational elements were regarded as sub-standard by reference to British standards. The lexical element was largely judged to be slang, and the pronunciation was condemned, parodied, or suppressed (as it was well into the 1960s by the **Australian Broadcasting Commission**).

The military disasters of World War II marked the need for a foreign policy independent of Britain, but the postwar immigration policy, with its emphasis on Europeans, and its assumptions that migrants would assimilate and speak English, underlined the monolingual imperative. Yet it is perhaps this postwar migration (especially as the White Australia policy was discarded), along with the decreasing confidence in Empire, which effected a radical shift in attitudes towards English in Australia. The stirrings of this change are signalled by the publication of five works in the mid-1960s—Arthur Delbridge and A.G. Mitchell, *The Speech of Australian Adolescents* (1965), which established the categories of Cultivated Australian, General Australian, and Broad Australian; W.S. Ramson, *Australian English: An Historical Study of the Vocabulary 1788–1898* (1966); the third edition of Baker's *The Australian Language* (1978); G.W. Turner, *The English Language in Australia and New Zealand* (1966); the revised edition (with Delbridge) of Mitchell's *The Pronunciation of English in Australia* (1966). Four of these works appeared in the year which marks the end of the **Menzies** era.

For Australian English, it would seem, 'it was almost time'. And it was almost time for a renewed interest in community languages. The requirement that ethnic newspapers obtain a publication permit from the Department of Immigration had been dropped in 1954, but it was not until the 1970s that governments actively encouraged the use of community languages. After the new **nationalism** of the **Whitlam** era (a period when the rules on Asian and African immigration were relaxed, opening up Australia to more languages), Australian-produced dictionaries appeared which included a good sampling of Australianisms within the body of the text. Up until this time the dictionaries used in Australia were British or American (sometimes with a supplement of Australian words). The first of these new Australian dictionaries was Grahame Johnston's *The Australian Pocket Oxford Dictionary*, published in 1976. This was followed five years later by *The Macquarie Dictionary*.

The major work on Australian English, W.S. Ramson's *Australian National Dictionary*, appeared in the Bicentennial year, 1988. Here, for the first time, were on public and scholarly display the more than 10 000 Australian words and expressions which make up Australian English, illustrated by more than 60 000 citations. There are terms which are primarily of historical significance (*Black Line*, *cabbage-tree mob*, *holey dollar*, **Vandemonian**), but all of them are bearers of Australia's history in some way. The 400 words borrowed from some 70 Aboriginal languages are mainly terms for flora, fauna, and physical objects, perhaps the standard lexical fare of

an invading culture, but they are nevertheless central to the lexicon (*billabong*, **corroboree**, *kangaroo*). Some words are part of the constructions of Australian notions of identity (**digger**, *Anzac*, **Aussie**, *mate*). Some define differences, including interstate rivalry (*banana bender*, *crow-eater*, **sandgroper**), social differentiation (**bunyip aristocracy**, *westie*, *bogan*, *silvertail*), or country of origin (*balt*, *pom*, *seppo*). Other words and phrases carry the history of names (*Buckley's chance*, **furphy**, **Goyder's line**, *jacky howe*, *lamington*, *do a Melba*, *game as Ned Kelly*) and folklore (*blind Freddie*, *Jimmy Woodser*, *the man outside Hoyts*, *send 'er down Hughie*). There are stereotypes (*Alf*, *Norm*, *ocker*), and phrases which sum up quintessential Australian attitudes (*no worries*, *don't come the raw prawn*, **tall poppy** *syndrome*).

The emergence of multilingualism did not cause the naturalisation of Australian English, but it was in the climate of an acceptance of other voices, of linguistic diversity, that Australian English was able to cast off the shackles of the post-colonial **cultural cringe**, and that Australia was able to accept and embrace its own distinctive voice.

BRUCE MOORE

Larrikins were members of gangs or **pushes** that arose amongst the working classes of Sydney and Melbourne from the 1870s onwards. The word has dubious origins: despite a popular claim that it derived from an Irish policeman's pronunciation of the word *larking*, it is generally believed to have an English origin. Journalistic accounts provided descriptions of the larrikin's typical physical appearance and habits, and condemned them as a public menace. Despite reports of their violent behaviour, the degree of danger that they actually posed to the public was probably exaggerated. Their recklessness, irreverent antics, and disdain for authority were generally criticised by visiting writers, although Mark Twain in 1897 credited the Australian larrikin with better manners and appearance than those of his English equivalent. C.J. **Dennis** enlivened his lyrical verse, particularly *The Sentimental Bloke* (1915) and *The Moods of Ginger Mick* (1916), with larrikins to whom he attributed sentimentality, humour, and charm. This won larrikins greater public acceptance, and they came to be regarded affectionately, even romantically, for displaying qualities representative of the **national identity**. Noel McLachlan's MA thesis (University of Melbourne, 1950) was an early study of the phenomenon, and James Murray's *Larrikins: A Nineteenth-Century Outrage* (1973) is a lively popular account. Clem Gorman, *The Larrikin Streak* (1990), celebrates and romanticises those typical larrikin qualities which are regarded as inherently Australian.

HD

Lasseter's Lost Reef was a fabled gold reef supposedly located in Central Australia, the search for which was prompted in 1930 by the fervent claims of adventurer Harold Bell Lasseter (1880–1931). A search for the reef by the Central Australian Gold Exploration Co. Ltd later in the same year was unsuccessful and confounded by the death of Lasseter. Ion **Idriess's** novel, *Lasseter's Last Ride* (1931, 1954), generated public interest in the story. While further unsuccessful searches suggested the falsity of the claim, Austin Stapleton in his *Lasseter Did Not Lie!* (1981) supports Lasseter's claims. Later studies include Billy Marshall-Stoneking, *Lasseter: The Making of a Legend* (1985).

HD

Latham, John Greig (1877–1964), lawyer turned politician, was called to the Bar in 1904. He served as head of naval intelligence during World War I and attended the Versailles Peace Conference, where he became highly critical of Billy **Hughes**. Although elected MHR in 1922 for the seat of Kooyong, Victoria, as an independent, he joined the **Nationalist Party** three years later and succeeded S.M. **Bruce** as leader after the federal election of 1929. A tall, aloof man of chilling propriety, he was incapable of wooing popularity. He stepped aside for Joseph **Lyons** in 1931. Latham held the portfolio of attorney-general 1925–29 and again 1932–35, when he was also minister for external affairs. In this capacity he led an important Asian mission in 1934. He introduced anti-strike legislation and was vigilant in surveillance of the **Communist** Party. In 1935 he was appointed chief justice of the High Court of Australia and held that position until 1952. He was the sole High Court judge to support the **Menzies** government's attempt to ban the Communist Party. Zelman Cowen wrote about him in *Sir John Latham and Other Papers* (1965).

KT

Law, Phillip Garth (1912–), scientist and Antarctic explorer, became entranced by **Antarctica** as a boy through the writings of pioneer explorers such as Shackleton and **Mawson**. After graduating in physics from the University of Melbourne, he went on to complete an MSc degree before joining the staff as a physics lecturer. His first trip to the Antarctic was as senior scientific officer on the 1947–48 Australian National Antarctic Research Expedition, Australia's first since the war. When a permanent Antarctic organisation was established, Law was appointed director, and remained in the position from 1949 to 1966. During this time he made frequent exploratory trips to the Australian Antarctic Territory, and oversaw the establishment of Mawson, Casey, and Davis bases. He chaired several committees on marine and Antarctic research and was president of the Royal Society of Victoria 1967–69. His achievements have been recognised by national and international geographical societies. His published works include *Antarctic Odyssey* (1983). Papers from a symposium held to honour his eightieth birthday (Janet Mentha and Graeme Watson, eds) were published in 1992. Kathleen Ralston has written a biography of his early years, *A Man for Antarctica* (1993).

KT

Lawler, Raymond Evenor (1921–) wrote the classic Australian play *Summer of the Seventeenth Doll*, first performed at the Union Theatre, Melbourne, on 28 November 1955. Set in 1953, the *Doll* portrays the decline of the **Australian Legend** through two Queensland canecutters, who arrive in Melbourne for their seventeenth consecutive summer lay-off and discover that the world has changed. Australian audiences recognised themselves in the play, Lawler's ninth, which triumphed in London (1957), but flopped in New York (1958). Lawler was born in Footscray, Victoria, and left school at 13, working in factories before taking up acting and playwriting. He appeared in the Melbourne and London productions of the *Doll*, then remained in Europe from 1957 to 1975, returning as a Melbourne Theatre Company director 1975–87. His *Kid Stakes* (1975), set in 1937, and *Other Times* (1976), set in 1945, combined with the original play to form *The Doll Trilogy* (1977, 1978). The *Doll* is a landmark in Australian theatrical history; adaptations, including a film (1959) and an opera (1996), testify to its enduring cultural significance.

DC

Lawrence, (David Herbert) D.H. (1885–1930) arrived in Fremantle, WA, with his wife, Frieda, on 4 May 1922. He had already published the novels that would establish his literary reputation, and was a minor, if controversial, celebrity. The decision to visit Australia was accidental: the couple were caught between an unsuccessful visit to Ceylon and Lawrence's time at an artists' colony in Taos, New Mexico. He spent two weeks in WA among Perth's exiguous literary circles, meeting Mollie Skinner, whose manuscript he would rework into the collaborative novel, *The Boy in the Bush* (1924). The Lawrences then continued the voyage to Sydney, arriving on 27 May and taking a house, Wyewurk, at Thirroul, 87 kilometres south, where Lawrence wrote the bulk of *Kangaroo* over the next six weeks. They left Sydney on 11 August. The novel was completed in New Mexico, and published in October 1923.

The visit attracted little public notice in Sydney at the time. Lawrence did not bask in the celebrity normally accorded the 'famous overseas visitor' by the local press and *Kangaroo* attracted little critical attention on publication, Australian booksellers initially turning it down. The lack of interest became something of an embarrassment to Australian literary circles as Lawrence's international reputation grew. We had had a brush with a modern genius and hadn't noticed. As a consequence, the novel and Lawrence have had a continuing notoriety as a touchstone of national culture.

Kangaroo is preoccupied with the vastness and emptiness of Australia as a metaphor for democracy and suburban life—Lawrence was revising his 'Essay on Democracy' in 1922. His evocative descriptions of **Sydney**, the **bush** and Australian social attitudes came to be seen as evidence of an artist's capacity to penetrate the soul of a place, seeing what the locals could not; his summations of Australia were increasingly quoted, with or without acknowledgment. While nationalists saw Lawrence's sense of the beauty of the bush positively—the *Bulletin*, which Lawrence read closely during his stay, reviewed the novel as 'a very beautiful book full of the sunshine and flowers of Australia'—they read his social criticism as that of a 'typical "pommy" neurasthenic'. On the other hand, critics of Australian 'philistinism' found sustenance in Lawrence's social commentary, and saw *Kangaroo* as the sum total of 'Australian literature'.

The plot of *Kangaroo*, revolving around an underground right-wing secret army, was assumed at first to be fantasy, or the weaving of Lawrence's knowledge of Italian fascism into an Australian setting. However, from the 1960s scholars inquired further into the history of **secret armies** in Australia. The research of Robert Darroch (*D.H. Lawrence in Australia*, 1981) and Andrew Moore (*The Secret Army and the Premier*, 1989) in particular suggests that the novel was not just uncannily prescient, but was based on Lawrence's acquaintance with a secret army connected to the king and Empire alliance, and its leaders, Charles Rosenthal and Jack Scott. However, Lawrence's biographer, David Ellis, disputes this claim with a detailed reconstruction of his subject's Australian itinerary.

Lawrence's popular reputation was based on his literary investigation of **sexuality**. He reinforced an Australian cultural stereotype which equated intellectualism with sexual deviance. Australia followed Britain in banning his 1928 novel, *Lady Chatterley's Lover*, a ban maintained by the minister for customs, against the advice of the Literature Censorship Board, on the eve of the famous English trial which saw the novel's release in Britain in 1960. The minister went further and banned the account of the trial, which A.W. Sheppard then published in Australia in 1965, an action which precipitated a significant relaxation of Australian censorship.

RICHARD WHITE

Lawson, Henry Archibald (1867–1922), balladist and short-story writer, was the most talented of the nationalist writers associated with the Sydney *Bulletin* in the closing decades of the nineteenth century. His stories of **bush** life, with their laconic humour and realism, exemplified the Australian code of **mateship** and became a touchstone for later writers and historians.

Lawson's life was unlucky almost from the first. His parents—a runaway Norwegian seaman, Niels (Peter), and Louisa **Lawson** (née Albury), the daughter of small farmers in the Gulgong area—were an ill-matched pair. Henry, their eldest child, grew up on their small selection, witnessing his father's unavailing struggle to make a living as a farmer and prospector, and the slow disintegration of his parents' marriage. At the age of seven his hearing became impaired and this accentuated his feelings of awkwardness and loneliness. He left school, after only about three years of interrupted tuition, and worked in the bush with his father until 1883, when Louisa, who had now fled to Sydney, called for him to join her.

His poem 'Faces in the Street', evokes his 'shabby, supersensitive, soul-starved bushboy's' view of the big city, while his 'Arvie Aspinall' short stories are a Dickensian reworking of his experiences at Hudson's ('Grinder Brothers') factory. Louisa's pent-up intellectual and religious impulses had meanwhile found new direction as a participant in Sydney's radical subculture of freethinkers, spiritualists, suffragists, socialists, and **republicans**. Her son's first published works were tub-thumping anthems such as 'The Army of the Rear' and 'Song of the Republic'. In 1887 his ballad 'The Wreck of the Derry Castle' attracted the notice of the editor of the *Bulletin*, J.F. **Archibald**, who became his principal literary champion. He was soon one of the paper's regular contributors.

But Lawson's economic and emotional equilibrium remained precarious. His *Bulletin* contributions brought fame but little fortune: in 1899 he calculated that 12 years' writing had yielded only £700. Already he was falling into the cycle of odd jobs, sporadic writing, and heavy drinking that characterised his adult life. Among the *Bulletin*'s stable of 'bush' writers he was the sardonic realist, Banjo **Paterson**, the sunny romantic. In their famous duel in verse in the *Bulletin* early in 1892, Lawson had dismissed his rival as a 'City Bushman'; but his own experience of the outback was still limited. In September he accepted Archibald's offer of £5 and a rail ticket out to Bourke in return for an undertaking to write about his travels through the drought-stricken outback—a journey retraced by Robyn Burrows and Alan Barton in *Henry Lawson: A Stranger on the Darling* (1996). He humped his swag a further 200 kilometres out to Hungerford, a purgatorial six-month journey from which emerged some of his finest stories, including 'The Bush Undertaker', 'Hungerford', and 'The Union Buries its Dead'. They offered a searing vision of the landscape and ethos of 'the grand Australian bush—the nurse and tutor of eccentric minds, the home of the weird, and of much that is different from things in other lands'—and of the stoic code of mateship by which its inhabitants lived.

In 1896 Lawson married Bertha Bredt, and his life briefly entered a new and more stable phase. With her support, he sought new opportunities away from the bars of Sydney, in WA and NZ, but these ventures were short-lived. As his literary reputation grew, admirers encouraged him to try his prospects in London, where he might find a larger readership. The couple left, with their two children, in April 1900; but in spite of some encouraging signs, the breakthrough did not come. Two years later they were back in Sydney, sick, penniless, and emotionally exhausted. In December 1902 Lawson attempted suicide; soon afterwards his marriage finally broke up. He was not yet 40, but it was the beginning of the end. Although friends tried to support him, his drinking got worse and the periods of depression longer and more intense. He became a familiar, pathetic figure on Sydney streets: David Low's 1911 caricature—beanpole body, crumpled suit, drooping moustache, tipsy salute—captured him best. With the outbreak of war in 1914, the bellicose streak evident in the young Lawson's revolutionary verse found a new outlet in jingoistic calls to arms. He continued to write but, as Brian Matthews shows in *The Receding Wave* (1972), the originality of his early work was gone. By the time he died, his reputation had long outlived his creativity.

Perhaps no Australian writer has exerted such a strong fascination for historians. As John Hirst showed in *The World of Albert Facey* (1992), Lawson was an acute observer of bush life with an almost intuitive grasp of the forces transforming his own society, of how 'the mighty Bush' was being 'tethered to the world'. His writings also contain a distinctive and influential vision of Australia's past. The **socialism** of the young Lawson was of a romantic visionary kind which looked backward to a golden age when men were braver and kinder, and forward to a future in which lost battles would be refought and won. In imagination he liked to revisit the great days of sea exploration ('the days when the word was wide') and the 'roaring days' of the 1850s **gold rushes**. Lawson's own knowledge of Australian history was also probably acquired through reminiscence and folklore; but he was conscious of the need to ensure that younger Australians were not denied a national past. In an 1887 article, 'A Neglected History', he called for the study of Australian history to be made an essential part of the school curriculum.

After his death, Lawson's life was soon absorbed into the legend he helped to create. In 1931 a statue by George Lambert was erected by popular subscription in the Sydney Domain. Members of a Henry Lawson Society began to gather each year to mark the writer's birthday with readings and commemorative addresses under a gum tree in Melbourne's Footscray Park. His friend J. Le Gay Brereton and daughter Gertrude edited a volume of reminiscences *Henry Lawson by His Mates* (1931) and his wife Bertha contributed a circumspect memoir of *My Henry Lawson* (1943). Readers of Lawson owe much to the heroic labours of Colin Roderick, whose scholarly edition of his writings (1967–72) is an indispensable guide to his sources. Lawson has been the subject of several major biographical studies: Denton Prout, *Henry Lawson: The Grey Dreamer* (1963), is the most concise; Manning **Clark**, *In Search of Henry Lawson* (1978), the most mystical; Xavier Pons, *Out of Eden* (1984), the most psychoanalytic; and Roderick, *The Real Henry Lawson* (1982) and *Henry Lawson: A Life* (1991), the most exhaustively factual.

Views of Lawson and his significance have been a touchstone of historical interpretation for three-quarters of a century. Ernest **Scott**, writing in the midst of the Great War, viewed 'The Star of Australasia' as a premonition of the Anzacs' trial of arms. By 1930 W.K. **Hancock** hailed him as the foremost writer of his generation, who had brought 'self-recognition' to the people of the outback. But his staunchest champions came from the Left, especially from the Popular Front **Communist** Party which found in his creed of mateship a foreshadowing of their own militant brand of socialism. Russel **Ward's** *The Australian Legend* (1958) presents Lawson's bushman as 'the national culture-hero on whose supposed characteristics many Australians tend, consciously or unconsciously, to model their lives'. Not everyone, however, agreed with this estimate. In 1943 Manning Clark had decried the 'myth of "mateyness"', which Lawson had preached to his generation as a 'vain comforter'. Humphrey **McQueen's** *A New Britannia* (1970), published in the midst of the **Vietnam War**, accused him of many of the tenets of fascism, such as racism, anti-intellectualism, militarism, and anti-Semitism. McQueen did not contest Lawson's status as a national icon, but used him to expose an alleged canker in the Australian psyche, a technique since repeated by feminists

such as Miriam **Dixson** (*The Real Matilda*, 1976), and Kay Schaffer (*Women and the Bush*, 1988), for whom he stands as a type of Australian misogyny. Historians will continue to reinterpret him; and his writings will outlive them all.

GRAEME DAVISON

Lawson, Louisa (1848–1920) was a writer, editor, publisher, and pioneer of the women's movement in Australia. When in 1902 the women of NSW received the vote, she was publicly acclaimed as the 'the mother of women's suffrage' in Australia, but she has since been better known as the unsympathetic mother of Australia's most famous writer, Henry **Lawson**.

The second of the 12 children of Henry Albury, 'a good old Kentish yeoman' as she afterwards described him, and his wife Harriet, Louisa was born near Mudgee, NSW, where her father worked as a station hand. Denied by her parents the opportunity to become a pupil teacher, she felt herself to be a drudge in the unhappy and impoverished parental home, from which she escaped by her marriage at the age of 18 to Niels 'Peter' Larsen, a 34-year-old Norwegian sailor who had jumped ship at Melbourne in 1855 to join the gold rush. The couple were ill matched, and in 1883, after 17 stressful years of marriage spent on goldfields and a poor selection near Mudgee, during which five children were born to them, they separated, and she moved to Sydney with her children. When registering the birth of her first-born, Henry, Louisa gave the family name as 'Lawson', an anglicised spelling of her husband's name always used thereafter.

In Sydney she found for the first time in her life a satisfying outlet for her intellectual energy. In 1887, with the help of Henry, she published the short-lived *Republican*, a monthly which undertook, in its own words, 'to observe, to reflect, and then to speak and, if needs be, to castigate'. From 1888 to 1905 she edited and published *The Dawn*, a monthly which proclaimed itself to be 'the Australian Women's Journal and mouthpiece'. In 1889 she established the Dawn Club, a Social Reform Club for Women, and began to campaign for women's suffrage.

Although Louisa Lawson's relations with Henry (he called her 'the Chieftainess') became hostile, even bitter, in later years, he owed much to her, including the publication of his first collection in 1894. Her own creative writing—verse and short stories—was overshadowed by that of her son, who appears to have found part of his inspiration in stories she told him in childhood.

A forceful woman ('I suppose I am taller and stronger than most women: I'd need to be, for what I've gone through'), Louisa Lawson believed in plain speaking, and other feminists did not always find her a comfortable colleague. There is as yet no biography dealing fully with her role in the women's movement. Brian Matthews's imaginative and playful study, *Louisa* (1987), vividly evokes aspects of her life and personality; *The First Voice of Australian Feminism* (1990), a selection from *The Dawn* between 1888 and 1895 made by her great-granddaughter, Olive Lawson, and the comprehensive index of the journal being prepared in

Adelaide, point to the growing contemporary appreciation of her significant contribution to Australian **feminism**.

JOHN BARNES

League of Rights is a right-wing political organisation inspired by the 1930s theories of Britain's Clifford Douglas, who believed economic problems resulted from the failure of banks to generate adequate purchasing power, but could be solved by government-issued 'Social Credit'. Douglas blamed Jewish financial power for rejection of his policies. His chief Australian disciple was Eric Butler, whose numerous tracts included *The International Jew* (1946). During the mid-1940s Butler established League of Rights branches in SA, Victoria, and elsewhere. In 1960 these joined under his national direction as the Australian League of Rights. Links were soon forged overseas. While upholding individual rights over capitalism and 'big' government, the league professed loyalty to God, Crown, and country. It opposed **communism**, **Aboriginal land rights** and, later, **multiculturalism**. Other characteristics identified by Andrew Campbell in *The Australian League of Rights* (1978) and Andrew Moore in *The Right Road* (1995) include subversive, anti-democratic tendencies and a fascist, anti-Semitic ideology. Butler responded to critics in *The Truth about the Australian League of Rights* (1985).

League cells have cultivated politicians, political parties, and other influential agents. Members are recruited by personal contact and front organisations, notably the Australian Heritage Society, Institute for Economic Democracy, Conservative Speakers' Clubs, and the Christian Institute for Individual Freedom. *Electors' Voice*, *Heritage*, *New Times*, *Intelligence Survey*, and *On Target* are among numerous league publications. Jeremy Lee has progressively succeeded the ageing Butler, while the league has gathered support in depressed rural areas crippled by harsh banking policies. David Greason in *I Was a Teenage Fascist* (1994) observes that it is 'not simply the disturbed and paranoid who attend League of Rights meetings up in Kaniva or the Eyre Peninsula … often it's very ordinary people with very real problems that no one else in politics is even talking about'.

DC

Lee, Bessie Harrison (1860–1950), working-class wife and temperance evangelist, became a prominent advocate of women's suffrage and 'voluntary motherhood' in Australia and NZ.

Born Bessie Vickery, her adult commitments were framed by the transcending experiences of her early life: the death of her beloved mother and her unhappy upbringing in the home of a drunken uncle and aunt; her conversion to evangelical Christianity, and her escape into marriage with the steady-going railwayman Harrison Lee. From a cottage in the back streets of Richmond, Bessie was gradually drawn into a wider world of evangelical reform, first as a door-step missionary, then as a preacher and temperance lecturer. Like other **evangelicals** she believed that a woman's place was in the home, submitted to her husband; but, fortified by her zeal on behalf of other women and their children (she was childless herself), and with the acquiescence of her husband, she effectively projected her maternal role into the larger sphere of the metropolis. In the late 1880s and 1890s she travelled widely as a speaker for the infant **Woman's Christian Temperance Union**, urging votes for women in the belief that women would exercise a civilising influence on men. In the 1890s Lee emerged as an advocate of 'voluntary motherhood', an ideal practised, not through artificial birth-control, but through sexual abstinence within marriage. Patricia Grimshaw (in Marilyn Lake and Farley Kelly (eds), *Double Time*, 1985) interprets Lee's outlook as working out traditional Christian ideals of sexual purity and prefiguring modern feminists' demands for control of their own bodies.

GD

Lee, Ida Louisa (1865–1943) was a historical geographer, born in NSW, whose research of previously unpublished records held in England of Australia's early history resulted in such works as *The Coming of the British to Australia 1788–1829* (1906), and *The Logbooks of the 'Lady Nelson'* (1915). She also contributed many articles to newspapers and journals. Initially well-received, the authority of some of her scholarship was later called into question.

KT

Legacy, a voluntary organisation, was founded in 1923 by World War I veterans who believed they had an obligation or 'legacy' of responsibility for the welfare of deceased comrades' dependants. Stanley Savige and other Melbourne founders were influenced by Major-General Sir John Gellibrand, who had started a Remembrance Club in Hobart. The Melbourne Legacy Club (established 1923) became the model for other autonomous clubs, eventually linked by a coordinating council in 1938. Members, called legatees, offered personal, practical assistance: advice, financial aid, health, housing, education, employment, and youth advancement. From the 1960s the emphasis has shifted from assisting youth to assisting ageing war widows. In 1997 Legacy comprised 51 clubs with 7400 legatees, and 123 000 widows and 2000 children were enrolled. Mark Lyons's *Legacy: The First 50 Years* (1978) is a general history.

DC

Legal history of Australia, whether conceived as the narrow study of the law and its institutions or as the study of its role in society, is largely a creature of the twentieth century. As A.C. Castles's *Annotated Bibliography of Printed Materials on Australian Law 1788–1900* (1994) shows, nineteenth-century histories, such as Henry **Melville**, *The Present State of Australia* (1851), sometimes included legal historical material, but not as their central concern. One exception was John **Quick**, *History of Land Tenure in the Colony of Victoria* (1883). Some of the many nineteenth-century works of **constitutional history**, such as Edward Jenks, *The Government of Victoria* (1891), also went beyond constitutional issues to touch on legal history generally. The university law faculties, which were established late in the nineteenth century, also paid some attention to legal history, but their concern was the history of English and even Roman law, rather than that of Australia. The assumption was that Australian law was a dependent part of that of England.

C.H. **Currey** wrote the first major work of Australian legal history. His 'Chapters in the Legal History of New South Wales 1788–1863' (n.d. [1929]) was a doctoral thesis submitted to the University of Sydney. Although largely descriptive, it was an extensive study of the development of substantive Australian law. Almost 30 years later, Currey published two biographies of early NSW judges, *The Brothers Bent* (1968) and *Sir Francis Forbes* (1968). In the meantime, others published books and articles on Australian legal history, particularly biographies and institutional histories. Most of this work was written by legal academics, lawyers, and judges rather than general historians, and little of it questioned the English origin of Australian legal doctrine or concentrated on the social impact of law. H.V. **Evatt's** remarkable *Rum Rebellion* (1938) was unusual in being a work of political and social history as much as legal history. On the High Court bench, he was also a reminder that even at the height of the pseudo-scientific period of legal reasoning, some resisted the imperial pressures to conform.

Over the past 30 years, Australian judges have begun to lose faith in the supposedly scientific method by which the common law was developed from largely English precedents. This positivist or legalist approach emerged in the middle of the nineteenth century, and was linked to a strict doctrine of precedent across the Empire. However, appeals from Australian courts to the **Privy Council** were abolished in stages between 1968 and 1986, and with them went the automatic deference to England as the true source of the law. In the same period, legal historians began to question whether Australian law stuck as closely to the law of England over the past 200 years as previously assumed. Historians and legal academics have developed new legal historiographies, which emphasise the social impact of law as much as its doctrinal development.

A hint of something new came in 1971, when John Bennett and J.R. Forbes published a paper in the *University of Queensland Law Journal* called 'Tradition and Experiment: Some Australian Legal Attitudes of the Nineteenth Century'. Bennett is one of the most prolific of the lawyer–historians. In 1982, A.C. Castles published the first general history of Australian law, *An Australian Legal History*, a book which looked at differences between Australian and English law. In the same year, the first of the annual Law in History conferences was held at La Trobe University, and these became the stimulus to a radical change in Australian legal historiography.

The approaches to legal history from then onwards question the supposed autonomy of legal development, the theory that law develops in isolation from social conditions. Legal academics and lawyers have been joined by general historians, such as Paula Byrne (*Criminal Law and Colonial Subject*, 1993), and Mark Finnane (*Police and Government*,

1994), in looking at law from the outside, questioning how it was administered or used and not merely what it said. Among the most influential was Henry **Reynolds**, whose *The Law of the Land* (1987), a historian's view of the **terra nullius** doctrine, had an effect on the **Mabo** decision of 1992. Legal academics also changed the nature of their legal history. One group, for example, published *The Emergence of Australian Law* (1989) as part of the surge of nationalism at the time of the Bicentenary, showing that England has not been the source of all legal ideas in Australia. Others attempt to blend the skills of social and legal historians, to show how the inherited law of England was changed to meet different circumstances, a theme of Bruce Kercher, *An Unruly Child: A History of Law in Australia* (1995). Australian legal historiography is now as diverse as historiography generally, and as much engaged in questioning imperialism and looking at institutions from below as well as from above. It is no longer monopolised by lawyers, and no longer subject to their version of the **cultural cringe**.

BRUCE KERCHER

Leichhardt, (Friedrich Wilhelm) Ludwig (1813–?48) travelled from Europe to NSW in 1842 to pursue an interest in natural science. He became a local celebrity after leading an expedition from Brisbane to Port Essington, near modern Darwin, during 1844–45. Leichhardt then planned an east–west crossing of the continent. His 1846 expedition from the Darling Downs in Qld to the coast of WA failed; on his next attempt in 1848 he left the Condamine River near the present town of Roma. This expedition disappeared and, despite many searches, no definite evidence of its fate was found. The Mitchell Library in Sydney holds many of Leichhardt's papers. His journal of the Port Essington expedition was published in 1847; Dan Sprod's *Proud Intrepid Heart* (1989) includes Leichhardt's journal of the aborted expedition, and his letters (translated by Marcel Aurousseau) appeared in 1968. Among the large body of works on Leichhardt are A.H. Chisholm, *Strange New World* (1941), reprinted as *Strange Journey* 1973); E.M. Webster, *Whirlwinds in the Plain* (1980); and Colin Roderick, *Leichhardt: The Dauntless Explorer* (1988). The enigmatic nature of the man and the mystery of his disappearance inspired poetry, plays, and novels—famously, Patrick **White's** *Voss* (1957).

KT

Leisure, see **Sport and leisure**

Lesbian history, like **women's history, feminist history, Aboriginal history**, and **gay history**, has both reflected and informed the demand that differences among people be recognised and valued. Writings in Australian history, whether produced in the past or the present, have almost without exception assumed the naturalness of heterosexuality. As a consequence, lesbians and their experiences have been rendered non-existent, irrelevant, or unworthy of attention. The women's liberation and gay liberation movements of the late 1960s and 1970s provided impetus for the development of lesbian history by highlighting and, to varying extents, theorising the significance of sex and **sexuality** in private and public domains.

By the early 1970s, lesbians in Australia and abroad had begun to assert the need for a history which recognised their lives and social positioning. The development of lesbian history, however, was hindered by a lack of resources and academic credibility and also by an urgent need to deal with more immediate social and political concerns. Those who sought to undertake research in this area were also confronted by distinct methodological problems. The task of even identifying lesbians of earlier generations proved difficult, for women whose primary emotional and sexual attraction was to other women had often closely guarded their personal lives for fear of social condemnation. Few left any record of their intimate lives. This evidential problem was mirrored in the public record. Whereas the criminalisation of sexual activity between men publicly acknowledged, albeit negatively, the existence of homosexual men and rendered them susceptible to official surveillance and public disclosure, the existence of lesbians was more often publicly denied and therefore less frequently discussed and documented. Those public records which did allude to lesbians also almost invariably did so in a negative manner, presenting same-sex desire as a problem, and the women and men who manifested it as individuals requiring salvation, punishment, or cure.

In the early 1980s, full-length studies in lesbian history began to be produced in the USA and the UK. In Australia, offerings were more modest. Given the paucity of historical documentation, some of the earliest endeavours in this area were directed to recording the past experiences of living lesbians. The 1987 publication, *Words from the Same Heart*, thus offered glimpses of lesbian history through the presentation of autobiographical essays. Similarly, 'History Inverted', a collective of lesbian historians founded in Melbourne in 1989, sought to remedy the lack of an historical record by launching a community-based oral history project.

The suggestion that lesbian history might constitute more than simply identifying and documenting lesbians and their lives was signalled by Jill Matthews in 1984. In *Good and Mad Women*, Matthews discussed women's same-sex desire in relation to changing meanings of femininity. In exploring the connections between **gender** and sexuality, she highlighted the constructed nature of sexuality and sexual categories and their importance to social ordering. Matthews's contribution remains a notable example of lesbian history as a specific approach to history; one which is characterised not merely by a recognition of lesbians but also by a relentless questioning of sexual categories and their normative effects. In succeeding years, this problematisation of sexuality, including heterosexuality, has come to characterise lesbian history. Drawing upon feminist, queer, and postmodern theories, writers in lesbian history have been increasingly concerned with how specific understandings of sexuality have emerged and shifted over time, and how these understandings relate to sex, gender, identity, practice, social order, and structure. This questioning has included a reconsideration of the previously taken-for-granted category of lesbian. Rather than resulting in a denial of same-sex desire between women across historical periods, it has led to a recognition that desire and its expression, along with forms of self-identification, have not always conformed to contemporary conceptions of lesbian.

In Australia today, lesbian history is researched within the lesbian community and the academy. Published works remain scarce. However, the burgeoning fields of women's studies, sexuality studies, and cultural studies have provided new academic forums for discussion and research. It has raised questions and addressed issues which have profound implications for broader understandings of the nature and significance of sex, gender, and sexuality.

SUSANNE DAVIES

Letters, in their different forms—personal and private, official, or printed and public—constitute a potent resource for the historian and biographer. The letter brings the historian as close to contemporary events as it is possible to get; while for the biographer, the letter, together with diaries or personal journals, gives the best overall sense of an individual voice and a personal style.

Before the telephone, the letter provided the means by which individuals and families, separated by distance, stayed in touch with each other. The letter was also the means by which formal and official business was transacted between individual citizens and between citizens and the various arms of government. Letters provide the means by which the first official transactions of the infant settlement at Port Jackson in 1788 may be known and understood, and many of the official despatches as well as other administrative correspondence was gathered in *Historical Records of Australia* and other publications. A similar pattern of documentation exists for each of the other Australian colonial settlements and offers the means by which much of the early European settlement of Australia and its expansion may be understood, sometimes in remarkable detail. For example, the *Gipps–La Trobe Correspondence* (1989), edited by A.G.L. **Shaw**, is an important source on the early history of the **Port Phillip District**. A cache of convict letters found in a fur pouch at Toodyay in WA provided the basis for Alexandra **Hasluck**, *Unwilling Emigrants* (1959).

Letters also provide an important source of **business history** and figure prominently in such major pastoral studies as P.L. Brown (ed.), *Clyde Company Papers* (7 vols, 1941–71), as well as mercantile and other enterprises. The use of letter-books to retain a copy of outward correspondence complements files of inward correspondence to constitute a fuller record than exists for most private letter-writers, who might have kept the mail they received but whose own letters were scattered among the recipients.

While official letters of various kinds continue to record the transactions of governments and business, the heyday of the private letter can be identified in Australia as extending from the early nineteenth century until the 1950s. Although letters continue to be written and letter-writing still has its devoted practitioners, it is apparent that advances in technology and the relative cheapness of long-distance telephone calls have removed the letter as the essential means by which Australians keep in contact with friends and families. Electronic mail represents the modern revival of the letter, but is seldom preserved. It is doubtful that communication as intimate as that between Henry **Parkes** and his daughter (A.W. **Martin**, ed., *Letters from Menie*, 1983), or as informative as that between *Walter Murdoch and Alfred Deakin on Books and Men* (edited by J.A. **La Nauze** and Elizabeth Nurser, 1974), will survive for publication in the future.

The survival of letters as a key historical source is partly due to a practice of families and individuals retaining material for sentimental reasons. There has also been a strong collecting tradition by Australian **libraries** seeking material for its long-term historical and research value. Notable among these are the state libraries and the National Library of Australia. Between them, major libraries hold vast quantities of letters which constitute a formidable resource for an understanding of Australia's social, political, and cultural development from the eighteenth century until the present. Specialised collections include the **Australian War Memorial** in Canberra; the University of Melbourne Archives, which includes major holdings relating to Australian business and commercial development; and the special literary collections in some university libraries such as the Baillieu Library, University of Melbourne, and the Australian Research Collection in the Australian Defence Force Academy in Canberra. Official repositories such as the Australian Archives in Canberra and the public record offices in each state house principally the records of government and public administration.

Australian scholars and readers alike have demonstrated a strong interest in letters as research material and for their sheer readability. Numerous collections of letters have been published, though editorial standards and practice vary considerably. Of special interest is *Letters from Victorian Pioneers*, edited by T.F. Bride (1898), and the later edition by C.E. Sayers (1969). Written by key figures in the early settlement of Victoria, the original letters are held in the State Library of Victoria and provide an unparalleled record in Australia of the motivations and early (though remembered) experiences of the pioneering generation. In NSW, the colonial letters of Rachel **Henning**, held in the Mitchell Library, give an invaluable picture of colonial life during the second half of the nineteenth century. Published in the *Bulletin* (1951–52), these letters have appeared in several later editions, though none has done editorial justice to this important material. Similarly, Alexandra Hasluck, *Audrey Tennyson's Vice-Regal Days* (1978), uses the letters of a governor-general's wife to illuminate her milieu. Patrick **O'Farrell** published an important collection of *Letters from Irish Australia 1825–1929* (1984), and in *Oceans of Consolation* (1994) David Fitzpatrick used the personal correspondence of 14 families of **Irish** immigrants to explore the nature of epistolary discourse between separated kith and kin. His book delivers a poignant record of the nineteenth-century immigrant experience. Brenda Niall and John Thompson have produced a wide-ranging anthology (1998).

The letters of writers, artists, and musicians have attracted considerable interest. Volumes have appeared for figures such as Miles **Franklin** (1993), Joseph **Furphy** (1995), Mary **Gilmore** (1980), Percy **Grainger** (1985), Joy Hester and Sunday Reed (1995), Norman **Lindsay**, (1979), Hugh McCrae (1970), Vance and Nettie **Palmer** (1977), Christina **Stead** (1992), Arthur **Streeton** (1989), Patrick **White** (1994), and Kathleen **Fitzpatrick** and Manning **Clark** (1996). F.J. Gillen's letters to Baldwin **Spencer** (1997) record the development of Australian anthropology and the social organisation of Aboriginal society in Central Australia. Published collections of Australian political letters are few, though the correspondence of R.G. **Casey** to S.M. **Bruce** in *My Dear P.M.* (1980) documents relations between Australia and Britain in the period 1924–29.

JOHN THOMPSON

Lewis, Essington (1881–1961), was an **iron and steel** industrialist. Born at Burra, SA, he was educated at St Peter's College, Adelaide, and learned self-reliance on outback stations. After training as a mining engineer, he joined **BHP** in 1904, and became general manager 1921–26, managing director 1926–38, chief general manager 1938–50, chairman 1950–52, and deputy chairman 1952–61. Whatever Lewis lacked in intellect, he compensated with hard work, observation, patience, perfectionism, rote learning, and attention to detail. He improved the efficiency of the Newcastle steelworks in the 1920s; secured control of associated industries; negotiated the acquisition of Australian Iron and Steel Ltd in 1935; and established shipbuilding and steelmaking at Whyalla. Wary of Japan, Lewis encouraged BHP to manufacture munitions and stockpile raw materials from the mid-1930s. He helped launch the Commonwealth Aircraft Corporation in 1936. As Director-General of Munitions 1940–45, Lewis exercised unprecedented powers and superb organisational skills that boosted Australia's war effort and facilitated industrial expansion. His vision culminated in Port Kembla's huge flat-products division 1947–55, which enabled large-scale manufacture of cars and consumer durables in Australia. A friend of Labor leaders John **Curtin** and Ben **Chifley**, Lewis refused a knighthood. The grey workman's sweatrag that he carried symbolised an identity with the workers he admired, and emphasised his belief that the laurels in life are won by the sweat of the brow. He is the subject of a biography by Geoffrey **Blainey**, *The Steel Master* (1971), and a play by John O'Donoghue, *Essington Lewis: I Am Work* (1987).

DC

Liberal Party (1901–17) was the name assumed by the progressive wing of the protectionists in federal politics at the establishment of the Commonwealth at the turn of the century. In Victoria, where the association of liberalism with **tariff** protection of local industry and other forms of ameliorative state action was clearly established, Alfred

Deakin and his colleagues established the National Liberal Organization. In NSW, where both protectionists and free-traders laid claim to the liberal mantle, George **Reid** let the opportunity pass: his free-trade party became identified nationally with conservatism. When the protectionists and free-traders came together in an anti-Labor **Fusion** in 1909, they adopted the title of the Liberal Party and operated under that name until 1917, when they merged with W.M. **Hughes's** pro-conscriptionist National Labor Party to form the **Nationalist Party**. The links between the original federal Liberal Party and that formed in 1944 are tenuous but commemorated in the annual Deakin lecture and episodic invocations of his legacy.

SM

Liberal Party of Australia was officially launched on 31 August 1945, two years after the **United Australia Party** virtually disintegrated following its annihilation in the 1943 federal election. R.G. **Menzies**, the former UAP prime minister, is usually credited with bringing some 18 non-Labor parties and groups together to form a national and permanent organisation subordinate to the parliamentary leadership. In fact, many men and women were involved in the drawn-out process. They were animated by the post-war idealism of ex-service personnel, a deep-seated fear of **socialism**, and a commitment to free enterprise balanced by an acceptance of government involvement in the economy.

The founders took three important decisions in relation to organisation. First, they established a federal structure where the federal executive, council, and secretariat provided a national framework but real power and responsibility resided with the state divisions. Second, the party resolved to raise its own funds so that, unlike the UAP, it was not beholden to outside finance committees. Third, the founders agreed that, while the extra-parliamentary organisation would formulate the party platform, the parliamentary parties (federal and state) would determine policy and not be subject to external dictation, as in the case of the **Australian Labor Party**.

After a severe setback in the 1946 federal election, the faithful regained their enthusiasm in 1947 when Ben **Chifley** attempted to nationalise the private trading banks. A well-planned and energetic campaign gave the Liberals, in coalition with the Country (later **National**) Party, an easy victory in the 1949 election, when they promised to remove the remaining wartime controls, ban the **Communist** Party, and promote free enterprise.

From this point, the Liberal Party became a machine for re-electing Menzies as prime minister, and for presenting Menzies as a national figure and international statesman. Frustrated organisational leaders complained of having no role in formulating federal policy. Centralist federal presidents objected when the near-autonomous state divisions continued to raise their own finance, select federal candidates, and run their own federal as well as state campaigns. The federal secretariat depended for its existence on donations from the NSW and Victorian divisions, whose general

secretaries carried more weight in the 1950s and 1960s than the federal director. Reliant on voluntary after-hours workers—many of them women who, in Victoria, enjoyed equal status with men as office-holders—the Liberal Party cast envious glances at the Labor Party's trade union base, at the greater emotional commitment of its supporters, and at its tighter internal structure. Nevertheless, the repeated federal and state victories convinced even the most sceptical within the organisation by the early 1960s that the Liberal Party had become a fixture in federal politics.

The Liberal Party exploited continuing material prosperity, anti-communism, the Cold War, and the Labor **split** to win successive federal elections until 1972. Liberals also held or shared power for some of this period in each of the states, while in Victoria the government of Henry **Bolte** gave the self-styled 'jewel in the Liberal Crown' an unaccustomed single-party rule. Menzies's retirement in 1966, however, signalled a general decline within the party at the federal level. Unable to find a substitute for the worn-out themes of 1949, led by the second-rate, and disadvantaged by the growing unpopularity of the **Vietnam War**, the Liberals were no match for a resurgent Labor under Gough **Whitlam**.

Malcolm **Fraser** led a Liberal revival in 1975, promising financial restraint and adopting the rhetoric of small government and economic rationalism. After its defeat in 1983, for which many party insiders blamed Fraser's failure to live up to his tough image, the Liberal Party moved further to the right in advocating extensive privatisation, enterprise bargaining, and the removal or reduction of **tariffs**. Demoralised, because Labor in government adopted several of these policies, and because their own dogmatic 'dries' were rendering them unelectable, the Liberals squabbled over leadership at both federal and state levels and lost ground everywhere except in NSW. At the same time, despite periodic attempts to strengthen the national organisation, the state divisions jealously guarded their fiefdoms while the federal parliamentary party continued to shut out organisational influence on policy-making.

The financial excesses of state Labor governments and the recession helped the Liberal Party to recover in the early 1990s. Yet, under Dr John Hewson, it lost the 'unloseable' federal election of 1993 when, without consultation with the organisation, the parliamentary party adopted a radical reform program, including a goods and services tax. After some more leadership contests, the Liberals returned to John **Howard**, the former 'dry' leader of 1985–89 who had become a cautious pragmatist. They regained federal office in the landslide of 1996. By then the party's national bodies had successfully obtained greater powers to intervene in the state divisions, developed a thoroughly professional approach to electioneering, and ensured that the grassroots—in the wake of the 1993 disaster—participated more in policy formulation.

Even so, the state divisions remained responsible for pre-selection, raising their own funds, and election campaigning. Each division had its own character and problems. Qld and Tasmania were always financial basket-cases while, in the former, and despite electoral success in the federal sphere, the Liberals were reduced to a mere rump behind the Nationals in state politics. In all the other divisions, traditional conservatives, economic rationalists, and liberals have periodically clashed with each other. Strong leaders in WA (Charles **Court** and his son Richard) and in Victoria, where Bolte and Jeff **Kennett** added a larrikin streak, contrasted with the progressive liberalism of Sir Rupert Hamer in Victoria and Steele Hall and Dean Brown in SA. Extreme right-wingers in NSW, allied to the 'dries', forced the more moderate within the party to organise as a **faction** to ensure their survival.

Although in the 1940s officials spoke of the Liberal Party being one 'for all Australians'—and not a class-based party dependent financially on big business—it was then predominantly middle-class, Anglo-Scottish, and Protestant. By the 1990s it had become the party 'for all of us', principally standing for small business, families, and 'the battlers', and seeking support from Catholics and the ethnic communities. The Liberal Party's support base is now much harder to define: its identity—so certain in the Menzies years—has become obscured in the face of globalisation, a market-driven approach to the economy, the revival of socially conservative elements, changing demographic patterns, and the growth of **multiculturalism**. The early Liberals worried that they lacked a 'soul-rousing gospel' and relied on Labor presenting them with election victories. The current generation confronts the same problem in more severe form though, having little sense of their own history—unlike Labor supporters—and lacking a preoccupation with ideas, they are not unduly worried.

There is no official or standard history of the Liberal Party. There are several accounts of its early years (J.R. Williams and Peter Aimer); a book of documents (edited by Graeme Starr, 1980); longer studies of the years before 1970 (Katherine West and Aimer); numerous political science analyses and texts; many autobiographies; forays into the party's philosophy; laments (*Is the Party Over?* by Chris Puplick, 1994); and biographies. Patrick O'Brien (*The Liberals*, 1985) tried to explain the various strands or positions in the Liberal Party; Gerard Henderson (*Menzies' Child*, 1994) ranged across its history, using mainly published material and interviews. Judith Brett in *Robert Menzies' Forgotten People* (1992) provides shrewd insights into Menzies's constituency and into the problems experienced after his departure. Ian Hancock has written *National and Permanent? The Federal Organisation of the Liberal Party of Australia 1944–1965* (2000).

IAN HANCOCK

Liberalism is the most durable political doctrine of the past two centuries. It has persisted through vigorous adaptation, and the variety of Australian liberalism is further complicated by the fact that there have been two national parties in this century bearing its name. Liberalism is a doctrine of freedom—freedom from the tyranny of superstition, tradition, hierarchy, and privilege. It drew on the ideas of the eighteenth-century Enlightenment and early-nineteenth-century political economy to emancipate the individual in the expectation that reason and virtue would guide personal conduct for the benefit of society.

In the penal colonies of NSW and Van Diemen's Land, liberals opposed the privileges of the **exclusives** and **squatters**, criticised the arbitrary powers of the governors, and condemned convict **transportation** because of the illiberal effects of the penal system. While these liberals sought representative government, they were not yet thoroughgoing democrats: they wanted a franchise restricted to those capable of exercising it, and feared the danger of mob tyranny as imperilling the rights of property on which they believed liberty depended. There was accordingly a barrier between the liberals and radicals influenced by the ideas of Chartism and other more egalitarian doctrines, which was sometimes bridged in common campaigns against conservatives but never disappeared. These distinctions are explored by Michael **Roe**, *Quest for Authority in Eastern Australia 1831–1851* (1965), and John Hirst, *The Strange Birth of Colonial Democracy* (1988).

When the Australian colonies achieved limited self-government in the middle of the nineteenth century, liberals mobilised popular support to defeat the conservatives and abolish privilege. They now accepted an equality of political rights, and used the manhood franchise to break the pastoral grip with land **selection** laws. The apparent triumph of the democratic principle, and its subsequent application to most aspects of public policy, has persuaded some historians to suggest that Australian liberalism meant nothing more than the satisfaction of popular aspirations. 'Australian democracy', wrote Keith **Hancock** in *Australia* (1930), 'has come to look at the State as a vast public utility, whose duty is to provide the greatest happiness of the greatest number.' He attributed this outcome to the 'levelling tendency of migrations which have destroyed old ranks and relationships and scattered over wide lands a confused aggregate of individuals bound together by nothing save their powerful collectivity'. Similarly, Hugh Collins argued (in Stephen R. Graubard, ed., *Australia: The Daedalus Symposium*, 1985) that Australian public life was dominated by the complete triumph of the ideas of Jeremy Bentham: a utilitarian, positivist legalism that attached little importance to principles and was quick to extinguish minority rights. According to Peter Loveday and A.W. **Martin**, *Parliament, Factions and Parties* (1966), the liberal fervour of the 1850s quickly subsided to 'vague attitudes of enthusiasm for progress and development'.

The liberalism of the self-governing colonies was shaped by the absence of familiar enemies. A conservative Victorian parliamentarian noted that whereas in Britain there was an established church, a hereditary aristocracy and large vested interests, here there was 'nothing to preserve and nothing to destroy' (Stuart Macintyre, *A Colonial Liberalism*, 1991). This conundrum of Australian **conservatism** was also a problem for liberals. Theirs was not a dissident but a dominant creed. They turned to the tasks of creation, after the victory of the 1850s, with a particular awareness of the need to realise the freedoms they had set loose and to augment the capacity of citizens to practise them. The creation of a system of public education, the **universities**, the **libraries**, galleries, and other civic institutions, were all part of this civilising endeavour.

Within this endeavour there were local variations. In NSW liberalism remained constant to the free-trade heritage of the British liberals; in Victoria, and to a lesser extent in other colonies, liberals embraced **protection** and other forms of state action to nurture self-sufficient independence. The reasons for the Victorian adoption of the **tariff** are usually attributed to its particular circumstances after the **gold** rush: a large population of energetic and acquisitive immigrants in need of an alternative livelihood; the absence of alternative public revenue in a small state with limited land to sell. Equally important was the strenuously interventionist liberal doctrine set out in David **Syme's** works of political economy and propounded through his newspaper, the *Age*. So strong was his influence that a liberal contemporary as resolutely independent as George **Higinbotham** and an English immigrant as intellectually distinguished as Charles **Pearson** accepted the protectionist argument. His protégé, Alfred **Deakin**, also bowed to the same imperative and carried it into the early Commonwealth. This liberalism was a rigorous doctrine, balancing the rights of the individual with stern duty.

By the end of the century the liberals had achieved enough of their program for the boundaries between liberalism and conservative to blur, a development fostered by the emergence of the **Australian Labor Party** and the threat of more radical collectivism. Most of the delegates to the Federal Conventions regarded themselves as liberals, and the pervasive influence of the doctrine is expressed in the claim by John **Quick** and R.R. **Garran** in their *Annotated Constitution of the Australian Commonwealth* (1901) that it 'embodies the best achievements of political progress, and realizes the latest attainable ideals of liberty'.

The new Commonwealth brought the two liberal traditions face to face. George **Reid**, the NSW free-trader who became leader of the opposition, was no less liberal than Edmund **Barton**, the protectionist prime minister. He was pushed into a more conservative stance after Deakin replaced Barton as leader of the protectionists, and he criticised Deakin's extension of state activity. The Deakinite program of **new protection**, national development and maintenance of living standards certainly represented a substantial departure from nineteenth-century rugged individualism in favour of an interventionist liberalism, as was occurring internationally, and is given its most positive description by Robert Birrell, *A Nation of Our Own* (1995). Both the free-traders and the protectionists were forced by the growth of the ALP into closer dependence on business support and middle-class votes, yet when they arranged the **Fusion** it was under the banner of the **Liberal Party**.

That Liberal Party lasted only until World War I, when partnership with W.M. **Hughes's** pro-conscription wing of the Australian Labor Party created the **Nationalist Party**. The **conscription** crisis and associated labour turmoil confronted Australian liberals with the perils of class. In Europe the war gave rise to two powerful new enemies of liberalism—communism and fascism—and the influence of both spilled over into Australia. Liberals searched for new sources of authority that would provide purpose and direction to national life: sometimes by recourse to repression of dissidents and enforcement of the rule of law (as in the case of one erstwhile Deakinite liberal, John **Latham**); or by restricting the role of the state (as with another, Frederic **Eggleston**); or by inculcating an appreciation of social responsibilities (as with the secular evangelists of the **Workers Educational Association**). These responses are explored from quite different perspectives by Tim Rowse, *Australian Liberalism and National Character* (1978), and Gregory Melluish, *Cultural Liberalism in Australia* (1995).

The responses were pursued also within, or in alliance with, the non-Labor side of politics. An alternative was to renew liberalism as a progressive force through association with the labour movement. In 1918 H.V. **Evatt** published a historical study of *Liberalism in Australia*; in the 1920s he entered the NSW parliament as a Labor representative, and after serving on the High Court bench from 1930 to 1940, went to the Commonwealth parliament where he became minister for external affairs. Evatt brought a concern for freedom, and for the law as a guardian of freedom, to his judicial responsibilities; in international relations he applied the same principles of self-determination to wartime diplomacy and postwar decolonisation. The NSW lawyer A.B. **Piddington** moved from state parliament to the Bar as a prominent civil libertarian. Brian **Fitzpatrick's** leadership of the Australian Council for Civil Liberties in close association with the union movement pursued a liberalism in the service of popular rights and social amelioration.

The decision by the non-Labor forces during World War II to re-establish themselves as the Liberal Party reasserted a more conservative liberalism. Under the leadership of Robert **Menzies**, this party accepted the responsibilities of government to maintain full employment, provide **social welfare**, and enhance opportunity. Like Latham, Menzies upheld the rule of law with rigour and especially in the Cold War was intolerant of radical dissent. His party remained broadly based, balancing the claims of powerful interest groups and encouraging individuals and families to help themselves. Menzies's successors proved less capable of holding that balance, and prominent Liberals (now distinguished as small-l liberals) such as Edward St John and Ian McPhee were casualties of a more illiberal conservatism. Malcolm **Fraser's** concern for human rights and opposition to racial intolerance became more apparent after he left office in 1983: the circumstances of his becoming prime minister in 1975 made him appear an aloof Tory. John **Howard** upholds the freedom of the individual in industrial relations and the freedom of vilificatory expression, but is timorously complacent about other abuses of power.

In the second half of the twentieth century liberalism was frequently under fire. James **McAuley** blamed it for the ills of secularism in early issues of *Quadrant* during the 1950s. **New Left** radicals roundly condemned liberals in the

1960s for their reluctance to take sides, and later the new social movements criticised the liberal blindness to particular identities. The attempts by such liberal theorists as John Rawls to work out a utilitarian concept of social justice suffered from the retreat of the state and the return to the market in the 1980s. More recently, communitarians have decried the absence of a moral centre in liberalism. Withal, it has persisted to assert the necessity of reconciling the individual with the social, and the necessity of tolerance and respect for human rights.

STUART MACINTYRE

Libertarianism is a minority, almost fugitive, tradition in Australia, and one that has re-emerged in strikingly different forms. Resistance to the harsh discipline of the convict colonies was channelled into demands for constitutional liberties. Even the defiance of the **Eureka** rebels and the occasional manifestoes of **bushrangers** (such as Ned **Kelly's** Jerilderie Letter) appealed to principles of justice and good government. The advent of representative government and speedy democratisation of public life fostered the extension of state activity: as Keith **Hancock** argued in *Australia* (1930), Australians turned almost instinctively to the state for remedy of their ills and realisation of their freedom. When the colonial governments crushed the strikes of the 1890s and imprisoned their leaders, the unions entered parliament and turned industrial relations into a new province for law and order. Nor did the opponents of colonial **socialism** challenge the legitimacy of the state; rather, these upholders of *laissez-faire* looked for an authority that could withstand the weight of numbers.

Libertarian attitudes were to be found at this time among dissident radicals: **free thought** was one stream, anarchism (surveyed by Bob James in *A Reader of Australian Anarchism 1886–1896*, 1979) another. In the early twentieth century the **Industrial Workers of the World** practised an anti-authoritarian form of working-class protest, but **communism** replaced it with a highly centralised and tightly disciplined style of left-wing politics. After his brief involvement with the Communist Party in the early 1930s, the Sydney philosopher John **Anderson** developed an influential critique of the conformist and consumerist values of the 'servile state'. Around him formed the self-conscious group of iconoclasts who became known as the Sydney Push, with links back into literary bohemian circles and forward into the counter-culture of the 1960s. These two milieux are treated by Peter Kirkpatrick, *The Sea Coast of Bohemia* (1992), and Ann Coombs, *Sex and Anarchy* (1996).

Their libertarianism was more aesthetic than political, an assertion of personal autonomy against repressive philistinism. The libertarianism that revived in the 1970s had some links with Andersonianism but drew also on Friedrich von Hayek and other international prophets of the New Right to contest social welfare, wage regulation, and other forms of state meliorism. These free-market libertarians, dubbed 'economic rationalists', combined uneasily with conservatives during the 1980s, divided on such issues as **migration** policy, **multicul-**turalism, **sexuality**, and euthanasia, but united in their hostility to government intervention in the economy.

SM

Libraries are collections of books, periodicals, manuscripts, and other sources of information. While new information technologies are changing forms of collection and access, Australian historians remain heavily dependent on the country's library system. That system consists principally of the national and state libraries, university libraries, local libraries, and a number of specialised collections.

The first libraries in the Australian colonies were private collections, subscription libraries, and libraries maintained by the **mechanics institutes** and schools of arts. These libraries concentrated on British and European publications, though most included local books, journals, and newspapers among their accessions. During the second half of the nineteenth century the colonial governments established public libraries in the capital cities, which eventually evolved into the present-day state libraries.

The State Library of New South Wales began when the government bought Sydney's principal subscription library in 1869. A new building was completed in 1889 and the trustees were incorporated in 1899 to receive D.S. **Mitchell's** unique collection of Australiana. The Mitchell Library was opened in 1910 and the Dixson wing added in 1929 to accommodate a further important Australian collection. The Tasmanian Public Library was established similarly in 1870 with endowments from the colonial and muncipal governments, and a grant from the Carnegie Foundation financed a building that was opened in 1907. In 1944 the state government assumed responsibility for the restyled State Library of Tasmania. Qld made the same arrangement with its Libraries Act of 1943. Victoria was most ambitious, establishing a major public library at the advent of self-government. The initial building (now Queen's Hall) was supplemented to accommodate a combined library, art gallery, and museum, and crowned in 1913 by a massive domed reading room. Adelaide's subscription library merged with the mechanics' institute library in 1856, and subsequently joined with the museum and art gallery; it became a department of the SA government in 1939. WA founded its public library in 1886, and also merged the library, museum, and art gallery in 1911; the State Library of WA was created in 1955. Most of these early state libraries gained powers of copyright deposit and built substantial state collections, which usually included manuscript and **archive** material.

Most also circulated books to smaller public libraries in the suburbs and hinterland, but the scale of such local libraries and the level of state and local government support remained limited. Subscription libraries and small commercial libraries were still of primary significance for most readers.

The reconstitution of the state libraries in the middle decades of the twentieth century and the augmentation of local public libraries was fostered by a major review of Australian libraries conducted by the American librarian Ralph Munn and the chief Victorian librarian, E.R. Pitt.

The Munn–Pitt report (1935) was outspoken in its condemnation of the paucity and backwardness of Australian library provision. Its emphasis on the civic role of the library reinforced a free library campaign, and the recommendation that local government should establish such libraries with state government assistance provided the model for subsequent development. Its valorisation of the specialist skills of the library profession improved training and library practice. Its recommendation that the Commonwealth National Library should build larger specialised collections and provide national leadership in bibliography and cataloguing assisted the evolution of that institution into the National Library of Australia.

The National Library of Australia had its origins in the Commonwealth Parliamentary Library, in Melbourne, whose first publication was *Historical Records of Australasia* (1914–25). Like the earlier colonial parliamentary libraries, it went some way beyond the working needs of legislators in its acquisitions policy. Its chair, Frederick Holder, who was the first speaker of the House of Representatives, went farthest in his assertion that it should be 'the home of the literature, not of a state, or of a period, but of the world, and all time'. This idea of an antipodean Library of Congress was never realised, but the library's acquisition of the Australiana collection of E.A. Petherick in 1911 and the deposit provisions of the federal Copyright Act in 1912 laid the foundations for a growing role. Its early history has been written by A. and M. Osborn (1988). When the library moved with the federal parliament from Melbourne to Canberra, it was renamed the Commonwealth National Library. Under the direction of Harold White, it grew rapidly after World War II, was established by statute as the National Library in 1960, and moved into its present building on the shores of Lake Burley Griffin in 1968. The National Library established major bibliographical and **reference** series. From 1936 its *Australian National Bibliography* listed all Australian publications. In 1988 the gap between this series and the *Bibliography of Australia* up to 1900 compiled by J.A. **Ferguson** was filled in a major retrospective publication, *Australian National Bibliography 1900–1950* in four volumes. The Australian Public Affairs and Information Service indexes serials and newspapers. Kinetica provides online details of Australian library holdings. C.A. Burmester's *Guide to the Collections* in four volumes offers helpful descriptions of many of the collections up to the early 1980s. To mark its centenary, a volume on the history of the library, *Remarkable Occurrence*, was published in 2001.

The state libraries also expanded significantly after World War II, and gave increased emphasis to state and national history. With the exception of Tasmania, all have secured major rebuilding programs in the past two decades, and the NT library shares a gargantuan new edifice with the parliamentarians of the territory. Most followed the State Library of New South Wales in establishing a separate state and Australian collection: the La Trobe Library in Victoria, the John Oxley Memorial Library in Qld, the Mortlock in SA, and the Battye in WA. All have extensive manuscript, picture, and oral history collections, and comprehensive newspaper holdings.

Benefiting from close relations with government ministers, and the public largesse of the postwar boom, Harold White acquired and built major international collections at the National Library, which supported the rapid expansion of research in Australian universities after World War II. By the end of the 1960s the National Library had clearly outstripped even the largest state libraries in its scale and resources—but it would soon be challenged by the far more dramatic growth of the academic libraries. Before World War II each of the six state universities maintained a cramped and inadequate library designed for undergraduate use. Increased research activity and the exponential growth of scholarly publishing, in serial and monograph, forced them to expand. The library was a commanding central presence on the campuses of the new universities built in the 1960s and 1970s. H. Bryan and J. Horacek (eds), *Australian Academic Libraries in the Seventies* (1983), gives a good picture of the transition at a mid-point. By the later 1980s the combined expenditure of universities on libraries far exceeded that of the national and state libraries. The University of Melbourne alone spends more on acquisitions than the National Library of Australia. The National Library has redefined its own collection policy on the principle of a National Distributed Collection, which sought to clarify the roles of major Australian libraries and facilitate access to their holdings.

Other specialist libraries are maintained by federal and state departments and agencies, and by learned and professional societies. Thus the law libraries of universities are supplemented by the libraries of courts and large legal firms, and in this field as well as others electronic information is rapidly replacing print. The Institute of Aboriginal and Torres Strait Islander Studies holds the primary library collection on that subject. Important collections of such specialist libraries as the **CSIRO** and the former Bureau of Immigration, Multicultural and Population Research have been dispersed. School libraries, which flourished in postwar years, are now under pressure, and the colleges of advanced education that trained librarians have merged into universities that have little regard for an activity of reduced enrolment. The values of information management, heritage, and cultural display jostle for attention, and the role of the scholar librarian is at a discount in line-management structures.

The Australian Library and Information Association seeks to maintain professional standards and principles against the insistent pressure of economic rationalism and the readiness of academics to criticise, from an aloof distance, highly complex institutions as they respond to rapid change and uncertainty. Library history remains an active field, and since 1984 the proceedings of the Forum on Australian Library History have been published by the library schools of the University of New South Wales and Monash University. Articles on the subject appear in the *Australian Library Journal* and *Australian Academic and Research Libraries*.

STUART MACINTYRE

'Light on the hill' was a phrase coined by the Labor prime minister Ben **Chifley** at the NSW state conference of the

Australian Labor Party in 1949. He used the metaphoric 'light on the hill'—cloaking the political ideals of **socialism** in homely comfort—to describe the party's 'great objective … which we aim to reach by working for the betterment of mankind not only here but anywhere we may give a helping hand. If it were not for that, the Labour movement would not be worth fighting for.' The phrase was revived in the title of Ross McMullin's history of the Labor Party (1991), and also invoked by Labor Prime Minister Paul **Keating**.

HD

Light, William (1786–1839) was recommended for the first governorship of SA on the basis of his military service in the Napoleonic Wars, but lost the post to John **Hindmarsh**. He did accept the position of surveyor-general in 1835 and arrived in 1836 with the power to select the site and design the capital. This power caused conflict with Hindmarsh.

Light faced major hurdles. He was expected to establish the capital and survey the surrounding country in a short period with limited equipment and funds, inexperienced surveyors, and drunken labourers, and without the support of Hindmarsh. He made inroads into the huge task of country settlement, and selected a suitable site and began planning the capital less than a year after his appointment. However, officials deemed his progress too slow. He was temporarily relieved of duties in 1838 and resigned in protest. His work was vindicated soon after: **Adelaide** gained world renown in the history of **town planning** for the grid design and large areas of parkland that were regular but sensitive to the natural contours of the area. Light refused further public involvement but worked in the colony as a private surveyor until his death of tuberculosis. According to his wishes, he was buried with a copper breastplate reading 'Founder of Adelaide'. There is a memorial in Light Square and a statue on Montefiore Hill. Geoffrey **Dutton** wrote a biography, *Founder of a City* (1960).

KELLIE TOOLE

Lighthouses were critical to the settlement of Australia by sea in the nineteenth and early twentieth centuries, assisting navigation at hazardous capes and promontories, and guiding vessels into ports and harbours. Australia's first lighthouse, designed by Francis **Greenway**, was built at South Head, Port Jackson, in 1817; the oldest surviving lighthouse, built by convict labour in 1833, is situated at Iron Pot Islet, near Hobart. The signalling code of each lighthouse was emitted by a large revolving lens, traditionally fuelled by whale oil. Lighthouse keepers, who were responsible for maintaining the signal, usually occupied separate living quarters. Lighthouses helped to reduce the number of **shipwrecks** along Victoria's south-west coastline and in Bass Strait, at Cape Otway (1848) and King Island (1861).

Lighthouses provided safety and refuge in an otherwise hostile environment of treacherous coast and wild seas, and they acquired a certain romantic image. However, with the development of sophisticated radio beacons and automated electrical lighting, as well as shipboard navigational aids, many lighthouses became redundant. They have been converted for other uses, including museums and private accommodation. With this obsolescence, a substantial literature of lighthouse history has emerged.

HD

Lilley, Charles (1827–97), premier and chief justice of Qld, arrived in Australia in 1856. He quickly completed legal studies that he had begun in England, and became a journalist for, later editor of, the *Moreton Bay Courier*. Lilley supported the movement for separation of Qld from NSW and became member for Fortitude Valley in the first Legislative Assembly in 1859. He held the position of attorney-general in two ministries before becoming premier in 1868. In 1870 he introduced free education, making Qld the first colony to take that step. An impulsive, erratic politician, Lilley withdrew to the Supreme Court in 1874 and became its chief justice five years later. By the late 1880s he chafed at the restriction of the bench and aligned himself with both **republicanism** and **socialism**. In 1893 he resigned his judicial post to contest the 1893 election on the Labor side, but was unsuccessful.

KT

Lindrum, Frederick (1888–1958) and **Walter Albert** (1898–1960) were taught to play billiards by their father who ran various billiard-halls, the best-known being Lindrum's in Flinders Lane, Melbourne. Fred won the Australian title in 1908, but it was Walter who received international recognition after his 1929–30 trip to England, during which he made 67 scores of a thousand points or more at billiards. He went on to win the world championship in 1933, a title he successfully defended in Australia the following year and retained until 1950. Andrew Ricketts relates his success in *Walter Lindrum* (1982). Walter's record-making skill in nursery cannons prompted a rule-change limiting their use. The memorial over his grave, depicting a billiard table with cue and balls, is one of the more striking in the Melbourne General Cemetery.

KT

Lindsay family was, in its heyday in the early twentieth century, Australia's best-known artistic family. Of the 10 children born to the medical practitioner Robert Lindsay and his wife Jane in the fading gold town of Creswick, Victoria, in the 1870s and 1880s, five became prominent in art and literature. PERCY (1870–1952), LIONEL (1874–1961), NORMAN (1879–1969), and DARYL (1889–1976) led long and—particularly in Norman's case—controversial lives. RUBY (1885–1919), a pen-and-ink artist and much-loved wife of the cartoonist and war artist Will **Dyson**, was a victim of the terrible influenza pandemic that ravaged her generation in the immediate aftermath of World War I. Her death highlights the good fortune of her prominent brothers in either escaping or, in Daryl's case, surviving the war and the deadly pandemic that followed. They stood out in a society that had lost so many talented young men and women.

Norman was the best known and most diverse of the Lindsays of his generation. His recruiting cartoons for the *Bulletin* during World War I are still cited as clear examples of the propagandist racism that war encourages. Students of Australian anti-Semitism and anti-modernism find strident examples of both in the writings of the Lindsays, though Daryl, as director of the National Gallery of Victoria 1941–56, encouraged the acquisition of modern art. With varying emphasis, the Lindsays extolled the artist as bohemian and made large claims for creative genius. They were often energetic critics of the wowser spirit, the churches, and the middle class, favourite targets in many of Norman's novels. Their creed might be summed up as vitalist. Norman's children's book, *The Magic Pudding* (1918), is one of his most enduring and endearing works; it is by turns funny, vulgar, unruly, and very Australian in tone and setting. Norman and Lionel Lindsay, for all their personal differences, were consistently opposed to the labour movement and the Labor Party, which they interpreted as the envious voice of the mob or mass mind. In characterisations of Australian cultural life, the Lindsays, despite their Victorian origins, have been seen as exemplars of a Sydney elitism as against the democratic **liberalism** and **socialism** that were thought to typify Melbourne's cultural commitments and practices.

Norman's second marriage to the voluptuous Rose Soady, his most famous model, brought a striking, and in some quarters unwelcome, personality into the family. When Daryl Lindsay married Joan à Beckett Weigall in 1922, the Lindsays were linked with another famous artistic family, the **Boyds**. JOAN LINDSAY (1896–1984) is best known as the author of *Picnic at Hanging Rock* (1967), which was made into an extremely popular film in 1975.

JACK (1900–90) and PHILLIP (1906–59), sons of Norman and his first wife Kate Parkinson, were the most prominent of the next generation of the Lindsays. Jack lived in England from 1926, where he established himself as a Marxist intellectual and an astonishingly productive translator, historian, classical scholar, art critic, novelist, and biographer. Phillip was best known as a prolific historical novelist. Like Jack, he contributed to the substantial body of Lindsay autobiography, a significant *oeuvre* in its own right. No Australian family has told its story so often and from so many different angles.

DAVID WALKER

Lingiari, Vincent, see Gurindji

Link-Up is an agency founded in Sydney in 1980 that assists thousands of Aboriginal people who were taken from their homes as children. The agency helps people both to re-establish links with their families and to feel pride in their Aboriginality. The removal of Aboriginal children from their parents by the Aborigines Protection Board was introduced through legislation in 1915 and continued until the 1960s. Link-Up was co-founded by historian Peter Read and Coral Edwards. Read was later commissioned to carry out a NSW government inquiry, in the report of which the term **Stolen Generations** was coined. The creation of similar agencies followed in the other states.

HD

Literature in Australia first took the form of official reports, annals, and semi-official accounts of settlement, such as Watkin **Tench's** *A Narrative of the Expedition to Botany Bay* (1789). The first literary efforts reflected the diverse backgrounds of the new arrivals, from *First Fruits of Australian Poetry* (1819) by the Supreme Court judge Barron **Field** to the *Memoirs* (1819) of the convict James Hardy **Vaux**. Another convict, Henry **Savery**, wrote the first **novel** published in Australia, *Quintus Servinton* (1830–31), a fictionalised autobiography.

The earliest significant poets, Charles **Harpur**, Henry **Kendall**, and Adam Lindsay **Gordon**, were dependent on English models, but responded in fresh, direct ways to Australia, especially its landscape. Gordon's reputation was the highest among contemporaries, but his work has not worn well. Colonial novelists included Henry **Kingsley**, Rolf **Boldrewood**, Marcus **Clarke**, Catherine **Spence**, Ada **Cambridge**, Catherine Martin, Rosa **Praed**, and Jessie Couvreur. Clarke, a brilliant, satirical writer, played a prominent role in the colony of Victoria as journalist, playwright, editor, and prolific writer of fiction. His greatest achievement is the novel of the convict system, *His Natural Life* (1874). The pastoral romances of Kingsley and Boldrewood, as popular in their day as *His Natural Life*, now appear relatively thin and dated. It became fashionable after the 1890s to discern the first essentially Australian writing in the novels of Boldrewood, Kingsley, and Clarke—an attitude that persisted until the 1970s.

Women writers, often grouped together although their writing is markedly diverse, were perceived as servile to English models and manners. The reverse opinion, that women writers were more true to the national life, was held by contemporary historians of the literature, such as H.G. **Turner** and Alexander **Sutherland**. Recently retrieved from obscurity, colonial women writers are now the subject of biographies, bibliographies, critical editions, and essays.

Drama began very early, with a performance of *The Recruiting Officer* by George Farquhar in mid-1789. After professional theatre began in Sydney with the opening of Barnett Levey's Theatre Royal in 1833, other colonial centres soon followed suit and were served by a vigorous tradition of pantomime and melodrama, some of it by Australian authors. Meanwhile there was an even more vigorous proliferation of first-hand accounts of colonial life from explorers' journals, diaries, letters, and reminiscences. The first substantial work of criticism was Frederick Sinnett's essay, 'The Fiction Fields of Australia' (1856), which took up what was to be a perennial issue—the difficulty of developing a native literature in a derivative culture.

The decade of the 1890s, when the *Bulletin* under the editorship of J.F. **Archibald** was dominant, stimulated a more radical national attitude to literature. The Red Page, instituted on 29 August 1896, and edited by A.G. **Stephens**, was an important critical forum, while the journal itself fostered such writers as Henry **Lawson**, Norman **Lindsay**, A.B. **Paterson**, Steele **Rudd**, Joseph **Furphy**, Barbara **Baynton**, John Shaw **Neilson**, and Randolph **Bedford**. Advertising itself as the 'premier literary journal' with an 'Australian national policy', the *Bulletin* advocated the yarn and ballad as the essential national genres. Few women writers appeared in its pages. Miles **Franklin**, whose early autobiographical novel, *My Brilliant Career*, created much interest when first published in 1901, was received by Henry Lawson and others as a celebration of real 'Australianness', ignoring the **feminism**, which led to the novel's retrieval in the 1970s as an internationally significant text. Much material, including poetry, short stories, and serialised novels, was published in newspapers such as the *Sydney Mail* (1860–1938) and the *Australian Town and Country Journal* (1870–1919). Angus and Robertson was almost the sole local publisher of Australian novels and books of poetry.

The 1890s are often presented as a golden decade, the beginning of a national literature based on indigenous egalitarian **bush** values, but since the 1970s the decade has been subject to much revisionist research. Feminist historians in particular have modified previous assumptions about the origins of the myths of bush and mateship. Other studies have emphasised the international interests of the so-called nationalists, including A.G. Stephens himself. The major figure of C.J. **Brennan**, who acknowledged a strong debt to the French symbolist poets, has always been seen as an anomaly.

The period between Federation and World War I is often perceived as an arid one for literature and criticism, although several significant magazines, such as the *Lone Hand* and the *Bookfellow*, continued to appear. A major novelist who began publishing in the period, however, was Henry Handel **Richardson**. *Maurice Guest* appeared in 1908; *The Getting of Wisdom* in 1910; and the first volume of *The Fortunes of Richard Mahony* in 1917. As an expatriate isolated from literary movements in Australia, Richardson had to wait many years for extensive critical appreciation in Australia, as did Christina **Stead** later. The 1920s and 1930s were also marked by several diverse literary movements in search of a truly indigenous literature. One of the most significant literary journals in the 1920s, reflecting the influence of Norman Lindsay, was *Vision* (1923–24). Lindsay's elitist, Nietzschean notions on the importance of the artist, loosely termed 'vitalism', had great influence on such later writers as Kenneth **Slessor**, Douglas **Stewart**, R.D. Fitzgerald, Hugh McCrae, and Kenneth Mackenzie, but have not had lasting effect. The **Jindyworobak** movement, promoted by Rex Ingamells and Ian Tilbrook in *Conditional Culture* (1938), argued for an indigenous response to the land similar to that of the Aborigines, expressing in extreme form much of the general sense that a national literature should be created from native experience. Social-realist writers, largely made up of those with Leftist political convictions, included Katharine Susannah **Prichard**, Vance **Palmer**, Marjorie **Barnard** and Flora Eldershaw (who combined their talents in several novels under the pseudonym M. Barnard Eldershaw), Frank Dalby Davison, Jean **Devanny**, Eleanor **Dark**,

and Miles Franklin. Xavier **Herbert**, whose massive novel, *Capricornia*, set in the north of Australia and dealing with white–black relations, appeared in 1938, was an idiosyncratic writer who found it difficult to establish a bent, ultimately publishing his most ambitious and thorough manifesto about Australia, *Poor Fellow My Country*, in 1975. John Morrison, Kylie **Tennant**, Judah Waten, and Alan **Marshall** also belong loosely in the social-realist tradition. Two writers who began publishing in the 1920s and 1930s but who remained outside mainstream movements were Martin **Boyd**, a member of a talented Anglo-Australian family, whose novels reflect his own predicament of living between two cultures, and Christina Stead. Stead's novels were very slow to win recognition in Australia, although she is often now perceived as having a talent second only to that of Patrick **White**, especially in *The Man Who Loved Children* (1940) and *For Love Alone* (1945).

The 1930s and 1940s saw the emergence of several major poets, such as A.D. **Hope**, R.D. Fitzgerald, Rosemary Dobson, Judith **Wright**, and James **McAuley**, whose work reflected both Australian and overseas influences. The residual strength of conservative attitudes, however, was manifested in the Ern Malley hoax, perpetrated by McAuley and Harold Stewart in 1944, in a largely successful attempt to expose as nonsense the modernist poetry sponsored by the magazine *Angry Penguins*, edited by Max Harris. The founding of the literary magazines *Southerly* in 1939 and *Meanjin* in 1940 provided a reliable forum for literary debate and anticipated a growing proliferation of little magazines. Emanating from Sydney and Melbourne respectively, *Southerly* and *Meanjin* reflect to some extent the opposing and opposite cultures of the two cities.

The Commonwealth Literary Fund was founded by Alfred **Deakin** in 1908 to dispense pensions to sick and distressed writers and their families, and from 1939 it offered fellowships and grants to a wider range of writers and literary publications. Unless, like the novelist Patrick White, they had independent means and strong connections with overseas publishers, it had been hard for Australian writers to establish an independent literary career. In 1973—the year of White's Nobel Prize—the functions of the Literary Fund were taken over by the Literature Board of the Australia Council, and more generous levels of support increased the volume and diversity of literary activity.

Among the figures of historical interest to emerge during this period are the poets David **Campbell**, Gwen Harwood, Vincent Buckley, Chris Wallace-Crabbe, Les **Murray**, and Bruce Dawe, and the short story writers and novelists Hal **Porter**, Rodney Hall, George Johnston, David **Malouf**, Thomas **Keneally**, Roger McDonald, Christopher Koch, Thea Astley, Frank Moorhouse, Gerald Murnane, Michael Wilding, and Peter **Carey**. Australian publishers have played a major role in creating a new market for Australian writing—University of Queensland Press, Penguin Australia, and McPhee Gribble have been especially notable.

Drama developed more slowly, despite the efforts of Louis **Esson** and Vance Palmer and the company they formed in

1921–22 to promote a national drama—the Pioneer Players. Ray **Lawler's** *Summer of the Seventeenth Doll* (1957) and Alan **Seymour's** *The One Day of the Year* (1962) were a brief flowering. In the 1970s, however, several young playwrights, mainly based in Melbourne and encouraged by the formation of the politically radical Australian Performing Group, began to win recognition. They included Jack Hibberd, John Romeril, Barry Oakley, and David **Williamson**.

Aborigines, writers from diverse ethnic backgrounds, and women have since emerged as successful playwrights, as they have in other fields of literature. Historical themes, sometimes merging fiction and fact, and memory and text, have become a strong preoccupation in the work of several prose writers, including Jean Bedford, Kate Grenville, and Drusilla Modjeska. Aboriginal literature in English has flourished since the 1970s and includes poetry, drama and fiction, although political writing, such as Kevin **Gilbert's** *Because a White Man'll Never Do It* (1973), and life histories, such as Ruby Langford Ginibi's *Don't Take Your Love to Town* (1988), predominate.

Literary history has been a prolific genre in this century, if probably less influential than such cultural studies as Russel **Ward**, *The Australian Legend* (1958), Vance Palmer, *The Legend of the Nineties* (1954), Richard White, *Inventing Australia* (1981), and Graeme Turner, *National Fictions* (1986). Literary magazines have also played an influential role in shaping opinion. Regionalism, which has always been a feature of Australian literature, has been reflected in such magazines as *Island* (Tasmania), *Westerly* (WA), *Northern Perspective* (NT), *LinQ* (north Qld), and *Australian Letters* (SA). Two particularly influential periodicals with national concerns are the monthly *Australian Book Review* and the twice-yearly *Australian Literary Studies*.

The most comprehensive account of Australian literature to the late 1920s was H.M. **Green**, *An Outline of Australian Literature* (1930). Nettie **Palmer**, *Modern Australian Literature* (1924), focused on contemporary literature, reflecting the Palmers' anxiety to see a truly national literature come to pass. Such anxieties were also aired in P.R. **Stephensen**, *The Foundations of Culture in Australia* (1936). Meanwhile, E. Morris **Miller** carried out much needed bibliographical documentation in *Australian Literature* (1940); revised and extended by F.T. Macartney in 1956, it remains a fundamental reference work. The numerous histories of Australian literature include the two Penguin *Histories* (1964, 1976) edited by Geoffrey **Dutton**, which were succeeded by the *Penguin New Literary History of Australia* (1988), edited by Laurie Hergenhan, and the *Oxford History of Australian Literature* (1981), edited by Leonie **Kramer**. *The Oxford Companion to Australian Literature* by W.H. Wilde, Joy Hooton, and Barry Andrews, appeared in 1985 and a second edition in 1994. Literary history is still overshadowed, however, by H.M. Green's two-volume *History of Australian Literature* (1961), expanded and revised by Dorothy **Green** in 1984–85. Green's comprehensive approach, including philosophy, science, economics, psychology, journalism, travel-writing, and

reminiscence, as well as histories and biographies, seemed too wide-ranging at the time of the book's appearance, when New Criticism was the dominant ideological critical theory. Although Green is often classed with the so-called radical nationalists, his approach is informed by wide reading in international literature and by an awareness that Australianness and literary excellence are by no means equivalent.

JOY HOOTON

Little Boy from Manly became a figurative representation of the Australian nation in the 1880s. In March 1885, as the NSW contingent was about to depart for the Sudan, a letter addressed to the Premier William Bede **Dalley** appeared in the *Sydney Morning Herald*, from Master Ernest Laurence, son of a Sydney merchant. 'How I longed to be with them, and help to punish the wicked Arabs who killed poor General Gordon', he wrote. He enclosed a £25 donation for the Patriotic Fund 'with my best wishes from a little boy at Manly'. As Ken **Inglis** has shown (*VHJ*, 1981, and *The Rehearsal*, 1985) in the patriotic frenzy surrounding the departure of Australia's first overseas military adventure, the little boy became a symbol of young Australia's sterling patriotism or, among opponents of the adventure, of its mindless chauvinism. The *Bulletin* cartoonist Livingstone **Hopkins** put the little boy in a cartoon, dressed in the pantaloons and frilled shirt associated with English storybook schoolboys of the namby-pamby kind. Over the following decades 'the little boy from Manly' became the *Bulletin's* stock symbol of Young Australia, appearing, for example, as a young cricketer during the first Test matches against England, and gradually becoming taller, sturdier, and less middle-class as young Australia itself grew up. **Gallipoli** marked his passage into manhood: in a *Bulletin* cartoon of May 1915 a picture of 'the little boy from Manly' looks down from the wall as a returning Anzac greets old John Bull with an expectant 'Well, Dad?'

GD

Liversidge, Archibald (1846–1927) was a geologist and promoter of science. Educated in England, in 1874 he became professor of geology and mineralogy at the University of Sydney, with few students and fewer facilities. Science had just become a matriculation subject in NSW, and Liversidge worked tirelessly to promote the discipline at both the secondary and tertiary level. He persuaded the university to create a faculty of science in 1879 and became its first dean; he was also one of the few who supported the admission of women to the university. He revived the local Royal Society, served as its secretary for 10 years, and initiated the **Australasian Association for the Advancement of Science** (ANZAAS). His major scientific work, *The Minerals of New South Wales*, was first published in 1876; enlarged editions appeared in 1882 and 1888.

KT

Living wage, see **Basic wage**

Loan Council is a Commonwealth–state body which authorises and coordinates Australian and overseas borrowings by state and federal governments. With the aim of preventing mutually detrimental competition for loan funds, the Australian Loan Council originated as a Commonwealth proposal at the 1923 **Premiers' Conference**. It first met in 1924 on a voluntary and advisory basis, but when the Financial Agreement became effective in 1929, the Loan Council assumed statutory authority and has since become an important vehicle of central economic policy. The council comprises the prime minister and state premiers (and usually the federal and state treasurers), with meetings normally held in Canberra to coincide with Premiers' Conferences at the end of the financial year. Each state is entitled to one vote, but the Commonwealth enjoys two votes and a casting vote, which usually ensures its dominance. (See also **Commonwealth–state relations**.)

DC

Loans affair was the name given to the unorthodox methods pursued by ministers in the **Whitlam** government to borrow money overseas. Rex Connor, minister for minerals and energy, was an old-style Labor man and economic nationalist. He planned to borrow large sums to keep the processing of **oil**, **gas**, and **uranium** in Australian hands. In 1974 he recruited a Pakistani, Tirath Khemlani, who claimed he could contact those who held the so-called petrodollars, the proceeds of the huge rise in oil prices. Connor's authority to proceed was given in an Executive Council minute which described the loan falsely as one for temporary purposes, which meant that the **Loan Council** did not have to be consulted. The Treasury, alarmed at the use of a shady intermediary, established that Khemlani could not do what he claimed. Connor's authority to seek the loan was withdrawn, but he continued to deal with Khemlani, though he told parliament the relationship was ended. When the press revealed that the contacts had continued, Connor had to resign. The leader of the opposition, Malcolm **Fraser**, declared that the affair constituted the reprehensible circumstance which warranted the deferring of supply to the government in the Senate. From this followed the **Dismissal** of the Whitlam government. Earlier Treasurer Jim **Cairns** had been dismissed by Whitlam for using another doubtful emissary in pursuit of the petrodollars.

JH

Local government has not been a necessity in Australia. It might be thought that in pioneering times local communities would have to provide for themselves, but this was not so. The colonial governments were for long periods after their foundation the only government in their territory. They then encouraged the formation of local government with very mixed success. Most of NSW was still without local government 100 years after the colony's foundation. Efforts to oblige local communities to form local government were fiercely resisted. This led to the formulation of a new principle in political philosophy: the right not to have local government.

The federal government had been created before, in 1906, local government was imposed on all the settled areas of NSW.

When established, local government performed a narrow range of tasks. Its chief business has been road-making and garbage collection, with a broadening since the 1970s into community services and leisure activities. It has not been responsible for police, education, public housing or, until recently, social welfare.

The weakness of local government in Australia was long ascribed to the sparseness of rural settlement. This might be convincing as an explanation for the absence of local bodies—as in NSW—but in some other colonies, Victoria and SA most notably, there was a much greater readiness to form councils and evidently no geographical impediment to their operation. The question is: why did they undertake so little? The answer lies, mainly, in the relative affluence of the colonial governments. They acquired their revenues from customs duties and the sale of Crown lands and until late in the nineteenth century did not impose any direct **taxation**. Local government gained its revenue from rates, a tax on land. There was thus little enthusiasm for transferring responsibilities from central to local government because the consequence would have been an increase in direct taxation.

Significantly, it was when colonial governments were short of funds that they obliged localities to incorporate and contemplated assigning them more responsibilities. Before the comprehensive state **education** systems were established, there had been some local control of schools and some local funds raised for them. But from the 1870s, when the colonial governments proposed to pay the full cost of a centralised system without imposing direct taxation, the cause of local control was hopeless.

The weakness of local government was also a tribute to the administrative reach and competence of the colonial governments. Isolated communities have to fend for themselves. But the pattern of Australian settlement did not produce isolated communities. From the beginning, goods were produced for export and the most distant inland settlers were regular users of imported goods. There was never in Australia a series of self-sufficient local economies and societies. The village was not replicated. Goods and people moved freely through the whole territory and likewise the writ of the colonial government. With the arrival of the telegraph and its rapid extension throughout the settled areas, the governments acquired the tool which made possible an efficient centralised **bureaucracy**, and this became the characteristic mode of Australian government. This explanation of the weakness of local government is developed in John Hirst, *Adelaide and the Country 1870–1917* (1973) and *The Strange Birth of Colonial Democracy* (1988).

Two patterns of local government development are discerned by John Power, Roger Wettenhall, and John Halligan in *Local Government Systems of Australia* (1981), which is the best guide to this subject. In Victoria and SA, where more councils were voluntarily formed early, they remained longer as narrow corporations elected by property-owners to provide property services. In Qld and NSW more of the territory was forced to incorporate by the central governments, which remained more interventionist: more ready to make councils their local agents and sooner providing that all adults could vote for them.

The narrow range of functions performed by local government meant that generally the political parties did not bother to contest elections, except that the **Australian Labor Party** frequently dominated the councils in its inner urban strongholds. They became famous not for policy innovation, for which there was little scope, but for petty corruption. On the fringes of the cities corruption took the form of capitalising on the rezoning of land from rural to urban. Planning is a significant power for local government and allows it to mobilise protest at unwanted developments promoted by the state or private corporations.

Brisbane is the only capital for which there is a metropolitan council dating from 1924. In the other capitals, subdivided into a multitude of local bodies, the state government organises city-wide services of water, sewerage, and public transport. The failure to create metropolitan councils for the other capitals in part reflected the reluctance of state governments to encourage an authority which might rival themselves. Brisbane contained a much lower proportion of the state population than the other mainland capitals.

State governments have regularly sought to improve local government efficiency by amalgamating councils into larger areas. The most outstanding success of local government has been its ability in almost every case to resist these moves in the name of small-scale democracy. However, this democracy has, if anything, a lower standing than the forms which operate at state and federal level.

JOHN HIRST

Local history, the history of local communities, small and large, often written for and by the locals themselves, is among the most vigorous fields of historical inquiry in Australia. There are almost 1000 local **historical societies**, numbering about 50 000 members, across the continent; their publications are among the most prolific, if often ephemeral, forms of history-writing.

Local history, along with natural history, was a tradition well established by amateur scholars in Britain by the time of Australia's foundation, and, as Tom Griffiths shows in *Hunters and Collectors* (1995), the methods of observation, collection, and classification characteristic of the field tradition were important to the awakening of an Australian sense of the past. Brief histories of local communities were sometimes appended to gazetteers and topographical surveys, but the publication of more formal local histories seldom occurred before the **gold rushes**. In the late nineteenth century, as the gold generation aged, Victoria experienced a mild nostalgia boom as **pioneers** began to write their reminiscences, and journalists attempted the first substantial histories of the gold towns. When W.B. Withers, a veteran of **Eureka** and long-time local journalist, published the first edition of his *History of Ballarat* (1870), many of the town's founders were still alive: he wrote 'for those who know the

place, and knowing it, are proud of it'. For the pioneer local historian there was no sharp line between history and memoir, research and recollection. Reading old newspapers, Withers remarked, was like 'making a pilgrimage ... through an old burial ground' where the names on the gravestones triggered a host of memories.

Local histories, like the colonial narratives they reflected and reinforced, were stories of material and social progress. Their long lists of firsts—the first European 'discovery', the first river crossing, the first pastoral station, the first land survey, the first church service—established a genealogy for communities still striving to be born. These histories did not obliterate the pre-European past—they often contained a rich store of information on Aboriginal place-names, sites and customs—but the Aborigines' later history is typically passed over in silence. Later historians have tended to dismiss these pioneer local histories as 'diffuse' and 'anecdotal', but the best of them, such as *The Land of the Lyre Bird* (1920), a remarkable collection of pioneering memoirs of the Gippsland forests, contain powerful evocations of past landscapes by men and women who knew the country intimately and enjoyed a natural narrative flair. In the city, as in the country, people's imagination tended to be most easily stirred by histories of small-scale, familiar places, such the popular sketches of Sydney's streets published in the daily press by the librarian C.H. Bertie.

One sign of the growing nationalism of the early Commonwealth was the foundation of historical societies devoted, not only to the study of state and national history, but also to the encouragement of local history. Progressive educationalists sought to bring the lessons of national history home to young Australians by inscribing their own localities with cairns marking the passage of heroic explorers. Charles Long, editor of the Victorian *School Paper*, recommended the study of 'local chronicles' in 'the guidance of future generations'.

During the years between the two world wars, as many small towns lost population to the coastal cities, local history sometimes became a means of shoring up the self-esteem of communities that had seen better days. When the district's sons and daughters returned for a 'back-to' celebration, the program would often contain a slim, hastily written history illustrated with old group photographs as an aid to reminiscence. Prosperous municipalities sometimes hired their own historians: the journalist J.B. Cooper, who wrote workmanlike civic chronicles of Prahran (1924), St Kilda (1931), and Malvern (1935), has since been followed by many others.

Not until the 1950s, however, did academically trained historians seriously enter the field. In 1954, a curly-haired young graduate named Geoffrey **Blainey**, who had just undertaken to write a history of Mount Lyell in Tasmania, contributed an article to *HSANZ* attacking the 'scissors-and-paste' methods of amateur local historians. The author of 'Back to Boomerang', he alleged, 'paved his history with slabs which other writers have constructed'—careless about how cracked or fragile the slabs might be or how poorly applied the mortar between them. A century after the foundation of local government in NSW and Victoria, a surge of municipal centenaries had opened up a new frontier of opportunity for young honours graduates. 'Enlightened councils', Professor Max **Crawford** noted in his introduction to Susan Priestley's *Echuca* (1965), would have 'the wisdom to turn to trained historians to help them in their task'. Weston **Bate**, another of Crawford's protégés, extended Blainey's critique (*HSANZ*, 1963) of the methods of local history. In his own histories of Brighton (1962) and Ballarat (1978, 1993) he sought, through a meticulous analysis of ratebooks and newspapers, to present a richly textured, complex portrait of a past society in action.

The path blazed by Blainey, Bate, and Priestley has since been followed by many other academically trained historians, including Max Kelly, Michael Jones, Carol Liston, Grace Karskens, John Turner, Don Garden, Bernard Barrett, John Lack, Andrew Lemon, Sally Wilde, Susan Marsden, Peter Donovan, and Tom Stannage. Sometimes it is a local, like Bill Gammage, who goes 'back to' Narrandera, to write the town's history; more often it is the city-based academic who answers an advertisement in the metropolitan press, and drives up with a sheaf of references to meet the local editorial committee.

Hiring a professional may guarantee that the job is well done, but it may leave the locals with the uneasy feeling that their history, like everything else, has been appropriated by the educated people from the city. Since the 1970s, however, local history has often played an important role in the efforts of residents' associations and other community groups to conserve historic towns and neighbourhoods. The numbers of local historical societies have multiplied more than fourfold since 1970, as have the numbers of published local histories. Carol Beaumont has published a valuable bibliography of local histories in Victoria (1980); Christine Eslick and others of NSW; and Ros Paterson of SA (1989). Some recent experiments in local history writing involve the locals themselves more fully in the process of making their own history. Janet McCalman's *Struggletown* (1984) is the history of a place—the Melbourne working-class suburb of Richmond—as well as an **oral history** of the generation who grew up there between the wars. Academic historians are now more likely to see themselves as helping local communities to write their own histories. The History and Heritage Committee of the Victorian Sesquicentenary (1985) sponsored *A Handbook of Local History for Enthusiasts* and the University of NSW's Local History Coordination Project, founded in the wake of the Australian Bicentenary, published *Locating Australia's Past: A Practical Guide to Writing Local History* (1988). The model of the monolithic, officially sponsored, single-author local history has been challenged by more open-ended, collaborative, and experimental approaches. More than 30 writers, including architects, journalists, and community activists as well as historians, contributed to *Fitzroy: Melbourne's First Suburb* (1989), while *Brunswick: One History, Many Voices* (1994) contained chapters, published in their own languages as well as English, from members of the Italian, Greek, Turkish, and Lebanese communities.

Most local histories end on an elegiac note, mourning the decline of the 'community' which, they imply, was once coterminous with their locality. Local councils, whose sense of identity and self-worth is bound up with a belief in the importance of local ties, are eager sponsors of such histories; but critics of the genre ask whether the 'local community', especially when it is a Sydney or Melbourne suburb with invisible boundaries, is just a myth. Some local histories, such as Grace Karskens's *The Rocks* (1997), and Clive Faro and Gary Wotherspoon's *Street Seen: A History of Oxford Street* (2000), celebrate the informal community of street or neighbourhood, rather than the officially defined town or suburb. In 1991, when the NSW Local History Coordination Project changed its focus from 'locality' to 'community', its founding director Patrick **O'Farrell** explained that 'community' was 'more than a place'; it was a 'state of mind, a disposition of involved neighbourliness'. Three of the best recent Australian local histories tackle this relationship between place and community head-on. John Lack's *A History of Footscray* (1991) probes the networks of local employment and institutional affiliation which undergirt the industrial suburb's intense local pride; Bill Gammage reconstructs the linkages of trade, communications, and migration which tied the destiny of *Narrandera Shire* (1986) to a wider world; and in *Camden* (1988), Alan Atkinson shows how the **Macarthurs**' attempt to create a patriarchal village community succumbed, as early as the 1860s, to the pressures of Sydney markets and the blandishments of Sydney politicians. 'Community', he concludes, may be a myth, but it is a valuable myth which local history helps to keep alive.

GRAEME DAVISON

Local option, or the right of localities to exclude bars or saloons, had been a central plank of **temperance** campaigns since the 1880s. Legislation in the early twentieth century gave municipalities the option of reducing or prohibiting liquor licences in their local area by a referendum. This followed considerable lobbying by the temperance movement. In NSW, where referendums were held in 1907, 1910, and 1913, most voters elected for no change to be made to the existing number of licences. In subsequent referendums in the other states, electors generally followed this position. The referendums held in Victoria in 1920, however, revealed strong opposition to licensed hotels in Melbourne's eastern suburbs. In the municipalities of Camberwell and Box Hill, where the influence of middle-class respectability and Methodist sobriety was particularly strong, residents voted for the removal of licences, thereby creating a 'dry area'. Despite significant changes to social drinking behaviour in the 1990s, attempts to abolish Melbourne's dry areas have been unsuccessful.

HD

Lodges, see **Benefit societies**

Logan, Patrick (1791–1830), a Scottish-born soldier, was appointed commandant of the **Moreton Bay** penal settlement in 1825. He improved the settlement and led several important exploratory expeditions, but was reputedly very harsh in his treatment of the convicts—the folksong 'Moreton Bay' portrays him as a tyrant. Under Logan's command the settlement was frequently subject to unrest and uprisings. His killing by Aborigines was reputedly encouraged by the convicts, but this was denied by a fellow soldier. He is the subject of a biography by Charles Bateson, *Patrick Logan: Tyrant of Brisbane Town* (1966), and is the central figure in Jessica Anderson's novel, *The Commandant* (1975).

KT

London Dock Strike of August 1889 was a pivotal event in the trend towards mass unionism of the 1880s which drew together workers of various backgrounds. The action received great support in the Australian colonies. Unionists and members of the public contributed a generous £30 000 in support of the London dockworkers—a gift which contributed significantly to the strikers' success. The strike provided a precedent for the **Maritime Strike** held in Australia the following year, to which sympathetic English strikers reciprocated the donation of funds. The dockers' leader, Ben Tillett, later toured Australia.

HD

Long boom identifies two periods of economic history: the first 1860–90, and the second 1945–73. The first saw sustained growth stimulated by large-scale immigration from Britain and population growth, and increased availability of British capital to underwrite the application of new technology. While the gold and pastoral industries led the export sector, population concentrated particularly in the cities which benefited from substantial construction as well as the production and consumption of manufactured goods and services. The first long boom ended in the **depression** of the 1890s.

The postwar boom was again aided by large-scale immigration and buoyant export conditions. The initial prosperity of farming and later mining were accompanied by the expansion of **manufacturing** and the service sectors. Unemployment was at a historic low, and comsumption reached unprecedented levels. High rates of home-ownership fuelled an increased demand for housing, which extended the boundaries of the **suburbs** and renewed enthusiasm for domesticity. Manufactured goods, such as **motor cars** and domestic appliances, defined the new postwar lifestyle. Australia's capital cities were transformed as the demolition of existing structures made way for multi-storey office buildings. Postwar immigrants provided the necessary labour, both for the postwar building boom and for national development programs, such as the **Snowy Mountains Hydro-Electric Scheme**. The postwar long boom ended when the international economy was shaken by the oil crisis of 1973–74, emphasising Australia's reliance on world trade and investment.

HD

Long, Gavin Merrick (1901–68), journalist, was general editor of Australia's official history of **World War II**.

Educated in Bathurst and Sydney, and a senior journalist with the *Sydney Morning Herald*, Long followed in the footsteps and shadow of Charles **Bean**, the editor of the **World War I** history. His extensive series (22 volumes, of which he wrote three himself) attracted far less attention than Bean's series, possibly because the themes of Long's history and the achievements of the Australians were less dramatic. His prose was elegant, well-paced; his capacity for critical comment was better developed than Bean's. His treatment of Churchill in *To Benghazi* (1952) is evidence of an independent mind. Long's instructions to the other war historians are fine essays in the historian's craft, showing what sensitivities they needed. Like Bean, Long wrote a synoptic account, *The Six Years' War* (1973), ignoring **Chifley's** advice to begin with the short history to give readers a taste for the longer work. The series had fewer readers than Bean's; although well-mined on commemorative occasions, it is mostly overlooked. Long wore himself out over the history, taking a much heavier load than the term 'general editor' might imply. He did not return to journalism when he completed the war history; from 1963 he worked on the staff of the *ADB*.

MICHAEL MCKERNAN

Longford, Raymond Hollis (1878–1959), born John Walter Longford, worked as a stage actor before entering the **film industry**. With actress Lottie Lyell (1890–1925) he made a succession of silent movies on Australian themes—*The Sentimental Bloke* (1919); *On Our Selection* (1920) and *Rudd's New Selection* (1921); *Ginger Mick* (1920); and *The Dinkum Bloke* (1923). Longford was a staunch believer in the local film industry: 'I would like to see the industry go ahead in leaps and bounds, particularly the good Australian stories … indigenous to Australia and full of sentiment.' Lyell's early death and increasing pressure from large film companies forced him out of the business, and he ended his working life as a nightwatchman on the Sydney wharves. The Australian Film Institute has recognised his contribution to the industry in the annual Raymond Longford award.

KT

Longstaff, John Campbell (1861–1941) achieved early recognition as an artist in 1887 when he won the first travelling scholarship offered by the National Gallery School, Melbourne, for *Breaking the News*, an indication of his penchant for narrative painting. On his return to Melbourne seven years later, he eked out a living as a portraitist until he received a commission from the trustees of the National Gallery of Victoria to paint the epic *Arrival of Burke, Wills and King at Cooper's Creek* (1907). This took him to London where he became established as a society portrait painter. He was appointed an official war artist during World War I, painting mainly prominent military figures. When he returned to Australia he was accepted as the nation's leading portrait painter, a position reinforced by his five prize-winning **Archibald** portraits. A biography,

Debonair Jack (1994), by a distant descendant, Prue Joske, explored what she saw as the contradictions of his life.

KT

Lowe, Robert (1811–92) exerted considerable influence as a politician, journalist, and orator during his comparatively short time in Australia. He practised law in London following a brilliant career at Oxford, but a medical warning that he could soon become blind caused him to migrate to NSW in search of a quick fortune. Within a year of his arrival in 1842 he was appointed to the Legislative Council by Governor **Gipps**, who underestimated Lowe's independence. This was soon demonstrated by his support for the separation movement of the **Port Phillip District**. He resigned from the Council to found and write satiric poems for the *Atlas* on behalf of the Pastoral Association. He later broke with the squatters over the question of land monopoly. Lowe was also a leader of the movement opposing transportation, when the **Colonial Office** sought to revive it in 1848, and elected to the Council with the support of the Sydney radicals.

After his return in 1850 to England, Lowe was elected to the House of Commons and served as chancellor of the exchequer in liberal governments, but opposed the extension of the franchise in the Second Reform Act. His *Poems of a Life* (1885) included several written in Australia, and *Speech on the Australian Colonies Bill* appeared in 1850. He has been the subject of several biographies, including Ruth Knight's *Illiberal Liberal* (1966).

KT

Lowenstein, Wendy (1927–) has been a pioneer of **oral history** in writings on popular culture, working life, and radical politics. She grew up in Melbourne and was drawn to the Left when she became active as a teenager in the New Theatre. Initially a journalist, she was directed into factory work after she joined the **Communist** Party, but studied journalism at the University of Melbourne and subsequently worked as a teacher and librarian. She and her husband, Werner, left the Communist Party following the 1956 revelations of Stalin's terror, but have remained active in the Left.

With Ian **Turner**, Lowenstein established the Folklore Society of Victoria and collaborated with him and June Factor in studies of children's play rhymes during the 1960s. After Turner showed her a copy of *Hard Times* (1970), Studs Terkel's oral history of the **Depression** in the USA, she began work on an Australian equivalent. It took her six years to prepare *Weevils in the Flour* (1978) and no publisher would accept it until she and Morag Loh used the interviews as the basis of an oral history, *The Immigrants* (1977). *Weevils in the Flour* drew on more than 200 informants from across the country and from varied backgrounds, but with a strong leaning towards activism, and transcribed their testimony into pungent prose. The work has passed through several editions, and historians have drawn freely upon it. She later produced a parallel study of contemporary unemployment. In 1982 she collaborated with Tom Hills, a veteran waterside worker and communist, on an account of 'working lives and class war' in Port Melbourne, *Under the Hook*. She has reflected on her life in 'Acquiring Class' (*Overland*, 1997).

SM

Lucky Country was the title given, ironically, to Australia by the journalist and historian Donald **Horne** in his book of that title published in 1964. 'Australia is a lucky country run mainly by second-rate people who share its luck', he concluded. He wrote in the midst of the postwar **long boom** when material living standards were high and Australians were becoming a complacent, suburban, middle-class society. Australia, he considered, had not deserved its luck and might not continue to enjoy it unless its leaders became 'clever' as well. His verdict was confirmed by the way in which the phrase was stripped of its ironical edge and used to reinforce the very complacency he had set out to disturb. In *The Lucky Country Revisited* (1987), Horne lamented its transformation into a 'phrase of self-congratulation', attributing it to the 'profound silliness' of sections of the Australian intelligentsia. His *Death of the Lucky Country* (1976) was not, as some readers had expected, a lament for the recently dismissed **Whitlam** government—though Horne was outraged by the manner of its going—but a review of the ways in which Whitlam had broken down the cushioned complacency of a country whose luck, he still feared, was running out.

GD

Lutheran Church, the world's oldest Protestant denomination, was founded by Martin Luther. The first Lutherans to emigrate to Australia were **Germans** escaping the religious persecution that had been sparked by the determination of King Frederick William to merge traditional with Calvinist branches of the Church. The first arrivals, led by Pastor Augustus Kavel, landed at Port Adelaide in 1838, and a second migration, led by Pastor Fritzsche, in 1841. These Lutherans built village settlements in the Barossa Valley, which they developed as a thriving farming and wine-growing district. They formed an independent Australian Church and established schools, churches, and **Aboriginal missions**, notably Hermannsburg. In 1846, however, personal and doctrinal disagreement between Kavel and Fritzsche led to a schism which lasted over 100 years and created two rival bodies: the United Evangelical Lutheran Church in Australia (led by Kavel) and the Evangelical Lutheran Church in Australia (led by Fritzsche). Lutherans were subject to anti-German sentiment expressed during both world wars (see **aliens**), and experienced continued dissension among factional groups until 1966, when the Lutheran Church of Australia was established as a unified national body.

HD

Lycett, Joseph (?1774–?1828) was a Staffordshire-born painter and engraver sentenced to 14 years' transportation for forgery, who arrived in Sydney in early 1814. Working as a police clerk, Lycett was soon convicted again of forgery and sent to Newcastle, where he worked on the planning and decoration of the church. A conditional pardon allowed him to work and travel in Van Diemen's Land and NSW. Governor **Macquarie** sent three of his paintings to Lord Bathurst in 1820. After receiving an absolute pardon, Lycett returned to England in 1822 and produced the series of engravings for which he is best known, *Views in Australia: Or New South Wales, and Van Diemen's Land Delineated*. Dedicated to Lord Bathurst, the series was designed to show the 'benign changes' wrought on 'the wild scenery of Australia [by] the arts and sciences of Britain'. Bernard **Smith** in *Australian Painting* (1962) noted Lycett's tendency to make his scenes conventionally picturesque with the comment that he became famous for 'forging landscapes'. Less well known are Lycett's watercolour sketches depicting Aborigines involved in traditional activities, published by the National Library of Australia as *The Lycett Album* (1990).

KT

Lyons, Joseph Aloysius (1879–1939) was prime minister of Australia and first leader of the **United Australia Party** 1932–39. In 1915, aged 35, he married Enid **Burnell** (1897–1981), a 17-year-old Methodist pupil teacher, who became an enthusiastic convert to her husband's Catholicism. Enid's subsequent life with Joseph has by common consent been regarded, as Kate White described it in the title of her book on the subject in 1987, as *A Political Love Story*.

Originally a schoolteacher from a middle-class but deprived background, Lyons entered the Tasmanian parliament in 1909, and at the time of his marriage was minister for education in John Earle's Labor government. When Labor split over **conscription** in 1916, Lyons's sentimental Irish nationalism, learnt from his mother, ensured that he would be on the anti-conscription side. The schism led to his becoming party leader and premier. Lyons lost the premiership after defeat at the state election of 1919, but regained it in 1923, with a minority government initially supported by some Labor members and a group of Nationalists.

In office until 1928, Lyons developed a style of consensual politics which offended his party's left wing as he wrestled with the economic difficulties of a small and marginalised state. Enid, by then the mother of five, stood unsuccessfully for state parliament in 1925. She closely shared her husband's political preoccupations and seconded his preference for compromise rather than confrontation. It was at her insistence, for example, that the couple cancelled their subscription to the *Australian Worker*, deciding it was a journal too bitter for their children to read.

Entering federal politics in 1929, Lyons won ministerial office in **Scullin's** government, but in 1931, when acting treasurer, he left the ministry and party in profound disagreement with their handling of the **Depression** crisis. As leader of a new party of orthodoxy and compromise, the UAP, Lyons was prime minister from 1932 until his death in 1939. To leave the Labor Party was acutely distressing but, as 'Honest Joe', Lyons caught the popular imagination and was a sure-fire election winner; to the end, he and Enid were convinced that 'we saved Australia from ruin'.

When visiting Australia in 1934, Maurice Hankey, Britain's celebrated cabinet secretary, found Lyons 'a frightfully decent old boy'. When congratulated on a 'delightful' speech he had made the evening before at a parliamentary dinner, Lyons 'at once told me that most of it had been written by Mrs Lyons—a wonderful woman, a good mother of twelve, and no mean politician'. A homely and popular public speaker, Enid was perhaps the more formidable and intelligent of the pair. However, her published reminiscences (especially *Among the Carrion Crows*, 1972), suggest that in her likes and dislikes, especially about people, she was also much the narrower of the two.

Lyons was not an effective cabinet chair, and few positive policies were developed during his prime ministership. Though it was understood that he would step down after his first term of office, party officials insisted that he hold his position in 1934 and in the shaky election of 1937. The cares of office were important in the subsequent deterioration of his health. By 1939, his government's failure to act resolutely on rearmament vexed those who thought war imminent, and observers like Keith **Murdoch** blamed Enid, whom he called 'an ardent, even a belligerent pacifist'.

After Joe's death, Enid entered the federal House of Representatives as its first woman member, having won the seat of Darwin, Tasmania. Somehow she managed to overcome the long-standing hostility to R.G. **Menzies**, which is revealed in her writings, to serve between 1949 and 1951 as his vice-president of the Executive Council—the first woman in the history of the Commonwealth to hold ministerial office.

A.W. MARTIN

M

Mabo, Eddie Koiki, see Mabo case

Mabo Case, officially known as *Mabo & Others v State of Queensland*, refers to a landmark High Court decision of 1992 concerning **Aboriginal land rights**. The plaintiffs were **Torres Strait Islanders** from Mer Island, including 'Eddie' Koiki Mabo (1936–92), who first brought their case before the Supreme Court of Queensland in 1982. The High Court's decision, handed down on 3 June 1992, overturned the doctrine of *terra nullius*—that at the time of European settlement, as nomads, Aborigines had no claim to the land—and recognised the Meriam people's common law rights to native title; Justice Dawson was the sole dissenter. The court's decision hinged largely on the Mer Islanders' demonstration of continued cultural ties with their land, but the judges extended the same principles to the mainland and cited the work of historian Henry **Reynolds**. A federal Native Title Bill was passed in 1993 in response to the decision, and this attempted to clarify the decision for the mainland. A further decision of the High Court in the **Wik** case suggested that native title could coexist with other land rights, and caused the federal government to seek a legislative settlement of native title. Numerous published works on the Mabo Case have appeared, including a legal commentary by Richard H. Bartlett in *The Mabo Decision* (1993), and Tim Rowse and Murray Goot (eds), *Make a Better Offer: The Politics of Mabo* (1994). (See also **Aboriginal land rights**.)

HD

Macarthur family played a leading role in early NSW politics, commerce, and **pastoral history**. JOHN (1767–1834), a lieutenant in the **New South Wales Corps**, arrived at Port Jackson in June 1790, accompanied by his new wife ELIZABETH (1766–1850), and with an air of arrogant self-confidence that would produce many enemies, but win enough friends in high places to ensure his wealth and influence. In 1792–93 Francis Grose appointed him regimental paymaster, then inspector of public works, and granted him land at Parramatta; there he established Elizabeth Farm, which survives today as a museum, its story told by James Broadbent in *Elizabeth Farm* (1984). By 1794 Macarthur was trading in grain and other produce. Grose assisted his promotion to captain in 1795, but John **Hunter** and P.G. **King** were wary of 'this perturbator', as King described Macarthur, whom he sent to England for court martial in 1801 after a duel with William Paterson. The trial was not pursued, allowing the ever-opportunistic Macarthur to promote NSW's prospects for fine **wool** growing. Lord Camden facilitated Macarthur's resignation from the army and return to NSW in 1805 with a grant of 5000 acres, which he took up at the Cowpastures, calling his property Camden Park. Macarthur's flocks were based on Spanish merinos and the term *pure merino* became a metaphor for colonial aristocracy. A key figure in the 1808 **Rum Rebellion**, Macarthur returned to England to give account and remained in exile until 1817. He manipulated J.T. **Bigge** and quarrelled with Lachlan **Macquarie** and Sir Ralph **Darling**. After 1817 he expanded wool exports, developed a wine industry, promoted the Australian Agricultural Company (1824) and Bank of Australia (1826), and was a legislative councillor before slipping into insanity in the 1830s.

M.H. **Ellis**, in his biography, *John Macarthur* (1955), claims Macarthur 'did the country greater material service than any other man', but 'was not, as he was prone to claim, the first man to see the advantages to the Colony of the development of the sheep industry'. Sibella Macarthur-Onslow's *Some Early Records of the Macarthurs of Camden* (1914) helped perpetuate Macarthur as father of the Australian wool industry, an image commemorated on Australia's $2 note in 1966. Macarthur's credibility as a breeder of pure merinos has since been strongly disputed by J.C. Garran and Les White in *Merinos, Myths and Macarthurs* (1985). The importance of Elizabeth Macarthur's role is now better recognised following Hazel King's work in *Elizabeth Macarthur and Her World* (1980) and

'Lives in Exile' (in Penny Russell, ed., *For Richer, For Poorer: Early Colonial Marriages*, 1994). The fate of the Macarthurs' attempt to create a patriarchal community around their estate is told in Alan Atkinson's *Camden* (1988).

Nine children were born to Elizabeth and John Macarthur. The eldest son EDWARD (1789–1872) pursued a military career and promoted Australian colonisation during the 1840s. He administered the Colony of Victoria in 1856. Second son JOHN (1794–1831) became a London lawyer who attended to his father's business affairs. Fourth son JAMES (1798–1867) was prominent in mid-nineteenth-century NSW politics. John Manning **Ward's** *James Macarthur: Colonial Conservative 1788–1867* (1981) portrays James's liberal conservatism as based on creation of 'a stable, hierarchical society, in which political and social authority would belong to an elite of educated, wealthy and responsibly minded landowners'. Fifth son WILLIAM (1800–82) enjoyed a minor political career, but mainly assisted James with management of the family estates. William achieved international recognition as a horticulturist and was a pioneer of the Australian wine industry. The daughter of James Macarthur, ELIZABETH (1840–1911), married Captain A.A.W. Onslow in 1867, which commenced the Macarthur-Onslow family. HANNIBAL HAWKINS MACARTHUR (1788–1861), a nephew of John Macarthur snr, shared in various business ventures, and became a legislative councillor and prominent member of the **exclusives**. He was chairman of the Bank of Australia from 1835 to 1843 and lost heavily in its collapse. His son GEORGE FAIRFOWL MACARTHUR (1825–90) was headmaster of the King's School, Parramatta, from 1869 to 1886. Important collections of records relating to the Macarthur family are held at the Mitchell Library, Sydney, the National Library of Australia, and the University of Newcastle Archives.

DAMIEN CASH

Macassans, also known as 'Malays', were from the Dutch port of Macassar (Udjung Pandang) in eastern Indonesia. They made seasonal visits to northern Australia, probably from the late seventeenth century, to collect trepang (also known as *bêche-de-mer*, sea slug, or sea cucumber—reputedly an aphrodisiac), which they traded with the Chinese. Other items they sought included pearl fish, turtle shell, and cypress pine timber, for which they bartered tobacco and other items with Aborigines. Macassans crossed the Arafura Sea each December in a fleet of small wooden vessels, called praus, and set up camp on beaches, particularly on islands in the Gulf of Carpentaria and in Arnhem Land. Here they boiled trepang in stone ovens, dried it and smoked it to enable preservation. They often employed Aborigines to work for them. After about three months' work, they returned to Macassar with their valuable dried product. In contrast with the violence of British settlement, the Macassan encounters were generally amicable, probably because their impermanency was seen as less threatening. The SA government, then responsible for the NT, ended the Macassan trade in 1906. The visits are remembered in the Aboriginal art and music of the northern coastal region. Remains of a trepanging camp are evident at Kuruwa Island in the Gulf of Carpentaria. The best account is C.C. Macknight, *The Voyage to Marege': Macassan Trepangers in Northern Australia* (1976).

HD

Macdonald, Louisa (1858–1949) was appointed first principal of the Women's College, University of Sydney, in 1891, from her position as fellow of the University College, London. She spent the following 28 years consolidating the Women's College financially and academically, as well as working to give women a voice in the wider university life. While she returned to her native Scotland, her papers are in the Sydney University Archives. In the 1890s she was active in the female suffrage movement in NSW.

KT

MacGregor, William (1846–1919) entered the British colonial service in the 1870s as a medical officer. His involvement with administration gradually overtook his medical duties and in 1888 he arrived in Port Moresby as Administrator of British New Guinea, where he remained until 1898, for the last four years as lieutenant-governor. His administration sought to protect Papuans from the depredations of Australian entrepreneurs and colonial governments. In 1909 he was appointed governor of Qld, a position he filled for five years before retiring and returning to Scotland. R.B. Joyce has written a biography (1971).

KT

Mackaness, George (1882–1968), a former pupil-teacher, gained master's and doctoral degrees from the universities of Sydney and Melbourne. His original specialty was English literature, and from 1924 until 1946 he was lecturer in charge of the English Department at Sydney Teachers College. A leading bibliophile, he amassed a substantial collection of Australiana, sat on the Board of Trustees of the Public Library, and was active in literary and educational circles. He belonged to that group of prewar Teachers College lecturers who, besides training teachers, enriched Australian cultural life.

Mackaness developed interests in Australian history and became a prominent member of the **Royal Australian Historical Society**. Marjorie **Barnard**, one of his critics, once described him as entering the Mitchell Library, which he frequented, 'smiling like a surprised but affable egg'. He proved adept at research and writing; he was unrivalled for his capacity to locate original sources, many of which he published. His reputation as a historian rests mainly on his monumental biographies, *The Life of Vice-Admiral William Bligh* (1931), a Melbourne doctoral thesis which took 10 years to write, and *Admiral Arthur Phillip* (1937). He portrayed both men in favourable terms, arousing opposition from those who denigrated Bligh. These and other writings were, nonetheless, thoroughly researched and carefully crafted. They stamp him as one of the pioneers of scholarly historical writing in Australia.

BRIAN FLETCHER

Mackellar, (Isobel Marion) Dorothea (1885–1968) wrote the lyric poem 'My Country', initially published in 1908 as 'Core of My Heart'. The poem, with its famous second verse beginning 'I love a sunburnt country', was reportedly inspired by the breaking of a drought at one of the family's rural properties. It gave voice and form to nationalistic feelings and, revised and published in her first book of poems, *The Closed Door and Other Verses* (1911), rapidly became part of the staple diet of Australian schoolchildren. Several of its phrases— 'the wide brown land' and 'a sunburnt country'—have entered the national lexicon. Mackellar produced several further volumes of poetry and three novels before ill-health caused her to cease writing. Her diaries, edited by Jyoti Brunsdon, were published in 1990; and a biography by Adrienne Howley, *My Heart, My Country*, appeared in 1989.

KT

Mackerras family has contributed significantly to cultural endeavour. Its progenitors were ALAN (1899–1973) who lectured in electrical engineering at the University of Sydney, and CATHERINE BREARCLIFFE (1899–1977), a history honours graduate, who was born into the Maclaurin family that was highly esteemed in Sydney medical circles. A descendant of the colonial musician Isaac Nathan, who came to Sydney in 1841, Catherine wrote his biography (*The Hebrew Melodist*, 1963), together with an unpublished history of her family, and *Divided Heart: The Memoirs of Catherine B. Mackerras* (1991), which appeared posthumously and traced at length the path that led her to Catholicism. Of their children, CHARLES (1925–), a noted orchestral conductor, did much to promote music overseas and in Australia. ALASTAIR (1928–99) made his name as a highly innovative headmaster of Sydney Grammar School. NEIL (1930–87), a founding member of the **Democratic Labor Party**, was a lawyer and prominent defender of the Aboriginal people. JOAN (1934–) was a violinist. ELIZABETH (1937–) began her professional career as a ballerina and then changed to interior decorating. COLIN (1939–) became an academic and leading China expert, while MALCOLM (1939–), also an academic, was well known for his commentaries on Australian elections. Here was a remarkable family, noted both for its talents and individuality.

BRIAN FLETCHER

MacKillop, Mary Helen (1842–1909), also known as Mother Mary of the Cross, was co-founder of the Josephites, an Australian order of nuns dedicated to a life of poverty and the service of the poor. Long revered by Australian Catholics, she was beatified by Pope John Paul II in January 1995.

MacKillop was born in Fitzroy, Melbourne, the daughter of Highland Scots immigrants. Her father Alexander had been educated for the priesthood in Rome, but did not proceed to ordination and emigrated to Port Phillip. Mary grew up in a pious but financially precarious and unhappy household, inheriting both her father's educational aspirations and the burden of his 'great refusal'. 'I will devote my life to the service of God, since my father failed', she resolved.

She worked as a shop-girl and governess in Melbourne and as a schoolteacher in Portland until 1866, when the dashing but wayward English priest Julian **Tenison-Woods**, then parish priest at Penola, SA, invited her to join him in the foundation of a new religious order. The Sisters of St Joseph of the Sacred Heart was modelled on the Sisters of St Joseph of Puy, a French penitential order observed during his travels by Tenison-Woods. He, like MacKillop, was inspired by an authoritarian, almost mystical, faith and a determination to rescue poor Catholic children, especially those in the outback, from the perils of a secular state education. The Josephites were poorer, more egalitarian, and less subject to episcopal control than other religious orders.

With the encouragement of Woods, the sisterhood expanded rapidly, establishing its head house in Adelaide. But it soon encountered difficulties. While MacKillop was absent in Brisbane, reports of strange happenings among some of the younger sisters—visions of saints and demons, mysterious conflagrations, self-inflicted stigmata—alarmed the local hierarchy. In September 1871, Bishop Shiel returned from Rome and excommunicated her for alleged insubordination. Several of the sisters fled the convent, and it seemed that the order might be disbanded.

Five months later, on his deathbed, Shiel repented his decision and the decree was removed. In 1872 MacKillop visited Rome and obtained papal approval of the Josephites' Rule, but in a revised form that, Tenison-Woods believed, compromised their original vision. The intense personal and spiritual relationship between MacKillop and her confessor cooled; thereafter his influence declined as her authority grew. In 1875 she was elected superior-general of the sisterhood, now comprising more than 200 nuns, and conducting over 40 schools and other institutions. Mary was revered by most of her followers, but criticisms of her financial administration and rumours of her alleged over-indulgence in alcohol (she took brandy on doctor's orders as a remedy for severe menstrual pains) emerged during an episcopal visitation in 1883. Rather than surrender her leadership, Mary transferred the order's headquarters to Sydney. In 1901 MacKillop suffered a stroke and she remained an invalid until her death in Sydney on 8 May 1909.

MacKillop was reared to venerate the saints, and lived in an era when saints of humble origin, such as St Therese of Lisieux, became a focus for popular devotion throughout the **Catholic Church**. It was as natural for her to aspire to sainthood as it was for her followers, once she died, to advance her cause for canonisation. The first hagiography appeared seven years after her death, and more than a dozen other lives have since appeared under official auspices. In line with papal requirements for canonisation, they stress the purity of her childhood; early intimations of her vocation, such as the prophecy of the Portland bootmaker Rodriguez ('I see you at the head of a long train of virgins in brown …'); her submission to the will of God and Rome; and her charismatic gifts. In the early 1960s the recovery of a woman with apparently incurable cancer was attributed to prayers offered by the Josephites for MacKillop's intercession; this was the authenticated miracle necessary for her beatification.

A 1926 biography by George O'Neill, written to advance her cause, actually set it back, by touching too directly on the 'problem' of MacKillop's drinking habits; it was only after Osmond Thorpe's more circumspect life of 1957 that her cause was again taken up by the Australian hierarchy. Paul Gardiner's 1993 biography is based on the lengthy *positio*, which he compiled as the official proponent of her canonisation. The Josephites themselves venerate a less submissive, more socially engaged, and proudly Australian founder. Marie Foale's scholarly *The Josephite Story* (1989) places MacKillop in the life of the community she helped to found; Margaret Press's life of Tenison-Woods (1979) sensitively explores the relationship with her co-founder; while *Mary MacKillop Unveiled* (1994), written on behalf of the order by Lesley O'Brien, a former *Vogue* journalist, hails MacKillop as 'before all else a great Australian', a feminist heroine more than a nineteenth-century saint. An art competition 'Mary MacKillop—A Tribute' (1995) reinforced this image; the winning entry, by Chinese-Australian artist Jaiwei Shen, depicted the saint seated in a Cobb & Co. coach amid bush children, swagmen, and Aborigines.

GRAEME DAVISON

Macnamara, (Annie) Jean (1899–1968) was involved, as a medical scientist, in work on eradicating two great scourges—poliomyelitis and rabbits. After she graduated in medicine from the University of Melbourne in 1922, she worked with Macfarlane **Burnet** and they discovered that several strains of the polio virus existed. She became involved with the treatment of child polio victims, for whom she established a clinic. Her methods brought her into conflict with Elizabeth **Kenny**, whose work she criticised vociferously. Philipa Martyr assesses their relationship in a re-examination of the Kenny controversy (*AHS*, 1997). Macnamara was a staunch advocate of the introduction of myxomatosis to arrest rabbit plagues, campaigning for 20 years before the worth of the virus was finally accepted. Desmond Zwar's 1984 biography portrays her as a 'medical pioneer'.

KT

Maconochie, Alexander (1787–1860), prison reformer, went to Van Diemen's Land in 1837 as private secretary to John **Franklin**. Before leaving England, he had been asked to prepare a report on the **convict** system. His criticisms of the **assignment system**, and the alternative system emphasising rehabilitation that he formulated, formed part of a parliamentary paper published by the House of Lords in 1838. Maconochie developed his proposals, published in 1839 as *Australiana: Thoughts on Convict Management* and *General Views Regarding the Social System of Convict Management*. In 1840 he was appointed superintendent of the penal settlement at **Norfolk Island**, where he implemented his 'mark' system, which rewarded good behaviour with a view to reforming prisoners. After his dismissal in 1844 the

scheme was abolished, but Maconochie published his influential *Crime and Punishment, the Mark System* (1846). He figures in several stories by Price Warung (William **Astley**), and is the subject of a study by J.V. **Barry** (1958).

KT

Macquarie, Lachlan (1762–1824) was governor of NSW from 1810 to 1821. He died in despair soon after returning to Britain; his achievements were not recognised and his most distinctive policies had been repudiated by a royal commission (the **Bigge** report). Now he is the best remembered and most highly esteemed of the colonial governors.

He came of an impoverished farming family in the inner Hebrides in Scotland. When he was 15, his uncle, a Highland laird, secured him a place in the army, in which he slowly advanced his position. Macquarie came with his regiment to NSW in 1809 to replace the **New South Wales Corps** and to re-establish legitimate authority after the rebellion against **Bligh**. Macquarie acted from the first as if this governorship was to be the crowning achievement of his life. He did not intend merely to administer the affairs of the colony; he set out to transform it. This is part of his attraction to modern Australia; he treated a ramshackle convict colony of 5000 people as if it were or could be a significant place. In his eye it could not be civilised until it had the appurtenances of civilisation, which were churches, schools, hospitals, and barracks. Macquarie was a great builder, turning a deaf ear to British ministers who were increasingly alarmed at the expense. Macquarie and his later defenders argued that public works had to be expanded to employ the rapidly increasing number of convicts. This may have been so, but Macquarie's commitment to building predated this rationale for it.

The buildings carried the inscription 'Lachlan Macquarie, Governor'; because so many survive, his mark, much more than other governors', is on the physical fabric of modern Sydney and the towns he established—Liverpool, Windsor, and Richmond. His name was also attached to rivers, lakes, harbours, mountains—bestowed either by himself or by the explorers he sponsored.

Macquarie was the last of the autocratic governors, and for him personal rule meant rule in person. As John Ritchie suggests in *Lachlan Macquarie* (1986), the governor acted the part of the benevolent, improving landlord, identifying the inhabitants of all degrees as his people and the colony as his personal estate. The Aborigines too were his people and clearly in need of improvement. He instituted an annual meeting between himself and the Aborigines at Parramatta, where he made his offers to set them up as farmers and fishermen, and to educate their children.

Macquarie is most famous for his **emancipist** policy. In the absence of suitable free people, other governors had used convicts and ex-convicts in positions of trust and responsibility; Macquarie transformed this expedient into a principle and carried it to the ultimate by appointing ex-convicts as magistrates. His insistence that the gentlemen of the colony should accord to the leading emancipists the same respect he showed them was responsible for much of the opposition to his rule. Judge Jeffery Bent, sent out to constitute the Supreme Court, refused to allow ex-convict lawyers to appear before him despite Macquarie's urging, even though this had the effect of keeping the court closed. Bent insisted that as a judge he was not subject to direction from the executive and he went on to question the legal basis of the governor's autocratic rule.

As his policy came under attack, Macquarie developed the view that the colony had been founded to promote the reformation of convicts and that the ex-convicts did much more for its advancement than the touchy free settlers, who should go elsewhere. In Whitehall this view created increasing alarm; the governor had, in modern parlance, gone native, accepting a local logic, and forgetting the purposes and standards of the metropolis. This is why he now attracts so much admiration. Macquarie must have a place in any account of Australian **nationalism**, and it is fitting that the name **Australia**, suggested by **Flinders**, owes its acceptance to his espousal.

No satisfactory explanation has been given for the governor's policy. He was an old-fashioned Tory, a stickler for due subordination, whose codes he knew so well as a poor man made good, and might have been expected to share the usual prejudice against former criminals. It was perhaps the exalted view of his own rank that made him careless of the honour of free settlers, and the high ambition he had for himself and the colony that attracted him to the vigorous enterprise of the ex-convicts.

In his attitude to convicts and their reformation he can seem a modern figure; in everything else he was traditional. The playwright Alexander Buzo, in his *Macquarie* (1971), could not sustain this paradox. He has the governor visiting a low tavern to question convicts on their conditions of work, and Macquarie then abandons flogging altogether!

A nation which saw its history as the gradual acquisition of civil and political liberties would not honour Macquarie. Marion Phillips shows this hesitation in *A Colonial Autocracy* (1909), which highlights the disadvantages of that mode of government and the corrupting effect it had on Macquarie. He did use his power arbitrarily, most notably when, without trial, he had three men flogged for trespassing on the government domain. On this view, Judge Bent, in refusing to pay a toll on the Parramatta road because Macquarie had no power to levy it, was striking a blow for Australian liberty. But this view of our history did not take root, and now the usual opinion on Bent is that he was a factious opponent of the good governor who stood up for convicts. Macquarie's opponents have difficulty in gaining sympathy as the society has become more comfortable with, even proud of, its convict origins. The full biographies of Macquarie, written much later than Phillips's study, are more sympathetic. Of these, Malcolm Ellis (1947) gives the fullest account of the governor's rule; John Ritchie is more concerned with his character.

In 1963 Sydney's third university was named Macquarie, and the dictionary which it produces, *The Macquarie*, has become the standard authority on Australian English. So the old viceroy continues to be honoured, and no-one takes offence that on his tomb in Scotland this British autocrat is called 'The Father of Australia'.

JOHN HIRST

Madgwick, Robert Bowden (1905–79) studied economics at the University of Sydney and completed a doctorate at Oxford. Appointed to a senior lectureship in economics at Sydney during 1936, he served as director of the Australian Army Education service 1941–46. A year later he became warden of the New England University College and first vice-chancellor of the university after it achieved independence. In 1967 he succeeded James Darling as chairman of the **Australian Broadcasting Commission**, where he remained until his retirement in 1973.

Madgwick was a distinguished administrator who was said to possess the skills of a diplomat. Fair and firm, he achieved much both for the university and for the Australian Broadcasting Corporation, whose independence he strongly supported. With E.R. Walker he published *An Outline of Australian Economics* (1931), but he described himself as 'an economist who saw the light and became a historian'. His book, *Immigration into Eastern Australia 1788–1851* (1937), was one of the few scholarly works on Australian history to appear before World War II. Its perceptive analysis of the machinery established to facilitate assisted migration to Australia and of the migrants who arrived before 1850 made the book a classic in its field.

BRIAN FLETCHER

Madness can be found in many different cultures and times, but how it is understood, how many people suffer from it, and the ways it is treated vary remarkably. In this sense, madness has a history.

European colonisation of Australia coincided with a momentous change in the understanding and treatment of madness in Britain. In the eighteenth century madness was seen as either animalism, best controlled by harsh restraint, or as imbalances in bodily humours, treated by bleeding. Most lunatics were kept at home or locked away in small, privately run 'mad-houses'. There were a few asylums, most notably St Mary Bethlehem Hospital in London, popularly known as Bedlam. Here lunatics were chained to walls and were the object of fascination for Londoners who paid to visit these institutions. But from the 1790s Evangelicals, Quakers, utilitarians, and liberals argued that madness was a consequence of a disordered moral environment. The new 'moral therapy' involved the removal of restraints, pleasant surroundings, ordered routines, religious instruction, education, work, and contact with moral exemplars who would inspire the mad to regain their moral will and hence their reason.

Moral therapy was slow to arrive in Australia. If anyone suffered from madness in the early years of the colony, they were more likely to be punished than reformed. The first

Magistrates

lunatic was not declared until 1805. Six years later there were sufficient numbers to warrant opening an asylum at Castle Hill. The first classic Victorian asylum was Tarban Creek, near Sydney, opened in 1838. By the 1860s there were similar sizeable lunatic asylums in all the Australian colonies. In appearance these institutions resembled the new British asylums, but through recurrent controversies, critics argued that they fell far short of the standards required for moral therapy. Inmates were kept in overcrowded, poorly maintained, understaffed wards, with little active therapy or occupation. From the 1860s concerted efforts were made by colonial reformers and doctors to bring the standards of care and treatment in Australian asylums up to those in Britain and North America. By the 1890s they had largely succeeded.

Although historians such as Kociumbas (*Oxford History of Australia*, vol. 2, 1992) have seen this development as part of a broader process of cultural transmission to Australia, they have failed to acknowledge the distinctive features of Australian madness. In Britain the majority of asylum patients were women, but in the Australian colonies they were men—a pattern that reflected the greater involvement of police in determining incarceration in Australia. Only in the 1930s did Australia begin to follow Britain, as more patients were referred to psychiatric care by family doctors and specialists. These developments were part of a new medical concept of mental illness. From the late nineteenth century, asylum doctors began to argue that madness was not a moral problem but an illness best treated by medical rather than moral intervention. They laid claim to medical expertise as psychiatrists, and urged that patients be treated in clinics and private practices in the early stages of their illness. They opposed the traditional safeguard of certification, which ensured that no person could be confined in a mental hospital without authorisation from two doctors. For psychiatrists, this meant that the mentally ill were denied medical assistance until their condition had become serious and in many cases incurable.

From the early twentieth century many psychiatrists began to establish private practices in the belief that asylums had become repositories for the incurable. As a consequence conditions in the old mental hospitals declined. There were fewer staff, poorer conditions, and a greater resort to restraints such as strait-jackets to control unruly patients. Patients in private practice received new psychotherapeutic treatments, while in the crumbling mental hospital system, doctors were beginning to experiment with new shock and convulsion therapies in the hope of a breakthrough for the 'incurably insane'. By the 1950s conditions in Australian mental hospitals were condemned by experts as hopelessly inadequate. Psychotropic drugs offered the first genuine hope for alleviating the symptoms of serious mental illness. From the 1960s reformers began to advocate the emptying of the old mental hospitals and the placement of the mentally ill in the community, a policy pursued with mixed motives and mixed results by most Australian governments in the 1980s. Inadequate community facilities often condemned released inmates to a twilight world of poorly maintained hostels and halfway houses, where staff administered high drug dosages to maintain order.

Mental illness has received little historical attention in Australia. The pioneering works of John Bostock, *Dawn of Australian Psychiatry* (1951), and C.R.B. Brothers, *Early Victorian Psychiatry* (1961), were really histories of the psychiatric profession. The major histories of psychiatry in Australia are Milton Lewis, *Managing Madness* (1988), and W.D. and Hilary Rubinstein, *Menders of the Mind* (1996). Jill Julius Matthews, *Good and Mad Women* (1984), examines personal histories of madness and institutionalisation from a feminist perspective. The main social history of madness is Stephen Garton, *Medicine and Madness* (1988).

STEPHEN GARTON

Magistrates are the judges in local courts of petty sessions. In the colonial period most of them were, as in England, unpaid, and the appointment to the magistracy was much sought-after as a sign of gentlemanly status. Magistrates were known as Justices of the Peace and could put the initials JP after their name. They also acted as the administrative arm of the colonial governments and until **local government** was established performed some of its functions. In the busier courts salaried (or stipendiary) magistrates were appointed. Governor **Arthur** upset the Tasmanian gentry by using them throughout the island to enforce his rule. Central control over convicts was hard to enforce with unpaid magistrates who themselves used convict labour. In the twentieth century the gentleman JPs have been totally superseded by salaried magistrates. Pat O'Shane became the first Aboriginal magistrate in 1986.

JH

Mahogany Ship, reputedly wrecked at Armstrongs Bay, between Warrnambool and Port Fairy, Victoria, was so named due to the reported dark colour and the hard, glassy quality of its timber. Recorded sightings between 1836 and 1880 by settlers in the area, anecdotal evidence by local Aborigines, and foreign coins found near Port Fairy were used as evidence of the ship's existence, and its presumed Portuguese or Spanish origin. George **Collingridge**, using the Dieppe Maps to argue the likelihood of **Portuguese discovery**, proposed that the Mahogany Ship was one of three Portuguese caravels under the command of Christóvão de Mendonça that was wrecked in 1529. This view was supported by Kenneth McIntyre in *The Secret Discovery of Australia* (1977). McIntyre demonstrated that the Dieppe Maps, if cartographically adjusted, bear a striking resemblance to the east coast of Australia, and the wreck site to the area of Armstrongs Bay. This theory has been dismissed by other historians, notably D.J. **Mulvaney**, owing to a lack of substantial evidence. Joseph Archibald, the father of J.F. **Archibald**, claimed to have seen the wreck in 1891; George McCrae in 1911. Local historian Jack Loney, in *The Mahogany Ship* (1974), and two symposia held at Warrnambool (1980, 1987), assessed these claims, but numerous searches, including those of 1976–77, 1981, 1987, 1991, and 2000, were unsuccessful.

HD

Major's Line was the path left by the wheel-tracks of Major Thomas **Mitchell** and his party in 1836 on their trip through **Australia Felix** to Portland Bay, Victoria. This became a well-worn, and in some parts deeply furrowed, track as **overlanders** from the 'Sydney side' and Monaro district used it to travel to the **Port Phillip District** in search of new grazing lands. Stephen **Roberts** claims it was 'a kind of internal boundary line for the province'. The route was developed by the Victorian government as the Major Mitchell Trail, a guide for which was published in 1988.

HD

Makarrata is a Yolngu word that refers to a ceremony held to mark the resolution of a conflict. It is derived from the word for thigh, owing to the practice of an opponent spearing the thigh of a wrongdoer in a traditional makarrata ceremony. In proposing a treaty between Aborigines and the Australian government in 1979, the National Aboriginal Conference committee on this subject chose the word 'makarrata', and defined it as 'the end of a dispute between communities and the resumption of normal relations'. The Aboriginal Treaty Committee—whose 14 members included H.C. **Coombs**, C.D. **Rowley**, Bill **Stanner**, and Judith **Wright**—was established to create awareness of the need for a treaty. The proposal was heard and examined by the Senate Standing Committee on Constitutional and Legal Affairs (1981–83). However, while Aboriginal groups held conflicting views about the desirability and substance of such a treaty, the Standing Committee accepted the Fraser government's refusal of that term on the grounds that it implied recognition of Aboriginal nationhood and Aboriginal sovereignty. The committee was disbanded in 1983. Stewart Harris's *It's Coming Yet* (1979) was a manifesto of the committee, and Wright's *We Call for a Treaty* (1985) gave an account of its endeavours. In 1987, in the lead-up to the bicentenary, Prime Minister **Hawke** reintroduced the concept of a treaty or compact, but proposed simply a statement of understanding, obligation and commitment, rather than a legally binding agreement. **Keating** continued the program for Aboriginal Reconciliation begun by Hawke, but only in the Native Title bill—and then only narrowly—did his government recognise any of the committee's objectives for more substantial recognition. (See also **Aboriginal land rights**.)

HD

Malayan emergency, a war between British authorities in Malaya and local communists, lasted from 1948 to 1960. Australian military forces were dispatched by the **Menzies** government for regional security and forward **defence**. An official history by Peter Dennis and Jeffrey Grey, *Emergency and Confrontation* (1996), examines this little-understood campaign, the longest in Australian **military history**.

A State of Emergency was declared in Malaya on 18 June 1948 after three estate managers in Perak were murdered by Malayan Communist Party guerrillas. Backed by a disaffected, downtrodden Chinese community, the guerrilla force became the Malayan Races Liberation Army, which aimed to overthrow British rule. The British general, Sir Gerald Templer, successfully isolated the insurgents by combining the resettling of Chinese fringe-dwellers with air and land assaults and security patrols which drove the enemy into the jungle. Britain also stepped up progress towards Malayan political independence.

Australia's participation began in June 1950 with deployment of **Royal Australian Air Force** bombers and transports at Britain's request. When Australian ground troops arrived in October 1955, the battle had already turned against the Liberation Army. Australian infantry mainly had a deterrent role in Britain's Far East Strategic Reserve, along with the **Royal Australian Navy** which attacked targets on two occasions in 1956 and 1957. Malaya gained independence in August 1957. By 1959 most of the Liberation Army had either died or fled to Thailand. On 31 July 1960 the emergency was declared over. It was three more years before all Australian forces returned, their success overshadowing earlier domestic criticism at the **Australian Labor Party's** 1955 Federal Conference. A key historical issue is whether participation was vital to Australian security or merely a gesture to Britain. Of the 51 Australians who died, only 15 were killed in action.

DC

Malouf, (George Joseph) David (1934–) first won attention as a poet, later as a novelist and short-story writer. His autobiographical novel *Johnno* (1975) vividly evoked the Brisbane of wartime and his childhood. It was followed by *An Imaginary Life* (1978), the account of Ovid in exile at Tomis that secured Malouf an international reputation. He has said that the past is interesting 'only in that it is inside the present; it's also going to be inside whatever future there is'. Increasingly his fiction has imagined key moments in Australian history, both obscure and familiar, from which national mythologies were forged. Thus *Fly Away Peter* (1982) treated the horrors of the Western Front for youths who had left behind an idyllic Australian life. In 1998 the Australian Ballet produced a version of this novel, *1914*. Malouf's nearest approach to modern epic, *The Great World* (1990), explored the effects of World War II on Australians, and in particular imprisonment by the Japanese. The colonial period is the setting of his two most recent novels: *Remembering Babylon* (1993) and *The Conversations at Curlow Creek* (1996), where exile from Britain and the physical and mental rigours of accommodating to Australia are paramount themes. A key to the pathos of Malouf's historical vision is the intimation of all that affiliates his characters to a past that is nonetheless lost forever. 'The matter of Australia'—all that is rich and strange in our history—is now his fertile preoccupation.

PETER PIERCE

Mann, Thomas (1856–1941), trade unionist and socialist, was influential in the Australian labour movement in the early twentieth century. He came to Australia in 1902, via NZ, with an established reputation as an industrial organiser and orator, and supported himself by speaking tours across the country. His greatest influence was in Victoria, where in 1906 he created the Victorian Socialist Party. With a strong emphasis on fellowship and a wide repertoire of activities, it sought to operate as a party within a party, the socialist conscience of the **Australian Labor Party**. The party attained a membership of 2000, and its influence was appreciable; but the tactic of permeating the Labor Party soon exhausted the patience of Mann, who turned to industrial activism and departed for Broken Hill at the end of 1908. His arrest and eventual acquittal on charges of sedition strengthened militant convictions that he took back to Britain in 1910 and pursued through syndicalism and then communism. His influence in the communist movement was minimal but Tom Mann became the grand old man of the Anglophone left, and retained the respect and affection of Australian labour activists. His account of his Australasian years was published in 1967.

SM

Manning, Frederic (1882–1935) was born in Sydney and educated privately, partly in England, where he later settled permanently and led a reclusive, literary life, publishing collections of his poetry and prose, and writing literary reviews for the London *Spectator*. He broke the pattern of this life in 1915 by enlisting as a private in the British Army and serving at the Somme. In 1929 he published anonymously an account of this experience, *The Middle Parts of Fortune*; an abridged version appeared in 1930 as *Her Privates We*. After a period of neglect, this work is now regarded as a classic account of World War I. A biography of Manning, *The Last Exquisite* by Verna Coleman, was published in 1990.

KT

Mannix, Daniel Patrick (1864–1963), Catholic archbishop of Melbourne, was for a half-century Australia's most dominant and controversial cleric, loved and reviled equally for his pungent Irish–Australian **nationalism**, political **Catholicism**, and unsparing wit. Certainly, no twentieth-century history of Australian Catholic education, the **Australian Labor Party**, or the shifting patterns of Catholic social and political allegiance can be written without comprehensive reference to the part played by this magisterial interventionist from Cork. The tall Munsterman intrigued poets; so enraged Australian Prime Minister W.M. **Hughes** that he accused Mannix of preaching sedition; and commanded the affection and loyalty of the Catholic faithful, who expanded in numbers from 150 000 to 600 000 in Victoria during his long episcopate.

Mannix was born in Ireland, on his father's tenant farm in Cork, near Charleville (named for Charles II), now called Rath Luirc in an Irish cultural resurgence that Mannix, no devotee of the Gaelic revival, did not stay to see. He was the eldest of his parents' five surviving children, a talented scholar who made rapid progress through Mercy and Christian Brothers' schools, then academies, to qualify for a doctorate in divinity, and finally Maynooth, where he took the chair of moral theology in 1895. By 1903 he was president.

In Ireland, Mannix was something of an enigma both as nationalist and religious leader. He did much to raise academic and administrative standards at Maynooth, winning a reputation for integrity but also for principled ruthlessness. Walter McDonald's *Reminiscences of a Maynooth Professor* (1925) conveys the astringent flavour of life in the shadow of his paradoxical superior. Theology and politics in Ireland were equally fierce: Irish nationalists did not appreciate Mannix's decorous reception of two English kings, Edward VII and George V, at Maynooth.

So it was with scant reputation as a nationalist that Mannix arrived in Melbourne on Easter Sunday, 1913, to become coadjutor to the ageing Archbishop Thomas **Carr** and intellectual successor to Sydney's Cardinal Patrick Francis **Moran**, who had died in 1911. The times did not permit a peaceful transition to scholarly or pastoral duties. Mannix, scarcely off the boat, took on himself the argument over state aid for Catholic schools, thereby aggravating the pervasive anti-Catholic and anti-Irish sentiment. By 1917 he had publicly denounced **conscription**, drawing down the maledictions of Hughes but also earning the cheers of an Irish Catholic Australia ripe, as Patrick **O'Farrell** notes in *The Irish in Australia* (1993 edn), for a hero. O'Farrell, never a historian to shirk complexity, is also sufficiently magisterial himself, and Irish-tuned, to judge the pitch of the man: 'Prodigiously out of place in a slow, conservative church, Mannix combined the hallowed virtues of religion, and the role of leadership thereby conferred, with the legacy of [Les] **Darcy**. From the popular Irish Catholic viewpoint … he was a fighter, and most of all he was a winner … And it was his swinging of Irish pugnacity away from sport and into politics that made him so formidable and dangerous to the establishment.'

The 1916 Easter Rising in Ireland further perplexed Irish and Catholic opinion in Australia. At the Maynooth Union, Mannix had encouraged debate on the contentious social issues of the day; in Melbourne, in the middle of his life, he came to embody them. His Empire loyalties were questioned; calls were made for his deportation. When he did voluntarily depart, in 1920 on his first *ad limina* visit to Rome, he was feted in New York and refused landing in strife-torn Ireland by the British government. Yet six years later, on his last visit to Ireland, nearly all of his brother bishops ignored him. At home in Australia, he encouraged education, promoted Catholic lay action, and had liberal relations with Labor governments. He voted against **Menzies's Communist** Party dissolution referendum in 1951, yet gave funds and encouragement to the Catholic Social Studies **Movement**. Mannix's support of B.A. **Santamaria's** crusade against communist influence in the trade unions was sustained during and after the Labor **Split** of 1954, by which time Rome, and many of Mannix's fellow bishops, had condemned the Movement.

There is no unified historical view of Mannix's profound influence on Australian politics or Australian Catholicism, nor even on Australian–Irish nationalism. Each account generates fiery reaction, even three decades after his death. Most famously, James Griffin's dense and authoritative *ADB* entry, published in 1986, caused a furore. Griffin revoked the canonisation conferred on Mannix by earlier hagiographers, and questioned his reputation both for exemplary scholarship and political nous. His evidence confirms at very least that the archbishop was not politically consistent. Edmund Campion has remarked that the Movement, of which Mannix was the essential patron, sacralised politics. Certainly, critique of Mannix is often interpreted as sacrilege. The man who for half a century hung in silver-framed images on Catholic parlour walls, who reputedly motored grandly up Swanston Street to stop outside Newman College and have his confession heard by his good friend, Jesuit Father Jeremiah Murphy, looms too large, some would have it, for the precisions of history. B.A. Santamaria, whose own *Daniel Mannix* was published in 1984, accused Griffin of trying to 'cut the Archbishop down to size' (*Quadrant*, 1991). 'A good thing, surely, if it's the correct size,' was Griffin's riposte. Bishop George Pell (also in *Quadrant*, 1991) called Griffin's entry jaundiced, snide, and unworthy.

Mannix lived for 99 years, long enough for legend to obscure him. But the evidence is gathered. Patrick O'Farrell's close-hatched histories of Australian–Irish Catholicism and politics, together with Griffin's brief biography, have kept Mannix human, not merely mythic, by deft analysis of the events he precipitated and of the great social movements with which he intersected. Others, like Edmund Campion (in *Australian Catholics*, 1987), Niall Brennan, and Vincent Buckley have preserved the psychological and political import of the man through their manifest understanding of the conflicts and seductions that Catholic triumphalism holds for a powerfully gifted liberal thinker. 'He stood for law and order and also rebellion,' Buckley wrote in *Cutting Green Hay* (1983); 'he represented the untamed part of the Irish in its effective and socially visible aspect'.

Every account of Mannix, be it from friend or enemy, is testimony to his titanic determination and complex legacy. 'He would have had a hard time composing himself for death', Vincent Buckley concluded. That is an Irish judgment, and one that does sympathetic justice to Daniel Mannix's prodigious life.

MORAG FRASER

Manufacturing has occupied an ambiguous position in Australian economic history. On the one hand, as an attraction for investment in the nineteenth century, manufacturing was overshadowed by the dynamism of industries directly exploiting natural resources. On the other hand, manufacturing has been a significant part of the Australian economy and from an earlier time than was originally acknowledged by Australian economic historians. In their seminal economic histories of Australia, Edward **Shann** and Brian **Fitzpatrick** paid little attention to manufacturing before the twentieth century. The detailed statistical estimates of Australian gross domestic product by N.G. **Butlin**

revealed a different picture. Largely because of two factors, the great distance of Australia from efficient manufacturing countries and the possibilities of processing local primary products, manufacturing was a significant contributor from 1860 at the latest; it increased its share of GDP to about 12 per cent at the end of the 1880s to be only a little under that of the pastoral industry. Manufacturing, to a large extent, took over from primary industry as the basis for the continuance of economic growth when the limitations on the availability of productive land became more apparent from about the 1920s. By the middle of the 1950s, manufacturing's share of GDP had risen to about 28 per cent.

In the twentieth century manufacturing became more important and more diverse. Nineteenth-century manufacturing could be categorised, in the main, as involving either the exploitation of local raw materials in such industries as food-processing and building materials, or simple fabrication, notably of clothing and boots and shoes, or so-called 'engineering' consisting mainly of small-scale repairs and servicing of machines. The most obvious mark of the changing nature of manufacturing in the twentieth century was **BHP's** steelmaking plant, established at Newcastle in 1915. It signalled the emergence of an Australian 'heavy industry' allied with a more elaborate engineering industry. Other important new industries, which gained a foothold soon after **World War I**, were **motor car** assembly, and certain chemical and rubber products. Textile plants also became larger and more numerous. Further diversification of Australian manufacturing occurred, particularly in the 1950s and 1960s, the most visible being associated with the progression from assembly to production of automobiles soon after the end of World War II. Production of a wide range of metal products and machinery and of electrical and electronic equipment, chemicals, and paper also grew fast. Although this development of manufacturing industry occurred in all the Australian states, largely in their main urban centres, it was Victoria, the most advanced manufacturing colony in the nineteenth century, which continued to lead the way. NSW was the main location for the metals and **engineering** industry.

Ambiguity as to the role of Australian manufacturing has continued to the end of the century. Its share of GDP has fallen from a peak of about 28 per cent to about 15 per cent in the first half of the 1990s and there has been an absolute decline in the numbers employed in the sector since the mid-1970s. This replicated a general trend in mature industrial economies, resulting from a secular switch in demand towards services accompanied by productivity improvement in manufacturing. But it has also coincided with a major change in economic policy. The **protection** of Australian manufacturing from overseas competition was being dismantled through the lowering of duties on imported manufactures. The Commonwealth **tariff**, which had its antecedents in pre-Federation Victoria, and to a lesser extent the smaller colonies, can be seen as a device, increasingly adopted up to the early 1970s, to enable Australian manufacturers to enlarge their share of the domestic market without having to subject Australian wage levels to the dictates of international competition. The drastic reduction of import duties that began in the 1970s could be seen, in part at least, as a recognition of the costs imposed by the growth of highly protected industries on less-protected ones. Manufacturing in the 1990s differs from that of the 1970s. It is not only a smaller part of the economy, but more economical in its use of resources and more oriented towards export markets.

Noel Butlin's *Investment in Australian Economic Development* (1964) first quantified the significance of colonial manufacturing. Godfrey Linge's mammoth *Industrial Awakening* (1979) delineates the geography of colonial industry. Colin Forster, *Industrial Development in Australia 1920–1930* (1964), and Helen Hughes, *The Australian Iron and Steel Industry 1848–1962* (1964), cover early twentieth-century developments. Recent changes are outlined in Rodney Maddock and Ian McLean (eds), *The Australian Economy in the Long-Run* (1987).

W.A. SINCLAIR

Maps and mapping of Australia have their origins in the earliest world maps to depict a large southern land-mass. The first map to show a part of the continent from actual discovery was Willem Jansz's chart of the west coast of the Cape York Peninsula in 1606. Other Dutch maps followed until **Tasman's** map of 1644 accurately depicted the western half of the mainland and southern tip of Tasmania. **Cook's** charts began to fill in the east coast; later those of **Flinders** and **King** recorded the remaining sections of the north, west and south. Exploration of the interior increased knowledge of the topography and resources of the country. Some maps were published locally; others were produced by well-known map publishers in Britain and Germany, such as Arrowsmith, Wyld, Stanford, and Petermann.

However, surveying and mapping technology failed to keep pace with demand until military needs provided an impetus. The army, through the Royal Australian Survey Corps, started to map at scales of 1:63 360 (1 mile to 1 inch) and 1:253 440 (4 miles to 1 inch). Later, these series were superseded by mapping at metric scales, on the basis, first of the Australian Geodetic Datum, then the Geocentric Datum of Australia from 1994. The tasks have been shared between military and civil mapping organisations, both state and Commonwealth, with a move in the 1990s towards private contracting.

JUDITH SCURFIELD

Maralinga, in north-central SA, was selected by the British government in the 1950s as a permanent site for **atomic testing**. Maralinga was chosen for its apparent isolation from human settlement, despite the Aboriginal communities in the area. The radioactive emissions from a series of atomic explosions between September 1956 and 1958 afflicted the Aboriginal inhabitants with critical health problems, including blindness, skin disease, and cancer, and left the land poisoned and permanently scarred. A royal commission, appointed by the **Hawke** government in 1985, acknowledged the damage caused by the explosions and

recommended that compensation payments be made to the Aborigines affected. The British government subsequently made an official apology to the Aboriginal people affected, and awarded compensation payments.

HD

Maritime history, see **Exploration by sea**

Maritime Strike of 1890 was a major confrontation between employers and **trade unions**. The immediate cause was the refusal of the marine officers to disaffiliate from the Melbourne Trades Hall Council, but behind this lay the unions' demand that employment be restricted to their members, and the employers' insistence on their right to choose their own labour. Industrial relations were further exacerbated by growing economic difficulties after a long period of prosperity, and the consequent pressure on wage costs. Both camps had recently achieved a high degree of organisation, and their respective principles of the 'closed shop' and 'freedom of contract' put them on a collision course. When the marine officers were refused work, other maritime unions refused to work the ships.

The consequent stoppage embroiled other transport workers; miners refused to produce coal to fire the ships' boilers; shearers would not produce wool for overseas shipment. It was by far the most serious industrial dispute in Australian history, and the spectre of class war alarmed middle-class opinion. Charles **Kingston** suggested **arbitration**; George **Higinbotham** publicly supported the unions against the employers' refusal to negotiate; but such prominent liberals as Alfred **Deakin** and Samuel **Griffith** were outspoken in their condemnation of the strikers. The governments of NSW, Qld, and WA used police and troops to break the picket lines and protect the strike-breakers, who defeated the maritime unions by the end of the year. There was another shearers' strike in 1891, but they and other unions were all defeated.

The Maritime Strike is commonly regarded as a turning-point in labour history, and was pivotal in Brian **Fitzpatrick's** *Short History of the Australian Labour Movement* (1940). Revisionist historians such as Bede **Nairn** and **New Left** critics such as Humphrey **McQueen** suggested that the heroic version of the Maritime Strike given by the **Old Left** exaggerated the extent of class conflict, and others have modified estimates of the unions and employers. Withal, the event undoubtedly fostered the turn to political action and the formation of the **Australian Labor Party**; and it prepared acceptance of industrial **arbitration** as an alternative to industrial conflict. For socialists such as William **Lane**, its significance was momentous—an irrevocable loss of the **workingman's paradise**.

SM

Marnalagenna, see **Aboriginal resistance**

Marsden, Samuel (1764–1838), known as the 'flogging parson', arrived in NSW in 1794 and after **Johnson's** departure in 1800 was the senior Church of England minister in the colony. He worked hard for his church, but soon after his arrival was also busy on worldly affairs. He was appointed a magistrate and so was involved in the punishment of convicts. He obtained grants of land and became one of the colony's leading farmers and graziers and a wealthy man. Coming from humble origins, he had obtained his education and position in the church from supporters of the new **evangelical** movement. Marsden shared to the full its sense of man's depravity, so that when the convicts refused to heed his puritan message, he fell into treating them with contempt and cruelty. His reputation as a severe magistrate was deserved. The **Aborigines** too were uninterested in his Christian message. Despairing of converts in Australia, Marsden threw himself into a mission to the Maoris in NZ, where he had much more success, for which he is still honoured. The contrast between his New Zealand and Australian reputations was a central theme in A.T. Yarwood's fine biography (1977). Manning **Clark** was a descendant of Marsden, whose character he explored sympathetically in the first two volumes of his *History*.

JH

Marshall, Alan William (1902–84) was a writer whose youthful experience as a victim of poliomyelitis formed the basis for his internationally successful autobiographical novel, *I Can Jump Puddles* (1955), which portrayed his determined fight to lead a normal childhood. Marshall had already written prolifically—short stories, newspaper articles, and articles for the communist press in the 1930s and later for the *AIF News*—but with limited popular recognition. The enormous success of *I Can Jump Puddles*, which was later made into a Czechoslovakian film and a television series in Australia, turned him into a national figure. He completed an autobiographical trilogy with *This Is the Grass* (1962) and *In Mine Own Heart* (1963). The latter recounts his experiences working in a shoe factory in inner-suburban Melbourne during the **Depression**, experiences which he drew upon earlier for the novel *How Beautiful Are Thy Feet* (1948). Other works ranged from *Ourselves Writ Strange* (1949)—an account of his visit to Arnhem Land, later published as *These Were My Tribesmen* (1965)—a history of the Myer Emporium, *The Gay Provider* (1961), and *Pioneers and Painters: One Hundred Years of Eltham and Its Shire* (1971). Common to all Marshall's writing was an optimistic belief in humanity and the joy of life. He is commemorated by several literary awards, including the Victorian Premier's Award for children's literature. *I Can Jump Oceans* (1976) by Harry Marks is an account of Marshall's life and work.

KT

Marshall-Hall, George William Louis (1862–1915) was a controversial composer and conductor. He was appointed from London as Ormond professor of music at the University of Melbourne in 1891, established the university's Conservatorium of Music, and founded an orchestra. He became notorious for his newspaper debates with music crit-

ics, and for a bohemian lifestyle. His publication in 1897 of two booklets of verse aroused controversy for their allegedly erotic nature. This was compounded a year later with the publication of *Hymns, Ancient and Modern* which were criticised in the *Argus* as lascivious and irreverent. These criticisms, combined with claims of immoral behaviour towards female students, resulted in 1900 in Marshall-Hall's dismissal. He established his own music conservatorium and continued to compose and conduct. He was reappointed to the Ormond chair shortly before his death. The Grainger Museum at the University of Melbourne holds the Marshall-Hall collection. Thérèse Radic wrote a biography, *G.W.L. Marshall-Hall: Portrait of a Lost Crusader* (1982).

KT

Martens, Conrad (1801–78), landscape painter, studied painting in England before joining the 1833 *Beagle* expedition. In 1835 he travelled to Sydney and it was there that he produced his large body of work, with Sydney Harbour as his favourite subject. He travelled widely on sketching expeditions and is represented in most state art galleries as well as a large collection held by the Mitchell Library, Sydney. He also painted pictures of the houses of many wealthy landowners. Lionel **Lindsay** gave an account of his work in *Conrad Martens: The Man and His Art* (1920; 1968). Recent studies are *Conrad Martens* (1993) by Susanna de Vries-Evans and Elizabeth Ellis, *Conrad Martens: Life and Art* (1994).

KT

Martin, Allan William (1926–), historian, trained at the University of Sydney. After appointments at the universities of New South Wales, Melbourne, and Adelaide, he was appointed foundation professor of history at La Trobe University in 1966. He built the department there into one of the largest and most distinguished in the country. From 1973 until retirement he was a senior fellow in the Research School of Social Sciences at the Australian National University. Martin's wide experience and equable disposition enabled him to mediate institutional rivalries in the history profession; he was greatly in demand as a supervisor of postgraduate research.

His own research falls into three principal topics. With Peter Loveday he pioneered the study of nineteenth-century parliamentary politics; their book on NSW, *Parliament, Factions and Parties* (1966), served as a model for subsequent work. He then embarked on a biography of *Henry Parkes* (1980), and brought to it an innovative interest in the psychological dimension (as he explained in James Walter and Raija Nugent (eds), *Biographers at Work*, 1984). An edited collection of *Letters from Menie* (1983), **Parkes's** daughter, followed in 1983. Since then he has been occupied on a biography of Robert **Menzies**. The first volume appeared in 1993 along with an edition of Menzies's 1941 war diary, *Dark and Hurrying Days*, both with the assistance of Patsy Hardy. Martin's work is deeply researched, nonpartisan, and shows an awareness of social science; his first wife was the distinguished sociologist, Jean Martin.

SM

'Marvellous Melbourne'

'Marvellous Melbourne', the title conferred by the visiting London journalist George Augustus Sala in 1885, epitomised the high optimism of the city in the 1880s. Sala had come on a lecture tour and first coined the phrase in a series of articles describing his travels in the London *Daily Telegraph*, which were later serialised in the Melbourne press. In the atmosphere of brash confidence and conspicuous display induced by the **land boom**, his boastful epithet caught on. In 1889 the dramatist Alfred Dampier used it as the title for a topical melodrama featuring representative scenes of Melbourne life. But the collapse of the property market in 1891 marked the end of Melbourne's heyday. Graeme Davison's *The Rise and Fall of Marvellous Melbourne* (1978) is a detailed study of this period. By contrast, *The Outcasts of Melbourne* (1985), edited by Davison et al., reveals the less affluent side of Melbourne during this period; derided as 'Marvellous Smelbourne', it was notorious for its slums, poverty, and pollution.

GD

Marxist history employs Karl Marx's concepts to interpret the past according to his materialist method and concerns. This legacy predisposes Marxist historians to look for explanations in terms of **class** and economic development. Marxist historians usually focus on questions concerning the relationship between economic development and class formation, or the relationship between class structure and class struggle on the one hand, and politics, law, and ideology on the other. In the field of Australian history, the first to address these themes on a grand scale was Brian **Fitzpatrick**. In *British Imperialism and Australia 1783–1833* (1939) and *The British Empire in Australia 1834–1934* (1941), he argued that British capital financed the rise of pastoral capitalism at the expense of small farmers, separating the bulk of the people from the land and creating a proletariat which became the basis of the labour movement. Much of his argument has stood the test of time and, together with the work of his non-Marxist critics like Noel **Butlin**, it has heavily influenced later historical materialist accounts like R.W. Connell and T.H. Irving, *Class Structure in Australian History* (1980), and Philip McMichael, *Settlers and the Agrarian Question* (1984).

Marxists have always explained the rise of class consciousness, trade unions and Labor parties in the later nineteenth century through processes of capitalist development, which increased the size of the working class and its ability to organise itself. This 'materialist' interpretation is supported by a wealth of evidence, set out most convincingly in Ray Markey's *The Making of the Labor Party in New South Wales 1880–1900* (1988). It has been accepted by most non-Marxists, as has the claim that politics soon became organised on class lines. Indeed, the most persuasive account of the emergence of a class-based party system is by John Rickard, whose *Class and Politics* (1976) employed the understanding that class was not a thing but a shared experience, along similar lines to the work of the English Marxist historian, Edward Thompson.

Marxist treatments of the twentieth century concentrated on the development of industrial capitalism, the struggles of trade unions, and the failure of socialist politics. A persistent theme was the role of the state in containing class conflict. A tradition of analysis starting with V. Gordon **Childe**, *How Labour Governs* (1923), pointed out how the democratic system integrates working-class leaders into the parliamentary club, tempts them to abandon **socialism** to buy middle-class votes, and confronts them with the reality that socialist governments lose support if they do not make capitalism work. Other historians placed legislation in its class context. Stuart Macintyre, *The Labour Experiment* (1989), explained **arbitration**, the **basic wage**, the protective **tariff**, and **social welfare** in terms of class and, where appropriate, gender. More controversially, Rob Watts, *The Foundations of the National Welfare State* (1987), has analysed welfare initiatives between 1939 and 1945 in the context of Keynesian economic theory, fiscal policy, and the need to legitimate capitalism.

By the 1970s the first generation of Marxist historians had been dubbed the **'Old Left'**. Members of the Old Left found little cheer in Australia's twentieth-century history, but identified easily with the late nineteenth century, seeing in it intimations of an alternative future. They found in the growing labour movement socialist tendencies linked to the **'mateship'** of the pastoral frontier; they celebrated the movement's **nationalism**, and they seldom dwelled on its racism. However, the publication of Humphrey **McQueen's** *A New Britannia* in 1970 brought to public notice a **New Left** critique which undermined the identification of Marxist historiography with the Australian radical tradition. Influenced by Antonio Gramsci's writings on hegemony and adapting research by non-Marxists, McQueen and others concluded that the labour movement was never socialist and that its nationalism was virulently racist. The New Left carried its argument about the pervasiveness of racism, but the publication of Verity Burgmann's *'In Our Time'* (1985) ensured that debate continues about the strength of late nineteenth-century socialism.

From the 1970s, too, Marxism was challenged by the rise of new social movements, emphasising gender and race as sources of personal and social identity. Attempts to reassert the priority of class were attacked as attempts to undermine the importance of these new alignments, and many Marxists capitulated. The second edition of Connell and Irving, *Class Structure in Australian History* (1992), for example, dismissed the view that class had priority as 'obsolete' and 'a hindrance to progressive politics'. From the 1980s materialism was further questioned as postmodernists denied that ideas can reflect a reality outside our minds, asserting instead that the only reality we know is one which we 'construct' through language. Even young historians, unconvinced by this claim, increasingly analysed dominant discourses rather than ruling classes, or explored the linguistic construction of 'reality'. Marxist history and even social history were no longer at the cutting edge of the discipline. Increasing numbers of historians, preoccupied with language and culture, had grasped the truth that people with different pre-existing beliefs can construct different versions of reality out of identical material circumstances. What some of them forgot was something just as important: that different material circumstances can produce radically divergent patterns of belief. It is this second truth that Marxist historians, among others, have proclaimed. In the long run, their insight is unlikely to be forgotten.

CHRIS CONNOLLY

Masculinity, the cultural expression of male identity, emerged as a topic of historical inquiry during the mid-1980s. This reflected wider shifts within **feminism**, from making women visible in history to considering **gender** as a relational category. Histories of how men were socialised into specific formations of masculinity, and of how they defended their interests as men, it was argued, would help bring a gender perspective to the mainstream of historical work.

However, myths of masculinity have long been a central, if implicit, theme of Australian historiography. In particular, the elevation of the bushworker to the status of a national hero has fascinated generations of Australian historians. Russel **Ward's** *The Australian Legend*, published in 1958, charted its rise from the convict era to the **Anzac** landing. Ward's 'typical Australian' is a 'practical man, rough and ready in his manners'. He 'swears hard and consistently, gambles heavily and often, and drinks deeply on occasion'. He is 'fiercely independent' and 'hates officiousness and authority', yet 'will stick to his mates through thick and thin'. From the late nineteenth century the myth began to take on a national dimension, assisted by its cross-class connotation and its significance as a pastoral myth in an increasingly urban nation.

David Walker showed in 'Modern Nerves, Nervous Moderns' (*ACH*, 1987) how early-twentieth-century 'racial pride movements' in the arts drew upon a long-standing tradition in which national achievement was perceived as a 'male endowment'. Writers such as Norman **Lindsay**, the poet Vance **Palmer**, and the socialist Frederick Sinclaire invoked metaphors of the male body to express the vitality of Australian culture. These writers were suspicious of the enervating effects of modernity, and contrasted Australian virility with the dulled manhood of Europe. This myth was further strengthened during World War I, with the official war historian C.E.W. **Bean** favourably comparing the Australian digger with the British Tommy because of the former's outback pedigree. Official and popular accounts transformed the failed campaign at **Gallipoli** into a story of the birth of the Australian nation through the heroism of its soldiers. Australia's performance in this 'test of manhood' was measured principally in relation to the 'drawbacks' of the British, rather than the Turkish, fighting forces.

Feminist historians in the 1980s and 90s situated nationalist projects such as this within the context of a wider gender politics. They showed how historians such as Ward contributed to the transformation of masculine attributes into touchstones of national identity. In 'The Politics of Respectability: Identifying the Masculinist Context' (*HS*, 1986), Marilyn Lake argued that concepts such as 'national character' had obscured 'one of the greatest political struggles in Australian history: the contest between men and women in the late nineteenth century for the control of national culture'. Lake coined the term *masculinism* to describe the ways in which groups such as the Bohemian radicals—widely celebrated as progenitors of the Australian legend—created a separatist politics to defend their interests as men. Publications such as the Sydney *Bulletin* and its Melbourne equivalent, the *Bull-Ant*, set forth a masculinist program which celebrated men's independence from domestic influences. In elevating the bushman into a national legend, the Bohemian men's press endorsed a male culture of drinking, tobacco consumption, and misogyny. Lake argues that early feminist campaigns on issues of social purity and temperance thus had particular resonance in Australia, because they directly confronted this masculinist code.

Lake's argument challenged the received image of Bohemian radicalism by stressing the profound conservatism of its sexual politics. It also broke new ground by emphasising the ways in which dominant ideals of masculinity change over time. The late-nineteenth-century Bohemian cult of the independent bushman was premised on a rejection of the mid-century, Evangelical, middle-class ideal of domesticity. Yet by World War I, the combined pressure of employers' needs for a more disciplined workforce, and feminist agitation, had placed the breadwinner ethos in the centre of ideas of masculinity. In the interwar era masculinity was defined principally in terms of a man's ability to support a family, rather than his independence from domesticity.

More recent work on masculinism has both extended and revised this analysis. Chris McConville (*HS*, 1987) pointed out that Lake assumes a close similarity between the practices of Australian men in general and the rhetoric of the *Bulletin* writers, despite the latter's atypical position as part of an emerging literary elite, and their 'endeavours to paint themselves as social pariahs'. Her analysis does not explore how the lived experience of this largely urban intelligentsia led them to idealise the 'carefree roaming life' of the bushman. Nor is it clear that the myth had diminished in significance by World War I. Annabel Cooper has shown in 'Textual Territories' (*AHS*, 1993) how popular literature of the war renewed the authority of the bush mythology, confirming its rejection of domesticity and hostility to women as public actors. In popular accounts such as the Ginger Mick stories of C.J. **Dennis**, the rejection of mother figures was a necessary precondition for becoming a true man and soldier. Similarly, in Bean's official history, prewar links with Britain were depicted in terms of a mother–son dependence from which the nation had been liberated by its 'entry into manhood' through battle (see Alistair Thomson, *Anzac Memories*, 1994). Moreover, as Stephen Garton argued in *The Cost of War: Australians Return* (1996), ex-soldiers were ambivalent about the transition to civilian life, perceiving it as a feminine world of 'dreary routine, of domestic responsibilities, of the burden of being a breadwinner'. Repatriation policies had to negotiate between codes of masculinity which stressed the idea of independence, and the perception of welfare as feminising in its effects. In this analysis the influence of earlier codes of masculinity—particularly the 'old' bush ethos—is regarded as equally significant for the shaping of repatriation policy as the 'more modern' ideal of the breadwinner. The separatist politics of the *Bulletin* writers continued to be influential well into the twentieth century.

The term 'masculinism' is distinctive to Australian historiography. It has contributed to a particular stress on public formations of masculinity—nationalist, military, socialist, bohemian libertarian, and trade union—and on the political movements through which men have defended their interests. This work has opened up the historical heartland to gender analysis by exposing the **Australian Legend** itself as a myth of masculinity. At the same time comparatively little work has been done on the socialisation of individual men into cultural formations such as that of the bushman; on the variability of ideals of masculinity across social categories of class and 'race'; or on the relationship of the psychic to the social and cultural meanings of masculinity.

MICHAEL ROPER

Massacres now refer to mass killings of defenceless Australians, but historically referred to the large-scale slaughter of Aborigines. Manning **Clark's** *History of Australia: The Musical* (1988) represented black–white frontier relations with a massacre, chillingly dramatised by strobe lighting.

Massacre was a feature of the **frontier**. Australia was settled by Europeans as Western ethnocentrism meshed with racial ideas. A desperate struggle for the land magnified these ideas into a dominant image of Aborigines as 'savages' and impediments to settler progress. After the 1860s, social Darwinism hardened such racial ideas, representing Aborigines as 'primitive' relics of social evolutionism who were destined to die out. Although Aboriginal populations were dramatically reduced by disease and economic disruption, killings played a significant part. Henry **Reynolds** in *Frontier* (1987) estimated Aboriginal deaths by white hands at 20 000. This accords with Richard Broome's overview of frontier violence, 'The Struggle for Australia: Aboriginal–European Warfare 1770–1930' in Michael McKernan and Margaret Browne (eds), *Australia, Two Centuries of War and Peace* (1988). Keith Windschuttle in **Quadrant** (2000), has contested these estimates as too high, without creating his own.

Aboriginal deaths by massacre formed a significant proportion of the total killings. No Australia-wide count has been made of massacre sites, but a map published by the Koorie Heritage Trust of Melbourne, and a recent detailed study of the Western District of Victoria by Ian Clark, show 68 and 110 massacre sites respectively. Records now list hundreds of alleged massacre sites around Australia, although many remain unscrutinised. Historians have traced massacres in particular regions: Geoffrey Blomfield for the Taree–Kempsey region; Peter Gardner for Gippsland; Roger Milliss for New England; Rory Medcalf for the northern rivers district of NSW; and Gordon Reid for central Qld. Accounts of particular massacres include Neville Green on the Forrest River massacre of seven Aborigines in 1926 by police and John Cribbin on the **Coniston massacre** of 31 Aborigines by police in 1928. Bruce Elder's *Blood on the Wattle* (1988) gives a popular account of major massacres.

Although John **West** (1852), James Erskine Calder (1875), and Clive Turnbull (1948) described massacres in the **Black War** in Van Diemen's Land, most twentieth-century historians failed to write about massacre until Charles **Rowley's** seminal *The Destruction of Aboriginal Society* (1970) gave the first details about white punitive expeditions against Aboriginal people. Robert Reece's *Aborigines and Colonists* (1974) contained the first extended treatment of a massacre, the notorious killing of 28 Aborigines at **Myall Creek** in June 1838. Roger Milliss's *Waterloo Creek* (1992) provides immense detail on this and related episodes. Since the late 1980s, many historians, journalists, and popularisers have described the massacre of Aboriginal people in colonial Australia.

The emotiveness of massacre and the moral dimensions of frontier history make for strong views. Aboriginal people have emphasised massacre in such works as *Koorie* (1991), and in oral evidence. Some of these accounts play loose with the numbers killed in massacre by referring to many 'thousands' slaughtered in small regions, or hundreds in single events. So too, do popularisers such as Bruce Elder, who claims that experts (unnamed) estimate over 100 000 Aborigines were killed by whites on the frontiers. On the other hand, Geoffrey **Blainey** in *A Land Half Won* (1980) argued that it is possible that Aboriginal groups suffered more deaths from Aborigines in pre-contact times than they did from the hands of Europeans after contact. Such conjecture downplays inordinate killings as much as Aboriginal sympathisers inflate the numbers. Significantly, some Aboriginal memories, with less of an eye to political outcomes, recount massacre as a fact of life no more remarkable than other frontier events. This is evident in unpublished oral history research by Reece on the Myall Creek massacre.

While massacre was frequent, albeit mostly small-scale, it threatens to dominate our view of the frontier, obscuring other themes. Sympathy for Aborigines and a focus on massacre can patronise them as simply victims of white violence, with no sense of them as complex historical characters. 'Victimology' also obscures the strong **Aboriginal resistance** first noted by Charles Rowley in 1970, first detailed by Noel Loos in *Invasion and Resistance* (1982), and recorded by many since. Thus, battles which were hard fought by Aboriginal warriors and lost have been described as massacres in works such as *Koorie*, which diminishes the efforts of Aboriginal warriors. The danger of over-emphasising massacre is that it places Aborigines back into the old stereotype of passiveness. Others like Michael Christie (1979) and Elder, out of shame and their enthusiasm to detect white barbarism, have accepted colonial gossip that Aborigines were shot by 'hundreds' in some episodes. By so doing, they have overlooked the impossibility of small parties armed with single-shot, muzzle-loading, pre-1850 rifles achieving such results. Politicised views of massacre have also obscured instances of black massacres of whites and all-Aboriginal (*inter se*) killings. The politics of massacre are discussed by Richard

Broome in 'Aboriginal Victims and Voyagers: Confronting Frontier Myths' (*JAS*, 1994).

Many Australians now see the recognition of massacre as a prerequisite for reconciliation. What was once unmentionable is now openly discussed. This surely is a measure of our maturity as a nation. Now, it needs to be discussed critically, as a measure of our impartiality.

RICHARD BROOME

Maternity as a social concept was born of the fertility transition of the last two decades of the nineteenth century. As Australian women began to fall pregnant less often, 'maternity'—the whole process of conceiving, carrying and delivering a new life—took on national significance for those concerned at the colonies' falling birth-rates. A number of historians, notably Jill Julius Matthews (in *Good and Mad Women*, 1984) and Lyndall Ryan and Margie Ripper (in 'Women, Abortion and the State', in Renate Howe, ed., *Women and the State*, 1993), have argued that women's reproductive duties were a central concern of the new Commonwealth, and that those duties have been 'more rigidly represented in discourses about national identity until the 1960s than in most other Western countries in the same period'.

Concern at the birth-rate was matched by a changing medical conception of pregnancy itself. When it was a near constant condition for sexually active women, it was 'normal' until complications arose, and therefore not a medical condition until it became 'abnormal'. Modest women dreaded intimate examinations, so that apart from the affluent with their family physicians, most saw the doctor for the first time when they were in labour and usually after something had begun to go wrong. Despite the everyday realities of sick and suffering women disabled by childbearing, doctors and society perceived reproduction as 'normal' and 'natural' and therefore not of itself dangerous for women. Danger came from unnatural interference in the process: poor physique, malnutrition, tight-lacing, tea and coffee, prevention of conception, mental over-excitement. Civilisation made affluent women sick, while poverty and sin blighted the parturient poor. 'Excessive' childbearing for the healthy was a contradiction in terms, and contraception by definition dangerous.

When childbirth went wrong, the doctor's duty was to save the mother, and it was to improve maternal health that ante-natal care first grew in significance. Medical supervision in pregnancy could anticipate threats from eclampsia, obstructed labour, abnormal foetal positions, infection, and haemorrhage. Adelaide claimed to have founded the first ante-natal clinic in the world in 1910, Sydney Women's Hospital the third, and the Women's Hospital in Melbourne, whose history is told in Janet McCalman's *Sex and Suffering* (1998), established its own in 1917. Ante-natal care did not become universal, however, until the 1950s when the public hospitals, determined to reduce the incidence of eclampsia, enforced attendance at clinics after research had established that it was those without ante-natal care who were most at risk from the complications of pregnancy and birth.

Maternal health and infant life protection commanded political and public support in a new nation, while state education in most states and territories languished. In 1912 the Commonwealth introduced the Maternity Bonus of £5 to enable women to engage a doctor or a good midwife; the unintended result was the blossoming of small, often low-standard, private hospitals where infection and ill-considered obstetrical interference flourished. Through the 1920s, the maternal death-rate caused continuing anxiety, even though almost twice as many women of child-bearing age were still dying of tuberculosis. In 1929 Dr R. Marshall Allan completed a report commissioned by the Victorian branch of the British Medical Association on maternal health. Aseptic midwifery, in practice since the 1880s, had dramatically reduced the death-rate in public hospitals from obstetric infection, but was imperfectly applied in private hospitals and home births. The increasing resort to induced abortion by women desperate to control their fertility kept the maternal death-rate in Australia high until the introduction of antibiotics after 1937.

Motherhood, even proletarian motherhood, was transformed in the early twentieth century from a private fate to a public duty. As Kerreen Reiger, *The Disenchantment of the Home* (1985), and Philippa Mein Smith, *Mothers and King Baby* (1997), show, a constellation of institutions and reformers—infant welfare centres, safe milk, **kindergartens** and crèches—now instructed mothers on how to raise better babies and **children**. The corollary was the construction of the unfit mother: a conception that dispelled moral qualms about depriving Aboriginal, poor white, and unmarried mothers of their babies and transferring them to 'fit' mothers by adoption (see Renate Howe and Shurlee Swain in *JAS*, 1993). But the discovery of the foetus as a patient in its own right did not begin until the period between the world wars, and did not come to prominence until after antibiotics had conquered sepsis in all areas of medicine. And in the cause of protecting the foetus, women experienced the most extensive interventions in pregnancy and delivery in human history.

'Maternalism' as a conception of female citizenship which incorporated women's maternal responsibilities was important in labour and **feminist** discourse in the first half of the twentieth century. Marilyn Lake examines its Australian exponents in Seth Koven and Sonya Michel (eds), *Mothers of a New World*, (1993). Patricia Grimshaw et al., *Creating a Nation* (1994), is the most comprehensive and original exploration of 'maternity' and citizenship.

JANET MCCALMAN

Mateship is not, as some claim, a term of Australian origin; but most examples of its use cited in the *Oxford English Dictionary* are from this country, and there are rich entries on *mate* and *mateship* in the *Australian National Dictionary*, which defines mateship as 'The bond between equal partners or close friends; comradeship; comradeship as an ideal'. For *mate* it distinguishes four usages, all found in the nineteenth century: 'An equal partner in an enterprise';

Mateship

'An acquaintance; a person engaged in some activity'; 'One with whom the bonds of close friendship are acknowledged'; and 'A mode of address implying equality and goodwill; freq. used to a casual acquaintance and esp. in recent use … ironic'.

Historians have put mateship at the centre of our national experience. W.K. **Hancock** in *Australia* (1930), explaining why the country had proportionately more trade unionists than any other, pointed to the underlying environment. 'It was a hard land if a man would be his own master on his own plot of soil; but it offered him self-respect and independence and even a master's pride as the member of a class. Thwarted individualism found consolation in the gospel of mateship.' Manning **Clark**, in *Select Documents* (1950–55), offered a valediction to the Australians of 1900: 'So we leave them, dumbfounded at their optimism, astounded that belief in material progress and mateship could be their only comforters against earth and sky, man and beast.' In 1953 Clark had edited Alexander **Harris**, *Settlers and Convicts* (first published 1847), with its classic account of the relationship between two men in the early days of British settlement, 'working … together in the otherwise solitary bush; habits of mutual helpfulness arise, and these elicit gratitude, and that leads on to regard. Men under these circumstances often stand by one another through thick and thin; in fact it is a universal feeling that a man ought to be able to trust his own mate in anything.' Harris was called as a witness for early bush attitudes by Russel **Ward** in *The Australian Legend* (1958). The 'typical Australian' of myth, Ward wrote, 'above all will stick to his mates through thick and thin'. Ward argued that a set of values, with mateship at their core, travelled from country to town and constituted our national tradition. For the later nineteenth century he called on Henry **Lawson**, laureate of the legend, who wrote in 'Shearers':

> They tramp in mateship side by side—
> The Protestant and Roman
> They call no biped lord or sir
> And touch their hat to no man!

Is mateship then a religion? Not in any 'serious philosophical sense, comparable with Christianity', wrote Ward. Yet W.G. **Spence**, organiser of shearers, declared in 1909: 'Unionism came to the Australian bushman as a religion … It had in it that feeling of mateship which he understood already, and which always characterised the action of one "white man" to another.' ('White man', the *AND* records, came to mean in Australia 'A person of impeccable character'.) And C.E.W. **Bean**, official historian of Australians at war, could see mateship as a national substitute for religion. 'The typical Australian', he wrote in *The Story of Anzac* (1921), 'was seldom religious in the sense in which the word is generally used. So far as he held a prevailing creed, it was a romantic one inherited from the gold-miner and the bushman, of which the chief article was that a man should at all times and at any cost stand by his mate.'

In his study of these soldiers, *The Broken Years* (1974), Bill Gammage concludes 'mateship was a particular Australian virtue, a creed, almost a religion'. It could be expressed in ways not easily accommodated in official history. After the horrors of Pozières in 1916, an ambulance man observed: 'The fellows shake hands with and congratulate their mates and brothers when they find that they have a wound that … will most likely keep them away for a few months.'

When Gammage asked 237 men of the old AIF to make general comments about their war service, the commonest response—by one in three—was that the quality of mateship had been incomparable. Incomparable, for an uncounted proportion of all returned men, with the culture of a nation at peace. Within old soldiers' organisations and especially the **Returned and Services League** they formed a brotherhood privileged to call each other 'Digger', while other men found mateship in **trade unions** or sporting clubs or associates at work.

When Australians went to war again in 1939–45, the old mateship revived, but never quite became what it had been in 1914–18. This time men rarely served together for such long periods; and this time, unlike last, many ex-servicemen were conscripts, who for long after the war were excluded from the RSL.

From the 1960s the notion came under sceptical scrutiny. How far was mateship a fact of life, how far a sentimental legend? Among the men in war, was it a peculiarly Australian quality or a locally accented version of a comradeship that sustained many, perhaps all, armies? John Douglas Pringle believed that the best description of mateship ever written was in Frederic **Manning's** novel *The Middle Parts of Fortune* (1929)—by an Australian, to be sure, but about Tommies, not Diggers. A strikingly revisionist view of digger mateship gets homely expression in a visitor's book at a French cemetery full of Australian graves: 'He should have stayed at home with his mates.'

In 1965 the literary scholar T. Inglis Moore observed that the frailties of mateship had lately been animated on stage by Richard Beynon, *The Shifting Heart* (1960); Ray **Lawler**, *Summer of the Seventeenth Doll* (1957); and Alan **Seymour**, *The One Day of the Year* (1962); and in print, by authors of fiction with otherwise little in common, John Morrison and Patrick **White** (whose *Riders in the Chariot*, 1961, he found an 'unconvincing burlesque' on the subject).

As **homosexuality** became a topic for public discussion, some observers of mateship reflected that the idea is charged with ambiguity; for 'mate' can mean not only cherished male companion but partner in marriage. Robert **Hughes** wrote in *The Fatal Shore* (1986): 'Because there were no white women in the bush, it meant—as some authorities grudgingly acknowledged, by the end of the 1830s—that "mateship" found its expression in homosexuality.' D.H. **Lawrence's** Australian novel *Kangaroo* (1923) had a steamy and obscure passage in which the socialist leader Willie Struthers fixed a 'glistening and half-sweet' gaze on Richard Lovat Somers, stirring 'the latent power that is in man to-day, to love his near mate with a passionate, absolutely trusting love'. Miriam

Dixson in *The Real Matilda* (1976) defined mateship as involving sublimated homosexuality. What would count as evidence for or against that view?

The mateship of Gammage's diggers certainly presupposed a womanless world. Women and possessions, wrote one of them looking back, 'came in between friends'. More generally, Judith **Wright** observed in 1965, 'The "mateship" ingredient of Australian tradition … left out of account the whole relationship with woman.' In politics, the NSW Labor parliamentarian Franca Arena complained in 1996, women are disadvantaged by their exclusion from the tradition. 'In my next life,' she vowed in 1995, 'I will ensure that I am married to a mate, have a brother who is a mate, and related to a mate one way or another.' Labor Party mateship, however, might not deliver the loyalty of legend. Conference delegates applauded Bill **Hayden** in 1983 as he recalled the idiom of a party functionary who was at the centre of the plot to remove him as leader: '"Oh mate, mate."' 'When they call you "mate" in the NSW Labor Party,' said Hayden, 'it is like getting a kiss from the Mafia.' The *AND* cites this remark as an example of ironic use.

In the gender-conscious 1990s a word putting down mateship began to circulate: certain regrettable male attitudes were 'blokey'. Geoffrey **Dutton** had actually made it up 40 years earlier, in a sardonic poem entitled 'Sour City', whose images included 'beery blokey faces'. In 1999 poet Les Murray enshrined mateship in a proposed preamble to the Constitution drafted for the Prime Minister, John **Howard**. The objections of feminists helped sink the plan and signalled that the idiom of mateship was being eroded. Sporting captains spoke of their 'guys', assimilating teammates to a new American model in which sporting heroes had no loyalty except to their profession, and even Ginger Meggs, the most deeply Australian of cartoon characters, speaks of his gang these days as 'the guys'. *Guys*, as a gender-neutral term, may ease out *mate*. Before long, it is tempting to conclude, mateship may survive only in our national museum. But at **Port Arthur**, one of its ancient nurseries, a clergyman invoked the concept in 1996 to comfort people grieving after the massacre; and later that year an Australian Opera singer, celebrating the company's ensemble work, attributed its strength to 'that fabled mateship'.

KEN INGLIS

Matra plan for the **settlement** of NSW was put to the British government by James Matra in 1783. He was a midshipman with **Cook** on his 1770 voyage and so had first-hand experience of the place. His plan was for the settlement of loyalists from the American colonies and is notable as the first proposal for the use of Britain's new possession. It includes an optimistic account of the land's resources and its strategic significance, and highlights its closeness to NZ and its flax and timber. These passages have been used by those in the settlement debate who argue that Britain was not simply ridding itself of convicts when it decided on the settlement of NSW in 1786. (See also **Settlement**.)

JH

Mawby, Maurice Alan Edgar (1904–77), mining engineer and mineralogist, was born into a poor family at Broken Hill, NSW, where he attended school barefoot. A brilliant metallurgy and geology student, he joined the Zinc Corporation in 1928 and developed an all-flotation, lead–zinc recovery process during the 1930s. As a member of the Commonwealth Minerals Committee during World War II, he identified the potential of King Island scheelite. He became director of research and exploration at the Zinc Corporation in 1946 and chairman of Consolidated Zinc Pty Ltd in 1955. As foundation chairman of Conzinc Rio-tinto of Australia Ltd (CRA) 1962–74, he fostered development of bauxite at Weipa, iron ore at Hamersley, and copper at Bougainville. Mawby's personal files are held at the Melbourne University Archives. His outstanding mineral collection was donated to the Museum of Victoria.

DC

Mawson, Douglas (1882–1958) led Australian exploration of **Antarctica**. He came to Australia as a young boy from Yorkshire, England, and graduated in engineering from the University of Sydney. From 1905 he lectured in mineralogy and petrology at the University of Adelaide and became the first professor of geology and mineralogy in 1921. As the first person to identify radium-bearing ore in Australia and the only expert on Australian radium and **uranium** occurrences he contributed much to economic geology and mineralogy.

Mawson was interested in Antarctic glaciation and joined Sir Ernest Shackleton as surveyor, cartographer, and magnetician on the 1907–09 expedition. He preferred scientific discovery to the journey to the pole and declined to accompany Robert Scott in 1910, choosing instead to lead the Australasian Antarctic Expedition in 1911. In *The Home of the Blizzard* (1915) he documented what is considered the greatest story of lone survival in polar conditions after his two companions on a trek north died far from the base camp. He then led the successful British Australian New Zealand Antarctic Research Expedition in 1929–30 and 1930–31, adding more territory than any other explorer. The Mawson Institute for Antarctic Research, established at the University of Adelaide, contains his papers; his eloquent diaries were edited by Fred Jacka and Eleanor Jacka (1988). Philip Ayres has produced a biography (1999).

KELLIE TOOLE

May, Phil (1864–1903) was working as a cartoonist in London when he was attracted to Australia in 1885 to work on the *Bulletin* by editor, W.H. Traill. During his three years at the *Bulletin* he worked with Livingston **Hopkins** and produced more than 800 drawings, of which the best-known were caricatures of politicians and the satirical series, 'Things We See When We Go Out Without Our Gun'. A selection of his *Bulletin* cartoons, published as *Phil May in Australia*, was edited by A.G. **Stephens** in 1904. James Thorpe wrote *Phil May: Master Draughtsman and Humourist* (1932).

KT

Mayo, (George) Elton (1880–1949) became interested in psychology after studying medicine. He graduated in philosophy and psychology from the University of Adelaide, and went on to become foundation professor of philosophy at the University of Queensland (1919–23) and a professor at Harvard (1926–47). His chosen field was that of industrial psychology, and he outlined his theories of 'scientific management' in *The Human Problems of an Industrial Civilisation* (1933) and *The Social Problems of an Industrial Civilisation* (1945). Mayo is regarded as a pioneer of industrial human relations; his contribution to the field is discussed in a biography by R.C.S. Trahair, *The Humanist Temper* (1984). A school of management bearing his name was established in Adelaide. His siblings had successful careers in medicine, law, and history.

KT

McAuley, James Phillip (1917–76), poet, was a young serviceman in Sydney when he helped create as a hoax a pastiche of modernist verse under the name of Ern Malley which was published in *Angry Penguins*. From dalliance with the Left, he moved after World War II to the Right, and in 1956 was founding editor of **Quadrant**. He also supported the anti-communist Catholic **Movement**, founded by Bob **Santamaria**. His fascination with PNG began with his wartime experience in the New Guinea Administration Unit, and increased during his lectureship at the Australian School of Pacific Administration (1946–60). He then became professor of English at the University of Tasmania. McAuley's earlier works drew heavily on classical themes; his later poems became increasingly personal. His major prose works are *The End of Modernity* (1959), a collection of essays; *The Personal Element in Australian Poetry* (1970); and *A Map of Australian Verse* (1975). Works on McAuley include a memoir by Peter Coleman, *The Heart of James McAuley* (1980), which is as laudatory as Cassandra Pybus's *The Devil and James McAuley* (1999) is hostile.

KT

McCrae, Georgiana Huntly (1804–90), artist and diarist, enjoyed a privileged upbringing as the illegitimate daughter of a Scottish aristocrat. Her father sent her to a private London school and indulged her talent for portraiture, but Georgiana's fortunes changed dramatically following her father's remarriage. A jealous stepmother thwarted her artistic endeavours, encouraged a bad match in her marriage to Andrew McCrae, and ensured that she was denied her promised inheritance. In 1841 Georgiana followed Andrew to Port Phillip, where his lack of success at farming exacerbated the difficulties of their marriage. Her disappointment was relieved somewhat by her art, with which she supplemented the family income, and by a wide circle of friends, notable among whom were Governor **La Trobe** and his family.

Georgiana's diaries, which provide a vivid picture of early Melbourne, were edited by her grandson, the poet HUGH MCCRAE (1876–1958), and published as *Georgiana's Journal* in 1934. Sixty years later, Georgiana's biographer, Brenda Niall, revealed a minor scandal in Hugh McCrae's apparent tampering with his grandmother's original manuscript. The former McCrae homestead at Arthur's Seat is a house-museum managed by the Victorian branch of the National Trust.

HD

McCubbin, Frederick (1855–1917), painter of bush battlers and mythologiser of the small settler, has long been one of Australia's most popular artists. Born in Melbourne, of humble Scottish and Yorkshire parentage, McCubbin's working-class background gave him the sympathy with ordinary people that is the distinctive mark of his art and life. He studied art in the evenings when his day job—first as a bread carter for the family business and then as a coach painter—was over. He took years to complete his studies at the National Gallery of Victoria and then, in 1886, became the school's drawing master, a job he retained for the rest of his life.

From George Folingsby, the Munich-trained head of the school, McCubbin learned a new style of **history painting** in which telling incidents from everyday life were used to illuminate a moment in the nation's history. McCubbin's *Home Again* (1884), depicting the return of a bush traveller to his wife and child, was his first essay in this new genre, which was gradually to dominate his work.

McCubbin became an early member of the **Heidelberg School**. After some early landscape studies of the dock and riverside areas near his home, he began to paint the surrounding countryside, often introducing historical or narrative themes. *The Lost Child* of 1886, his earliest essay in this vein, reflected the ideas and practice of the English Newlyn School as well as the sentimental preoccupation of Australian writers and readers with the fate of children lost in the bush. (See **Bush searches**.)

The combination of closely observed landscapes and late Victorian subject-matter led McCubbin to the painting of large-scale bush subjects in the late 1880s and 1890s. *Down on his Luck* (1889), *Bush Burial* (1890), *On the Wallaby* (1896), and finally the triptych, *The Pioneer* (1904), elevate popular narrative themes into myth. In this series McCubbin captured a moment in Australian history when the age of the **pioneer** had given way to urban settlement, but the Australian soul still seemed to reside in the bush ethos of struggle, perserverance, and eventual triumph. His art captured the emotion of a nation on the eve of Federation. The overwhelming popularity of *Bush Burial*, when it was shown at the new Geelong Art Gallery, led to a clamour for its purchase which was achieved by public subscription. *The Pioneer* was acquired by the **Felton Bequest** for the National Gallery of Victoria not long after its creation, while *Down on his Luck* was one of the earliest acquisitions of the Art Gallery of Western Australia.

The series ended with *The Pioneer*, yet McCubbin continued to interpret the landscape imaginatively, peopling it with children and fairies, nymphs or woodcutters and rendering it with a subtlety of colour and technique beyond his contemporaries. J.A.S. MacDonald's *The Art of Frederick McCubbin* appeared only a year before he died, but there was generally little interest in his art during the period of early modernism in

Australia. The first retrospective was held in 1955, largely at the instigation of his son Hugh, but further critical writing on him did not appear until the 1980s: Ann Galbally, *Frederick McCubbin* (1981); Leigh Astbury, *City Bushmen* (1985); Geoffrey **Dutton**, *Frederick McCubbin 1855–1917* (1989); and Andrew Mackenzie, *Frederick McCubbin: The 'Proff', and his Art* (1990).

ANN GALBALLY

McEwen, John 'Jack' (1900–80) became involved with politics through his association with the Victorian Farmers Union in the 1920s, after he established a dairy farm on a soldier-settlement block. He became the Country Party (**National Party**) member for Echuca in 1934 and quickly acquired the sobriquet of 'Black Jack' as testament to his toughness and persistence. He served in coalition ministries during the internecine conflict in the Coalition parties of the late 1930s and was expelled from the Victorian branch of his party until 1943. Following the Coalition victory in 1949, McEwen held the portfolios of commerce and trade, and established an unprecedented command of national policy. A committed protectionist, he championed agriculture, mining, and manufacturing as the 'basic wealth-producing industries' on which national prosperity rested. He drove hard bargains in international negotiations and resisted as long as he could the loss of trade preferences following Britain's entry into the European Economic Community.

Especially after he succeeded **Fadden** as leader of the Country Party in 1958, McEwen challenged the advice of Treasury and the Tariff Board to champion economic nationalism. His own experience as an impoverished soldier-settler and memories of Australian vulnerability in World War II intensified a commitment to protection of local industry that was so personally obdurate it became known as 'McEwenism'. His relations with Menzies were good, but those with William McMahon, who was treasurer from 1966, bad. After the death of Harold **Holt** in 1967, he served briefly as acting prime minister and vetoed McMahon's succession. The constant battle took a severe toll on his health. He retired to his farm in 1971 and died in 1978.

Peter Golding's biography, *Black Jack McEwen: Political Gladiator* (1996), suggests a far more complex figure than emerges from McEwen's autobiography, published in 1983 from transcripts of tapes recorded in 1974, held in the National Library of Australia.

KT

McIlwraith, Thomas (1835–1900) was a force in Queensland politics for more than 25 years, serving several terms as premier. Born in Scotland, he migrated to Victoria in 1854 where he mined at Bendigo and worked as a surveyor in the railway department before taking up pastoral runs in Qld. He entered the Queensland parliament in 1870. He continually advocated the expansion of the **railway** system, borrowed to finance comprehensive public works, and aroused opposition with his support of the introduction of non-European labour. His annexation of south-eastern

New Guinea in 1883 was disallowed by the British government. McIlwraith had extensive financial interests and resorted to malpractice to save them during the **depression** of the early 1890s. He was forced to resign in 1897 after an inquiry into his directorship of the Queensland National Bank condemned his conduct.

His elder brother JOHN (1828–1902) preceded him to Australia by a year and established a successful manufacturing business in Melbourne, but was forced to sell up in the depression of the 1890s. The youngest brother, ANDREW (1844–1932), established the London-based shipping and mercantile firm of McIlwraith, McEacharn & Co., with a profitable Melbourne operation.

KT

McKay, Hugh Victor (1865–1926), contrary to the legend that asserted that he invented the Australian combine harvester that stripped, threshed, cleaned, and bagged the grain, was one of a number of farmer-mechanics who experimented with the idea in northern Victoria from the mid-1880s. The legend (see John Lack, 'The Legend of H.V. McKay', *VHJ*, 1990) backdated his first trial and patent to claim precedence over those who came before him. McKay is more significant as an entrepreneur and anti-unionist than as an inventor. His major achievement was to induce established agricultural machinery manufacturers in Melbourne, Bendigo, and Ballarat to build his harvester, which he promoted and sold to farmers before he commenced manufacture and distribution on his own account in Ballarat from 1888. His firm collapsed in the 1890s **depression**, but in 1895 he launched an improved and very successful 'Sunshine Harvester'. Annual output rose from 12 machines in 1895 to 2000 by 1906, when McKay moved the business near Melbourne at Braybrook Junction (soon renamed Sunshine). There the Sunshine Harvester Works, the largest factory in Australia, became the locus of conflict between an owner implacably opposed to unionism and to state regulation of wages and conditions, and a workforce that had campaigned for high federal **tariffs** to protect their employer's business and their jobs. The 1907 Harvester Judgment established **basic wage** principles in Australia. McKay, fearful of the implications of judge Henry **Higgins**'s insistence on recognising and paying margins for skill, challenged the legislation in the High Court. McKay's win undermined **New Protection**, exposed Liberal leader Alfred **Deakin**'s essential conservatism, and provoked the two-party federal divide. McKay alienated his Sunshine workforce, and when they unionised and campaigned for the closed shop, he destroyed the union during a 13-week strike and lockout in 1911. Victorious, McKay then changed his tactics. Offering land and housing to dependable workers, and implementing the piecework system, McKay created a model company town to which his workforce became tied by a blend of gratitude, necessity, and cupidity. In 1922 McKay helped form the Single Purpose League to combat arbitration and foster 'free' (non-union) labour. After his death, McKay's family installed at Sunshine the farm smithy in which the boy inventor had allegedly originated a world revolution in grain harvesting. C.J. **Dennis** sentimentalised this shrine in his poem 'The Old Farm Smithy' (1926). When the McKays sold out to their Canadian competitors in 1955, the smithy was removed to the Museum of Victoria as a tribute to Victorian **pioneer** ingenuity.

JOHN LACK

McKell, William John (1891–1985) was a labour leader. He was Labor member for Redfern, NSW, in 1917 and from 1920 held various portfolios. During this time he also studied law and was called to the Bar in 1925. He replaced Jack **Lang**, whose style he deplored, as state leader in 1939; two years later he took Labor to a long-denied electoral victory, serving as premier and treasurer of NSW until 1947. His appointment to the position of governor-general by Ben **Chifley** was doubly controversial—he was not only a Labor Party member, but was still premier at the time. Further controversy followed his 1951 decision to allow the Liberal **Menzies** government a **double dissolution**. Michael Easson edited *McKell: The Achievements of Sir William McKell* (1988), and Chris Cuneen's biography appeared in 2000.

KT

McLeay, Alexander (1767–1848) was a colonial official who fostered the development of science in the colony. He arrived in NSW in 1826 as colonial secretary and was appointed to the Executive Council under Governor **Darling**. However, as a leading **exclusive**, he and the liberal governor, **Bourke**, did not work well together and McLeay was forced to retire in 1837. He was elected to the Legislative Council in 1843 and was speaker until his retirement three years later. His early interest in entomology was extended to ornithology after his arrival in the colony, and he sent many specimens back to England. McLeay supported the establishment of the Australian Museum and was its first president.

His third son, GEORGE (1809–91), came to the colony a year after his father. In 1829 he accompanied Charles **Sturt** on the expedition to the mouth of the Murray, during which they became close friends. George took up farming, and although he appears to have shared his father's interest in zoology, was not an active collector. At the first election for a Legislative Assembly in 1856 he was returned for the electorate of Murrumbidgee. He went back to live in England three years later.

KT

McLeod, Don, see **Pilbara walkoff**

McMahon, William 'Billy' (1908–88) entered federal politics in 1949 after establishing a career as a solicitor in Sydney. As Liberal MHR for Lowe he quickly entered the ministry and rose, upon **Menzies's** retirement in 1966, to become Australia's first treasurer with an economics degree. This did not satisfy him, and in the final phase of the Liberal hegemony he was a prominent intriguer, dubbed 'Tiberius

with a telephone' by Gough **Whitlam**. A veto by Jack **McEwen** prevented him from becoming prime minister after the death of Harold **Holt**, but by 1971 he was able to replace John **Gorton** as leader and prime minister. That gave him the unenviable task of leading the Liberals in their 1972 election campaign against a rampant Whitlam, a contest from which McMahon emerged looking both physically and intellectually insignificant. He resigned the party leadership after the 1972 defeat but remained another 10 years in parliament.

KT

McNair, William Allan (1902–79) was born, educated, and worked in NZ, before moving to Sydney in 1931 as director of an advertising company. He is known for the pioneering company that he founded in 1944, McNair Survey Pty Ltd, which became Australia's largest market-research organisation. McNair wrote several books on the media, including *Radio Advertising in Australia* (1937). (See **Polls, public opinion**.)

KT

McNamara, (Matilda Emilie) Bertha (1853–1931), socialist and feminist, migrated from Prussia to Australia in 1869 to live with an uncle. She had six children from her first marriage when widowed, and made a precarious living as a travelling saleswoman. It was then that she turned to **socialism** and published the first of her pamphlets, *Home Talk on Socialism* (1891). In the following year she married WILLIAM HENRY (1857–1906) and they opened a bookshop in Sydney that became the unofficial headquarters of socialist, radical, feminist, and bohemian activity. William had been one of the Australian Socialist League; he later resigned over the decision to support the Labor Electoral League which compromised his socialist principles. After a short time as correspondent for the Melbourne *Truth*—during which editor John **Norton** called his style 'too fiery'—he and Bertha established the Castlereagh Street bookshop. Late that year William formed the Social Democratic Federation of Australasia.

During the 1890s Bertha was a leading figure in socialist and female suffrage movements. Even after World War I she strove to turn the Labor Party to socialism, and led many women's deputations to Premier Jack **Lang**, her son-in-law. Another daughter married Henry **Lawson**. Bertha's publications included *Paper Money* (1910) and *Shylock Exposed* (1920), her critique of money-power. She was also an enthusiastic supporter of the *Labor Daily*. She died of pneumonia after visiting her former colleague, Adela **Pankhurst** (Walsh), to upbraid her for abandoning the socialist cause.

KT

McQueen, Humphrey (1942–), has been one of Australia's most prolific and controversial historians and cultural commentators. McQueen's early reputation rested primarily on *A New Britannia: An Argument Concerning the Social Origins of Australian Radicalism and Nationalism* (1970), which was the foundation historical text of the **New Left**. It contained a reinterpretation of Australian history which, in its emphasis on racism, militarism, and the pervasiveness of bourgeois values in Australia's past, was congenial to a rising generation of radical Australian historians, university students, schoolteachers, and intellectuals. They were often influenced, like McQueen himself, by new streams of Marxism, and involved in demonstrations against the **Vietnam War** and other protest movements of the period. McQueen's attacks on the **Old Left**, however, poisoned relations between him and some established radical historians. In the 1970s he moved towards a Maoist position and criticised US imperialism in Australia.

McQueen taught at the Australian National University and the Canberra School of Art in the 1970s before becoming a freelance writer. His research interests since *A New Britannia* have been diverse, encompassing labour, social, and cultural history, and Australia's relations with Asia. He has published numerous books and articles on Australian literature, media, and art, including a monumental biography of Tom **Roberts** (1996) and a defence of Manning **Clark**, *Suspect History* (1997).

FRANK BONGIORNO

Mechanics institutes originated in Britain as a means of spreading popular education among skilled working men, or 'mechanics' as they were known. The Sydney Mechanics Institute was founded in 1833 with the support of Governor Richard **Bourke**, who, as George Nadel showed in *Australia's Colonial Culture* (1957), conceived it as the spearhead of a campaign by moral reformers to counter the effects of convictism. 'Sound and cheap education is the great moral lever', the institute declared in an early report. It had been preceded by the Hobart Town Mechanics Institute (1827) and was followed by institutes in Adelaide (1838)—where they were usually known simply as 'Institutes'—Melbourne (1839), Brisbane (1842), and Perth (1851). Mechanics institutes typically provided a free lending **library** and a venue for touring lecturers on moral philosophy, self-improvement, natural history, and technical subjects. Founded for the improvement of working men, they quickly became the stamping-ground of clerks, schoolteachers and professional men. Throughout much of Australia the mechanics institute was the largest secular building in town, and improving lectures and debates were gradually edged out by town meetings, dramatic and musical performances, and other community activities. In keeping with their founding ideals, mechanics institutes, or 'athenaeums' as they were sometimes called, were typically housed in simple classical buildings with triangular fascias, artificial columns, and pediments. These remain a prominent feature of the landscape, particularly on the Victorian goldfields where the spirit of thrift and self-improvement was once strong, and where they sometimes continue to function as local libraries or **museums**. Catherine Milward-Bason has compiled an annotated bibliography of secondary sources, *Mechanics' Institutes and Schools of Art in Australia* (1995).

GD

Medicine, see **Health**

Melba, Nellie (1861–1931), first Australian prima donna and, with the gramophone, the first Australian woman to achieve world fame, contributed uniquely to Australian pride, musicality, language, and confusion as to Australian identity. She also bequeathed and provoked a pot-pourri of small lies and sensational legends about herself, which, despite John Hetherington's popular *Melba* (1967), were not plumbed historiographically until Thérèse Radic's biography and Jim Davidson's *ADB* entry, both in 1986.

She was born Helen Porter Mitchell in the Melbourne suburb of Richmond, the eldest daughter of David and Isabella Ann Mitchell, migrants from Forfarshire, Scotland. Father and daughter were both ruthless and painstaking exemplars of the colonial Calvinist dynamic. She enjoyed the privileged childhood conferred by her father's rising wealth as a contractor who built Scots Church (he was a lifelong choir member), Charles **Pearson's** Presbyterian Ladies College (where Nellie became a day student), Menzies Hotel, and the 1880 Royal Exhibition Building, as well as Doonside, where she grew up. Her high spirits already showed, but the tale told by her organ teacher and flourished by Jack Hibberd in his play *A Toast to Melba* (1976), that she used to swim naked in the Yarra with Richmond boys after school, still looks tall.

In contrast to Ethel ('Henry Handel') **Richardson**, also a product of PLC, who was taken, fresh from school, by her mother to Leipzig music studies and marriage to an English academic, but felt obliged to write her expatriate novels under a man's name, Melba took longer to escape. In 1882 she had a swiftly breaking marriage to Charles Armstrong, genteel Anglo-Irish sugar plantation manager, in humiliatingly uncouth and humid Port Mackay, and a son (George, born in 1883). She then returned to Melbourne for seven years of singing classes with Pietro Cecchi before her début at a Liedertafel concert in the Melbourne Town Hall on 17 May 1884. She was almost 25 by the time she went to London in March 1886 with her husband, son, and father, who was Victoria's Commissioner to the Indian and Colonial Exhibition.

Unlike Richardson, Melba was able to brandish her sex, and her comeliness clearly helped her voice get a fair hearing in a cut-throat competition where patronage could be decisive. Australian artists of all kinds had to grapple with the severest anti-colonial prejudices in London. Unsinkable, she weathered her dismal first recital on 1 June and the lukewarm listening of Sir Arthur Sullivan, and went off to Paris where her audition with Mathilde Marchesi proved the turning-point: 'If you are serious, and if you study with me for one year, I will make something *extraordinary* of you', she declared and rushed upstairs to tell her husband: '*Salvatore, j'ai enfin une étoile!*'

Madame Nellie Melba ('my operatic *nom de guerre*') was introduced to the world at Marchesi's *matinée musicale* on 31 December 1886, saluting what George Sala had nicknamed **Marvellous Melbourne** in 1885. She was an apt pupil ('It was her brain that made Melba's voice', insisted Marchesi), and refined her birdlike 'Melba trill', pianissimo touch, and Australian French. Her exhilarating opera début was at Brussels as Gilda in *Rigoletto* on 13 October 1887: the start of her phenomenal 38 years on the world stage. But Covent Garden did not warm to her on 24 May 1888; not until her triumphant Paris Opera début as Ophélie in Thomas's *Hamlet* on 8 May 1889 did her English patron, Lady de Grey, persuade her to return. After more apathy, the Prince of Wales and Princess Alexandra were in the ardent audience when she sang Gounod's *Juliette* in French on 15 June and captivated Covent Garden for a whole generation. In 1891 the Tsar invited her to St Petersburg, and in 1893 she graduated grandly as Lucia at La Scala, Milan.

Offstage, she began an affair with the young Duc d'Orléans, Pretender to the French throne, in 1890—abruptly ended in 1892 when her husband cited him in divorce papers, the embarrassing scandal explaining why the *Westminster Gazette* blithely called her 'an artist and a woman of the world'. She began two decades at the Metropolitan Opera House, New York, in 1893, but switched to Oscar Hammerstein's Manhattan Opera House in 1907. She made her first recording in 1904. In 1974 J.B. Steane ranked her in important respects the best of all the recorded singers: 'Hers was the purest and firmest of voices, the most perfect scale, the most exact trill', and her records 'the crowning glory of the age called golden'.

In 1962 Geoffrey Hutton quoted an estimate of £500 000 for her earnings, plus £200 000 for charity. She found an excellent business manager in Australian flautist John Lemone, and controlled her finances cannily—and from 1910 she was free of her husband, who obtained a Texas divorce for desertion. Percy **Grainger's** father had built Melba's Coombe Cottage at Coldstream, outside Melbourne, following her extraordinary 16 000-kilometre bush concert tour in 1909. Melba lived there during most of the Great War, which she spent singing to troops, and raising money and morale by means that included a film clip with Charlie Chaplin in Hollywood. Her reward was a DBE in 1918 and a return to Covent Garden for the first postwar season.

Chewing wattle-gum at Covent Garden, she boasted that 'I put Australia on the map'; this reflected real pride in her country, even if there is no reason to doubt Clara Butt's word that, about to tour Australia, Melba advised her: 'Sing 'em muck; it's all they can understand.' She was also proud of being very modern; on each return visit she gave classes on the Marchesi teaching method, and she published *The Melba Method* (1926). She also helped both the university and **Marshall–Hall** orchestra introduce normal pitch instruments, laid the foundation-stone of Melba Hall in 1913, established the Albert Street Conservatorium in 1915, and bequeathed £8000 to it for a singing scholarship 'in the hope that another Melba may arise' as well as possibly 'the purchase or building of an Opera House'. In 1920 she took part in direct radio broadcasts of music (possibly the first international artist to do so). Inevitably, she sang at the 1927 opening of the new Parliament House in Canberra.

Her aggressively Australian jokes could be near the bone as demonstrated by her shipboard *bon mot* in 1908 (when offered a limp jelly at table): 'No thanks, there are two things I like stiff, and jelly's one of them.' Linguistically not hers were *pêches Melba* and Melba sauce; 'to do a Melba' posthumously celebrated the diva's prolonged and repeated international adieus that began in October 1924 with a farewell to grand opera in Melbourne and ended there on 27 September 1927—the year she was promoted to Dame Grand Cross of the British Empire. She died at St Vincent's Hospital, Sydney, following infection from a face-lift in Europe, and she was embalmed and buried (next to her father) in Lilydale Cemetery after a huge funeral at Scots Church and a marathon procession, flatteringly patronised by many thousands of ordinary Australians, partners of this strange love–hate relationship—a fitting finale.

NOEL McLachlan

Melbourne, the capital city of **Victoria**, had its origins in an illegal frontier trading post of the 1830s, a doubly questionable settlement. The pastoralists and traders who sailed from Van Diemen's Land into Port Phillip Bay in 1835 had no official sanction from the NSW government in Sydney. As well, they stepped ashore, uninvited, onto land belonging to the Kulin people, seizing an elevated slope along the north-western bank of the River Yarra, above its junction with the Saltwater (Maribyrnong) River.

In this rough and illegal township—The Settlement, or Bearbrass, as it was first known—parties headed by John **Batman** and John Pascoe **Fawkner** threw together crude buildings above a rocky fall in the River Yarra. The government in Sydney, accepting that it could not remove the settlement, began to regulate it. In November 1836 the first official administrator, the police magistrate William Lonsdale, set up office in a wattle-and-daub hut. Government surveyors Robert Russell and Robert Hoddle were sent from Sydney to mark out a street grid of alternating 30-metre main roads and 10-metre lanes, a framework for the twentieth-century town centre. In 1840 George Cole built wharves along the northern bank of the Yarra. By 1842, The Settlement had become Melbourne (named after the British prime minister), with a rudimentary civic life centred on a town council, market, hotels, men's clubs, a library, a customs house, and the flagstaff at Flagstaff Hill, where townspeople could watch for ships sailing up the Bay. Locally quarried basalt blocks and bricks from claypits in Hawthorn and Brunswick brought a solidity to warehouses and government buildings. This more substantial Melbourne became the capital of a separate colony of Victoria in 1851.

Between 1851 and 1855, in a mass migration which overwhelmed the township, gold diggers poured into Melbourne from around the globe, although principally from the British Isles. Prominent among the crowds of eager diggers were the young and the educated—Irish nationalists and Chartists, for example, men and women alive to the political and moral questions of the day. The **gold rushes** also ensured a lasting place for Nonconformist religion in the social conscience of

Melbourne. In both colonial and local politics, these migrants brought an enduring radical voice, heard initially in 1856 when Melbourne stonemasons demanded, and won, an **eight-hour day**. The gold-rush generation proudly supported churches, a university, and a public library. They petitioned for local municipal councils. The thousands of young, male gold diggers centred much public life on **sport**. **Australian Rules football** was first codified by members of the Melbourne Football Club in 1859. The **Melbourne Cup** horse-race ('The Australasian Nation Day', according to Mark Twain) was first run in 1861.

Between 1851 and 1861, Melbourne grew from 29 000 residents to 125 000, and then to 268 000 in 1881. In the decade of the **land boom**, 1881–91, **'Marvellous Melbourne'** again doubled in population. New railway routes had enabled suburbs to spread far beyond the gold-rush city, so that, by 1891, Melbourne encompassed twice the area of **Sydney**. By then there were recognisable precincts in the central city grid. The western streets were given over to trade, with warehouses in narrow Flinders Lane and King Street and florid commercial offices in Collins Street West. The Eastern Hill acquired a patrician tone, especially when medical men colonised Collins Street East, 'Melbourne's Harley Street'. The gold rushes ensured a lively theatrical life for Melbourne. The city was the centre for nineteenth-century Australian stage production, with theatres lining at least one block in Bourke Street East. Gathered at the rear entrances of these theatres in the 1880s were 'the back slums', a red-light zone, and the Chinese quarter, sharing space in a tangle of laneways.

With the bank crash of the 1890s vanished much of the hubris of the land-boom city. The **depression** forced thousands from their livelihoods and homes so that the metropolitan population fell. In place of the 1880s land-boomer, the Melbourne **'wowser'** emerged as an over-simplified, but nonetheless telling symbol, of the city's underlying moral conservatism.

Melbourne's suburban expansion, renewed gingerly in the later 1890s, proceeded with greater speed up to and beyond World War I. Even the Depression of the 1930s failed to entirely halt suburban home-builders. A ring of new **suburbs** filled gaps left by failed subdivisions of the 1880s and were typically placed close to the now-electrified tram and train routes of the land boom. Spanish Mission villas and nostalgic 'Tudorbethan' cottages shared a consistent decor, regardless of the economic class for whom they were intended and their scale. Nonetheless, the interwar suburbs did cement the nineteenth-century social divide between wealthier suburbs to the east of the Yarra—where local covenants often demanded brick construction and local by-laws excluded factories, and sometimes even hotels—from the industrial and working-class north and west.

Shaped by the **motor car**, postwar suburbs have exaggerated the low densities of Melbourne and only marginally altered the class disparities. The suburbs of post-1945 Melbourne, like those of the interwar years, the 1880s, and even the 1850s, responded to the demand for single-storey detached dwellings each on its own block of land, in an environment where housing and industry were segregated. Only in inner Melbourne, where, after World War II, the Housing Commission of Victoria had bulldozed cottages to make way for high-rise public housing towers, was there any radical departure from the standard low-density suburb. Height limits restricted skyscraper development in Melbourne's central grid until 1958. The first of the modern postwar towers, ICI House, was built in that year immediately beyond the central grid. Its completion launched a rebuilding of the city centre itself, as modernist towers rose along Collins and other major streets. Apartment-building, restricted to a few inner suburbs like St Kilda between 1900 and 1961, eventually brought a new compactness to the whole of inner Melbourne. During the mass migration of the years 1945–80, Melbourne emerged as Australia's most European and multilingual city. Italians and Greeks took over decayed inner-city terraces, and transformed the streets with their cafés and restaurants.

Melbourne's economic vitality has depended centrally on the strength of the building industry. Significant also has been the city's strong **manufacturing** sector, in the nineteenth century most typically seen in the many finishing trades of the city, clothing, leathergoods, and food processing. Clothing and boot factories operated in the inner northern suburbs; the woolworks, tanneries, and slaughterhouses clustered near to the port and railyards in the inner west of the metropolis. The **tariffs** that protected these industries also encouraged heavy manufacturing, so that giant car plants were located on the fringe of the postwar city. Suburban shopping malls, such as that promoted by Myer at Chadstone in 1960, weakened the ties between suburb and city and forced changes on those shopping strips which once thrived along the tram routes of Melbourne.

Liberalised drinking and gambling laws have become central to a refashioned Melbourne imagery. In casting off its wowserish restraint, questioning the worth of its Melburnian virtues of solidity, and making up for the demise of industries once protected by tariffs, Melbourne has been revolutionised. From this revolution, a different city must eventually emerge. The highly localised municipal governments, many of them dating back to the gold-rush decade, have vanished. The public sector suppliers of gas, electricity, rail transport, and water have been sold to private corporations. A vast entertainment complex has arisen on the south bank of the Yarra, intended to exploit new markets in **gambling**, dining, and retailing, challenging Melbourne's traditional city centre. Melbourne's distinctive theatrical, literary, and visual arts traditions have been exploited to become capital for commercial festivals. Radical politics, with which Melbourne and its artistic circles were long identified, seems weaker at the end of the twentieth century than at any time since the 1840s.

The cultural sensibilities of Melbourne, and their debt to nineteenth-century economic and social contours, have been intensively studied by a small group of historians, aware both of Melbourne as an Australian variant of the global commercial city and of its unique cultural and material qualities. Graeme Davison, *The Rise and Fall of Marvellous Melbourne* (1978), is the foundation work which set a new standard in the writing of **urban history**. The fragmented political structure of the city is charted in David Dunstan, *Governing the Metropolis: Melbourne 1850–1891* (1984), while Andrew Brown-May, *Melbourne Street Life* (1998), views the process of municipal improvement from the more intimate vantage point of the street. Much of the emphasis in these urban histories remains with the nineteenth rather than the twentieth century, and they are firmly grounded in an understanding of the city's economy. The most distinctive and most undervalued historiography of Melbourne is a meticulous **local history**, which, as in John Lack, *A History of Footscray* (1991), and Janet McCalman, *Struggletown: Public and Private Life in Richmond, 1900–1965* (1984), explore class, community, and domestic life with more acuity than is apparent in any broad national survey. A large-scale *Encyclopedia of Melbourne* is in preparation.

CHRIS MCCONVILLE

Melbourne, Alexander Clifford Vernon (1888–1943) was a historian and author of the classic study, *Early Constitutional Development in Australia* (1934), written for a PhD in history at the University of London 1928–30. Melbourne was then on leave from the University of Queensland, to which he had been appointed in 1913 after taking honours in history at the University of Adelaide, and where he remained for the rest of his academic career. The book is still the authoritative account of its subject. Its title is somewhat misleading, for it gives close attention to the social and political forces that shaped constitutional development. Melbourne did not have access to all the **Colonial Office** records, but he was a shrewd judge of what guided British policy. The 1963 reprint of the work includes his study of constitutional development in Qld, the subject of his MA thesis (1921).

Melbourne had a disappointing academic career, being passed over for chairs in history at Queensland, Sydney, and Adelaide. In the 1930s he wrote two official reports on the prospects of Australian trade in Asia and took the unorthodox position of questioning the value of the British connection in **trade** and **defence**. His life and work have been examined by Geoffrey **Bolton** in Stuart Macintyre and Julian Thomas (eds), *The Discovery of Australian History* (1995).

JH

Melbourne Cup is a handicap horse-race run over 3200 metres that is conducted at Flemington by the Victoria Racing Club on the first Tuesday in November each year. After it was first run in 1861, the popularity of the Melbourne Cup grew rapidly; the day was made a public holiday in Melbourne in 1879. It became a national event as the telegraph carried the result throughout the continent. The whole country now stops when the race is run; sweeps are organised and bets laid across the country. Well-known winners include Archer (1861), Carbine (1890), **Phar Lap** (1930), and Peter Pan (1932, 1934). Trainer Bart Cummings holds a record number of 11 Melbourne Cup winners. Overseas horses were first invited to enter in 1993, with Irish stayer Vintage Crop taking first place that year. The race's popularity with all classes has been used as evidence for a democratic Australian spirit; at the same time **wowsers** have bemoaned its overt frivolity and others have lamented the social prestige attached to the members' enclosure.

HD

Melbourne School of History refers to the evolution, beginning with Ernest **Scott** but associated particularly with R.M. **Crawford**, of a singularly successful and influential program, primarily undergraduate, of historical training. It refers as well to a presumed approach to historical study.

Soon after his appointment to the first chair of history in 1913, Scott brought historical study out of the relative depression it had experienced under J.S. Elkington. Although his curriculum emphasised the British Empire, Australian studies achieved very high visibility within that framework. Scott also revitalised teaching methods and, in particular, established a strong honours program. But it was the achievement of Crawford to build on Scott's foundations a major enterprise in teaching and in the exploration of historical theory.

Under Crawford, who was appointed Scott's successor in 1937, the School of History expanded greatly from its three fulltime members at Crawford's accession to 15 tenured historians and a number of assistants. There were 575 honours graduates from 1937 to 1966, and a 1971 survey (by Geoffrey **Serle** in *HS*) revealed that 43 per cent of them had become academics; Melbourne graduates occupied more than one-third of the chairs in history in Australian universities at that time. The key to this success was a tightly defined honours program, made into a four-year program after 1949, which, in its later evolution, students entered directly from Year 12 in secondary school and pursued in special streams throughout the degree. The honours curriculum was constructed out of a small number of electives which fell into three broad strands: one for students attracted to ancient studies, later archaeology and Pacific studies; a second for students of British and Australian history, and a third for those with substantial American and European interests. There was a critically important common course on the theory and method of history.

From the 1940s, graduates of this program flowed in steady annual streams to Oxford, Cambridge, London, and from the 1960s to the USA, returning in many cases to staff history departments throughout Australia. The department acquired a distinctive reputation for its preparation of these graduates, for the sophistication of their approach to historical inquiry, and for their approach to historical theory.

It is on this last point that the concept of a Melbourne 'school' is both important and elusive. As Robert Dare has shown (in Stuart Macintyre and Julian Thomas, eds, *The Discovery of Australian History*, 1995), Crawford had sketched out a plan for a transdisciplinary approach to historical teaching and study before he was appointed at Melbourne. The practical logistics of building an honours school occupied most of his immediate attention, but he worked at clarifying the content of his historical thinking and gave important expression to it in *The Study of History: A Synoptic View*, the presidential address to the **Australian and New Zealand Association for the Advancement of Science** for 1939.

A conjunction of appointments in the Arts Faculty at Melbourne (notably George Paul and Douglas Gasking in philosophy) gave Crawford particular stimulus to explore topics concerning history's meaning more systematically. Crawford and these colleagues, joined by a number of students, made the Melbourne Faculty of Arts for about a decade one of the most lively and focused scenes of debate about the logic of explanation, narrative, moral judgment, and causality in history to be found anywhere in the English-speaking world.

From these discussions, which were largely completed by the 1950s, there evolved a style of reflexivity which suffused major offerings in the department. Students could not avoid being confronted with a sense of historical understanding itself as contingent and needing to be 'theorised', as a later generation puts it. This meant an early involvement in historiography, not as an arid exercise in mapping a succession of technical positions, but as a historically grounded inquiry itself. Crawford's school was identifiable not through its published research or a body of monographic writing based on a discrete set of questions and approaches; rather, it was embodied in an intellectual style, a high seriousness about the intellectual and moral activity of exploring past life expressed principally through the education of undergraduates.

The success of the Melbourne School of History had much to do with the remarkably talented generations of students attracted to the Faculty of Arts at the University of Melbourne. At various points in the 1950s and 1960s a better performance in the old Victorian matriculation exams was required to enter the honours stream in Arts than to secure entry into Medicine or Law. It was this stream of students, many sent enthusiastically by former students in the outstanding Victorian secondary system, both public and private, who provided the talent that Crawford and his colleagues served so well.

The diaspora of the 1960s took numbers of Crawford's team to other institutions, and Greg Dening, the Max Crawford Professor at Melbourne from 1974, systematically pursued the appointment of non-Melbourne graduates. Major new departments emerged at Monash and La Trobe Universities, while older departments such as Adelaide and Sydney were invigorated by growth and new appointments. The more recent history of the Melbourne school has seen its teaching and research enter into a wider range of specialist sub-fields than was ever envisaged by Crawford; the elaboration of a very large postgraduate commitment; and, in particular, the achievement of high visibility for the published research of its staff. Earlier Melbourne publishing had rested on the rather occasional special event of a major book.

A mark of change is the recent usage in the USA of the phrase 'Melbourne group of historians'. This refers to the influential work of Dening, Rhys Isaac, Inga Clendinnen, and Donna Merwick, which variously explores dimensions of cultural change, especially at the margins of contest between local and metropolitan societies. Although all these scholars have had extended involvement in different ways at the University of Melbourne, this 'Melbourne School' has been associated with La Trobe rather than the older university. (See **Ethnographic history**.)

PAUL BOURKE

Melville, Henry Saxelby Melville Wintle (1799–1873) was a journalist and publisher, thought to have arrived in Hobart from England in 1827. Within a year of purchasing the *Colonial Times*, he published Henry **Savery's** *Quintus Servinton* (1830–31), the first Australian novel published in Australia. He later founded Tasmania's first literary monthly, the *Hobart Town Magazine*, and became involved in running the *Tasmanian* and the *Trumpeter*. Melville's criticisms of the government, published anonymously in a pamphlet *Two Letters Written in Van Diemen's Land* (1835), and an article commenting on a decision made by the Supreme Court, resulted in his imprisonment for contempt of court. In prison he wrote 'A Few Words on Prison Discipline', later published in *The History of the Island of Van Diemen's Land, from the year 1824 to 1835* (1835). He returned to England where, in 1851, he published *The Present State of Australia*. His journalistic and publishing activities in Tasmania are discussed in E. Morris **Miller**, *Pressmen and Governors* (1952).

KT

Mennell, Phillip Dearman (1851–1905) wrote *The Dictionary of Australasian Biography* (1892), which comprised nearly 2000 biographies of 'eminent Australasian colonists' who flourished between 1855 and 1892. His work improved on earlier **biographical dictionaries** by J. Henniker **Heaton** and David **Blair**. Born at Newcastle-on-Tyne, England, Mennell was a qualified solicitor who pursued journalism in England and Australia. He edited the *Bairnsdale Advertiser* 1877–82 and was London cable agent for the Melbourne *Age* in the late 1880s. During the 1890s he became Australian correspondent for several London newspapers. He was editor–owner of the *British Australasian and New Zealand Mail* from 1892. Mennell was an ardent advocate of Imperial Federation who hoped his *Dictionary* would satisfy the heightened English and Australian desire for knowledge about the Australasian colonies. During the 18 months he took to complete it, Mennell obtained information from a wide range of sources, including the colonial agents-general in London, and especially from his extensive newspaper and personal contacts in Australia and NZ. He quarried major histories, previous biographical collections, and standard handbooks and directories. Among those who provided personal assistance were G.W. **Rusden**, Alexander **Sutherland** and Fred **Johns**. Mennell also wrote *Lord John*

Manners: A Political Biography (1872) and *The Coming Colony* (1892); and edited *In Australian Wilds* (1889) and *Australian Crisis of 1893* (1894).

DC

Menzies, Robert Gordon (1894–1978) is undoubtedly the most successful and probably the most controversial of conservative politicians. As prime minister from 1939 to 1941 he was a failure; back in office from 1949 to 1966, he retrieved initial humiliation to rout his opponents. When he retired from parliament (the last prime minister to do so while still secure in office), he dominated public life. His supremacy was such that contemporaries argued only over the merits of his success, and these arguments still linger in the estimates of biographers and historians.

In a perceptive analysis of the imagery and reference points of his appeal to *Robert Menzies' Forgotten People* (1992), Judith Brett distinguishes three ways in which Menzies was regarded. First, there was Menzies the statesman, who presided over two decades of growth and prosperity, stalwart in defence of the nation's security, the grand old man of conservative politics. Second, there was the Menzies who was reviled by the left. He was 'Pig-Iron Bob', the appeaser who had fought the unions in 1939 over their refusal to ship war materials destined for the Japanese war machine; the man who had not served in World War I but presumed to lecture humbler Australians on their duty in World War II and then conscripted Australians once more into the Cold War. This Menzies was a deceiver, an illiberal servant of the ruling class, and an opportunist who fomented division for partisan advantage. Finally, there was Menzies senescens, the ageing Anglophile anachronism who clung to the values and assumptions of the past.

The publication of his disappointingly slight memoirs, *Afternoon Light* (1966) and *Measure of the Years* (1970), did little to soften these sharply opposed evaluations. Nor did the admiring early biographers subject him to serious scrutiny. That process began with the publication of Cameron Hazlehurst's *Menzies Observed* (1979); it advanced with the appearance of the first volume of Allan **Martin's** authorised biography (1993), as well as Brett's more critical study, and still continues. If there is no agreement on important aspects of his life and career, the disappearance of the verities he established at least makes it possible to appreciate the magnitude of his achievement.

The life of Menzies can be seen as a journey from the margins towards the centre. He progressed from the tiny township of Jeparit on the Wimmera wheatlands where he was born in 1894, via the regional centre of Ballarat where he attended school, and then by scholarship to further study at Melbourne. Success at the Bar inducted him into the professional and business elite of the nation's temporary capital, and success in state politics prepared the transition in 1934 to federal parliament. As attorney-general he represented his country in London, the heart of an empire which he already knew so ardently from a distance and which always remained dear to him. His devotion to the monarchy was absolute.

During his long postwar supremacy he travelled regularly to the UK for meetings, Test cricket at Lord's and affirmation of the links with an idealised England that provided him with tradition, order, and value. Investiture as a Knight of the Thistle in the twilight of his career, and later his succession to Winston Churchill as Warden of the Cinque Ports, symbolised a reputation as the last of the Queen's men.

Yet Menzies began with greater advantages than this success story allows and the course of his career did not run smooth: His father and uncles were parliamentarians, and he married into a political family; the decision not to volunteer for military service in World War I was frequently used against him. He made his way in conservative circles between the wars as a stern critic of political expediency and upholder of the rule of law. He was gifted with intelligence and eloquence, handicapped by inordinate ambition and an incapacity to disguise it. As prime minister on the outbreak of World War II, he was unable to command party loyalty, coalition unity, or national consensus. From abject defeat in 1941 he retired to the backbenches to reconstruct the non-Labor forces into the new **Liberal Party**, provide it with policies and organisation to recapture the middle ground, and rehabilitate his own reputation. Henceforth Menzies ensured that the Liberal Party maintained cooperation with its coalition partner, the Country Party (later **National Party**). He infused its ranks with young ex-servicemen, reduced the dependence on big business, and cast himself as the champion of the thrifty and self-reliant 'forgotten people'. Accepting the expanded economic and social role of government, Menzies benefited from the postwar prosperity and made timely increases in public outlays designed to reward the provident. Recognising the shift in the balance of world power, he cultivated the USA as a 'powerful friend' that could underwrite Australia's regional security.

His political supremacy owed much to skilful exploitation of Cold War fears. The attempt to outlaw the **Communist** Party was rejected by the High Court in 1950 and by a national referendum in 1951, but brought electoral rewards. He continued to allege communist influence over the labour movement, and the **split** in the Australian Labor Party following the **Petrov Affair** in 1954, brought him the decisive electoral advantage of **DLP** preferences. In contrast to the difficulties of the Labor leaders, H.V. **Evatt** and A.A. **Calwell**, with the Australian Labor Party federal conference (which he characterised as '36 faceless men'), he dominated his own party. Parliamentary colleagues who might have challenged his leadership were removed, leaving a dearth of talent in his later ministries. Menzies cultivated a magisterial manner of effortless superiority, which belied his attention to public presentation and administrative detail. He could be arrogant in dealings with colleagues as well as opponents, but not duplicitous—had he suffered fools more gladly, he would have been remembered more fondly. His personal probity was absolute, his standard of public duty high.

Evaluations of his achievement are offered in Scott Prasser et al. (eds), *The Menzies Era* (1995) and Frank Cain (ed.), *Menzies in War and Peace* (1997). Gerard Henderson's critical assessment of *Menzies' Child* (1994) both magnifies his mastery and suggests its impermanence, as Menzies's own occasional indiscretions during his retirement recognised.

STUART MACINTYRE

Mercury is a **newspaper** founded in Hobart in 1854 by John Davies, formerly a journalist in Calcutta, and George Aubey Jones. Davies and Jones had acquired the *Hobarton Guardian* in 1852 and used it to model their new paper— originally published bi-weekly as the *Hobarton Mercury*. By 1860 it was published daily as the *Mercury*. The paper remained under the control of the Davies family until a public company was formed in 1895. For most of the twentieth century the conservative views offered by the *Mercury* held a virtual newspaper monopoly in Hobart, and the paper had a consistently high circulation. In 1987 Rupert **Murdoch's** News Corporation gained a controlling interest.

HD

Meredith, Gwenyth Valmai (1907–) wrote the outstandingly successful series *Blue Hills*, which was broad- cast four days a week on Australian Broadcasting Corpora- tion radio 1949–76. This series had developed from *The Lawsons* (1943–49), which was also set in a farming commu- nity. Meredith recognised the urban Australian nostalgia for an apparently simple bush life, and developed her stories of ordinary people dealing with universal issues in this setting. As well as other plays, Meredith produced several novels based on the radio serials, including *Blue Hills* (1950) and *Beyond Blue Hills* (1953).

KT

Meredith, Louisa Anne (1812–95), writer and artist, came to NSW from England in 1839 after her marriage. The couple soon moved to Tasmania, where her husband, Charles, later became a member of parliament. She wrote vividly of colonial life in *Notes and Sketches of New South Wales* (1844), *My Home in Tasmania* (1852), and *Over the Straits: A Visit to Victoria* (1861). She also produced and illus- trated many volumes of poetry and several novels. Her paint- ings of native flora and fauna won prizes. The title of Vivienne Rae Ellis's biography, *Louisa Anne Meredith: A Tigress in Exile* (1979), suggests the force of her personality.

KT

Methodist Church was founded in the mid-eighteenth century by the Rev. John Wesley as a network of societies within the Church of England and became a separate denomination after his death. Methodists, so called because of their methodical pursuit of personal holiness, were also inspired by the apostolic command to 'make disciples of all nations'. Their converts included even the 'harlots and publicans and thieves' addressed in one of the famous hymns by Wesley's brother Charles and prominent among the convict settlers of Australia. These impulses—inward and outward, towards the reformation of character and towards the transformation of society—were finely balanced in the

Church's character and history. Methodist members of the London Missionary Society had visited the Pacific in 1796 and the first Methodist class meeting was held in Sydney in 1812. The Church became strongest in SA and Victoria, especially in mining communities where many had come from Methodist strongholds in Cornwall and South Wales. Except for a brief period in the early 1860s, when the Amer- ican **evangelist** California Taylor won converts on the Victorian goldfields, Australian Methodism was little touched by revivalism. But its organisation through itinerant ministers and lay preachers directed by a central conference was well adapted to frontier conditions, making it, as J.D. Bollen argued, 'the most Australian of the churches'. Its stress on ideals of self-improvement also harmonised with the ideals of a liberal democratic society.

Yet self-improvement, and the respectability it often produced, gradually transformed Methodism. The class meetings in which Wesley had gathered his followers for prayer and mutual support declined as Methodists adopted the congregational pattern characteristic of other Protestant churches. They continued to uphold an austere moral code, keeping the Sabbath and eschewing dancing, gambling and drinking. Critics labelled them **wowsers**. They led the public campaigns to curb drinking and gambling; but also to improve factory conditions, abolish slums and 'rescue' neglected children. The various branches of Methodism— Wesleyans, Primitive Methodists, and Bible Christians— united in 1902, ahead of a similar union in Britain. By the early twentieth century many Methodists had become ardent followers of the social, as well as the personal, gospel. The Rev. Alan **Walker**, evangelist, social reformer and anti- war campaigner, was a representative figure. Methodism left its imprint on conservatives like Garfield **Barwick** and John **Howard**, as well as social reformers like Oswald **Barnett** and Brian Howe. In 1977 the Methodists joined with the **Congregationalists** and most **Presbyterians** to form the **Uniting Church**. There is no recent national history of Methodism, but studies of SA by Arnold Hunt (1985) and NSW by Don Wright (1993), and of Melbourne's Wesley Central Mission by Renate Howe and Shurlee Swain (1993) develop significant themes.

GD

Métin, Albert, see *Socialisme sans doctrines*

Miklouho-Maclay, Nikolai (1846–88), a Russian scientist, came to Australia because of his interest in anthro- pology. For seven years he studied the people of the Astro- labe Bay area of New Guinea, and also made expeditions into Papua and the Malay Peninsula. Weakened by fever, Maclay went to Singapore with the intention of returning to Russia, but was unable to do so. He travelled instead to Australia and arrived in Sydney in 1878. Maclay was welcomed by the local scientific community, and became an active member of the Linnaean Society. His campaign for a local laboratory of marine science eventually bore fruit in the Watsons Bay laboratory. He promoted the welfare of

Pacific peoples, especially indentured labourers (see **Pacific Island labourers**). Qld's announcement that it intended to annex eastern New Guinea deepened his concern. Maclay returned to Russia in 1886. After his death, his Australian-born family returned home with copies of his New Guinea diaries which were eventually translated and published by C.L. Sentinella (1975). E.M. Webster has written a biography, *The Moon Man* (1984).

KT

Military history as an intellectual discipline in Australia has attracted more direct government funding than perhaps any other branch of Australian history. This has resulted in an impressive series of publications, the organisation and retention of a major government archive, and the development of a distinctly Australian way of writing about war. For many years, however, military history was regarded as a sideline for enthusiasts rather than a major branch of the historical discipline in Australia.

Charles **Bean**, appointed official Australian war correspondent at the outbreak of **World War I**, revealed himself to be an indefatigable writer and note-taker. Already practised in the art of turning a series of newspaper articles into published books, Bean left Australia with the first contingent of the **AIF**, determined to write a solid history of Australia's role in the war on his return. In 1919 the government accepted Bean's plan, which was wildly optimistic, and then watched with some impatience while Bean, working with extraordinary diligence, turned out six solid volumes of his own and substantially wrote and rewrote five volumes of the work of others.

The first of Bean's volumes in this *Official History of Australia in the War of 1914–1918* was published in 1921, the last in 1942. So thorough was his work, and so massive, that Bean has still not been superseded. He devoted a lifetime to sifting the records and writing a narrative that depended entirely on those records and other personal accounts. What was distinctive about his approach was his concern to know how the battle unfolded on the front line; to follow the common soldiers rather than the commanders: 'what actual experiences, at the point where men lay out behind hedges or on the fringe of woods, caused those on one side to creep, walk or run forward, and the others to go back'.

Bean had his critics: at the highest levels of the military, practitioners who refused to believe that he, an amateur, could readily penetrate the arcane science of the profession of arms; at the highest political levels, where men believed that he was simply producing too much to be readable; and among accountants, who doubted that the public was sufficiently interested in his work to justify the expense. It is doubtful that these concerns even registered with Bean, who was inspired by a sense of mission to complete his work. It was a tragedy for him, and for the discipline, that his last volume describing the Australian triumphs of 1918 lay largely unread, published in 1942 when the life of the nation was at risk from a far more pressing foe.

Others, of course, also told the story of Australia at war—no-one more promptly and forcefully than John **Monash**, whose *The Australian Victories in France* (1920) appeared within months of the events he describes. Bean deprecated Monash's account as self-serving and propagandistic, but it was the account that held sway, if only because of the lack of any alternative. Battalion historians attempted to write at the local level where the official history aspired to the global, but for most part these books did little to alert serious historians to the possibilities that military history presented. The best of the battalion historians explained the emergence of that peculiar group loyalty that appears to bond men in war. There were also modest efforts in hagiography, although such was the cohesion of the First AIF that most deplored any tendency to single out individuals from the mass. It may be that Bean's response to Monash's account suffered from this democratic impulse as if, somehow, it was improper for an Australian commander to tell the people what their troops had achieved at war.

When Bean engineered the appointment of Gavin **Long** as the official historian of **World War II**, he expected to play a mentoring role to ensure that Long followed his model closely. Despite strong advice that other methods might be attempted, Long adopted Bean's method, even down to the detailed note-taking in diaries that would become the historian's most prized possession. So vast was the scope of the history Long devised that it was not possible for him to take the central role that Bean had carved out for himself; he was designated 'general editor', writing only three of the 18 volumes of *Australia in the War of 1939–45* himself. There were also four volumes in a medical history series. Long's history has been mined by subsequent historians and speechwriters, but there must be only a small minority of serious students of history who can claim to have read it all. Designed, like Bean's, for the men who served, it is more than likely that its fate was that of Bean's. A relative of a veteran will say, 'Dad was mentioned in the official history'—almost as important a distinction as 'mentioned in despatches'.

Subsequent official histories have covered Australian military activity from **Korea** to **Vietnam** with a similar level of detail. Commercially, they have always been a doubtful proposition. His publishers could not even make Bean's history work and it was saved only by the commercial genius of John Treloar of the **Australian War Memorial**. If part of the historian's responsibility is to find and reach a readership, then the fate of official histories should have caused concern to more than the accountants. In fact sales performance indicates that the sponsors have seen the histories as having a memorial role, rather than the conventional 'read, debate, and develop' notion of standard historical work.

Broader and more accessible military history in Australia developed a genuine readership and interest during the 1980s and 1990s; in part this has relied on the discovery of military history by academic historians. The interest is part of a wider interest in Australian history generally; and it has depended upon the opening of archives which were previously restricted to the official historians. K.S. **Inglis**, John

Robertson, Lloyd **Robson**, L.F.C. Turner, David Horner, and others have shown what insights military history can offer the generalist historian and have demonstrated, Horner in particular, the intrinsic interest and drama of well-written military history.

It is possible to identify three main approaches to the contemporary writing of Australian military history: a social-democratic model, inherited from Charles Bean; a 'war and society' approach, derived from mainstream Australian social history; and a technical-analytical model, derived from an international perspective, dependent for its inspiration on contemporary work in America and Europe.

Bill Gammage reanimated the Bean model, and it would be difficult to overemphasise the seminal importance of his outstanding and often-republished book, *The Broken Years* (1974). Gammage learned Bean's method from Arthur Bazley, Bean's batman during the war years and his factotum thereafter. The success of Gammage's work inspired similar approaches in other areas of Australian history, and thus Bean entered general historical discourse for the first time. A later and highly successful follower of this approach was Alistair Thomson, whose *Anzac Memories* (1994) was recognised as a major work in memory and meaning. Many battalion historians derived their inspiration from these models, including David Hay's eloquent *Nothing Over Us* (1984) and Margaret Barter's thoroughly researched *Far Above Battle* (1994). Memoirs and reminiscences multiplied as the World War II generation entered the leisure years necessary for this kind of writing. Outstanding among these books was Barney Roberts's *A Kind of Cattle* (1985).

Lloyd Robson dominated the 'war and society' approach to Australian military history in the 1970s and 1980s, as both a teacher and a writer. His encouragement drew many younger historians to military themes and is perhaps best exemplified in Jan Bassett's deeply moving *Guns and Brooches* (1992), a history of Australian army nursing. From Sydney, where Robson's influence was slower to penetrate than in his home academy at Melbourne, Peter Cochrane made a major impact with his re-examination of the **Simpson** story, *Simpson and the Donkey* (1992).

The third approach has received significant promotion at the Australian Defence Force Academy: through the work of historians like Peter Dennis and Jeffrey Grey; through formal links with the army, whose support for military history with grants and publications programs has been influential in the 1990s; and through the development of networks with military historians in other countries, particularly the USA and Canada. Outstanding interpreters of World War I have been Trevor Wilson and Robin Prior, whose *Passchendaele* (1996) and *Command on the Western Front* (1992) are among the most acclaimed studies of the Great War written in the 1990s. The most prolific producer within this category has been David Horner, firstly as a serving officer in the Australian army, and more recently as a member of the staff of the Australian National University. Horner's output is impressive, ranging from early works like *High Command* (1982) to studies of

aspects of the military, such as *The Gunners* (1995) and *Duty First* (1990).

MICHAEL McKERNAN

Miller, Edmund Morris (1881–1964) compiled the two-volume descriptive bibliography *Australian Literature from its Beginnings to 1935* (1940), which remains an important reference work. Miller began his working life at the Public Library of Victoria. In 1913 he went to the University of Tasmania as lecturer in mental and moral science, rising to become professor of philosophy and psychology, and later vice-chancellor. The University of Tasmania's library, where he was honorary librarian, was named after him. His other publications, which include philosophy, librarianship, and Australian literary history, demonstrate the breadth of his interests.

KT

Mills, Richard Charles (1886–1952), graduated from the universities of Melbourne and London, served as a chaplain in the British army during World War I and was wounded and mentioned in despatches. He then taught economics at the University of Sydney. Chairman of the Commonwealth Grants Commission 1939–45, he took charge of the Commonwealth Office of Education after the war. He helped guide the Commonwealth through the early stages of involvement in tertiary education and in 1950 chaired a committee of inquiry into the needs of the universities which took the process a stage further.

Mills's academic interests centred on money and public finance, and he published several works in these fields, including *Money* (1936), which he co-authored. He served on the 1935 royal commission on banking, and in 1942 chaired the Uniform Tax Committee, which helped reshape the financial aspects of Commonwealth–state relations.

Mills appreciated the importance of Australian history, and stressed the need for it to be approached more scientifically. G. Arnold **Wood** rated him one of Australia's leading historians and 'perhaps the handsomest man in the University', recommending him for the editorship of the *Historical Records of Australia* when Frederick Watson retired. Mills's major contribution to historical writing, however, was his London doctoral thesis, published as *The Colonization of Australia 1829–1842* (1915, 1968). It stood out as a meticulous critique of Edward Gibbon **Wakefield's** ideas and their impact on WA and SA. Mills exaggerated Wakefield's importance as a colonial theorist, but his book was long regarded as authoritative.

BRIAN FLETCHER

Miner's right is a government-issued document or permit entitling its holder to prospect and extract minerals, together with associated privileges. Geoffrey **Blainey**, *The Rush That Never Ended* (1963), describes its origins during the **gold rushes** in mid-1855, when Victoria reformed goldfields legislation after discontent with the expensive licence-fee system had culminated in the **Eureka** rebellion of 1854. For £1 per year, a miner's right not only allowed miners to dig for gold, but also to vote at parliamentary elections; to elect delegates to local courts which settled mining disputes; and to reside on land claimed for mining purposes. Miner's right thus contributed towards eventual manhood suffrage in Victoria, and to land reform. Weston **Bate**, *Lucky City* (1978), notes many Ballarat properties are still held under formal registration of miner's right claims, which were first allowed in 1857. Miner's right was rapidly adopted in other Australian colonies and in NZ. *The Miner's Right* was the title of an 1890 novel by Rolf **Boldrewood**.

DC

Mining has been practised in Australia for at least 20 000 years. For most of this time it involved quarrying stone and ochre, and mining flint for Aboriginal tools and weapons. Since white occupation it has diversified to include nearly 40 principal mineral commodities, and has influenced almost every aspect of economic, social, and political life. European mining began at the **penal settlement** of Coal River (Newcastle) in 1804 and within 10 years coal was being exported to India (in exchange for Bengal rum). South Australians opened the earliest significant metal mines; silver–lead at Glen Osmond from 1841, and copper from the Kapunda lodes discovered the next year. Early ventures were characterised by features that typified later mining: amateurish **prospecting** and long delays while ore samples were assessed in Britain. Transport was expensive and metallurgical experimentation sporadic and improvised. As bigger mines opened, first at Burra (1845) and later in the Moonta–Kadina–Wallaroo triangle (early 1860s), they attracted money and migrants, and became durable centres of population.

The **gold rushes** that began in NSW and Victoria in 1851 continued this process in other colonies. By the 1860s **diggers** were prospecting Qld and NT; they reached Tasmania and the Kimberley Plateau in WA in the 1880s. Gold was rare on the coast and, while many mining settlements were ephemeral, the rushes created significant inland towns: Ballarat and Bendigo (1851) in Victoria; Charters Towers (1872) and Mount Morgan (1885) in Qld; and Coolgardie–Kalgoorlie (1892–93) in WA. Indeed, gold financed **development** throughout the colonies. While early mining was the province of diggers, syndicates, and small companies, governments quickly revamped company legislation to encourage overseas investment. Many, perhaps most, British shareholders were disappointed with dividends, but their capital underwrote Australian **agriculture**, industry, **transport**, and construction.

Gold dominates writing about the history of mining. This reflects both the excitement it generated and its enduring influence on mining law, prospecting, and investment. Colonial governments framed early legislation with the digger in mind; political imperatives took precedence over efficient mining practice. Gold seekers usually worked independently and, where possible, in secret. Their style contributed to the late development of large-scale, scientifically based mineral prospecting. Gold influenced attitudes to investment, encouraging hopes of early dividends and expectations that development could be financed by easy pickings from the surface shows. But its influence on base metal mining was not entirely negative; prospecting often led to discovery of other minerals. The Peak Downs rush of 1861, for example, led to the opening of Qld's first copper mine. Gold lured diggers to Mount Lyell and Rosebery in Tasmania in the early 1880s, opening these fields for the next generation of base metal miners.

By the early twentieth century, tin and silver–lead were challenging the supremacy of precious metals, despite Australia's rank as the world's top gold producer from 1903 to 1913. The tin industry began with alluvial workings at Inverell (NSW) in 1871. The next year, discovery of huge tin runs on the Queensland border (Stanthorpe–Tingha), in Tasmania (Mount Bischoff), and in north Qld at Herberton made Australia, for a decade, the world's premier supplier. More significantly, Charles **Rasp** found silver–lead at Broken Hill in 1883. The Broken Hill companies imported American expertise, and funded experimentation that brought Australia to the forefront of international metallurgy. Different aspects of this field have been documented by Leonard Curtis, *The History of Broken Hill* (1908); Roy Bridges, *From Silver to Steel* (1920); Geoffrey **Blainey**, *The Rise of Broken Hill* (1968); Ruth Fischer, *The Hog's Back* (1970); and Brian Kennedy, *Silver, Sin and Sixpenny Ale* (1978). Coal production was also significant at this stage; in the nineteenth century deposits were exploited intensively in Qld (Ipswich and the Bowen Basin) and NSW, particularly after the discovery of the Greta measures in 1886. WA's only commercial field opened at Collie in 1889, and work slowly commenced at the as yet underdeveloped fields of Leigh Creek (SA), and Yallourn and Wonthaggi (Victoria).

War had a mixed impact on Australian mining. Transport problems and the loss of German smelting facilities crippled tin, lead, and zinc extraction. On the other hand, coal was at a premium and the price of copper was fixed at £100 a ton. The removal of British guarantees after World War I caused an immediate collapse of this industry. Mining ceased on the Cloncurry copper field in 1918, followed by Moonta–Wallaroo and Mount Morgan in the 1920s. Tin failed at Mount Bischoff in 1935, but in this decade Mount Isa Mines came into lead production. Geoffrey Blainey has written a history of the field, *Mines in the Spinifex* (1960), and Kett Kennedy covers the rise of the company in his biography of its first chairman, Leslie Urquhart, *Mining Tsar* (1986). Like the Broken Hill companies, this silver–lead–zinc producer also owned huge reserves of copper, which it began to exploit towards the end of World War II. This war also increased coal sales, though most mines stepped up production at the expense of development and forfeited profits in peacetime. Indeed, the company that benefited most from war was the one that diversified away from mining: **BHP** had won a monopoly of the Australian **iron and steel** industry in 1935.

When the **Chifley** government surveyed the industry for **postwar reconstruction**, it found it to be run down.

However, Australia was about to enter a resources boom that spanned three decades. The key was investment which underwrote new methods of copper and coal extraction, and the discovery and development of 'new' metals. In 1947 the town of Wittenoom (WA) was built to house miners of the asbestos deposits in the gorge found by Lang **Hancock**. **Uranium** was found at Rum Jungle (NT) (1949) and Mary Kathleen (Qld) (1954). In the early 1950s the Gove (NT) bauxite deposits were recognised as commercially viable, followed by Weipa (Qld) in 1955. Hancock aerially prospected iron deposits in the Pilbara (WA) at the end of the decade. Australia's **oil** industry began at Moonie (Qld) in 1961, and the major oil and gas fields off the coast of Victoria in Bass Strait were opened in 1965. Nickel, tungsten (wolfram and scheelite), and titanium (rutile and ilmenite) were other new mining industries. Important to many of these developments was the introduction of new prospecting techniques and the increasing use of heavy machinery and open-cut methods of mining.

Capital for postwar expansion came from a few large companies which, in different permutations, controlled every phase of production across the various mineral sectors. For example, Western Mining Corporation, a multinational originating with the **Collins House Group**, combined with British and South African gold interests to mine and treat gold, bauxite, iron, and nickel. Conzinc Riotinto Australia (CRA), two international mergers onwards from Broken Hill's Zinc Corporation, became a member of consortia involved in all stages of coal, gold, bauxite, uranium, and iron production. Typically, they explored and developed their mines, and constructed towns and other expensive infrastructure, such as **railways** and ports, before attempting production. In 1984, the group that opened the Blair Athol coal mine in the Bowen Basin spent $450 million before mining started. Four years earlier the development budget for the North-West Shelf oil project was $11 000 million. Even those traditional resources of the small miner, gold and precious stones, were taken over by multinationals. The price of gold rose 1800 per cent between 1968 and 1980, allowing exploitation of low-grade ores, while the huge harvest from the Argyle diamond field (discovered on the Ord River in 1979) raised fears of a destabilised world market.

The increased pace and scope of mining, combined with a changing political climate, forced examination of problems that had long dogged the industry. Stock market scandals that had plagued investors since the first SA copper companies, assumed, in the Poseidon nickel ramp of 1970, a prominence that led to government intervention to regulate markets and restrict foreign ownership. Aboriginal dislocation, which had accompanied every mineral project since European occupation, demanded attention when Nabalco prepared to extract bauxite on an **Aboriginal mission** on the Gove Peninsula in 1972. In that year, too, long-term competition between states led the federal government to establish a Department of Minerals and Energy to coordinate fuel production. In 1975 Australians confronted the **environmental** degradation that had scarred outback

mineral fields for more than a century, when rutile and ilmenite extraction (sand mining) began at Fraser Island, on the more heavily populated and diversified east coast. The Fox Inquiry (1976–77) into proposed exploitation of the Ranger uranium deposits urged governments to exert considerably more control over this mineral, and compensation claims by ex-asbestos miners from Wittenoom gave a new edge to mining health and safety issues.

Despite its importance, the mining industry has attracted relatively little historical attention. Geoffrey Blainey's *The Rush That Never Ended* (1963, 1978) remains the best overview, though individual minerals and specific fields have a far richer literature. Apart from the gold rushes, publishers have been wary of work on mining history; much of the available material was commissioned by mining companies, institutes, trade unions, and local historical groups. On the whole this sponsorship has been benign. An Australian Mining History Association was formed in 1994.

DIANE MENGHETTI

***Mirror* (Sydney)** was first published in August 1915 by the Australian Pictorial Newspaper Company as a penny paper featuring war photos. The paper was modelled on the London *Mirror*, and described itself as 'The Brightest and Best Picture Paper'. As well as war pictures, the *Mirror* featured a comic strip, a women's section, and sport illustrations. The paper was also ferociously anti-German in sentiment and called for the **internment** of all German residents. It absorbed the *Globe* in 1917 but ceased publication in September 1919, possibly affected by the inception of *Smith's Weekly* earlier that year, or by a reduced interest in war photos. (See also **Newspapers**.)

KT

Mitchell, David Scott (1836–1907) was an ardent Sydney bibliophile with a substantial private income. He qualified in law and was admitted to the Bar but never practised, living a reclusive life that centred on his collection. Although initially interested in English literature, from around 1886 he turned his attention to Australia, the Pacific, and Antarctica. He attempted to collect every significant manuscript and publication relating to these areas, as well as pictures, coins, and medals. He bequeathed his collection, with a large endowment, to the State Library of New South Wales, and this formed the basis for the Mitchell Library collection, which opened in 1910. Anne Robertson's *Treasures of the State Library of New South Wales* (1988) includes a description of the collection.

KT

Mitchell, James (1866–1951), WA **Nationalist** politician, used his position as minister for agriculture, and later, as minister for railways and industry, to advance the **group settlement scheme**, which promoted **immigration** as a means of developing **agriculture**. During his two periods as premier of WA (1919–24, 1930–33), he was instrumental in placing 15 000 British settlers on farms in the state's south-west, nearly half of whom later walked off. His determination to develop the south-west into a centre of dairy farming resulted in his nickname 'Moo-cow Mitchell'. He allowed a referendum on WA **secession** at the 1933 general elections; 68 per cent voted 'yes' but Mitchell lost his seat, as did every National member of Cabinet. He remained a popular figure who served as governor of WA 1948–51.

KT

Mitchell, Roma Flinders (1913–2000) barrister, judge, and governor, was admitted to the SA Bar in 1934. In 1962 she became Australia's first female Queen's Counsel, the first of her many firsts. In 1965 she became a judge of the Supreme Court of South Australia, the first woman in Australia to hold such a position. On two occasions she served as acting chief justice. She chaired the Human Rights Commission (1981–86). In 1983 she was elected chancellor of the University of Adelaide, the first woman to hold that position in any Australian university.

In 1991 she became SA's first woman governor, finishing her term in 1996. It was spectacularly successful. She was at ease with protocol and ceremony, and clearly enjoyed her position and the opportunities it gave her. She could talk about the state's history and economy, but her special interest was in the arts. She hosted many musical events, invited writers and artists to visit Government House, and attended as many plays, launchings, and openings as possible. Mitchell has a strong sense of duty, a determination to succeed, and an uncompromising commitment to truth and justice which led her to **feminism**.

JEAN WHYTE

Mitchell, Thomas Livingstone (1792–1855), Scottish-born surveyor, served in the army before his appointment as surveyor-general of NSW in 1827. From his arrival he did much to improve the quality of the survey of the colony with systematic new measurement and calculation of the topography. His first and second expeditions were westwards along the interior rivers of NSW. In 1836 Mitchell set off on his third major exploratory expedition: to trace the course of the **Murray River** upstream from its junction with the Darling. On climbing the summit of Mount Pilot, just south of the Murray, however, Mitchell was so enthused by the vista of verdant pastureland that he disregarded official orders and continued south through the **Port Phillip District**. His delight with this country, which he labelled **'Australia Felix'**, encouraged a rush of overlanders. Early accounts of Victorian history that celebrate Mitchell's pioneering journey are echoed in the countless historic markers across western Victoria that meticulously record his route.

Mitchell's travel journals, published in two volumes in 1839 with a third volume in 1848, are a rich source for historians. Gregory C. Eccleston (1992) examined these closely in relation to Mitchell's 1836 expedition, as did Paul Carter, from a postmodern position, in *Living in a New Country* (1992). In *The Civilised Surveyor* (1997), D.W.A. Baker

contrasts Mitchell's close and at times affectionate relationship with the Aborigines with whom he travelled, and the ultimate effect of his expeditions which was to encourage white settlement and further hasten dispossession.

HD

Mob originally described a noisy and usually threatening crowd of people, but in Australia, despite its use in reference to town gangs or ***pushes***, it was applied more broadly to non-threatening animal and human collectives. For shepherds and stockmen, many of whom were convicts and ex-convicts, *mob* was perhaps the most familiar term for any unruly collective. They subsequently adopted it when referring to sheep and cattle, as a substitute for *flock* or *herd*, and also to groups of indigenous animals, such as kangaroos and emus. *Mob* was also used by whites as a general collective for Aborigines. Large numbers of Aborigines working in the pastoral industry, who learned the word as a collective for stock, and also heard it applied to themselves by non-Aboriginal stockmen, subsequently adopted the word as their own. As well as applying it to animal collectives, Aborigines developed the word as a means of differentiating between clans and familial groups. Membership of such 'mobs' requires recognition of that group's particular responsibilites and behavioural code. The word has since become synonymous with self-identity, as evident in Mudrooroo's title *Us Mob* (1995). White Australians also commonly used the word to identify family- or place-specific groups, as popularised in John **O'Grady's** *They're a Weird Mob* (1957), but this use has dwindled in the late twentieth century.

HD

Molloy, Georgiana (1805–43), amateur botanist, arrived in Swan River colony in 1829 following her marriage to Captain John Molloy. They settled at Augusta on the Blackwood River, 320 kilometres south of Perth, where Georgiana endured the privations and social isolation of pioneer life and the tragic deaths of two of her four children.

Georgiana was sustained by her religion and her love of plants. A chance gift of seeds from Captain James Mangles, horticulturalist, accompanied by the request to supply native specimens in return, prompted her to botanise in earnest. Although doubting her ability, Georgiana soon won praise for her meticulously prepared specimens. Botany gave Georgiana an interest beyond the 'domestic drudgery' that filled her days, and increased her appreciation of the beauty and diversity of the native flora. Her correspondence with Mangles reveals her to be articulate, intelligent, and sensitive; later scholars credit her with much of the work for which he gained credit.

In 1839 the Molloys moved 100 kilometres north to the Vasse River, where farming was easier. Georgiana experienced increasing difficulties with childbirth, and died after the birth of her sixth daughter. Her correspondence has formed the basis of biographies by Alexandra **Hasluck** (1955) and, more recently, William Lines (1994).

JUDY SKENE

Monarchy, the system by which the state is personified by a single figure, normally a king or queen, was integral to Australian government from the beginning of British settlement in 1788.

At this time the monarchy in Britain was enjoying a resurgence of popularity, and the challenge of revolution in North America and Europe seems, by a profound reactionary process, to have given the image of the sovereign a new diversity and power. George III (1760–1820) thus became an important national rallying point during the wars with revolutionary and Napoleonic France. Also, by the end of the eighteenth century public opinion had newly focused on the relationship between public and private life. Daily events within the royal family—the activities of royal women, in particular—offered a new challenge to common imagination throughout the British Empire. Queen Charlotte, wife of George III, was the first of a series of queens to enjoy a type of mass appeal in their own right. Royalty was successful on these terms, in Britain and Australia, for as long as the Empire lasted.

From the beginning of settlement, the monarchy served two distinct purposes among the British population in Australia. On the one hand, it symbolised power: the power of the Empire, of British arms, commerce, language, and culture. But it was also thought of as a guarantor of common liberties. Early colonial radicals, such as John Grant and Joseph Holt, wrote of George III in reverential terms, while arguing that common rights were being undermined by the false representatives of the king in NSW. Edward Smith **Hall**, the radical editor of the Sydney *Monitor* (founded 1826), wrote as if George IV (whose real knowledge of Australia was nominal) watched over both the daily welfare and the liberties of his people in the antipodes. Three generations later, a similar argument can be seen in lines by Henry **Lawson** (at times a keen republican), who wrote on the death of Edward VII that 'He shamed, by manliness and truth, / The lies that beat about a crown'. Such 'shaming' was the perceived task of kings. Soon afterwards Lawson hailed the coronation of George V, 'the only British King / To see the Southern Hemisphere', as a promise of continued liberties.

The notion of the monarch as a guardian of traditional rights flourished among large numbers of Australians even into the last decades of the twentieth century. In a peculiar way the monarchy was thus a means of reconciling notions of British power and of British freedom, two things which might otherwise have seemed contradictory. The splendour of the Crown seemed to prove that monarchs had all the power they needed in doing their duty by the people.

The moral authority of the monarchy in Australia has thus been based to some extent on a common understanding of the personal power of the monarch; or, it might be argued, a common misunderstanding, given the way government really works. This pattern of belief has frequently shown itself in individuals and groups who have lost hope of securing their rights except by going to the top. One of the earliest appeals sent from Australia directly to the monarch was that of Walter George Arthur, the Tasmanian Aborigine who wrote to Queen Victoria in 1846 on behalf of his people on Flinders Island. In 1993, 700 Aborigines meeting in Canberra similarly agreed to ask Elizabeth II to take their side in deliberations over **Aboriginal land rights**. Even the speaker of the House of Representatives, in November 1975, wrote to the queen with the hope of reversing Governor-General Sir John **Kerr's dismissal** of the **Whitlam** government.

The monarchy in Australia has thus operated as the focus of common ideas about public faith, ideas implicit and often overlooked from day to day, but vital in times of crisis. Indeed, the moral authority of the Crown within the population at large, and therefore even its success in a narrow constitutional sense, can be said to have depended in the last resort on an unrealistic and even whimsical pattern of common belief. It may be doubtful whether the constitution of a nation such as Australia ought to rest on such simple idealism, and differences on this point played a large part in the **republicanism** debate of the 1990s.

The main distingishing aspect of the monarchy as an Australian institution has been the absence of the monarch. In the colonies, and later states, the gap was easily filled by **governors**, and **governor-generals** have played a similar role throughout Australia from 1901. However, Federation created a political community, like that of India or Canada, of peculiar vastness and diversity, an empire within the Empire, which has often seemed to need something additional, and even some kind of personal monarchy. This need was confronted in a variety of ways during the twentieth century. To begin with, the governors-general were Englishmen whose distinguished background made it possible for them to be seen as the personal as well as the constitutional representatives of the monarch. The king's brother, the Duke of Gloucester, served for a period during World War II. The appointment of Australians, at intervals from 1931 and continuously from 1965, broke this link. But at the same time **royal visits** became progressively easier, and from 1954 to 1991 Elizabeth II frequently undertook the duties of personal monarchy in Australia. However, with the exception of the first coronation visit, her tours were always very brief. A proposal by Prime Minister **Fraser** that Prince Charles should become governor-general was not supported by the Labor opposition and lapsed. Finally, during the 1990s, the non-residence of the Queen became the central point of the campaign for a republic. This simple, negative, but undeniable argument—'she is not Australian'—distinguished the republican campaign of the 1990s from all similar movements in the past, and explained its unprecedented appeal.

Historians of the monarchy in Australia have thus for the most part been concerned with one of three things: the powers of the monarch as exercised by governors and governors-general; royal tours (especially those of Prince Alfred, the first royal visitor, 1867–68, and of Elizabeth II in 1954); and issues arising from demand for a republic, especially in the 1990s. The classic examination of vice-regal powers is H.V. **Evatt's** work of constitutional law, *The King and His*

Dominion Governors: A Study of the Reserve Powers of the Crown in Great Britain and the Dominions (1936). Evatt explored the question of the divisibility of the Crown within the Empire, or nascent Commonwealth of Nations, concentrating especially on the significance of the royal prerogative as used by the monarch and by vice-regal figures. He was fundamentally concerned with government sovereignty among the Dominions, including Australia. Though he was essentially a republican, his understanding of the monarchy was therefore integral to his beliefs about national independence.

The public debate during the 1990s on the need for a republic included some detailed appraisal of the way the monarchy has worked in Australia. Most of the discussion centred on the question of the constitutional powers of the monarchy and on the way in which such powers might or might not be transferred to a republican head of state. This was one of the main issues tackled by the Republic Advisory Committee appointed by Prime Minister **Keating** in 1993 (reporting in October that year), and by the chair of that committee, Malcolm Turnbull, in *The Reluctant Republic* (1993). Broader issues relating to the popular appeal of the monarchy were dealt with by Alan Atkinson, *The Muddle-Headed Republic* (1993); John Hirst, *A Republican Manifesto* (1994); Tony Abbott, *The Minimal Monarchy: And Why It Still Makes Sense for Australia* (1995); and Mark McKenna, *The Captive Republic: A History of Republicanism in Australia 1788–1995* (1996). Atkinson's work was largely historical, though informed by an ethnographic understanding of public ritual and symbolism. Slight as it was, it was unusual as a sympathetic study of the impact of monarchy on Australian ideas of community, state, and citizenship (and in its scant reference to legal issues). Hirst's book was not meant as a connected piece of history, except insofar as it argued for the evaporating authority of the Crown in Australia. Abbott's was partly historical, with particular emphasis on the recent past and on his work as executive director of Australians for Constitutional Monarchy, a body formed in Sydney in 1992. McKenna's work is particularly enlightening insofar as he gives a history of republicanism in Australia within a context of widespread popular support for the monarchy. On the whole, however, and despite its fundamental place in Australian civic attitudes since 1788, historians have been much more interested in movements for ending the monarchy than they have been in the institution itself.

In 1999 Australians had the chance in a constitutional referendum to reject the monarchy and adopt a republic. A president appointed by parliament did not seem to most an adequate replacement for the Queen and the proposal was defeated, with 55 per cent voting No.

ALAN ATKINSON

Monash, John (1865–1931), soldier and administrator, was born in West Melbourne of German Jewish parents. His was a somewhat turbulent childhood in which he knew both moderate wealth and poverty. His final schooling was at Scotch College whence he matriculated at the age of 14; he retained a lifelong affection for the school. Despite a prodi-

gious intellectual capacity, he did not triumph at the University of Melbourne. His mother's long illness and early death in 1885 seriously unsettled him, although he graduated eventually with degrees in engineering, law, and arts.

Monash's early years in business, engineering, and the construction industries were influenced by what he termed his 'cursed bad luck', and again he endured alternately modest wealth and substantial debt. But hard work, extraordinary energy, and an eagerness to strike out in new directions repaired his fortunes and by the time World War I broke out, Monash was a Melbourne man of substantial means.

It was at university that Monash had first determined to combine a career in engineering with the profession of arms. Although his rise in part-time soldiering was by no means spectacular, Monash made his way and seemed to enjoy the military environment. He was not one of the first officers chosen for appointment to the Australian Imperial Force but in September 1914 he was given command of the 4th Infantry Brigade and sailed with the Second Contingent on 22 December 1914. His strength as a soldier was in training and in the minute preparation of his troops for battle. All the skills that he had developed in business and science supported him, and he shone in the company of generals whose previous experience gave no such rigorous schooling in problem-solving. For all that, Monash was not a loved general, either by the troops or by his peers. **Bridges** or **Birdwood** moved among their men, seeking to inspire them; Monash worked at his battles, seeking to prevent the carnage which had become synonymous with the Western Front.

Landing at **Gallipoli** on 26 April 1915 with his 4th Brigade, Monash's reputation suffered from the bungled attack on Sari Bair and Hill 971. His men lost their way in the gullies, and Monash took to heart the lessons of inadequate preparation. Yet his brigade performed at least as well as any other, and Charles **Bean's** assessment that Monash would 'command a division better than a brigade and a corps better than a division', though unkind, would be proved correct in France. It must not be forgotten that Monash laboured under the double disadvantage of Jewish and German ancestry.

In July 1916, promoted major-general, Monash was given command of the 3rd Division then training on Salisbury Plain. He developed the new division to a high pitch of readiness, indeed it is likely that no Australian division had ever been better prepared for battle. Monash and his division made their mark at Messines in 1917, at Broodseinde and at Polygon Wood, but no general on the Western Front could escape criticism and Monash's career showed that he developed skills on the job. By 1918 as corps commander—an appointment strenuously and unfortunately contested by Bean and Keith **Murdoch**—Monash brought all his considerable intelligence and military skill into play. Perhaps still remote from the frontline troops, nevertheless Monash saw his job as devising ways of attacking the enemy without squandering lives and causing huge casualties. He was ambitious and aggressive; if he drove the corps too hard, he and they were also magnificently successful. His period in command was, without any doubt, the AIF's finest hour.

A self-promoter, Monash wrote *The Australian Victories in France* (1920), his only substantial book, in a month following the cessation of fighting. Curiously, Bean does not refer to this account in the official history. Monash returned with his men, whom he had done so much to bring home quickly, expecting a hero's welcome. But in many senses the 1920s was not the decade of the returned man that some have assumed it to be; Monash could not translate his supreme authority and achievement at war to civilian Australia. He became general manager of the State Electricity Commission of Victoria, overseeing the introduction of brown coal generation in the LaTrobe Valley—important work in the industrialisation of Australia but not perhaps what Monash might have expected.

He was busy for his remaining years, but became an early example of how poorly Australians find work and meaning for their greatest citizens. When the Prince of Wales arrived in Melbourne in 1920 as part of an Empire-wide tour to honour the people's commitment to war, Monash watched proceedings from among the crowd in Swanston Street. The snub set the pattern for his remaining years. Extraordinary ability, determination, and extreme hard work had taken John Monash to pre-eminence in Australia. But his background and a perception that he was ambitious and self-seeking denied him the affection or advancement of those who called the shots. Geoffrey **Serle's** *John Monash* (1982) is the definitive biography.

MICHAEL MCKERNAN

Moncrieff, Gladys Lillian (1892–1976) gained immense popularity in Australia and NZ in musical comedy and Gilbert and Sullivan opera. Her ability to generate warmth and enthusiasm from her capacity audiences was developed as a teenager in Qld, performing popular songs, ballads, and Gilbert and Sullivan in a touring family road show. From 1912 she honed her repertoire of popular operetta with J.C. **Williamson's**, achieving Australia-wide success in the title role of *The Maid of the Mountains*. Her voice was a light and flexible soprano, which could develop a rich, warm tone complemented by excellent diction. In 1938 she was seriously injured in a car accident, and it was reported in the *Australian Musical News* that 'an almost personal sense of anxiety which only the well-beloved can inspire was felt ... not since Nellie **Stewart** has any musical stage favourite established so warm a regard'. 'Our Glad', as she was popularly known, returned to the stage in 1940, and consolidated her hold on the popular imagination with wartime concerts at home and for troops in the Pacific. In 1951 she again entertained troops in Japan and Korea, but retired from singing while on tour in NZ in 1959. She published her memoirs in 1971 as *My Life of Song*.

WARREN BOURNE

Monk, Albert Ernest (1900–75) was a leading figure in the trade union movement. By 1939 he held its 'triple

crown'—simultaneous presidencies of the **Australian Council of Trade Unions**, the Victorian branch of the **Australian Labor Party**, and the Melbourne Trades Hall Council—a situation which he reportedly said he 'wouldn't wish on my worst enemy'. Monk, whose family emigrated to Australia from England in 1910, began his trade union career as a clerk for the Transport Workers Union. During the Depression he was secretary of the organisation established by the Trades Hall Council to help the unemployed, a position which frequently brought him into conflict, sometimes physical, with members of a rival communist organisation. He saw that Australian trade unions needed to develop a more international outlook, especially towards South-East Asia, and be involved with the 'great problems of our time'. To this end he cooperated with the Menzies government in the 1950s and became a member of the governing body of the International Labor Organization and of the executive of the International Confederation of Free Trade Unions. His support for postwar **immigration** was important to the policy's success.

KT

Montez, Lola (1818–61), born Maria Dolores Eliza Rosanna Gilbert in Limerick, Ireland, toured Australia as a dancer in 1855–56. Her elopement in 1837 was the first in a long series of romantic entanglements for which she became notorious. After training as a dancer in Spain she returned to England as Donna Lola Montez, to be hissed off the stage for her immorality. She fled to Europe and became the mistress, at various times, of Franz Lizst, Alexandre Dumas, and King Ludwig of Bavaria. It was on a tour of the California goldfields that she developed the notoriously provocative 'Spider Dance', which was a feature of her Australian tour. After seasons in Sydney, Melbourne, and Adelaide, Montez took her show to Ballarat. She responded to a critical article in the *Ballarat Times* by horsewhipping the editor, Henry Seekamp, who retaliated in kind. Raymond A. Bradfield's *Lola Montez and Castlemaine* (1980) includes a colourful account of her time on the goldfields. Her notoriety spawned other accounts, including Doris Foley, *The Divine Eccentric* (1969), a musical in 1958, and Bruce Seymour, *Lola Montez: A Life* (1996).

KT

Monuments are the public memorials of past people, movements, and events. They are significant to the historian in conveying something both of their subjects, and of their makers; of those commemorated and of changing attitudes towards the act of commemoration itself.

To the first British colonists Australia was, as Barron **Field** observed, a 'land without antiquities'. Three decades after the foundation of Sydney, Field recognised only one significant monument, the small brass plaque which had recently been affixed to Cape Solander by the gentlemen of the Royal Society of New South Wales to mark the landfall of James **Cook** and Joseph **Banks**, 'the Columbus and Maecenas of their times'. Other monuments, he believed, must await future deeds of glory. In fact there were other monuments in

NSW, but it is unlikely that Field and his friends would have recognised either the antiquity, or the monumentality, of the sacred sites and rock paintings which Aborigines had created across the continent over thousands of years.

Since classical times, monuments in the form of ceremonial arches, columns, obelisks, and statues had contributed to the grandeur of cities, especially those which were sites for the display of state power. Australia was founded in an age of classical taste, and public statues were often erected as a form of civic beautification as well as homage to the colonies' notable public men. The inscriptions placed on public buildings by 'Lachlan **Macquarie**, Governor' were a discreet way of claiming the admiration of posterity for both the edifices themselves and their author. But it was not until the 1830s, under the liberal regime of Governor Richard **Bourke**, that the creation of a public sphere of free institutions was given tangible expression in the impressive buildings and monuments around Sydney's Domain and Hyde Park. In 1842 George **Gipps** dedicated a public statue of Bourke in a speech which highlighted the combination of patriotic, educational, and aesthetic motives which had moved the people of NSW to contribute to its erection.

Statues were seen as aids to the **hero**-worship which patriots hoped to instil among Australia's youth. In 1879, as he unveiled a statue of Captain Cook, the governor of NSW, Sir Hercules Robinson, reflected that 'many a child in the future will learn at the foot of this statue how a faithful, patient attention to the details of daily duty … will bring its own reward'. He was speaking on the threshold of what was to be the heroic age of Australian public monuments: over the next half-century, hundreds of public monuments were erected in Australia's cities. Memorial statues, cairns, and plaques commemorated the **foundation** of the various colonies: the most notable is the statue of Colonel **Light**, first erected in 1905 at Victoria Square and moved in 1938 to a site overlooking Adelaide from the parkland he planned. All the capitals honoured Queen Victoria with public statues: Sydney in 1888; Adelaide in 1894; Melbourne, belatedly but most magnificently, in 1907. Scots erected statues of Robbie Burns, Irishmen of Daniel O'Connell. When NSW sent a contingent to help British troops avenge the death of General Gordon in Khartoum in 1885, the Victorians, whose similar offer of troops was turned down, demonstrated their patriotism by erecting a statue of the dead hero (1889). Glorious death was an irresistible subject for statuary, most strikingly expressed in Charles Summers's statue of **Burke** and Wills, erected in Melbourne in 1865.

In the early twentieth century Australian patriots, led by schoolteachers and amateur historians, erected monuments in places associated with the early history of Australian discovery and **exploration**. Tablets and cairns now mark the routes of **Hume and Hovell**, **Mitchell**, **Sturt**, and **Strzelecki**, and the landing places of **Tasman**, **Cook**, **Flinders**, and other notable explorers. Their austere non-representational form indicated a subtle shift from the heroic character of the explorers to the deed of exploration itself, from venerating the mighty dead to historicising the landscape they traversed, although the mammoth statue of Strzelecki overlooking Lake Jindabyne, erected by the Polish government in 1986, is a striking exception.

The enormous outpouring of grief and admiration elicited by the slaughter of young Australians in World War I demanded a fitting monumental response. Yet, the manner of their dying was often more tragic than glorious. They gave their lives in a vain assault on the heights of **Gallipoli** or bogged down in the trenches of the Western Front; they were buried in graveyards far from the homes of those who mourned them. Australian **war memorials**, Ken **Inglis** suggests in *ACH* (1987), were shaped in part by the need to accommodate acts of mourning which distance had denied to those who had sacrificed their husbands, sons, and brothers. Every **Anzac Day**, in towns and cities across Australia, their countrymen paid tribute at the foot of a local monument: sometimes a simple obelisk; sometimes, as at Yackandandah, Victoria, a memorial garden; but often and most memorably, a small marble statue of a Digger, head bowed, arms reversed, and standing to attention. This was a democratic kind of monument: like Charles **Bean's** war histories it honoured the citizen soldier rather than the generals on horseback. Paul Montford's miniature bronze of **Simpson and his donkey** (1936) had a more lasting impact than the nearby equestrian statue of John **Monash**. The grandest Australian war memorials, such as Melbourne's Shrine of Remembrance (1934) and Canberra's **Australian War Memorial** (1941), are modelled on Greek temples, and evoke an atmosphere that is Stoic rather than Christian, funereal rather than triumphant.

In the aftermath of the war many Australians expressed a revulsion from monumental architecture. 'By building temples of memory they were perpetuating sentiments of enmity and strife', one observer of Sydney's War Memorial (1934) suggested. Aesthetic functionalism reinforced a growing preference for useful memorials, such as public halls, hospitals and swimming pools, over grand but useless statues. During the 1930s the Pioneer Women of Victoria and SA were honoured by the dedication of memorial gardens, while Victoria's tribute to the dead servicemen of World War II assumed the modest form of a ceremonial forecourt to the Shrine of Remembrance, rather than another granite temple. By the time Australians at last honoured the veterans of the **Vietnam War**, it seemed as though the age of monuments, like the age of heroes, was all but dead. Like its famous American counterpart, Canberra's Vietnam War Memorial is notable for the almost total absence of figurative or iconographic content.

By the 1980s the nation's attention had returned to the memory of battlefields closer to home. In 1883 local protector of Aborigines James Dawson had erected a headstone over the grave of the local Aboriginal chief, Wombeetch Puuyuun, in Camperdown, Victoria. Such monuments were unusual in the colonial period; occasional references to the unnamed Aboriginal killers of white pastoralists or to their 'faithful' Aboriginal guides were the only monuments to the intermittent warfare between white and black. As Chilla Bulbeck has shown (*AHS*, 1991), one aspect of the historical rediscovery of the Aboriginal past was a movement, from the 1980s onwards, to conserve such marks of the Aboriginal presence as canoe trees and fish traps, to build new monuments commemorating its unmarked battlefields, and to correct the errors inscribed on some old ones. A proposal in 1978 to erect a statue in Perth to honour the Aboriginal leader **Yagan** polarised local historical opinion. A decade later historians from Murdoch University led a campaign to correct the interpretation in a local monument to white settlers killed by 'treacherous' Aborigines. Some locals proposed to demolish the old statue and erect a 'correct' new one; but the historians argued successfully for a new monument which would stand in a critical relationship to the old.

The 1990s has brought a modest revival of monumental history. The erection of new war memorials along Canberra's Anzac Parade and of statues in honour of 'Weary' **Dunlop** in Melbourne, Benalla, and Canberra—the first erected by public subscription in honour of an individual Australian for decades—suggests that the age of heroes may not be quite dead. Yet the new monuments, which often incorporate a strong pictorial-narrative element, are subtly different from the old. They are stories in bronze or stone rather than objects of veneration.

The 1988 NSW Bicentennial Authority sponsored a useful but incomplete survey of monuments in that state, Beryl Henderson (ed.), *Monuments and Memorials* (1988), while the Australian Bicentennial Authority carried out a national study of 'unusual monuments'. The principal monuments in each city are listed in Ronald Ridley, *Melbourne's Monuments* (1996); Simon Cameron, *Silent Witnesses: Adelaide's Statues and Monuments* (1997); the National Capital Development Commission, *Works of Art in Canberra* (1980–); and the Society of Sculptors, *Brisbane Sculpture Guide* (1988).

GRAEME DAVISON

Moorehead, Alan McCrae (1910–83), was a journalist, historian, and biographer. After working on the Melbourne *Herald*, in 1936 he sailed for Europe: 'To stay at home was to condemn yourself to nonentity.' He soon found work on Lord Beaverbrook's *Daily Express* as foreign correspondent in Spain, France, and Italy, and from 1940 North Africa.

Moorehead's frank dispatches as war correspondent from there and Italy and France, backed by three books and a biography of Field Marshal Montgomery (1946), won him great fame. He was a born writer, and after the war followed a very successful literary career while living mainly in Italy, often writing for the *New Yorker*. *The White Nile* (1960), *The Blue Nile* (1962), and *Gallipoli* (1956) were perhaps the most successful of his 20 books including two novels. He enjoyed returning to Australia several times, especially to gather material for *Rum Jungle* (1953); *Cooper's Creek* (1963), an account of the **Burke** and Wills expedition; and *The Fatal Impact* (1966), which deals with the Europeans in the Pacific. His writing was of the highest quality, his historical works not scholarly

but reputable. He wrote an autobiography, *A Late Education* (1970), and Tom Pocock has written a biography (1990).

GEOFFREY SERLE

Moran, Patrick Francis (1830–1911), Catholic archbishop of Sydney and cardinal, was born in Carlow, Ireland. Orphaned at 12, he was raised by his uncle, Paul Cullen, who was rector of the Irish College, Rome. Moran was ordained in 1853 and subsequently held clerical positions in Rome and Ireland. His arrival in Australia as archbishop of Sydney in 1884 (he was a cardinal from 1885) brought a distinctly Irish character to the **Catholic Church** in NSW, and at the same time established a role for the Church in Australian public affairs. Moran remedied the previous disharmonious relations between English-born clergy and Irish laity by developing a united Australian Church, and encouraging nationalist loyalties to Australia rather than to Ireland. In promoting a peculiarly Catholic Australian **nationalism**, such as his vigorous defence of the 'Catholic' discovery of Australia in 1606 by Spanish explorer De Quiros, Moran brought church and nation closer together for the Catholic population. He oversaw an extensive building program, which included the establishment of St Patrick's Seminary at Manly, and in 1900 headed the First Australasian Catholic Congress.

While he supported **Federation**, he aroused a Protestant storm when he stood as a candidate at the Federal Convention, which ensured his defeat. He did not attend the inaugural celebrations in 1901 because the Anglican archbishop was given precedence over him, even though he was a cardinal. Moran's desire to integrate Catholics into Australian society is reflected in his major historical work, *The History of the Catholic Church in Australasia* (1895), which, although comprehensive, was criticised for its unscholarly approach and overly triumphal note.

HD

Morant, Harry Harbord 'Breaker' (?1864–1902) was court-martialled and executed in February 1902 for killing prisoners during the **Boer War**. His origins are hazy; he claimed to have been born in Devon, son of Admiral Sir Digby Morant; however, Margaret Carnegie and Frank Shields, *In Search of Breaker Morant* (1979), indicate that he was Edwin Henry Murrant of Somerset who landed in Townsville, Qld, in 1883. He worked in a travelling rodeo which took him to Charters Towers, where he married the woman who would become widely known as Daisy **Bates**. After only a few weeks Morant resumed his wandering life of droving and horse-breaking; it was his skill with horses that earned him the nickname 'The Breaker'. This was the name with which he signed his first published poem, 'A Night Thought' (*Bulletin*, 1891). About 60 more of his poems were published in the *Bulletin* in the ensuing years, including one written on the eve of his execution, 'Butchered to Make a Dutchman's Holiday'. A collection of these was published in 1980.

Although his execution caused a dispute about British authority over Australian troops, Morant was not immediately accorded his later semi-heroic status. At the time of his death, he was condemned by the Australian press. The colourful image of an independent, laconic bushman crushed by English wrong-headedness took decades to develop. The view espoused by one of his fellow prisoners, George Witton, in *Scapegoats of the Empire* (1907), was developed in Kit Denton's romantic novel *The Breaker* (1973), upon which was based the 1980 film, *Breaker Morant*. Denton's later account of the Morant case based on official records, *Closed File* (1983), is a more critical view of the man.

KT

Moratorium refers to the mass public demonstrations against Australia's involvement in the **Vietnam War**. Australian opposition to US military action in Vietnam was evident in October 1966, when US President Lyndon Johnson was met by angry protesters on his visit to Australia. Opponents were initially regarded with suspicion, but support grew. Public demonstrations opposed the **conscription** of Australian men to a war that was regarded increasingly as unwinnable and immoral, and condemned the lottery method of selecting conscripts as the 'blood ballot' or the 'lottery of death'.

The anti-war movement gathered strength as part of a wave of social protest in the late 1960s. In an effort to establish a broader constituency, the Moratorium movement was created by representatives of the peace movement, women's groups such as Save Our Sons, and campus radicals. Jim **Cairns** was the chair of the Melbourne organising committee and the leading national figure. The first Moratorium, held in May 1970, attracted hundreds of thousands in the capital cities and, despite predictions of violence from federal and state governments, was remarkably peaceful. Later Moratorium marches drew smaller numbers, but affirmed the growing anti-war sentiment. Following his election as prime minister in 1972, Gough **Whitlam** authorised the release of those imprisoned for defying conscription. The Moratorium movement is discussed by Greg Langley in *A Decade of Dissent* (1992).

HD

Moreton Bay lies at the mouth of the Brisbane River in southern **Queensland**, and was the name of the penal settlement established there in 1824 which lasted until 1842. Until the separation of Qld from NSW in 1859, the whole of the region was known as the Moreton Bay District, and the same name was bestowed on local trees, birds, oysters, and crustaceans. Its primary connection with the penal colony under the command of the notorious Captain **Logan**, from 1826 until his violent death in 1830, gives it sombre associations.

SM

Morgan, Sally (1951–   ), artist and writer, was born and lives in Perth. Morgan gained a national and an international reputation with the publication of her autobiographical work, *My Place* (1987). In it she uses her own voice and those of her mother, great-uncle, and grandmother to tell the story of her search for her origins and discovery of her family's Aboriginal history. The book was by far the most successful of writings that sought to reclaim and reflect upon

an indigenous identity. Criticism of its authorial identity by Bain Attwood in *AHS* (1992) stimulated further discussion in the following issue of that journal.

Since *My Place*, Morgan has published *Wanamurraganya: The Story of Jack McPhee* (1989) and three children's books: *The Flying Emu and Other Australian Stories* (1992) and *Pet Problem* (1994), both with indigenous cultural significance; and *Hurry Up, Oscar!* (1993). Painting is Morgan's primary creative activity, and her work is held in many of the major galleries in Australia. Using a silkscreen process, and forms and colours as well as stories derived from her Aboriginal country and people, Morgan produces striking art works that are enmeshed in indigenous politics. An arts activist, Morgan speaks against the economic and cultural exploitation of Aboriginal artefacts and artists and for ownership by Aboriginal artists and groups both of their own work and of their cultural heritage. In 1997 she was appointed professor and director of a new Centre for Indigenous History and the Arts at the University of Western Australia.

Delys Bird

Morrison, George Ernest 'Chinese' (1862–1920) began his journalistic career with the Melbourne *Age*, reporting on New Guinea, after he failed his medical studies at the University of Melbourne. He eventually qualified at Edinburgh in 1887, after which he continued his travels, which included a monumental walk in 1894 from Shanghai to Rangoon. His story of that experience, *An Australian in China* (1895), and his accurate and often prescient reports on events in the troubled area, led to his appointment with *The Times* as permanent correspondent in Peking. He resigned in 1912 to become adviser to the new Chinese government. His colourful life has attracted several biographers, including Frank **Clune** (1941) and Cyril **Pearl** (1967). His correspondence, edited by Lo Hui-Min, was published 1976–78. In Australia he is commemorated by the Morrison lectures on China at the Australian National University.

KT

Morrison, (Philip) Crosbie (1900–58) worked as reporter for the Melbourne *Argus* after graduating in science from the University of Melbourne. He contributed enormously to public understanding of natural history issues as editor of *Wildlife* magazine (1938–54), and through his radio series of the same name. He organised natural history lectures and was very involved in the development of Victoria's national parks. His contribution was recognised in 1947 when he was awarded the Australian National History medallion. A fellow natural historian, Graham Pizzey, produced a biography of Morrison in 1992.

KT

Morshead, Leslie James (1889–1959), army general, distinguished himself in World War I at **Gallipoli** and in France. He remained in the **CMF** after the war and, at the outbreak of World War II, was chosen to command the 18th Brigade. When the command of the 9th Division became vacant, Morshead was appointed and went with the division to Libya where, under strong German attack, it withdrew to Tobruk and he became fortress commander. Known to his troops as 'Ming the Merciless' and jeered at as 'Ali Baba Morshead and his 20 000 thieves' in Axis propaganda, Morshead developed a policy of active defence that included frequent night patrols. His leadership during the siege made him one of the best-known and admired of the Australian commanders. After they were eventually relieved, Morshead and the 9th Division took part in the battles for El Alamein before their return to Australia. He was soon appointed commander of the Second AIF and went on to command the troops training for an assault on Borneo, which he led. He retired from the army after the war but was called upon in 1957 by the **Menzies** government to head what became known as the Morshead committee of inquiry into the defence departments. A biography by John Moore appeared in 1976.

KT

Mort, Thomas Sutcliffe (1816–78), entrepreneur and refrigeration pioneer, was born at Bolton in Lancashire, England. He migrated to NSW in 1838 and established a system of regular **wool** auctions in Sydney in 1843, then moved into London consignments, the stock and station agency business, railway promotion, mining, and sugar-growing. Successful pastoral investments in the 1850s financed his development of an extensive model **dairy** farm at Bodalla, NSW, where he also experimented with cotton and silk cultivation. He converted a cottage into a neo-Gothic mansion, Greenoakes, at Darling Point, Sydney, and indulged passions for art, antiques, and horticulture. In 1855 he established Mort's dry dock at Balmain, and progressed from shipbuilding to locomotive manufacture and general engineering. The business became Mort's Dock and Engineering Company in 1872 and **Goldsbrough**, Mort & Co. in 1888. It experimented with profit-sharing in the early 1870s, but like Bodalla, Mort's Dock was overcapitalised and struggled to survive. Mort, the patriarch, interfered excessively. Between 1866 and 1878 he backed refrigeration experiments by Eugene Nicolle and incorporated his systems in the NSW Fresh Food & Ice Company. Mort spent over £100 000 and died before a successful overseas shipment of refrigerated Australian meat, but he saw the process proved locally.

Alan Barnard noted in *Visions and Profits* (1961) that Mort's major schemes were economically unjustified and that he 'grossly underestimated' development costs for ventures which proceeded more by accident than design. Barnard suggested Mort's Anglican ethics encouraged him to subordinate profit to loftier ideals of community service and creation of lasting enterprise. Mort remains a complex and little-understood character—perhaps a 'wise steward', but also a speculator who accumulated vast personal wealth and status, and whose image as a far-sighted industrial pioneer must be balanced with that of a dreamer and dabbler in Gothic follies of his day.

DC

Mosquito was a name by which at least two Aboriginal men were known. The most prominent of these was a Kuring-gai from NSW who was sent to **Norfolk Island** in 1805, probably as punishment for having resisted the advance of white settlement along the Hawkesbury River. Ten years later he was sent to Van Diemen's Land, where he received a ticket-of-leave and apparently worked as a stockman. In 1817 he was commended by Lieutenant-Governor Sorrell for his help in tracking down bushrangers. Some time around 1820 he joined the Oyster Bay people in resisting expulsion from their land and led raids on outlying farms. A reward was offered for his capture and he was executed in 1825.

Mosquito was also the name given to one of the men in the Aboriginal cricket team that toured England in 1868. He probably came from the Western District of Victoria, and his traditional name was recorded as Grongarrong. The account of the tour by John **Mulvaney**, *Cricket Walkabout* (1967; revised in conjunction with Rex Harcourt, 1988), contains the known details of his cricketing exploits and later life.

KT

Motor car manufacture established an important Australian industry and transformed the Australian way of life. Though the first models were assembled overseas in the 1890s, automobiles were not imported from the USA and Europe until the 1910s and 1920s, when they were strictly the preserve of the wealthy. The Ford company established an assembly plant at Geelong in 1926, where in 1934, local engineer Lew Bandt invented the 'ute' (utility), which he designed specifically for the needs of rural Australians. As a Commonwealth government initiative, 20 hectares of Crown land at Fishermens Bend, near Port Melbourne, was granted to General Motors–Holden Ltd in 1935 to establish a car manufacturing plant. The first **Holden** was produced there in 1948. Laurence Hartnett, former managing director of GMH, relates the fortunes of the plan to build an Australian car in *Big Wheels and Little Wheels* (1964). Volkswagen, Plymouth, and later Nissan and Toyota also established Australian manufacturing or assembly plants. Since the 1980s, Australian car manufacture has been increasingly integrated into the global manufacturing strategies of multinational companies.

From the 1920s onwards Australians achieved higher levels of car ownership than any nationality except Americans and Canadians, a social and political transformation perceptively explored by John Knott (*AHS* 1994, 2000). Surveys during World War II showed that, next to a house, a family car was high in Australian families' postwar priorities, as R.G. **Menzies** shrewdly recognised in his 1949 election promise to abolish petrol rationing. Cars were still expensive and in short supply until the mid-1950s, when a Holden cost £1000, or twice a workingman's annual income. Ten years later it cost £1200, but average incomes had quadrupled. In 1950 only about one Australian in eight owned a car; by the mid-1950s it was one in five, and by the early 1960s one in three. Until the late 1960s the family car and the male driver were the norm, but by the early 1970s the proportion of female drivers was rising quickly. The early postwar years were a dangerous time on Australian roads: the risk of death and injury was higher in the early 1950s than ever before or since. While strong in their desire to own a car, Australians have been readier than some other high car-owning nations to accept safety regulations, such as compulsory seat-belts and compulsory alcohol breath-testing.

Motor cars and motor trucks transformed postwar Australia. They freed industry from the old patterns of centralised location based on rail and coal. They enabled the **suburbs** to sprawl, filling the wedges of open country between the tentacles of rail with new car-based commuter suburbs ('Kingswood Country'). They created new forms of leisure, car-racing and drive-in picture theatres; new forms of holidaying, caravans and motels; new forms of shopping, drive-in bottle-shops and car-based shopping-towns; and new social rituals, the Sunday drive and the teenage drag race. Cars also created a new politics, as motorists were mobilised to resist higher fuel taxes and to campaign for better roads, a movement which culminated in the early 1970s in the conflicts between the road lobby and environmentalists over the introduction of metropolitan freeway systems in Sydney and Melbourne. Enthusiasts have written evocative histories of some famous Australian cars, such as the FJ Holden and the Ford Falcon. Susan Priestley, *The Crown of the Road* (1983), and Rosemary Broomham, *On the Road* (1996), examine the history of two leading motoring organisations, the RACV and the NRMA. Ian Manning, *The Open Street* (1991), examines the political economy of motoring, while Charles Pickett (ed.), *Cars and Culture* (1998), approaches the still largely unwritten cultural history of the car.

GRAEME DAVISON

Mount Rennie rape was a crime committed in Sydney in 1886. Mary Jane Hicks, aged 16, was picked up in town by a cab-driver, Charles Sweetman, and driven to Mount Rennie, near Moore Park, Sydney, where he assaulted her. She was then 'rescued' by some young men who, joined by several others, committed serial rape. A large-scale police search led to the arrest of 15 men; 11 were subsequently tried for criminal assault. After unusually lengthy proceedings before Judge William **Windeyer**, and a stormy press coverage, nine of the youths were sentenced to death. However, fierce public opposition put pressure on the state government to commute the sentences of five of the men. The remaining four, Duffy, Martin, Read, and Boyce, were executed on 8 January 1887. The case is examined by Frank **Clune** in *Scandals of Sydney Town: The Mount Rennie Case* (1957) and by Michael and Anne Tuffley in *The Mount Rennie Gang* (1989). David Walker, in his article 'Youth on Trial', *LH* (1986), examines the debate on colonial youth which the crime and trial sparked off, while a more recent feminist analysis by Juliet Peers, *ACH* (1993), examines the impact of the crime on the victim.

HD

Mountford, Charles Pearcy (1890–1970) became a prominent ethnologist without any formal training. His first contact with the Aborigines of Central Australia as a post-office mechanic in the 1920s sparked a lifelong interest in their culture. From 1938 he frequently led expeditions into the inland, mainly from the University of Adelaide. He produced numerous books on Aboriginal art and culture—often illustrated with his own photographs—including *Brown Men and Red Sand* (1948), *The Tiwi* (1958), *Ayers Rock* (1965), and a series illustrated by Ainslie Roberts, collectively published in 1973 as *The Dreamtime Book*. He also produced two films. In later life he graduated from Cambridge and the University of Adelaide; the latter institution recognised his contribution to the field with an honorary doctorate, as did the University of Melbourne. A biography, *Monty*, by Max Lamshed appeared in 1972.

KT

Movement, the was a secret **Catholic** political organisation founded in 1939 by Daniel **Mannix**, the archbishop of Melbourne, and administered by B.A. **Santamaria**. Known in full as the Catholic Social Studies Movement, it encouraged lay involvement in church life but was chiefly concerned with combating the growth of **communism** in Australia. The Movement formed industrial Groups within the **trade unions** in the 1940s and 1950s. It flourished particularly in Melbourne under the influence of Mannix, but H.V. **Evatt**, the leader of the federal Labor Party, became an opponent. Through the success of industrial Groups in unions affiliated to the Australian Labor Party, the Movement gained control of the Victorian Labor executive in the early 1950s. The bitter struggle for power played out, most dramatically in Victoria, between the Catholic and communist factions of the Australian Labor Party, led to the Labor **Split** of 1955 and the formation of the **Democratic Labor Party**.

HD

Moyal, Ann (1926–   ), historian of science, studied history at the University of Sydney. Following a period of postgraduate study in England she worked as a research assistant, notably for the newspaper magnate, Lord Beaverbrook, as he wrote *Men and Power*, about World War I. At the invitation of Keith **Hancock** at the Australian National University, she returned to Australia (as Ann Mozley) to help establish the *ADB*. Her frank autobiography, *Breakfast with Beaverbrook* (1995), provides a detailed account of these early days of the *ADB*, in particular the turbulent impact of Malcolm **Ellis**. During this time she also worked on Earle **Page's** autobiography.

Moyal left the *ADB* in 1962 to move into 'a new career in the history of Australian science'. She compiled the bibliography *A Guide to the Manuscript Records of Australian Science* (1966), wrote *Scientists in Nineteenth-Century Australia* (1976), then returned to take up a teaching position at the New South Wales Institute of Technology (later University of Technology, Sydney). After completing a study of atomic energy in Australia (1977), Moyal became director of the Science Policy

Research Centre at Griffith University. Her resignation after a critical finding by a disciplinary review became an academic *cause célèbre*. She then returned to freelance research to produce *Clear Across Australia* (1984), a history of telecommunications, and became honorary editor of the journal of the **Australian and New Zealand Association for the Advancement of Science**. She developed her work on colonial scientists in *A Bright and Savage Land* (1986). Moyal is now a leading member of the Association of Independent Scholars.

KT

Mudie, James (1779–1852) was a leading antagonist of Governor **Bourke** and the author of a scathing account of the colony under his administration. He had a shady past in Britain in the marines and as a promoter of a scheme to issue medals in commemoration of the Napoleonic wars. He arrived in 1822 and was given a land grant in the Hunter Valley. The free settlers in this area were the leading opponents of Bourke's liberalism and his favouring of the **emancipist** cause. They attempted to discredit him by claiming that his limitations on magistrates' powers had undermined **convict** discipline. In the midst of this controversy, six convicts on Mudie's property rebelled and attempted to shoot the overseer, claiming that they had been starved and repeatedly flogged. Bourke's supporters could now depict Mudie as a tyrant. Mudie was outraged when the governor ordered an inquiry into the running of his property as the rebels had called for at their trial. The inquiry gave Mudie a grudging exoneration, which the governor refused to publish. Mudie published it himself and went to London to seek the governor's recall. There he published *The Felonry of New South Wales* (1837), which mocked the attempt to apply liberal principles to the government of convicts and ex-convicts, a group for whom Mudie coined the term *felonry*. This approach confirmed his reputation for harshness, which most historians have endorsed, overlooking the contrary evidence collected by the inquiry into the running of his property. His book shows him as a close and not unsympathetic observer of the convicts, with a good ear for their talk.

JH

Mudrooroo (Colin Johnson), see **Aboriginal narratives**

Mueller, Ferdinand Jakob Heinrich (von) (1825–96), botanist, was born Ferdinand Müller in Rostock, Mecklenburg, Germany, and arrived in SA with his two sisters in 1847. Although he had trained as a pharmacist, his botanical knowledge so impressed Victorian Governor **La Trobe** that Müller was appointed government botanist for that colony in 1853; in 1857 he became director of the Melbourne Botanic Gardens. Mueller (as he then became) was a formidable correspondent, and supplied vast quantities of plants and seeds to public gardens and individuals throughout the colonies and overseas. His exchange of plant specimens led to the widespread plantation of Australian species—for example, of Blue Gum in California and Italy. In addition to acclimatising exotic species, Mueller contributed significantly to the study of Australian flora; his research provided the basis for the publication of George Bentham's *Flora Australiensis* (1863–78).

The Mueller Correspondence Project, based at the University of Melbourne, forms the basis of a forthcoming biography and published *Regardfully Yours* (1998), a selection of his correspondence.

HD

Multiculturalism, as word and idea, has inspired much discussion and debate, confusion and heat, over the past 25 years. The term was taken from Canada, where, as a counter to French Canadian demands for the official recognition of Canada's cultural dualism, the federal government in 1971 declared a policy of multiculturalism that recognised the desire among all groups bound by common ethnic origins to preserve their linguistic and cultural heritage. In Australia multiculturalism was enlisted, not to contain ethnic division, but to recognise ethnic diversity.

The **Whitlam** Labor government's minister for immigration, Al Grassby, invoked multiculturalism in 1973, as both a simple descriptor of Australian ethnic diversity, and a valued social ideal. His attempt to win positive acknowledgment of the changes resulting from the postwar **immigration** program led him to attack what he called 'a conspiracy of silence'. Challenging the notion that there was a single Australian way of life, Grassby argued that Australia was a mosaic of cultures. Multiculturalism thus displaced the earlier official policy of **assimilation**, which since 1945 had described, more as an act of faith, the absorption of European immigrants into a British Australia. Both assimilation and multiculturalism were settlement ideologies developed to manage the consequences of postwar immigration, rather than sociological terms or analytical tools for describing change and investigating processes of adaptation.

The Whitlam government had embraced multiculturalism as part of Labor's clean break from the Liberal–Country Party's lingering identification with an Anglo-Australian monoculture. Returning to power in 1975, the conservative coalition adopted the policy of multiculturalism and conducted a Review of Migrant Services (under chairman Frank Galbally QC). The Galbally Report (1978) supported existing services, such as the Telephone Interpreter Service and the Special Broadcasting Service, and recommended others, including the establishment of the Australian Institute of Multicultural Affairs (which was succeeded by the Office of Multicultural Affairs in 1987). Multiculturalism became a policy for delivering services to migrant constituencies.

Nevertheless, scepticism mounted. Critics on the left argued that the policy disguised serious social inequities, and that migrant access to mainstream services, such as education and welfare, remained unequal. The **Hawke** Labor government, committed to achieving greater social justice for migrants, required government agencies to recognise and respond to the diverse ethnic backgrounds of their clientele.

Critics on the right, notably Lauchlan Chipman in *Quadrant* (1978, 1980) and Frank **Knopfelmacher** (in Robert Manne, ed., *The New Conservatism in Australia*, 1982), argued that multiculturalism blocked immigrant integration into mainstream Australian life. Others, like historian Geoffrey **Blainey**, saw in multiculturalism, not the promise of a cosy cosmopolitanism, but a threat of national fragmentation. The debate over multiculturalism suddenly became public, populist, and polarised. Opponents saw multiculturalism not as a benign attempt to encourage tolerance in an ethnically diverse society and to ensure the equitable provision of services, but as a policy deliberately aimed at diversifying the migrant intake and championing ethnic separatism. Migrants had always been expected to 'leave their troubles at home'; multiculturalism seemed, in the context of ethnic and religious conflicts overseas, to threaten to entrench cultural differences which might create a fertile breeding-ground for social strife.

The report (1988) of the Committee to Advise on Australia's Immigration Policies, chaired by Dr Stephen FitzGerald, acknowledged that 'the idea of Australia as a country of immigration' was imperilled by community confusion, faltering public support, and collapsing consensus. The original ideals of multiculturalism ('justice, equality and esteem') had become obscured by a multiplicity of meanings. The report suggested that the term *multiculturalism* be abandoned.

When John **Howard** declared himself in favour of replacing the policy of multiculturalism with the idea of 'One Australia', and slowing Asian immigration in the interests of 'social cohesion', his perceived abandonment of a racially non-discriminatory immigration policy cost him the Liberal and Opposition leadership. In 1989 the Advisory Council on Multicultural Affairs, under Sir James Gobbo, produced a carefully worded *National Agenda for a Multicultural Australia*. The statement guaranteed cultural rights and social justice to all Australians, 'whether [of] Aboriginal, Anglo-Celtic or non-English-speaking background' and wherever they were born, subject to 'an overriding and unifying commitment to Australia'. This even-handed approach was not maintained by the **Keating** Labor government (1991–96). The prime minister certainly projected multicultural Australia as resource-rich in its ethnic and linguistic diversity, assets vital to Australian prospects in a sophisticated regional and global economy. But Keating's devaluing of Anglo-Australia and of the links with Britain rankled with sections of the British-descended majority. There was also mounting criticism of the patterns of patronage in multicultural programs.

The Howard government abolished the Office of Multicultural Affairs and the Bureau of Immigration, Multicultural and Population Research. Such policy reversals, together with the prime minister's declaration 'I'm a one-nation man', encouraged resurgent right-wing racism, notably the campaign by Independent MHR Pauline Hanson against 'Asian' immigration and in favour of 'One Nation'. Certainly the inclusivist language of cultural pluralism was swiftly replaced by rhetoric stressing national homogeneity.

Ann-Mari Jordens (*Redefining Australians*, 1995) concluded that 'Bipartisan consensus since [1975] has made multiculturalism an issue which produces unity rather than division.' But few other analysts of immigration and settlement policies regard multiculturalism as non-problematic and doubts mount to divide even those most disposed to be sympathetic to the ideals of the policy: to accord dignity to all Australians whatever their cultural backgrounds; to achieve harmony, tolerance and inclusiveness; and to respond in practical ways to the needs of migrants. Some of the most penetrating critiques of multiculturalism have come from the Centre for Multicultural Studies at the University of Wollongong (*Mistaken Identity: Multiculturalism and the Demise of Nationalism in Australia*, 1988). Stephen Castles, director of the centre, continues to identify the philosophical tensions and contradictions in multiculturalism, but argues (in Gary Freeman and James Jupp, eds, *Nations of Immigrants*, 1992) that it remains probably the best possible formula for managing Australia's cultural diversity. For James Jupp, Director of the ANU Centre for Immigration and Multicultural Studies, who believes that ethno-cultural variety will persist, the 'most desirable national identities … combine democratic and egalitarian principles with multicultural and cosmopolitan outlooks' ('Identity' in Richard Nile (ed.), *Australian Civilisation*, 1994). Critics of multiculturalism, however, consider that a policy which has no commonly understood meaning, and which has never enjoyed widespread public support, cannot be satisfactory, however laudable its aims. It is significant that the Centenary of Federation Advisory Committee chaired by Joan Kirner, searching for a formula to embrace unity and diversity, emphasised tolerance and pluralism, but avoided multiculturalism in its 1994 report: 'The motto of 1901 was: "One people, one destiny". For 2001 it must be: "Many cultures, one Australia".' James Jupp, concerned about the problems and anomalies arising from the adoption of ethnicity as a definer, argues for an ethnicity-blind policy which will seek to identify and meet the special needs of Australians, regardless of background. Nancy Viviani, in *The Indochinese in Australia 1975–1995* (1996), suggests, as more appropriate for Australia in the 1990s, an emphasis on equality and a shift to a 'substantive citizenship' under which multicultural values are best subsumed: 'Citizenship and equality can encompass the multiple identities that all Australians share.' The reconstituted National Multicultural Advisory Council, charged in 1997 with reviewing the policy and practice of multiculturalism, issued a discussion paper that canvassed dropping the term altogether.

Multiculturalism, having failed to command consistent, broad political and popular support, has become something of a rallying point for those opposing tolerance and pluralism, and may now be a serious liability to those who feel the need to prove cultural diversity compatible with national unity. The claim of Ghassan Hage (*White Nation: Fantasies of White Supremacy in a Multicultural Society*, 1998) that multiculturalism was government's response to the reality of ethnic diversity is flatly contradicted by Mark Lopez in *The Origins of Multiculturalism in Australian Politics 1945–1975*

(2000), who argues that the policy was the work of a small lobby of academics, social workers, and political activists. This seems bound to fuel suspicions that multiculturalism was foisted upon indifferent migrant communities and an unsuspecting nation.

JOHN LACK

Mulvaney, Derek John (1925–), archaeologist and historian, was foundation professor of prehistory at the Australian National University, Canberra (1971–85). He was the first university-trained prehistorian to make Australia his subject, and has revolutionised scholarly and popular understandings of the Aboriginal past.

Mulvaney completed a history honours degree and a Master's thesis on Roman Britain in Max **Crawford's** department at the University of Melbourne. He then studied **archaeology** at Cambridge, where he was inspired by Grahame Clark's global approach to prehistory, but determined to apply his training in Australia: 'I hankered after the Iron Age but knew I must return to Stone.' Mulvaney conducted his first Australian fieldwork (at Fromms Landing on the Murray River), using the sciences of stratigraphy and radiocarbon dating to illuminate what, in 1961, he called 'the dark continent of prehistory'. He championed and built upon the pioneering archaeological work of Norman **Tindale** and Frederick McCarthy. At Kenniff Cave in southern Qld in 1962, Mulvaney confirmed the Pleistocene occupation of Australia with a minimal radiocarbon date of 13 000 years, a discovery soon eclipsed by others 20 000, then 30 000 years old and more. 'No segment of the history of *Homo sapiens*', he wrote, 'had been so escalated since Darwin took time off the Mosaic standard.'

Mulvaney brought a new vision of Australian history that deepened it greatly in time, and demanded that it be cross-cultural. In the late 1950s, he wrote a pioneering survey of changing European perspectives of Aborigines (*HSANZ*, 1958), and a decade later began his book *The Prehistory of Australia* (1969) with the words: 'The discoverers, explorers and colonists of … Australia, were its Aborigines.' He rejected the paradigm of **Aborigines** as 'an unchanging people in an unchanging environment'; he placed great emphasis on Aboriginal cultural change, adaptability, and diversity, an approach also evident in *Aboriginal Man and Environment in Australia* (edited with Jack Golson, 1971) and *Australians to 1788* (ed. with J. Peter White, 1987). In his studies of culture contact, such as *Cricket Walkabout* (1967), his biography of Baldwin Spencer ('*So Much That Is New*', written with John Calaby, 1985), *Encounters in Place* (1989) and *Commandant of Solitude* (with Neville Green, 1992), and his many articles on the history of Australian anthropology, he emphasised accommodation and acculturation rather than conflict. He was keen to articulate a humanitarian tradition in Australia, a positive, moral vision of race relations, and to understand and overturn the strait-jacket of Social Darwinism that had gripped Aboriginal studies for nearly a century. He considered racism 'a fatal flaw in the Australian psyche'.

From the 1970s, Mulvaney held many public positions in the fields of heritage and environment. He was an early advocate (from the 1950s) of the conservation of Aboriginal sites; a champion of the National Museum of Australia; a vigorous critic of the proposed Franklin River Dam in Tasmania (1981–83); a defender of the First Government House site in Sydney (1983); and an opponent of the Museum of Victoria's unconditional return of ancient skeletons from Kow Swamp to the local Koori community for reburial (1990). A pioneer of scientific archaeological techniques, he firmly aligned himself with the humanities and continually argued the imaginative, language-based character of his craft.

In 1986 he wrote a brief 'Archaeological Retrospect' (*Antiquity*), and many of his essays were gathered in *Prehistory and Heritage* (1990). His *oeuvre* was directly assessed in *Archaeology in Oceania* (1986) and *Prehistory to Politics* (edited by Bonyhady and Griffiths, 1996).

TOM GRIFFITHS AND TIM BONYHADY

MumShirl (1921–98) is the better-known name of the Aboriginal social worker Shirley Colleen Smith, of Wiradjuri descent. Her work assisting Aborigines in gaol began with visits to her brother in prison in the 1940s. She subsequently visited hundreds of other Aboriginal prisoners throughout Australia and took countless needy Aboriginal children into her own home. By the 1970s MumShirl had become an important figure in the provision of Aboriginal welfare in Redfern, Sydney, where she helped set up a children's welfare agency, and helped establish Aboriginal legal and medical services. Roberta Sykes co-wrote her autobiography (1981).

HD

Mundey, Jack (1932–) environmentalist and trade union activist, was the principal leader of the **green bans** movement in Sydney, 1971–74. Mundey moved to Sydney from Qld in 1951 to play Rugby League for Parramatta and, as a manual worker, became a trade union activist. He joined the Communist Party of Australia in 1955 and was elected president of its Sydney District Committee in 1966, though he was always critical of communist regimes.

In March 1957 he joined the NSW Builders Labourers Federation and was important in the rank-and-file movement to remove the corrupt, conservative leadership of the union, and to promote Aboriginal rights and oppose the **Vietnam War**. In 1968 he became acting secretary and was elected secretary in 1970. The union became famous for its refusal to demolish buildings of historical and architectural significance, such as the **Rocks**, or to build on parkland such as Centennial Park. Its history is explored in Meredith Burgmann and Verity Burgmann's *Green Bans, Red Union* (1998). Berated by the media, politicians, and business interests, Mundey asserted the builders labourers' right to use their labour only in a manner that was socially useful and responsible. He did not seek re-election in 1973, and returned to work as a builders labourer, because he believed in limited tenure of office for union officials, a principle that was not well received by other trade union officials. Since this period Mundey has remained a prominent environmental activist, concerned to forge links between middle-class **conservationists** and working-class activists. He became an executive member of the Australian Conservation Foundation. His dream, outlined in his autobiography *Green Bans and Beyond* (1981), is to achieve a socialist and sustainable society, 'with a human face, an ecological heart and an egalitarian body'.

VERITY BURGMANN

Munro Ferguson, Ronald Craufurd (1860–1934) was appointed governor-general of Australia in 1914 after a political career in Britain in the Liberal Party. His determination to uphold the role of his office as sole channel of communication between Britain and Australia caused friction with state governors, and he was privately caustic about Australian politics. The onset of World War I gave him enhanced status and he took an active role in defence decisions. He came to believe that Billy **Hughes** was essential to the war effort and supported him through the crisis over **conscription**. Munro Ferguson returned to Scotland in 1920, leaving behind state governors so irritated by his insistence on federal precedence that they requested the **Colonial Office** to never again appoint such an overbearing governor-general, but he was widely respected and probably the most capable of the earliest governors-general. Ernest **Scott** drew extensively on his diaries and testimony for the **official history** of *Australia During the War* (1936), and Chris Cuneen gives a sympathetic portrayal in *King's Men* (1983).

KT

Murdoch family has become an international media dynasty. (KEITH) RUPERT MURDOCH (1931–) is a creature of the information highway, a robber baron of the new era. Wherever his private jet lands, whether it be New York, Singapore, London, or Sydney, he commands attention. There has been no more powerful Australian.

His drive and ambition almost certainly came from his father, KEITH ARTHUR (1886–1952). Sir Keith believed that if he controlled newspapers and radio stations, he could also influence politicians. Keith Murdoch's father and grandfather were clergymen. Both his father and mother were children of Presbyterian ministers. He grew up in Camberwell, comfortable suburban Melbourne. He went into journalism and became Commonwealth parliamentary reporter for the *Age*. Here he fathomed the sources of power. He became friendly with Andrew **Fisher** and W.M. **Hughes**. In 1915 he was appointed managing editor of the United Cable Service in London. Before Murdoch sailed, Fisher, now the Australian prime minister, gave him an official commission to report on the progress of the **Gallipoli** campaign. Many thought the report both inaccurate and over-emotional, but there were no doubts about its effects. Almost certainly it resulted in the withdrawal of the Gallipoli commander, General Sir Ian Hamilton, and it influenced the ultimate withdrawal of the Allied troops.

After the 1914–18 war, Murdoch returned to Australia to become editor of the *Herald* in Melbourne, an important but unremarkable afternoon daily. He poured life into it, made it sell, with the result the *Herald* was always the flagship of the Herald & Weekly Times chain. His company accumulated controlling powers over newspapers and radio stations in every capital city except Sydney. Murdoch himself was a grand figure, who liked to think of himself as a kingmaker and a master of politics. He did not marry until late. In 1928, at 42, he married 19-year-old ELISABETH GREENE (1909–). They had four children, three daughters and a son, Rupert.

Keith Murdoch died in 1952, when Rupert was 21 and just out of Oxford. His father had no equity in the Herald & Weekly Times Ltd, but after probate, Rupert, through the family company Cruden Investments, won control of the Adelaide *News*. He was impetuous and unfrightened of rivals like Sir Lloyd Dumas, chairman of the Advertiser Newspapers Ltd, the newspaper grandee of Adelaide, or Frank Packer, the tiro of Sydney's *Daily Telegraph*. Keith Murdoch could be ruthless, but with his Presbyterian background was constantly nagged by conscience. Rupert was ruthless and unfettered by Presbyterian sensibilities. He sacked those who got in his way.

His father was always timid about being in debt. Not Rupert—he borrowed to every banker's limit, but always with uncanny judgment for a good thing. In 1960 he bought Sydney's *Daily Mirror* and in 1964 he started the *Australian*, the nation's first national newspaper. In 1968 he went to London and bought the racy *News of the World*. He took over the ailing tabloid the *Sun*, and turned it into the top-circulating newspaper in Britain. From here on, he soared, gathering newspapers everywhere, including the *New York Post*, the *New York* magazine, and three newspapers in San Antonio. He bought *The Times* and the *Sunday Times* in London. In the mid-1980s he won control of Hollywood's 20th Century Fox, the publisher Harper & Row, plus, for $3 billion, a huge American company which published the *TV Guide*. He launched Sky TV in Britain and Star TV in China. Rupert's son, LACHLAN (1971–), returned to Australia to assume control of the Australian publications in 1995.

Pragmatic was a word almost invented for Rupert. From the 1960s he lent support to, and withdrew support from, both Labor and non-Labor governments. He ceased to be an Australian and became a US citizen so that he could escape foreign ownership laws in the USA. But he remained Australian in spirit and was close to his mother, Dame Elisabeth, a remarkable character in her own right. She was on the board of Melbourne's Royal Children's Hospital for 33 years, and was president 1956–65. Her energy and drive were responsible for the creation of the grand new hospital in Royal Park in 1963.

An unpublished biography of Keith is in the National Library; the later, published life by Desmond Zwar (1980) is anodyne. The discussion of the good and evil of Rupert Murdoch has been debated in at least six biographies and innumerable newspaper articles. Yet he saved more newspapers than he closed; and the man who fed the English sleaze through the *News of the World* also published the august *Times* and, through Harper & Row, was the world's largest printer of Bibles.

KEITH DUNSTAN

Murdoch, Walter Logie Forbes (1874–1970) was educated at the University of Melbourne and in 1912 became foundation professor of English at the University of Western Australia. He was a prolific essayist and widely syndicated newspaper columnist. As a university teacher, he embraced the Horatian dictum of 'teaching by seeming not to teach'. He edited a number of anthologies of Australian short stories and poetry, and wrote of his mentor in *Alfred Deakin: A Sketch* (1923). A certain defensiveness is evident in his description of himself as a writer of 'occasional verse … but not a poet' and a 'Professor of Things in General'.

Murdoch was chief public examiner of secondary school English, and his literary canon could be seen in WA syllabuses for over two decades from the 1920s: the works of Chaucer, Shakespeare, Scott, and Tennyson were all-pervasive, with 'occasional adventures into George Eliot, Hardy and Swinburne'. During the same period, Murdoch wrote that he 'would gladly praise the great West Australian masterpieces, if someone would kindly tell [him] where to find them'. His student J.A. **La Nauze** wrote *Walter Murdoch: A Centenary Tribute* (1974) and *Walter Murdoch: A Biographical Memoir* (1977).

PETER McCLELLAND

Murphy, Lionel Keith (1922–86) introduced major legal reforms during his time as attorney-general in the **Whitlam** government of 1972–75. After graduating in law in 1949, Murphy became known at the Sydney Bar for his work on industrial cases. He was elected as NSW senator for the Australian Labor Party in 1962. As opposition leader in the Senate he did much to develop the upper house's significance through the use of committees to scrutinise government actions. Once in government, he introduced significant legal reforms which included the Family Law Act, the Law Reform Commission, and the Legal Aid Office. His decision to order a raid on the headquarters of the **Australian Security Intelligence Organisation** was extremely controversial.

Murphy retired from politics in 1975 to take up an appointment to the High Court, where his judgments (frequently dissenting from the majority) reflected his reforming zeal. He favoured the extension of Commonwealth power over states' rights, and championed the rights of individuals. In 1984 he was charged with attempting to pervert the course of justice on behalf of a friend who was a Sydney solicitor. His alleged overture to the NSW chief magistrate—'What about my little mate?'—entered the Australian lexicon. A protracted trial ensued, during which Murphy took leave from the High Court. He died of cancer soon after he was exonerated. Jocelyn Scutt edited a volume of appreciation, *Lionel Murphy: A Radical Judge* (1987), and Jenny Hocking produced a sympathetic biography (1997).

KT

Murray, (George) Gilbert (1866–1957) and his brother **(John) Hubert** (1861–1940) were born and educated in NSW before studying at Oxford University, where Gilbert achieved such brilliant results in classics that he was appointed professor of Greek at Glasgow at the age of 23 and later became Regius professor of Greek at Oxford. He was internationally recognised for his translations of Greek literature. Gilbert discusses his Australian childhood in *An Unfinished Autobiography* (1960), and Francis West discusses Gilbert's responses to Australia in his 1984 biography.

Hubert qualified in the law and returned to Australia, where he was appointed NSW prosecutor in 1896. After service in the **Boer War**, he was appointed chief judicial officer in Papua, where he remained for 35 years—from 1908 as lieutenant-governor. He promoted economic development while protecting the indigenous people from expatriate exploitation. The combination of compulsion and benevolent paternalism brought criticism and ultimate disappointment. He wrote *Papua or British New Guinea* (1912) and *Papua of Today* (1925). Francis West has also written Hubert's biography (1968) and edited a collection of his letters (1970).

KT

Murray, Leslie Allan (1938–   ), poet, has the most distinctive style of any Australian poet of the late twentieth century. Rooted in landscapes, particularly those of northern NSW, his poems recurrently explore historical themes of ancestry, pioneering, and the two world wars. In verse, prose, and polemic, he has taken a stand against a number of modern ideological developments, and spoken up for indigenous, rural, and conservative values, most vehemently in *Subhuman Redneck Poems* (1997). Among his most brilliant reimaginings are 'A New England Farm, August 1914' and 'The Ballad of Jimmy Governor'. One sequence in *Ethnic Radio* (1977) attempts a historical invention of the future.

CHRIS WALLACE-CRABBE

Murray River rises in the Australian Alps and flows broadly north-west before turning south and entering the Southern Ocean in SA. Charles **Sturt**, who charted its course in 1830 below the junction with the Murrumbidgee, named the river in honour of George Murray, British secretary of state for the colonies. Six years earlier, **Hume and Hovell**, who named the river after Hume, had crossed it higher up on their journey to Port Phillip. From 1836 the Murray formed the northern boundary of the **Port Phillip District**, and from 1851 the NSW–Victoria border. The main Sydney–Melbourne route crossed the Murray at Albury, following the well-trodden path of the overlanders.

The Murray provided an important link for settlements in the Riverina and northern Victoria. The port town of Echuca, linked by rail to Melbourne from 1864, dominated **river transport**. The romance of the river-boat age, as epitomised by Nancy Cato's *All the Rivers Run* trilogy, has become a mainstay of Echuca's local heritage and tourism industry. Historical accounts of the Murray include Allan

Morris's study of river boats, *Rich River* (1953), and G.W. Broughton's *Men of the Murray* (1966).

The Murray–Darling river basin has since the nineteenth century been Australia's most important agricultural region, of sufficient importance that its inhabitants who were separated by state borders gave major impetus to **Federation**. **Irrigation** projects augmented its productivity, but increasing salinity now constitutes a major problem.

HD

Murri, see Aboriginal nomenclature

Museums were among the earliest cultural agencies of European colonisation in Australia. By collecting, classifying, studying, and displaying specimens of Australia's natural history, and of the material culture of its indigenous peoples, they were at the forefront of the process by which the colonisers sought to bring an unknown continent within the compass of European science. In each of the Australian colonies a similar history unfolded. The first museums were often private collections, begun by amateur scientists, but these were quickly incorporated into public collections, established often under vice-regal patronage and with state funding. Australia's first public museum, the Colonial (later the Australian) Museum was founded by Governor **Darling** in 1827 with support from the **Colonial Office**, and placed on a permanent footing by Governor Richard **Bourke** in 1835. Sir John and Lady **Franklin's** private Ancanthe Museum (1842) became the nucleus of a museum established by the Royal Society of Tasmania and brought under government auspices in 1885. In Victoria the establishment of the National Museum in 1854 coincided with the foundation of the University of Melbourne. Although governed and funded by the colonial government from 1863, its long-serving directors Frederick McCoy (1854–99) and Baldwin **Spencer** (1899–1928) were professors of the university. In Qld, a private museum established in 1855 by Charles Coxen, brother-in-law of the famous naturalist John **Gould**, was brought under government control as the Queensland Museum in 1876.

Like the Natural History Museum in London, on which they were modelled, these colonial museums took as their province the entire created universe, which they conceived as animal, vegetable, and human kingdoms, each organised taxonomically into species and genera. Sometimes they also incorporated mineral collections, although these were often established separately through schools of mines or government geological surveys. The publication of Charles Darwin's *The Origin of Species* (1859) gave new impetus to the collection of these specimens: they could now be interpreted both synchronically, as members of the various natural kingdoms, and diachronically, as moments in the history of the natural world. In this scheme of things, ethnological materials, such as Aboriginal skeletal remains, totemic objects, and weapons, sat alongside dinosaur bones, birds' eggs, and stuffed animals as pieces in a larger evolutionary jigsaw. Tom Griffiths's *Hunters and Collectors* (1996) illus-trates the fertile yet troubling connections between science and superstition, natural history and anthropology which shaped the colonial museums. Their collections of ethnological materials, such as the New Guinea materials collected by Sir William **MacGregor** and given to the Queensland Museum, reflected a story of cultural imperialism that reached beyond Australia's shores.

While the natural history museum displayed the works of nature, a new kind of museum had meanwhile appeared to display the works of civilised man. Inspired by the same imperatives as the international **exhibitions** and modelled on London's Victoria and Albert Museum, colonial museums of science and technology were designed to spread the gospel of industrial progress in the new land. Victoria's Museum of Applied Science was founded in 1870 and housed in the building erected for the 1866 exhibition. Sydney's Museum of Applied Arts and Sciences was founded in 1880; it occupied the Garden Palace, erected for the international exhibition of the previous year, until the building was destroyed by fire in 1882. While the natural history museum evolved in response to the outlook of the gentleman collector, the industrial museum was designed with a more popular audience and a more didactic purpose in mind. 'We believe that an institution of this sort, devoted to industry and art, is essential, if it is expected that the mechanics or artisans here are to compete with those in England', said the founders of the Victorian institution. They aimed to show, through practical examples, how technology worked and how it was applied in such colonial settings as the gold mine, the railway, and the wheat farm. They also included such icons of industrial progress as the great beam engine designed by James Watt (1785), which now dominates the entrance hall to Sydney's Powerhouse Museum.

The nineteenth century was a golden age for the state museums; in the early twentieth century they continued to build their collections, publish scientific papers, and make modest advances in exhibition technique. In the 1930s, for example, the Museum of Victoria, an amalgamation of the old National and Applied Science Museums, was displaying stuffed animals in dioramas depicting their natural habitat, and powering model steam-engines with electric motors so that visitors could visualise how they worked. But by the mid-1970s when the **Whitlam** government appointed a committee, headed by P.H. Pigott and including the historians Geoffrey **Blainey** and John **Mulvaney**, to survey Australia's museums, it found more to lament than to praise. Museums were under-funded, and important collections were being sadly neglected. The report *Museums in Australia 1975* appeared on the eve of a dramatic cultural shift which would push museums, especially historical museums, into a new phase of growth.

Like the **heritage** movement and the study of **genealogy** and **local history**, which underwent a similar boom, the new museums reflected a desire, not merely to learn about the past, but to re-enter it imaginatively. In SA the state government, eager to attract tourists, established a suite of innovative social history museums. In the former Parliament

House, now a Constitutional Museum, visitors sit in the places once occupied by colonial politicians, listening to actors reproduce their words and supplying the gestures themselves. In the Port Adelaide Maritime Museum they could re-enter the world of the colonial migrant, and even sample the rocking motion and claustrophobia experienced by steerage passengers on the long voyage out. A study of these new museums, Bennett et al., *Accessing the Past* (1991), found that visitors were motivated most strongly by a desire to know 'what life was like in the past', especially for 'ordinary people'.

Many of the new museums established in the 1980s and 1990s have sought to meet that expectation. They include such places as Calthorpe's House, a house-museum exemplifying 1920s middle-class life, in Canberra; the Museum of Childhood in Perth; the Pioneer Women's Hut in Tumbarumba, NSW; the Jewish Museum in Melbourne; and the New Norcia Museum, illustrating the life of a Benedictine abbey, in WA. The state museums, beginning with the Western Australian Museum in 1970, have also grafted new social history sections onto their original natural history and technological divisions; some, such as Sydney's Powerhouse Museum and Melbourne's Scienceworks, enable visitors to interpret technology in a social, as well as a scientific, context. In the two newest—the Melbourne Museum (opened 2000) and the National Museum of Australia (2001)—the history of European Australia is brought into a more critical relationship with that of Aboriginal Australia, and with the Australian environment.

Canberra, the nation's capital, is the home of Australia's largest and most successful history museum, the **Australian War Memorial**. A 1991 study by Margaret Anderson of *Heritage Collections in Australia* found that over half of Australia's inventory of 'heritage items' belonged to this one museum. A key recommendation of the 1975 Piggott Report had been the establishment of a Museum of Australian History in the national capital. By the late 1980s, in consultation with historians, prehistorians and other interested groups, the museum had developed collection policies round three themes: Aboriginal and Torres Strait Islander people and culture, Australian society and history, and people's interaction with the environment. A fourth theme, Nation, was added in the early 1980s. A site suitable for a mixture of indoor and outdoor exhibits was selected on Yarramundi Reach on Lake Burley Griffin. But little was done until the **Howard** government decided in 1997 to move the projected museum to a new site on Acton Peninsula. Architects Ashton, Raggatt, and McDougall's winning design follows the lakefront, its four galleries encircling a symbolic 'Garden of Australian Dreams'. As the exhibits took shape, conservative members of the museum's council, including the prime minister's biographer and former speechwriter, accused curators of 'political correctness' and lobbied for a more relaxed and comfortable version of the national past.

History could not become more important as a subject for museums without soon turning attention to the past of the museums themselves. Young historians schooled in the 'new social history' and eager to exploit the possibilities of communicating a sense of the past through material culture, often found themselves caught in institutions still organised around nineteenth-century traditions of taxonomy and cultural imperialism. Many of the new curators were women, some Marxists, with a commitment to the study of material culture as a means of retrieving pasts invisible in print. A central issue, which agitated museum directors and curators in the 1980s, was the problem of whether, and how, to preserve the large collections of Aboriginal skeletal remains and ceremonial objects acquired in the past, sometimes in shameful ways, by collectors, anthropologists, and prehistorians. *Who Owns the Past?* the Academy of the Humanities asked in a symposium on the topic in 1983. Should these objects be returned to the descendants of those to whom they belonged, or did the universal claims of science outweigh those of kinship and descent? By the late 1980s most Australian museums had evolved policies for the return of such objects to Aborigines, either for safe-keeping in special keeping-places or, in the case of skeletal materials, for reburial. The question remains: how should museum curators and historians interpret those trophies of cultural imperialism that remain in their keeping? Perhaps the boldest and most controversial answer to that question is the new Museum of Sydney, erected on the site of First Government House close to Circular Quay. Its director, Peter Emmett, has created Australia's first postmodern, post-colonial museum. In abandoning story-lines and didactic captions, the Museum of Sydney is both an inversion of the nineteenth-century museum and a radical, often baffling, commentary on history itself.

The history of Australian museums remains a neglected topic. The Museum of Victoria is the best served with studies by David Goodman (*Continuum*, 1990), Sally Kohlstedt, *Historical Records of Australian Science* (1983), Warren Perry, *The Science Museum of Victoria* (1972), and Carolyn Rasmussen, *Nature and Man Mirrored in Our Museum* (2001). Patricia Mather et al., *A Time for a Museum* (1986), covers the Queensland Museum. Essays by Ian McShane (*Public History Review*, 1998) and Margaret Anderson (in F.E.S. Kaplan, *Museums and the Making of 'Ourselves'*, 1994) outline the genesis of the National Museum of Australia, while Darryl McIntyre and Kirsten Wehner (eds), *Negotiating Histories* (2001), sets historical interpretation in Australian museums in international context.

GRAEME DAVISON

Music from the fife-and-drum corps at Botany Bay in 1788 signalled a rather prosaic beginning for the new colony. First Fleet marine officers and settlers clung to the few musical instruments they had brought with them, dragging battered pianos overland to their new homes, their wives treasuring tattered volumes of parlour songs and quadrilles that passed from hand to hand. From 1800 the regimental band stationed at Sydney gave open air concerts and played at the governor's occasional balls, but aside from crude carousing in hotels there was no other public music-making for 30 years. The earliest governors had little time for it, and only the dimmest awareness of the Aboriginal culture which already filled the country with a music of the greatest subtlety and antiquity.

The convicts could not be stopped from singing. Those such as Francis Macnamara, who composed original ballads with lines critical of their captors, were flogged. Nevertheless, anguished, seditious, or satirical convict ballads circulated, and songs like 'Jim Jones', 'Van Diemen's Land', Macnamara's 'Moreton Bay', and hymns to those who escaped to become bushrangers, like Bold Jack **Donohue**, passed into common currency. They became the foundation of Australia's folk-music and its first original compositions.

Public concerts were mounted at Sydney and Hobart from 1826, churches began installing organs, and in 1833 the makeshift Theatre Royal of the Royal Hotel, Sydney, assembled a tiny 'orchestra' for its entertainments. The music was a roughshod affair—instrumental trifles, Sir Henry Bishop's butchered version of *Don Giovanni*, or his *Maid of Milan*, from which the evergreen 'Home Sweet Home' became popular. Even when the permanent Victoria Theatre opened at Sydney in 1838, its operatic productions were at first brutally abridged, translated, and arranged with music more easily at hand.

The wealth and growth of the **gold rushes** brought improvement: visits by star performers, the building of music halls, and the foundation of British choral societies. Gold diggers and the growing nomadic class of shearers and drovers produced more ballads, and songs such as 'The Wild Colonial Boy', 'The Eumeralla Shore', and 'Ladies of Brisbane', followed the convict songs into folk-music. Many of these were later assembled and published by Banjo **Paterson**, himself the author of the most famous ballad of the colonial era and the most popular **national song**, 'Waltzing Matilda'.

W.S. Lyster's Opera Co., which toured the capitals from 1861, provided two dazzling decades of **opera**; his example inspired local theatre entrepreneurs J.C. **Williamson** and George Musgrove (1854–1916), who from 1880 began importing the new Gilbert and Sullivan operettas and musicals from Britain. In the 1900s the Tivoli circuit and Fuller's became vast national networks for vaudeville, also producing native stars with significant success abroad, notably Florrie Ford (1876–1940) and later Gladys **Moncrieff**.

The centenary of Australia's settlement in 1888 brought centennial choirs and orchestras; distinguished visiting players gave recitals, and large cathedral and town hall organs were built, notably the five-manual Sydney Town Hall organ, then the largest organ in the world. In the 1890s several capital cities opened permanent music schools, and, following the popular Welsh pattern, musical Eisteddfods sprang up in many cities and towns. Symphony orchestras began to be formed: G.W.L. **Marshall-Hall's** Orchestra in Melbourne (1892–1912); August Heinecke's Grand Orchestra in Adelaide (1893–1910); Roberto Hazon's Amateur Orchestral Society in Sydney (from 1888); then Henri Verbrugghen's NSW State Orchestra (1919–21). Most had a mix of amateur

and professional players which would lead eventually to their disintegration amid fights with the Musicians Union.

By Federation in 1901 Australia had made its place in the musical world, at least in the sense that a number of its own musicians had become international celebrities—Nellie **Melba**, Percy **Grainger**, violinist Johann S. Kruse, and pianist Ernest Hutcheson. These were soon to be joined by singers Peter Dawson, John McCormack, John Brownlee, and Browning Mummery. But enthusiasm for Australian music and musical life went with deference to received models. The first operas written in Australia—Isaac Nathan's *Don John of Austria* and John Howson's *The Corsair* (premiered 1847–48)—were frankly derivative, deaf to the sounds or atmosphere of the new land. There were Victorian songs of stilted enthusiasm for the innocence and clear sunny skies of the new country, hymned in the English art song idiom. In the years before World War I, the full-scale symphonies and dramatic works by Marshall-Hall, Alfred Hill (1870–1960), and Fritz Hart (1874–1949) were no more original, although at least one (Marshall-Hall's *Stella*, 1910) had an Australian subject. As late as 1948 directors of the conservatoria like Edgar Bainton were emphatic that Australian music would have to be based on the British. Australian music examination standards long continued to be based on British practice. Only a few composers achieved more independence: the bitonality of Dorian Le Gallienne, the Aboriginal-inspired primitivism of John Antill's *Corroboree* (1946), or the athletic linear voice of Margaret Sutherland.

The arrival of regular radio broadcasts in 1923 was to prove the agent of profound change. Several commercial stations established ensembles for light music, while the national government network, the **Australian Broadcasting Commission**, formed wireless choruses and studio orchestras from its foundation in 1932. From 1936, with Bernard Heinze (1894–1982) as its adviser, the Australian Broadcasting Corporation began a much grander project—to create permanent symphony orchestras in all capital cities. ABC Celebrity Concerts were begun, and after World War II the ABC moved quickly, completing an immense radio-orchestral network 20 years before most other countries had attempted it. Rapid European immigration in the postwar years brought the ABC an urbane audience, as well as patrons for first-class chamber music, for which Musica Viva (from 1955) developed a unique national concert network, still the largest of its kind in the world. A remarkable harvest of outstanding operatic voices appeared, and the Elizabethan Theatre Trust Opera Company (established 1956) became the first full-time opera company, evolving into the Australian Opera (now Opera Australia) in 1970.

With radio, jazz reached Australia. The influence spread largely through recordings, and the response was therefore delayed: even as the international fashion for swing bands was giving way in the war years to modern jazz, Australia had a late and lush flowering of Dixieland, producing a host of 'trad' bands, led by Graeme Bell. Through radio and recordings, country music of astonishing resilience and intensity also developed in rural centres. Tex Morton and Smoky Dawson, who had been performing American hillbilly songs, began singing of the Australian outback; presently Buddy Williams and then Slim Dusty came to prominence, travelling the length and breadth of the country as well as appearing on country radio, and inspiring many imitators.

The American rock and roll explosion of the late 1950s inspired local singers; and with daemonic energy Johnny O'Keefe drove Americans from domination of the local 'Top 40', paving the way for Australians to become pop music stars in their own land. In his wake numerous local artists followed: the Mersey-style Easybeats and the folk-singing Seekers in the 1960s achieved substantial European success. With the development of independent Australian record labels, a local popular music industry gathered momentum which, in the 1970s and 1980s, delivered into the European and American spotlight first Helen Reddy and Olivia Newton-John, then the Little River Band, AC/DC, Midnight Oil, INXS, Men At Work, Kylie Minogue, and many others.

The ABC had always broadcast Australian composers, but the number successful internationally remained small—Grainger, Arthur Benjamin (1893–1960), Peggy Glanville-Hicks (1912–90), and few others. When British conductor John Hopkins became its music director in 1963, the ABC's work with composers was suddenly transformed: new scores were commissioned, old works were revived, and all were performed and recorded by the Australian Broadcasting Corporation orchestras in considerable quantity. Younger composers were aired, revealing the neo-European structuralism they had adopted, again through recordings, and much more original musical composition was stimulated. Peter Sculthorpe's *Sun Music* (1965–67) captured the heat of the Australian desert in the way that **Drysdale** had on canvas, while Richard Meale, Nigel Butterley, Don Banks, and Malcolm Williamson surprised listeners with the sudden independence of their voices. Through the **Australia Council**, the **Whitlam** government created the largest government-supported commissioning program ever mounted in a Western country: Australian works were published and recorded, and ensembles were enticed to perform them. A plurality of influences became audible, embracing not just European traditions but also American experimentalism and a vein of South-East Asian and Japanese ideas and sonorities as well.

Meanwhile, tribal Aboriginal music continued to be heard in the central and northern deserts where its traditions had been preserved. Sporadic collection and documentation had revealed an ornate vocal music, accompanied by very few instruments (in only a few locations by didgeridoo), often integrated with dance, and manifest in secular, sacred, and secret repertoires. By the 1960s hybrid forms had appeared in many Aboriginal communities, which mixed traditional music with Christian missionary hymns or with country music. In the 1970s and 1980s indigenous youth, even in the most remote communities, had adopted folk-music, rock, and reggae, and began delivering their own artists into the international arena, like Yothu Yindi and Archie Roach.

In the late 1970s, many Australian composers overtook the terse European models they had previously followed and set their sights on more independent goals. Meale's *Viridian* (1979) surprised audiences with its lyrical evocation of the tropical rainforests, and his opera *Voss* (1986), after Patrick **White's** novel, spoke a warm post-Romantic language. Ross Edwards presented an attractive voice with the meditative, Asian-influenced *Mountain Village in a Clearing Mist* (1973), the buoyantly rhythmic *Piano Concerto* (1982), and the diatonic repeating nonsense syllables of his Maninyas series (1981–88). Butterley's *From Sorrowing Earth* (1991) was another newly lyrical work. Sadly, the new confidence of the composers has coincided with an increasing conservatism among their audience, and in the late 1990s the opportunities of the previous 20 years seem to be diminishing once more.

Roger Covell, *Australia's Music: Themes for a New Society* (1967), pioneered the history of Australian music. Warren Bebbington (ed.), *Oxford Companion to Australian Music* (1997), is a comprehensive reference work; and a major new history is currently in preparation by Thérèse Radic.

WARREN BEBBINGTON

Myall is an Aboriginal word originating from the Dharuk language of the Sydney region which signifies a person from a foreign tribe and, by implication, a stranger and an enemy. An area of land thought inhospitable was described by Aborigines as 'myall country'—a term later adopted by European settlers. *Myall* also refers to an Aboriginal who is unfamiliar with European ways, regarded as inferior, lacking in skills, and dangerous. The word has also been ascribed to several indigenous plants.

HD

Myall Creek massacre was unusual among **massacres** of Aborigines in that some of the perpetrators were punished. It occurred in June 1838 at Henry Dangar's station at Myall Creek, near Inverell in the New England District of NSW. At the encouragement of local squatter's son, John Fleming, a party of 11 white ex-convict station hands drove a group of Aborigines who were peaceably camped at the station into the bush and battered them, on the pretext that they had been involved in cattle-stealing. The burnt bodies of at least 28 victims were subsequently discovered. On the order of Governor **Gipps**, the 11 white men were arrested for murder and tried in the NSW Supreme Court, but all were acquitted. In response to growing humanitarian concerns, especially on the part of British authorities who were keen to demonstrate that such outrages would not go unpunished, Gipps ordered a retrial. Seven of the men were sentenced to death. The case's significance rests on this unexpected judgment, emphasised by the angry reaction from those who regarded Aborigines as 'savages'. Those who defended the Aborigines as victims of persecution welcomed justice, though critics described the punishments as merely token compensation for past injustices committed against Aborigines. Charles **Harpur's** sentimental poem, 'An Aboriginal Mother's Lament', appeared shortly after. An account of the massacre is given in Laurie Barber's *Massacre at Myall Creek* (1993).

HD

Myer family built Australia's largest department store. SIDNEY MYER (1878–1934) was the founder of the business and a notable **philanthropist**. Born Simca Baevski, the son of a Hebrew scholar, at Kritchev in the Russian Pale, Myer emigrated to Melbourne in 1898 and joined his elder brother ELCON (1875–1938) in business, adopting the name Myer. Beginning as travelling salesmen, the brothers later established a drapery store in Bendigo. Sidney, a marketing virtuoso, soon eclipsed local competitors; in 1911 he purchased the Bourke Street drapers Wright and Neil, whose manager, the paternalistic Lee Neil, became Myer's long-time partner and foil. Myer travelled frequently to Europe and the USA to observe the latest marketing trends, making the Myer Emporium the Australian pioneer of the bargain basement, the self-service cafeteria, motorised home deliveries, the cash-and-carry grocery, and other advanced selling techniques. In America he also converted to Christianity and in 1920 married his second wife, Merlyn **Baillieu**, daughter of another Melbourne business dynasty. During the Great Depression Myer continued to expand; its profits sustained generous benefits to store staff and benefactions to cultural and charitable causes, including the Melbourne Symphony Orchestra and, in 1930, a Christmas Day party for the unemployed. Sidney Myer died suddenly in 1934; one-tenth of his million-pound fortune was willed to a trust for charity and philanthropy.

His place at the head of the Myer business later passed to his nephew NORMAN (1898–1956) and to his sons KENNETH BAILLIEU (1921–92) and (SIDNEY) BAILLIEU (1926–). Like Sidney, they were strongly influenced by American contacts and marketing techniques. Kenneth established Myer Chadstone in Melbourne's suburbs in 1961, led take-overs of Farmer Brothers and Boans Stores (WA), and founded the Target chain. He was influential in civic affairs, especially in pressing for modern solutions to problems of traffic and congestion. In 1958 he became founding president of the Myer Foundation and during the 1960s and 1970s he headed a number of cultural and philanthropic bodies, including the National Library and the **Australian Broadcasting Corporation** (1983–86). After 1985, when Myer merged with the **Coles** chain, he largely retired from public life. He and his second wife Yasuko Hiraoko were killed in a plane accident in Alaska in July 1992. The Myer family remain substantial, though not controlling, shareholders in Coles–Myer and prominent contributors to Melbourne's civic and cultural life.

An admiring life of Sidney Myer, by his contemporary Ambrose **Pratt**, was published, 40 years after it was commissioned by his family, in 1978. A history of the company, *The Gay Provider* by Alan **Marshall**, appeared in 1961.

GD

Myxomatosis, see **Pests**

N

Nairn, (Noel) Bede (1917–), historian, was born in Turill, NSW, into a working-class Catholic family that was active in the **Australian Labor Party**. His Master's thesis, completed in 1955, was a study of the NSW labour movement in the nineteenth century and the early Labor Party. Nairn taught at the University of New South Wales before appointment to the staff of the *ADB* in the mid-1960s. He later became joint editor with Geoffrey **Serle**.

Nairn published many articles on the nineteenth-century NSW labour movement before the appearance of *Civilising Capitalism:The Labor Movement in New South Wales 1870–1900* (1973). In this book, which is much admired by influential figures on the Right of the NSW ALP, Nairn emphasised the strength of the moderate reformist element within the emergent party. He endorsed **labourism**, while playing down the impact of **socialism** and anarchism. Nairn later produced a critical appraisal of *The Big Fella: Jack Lang and the Australian Labor Party 1891–1949* (1989). His work is characterised by a strong belief in the progressive role of the labour movement in Australian history, a greater interest in the leaders of the movement than the led, and a profound scepticism about the usefulness of **class** as a tool of historical analysis. *Bede Nairn and Labor History* (1991) was a tribute to his achievements as a historian and also contains useful biographical information.

FRANK BONGIORNO

Namatjira, Albert (1902–59) achieved immediate popular success with the first exhibition in 1938 of his luminous water-colour paintings of the landscape surrounding the Hermannsburg Lutheran Mission in Central Australia. He was an initiated member of the Western Arrernte people as well as a baptised member of the Lutheran Church in whose mission school he was educated. In the late 1920s Namatjira was introduced to watercolour by visiting artist Rex Battarbee, who later became his agent. His consequent success brought public recognition in many forms—a biography in 1944 by C.P. **Mountford**; a film, *Namatjira the Painter*, in 1947. He was flown to Canberra to meet Queen Elizabeth in 1954 and was awarded citizenship status in 1957. His arrest in 1958 for supplying alcohol to a fellow Arrernte showed the limits of that status. As a citizen he could legally buy alcohol, yet it was an offence to share it with other Aborigines as custom required. A biography by Joyce Batty (1963) and a pamphlet by T.G.H. **Strehlow**, *Nomads in No-Man's Land* (1961), put forward a tragic picture of Namatjira as torn between two cultures. Initially he was regarded as outside Aboriginal tradition for his choice of medium, but later reassessment of his work recognised its spirituality and identification with the landscape as essentially Aboriginal. Jane Hardy et al. (eds), *The Heritage of Namatjira* (1992), was published in association with a touring exhibition of his work. Nadine Amadio (ed.), *Albert Namatjira* (1986), looks at both the life and work. (See also **Aboriginal art**.)

KT

Nan Kivell, Rex de Charembac (1899–1977) was a New Zealand-born art dealer, collector, and benefactor. He lived for the whole of his adult life in England where, in partnership with the Australian Harry Tatlock Miller, he ran the influential Redfern Gallery from the early 1930s until his death. Nan Kivell's antipodean reputation is based on the large collection of historical and topographical paintings, prints, and drawings relating to Australia, NZ, and the Pacific, which he built up following his demobilisation from wartime service in 1919.

In 1946, probably prompted by Maie **Casey**, Nan Kivell commenced discussions with the Commonwealth National Library to find a permanent home for his extensive Australasian and Pacific collection, which also included a fine collection of books and manuscripts. Prime Minister **Menzies** supported its purchase by the Australian government for what now seems the modest sum of £70 000; Nan Kivell used the proceeds to buy other items which he later donated to the collection. The core of the collection is housed in the National Library of Australia, although in 1992 a number of major paintings were placed on permanent loan with the National Gallery of Australia.

Nan Kivell attributed his interest in history and in collecting to the encouragement he was given as a boy in Christchurch, NZ, by an antiquarian book-dealer. In later life, he pursued this interest with a keen eye both to provenance and to quality. He built his collection at a time when there was little active competition and when the appreciation of so-called historical works relating to Australia and NZ was limited. It has since provided the means for later generations to come to a new appreciation of an antipodean visual arts tradition dating from the late years of the eighteenth century.

JOHN THOMPSON

Nation; Nation Review began in Sydney in 1958 as the *Nation*, subtitled 'An independent journal of opinion', a fortnightly magazine of politics and culture that was edited by Tom Fitzgerald and George Munster. From the heyday of **Menzies** to the eve of **Whitlam** it provided an informed and critical commentary on domestic and foreign issues. Contributors included Cyril **Pearl**, K.S. **Inglis**, Manning **Clark**, Sylvia Lawson, and Robert Hughes. Inglis has edited an anthology, with a substantial retrospective commentary (1989).

In 1972 the *Nation* merged with the Sydney (Sunday) *Review*, founded two years earlier, to create the weekly *Nation Review*, published by Richard Walsh. This was a disrespectful, sardonic platform of young intellectual radicals; contributors included John Hepworth, Mungo MacCallum, Bob Ellis, and the cartoonist Michael Leunig, whose wayward and often irreverent drawings captured the tone of the paper. Publication of the *Nation Review* was suspended in October 1979, then resumed briefly in a smaller format (1980–81). (See also **Newpapers**.)

HD

National Council of Women was formed in NSW in 1896, Tasmania in 1899, Victoria and SA in 1902, Qld in 1905, and WA in 1911. The national organisation was founded only in 1931. The guiding principle of the International Council of Women was inclusiveness; women's organisation of all kinds, not just those with feminist objectives, were encouraged to affiliate. The council was effective as a lobbyist for legislation and representation on all boards and committees relating to the welfare and legal rights of women and **children**. Its guiding philosophy—strength in unity—rested on the assumption of a common and universal female interest superseding differences of class, race, nationality, and political allegiance. The network of women who led the council in its early years were mostly wealthy, with powerful family connections and conservative political affiliations. The other major source of leadership and policy was the universities, which provided the 'scientific expertise' that underlay the council's claims to be modern and rational.

After International Women's Year in 1975, however, it lost its once undisputed leadership of the women's movement.

JUDITH SMART

National Estate, Register of the, administered by the Australian Heritage Commission, is an inventory of places classified as significant to Australia's natural, Aboriginal, and post-contact **heritage**. It was established in accordance with the *Australia Heritage Commission Act 1975*, and listed its first site, Fraser Island, Qld, in 1977. Nominations to the register usually follow recommendations from the **National Trust**, local historical societies, or commissioned heritage studies. In addition, the Heritage Commission carries out its own assessments, usually regional or thematic, which fill particular gaps in listings. In 1997 the register listed over 11 000 places. An illustrated compendium of registered places, *The Heritage of Australia*, was published in 1981, and current listings appear online through the commission's HERA database.

HD

National identity is the most recent and popular of the concepts by which Australians have defined their selfhood as a people. Imported from the USA in the 1960s, it is now deeply embedded in political and cultural discourse: national identity is something both attained and constantly renegotiated, something derived from the past yet still to be discovered.

Colonial Australians defined themselves primarily in relationship to Britain, the land from which they or their parents came, but which most would never see again. They were sons and daughters of Empire—rebellious ones, perhaps, if they happened to be Irish—but caught for good or ill in a filial relationship they could not easily imagine away. Henry **Parkes** spoke of the 'crimson thread of kinship' binding those of British descent, others pictured the colonies as sons of John Bull and daughters of Queen Victoria. As Douglas Cole argued (*HS*, 1971), the language of colonial nationalism was deeply imbued with ethnocentric concepts of Anglo-Saxon or White 'race' and 'blood', although these shaded imperceptibly into notions of cultural inheritance. 'We are all one family, one blood, one race ... We are one in the inheritance of all the achievements of our great forebears', Parkes declared in 1893. In *The Australian Colonists* (1974), Ken **Inglis** reviewed the diverse forms of colonial **nationalism**: celebrations of the monarch's birthday, the eating of plum pudding at Christmas, the English Sabbath, and the eager longing for news from Home.

Imperial and colonial observers had long speculated about the modifications which a sunny climate, ample diet, and egalitarian social relations might make to the parent stock. Charles Darwin's theory of evolution provided one convenient metaphor for understanding this process. Contemporaries, as David Walker shows (in James Jupp, ed., *The Australian People*, 1988), held a baffling variety of views on the subject, although the balance of opinion was towards improvement rather than the reverse. They also divided over the relative contributions of heredity and environment in the Australian type, although environment increasingly won out. For example, Charles **Bean**, war correspondent and historian, traced the character of the 'typical Australian' not only to the mixed blood of Anglo-Saxon races and 'the open-air life in a new climate', but to the 'independence of character' and **egalitarianism** nurtured by the hardships of the bush and mining frontiers. The code of **mateship** was 'bred in the child and stays with him through life'.

Those, like Bean and the young Keith **Hancock** who had grown up within the bosom of Anglo-Australia, resisted the idea that being Australian and being British were incompatible. 'Among Australians,' Hancock wrote in *Australia* (1930), 'pride of race counted for more than love of country ... Defining themselves as **"independent Australian Britons"** they believed each word essential and exact, but laid most stress upon the last.' Irish-Australians, even when Hancock wrote, would likely have reversed that emphasis. The **conscription** campaigns of 1916 and 1917 were a severe test of their loyalties. 'Some people are fond of calling England the motherland', observed their champion Daniel **Mannix**. 'It is not my motherland ... indeed it is my stepsister.' This sense of difference, argued Patrick **O'Farrell** in *The Irish in Australia* (1986), provided Australian nationalism with its essential dynamic: 'Australian identity was not born in the bush, nor at Anzac Cove, [but] in Irishness protesting against the extremes of Englishness.'

Among Left historians the conflicts between heredity and environment, Englishness and Irishness, rested on a more fundamental dialectic, the international **class** struggle. In the 1940s, when the causes of international Marxism and national defence converged, the Australian Left incorporated the legacy of **Lawson**, **Furphy** and bush folklore into a radical interpretation of what its leading exponent, Russel **Ward**, later called the *The Australian Legend* (1958). Ward's portrait of the 'typical Australian'—rough-and-ready in manner, independent and egalitarian in outlook, true to his mates—was unambiguously male and working-class, traits which he traced from the country's convict origins and from the 'nomad tribe' of pastoral workers who were the authentic Australian frontiersmen. While the USA, a frontier of small farmers, developed an ethos of liberal individualism, Australia—a big man's frontier—developed a more polarised class system and a more proletarian national outlook.

The legend, in Ward's eyes, was both something imagined—'a people's idea of itself'—and something real—it was 'always connected with reality'. His critics, who appeared in increasing numbers in the 1970s, questioned both his characterisation of the Australian national type and his explanation of its origins. Michael **Roe** (*Meanjin*, 1962) and John Hirst (*HS*, 1978), among others, identified other national types that were more conservative and less proletarian, such as the **'pioneer'**. Graeme Davison argued (*HS*, 1978) that the legend derived as much from the dreams of disenchanted urban intellectuals as the experience of outback workers, from the boarding-houses of Sydney as the shearing sheds of the bush. Ward's language—'legend', 'mystique', 'ethos'—invited a more sceptical interpretation than he himself had

contemplated. And a more suburbanised, prosperous Australia identified less closely with the bush ethos in which he had located its origins.

The concept of 'national identity', derived from the writings of the American psychoanalyst Erik Erikson and imported to Australia in the mid-1960s, provided a useful framework for this more contingent understanding of national selfhood. Erikson's theory of development proposed that individuals matured through stages: identity was not fixed or permanent but had to be established through a process of constant renegotiation. Thus Geoffrey **Serle** could write, in *From Deserts the Prophets Come* (1973), of Australians pursuing 'a search for national identity'. Identity was something *both* residing in individuals *and* ascribed to them by others. As Ken Inglis argued (*Multiculturalism and National Identity*, 1988), 'national identity' had the merit of avoiding the evolutionary and racialist assumptions that had tarnished nineteenth-century ideas of national becoming, while conveying a sense of nationality that was both coherent and more than skin-deep.

As Miriam **Dixson** observed in *The Real Matilda* (1976), concepts of 'identity' implicitly introduced questions of sexual, as well as class and ethnic difference. Dixson herself offered an account of the origins of Australian **gender relations** which blended psychoanalytic and frontier themes. At first feminist historians emphasised the influence of the state on the formation of gender roles; only later did their attention turn to the influence of gender in 'creating a nation'. 'The creation of nations', wrote Patricia Grimshaw and her co-authors of *Creating a Nation* (1994), 'has traditionally been seen as men's business.' Their response was twofold: to deconstruct the gendered language of nation-building (Why was the nation represented as feminine? And how could male soldiers 'give birth' to a nation?) and to celebrate the unacknowledged role of women in the national history.

Postwar immigration had produced an Australia that was too diverse, ethnically and religiously, to fit either the old British imperial or the Australian bush paradigm. There had always been more than one way of being Australian; but **'multiculturalism'** gradually supplanted assimilation as the goal of official policy and government cultural agencies consciously promoted a pluralist sense of national identity. Bruce Woodley's 1988 Bicentennial anthem nicely caught its tone:

> We are one, but we are many,
> And from all the lands on earth we come.
> We'll share a dream and sing with one voice,
> I am—you are—we are Australian.

National identity became something chosen or made, rather than something inherited or given. One could be Italian, or American, and 'still call Australia home'. Whites could appropriate elements of Aboriginal culture, often without the authors' permission, into a composite Australian identity.

Historians, embracing the new ethos, increasingly saw Australia itself as a historical fiction. 'There is no "real" Australia waiting to be uncovered', declared Richard White in 1981. 'A national identity is an invention. There is no point in asking whether one version of this essential Australia is truer than another, because they are all intellectual constructs, neat, tidy, comprehensible—and necessarily false.' *Necessarily* false? There was something uncomfortably solipsistic about such a formulation, and by 1997 White had qualified himself:'to say that "Australia" is an invention is not to say that there are not "realities" connected with Australia'.

Nations, Benedict Anderson argues, are 'imagined communities', present in the mind before they are 'built', 'born', 'baptised', or 'founded'. But nations also define themselves in relation to an 'imagined audience' of parents and rivals. Colonial Australians had projected their identity through international exhibitions, Test matches, and the great theatre of war. Their self-image was reflected back to them in the reports of visiting journalists and the speeches of visiting dignitaries. In the late twentieth century, however, Australian identities have become commodified, made tangible in Akubra hats and Drizabones, and distributed worldwide through films, novels, and video clips. Once, it seemed, national identity was in-born. Then it was said to have been made through an encounter between people and the land, or one tribe of Australians and another. Now it is formed by a new dialectic, the restless craving of international tourists for ethnic and local colour, and of Australians themselves for a bulwark against the incursions of a homogenising global culture.

GRAEME DAVISON

National parks are large public reserves which were first gazetted in Australia at the end of the nineteenth century, primarily for public recreation and enjoyment, but also, with similar purposes to **acclimatisation societies**, as a means of improving nature. Royal National Park, south of Sydney, gazetted in 1879, became the first Australian national park and the second in the world after Yellowstone in the USA. This was followed by Ferntree Gully National Park, east of Melbourne, gazetted in 1882. By the early twentieth century, utilitarian attitudes to the natural landscape were replaced by a growing interest in indigenous plants and animals and natural landforms, and national parks became important sites for the preservation of Australia's natural environment. The National Parks and Primitive Areas Council was established in 1932. Many new parks were reserved in the postwar period, the first being Kosciuszko National Park in 1944. Aside from their significance to **natural history**, national parks have come to be viewed as important internationally to the history of **conservation** and of human interaction with the environment.

HD

National Party of Australia is one of the world's few remaining agrarian political parties. First established in WA by the Farmers and Settlers Association in 1913, the party was represented in all seven Australian parliaments by 1920. For most of its history it was known as the Country Party, but the Queensland branch adopted the current title in 1974 as a tactic to broaden its electoral appeal. The discarding of the traditional rural title proved controversial, and it was not uniformly adopted by the party until 1982.

Throughout its history the National Party has sought to represent rural and regional dwellers, and has advocated policies—such as subsidies to primary industry, organised marketing, reduced freight charges, and fuel rebates—to advance their interests. Changing circumstances have sometimes produced major policy adjustments, as in the 1960s when the federal leader and deputy prime minister, John **McEwen**, abandoned the party's long-standing commitment to low **tariffs**, and sought an alliance with secondary industry. Ideologically right of centre, the National Party has been socially conservative, but its attachment to free enterprise has been tempered in the past by a willingness to support government intervention in the economy—but less so in the 1990s.

Because of its minority constituency, the National Party could not usually aspire to form governments in its own right—though it did so with the help of other parties in Victoria in the 1930s, 1940s, and early 1950s, and independently in Qld from 1983 to 1989. Federally the party preferred a coalition arrangement with the **Liberal Party** and its predecessors. The first such coalition was formed by the Country Party with the original and urban-based National Party in 1923, and held office until its electoral defeat in 1929. Another coalition was formed in 1934 with the **United Australia Party**, but relations between the two parties deteriorated after 1939 and they suffered a major electoral rebuff in 1943.

By cooperating closely, the Liberal and Country Parties won the 1949 election and formed continuous administrations until defeated in 1972. Further coalitions governed from 1975 to 1983 and from 1996. Despite its minority status, National Party ministers regularly exercised influence beyond their Cabinet representation. In this respect the party was well served by forceful and adroit leaders in Earle **Page** (1921–39), Arthur **Fadden** (1940–58), John McEwen (1958–71), and Doug Anthony (1971–84). Anthony and his colleagues Ian Sinclair and Peter Nixon were especially influential in the governments of Malcolm **Fraser** (1975–83), but the National Party has not been so significant in John **Howard's** ministry (1996–), despite the efforts of Tim Fischer, who was party leader from 1990.

The demise of the National Party has often been predicted, but it has survived for more than 80 years despite adverse demographic trends and aggressive electoral competition from both the Labor and Liberal Parties. While maintaining an organisational presence in all states, the party now has federal parliamentary representation from only NSW, Qld, and Victoria, and no parliamentary representation at all in SA and Tasmania. After a very poor result at the 1990 federal election, a merger with the Liberal Party loomed as inevitable. Again the National Party survived intact, and a modest seat improvement in 1996 secured at least its medium-term future.

For a minority party, the National Party has generated a sizeable literature. The origins and early history of the party are authoritatively analysed in B.D. Graham, *The Formation of the Australian Country Parties* (1966). Party member Ulrich Ellis provides sympathetic but useful accounts in *A History of the Australian Country Party* (1963) and *The Country Party in NSW* (1958). Don Aitkin's *The Country Party in New South Wales* (1972) gives a detailed regional perspective. A more contemporary account of the party is Brian Costar and Dennis Woodward (eds), *Country to National: Australian Rural Politics and Beyond* (1985).

BRIAN COSTAR

National songs, giving musical expression to patriotic sentiment, have taken various forms, including folksongs, songs composed to mark momentous occasions, and popular songs disseminated through print, sound recordings, radio, and television.

Alongside the oral tradition, a published tradition soon developed. Perhaps the first national song to be published in Australia, 'Song to the tune of Rule Britannia', was printed in the *Sydney Gazette* (1817). Although the words of the song praised the potential of the newly settled country, its musical setting implied a continuing link to England. As the colonies became established and populations grew, the demand for printed music to be performed in the parlours and at the balls of the colonists increased. Local compositions reflected the prevailing British fashion of ballads and salon music, but their words introduced subjects and sentiments more reflective of the landscape, flora and fauna of the new land. 'A Garland for Australia' (by L.Y. Ball, c.1840s), 'Our Australian Sky' (Bryant and Astbury, c.1850s), and the current national anthem, 'Advance Australia Fair' (Peter Dodds McCormick, 1878), are representative of this phase of colonial song-writing. The **Australian Natives Association**, which sought to cultivate patriotic feeling among native-born Australians, inspired songs of a more robustly patriotic kind such as 'Australians True' (Henry Walton and Hume Cook, 1900) and 'Australia for Ever' (Henry Rix, 1900). In the age of high **nationalism**, brass bands and rousing songs became weapons in the armoury of the electioneering politician and the military recruiting officer. **Federation**, the **Boer War**, and the world wars each prompted the composition of new songs, exciting national feeling in support of celebrations and fundraising events, and for propaganda and boosting morale. 'Australia' (Charles Kenningham), written for the Federation celebrations in 1901, 'For Auld Lang Syne! Australia Will be There' (W.W. Francis, 1914), written to pledge Australia's loyalty to Britain at the beginning of World War I, and 'Wake Up! Wake Up! Australia' (Alfred Hill, 1942), written when the Japanese were at Australia's gates, express this heightened sense of national endeavour.

The conventional sentiments of national songs are elevated and optimistic, and hence perhaps in conflict with an Australian ethos often characterised as unsentimental and sardonic. The most popular of Australian songs, Banjo **Paterson's 'Waltzing Matilda'**—a ballad about the violent death of an itinerant labourer—drew upon Paterson's knowledge of folk tradition but owed some of its popularity to the promotional efforts of a tea company. The **bush**, often conceived nostalgically as a loved but departed place, remained a favorite subject of Australian songs. The most famous song of the interwar period, when the drift from country to city gathered pace, was Jack O'Hagan's 'On the Road to Gundagai' (1922). Roger Covell writes of this genre in 'Winding Back Along the Track' (*Quadrant*, 1977). National **heroes** also inspired composers to create songs, such as 'Our Don Bradman' (O'Hagan, 1930).

The quest for a definitive national song has inspired almost as many competitions as memorable songs. In 1859 the German-born composer Carl Linger won a competition for 'Song of Australia', a setting of words by an English immigrant poet, Caroline Carleton. The Women's Work Exhibition of 1907 awarded a prize to 'God Guide Australia' (Florence Ewart and Annie Rentoul, 1907) and in the following year the *Bulletin* magazine announced a competition for 'an Australian song'. 'The Cross and the Great White Star' by 'Gum Tree' (the allusion in the title was to the new Commonwealth flag) and 'An Australian Battle Hymn' by J. Alex Allan shared the prize, but a special award was made to C.J. **Dennis** for the more jocular 'The Australaise', later adopted as a favorite song by soldiers of the **AIF**.

> Fellers of Australia
> Blokes and coves and coots,
> Shift your [bloody] carcases,
> Move your [bloody] boots.

The choice of an official national anthem has been determined as much by politics as popularity or musical quality. The British anthem 'God Save the King/Queen' was also Australia's anthem from 1788 to April 1974. In 1973 Prime Minister **Whitlam** held another competition for a new anthem which drew 1500 entries, none of them good enough to merit a prize, much less official adoption. Sixty thousand Australians were then polled to make a choice between 'Advance Australia Fair', 'Waltzing Matilda', and 'Song of Australia'. 'Advance Australia Fair' drew 51 per cent of the vote and was duly adopted as the National Anthem in 1974, although both it and 'God Save the Queen' were to be played at Australian state occasions when the Queen was present or to acknowledge her role as Queen of Australia and the Commonwealth at other appropriate occasions. Prime Minister **Fraser**, critical of Whitlam for imposing change, conducted a plebiscite on the anthem which included 'God Save the Queen' as an option. It confirmed the choice of 'Advance Australia Fair'. In 1984 Prime Minister R.J. **Hawke** declared 'Advance Australia Fair' as the national anthem, to be played at all official and ceremonial functions. It is an acceptable rather than a popular anthem. Older Australians have difficulty remembering the words, but elite athletes, who have mostly grown up learning it at school, at least now seem able to mouth them on the victory dais. John **Howard**, a professed royalist, has not attempted to displace it.

Meanwhile new moments in the life of the nation continue to inspire songs. Often now it is advertisers and television moguls who pay the piper and pop musicians who play the national tune. 'C'mon Aussie' (Allan Johnston and Alan Morris, 1978), the promotional jingle for Kerry **Packer's** World Series cricket, became an unofficial sporting anthem. Peter Allen's 'I Still Call Australia Home' (1980), written by the home-coming singer for an Australian concert tour, became an anthem for expatriates. And Bruce Woodley's 'We are Australians', commissioned for the 1988 Bicentenary, was taken up as a jingle by the government's Office of Multicultural Affairs. The Sydney 2000 Olympics gave indigenous musicians a high profile and reinforced the popularity of songs such as 'My Island Home' by Neil Murray, widely adopted by younger Australians as an anthem of national **reconciliation**.

For an overview of the genre, refer to Covell, 'Patriotic Songs: An Australian Disease' (*Quadrant*, 1977), and Georgina Binns, 'John Bull Jnr vs Blinky Bill: Music for an Australian Republic', in Brenton Broadstock (ed.), *Aflame with Music* (1996).

GEORGINA BINNS

National symbols have been effective to the extent that they are seen to evolve naturally from an agreed **national identity**. Yet national identity is rarely fixed or agreed, so symbols also need a certain ambiguity if they are to have wide appeal. The result is that the legitimacy of particular national symbols can increase or decrease over time, according to the emotional power derived from their growing familiarity, the extent to which they are formally recognised by government, their identification with sectional interests, and their perceived relevance to a changing society. The function of a national symbol can also vary. The role of the nation-state itself has changed considerably in the last two centuries; globalisation increasingly brings nations and their symbols in contact; and the technological capacity to reproduce visual symbols has transformed the world we see around us.

Of the formal symbols that require legitimation by government, **flags**, coats-of-arms, seals, and **national songs** are conceived as singular and permanent, whereas the design of **currency** and postage stamps has more scope to reflect a range of changing national concerns. Usually they reflect a bipartisan, if banal, consensus. In *Lion and Kangaroo* (1976), Gavin **Souter** showed how, when the Commonwealth of Australia came into existence in 1901, the new government contrived a set of symbols reflecting a dual loyalty, and combining relatively neutral symbols of Australia—the Southern Cross and Australian flora and fauna—with symbols of the British connection, such as the Union Jack, the lion, and the crown. Most had their critics. Use and familiarity generally led to broad acceptance, though Elizabeth Kwan (*AHS*, 1994) has demonstrated that the flag was not unquestioningly accepted even in the 1920s; particularly since Canada adopted a new flag in 1965, flag debates have regularly erupted around **Australia Day**. On the one hand,

the flag has, with time, symbolised a more shared national experience, and acquired a special emotional intensity from the fact that the nation has 'gone to war' under it; on the other hand, the presence of the Union Jack on the Australian flag has been seen as increasingly irrelevant to a population with a declining attachment to Britain. In the many proposals for a new flag, from Ausflag Ltd since 1993, the **Southern Cross** remains the most commonly featured symbol.

Other formal symbols have proved less controversial. The Australian coat-of-arms, granted in 1912 to replace a 1908 version, made use of the kangaroo and emu, and the wattle blossom, as well as the emblems of the six states. Coinage commonly used native animals on the reverse (the monarch's bust was on the obverse), but have also used symbols of produce (ears of wheat, the ram's head) and busts of Aborigines. Postage stamps have increasingly widened their range of subjects from these basic symbols to a multiplicity of subjects, most of which could not be thought of as national symbols.

Well before Federation, Australians had used this same range of symbols in a variety of less official contexts, from stained glass and cast iron to cartoons, to express a specifically colonial identity pictorially, and in this vernacular use of symbols there was usually no overt reference to the British connection. The Southern Cross appeared on flags from the early 1820s, most famously on the flag raised by the miners at the **Eureka Stockade** in 1854. The kangaroo has been the most enduring and widely recognised of all Australian national symbols, but the emu, the lyrebird, the koala, the platypus, and the kookaburra have also had their moments.

Flowers were widely used in design, particularly from the 1880s, when motifs based on the waratah, wattle, bottlebrush, and eucalyptus were popular. Margaret Betteridge, *Australian Flora in Art* (1979), showed the influence of Lucien Henry and R.T. Baker in technical colleges, where they encouraged the use of native flowers in Australian design. Such decorative work was prominent in the international **exhibitions** from 1879, in the arts and crafts movement of the 1900s, art deco design in the 1920s, and in the revived crafts movement of the 1970s. The coming of **Federation** encouraged national self-consciousness, and provoked a debate as to whether the wattle or the waratah should be adopted as the national flower. The wattle won. It also had associations with purity and cheerfulness, values which were vigorously promoted at the time as being representative of white Australia. At the turn of the century another popular natural symbol was the rising sun, which identified Australia with the future, unlike other nations' symbolic preoccupation with the past. It appeared on the NSW and South Australian coats-of-arms, was an element in **Federation architecture** and found favour with Australian military forces from 1902.

Other symbols moved beyond natural phenomena, and were more explicit politically. The Australian equivalent of Britannia or Columbia fitted the classical convention of an idealised woman. Usually blonde, befitting the land of the wattle, often with a shepherd's crook representing the wool industry, she was always young, clear-eyed, and innocent. In cartoons she often appeared vulnerable to foreign threats, or as the daughter of John Bull, balancing a continuing filial duty to Britain with a growing independence. The **Little Boy from Manly**, who first appeared in *Bulletin* cartoons in 1885, provided a similar balance.

Just as value-laden was the use of particular products to represent the nation. The golden fleece, the miner's pick, or the stook of wheat represented particular sectors of the economy, and grouped together they equated the nation with its economic resources. A more general pastoral image of sheep and gum trees popularised by the **Heidelberg School** became widely accepted as standing for the 'real' Australia by the end of the nineteenth century, despite the fact that Australia was highly urbanised. In general, the imagined landscape, rather than the imagined community, has supplied the majority of Australia's national symbols.

The use of national symbols became particularly popular as a way of delineating the emerging national market. With the development of packaging and illustrated advertising, trade marks, brand names, and marketing ploys of Australian-based companies exploited and elaborated an immense range of symbols, often humorously, as demonstrated by Mimmo Cozzolino in *Symbols of Australia* (1980). They appealed to the consumer's national sentiment, but also defined the Australian domestic market, particularly against imports from overseas. This symbolic definition of Australia as a market contributed critically to the development of national identity.

Many small manufacturers disappeared along with their trade marks, and heavy industry, expanding from the 1920s, challenged the bias towards rural symbolism. The lifesaver provided a popular national symbol between the two world wars, combining the bushman's mateship with the Anzac's bravery and voluntary sacrifice in an urban context. The **Sydney Harbour Bridge**, completed in 1932, symbolised industrial progress, while the **Sydney Opera House**, opened in 1972, became a readily recognisable symbol of urban sophistication. Beach imagery, backyard barbecues, and sport also became symbolic of a leisured lifestyle, and were reinforced with the rise of international **tourism**.

National symbols were further commercialised with television and advertisers' increasing sophistication in manipulating images. By the 1980s, as products developed new national markets (beer, sport, and media particularly), and the relative importance of Australian manufacturing in the domestic market declined, there was a revival of outback imagery. The successful 1983 America's Cup challenge used a boxing kangaroo, *Crocodile Dundee* revived a conservative version of the bushman, and **Uluru** came to symbolise the heart of Australia. By a curious process of back-formation, a number of brand names, products and logos—Aeroplane jelly, Arnott's biscuits, **Holden** cars, **Vegemite**, the **Qantas** kangaroo—became national symbols in their own right. While national symbols proliferated commercially, formal attempts to develop national symbolism appropriate to **multiculturalism** foundered. The Australian Bicentennial

Authority had trouble finding a logo and a slogan to satisfy everyone. As with **Anzac**, words associated with the Bicentenary were protected by legislation, but in this case so that commercial sponsors could exploit them more effectively. The search for a mascot for the 2000 Olympic Games inevitably returned to traditional fauna; the choice of three animals as mascots reflects both the difficulty of agreement on a single symbol as well as an awareness of commercial possibilities.

While native plants and animals supplied a constant stream of national symbolism over two centuries, the possibilities of Aboriginal culture were largely ignored, perhaps because white nationality was built on a denial of prior Aboriginal ownership of the land. Aboriginal figures were often used in trademarks before World War I, but usually in a humorous and derogatory context. The craft movement between the wars had shown an increasing interest in Aboriginal motifs, and in the 1950s Aboriginal figures and artefacts provided popular ornaments, garden statuary, souvenirs, and national decoration—for example, in the official account of the Commonwealth jubilee in 1951. Boomerangs particularly were a common symbol of Australia. They dominated the souvenir market but had wider use in the Buy Australian campaign launched in 1961.

The use of Aboriginal symbols as Australian national symbols has increased since the 1970s. They are often called on to fill the symbolic vacuum left by the breaking of monarchical ties. They have been stimulated by a new market for **Aboriginal art** and the development of the tourist industry, symbolised by the handover of **Uluru** to its traditional owners in 1985. The shift to the 'Red Centre' as symbolic heart is also evident in the (intentionally) under-stated symbolism of the new Parliament House. The Aboriginal flag has found a wide acceptance in the non-Aboriginal community and is probably the most frequently used symbolic source of proposals for a new flag after the Southern Cross. A new attitude to Aboriginal culture has opened up a whole new quarry of national symbolism, though whether it is driven by a spirit of reconciliation or appropriation is not always clear.

RICHARD WHITE

National trusts were formed in NSW in 1947, SA in 1955, and Victoria in 1956, followed by WA, Tasmania and Qld. Campaigns to conserve native bushland, like Sydney's Kuring-Gai National Park, and old mansions, like Melbourne's Como, provided the spur for the foundation of branches of the National Trust, on the model established in England in 1894. Their founders were mostly members of the local landed and professional elite united by a conception of the natural and built **heritage** as a 'trust' held by the present for posterity. The trusts acquired historic properties, such as Rippon Lea in Melbourne and the old Sydney Observatory, usually by donation, and opened them to the public. An Australian Council of National Trusts was formed in 1965. In the 1970s the trust became a vigorous heritage advocate, supporting the **green bans** placed on endangered historic buildings and neighbourhoods by militant trade unionists, such as Jack **Mundey** and his Builders Labourers Union. Financial and administrative crises in the late 1980s and early 1990s brought a consolidation of the trusts' primary role as fund-raisers and managers of historic properties, and decreased emphasis on its role as a heritage advocate, which was increasingly assumed by the new state heritage bodies. The founding years of the NSW National Trust are recalled in Ian Wyatt, *Ours in Trust* (1987), and pioneers of the Victorian Trust contributed their recollections to Mary Rhyllis Clark, *In Trust* (1996).

GD

Nationalism, always a difficult subject to analyse, presents peculiar problems in its Australian manifestation. To separate feeling for Australia as a whole, as distinct from attachment to some particular place within it, is one such problem; another is that, whereas for some nationalists a major source of joyous pride has been Australia's link with Britishness, for others the great aim has been separation from Britain. These complexities help explain why Australian nationalism has never attained vast strength.

On the deposition of Governor William **Bligh** on 26 January 1808, one of the rebels displayed a rudimentary coat-of-arms featuring kangaroo and emu. Presumably this sought to identify the deposition as an act of local patriotism, as also might have the choice of date for the coup. Such use of local fauna establishes that the physical environment has always sustained nationalist sentiment.

Consciousness of kind early developed among convicts and ex-convicts in NSW, along with their claims to improved status. Governor Lachlan **Macquarie** fostered this 'emancipist party', which came to include convict progeny, and liberals hostile to free-settler **exclusives**. Emancipist Australianism survived at least into the 1850s. W.C. **Wentworth** was its surpassing voice, particularly through his *Australian* newspaper, while its political arm in 1835 took the title, **Australian Patriotic Association**. James Martin's *Australian Sketch Book* (1838) brimmed with this liberal, nativist sentiment.

Such early nationalism was informed by movements of national liberation and unification that formed in Europe after 1815 in response to the Treaty of Versailles, and its restoration of autocratic, imperial regimes. This nationalism drew on romantic and advanced liberal sources to construct the nation as a progressive force. While resident in Van Diemen's Land 1826–29, the feminist Mary Leman Grimstone wrote in praise of that place and nativist attachment, themes she resumed in the 1840s when associated with the Italian nationalist, Giuseppe Mazzini. In NSW Mazzinian ideas (mixed with American Transcendentalism) were proclaimed by Charles **Harpur** from the 1830s, with J.D. **Lang** adding a republican edge after 1850. Whereas emancipist patriotism drew from the convict past, Grimstone, Harpur, and Lang all repudiated that legacy. The latter pair became active in the **anti-transportation** cause, which developed inter-colonial organisation and sported a flag featuring the **Southern Cross**. John **West**, supreme anti-transportation publicist, pioneered intellectual debate as to **Federation**.

The same European nationalism that exploded in revolution in 1848 helped foment the discord which led to **Eureka** in 1854. Dissident miners followed anti-transportationists in invoking the Southern Cross. Also potent in this situation was Irish assertiveness, which already had had some part in emancipism, and long continued to take a nationalist bearing. Through the generation ahead, Victoria contributed much to nationalism. Charles Gavan **Duffy**, fresh from the Young Ireland movement, used his position as a cabinet minister there to prompt inter-colonial discussion of federationist ideas. More important was Victoria's style of economic nationalism, centred on tariff **protection**, as advanced by the Scottish David **Syme**. Victoria's many Presbyterians, conscious of their church's missionary interests, fostered geo-political awareness within Australia as France and Germany pushed into the South Pacific.

Several further elements, very different among themselves, made for nationalist vigour in the 1880s and 1890s. In Qld a nationalist party led by Thomas **McIlwraith** seized eastern New Guinea after Britain refused to, and insisted on being consulted on the appointment of governors. Federation became a constant, if problematic, point of reference for the nation that was to be. One dynamic towards its achievement was intent to have a louder voice in world and imperial affairs. Interlocked with that was a surge of liberal nationalism, which had its major mass support from the **Australian Natives Association**—which started as a **benefit society** but became an engine of nationalist ideas and practice. Alfred **Deakin** was the ANA's hero, while others to extol Federation in a liberal-nationalist way included R.R. **Garran** and W. Jethro **Brown**.

Some bourgeois liberals, H.B. **Higgins** and A.B. **Piddington** among them, opposed the proposed scheme of Federation, believing it would thwart true nationality by sustaining archaic state interests. Similar views prevailed on the radical left. **Republicanism** had its heyday in the 1880s, allied with variants of **socialism**. Similar feeling tinctured the early labour parties, but the view that prevailed, argued most fervently by William **Lane** and most effectively by W.G. **Spence** and W.M. **Hughes**, was that Australia's destiny was to spearhead white-race leadership in Darwinian evolution towards national-socialist fulfilment.

The *Bulletin* fostered nationalist writing and art which presented the bushman as a distinctive Australian figure—capable, resolute, independent, yet altruistic. That shearers and miners were ardent trade unionists made such ideas attractive to Labor. Supreme among the expositors was Joseph **Furphy**, but Francis **Adams's** *The Australians* (1893) had more immediate impact. Tom **Roberts** and Arthur **Streeton** were the period's outstanding artists of nationalist thrust.

The reality of Federation and the world's deepening crisis together sharpened nationalism after 1901. **White Australia** legislation affirmed the pervasiveness of racial thought. Defence preparations brought Hughes–Spence Laborites to support programs of national efficiency and helped reconcile them to Empire. Major nationalist writing now came from two **bush** mythologists, C.E.W. **Bean** and Bernard **O'Dowd**. Bean extolled bush influence and bush people as elements that would mould Australia's creative evolution; his thought combined elements from his Anglo-Australian classical education with ideas akin to those of Henry Bergson and George Sorel. O'Dowd drew from Walt Whitman and leftist republicanism as he imagined how the bush might inspire psychic and spiritual energy for Australia's advance. From London the Qld-born William Baylebridge, much influenced by **eugenics**, developed ideas as to Australia's future which prefigured interwar fascisms.

Bean and Baylebridge were among the many who saw World War I as consummating Australian nationalism. Subsequently, they wrote books to further that outcome, while celebration of **Anzac Day** and much rhetoric instilled like views into everyday thought. Non-Labor was ardent for Anzac and Empire, although some feared that Britain might no longer be able and willing to protect Australia. On the Labor side, isolationism and introversion went deeper.

Congruent attitudes affected cultural practice. In the 1920s Henry Tate and Percy **Grainger** sought musical inspiration from the sounds of Australian nature, and Margaret **Preston** used Aboriginal motifs in her nationalist-cum-modernist art. Such trends deepened and darkened in years ahead. **Jindyworobak** ideas, led by Rex Ingamells, upheld the creative harmony between Aborigines and the environment as a model for European Australians, while P.R. **Stephensen** yearned to destroy links with Britain, cultural and political. Stephensen became a leader in the **Australia First Movement**, fascistic in style and hostile to involvement in World War II; earlier he had worked with Norman **Lindsay** and the *Bulletin* to publish Australian works, and had some (tortuous) connection with Xavier **Herbert's** writing of *Capricornia* (1938).

After 1940 nationalism's impact diminished, as was evident for example in failure to add to the **Anzac Legend** and slowness in approaching republican status. Explanation might lie in the fact that Australia had now achieved such autonomy, in both politics and culture, that deliberate and self-conscious nationalism became otiose. Arguably, Australian nationalism was so much a factor of European hegemony that it could not but wither as that hegemony did. The new immigration and consequent **multiculturalism** called for different approaches to **national identity**. Various intellectual forces ran against the old ideas. Humphrey **McQueen's** *A New Britannia* (1970), written from a **New Left** stance, presented traditional nationalism as morally and ideologically degenerate; influenced by postmodernism, Richard White in (*Inventing Australia*, 1981) argued that there was no Australia, only different images of it created to serve particular purposes. Feminist historians, led by Patricia Grimshaw, presented their sex as crucial and even dominant in *Creating a Nation* (1994), but 'nationalism' had no place in that book's index.

Perhaps the remarkable phenomenon is that anything like the old nationalism echoed at all. *Meanjin* and *Overland* were two literary journals of acclaim and influence which confirmed the tie between radical politics and this tradition in the 1950s and 1960s. Communist influence also went in this direction from the 1930s. Thus Russel **Ward's** *The Australian Legend* (1958) synthesised Francis Adams, C.E.W. Bean, the *Bulletin* tradition, and Vance **Palmer**, and the book has found ready audiences ever since. Manning **Clark**, once sceptical of old-style nationalism, came increasingly to uphold it as his *History* advanced. Patrick **White** in fiction; Judith **Wright** and Les **Murray** in poetry; Arthur **Boyd**, Sidney **Nolan**, and Fred **Williams** in art—these are foremost among creators who have explored and defined Australia with passionate commitment. Clark and White helped lead the republican surge which followed John **Kerr's dismissal** of the **Whitlam** government in 1975. Humphrey McQueen himself, together with radical feminist Kay Daniels, joined in the Committee to Review Australian Studies in Australian Tertiary Education, which in its 1987 report argued that Australianist elements should pervade virtually all such curricula. Conceivably, the nationalist tradition will revive in the third millennium.

The history of nationalism has been explored by Stephen Alomes, *A Nation at Last?* (1988); Noel McLachlan, *Waiting for the Revolution* (1989); and W.G. McMinn, *Nationalism and Federalism in Australia* (1994).

MICHAEL ROE

Nationalist Party (1917–31) was formed during World War I as a union of the anti-Labor forces and those members of the Labor Party who followed W.M. **Hughes** into the pro-conscription National Labor Party. It took its name from the National Federation, the party organisation, and was in turn heavily dependent upon the National Union, an association of businessmen who financed conservative politics. The Nationalist Party held office in federal politics from its formation until 1929. It cultivated an aggressive imperial nationalism, and in the elections of 1922 and 1925 successfully impugned the loyalty of the Australian Labor Party and the labour movement. Its own centre of gravity was unstable. Conservative opposition to Hughes's populist state interventionism culminated in his replacement as prime minister by S.M. **Bruce** in 1923, but divisions between the protectionist manufacturing interests and the market-oriented pastoral and finance sectors remained endemic. In state politics the electoral pragmatism of Nationalist leaders was repeatedly challenged by conservative dissidents. Following the defeat of the Nationalists in the 1929 federal election and the replacement of Bruce by J.G. **Latham**, these internal tensions became unmanageable and a new political party, the **United Australia Party**, was formed in 1931.

SM

Native police, sometimes called Black Police, were corps of Aborigines, generally mounted, as distinct from the individual **black trackers** employed by the colonial police forces. Usually the native police operated on the frontiers of white settlement.

The earliest, short-lived force, established in the late 1830s in the **Port Phillip District**, was formed with the dual purpose of utilising Aboriginal bush skills and 'civilising' the men. A second corps operated in Melbourne 1842–53; it is the subject of Marie Fels's *Good Men and True* (1988). The prestige of a smart uniform and opportunity to ride attracted an influential group of recruits, many of whom were clan heads. William **Strutt** captured their pride and elegance in a series of portraits. This corps was never involved in the brutalities associated with other native police. They were reformed briefly to assist in the hunt for Ned **Kelly**.

A similar body, formed in NSW in 1848, operated mainly in the north of the colony. This corps became known for its brutality towards local Aborigines and was implicated in several **massacres**. Qld took over responsibility for the corps in 1859, following its separation from NSW, and it was regularly used to 'disperse' Aborigines who hindered white settlement until disbanded in 1900. SA had a force between 1852 and 1856 and, in 1884, formed another for use in the NT, then under its control. This force also became notorious for atrocities, and was eventually disarmed and used solely for tracking. Although WA made use of armed trackers, it never formed an Aboriginal police corps. Native police figure in A.L. Haydon's early general study, *The Trooper Police of Australia* (1911). Bill Rosser's *Up Rode the Troopers: The Black Police in Queensland* (1990) is an impassioned account of the violence so frequently perpetrated by these forces. Fels's revisionist argument in *Good Men and True* seeks to explain why Aborigines were prepared to serve as native police.

KT

Native Title, see **Aboriginal land rights**; **Mabo case**; **Wik decision**

Natural history is the descriptive study of animals, plants and minerals. It originated in medieval times when it was primarily concerned with the uses, 'wonders', or edifying properties of nature. During the era of European expansion, exploration and the discovery of new species led to more detailed classificatory systems. The natural history of Australia was little recorded in early Dutch voyages of the seventeenth century, although there were observations of wallaby, quokka, and black swan. William **Dampier's** account of his 1699 voyage in the *Roebuck* to WA was unusually rich in its natural history descriptions for this early period.

The European invasion of Australia, where 'all things [were] queer and opposite', came at the height of classificatory mania following the emergence of Linnaean 'binomial' nomenclature in 1753. Taxonomy was the 'new science' that Joseph **Banks** and his scientific colleagues on the *Endeavour* brought to the botanical investigation of the east coast of Australia in 1770. Bernard **Smith**, *European Vision and the South Pacific* (1960), and C.M. Finney, *To Sail Beyond the Sunset* (1984), who quotes the puzzled response to the new land, describe the scientific framework of imperial exploration. Banks's testimony in 1779 at a Select Committee of the House of Commons on the location for a penal settlement probably influenced its choice of Botany Bay. As director of the Royal Botanic Gardens at Kew from 1772, Banks saw the natural history of the 'new' land as an urgent task: he personally financed early botanical collections, paying for the salaries of collectors and for modifications to ships to transport specimens, sometimes with disastrous effects on their seaworthiness.

French–British imperial rivalry often took a natural history dimension. The French scientific expeditions of d'Entrecasteaux (1793) and **Baudin** (1801–03) (see F.B. Horner, *Looking for La Pérouse*, 1995, and *The French Reconnaissance*, 1987) were also important in early understandings of Australia's natural history. 'Cabinets of curiosity' were a mark of class and civilisation, a cultural rather than an economic resource of Empire. The visual dimensions of natural history were important to the collectors, and the artistic works—formal and informal alike—a key to understanding early natural historians, as Ann **Moyal** argued in *A Bright and Savage Land: Scientists in Colonial Australia* (1986).

Perhaps the excitement about the 'curious' was compensation for the scenery, with its 'eternal gum trees', which many found dull. 'There is not the slightest variation whatever in the foliage for mile after mile: no light and shade for the leaves hang straight down', said Professor Baldwin **Spencer** on his arrival in 1887. Victoria's government botanist, Ferdinand von **Mueller**, spent his first 15 years collecting with a passion, gathering 350 000 plant specimens—the core of the National Herbarium of Victoria—on arduous expeditions in the 1850s and 1860s. Like Spencer, he came to love the Australian environment, and was one of the champions of its **conservation** and study. In the 1850s in Victoria (and later in WA), the discovery of gold brought a new urgency to the mineralogical exploration of Australia.

Physiologically based biology and geology took over from natural history towards the end of the nineteenth century. One example of this was the approach to the platypus, which was initially thought to be a taxidermist's hoax, since it appeared that a duck's bill had been attached to a mammal. British classifiers doubted the evidence of colonial collectors until Cambridge scientist W.H. Caldwell, working with Aboriginal collectors, obtained eggs of both platypus and echidna in 1884. His famous technical telegram, 'Monotremes oviparous ovum meroblastic', was received at the British Association for the Advancement of Science meeting in Montreal, moving the platypus out of natural history and into the physiologist's laboratory. Colin Finney, *Paradise Revealed* (1993), and the biography of Spencer, '*So Much That Is New*' (1985), by D.J. **Mulvaney** and John Calaby, provide historical context for the transitional era of the late nineteenth century.

The older tradition of natural history, which documented the social and cultural contexts of living things, was marginalised by professional science. Nature writers like Donald Macdonald and Charles Barrett maintained an interest in natural history 'with a human touch' in the early twentieth century. Groups such as **field naturalists' clubs** also fostered emotional attachments to nature. In this way, natural history was a cornerstone of 'the sense of place' which Tom Griffiths links to early historical consciousness in *Hunters and Collectors* (1996).

Despite growing pride in Australian flora and fauna—for example, the kangaroo and emu on the national coat of arms—the image of Australia as the 'stock farm of the Empire' dominated the emerging sciences. The **Australian and New Zealand Association for the Advancement of Science** (ANZAAS), inaugurated in 1888, advocated 'biological surveys', but the funding for such ventures was not forthcoming. Scientific research was dedicated to improving imported food and fibre species, and dealing with associated **pests**. Research on indigenous flora and fauna remained the realm of amateur natural historians until the second half of the twentieth century.

LIBBY ROBIN

Neilson, John Shaw (1872–1942) was, like Robert Burns, a labouring man and a poet. He was born into a poor selector's family, which moved from Penola, SA, to the harsh Wimmera and Mallee areas of Victoria. Neilson's appreciation for the beauty of this sparse landscape is embodied in his lyrical verse. He published regularly in the *Bulletin* from 1896 and A.G. **Stephens** became a trusted mentor. The first published collection, *Heart of Spring*, appeared in 1919, followed in 1923 by *Ballads and Lyrical Poems*, which contained 'The Orange Tree', probably his best-known poem. Neilson was subject to failing eyesight from the early 1900s, though he continued to work as a labourer until 1928 when he was given an office job in Melbourne, after which he wrote little more. His autobiography was published in 1978. Hugh Anderson produced a revised bibliography in 1964, and Cliff Hanna has written several studies of Neilson.

KT

Never-Never refers to the seemingly never-ending expanse of land, of unknown area and imprecise boundaries, in the arid Australian **outback**. The expression suggests the inaccessibility and inhospitability of this country, and the vulnerability of white people's place in it, but generally ignores its occupation by Aborigines. The term originally meant a vast tract of 'unoccupied' land and referred specifically to a remote area of north-west Qld and eastern NT. One explanation of its origin, given by F. de B. Cooper in *Wild Adventures in Australia* (1857), suggests a corruption of the Aboriginal word *nievah vahs*, which meant 'unoccupied land'. The term was popularised through Jeannie **Gunn's** novel, *We of the Never Never* (1907), in which Gunn provided an explanation: 'they who have lived in it and loved it, Never Never voluntarily leave it [while] others—the unfitted ... swear they will Never Never return to it'. Earlier, Henry **Lawson** had used the term in his poem 'Marshall's Mate': 'Beyond the farthest Gov'ment tank, and past the farthest bore — / The Never-Never, No Man's Land, No More and Nevermore'. As with their treatment of

the outback, writers and artists have been both enchanted by its romance and alienated by its harshness.

HD

New Australia was the name of a utopian socialist settlement established by labour figure William **Lane** on a large area of land in Paraguay donated by the Paraguayan government. Lane founded the New Australia Movement in despair at the prospects of social reform in Australia in 1892, following the **maritime** and **shearers' strikes**. He gathered a large number of supporters, including the poet Mary **Gilmore**, who travelled with him to Paraguay the following year aboard the *Royal Tar*. The settlement was envisaged as a communal, self-providing cooperative, but difficulties soon emerged as a result of members' poor farming skills and unfamiliarity with the country. This exacerbated internal dissension and led, in 1894, to a split in the movement. Lane established a second, breakaway settlement nearby, named Cosme, but this was largely broken up by 1905. Some of the settlers returned to Australia, but others stayed. Gavin **Souter** provides the best account of the settlement's establishment and its failure in *A Peculiar People* (1968). The settlers who remained are the subject of Anne Whitehead's *Paradise Mislaid* (1997). Michael Wilding has written a fictional account, *The Paraguayan Experiment* (1984).

HD

New Australians was a term first used in the 1890s in reference to those who accompanied William **Lane** to his **New Australia** settlement in South America. The term gained a new meaning in 1949, when the minister for immigration, Arthur **Calwell**, proposed that the large numbers of recently arrived European migrants be known as 'New Australians', rather than by the various derogatory names then in common use. Calwell believed this would encourage a feeling of belonging on the part of the migrants, and would engender their acceptance. It coincided with the creation of Australian citizenship in 1948, and the encouragement of migrants to acquire this status. (See also **Assimilation**; **Immigration**.)

HD

Newcomb, Caroline, see **Drysdale, Anne**, and **Newcomb, Caroline**

New chum was a term recorded in convict J.H. **Vaux's** 1812 dictionary of criminal slang to describe a recent arrival to gaol or the prison hulks. Newly arrived convicts to Australia were thus termed *new chums*. By the 1840s its meaning had extended to free settlers recently arrived in the colonies, usually English, who were unfamiliar with colonial life. New chums' ignorance and inexperience became a source of amusement for 'old chums' or old hands, especially for **emancipists** and **currency** folk, who were proud of their own colonial expertise and intolerant of less experienced settlers. The distinction between the old chums and new chums—the same meaning was also originally attached to the word *jackeroo*—was especially pronounced in the bush. Popular literature frequently portrayed new chums as comical figures. Percy Clarke wrote as *The New Chum in Australia* (1886) and J.D. Hennessy published a farmer's guide, *The New Chum Farmer* (1897); Paul Wentz's humourous account, *The Diary of a New Chum*, appeared in 1908. Russel **Ward** claimed that this scorn for new chums helped formulate a nationalist tradition.

HD

New Guard, see **Secret armies**

New Guinea, see **Papua New Guinea–Australian relations**

New Holland, the name by which Australia was commonly known from around the mid-seventeenth century, signalled the leading role of Dutch navigators in its exploration. Alternative names, such as Terra Australis, were also in use and **Australia** was proposed as the official name in 1817. The name New Holland nevertheless persisted into the early nineteenth century.

HD

New Left was a radical political movement of the late 1960s, and a radical historiography of the 1970s, the former defining itself against the consumer capitalism of the **long boom**, and the latter against the **Old Left** historians. There had been an earlier New Left, which broke from the **Communist** Party over the invasion of Hungary in 1956, was disenchanted with the Soviet model, and placed its faith in humanist **socialism**. It was represented in Helen Palmer's *Outlook* (1982), and described in Alan Barcan's *The Socialist Left in Australia* (1960). One of the few threads connecting this and the late 1960s movement was anti-racist activism in the mid-1960s, over Aboriginal rights and the **White Australia** policy.

In an accelerated radicalisation after 1966, student radicals, younger members of the Communist Party, and counter-culturalists formed a second New Left, made up of disparate elements ranging from the libertarianism of Students for a Democratic Society to the Bolshevism of Maoists. If they were united, it was by two themes. One was the critique of Australian racism and **nationalism**, which became principal motifs of New Left historiography. A second was the critique of Australian capitalism, characterised as imperial subservience and pervasive liberalism. Inspirations were varied, but included the Frankfurt School of neo-Marxism and, most importantly, Gramsci's analysis of **bourgeois hegemony**. These, among other inspirations, are seen in Richard Gordon's collection *The Australian New Left* (1970), which also illustrated the importance of the **Vietnam War** as a catalyst for the New Left's development. As a movement, the New Left remained campus-bound, the peak of its influence being its part in the **Moratorium** movement, though its analysis flowed through radical politics in the 1970s. Largely because **gender** was beyond the New Left's horizons, the feminist movement of the early 1970s developed against, as much as within, its ambit, a relationship reflected autobiographically by Ann Curthoys in *For and Against Feminism* (1988).

Where the Old Left glorified working-class traditions as inherently radical and egalitarian, the New Left's historiography disputed the claim. A subtle version was Terry Irving and Baiba Berzins, 'History and the New Left' (in Gordon's collection), describing the Old Left as 'vulgar Marxists' unable to see that 'middle-class hegemony' had progressively absorbed working-class radicalism. But the point was sharpest in Humphrey **McQueen's** *A New Britannia* (1970), an excoriating critique of Russel **Ward**, Geoffrey **Serle**, Ian **Turner**, Robin **Gollan**, and Brian **Fitzpatrick**. The **Australian Legend** they had constructed during the Cold War was now 'counter-revolutionary', a nostalgic and populist fancy which lacked class analysis. McQueen wrote with iconoclastic verve. Australian labourist sentiments had been racist, imperialist, petit-bourgeois, and acquisitive; labourism was more racist than socialist, and the **Australian Labor Party** 'fog-bound within capitalism'. The apogee of this iconoclasm was McQueen's description of Henry **Lawson** as a fascist, a view later recanted. Manning **Clark's** foreword was remarkably restrained: the New Left were 'latter-day Robespierres', the book illustrated 'the New Left as judges'. While not all shared its censorious exultation, McQueen's history was highly influential, insisting on the theme of racism and marking a distinct rupture with the Old Left. Yet with its emphasis on attitudes at the expense of social relations, and its absences of gender, culture, and Aborigines, perhaps *A New Britannia* was, as McQueen disarmingly put it, the last Old Left history.

Through the 1970s, New Left historians developed, with more finesse, similar themes. Stuart Macintyre's 'Radical History and Bourgeois Hegemony' (*Intervention*, 1972) continued the Gramscian critique of the Old Left, while 'The Making of the Australian Working Class' (*HS*, 1978) criticised McQueen's excessive concern with consciousness at the expense of lived class experience, and signalled the influence of radical social history. The omnipresence of liberalism was the theme of Tim Rowse's *Australian Liberalism and National Character* (1978). Explorations of racism took a more central place in **labour histories**, such as the collection by Ann Curthoys and Andrew Markus, *Who Are Our Enemies?* (1978), though Aboriginal histories of the 1970s were less obviously indebted to the New Left. Bob Connell, combining sociology and history, extended the analysis of hegemony in *Ruling Class, Ruling Culture* (1977); while Ian Turner's measured response to the critics in 'Temper Democratic, Bias Australian' (*Overland*, 1978), defended the radical nationalists in their Cold War context. In 1980, Connell and Irving published the first and last general history from a New Left position, *Class Structure in Australian History*, a history of class as a social relation, influenced by E.P. Thompson, Gramsci, and Althusser. The length of its gestation suggested the difficulty of writing a history while the New Left's theory was changing, first with structuralism, then with the emerging crisis of Marxism. By 1980 the New Left was not so much over as dispersed, but its traces remained in the shape of radical histories, particularly labour, **social**, and **feminist histories**.

JOHN MURPHY

New Protection was the policy introduced by the Commonwealth in 1906 that laid the foundations of the **basic wage**. The protectionist government led by Alfred **Deakin** relied on the support of the **Australian Labor Party**, which was initially divided over the merits of **protection**. Deakin thus coupled the device to the protection of working-class living standards by combining a tariff on imported goods with an excise duty on locally produced ones; the duty would be waived if the local producer paid his workers a 'fair and reasonable wage'. In response to an application for such relief from H.V. **McKay's** Sunshine Harvester company, H.B. **Higgins**, the president of the **Arbitration Court**, determined the level of a fair and reasonable wage for a male breadwinner, and this standard was subsequently extended across the workforce.

SM

New South Wales, founded as a convict settlement in 1788, was the mother colony of the Australias; its inhabitants continue to believe that it is the heartland of the nation. Historians have supported them in this; since World War II they have written histories of every state except NSW. The history of NSW has to be found within the histories of Australia.

The pre-eminence of NSW has a substantial basis. At its foundation it encompassed two-thirds of the continent. Four other colonies were carved from it: **Tasmania**, 1825; **South Australia**, 1836; **Victoria**, 1851; **Queensland**, 1859; and the **Northern Territory** in 1863. Three of today's capital cities—**Hobart**, **Brisbane**, and **Melbourne**—were first ruled from **Sydney**. When NSW assumed its present dimensions in 1863, it was second in population to gold-rush Victoria whose capital, Melbourne, had become the country's largest city. In the long term, its more abundant resources in land and possession of iron ore and black coal enabled it to overtake its upstart rival. In the early 1890s NSW resumed its position as the most populous colony and 10 years later Sydney again became, as it has remained, the country's largest city.

While Victoria pioneered the policy of **protection** for local industry; NSW became the standard-bearer for free trade. Victoria adopted protective duties in part to raise revenue as returns from land sales declined; NSW continued to reap large sums from land sales until the 1880s. It also had less need to promote **manufacturing** to provide employment because economic growth came from the further development of the pastoral industry. In 1892, just before the great drought, NSW carried more than 50 million sheep, over 60 per cent of the continent's total. The colony had passed the most radical of the **Selection** Acts in 1861 but small holdings made fewer inroads into pastoralism than in Victoria and SA. NSW did not grow enough grain to feed

itself until around 1900. Until the railways crossed the Great Dividing Range, **wheat** growing on the western slopes and plains was not viable except for the small local market. The railways arrived in the 1880s and 1890s when the modern wheat belt began to take shape. At the same time **dairying**, **sugar**, and maize production became well established on the well-watered coastal lands.

Good-quality black coal was discovered in the Hunter Valley, 150 kilometres north of Sydney, in the 1790s. The coal was within easy reach of the sea and this basic **energy** source was shipped from Newcastle to the other colonies for their factories, **railways**, and gas works. There was a substantial foreign export trade as well. In 1915 **BHP** established its first steelworks at Newcastle, with the iron ore being shipped from Whyalla in SA. The colony's first iron- and steelworks had been established 40 years earlier at Lithgow, just west of the Divide, where iron and coal were found together. In the 1920s they were transferred to Port Kembla, another coal-mining centre on the coast 80 kilometres south of Sydney. The state's two centres of heavy industry, Newcastle and Port Kembla–Wollongong, are now the northern and southern outliers of the greater Sydney conurbation.

The confidence of NSW in its economic capacity partly explains its reluctance to join the Australian **federation**. In the 1890s the colony moved more decisively to free trade and so differentiated itself more sharply from the other colonies that had followed Victoria into protection. If an Australian federation were formed, it seemed likely that it would adopt a protectionist policy and hence Sydney would lose its advantage as a free port. It was to compensate for this and to honour its foundation role that NSW claimed the federal capital for itself. The other colonies refused to make Sydney the capital, but agreed that it should be in NSW, at least 160 kilometres from Sydney. Such is the speed of modern travel that **Canberra**, almost twice that distance from Sydney, may yet become one of its dormitory suburbs.

Sydney supplanted Melbourne as the country's commercial and financial capital from the 1960s. The older city is oriented to the Pacific, the new source of trade, investment, and migrants, and its more central location has made it the hub of air traffic. The abandonment of the national protection policy in the 1980s represented the final victory of Sydney over Melbourne. From the 1980s Sydney also became the pre-eminent cultural and media centre.

The pre-eminence of NSW in age, resources, and people and the dominance of its capital city means that it is difficult to deny it a central place in the nation's history. Australian history, especially before 1851, is frequently written as NSW with the other bits tacked on. Each state does have its own distinctive history which would be better recognised if John McCarty's suggestion were followed and Australian history were conceived federally, so that the interconnections between its various states and regions were made the central object of analysis. But to consider NSW as no more than the first among equals would miss much of what has assumed general significance in Australia's past. Its more diverse, complex, and fractured society has given the nation its defining moments and symbols.

A founding population of **convicts** made NSW unique and its **convict history** has been a national preoccupation. There were other convict settlements in Australia, but only in Sydney and its hinterland did ex-convicts quickly acquire wealth, staff the professions, and assume public responsibilities. Their progeny were found in the ranks of good society. In the nineteenth century the free settlements of Victoria and SA were reluctant to acknowledge descent from this anomalous society. But as shame at the 'convict stain' has given way to pride, Sydney and its harbour are more willingly accepted as the **foundation** site of the nation, and the national imagination dwells on the contrast between the barbarism of convict punishments and the beauty of the locale. The difficulty in celebrating 26 January as **Australia Day** now lies more in the offence it gives to Aborigines than in the slight to the other states.

NSW was an eighteenth-century foundation. This as much as its convict origins determined the nature of its early society. Its people came from a Britain and Ireland, where **liberalism** had not touched the middle class or self-improvement and **democracy** the lower orders. The odd assortment of settler adventurers made their money and disputed precedence in a society of ranks where the landed gentlemen assumed they would hold the commanding position. In the 1850s, when the colony was allowed to draw up a **constitution** for self-government, William **Wentworth**, the leader of the landed gentlemen, planned an upper house to be composed of a colonial nobility. By this time there was a liberal and radical movement which succeeded in removing this part of Wentworth's plan. An Australian nobility, only attempted in NSW, received a memorable Australian reply. The radical Daniel **Deniehy** denounced it as a **bunyip aristocracy**.

The liberal-radical movement bundled the landed gentlemen from power as soon as the new constitution came into force. This was the first of the two rapid transformations which have marked NSW political history. The new rulers introduced manhood suffrage and passed a radical land law, but much of the driving force for democracy came from a desire to claim the rewards of a society of ranks. Who should gain the gentlemanly post of justice of the peace long continued an important issue.

Liberal politics settled into **factional** manoeuvring where roads, bridges, and government jobs were the rewards; Henry **Parkes** was a master at this. In the 1880s a new trade union and radical movement mobilised outside these structures. It was enlivened by a fresh wave of working-class migrants who brought **socialism** and **republicanism** with them. A new dissenting voice appeared in the Sydney *Bulletin*, the first national publication, which scorned the stuffiness, pettiness, and toadying loyalty of the established politicians. On the defeat of the unions in the 1890 **Maritime Strike**, politics underwent its second transformation. A newly formed Labor Party gained a quarter of the seats at its first election, its most spectacular

Australian debut. It marked its contempt for parliamentary politics by insisting that its members vote as caucus directed, a discipline which was adopted by all the Labor parties. NSW Labor established itself as the natural party of government because, as well as appealing to city workers and to miners, it gained support in the countryside from pastoral workers and struggling selectors who wanted better opportunities on the land.

The survival of pastoralism represented a failure for the liberal-radical movement of the mid-nineteenth century which had planned to establish yeoman farmers throughout the bush, but paradoxically this 'failure' supported a society which came to be regarded as typically Australian. Here the ordinary working man acquired greater self-confidence and dignity. His labour in demand, frequently mounted on his own horse, he moved confidently through these vast untamed spaces. Outside his work little control was exercised over him. The state and the institutions of civil society were weak; his employers were content if they protected their cattle from theft and got their sheep shorn. The state actually encouraged frontier anarchy by allowing the selector under 'free selection' to locate himself unannounced on the pastoralist's run. The state was humiliated in the 1860s by a spectacular revival of **bushranging**, when bushrangers for the first time became national heroes, their exploits carried by telegraph and newspaper Australia-wide. In the 1880s and 1890s this pastoral world was celebrated by two NSW writers, Henry **Lawson** and Banjo **Paterson**, who more than anyone else have defined Australian types and values.

In the great twentieth-century crisis of the **Depression**, society divided more sharply in NSW than in the rest of the country. The demagogic Labor premier Jack **Lang** frightened not only Sydney's but also the nation's bourgeoisie with his plans to default on payment to British bondholders. Working people in Sydney came close to worshipping Lang; in the affluent suburbs on the other side of the harbour a private army, the New Guard, was formed which was to combat Lang and his red allies. When Lang stepped forward to open the Sydney Harbour Bridge, Captain de Groot, an officer in the New Guard, beat him to the ribbon and opened the bridge in the name of the decent citizens of NSW. Lang was dismissed by the governor when he defied federal law which was to force NSW to pay the interest on its debt.

After the Labor Party had rid itself of Lang, it developed into a ruthless pragmatic machine avoiding extreme measures in order to hold on to the fruits of office. With a strong Catholic element, it maintained good relations with the Catholic hierarchy, which were not disturbed by the **split** over **communism** in the 1950s. Long periods of rule by this party have helped make Sydney now the quintessential Australian city, raffish, hedonistic, where old wealth means little and new wealth is admired and ostentatiously displayed. In the nineteenth century Melbourne was regarded as the American city and Sydney as more English. The reverse is now true. It was in Sydney in 1991 that the modern republican movement was founded and attracted for the first time wealthy and influential supporters.

JOHN HIRST

New South Wales Corps was a British regiment formed in 1789. Its first detachment sailed with the Second Fleet and arrived in Sydney in 1790. Officers of the corps quickly became involved in local trade. For a short period (1792–95) it had virtual administrative control over the colony, and its members, who included John **Macarthur**, gained large land grants. By exploiting its position, notably through its control of the rum trade—hence its later name 'Rum Corps'—the regiment developed a reputation for corruption. Convicts feared and despised the 'redcoats' for their bullying tactics. Criticism of the corps intensified with the notorious **Rum Rebellion** of 1808, when the corps deposed Governor **Bligh**. On the arrival of the reformist governor, Lachlan **Macquarie**, in 1810, the officers of the corps were requested to return to England. The corps' abuse of authority was inflated somewhat in later accounts of the period, including that by John Dunmore **Lang**—and this view has endured. However, many members of the regiment brought specialised skills to NSW, and contributed constructively to the development of the colony. Pamela Statham published *A Colonial Regiment* in 1991.

HD

New states have been regularly proposed within the boundaries of the colonies and the states. The most persistent claimants have been north Qld, New England, and the Riverina. The desire for new states has been fuelled by rural resentment at metropolitan domination and neglect, though the wish to escape from a particular state policy has often been the spur for action: north Qld in the 1880s to preserve its **Pacific Island labour** force; the Riverina in the 1860s to escape free **selection** and, in the 1930s, Jack **Lang**. New states were promoted by the Country Party (later **National Party**); in New England, a party stronghold, the most determined effort for a new state was made. In 1967 a referendum was held in the region; it was defeated chiefly because of strong opposition in the Hunter Valley, which had been included to make a more viable state. The federal **Constitution** provides for the formation of new states, but to allay state fears of dismemberment, a proposed new state has to be supported by the parliament of the state affected. Since the 1970s a new state across the north of Australia has sometimes been proposed to take in north Qld, the NT, and northern WA.

JH

New Zealand–Australian relations before 1901 linked seven colonies commonly thought of as a single group—**Australasia**—and whose destiny was political union. Australasia was not only a topic in its own right and an embryonic nation, but it shaped the writing of colonial history. Most significantly, before colonisation began, Edward Gibbon **Wakefield** spelt out a vision of a British New Zealand as Australia's Other, designed to avoid the pathological characteristics of the penal colonies and pastoralism. His *Letter from Sydney* (1829) constituted the penal/pastoral colonies as a negative referent for the yet-to-be imagined New Zealand/New Britain. In the course of the 1830s, especially once disillusioned with South Australia, he shaped his imaginary New Zealand as the site for his experiment. Britain's colonial policy, which resulted in the annexation of NZ in 1840, was also shaped by a desire to limit the evil effects of the **felonry** on Maori.

Wakefield wrote extensively to attract emigrants and influence imperial policy. Others built on his belief that NZ would be unique, and wrote accordingly. A veritable library appeared, notably: Thomas Cholmondeley, *Ultima Thule* (1854); Richard Taylor, *Te Ika a Maui* (1855); Charles Hursthouse, *New Zealand … The Britain of the South* (1857); and Arthur Thomson, *The Story of New Zealand … Savage and Civilized* (1859). The six colonies of NZ also soon boasted their own histories. Some were written for a British market, others to celebrate provincial identity. All shared a sense of a distinctive and unique New Zealand future, based on 'superior British stock' settling a fertile land blessed with a temperate climate; all tended to ignore the Australasian context. In the 1860s and 1870s, however, a succession of British visitors brought Australasia into focus as part of an English-speaking Anglo-Saxon empire. The influx of Victorian miners and the development of Australasian labour markets, not to mention regular steamship links, gave substance to the claim. Charles Dilke's *Greater Britain* (1868) was symptomatic, mocking New Zealand claims to superiority and portraying the colony as an outpost of Australia. Many others published accounts of Australasian tours. The attempt to elide difference culminated with the Melbourne-based George **Rusden's** *History of New Zealand* (1883)—a caustic attack on NZ's claim to superiority.

In the last decades of the nineteenth century, the idea of an Anglo-Saxon 'race' made Australasia more fashionable. NZ participated in most of the conferences to discuss **Federation** but the growth of radical colonial nationalism complicated the flirtation. William Pember **Reeves** wrote a brilliant one-volume history of NZ in which he did justice to NZ's Australasian past—whaling, sealing, missionaries, goldmining, pastoralism—but promptly contextualised that history in his two-volume masterpiece, *State Experiments in Australia and New Zealand* (1902). Others followed, notably Robert McNab, a southern runholder and Liberal politician. He began gathering materials for a history of Southland but the project grew, culminating in the first of his Rankean volumes, *Murihiku* (1905). Dissatisfied with this, he kept researching, visiting libraries and archives in Australia, especially Sydney and Hobart, the USA, Britain, and Europe. He published a fuller volume in 1907 and another in 1909, both also entitled *Murihiku* (although the sub-titles varied); the last covered the history of the entire 'contact' period in the South Island from **Cook's** first visit until the establishment of the first shore-whaling station in 1829. McNab's documentary evidence made it clear that southern NZ had begun its European history as a frontier of the penal colonies. His *Historical Records of New Zealand* (2 vols, 1908, 1914) was a frank imitation of *The Historical Records of New South Wales* (1892–1901)—the first volume consisted largely of material contained in the latter work—and also emphasised that the senior colony had played a major role in NZ's history. *The Old Whaling Days* (1913), a scissors-and-paste narrative, made the same point.

On both sides of the Tasman, Australasia possessed a social and cultural unity between the 1890s and World War I. That unity did not preclude vigorous inter-colonial rivalry, especially during the **Boer War** and on various sporting fields. Nor were all New Zealanders equally happy (Wakefield's self-conscious heirs were most unhappy). Between 1895 and 1914 a flood of Australians emigrated to NZ, including William **Lane** and most of NZ's first Labour Cabinet (1935–39). The *Bulletin* sold widely in NZ during this period. In 1905 the first edition of *New Zealand Truth* appeared, soon followed by various provincial editions. Australasian popular culture culminated with the **Anzacs** at **Gallipoli**, but the same event re-emphasised NZ's distinctiveness. As ever, the Maori both symbolised and defined that difference (indeed the 'shaky isles' were widely known as Maoriland in Australia). Australasian popular culture survived World War I but succumbed to imperial nationalism among the educated. Historians between the wars worked on two fronts, reviving the idea of NZ as a new and better England or conceptualising its past within an imperial, rather than an Australasian, context. The two projects were complementary and mirrored the indifference of the two dominion governments. Young historians now went to England to undertake further study, stopping in Sydney briefly en route, and tackled topics which emphasised NZ's links with the imperial heartland. J.C. Beaglehole worked on European 'discovery' of the Pacific and began his lifelong work on James Cook; W.P. Morrell worked on Britain's colonial policy in the age of Peel and Russell; A.H. McLintock studied Newfoundland's long march to Dominion status. The New Zealand volume of *The Cambridge History of the British Empire* (1933) and Morrell's *New Zealand*, published in London in 1935, marked the apogee of imperial nationalism.

World War II briefly witnessed a renewed flurry of trans-Tasman communications, many of them born of an anxious desire to prevent the USA from eclipsing Britain in the Pacific. American scholars treated Australia and NZ as one, but on both sides of the Tasman new nationalisms flourished. In NZ a small avalanche of works set out to explain NZ's history in New Zealand terms. Keith Sinclair's *A History of New Zealand* (1959) both expressed and defined the new and cocky mood. Both Empire and Australasia receded to the periphery, although he emphasised the importance of Australia before 1840 as a device to limit imperial influence. E.J. Tapp's dry monograph, *Early New Zealand: A Dependency of New South Wales 1788–1841* (1958), was published in Melbourne and little known in NZ. Yet *HSANZ* remained the major scholarly journal for work on New Zealand history and the Historical Section of

the **Australian and New Zealand Association for the Advancement of Science** the major conference. In some senses, however, both institutions presupposed an unspoken English background.

In 1966 the New Zealand Historical Association was formed, organised its first conference, and agreed that Sinclair's History Department at the University of Auckland should publish the *New Zealand Journal of History* on its behalf. The first issue appeared in 1967. The retirement and death of the doyens of the older imperial tradition, all of whom instinctively grasped NZ's Australasian identity, coincided with a rapid expansion of the universities and a growing hunger for work on NZ. A.H. McLintock (ed.), *The Encyclopaedia of New Zealand* (3 vols, 1966), almost ignored Australia and historical links with it. There were entries on 'Seals, Public and Provincial', but hardly a word about sealing, whaling, or Sydney's traders. Autochthonous self-absorption began to fray, however, when the UK joined the Common Market and the idea of an Australia–NZ market emerged as a goal. Closer Economic Relations provided an economic framework for the process of cultural rediscovery, and thousands of New Zealanders migrated across the Tasman, including many Maori.

A new generation was to rediscover NZ's Australian past and the Australasian dimension to popular culture (the same generation also had to rediscover the country's imperial past). Labour historians led the way, but the whaling industry, pastoralism and even the gold rushes again attracted scholarly attention and were studied within an Australasian or a Pacific context. The reasons why NZ refused to join the Australian Commonwealth became contentious among scholars. Gallipoli, war, and foreign policy were studied from the Australasian perspective. Nor were literary links and popular culture ignored. The doyen of the nationalist school, Keith Sinclair, brought much of this work together when he edited *Tasman Relations: New Zealand and Australia 1788–1988* (1987) as NZ's contribution to Australia's Bicentenary. This volume reveals the new balance that has emerged, in which different New Zealands—predominantly (but not exclusively) Maori and Pakeha—can be seen within their Australasian and Greater British contexts without diminishing or denying an autochthonous identity.

ERIK OLSSEN

Newspapers were initiated in the colonies by enterprising printers, journalists, storekeepers, and others. The first newspaper printed in NSW was the *Sydney Gazette* in 1803. In Tasmania the *Derwent Star* appeared in 1810, in Hobart. In WA the *Perth Gazette* was published in 1833. In SA the second number of the *South Australian Gazette* came out in 1836 in Adelaide (the first having appeared a year earlier in London). In Victoria the tenth issue of the *Melbourne Advertiser* was printed (earlier ones were handwritten) by John Pascoe **Fawkner** in 1838. In Qld the *Moreton Bay Courier* was first published in 1846 in Brisbane.

The *Moreton Bay Courier*, with mergers and title changes, has survived to the present as Brisbane's daily paper, the

Courier Mail. The other major dailies also had nineteenth-century origins. The *Sydney Morning Herald* began as the *Sydney Herald* in 1831. The Perth *West Australian* may be traced back to the *Perth Gazette* started in 1833, the Melbourne *Herald-Sun* to the *Port Phillip Herald* in 1840, and the Hobart *Mercury* to the *Hobarton Guardian* (1847) and the *Hobarton Mercury* (1854). The Melbourne *Age* began publication in 1854. The Adelaide *Advertiser* started as the *South Australian Advertiser* in 1858, the Sydney *Daily Telegraph* in 1879.

The first provincial paper on the Australian mainland, the *Geelong Advertiser*, appeared in 1840 and was still being published in the late twentieth century, one of numerous strong regional dailies. The **gold rushes** greatly stimulated newspaper publication. With land **selection** and **agriculture** came towns and, inevitably, local newspapers—often two or more in competition in the same locality.

For several decades most newspapers had the same format, derived from British newspapers of the time: a single sheet folded to four pages, with advertisements occupying the outer two. The inner pages were dominated by an editorial that, more often than not, took a partisan stand on a burning political question and was typically lengthy, verbose, and sententious, albeit sometimes jocular. While papers were crucial and influential in the introduction and functioning of representative democracy, relations between press and parliament were often fiery.

Improvements in printing technology brought large increases in the size and circulation and decreases in the price of capital-city newspapers, and the introduction of **railways** facilitated extensive and timely distribution. Country papers in all but large regional centres became subordinate and more parochial. With developments in **communications** came intercolonial and overseas cable news agencies, and the replacement of randomly selective extracts from foreign newspapers by packages of current, tersely worded news. These ushered in crisp journalism, and syndication services, and they prompted the start of competing alliances of powerful newspaper proprietors to resist the imperial monopoly on cable news of the London-based Reuters.

By 1888, as the advertising agency Gordon and Gotch records in its *Australasian Newspaper Directory*, almost 600 newspapers were being published in the Australian colonies. There were clearly differentiated types: country papers for regional centres and small towns, suburban papers (in Melbourne and Sydney), metropolitan dailies, and metropolitan weeklies that were 'companions' to dailies. These weeklies were particularly important in the late colonial period in publishing Australian creative writing. With free **education**, a generally high level of literacy, an increase in train travel, the advent of gas and electric lighting, and more leisure, Australia had become, as Richard **Twopeny** observed in *Town Life in Australia* (1883), 'essentially the land of newspapers'.

For three decades from 1890 a prolific and diverse press flourished without competition from other media. A new popular style of journalism, partly influenced by the English papers of Lord Northcliffe, partly by assertive Australian **nationalism** exemplified from 1880 by the *Bulletin*, livened the appearance of some established papers. The Melbourne *Herald* in 1889, one of the first to change, took advertisements off the front page, providing instead bold headlines and illustrations. Many new papers were started—lively and sometimes brash, satirical, and sensationalist—such as the weekly Sydney *Truth* in 1890, the daily Sydney *Sun* in 1910, *Smith's Weekly* in 1919, and the Melbourne daily *Sun–News Pictorial* in 1922. With a labour movement gathering force in the 1890s came a host of newspapers in support, most notably the Brisbane *Worker* in 1890 and the Sydney *Labor Daily* in 1924. Continuing to resist complete domination by Reuters, formerly competing newspaper interests joined forces to establish cable news services, the first and strongest being the Australian Press Association in 1895. While World War I brought newsprint shortages and press **censorship** for a time, newspaper expansion resumed after the armistice: both numbers of papers and their circulations increased, and a continuing diversity of ownership peaked in 1923, with 26 metropolitan dailies having 21 owners.

In the 1920s and 1930s, however, came the growth of country newspaper chains and the building of metropolitan newspaper empires, such as the Herald & Weekly Times Ltd, substantially the creation of Keith **Murdoch**. While there were some significant new city papers, notably the *Canberra Times* in 1926 for the new federal capital, the clear trend, and one which was influenced by the advent of **film** and **radio**, was to mergers and closures, especially of country papers. The joining of the two main cable news services in 1935 to form Australian Associated Press was prompted as much by the news needs of the **Australian Broadcasting Commission** as by those of the print media. **World War II** brought sometimes severe newsprint rationing and a degree of censorship that elicited powerful press protest actions. It also saw the disappearance of the last vestiges of the old journalism, with news and photographs displacing advertisements on the front pages of even the most conservative papers.

Postwar **immigration** led to a steady increase in the range and numbers of newspapers published, mostly in Sydney and Melbourne, for **ethnic groups**. The 1960s saw the establishment of national dailies whose circulations would steadily increase—in 1963 the *Australian Financial Review*, which had been a weekly magazine for investors, and in 1964 Rupert **Murdoch's** *Australian*. However, it was during this decade that **television**, along with other competing media, began to reduce advertising and readers, resulting in a continuing trend to fewer papers and lower circulations. In the 1990s roughly the same number of papers were being published as a century earlier, for a population almost six times greater, while circulations continued to decline. Of the 600 or so daily to weekly newspapers appearing in 1996, the majority were free suburban and country papers that sprinkled some local news among real estate and supermarket advertising. Sydney's *Sunday Telegraph* sold over 100 000 in 1997, and the Melbourne *Herald-Sun* had the highest weekly circulation of 566 484; but most were under 30 000 and only five above 500 000. The concentration of ownership of the 12 national and capital-city dailies was greater than ever. After the advent of computer typesetting in the 1970s, which gave journalists more direct control over their copy, all papers abandoned anonymity for featured bylines in domestic reporting. Technological change also led to newspaper content being made available on CD-ROM and the Internet, thus putting into question the future of the traditional hard-copy paper in Australia and elsewhere. Media specialists have suggested that, because a core demand for the printed product continues, newspaper providers may consider 'unbundling' and making separately available the several distinct and often separately paged news, advertising, lifestyle, and other sections.

Nineteenth-century newspaper proprietors such as David **Syme** used papers to promote their political views. While the papers profess objectivity and freedom from bias, it has been generally accepted that twentieth-century owners and corporate managers have thrown their weight behind particular parties. The extensive media interests of the Murdoch and **Packer** families have augmented their influence over government policy, especially concerning newspaper ownership and cross-media rules.

Australian newspapers are vital sources for Australian general and media history. Major collections are held in the National Library and in the respective state libraries, and listed in *Newspapers in Australian Libraries: A Union List* (1985). Because no copies have survived of an estimated one-quarter of newspapers published in the middle decades of the nineteenth century and there are sizeable gaps for many later titles, the newspaper historian often has to reconstruct through a range of registers, directories, and miscellaneous clues. The *Koori Mail*, published from 1991, and earlier newspapers for Aborigines are listed in Michael Rose's anthology *For the Record: 160 Years of Aboriginal Print Journalism*. Newspaper indexes are noted in **reference works**.

Numerous **local histories** of the colonial period feature romanticised legends of the early press of their district, while memoirs of many itinerant talented journalists of the turn of the century convey bohemian excitement and give glimpses of the workings of newspaper offices and proprietorial dealings—by Randolph **Bedford**, for instance, and the recently published memoirs of Monty Grover, *Hold Page One* (1993), edited with an informative introduction by Michael **Cannon**.

R.B. Walker has written the history of newspapers in NSW to 1945, and Gavin **Souter's** history of the *Sydney Morning Herald, Company of Heralds* (1981), is the best treatment of a single paper. Henry Mayer, *The Press in Australia* (1964), was a landmark study of mid-twentieth-century newspapers that gave some historical context and made accurate forecasts of future trends. Newspaper influence and political involvement are studied in Denis Cryle, *The Press in Colonial Queensland* (1989); in C.J. Lloyd, *Parliament and the Press* (1988), which looks over time at the workings of the federal press gallery and its colonial antecedents; and in Derek Parker, *The Courtesans* (1991). The implications of concentrated foreign ownership are explored in David

Bowman, *The Captive Press* (1988), and in other books cited in John Henningham's chapter 'Media' in *Institutions of Australian Society* (1991), which also gives a concise, comprehensive overview of Australian newspaper history, some notes on further reading, and a short bibliography of key books and periodicals.

ELIZABETH MORRISON

Nicholls, Henry Richard (1830–1912) was a committed Chartist who came to Victoria in 1853 where he edited the *Diggers' Advocate*. He joined the diggers at the **Eureka Stockade**, but was absent at the time of the attack and campaigned vigorously for the release of the rebels. Nicholls wrote subsequently for the *Ballarat Times*, was editor–owner of the *Ballarat Star* 1875–83, and editor of the Hobart *Mercury* 1883–1912. During this time he wrote for the *Australasian* and *Argus* as 'Henricus', and also produced the satirical piece, *An Essay on Politics in Verse* (1867). Nicholl's criticism of H.B. **Higgins** in 1911 for his role as president of the Arbitration Court led to his being charged with contempt; he appeared before the High Court but the case was dismissed. For this defiance, the members of the Australian New Right adopted this old radical as their hero when the H.R. Nicholls Society was formed in 1986.

KT

Niemeyer, Otto (1883–1971) came to Australia in 1930 at the beginning of the **Depression** as a leading member of a mission from the Bank of England, invited by the Commonwealth government to assess the nation's parlous credit and formulate advice about restoring it. Niemeyer's report to the **Premiers' Conference** of that year was unequivocal: Australians enjoyed a **standard of living** beyond what their economy could support. The conference accepted his findings, and Prime Minister **Scullin** left for England immediately in an attempt to repair Australia's financial standing. Following the publication of his report, Niemeyer was regarded by some as having done Australia a great service, by others as a symbol of foreign financial oppression. Peter Love, *HS* (1982), published part of Niemeyer's diary of his visit with an explanatory preface. W.F. Mandle, *Going it Alone* (1977), considers the popular impact of the Niemeyer mission.

KT

Nineteen Counties marked the official limit of location, or settlement, in the Colony of **New South Wales**. This area extended to Kempsey in the north, Batemans Bay in the south, and Wellington to the west. The survey, authorised by Governor **Darling**, was carried out by John **Oxley** and his successor Thomas **Mitchell**, who completed the work in 1829; the boundaries were formally proclaimed in 1835. While the NSW colonial government prohibited permanent settlement beyond the boundaries of these counties, pastoralists and land spectulators successfully evaded this ruling, notably in the **Port Phillip District** 1834–35.

HD

Nolan, Sidney Robert (1917–92) was an artist and stage designer, whose powerful lyrical gifts and spontaneous technique gave expression to a sense of the tragic nature of Australian history in themes that included **bushranging**, **exploration**, and the doomed heroes of the **Gallipoli** campaign, as well as reinvigorating the tradition of Australian landscape painting. Perhaps the most original and best known of the generation of Australian modernists to emerge from the 1940s, he did much to establish an international prominence for Australian art.

Nolan was born into a Melbourne working-class family of Irish descent. His formal art training was limited to night classes at the National Gallery School. In 1938 he met his future patrons, John and Sunday Reed, and became a leading member of the newly established Contemporary Art Society. He later left his first wife, Elizabeth Paterson, to establish an intense relationship with Sunday Reed. From the beginning his work, with its roots in French symbolist poetry, post-impressionist, primitivist, and early-twentieth-century art, shocked even many of his modernist contemporaries. While serving in the army between 1942 and 1944, he painted a major series of landscapes of the Wimmera. In 1946–47 he painted the first Ned **Kelly** series, one of the high points in his own and of Australian twentieth-century art. In 1947 Nolan left Melbourne and travelled throughout outback Qld. He married Cynthia Hanson (sister of John Reed) in Sydney in 1948. After further extensive travels throughout outback Australia, which furnished him with material for an unprecedented series of paintings on inland Australia, Nolan went overseas for the first time in 1950.

From 1952 Nolan made London his home, returning to Australia only for brief visits. He became a relentless traveller, sparing no continent and few countries in quest of subjects and themes. His output was matched by no other Australian artist. Following the suicide of Nolan's wife Cynthia in 1976 and his subsequent remarriage to Mary Perceval (née Boyd) in 1978, Patrick **White** initiated one of Australia's more notorious public feuds with his one-time friend. Nolan received a British knighthood in 1981 for services to British art, and the Order of Merit in 1983.

Nolan's Australian reputation dates from his move to Sydney in 1948. Wider acclaim came with the first monograph, published in England in 1961, and with a celebratory tribute by Kenneth Clark. Elwyn Lynn's *Sidney Nolan: Myth and Imagery* (1967) appeared in the same year as his first retrospective exhibition at the Art Gallery of New South Wales. His fame was then at its zenith, although he was already being criticised for work that, as John Olsen noted, was too often 'contaminated with the over-ripened atmosphere of Bond Street'. In the 1980s, new appraisals culminated in a 1987 retrospective exhibition at the National Gallery of Victoria. By his death, in 1992, his reputation—in spite of an excess of mediocre work—was confirmed.

RICHARD HAESE

Norfolk Island, a volcanic island situated 1500 kilometres east of Australia, was settled in 1788. In his instructions for settling Botany Bay in 1786, Lord Sydney had acknowledged **Cook's** reports of the island's abundance of flax and pine trees, and recommended settlement. In *The Tyranny of Distance* (1968), **Blainey** argued that the availability of flax and pines—valuable materials for shipbuilding—on Norfolk Island was a critical factor in establishing NSW. The island was abandoned in 1814, but re-established in 1825 as a **penal settlement** for second offenders. Its harsh conditions were alleviated somewhat by the reforms of Captain Alexander **Maconochie** 1840–44, but his notorious successor John Price re-instituted brutal punitive measures. With the end of transportation in 1852, the penal settlement was abandoned. In 1856 descendants of the *Bounty* mutineers from Pitcairn Island were settled at Norfolk Island, and a community of hybrid ethnicity and language subsequently developed. Heritage and tourism are major industries, and are discussed by John Rickard in *AHS* (1995). Novelist Colleen McCullough is a resident.

HD

Northern Myth, a phrase describing the erroneous belief that the tropical north of Australia was capable of supporting a vastly increased European population, was coined by the agricultural scientist B.R. Davidson in his book of that name in 1965. But the belief has a longer history. During the early years of colonisation, imperial strategists saw outposts on the northern coasts as a bulwark against European rivals and a conduit for trade with lands to the north. The idea of 'the empty north', a phrase coined in the early twentieth century, expressed the neo-Darwinian conviction that the 'higher' races had a mission to fill up the 'empty spaces' of the earth. Believers expounded the need for increased population to defend the coast, to justify the white man's claim to the soil, and to feed the under-nourished populations of Asia. There was no medical reason, Raphael **Cilento** argued in 1925, why the white people could not survive in the tropics. Sceptics, such as Griffith **Taylor**, described northern development as a white elephant; they pointed to the intrinsic aridity of the region and hammered the unpalatable truth that anything that could be grown in the tropical north could be produced in temperate Australia at a fraction of the cost. The debate was central to wider discussions of Australia's future in the period between the two world wars. '"But what's goin' to happen to the place if we don't do something with it?"', a character in Xavier **Herbert's** *Capricornia* (1938), asks. '"It'll look after itself, Sonny, till it's really needed"', his companion replies. The dire results of the German quest for *lebensraum* helped to undermine the myth of empty lands in the postwar period. 'The real need is not open spaces, but open doors', wrote W.D. Forsyth in 1942. Since the 1970s environmentalists, recognising the 'limits to growth' and the fragility of the region, have reinforced the view. In the 1920s, people believed, Australia must 'populate or perish'; in 1984 Robert Birrell and his colleagues wondered if Australia might 'populate and perish'.

GD

Northern Territory had its present boundaries fixed in 1863 when the colonies of **South Australia** and

Queensland reached agreement on their boundaries. The NT was officially annexed by SA in 1863, having been part of **New South Wales**. In 1911 the territory passed to the Commonwealth, and it was granted self-government in 1978.

Climate and weather patterns separate the territory's regions as much as landform. Aboriginal people refer to themselves as belonging to one of three major groupings: salt water, river country, or desert. Tropical Darwin is affected by two major wind systems, the north-west monsoon (which brought destructive cyclones in 1897, 1937 and **Cyclone Tracy** in 1974) and the south-east trades. Central Australia experiences a desert climate, night-time temperatures in winter sometimes dropping below freezing.

Early settlement was attempted by the British at Melville Island (Fort Dundas, 1824–27), and on Cobourg Peninsula (Fort Wellington, 1827–29; Victoria Settlement, 1838–49). Before SA settled in 1869 on Palmerston (now **Darwin**) as the capital, it attempted settlement at Escape Cliffs on Adam Bay. All were abandoned. A pattern of transient European presence was set which overshadowed European settlement well into the twentieth century.

Relations between Aboriginal communities and the British were strained on Melville Island. **Aboriginal resistance** to the British was a determining factor in the abandonment of Fort Dundas. At other settlements the Aboriginal response was more welcoming, perhaps based on previous experience of good relations with **Macassan** trepangers who had visited the coast annually since at least the eighteenth century.

From the mid-1840s the territory was explored overland from the south. Chief among the explorers were Ludwig **Leichhardt** and John McDouall **Stuart**. The **Overland Telegraph**, the Stuart Highway, and the old Port Augusta to Alice Springs railway follow the track taken by Stuart. His endeavours contributed to the opening up of the inland. Permanent European settlement after 1869 brought considerable change to Aboriginal lives as settlers and cattle spread inland. Mining also brought a permanent European presence. European numbers have never been great, and were still only 173000 in the mid-1990s. Their impact has been substantial. **Massacres** of Aborigines on the Daly River in 1884, and at Coniston in Central Australia in 1928, are among events which have marred race relations and contributed to the territory's reputation as a violent frontier.

Modern towns are relatively small in size and population. They are widely separated and people are likely to relate outwards to neighbouring states, or to Asia, as much as to each other. Populations are markedly multicultural, and the heritage of early **Chinese** and **Greek** settlers in the north, and **Italian** settlers in the centre, is celebrated. Recent arrivals have included East Timorese refugees and South-East Asian **boat people**.

Boundaries and borders, definition of place and space, continue to be important factors in social, economic, and political development. The Land Rights Act (NT) 1976, and the Native Title Act 1993, have provided Aboriginal people with an opportunity to seek redress for racial violence and land appropriation. The first claims under the 1976 act were the Borroloola claim lodged by the Northern Land Council, and the Warlpiri–Kartangarurru–Kurintji claim lodged by the Central Land Council, both in 1977. In November 1994 the Northern Land Council lodged the first sea claim under the Native Title Act: *Mandilarri-Ildugi and others*, for traditional territory in waters off Croker Island. Aboriginal clans are involved with government in joint management of conservation and tourism in three national parks on Aboriginal land: Kakadu in Arnhem Land, **Uluru** in Central Australia, and Nitmiluk in the Katherine district. **Uranium** and gold mining occurs in areas exempted from Kakadu. Mining has attracted opposition from conservation groups, and recently Aboriginal landowners have objected to the proposed extension of uranium mining.

The presence in modern times of **Indonesian** fishers in territorial waters reflects historical links between coastal communities and trepangers. An international agreement between Indonesia and Australia permits fishers to follow traditional practice in the vicinity of Ashmore and Cartier Islands in the Indian Ocean. The islands, territories of the Commonwealth, were administered by the NT between 1942 and 1978.

The NT elected members to the SA parliament, but lost political representation when it passed to the Commonwealth. There was a non-voting member of the House of Representatives from 1992. It has participated fully in federal elections since 1968, and from 1975 has been represented by two senators and one member in the House of Representatives. Following self-government in 1978, the NT has a 26-member Legislative Assembly which sits in a controversially grandiose building completed in 1994. At other levels there are elected local government and community government councils, four Land Councils, and regional councils of the **Aboriginal and Torres Strait Islander Commission**.

There is a good general history of the NT, Alan Powell's *Far Country* (1982, 2000), and several regional or specialist histories. Ann McGrath, *Born in the Cattle* (1987), Lyn Riddett, *Kine, Kin and Country* (1990), and Deborah Bird Rose, *Hidden Histories* (1991), discuss Aboriginal–settler relations. Prehistorian John **Mulvaney** has also made a major contribution to the field in *Encounters in Place* (1989). Since the early 1980s a series of monographs published by the North Australia Research Unit at the Australian National University have dealt with economic and political topics. Claim books lodged by Land Councils under the Land Rights Act contain valuable Aboriginal perspectives on contact history.

LYN RIDDETT

Norton, John (1858–1916), long-term editor of the sensationalist newspaper *Truth*, travelled to Sydney from England in 1884. Through his reporting work on the *Evening News* he became involved with the emergent labour movement. He was the Sydney delegate to inter-colonial trade union congresses and author of a pamphlet, *The Australian Labour Market. Startling Disclosures. Distress and Destitution in New*

South Wales (1886)—an early example of his propensity for alliteration and histrionics. He went to the newly established *Truth* in 1890 and soon became editor and part-owner. He was removed as editor by a court injunction in 1892, but returned four years later in full control. Norton marked his return with a description of Queen Victoria as 'flabby, fat, and flatulent' and the Prince of Wales as a 'card-sharping, wife-debauching' cad. His subsequent trial for sedition turned him into a hero of the working classes. The scandalous nature of the paper, reflected in his own life, often involved him in court actions. In spite of this, he was elected to the NSW parliament in 1898. Cyril **Pearl** examined Norton and his cohorts in *Wild Men of Sydney* (1958). Michael **Cannon's** *That Damned Democrat* (1981) includes selections from his editorials.

When Norton's son EZRA (1897–1967) took control of the *Truth* he continued its focus on sport and sensationalism. He established the tabloid *Daily Mirror* in 1941, but divested himself of all his newspaper interests in 1958.

KT

Novels presented influential interpretations of the Australian past well before history had become consolidated as an academic discipline. Henry Handel **Richardson's** trilogy, *The Fortunes of Richard Mahony* (1917–29, 1930), described, through the experiences of a restless Protestant Irish immigrant, the Victorian **gold rushes** (including the emblematic episode of the **Eureka Stockade**), the development of a colonial middle class and its susceptibility to material gain, and the ambivalent notions of home of those who had come from Europe to make lives in Australia. Eleanor **Dark**, whose trilogy of novels of the first decades of European settlement began with *The Timeless Land* (1941), declared a patriotic responsibility: 'Without history we should be unable to learn our past experience, and a knowledge of its history is in the same way indispensable to a nation.' Her work belongs to the saga literature that was the dominant form of the Australian historical novel between the wars. Some of these were costume drama, such as G.B. Lancaster's *Pageant* (1933) or Ernestine **Hill's** tale of Matthew **Flinders**, *My Love Must Wait* (1941). Others were more complex and iconoclastic. The pioneering of Australia was a dominant subject, whether atypically through the growth of a Sydney mercantile firm in Marjorie **Barnard** and Flora Eldershaw, *A House Is Built* (1929), or—more often—in rural, remote areas of the country. Brian **Penton's** *Landtakers* (1934) and Katharine **Prichard's** *Coonardoo* (1929) are two examples of this essentially parochial fiction. Fire, flood, and drought are natural forces that test these pioneers. The world beyond Australia is scarcely a rumour.

Historical novels of the nineteenth century were inward-looking, necessarily so, for their intention was the appropriation for fiction of a history that European Australia had scarcely had time to have. Marcus **Clarke's** *His Natural Life* (1874) was the most famous depiction of the convict era. It had been preceded by Caroline Leakey's *The Broad Arrow* (1859) and has had successors—imitative and revisionary—for more than a century. The transmuting of recent historical events into those

of a legendary past was also the project of Rolf **Boldrewood** in *Robbery Under Arms* (1888), as it was for such balladeers as Banjo **Paterson**. These enterprises were validated by Mark Twain; writing in *More Tramps Abroad* (1897), he praised Australia's history as its 'chiefest novelty' and admired its 'incongruities, and contradictions, and incredulities'.

Following Twain's example, Australian novelists have, in recent decades, shown themselves to be revisers not only of the national history, but also of literary history. Thus Patrick **White** confronted 'the dreary, dun-coloured offspring of journalistic realism' (his contentious view of the saga) with a transformation of that tradition in *The Tree of Man* (1955) and his legendary reshaping of the story of the lost explorer **Leichhardt** in *Voss* (1957). The respectful hero-worship of Governor Arthur **Phillip** in J.M.H. Abbott's *Castle Vane* (1920) is superseded by the droll portrayal of H.E. (His Excellency) in Thomas **Keneally's** *The Playmaker* (1987). Many of the latter's novels have been historical, whether set in Australia or overseas. Keneally attests to belief in 'a direct fuse line, a fuse that is still burning between the past and the present'. In *Illywhacker* (1985), Peter **Carey** presented a narrator who believed—in Twain's words—that Australia's history comprised 'the most beautiful lies'. His are veritably 'all of a fresh sort', in this narrative of an anti-historian who poses as the appropriate chronicler of his country. The 'illy-whacker', Herbert Badgery, contests meliorist notions of national history, as well as determinist, generative authority of significant events that saga prefers.

Recent historical novels have frequently been revisionist treatments of legendary figures and periods. Ned **Kelly's** Sister Kate appeared in a novel of that name by Jean Bedford (1982), Ned himself in Robert Drewe's *Our Sunshine* (1991). A re-examination of the Great War, and of the supposed loss of national innocence that it occasioned, has been intensively conducted in poetry and such novels as Roger McDonald's *1915* (1979), David **Malouf's** *Fly Away Peter* (1982), and Geoff Page's *Benton's Conviction* (1985). Several modern historical novels are **captivity narratives**: White's version of the Eliza **Fraser** story in *A Fringe of Leaves* (1976); tales of the **convict** system by Jessica Anderson in *The Commandant* (1975) and by Keneally; the Rodney Hall trilogy that began with *Captivity Captive* (1988), thence to explore the torments of those ensnared by ties of family and history, blood, and the burden of the past. The history of convictism in **Van Diemen's Land**, theme of many of Roy **Bridges's** novels in the first half of last century, has recently and vividly been revisited by Tom Gilling, *The Sooterkin* (1999), Christopher Koch, *Out of Ireland* (1999), and by British authors Andrew Motion, *Wainewright the Poisoner* (2000), and William Kneale, *English Passengers* (2000).

Nor has the saga been extinguished. Its territory was ceded to radio serials such as Gwen **Meredith's** 'Blue Hills' (1949–76), and then to television mini-series; but Colleen McCullough's *The Thorn Birds* (1977) is one of the best-selling of all Australian novels. Malouf's *The Great World* (1990)—also in part a captivity narrative with episodes in Japanese **prisoner-of-war** camps—ranges across half a century to probe the ambiguous returns for Australia of those times when it has broken out of isolation and sought to enlist in history by going to war. If there is continuity between the patriotic annals of the saga tradition and the sceptical revisionism of contemporary Australian historical novels, it may lie in a humanist faith in the efficacy of narrative, a belief that—however their evidence or intentions are contested—stories are best told and not forgotten. As Digger Keen remarks in *The Great World*: 'Even the least event had lines, all tangled, going back into the past … and other lines, leading out, also tangled, into the future. Every event was dense with causes, possibilities, consequences …'

PETER PIERCE

Nuclear industry, see **Uranium**

O'Brien, Eris (1895–1974), historian and bishop, born in NSW, entered the Catholic priesthood in 1918. After studying in Louvaine in Belgium, he was awarded a doctorate for *The Foundation of Australia 1786–1800* (1937). His other publications reflect his interest in the role played by **Irish** Catholics in Australia: a biography of John Joseph Therry (1922), *The Dawn of Catholicism in Australia* (1928), and *The Establishment of the Hierarchy in Australia* (1942). He also wrote a play, *The Hostage* (1928), about Jeremiah O'Flynn, an Irish priest expelled by Lachlan **Macquarie**.

KT

O'Brien, John, see **Hartigan, Patrick Joseph**

O'Connor, Charles Yelverton (1843–1902) is remembered for the design and construction of the Perth–Mundaring water pipeline and of Fremantle Harbour and, carried out with equal efficiency, his seaside suicide. In the commercially released *From Success to Success: A Film History of Fremantle* (1987), the re-enactment of O'Connor's suicide shocked viewers, even as many thousands of people stood appreciatively before his harbourside statue during the America's Cup defence of that year. In widely used school texts, especially C. Eakins and A.E. Williams, *Social Studies Through Activities* (1940s to 1970s), O'Connor was presented as a heroic and tragic figure of Empire and nation.

O'Connor was born in Ireland into a family of affluent Anglo-Irish landowners, and was articled to the local resident engineer. From 1865 he worked as a government engineer in NZ, rising to the position of under-secretary for public works. In 1891 Sir John **Forrest**, the first premier of WA, offered him the new position of engineer-in-chief. And 'the Chief' he became. O'Connor, 48 years of age and vastly experienced, matched Forrest well in all but size. He surprised Forrest by recommending the construction of an inner harbour at Fremantle rather than the favoured alternative of an open harbour further south. After 12 months of debate it was O'Connor's proposal that went ahead. By the late 1890s he had completed the south and north moles, and the new harbour was ready to receive the great P & O liners. For the next 70 years Fremantle Harbour would be the first sighting of Australia for generations of migrants, as well as the state's principal trading port.

O'Connor became embroiled in a debate over the provision of water for the eastern goldfields, centred on Coolgardie. Some powerful Westralians, including the premier's brother Alexander **Forrest**, wanted a series of deep bores placed alongside the railway line. O'Connor, however, favoured the construction of a 560-kilometre pipeline from the watered coast to the dry goldfields, with pumping stations along the way. Not until 1896 was the premier won over by his engineer-in-chief, and then partly because he could see that the regular supply of water could be used for new farms along the route. But still the critics of the scheme pounded O'Connor. Forrest's 1901 departure for federal politics left O'Connor exposed. Premier Leake was lukewarm about the scheme, despite its advanced state by early 1902. And the *Sunday Times* was relentless in its criticism. Finally the scheme was made subject to a royal commission. O'Connor had been wanting to take leave but had to prepare his 'defence'. On Monday morning, 10 March 1902, he saddled his horse, rode into the sea at South Fremantle, and shot himself. Earlier that morning he had written: 'I have lost control of my thoughts'.

The Coolgardie Water Scheme was a brilliant success, one of the greatest engineering feats in Australian history. O'Connor's holistic vision for economic development in WA was high art indeed. Even in a more critical age, his heroic status is secure. Merab Tauman captures his vision well in 'The Chief' (1978).

TOM STANNAGE

O'Connor, Richard Edward (1851–1912) was an influential figure in the movement for **Federation**. With a successful career in the law and politics, he was a founder with Edmund **Barton** of the **Federation League** (1893) and Central Federation League (1896) before his election as a NSW representative to the 1897 Australasian Federal Convention, at which he helped draft the Federation Bill upon which the Constitution was based. He was the leading Catholic among the promoters of Federation and perhaps the most widely respected.

O'Connor served as a senator for NSW in the first federal parliament before accepting an appointment as judge of the High Court in 1903. His appointment in 1905 as president of the Commonwealth Court of Arbitration and Conciliation added to an already heavy workload and he retired from this position in 1907. He twice refused a knighthood.

KT

O'Dowd, Bernard Patrick (1866–1953) was a key figure in Melbourne's radical political culture at the end of the nineteenth century before he built up a substantial reputation as a poet. O'Dowd was born at Beaufort, Victoria, the son of Irish Catholic immigrants; he was educated at state schools and the University of Melbourne, where he graduated in arts and law, before becoming Supreme Court librarian. After abandoning the Catholic faith, he experimented with spiritualism, secularism, and **socialism**, and contributed to many newspapers and journals. From about 1902, O'Dowd mixed with members of Melbourne bourgeois intelligentsia, such as F.W. **Eggleston**, John **Latham**, and Herbert **Brookes**, and continued to experiment with various belief systems, including theosophy, Christian Science, and New Thought. He briefly returned to the Catholic Church. Meanwhile, the publication of several books of verse in the years between 1903 and 1921 secured his literary reputation. His long allegorical poem 'The Bush', expressive of an apocalyptic sense of nationhood, is the best-known of his works.

There was an early biography of O'Dowd by Victor Kennedy and Nettie **Palmer** (1954), and a later study by Hugh Anderson (1968). Cultural historians have also given O'Dowd considerable attention. His reputation as a poet, however, has declined dramatically since his death. John Docker has suggested that he was a victim of the tendency among Australian critics to consign 'political' verse such as O'Dowd's to a low rank in a hierarchy of genres. His verse was collected in a volume first published by Lothian in 1941, and individual poems appear in many anthologies.

FRANK BONGIORNO

O'Farrell, Patrick (1933–   ), historian, was born in NZ and studied history at the University of Canterbury, and the Australian National University, where he made the trans-Tasman socialist Henry Holland the subject of his doctoral thesis. His membership of the **Catholic Church** inspired a major study of Australian Catholic historiography, from which emerged two publications: *The Catholic Church in Australia: A Short History 1788–1967* (1968) and *Documents*

in Australian Catholic History 1788–1968 (2 vols, 1969). Subsequent research on the immigrant **Irish in Australia** provided material for a collection of letters (1984), and formed the basis of his major work, *The Irish in Australia* (1986), which examines the nature and extent of Irishness in Australia. The turn from a clerically centred history of Catholicism to a broader cultural history of the Irish, one impatient with the comfortable and enclosing myths, signalled a shift that other Catholic historians have followed. O'Farrell further examines this theme in *Vanished Kingdoms* (1990), a personal discovery of his family's Irish Catholic connections. Although a founding member of the Oral History Society of New South Wales, he has been a prominent critic of **oral history**. He was visiting professor of history at University College, Dublin (1965–66), and was a professor of history at the University of New South Wales.

HD

O'Grady, John Patrick ('Nino Culotta') (1907–81) began writing while working as a commercial traveller. After service in World War II he held a number of jobs, including as a builder's labourer—experience he drew upon in writing his popular novel, *They're a Weird Mob* (1957). Purportedly written by Nino Culotta, a Northern Italian migrant, the story offered a warmly sympathetic view of Australian society by an outsider, and made full play of the humorous possibilities to be found in misunderstandings of Australian idiom and mores. It was made into a film in 1966. He wrote two further books as Culotta: *Cop This Lot* (1960) and *Gone Fishin'* (1962). At a time of migrant influx, Nino Culotta affirmed both the worth of the Australian way of life and the prospect of migrant **assimilation**.

KT

O'Malley, King (?1858–1953), member of the first federal parliament, claimed two notable achievements—the foundation of the Commonwealth Bank, and selection of the site for a national capital. Although apparently an American, O'Malley purported to be Canadian, possibly in order to meet the British citizenship requirements for the SA parliament to which he was elected in 1896. He entered the 1901 federal parliament as an independent member from Tasmania but joined the Australian Labor Party in June 1901. As minister for home affairs (1910–13 and 1915–16), he oversaw the selection of Walter Burley **Griffin** as architect for **Canberra** and drove in the first survey peg for the construction of Parliament House. A colourful figure, O'Malley is the subject of a biography, sub-titled 'The American Bounder' (A.R. Hoyle, 1981), and a burlesque by Michael Boddy and Bob Ellis, *The Legend of King O'Malley* (1974).

KT

O'Reilly, John Boyle, see **Fenianism**

O'Shane, Patricia June (1941–   ) is known for her outspoken comments on legal and social issues, particularly those relating to the welfare of **Aborigines** and women. Born of an Aboriginal mother and Irish father in north Qld, O'Shane taught for a time before completing a law degree at the University of New South Wales. She was admitted to the NSW Bar in 1976, in 1981 became head of the NSW Department of Aboriginal Affairs, and was appointed a magistrate in 1986. Her decisions have sometimes aroused controversy, as did her dismissal of charges in 1993 against women accused of defacing an advertising billboard that showed a lightly clad woman being sawn in half, on the grounds that the creation of such advertisements was the 'real crime'. O'Shane was appointed chancellor of the University of New England (NSW) in 1995.

KT

Official history is sponsored, authorised, or endorsed by its subject. A wide range of organisations have generated such histories, and they are considered in the entry for **commissioned history**. In its more particular sense, official history is created at the behest of government as a record of its activity.

Official history of this kind was commonly initiated by the colonial administrations in the nineteenth century as a way of publicising the attractions of the Australian colonies to investors and immigrants. Government statisticians frequently incorporated historical material in yearbooks and other compilations, and T.A. **Coghlan** went further with a series of historical studies that culminated, when he was NSW agent-general in London, in the four-volume *Labour and Industry in Australia* (1918).

Such promotional uses of official history were joined at the end of the century by commemorative publications. James **Bonwick** was employed during the 1880s by the governments of NSW, Qld, SA, and Victoria to transcribe official records in London on their settlement and early administration. Bonwick's work formed the basis for the commissioned work by G.B. **Barton** and Alexander Britton, *History of New South Wales* in two volumes (1889, 1894), and eight volumes of *Historical Records of New South Wales*, edited by F.M. Bladen (1892–1901). These served in turn as the precedent for *Historical Records of Australia* (1914–25) in 33 volumes, regarded by their editor, Frederick Watson, as 'the birth certificates of a nation'. Watson, a medical practitioner and antiquarian, was commissioned by the library committee of the Commonwealth parliament, and fell into dispute with its members; the series was abandoned after two academic historians, Ernest **Scott** and G.A. **Wood**, reviewed his work. His work is assessed by Ann M. Mitchell in *HS* (1982). A similar project was created by the Victorian government in the 1970s.

World War I initiated a new genre, **military history**, which tellingly became the most substantial form of official history throughout the twentieth century. When C.E.W. **Bean** was elected by the Australian Journalists Association as the official war correspondent in 1914, the minister for defence suggested to him that he should write a history of the conflict. Bean thought at the time (as he recalled in *JRAHS*, 1938) that this would require 'a small one-volume work'. After the Armistice he submitted a scheme for 12 volumes to the Commonwealth government, which accepted and supported it for the next 20 years. Bean wrote six of the volumes and edited the others. It was agreed that the official war historians (most of them with backgrounds in journalism) would enjoy freedom from censorship: the draft of each volume was submitted to the minister for defence, who could suggest amendments, but Bean was to exercise final judgment. He later claimed that only one 'discussion of importance' arose from this arrangement during the entire series. On the other hand, both the publisher, George **Robertson**, and the retired University of Melbourne professor, T.G. Tucker, who served as 'literary adviser', intervened frequently. Bean's work is discussed by K.S. **Inglis** and his biographer, Dudley McCarthy, while Michael McKernan's introductions to the reprint of the official history by the University of Queensland Press provide a detailed commentary on its preparation.

Similar arrangements were made for the official histories of World War II, in 22 volumes, edited by Gavin **Long**; and the **Korean War**, in two, undertaken by R.J. O'Neill (1981, 1985). In both cases the writers had free access to the official records (including records closed to other historians) and were unrestricted in using them except for material deemed of continuing strategic significance. Long, like Bean, was a journalist; most of his contributors brought specialist expertise, though Paul **Hasluck** began the two domestic volumes as a fellow of the history department at the University of Western Australia, and the economic historians S.J. **Butlin** and Boris Schedvin wrote on the war economy. O'Neill combined military and academic training. They were supported by substantial research establishments and published by the Australian Government Publishing Service through the Australian War Memorial. The fourth official war series on Australian involvement in South-East Asian conflicts from 1948 to 1975, on the other hand, reverted to a commercial publisher, was undertaken by academic researchers, and created controversy. The principal historian, Peter Edwards, fell out with two of his colleagues, Greg Pemberton and Ann-Mari Jordens, both of whom resigned after complaining of interference.

Complementing the war histories was a series of volumes of *Documents on Australian Foreign Policy 1937–* (1975–), commissioned by the Department of Foreign Affairs. The present editor, W.J. Hudson, is a former academic and has also published other compilations of correspondence bearing on interwar Australian diplomacy and trade. Other federal departments and agencies have been slower to embark on official histories. David Day wrote a history of Australian customs services (2 vols, 1992, 1996); Clem Lloyd and Jacqui Rees, a history of **repatriation**.

Meanwhile, state governments and instrumentalities took up official history from a variety of motives. For some, it was a way of reflecting on former practice; for others, a form of public relations. Sometimes an administrator commissioned an official history to salve staff morale in a period of rapid change in previously stable and monolithic organisations; sometimes the new chief executive officer expected that a revelation of outmoded former practice would help to sweep out the detritus of the past. These commissions raised similar issues to those that bedevilled historians of business or voluntary organisations, and just as frequently strained ethical codes. Hugh **Stretton** argued vigorously to maintain the independence of Susan Marsden's *Business, Charity and Sentiment* (1986). From the 1980s much official history turned away from the inward study of organisational practice to more contextualised studies of the impact and effects of a public authority, frequently drawing on oral and social history techniques to develop a thematic treatment. Examples are the account by Clem Lloyd and Pat Troy of the Hunter Valley Water Board (1992); Renate Howe's edited collection on public housing in Victoria (1988); the history by Tony Dingle and Carolyn Rasmussen of the Melbourne and Metropolitan Board of Works (1991); and the study of the wheat industry by Greg Whitwell and Diane Sydenham, commissioned by the Australian Wheat Board (1991).

In the past quarter-century official history has also returned to commemoration. The national sesquicentenary in 1938 was celebrated chiefly in NSW with **pageants** and spectacles; the other mainland states marked their centenaries during the 1920s and 1930s with a thin sprinkling of official histories. By contrast, their sesquicentenaries brought a rash of publication. WA led off in 1979 with a series of books of mixed quality, the best of them a documentary history edited by Marian Aveling (Quartly) and *People of Perth* by Tom Stannage; Stannage edited the *New History of Western Australia* which followed in 1981. SA's historians contributed to that state's anniversary with edited collections of studies of political, social, and economic history (1986). Victoria was more adventurous with three thematic volumes on *Arriving, Settling,* and *Making Their Mark,* written by Richard Broome, Tony Dingle, and Susan Priestley (1984). The large audience, handsome format, and substantial budgets of these projects attracted historians; the management committees brought them into negotiation with government representatives with divergent expectations, though differences were generally resolved.

By contrast, the principal energies of the profession were occupied in the lead-up to the Bicentenary in an unofficial enterprise that they initiated, the **Bicentennial History Project**. The government's Bicentennial Authority sponsored a range of more popular publications, and the Commonwealth parliament commissioned three significant works: Gavin **Souter's** narrative history, *Acts of Parliament* (1988); an analytical study by G.S. Reid and Martyn Forrest of *Australia's Commonwealth Parliament 1901–1988* (1989); and Clem Lloyd's *Parliament and the Press* (1988), a history of the press gallery. In similar vein, Ray Wright of the Victorian parliamentary library wrote a history of that state's legisla-

ture, *A People's Counsel* (1992). The centenary of the Commonwealth was marked by the preparation of a comprehensive list of archival sources, *Federation: The Guide to Records* (1998), and a CD-ROM, *One Destiny: The Federation Story* (1998). The authority established to organise the commemoration assisted a number of projects but did not attempt an official history.

STUART MACINTYRE

Oil and gas are Australia's primary **energy** source. The demand to fuel kerosene oil lamps sparked oil exploration in Australia, with the first oil well drilled in 1866 at Coorong, SA. In the following years numerous wells were drilled across Australia without success, including a non-commercial gas deposit at Roma, Qld, in 1899, and a minor oil deposit in 1928. In WA oil exploration began in 1919 at Fitzroy Crossing. In the 1920s and 1930s attempts to find the source of oil seeps in the Gippsland region of Victoria produced 785 000 litres of oil between 1930 and 1952.

This lack of success in exploration led to the mining of oil shale to help satisfy Australia's growing oil needs. One of the world's largest oil shale deposits, near Bathurst, NSW, was mined in the early 1860s. The first commercial oil shale works were constructed at Port Kembla in 1865. The first oil refinery in Australia to contain a catalytic cracking unit was at Glen Davis, producing 160 000 barrels a day of crude shale oil. Oil shale produced only 3 per cent of Australia's needs during World War II, and was discontinued in 1952, unable to compete against cheap imported oils. The technical knowledge gained at Glen Davis allowed the formation of the modern refining industry, which grew rapidly after the war along with consumption and today consists of eight major refineries operated by four major marketing companies: Ampol (USA), BP (UK), Mobil (USA), and Shell (Dutch/UK).

In 1957, in an attempt to reduce Australia's reliance on oil imports, the federal government made generous tax concessions for petroleum exploration. The first commercial oil discovery was made at Moonie, Qld, in 1961, with later discoveries in Central and Western Australia. These discoveries sparked renewed exploration interests in Australian sedimentary basins, long thought too old to contain oil. On the advice of American geologist Lewis Weeks, the Australian company **BHP** formed a joint venture with the American company Esso, and commenced exploration in Bass Strait in the early 1960s. By 1967 the giant oilfields of Kingfish and Halibut had been discovered. Their production of crude oil and natural gas began in 1969, greatly reducing Australia's dependence on imported oil.

The 1989 agreement between the Australian and Indonesian governments for joint administration of a Zone of Cooperation of the Timor Gap allowed exploration there after a 15-year moratorium. BHP began oil production in the Timor Sea in 1986 and has developed worldwide petroleum interests. The North-West Shelf joint venture near

Dampier, WA, first supplied gas in 1984 and is Australia's biggest resource development.

The government had encouraged exploration by allowing an incentive margin on locally produced crude oil, set by the Tariff Board at $US4.72 per kilolitre, and from 1968 by setting prices of local production at 'import parity'. But this kept Australian oil prices too low when international prices increased dramatically during the first oil crisis of 1973–75. The price of domestic crude oil remained at one-third of the imported price, thereby protecting Australia's manufacturing and **motor car** industries from escalating costs, but deterring exploration.

To ensure that the Commonwealth government received a larger share of the profits generated by Bass Strait production without retarding exploration in other areas of Australia, the **Whitlam** Labor government announced in September 1975 that 'new' oil would attract import parity prices with no production excise. In August 1977 a proportional pricing scheme for 'old' oil was introduced, and a progressive excise system in 1983. The **Hawke** Labor government legislated a resource rent tax in December 1987 to replace royalties and the crude oil excise levy for new offshore fields. This increased the government's share of oil profits on large fields, without discouraging the development of marginal production projects.

On 1 January 1988 the government deregulated the oil refining industry and dropped the crude oil allocation scheme, which had required local refineries to take a proportion of their feedstock as local crude at import parity prices. Deregulation allowed domestic oil producers to export their production, and refiners to import all their oil requirements, without government interference. In 1997 the petroleum products industry was deregulated to increase competition and benefits to customers.

Oil production peaked in 1996, but the decline in Bass Strait has been offset by new production in the West. Only two of the six major oil producers are Australian-owned, BHP and Santos, and local producers face aggressive competition from South Korean refineries. Australia is under pressure to yield more of the Timor Gap reserves to independent **East Timor**. It will increasingly rely on foreign corporations for its investments in the industry and for its crude oil and petroleum products. The best guide is *Australia's Oil Industry* (1997), produced by the Australian Institute of Petroleum.

GRAHAM E.L. HOLTON

Old age was a novelty in colonial Australia, an immigrant society that was young both historically and demographically. In the mid-nineteenth century only about one Australian in a hundred was over the age of 65, whereas in Britain the proportion was more than four times that figure. A pioneer of the 1830s recalled that anyone over the age of 30 was known in those days as 'old So-and-so'. Old age caught up with the gold-rush generation in the 1890s, a depressed decade when building society closures and bank crashes robbed many **pioneers** of the nest-eggs they had gathered for their retirement. Benevolent homes and other charities were unable to cope with the sudden influx of indigent old people. This, Australia's first crisis of aged care, spurred the introduction of non-contributory old-age pensions in Victoria (1899), NSW (1900), Qld (1907), and later in the Commonwealth (1908). Long regarded as a sign of Australia's progressive social attitudes, the old-age pension is better seen as a special form of compensation for those who, as a Victorian parliamentarian noted, had 'played their part in assisting to build up the State, who have discharged all their obligations as citizens, and who now find themselves unable to obtain a livelihood'. Only a small fraction of old people qualified for the pension; it was restricted to the poor and virtuous. But by legally defining the threshold of old age, the pension helped to reinforce the concept of 'retirement' as a period of compulsory abstention from paid work. In the early twentieth century Australians generally preferred to think of themselves as a young nation, and took a negative view of old age. Many doctors, influenced by theories of ageing as a depletion of vital energy, reinforced their view.

Not until the 1940s and 1950s, when the proportion of people aged 65 and over rose to about seven per cent, did old age again become a subject of public discussion. In an over-crowded housing market, old people were often the worst housed of all. In 1954 the sociologist Bertram Hutchinson reported that 'old age, both in prospect and in actuality, is felt to be a distasteful necessity with few pleasing features to redeem it'. In the same year the **Menzies** government passed its Aged Persons Homes Act, the first of a series of measures extending Commonwealth assistance to the aged, usually through church and other voluntary agencies on the basis of a pound-for-pound subsidy. In the 1970s the aged had become a vocal pressure group, helping to secure the abolition of death duties and a gradual relaxation of the means test for the pension. There followed a period of unrivalled financial security for Australia's old people, most of whom now owned their own homes and could secure access to a wide range of concessional benefits through seniors' cards.

This golden age of aged care was short-lived, for by the 1990s the steeply rising numbers of old people, especially in their eighties and beyond, combined with the rising costs of pensions and medical and residential care, had made ageing once again a national problem. In 1998, 12 per cent of Australians were over 65 years and by 2051 the proportion is expected to approach 25 per cent. Just as compulsory retirement was about to be abolished, old people faced longer queues for elective surgery and larger fees to enter nursing homes. They experienced less stigma but could expect less government support.

Compared with the historical study of women, children, and the family, the history of ageing in Australia is only in its infancy: a first collection of essays on the theme appeared in *ACH* (1995).

GRAEME DAVISON

Old Left is the name conferred by the self-styled **New Left** during the late 1960s and early 1970s on their predecessors as part of the impatience with established forms of radicalism. More particularly, it refers to the generation of left-wing intellectuals who were associated with the **Communist** Party, and especially the historians Russel **Ward**, Robin **Gollan**, Ian **Turner**, Lloyd Churchward, and Eric Fry. Strictly, the term is a misnomer. Most of these historians had broken with the Communist Party after 1956, along with Ken Gott, David Martin, and Jim Staples, to seek a new left position through the journals *Outlook*, edited in Sydney by Helen Palmer, and *Overland*, edited by Stephen Murray-Smith. As the entry on the New Left notes, they had much in common with their counterparts in Britain such as E.P. Thompson, who established the New Left there. Insofar as there was an Old Left historiography in Australia by the late 1960s, it was represented by ageing Communist Party members such as E.W. Campbell, whose *History of the Australian Labour Movement* (1945) still remained an authoritative party text. But these ex-communist, university-based scholars were made to carry the incubus of the past.

Behind the Old Left historians lay an earlier literature on Australian history produced by communists between the world wars—Lloyd Ross, James Rawling, and Esmonde Higgins—all with university training, who cultivated a knowledge of and respect for past struggles, from **Castle Hill** and **Eureka** to the anti-conscription campaigns of World War I. Their work is discussed in Stuart Macintyre, *The Reds* (1998), and also in Stephen Holt's 1996 biography of Ross.

Between that form of labour history and their own came Brian **Fitzpatrick**, who pioneered a different kind of history—the history of Australian capitalism. Both in his early publications on **economic history** and later, more popular works on the labour movement, *The Australian People* (1946) and *The Australian Commonwealth* (1956), Fitzpatrick combined analysis of capitalist exploitation and **class** conflict with a broader sympathy for the people. His emphasis on the imperial dimension of capitalism had a strong nationalist element. A lifelong civil libertarian, he portrayed the Australian people contending with vast, coercive forces and drawing on indigenous values as they sought a measure of independence, comfort, and fellowship. A similar assertion of nativist, egalitarian creativity was apparent in Vance **Palmer's** evocation of *The Legend of the Nineties* (1954); A.A. **Phillips's** re-evaluation of *The Australian Tradition* in literature (1958); the productions of the New Theatre, especially *Reedy River* (1953); John Manifold's collection of popular ballads; and the heroic depiction of workers by artists such as Noel Counihan.

The Old Left group of historians discovered that cultural tradition as young men in uniform. Their military service during World War II was formative. Mostly from middle-class backgrounds, they were brought into contact with the diversity of social experience and individual capacity at a time of national emergency when Australia's reliance on Britain ended. After 1941, when the Soviet Union was an ally, communism had an unprecedented appeal. For them the fight to defeat fascism became a 'people's war' that included the creation of a new national and international order. They returned in 1945 to complete their studies as part of this process.

Most turned to **labour history**, seeking through the study of the working class and the labour movement to realise its potential as an agent of radical change. They were responsible for the formation of the Australian Society for the Study of Labour History in 1961. Their academic careers were delayed partly by political duties (both Turner and Murray-Smith worked as organisers for the Communist Party) and partly by the changing political circumstances, for they conducted their research just as the Cold War brought a sustained intellectual offensive against the Left.

Gollan's doctoral studies at the London School of Economics brought him into contact with the historians group of the Communist Party of Great Britain, and yielded *Radical and Working Class Politics* (1960, 1967). Turner completed a doctorate at the Australian National University, published as *Industrial Labour and Politics* (1965). Fry's doctoral thesis was on 'The Condition of the Urban Wage-Earning Class in Australia in the 1880s' (Australian National University, 1958). Churchward produced a synoptic essay for the posthumous publication of documents on *The Australian Labor Movement 1850–1907* (1960), collected by Noel Ebbels. Miriam Rechter studied the maritime and coalmine strikes of the late 1920s in an MA thesis at the University of Melbourne in 1957, and as Miriam **Dixson** wrote a PhD thesis on 'Reformists and Revolutionaries' in NSW in the 1920s (Australian National University, 1964). Murray-Smith's Melbourne doctoral thesis was on technical education, while Ward ranged most widely in his Australian National University doctorate, which became *The Australian Legend* (1958).

These works traced a line of radical protest from the **convicts** and **bushrangers** to the contemporary labour movement at a time when economic prosperity was altering class relations and throwing up new forms of social protest largely disconnected from the themes of the Old Left. Responses to the often intemperate criticism from the New Left came from Turner in Leonie Sandercock and Stephen Murray-Smith (eds), *Room for Manoeuvre* (1982), Eric Fry in *Common Cause* (1986), and Ward in *HS* (1978). Ward's *A Radical Life* (1988) is the fullest autobiography. Reappraisals of the Old Left historians include John Merritt in G. Osborne and W.F. Mandle (eds), *New History* (1982); Andrew Wells in Brian Head and James Walter (eds), *Intellectual Movements and Australian Society* (1988); and Stephen Garton in Terry Irving (ed.), *Challenges to Labour History* (1994).

STUART MACINTYRE

Oliphant, (Marcus Laurence Elwin) 'Mark' (1901–2000) distinguished himself as a student of physics at the University of Adelaide and in 1927 joined scientists at

Cambridge University working to split the atom. In World War II he advised the British government on defence science and assisted American scientists with the development of the atomic bomb. However, Oliphant always harboured reservations about the military applications of nuclear technology, and after the attacks on Japan he became a 'belligerent pacifist'. To the detriment of his career, he became a public critic of nuclear weaponry. He returned to Australia in 1950 to the National University and became foundation president of the Academy of Science. Appointed governor of SA in 1971, he continued to speak his mind. His social and religious commentary sparked controversy. There is a biography by Stewart Cockburn and David Ellyard (1981).

KELLIE TOOLE

Olympic Games have played a growing role in projecting Australia's **national identity** to the world. Since the nineteenth century, when sporting achievement first became a measure of national prowess, Australians worshipped athletes as national **heroes**. But it is only from the midtwentieth century, as jet planes and satellites revolutionised international travel and communications, that the Olympics emerged as the pre-eminent festival of **nationalism**.

The modern Olympics were the creation of a French aristocrat, Baron Pierre de Coubertin, who had been attracted to the muscular Christianity and Hellenic ideals of bodily perfection upheld by English public schools, especially Thomas Arnold's Rugby. His movement was long dominated organisationally by aristocratic Europeans and rich Americans. Australia, far from Europe, more democratic in outlook but hungry for international recognition, became an eager junior member of this exclusive club. In 1894, when the Olympic movement was coming into being, the Melbourne lawyer and amateur athlete Basil Parkinson had urged the new body to adopt a strict, but socially more inclusive, code of amateurism. 'No distinction should be made between manual labourers and any others', he urged. Olympic athletes could not be paid, take admission money for prizes, or wager on their performances, but they might accept travelling expenses to get to distant destinations. Australia boasts of having been represented at every Games of the modern era, but Edwin Flack, the Melbourne accountant who won the 800- and 1500-metre races in Athens in 1896, entered as an individual through a London athletic club and stood under the Union Jack to receive his medal. His win caused little excitement at home: 'the average Victorian football team' surpassed the athletic feats of those performing under the shadow of Mount Olympus, the *Argus* declared.

Like Flack or Wilfrid **Kent Hughes**, Australia's first Olympians were often ex-public schoolboys competing as individuals or as members of combined British Empire or Australasian teams, or participating in the Games while overseas as students, businessmen, or soldiers. The first state Olympic Councils were formed in Sydney and Melbourne

in 1911 and an Olympic Federation linked Australia and NZ in 1914 before an independent Australian Olympic Council was formed in 1919. Organised teams, with accredited team managers, uniforms, and government sponsorship, date from the 1920 Antwerp Games. Australia has been represented on the International Olympic Council through a self-perpetuating oligarchy of wealthy ex-sportsmen, with the money and leisure to attend meetings: hardware millionaire Harold Luxton (1933–51), his son and Shell Australia chairman Lewis Luxton (1951–74), shipping executive Hugh Weir (1946–75), and Shell chairman Kevan Gosper (1977–) have been long-serving influential figures. Harry Gordon surveys Australia's Olympic organisations as part of his more general history of *Australia and the Olympic Games* (1994).

Increasingly, Australian Olympians came from humbler backgrounds, especially in sports such as swimming where Australia enjoyed growing success through working-class champions like Freddie Lane (1900), Frank **Beaurepaire** (1908, 1920, 1924), and Andrew 'Boy' Charlton (1924, 1928). In 1912 swimmer Fanny Durack won a gold medal at Stockholm, the first Olympics open to women, thus founding a remarkable line of Australian women swimmers that includes such multiple medallists as Dawn **Fraser** and Shane Gould. Although the Olympic code then forbade professionalism, some former Olympians, such as Beaurepaire, Herb Elliott, Ron Clarke, Jon Konrads, Kevan Gosper, and Murray Rose, have launched successful business careers through the fame and contacts acquired through amateur sport. Famous women Olympians, such as Dawn Fraser and Shirley Strickland, have won political office, but seldom business success.

Since the 1890s Australian Olympians had hoped that one day Australia might host the Games. In 1947 the Victorian Olympic Council initiated a bid to hold the 1956 Games in Melbourne and in 1948 a delegation led by ex-Olympian and industrialist Frank Beaurepaire lobbied IOC delegates in London, arguing that it was time for the southern hemisphere to have a turn. The vote was postponed until 1949 in Rome, when Melbourne won by one vote from Buenos Aires. The bid had united Olympic officials, eager to promote amateur sport, and Melbourne businessmen and others, eager to promote their city. But the challenge of organising the Games almost fractured this alliance, as businessmen, athletic officials, and politicians quarrelled over the site of the main stadium (should it be the Melbourne Cricket Ground, the Showgrounds, or the Carlton Cricket Ground?) and leadership of the Games organisation. In 1953 the president of the IOC, Avery Brundage, threatened to take the Games away. Melbourne's self-confidence, never strong, was badly dented: the fear of becoming 'the laughing-stock of the world' briefly eclipsed Melbourne's hope of winning the world's approval. In fact, as Graeme Davison argues (*AHS*, 1997), the world knew little and cared less about Melbourne's performance. Bungled negotiations for the television rights meant that pictures of the triumphs of Betty **Cuthbert** and Vladimir Kuts failed to reach American living-rooms. Melbourne's reputation as 'the Friendly Games' derives largely from the last-minute adoption of the suggestion of a young Chinese correspondent that athletes at the closing ceremony should walk together rather than march in national teams, a custom maintained at every subsequent Games.

In 1988 Melbourne again sought to host the Olympics but lost to Atlanta, a campaign that served nevertheless as a valuable trial run for Sydney's successful campaign in 1993 for the 2000 Olympics. Liberal premier John Fahey promised the first 'Green Games', with most of the events to be held at a massive complex of sporting stadia on reclaimed industrial land at Homebush. The Sydney Organising Committee for the Olympic Games (SOCOG), headed by Olympics Minister Michael Knight, survived internal dissension, ticketing scandals, and sinking public confidence to complete the project on time. Eleven thousand runners carried the Olympic torch across the continent to Sydney, where Aboriginal sprinter (and subsequent gold-medallist) Cathy Freeman lit the cauldron in a spectacular ceremony watched by 3.5 billion people worldwide. Thousands of volunteers helped Sydney maintain the tradition of the 'Friendly Games'. But the ceremony itself, with its gestures towards Aboriginal **reconciliation**, tributes to women athletes, and playful parodies of the old Australia of sheep and suburbs, showed how far the nation had travelled since Melburnians welcomed the world with 'God save the Queen' in 1956. No one was surprised when IOC chairman Juan Antonio Samaranch declared Sydney's 'the best Games ever'.

Australia's record in Olympic competition is generally reckoned to be a strong one, especially if medal tallies are computed, as Australian journalists often suggest, on a per capita basis. In the period between the world wars its natural advantages—warm climate, high living standards, strong sporting traditions—were offset by the high costs of competing out of season in distant locations. Most medals were won by swimmers, whose access to seabaths, mainly in the Sydney area, probably enabled them to train more easily than their competitors in colder climes. After World War II, air travel allowed Australian athletes, such as the 'four-minute miler' John Landy, to compete overseas more regularly. The Indian summer of lily-white amateurism was the golden age of Australian Olympianism: the peak was 1956 when Australia, competing at home, achieved its then all-time best of 35 medals. Runners, especially women such as Marjorie Jackson and Betty Cuthbert, and swimmers, now coached through the year by professionals like Forbes Carlisle and Don Talbot, won most of Australia's medals; cyclists and rowers also made a significant contribution. Half the medals won between 1948 and 1968 went to swimmers, about 40 per cent to women. In the 1970s the rest of the world caught up and overtook Australia, especially in the adoption of scientific training techniques. The low point was in Montreal in 1976 when Australia won only five medals, a 'disgrace' that prompted the Fraser government to create the Australian Institute of Sport, a new training centre for elite athletes in the national capital. This decision, coinciding with a changing of the guard within the Australian Olympic movement, laid the foundations for the nation's improved medal-winning performance in the 1980s and 1990s. The 1992 Barcelona Games were the first at which Australian athletes received cash prizes for winning medals. Hometown advantage, an intense training program, and commercial sponsorship produced 58 medals (16 gold) at the Sydney Olympics. The code of democratic amateurism outlined by Parkinson in 1894 had been supplanted by the dominance of the elite professional.

GRAEME DAVISON

One Nation, an anti-political political party, was formed in 1996. Its leader, Pauline Hanson, had won a Queensland seat in federal parliament earlier that year after her endorsement by the Liberal Party was withdrawn because of her racially inflammatory statements. In occasional parliamentary speeches and frequent public appearances she won considerable support by attacking economic rationalism, **multiculturalism**, government assistance to Aborigines, gun law reforms, and the 'Asianisation' of Australia. One Nation is a **populist** party with a corporate structure tightly controlled by Hanson and her close associates. Despite the endemic conflict this has caused, One Nation has been able to capitalise on dissatisfaction with the major parties. It has inflicted particular electoral and political damage on the coalition.

SM

Oodgeroo Noonuccal (Kath Walker) (1920–93), poet, grew up in Qld and was employed as a housemaid for the **Cilento** family in Brisbane. She obtained work as a switchboard operator during World War II, and soon after joined the **Communist** Party. Through her work with the Federal Council for the Advancement of Aboriginal and Torres Strait Islanders in the 1960s, she became increasingly active in the struggle for Aboriginal rights. Her first collection of verse, *We Are Going* (1964), was a poignant response to Aboriginal dispossession. Walker became a strong advocate of land rights and reconciliation; in this respect, she shared an affinity with fellow poet Judith **Wright**, who was a notable supporter of her work. In the Bicentennial year, 1988, Walker returned the MBE medal she had been awarded in 1970 and assumed her traditional name, Oodgeroo Noonuccal. Through educational programs offered on her native North Stradbroke Island, she attempted to teach Aboriginal and non-Aboriginal children a spiritual appreciation of the land and the natural world, and to bring indigenous and white Australians closer together.

HD

Opera put down deep roots early in Australia and has never ceased to flourish. Its history can be divided into pioneering, entrepreneurial, imperial, and state-fostered phases. Pioneering began with the introduction of English semi-operas into the repertories of colonial theatres. By the 1840s a group of singers originally recruited for Hobart's Royal were offering Sydney cut-down English-language versions from the pre-Verdian repertoire. In the mid-1850s the construction of the enormous gold-boom theatres permitted more ambitious productions. A Melbourne season of 1856, bankrolled by George Coppin, featured a genuine star of the age in Anna Bishop.

Having lost heavily, Coppin was happy to surrender the field to William Saurin Lyster (1828–80), an Irish soldier of fortune turned entrepreneur. Lyster's company of American principals (bands and choruses were recruited locally for each season) came fresh from a successful residence in San Francisco. Effectively the first Australian Opera, it toured from March 1861 to August 1869, giving 42 operas in 1459 performances. Lyster made a profit despite an absence of subsidies. From 1870 to 1880 he alternated seasons by Italians imported via Suez with the work of a new, 'English' company, whose chief drawcard was the Frenchman, Offenbach.

After his death in 1880, Lyster's role as an opera importer was assumed by the various J.C. **Williamson** organisations. Williamson had staged successful productions of Gilbert and Sullivan, and other popular operas, before bringing an Italian company in 1893. Touring companies were usually assembled in Britain or Italy, though a German company gave a stunning *Walküre* in 1907. Local singers, less considered than in Lyster's time, could either soldier on in Gilbert and Sullivan, or seek fame overseas. This option, first taken by Lucy Chambers in the 1860s, was made irresistible by the world ascendancy of Nellie **Melba**, and continued through a long line of Australian performers at Covent Garden, down to Joan Hammond and Joan **Sutherland**. Its negative effect was in further entrenching opera in the imperial touring system, which in the interwar period treated Williamson's (then run by the **Tait** brothers) very much as branch managers for London. The Williamson–Melba company of 1928 imported its scenery as well as its singers.

The Williamson–Sutherland company of 1965 (including a young Pavarotti), as well as being the last of these importations, marked the evolution of the form from middle-brow to highbrow culture. The Taits complained that there was too little Puccini; but Sutherland and Richard Bonynge (as later with the Australian Opera) specialised in the more recondite *bel canto* repertoire. Under their influence, Auber's somewhat moth-eaten *Fra Diavolo* was revived by the Australian Opera in a production with Regency-style cut-out scenery that slid on from the wings! The Australian Opera (today largely a NSW company that has merged with the Victorian company as Opera Australia—the other states retain their own) developed from the 1956 Elizabethan Trust Opera Company, itself the successor to strong, part-professional Melbourne and Sydney companies. Its growth coincided with acceptance of the reigning international pattern of state-subsidised companies working in state-constructed palaces of culture. Thanks to this, a number of outstanding performers, among them the sopranos Joan Carden and Marilyn Richardson, and a succession of splendid baritones and basses—but not too many tenors after Donald Smith—have chosen to base their careers in Australia rather than elsewhere.

Serious study of the heritage of opera production in Australia began only in the 1970s and is still far from satisfactory. While there are reputable narrative histories and many biographies and autobiographies of singers, little information is currently available about orchestras, pre-Meale composers, companies (including the current high-flyers) or, most significantly, audiences, of whom the majority attend now as subscribers. Nineteenth-century opera-goers expected sung versions of the dramas that were performed in the same theatres on other occasions. Since the music was familiar from band concerts and pantomimes, opera was still part of popular culture. The next phase, as mentioned, was the middle-brow one, sustained by the glamour of Melba and the seductive scores of Puccini. Today's audiences go consciously to experience high culture, but want it to be glamorous, theatrically virtuosic, and entertaining. Though companies fret over the high average age of audiences, subscription attendance at opera has traditionally been an enjoyment of the middle-aged and elderly in this country, and new generations will continue to find their way to it.

HAROLD LOVE

Opperman, Hubert Ferdinand 'Oppy' (1904–96),

also known as the 'Tin Hare' and the 'Human Motor', was a racing cyclist in the 1920s and 1930s. He established or broke 57 world records and 68 Australian records, some of which still stand. Opperman initially worked as a bicycle messenger and telegram boy. In 1922 he forged a lifelong link with Bruce Small, the entrepreneurial proprietor of Malvern Star Bicycles, who became his manager and business partner. Opperman was Australian Road Champion on four occasions, and captained Australia's Tour de France teams 1928–31. His finest wins were probably the 24-hour French Bol d'Or in 1928 and the 1931 Paris–Brest–Paris marathon (1162 km). In 1937, on a record-breaking 13-day solo journey from Fremantle to Sydney, he carried the bike over sand for 16 kilometres. Nearly 30 000 people greeted him in Adelaide, and parliament was suspended as he passed through Melbourne. His record ride from Albany to Perth in 1938 was three hours faster than the train. In his last big race, over 24 hours at Sydney in 1940, he broke 101 NSW, Australian, and world records.

Opperman served in the RAAF 1940–45. As Liberal MHR for Corio, Victoria (1949–67), he held several ministerial appointments and defended his seat against Bob **Hawke** in 1963. From 1967 to 1972 he was Australian high commissioner in Malta. Opperman's life is revealed in his autobiography, *Pedals, Politics and People* (1977); Sandra Fitzpatrick's biography, *Hubert Opperman* (1996); Tracy Gibson's bibliography, *Guide to the Literature and Resources on Sir Hubert Opperman* (1989); and personal papers held by the National Library of Australia. In 1994 Opperman unveiled a statue of himself at his birthplace in Rochester, Victoria, opposite the 'Oppy Museum', where his old Malvern Star now rests.

DC

Oral history

Oral history is usually defined as a form of memory collection through a planned interview or collaboration between two people (sometimes more). The interview is recorded in some form, either handwritten notes or, more usually, audio or video tape. Oral history is a way of 'harnessing talk': some of the countless stories that are told both formally and informally between people every day that make sense of their experience in narrative form through spoken language.

As a historical source, oral history is akin to others, such as autobiography or written reminiscence, which are generated some time after a historical event, or at a later stage in life, and involve personal reflection. It is distinct from these other forms of remembering because of the collaborative nature of its creation. Some scholars argue that the interviewer, who initiates and develops the project, is implicated in the constitution of what is defined as historical evidence.

Oral history is always a personal account, an 'eyewitness to events of the past', and its value depends upon many factors: the quality of the subjects' memory, their proximity to the event, and their capacity to observe, describe, and relate it. Good oral history depends on the subject's ability to tell a story and the interviewer's ability in shaping it. Like all sources, it has limitations and strengths. As a spoken form it is less formal than the written composing of an autobiography, more emotive, often more revealing. Yet, oral history inevitably suffers from the narrowness of personal meaning—some argue that it cannot be regarded as a representative form of information and its value is rather for insight into personal experiences and attitudes in the past. Others gather large numbers of individual stories for particular projects, believing that these 'innumerable biographies' do tell us something of collective mentalities or commonsense views of the world that are no longer in existence.

Many of the features of oral history in Australia derive from its emergence during the 1960s and 1970s as a primary tool of the new **social history** or 'history from below' to investigate the lives of those previously 'hidden from history', particularly the oppressed in society. Practitioners saw increased accessibility to the past through publication as central to a more democratic history-making. Some of the important published works in the 1970s had this effect, particularly Kevin **Gilbert's** *Living Black* (1977); Wendy **Lowenstein's** *Weevils in the Flour* (1978), which sold over 9000 copies and is still in print 20 years later; and Patsy **Adam-Smith's** series of popular histories. The areas tending to dominate in both oral history collections and publications are migration and ethnic community histories, work by and with indigenous peoples, the working class in particular industries or occupations, and local histories. Feminist historians in Australia have been slower to utilise oral history in their research, despite a large number of community projects exploring aspects of women's experience in the 1970s and 1980s.

Since the 1970s the oral history movement has combined a strong community orientation with a national organisational framework with the formation of the Oral History Association of Australia in 1978. The association aims to encourage the development of skills through regular workshops, with a national conference every two years. A distinctive feature of the Australian scene has been the influence of government in sponsoring the collection and archiving of oral histories. Among the most important institutional supporters of such projects have been the National Library of Australia, which has a long-running scheme to interview prominent Australians about their lives and times, the **Australian War Memorial**, the Institute of Aboriginal and Torres Strait Islander Studies, the NSW Ethnic Affairs Commission, and the state libraries. There are also extensive research collections in local and university libraries, and some museums.

Oral history was at first regarded with suspicion by some academic historians. Their concern about the 'unreliability' of memory reflected the widespread assumption, among both advocates and critics, that oral history was a transparent representation of experience. This led to the belief that oral history could only be used in conjunction with written evidence in order to have its 'truthfulness' verified. However, Michael Frisch, the noted American oral historian, argues in *A Shared Authority* (1991) that oral history should not simply add more evidence—'more history'—or fill in the gaps of the written. In doing oral history, he says, we are 'involving people in exploring what it means to remember'. As they examined the conditions under which historical knowledge is produced, scholars realised that the stories told by others are not simply 'the source of explanation but *require* explanation'.

From the 1980s some historians began utilising oral history in a more sustained way and writing histories for wider audiences. The most important of these was Janet McCalman's *Struggletown* (1984), a study of working-class life in the Melbourne suburb of Richmond, which marked a new direction by combining sensitive analysis with a widely readable text. Scholars working in Aboriginal history, such as Heather Goodall and Peter Read, also utilised oral histories and combined their scholarship with strong community involvement. The 1938 volume of the **Bicentennial History Project** made oral history its primary method of inquiry. Hank Nelson was perhaps the first Australian historian to recognise the potential of radio as the natural form of oral history publication. His powerful Australian Broadcasting Corporation series on the colonial era in New Guinea, 'Taim Bilong Masta' (1982), and on the POW experience, 'Prisoners of War: Australians Under Nippon' (1985), opened the way for the more regular oral history programs produced by the Social History Unit of Australian Broadcasting Corporation Radio National. Since 1986, when it began a weekly program, the unit has conducted hundreds of interviews and established a vast regular audience for oral history.

At the 'Narratives, Stories, Lives' conference at Monash University in 1997, Janet McCalman argued that oral history has 'humanised history and brought it to wider audiences'. Certainly it has changed the practice of some academic historians, by strengthening links with communities and groups, and deepening their appreciation of the historical dimension of the culture. In turn, oral history has become more integrated into the discipline of history. Reflective oral history practice, for example, is a vital component of the skills training for **public historians** in Australia and has assisted extension of its use in areas such as heritage studies, museum exhibitions, CD-ROMs, films, and in legal arenas, such as native title claims. Some oral historians have now embarked on studies of social memory, particularly in relation to what is remembered and how, at the collective or public level. They have become increasingly aware of the central role of memory in public debates about the nature and place of historical knowledge in Australian life. Key contributions to that new debate are John Murphy (*AHS*, 1986); Kate Darian-Smith and Paula Hamilton (eds), *Memory and History* (1994); Alistair Thomson, *Anzac Memories* (1994); and Peter Read, *Returning to Nothing* (1996).

PAULA HAMILTON

Oratory has been practised in Australia in sermons, at weddings and funerals, in large political meetings and local protests, in unions and parliaments, in the meetings of innumerable voluntary societies, and on the lecture circuit.

British traditions of public meetings and public speaking retained their importance in the Australian colonies. Nineteenth-century **liberalism** regarded the capacity of citizens to meet together and discuss the great questions of the day as one of the defining characteristics of democracy. Public meetings ideally were scenes of debate, at which public opinion was formed in conversation, and oratorical performance was quite central to their function. Before the invention of amplification, considerable experience and skill was needed to convey both voice and meaning to large crowds, whether indoors or out. Citizens at public meetings witnessed oratory seeking to speak for the community, a series of rhetorical contests over who could truly speak for 'the people'. Debates in public meetings at mid-century were often reported verbatim in newspapers—as was debate in the colonial parliaments.

The **mechanics institutes** which proliferated in the second half of the nineteenth century provided one kind of venue for the lecture circuit—a surprisingly popular form of entertainment in the colonies. Frank Fowler in 1856 described 'the patent or current style of lecturer—two candles on the desk, spectacles, bundle of papers, etc., etc.'. Lecturers spoke on literary, scientific, political, or historical topics—and often for much longer than modern audiences would be expected to tolerate.

Colonial Australians were more often than their twentieth-century counterparts taught the elements of formal rhetoric. Children, at school and in families, were taught recitation and elocution from school or home readers, which contained prose excerpts and poetry suitable for reading aloud. British and American rhetorical primers were in circulation, but there was also an Australian advice literature. Thomas Padmore Hill's *The Oratorical Trainer* (1862) went

through at least eight Australian editions. Hill, who described himself as a 'Professor of Elocution', argued, as did almost all of the guides to public speaking, that speech-making could be learnt. If we are to fix our ideas and feelings upon the hearts and minds of others, he argued, our voices must be 'strongly impregnated with the warmth of genuine emotion'. T. Kingsland, a student of Hill, published his *Comprehensive System of Elocution* at Brunswick, Victoria, in 1891—the book would, he said, enable everyone to speak in 'a clear and earnest manner'.

Formal oratorical training was then supplemented by a range of self-help books which promised, democratically, to make anyone into a polished public speaker. From the 1930s, these books became more common. William Bottomley's *How to Become an Effective Public Speaker* (1931) reflected characteristic twentieth-century concerns when it argued that the 'personality' of the speaker was a crucial consideration for effective public speech, but that even personality could be acquired by proper training. J.P. Monro's *Speeches and Toasts For Every Occasion* (1934) offered model speeches and toasts for occasions such as weddings ('It is almost superfluous for me to say that we wish the recently-united pair the very best of health, wealth, and happiness …') and presentations, and sporting, municipal, and political speeches. By the 1930s, it was increasingly insisted that everyone ought to make themselves into an orator, in order to carry off successfully the innumerable small ceremonial occasions which marked even an ordinary Australian life.

There were also more institutional modes of learning oratorical skills through practice. Important among these were the traditions of competitive public recitation and debating. At Ballarat, from 1879, the South Street Debating Society ran competitive debates, and from 1890 annual competitions in which hundreds competed in categories which included reciting, debating, and speech-making. Debating became in Australia a characteristic part of elite education. Alan Missen and Brian Bourke's *The Australian Debater* (1963) argued that there was an 'urgent' need for debaters in Australian society, in order to combat communism—'the debater who is acute will be ready to answer its arguments'. More informally, the outdoor speakers' corners in Australian cities provided another context for oratorical performance and training. The Sydney Domain was a site for popular oratory on Sundays from 1878, after the colonial government closed Hyde Park to public speaking. The Yarra Bank was similarly used in Melbourne from the 1890s—John **Curtin** is said to have learnt his speaking skills there.

Women in Australia seem rarely to have spoken publicly until the 1890s. Caroline **Chisholm** was an exception—she spoke forthrightly at large public meetings in the 1850s, though still with a sense that her appearance before the public needed special justification. Late nineteenth-century feminist leaders such as Catherine Helen **Spence**, Rose **Scott**, and Vida **Goldstein** spoke in public frequently. By the 1890s women's names were more common among the sponsors of and speakers at public meetings, especially in connection with the **temperance** and women's suffrage movements, but still resolutions were usually proposed by men. In the early twentieth century, resistance to women speaking in public was still strong: Joy Damousi has written of the particular hostility which met women anti-conscription speakers during World War I. One of the most frequent objections to women's speaking was their reputed dislike of being the focus of the gaze of a mixed audience. Men feared, too, that women would demand higher levels of decorum in public debate. 'The average working-man politician must not be expected to comply with the rules of drawing-room etiquette', asserted a letter to the Melbourne *Argus* in 1895.

The quality of local oratorical performance was clearly measured against metropolitan standards. Locally produced readers contained mainly non-Australian texts for emulation. The literary tradition provides some striking depictions of everyday Australians as orators—think of the elaborate story-telling in **Furphy** and **Lawson**. Frank Fowler in the 1850s thought that 'the great fault of all the antipodean orators is the rapidity of their utterance'. It is difficult to say when the idea of Australians as an inarticulate and laconic people took hold, but by the twentieth century this had become a staple of Australian cultural criticism. W.K. **Hancock** argued in *Australia* (1930) that 'there is practically no propaganda except that of the political parties'. 'By any standards public oratory is appalling', claimed Donald **Horne** in *The Lucky Country* (1964).

The broadcasting of the proceedings of political meetings from the 1920s, and of federal parliament on **Australian Broadcasting Commission** radio from 1946, perhaps gave Australians an unusual level of exposure to political oratory. Radio certainly benefited those politicians, such as Robert **Menzies**, whose attention to language and oratorical style marked them as good radio performers. Television had different demands, and boosted other careers—John **Gorton** and Bob **Hawke** in federal politics, for example. The rapid development of both media, however, meant that from mid-century oratory was probably most often experienced at home.

Recent Australian works on oratory have quite distinct emphases. Public speaking is now an economic tool for many, and the titles of the recent books represent some of the urgency felt. There is less of the leisurely tone of earlier manuals, which were aimed at the person who might occasionally have to speak at a wedding or sporting club function, or chair a committee meeting. Now Australian books with titles such as *Excellence for Communicators*, *How to Create and Deliver a Dynamic Presentation*, and *Switch on Your Magnetic Personality: Communication in the 1990s* jostle in the marketplace. If in the nineteenth century oratory was primarily prized as a way of articulating communal consensus on important issues, it was now clearly most valued as a display of the personality and effectiveness of the individual.

There is as yet little historical work directly on the Australian oratorical tradition, though Ken **Inglis's** published lecture *'Men and Women of Australia': Speech Making as History* (1993) makes an important beginning. A good sense of the changing rhetoric of Australian public life can be gained from a reading of Manning **Clark's** *History of Australia* (1962–87), which throughout follows attentively the rhetorical dimensions of its subjects.

DAVID GOODMAN

Ord River Scheme is an expensive, controversial, large-scale agricultural **irrigation** project in north-eastern WA. The seasonal Ord River drains 45 000 square kilometres and is one of the greatest flooding rivers on earth. Its irrigation potential, recognised by the Fyfe royal commission (1939), attracted political support after the Japanese advance and the bombing of Darwin emphasised the vulnerability of isolated, unpopulated northern frontiers. Feasibility studies of the project convinced the WA government, and Commonwealth assistance in 1959 facilitated Stage 1, the Kununurra Diversion Dam, which commenced irrigation in April 1963. Stage 2, the Ord River Dam, was completed in June 1972. Hydro-electricity and further expansion were planned, but cotton-growing, the mainstay, ceased in 1974 because of rising costs, ineffective pesticides, and falling yields and quality. Zinc deficiency destroyed rice crops; peanut yields were erratic; safflower quality was poor; wheat and sugar proved non-viable. Government reports, *An Outline of the Ord Irrigation Project* (1976) and *Ord River Irrigation Area Review: 1978* (1979), describe this history. B.R. Davidson, *The Northern Myth* (1972), saw politics overriding economics in the Ord. Susan Graham-Taylor (with B.R. Davidson), *Lessons from the Ord* (1982), argued that research was too late and competing government bodies stymied planning. By the early 1980s, 35 farms were obtaining mixed commercial results with sorghum, soya beans, rice, maize, millet, bananas, cucurbits, mung beans, sunflowers, and pasture. After paying out $100 million in subsidies, Davidson observed, it would have been cheaper for the government simply to pay people to live in the area and let the Ord flow out to sea.

DC

Order of Australia, see **Honours**

Orr case involved the dismissal of Sydney Sparkes Orr (1914–66), foundation professor of philosophy at the University of Tasmania, in 1956. The alleged affair between Orr and his female student, Suzanne Kemp, caused a scandal in conservative Tasmania, but opinion was divided over whether his dismissal was just.

Orr was an erratic individual who caused controversy, and his supporters argued that his critics had framed him. The academic community generally abhorred the dismissal as a matter of principle; this was expressed in an international ban on the chair of philosophy to which Orr had been appointed. The lack of natural justice in the university's disciplinary procedures and the collusion of the state government and judiciary in subsequent events affronted many observers. Prominent church leaders sided with him. Orr found notable supporters in Douglas 'Pansy' Wright, who was later chancellor of the University of Melbourne, and W.C.H. 'Harry' Eddy, who published an account of the case in 1961. His supporters also launched a virulent attack on Kemp. The university finally succumbed to public pressure and agreed to pay Orr his missed salary, but refused to reinstate him. He died shortly after.

In *Gross Moral Turpitude* (1993), Cassandra Pybus defended Orr's dismissal on the grounds that he had abused a position of power—a factor which by the 1980s had come to be seen as typical of university sexual harassment cases.

HD

Osburn, Lucy (1835–91) was chosen by Florence Nightingale to introduce her nursing principles to the Sydney Infirmary. Osburn was appointed lady superintendent and she arrived in Sydney with five other nurses in 1868. Horrified at the decrepit and unsanitary conditions of the old hospital, and by the untrained local staff, she immediately instituted reforms. She soon gained the support of the governor and his wife when they asked her to nurse the visiting Duke of Edinburgh after he was shot in an **assassination** attempt. Her reforms were opposed by the infirmary's board of management and doctors, however, and the ensuing disputes resulted in the establishment of a royal commission in 1873. Its report vindicated Osburn and was critical of many aspects of the hospital. This led to the 1881 Sydney Hospital Act, which provided for a new building and an altered management structure. These changes were under way in 1884 when ill-health prompted Osburn to resign and return to England; her position was filled by one of her Australian graduates. Freda MacDonnell provides a sympathetic account in *Miss Nightingale's Young Ladies: The Story of Lucy Osburn and Sydney Hospital* (1970).

KT

Ottawa Agreement, see **Tariff**

Outback, deriving from the term *out back* in the latter half of the nineteenth century, refers to the wide expanse of harsh, dry, sparsely populated land which, aside from the fringe of settlements around the coastal areas, forms the bulk of the continent. The outback came to be seen as a place of distinctly Australian forms, but in reality most Australians, being urban, rarely venture far into the **bush**. Like the *Never-Never*, the outback has imprecise boundaries; in collocations such as *back country*, *back of Bourke*, and *back of beyond*, it alludes as much to an idea as to a place. More recently, the Great Australian Outback has been promoted for tourism. (See also *Dead Heart*.)

HD

Outstations are small settlements of **Aborigines**, usually close kin, who have left the large artificial 'communities' which

had been gathered together at missions, reserves, and cattle stations. They wish to escape feuding and the effects of alcohol abuse, and to re-establish traditional life on their own land. The movement to outstations began in the 1960s and has become widespread, chiefly in WA and the NT. The movement has been one of the most positive results of the policy of self-determination, though it has its own problems. Health services and education can be supplied to outstations only with great difficulty and extra cost, and the Aborigines still depend on social welfare benefits, though more bush tucker is consumed at outstations than at the older settlements. The isolation of outstations is mitigated by new communications technology. The Australian Electoral Commission goes to extraordinary lengths to provide voting facilities in outstations.

JH

Overland Telegraph, the telegraph line from Darwin to Adelaide completed in 1872, established direct electronic **communication** between eastern Australia and Europe for the first time. Telegraphs between the eastern capitals had been completed by the late 1850s and from London to India by the late 1860s, but it was not until the undersea link between Java and Darwin was undertaken in 1870 that the cross-continental line became feasible. Charles **Todd**, SA's superintendent of telegraphs and government observer, supervised the project; it was completed in a little under two years, in spite of natural hazards and political obstruction, especially from Qld, which had sought a rival route through Normanton. In her history of Australian telecommunications, *Clear Across Australia* (1984), Ann **Moyal** hails it as 'the greatest engineering feat carried out in nineteenth-century Australia'. Communication at first was too expensive—10 shillings a word—for all but the most urgent messages and wealthiest customers, but by 1901, as new cables were laid, the price dropped to just one shilling a word. The telegraph, like the railway, strengthened links between the colonies and between a federating Australia and its motherland. Ken **Inglis's** essay 'The Imperial Connection' (in A.F. Madden and W.H. Morris, eds, *Australia and Britain*, 1980) explores the imperial dimension, while Kevin Livingston in *The Wired Continent* (1996) argues for 'technological federalism' as an important strand in the story of Australian Federation.

GD

Overlander was the name given to settlers who drove stock over long distances to new pastures. The discovery of new territory for pastoral occupation sparked a steady flow of overlanders and their stock. The first overlanders crossed the Murray River near Albury in the 1830s, and headed south into the **Port Phillip District**; some continued on to SA. Their route followed the earlier tracks worn by the explorer Major **Mitchell**. In the 1840s settlers from NSW pushed northwards into the Darling Downs in southern Qld. The overlander's rough bush style, with his penchant for freedom and male fraternisation—as expressed in the ballads of the period—fits Russel **Ward's** model of the typical Australian bushman. Overlanders are celebrated as key figures in local **pioneer** legends, which, typically, emphasise the perils of travelling unprotected through unsettled country and their bravery for doing so. The name was given to the Melbourne–Adelaide railway service.

HD

Oxley, John Joseph (1783–1828), explorer, came to NSW as a sailor in 1802. He was appointed surveyor-general to the colony in 1812 and in 1817–18 explored the Macquarie, Lachlan, Castlereagh, Peel, and Hastings Rivers. His inability to trace the course of some of these rivers led him to accept the popular theory of a large inland sea. An account of these expeditions was published as *Journals of Two Expeditions into the Interior of New South Wales* (1820). In the course of later surveying work, he named the Tweed and Brisbane Rivers, and his exploration of the **Moreton Bay** area led to the establishment of a new penal settlement there. He is commemorated in the name of a township and highway.

KT

P

Pacific Island labourers, also known as Kanakas, were used as indentured labour in the last decades of the nineteenth century. The technique of recruiting them, sometimes by fraud or force, was known as *blackbirding*—the term *blackbird* was originally used to describe inhabitants of the West African coast, who were sold as slaves in America and the West Indies. From 1863 to 1904, 62 000 Pacific Island labourers—mostly from Vanuatu and the Solomons—were imported to Australia to work on **sugar** and cotton plantations in Qld. The practice aroused opposition from the trade union movement and was condemned by religious and humanitarian reformers. Contemporary accounts included George Palmer's *Kidnapping in the South Seas* (1871) and newspaper articles by George **Morrison** in 1883. The new Commonwealth parliament legislated in 1901 to outlaw the practice and repatriate the labourers. While more recent studies have confirmed that recruitment practices were sometimes brutal, and employment conditions exploitative, many of the Pacific Island labourers entered willingly into indenture contracts and formed local attachments. Peter Corris, *Passage, Port and Plantation* (1973), and Clive Moore, *Kanaka* (1985), are the principal studies.

HD

Pacific Islands–Australian relations differ profoundly from Australian relations with other regions. This is the only place on earth outside Australia where Australian policies and practices are expected to have predominating influence.

Australian-based venturers harvested sandalwood and shell in the nineteenth century, opening the Pacific region to missionaries and gold prospectors, many of whom were also Australian-based. In 1906 the new Commonwealth assumed government in Papua, and World War I was the occasion for seizing German New Guinea, which was then administered under a League of Nations mandate. After World War II these two dependencies were administered as a single entity, which became the independent state of **Papua New Guinea** (PNG) in 1975. Apart from Nauru, which was also an Australian dependency, no further territorial gains were made—despite sporadic interest in taking over the British Solomon Islands.

The Islands were major fields of Australian missionary endeavour, maritime trade, exploration, mineral prospecting, and archaeological and ethnographic research. During nearly a century of colonial administration in PNG, political, economic, and academic networks linked institutions and individuals in ways that survived decolonisation; this is rather less true in Nauru, where external influences are diluted by Nauru's affluence. Through the South Pacific Commission (a consultative body of Western countries established in 1947 with headquarters in New Caledonia), Australian influences touched the whole Islands region. Australian armed forces played decisive roles in New Guinea in both world wars, reflecting and intensifying Australia's strategic interests. After decolonisation, Australia continued to be involved as chief source of aid and technical and specialist services. The nine-year civil war in Bougainville, for example, was almost as much an Australian as a Papua New Guinean issue. Although New Zealand took the lead in brokering a truce, Australia contributed most of the 'peace dividend' and Australian personnel are the largest component of the peace-monitoring teams. The collapse of government in Solomon Islands in 2000 prompted similar Australian involvement in a cease-fire and disarmament initiative, and in monitoring the peace. Prompted by interventions there and in **East Timor**, some Island governments want to commit Australia to take an active role in Irian Jaya.

Australian scholars have therefore made notable contributions to the literature on the Pacific Islands, to an extent that shapes the self-image of many governments and individual Islanders. Much of the research was and is conducted through the Research School of Pacific Studies at the Australian National University, founded in the 1950s.

During the 1960s, tertiary education began in PNG and in Fiji, the former starting as an Australian institution. Graduate studies have brought large numbers of Island scholars to Australian universities, and few are untouched by these connections.

The trope of 'cargo cultism' was delineated by Peter Lawrence, *Road Belong Cargo: A Study of the Cargo Movement in the Southern Madang District* (1964), as an ancient tradition of Melanesian innovation, and by Peter Worsley, *The Trumpet Shall Sound* (1957, 1968), as embryonic anti-colonial nationalism. More conventional religious history builds on the pioneer research of W.N. Gunson, *Messengers of Grace: Evangelical Missionaries in the South Seas 1797–1860* (1977), through David Hilliard, *God's Gentlemen: A History of the Melanesian Mission 1849–1942* (1978), and Hugh Laracy, *Marists and Melanesians: A History of Catholic Missions in the Solomon Islands* (1976), to Diane Langmore, *Missionary Lives: Papua 1874–1914* (1989). Most of the revolutionary archaeological research in Melanesia has been carried out by Australian-based scholars, the most remarkable of which traced the origins of agriculture in the highlands back more than 6000 years. This work is summarised by Matthew Spriggs et al., *A Community of Culture: The People and Prehistory of the Pacific* (1993). Similarly, Norma McArthur's *Island Populations of the Pacific* (1968) is the base-line for most demographic studies. An equally influential literature is now evolving, from research in issues of governance, and law and order.

Some monographs dominate the literature on whole nations—for example, Azeem Amarshi et al. (eds), *Development and Dependency: The Political Economy of Papua New Guinea* (1979), which applied dependency theory, and James Griffin et al., *Papua New Guinea: A Political History* (1979), which is a more conventional political narrative. Equally seminal were James Davidson, *Samoa mo Samoa: The Emergence of the Independent State of Western Samoa* (1967); Nancy Viviani, *Nauru: Phosphate and Political Progress* (1970); and Judith Bennett, *Wealth of the Solomons: A History of a Pacific Archipelago 1800–1978* (1987). Fiji's historiography is shaped by Brij V. Lal, *Broken Waves* (1992), and Deryck Scarr, *Fiji: A Short History* (1984) and *Fiji: Politics of Illusion* (1988). The economic history of the western Pacific Islands is dominated by Ken Buckley and Kris Klugman, *The History of Burns Philp* (2 volumes, 1981, 1983); Dorothy Shineberg, *They Came for Sandalwood: A Study of the Sandalwood Trade in the Southwest Pacific 1830–1865* (1967); Hank Nelson, *Black, White and Gold: Gold Mining in Papua New Guinea 1878–1930* (1976); and Peter Corris, *Passage, Port and Plantation: A History of Solomon Islands Labour Migration* (1973).

Military and strategic issues have commanded much attention. In scholarly terms the most remarkable overview is Oskar Spate's trilogy, *The Pacific Since Magellan* (1979, 1983, 1988), although it ends before Australian influence properly began. Dudley McCarthy and David Dexter wrote volumes on New Guinea for the official history of World War II, while Stewart Firth, *Nuclear Playground* (1987), and Roger Keesing and Peter Corris, *Lightning Meets the West*

Wind: The Malaita Massacre (1980), extend the normal range of military studies.

The attempt to separate the Australian Commonwealth from the Pacific Islands had scholarly as well as political dimensions. The promiscuous anarchy of the pearl and labour trades in Torres Strait and the Coral Sea offended '**White Australian**' sentiment, and initiated a sustained attempt to separate Australia from the region. Bounded political and cultural domains were proposed by officials and anthropologists, as part of the delineation of the Australian community at the time of Federation. Legislation arrested immigration and repatriated Pacific Island labourers. The strategy was only partly successful. Torres Strait Islanders formed an awkward part of 'white Australia', whose economic history is reconstructed by Regina Ganter, *The Pearl-Shellers of Torres Strait* (1994). Not all South Sea Islanders were repatriated in 1906, and the experience of those who remained is recovered by Patricia Mercer, *White Australia Defied: Pacific Islander Settlements in North Queensland* (1995), and Clive Moore, *Kanaka: A History of Melanesian Mackay* (1985).

There is no complementary research on Australia by Islanders, though much has been published on themes of direct relevance to the Islands. Such academic dominance begs questions of intellectual colonialism and the politics of representation. Perversely, Australian scholars have made notable contributions here as well, beginning with Bernard Smith, *European Vision and the South Pacific* (1960, 1985), and elaborated by Greg Dening in *Islands and Beaches* (1980) and *Mr Bligh's Bad Language* (1992). Margaret Jolly and Nicholas Thomas extend these revisions to address issues of gender and colonialism, in a special issue of *Oceania* (1992) on 'The Politics of Tradition in the Pacific', which they edited. As in these examples, the themes of post-colonial literature have been addressed mainly in Polynesia, while the empirical and strategic literature is mainly concentrated in Melanesia. A bibliography is provided in Donald Denoon (ed.), *The Cambridge History of the Pacific Islanders* (1997), and for an introduction to many topics, see Brij V. Lal and Kate Fortune (eds), *The Pacific Islands: An Encyclopedia* (2000).

The Islands are too close to ignore, but too different to be relaxed neighbours. Infinitely more Australian ink has therefore been spilt on Island topics than (for example) NZ. This is only partly attributable to Australian strategic and material interests: equally important is the power imbalance between a relatively advanced industrial economy and a stable polity, and a dozen island states whose increasingly turbulent polities and economies rest on primary production. Post-colonial relations carry historical baggage, so that Australian journalists and even scholars continue to offer condescending images of the Islands as both exotic and familiar, remote and immediate.

DONALD DENOON

Pacifism is the doctrine that war and violence are unjustifiable and morally unacceptable. Christian pacifists further believe that the taking of human life is utterly contrary to

God's will. Many of Australia's earliest pacifists, such as the Rev. Charles **Strong**, came from the church. But despite opposition to the **Sudan campaign** (1885), the **Boer War** (1899–1902), and the introduction of compulsory military training in 1911, it took the enormous loss of life in World War I to give pacifism *per se* greater impetus. Throughout the 1930s it enjoyed an unprecedented popularity, but strains were already apparent. While thoroughgoing pacifists were opposed to all military activity, the **communist**-led Movement Against War and Fascism called for action against fascist belligerence in Spain, China, and other theatres of conflict. Carolyn Rasmussen records the efforts of these opponents of war in *The Lesser Evil?* (1992). Support for pacifism declined during World War II, especially after Japan entered the war. Pacifists and conscientious objectors were, however, tolerated, and organisations like the Federal Pacifist Council continued to work for reconciliation and reconstruction. Bobbie Oliver provides details of this phase in *Peacemongers* (1997).

Following the war pacifism again became more strongly associated with the left, but continued its involvement with Christian leaders, in particular the 'peace parsons', about whom Valerie O'Byrne wrote her MA thesis (Monash University, 1984). The use of **conscription** for the war in **Vietnam** galvanised pacifists, and they joined with others in opposition to what many thought was an unjust war. In the 1980s and 1990s they concerned themselves with nuclear disarmament, while pacifism as a credo has become more humanist than religious in outlook. Malcolm Saunders and Ralph Summy, *The Australian Peace Movement* (1986), gives an overview.

JANE YULE

Packer family, a media dynasty, have for three generations shown an aptitude for detecting new openings in the mass culture industries, a selective indifference to Establishment standards, a capacity both to bully employees and to inspire an almost feudal sense of loyalty, and a genius for pulling off coups in a vigorous pursuit of personal advantage.

The founder of the family style, ROBERT CLYDE PACKER (1879–1934), after working as a labourer and then a provincial journalist, gatecrashed the Sydney newspaper scene in 1908. As an editor of weekly, daily, and Sunday newspapers, he was imbued with the Northcliffean spirit of catchy headings, simple style, and circulation stunts, to which he added comic strips and American tabloid sensationalism. Partly through astute business deals with, and then against, his two business partners, he made himself a rich man, with a waterfront mansion, a limousine, and a yacht; he then moved to a rival firm, and in a commercially heroic saga, saved it during the Depression with an energy seen by his admirers as causing his early death.

His son, (DOUGLAS) FRANK HEWSON (1906–74), founded his magazine and newspaper business on two successive coups, both based on bluff, and later extended his television holdings in the same way. Though lacking his father's flair in popular journalism, he proved a skilful and bold publishing entrepreneur, in 1933, with the launch of the *Australian Women's Weekly*, a new concept in women's journalism (devised by an employee); he boasted of this as a gamble which came off—an approach extended, later, to his entry into **newspapers** and, later still, **television**. Although he was at times impelled by fear of failure, Packer's main prompting (other than making money) was a continuing need for new excitement. At first, the *Daily Telegraph*, under strong editors, had been determinedly liberal; however, when he took a firm grip on his daily newspapers, he became so addicted to the pleasure of using it as a personal mouthpiece that its sales declined. Bridget Griffen-Foley has written a study of *Sir Frank Packer: The Young Master* (2000).

Frank's elder son, ROBERT CLYDE (1934–2001), emigrated to USA after falling out with his father. The younger son, KERRY FRANCIS BULLMORE (1937–), reached heights of wealth, power, and personal indulgence his father had never dreamed possible. Among the speculators of the 1980s he maintained a calm intention of always buying cheap and selling dear so successfully that he came out of the 1980s as Australia's richest man. Gerald Stone, *Compulsive Viewing* (2000), comments on the success of his Nine network. Some of his biggest holdings were outside the media industry and, unlike his father and his grandfather, he added little to the media industry itself. The exception was the setting up of World Series Cricket as television entertainment in 1977—an instructive reminder of the talent for coups of three generations of Packers outlined in Paul Barry's *The Rise and Rise of Kerry Packer* (1993) along with other elements in that family's history: he had detected a new opening in mass entertainment; he had put his head down and butted his way to success; he had made a lot of money; and, as his father would have said, he had put a cat among the pigeons. Griffen-Foley's *The House of Packer* (1999) explains how his son JAMES (1967–) has been assuming responsibilities in the business, which has now passed through four generations.

DONALD HORNE

Page, Earle Christmas Grafton (1880–1961), a surgeon of Grafton, NSW, was leader of the Country Party (**National Party**) and almost without question the most inventive federal politician of the twentieth century. His virtue lies in the longevity of his principal creations; the effect of most of them has been to increase the power of the Commonwealth at the expense of that of the states, which was, at least in principle, the opposite of his intent.

Page achieved power quickly and he held on to it for a long time: 42 of his 81 years were spent in parliament, which he entered in 1919 as one of the founding members of the Federal Country Party. His political weapons—audacity, a quick mind, and an intuitive feel for issues—he used almost at once to achieve the leadership of the new party. After the 1922 elections gave his party the balance of power, they were called into play again as Page negotiated to remove W.M. **Hughes** as prime minister in favour of S.M. **Bruce**, with Page himself as deputy prime minister and treasurer. The period of the Bruce–Page government (1923–29) produced three more achievements: the formation of the **Loan Council**, whereby the Commonwealth gained control over the borrowing of the states; the use of tied grants under Section 96 of the **Constitution** to allow the Commonwealth to enter fields of expenditure reserved by the Constitution to the states (roads, in this first case); and the extension of protection to primary producers, through export subsidies, bounty schemes, and financial credits.

Page and his party re-entered government in 1934 in a coalition with J.A. **Lyons**, which lasted until Lyons's death in April 1939. Page established regular meetings with state ministers to coordinate policy in **agriculture**, an arrangement later extended to most areas of the administration. Page became interim prime minister on Lyons's death, and then refused to serve under R.G. **Menzies**, who had been elected by the UAP to replace Lyons. Page's subsequent personal denunciation of Menzies in parliament was a major error of judgment; although Menzies took him back into Cabinet the following year, it marked the end of his dominance in his own party. Page was to have yet another productive period in office, as minister for health (1949–56) when Menzies regained power. The principal product of this period was a National Health Scheme, the forerunner and foundation on which all subsequent health schemes have been based.

Page's policy productivity had no obvious ideological underpinning, and even his belief in country virtues and the importance of country people in the Australian scheme of things seems in retrospect to have been yet another intuitive response to a political situation. He simply enjoyed planning and scheming, and saw possibilities and opportunities everywhere.

Page's autobiography, *Truant Surgeon* (1963), was built on chapter drafts written by his long-serving private secretary, Ulrich Ellis, and benefited from the editing skills of Ann Mozley (**Moyal**). It is, nonetheless, an unsatisfactory account of the man. It fails to bring out his quirky appeal, his capacity to provide vision and attract political support, his merriness, and a certain buccaneering quality that was as evident on the tennis court as it was in backroom negotiations in parliament. By and large historians and political scientists have ignored Page, who remains through that neglect the most under-regarded politician of the federal arena.

DON AITKIN

Pageants are public spectacles. They dramatise the past in popular ways, and include ritual displays, parades, and re-enactments. Pageants are theatrical, purposeful, and often contentious. They are created, ostensibly for the public benefit, at the intersection of government, bureaucracy, public bodies, associations, and business; and they are politicised, because of their proximity to government and because their representations of the past are always partial. They represent the past in non-academic, ephemeral ways, but they are of sufficient cultural significance to demand serious historical attention in their own right.

Pageants are usually associated with the anniversaries of historical events. In Australia and other modern settler soci-

eties, the colonial **foundations** which are seen as constitutive of the nation have been the basis of recurrent retrospective celebrations. These have become more sophisticated, expensive, and contentious over time. The date of Arthur **Phillip's** colonisation in 1788 was made a public holiday and the occasion for a military review by Governor **Macquarie** in the early nineteenth century. By the centenary of colonisation in 1888—which is discussed in Graeme Davison et al. (eds), *Australians 1888* (1987) and compared with the centenary of the USA by Lyn Spillman, *Nation and Commemoration* (1997)—elaborate and extended celebrations set a pattern for subsequent anniversaries in NSW and the other colonies. More solemn commemorations, notably **Anzac Day**, have been organised to cultivate the memory of soldier-heroes. Beginning with the dawn service, distinctive rituals and processions are central to Anzac Day. Characteristic festivities also have a place in the political culture of labour, extolling past victories from the **eight-hour day** to **equal pay**. But Australian pageants are typically perspicuous celebrations of progress and prosperity, and their theme has been the rapidity of change over the brief span of European occupation: colonisation, settlement, free immigration, population growth, and economic development.

From the local to the national anniversary, pageants of this sort have the capacity to tell us a great deal about Australian attitudes to the past. First, although these events have been organised by governments, they have usually represented more than merely an official view of history, because they have drawn on expertise from an expanding field of **historical societies**, **libraries**, publishing, **museums**, and schools. So the appearance and organisation of pageants help to demonstrate the development and diffusion of history before its emergence as a field of academic scholarship. Second, the organisation of pageants in public spaces, as theatrical spectacles in the form of re-enactments or processions, has formed part of the creation of an Australian public history, putatively both shared and representative. Finally, these events have dramatised a culturally specific sense of historical events and progress, organised around pioneering heroics and foundational moments of revelation and promise, all presented as central to national historical experience. These aspects are explored in Julian Thomas's doctoral study of the Australian sesquicentenary (Australian National University, 1992) This sense of history departs from standard accounts of modern Western historical consciousness, and therefore helps to delineate particular aspects of historical consciousness in a settler society.

Unlike their European and American colleagues, Australian historians have rarely paid detailed attention to pageants and events like them. Such events have a marginal place in the new discipline of **public history**; nor do they fit easily into the explanatory frameworks of national cultural historiography, which have often depended on themes of an emergent national consciousness or resistant popular culture. A notable exception is K.S. **Inglis's** innovative social history, *The Australian Colonists* (1974), which explored the construction of heroic history in nineteenth-century Australia. The 1988 Bicentenary was the subject of extended analysis and comparison in a special issue of *AHS* (1988), *Making the Bicentenary*, while more recently Chris Healy's *From the Ruins of Colonialism* (1997) has drawn re-enactments and celebrations into a wider context of **post-colonial** historical questioning. These texts aside, since the early 1980s historical scholarship on the subject has tended to pursue the influential, but ultimately circular, approach of Terence Ranger and Eric Hobsbawm in their 1983 collection, *The Invention of Tradition*, which emphasised the novel political role of modern representations of tradition in maintaining social order in a new era of mass democracy.

JULIAN THOMAS

Painting, history records contemporary events with an eye to the future and celebrates significant past events. The earliest European depictions of Australia's history were made in the form of small water-colour drawings which recorded momentous events, such as the wrecking of the *Sirius* on Norfolk Island in 1790, and significant encounters with Aboriginal people, such as the wounding of Governor **Phillip** and the subsequent meeting with **Bennelong**, also in 1790.

Encounters with Aborigines continued to be painted throughout the nineteenth century by colonial artists. The painting which is often described as Australia's first history painting —one which attempted to cast a contemporary event into a heroic mould—is Benjamin Duterrau's *The Conciliation* (1840). This painting was the largest of several in which the artist recorded the activity of George Augustus **Robinson** in contacting Tasmanian Aboriginal people in the bush and persuading them to leave with him for the settlement on Flinders Island. Duterrau's purpose was twofold—to celebrate Robinson as a man of exemplary principle, and to record for posterity the Tasmanian Aborigines, widely regarded in the 1830s as a 'doomed race'.

Duterrau's work was certainly the most sustained of early contact imagery. Late in the century the Aboriginal artist Tommy McRae (c.1824–1901) made pen-and-ink drawings which depicted the other side of contact—Aboriginal reaction to the arrival of ships in Victoria and the story of William **Buckley**, the **'wild white man'**. As an Aboriginal artist working with non-traditional mediums and for a European art market, McRae prefigured urban artists of the late twentieth century; the history of Aboriginal–settler relations has been an important subject for many Aboriginal artists of the 1980s and 1990s. Artists such as Robert Campbell Junior, Gordon Bennett, and Fiona Foley have offered ironic post-colonial commentaries on nineteenth-century attitudes, while Rover Thomas painted a series of works recording massacres which took place in the Kimberley in the first quarter of the twentieth century.

Foundation imagery—the most deliberate historical imagery in Australian art—makes its earliest appearance in the 1850s. J.A. Gilfillan's *Captain Cook Taking Possession of New South Wales, 1770* was painted in 1859 and given by the artist to the Royal Society of Victoria. This fanciful image became well known through prints. The classic **Cook** painting, again widely available in print form, was E. Phillips Fox's *The Landing of Captain Cook at Botany Bay, 1770*, commissioned by the trustees of the National Gallery of Victoria in 1901 in fulfilment of the Gillbee Bequest, which specified two subjects—the landing of Cook, and the **Burke** and Wills story. While Cook could be claimed to be a significant figure for both NSW and Australia, each of the other states celebrated their own founding landfalls in art, Victoria in the **Batman** and **Fawkner** paintings by Woodhouse, and later Blamire Young; SA in Charles Hill's *The Proclamation of South Australia* (1855–70); Qld in a work of 1928 by the marine painter John Allcot; and WA in a large work by George Pitt Morison, painted in 1929 and now in the Art Gallery of Western Australia. These foundation set-pieces are characterised by an air of stagey unreality and they have seldom been considered satisfying works of art. Paintings of the openings of governments tend similarly to be stiff and undistinguished other than for their documentary interest. The English painter William **Strutt** was commissioned to paint members of the Victorian parliament but the largest and best-known of such paintings is Tom **Roberts's** laborious sea-of-heads painting (completed in 1903) of the opening of the first parliament of a federated Australia.

Of far greater interest are paintings which record individual pioneering endeavour, exploration, or bushrangers. Strutt's arrival in Victoria in 1850 coincided with the separation of Victoria from NSW as a self-governing colony, and the progress of 'Victoria the Golden' provided him with themes for historical painting. His major Australian subject was the bushfire of **Black Thursday**, 6 February 1851, which he began painting after his return to England in 1862 and completed in 1864. Strutt was the first artist to make a significant work on a bushranging theme with his *Bushrangers, Victoria, Australia, 1852*, painted in 1887. He was one of many artists to paint episodes from the Burke and Wills story. As a witness to the start of the Burke and Wills expedition, he had hoped to secure the Gillbee Bequest commission for a commemorative painting. But it went to Longstaff who completed his monumental *Burke, Wills and King at Cooper's Creek* in 1907; Strutt completed his own *The Burial of Burke* in 1911.

The painters of the **Heidelberg School** engaged in a type of history painting, but could be said to have been more interested in the relationship of figures, historical types, and stories to the landscape than in illustrating historical incidents. The three panels of Frederick **McCubbin's** *The Pioneer* (1904) encompass a family saga, which symbolises civic progress from selection to urbanisation. Tom Roberts's two 1895 works, *Bailed Up* and *In a Corner on the McIntyre*, are both bushranging pictures which prefigure Sidney **Nolan's** Ned Kelly series (1946–47) in that they embed historical dramas in distinctive landscape settings.

Several artists of the generation of the 1890s were involved in the most sustained attempt to develop history painting in Australia—in the **Australian War Memorial**. Towards the end of World War I the aspiration of the historian C.E.W. **Bean** to record Australia's wartime activities led to the appointment of official war artists, and throughout the 1920s artists such as George Lambert and John Longstaff were commissioned to produce major battle pieces. This practice continued after World War II, and the Australian War Memorial amassed a vast art collection. Much of the collection is documentary in nature, but in works such as Lambert's *Anzac, the Landing, 1915* (1920–22) it rises to the status of important art. Lambert's Gallipoli works were the result of extensive research, including a field trip with Bean in 1919.

Perhaps inspired by a need to establish a historical basis for the Australian character which had been highlighted during the war years, the 1940s saw a renewed interest in nineteenth-century subjects. In Sydney a number of artists such as Donald Friend were captivated by the more theatrical and colourful elements of colonial life, while in Melbourne the young Sidney Nolan's interest in Ned Kelly was motivated by a desire to explore a mythical dimension in Australian folklore, rather than to paint history literally. He later explored other Australian historical themes, including Burke and Wills, the story of Eliza **Fraser**, the convict drama of Marcus **Clarke's** *His Natural Life*, and Gallipoli. Several of Nolan's contemporaries in the 1940s and 1950s, including Albert Tucker and David **Boyd**, also tackled historical and mythical subjects, such as **Lasseter** and **Truganini**.

The late twentieth century has not produced much significant history painting. This is partly to be explained by the decline of narrative painting as a vigorous art form in Australia; the medium of film has to a large degree superseded this art form. The 1980s and 1990s have, however, seen the exploration of historical themes by contemporary artists, particularly those who have taken an ironic, postcolonial, or anti-racist stance on Australia's history.

ANDREW SAYERS

Palmer, Janet Gertrude 'Nettie' (1885–1964) and **Edward Vivian 'Vance'** (1885–1959) were writers who in a range of activities sought to develop a national culture in Australia. She was born and educated in Victoria, he in Qld, and they spent most their lives in the two states after extensive travel in Europe before World War I. Their socialist politics yielded to a more chastened left liberalism, charted by David Walker, *Dream and Disillusion* (1976), though they were active in the campaign against fascism during the 1930s and Vance was attacked by the right when chair of the Commonwealth Literary Fund 1947–53. Vance was a prolific writer of fiction and verse, and his Golconda trilogy (1948–59) was inspired by the career of E.J. **Theodore**. Nettie was a leading critic whose role in the promotion of Australian writing is assessed by Drusilla Modjeska, *Exiles at Home* (1981). Nettie's biography of her uncle, H.B. **Higgins**, and the diary *Fourteen Years* (1948) are both notable historical sources, while Vance's *National Portraits* (1940) and *Legend of the Nineties* (1954) were important contributions to the **radical nationalist** interpretation of Australian history.

SM

Pankhurst Walsh, Adela Constance (1886–1961) was the youngest daughter of the British suffragette Emmeline Pankhurst. Schooled in the suffrage campaigns organised by her mother, Adela entered public life with all the passion and flamboyance which characterised her politically active family. After an altercation with her mother Emmeline and sister Christabel, she was invited by feminists and socialists to Australia. Arriving in April 1914, she was welcomed by Vida **Goldstein** and became organiser for the **Women's Political Association** and the Victorian Socialist Party. In 1920, she was one of the founding members of the **Communist** Party of Australia with her husband Tom Walsh. Together, they formed a formidable political partnership which was combined with rearing six children. Increasingly, she expressed disillusionment with the Left and by 1925 became a rabid anti-communist. In 1929 she formed the Women's Guild of Empire and in 1940 stood as an unsuccessful independent candidate for the Senate. During World War II, she gravitated towards the neo-fascist **Australia First Movement**. In 1942 she was accused of espionage and interned. Following Tom Walsh's death in 1943 and the end of the war, she retreated from public life. Verna Coleman published a biography in 1996.

JOY DAMOUSI

Papua New Guinea–Australian relations have changed sharply over a century. From the foundation of white settlement on the east coast of Australia, ships going north to Asia passed through New Guinea waters. New Guineans living on the main routes became accustomed to ship-to-canoe trading, and parties of seamen coming ashore for wood, food, and water. Whalers and survey vessels continued sporadic contact to the late 1870s when Australian pearlers, *bêche-de-mer* fishers, and labour traders began pushing north into Torres Strait, the Louisiades, Bougainville, New Britain, and New Ireland. Australian miners looked on New Guinea as another prospecting frontier, and especially after an abortive rush inland of Port Moresby in 1878 they treated New Guinea as an extension of the north Qld fields.

New Guinea's reputation for fever and violence inhibited traders and settlers, and it was partly to impose law and order and protect what was thought might become a significant shipping route that the Queensland government in 1879 extended its border to enclose Torres Strait. Later, that made some Melanesians in the Torres Strait islands Australians, and resulted in a complex border settlement of 1978 when Australia attempted to retain all inhabited islands and grant freedom of movement and access to marine resources to Papua New Guineans. The border between Australia and PNG is now a set of circles and lines dividing seabed resources, territorial seas, and the protected environment zone.

Alarmed that a European power was about to annex east New Guinea, the eastern Australian colonies pressed Britain to act first. Qld's attempt to assert sovereignty was rejected by Britain, and by the time the British raised the flag in Port Moresby in 1884 the Germans were claiming the northeast. The eastern colonies contributed to the cost of administering British New Guinea and the lieutenant-governor in

Port Moresby reported to them as well as to the imperial government. Some basic laws, such as the Queensland criminal code and mining laws, were re-enacted in Port Moresby. Roger Thompson, *Australian Imperialism in the Pacific* (1980), covers these early relations.

One of the first decisions taken by the new Australian parliament meeting in Melbourne in 1901 was to accept British New Guinea as a territory. When World War I broke out in Europe in 1914, the Australians faced the situation they had long feared: Britain was at war, and the enemy, with a wireless station, ports, and naval vessels, was across Australia's north. An Australian expeditionary force went there and occupied German New Guinea. Granted a League of Nations mandate over north-east New Guinea in 1920, Australians held the Territory of New Guinea as a prize of war, and they believed they had the same right to make laws for the new territory as they did for Papua. They dispossessed German planters and German companies. But the Australians had accepted German New Guinea as a 'sacred trust' and they were committed to promote to the 'utmost' the progress of New Guineans.

From 1908 until his death in 1940, Lieutenant-Governor Sir Hubert **Murray** dominated the administration of Papua. Initially committed to the dual policy of promoting white settlement and at the same time recognising Papuan land rights and protecting and 'raising' Papuans, Murray found his task easier after 1914 when it became apparent that economic and geographic conditions meant that few Australians were going to live in Papua. Francis West, *Hubert Murray* (1968), examines his policies. Murray instilled into his officers that Papuan labourers were to be protected from employers who would bash or rob them, and Papuans were allowed to give evidence in courts against whites. But Murray also allowed the passing of petty discriminatory laws: preventing Papuan labourers from being outside their quarters after 9 p.m.; making illegal the use of 'jeering or disrespectful language to a European'; reserving certain beaches for whites; and, through the White Women's Protection Ordinance, accommodating the white community's fears that black men were likely to violate white women. Amirah Inglis, *Not a White Woman Safe* (1974), examines this latter aspect.

In the neighbouring mandated territory, the administration, headed by a succession of ex-AIF officers, had to deal with slightly more settlers who wanted assurance that their interest would not be sacrificed to what they saw as an international body of do-gooders in Geneva, a resurgent Germany wanting its colonies returned, or the threat of the Japanese just over the horizon in Micronesia. In Rabaul the Australians maintained strict divisions between Europeans, Asians, and Melanesians; they had separate hospitals, schools, and cemeteries. The opening of the goldfields at Wau and Bulolo from 1926 protected New Guinea from the impact of the Depression, and the exploratory patrols through the highland valleys increased the excitement, obligations, and possibilities for Australians in New Guinea. Australians had responsibility for the introduction of nearly a million new people to the outside world, and they had to decide whether they would foster settlement in the temper-

ate highlands. That decision was not made finally until the 1950s, and then it was decided that there would be just a scatter of plantations though the highlands. The Australian population in Papua and New Guinea reached its maximum of 30 000 in 1971 when PNG was being prepared for self-government, and most of the Australians were transitory.

World War II came suddenly and violently to New Guinea in January 1942. Nearly all white women and children were evacuated; Chinese women and children were left to face the Japanese; many Australian men in the public service, the missions, and private enterprise were interned by the Japanese, and over 400 died. Initially finding the terrain hostile and alien, by the end of the war the diggers were proud of their reputation as jungle fighters. By August 1945 more than 300 000 Australians had been in New Guinea, and most Australians had a familiarity with the map; they had a sense of debt to the **fuzzy-wuzzy angels** who had aided Australians on the **Kokoda Track** and in other battles; and they were prepared to pay to support more progressive policies. Although the postwar reforms in health, education, and wages were significant, they left Papua New Guineans who thought they had demonstrated their abilities in war, who heard praise and promises, with modest gains. Ian Downs, *The Australian Trusteeship: Papua New Guinea 1945–75* (1980), is a comprehensive official history of the postwar Australian administration.

For 20 years after World War II government and opposition parties supported a general policy of self-determination for PNG, and agreed to subsidise development. By 1960 over two-thirds of the territory's revenue came in grants from Australia. In statements of 1966 and 1968 the Australian government made it clear that no part of the Territory of Papua New Guinea could choose a separate constitutional future and the whole was to be self-governing. As leader of the opposition, Gough **Whitlam** briefly broke the bipartisan policy in 1970 by announcing that a Labour government would make PNG independent: it was 'not negotiable'. But the Liberal–Country Party government of John **Gorton** and the Australian administration were already preparing to transfer power. Michael Somare, leader of the minority Pangu Pati with a policy of home rule, put a coalition together following the 1972 general election. By independence day, 16 September 1975, many Papua New Guineans welcomed their new nation with enthusiasm, but Bougainvilleans had misgivings, and others feared submergence in more numerous groups. Australians made their formal departure with goodwill, and a commitment to continue financial and other aid.

Post-independence PNG initially defined itself as a South Pacific island-state but, while it has retained that identity, it has increased its engagement with South-East and East Asia. In the face of reports of increased crime, inefficiencies in government, and a violent secession movement on Bougainville, Papua New Guineans have blamed Australians for a legacy of deficiencies—a majority of the population illiterate, low life-expectancy, arbitrary borders, and a late rush to create a sense of nationhood. Sean Dorney, *Papua New Guinea* (1990), reported post-independence PNG, and

Dorney, *The Sandline Affair* (1998), and Mary-Louise O'Callaghan, *Enemies Within* (1999), have written on the failed attempt to hire mercenaries to fight on Bougainville.

Australians, while claiming a 'special relationship' and continuing to be generous with aid funds, have been uncertain how to influence events in PNG without being accused of a return to colonial policies and attitudes. Australian mining companies (or the Australian subsidiaries of transnational companies), churches, and aid agencies have retained close relationships with a turbulent independent PNG as Australian administrators and settlers have retreated. Papua New Guineans, so rarely seen in Australia before the mid-1960s, are now more numerous in Australia than Australians in PNG. In 1992 Prime Minister Paul **Keating** claimed to have found the spiritual basis of Australia at Kokoda. The 'special relationship' continues, but with movement north being replaced by a complicated north and south traffic of people, capital, and perceptions.

Donald Denoon (ed.), *The Cambridge History of the Pacific Islanders* (1997), considers PNG history in a Pacific Island context and includes bibliographic essays. Missionaries (see Diane Langmore, *Missionary Lives: Papua 1874–1914*, 1989) and government officers (for example, J.K. McCarthy, *Patrol into Yesterday*, 1963) have been studied extensively; but miners (Hank Nelson, *Black, White and Gold*, 1976), planters (D. Lewis, 'The Plantation Dream', *Journal of Pacific History*, 1996), and traders (Ken Buckley and Kris Klugman, *The History of Burns Philp*, vol. 1, 1981, and vol. 2, 1983) have been less conspicuous. Hank Nelson's radio series *Taim Bilong Masta* was also published (1982). Papua New Guineans, beginning with Albert Maori Kiki, have written illuminating autobiographies, and John Waiko has produced *A Short History of Papua New Guinea* (1993).

HANK NELSON

Parer, Raymond John Paul (1894–1967) began his career in aviation as a pilot with the Australian Flying Corps during World War I. Although lack of funds prevented him from participating in the 1919 England–Australia air race, he and John McIntosh made the first single-engine flight from England to Australia the following year. Parer's book, *Flight and Adventures of Parer and McIntosh* (1921), describes the innumerable problems they encountered during the 208-day flight. He formed a small commercial aviation service in Melbourne and continued air-racing. His plane crashed in an attempt to encircle the continent, but he survived. He later flew in New Guinea, where he established an airline, prospected for oil, and ran a pearling boat. 'Battling Parer' as he became known, figures in Ion **Idriess's** romantic account of the New Guinea goldfields, *Gold Dust and Ashes* (1933).

KT

Park, Ruth (1923–) is the author of several popular historical novels. Born in NZ, Park moved to Sydney where she worked as a journalist and found the inspiration for her first two novels, *The Harp in the South* (1948) and its sequel, *Poor Man's Orange* (1949). In these works Park paints a grim picture of the struggle for survival of the inner-Sydney poor, mostly those of Irish background, during the 1920s and 1930s, but her stories are enlivened by a colloquial larrikin spirit. The later *Swords and Crowns and Rings* (1977) recreates social change during the early decades of the century. Her historical novel for children, *Playing Beattie Bow* (1980), re-creates Sydney's convict period. Park has also produced two autobiographical volumes, *A Fence Around the Cuckoo* (1992) and *Fishing in the Styx* (1993). She was married to fellow writer, D'Arcy Niland (1917–67).

HD

Parker, Catherine Langloh 'Katie' (1856–1940) was a rare example of a white woman studying Aboriginal culture, and became a respected contributor to Australian literature and anthropology, an area traditionally dominated by male writers. She grew up on a pastoral station in western NSW and developed close relations with **Aborigines**. After marrying pastoralist Langloh Parker, she lived on several stations in northern NSW and southern Qld, where she pursued an interest in Aboriginal culture and Dreamtime stories. As a woman she was able to record Aboriginal women's stories which had previously been denied to male anthropologists and collectors of Aboriginal culture. In *The Euahlayi Tribe* (1905) she documented this information, and provided an insight into the intimate relations between pastoralists' wives and Aboriginal women in frontier rural Australia. She was quick to defend the people she wrote about and testified to her deep respect for them. Her *Australian Legendary Tales* (1896) and *More Australian Legendary Tales* (1898) were pioneering works in traditional **Aboriginal narratives**. After her husband's death she remarried and, as Katie Stow, published *Woggheeguy: Australian Aboriginal Legends* (1930). An account of her life at Bangate was published posthumously as *My Bush Book* (1982). Her role as a woman writer on the frontier is considered by Patricia Grimshaw and Julie Evans in *AHS* (1996).

HD

Parkes, Henry (1815–96) is the best known of Australia's nineteenth-century politicians. He owes this to durability, his career of nearly half a century in NSW politics culminating in well-timed advocacy of the 1890s **Federation** movement. Vestiges of his early radicalism survived into old age as Australia's first Knight Grand Cross of the Order of Saint Michael and Saint George, but he flourished largely as a master of **faction** politics until party lines solidified in his last years.

Son of a tenant farmer dispossessed for rent arrears, Parkes served an apprenticeship in Birmingham to an ivory and bone turner, but failed to establish his own business. Having married Clarinda Varney in 1836, he emigrated to NSW in 1839. Initial struggle was followed by security as a customs official, 1840–45; he then set up business as an ivory turner and importer of toys. Politically engaged since his Birmingham days, he was active in the **anti-transportation** movement of the 1840s and joined the radical Constitutional Association in 1848. In 1850 he was a campaign manager for the republican Dr J.D. **Lang**, and established a newspaper, the *Empire*, as democratic competitor to the *Sydney Morning Herald*. Prominent in the 1853 Constitution Committee demanding an elected Legislative Council under responsible government, Parkes gained election as a member of the old Council at his second attempt in 1854, transferring to the new Legislative Assembly in 1856.

Parkes sat in the Assembly from 1856 to 1895, representing nine different constituencies, with breaks totalling six years because of overseas travel or bankruptcies. His finances were usually precarious. In 1858 bankruptcy ended his editor-proprietorship of the *Empire*. He was again insolvent in 1870, and several times later ran close to the wind, but he flourished in politics. Originally one of the large number of colonial **liberals** united in little more than opposition to the pre-1856 hierarchy of landowning conservatives, Parkes survived through his skill in cobbling coalitions from disparate factions in the Assembly. He was six times colonial secretary (1866–68, 1872–75, 1877, 1878–83, 1887–89, and 1889–91), the first time in James Martin's ministry, the others as premier.

His first term under Martin was productive. During the 1860s and 1870s the major issues of colonial politics were shaped around the provision of opportunity and basic services for a society of immigrants and their children. Parkes reformed Sydney's hospital system by introducing Nightingale-trained nurses and modernising the lunatic asylum. In 1866 he was architect of legislation setting up a Council of Education to administer and fund all schools, government or denominational. The **Catholic** bishops were never happy with it and their mistrust of Parkes deepened when he took a stridently anti-Irish line after the attempted **assassination** of the Duke of Edinburgh in 1868. Although during the 1870s Parkes tried to cultivate Catholic allies, the rift never healed, and in 1880 Parkes committed NSW to **'free, secular, and compulsory'** education.

The 1870s were more barren because faction politics led to frequent changes of ministry, until in 1878 Parkes formed his strongest government in coalition with his major competitor, Sir John **Robertson**. As well as resolving the education issue, this ministry reformed the licensing laws, antagonising the publicans but courting the considerable church and **temperance** vote. The Royal National Park south of Sydney was conserved for recreational use, Parkes having already shown environmental awareness with the declaration of a reserve at Jenolan Caves. Anticipating the **White Australia** policy, legislation was passed to curb Chinese immigration. This issue led to an inter-colonial conference in 1880–81, providing Parkes with the opportunity to resurrect a proposal for the Australian colonies to form a **Federal Council**. Nothing followed immediately, but his credentials were established as Australia's elder statesman urging closer national unity.

Following the coalition's defeat in 1883, NSW politics evolved towards the contemporary British two-party model, with a nascent protectionist party confronting a **free-trade** party whose leadership Parkes had resumed in 1886. His career was in no way impeded by his opposition to the **Sudan** expedition of 1885. Premier once more in 1887, he celebrated the centenary of white settlement by the creation of Centennial Park as site of a projected national pantheon, and sponsored an abortive scheme to rename NSW 'Australia'. Too autocratic and secretive to feel at ease with evolving conventions of party discipline, he sought to seal his career with the Federation of the Australasian colonies, although he had been among those who successfully kept NSW out of the Federal Council formed in 1885. An 1889 report on Australia's need for coordinated defence gave him an opening to confer with fellow-premiers in 1890 and set up the first Federal Convention in 1891. Patriarchally bearded, he presided over the gathering picturesquely, but the real work of devising the draft constitution fell to others such as **Griffith**, Inglis **Clark**, **Barton**, and **Kingston**.

It was his swan-song. Although at first Parkes was able to accommodate the appearance in NSW in 1891 of the Labor Party as a third force offering support in return for concessions, he failed to retain their backing. Losing office in October 1891, he was replaced as free-trade leader by George **Reid**. It was a reluctant yielding to a younger generation who were at home with the new style of party management. He remained in parliament until 1895 (and contested two by-elections in the 10 months before his death), sniping at Reid's leadership of the free-traders and Barton's of the federal movement. Twice remarried after his seventieth birthday to much younger women (and a father at 77), he was a 'character', but no longer a political force. His was a vigorous, at times tempestuous, and uneven record, but Alfred Deakin's verdict may stand: 'He had always in his mind's eye his own portrait as that of a great man, and … there was in him the substance of the man he dressed himself to appear.'

In addition to too much third-rate verse, Parkes wrote his own account of his life and times in *Fifty Years in the Making of Australian History* (1892), and a respectful biography by the journalist Charles Lyne, *Life of Sir Henry Parkes, GCMG, Australian Statesman*, appeared in Sydney on his death in 1896. The essential modern study is A.W. **Martin**, *Henry Parkes: A Biography* (1980), a subtle, thorough, and illuminating account. The portraits in old age by Tom **Roberts** and Arthur **Streeton** also repay contemplation.

GEOFFREY BOLTON

Pastoral history until recent decades was the central component of the general history of Australia. Australia was said to ride on the sheep's back, and the history of the nation rode on the back of pastoral history.

Long before the wool industry achieved its later prominence, pastoralism was seen as the distinctive and major force in the colony of NSW. William Charles **Wentworth** in his *A Statistical, Historical and Political Description of the Colony of New South Wales* (1819) was enthusiastic about the prospects for investment in 'fine woolled sheep' and praised the early work of John **Macarthur**. John Dunmore **Lang** in *An Historical and Statistical Account of New South Wales* (4th edn, 1875) also acknowledged the importance of fine wool to the economy but he decried the 'sheep and cattle mania' of the 1820s and the ascendancy which the squatters, 'Shepherd Kings' as he called them, later acquired. He looked to the day when the pastoral stage of development would be succeeded by the superior agricultural stage.

Perhaps the most extravagant statement of pastoral dominance was James Collier's *The Pastoral Age in Australasia* (1911). In addition to a comprehensive history of sheep and cattle, he included chapters on the importance of pastoralism for morals, science, art, literature, and politics. Pastoral dominance of economic history continued after World War I with a new generation of academic historians. Stephen **Roberts** wrote *History of Australian Land Settlement 1788–1920* (1924) from an early interest in 'the romance of Australia's squatters', a theme he developed further in *The Squatting Age in Australia 1835–1847* (1935). In Edward **Shann's** *An Economic History of Australia* (1938) the squatters appear as exemplars of economic enterprise, and the industry itself as 'the principal activity and support of the white man's Australian economy'.

W.K. **Hancock** and Brian **Fitzpatrick**, opposed in their views of British imperialism, were at one in their recognition of the central economic importance of wool. Yet it was Hancock, through his role in establishing the inter-disciplinary Wool Seminar at the Australian National University in the 1950s, who laid the groundwork for the most significant challenge to the dominance of pastoralism in Australian history. One of the participants, Alan Barnard, would make major studies of the marketing and financing of wool. More significant still was the role of Noel **Butlin**, whose estimates of Australian domestic product and investment revised traditional understandings of wool's importance. His dramatic statement, 'Australian economic history was not a footnote to the industrial revolution nor was Australia a sheep-walk for the benefit of British imperialism', was aimed most immediately at Fitzpatrick, but it overturned all previously received wisdom. He argued that, although the Australian dependence on British capital and markets suggested 'a special dependent relationship', 'the critical decisions in capital formation and in the orientation of the economy were taken in Australia, by Australians and in the light of Australian criteria'. While acknowledging that pastoral activity was 'unquestionably one of the main sources of Australian growth', especially in its heyday from 1861 to 1876, he stressed that the Australian economy had 'two other special characteristics' in the second half of the nineteenth century—a mixed economy and a high rate of urbanisation. Butlin's influence was immediately seen in the detailed regional studies of former doctoral students at the ANU, such as G.L. Buxton, *The Riverina 1861–1891* (1967), and Duncan Waterson, *Squatter, Selector and Storekeeper: A History of the Darling Downs 1859–1893* (1968), which connected pastoral activity to previously neglected sectors of transport, towns, and mining.

Pastoralists had long developed their own forms of history-writing, including reminiscences, biographies, and family and station histories. Pioneering experiences from the 1830s were recalled in W.A. Brodribb's *Recollections of an Australian Squatter* (1883), and from the 1840s by Alan Macpherson, *Mount Abundance* (1878), and Alfred Joyce, *A Homestead History* (ed. G.F. James, 1942). Often the role of pastoral chronicler or historian was assumed by women: one of the first published accounts was A Lady (Mrs Macpherson), *My Experiences in Australia* (1860), while some of the most lively, by Annie **Baxter**, Sarah Davenport, and others, have been collected by Lucy Frost in *No Place for a Nervous Lady* (1984).

In their heyday the great pastoral families had aspired to the status of an Australian aristocracy, a self-image which found expression especially in the building of impressive homesteads. By the end of the nineteenth century, portraits of the Australian squattocracy often incorporated illustrated histories of their properties. A series in the *Pastoral Review* (1909–14 and 1926–31) celebrated over 300 homes. Since the 1950s interest in the architecture of pastoralism has quickened further, with volumes by G. Nesta Griffiths on the southern (1952) and northern (1954) homesteads of NSW, Maurice Cantlon on Victoria (1967), a general study by Phillip Cox and Wesley Stace (1972), and several pictorial volumes produced by the National Trust.

The most devoted, yet often scholarly, historians of the pastoral **pioneers** have been their descendants, especially their daughters and grand-daughters. The novelist Mary **Durack** wrote a popular saga of her ancestors, cattlemen from the Kimberleys, in *Kings in Grass Castles* (1959). The poet Judith **Wright** commemorated her Hunter River and New England forebears in *The Generations of Men* (1959), a story she subsequently revisited in a mood more mournful than elegiac in *The Cry for the Dead* (1981). Margaret **Kiddle's** *Men of Yesterday* (1961) was both a 'social history' of the Victorian Western District and a tribute to her own ancestors—Scots pastoralists in the main. The genre continues in to the 1980s and 1990s with station histories by Judy White (Belltrees, 1981), Suzanne Falkiner (Haddon Rig, 1981), Anne Harris (Abington, 1982), and Jillian Oppenheimer and Bruce Mitchell (Ohio, 1989).

Pastoral history has not remained immune from the gusts of reinterpretation which have blown through Australian history since the 1970s. John Macarthur's claims to be the 'father' of the sheep industry are now displaced, not only by his wife, Elizabeth, whose feats as a sheepbreeder are now seen to have been greater than her husband's, but by other notable women, such as Eliza Forlonge and Janet Templeton. Older versions of pastoral history had rested upon the idealisation of the pioneer squatters as 'founders' and 'settlers'—an ideal which has been sharply contested by students of Aboriginal–white relations. Henry **Reynolds** (*The Law of the Land*, 1987) documented the crucial part played by pastoralists in combating, and finally defeating, imperial attempts to safeguard Crown land for Aboriginal reserves, while Ann McGrath (*Born in the Cattle*, 1987) and others have demonstrated how vital has been the continuing role of

Aboriginal stockmen to the viability of pastoralism in the far north. The self-image of the pastoralist as 'improver' has also been challenged by environmental historians, beginning with W.K. Hancock's *Discovering Monaro* (1972), which traced the long-term damage of grazing on trees, soils and rivers. Eric **Rolls**, himself a pastoralist, tells a less dismal story in his *A Million Wild Acres* (1981), a history of how pastoralism created a forest where a desert had been.

Yet, in spite of historiographical shifts, and the steady drift of population to the cities, pastoral Australia retains a treasured place in the national imagination. Ideas of pastoral peace and solitude had influenced literary ideas of Australia from mid-nineteenth-century British novelists to the poets of the *Bulletin* school, such as Banjo **Paterson**. It was the pastoral worker—the shearer, the stockman, the swagman—who came to be seen as the quintessential Australian. In *The Australian Legend* (1958) Russel **Ward** argued that 'a specifically Australian outlook grew up first and most clearly among the bush workers of the pastoral industry', a view which, in spite of Ward's academic critics, remains a fruitful source of popular myths. In 1990, for example, when the Labor Party celebrated its centenary, it traced its origins to the shearers' strikes of the outback rather than industrial and parliamentary conflicts along the coast. Pastoral history of a demotic kind lives on in the musical tradition of country and western, exemplified by the annual Tamworth Festival, and in the tourist industry of inland Australia, most notably in the Stockman's Hall of Fame at Longreach.

BRUCE MITCHELL

Pastoralist refers to someone whose income derives principally from grazing beef, cattle, and sheep on large areas of land. As **squatters**, many pastoralists initially occupied territory illegally, beyond the **Nineteen Counties** of NSW. The adoption of the title *pastoralist* from the 1880s is indicative of a desire to throw off the pejorative associations of *squatter*, and was institutionalised in the foundation of the Pastoralists Association and *Australian Pastoralist's Review* of the 1890s. Despite failures, generally good returns on a modest capital outlay enabled pastoralists to accumulate extensive holdings. Favourable terms for the purchase or lease of large acreages, and the availability of cheap labour—or free labour in the case of Aborigines and convicts—helped considerably. In the 50 or so years before World War I, when revenue from wool sales largely determined Australia's wealth, pastoralists formed a bastion of political power and social conservatism. Perhaps the most successful pastoralist was Sidney **Kidman**. Pastoralists' interests conflicted with those of rural labourers, most dramatically in the 1891 **shearers' strike**. Many pastoral estates were subdivided under various **closer settlement** schemes in the twentieth century; surviving holdings, now relatively more costly to maintain and yielding smaller profits, have often been consolidated. In 1997 pastoralists opposed the High Court's **Wik decision**, which held that pastoral leases did not extinguish native title on areas of Crown land.

HD

Paterson, Andrew Barton 'Banjo' (1864–1941), solicitor, bush balladist and journalist, was a prominent member of the *Bulletin* school of writers and author of the most popular of Australian **national songs**, 'Waltzing Matilda'. He is often, and too readily, portrayed as the horse-back squatter in contrast to Henry **Lawson's** footslogging swagman; but his was nevertheless the more joyous and—at the time—the more popular voice of bush **nationalism**.

Paterson's earliest memories were of growing up on his father's pastoral properties, Buckinbah Station in western NSW and Illalong Station near Yass. Paterson senior was often away managing the family's other properties and, while his wife was occupied in the kitchen, their son resorted to the men's hut, where he listened to the songs and stories of an old shepherd, Jerry the Rhymer. Paterson's own ballads and stories spring from this oral folk tradition, and from the sense of an idealised past ('the days of old') and a place ('the land o' lots of time') before or beyond the coming of the telegraph and the railway. In his 'Song of the Future' (1889) he mourned its passing and hinted at his own role, as a bush poet, in commemorating its otherwise unsung heroes.

> But times are changed, and changes rung
> From old to new—the olden days,
> The old bush life and all its ways
> Are passing from us all unsung.

After attending primary school at Binalong, he lived with his widowed grandmother at Gladesville while attending Sydney Grammar. He then served as an articled clerk until his admission as a solicitor in 1886. Working long hours in a 'dingy little office' on the threshold of the **Rocks**, he observed regretfully the contrast between the 'rush and nervous haste' of the city and the freedom of the man on horseback. This cityman's backward view of the bush became the theme of one of his first, and most successful, ballads, 'Clancy of the Overflow', contributed to the *Bulletin* under the pseudonym 'The Banjo' in 1889.

A fine horseman and a keen racing man, Paterson celebrated colonial Australia's worship of the **horse**. In lolloping ballads such as 'The Man from Snowy River' and 'Old Pardon, the Son of Reprieve', he evoked the mysterious bond between horse and rider, their feats of physical endurance and courage, and the raffish fellowship of the race track and the polo field. The social and political sympathies of the young Paterson were wider than those of his own class. In *Australia for the Australians* (1889) he called for land and tariff reforms that would reverse the fatal drift to the city and settle Sydney's growing unemployed on the 'great rolling fertile plains' of the interior. In 1892 he responded to Henry **Lawson's** catalogue of outback horrors, 'Borderland', with a poem 'In Defence of the Bush'. 'Did you hear no sweeter music in the music of the bush / Than the roar of trams and buses, and the war whoop of "the Push"?' he asked his maudlin opponent. Yet by pitting Paterson the romantic against Lawson the realist, the *Bulletin* had simplified the outlook of both writers. In 'On Kiley's Run' and 'A

Bushman's Song', Paterson showed a sympathy with debt-stricken farmers and itinerant shearers less grudging than Lawson's admiration for the squatters in 'The Fire at Ross's Farm'. Paterson's knowledge of the outback was much more extensive than Lawson's, ranging from the NT to the Riverina; his ballads certainly enjoyed a wider readership in the bush, where they gradually merged with the folk traditions which inspired them. They are perhaps the classic expression of the '**pioneer** legend', as Lawson's short stories are of the **Australian Legend**.

Paterson's reputation as the most popular of *Bulletin* writers dates from the publication and prodigious sale (7000 copies) of *The Man from Snowy River, and Other Verses* in 1895. In the same year, while holidaying at Dagwood Station near Winton in Qld, he wrote the verses of 'Waltzing Matilda', destined to become the most popular of Australian songs. In the late 1890s he gradually abandoned the law for journalism, and during the following decade he travelled extensively as a freelance correspondent for various Sydney papers. His despatches from the **Boer War** (1899) (edited by R.W.F. Droogleever, 2000) and China (1901) brought international recognition; they opened contacts with famous contemporaries, including the master balladist Rudyard Kipling, and led to his appointment in 1903, the year of his marriage, as editor of the *Sydney Daily News*. *Old Bush Songs*, the fruit of his long interest in collecting and transcribing traditional Australian ballads, appeared in 1905. During World War I he served as an officer with the Australian Remount Squadron.

Handsome, personable, and well-connected, the Banjo became a popular and respected figure in Australian life. Clement Semmler's *The Banjo of the Bush* (1966) remains the most readable biography; it may be supplemented with new material in the 1983 two-volume edition of his *Collected Works*, edited by his grand-daughters, Rosamund Campbell and Philippa Harvie, and by Colin Roderick's *Banjo Paterson: Poet by Accident* (1993).

GRAEME DAVISON

Paterson's Curse, see Pests

Paton family JOHN GIBSON PATON (1824–1907), missionary, was a minister of the Presbyterian Church who went to the New Hebrides in 1858 to establish a mission. He worked in the New Hebrides for most of the rest of his life, and was a frequent visitor to Australia on fundraising tours. Paton wrote several books on the welfare of the New Hebrideans, including *The Kanaka Labour Traffic to Queensland* (1892), and a best-selling autobiography, *John G. Paton, Missionary to the New Hebrides* (1889). One of his five sons, FRANCIS HUME LYALL (1870–1938), who was also a missionary in the New Hebrides, published *John G. Paton, Later Years and Farewell* (1910), as well as a history of the missions, *The Kingdom in the Pacific* (1913). Frank served as Moderator of the Presbyterian Church in Victoria 1922–23. His son, GEORGE WHITECROSS (1902–85), was professor of

law at the University of Melbourne (1931–51) and went on to serve as vice-chancellor (1951–68).

KT

Peacocking, also known as 'spotting' or 'eye-picking', was a practice for which **squatters** were notorious in the second half of the nineteenth century. After being granted a preemptive right—the option to purchase part of a previously leased run—squatters would select the choicest land offered for sale by the colonial governments, usually river frontages and other watered areas. Without access to water, squatters knew, the remaining land would be made virtually useless and would become available at a much lower price. Squatters continued this practice following the introduction of the **Selection** Acts in the 1860s, when they purchased the best allotments by **dummying**.

HD

Pearce, George Foster (1870–1952), a politician, was born at Mount Barker, SA, and finished schooling at the age of 11. In 1894, an unemployed carpenter, he joined the gold rushes to Coolgardie. He returned to Perth in 1901, unsuccessful as a gold digger, but with the status of president of the United Trades Council. He was elected to the Senate in 1901 and remained a member until 1937.

As minister for defence in the **Fisher** government, Pearce attended the 1911 Imperial Conference in London where he assured the British government that a military force would be raised in Australia to serve overseas if called upon. When **Hughes** was expelled from the Labor Party, Pearce went with him to the new **Nationalist Party**, but subsequently deserted Hughes for the **Bruce–Page** ministry. He later joined Joseph **Lyons's** United Australia Party. Pearce was dubbed 'Vicar of Bray' because of these changes of allegiance. He was minister for defence 1914–21 and again 1932–34, and also held the portfolios of Territories and External Affairs in a long, unobtrusive, and increasingly conservative political career. Finally defeated in 1937, he left political life. His memoirs, *Carpenter to Cabinet* (1951), appeared a year before he died, and his former secretary, Peter Heydon, published a biography, *Quiet Decision*, in 1965.

PATRICIA M. BROWN

Pearl, Cyril Alston (1906–87) was a journalist who wrote a number of books on colourful aspects of Australia's past. He was educated at the University of Melbourne and associated with the progressive literary circles in that city during the 1930s. After he moved to Sydney in 1939 as foundation editor of Frank **Packer's** *Sunday Telegraph*, his iconoclasm was directed at safer targets. He remained a critic of censorship, a *bon viveur*, and a raffish wit.

Pearl's writing included fiction, but his best work took up notorious figures, eccentrics, and troublemakers. *Wild Men of Sydney* (1958) arraigned the muckraking editor, John **Norton,** and his associates. He wrote stylish literary biographies of Daniel **Deniehy**, Gavan **Duffy**, R.H. **Horne**,

Ernest **Morrison**, and Hardy **Wilson**, accounts of the **Shenandoah incident** and the *Dunera* boys, an idiosyncratic history of *Beer, Glorious Beer* (1969), and an engaging pictorial account of *Our Yesterdays* (1954), revised as *Australia's Yesterdays* (1974). Pearl's work is distinguished by his skill as a raconteur; he usually disdained any scholarly apparatus but researched his topics and wrote with feeling for the past.

SM

Pearling became a viable commercial industry in northern Australia from the mid-nineteenth century, though pearlshell had long been collected and used by Aborigines, chiefly for ornamental purposes. Pearls were harvested for their high value and pearlshell was used commercially for button-making and for mother-of-pearl. Pearl was collected from the sea-bed by diving, with the aid of manually operated air pumps and, later, power compressors. Nickol Bay, WA, the first important pearling area in the 1860s, was overtaken by Broome on Roebuck Bay in WA in the 1890s. The industry slumped after the late 1930s, by which time pearlers had exhausted the sea-beds.

Diving for pearlshell was notorious for its high mortality rate. Divers not brought to the surface at the correct speed were likely to be afflicted with the bends. The industry relied on the labour of **Aborigines** and, later, **Torres Strait Islanders**. Many indigenous women working as divers were forced into **prostitution**. When legislation in WA in 1905 prohibited Aboriginal women from coming into proximity of pearling boats, Timorese and Javanese divers were recruited as divers. The Japanese played an important part in the industry from 1885, but withdrew during World War II. Regina Ganter, *The Pearl-Shellers of Torres Strait* (1994), examines the industry and its racially mixed workforce.

HD

Pearson, Charles Henry (1830–94), historian, politician, and **education** reformer, was professor of modern history at King's College, London (1855–64), and lecturer in modern history at Trinity College, Cambridge (1869–71), before migrating to SA for health reasons. He lectured in history at the University of Melbourne in 1874, then became first headmaster of Melbourne's Presbyterian Ladies College 1875–77, where his inaugural lecture, 'The Higher Culture of Women', advocated the rights of women to compete equally with men for 'the career open to talents'. His resignation was forced after controversial lectures advocating a land tax in December 1876 and February 1877. Pearson was a member of Victoria's Legislative Assembly 1878–92. His one-person royal commission into Victorian education in 1878 recommended a major expansion of secondary and tertiary education, but was many years ahead of its time. As minister for public instruction (1886–90), he successfully fostered secular, technical, and teachers' education.

John Tregenza's biography, *Professor of Democracy* (1968), showed that Pearson's **liberalism** significantly shaped public opinion, especially through his role as an editorial writer for the *Age* 1874–85. He opposed blackbirding, campaigned on behalf of neglected children, and advocated Sunday opening of cultural institutions, women's rights, plebiscites, **trade unions**, state insurance, and housing controls. Stuart Macintyre's *A Colonial Liberalism* (1991) studies Pearson in the context of contemporary liberal 'visionaries' David **Syme** and George **Higinbotham**. A high-minded hypochondriac, his liberal convictions were constantly frayed by the vulgarity of colonial life. Pearson returned to England in 1892. His most significant publication, *National Life and Character* (1893), forecast the decline of Europe, the family, and the church against the rise of China, the working class, and the state. In *The Great Seesaw* (1988), Geoffrey **Blainey** observed that Pearson foreshadowed a revival of cyclical historical interpretation by predicting Western decline long before its more famous prophet, the German writer Oswald Spengler.

DC

Pemulwuy, see **Aboriginal resistance**

Penal settlements were places to which **convicts** were sent as a form of secondary punishment for crimes committed in the colony. The first was established at Newcastle (1804), followed by Port Macquarie (1821) and **Moreton Bay** (1824). **Norfolk Island** was used as a penal settlement from 1825. In Van Diemen's Land penal settlements were founded at Macquarie Harbour (1823), Maria Island (1825), and **Port Arthur** (1830). The sites were usually chosen for their natural isolation and near-impossibility of escape. Convicts were generally employed as labourers at the settlements themselves or in nearby areas, and were usually responsible for the construction of buildings, which at Norfolk Island and Port Arthur were penitentiaries. Conditions were notoriously harsh, often brutal, with subsequent offences leading to solitary confinement or execution. Marcus **Clarke's** *His Natural Life* (1874) provides a gruesome account of punishment at Macquarie Harbour. When **transportation** ended in 1868, the only remaining penal settlement was at Port Arthur.

HD

Pentecostalism, a branch of the Christian church which emphasises the 'baptism of the Holy Spirit' and its evidence in the form of charismatic gifts of inspired utterance, physical healing and the speaking of tongues, has been among the fastest-growing religious groups in Australia in recent years. Pentecostals have formed some 28 separate denominations and are also present within several of the mainstream churches, including the Catholic Church. By casting off some of the emotional reserve and institutional rigidity of traditional Protestantism, they have created religious communities arguably more consonant with the structures of a mobile but insecure post-industrial society.

Australian pentecostalism has been strongly shaped by developments elsewhere, especially in the USA, although the traffic in religious ideas has not been all one-way. The evangelist John Alexander Dowie conducted healing missions in Australia in the 1880s before becoming a national celebrity in the USA. Women played a significant founding role. The Good News Hall, founded by an ex-Methodist, Janet Lancaster, in North Melbourne in 1909, was the first organised pentecostal church in Australia. The tour of the American evangelist Aimée Semple McPherson in 1922 was followed by the foundation in Richmond of the Pentecostal Church, the forerunner of the Assemblies of God, which now claim approximately half of Australia's pentecostals. The visit of the American evangelist Oral Roberts in 1956 spurred public controversy but paved the way for the more recent explosion of pentecostal churches, especially in the frontier states of Qld and WA. Barry Chant's sympathetic *Heart of Fire: The Story of Australian Pentecostalism* (1973) is the only history, while Rowland Ward and Robert Humphreys, *Religious Bodies in Australia* (3rd edn, 1995), contains a comprehensive guide to the main pentecostal groups.

GD

Penton, Brian Con (1904–51) enraged politicians of all factions with his daily column, 'From the Gallery', for the *Sydney Morning Herald*, in which he reported on federal parliament. He resigned from the paper soon after his recall to Sydney, and went to London where he wrote *Landtakers* (1934), the first of an intended trilogy. In following the life of a pioneering Queensland family, this novel, and its sequel, *Inheritors* (1936), chronicles early rural life in that colony, and condemns the ruthless greed of the first settlers. His later works, *Think—or Be Damned* (1941), which critically examines some of the myths of Australian history, and *Advance Australia—Where?* (1943), were both provocative studies of contemporary Australian society.

Penton's position as editor of the Sydney *Daily Telegraph* brought him into conflict with government censors during World War II. He led the campaign against what he saw as excessive **censorship**, and later wrote about the issue in *Censored!* (1947). The aggression that made him such a highly regarded journalist and editor could also make him difficult to work for, as Don Whitington recorded in *Strive To Be Fair* (1977). Patrick Buckridge has written a biography, *The Scandalous Penton* (1994).

KT

Pentonvillians, a composite of *Pentonville* and *villain*, were **convicts** who had served briefly at Pentonville Prison in England, before being transported to Australia. Many such convicts came from Van Diemen's Land to the Port Phillip District in the 1840s to satisfy the growing demand for labour, much to the ire of free settlers intent on keeping that colony 'untainted' by convictism. At Port Phillip they were condemned by the local press as criminals and trouble-makers; appeared regularly before the police magistrates on petty charges; and were blamed for various unsavoury aspects of social life. However, colonial authorities at Port Phillip defended the scheme on account of the relatively good behaviour demonstrated by Pentonvillians—an observation shared by some contemporary accounts. Its defendants praised the reformatory emphasis of Pentonville, its generally softer punishment regime, its system of solitary confinement, and its emphasis on prisoners' self-development. Reports of the successful assimilation of prisoners into free society, however, were perhaps exaggerated by colonial authorities in order to justify the function and purpose of the reformatory system. Though convict transportation to WA from 1850 to 1868 drew on the Pentonville penitentiaries, the term was not used there. Ian Wynd published *The Pentonvillians* in 1996. (See also **Vandemonians**.)

HD

Periodisation in the earliest histories of the colonies was by term of office of governors, a principle which can still be found in the writing of colonial history. The title of the first volume in Manning **Clark's** *History* (1962) was *From the Earliest Times to the Age of Macquarie.*

In the second half of the nineteenth century, the convict era was identified as a shameful foundation period for which it was imperative to find a decisive conclusion. The transformation was ascribed in popular consciousness, more than in the formal histories, to the **gold rushes** of the 1850s, even though they occurred 10 years after transportation to mainland eastern Australia had ceased. Since the convict taint was thought to be in the blood, the infusion of so much good stock was the most beneficial effect of the rushes.

In the early twentieth century when the **pioneers** were being celebrated, James Collier's *The Pastoral Age in Australasia* (1911) identified the escape from convictism in the spread of the pastoralists, a new enterprising group casting off the shackles of the convict colony (even though they employed convicts). This perspective was present in **Hancock's** classic *Australia* (1930) ('Wool made Australia a solvent nation, and, in the end, a free one'); and in Stephen **Roberts's** romantic account of the pastoralists, *The Squatting Age in Australia* (1935). However, at the hands of G.V. **Portus**, the Australian volume of *The Cambridge History of the British Empire* (1933) put an official seal on gold as a turning-point.

That the gold rushes were not a turning-point was one of the conclusions of the new history profession in the 1940s and 1950s. It saw the lineaments of Australia established before the gold rushes: a pastoral economy and an urbanised society with the beginnings of trade unions and radical movements against the squatters. On this view, the renunciation of the convict era was made by the anti-transportation movement of the late 1840s and early 1850s (most tellingly put in Michael **Roe's** *Quest for Authority in Eastern Australia*, 1965). Geoffrey **Serle's** *The Golden Age* (1963) was in part a reaction to the down-playing of the gold rushes: NSW might not have been transformed by gold, but Victoria was.

At the same time, the profession debated whether 1890 was a turning-point. It was the year of the **Maritime Strike**, traditionally regarded as the cause of the labour movement's turning from industrial to political activity. The case against 1890 had two aspects: the prior interest of the movement in politics; and the denial that it was the only radical force and the first to organise itself as a party. The year 1890 now is not given high significance, but the **depression** of the late nineteenth century, the great strikes, the rise of Labor and other radical forces, and the strengthening of nationalism are generally regarded as marking a new period. This was brought to an end by World War I, which gave the nation its baptism of blood, ended the broad consensus over social reform, and dissociated nationalism from it.

World War II is regarded as marking another divide: the end of British supremacy in the region, the turn to the USA, the growth of manufacturing industry, the ascendancy of the federal government and, as a response to the threat of invasion, the inauguration after the war of a large-scale immigration program which included non-British people.

For the years after the war, there is a tendency to return to the principle of defining periods by the government in office. So there is the **Menzies** era 1949–66, the **Whitlam** years 1972–75, and the Labor Ascendancy 1983–96. Here periods are multiplying, but for the broad course of the history they are being reduced in response to fundamental reappraisal of the character of Australian society and its future direction. The economic rationalists propose two periods: an unregulated economy of rapid growth and the highest living standards in the world until circa 1890; regulation and decline thereafter. **Multiculturalists** also conceive of two periods: British Australia (commonly assumed to be homogeneous) until the end of World War II; multicultural Australia thereafter.

Since the 1950s Aborigines have sometimes been called the First Australians, and more recently historians have begun to treat their subject as the human occupation of the continent. Australian history thus does not begin with European settlement in 1788 or with European exploration from 1606, the date of Jansz's visit. What was previously 'prehistory' is now history. Given the radical difference between Aboriginal society and that of the European invaders, the attempt to posit continuity is frequently strained (a chapter on Aboriginal science began the Academy of Science's Bicentennial history) except in the matter of human interaction with the land. As the extent of the Aborigines' transformation of the environment becomes known, they become closer kin to the Europeans who displaced them. Such a perspective again simplifies the history into two periods: before and after the coming of man.

JOHN HIRST

Perkins, Charles Nelson (1936–2000) was an outspoken, often controversial, Aboriginal rights activist since the 1960s. Born in the NT, he was taken to Adelaide for his education and then played professional soccer to finance his way through an arts degree at the University of Sydney. A period as a professional footballer in England highlighted Australian racism for him. In 1965 he received national attention, frequently hostile, as an organiser of, and

spokesman for, the **freedom ride** through country NSW, which successfully highlighted racial discrimination against Aborigines. Perkins was recruited to the federal Office of Aboriginal Affairs in 1969; he became manager of the Aboriginal Development Corporation in 1981, and secretary of the Department of Aboriginal Affairs in 1984. During his time with the department he campaigned vigorously for Aboriginal rights, and was often reprimanded for his willingness to criticise superior officers and ministers. His advocacy stressed Aboriginal home ownership, business enterprise, and sporting associations. A charge of maladministration in 1988, later quashed, forced his resignation. Subsequently he was involved in the native title issue, chaired the Arrernte Council of Central Australia (1991–94), and was appointed deputy chair of ATSIC. The provocative title of his autobiography, *A Bastard Like Me* (1975), mirrored his often aggressive stance. Peter Read provides a more complex analysis in *Charles Perkins* (1990, 2001).

KT

Perth, the capital of **Western Australia**, is situated on a wide expanse of the Swan River on the coastal plain west of the Darling Ranges. Settlement originally followed the course of the river, but today suburban sprawl stretches north and south along the coast for almost 75 kilometres. Perth's distinctive sense of place has been well analysed by George Seddon in *Sense of Place* (1972). It is frequently characterised as the most isolated city in the world.

The city was proclaimed capital of the Swan River Colony by Captain James **Stirling** on 12 August 1829. Its history is best understood through C.T. Stannage's powerful *The People of Perth* (1979), one of Australia's ground-breaking city biographies. As he argued, the gentry colonists of the Swan River were motivated to emigrate from Britain by a fierce desire to possess land and, through this, power. Their need for labour, as well as the British government's need for a penal colony, led to the introduction of **convicts** in 1850. When transportation ceased in 1868, an infrastructure of roads, bridges, and public buildings remained, as well as a legacy of deep shame. Perth had been proclaimed a city (1856) and its population had swelled to nearly 5000.

Self-government in 1890 and the rush for gold in the eastern goldfields in the early 1890s had a spectacular impact on the city. Perth's population quadrupled in a decade, with many newcomers fleeing the depression in the eastern states. It reached almost 44000 in 1901, and by then a host of public and commercial buildings were changing the face of the city, but the provision of housing and urban infrastructure lagged behind the growth. In the early 1900s Town Clerk W.E. Bold moved to combine municipalities into a Greater Perth Authority. Influenced by the British town planning movement, he was only partially successful, leaving the city with unwieldy municipal boundaries that spanned the river and were not redrawn for almost 100 years. Through Bold's influence and the work of architect–planner Harold Boas, the city's first **Town Planning** Act was enacted in 1928. Suburbia developed rapidly in the 1920s, fed by immigration from Britain and natural population growth, and shaped by new tramways, bus routes, and the motor car. Perth suburbs increasingly reflected a pattern of residential segregation by class.

The impact of the **Depression** was mixed, even though nearly 30 per cent of trade unionists were unemployed in 1932 and violence erupted in protest marches on the city. Sustenance men were employed on major public works, such as the building of Canning Dam, and on public relief projects. G.C. **Bolton's** *A Fine Country to Starve In* (1972) remains the major work on the Depression, although critics such as the contributors to Jenny Gregory's edited collection, *Western Australia between the Wars* (1990), have argued that he minimised the divisive nature of its impact. It has been common for the eastern states to be blamed for any economic downturn in the west; the **secession** movement of the 1930s, which fed off a sense of isolation and a feeling of neglect, typifies this pattern.

Between 1947 and 1961 Perth's population more than doubled to 420 000. The construction of a major industrial area at Kwinana to the south was facilitated by the government's **development** policies (the best analysis of which remains a 1982 article in *HS* by Lenore Layman) and many migrant workers were housed in new suburbs nearby. Although most of the numerous suburban histories that have emerged recently, including Geoff Bolton and Jenny Gregory's *Claremont* (1999), have focused on the period before World War II, some like Cathie May's *History of Bayswater* (1997) have begun to tackle postwar development. A major freeway system was developed under the Stephenson Plan of 1956, discussed by Leigh Edmonds in *Vital Link: A History of Main Roads, Western Australia 1926–1996* (1997) and C.T. Stannage in *Lakeside City: The Dreaming of Joondalup* (1996). The river was spanned by a new bridge at the Narrows in 1959, facilitating the growth of Perth's southern suburbs. During this period the appearance of the city was again transformed by the erection of high-rise office blocks. Events in 1962 marked a coming of age for modern Perth. The city hosted the Commonwealth Games and astronaut John Glenn dubbed it City of Lights.

The sesquicentenary of the foundation of WA in 1979 was marked by a surge of historical writing, most of which concentrated on the nineteenth-century history of the state. The buoyant economy that began with the mineral boom of the 1960s and 1970s again remade the city, as George Seddon and David Ravine show in *A City and its Setting* (1986). By the mid-1980s glass towers dominated St George's Terrace; inner-city suburbs like Subiaco had been gentrified or, like Northbridge, invented and filled with restaurants and nightclubs. Suburban sprawl continued to dominate the metropolitan area, even though urban renewal had become the rationale for the sale of inner-city industrial land for housing .

Perth has produced more than its share of corporate 'cowboys' and future historians will find a rich field for research in the follies of WA Inc., the name given to Labor's Brian Burke's accommodation of entrepreneurial excess in the 1980s. Local bravado and sporting skill prised the America's Cup from the old-moneyed elite of the yachting world in 1983, but just four years later Perth's entrepreneurial dash and daring were badly shaken in the 1987 Stock Market crash. A conservative government dominated the 1990s, but the building of a huge bell tower on Perth water came to symbolise its disregard of the needs of the people, and the scandals of the 1980s were finally nullified when the Labor Party galloped to a historic victory in 2001.

JENNY GREGORY

Pests introduced from elsewhere have been a potent influence in modifying the Australian **environment**. Like **drought** and **flood**, the word *pest* is defined culturally as well as biologically, as a reflection of settler preferences as well as biological sustainability. Thus rabbits, thistles, and cane toads, which caused economic loss to settlers, were often described as pests, while willow trees, cattle, and imported grasses were not, even though each brought significant change to the native environment. During the second half of the twentieth century ecological studies of the relationship between species, humans, and the environment have produced a more sophisticated understanding of the complex interactions unleashed by the introduction of new species.

The importation of exotic species preceded the coming of Europeans. The arrival of the **dingo** from South-East Asia, sometime within the past 4000 years, and its use as a hunting animal by Aborigines, might have brought the extinction of several native species from the mainland, such as the Tasmanian devil and the thylacine. But these changes pale beside the catastrophic impact of importations since 1788. In the eyes of colonial settlers, the Australian environment often seemed barren and in need of improvement through the introduction of imported, largely European, species. One of the main preoccupations of natural scientists in the mid-nineteenth century was **acclimatisation**—the scientific study of how imported species adapted to the new environment, or native ones to environments elsewhere in Australia or abroad. Edward Wilson, a founder of the Victorian Acclimatisation Society (1861), defined its mission expansively as 'the introduction, acclimatisation, and domestication of all innocuous animals, birds, fishes and vegetables whether useful or ornamental'.

The objective was commonly to re-create the Australian landscape in a European idiom, with groves of oaks and elms, pastures sown with English grasses, and gardens full of roses and foxgloves. Homesick Scots planted Scotch thistles. The English, longing for the sounds of their native countryside, introduced blackbirds and thrushes. Sportsmen, seeking the thrill of the chase, released rabbits, hares and foxes. Sometimes the experiment failed: the imported species failed to thrive or were devoured by natives. Sometimes they survived in balance with the new environment. And sometimes, as Eric **Rolls** suggests in his definitive history of the problem, *They All Ran Wild* (1969).

The most notorious of these experiments was the release of the European rabbit and its increase to plague proportions throughout much of the continent. Rabbits, a notoriously prolific animal, were among the animals brought on the First Fleet, but they became a pest only in the later nineteenth century when the clearance of the great inland plains for pasture offered them an ideal habitat in which to multiply. The origin of the plague is commonly traced to the 1859 release of rabbits for game by the squatter Thomas Austin on his property Barwon Park near Winchelsea, Victoria. In fact, as Rolls argues, there were probably many such releases, and the plague, rather than spreading from a single centre, was really a combination of many localised outbreaks. Two decades later they had crossed the border into NSW and SA; by 1888 they had penetrated the 'rabbit-proof' fence erected by the NSW government between Bourke and Barringun and were running wild in southern Qld. At their worst, as in the great drought of the late 1880s, rabbits became a major threat to the economic viability of pastoralists. Farmers and scientists tried many remedies—shooting parties, digging up burrows, poisons, fences, imported predators, imported diseases—but none was really effective until the **CSIRO** was bullied by the biologist Jean **Macnamara** into releasing strains of the South American rabbit disease myxomatosis at Gunbower, Victoria, in 1950. The disease spread almost as fast as the rabbits had once done, killing more than 90 per cent of those in its path. It gave pastoralists and farmers a 30-year breathing space until, by the 1980s, the rabbits had acquired an immunity and began to breed again. Again the scientists looked for a new disease to curb the rabbits' spread. In October 1995 the CSIRO attempted a 'controlled release' of the calicivirus on Wardang Island, SA, but the disease quickly spread to the mainland. Despite some public alarm about the possible effect of the disease on native animals, the scientists claimed substantial success in reducing rabbit numbers, especially in Central Australia, and negligible effect on other species.

While the rabbit was in a class of its own, some other imported animals, such as foxes, hares, deer, goats, pigs, starlings, and Indian mynahs have all become pests, because they not only cause direct damage to stock or pasture but also act as hosts for other pests, such as the cattle tick, which attack stock or native animals. One of the most troublesome has been the mouse, which regularly assumes plague proportions in wheat-growing regions. The 1996 *State of the Environment Report*, commissioned by the Commonwealth, drew attention to the impact of introduced feral species, such as cats and foxes, on the decline and near-extinction of some native fauna.

The introduction of imported plants, fish, and insects has been a less remarked, but equally significant, dimension of the problem. The European carp and trout have driven many native species of fish from our streams. The European wasp, first seen in Sydney in 1978, has now spread widely, killing many native insects and attacking fruit crops. Introduced plants now comprise approximately 15 per cent of total flora; about one-quarter are, or have potential to be, serious environmental weeds. The blackberry and the gorse, imported into Tasmania in the early nineteenth century as fruiting or ornamental plants, soon became pests. In Victoria

government botanist Ferdinand von **Mueller** hastened the spread of blackberry by dropping seeds along bush tracks to provide sustenance for hungry walkers. Paterson's Curse, the fast-growing purple-flowered bush, was named for a squatter in the Albury district, where it first invaded pastures, though farmers in dry areas of SA welcomed the weed as Salvation Jane—a sign of coming rains. The rubber vine, imported as a decorative plant, is now strangling trees and native vegetation along Qld's rivers. When hopes of taming the Australian environment were high, politicians looked confidently to scientists to provide the chemical and biological controls to keep these pests at bay. They pointed to success stories, such as the introduction in 1925 of the Argentine insect cactoblastis, which eradicated another imported pest, the dreaded prickly pear, from central Qld. But there were failures as well, like the cane toad, introduced in 1935 to control the cane beetle, which then ran wild across north-eastern Australia, killing native predators such as snakes and goannas. By the 1970s galloping rates of infestation and growing awareness of the untoward effects of chemical and biological controls made scientists less confident of their ability to manipulate nature benignly.

A hundred years ago, European Australians looked to the importation of animals, birds, plants, and fishes to make the wilderness a home. This, writes Tim Flannery in his ecological history of Australasia, *The Future Eaters* (1994), was 'one of the saddest chapters in the history of our continent'. His verdict is perhaps too harsh—how many Australians could imagine their land without the sight, and economic contribution, of sheep, pine trees, and European cereals and grasses? But it reminds us that the story of European conquest had its ecological as well as its human costs.

GRAEME DAVISON

Petrov Affair refers to the defections of a Soviet diplomat, Vladimir Petrov, and his wife Evdokia, on the eve of the 1954 federal election. The defections, the subsequent Royal Commission into Espionage, and the reaction to these events by the leader of the **Australian Labor Party**, Dr H.V. **Evatt**, have become known as 'the Petrov Affair'.

Since the Bolshevik Revolution, anti-communism had linked communists as an internal enemy of social order with the external enemy of a hostile foreign power. The defection of a Soviet spy who promised evidence of espionage activities in Australia gave new to life the Cold War debate about **communism** in Australia. The **Menzies** government's attempt to ban the Communist Party had been finally defeated in the 1951 **referendum**, but hostility to communism was still strong and the Australian Labor Party was deeply divided over appropriate methods of containing its influence, particularly within the union movement.

The defection could not help but harm the ALP's chances in the forthcoming election. Labor had done exceptionally well in the Senate election the previous year, and Evatt had high hopes that his ambition to become prime minister would at last be fulfilled. Now, it seemed, his old enemy Menzies had pulled a defector from the hat. The election result was very close, with Labor winning the majority of the primary votes but not the majority of seats, and Evatt became convinced that the defections had been stage-managed by Menzies. Menzies always denied this, saying he knew nothing about the planned defection when he set the election date. Subsequent research by Robert Manne (*The Petrov Affair*, 1987), after the files of the **Australian Security and Intelligence Organisation** (ASIO) were opened in 1984, bears him out.

Evatt's suspicions of a conspiracy were fuelled further when the Royal Commission into Espionage named members of his staff as implicated in the Petrovs' evidence of Soviet espionage activities in Australia. Evatt was outraged, and appeared as counsel for his staff before the royal commission. He became increasingly preoccupied with his theories about the conspiracy behind the Petrovs' defection, and his intemperate behaviour eventually led to his being barred from the hearings. The royal commission dragged on throughout 1954, causing much grief to the many people, mostly minor left-wing activists, who were called before it. It uncovered evidence of successful Soviet espionage in Australia between 1945 and 1948, but nothing sufficient to justify the laying of charges against any Australian citizen. It also fuelled a long-lived resentment of the left towards ASIO.

Evatt's behaviour during the royal commission inflamed the already acute tensions within the ALP over communism. Many anti-communist ALP members resented deeply Evatt's role in defeating the referendum on banning the Communist Party, and here he was again defending suspected communist sympathisers. As well, his increasingly erratic and suspicious behaviour and obsession with proving that a conspiracy had robbed Labor of government cast doubts over the soundness of his judgment and his capacities as party leader, let alone as prospective prime minister. By October his preoccupations with conspiracy had widened to include members of his own party, and a public attack on a small group within the party precipitated the events which led to the **Split** in the ALP, and the formation of the **Democratic Labor Party**.

A year later, in the parliamentary debate on the royal commission, Evatt reached the nadir of his political career when, to the ridicule of his parliamentary opponents and the despair of his colleagues, he cited a letter from the Soviet Foreign Minister Molotov in support of his claims that key documents in the Petrov case were forgeries. Menzies's reply was measured as he defended the institutions and authority of the state against Evatt's wild accusations. Menzies called an early election the next day, which he won decisively with Anti-Communist Labor preferences.

As the ALP limped on through the remainder of the 1950s and into the 1960s, the Petrov Affair came to stand for the manifold injustices which kept it from government: the concentration of its votes which meant that it could win a majority of votes and still lose an election; the conservative press that never gave Labor a fair go; the duplicity of Menzies; the role of ASIO in its surveillance of innocent Australian citizens; and, most of all, the use of communism

by the Liberal and Country parties to frighten voters away from Labor. This version appeared in a number of publications, including Nicholas Whitlam and John Stubbs, *Nest of Traitors* (1974). Only when the effectiveness of kicking the communist can declined in the early 1970s did the symbolic power of the Petrov Affair start to wane. It was soon replaced by an even more potent symbol of the forces arrayed against Labor, the **Dismissal** of the **Whitlam** government in 1975.

JUDITH BRETT

Petty, Bruce Leslie (1929–), cartoonist, began as a freelance contributor to magazines in London and New York when he was travelling and studying overseas. From 1965 to 1975 he was cartoonist for the *Australian*, and then joined the Melbourne *Age*. His individual, often frenetic, style conveyed the chaos he saw in much of the Australian political and social systems. Petty created fantastic machines to represent intangibles such as the economy, some of which he made into sculptures. There are numerous published collections of his work, and he has also produced animated films, including *Australian History* (1972).

KT

Phar Lap was a New Zealand racehorse brought to Australia as a 3-year-old. Under trainer Harry Telford, he enjoyed remarkable success in Victoria and NSW. His easy victory as favourite in the 1930 **Melbourne Cup**, run in the midst of the Depression, captured the heart of a nation. His bright chestnut coat earned him the nickname 'Red Terror'. In 1932 he was shipped to America for the prestigious Agua Caliente in Mexico, but afterwards died in California, reputedly poisoned. For strapper Tommy Woodcock, it was a great personal loss. As the nation mourned, Phar Lap assumed abnormal, heroic proportions. His early death was made worse by his lack of progeny, and magnified his greatness; like Les **Darcy**, his unfulfilled potential and death overseas intensified feelings of national loss. The close, affectionate relationship between Phar Lap and Woodcock, who gave him the pet name 'Bobby', added a human dimension to the legend. Phar Lap was a large horse with great staying power which, following a post-mortem examination, was attributed to his unusually large heart. His carcass, stuffed and mounted in a glass display box at the Museum of Victoria, continues to be saluted, mostly by those too young ever to have witnessed him race. His heart is displayed separately in Canberra, and his skeleton in NZ. His story has inspired poetry and fiction, and a feature film (1983).

HD

Philanthropy in Australia has been largely synonymous with charity. Born out of a class-divided society, it was seen as an individualistic exchange in which the rich were expected to give of their money and their time in relief of the poor. Where British philanthropy sought to rescue the deserving from the indignities of the workhouse, the determination of the Australian colonies to avoid a Poor Law meant that philanthropic organisations, often heavily dependent on government funding, became the primary source of relief.

The foundation of the first charities in NSW was celebrated as evidence of the British character of the settlement. A mere 25 years after the arrival of the First Fleet, the Society for the Promotion of Christian Knowledge was able to report that 'even in this distant and obscure corner of the world, the British character does not degenerate ... Englishmen, in every clime and on every shore, cease not to remember the characteristic benevolence of their native land.' Historians have been less generous in their assessment, following Elizabeth Windschuttle (in Richard Kennedy, ed., *Australian Welfare History: Critical Essays*, 1982) in arguing that philanthropy was central to the establishment of **bourgeois hegemony** in the colonies.

Philanthropic activity was highly gendered. Men dominated public giving and sat on the committees controlling high-status charities (hospitals, for example). Large endowments were rare, but institutions run by men were able to set high subscription rates and to use business and political networks to build a large list. Few women had access to such resources, but their contribution was central to face-to-face relief. Where other European societies were developing a welfare bureaucracy, in Australia the critical decisions as to who should be relieved and how were made by women.

Colonial women were attracted to philanthropy because it mimicked the activity of bourgeois women 'at home'. Philanthropy, Judith Godden observed in the book edited by Kennedy, 'was one of the few public and highly visible activities allowed women'. As the numbers of bourgeois women free of domestic and child-care responsibilities grew, so too did philanthropic activity. Like Jesus Christ, charitable women were 'seeking and saving the lost'. By couching their activity in religious terms, they were able to extend the boundaries of their accepted sphere without publicly challenging their subordinate role.

Nineteenth-century philanthropy could be alleviatory and oppressive at the same time. Where Richard Kennedy sees 'a ritual of stigmatization and humiliation in the process of inquiry', others, such as Shurlee Swain ('The Victorian Charity Network in the 1890s', PhD thesis, University of Melbourne, 1977) see a more discerning process in which the ability of the donor to identify with the recipient was critical to the way in which aid was dispensed. The dominant culture, **masculinist** and **egalitarian**, was opposed to any such display of *noblesse oblige*. Both radicals and conservatives accepted that to be a man was to be a breadwinner and that to resort to charity was a sign of weakness. Conservatives condemned the man who chose to beg. Radicals condemned both the society which drove him to do so and the women who administered relief, classing them with the men whose interests philanthropy sought to uphold.

The gendered nature of the **social welfare** system, established after Federation, preserved a space for philanthropy, but it was increasingly marginalised, seen as retrograde and judgmental when compared with the progressive, benevolent, and supposedly universalist state. Yet, as fundraisers and direct service providers, philanthropic women were involved in identifying needs and filling the gaps in state provision. As Anne O'Brien argues in *Poverty's Prison* (1988), the continuing success of voluntary charity explains why the early state provision, which in retrospect appears so meagre, was so widely acclaimed.

Large charitable bequests and foundations are not a prominent feature of Australian philanthropy. The nineteenth-century benefactions of pastoralist's widow Elizabeth Austin set an uncomfortable example. Although her liberality was extolled as 'an honourable example of practical Christian widowhood ... affording through future times to the multitude of rich dwellers in the land an illustration of the power of individual sacrifice', few were willing to risk their family's slender hold on gentility by following biblical injunctions so explicitly. Early fortunes were more likely to be used to finance a family's return to England to live as minor aristocrats than to be invested locally. Churches and universities were among the main beneficiaries of the few large philanthropists there were: Robert Barr Smith and Thomas **Elder** in Adelaide, Francis Ormond, John Wyselaskie, and Samuel Wilson in Melbourne, T.S. **Mort** and J.H. Challis in Sydney. Alfred Felton, creator of the National Gallery of Victoria's **Felton Bequest**, is almost alone among great colonial patrons of the arts.

Some trusts and foundations have been established in the twentieth century, but neither the large fortunes nor the deep suspicion of the state which motivated philanthropists in the USA has ever gained ascendancy. A notable exception is the prominent role played by Jewish patrons of the arts. Although government is increasingly looking to philanthropy to fill the gaps left by a retreating welfare state, levels of giving remain low, and charities, both secular and religious, continue to look to government for their base support.

SHURLEE SWAIN

Phillip, Arthur (1738–1814) was the first governor of NSW. Born in London, he was commissioned in the navy and served in the Seven Years' War. In breaks from active service, he farmed in Hampshire, took employment with the Portuguese navy, and was briefly employed as a spy among the naval bases in southern France. In May 1787 he left England as commodore of the **First Fleet**.

Phillip spent nearly five years in Australia, from January 1788 to December 1792. The people under his government were divided between Port Jackson (on the mainland) and Norfolk Island. His principal achievement as governor was their survival and good order, in spite of extreme shortages of food and all the psychological effects of extreme isolation. He was keenly interested in the Aborigines: his was the most creative period of Australian race relations before the late twentieth century. He formed towns at Sydney and Parramatta, and made some progress with inland exploration. He was a man of significant intellectual authority and his ideas about government, including penal discipline, were to be fundamental to the system maintained in NSW during at least the next 60 years.

For many years after his death little was known of him. The NSW government made the details of his work widely available for the first time by its publication of the *Historical Records of New South Wales* (beginning 1892). In 1897, thanks largely to the earlier efforts of Henry **Parkes** as premier, his tomb was discovered near Bath in England and a massive monument was completed in Sydney. In 1899, a full-length biography by Louis Becke and Walter Jeffery was published in London as one of a series entitled *Builders of Greater Britain*.

There was renewed interest during the 1930s, partly as a result of the sesquicentenary of settlement but also due to contemporary concern for issues of race and for the moral basis and authority of the state. *Admiral Arthur Phillip: Founder of New South Wales 1738–1814* (1937), by George **Mackaness**, published much new detail. Marjorie **Barnard** and Flora Eldershaw, in *Phillip of Australia: An Account of the Settlement at Sydney Cove 1788–92* (1938), wrote less but they were more radical and imaginative, and they wrestled more effectively with Phillip's character. They had a profound admiration for him but they were still able to suggest (perhaps with undue harshness) that 'He had no gift with people, no emotional gift at all.' Their achievement was carried forward by Eleanor **Dark**, whose fictional work, *The Timeless Land* (1941), includes what is still the most subtle and satisfactory portrait of this enigmatic man.

The copious scholarship of the 1950s to the 1980s shed less new light on Phillip than might have been expected. There was one good full-length biography, Alan Frost's *Arthur Phillip 1738–1814: His Voyaging* (1987), which offered some important new discoveries, but its attempt to present Phillip as a wanderer—only one-third of the book deals with NSW—was symptomatic of a generation for whom introspection and individuality were the touchstone of character. The concerns of the 1990s, especially public legitimacy and race, may well help to revive the profound questions asked of the first governor by Barnard, Eldershaw, and Dark.

ALAN ATKINSON

Phillips, Marion (1881–1932), born and educated in Melbourne, worked in England as a researcher for Fabian socialists Beatrice and Sidney Webb during the early 1900s while completing a thesis at the London School of Economics; this was published as *A Colonial Autocracy: New South Wales Under Governor Macquarie* (1909). She became active in British labour and women's movements, and negotiated the incorporation of the Women's Labour Leagues into the British Labour Party. In 1929 she became the first Australian woman to win a seat in the House of Commons, but lost it at the following election.

KT

Photography often captured a moment in the process of colonisation. It recorded oppositions—between civilisation and wilderness, coloniser and colonised. The invention of photography coincided not only with the rise of Victorian theories concerning ethnology and race, but with the democratic age.

Changes in photographic technology made portraiture available to all. In 1859, with the advent of the *carte de visite*, the calling-card of the leisured classes became the name for cheap photographic portraiture and served as an important means of maintaining contact between families in Europe and the colonies, and of promoting the colonies themselves. Thomas Foster Chuck's *The Explorers and Early Colonists of Victoria* (1872), a framed assemblage of photographic portraits, suggested that pioneering squatters were as good as English squires, and the colony a superior forcing-ground for nineteenth-century virtue. Similarly, photographs of crowds involved in civic and cultural activities created a vision of social cohesion.

By their incorporation into illustrated journals, photographs became a part of middle-class literacy. Those of Charles Walter and Charles Beaufoy Merlin appeared as engravings in the Melbourne *Illustrated Australian News* and the Sydney *Town and Country Journal*, while the *Tarnagulla Courier* anticipated modern photo-journalism in 1866 by pasting photographs on its front page. Not until 1900, however, did half-tone photographic images become a regular feature of newspapers and magazines.

Colonial and international **exhibitions** provided another mass audience for photography. In the 1870s Bernard Otto **Holtermann** mounted a private photographic exhibition to advertise the progress of NSW. At the direction of Judge Redmond **Barry**, commissioner of the 1866 Melbourne exhibition, the Victorian colonial government carried out a photographic survey of nearly every Victorian municipality. By showing their civic, religious, and cultural institutions, Barry aimed to demonstrate the rise of civilisation in the wilderness. The practice continued until the 1880s, photographs being shown at the Paris, Vienna, Philadelphia, Calcutta, and London international exhibitions. Until Nicholas **Caire** and J.W. Lindt in the 1880s, colonial photography was more likely to record the frontier rather than urban imaginings of nature.

Scientific exploration also played a role in creating a pictorial understanding of the Australian colonies. Photographer and geologist Richard **Daintree** created the Victorian Geological Survey's quartersheets with the aid of photography; his 1863 visit to Gippsland was described by contemporaries as a scientific expedition. This interplay of mapping, photography, and expedition is also evident in the inclusion of Merlin as a member of the 1873 survey by HMS *Basilisk* of the coastline of New Guinea.

The development of the photographic dry plate in 1878 cut exposure times and made cameras simpler and more portable. It enabled city photographers like Lindt to capture the ever-moving life of the street. It also allowed explorers like W.H. Tietkens to take the first photographic view of Ayers Rock (**Uluru**) in 1889; anthropologist and honorary director of the Victorian National Museum Baldwin **Spencer** to photograph Central Australia and Arnhem Land

and their people; and Frank **Hurley** to photograph Douglas **Mawson's** 1913 expedition to Antarctica.

The title of Spencer's 1928 volume of travel writing, *Wanderings in Wild Australia*, reinforced the conception of wilderness as untamed by European science and culture. Aboriginal people and their knowledge were seen as 'the other' of European vision. The camera's claims to veracity strengthened these representations. Both Charles Kerry's photograph *Aboriginal Bora* (c.1908), and Baldwin Spencer's photographs of Aboriginal rituals, misleadingly suggested that the camera ensured spontaneity, wholehearted participation, and a willingness to allow ritual practices to be seen. In reality, Aboriginal people both negotiated and resisted European photography. For example, the Aboriginal artist Yackaduna (Tommy McCrae) once sued a European photographer in the Cowra small debt court for the non-payment of a fee negotiated for allowing Aboriginal people to be photographed at Wahgunyah in 1894.

In the twentieth century, photographers challenged this divided vision of Australia's past. Anthropologist Donald **Thomson's** photographs of the Aboriginal people of Arnhem Land during the 1930s, and Axel Poignant's 1950s photographs of Arnhem Land, where the seating arrangements of the Aboriginal people being photographed reflect an understanding of kin relationships, suggest new European understandings and photographic portrayals of Aboriginal people.

When the Australian Tourist Board decided to launch a photo-journal to popularise Australian **tourism** in 1934, it named the magazine *Walkabout*—the pejorative European-Australian term to describe Aboriginal people's nomadic wanderings. Yet the photography in *Walkabout* developed new paradigms of scenic beauty, including depictions of Central Australia. What was represented in the 1960s as the 'true blue' outback had become a different sight by the 1980s. European seeing accepted (in some limited way) the Aboriginal perception of their land. The old colonial paradigm which underlay colonial photography had finally begun to break down in time for the internationalism of the digital age.

The first history of Australian photography, Jack Cato's *The Story of the Camera in Australia* (1955), has been superseded by specialised studies, including Keast Burke, *Gold and Silver* (1973); Alan Davies and Peter Stanbury, *The Mechanical Eye in Australia 1841–1900* (1985); Barbara Hall and Jenni Mather, *Australian Women Photographers 1840–1960* (1986); Gael Newton, *Shades of Light* (1988); Anne-Marie Willis, *Picturing Australia* (1988); Joan Kerr (ed.), *The Dictionary of Australian Artists, Painters, Sketchers, Photographers and Engravers to 1870* (1992); and Michael D. Galimany (ed.), *'Australia', History of Photography* (1999).

PAUL FOX

Piddington, Albert Bathurst (1862–1945) qualified in law but chose to teach, including five years at the University of Sydney where his circle of friends included Christopher **Brennan**. In 1895 he was elected to the NSW Legislative Assembly as an advanced liberal. He campaigned strongly against the proposed **Federation** bill because of its insufficiently democratic character, and lost his seat in 1898. He went to the Bar and was appointed to the High Court by W.M. **Hughes**, but withdrew after allegations that his was a political appointment. Piddington served on both state and federal royal commissions, principally on labour issues, before and after World War I. In 1926 J.T. **Lang** appointed him industrial commissioner, and they worked together to introduce child endowment. Later, Piddington argued against Lang's dismissal and resigned from the Industrial Commission in protest. He remained busy after retirement, advocating child endowment, representing Egon **Kisch** in the High Court, and defending the right of married women to remain teaching. His memoirs, *Worshipful Masters* (1929), were mainly concerned with his legal profession. Morris Graham, *A.B. Piddington: The Last Radical Liberal* (1995), is a fuller record.

MARION LOUISA (1869–1950) shared her husband's enthusiasm for eugenics. She argued that women unable to find fit husbands after World War I should be artificially inseminated to fulfil their destiny as mothers and to their race. She also advocated acceptance of unmarried mothers. In addresses and publications on sex education she urged parents to talk openly and honestly to their children but also suggested boys be given pocketless trousers to prevent masturbation. Her belief in the importance of birth control as a means to improve the race resulted in her helping establish the Racial Hygiene Association of New South Wales and the Institute of Family Relations. Michael **Roe**, in *Nine Australian Progressives* (1984), discusses the impact of their views.

KT

Pike, Douglas Henry (1908–74), historian, was the first editor of the *Australian Dictionary of Biography*. He came to the academy in middle life after working on the land and as a minister in the Church of Christ. He took honours in history at the University of Adelaide in 1947 and was appointed reader there in 1950. In 1957 he published *Paradise of Dissent: South Australia 1829–1857*, which caused some controversy locally because Pike was thought insufficiently reverential to the founders. Actually he served them well by taking their ideals seriously. The book was then unusual in its close attention to the social and political environment in which the plan for a new colony developed. The book's theme was of a radical vision turning conservative with success, to sustain which Pike gave a rather misleading account of the state's history after 1857. While holding the chair in history at the University of Tasmania, he wrote *Australia: The Quiet Continent* (1962), often criticised because its title suggests that Australia had known no violence. In fact the slaughter of the Aborigines is treated in the book. The quietness was a comparative judgment and its sources were explored in a penetrating analysis at the end of the narrative account. He became editor of the *ADB* in 1964, producing the first five volumes to critical acclaim. All the entries were subject to his scrutiny and he was responsible for their crisp, spare style.

JH

Pilbara walkoff occurred in May 1946 when Aboriginal pastoral workers at Pindan in the Pilbara region of northern WA took strike action over their low rate of pay. The strikers were led by Don McLeod, a white man and former member of the Communist Party, and two Aborigines, Dooley Bin Bin and Clancy McKenna. They were supported by trade unions and church organisations. At the end of the three-year strike, the workers had achieved significant gains; McLeod and the strikers, known as the Group, were able to purchase a station for the use of the local Aboriginal community, using as funds the proceeds they had received from mining. Their action prompted a similar walkoff at Red Hill station in 1949, led by Daisy Bindi. The walkoff has generated extensive literature, including Max Brown, *The Black Eureka* (1976), and Kingsley Palmer and Clancy McKenna, *Somewhere between Black and White* (1978).

HD

Pinjarra, Battle of, between the Nyungar people and a government party under Governor **Stirling**, took place in October 1834 at Pinjarra on the Murray River, about 80 kilometres south of Perth. Conflict began when colonist Thomas Peel attempted to settle the fertile Mandurah–Murray area and met a hostile reaction from Nyungar leader, Calyute. At Peel's urging, Governor Stirling mounted an expedition of 24 police, soldiers, and civilians to put a stop to the **Aboriginal resistance** to European settlement. It was claimed by Europeans that the ensuing affray was accidental, but later research pointed to a planned ambush by Stirling and the party's organiser, Captain Ellis. The party surrounded the camp of about 80 Aborigines on the morning of 28 October 1834 and opened fire, killing at least 35 men, women, and children. Calyute escaped, but his wife was killed and his son wounded. Only two of Stirling's party were killed. As D.J. **Mulvaney** points out, the loss of so many of the tribe, especially the men, 'virtually terminated the Pinjarra clans as social units'. The **massacre** has been traditionally regarded as marking the end of Aborigines' effective armed resistance to European colonisation in the south-west of WA.

HD

Pioneer, the word denoting the first comers to a land or region, was in common use in Australia by the 1840s, perhaps arriving by way of the USA. While pioneers were sometimes seen by contemporaries as bringers of civilisation to the wilderness, it was not until the closing decades of the century, as the gold generation neared the end of their lives, that 'the pioneer legend', as John Hirst has called it, was born. 'It is a nationalist legend which deals in a heroic way with the central experience of European settlement in Australia: the taming of the new environment to man's use', he wrote in *HS* in 1978. Unlike Russel **Ward**, whose **Australian Legend** was collective and proletarian in spirit, Hirst emphasised the conservative, individualistic, and nostalgic features of 'the pioneer legend'. It was a legend more resonant with the history of Victoria and SA than NSW or Qld, he believed; it found expression not only in the literature of *Bulletin* writers but especially, as Leigh Astbury later showed in his *City Bushmen* (1985), in the paintings of Frederick **McCubbin**. The final panel of McCubbin's famous triptych *The Pioneer* shows a burial and, by 1904, when it was painted, the pioneer was often pictured as an old man. As Graeme Davison argues (*ACH*, 1995), the pioneer legend both endorsed the moral claims of the old—for old age pensions, for example—and relegated them to the past. In the twentieth century, the pioneer became a central figure in the morally inspiriting versions of nationalism favoured by governments and promoted through state school readers and public **monuments**, although the Left also attempted to appropriate him, as for example in Katharine Susannah **Prichard's** novel, *The Pioneers* (1915), and Louis **Esson's** *Pioneer Players* (1921–22). By the 1930s, the pioneer legend had been broadened to incorporate women—usually as faithful helpmeets of their brave menfolk; monuments to pioneer women were dedicated as part of the Centenary celebrations in both Victoria and SA. In the 1970s, when the pioneers themselves had long passed, and even their memory was faint, the legend lived on in the form of **pioneer settlements** devoted to the display, and increasingly to the fabrication, of slab huts and rough-hewn artefacts reflective of hardships long passed and—it was hoped—never again to be endured.

GD

Pioneer settlements are open-air museums which illustrate and celebrate the lives of local **pioneers**. Swan Hill Pioneer Settlement, established on the banks of the Murray in 1966, was the first of many similar open-air museums and historical theme parks, ranging from the West Coast Pioneer and Mining Museum in Zeehan, Tasmania, to the Qantilda Centre in Wilton, Qld, and from Old Sydney Town near Gosford, to the Yilgarn History Museum in WA. A few local museums, such as Burnie's Pioneer Village Museum, founded in 1942, and Beechworth's Burke Museum, had previously incorporated indoor 'historical streets'; the advent of the open-air pioneer museum was suggestive of greater ambition and realism in local historical endeavour. As the words *pioneer* and *settlement* suggest, the new museums often reflected a nostalgic, consensual view of the Australian rural past.

Like other manifestations of the **heritage** movement, pioneer settlements were a response on the part of small communities to the contradictory pressures of social change: a desire, on the one hand, to preserve and understand the local past and, on the other, to secure an economic future for their town by putting that past on display to visitors. Community leaders were aware that the pioneers of the district were ageing, and that the relics of their way of life were disappearing. The founders of Ballarat's Sovereign Hill Historic Park, established in 1970, aimed to provide 'a worthy visual reminder of the lives of the men and women who … pioneered this great city' but also to create 'one of the great tourist attractions' of the state. Most of the new museums were strongly linked to their local communities through ownership or management. Businessmen with influence in local government or state parliament often played an important part in raising capital and acquiring suitable sites. Eric **Reece**, former union official, local MP, and Tasmanian premier, was instrumental in enabling Zeehan to turn its old School of Mines into a museum.

Pioneer settlements usually offered a thematic presentation of local history. Swan Hill Pioneer Settlement, Flagstaff Hill Maritime Museum at Warrnambool, and Old Gippstown each gathered buildings and artefacts from scattered locations around the district and asssembled them in make-believe villages illustrative of the material life of the pioneers. Their collections of bark huts, **stump-jump ploughs**, harvesting machines, Coolgardie safes, mining implements, and kitchen utensils conveyed, at least to modern eyes, a sense of the hardship and simplicity of pioneer life. Interpretation was often fairly rudimentary and careless of chronology, since the objective was not usually to document or explain the course of local history, but to reinforce the nostalgic contrast between the 'pioneer era' and our own technologically sophisticated yet perplexing present. Sovereign Hill, built on the site of disused alluvial and quartz mines, was unusual in maintaining a definite chronological focus, the gold decade of the 1850s.

The fortunes of the pioneer settlements, like those of the pioneers themselves, have always been precarious. They are reliant on the whims of an increasingly sophisticated tourist clientele. Several have recently closed or have been forced to drastically reduce their opening hours. Most, with the exception of Old Sydney Town, are publicly owned, and many rely on subsidies from local government to survive. Ballarat's Sovereign Hill, which draws almost half a million visitors each year, is the only Australian open-air museum to run at a profit without subsidy.

Some Australian outdoor museums have followed the lead of successful American and British theme parks by introducing 'living history' techniques, such as activated technological displays and re-enactments of past events. The objective is to enable the visitor imaginatively to visit the past. At Old Sydney Town 'convicts' are flogged with a cat-o'-nine-tails. At **Port Arthur**, a candle-lit 'Historic Ghost Tour' offers a 'gripping and spine-chilling narration of sightings and apparitions' in the settlement's grisly past. At the Central Deborah goldmine in Bendigo, visitors may experience the thrill of plummeting down a darkened mine-shaft to the workings hundreds of feet below. At Sovereign Hill, tourists pan for gold; schoolchildren dressed in period costume take part in make-believe lessons; and volunteer guides assume the dress and identity of well-known characters from Ballarat's golden days.

Since its foundation, when the historian Weston **Bate** advised on the re-creation of Ballarat's Main Street, Sovereign Hill has taken pains to ensure a high degree of histori-cal integrity in both the physical accuracy of its exhibits and the scripting of its historical vignettes. In the wheelwright's workshop and the gold-smelting works, visitors can see old crafts and technologies practised in something like their original setting. This form of interpretation is popular but labour-intensive, sustainable only through the revenue from ancillary gift shops, visitor accommodation, and conference facilities. Modern requirements for hygiene and tourist amenity mean that visitors to Sovereign Hill necessarily experience a selective version of the colonial past. Yet, as Michael Evans argues in *AHS* (1991), it reflects an increasingly sophisticated interpretation of the goldfields experience. There are affinities, he argues, between the objectives of living history presentation and those of **ethnographic historians**, who seek an understanding of past societies through the drama of everyday life.

The first pioneer settlements relied on the relics of the past to speak for themselves. But the living history museums and theme parks which succeeded them have increasingly sought to 'activate' these static exhibits: first with human actors, such as craftsmen and guides who dress in period costume and play contemporary roles; and increasingly with big-screen 'orientation experiences' and electronic sound-and-light shows like Sovereign Hill's interpretation of the **Eureka** story, 'Blood on the Southern Cross'. In an electronic age historical reality may be mediated and validated as much by convincing simulation as by faithful historical reconstruction. (See also **Museums**.)

JAN PENNEY

Playford, Thomas (1896–1981), premier of SA from 1938 to 1965, was the longest-serving premier in the history of Australia. Playford is popularly regarded as the greatest SA premier because his incumbency oversaw the state's economic transformation from pre-Depression dependency on agricultural production to post-World War II optimism of industrial development. He is particularly remembered for the development of low-cost workers' housing which attracted manufacturing investors; the establishment of Whyalla; the opening of the Leigh Creek coalfield; the relief of semi-arid country areas by water piped from the River Murray; centralising the state's power supply; and encouragement of a variety of manufacturers, especially in motor cars.

Recent commentators recognise that a premiership spanning the end of the Depression, massive Commonwealth investment in war industry, and the postwar consumption boom would have inevitably encompassed these or similar developments, and that the projects listed were mooted before Playford's regime began. His government came under increasing attack because the economic growth of government-favoured industry was not matched by social and welfare development opportunities for the growing and diverse population, and eventually lost office to the Australian Labor Party. Playford, who had entered the House of Assembly as member for Gumeracha in 1933, served as opposition leader until his retirement in 1967. There are biographies by Stewart Cockburn (1991) and Walter Crocker (1982).

Poetry

Bernard O'Neil et al. (eds), *Playford's South Australia* (1997), surveys many of his policies and their impact on the state.

CAROL FORT

Poetry has an immemorial association with history, which finds its most notable expression in epic, traditionally the celebration of heroic events which have defined the poet's native land. In Australia historical poetry came into being within the new subjectivity inscribed in European literature by the Romantic movement; it emerged only slowly, in the wake of many topographical and reflective poems about perceptions of a continent whose leading characteristic was its apparent newness.

Charles **Harpur** wrote the first historical poem on an Australian subject, 'The Creek of the Four Graves' (1853), already having the imagination to locate a settler in 'olden times'. The *Bulletin* poets looked back to a heroic Australian past—'the Roaring Days', as **Lawson** called them—but it was through folk memory rather than history that they usually retrieved it. One popular Australian genre which dabbled in history was the bushranger ballad. Although these popular songs were often only set a short half-generation back, they were often designed to engage rogue sentiment and to historicise outlaws. They can be compared with the Robin Hood ballads, and were in time to feed into Douglas **Stewart's** verse-play *Ned Kelly* (1942; 1943), which began a short flurry of historical verse-plays that included his Antarctic drama, *The Fire on the Snow* (1941, 1944), and *Shipwreck* (1947), his romantic presentation of the wreck of the *Batavia* and Captain Pelsaert's heroism.

Apart from *The Great South Land* (1951), a national epic by the leading **Jindyworobak**, Rex Ingamells, and a scatter of historical references in Mary **Gilmore's** lyrics, awareness of the past as material for poetry was the property of the followers of the anti-modernist Norman **Lindsay**. In the 1930s, Kenneth **Slessor** turned from a lushly glamorised European past and imaginary maps to dramatise Captain **Cook** and Samuel **Marsden**. Himself a New Zealander, Douglas Stewart was a continuing presence in these national history projects and he memorialised them in his anthology, *Voyager Poems*, of 1960, which contains extended historical poems by Slessor, R.D. FitzGerald, Francis Webb, Bill Hart-Smith and Stewart himself. Webb's poetic studies of **Eyre** and **Leichhardt** are complex lyrical psychodramas, which can be said to look forward to Patrick **White's** *Voss* (1957). The naturally noble imagination of FitzGerald turned successively to examples of masculine action or decision-making: his 'Heemskerck Shoals' turned on a decision of **Tasman**; 'Fifth Day' represented the pomp and tension of Warren Hastings's trial in London; 'The Wind at Your Door' reflected on an early convict flogging that one of the poet's ancestors had witnessed; while the book-length poem, *Between Two Tides* (1952), had its focus on a nineteenth-century Tongan hero, Finau.

Historical poetry, perhaps, implies more than fleeting reference to the past. Many Australian poets turn back from time to time, imagining themselves for a moment in the psyche of some creative artist from the past; but such lyrico-dramatic moments seem less than historical poetry, which should ally itself to some extended story. A.D. **Hope** approached such a mode, in his customarily subversive or personalised way, with his dramatic monologue 'Edward Sackville to Venetia Digby' (1959). In 1969 J.M. Couper, who had emigrated to Australia from Scotland, returned to the themes of the 'Voyager' poets with his long narrative, *The Book of Bligh*.

Few poets have turned to events in history of **science**: the rare exceptions include Douglas Stewart in 'Rutherford', Hope in 'On an Engraving of Casserius', and Jennifer Strauss's more recent celebration of Simmelweis, who identified the causes of septicaemia. In the 1970s and 1980s a number of poets brought into renewed focus the events of **World War I**, among them Geoff Page, Les **Murray**, and Chris Wallace-Crabbe. But the distant past can still have its attractions for a poetic imagination: Geoffrey Lehmann followed his earlier classical monologues by one Marcus Furius Camillus with his dramatisations of a notorious emperor's character in *Nero's Poems* (1981); Dorothy Porter published the book-length *Akhenaten* in 1992; and, from his vantage point at Queenscliff, Victoria, Barry Hill reached back to **captivity narratives** with his 1993 long poem, *Ghosting William Buckley*, **Buckley** being the '**wild white man**' who escaped from the short-lived Sorrento settlement and lived among the Aborigines for three decades, before turning up at the new village of Melbourne. Another such regional history was Laurie Duggan's 250-page poem-in-collage, *The Ash Range* (1987), dealing in remarkable detail with the settlement of Gippsland.

CHRIS WALLACE-CRABBE

Polding, John Bede (1794–1877), Catholic bishop, was born at Liverpool, England, and entered the Benedictine order, in which he became a novice-master and subprior. He arrived in Sydney in 1835 as Australia's first bishop. Displaying enormous missionary zeal, he heard confessions from the convicts, and sought to remedy the shortage of priests by attracting other English Benedictines to join his ministry. The success of his early ministry was evident in the substantial increase in building works and church attendances. In 1842 he was appointed archbishop of Sydney and metropolitan of Australia. Polding was responsible for planning and overseeing new hierarchical structures for the **Catholic Church** in Australia. This role was constrained by his own failings as an adminstrator, and his long-held dream to found a flourishing Benedictine monastery in NSW was never realised. His monastic school struggled in a Catholic community that was predominantly Irish and working-class, whose members distrusted what they perceived as the authoritarian manner and elitist interests of the English Benedictines. When the pope refused to declare Sydney a strictly Benedictine diocese, Polding resigned. His resignation, however, was rejected. Criticism of Polding's leadership, voiced most strongly by Sydney laity in the *Freeman's Journal*, came to a head in a debate over lay versus clerical leadership of St John's College at the University of Sydney in 1858, when Polding's ambition for a key role in governing this centre of Catholic cultural and intellectual activity was ultimately frustrated. He attended the First Vatican Council of 1870. The fate of the 'Benedictine dream' embodied in Polding's career has been a subject of sustained debate among Catholic historians, most notably Patrick **O'Farrell**.

HD

Police have played a critical role in Australia's modern history. As one of the earliest offices of government in the colonies, police provided an essential aid to administration. Their functions were not restricted to catching thieves and keeping the peace on the streets. In colonial Australia they collected statistics, carried out the Census, administered elections, licensed pubs, and looked for lost children. In the twentieth century they divested some of these functions but acquired others, especially the management of traffic. Police were of increasing importance to the settler colonies' dispossession of Aborigines, and came to have a central role in the administration of the 'protected' Aboriginal populations. Their role in maintaining public order has required them to play an often controversial part in government's response to industrial and political dissent. But police have also been the focus of intense political scrutiny, their actions sometimes provoking political change of an unexpected kind.

Although the authority to appoint constables was first vested in Governor **Phillip**, the organisation of early colonial police imitated English practice in the subordination of police to magistrates and a tendency to localised jurisdiction. In NSW before 1850 there were a large number of separate police, with jurisdictions defined by region or function— Mounted Police, Water Police, Sydney Police, and so on. The enactment of self-government consolidated a movement to dispense with magistrates' control. By the 1860s most colonies had decided to centralise police functions in a single office of Inspector-General (in NSW) or Commissioner (elsewhere). Only in Tasmania did the tradition of a local police persist for some decades, until it too adopted a single police force after 1899. The police were governed in each jurisdiction by special legislation which typically made the commissioner responsible to a minister of the government. In spite of this provision, by turn of the century police leaders had created a strong tradition of independence of government and increasingly insisted that their overriding responsibility was to uphold the law. In doing so, they built strong police departments which influenced the shape of criminal law and debates on crime and punishment.

Police work in the nineteenth century was attractive for its relative security at a time when labour markets in Australia were subject to boom and slump. It appealed particularly to male immigrants without assets—a high proportion of the police forces was made up of **Irish** migrants, many of them with the decided advantage of prior service in the Irish Constabulary, which was also an influential model of police organisation and discipline. Yet police work had other less endearing features. In the cities and large towns, colonial police were housed in barracks; constables were forbidden to marry for their first few years of service; police were excluded from the franchise while it was extended to other males of their age and class; and, before World War I, they could not unionise. Control was through a rigid hierarchy with the police commissioner at its apex; officious and often severe discipline was exercised by inspectors and sergeants. From early in the twentieth century many of these conditions began to change, as other employers attracted potential recruits from policing. Police organised themselves in defence of economic, political, and industrial rights, most of which they gained by or during the interwar years. The 1923 **Police Strike** in Melbourne was the most eloquent demonstration of the rising militancy of police as workers, a strike which cost hundreds their jobs but in the long run probably made governments wary of antagonising police.

Other kinds of change to the police workforce were much longer in development. From the 1890s feminists argued that women and children should have women police available when they came in contact with the police department. This argument found favour around the time of World War I, and a number of departments began employing women police officers. Their duties were for many decades restricted to the management of women and children in custody, and preventive work on the streets and in domestic situations. Only in the 1960s did women police start to achieve equal status as fully sworn officers and only since the 1980s have they been promoted into higher ranks. In 2001 Christine Nixon became the first woman to head an Australian police force, in Victoria. The police forces have been not only very male but also very white Australian institutions. After the demise of the **native police** (mostly involved in aggressive frontier policing) Aboriginal people were policed by officers remote from them in background, culture, and disposition. Again, it was not until the 1980s that the ethnic and cultural make-up of Australian police has broadened slightly as a result of policy.

The functions of police derived from traditional common-law powers of peace-keeping, as well as from a growing number of statutes, including the Police Acts and Vagrancy Acts. While all police have been responsible for dealing with offences under such legislation, in practice the twentieth century has seen the consolidation of a significant division of labour in policing. The existing distinction between plain-clothes detectives and uniformed police was amplified as police departments formed specialised squads of detectives who were responsible for administering areas such as licensing, vice, armed robbery, and intelligence. In the postwar era the role and functions of these specialised branches of police forces generated great political controversy. The corruption of the licensing branch in Qld eventually led to the demise of the National Party government in the wake of the Fitzgerald Inquiry established in 1987, which explored the generation of corruption in police and government, while from 1994 the Wood Royal Commission into the NSW Police Service unveiled similar levels of corruption in police squads, though without the same political connections. These latter-day inquiries confirmed earlier historical critiques of police organisation of corruption, especially in the 'vice' and drugs trades (Alfred McCoy, *Drug Traffic*, 1980, and Judith Allen, *Sex and Secrets*, 1990).

The function of police in relation to political intelligence proved controversial. Much of this work was organised at a Commonwealth level after Prime Minister **Hughes** initiated an intelligence operation during the World War I conscription and industrial conflicts, but the state police forces established 'Special Branches' which maintained more localised political surveillance (Frank Cain, *The Origins of Political Surveillance in Australia*, 1983). The questionable practices of such operations came to the fore during the political conflict over the **Vietnam War**, in the aftermath of which commissions of inquiry into the Special Branch in SA, and later into the role of **ASIO**, helped to make these organisations more accountable.

The history of police in Australia did not attract much notice until the 1980s, except in the passing observations of Russel **Ward**, who postulated a popular tradition of anti-authoritarianism epitomised in antagonism to police, or of Humphrey **McQueen**, for whom the readiness of ex-convicts to enlist in the early constabularies signalled their reprobate and petit-bourgeois character. A 1960 survey of police by G.M. O'Brien, *The Australian Police Forces*, included useful reviews of the early colonial formation of police in the different jurisdictions. The first major history of an Australian police was by a serving police officer, Robert Haldane, *The People's Force* (1986, 1995), a history of the Victoria Police, in which he explored the theme that the people get the force they deserve, in a broad-ranging narrative of the forces shaping the police under successive commissioners. Robert Clyne, *Colonial Blue* (1987), covers the nineteenth-century history of the SA police, while W.R. Johnston, *The Long Blue Line* (1992), gives a more comprehensive history of the Qld police. Growing interest of historians in the role of police in Australian history was evident in Sydney Labour History Group, *What Rough Beast?* (1982), a series of essays on 'the state and social order'; Mark Finnane (ed.), *Policing in Australia: Historical Perspectives* (1987); and David Philips and Suzanne Davies (eds), *A Nation of Rogues* (1994). In *Police and Government* (1994), Mark Finnane provides an overview of the history of police forces and of the social history of policing. The histories of police forces in NSW, WA, Tasmania, and the NT are yet to be the subject of a major published study. M.H. Fels, *Good Men and True* (1988), is the best history of native police but confined to the Port Phillip District, 1837–51. A different kind of picture of the policing of Aborigines and the role of the native police is evident in the north of Australia, as depicted in Bill Rosser, *Up Rode the Troopers* (1990); Noel Loos, *Invasion and Resistance* (1982); and N. Green, *The Forrest River Massacre* (1995). The Victorian police continue to receive more detailed attention with Gavin Brown and Robert Haldane, *Days of Violence: The 1923 Police Strike in Melbourne* (1998), analysing that memorable event, and Colleen Woolley, *Arresting Women* (1997), documenting the history of women police in Victoria.

MARK FINNANE

Police Strike (Melbourne) began on 29 October 1923, when one-third of Victorian police went on strike. The major catalyst was the policemen's strong objection to plain-clothes senior constables being appointed to act as inspectors of police in the metropolitan areas. With the police off the streets, there was looting, rioting and other petty crime, which was exacerbated by the carnival atmosphere of Melbourne's spring racing season. To avert public danger, the government passed a public safety bill after a week, which authorised the formation of a special force to replace the strikers. A subsequent royal commission acknowledged the strikers' grievances but refused to justify their action; the strikers were not reinstated. The Victorian police force was subsequently re-formed by Thomas **Blamey**, who became chief commissioner of police in Victoria in 1925. The strike is discussed by Jacqueline Templeton in John Iremonger et al. (eds), *Strikes* (1973), and Robert Haldane, *The People's Force* (1986, 1995).

HD

Political history is a long-standing interest of Australian historians. The early colonial histories of W.C. **Wentworth**, James **Macarthur**, J.D. **Lang**, Herman **Melville**, and John **West** were concerned with the policy of British officials and its implementation by local administrators; their works were interventions into contemporary debates that sought to draw out the lessons of the past in order to shape the future. After the advent of self-government in the 1850s, later nineteenth-century historians such as G.W. **Rusden** and H.G. **Turner** took the actions of parliaments and ministries as the central dynamic of their narrative accounts.

The early academic historical profession reinforced this preoccupation. 'History is past politics, politics are present history', pronounced the English constitutional historian E.A. Freeman at the end of the century. He and his Australian counterparts traced the growth of freedom from monarchy to democracy, and trained their students in the lessons of statecraft by attending to the record of representative government. Politicians and politics were at the forefront of twentieth-century national record as related in the textbooks and short histories of Ernest **Scott**, Gordon **Greenwood**, and Frank **Crowley**: Alfred **Deakin** and the making of the early Commonwealth, W.M. **Hughes** and the conscription crisis of World War I, S.M. **Bruce** and national development, James **Scullin** and the Depression, John **Curtin** and national survival in World War II, Ben **Chifley** and postwar reconstruction, R.G. **Menzies** and the conservative supremacy of the 1950s. The same technique is apparent in Manning **Clark's** *History of Australia* (1962–87), where leading figures in public life contend for supremacy as they seek to impose their will on national life: thus the detailed portraits of Macarthur and Macquarie in volume 2, and the polarisation of Curtin and Menzies in volume 6.

Political history has frequently been treated biographically, and is present in constitutional, economic, and social history; but it was slower to develop as a subject in its own right, and historians still commonly depend on journalism and other contemporary commentary for an understanding of the political dimension. F.W. **Eggleston's** elucidation of early-twentieth-century Victorian politics in the 1931 biography of *George Swinburne* remains the best guide to that phenomenon; the Canberra reporter Warren Denning's narrative, *Caucus Crisis* (1937), remains the standard account of the failure of the Scullin government, just as Paul Kelly's *The Dismissal* (1983) and *November 1975* (1995) offer the fullest record of the **Whitlam** government's demise. Nor is the neglect of politics confined to the political historians. In a survey of political history (in Don Aitkin, ed., *Surveys of Australian Political Science*, 1985), Peter Loveday observed that historians of land settlement, immigration, or education could not avoid dealing with political history but typically failed to undertake the 'in-depth research in its own right' necessary to provide an understanding of 'the struggle for power within the field in question'. He contended that 'the politics in history is, on the whole, left to the political scientists'.

Loveday was able to look back on a substantial corpus of work on the Australian political system built up by the pioneers of his discipline—L.F. Crisp, *Australian National Government* (1965); Sol Encel, *Cabinet Government in Australia* (1962); S.R. Davis (ed.), *The Government of the Australian States* (1960); R.N. Spann, *Government Administration in Australia* (1979); and state studies by R.S. Parker on NSW, C.A. Hughes on Qld, Dean Jaensch on SA, W.A. Townsley on Tasmania, Jean Holmes on Victoria, Ruth Atkins on the ACT, and A.J. Heatley on the NT—all with substantial historical coverage.

His censure of the historians was too sweeping, but later trends might seem to confirm it. The shift to **social history** turned historians' attention away from decision-making to lived experience; 'history from below' rejected the institutional. 'Why does social history ignore politics?', asked two of its prominent British exponents (Geoff Eley and Keith Neild, *Social History*, 1980). The further shift to cultural history brought a new understanding of politics, the politics of discourse in which every form of knowledge was a field of power relations and governmentality a technique for controlling marginality and difference; but cultural historians seldom attended to formal political processes—three case studies presented as examples in *AHS* (1993) dealt with kindergartens, civics, and the 1954 **royal tour**.

The earlier political history worked with more narrowly defined boundaries. It took the business of government as legislation, administration, and judicial review, and studied it through the official record. It sought to identify the forces that linked elected representatives to their bases of support, typically by positing their expression of competing interests, and to show the means whereby they secured election through the articulation of policies and programs, typically by public opinion studies based on the press. This methodology suited the requirements of the postgraduate thesis, since a given period of colonial, state, or federal politics or a particular political issue could be subjected to close study, but it largely assumed its terms of analysis.

Peter Loveday and A.W. **Martin** combined a more rigorous conceptual framework with a quantitative methodology in *Parliaments, Factions and Parties* (1966), which showed how the advent of responsible government in NSW preceded the party system. They demonstrated that a shifting pattern of **factions** characterised parliamentary life. Their identification of the factional nature of colonial politics was widely imitated in other colonial studies. With the assistance of other scholars, Loveday extended the examination to *The Emergence of the Australian Party System* in the states and early Commonwealth (1977). John Rickard's *Class and Politics: New South Wales, Victoria and the Early Commonwealth 1890–1910* (1976) looked more closely at the transition to **class**-based parties. **Federation** itself has been widely studied, but more often in its constitutional and cultural dimensions (as in J.A. **La Nauze**, *The Making of the Australian Constitution*, 1972 and Helen Irving, *To Constitute a Nation*, 1997) than to elucidate the political alignments.

There has been a revival of attention to the earlier forms of colonial politics. David Neal suggested in *The Rule of Law in a Penal Colony* (1991) that, in the absence of representative assemblies, politics was displaced into the courts; the first volume of Alan Atkinson's *The Europeans in Australia* (1997) argued that 'the establishment of a community of convicts and ex-convicts raised, almost by accident, profound questions about common rights … [and] the responsibilities of power'.

The distinctive forms of colonial politics outside NSW were studied by Douglas **Pike**, *Paradise of Dissent* (1957), and J.B. Hirst, *Adelaide and the Country* (1973), for SA; and Geoffrey **Serle**, *The Golden Age* (1963) and *The Rush To Be Rich* (1971), and Stuart Macintyre, *A Colonial Liberalism* (1991), for Victoria. The political history of other colonies was pursued through biographies of leading politicians, such as Frank **Crowley** on John **Forrest**, R.B. Joyce on Samuel **Griffith**, and A.W. Martin on Henry **Parkes**, or in general histories such as Lloyd **Robson** on nineteenth-century Tasmania.

The history of state politics in the twentieth century has suffered an equal neglect. In the rash of sesquicentennial publications in the 1970s and 1980s, it was notable that only SA produced a volume concerned with the subject. In 1992 Ray Wright produced a first-class narrative history of the Victorian parliament, *A People's Counsel*.

There is an extensive literature on twentieth-century parliamentary affairs. C.A. Hughes has produced three volumes of the essential handbook, *Australian Government and Politics* (1968, 1977, 1986), which lists ministries and election results. Geoffrey Sawer's *Australian Federal Politics and Law* in two volumes (1956, 1963) summarised the party policies, legislation, parliamentary business, and constitutional issues of each of the first 18 Commonwealth parliaments up to 1949. While successor digests are still needed, the *AJPH* has published since 1955 political chronicles of federal and state politics. Gavin **Souter's** *Acts of Parliament* (1988) offered a large-scale narrative of federal politics, enlivened by sharp evocations of the leading personalities and incidents.

The principal histories of political parties are covered in entries on the **Australian Labor Party**, the **Democratic Labor Party**, the **Democrats**, the first **Liberal Party** and **National Party** (1917–31), the **United Australia Party**, the post-World War II **Liberal Party**, and the former Country Party. **Labour history** has produced an abundant literature on the left, and Andrew Moore, *The Right Road* (1995), brings together substantial research on the far right. Yet while rural politics is well served by the histories of Don Aitkin, B.D. Graham, and Ulrich Ellis, urban conservatism is a neglected field. The essays on *Australian Conservatism*, edited by Cameron Hazlehurst in 1979, provided some insight into conservative ideology and organisation between the world wars. Judith Brett's reading of *Robert Menzies' Forgotten People* (1992) opened up the rhetorical and psychological dimensions of Australia's pre-eminent conservative leader. While there are substantial studies of political attitudes and voting behaviour, the history of **elections** and electioneering remains sadly neglected.

STUART MACINTYRE

Political parties in Australia were among the earliest of the modern parties, defined as an organised force with a platform or doctrine and a parliamentary presence. Peter Loveday and Allan **Martin**, in their seminal study of the first 30 years of the NSW government, *Parliament, Factions and Parties* (1966), convincingly argued that the Freetrade and Liberal Association of New South Wales and the Protection Union of New South Wales both met these criteria by 1889. The prototype of the modern party is generally agreed to be the English Liberal Party as created at the Birmingham meeting of 1868. There is, equally, general agreement that modern parties only come into widespread existence in many countries in the years after World War II. In this sense, as in many others, there is further evidence that Australia was 'born modern'.

Modern parties tended to emerge as the suffrage expanded. Max Weber has classically referred to this process as the advent of 'plebiscitarian democracy'. Under this model, modern parties provide the 'managerial pattern' and developed from earlier 'aristocratic cliques and groups of political notables'. Maurice Duverger, in *Political Parties* (1951), developed a more extended typology of modern parties based on Weber's analysis. His fundamental distinction was between interior and exterior parties; in the former the impetus springs from among the parliamentarians themselves, who are involved in the creation of organisations to ensure their election and re-election. With the competitive pressure of an expanded electorate, interior parties are forced to adopt some of the characteristics of exterior ones. Both are best understood as components of a party system. This contrast is usually made with exterior parties; formed by the pressure of groups outside the parliament, and lacking representation within, they find it difficult to gain access to political power. The two early Australian political parties, the Freetraders and the Protectionists, are classic examples of so-called interior parties (sometimes called parties of 'notables' or 'bourgeois' parties).

In Australia the two examples of exterior parties are the Labor Party and the Country, later **National**, **Party**. The **Australian Labor Party** first emerged in NSW and Qld in 1891, and soon imposed an unusually rigid discipline on its parliamentarians. On matters concerning the platform, they had to vote as the majority of Labor members, meeting in **caucus**, determined. The ALP is an excellent example of another of Maurice Duverger's types, namely an 'indirect' party; whereby a large proportion of the party comes from affiliated organisations. In the case of the ALP, individual unions typically affiliate to state branches, and in general have constituted about 60 per cent of the attendance at state conferences. In other words representation from the ordinary branches of the party has been a numerical minority. It was never instituted along the same lines as the mass membership parties of the Western European type, although the ALP as an exterior party has shared their theoretical commitment to internal party democracy and the sovereignty of the external party over its parliamentary wing. The organisational wing of the party has its legitimate right to authority enshrined in the party's federal and state constitutions.

The Country Party, as the National Party of Australia was known until 1976, in its first incarnation grew out of various farmers' and settlers' associations in NSW in the early 1890s. In its second incarnation it emerged federally in 1918 and immediately sought to ensure its future by amending the Commonwealth Electoral Act to implement the preferential voting system. The Country Party throughout most of the twentieth century maintained a strong extra-parliamentary organisation. After it went federal in 1918 it maintained, at least in the formal constitutional sense, a strong commitment to the sovereignty of the extra-parliamentary wing over the parliamentary. Yet on closer examination (see Peter Loveday et al. (eds), *The Emergence of the Australian Party System*, 1977) in its early years, before 1918, it also had characteristics of an interior party. In NSW in the 1890s, for example, a Country 'party' emerged from within the parliamentary Protectionist Party at about the time the Farmers and Settlers Association was born. Similarly, in Victoria, the Farmers, Property Owners and Producers Association allowed its parliamentary representatives in the Victorian state house a relatively free hand.

The ALP's boundaries have also at times been blurred. L.F. Crisp, in his detailed history of the party, *The Federal Parliamentary Labour Party 1901–1951* (1955), described the dominant role of the Parliamentary Labor Party or 'caucus', particularly when the party was in office. There was also a parallel tendency for the Cabinet to dominate the caucus on policy questions. In fact, given the weight of the historical precedents to the contrary, the strength of the ideological commitment within the ALP towards the organisational sovereignty model remains almost as a contradiction.

The modern **Liberal Party**—formed in 1945—emerged from among the heirs to the original interior parties. Partly as a consequence of this, it adapted the rhetoric of parliamentarianism. Under this model, individual members of parliament are considered as representatives of their constituencies rather than as delegates of their party. In this the Liberals boast of their difference from the ALP, but in practice the overwhelming majority of Liberal parliamentarians have followed the party line. Don Chipp provided one notable exception; policy disagreements led him to form his own political party in 1977, the **Australian Democrats**. This can also be seen as the exception that proved the rule, demonstrating the limits to ideological toleration within the Liberal Party. The party's commitment to parliamentarianism is reflected in the relative weakness of its organisational machinery compared with that of the ALP. The ALP's national executive has intervened in the internal affairs of state branches on various occasions and has also determined pre-selections. The Liberal Party adopted changes to its organisational constitution in 1995 at its 50th anniversary Federal Council meeting, which gave its federal executive limited powers to involve itself in certain financial and pre-selection issues of its state divisions.

After the defeat of the coalition **Fraser** government in 1983 and the consequent promulgation of the Valder Report the same year, the Liberal Party's federal election campaigns have been based upon more central planning and coordination. In its 1996 campaign, when the coalition routed the ALP to win office after 13 years in opposition, the party ran a brilliant, centrally conducted campaign, also in concert with the National Party.

Clever campaigning had underpinned the longevity of the **Hawke** government (1983–92). At the organisational level, however, the ALP functioned smoothly on the basis of the system of national **factions**, which were formalised in 1984. Labor factions had new elements, but also to a degree formalised the divisions which had existed in the party from its inception, namely the right, the left, and the moderates. The factional system in the 1980s still bore the imprint of the **Split** of the 1950s. Labor was always weaker in Victoria, and then was marginalised in the aftermath of the Split. In NSW, and to a lesser degree in Qld, the party emerged relatively unscathed by the sectarian divisions that tore Victoria apart. NSW had been badly scarred during the Great Depression by the trauma of the **Lang** Labor Party, and emerged with a healthy pragmatism.

In international terms the Australian party system looks stable and has been remarkably durable. This has been partly aided by changes to the electoral and voting systems to entrench the position of the three key players in the party system. The preferential vote (adopted in 1918) has allowed the Country Party to become a niche party. Compulsory voting (adopted in 1924) was supported by the three parties to their mutual advantage. Public funding of **elections** was introduced by Labor in 1984, with the coalition parties opposing, but by 1991 when the original legislation was amended all three parties were in support (see Scott Bennett, *Winning and Losing: Australian National Elections*, 1996). In institutional terms, the Senate, designed as a states' house, has become, as the result of the adoption of propor-

tional representation in 1948, a place for the Australian Democrats and other minor parties and independents to find expression. The share of the first-preference votes going to the three major parties in the House of Representatives has declined. In the 1970s and 1980s they attracted over 90 per cent; in the 1990s this slipped to just below 85 per cent. Even before the advent of Pauline Hanson's **One Nation** Party in the 1998 elections, the three-party hegemony had been challenged by the rise of independents, particularly in rural and regional Australia.

MARIAN SIMMS

Polls, public opinion commissioned by the media to sample systematically the views of particular populations, first appeared in Australia in the early 1940s. Since then they have played an increasingly prominent part in Australian political life.

The first regular poll, Australian Public Opinion Polls (the Gallup method), was established by the Herald & Weekly Times in July 1941. In 1940, the director of APOP, Roy Morgan, had been sent by Sir Keith **Murdoch** to the USA to learn the art of polling from George Gallup. The poll's findings were published by the Melbourne *Herald*, the Brisbane *Courier-Mail*, the Adelaide *Advertiser*, the *West Australian*, and the Hobart *Mercury*; and, in Sydney, by the *Daily Mirror*.

In 1971, the monopoly of the Herald & Weekly Times was broken by **Fairfax** and by Rupert **Murdoch's** News Ltd. First, the *Age* and the *Sydney Morning Herald* decided to commission surveys through the Australian Sales Research Bureau (subsequently Irving Saulwick & Associates). Then Murdoch, keen to see the **Australian Labor Party** win the 1972 election and suspicious of Morgan's Liberal leanings, established Australian Nationwide Opinion Polls. In late 1977 ANOP—now wholly independent and used by the *National Times*—ceased its press work to concentrate on other activities, notably its polling for Labor.

From 1973 the Morgan poll shifted to the *Bulletin*; in 1992 it moved to *Time Australia* but returned in 1995. Having cut its ties with Morgan, the Herald Group commissioned **McNair** Anderson & Associates to run APOP; but in 1987, after Murdoch bought the group, the poll was dropped. That year News Ltd co-founded Newspoll to service its most prestigious daily, the *Australian*. Between 1992 and 1995, McNair (now owned by Audits of Great Britain) replaced the Morgan poll in the *Bulletin*; from 1996, Morgan returned to the *Bulletin*, and AGB McNair (later, A.C. Neilsen McNair) replaced Saulwick at the *Sydney Morning Herald*; the *Age*, however, pulled out of the arrangement. Under Morgan and McNair Anderson, the Gallup poll was conducted face-to-face. But with the spread of telephone ownership and pressures to publish early, interviews have been conducted increasingly by phone since the late 1970s.

As the two-volume index to *Australian Opinion Polls 1941–1990* compiled by T.W. Beed et al. (1993) makes clear, the output of the polls has grown at an exponential rate: over

6300 items between 1941 and 1977; more than twice that number between 1977 and 1990. Until the late 1960s, the polls were overwhelmingly concerned with the issues of the day. Since then, federal and state voting intentions and party leaders have moved to centre stage. The all-too-brief histories of polling in Australia by T.W. Beed (in Howard R. Penniman, ed., *Australia at the Polls*, 1977), Ian McNair and Frank Teer (in R.M. Worcester, ed., *Political Opinion Polling: An International Review*, 1983), and Stephen Mills, *The New Machine Men* (1986), focus on elections. Conversely, since 1972 most election monographs have included chapters on the polls.

Poll data have been used by political scientists for wider purposes: to test claims about electoral differences, representation, and political change. In *Policies and Partisans: Australian Electoral Opinion 1941 to 1968* (1969), Murray Goot compared patterns of opinion among Labor and Liberal–Country Party voters and support for the parties' policy positions. A long line of research, from R.W. Connell and Goot on federal politics (*Australian Quarterly*, 1972) to work on state politics (Goot in *Australian Studies in Journalism*, 1996), challenges the view that electoral choice has been 'presidentialised'. A series of studies, running from R.R. Alford, *Party and Society* (1963), through D.A. Kemp, *Society and Electoral Behaviour in Australia* (1978), to Goot on 'class voting' (in Judith Brett et al., eds, *Developments in Australian Politics*, 1994), offers conflicting accounts of changes in the occupational distinctiveness of the Labor vote.

The polls have influenced political journalism, the fortunes of party leaders, and the strategic thinking of the parties—though each of these changes awaits its historian. The influence of polls on journalism is discussed, in quite different ways, by Philip Bell et al., *Programmed Politics* (1982), and Derek Parker, *The Courtesans* (1991). The impact on the fortunes of leaders is noted by Goot (in Ernie Chaples et al., eds, *The Wran Model*, 1985). Some sense of the growing importance of the public polls—and of the parties' own research—on the way parties plan and prosecute their campaigns can be gained most readily through the works of journalists such as Laurie Oakes and David Solomon, *The Making of an Australian Prime Minister* (1973); Stephen Mills, *The New Machine Men*; and Pamela Williams, *The Victory* (1997). Caught between the conflicting demands to show leadership and to reflect public opinion, political leaders are regularly upbraided for being 'out of touch' or 'poll-driven'.

While polls are widely regarded as reliable guides to public opinion, they have also been seen as political constructs shaped by the assumptions of the pollsters themselves. This is especially true of Goot's work: for example, on **Vietnam** (with Rodney Tiffen in Peter King, ed., *Australia's Vietnam* 1983); **Mabo** (in Goot and Tim Rowse, eds, *Make a Better Offer: The Politics of Mabo*, 1994); and **republicanism** (in George Winterton, ed., *We, the People*, 1994).

The 'poverty of meaning' in mass surveys had earlier been attacked by R.W. Connell (*Meanjin*, 1972). The indifference to survey evidence displayed by most professional historians suggests widespread sympathy for this view.

Murray Goot

Pommy originally referred to English immigrants to Australia, but later became a slang term used by Australians (and others) for the English in general. The most popular theory of its origins claims the word derived from rhyming slang: *pommy*, a diminutive of *pomegranate* or *pommygrant*—supposedly chosen because of its likeness to the rosy cheeks of English immigrants—was used as an alternative for *jimmy*, a shortened and slightly more derogative form of *Jimmy Grant* or *Jemmy Grant*, which was rhyming slang for *immigrant*. A second, less substantiated suggestion is that it was a play on the acronym POME (Prisoner of Mother England), which was carved into the walls of several convict cells during the penal period in Tasmania. The first recorded usage is in the popular press in the early twentieth century. The term *pommy bastard* developed later in response to Australians' persistent, though partly affectionate, disdain for the English.

HD

Poppy, tall, see **Tall poppy**

Population has been the foundation of Australia's development, and a recurrent topic of political debate since 1788.

Scholars have made several attempts to estimate the Aboriginal population before 1788. These are derived in two main ways: by using early colonial tallies of Aboriginal populations in specific regions as a benchmark, and multiplying them to take account of a larger area and the effects of disease and killing by the invading Europeans; or by reconstructing the potential population from a study of the Aboriginal way of life and the capacity of the land to support it in various regions. These estimates have varied widely, in accordance, partly, with the authors' appraisal of the extent of frontier violence and the casualties from smallpox, measles, and other exotic diseases on the Aboriginal population. The long-accepted estimate by Radcliffe-Brown of 200 000 was challenged in 1983 by Noel **Butlin**, who proposed a pre-1778 population of 900 000. The consensus of scholarly opinion favours an estimate of around 400 000.

Australia was settled by the British largely as a means of solving its own population problems. The gloomy theories of the Rev. Thomas Malthus, and his anticipations of overpopulation and starvation, cast a long shadow over early-nineteenth-century debates over crime, emigration and colonisation. Transporting **convicts** and shovelling out paupers were ways of relieving Britain's surplus population and became the most important factor in Australia's demographic growth. For the first 70 years of settlement, the Australian population more than doubled itself every decade, rising from 2000 in 1790 to just over one million in 1860, with growth greatest in the 1810s, the 1830s, and especially in the 1850s, when population increased from 437 000 to 1.1 million. Most of these immigrants were young, usually in their twenties and thirties, and predominantly male. Males outnumbered females by three to one in 1828, by more than three to two in 1851, and achieved approximate parity only in the first quarter of the twentieth century. South Australia, influenced by the colonising ideals of Edward Gibbon **Wakefield**, came closest to achieving a demographic parity, just as it later led the colonies to the achievement of female suffrage.

Being young, these immigrants also had a high propensity to marry and have children; the colonial spinster was a rarity. Women marrying in the 1850s had large **families**— an average of seven live births each—but infant mortality was also high. In the 1860s and 1870s, as the gold-rush generation settled down, natural increase (the predominance of births over deaths) took over from immigration as the main factor in population growth, which was now running at barely half the rate of the pre-1850 period. In Victoria especially, where the gold-rush influx had been greatest, the population had assumed a distinctive kinked age distribution, with large cohorts of young parents and children, and relatively few middle-aged and old folk. By the 1880s, however, those gold-rush children were themselves growing into adulthood and forming families of their own, a new demographic impulse which, some historians argue, was a powerful underlying factor in the economic upsurge of the **land boom**. Much of this growth was now concentrated in the coastal cities, which had begun to acquire some of the deadly characteristics of their European counterparts. While Australian death-rates were generally low by European standards, some characteristically urban diseases, such as typhoid, took heavier toll in Australian cities than in British ones.

By the end of the 1880s Australia had also begun to feel the effects of a rapid decline in the birth-rate. 'Why don't the young men marry?' contemporaries had begun to ask in the 1880s. Prompted in part by the desire to establish themselves economically, couples had begun to defer marriage and child-bearing to a later stage of life. The economic crash of the 1890s may have forced some men and women to give up matrimony altogether; for the first time, older bachelors and spinsters became a significant component of the Australian population. But, as recent research in Australian **demographic history** has shown, the decline in the birth-rate was chiefly caused by a decline in the propensity of already married couples, including newly-weds, to restrict the size of their families. Between 1891 and 1901 the number of births per 1000 married women aged 15 to 45 fell by 22 per cent. Contemporaries were alarmed by the appearance of such trends in a nation that considered itself still young and expansive. A 1904 NSW Royal Commission on the Decline of the Birthrate was driven, reluctantly. to the conclusion that people had been 'led astray by false and pernicious doctrine into the belief that personal interests and ambitions, a high standard of ease, comfort and luxury, are the essential aims of life, and that these aims are best attained by refusing to accept the consequences which nature has ordained shall follow from marriage'. The commission had noted evidence of the widespread dissemination of information and technology about artificial birth-control, although sexual abstinence and the long absences of husbands looking for work during the **depression** may also have contributed to the decline in fertility.

By 1901 Australia had reached a population of 3.7 million but it was growing only half as fast as it had in the 1870s, and at a quarter of the rate in the period 1790–1860. In their anxiety over the falling birth-rate, contemporaries often failed to notice that the nation's death-rate had also begun a marked decline. Infant mortality was reduced by more than half between the 1890s and the 1920s, thanks largely to improved ante-natal and post-natal care, while adult mortality also began to fall as the major killer diseases, such as tuberculosis, were brought under control. The life-expectancy of males at the age of five rose from 53 years in the 1880s to 60 in the 1920s. This fall in deaths, however, did not compensate for the even more precipitous fall in births. Nationalists renewed calls for a program of assisted immigration to fill the 'empty spaces' of the continent. Estimates of Australia's optimal population varied widely, from Prime Minister W.M. **Hughes's** bold projection of 100 million to the more cautious 20 million of the geographer Griffith **Taylor**. More fundamental even than the belief that Australia's population should be larger was the conviction that it must be European. 'It is as a free, white democracy that Australia can best make its contribution to the peace and well-being of the world as whole', said J.G **Latham** in his introduction to *The Peopling of Australia* (1928). Official definitions of whiteness remained too stringent to admit more than a handful of non-Anglo-Saxons until the end of World War II.

Net migration, which had fallen below zero in the early years of the Commonwealth, reached a new peak in the years just before World War I, slumped during the war itself, then flowed strongly through the 1920s. This recovery was only temporary, however, for with the onset of the Great Depression, the birth-rate slumped to a new low. While women born in the 1870s, reaching marriageable age in the 1890s, would give birth to an average of four live children, those born around the turn of the century, and marrying in the late 1920s would have only about 2.7 births. Between 1930 and 1937 more people left the country than arrived. Only on the eve of World War II, with the arrival of refugee settlers and the cautious resumption of assisted immigration, was the flow reversed.

Australia ended World War II with a population of about seven million people, many of whom had been obliged to defer their hopes of family life until the return of peace and prosperity. The marriage rate had already begun to rise during the war years and after 1945 Australia experienced its biggest 'baby boom' since the 1860s. Families remained small by nineteenth-century standards (about 3.2 live births for each married woman) but slightly larger than among either their mothers' or daughters' generations. The advent of penicillin and other medical advances contributed to a steady decline in mortality; between 1945 and 1982 the life expectancy of men increased from the mid-sixties to the early seventies, and of women from the early to the late seventies. The natural growth of the population was strongly reinforced by the decision of the **Chifley** government to resume large-scale immigration. Between 1946 and 1970 over two million assisted immigrants arrived in Australia. In the 1950s the Australian government continued to exercise a preference for settlers from the British Isles and Northern Europe, but by the 1960s the balance had swung towards Southern Europe and the Middle East.

Between 1947 and 1971 Australia's population had grown from 7.5 million to 12.6 million, an annual rate of almost two per cent. But in the early 1970s it again began to slow. Assisted immigration in the mid-1970s was running at less than a quarter of the rate in the mid-1960s. As in the 1890s, adverse economic conditions—the oil price crisis of 1974, inflation, rising interest rates, and growing unemployment—had helped to precipitate a major demographic shift. Women were now entering the workforce in greater numbers. The advent of the oral contraceptive in the mid-1960s offered many women greater discretion in planning their careers and families. By the early 1980s those in their twenties were reproducing at only half the rate of their counterparts in the early 1960s. Responding to the fears of environmentalists about the depletion of natural resources and the limits to economic and population growth, governments had retreated from the expansionist outlook which had inspired the pro-natalist policies of the interwar years and the mass immigration of the 1950s and 1960s. Immigration revived in the late 1980s to a level as high, in numerical terms, as at any previous period in Australian history, but the recession which followed left many of the newcomers unemployed, a factor which prompted governments in the early 1990s to cut the intake.

In 1996 Australia had a population of 18.3 million. The postwar baby boom, followed by three decades of low fertility, reduced immigration; together with low mortality, this produced a population that was growing more slowly (just over one per cent per annum in 1997) and ageing more quickly than that of any previous generation. The Aboriginal population, which had continued to fall until the 1930s, was now rising faster than the population as a whole. By the year 2021, it is estimated, 18 per cent of Australians could be over the age of 65, more than twice the proportion in 1961. For the first time in Australia's history, zero population growth is both an aspiration and a looming possibility. With zero net immigration, Australia's population would begin to decline from about 2030, unless fertility again begins to rise.

GRAEME DAVISON

Populism connotes invocation of mass feeling in support of presumed general rights and benefit. Characteristically, the latter is postulated in over-optimistic terms, while conspiratorial malice is attributed to interests and elites allegedly thwarting its fulfilment. In Australia populism has appeared in staccato phases, that style being appropriate to its nature. Being hostile to liberal academicism, populism bears a pejorative taint in most liberal and academic analysis. Withal, it is a sibling of **democracy**, and has served democratic purposes.

Its origins can be traced to the **emancipists'** stress on the convicts' role in building the older colonies and on the greed of their **exclusive** enemies. That feeling waxed strongest in Sydney, where too a coalition of small interests, organised by Henry **Parkes** and pursuing populist ends, developed before 1850. That group expressed Utopian hopes for small-farm settlement, and hatred for the **squattocracy**. These themes swelled throughout Australia in the 1850s, and long continued. During the first generation of self-government, such alliances as that structured by the young Parkes often affected colonial politics.

Admiration for outlaws as heroic challengers of authority found its Australian version in idolatry of several **bushrangers**. Ned **Kelly's** establishment in that pantheon joined other forces in making the 1880s notable for populism. NSW was again to the fore in efforts (fairly described as populist by B.E. Mansfield (*Australian Democrat*, 1965)—to establish political organisations consolidating small interests. Associated in this was A.G. Taylor, active in other populist jousts. One was oratory in Sydney's Domain, a mode which had counterparts throughout Australia; another, support for the **Tichborne Claimant**, which crusade Michael **Roe** has presented (*Kenealy and the Tichborne Cause*, 1974) as archetypal populism; and a third, founding *Truth* newspaper. Under John **Norton**, *Truth* was to combine smut-and-scandal with perfervid populist radicalism.

For many years from the 1880s, trade unions and Labor parties embraced two populist themes: racism and hate/fear of 'the money power', which is analysed by Peter Love in *Labour and the Money Power* (1984). However, the Labor parties were not otherwise especially populist, and by giving underdogs a political voice sapped that alienation which fosters populist extremism. The Country Party's later success served farmers similarly.

Imperial nationalism became jingoistic with the **Boer War**; it intensified with World War I, W.M. **Hughes** then best displaying its populist potential. Hughes among those characterised by Sol Encel (*Nation*, 25 May 1968) as 'Larrikin Leaders', pinpointing an Australian populist style. Adulation of the ex-soldier was prime in *Smith's Weekly*, outstanding in the interwar heyday of populist journalism. In presenting a glorious future for Australia, *Smith's* scorned sceptical experts and applied xenophobia even to British immigrants.

In the 1920s, too, populism had play in regional moves to create **new states** while also being deployed by State Rightists against the Commonwealth centre. J.T. **Lang** took this further in his assertion of Australian interests against British bondholders, and Frank **Anstey** added an anti-Semitic note to that campaign. **Douglas credit** also belonged here, and the **League of Rights** had its origins in this experience. The Depression stimulated not only such monetarist populism but broader 'anti-political political thought', discussed by Peter Loveday in *LH* (1970), in which populism and fascism mingled.

R.G. **Menzies** based his creation of the Liberal Party in the 1940s on arousing 'forgotten people' and in similar style campaigned against bank nationalisation, thereby revealing how inexorably democratic politics requires use of populist vernacular. Menzies was no 'larrikin', but that term did apply to several of his prime ministerial successors: John **Gorton**, Robert **Hawke** (whose physical and psychological transformation were alike extraordinary), and Paul **Keating**. Meanwhile, as premier of Qld, Joh **Bjelke-Petersen** synthesised and surpassed various populist traits, including hostility to Canberra, contempt for intellectuality and legalism, and exaltation of the smallholder. The notion of populism has been best refined in the Australian literature by reference to Bjelke-Petersen by P. Mullens, in B.W. Head (ed.), *The Politics of Development in Australia* (1986), and Alan Patience (ed.), *The Bjelke-Petersen Premiership* (1985).

The upsurge of support for Pauline Hanson's **One Nation** at the 1996 federal and 2001 Queensland elections demonstrated that considerable populist hostility prevailed throughout Australia, especially in rural and regional areas. Its targets were the traditional populist targets: banks, mainstream politicians, welfare dependants, and ethnic minorities, including Aborigines. Its supporters sometimes joined with gun lobbies, pursuing tactics that echoed their counterparts in the USA. Demanding recognition too is the continuing variety of populist-disposed media, replacing erstwhile Domain orators and the journalism of *Truth* and *Smith's*. Especially in talkback radio has that old spirit continued: John Laws, Alan Jones, Derryn Hinch, Ian MacNamara, and others claim to uphold the people against bureaucracy, elites, experts, cruel fate, and harassing change.

STEPHEN ALOMES AND MICHAEL ROE

Port Arthur, situated on the Tasman Peninsula, south-east of Hobart, was the site of a **penal settlement** established for secondary offenders by Lieutenant-Governor George **Arthur**. The prison buildings, built by convict labour from the 1830s, incorporated yards for hard labour, facilities for constant surveillance, and solitary confinement cells. A notable feature is the chapel, designed to separate the prisoners from one another while providing the minister with a clear view of the congregation. Port Arthur was notorious for its harsh treatment, especially of boy convicts at Point Puer. Its natural features impeded escape. Soldiers and guard dogs stationed at the Eaglehawk Neck isthmus kept watch over the only land bridge; several escapees who attempted to swim to freedom were drowned.

After the penitentiary closed in 1877, Port Arthur was briefly renamed Carnarvon to dissociate it from the convict past. Extensive fires left the burnt-out Gothic shells that remain today. These were redeveloped by the Tasmanian government in the 1970s as a historical site that became Tasmania's premier tourist attraction. Several historians, however, questioned the romanticisation of picturesque ruins and their effacement of punitive brutality at Port Arthur, and the site became the subject of a debate over the merits of historic preservation. On 28 April 1996 a gunman opened fire on tourists at Port Arthur, leaving 35 dead and many others injured, and sparking a national debate on gun control.

HD

Port Phillip Association, a speculative private company headed by John **Batman** (and including Gellibrand and others), was formed in **Van Diemen's Land** in 1835 for the purpose of acquiring grazing lands at Port Phillip. In May 1835, Batman sailed to Port Phillip to investigate the suitability of the land and made his infamous treaty with the Wurundjeri people. On this pretext, the association claimed possession of the site of **Melbourne**, as well as all the land from Melbourne to Indented Head in the south-west, and to Gisborne in the north, in exchange for some blankets, knives, mirrors, axes, trinkets, and a yearly tribute. Governor **Bourke** declared the treaty void. In 1982 the Library Council of Victoria published *Trespassers and Intruders: The Port Phillip Association and the Founding of Melbourne*.

HD

Port Phillip District, an area which extended south of the Murray River to the coast and westwards past Portland Bay, was declared the Colony of **Victoria** in 1851. The district was settled as a result of private action rather than government policy. John **Batman**, representing the **Port Phillip Association**, and John Pascoe **Fawkner**, a private speculator, had arrived at the future site of **Melbourne** in 1835; the **Henty** brothers and others had settled illegally at Portland Bay a year earlier. An official settlement at Sorrento, near the opening to Port Phillip, had been abandoned in 1803. In 1839 C.J. **La Trobe** was appointed superintendent under the governor of NSW. Early accounts include James **Bonwick**, *Discovery and Settlement of Port Phillip* (1856), and John Shillinglaw, *Historical Records of Port Phillip* (1879, 1972): the most systematic treatment is A.G.L. **Shaw**, *A History of the Port Phillip District* (1996). Records of pastoral settlement in the district are collected in Billis and Kenyon, *Pastoral Pioneers of Port Phillip* (1932, 1974).

HD

Porter, Harold 'Hal' (1911–84), author, began his early working life as a journalist and later trained as a schoolteacher. Although he was always interested in writing, his first published works appeared relatively late in life. He published a collection of short stories in 1942 and a collection of verse in 1956. After returning to his boyhood town of Bairnsdale, Victoria, to work as a librarian, Porter found the inspiration and the material for his evocative memory of childhood, *The Watcher on the Cast-Iron Balcony* (1963); he subsequently turned to full-time writing. Later works included two more autobiographical volumes, three novels, volumes of poetry, and several plays. He also wrote and illustrated a highly personal local history of Bairnsdale. Mary Lord's 1993 biography is the product of a long personal association, but one that was ultimately fractured by her belief that Porter had a paedophilic relationship with her son.

HD

Portuguese discovery of Australia in the early sixteenth century has long been proposed by maritime historians, but claims have so far been unsubstantiated. The Dieppe maps, which are French copies of early sixteenth-century Portuguese charts, depict a southern continent that is thought to represent Australia. One of these, the Dauphin map, charts a coastline which, when cartographical differences have been accounted for, closely resembles the eastern coast of Australia. At the time this map was drawn, the Portuguese were the world's leading seafaring nation and the only European power in the East Indies.

Artefacts linked to an early Portuguese presence in Australia include cannons found on an island off WA, and the lost **Mahogany Ship**, reputedly a Portuguese caravel wrecked near Warrnambool, Victoria, under the command of Christóvão de Mendonça. Several symposia held at Warrnambool in the 1980s and 1990s failed to find conclusive evidence for Portuguese discovery, but popular interest in the theory persists. A memorial to the perhaps mythical Portuguese sailors was erected near the beach at Warrnambool in the 1980s and the city also holds an annual Portuguese festival.

Sydney historian George **Collingridge** argued the case for Portuguese discovery in *The Discovery of Australia* (1895). Kenneth McIntyre strongly supported the theory in *The Secret Discovery of Australia* (1977), but W.A.R. Richardson disputed it in *The Portuguese Discovery of Australia: Fact or Fiction* (1989). (See also **Exploration by sea**.)

HD

Portus, Garnet Vere (1883–1954), historian, was born in Morpeth, NSW, and studied arts at the University of Sydney. He continued his studies at Oxford after winning a Rhodes scholarship in 1907; while there, he also represented England at rugby union. Several years after returning to Australia, he abandoned his plan to join the Anglican ministry and instead turned his energies to teaching—a profession he practised for 40 years. He taught initially at the University of Adelaide and then fostered the early **Workers Educational Association** at the University of Sydney for 17 years; he subsequently returned to Adelaide to take a chair in political science and history (1934–48). Portus was remembered as a dedicated and enthusiastic teacher who always encouraged student participation. He adopted a global perspective in his teaching, drawing inspiration from a broad range of cultures and historical periods; an obituary in *HSANZ* (1955) described him as 'one of the pioneers of the subject now known as World History'. His publications included a short history for school students entitled *Australia Since 1606* (1932); *Free, Compulsory, and Secular* (1937); and the edited collection, *Milestones in Economic History* (1949). His autobiography, *Happy Highways*, appeared the year before his death.

HD

Post-colonialism refers to theories of culture and modes of analysis which dissect colonial discourses and structures of power. Such critiques highlight the legacies of European imperialism in readings of cultural production and the politics of resistance and identity in both the past and present. The term *post-colonial* (or *postcolonial*) suggests a chronological phase that follows the processes of decolonisation and the end of formal colonial rule. But the continuation of the inequalities of political and economic power that marked European colonialism, as well as the enduring legacy of its cultural effects, make it problematic to suggest that colonialism has been transcended. A broader definition of post-colonialism, and one used more frequently in relation to Australia, examines the impact of European colonisation on non-European societies from first contact, and the complex interchanges between colonised peoples and their European colonisers. In this sense, the 'post-colonial moment' can be seen to encompass all of Australia's history from white settlement or **invasion** to the present day. Post-colonial analyses of the entanglements between historical and contemporary structures of power, events, and representations have brought new insights to the studies of **race relations**, imperialism, and nationalism; to the practices of museology and **public history**; and to commentaries on topical issues such as **republicanism**, **multiculturalism**, **reconciliation** and **black-armband history**.

The term *post-colonialism* came into common academic usage by the mid-1980s. It was heavily influenced by the Palestinian literary scholar Edward Said, and especially his notion of *Orientalism* (1978), the process whereby the West constructed other cultures as its dark 'other'. However, post-colonial interests in the dynamics of the relationship between European metropolitan centres and their colonial peripheries, and in the development of colonial nationalisms, build upon and offer revisionist interpretations of earlier **imperial** and national histories. Particularly influential here has been the work of the Indian 'subaltern studies' group, among them Ranajit Guha of the Australian National University.

Imperial histories published in the interwar period situated Australia within the context of the British Empire. Although acknowledging local innovations, such histories celebrated the triumph of British imperialism as demonstrated by the dependence of Australia on British culture, economies, and institutions. The more radical national histories that proliferated from the 1950s told of a nation which had thrown aside its imperial origins to create a new and distinctive society, although this model of independence still operated within, as much as against, the framework of the colonial relationship between the centre and the periphery.

By the 1970s, the political activities of the Aboriginal rights movement drew attention to contemporary racial inequality, while the publication of histories of Aboriginal–

white relations turned attention to colonial racism and frontier violence. In the subsequent two decades, a spate of historical texts, autobiographical writing, and **oral histories** brought the experiences of indigenous peoples into the historical record. These accounts have opened new avenues of inquiry and posed different questions about the processes of colonialism in Australia. One aspect of rethinking the colonial project has been to acknowledge the diverse attitudes of white settlers to Aborigines, and to reject the reductiveness of the coloniser–colonised relationship. Feminist historians, including Ann McGrath and Marilyn Lake, have argued that **gender relations** and **sexuality** were, and are, integral to the power structures of European imperialism and colonial ideologies. New works that compare colonialisms within the British Empire provide different perspectives on issues of race, ethnicity, and cultural nationalism. Comparative studies of colonialisms within the British Empire have emphasised distinctive Australian responses to issues of race, ethnicity, and cultural nationalism. An example is Klaus Neumann et al. (eds), *Quicksands* (1999), which probes the differences and similarities between the histories of Australia and New Zealand.

One of the strategies of post-colonialism has therefore been to contest the dominant histories of imperialism by the inclusion of oppositional histories and alternative voices. But post-colonialism also seeks to interrogate those forms of cultural representation and power embedded in the historical narratives of colonialism. European annexation of 'new worlds' and the subjection of the non-European peoples who inhabited them coincided with the development of the modern Western discipline of history. The nineteenth-century construction of history as an objective narrative with Europe at its centre was crucial in legitimising European colonialism and in constructing non-European people as the inferior 'other'.

Art historian Bernard **Smith's** *European Vision and the South Pacific*, first published in 1960, provided an early analysis of how European philosophical, artistic and scientific knowledges were reflected in and projected upon colonial discourses, in Smith's case in the field of pictorial representation. This imaging had powerful implications for the ideological and material patterns of race relations in Australia.

Paul Carter's influential *The Road to Botany Bay* (1987) argued that the imperial landscape of Australia was created by the naming and mapping of its geographical features by white explorers and settlers. Carter's spatial history—the history of places, roads, journeys—is a radical alternative to imperial histories of Australia which 'reduce space to a stage' where the theatre of the imperial conquest creates 'order from chaos'. A layered spatial history, Carter argues, incorporates competing or overlapping histories which may be silenced or made present through colonial maps, boundaries, and place-names. Chris Healy's *From the Ruins of Colonialism* (1997) contributes to debates about the processes of history-making and the meanings of historical narrativity, suggesting that the social memory of historical events which chart the disintegration of colonialism offers possibilities for

Australians to 'learn to belong' in the ruins of colonial histories. Peter Read, in *Returning to Nothing* (1996) and *Belonging* (2000), explores how non-indigenous Australians express their attachments to places from which Aborigines have been violently dispossessed.

In Australia the post-colonial field has been embraced enthusiastically by scholars in literary studies, especially in the comparative frameworks previously known as 'Commonwealth literatures' or 'new literatures in English'. *The Empire Writes Back* (1989) by Bill Ashcroft et al. proposes a model for theorising post-colonial literature, although one that disregards many of the historical and cultural differences between white settler and black post-colonial societies. Bob Hodge and Vijay Mishra in *The Dark Side of the Dream* (1990) re-evaluate the literary history of Australia to explore the 'post-colonial mind'. Drawing on the **fragment thesis** whereby culture is transformed by colonialism, they maintain that white Australian identity has been shaped by its duality as colonised and coloniser. Other literary histories exploring the responses of white Australians to the Aboriginal presence, and the forms and strategies of Aboriginal writing (including Mudrooroo Narogin's manifesto, *Writing from the Fringe*, 1990) have emphasised post-colonial questions. The work of cultural critics such as Ross Gibson and Stephen Muecke has enriched the field considerably.

In the public sphere, post-colonial concerns have informed interventions in the way the past is represented, particularly in regard to Aboriginal experiences—hence the challenge to the politics of exclusion and inclusion in the 1988 Bicentennial commemorations. In other disputes regarding the use of indigenous place-names, the status of colonial explorers as **heroes** or the appropriation of Aboriginal culture, the colonial legacy has been variously invoked. Jane M. Jacobs's *Edge of Empire* (1996) explores some of these issues in the context of urban planning and heritage conservation.

There has also been a reassessment of the institutional role of the colonial **museum** in authorising racial and cultural hierarchies. Historians and anthropologists including Paul Turnbull, Roslyn Poignant, and Tom Griffiths have documented the colonial practices of collecting and exhibiting indigenous culture and bodies. Within state and regional museums, policies for cultural repatriation and consultation with indigenous communities have contributed to a museological reinterpretation of colonial histories. This shift in curatorial practice can be readily seen in the design and interpretative devices of the Museum of Sydney. Opened amid controversy in 1995 on the site of Australia's first Government House, the Museum of Sydney presents history as an open-ended series of disruptions and dialogues between colonising and colonised peoples. An exhibition entitled 'Colonial Post Colonial' at the Museum of Modern Art at Heide, Melbourne (1996), was significant for its critical engagement with the aesthetics of colonial representation and the hybridity of post-colonial cultural forms. The Bunjilaka Gallery at the Melbourne Museum (1999) is notable for employing post-colonial approaches in interpreting the entangled histories of Aboriginal and settler Australia. Some of the most striking responses to the pervasiveness of colonial legacies in contemporary Australia can be seen in the responses of leading visual and performing artists, many of whom are indigenous. Those drawing explicitly upon historical material include visual artists as diverse as Fiona Foley, Gordon Bennett, Leah King-Smith, and Imants Tillers; film-makers such as Tracey Moffatt; and, in theatrical works, Wesley Enoch, Leah Purcell, and Jimmy Chi.

With the new century, Prime Minister John **Howard**'s continued refusal to apologise to indigenous Australians for past injustices only illustrates the immediacy of post-colonial questions to debates about history, politics, and identity in Australia.

KATE DARIAN-SMITH

Postal services have been a government monopoly through most of Australian history. Government despatches were at first the main form of correspondence, delivered by constables who were permitted at times to carry private correspondence as well. But it was not until 1809 that Lieutenant-Governor Paterson issued an order establishing a central office for the collection of mails under an appointed official, Isaac Nichols. In 1825 the NSW Legislative Assembly passed an act regulating postal services which shortly led to the establishment of a general system of post offices and mail deliveries throughout the colony. The other colonies appointed postmasters and passed similar acts, establishing uniform rates of postage by 1849. The 'penny post' and the halfpenny postal card enabled even poor people to communicate relatively cheaply over great distances. In the capital cities mail was often delivered three times a day by the 1880s. While the government held a monopoly on the collection and delivery of mails, carriage was often entrusted to private contractors, such as coastal shipping lines and the famous coach service of **Cobb & Co**. The Post Office became the linchpin of the colonial communications system and a large state bureaucracy. From the 1870s it also held a monopoly of telegraph services, and from the 1890s of telephone services. It issued postal notes, an important means of transmitting money especially for poor people. From 1901, when the Commonwealth government took over the running of posts and telegraphs, the Post Office also paid pensions, collected licences and some taxes, and ran sub-branches of the new Commonwealth Bank. The first airmail was carried between England and Australia in 1919 and services became regular in 1934. In 1975 postal and telecommunications services were split into two separate commissions, Australia Post and Telecom (later Telstra). Since the 1980s, Australia Post has had to compete with private parcel and courier services, and increasingly with electronic mail. Corporatisation has slimmed the size of the postal service and forced the closure of many old post offices. Since the

1930s, when it first began to produce commemorative postage stamps, Australia Post has played a significant part in the popularisation of Australian history.

GD

Postwar reconstruction was the term applied to the plans of the **Curtin** and **Chifley** governments (1941–49) to provide a new postwar economic and social order. The prewar record of private enterprise and of conservative governments endeavouring to sustain it contrasted miserably with the full employment flowing from wartime government intrusion into every sector of the economy. The democratic political imperative of peacetime full employment, supported intellectually by the 'Keynesian revolution', demanded continued government intervention. The process began with the establishment in December 1942 of the Department of Post War Reconstruction. Treasurer J.B. Chifley was minister in charge until February 1945, when J.J. Dedman took over. The department's planning staff, headed by H.C. **Coombs**, were mainly enthusiastic young economists newly drafted to the wartime public service.

The **Australian Labor Party** had unprecedented scope to inaugurate change. From July 1944, Labor controlled the Senate and the emergency National Security Act bestowed extraordinary powers on the Commonwealth, many lasting until 1947–49. These were fortified by the wartime establishment of certain patterns of economic management—notably in **banking** and **taxation**—which demonstrated the practicability and efficiency of federal control. On the other hand, the government had failed in 1944 to obtain an extension of its constitutional powers by referendum and, as the national emergency receded, the High Court, the states, and the private sector were less ready to accept its intrusions. Again in 1946 and 1948 the electorate refused to extend the Commonwealth's peacetime economic powers—although in 1946 the voters did widen and secure its social security powers.

In *War Economy 1942–45* (1977), S.J. **Butlin** and C.B. Schedvin analysed the Bretton Woods discussions which shaped a new world order. Domestically, there was an immense backlog of consumer demand and severe shortages of building materials and coal. Methods of war-financing posed serious inflationary dangers. The government's reconstruction program consisted of six major elements.

(1) The maintenance of full employment—largely by means of creating a stand-by 'shelf' of public works ready to be initiated when unemployment rose. This proved redundant in the subsequent international 'long boom'—although the Commonwealth did facilitate the **Snowy Mountains Hydro-Electric Scheme**.

(2) A **housing** program designed to protect low-income earners. This necessitated state cooperation and the outcome was disappointing. Commonwealth controls were relaxed in a manner which worked against low-income earners. Not until 1951 did the number of new houses and flats begin to exceed family formation.

(3) Phased demobilisation plus training schemes for service personnel. In 1947 a peak of 42 per cent of university students were ex-servicemen. Tradesmen's opposition and shortages of building supplies kept adult craft training down to about 60 per cent of original estimates.

(4) Bolstering of **manufacturing** employment behind the traditional **tariff** wall, notably by reaching agreement with General Motors to produce an all-Australian **motor car**, but also by giving assistance to shipbuilding for strategic reasons.

(5) Avoidance of uneconomic **agricultural** development while placing 9000 ex-servicemen on the land.

(6) **Immigration** aimed to stimulate overall development. Here the government unprecedentedly recruited continental Europeans who in 1949, the scheme's first full year, constituted two-thirds of net immigration.

The government used controls covering trade, money supply, prices, building materials, capital issues and primary produce marketing but price control was the linchpin of its economic strategy—and wage control as the *sine qua non* of price control. The government long concealed this, culling from drafts of the landmark 1945 White Paper on Full Employment any reference to its determination to hold down wages. Price control was dismantled after the 1948 referendum but Tom Sheridan, in *Division of Labour* (1989), demonstrated how government attempts to suppress wage costs had produced turbulent industrial relations, culminating in unprecedented state repression of coalminers' legal efforts to improve their conditions of employment.

The government's primary goal was to raise living standards via full employment. Social security was secondary, being compared by Chifley to a trapeze artist's safety-net. Rather than establishing the welfare state, the National Welfare Fund unveiled in February 1943 represented a move away from Australian Labor Party principles of non-contributory social insurance. The scheme was launched at a time when little would be paid out in benefits—particularly unemployment—but, under the guise of paying for them, extended the tax threshold to people earning only 41 per cent of the 1943 basic wage, thus raising two-thirds of the new tax receipts from very low to low-middle incomes. Stuart Macintyre, *Winners and Losers* (1985), Carol Johnson, *The Labor Legacy* (1989), and Paul Smyth, *Australian Social Policy* (1994), have emphasised the conservative and subordinate nature of Chifley's welfare policies.

Despite L.F. Crisp's laudatory evaluation, *Ben Chifley* (1963), and the coincidental furore over banking, later scholars have emphasised the moderation of Australian Labor Party policy. Bob Catley and Bruce McFarlane, in *Australian Capitalism in Boom and Depression* (1981), concluded that it was less interventionist than either the contemporary Labour government in Britain or the subsequent **Menzies** ministries in Australia. Dave Clark, in 'Political Economy of Labour in Office' (in Paul A. Samuelson, ed., *Economics*, 1975), pointed to the fact that no capital gains tax was introduced and that the percentage of GNP 'controlled by the

state' only rose from 13.0 per cent in 1941 to 14.9 per cent in 1949—when indirect taxes still accounted for an 'inordinately high' 44.7 per cent of tax revenue and the degree of income tax progressiveness was 'very much below' the British or Scandinavian scales. Rob Watts, in 'Revising the Revisionists' (*Thesis Eleven*, 1983), detected a 'Faustian pact' between government and the 'liberal' economics of the planners which ensured the freedom of private enterprise from any postwar socialist inroads.

TOM SHERIDAN

Poverty has been a constant, but reluctantly acknowledged, feature of Australian society since 1788. Imperial statesmen conceived Australia as a place that could relieve the poverty of the Old World by drawing off its surplus population and providing it with a happy livelihood in the New. In the 1820s British statesmen had urged 'shovelling out paupers' as a remedy for the rising tide of poverty at home. Poverty was also the spur for many famine-stricken Irish to migrate: 'The grey shades of poverty darkened our door / I was forced to leave Ireland because I was poor.' By contrast, their destination, Australia, was often characterised as a land almost without poverty. In the 1880s Richard **Twopeny** considered that 'poverty in Australia may fairly be considered a reproach. Every man has it in his power to earn a comfortable living.' Australia was called the **'workingman's paradise'**. Yet poverty remained a fact of life for many Australians, perhaps as many as one in five, for most of our history.

In Britain, people had a ready-made way of measuring poverty through the operations of the Poor Law, the statute passed by Westminster, administered by local magistrates and Poor Law Guardians and supported by rates levied on local landowners, to provide relief to those in need. The New Poor Law passed in 1834 instituted rigid tests on the eligibility of the poor for relief. It was designed to prevent people sponging on the system (becoming 'pauperised') but it also stigmatised and humiliated those who applied for relief. It was hated by most working people. One of the new freedoms of Australian society, as John Hirst argued in *HS* (1984), was the absence of such an unpopular poor law. 'As far as the law is concerned,' Anthony **Trollope** observed in 1873, 'any man who cannot feed himself may lie down and die.' But, as he admitted, by abolishing a poor law the Australian colonies had not abolished poverty.

Poverty means different things at different times and in different societies. Modern students of poverty, following the classic British studies by Charles Booth and Seebohm Rowntree, defined poverty in terms of a 'poverty line', the divide between decent sufficiency and outright want. The poor were unable to afford fuel for heating and cooking, or nourishing food, or weather-proof shelter and housing, or clothing or shoes, or (for the first 100 years) elementary education and certainly not secondary schooling. But poverty was also a matter of opportunity and outlook. It meant limited horizons and limited expectations. The circle of poverty was made of iron; or, to alter the image,

Australian history for the poor was characterised by blocked rather than open mobility.

Poverty was both an endemic and a recurrent feature of Australian society. Visitors were probably correct in their view that colonial Australians enjoyed a high **standard of living** relative to their British counterparts. But they too easily assumed that this high average meant that few individuals were poor. A list of the identifiable poor in Australian history includes a wide range of people: the unemployed, seldom less than 10 per cent and, if casual and part-time employment is added, a far higher percentage; large families on low and/or irregular incomes; the aged, chronically ill, and disabled; outcast and destitute people (like drunkards and Aborigines); orphans and other neglected or abused children; widows and unmarried mothers. Well into the twentieth century, a large number of Australians depended for their livelihood on primary, extractive, or construction industries that varied in their demand for labour. Poverty peaked in periods, such as the **depressions** of the 1890s and 1930s, when these industries collapsed. Migration could also be considered a risk factor in generating poverty. Newcomers often had to overcome the handicaps of mismatched skills and lacked the support network of kin and friends. Trollope noticed that few of those who applied for charitable relief were native-born. More than a century later a study of poverty showed that more than half the first-generation migrants from Europe and Asia after World War II and the Vietnam War were classified as poor. Sometimes poverty was the consequence of personal crises or catastrophes (bereavement, injury, unemployment, bankruptcy), sometimes of unalterable long-term conditions (physical or mental **disability**). Stephen Garton's moving book, *Out of Luck: Poor Australians and Social Welfare* (1990), is a catalogue of the human stories of poverty.

In the absence of a poor law, Australia's poor depended for relief on the ministrations of charities, such as immigrants' homes, benevolent asylums, and orphanages, which were supported by private donations and topped up with grants from the colonial governments. Recent historians have used the evidence furnished by the case-records of these institutions to build up a detailed portrait of the nineteenth-century poor and their dealings with those who administered relief. Shurlee Swain in Graeme Davison et al. (eds), *The Outcasts of Melbourne* (1985), and Anne O'Brien, *Poverty's Prison* (1988), illustrate this approach. During the depressions of the 1890s and 1930s this system of private charity virtually broke down. Geoffrey **Bolton**, *A Fine Country to Starve In* (1972), and Ray Broomhill, *Unemployed Workers* (1978), studied the effects of poverty in WA and Adelaide; but David Potts, PhD thesis (La Trobe University, 1987), challenges the standard view by arguing, largely from Victorian evidence, that poverty was an exceptional rather than a typical depression experience.

In the period after World War II, as living standards rose, the poor once again disappeared from public view, if not from Australian life. Full employment and the growth of the welfare state led many people to assume that poverty had been all but abolished. In 1966 a journalist, John Stubbs, published *The Hidden People: Poverty in Australia*, which claimed that over 600 000 Australians were living below a rather austere poverty line, but his estimate was widely questioned. A decade later Professor Ronald Henderson and his colleagues completed the massive National Inquiry into Poverty, which drew the even more pessimistic conclusion that over one million Australians still lived in 'extreme poverty'. Henderson, a direct heir to the Booth–Rowntree tradition of British poverty research, argued that 'poverty is not just a personal attribute; it arises out of the organization of society'. He urged that measures should be taken 'to increase the capacity of poor people to exercise power'.

His report was probably the historical high-water mark of Australian concern with poverty. Paradoxically, it was one of the most prosperous periods in Australian history that generated the most intensive inquiry into poverty. In the 1980s and 1990s, when unemployment increased, income differences widened, and confidence in state-provided welfare receded, the issue of poverty, like the word itself, quietly dropped off the political agenda. Prime Minister **Hawke** was mocked for his promise in the 1984 election that by the year 1990 'no Australian child shall live in poverty'—not because the objective was unworthy, but because he should have known that the promise could not be kept. Poverty, in relative if not absolute terms, was probably worse in the late 1990s than at any time since the Depression; politically, its alleviation has never been such a low priority.

TOM STANNAGE

Praed, Rosa Caroline, née Murray-Prior (1851–1935), novelist, was born in Qld, the daughter of a landowner. Encouraged by her mother, Praed began writing as a child. Following her marriage to Campbell Praed and their subsequent life in England, she published prolifically. Praed's novels, which drew on her experiences of frontier station life and Australian landed society, held great exotic appeal for her English readers. Many of her works also relied heavily on historical events, such as the Qld shearers' strikes.

Her autobiographical work, first published in 1885 as *Australian Life: Black and White* and revised in 1902 as *My Australian Girlhood* (1902), provided first-hand descriptions of Aboriginal life, rare for a woman writing at the time and, when Aborigines were considered to be a 'dying race', it argued for the preservation of Aboriginal culture. Praed's childhood memory of the Hornet Bank massacre, and of the extreme retaliatory action taken by the squatters, left her with an enduring horror of the impact of white settlement on Aboriginal society and grave doubts as to its justice. Her sentiments about the **Myall Creek massacre** echoed those of her uncle, the poet Charles **Harpur**. The most comprehensive study of Praed is Colin Roderick, *In Mortal Bondage: The Strange Life of Rosa Praed* (1948). Patricia Grimshaw and Julie Evans consider her role as a writer about the Australian frontier in *AHS* (1996).

HD

Premiers' Conference is an extra-constitutional device for consultation and cooperation between the state and Commonwealth governments. Before 1901 there were **inter-colonial** conferences to discuss matters of common interest, and these facilitated the process of Federation. After 1901 they continued, initially as a means of transferring state departments to the Commonwealth. At first the practice was for the premier of NSW to summon an annual meeting, to which the prime minister was also invited; after World War I the Commonwealth government usually summoned meetings and held the initiative. From 1928 the Premiers' Conference was held in conjunction with meetings of the Loans Council, and in the **Depression** the gatherings provided the forum whereby the Premiers' Plan for reduction of public expenditure was adopted. Subsequently, as the Commonwealth acquired increasing control over public revenue, a ritual of annual meetings of the prime minister and treasurer with their state counterparts was established in which the Commonwealth would announce the federal grants to the states amid mutual recrimination. Since 1992 an enlarged Council of Australian Governments has assumed many of the functions of the Premiers' Conference. (See also **Commonwealth–state relations**.)

SM

Presbyterian Church is a Protestant denomination which follows the teachings of the French reformer John Calvin. Established in Scotland in the sixteenth century, it is organised through ministers and elected elders, with each church answering to its respective assembly. Australia's first Presbyterians came predominantly from Scotland, and to a lesser extent from Ulster. Services began in NSW in 1809 and the first ministers arrived in the 1820s. The Church established home missions, and built schools and theological colleges. Critical to Calvinism was the doctrine of predestination, which regarded the salvation or damnation of each soul as preordained. The argument of sociologist Max Weber that a resulting salvation anxiety produced high moral seriousness, self-improvement, hard work, thrift and learning, and encouraged capitalism is evident to some extent in Australian Presbyterian circles. When the various Presbyterians in Victoria united in 1859 (the other states united in 1865), this effectively established the state's wealthiest and most influential church; its adherents' commercial, pastoral, and professional influence helped shape the Melbourne Establishment. The various doctrinal schisms within the Church of Scotland had reverberations in NSW and Victoria, where disputes arose over the colonial hierarchy of authority. J.D. **Lang** led the move to establish the independent Free Church of Scotland in the 1840s. Two other churches emerged: the Presbyterian Church of Eastern Australia and the Reformed Presbyterian Church. The state bodies united as the Presbyterian Church of Australia in 1901. Plans for a united Protestant church in Australia failed to attract adequate Presbyterian support until 1977, when, despite dissension from the NSW state assembly

and considerable resistance in Victoria, most Presbyterians joined **Methodists** and **Congregationalists** to form the **Uniting Church in Australia**. Many churches and schools in NSW and Victoria remained autonomous. Among its historians, the work of Ian Breward is noteworthy, while Rowland S. Ward, *The Bush Still Burns* (1988), examines the continuing Presbyterians.

HD

Preston, Margaret Rose (1875–1963), artist, studied in both Melbourne and her native Adelaide before she travelled to Europe in 1904 for further study. She returned to Adelaide several years later, where she taught and exhibited. During further travel in Europe and England, she first saw work of the post-impressionists whose influence became apparent in the increasingly strong designs and glowing colours of her own work. Preston produced oil paintings, linocut prints, and woodcuts that were often still-lifes of Australian flora and fauna. Her recognition of the depth of Aboriginal culture, unusual for the time, is reflected in her inclusion of Aboriginal figures and motifs in her later work. She wrote for Sidney **Ure Smith's** influential *Art in Australia* and *Home*, and worked with other female artists, including Thea Proctor and Grace Cossington Smith, in a range of mediums. Her work is widely represented in Australian galleries, and studies include an 1985 biography by Elizabeth Butel and an overview of her prints by Roger Butler (1987). Humphrey **McQueen** discusses her contribution to modernist art in Australia in *The Black Swan of Trespass* (1979).

KT

Price, Archibald Grenfell (1892–1977) and his son **Charles Archibald** (1920–), respectively geographer and demographer, have both made substantial contributions to historical scholarship. 'Archie' taught at St Peter's College, Adelaide, where he had studied, before becoming foundation master of St Mark's College at the University of Adelaide in 1925. Strongly influenced by Griffith **Taylor**, his *Foundation and Settlement of South Australia 1829–1845* (1924) and later studies of northern Australia, including *White Settlers in the Tropics* (1939), have a strong emphasis on colonial adaptation to environmental constraints. *The Western Invasions of the Pacific and its Continents* (1963) is unashamed in its vindication of the imperial enterprise. He was prominent in conservative responses to radical unrest during the political crisis of the **Depression**, later served briefly in state parliament, and was knighted in 1963. Archie Price was an influential first chairman of the Council of the National Library of Australia from 1960 to 1971 as it built major research collections. There is a biography by Colin Kerr.

Charles followed him to St Peter's and Oxford, and in 1953 became a fellow of the Research School of Social Sciences at the Australian National University. In a number of studies of **ethnic groups** in Australia, including *German Settlers in South Australia* (1945) and *Southern Europeans in Australia* (1963), he pioneered **ethnic history** from an assimilationist perspective. He also wrote a major study of the origins of the **White Australia** policy, *The Great White Walls Are Built* (1974).

SM

Prichard, Katharine Susannah (1883–1969) was perhaps the most significant of the social realist school of novelists and for nearly 50 years a communist. In 1936, Prichard deplored the fact that there were people in Australia who not only lacked 'sufficient food or clothes', and were 'unable to enjoy the beauty and natural wealth about us … forced to live in filthy slums', but who also 'in the bitter struggle for existence cannot afford to buy books, to know anything of the art and poetry of their native land'. This dual concern with both the material conditions of existence, and with the positive power of education and culture, marked Prichard's long life of activism and writing.

Born in Fiji, the daughter of a journalist, she was educated in Melbourne. She was part of a socialist study circle in Melbourne that would help form the Communist Party in 1920; at the end of that year she was one of a handful of people who formed the Perth branch (see **Communism**). Prichard had moved there in 1917 and two years later had married the war hero Hugo Throssell, who more or less shared her Marxist views; he would commit suicide in 1933 while she was visiting the Soviet Union.

The struggle for socialism in Australia was dominated in many areas by the Communist Party, especially from the 1920s to the 1950s, and Prichard's contribution to it took several forms, all providing an interesting comparison with the similar—and different—situation of her comrade Jean **Devanny**. In Perth Prichard worked with Cecilia Shelley to build the Unemployed Women and Girls Association in the 1920s, and was instrumental in the Spanish Relief Committee in the 1930s. She was active on the east coast as well: in the **Kisch** defence campaign and the Movement Against War and Fascism, and in setting up organisations of Left writers in Sydney in the early 1930s. Back in Perth, she was associated with the New Theatre, which performed some of her plays, including *Women of Spain* in 1937.

Prichard's literary reputation bolstered the prestige of the party. *The Black Opal* (1921) has been labelled Australia's first industrial novel; Jack Beasley suggests that her subsequent trilogy of the WA mining industry—*The Roaring Nineties* (1946), *Golden Miles* (1948), and *Winged Seeds* (1950)—was a larger development of the same theme: 'Black Opal writ large'. Between Prichard's novels of the 1920s—the most famous are *Working Bullocks* (1926) and *Coonardoo* (1929), the latter a radical depiction of inter-racial sexuality—and her later work, she visited Russia. She returned in 1933 armed with ideas about socialist realist writing, a subject of considerable debate in the party until the 1960s about how committed writing in the interests of the working class might best be produced.

Little substantial writing about Prichard's life has followed the publication of a rather guarded biography by her son Ric Throssell, *Wild Weeds and Wind Flowers* (1975). Her letters offer insights into her public, private, and writing selves, and a number of these have been published in Carole Ferrier's *As Good as a Yarn With You* (1992). Those papers that have survived her instruction that they be destroyed are in the National Library of Australia.

CAROLE FERRIER

Prickly pear, see **Pests**

Prisoners of war of the Japanese in **World War II** suffered a death-rate of one in three, and images of the 12 000 gaunt surviving ex-prisoners profoundly influenced Australian attitudes in the postwar period. The horror of the camps and the endurance of the prisoners, re-created in the arts and popular media and recalled at times of public remembering, have been absorbed as defining experiences of Australians at war.

In the **Boer War** only about 104 Australians became prisoners of war, but sometimes mobile Boer troops avoided the impediment of prisoners by stripping captured Australians of weapons and clothes and letting the naked soldiers find their own way to friendly forces.

Early in World War I the crew of the submarine *AE2* was captured by the Turks; and by the end of the war just over 4000 Australians were prisoners, about 3850 having surrendered to the Germans. Many prisoners were victims of their own daring; they broke through enemy lines and lost contact with supporting troops. At First Bullecourt in 1917, 1770 Australians surrendered, the largest number of Australian prisoners taken in a single battle.

Conditions in Turkish prisoner-of-war camps were harsh and the death-rates high, reflected in the title of T.W. White's reminiscences, *Guests of the Unspeakable* (1928). But as only 232 Australians were captured by the Turks, their deprivations had little public impact, especially when measured against the 7600 killed or mortally wounded at **Gallipoli**. In the German camps, food was short and working conditions poor; the death-rate of nine per cent was unacceptably high, but many of the deaths resulted from severe battle wounds received before capture. In World War I the incidents in which prisoners were captured, the relative number of prisoners to other battle casualties, and enemy treatment of prisoners did little to prepare Australians for events in World War II.

The dominance of offence and the mobility of attacking forces in World War II resulted in the taking of millions of prisoners. As the Allies were on the defensive early in the war, most Australian soldiers who became prisoners were captured before mid-1942. The first Australian soldier was taken prisoner in North Africa in December 1940, but the main surrenders began after March 1941 with the retreat east and the siege of Tobruk. The Australians suffered greater losses with the disastrous campaigns of April and May in Greece (2065 prisoners) and Crete (3109). More prisoners were taken in 1942 in the fighting at El Alamein, making a total of 1941 Australians captured in North Africa. Australians in the **Royal Australian Air Force** in flights over enemy territory continued to be vulnerable to capture throughout the war, and by the end of the war 1476 members of the RAAF were in German and Italian prisons. Successful escapes, so popular in fiction, were rare. Of the 41 airmen who escaped from German camps, only five reached England. Evasion of capture by aircrew forced down over occupied territory was far more common and, assisted by local sympathisers, men made the long journey from Holland and Belgium to Gibraltar. Others took less orthodox routes or stayed with partisans until liberation.

For many prisoners the most dangerous period was soon after capture. Those from North Africa risked being sunk by Allied fire when being shipped across the Mediterranean; those captured in Crete and Greece endured harsh conditions, then a long, cramped train journey to Germany. When Italy surrendered in September 1943, some 400 Australians escaped into Switzerland and others joined anti-fascist villagers and guerrillas before the Germans took over and transported the remaining prisoners to Germany.

Most of the German camps for officers (*oflager*) and men (*lager*) were in the east on or beyond the German border. In the largest camps, such as Lamsdorf and Wolfsberg, Australians numbered around 1000 among 25 000 to 30 000 prisoners. Men allocated to farms as labourers lived close to farming families, and a few formed friendly relationships that survived the war. Conditions for workers in mines and factories were sometimes harsh. In spite of frequent distribution of Red Cross parcels, hunger was common, and cold and boredom were hard to combat. As the Russians advanced, prisoners were forced to join the columns of German troops and civilians trudging hundreds of kilometres west. By March 1945 prisoners who had been liberated by the Russians were on the way home through Odessa, and from April other prisoners were escaping west to join the Americans.

In all, 8184 Australians were prisoners of war of the Germans and Italians, and 269 of them died. Neglect and arbitrary acts of violence had caused or contributed to deaths, but a rate of three per cent was relatively low.

Within weeks of the Japanese entering World War II, Australians were taken prisoner: about 1000 around Rabaul, just under 1000 on Ambon, 15 000 in Singapore and Malaya, over 1000 on Timor, 3000 on Java, and others on Sumatra, New Ireland, Nauru, at sea, and at scattered points. From January to March 1942 over 22 000 Australians became prisoners of war. After that time only aircrew, coastwatchers, and isolated servicemen were captured. The Rev. Len Kentish, a Methodist missionary, was plucked from Australian waters off Arnhem Land and executed on Dobu Island. More than 400 other civilians interned in Papua and New Guinea died, 208 of them when the *Montevideo Maru* was sunk by an American submarine.

In separate incidents at Paril Sulong, Tol Plantation, and on Ambon over 100 Australian prisoners of war were executed, but most died of malnutrition and disease. The Burma–Thailand Railway was the common place of death. Sent in cramped ships or trains to work on the Burma or Thai ends of the railway, those Australians who worked through the 1943 wet season on the distant camps at the end of attenuated supply lines suffered the most. Of 13 000 Australians who laboured on the railway, 2800 died. Of another 2000 Australians shipped from Changi on Singapore to Borneo, just six survived: the prisoners died in the camp at Sandakan, on a death-march to Ranau, or at Ranau itself. Ambon and Rabaul were other camps where more than half the prisoners died. Travelling as a prisoner was nearly always uncomfortable and often dangerous: 1600 Australian prisoners died at sea as a result of American attacks on Japanese shipping. But some camps, such as Zentsuji in Japan and even Changi, had death-rates comparable to those of British prisoners in German camps.

As prisoners, women suffered equal brutality. Under fire, members of the Australian Army Nursing Services escaped from Greece and Singapore, but the *Vyner Brooke* carrying the last 65 Australian nurses from Singapore was sunk by the Japanese, and 12 nurses died in the attack or were drowned. On the beach at Banka Island in the Dutch East Indies 21 survivors were executed; of the 32 who went into prison camps, 24 survived. Another six army nurses, 11 civilian nurses, and one other Australian woman were captured in Rabaul and shipped to Japan, where they suffered deprivation. All survived captivity, but one died soon after liberation.

By August 1945, 8000 Australians had died as prisoners of war of the Japanese, half of the Australians who died in the war against Japan. Interviews with returning ex-prisoners, the war trials that continued to 1951, and the publication of best-selling first-hand accounts by Rohan Rivett, *Behind Bamboo* (1946), and Russell Braddon, *Naked Island* (1952), sustained public knowledge of the prisoner experience. A later generation learnt of the prisoners through films (*A Town Like Alice*, 1956) and television series (*Blood Oath*, 1990; *Paradise Road*, 1997), novels (David **Malouf**, *The Great World*, 1990), plays (John Romeril, *The Floating World*, 1975), and published reminiscences and diaries, particularly those by Stan Arneil (1980) and Sir Edward 'Weary' **Dunlop** (1986). Dunlop's elevation to folk hero by the time of his death in 1993 was a powerful factor in the spread of popular knowledge of the prisoners of war.

Less prominent in Australian memories were the 25 720 enemy prisoners of war held in Australia during World War II. Most of these were Italian troops transferred at the request of the British government at the end of the Middle East campaign, and employed, usually without guards, as farm labourers. There were a number of escapes by POWs, the most famous being the **Cowra breakout**.

Of 29 Australians captured in the **Korean War**, only one died. But, as well as cold, lack of medical attention, and little food, the prisoners were harrowed by communist propaganda. The Australians resisted 're-education', and most remained hostile to Wilfred Burchett whom they saw as assisting their enemies. No Australian servicemen became prisoners of war in Vietnam, and Australia escaped the anger of Americans about the reality of prisoners being mistreated and the delusion that they were held in some secret location.

Many ex-prisoners have written reminiscences. Besides those noted, Ray Parkin's trilogy and Barney Roberts, *A Kind* of Cattle (1985), are evocative of Japanese and German camps. The official histories by Wigmore, Herington, Walker, and O'Neill have summaries. Many of the unit histories, such as those of the 2/19th, 2/30th, and 2/40th battalions, have much detail. Scholarly studies are Joan Beaumont, *Gull Force* (1988), Gavan Daws, *Prisoners of the Japanese* (1994), and Hank Nelson, *POW: Australians Under Nippon* (1985).

HANK NELSON

Prisons became the central institution of punishment following the abolition of **transportation**. **Capital punishment** was for long the most serious penalty, the fine always the most common—but imprisonment has persisted as the archetypal consequence of serious offending. The founding of NSW as a convict colony, initially a 'prison without walls', coincided with a great historical movement in Europe and North America for the founding of the penitentiary—an institution which would reform rather than simply detain the convict. In both architecture and the discipline of its inmates, the penitentiary would effect its reforms by breaking the prisoners' associations with a criminal past, separating them from each other, and subjecting them to a rigid custodial discipline including hard labour.

The earliest applications of this idea in Australia included the buildings at **Port Arthur**, the gaol at Darlinghurst, and the **Female Factories** at Parramatta and Hobart. For the most part these were buildings constructed to house the most intractable of the transported convicts. But as free populations grew and the numbers of offenders increased, the colonial governments constructed prisons at an increasing rate.

From 1850 to 1890 Victoria and NSW undertook public works programs which produced prisons for the succeeding century: Pentridge, Bathurst, an expanded Darlinghurst, and a host of smaller prisons in rural districts. Other colonies followed: Fremantle Prison, built by and for the last of the country's transported convicts, transforming WA's major prison for over 100 years; the Dry Creek Stockade at Yatala in SA; St Helena Island in Moreton Bay, and then Brisbane's Boggo Road Gaol and the Stuart Creek Prison in Townsville. Tasmania avoided the expenditure, using buildings which dated back to 1818 until the 1950s. The prisons typically consisted of a number of cell blocks, sometimes in a radial organisation branching off a central hall, but the famous Panopticon of Bentham was of limited influence in the prison architecture in Australia.

By the early twentieth century, many cells were empty. Few institutions were closed, however, as a program of increasing classification of prisoners multiplied the accommodation required. In the larger states separate women's prisons were built, occasionally according to distinctive design and regime, as at the Female Penitentiary at Long Bay in Sydney (1908), but in other cases adapting old institutions to new purposes, as with Fairlea Women's Prison in Melbourne (1956–96). In some regions there was another kind of classification—a special prison for Aborigines was established at Rottnest Island in WA in 1840 and in the northern parts of WA a number of institutions were almost wholly occupied by Aborigines in the 1890s. So too were there special prisons for juveniles—sometimes in hulks, as in Sydney's *Sobraon* and *Vernon*—while the construction of special reformatories and prison farms proceeded well into the twentieth century.

Prisons were the product and responsibility of government, but in recent years policies of privatisation have invaded the prisons domain, especially in Qld and Victoria, and are the subject of a study by Paul Moyle, *Profiting from Punishment* (2000). The functions of imprisonment as an instance of the continuing disadvantages of Aboriginal people in Australia received prolonged attention in the reports of the Royal Commission into Aboriginal Deaths in Custody (1987–91). Prison architecture is the subject of J.S. Kerr, *Out of Sight, Out of Mind* (1988), while Mark Finnane, *Punishment in Australian Society* (1997), discusses the history and politics of punishment between the convict era and the 1970s. George Zdendkowski and David Brown, *The Prison Struggle* (1982), is essential reading on the stormy period of NSW prisons history that led to the burning of Bathurst Prison in 1974 and the subsequent Nagle Inquiry. J.E. Thomas and Alex Stewart, *Imprisonment in Western Australia: Evolution, Theory and Practice* (1978), John Ramsland, *With Just but Relentless Discipline: A Social History of Corrective Services in New South Wales* (1996), and Peter Lynn and George Armstrong, *From Pentonville to Pentridge* (1996), document prison history in three states. The short-lived history of a modern women's prison is examined in Emma Russell, *Fairlea: A History of Victoria's First Women's Prison* (1998). (See also **Crime and punishment**.)

MARK FINNANE

Privy Council in London was the ultimate court of appeal for the Australian legal system. Its rulings include a 1936 decision protecting interstate commerce from Commonwealth interference, which was applied in 1949 to invalidate Ben **Chifley's** nationalisation of the banks. The Privy Council began as a body of advisers to the British sovereign and evolved to incorporate Cabinet members and a Judicial Committee, established in 1833, which has mainly comprised judges and legal experts. From their 'dingy den in Downing Street', Isaac **Isaacs** observed, Judicial Committee members were 'as unable to interpret our statutes as if they were living on the planet Mars'. Alex Castles in *An Australian Legal History* (1982) examines Privy Council influence in the nineteenth century, while Bruce Kercher's *An Unruly Child* (1995) includes recent **legal history**.

Early NSW civil cases involving £300 or more enjoyed automatic right of appeal to the Privy Council, and provided a means of evading justice when it took two years before results were received in Australia. These appeals ruined colonial credit, according to judge-advocate Ellis Bent in 1811. Their number declined after reforms in 1814 increased the monetary threshold and forced appellants to provide security. In 1867 the Privy Council ruled it had authority in criminal appeals. Castles and Kercher agree that in constitutional matters, appeals strengthened the 'bonds of

Empire' in both symbolic and practical terms.

Vigorous debate before **Federation** over the Privy Council's role resulted in a compromise whereby the **High Court** became the final court of appeal on *inter se* matters relating to the demarcation of Commonwealth and state powers. The Privy Council retained other appeal rights, but the Commonwealth parliament was authorised to make laws limiting such appeals. Over several stages beginning in 1968, parliament progressively abolished Privy Council appeals until Australia's judicial independence was finally gained with the simultaneous passage of *Australia Acts* in the Australian and British parliaments on 3 March 1986.

DC

Probation system was a penitentiary scheme for convicts introduced in Van Diemen's Land in 1842 that replaced the **assignment** system. Instead of being assigned into private service, **convicts** served in government gangs for a probationary period; they were subsequently permitted to live as they liked, but were prohibited from returning to Britain before the sentence expired. A convict bound by this code was termed a probationer. The system was highly unpopular with free settlers, whose opposition contributed to the **anti-transportation** movement.

HD

Professions and professionals have exercised strong influence since the foundation of European Australia, and have assumed increasing importance in the twentieth century as higher education and credentialism have grown.

Professions, such as the church, medicine, and the law, have traditionally distinguished themselves from other skilled occupations in several ways: by their command of some specialised theoretical knowledge or skill, acquired either through higher education or through a process of pupillage to a senior practitioner; by the creation of a framework of ethical obligation towards clients and fellow practitioners; and by the establishment of professional associations and laws designed to protect the right to exclusive practice. The prestige of the professions, old and new, has rested in part upon a sense of continuity and tradition; more than most callings, professions cultivate a consciousness of their own history.

In early colonial Australia, a society based as much upon paternalism as freedom, in which the pool of educated men was small, professional men often acquired authority well beyond their professional sphere. Clergymen like the Rev. Samuel **Marsden**, Presbyterian ministers like John Dunmore **Lang**, doctors like Balmain, **Redfern**, and Bland, and lawyers like Francis Forbes and William Charles **Wentworth** were powerful in virtue of their professional standing as well as their native abilities. More than in Britain, professional recognition and employment derived from the government: many doctors had been employed as surgeons aboard convict or immigrant ships or at government hospitals, while the professional status of lawyers derived, ultimately, from their recognition by the courts, an issue which was much disputed in the 1810s, when the NSW judge-advocate Jeffery Bent opposed the appointment of ex-convicts as advocates or **magistrates**.

In the free society which emerged after the 1840s, professional status was increasingly based upon the award of university degrees or other standardised credentials and reinforced by protective legislation. In 1862 the University of Melbourne established Australia's first medical school. (Most doctors had previously been immigrants trained in the great London or Scottish hospitals.) Sydney followed in 1883, Adelaide in 1885, and Queensland in 1936. The 1858 British Medical Act had already established the legal foundations for the practice of medicine, making it an offence for unregistered practitioners to charge for their services and restricting employment in government-funded hospitals to qualified professionals. This legislation was copied, almost word for word, by the Australian colonies, but the monopoly it created was not unchallenged. Throughout the century, homeopathists, herbalists, practitioners of electro-magnetism, and other unorthodox healers continued to attract patients and test the reach of the law. The standard defence of the doctors' monopoly was utilitarian and humanitarian: unqualified practitioners, it was argued, might cause more harm to their patients than those who had undergone a prolonged training. This was a plausible, but by no means unassailable, argument, since the methods of the herbalist or the homeopath were often less risky, if also less effective, than those of the heroic surgeon or physician.

Medicine became the template for the legislative protection of other professions, beginning with pharmacy and dentistry which were close to medicine, and later extending to others where the utilitarian argument was more tenuous, such as architecture and accountancy. All these professions had achieved registration in Victoria by 1900. **Engineering** had been taught at the University of Melbourne since 1862, but it was not until the twentieth century that courses in architecture developed, first in technical colleges and eventually in universities. From the beginning, professions mobilised themselves in their defence against quacks and impostors through associations or institutes. Some of these, like the early medical societies, were originally formed for scientific purposes, such as the presentation of papers on clinical topics; but their role was always political as well, since recognition by the circle of eminent practitioners who acted as 'honoraries' in the public hospitals was always the gateway to professional success. By the late nineteenth century the younger generation of Australian-born and Australian-trained doctors had formed branches of the British Medical Association and were adopting a more militant stance in defence of their professional status. By the early twentieth century a degree of specialisation had developed, as doctors formed Colleges of Surgeons (1928) and Physicians (1938), and Obstetricians and Gynaecologists (1929). Barristers, perhaps the most fiercely independent professionals, were loosely affiliated through a Bar Council; in spite of the efforts of reformers to unify the profession, they resisted any association with the mass of solicitors, whose collective interests were pursued through Law Institutes.

Progress associations

The professions, especially the most prestigious and traditional ones such as law and medicine, were once very much a family affair. Of Australian-born doctors commencing practice in Melbourne during the 1880s, three-quarters were themselves the sons of professional men, mainly doctors. Where entry to the profession was through indenture as an articled clerk or pupil, family connections were also important, as they were in obtaining business. 'As nearly every attorney has a son or a son-in-law at the bar, parental affection has much to do with the distribution of business', one young lawyer ruefully observed. The history of the professions, especially in the early twentieth century, is full of famous dynasties, such as the legal **Duffys**, **Windeyers**, **Streets**, Starkes, and **Evatts**. Women made their way only slowly into the 'learned professions', although they were strongly represented in the 'lesser professions' such as teaching and nursing. The first women were admitted to the University of Melbourne medical school in the late 1880s, but women doctors were long confined to those branches of the profession, such as gynaecology and paediatrics, which accorded with their traditional roles. **Sectarianism** was also a strong, though subterranean, force in the recruitment of the professions. Elite professionals could become rich men. By the early twentieth century, leading barristers or surgeons commanded incomes of £3000, or almost 20 times a working man's wage, although incomes of £500–1000 were closer to the norm among suburban solicitors and GPs, engineers, and accountants. Lawyers, doctors, and even bank managers enjoyed particular prestige in country towns in the absence of a landed class on the English model.

In the course of the twentieth century the list of occupations claiming professional status has grown prodigiously. The proportion of the Australian workforce in 'upper professional' occupations grew from 1.7 per cent in 1911 to 4.4 per cent in 1981, most of that growth occurring since World War II. Professional qualifications carried status, even if they did not always bring wealth. In 1966 a Sydney sociologist asked people to rank a list of 100 common occupations. The highest scores went, in order, to doctors, university professors, solicitors, architects, professional engineers, company directors, dentists, veterinarians, and clergymen. But the professions have also been enlarged as old occupations have been professionalised and as new professions have emerged in response to the need for more specialised expertise. Almoners have been turned into professional social workers. Physiotherapy emerged, originally to meet the challenge of rehabilitating wounded soldiers, and then car-accident victims and footballers. Nurses have turned themselves from a form of menial service into self-conscious professionals. Soon masseurs became chiropractors, chiropodists became podiatrists, and short-order cooks won diplomas in hamburgerology. In 1964 an American sociologist anticipated the trend when he jocularly entitled an article, 'The Professionalisation of Everyone'. Between 1911 and 1981 the proportion of the workforce in these mainly new, feminised 'lower professions' grew from 3.1 to 10.3 per cent.

The English historian Harold Perkin sees this trend, *The Rise of Professional Society* (1989), as one of the hallmarks of twentieth-century society, although, as he suggests, it is a trend that has weakened since the 1980s as the professional 'service' ethic has come into collision with the 'enterprise' ethic of free-market capitalism. In the 1990s professional registration and protection, along with other forms of restrictive practice, have been subjected to a more rigorous scrutiny, as for example in the 1995 Victorian report, *Reforming the Legal Profession*, though without as yet dislodging the upper professionals from their powerful position in Australian society.

Since tradition is a key component of the professional mystique, practitioners have been keen, though often uncritical, custodians of their history. Tony Pensabene, *The Rise of the Medical Practitioner in Victoria* (1980), and Evan Willis, *Medical Dominance* (1983), are the best historical introductions to the professionalisation of medicine. John and Judy Mackinolty in *A Century Downtown* (1991) view the NSW legal profession through the history of the University of Sydney Law School. J.M. **Freeland**, *The Making of a Profession* (1971), surveys the architectural profession. Writing one's history has often been an important phase in establishing or redefining a profession, as Bob and Judith Bessant's study of recent nursing history, *The Growth of a Profession* (1991), shows. Yet 'the rise of professional society' in Australia has still to find its historian. Much has been written about the Australian working class, and almost as much about sections of the 'ruling class', such as squatters or businessmen, but, as John Rickard noted in *HS* (1981), little has been written about professionals collectively as professionals. Where they do appear in general histories, the historians often seem unsure how to deal with them. Sometimes they are **heroes**—doctors and engineers cleaning up slums, lawyers fighting for the rights of oppressed minorities; and sometimes they are villains—stooges and lackeys of the ruling class. Any list of radical heroes—from Dr Redfern to Bertram Wainer and Fred **Hollows**, and from Daniel **Deniehy** to Gough **Whitlam**—would include its quota of professionals. Yet professionals have also been prominent among the forces of conservatism. While a minority of radical doctors has belonged to the Doctors Reform Society, the majority has affiliated with the more conservative Australian branch of the British Medical Association and its successor, the **Australian Medical Association** (1962). Yet, in the power structure of Australia, these ideological differences were perhaps less significant than we suppose. After all, Evatt and Menzies, Whitlam and Kerr, were class enemies only by proxy; more significant, perhaps, were the professional loyalties, and rivalries, that they shared.

GRAEME DAVISON

Progress associations were voluntary non-political bodies formed from among local residents in order to press for the improvement of basic services and community facilities in their own neighbourhoods. The first associations were formed in the early 1910s, often among ex-servicemen pioneering new suburbs in Melbourne's west, but their heyday was the late 1940s and 1950s when the marriage and baby boom following World War II created a new surge of suburban expansion. Young married couples, often owner-builders, were living in garages or half-completed houses along unmade streets. Progress associations sought to exert collective strength in support of their aspirations for better roads, schools, pre-schools, transport facilities, parks, and other recreational facilities, or to agitate against some community detriment, such as an abattoir or aircraft noise. In some neighbourhoods they also built Community or Progress Halls. Diane Sydenham, whose *Windows on Nunawading* (1990) contains a valuable discussion of their organisation and role, argues that they declined from the late 1960s when local community concerns swung from development to conservation, and from a focus on community-building to a concern with specific issues.

GD

Progressivism, a political and social movement of American origin, strongly influenced Australian intellectuals, politicians, and public administrators between the 1890s and the 1920s, although the name 'progressive' was less frequently used here. The American Progressives believed that 'science' and 'efficiency' should be the watchwords of reform, and they developed an ambitious program extending from national parks to kindergartens, and from town planning to 'scientific motherhood'. In the debate unleashed by Darwin's theories over the relative influence of nature and nurture on human development, the Progressives were firmly on the side of nurture (see Bacchi in *HS*, 1980), a stance which distanced them and their Australian followers from the more radical **eugenic** ideas gaining ground in Europe. Support for progressive ideas was strongest among the professional middle classes who parted company with classical liberals in their belief in a more extensive use of state power. Many of its ideals found expression through the Deakinite wing of the **Liberal Party**. Michael **Roe's** *Nine Australian Progressives* (1984) drew a collective portrait of some prominent Australian progressives, including William Jethro **Brown**, James **Barrett**, and A.B. **Piddington**, and stressed their intellectual affiliations, not only with democratic liberalism, but—more sinisterly—with European vitalism and fascism. Graeme Davison (in Peter Williams, ed., *Social Process and the City*, 1983) has delineated the progressive contribution to urban reform in early-twentieth-century Melbourne.

GD

Prospecting is searching for minerals in the hope of locating a deposit with the potential or prospect of profitable exploitation. Thus a mineral seeker is known as a 'prospector', a mineral find is a 'prospect', and a 'prospectus' is a document issued by a company to raise working capital. The term derives from the USA and was popularised in Australia during the 1850s **gold rushes**. Geoffrey **Blainey** in *The Rush That Never Ended* (1963) showed most of Australia's major nineteenth-century mineral discoveries were made by prospectors. His 'Theory of Mineral Discovery' (*EHR*, 1970)

suggested these finds were less 'accidental' than commonly imagined and were often linked to economic conditions and other factors. Before modern **mining** clashed with **Aboriginal cultural ownership** and the **environment**, prospecting was a somewhat romantic pursuit that created vast wealth, but not always for the prospector. 'Paddy' **Hannan** made little from Kalgoorlie's gold, while Charles **Rasp** earned a fortune from **Broken Hill**. Prospectors were often skilled in bushcraft, like Campbell Miles, discoverer of Qld's Mt Isa in 1923, and James 'Philosopher' Smith, who found the richest tin-mine in the world at Mount Bischoff, Tasmania, in 1871. The discoverers of Mt Morgan, Qld, in 1882 were gamblers who searched where others passed by. Some prospectors, like Harold **Lasseter**, were dreamers; others, like Edward **Hargraves**, were tricksters. Most were losers, and before the 1930s most were also amateurs, capable of identifying only common, easily observed minerals. In 1946 the Commonwealth Bureau of Mineral Resources supported a new era of scientific prospecting by companies using such techniques as geological and geophysical surveying, geochemistry, seismic data, aerial mapping and satellite photography, and metal detectors. The Hamersley iron ore discovery by Lang **Hancock** is a modern exception.

DC

Prostitution in its narrowest sense refers to the sale or barter of sexual services on a commercial basis. In this sense, it has provided an important occupation for women (and some men) in Australia since the arrival of the First Fleet. However, prostitution has also assumed a rhetorical and symbolic significance far beyond its importance to the history of women's work: the idea of prostitution has been used as a term of abuse and as a metaphor for corruption; as a gauge of the worth of colonial women and, by extension, colonial society; and as an instrument of social control. Prostitutes and prostitution have also been major targets of religious, social, and health reformers as well as important elements in a number of criminal networks.

It is a conventional wisdom that prostitution is the oldest profession and that it has existed in all societies in all times. The case of Aboriginal society before the European invasion refutes the latter claim. As far as we know, prostitution, in the sense of the commercial exchange of sexual services, did not exist in traditional Aboriginal society. The earliest hints we have of commercialised sex are with the **Macassan** fishermen who visited the northern shores of Australia from at least the 1670s.

Feminist historians have argued that prostitution was an integral part of the social and economic system of the early **convict** colonies. According to Anne **Summers** in her influential book, *Damned Whores and God's Police* (1975), this amounted to a system of 'enforced whoredom': prostitution provided one of the few economic options for women, who supplied a high level of demand for sexual services in a disproportionately male population. Deborah Oxley, in her account of convict women in Stephen Nicholas and Peter Shergold (eds), *Convict Workers* (1988), identifies prostitution as a structural part of the capitalist patriarchy that characterised the colonising society.

While prostitution of European women flourished in the penal settlements, wherever the white colonisers intruded on Aboriginal lands, sexual contact between white men and black women occurred soon after. In the aftermath of dispossession, Aboriginal women were often left with little choice but to engage in sexual barter in order to survive as individuals and to contribute to the survival of their kin. They formed the pivot of what Deborah Bird Rose in *Hidden Histories* (1991) calls 'an economy of sex'.

It was not just Aboriginal women who were engaged to satisfy the lusts of men in the North. C.D. Sissons, Su-Jane Hunt, Clive Moore, Raymond Evans, and Raelene Davidson have investigated the involvement of Japanese and European brothel-keepers and sex workers in northern Australia in the nineteenth century, especially in ports and mining centres. The more southerly the location, the greater proportion found of Australian and European women, and the fewer number of Japanese. Officials generally tolerated prostitution in mining centres, especially in more remote locations. This attitude persisted into the late twentieth century and found its most notorious expression in Hay Street, Kalgoorlie, where the brothels were run under virtual police supervision until the 1990s.

The sale of sexual services was not, however, simply a product of the sex imbalance in convict society or on the frontiers. On the contrary, prostitution flourished even where the sex ratios were more evenly matched. A double standard of morality which valued female chastity and tolerated male promiscuity, combined with limited work opportunities for women, ensured that prostitution operated in all Australian cities and towns throughout the nineteenth and twentieth centuries. As Kay Daniels and other contributors to *So Much Hard Work: Prostitution in Australian History* (1984) have shown, urban prostitution caused increasing concern to colonial authorities for reasons both of health and of social order. These concerns led to legislative changes in the late nineteenth and early twentieth centuries aimed at reducing the visibility of prostitutes and regulating their health. Such issues continued to influence official treatment of prostitution in the twentieth century, especially during times of war. Hilary Golder and Judith Allen have argued ('Prostitution in New South Wales 1870–1930: Restructuring an Industry', *Refractory Girl*, 1979–80) that these legislative changes led to the proletarianisation of sex workers, who were increasingly vulnerable to harassment from police and criminals. It is only since the 1980s that agitation from sex workers, feminists, and other civil liberties groups has seen serious re-evaluation of the legal status of prostitution. These initiatives and their results are surveyed by Roberta Perkins et al. in *Sex Work, Sex Workers in Australia* (1994), and by Barbara Sullivan in *The Politics of Sex* (1997).

RAELENE FRANCES

Protection of local production of goods by **tariff** barriers was national policy from the early years of the Common-

wealth until the 1980s. The policy was first adopted in Victoria in the 1860s, where it was a central plank in the liberal program, supported by farmers seeking protection from cereal imports and by urban workers and gold-diggers who hoped for employment in **manufacturing** industries. Its opponents were large landowners (producing wool for export rather than grain), importers, and bankers, all well-represented in the Legislative Council, which only agreed to the policy in 1867 after a prolonged dispute with the liberal Assembly which developed into a **constitutional** crisis.

Liberals in Britain were opponents of protection; the great liberal triumph in mid-century was the removal of import duties on grain, the last of the protected industries, and the establishment of *laissez-faire*. Hence in a British colony, protection was treated as a sort of heresy by supporters of free trade who regarded protectionists as merely ignorant or panderers to mob prejudice. What else could explain their defiance of the 'laws of political economy'? Indeed, those who took their liberalism seriously did have intellectual difficulties with the policy and they relied heavily on John Stuart Mill's concession that temporary protection was admissible to promote infant industries. But when protection became permanent, Mill warned that in Victoria, as everywhere else, it created vested interests which were the enemy of the common good. The protectionists came to rest their case on a proto-nationalism: it might in the abstract be best for each country to produce what it could most efficiently and trade with other countries for the rest, but if this kept Australia a sheepwalk, it would not have the industrial strength to defend itself or the diversity of employment to occupy an intelligent and resourceful people. David **Syme**, the editor of the *Age*, gave a fully worked defence of protection in *Outlines of an Industrial Science* (1876), which challenged the *laissez-faire* assumption that the state had no right in economic affairs to protect the common good. After a cautious endorsement of protection in the early 1860s, Syme's *Age* came to treat it as an article of faith. The longest and most bitter newspaper war in the nineteenth century was between the protectionist *Age* and the free-trade *Argus*. The pamphlet war on the issue is assessed in Craufurd D.W. Goodwin, *Economic Enquiry in Australia* (1966).

NSW, with some occasional aberrations, kept to the British policy of free trade, which did not deprive it of a manufacturing industry. Since the differences in industrial development between the two colonies were so slight, the dispute between them over which had the better policy was more bitter, and extended beyond the counting of factories and jobs to the numbers of lunatics and suicides. The dispute over the effects of the Victorian tariff is now carried on by historians. Clearly protection was not as crucial to the establishment of manufacturing as its proponents claimed, but manufacturing may have developed sooner and have been biased towards labour-intensive industries. The debate is assessed in Stuart Macintyre's study of Syme in *A Colonial Liberalism* (1991).

One of the reasons NSW could maintain free trade was that its ample land revenue did not oblige it to look for new sources of **taxation**. Tariffs, so long as they are not prohibitive, raise revenue. Noel **Butlin** noted the correlation in Victoria between government deficits and the rise in protection levels. The raising of revenue was certainly a motive for the imposition of tariffs, but Butlin appeared to imply that there were no genuine protectionists, for which he was justly rebuked by G.D. Patterson, *The Tariff in the Australian Colonies 1856–1900* (1968), who nevertheless concedes that the 1892 increase in the Victorian tariff, the last of eight increases, was prompted solely by the need for revenue. The raising of revenue was a more prominent consideration in the adoption of protection in the smaller colonies. The organised protectionists were much weaker than in Victoria and the levels of protection adopted were not as high.

When NSW faced financial difficulties in the 1890s it remained true to free trade, which was actually brought to purer form by the abolition of duties on all but three items and the raising of revenue by direct taxes on land and income. This was strenuously opposed by the Legislative Council, where protection was embraced as a better alternative to the taxing of wealth. Protection thus came to wear a conservative aspect in NSW, the opposite of Victoria. It did have genuine supporters in NSW, chiefly in the country, where the growing agriculture sector, a late developer in this colony, was looking for protection against grain imports.

That the largest colony was committed against protection, the policy adopted in various degrees by the rest, was a huge obstacle to **Federation**. Supporters of free trade in NSW had to assume that the policy of the new nation would be protectionist, for which the only compensation would be the operation of free trade between the colonies. But the issue was still vigorously fought out in the new arena. The two major parties at the first federal elections were free-traders and protectionists, with the latter securing a narrow victory, though not a parliamentary majority. The first federal tariff in 1902 was a compromise: designed to raise revenue but with protection to industries already established. The Labor Party was neutral on the tariff issue until the protectionists under **Deakin** developed the doctrine of **New Protection** by which industries were only to receive protection if they paid fair and reasonable wages to their employees. With Labor support, the Deakin government established the first protectionist tariff in 1908. When the protectionists and free-traders coalesced in 1909 to fight the Labor Party, the free-traders were obliged to drop their objection to protection, which became one of the settled policies of the nation and regarded as essential to nation-building. Keith **Hancock** wrote in *Australia* (1930): 'Protection … has been more than a policy: it has been a faith and a dogma … interwoven with almost every strand of Australia's democratic nationalism.'

In the 1920s a new political force, the Country Party (**National Party**), challenged this consensus. When farmers were establishing themselves, they needed protection from grain imports; once they were fully supplying the local market and relying increasingly on export sales, protection of local manufacturing raised their costs. The Country Party's challenge was short-lived; it formed coalition governments with the non-Labor parties and, instead of securing a reduction in tariffs, it gained protection for its own supporters in the form of subsidies, grants, and state-supported marketing schemes. This was the policy of protection-all-round.

Opposition to protection was left to academic economists who, knowing outright opposition to the policy was fruitless, urged caution in its application. The most notable academic defence of the policy was propounded by J.B. Brigden as chair of an official inquiry into the tariff in 1929. He argued that it promoted employment in manufacturing at wage levels acceptable to Australians and attractive to migrants. Without it, there was no prospect of Australia's population continuing to grow, since rural production had reached its physical limits. The cost which it imposed on rural producers was a justifiable redistribution of income. But Brigden, like his colleagues, wanted the tariff applied cautiously and warned there was a point beyond which it was counter-productive. The **Scullin** government ignored the warning and rushed through large increases in the tariff as a response to the **Depression**. The **Lyons** government that replaced it at the end of 1931 modified the tariff to provide for **imperial preference** but did little to reduce protection in a world economy that had abandoned free trade.

After World War II Australia did not follow the rest of the developed world in reducing levels of protection. In its eyes it was still developing and needed to promote a larger manufacturing sector. The policy of protection-all-round was carried to its ultimate just prior to its demise. Trade policy from 1956 to 1971 was in the hands of John **McEwen**, leader of the Country Party, who protected manufacturing so enthusiastically that he could collect from it large sums to fund his own party's election expenses.

McEwen met his nemesis in Alf Rattigan, from 1963 the chair of the Tariff Board, a body established to give independent advice on tariff levels. Rattigan used this independence to mount a crusade for free trade by highlighting in the board's reports the costs of protection. The work of the economists in the board was picked up by a new generation of economic commentators in the press and by Gough **Whitlam**, the leader of the Labor opposition, who now saw protection not as a preserver of jobs but of the business interests which backed his opponents. As prime minister in 1973, Whitlam made the first attack on the hallowed policy by a 25-per-cent across-the-board tariff cut.

The final attack on protection was launched by the proponents of 'economic rationalism' or neo-classical economics. After a bitter struggle, they converted the Liberal and National parties in the 1980s. The Labor Party at first rejected these doctrines, but the **Hawke** and **Keating** governments succumbed and it was they who carried through the abandonment of protection. The growing internationalisation of the economy and the revival of the General Agreement on Trade and Tariffs in the late 1980s were important external factors. Only a few industries still enjoy tariff protection—motor vehicles and clothing, textiles, and footwear—and the major parties argue over only how rapidly it should be phased out. This reversal of national policy has been traced by Paul Kelly in *The End of Certainty* (1992).

Hancock wrote that the very word *protection* appealed to Australians 'because they believe in their hearts that both their enjoyments and their existence need to be protected against extraordinary dangers'. Protection was part of a broader mindset, now sometimes called protectionism, which included the **White Australia** policy and wage regulation. For Kelly these are now all equally discredited. Protection is not nation-building but xenophobia. However, it did create a large manufacturing sector, the costs of which are debated in Rodney Maddock and Ian McLean (eds), *The Australian Economy in the Long Run* (1987).

JOHN HIRST

Public history is the term, first coined in the USA, and adopted by Australian historians since the mid-1980s, to describe the practice of history by academically trained historians working for public agencies or as freelancers outside the universities. There had been public historians in Australia long before the term was coined: Charles **Bean** and Geoffrey **Blainey** were notable examples. In the 1960s, as the universities expanded, the attention of academic historians had turned inward as they developed their own professional systems of specialisation and accreditation, and strengthened links with the international academic community. The introduction of the term *public history* a decade later signified the distance which had opened up between the academy and the Australian public, and expressed a determination to bridge it.

In the 1970s, as university expansion began to wane, many of the ablest history graduates sought employment as **heritage** advisers, **museum** curators, and writers of **commissioned histories**. The environmental movement had stimulated a new interest in historic environments, buildings, and objects and a demand for new kinds of historical interpretation and writing. Often, though not always, public history meant history performed in public employment or at public expense: the heritage and cultural bureaucracies of the state and federal governments were probably the largest employers of young historians. Non-academic employment grew during the late 1970s, but it was not until the 1980s that the movement found institutional expression through the formation of professional historians' associations in SA, 1981; Victoria 1983 (as part of the History Institute of Victoria; self-determining from 1991); NSW, 1985; Qld, 1990; WA, 1989; and Tasmania, 1992. By the mid-1990s their combined membership was approaching 400. In an effort to raise the public image and remuneration of professional historians, they drew up codes of professional ethics and scales of remuneration, and voiced their members' concerns with freedom of archival access and the protection of authorial copyright. Sometimes they did battle with rival professionals, such as architects and archaeologists, for fair shares of the heritage business.

Public historians are often women; the fight for professional recognition has been, in part, a fight for gender equality. A regular feature of the NSW Professional Historians' Association newsletter was a satirical column recounting the adventures of the fictional 'Phyllis Phame, Girl Historian'. When Phyllis's adversary was not a moonlighting male academic, he was likely to be a male journalist or architect, for the professional historians' battle to secure contracts and commissions was often a battle to get the male businesspeople and government officials who commissioned historical work to select an academically trained woman historian, often in part-time employment, rather than a male non-historian with impressive paper credentials or a well-recognised journalist's byline.

Although the links between the universities and the professional associations were sometimes close, half a decade passed before the universities registered the changed employment market for historians through the establishment of new graduate programs in public or applied history. The first, at Monash University and the University of Technology, Sydney, were established in the Bicentennial year, 1988. Other programs began at Murdoch University in 1991; the University of Queensland in 1994; University of Sydney in 1994; and the University of Adelaide in 1996. In 1989 the visit of Philip Cantelon of History Associates, a Washington-based consultancy firm, became the focus for the first conference of public historians, held in Melbourne under the auspices of the History Institute, Victoria. In 1991 *AHS* recognised the movement with a special issue entitled 'Packaging the Past: Public Histories', and in 1992 the Professional Historians' Association of New South Wales launched *Public History Review*, with articles on a wide range of public history topics, from historic buildings and landscapes to Aboriginal history and historical museums.

Australian public historians, argues Graeme Davison (*AHS*, 1991), drew inspiration from at least three international paradigms. The American public history movement sees the historian as a disinterested expert at the service of the public, putting his or her skills in historical analysis to work as one of a team of professional advisers or consultants. This model, which resonates strongly with American concepts of public interest, was grounded in a liberal consensus model of society and a pragmatic conception of social reform. Among Australian historians, it competed with another equally influential conception of popular historical activity, that offered by the British people's history movement associated with Ruskin College, Oxford, and the *History Workshop Journal*. People's history assumes a society where conflict and social injustice are the norm; where historical judgments are inseparable from value judgments; and where the historian adopts the vantage-point of an advocate for history's losers, rather than the stance of an impartial expert. Less commonly invoked was a third model, that of applied history—the brave attempt of some American historians to apply historical analogies to the solution of public policy dilemmas. By plotting historical trends, or analysing the conduct of old battles, applied historians, it was argued, might improve the analytical skills of present-day decison-makers. Australian historians such as Noel **Butlin**, Hugh **Stretton** and D.J. **Mulvaney** have often played a vigorous and influential role in debates on public policy, but more often as public intellectuals—disinterested writers with a public conscience—than as public historians.

Public history also sought to enhance communication between historians and the general public. 'Commitment to the idea of public history is a commitment to a concern with audience, and an awareness of the complex relationship between audience, historical practice and institutional context', declared the editors of *Public History Review* in their first issue. Within the universities, they noted, historians had become more concerned with issues of textual and visual communication; public historians would seek to bring history to the new audiences created by electronic communication.

The 1990s brought fresh challenges to the role of the public historian. In relations with potential clients, historians often portrayed themselves as objective experts, yet among themselves they were unashamed relativists. Historians who had read their Foucault and Derrida were all too conscious of the politics of knowledge; but their employers were baffled when the 'expert' turned out to be the bearer of just another point of view. When Ann McGrath, employed as a consultant on the inquiry into Aboriginal deaths in custody, asked to attend a conference 'to become familiar with the most up-to-date debates relating to Aborigines and justice', her employer declined to support her on the ground that '"debates" or "controversies" would not be of any interest to the Commission; they were only concerned with "incontrovertable facts", nothing in dispute'(*Public History Review*, 1994). In a time of rapid change, ambitious managers were also inclined to place a low value on history, regarding corporate or community memory only as a brake on innovation. So when the public historian is called in, it is often to carry out a limited commemorative brief, to obituarise the past, rather than to engage in the kind of wider, critical reflection that public historians saw as their distinctive contribution. Since the 1980s the winding back of the public sector, and of cultural agencies such as the Australian Heritage Commission, has further limited the scope for the employment of public historians. Victoria has terminated the position of state historian, although the foundation of the **History Council of New South Wales** is a more hopeful sign. It is hard to be a public historian unless the public is prepared to pay for your services; and harder still when the very idea of public good is subverted by doctrines of privatisation and the assertion of private over public interests.

GRAEME DAVISON

Public opinion polls, see **Polls, public opinion**

Public service, see **Bureaucracy**

Public works, see **State socialism**

Publishing, see **Books**

Pubs have played a major role in the creation of Australian culture. They have been the centres of neighbourhood social activity, and the focus of an imagined unique **national identity**.

Pub is short for *public house*, meaning a place licensed to sell alcoholic liquor to the passing trade. In England pubs were either inns, providing accommodation and food to wealthy travellers; or taverns, providing only wine and spirits to the local neighbourhood; or alehouses, selling only beer to a poorer clientele. Drinkers were served in the taproom, a large single room furnished with trestle tables and benches. Beer, frequently brewed on the premises, was ladled from a barrel into mugs and carried to the taproom by servants of the household, who treated the customers as guests of the landlord. Men, women, and children drank, either on the premises or by filling a jug to take home or into the street. Changes in the law and the development of gin shops in the early nineteenth century transformed this relationship. Gin shops brought in the bar, a counter from behind which bottles of gin were sold.

The three distinctive types of public house fused in the Australian colonies to become a new institution, created in large part by government regulations. First, these separated the sale of beer from its brewing, and required all licensees to sell both beer and spirits. The colonial public house thus provided customers with a choice of drinks; patronage was not determined by the type of drink available, but the kind of service that was provided or the proximity of the pub to home or work. A further requirement in 1830 made licensed houses provide accommodation for guests and separated the retailing of other household goods from that of liquor. From now on licensed premises sold all kinds of **alcohol** to the passing street trade, and always had rooms available to anyone wishing to stay.

The large single taproom had also been differentiated into rooms for different clientele, and the single long counter, the bar, became the space behind which staff now served the public. No longer guests of the landlord, they had become customers; they drank either in the saloon bar, the lounge, the private bar, or the public bar, which was always closest to the street. This was 'the pub' as subsequent generations of Australians came to know it. This history was told in J.M. **Freeland**, *The Australian Pub* (1966), which is still the only history of pubs in Australia. Afterwards, with the transformation wrought by the **motor car**, came the gargantuan beer barns of the suburbs and the drive-in bottle shops. The pub has been shaped in part by patterns of work and leisure, in part by the breweries which, through ownership, contract or other arrangements, bound pubs to sell their products.

Pubs spearheaded settlement into previously uncolonised parts of the continent. Many of these were family businesses. Keeping a pub or selling sly-grog was a means of livelihood for women when other avenues of employment were not available. Many of them were cleaning and cooking staff. Some began to serve behind the bar. Over time 'the barmaid' became a popular figure of Australian folklore.

This history has been discussed in Diane Kirkby, *Barmaids: A History of Women's Work in Pubs* (1997).

Pubs proliferated in the colonies: in the inner suburbs of the cities there was a pub on every corner and several in between. In isolated rural areas they provided the nucleus of social life. Over the course of the nineteenth century, as cities grew larger, public drinking practices changed and concerns about public drunkenness grew. The idea that women might drink in a public bar became unacceptable and finally, at the turn of the century, laws were passed by state legislatures which restricted hours of trading and prevented a woman working there unless she was a member of the licensee's immediate family. These laws also confirmed and reinforced the **masculinity** of pub culture. Aboriginal people were also forbidden to drink in pubs, through legislation which stayed in place in most states until the 1960s.

Pubs therefore became identified with a quintessentially Australian national identity that was both racially and sexually specific. By the middle of the twentieth century they were being celebrated in popular culture: excessive drinking in the company of other (white) men at the pub became a measure of 'the Australian way of life'. Having to close at 6 p.m., pubs were designed to serve drinks at a rapid rate during the **six o'clock swill**; walls were often tiled inside and out so that the mess could be more readily cleaned up. Feminists in the 1970s attacked this culture as they demanded the right for women to drink in the public bar. By then pubs were already on the decline as motels provided low-cost accommodation and licensed clubs provided more luxurious drinking facilities. Pubs responded by transforming bars into bistros and restaurants, made possible by the easing of restrictions on drinking hours. By the 1990s the loss of old-style pubs to Australian culture was frequently lamented in the daily press. (See also **Temperance**.)

DIANE KIRKBY

Pure merino, or simply *merino*, was a term in use at least by the 1820s to describe one who had come to Australia from Britain as a free settler rather than as a convict. Later the term also applied to the descendants of pure merinos. The name is taken from the breed of fine-wool sheep intro-duced into NSW from 1797 that was prized over the otherwise inferior coarse-grade wool of sheep in the colony. Pure merinos, like **exclusives**, prided themselves on having no 'taint' of convict blood. They affected genteel social pretensions and set themselves apart from the convict and **emancipist** classes, to whom they believed themselves superior, and as a result were resented and mocked by those of **currency** status. In the earliest settled districts of eastern Australia, *pure merino* came to mean a member of a set of particularly wealthy, well-connected **pastoralists** who were served by convict labour and whose grand lifestyle emulated that of American planters or the European landed gentry. They wielded considerable power in colonial parliaments and were the proposed parliamentary representatives of W.C. **Wentworth's 'bunyip aristocracy'**.

HD

Push was a word first used in Sydney in the early 1800s in reference to a group of people at a public sporting or theatrical event. In the later 1800s, it more commonly referred to a group or gang of **larrikins** who gathered on street corners in Sydney and Melbourne to harass passers-by and generally make a nuisance of themselves. Generally the word was preceded by the locale of the particular group—for example, the Woolloomooloo push or the Fitzroy push. Phrases such as 'the captain of the push' and 'the cuff and collar push' came into vogue in the 1890s and were common to poetry and fiction of the period, notably that of Henry **Lawson** and C.J. **Dennis**.

While these early uses alluded mainly to the element of physical force associated with the word, later uses of *push* implied a political or social movement, or a force of ideas. In the 1960s the 'Sydney Push' was the more popular name of the influential Sydney University Libertarian Society, which is the focus of Anne Coombs's study, *Sex and Anarchy* (1996). Its members, who included Germaine **Greer**, Robert **Hughes**, Clive James and Jill Kitson, were associated with the controversial *Oz* magazine. A later journal of early colonial social history, *The Push from the Bush*, was published 1978–88, and continued, retitled as *The Push*, until 1992.

HD

Q

Qantas, an acronym for Qld and NT Aerial Services, is an airline company founded at Longreach, Qld, in 1920 by Hudson Fysh and P.J. McGuinness, with W.A. Baird as mechanic, and registered in Brisbane. It began a government-subsidised service between Charleville and Cloncurry in 1922. Qantas Empire Airways Ltd launched Australia's first international flight in 1934, which flew from Brisbane to London in 13 days, and a regular round-the-world service operated from 1958. The company was acquired by the Commonwealth in 1947. Renamed Qantas Airways Ltd in 1967, it purchased a fleet of Boeing 747s in the 1970s and introduced the world's first 'business class' in 1979. John Gunn has written a history to 1970 in three volumes. Due to the federal government's two-airline policy, Qantas was barred from domestic flights until deregulation in 1990. In 1993 it merged with the domestic carrier Australian Airlines. In 1995, its 75th anniversary year, Qantas launched a commemorative history and was floated as a public company. It has formed a close relationship with British Airways, a principal shareholder. (See also **Aviation**.)

HD

Quadrant, a right-wing journal of literature and commentary, was established in Sydney in 1956 by Richard Krygier, with the Catholic poet James **McAuley** as its editor. A product of the Cold War, *Quadrant* was sponsored by the Association for Cultural Freedom, which was funded by the US government. As founding editor, McAuley gave space to writing that espoused intellectual freedom, challenging the Left intellectual tradition in Australia. McAuley's religious and classical convictions were hostile to the nineteenth-century ideologies of liberalism and romanticism. Subsequently *Quadrant* was supported by Clyde **Packer** and took on a closer alignment with **conservatism**. Later, under the editorship of Robert Manne (1989–97), it broadened its range to encompass a more progressive position on social issues, particularly on Aborigines. This was sharply reversed

under the editorship of Paddy McGuinness (1998–). Peter Coleman, a former editor, co-edited the collection *Quadrant: Twenty-Five Years* (1982).

HD

Queensland was created as a separate colony in 1859 from a straggling former convict settlement on the Brisbane River and the ever-expanding pastoral occupation of the Darling Downs, Warrego, Burnett, and Fitzroy districts. Successive waves of graziers, miners, and small farmers pushed the frontier steadily north and west until by the end of the nineteenth century an attempt had been made to claim Papua and exploit the islands of the South-West Pacific for Qld. Though officially self-governing from 1859, much of Qld's trade and development was in fact controlled from Sydney, Melbourne, or London, so it was more a branch office than a colony. Its size, remoteness, tropical location, and late development made for a raw, vigorous, unsophisticated version of the Australian experience. The most vibrant version of the **Australian Legend** had its roots in Qld's pastoral and mining industries. The most desperate of the clashes between capital and labour occurred at Barcaldine in 1891. It was in Qld that the Labor Party first achieved government, when Andrew Dawson formed the first Labour ministry in 1899, while some of the most bitter struggles between Aborigines and settlers occurred on remote mining fields from the Palmer River to Mount Isa and in the northern rainforest.

Although the attempt to sustain large-scale European settlement in the tropics fostered significant political and social innovations with a wide-ranging impact on the rest of Australia, the special problems created by that enterprise were not always understood or easily accommodated in the south. Just as Qld has produced the broadest version of the Australian accent, so it has also been the source of the most aggressively masculine versions of the politics of development and the work ethic, as well as the crudest forms of states' rights. Socially conservative attitudes, which from the mid–nineteenth century sought to end prostitution and inter-racial marriage, and refused to acknowledge the existence of sexual deviance or abortion, have resulted in countervailing forms of dishonesty and hypocrisy. Qld acquired a reputation as Australia's 'deep north', though in recent years the flow of tourists and retirees has lessened its isolation and improved understanding. Tension has never been far below the surface, however, especially as **Aboriginal land rights** have become part of the national agenda and as the claims of **conservation** against development and tourism come more sharply into focus.

Nineteenth-century pastoral expansion was followed by the discovery of gold and tin, which attracted miners (many of them Chinese) from the south and elsewhere. In the search for farmers and labour, other settlers were recruited in Denmark, Germany, Scandinavia, and Italy, as well as Britain and Ireland, and labour for the cane-fields in the coastal valleys was brought, often by unscrupulous traders, from the Pacific Islands. Local Aborigines were increasingly employed in beef production, agriculture, and coastal fisheries. By the early twentieth century, Qld had the most diverse and polyglot population of any of the Australian states, though Brisbane itself was comfortably and conservatively British and Irish. The tensions between the competing regional claims of its vast rural hinterland and Brisbane's staid, even backward, attempt at urban liberalism explain much of Qld's history.

For most of the 1890s it seemed possible that Qld might be excluded from the federation of the Australian colonies, despite the leading role played by Premier S.W. **Griffith** in drafting the Constitution of 1891. By 1901, however, Griffith had transformed the plantation economy by which sugar was produced into a cooperative model, allowing for the abolition of the **Pacific Island labour** that was regarded as anathema by the other colonies. Qld became a small man's frontier during the first half of the twentieth century, and a semblance of order and coherence was maintained by two powerful organisations: the **Australian Workers Union**, which held sway not only in the woolsheds of the interior and the cattle industry of the north, but in the labour-intensive sugar, maize, and dairying industries near the coast; and the Catholic Church, which commanded the allegiance of a more than one-third of the population in the 1920s. This alliance returned a succession of Labor governments through which the simple idealism of the 1890s, as expounded by William **Lane** and the Queensland *Worker*, was transformed in practice and carried into federal politics as the Australian Labor Party's socialisation objective in 1921. Under the leadership of T.J. **Ryan** and E.G. **Theodore**, Queensland Labor governments embarked on a series of state-owned enterprises in the 1920s, set up a government insurance office to pay workers' compensation, paid unemployment relief, and abolished the upper house of the state legislature in 1922. Later initiatives included the approval of subsidies to Catholic schools, and a free public hospital system financed by a state-run lottery. In part this was a reflection of the difficulties Qld now experienced in

attracting investment for the kind of infrastructure acquired by the more populous southern states prior to the borrowing constraints imposed by Federation and World War I, but as well, socialist rhetoric and militant unions discouraged investors. Though agriculture and mining continued to support the welfare provisions of the government, there was little room for expenditure on education or cultural development. Increasingly, services were run-down or became trapped in their own isolation.

World War II revealed the primitive level of investment in the far-flung parts of Qld. It also left visible marks, literally, in the form of air-raid shelters, air-strips, and all-weather roads, though not even the Americans succeeded in building a high-level bridge across the Burdekin River or a parallel set of rails between Brisbane and Cairns. Many Queenslanders believed that invasion was imminent and that the **Brisbane Line** would sacrifice them to the Japanese forces. There was effectively a military occupation, especially visible in Brisbane, Townsville, and further north. Significantly, a substantial proportion of the population of these northern areas was Aboriginal, Chinese, or of mixed Islander descent. For many years Qld carried the burden of finding resources to care for this diverse population, with its special needs. Because federal funding was based on Census figures and the Aboriginal people were not officially counted, the people of Qld paid dearly for national apathy, neglect, ignorance, or inability to face facts.

While the rest of Australia tried to industrialise and modernise after World War II, Qld remained dependent on inefficient rural industries and industrially troubled mines. Much of the stimulus of postwar immigration passed Qld by. Italian migration had been encouraged from the 1890s as a way of providing much-needed labour on the cane-fields, but these migrants became a source of great anxiety during World War II when Italy was an enemy state, and many, both pro- and anti-Fascist, were interned. Tensions between Catholicism and communism in the labour movement, which produced the **Split** of 1954, were complicated in Qld by the additional challenge of Italian Catholicism to a deeply entrenched and powerful Irish Catholic conservatism. The Split in Qld resulted in a new political party, the Queensland Labour Party, led by Vince **Gair**, which merged after a while with the **Democratic Labor Party**. It also destroyed the long-standing domination of Queensland politics by the Australian Labor Party. At the same time, mechanisation in agriculture greatly lessened the need for labour in the cane-fields and on the wharves. Power passed from the trade unions in most coastal centres to local businesspeople and farmers, and the Country Party, later renamed the **National Party**, strengthened its position to dominate the coalition governments elected after 1957. Rural Qld, revitalised by demand for the twentieth-century minerals—coal, oil, uranium, and bauxite—maintained its hold on politics through a gerrymander originally designed to favour the AWU, but which now maximised the conservative vote. Though Brisbane was transformed into a lively modern city—no longer a branch office, but able in its own right to command the Commonwealth Games and a World Expo in the 1980s—it remained a remote source of suspect ideas to the rest of the state.

Since the 1950s, Qld has seen the return of the kind of development it experienced before Federation, with an emphasis on mining and associated industries. Retirees, encouraged by the abolition of death duties, came from the south to strengthen a conservative element in the population, while developments associated with the growing holiday traffic made for a kind of brash, lively modernity. Money for development—new mining projects, canal-style luxury housing on the Gold Coast, new airports and hotels at Barrier Reef resorts—flowed into Qld, as did controversial American and Japanese entrepreneurs, and a great many small-time operators. As premier for 19 years, Joh **Bjelke-Petersen** brought to politics the pragmatism and energy with which he had cleared brigalow scrub and flown crop-dusting planes. An old-fashioned **populist**, he played on Qld's sense of its own superiority and grievance at being seen as out of step with the rest of Australia. Traditional means of managing Qld's disparate interests—the bribe and the payback—also flourished.

Since 1 January 1860, when a Sydney syndicate secured preferential treatment in the matter of pastoral leases in the Burdekin Valley, entrepreneurs in Queensland politics have furthered their own interests for the greater good. Names like Macalister, Palmer, McIlwraith, Macrossan, and Philp were linked to land grants, railways, shipping facilities, and mining concessions. Labor politicians, it seems, were less successful entrepreneurs, as E.G. Theodore learnt at Mungana. By the 1980s, corruption involving drugs, prostitution, and the police at street level ran all the way through to the chief commissioner, the premier's office, and the Cabinet. During 1989 a commission of inquiry, headed by Tony Fitzgerald, hastened the defeat of the Bjelke-Petersen government, with the gaoling of several senior figures. Qld appeared to be undergoing modernisation at the hands of a new, young, university-educated, managerially slick Labor government. However, a **populist** reaction led by disgraced former federal Liberal candidate for Ipswich Pauline Hanson and her **One Nation** Party helped restore some of the more traditional rough values to Qld politics.

As in the late nineteenth century, when Qld was required to transform its sugar industry at the insistence of southern opinion, in the late twentieth century its mining and pastoral industries were at odds with federal moves towards Aboriginal land rights. The strength of the Aboriginal people in the north relates to their historic isolation, while some of Australia's greatest tourist attractions—the Barrier Reef, the rainforest and the beaches of the far north—survive only because of Qld's failure to develop earlier. Now it is environmental arguments about the protection of these resources that are balanced against a desire to exploit, develop, and possibly destroy them.

Because of its diversity, Qld has produced many local and regional histories by industrious amateurs and sophisticated scholars. The state centenary in 1959 saw the publication of *Triumph in the Tropics* by Raphael Cilento and Clem Lack, its title a clear statement of its celebration of white settlement. Ross Fitzgerald's two-volume state history (1982; 1984) explicitly challenged this view, while Ross Johnston's *The Call of the Land* (1982) is a thoughtful general history closely attuned to the importance of environmental factors. Jamie Walker, *Goss: A Political Biography* (1995), is a good bridge to the 1990s, while Margo Kingston's book on Pauline Hanson, *Off the Rails* (1999), gives a useful insight into a political style.

Beverley Kingston

Quick, John (1852–1932) was a poor boy made good, a second-order lawyer and politician, who entered the nationalist pantheon because of two signal contributions to **Federation**. He was a fervent nationalist and was allowed honorary membership of the **Australian Natives Association** because he arrived in Victoria from England when only two years old. His father died on the Bendigo goldfields, his mother remarried, and at the age of 10 he was earning his living. Quick moved from journalism into law and then politics. He was a delegate of the Bendigo Natives to the **Corowa** Conference on Federation in 1893. The novel plan for a new popular basis for Federation was embodied in a motion moved by him, though he may not have been its sole originator. He did much to bring it to public notice by lobbying in Sydney with the Federal League and George **Reid**, then leader of the opposition. At Corowa he met Robert **Garran**, with whom he collaborated to produce *The Annotated Constitution of the Australian Commonwealth* (1901), still the authoritative guide to the document's formation and containing a substantial history of the federal movement. Quick was knighted for his services to Federation on the day of the Commonwealth's inauguration; he was returned unopposed to the first parliament, but did not have a distinguished career there and increasingly dwelt on his part in Federation. L.E. Fredman (ed.), *Sir John Quick's Notebook* (1965), gathers some of his frequent reminiscences. His other historical works included *The History of Land Tenure in the Colony of Victoria* (1883) and *The Inauguration of Parliamentary Government in Victoria* (1886).

JH

Quong Tart, Mei (1850–1903), was an entrepreneur and philanthropist, notable among early **Chinese in Australia** for his social, cultural and economic integration into the European-Australian community. Quong Tart was born in Canton, China, and arrived in NSW in 1859, aged 9, with an uncle who took him to the Braidwood goldfields. He lived with an Anglican family, who converted him to Christianity. From local Scots he learned to speak English with a Scottish lilt and developed a love for the poetry of Robert Burns. Hard work and a talent for goldmining made him wealthy by 21, when he was naturalised. For a Chinese-born Australian when **White Australia** was becoming the norm, Quong enjoyed unusual acceptance. He was prominent in clubs and societies; raced horses, played cricket; was elected to an Oddfellows Lodge in 1871; and became a Freemason in 1885. In the 1880s and 1890s he ran restaurants and tea and silk shops in Sydney. Quong's imports of Chinese tea from 1881 created his second fortune, but he generously provided free 'feasts' for Sydney's poor. He published *A Plea for the Abolition of the Importation of Opium* (1887).

Quong became an unofficial Chinese ambassador after his intervention in various disputes, including the '*Afghan* riot' of 1888, when Chinese on the ship *Afghan* were prevented from landing in Sydney. He petitioned colonial premiers to consider 'equity, justice and brotherly love' in **immigration** policy. He returned to China several times and was made a mandarin in 1888. The highlight of many a Sydney social gathering was Quong in ceremonial dress, bubbling with Oriental charm and wit, then bursting forth with a rendition of 'Annie Laurie'. Sydney rallied to Quong's support after he was brutally bashed by an intruder in August 1902. Robert Travers wrote his biography, *Australian Mandarin* (1981), and Quong's English-born wife Margaret published *The Life of Quong Tart: Or How a Foreigner Succeeded in a British Community* (1911).

DC

R

RAAF, see **Royal Australian Air Force**

RAANC, see **Royal Australian Army Nursing Corps**

Rabbits, see **Pests**

Race relations have a wide meaning in today's **multi-cultural** Australia. However, until the 1940s Australians were predominantly of British and Irish descent, and from this dominant Anglo-Celtic position race relations in colonial and early-twentieth-century society meant maintaining their superiority over the indigenous population and controlling immigration from Asia and the Pacific Islands. The historical literature carries a similar emphasis. The two major texts are A.T. Yarwood and M.J. Knowling, *Race Relations in Australia: A History* (1982), and Andrew Markus, *Australian Race Relations 1788–1993* (1994).

Darwinian beliefs shaped perceptions of racial difference in the nineteenth century. Dispossessed of their lands and natural rights, indigenous Australians were marginalised within the European society, an embarrassment quite purposely lost from history. Until Charles **Rowley's** seminal three-volume study of *Aboriginal Policy and Practice* (1970–71), most literature on indigenous Australians remained the province of anthropologists. Rowley was followed by a series of historians in the 1970s and 1980s, particularly Henry **Reynolds**, Raymond Evans, Michael Christie, Lyndall Ryan, and Bob Reece. They saw the immigrants as invaders and frontier conflict as warfare. This interpretation of frontier history continues today, slowly retrieving knowledge of the early contact period, which has been shown to vary regionally. This 'conflict' interpretation has percolated into the school and tertiary curricula and is now a standard approach to the history of early settlement.

Writers such as Peter Read, Heather Goodall, Peggy Brock, Dawn May, Anna Haebich, and Ann McGrath, using documentary sources and oral testimony to give an indigenous voice, have partly restored a sense of 'agency' to show Aborigines as participants in shaping their lives. Their more regional approaches have helped to focus on the twentieth century, and on Aborigines institutionalised on missions and reserves. However, there still is a lack of stress on the way indigenous Australians have been incorporated into the capitalist economy: most Australian still see Aborigines and Torres Strait Islanders as outside the mainstream economy, society, and history. Indigenous Australians are increasingly using **autobiography** and narrative (see **Aboriginal narratives**) as a way of putting their views, but none has yet challenged the post-Rowley history of race relations.

Controlling and excluding Asian immigrants was a periodic theme in Australian history from the first antagonisms on the 1850s goldfields, renewed attempts in 1888 and the formulation of a whites-only Australian policy by several colonies in the 1890s, to the legislation of the new federal government in 1901. Relations with indigenous Australians were viewed quite differently from relations with Asians. Aborigines could be decimated and marginalised, but the remnant community would always remain in some form. The British settlers saw their island continent as able to be protected from incursions from Asia and the Pacific. Immigrants of European origin united against Asians for racial and economic reasons. **Chinese** were competitors for gold and soon moved into rural and urban industries. Other Asian groups—Indians, Sri Lankans, Japanese, Malays—more confined to northern Australia, impinged less on the national consciousness. Sandy Yarwood's detailed studies of Asian migration (1964, 1968) were the forerunners of regional studies by D.C.S. Sissom, Andrew Markus, Kathy Cronin, and Cathy May. The emphasis has been on the restrictive legislation and the Asian reaction. Very little has been written on Asian-Australians in the twentieth century. The same is true of Pacific Islanders.

Pacific Islanders entered Australia from the 1790s, first on board ships from Polynesia, then later from Melanesia as part of an organised labour trade into Qld from 1863 to 1904. There is a substantial literature on the Qld labour trade, which supplied mainly young Melanesian men as labourers to the pastoral, maritime, and sugar industries (see **Pacific Island labourers**). Just as with the literature on Aborigines, the emphasis is on the colonial period. Scholars such as Peter Corris, Kay Saunders, Ralph Shlomowitz, and Adrian Graves have written on the 'Kanaka era', which ended with forced deportation in 1906–08. Clive Moore, and particularly Trish Mercer and Carol Gistitin, have traced the community into the twentieth century. Four Islanders, Faith **Bandler**, Mabel Edmund, Noel Fatnowna, and Cristine Andrew have published substantial books about their own families. Racial discrimination, both by governments seeking to control the Islanders' working and private lives, and antagonism from other Australians against this black immigrant group, are central to the literature.

With the official abandonment and subsequent prohibition of racial discrimination in the second half of the twentieth century, the preoccupation with race shifted to ethnicity and culture. Within the official policies of multiculturalism and recognition of Aboriginal culture, the concepts have affirmative meanings, treating a separate ethnic identity as both a right and a national benefit. Much recent writing follows this semantic shift, treating race relations and cultural relations as negative and positive poles of Australian history; but the full implications have yet to be registered.

CLIVE MOORE

Radical nationalism combines national sentiment with radical politics. The combination can be traced back to early colonial anticipations of a new nation that would leave behind the evils of the Old World, but is usually seen to commence in the late nineteenth century when popular mobilisation coincided with imminent Australian nationhood. Joseph **Furphy's** description of his novel *Such Is Life* (1903)—'temper democratic, bias offensively Australian'—in a letter to his publisher in 1897 is emblematic of this radical nationalism, and it became the epigraph for a later generation of radical nationalists who created the journal *Overland* in 1954.

Radical nationalism has a strong mytho-historical component. Its late-nineteenth-century exponents celebrated the convicts, diggers, and bush workers as bearers of a tradition of egalitarian, masculine solidarity. Even as it was formulated by urban intellectuals caught up in the transition to industrial modernity, there was a clear nostalgic tone that is caught in Vance **Palmer's** retrospective account of *The Legend of the Nineties* (1954). Palmer's book appeared at a time when the Cold War, growing suburban affluence, and increasing influence of an international mass consumer culture threatened radical nationalism. Through such works as Russel **Ward's** *The Australian Legend* (1958), the historians associated with the **Old Left** attempted to restore continuity with an indigenous left tradition. That tradition faded as nationalism lost its radical connotations and radicalism became more international in its language and concerns, a

process fostered by the **New Left**; but it remains a strong theme in Australian historiography.

SM

Radio attracted many interests that imagined it operating in very different ways. Two visions of the technology competed: was radio to be a two-way, point-to-point process or a point-to-multipoint means of mass communication? Marconi had pursued the commercial application of his invention of radio telegraphy chiefly as a means of point-to-point maritime communication. In Australia, others interested in the two-way possibilities included experimenters and professional **engineers**, drawn to radio as a field of science and invention. However, radio traders, manufacturing and engineering companies, retail stores, newspaper, theatrical, and entertainment interests saw greater commercial possibilities in providing regular content on a point-to-multipoint basis. Prevailing on government to require more elaborate and more expensive transmitting equipment, the big business group effectively forced the hobbyists and amateurs from the field and radio became synonymous with broadcasting.

Government and politicians had their own interest in the technology. As early as 1925, the **Ryan** Labor government in Qld established its own radio station, 4QG, thereby creating a means of addressing voters that bypassed the press. Between 1926 and 1932, federal politicians achieved a *rapprochement* with the commercial interests which resulted in a public service broadcasting body, the **Australian Broadcasting Commission**, existing in an arm's-length relationship with the state, and a group of privately owned broadcasting stations, financed by selling air-time to advertisers. The Australian Broadcasting Corporation's formation in 1932 amalgamated capital city stations (including 4QG) that initially had little in common other than powerful transmitters. However, by 1935, it was fully functioning, operating two national radio networks. Meanwhile, commercial interests sought to create national markets for manufactured goods and services; in 1938 the Macquarie Network, founded on the model of American commercial national networking, was established.

By 1939, this transformation into a dual system of commercial and public service sectors was complete. This was later the pattern for aviation and television. The dual system for radio remained intact until 1975, when a third sector was established. In these years in particular, radio meant radio broadcasting, on a national or regional basis, with Australian society imagined as a single consumerist and political whole. Ian Mackay's *Broadcasting in Australia* (1957) deals with structure and ownership in this period.

The dominant feature of the period was the stability of the radio dual structure. It endured changes in station ownership, audience demographics, listener preferences, regulatory regimes, production patterns, and even in receiver technology. Where radio licences had once been easy to obtain, now, on a claim of technical scarcity, the Postmaster-General's Department refused to increase the number of transmitting frequencies on the air. Thus, residents of Sydney could listen to eight stations in 1975, the same number as in 1939. The period, especially 1939 to 1956, was radio's golden era, a time when radio was the sole domestic source of electronic information and entertainment. For the commercial stations, this meant that radio broadcasting was a profitable affair with none of the financial uncertainties of the 1920s and early 1930s. The high point of the radio listening week is dealt with in *The Golden Age of Australian Radio Drama* (1994) by Richard Lane.

While there was limited overlap between press and radio ownership, the dominant force in commercial radio was nevertheless the large advertising agencies that controlled the airwaves on behalf of major clients, and frequently forced individual radio stations to act as network affiliates for the purposes of national marketing. Always weaker in financial resources and popularity, the ABC complemented the commercial stations, catering to both the mass audience and to rural and high-culture minorities. It also performed a national ideological function with programs such as the broadcast of federal parliament and English for 'new Australians'. Ken **Inglis's** *This Is the ABC* (1983) is a lively account of its first 50 years.

Television caused a brief hiccup, taking control of radio's programming schedule, program genres, artists and personnel, many advertisers and, most especially, the family audience. However, by concentrating on particular segments within the listening public and switching to cheaper forms of content such as popular recorded music and talkback, radio soon achieved a profitable complementarity with television.

The closely controlled system of Australian radio began unravelling in the late 1960s, and from 1975 the duopoly was replaced by diversity. The technological arguments about scarcity of transmitting frequencies were abandoned and a large number of new AM and FM stations came on the air. In Sydney by 1997, there were at least 50 different radio services. While the new stations included both public service and commercial, most were based on the principle of community access. The community stations represented special-interest groups who marked themselves off through differences of language, religion, ethnicity, sexuality, age, geography, taste, hobby, and so on, and could be found broadcasting on a national, regional, and even local basis. Once again, radio broadcasting became increasingly low-budget, both because of the often minimal resources that new broadcasters could muster and because existing broadcasters faced the continued erosion of their audience. The limited pluralism evident in the previous period mushroomed so that the needs of Australia's increasingly multicultural population were both served and further fuelled by radio.

The best general guide to radio is *Radio in Australia* (1986) by John Potts. Lesley Johnson provides a sophisticated account of program content, especially performers' voices, in *The Unseen Voice: A Cultural Study of Early Australian Radio* (1986).

ALBERT MORAN

Railways harnessed the **energy** of steam and the smoothness of iron rails to ease and speed the carriage of people and goods across inland Australia. They influenced the fortunes of towns and regions; became the colonies' largest employers; transformed the relationship between town and country; sometimes influenced the fortunes of politicians and governments; and introduced new conceptions of distance, **time**, and comfort. In the twentieth century their significance declined, although they remain an important form of transport for freight and for suburban commuters.

Railways had appeared in Australia within a decade of the first great British railway boom of the 1840s. 'Without the means of internal communication no country can advance', declared the promoters of the Sydney Railway Company in 1851. 'The cheapest and incomparably the best description of roads that can be made are Railways.' The company experienced several setbacks before its first line, from Sydney to Parramatta, opened for regular service in 1855. In the meantime, the Hobson's Bay Railway Company had established the first Australian railway between Melbourne and its port for ocean-going vessels at Sandridge (Port Melbourne) in September 1854. Lines between cities and their ports, such as the similar line from Adelaide to Port Adelaide (1856), were highly profitable. Geoffrey **Blainey** argued in *The Tyranny of Distance* (1966) that they were perhaps the only services capable of returning the high costs of construction quickly enough to justify private operation. Early railway entrepreneurs recognised that Australia's sparse inland population made the economics of railways less favourable than in thickly populated countries like England, but believed that by stimulating the growth of settlement in the interior 'they [would] tend to create the very means of their support'. This hope proved vain; by the 1860s the colonial governments had taken over the operation of all the main railways outside the cities themselves.

Each Australian colony now built its own railway system, centred, usually, on its capital city and principal port, its network extending like unfolding tentacles towards its borders where, as in the Riverina for example, rival colonies sought to capture the commerce of each other's borderlands. Qld, where the railways extended westwards from the coastal ports of Rockhampton and Townsville as well as from Brisbane, was the main exception to this radial pattern. The colonies built their lines with different gauges. Victoria, the richest and most densely populated colony, chose the wide Irish gauge of 5 feet 3 inches, with magnificent bridges, tunnels, and viaducts built to the highest European standards. NSW chose the English system of 4 feet 8½ inches. Qld opted for the narrow gauge of 3 feet 6 inches that was becoming common in the USA and India; Tasmania, WA, and eventually SA, which had initially opted for the Victorian system, eventually followed the Queensland example. Later generations would deplore the blind parochialism that bequeathed such a disjointed system to a federated Australia, but each colony had chosen sensibly according to its interests at the time. Wide tracks, with their gentler curves and grades, were more expensive to build but they enabled trains to travel faster and with heavier loads. Narrow tracks were much cheaper to build, and more suitable, therefore, for servicing sparsely populated, developing regions. Under the influence of their English-trained managers, Australian railways probably built too many wide-gauge and too few narrow-gauge railways.

Railways were by far the largest colonial development projects, absorbing more than half of public investment in the 1870s and 1880s, and employing thousands of men as surveyors, engineers, navvies, carriage builders, sleeper cutters, and quarrymen. Banjo **Paterson** recalled the devastating impact of the Great Southern Railway upon his childhood home at Illalong in southern NSW. 'Civilisation … hit us with a bang', he wrote. 'For miles to the north and miles to the south there were nothing but torn earth and navvies' camps, and blasts going off, and the clang of temporary rails.' Arthur **Streeton's** picture *Fire's On*, depicting railway gangs blasting their way through the Blue Mountains, was the most famous visual record of the scene. Between 1871 and 1891 Australia's railways grew from 1657 to 15 290 kilometres, and the numbers of passengers from 5 million to nearly 1000 million a year. Railways dramatically changed the equations between time, money, and distance. In 1854 it had taken 23 days and cost over £15 a ton to send freight from Sydney to Bathurst, NSW, by road; by 1871 it could be carried in 16 hours at one-sixth the cost. In 1871 it took 13½ hours and cost 50 shillings for a coach passenger to travel the 142 kilometres between Penrith and Bathurst; by 1886 a second-class railway passenger could make the journey in half the time for a little over one-third the price. The railway had been preceded by the **telegraph**; together they imposed common timetables on the whole colony, and eventually on the nation. 'The mighty Bush', as Henry **Lawson** had famously written, was being 'tethered to the world'.

Railways were seen almost from the first primarily as agents of colonial development, rather than profit-making businesses. Railway policy, including decisions on where new lines should be built, how much should be borrowed to build them, and who employed to run them, became political questions, subject to the vagaries of factional alliances and the pressures of local lobby groups. Missing out on a railway could turn a flourishing centre into a ghost-town; but so could getting one, if local industries could not meet the competition of city-based manufacturers. Ministers and members of parliament were subjected to a constant barrage of petitions for new lines to suit the convenience of influential constituents. In Victoria, these pressures culminated in the passage of the 1883 Railway Act, the so-called 'Octopus Act', under which log-rolling politicians granted each other more than 1500 kilometres of railways, many of them, such as Melbourne's notorious 'Outer Circle', with an eye to the speculative land ventures of the politicians and their friends rather than to the transport needs of the colony. To remove such temptations, and to shorten the queues of job-seekers at its doors, the parliament decided to place the railways under a board of appointed commissioners, at one remove from the political process. This, the first of the statutory commissions which were to become a notable feature of Australian public administration, was later emulated by each of the other colonies. Ironically, in Victoria, it did little, at least immediately, to curb the railway-building mania: the new chief commissioner, the ex-Midlands Railway official Richard Speight, turned out to be even more blithely expansionist than his predecessors. Noel **Butlin** argues that by the late 1880s excessive government borrowing, especially for railways, had seriously distorted the colonial economies and was a major factor in the **depression** of the early 1890s, when the railway boom came to a sudden and catastrophic end.

The movement towards a unified railway system was one of the forces promoting **Federation**. The NSW and Victorian systems were joined at Albury–Wodonga in 1883, Adelaide was joined to Melbourne via Bordertown in 1887, and Brisbane to Sydney in 1888. The first rail link between east and west, from Port Augusta to Kalgoorlie, was constructed under Commonwealth auspices in 1917. But the completion of a standard gauge line enabling trains to run continuously from Sydney to Melbourne did not come until 1962. In the 1930s streamlined express trains like 'The Spirit of Progress' introduced new standards of air-conditioned comfort and dining-room service. Under powerful commissioners like Harold **Clapp** in Victoria and James Fraser in NSW, the railways also pioneered modern systems of scientific management. Passenger traffic reached an all-time peak during World War II, when petrol rationing and the rail-based troop movements boosted demand. But it fell thereafter as road and air transport increased. Rail remains an important form of transport, especially for long-haul bulky freight, such as coal or iron ore, much of which is now carried on private lines constructed by mining companies. Dreams of transcontinental railways have an enduring appeal. Plans to build a VFT (very fast train) rail link between Sydney and Melbourne via Canberra were shelved in December 2000, but an Alice Springs–Darwin railway is still planned at a cost of A$1.2 billion.

Railways are also still important for intra-urban transport. In the late nineteenth century Melbourne built the largest suburban system, in an often wasteful competition with a privately run cable tram system. By the end of the 1880s Melburnians were among the world's most frequent commuters and the city had become one of the most **suburbanised** in the world. The development of Sydney's suburban system was initially handicapped by an awkward gap between the city centre and the Redfern terminal which was not satisfactorily overcome until the construction of an underground railway in the 1920s. The electrification of suburban railways during the interwar period greatly increased the speed, comfort, and flexibility of suburban railways. Trains were able to accelerate and stop faster, intervals between stations could be shortened without increasing overall journey times, and thus the potential catchment area for commuters was increased. In the long term Sydney's denser population provided a firmer foundation for a suburban system than Melbourne's sprawl which was more vulnerable to the challenge of the **motor car**. By the 1990s Sydneysiders were almost twice as likely as Melburnians to take a train to work.

Railways now attract historians as strongly as they once attracted small boys and would-be engineers. Like **genealogy**, railway history is about lines and branches, and displays a similar blend of hard facts and nostalgia. The National Library lists more than 100 works on the history of Australian railways, many of them tracing the history of individual lines, types of locomotive, signalling systems, or other technical features of railway operation. Since its foundation in 1937 the Australian Railway Historical Society *Bulletin* has carried valuable historical articles. Noel Butlin, *Investment in Australian Economic Development* (1964), is the departure point for discussion of the macro-economics of railways, as Blainey's *Tyranny of Distance* (1966) is for their micro-economics. In Robert Lee, *The Greatest Public Work* (1988), and John Gunn, *Along Parallel Lines* (1989), NSW has the best official histories. Leo Harrigan, *Victorian Railways to '62* (1962), and Marc Fiddian, *Trains, Tracks, Travellers* (1997), are less-impressive studies of the Victorian Railways, although Patsy **Adam-Smith**, *The Romance of Victorian Railways* (1980), is a valuable record of railway folklore. J.B Hirst, *Adelaide and the Country* (1973), illuminates the role of railways in the development of SA. John Kerr, *Triumph of Narrow Gauge* (1990), and Fred Affleck *On Track* (1978), deal with aspects of the Queensland and WA stories. Mark Hearn and Eddie Butler-Bowden have told the stories of the once-powerful railway unions in NSW and Victoria.

GRAEME DAVISON

Rainbow Serpent, see **Dreamtime**

Rasp, Charles (1846–1907) pegged the first mineral lease at Broken Hill, NSW, while working as a boundary rider at Mt Gipps Station in September 1883. Roy Bridges in *From Silver to Steel* (1920) described Rasp's **prospecting**, his involvement in early syndicates, and his eventual discovery of rich silver chlorides that led to establishment of **BHP** in August 1885. Rasp retired to enjoy his wealth in Adelaide, but his background remained mysterious. W.S. **Robinson**, *If I Remember Rightly* (1967), revealed that Rasp was an educated German edible-oil technologist who migrated to Victoria in 1869. Later research by Maja Sainisch-Plimer (*Good Weekend*, 1992) suggests Rasp was in fact Hieronymus Salvator Lopez Von Pereira, a Saxon military officer of noble birth who deserted in the Franco-Prussian War and fled to Australia in 1871.

DC

Rats of Tobruk was the name bestowed on the Australian soldiers who withstood a seven-month siege of the port town of Tobruk on the Libyan coast during 1941.

Accounts of the siege are given in Gavin **Long's** official history and in Chester Wilmot's *Tobruk* (1944). The siege provided material for two feature films, *The Rats of Tobruk* (1944) and *Desert Rats* (1952); a controversial novel by Lawson Glassop, *We Were the Rats* (1944); and Eric Lambert, *The Twenty Thousand Thieves* (1951). After the war, ex-servicemen formed the Rats of Tobruk Association, with headquarters in Melbourne.

HD

Reade, Charles Compton (1880–1933) was born in NZ and, on moving to England, became an influential proponent of **town planning**. He published *The Revelation of Britain* (1909). Reade became active in the Garden Cities and Town Planning Association, and travelled to NZ and Australia in 1914 to deliver lantern lectures on town planning. In 1916 he was retained as adviser by the government of SA, where he planned a new garden suburb and spoke at Australia's first Town Planning and Housing Conference and Exhibition.

KT

Reconciliation was the key term in a Commonwealth program of civic education about the relationships between indigenous and non-indigenous Australians. A statutory Council for Aboriginal Reconciliation, initiated by the **Hawke** government in 1991 and terminating in January 2001, envisaged 'a united Australia which respects this land of ours; values the Aboriginal and Torres Strait Islander heritage; and provides justice and equity for all'.

Two contrasting understandings of these words emerged. One saw reconciliation as dissolving distinctions between the rights, institutions, and identities of indigenous and non-indigenous Australians. Labelling policies of separate programs and institutions for indigenous and non-indigenous Australians as divisive, radio talk-back host Alan Jones rejected the possibility of 'identifiable groups determining their own destinies'. The competing ideal of reconciliation sought to build on various governmental recognitions that indigenous Australians suffered distinct problems and enjoyed distinct rights. In this view, a treaty between indigenous and non-indigenous Australians was necessary to give permanent form and a just base to a relationship in which indigenous Australians would determine their futures.

In the weeks preceding the Council's climactic ceremony, 'Corroboree 2000', in May 2000, it became clear that the contest between these two senses of reconciliation had been deferred by the emergence of a third meaning: 'reconciliation' as personal and national 'journey' towards an apology to the **Stolen Generations**. Large demonstrations attested a popular will to apologise. Until the Prime Minister offered his own apology to the Stolen Generations, it was claimed, reconciliation was impossible.

TIM ROWSE

Red Centre, see *Dead Heart*

Red Flag riots occurred in the aftermath of World War I in public clashes between the right and left. The flying of the red flag, a symbol of the labour movement, had been banned under the War Precautions Act, and various attempts to defy the ban at public rallies brought police action and prosecution. One such left-wing demonstration in Brisbane in 1919 was answered by a counter-demonstration of ex-servicemen who attacked the city's Russian community; it is the subject of a study by Ray Evans (1988). Another red flag demonstration in the Sydney Domain on May Day 1921 was disrupted by a group of ex-soldiers carrying a Union Jack. The demonstrators seized and burned it, and on the following Sunday a large crowd attacked the left-wing speakers and laid siege to the **Communist** Party's hall.

SM

Redfern, William (?1774–1833) was a naval surgeon sentenced to transportation for life after sympathising with mutineers. He arrived in NSW in 1801 and worked as assistant surgeon on Norfolk Island. He received a pardon in 1803 and was later granted a licence to practise medicine, which he did at Sydney Hospital until 1819, when he resigned because he was not appointed chief surgeon. His 1814 report on deaths on convict ships, containing the recommendation that all convict ships carry a surgeon responsible for convict welfare, was crucial to the improvement of conditions and reduction in the convict death-rate. He was also instrumental in improving the status of **emancipists** with a petition to the king resulting in an act decreeing that pardons restored people to the full rights of a free person. Governor **Macquarie** appointed him a magistrate in 1819. The Sydney suburb of Redfern includes the area of his country estate.

KT

Reece, Eric Elliott (1909–1999), premier of Tasmania, became known as 'Electric Eric' because of his support for the development of hydro-electricity. Reece began working in a mine at the age of 13 and soon became involved with the **Australian Workers Union**. In 1946 he won the state seat of Braddon for the **Australian Labor Party**. He became the most prominent Labor figure in Tasmanian politics, serving as state president of the Australian Labor Party for nine years, and two terms as federal president. During most of his two terms as premier, 1958–69 and 1972–75, he was also treasurer.

KT

Reed, Joseph (1823–90) is considered by many as the architect who made Melbourne. Reed won the competition to design the Melbourne Public Library soon after his arrival in 1853. He worked almost exclusively on large, public buildings; the Sargoods' Rippon Lea mansion was a notable exception. Much of Reed's work remains, and helps to define Melbourne as a distinctive Victorian city. This includes the Town Hall, the Exhibition Building, the Trades Hall, and many of the central city churches and banks. Appointed University of Melbourne architect, Reed designed Ormond College and old Wilson Hall. The facade of his Bank of New South Wales building in Collins Street found a new home on the university's Commerce Building. Reed went into partnership with Frederick Barnes in 1862; the firm continues today

as Bates Smart. Reed and Barnes won the public competition to design Melbourne's Government House in 1864, but their design was never built. The job was eventually given to the Public Works Department under William **Wardell**. Historians have offered sharply opposed views of Reed's work. Robin **Boyd**, in *The Australian Ugliness* (1960), called him 'the supreme eclectic, the master Featurist'. Recent judgments have been more favourable: J.M. **Freeland** (*Architecture in Australia*, 1968) regarded him as the best, as well as the most prolific, of Australia's late colonial architects.

KT

Reeves, William Pember (1857–1932) was a New Zealand radical who surveyed the *State Experiments in Australia and New Zealand* in an influential two-volume study published in 1902. The Oxford-educated son of a South Island businessman, he became minister for education and justice in the Liberal ministry of John Ballance in 1890, and was responsible for the introduction of industrial **arbitration**. Considerably more radical than Richard Seddon, who defeated him for the premiership when Ballance died in 1892, Reeves accepted appointment as agent-general in London in 1896. He held the post until 1908, became an important member of the Fabian Society and first director of the London School of Economics. Keith Sinclair has written a biography (1965).

Reeves had already written a history of NZ, which he expanded in London into *The Long White Cloud* (1898). His 1902 assessment of the state experiments was based on limited direct knowledge of Australia but close consideration of the literature. He surveyed the industrial legislation, old-age pensions, immigration restriction, and democratic reforms; the emphasis on enfranchisement of women and land reform had particular New Zealand salience. It was published in England and probably had greatest impact there, though labour historians have frequently drawn on it and repeated the title's characterisation as a variant on the **social laboratory**.

SM

Reference works, the essential tools of historical research, include atlases, bibliographies, chronologies, compilations, dictionaries, directories, encyclopaedias, gazetteers, guides, handbooks, lists, indexes, registers, and other sources of information or navigational aids.

State atlases include the *Atlas of Tasmania* (1965), the *Atlas of Victoria* (1982) and *Western Australia: An Atlas of Human Endeavour 1829–1979* (1979), all with historical components. *Australians: A Historical Atlas* (1987) was prepared by C.R.J. Camm and John McQuilton as part of the **Bicentennial History Project**. It consists of three parts: Place (including Aboriginal landscapes, European exploration, rural and urban landscapes); People (including immigration, demography, and religion), and Landscapes. The Division of National Mapping in Canberra (now the Australian Surveying and Land Information Group) has produced a range of topical atlases and, in conjunction with the Australian

Bureau of Statistics, social atlases of Australian cities based on Census data.

The bedrock of national bibliography is the work of the private collector and scholar, J.A. **Ferguson**; his *Bibliography of Australia* in seven volumes (1941–69) covers the period from 1784 to 1900, though it omits some categories of publication; an addendum was published by the National Library of Australia in 1986. From 1961 to 1996 the National Library published a comprehensive annual, *Australian National Bibliography*, and in 1988 it filled the 'Ferguson gap' with a retrospective *Australian National Bibliography 1901–1950* in four volumes. Since 1956 *Australian Books in Print* has appeared annually. Lurline Stuart's annotated bibliography of *Nineteenth-Century Australian Periodicals* appeared in 1979.

Subject bibliographies are more uneven. D.H. Borchardt and Victor Crittenden (eds), *Australians: A Guide to Sources* (1987), and John Arnold et al. (eds), *Australia: A Reader's Guide* (1996), are both organised thematically. There are some state guides to historical literature: F.K. **Crowley**, *A Guide to the Principal Documents and Publications Relating to the History of Western Australia* (1947); E.D. Flinn, *The History, Politics and Economy of Tasmania in the Literature 1856–1959* (1961); F.K. Crowley, *South Australian History* (1966); W.R. Johnston, *A Bibliography of Queensland History* (1981); Carol M. Mills, *A Bibliography of the Northern Territory* (1977–83); Joanna Monie, *Victorian History and Politics* (1982); and the Monash Public History Group, *Straight to the Source* (1995). Noteworthy topical bibliographies are Margaret Bettison and Anne **Summers**, *Her Story: Australian Women in Print 1788–1975* (1980), and Kay Daniels et al., *Women in Australia: An Annotated Guide to Records* (1977); Victor Crittenden, *A Bibliography of the First Fleet* (1982); Ian McLaren's massive guide to *Australian Explorers* in nine volumes (1988–91); Gavan McCarthy, *Guide to the Archives of Science in Australia: Records of Individuals* (1991); Alex Castles, *Annotated Bibliography of Printed Materials on Australian Law* (1788–1900); Beverley Symons, *Communism in Australia* (1994); and the guide to **Federation** published by National Archives of Australia (1998).

Chronologies were frequently included in older histories and **school histories**. Among recent works are A.C. Castles, *Australia: A Chronology and Fact Book 1606–1976* (1978); the *Macquarie Book of Events* (1983, 1997); the *Australian Almanac* (1985); *Collins Milestones in Australian History* (1986); *Australians: Events and Places* (1987); and Anthony Barker, *What Happened When* (1992).

Compilations include such works as official yearbooks produced by the states (Victoria from 1873, NSW from 1886–87, WA from 1886, and the other states from this century) and the Commonwealth (from 1908). Reports of the **Census** and other compilations of data also go back to the nineteenth century and are now produced by the Australian Bureau of Statistics in electronic as well as hardcopy form; A.E. Miller, *Checklist of Nineteenth-Century Australian Colonial Statistical Sources* (1983) lists early censuses, blue books, and statistical registers. Wray Vamplew

(ed.), *Australians: Historical Statistics* (1987), collates these and later statistical series. Notable among other compilations are the three volumes of *A Handbook of Australian Government and Politics* (1968, 1977, 1986) compiled by Colin A. Hughes (the first with B.D. Graham), which list Commonwealth and state ministries, and election results from 1890 to 1983, as well as the companion volumes of voting details.

Dictionaries range from language guides to handbooks of information arranged alphabetically on a range of topics. Of the first, while the *Macquarie Dictionary* (3rd edn, 1997) is based on contemporary Australian usage, the *Australian National Dictionary*, first published in 1988, gives extensive historical examples of all Australianisms. From its rich database, more specialised dictionaries have been generated on military terminology, regional variations, underworld slang, and most recently a compilation by J.M. Arthur of *Aboriginal English* (1997). G.A. Wilkes, *Dictionary of Australian Colloquialisms* (1978, 1996), Stephen Murray-Smith, *The Dictionary of Australian Quotations* (1984, 1992), and the *Macquarie Dictionary of Australian Quotations* (1990) are indispensible auxiliaries.

Biographical dictionaries are considered elsewhere. The dictionary format is also followed by other reference works, such as Jan Bassett, *Concise Oxford Dictionary of Australian History* (1986), and *Australians: A Historical Dictionary* (1987), and particularly by the Oxford Companions. Besides this present work, there are companions to Australian history, literature, children's literature, feminism, folklore, cricket, jazz, music, military history, and sport. So far there is no Oxford Companion to Companions.

The major Australian encyclopaedia was edited by H.J. Carter and A.W. **Jose** in two volumes (1925–26) and by Alec Chisholm in 10 (1958); the sixth edition of nine volumes, edited by Tony Macdougall, appeared in 1996. Both the Jose and Chisholm encyclopaedias provided detailed historical data that is missing from the latest. James Jupp (ed.), *The Australian People* (1988), is an encyclopaedia of the peopling of Australia; Susan McCulloch revised her father's *Encylopaedia of Australian Arts* in 1994; and David Horton (ed.), *Encyclopaedia of Aboriginal Australia* in two volumes (1994), is a comprehensive guide to its subject.

Numerous gazetteers were published from the nineteenth century onwards, mostly on a colonial basis, and the motorists' street directories have been published for the greater part of this century. Richard and Barbara Appleton, *The Cambridge Dictionary of Australian Places* (1992), is a useful handbook; and A.W. Reed, *Aboriginal Place Names and Their Meanings* (1967), and Aldo Massola, *Aboriginal Place Names of South-East Australia and their Meanings* (1968), are standard reference works. The former Division of National Mapping published the official gazetteer of Australian place names in 1975; in 1989 the Australian Surveying and Land Information Group produced a gazetteer in computer form. An authoritative historical gazetteer has still to be produced.

Post-office and commercial **directories**, such as Sand's, were published from the nineteenth century, and are extensively consulted by genealogists since they provide a precise address for householders. More recent directories for business, non-profit organisations, professions, the Commonwealth government, and municipal governments are important guides.

Guides and aids for finding manuscripts are produced by the major **archives**, and galleries and **museums** publish guides to their holdings. D.H. Borchardt's *Australian Official Publications* (1979) has been rendered obsolete by the passage of time but remains the only survey of this important source. He has also compiled the *Checklist of Royal Commissions, Select Committees of Parliament, and Boards of Inquiry* for the Commonwealth, NSW, Qld, Tasmania and Victoria, as Elmar Zalums has for SA and WA (1958–80). Henry Mayer's idiosyncratic *ARGAP: A Research Guide to Australian Politics and Cognate Subjects* (1976) and second Guide in 1984 contain substantial historical references. Volumes of parliamentary debates and parliamentary papers usually incorporate an internal index but lack cumulative indexes. A Victorian consolidated index now exists. The recent move to electronic publication creates new problems of preservation but does allow searching.

The handbook is a portmanteau category that covers the contemporary publications of sporting bodies, professional and trade associations, churches, universities, etc. University calendars present the student of education, for example, with regulations, subject details, details of staff, and class lists. Cricket almanacs, on the other hand, include lengthy lists of past players and results. Municipal directories are a neglected source for **local government**.

The two principal published newspaper indexes are for the *Sydney Morning Herald* (1842–45; 1927–61; Oct. 1961–Feb. 1962; Apr. 1963–1978; 1979–87) and the Melbourne *Argus* (1846–59, 1910–49). A project to index the *Argus* for the intervening years has produced remarkably detailed volumes for 1860–69, but awaits completion. The *Sydney Gazette* (1803–42) and *Australian* (1824–42) have been retrospectively indexed. *Newspapers in Australian Libraries: A Union List* (1975) is a useful guide to holdings.

There are topical indexes to the serial literature on business, education, law, science, and other subjects but the indexes to **historical journals** are seriously deficient. Trevor Hogan et al., *Index to Journal Articles on Australian History* (1976), compiled a retrospective listing to 1973, and from then until 1983 an annual *Index to Journal Articles on Australian History* was prepared by Victor Crittenden and colleagues. After that date the researcher is forced to rely on *APAIS*, the acronym for Australian Public Affairs Information Service, published by the National Library from 1945, in annual cumulations since 1955, and in electronic form back to 1978. It provides only a partial index of Australian history journals, as do the international citation indexes. *Australian Literary Studies* publishes annual bibliographies of publications, including journal publications, on literature and literary history. These are cumulated in Martin Duwell (ed.), *The ALS Guide to Australian Writers* (1992, 1997).

Research theses were recorded from 1959 to 1988 by the University of Tasmania's *Union List of Higher Degree Theses*.

Andrew Pike and Ross Cooper, *Reference Guide to Australian Films 1906–69* appeared in 1981. The Australian Heritage Commission maintains a register of the **National Estate**, and its book, *The Heritage of Australia* (1981), lists 6600 places of 'aesthetic, historic, scientific or social significance'.

Many of these reference works are being supplemented, or partly superseded, by electronic forms of data collection and information management. Thus the *Guide to Collections of Manuscripts Relating to Australia*, published irregularly by the National Library from 1965 to 1995, has given way to RAAM, the Register of Australian Archives and Manuscripts, which is available at <http://www.nla.gov.au/raam>. A library user is presented with an array of other online and CD-ROM products, some offering abstracts or full-text retrieval. It is not clear whether the advance in technology has kept up with the variety of information, nor that the bibliographical quality of reference works has been maintained.

Stuart Macintyre

Referendum is the apotheosis of constitutional democracy. It is the device which registers the opinion of citizens on law or policy. The Australian **Constitution**, endorsed by referendums, was among the first to use this method for the approval of constitutional change.

The first Australian enthusiast for the referendum was David **Syme**, the editor of the Melbourne *Age*; he proposed it as a means of resolving deadlocks between the two houses of parliament, which in Victoria had led to **constitutional crises**. It became part of the program of Victorian liberals. The early **Australian Labor Party**, highly critical of the game of ins and outs in colonial politics, wanted the people to rule more directly. It supported the initiative (the submission of measures to parliament by citizens) and the referendum. The referendum was well known to those involved in **Federation** because of its use in the Swiss federation.

The framers of the 1891 constitution adopted the US model of State Conventions for approving constitutional amendment. A bill to amend the constitution required an absolute majority in each house. The proposal was then submitted to State Conventions, elected by those eligible to vote for the House of Representatives, but otherwise convened under conditions determined by the Commonwealth parliament. Any alteration to the proportions of state representation required the assent of the affected state, and amendments could be disallowed by the Queen. Opponents of the model complained of double jeopardy as both the Senate (the states' house) and the State Conventions had veto power.

By the 1897–98 Convention, sentiment favoured constitutional amendment by referendum. This round of constitution-making itself involved popular participation in the election of Convention delegates and the approval of their draft by referendum. At the Adelaide session of the Convention, **Deakin** described the federal character of the scheme adopted: an 'amendment of the Constitution requires an absolute majority of the Senate and the House of Representatives, a majority of the whole of the people and a majority of the states of which the Commonwealth is composed'. The referendum was commonly regarded as ultra-democratic, but these arrangements satisfied the conservative Tasmanian premier Edward **Braddon**, who said it 'should be made as difficult as possible to amend the Constitution'. Deakin's attempt at the 1898 session to allow for a simple rather than an absolute majority failed.

After the constitution failed to obtain sufficient 'yes' votes in NSW at the 1898 referendum, the premiers agreed to changes to win over that colony, including one designed to make constitutional amendment easier. A proposal could be put to the people with the assent of one house, provided it had been submitted to the other house, then resubmitted to that house and still failed to pass. The amending provision, Section 128, was itself altered in 1977 to permit electors of the territories to vote at referendums, but the required majority of states remained. A curiosity persists concerning the franchise. Section 128 allowed that, until the Commonwealth adopted a uniform franchise, only half the votes would be counted from a state with the adult franchise, which, at Federation, only SA and WA had adopted.

Since Federation, 110 referendum bills have lapsed, failed in the parliament, or been rejected. Forty-four questions have been put on 19 separate occasions. Eight of the 44 have passed. Only two (1946 and 1967) have clearly expanded Commonwealth powers, over social security and Aboriginal affairs respectively. The remainder are either housekeeping or the formalisation of accepted convention: rotation of senators (1906); state debts (1910, 1928); casual Senate vacancies; territorial votes in constitutional amendment; retiring age of judges (1977).

Twenty-five questions, many concerning the expansion of Commonwealth power, have been put by Labor, with only one success. The seven other successful proposals were put by non-Labor. The largest win was in 1967 (when 90.7 per cent voted in favour). The closest losses were on Commonwealth power over industrial employment (supported by 50.30 per cent of the national electorate) and marketing (50.57 per cent) in 1946, with three states voting 'yes'. The most controversial was the failed 1951 attempt to empower the Commonwealth to ban the Communist Party (49.44 per cent). Three states voted 'yes'. The worst losses were in 1988: parliamentary terms (32.92 per cent), fair elections (37.60 per cent), local government (33.62 per cent), and rights and freedoms (30.79 per cent). The 1999 republican referendum was a middling loss at 45 per cent.

Referendums are now required to amend some state **constitutions**. They have been used in the states to test opinion on a range of issues: Bible reading in schools, drinking hours, and daylight saving. Two national votes were taken by the Commonwealth government on **conscription** in 1916 and 1917. Referendums are sometimes referred to as 'plebiscites' (advisory polls), when they have no legal force and entail no constitutional change. There has recently been a revival of interest in the initiative and referendum, usually from right-wing groups.

JAMES WARDEN

Reffo, or *refo*, was a diminutive form of *refugee* that was first used around 1941 in reference to European refugees of non-British origin. It developed a much wider usage in the 1940s and 1950s, and became a generic term for immigrants to Australia, refugee or otherwise, who were from a non-British background. Its use carried with it a range of sentiments, varying from affectionate to hostile, but, generally, *reffo* became a derogatory label that was applied to anyone of 'foreign' appearance—particularly **Jews**, who arrived in large numbers during and after World War II, and who were also derided as *refujews*. This reflected the intolerant and superior attitude that was commonly shown towards people of non-British background.

HD

Refugees, see **Boat people**; **Immigration**

Regional history is often confused with state and **local history**. The general homogeneity of Australia's geography and peoples, the low impact of sectionalism, and the metropolitanisation of the nation-continent have all tended to blur regional differentiation, while the absence of a powerful hypothesis, such as F.J. Turner's **frontier** thesis provided for the study of American regions, has left regionalism without the powerful explanatory force it has had in some other new countries.

The first Australian regional histories originated in a simple desire to 'preserve the past' rather than investigate a problem. Margaret **Kiddle's** evocative *Men of Yesterday: A Social History of the Western District of Victoria 1834–1890* (1961) aimed to recapture the lives of colourful pioneering pastoralists, while G.C. **Bolton's** *A Thousand Miles Away: A History of North Queensland to 1920* (1963) resulted from a commission by a like-minded Local Government Association. Similarly, a number of NSW regional histories in the 1960s benefited from materials gathered and presented by a 'local history project' launched in NSW schools in the 1920s. Most of these early works were social histories constructed around occupational sequences rounded out by political synthesis.

The publication of the American historical geographer D.W. Meinig's *On the Margins of the Good Earth: The South Australian Wheat Frontier 1869–1884* (1962) inspired focused doctoral theses based on an analysis of land legislation. They included R.L. Heathcote's *Back of Bourke* (1965), G.L. Buxton's *The Riverina 1861–1891* (1967), and D.B. Waterson's *Squatter, Selector, Storekeeper: A History of the Darling Downs 1859–93* (1968). Each explored the clash of competing rural ideologies against the distant interests of European capital.

This flowering of regional history in the 1960s prompted a concern with the definition, methodology, and purpose of studying regions. In 1978 J.W. McCarty (*HS*), drawing from geography, distinguished formal and functional regions as organisational units for analysis. Formal regions were characterised by a single feature (e.g. pastoralism) or several (e.g. mining and agriculture), and further prescribed by physiography (e.g. a river valley) or politics (e.g. state boundaries) or society (e.g. squatterdom). All the works mentioned above fell into this category. Functional regions incorporated several formal regions, including the nearest metropolitan area, necessitating an understanding of their inter-relationships. J.B. Hirst, *Adelaide and the Country 1870–1917: Their Social and Political Relationship* (1973), largely concerned with the formation of political parties, still stands as the prime example.

While McCarty's article essentially reflected the state of regional history, he had earlier attempted to shape the study. Drawing on Marc Bloch's 'comparative history' and Ragnar Nurkse's 'regions of recent settlement', he posited that Australia itself constituted a region best understood by comparison with similar societies such as Argentina, the USA, and South Africa. Each was a region of sparse or 'primitive' indigenous populations and vast natural resources, substantially settled in the nineteenth century by the transfer of European capital, technology, and labour paid for by the export of raw materials to feed industrial capitalism. Each, however, had developed differing social and political institutions. Whereas McCarty advocated **staple theory** as the relevant analytical tool, Donald Denoon (*HS*, 1979) espoused class analysis while John Fogarty (*HS*, 1981) questioned the nation-as-region concept. Denoon and Fogarty elaborated their respective views in *Settler Capitalism: The Dynamics of Dependent Development in the Southern Hemisphere* (1983) and *Australia and Argentina: On Parallel Paths* (1984). Subsequently, this comparative approach has been pursued more by economists than historians and edged tentatively towards Immanuel Wallerstein's world system theory.

Much of the early work—the 'old regionalism'—had been produced by historians with cognate skills in geography, economics, and politics, and informed, if not influenced, by geographical determinism and proto-Marxism. Most regional histories of the 1980s and 1990s have continued the socio-economic study of a formal region but now reoriented to incorporate new concerns of race, gender, and environmentalism, the last being signalled as early as 1972 with W.K. **Hancock's** personal odyssey, *Discovering Monaro: A Study of Man's Impact on his Environment*.

The purpose of regional history was stated, by G.C. Bolton in J.A. Moses (ed.), *Historical Disciplines and Cultures in Australasia* (1979), to reflect national and world events in the region while identifying its own unique contribution to 'sense of place'. The extensive use of pictorial material and travel literature, as in Maurice French, *Travellers in a Landscape: Visitors' Impressions of the Darling Downs 1827–1954* (1994), reflects this new approach. Alan Frost, *East Coast Country: A North Queensland Dreaming* (1996), is a novel perspective on childhood memory interwoven with history to construct a personal and regional identity.

In the meantime, the 'old regionalism' needs to be further revised—extended into the twenty-first century, broadened to a functionalist approach (including greater attention to provincial cities) and placed within a comparative perspective to test regional attachment, particularly against the weight of homogeneous nationalism. Australia still awaits a 'new regionalism'.

MAURICE FRENCH

Reibey, Mary (1777–1855), ex-convict business owner, was born at Bury in Lancashire, England. According to her biographer Nance Irvine, *Mary Reibey: Molly Incognita* (1982), Reibey was christened Molly Haydock and ran away from home at 13 disguised as a boy. She was caught trying to sell a stolen horse, and sentenced to seven years' transportation in 1791. At Sydney in 1794 she married an entrepreneurial free settler, Thomas Reibey, who with Edward Wills had developed interests in property, trade, retailing, shipping, and sealing in NSW and Van Diemen's Land. Both men died within weeks of each other in 1811, leaving Mary to manage the business network while raising seven children. With extraordinary energy and competence she acquired new ships and properties, and established her sons in Van Diemen's Land. Hard-nosed and spirited, in 1817 she was convicted of assaulting an evasive debtor. Her portfolio of central Sydney real estate included the first premises of the Bank of New South Wales. She was supposedly worth over £20 000 by 1816–17, and became active in charitable work. Richard Cobbold's *History of Margaret Catchpole* (1845) led to incorrect assumptions that Reibey was the convict Margaret **Catchpole** in his story. Catherine Gaskin's novel *Sara Dane* (1955) was inspired by Reibey's life, though details differ. Portia Robinson's *The Women of Botany Bay* (1988) and *The Hatch and Brood of Time* (1985) show Reibey was not the only successful female ex-convict. As part of her 'rediscovery', Reibey's letters (held in the Mitchell Library, Sydney) were published in Nance Irvine (ed.), *Dear Cousin: The Reibey Letters* (1992). Her portrait on Australia's $20 note (1995) depicts the somewhat stern, bespectacled woman of the world who climbed to the high ground in masculine, **emancipist** society.

DC

Reid, George Houstoun (1845–1918) was the leader of the free-trade party in the early Commonwealth parliament and Australia's third prime minister. As premier of NSW 1894–99 he played a vital, if controversial, role in the **Federation** movement. Reid worked in the NSW public service and as a barrister before entering the colony's parliament in 1880 as a liberal free-trader. He was a gifted public speaker with a close feel for the popular mood who affected a self-deprecating cynicism. His corpulent figure and indolent manner belied ambition and a keen political intelligence. As premier he overcame upper house resistance to reform the colony's public service and **tax** system. He established free trade by raising revenue from direct taxes on land and income.

Reid initially resisted Henry **Parkes's** initiative to revive Federation. He criticised the proposals formulated at the 1891 Convention, principally because he feared that NSW would be forced to give up free trade; as he put it, the colony would be acting like a reformed alcoholic who set up house with five fiscal drunkards. In 1894, however, he took up the scheme proposed at the **Corowa Conference** to revive Federation by popular participation, and with C.C. **Kingston**, had it adopted at the Hobart meeting of colonial premiers that he initiated in early 1895. He claimed to have picked Federation out of the gutter. He was a key figure in the 1897–98 Convention, but was disappointed with the concessions it made to the less populous colonies and voiced his objections in the ensuing referendum. The failure to carry the proposal in NSW was blamed on the vacillations of Reid, who criticised the proposal but said he would vote for it, and so earned the nickname 'Yes–No Reid'. The critical account of his role given by Alfred **Deakin**, B.R. **Wise**, and other ardent federalists still lingers over his historical reputation. NSW did obtain concessions in subsequent negotiation and Reid campaigned in favour of Federation when NSW approved it in 1899.

By this time Reid had lost the support of the Labor Party and was turned out of office. He became the leader of the free-trade party in the Commonwealth parliament in 1901 and, while uncomfortable with the loss of the middle ground to his protectionist opponents, found himself aligned with the conservatives. He formed a coalition ministry in 1904 and sought to fashion a popular anti-socialist alliance, but was given notice to quit by the Liberal leader Deakin in 1905, who then governed in collaboration with the Australian Labor Party. Reid responded with an anti-socialist crusade in the 1906 election, which weakened but did not remove the government. The eventual **Fusion** of the liberals and conservatives in 1909 required conservative acceptance of protection and the retirement of Reid. He became the first high commissioner to London, an appointment terminated by the wartime Labor government, and shortly before his death was elected to the British parliament. Reid's own reminiscences, published in 1917, are perfunctory. The substantial biography by W.G. McMinn (1989) has helped to restore appreciation of his political substance.

STUART MACINTYRE

Religion suffused Aboriginal society so that there was no clear distinction between the 'sacred' and the 'profane', or between the spiritual and secular realms. White settlers brought quite different ideas of religion to Australia. Christianity, both **Catholic** and Protestant, was apparent in its organisation and ceremony, in sacred time and places, and religious and secular callings. All this was not so obvious in the earliest years of NSW, when the colony lacked a church building and had only one clergyman. Not until the second decade of British settlement did a few permanent church buildings rise to denote a religious presence on the colonial landscape. It took much longer for historians to take the religious aspect of colonial society seriously.

Douglas **Pike**, in his study of SA, *Paradise of Dissent* (1957), was the first modern historian to recognise the role of religion in the formation of Australian society. Manning **Clark** is better known for the prominence he gave to religion in the first volume of *A History of Australia* (1962), casting Catholicism, Protestantism, and the Enlightenment as contesting forces in the shaping of Australian society. Michael **Roe** developed these themes in *The Quest for Authority in Eastern Australia 1835–1851* (1965), arguing that 'moral enlightenment' was 'the new faith' that supplanted traditional Christianity and became the basis of a secular society.

Some measure of religious belief and practice may be obtained from the wide range of official statistics in censuses and church attendance returns, and from various surveys of religious attitudes and behaviour in the period after World War II. Most notable is the sociologist Hans Mol's 1966 survey on religion in Australia, which was published as *Religion in Australia* (1971) and updated in *The Faith of Australians* (1985). Some basis for comparison between the nineteenth and twentieth centuries exists in Walter Phillips, 'Religious Profession and Practice in New South Wales 1850–1901: The Statistical Evidence' (*HS*, 1972).

Australia was overwhelmingly Christian and predominantly Protestant from the beginning of British settlement to the early postwar years. **Immigration** reinforced the ratio of the various denominations. The **Anglican Church** (Church of England to 1981), with a high nominal component, was the largest, but less strong in SA and Victoria. Catholics were the next largest denomination, but less numerous in SA and Tasmania. SA was the most Protestant, with a high proportion of **Methodists** and other Dissenters or Nonconformists, particularly **Baptists** and **Congregationalists**. **Presbyterians** were generally about as numerous as Methodists, but were stronger in Victoria. Most denominations were of British origin, apart from German **Lutherans**, concentrated mainly in SA and south-east Qld, the Victorian Wimmera, and the Riverina. There were also small numbers of other Christians and various sects from Britain and the USA. No new religious movement arose in Australia. The overwhelming proportion of Protestants adhered to the Anglican, Methodist, and Presbyterian Churches.

Sectarian conflict shaped **church and state** relations in the nineteenth century, in the opposition of both Catholic and non-episcopal Protestants to the Church of England's claim to be the established church, and in disputes, largely between Catholics and Protestants, over denominational versus comprehensive state **education**. For a time colonial governments gave financial aid for religion and education to the four larger denominations—Anglicans, Catholics, Presbyterians, and Wesleyan Methodists. Opposed by religious voluntarists and political liberals, state aid was abolished in all colonies during the second half of the century and free, compulsory, secular education introduced, leaving Catholics to maintain their separate school system. Sectarian opposition also silenced prayers in most colonial parliaments, giving a secular appearance to Australian society.

Anglicans and Catholics have generally lamented this apparent separation of church and state, some Catholic historians attributing it to the ascendancy of secular liberalism. Douglas Pike, however, in *Paradise of Dissent*, wrote that 'The separation of church and state was neither son nor father of secularism', while J.S. Gregory, in *Church and State* (1973), concluded that this separation was 'less absolute in practice than in theory'. Ideological secularism had few followers in Australia, although some historians have asserted a decline in religious belief in the nineteenth century as a result of the conflict between religion and contemporary science; but the casualties of this confrontation were few. Nominal adherence to Christianity remained high and stable from the mid-nineteenth to the mid-twentieth centuries.

Regular churchgoers represented a smaller proportion of the population, although the churches received substantial support in the late nineteenth century. During his visit in 1887 the English Congregationalist R.W. Dale found 'remarkable proofs of religious liberality and energy', apparent in substantial church buildings and church attendance, and evangelistic activity (*Impressions of Australia*, 1889). Available figures suggest that about 45 per cent of the population in south-eastern Australia attended church or Sunday school regularly in the late nineteenth century—a significantly higher proportion than in the second half of the twentieth century, contrary to the claims of some modern religious sociologists. Postwar surveys suggest a decline in regular church attendance from 30 per cent of the adult population in 1960 to 17 per cent in 1990.

Despite the separation of church and state, Australia remained 'a Christian country', although, following his visit in 1885, the historian J.A. Froude observed in *Oceana* (1886) that church and creed had 'ceased to be factors in the commonwealth', while conceding that religion still transformed individual lives. Some contemporary churchmen would have endorsed this judgment, but the churches continued to enjoy some privileges and protection. Protestants exerted significant influence, especially in enforcing strict Sunday observance, promoting temperance reform, and restricting facilities for gambling. Never as successful as they wished, they still managed to impose **wowserish** social morality through legislation that endured to the 1960s. At Federation they won the recognition of Almighty God in the preamble to the Australian Constitution and secured the observance of prayers in the Commonwealth parliament, and subsequently in all state parliaments, without infusing a religious spirit into political life.

The Catholic Church remained aloof from Protestant moral crusades, but supported the campaign for the public recognition of God. Catholics generally supported the **Australian Labor Party**, while Protestants mostly adhered to liberal and conservative parties. Political differences and the Catholic grievance over the denial of state aid for church schools intensified sectarian conflict, keeping Catholics and Protestants apart until the 1960s. While Catholics looked to their schools to inculcate religious faith, Protestants relied on their Sunday schools, but also campaigned to get religious instruction in state schools or to strengthen it where it was permitted. By the mid-twentieth century all state schools allowed religious instruction, and from 1974 all church schools began to receive substantial state funding. Thus the trend towards secularism begun 100 years earlier appeared to be reversed. But other changes suggest that Australia was becoming a less religious society.

The religious configuration of Australia changed from the 1960s, partly through immigration. Orthodox Christians, Jehovah's Witnesses, Latter Day Saints (Mormons), Pentecostalists, Judaism, **Islam**, and Buddhism have increased their followings, but these changes altered the religious balance only slightly. The most significant change since 1966 has been the decline in the proportion of Protestants (including Anglicans)—from 60 per cent of the population in 1966 to 41 per cent in 1996. The **Uniting Church**, formed in 1977 by the union of Congregationalists, Methodists, and a number of Presbyterians, has hardly grown since its inception; it fell from a peak of 8.2 per cent in 1991 to 7.5 per cent in 1996. The combined percentage of the Uniting Church and Presbyterians (11.2 per cent in 1996) is significantly less than the aggregate of the three denominations (19.4 per cent) in 1966. The Catholic Church is now the largest denomination, having grown largely through migration during 1947–66 from 21 to 26 per cent of the population; Catholics were 27 per cent in 1996 and Anglicans 22 per cent. The other notable change is in the increase of those professing 'no religion'—6.7 per cent in 1971, when the Census first specifically invited such a response, to 16.5 per cent in 1996; and those not answering the religious question—6.1 per cent in 1971, 8.7 per cent in 1996. These statistics and recent surveys of church attendance seem to point to a significant decline in religious belief or commitment among Australians.

Despite this decline, Christianity remains the professed faith of almost three-quarters of the Australian population. The decline has been mainly within Protestantism. It may be attributed in a large part to the theological ferment and moral revolution of the 1960s and 1970s, and is reflected in the waning influence of religion in social and political life. The principal Protestant churches have retreated from their policing role over a supposedly Christian society; and the Catholic Church has not filled their place. With the demise of the old **sectarianism**, Protestants and Catholics cooperate freely, but they are unlikely to assert the Christian character of Australian society in the former manner. In a multicultural Australia they must also recognise and cooperate with other faiths. This religious unity is to be welcomed; but it is not likely to stem the ebbing tide of religion on this continent.

WALTER PHILLIPS

Religious history has been one of the most popular and widely read genres of Australian historiography. It is often argued, nevertheless, that religion has been neglected by writers of mainstream Australian history who err in representing Australia as a secular and masculinist country without a significant religious culture.

For early historical commentators with an interest in religion, such as J.D. **Lang** and John **West**, the planting of denominational Christianity upon the barren and anti-clerical ground of convict society was one of the great achievements of the early colonies. Yet after its colonial phase, religious history became the domain of cleric-historians celebrating their own denominational achievements. Cardinal Patrick Francis **Moran**, *History of the Catholic Church in*

Australasia (1894), while triumphalist in tone, was the first national study of a single denomination. It was not until the 1960s, when Patrick **O'Farrell** began his transformation of Catholic history from memorial to scholarly practice, that the academic pursuit of Australian denominational history can be said to have begun. The first edition of O'Farrell's *Catholic Church in Australia* appeared in 1968, and continued to gather depth with new and retitled editions in 1977, 1985, and 1992. O'Farrell's work remains rooted in the history of Ireland in the eighteenth and nineteenth centuries, and delineates the complex interactions of Irish ethnicity, community, clergy, and hierarchy.

The pioneering study of religious issues in colonial society was John Barrett, *That Better Country* (1966), and it was followed by studies of the colonial struggle between **church and state**, Christian **sectarianism**, and the **education** question, many of them published by Melbourne University Press. Michael **Roe** defined 'moral enlightenment', a concept which included a large component of Protestant values, as the answer to the *Quest for Authority in Eastern Australia 1835–1851* (1965). Other studies which wrestled with the formation of sectarian identities included T.L. Suttor, *Hierarchy and Democracy in Australia 1788–1870* (1965); J.S. Gregory, *Church and State* (1973); and, of course, O'Farrell, the major historian of Catholicism. Walter Phillips, *Defending a 'Christian Country'* (1981), and Richard Broome, *Treasure in Earthen Vessels* (1980), looked at the way in which Protestant churchmen sought to enshrine their model of society in legislation. By 1980 a body of work had been produced which placed sectarianism and denominational politics squarely in the centre of colonial culture. The entanglement of religion and politics also featured in much that was written in the same period about the twentieth century. Bruce Duncan's *The Movement: Crusade or Conspiracy?* (2001) brought a new detachment to the most divisive issue in postwar political history. Michael McKernan in *Australian Churches at War* (1980) and *Padre* (1986) profitably explored the theme of the churches and war.

The *Journal of Religious History*, first published in 1960 under the editorship of Bruce Mansfield, reflected a new confidence in the sub-discipline. It published articles on Australian and NZ religious history together with historical studies of all religions, places, and times. The major declared influence was the French journal *Annales*, and there was a conscious resistance to the purely Christian focus of the US *Church History* and the British *Journal of Ecclesiastical History*.

Despite this scholarship, a new generation of historians continued in the 1970s to feed the myth of Australia as an anti-clerical state whose people were indifferent to religion. Secular histories of Australia ignoring, or perhaps simply blind to, the Protestant hegemonic influence on Australian identity affirmed the secularist vision of Australia as a country without religion—or the mere form of Protestant ascendancy, which amounted to the same thing. The weakness of specifically Protestant historiography may be a factor here, despite the strength of regional studies. There remains no national history of the Church of England in Australia, and the first survey of the highly successful **evangelical** tradi-

tion, Stuart Piggin, *Evangelical Christianity in Australia: Spirit, Word and World*, appeared only in 1996.

Assessing the state of the field of Australian religious history in the 1960s, and again in the 1970s, O'Farrell and Mansfield worried most about whether denominational adherence influenced the scholarly judgment of religious historians. Yet, arguably, the domination of Australian religious history by mainstream Christian denominationalism has been a source of both strength and weakness. Although there are few national histories of denominations, there are many studies of individual dioceses, parishes, schools, and church organisations produced by practising pastors or communicant scholars who write the careful narrative history of sympathetic insiders. Works in this category, such as A.P. Elkin, *History of the Diocese of Newcastle* (1955), are notable for their loving attention to archival detail. More ambitious diocesan histories include, for Anglicans, David Hilliard, *Godliness and Good Order: A History of the Anglican Church in South Australia* (1986); Stephen Judd and Kenneth Cable, *Sydney Anglicans* (1987); and Brian Porter (ed.), *Melbourne Anglicans* (1997); and, for the NSW Methodists, Don Wright and Eric G. Clancy, *The Methodists: A History of Methodism in New South Wales* (1993); such works demonstrate the importance of the religion practised at the local level, where religious engagement was often felt and expressed most intensely.

Biography has also been a major vehicle for the scholarly investigation of religious issues in Australian history; notable contributions include A.T. Yarwood, *Samuel Marsden* (1977); B.A. **Santamaria**, *Daniel Mannix* (1984); D.W.A. Baker, *Days of Wrath: A Life of John Dunmore Lang* (1985); T.P. Boland, *James Duhig* (1986); Peter Hempenstall, *The Meddlesome Priest: A Life of Ernest Burgmann* (1993); and Edmund Campion, *Rockchopper: Growing Up Catholic in Australia* (1994). For actual hagiography there can be only one Australian subject, Mary **MacKillop**, who has received substantial treatment by Paul Gardiner (1993) and Lesley O'Brien (1994).

Religion as social practice divorced from a specific denominationalism did not emerge as a topic for historical discussion until the 1980s. Hugh Jackson opened up the topic of popular religious culture in the nineteenth century in a single, lively, and polished volume, *Churches and People in Australia and New Zealand 1860–1930* (1987), which was unusual in treating both Catholics and Protestants, and Australia and NZ, in the same study. Sally Kennedy's ground-breaking account of Catholic women's religious organisations, *Faith and Feminism* (1985), is another important foray into the field.

Judaism has been thoroughly treated by W.D. Rubinstein, *The Jews in Australia* (1986), Hilary Rubinstein, *The Jews in Australia: A Thematic History* (1991), and Suzanne D. Rutland, *Edge of the Diaspora* (1988). But historical accounts of other major world religions remains patchy, with the exception of Paul Croucher, *Buddhism in Australia 1848–1988* (1989), and the asides of religious sociologists, such as Hans Mol on secularisation, Gary D. Bouma on Islam, and Alan D. Black on minority religious practice. Despite the presence of large communities of Muslims and Orthodox believers, the history of these faiths in Australia remains practically unexplored.

Outside denominational Christianity and the world religions, there has been even more limited scholarship. Radical religion has had few historians, as indeed it secured few adherents in the founding period of the Australian churches. Jill Roe, *Beyond Belief* (1986), is a notable exception—notable too for its discussion of the place of women. On religion more esoteric even than theosophy there is N. Drury and G. Tillett, *Other Temples, Other Gods: The Occult in Australia* (1980).

Since the late 1980s there has been a major advance in the discipline away from a narrow emphasis on the political engagements of denominational Christianity with the state. The history of Aboriginal missions is a flourishing field, with surveys by John Harris, *One Blood* (1990), and Tony Swain and Deborah Rose (eds), *Aboriginal Australians and Christian Missions* (1988). Historical writing about Aboriginal religions has emerged as part of the **post-colonial** fascination with the construction of indigenous and national identities. In a controversial thesis, Tony Swain, *A Place for Strangers: Towards a History of Australian Aboriginal Being* (1993), argued that a number of the defining features of traditional religious belief in many of the major cultural blocs of Aboriginal Australia are artefacts of historical contact with outsiders. The influence of Swain is already being felt in new writing about the contact history of European Australia, such as Alan Atkinson, *The Europeans in Australia* (1996), a book which makes, almost for the first time, a full and nuanced engagement with religious themes as part of a general history of Australia.

The richness of the Australian religious landscape is emerging in specialist writing, such as that of Katharine Massam on Catholic spirituality, David Hilliard on the intersections of suburban life and secularism, and Anne O'Brien on gender and nineteenth-century religious life. A flurry of short, one-volume histories of Australian religious history appeared in the 1990s and sparked excited critical attention reflecting new expectations of practitioners. Ian Breward, *History of the Australian Churches* (1993), was the first national history of the Christian denominations with full coverage of neglected themes such as Orthodoxy, women, and Aboriginal Christians. There was dissatisfaction with the content of Roger Thompson, *Religion in Australia* (1994), who defended an older tradition of denominational history writing, one which focused on sectarian and political issues. More wideranging than these, Hilary Carey, *Believing in Australia* (1996), sought to open the full range of religious experiences in Australia to historical scrutiny. There was an extensive review of work up to 1980 in the *Journal of Religious History* (1980), and a subsequent review in the same journal (2000–01). Whether religious history can escape from the confines of denominational historiography which has contributed to its marginality within mainstream Australian historiography remains to be seen.

HILARY M. CAREY

Remittance man was a nineteenth-century male immigrant to Australia who was financially supported by regular remittance of funds from his wealthy or aristocratic family back home. Commonly a 'black sheep', he lived in subsidised colonial exile because his character, behaviour, or past indiscretion threatened family respectability. He was paid to stay away where he could only embarrass himself, and usually did, on drinking sprees or chasing women, or wasting his money and talent. *Remittance man* became a byword for a ne'er-do-well. The journal of Quaker missionary Frederick Mackie, republished as Mary Nicholls (ed.), *Traveller Under Concern* (1973), described a Melbourne example in 1854: 'the son of highly respected friends in England … spending his life in riot and intemperance … his indulgent father continually sends him supplies'. Remittance men feature in the writing of Henry **Lawson**, Joseph **Furphy**, Ambrose Pratt, and others. Judith **Wright's** poem 'Remittance Man' (1946) captures the contradictions of the disinherited, graceless spendthrift, so tragic and pathetic as he tramps the back tracks in the summer haze, but who is also liberated from the formal restrictions of an older, darker past.

DC

Rene, Roy 'Mo' (1891–1954) was the professional name adopted by Henry van der Sluys (or Sluice), regarded by many as Australia's finest comic performer. He took on the 'Mo' persona when he teamed up with Neil Phillips in 1916 and formed the 'Stiffy and Mo' duo. It was as part of this successful vaudeville act that he developed his distinctive black-and-white face paint and lisping delivery of his trademark phrase, 'Strike me lucky'. This was later used as the title of his only film (1934). His success continued in his radio career during the 1940s when, as Mo McCackie, he starred in the popular series *McCackie Mansions*. *Mo's Memoirs* (1945) were ghosted by Max Harris and Elizabeth Lambert. Fred Parsons, Mo's scriptwriter, wrote a celebratory biography, *A Man Called Mo* (1973).

KT

Repatriation, a distinctively Australian usage, signifies the responsibility assumed by the nation for enabling those who served it in war to be returned to peacetime society. First used during World War I, the word reflects a conviction that the 'returned serviceman', whose heroic sacrifice had constituted the nation, deserved to be assisted in reclaiming an honoured place in civilian life. Together, the services provided to assist returned soldiers ('the Repat') constituted, as Stephen Garton argues in *The Cost of War* (1996), 'a second welfare state' whose influence on Australian society is too little appreciated.

Australian policy towards its veterans was decisively shaped by official responses to the Great War, when in addition to the 60 000 who died, 166 000 (together more than two-thirds of those who had served overseas) suffered casualties or illness. The first Repatriation Act of 1917, passed by the **Hughes** government, placed responsibility for the scheme under a Repatriation Commission with a Department of Repatriation to administer it. The act established a wide range of benefits and services: war service, and war widows' pensions; assistance in finding work through labour bureaus; education and retraining; physical rehabilitation; free prostheses; free hospital care or hostel accommodation; war gratuities; war-service home loans; **soldier settlement** schemes; and assistance with children's education. Public and private employers were required to give preference to returned soldiers seeking work, although no-one knew quite how, or even when, such preference should be given. Central to these policies was the idea that returned soldiers deserved help to regain their independence, but should not be subjected to the humiliation of charity. According to Edward Millen, the first minister for repatriation, the state acknowledged an obligation to the returned soldier and 'aimed to redeem the debt as far as redemption was possible'.

The financial obligation which the nation undertook in the immediate aftermath of war grew in peacetime as the human costs of war accumulated. By 1938 benefits and services dispersed through Repatriation accounted for almost one-fifth of Commonwealth outlays. While repatriation benefits were ostensibly given as a matter of right, claimants for war disability pensions, for example, had to run a gauntlet of doctors and officials charged with a responsibility of weeding out malingerers and impostors. Various ex-servicemen's organisations, especially the **Returned and Services League**, strove to widen the scope of eligibility, while the rest of the community, increasingly suspicious of the lurks and perks of 'the Repat' system, called for increased vigilance.

More than 82 000 ex-servicemen were still in receipt of pensions when World War II broke out. This time the level of casualties was lower but the numbers of enlisted men, and the consequent pressure on the Repatriation scheme when the conflict was over, were much higher. By 1950 over 180 000 were receiving war or service pensions. It was probably the taxing powers by the Commonwealth that enabled it to meet the costs of the scheme. The broad scope was unaltered, although Australia, like other combatant nations, now placed more emphasis upon university education, occupational therapy, and other scientific forms of physical and emotional rehabilitation. The **Vietnam War** posed new problems of repatriation, if only because the society which the veterans re-entered had been so divided by the conflict itself. Veterans' organisations fought hard, and with some success, to secure recognition of the special health and emotional problems of their members. The proportion securing pensions and other benefits was broadly comparable to those in earlier wars. In 1976 the old division between the Repatriation Commission and the Department was abolished with the creation of the new Department of Veterans' Affairs.

In their official history, *The Last Shilling: A History of Repatriation in Australia* (1994), Clem Lloyd and Jacqui Rees see the generous level and scope of Australia's repatriation scheme as evidence of its democratic welfare tradition, a verdict which is qualified, however, by the more systematic comparisons in Stephen Garton's *The Cost of War*. While Australians were generous in extending their assistance to more ex-servicemen, and made fewer distinctions of rank or proportional assistance between them, the average purchasing power of those benefits was less than that offered in some other countries.

GRAEME DAVISON

Republicanism is a crucial, but neglected, topic in Australian historical writing, partly because Australian republicanism has often been conflated with working-class radicalism by historians influenced by Marxism. Today, Australian republicanism needs to be studied in its own terms without the hints of imminent insurrection that distort both Noel McLachlan's *Waiting for the Revolution: A History of Australian Nationalism* (1989) and Robert **Hughes's** *The Fatal Shore* (1987).

Although the term *republicanism* is often associated in Australia with anti-royalist nationalism and with demands for Australian independence from Britain, this was only one of the republican strands in nineteenth-century Australian culture, and not the most important one. In colonial NSW republicanism was associated with the bloody outcome of the French Revolution and with the works of Tom Paine. Another aristocratic and agrarian strand of Australian republicanism was indebted to classical Roman and Greek republican thought of Polybius, Solon, and Cicero. Thus the colonial conservative James **Macarthur** cited Polybius and used classical republican notions of civic virtue to justify the need for a colonial aristocracy. Yet another strand in Australian republicanism associated republican government with the English constitution, the sovereignty of parliament after 1688, and the birthright of British subjects. All sides used this rhetoric in the lead up to **responsible government** in 1856. Republicanism in this sense was associated with opposition to tyranny, not opposition to **monarchy**, although this could pass over into possible independence from Britain when a governor seemed despotic (for example, **Gipps** in the 1840s), or if the British government attempted to reintroduce **transportation** or was reluctant to protect Australian interests by keeping other powers out of the Pacific. Colonial republicanism was often a bluff to persuade the British government to accept colonists' demands.

A more virulent republicanism demanding separation from Britain was promoted by John Dunmore **Lang**, the notorious Presbyterian clergyman. Lang, however, insisted that he was loyal to Britain; he also referred to 'the Australian Empire'. He was the most articulate republican in nineteenth-century Australia, and the only one to advance a detailed republican scheme. He was not a secular republican. His ideals of independence and self-government were Biblically based, and he argued for the independence of Australia and of each colony from one another on strict Presbyterian theological grounds. Lang wanted 'godly Commonwealths' in which there was no sharp distinction between the sacred and the secular; he also spoke of representative democracy under the universal government of God. Lang's attempt to link republicanism with independence from Britain, however, was unsuccessful, partly because of the efforts of Henry **Parkes**, who argued in the pages of his paper *Empire* that republicanism, in fact if not in name, was consistent with the British constitution, not incompatible with it.

As colonial **liberalism** developed, it incorporated much of the 'commercial republic' version of republicanism advanced by Thomas Madison in the USA. Republicanism in Australia came to mean representative government in the interests of the people, not participation of the people. A case can also be made for republican elements in the social reformism of Victorian liberals such as George **Higin-botham**, C.H. **Pearson**, and Alfred **Deakin**, but there is no strong tradition of the sovereignty of citizens in Australia.

Many later nineteenth-century republicans advocated separation from Britain, but they were mostly British and only recently arrived. Irish and the native-born were not over-prominent in separatist activities, and many of the British who promoted separatism were originally cosmopolitan republicans, or were Welsh or Scots, bearing the grudges of subject populations. There was also a labourist republicanism oriented to social reform and workers' rights rather than to separation from Britain. The peak of activity occurred in the 1880s when 15 republican organisations and 20 newspapers or journals appeared in cities and major country towns. Studies of this outburst, however, confirm its involvement with struggles between capital and labour, as well as the absence of developed republican ideas. The Charters Towers Republican Association, for example, was made up of workers and miners united against British capitalists. A republicanism hostile to social inequality spread to outback workers, but republican issues were down-graded as potentially divisive by labour leaders seeking success in strikes and social struggles. Even William **Lane** was not sympathetic to republicanism without social reform, and emphasised that republicanism in Australia needed to be socially radical, thoroughly progressive, and democratic politically.

In 1887 the Australian Socialist League was republican, and there were republican riots at the time of Queen Victoria's jubilee. But republicans remained a largely secularist minority with little support from the bulk of the population. Even Catholic bishops remained in favour of the monarchy, as did vulnerable ethnic minorities, such as the Chinese. The nationalist republicanism associated with the *Bulletin* was more significant, not because it was anti-royalist and anti-British, but because it implied that what was original about Australia fitted better with a republic. This insight also coloured the views of Louisa and Henry **Lawson**, and their paper, the *Republican*. The Lawsons argued that independence from Britain was essential if Australia's **national identity** was to emerge fully. This theme was taken up by later writers and artists, including Les **Murray**.

At Federation there were theoretical republicans, such as Charles **Lilley**, W.H. Traill, and Andrew Inglis **Clark**, as well as a few republican extremists. But the crucial voices were sympathetic to constitutional liberalism and to the Empire tie. After Federation, the **Australian Labor Party** came to support the monarchy and the Empire as the only realistic option. Indeed, loyalty to the Empire was the dominant note well into the twentieth century, partly because the Empire was a multinational organisation committed to parliamentary government. Even the *Bulletin* came round to this view.

Despite the activism of individual republicans, such as Geoffrey **Dutton** and Donald **Horne**, the separatist republicanism made little progress in Australia until the **Whitlam** crisis of 1975. In 1991 the Australian Republican Movement was set up by prominent individuals. Its republicanism was minimal and limited to a single issue: changing to an Australian head of state. In the 1990s Paul **Keating** and his speechwriter, Don Watson, revived the patriotic nationalist republicanism of Henry Lawson, as if the only authentic Australians were those who wished to separate from Britain. The Keating government committed itself to the creation of an Australian republic on minimalist lines at the 1996 election, which it lost, but the incoming Liberal government, though officially monarchist, promised to give the people a chance of expressing their views on the issue. In February 1998 a half-elected, half-nominated constitutional convention resolved in favour of a republic with a president elected by a joint sitting of the parliament. This proposal was put to the people in 1999 and defeated with 55 per cent voting No. The modern republican debate has prompted polemical works by two historians: Alan Atkinson, *The Muddle-Headed Republic* (1993), and John Hirst, *A Republican Manifesto* (1994).

Today the neglect of the Australian republican heritage is belatedly being remedied, sometimes at the risk of finding republican influences everywhere: from the writings of colonial governors to the dicta of High Court judges. Mark McKenna's *The Captive Republic: A History of Republicanism in Australia 1788–1996* (1996) now provides an overview which emphasises the importance of monarchist republicanism in the nineteenth century. McKenna argues that Australian separatist republicans had few republican political ideas and virtually no program. They were often markedly less republican than the constitutional liberals who remained loyal to the monarchy; they were also less effective in bringing about political and social change.

It may also be misleading to treat Australian republicanism as merely one part of a pluralist British legacy. There were isolated receptions of German and Central European ideas, as well as considerable interest in twentieth-century Spanish republican debates. Much is often made of a French republican tradition in Australia, but the evidence is thin. Lawson celebrated French revolutionary traditions in some of his poems, but mainly to offend loyalists. He was not a student of French republican thought, and ended up a monarchist. There was one Italian republican at **Eureka**, but the rising was guided by Chartist, not republican, ideas.

There was also some reception of American political thought. The Tasmanian republican Andrew Inglis Clark cited Jefferson and enthused about natural rights, just as earlier Australians had noted that the Confederacy had a case against the Union. Irish voices were also heard. Ned **Kelly** was an Irish nationalist with a notion of an autonomous Victorian regional republic, while Daniel **Deniehy** derived his political ideals from English and European sources. Irish republicanism remained important, but there were few attempts to propose foreign republican models for Australia. The indigenous tradition was inclined instead to appeal to inarticulate notions of democracy, national development, and fairness. This tradition now deserves extended treatment. The major figures need to be studied in depth, and a much greater appreciation of the originality and diversity of Australian republicanism needs to inform our historiography and public debate.

WAYNE HUDSON

Reserve Bank of Australia, which commenced operations in 1960 following federal legislation the previous year, is Australia's central monetary authority and controls Australian **banking** practices. This function, a postwar Keynesian measure introduced through legislation in 1945, had been initially carried out by the central banking arm of the Commonwealth Bank, but a conflict of interest between its trading and regulating roles highlighted the need for an independent authority. The Reserve Bank is controlled by the federal government and administered by a board and governor. H.C. **Coombs** served as the first governor. Its legislation specified that it should encourage a stable currency and full employment, and promote 'the economic prosperity and welfare of the Australian' people. Until the Australian dollar was floated in 1983, the Reserve Bank also managed the exchange rate. Following the election of the **Howard** government in 1996, the primary commitment to full employment gave way to control of inflation. While the Reserve Bank gained greater independence from government, it lost some of its traditional supervisory functions to a new regulatory body, the Australian Prudential Regulation Authority. Boris Schedvin published a history in 1992.

HD

Responsible government is the system of parliamentary government under which ministers hold office only so long as they command a majority in the lower house of the parliament. It was introduced in the mid-1850s to the Australian colonies (except WA which acquired it in 1890) and replaced the rule by governors and officials appointed by the Colonial Office. It was provided for in the federal **Constitution**, but only awkwardly because a strong upper house like the Senate threatens the system by making the government dependent on the support of two houses which may take different views. To ensure that the government could rely on its taxation and spending measures being passed (without which it cannot operate), the Senate was prevented from amending these, though it could suggest alterations. However, the Senate was left with the power to reject these measures outright. This power was not used until 1975, when the Senate created the impasse which led to the **Dismissal** of the **Whitlam** government. In his advice to the governor-general on this occasion, Chief Justice **Barwick** declared that the government was ultimately responsible to both houses, a novel doctrine at the time, but one which the outcome of the episode appears to confirm.

JH

Returned and Services League was formed in Brisbane in September 1916 as a federal body representing the interests of 'returned men'—an expression meaning veterans of wars who had served overseas. Its original name was 'Returned Sailors' and Soldiers' Imperial League of Australia', to which 'Airmen's' was added during World War II. Extravagant promises had been made to induce men to enlist, and men returning to Australia while World War I still continued, many of them badly injured, found a level of indifference to their plight and an uncertainty about them in civilian society. So the RSL began as a protective organisation for men fearful for their place in Australian society as a result of their war service.

When the war concluded, Australia was swamped with returning soldiers looking to resume their civilian lives. They wanted jobs and security, and they expected governments to honour pledges about pensions and medical treatments. Some returning men also believed that service at war gave them a greater entitlement to determine Australia's future, and in the tense political environment caused by the **conscription** debates and **sectarianism**, 'loyalist' ex-soldiers questioned the right of their opponents to be heard at all. Recognising that veterans had a variety of political allegiances, the RSL attempted to stand apart from politics, with little apparent success. To advance its causes, the RSL necessarily had to be involved with elected government.

The RSL adopted a broadly based structure designed to ensure that the organisation was firmly in the control of its members. Sub-branches were established in each local community, controlled by a state branch, to which the sub-branches sent delegates. In turn, state branches elected delegates to a national congress—the supreme policy-making body. Each state branch elected a state president, and together these presidents and the national president formed a national executive to guide the affairs of the RSL between congresses. The structure, unless monitored by constant vigilance on the part of the members, reposed a great deal of power in the elected and paid state and national officials. Membership reached its peak in 1919 with about half of the eligible veterans enrolling, usually on the troopships as they returned to Australia, or immediately thereafter. Membership then declined rapidly, with only about nine per cent of eligible veterans retaining their interest in the RSL by 1924.

Such a collapse of membership requires explanation, as does the continuing influence of the RSL while representing only a minority of veterans. The 1920s were a confused time for those who had served overseas. Many veterans wanted to forget war, others needed assistance to re-establish themselves after the torment of war. At the local level the RSL was a major and successful welfare agency, caring for veterans, assisting them in all matters relating to **repatriation** entitlements, and establishing programs to assist widows and dependants. Its clubhouses became important social centres where the drinking was interrupted for one minute's silence in honour of the fallen. The organisation of the ceremonial of **Anzac Day** was an important part of the league's activities at branch and state level.

Conflict was endemic in the higher reaches of the organisation. The national president from 1919 to 1946, Gilbert Dyett, had been badly wounded in the fighting at Lone Pine on Gallipoli and, repatriated to Australia in 1915, saw none of the fighting on the Western Front. Dyett was a skilled diplomat who worked carefully behind the scenes with politicians—too quietly for some of his more strident opponents. Each election he contested for the national presidency was hard-fought, a substantial clique of members believing that the senior position should be reserved for a person of high military rank. Dyett's troubles within the organisation culminated in 1930, when he had to rely on his own vote and the casting vote of the national secretary to survive.

The model that Dyett established continues to prevail in the RSL. Attracting demagogues from time to time, the RSL has prospered under conciliatory and skilful negotiators. William Keys, whose length of service for the RSL — first as national secretary and then for a decade as national president—matches that of Dyett's, was the exemplary RSL leader. Always willing to talk to the media, and skilled in putting his view across, Keys reserved most of his energies for negotiations at the highest political levels. Observers noted with admiration his capacity to develop close and effective relations successively with Prime Ministers **Fraser** and **Hawke**. Keys would fight with great determination for the interests of his members, and would comment on matters affecting Australian defence and security, always an RSL concern, but he recognised the need to modernise the organisation and reform membership requirements as the number of veterans of both world wars declined significantly. At first strictly limited to those who served overseas, membership has now been widened to all former and present members of the defence forces.

The RSL still benefits from respect and admiration for increasingly aged veterans and their contribution in war. For the 'Australia Remembers' program to commemorate the 50th anniversary of the end of World War II, the RSL worked closely with the federal government on a program of activities that involved large numbers of people. But increasingly strident and plainly silly responses to issues well outside the RSL's stated charter on the part of officials, even at the level of national president, have disturbed some members of the RSL and the wider public. It is possible that RSL influence on national life was one of the great myths of twentieth-century Australia. A rapidly reducing membership may cause less influential officials to shout even louder to be heard.

G.L. Kristianson's history of the RSL, *The Politics of Patriotism* (1966), is particularly concerned with its pressure-group activities.

MICHAEL MCKERNAN

Reynolds, Henry (1938–), historian, graduated from the University of Tasmania with an MA. His ground-breaking work, *The Other Side of the Frontier* (1981), which won the Ernest Scott Prize, was an examination of Aboriginal responses to British colonisation that included previously little-discussed issues, such as guerrilla warfare and the exploitation of Aboriginal women by white frontiersmen, and launched a stream of publications on post-colonial Aboriginal society by Aboriginal and white historians. His subsequent works, which included *Frontier* (1987) and *This Whispering in Our Hearts* (1998), brought a new subtlety to the examination of black–white relations. *The Law of the Land* (1987) drew attention to British commitment to land rights in the 1830s, and *With the White People* (1990, reprinted as *Black Pioneers* 2000) showed how Aborigines adapted to the European settlers. He was the first academic historian to argue for the justice of **Aboriginal land rights** and, later, sovereignty. His *Fate of a Free People* (1995) investigates claims to Tasmanian Aboriginal sovereignty—an issue that he covers nationally in *Aboriginal Sovereignty* (1996). Reynolds was an associate professor of history at James Cook University of Northern Queensland and then took up a research fellowship. His work with Eddie Mabo on an oral history project in the 1970s contributed to the High Court's recognition of land rights.

HD

Richardson, Henry Handel was the pen name of Ethel Florence Lindesay Richardson (1870–1946), novelist and short-story writer. Although she left Australia at the age of 18 and returned only once for a brief visit, much of her important work was Australian in setting and in complex ways autobiographical. She is regarded as one of the major figures of Australian literature.

Richardson was born in Fitzroy, Melbourne, the elder of two daughters of Walter Richardson and his wife Mary. Although Walter died when Ethel was only nine years old, critical and biographical studies of her have always devoted considerable space to the story of his life—in part because her trilogy of novels, *The Fortunes of Richard Mahony*, undoubtedly her major work, was based upon her father's life. There are, however, a number of differences—Richardson was a significant figure in the intellectual and social community in Ballarat and Melbourne, while Mahony was a restless figure increasingly at odds with colonial society. Walter Richardson was also an enthusiastic spiritualist at a time when many of his progressive contemporaries were similarly exploring psychic phenomena. Ethel Richardson was herself an active member of the spiritualist movement in Britain.

Ethel Richardson lived as a child in Chiltern, Queenscliff, Koroit, Maldon, and as a boarder at Presbyterian Ladies College, Melbourne. She excelled at music, and in August 1888 left Melbourne with her sister Lillian and her mother for Leipzig, Germany, where she studied piano at the conservatorium. There she met and in 1895 married John George Robertson, a major English scholar of German literature. They lived in Germany until 1903, when Robertson accepted the chair of German at the University of London; thereafter Richardson lived and wrote in England.

Richardson adopted the pen-name Henry Handel Richardson for her first novel, *Maurice Guest* (1908), about the lives of music students in Leipzig, and thereafter always published under this name. *The Getting of Wisdom* (1910) was set in a girls' boarding school, based in part upon her own experiences at PLC. The Richard Mahony trilogy (*Australia Felix*, 1917; *The Way Home*, 1925; *Ultima Thule*, 1929) told the story of Mahony from store-keeper on the Ballarat fields to his tragic madness and death—critics and biographers have argued that Richardson knew her father had died of the effects of syphilis, and that she wrote into the novel an accurate account of the effects of the disease. It was the third volume of the trilogy which received the greatest popular and critical acclamation at the time of publication. Later works included *The Young Cosima* (1939), a novel about Wagner and his circle, and a short-story collection, *The End of a Childhood* (1934). Her last work was *Myself When Young* (1948), an unfinished autobiographical narrative—Axel Clark's study, *Henry Handel Richardson: Fiction in the Making* (1990), also covers these early years.

The reception of Richardson's work in Australia has generally been related to two major clusters of issues—nationalism and realism. Her work met with a somewhat muted response from nationalist critics, who remained troubled by her expatriate status. 'Though most of her work is Australian in subject,' H.M. **Green** wrote in his *History of Australian Literature* (1962), 'none of it is Australian in tone.' Richardson's work then found criticism from the more cosmopolitan and evaluative tradition in Australian criticism, for its commitment to realism—'a victim of the dictatorship of facts', wrote Leonie Gibson (Kramer) in *Henry Handel Richardson and Some of Her Sources* (1954); 'distrusts her powers of invention', argued Adrian Mitchell in *The Oxford History of Australian Literature* (1981). Dorothy Green's *Henry Handel Richardson and Her Fiction* (1973, 1986) is devoted to refuting these charges, and to stressing Richardson's context in European intellectual history. Three volumes of her correspondence have been edited by Clive Probyn and Bruce Steele (2000).

Contemporary critics are now beginning to locate new topics of interest in Richardson's work—in particular exploring issues of gender and sexuality, and reasserting the importance of her more exploratory short fiction. Current work on her unpublished correspondence is making possible a more complete assessment of the biographical and historical sources of her fiction. She remains an emblem of the cosmopolitan possibilities of Australian literature.

DAVID GOODMAN

Ricketson, Staniforth (1891–1967) entered the financial world in 1911 as a stockbroker with the firm established by his great-grandfather, J.B. Were & Son. After war service he returned to Weres as senior partner, and turned it into Australia's largest stockbroking firm. Conservative and outspoken, Ricketson was extremely influential in the finance industry as he pushed for **banking** law reforms and helped establish the short-term money market. He played a central role in the recruitment of J.A. **Lyons** to head the new **United Australia Party**. Ricketson figures in *Australian Financiers: Biographical Essays* (ed. R.T. Appleyard and C.B. Schedvin, 1988).

KT

Ripon Regulations, introduced in 1831 by the Earl of Ripon (then Viscount Goderich), instigated a new system for the sale of Crown land in the Australian colonies. Crown land had previously been acquired through grants or sale by tender. The Ripon Regulations standardised the sale process by introducing compulsory sale by auction and by setting a minimum sale price of 5 shillings per acre; this rose to 12 shillings per acre in 1839 and to £1 in 1842. The proceeds from land sales were used to fund the assisted **immigration** of labourers and servants into the colonies. The Ripon Regulations pre-dated settlement in Victoria, SA and Qld; in Tasmania and NSW much land had already been disposed of through large land grants.

HD

Rischbieth, Bessie Mabel (1874–1967) was arguably the most important figure in the Australian women's movement during the 1920s and 1930s. A former Adelaide society beauty who had been raised by a progressive theosophist uncle, Bessie moved to WA with her husband in 1899. She soon became an activist and was founding vice-president of the Women's Service Guild of WA in 1909. An expert lobbyist, political tactician, and networker, Rischbieth used her skills to promote the guild's principal aim: absolute equality between men and women.

In 1921 she formed the Australian Federation of Women Voters, and served as its president for 21 years. She frequently crossed the country at her own expense, energising this coalition with visits, meetings, and lecture tours. Her main aim in creating the federation was to enable Australian women's voices to be heard overseas, and she immediately arranged for its affiliation to the International Woman's Suffrage Alliance. She led the Australian delegations to nearly all the alliance's triennial congresses, and also to the inaugural Pan-Pacific Women's Conference in Honolulu. A committed supporter of Empire, she was a co-founder of the British Commonwealth League of Women. After the early death of her husband Henry in 1926, Bessie was left independently wealthy and able to move freely on the international stage: after each trip overseas she brought back to Australian women news of the latest developments.

Rischbieth's prominence waned after World War II, partly because of her aversion to party politics. She became a passionate environmentalist, and attracted widespread public attention at the age of 89 when, characteristically well-dressed except for her bare feet, she confronted the bulldozers filling in the Swan River for a freeway. In the same year she published *The March of Australian Women* (1964) as a record of her life's work. Feminist histories such as Marilyn Lake, *Getting Equal* (1999), and Fiona Paisley, *Loving Protection?* (2000), have more recently paid her increasing attention.

DIANNE DAVIDSON

River transport developed soon after Europeans established each colony and used the rivers nearest them. Numerous little port towns grew up at river mouths and these became linked by intra-colonial and later inter-colonial shipping. Initially, river transport was by sail and rowboat; mechanical means did not appear until the arrival of paddle-steamers in the early 1830s. These were the high technology of their day, and were first introduced into Sydney Harbour, the Hunter River, and the Brisbane River, with the Melbourne area following in the 1840s. Inland navigation on the **Murray**, Darling, and Murrumbidgee Rivers was established in the 1850s using the same technology, and considerable areas of pasture and arable land were opened up as a result. Similar services commenced in SA, WA, and the NT and, unlike those in the east, they carried both freight (primary produce, supplies, etc.) and passengers on most journeys. The standard history of shipping in Australia, *A Maritime History of Australia* (1976) by John Bach, does not devote much space to river transport; a better appreciation is obtained from Barry Pemberton's *Australian Coastal Shipping* (1979), where the narrative of river operation is blended with the wider story of that along the coasts. The fullest account of riverboat operations on the Murray, Darling, and Murrumbidgee Rivers is still Ian Mudie's *Riverboats* (1961).

The advent of steamships as the successor to paddle-steamers enabled an expansion of most river services and an increase in their number and frequency, especially in NSW. There were individual steamship companies for nearly all the rivers from Shoalhaven in the south to the Richmond in the north. The Hunter River company dated from the 1840s; most of the others began between the 1850s and the 1870s. Many of the rivers had bars at their mouths and navigation was hazardous: over the years a number of ships were lost as a result. The best regional history of a river is that by L.T. Daley, *Men and a River* (1966).

In 1891 the river companies from the Hunter north amalgamated and formed the North Coast Steam Navigation Co., which then dominated the whole northern area, providing river services until rising labour costs and serious competition from road transport forced it to be wound up in 1954. The principal account of this firm is by M.P. Richards in *The North Coast Run* (3rd edn, 1996). Services on the Hawkesbury were not affected and, although they changed in nature at different periods, some still operate on at least a weekly basis. The most recent writing is Jean Purtell, *The Mosquito Fleet: Hawkesbury River Trade and Traders 1794–1994* (1995). Tourism plays an important part in sustaining the services on this river.

The long-distance trades were maintained along the Murray, Darling, Barwon, and Murrumbidgee Rivers throughout the nineteenth century and until World War I. At the peak in about the 1880s, some 6500 kilometres of waterway were serviced, and more than 200 steamboats and barges were being employed. However, it was a relatively slow form of travel, and both colonial and state governments invested small amounts in river improvements or the development of the ports serviced by the shipping. For example, Goolwa, Port Elliot, and Victor Harbor in SA did not even realise their limited potential. Victoria and NSW built railways to divert the river trade away from SA. The trade had

declined significantly by World War I, when a series of droughts caused great inconvenience. The lock-building program on the Murray had just commenced, but was too late to stimulate the trade. Gwenda Painter's *The River Trade: Wool and Steamers* (1979) contains evocative illustrations of this era as well as useful commentary. Other useful histories include *Echuca: A Centenary History* (1965) by Susan Priestley and *Rich River* (1953) by Allan Morris.

The interwar period saw the gradual demise of the remaining river services in Australia; many ran weekly or less often. After World War II the ever-increasing number of motor trucks made it even more difficult for river services to survive. The small non-capital ports which had largely developed as a result of the initial river services had reached their peak well before that war, and their value was subsequently realised and maintained through **tourist** development, encouraged by the conservation movement and concern for **heritage** and the National Estate. New riverboats were constructed to meet these new tourist markets, and much effort was also expended on the restoration of surviving nineteenth-century boats, either for tours or as moored museums. The waterfront precincts of the River Murray towns—Echuca, Swan Hill, Mildura, Renmark, and Mannum—have taken on new life.

G.R. HENNING

Rivett family practised religion, medicine, philanthropy, science, and journalism with a strong sense of social responsibility. ALBERT (1855–1934) was a Congregational minister of progressive sympathies, who died while speaking at a protest meeting at the Sydney Domain in support of Egon **Kisch**. Of his children, ELEANOR CHRISTINE (1883–1972) was a missionary and educationist in India; ELSIE GRACE (1887–1964) promoted children's libraries; AMY CHRISTINE (1891–1962) was a doctor and disciple of Marie Stopes; and DORIS MARY (1896–1969), a psychologist, joined with Elsie in promoting children's welfare.

All achieved educational distinction, but (ALBERT CHERBURY) DAVID (1885–1961) was the most distinguished. From a degree in chemistry at Melbourne he proceeded to Oxford with a Rhodes scholarship and then returned to Melbourne, where he married Stella, a daughter of Alfred **Deakin**, and became professor of chemistry in 1924. From 1927 he was the head of the newly formed Council for Scientific and Industrial Research (later the **CSIRO**). His successful leadership is documented by C.B. Schedvin, *Shaping Science and Industry* (1987), though Cold War political controversies overshadowed his final years. A biography was written by his son, ROHAN DEAKIN (1917–77), who became a journalist. From his experiences as a prisoner of war after capture in 1942 at Singapore, where he was a war correspondent, Rohan Rivett wrote *Behind Bamboo* (1946). Eleanor Rivett's memoirs, *Memory Plays a Tune*, appeared in 1965.

SM

Roberts, Stephen Henry (1901–71) was a most significant historian and educator in twentieth-century

Australia. Born of humble migrant parents in Maldon, Victoria, and educated largely in Ernest **Scott's** history department at the University of Melbourne, he made his name as Sydney's second Challis Professor of History (1929–47) and was later its vice-chancellor (1947–67) in critical years of development.

Grounded in the empiricism of the Scott department, he also acquired its professional concern with research, together with its related concern for citizenship and an outlook of internationalism. As a postgraduate student at the London School of Economics, he studied French colonial policies. At Sydney he stamped his European outlook on the department and stressed research. In a remarkable burst of energy, he wrote six books of significance in a decade; several are still in use today, notably those to do with Australian **pastoral history**. These pioneer studies of early white land settlement reflected a romantic and nascent sense of Australian nationality, while his European studies captured a contemporary interest in the role of the colonial empires then at their apogee. He also expanded his concept of history into the contemporary period through a fascination with international affairs. A study of German Nazism, *The House That Hitler Built* (1937), courageously exposed national socialism and its racist ideologies, making Roberts both famous and affluent. Roberts wrote extensively for the newspapers, and provided pioneer communications in the new medium of **radio**.

Within NSW he wrote the key texts for schools and chaired the Examinations Board. His conviction that history was a preparation for intelligent citizenship characterised his school and university curriculum design. A firm believer in the idea of progress through economic and scientific development, he took a traditional view towards indigenous societies, such as Australian Aboriginals, presuming that their culture would be submerged by development and **assimilation**. Education would be a key catalyst of that process. As University of Sydney vice-chancellor after World War II, he supported an outreach for educating Pacific Islanders and PNG citizens, and delighted at Charles **Perkins's** becoming Sydney's first Aboriginal graduate. He failed to value indigenous Aboriginal culture, but wrote about Australia with a notable non-British bias: he encouraged a broad international view and he pointed to the significance of the Asia–Pacific in Australia's future. There is a memoir by an administrative colleague, David Wood, and an appraisal by Deryck Schreuder in Stuart Macintyre and Julian Thomas (eds), *The Discovery of Australian History* (1995).

DERYCK SCHREUDER

Roberts, Thomas William 'Tom' (1856–1931) was a painter who has come to be regarded as the key figure of the **Heidelberg School** in its evocation of the Australian landscape, yet, English-born and spending almost half his life in England, he saw himself as much an Englishman as an Australian. He left England as a child and returned in 1881 to attend the Royal Academy of Art and again from 1903 to complete what he called the 'Big Picture' of the opening of the first federal parliament.

During his lifetime Roberts never gained recognition on the scale accorded his friend Arthur **Streeton**. But with the publication in 1935 of R.H. Croll's *Tom Roberts: Father of Australian Landscape Painting* the Roberts myth began to take shape: how, travelling in Spain in 1884, he had met at Granada two Spanish painters who preached the gospel of impressionism which Roberts brought back to Australia, where it was to inspire the Heidelberg School. Art historians now agree that the application of the term *impressionism* to the Heidelberg painters is inappropriate, and the Spanish story largely a colourful irrelevance, but Roberts's European training and experience combined with his enthusiasm and organisational skills made him a crucial figure in stimulating the Melbourne art scene, the most notable example being the celebrated '9 by 5' exhibition of 1889.

Although his own background was shabby-genteel, Roberts cut a dashing figure in society and was an articulate spokesman for the artistic community. As the founding president of the Society of Artists in Sydney, he signed his name in the visitors' book at Government House, thus affirming the position of the professional artist in colonial society. When painting the 'Big Picture', he enjoyed meeting royalty, the vice-regal set and political leaders, striking up a number of friendships, particularly with attorney-general and later prime minister, Alfred **Deakin**.

The years spent painting the 'Big Picture' are often seen as debilitating Roberts's artistic talent, but for him the project helped define his sense of Anglo-Australian identity: 'The royalty and its suite of Governors of states and—the members, democracy—with the people— / that's the Empire and this all meets under the one roof.' If in England Roberts was a great one for nostalgically burning gum leaves, he had also 'longed and longed' to return to 'the centre of our race'. His nickname, 'Bulldog', confirmed his Britishness.

Tom Roberts's big rural set-pieces, such as *Shearing the Rams* (1889–90) and *Bailed Up* (1895), have become national icons, but his work also encompassed urban and beach scenes. He was, furthermore, an accomplished portrait painter and one of the few of his generation to paint Aborigines. In all his work he was sustained by a belief in the role of the artist in society. Helen Topliss rightly asserts that Roberts was 'heroic in his claims for art and as a patriot' (*ADB*), but his overriding loyalty was to the Empire. A biography by Humphrey **McQueen** appeared in 1996.

JOHN RICKARD

Robertson, George (1860–1933) became an influential Australian bookseller and publisher in the late nineteenth century. After migration from England via NZ, he first opened a bookshop in Melbourne but transferred to Sydney in the 1870s. With David Angus he established his most successful partnership, and by the end of the century Angus & Robertson was the most important Australian firm of publishers. Henry **Lawson**, Banjo **Paterson**, and Mary **Gilmore** were among the writers he published. Robertson's interest in Australiana brought him in touch with such major collectors as David **Mitchell** and William **Dixson**. His evidence to a parliamentary committee on the worth of the former's collection was influential in the establishment of the Mitchell Library. The early history of the firm is outlined in *Some Early Australian Bookmen* (1978), by Robertson's grandson, George Ferguson. *Dear Robertson* (1982) is a selection of his correspondence edited by A.W. Barker, a revised version of which was published in 1993 as *George Robertson: A Publishing Life in Letters*.

KT

Robertson, John (1816–91) designed, fought for, and implemented the land policy of **selection** before survey in NSW. He was, unusually, both a politician and a popular hero. A ballad celebrated the adoption of his policy in 1861: 'Come all you Cornstalks, the victory's won, / John Robertson's triumphed, the lean days are gone.' Henry **Lawson** wrote a poem in his honour in the 1880s. There are statues in the Sydney Domain and at the Land Office.

The man who opened the whole of the **squatters**' holdings to settlement by the small man was himself a squatter. From a base of freehold land in the Hunter Valley, he had been part of the squatting rush over the divide into the Liverpool Plains, and had explored the new country as far as Bourke on the Darling. He was an accomplished bushman, a great drinker and swearer, short-tempered and generous-hearted, a man not to be contained by parliamentary etiquette.

He arrived in NSW as a child of five and always thought of himself as Australian. One of his teachers was J.D. **Lang**, who remained a mentor and from whom he seems to have imbibed his radicalism. In the debate over the **Constitution** in the 1850s he was unusual in showing no respect for British precedent. He wanted a constitution of republican simplicity: a single house, manhood suffrage, and absolutely equal electorates.

He entered the first parliament in 1856 as radical **liberal**. He was responsible for the rejection of the land bill of the first liberal government. It provided that land be resumed from the squatters as need arose, surveyed, and sold at auction. Robertson insisted that land must be sold at a fixed price, on time payment, and that selectors should, without waiting for surveyors, be able to mark out their farms anywhere they chose. He rallied great popular support for his scheme. **Cowper**, the liberal leader, gave up his objections to it; liberals who would not yield were defeated at the polls; and finally Cowper and Robertson coerced the conservative majority in the Legislative Council into acceptance by reconstituting the Council with fresh nominees. D.W.A. Baker, in his influential article, 'The Origins of Robertson's Land Acts' (*HSANZ*, 1958), was mistaken in seeing the acts as the victory of middle-class liberals over the squatters. It was only after the solid middle-class liberals were replaced by more radical members that the acts were carried.

The objection to selection before survey was that it would needlessly bring insecurity to all squatters and lead to warfare on the land between selectors and squatters. These fears were amply realised, but Robertson had made free selection such an article of faith that it was impossible to touch it for two decades. Whatever its failings, Robertson's

measure had given many small men their chance and they provided a grateful constituency for him.

He was premier of the colony five times, retiring from politics in 1886, two years after his acts were repealed. In his declining years he became the leading opponent in his colony of **Federation**. He was scornful of that cabbage garden, Victoria, and said union should come by the other colonies rejoining NSW, which he thought of as Australia.

The *ADB* carries an extensive entry by Bede **Nairn**.

JOHN HIRST

Robinson, George Augustus (1788–1866), protector of Aborigines, arrived in Hobart from London in 1824. In 1829 he was commissioned by Governor **Arthur** to make contact with the remaining Tasmanian Aborigines, and to settle them at a specially designated reserve. As claimed in Vivienne Rae-Ellis's biography, *Black Robinson* (1988), Robinson's desire for public recognition and material reward led to breaches of trust with the Aborigines. He eventually arranged for the group whom he had enticed to join him, and whose claims to land rights he had promised to support, to be transferred against their wishes to the Wybaleena settlement on Flinders Island. Here sickness and despair were rife, and many died. Robinson was subsequently appointed chief protector of Aborigines in Port Phillip District in 1839. Taking with him several Tasmanian Aborigines, including **Truganini**, Robinson made contact with Aborigines at Port Phillip, but the rapid advance of pastoralism made the notion of an Aboriginal protectorate a farce and Robinson's work a failure. His Tasmanian journals and papers were published by N.J.B. Plomley as *Friendly Mission* (1966) and *Weep in Silence* (1987), and his Port Phillip journals have been edited by Gary Presland (1977, 1980) and Ian D. Clark (1988, 2000).

HD

Robinson, William Sydney (1876–1963), industrialist and government adviser, was a key figure in the development of Australian non-ferrous mining and smelting. His father was a financial journalist and his mother was a sister of Edmund **Barton**. At 23 he became financial editor of the *Age*. A visit to Broken Hill in 1905 introduced him to influential members of the **Baillieu** family, who later became his colleagues in the **Collins House Group** of companies. Robinson gained financial experience as a partner in his brother Lionel's London stockbroking firm between 1908 and 1914. When World War I jeopardised Broken Hill's markets in 1915, he joined W.L. Baillieu to organise the cooperative, Broken Hill Associated Smelters, based at Port Pirie, SA. Robinson was managing director 1915–35. He joined the Zinc Corporation board in 1920, then steered its worldwide expansion as managing director 1926–47 and became president of its successor, Consolidated Zinc Corporation, from 1949 to his retirement in 1951. Robinson combined financial acumen and mining expertise with wisdom, energy, integrity, and creative vision. In the 1930s he played pivotal roles in the formation of the Commonwealth Aircraft Corporation, Western Mining Company, and Gold Mines of Kalgoorlie. His advice to British and Australian governments on metals supply and distribution in World War II was such that Winston Churchill described Robinson's services as 'beyond computation'. His counsel also benefited Australian political leaders from W.M. **Hughes** to R.G. **Menzies**. Following Robinson's death in 1963, Geoffrey **Blainey** edited his memoirs, *If I Remember Rightly* (1967). The University of Melbourne Archives holds a major collection of Robinson's personal and business records.

DC

Robson, (Leslie) Lloyd (1931–90), historian, was born at Ulverstone, Tasmania, and grew up near Penguin, where he is buried. After Devonport State High School he attended the University of Tasmania, London University, and the Australian National University. He was a member of the history department at the University of Melbourne from 1964 until retirement in 1988. A natural teacher, Robson was an enthusiast with a rare capacity to inform, inspire, and entertain. His marvellous sense of humour spiced highly disciplined lectures in broad, well-grounded courses. With a wry grin, Robson told students at the end of every year that he liked them so much he hoped they later received a little more than they deserved. It was more than he deserved to be cut down by cancer early in his retirement.

In *The Convict Settlers of Australia* (1965) and *The First AIF* (1970), Robson pioneered the application of statistical sampling techniques in Australian History. Yet he did not allow rigorous methodology to overwhelm his sensitivity. Robson was a published poet. He influenced generations of school students through special lectures and publications. He edited *Australian Commentaries* (1975), an anthology of articles on Australia from the *Round Table* journal, and joined Nick Dawes to edit *Citizen to Soldier* (1977). Robson won major literary awards with his encyclopaedic *A History of Tasmania* (vol. 1, 1983; vol. 2, 1991), which he began under a Nuffield Fellowship in 1969 and finished a few months before his death. It maintained the same moral passion as John **West** in its condemnation of frontier violence and convict discipline, and cast an expatriate's sardonic eye on the insular conservatism of later Tasmanians. In the last words of a lifetime's work, Robson concluded that, despite all the gloom and tragedy of Tasmania's past, 'it is possible to go forward with hope'. A new edition of his *Short History of Tasmania* appeared in 1997 with a final chapter by Michael **Roe**.

DC

Rock art, see **Aboriginal art**

Rocks, the, one of Sydney's oldest and most historic neighbourhoods, are built into the steep sandstone cliffs that rise on the western side of Circular Quay. Governor **Phillip's** town plan of 1792 separated the government precinct around his own house on the eastern side of the quay from the convict quarters and soldiers barracks to the west. By the 1820s contemporaries likened the Rocks to London's notorious St Giles slum, in contrast to Sydney's St James, the fashionable zone along Macquarie and Pitt Streets. In fact, the Rocks was not entirely plebeian: from the rows of waterside pubs and cheap lodging-houses, inhabited by lumpers and seamen, it rose through tiers of narrow streets and steep sandstone stairs to streets of comfortable terraces inhabited by sea captains and stevedores near Millers Point. The early history of the area is studied in Grace Karskens, *The Rocks: Life in Early Sydney* (1997). By the late nineteenth century the area was notorious for drunkenness, theft, and **larrikinism**: Henry **Lawson** makes it the home of 'The Captain of the Push'. An outbreak of bubonic plague in 1900 led to large-scale clearance and rebuilding by the main landowner, the Maritime Services Board. Plans for further redevelopment, and the replacement of the area's remaining historic fabric with high-rise offices and apartments, were shelved when residents enlisted trade union and conservationist support for a **green ban** on the area. It is now promoted as one of the city's main tourist destinations, largely through the link to its once disreputable convict past.

GD

Roe, (Owen) Michael (1931–) is an original, penetrating and precise analyst of key elements in the intellectual and cultural formation of modern 'bourgeois' Australia. His *Quest for Authority in Eastern Australia* (1965) identified 'moral enlightenment' as the body of ideas which sustained the transformation of penal colonies into civil societies. Exploring its roots in utilitarianism, **evangelicalism**, and American transcendentalism, Roe charts its struggle against, and triumph over, more conservative forces and visions. In *Nine Australian Progressives: Vitalism in Bourgeois Political Thought* (1984), he presents **progressivism** as the dominant paradigm at the beginning of the twentieth century, and examines in nine case studies the role of ideas and of visions of the 'good society' in shaping civic endeavour and government policy in Australia. His *Kenealy and the Tichborne Cause* (1974) represents a pioneering engagement with **populism** in nineteenth-century British politics, while his most recent book, *Australia, Britain, and Migration 1915–1940* (1995) provides echoes of his early, incisive contribution to the 'reasons for settlement' debate (see **Settlement**).

Roe was born in Melbourne and studied at the University of Melbourne, Cambridge, and the Australian National University. He joined the University of Tasmania in February 1960, where he was professor of history from 1975 until his retirement in February 1996. He has been active in the broader cultural life of Tasmania and brings a provincial perspective to the study of the Australian nation. David Walker and Michael Bennett (eds), 'Intellect and Emotion', *ACH* (1998), includes appraisals and a bibliography.

MICHAEL BENNETT

Rolls, Eric Charles (1923–), farmer, poet, and historian was among the pioneers of Australian **environmental history**. Born, like Henry **Lawson**, in Grenfell, he was brought up in north-west NSW where he has farmed his own land since 1948. His histories combine deep archival research, close observation of nature, and a poet's eye and ear for the sights and sounds of the Australian bush. *They*

All Ran Wild (1969) began as a history of the rabbit in Australia but grew into a more general study of the impact of imported **pests** on native landscapes and fauna. It ends with a moving plea for the preservation of Australian wildlife. 'It is not too late to stop the destruction which our ancestors began directly by axe and poison, indirectly by importations of pests … Men cannot so change that they will be satisfied in a world of machines with only a clipped poodle or a flock of pigeons in a park to show what animals are.' A conservationist before it was fashionable to be so, Rolls was also quicker than most to recognise the paradoxes of environmental change. *A Million Wild Acres* (1981) told the surprising story of the creation, largely through human intervention, of a unique environment, the Pilliga scrub of his own north-west NSW. More recently he has turned to the subjects of migration, in a two-volume history of the **Chinese in Australia**, *Sojourners* (1993) and *Citizens* (1996), and sport, in *A Sporting Nation* (1999). The first volume of a projected environmental history of Australia, *Australia, A Biography* (2000), covers the period before the arrival of Europeans.

GD

Rose, Lionel Edmund (1948–), Aboriginal boxer, who became world bantamweight champion in 1968, was living proof that hard times breed the best fighters. Born at Warragul, Victoria, the eldest of nine children, he lived in shanties at Jacksons Track, Gippsland, learning to punch on a flour bag filled with sawdust. He won his first fight at Festival Hall, Melbourne, aged 15, on the day of his father's funeral. A whip-round at the Warragul Hotel sent him to Hobart, where he won the Australian amateur flyweight title in 1963. After missing selection for the Tokyo Olympics, he turned professional under Melbourne trainer–manager Jack Rennie, who raised him with his own family. In 1966 Rose won the Australian professional bantamweight title from Noel Kunde, and in 1968 in Tokyo he outpointed 'the unbeatable one', Masahiko 'Fighting' Harada, to claim the World Boxing Association bantamweight title. Earning up to $75 000 per fight, he defended his title against Takao Sakurai and others, but lost to Ruben Olivares in 1969. As a junior lightweight in the early 1970s, he lost on points against Yoshiaka Numata for the world title.

Peter Corris, *Lords of the Ring* (1980), observes that the sport has long been an avenue of Aboriginal advancement, and that Rose was the most successful of many accomplished boxers. Renowned for his speed, poise, and lightning lefts, Rose won 42 of 53 bouts. He produced an autobiography, *Lionel Rose: Australian* (1969). A television mini-series, *Rose Against the Odds* (1991), was based on his life. In retirement he has enjoyed success as a country-and-western singer, and has discovered the old ex-boxer's adage: 'It's the fight after the fight that's hardest.'

DC

Rotary hoe was invented by Arthur Cliff Howard, who first experimented with mechanised hoes as an apprentice

engineer while working on his father's farm in Gilgandra, NSW. He had little success until 1919, when he fitted a machine to the rear of a steam-engine. The engine drove the rotary action of L-shaped blades that broke up the soil as they turned. He demonstrated the invention—the first of its kind in the world—to the people of Gilgandra the following year. Compared to tilling the soil by manual labour, the rotary hoe was a great improvement, and on larger farms it offered a more thorough cultivation than the plough. Howard patented the invention, and established a company in NSW, which also manufactured other agricultural implements, including tractors to which the rotary hoe could be attached. He moved to England in 1938, where he operated a successful business. Frances Wheelhouse used first-hand communication with Howard as the basis for her discussion of the invention in *Digging Stick to Rotary Hoe* (1966). (See also **Invention and improvisation**.)

HD

Rothbury incident occurred in the Hunter Valley of NSW when police opened fire on miners during the lockout of 1929–30. The owners had locked out the miners on the northern coalfield in March 1929 when they refused to accept lower wages, and at the end of the year the **Nationalist** state government arranged to reopen the Rothbury mine with non-union labour. On 16 December a march of several thousand mineworkers converged on Rothbury in an effort to prevent the resumption of work, but were refused admission to the mine. One group crossed the fence and the police opened fire. Forty miners were wounded; one—Norman Brown—was fatally shot in the stomach. Seven thousand attended Brown's funeral in Greta, but police reinforcements were stationed on the coalfield and prevented further gatherings until the miners surrendered in May 1930.

SM

Rowley, Charles Dunford (1906–85) made a major contribution as a scholar and educationalist to the understanding and rectification of Australian colonial policy in **Papua New Guinea** and Aboriginal administration in the Commonwealth territories. He was born in rural NSW, and through scholarships graduated from the University of Sydney to become a secondary-school teacher. After serving in PNG during World War II, he became principal of the Australian School of Pacific Administration, and also worked as an educationalist for UNESCO in East Asia; from 1968 to 1974 he was foundation professor of politics at the university established at Port Moresby. His writings on the region include a study of *Australians in German New Guinea 1914–1921* (1958) and *The New Guinea Villager* (1965).

In 1964 Rowley became director of a major research project on Aboriginal policy by the Academy of the Social Sciences, sponsored by the Myer foundation. He wrote three volumes—*The Destruction of Aboriginal Society* (1970), *Outcasts in While Australia* (1971), and *The Remote Aborigines* (1971)—that did much to increase awareness of the historical legacy of maltreatment and discrimination. These were pioneering works that provided a detailed record of abuse by pastoralists and governments. While their emphasis on destruction and the plea for ameliorative intervention were superseded, they are imbued with an impassioned liberalism that Rowley carried into later activities more attuned to recognition of Aboriginal autonomy and the need for negotiation of reconciliation. From 1975 to 1980 he chaired the Aboriginal Land Fund Commission, and was also a leading member of the Aboriginal Treaty Committee.

SM

Royal Australian Air Force (RAAF) began in 1921 as the Australian Air Force. An earlier air force had served in World War I as the Australian Flying Corps. Using British aircraft the RAAF operated from two airbases, built near Sydney and Melbourne. Increased personnel and equipment in the 1930s provided an expanded but inadequate force by the outbreak of war in 1939. Additional airbases were also opened in WA, NT, and Qld. The RAAF expanded dramatically during World War II, particularly during the war in the Pacific. It subsequently served in East and South-East Asia. It also carried out a range of non-defence tasks at home, including comprehensive aerial photography and public aerobatic displays. George Odgers has written a history (1989, 1993). (See also **Defence**.)

HD

Royal Australian Army Nursing Corps (RAANC) formed in 1951 with the union of the Australian Army Nursing Service and the Australian Army Medical Women's Service, was composed of voluntary aids. Subsequently army nurses served in **Malaya** and **Vietnam**, and a small number served on a US support ship during the 1991 Gulf War.

The first Army Nursing Service was established in the late 1890s and Australian nurses went to the **Boer War**. The Australian Army Nursing Service Reserve was created in 1902. In World War I over 2000 nurses served overseas, more than 20 of whom died on active service. During World War II, nurses served in many theatres of war; 71 were killed. Their exposure to all the dangers of warfare was exemplified in the infamous machine-gunning of a group of Australian nurses on a beach on Bangka Island in the Dutch East Indies, the story of which was told by its sole survivor, Vivian Bullwinkel. In 1948 the service acquired the title 'Royal', and the following year it became part of the Australian regular army. In 1951 the title was altered to its final form, with 'Corps' replacing 'Service'.

The Medical Women's Service had its origins in World War I with volunteers from the Australian Red Cross and the Order of St John. With the need to release men for military service in World War II, voluntary aids were introduced into military hospitals. The service was formed in late 1942 to distinguish these aids. They served in hospitals in northern Australia and New Guinea, and in Japan as part of the Occupation Force. Jan Bassett relates the history of Australian Army nurses in *Guns and Brooches* (1992).

KT

Royal Australian Historical Society, founded in Sydney 1901, is the parent body of a network of local historical societies in NSW. Similar societies were subsequently formed in the other states (see **historical societies**). The charter of the society is to promote interest in the study of Australian history, particularly the history of NSW, which it does through its publications: *Journal of the Royal Australian Historical Society*, first published in 1901, and the magazine *History*. The society has greatly raised awareness of history at a popular level. It acts as a resource centre for Australian and NSW history, through its library of publications and primary documents, such as journals, maps and ephemera, and also through its educational programs, conferences, and excursions. The society also promotes the study of Australian history in schools by offering prizes to secondary school students. In 1969 the society took up residence in an 1871 townhouse at 133 Macquarie Street, now known as History House.

HD

Royal Australian Navy was formed in 1911, when despite its status as a dominion, Australia claimed the right to its own navy. The small naval forces taken over from the colonies in 1901 were known previously as the Commonwealth Naval Forces. The RAN was created in a substantial building program before World War I. It saw action in all wars in which Australia has participated since World War I. Its history in World War I is covered in volume 9 of **Bean's** official history, written by A.W. **Jose**; a volume by G. Herman Gill details the RAN's involvement in World War II. (See also **Defence**.)

HD

Royal tours became popular as imperial administrators began to look beyond military and economic administration and toward the 'distant sympathies' that would bind their far-flung colonies into a 'family of nations'. It was considered that Queen Victoria's own, extensive family might play a useful role in personifying such sympathies, and so, from the 1860s, its members were despatched on lengthy tours round the globe.

The first royal visitor to Australia was the Queen's son, the Duke of Edinburgh, who enjoyed five memorable months here in 1867–68. Organisers had not anticipated the overwhelming interest in this little-known prince, and under-preparation resulted in a series of stampedes and accidental deaths. The tour was also beset by political and sectarian brawling, and was capped by an attempted **assassination** on Clontarf Beach in Sydney, when the Prince was shot by an Irishman falsely claiming the imprimatur of the **Fenians**. The gunman was tried and hanged in haste, in the midst of public outrage and shame. This dramatic episode has attracted the passing attention of many historians interested in religious and nationalist tensions of the nineteenth century, but the only full chronicle remains that of Brian McKinlay, *The First Royal Tour 1867–1868* (1970).

Subsequent royal tours in 1881, 1901, 1920, 1927, and 1934 followed much of the pattern laid down in 1867–68.

While each drew record-breaking numbers—the arrival of the Duke and Duchess of York in Sydney Harbour in 1927, for example, was witnessed by the first Australian congregation of one million—journalists and other commentators either marvelled or despaired at the passionate reception accorded to such visitors. The *Bulletin* observed with anger that the immense crowds attending the **Federation** celebrations in Melbourne in 1901 were more profoundly stirred by the presence of a 'small, accidental prince' than by the actual milestone in indigenous democracy. This phenomenon of Anglo-Australian crowds pouring their hearts out to members of the British royal family persisted, and the continuing fervour of welcome suggests a profound and enduring sense of isolation from the mother country.

These features were still apparent in early 1954, when the newly crowned Queen Elizabeth II became the first British monarch to set foot on Australian soil. Contemporary police and media estimates suggested that the Queen was seen by some six or seven million people during her two-month tour, making it the best-attended and most elaborate event ever staged in this country. Building on postwar optimism—of which the Queen herself was regarded as symbolic—Australia's progress from eighteenth-century wilderness to modern nation was demonstrated through the presentation of industrial, agricultural, and social achievements to the validating gaze of the royal visitor. **Jindyworobak** poet Rex Ingamells was one of many to draw a glittering thread of historic connection between the throne and its distant subjects: the chronicle of royal visits, he wrote, was the record of Australian 'growth and advancement'. Certainly, in popular reminiscence today (enhanced by the profuse extant memorabilia) the 1954 Royal Tour has itself become the most immediately redolent event of its era—though the associated sentiment may be either fond or rueful.

Although there had been limited visible dissent from royal tours prior to 1954, it was not until the 1970s that opposition could be said to have become widespread or respectable. Diminution in support for the monarchy was obvious in the smaller crowds for the Queen's second visit in 1963. Despite the stubborn popular ascription to 1954, it was on this tour that Prime Minister Robert **Menzies** embarrassed Her Majesty with an adoring recitation of 'I did but see her passing by / And yet I love her till I die.' It was the anachronistic feature of this effusion in the swinging sixties that made it memorable. The tour models developed in the nineteenth century were finally modified in the late 1960s, since when visits from royalty have been paid with unprecedented frequency, but are generally brief and based on a specific ceremonial duty. While many Australians have continued to turn out for royal tourists, especially for Diana, the Princess of Wales, these occasions have also become an occasion for protest (during the Bicentenary in 1988) and satire (from the drag queens of inner-city Sydney).

Despite their immense contemporary impact, the literature on royal tours is sparse. Philip Pike's *The Royal Presence in Australia* (1986), a straightforward compendium aimed at a general market, is the only work of its kind. Kevin Fewster surveys the 1920 visit of the Prince of Wales in *LH* (1980). Peter Spearritt in *ACH* (1986) and Jane Connors in *AHS* (1992) examine the 1954 tour. This curious neglect is of a piece with the slender historiography on **monarchy** and royalty. Australian historians have had little time for the popular attachment to the occupants of the British throne—strict constitutionalists and radical nationalists have had equal distaste for such sentiment—and even less for the royal tours, such spectacular manifestations of this discomforting phenomenon.

JANE CONNORS

'Rudd, Steele' (Arthur Hoey Davis) (1868–1935) was the creator of short stories which ironically, humorously, and with increasing pathos, chronicled the harsh and demanding life of small selectors on the Darling Downs of south-eastern Qld. He was the son of an ex-convict Welsh selector and worked on his father's and neighbouring selections. At 17 he became a government clerk in Brisbane, rising to under-sheriff in 1902 before being dismissed in 1904 through a combination of retrenchment and jealousy.

Rudd's first Darling Downs sketch, 'Starting the Selection', appeared in the *Bulletin* on 14 December 1895. It was followed by a stream of short stories culminating in his finest collections, *On Our Selection* (1899) and *Our New Selection* (1903). Twenty-two works followed, ranging from farces, such as *Dad in Politics*, to repeats of episodes on Dad's Emu Creek selection. Between 1904 and 1907 he produced *Steele Rudd's Magazine* in Brisbane and Sydney. After its collapse he purchased a farm at Nobby on the Darling Downs. This failed venture replicated the deepest problems of Rudd's farmers. Thereafter he produced *Steele Rudd's Annual* (1917–23) which went through several metamorphoses. His private life was unhappy. His wife, after bouts of mental illness, was hospitalised as incurably insane in 1919. In spite of the mammoth sales of his books, Rudd was constantly in financial difficulties before his death in Brisbane in 1935.

In 1912 Bert Bailey's stage adaptation of *On Our Selection* premiered in Sydney. It was succeeded by four other productions, three silent films in 1920, 1921 and 1927, and five further motion pictures. The last, starring Leo McKern and Joan **Sutherland**, appeared in 1994. From these extraordinarily popular adaptations, as well as several **'Dad and Dave'** radio serials, a television series, and even comic strips, Rudd and his family derived but meagre royalties. Indeed, he had the mortification of observing, in his lifetime, the transformation of his seminal characters from authentic literary creations with historical resonances into bastardised stereotypes of little depth and gormless responses. This was a dual loss. The often coarse, complicated, and careworn lives of the selectors, as well as the agrarian myths associated with family farm settlement in the fertile crescent, deserved more than slapstick. Rudd was aware of this. Introspectively, he once said, 'I don't think comedy's my line … if I would let myself go I'd be gloomier than Lawson at his worst.' But he seldom explored further. There was an increasing divergence between realism and romanticism in his writing.

His own childhood and adolescent experiences and composite observations of storekeepers, politicians, lawyers, doctors, and farmers, with all their patriarchal appurtenances, his awareness of cruelty and his penetrating visual literary gifts, ultimately succumbed to surface reactions. The gifted illustrators of his work, particularly the **Lindsays**, finally overwhelmed the text. A pictorial guide by Peter Putnis, *Steele Rudd's Australia*, was published in 1988. D.B. Waterson, *Squatter, Selector and Storekeeper: A History of the Darling Downs 1859–1893* (1968), analyses the regional background. His son E.D. Davis published a biography, *The Life and Times of Steele Rudd*, in 1976, while the scholarly work by Richard Fotherington, *In Search of Steele Rudd* (1995), combines fresh biographical material with solid literary criticism as well as an examination of the Dad and Dave phenomenon.

D.B. WATERSON

Rugby, a major winter sport in NSW and Qld, is named after the style of football played at Rugby School, near Leicester, England. A stone tablet erected there in 1895 commemorates William Webb Ellis, 'who, with a fine disregard for the rules of football as played in his time, first took the ball in his arms and ran with it, thus originating the distinctive feature of the Rugby game A.D. 1823'. The Ellis legend is questionable. Eric Dunning and Kenneth Sheard in *Barbarians, Gentlemen and Players* (1979) identified the origins of rugby in the winter games of pre-industrial Britain. Their title reflects key stages in rugby's progress under the influence of increasing demands for orderliness, restraint, and democratisation, which resulted in a split between amateurs and professionals at the end of the nineteenth century.

Rugby's origins in Australia remain obscure. The game seems to have arrived by July 1829, when the Sydney *Monitor* reported a version of Leicestershire-style football being played by soldiers. As in England, rugby had its foundations in the private schools. Gentlemen's clubs upheld these traditions, but early competition was largely confined to an upper-class social elite. Games were occasional rather than regular. Thomas Hickie's *They Ran with the Ball* (1993) cites 1865 as the year rugby was played on a continuing basis in Sydney. By 1877 there were 23 clubs in the Southern Rugby Football Union, which was established in 1874 and became the NSW Rugby Union in 1892. Hickie notes that the 1874 title reflects how the rugby fraternity in Sydney saw themselves—not so much as an indigenous football body, but the southern offshoot of England's Rugby Football Union.

Inter-colonial competition during the 1880s boosted the game in NSW and Qld, but not in Victoria, where a desire to 'improve' rugby had fostered **Australian Rules football** in the 1850s. The potency of class factors tended to be diluted in Australian Rules by early adoption of suburban and district-based competitions. Rugby remained aloof and undemocratic. A metropolitan union was not established in Sydney until 1896, despite the city's suburbanisation in the 1870s and 1880s.

As a wider cross-section of players emerged, pressure grew for payment at senior levels. While gentlemen could afford to be amateurs, working and lower-middle-class men were at a disadvantage. The issue flared in England in 1895, when a breakaway Northern Rugby Football Union was established by working-class players seeking payment. This was followed in Australia in 1907 by the formation of the NSW Rugby Football League, which embraced professionalism and various rule modifications similar to the English body. Qld formed a Rugby League Association in 1908. Australia's distinguishing 'League' title was adopted by Britain's Northern Rugby Football Union when it became the Rugby Football League in 1922.

The Union/League split in Australia was complex. League had links to the **Australian Labor Party** and Catholic schools, as Chris Cunneen observes in 'The Rugby War: The Early History of Rugby League in New South Wales 1907–15,' in Richard Cashman and Michael McKernan (eds), *Sport in History* (1979). League outstripped Union after H.H. 'Dally' Messenger and other champions defected in 1908–09. Both codes failed to match the popularity of Australian Rules outside NSW and Qld, although international competition was a major advantage that rugby enjoyed over the Australian game. Control of national and international competition was vested in the Australian Rugby League (ARL), which originated in 1924, and the Australian Rugby Football Union (1949).

In 1903 NZ defeated Australia in the first of a series of Rugby Union Tests, now called the Bledisloe Cup after a trophy presented by Baron Bledisloe in 1931. Australia's Rugby Union 'Wallabies' won gold at the 1908 **Olympic Games**, and in 1909 they clinched the inaugural Rugby Union Test against England. League's 'Kangaroos' drew their first Test against England in 1908, and South Africa's Rugby Union 'Springboks' first toured Australia in 1921. The Springboks' six-week tour in 1971 was disrupted by violent anti-apartheid protests.

Declining public interest in Rugby League was reversed in the 1980s and early 1990s by state-of-origin clashes and a massive marketing campaign featuring American singer Tina Turner. The ARL took over the Sydney premiership, which progressively accepted sides from Wollongong, Newcastle, the ACT, Qld, WA, NZ, and Melbourne. The wider potential of this expansionary phase attracted Rupert **Murdoch**, who saw huge profits in cable television rights to an international competition under private management. In 1994–95 he began to engineer his breakaway Super League, which eventually opposed the ARL competition in 1997. ARL chief Ken Arthurson lamented in *Arko: My Game* (1997) that 'greed and corporate ambition' dismantled the game he loved. But money had been talking in rugby circles for a long time. Even Rugby Union finally turned professional in 1996. And in the end, money motivated a peace deal between the ARL and Super League in December 1997, which provided for a united competition in 1998. From barbarians, gentlemen, and players, to 'products', the sport had moved deep into an age of control. Ian Heads has written a history of the NSW Rugby League, *True Blue* (1992), and David Headon and Lex Marinos edited *League of* *a Nation* (1996). Andrew Moore's *The Mighty Bears!* (1997) is an accomplished study of the North Sydney team.

DAMIEN CASH

Rum Rebellion refers to the uprising in Sydney by members of the **New South Wales Corps** on 26 January 1808. Power in the colony rested largely with the military and wealthy settlers, John **Macarthur** prominent among them, who together amassed large profits from their control of the rum trade. When William **Bligh** was appointed governor in 1805, he confronted Macarthur and took action to end the corrupt trade in rum. In 1808 he refused Macarthur bail when he faced trial on a commercial matter. Macarthur's military colleagues immediately reversed the situation, arresting Bligh and releasing Macarthur from detention. The senior officer George Johnston became nominal commander while Bligh was held captive until June 1808 at Government House. In December 1809 Governor **Macquarie** brought with him his own troops and sent the NSW 'Rum Corps' home to England. H.V. **Evatt** put the case for Bligh as a champion of the small settler in *Rum Rebellion* (1938), while M.H. **Ellis's** 1955 biography of Macarthur is the most robust defence of the rebels. Ross Fitzgerald and Mark Hearn reconsidered *Bligh, Macarthur and the Rum Rebellion* (1988).

HD

Rusden, George William (1819–1903), educationist and civil servant, wrote the most ambitious nineteenth-century history of Australia. He was one of a large family of an English clergyman that emigrated when George was in his teens (his brother Henry became a leading Melbourne rationalist). George tried pastoralism and trade in China before he became agent for the establishment of government schools in NSW. Following the separation of Victoria, he became a government official there and from 1856 to 1882 was clerk of the Legislative Council. He retired to England until 1893, when he returned to Melbourne. His substantial papers are held by Trinity College, University of Melbourne.

Rusden had already published literary and educational works as well as works on the settlement of Victoria. In 1883 his *History of Australia* and *History of New Zealand*, both in three volumes, appeared in London. Each was a long, highly literary, digressive, and polemical account of the failure of the colonists to make good their British patrimony. Drawing on his involvement in the Victorian **constitutional crises**, Rusden condemned both countries for democratic excess. One part of his arraignment was the mistreatment of the indigenous inhabitants. A suit for libel brought by a NZ minister for native affairs brought heavy damages and forced a retraction. Australian historians are more sympathetic to Rusden's criticism of the injustices to Aborigines. A.G. **Austin**, *George William Rusden and National Education* (1958), assessed him favourably.

SM

Russian–Australian relations began in 1807 when the naval ship *Neva* visited Port Jackson. During the period 1807–35 there were 17 naval visits, described by Glynn Barratt in *The Russians and Australia* (1988). Until the 1830s relations were harmonious and Russian perceptions of the colonies were enthusiastic. Australian hostility towards Russia emerged in the 1830s and intensified during the Crimean War, 1853–56. Australia experienced scares of Russian invasion and espionage in 1863, 1871, 1878, 1882, and 1885. Popular mythology still associates the Australian coastal defence system with fears of Russian invasion.

In 1857 Russian honorary consuls were appointed to Melbourne and Sydney. In 1894 the first regular consular representation, headed by career diplomat Aleksei Putiata, was established in Melbourne. Putiata and his successors championed direct Russian–Australian trade, leading to the creation in January 1917 of the Russian–Australian Bureau of Commerce and Information. Russians contributed much to the study of Australia. Considerable collections of Aboriginal artefacts were gathered by the early naval visitors and by Aleksandr Iashchenko in 1903. The Russian scientist and anthropologist Nikolai **Miklouho-Maclay**, whose life has been explored by E.M. Webster, *The Moon Man* (1984), lived in Australia from 1878 to 1886, founding the first biological station in Sydney. He also championed an increasing Russian presence in the Pacific and provided information about Australia for the Russian Ministry for Foreign Affairs. The visitors praised new, democratic, 'un-English', as they believed, features in the emerging nation. Russian attitudes appeared especially enthusiastic at the beginning of the twentieth century, when Australia was perceived by Russian writers and visitors as an example for Russia—a 'Workers' Kingdom' distinguished by social reforms and respect for the working man. This interpretation was contested by Russian revolutionaries who found exile in Australia after 1905.

The first ethnic Russian to settle in Australia was a convict, Constantine Milcow, who arrived in 1816. Initially immigrants from Russia were mainly of Jewish, Finnish, and Polish descent. Ethnic Russians began to arrive in considerable numbers in the early twentieth century, mainly from the Far East. By 1917 they numbered at least 2000. Political refugees numbered around 500 and they organised the Union of Russian Workers led by Bolshevik Artem. Early immigrants were sympathetic to Australian conditions to the extent that in 1912 the federal government sent Russian delegates—Leandro Illin and Constantine Vladimirov—to the NT to explore the possibilities of establishing a Russian colony there. The economic and political situation of the Russians deteriorated during World War I simultaneously with an increase in the influence of Russian radicals, which made the Russian community one of the most radical by 1919, when the **Red Flag riots** occurred. The history of pre-revolutionary attitudes and contacts is explored by Elena Govor in *Australia in the Russian Mirror: Changing Perceptions 1770–1919* (1997).

After the Russian Revolution of 1917 the imperial consul resigned in 1918 and Soviet consul Petr Simonov, unrecognised by Australia, held office 1918–21. Australian troops served in a British force which intervened in the

Civil War. Russians participated in the creation of the Communist Party of Australia. The association of Russia with **communism** during the period between the two world wars gave rise to extreme support and opposition by Australians. Popular Australian attitudes to Russia were also influenced by Russian cultural achievements, especially in the performing arts, which were highly praised in Australia following the visits of the Russian Ballet with Anna Pavlova and singer Fedor Chaliapin in 1926. Russian migrants between the wars were mainly White Russians who had fought the revolutionary Russian forces.

During World War II, when the USSR and Australia were allies, both official and popular attitudes became more sympathetic, and in 1942 diplomatic relations were established. The Cold War period was marked by the **Petrov Affair**, which led to a breach in diplomatic relations between 1954 and 1959. In the period of *détente*, and especially under the **Whitlam** government, Russian–Australian contacts strengthened, to be followed by further confrontation until *perestroika*. Since *perestroika* and the collapse of the USSR, diplomatic relations have steadily improved. Now that Russia and Australia consider themselves to be part of the Asia–Pacific rim, further *rapprochement* and deeper contacts between the Russian Far East and Australia are developing, although current economic difficulties in Russia prevent significant growth of economic relations.

After World War II Australia accepted many Russian displaced persons from Europe as well as Russians from China. Although Soviet propaganda depicted working-class hardships and blackened Australian capitalism, popular Russian attitudes remained sympathetic. This was reflected in the aspiration of many Russian Jews to emigrate to Australia from the early 1970s. In contrast to Stalin's period, since the late 1950s Russian academics have made contributions to the fields of Australian ethnography, history, literature, and natural sciences. Over 1000 works of Australian fiction have been translated into Russian. The Russian community in Australia—recently studied by Maria Frolova, *Russians in Australia* (1996, in Russian), and Artem Rudnitsky, *Another Life and Land So Far Away* (1991, in Russian)—numbers at least 45 000 people. Different aspects of Russian–Australian relations are explored in the collection *Russia and the Fifth Continent* (ed. John McNair and Thomas Poole, 1992). Other works include Elena Govor, *Australia in the Russian Mirror* (1997) and *Russian Sources on Australia* (ed. Poole et al., 1993).

ELENA GOVOR

Ryan, Edna Minna (1904–97), the godmother of late twentieth-century Australian feminism, is most famous for her work to improve conditions of work for women. Her greatest achievement was the submission by the **Women's Electoral Lobby** on the National Wage Case in 1973, in which she advocated a uniform minimum wage for women and men, after which the Arbitration Commission extended the minimum wage to women.

Born in Sydney, the tenth of 12 children, she pursued her education through adult education classes and activism, with her husband Jack Ryan. Both were leading members of the **Communist** Party of Australia in the 1920s; he was expelled in 1930, she subsequently refusing to denounce him. She became prominent in the **Australian Labor Party**, campaigned for election to the Senate in 1953, and from 1956 to 1965 served as an ALP councillor and alderman in local government. In 1962 she was elected the first woman president of the clerical branch of the Municipal Employees Union, and when she retired from the workforce in 1972 she became an active member of the Women's Electoral Lobby.

Ryan was, with Anne Conlon, the author of *Gentle Invaders: Australian Women at Work* (1975), a ground-breaking and influential study of women's work and wages since 1788. Her second book, *Two-Thirds of a Man* (1985), examined the origins of compulsory arbitration and its disadvantageous effects on women workers. Her achievements were recognised by the award of honorary doctorates by the University of Sydney in 1985 and Macquarie University in 1995, and life-membership of the ALP, her union, and WEL. A book of essays about her appeared in 1997.

SUSAN MAGAREY

Ryan, Thomas Joseph (1876–1921) was admitted to the Queensland Bar after a childhood in rural Victoria. He became an expert in trade union law and joined the Labor Party. In 1909 he won a seat in state parliament; six years later he became premier when Labor was swept to power. Ryan proved a popular and successful premier with a strong team of ministers. During World War I his anti-conscription views brought him into conflict with W.M. **Hughes**, the bellicose prime minister, and as the only premier opposed to **conscription** he played an important role in the referendums. He was drafted into federal politics in 1919 and was widely expected to assume the Labor leadership, but died of bronchial infection two years later. Denis Murphy has written a biography (1975).

KT

S

Sacred sites are places that hold religious significance for **Aborigines** because of their connection with the ancestral spirit beings of the **Dreamtime**. They may cover a large area, such as **Uluru**; more commonly, they are confined to a waterhole, a rock painting, a burial site, a shell midden, a carved tree, or a scattering of artefacts. Sacred sites are believed to hold special powers, with a consequent danger to those who transgress them or neglect their responsibilities to them. Sacred sites can also be secret, in which case access is strictly confined to certain individuals.

The first legislation to protect sacred sites was the 1976 **Aboriginal Land Rights** (NT) Act, which protects a site that is 'sacred to Aborigines or is otherwise of significance according to Aboriginal tradition'. Under federal legislation sacred sites are recorded on a register, governed by the Aboriginal Areas Protection Authority, which facilitates the protection, access control, and appropriate management by the site's traditional owners. Similar legislation was subsequently adopted by the states and the ACT. The federal Aboriginal and Torres Strait Islander Heritage Protection Act (1984) overrides state and territory legislation. Legal recognition of sacred sites gave Aborigines a stronger position from which to mount land rights cases and oppose mining developments.

HD

Salvado, Rosendo (1814–1900) was a Spanish Benedictine monk who, with several other members of the order, arrived in WA in 1846 to establish a mission. In 1847 they settled on a site approximately 130 kilometres north of Perth, which they called New Norcia, and began building a monastery. A farm was established and local Aborigines were taught farming, handcrafts, and Christianity. During four years in Europe raising funds, Dom Salvado wrote his account of the mission (1851). He returned to WA in 1853 and in 1859 was appointed administrator of the mission, reporting directly to Rome. He gained greater freedom in 1867 when the monastery was made an abbey and he was appointed abbot as well as a local bishop. In 1887 he was appointed protector of Aborigines. Three years after Salvado's death in Rome his remains were returned to WA and reburied at New Norcia. George Russo has written two accounts of Salvado and New Norcia (1979, 1980).

KT

Salvation Army, an evangelistic and welfare organisation run on military lines, was founded in England by William and Mary Booth in 1865, and transplanted to Australia by two immigrant salvationists, John Gore and Edward Saunders, who founded the first corps in Adelaide in 1880. The army grew quickly and in 1882 Major James Barker was appointed to take command in the colonies; he established his headquarters in Melbourne. Three years later the army attracted an attendance of over 20 000 at its Sunday services in Melbourne, making it the third best attended Protestant denomination. Salvationist converts entered a life of strict personal discipline, which was in sharp conflict with the mores of the working-class communities from which they had mainly come and out of which they now commonly rose. In 1901 the Salvation Army was still the most proletarian religious group in Australia but it included an increasing number of small shopkeepers and tradesmen. While placing primary emphasis upon its evangelistic mission, the army sought to reach the poor through a variety of charitable agencies, extending from homes for fallen girls and dosshouses for vagrants to labour bureaus and disaster services. In the late twentieth century it maintains one of the largest and most well-regarded welfare organisations in the country, and many Australians, oblivious of its religious orientation, 'Thank God for the Salvos'. Barbara Bolton, *Booth's Drum* (1980), is a popular history.

GD

Salvation Jane, see **Pests**

Samuel, Sidney (1813–83) came to be regarded as an expert on Australian emigration without ever leaving England. A journalist, he wrote *A Voice from the Far Interior of Australia* (1847) under the pen-name of 'A Bushman'. This was based on material from his brother John, who had been in NSW for six years. It was followed by the popular *Sidney's Australian Handbook* (1848), the success of which prompted the brothers to establish *Sidney's Emigrant's Journal* (1848–50). His other writings included *The Three Colonies of Australia* (1852) and a novel (1854), and he wrote about Australia for Charles Dickens's journal, *Household Words*. Coral Lansbury considers his influence on the popular myths of *Arcady in Australia* (1970).

KT

Sandgroper is a colloquial term to describe a person from WA, derived from the tendency to grope with one's toes when walking through soft sand. The term first emerged with the large immigration influx from the eastern states during the 1890s gold rush. It was used, for example, by Henry **Lawson** in 1896. *Groperland* and *Sandgroperland* were subsequently adopted as colloquial names for WA. While *sandgroper* is used affectionately by Western Australians, there is an element of mockery in its use by those from the eastern states, both in its allusion to the sandy soil of the state capital and in the suggestion that Western Australians spend a considerable amount of time walking through sand and not doing much else.

HD

Santamaria, Bartholomew Augustine 'Bob' (1915–98) was a controversial **Catholic** intellectual, writer, and political activist best known for his opposition to **communism**. Santamaria's immigrant Italian parents ran a fruit shop in the Melbourne suburb of Brunswick. He was educated at Christian Brothers schools and at the University of Melbourne, where he studied arts and law in the early 1930s. The **Depression** sharpened Santamaria's social consciousness, but he rejected Marxism, especially after the **Spanish Civil War** emphasised the vulnerability of religious and political freedom. He became part of Catholic intellectual life as a member of the Campion Society. In 1936 he played a prominent role in establishing the *Catholic Worker* newspaper, which was influenced by the papal encyclicals *Rerum Novarum* (1891) and *Quadragesimo Anno* (1931). In 1937, at Archbishop **Mannix's** request, he joined the National Secretariat of Catholic Action, a collaborative lay apostolate to the working class, for which he produced numerous social and political statements. After 1941, when Victorian Australian Labor Party leader H.M. Cremean persuaded him to oppose communism in trade unions, Santamaria created an effective anti-communist organisation known variously as the Catholic Social Studies Movement, Catholic Social Movement, or simply the **Movement**.

Santamaria was the Movement's president 1943–57 and was president of its successor, the National Civic Council, from 1957. The Australian Labor Party broke with the Movement in 1954, as did the Church in 1957. Santamaria explained his contentious role in the 1950s ALP **split** in *Santamaria: A Memoir* (1997), a revised edition of *Against the Tide* (1981). Paul Ormonde (ed.), *Santamaria: The Politics of Fear* (2000), and Bruce Duncan, *Crusade or Conspiracy?* (2001), make serious criticisms. His superb oratory, convictions, and sense of urgency inspired James **McAuley's** poem 'In a Late Hour' (1955). In his later years, through newspaper columns and the Civic Council publications *News Weekly* and *AD 2000*, Santamaria championed traditional family and religious values, and amplified his 1930s thesis that democracy and Australian economic sovereignty are more threatened by capitalism than communism.

DC

Savery, Henry (1791–1842), generally considered to be Australia's first novelist and essayist, was born at Butcombe in Somerset, England. For a banker's son, Savery was tragically deficient in the banker's prime virtue of prudence. A bankrupt sugar-refiner in 1819, he edited the *Bristol Observer* 1819–22, dabbled in insurance broking, then returned to sugar-refining. He forged bills to escape another bankruptcy in 1825 and was sentenced to death. At the last minute this was commuted to transportation for life. After landing at Hobart Town in December 1825, Savery worked as a government clerk before being assigned to Captain Bartholomew Thomas. His wife Eliza arrived from England in 1828, having survived a shipwreck, but not apparently the attentions of her 'protector' on the voyage, attorney-general Algernon Montagu. Believing the pair had formed a relationship, Savery attempted suicide by cutting his throat. Yet again, his life was saved, but soon afterwards he was gaoled for debt. During imprisonment in 1829–30 Savery wrote about Van Diemen's Land for the *Colonial Times*, using the pseudonym Simon Stukeley. The republished series formed the first collection of Australian essays, *The Hermit in Van Diemen's Land* (1829). On release, Savery wrote a three-volume, semi-autobiographical novel, *Quintus Servinton* (1830–31), which was reissued in England in 1832. Mary Grimstone's *Woman's Love* (1832) may have been written earlier, but as Cecil Hadgraft argues in his biographical introduction to the 1962 edition of *Quintus Servinton*, Savery's work has greater claims as the first 'Australian' novel by virtue of its setting, date of publication, and author's residence. Like Savery, the main character in *Quintus Servinton* fails in business and resorts to forging bills, resulting in his transportation to Australia, where he learns his lessons and proves a model prisoner. Unfortunately, *Quintus Servinton* did not change Savery's life. He attempted farming, but was again caught forging bills when he fell into debt. In a final indignity, Algernon Montagu sentenced Savery to imprisonment at Port Arthur in October 1840.

DC

Scab or *scabby* is a derogatory term for non-union labour, which takes its name from a disease common in sheep that attacks the fleece and renders it less valuable. The term emerged in Qld during the strikes of the early 1890s, when unionists taunted the non-union · labour employed by pastoralists and other non-striking workers for betraying the cause of the labour movement.

HD

Scantlebury Brown, Vera (1889–1946) is credited with establishing the network of infant welfare services that developed in Victoria between the wars. After qualifying in medicine at the University of Melbourne, she travelled to London in 1917 to work as an assistant surgeon in the Royal Army Medical Corps. Shortly after her return to Melbourne she was appointed medical officer to the newly established Victorian Baby Health Centres Association. Her growing involvement with child welfare took her on tours to examine the systems of NZ, Canada, and the USA. She helped prepare a comparative report on the infant and welfare services in NZ and Victoria, which was presented in 1926 and recommended establishing the position of Director of Welfare Services. She was offered the position (in a part-time capacity to overcome her married status) and held it for the rest of her life. Much of her time was spent in attempting to reconcile conflicting views held by organisations over various aspects of child development. Her *Guide to Infant Feeding* (1929) is an example of her concern to support mothers with advice that was acceptable to all parties. The birth of her own children sharpened her understanding of the difficulties of mothering, particularly when pursuing a career. She worked on revisions of her *Guide to the Care of the Young Child* (1947) during her final illness.

KT

School history consisted of the most widely circulated versions of Australian history: those found in school textbooks and taught to the nation's youth. Between the turn of the century and the 1960s, history, with a steadily increasing Australian emphasis, became an essential component in the curriculum of both primary and secondary schools. Whether school history was the most influential form of Australian history is more doubtful, since the circumstances under which it was disseminated—rote learning in crowded classrooms under sometimes poorly trained teachers—may also have made it the most quickly forgotten version of the nation's past.

Schoolteachers had long promoted history as a foundation for morality and patriotism. According to S.G. Firth (*Melbourne Studies in Education*, 1970), late colonial primary texts emphasised the link between Protestant morality and imperial expansion. The **heroes and heroines** held up to Australian schoolchildren were usually British rather than Australian. In 1888 Henry **Lawson** had complained that not one in 10 of the public schoolchildren in NSW was acquainted with a single historical fact about Australia. Boys in the upper classes might be able to parrot the names of English monarchs, but of the main events of Australian history—Captain **Cook's** 'discovery', the **Black Wars**, the **Eureka Stockade**—they knew nothing.

Australian topics began to appear in the school curriculum in the early 1900s as chapters in the grand story of Britain and its Empire. Teacher-educators influenced by the ideals of the 'new education', with its emphasis on child-centred, environmental learning and civic duty, sought to ground the child's love of country in a local and visible past. The objective, according to the 1904 NSW primary syllabus, was to 'give such an account of the past as will enable the pupil to have some insight into the present and furnish him with noble ideals of life and character upon which he may model his own'. As British children learned to admire the valour of Drake and Nelson, so young Australians were taught to honour the **explorers** and **pioneers**. Their teachers joined the movements to inaugurate 'foundation' and 'discovery' days, and to mark the passage of the explorers across the land with cairns and obelisks. These became the shrines and saints' days of the secular state school system.

The Great War reminded statesmen and educators how fragile were the foundations of national unity. ' "History" is a record of the doings of men living in communities', declared Ernest **Scott** in his widely used textbook, *A Short History of Australia* (1916). As Stuart Macintyre has argued (*A History for a Nation*, 1994), the shape of Scott's narrative—beginning with the European discovery of Australia and culminating in its emergence as a self-governing nation within the Empire—invested that imagined community with the aura of historical destiny.

Although professors already influenced school history through their role as public examiners, Scott was the first to write a text for schools. His lead was soon followed by others, including G.V. **Portus**, R.M. **Crawford**, N.D. **Harper**, and A.G.L. **Shaw**. There is much a modern reader might criticise in these texts. Portus dedicated his *Australia Since 1606* (1932) to the succeeding generation of Australian *boys*, likened war to a rugger scrum, and treated Aborigines, when they entered his narrative at all, as remnants of the Stone Age. But his book is entertainingly written and explains events in an international, as well as national, context. That international context was constantly changing, and Max Crawford's *Ourselves and the Pacific* (1941) and *Our Pacific Neighbours* by George Browne and Norman Harper (1953) registered the abrupt shift in the focus of Australian **foreign relations** following World War II.

There was always a tension between the political and scientific aims of school history. Was history valuable mainly for the lessons it taught, or for the skills it instilled? By the 1960s and 1970s, the link between academic history and school history was growing weaker everywhere. 'The history of a historian is not the history of an educator', a Melbourne schoolteacher declared in 1976. Academic historians were increasingly oriented to the international world of historical scholarship, while school history was being 'integrated'—some said submerged—in a general social studies curriculum.

Some conservatives believed that the distinction between school history and academic history had been pushed too far. In 1975 Alan Barcan, the most persistent critic of school history, lamented that 'history as an intellectual subject is weakened when education is concerned with personal development, entertainment of pupils and physical movement about the classroom or outside the school'. By the 1990s, when he and Stuart Macintyre debated the dramatic decline of school history enrolments in the *Australian Journal of Education* (1997), Barcan's forebodings had been realised. The analytical, literary skills taught by history seemed irrelevant to the vocational requirements of the computer age. But in giving up history young Australians were perhaps missing out on something other than vocational skills. 'We believe that a knowledge and understanding of the history of Australians is an essential foundation for Australian citizenship', declared the Civics Expert Group appointed by Prime Minister **Keating** and chaired by Ernest Scott's biographer in 1994. Purged of racism and sexism, and leavened by a generous understanding of national identity, citizenship might again become the keynote of school history. The **Howard** government expanded the expert group and commissioned it to prepare school courses in civics in which history was a central component. In 2000 the report of a National Inquiry into School History, *The Future of the Past*, recommended the establishment of a National Centre for History Education with a mission to strengthen history curriculum development and training. The centre, based at the University of Melbourne, opened in 2001.

GRAEME DAVISON

Schools of art, see **Mechanics institutes**

Science, history of is a field intimidated by its subject. Historians have been too slow to examine the local context of knowledge production and use, deferring to scientists and their uncritical catalogues of the past. Historical analysis has given way too often to the antiquarian plod or the celebratory frolic.

In nineteenth-century Australia, 'progress' was a popular theme whenever the scientifically inclined paused to reflect on their discipline. By the latter half of the century, science was developing an institutional base with the establishment of universities, societies, and government posts. History helped locate this fledgling enterprise within a grand progressive tradition. Catalogues of scientific achievement provided a preface to current endeavours. Obituaries of local workers portrayed them, stuffed and mounted, within a gallery of revered pioneers; there were no Darwins or Newtons among them, but their lives were still dedicated to the same glorious ideals. Collecting historical facts paralleled the collecting of specimens—the main scientific activity within the colonies. Science progressed by the steady accumulation of plants, platypuses, and people.

By the end of the century, science was changing. Experimental science was beginning to displace **natural history**; professional scientists were edging amateurs out of the vanguard of progress. With more scientists, more societies, more publications, and a never-ending parade of anniversaries to be commemorated, disciplinary and institutional studies became commonplace in the twentieth century—

predominantly in scientific journals. As science fractured into increasingly narrow specialisations, history filled the cracks, smoothing the narrative flow of scientific progress. Many of these historical efforts were of the 'amateur–antiquarian' variety identified by Michael Hoare in *Newsletter of the Australasian Association for the History and Philosophy of Science* (1974), but some disciplines have been better served. T.G. Vallance and David Branagan (in Roy MacLeod, ed., *The Commonwealth of Science*, 1988) and R.W. Home (in Nathan Reingold and Marc Rothenberg, eds, *Scientific Colonialism: A Cross-Cultural Comparison*, 1987) have helped us to understand how the disciplinary communities of geology and physics coalesced and changed. **Astronomy** has been remarkably well endowed, with detailed institutional histories, *Beyond Southern Skies: Radio Astronomy and the Parkes Telescope* (1992) and *The Creation of the Anglo-Australian Observatory* (1990), as well as a recent general work, *Explorers of the Southern Sky* (1996).

Significantly, much of this work has been undertaken by scientists. Despite the oft-heard protest that scientists look forward, not backward, scientific institutions have been major supporters of historical research in Australia. In 1962, the Australian Academy of Science established the Basser Library as a 'centre for the study of the history of Australian science'. Ann **Moyal** and Michael Hoare used research positions within the library to pioneer the field, create bibliographical resources, and outline many of the broad historiographical questions. The academy continues to publish the only specialist journal in the field, *Historical Records of Australian Science*. Within this journal, however, scholarly historical articles are juxtaposed with biographical memoirs of deceased academicians, written almost exclusively by Fellows. The memoirs are far advanced beyond the taxidermic tributes of the nineteenth century, but the relationship between the articles and the memoirs is uneasy. Such biographies, as with many disciplinary histories, do not just comment on science past: they help to define science present. Scientists writing history are helping to establish, within both the scientific and broader communities, what makes a scientist and what counts as knowledge. In a powerful sense, the history of science is science. This nexus has been largely ignored, robbing the field of much analytical insight.

A lack of access to sources has sometimes been blamed for this historical inertia. But no more. The Australian Science Archives Project provides details of **archival** and published sources through its online database, Bright Sparcs <http://www.asap.unimelb.edu.au/bsparcs/>. Few other fields of Australian history are so well served. In addition, some naturalists' journals have been published, and collections of correspondence are appearing. A major project is under way to collect and selectively publish the voluminous correspondence of eminent nineteenth-century botanist, Ferdinand von **Mueller**. Over the past few decades, tools such as these have been put in place to support an active research community, but where is the activity?

Biographies have appeared for major scientific figures, though there are notable omissions and inadequacies. The

ADB has paid increasing attention to scientists over the years, and its entries remain the authoritative sources for many significant workers. Scientist-cum-explorers have fared rather better, as in E.M. Webster's biography of Ludwig **Leichhardt**, *Whirlwinds in the Plain* (1980). Recent years have brought a mixed bag of scientific biographies, with subjects including Macfarlane **Burnet**, Crosbie **Morrison**, and Ian **Clunies Ross**, but none really manage to blend the scientist with the person. The dilemma is revealed most clearly in Lyndsay Gardiner's biography, *E.V. Keogh: Soldier, Scientist and Administrator* (1990)—Keogh's scientific work is dealt with separately in an appendix by a scientist. Scientists will remain divided figures as long as biographers are intimidated by science.

Science has been quarantined within Australian history. W.K. **Hancock**, however, thought differently when he emphasised the economic significance of William **Farrer's** wheat-breeding heroics in *Australia* (1930). In the 1950s and 1960s science seemed to provide healthy fodder for historians exploring the boundaries of their discipline. Geoffrey **Blainey** recognised its importance within economic history, Geoffrey **Serle** mapped its development alongside other cultural markers, while George Nadel and Michael **Roe** began to explore the meanings and uses of science within Australian cultural history. An exciting program of research was unfolding, and yet faltered. Why?

The 1960s and 1970s brought a loss of faith in the benevolent bounty of science. Significantly, the same period saw the rapid growth of the history of science as a separate discipline. The interests of such historians generally lay in the grand themes of science, such as the Scientific Revolution. Their models and mentors were international, not local. When attention finally turned towards the history of Australian science, it was within such an international framework; Australia became a case-study in the diffusion of scientific knowledge. International conferences on 'Scientific Colonialism' (1981) and 'International Science and National Scientific Identity' (1989) explored, in a cross-cultural context, the development of the colonial scientific community and its interaction with Europe. Analyses of 'colonial science' extensively modified the crude diffusionist models. Roy MacLeod, for example, in *Historical Records of Australian Science* (1982), offered an alternate taxonomy that recognised the complex trajectories of science and imperialism. Nonetheless, conceptions of Australian science have largely remained bound by the top-down perspective assumed by the diffusionist model. Blainey's clichéd 'tyranny of distance' is wielded as a causal mechanism, without reflection upon the actual meaning of isolation within an Australian setting. Wade Chambers provides some antidote in 'Does Distance Tyrannize Science?' (in Rod Home and Sally Hohlsedt, eds, *International Science and National Scientific Identity*, 1991), exhorting historians to challenge the 'metaphorical power' of 'the myth of "tyrannical distance" '. But his call to arms has brought forth few eager combatants.

Important contributions to our understanding of science in Australia have come from outside the mainstream discipline. Bernard **Smith's** *European Vision and the South Pacific 1768–1850* (1960) drew attention to the way the land and its inhabitants were perceived by European scientists. Tom Griffiths in *Hunters and Collectors* (1996) revealed how amateur scientists and collectors were involved in the construction of Australia's past. **Environmental history** has similarly explored the role of science in the complex relationship between people and environment. 'Australia' is revealed as a participant in this process, not merely a receptacle for transplanted institutions.

In 1988, Roy MacLeod noted that 'we await works of synthesis: a new Hancock, who will convey and interpret for us the scientific enterprise, from colony to Commonwealth in the making'. And beyond. Only Ann Moyal, in *A Bright and Savage Land* (1986), has dared to move towards such a broadly integrative project. But hers is the work of a pioneer—a sketch rather than a detailed analysis. The 1988 Bicentenary prompted a surge in history of science publications. However, the main works, *The Commonwealth of Science* and Rod Home (ed.), *Australian Science in the Making* (1988), were collections of articles—hors-d'œuvres at the history-of-science banquet. The pickings are sparser still in relation to twentieth-century science. Rod Home in the above volume rightly directed attention towards the impact of World War II on the scientific community, but D.P. Mellor's volume of the official history, *The Role of Science and Industry* (1958), remains the most comprehensive account. Boris Schedvin's history of the **CSIRO**, *Shaping Science and Industry* (1987), stands out as the story of a scientific institution within its political and economic context and as a history of Australian science in the early twentieth century. However, the companion volume on the CSIRO has never eventuated.

While historians may have successfully occupied territory on the other side of World War II, scientists largely remain in control of the recent past. Academic interest in modern Australian science has typically been within the realm of science policy or sociology of science, although with some interesting results. Max Charlesworth, *Life among the Scientists* (1989), for example, is a quasi-anthropological study of the Walter and Eliza Hall Institute for Medical Research. Such studies should give historians cause for reflection. Methodologies and insights drawn from the social studies of science can, and should, inform the practice of historians. In the same way, historians of Australian science need to explore the cultural context of their studies, moving beyond an examination of the culture of science, towards an understanding of science as culture. Our knowledge of science, as well as of Australian history, will greatly benefit.

TIM SHERRATT

Scots in Australia formed, until the last half-century, the third-largest immigrant intake after the English and **Irish**. Australia's Scottish-born population oscillated around 100 000 during the century after 1861, peaking at 124 000 in 1891, 132 000 in 1933, and 160 000 in 1971. Australia's rapid growth of population ensured, however, that the Scottish presence became less and less visible. In the mid-nineteenth century, about one Victorian in 10 had been in Scotland, with rather lower proportions elsewhere. By 1971, Australia's record population of Scots amounted to scarcely one in 80 of the total population. Scottish accents could still be heard amid the Australian babel, but the immigrants were far outnumbered by the Australian-born claiming Scots origin. As with all 'ethnic' groups of Australian birth, these 'Scots' were typically descended from ancestors of several nationalities, having selected the Scottish strain because of a surname, schooling, religious affiliation, or simply sentiment. Australia's **Presbyterian** population provides a rough index of the importance of the Scots in this broader sense, most Scottish immigrants having been Presbyterian and most Presbyterian immigrants Scottish (along with a substantial minority from Ulster). By 1911, Presbyterians made up over one-sixth of the Victorian population, one Queenslander in eight, and one-ninth of the people of NSW. Only in SA did the proportion fall far below one in 10. As the generations multiplied in Australia, the equation of Presbyterianism with Scottishness matched that of Catholicism with Irishness.

Movement to the antipodes accounted for only about 30 per cent of Scottish emigration between 1853 and 1880, although in five years, during the Victorian gold rush and the American Civil War, the majority chose Australia or NZ. The Scots who peopled Australia have generally been depicted as an elite among nineteenth-century immigrants, whose superior access to capital allowed them to travel in family groups, often without government subsidies. Even among assisted immigrants, the Scots were more likely than the English, and especially the Irish, to be literate, skilled, and also male. The Scottish-Australian reputation for respectability was enhanced by the reluctance of Scottish courts to sentence minor offenders to transportation, so that only 8700 of Australia's 160 000 transported convicts were Scots. The vast majority of Scottish immigrants came from the lowland and industrialised regions (especially Lanarkshire, Edinburgh, and Midlothian), which already accounted for seven-eighths of the Scottish population in 1841. In marked contrast with the Irish, the immediate background of the Scottish immigrants tended to be urban, though movement to Australia was often the latest in a sequence of migrations from country to city and between Scottish towns. Yet the Scottish comparative advantage within urbanising Australia should not be exaggerated: among those assisted to NSW in the 1850s, about one adult Scot in five was illiterate. Many Scots, like Irish, were poor and ill equipped for Australia's alien environment; but failure and poverty have been largely erased from the dominant Scottish-Australian myth. Don Watson, *Caledonia Australis* (1984), explores this relationship.

The flattering stereotype of the Scottish newcomer, with his capital, skills, family responsibilities, industriousness, and entrepreneurial flair, was undermined from the late 1830s by the immigration of highland 'Celts'. Though they were always a tiny fraction of the intake from Scotland, assisted movement from the highlands and islands was significant in the aftermath of the famines of 1836–37 and 1847–49, which resulted in extensive 'clearances' involving both private and public schemes for systematic emigration. The highland Celt was deemed by English officials (like Trevelyan of the Treasury) to share the negative attributes of his Irish cousins, such as sloth, passivity, reliance on charity, ignorance, marital imprudence, and personal filthiness. Trevelyan, who had opposed systematic colonisation during the Irish Famine for fear of discouraging 'voluntary' emigration, made Australia the focus of an ambitious scheme of social engineering which elicited strong support from lairds and tacksmen. Between 1852 and 1858, Trevelyan's Highland and Island Emigration Society sent 5000 'surplus' Celts to Australia, one-eighth of the intended outflow which was to have provided a final solution to the Celtic problem. Highland emigration was also promoted energetically by John Dunmore **Lang**, the fearless if bigoted radical who became Australia's first and most controversial Presbyterian minister. For Lang, transplantation to Australia gave Scottish crofters an opportunity to demonstrate their moral superiority over Irish Romanists in the land of promise. The highlanders, with their visible poverty and audible oddity of speech, met with a mixed reception and often sent home unfavourable reports. Australia's Scottish reputation was not enhanced by the spectacular failure of Macdonnell of Glengarry, who transplanted much of his tenantry to found a Gippsland dairy farm in 1842, only to return home, ruined, in the following year. Yet the emigration of other landowners, accompanied or followed by their redundant crofters, built up significant chains of migration, especially from the islands to Victoria. To a surprising degree, Scottish identity in Australia was shaped by the tragic origins of the relatively minor outflow from the highlands and islands, just as the famine exodus was assigned an exaggerated role in defining Irish-Australia.

As with most ethnic groups, historians of the Scots in Australia have concentrated on their collective 'contribution' to national development, particularly as governors, politicians, pastoralists, explorers, businessmen, bankers, academics (in Sydney more than in Melbourne), schoolmasters, doctors, and clergymen. This Companion is replete with Scottish names such as governors **Hunter**, **Macquarie** and **Brisbane**, prime ministers from **Reid** and **Fisher** to **Menzies**, pastoralists such as **Macarthur** and **Elder**, and the explorers **Mitchell** and **Stuart**. The Scottish economic influence was evident not only in local business, but also in the contribution of capitalists such as the Aberdeen-based Scottish Australian Investment Company to developing mercantile shipping and the pastoral industry. The over-representation of Scots in colonial parliaments symbolises their successful assimilation as an immigrant group, joining (even dominating) rather than subverting the colonial establishment. This record of efficient adaptation sits rather uneasily with the proliferation from the mid-nineteenth century of Caledonian societies, celebrating Scottish and often highland culture through caber-tossing, pipe bands, whisky, haggis, kilts, and Celtic kitsch. Such ethnic exhibitions, by contrast with their Irish equivalents, are usually interpreted as a harmless freemasonry. Even so, the persistence in Australia of a defiant

Scottishness, however artificial in form, betokens a deeper failure on the part of Scots colonists. Lang's puritan dream of a godly community, gladly submitting to a rigorous moral jurisdiction, was never fulfilled outside a few sober suburbs.

Malcolm Prentis, *The Scots in Australia* (1983), is a history of the period 1788–1900 in NSW, Victoria, and Qld. This may be supplemented by Eric Richards (*HS*, 1985) and the relevant sections of James Jupp (ed.), *The Australian People* (1988).

DAVID FITZPATRICK

Scott, Ernest (1867–1939) was professor of history at the University of Melbourne, with a broad influence in shaping a generation of scholars and public intellectuals from S.H. **Roberts** to Manning **Clark**.

Born illegitimate, raised by his grandparents, and enjoying no higher education, he trained on the job as a journalist in London. As a young Fabian and Theosophist, he married the daughter of Annie Besant and migrated to Melbourne in 1892. He made a career in journalism and as a Hansard reporter, ultimately leading to the Melbourne academic chair in 1913. He might have had no formal qualifications or degrees or research training, but he did have definite ideas about useful knowledge and its dissemination, in particular knowledge about the past as the guide to the present, and especially as a key factor in the making of a new nation. An early antiquarian interest in European explorers—leading to the writing of *Terre Napoléon* (1910), *Lapérouse* (1912), and *The Life of Matthew Flinders RN* (1914)—deepened with the reading of von Ranke and the German scientific school. An unreflective empiricism distinguished his historical method and teaching ideas but, within its times, it made Scott into a professional among amateurs and antiquarians. He inspired his students to do archival research and to ask critical questions of popular historical mythologies. His notable *Short History of Australia* (1916) was a key text, 'an artefact of a nation at its lessons', in the words of his biographer and Ernest Scott Professor, Stuart Macintyre.

Between World War I and his death on the eve of World War II in 1939, Scott wrote or edited eight books. He reformed the history syllabus at his university to make it more European (and less British) as well as more Australian. He developed the honours programs and tutorial work, lectured and marked papers on a large scale, encouraged talent among his students (who included the main historians of Australia in mid-century, notably, Stephen Roberts, Keith **Hancock**, Fred **Alexander**, Norman **Harper**, and Manning Clark), and he played a valued role in faculty life. Above all, he established the idea of seeing Australia in a wider world, rather than merely as an imperial projection. He began to teach and research in Australian history, as well as progressively supporting state and federal collections, regional histories, and memorials for major figures; and he combined these activities with increasing involvement in the work of the **Australian Institute of International Affairs**, the Institute of Pacific Relations, and their associated bodies. His major contribution to the *Cambridge History of the British*

Empire (1933) revealed the enduring imperial sentiment in his thought, but this lived alongside his prescient sense of Australia's regional and international future relations.

This remarkable and successful career was based on a quick intelligence which made Scott an excellent journalist, able to synthesise ideas and data, to ask good questions, and to develop his position in a changing world of early-twentieth-century Australia as a new federated nation. Never profound or original as a writer, teacher, or propagandist, he yet had considerable impact as a disseminator of historical and political knowledge, in which he addressed the popular issues of the day. It was this role as a historical Everyman which was significant, rather than his published scholarship, which has not worn well—except as remarkably revealing of common ideas and preoccupations of its age.

DERYCK SCHREUDER

Scott, Rose (1847–1925), was a central figure in campaigns for women's rights. Born on a large pastoral property called Glendon, near Singleton, NSW, she was educated at home and in the households of other family members. Her fine and extremely feminine looks matched prevailing views of female beauty: she once observed of herself, self-mockingly, 'I have the misfortune to be passably good looking, my hair waves, my eyes are blue, my cheeks are pink'. There was an array of suitors and a close relationship with her cousin, David Scott **Mitchell**. When Mitchell died in 1907, he left £5000 to Scott. In the 1860s and 1870s, his intellectual companionship and the development he offered were incomparable gifts, shaping the critique of conventional sexual relations that was the foundation of her public career after 1890. The paradox was that he taught her what men were—'the animal in man' as she called it—while subverting conventional manliness in his life choices and in his intellectual relationship with her.

Scott's father had died, leaving her £500 a year. In 1880 Rose Scott moved to Sydney where members of the family in need of nursing or other forms of succour came to stay from time to time. Five years later, the household moved to a picturesque cottage in Woollahra. As a woman of independent means, Rose Scott was a member of a class in which the women, when not ministering to their families, undertook public philanthropic work. She learned to see such work as similar to cutting the heads off weeds without digging out and destroying their roots. Accordingly, when she began to look beyond her family, it was to a world that she saw as being in need of radical social reform.

At Woollahra during the 1880s Rose Scott built the community beyond her family in which she formulated her feminism. She did this by holding the Friday night at-home gatherings at which the great questions of the day were debated and the direction of particular social and cultural reforms were set. The 1898 Early Closing Bill was drafted on her rosewood dining table; shopgirls told politicians of the conditions in which they worked; and Rose Scott established the serious friendships with powerful men which ensured that they would take her seriously in her subsequent political work. From such commitment and activity it was but a short step to the Women's Literary Society, formed in 1889, and the Woman's Suffrage League (WSL), established in 1891.

The causes that she took up, and worked for energetically, embraced raising the age of consent for girls; challenging sexual and financial inequality between women and men in marriage; improving working women's wages and conditions; giving women better access to education; politicising rape and abortion; combating **prostitution**; abolishing contagious diseases legislation; promoting women's work in literature, art, and music; and achieving political rights for women. The range of her concerns and the nature of her feminism are explored in a major biographical study by Judith Allen, *Rose Scott: Vision and Revision in Feminism* (1994). Scott became an inspiring public speaker. Her dominance of the suffrage campaign in Sydney, through her position as secretary of the Central Sydney branch of the WSL, encountered challenge from suburban branches and suffragists more closely identified with working women, who formed the Women's Progressive Association in 1902. But this did not prevent the NSW parliament enfranchising women in that same year.

At the end of 1902 she founded the non-party Women's Political and Educational League which, at its peak, had branches state-wide. But this effort to establish political solidarity on the basis of sex was gradually eroded by political alignments based on class and party; it was disbanded in 1910. Scott increasingly turned to **pacifism** and prevention of war; she established a NSW branch of the London Peace Society in 1907 but felt its efforts rendered useless by the eruption of World War I. In 1921, she announced her retirement from public life with a speech ending in an exhortation that could represent the encompassing determination of her whole public life: 'Be passionate in earnest and loyal to your womanhood and to your sex and in the end you will certainly win.'

SUSAN MAGAREY

Scottish Martyrs were Thomas Muir (1765–99), political leader and lawyer; Thomas Fysche Palmer (1747–1802), Unitarian minister; William Skirving (?–1796), secretary of the Edinburgh Friends of the People Society; Joseph Gerrald (1760–96); and Maurice Margarot (1745–1815). They were arrested in 1793 following their promotion of political and economic reforms inspired by the French Revolution. They were tried for sedition in Edinburgh by the infamous Justice Braxfield, who dismissed doubts as to the authority of British transportation laws in the Scottish judicial system, and handed down a sentence of transportation to NSW. Braxfield's critics, who included members of the House of Commons, condemned his harsh treatment. The poor conditions the men endured on board the *Surprize* en route to NSW were recounted in *A Narrative of the Sufferings of T.F. Palmer, and W. Skirving* (1797). Four of the five died as an indirect result of their punishment. Muir escaped on an American ship, but died later in France; Palmer died on the voyage back to England; and Skirving and Gerrald died in

Sydney. Margarot was suspected of involvement in the ill-fated **Castle Hill Rising** of 1804, but later returned to Scotland. Frank **Clune** provides an account in *The Scottish Martyrs* (1969).

HD

Scullin, James Henry (1876–1953), prime minister from October 1929 to January 1932, bore the burden of national leadership during the most difficult years of the **Depression**.

He was born at Trawalla, Victoria, to Irish Catholic parents. When he was about 10 the family moved to the Ballarat area where, after leaving school, he combined part-time work with earnest self-improvement at night school, debating societies, and the public library. Like many young Irish Catholics, he was attracted to the **Australian Labor Party** as the only party that respected his heritage. He joined around 1903 and, after contesting Ballaarat against Prime Minister **Deakin** in 1906, finally won the House of Representatives seat of Corangamite in 1910. Despite a creditable parliamentary performance, he was defeated at the 1913 election and moved to edit the Ballarat *Evening Echo*.

Along with most of the labour movement, Scullin was radicalised by World War I. He opposed **conscription** for overseas service in 1916–17, supported the Irish nationalist struggle against Britain, and argued for the adoption of Labor's 1921 socialisation objective; but after winning the seat of Yarra in 1922, the sober and resolutely respectable Scullin adopted less radical positions. He became one of Labor's leading advocates of economic and fiscal respectability. After a year as deputy, he was elected leader of the Federal Parliamentary Labor Party in April 1928 and significantly reduced the **Bruce–Page** government's majority at the November 1928 election. By October 1929 he was prime minister after Bruce and his government were defeated in a House of Representatives vote and then an election fought on the issue of industrial relations.

The Scullin government was quickly overwhelmed by the Depression. On taking office it was confronted by the shock waves of the Wall Street collapse and soon faced a crisis in government finance. As unemployment escalated and loans fell due, Scullin had a cruel choice between a moral responsibility to distressed Australians and a legal obligation to foreign bond-holders. Confronted by a hostile Senate and unhelpful bankers on one side, and a rebellious Labor Party on the other, he aged visibly as he struggled to formulate a compromise plan that would ensure economic recovery with 'equality of sacrifice'. By mid-1931 Labor had split into three factions centring on contending fiscal policies as a dispirited Scullin tried to implement the deflationary Premiers' Plan. The government was defeated in parliament by the **Lang** Labor faction and subsequently trounced by the **Lyons**-led Opposition at the December 1931 election.

After another demoralising defeat in 1934, Scullin relinquished the leadership to **Curtin**, thereafter playing the role of benign elder statesman until his retirement in 1949.

In 1937 Warren Denning's *Caucus Crisis* concluded that, 'Of James Henry Scullin it can be said that he brought character, honesty and sincerity of purpose to the Labor party and to his political life.' John Robertson's standard *J.H. Scullin* (1974), offered a generous and solid case for the defence against critics on the left. C.B. Schedvin's *Australia and the Great Depression* (1970), and most general historians, have seen Scullin as a decent but largely ineffectual figure overwhelmed by forces beyond his grasp.

PETER LOVE

Sealing long provided an important food source for coastal Aborigines. Like **whaling**, the exploitation of seals for commercial gain coincided with the beginnings of European settlement of Australia, when roving parties of English and American seamen discovered vast colonies of these semi-aquatic mammals along the coastlines and on the islands of Australia and NZ. In October 1798, in the first major haul of seal skins in Australia, crewmen of the English brig *Nautilus* clubbed and killed 9000 seals in the Bass Strait islands; in 1809 three ships collected 45 000 skins in Foveaux Strait in a single week. Over the next 50 years seals were hunted extensively in the colonies; the skins and oil provided a lucrative source of export income. Semi-permanent sealing camps were established at vantage points along the southern coastline and on the Bass Strait islands off northern Tasmania, where Aboriginal women were often exploited. Sealing in Bass Strait continued as a way of life well into the twentieth century. Following near-extinction of several species, seals were protected in the 1950s and sealing ceased as a commercial venture.

HD

SEATO was the South-East Asian Treaty Organisation, established in 1954 by the USA, Britain, France, Thailand, the Philippines, Pakistan, Australia, and NZ. Its signatories agreed to mutual resistance to aggression, but the USA amended the treaty so that it was obliged to render assistance only in response to communist aggression. With the earlier **ANZUS** treaty, SEATO provided the framework of Australia's regional foreign policy during the Cold War, but was weakened by changes in the region and the increasingly critical domestic response to Australian participation in the **Vietnam War**. SEATO was disbanded in 1977.

SM

Secession from the Commonwealth is precluded by the **Constitution**, which established 'one indissoluble Federal Commonwealth under the Crown of the United Kingdom'. Efforts to secede therefore required an approach to Westminster until the Australia Acts of 1986 removed that possibility. The most serious attempt to do so occurred in WA during the **Depression** of the 1930s. The **Nationalist** government conducted a state referendum in 1933, in which the electors voted two to one in favour of separating from the Commonwealth. The federal government despatched three ministers to the west, who were badly received. The new state govern-ment (Labor defeated the Nationalists in 1933) allowed a committee to prepare a detailed *Case of the People of Western Australia*, which went to London at the end of 1934 with a petition eight metres long. The British parliament rebuffed the approach. The event is discussed by E.D. Watt in *University Studies in Western Australian History* (1958) and by Geoffrey **Bolton** in *A Fine Country to Starve In* (1972).

While constitutionally debarred, the threat of an aggrieved state occupied the Commonwealth government then and at other times. The system of adjusting public expenditure by the states through Commonwealth assistance devised between the world wars to equalise the national standard of living was a response to this fear. It is revived periodically by populist politicians in the resource-rich states of Qld and WA who capitalise on discontent with Canberra. The constitutional status of secession is examined in Gregory Craven, *Secession: The Ultimate States Right* (1986).

SM

Second AIF, see AIF

Second Fleet of British ships transported the second shipment of **convicts** to NSW under notorious conditions. The brutal treatment of convicts on these vessels, the high rates of disease and mortality, the excessive use of leg-irons, and the convicts' struggle ashore at Sydney Cove in June 1790 were reported in gruesome tones by the Rev. Richard **Johnson**. Blame was levelled at the private shipping contractors who sought to maximise their cargo and minimise expenditure on food and medicine in order to make a profit. Public outcry led to some improvements in the **transportation** system.

HD

Second World War, see **World War II**

Secret armies were the right-wing military organisations formed after World War I that flourished during the **Depression**, notably the Old and New Guard in NSW and the White Army in Victoria. Alarmed by the leftward trend in the labour movement, and especially the policies of Labor Premier J.T. **Lang**, members prepared themselves to raise arms in the defence of King and Country. The enemy, they believed, was composed of the unemployed, the Bolsheviks, and even Catholics. The secret armies had a particularly strong following among ex-servicemen, especially those in farming communities. Their fear reached a peak across the Victorian countryside on the evening of 6 March 1931, when thousands of White Army members mobilised themselves in readiness for an attack—one which never eventuated. Michael Cathcart illuminates something of the absurdity of their defence strategy in *Defending the National Tuckshop* (1988). Cathcart claims that **Blamey** was the White Army's commander-in-chief, but this is denied in Hetherington's biography. Edmund Herring, later chief justice of Victoria, was also a leader.

The NSW Old Guard had formed after World War I and is the subject of Andrew Moore, *The Secret Army and the Premier* (1989). The New Guard, formed in February 1931 and led by Eric Campbell, was a fierce opponent of J.T. Lang. This was demonstrated most dramatically at the opening ceremony of the **Sydney Harbour Bridge** in 1932, when a member, Captain Francis de Groot, rode forth on a horse and slashed with his sword the ceremonial ribbon, depriving Lang of the honour. There was extensive street violence in Sydney during this period. Enthusiasm for the New Guard waned after Lang's dismissal and its own embrace of fascism; by the mid-1930s it was largely irrelevant. Its history is discussed in Robert Darlington, *Eric Campbell and the New Guard* (1983), and in Campbell's own book, *The Rallying Point* (1965). A later secret army, known as the Association, was formed in the 1940s, with Blamey as its commander.

HD

Sectarianism in Australia refers to the mutual antagonism between **Catholics** and Protestants, which was a regular feature of social and political life from the 1860s to the 1920s. It had appeared occasionally before the 1860s; its effects persisted until the 1960s.

Sectarianism was most obviously manifested in fiery speeches by sectarian champions, almost invariably clergymen, Catholic or Protestant, denouncing or ridiculing the beliefs of others and attributing to them complex conspiracies against the speaker's religion. Sectarianism was sometimes manifested in political organisations of Catholics or Protestants; more frequently, sectarian fears and grievances were played on by politicians seeking votes. Sectarianism was manifested and reproduced by organisations such as Orange Lodges and the Irish national associations, and in the commemoration of the Battle of the Boyne and St Patrick's Day.

Anti-sectarianism became a central tenet of colonial **liberalism**, the dominant political creed during the second half of the nineteenth century. Colonial liberals viewed sectarianism as a vice of the Old World which had no place in the new. Government schools, organised along the lines of the Irish national schools and teaching the common beliefs of all Christian denominations, were to be the means for preventing sectarianism from taking root. At first prominent Catholics were among those espousing this view.

A predisposition to sectarianism came to Australia in the mental baggage of many migrants. For Protestants of fundamentalist or evangelical faith, particularly those from the north of Ireland, Catholicism was not only an erroneous and superstitious creed, but one whose adherents actively sought to force Protestant nations back under the rule of Rome. From the 1840s, the attitudes of many Catholics were shaped by the popular movement for Irish independence, which wove nationalism and religion into a single identity, and by the hardening opposition in Rome to European liberalism and nationalism. Pope Pius IX, determined to exert a high degree of control over the church, insisted that Catholic children be educated in Catholic schools. In the Australian colonies, earlier Catholic clerical support for national schools turned to opposition in the 1860s. This in turn exasperated colonial liberals and hardened their resolve to educate all children in national or state schools. Government support for denominational schools was gradually withdrawn. The Catholic Church alone remained committed to educating all its children and demanded the return of state aid.

In the 1860s, the **Fenian** rebellion in Ireland and subsequent bombings in England raised the spectre of an Irish threat to social order in the colonies. In Sydney, in 1868, an Irishman claiming to be a Fenian attempted to assassinate the Duke of Edinburgh, Queen Victoria's second son. Many colonists wondered if the Protestant sectarians might not be right. Protestant sectarianism flourished. This in turn helped sectarian Catholics, especially the clergy, to persuade other Catholics that colonial society was hostile to them.

Hostility to sectarianism and the general openness of Australian society continued to contain sectarianism. For the next 50 years, periodic bursts of sectarian clamour were succeeded by longer periods of quiet, but a barrier grew between Catholics and their fellow Australians. Sectarian outbursts were sometimes occasioned by Protestant sectarians, but most often, sectarianism was ignited by the forays of Catholic episcopal leaders. Convinced of their moral and intellectual superiority, they demanded state aid for their schools while denouncing public schools, Protestantism and, later, the British Empire in deliberately provocative language. Catholic sectarianism inevitably engendered a furious response from Protestant sectarians and weary denunciations by the majority of opinion leaders who remained firmly anti-sectarian.

On several occasions between the 1860s and 1920s, Protestant political organisations formed to support Protestant candidates and oppose Catholics. In 1911, a Catholic Federation formed in the eastern states to organise the Catholic vote and fight for 'educational justice'. But lay Catholics were generally reluctant to have their vote determined by their bishops. Rather, by the early twentieth century, many Catholics were turning to the **Australian Labor Party**, forging a link which survived until the 1960s. This link was strengthened during the 1916 and 1917 controversy over **conscription**, which most Catholics and most Labor supporters opposed, urged on by the Catholic Archbishop **Mannix**. That controversy was marked by a high level of sectarianism which continued until the mid-1920s.

Thereafter, sectarianism declined. Its legacy lived on in common forms of low-level discrimination. Catholic and state school children going to and from school frequently exchanged insults and, occasionally, blows; Catholic and non-Catholic parents alike sought to prevent their children contracting a 'mixed marriage'; certain government departments and certain firms would never employ Catholics; others would employ only Catholics. But the natural resistance of Australian society to sectarianism continued. By the end of the 1960s, the factors which caused sectarianism had been removed. Most of Ireland attained independence in 1922; state aid to church schools was granted in the 1960s;

Catholicism was transformed by the Second Vatican Council; and the ecumenical movement encouraged Catholics and Protestants to set aside past differences in the face of an increasingly irreligious world.

The comprehensive study of Australian sectarianism has yet to be written. It has been studied mainly by Catholic historians. Michael Hogan, *The Sectarian Strand: Religion in Australian History* (1987), provides the most extensive survey. Mark Lyons is critical of the conventional Catholic interpretation in 'Aspects of Sectarianism, New South Wales c.1865–1880' (PhD thesis, Australian National University, 1972).

MARK LYONS

Selection originally meant the choosing of any Crown land available for grant or sale. From the 1850s it referred to small farmers settling on Crown lands occupied by squatters. These smallholders (or selectors) were to pay for their land in instalments; they had to reside on the land and improve it. In NSW the selector could settle on land in the pastoral domain without prior notice or official survey: this was free selection by free selectors. Elsewhere the land was withdrawn from the pastoralist and surveyed before it was open for selection.

Selection Acts were passed in all colonies. The first in Victoria (1860) and NSW (1861) were the outcome of sustained popular agitation. Gold-diggers and town workers rallied to break the squatters' monopoly and give the poor man his chance; their leaders promised an Australia transformed into a pre-industrial utopia of smiling homesteads. D.W.A. Baker argued in 'The Origins of Robertson's Land Acts' (*HSANZ*, 1958) that the middle class, committed to equality of opportunity and resentful of the squatters' aristocratic pretensions, were in charge of this movement and its chief beneficiaries. However, the acts were only carried in NSW after the sober middle-class reformers had been pushed aside for more compliant politicians.

In their first years the Selection Acts had exactly the opposite effect from their intention: over wide areas the squatters became the owners of lands they had formerly leased and very few smallholders established themselves. This was the first bitter failure of Australian democracy. Squatters used agents (or dummies) to select land on their behalf, they arranged for the declaration of reserves to preserve land from selection, they paid cash for land at auction sales (which continued alongside the instalment schemes), and generally exploited every legal loophole and administrative opportunity to retain their lands. This greed and cunning and the short-sightedness and carelessness of legislators were prominent themes in the first histories of these events, including S.H. **Roberts's** *History of Australian Land Settlement* (1924)—still the only volume to describe the acts and their numerous amendments in all colonies.

Manning **Clark** rejected this interpretation in his *Select Documents*, vol. 2 (1955) and attributed early failure to the smallholders' lack of capital and equipment, their ignorance of agriculture, and inadequate transport. Factors such as these, to which should be added the small market for **agriculture** in the interior until the arrival of **railways**, have been stressed much more in subsequent accounts. Numerous local studies (most notably G.L. Buxton on the Riverina, J.M. Powell on western Victoria, and Duncan Waterson on the Darling Downs) have explored the complex uses to which the acts were put and the play of local circumstances and opportunities. What counts as agricultural failure might be success when a selector sold out with advantage to a squatter and selected more land elsewhere or accumulated enough land to be a small grazier. To get sufficient land, all the members of a family took up a selection, a loophole which worked in the small man's favour. The role of **family** in securing land and providing labour (unpaid) to work it has been highlighted in recent studies of gender and family.

The emphasis on the preconditions for agricultural success has had the unfortunate consequence of downplaying the significance of amendments to the legislation which put the smallholder in a stronger position. Without them, it would have been the pastoralists who exploited the new opportunities for agriculture and farmers would have been their tenants. The amendments abolished or limited open sales at auction, made **dummying** more difficult, gave more generous terms for repayment, and subjected the whole process to close administrative surveillance. This at last solved the dilemma which had beset legislators: if they made it easy for the small man to get land, it was also easier for the squatter's dummy. Under such provisions the modern wheat belt in SA and northern Victoria took shape in the 1870s with the cultivators being small freeholders. In NSW agriculture developed later, after the squatters had secured much of the good land, with the consequence that more of the wheat farmers were tenants or share-croppers. **Closer Settlement** Acts later provided more land for owner–cultivators.

In NSW free selection meant that selectors arrived unannounced on the squatters' runs. Without surveyed boundaries or fences, squatter and selector fought each other over water, access roads, and the straying of horses and stock. Selectors were hounded off the land by squatters or eked out a precarious existence in a place and time unsuited to agriculture. These were the experiences treated by Henry **Lawson** in his verse and stories. Steele **Rudd** in *On Our Selection* (later popularised as **'Dad and Dave'** on film and radio) also depicted poverty-stricken and blighted selectors in Qld's Darling Downs. These powerful images helped to disguise the success achieved in SA and Victoria from the 1870s, and subsequent success elsewhere. (See also **Land settlement**.)

JOHN HIRST

Selector, see Selection

Separation was the means whereby new settlements attained the status of separate colonies. Van Diemen's Land first formally requested status as a separate colony in 1824. The **Port Phillip District** attained independence from NSW as the Colony of Victoria in 1851; Qld followed in 1859. Great festivities marked the occasion in each new colony.

Following the **Federation** of the colonies as states of the new Australian Commonwealth, **secession** movements became part of a continuing tradition in the state politics of Qld and WA, though they have so far proved unsuccessful. Regional districts, usually those rich in natural resources or disadvantaged by distance or politics, have also demanded independence as **new states**. Far north Qld continues to regard itself as a separate social and geographic entity with inadequate representation. In a radical move in 1970, WA farmer Leonard George Casley declared his property a sovereign state, under the name Hutt River Province, and styled himself Prince Leonard.

HD

Serle, (Alan) Geoffrey (1922–98) was the doyen of Victorian historians. His first book on Victoria during the 1850s, *The Golden Age* (1963), was dedicated to his four grandparents and four of their parents who settled in Victoria during that decade. His father, Percival Serle, was a student of Australian literature and compiler of a **biographical dictionary**, vocations his son inherited. Study at the University of Melbourne was interrupted by service in New Guinea during World War II. Serle returned to the history department at Melbourne after postgraduate study at Oxford, moved to Monash University in 1961, and worked towards the end of his career at the Australian National University as editor of the *ADB*, but resided in the Melbourne suburb of Hawthorn all his life.

Serle's *Golden Age* and subsequent *The Rush To Be Rich* (1971) were detailed and panoramic studies based on an unrivalled knowledge of Victorian history. Liberal and egalitarian in sympathy, they eschewed class analysis for civic meliorism, in keeping with his own social democratic values. His later biography of *John Monash* (1982) also discerned a life of service from an ambitious engineer-turned-general. Serle's cultural history, *From Deserts the Prophets Come* (1973), traced the growth of national creativity in literature, art, music, theatre, and architecture; when he revised it as *The Creative Spirit in Australia* (1987) he observed that it was no longer possible to keep abreast of these fields, as he had once been able to do when they were enlarging national life. The later biography of *Robin Boyd* (1995) affirmed the impact of the modernist aesthetic on postwar Australia. 'I write in the liberal humane tradition', he stated in David Duffy et al. (eds), *Historians at Work* (1973), and 'any discerning reader may see that I stand for a hundred things, though I must not assert them too strongly; distaste for the corruption of the market-place; the prime place of the artists, tolerance, humanism, egalitarianism, liberal social democracy'. The National Library of Australia published a tribute in 1994.

SM

Settlement of Australia by the British began in 1788. Its impulse is the subject of a long-standing debate. The conventional explanation, accepted by most historians, was that the British government needed an alternative outlet for disposing of its criminals after the loss of the American colonies in the 1770s, and turned accordingly to NSW, which had been described favourably by James **Cook** in his voyage of exploration in 1768–71. The result was the despatch of the **First Fleet** to **Botany Bay** in 1787, under the command of Captain Arthur **Phillip**. **Convicts** and their custodians made up the settlement he established at Sydney Cove, and for some time afterwards the penal function shaped its development. Historians paid considerable attention to the circumstances that created this unwanted felonry—and, with varying shades of sympathy or distaste, to the background and subsequent experience of the convict settlers of Australia—but they were less interested in the details of the decision to ship them here. The concern was with the new nation that emerged from such unlikely materials. Since British colonisation began with convicts, it was generally assumed that its purpose was to create an open-air gaol. Thus, in *The Foundation of Australia* (1937), Eris **O'Brien** took it as axiomatic that the country was settled because the British gaols were 'unwontedly full'.

The assumption was challenged by K.M. Dallas, who suggested in *PPTHRA* (1952) that 'the dumping of convicts view is too simple'. He surmised that a base for trade in Asia and the Pacific was envisaged, a hypothesis developed in *Trading Posts or Penal Colonies* (1969). Dallas's arguments had limited currency until 1966, when Geoffrey **Blainey** worked the British settlement into his iconoclastic interpretation of *The Tyranny of Distance*. Because NSW was so far from Britain, he argued, there had to be some compelling reason to choose it as the site for settlement. Blainey suggested that bases were established at both Sydney and Norfolk Island in 1788 because New Zealand flax and Norfolk Island pine could provide ropes, sailcloth, and masts for the British navy. For confirmation he relied particularly on the 'Heads of a Plan'—a document enclosed with correspondence in 1786 of Lord Sydney, the minister for the Home Office with responsibility for colonial affairs—which set out the scheme for 'effectually disposing of convicts, and rendering their transportation reciprocally beneficial to themselves and the State'. Blainey concluded that Australia 'was not designed simply as a remote gaol' but was expected to develop its own export trade.

His theory was challenged by Geoffrey **Bolton** in *AEHR* (1968) and A.G.L. **Shaw** in *HS* (1968), and generated an extended debate. Both critics drew on substantial knowledge of eighteenth-century British colonial policy to argue that Blainey's emphasis on naval supplies was excessive and that other sources for them were available. Bolton queried whether the 'Heads of a Plan' determined the British decision; Shaw noted that the paragraphs mentioning flax and timber were tacked on at the end; David Mackay in *Historical Journal* (1974) questioned if it was even an official document; and in *JRAHS* (1976), Alan Atkinson demonstrated the need to distinguish among the attitudes of different parties and factions toward the foundation of a penal settlement.

If the direct evidence for Blainey's claim that naval supplies provided the motive for settlement of NSW was fragile, it was by now accepted that the choice of NSW as a penal colony required explanation. Several contributors to a growing literature that was gathered together by Ged Martin in *The Founding of Australia* (1978) demonstrated that other locations were considered, and these strengthened the argument that geopolitical considerations influenced the final decision.

In his first articles on the subject, in *AEHR* (1975) and *HS* (1975), Alan Frost followed Blainey in stressing the importance of naval supplies, and tied the decision to colonise NSW with British needs in the Indian Ocean. Frost developed this argument in *Convicts and Empire: A Naval Question* (1980), and has held fast to it in subsequent publications, including his biography of Phillip, his contribution to the **Bicentennial History Project** volume, *Australians: To 1788* (1987), and more polemically in *Botany Bay Mirages: Illusions of Australia's Convict Beginnings* (1994). In these works the predilection for more auspicious national origins finds expression in providential imperial foresight.

The sceptics remain. David Mackay extended his criticisms of the 'flax and timber' argument in *A Place of Exile* (1985). Mollie Gillen made a closely argued case for 'The Botany Bay Decision 1786: Convicts not Empire' in *English Historical Review* (1982). Alan Atkinson attempted to shift the debate through consideration of 'The First Plans for Governing New South Wales' (*AHS*, 1990), which suggested that convicts were uppermost in the initial planning up to October 1786 but that the scheme then expanded to give the settlement 'a new, more elevated and also more expensive status'. The first volume of his general history, *The Europeans in Australia* (1997), provides a larger context for the British decision. Following Cook's voyage, various people (including Joseph **Banks**) suggested that Australia should be used to establish a settlement of convicts. NSW was chosen after African alternatives were found unsuitable. Atkinson concludes that NSW was to be 'an addition to the old empire', but a distant place where 'the convicts would be peasants in a country of their own. Their labour would serve no great imperial purpose.'

Ged Martin (in Pamela Statham, ed., *The Origins of Australia's Capital Cities*, 1989) suggests that there were 'layers of incentive' in the decision to settle NSW. The desire to deter and reform criminals, and need to relieve the pressure on Britain's prison system after the loss of the American colonies, constitute a necessary but not sufficient decision for the despatch of the First Fleet to Botany Bay. Considerations of imperial strategy, trade, and naval supplies seem to provide the additional explanation for the location of the penal settlement. But the settlement debate remains remarkably polarised, no closer to resolution than it was during the spirited argument over Blainey's *Tyranny of Distance*. This is partly due to the reluctance of the participants to concede ground to their adversaries, partly to the attenuated nature of the documentary record and the disputed provenance of the documents that do remain. Most of all, it is caused by the different purposes and dispositions of the disputants, and the foundational significance of the subject. (See also **Invasion**.)

STUART MACINYTRE

Settlement, land, see **Land settlement**

Sexuality was understood as a powerful and independent force in colonial Australia. It could be expressed legitimately within marriage (in accordance with Christian morality) but, unleashed outside this institution, its consequences could be dire. From an early age, girls were urged to guard their purity lest they should excite men's 'instinctively forceful' sexual passions. Despite such warnings, annual registered illegitimate births imply a high level of premarital sexual intercourse: about one Melbourne bride in six was pregnant on her wedding day in the 1880s. Although this suggests that some young people contravened social prescriptions, it does not follow that they were impervious to contemporary sexual mores. Many of the single women involved in cases of abortion and concealment of birth, for example, spoke of their desperate attempts to hide their (and their family's) 'shame'. They were well aware that, in order to retain social respectability, their sexual behaviour had to be beyond reproach.

In the late eighteenth and nineteenth centuries, sexuality was also understood as a *limited* energy source. Sexologists discussed the dangers of seminal loss, emphasising the ill-effects of masturbation on the male population. By the late nineteenth century, sexologists such as Robert von Krafft-Ebing (1892) challenged earlier views that masturbation could lead to **madness**, paralysis, and even death, but they still feared energy loss and general physical debilitation. What is more, these concerns reverberated within the prevailing discourse of national greatness. In *LH* (1985), David Walker argues that, in this period, semen was considered a national resource; unless deposited within socially sanctioned parameters its 'loss foreshadowed national decline'.

There was considerable anxiety in late-nineteenth-century Australia about the declining birth-rate, with its implications for national efficiency and security. Married women were exhorted to do their national duty—to populate the country and ensure the dominance of the white race. In 1888, when Justice **Windeyer** ruled that Annie Besant's popular birth control literature was not obscene, alarm intensified and state agencies moved to censor newspaper advertisements for contraceptives and to check what they saw as the rising tide of abortion, child abandonment, and infanticide cases. A number of historians, most recently Kerreen Reiger in *The Disenchantment of the Home* (1985) and Stefania Siedlecky and Diana Wyndham in *Populate and Perish* (1990), have examined these **population** debates. They argue that state agencies, clergymen, and members of the medical profession believed that women were deliberately limiting the size of their families and that such 'selfishness' was threatening race suicide and economic decay.

Evidence for the Royal Commission into the Decline of the Birth Rate in New South Wales in 1903–04 indicates that there was indeed an increase in contraceptive knowledge and use in the nineteenth century. When one witness, Dr Robert Scot Skirving, was asked if he knew of any women seeking abortions he replied, 'Oh, it is awfully common … A woman will come to you and say, "I am in the family way: I want to have an abortion produced." "Well," you say, "I can do nothing for you." "Oh, very well, I will go somewhere else, where they will do it." And they do, and you meet them a month or six weeks afterwards, smiling, and no longer pregnant.' While Skirving may have exaggerated, it is clear that many women were prepared to abort unwanted pregnancies (and they were assisted by their sexual partners in about half of all cases). The women interviewed by the royal commission often stated that they sought abortions out of economic necessity.

Fears of race suicide continued well into the twentieth century. However, according to Anne Curthoys in *Hecate* (1989), the fact that many highly populated countries collapsed during World War I ensured that it was 'the quality and not the quantity of the population' which became the issue by the 1920s. This change in emphasis reduced some of the pressure on women to bear children (although, as Marilyn Lake suggests in Joy Damousi and Lake, eds, *Gender and War*, 1995, this pressure was still immense). As **eugenists** recognised the importance of maternal and infant health, they eased their opposition to contraception and the birth control movement gained in strength.

Ironically, at this time there was increasing public support for **censorship** of contraceptive information on the grounds of obscenity. In their oral history *Generations: Grandmothers, Mothers, Daughters* (1987), Diane Bell and Ponch Hawkes conclude that such censorship was effective; women reaching maturity in the 1920s and 1930s knew little about 'the facts of life'. They turned to household manuals, medical texts, and true love novels for information about sexuality. Bell and Hawkes suggest that women did not even share information among their peers, and therefore 'the anguish arising from the fear of pregnancy from an innocent touch or kiss was real'.

But this picture of overwhelming sexual ignorance is exaggerated. Supreme Court depositions suggest that, while *middle-class* women may have possessed little sexual knowledge in the early twentieth century, information networks set up in the nineteenth century were still available to *working-class* women. Indeed, working-class women were not only well informed and sexually active but were quite prepared to share their experiences of menstruation, contraception, abortion, and childbirth. For example, when a 21-year-old domestic servant named Lilian G. was tried in WA in 1931 for concealing the birth of her child, she told the court that she sought no assistance during the birth; she attended to her own 'confinement'. She explained, 'I knew all about the birth of babies. I have helped in several cases.' The more convincing historical accounts of women's sexual knowledge in this period incorporate the experiences and understandings of women such as Lilian G.—women who attended births, spoke freely of their 'floodings', shared contraceptive advice, and assisted friends and relatives to seek out abortionists.

With the 1930s **Depression**, women (often, although not always, in conjunction with their partners) tried desperately to limit their families. They turned to abstinence, the rhythm method, contraceptives, and abortion to ward off unwanted pregnancies. Sometimes as a last resort, they adopted babies out, abandoned them in parks, or smothered them and concealed their bodies. The result was that the birth-rate fell to its historically lowest point in 1934.

Around this time too, there was growing debate about single women's sexuality. As Katie Holmes argues in *Spaces in Her Day* (1995), single women of the years between the two world wars were allowed to engage in 'the adventure of romance' and cultivate their (hetero)sexual desirability. But strict rules of play applied. In the story of romance, for instance, men were the pursuers and women the pursued. These new freedoms to cultivate desirability encouraged and reified changing understandings of women's bodies. In *AFS* (1987), Jill Julius Matthews argues that, while understandings of women's bodies in the late nineteenth and early twentieth centuries were firmly 'uterine', emphasising reproduction and motherhood, around 1930 there was 'a fragmenting of the exclusive meaning of women as wombs'. Health and beauty took on new meanings and became central to changing conceptions of women's sexuality.

The most radical challenge to established sexual mores, though, came in the 1960s, no doubt assisted by the introduction of the contraceptive pill. Sexual liberation was heralded (by left-wing student groups at least) as a political statement, as an attack on 'bourgeois morality'. While feminists began to question the 'liberating' effects of the 'sexual revolution' for women, the 1970s were also years of consolidation of the new sexual freedoms—freedoms which extended beyond heterosexuals. It was in the 1970s that a strong homosexual self-identification emerged, and male **homosexual** and **lesbian** subcultures were established. During the 1980s and 1990s, homosexuality and lesbianism have received increasing attention from historians. Works such as Michael Gilding, *The Making and Breaking of the Australian Family* (1991), Sylvia Martin (in *Women's History Review*, 1993), and Ruth Ford (in Diane Kirkby, ed., *Sex, Power and Justice*, 1995), have offered valuable insights into the ways in which male homosexuals and lesbians have made spaces for themselves within Australia's heterosexual society.

There are still, however, a number of sexual issues which historians have neglected. More could certainly be said, for instance, about Aboriginal sexuality. In the 1980s, a number of histories were written about the sexual exploitation and the sexual understandings of Aboriginal women, but there has been no equivalent attention to the sexuality of Aboriginal men. Perhaps this lack of attention is due as much to gender as to race. For although there is growing interest in historical constructions of (white) **masculinity**, writers in this field have barely touched on issues of *sexuality*. They have concentrated instead on revisiting the **Australian Legend**, and analysing the role of **sport** and war in constructing and perpetuating notions of masculinity.

JILL BAVIN-MIZZI

Seymour, Alan (1927–) wrote *The One Day of the Year*, a controversial play about generational conflict between a father and his son, who challenges the celebration of **Anzac Day**. After being banned by the Adelaide Festival Board for fear of offending the **Returned and Services League**, it was premiered by the Adelaide Theatre Group on 20 July 1960 and has become one of Australia's most successful plays. Seymour was born in Perth, WA. As a young man he moved to Sydney, where he worked as a film and theatre critic. He was also a director for the Sydney Opera Group 1953–57. In 1961 Seymour left for London, swearing he would never return. Contrary to popular belief, the catalyst was not so much Australia's reaction to *The One Day of the Year*, but a dispute over his play *Lean Liberty* (1962), which the Australian Broadcasting Corporation commissioned, then rejected when Seymour refused to modify the lead character's sympathy with **communism**. Seymour was theatre critic for *London Magazine* 1963–65, and then lived in Turkey 1966–71. Political themes permeate his best writing, which includes his play against the **Vietnam War**, *The Gaiety of Nations* (1965), and *The Coming Self-Destruction of the United States of America* (1969), a novel portraying America's disintegration due to racial violence. After returning to London in the 1970s, Seymour worked as a BBC script editor and television writer and producer. In 1978 he adapted David Ireland's novel *The Unknown Industrial Prisoner* (1971) for Film Australia, but in an echo of earlier controversies the project was vetoed as 'uncommercial' by Home Affairs Minister Robert Ellicott. In recent years Seymour has specialised in writing radio and television dramas, and he has produced several critically acclaimed adaptations for British television.

DC

Shann, Edward Owen Giblin (1884–1935) studied at the University of Melbourne and the London School of Economics before accepting an appointment as foundation professor of history and economics at the University of Western Australia in 1913. It was here that he pioneered the development of economics as an academic study in Australia and made a major contribution to the developing university, serving as vice-chancellor 1921–23. His youthful socialism moderated to a respect for the exigencies of the market, tempering a social responsibility which he communicated to his students, who included H.C. **Coombs** and Arthur Tange—later influential figures in the public service—and historian John **La Nauze**. Shann was a member of the Copland Committee which, in response to the **Depression**, developed the Premiers' Plan. His *Economic History of Australia* (1930) countered the dominant interventionist assumptions. C.B. Schedvin appraised his growing faith in the market in Stuart Macintyre and Julian Thomas (eds), *The Discovery of Australian History* (1995). Shann's *Cattle Chosen* (1926) is a history of the pioneering WA family, the **Bussells**.

KT

Sharkey, Laurence Louis 'Lance' (1898–1967) was president and later general secretary of the Communist Party of Australia. A country boy who drifted to Sydney and worked as a lift-operator in a city store, he was drawn to **communism** as a delegate to the NSW Labor Council of the Miscellaneous Workers Union. An awkward, scruffy, unsociable comrade, Sharkey emerged as a leading critic of the leadership that was defeated at the end of 1929 in the turn to sectarian extremism. As editor of the national newspaper, Sharkey was second only to the general secretary, J.B. Miles, whom he eventually replaced in 1948. *An Outline History of the Australian Communist Party* (1944) and *The Trade Unions* (1942) were among his more important publications. In 1949 Sharkey was gaoled for sedition when he claimed that Australian workers would welcome a Red Army if it pursued an imperialist aggressor here. He was an utterly obedient servant of the Communist International, and its Australian representative after 1935. Attempts to invest him with the qualities of a model proletarian, most notably in W.A. Wood's biographical sketch (1950), were handicapped by his conspicuous deficiency of these qualities; but he was shrewd, determined and, at least until Khrushchev's denunciation of Stalin in 1956, would do whatever Moscow asked.

SM

Shaw, Alan George Lewers (1916–), historian, was a graduate of Melbourne and Oxford. He taught at Melbourne and Sydney Universities before being appointed professor of history at Monash University in 1964. His first book, *The Economic Development of Australia*, appeared in 1944, followed by *The Story of Australia* (1955), a widely used textbook. In 1950 he turned his attention to penal administration, and his most important work, *Convicts and the Colonies*, a history of the transportation system, was published in 1964. Lloyd **Robson's** *The Convict Settlers of Australia* appeared a year later and, although Shaw's is the more thorough and discriminating study, both were pioneering attempts to elucidate some of the vast mass of administrative records of the convict period then becoming available to scholars. Shaw's book remains a standard text. It was followed in 1980 by a biography of Governor **Arthur**, one of the moulders of the convict system. Shaw's research focused henceforth on early Victoria and led to the publication of *A History of the Port Phillip District* (1996). No other Australian historian has demonstrated such a high level of productive scholarship over more than 50 years. His leading concerns throughout have been the creative use of power and the significance of duty in public life.

Alan Atkinson

Shearers, the workforce of the **wool** industry, have played a key role in the development of an Australian **national identity** by representing the egalitarian and democratic Australian character. Popular figures of Australian bush folklore, shearers are celebrated in the work of painter Tom **Roberts** and in bush ballads such as 'Click Go the Shears'; the hero of **'Waltzing Matilda'** is believed to have been a shearer. For Henry **Lawson**, mateship between shearers was at odds with an otherwise sectarian, class-ridden society:

> They tramp in mateship side by side,
> The Protestant and Roman
> They call no biped lord or sir,
> And touch their hat to no man!

A Shearers Union was established in the 1880s to oppose a wage cut and improve working conditions; in the 1890s it struck in support of the closed shop. Unionism has continued to be strong and opposition to **scabs** has continued. Russel **Ward** argued in 1958 that the seasonal and itinerant nature of the work, and the poor working conditions in nineteenth-century sheds, encouraged loyalty and camaraderie among shearers.

Shearers competed fiercely—individual tallies and shed records were strictly kept and religiously remembered. The status of ringer, who shore the highest number of sheep, was esteemed. The introduction of machine shears allowed for higher tallies, but divided shearers over their use. The non-compliance by some pastoralists with the closed-shop rule led to scab labour and this has been a source of continuing conflict both among shearers themselves, and between shearers and pastoralists. Patsy **Adam-Smith's** *The Shearers* (1982) evokes the occupation.

HD

Shearers' strikes occurred in Qld and NSW as a result of increasingly bitter relations between shearers and pastoralists in the late nineteenth century. Before 1886, working conditions for shearers were of a poor standard; pastoralists paid relatively low wages and frequently provided unsatisfactory rations and accommodation. Shearers formed the Amalgamated Shearers Union under the leadership of W.G. **Spence** in 1886 (the Queensland Shearers Union remained a separate organisation). Initially some gains were made, largely owing to support from maritime workers who refused to handle 'black' wool. However, pastoralists, through their own national organisation, the Pastoralists Union, refused to concede the union demand that they employ only union labour and instead insisted on 'freedom of contract'.

NSW members of the union stopped during the **Maritime Strike** of 1890 in support of their fellow unionists. In January 1891 the Queensland Shearers Union became embroiled in a dispute with the Pastoralists Union over terms of employment. The colonial governments assisted the employers to introduce non-union labour, and used special powers against the camps of strikers; twelve Queensland leaders were convicted of conspiracy. A second and shorter strike in 1894 again brought clashes between shearers and the militia; the steamer *Rodney* was burnt by unionists on the Darling River. Along with the Maritime Strike, these events fractured social consensus and led Henry **Lawson** to wonder 'if blood should stain the wattle'. The

best account is given by John Merritt, *The Making of the AWU* (1986). (See also **Strikes and lockouts**.)

SM

Shearing machines were first exhibited in Australia in the 1860s. James Higham took out the first patent for such a machine, comprising a hand-held comb and mechanised cutter, in 1868. Other versions were introduced and patented in Australia and Britain in the 1870s, including that invented in 1877 by Frederick Wolseley and Robert Savage. Irish-born Wolseley developed his plan for a shearing machine while managing a sheep property in Victoria. He patented other machines with the assistance of R.P. Park and later John Howard and William Ryley, from which evolved a commercially successful product. Wolseley subsequently moved to England, where his shearing invention led to his development of the Wolseley **motor car** in 1895; Lord Austin, also a British motor car manufacturer, had worked with Wolseley in developing shearing machines in Australia. Although the first electric machine was invented in 1906, other forms of energy—steam, oil and petrol—were favoured for many years. The Lister shearing machines subsequently proved particularly popular.

The introduction of machine shears into sheds from 1888 led to opposition from newly unionised **shearers**, who felt their labour threatened, as well as from conservative pastoralists. Despite their recognised efficiency, machine shears also represented a break with popular romanticised perceptions of the bush and of rural labour in the 1890s; they are noticeably absent in Tom **Roberts's** *Shearing the Rams*, painted in 1888–90.

HD

Sheep, see **Wool**

***Shenandoah* incident** occurred in 1865 when a war vessel of that name flying the flag of the Confederate states docked at Melbourne. Despite the protests of the US consul, the officers of the *Shenandoah* were entertained at the Melbourne Club. They also took on provisions and crew, and later resumed depredations against US ships. The colonial government had no authority to act but the governor, as the official of the British government, did and took advice from the attorney-general, George **Higinbotham**, in a significant demonstration of the artificiality of the restrictions on responsible government in the Australian colonies. An international tribunal subsequently ordered the British government to compensate the USA. The incident provided the basis for Cyril **Pearl's** *Rebel Down Under* (1970).

SM

Shipping was crucial to both the discovery and the development of the Australian continent. The subsequent international flows of investment, trade, and migration have never ceased to be important. Much of the narrative on this subject can be gleaned from John Bach's *A Maritime History of*

Australia (1976), the first general history of its kind. Most recently there is the thoughtful and wide-ranging book by Frank Broeze, *Island Nation* (1998), which discusses how Aborigines and European settlers have been influenced by and interact with the sea around their continent. In the 1810s and 1820s sailing ships which averaged less than 300 tons arrived in their tens; by the 1830s ships which averaged about 450 tons arrived in their hundreds as the volume of both exports and imports increased rapidly. Prior to 1846 non-British shipping which called at the Australian colonies was in breach of the East India Co. monopoly over the Eastern trade. Thereafter the colonists could trade with any country they wished. Shipping services were improved further by the advent of clipper ships, used by British firms for fast passenger voyages out and backloaded with wool cargoes in the late 1840s, and subsequently the great upsurge in all shipping activity associated with the Australian **gold rushes**. Sailing vessels continued to service both passenger and cargo trades to and from Australia throughout the nineteenth century and were gradually replaced by steamers after Federation.

Steam communication really began in the 1850s; British firms such as Peninsula and Oriental Steam Navigation Co. (P & O), which had the mail contracts, Gibbs, Bright & Co. and other British, French, and German lines followed. There are a number of brief histories of participating companies in John M. Maber, *North Star to Southern Cross* (1962). The passenger and cargo trades increased in volume until World War I, which disrupted overseas shipping services and their development. Most mercantile fleets did not build diesel motorships until the period between the two world wars, and other improvements were adopted in order to remain competitive. This was also the period in which the federal government first acquired a mercantile shipping fleet. With 56 ships by 1924, it maintained passenger and cargo services between Australia and Britain, but escalating costs and accumulating losses resulted in all the ships being sold by 1928. There is an account of the Commonwealth Government Shipping Line in Ralph McDonell, *Build a Fleet, Lose a Fleet* (1976). Throughout the period the size and speed of overseas ships were increasing. The trades were also becoming more competitive and most firms dealing with Australia belonged to the appropriate shipping conferences for Europe or Asia. Trade with East Asia, especially Japan, expanded in the nineteenth century and continued to be developed by firms such as the Eastern and Australian Mail Steamship Co., Nippon Yusen Kaisha, and Osaka Shosen Kaisha. Closer to Australia, Burns Philp & Co. and Dutch shipping companies developed services to South-East Asia and PNG. Other Pacific trades begun in the nineteenth century were with Canada and the east coast of America. There is a useful analysis of the inter-war period in Kevin Burley's *British Shipping and Australia 1920–1939* (1968).

During World War II the maritime participation was on a much greater scale than previously and the world's largest liners were used for troop movements. There was very considerable disruption to Australia both during and after the war. Ships had been lost and normal passenger and cargo services were not restored, especially on the Britain–Australia run, until the end of the 1940s. The overseas firms built the most modern and efficient ships, prompted by Australia's large-scale migration scheme: the ships were now likely to exceed 20 000 tons, 25 knots in speed, and £4 million in cost. The various Pacific shipping trades also took time to recover from the war; until the Japanese and German fleets re-emerged, the trades were dominated by the British and American lines. Migration was eventually reduced: the passenger trade centred on tourists and the new ships reflected that. With respect to cargo, there has been greater emphasis on specialist shipping such as container ships and tankers, which have helped maintain a competitive position against alternatives. Broeze discusses the postwar industrial disputes and the organisational forms of the major players—shipowners, cargo shippers, stevedores, and maritime labour. He also charts recent attempts by federal governments to effect waterfront reform.

Coastal shipping was also important for many decades after European settlement, along with **river transport**. The first trades were to the Hawkesbury River and later to Newcastle. A newly arrived paddle-steamer inaugurated coastal steam navigation in 1831 and the Hunter River Steam Navigation Co. (HRSN) was a company first in 1839. The general overview of coastal shipping development is also covered by Bach in *A Maritime History of Australia*, and there is a stimulating chapter on it in Frank Broeze's *Island Nation*. A detailed, static analysis of firms and trades is contained in Barry Pemberton's *Australian Coastal Shipping* (Melbourne, 1979). When shipping services first began in each colony, they covered short distances to intracolonial outports or around harbours. Eventually these became inter-colonial runs. The HRSN Co. became the Australasian Steam Navigation Co. in 1851 and extended its services around the coasts and east to Pacific ports. There is a comprehensive history of the firm and its successors, entitled *From Derby Round to Burketown* (1977) by N.L. MacKellar; it also contains a considerable amount of detail about the other inter-colonial companies. For all the firms, the most frequent coastal sailings were between capital city ports and from the 1860s these included the New Zealand ports. The dominant New Zealand company, and also a strong competitor in some of the Australian trades, was the Union Steam Ship Co. of N.Z. Its history, *The Southern Octopus* (1990) by G.J. McLean, also includes some of the history of the Tasmanian Steam Navigation Co. A few coastal companies began with sailing ships, while others did so with steamers. William Howard Smith and Sons were established in 1854; Adelaide Steamship Co. in 1875 (its history is *Fitted for the Voyage*, 1975, by Michael Page); Huddart, Parker & Co. 1876 (in sail); TSN Co. 1852; and the Australasian United Steam Navigation Co. (AUSN) 1887. There were also smaller intracolonial firms along the southern and eastern coasts, except for Qld where the AUSN and Burns Philp dominated. In WA the government played an important role in the development of the coastal trades through the State

Shipping Service, which was commenced in 1912 to service ports from Wyndham to Eucla.

Prior to the mid-1890s the coastal companies competed strongly against each other and adopted new technology quickly. By the late 1890s the larger firms had formed a cartel which controlled most of the coastal trades and had secured vertical integration with the NSW collieries. Services were disrupted during World War I and the interwar period witnessed few new developments except for the introduction of diesel motorships. The adoption of new technical changes was slow and, together with labour demands and disputes, helped contribute to the rising cost levels. However, it was World War II that caused the major disruption: ships were commandeered for war service and there was no restoration of services or replacement of tonnage until the late 1940s. The passenger trade by sea, which had been reduced steadily since the late nineteenth century, firstly by railways and then by road and air transport, declined rapidly in the postwar years. The cargo trade was also seriously affected. Almost all those intrastate shipping companies which had survived beyond World War II ceased to operate in the 1960s. There was a shortage of coastal ships in the postwar years, and those operating were old and inefficient. The only profitable trades were coal, ores, and sugar, where bulk ships were used. The cargo-handling facilities were inadequate and labour costs were high and rationalisation was necessary if interstate companies were to remain. Three of the oldest companies had disappeared by the mid-1960s and the rest went by the late 1970s. Only the new bulk and container ships and the roll-on, roll-off vessels have enabled any coastal trades to survive. Even government intervention did not achieve much success, with the Australian Shipping Board accumulating losses in the 1950s. By 1956 when the Australian Coastal Shipping Commission and the Australian National Line were created, the federal government owned 44 ships. The commission built new and appropriate ships for the coastal trades, especially those between Tasmania and the mainland, and the Australian National Line continues to provide services for passengers, vehicles, and cargo. Broeze also discusses the role the line played in penetrating the overseas conferences and assisting the overseas services, in addition to the most recent developments in government policy with respect to coastal operations.

G.R. HENNING

Shipwrecks occurred regularly in colonial times. They were caused by human error, the negligence or drunkenness of ships' masters, inadequate or faulty navigational aids, bad weather, and structural defects. Gradually the number of wreckings decreased as navigational aids (including **lighthouses**) and pilot services were improved. Wooden sailing vessels were slowly replaced by iron and steel steamers which were more manoeuvrable and less vulnerable to fire. However, wreckings still occur today, human error or folly often being the cause. All told, more than 6000 vessels are known to have been lost in Australian waters.

Shipwrecks were the grand **disasters** of colonial life. Communities were closely involved in them because the

rescue and support of survivors was largely a voluntary effort. Relief funds for shipwreck survivors were regularly collected and often generously supported. In 1886 the steamer *Ly-ee-moon* was wrecked in southern NSW. Even in far-off Bathurst money was collected for the destitute widows and orphans.

The danger produced **heroes and heroines**. Lifeboat crews and others often performed acts of bravery to save lives in frightful conditions. Grace **Bussell's** rescue of women and children from the steamer *Georgette* in 1876 and Tom Pearce's rescue of Eva Carmichael after the wreck of the *Loch Ard* in 1878 thrilled the press and the public. Yet in other instances criticism was levelled at male survivors. Often it was the women and children who were lost. When the immigrant ship *Cataraqui* was wrecked off King Island in 1845, with the loss of 400 lives in the worst shipping disaster in Australian waters to date, none of the women and children on board was saved. But in the nineteenth century women were difficult to save: their voluminous clothing was a dead weight in water, and modesty usually prevented their shedding their apparel, even when in danger of drowning. The class distinctions that permeated life at sea could also still prevail in times of crisis. When the *Cheviot* was wrecked outside Port Phillip Heads in 1887, 35 lives were lost. The ladies travelling first class were all rescued, but the women in steerage were not even issued with lifebelts. All were lost.

The horror of shipwrecks frequently inspired dramatic verse: Charles **Harpur** wrote 'The Wreck' in 1833; Henry **Kendall** mourned the wrecking of the *Dunbar* at Sydney Heads in 1857 with 121 lives lost; in 'From the Wreck', Adam Lindsay **Gordon** wrote of his ride for help when the steamship *Admella* was lost in SA in 1859 with 24 survivors from a total complement of 113. The legendary **Mahogany Ship** has fascinated some modern poets, including Philip Martin, Francis King, and Judith Rodriguez.

Shipwreck survivors sometimes suffered under Australia's restrictive immigration laws. When the *Petriana* was wrecked at Port Phillip Heads in 1903, the Asian crew members were not allowed to land and were confined to a tug until they could be shipped home. The following year, the Lascar crew of the *Australia* were locked in a shed on a Melbourne wharf under guard until they too were shipped out.

Maritime **archaeology** is now a well-established discipline in Australia. Though it often only confirms the historical record, in some instances it has added another dimension to the written record and has the potential to challenge it. Maritime archaeology can also produce information about the past where records are otherwise deficient or absent. The research design for the underwater excavation of the wreck of the **First Fleet** flagship, *Sirius*, at **Norfolk Island**, was to address the historical debate about Britain's political intentions regarding the permanency and function of the new colony at Port Jackson. A comparison with available records from other British ships sent on similar expeditions points to a long-term, well-planned strategy. Scientific analysis of the quality of shipbuilding, maintenance materials, and the technology used in and on the ship supports this view, although testing is not complete. The analysis of remains of the Australian-built *Clarence* (1841–50) provided information about the quality of early Australian shipbuilding which was unavailable in the scant historical records: in this instance it revealed poor construction and the use of second-hand materials.

Although the raising of wrecks is a matter of debate among maritime archaeologists, the raising and display of the **Batavia** by the Western Australian Maritime Museum has attracted enormous popular interest. The growth of scuba diving has led to greater access to wreck sites. Damage to wreck remains and souveniring by treasure hunters have led the Commonwealth and state governments to introduce Historic Shipwrecks legislation, which protects shipwrecks as part of our cultural heritage. Australia has become the international leader in shipwreck protection and preservation.

LEONIE FOSTER

Shopping began in make-do quarters in towns, on the goldfields, and in farming centres, and proliferated with mass immigration in the mid-nineteenth century. The corner shop and general store had become regular features of Australian towns by the late nineteenth century. Essential items were available in small country towns, though perishables were more likely to be obtained from pedlars or markets; luxury items were usually purchased in larger towns or, by the very wealthy, through overseas mail order. Higher wages gave the working classes greater consuming power than they had had in Britain. With the land boom, mass consumption, and frivolity of the 1880s, shopping became fashionable and, increasingly, a woman's role. Emulating developments in Europe and the USA, arcades and large department stores, notably Myer (Melbourne), and Horderns and David Jones (Sydney), opened in the main cities to serve the shopping needs of the growing middle class. In Melbourne, 'doing the Block' became popular. In the 1920s and 1930s the mass production of cheaper products marked the emergence of penny stores and chain stores, such as those of the **Coles** brothers, and in the 1950s refrigeration fostered the growth of food supermarkets. Large suburban shopping complexes appeared in the 1960s and 1970s, largely a result of Australia's growing reliance on the **motor car**, but subsequent decades saw a revival of inner-city shopping strips. Beverley Kingston's shopping history, *Basket, Bag and Trolley*, appeared in 1994. In *Temptations* (1993), Gail Reekie explored the sexual culture of the department store in the early twentieth century.

HD

Shute, Nevil (1899–1960) was the pen-name of the popular writer, Nevil Shute Norway. His works draw upon his own experiences as an aeronautical engineer in England and World War II work in the Royal Navy Volunteer Reserve. He achieved popular recognition with the publication of *Pied Piper* (1942), based on war experiences. In 1950, after a visit to Australia, Shute published *A Town Like Alice*, the work for which he is possibly best known. Shortly after its

publication, he returned to live permanently in Australia, where many of his later novels were partly or fully set. These include *The Far Country* (1952); *Beyond the Black Stump* (1956); and the nuclear holocaust story *On the Beach* (1957), a film version of which appeared in 1959. *A Town like Alice*, produced as a film in 1958 and television mini-series in 1981, portrayed its Australian hero as the archetypal bushman— laconic, kind and brave—and the country as harsh but potentially rewarding. Shute produced an autobiography of his early years in *Slide Rule* (1954), and Julian Smith has written a critical biographical study, *Nevil Shute* (1976).

KT

Simpson and his donkey are the best known **heroes** of the **Anzac Legend**. John Simpson Kirkpatrick (1892– 1915) was an Englishman working in Australia, who on the outbreak of World War I planned to get a free passage home by joining the army. At Perth in August 1914 he enlisted in the **AIF** under the name John Simpson. He landed at **Gallipoli** with the first troops as a stretcher-bearer. He found a donkey, on which he ferried injured men down to the beach, and was allowed to work on his own. For three weeks he journeyed up and back, fearless of bullets and shells. He was shot through the heart on 19 May. He was not the only brave stretcher-bearer nor the only one to use a donkey, but generations of schoolchildren learned of his courage. How his exploits became known and turned into legend is the subject of Peter Cochrane, *Simpson and the Donkey* (1992), which reveals the distortions of an earlier biography (1965) written by Irving Benson, a Methodist minister. Benson hid his subject's rough ways and his radical politics as unfit for a man who was held up as a model to generations of schoolchildren. There are statues of Simpson supporting an injured man on the donkey at the war memorials in Melbourne and Canberra.

JH

Single tax was a proposal of the American reformer Henry George (1839–97) to place a heavy tax on land, to the full extent of its unimproved value, as a remedy for social ills. No other taxation was necessary—hence the term *single*. The scheme was outlined and defended in his book *Progress and Poverty* (1879). Liberal and radical reformers in Australia were attracted to the scheme, leagues were formed to promote it, and the cause received a great boost by the highly successful tour of George himself in 1890. George struck a chord in a country where the breaking of monopoly on the land had been a reforming cause for several decades. Single-taxers were a strong force in the early **Australian Labor Party** (as Bruce Scates argued in *HS*, 1984), but a disruptive one finally because they opposed other taxation (including a protective tariff) and insisted that all landholders must be subject to the tax, even small farmers whom Labor had to attract to win country seats. The **Fisher** Labor government introduced a land tax in 1911, but it applied only to holdings worth over £5000.

JH

Six o'clock swill, a result of six o'clock closing of hotels, describes the phenomenon of patrons' hurried last drinks. Legislation for six o'clock closing was first introduced in 1915 in SA as a war austerity measure, and adopted by NSW, Victoria and Tasmania the following year (Qld introduced eight o'clock closing in 1923). The legislation, which was made permanent in 1919, also came in response to the influential **temperance** movement; the lobbying of the **Woman's Christian Temperance Union** was largely responsible for the decision in Victoria. Early closing failed to discourage excessive drinking; instead, hotels gained notoriety as swilleries. After finishing work at around five o'clock, men would rush to the **pub** to consume copious quantities of alcohol before six o'clock, then stagger home inebriated to wives and families. Closing time was eventually extended to 10 o'clock, firstly in Tasmania (1937), and later in NSW (1954), Victoria (1966), and SA (1967). Walter Phillips examines the introduction of early closing in *HS* (1980).

HD

Slessor, Kenneth Adolf (1901–71), poet and journalist, is often seen as Australia's first poet to embrace modernism. His beginnings, however, were firmly in the exotic, swashbuckling school of historical fancy developed by Norman **Lindsay**. The lyrics of *Earth Visitors* (1926) are coloured by pagan romance and Rubensesque colour. His mature poetry of the 1930s turns to imaginings of Australian history, along with expressive landscapes. A central sequence is 'Five Visions of Captain Cook', which sees **Cook** as the source of our poetry. 'Five Bells', an elegy for a friend drowned in Sydney Harbour, has inspired a mural by John Olsen in the **Sydney Opera House**. He worked as a journalist in Sydney, and from 1940 to 1944 was official war correspondent; 'An Inscription for Dog River' is a savage indictment of the Australian commander, Thomas **Blamey**. There are biographies by Herbert C. Jaffa (1971) and Geoffrey **Dutton** (1991).

CHRIS WALLACE-CRABBE

Slums have been a target of social reformers since the word was first applied to the mean streets of Sydney in the 1870s. 'By slum I mean dirty, neglected houses, streets or portions of streets inhabited by disorderly persons', a policeman replied to a 1917 inquiry into housing in Melbourne, parroting the Oxford dictionary and reflecting the theories about environment and morality which had given the word currency in mid-Victorian London. Over-crowding was believed to break down the moral bonds between family members and neighbours, and increase the incidence of contagious disease. As Alan Mayne has shown in *The Imagined Slum* (1993), crusading journalists developed a rich repertoire of imagery to describe, and stigmatise, the dangerous and exotic world of the slum-dweller. The *slum* label reinforced the territorial and social division between rich and poor and, historians have argued, diverted attention from the underlying connection between low wages, **sweating**, and sub-standard housing. Australians were often reluctant to acknowledge the existence of slums, which they considered more characteristic of the cities of the Old World. Reformers sought to cure them by moralising or evangelising their inhabitants, improving sewerage and water-supply, or simply demolishing the sub-standard houses themselves. In the early twentieth century fears of **eugenic** catastrophe inspired campaigns to rescue slum children from their 'slum-minded' parents. Only after the 1930s did Australians embrace large-scale programs of slum clearance, when 'slum abolition' campaigns led by Protestant reformers such as Oswald **Barnett** and N.H. Dick inspired the creation of state housing commissions. The history of these campaigns is covered by Peter Spearritt in *LH* (1974); Graeme Davison in Peter Williams (ed.), *Social Process and the City* (1983); and Renate Howe (ed.), *New Houses for Old* (1988).

GD

Smith, Bernard William (1916–   ), art critic and cultural historian, is one of our most variously influential thinkers. In his autobiographical *The Boy Adeodatus* (1984), he related his Sydney childhood that led him to the Sydney Teachers College and the **Communist** Party. As a young schoolteacher, he painted but soon turned to **art history**; from 1944 to 1952 he was education officer at the Art Gallery of New South Wales, and made his name with *Place, Taste and Tradition* (1945), a Marxist interpretation of Australian art. In 1955, when he moved to the University of Melbourne, he had left the Communist Party but was a key figure in the 1959 Antipodean Manifesto, which attacked modernism from a social realist standpoint. From 1966 to 1977 he was professor at the Power Institute, Sydney.

Smith's most important book is *European Vision and the South Pacific 1768–1850* (1960), a study of the relations between soft and hard primitivism, showing how they shaped the romantic movement of thought. This is a central text in **post-colonial** thought. *Australian Painting 1788–1960* (1962, 1979, and 1990 edition with Terry Smith) was a formative work for the **Old Left** interpretation of national history. His 1980 Boyer lectures, *The Spectre of Truganini*, extended that concern to other aspects of Aboriginal–white relations. Smith wrote a study of the inner-Sydney suburb of Glebe, which was influential in the **conservation** movement, and with Rüdiger Joppien has collected *The Art of Captain Cook's Voyages* in three volumes (1985–87). An important study of the continuity in Smith's ideas is Peter Beilharz's *Imagining the Antipodes* (1997).

CHRIS WALLACE-CRABBE

Smith, Charles Kingsford, see **Kingsford Smith, Charles**

Smith, Christian Brynhild Ochiltree Jollie (1885–1963) served as solicitor to the revolutionary labour movement for more than 30 years. The daughter of a Presbyterian minister and professor of theology, she was educated at Presbyterian Ladies College in Melbourne, where Nettie **Palmer** was a close friend, and studied law at the University of Melbourne, where Guido Baracchi introduced her to socialism. During World War I she had to resign from a post in the Crown solicitor's office for divulging details of the prosecution of Adela **Pankhurst**. In 1920 she moved to Sydney to teach at the Labour College with her lover, W.P. Earsman. The two were founders of the **Communist** Party of Australia. Smith served on its early executive but later stood down to establish her legal practice in Sydney. She represented the Communist Party and its various front organisations in their numerous court appearances, and during the Depression handled hundreds of defences for the Unemployed Workers Movement and International Class War Prisoners Aid. She also briefed A.B. **Piddington** to defend Egon **Kisch** from deportation in 1934 and H.V. **Evatt** to represent unions in the High Court against R.G. **Menzies's** Communist Party Dissolution Act in 1951. A small fraction of the records of her extensive legal practice are held in the Noel Butlin Archives at the Australian National University.

SM

Smith Family is a welfare agency which had its origins in Sydney in 1922, when a Christmas party was held for 40 children who were residents of a home for the underprivileged. The function was arranged by five Sydney businessmen who, wishing to remain anonymous, each claimed the name Smith; as a result, the group called itself the Smith Family. The organisation provides food, clothing, and accommodation to underprivileged people in the eastern states. (See also **Social welfare**.)

HD

Smith, Keith Macpherson (1890–1955), and **Ross Macpherson** (1892–1922), **aviation** pioneers, were brothers who in 1919 piloted the first England–Australia flight. In a Vickers-Vimy bomber crewed by James Bennett and Walter Shiers they completed the flight in 28 days. For this, the first flight across the world, they won a £10 000 prize from the Australian government. Ross Smith's *14 000 Miles Through the Air* (1922) understates the deficiencies of their aircraft. A more rounded account is A. Grenfell **Price**, *The Skies Remember* (1969), based on the Smith Papers at the University of Adelaide and State Library of South Australia. An oral history recording by Shiers (1966) is held in the National Library of Australia. The flight made **postal services** history by carrying the first England–Australia airmail, which Nelson Eustis documents in *The Ross Smith Air Stamp* (1979). Both Adelaide-born pilots were educated locally and in Scotland. Keith joined the Royal Flying Corps in 1917. Ross went to **Gallipoli** and won the Military Cross twice before joining the Australian Flying Corps in 1917. He won the Distinguished Flying Cross three times and was reputedly the finest flier in the Middle East during World War I. His bravery as pilot for T.E. Lawrence ('Lawrence of Arabia') was described in Lawrence's *Seven Pillars of Wisdom* (1926). Ross Smith and Bennett were killed in a test-flight crash in England on 13 April 1922. Keith Smith became

chairman of several Vickers companies and served on the board of **Qantas**, but declined the chairmanship of Trans-Australia Airlines (TAA). The Vimy was permanently displayed at Adelaide Airport in 1958. There are Smith memorials in Darwin, Adelaide, and elsewhere. Many babies born in late 1919 were named after the heroes, including the pilot and champion cricketer Keith Ross Miller.

DC

Smith, Shirley Colleen Smith, see MumShirl

Smith, Sydney Ure, see Ure Smith, Sydney George

Smith, William Forgan (1887–1953), premier of Qld from 1932 to 1942, was active in the Labour Party in Scotland before he migrated to Qld in 1912. He served as president of the local branch of the **Australian Workers Union** before winning the seat of Mackay in 1915. He served in several ministries before the government defeat in 1929, after which he became leader of the opposition. Back in government, Forgan Smith encouraged public works in an attempt to mitigate the social impact of the **Depression**. These included the Storey Bridge and the university buildings on the St Lucia campus, but he placed principal emphasis on works to assist primary industries. A vehement and authoritarian moderate, Forgan Smith stamped his control on the **Australian Labor Party** in Qld and held office until 1942. A chapter of D.J. Murphy and R.B. Joyce (eds), *Queensland Political Portraits* (1978), lists his achievements; Ross Fitzpatrick's treatment in *A History of Queensland from 1915 to the 1980s* (1985) is less complimentary. He became chancellor of the University of Queensland in 1944.

KT

Smith's Weekly was a populist left-wing weekly broadsheet, predominantly graphic, founded in Sydney in March 1919 and named after Sir James Joynton Smith who funded the first issue. The first editors were Claude McKay, R.C. Packer, and J.F. **Archibald**. *Smith's Weekly* set a radical nationalist tone, fervently anti-communist yet disrespectful of authority. It upheld the digger ethos, and gave prominence to war stories and digger **humour**. It was particularly known for its high quality, broad-ranging cartoons, most notably Stan Cross's 'For gorsake, stop laughing—this is serious!' of 1933. The paper ceased publication in October 1950 although it was briefly revived in 1967. A history is George Blaikie's *Remember 'Smith's Weekly'?* (1966).

HD

Smyth, (Bridgetena) Brettena (1842–98) was middle-aged before she began her political activity: she had worked to support her four children after her husband died. Then she became involved in the Victorian Women's Suffrage Society and, in 1888, helped to found the Australian Women's Suffrage Society. Smyth considered birth-control integral to the well-being of women and families, and published her lecture *Limitation of Offspring* (1893) to provide clear information on the subject. In her lectures and pamphlets she drew on current **eugenic** arguments relating to the 'improvement of the race'. Her book, titled *What Every Woman Should Know* (1895), was a further attempt to make information about their physical selves and potential diseases more readily available to women.

KT

Snowy Mountains Hydro-Electric Scheme was a Commonwealth public works project instigated by the **Chifley** Labor government in 1949 and continued under **Menzies**. Its chief purpose was to capture the waters of the Snowy River in the Alps, use them to generate electricity, and divert them to the Murray–Murrimbigee rivers flowing inland for use in **irrigation**. This was Australia's greatest **engineering** feat, straddling the two states of NSW and Victoria, and employing thousands of workers, principally newly arrived European immigrants. It was also a great managerial feat by Sir William **Hudson**, commissioner of the Snowy Mountains Scheme Authority, 1949–67. At its fiftieth anniversary, there was whole-hearted celebration of the scheme's **multicultural** achievement in bringing together workers of so many nationalities, but conservationists now doubted the benefits of irrigation and called for water to be diverted back to the heavily depleted Snowy. Siobhan McHugh tells the human story in *The Snowy* (1989); George Seddon's *Searching for the Snowy* (1994) is an environmentalist study.

HD

Social history covers a broad spectrum of approaches, from a history defined by its subject matter, the society, or the social group which is studied, to one determined by its theoretical orientation, often derived from neighbouring disciplines, including sociology or social psychology, anthropology, or some variety of Marxism. An example of the first approach is Geoffrey **Bolton**, *A Fine Country to Starve In* (1972), a social history of WA during the Depression; of the latter, R.W. Connell and T.H. Irving, *Class Structure in Australian History* (1980), attempted to apply an aggressively radical sociological analysis to the past. A wide definition of social history would encompass virtually the whole corpus of Australian history with the exception of its straightforwardly political and military history and its biography. A narrower definition, based on the more self-conscious social history that emerged internationally from the 1960s, admits a more restricted literature.

Social history achieved distinct status following the appearance of G.M. Trevelyan's *English Social History* during the depths of World War II, a bestseller published at a particularly fraught period in the life of the nation whose democratic and popular antecedents he sought to capture. Trevelyan wrote that 'Social history might be defined negatively as the history of a people with the politics left out … Without social history, economic history is barren and political history is unintelligible.' This phrase 'history with the politics left out', which Trevelyan used deliberately as a nega-

tive characterisation, was to be used by subsequent radical historians to condemn him out of hand, to the severe loss of those who have not read his coruscating prose.

In the 1960s, with the expansion of university education around the globe, that social history established an independent momentum and became a self-conscious offshoot of the discipline of history. Journals supporting research in the area appeared in the USA and the UK, drawing some inspiration from the pioneering work of the French *Annales* school of social, demographic, and cultural historians. These included *Past and Present* (1952), the *Journal of Social History* (1967), and the *History Workshop* (Journal) (1976).

Social history built close, if uneasy, relationships with social science disciplines from the 1960s to the 1980s. Conceptions of **class**, of social control, of social structure were borrowed, refined, rejected, or re-exported. Anthropology, particularly through the work of Clifford Geertz, began to be influential. More fruitful alliances with demographers, pioneered in France, produced new quantitative evidence through family reconstitution, for example, and more recently through studies of specific groups, including convicts and migrants from particular parts of Europe. More recently, social history has also taken the 'linguistic turn' to appear as a **cultural history** more concerned with readings, discourses, and other obfuscatory neologisms of a fashionable postmodernism.

Australian social history never really established the degree of independence and self-confidence noted in other parts of the English-speaking world. When he surveyed the state of the history profession in Australia in *HS* (1973), Geoffrey **Serle** did not specifically mention social history, though he produced some of the best examples of the genre himself. In the same issue of *HS*, Greg Dening reflected on the links between history, sociology, and anthropology, without explicitly taking up any concept of social history. The almost coincidental diversification of history into a range of sub-disciplines undermined the peculiar role of social history as an integrating praxis, as **labour**, **oral**, **family**, **urban**, agricultural, **demographic**, **sports**, **Aboriginal**, cultural, and **women's history** appeared and thrived. No separate journal of social history appeared, though *LH* adopted the subtitle 'a journal of labour and social history' in 1981 and most mainstream Australian historical periodicals welcomed and carried extensive writing in social history.

Australian social history has been essentially pragmatic, usually burying its theory deeply if it has been theoretically engaged, whereas its ideology has often been transparent. Much of the best-known Australian social history has been informed by a left-of-centre, **egalitarian** sentiment, half-proud and half-ashamed of the society and its heritage which it tries to illuminate. There has also been a 'conservative' social history, though this has more often been identified by the readers than the authors.

While social history has struggled to establish itself as a separate genre in Australian historiography to the same degree as in other countries, there is a powerful strain of indigenous writing within the general area which merits comparison with the best of overseas output. Classics of

Australian social history include Margaret **Kiddle**, *Men of Yesterday* (1961). This evocation of the life of the first generations of squatters, critical, sympathetic, wise and occasionally poetic, set a standard for everything which followed in the postwar years, though some of its emphases and omissions may not be congenial to modern tastes.

Geoffrey Serle, in *The Golden Age* (1963) and *The Rush To Be Rich* (1971), developed a broad-ranging approach which married the social and political history of Victoria in the second half of the nineteenth century, while Graeme Davison in *The Rise and Fall of Marvellous Melbourne* (1978), and Weston **Bate** in *Lucky City* (1978), demonstrated a social history approach to two of the colony's urban centres, deriving inspiration both from the developing sub-discipline of urban history and from recent work in demography, but still relying heavily on traditional historical skills. A thematic treatment of the sesquicentenary of Victoria appeared in three volumes, largely from a social history perspective— *Arriving*, *Settling*, and *Making their Mark* (1984). In the next phase, Janet McCalman's works *Struggletown: Public and Private Life in Richmond 1900–1965* (1984) and *Journeyings: The Biography of a Middle-class Generation 1920–1990* (1993) pushed the boundaries of social history into an area which might be described as the collective biography of a social group.

If social history was active in Melbourne, it also had strong exemplars throughout Australia. Ken **Inglis** in *Australian Colonists: An Exploration of Social History, 1788–1870* (1974), provided a fascinating overview, while Beverley Kingston in *My Wife, My Daughter, and Poor Mary Ann* (1975) opened a major area of research. In a similar way, Henry **Reynolds**, *The Other Side of the Frontier* (1982), set the agenda for a committed social history of the clash between Aboriginal and European Australians, from which the politics was never left out. Tom Stannage (ed.), *A New History of Western Australia* (1981), was strongly imbued with social history, and Eric Richards edited a volume of social history for the South Australian sesquicentenary in 1986.

The **Bicentennial History Project**, conceived in 1976 and published in 1987–88, was a major attempt at total social history. Graeme Davison, editor of the volume on 1888, explicitly acknowledged the influence of European approaches, particularly that of Braudel: 'insofar as we have a specific model, it is perhaps the kind of fully textured detailed portrait of environment, economy, society and politics that one finds in Fernand Braudel … We aim to portray, more fully than hitherto, the regional and social diversity of Australia in 1888 and the ways in which different environments and regional economies were mediated in family structure and class relations.' The volume on 1838 conceived by Alan Atkinson and Marian Aveling (Quartly) was explicitly an attempt to write 'history from below' in the style of Edward Thompson, while the 1938 volume drew heavily on oral history interviews as the basis for a contemporary social history.

The Bicentennial History provoked a series of reactions in the ranks of Australian historians, and a group of younger radicals produced the four-volume series, *A People's History of Australia Since 1788*, edited by Verity Burgmann and Jenny

Lee, and published in 1988, which aimed at providing the view from the laundry or the kitchen rather than the front room, its touchstone being 'the experience of everyday life'.

One of the greatest strengths of Australian social history has been the popular and accessible style of writing typified by Patsy **Adam-Smith**, Geoffrey **Blainey**, Michael **Cannon**, Andrew Lemon, Robert **Hughes**, Wendy **Lowenstein**, and Eric **Rolls**. Scrupulously researched and presented in an open, flowing prose, these works have reached a far wider audience than those of the majority of academic social historians. Frequently, they have carried some of the findings of detailed scholarship into the wider community, but at least as often they have been the products of individualistic pioneering, paving the way for more traditional research to follow.

The surface of wide areas of social history has hardly been touched. Generalisations of doubtful validity still hold the field in many instances, crying out for a new generation of detectives, scholars, and writers. Modern technology has enormously eased some of the hurdles to research. Nevertheless, a word of caution, from Trevelyan again, is salutary. Doing social history is a task which requires skill, training, and vision. 'Thus the age of Chaucer speaks to us with many voices not unintelligible to the modern ear. Indeed we may be tempted to think that we "understand" more than in fact we do. For these ancestors of ours, in one half of their thoughts and acts, were still guided by a complex of intellectual, ethical and social assumptions of which only mediaeval scholars can today comprehend the true purport.' Any reading will not do. It has to be informed by a deep understanding of the period and its cosmology. The comment remains true of periods of the much more recent past, including Australian social history of the modern period.

ROY HAY

Social justice has always been at the core of Australian political language. Dominated by notions of the '*fair go*' and equality, social justice issues have originated from the problems of coping—politically, socially, and morally—with the problems generated by a market society. The Australian political tradition has seen state action as the means to redress the resulting inequalities between individuals, classes, and regions. The groups singled out for attention (or excluded) have varied according to prevailing assumptions about race and gender. Until the 1980s, however, many of the core assumptions were remarkably constant.

In the mid-nineteenth century, notions of social justice revolved around an agrarian ideal of economic independence. As David Goodman argued in *Gold Seeking* (1994), demands for unlocking the lands, for a democracy based on agricultural smallholding, emerged as the main opposition to the market-based nostrums of liberal political economy. The movement for free **selection**, as well as twentieth-century agrarian experiments such as **soldier settlement**, were guided by this conception of social justice.

The state has been seen as the arbiter of competing claims. In Keith **Hancock's** influential but critical account in *Australia* (1930), Australians expected 'the right to work, the right to fair and reasonable conditions of living, the right to be happy—from the State and through the State … collective power at the service of individualist "rights"'. A just social order required state action to redistribute resources. As Stuart Macintyre argued in *The Labour Experiment* (1989), **tariff** protection shifted some of the earnings of rural export industries to urban manufacturing. In turn, the **arbitration** system ensured that workers shared this bounty. These notions of fairness underpinned the whole wages system. Capacity of the employer to pay was secondary to comparable wage justice: the **basic wage** was based on the needs of a family dependent on a male breadwinner. Francis G. Castles in *The Working Class and Welfare* (1985) called Australia a wage-earner's welfare state. The pensions and benefits of the welfare state were reserved for those who had fallen outside this wages system through no fault of their own. Women were excluded from a full place in the wages system, so were protected, more or less, by a minimal safety-net.

This model of comparative justice was so strong that when rural interests organised politically their prime demand was not to end the system of redistribution, but to extend 'protection all round' to rural industries. **Secessionist** movements in the smaller states were concerned that the benefits of **Federation** had been monopolised by the manufacturing states. However, they did not demand the dismantling of the system of redistributional justice, but compensation on the same principle. 'Horizontal equalisation' between states, guaranteeing the citizen of a poorer state the same services as those of the most wealthy, became a distinctive feature of Australian federalism from the formation of the Commonwealth Grants Commission in 1933.

While advanced liberals and socialists shaped these initiatives, Catholicism provided another source for the mildly redistributive notions of social justice. The Catholic bishops' annual Social Justice Statements commenced in 1940. Vehemently anti-communist, they adapted the Catholic social tradition, from the encyclicals *Rerum Novarum* (1891) to *Quadragesimo Anno* (1931), to the established traditions of working-class politics. The early statements were hostile towards class inequality and the corrosive effects of market relations on social cohesion, supporting a rural utopia based on strong communities founded on religious belief.

By the 1970s established patterns were under attack. The **Whitlam** government experimented with a new egalitarian politics, drawing heavily on European models, and rejecting many of the main planks of the Australian social justice tradition—especially its reliance on the male wage-earner. It displaced the individualism of earlier approaches to social justice, bringing a new stress on group rights: those of women, immigrants, Aborigines. The more recent dominance of free-market economic policies has seen the rapid disappearance of many of the landmarks of the Australian social justice tradition, such as comparative wage justice and horizontal equalisation in relations between the states. More fundamentally, the legitimacy and capacity of state intervention to achieve social justice objectives has been challenged.

One reaction has been the recrudescence of earlier notions of social justice, with those drawing on the Catholic and left traditions coming together, especially over questions such as **Aboriginal land rights**. In the dying days of the **Hawke** government a 'social justice branch' was established in the Department of Prime Minister and Cabinet, and Australian Labor Party governments at state and federal levels vied to establish 'social justice strategies'. Historians have also given more attention to social justice issues, although usually confined to particular contexts, especially the welfare state, as in Stephen Garton, *Out of Luck* (1990). The most wide-ranging account is Stuart Macintyre, *Winners and Losers: The Pursuit of Social Justice in Australian History* (1985).

JIM GILLESPIE

Social laboratory has been a term broadly used to denote the adoption of innovative political and policy ideas in Australia and NZ in the latter decades of the nineteenth century and early decades of the twentieth. The notion of **Australasia** as the site of social experimentation was predominantly, although not exclusively, an outsider's notion, with overseas commentators identifying, praising and, more rarely, decrying developments and reforms current in progressive thinking in their own countries but yet to come to fruition there. Commentary on the experimental character of reform initiatives was rarely clear-cut but shaded into accounts of Australasian exceptionalism.

Four main areas tended to feature in discussions of the Australasian social laboratory. The first was the early adoption of the institutions of representative democracy, including the secret ballot (known as the 'Australian ballot' in the USA), the abolition of plural voting ('one man, one vote'), the payment of MPs, and female suffrage. The standard commentary on these developments was to argue that the Australasian colonies were the first in the world in which the demands of the English Chartists had been realised. A second area was labour relations, with an initial emphasis on early working-class mobilisation for the **eight-hour day**, some later interest in factory legislation and, from the last decade of the nineteenth century, a vast degree of attention to the enactment of provisions for compulsory conciliation and **arbitration** of industrial disputes, wage regulation, and the judicial enunciation of a minimum wage. The third area of interest was the size and ubiquity of the role of the state as an employer, as a provider of services, and as an agency of **social welfare** and equality. Finally, most commentators were fascinated by the unusual strength of the industrial and political wings of the labour movement, their success in achieving power and influence, and the extent to which this facilitated achievements in the other areas of reform.

Given that reform initiatives in many of these areas—the start of the eight-hour movement, the female suffrage, industrial arbitration, and the age pension—occurred somewhat earlier in NZ than in the Commonwealth of Australia (although not always earlier than in individual states), it is not surprising that the best-known 'local' protagonist of the social laboratory idea was a New Zealander, William Pember

Reeves, who, on his retirement as minister for labour in the reforming Liberal government of the 1890s, wrote a two-volume study entitled *State Experiments in Australia and New Zealand* (1902). This book laid out both the case for, and the course of, legislation in both countries in all the main areas of reform. In addition, it offered a strong and (by modern standards) unashamedly racist advocacy of a further strand of contemporary colonial reforms—the exclusion of **aliens** and other 'undesirables'—illustrating, as John Child noted in an introduction to the new edition (1969), 'the limitations of the sort of liberalism which Reeves professed'.

Given the links of economic interest and intellectual sympathy between Britain and its colonies, it is not surprising that many of those interested in colonial reforms were British and not a few were eminent or to become eminent. In 1868, referring to a report of a debate on female suffrage in the Victorian parliament, John Stuart Mill commented that 'it would not be the first time a colony has outstripped the mother country in the introduction of improved principles of legislation'. Anthony **Trollope**, in his travels through *Australia and New Zealand* (1873), cites respondents ready to concede the success of the secret ballot in an Australian context, but quite unwilling to allow the applicability of attempting to repeat the experiment in Britain. Active figures on the British political stage were no less interested, with Herbert Asquith describing NZ of the 1890s as 'a laboratory in which political and social experiments are every day made for the information and instruction of the older countries of the world', and Sidney Webb writing to Graham Wallas from Australia in 1898 that 'you have here a genuine Democracy, the people really getting what it wishes to get'. As late as 1921, no less eminent a commentator than Viscount Bryce in *Modern Democracies* identified Australia as the country 'which has travelled farthest and fastest along the road which leads to the unlimited rule of the multitude' and in which 'the tendencies that rule displays' may be better studied than anywhere else.

However, the British were not the only ones interested in social and political reform in the South Pacific. The first and best-known French commentator on Australasian developments was Albert Métin in *Le Socialisme sans Doctrines* (1901). (See *Socialisme sans doctrines*.) Métin's thesis differed from the thrust of British commentary in attributing Australasian reforms not merely to the unfolding of the democratic principle, but rather to the victory of the labour movement working through democratic institutions. In Métin's view, what distinguished the colonial reformers from socialists in Europe was the former's greater pragmatism and empiricism, which made them value practical aims, such as guaranteed minimum wages, far more than collective ownership and other similar 'utopian' principles. Métin's conclusion was that the empirical colonial labour movements had achieved far more than the principled socialists of the Old World. To Métin that was a reason to applaud socialism as practised in Australasia. For other compatriots, it was a cause of deep concern, and Bryce cites later books by Louis Vossion (*L'Australie Nouvelle*, 1902) and Georges Biard d'Aunet

(*L'Aurore Australie*, 1907) as coming to deeply pessimistic conclusions on the basis of similar observations, including predictions of the imminent usurpation of capital, the destruction of enterprise, and the onset of revolution.

American commentary was divided between those who focused on the unfolding of democracy and those who saw the Australian nations as pioneers of social democracy. Henry Demarest Lloyd's *Newest England* (1900) was subtitled 'Notes of a Democratic Traveller in New Zealand, With Some Australian Comparisons', and concentrated on the experimental nature of colonial reform initiatives. Victor Clark's *The Labour Movement in Australasia* (1907) was subtitled 'A Study in Social Democracy', and sought to explain why 'wage-earners had relatively more political strength in the Australasian colonies than in the American Union'. To Clark, the answer to that question lay in the fact that the long series of industrial and political problems that were resolved successively in the USA occurred simultaneously in Australia. The social democratic credentials of the reform occurring in Australia were a theme also stressed in an assessment of the achievements of the arbitration system appearing in the *Annals of the American Academy of Political and Social Science* in 1913, which saw 'judicial interpretation of the minimum wage in Australia' as 'the most notable experiment yet made in social democracy'. In 1918, a Columbia doctoral dissertation by Clarence Hunter Northcott could claim Australian social development as the working out of the ideal of progressive social democracy.

Although Australian writers were not those who first and foremost elaborated the social laboratory notion, a paper by Helen Bourke on 'Sociology and the Social Sciences in Australia 1912–1928' (*Australian and New Zealand Journal of Sociology*, 1981) suggests that 'the glowing terms "social laboratory" and "political and social experiment" were almost invariably used to describe the cycle of social legislation which characterised the **Deakinite** new liberalism'. Nor were local commentators wholly innocent in propagating the idea of an Australasian model of progressive reform. As New Zealand agent-general, Pember Reeves was a tireless activist of that message in Britain, and feminists in both Australia and NZ were most happy to attach their own program to it. More generally, the wider literature that lauded Australasian economic and social progress fed into the stream which for many decades nurtured the concept of an Australasian social laboratory.

By the time of World War I, however, the high point of enthusiasm for the results of Australian reform initiatives was past. In 1915, Meredith Atkinson, Australia's first director of the **Workers Education Association**, was already suggesting that Australia's experimental social reform was a thing of the past. Later, W.K. **Hancock** encapsulated much of the social laboratory ethos in his view that, in Australia, the state was regarded 'as a vast public utility, whose duty is to provide the greatest happiness for the greatest number'. But the reformist optimism of the past was long gone by 1930, and Hancock was doubtful that this had, in fact, been the outcome. As time went on, and particularly as the exhaustion of the reform initiative became still more apparent, the social laboratory era was gradually transformed into a negative reference point for Australian radicals, who increasingly bemoaned the fact that Australia was a laggard in the arena of progressive policy innovation, where once it had been an exemplar to the world.

FRANCIS G. CASTLES

Social welfare encompasses efforts to ensure that those less well-off in society are assisted in their time of need. Historians, however, have defined social welfare more specifically as those organised initiatives of governments and welfare organisations aimed at alleviating **poverty** and social disadvantage, and their consequences.

European colonisation of Australia created a welfare society. By encroaching on Aboriginal cultures, colonists attacked indigenous social networks, forcing Aborigines to rely on colonial systems of support. For the colonists themselves, the establishment of early settlements involved extensive public provision to ensure their survival. The British government was responsible for housing, clothing, feeding, and caring for all colonists in the first decades of settlement. But the beginnings of a market economy brought wage labour and demands and desires for self-sufficiency. Such imperatives sometimes foundered on the rocks of ill-health, injury, **old age**, death of a breadwinner, drought, crop failure, **unemployment**, and other events which precipitated the fall into the class of destitute poor. Some colonists believed that efforts were necessary to alleviate poverty and debated the virtues of a public system, modelled on the British Poor Law, versus **philanthropy**, where private citizens dispensed charity.

The advocates of charity won. There was no extensive system of public provision in colonial Australia and it is for this reason that some historians argue that social welfare really begins in the twentieth century with the creation of a system of publicly funded benefits for the disadvantaged. In this argument charity is private benevolence and social welfare is public. But such conclusions ignore the fact that much private philanthropy was supported by the public purse. The number of wealthy colonists willing to donate to charities was small, and most charitable organisations depended on government subsidies for their survival. This gave public officials considerable say in who received assistance and the type of assistance provided, although philanthropists insisted that charity administered by respectable citizens was the best means for ensuring that only the deserving poor were helped.

By the 1860s, however, colonial governments were becoming more directly involved in the provision of social assistance. By then it was clear that charities had little interest in assisting some groups, such as the aged poor and the insane, or had insufficient resources to tackle important social problems such as orphaned, neglected, and delinquent children. Equally, governments faced intense challenge from groups such as unemployed workers, who were traditionally denied charity on the grounds that they were able-bodied and hence capable of supporting themselves. They claimed that their plight was due to the state of the economy and demanded work. Such problems required greater public provision. Government asylums were built for the aged and insane, orphanages and industrial schools were provided for children, and labour camps, labour bureaux, and public relief systems for the unemployed.

These public efforts began to flag in the late nineteenth century. On the one hand, institutions and asylums for the poor strained the public purse. On the other hand, voices of opposition to the demeaning and moralistic imperatives of philanthropists grew louder. The organised labour movement asserted that workers had economic entitlements by virtue of their citizenship. Women's rights organisations argued that women were being forced into penury because they were supposedly dependants, yet many men were unable or unwilling to support them and their children. Although the Australian colonies had a reputation as a **workingman's paradise**, and undoubtedly the extent of poverty and destitution was less than in other comparable countries, the extent of distress was evident, the discontent with the remedies provided palpable, and the capacity of governments to deal with it hampered by a reliance on inefficient charities and expensive institutional solutions. The severe 1890s depression sharpened these lines of material stress and social tension.

In this climate of upheaval, prominent liberals sought to broker a new social contract that would ensure greater prosperity and progress. Federation provided a context to further their efforts. Their solution was to harmonise the relations between capital and labour by ensuring that employers paid workers a living wage (see **Basic wage**), and compensating employers by erecting **tariff** barriers to guarantee adequate prices for produce. Both employers and workers were to be further protected from unfair competition by restrictive immigration regulations. Through these means, employers would be guaranteed a reasonable profit and part of that profit would be passed onto workers, who would be able to support themselves and their families in reasonable comfort. This would provide a measure of welfare for the majority.

For the minority who fell outside this relationship, governments would provide assistance through social security payments. Throughout the 1890s and 1900s there was much debate over who would receive such payments and how such a system was to be funded. The groups thought most worthy of assistance were invalids and the aged, whose plight was no fault of their own. By 1908 there were comprehensive federal invalid and old age pensions schemes. These payments were funded from Commonwealth consolidated revenue. The alternative was to ask workers to contribute to an insurance scheme throughout their working life which supported them when they succumbed to invalidity or the infirmities of age. Insurance was rejected because many Australians had only casual and seasonal work, preventing them from maintaining regular payments. In the end it was thought that payments from general revenues, raised by duties and taxes, was both fairer and more efficient. But to limit the call on such revenues, governments restricted access to pensions to those most in need. Entitlement was based on stringent income and asset tests.

The one group effectively excluded from this compact were indigenous Australians. While governments acted to ensure the transfer of the disadvantaged from asylums to the community to be maintained by social security payments, Aborigines were increasingly subject to harsher forms of confinement and dependency on reserves and missions, denied even a basic right to keep their own children. It was not until the 1970s, after decades of Aboriginal protest, that governments saw fit to extend the social security system to Aborigines, as the most impoverished group in Australia. Later, land was added to their list of entitlements to compensate them for their dispossession.

These reforms provided the basic framework for the social welfare system we have today—a basic wage to ensure a decent income for workers and a social security system funded from consolidated revenue for those in need. Because Australia was one of the first countries to develop a comprehensive social welfare system, it earned a reputation as a **social laboratory**. But when other countries came to develop their own social welfare systems, they took a different course. The majority of Western nations opted for insurance-based social security; because insurance provided a guaranteed source of revenue, most of these countries were able to provide a greater range of benefits for such groups as the unemployed, the sick, widows, deserted wives, and their children. Australia, in the apposite phrase of historian Jill Roe (*Social Policy in Australia*, 1976), was 'left behind'. After **World War I**, Australia was further burdened by an extensive **repatriation** system, which made it even more difficult to find sufficient revenue to maintain the civilian welfare system. In this context, conservative governments sought to transform social security into an insurance-based system. Their efforts were stalled by the onset of another war.

World War II, however, provided a context for a renewal of the social security system. The **Curtin** and **Chifley** Labor governments expanded the tax base and introduced new benefits such as widows pensions, **child endowment**, unemployment, sickness and pharmaceutical benefits—all funded from consolidated revenue. The one major area of social welfare missing from this package was a comprehensive medical benefits scheme. Doctors refused to participate in such a reform, defending their traditional practice of providing free medical assistance to those they deemed in need. They preferred an older ethic of philanthropic benevolence, and while some Australians undoubtedly benefited from such charity, it left others unprovided for. This problem was not addressed until the introduction of a government medical and hospital benefits scheme in 1975.

The social welfare system has been a vital part of Australia's political culture and an enormous benefit to its citizens. But it has also been much criticised. Some believed it was too generous, giving benefits to those thought undeserving, encouraging dependency, promoting idleness, and undermining self-sufficiency. Some charged that it was a bloated and inefficient bureaucracy, delivering few actual benefits. For others, a welfare system predicated on a basic wage favoured some groups, notably male breadwinners, at the expense of more needy groups, such as indigenous people, women, and ethnic minorities. Some have pointed to the fact that many forms of disadvantage and need have not been adequately provided for. Since 1945 most governments, however, have sought to expand the range of welfare benefits, and sometimes counter the biases in entitlement. The period of greatest expansion was in the late 1960s and early 1970s. Since then anxieties about supposed welfare cheats and greater concern with balanced budgets have led to restrictions on entitlements and benefits. From the late 1990s a coalition government has wound back social security by contracting out services to religious groups, and by promoting policies of mutual obligation and work for the dole, seemingly ignorant that a century before it was liberals who had seen that such a philosophy underpinned serious destitution and increasing social tension, and acted to correct such problems by promoting **social justice**.

STEPHEN GARTON

Socialism is both a political program and a creed that seeks to replace capitalism with an alternative order of value. It arose in early-nineteenth-century Europe in response to the disruptive effects of the market, when various reformers sought a substitution for competition and exploitation in model communities based on cooperation and social control of economic activity. This tradition, with a strong ethical component, has been overshadowed by the self-styled scientific socialism strongly influenced by Marx and Engels, which discerned in history a **class** struggle that required the conquest of state power. Not all followed the revolutionary strategy of Marxism, but even in its most tepidly reformist forms, **state socialism** has been the dominant tradition in Australia.

Socialist ideas and socialist literature came to Australia in the late nineteenth century, and flourished as part of a diverse radical culture that spanned secularism, **republicanism**, anarchism, and other schemes of redemption. Small socialist groups formed in the principal urban centres, held indoor and street meetings, produced and sold tracts, argued among themselves, and maintained a largely self-enclosed circle of fellowship. Bruce Scates, *A New Australia* (1997), evokes the milieu and enthusiasms of this *fin de siècle* subculture. While their presence in the trade unions was marginal, the socialists played a major role in the establishment of the **Australian Labor Party** in the early 1890s, especially in NSW and Qld. In Sydney the Australian Socialist League, reformed in 1890, contributed such prominent early Labor parliamentarians as George **Black**, William **Holman**, and W.M. **Hughes**. In Brisbane, William **Lane** launched the *Boomerang* weekly newspaper in 1887, and in 1890 became editor of the new Labor organisation's *Worker*; that party adopted the objective of socialism in the same year. His novel, *The Workingman's Paradise* (1892), first serialised in the *Worker*, presented socialism as the only possible salvation from capitalist degradation. Lane, however, almost immediately abandoned hope in parliamentary socialism and left for his **New Australia** socialist colony in Paraguay.

'Socialism', wrote Lane, is 'being mates'. The heroes of his novel were Ned and Nellie, two flowers of the Australian bush, and the bush socialism of the shearers' union, the **Australian Workers Union**, was less doctrinaire than that of the city socialists. 'Socialism is more of a spirit and a temper than a system', claimed the AWU paper, the Queensland *Worker*, in 1892. Yet the AWU quickly moderated the aggressive militancy that had marked the **shearers' strikes** of the early 1890s, and turned to parliamentary action and industrial **arbitration**. Through its strong presence in the Australian Labor Party, it also tempered that party's socialist inclinations. Raymond Markey, *The Making of the Labor Party in NSW* (1988), argues that an alliance of professional politicians from the Australian Socialist League and the union organisers of the AWU fostered Labor's commitment to gradualist reform through state activity. The result was an electorally expedient pragmatism that the visiting Frenchman Albert Métin discovered in 1899, when he asked an Australian worker to explain his program: 'Ten bob a day'. In her account of the early socialists, *'In Our Time'* (1985), Verity Burgmann suggests that Métin did not appreciate that his leg was being pulled. She shows the pervasive influence of socialist ideas on the labour movement, as well as continuing resistance of socialists to the ALP's expediency.

Socialists worked both outside and inside the ALP and the unions. A shifting constellation of doctrinaire socialist groups condemned Labor moderation during the first two decades of the twentieth century, a role assumed upon its formation in 1920 by the **Communist** Party in 1920. A wave of syndicalism spread in the years before World War I, impatient with the limits of arbitration. The **Industrial Workers of the World** condemned both the ineffectiveness of sectional unions and the insincerity of 'Labor fakirs'. Their program of *Revolutionary Industrial Unionism*, the title of Burgmann's 1995 study of the IWW, rejected state socialism for direct control of industry by the workers—an objective adopted by a national union conference in 1921. The campaign to win the ALP to socialism was pursued by organisations such as the Victorian Socialist Party, and resisted by the Labor leadership. George **Reid**, the leader of the federal free-trade party, strengthened their caution with his national anti-socialist crusade in 1906 and they would go no further than calling for the nationalisation of monopolies. Following the 1921 union resolution, a federal conference of the ALP narrowly adopted a compromise resolution formulated by Maurice **Blackburn** that bound the party to 'collective ownership for the purpose of preventing exploitation', with the proviso that it did not seek to abolish private ownership 'of any of the instruments of production where such instrument is utilised by its owner in a socially useful manner and without exploitation'.

Subsequent ALP conferences proposed nationalisation of specific industries (broadcasting in 1927, banking in 1937, 'essential industries' during World War II), and the details of Labor's Socialist Objective are given in the book of that name edited by Bruce O'Meagher in 1983, and L.F. Crisp, *The Australian Federal Labor Party* (1955). Conspicuously absent from these later glosses was any attention to the organisational forms of collective ownership. The earlier interest in voluntary associational schemes, such as land settlement communes and cooperative enterprises, lapsed. The government-controlled corporation or directly administered public agency was almost invariably used whenever the federal or state governments embarked on a public enterprise. **Social welfare** provision was administered similarly, and its level lagged behind other countries, for reasons suggested by Francis Castles in *The Working Class and Welfare* (1985): the Australian labour movement preferred to underwrite the employment and wages of male trade unionists than to find a public alternative to market earnings.

Socialist criticism of these arrangements began with V.G. **Childe's** trenchant condemnation of *How Labour Governs* (1923): 'The Labor Party, starting as a band of inspired socialists, degenerated into a vast machine for capturing political power, but did not know how to use that power when attained except for the profit of individuals.' Socialism revived at moments of crisis. Socialisation Units formed in NSW during the **Depression** and spread to other states, but were defeated and disbanded; the national Labor governments of **Curtin** and **Chifley** used wartime powers to increase public control of the economy and expand welfare provision, but failed in the attempt to nationalise the banks.

Socialism became a principal point of contention in the factional and ideological contest for control of the Labor Party initiated after World War II by the anti-communist **Movement**, a schism which led eventually to the formation of the **Democratic Labor Party**. In 1951 the federal conference wrote an interpretation into the 1921 Socialist Objective: 'The ALP proposes socialisation or social control of industry and the means of production, distribution and exchange to the extent necessary to eliminate exploitation and other anti-social features.' The rubric had little practical import for a party which would remain out of office at the federal level for two decades, and had in any case long since accepted the mixed economy. Its significance was chiefly symbolic: both for the Liberal Party, which conflated socialism with communism to exploit the Red menace, and for traditionalists in the labour movement, who clung to the Socialist Objective as a solace for electoral failure. The Labor revisionists who sought to replace it were long denied. In 1957 the qualification 'democratic socialisation' was introduced; in 1981 the implications of democratic socialism were set out. The modification had minimal influence on the **Whitlam** Labor government of 1972–75, which expanded the public sector without any attempt to democratise industry, or the **Hawke** and **Keating** governments of 1983–96, which held public expenditure steady while dismantling most controls over the market. Even the Socialist Left faction of the party was unable to articulate a plausible socialist alternative; its vestigial commitment was bereft of the transformative zeal of earlier forms of socialist fellowship.

Socialisme sans doctrines

The global abandonment of socialism in the last quarter of the twentieth century came as a dramatic surprise. The economic inefficiency and traumatic social effects of *laissez-faire* capitalism were judged intolerable at the end of World War II. The apparent triumph of the Soviet Union served as a spur to amelioration of the market economies. Keynesian economic management, state planning, public enterprise, and social welfare brought stable growth, freedom from want, and an enhancement of capacity. But from the mid-1970s Keynesianism was powerless to prevent stagnation, inflation, and public sector deficits; deregulation, privatisation, and withdrawal from welfare followed. Meanwhile the command economies of the communist bloc collapsed or were dismantled. In both cases large, impersonal, bureaucratic structures proved incapable of responding to the needs of a more diverse population and their non-material aspirations. If neither of these alternatives to capitalism was genuinely socialist, then that socialism has yet to be found.

STUART MACINTYRE

Socialisme sans doctrines (socialism without doctrine) is the title of an influential survey of reform movements in Australia and NZ published in 1901 by Albert Métin. Métin, a young French radical, had visited Australia between April and August 1899, observing social and political conditions. His title drew attention to an apparent puzzle: the expansion of social and industrial legislation in Australia and NZ in an environment where socialist doctrine, of the kind familiar to him in Europe, had apparently yet to take root. 'Australian politics', he concluded, 'are concerned with practical affairs. They may be socialist in their results, but they are not always so in inspiration.' Métin was an admirer of English moderation, and his paradox—socialism without doctrine—carried an implied message to his French readers. Few Australians read Métin's book, which was not translated into English until 1977 (by Russel **Ward**), but *socialisme sans doctrines* became a stock phrase in Australian social criticism for the next half-century. W.K. **Hancock** (1930) treated it as a synonym for the tendency of Australians to look upon the state 'as a vast public utility' and emphasised the individualistic rather socialistic rationale which underlay it. Brian **Fitzpatrick** (*The Australian People*, 1946) concurred: the Australian labour movement was 'no more socialist than it was doctrinaire'. While historians of the Australian labour movement have generally concurred with Métin's view of Labor politics, Verity Burgmann ('*In Our Time*', 1985) is a vigorous dissenter: 'Métin was as wrong about the untheoretical nature of Australian socialism ... as he was about Australia being a workingman's paradise.' (See also **Social laboratory**.)

GD

Soldier settlement was a **closer settlement** scheme established during **World War I** to settle ex-servicemen on the land. Over 37 000 returned soldiers were **repatriated** in this way. British soldiers also took up Australian land under the scheme in the 1920s. New technology enabled many soldier settlers to pursue dairying, intensive cropping, or fruit-growing. Closer settlement was a new version of the recurrent dream that increased population was necessary, and a healthy, rural life desirable. However, small allotments of poor-quality land, insufficient agricultural training, and shortage of working capital contributed to a high failure rate among soldier settlers. In *The Limits of Hope: Soldier Settlement in Victoria, 1915–38* (1987), Marilyn Lake showed how the dream of land-ownership too often turned sour; her assessment was challenged by Jacqueline Templeton in *VHJ* (1988). Smaller-scale soldier settlement, more closely managed, was carried out more successfully after **World War II**. (See also **Land settlement**; **Selection**.)

HD

Souter, Gavin Geoffrey (1929–) is a journalist and historian. Born in Sydney and educated at the University of Sydney, he worked for the *Sydney Morning Herald* as a foreign correspondent and feature writer. His first historical works were a pioneering study of *New Guinea* (1963) and an account of the socialist colony in Paraguay established in 1893 by William **Lane**, *A Peculiar People* (1968). *Lion and Kangaroo* (1976) was an innovative study of the early Commonwealth that paid particular attention to the ceremonies, the new institutions and the interplay of national and imperial consciousness. As company historian for John Fairfax Ltd, he wrote a history of his paper, *Company of Heralds* (1981), by far the most accomplished **newspaper** history and one that did not shy from the **Fairfax family's** peccadilloes. The subsequent calamities of young Warwick provided the basis of a sequel, *Heralds and Angels* (1991, 1992).

From 1983 to 1987 Souter was a visiting fellow in the history department of the Institute of Advanced Studies at the Australian National University while he prepared a history of the federal legislature for the Bicentenary. *Acts of Parliament*, which appeared in 1988, was subtitled *A Narrative History of the Senate and House of Representatives*, but it was enlivened by felicitous evocations of parliamentarians and political dramas. He wrote of his childhood in *The Idle Hill of Summer* (1972).

SM

South African–Australian relations were fostered by the sailing route from Britain via the Cape of Good Hope, especially in the years before the Suez Canal, steamships, and cables opened other **communications**. Trans-migration occurred at several levels as British governors transferred between the two countries, and colonists sought gold in both. The largest movement was to the Witwatersrand in the 1890s, and the **Boer War** (1899–1902) drew many more Australians, including Breaker **Morant**; thereafter, direct links dwindled.

Imperial statesmen applauded the Australian Commonwealth and the South African Union (1910) as apotheoses of British policy and buttresses of Empire; and for some decades imperial (later Commonwealth) conferences allowed significant exchanges of information and opinion among the Dominions. Prime ministers from **Deakin** to

Menzies found common ground and personal pleasure in the company of Smuts. However, in the imperial economy, and in global markets, Australia and South Africa exported very similar agrarian produce and minerals and, although some expertise was shared, rivalry was more common. Sporting competition (in **rugby** union, **cricket**, and netball) generated similarly ambivalent relations.

Official relations cooled after 1948, when Afrikaner nationalists came to power, with apartheid as the goal of policy. South Africa withdrew from the Commonwealth in 1961 in the face of criticism from 'old' as well as 'new' Commonwealth leaders, and became a republic. Increasingly violent repression prompted first **Whitlam's** Labor and then **Fraser's** Liberal government to impose cultural sanctions and to voice diplomatic criticism. Meanwhile, popular revulsion against apartheid (focused first on sporting contacts) gave rise to informal boycotts of South African products. The South Africa government came to symbolise everything that was embarrassing to a self-consciously multicultural Australia in an Asian region. For that reason, a trickle of die-hard white Australians chose to migrate to South Africa. For the families of white South African professionals, Australia symbolised harmony and freedom from military conscription, and they voted in large numbers with their airline tickets.

Responses to apartheid therefore meshed with Australian domestic politics. The **ACTU** gave increasing material support to the free 'black' unions which formed from the 1970s: the Building Workers Industrial Union developed close links with unions aligned with the African National Congress, while the Builders Labourers Federation chose to endorse unions aligned with the Pan-Africanist Congress. The ANC and South-West African People's Organisation opened quasi-diplomatic information offices (in Sydney and Melbourne respectively) in the 1980s, while the BLF supported a PAC information office in Canberra. Equally significant were links between Catholic, Anglican, and Uniting Church hierarchies in the two countries, since clerical leadership was critical to the South African liberation movement, especially in the 1980s.

The release of Nelson Mandela in 1991, the dismantling of apartheid thereafter, and the democratic election of an ANC-dominated coalition, led to enthusiastic diplomatic support and a measure of technical assistance from both government and non-government sources, building on informal links created during the anti-apartheid struggle. In the 1990s, when the Western Australian government introduced legislation to curb trade union powers, there was even some talk of a South African trade union boycott of Western Australian goods and services.

Scholarly interaction largely reflects these political trends, and has been mainly in one direction. C.W. de Kiewiet's pioneering economic and political histories of South Africa in the 1930s acknowledged his debts to Australian scholarship. Keith **Hancock's** vision of the Commonwealth inspired a full-dress biography of Smuts in the 1960s, while Geoffrey **Blainey's** mastery of the technol-

ogy and politics of mining earned him accolades as the progenitor of materialist explanations in South African history. By contrast, Arthur Davey's study of Breaker Morant, undercutting the credibility of the Australian film of the same name, is almost unique in South African scholarship. Similarly African Studies from the 1960s has relayed South African scholarship to Australian universities, and produced a trickle of research projects, whereas Australian Studies have found no niche in South Africa. More diffusely, however, South African academic critiques of race, class, and gender relations have had some influence on Australian scholarship on parallel topics. Colin Tatz and Norman Etherington have been the most prolific and influential mediators of these ideas into mainstream Australian scholarship.

DONALD DENOON

South Australia shares boundaries with all of the other mainland states and the **Northern Territory**, and has a long, deeply indented southern coastline bordered by the Southern Ocean. The state occupies 984 377 square kilometres of desert, plain, and ancient, eroded ranges, one-eighth of the continent, and its driest region. The average annual rainfall is 528 millimetres, but 80 per cent of the state receives less than 250 millimetres. This vast and arid environment is the central fact of SA's history. The Aboriginal population had adapted to the dry climate by wide-ranging hunter–gathering and by concentrating near the wetter coast and the **Murray**, the region's only river. It took more than a century for settlers of British origin to accept the same limitations on occupying the arid inland, where Aborigines could live well but European agriculture would prove a complete failure.

From the first recorded visit, by a Dutch ship in 1627, European views of southern Australia were negative. **Flinders** and **Baudin** in 1802 gave no encouragement to official settlement but their discoveries prompted visits by whalers and sealers, who, with escaped **convicts** and Aboriginal women from Van Diemen's Land, formed a 'den' on Kangaroo Island after 1810. For a short but crucial period, opinions of the land changed. Sealers praised the mainland near Kangaroo Island; **Sturt** admired its 'promising aspect' in 1829–30. These reports were sufficient to justify the choice of southern Australia, at a respectable distance from convict **New South Wales**, as the place for a free British colony.

SA was the product of a combination of English liberal reformism and speculation. **Wakefield's** concept of 'systematic colonisation' proposed that a 'contrived' balance between invested capital and labour, combined with concentrated agricultural settlement and freedom from government interference, would ensure maximum returns for England's investors and enhance opportunities for its labourers. There would be neither an established church nor convicts. Using Wakefield's ideas, promoters negotiated a compromise in which the British government would control the colony but colonisation commissioners would manage the survey and sale of land, using the proceeds to select and transport the labourers. The Province of South

South Australia

Australia was established by Letters Patent in February 1836 and surveyor-general **Light** was sent to St Vincent Gulf, where he sited **Adelaide**, the capital city, and then surveyed the adjacent country.

Government was proclaimed in the summer of 1836 to colonists eager to take up country not yet seen or surveyed. Men rode inland to find water, pasture, and stock routes, establishing runs as far north as the Flinders Ranges by the 1850s and following **Stuart** up into northern Australia in the 1860s. From 1853 paddle-steamers plied the Murray as a route into the interior, bringing down cargoes of wool from inland NSW. In SA remote districts were opened up from numerous small coastal ports, served by ketches. Ships sailed deep into the outback up Spencer Gulf to Port Augusta, and in 1865 off-loaded camels and men from British India and Afghanistan. Camel trains, under the management of 'Afghans' such as Faiz and Tagh Mahomet, provided Central Australia's essential transport until the 1930s.

Success attended **wheat**-farming in the south, and by the mid-1850s SA had surpassed **Tasmania** as Australia's major producer. Farming practices also reflected cultural differences. The main contrasts were between the principal European groups: British and **German**. By contrast to the British, who aimed to exploit the land for commercial return, the German Lutherans, who first arrived in 1838, were peasants who pursued a subsistence agriculture, husbanding the land and creating self-sufficient communities in the hill country encircling the Adelaide Plain. These distinctive communities have survived, but many in the second generation, both British and German, adopted a form of shifting agriculture, trekking north, east, and west into lands of ever-increasing aridity, fervent in the belief that rain followed the plough. Savage **drought** in 1864–65 destroyed many pastoral runs, except in the swampy south-east; 30 years later, another drought defeated the farmers who had moved in the 'great wheat rush' beyond **Goyder's Line**. Drought intensified the destructive effects of over-stocking, deep-ploughing, and feral rabbits.

From the turn of the century renewed attempts to farm 'marginal lands' were promoted by the SA government in **irrigation** schemes along the Murray, drainage works in the south-east, and an extension of developmental **railways**. The most marginal land of all, the NT, was gratefully relinquished to the new Commonwealth administration in 1911. After World War I, **soldier settlers** were encouraged to take up irrigation blocks and Mallee farms but in the 1930s, further drought, compounded by the **Depression**, forced many of these settlers off the land. The government finally acknowledged the limits to agricultural expansion and, while maintaining its support, began to promote secondary industry and urbanisation. SA's climate also constrained industrialisation, and from the 1940s the government constructed pipelines from the Murray to Whyalla and other developing towns, and to suburban Adelaide. The rural population had reached a peak of almost 75 per cent of the total in SA in 1871, but in the retreat from the frontier

Adelaide regained the majority by 1921. Industrialisation accelerated rural out-migration, and together with high levels of European **immigration** in the 1950s and 1960s, further increased Adelaide's majority. Most South Australians are now employed in manufacturing and service industries, and in 1996, 73 per cent of the state's population of 1 474 000 lived in Adelaide.

There were successes as well as defeats in the European response to the Mediterranean climate, and both have left an enduring heritage. Wheat, grapevines, almonds, olives, and oranges were planted from the beginning. More than 40 per cent of Australia's vineyards are in SA. Sheep breeders developed a large-framed merino suited to dry conditions, and farmers eventually developed a productive dry-lands system that integrated cereal crops and stock. **Wool**, wheat, and wine are the state's most valuable commodities. Minerals are another. **Mining**, one of few industries not constrained by climate, rescued the colony's failing economy in the 1840s, when copper was discovered at Burra and Kapunda, producing Australia's first mining boom. By the 1890s SA was one of the largest copper producers in the world. The major mines, in northern Yorke Peninsula, were closed in the 1920s but copper production started again in 1988 at Roxby Downs in the far north. South Australian businessmen and diggers also exploited the bonanzas in silver–lead and gold that developed in desert country beyond the borders at Broken Hill and Kalgoorlie, and, in the twentieth century, in coal, opals, iron, and natural gas.

The challenges of the environment encouraged cooperation between producers, between capital and labour, and between the public and the private sector. Primary and secondary industries depended upon government-funded services, infrastructure, and immigration. The relationship between public and private sectors was continually renegotiated after the 'self-supporting system' of the founding Board of Colonisation Commissioners failed and the British government assumed sole responsibility for the colony in 1842. This is a society which has had to continually reinvent itself in order to prosper in an arid environment—modestly endowed and physically isolated. There are long antecedents for efforts by state and business in the early 1900s to redefine SA as a 'multi-function polis', in place of its identification as 'Festival State', based on Adelaide's Festival of Arts, held since 1960.

Historians have often debated the theme of social experimentation in South Australian history. Most have followed Douglas **Pike** in *Paradise of Dissent* (1957) and focused on Wakefield, the commissioners, and the **South Australian Company**, the freedom from convictism and the creation of a 'paradise of dissent' where religious Nonconformism flourished. Where historians have disagreed has been whether SA continued after the 1840s as a **social laboratory**. Proponents of continuing experimentation point to the early achievement of self-government (1856), use of the secret ballot, granting women the right to vote in local government elections (1861) and to vote and stand for parliament (1894); then (leaping half a century) they emphasise the innovative industrial policies associated with Premier **Playford** in the 1940s and Don **Dunstan's** radical social and environmental legislation of the 1970s.

Another strand in the theme of social experiment was the commitment to establishing a family-based society comprising equal numbers of young British men and women. Wakefield's scheme specified not only sale of land and use of the proceeds to convey labourers to the colony, but also that emigrants be selected giving 'absolute preference … to young persons, and … no excess of males', so that fertile young couples might quickly increase the colonial population. This Wakefieldian aim has been steadfastly maintained, especially through government policies which successfully favoured family-based rural settlement and established hundreds of towns and schools within walking distance of every farming family. Women as artists, writers, mothers, farmers, and social reformers were prominent from the first, and their presence pervades South Australian history, contrary to the masculine images which still prevail in the history of Australia. A series of sesquicentennial histories, including Eric Richards (ed.), *The Wakefield History of South Australia*, appeared in 1986; a *Wakefield Companion to South Australian History* is scheduled for publication in 2001.

SUSAN MARSDEN

South Australian Company was formed in London in 1835 for the purpose of financing British settlement in the province of **South Australia**. The establishment of SA was to be a joint undertaking between the British government and a nominated board of commissioners, who would be responsible for raising the necessary capital by land sales. In order to do so, the commissioners formed a private company, chaired by George Fife **Angas**, to buy large quantities of land at a discounted price. The scheme was based on the **Wakefield system**. In the climate of heady optimism that followed, however, land prices escalated rapidly and the South Australian Company instead became the central player in a flurry of speculative property dealings. Such activities, unrelated to Wakefield's original concept, contributed largely to the failure of his scheme in SA.

HD

South Australian Register was founded in London in 1836 by George Stevenson and Robert Thomas as the *South Australian Gazette and Colonial Register*. The subsequent issue was printed in Adelaide the following year. Increasing outspokenness against the government led to the withdrawal of government gazette notices, which ultimately led to the paper's cessation in 1842. Stevenson re-established the paper in 1845. It became a daily in 1850, with a weekly supplement, the *Observer*; from 1858 the *Advertiser* became a long-term rival. While the *Register* supported free trade and became firmly anti-Labor, the more radical *Advertiser* pushed for protection. The *Register* developed a successful literary reputation in the early 1900s. The paper's conversion to a pictorial format in 1929 heralded its ultimate decline; J.L.

Bonython, the owner of the *Advertiser*, purchased it in 1931, and it was merged with its former rival.

HD

Southern Cross flag, also known as the Eureka flag, features the Southern Cross constellation on a broad white cross on a dark blue background. Miners first unfurled it at Bakery Hill, Ballarat, Victoria, in 1854, as a symbol of liberty and democracy; on 3 December 1854 they fought under it at the **Eureka Stockade**. Various early forms of the flag were used in Australia prior to Eureka, most notably by the anti-transportation league of the 1840s. In the 1970s the Eureka flag was adopted as the standard of the Builders Labourers Federation, and right-wing nationalist groups have also used it. The original Southern Cross flag was donated to the Ballaarat Fine Art Gallery by the King family, whose ancestor John King fought with the military at Eureka. After years of controversy over the flag's authenticity, it was officially unveiled by Prime Minister Gough **Whitlam** at Ballarat in 1973. (See also **Flags**.)

HD

Spanish Civil War was fought from 1936 between the republican government and right-wing rebels led by General Franco who prevailed in 1939. The rebels were assisted by the German and Italian military, the republicans by volunteers in the International Brigades. More than 30 Australians enlisted in the International Brigades (of whom at least 14 died), and perhaps as many more nurses, administrators, drivers, and journalists worked on republican territory; one Australian is known to have fought for Franco. The Commonwealth government of Joseph **Lyons** maintained a policy of strict neutrality, the **Australian Labor Party** was deeply divided between anti-fascist supporters of the Spanish republic, **Catholic** supporters of Franco, and isolationists.

While the Catholic Church was most forthright in support of the rebels, Australian **communists** led the defence of the republic. Broader organisations such as the Movement Against War and Fascism and the Spanish Relief Committee raised funds and publicised the democratic cause. Nettie **Palmer** and Len Fox published an account of *Australians in Spain* in 1938, and Amirah Inglis wrote the fullest history of *Australians in the Spanish Civil War* (1987). Inglis also edited the *Letters from Spain* (1985) of an Australian volunteer truck-driver, Lloyd Edmonds, while Judith Keene wrote of the experiences of an Australian nurse, Agnes Hodgson (*The Last Mile to Huesca*, 1988). In 1993 a memorial to the Australian volunteers was established in Canberra.

SM

Spence, Catherine Helen (1825–1910), called the 'Grand Old Woman of Australia' at the end of her long life, was one of SA's most progressive, energetic, and active public figures. Well-educated in Melrose, Scotland, Spence arrived in Adelaide on her fourteenth birthday, in 1839. After the death of her father seven years later, she drew upon this intellectual capital to support herself and her mother. From governessing at sixpence an hour, she progressed to paid journalism as outside contributor to the Adelaide *Register* from 1878, published five novels and two polemical works, and was gradually drawn into public life through volunteer philanthropic activities. The work she considered most important was electoral reform. Her lifelong campaign for the introduction of proportional representation, or Effective Voting as she called it, brought her into contact with influential figures such as John Stuart Mill and Oliver Wendell Holmes.

Perhaps the foundation of her growing radicalism was her abandonment, about 1856, of the Calvinist Presbyterianism of her youth for the freedom of Unitarianism. She became SA's first woman preacher, her sermons expressing an optimistic, sometimes utopian, belief in human progress.

Spence was a 'new woman' even before the phrase came into vogue. She led the campaign that made SA, in 1894, the first Australian colony to grant female suffrage. She later became the first female political candidate in Australia when she stood, unsuccessfully, for the 1897 Federal Convention. Yet she has never enjoyed a national reputation—perhaps because she was identified with Adelaide rather than Sydney or Melbourne, or because the electoral reforms she championed were defeated by party interests. A brief sketch of her life and influence ('The Veiled Maid of Adelaide') appears in Geoffrey **Blainey's** *A Land Half Won* (1980), but Susan Magarey's *Unbridling the Tongues of Women* (1985), the tribute of a second-wave South Australian feminist to a nineteenth-century pioneer, is the first scholarly biography.

Spence's literary reputation, partly revived by the republication in the 1980s of some of her fiction, has also fluctuated. In her novels, Australian settings, themes, and characters are confined within the perimeters of the conventional romance plot, the settings are domestic and urban, and ideas are more conspicuous than imaginative power. Nevertheless, the 1854 novel *Clara Morison: A Tale of South Australia during the Gold Fever* and the posthumously published *Autobiography* (1910) are vividly written, realistic in detail, and everywhere informed by energetically expressed and intelligent opinion.

Catherine Spence represented the best qualities of the respectable middle classes of her time—their belief in the value of education, public as well as private probity, hard work, justice, concern for those less fortunate, and close family ties. Such people were, she believed, ideal colonists, their fictional representations in her novels effectively contesting other, and ultimately more successful, claims for national identity, dominated by associations with **masculinity**, the working class, and the **bush**.

HELEN THOMSON

Spence, William Guthrie (1846–1926), had become the best-known union leader in Australia by the 1890s. His Scots parents came to Victoria in the gold rush and settled near Creswick. Spence, who had no formal schooling, became a mine worker while still in his teens. He was a teetotaller, a self-improver, and a ubiquitous presence in

Creswick's public life as office-holder in the Presbyterian Church, a borough councillor, a justice of the peace, and member of the militia and the debating society.

He became involved with miners' unionism in 1874. In 1878, he took the Creswick Miners Union into the recently formed Amalgamated Miners Association and, by determined and resourceful leadership, made it into a large inter-colonial union. He was asked in 1886 to help form a shearers' union and within a year was president of the Amalgamated Shearers Union of Australasia (ASU). His good name contributed to its rapid growth in the late 1880s, but three unsuccessful **shearers' strikes** between 1890 and 1894 led to an equally rapid decline. The extent of his responsibility for the 1890 **Maritime Strike** has been a matter of historical dispute. Spence knew considerably less about **shearers** and **pastoralists** than he did about miners and mine owners, and could never find a way of countering the pastoralists' unions' refusal to negotiate. The revival of shearers' unionism in the early 1900s owed little to him. John Merritt discusses this phase of his career in *The Making of the AWU* (1986).

The ASU, which became the **Australian Workers Union** (AWU) in 1894, played an influential role in shaping and sustaining the NSW Labor Party; the greater public prominence that came Spence's way 'enlarged his populist longings'. He wrote a verbose pamphlet on *The Ethics of New Unionism* (1892), and formulated an ambitious plan to bring unions into one large political–industrial organisation, which came to nothing. He entered the NSW parliament in 1898 and was a federal member 1901–17. Denied a ministry until the war years, he then became known as the mouthpiece of his departmental heads.

After 1900, a new group of AWU officials centralised the union and suppressed dissent. Spence lent his weight to this process by distorting history, particularly in his two books, *Australia's Awakening* (1909) and *History of the AWU* (1911), and by deserting former, loyal colleagues who were now out of favour. His reward was to remain president of the AWU and to be exalted as the grand old man of the Australian labour movement, but the myth-makers were embarrassed when the old man supported **conscription** in 1916. They allowed him to resign from the union rather than face expulsion, claiming that he had been too ill to resist the wily W.M. **Hughes**. Spence's obsession with place and status had brought his career to an ironic and tragic end. He had worked hard and selflessly in the 1870s and 1880s to improve the lot of his fellow miners, but if he is now remembered as a vain man of doubtful ability and integrity, the blame is as much his as it is that of the bureaucrats who used him.

His account of the origins of his creation—'Unionism came to the Australian bushman as a religion'—was a key element in the **Australian Legend**.

JOHN MERRITT

Spencer, (Walter) Baldwin (1860–1929) came from England in 1887 as foundation professor of biology at the University of Melbourne. As a member of the 1894 scientific expedition to central Australia, led by W.A. Horn, he began the anthropological work for which he is best known. This was also where he met his partner in this work, Francis Gillen, the Alice Springs postmaster who was sub-protector of the Alice Springs Aborigines. Gillen was a trusted ally of the Aranda (Arrernte) people, and he and Spencer were able to spend long periods with them. The results of their study were published in 1899 as *The Native Tribes of Central Australia*, published in a revised and extended form as *The Arunta* (1927). They later made film and sound recordings of Aborigines in the Oodnadatta area and, in their final collaboration, produced *The Northern Tribes of Central Australia* (1904). Spencer worked as special commissioner and chief protector of Aborigines for the NT in 1912, the same year he produced his report to federal government about possible development of the north with paternalist, segregationist policies.

Spencer was a trustee of the National Gallery of Victoria, and he encouraged and befriended young Australian artists, including Norman **Lindsay**, Arthur **Streeton**, and Tom **Roberts**. As honorary director of the Museum of Victoria, he oversaw the establishment of the ethnographic section, to which he eventually donated his own extensive collection of Aboriginal artefacts. His biography, '*So Much That Is New*' (1985), was written by D.J. **Mulvaney** and J.H. Calaby. Mulvaney has also edited Gillen's correspondence with Spencer, collected in *My Dear Spencer* (1997), and letters from other correspondents, collected in *From the Frontier* (2001).

KT

Spender, Percy Claude (1897–1985) was a lawyer before becoming MHR for Warringah, NSW, in 1937 as a member of the **United Australia Party**. He held a number of ministerial posts including minister for army (1940–41) and minister for external affairs (1949–51). He took a leading role in the **Colombo Plan** and **ANZUS Treaty**. Following his retirement from politics, he served as ambassador to the USA (1951–58) and as president of the International Court of Justice (1964–67). He published his autobiography, *Politics and a Man*, in 1972.

KT

Splits refer to the break-up of a political party, usually of the **Australian Labor Party** because its discipline is so strict that a group defiance of it leads to an unhealable breach. The first Labor split occurred in NSW in 1894, soon after the party's formation, over the issue of tariff policy. This led to the introduction of the requirement that Labor members vote as caucus directs. National splits occurred in 1916 over **conscription**, in 1931 over the response to the **Depression**, and in 1954 over **communism**. After the first two of these, the Labor rebels joined the non-Labor parties; after the third, the rebels formed the **Democratic Labor Party**, which at elections directed its preferences to the non-Labor parties. Splits have occurred more frequently in the non-Labor parties, but with less disastrous consequences because those involved have been more inclined to cooperate in parliament and at elections

and have usually reformed a new, united party. Labor has taken an unforgiving attitude to its 'rats'.

JH

Spofforth, Frederick Robert (1853–1926), cricketer, became widely known as the 'Demon Bowler' while touring with the first white Australian **cricket** side in England, where in 1878 he achieved a hat-trick and figures of 6/4 and 4/16 against the Marylebone Cricket Club at Lord's. In the historic **Ashes** Test in 1882, he steered Australia's victory, taking seven wickets in each innings (14/90). Richard Cashman in *The 'Demon' Spofforth* (1990) calls him 'the father of modern fast bowling'. Initially a tearaway, Spofforth developed the art of mixing speed with 'control, cunning and variety'. His cleverly disguised off-cutters terrified batsmen, and a legend grew as cartoonists captured his Mephistophelean physiognomy and writers relished his deadly deeds. Born at Balmain, NSW, Spofforth learned to play cricket with Sydney's Newtown and Albert clubs in the early 1870s. In 18 Tests against England (1877/78–1886) Spofforth's record was 94 wickets at an average of 18.41. His first-class career figures (1874/75–1897) are 853 wickets at 14.95, and his best bowling was 9/18 when playing for Australia against Oxford University in 1886. From 1888 Spofforth lived in England. He became managing director of the Star Tea Company and grew gum trees in Surrey.

DC

Sport and leisure have offered entertainment for generations of Australians, helped in the development of social relationships, and contributed to the economy by providing employment and encouraging investment. They have also reflected contemporary society and cultural attitudes, so that historically Aborigines have been excluded from most mainstream recreational activities, women discriminated against, and 'minority' ethnic groups marginalised. Hence the much-vaunted egalitarian sporting or leisure culture has always been incomplete. Social segregation was pervasive: the timing and location of organised recreational activities, the costs of participation and viewing, and competing codes of 'respectability' and 'style', made certain leisure pastimes the preserve of particular social classes and groups. The polo club and the orchestral ensemble, the dockside tavern and the two-up school, each had distinct adherents according to socio-economic status.

The first recorded organised sporting event in Australia was a race meeting at Hyde Park in 1810—a crude replica of what the participating military garrison had left behind in England. Not till the mid-nineteenth century did Australians begin to modify their imported cultural baggage, adapting British sporting practices to local conditions rather than merely adopting them wholesale. The genesis of **Australian Rules football** in the late 1850s was a step along the road of sporting self-confidence, although this game was partially inherited as an amalgamation of rules of various styles of English and Irish football. In the following decades the colonists' defeat of British teams in various sports was said to demonstrate that Australia's social and physical climate was especially conducive to athletic excellence. It was also claimed that such sporting victories were fostering a sense of colonial **nationalism**. However, this 'unifying' nationalistic sentiment was associated narrowly with white Anglo-Celtic male Australians. Similarly, the so-called unifying role of sport within Australia was not self-evident; intercolonial and suburban sporting rivalries often produced collective intolerance rather than solidarity, and ill-feeling instead of goodwill.

Public houses were the most important indoor recreational venues in the colonial period. **Pubs** provided food, drink, entertainment, and they acted as meeting houses in both urban and rural townships. Common tavern sports included skittles, darts, and billiards, while some publicans set up areas adjacent to their premises for wrestling, boxing, or animal baiting. Singalongs, comedy acts, and 'variety' performances were staged in pubs regularly before music halls and vaudeville theatres became firmly established from the mid-nineteenth century. However, while the nomenclature and the culture of pubs were typically Anglo-Celtic, the minstrel shows and song-and-dance routines of the late nineteenth century were strongly influenced by American vaudeville tradition. J.W.C. Cumes provides an account of colonial recreation in *Their Chastity Was Not Too Rigid* (1979) and Richard Waterhouse deals with the popular stage in *From Minstrel Show to Vaudeville* (1990).

American influence was also apparent in the form of major travelling circus acts from the 1870s. Like most organised **entertainment**, circuses were launched in Australian cities and then spread, where possible, to rural areas. **Agricultural shows** were an exception to this pattern. They began as country fairs, and became popular annual demonstrations of the rural economy and bush culture in most capital cities from the early 1900s. Over time, these city-based 'royal shows' have incorporated theme-park attractions more consistent with American popular culture; so much so that farming and agricultural displays now play second fiddle. However, in rural and outback regions the shows still retain their traditional emphasis on agriculture, pastoralism, and 'country' hospitality.

The introduction for most urban workers of a free Saturday afternoon from the 1880s provided a uniform time for working-class players to take part in organised team sports on a regular basis—although the 'black-ball' test kept labourers from many amateur rowing and sailing clubs, which were dominated by middle-class 'gentlemen'. Given Sabbatarian opposition to Sunday recreation, Saturday afternoon was also a period for informal leisure practices, such as bathing at the beach, or visiting public amenities such as museums, art galleries, and libraries. During the twentieth century the amount of available time for leisure improved steadily for most workers, with trade unions winning reduced hours of labour, and governments allowing recreational activities on Sundays. From the 1960s there has also been a more liberal approach to sports participation among various social groups: an increased importance attached to player performance, rather than skin colour, has seen Aborigines take a prominent

position in professional versions of Australian Rules football and rugby league, while an acceptance of new social roles for women has opened up many athletic and leisure activities on a less gender-biased basis. The nature of 'play' and 'spectating' have also undergone reforms: altered attitudes towards violence have transformed bloody prizefighting into the highly regulated sport of boxing, while the introduction of all-seater sporting arenas and alcohol restrictions among fans has reduced spectator violence and disorder.

Geographical factors have strongly influenced the development of Australian sport. Although transport improvements have enabled the formation of national leagues, many teams are still based on the suburban community, which was at the heart of the nation's sporting development when transport difficulties restricted competition to the intra-metropolitan. Associated with this pattern has been a reluctance among Australians to embrace private ownership in sport: local authorities have been major providers of sports facilities, even at the elite level. State and federal governments also have backed Australians at play; initially for military purposes, later for health, and more recently for international prestige. While early sports such as ploughing matches, digging contests, and watermen's rowing races were recreational adaptations of participants' work tasks, sport has now become an economic activity in its own right. In the 1980s and 1990s commercial sponsorship and television broadcasting have become integral parts of sport's financial infrastructure; 'true' amateurism has been abandoned at the elite level (though few sports have yet to embrace full-time professionalism); while state governments have vied with each other to attract international sporting events for their effects of employment and revenue.

While Australian sport has had an ambivalent profit-taking role, many other forms of leisure in Australia have been unquestionably commercial. Ownership of bicycles, for example, became popular among both men and women during the 1890s after manufacturers promoted cycling as a pleasurable recreational pastime for both sexes. Jim Fitzpatrick, *The Bicycle and the Bush* (1980), records its rural uses. Leisure consumers were also a cornerstone of the **film industry**, with cinema attendance to see the 'moving pictures' a weekly ritual for many couples in the 1930s. At about the same time commercial and public **radio** stations were introduced in Australia, with many living-rooms boasting the latest 'wireless', which enabled the population to receive news broadcasts, hear music, and listen to radio plays. **Television** now occupies a considerable amount of Australians' leisure time, a situation that is likely to continue with the introduction of cable and satellite channels. The multi-functional role of the home computer suggests, however, that private leisure time may become more active, with Internet users scanning the World Wide Web to uncover their personal interests.

Tourism has grown to become Australia's biggest leisure industry. The number of short-term visitors to Australia has increased significantly during the 1980s and 1990s, with the volume of tourists from Asia particularly high. While many Australians have travelled abroad, most of their holidays have been taken domestically—whether in a rudimentary riverside caravan park or in a plush suite on the Gold Coast—with obvious spin-off effects to the local economy. 'Short-break' vacations have been of special importance to Australians, blessed as they are with a good number of public holidays. Additionally, Australia has boasted a wide variety of cultural events to attract tourists: Melbourne's Moomba festival and Adelaide's Festival of Arts have offered carnival and drama respectively; celebrations of national origin like St Patrick's Day, Glendi, and the Schutzenfest have enabled a 'coming together' of Australians with similar ancestral backgrounds; various wine-making festivals have been held regularly in the south-east of Australia; the spring racing carnival in Melbourne has been a parade of fashion and glamour as much as horseflesh; while other tourist successes of more recent times have been Sydney's spectacular Gay and Lesbian Mardi Gras and the Australian Formula 1 Grand Prix.

Clearly, Australians now have more sport and recreation options than in the past. However, socio-economic differences still govern the direction in which certain groups take part in leisure activities. Not all families can afford a home computer, a video player, or a backyard swimming pool, so they make use of public facilities in libraries and recreational centres. Hence community-based, publicly funded, leisure resources continue to be central to Australians' participation in organised sport and recreation.

Richard Waterhouse, *Private Pleasures, Public Leisure* (1995), surveys the role of sport and entertainment in Australian popular culture since 1788, especially in its urban context, while Richard Cashman, *Paradise of Sport* (1995), is the most comprehensive history of Australian sport. The Australian Society for Sports History holds regular conferences and publishes the journal *Sporting Traditions*. The second edition of the *Oxford Companion to Australian Sport* (1994) is a useful general guide.

WRAY VAMPLEW AND DARYL ADAIR

Sporting history, according to Ian **Turner's** prediction in *HS* in 1973, would inevitably cause the 'older history pros [to] suggest that their younger colleagues, having run out of all significant subjects to write about, are now descending to trivia'. Thus he articulated the stigma that has surrounded this subject, and foreshadowed the grouping of those keen to establish and maintain the discipline's academic credentials. In response, sports historians have tended to overemphasise Australia's obsession with sport and its role in constructing (male) **national identity**.

Reflections on Australia's sporting history, which included organised sport as well as pastimes and amusements, began in colonial times as the published impressions of visitors like Anthony **Trollope** (1873) and immigrants like Richard **Twopeny** (1883). These bore the marks of their origin—preoccupation with British sports, notably shooting, horse-racing and hunting, with a strong emphasis on gambling. As the largely British and Irish sports developed in the colonies, the analysis expanded to incorporate football and **cricket**, the latter emerging as the best-docu-

mented and most popular strand of sporting history. From the late nineteenth century, sporting history was expounded and practised by disparate groups, the most prominent being newspaper journalists and devoted amateur historians of individual sports and clubs. To these were added hagiographic accounts of sportsmen and anniversary histories of sport associations. Antiquarian chronicles were dominant in the first half of the twentieth century.

The readership and writing of sporting history broadened after 1956 with the popularity of Olympians and Olympic sports, but the genre remained descriptive rather than analytical, anecdotal rather than substantial. Three notable exceptions were Gordon Inglis, *Sport and Pastime in Australia* (1912); John **Mulvaney**, *Cricket Walkabout* (1967); and Keith Dunstan's irreverent *Sports* (1973). Consequently, there were few reliable resources to inform the inclusion of sport in general histories.

A major change occurred in the late 1970s with the embrace of **social history**. This distilled in the July 1977 conference, 'Making of Sporting Traditions', held at the University of New South Wales, which brought together academics who shared a common interest in sporting history. The proceedings of this conference were published as *Sport in History* in 1979. This and subsequent scholarly conferences and publications serviced the emerging tertiary discipline of sport and human movement studies. Interest was strong enough at the fourth conference in 1983 to support the foundation of the Australian Society for Sports History, followed by the publication of the society's journal, *Sporting Traditions*, from November 1984. The journal and conferences encouraged a multi-disciplinary approach to sporting history, but the product often lacked diversity and failed to encompass the issues of gender, race, ethnicity, or class.

At the same time, a market-oriented publishing industry brought increasing numbers of popular sporting 'histories' to the public—including biographical (now both hagiographic and warts-and-all), anecdotal, humorous, photographic, coffee-table, and reference works, along with compendiums and nostalgic albums. Many made the best-seller lists, but were informed more by journalism than by history.

The sources for sporting history, as observed by Bill Mandle in *New History* in 1982, are not to be found in the Blue Books. Little sporting history bears the mark of archival investigation; rather, it relies on newspapers, sporting magazines, journalism, and ephemera. Much of the documentary and material evidence of sport history is located not in libraries and archives but within **museums**. From the early 1970s museums in Australia recognised the importance of collecting and curating sporting history as part of the new social history. However, the collections remain largely neglected by sporting historians. The emphasis of collecting was Anglocentric and it neglected the sporting history of women, indigenous people, and recent migrants. Its focus was on famous sportspeople, although more recently it has broadened to include popular recreation and the sport of 'ordinary people' as well as serious sporting endeavour.

Squatting

By 1987 the *Sporting Traditions* journal listed dissertations, reflecting the growing number of students embarking on sporting history within tertiary institutions. These dissertations increasingly examined the influence of sport in modern industrial society and within cultural history. By the early 1990s greater attention was paid to indigenous (Colin Tatz), women's (Marion Stell), and migrant sport, as well as to the Olympics (Harry Gordon).

This period also witnessed market-oriented publications from scholarly houses. Landmark publications included *The Oxford Companion to Australian Sport*, written by members of the Australian Society for Sports History in 1992 (revised 1994); a selection of entries from the *ADB*, entitled *The Makers of Australia's Sporting Traditions* (1993); and the Cambridge *Sport in Australia* (1995). A proliferation of sporting history emerged from 1996 on the Internet, contained on the homepages of individuals, associations, sports, and clubs—a new format that will, without doubt, help shape the future of sporting history.

MARION STELL

Squatting—originally, in a pastoral context, the unauthorised creation of stock stations on vacant Crown land—arose only when and where a landowner's increasing stock numbers out-grazed the land available to him by grant, purchase, lease, or permit. In eastern mainland Australia, the original impetus for squatting in the early 1820s was primarily an expanding Sydney meat market and secondarily an experimentation with **wool** production, with added impetus from **emancipist** and native-born families in search of social and economic freedom. Squatting took on fresh vigour (and its actual name of squatting) in 1836 with a British wool market that strengthened pastoral diversification and drew new pastoralists from **Van Diemen's Land** and from Britain itself. In turn, the creation of **Melbourne** and **Adelaide** expanded the meat markets for the 'Sydneyside' cattle holders, just as the goldfields populations would do on a grander scale in the 1850s. Despite a pastoral myth which sees wool as the creator of squatting (an idea encouraged by the faulty organisation of S.H. **Roberts's** *The Squatting Age in Australia 1835–1847*, 1935), it is possible that sheep grazed no more land than did **cattle** in eastern Australia even as late as 1860.

In the meantime, the term *squatting* had changed its meaning—almost as soon as the word was applied to pastoralism. First, in 1837 in NSW, Governor Richard **Bourke** made squattages subject to an annual licence fee. With this *de facto* recognition of squatting, the word quickly came to mean simply that the tenurial status of the occupied land remained unresolved. Consolidation of this meaning came in 1846 when the British government foreshadowed replacement of the annual fee with a three-level lease system, a move seen as a half-way step to resolving the issue.

In NSW, formidable obstacles to this resolution existed. Despite a popular belief that squatting was a general Australian experience, squatting as a problem hardly existed in the other colonies. In Van Diemen's Land (a place of few cattle), lax land administration on the island in the 1820s had allowed sheep owners all the freehold land they wanted, and in due course the owners had found their squatting outlets in the **Port Phillip District** of NSW. In **Western Australia**, a late foundation date of 1829, sometimes massively liberal land grants, low initial stock numbers, and a tiny domestic market, deferred for many years any perceived need to graze the Crown lands. In **South Australia** in 1836, the founders' **Wakefieldian** agriculturalist philosophy of settlement—reinforced in the 1840s and 1850s by the province's emergent agricultural and copper-mining dynamics—ensured that squatting in the province would remain a fringe activity. In effect, Van Diemen's Land, WA, and SA were to remain spectators of the eastern mainland's resolution of squatting.

This resolution was difficult. Coincidentally with their squatting march, the leading Sydneyside landowners acquired the magisterial, executive, and legislative power to preserve their hold on the land; the newer immigrant squatters brought with them the matching political power of family connection and patronage. Ironically, British government land policy, developed from the **Ripon Regulations** during the 1830s (and including a land purchase price of £1 per acre), gave the squatters added incentive to preserve their status quo, for at that price most of their land would be unattractive to buyers.

Foreshadowed in the late 1840s, excision from squattages of town agricultural reserves began the process of resolving the fate of the Crown lands. In the 1850s and early 1860s, the then new eastern mainland parliaments of Victoria, NSW, and **Queensland** advanced the process with **selection** schemes designed to open the Crown lands—by purchase on time payment—to agricultural settlement.

These plans had some localised successes, particularly in Victoria. But on a larger scale, with great differences in detail according to time and place (demonstrated in recent years through a mass of regional and local studies), the squatters secured their holdings against prospective farmers—by law and by chicanery where the land warranted a buying duel; by the buying out of failed farms; and by long leaseholds where the land would never sustain agriculture.

On the purchased lands, the pastoral victory was often pyrrhic. At the price of at least £1 per acre, many of the new estates were overcapitalised, falling to bank interest and bad management. Despite the economic pastoral boom of the 1870s and 1880s, which helped to build the survivors' mansions, many of these survivors in turn fell in the 1890s to over-reaching ambition, worldwide depression, and the great Australian **drought** of 1895–1903. As is usual, only the level-headed survived. Most of these then sold out to—or were bought out by the government for—farmers, when new population pressures, new markets, and new technologies made agricultural land use more economically possible.

From this age of squatting in eastern Australia came two opposing—and probably equally silly—images of the squatter and **pastoral history**: one as the robber baron who stole the colonial earth, the other as the romantic civiliser of the bush. The first was created by men and women from failed farms; the second by people from failed squattages. (See also **Land settlement**; **Pastoral history**; **Pioneer**.)

DAVID DENHOLM

Squattocracy is a tongue-in-cheek reference to the aristocratic pretensions of squatters, whom the colonial governments permitted to graze stock on vast areas of land from the 1830s in exchange for a trifling fee. According to Sidney **Baker**, the expression first came into use in 1846 as a mocking term of derision.

In the 1830s and 1840s squatters were often depicted as wild young men, prone to hard drinking and fighting; but as they married and amassed wealth, they increasingly presented themselves as members of a landed establishment on the English model, maintaining large country and town houses and dominating the upper houses of colonial parliaments. Their children were educated at exclusive private schools, and their sons often attended Oxford or Cambridge, before settling on the land themselves. (See also **Squatting**.)

HD

St Vincent de Paul, Society of is a lay charitable organisation of the Catholic Church, founded in 1833 by Frederic Ozanam and fellow students at the Sorbonne, Paris. Branches were soon after established throughout the world, including Australia. Following in the tradition of its namesake, St Vincent de Paul (?1581–1660), the society works towards relieving sickness and suffering among poor and homeless people. Relying largely on a network of voluntary labour, the society makes contact with and offers assistance to people in need of food and shelter, and more recently to those suffering from alcohol and drug abuse.

HD

Standard of living, as a measure of individual and community well-being, was a social objective deeply grounded in Australian experience even before statisticians gave it formal definition early in the twentieth century. 'Australia's religion is its standard of living', said Lloyd Ross in 1932. For almost a century it has been continuously monitored and debated through a unique national institution, the **arbitration** system.

Long before Europeans arrived, it has been suggested, Australia was a prosperous land, with a high material standard of living. Aborigines enjoyed an abundance of fresh food and could support themselves in only a few hours' work a day. If an Aborigine had toured late-eighteenth-century Europe and saw how people struggled to survive, he would have concluded that he had descended to a kind of Third World, Geoffrey **Blainey** claimed in *Triumph of the Nomads* (1975). While countering stereotypes of Aborigines as primitive, such picturesque comparisons may mislead as much as they inform. In *Economics and the Dreamtime* (1993), Noel **Butlin** agreed that Aborigines were indeed better fed than the first generation of European settlers of Australia, although he questioned whether a society in which food

supplies were so seasonal, and cultural norms so different from Europe's, should be called 'affluent'.

Among European newcomers the comparison that mattered was not between Aborigines and themselves, but between how well they lived in Australia and how poorly they lived back home. It was a common criticism of **transportation** that, so far from deterring wrong-doers, it actually improved their living conditions. Contemporaries contrasted the abundance, freshness, and cheapness of food in NSW ('meat three times a day') with the mean and costly diet of English town-dwellers or Irish peasants. Gentleman travellers and colonial immigration agents assiduously promoted the idea of Australia as a **workingman's paradise**. 'In no other land', declared the NSW statistician Timothy **Coghlan**, 'can a better-dressed, better fed, and more contented-looking class than the working people of New South Wales be found. This fact is plainly revealed whenever a holiday attracts crowds to the streets of the metropolis or to the numerous resorts of amusement in and around the city.' Almost a century later, the economic historian Noel Butlin confirmed Coghlan's impressions when he estimated that colonial Australians had the highest real per capita incomes in the world (Keith Hancock, ed., *The National Income and Social Welfare*, 1965).

Comparing Australian and English wage rates and prices, or observing the dress and demeanour of holiday crowds, were simple, but possibly misleading, ways of measuring economic well-being. It was hours of work, not just wage-rates, which determined the size of the workingman's pay packet. Australia's staple industries—wool, wheat, mining, and construction—were cyclical in character, with a fluctuating and unstable workforce. Their ups and downs, argues Shirley Fitzgerald in *Rising Damp* (1987), were also reflected in the seasonal peaks and troughs of activity in the warehouses, workshops, and abattoirs of the coastal cities. Thomas Dobeson, an emigrant artisan, found himself trapped in a cycle of short-term jobs, uncertain earnings, and poverty. He railed against those 'lying vipers' the emigration agents who had enticed him to 'sunny new South Wales the workingman's paradise'. Dobeson's situation was not unusual: as Charles Fahey and Jenny Lee showed (*LH*, 1986), workers in many colonial trades earned wages no more than two-thirds the nominal rate.

When people talked about the colonial standard of living, they generally thought of a white working-class male supporting a wife and at least two or three children. Largely omitted from consideration were such significant minorities as Aborigines, Chinese, single women, old people, and children. In 1907 in his famous Harvester Judgment, Justice H.B. **Higgins** institutionalised this concept when he based his definition of a **'fair and reasonable'** wage (seven shillings a day) on the needs of a man, his wife and three children living in 'frugal comfort'. Besides food and shelter he made allowance for furniture, utensils, rates, life insurance, savings, a benefit society subscriptions, union dues, books and newspapers, a sewing machine, school requisites, and modest amounts for amusements, holidays, liquor, tobacco, and charity. Later commentators questioned and refined Higgins's definition, but it remained the benchmark for Australian wage-fixing for more than half a century.

The requirement of the Arbitration Court for more rigorous indices of living standards coincided with a worldwide interest in developing comparative cost-of-living statistics. Coghlan had deployed crude indices of Australian well-being, such as per capita consumption of various foods, with that of other nations, but the Commonwealth Statistician George Knibbs, a close student of international statistical developments, was possibly the first Australian to use the phrase *standard of living* regularly. It became an indispensable part of Australian political discourse, and continues to appear in Australian economic dictionaries even though it is seldom listed elsewhere. In *Australian Standards of Living* (1939), F.W. **Eggleston** had recognised the concept as 'a dynamic political factor'. Preserving the 'standard of living' became the basis on which the state secured the well-being of the individual, not only by arbitrating a 'living wage', but through pensions, maternal endowment, and an ever-growing list of state-funded benefits. 'The ideas which men form as to the living standard to which they are entitled are a determinant of their actions as self-conscious members of the community', Eggleston argued.

The **depression** of the 1890s marked a break in the history of Australian living standards. In the previous three decades per capita incomes, Butlin estimated, had risen steadily; but over the next five decades, from 1890 to 1940, they scarcely rose at all. Australia, which had once outpaced the world, now lost ground to the USA and Canada, and even Britain began to catch up. Later studies have modified this picture a little: stagnant real wages were substantially offset by shorter working hours, increased government benefits, and longer life-expectancy (Ian McLean in Rodney Maddock and McLean, eds, *The Australian Economy in the Long Run*, 1987). During the Depression of the 1930s the nominal basic wage was cut by 10 per cent, but thanks to an even steeper fall in prices, real wages (wages adjusted to reflect prices of basic items of consumption) actually *rose*. But such statistics had little meaning in a society where about one male wage-earner in three was out of work and many others lacked full-time employment.

Not until the **long boom** of the 1950s and 1960s did the Australian standard of living again improve. From 1939 to 1970 real GDP per head more than doubled while standard working hours continued to fall. This was the age of the brick veneer, the owner-occupied home, the Holden station wagon, the washing machine, the fridge, the TV, and the motor mower. Skilled workers, who were successful in securing 'margins' over the basic wage and had access to plentiful overtime, fared better than unskilled workers. Until the achievement of **equal pay** in 1974, men fared better than women. But for many families the postwar years brought unparalleled levels of material prosperity. 'The working man was never better off than he is now', the wife of a suburban butcher observed in the mid-1960s.

In the early 1970s Australia, like the rest of the developed world, entered a new period of difficulty precipitated by the oil-price rise of 1974. Living standards, as measured by per capita GDP, have since risen much more slowly than previously, and more slowly than the rest of the world. From tenth place in 1970, Australia has slumped to fourteenth in 1990. Such narrowly economic indices, some scholars argue, fail to capture anything like the full range of factors, both subjective and objective, which contribute to people's standard of living. In *Living Decently* (1993), Peter Travers and Sue Richardson show that, if life-expectancy and education levels are also taken into account, Australia jumps from fourteenth to seventh place on the league table. But people's sense of well-being is perhaps more strongly influenced by their standard of living relative to others in their own society. Since the early 1980s there has been a tendency for both the very rich and the very poor (those on pensions and other state benefits) to gain at the expense of lower-paid workers (Phil Raskall and Robert Urquhart, *Inequality, Living Standards and the Social Wage During the 1980s*, 1994).

The Australian standard of living was a political as well as a statistical ideal, reflecting the belief, formed in the founding years of the Commonwealth, that community standards, as well as market pressures, should determine people's well-being. With the resurgence of free-market ideology in the 1980s, wages were increasingly determined by the capacity of industry to pay, rather than the maintenance of workers' living standards. The poor came to depend increasingly upon a 'social wage' delivered through the welfare system. But the **ACTU's** 1996 claim for a 'living wage' sought to reverse this trend by demanding a 12-per-cent increase in the minimum wage. Returning to the principles first enunciated by Higgins, it proposed that, as well as food and shelter, a staple living standard in the late 1990s should include such items as a second-hand car, a telephone, a television, perhaps a video or second-hand computer, childcare, holidays, heating, and occasional visits to a restaurant or cinema. But in the 1990s governments no longer promised even a 'frugal' standard of living for all; just a safety-net for those who fell disastrously below it.

GRAEME DAVISON

Stanner, William Edward Hanley (1905–81) the slightly formal, 'naturally conservative', cricket-loving, academic, soldier, and administrator, and Bill Stanner the irrepressibly radical thinker with a common touch were two sides of the same person. It was his seriousness, the clarity and measured tone of his writings, and his respectability that enabled him to play an important role in Australian political life; it was his radicalism, his capacity to change with the times and to retain a youthful enthusiasm for life and justice that enabled his influence to be so positive. He worked his way through the University of Sydney in the late 1920s as a journalist. Under the influence of A.R. Radcliffe-Brown he became an anthropologist and eventually professor of anthropology at the Australian National University. He also spent many years in British and Australian government service and was an adviser on colonial administration in Africa and Borneo during the period of decolonisation, an experience which informed his work on the Council for Aboriginal Affairs, 1968–76.

Stanner's lifelong research was with the peoples of the Daly River region of the NT. By emphasising from the beginning the possibility of continuity through change, Stanner's anthropology was always relevant to the political context of the times. His writings on the Aboriginal concept of **Dreamtime** and his insights into Aboriginal religion through his own form of structural analysis were among his most important intellectual contributions. He played a major role in the Gove land rights case as a witness and in preparing the case for the Yirrkala community. From 1967 to 1976 with H.C. **Coombs** and Barrie Dexter he was a member of the Council for Aboriginal Affairs, which played a major role in changing government policy towards self-determination and in advancing land rights. His 1968 Boyer lectures helped break what he described as 'The Great Australian Silence'. A collection of his essays appeared in 1979 as *White Man Got No Dreaming*.

HOWARD MORPHY

Staple theory, an explanation of economic growth in new countries of European settlement, was first developed by the Canadian historian Harold Innis, refined by the Americans R.E. Baldwin and Douglas North, and introduced to Australian economic history by J.W. McCarty (*Business Archives and History*, 1964, and *AEHR*, 1973). The choice of a staple—a major export product—was crucial, not only to the pattern of economic development in a new region, but—said McCarty—to 'its social and even its political structure'. In Australia, **wool** and **wheat** became the main staples, and through 'backward' and 'forward linkages' to other industries, such as agricultural implement making and flour milling, they influenced the shape of the whole colonial economy. Staple theory enabled Australian historians to move beyond the simple export model of growth adopted by **Fitzpatrick** and **Shann** and it became an important building block in McCarty's broader interpretation of capital city and regional growth (*AEHR*, 1970) and the main organising principle of W.A. Sinclair's *The Process of Economic Development in Australia* (1976). Staple theory was a useful tool for explaining the structural features of an economy or region, but its capacity to explain the changes flowing from such apparently fortuitous events as mineral discoveries or technological breakthroughs was more limited. Rather than being overthrown, it has been absorbed into the interpretative tool-kits of many historians who may not even recognise its origins.

GD

State aid, see **Church and state**

State socialism was the preferred form of **socialism** of the **Australian Labor Party** and was adopted as the party's official objective in 1921. The term is also used to describe the extensive intervention by the state in the economy which long predated the Labor Party and owed nothing to socialism.

That the state played a strong role in the colonial economies had always been acknowledged, but the full extent of its operations was not revealed until Noel **Butlin** published his research based on estimates of the national accounts. His conclusions on the nineteenth century are usefully summarised in his chapter in H.G.J. Aitken (ed.), *The State and Economic Growth* (1959). His analysis of the interaction of the public and private sectors in the twentieth century occurs in *Government and Capitalism* (1982). Butlin used the term *colonial* rather than *state* socialism for this public intervention which attained such a scale between 1860 and 1900 that (in his words):

- government had been directly responsible for securing the inflow of half the total foreign capital imports
- government had accounted for approximately 40 per cent of total domestic capital formation, essentially in the areas of transport and communications
- government by 1900 owned approximately half the total fixed capital (excluding land) of Australia
- government by 1900 conducted the largest enterprises in the economy primarily in transport and communications and in water and sewerage, thereby absorbing approximately five per cent of the total workforce in the economy and generating some six per cent of gross domestic product.

This amazingly high degree of government involvement occurred in British colonies where *laissez-faire*, if not proclaimed with such vigour as in the mother country, had not been disavowed. The problem for historians has been to explain a phenomenon for which there seems to have been little ideological support. Charles **Pearson** went so far as to say that the colonists were often acting against their will. What constrained them? One suggestion has been that the great distances of Australia and the sparseness of population made **railways** (the largest of the state enterprises) uneconomic, leaving no alternative to state action. Butlin rightly rejects this view, pointing to the profitable operation of state railways until political pressure for lower freight rates was applied. In WA a private company built and ran the main railway from Perth to Albany in return for grants of large areas of land along its route, the standard form of private construction in the USA. Butlin considers that the state take-over of railways in the eastern colonies in the 1850s was to some extent fortuitous. Private companies had begun construction when their operations were thrown into disarray by the gold rushes, which led to huge increases in labour costs, and they had trouble raising extra capital. In these circumstances, to draw on the state's advantage of being able to raise overseas capital more cheaply was the way to guarantee that the lines would be built. It was an 'undoctrinaire', 'ad hoc' decision—terms along with 'pragmatic' that are often reached for in this case. Whatever it was, the decision was not innovative. Though private companies constructed railways in Britain, some governments did so in Europe, as they had done in the USA in the early nineteenth century. Furthermore, as Butlin acknowledges, the state was already omni-competent in the Australian colonies, supervising land settlement, sponsoring migrants, and constructing public works. Having taken responsibility for roads, it was in principle doing nothing more in becoming responsible for this new alternative. There were, in short, respectable precedents and local practice and tradition to guide and encourage these pragmatists, who needed guidance and encouragement as much as anyone else. Some writers have gone further and claimed that the 'pragmatism' had a theoretical underpinning in a Benthamite utilitarianism, which in Britain worked for the dismantling of an old state apparatus, but in Australia (as in Ireland and India) worked to create a new one.

The puzzle of the large colonial state lessens when it is realised that the aim of state activity was to facilitate private enterprise. As Keith **Hancock** notably proclaimed in *Australia* (1930): 'To the Australian, the state means collective power at the service of individualistic "rights".'

With the emergence of the Labor Party, state action had vigorous ideological support. Labor's opponents differentiated themselves as the protectors of free enterprise, but there was no slackening in state activity. In fact there was an extension: banks, irrigation schemes, and marketing boards for the further encouragement and protection of rural settlement; state trams in addition to state trains. Labor was far from being the sole initiator of these extensions—in Victoria where state socialism was most extensive, Labor was weakest—but where it was the initiator, its opponents did not undo its work.

Far more contentious was Labor's establishment in the states of manufacturing and retail businesses in direct competition with the private sector: brickworks, sawmills, hotels, butcher-shops, even tobacconists. These were vigorously opposed and constantly criticised by the non-Labor parties, which dismantled them when they returned to office. The only socialism Labor could effect was the extension of what had been established before its arrival: the operation of government business and services as monopolies in support of private development. In NSW the Labor government had developed plans in the early 1900s for the operation of a government steel industry, but it dropped these in favour of facilitating the establishment by **BHP** of steelworks at Newcastle.

At the Commonwealth level, Labor's aim of nationalising private corporations was blocked by the federal Constitution or, more particularly, its interpretation by the High Court. In 1911 and 1913 Labor sponsored referendums to give the Commonwealth power to nationalise monopolies, but they were defeated. The **Chifley** government's nationalisation of the banks and the airlines were declared unconstitutional by the court after World War II. The Labor Party had to be satisfied with government enterprises competing with private: the Commonwealth Bank (established in 1911 by the **Fisher** Labor government) and Trans Australian Airlines (established in 1945, later renamed Australian and then amalgamated with **Qantas**). These bodies were revered by Labor people; the socialists among them saw them as only the first step to a transformation of the economy, but all were delighted with the demonstration that businesses could operate efficiently without the motive of private profit. This was a better record than the state railways, which did not have the spur of competition.

In the first three decades of the twentieth century the proportion of public sector investment remained as high as in the nineteenth century and sometimes exceeded that level. With the **Depression** of the 1930s a long-term decline began. So much had been borrowed without securing an economic return that governments thereafter became more cautious. By this time, the railways, which had been the chief absorber of capital, were being supplanted by road transport; governments had to provide the roads, but the private sector provided the vehicles.

In the midst of the Depression, state socialism was subjected to a searching critique by Frederic **Eggleston**, an intellectual who had served briefly as a Victorian Cabinet minister. He published *State Socialism in Victoria* (1932) to warn of its perils, for he saw that progressive opinion in the English-speaking world was still enamoured of state action. Victoria had tried state action on a large scale—'the largest and most comprehensive use of state power outside Russia'—and the world would be foolish to ignore the results. Eggleston concluded that managers of state enterprises were competent, efficient, even outstanding; what undermined their labours were political pressures from the customers/citizens. Farmers wanted lower rail freights or lower irrigation charges or lower repayments on their land purchase. Politicians had attempted to shield the enterprises from these dangers by placing them under independent boards, beginning with the Railways Commissioners in 1883. But none of these bastions was proof against political interference; indeed, citizens could see no point in having these enterprises if they were not subject to their will. The Labor Party was always interested in making the state enterprises pace-setters in wages and conditions of work.

Eggleston had no principled objection to state action. It had to be tested by results and in Victoria these were: protection of inefficient producers; the misallocation of resources; a drain on state finances; and the corruption of the citizenry. He recommended the sale of state businesses or contracting out of their operations in order to liberate society's 'constructive and progressive qualities'. Hancock relied heavily on Eggleston, for his chapter on state socialism in *Australia* shared his concerns, but thought him too severe on state enterprise which had clearly been beneficial.

Eggleston's book was against the spirit of the age; the rest of the free world did move to a larger public sector and state planning (which he had also opposed). No longer was Australia distinctive; it was just one of the mixed economies and far from possessing the largest public sector. It was only in the 1980s that the English-speaking world was ready to listen to Eggleston's message, though now it came from ideologues committed against state action. In Australia governments of all persuasions sold off and contracted out. The federal Labor government sold the Commonwealth Bank and Qantas. The Liberal government in the 1990s aimed to sell Telstra, but because of growing misgivings about privatisation had to be content with a partial sale.

JOHN HIRST

Statistics, see Historical statistics

Statute of Westminster was an act of the British parliament in 1931 which declared that the self-governing Dominions of the Empire were fully independent states, free from any British control, and able to form their own defence and foreign policies. Britain and the Dominions were, in the words adopted at the 1926 Imperial Conference, 'autonomous communities within the British Empire, equal in status, in no way subordinate one to another in any aspect of their domestic or external affairs, though united by a common allegiance to the Crown'. The claim to independence had been made by South Africa, Canada, and the Irish Free State. Australia, keen to have British support in defence, was wary of these moves and arranged that the statute was not to apply to Australia until it chose to adopt it. Australia did not do so until 1942. The delay in accepting the grant of freedom makes it difficult to determine when Australia did become an independent state. This matter is explored in *Australian Independence: Colony to Reluctant Kingdom* (1988) by W.J. Hudson and M.P. Sharp. (See also **Constitutional history**.)

JH

Stead, Christina Ellen (1902–83) novelist, was born in Sydney, the only child of David Stead, a naturalist, conservationist, and socialist, and his first wife, Ellen Butters, who died when Christina was aged two. At five she acquired her first stepmother, and subsequently a step-family. Her first collection of stories, *The Salzburg Tales*, was published in 1934. Of 14 subsequent volumes of fiction, two novels, *Seven Poor Men of Sydney* (1934) and *For Love Alone* (1944), were based loosely on the life of the Stead family at Watsons Bay and Sydney itself, with characters drawn from family acquaintances, Christina's time at Sydney Teachers College and as an office-worker saving desperately to see the world and find love. A third novel, *The Man Who Loved Children* (1940), though set in Baltimore (USA), was drawn largely from Stead family life. In 1928 she left Australia, and thereafter lived a wandering life with an urbane Jewish Marxist writer and banker, William Blake (Blech), whom she met in London. Most of her other novels arose from their work and travel in Europe, the USA, and England. After Blake's death in 1968 she returned to Australia for the first time since 1928, settling permanently in 1974.

Australia was reluctant to recognise her writing. An expatriate with Stalinist politics and an experimental approach to writing was not easily accommodated during the Cold War years. American critics began to rediscover her in the late 1960s, though she was rejected for a Britannica–Australia award in 1967 because she was no longer an Australian citizen. In 1974, however, she received a Patrick White award. Ron Geering's critical studies of her work and his edition of her letters, a film of *For Love Alone*, and a biography by Hazel Rowley in 1993 have since helped to make her accessible to a more receptive readership.

BEVERLEY KINGSTON

Stephen family were influential in the development of the colonial legal structure. ALFRED STEPHEN (1802–94), chief justice and legislator, was the principal draftsman of much civil and criminal law during his time as chief justice of NSW (1844–73). He arrived in Hobart in 1825 with a recommendation from his uncle to Governor **Arthur**, who soon appointed Stephen solicitor-general. He was instrumental in reform of the land grant system, and became attorney-general before in 1839 accepting a judgeship in Sydney, where he later became chief justice. An advocate of an upper house in NSW, Stephen accepted a position on the new Legislative Council and in two years (1856–58) introduced 14 law reform bills. After his retirement from the law he was again nominated to the Legislative Council. He was also active in philanthropic causes. JAMES WILBERFORCE (1822–81) persuaded his father GEORGE (1794–1879) to migrate to Victoria with him in 1855. They were both admitted to the Bar; George became a QC in 1871. James taught the new law course at the University of Melbourne, where he was later a member of council. He was elected to the Legislative Assembly in 1866 and became attorney-general six years later. After seeing through the **education** bill, he became the first minister of public instruction in 1873; he oversaw implementation of the legislation until his 1874 resignation, upon his appointment to the Supreme Court. MATTHEW HENRY (1828–1920), son of Alfred, was admitted to the Bar in 1850 and established a successful practice before his 1869 election to the Legislative Assembly. In 1887 he became a judge in the Supreme Court, where he remained for 17 years. He is remembered for a gaffe in a horse-stealing case when he asked that 'Mr Brumby' be called—the genesis of Banjo **Paterson's** ballad 'Brumby's Run'.

MONTAGU CONSETT (1827–72) and SEPTIMUS ALFRED (1842–1901), second and seventh sons of Alfred, also followed in the family tradition of entering the NSW legislature after establishing successful legal careers. Septimus's son COLIN CAMPBELL (1872–1937) joined the family firm of Stephen, Jacques & Stephen in 1896. He was a keen amateur jockey and horse breeder who used his time as chairman of the Australian Jockey Club to revise the rules of racing—revisions that were later adopted nationally.

KT

Stephens, Alfred George (1865–1933) exercised considerable influence on Australian writing between 1894 and 1906 through the ***Bulletin***, where he combined the roles of editor of the Red Page (the literary section to which the inside front cover was devoted) and publications manager of the Bulletin Library.

Vance **Palmer**, whose own perspective on Australian literature owed much to Stephens, saw him as giving the *Bulletin* 'a literary centre'. By the 1890s the Sydney weekly, under **Archibald's** editorship, was encouraging local writers; in reviews and articles, Stephens identified the beginnings of a 'national school' of writing. His tendency to pontificate about writing that was 'Australian in spirit' may have merited Victor Daley's satirical characterisation of him: 'I am the Blender of the pure / Australian Brand of Literature', but it was very much in keeping with the whole *Bulletin* enterprise.

Despite his prescriptively nationalistic attitude, and his commitment to the notion that 'the **bush** is the heart of Australia', Stephens himself was cosmopolitan in his literary tastes. Given a free hand in running the Red Page, he ranged widely over recent English and foreign writing. With the scholar–poet, Christopher **Brennan**, a most atypical *Bulletin* contributor, whom he admired and encouraged, he shared an enthusiasm for the French Symbolist poets.

Stephens is perhaps best seen as a performer in 'the Great Print Circus', as Sylvia Lawson describes the *Bulletin* (in *The Archibald Paradox*, 1983). Born in Toowoomba, Qld, he was the eldest of the 13 children of a Welsh storekeeper and his Scottish wife. Although he served a double apprenticeship in printing, he chose to make a career in journalism and within a few years his talent was widely recognised. With his quick intelligence, readiness to question established attitudes, breadth of reading, and terse, salty, epigrammatic style, he was a star performer, and under his direction the Red Page was the outstanding literary column in Australia.

Stephens, however, was restless, dissatisfied, and erratic, even at the height of his success. So far only Valerie Lawson—in her biography of his daughter, *Connie Sweetheart* (1990)—has revealed the insecure and troubled personality behind the confident and urbane persona of 'The Bookfellow', as Stephens presented himself in the pages of the *Bulletin*. In his later years, as he struggled to earn a living as a writer, publisher, and literary agent, and to build upon the reputation he had made on the Red Page, he persisted to the point of obsession in his attempts to edit and publish his own literary periodical. The *Bookfellow* had a chequered existence, and never exerted an influence comparable to that of the Red Page.

As critic and editor, Stephens showed a partiality for minor lyricists, like Daley and Quinn, and allowed personal feelings to cloud his judgment on occasions. However, two of his judgments which would have seemed extravagant when they were made—that **Furphy's** *Such Is Life* (which he published in the Bulletin Library) was 'fitted to become an Australian classic or semi-classic', and that John Shaw **Neilson** (whom he edited and published) was 'First among Australian poets'—now stand as testimony to his powers of discernment.

John Barnes

Stephensen, Percy Reginald (1901–65), also known as 'P.R.' or 'Inky', was an influential writer, editor, publisher, critic, and promoter of Australian writing. Following his early education in Qld, he went to Oxford in 1924 as a Rhodes scholar, where he was threatened with expulsion for his communist activities. After several years working in publishing in London with Jack **Lindsay**, Stephensen returned to Australia and worked at the Endeavour Press until he established his own firm. Authors he published

before the press went into liquidation in 1935 included Eleanor **Dark** and Henry Handel **Richardson**. In 1936 Stephensen published his call for a distinctive Australian culture, *The Foundations of Culture in Australia*. His increasingly isolationist, anti-Semitic and pro-fascist attitudes were reflected in his work for the right-wing journal, the *Publicist*. In 1941 he helped found the **Australia First Movement**, for which he and other members were later interned and not released until late 1945.

Stephensen was a prolific writer, sometimes in his own name, sometimes as a co-writer or ghost writer. He helped Xavier **Herbert** revise *Capricornia* (1938), and began a long collaboration with Frank **Clune** in the mid-1930s. His later work included books on the history of the sea around Sydney, a memoir of his time in London, and *Kookaburras and Satyrs* (1954). Craig Munro has written an extensive biography, reprinted in 1992 as *Inky Stephensen: Wild Man of Letters*.

KT

Sterling, recorded as early as 1827, was a term that denoted a free settler in NSW, who, like the self-styled *pure merinos*, assumed an upper-class rank in the predominantly 'lower-class' society of penal NSW, but relied considerably on social pretension and self-conceit to do so. Sterling were typically English-born, of modest capital, and occupied as landowners, politicians, magistrates, and other professionals. Derived in the same manner as the plebian counterpart *currency*, *sterling* was a reference to the form of money in circulation in NSW. Whereas *currency*, or lower-value colonial coins, alluded to the Australian-born and the children of convicts and emancipists, *sterling* referred to the more valuable British money, and so became a synonym for the free, generally wealthier British immigrant.

HD

Stevens, Bertram Sydney Barnsdale (1889–1973), premier, was a NSW public servant who entered parliament as a Nationalist MLA in 1927. He became state leader of the **United Australia Party** in 1932, won the election that followed the dismissal of Jack **Lang**, and led the UAP into government. While Stevens implemented many economies of the Premiers' Plan as a response to the **Depression**, his knife did not cut deep enough for many business leaders. He held power through a firm alliance with the Country Party (**National Party**) and ruthless treatment of his own party rivals. In 1939 his critics defeated him in a parliamentary vote.

KT

Stewart, Douglas Alexander (1913–85), editor and poet, came to Australia from NZ in 1938 to work on the *Bulletin*. In 1940 he became editor of the literary section of the magazine, the Red Page. His 20 years in that position and subsequent work as editor for the publishers Angus & Robertson gave him considerable influence, and he was generous in his encouragement of young writers. Stewart's lyrical poems and ballads expressed his love of landscape. He published historical **drama** in verse on Ned **Kelly**, on the wreck of the *Batavia*, and on Robert Scott's fatal expedition to the South Pole. He was also important to the collection and appreciation of bush ballads. His *Springtime in Taranaki* (1983) is an account of his youth in NZ; *Douglas Stewart's Garden of Friends* (1987) consists largely of extracts from his diaries, which discuss other writers.

KT

Stewart, Eleanor Towzey 'Nellie' (1858–1931), actor and singer, made her stage debut aged 3 in *The Stranger* at Melbourne's Haymarket Theatre. Born into a theatrical Sydney family, she trained in ballet and singing, and obtained minor *opéra-bouffe* roles before touring Australia and overseas in *Rainbow Revels* (1877–79). George Coppin recalled her to Melbourne's Theatre Royal, where as principal boy in the pantomime *Sinbad the Sailor* (1880) she became a star. Specialising in comic opera from 1881, her autobiography *My Life's Story* (1923) notes she was prima donna in 18 comic operas and two pantomimes between 1884 and 1887. She played Yum Yum in *The Mikado* at the 1886 opening of Melbourne's Princess Theatre, and sang the ode 'Australia' at the first federal parliament's celebratory concert in 1901. Her soprano voice deteriorated early, perhaps from overwork—as Marguerite in *Faust*, she once performed 24 consecutive nights. After playing Nell Gwynne in the Melbourne premiere of *Sweet Nell of Old Drury* (1902), she became identified with the role, touring every state as well as NZ and the USA, where critics admired her freshness, facial expression, well-modulated speech, and dancing talent. She appeared in Raymond **Longford's** film version in 1911, and afterwards concentrated on charitable appearances, teaching, and following her actor daughter Nancye, who was fathered in 1893 by her manager and companion, George Musgrove. An 1884 marriage to Richard Row ('a girl's mad act') lasted two weeks.

DC

Stirling, James (1791–1865), first governor of WA, joined the Royal Navy as a boy of 12 and was promoted through officer ranks. As captain of the *Success*, he sailed for NSW in 1827 and later explored the continent's west coast, where he became convinced of its suitability for colonisation. In London, Stirling—related by marriage to a director of the East India Company—attracted investors and eventually won British government support for his plans. He sailed with wife Ellen and family on the *Parmelia*, and on 18 June 1829, the new colony was proclaimed. Stirling ruled as lieutenant-governor at first, and as full governor from 1831. With a grant of 100 000 acres from the Crown, his own fortunes were inextricably entwined with those of his settlers. In 1834 he personally led a bloody raid against a Nyungar group near **Pinjarra**, which left 15–30 people dead. The once-popular governor suffered increasing criticism for his imperious and autocratic administration. Frustrated by the apparent lack of progress, he resigned his post and sailed from Fremantle in 1839, never to return. He resumed his naval career and, after long and distinguished service, was made an admiral. Stirling retired to Guildford, in Surrey, England, where he died.

MATHEW TRINCA

Stolen Generations was Peter Read's title for a 1981 study of NSW government removal of 5625 Aboriginal children from their families between 1883 and 1969. Those removed became more visible in the 1990s, after the 1991 Report of the Commonwealth Royal Commission into Aboriginal Deaths in Custody highlighted the pervasive psychological morbidity of indigenous Australians. From 1995 to 1997, the Human Rights and Equal Opportunity Commission reviewed all governments' 'separation' programs. Its report, *Bringing Them Home* (1997), found that indigenous children had been forcibly separated from their parents since Europeans first colonised Australia. From 1910 to 1970, between one-tenth and one-third of Australia's Aboriginal children were so treated. Testimonies from 535 indigenous people who had experienced removal revealed that many children, after separation, suffered physical (including sexual) and mental abuse.

By 1997 the phrase *Stolen Generations* evoked the increasingly public grief and pain of Aboriginal Australians. Narrating their life stories as members of the Stolen Generation, individuals positioned themselves—tragically, honourably, and pathetically—within a new story of national **'genocide'**. However, the conflicting non-Aboriginal responses to this shaming account of Australia made the senses of both 'stolen' and 'generations' subject to dispute.

Bringing Them Home recommended a politics of collective memory: maintenance of archives, further historical inquiry, and disseminating that history through curricula, monuments, and days of commemoration. The inquiry's chair, Sir Ronald Wilson, later explained that he had not been obliged 'to identify offenders for prosecution or as possible respondents to civil litigation'. He hoped that this had enabled the process of storytelling to be the beginning of a healing process. It worried some critics that Wilson had not tested the truth of testimonies, or explored the intentions, methods, and rationales of 'genocidal' authority with due sensitivity to their moral and factual complexities.

In recent litigation by the Stolen Generations, the intertwined stories of governments and the people they removed have been subjected to public cross-examination. In July 1997, the High Court rejected Alec Kruger's claim that the laws under which he had been taken were unconstitutional. In 1999, Joy Williams did not persuade the New South Wales Supreme Court that Aboriginal Welfare Board officials had breached their duty of care for her as the state's 'ward', nor could Lorna Cubillo and Peter Gunner prove before the Federal Court of Australia that their removal and mistreatment had been an unlawful exercise of Commonwealth power.

Adversarial processes, pitting the Stolen Generations' 'healing' testimonies against official defensiveness and judicial literalness, have weakened the emergence of the moral order implied by Peter Read's words: 'Perhaps in time the whites will suffer in the knowledge of what they have done. But they cannot expect forgiveness'.

TIM ROWSE

Stone, Louis (1871–1935), schoolteacher and writer, was the creator of the novel *Jonah*, a notable experiment in Australian urban fiction. Born in Leicester, England, Stone emigrated with his parents in 1884, grew up in the inner Sydney suburbs of Redfern and Waterloo, and trained as a pupil-teacher at the Waterloo School from the late 1880s. After a brief period in the country, Stone returned to Sydney, where he continued as a teacher at inner-city schools until his retirement in 1931. *Jonah*, which he began writing around 1908, was modelled on the slum fiction of late Victorian London, especially Frank Morrison's *A Child of the Jago*, but drew upon Stone's own detailed observations of inner Sydney life. It reflects, in its tone and themes, the growing anxiety of progressive intellectuals about the physical and moral destiny of urban youth. Stone's schoolteacher's interest in language comes through in the dialogue, with its careful rendition of larrikin vocabulary and speech patterns. Published in London in 1911, *Jonah* had a tepid Australian reception; Stone's later attempts to write for the theatre enjoyed little success. Late in life, his reputation began to rise; a brief critical and biographical study by H.J. Oliver appeared in 1968.

GD

Street, Jessie Mary Grey (1889–1970) was a leading feminist campaigner and pro-Aboriginal activist. She was born into the Livingstone family in India, where her father worked in the Indian Civil Service. In 1896, the family moved to NSW, to the pastoral station Yulgilbar, on the Clarence River, which had been inherited by her mother. Street enrolled at the University of Sydney, where she met her future husband Kenneth Street, who was studying law. She graduated with an arts degree in 1910. Although they had four children, her family's relative wealth enabled Street to devote herself and her resources to political work on behalf of women. In 1918 she joined the League of Nations Union; in 1920 she became secretary to the **National Council of Women**. She then joined the Sydney Feminist Club in 1929 but, wanting greater political reach, Street helped form the United Associations of Women, an amalgamation of three earlier women's groups.

Perhaps because she herself enjoyed economic independence, Street was insistent on its importance for all women, for mothers and wives as well as women in the workforce. In pamphlets, public speaking, and radio broadcasts, she publicised numerous schemes to win 'the economic independence of the married woman', ranging from a legal requirement that husbands share their wages with their wives, and schemes for child and motherhood endowment, to a proposal that women be legally entitled to household savings. Mothers as citizens, she argued, should be paid for their service to the state. At the royal commission established in 1927 to inquire into the feasibility of introducing motherhood and **child**

endowment, Street incurred Labor men's wrath by suggesting that the very large number of single men who received a breadwinner's wage on 'false pretences' were likely to waste the money on drinking and gambling.

Street's fearless opposition to male privilege together with her own privileged background often strained her relations with men and women in the labour movement, but by World War II she had joined the **Australian Labor Party**, standing (unsuccessfully) as an endorsed candidate for the House of Representatives in the 1943 and 1946 elections. She moved increasingly to the left in her support for the Soviet Union and involvement in the Sheepskins for Russia campaign. By the early 1950s, in the context of the Cold War, Street and the United Association of Women were increasingly criticised as **communist** sympathisers, attacks which influenced her decision to live abroad for six years. An ardent idealist, Street focused much of her energy on preparing for a new postwar social order in which men and women would be equal participants. She organised national conferences in 1943 and 1946 that formulated the Australian Women's Charter, and she championed the United Nations Commission on the Status of Women. Her autobiography, *Truth or Repose* (1966), emphasises these commitments.

While overseas in the 1950s, Jessie Street became increasingly involved in demands for justice for Aboriginal people, and she reactivated the campaign to make Aboriginal welfare a national and federal responsibility. She was present at the meeting in 1958 in Sydney which brought together Aboriginal and non-Aboriginal activists on the Federal Council for Aboriginal Advancement (later the Federal Council for the Advancement of Aborigines and Torres Strait Islanders).

In his 1978 biography, *Jessie Street*, Peter Sekuless calls her involvement in the cause of Aboriginal advancement her 'crowning achievement'. This assessment has been corroborated. It calls into question the charge elaborated in Kay Saunders and Raymond Evans (eds), *Gender Relations in Australia* (1992), that white Australian feminists did not usually express 'gender affinity' with women from other races. Her activities, on the contrary, were the culmination of a long tradition of feminist anti-racist politics in Australia begun in the 1920s.

An important collection, *Jessie Street: Documents and Essays* (1990), edited by Heather Radi, demonstrated the range and generosity of Street's commitments.

MARILYN LAKE

Streeton, Arthur 'Smike' (1867–1943) was an artist who created a romantic vision of a sunlit pastoral landscape which has had enduring appeal for Australian audiences. He was born in Victoria and attended night classes at the National Gallery while apprenticed to a lithographer. He was an original member of the **Heidelberg School** of artists who, in the late 1880s, painted in the open air in the suburban bush surrounding Melbourne.

After he moved to Sydney in the early 1890s, Streeton painted some memorable interpretations of a heroic pastoral landscape in his Hawkesbury River series (1896). In pictures such as *The Purple Noon's Transparent Might* (1896), the blue and gold palette and the panoramic view are employed with subtlety, tempered by the artist's close observation of the scene. This proved to be a convenient formula, repeated frequently in his landscapes of the period between the two world wars. Streeton also utilised the panoramic convention in his portrayal of Sydney Harbour, emphasising its light-filled atmosphere and deep blue expanses of water and sky. Critics and writers have long recognised that such an ability to establish his own 'patent' to certain artistic subjects was instrumental in Streeton's popular success. Encouraged by the National Gallery of Victoria's purchase of *The Purple Noon's Transparent Might*, he sailed for England in 1897, intent upon winning a reputation as an artist in the heart of the Empire.

He struggled to succeed financially and artistically, and on his first return trip to Australia in 1907, he discovered where his real market and reputation lay. After serving as an official war artist in 1918, Streeton finally returned to Australia in 1923. By this time he was already considered 'something of a national institution'. He represented the strongest link with the earlier Heidelberg era, which was seen to mark the 'beginning' of an Australian school of landscape painting. William Moore duly accorded Streeton the accolade of being the founder of the school in his pioneering study, *The Story of Australian Art* (1934). Streeton himself did much to foster this interpretation by contributing his reminiscences to newspapers and by publishing *The Arthur Streeton Catalogue* in 1935. While there were private mutterings that Streeton's interwar landscapes reeked of commercialism and a slick, meretricious technique, few critics were prepared to state this publicly. Instead, most writers interpreted them as evidence of the distillation of his ideas and mastery of his craft.

Bernard **Smith**, in *Place, Taste and Tradition* (1945), was the first to be critical, characterising them as 'a national vice' which supported a conservative, isolationist nationalism. Towards the end of his life, Streeton affected a magisterial indifference towards both the Establishment and art politics in general, refusing to join the conservative Australian Academy of Art, founded by **Menzies** in 1937.

Christopher Wray's *Arthur Streeton: Painter of Light* (1993), is the first full-scale biography. Measured and even-handed, it addresses hitherto neglected areas of Streeton's art—the war paintings and the late landscapes which reveal an environmental concern—while tracing the artist's passage from young visionary, fond of quoting Keats and Shelley, to hard-headed businessman.

Leigh Astbury

Strehlow, Carl Friedrich (1871–1922), and his youngest son, **Theodor George Henry 'Ted'** (1908–78), between them documented the most complete picture of Aranda (Arrernte) culture ever recorded. Carl, born in Fredersdorf, Germany, was the Lutheran missionary at Hermannsburg in Central Australia from 1894 until his death in 1922. Early in the twentieth century he began writing a major cultural study of the Arrernte and Luritja people—*Die Aranda- und Loritja-Stämme in Zentral Australien*—

which was published in seven volumes in Germany between 1907 and 1920. Although his findings were accepted by his European contemporaries such as Durkheim, Freud, Malinowski and Roheim, controversy arose as a result of an attack by Baldwin **Spencer** (then director of the National Museum of Victoria) on Strehlow's overall approach. The differences were between the Christian linguist Strehlow, and the empirical scientist Spencer, and were a part of what **Mulvaney** and Calaby in *'So Much That Is New'* (1985) described as 'an international debate over religious origins'. As a result of this controversy, but more substantially because of the fact that his work was published in German, Strehlow's study fell into anthropological literature's 'great silence'. Ted Strehlow re-established its importance in his *Journey to Horseshoe Bend* (1969), and *Songs of Central Australia* (1971). Carl Strehlow's other works concentrated on Arrernte translation material such as a teaching book, a school primer, and a largely unpublished translation of parts of the New Testament.

Ted was educated at Hermannsburg by his father until he was 14. The holder of a personal chair at the University of Adelaide, he was the author of hundreds of books, articles, reviews, addresses, and lectures. His work was initially linguistic rather than anthropological, and despite the fact that anthropologists and linguists still cite his publications, much of his material has been unfairly relegated to the periphery of discussions of Aboriginal culture. His *Aranda Phonetics and Grammar* (1944) was the first published complete study of an Aboriginal language. Ronald **Berndt** regarded his *Aranda Traditions* (1947) as a classic work. It was Strehlow's linguistic, or rather literary, talents—revealed in his *Songs of Central Australia* (1971)—which prompted Berndt in his 1972 review to recognise 'a poetic quality … which seeps through from the original'. It received acclaim from those who recognised that, largely due to the strengths of its comparative perspective, such a work could never be duplicated.

Controversy was never far from Ted Strehlow, especially in the latter half of his life, when he spent much of his time arguing publicly and vociferously with academic colleagues and the then Institute of Aboriginal Studies. He was allegedly rebuked by Aboriginal men at Hermannsburg in 1977 because of persistent rumours that he was revealing men's secret information to women. In early 1978 he again aroused criticism when ceremonial photographs that he had taken, and allowed to be used in an article in the German magazine *Stern*, appeared in Australia. The protracted dispute after his death over the ownership and disposition of his personal papers, research materials, and Aboriginal artefacts extended the controversy. Ward McNally's *Aborigines, Artefacts and Anguish* (1981) remains to date the only published biography, but it is inaccurate and does little to shed light on the complex nature of the man or his work in Central Australia.

Through the work of Carl and Ted Strehlow, much of the culture of the Aboriginal people of Central Australia, which would have been lost, has survived. Ted's expressed desire during his lifetime to have his and his father's work (amassed over 85 years) take a prominent place in discussions of Central Australian Aboriginal culture led eventually to the establishment of the Strehlow Research Centre in Alice Springs in 1991.

DAVID HUGO

Stretton, Hugh (1924–) is the author of the most influential book written on Australian **town planning**, *Ideas for Australian Cities* (1970), and a social-democratic theorist of international importance. Stretton's outlook, a distinctive blend of the egalitarian and the patrician, is an amalgam of several influences, especially his family and his education. His father Leonard Stretton was a humane judge and author of a brilliant report on the 1939 bushfires. Hugh attended Scotch College (Melbourne), University of Melbourne, and Balliol College Oxford, where he became a Fellow and began his studies of social philosophy. Another influence was the transition from Attlee's Britain to **Menzies's** Australia, where he began to formulate his ideas. He became professor of history at Adelaide in 1954, but stepped down to a readership in 1968 to make more time for writing. Stretton's abiding concern is the moral and political basis of public policy. *The Political Sciences* (1969) challenges the ideal of social scientific neutrality in the name of a moralising social science. *Ideas for Australian Cities* (1970), 'an amateur book' first published by the author, became a best-seller and the unofficial manifesto of the **Whitlam** government's urban reforms. Australians were sensible to like **suburbs**, and to want to own their own houses, he argued, but those benefits needed to be spread more widely and evenly. Here, as in his other writings—such as *Housing and Government* (1974), *Capitalism, Socialism and the Environment* (1976), *Political Essays* (1987), and *Public Goods, Public Enterprise, Public Choice* (1994)—Stretton is a lucid, persuasive defender of state instrumentalities, such as the South Australian Housing Trust, of which he was a long-serving deputy chairman. Lionel Orchard and Robert Dare (eds), *Markets, Morals and Public Policy* (1989), contains a bibliography and assessments of his writings.

GD

Strikes and lockouts are a recurrent feature of **industrial relations**. Strikes have occurred when groups of workers have withdrawn their labour from employers in pursuit of better pay or conditions, or as the result of a grievance. As unions expanded their reach and membership, so the scale of strikes increased. Lockouts of workers have been less common because employers have usually been able to alter pay and conditions without recourse to such action; but they increased after the introduction of **arbitration** as a mean of circumventing an award.

The history of nineteenth-century strikes and lockouts has suffered from neglect, but the detailed research of Michael Quinlan suggests a high frequency, usually local and short-lived. His article in *Labour and Industry* (1987) provides a sample of his large database. The NSW coalmines were particularly prone to both strikes and lockouts (described by Robin **Gollan**, *The Coalminers of New South Wales*, 1963) because of the formal bargaining procedure in a vital industry. In other occupations the attempt to organise a previously non-unionised workforce often precipitated conflict, as in the Melbourne tailoresses' strike of 1882 (Raymond Brooks in *LH*, 1983).

The **Maritime Strike** of 1890 was unprecedented in scope and duration. It drew in miners, **shearers**, and other workers; paralysed trade and industry across most of Australia and NZ; and was defeated by the actions of special police and troops as well as criminal prosecutions. From this turmoil emerged the system of industrial conciliation and arbitration that was meant to secure industrial peace. The efficacy of the device is difficult to test: comparisons with other countries are complicated by differences in the collection of statistics, but studies suggest that while Australia's twentieth-century record is of relatively frequent industrial disputation, the stoppages were usually brief: many stoppages were intended to bring a dispute to early settlement by an industrial tribunal.

Major strikes and lockouts occurred in the early years of the century in an initial trial of strength as new unions were formed. The Victorian railways (1903), the Broken Hill mines (1908–09), the NSW coalmines (1909), the Queensland sugar mills (1911), and the Brisbane tramways (1912) were sites of particular conflict; the first two are treated in John Iremonger et al. (eds), *Strikes* (1973); the last two in D.J. Murphy (ed.), *The Big Strikes* (1983). They were overshadowed by the NSW rail strike of 1917, which again took on the dimensions of a general strike, and a further wave of disputes in mining and maritime transport at the end of World War I.

The principal interwar confrontations came with the downturn of the economy at the end of the 1920s. Waterside workers in several ports struck against a new award from 1928 to 1929; timberworkers responded similarly in 1929; and the coalminers were locked out from 1929 to 1930 for their refusal to accept pay cuts. These were epic confrontations that largely broke union resistance during the **Depression**. With the recovery, a new generation of largely **communist** union officials in key industries—transport, mining, iron and steel, building and construction—organised strikes to regain lost ground. Over the following decade these unionists transformed insecure, poorly paid, and unsafe occupations. They were frequently condemned as strike-happy wreckers; in fact they abandoned the older strategy of indefinite stoppage for calculated militancy in pursuit of carefully formulated objectives. The most important of the strikes after World War II, that of the coalminers in 1949, is interpreted by Tom Sheridan, *Division of Labor* (1989), as a miscalculation on their and the Labor government's part.

From the 1960s, strikes among traditionally militant manual workers declined, and those in new key industries such as electricity and communications increased. Professions such as teachers, nurses, and, in 1989, airline pilots, adopted a practice that had hitherto been unthinkable—though as early as 1923 the Victorian police had discovered its hazards when they struck unsuccessfully and suffered victimisation (see **Police Strike**). The political strike, designed to secure a non-industrial demand, also has a long history that includes the refusal to load pig-iron to Japan in 1938, the strike to release the tramworkers' leader Clarrie O'Shea in 1969, and the **green bans** of the 1970s. Strikes among Aboriginal pastoral workers in the **Pilbara** region of WA in the 1940s and at Wave Hill station, NT, in 1966 were more concerned with reclaiming traditional ways than with wage rises. The unsuccessful dismissal of members of the Maritime Workers Union from the wharves in 1998 was actively encouraged by the Commonwealth government, as Helen Trinca and Anne Davies show in *Waterfront* (2000).

Strikes have been studied extensively by **labour historians**, both for the information they provide about working conditions and the forms of occupational and communal solidarity they evoke. They lend themselves to dramatic narrative, and particular incidents—the ritual funeral for scabs at Broken Hill; the chaining of the coalminers' leader, Peter Bowling; the burning of strike ballots by the timberworkers; the shooting of a coalminer at **Rothbury** in 1929—have entered into labour mythology. Among novels based on strikes are those by William **Lane**, Jean **Devanny**, Vance **Palmer**, Frank **Hardy**, Betty Collins, and Barry Hill. The film *Strikebound* (1984) dramatised a stay-down action at a coalmine near Wonthaggi in 1937; *Sunday Too Far Away* (1975) recalls a shearers' strike in 1954.

STUART MACINTYRE

Strine is a satiric creation of a form of spoken Australian English that results from lazy pronunciation, and characterised by dropped consonants, vowels, and syllables, and transliteration; typical examples are *owyergoin* and *orright*. The term was coined by Alastair Morrison in an article in the *Sydney Morning Herald*, 'New Light on the Strine Language', written under the pseudonym Afferbeck Lauder, Professor of Strine Studies, University of Sinny, and followed up with *Let Stalk Strine* (1965) and *Nose Tone Unturned* (1966).

HD

Stripper was an **invention** for the harvesting of **wheat** that was developed in SA in 1843. Its novelty was that only the heads were removed; other harvesting machines in Britain and the USA mimicked hand harvesting in removing stalk and head. The machine was pushed into the crop by horses harnessed behind it; a comb separated the stalks, and rotating wooden beaters took off the heads and carried them into a box. When the box was full, its contents were shovelled out onto a tarpaulin and then put through a hand-driven winnowing machine. Its successful operation depended on hot, dry conditions so that the heads would snap off the stalks. It was used extensively in SA and in Victoria, but only to the north of the Great Dividing Range. The stripper was superseded by **McKay's** harvester, which placed a winnower within a stripper so that the harvesting was completed in one operation. Two men are claimed as the inventor of the stripper: J.W. Bull, who first had the idea, displayed in an Adelaide competition for a harvester; and John Ridley, who manufactured the first effective machine.

JH

Strong, Charles (1844–1942), born and educated in Scotland, was the Presbyterian minister appointed to Melbourne's Scots Church in 1875. Formally charged with heresy because of his liberal theological views, he resigned and returned to Scotland. However, in 1884 he returned to Melbourne and founded the Australian Church, through which he espoused his vision of a loving rather than a punitive God. Strong's commitment to social justice and peace found expression in his work on the Council of the Working Men's College, and in his anti-**conscription** stand in 1917 as well as in the social mission of his church. His published works include *Christianity Reinterpreted and Other Sermons* (1894). The Australian Church was dissolved in 1957. Colin Badger wrote *The Reverend Charles Strong and the Australian Church* (1971).

KT

Strutt, William (1825–1915), artist, left his career in Europe as a book illustrator in the hope that colonial life would restore his health. He arrived in Melbourne in 1850 and almost immediately had work published in the *Illustrated Australian Magazine*. His interest in the history of the colony was fostered by John Pascoe **Fawkner**, who acted as a mentor and encouraged him to depict events in the developing colony. Strutt also maintained a detailed journal, of which the entries for 1850–62 were edited and published by George **Mackaness** in 1958. His portraits include notables, such as Fawkner and Robert O'Hara **Burke**, as well as his miniature watercolours of **native police**. He made many sketches of the departure of the Burke and Wills expedition and later used them for his oil painting, *The Burial of Burke* (1911). Other notable historical works are *Black Thursday* (1862–64), housed in the State Library of Victoria, which records the devastating Victorian bushfires of 1851, and *Bushrangers, Victoria, Australia, 1852* (1887).

Strutt was part of a group of local artists, including von **Guérard**, **Becker**, and **Chevalier**, who attempted to form a Fine Arts Society in Victoria. He returned to Melbourne following a brief sojourn in NZ, and later returned to England. Collections of his manuscripts, sketches, and paintings are held in the Dixson and Mitchell libraries, Sydney; the Australian National Library, Canberra; and the state and parliamentary libraries, Melbourne. Marjorie Tipping added a narrative section to the volume of his work published by the Victorian Parliamentary Library in 1980, *Victoria the Golden*.

KT

Strzelecki, Paul Edmund de (1797–1873), explorer and geologist, was born into a poor family with noble ancestry at Gluszyna, Poland. His right to the title 'Count' is dismissed by many historians, and there is debate concerning his involvement in romantic and financial scandals in Poland. When Strzelecki arrived in NSW in April 1839, he had a working knowledge of geology and had travelled in Europe, America, and the Pacific. In early 1840 Strzelecki led an expedition which explored the Australian Alps. On 12 March 1840 he ascended what he believed to be the highest 'peak', naming it Mount Kosciusko in honor of Polish patriot Tadeusz Kosciuszko (1746–1817). Some inconsistencies and inaccuracies in Strzelecki's accounts have contributed to confusion as to whether this mountain was the present Mount Kosciuszko. Strzelecki's party almost starved to death in Gippsland, which he named, although Angus McMillan preceded his explorations there. At times, Strzelecki inched ahead on hands and knees through almost endless scrub and rain. After seven weeks' rest in Melbourne, on 10 July 1840 he sailed for Van Diemen's Land, and spent the next two years making a geological and topographical survey of the island. In 1843 Strzelecki moved to England, where he published his *Physical Description of New South Wales and Van Diemen's Land* (1845). Many Australian places are named after Strzelecki, and he is the subject of several biographies and numerous articles. Lech Paszkowski's *Poles in Australia and Oceania 1790–1940* (1987) is a wide-ranging introduction. An impressive monument erected by the Polish government overlooks Lake Jindabyne. In 1997 the NSW Geographical Names Board changed the spelling of Mount Kosciusko to follow that of Tadeusz Kosciuszko.

DC

Stuart case arose from the disappearance in 1958 of 9-year-old Mary Hattam from the small isolated town of Ceduna on SA's west coast. An all-night search discovered her body early the next morning. She had been raped and murdered. Rupert Max Stuart, a 27-year-old Aboriginal man, was arrested, charged with, and convicted of the crime, despite his insistence that he was innocent. He was sentenced to be hanged.

Stuart's trial aroused deep passions on the issues of race and capital punishment. The violence of the crime and Mary's extreme youth induced the public to hatred of Stuart, heightened by horror of his Aboriginality. Opponents of capital punishment and promoters of Aboriginal rights feared Stuart had been treated unfairly. Some, especially prison chaplain Father Dixon, were convinced that he was innocent. The state government was pressured from all sides and ordered a royal commission which concluded that a retrial was unnecessary. Partisan interest in the case was inflamed by libel charges laid against the editor of the *News* and by a series of appeals to the Supreme Court, High Court, and Privy Council. Stuart's sentence was commuted to life imprisonment. The episode is treated in Ken **Inglis**, *The Stuart Case* (1961).

CAROL FORT

Stuart, John McDouall (1815–66) arrived in SA in 1839 and undertook work as a **surveyor**. He accompanied

Charles **Sturt** on expeditions in the 1840s that yielded little. However, he experienced greater success than any other South Australian **explorer** when he led northern expeditions in search of gold, pastoral land, and stock routes in the 1850s. He crossed the salt lakes that had isolated the colony since settlement, and provided access to Central Australia. In 1861–62 he became the first explorer to cross the continent from south to north and return alive.

His expedition provided access to land in Central Australia and the NT that South Australian officials were eager to control. The stock route he discovered was subsequently consolidated by road and rail, and served as a foundation for the **overland telegraph** line to Darwin that led to further western exploration. Stuart left Australia in 1864, embittered that the South Australian authorities did little to financially reward his efforts.

KELLIE TOOLE

Stuart, Max, see **Stuart case**

Stump-jump plough was an **invention** of South Australian farmer R.B. Smith in 1876 that enabled land to be ploughed before stumps had been grubbed from the ground. When the plough came in contact with a stump, it rode over it and then returned to the ground. It enabled huge areas of Mallee scrub to be brought rapidly into production, though condemned by agricultural experts as encouraging slovenly farming.

JH

Sturt, Charles (1795–1869) embarked on exploratory expeditions shortly after his arrival in Sydney in 1827 as an army captain. He achieved fame for his extensive exploration during 1828–30 of the NSW river systems, during which he traced the course of the Murray, Darling, and Murrumbidgee Rivers, and theorised that many other rivers were part of that system rather than running into an inland sea. After retiring from the army, Sturt published *Two Expeditions into the Interior of Southern Australia* (1833), which was influential in Edward **Wakefield's** choice of SA for a new settlement. During 1844–46 he led an arduous, ultimately unsuccessful expedition from Adelaide to the centre of Australia, which he recorded in *Narrative of an Expedition into Central Australia* (1849). Numerous published works on Sturt include Henry **Kingsley's** essay (1872) on his river journeys, and J.H.L. **Cumpston's** celebratory biography of 1951. Edgar Beale is more critical in *Sturt, the Chipped Idol* (1979). Sturt is commemorated by SA's floral emblem—Sturt's Desert Pea—as well as the Sturt Highway, Sturt's Stony Desert, and the Charles Sturt University.

KT

Suburbs are almost as old as town life in Australia. In laying out **Sydney** in 1790, Governor Arthur **Phillip** divided land into allotments of 60 by 150 feet—close to the dimensions of the modern quarter-acre block—and required houses to stand free of their neighbours. Early observers of the

Australian coastal towns were struck by the almost universal preference for houses standing alone in their own gardens.

It was not until the 1830s that the word *suburb* was regularly applied to Australian towns. Occasionally colonists used it in its traditional European sense, 'land beyond or below the formal boundaries of the town'. Sydney and **Hobart** had no walls, but officials still banished undesirable people and functions such as hospitals, prisons, and cemeteries beyond the town limits. Under the **Ripon Regulations** (1831), land on the fringes of the towns was often divided into so-called suburban allotments, usually of 10–30 acres and intended for small-scale agriculture.

This traditional idea was rapidly being eclipsed by the modern idea of the villa or cottage suburb as a place of retreat from the sanitary and social ills of the city. The suburban idea drew on four great contemporary beliefs; evangelicalism, which sanctified domestic privacy; sanitary science, which preached the importance of fresh air; Romanticism, which inculcated a reverence for nature; and class-consciousness, which fed the demand for exclusive bourgeois neighbourhoods. First popularised in London by landscape designers such as John Claudius Loudon, the idea of the romantic suburb soon made its way to Australia, where it gained favour among the circle of wealthy, often **evangelical**, free settlers known as the **exclusives**. In 1829 their ally Governor **Darling** authorised the subdivision of Woolloomooloo hill into villa allotments for the 'ornament and improvement of the suburbs of Sydney'.

The exclusives fled to the suburbs to avoid the convict associations of the towns; but the rest of the population soon followed them and by the 1840s most of the infant Australian capitals were surrounded by a penumbra of villa and cottage suburbs. Working-class immigrants, imbued with the dream of three acres and a cow, settled for a quarter-acre suburban block and a pen of chooks. In 1858 a perceptive young Englishman glimpsed the new suburb of Redfern and observed: 'Almost every labourer and mechanic here has his own residence on freehold or leasehold land, and unpretending as it is to any conveniences or beauties, it yet satisfies him better than the brick-built, closely packed, and rented houses of English towns.'

By 1890 Australia was already more suburbanised than any other country in the world. Melburnians and Sydneysiders were more likely to live in free-standing houses on their own freehold allotment than city-dwellers in Britain or the USA. They used the word *suburb* to describe almost any part of the city except the central business district, a distinctive usage which reflects this demographic reality. High wages and cheap freehold land partly account for this pattern. Immigration, which severed extended family links, may have reinforced nuclear family ties, and with them, the preference for the single-family suburban house. Getting to the suburbs called for fast, cheap transport, and Australian cities were able to build **railways** and tramways almost from the outset rather than superimpose them on towns already formed. Melburnians were already more likely to ride a train or tram to work than Londoners

or New Yorkers. The Australian tradition of strong central government also aided suburban growth, not only by centralising white-collar work in the coastal cities—clerks and public servants were keen suburbanites—but by providing the schools, police stations, railways, and other services that new American and British suburban communities had to provide out of local rates.

Australian intellectuals, echoing their Edwardian British counterparts, often sneered at the suburbs. 'The suburban home must be destroyed. It stands for all that is dull and cowardly and depressing in modern life', declared the socialist playwright Louis **Esson** in 1909. There was more common ground between critics and defenders of the suburbs than at first appeared: both were environmental determinists, convinced that fresh air, domestic privacy, and horticulture had a moral effect, and differing only in the value they put upon it.

Australian suburban growth slowed in the early twentieth century. Public transport patronage in Sydney and **Melbourne** more than quintupled between 1890 and 1930 but slumped in the 1930s. Motor buses extended feeder routes to the rail and tram networks, although automobile ownership lagged well behind North American levels. Some of the old inner suburbs, crammed with factories and broken-down cottages, were now called '**slums**'. The political conflicts of the 1930s gained some of their bitterness from the geographical division between depressed, immobile inner suburbs and well-to-do, automobilised villa suburbs. 'North Shore' was becoming the name of an attitude as well as a place.

The suburban surge of the postwar years was fuelled by the accumulated hardships and frustrations of the Depression and war. 'Now for the Big 3—the wedding, the honeymoon and the house and where to build it', a returning POW wrote to his fiancée in 1945. Many returning soldiers built their dream homes with their own hands, although by the late 1950s the owner–builders of fibro or weatherboard cottages had been overtaken by the project-builders of triple-fronted **brick-veneer** ranch houses. The suburbs of the 1950s and 1960s were the incubators of the postwar baby boom, their family ethos inseparable from the generation that gave them shape. Robert **Menzies's** Liberals reflected and reinforced their aspirations with road grants and subsidies for home-ownership, which peaked at over 70 per cent in the mid-1960s. The suburbs returned the compliment, providing the electoral base for the long rule of Menzies.

The suburbs that grew fastest lay beyond the reach of the rail and tram, and were reliant almost entirely on cars for personal transport. The **Holden** station-wagon and the telephone were as indispensable to the growth of the suburbs as the **Jennings** house and the Hills hoist. Industry suburbanised too, freed by electricity, fork-lift trucks, and semi-trailers from the waterfront and railways. By the 1960s, when Donald **Horne** proclaimed Australia 'the first suburban nation', a clear statistical majority of Australians were living in the suburbs of the capital cities. **Canberra**, the nation's capital, was the most suburban of all.

Sudan campaign

Postwar suburbs were strongly influenced by American fashions. The supermarket, the motel, the freeway, and the ten-pin bowling alley all made their appearance in the 1950s. Even Australian critics of the suburbs slavishly followed the diagnoses of American sociologists and planners, anticipating the disappearance of the working class, deploring the visual pollution of the billboard and the neon sign, watching for symptoms of 'suburban neurosis'. It was the historian Hugh **Stretton**, in his *Ideas for Australian Cities* (1970), who offered the most robust defence of the suburbs. 'You don't have to be a mindless conformist to choose suburban life', he declared. 'It reconciles access to work and city with private, adaptable, self-expressive living at home.'

With the new appreciation of the suburbs came a new curiosity about their history. Weston **Bate's** *A History of Brighton* (1962), Geoffrey **Blainey's** *A History of Camberwell* (1964), and Max Kelly's *Paddock Full of Houses* (1978) were among the first of a line of scholarly suburban histories. Graeme Davison, *The Rise and Fall of Marvellous Melbourne* (1978), and Peter Spearritt, *Sydney Since the Twenties* (1978), place the suburbs in a metropolitan frame, while Lionel Frost, *The New Urban Frontier* (1991), and Graeme Davison, 'Australia—The First Suburban Nation?' (*Journal of Urban History*, 1995), establish the international context. Suburbia has also attracted the attention of cultural theorists, notably the contributors to Sarah Ferber et al. (eds), *The Beasts of Suburbia* (1994), and Louise Johnson (ed.), *Suburban Dreaming* (1994).

In the 1990s the long suburban boom shows signs of flagging. Home-ownership rates and house values are falling. Lower immigration, declining fertility, depleted energy sources, and smaller government have produced a new urban agenda in which consolidation, rather than sprawl, seems virtuous as well as economic. The old pattern of rich outer and poor inner suburbs is being reversed as old inner-city neighbourhoods gentrify and postwar working-class suburbs lose their industrial base. Mark Peel's *Good Times, Hard Times* (1995) illustrates the latter theme. Yet residents of most suburbs continue to express high satisfaction with their lot and, as Miles Lewis shows in *Suburban Backlash* (1999), pressures for intensive redevelopment meet with more opposition than support. The suburban dream is still alive, if not completely well.

GRAEME DAVISON

Sudan campaign was fought by the British in retaliation for the death of General Gordon and his men at Khartoum in February 1885. A contingent of soldiers from NSW, offered by acting premier W. B. **Dalley**, following Canadian offers of assistance, sailed for the Sudan the following month to serve under British command. Despite their enthusiastic send-off, the Australians saw little or none of the real fighting. The bulk of the contingent returned to Sydney by June that year, leaving some men behind in hospital suffering from fever. Francis **Myers** co-wrote a contemporary account with Frank Hutchinson (1885); later accounts of the campaign are given by Stanley Brogden in *The Sudan Contingent* (1942) and Ken **Inglis** in *The Rehearsal* (1985).

HD

Sudds–Thompson case followed the arrest of two privates, Joseph Sudds and Patrick Thompson, who belonged to the 57th Regiment stationed in NSW. In 1826 both deliberately committed theft to obtain a discharge. In an attempt to discourage this practice, however, a shrewd Governor **Darling** decided to make Sudds and Thompson an example to the rest of the colony by commuting their sentences to seven years' hard labour in chains. Sudds's death five days later, seemingly as a result of the harsh treatment to which he was subjected, sparked great public outcry against Darling's action. The incident offered a prime opportunity for Darling's opponents. In a long-running attack, fuelled by W.C. **Wentworth's** angry comments in the *Australian*, they accused him of responsibility for Sudds's death. A subsequent parliamentary inquiry found him blameless. Sudds had apparently been suffering from a preexisting medical complaint, which was thought more likely to have caused his death.

HD

Suez crisis was a military attack on Egypt by Britain, France, and Israel in 1956, which aimed at restoring international control of the Suez Canal. It received exceptional diplomatic support from Australian Prime Minister R.G. **Menzies**, who headed an unsuccessful delegation to Egypt. Hugh Thomas's *The Suez Affair* (1970) summarises the crisis, which began on 26 July 1956 when Egyptian President Gamal Abdel Nasser announced the nationalisation of the Suez Canal Company. British troops had recently been withdrawn from the Canal Zone, and Western powers feared Nasser's links with the USSR. When both Britain and the USA refused to help finance the Aswan Dam, Nasser declared canal tolls could build it instead. The leading Suez shipping powers, Britain and France, planned military occupation to restore their control, but the USA refused to join them. In August 1956 Menzies presented Nasser with a plan for international control of the canal, which Egypt not surprisingly rejected as reimposition of colonial rule. Israel invaded Egypt in late October, soon followed by Britain and France, before US pressure and UN intervention ended the dispute and the canal reopened under Egyptian control in March 1957.

Australia's role caused domestic controversy and historians have frequently argued over it. Menzies blamed US President Eisenhower for undermining Anglo-French resolution. According to W.J. Hudson's *Blind Loyalty* (1989), Menzies failed to separate loyalty to Britain from Australian interests and was deceived when Britain did not warn Australia of the invasion. Menzies's own Cabinet members, including foreign minister Richard **Casey** and defence minister Philip McBride, were critical of Britain. In Frank Cain (ed.), *Menzies in War and Peace* (1997), Wayne Reynolds noted that Menzies also contemplated military involvement. Those who argue that Suez showed Australia's immaturity in **foreign relations** see the statement that Hudson attributes to Menzies as revealing his antiquated imperialism: 'These Gyppos are a dangerous lot of backward adolescents ... full of self–importance and basic ignorance.'

DC

Sugar industry developed in the mid-nineteeenth century mainly in Qld and northern NSW. Sugar cane, indigenous to PNG and the Pacific Islands, was first grown in Sydney in 1817, and later became a successful crop in northern districts of the colony. It was introduced into Qld in the 1860s, where the number of cane-growers and the size of their acreages grew rapidly over the next 20 years. The success of cane-growing in Qld and NSW in the 1860s and 1870s hinged largely on the indentured labour of Kanakas or **Pacific Islanders**. Experimental cane-growing in other colonies met with little success, although sugar beet was grown for a brief period in Victoria. With the advent of steam power and other improved technology in the late nineteenth century, the refinery process was concentrated at a few centralised mills, and was increasingly managed by large companies, notably the Colonial Sugar Refinery Co. Ltd. The industry benefited at this time from the publication of technical reports such as Angus Mackay's *The Sugar Cane in Australia* (1870).

With the repatriation of the Pacific Islanders in 1906, the growers employed a unionised workforce. These cane-cutters practised an itinerant, aggressively masculine lifestyle which formed the basis of Ray **Lawler's** play *Summer of the Seventeenth Doll* (1957). Their industrial militancy culminated in major strikes during the 1930s, which Diane Menghetti has described in D.J. Murphy (ed.), *The Big Strikes* (1983); they are also the subject of Jean **Devanny's** novel, *Sugar Heaven* (1936). The industry benefited from government assistance and **protection** to establish substantial export markets during the twentieth century.

HD

Sulman, John (1849–1934), architect and town planner, was born in England to artistic parents; his eldest daughter, Florence, also shared the family's artistic talent. After training in architecture, Sulman won the coveted Pugin travelling scholarship in 1871. Despite a successful practice in London, his own and his wife's illnesses compelled the family to move to Australia in 1885. Sulman worked in private practice in Sydney, where his commissions included numerous churches and public buildings. He contributed significantly to the development of the Australian profession through his office as vice-president of the Institute of Architects of New South Wales and his lectures at the University of Sydney.

The fashion in Europe for **town planning** coincided with Sulman's arrival in Sydney, and in 1890 Sulman delivered an influential paper, 'On the Laying Out of Towns'. He was a leading figure in the formation of the Town Planning Association of New South Wales in 1913, the first of its kind in Australia. He became a key proponent of the Garden City ideal, which promoted progressive urban planning through the integration of modern design, curvilinear roadways, and garden reserves. In 1924 he represented Australia at the conference of the International Garden Cities and Town Planning Federation in Amsterdam. The Sir John Sulman prize for art is awarded annually by the Art Gallery of New South Wales.

HD

Summers, Anne Fairhurst (1945–   ), feminist historian and journalist, wrote *Damned Whores and God's Police: The Colonization of Women in Australia* (1975), which became one of the key texts on Australian **feminism** and **women's history** published in the 1970s. It explained women's identity as subject to a perceived dichotomy: the stereotypes of 'bad' women, such as prostitutes, who were regarded as harbingers of immorality and evil, and of 'good' women, such as Caroline **Chisholm**, who were regarded as prim upholders of morality. Summers later worked as editor-in-chief of the US *Ms* magazine, and served in the Office for the Status of Women and as adviser to Paul **Keating** on women's affairs. She was editor of *Good Weekend Magazine* 1993–97. A second edition of *Damned Whores*, published in 1994, included a new chapter, 'Letter to the Next Generation', in which Summers discussed the progress made by Australian feminists since 1975 and pointed to future concerns.

HD

***Sun* (Melbourne)**, morning **newspaper**, properly titled the *Sun–News Pictorial*, was Australia's first daily picture tabloid. Launched in 1922 by Hugh Denison, proprietor of the Sydney *Sun*, its open, attractive style was influenced by the London *Mirror*. Pictures predominated; stories were brief, numerous, and wide-ranging. The Herald & Weekly Times Ltd acquired the *Sun* in 1925, and while chief executive Sir Keith **Murdoch** preferred the *Herald*, the *Sun* became the biggest-selling newspaper in Australia by the late 1930s. Sales of around 240 000 in 1938 increased to 550 000 in 1957 and 650 000 by 1971. Both papers lost circulation in the 1980s and in 1990 were amalgamated by Rupert **Murdoch's** News Ltd into a new '24-hour paper', the *Herald Sun News Pictorial*.

DC

Surveying could be said to have been first practised in Australia with the naval surveys of Captain James **Cook** in 1770. Nautical surveying remained an important source of information about the Australian coast and nearby waters through the work of Matthew **Flinders**, Phillip Parker King, various French explorers, and later the British Admiralty. The individual states and, after Federation, the Commonwealth through the Royal Australian Navy gradually took over responsibility for charting Australian waters, as documented by Geoffrey Ingleton in *Charting a Continent* (1944).

The survey of inland Australia began with the **explorers**, some of whom were professional surveyors. While explorers are often credited with being the first to enter new territory, surveyors rarely are—a point made by F.M. Johnston in *Knights and Theodolites: A Saga of Surveyors* (1962), and Gordon and Judith Scurfield in *The Hoddle Years: Surveying in Victoria 1836–1853* (1995). Perhaps a stronger incentive than curiosity was that of being credited with the discovery of rich grazing or agricultural lands, achieved by surveyors Evans and **Oxley** in New England (1818), Thomas **Mitchell** in 'Australia Felix' or Victoria (1835–36), and **Light** in parts of SA (1834–36). Trained in military or naval techniques, these early surveyors were required to use their skills first in the subdivision of land for sale and the laying out of towns, and later for building roads, bridges, and railways.

One of the most striking visual legacies of colonisation was the imposition of the straight line: so claims David Denholm in *The Colonial Australians* (1979), which explores the cultural logic behind the surveyors' practice. The techniques used in carrying out trigonometrical surveys such as that instigated by Mitchell in 1828, and subsequently used during much of the nineteenth century, were described in Alan Andrews's detailed study, *Major Mitchell's Map 1834* (1992). However, because of the disjointed nature of the work, topographic surveys could not be carried out across the vast areas of the continent or across state boundaries until after Federation. Ian Williamson, in articles in *The Australian Surveyor* (1982–84), called this 'an isolated survey system'. A general geodetic survey (i.e. one based on the accurate measurement of the earth's surface) across the whole country was needed to link separate surveys begun at various times: in NSW in 1828, Victoria in 1839, Tasmania in 1847, Qld in 1879. This was called for in 1912, but positive steps were not taken until World War II, and the final result not achieved until 1966 with the adoption of the Australian Geodetic Datum, a system of coordinates on which all surveys and mapping could be based.

The military also had an interest in mapping for defence purposes, and an Intelligence Corps, then a Survey Section of the Royal Australian Engineers, was formed before the establishment of the Australian (later Royal Australian) Survey Corps in 1915. The corps continued to work under this name until 1996, when it was reabsorbed into the Royal Australian Engineers.

Surveying of land with mining potential began with the first exploitation of coal in NSW in 1797, and has been a necessary adjunct to mining exploration from the gold rushes of the 1850s to the mining boom of the 1960s and 1970s, and beyond. Major projects, such as the **Snowy Mountains Hydro-Electric Scheme** and the hydrographic survey of the continental shelf, have required extensive surveying programs. Offshore, some responsibility has been taken for the survey and mapping of PNG and the Australian **Antarctic** Territory by Australian mapping authorities.

What John Lines in his history of Australian mapping, *Australia on Paper* (1992), has called 'the third dimension … the vertical component of the spatial co-ordinate' could not be adequately incorporated into surveying practice until the advent of aerial photography. This began systematically in 1924 after the formation of the RAAF, which continued to carry out aerial surveys for the Commonwealth until the 1950s, when such surveying was progressively taken over by the states and by private contractors. New technologies based on radar, satellite imagery, global positioning and geographic information systems have radically altered the tasks of surveyors, while cartography is increasingly practised in a computerised environment.

A rethinking of the concepts of land and boundaries has been necessary in the 1990s in order to deal with the issues of sustainable development, land use, and land-ownership, particularly with respect to **Aboriginal land rights**. This demands a greater sensitivity and responsibility on the part of surveyors towards land claimants and the land itself, as its resources are perceived to be finite, and its original inhabitants to have a relationship with the land which cannot be mapped in the conventional sense. Such areas of survey work also rely more on modern techniques, such as satellite imagery, digital photogrammetry (making of maps from aerial photographs), and global positioning systems.

JUDITH SCURFIELD

Sutherland family made diverse and distinguished contributions to Australian intellectual life. Children of a Glasgow wood-carver, George Sutherland, they arrived with their parents in Sydney in 1864, but later moved to Melbourne where they became the centre of a close-knit circle that exhibited something of the intellectual range and high seriousness of the Scottish Enlightenment. ALEXANDER (1852–1902) and GEORGE (1855–1905), schoolmasters and journalists, helped establish the study of Australian history in the era before universities. Alexander's success as founder and headmaster of Carlton College in the 1880s launched him into Melbourne society where, along with his fellow Unitarian and historian, Henry Gyles **Turner**, he was one of the circle of intellectuals who gave Victorian liberalism its distinctive meliorist character. With George, who had turned from teaching to journalism in Adelaide, he had already written a *History of Australia …* (1877) for schools, a concise, judicious narrative constructed around the founding deeds of **explorers** and **governors**; it remained in print, in various editions, for almost 50 years. In 1888 he edited *Victoria and its Metropolis*, a 1500-page encyclopedia of the colony's past and present, which expresses and embodies the overweening confidence of **Marvellous Melbourne**. 'To some there may seem a sense of disproportion in the size of this volume', he began apologetically, before warming to his theme—the civilising genius of 'the English-speaking race' as demonstrated in Victorian history. In the 1890s, when Melbourne's bubble burst and his personal fortunes declined, he turned to journalism, mainly for the *Age*; he made unsuccessful forays into politics and completed his most ambitious work, *The Origin and Growth of the Moral Instinct* (1898), an attempt to harmonise moral philosophy with Darwinism, published in the same year as George's major work, *The South Australian Company*.

Their sister JANE (1853–1928) was a member of the **Heidelberg** group of artists but never achieved the public recognition her male colleagues enjoyed. She studied at the National Gallery School, Victoria, from 1871 to 1886 and for many years shared a studio with Clara Southern. Her landscapes were gentle, often romantic, and she eschewed the subjects of many of her male contemporaries, preferring domestic scenes. An exhibition of her work was held in 1977.

WILLIAM (1859–1911), the youngest son, graduated from the University of Melbourne in natural science; he studied experimental physics at University College London before returning to Melbourne, where he devoted himself to private reading and research. Over the next 30 years he contributed 78 papers to international journals, many of them expounding his own theory of molecular attraction. Disputed at the time, 'the Sutherland model', as it became known, is now widely accepted. Shy and unassuming, he shared the family passion for music and bushwalking.

MARGARET (1897–1984), a daughter of George, won scholarships to study music in London and Vienna, before returning to Melbourne in 1925. She was the first Australian composer to work in the style of her European contemporaries, although her work, which includes an opera on Daisy **Bates** and song-settings of poems by John Shaw **Nielson** and Judith **Wright**, also reflects an appreciation of Australian idioms.

GRAEME DAVISON

Sutherland, Joan (1926–) is Australia's best-known diva. After premiering Goosens's *Judith* at the NSW State Conservatorium in 1951, she went to London to study with Clive Carey at the Royal College of Music. At Covent Garden in 1952 she made her debut as the First Lady in *Die Zauberflöte* and soon sang the standard repertoire. Conductor Richard Bonynge, her husband from 1954, guided her towards Italian *bel canto*, and she gradually added long-neglected roles by Bellini, Donizetti, Meyerbeer, Gounod, and Massenet. In 1959 her stunning performance in the title role of the Zeffirelli production of Donizetti's *Lucia di Lammermoor* at Covent Garden brought her worldwide acclaim. Appearances in the principal houses of Europe and America followed; and after performances at La Fenice, Venice, the accolade 'La Stupenda' was bestowed on her. She revisited Australia in 1965 with the Sutherland–Williamson Grand Opera Co., and from 1976 returned regularly until her retirement in 1990 as the inspirational principal artist at the Australian Opera.

Sutherland's repertoire was immense, ranging from Handel and Mozart to Rossini, Verdi, and Puccini. She had a distinctive voice of intense warmth and startling range, and a technique seldom matched in the history of opera. She recorded more than 40 complete operas (chiefly for Decca), and her recordings, *The Art of the Prima Donna* (1960) and *The Age of Bel Canto* (1963), are permanent records of the pinnacle of operatic singing.

WARREN BEBBINGTON

Sutherland, Selina (1839–1909) was a pioneer of the child welfare movement in Victoria from the early 1880s. She came from Scotland via NZ, where she utilised her self-taught medical knowledge in helping local settlers. She became matron of the Wellington Hospital, from which she resigned over a disagreement with the management committee—a continuing motif of her working life. Sutherland settled in Melbourne in 1881 and became friendly with Maria Armour, who was working with the city's neglected children. With the support of Scots Church they established an aid society which placed slum children with foster families in the country. From this developed the Maternity Aid Society and the Melbourne District Nursing Society. By the early 1890s she was lady missionary for the Presbyterian Church of Victoria and, as the colony's first licensed 'child rescuer', she was credited with having rescued 879 people. Conflict between Sutherland and management committees resulted in her leaving the church auspices and establishing the Victorian Neglected Children's Aid Society, still in existence as Oz Child. Her work there is documented in *Selina's Legacy* (1993), by Della Hilton. Eventually Sutherland was dismissed in contentious circumstances, following which she established the Sutherland Home for Children. Although she considered that women and children were victims and that men were to blame for the sins of society, Sutherland never became closely involved in the women's suffrage movement.

KT

Swagman and the less common swagwoman were itinerant workers, named after the swag, or bundle of belongings and bedding that they carried on their shoulder. Swagmen and swagwomen tramped the country roads alone or in pairs in search of seasonal work, a situation referred to as 'on the wallaby'. They were distinguished by the corks that dangled from their hat to keep the flies out of their eyes, and the billy that hung from their swag. Mostly they camped along the road, but frequently obtained food and shelter from farmers in return for labour. Their routine of seeking shelter and a meal from farmers just before nightfall led to the term *sundowners*. Swagmen became numerous during the **depressions** and high unemployment of the 1890s and 1930s. They have been romanticised in fiction, such as D'Arcy Niland's *The Shiralee* (1955), and in folksongs, notably **'Waltzing Matilda'**. The experiences of Joseph Jenkins are recorded as *Diary of a Welsh Swagman 1869–1894* (1975). Swagman 'Scotty the Wrinkler' (pen-name of Phil Mowbray) published a short book entitled *The Swag: The Unofficial Flute of the Sundowners and other Colonial Vagrants …* in about 1900 as an unsuccessful attempt to gain representation for swagmen in the official conventions and discussions leading to Federation.

HD

Swan River settlement was established in 1829 at the mouth of the Swan River on the site of present-day **Perth**. On an exploratory voyage to the Swan in 1827, Captain James **Stirling** had been impressed by its fertile valleys, and he eventually won the support of Governor **Darling** and British authorities to establish a permanent settlement. Stirling was appointed lieutenant-governor, and arrived with the first colonists in 1829. The settlement was to be funded by private investment, and those willing to improve the land were to be awarded land grants. The granting of an enormous area of 250 000 acres to Thomas Peel, a cousin of the British prime minister, brought accusations of favouritism, but Peel subsequently failed as a settler. Problems such as physical isolation, unsurveyed land, and food and labour shortages impeded initial development and threatened the settlement's survival. Attacks and reprisals between whites and Aborigines were frequent, and culminated in the Battle of **Pinjarra**. Development during the early period is discussed in J.M.R. Cameron's *Ambition's Fire: The Agricultural Colonization of Pre-Convict Western Australia* (1981).

HD

Sweating, a pejorative term for the excessive exploitation of labour, refers particularly to the practice of piece-work that was common in the clothing and footwear industries in the nineteenth century. In the absence of industrial legislation, women and children laboured sometimes more than 10 hours per day in their own homes, receiving in return a meagre remuneration for each completed garment or shoe. 'Outwork', as this form of employment was called, was one of the few sources of paid work for poor women with domestic responsibilities.

In Victoria, the major manufacturing colony, agitation for improved conditions for employees resulted in the Factory Act of 1873, which was designed to put an end to sweating. Conservatives opposed the act, arguing for the 'natural' right of capital and free enterprise, as did factory owners themselves, who saw it as threatening their business interests. The legislation left many loopholes and was weakened by subsequent amendments in 1885. In the early 1890s the Victorian Anti-Sweating League, led by Samuel Maugher, united trade unionists, churchmen, and liberal politicians in a vigorous campaign to abolish the system. A more effective act, passed in 1896, introduced compulsory registration of outworkers. Similar legislation was passed in NSW, and later in SA and Qld. Minimum industrial controls in clothing production and the out-sourcing of garment finishing, particularly in Victoria, has allowed sweating to persist into the 1990s. Raelene Frances, *The Politics of Work* (1993), places sweating in the broader history of women's work in Victoria.

HD

Sweet, Georgina (1875–1946) became Australia's foremost parasitologist, noted for her work on worm nodules in cattle, after she was awarded a DSc from the University of Melbourne in 1904. She had previously taught in secondary schools and as a demonstrator at the university. Her postgraduate work was undertaken in the biology department headed by Professor Baldwin **Spencer**. Although by 1919 she was a popular and respected teacher and administrator at the University of Melbourne, Sweet was passed over to succeed Spencer when he retired. In the following year she became the university's first female associate professor. She was active in ensuring that women were represented as widely as possible in the university. Her outside interests included the Royal Society of Victoria, the Field Naturalists Club of Victoria, the YWCA, and the establishment of the Women's College at the university.

KT

Sydney is Australia's first-established and most populous city. From a high-rise central business district (CBD) at the edge of Sydney Harbour it sprawls through successive rings of suburbs to the foot of the Blue Mountains in the west, and to the once-distant cities of Campbelltown in the south and Gosford in the north. Shaped by a topography of waterways, ridges, and gorges, which provided both barriers and access routes, it is what Paul Ashton calls an 'accidental city', where attempts at town planning have largely been absent, ignored, or compromised.

Sydney was founded in 1788 when Captain Arthur **Phillip** selected a site overlooking a cove on the southern shore of Port Jackson for a colony of transported convicts. A crude settlement was scratched out and pegged down on land already occupied by Aboriginal people of the coastal Cadigal band. Although envisaged as a kind of gaol, the town emerged and operated like a free society in these early years, with civil and military precincts, and neighbourhoods of shopkeepers, tradespeople, and publicans, the most distinctive being the **Rocks** on the west side of the cove. A maritime town, Sydney was driven by private enterprise, and shaped by the pre-industrial culture of its convict and ex-convict inhabitants.

From the 1820s wealthy free immigrants built fine villas, both close to the town (Millers Point) and set apart from it (Woolloomooloo Ridge) in the city's earliest **suburbs**. After the end of transportation in 1840, and with the rise in free immigration, the growing population of middling and working people lived mostly in and around the older centre, and later in new suburbs some distance away, such as Paddington, Redfern, and Surry Hills. There were stirrings of long-standing anti-urban sentiment, as journalists and social investigators (the most famous being W.S. Jevons) expressed disgust and fear of the old city precincts, where alleged filth, disorder, and disease were inextricably bound up with the moral degeneracy of inhabitants.

Between 1851 and 1900 Sydney grew from a population of 54 000 to 400 000. The terrace house became the norm, spreading rapidly over older gardens and yards, or newly subdivided land. An emerging industrial landscape comprised mostly small-scale factories and workshops, both at the periphery and amid residential areas. Wharves, warehouses, and workshops lined the foreshores from Woolloomooloo to Darling Harbour and Balmain and, until the advent of container ships in the late twentieth century, the waterfront with its pubs, homes, and lodging-houses was the centre of a distinctive maritime culture. Meanwhile, shops evolved from front rooms in private houses, to stylish purpose-built specialist shops, and thence to elaborate arcades (the Strand and later the Queen Victoria Markets) and great department stores like that of Anthony **Hordern**.

A system of tramways, built from the 1880s, linked the city to outlying suburbs. Railways extended from the great city terminuses at Redfern and Central to the rural hinterland, adding new stations almost as an afterthought. More suburbs grew up around them, from the stucco and iron of the 1880s, through the brick and tile of the 1920s, and thence through corridors of fibro and brick veneer before the ever-shifting, ragged hinterlands where Sydney met the bush.

Sydney suffered the complaints of great cities everywhere: until the construction of the Upper Nepean Water Scheme (completed 1886) there were frequent water shortages and that water was often unspeakably dirty. The limited sewers discharged straight into the harbour; before the introduction of wood-paving in 1880, the streets were often mires of mud, fly-infested horse-droppings, and rubbish. The improvements had only limited impact on urban diseases which killed thousands. An outbreak of bubonic plague in 1900, although claiming relatively few victims, shocked authorities into action. The waterfront districts were quarantined and then resumed; a city-wide clean-up removed mountains of accumulated rubbish; hundreds of buildings were demolished and some rebuilt. The plague reinforced the shift in allegiance from urban to suburban life; the twentieth-century suburbs, with their grid-patterned streets and detached houses on quarter-acre blocks, were as different as possible from old city neighbourhoods.

Sydney's population boomed after both world wars. It reached one million in the late 1920s, stagnated through the 1930s, but passed two million in the late 1950s. The 1950s were marked by severe shortages in building materials and enormous demand for housing: it was the era of the owner-builder, and doing-it-yourself. This period was also seen as an opportunity to plan rationally and responsibly for the future of Greater Sydney. But attempts at farsighted **town planning** by the Cumberland County Council were bedevilled by lack of funding and cooperation, and the unforeseen explosion in population. The NSW Housing Commission built thousands of homes for low-income earners. Some of these estates were successful, attractive, and accessible; others were appalling in their drabness and isolation. The spread of motor transport in this period meant that suburbs were no longer tethered to trains and trams: by 1978, 85 per cent of Sydney people made the journey to work by car. Industries were freed from railways and waterways, and modern industrial landscapes proliferated from the 1960s, particularly in western Sydney. But the boom soon added to the city's problems with pollution, traffic congestion, a horrific road-accident toll, and the ever-increasing demand for expensive new roads.

Any close examination of Sydney tends to dissolve the idea of the city as a single entity, for Sydney is a fractured city of myriad worlds, networks, and perspectives. It fosters diversity along the lines of economic, social, and cultural status; ethnic allegiances; religious, moral, and sexual identities. Sydney has the world-famous annual Gay and Lesbian Mardi Gras; and also tiny communities of Plymouth Brethren who prefer to mix only with their own. Sydney people tend to remain in their own suburbs or districts; residents of the Manly–Warringah Peninsula, Sutherland Shire, or the West may be completely unfamiliar with the Sydneys beyond, except for the CBD.

While suburban life was fundamental to the culture of Sydney people, the sprawling suburbs were not part of the public image of the city, and until the 1970s they attracted mostly satirical or derogatory comment from intellectuals. The CBD remains symbolic Sydney, particularly the vistas over and from the harbour, dominated by the **Sydney Harbour Bridge** and the **Sydney Opera House**. These vistas and structures transcend the facts that they are of little use and inaccessible to the majority of Sydney people. They have become admired and inspiring Sydney icons.

Sydney has been a perennial source of inspiration for writers, from Henry **Lawson** to Patrick **White**, painters from Conrad **Martens** to Brett Whiteley, and photographers such as Harold Cazneaux and Max Dupain. The city's complexity is reflected in historical writing, much of which examines particular locales, aspects, or periods. The Sydney History Group, formed in 1978, produced several books of pioneering essays. Peter Spearritt in *Sydney Since the Twenties* (1978) presented a broad view of a radically realigned Sydney, while Shirley Fitzgerald in *Rising Damp: Sydney 1870–1890* (1987) examined everyday life and work in late-nineteenth-century Sydney. Alan Mayne in *Representing the Slum* (1991) dissects contemporary images of city slums. Interest in the city's history also produced a number of commissioned works. Shirley Fitzgerald's *Sydney 1842–1992* (1992) and shorter books on Chippendale, Surry Hills, Millers Point, and Pyrmont were a major part of Sydney City Council's sesquicentenary celebrations. Local councils also commissioned histories of western Sydney, a region long neglected by academics: Carol Liston's *Campbelltown* (1988), Grace Karskens's *Holroyd* (1991), and Christopher Keating's *On the Frontier* (1995) (Liverpool) are examples.

The 2000 **Olympics** marked Sydney's debut as a self-conscious world city, and occasioned a plethora of celebratory histories. Lucy Turnbull's was the most lavishly illustrated, English travel writer Geoffrey Moorhouse's *Sydney* the most chattily readable, John Birmingham's 'unauthorised biography' *Leviathan* the grungiest, and Peter Spearritt's revision of his 1978 book, *Sydney's Century*, the most consistently informative.

GRACE KARSKENS

Sydney Harbour Bridge, a single-arch steel bridge framed by four decorative towers of granite-faced concrete, spans Sydney Harbour. It connects **Sydney** with North Sydney, and provides for rail, road, and pedestrian transport. Proposals for a bridge were made from the late nineteenth century, and designs conceived as early as 1912. The design tender was won by railway engineer John **Bradfield**, and construction began in 1923. Ceremonies marked various stages of the construction process, the most dramatic being the opening ceremony on 20 March 1932, when Captain de Groot, a member of the New Guard, unexpectedly charged forth on horseback and sliced the official ribbon with his sabre, thus depriving Premier Jack **Lang** of the honour. Whilst the construction process was meticulously recorded by artists and photographers, such as Grace Cossington Smith and Harold Cazneaux, conservative artists sought to capture views of the historic Sydney that was about to be obliterated. Its completion, at a cost of £9 577 507, marked the progress of Sydney and the nation. Hailed as the world's largest arch bridge on its completion, it became, more than any other built structure, the most universally recognised symbol of Sydney. Peter Spearritt recounted its life in a 50th anniversary publication.

HD

Sydney History Group, see **Sydney**

Sydney Morning Herald was jointly founded by William McGarvie, Alfred Ward Stephens, and Frederick Michael Stokes, who launched the weekly *Sydney Herald* in 1831. A month after the first issue appeared, McGarvie sold his share in the venture to Stephens and Stokes. In its early years, the *Sydney Herald* established itself as a voice of moderation, **liberalism**, and reform. It was renamed the *Sydney Morning Herald* in 1842, two years after being purchased by John **Fairfax** and Charles Kemp, and subsequently developed a conservative tone. Fairfax assumed sole control in 1853, with historian and journalist John **West** appointed editor. During the long period under control of the Fairfax family, the *Herald* developed into Sydney's major daily broadsheet. With the collapse of the Fairfax empire in 1991, the paper was controlled by Canadian newspaper magnate Conrad Black, but subsequently he withdrew. The *Sydney Morning Herald* has long been regarded as Australia's pre-eminent newspaper. Gavin **Souter's** comprehensive accounts, *Company of Heralds* (1981) and *Heralds and Angels* (1991, 1992), supplanted an earlier centenary history produced by the Fairfax company in 1931.

HD

Sydney Opera House, a complex of theatres and performance space, built at Bennelong Point, comprises two clusters of sail-like forms covered in white ceramic tiles that are suggestive of the yachts that sail on Sydney Harbour. Like the **Sydney Harbour Bridge**, the Opera House has become a dominant feature and popular symbol of its city. The idea for an opera house was first proposed by Eugene **Goossens** in 1947; a design competition, held in 1957, was won by Danish architect Joern Utzon. Construction was financed by a state lottery. A scaled-down adaption of the original plan was finally completed and officially opened in 1973 by Queen Elizabeth II. However, controversies over the building design interrupted the construction process in the mid-1960s, and caused Utzon's resignation. He left Australia and never saw his completed masterpiece. An opera entitled *The Eighth Wonder*, which dramatises the building's history, premiered at the Sydney Opera House in 1995.

HD

Sydney School of History dates from the appointment of of G.A. **Wood** as the first Challis professor of history at the University of Sydney in 1891. An Oxford man and a liberal radical, Wood instituted a syllabus concentrating on European culture and British heritage. It proceeded via the Renaissance and Reformation to the rise of the British Empire, thus allowing for ample emphasis on the rights of the individual and the growth of liberty. As befitted Wood's Balliol origins, history at Sydney was a humane, literary and moral subject: 'a study', as he put it, 'of the human spirit in its noblest manifestations', which offered an ideal training for future public men. Australian history appeared late in the course and only in imperial context. Wood's single major published work, *The Discovery of Australia* (1922), is a romantic treatment of the great maritime explorers from de Quiros to Cook. He never managed to teach a course on Australian history since 1788, but he did further the production of the *Historical Records of New South Wales* and the *Historical Records of Australia*, and in a notable journal article in 1922 he argued that the **convicts** were wronged village Hampdens and the direct antecedents of the heroes of Gallipoli. Several of Wood's students became Australian historians of note: Marjorie **Barnard**, Max **Crawford**, Charles **Currey**, W.G.K. Duncan, G.C. **Henderson**, G.V. **Portus**, Charles **Rowley**, and Myra **Willard**.

Wood's successor, S.H. 'Swotty' **Roberts**, was a product of the University of Melbourne and the London School of Economics. He replaced the heart with the head by introducing a cool social-science professionalism—humourless, hard-headed, utilitarian. Roberts wrote seven books in 14 years, nearly all of which put data and analysis above sentiment and narrative. He was also a pragmatic nationalist rather than a romantic imperialist. A student of continental Europe and its empires, he focused the Sydney syllabus more on twentieth-century concerns, and extended it into contemporary problems in Africa, Asia, and the Pacific. In 1940 he also introduced a separate honours year with a research thesis, the first of its kind in Australia. Sydney historians now trained to be social engineers and administrators: several, including Roberts himself, became vice-chancellors. The Roberts years spawned several Australian historians of distinction—Alan Barcan, Robin **Gollan**, Gordon **Greenwood**, Allan **Martin**, Bede **Nairn**, and Roberts's successor J.M. **Ward** (1949–79).

Ward was the first head who was wholly a Sydney product. More conservative than his two predecessors, he was also trained in the law and had been secretary to the former UAP premier of NSW, Sir Bertram **Stevens**. Ward presided over the enormous growth of his department in the 1950s, 1960s, and 1970s: student numbers almost doubled to 2000 and the staff grew from six to 52. British and European history were boosted when a second chair was established in 1960; and in 1969 Marjorie Jacobs was promoted to the third chair and became the department's first (and still only) female professor. Under Ward, major strengths were added in Asian, American, and early modern European history. Ward

HD

himself wrote a rather dry brand of British imperial history which stressed constitutional evolution and administration. He described a perfect style as 'balanced', 'cautious', 'meticulous, reasoned and restrained'. But as head he was against prescription: 'I deliberately set my mind against any attempt to build up a School of History in the sense of … shared views on how to approach the study of history and how to interpret it', he remarked, in an oblique and muted criticism of the more self-conscious theorising of Max **Crawford's Melbourne School**.

Much of the Australian history written in Sydney from Wood to Ward was done outside the department by the lawyer H.V. **Evatt**, the journalist Malcolm **Ellis**, and the economists R.B. **Madgwick**, R.C. **Mills**, and S.J. **Butlin**. However, they too bore the Sydney stamp of solid empirical scholarship and a preference for hard data over ideas. Evatt aside, the radical approach of the **Old Left** had no place in this austere Sydney tradition.

Until the 1970s the Sydney syllabus remained within the grand European tradition established under Roberts: European history (mostly political) was traversed in the first and second years, and Australian, American, and Asian history might be ventured in the third. Honours theses were solely on Australian topics until the 1960s. Since then the department has become too diverse to be readily characterised as a school. Continuities with the era of Roberts and Ward are most apparent in the work of its senior Australian historians, such as Brian Fletcher, Heather Radi, Ken Cable, and James Waldersee. Fletcher and Cable show a fine-grained, pragmatic approach, an interest in early colonial NSW, and a dislike for ideology that appealed to the amateur scholars, especially local historians and genealogists, with whom they often worked. This emphasis was further entrenched when Fletcher became the first Bicentennial Professor of Australian History in 1988.

Useful analyses appear in Barbara Caine et al. (eds), *History at Sydney 1891–1991: Centenary Reflections* (1992); Brian Fletcher, *Australian History in New South Wales 1888–1938* (1993); and Stuart Macintyre and Julian Thomas (eds), *The Discovery of Australian History 1890–1939* (1995).

CARL BRIDGE

Syme, David (1827–1908), self-made newspaper proprietor and ideologue, was probably the most powerful man in Victoria in the last quarter of the nineteenth century. Born at North Berwick, Scotland, he was rigorously educated by his stern schoolmaster father. In 1851 he migrated to the Californian goldfields, then to Victoria, where he prospected for three years before taking up road contracting. His brother Ebenezer, while editor, bought the struggling *Age* daily in 1856, with David's financial support. David took control of the paper and its weekly *Leader* in 1859 (Ebenezer died in 1860), and eventually,

after much recrimination, was able to buy out Ebenezer's widow and children.

Detesting the privileged, especially the **squatters**, Syme fervently supported 'land for the people' and full rights of self-government. He was not, as he later claimed, the 'Father of Protection', but gradually came to adopt it by 1864 as a means of developing manufacturing and holding the transient population in the colony. He managed to beat off sabotage by free-traders and conservatives, and reduced the *Age's* price to one penny in 1868; circulation rose to 40 000 in 1880 and 100 000 about 1890, huge by world standards, five times that of the conservative twopenny *Argus*.

Syme backed the **Berry** government of 1877–80 during its **constitutional crisis** with the Legislative Council. He ruthlessly built up and destroyed politicians (especially Irish Catholics), such was the dominance of his newspaper, bludgeoning and praising, manipulating the news. He admitted that the *Age* 'does not ask the man in the street what he thinks, but it tells him what he ought to think'. Yet he was consistent in his radicalism, supporting farmers, trade unionists (but not the eventual Labor Party), the have-nots, enlightened state action, and the anti-**sweating** movement. His support had much to do with the lasting strength of radical **liberals** in Victoria, such as **Deakin** and C.H. **Pearson** who wrote prolifically for the *Age*; Deakin was one of the very few to maintain a long, affectionate friendship with Syme. Strong coalition governments of 1883–90 reduced Syme's impact, but in the 1890s he was at the peak of his dictatorial power. Bewildered by boom and depression, he had little positive to offer, yet in 1897 the *Age* ticket for the Federal Convention was elected to a man and the *Age* support was crucial for the eventual strong vote in favour of **Federation**. Of many libel cases, the successful tussle in 1892 with R. Speight, former railways commissioner, was outstanding.

Syme wrote little for the paper, but earned a minor international reputation as an unorthodox political economist. *Outlines of an Industrial Science* (1876) defended **protection** and **state socialism**, while *Representative Government in England* (1881) was a general attack on his subject. While unsuccessful, his campaign that ministries should be elected, rather than composed by the party with a parliamentary majority, was a notable extension of colonial democratic inventiveness. He published two other books, and articles on political economy in English and Melbourne journals.

Syme left an estate of nearly £1 million. He had been a serious farmer on properties in the Yarra Valley. Three of his sons carried on the *Age* until 1948, when it became a public company, which was bought out by **Fairfax** interests in 1972. Ambrose Pratt had written an official, hagiographical biography (1908); C.E. Sayers contributed a much more objective version (1965); and Stuart Macintyre has studied him at length in *A Colonial Liberalism* (1991).

GEOFFREY SERLE

T

TAB, or Totalisator Agency Board, known colloquially as 'the tote', is the most popular form of legal **gambling** on horses and other sporting events in Australia. The original tote *pari-mutuel* was invented by a Parisian bookmaker in 1873 and a similar machine was introduced to Melbourne at about the same time, by Seigfried Francks. Unlike a bookmaker, who quotes odds and backs his own judgment against the field, the totalisator takes bets, and after deducting a set percentage for the proprietor, distributes the takings to the winners. Primitive mechanised totes were used on nineteenth-century racecourses, the first in SA at Morphettville in Adelaide in 1879 and the first in Victoria at Bealiba in 1881. The Tasmanian Turf Club banned bookmakers and confined betting on the island to the on-course totalisator in 1897. In Victoria, in contrast, race clubs had legalised bookmakers and banned the tote. As a result, illegal off-course totes, such as John **Wren's**, became popular among Melbourne's working-class gamblers in the 1890s. In 1912, George Julius converted his invented mechanical vote counter into a mechanical totalisator. The first of these new machines were used at a trotting meeting in WA in 1916 and at Randwick racecourse in Sydney in 1917. The new tote was used on-course in Melbourne in 1931.

At the same time radio broadcasts of races spawned an illegal off-course SP bookmaking industry. A Victorian royal commission exposed the massive growth in this industry in 1958 and, in response, the Victorian government established the Totalisator Agency Board in March 1961. Other states copied the Victorian experiment, with a state-controlled TAB set up in WA one week after Victoria, in Qld 1962, in the ACT 1964, in NSW 1965, and in SA 1967. At first restricted to a few outlets, with minimal comforts for punters and slow uncertain betting opportunities, all TABs, largely through sophisticated electronic networks, have been able to offer complex 'exotic' bets with which bookmakers cannot compete. TAB turnover has grown while that of bookmakers has stagnated. The tote punter can now bet on most sports, in some states buying lottery tickets at the TAB, and those with cash reserves can bet by phone or on the Internet. The TABs in both Victoria and NSW have moved into the fixed-odds market, once the exclusive province of the bookmaker. In 1994, the Victorian government sold its TAB, which has become Tabcorp, a private-sector corporation in which the racing industry is a shareholder.

CHRIS MCCONVILLE

Tait family were enormously influential theatrical entrepreneurs from the early 1900s when JOHN HENRY TAIT (1871–1955) and (JAMES) NEVIN (1876–1961), with the assistance of their older brother CHARLES (1868–1933), began concert promotion. They were later joined by brothers EDWARD JOSEPH (1878–1947)—who worked previously for J.C. **Williamson's**, another renowned theatrical firm—and FRANK SAMUEL (1883–1965). They presented international celebrity artists in concerts which also included short films, an interest which involved them in the production of the innovative and popular *The Story of the Kelly Gang* (1906), Australia's first full-length feature **film**. The Taits expanded into theatrical productions and, in 1920, combined with Williamson's, 'The Firm', to become the pre-eminent force in Australian theatre. They were also involved in the early days of Australian **radio**, gaining the licence to operate 3LO, and later 3AW. The Taits dominated live entertainment in Australia for over half a century. VIOLA TAIT, Frank's wife, produced an affectionate history of the family and firm in *A Family of Brothers* (1970).

KT

Tall poppy refers to a person who has achieved considerable, possibly unwarranted success. Australia's tall poppy syndrome refers to a tendency for Australians to downplay achievement to the extent of being disdainful of such people, and so to cut them down to size. Its origins probably lie in the Greek parable, related by Livy, of the tyrant who was advised to cut down the higher growth in a field of corn. The first recorded Australian uses of the term, in the early twentieth century, applied it to senior public servants, but from the 1950s it spread to other forms of eminence as part of the growing resistance to **knockers** and levelling **egalitarianism**. While originally pejorative, it has come to acquire affirmative connotations. Susan Mitchell has published two accounts of successful Australian women entitled *Tall Poppies* (1984) and *Tall Poppies Too* (1991).

SM

Tariff, the imposition of duties on imports, was the first form of **taxation** in the infant colony of NSW and became the mainstay of the public revenues of all the colonies. Since tariffs affected trade, this was a matter which the imperial authorites supervised closely. With **responsible government**, the colonies gained the right to set their own tariff levels. Free-trade Britain did not prohibit Victoria in 1866 from adopting **protection**, the imposition of duties designed to discourage imports (in this case, British imports) and to nurture local industry. However, Britain refused to allow the colonies to impose discriminatory tariffs, the setting of different rates according to country of origin. This prevented the colonies from establishing bilateral trade agreements among themselves, which seemed a way of mitigating the evils of six different tariff systems since agreement on a common tariff always proved impossible. As a result of colonial lobbying, in which NZ played a prominent part, Britain withdrew its objection to discriminatory tariffs in 1873. Several attempts were subsequently made to secure trade agreements, but none succeeded. The six colonies maintained different tariffs until **Federation**, for which one of the prime motives was the abolition of the border duties between them.

Victoria's protectionist policy was followed by the smaller colonies in the 1880s and 1890s, though their tariff levels were not set as high as the Victorian. The duties were not so high as to be prohibitive and hence protection raised revenue, which was one reason why it was adopted. NSW, with a more abundant land fund, had less need of extra revenue; it maintained a policy of free trade, which did not mean that there were no import duties, but that they were fixed solely to raise revenue. The tariff policies of the colonies are studied in G.D. Patterson, *The Tariff in the Australian Colonies 1856–1900* (1968), which provides a guide to the level and incidence of the imposts.

The federal **Constitution** required that a uniform tariff be established within two years and that for 10 years three-quarters of the customs revenue collected be returned to the states. The first tariff in 1902 was designed to raise revenue and protect existing industries; hence it concentrated on manufactured items. The Commonwealth adopted a clearly protective tariff in 1908, which was substantially increased in 1921 (the Greene tariff) and in 1929–30 (the **Scullin** tariff). From 1908 Australia gave preference to British goods, which Britain reciprocated from 1919. After Britain abandoned free trade in 1931, an Empire-wide tariff regime was established at the 1932 **Ottawa** Conference. Under its terms,

Australia undertook to lower or restrict tariffs on imports of British manufactured goods in return for free access of its primary products to Britain. During World War II import restrictions virtually replaced tariffs as the means of control over trade. These were continued until 1960, when highly protective duties were reinstated.

From 1921 a Tariff Board gave independent advice on tariff levels. The aim was to protect ministers from the importunities of lobbyists and to produce a 'scientific' tariff. Needless to say, politics could not be easily removed from an issue where so many interests were vitally concerned. Leon Glezer produced a subtle study of the operation of the board in *Tariff Politics* (1981). From the mid-1960s the board, created to administer protective duties, became an advocate of free trade. It was renamed the Industries Assistance Commission in 1974 and the Industry Commission in 1990, and in these forms was a powerful force in the dismantling of protective duties which began in the 1970s and was almost complete in the 1990s.

Nineteenth-century customs houses, which were buildings of some distinction, survive in the capital-city ports, where they were once the centre of mercantile activity and the chief collectors of government revenue. David Day has written a two-volume history of Customs in Australia (1993, 1996).

JOHN HIRST

Tasman, Abel Janszoon (?1603–59) undertook many voyages of exploration for the Dutch East Indies Company, including two—1642 and 1644—which brought him to Australia. He named the place where he landed in 1642 **Van Diemen's Land**, after the governor of the Dutch East Indies. The name was used until the mid-nineteenth century, when it was replaced by Tasmania. Tasman's journals were first published soon after the voyages; Edward Duyker's edited version of journal extracts appeared in 1992.

KT

Tasmania was settled by Aborigines about 40 000 years ago. They spread throughout that area and more than 20 000 years ago lived further south than any other people. The sinking of Bass Strait (around 12 000 years ago) must have presented many challenges and contributed to the continuing simplicity of the Tasmanian tool-kit. Various commentators have seen the Tasmanians as ultra-primitive, even as facing genetic doom irrespective of European contact. Counter-argument proposes that their life-ways were efficient rather than impoverished. Their funeral ceremonies suggest a developed cultural life. About the year 1800 numbers probably approximated 6000.

Abel **Tasman** saw and named **Van Diemen's Land** in 1642 and landed a party on the south-east coast. From the late eighteenth century, visitors included several British and French explorer–scientists, notably those led by Nicolas **Baudin** and Matthew **Flinders**. British exploitation began with Bass Strait **sealing** in the 1790s; formal colonisation followed in 1803–04 in both south and north, served by the towns of **Hobart** and Launceston respectively. Strategic concerns were more significant in motivating this settlement than that in NSW, yet the Napoleonic Wars contributed to the imperial government giving the colony little heed for years. The first (lieutenant-)governor, David **Collins**, lost purpose well before his death in 1810. Residents—many of them convicts from Sydney—survived as the Aborigines did, by hunting in the bush. In 1812 the northern and southern sub-colonies amalgamated. Thomas **Davey**, governor 1813–17, did only a little to modify anarchic modes. Their chief expression was **bushranging** by escaped or erstwhile convicts. Michael **Howe**, most famous of them, conjured a possible alliance between bushrangers and Aborigines.

Van Diemen's Land shared in that furbishing of Empire which followed the Napoleonic Wars. Governors William Sorell (1817–24) and George **Arthur** (1824–36), both very able, oversaw the establishment of a **gentry** whose granted estates were tended by convict labour. Direct **transportation** from Britain commenced. **Wool** became a significant export, local pastoralists sponsoring the settlement of the **Port Phillip District** in the mid-1830s. Maritime industry continued to flourish, and tertiary services became quite sophisticated. Such growth, especially that of pastoralism, fell heavily on the Aborigines, who fought hard against the intruders. Arthur's attempt to capture and resettle the Aborigines by the Black Line failed. G.A. **Robinson** later gathered the remnants together, but the full-blood race did not survive.

The governors who followed Arthur were less commanding figures: John **Franklin** (1836–43), John **Eardley-Wilmot** (1843–46), and William **Denison** (1847–54). While the economy ebbed in these years, cessation of transportation to NSW meant that the island now reached its peak importance as a gaol, underpinning Britain's structures of authority and rule. Early cultural activity was exemplified in the writings of Henry **Savery**, a convict, and from slightly later still survive such institutions as Hobart's Theatre Royal (1837), the Royal Society of Tasmania (1843), and Anglican schools in both Launceston and Hobart (1846, 1847). Seeing transportation as a moral evil and an impediment to self-government, many colonists—most famously John **West**—crusaded for its abolition, which occurred in 1852–53. The end-point of West's excellent *History of Tasmania* (1852) is the success of the **anti-transportation** movement. The name-change to Tasmania came with self-government in 1855–56. The population was then around 80 000.

The end of transportation failed to bring the prosperity its abolitionists had forecast. Rather the truth now became apparent that Britain's expenditure on convict services had upheld the economy. Concurrent **gold rushes** in Victoria drew manpower from the island. Tasmania now entered upon its role as Cinderella of the Australian colonies. Conservative men and attitudes dominated its politics. The stigma of convictism diminished but little, partly because of the vehemence with which anti-transportationists had denounced it.

On the margins of this society were the Bass Strait islanders, the descendants of the sealers and Aboriginal women; timber gatherers, especially 'piners' in the south-west; small farmers—in the south-east growing those apples which became emblematic of Tasmania, in the north-west specialising in the potato; and trappers and shepherds of the central plateau. From the 1870s mining developed, tin at Mount Bischoff being followed by gold at Beaconsfield and then by the riches of copper, silver, and gold of the further west. Difficult terrain gave work in the latter fields a heroic cast. The economy achieved new strength, but unevenly in both geographical and social terms. Regional identities crystallised, resulting jealousies becoming a dominant force in Tasmanian politics and life.

Liberalism quickened in the later nineteenth century, bringing the colony towards Australian norms of social democracy. An outstanding reformer was Andrew Inglis **Clark**, famous both for impelling the adoption of proportional representation in Tasmania's lower-house elections and for his advocacy of **Federation**. Liberals such as Clark achieved the foundation of the University of Tasmania around 1890. Dynamic bureaucrats worked for better public health and education in the early 1900s. Launceston won acclaim as a model progressive municipality. The **Australian Labor Party** developed later than elsewhere but held office briefly in 1909 and longer 1914–16. In 1910 population stood at 193 803.

Tasmania was even more whole-hearted than the nation generally in support of World War I, and had its due share of subsequent ambiguities and disillusions. The 1920s saw some industrialisation underpinned by hydro-generation of electricity; zinc-smelting and confectionery at Hobart, textiles in Launceston, cement on Maria Island and in the north-west were the chief industries. Primary industry had little growth, however, and out-migration remained high. Many Tasmanians came to see Federation as having doomed the state.

The longest-serving premier of the time was Labor's J.A. **Lyons**, who held office 1923–28 and then proceeded to federal politics and (having crossed from Labor) the prime ministership. Lyons's successor as head of Tasmanian Labor was A.G. Ogilvie, who after becoming premier in 1934 showed dynamism and flair in both social and developmental policies. He was also forthright in calling for military preparedness against the Axis powers. He and Lyons, long antagonistic rivals, died within a few weeks of each other in mid-1939.

Alan Villiers lived and wrote in Tasmania in the later 1920s, launching his career as a superb depictor of the seas. Other journalists of the time and place included modernist critic and poet Clive Turnbull, and Robert Atkinson, whose compositions appealed to Percy **Grainger** as heralding 'the music of the future'. Two novelists of romance and adventure, Marie Bjelke-Petersen and N.W. Norman, sold well on international markets: Bjelke-Petersen extolled the virtues of Tasmania, while Norman was enthralled by Central Australia and urged his compatriots to find the national spirit there.

World War II dealt death and upheaval, but also heralded a generation of high material progress. In the inter-censal period 1947–54 Tasmania's population growth-rate exceeded the nation's, numbers then reaching 308 752. Industrialisation grew, aluminium smelting and paper processing to the fore; the Hydro-Electric Commission became the state's directing force. Primary produce found generally good markets. Tertiary employment rose fast, services in education and health sometimes excelling national standards. Labor held office continuously 1934–69; Premiers Robert Cosgrove and E.E. **Reece** showed vast political skills and commitment.

Two major poets lived in Tasmania after the war: Gwen Harwood 1945–95 and James **McAuley** 1961–76. Christopher Koch and Vivian Smith, both locally born in the early 1930s, early displayed their talents in creative writing. The latter pair were among many local graduates of the 1950s who were to achieve distinction. The university generally achieved much at this time despite the concurrent agony of the **Orr case**.

From about 1970 Tasmania changed in much the same degree as the rest of the industrialised world, but in its own distinctive way. Central in this was failure of industrial manufacturing to sustain momentum and employment. Population growth slackened to some 472 000 in 1994. Social balance and ease faltered, while such was the political flux that nine persons held office as premier 1972–96. Interacting with all these trends the Green environmental movement waxed passionate. Reacting especially against the flooding of Lake Pedder (completed 1972) by the Hydro-Electric Commission, environmentalists fought many campaigns, most famously and successfully that against damming of the Franklin River (early 1980s). Leaders included the charismatic Bob Brown; he and other members of the **Greens**, helped by proportional representation, held the balance of parliamentary power 1989–92 and from 1996. Warwick Fox, Robyn Eckersley, and P.R. Hay contributed notably to ecological theory, while B.C. Mollison developed his ideas and practice of 'permaculture'. Some could see Tasmania as equipped by both its glorious topography and its strange history to guide the world towards beneficent post-industrial ways.

A second transforming power came from the part-Aboriginal, Palawa, people. Official figures recorded 38 Aborigines in 1961, 10 113 in 1994, an expansion prompted by an eagerness to claim both an identity so long suppressed and the new welfare available to Aborigines. From 1972 the Tasmanian Aboriginal Centre provided leadership of great skill and tenacity. Its driving force, Michael Mansell, became a national leader in the call for Aboriginal sovereignty. In 1995 parliament recognised land rights over selected areas.

The generation saw much cultural achievement by Euro-Tasmanians. Outstanding were novels by Christopher Koch, Amanda Lohrey, James McQueen, and Richard Flanagan. The dominant tone was contemplative, often anguished in pondering grimmer Tasmanian experience. Meanwhile, scholars reared and educated in Tasmania contributed decisively to wider debates: Marilyn Lake to feminism; Henry **Reynolds** in Aboriginal matters; Dennis Altman on homosexual issues. Peter Conrad returned from England to offer Bicentennial reflections on his island home. Not only in

relation to environmentalism and the Palawa could it seem that, as Tasmania's share of the nation's population diminished, the place became more rather than less remarkable.

Tasmanian-born Lloyd **Robson** has written a two-volume *History of Tasmania* (1983, 1991), and so too his erstwhile teacher W.A. **Townsley** (1991, 1994).

MICHAEL ROE

Tattersalls, now widely known as Tatts, was established in Australia in 1858, with the opening in Sydney of Tattersall's Club, based on the English sporting club of the same name. Initially the sweepstakes were for members only; however, by 1881 so many other people wanted to participate that George Adams (1839–1904), the licensee of O'Brien's Hotel where Tattersall's was based, ran his first public Tattersall's sweep on the Sydney Cup. The success of these sweeps and their consequent growth attracted the attention of the churches, which pressured the government to ban sweeps and lotteries. Adams went to Brisbane but similar legislation forced him to Tasmania, where the premier, Sir Edward **Braddon**, supported the introduction of legislation that made Tattersall's the only lottery permitted to operate in Tasmania. With the eventual acceptance of state lotteries as revenue sources for hospitals and charities in Qld and NSW, the Victorian premier, John Cain, persuaded Tatts to move its headquarters to Melbourne in 1954. A need for greater revenue led to a move away from the sweeps and the introduction, in 1972, of Tattslotto. Other styles of gambling including poker machines have followed. Trevor Wilson and Eddie Dean, *The Luck of the Draw* (1996), chronicles the development of Tatts.

KT

Taxation lay very lightly on colonial Australian society. Until late in the nineteenth century there was no taxation of income or of company profits. All that was earned was kept. The chief form of taxation was a customs duty on imported goods, scarcely felt by the taxpayer, and easily collected since all the colonies faced the sea by which the great majority of imports arrived. The second chief source of revenue for colonial governments was not a tax at all—this was the receipts from the sale of Crown land. It was because colonial governments were able to acquire large revenues with so little pain that they took on so many functions, many of which—like police and education—in other countries were the province of local government.

The customs duty on imports was at first designed only to raise revenue. From the 1850s in Victoria there was a demand that duties be raised to protect local farmers and manufacturers. Victoria adopted a protective **tariff** in 1866, but it was not so protective that it did not raise more revenue, and indeed this was one of its purposes (see **Protection**). Other colonies, except NSW, moved to higher or protective duties for similar mixed motives. More revenue had to be raised from customs as receipts from land sales tapered off. In NSW land receipts remained buoyant, which enabled it to keep to the policy of low import duties and free trade.

Taxation

In the **depression** of the late nineteenth century, revenues declined; governments finally imposed direct taxes on personal income, company profits, and land, beginning with **South Australia** in 1884. The details can be found in the useful compendium *Taxation in Australia* by Stephen Mills (1925). Since the income of workers was excluded from income tax, the imposition of direct taxation partially offset the regressive effect of indirect taxes on consumption and was advanced as a democratic and radical cause, frequently resisted by legislative councils. Customs and excise remained the chief form of taxation, though the imposts which most directly affected the workers' standard of living now came under attack—those on tea, sugar, and kerosene.

Federation fundamentally disrupted the taxation regime: because control of imports was to pass to the Commonwealth, it would acquire the customs and excise duties which were the states' chief source of income. The drafters of the Constitution envisaged a small central government, but they could not help making it rich. Much argument at the Constitutional Conventions of the 1890s concerned how its surplus revenue would be returned to the states. The states wanted a guaranteed return, but free-trade NSW did not want the guarantee to be too high for fear that the new Commonwealth would have to establish very high customs duties to pay for it. To secure the adhesion of NSW after the failure of the 1898 referendum, the guaranteed return to the states was to operate for only 10 years. This prompted **Deakin's** prophecy that thereafter the states would be bound to the chariot wheels of the Commonwealth.

It took other developments before the prophecy was fulfilled. The states still had open to them income tax, land tax, and sales tax. The Commonwealth Labor government imposed its own land tax in 1911 in order to break up large estates. It partly achieved this aim; it also collected a substantial revenue and trespassed on what had been thought a state preserve. The **High Court** upheld the Commonwealth's right to do so.

The Commonwealth introduced its own income tax in 1915 to pay for World War I, and retained it after the war at a lower rate. In the 1920s and 1930s there were thus two income taxes, state and federal, calculated on different bases, with the Commonwealth tax being collected by the states, except in WA where the Commonwealth collected both taxes.

In the 1930s Depression the income of the working class was subject to income tax for the first time when states imposed special levies to pay for job-creation schemes. In World War II the Commonwealth needed to tax all incomes heavily to pay for the war and to reduce private consumption. It achieved what no-one had previously thought possible: the exclusion of the states from income-taxing. The Commonwealth set a high tax rate—equal to the previous Commonwealth and state taxes combined—and undertook to return some of this revenue to the states on condition that they abandoned their own income taxes. Legally they were still free to impose income tax; but if they did, they would forgo the Commonwealth grant and any tax they imposed would be in addition to the new combined high rate. Politically it was impossible for them to do so.

The imposition of the new income tax on the workers by a Labor government aroused some opposition in the party. To soften the blow, some of the revenue was earmarked for an expanded **social welfare** system. The Labor Party had always insisted that the rich and not the workers should be taxed for this purpose. The departure of a Labor government from this policy has featured in recent reassessments of the value to the workers of the welfare state: the workers were taxed to pay for the welfare (see Rob Watts, *The Foundations of the National Welfare State*, 1987). To ensure that workers did pay their tax, pay-as-you-earn deductions were introduced.

Uniform taxation, as the Commonwealth take-over was called, was upheld by the High Court without reliance on the defence power. It could thus be continued in peacetime. The states were now dependent on the Commonwealth for a large part of their revenue. Over time more of this came as tied grants, the Commonwealth directing the states how it should be spent.

The states might have been able to secure a large income for themselves by expanding their sales taxes into a broad-based goods and service tax, but the High Court, in the most perverse of all its judgments, blocked the way. Since 1926 it has ruled that 'excise', reserved to the Commonwealth, means any form of sales tax. No matter how the states dressed up a sales tax, the High Court declared it an excise and struck it out. The other growth tax to which the states have resorted is a tax on **gambling**.

The Commonwealth income tax collected a rapidly rising revenue in the 1950s and 1960s as inflation carried taxpayers into higher brackets on the graduated scale. In the 1970s evasions and avoidance became widespread, assisted by a High Court which shared the values of the evaders and avoiders. Following a 'tax summit' in 1985, the **Hawke** Labor government reduced the tax rates, abolished many concessions and exemptions, and tightened compliance, adding a capital gains tax and a fringe benefits tax to close off escape routes. Direct tax on income was becoming harder to sustain politically—indeed, the parties were outbidding each other to lower tax—which left revenue-raising particularly vulnerable in the absence of a goods and services tax (GST).

Labor proposed a GST at its tax summit in 1985 but did not persist with it. The Liberal Party offered a GST at the 1993 election and lost. In 1996 the Liberals under John **Howard** won an election with a GST as the centrepiece of a program of tax reform. The tax is set at a rate of 10 per cent. Food had to be excluded to ensure its passage through the Senate. The revenue raised by the GST flows to the states, the first significant redressing of the mismatch between their responsibilities and their taxing capacity since the adoption of uniform taxation.

The Labor Party opposed the GST and historically has preferred direct to indirect taxes, but it shows no sign of being able to persuade the electorate to adopt new direct taxes. Australia is notable for not having a wealth tax of any sort. The states used to levy death duties, but when Qld abolished its tax in 1977, partly to lure retirees, the other states followed. The Commonwealth then abolished its duties. They were very unpopular, which suggests that egalitarian Australia is more upset at taxing the person who has made good than it is worried at the adverse consequences of inherited wealth.

The leading critic of the taxation system—of both its inequities and inefficiencies and the imbalance between Commonwealth and the states in taxing capacity—has been R.L. Mathews. He examines the origins of the present system in *Federal Finance: Inter-Governmental Financial Relations in Australia Since Federation* (1972), a more wide-ranging study than its title suggests. Julie P. Smith, *Taxing Prosperity* (1993), outlines the story of taxation in Australia.

JOHN HIRST

Taylor, George Augustine (1872–1928), artist and craftsman, and **Florence Mary** (1879–1969), architect, were husband and wife. George worked as an artist in the 1890s, contributing cartoons to several magazines, including the *Bulletin*. He also developed an interest in radio technology and aircraft manufacture. George and Florence shared an interest in the then new field of **town planning**. George played a part, with John **Sulman**, in the formation of the Town Planning Association of New South Wales in 1913. He published several trade journals of construction, including *Building*. Florence, who was the sole female student of architecture at the Sydney Technical College, became Australia's first woman architect and engineer; she was, however, granted professional membership of the Institute of Architects of New South Wales only in 1920. She continued her work long after her husband's death.

HD

Taylor, (Patrick) Gordon (1896–1966) was one of the pioneers of long-distance **aviation** and flew with both Charles **Kingsford Smith** and Charles Ulm during the 1930s. He is best remembered for an extraordinary incident during a 1935 flight with Kingsford Smith in the *Southern Cross*. Engine damage forced Smith to turn back at the halfway point between Australia and NZ. When dropping oil pressure caused one of the remaining two engines to fail, Taylor climbed along the strut, collected oil from the damaged engine, and transferred it to the failing engine. He repeated the feat several times. Taylor re-enacted this incident for the film *Smithy* (1946). Taylor operated a flying business, and then ferried flying-boats from the USA until joining the **Royal Australian Air Force** in 1943. He soon transferred to the RAF as a civilian captain and ferried aircraft from Canada across the Atlantic Ocean. Taylor wrote extensively about his experiences as well as recording them in an Australian Broadcasting Corporation film, *An Airman Remembers* (1963).

KT

Taylor, (Thomas) Griffith (1880–1963) was a pioneer of university geography in Australia and Canada, and a vigorous proponent of geography's role in citizenship education. He provided analytical studies of selected national issues—including population predictions, tropical settlement, transcontinental railways, the multi-faceted question of race, and further expansions of crop and livestock frontiers—and the boosters of an '**Australia Unlimited**' disputed his allegedly pessimistic stance. He was appointed as foundation head of the department of geography at the University of Sydney in 1920, but his pugnacious personality and increasing notoriety as a purported 'environmental determinist' eventually left him dangerously exposed. Resigning from Sydney in 1928, he built an international career at the Universities of Chicago and Toronto. Taylor's early campaigning is discussed in J.M. Powell, *Griffith Taylor and 'Australia Unlimited'* (1993) and *An Historical Geography of Modern Australia* (1988, 1991).

Taylor is probably best-remembered in Australia for his remarkably accurate forecast of a total national **population** of approximately 19 million in AD 2000. That understates his broader contributions to national planning strategy and **conservation**. His major books include *A Geography of Australasia* (1914), *Environment and Race* (1927), *Australia* (1940), *Canada* (1947), and *Urban Geography* (1949). His disappointing, partly ghost-written autobiography is *Journeyman Taylor* (1957), and a useful if uncritical modern biography is Marie Sanderson, *Griffith Taylor* (1988).

J.M. POWELL

Telegraph, see **Communications**; **Overland Telegraph**

Telephone, see **Communications**

Television transformed Australian social and political life in the second half of the twentieth century. Introduced to Sydney and Melbourne by the **Menzies** government in 1956, it had spread to all capital cities by 1960. Regional access followed rapidly. With satellites complementing terrestrial transmission, and colour introduced in 1975, there were few homes that could not be reached by the late 1980s. About 99 per cent of Australians own at least one television and, on average, they spent over 20 hours a week watching television programs in 2000.

Australia's dual commercial and national **radio** system was the model for television. The **Australian Broadcasting Corporation**, and the multicultural SBS from 1980, provided public service broadcasting. Until restrictions on cross-media ownership were imposed in 1987, commercial (advertiser-funded) television was dominated by newspaper interests. A policy of 'localism' and a two-station ownership limit restricted the penetration of metropolitan commercial networks into regional areas. The **Hawke** government's 'aggregation' and 'equalisation' initiatives undid the local monopolies. De facto national networks, now implicitly recognised, became practical realities. Attempts to stimulate diversity in ownership of both metropolitan and country commercial television yielded mostly unintended consequences. The Australian Broadcasting Corporation's country audience share was substantially diminished by the presence of additional competitors. Two metropolitan networks went into receivership. The **Fairfax** newspaper group was a collateral casualty. Eventually, underlying market forces produced more effective integration of capital city and regional groupings. Australia's richest man, Kerry **Packer**, sold and re-acquired the Nine network. The Canadian Canwest company has remained successful, persuading regulators that its dominant financial position in Ten did not translate into operational control. The Seven network, after an inglorious episode in the portfolio of disgraced adventurer Christopher Skase, was bought by one of the few enduring entrepreneurs of the 1980s, Kerry Stokes.

Governments from the 1970s onwards were criticised for television industry policies which were supposedly technology-driven—by spectrum scarcity or satellite abundance, for example. In fact, the role of the ABC as well as the successive frameworks for commercial ownership and control were also substantially shaped by concerns about the influence of existing and emerging media interests. After a first decade dominated by foreign (mostly American) programs, Australian audiences were increasingly receptive to locally produced drama and comedy. Thirty years later, with three-quarters of a billion dollars' worth of Australian programs being made each year, the television industry was seen as having significant employment implications as well as cultural potency.

Stimulation of local production and maintenance of an Australian cultural identity were contingent on the exercise of regulatory authority. But domestic arrangements could not be permanently shielded from global ideological and commercial forces. Regulatory power over television content as well as ownership was progressively attenuated as the Broadcasting Control Board of the 1940s gave way to a Tribunal and then an Authority. The implicit recognition that television required unique regulatory consideration and protection was all but abandoned in the late 1990s, with the transfer of major functions from a reconstructed Authority to the Australian Competition and Consumer Commission. But the incoming **Howard** government's plan in 1997 to relax limitations on both cross-media ownership and foreign control foundered on Coalition back-bench reluctance to endorse dispensations blatantly favourable to Kerry Packer and Rupert **Murdoch**, and it has remained in policy limbo ever since. Pay television meanwhile had been introduced in a supposedly pro-competitive telecommunications environment which ensured that few of the players would be viable until most of them were bankrupt. It seems that only those with deep pockets will survive. Meanwhile, the policy of technology neutrality has gone out the window with the government's digital agenda legislation of 1999, which seeks to micro-define and control what new players may be able to do with the new technologies of carriage and transmission.

With the notable exception of Sandra Hall's *Supertoy* (1976), there was little serious historical inquiry into television's Australian history until the 1980s. The political origins of television and the technical telecommunications dimension attracted early interest. A magisterial commissioned history of the ABC by K.S. **Inglis** (1983) placed national television broadcasting in context. Cultural and media studies examining audiences, programming, and advertising brought multi-disciplinary insights to bear; a good example is Tom O'Regan's *Australian Television Culture* (1996). There remain significant gaps in knowledge and understanding. The biographies of media entrepreneurs are useful (for example, Bridget Griffen-Foley's *Sir Frank Packer: The Young Master*, 2000, and William Shawcross's *Murdoch: Ringmaster of the Information Circus*, 1992) but no substitute for the detailed studies of particular stations and networks which are yet to be written. Though there is well-informed journalism on communications since the mid-1980s, there is no adequately researched account of the business development of the industry or of its political context. An admirably compact historical summary by Terry Flew, in Stuart Cunningham and Graeme Turner (eds), *The Media and Communications in Australia* (2001), is the best available introduction.

CAMERON HAZLEHURST AND STUART CUNNINGHAM

Television, historical has generally operated at a remove from historical research. There have been occasional popular series such as the newsreel compilation *This Fabulous Century* (1978), but no Australian equivalent to the American PBS network's history of the American Civil War, or the BBC's monumental study of British participation in World War II. In general, Australian television has dealt with history in one of two ways: as occasional topics within general documentary or current affairs series (such as Chris Masters's 1995 *Four Corners* story on **Gallipoli**, 'The Fatal Shore'); or, more commonly, as the theme for dramatic series or mini-series.

Television historical drama in Australia began in the early 1960s with the **Australian Broadcasting Commission's** series *Stormy Petrel* (1960), *The Outcasts* (1961), and *The Patriots* (1962). These were set in early colonial Australia and aimed at a high level of historical accuracy in the narratives and the settings. There was little Australian expertise in writing for television, and Australian costume dramas looked amateurish in comparison with the slick American productions on the commercial channels. With the exception of ATN7's production of *Jonah* (1962), the commercial channels largely left history to the ABC until well into the 1970s. Colonial history, when it did appear on commercial channels, merely offered a novel backdrop for that familiar American genre, the western—as in the series based on Cobb & Co., *Whiplash* (1961)—rather than an opportunity for a respectful, let alone critical, dramatisation of Australian history. Audiences largely agreed, their tastes formed by Hollywood melodrama and thus insufficiently satisfied by the relatively unexciting narratives of the historical series.

It was not until the late 1960s that Australian drama started to attract substantial audiences. The contemporary police drama *Homicide* (1967) was the first Australian drama series to achieve a place in the top 10 programs. The gradual acceleration of interest in Australian material, which supported the push for the establishment of the Australian Film and Television School and the Australian Film Development Corporation between 1969 and 1972, seems to have had an effect on the Australian television audience's enthusiasm for the local product. Government investment in the film industry stimulated a brief 'bushranger-led' recovery of local historical drama. The screening of Homestead's *Cash and Company* (1975) and *Tandarra* (1976), the Australian Broadcasting Corporation's *Rush* (1973–74; 1975–76) and *Ben Hall* (1974–75), and Channel Nine's *Luke's Kingdom* (1976) showed that it was possible to make historical drama that retained a degree of historical accuracy (certainly this was a concern for *Rush* and *Ben Hall*) while acknowledging the need to provide high drama in conventional form (*Luke's Kingdom* and the rest). The commercial success of the period drama on both the big and little screens seems to have encouraged Channel Nine to embark on its only successful venture into serial drama. *The Sullivans* (1976), was a soap opera–cum–serial set between the two world wars and promoted on the basis of its attention to historical accuracy, a discipline which, as its historical adviser Donna Hellier noted (in *AHA Bulletin*, 1988), was more rigorously applied to props and costumes than to speech and mores.

The most significant contribution to Australian television's representation of Australian history was the development of the local mini-series. Usually seen to begin with the American *Roots*, a sweeping dramatisation of the history of black Americans, the mini-series was programmed as an event rather than as a continuing series and usually shown on consecutive nights in two-hour blocks. The first Australian production of this kind was *Against the Wind* (1978), a colonial melodrama focused on the life of an emancipated convict played by Jon English. (A review article on this series in *HS*, 1979, signalled that television history had at last caught the attention of academic historians.) Other historical mini-series followed, including an adaptation of Eleanor **Dark's** *A Timeless Land* (1979–80).

Changes to the regulatory structure of the Australian film industry in 1980 had a significant effect on Australian mini-series production during the rest of the decade. Most television production had been ineligible for Australian Film Commission and other state funding assistance until 1980, so the big budgets necessary for mini-series were rarely attainable. The change in the funding climate and the introduction of tax concessions for investors made the mini-series a much more realistic proposition. Mini-series became a dominant production mode. Mainstream period melodramas, such as *Sarah Dane* (1982) and the Crawfords' production *All the Rivers Run* (1983), proliferated. Adaptations of Australian fiction flourished, building their appeal partly on the work upon which they were based and partly upon their setting within a key point in Australian history: examples include *A Town Like Alice* (1981), *1915* (1982), *For the Term of His Natural Life* (1983), and *Waterfront* (1984).

However, the most significant development was the contribution of a new production company, Kennedy Miller.

Established by the late Byron Kennedy and George Miller to produce the *Mad Max* movies, Kennedy Miller is one of the few production companies in Australia which had a continuing existence. Kennedy Miller's mini-series productions were about key moments in Australian history. They include *The Dismissal* (1983), a documentary drama examining the dismissal of the **Whitlam** government in 1975; *Bodyline* (1984), on the infamous **bodyline** cricket Test series between Australia and England in the 1930s; *The Cowra Breakout* (1985), which told of a mass escape from a Japanese prisoner-of-war camp at **Cowra** during World War II; and *Vietnam* (1987), a powerful analysis of the social effects of Australia's participation in the **Vietnam War**. Kennedy Miller's productions were remarkable for their explicit commitment to historical construction. Miller, in particular, understood the potential for television to create national mythologies through its presentation of history. Kennedy Miller respected the source material, often incorporating documentary footage and applying exacting standards of accuracy. The documentary style of *The Dismissal* makes few concessions to the conventions or demands of television narrative melodrama. *Vietnam* approached its subject through a fictional group of participants, but took the radical step of treating the Vietnamese participants in similar detail and with similar sympathy and identification to the Australians, thus provoking a fresh perspective on the experience of the war.

The influence of the Kennedy Miller mini-series has been profound, spawning what has become probably the dominant, revisionist, mode of representing Australian history on television. Stuart Cunningham (in John Tulloch and Graeme Turner, eds, *Australian Television: Programs, Pleasures and Politics*, 1989) has argued that these mini-series, unlike the period films that dominated the first decade of the revival of the film industry, did not represent the past in a nostalgic manner. They were 'critical and interventionary', so that viewers could regard the mini-series as 'significant historical arguments'. *Vietnam*, for example, offers a contemporary, critical, but reconciliatory, re-reading of that period in Australian history, while *The Cowra Breakout* challenges the conventional opposition between wartime combatants in order to understand the attempted mass escape of Japanese prisoners from an Australian internment camp, and to retrieve that story for the national history. The point also holds for other commercially produced historical mini-series. Even the highly commercial narrative of the Burrows–Dixon production of *Anzacs* (1985), for instance, was structured around the polemical argument that the core experience for the **AIF** in World War I was in France, not at Gallipoli. While mini-series declined in number and scale after the establishment of the Film Finance Corporation in 1988, the practice of using them as vehicles for historical argument has continued. The Australian Broadcasting Corporation mini-series *The Leaving of Liverpool* (1993), for instance, focused on the abuse of British children put into Australian church and charity care during the war, and was directly responsible for the pressing of claims for compensation from some of the victims.

Temperance

It is through such strategies that Australian television has made its most significant contribution to Australians' understanding of their history. This has not occurred through a direct engagement with the discipline of history, but through the mining of history for stories suitable as the building blocks of national mythologies or, alternatively, for evidence of the inadequacy of existing mythologies to accurately reflect the reality of many Australians' experiences.

GRAEME TURNER

Temperance took root in Australia in the 1830s, as in other English-speaking countries. Directed first at spirits and not at wine and beer, temperance meant moderation in opposition to drunkenness; but it soon came to mean total abstinence from all **alcoholic** beverages. Temperance societies formed in all colonies with the support of both Protestant and Catholic clergymen, although the denominational bodies did not endorse it immediately. The idea that social regeneration might come through the adoption of temperance, as temperance advocates argued, encountered some criticism from a minority of churchmen, particularly High Anglicans. Some objected to the identification of temperance with total abstinence, while others saw the temperance movement as 'substituting the gospel of teetotalism for that of Christ' (John Barrett, *That Better Country*, 1966). Michael **Roe** in *Quest for Authority in Eastern Australia 1835–1851* (1965) sees the early temperance movement as the example *par excellence* of the doctrine of moral enlightenment which, he argues, was supplanting traditional Christianity in the mid-nineteenth century. It appealed to mind and will, placing the emphasis on human effort rather than divine grace, contrary to the prevailing **evangelical** theology of most Protestants. Within a generation, however, the Protestant denominations adopted temperance officially, forming their own denominational societies as well as cooperating in the Temperance Alliance or Local Option Leagues. The Catholic Church encouraged the formation of temperance societies under its influence, and discouraged Catholics from participating in the broader temperance movement, dominated by Protestants.

A variety of organisations promoted temperance: friendly societies, such as the Rechabites and the Sons of Temperance; the Good Templars; and for children the Band of Hope, founded 1847. The **Young Men's Christian Association** preached total abstinence in its evangelistic campaigns; and the succession of visiting **evangelists** to Australia in the last quarter of the nineteenth and the early twentieth centuries reinforced the temperance message. Several temperance evangelists also came to Australia; one of them was the American Eli Johnson, whose wife introduced the **Woman's Christian Temperance Union** to Australia in 1882. Matthew Burnett, an English Wesleyan Methodist, spent some 25 years preaching temperance around Australia, claiming to have persuaded 140 000 to sign the pledge. Women temperance lecturers, like Bessie **Lee**, were prominent in campaigns for women's suffrage.

Like the earlier temperance advocates, these evangelists relied on moral suasion in their effort to secure pledges. But their campaigns also assisted the temperance movement in its quest to curb intemperance. The movement encouraged the establishment of temperance hotels and coffee palaces, which proliferated in the 1880s. The movement's main thrust, however, was to seek legislative restriction of the liquor traffic. Emanating largely from the Protestant Churches, this became a middle-class campaign against the public house (see **pubs**) and the working men who drank there. It sought a reduction in the hours of trading, Sunday closing, the abolition of barmaids, and the limiting of licensed houses through local option. **Liberal** governments, which drew much of their support from middle-class Protestants, were generally more sympathetic to temperance reform than colonial conservatives or the **Australian Labor Party** when it emerged in the 1890s, although some of the first Labor MPs were staunch temperance men. The conservatives had more rapport with the Licensed Victuallers Association, while the Labor Party objected to the temperance emphasis on the drinking habits of the working class, taking the effect for the cause of social problems. Evangelical Protestants, however, were mostly wedded to *laissez-faire* economic principles, and the minority which sought a more just social order was just as committed to temperance reform. J.D. Bollen, *Protestantism and Social Reform in New South Wales 1890–1910* (1972), judges that temperance became '*the* Protestant reform'.

Temperance reformers achieved the introduction of local option laws in most colonies in the late nineteenth century, but the reformers did not obtain the choice of 'no licence' until the early twentieth century, when certain middle-class suburbs in Sydney, Melbourne, and Adelaide became 'dry'. Temperance reformers took up the campaign for six o'clock closing of hotel bars after the introduction of early closing of shops. The outbreak of World War I provided the opportune moment for this campaign, when abstinence became part of patriotism. SA carried a referendum in favour of six o'clock closing in March 1915, after an intense campaign. Success in SA encouraged temperance reformers in other states but the Victorian and NSW governments resisted for a time, Tasmania adopting six o'clock closing in May 1916, NSW in June 1916, and Victoria only later in 1916. As Walter Phillips showed in *HS* (1980), the infamous **six o'clock swill** was a phenomenon of south-eastern Australia; Qld and WA compromised with eight and nine o'clock closing respectively.

The temperance reformers saw six o'clock closing as the last step before prohibition. They never achieved that, but temperance sentiment was strong enough in several referendums to keep six o'clock closing, supposedly a wartime measure, on the statute books throughout the interwar years on mainland Australia. It was not abandoned in NSW until 1954; it survived in SA and Victoria until the 1960s.

Postwar migrants helped to change Australian culture and drinking habits to some extent. But adherence to temperance principles was also weakening within the Protestant Churches, especially among **Methodists**, who had sworn undying hostility to the liquor traffic. As in other matters, lay conduct influenced changes in official policy. Thus the main Protestant denominations formally abandoned defence of six o'clock closing during the Victorian Royal Commission on the liquor industry in 1964, and in the Methodist Church opposition to moderate drinking weakened. Conservative evangelicals, and the smaller Protestant denominations, upheld the old policy, while a new generation of ministers and lay folk drank in moderation.

WALTER PHILLIPS

Tench, Watkin (?1758–1883) wrote the most accomplished of the **First Fleet** narratives, *A Narrative of the Expedition to Botany Bay* (1789) and *A Complete Account of the Settlement at Port Jackson* (1793). Tench early received a literary education. He joined the Marines as a teenager, and saw service in the wars of 1776–83. He therefore came to NSW with an awareness of colonial ventures elsewhere. Though the First Fleet officers complained bitterly about the inconveniences of the new settlement, they understood the venture's historical significance and began recording its history.

Tench was curious about many features of his new environment; his ability to empathise with those about him meant that he largely avoided the common prejudices against **convicts** and **Aborigines**, and he wrote in a lively manner. He inspected the landscapes about Sydney, and became familiar with their plants, animals and birds, and Aboriginal inhabitants. Before he left the colony, he recorded the efforts of James Ruse and others in agriculture. His descriptions provide invaluable details of the beginnings of European horticulture in Australia and, therefore, also of the ecological transformation of the continent.

Tench powerfully evokes in his books the early struggles to establish the settlement, the despair that accordingly set in, and the relief as it became clear that it would survive. L.F. Fitzhardinge produced a fine scholarly edition of Tench's books in 1979; there has since been a more popular edition by Tim Flannery (1996).

ALAN FROST

Tenison-Woods, Julian Edmund (1832–89) is possibly best known now as co-founder with Mary **MacKillop** of the Sisters of St Joseph of the Sacred Heart in 1866 at Penola, SA. Educated in England, Woods also studied at Marist seminaries in France. He came to Australia with Bishop R.W. Willson, but soon parted with him and went to SA, where he trained for the **Catholic** priesthood. In 1857 he was appointed to Penola. In 1866 he joined with MacKillop to establish the Sisters of St Joseph, but later clashed with her, as he did with other members of the Church.

Tenison-Woods's interests spanned science, writing, and education. He published *Geological Observations in South Australia* (1862). He was appointed as director-general of Catholic schools in 1867, and edited various religious magazines between 1867 and 1871. A mystic, Tenison-Woods was also an acute observer of the natural world who frequently contributed papers to Australian and overseas journals, and wrote scientific articles for the newspapers. *A History of the Discovery and Exploration of Australia* (1865) and his survey *Australian Bibliography*, serialised in the *Australian Monthly*

Magazine (1866–67), are regarded as his most significant works. The autobiographical *Ten Years in the Bush 1857–1867* was published in 1982. Biographies include those by Margaret M. Press (1979) and Erik O. Eriksen; the latter, *The White Flower of Blameless Life* (1996), is described as a 'synoptic biography'.

KT

Tennant, (Kathleen) 'Kylie' (1912–88) wrote novels about people she described affectionately as the 'vagabonds, failures and criminals'. *Tiburon* (1935) and *The Battlers* (1941) epitomise this interest. She worked in a variety of jobs ranging from barmaid to journalist and—in her desire to write from first-hand experience—spent time in gaol, travelled with itinerant bee-keepers, lived with Aboriginal communities, and took to the roads with the unemployed during the **Depression**. Her sympathy for the 'battlers' never blunted her awareness of human absurdities and idiosyncracies, and her work is imbued with a strong sense of the value of life, in spite of its frequent tragedies. Tennant's novels are discussed in a 1966 study by Margaret Dick.

Ride On Stranger (1943) has a strong autobiographical element and is evocative of the Depression years leading up to World War II. Apart from the fiction her work included a popular history, *Australia: Her Story* (1953); a biography of H.V. **Evatt** (1970); a children's book, *All the Proud Tribesmen* (1959); a play about Alfred **Deakin**, *The Man On the Headland* (1971); and an autobiography, *The Missing Heir* (1986). An active figure in the Australian literary world, she was a member of the Commonwealth Literary Fund Advisory Board (1961–72) and a patron of the Fellowship of Australian Writers.

KT

Tennis, also known as lawn tennis, has been popular in Australia as a pastime and **sport** virtually since the game's invention in England in the 1870s. Australia has been a leading tennis nation for much of the sport's history, and dominated the major championships in the 1950s and 1960s. While Australians no longer rule the world scene, the all-time world record tennis crowd is still the 25 578 spectators who watched Australia play USA in the Davis Cup challenge round in Sydney on 27 December 1954; and the Australian Open, one of the world's four pre-eminent (Grand Slam) tournaments, is undoubtedly Australia's biggest and best-known event on the world sporting calendar.

In his excellent article, 'Lawn Tennis' in Wray Vamplew and Brian Stoddart (eds), *Sport in Australia—A Social History* (1994), Graeme Kinross-Smith describes well the game's early development in Australia. Initially, it was played more by women than men and was largely the preserve of the upper and middle classes, especially in the cities. Elsewhere in the world, tennis remained a sport for the well-to-do until recent decades. In Australia, by comparison, top tennis players have come from a wide social stratum and tennis clubs, especially in rural districts, have often been at the centre of local social life. In the middle decades of the twentieth century, the local tennis club (often linked to a church) was the next best thing to a marriage bureau!

Australia's first international tennis champion was Norman Brookes, who in 1907 became the first non-British resident to win the Wimbledon men's singles championship, the world's premier title. He then teamed with New Zealander Anthony Wilding to win the world men's team championship, the Davis Cup, the first time it had been won by a country other than Britain or USA. The son of a wealthy Melbourne businessman, Brookes (later Sir Norman) dominated the administration of Australian tennis (both men's and women's) for the next 50 years.

Sporadic success was enjoyed internationally over the following decades by Australia's leading men players such as Patterson, Crawford, Bromwich, and Quist. This was converted to world supremacy by a seemingly endless stream of Australian champions in the 30 or so years following World War II, as Frank Sedgman, Ken McGregor, Lew Hoad, Ken Rosewall, Mervyn Rose, Ashley Cooper, Mal Anderson, Neale Fraser, Rod Laver, Roy Emerson, Fred Stolle, Bill Bowrey, John Newcombe, and Tony Roche won more than half of all Grand Slam singles championships (the Australian, French, Wimbledon and USA titles). Concurrently, wily coach Harry Hopman guided Australia to 15 Davis Cup victories in 20 years. No nation had ever previously so dominated men's tennis. Rod Laver stands arguably as the world's greatest ever player; the only man to have won all four Grand Slam titles in the same year twice in his career. Laver, like almost all the top Australian players of the era, turned professional at the height of his career. An explanation of Australia's golden era, both the broad base of participation and the unusual level of support for top players, is provided by Kevin Fewster in his article, 'Advantage Australia: Davis Cup Tennis 1950–1959' (*Sporting Traditions*, 1985).

Australia's Margaret Court (née Smith) became the first woman to achieve the Grand Slam in 1970. Before World War II Australia's leading female players were given fewer opportunities than the men to tour overseas and no Australian woman had won an overseas Grand Slam title. Court dominated women's tennis in the 1960s and early 1970s, winning 62 Grand Slam championships. She lost the 1971 Wimbledon singles final to another Australian, Evonne Goolagong (**Cawley**), who won another six Grand Slam singles titles. A women's international teams' competition, the Federation Cup, was instituted in 1963 and Australia won seven of its first 12 years.

Australia's stranglehold on world tennis was broken when the distinction between amateur and professional players was abolished in 1968. Australia's liberal interpretation of the amateur code and the financial riches achieved through its many Davis Cup successes were advantages which soon disappeared with the advent of 'open' tennis. Rod Laver returned to win his second Grand Slam in 1969, but when he helped win back the Davis Cup in 1973 the average age of the Australian team was a creaky 35. Since then only one Australian, Pat Cash, has won a Wimbledon singles title, but Mark Woodforde and Todd Woodbridge have won many Grand Slam doubles titles, including five

consecutive Wimbledon men's doubles championships. Pat Rafter won the US Open in 1997.

Despite this fall from pre-eminence, tennis remains popular in Australia both as a participatory and spectator sport, although soaring real estate values have significantly reduced the number of courts in urban areas. In 1988 the world's most modern tennis centre, with a hardcourt playing surface and unique retractable roof over centre court, opened in Melbourne as home for the Australian Open. Surprisingly, no definitive history of Australian tennis has been written, but Alan Trengrove's *The Story of the Davis Cup* (1985) provides a comprehensive account of Australia's involvement in this important competition.

KEVIN FEWSTER

Tent Embassy was pitched on the lawn outside Parliament House, Canberra, by Aboriginal activists on Australia Day 1972, in an attempt to raise public awareness of the injustices experienced by Aborigines and to demand political recognition from the federal government. Their action had been sparked by Prime Minster Billy **McMahon's** announcement of a general-purpose lease for Aboriginal people that denied them any manner of land rights. Gary Foley and Kevin **Gilbert** were prominent in setting up the embassy; others involved were **Burnum Burnum** and Roberta (Bobbi) Sykes. The tent was pulled down several times after clashes with the police in 1972. It was finally removed in 1975 but later re-established and the earlier canvas shelters replaced by more permanent structures. In 1995 the area was declared a component of the parliamentary vista, but in 1999 the **Howard** government gazetted laws to prohibit vehicles and other structures from the site.

HD

Tenterfield Oration was given by Henry **Parkes**, premier of NSW, at the town of that name on the NSW–Qld border in October 1889. In it he called for the **Federation** of the colonies and the formation of a strong national government. He proposed that delegates from the colonial parliaments meet forthwith to draft a constitution. In itself the speech was not particularly arresting; it contains nothing as memorable as 'the crimson thread of kinship runs through us all', which appeared in a speech of the following year. Nor did it make clear Parkes's strategy of avoiding the differences between NSW and the other colonies on **tariff** policy by allowing the issue to be settled by the new national parliament and not by negotiation beforehand. This was spelled out in the series of speeches which he gave in the next few weeks. The speech was notable because NSW had hitherto stood apart from the incipient federal organisation, the **Federal Council**. The other premiers greeted Parkes's call warily and urged him to join the Federal Council. Parkes refused, insisting that the colonies were ready for union. In 1890 Parkes and the representatives of the other colonies on the council met in Melbourne and decided to call a convention to draft a constitution.

JH

Terra Australis, see **Australia (the name)**

Terra nullius has two meanings, according to Henry **Reynolds**: 'both a country without a sovereign recognised by European authorities and a territory where nobody owns any land at all, where no tenure of any sort existed'. The distinction between senses is politically significant: to assert **Aboriginal land rights** is not necessarily to challenge Australian sovereignty.

These distinct meanings of *terra nullius* structure Reynolds's revision of Australia's history in *The Law of the Land* (1987). Reviewing the policies and practices of British colonisation from 1788 to the 1840s, he did not question British sovereignty, but reinterpreted its significance. Colonial practice did not live up to British law in that Aboriginal people were not attributed property rights but were gradually, and controversially, dispossessed. Correspondence between the British **Colonial Office** and colonial governors and administrators in the 1830s and 1840s showed London's unsuccessful effort to bring Australian colonial practice into line with British understanding of international law, and with practices elsewhere in the Empire.

As Australian common law developed in the second half of the nineteenth century, it was as if 'no tenure of any sort existed' before colonisation. **Blackburn's** judgment in the NT Supreme Court in 1971 reaffirmed this common law tradition. Admitting that the Aborigines of Yirrkala mission had a system of law, Blackburn found that this system had no legal significance. Blackburn applied the legal fiction that Australia had been 'a tract of territory practically unoccupied, without settled inhabitants or settled law', in the words of the **Privy Council's** binding judgment of 1889. As Blackburn pointed out, legal fictions can be unconvincing without losing their binding force.

Though Blackburn did not invoke the doctrine *terra nullius*, he felt bound to insist that Australia had been 'settled', a classification in law which accords no consequence to indigenous customs. Until the 1970s, Australian historical writing contained little to question this view of the colonial process. Subsequent scholarship on **Aboriginal resistance** highlighted the use of force in colonial dispossession. Lawyers began to point out that it would be beneficial to indigenous rights, and more consistent with revisionist history, were Australia reclassified (in law) as 'conquered' territory. Sovereignty derived from 'conquest' is obliged to recognise the customs of those conquered. In 1977, the Wiradjuri lawyer, Paul Coe, went further, denying Australian sovereignty. He sought leave in the **High Court** to argue that Captain **Cook** and Captain **Phillip** had 'wrongfully treated the continent now known as Australia as *terra nullius*'. He claimed that 'conquest' had not extinguished Aboriginal sovereignty.

The High Court has refused to entertain challenges to Australian sovereignty. Without dissenting from that axiom, Justice Lionel **Murphy** in 1979 and 1982 cited anthropological and historical scholarship and a recent advisory opinion by the International Court of Justice to throw doubt on *terra nullius*. He seemed to invite litigation to test whether the legal fiction 'settled' should be overturned in favour of 'conquered'. Although such remarks did not clearly explain how the two meanings of *terra nullius* could be considered separately, Reynolds's distinction helps make sense of Murphy's comments.

When the High Court ruled in 1992 (the **Mabo case**) that 'native title' was protected by Australian common law, the judges reiterated that Australian sovereignty was not justiciable. While deploring forceful dispossession, their judgment did not, however, reclassify Australia as a 'conquered' colony. Rather, the court reinterpreted the essential prerogatives of Australian sovereignty, denying that it entailed wholesale dispossession. The High Court has not 'decisively rejected the concept of *terra nullius*', as Reynolds claimed in 1992. The first meaning of *terra nullius* is respected in the Mabo judgment's reaffirmation of Australian sovereignty. The Crown can lawfully extinguish native title, but some native title has yet to be extinguished. In 1996 Reynolds in *Aboriginal Sovereignty* questioned whether the High Court could affirm native title without implying residual indigenous sovereignty.

Popular reference to *terra nullius* does not necessarily honour the niceties of legal usage. In a letter to the *Age* on 29 March 1986, the mining executive Hugh Morgan denied that Captain Cook was the vanguard of an illegal occupation of Australia. Cook, Morgan insisted, had taken care to establish that Australia was *terra nullius*. Observing **Aborigines**, Cook found 'no agriculture, no animal husbandry, no social or political or religious institutions that could be recognised'. Its potency as a legal fiction much reduced, *terra nullius* lives on, sometimes in such apologetics, more usually as a summary image of any tendency to diminish, or ignore, the indigenous interest and presence. *Terra nullius* is a trope, lurking in once unquestioned usages, such as 'Captain Cook discovered Australia' or describing as 'wilderness' parts of the continent little used by those who have arrived since 1788. It is in this sense that the Nyungar leader, Rob Riley, referred with dismay to 'this *terra nullius*, the notion that Aboriginal people didn't exist before 1788'.

TIM ROWSE

Theatre, see **Drama**

Theodore, Edward Granville (1884–1950), Qld premier, federal treasurer, company director and administrator, forged a remarkable career from talent, energy, and ambition to become one of the most controversial figures in Australian public life.

Theodore was born at Port Adelaide into the large and improvident family of a Romanian father and English–Irish mother. After a rudimentary education he became an itinerant miner, who learned labour politics in Broken Hill and applied that knowledge in establishing a militant union at Chillagoe in northern Qld. A large, forceful man, he entered the Qld parliament in 1909, the same year as his marriage to the handsome but unstable Esther Mahoney. In 1912 he was elected deputy leader of the Labor Party; when the **Ryan** government took office in 1915, he became deputy premier and treasurer. He implemented vigorously interventionist and pro-**development** policies. After taking a prominent role in the anti-**conscription** campaigns of 1916–17, he used his power base in the conservative **Australian Workers Union** to become premier when Ryan moved to the federal parliament in 1919.

During his tempestuous premiership (1919–25), Theodore fought **socialism** in the **Australian Labor Party**, radicals in the trade unions, pastoralists and their associates in the London money market, as well as his conservative opponents in the Qld parliament, the more recalcitrant of whom he defeated by abolishing the Legislative Council in 1922. He resigned in 1925 to contest a federal seat, but lost and moved to Sydney; there he became embroiled in factional struggles with the emerging **Lang** Labor machine, eventually winning the federal seat of Dalley in 1927 amid accusations of bribery involving his friend John **Wren**.

After a brief period as a prominent opposition frontbencher, he was elected treasurer and deputy prime minister in 1929 when the **Scullin** government was elected to combat the **Depression**. He began to grapple with the crisis in government finance but soon stepped aside to answer royal commission findings that, as Qld treasurer, he had acted corruptly in a mining deal. After clearing his name in the courts, he was reinstated as treasurer in January 1931 and quickly introduced a sophisticated, counter-cyclical plan in answer to Sir Otto **Niemeyer's** orthodox deflationary policies. Soon after NSW Premier Lang tabled his populist program, Labor Party supporters of each plan split into three hostile factions, leaving Theodore to implement a compromise, the deflationary Premiers' Plan. Using the pretext of further corruption allegations against Theodore, the Lang Labor faction pushed the Scullin government to an electoral drubbing in December 1931.

Defeated by a Lang Labor candidate, he turned from politics to business, making his fortune, first with Frank **Packer** in Consolidated Press and later in Fiji goldmining with John Wren. He returned, without pay, to public life in 1942 as director-general of the Allied Works Council, where he earned official gratitude despite some popular resentment of his administration. He died in 1950, leaving an estranged wife, two daughters, two sons, and an estate valued at £629 915.

The relationship between Theodore's political and business careers is a central theme in the biographical and general historical works. C.B. Schedvin, *Australia and the Great Depression* (1970), and K.H. Kennedy, 'E.G. Theodore', in R.T. Appleyard and C.B. Schedvin (eds), *Australian Financiers* (1988), are critically appreciative of Theodore's, economic acumen as federal treasurer; but Kennedy, *The Mungana Affair* (1978), thinks the royal commission's adverse finding was correct. Irwin Young's *Theodore* (1971) is a self-consciously even-handed study, while Ross Fitzgerald's *'Red Ted'* (1994) is sympathetically critical with lapses into partisan advocacy.

PETER LOVE

Thomson, Donald Finlay Fergusson (1901–70) trained in anthropology after graduating in botany and zoology. Between 1928 and 1933 he undertook several scientific expeditions to Cape York. In 1932 he became a staff member of the University of Melbourne; in 1962 he became the professor of anthropology. Thomson went to Arnhem Land in 1935 to investigate the causes of conflict between Aborigines and others, notably the 1933 killing of some Japanese trepang fishermen. His 1938 report to the federal government recommended strongly that a reserve be established for the unhindered use of the Aborigines of the region. During World War II Thomson served in the **Royal Australian Air Force**, liaising with local indigenous communities in the Pacific, including Arnhem Land where he recruited Aboriginal men as coast-watchers.

In later years he strongly opposed the Woomera missile-testing facility and made an extensive study of the Pintupi people of that area. His extensive writings include *Bindibu Country* (1975), *Donald Thomson in Arnhem Land* (with an introduction by Nicholas Peterson, 1983), and *Children of the Dreamtime* (1989, published in 1983 as *Children of the Wilderness*). Thomson's collection of field-notes, artefacts and photographs, film and tapes, natural history and botanical specimens—now held by the Museum of Victoria—is regarded as one of the most important ethnographic collections in Australia. His career is documented in *Thomson of Arnhem Land* (2000).

KT

Thomson, Edward Deas (1800–79) began his notable career in the NSW public service in 1829 as clerk of the Executive and Legislative Councils. He became colonial secretary in 1837, and served five governors before his retirement in 1856. He was involved with the movement towards responsible government and the development of the licence system to control the **gold rushes**. Under **Gipps**, Thomson was forced to speak in the Legislative Council for an unpopular administration which he found very trying. He presented and supported Earl **Grey's** proposal for federal union to the Legislative Council in 1848. He was also a strong advocate of **free trade** between the colonies. Thomson realised the long-term effects of the discovery of gold for the colony and opposed heavy-handed attempts to control gold diggers. He was chosen, with W.C. **Wentworth**, to see the Constitution Bill for NSW through the British parliament. Upon Thomson's return to Australia, Governor **Denison** asked him to form a ministry, but he could not gather sufficient support either then or on a subsequent attempt.

Thomson was strong in his support for the University of Sydney, serving as vice-chancellor and chancellor from 1863 to 1878. His papers are held in the Mitchell Library, Sydney. A biography, *Colonial Improver* by S.G. Foster, appeared in 1978.

KT

'Three elevens' was an analogy used in 1904 by the prime minister, Alfred **Deakin**, to express his frustration at the lack of a parliamentary majority. In the election at the end of 1903 the three parties—Deakin's protectionists, George **Reid's** free-traders, and the Labor Party—obtained almost equal representation in the House of Representatives. Deakin therefore relied on the Labor Party to remain in office, but Labor insisted on amendments to the government's **arbitration** legislation as a condition of support. In January Deakin attended the **cricket** Test match in Adelaide, and when he spoke at a public meeting in Melbourne a fortnight later he asked: 'What kind of a game of cricket, compared with the present game, could they play if they had three elevens instead of two, with one playing sometimes with one side, sometimes with the other, and sometimes for itself? … It was absolutely essential that as soon as possible the three parties should somehow be resolved into two.' They were in 1909 when the free-traders and protectionists came together in a **Fusion** as the **Liberal Party**.

SM

Threlkeld, Lancelot Edward (1788–1859), missionary to the Aborigines, began his work in Australia after seven years in the Society Islands. With the support of the London Missionary Society, in 1825 he was established at Lake Macquarie, NSW. He came into conflict over finances with the London directors of the society and, more immediately, Samuel **Marsden**, the society's agent. After the society decided to close the mission in 1828, Threlkeld obtained land and an appointment from the NSW Executive Council to continue the work. He established a new mission on Lake Macquarie, Ebenezer, and, during the next 10 years, conducted a study of **Aboriginal languages**. He published *An Australian Grammar* (1834), *An Australian Spelling Book* (1836), and *A Key to the Structure of the Aboriginal Language* (1850). Ebenezer became a show mission visited by many observers, including James **Backhouse**, although the small number of converts caused Threlkeld to regard the venture as a failure. He remained an active advocate for Aboriginal welfare after the mission closed in 1841, while preaching in various capacities in Sydney.

KT

Tichborne Claimant was an opportunistic butcher from Wagga Wagga, NSW, named Arthur Orton, alias Thomas Castro, who professed to be the son of Sir Alfred and Lady Tichborne of County Hampshire, England. Their son and heir, Roger Charles Tichborne, was well educated and had had a short military career before setting sail for South America. When his vessel was wrecked and Tichborne apparently lost at sea, Lady Tichborne refused to believe her son was dead and advertised for his return. On Sir Alfred's death in 1866, Lady Tichborne was convinced her son would return to claim his inheritance. In response to the advertisement, Arthur Orton visited her and claimed to be her lost son. While Lady Tichborne believed him, suspicious family members demanded a court hearing. After a sensational court case, Orton was exposed as an impostor,

convicted for perjury, and sentenced to 14 years' penal servitude. Aspects of the case were borrowed for various works of fiction, including Marcus **Clarke's** *His Natural Life* (1874). Accounts include D. Woodruff, *The Tichborne Claimant* (1957), and Michael **Roe**, *Kenealy and the Tichborne Cause* (1974).

HD

Ticket of leave was a licence given to **convicts** which allowed them to earn their own living and live independently. Until they had served out their time, they were still subject to official surveillance and the ticket could be withdrawn for misbehaviour. This sanction worked better in securing good behaviour than the threat of flogging. Developed first as an expedient to save money, the ticket became a central part of the convict system and provided the model for later systems of probation.

Governor **King** first issued tickets to any convicts who seemed able to support themselves, in order to save the expense of providing them with food from the government store. The tickets were then used as a reward for good behaviour and special services, such as informing or the capture of **bushrangers**. Gentlemen convicts were issued with tickets on their arrival. After tickets had been identified in London as contributing to the laxity of the convict system, Governor **Macquarie** ordered that a convict had to serve three years before being eligible for one. Under Governor **Brisbane** the regulations reached their final form: the period of eligibility was set at four years for those sentenced for seven years, six years for those sentenced for 14 years, and eight years for those sentenced for life.

JH

Timber industry took shape within a few short years of European settlement. Watkin **Tench** wrote in 1789, 'the wood [is] universally of so bad a grain, as almost to preclude a possibility of using it'. From the beginning eucalypts were discounted as good only for firewood and rough bush carpentry, and farmers realised it was quicker to clear by burning than by cutting.

In the short term the shortage of good timber was solved by the discovery in 1789 of Red Cedar (*Toona australis*) along the banks of the Hawkesbury River. A soft hardwood, it was similar to other cedars familiar to the Europeans and was easily cut and worked. The cutting of cedar quickly developed as a major industry, though not a **staple**, as most of the cedar was consumed domestically. Cedar-cutters became the first pioneers of many parts of coastal NSW and Qld.

The colonial government found timber-cutting almost impossible to control (a predicament repeated with pastoralism and gold-mining). The first regulations limiting cutting were issued in 1795 and had no effect, for the notion of common rights to **forests** was deeply ingrained in British tradition. The eighteenth century was notable for clashes between authorities and local people over rights to timber. These rights were carried into Australia as part of the cultural baggage of the convicts and settlers. With limited resources and will, the authorities were unable to enforce their rights to exclude access to timber.

The coastal supplies of Red Cedar and other valuable rainforest species were quickly exhausted. By the 1830s the most accessible stands were gone, and Australia was increasingly relying on imports. As settlement spread inland, vast forests of eucalypts and other sclerophylls were discovered, but no further easily worked species. American techniques of ringbarking and clearing by burning were adopted to clear eucalypts for grazing and agriculture. With the discovery of gold, mining became a major consumer of firewood and rough timber. Mechanised sawmills became common. In a roundabout way, mining saved forests. To protect potential mining sites and timber supplies, the Box-Ironbark eucalypt forests which characterised auriferous soils were held back from agricultural settlement.

Mining and the booming economy of the late nineteenth century increased demand for timber imports. At Broken Hill the problem of ground creep led to the development of elaborate square-set timber supports made of imported Oregon. The suburbs of **Marvellous Melbourne** and the other rapidly growing cities were built of Oregon and Baltic Pine. Local timber continued to be seen as second-rate, except for River Red Gum, Jarrah, Karri, Tasmanian Blue Gum, and the increasingly scarce rainforest species. Indeed, a small export trade developed in Jarrah, Karri and Blue Gum for railway sleepers, blocks for road-making, and general construction timber. Late in the nineteenth century the wastefulness of agricultural clearing and timber-cutting led to repeated calls for better management of forests. (See **Conservation**.)

Forestry grew slowly in the first two-thirds of the twentieth century. Plantations of introduced softwoods, particularly Radiata Pine, were established, often on abandoned agricultural land. Especially after World War II, the timber industry, like all primary sectors, became more mechanised. Industrial growth spurred the development of pulp and paper. However, overall growth lagged behind increased demand and Australia continued to import timber. The low value of native timber, and the deeply ingrained belief that access to forest timber should be free and cheap, both discouraged private investment in native plantations.

In 1968 Australia began exporting eucalypt woodchips to Japan, where they were processed into paper and similar products. In those heady days of the resource boom, it was hoped that exports and jobs would finally begin to flow from Australia's difficult forests (the major forestry states—NSW, Victoria and Tasmania—had missed out on the mining boom). It was even hoped that eventually much of the processing would occur in Australia. Woodchips came from publicly owned forests, for private plantations of natives were almost non-existent. To keep costs low, forests were clearfelled, the best logs chipped, and the remainder burnt. Public outrage placed woodchipping with the farming of the Little Desert, sand-mining on Fraser Island, and the damming of Lake Pedder as the key environmental battles of the 1960s and 1970s.

Initial concern about woodchipping identified the environmental impact. However, it also slowly became apparent that woodchipping was economically unviable. The chips were low-value exports, processed overseas. The revenue from the felling of publicly owned and managed forests was low. Forestry employment actually fell (and continues to fall) after the introduction of woodchipping. Erosion, damage to water catchments, the spread of dieback, and the failure of regeneration all increased the public costs of an economic activity which benefited only a few. However, in the 1990s, the Labor and Liberal–National federal governments continued to support a subsidised woodchipping industry, and the conflict over how best to manage Australia's forests remains unresolved.

WARWICK FROST

Time and time-measurement were powerful, though seldom recognised, factors in Australian history. Since 1788, when Lieutenant William Dawes erected a chronometer on the point overlooking Sydney Cove which bears his name, shifts in time-consciousness have often underlain wider changes in social organisation and culture.

Australia before the coming of Europeans was famously characterised by the novelist Eleanor **Dark** as *The Timeless Land* (1941). But Aborigines, who owned no mechanical clocks, were not strangers to measured time. They observed the subtle changes of winds, tides, and bird migrations which indicated the passage of the seasons with an exactness unknown to their European successors. Measuring time, in fact, was also among the motives which first brought European navigators into the Pacific: James **Cook** had voyaged to Tahiti in 1770 to observe the transit of Venus and hence to check by astronomical observations the acccuracy of the new ship's chronometer invented by John Harrison. Accurate time, which enabled seamen to establish their longitudinal position, was among the preconditions for safe and regular passage to Australia.

Early colonial Australia inherited the new and more urgent sense of time associated with the **evangelical** revival and the Industrial Revolution. Time, people were coming to believe, was a precious resource which must be carefully measured and conserved. Reforming convicts, for example, was thought to be largely a matter of teaching them to observe the value of time. Governor **Arthur's** purchase of public clocks, to be installed in church towers across Van Diemen's Land, like the introduction of new 'watch clocks' in his model prison at Port Arthur, were symptomatic of this concern with time-based discipline.

A second important shift in time-consciousness occurred in the closing decades of the nineteenth century when the coming of the **railway** and the **telegraph** enabled communities across Australia, which had previously kept their own time, to be linked into a system of centralised or standard time. School inspectors now expected teachers to teach and observe a common time—a reform which the children of scattered farming communities often resisted. In factories and offices, work was increasingly organised around a regular **eight-hour day** with timetables with set times for signing on and off. The advent of the mass-produced American pocket watch put accurate time within reach of every man, if not every woman. Its fob chain, stretched across the workingman's waistcoat, became a new symbol of respectability. Centralised clocks, set by government astronomers, were now linked by telegraphic cable to public clocks on railway stations and post offices throughout the colonies. Charles **Todd**, builder of the overland telegraph, urged the adoption of a system of Australian standard time, a campaign which culminated on 1 February 1895 with the adoption of standard time zones for eastern, central, and western Australia. Common time, as much as common tariffs and common immigration policies, hastened the **Federation** of the colonies.

As the railway and the telegraph had centralised time, so the arrival of the radio and the automobile in the early twentieth century introduced a new and more flexible time regime. A car driver could now travel independently of the timetable, and a radio listener could check the time without reference to a public clock. World War I, which had required the mobilisation of millions of troops, hastened the introduction of time-based techniques of scientific management, based on the use of punch-card clocks and stopwatches. Scientific management had its counterpart in the home in Dr Truby King's new methods of baby-care, with regular four-hourly feeds.

Throughout this period, there had always been a minority of rebels who challenged the rule of the clock. In the early 1970s new technologies—the jet plane, the communications satellite, and the computer—once again heralded an abrupt shift in time-consciousness. In schools teachers threw out timetables and introduced open classrooms in which, it was suggested, children might learn in their own time. After half a century of debate most Australian states introduced daylight-saving time, a simple reorganisation of summer time-measurement that lengthened available hours of daylight. Flexibility and autonomy became the new mantras of management. At home, the microwave oven enabled families to abandon set meal-times—as, indeed, they were almost bound to do as retailers and other businesses opened around the clock. The eight-hour day, once an Australian article of faith, was abandoned in favour of flexi-time. The free-market ideologies which now permeated the nation's public life were inseparable, perhaps, from the dubious freedom to work, play, buy, or sell at any time one pleased. Mike Donaldson's *Taking Our Time* (1996) is a critical examination of the human implications of that new temporal order. Graeme Davison, *The Unforgiving Minute* (1993), surveys the longer history of 'how Australia learned to tell the time'.

GRAEME DAVISON

Tindale, Norman Barnett (1900–93) was one of a handful of Australian anthropologists whose conclusions were informed by direct experience with traditionally oriented **Aborigines** across the continent. Trained in natural history, he began his career as an entomologist's assistant at the South Australian Museum in 1919. Although he maintained an international reputation as an entomologist specialising in the Hepialidae moths, Tindale's 1921–22 expedition to Groote Eylandt directed his attention to anthropology. From that time he kept a daily scientific journal which has become a key research source. He published widely on aspects of art and technology, mythology and social structure, **archaeology** and ecology, and assembled data for his major project, the famous Tindale map and inventory of more than 250 Aboriginal Tribes of Australia (published in 1940, revised as a book in 1974).

Tindale undertook Australia's first scientific archaeological excavation, at Devon Downs on the Murray River in 1929. He helped to pioneer ethnographic film-making and sound-recording during the 1930s expeditions of the Board for Anthropological Research among Central Australian Aboriginal groups. Working with his friend and informant Clarence Long (Milerum), Tindale produced a comprehensive record of the traditions of the Tangane people of SA's Coorong. His 1938–39 and 1952–53 expeditions with the American physical anthropologist Joseph Birdsell resulted in an extensive national survey of Aboriginal mission stations and communities; the photographs and genealogies are heavily used by Aboriginal people today.

Tindale's military career as an intelligence officer based in the US Pentagon during World War II is little known. Having spent 10 years of his childhood in Japan, Tindale was one of the few Westerners with fluent Japanese. Promoted to wing commander, he and his unit were credited with breaking the Japanese naval code and aircraft production codes. Tindale received several natural history awards, and honorary doctorates from the University of Colorado (1967) and the Australian National University (1980).

PHILIP JONES

Tobruk, see **Rats of Tobruk**; **World War II**

Todd, Charles (1826–1910) supervised the building of the **Overland Telegraph** Line from Port Augusta, SA, to Darwin, NT, between 1870 and 1872. Born in London, Todd was head of the Galvanic Department at Greenwich when invited to SA as government astronomer and superintendent of telegraphs. He arrived in November 1855, 28 years old, short, slight, and energetic. He immediately erected the colony's first telegraph line, from Adelaide to Port Adelaide, and within a few years had overseen connection to Melbourne (1856) and Sydney (1866).

The Overland Telegraph Line was an enormously significant achievement. The Australian colonies were a long sea-voyage from Britain, their major trading partner, source of news, and provider of defence. The telegraph reduced communication time to only a few minutes and was described by **Parkes** as 'uniting us hand-in-hand … with the parent land'. Surveying and building the line pioneered the route that would eventually link north and south Australia and open its remote heart. Locally, relaying the line through SA (thanks to Todd's lobbying of government and private investors) attracted valuable revenue to the colony's treasury. Todd is memorialised in the Central Australian town of Alice Springs, named after his wife, and the nearby Todd River named after him.

CAROL FORT

Tolpuddle Martyrs were a group of six agricultural labourers from Tolpuddle, near Dorchester, England, namely James Brine, James Hammett, James and George Loveless, and John and Thomas Stanfield, who were convicted under the Combination Acts in 1834 and sentenced to seven years' transportation for establishing a **trade union** known as the Friendly Society of Agricultural Labourers. Their leader, George Loveless, was sent to Van Diemen's Land and recounted his experiences in *The Victims of Whiggery* (1837); the others were sent to NSW. All were subsequently released and returned to England, where they became heroes and were commemorated a century later. The Tolpuddle Martyrs were also adopted by the labour movement as part of Australia's trade union tradition, as presented by H.V. **Evatt** in *Injustice within the Law* (1937).

HD

Top End refers to the northernmost part of the **Northern Territory**, including the capital, **Darwin**. The term came into popular usage in the 1930s but colloquial use was probably older. The 'top' originally referred to the northern end of the major communication channels stretching up from Adelaide, such as the railway line, telegraph line, stock routes, and roads.

HD

Torrens title was a simplified system of recording title to land devised by politician Robert Richard Torrens (1814–84) who was a supporter of the **Wakefield** system. Torrens introduced his measure in 1857 to the SA parliament in a bill which was passed the following year; it was subsequently introduced into the other Australian colonies. The Torrens system recorded land-ownership on a public register, which detailed when the land was first sold by the Crown and listed all subsequent owners. This replaced an older method that relied on the execution of deeds and required individuals to prove ownership. Most Australian land has now been converted to the Torrens system.

HD

Torres Strait Islanders are recognised as having an ethnic identity and culture distinct from mainland **Aborigines**. Virtually all federal and Qld government initiatives concerning Australia's indigenous people now refer to two indigenous groups, 'Aborigines and Torres Strait Islanders'.

The Torres Strait, previously part of the Australian–Papuan land-mass which included the Arafura Sea, has been in its current geographical shape for at least 4000 years. At the time of European colonisation commencing in the 1860s, some regional cultural differences had emerged, both between Torres Strait Islanders of various regions and between them and mainland Aborigines. The material culture, though very distinctive, includes elements of Papuan horticulture and Australian hunter–gathering to varying degrees according to region; the languages of the Torres Strait also comprise elements of both Papuan and Australian **Aboriginal languages**. A lively trade circle linked both mainlands and the islands of the strait, and entrenched regional divisions of labour based on gardening, trading, and marine use. Today the cultural differences between these regions are submerged beneath a regional identity and a linking language, Kriol.

The separate political recognition of Torres Strait Islanders owes much to the colonisation of Torres Strait as the labour-intensive **pearling** industry arrived from the Pacific. Islanders traditionally dived for pearl-shell and other shells, and became sought after as labour. Jeremy Beckett, *Torres Strait Islanders* (1987), emphasises that, rather than being displaced by white settlement, they were tied into capitalist production as an unfree workforce. The industry also entailed a massive and sudden influx of Pacific Island labourers—some 500 in 1872 compared to a local population of 3000–4000. The London Missionary Society, too, introduced Polynesians as preachers.

The cultural and social infiltration from the Pacific magnified cultural differences from the mainland. When comprehensive Aboriginal protection legislation was introduced in Qld in 1897, pearl-shell masters and colonial agents argued for a separate legal status of Torres Strait Islanders to exempt them from its provisions, which included restrictions on employment. It was argued that their settled communities, cultivation of the soil, construction of canoes, and use of bows and arrows demonstrated that these people were 'advanced several stages in mental evolution' beyond mainland Aborigines, and that therefore 'different methods of management' were required. These arguments were initially successful in exempting Torres Strait Islanders from the Protection Act, for the convenience of master-pearlers (Regina Ganter, *The Pearl-Shellers of Torres Strait*, 1994).

Gradually they were drawn under the administration by means of a community lugger scheme, which from 1904 enabled communities to acquire pearl-shell luggers on hire purchase and guaranteed a market and fair prices for pearl-shell, rubber, and copra. By 1908 compulsory deductions of up to 50 per cent were made from the earnings, and the government teachers, acting as superintendents on the islands, encouraged able-bodied men into wage labour. In 1930, as three-quarters of the total Torres Strait Islander labour force were employed in the lugger scheme, the department took control of it, and made it the pillar of successful native administration in Qld. The department's rule was now entrenched. The islands were government reserves and movement between them was subject to a permit from the government teacher, while a curfew on Thursday Island prevented Torres Strait Islanders from seeking employment there. Funds from the Torres Strait region, now financially self-supporting, were diverted towards the support of mainland reserves.

Participation in the pearl-shell industry had become a firm tradition in Torres Strait, a source of pride and status. Contesting the paternalistic grip of the department, a lugger strike in 1936, which lasted several months, resulted in a devolution of responsibilities from the protector to the island councils, the abolition of the permit system for inter-island visits, and the first inter-island conference of island councillors in 1937. Nonie Sharp's *Stars at Tagai* (1993) identifies this as a significant step in the formation of a regional, rather than island-based, political force.

During World War II some 900 Torres Strait Islanders served in the Torres Strait Defence Force, paid at two-thirds the rate of white soldiers, an experience that sharpened their perception of exclusion from citizenship. After the war, Torres Strait Islanders rehabilitated Qld's pearling industry, excelling at deep-sea diving which had been the domain of Japanese indents.

In the 1960s, as the pearling industry collapsed, a mass migration to the mainland was set in train. In 1991 only 5680 of 26 883 Torres Strait Islanders were domiciled in Torres Strait, but island custom, a blend of old and recognisably newer elements, still binds Torres Strait Islanders, who have continued to set keynotes in Aboriginal politics, of which the **Mabo case** is the best known. Torres Strait Islanders were active in the Federal Council for the Advancement of Aborigines and Torres Strait Islanders, lobbying for citizen rights and social service benefits in the 1950s. In the lead-up to independence for **Papua New Guinea** (1975), they became players in international politics, conducting negotiations with their Papuan neighbours, and insisting that they would not be divided. The voices of secession, independence, or self-government for Torres Strait have periodically brought media controversy. Throughout the range of strategies proposed by various spokespersons, they have clearly insisted on a unifying regional identity and demanded to be in charge of their own destiny.

REGINA GANTER

Tourism was slow to develop in Australia. NZ, with more spectacular natural features, was quicker off the mark; but neither country—separately or together, and unlike Canada—was seen to warrant one of the famous pre-World War I Baedeker guides. Even so, the first tourists (as distinct from travellers) began to arrive in the 1880s, carried on faster steamships and in part lured by the colonial **exhibitions**. The first sustained publication of guidebooks dates from this time. In an age when armchair travel often preceded the real thing, the literature of tourism overlapped with the prolific works of **travel writers**, both local and overseas.

Tourist bureaus were private ventures initially. Governments became involved because the encouragement of tourism was seen as a natural extension of their other activities. In NSW, the first comprehensive guidebooks were produced by the **railways**, in the hope of making services more profitable. In the early twentieth century, they were linked to the projection of the states generally, a component of varying combinations involving the railways, information,

and immigration. The assumption of the day appears to have been that anybody who was prepared to come so far as a visitor could probably be induced to remain as a settler.

Travel within Australia was relatively difficult until after World War II. It was not till the 1880s, with the link-up of the rail systems, that there was much of it at all; until the interwar period, a significant proportion was by coastal steamer. The liners of P & O and the Orient Line, among others, connected Australia with the rest of the world.

For a long time the travelling public was quite limited. Although public servants and other professionals enjoyed paid annual leave from around the turn of the century, it was not stipulated in an industrial award till 1936—and that was not mandatory. Even so, annual leave was spreading more generally through society, as was the use of the car and other motorised forms of transport such as the charabanc. The constituency for tourism was thus broadening at the same time as travel was extending beyond fixed-route transport. State governments responded to the growing volume of inquiries, and a growing competition for custom, by setting up tourist bureaus as separate state departments. The interwar years saw massive headquarters arise in the capital cities, with large branches, rather like state embassies, in other capitals.

Traditionally, tourist accommodation was largely of two kinds. First was the guest-house, which differed from the traditional urban boarding-house only in its salubrious setting; family atmosphere and home cooking were its strong selling points. Then there was the hotel, which could vary from being extremely rough in the outback to a degree of luxury in the cities. From Melbourne's Federal Hotel in the 1880s, which modelled its foyer on the recent Paris Opera, right down to Phillip Cox's sails for the Yulara Sheraton, hotels have often drawn on the latest architectural fashions.

Motor car ownership, which grew fourfold from the late 1930s to the mid-1960s, also radicalised accommodation. Camping grounds now played second fiddle to caravan parks, while for a long time after the first motels appeared in the 1950s they were built around the guests' parked cars. Twenty years later, no Australian country town with a population of more than 1000 was without at least one motel. The individualised unit was the basic component now, marking the end of the communal style of the guest-house. Meanwhile, well into the 1960s, governments continued to spend money on upgrading rail facilities and building new passenger terminals for the ocean liners. But air travel began to boom beyond the wildest expectations. In 1950 there were 1.5 million passengers on domestic flights; in 1970, 6 million. Airlines built their own resorts, such as Ansett's at Hayman Island. The package tour was the rationale here, just as it had been half a century earlier when the Victorian government opened Mount Buffalo Chalet as an adjunct to its rail network.

Changing travel patterns have had their effect on tourist destinations, both for good and ill. Albany was stranded when it no longer functioned as WA's leading port, after being superseded by Fremantle. Much more important, though, has been the change in tourist fashions. In 1910

Tasmania, rugged and green and even endowed with one or two ruins, functioned as a substitute England: it was therefore the most popular long-range tourist destination in Australia. Since World War II tourists have been more likely to look north. The first organised tour parties were regularly taken to Ayers Rock in 1957, but by 1996 **Uluru** drew 337 018 visitors.

Special events, often organised by governments with the aim of attracting tourists, have always loomed large in tourist promotions and in the way people come to see particular destinations. All Australian states marketed their centenary celebrations (in the case of NSW its sesquicentenary celebration) in the interwar years. In the era before mass car ownership and discount air travel, such events rarely attracted more than a few thousand interstate, let alone international, guests. By the 1980s the competition had become so intense that state governments plotted against each other for sporting and cultural events. Melbourne bid, unsuccessfully, for the 1996 **Olympics**; Sydney won the 2000 Olympics. Melbourne, with the active support of the **Kennett** state government, persuaded the promoters of the Formula One Grand Prix to relocate the race there from Adelaide. Sydney's gay and lesbian Mardi Gras has become an international tourist event. **Tennis** competitions are huge drawcards, while the Australian Football League has deliberately created new teams in the other states, most notably the Sydney Swans, to give their game an interstate as well as a Victorian focus (see **Australian Rules football**). Airlines have restructured their inter-capital schedules accordingly.

The coming of the wide-bodied jets, such as the 747, enabled Australia to compete directly in the international tourist market. Sydney has become the major South Pacific gateway for Asian tourists, while Cairns, which gained international airport status in 1984, secured vast amounts of Japanese investment to build five-star hotels, a casino, and grand new golf courses. The new five-star hotels and resorts, predominantly in the Qld coastal resorts and Sydney, are fed by over four million international tourists a year. Victoria manages to attract about one-fifth of them, while the other states struggle to get on to the mental, let alone the actual, map of international tourists.

While the number of international tourists was negligible until the 1970s, the domestic tourist market has been adventurous and innovative, and often had a notable impact on both coastal and rural landscapes. Queenscliff and Marysville in Victoria and Katoomba and Manly in NSW offered grand hotels and guest-houses aimed at both metropolitan and country dwellers. Holiday shacks appeared in hundreds of coastal settings from the late nineteenth century. With the coming of fibro in the 1920s, they could be built cheaply and quickly almost anywhere, and they were.

Visitors from NZ, UK and USA continued to increase in the 1980s and 1990s, but numbers from Japan and elsewhere in Asia more than quadrupled between 1984 and 1994. The Japanese were most numerous, but stayed an average of only eight nights; Scandinavians, including many backpackers, were fewer, but stayed an average of 49 nights. By 1995 over

six per cent of the Australian workforce was employed in tourism and hospitality. The importance of the industry, and its volatility, were illustrated in 1989, when a seven-month pilot strike saw passenger numbers plummet, and in 1998, when an Asian currency crisis brought about the collapse of the highly promoted South Korean tourist market.

Such tourist developments, and the growth of the travel agency industry that serviced them, went virtually unremarked not only in general histories but also in state histories. Historians have failed to recognise that domestic tourism was one of the fastest-growing, hidden industries in Australia this century. The first major studies of tourism in Australia were undertaken in the 1970s not by historians, but by geographers. Textbooks on tourism, usually written by people with business backgrounds, appeared in the 1980s, aimed at the TAFE market, while a number of the new universities hopped on the tourism bandwagon. The first serious Australian textbook, *Introduction to Tourism in Australia* (1991), was written by the New Zealand-born geographer Michael Hall. Jennifer Craik's *Resorting to Tourism*, a Queensland-based study of the cultural politics of tourism, appeared the same year. A history by Davidson and Spearritt, *Tourism Business*, appeared in 2000. Tourist icons, especially those with rich cultural or landscape settings, have received more attention. The **Sydney Harbour Bridge**, **Uluru**, **Port Arthur**, and the Melbourne Exhibition Buildings have all been the subject of historical analysis.

JIM DAVIDSON AND PETER SPEARRITT

Town planning is the purposeful intervention by government into the processes of urban development in order to achieve social goals, such as public health, harmonious and efficient land-use arrangements, environmental protection, and economic development. It has been a significant state function since the beginnings of European settlement, although the comprehensive, self-conscious quest for social and spatial order dates only from the early twentieth century.

The cause of physical planning had inauspicious beginnings. Governor **Phillip's** first plan for **Sydney**—configured according to the imperialistic 'Laws of the Indies'—was ignored. The Australian penchant for property speculation won out, both inside and outside the unremitting gridiron plans favoured by early surveyors. William **Light's Adelaide** plan (1837) was the major achievement of the colonial era and the model for 'parkland' towns throughout SA. But even conspicuously 'planned' towns were marred by substandard housing, pollution, and chaotic land subdivision.

The decade before World War I saw more concerted moves toward improving urban health, efficiency, and beauty. John **Sulman**, Charles **Reade**, James **Barrett**, and George and Florence **Taylor** emerged as leading town planning missionaries, and voluntary associations were formed in every state between 1913 and 1916 to push for effective legislation. The vision of reform proffered by the City Beautiful movement was of grand civic buildings, parks, boulevards, and height restrictions to maintain decorum in the civic skyline. Such images featured in the first comprehensive plan for an Australian city produced by the *Royal Commission for the Improvement of the City of Sydney and Its Suburbs* (1909). More enduring was the house-and-garden environmentalism of the Garden City movement, its major contemporary impact being showcase garden **suburbs** like Daceyville (1912) in Sydney and Colonel Light Gardens (1920) in Adelaide.

In the 1920s the priorities of town planners were more pragmatic, with functional schemes of zoning and traffic management to the fore. The Town Planning Commissions in Melbourne (1922–33) and Perth (1928–30) undertook landmark civic surveys. In the wake of the **Depression**, slum clearance issues came to the fore. State housing agencies, like the Victorian Housing Commission (1938), evolved into quasi-metropolitan planning agencies. Permanent administrative machinery for planning in most states came only in the early postwar years, spurred on by reconstructionist idealism, modernist dreams of rational urban environments, and the requirement of the visionary Commonwealth Housing Commission (1944) that federal housing finance be allocated within a sound framework for community planning.

As planning moved from theory to institutional practice, master plans emerged as metropolitan blueprints. The seminal document was the 1948 Sydney scheme, described by Denis Winston as *Sydney's Great Experiment* (1957). A British-inspired amalgam of planned decentralisation, freeways, green belt, and rebuilt city centre, the plan could not cope with Sydney's growth, but it did check fringe subdivision and secured significant tracts of open space. Master plans embodying similar ideas for Melbourne (1954) and Perth (1955) followed. The transitional 1962 Adelaide plan pointed the way towards a new crop of expansionist 'corridor' plans, notably the *Sydney Region Outline Plan* (1968).

By the late 1960s, the results of postwar planning were being widely questioned on many levels: the commitment to both low-density suburbanisation and disruptive redevelopment of older neighbourhoods; rising backlogs in public utility provision; and the narrow focus on land use, an increasingly technocratic approach. An enormously influential and sympathetic critique was *Ideas for Australian Cities* (1970) by Hugh **Stretton**. The rise of resident action groups and the **green ban** movement in Sydney and Melbourne showed the need for new plans incorporating environmental and participatory provisions.

Responding to calls for a national approach to urbanisation problems, the federal Labor government of 1972–75, for the first time since the 1940s, developed an ambitious federal program embracing growth centres, stabilisation of land prices, sewerage schemes, improvement grants, and historic rehabilitation. Later conservative administrations retreated from national urban policy, but the **Hawke** and **Keating** governments of 1983–96 gradually re-established an urban agenda, driven now by concern with the high financial costs of traditional urban developments and the vision of Better Cities projects in every state.

In the 1990s planning has become increasingly fragmented, pulled in different, often contradictory, ways by the demands of postmodern urban society. It has shifted from its historic preoccupation with growth control toward encouraging development projects, managing public–private ventures, and brokering deals. Urban design has experienced a renaissance. Contemporary rhetoric at all levels of government revolves around increasing housing densities through 'urban consolidation', and conserving natural resources via 'environmental sustainability'.

The outstanding open-air museum for twentieth-century planning ideas is **Canberra**. The original 1912 plan by Walter and Marion Mahony **Griffin** synthesised City Beautiful and Garden City ideals. But its urban landscape now records the planning ideals of a succession of later planners, starting with Griffin's pragmatic successors, Sulman's Federal Capital Advisory Committee (1921–24), and continuing through the **Menzies** era under the National Capital Development Commission.

The history of Australia's suburban cities is really 'a multiplicity of plans', wrote Peter Harrison in 1977. Yet the historiography of urban planning—with the exception of Canberra—is surprisingly modest. John Tregenza has suggested that planning has been shunned by historians in favour of greater success stories, and Leonie Sandercock's path-breaking *Cities for Sale* (1975) is a history of 'failure'. More forgiving specialised accounts appear in Alan Hutchings and Ray Bunker, *With Conscious Purpose* (1986), and Robert Freestone, *Model Communities* (1989). The bibliographic review of 'the state of the art' by Freestone and Hutchings (*Planning Perspectives*, 1993) reveals a growing interest in the history of ideas, individuals, and institutions from cross-disciplinary perspectives.

ROBERT FREESTONE

Trade has been a principal component of the Australian economy for the past two hundred years. With a restricted domestic market, the country's prosperity has ever since depended upon overseas customers; the same economies of scale have made it dependent upon imported products and technologies.

From soon after the first settlement, whites in Australia looked for products which would be of value to people in other regions. They soon demonstrated that it was profitable to ship Australian **wool** to English textile mills. Wool was an ideal export product: the principal investment required was the natural build-up of the sheep numbers. Little labour was needed, and the product did not deteriorate on its way to the market. While a number of other exports enjoyed periods of importance, such as seal and whale products in the early years and copper in the 1840s, wool dominated Australian exports until the **gold rushes** of the 1850s. Gold trebled the value of Australian exports and was not surpassed again by wool for more than 20 years. The other important exports in the nineteenth century were animal products (14 per cent) and other **mining** products (10 per cent). The goods which were imported with the revenues generated from exports moved progressively from fabrics, clothing, and foods, towards machinery. Most of Australia's nineteenth-century trade was with Britain, although that country's share progressively declined to just over one-half by the turn of the century. The remainder of the export trade was split fairly evenly between British colonies and others. The British dominance of imports to Australia was similar, with Germany and the USA also important.

At the beginning of the twentieth century the new Commonwealth imposed tariff duties on a wide range of imports, and the level of protection was subsequently increased. A relatively open trading economy sought to insulate itself from external shocks, and the new arrangements slowed growth rates. For the first half of the century wool remained the dominant export, although its share of the total fell progressively to around one-third by mid-century. The ground it lost was made up by other agricultural products, including **dairy** products (mainly butter) and grains (mainly **wheat**). Mining gradually declined in importance. The patterns of trade were more volatile. Britain remained the major trading partner, taking between 30 and 40 per cent of exports, but Japan and France took 10 per cent each in the 1920s. The pattern with imports was more balanced, with USA gradually building up its trade to some 25 per cent relative to Britain's 40 per cent. Motor vehicles and manufactured goods made up almost one-half of these goods flowing into Australia, with textiles and chemicals dominating the remainder.

During World War II, North America became temporarily the dominant source of imported goods, mainly in the form of machinery, tools, vehicles, and fuels. This was financed by a jump in exports, led importantly and for the first time by manufactured exports, while wheat was the major category to decline.

In the second half of the twentieth century the long-term structure of Australian trade changed significantly. With Britain's entry into the European Economic Community, its share of exports fell from around one-third in 1959 to less than one-twentieth in 1979. Trade with the remainder of Europe grew from almost nothing immediately after the war to a quarter by the 1980s. Asia, dominated for much of the period by Japan, grew from 10 to 60 per cent, and the USA doubled its share to 12 per cent. Australia had thus become a supplier to the globe. It also managed to reduce its reliance on wool. Wheat, coal, and iron ore exports attained similar values to wool by the start of the 1980s; nickel and aluminium overtook wool by the 1990s, and meat was not far behind. Thus while Australia still exported raw materials, the range had spread. As a proportion of national income, Australian trade shows a long decline from first settlement to its low point around 1970, from which level it has now risen. The recent upward trend might be explained by the increasingly open world economy. As part of a process of trade liberalisation, Australia cut tariffs and reduced assistance to export producers. Australia has remained a significant exporter of commodities, but there are strong competitive pressures on its primary producers. **Manufacturing** exports have been revitalised, but they operate at a low level. The trade in services (**tourism**, transport, consultancy, construction, and education) has grown, and the range of markets has expanded, particularly within Asia. These changes indicate a move from reliance on land to greater use of human capital.

For imports the direction of trade has changed, with the USA, Japan, and the European Union each providing some 20 per cent of imports, compared with Britain's seven per cent. The bundle of goods imported into Australia is dominated by inputs into production—machinery, chemicals, and fuels—with less than one-quarter being consumption goods.

RODNEY MADDOCK

Trade diversion dispute between Australia and Japan followed a policy announced by Sir Henry **Gullett** in the House of Representatives on 22 May 1936. Australia was committed to **imperial preference** as a result of the 1932 Ottawa Agreement and Britain was Australia's largest customer for many goods, especially **wool**. Japan was Australia's second-biggest customer, but exports of Japanese textiles were threatening Britain's worldwide markets. Whether or not direct pressure from Lancashire was brought to bear on Australia, Gullett understood that if Australia wanted to continue enjoying its expanding export trade with Britain, it also had to buy more British products. After failing to persuade Japan to curtail exports to Australia, he attempted to divert Australia's import trade away from Japan in favour of Britain by adopting a licensing system and higher duties. Britain deserved protection, Gullett argued, for being a 'good' customer that absorbed Australia's surplus of 'difficult selling' commodities.

Both Japan and the USA resented the implication that they were not good customers too. America withdrew most-favoured-nation status from Australia. Japan retaliated by licensing Australia's main export commodities and by applying such heavy surcharges on others that imports of Australian products to Japan were effectively prohibited. The dispute was theoretically settled in December 1936, when Japan agreed to adopt 'orderly marketing' in Australia, but the long-term effects were disastrous. Sandra Tweedie argues in *Trading Partners* (1994) that any British market gains were insignificant compared to the loss of goodwill between Australia and Japan, which increased synthetic fibre production and acquired new wool suppliers in South Africa and South America. Total Australian exports to Japan dropped from £17.7 million in 1935/36 to £4.9 million in 1938/39.

DC

Trade unions are continuous associations of wage earners concerned to protect and enhance their conditions of employment and living standards, a standard definition adapted from Sidney and Beatrice Webb, *The History of Trade Unionism* (1894). Trade unions were a product of the development of wage labour and the associated concentration of capital in the early modern period. Unions first emerged in Britain well over 300 years ago as journeymen's associations in particular crafts or trades—hence the name.

In Australia the first unions were formed by free workers in Sydney and Hobart in the second half of the 1820s. From the late 1830s unions were also formed in Adelaide and Melbourne, and progressively spread to other towns in the following decades. About 100 unions were formed in the period up to 1849, and about 400 in the years 1850 to 1869. Early unions followed the British model of craft-based associations among printers, tailors, cordwainers, cabinet-makers, shipwrights, carpenters, and stonemasons. However, there were also more informal combinations of workers which included both craftsmen and other occupations, such as shop assistants, labourers, seamen, and miners. Indeed, the bulk of strikes prior to 1860 occurred outside unions. Further, many unions were very short-lived. The gold rushes of the 1850s represented no turning-point and this pattern of volatility continued until the early twentieth century. While more resilient organisations were slowly built, many unions continued to collapse after a short time and sporadic combinations continued to occur, although declining in relative importance. These points suggest weaknesses in the Webbs' emphasis on institutional survival, and therefore in general overviews of Australian union history which implicitly adopt the Webbs' model, and also in many single union histories in Australia, which usually consider only one or two failed efforts at organisation as setting the scene for the final triumphant effort.

Most early union struggles were linked to wages, but in 1856 Melbourne stonemasons became the first workers in the world to secure the **eight-hour day**. Their success soon spread to workers in other trades, towns, and colonies. The eight-hour principle became a major rallying point for workers in the Australian colonies, leading to eight-hour-day processions and committees. These were, in turn, the precursors of the trades and labour councils established in every major town. From the 1850s some non-craft occupations, such as road transport workers and miners, began to organise, followed by seamen, wharf labourers, construction labourers, shearers, rouseabouts, and later, from the 1880s, teachers, meatworkers, domestic servants, waiters and other groups. Women began to unionise from the 1870s, often in separate unions (such as the tailoresses), but unionism remained male-dominated—a situation which altered only slowly in the first half of the twentieth century but more rapidly thereafter.

Union growth accelerated in the 1880s, aided by the trades and labour councils, which also began playing an increasingly important role in mediating disputes. Union numbers peaked at over 1400 with around 200 000 members in 1890. Organisation was strongest among workers with craft skills and those associated with key export industries (wool, meat, coal, and minerals). A number of these unions of non-craft workers defied the Webbs' typology by adopting the practice of unilateral regulation (i.e. specifying the minimum wages, union membership, and other conditions that members could accept). Although there was some collective negotiation and also schemes for voluntary **arbitration** (among Newcastle coalminers, for example), stable forms of collective bargaining were exceptional. Labour councils had established inter-occupational and inter-colonial linkages (which included NZ) that became increasingly important in providing financial and industrial support to unions engaged in strikes or campaigns. The decisive financial assistance offered to the London dockers in 1889 reflected the broad notions of solidarity—based as much on pragmatism as on idealism—that had developed.

In the early 1890s employers challenged the shearers, maritime, miners, and other unions, demanding 'freedom of contract' or the right to avoid negotiations with unions. Beginning with the **Maritime Strike**, a series of titanic **strikes** was resoundingly lost by unions; this gave birth to political radicalism (such as the doomed **New Australia** experiment), numerous legends, and a national song, '**Waltzing Matilda**'. Amid defeat and a severe economic depression, union membership fell sharply; many of the smaller and recently formed bodies collapsed. The union movement only slowly recovered, a process assisted by the introduction of compulsory arbitration at state and federal levels.

The introduction of compulsory arbitration was itself a product of growing union involvement in the political arena. Workers had long demonstrated an interest in political issues such as **immigration** and **tariffs**, and union involvement in politics grew significantly from the 1880s. During this period, labour councils formed electoral leagues that ultimately gave rise to the **Australian Labor Party**. In the first 20 years of the twentieth century Labor achieved government federally and in almost every state. The arbitration system established awards specifying minimum wages and conditions, and encouraged employers to deal with unions. With this assistance, by 1920 male union membership density was again among the highest in the world.

Federal arbitration also added an additional impetus to the establishment of national unions, but national coordination of union peak councils took longer to achieve, principally because of the hostility of the omnibus **Australian Workers Union**. It was not until 1927 that a national union body, the Australian Council of Trade Unions (**ACTU**) was established.

The onset of **Depression** in the 1930s was associated with industrial defeats and significant losses of membership (but not union collapses), from which unions only fully recovered with the onset of World War II. The revival of unions was associated with both more militant strategies based on the rank-and-file and increasing influence from the **Communist** Party. During the next 20 years there was a political bitter struggle, which ultimately weakened communist influence. Divisions over industrial strategy were more enduring, reflecting historical differences in organisation and bargaining strength, business-cycle effects, and revolts against wage outcomes constrained by government pressure on arbitration tribunals.

During the postwar boom unions made a series of important industrial gains, such as reduced hours and equal pay. After the boom collapsed, unions entered in corporatist arrangements with two federal Labor governments by which wage movements were constrained in an effort to boost employment. The first of these broke down fairly rapidly, but the second lasted well over a decade (see **Accord**). This was a result of the longevity of the **Hawke** and **Keating** governments, the strong role of the ACTU, and the linking of social wage gains to pay restraint. The ACTU also took a strong role in accelerating union amalgamations and in winning union acceptance for a shift away from awards towards enterprise bargaining. Both measures proved to be problematic: they consumed considerable resources; they contributed to intra- and inter-union friction; they failed to arrest a decline in union membership (and probably exacerbated the loss); and, in the case of bargaining, they led to less equitable wage and other outcomes, especially for women and migrant workers. Changes to industrial laws by state and federal conservative governments in the 1980s and 1990s, and shifts in employment structures—such as the growth of casual and part-time employment and subcontracting—represent major challenges for the union movement in the future.

For much of its history unionism has been a critically important social movement in Australia, and one which has commanded considerable interest among academics and others. The Noel Butlin Archives at the Australian National University are the repository for national union records. For a long time, the historiography of the movement largely consisted of a few brief general histories, notably J.T. Sutcliffe, *A History of Trade Unionism in Australia* (1921), and Ian **Turner**, *In Union Is Strength* (1976); a larger number of single union histories; and published papers on particular disputes (many, for example, in the journal *Labour History*). Single union histories tended to concentrate on leading craft unions—although building workers have been neglected—and those involved in key export and transport industries. With notable exceptions, such as Tom Sheridan's *Mindful Militants: The Amalgamated Engineering Union in Australia* (1975) and John Merritt's *The Making of the AWU* (1986), union histories are largely institutional and give few insights into the views of rank-and-file members. Likewise, apart from Bradon Ellem's *In Women's Hands? A History of Clothing Trades Unionism in Australia* (1989), there have been few examinations of unions with strong female memberships or those in the service sector.

From the late 1960s onwards, the **New Left**, and later the influence of social history on **labour history**, led to more critical and less institution-bound accounts of unions in the context of their communities and Australian society as a whole. There was increased recognition of the need to analyse union performance in areas such as Aboriginal issues, racism, and gender, as well as to assess the role of management strategies and legal and political structures. *Labour History* provided a focal point for these shifts. The relationship of unions to other groups of workers, such as the Chinese and Pacific Islanders in the nineteenth century, and postwar immigrants, have also been the subject of more critical attention.

MIKE QUINLAN

Transport, see **Aviation**; **Motor car**; **Railways**; **River transport**; **Shipping**

Transportation refers to the system of transporting **convicts** to the Australian colonies. Beginning with the **First Fleet** in 1788, more than 150 000 convicts were transported to the Australian colonies. Conditions on convict vessels were generally good, though the voyage of the **Second Fleet** was horrific. From 1815 a surgeon-superintendent travelled on each ship to monitor conditions and attend to convicts' health. A campaign to abolish transportation was conducted by the **anti-transportation** movement, which was active from the mid-1840s. Transportation to NSW ceased in 1840 but resumed briefly in 1848, and transportation to Tasmania ceased in 1853. Transportation was abandoned completely after 1867, when the last convict ship departed for WA, to which convicts had been sent from 1850.

HD

Travel and travel writing, domestic has been one of the most significant ways of creating European views and impressions of Australia. In their published writings, explorers, residents, **visitors**, botanists, artists, and others have often used the genre of travel writing to observe Australia, to describe the social and cultural aspects of its population (including Aborigines), its **natural history**, and the political and economic dimensions of antipodean society. Where possible, argues Paul Carter, *The Road to Botany Bay* (1987), they have translated these into European frameworks. First intended for audiences outside Australia, where publishers might expect to sell a larger number of copies, these writings soon became an important basis for self-definition by many European and British residents in Australia, and have continued to be consulted by historians, if somewhat more critically. Whereas historians have long referred to travel writing by the likes of Anthony **Trollope**, James Froude, and Richard **Twopeny**, more recently they have turned to the significant volume of travel writing produced by women (for example, various books by Louisa **Meredith** and articles by Louisa Atkinson). Their observations have been used to chart particular women's perspectives on Australia, details of which have been collected in various anthologies and bibliographies of women's writing, such as Debra Adelaide, *Bibliography of Australian Women's Literature 1795–1900* (1990), and Robin Lucas and Clare Foster, *Wilder Shores: Women's Travel Stories of Australia and Beyond* (1992). Jan Bassett's *Great Southern Landings: An Anthology of Antipodean Travel* (1995) includes writings by both men and women and illustrates well the different reasons for travel.

Nineteenth-century writers on travel and **exploration** saw the Australian colonies as part of a growing Empire, with England at the helm. England was the usual collection point for information gathered by travellers and other exploring parties (unless, of course, they were French or another nationality), where observations from different parts of the world could be arranged and conclusions drawn, perhaps resulting in the naming of a new botanical species or a discussion about the possibilities for a convict society. Observations from colonial travels challenged much conventional European knowledge, a point discussed by Bernard **Smith** in *European Vision and the South Pacific* (1960; 1985). There emerged in Australia an increasing interest, even pride, in natural wonders and unusual phenomena. From the middle of the nineteenth century travel accounts about Australia were not only available to residents as part of a market extending across the British Empire, but also to a specifically local audience, and were published in newspapers and periodicals. Australian travel, then, was no longer primarily an imperial activity, one where the outcomes of observations were determined elsewhere, but also had local uses, especially in helping to educate Australians about Australia. By the second half of the nineteenth century, guidebooks like *Guide for Excursionists from Melbourne* (1868), as well as substantial volumes published by the colonial railways, provided descriptive and learned articles about interesting places along with practical information on how to get there. Travel, it was assumed, was something one could read about, but also undertake for oneself.

Travel accounts published in Australia urged residents to undertake tours so that they might see for themselves these natural and social phenomena, the geological curiosities of underground caves, the magnificence of treeferns, the bountiful colours of delicate wildflowers, prominent public institutions in major towns and cities, poor areas, rich areas, Aboriginal communities, town life, country life. In these accounts Australia was a place where nature, the picturesque, and the sublime might be studied as might the workings of a modern society, its democratic principles, the outcomes of public welfare, its cultural interests and commercial enterprises. And the occasional adventure helped the story along.

In the first half of the twentieth century, this type of travel writing continued to be published for an Australian audience not only in newspapers and magazines but also as books by a stronger local book publishing industry. William Hatfield, *Australia through the Windscreen* (1936), Ernestine **Hill**, *The Great Australian Loneliness* (1937), and numerous titles by Frank **Clune** described the remote parts of Australia to readers in the coastal cities. Following a genre well-established by the nineteenth century, they offered scientific explanations for unusual natural phenomena and the odd adventure, as well as social commentary. Travel magazines such as *Walkabout* were also bringing Australia to Australians in pictures as well as words.

From the 1950s, travel writing for a local audience began to decline, partly because **tourism** was by then well established and there was less reason for entrepreneurs to promote independent travel. Whereas travellers' tales were once an important way of conveying information about a place (and travel was the means to collect it), that role was now performed by historians, sociologists, political scientists, and other experts. The sense of wonder and adventure, elements central to travel writing, translated so well to the screen that television travellers like Bill Peach, the Leyland Brothers, and Bob Raymond had soon supplanted the traveller who relied on words alone.

JULIA HORNE

Travel and travel writing, overseas was concerned first with the homeward journey, the return to Britain, the place of birth; and for later generations, the site of family memory and ancestral graves. To travel to Britain was to voyage to the centre of the Empire, to the place of authority and authentication. Because Britain was the place of family origins, history, and culture, the voyage of colonials to the sacred centres was a form of pilgrimage. Australian travel in Europe also contained elements of the eighteenth-century Grand Tour: the provincial travellers sought culture at first hand among the galleries and ruins of Europe, a culture that conferred status and privileged speech when the traveller arrived home. Yet Australian Grand Tours differed from the original in that women's participation was as prominent as that of men.

The trip to Europe may have been the predominant form of overseas experience until well into the twentieth century, but from the earliest days Australians were to be found in the Pacific, Asia, America, Africa, and the Antarctic, as adventurers, explorers, traders, missionaries, reformers, soldiers, colonists, proconsuls, wives, and tourists.

Australians have also written about their travels at length. An identified listing of 867 published travel books written by 690 authors between 1850 and 1970 is but a fragment of a vast corpus of Australian travel writing which extends from jejune diaries of the 'what I did in the school holidays' genre to the literary travel book. The extent of the record— letters, diaries, books, newspaper and magazine articles— points to customs that associated travel and writing, to the significance of the travel experience, and to a wide audience for the tale. The satirical work by Victorian schoolteacher Nathan Spielvogel, *A Gumsucker on the Tramp*, first published in 1905, sold 20 000 copies.

While in relative terms the proportion of Australians who travelled abroad was high, until the 1970s, they were still a small minority—middle-class people with the money and leisure to undertake the five-week sea voyages that took them to Europe and then back. As late as 1953, fewer than 40 000 Australian residents made temporary departures overseas. Twenty years later, the number was well over 600 000. The late 1960s witnessed the take-off of the jumbo-jet and the beginning of an era of mass travel. Television brought abroad into everyone's living-room. And the nature of travel writing changed. While many travellers still felt the impulse to tell—and publish—their tale, in the marketplace the focus shifted from object to subject, to the writer's journey and location in place. And much contemporary writing situates Australians in other places.

The range of travel experience and the diversity in the manner of its recording make it difficult to establish a clear-cut genre. The boundaries have always been blurred between fiction and traveller's tale, as are those between **autobiography** and travel writing. Overseas travel experiences usually occupy a disproportionate amount of space in Australian autobiography. Other genres present similar problems. At what point does the social commentary of C.P. Fitzgerald in China or the **war reports** of Alan **Moore-**

head in North Africa spill over into the literature of travel? And as Richard White has asked (in 'The Soldier as Tourist', *War and Society*, 1987), where is the border between war memoirs and travel?

The colonial condition in Australia has led to far more interest being displayed in what visitors to Australia have thought about us than in what we have thought and written about others. Yet the corpus of Australian overseas travel writing reveals much about Australian engagement with other people and places over the past 200 years. But Australians travelled with their eyes fixed on home as well as abroad. In the midst of cathedrals and ivy-covered walls, they saw their own society as deficient in culture and history, but there were compensations—less poverty, hierarchy, oppression of women—and less dirt. The sun, light, and warmth of Italy made Australians feel at home, but also created anxiety about the future of the British race in an Italianate climate. It was particularly in Britain that Australians were prone to contemplate problems of identity, to make comparisons to measure themselves. Historian Kathleen **Fitzpatrick**, a student at Oxford in the 1920s, found that English indifference to 'dreary provincials' had 'a salutary effect in informing me of my own identity, not as a long-lost cousin of the people at home but as an Australian, a member of a new nation in the making' (*Solid Bluestone Foundations*, 1986).

The tendency in considering Australian travel and travel writing has been to anthologise rather than analyse. More critical assessments appear in the introductions to Robin Gerster (ed.), *Hotel Asia* (1995), and Ros Pesman et al. (eds), *The Oxford Book of Australian Travel Writing* (1996), and in *ACH* (1996); Alison Broinowski, *The Yellow Lady* (1992); and Ros Pesman, *Duty Free: Australian Women Abroad* (1996). Ros Pesman et al. (eds), *An Annotated Bibliography of Australian Overseas Travel Writing* (1996), is a valuable listing.

ROS PESMAN

Trollope, Anthony (1815–82), the novelist, visited Australia twice. On his first visit (with his wife Rose) he stayed 12 months (27 July 1871–29 July 1872) plus two months in NZ. He later came to visit his younger son Fred (the model for *Harry Heathcote of Gangoil*, 1873) at his Mortray sheep station near Grenfell, NSW, and write a travel book for which Chapman & Hall contracted to pay him £1250, following 11 lengthy letters which the *Daily Telegraph* agreed to publish.

Trollope had written *The New Zealander*, a Macaulayan diatribe against English dishonesty, in 1855. Disarming honesty distinguished *Australia and New Zealand* (February 1873), no less than Trollope's other three travel books, but it displayed heartless racial prejudice about Aborigines and Maoris (despite his cavorting with three 'Maori damsels' in the hot springs at Rotorua)—similar to that shown against Africans in *South Africa* (1878). The task of writing the book even prevented the Trollopes from attending Fred's wedding on 14 December and may explain why Rose hated the country.

There were also revealing contrasts between Trollope's public affability and private peevishness: 'He complained of everything, found fault with everything, and hectored everybody unmercifully' on the ship to Tasmania, we learn from Sir Ralph Williams. But he was back in Australia for several months in 1875 to sort out Fred's affairs—the Mortray investment apparently cost him as much as all the Barchester novels earned—and stomach the embarrassing criticism of the book. This time he contented himself with 20 letters in the *Liverpool Mercury*, published as *The Tireless Traveller* in 1941. His *Australia and New Zealand* was probably the most influential of nineteenth-century **visitors'** accounts of Australia, obviously regarded as essential reading by the many others who travelled in his wake and echoed his opinions. A critical edition of the Australian section by Roger Joyce and P.D. Edwards appeared in 1968.

NOEL MCLACHLAN

'True believers' were invoked by the prime minister, Paul **Keating**, as he claimed victory in the 1993 federal election: 'This was a victory for the true believers.' He took the phrase from a television series of that name which dealt with the heated battles for control of the **Australian Labor Party** in the 1940s and 1950s. The term entered the lexicon of the labour movement to affirm the continuity with its traditions of an aloof politician with expensive tastes who had considerable regard for what he had called 'the big end of town'. While Keating had done much to reorient the economic and social policies of the ALP, he identified strongly with its myths and legends. In contrast to the earlier terminology for its membership and constituency—*workers, toilers*, or even *wage slaves*—the true believers were socially imprecise. Like others on the right of the party, Keating avoided the language of **class** in favour of tribal loyalty. John Faulkner and Stuart Macintyre took the term as the title of the centenary history of the Federal Parliamentary Labor Party in 2001.

SM

Truganini (Trukanini) (1812–76), also known as Lalla Rookh, is the most famous Aborigine in white Australian history. She was born at Recherche Bay in Van Diemen's Land; her father was Mangerner, of the Lylequonny band from the South-East tribe, whose territory covered the D'Entrecasteaux Channel. She grew up on the margins of British settlement; by the time she was 17, her mother had been murdered by sealers, her uncle shot by a soldier, her sister abducted by sealers, and her fiancé, Paraweena, killed by timber-getters.

In 1829 she met the government agent, G.A. **Robinson**, on Bruny Island. With her partner, Woorredy, she joined the 'mission' Aborigines who guided Robinson on four epic journeys around Van Diemen's Land to 'conciliate' over 300 Tasmanian Aborigines who had been engaged in a guerrilla war with the settlers over possession of their country. She was a member of the party that negotiated with Robinson for the Aborigines to leave Tasmania in exchange for sanctuary on Flinders Island in Bass Strait.

On Flinders Island, Truganini became a leading critic of the Aboriginal Establishment. In 1839 she and 14 other Tasmanian Aborigines accompanied Robinson to Port Phillip, where in 1841 she was convicted with four of her compatriots, two men and two women, of the murder of two whalers in Western Port Bay. While the two men were hanged, Truganini and the other two women were deported to Flinders Island. In 1847 Truganini and 47 other Aborigines were repatriated to the Tasmanian mainland at Oyster Cove, 32 kilometres south of Hobart. She spent 25 years there until 1872, when she moved with her guardian, Mrs Dandridge, to Hobart, where she died on 3 May 1876, aged 63. Truganini was buried in the grounds of the Old **Female Factory**, but, because she was considered 'the last Tasmanian', the government exhumed her skeleton two years later and placed it on public display at the Tasmanian Museum between 1904 and 1947, as proof that she was 'the last of her race'.

As a young woman, Truganini was represented as the exotic princess, Lalla Rookh, after the heroine of the poem by Thomas Moore. As an old woman, she was represented as the Victorian widow. In the century following her death, she was represented in novels, plays, postage stamps, and films as 'the last Tasmanian', whose people had become extinct as a sad but necessary part of the white settlement of Australia. On the centenary of her death, these representations were fractured. First, the government cremated Truganini and returned her ashes to the Tasmanian Aboriginal community to scatter over the D'Entrecasteaux Channel. Truganini now became a symbol of survival of the Tasmanian Aborigines in the twentieth century. But this view was challenged by Vivienne Rae-Ellis who, in a new biography (1976), sexualised Truganini as a *femme fatale* who betrayed her own people.

In the 1990s Trukanini, as she is known to the Tasmanian Aborigines, is a political agent who fought for the survival of her people. For non-Aboriginal Australians, she is a symbol of reconciliation between a colonising power and a proud indigenous people. This was symbolised in 1997 by the return from a British museum of a shell necklace belonging to her.

Lyndall Ryan

Trugo is a game that contains elements of croquet and bowls and was invented by workers at the Newport Railway Yards in Melbourne in the 1920s. The first club was formed at nearby Yarraville, and since then competition has scarcely spread outside a ring of Melbourne working-class suburbs. The game is played on a lawn court and wooden mallets are used to hit small rubber disks, originally the discarded buffer washers from railway carriages, through goal posts. Its name is believed to have derived either from the player's call 'true go', or from the initials 'T.G.', after Tom Greaves, a Newport Railway worker who is regarded as the father of the game. In competition organised under the Victorian Trugo Associ-

ation, trugo is played by both men and women, but competitors must be pensioners or aged over 66.

HD

Trumper, Victor Thomas (?1877–1915), outstanding batsman of the golden age of **cricket**, scored 16 939 first-class runs from 1894 to 1914 at an average of 44.57 with 42 centuries. Always attacking, Trumper spoiled bowlers' lengths by advancing down the pitch, perfectly poised, armed with a flawless, fluent, seemingly endless range of strokes. A modest, shy, and generous man from a large working-class family in Paddington, NSW, he owned a sports shop in Market Street, Sydney. His early death at the age of 37 added to a legend which included several centuries scored before lunch; 300 not out at Sussex in 1899; 11 centuries on English sticky wickets in 1902; and 335 runs in 165 minutes on a magical day in 1903, when his big hits smashed factory windows all around Redfern Oval.

DC

Truth was the name of a **newspaper** founded in Sydney in 1890. Subsequently, local versions appeared in most other states. All were modelled on the English *Truth*, established by the radical politician Henry Labouchère to expose the iniquities of wealth and privilege. A New Zealand *Truth* took a similar approach. John **Norton** was editor and part-owner of the Sydney paper. Following its English precedent, Norton's *Truth* was notorious for its muckraking and scandal-mongering. It went one step further in its irreverence towards British royalty. After John's death in 1916 his papers were operated by his son Ezra until he sold out in 1958. Norton and his paper are the subject of Cyril **Pearl's** *Wild Men of Sydney* (1958) and Michael **Cannon** recalled *That Damned Democrat* (1981) in an anthology of his journalism. The Melbourne *Truth* was under the control of newspaperman Rupert **Murdoch** until 1960 and was acquired in 1980 by Associated Communication Enterprises Ltd. It ceased publication in 1994.

HD

Tucker, Gerard Kennedy (1885–1974), was the founder of a well-known Victorian charity, the Brotherhood of St Laurence. The son of Horace Finn Tucker, an Anglican priest who established rural settlements for the unemployed during the 1890s **depression**, Gerard shared his father's commitment to practical Christianity. After his ordination, he offered to work among the urban poor with a group of celibate priests. His offer was rejected but he retained his vision. Although he was frail and nervous in appearance, Tucker's determination can be judged by his enlistment as a private soldier in 1915 after his request to be posted overseas as an army chaplain was refused. The brotherhood was established in NSW and moved to Melbourne in 1933, where it operated hostels for homeless men in Fitzroy. Later, Tucker established the Carrum Downs resettlement project, designed to move poor families out of the slums. The Community Aid Abroad organisation evolved from his encouragement to the Carrum Downs residents to contribute money for rice shipments to India. Among other works, Tucker wrote his autobiography, *Thanks Be* (1954), and the story of the brotherhood, *How it Began and How it Goes On* (1940). John Handfield wrote about Tucker and the brotherhood in *Friends and Brothers* (1980).

KT

Turner, Ethel Mary (1870–1958), novelist, migrated to Sydney with her mother and sisters in 1879. While at high school she established a magazine, which was followed by the *Parthenon*, produced with her sister Lillian. For three years Turner wrote the children's page for this publication, and the stories show a developing authorial voice. She later wrote the children's section of the *Illustrated Sydney News* and contributed to the **Bulletin** while working on larger projects, one of which was *Seven Little Australians* (1894). This immensely popular book, with its believable children and an urban, middle-class setting with which readers could identify, was soon followed by a sequel, *The Family at Misrule* (1895). These works have remained popular; *Seven Little Australians* was made into a film (1939), a BBC television series (1953), an **Australian Broadcasting Commission** television series (1973), and a musical (1988). A prolific writer, Turner produced 27 novels as well as numerous short stories and verse. Her *Three Little Maids* (1900) follows very closely the story of her family's move to Australia and her mother's remarriage. Brenda Niall examines her work in relation to that of Mary Grant **Bruce** in *Seven Little Billabongs* (1979), and A.T. Yarwood has written a biography, *From a Chair in the Sun* (1994).

KT

Turner, Henry Gyles (1831–1920) was a banker, literary scholar, and historian. As general manager of the Commercial Bank of Australia from 1870 he achieved wealth and prestige. The bank took full advantage of the borrowing and lending opportunities in the boom of the 1880s, and was hit hard in the subsequent crash, when Turner was president of the Melbourne Chamber of Commerce; it suspended trade in 1893 and was slowly reconstructed until his retirement in 1901. Turner was a leading member of the Unitarian Church (his sister MARTHA was minister of the Melbourne congregation), a founder of the *Melbourne Review*, and with Alexander **Sutherland** wrote *The Development of Australian Literature* (1898).

Retirement allowed him to pursue long-established historical interests. The two-volume *A History of the Colony of Victoria* (1904) seeks to impress the lessons of experience on a reckless younger generation, but is marred by a violently partisan treatment of Victorian politics and a remarkably selective account of events (such as the financial crash) in which he had been involved. R.M. **Crawford** judged it to exhibit 'a ludicrously conservative bias', and the same prejudice runs through his account of *The First Decade of the Australian Commonwealth* (1911). Despite its lilliputian

title, *Our Own Little Rebellion* (1913), his history of the **Eureka** rising is surprisingly sympathetic.

SM

Turner, Ian Alexander Hamilton (1922–78) was the most versatile and responsive of the **Old Left** historians. From middle-class origins and education, he joined the **Communist** Party as an ex-service undergraduate at the University of Melbourne. The party directed him into work as a railway cleaner and in 1955 he became organiser of the Australasian Book Society, but was expelled along with his close friend Stephen Murray-Smith in 1958 for criticism of its Stalinist leadership. Keith **Hancock** provided him with the opportunity to study for a doctorate at the Australian National University, and he then taught at Monash University. While his earlier political activism declined, he became an influential member of the **Australian Labor Party** in Victoria.

Turner's doctoral thesis, published as *Industrial Labour and Politics* (1965), applied a Marxist analysis of **class** to the labour movement in the first two decades of the twentieth century. Although he later wrote a vivid account of the repression of the **Industrial Workers of the World** (*Sydney's Burning*, 1967) and a general history of Australian trade unions (*In Union Is Strength*, 1976), his interests turned increasingly to the study of culture and especially popular culture. *The Australian Dream* (1968) was an anthology of 'visions and dreams about Australia's future'. *Cinderella Dressed in Yella* (1969) broke new ground in its collection and interpretation of children's rhymes; he was assisted by June Factor and Wendy **Lowenstein**, whose own interests in folklore he encouraged. His passion for **Australian Rules football** found an outlet in the annual Barassi Memorial Lecture on the game and its larger significance. *Up Where Cazaly?* (1981), a history of football written with Leonie Sandercock, was more troubled by the growth of commercialism.

Some of his finest writing was in essays and reviews, especially for *Overland* magazine where he responded generously and perceptively to new political and artistic forms, always maintaining his commitment to a democratic and accessible culture. Some of this writing was gathered by Leonie Sandercock and Stephen Murray-Smith in *Room for Manoeuvre* (1982), where his political memoir, 'My Long March', appears.

SM

Turner, Martha (1839–1915), woman preacher, travelled to Melbourne from England in 1870 to visit her brother, H.G. **Turner**. He described her as having 'high intellectual qualities' and was happy to have her assistance in his occasional role of preacher to the Melbourne Unitarian congregation. In 1873 the congregation elected Martha as a regular minister, a novelty that attracted much public attention. She intended to resign on marrying John Webster in 1878, but was persuaded to continue until her replacement arrived two years later. He resigned after three months, and she resumed preaching until 1883. She was also an active member of the Australian Women's Suffrage Society. After a period of travel and preaching in Europe, she and her husband lived in Gippsland.

KT

Two-up or 'swy' (German *zwei*: two), sometimes called the 'Australian national game', has until recent years been a popular, illegal **gambling** activity, mainly among men, in which bets are laid on whether two coins spun in the air will both fall heads or tails uppermost. Two-up jargon has enriched Australian language and metaphor, described in S.J. **Baker**, *The Australian Language* (1966), while the game is revealed in poems by C.J. **Dennis**, and novels including Lawson Glassop, *Lucky Palmer* (1949); Dymphna Cusack, *Come in Spinner* (1951); T.A.G. Hungerford, *Riverslake* (1953); and Kenneth Cook, *Wake in Fright* (1961).

Two-up's origins remain vague. In April 1804 the *Sydney Gazette* criticised a 'chuck farthing mob' on the wharves. A two-up game was mentioned in the *Adelaide Observer* (4 October 1884), and the *Argus* (7 August 1905) described it as an Australian variant of the old English game, pitch-and-toss, adding 'every part of Melbourne, and indeed, of Australia, has its "two-up" school, and in most of them large sums of money change hands'. Australian soldiers played two-up in wartime, and diggers' games on **Anzac Day** became traditional. With notable exceptions, police have generally turned a blind eye towards two-up, partly from the difficulty of laying charges, but also due to its wide cultural acceptance. The famous Kalgoorlie school, now legalised, is a tourist attraction. Progressive legalisation of modified two-up began at Hobart's Wrest Point Casino (1973) and coincides with its decline in the wider community.

DC

Twopeny, Richard (1857–1913), journalist and exhibition promoter, was the author of *Town Life in Australia* (1883), an informative and penetrating account of Australia's colonial cities.

Twopeny was educated at Marlborough College and in France and Germany before joining his family in Adelaide in 1876. His knowledge of French got him a job as secretary to the South Australian Commissioner to the 1879 Paris Exposition. He later became an official at **exhibitions** in Sydney (1879) and Melbourne (1880–81), and organiser of privately sponsored exhibitions in Adelaide, Perth, Christchurch, and Dunedin. In 1883 Twopeny proposed a permanent Australasian exhibition in London. Visitors would be given pamphlets describing the living conditions of various classes of Australian town-dweller. The scheme came to nothing, but the pamphlets were reborn as *Town Life in Australia*. Twopeny had married in 1879, and his vivid descriptions of house-hunting, the servant problem, colonial furniture, and household budgeting drew on his own domestic life. 'There is an unpleasant air of patronage running through [this] book', one reviewer complained. But no other book of the period offers such a perceptive account of how the colonial bourgeoisie lived and thought. Twopeny became a newspaper editor in Christchurch and Dunedin before returning to Australia in 1890 to become editor of the *Australasian Pastoralists' Review*, the mouthpiece of the pastoralists in the looming struggle with organised labour.

A reprint of *Town Life in Australia* with an introduction by J.M. **Ward** appeared in 1973; Graeme Davison discussed its author's life and writing in *HS* (1974).

GD

Tyson, James (1819–98), pastoral entrepreneur and first native-born millionaire, was born at the Cowpastures, NSW, the son of a freeman and a convict woman. Tyson began his pastoral career working for Henry O'Brien of Douro, supervising stations between modern Griffith and Hay, and for John Buckland on the Ovens River. Tyson and one brother then set up their own station on the Billabong Creek in the Riverina. From here, three of the five Tyson brothers moved in 1846 to the Lachlan at Geramy. News of the gold find at Bendigo in late 1851 induced them to drive all their stock to the Victorian goldfields. James Tyson's pastoral empire was founded on the profits of the butchering of this first mob. He eventually owned or leased runs totalling 5 329 214 acres, from Glenormiston on the Qld–NT border to Heyfield in Gippsland, Victoria. From his headquarters at Felton near Toowoomba, Qld, he supervised a massive vertical integration of meat and wool production, which was sold after he died intestate. He also had investment in sugar lands near Tully and in allotments and buildings in Brisbane and Sydney and several country towns. Around him in his lifetime grew legends of wealth, miserliness, misogyny, and efficiency, some of which had a basis in truth. The *Bulletin* dubbed him 'Hungry Tyson'. He remained unmarried and is buried in a family vault of St John's Church of England cemetery, Campbelltown.

ZITA DENHOLM

U

Uluru, formerly known as Ayers Rock, is Australia's largest rock formation and is situated about 300 kilometres southwest of Alice Springs. The giant sandstone monolith reaches a height of 335 metres and measures 8.8 kilometres in circumference. Like Mount Connor and nearby Katatjuta (formerly known as Mount Olga), it was formed when upfolding of the land surface of **Gondwanaland** created the ancient Petermann Mountains. Explorer Ernest **Giles** became the first European to view the rock in 1872 while on an overland trip from Charlotte Waters, NT, in search of Lake Amadeus. The following year, explorer William Gosse came upon the rock while leading an expedition through Central Australia and named it after the South Australian premier Henry Ayers. In September 1985 the land title to an area of over 1324 square kilometres, including the Rock and the Olgas, was returned to its traditional owners, the Mutitjula people, and the Aboriginal names, Uluru and Katatjuta, were officially reinstated. The area was subsequently leased to the Australian government for a 99-year period. Uluru displays a spectacular transmission of light at sunrise and sunset, and is Australia's best-known **tourist** destination. Many people have also come to regard it as a place of primordial mystery for New Age pilgrimage.

HD

Unaipon, David (1872–1967) served as a spokesperson for the Aboriginal community for more than 50 years. Of Ngarrindjeri descent, born and educated at the Point Macleay mission in SA, Unaipon preached Christianity to Aboriginals as a means of self-improvement and urged white authorities to support education as a means to Aboriginal assimilation. His collection of *Native Legends* (1920) seeks to demonstrate the similarity of Christian and Aboriginal values. This approach brought him into conflict with the Australian Aborigines' League, in particular over the 1938 Day of Mourning. An unacknowledged collection of his work was published as *Myths and Legends of the Australian Aborigines*

(1930) by W. Ramsay Smith. Unaipon was also an inventor; he produced an improved mechanical handpiece for sheep shears and developed a sophisticated understanding of aerodynamics through experiments with the boomerang. His contribution to Aboriginal literature was recognised in 1988 with the establishment of the annual David Unaipon Award for unpublished work by Aboriginals or Torres Strait Islanders, and in 1995 he was depicted on the Australian $50 note.

KT

Unemployment has long been a feature of the Australian economy. From early colonial times to well into the twentieth century, work was seasonal and task-oriented in character. Through spring and summer, farming, fruit-picking, shearing, and maritime industries generated employment in city and country alike. Winter, by contrast, meant long periods of enforced idleness for a vast pool of casual labour. The development of manufacturing industries in the late nineteenth century modified this pattern only slightly. In the clothing industry, for instance, seasonality was notorious, changing consumer demands driving a cycle of busy and slack periods.

Cyclical movements in the economy were equally important in determining the demand for labour. Work by Charles Fahey and Jenny Lee in *LH* (1986) identified a recurrent period of boom and bust, even in periods once thought to be prosperous. Australia's continued dependence on foreign markets means that both primary industries and the service sector remain extremely vulnerable to these cyclical variations.

Although unemployment is usually seen as a working-class experience, the depressions of the 1890s and 1930s saw its effects being felt in a variety of middle-class occupations, particularly the clerical and retail trades. Always vulnerable to fluctuations in the labour market, craftsmen in the 1890s found that technological and productive innovation compromised the skills on which their livelihoods had once depended. The recent restructuring of the Australian **economy** has had similar consequences, the merger of banks and businesses destroying the security of even white-collar occupations. It has also contributed to a dramatic rise in youth and rural unemployment.

The experience of unemployment differed with every individual. Before the introduction of universal unemployment benefits, the workless relied on private charity (keen to distinguish between deserving and undeserving cases) and equally punitive systems of relief work. The latter in particular disadvantaged women, despite the manifest failure of the ideal of the male breadwinner. Governments insisted that women could not be unemployed because they were by definition 'dependants'. Charlie Fox has argued that the **Howard** government's 'Work for the Dole' scheme is a return to this 'punitive mindset' (*Fighting Back*, 2000). Similar discrimination was practised against Aboriginal people. For many men (particularly those who were single), unemployment meant forced mobility as they tramped city and country in hope of work or handouts. In the home, unemployment highlighted women's importance in maintaining the 'social economy', the domestic skills of recycling, thrift, sharing, and scavenging keeping many families from starvation.

It is the politics of the unemployed which has most interested historians. Graeme Davison and John Hirst's studies of the 1890s (*The Rise and Fall of Marvellous Melbourne*, 1978; 'Keeping Colonial History Colonial: The Hartz Thesis Revisited', *HS*, 1984), and Geoffrey **Bolton** and Ray Broomhill's studies of the 1930s (*A Fine Country to Starve In*, 1972; *Unemployed Workers*, 1978) argue that the unemployed quickly exhausted the possibilities of effective political protest. Demoralising idleness and the humiliation of charity or relief work left the unemployed dispirited, apathetic, or divided. These views have been challenged by Verity Burgmann and Bruce Scates's work on the 1890s (*In Our Time*, 1985; *A New Australia*, 1997) and various studies of the 1930s Depression. All these writers emphasise the resilience and diversity of unemployed protest, from the peaceful petitioning favoured by moderates to the mass resistance of anti-eviction struggles and dole strikes.

From World War II to the early 1970s Australia achieved close to full employment; since then economic change has thrown many out of work. The closing years of the twentieth century saw abandonment of full employment as the principal goal of economic policy, the weakening of industrial awards, and the increase of part-time and casual employment. Labour economists now identify underemployment as well as unemployment. The right to work remains a prerequisite of meaningful citizenship. Securing that right may well mean fundamental changes to the way society is organised.

Bruce Scates

United Australia Party was formed during the political crisis of 1931. It united the exhausted **Nationalist Party** with former members of the **Australian Labor Party** whose commitment to the financial economies introduced during the **Depression** had caused a second Labor **Split**, and new popular movements such as the All for Australia League that mobilised during the Depression to uphold financial and national honour. While the party's name signified a rejection of party and class divisions, its formation and composition reveal a conservative purpose. Behind the All for Australia League and other civic associations that denounced orthodox politics lay right-wing bodies whose acceptance of democratic principles was conditional on the maintenance of God, King and Empire.

It was a group of Melbourne businessmen who arranged for the former Labor federal treasurer, J.A. **Lyons**, to assume leadership of the new party from J.G. **Latham**, who had succeeded S.M. **Bruce** as the Nationalist leader. This transition is illuminated by the contributors to C. Hazlehurst, *Australian Conservatism* (1979). The creation of the new party brought an infusion of new faces into federal parliament in 1932, when the UAP took office with an absolute majority, but the older patterns of conservative politics were quickly resumed. Like its predecessor, the UAP began to break up as soon as it lost office in 1941; it dissolved upon the formation of the **Liberal Party** in 1944. The broad base and durability of that ultimate reincarnation of non-Labor politics is unique.

SM

United Kingdom, see **British–Australian relations**

United States of America, see **American–Australian relations**

Uniting Church, the third-largest religious denomination in Australia, was formed in 1977 when members of the **Congregational**, **Methodist** and **Presbyterian churches** united. The church's beliefs, expressed in the 'Basis of Union', place it in the maintream of liberal Protestantism: it treats the Bible and historic creeds as authoritative statements of the faith which are to be interpreted in the light of a later age. The architects of the church drew inspiration from the international ecumenical movement which had already produced similar unions of churches in Canada and South India; the choice of the word *uniting* indicated a desire for a progressive joining with other churches in accordance with Christ's injunction that 'they all should be one'. While Methodists, whose affairs were governed by a central conference, joined the new church as a bloc, and Congregationalists almost universally voted to join, a section of the Presbyterian Church, largest in NSW and Qld, remained outside the union. The Uniting Church gives prominence to issues of social responsibility and maintains the largest non-government social welfare agency in Australia. Membership of the church is predominantly Australian-born and increasingly aged; its affiliates, as measured by the Census, have declined from approximately 12 per cent of the population at the time of union to about eight per cent today. There is no comprehensive history of the church, but Ian Breward's *A History of* *the Australian Churches* (1993) provides a useful commentary. Both the NSW and Victorian branches of the Uniting Church Historical Society publish journals.

GD

Unity tickets are alliances of candidates from different parties for electoral advantage. The original unity tickets consisted of members of the **Australian Labor Party** and the **Communist** Party standing together in elections for union positions against right-wing or anti-communist rivals. There had been such alliances from the 1930s, but they became more common in the 1950s after the Industrial Groups of the Catholic Social Studies **Movement** began to win control of communist-led unions and to extend their influence within the Labor Party. These unity tickets were thus essentially defensive devices during and immediately after the Labor **Split** of 1955. Conservative politicians exploited the industrial alliance to discredit their Labor opponents as beholden to communists, and they were eventually declared contrary to the rules of the ALP.

SM

Universities were established in NSW in 1850 and Victoria in 1853, primarily as important symbols of colonists' cultural heritage. They assumed that a 'liberal education' would nurture the moral and social improvement necessary to mediate the transition to social and political maturity. As each of the other colonies reached a critical stage of development, a similar coalition of private and public interest led to the establishment of universities in Adelaide (1874), Tasmania (1890), Qld (1909), and WA (1910).

The founders accommodated colonial circumstances by drawing on English, Scottish, and Irish models, though it would be Oxford and Cambridge against which universities mainly judged themselves. The new universities were urban in character, largely non-residential, and meritocratic; they were more concerned with the communication of knowledge and professional training than induction into a privileged culture or the development of character. They were explicitly secular and predominantly state-funded and, in combining examining and teaching functions, they gave considerable scope to individual professors to shape future development.

Enrolments at the foundation universities were embarrassingly low until growth in secondary education in the 1880s provided them with a broader stream of students, both male and female. Greater community interest in education encouraged a steady expansion in courses offered, most of them in 'functional areas' such as engineering, science, and professional training, in line with 'modernising' trends elsewhere. Government grants, however, remained tightly circumscribed and, since fees were relatively low, most major initiatives depended on a generous benefactor. Until 1939 Australian universities were small and essentially undergraduate, sending their best and brightest off to revered British institutions and preferring the products of those universities to head their own faculties. They were dominated by professors who taught the majority of students, aided by only a handful of staff, often part-time. Professors carried out most of the administrative work.

Research was confined to a rare few, and there were no restrictions on entry for those who negotiated the relatively undemanding secondary curriculum.

World War II was a turning-point in the history of Australian universities, which up to that time could fairly be characterised as professional training institutions, elite, provincial, and peripheral, catering to 0.2 per cent of the population. Notwithstanding their dependence on government funding, they were autonomous, self-governing institutions, but the price of that independence was chronic insufficiency of resources—a situation that became critical as student numbers began to rise. The war transformed public opinion on the value of scientific research and an educated workforce. Once education and research became matters of national interest, governments, especially the Commonwealth government newly endowed with income-taxing powers, took an increasing interest in universities, and graduates began to play a larger role in Australian society. The establishment of the Australian National University with a strong research focus in 1946 symbolised the changed relationship between government, community, and universities, but the full implications of that changed relationship took longer to emerge. For the first time, during the war, there was some restriction on entry to university, harbinger of several decades of rising academic entrance requirements as demand for places rose dramatically. Increasingly self-confident universities began to offer postgraduate research degrees, and from 1951 Commonwealth scholarships further enhanced academic standards.

By the end of 1950s the Commonwealth had acquired control over policy and universities were drawn reluctantly into a national system. Six new universities were established (New South Wales, 1958; Monash, 1958; Macquarie, 1963; La Trobe, 1964; Newcastle, 1965; Flinders, 1966), some of them experimenting with new models of organisation. Student numbers trebled before the Commonwealth government's desire to curtail expenditure led to the introduction of the 'binary system' in 1965. Intended to protect the universities' elite status as research institutions by channelling most of the growth in student numbers into more applied or vocational courses, it failed to contain costs or dampen the aspirations of the new colleges of advanced education to become universities in their own right. In 1973 the states handed complete control of higher education over to the federal government, which abolished fees and introduced a system of living allowances intended to increase access.

By the early 1980s the artificial walls of the binary system were collapsing and the proliferation of small institutions was deemed unsustainable. In 1988 the coveted title 'university' was extended to a large number of new institutions, but a cost-conscious federal government imposed a program of amalgamations and reintroduced fees. This broadened university sector now consists of 37 public and two private institutions, with a total of 693 000 enrolments in 2000. Australian universities have rapidly expanded their international recruitment and tapped other sources to make good the shortfall in public funding.

After the war, universities became the subject of research and writing from inside and out, much of it concerned with function and organisation. A 1965 bibliography listed 13 000 items published since 1950 and there has been no slackening of interest. Since the 1980s there has been a steady stream of institutional histories prompted by a combination of renewed community interest in history and a need to reconsider the nature of universities in a period of change and challenge.

CAROLYN RASMUSSEN

Uranium is a radioactive metal that was first isolated in 1841. It was discovered in Australia in 1894, but not mined until the 1940s, when it became sought for its use in the generation of nuclear power. Following financial support from Britain, the Australian government offered tax-free incentives to encourage uranium mining in the late 1940s and 1950s. The major mines were developed at Rum Jungle, NT (from 1949), and Mary Kathleen, Qld (from 1954). These rich deposits made Australia a major supplier. The initial boom petered out in the early 1960s but production rose significantly in the early 1970s, following the international oil crisis and discovery of several large deposits, including Roxby Downs in SA, and the Jabiluka and Ranger mines in the NT. Uranium mining faced growing opposition in the 1980s from environmentalists and supporters of nuclear disarmament. The **Hawke** and **Keating** Labor governments restricted mining to two mines (Ranger and Nabarlek, NT, later Olympic Dam, SA), but maintained export contracts. The **Howard** government abandoned the two-mine policy in 1996.

HD

Urban history was a late developer in the writing of Australian history. Writing about cities generally meant concentrating on their future, not their past. By the 1870s, Richard **Twopeny** was already impressed by the growth of Sydney, Melbourne, and the other colonial ports; within 30 years Adna Weber (in *The Growth of Cities in the Nineteenth Century*, 1899) argued that Australia's urban concentrations placed it at the 'forefront of the modern world'. Celebrations of colonial or national prospects—notably the grand designs of Henry **Parkes** for a centennial Sydney in 1888—invariably focused on remaking the cities with exhibition halls, monuments and edifices, while turn-of-the-century reformers demanded the eradication of Old World eyesores like **slums** from the cities of a new nation.

In the nineteenth and early twentieth centuries, inventing the nation generated a desire for national history, but one in which the great port cities were simply the most visible emblems of links to the Empire and the world. Cities rarely featured in twentieth-century historical scholarship most interested in political conflicts and ideas. There were descriptive histories of local culture and society, including Geoffrey **Blainey's** *History of Camberwell* (1965) and Weston **Bate's** *History of Brighton* (1962). But, by and large, cities were incidental backdrops for the more important political and ideological dramas.

The growth of explicitly 'urban history' in the 1970s is a good example of how individual research interests—and eclectic borrowings from North American and European

scholarship—can have a dramatic impact within Australia's relatively small intellectual culture. The sources were varied, including British historian Asa Briggs's advocacy of 'urban studies' and his inclusion of Melbourne in *Victorian Cities* (1964). Meanwhile, following American and British scholars into a self-consciously 'new social' history, others rejected a focus on elite politics and insisted that historians attend to the finer patterns of social life. Economic historians—notably Noel **Butlin**—showed the importance of urban economies, while John McCarty explored the comparative dimensions of Australia's colonial commercial cities in 'Australian Capital Cities in the Nineteenth Century' (*AEHR*, 1970). Hugh **Stretton's** path-breaking *Ideas for Australian Cities* (1970) is remembered for championing the **suburb** against its detractors, but it was just as important for showing that Australians lived in urban worlds profoundly shaped by the ideas and the actions of people in the past, a project given further momentum by Leonie Sandercock's *Cities for Sale* (1975).

Hopes for a comparative and generalising history of Australian cities were not fulfilled; even in the 1990s, 'Australian' urban history tends to mean extrapolation from Sydney and Melbourne. Histories of provincial cities (including Bate's work on Ballarat in *Lucky City*, 1978, and *Life After Gold*, 1993) and of the relationships between cities and hinterlands—first explored in John Hirst, *Adelaide and the Country*, 1973—were sporadic. Lionel Frost's *Australian Cities in Comparative View* (1990) explored the implications of different settlement and development patterns in all the major cities, but most historians remained loyal to their 'own' metropolis. And within it, few ventured far beyond the physical boundaries of the nineteenth-century city; Peter Spearritt's *Sydney Since the Twenties* (1973) was an exception, but the suburbs of the 1920s and the 1950s generally awaited writers who saw them as 'fit' subjects for history.

In the 1970s and 1980s, Australian urban historians participated in overlapping conversations about power, reform, and the making of cities; they revealed the sharp conflicts which had marked the urban landscape. One conversation—strongest among Sydney historians like Max Kelly—examined the production of the city, tracing the imprints of power and conflict in planning regulations and land development. Others explored the evolution of urban government and nineteenth-century compromises between property, public interest, and amenity. As ever, the themes of urban history reflected the concerns of the present, in this case, 1970s demands for governments to protect the urban environment and urban heritage from developers' bulldozers.

Another conversation—best realised in Graeme Davison's *The Rise and Fall of Marvellous Melbourne* (1978)—traced the making of a city's everyday world of homes, transport, and jobs. Yet Davison also insisted that 'making Melbourne' was never simply a matter of bricks and tramtracks. People lived in cities with names and reputations, built from images and ideas, and giving physical expression to the dreams—and sometimes the fears—of those powerful enough to imagine that they could shape a city's destiny. The argument that cities were creations of culture and belief, not just technology, was also reflected in the energetic history of Canberra's planning, even if some coastal historians found it difficult to acknowledge Canberra as a 'city'.

While Tom Stannage recorded *The People of Perth* (1979) and Adelaide historians worked forwards from pioneer planner Colonel **Light**, Melbourne and Sydney historians were also exploring their cities' social margins: the back lanes, tanneries, and cramped cottages in which many of the poor lived a very different kind of urban experience. Shirley Fitzgerald's *Rising Damp* (1987) and Alan Mayne's *Fever, Squalor and Vice* (1982) placed poverty, poor housing, and disease at the centre of Sydney's history, while *The Outcasts of Melbourne* (1985) and rich local studies like Janet McCalman's *Struggletown* (1984) or John Lack's *History of Footscray* (1991) spoke of those on Melbourne's economic and social peripheries. Yet if poverty and misery were rediscovered, so too was the reformist tradition they helped to inspire. Almost at the very moment that late-twentieth-century governments were exploring every avenue for privatising urban infrastructure and selling off what they could of public housing and public services, these histories reminded us why such urban services had been taken under public control in the first place.

These first explicitly urban history ventures were often collaborative. The Sydney History Group, Melbourne's Urban History Seminar, and the Brisbane History Group showed the benefits of intellectual exchange, and the principle of collaboration continued into the 1990s with the Postwar Melbourne project. For all that, urban history had never really staked out its own turf: if this frustrated people with a need for boundaries, it made engagement with new kinds of urban studies much easier in the 1980s and 1990s. The urban story fragmented in an exciting jumble of feminist geographies, cultural studies, oral testimonies, public and 'amateur' local histories. Sometimes following the leads of overseas theorists and generalisers, Australian historians studied urban space and urban culture as fundamental products of modern life, turning more and more to the everyday experience of the city and the living of city life, whether on the streets (as in Andrew Brown-May, *The Itinerary of Our Days*, 1998) or amid the quiet satisfactions and hidden anxieties of middle-class suburbs (Janet McCalman, *Journeyings*, 1994). Local histories traced the impact of social and economic change, and the ways in which the particularities of local action and reaction shaped general processes. The grand dramas of urban planning (as in Robert Freestone, *Model Communities*, 1989) were not ignored, but panoramic perspectives were often supplanted by a finer focus, an eye for the to-ings and fro-ings of the 'city people' who made urban worlds.

Focusing on how cities shape the possibilities of everyday life—and on the small-time dramas of living in the city—historians also offered imaginative reconstructions of how different people inhabited, identified and remembered their own urban territories. This increasing emphasis on the experience and texture of place also stretched back into tracings of the colonial past, most successfully in the urban archaeology of Grace Karskens (*Inside the Rocks*, 1999) and the rich story-telling of Robyn Annear (*Bearbrass*, 1995). Other works focused on experiences hidden by neglect as

much as time. *Inner Cities: Australian Women's Memories of Place* (Drusilla Modjeska (ed.), 1989) gave writers like Jenny Gregory, Carolyn Allport, Jill Roe, and Jennifer McCulloch an opportunity to show how women, as homemakers, workers, neighbours, and activists, had inhabited and sometimes changed urban spaces built largely by men. Australian cities had accommodated millions of migrants; those migrants had also reshaped the appearance and the culture of the cities. The wealthy and the poor knew different Melbournes or Brisbanes. And each park, each riverbank, held profoundly different meanings and experiences for European and Aboriginal people. The 'city' was broken down, and with it the idea that there was one urban past, one 'urban man', or one urban culture (see Ruth Fincher and Jane Jacobs (eds), *Cities of Difference* 1998).

Within the broader framework of urban studies, Australian urban history is increasingly concerned with the variety of encounters which give shape and meaning to the experience of city life. Historians look less to the town hall and the parliament, more to the shopping mall and the suburban street. We examine how cities are structured by technologies of time (Davison, *The Unforgiving Minute*, 1993) and technologies of service or consumption. Cities are pipes and meters and clocks, cars and footpaths, telephones and televisions, drive-ins, amusement parks, and graffiti. This is an emerging history of city living, of smells and sounds and pleasures, a history of urban culture and urban communications which makes us all characters in a shared story.

But, as the contributors to Katherine Gibson and Sophie Watson (eds), *Metropolis Now* (1995) show, the city is also a place of differences and hard edges. Cities have walls, some real and others imagined. Urban life brings disadvantages and discriminations, destruction and loss, as shown by Peter Read, *Returning to Nothing* (1996), and Mark Peel, *Good Times, Hard Times* (1995). It is about miseries and privations which are neither new nor disappearing. At the end of the twentieth century, urban historians have special opportunities: to dramatise the story of how Australian cities have come to be, and to continue writing an evocative history of urban life and urban culture. And they have a special responsibility: to show that knowing the urban past is also about shaping a better urban future.

MARK PEEL

Urbanisation was pronounced from the beginning of European settlement, but the forces which made it so were different in important ways from those which propelled urbanisation in Europe.

During the nineteenth century, capital, labour, technology, and institutions were transferred from industrial Europe to the resource-rich regions of Australasia, southern Africa, Latin America, and North America. Wherever European traders and settlers produced a surplus for market, towns grew; the larger the surplus and the more productive the activity which created it, the greater the expansion of urban jobs. As frontiers expanded, towns provided bases for settlement of the surrounding hinterland. Each of these towns was part of a global urban system which directed international flows of commodities, capital, and labour. Cities as diverse and geographically distant as Chicago, Calgary, Johannesburg, and Buenos Aires were linked by a common characteristic, their involvement in the world economy.

Australian urbanisation was part of this transnational process. But there were differences in the pattern of Australian economic development which affected the pace of urbanisation. The first Australian towns were convict settlements, with large numbers of soldiers and administrators. The production and export of **wool** was a further stimulus to urban growth. This early development of a high-productivity primary export industry and the associated level of demand for urban goods and services created a much higher initial urban population than in any other region of recent settlement. In 1850, 40 per cent of the Australian urban population lived in towns of at least 2500 inhabitants, compared with only 14 per cent in the USA and 12 per cent in Canada. Thereafter, the Australian urban population grew more slowly, but by 1870, with 37 per cent of the population in towns, Australia was still significantly more urbanised than NZ (28 per cent), and the USA and Argentina (both 26 per cent).

During the gold rushes, **Melbourne** grew to be one of the great cities created by European colonisation, with an 1860 population (129 000) double that of San Francisco, which had also been stimulated by gold discoveries. **Sydney** was not far behind Melbourne, and it and **Adelaide** were the capitals of large, prosperous rural hinterlands. During the **long boom** from around 1860 to 1890, these major capitals increased their share of their respective colony's population: Melbourne from 23 to 41 per cent, Sydney from 27 to 35 per cent, and Adelaide from 35 to 42 per cent.

The growth of Australian cities during the nineteenth century, particularly the capitals, worried contemporary observers. Cities were widely seen as consumers rather than producers, with the countryside being the true source of all wealth. The NSW government statistician, T.A. **Coghlan**, wrote of a 'most unfortunate … abnormal aggregation' of population in the capitals. Accordingly, governments attempted to counter the trend by adopting rural development policies which promoted **closer settlement** and **decentralisation**, but these were largely ineffective.

Australia was heavily urbanised but this is not to say that its cities were abnormally large or that their size retarded economic growth in general. As J.W. McCarty argued (*AEHR*, 1970), the Australian capitals dominated their hinterland because they were the best location for seaports and rail hubs and thus for commerce and industry. This was the typical situation in regions where the hinterland was fairly compact and hugged a coastline with few natural harbours. A few large cities exerted similar dominion over North America's Pacific slope. Furthermore, these cities stimulated agricultural change, boosted rural incomes, and provided economies of scale and investment opportunities which created a wide range of products and amenities. The parallels between urbanisation in Australia and the American

West are developed by Lionel Frost in *The New Urban Frontier* (1991).

In the twentieth century, governments have taken a larger and more active role in promoting urban growth by **protection** of industry from foreign competition, assisted immigration, subsidisation of home ownership, and the building of infrastructure in new **suburbs**. During this century, the Australian capitals have increased their populations about sixfold on average, and have been the location of most of the new jobs which the economy has created. By the early 1970s, Australia, like most developed countries, had become virtually fully urbanised, with 86 per cent of the population living in towns.

LIONEL FROST

Ure Smith, Sydney George (1887–1949) studied with Julian Ashton, then established an innovative commercial art studio with cartoonist Harry Julius, before becoming co-founder in 1916 of *Art in Australia*, Australia's leading art journal for many years. The firm Ure Smith Pty Ltd developed into an influential publisher with such works as Bernard **Smith's** influential *Place, Taste and Tradition* (1945). He also fostered art and artists in his role as president of the Society of Artists (1921–48) and as a trustee of the Art Gallery of New South Wales (1922–47). Nancy Underhill discusses his importance to Australian art in *Making Australian Art 1916–49: Sydney Ure Smith* (1991).

KT

Uren, Malcolm John Leggoe (1900–73), journalist and historian, was born in Adelaide and went at an early age with schoolteacher parents to WA. Employed from 1920 to 1965 by WA Newspapers Ltd, he was an editor of the *Western Mail*, 1941–53, the *Broadcaster*, 1942–53, and *Milady*, 1948–52, as well as serving as a war correspondent in the South-West Pacific, 1944–45. From 1953 he was assistant to the managing editor, serving as media organiser for the Perth Commonwealth Games and for early tours to the promising mineral regions of the north-west. During his middle years he was a productive writer in the then underresearched field of Western Australian history. *Sailormen's Ghosts* (1940) described attempts to locate the seventeenth-century Dutch wrecks off the Western Australian coast, and was reprinted five times. This was followed by *Waterless Horizons* (1941) (with Robert Stephens), an account of Edward John **Eyre**; *Land Looking West* (1948) on Captain Sir James **Stirling**; and *Glint of Gold* (1948), in which oral history was used to enliven the story of the 1890s gold rushes. Isolation denied Uren contracts and recognition, and his later years were less productive. A colleague described him as 'heavy, sometimes sombre, but easy-going', and notably helpful to younger writers. His son, Malcolm (Bon) Uren, was also a noted journalist.

GEOFFREY BOLTON

Utzon, Joern, see **Sydney Opera House**

Van Diemen's Land, also known as Vandemonia, the island south of mainland Australia, was named in 1642 by Abel **Tasman** after Antonio van Diemen, the governor-general of the Dutch East Indies. Following British colonisation, Van Diemen's Land was settled in 1803 and became a separate colony in 1825. In 1851 its Legislative Council was changed into a partially elected body with power to draw up a constitution for self-government; this took place in 1856. The colony's name was changed to **Tasmania** in 1853. This move was strongly supported by Rev. John **West**, a leader of the **anti-transportation** movement, who used the word *Tasmania* in the title of his 1852 history in the expectation that it would dispel the notoriety associated with convictism and penal servitude.

HD

Vandemonian, derived from an earlier form, V*andiemener*, emerged in the 1830s as a general term for a non-Aboriginal person born in, or a resident of, **Van Diemen's Land**. Increasingly, however, it referred to a convict from that colony, and the evident pun encouraged this use: Tasmanian convicts were also known as *demens* or *demons*. This use carried a derogatory implication, particularly at Port Phillip, where free settlers abhorred the arrival of large numbers of so-called Vandemonians, or **Pentonvillains**, in the 1840s and 1850s, many of whom were **ticket-of-leave** men. Contemporary accounts emphasised the convict background of these men and encouraged their reputation for wild, unruly behaviour.

HD

Vaux, James Hardy (1782–?) began his colourful association with Australia in 1801 when he was first transported from England for theft. Despite having forged Governor **King's** initials on commissariat orders, he accompanied the governor home to England in 1807. Convicted again of theft, he was transported for life and arrived in Sydney in 1810. Within a year of his return he was sentenced to hard labour at Newcastle for receiving stolen property. It was here that he wrote his *Memoirs of James Hardy Vaux*, published in London in 1819 under the auspices of Barron **Field**, which included a dictionary of slang from the London underworld—the 'flash' language. This was republished in 1964, edited by Noel McLachlan, and has formed the basis for much of the early lexicography of Australian English. In 1829 Vaux broke his conditional pardon and fled to Dublin, where he was once again arrested, this time for passing forged bank notes. He was transported in 1830 and lost to public notice after the early 1840s. A ballad opera based on his eventful life, *Flash Jim Vaux*, by Ron Blair, was first produced in 1971.

KT

Vegemite, a spread produced from brewer's yeast, was created by the Melbourne food manufacturer Fred Walker & Co. in 1923 to compete with the popular British product Marmite. In order to create a similar product, Walker's chemist D.P. Callister determined Marmite's chemical composition, the research for which earned him a DSc from the University of Melbourne. Walker's product, manufactured from leftover yeast from the Carlton Breweries, was named 'Vegemite' after a public competition for a name and promoted as a health product. However, it was regarded as inferior to the British product, and its market-share remained small. In 1928, in an endeavour to recoup sales from Marmite, Vegemite was renamed 'Parwill'—relying on the slogan 'if Ma might, Pa will'—but this proved unsuccessful. A boost to sales from the inclusion of Vegemite in soldiers' rations during World War II was augmented by intense commercial promotion in the postwar period. The US company Kraft, which had become a part-owner in the 1930s, gained full control in 1950. The popular advertising jingle that Vegemite 'put a rose in every cheek' coincided with its growing popularity with children in the 1950s. Though unappreciated outside Australia, Vegemite has become a national institution.

HD

Victoria was the only colony where permanent European settlement began without the sanction of British authority. Four naval investigations explored Western Port, Wilsons Promontory, and Port Phillip Bay between 1797 and 1802. A party was despatched from Sydney during the summer of 1802–03 to find a site for a military camp to forestall anticipated French occupation, but it gave negative reports. London authorities despatched another party under Lieutenant-Governor **Collins**, who after six months at desolate Sorrento, withdrew to the Derwent River in Van Diemen's Land.

Whalers and sealers had long operated along the southern coast and in the islands of Bass Strait when the **Henty family** initiated pastoral settlement at Portland Bay in 1834. Explorer Thomas **Mitchell** named the western plains 'Australia Felix' in 1836, thereby strengthening the tentative southward movement of NSW graziers. These 'overlanders' were preceded by 'overstraiters' from Van Diemen's Land, following the examples of parties led to the head of Port Phillip Bay by John **Batman** and John Pascoe **Fawkner** in 1835. Official recognition came in 1836, when some 224 Europeans were living in huts along the Yarra River, and the district held 40 000 sheep on stations as far as 130 kilometres inland. **Melbourne** and Geelong grew rapidly to serve the pastoral advance: within a decade, almost three-quarters of the area south of the Murray River was taken, and the squatter occupation was licensed; by 1850, some 76 000 free migrants had arrived.

European economy and society in **Port Phillip** were thus founded on pastoral leaseholds. The gentlemen settlers among them attempted to reproduce polite society on the model of 'home' in a manner described by Paul de Serville, *Port Phillip Gentlemen* (1980), but they were decimated by **drought** and **depression** in the early 1840s. Conspicuous among the survivors were the single-minded Scottish tenant farmers and their sons, whose economic success, political power, and social prestige as a sort of country gentry were celebrated by Margaret **Kiddle's** *Men of Yesterday: A Social History of the Western District of Victoria 1834–1890* (1961). The myth of the squatters' peaceful dispossession of the Aborigines, which had its origins in John Batman's claim to have negotiated a settlement with them, was little disturbed by the subsequent publication of pioneer reminiscences by Rolf **Boldrewood**, W.A. Brodribb, and E.M. **Curr**; the full enormity of the white assault was exposed only by the contributions to regional history of professional historians such as Peter Corris's *Aborigines and Europeans in Western Victoria* (1968) and Don Watson's notable *Caledonia Australis: Scottish Highlanders on the Frontier of Australia* (1984). The definitive modern general account of Victoria before separation is A.G.L. Shaw, *A History of The Port Phillip District* (1996).

The late-1840s movement for the separation of Port Phillip from NSW coalesced around urban resistance to transportation and pastoral resentment of Sydney's control of land revenue. This alliance barely outlasted the bonfires lit to celebrate the proclamation of the Crown Colony of Victoria on 1 July 1851, for later that month the colony was convulsed by the discovery of **gold**. During the next decade Victoria produced more than one-third of the world's gold, and some 600 000 migrants—half of them from Britain and Ireland, 50 000 from Europe and North America, and the rest from Victoria's neighbouring colonies—swamped the old Port Phillip society. Population grew from 80 000 (1851) to 300 000 (1854), and to 540 000 in 1861, when alluvial mining by individual diggers had yielded to deep mining by companies. Self-government was conceded in 1852, and Lieutenant-Governor **La Trobe** and his partly elected, partly nominated Legislative Council drew up a **constitution**. It created a bicameral parliament that replicated the colony's great social and property divide: a popularly elected lower house (soon extended by votes for those holding miner's rights) faced a property-based upper house. The reformism expressed in agitation against the gold licence system, which exploded at the **Eureka Stockade** in 1854, quickly flowed into democratic reform of the Legislative Assembly: secret ballot (1856), manhood suffrage (1857), abolition of property qualifications for members (1857), and triennial parliaments (1859). The Legislative Council, dominated by a squatter and merchant oligarchy, remained unreformed. Geoffrey **Serle**, *The Golden Age* (1963), is the authoritative account.

The gold migrants of the 1850s dominated Victoria for a generation. Their political representatives battled to break the squatters' land monopoly and create a small farming community, a goal initially frustrated by squatter manipulation of the first **Selection** Acts, but achieved on the northern plains and in central Victoria by the acts of 1865 and 1869. State-owned railways and state-funded **irrigation** schemes helped make farming viable on this far-flung frontier. In turn, Victoria's larger and relatively denser population encouraged the growth of processing and **manufacturing** industries. Consumer-driven import-replacement, and government contracts, were probably more important in encouraging native industry and discouraging imports than were Victoria's much-vaunted **tariffs**.

By 1880 the colony boasted a varied economy, grounded on goldmining, wool-growing, and a strong agricultural sector. **State socialism**—the provision of roads, railways, and water supply, a system of secular primary schools, and a network of subsidised mechanics institutes and schools of mines—was a significant contributor to this prosperity and sense of well-being. The blend of private enterprise and state assistance was not uniquely Victorian, but in some respects Victoria led the Australian colonies. Serle, *The Rush To Be Rich* (1971), establishes the distinctive features.

The prosperity of the 1880s largely dissolved the old divide between radical and conservative, Assembly and Council, and a liberal–conservative coalition governed Victoria from 1883. Melbourne, with a population of almost half a million in 1891, surpassed Sydney in size and wealth, and became for a time Australia's financial centre. Much of the continent's 1880s outback mining and tropical agriculture were planned and financed from **Marvellous**

Melbourne. If Melbourne's confidence created and sustained the boom, Melbourne's profligacy brought it to a spectacular end. A land and building crash culminated in the bank smash of 1893, and the worst **depression** in Victoria's history. However, the crisis renewed Victorian interest in Australian **Federation**, as farmers, manufacturers, and merchants looked to wider markets under a colonial tariff union. Victorians voted overwhelmingly in favour at every opportunity.

Melbourne remained the temporary capital of the Federation until 1927. Alfred **Deakin** and his followers took their brand of British–Australian imperial-nationalism into the early Commonwealth, sanctifying it with the peculiarly Victorian pioneer legend; this blend of the mythologies of pastoralists, goldseekers, and small farmers exalted as the national day, not Victorian separation or the Eureka Stockade, but, magnanimously, 26 January 1788. Victoria regained its respectability by demonstrating financial probity: it paid its way with booming exports of meat, wheat, and butter from industries revolutionised by the technology of refrigeration, the combination harvester, and the cream separator. Under federal protection, manufacturing boomed in Melbourne; employers and employees negotiated wages through a system of **wages boards** designed to eliminate unions and strikes. Manufacturing industry was supplied with power (black coal from Wonthaggi after 1908, electricity generated from brown coal at Yallourn in the 1920s), and with labour (a vigorous assisted immigration scheme in cooperation with the Commonwealth). Victoria's factory workforce doubled between 1901 and 1918.

World War I ultimately strengthened these developments. When conservative and radical nationalism parted ways over **conscription** and commitment to the war effort, Melbourne was the cockpit. Victoria was the only major state to vote 'yes' to conscription, and the vote turned marginally against compulsion at the second referendum. The crisis produced an alliance between trade unions and Irish Catholics in opposition to the Protestant, Masonic and Australian nativist goldtown and suburban-worker culture, a divide which conditioned politics for 50 years.

Labor, weakly established in Victoria because of the liberal legacy and state socialism, and disadvantaged by a gerrymandered state parliament and blatantly undemocratic upper house, seldom governed at state level, and was rarely a stronghold of federal Labor. It is striking that, while nine of Australia's 21 prime ministers (omitting caretakers) originated in Victoria, the state has supplied only three (**Scullin**, **Curtin**, and **Hawke**) of nine Labor leaders.

Prime Minister Stanley Melbourne **Bruce**, businessman, war hero, and quintessentially a Melbourne man, presided over a Nationalist–Country Party coalition 1923–29. Immigration and soldier settlement were stimulated on a grand scale. Urbanisation accelerated: Melbourne held 55 per cent of the state's population in 1933; the eastern suburbs of Camberwell and Caulfield had larger populations than Geelong, Ballarat, and Bendigo combined. When the boom collapsed, and seasons turned bad, Victoria and Australia

were sucked into the worldwide Depression. In these circumstances, the Hogan Labor government of 1929–32 gradually disintegrated. The conservative Argyle government (1932–35) made even more severe cuts, and savagely suppressed unemployed protest, earning the loathing of both Country and Labor Parties, whose informal alliance saw Australia's most urbanised and industrialised state governed for more than a decade by Albert **Dunstan's** Country Party government 1935–45.

Recovering from the Depression, Victoria was confirmed as Australia's centre for naval construction, and the aircraft and motor vehicle industries. These, together with well-developed fertiliser, chemical, explosives, rubber, munitions, and small arms industries, made the state a key to the national war effort, especially when Japan entered the war in 1941. Melbourne for several years was Allied headquarters for the South-West Pacific. The surge in rural and industrial production continued after the war, labour demand far outstripping supply. Victoria attracted a major share of refugees and migrants gathered from Europe and Britain by Australia's postwar population-building program.

A period of political instability (1945–52) was followed by the first majority Labor government under John Cain (1952–55); but it was destroyed by the **Split**, and the Liberals governed for 17 years straight (1955–82). The theme, notably under (Sir) Henry **Bolte** (1955–72), was development and growth. The exploitation of gas and crude oil reserves off Gippsland, and industrial development at Western Port and in the Latrobe Valley, further underlined the swing of population and development away from western and central Victoria.

The state was 'the jewel in the Liberal Party's federal crown' until 1972, when not even Victoria could prevent the election of the first Labor government since 1949. Labor only returned to power in Victoria in 1982, under John Cain junior, and Cain's third term was beset by crises of party and public confidence in a deteriorating national economic climate caused by the slashing of federal tariffs, development mania, and property speculation rivalling those of the 1880s, and major haemorrhaging in the building society and banking sectors. Labor's Joan Kirner became Australia's first woman premier, but under impossible conditions, and the Liberals swept to power in 1992 under Jeffrey **Kennett**.

Victoria, now widely regarded as the buckle on Australia's rust belt, seemed a suitable case for treatment by the economic rationalists. A program of 'credit rating restoration' ensued: drastic cuts in the public service, extensive privatisation of government utilities, enforced amalgamation of local government, and reduction of services. Kennett aimed to make Melbourne the national sporting and entertainment centre. Nothing of conservative brutality, and little of the strategy of surface boosterism, was new. Victoria had been there and done it before—in the 1890s, the 1900s, and the 1930s. What *was* new in the 1990s was the premier's openly expressed contempt for the social forces, centred on the trade union movement and the (mainly Protestant) churches, that had made Victoria a pioneer of public culture and civilised living standards exactly a century before. It was provincial Victoria, however, that revolted against Kennett's privatisation and Melbourne-centredness, sweeping him from office at the 1999 general election and installing a minority Labor government under Steve Bracks.

Joanna Monie, *Victorian History and Politics* (1982), is a comprehensive bibliography to 1939. The sesquicentenary in 1984 brought three volumes, *Arriving* by Richard Broome, *Settling* by Tony Dingle, and *Making Their Mark* by Susan Priestley. Geoffrey **Blainey** and Don Garden have written general histories.

JOHN LACK

Vietnam War was the longest and most divisive of Australia's military engagements. For a decade from 1962, Australian forces were involved in a complex conflict which was in part civil war, and in part a proxy conflict in the Cold War. These complexities generated intense dispute in Australia, and are reflected in divisions in the historical literature.

The French made Vietnam a colony by military conquest in the 1860s and promptly put the people to work producing exports of rice and rubber. By World War II, nationalist groups had been crushed, leaving the Vietnamese Communist Party as the main force opposing Japanese occupation and the reimposition of French rule after the war. With the defeat of the French in 1954, the great powers applied a classic Cold War device: division into a communist north and a pro-Western south. The regime in the south was politically weak, and increasingly dependent on American support, while the Vietnamese Communist Party gave up neither its claim to reunify the country, nor its hold on nationalist sentiment. By the early 1960s, American resolve that Vietnam was where the line had to be held against communist expansion meshed with the Australian government's enthusiasm to promote Western intervention, motivated, as Gregory Pemberton demonstrated in *All the Way* (1987), by a desire to interpose American force between Australia and Asia. On 24 May 1962, Australia announced the first token of this desire, a small force of army instructors to assist the South Vietnamese army.

Australian foreign policy, under Richard **Casey** and Paul **Hasluck** as ministers for external affairs, persisted in seeing Vietnam as a case of communist aggression. When, on 29 April 1965, the government committed the first regular force of some 1500 military, R.G. **Menzies's** language was dramatic: 'The take-over of South Viet-Nam would be a direct military threat to Australia and all the countries of South and South-East Asia. It must be seen as part of a thrust by Communist China between the Indian and Pacific Oceans.' This Cold War interpretation was argued by Alan Watt in *Vietnam: An Australian Analysis* (1968), and was a view which found a popular response. Opinion polls recorded substantial majorities in favour of Australia's involvement until late 1968, by which time the Australian force had been expanded to over 8000, a tiny group alongside over 500 000 Americans.

From mid-1966, the Australian force had responsibility for Phuoc Tuy province. The most intense battle of Australia's war followed in August, when Vietnamese guerrillas laid an ambush at Long Tan; 18 Australians died, and 245 Vietnamese. Thereafter, the guerrillas were more cautious, and Australian strategy focused on denying them access to the supplies and political contacts of the villages. When the Australians withdrew in late 1971, some 500 had been killed, and Phuoc Tuy quickly returned to guerrilla control.

The movement in Australia against the war struggled to make an impact until 1969. The criticism of the **Australian Labor Party**, after Arthur **Calwell's** resounding defeat in the 1966 election, became more cautious under E.G. **Whitlam**. It was **conscription** that first mobilised opposition. Announced on 10 November 1964, the conscription scheme required males turning 20 to register for National Service. For the first time in Australia's fraught history of conscription, national servicemen could be sent overseas, without restriction. In a bizarre ritual which Calwell quickly dubbed 'the lottery of death', the annual intake was selected by drawing marbles from a Tattersalls barrel. Although conscription in the abstract was popular, a majority opposed sending conscripts to Vietnam. From 1965, the women's group Save Our Sons held lonely vigils against conscription; by 1968, their demure forms of moral protest were surpassed by the radical students' movement, with its emphasis on overt defiance.

By late 1969, the movement against the war had gathered strength, buoyed by the turn in popular opinion, which was itself shaped by the televised brutalities of the war. This shift culminated in the **Moratorium** campaign, which, in its first national demonstration on 8 May 1970, presented some 150 000 protesters on the streets. Subsequent marches were never as large, but that first success fostered the impression that it had stopped the war, despite the fact that the Americans were seeking ways to withdraw by mid-1969. The first step in the Australian withdrawal was announced on 22 April 1970; only 179 troops remained in December 1972, when the incoming Whitlam government ordered them home and abolished conscription.

Of the voluminous American literature, good overviews are Gabriel Kolko's *Anatomy of a War* (1985) and George McT. Kahin's *Intervention* (1986). In Australia, there is more foreign policy and military history than social history on the war. The official history presents the view from the commanding heights of policy, the key volumes being Peter Edwards, *Crises and Commitments* (1992) and *A Nation at War* (1997), the former written with Gregory Pemberton. A more critical overview is in John Murphy's *Harvest of Fear: A History of Australia's Vietnam War* (1993), while there are several edited collections, notably Pemberton's *Vietnam Remembered* (1990). The war has been fertile ground for **oral histories**, with both their riches and deficiencies. Gary McKay's *Vietnam Fragments* (1992) represents returned soldiers, while Greg Langley's *A Decade of Dissent* (1992) records the anti-war movement and Siobhan McHugh's *Minefields and Miniskirts* (1993) recounts women's experience.

JOHN MURPHY

Vigoro, a game resembling cricket and played exclusively by women, was first introduced to Australia by an Englishman, John George Grant, in 1908; it gained few followers in Melbourne and its popularity dates from Grant's second visit, to Sydney, in 1919. It continued to be played as a summer sport, especially in Qld and NSW.

GD

Villers-Bretonneux was a small French village on the Western Front of **World War I**, which became an important step towards the rail junction of Amiens. In early April 1918, Australian troops repulsed a strong German attack on the village; however, the inexperienced British troops who replaced them were unable to withstand another attack in late April and the Australian troops were brought back into the line. The bitter fighting that followed, recounted in C.E.W. **Bean's** *Anzac to Amiens* (1946), included what was claimed as the first encounter between tanks. By the 25th, Australian troops under the command of General Glasgow and 'Pompey' **Elliott** had secured the village and saved Amiens from attack. After the war, in Victoria the schoolchildren were urged to 'adopt' Villers-Bretonneux and donate money to build a new school. The Victoria School was opened in 1929 with the admonition 'Never forget Australia' painted above every blackboard. It houses a small museum commemorating the Australian involvement in Villers-Bretonneux; the assembly hall is decorated with acacia panels carved with Australian animals. The village has become a memorial to Australia—the school holds an **Anzac Day** ceremony, and local streets are named 'Australia', 'Victoria', and 'Melbourne'. The nearby National Military Cemetery includes a memorial to the nearly 11 000 Australian soldiers killed in France with no known graves. The campaign and continuing Australian relationship with the town is detailed in A. Blankfield and R.S. Corfield (eds), *Never Forget Australia* (1994), produced to commemorate the 75th anniversary of the battle.

KT

Visitors have been an important source of both Australia's reputation in the outside world and Australians' attitudes to themselves, their country, and their culture.

By contrast with American settlement, the Australian one was a weird experiment in government colonisation, the remotest dependency in the world. In 1770 James **Cook** and Joseph **Banks** were arguably the most influential visitors of all, and the planting of the Sydney Cove penal settlement in 1788 led to the publication of six naval officers' accounts (including that of Arthur **Phillip**), which took advantage of public curiosity in both the **convicts'** fate and their strange new world. They were part of the teeming, new, English

print capitalism and the burgeoning fashion for travel books fired by the first, important visitor writing in English: William **Dampier**, a scientifically minded Somerset privateer, whose *A New Voyage Round the World* was published in 1697. Before the English colonists came other first sightings of places, people, and animals, chronicled in 1995 by John Kenny in *Before the First Fleet*.

None of the early travel writers dared treat the convicts light-heartedly. Nor did the humourless royal commissioner, John Thomas **Bigge**, who published the first comprehensive (three-volume) report on the colony in 1822–23, suggesting how it could be run more cheaply. Outstanding in humanity and lightness of touch was Peter Cunningham's *Two Years in New South Wales* (1827), written after five voyages as surgeon–superintendent on convict transports, with its rare glimpse of native-born national pride: 'The Currency youth are warmly attached to their country, which they deem unsurpassable, and a few ever visit England without hailing the day of their return as the most delightful of their lives.' That tallies with Baron Carl von Hügel's impressive judgment of them in Sydney in 1834 after months in their company (in his *New Holland Journal*, translated by Dymphna Clark in 1994): 'They are an educated, powerfully built and fine-looking race of men, open-hearted and clear-headed, friendly, good-natured, yet vigorous in word and deed.'

Most convicts, transported for at least seven years, cannot count as visitors, but a few **Irish** political offenders lost no time in escaping and richly reinforcing Australia's reputation as a convict hell: Young Irelander John Mitchel's exciting *Jail Journal* (serialised in his *New York Citizen* in 1854) legendised Van Diemen's Land for a whole generation of Irish; ebullient **Fenian** escapee John Boyle O'Reilly's fascinating *Moondyne* (serialised in his immensely successful *Boston Pilot*) did the same for WA. Like the peevish Mitchel, high-minded **Tolpuddle Martyr** George Loveless (*Victims of Whiggery*, 1837), pardoned after three years, felt contempt for ordinary criminals, and his pamphlet enjoyed mass circulation in England.

With the gold rushes, the influx onto the mainland of sometimes violent **Vandemonian** convicts tarnished the fresh imagery brought by a flood of much more cosmopolitan visitors, most of them probably hoping to make their fortune and go home, but reconciling themselves to becoming colonists when they failed. Intense curiosity in London about fortune-finding prospects was fed by William Howitt's *Land, Labour and Gold* (1855); Ellen Clacy's no less delightful *A Lady's Visit to the Gold Diggings of Australia* (1853); Californian veteran William Kelly's chatty, surprisingly neglected two-volume *Life in Victoria* (1859); the *Gold Fields' Diary* of young Lord Robert Cecil (the future British Prime Minister Lord Salisbury) (1935); and Raffaello **Carboni's** memorable first-hand account of the **Eureka Stockade** (1855). Another foreigner, the bustling Young American apostle George Francis Train (1829–1904), was a Melbourne merchant for three years, though his autobiography did not appear till 1902; his lively, sharp-eyed letters have been collected by E. Daniel Potts and Annette Potts (1970).

During the second half of the nineteenth century, steam cut the long voyage to a few relatively comfortable weeks, and the soaring renown of the healthy climate added allure to northern Europeans. Following the North American fashion created by Dickens in 1842, Australia was now exploited by a succession of professional **travel writers**, some already celebrated men of letters and several (William Howitt, Samuel Clemens, and Michael Davitt) recently bankrupt. They usually combined journalising with public lectures here and were able to compare the country with other places on world tours, feeding the still burgeoning market (with rising literacy) for travellers' tales. Despite the flaws of hurried impressions and breathless, hopscotch itineraries, they left a rich harvest of brightly written reports. These visitors provided the foundations for New World comparison not only of events and institutions but of ideas and attitudes. With the increasing vogue for world history, this is probably the most fruitful perspective for assessing the significance of Australian experience.

Actor and impresario George Coppin brought over Americans J.C. **Williamson** and Maggie Moors, who returned here in 1879 for good with profound impact on Australian theatre. But it was Robert Smythe (1833–1917) from Lambeth who, in the early 1870s, set himself up in Melbourne as 'the only Lecture Manager at the Antipodes', dealing 'exclusively with Celebrities—Artistic, Scientific, Literary'. Among others, he brought explorer H.M. Stanley, astronomer R.A. Proctor, journalists Archibald Forbes and G.A. Sala, American preacher Thomas De Wit Talmage, French writer Max O'Rell (Paul Blouet), and in 1895 Mark Twain (Samuel Clemens)—but Michael Davitt could not afford his fees (half gross receipts).

The gold rushes of the 1850s radicalised Australian politics, and it was young Charles Dilke's brilliantly titled *Greater Britain* (1868) which set the fashion for turning a world tour into a highly successful book (eight editions) contrasting Australian and American democracy. Anthony **Trollope** (travel writer *par excellence* of the English-speaking world) in 1871 rejoiced in the imperial loyalty (after the attempted **assassination** of our first legitimate royal visitor, the Duke of Edinburgh, in 1868), but painted a 'halcyon view which I entertain of the closing days of the connection between England and Australia'. Despite their optimism, these visitors did not ignore the convict stain, even if Trollope did not get round to the 'difficulties' with which 'our Australian empire' commenced at Sydney until page 128. He detected the inferiority feelings, and his parting advice was 'Don't blow.' 'Englishmen think of the colonials as an inferior race', observed French *bon vivant* E. Martin La Meslée in 1883; but 'the Australians believe themselves every bit as good'.

The celebrated conservative English historian J.A. Froude, after observing Australia largely from the Melbourne Club and squatters' estates, wrote *Oceana* (1886) to champion Imperial Federation. Lord Rosebery, Liberal politician and prime minister, advocated 'a commonwealth of nations' after visiting Australia and NZ in 1881, while in 1893 Reginald Brabazon, 12th Earl of Meath (and inventor of **Empire Day**), compared America and Australasia in the *Nineteenth Century*, preferring the latter. But it was radical Irish nationalist Michael Davitt who described Australia and NZ in *Life and Progress in Australasia* as the most progressive countries in the world in 1898—and with more enthusiasm than Sidney and Beatrice Webb, though their French protégé, Albert Métin, coined the phrase '*Le Socialisme sans doctrines*' (1902) to describe the politics of the '**working-man's paradise**'—a notion also discussed in German Robert Schachner's letters of 1906–07. Davitt also good-humouredly advised Sydney not to be ashamed of its convict past and quoted the extraordinary view of Breton priest, Father Pierre Marie Bucas, at Mt Morgan, disputing, like von Hügel in 1834, 'the generally-accepted theory that the native Australian is the lowest in intellectual development of the known human species'.

The discreet English visitor (ironically, even Charles Darwin in 1835) had much to answer for in not confronting the fulfilment of Alexandro Malaspina's 1794 forecast about the Aborigines for the Spanish government that 'what will be easier and sooner will be the destruction rather than the civilisation of these unhappy people', and cheerful Mark Twain devoted a whole, caustic chapter to the extinction of the Tasmanians. In the twentieth century foreign insights continued, with Californian anthropologist, W. Lloyd Warner, telling the *Sydney Morning Herald* in 1927, after eight months in Arnhem Land, that he had 'never met finer people, nor better people, nor people more innately gracious', and in 1960 Paul Robeson drawing embarrassing world attention to the Aborigines and showing them the model of Negro militancy in securing justice and self-respect—condign counsel.

Three of the most influential visitors between the world wars were D.H. **Lawrence**, Egon **Kisch**, and H.G. Wells. Lawrence, who published *Kangaroo* in 1923, transformed Australians' attitude to the bush, and his short stay was examined by Robert Darroch in *D.H. Lawrence in Australia* (1981). Kisch (*Australian Landfall*, 1937) was impressed with the democratic exuberance of the Australian people, mordant in his observations of the insular ruling class. Wells, in the summer of 1938, incurred censure from the prime minister for calling Hitler ('a friendly Head of State') 'a certifiable lunatic'; he published his *News Chronicle* articles as *Travels of a Republican Radical in Search of Hot Water* (1939).

After World War II there was J.M.D. Pringle, who came to the *Sydney Morning Herald* as editor from the London *Observer* in 1952. His *Australian Accent* essays (1958), with brilliant Molvig cartoons, evoking Sydney metropolitan culture with English middle-class sensibility, probably did more than any book since the war to both transform Australian self-confidence and to kill English condescension. In the 40 years since, the almost apologetic defensiveness has vanished and visitors have lost their significance.

NOEL McLachlan

Visual arts, see **Aboriginal art**; **Painting, history**

Voluntary services

Voluntary services have been provided by a range of charitable and benevolent organisations, supported by church and community groups. The origins lie in the Christian practice of charity, supplemented by civic responsibility. In addition to the practical work of caring, feeding, and sheltering, committees of volunteers have generated considerable revenue through charity fairs, church bazaars, and lamington drives. Women have carried out the bulk of voluntary service work in Australia, especially during the two world wars, when 'women's work' was knitting socks, making blankets, nursing, and providing meals. With women's increased mobility and greater presence in the paid workforce, their involvement in voluntary services declined.

In times of emergency or disaster, voluntary bodies—the St John's Ambulance, the Country Fire Authority, local branches of the Red Cross, **Legacy**, and the surf life-saving associations—assist with the saving of lives, and with the provision of medical support and other relief. Other civic service is provided by bodies such as Rotary, Apex, the Lions Club, and the Boy Scout and Girl Guide movement. Many services, such as Meals on Wheels, are increasingly managed on a user-pays system or have been absorbed into the public welfare sector. Many government-funded welfare agencies evolved from voluntary service organisations.

Nineteenth-century governments supported philanthropic organisations. After a shift to public provision in the twentieth century, governments are again making increasing use of voluntary organisations for the delivery of welfare services. Yet as the voluntary organisations take on this role, they become managers and employers little different from the agencies to which they are contracted.

HD

Voting systems, see **Elections**

Voyager disaster occurred on the evening of 10 February 1964, when the destroyer HMAS _Voyager_ and the aircraft carrier HMAS _Melbourne_ collided in the navy's exercise area off Jervis Bay, NSW. The collision resulted in the deaths of 82 members of the _Voyager_'s crew, including the commander, Captain Duncan Stevens, and the sinking of part of the vessel. It was Australia's worst peacetime naval disaster. The first royal commission found that the main reason for the collision was that the _Voyager_ turned across the _Melbourne_, but concluded that the captains of both vessels had been guilty of negligence. Stevens was alleged to have consumed alcohol. Dissatisfaction with the inquiry forced the creation of a second royal commission (1967–68), which found that Stevens was not fit to command the ship because of ill-health. In the 1990s survivors of the disaster claimed to be among its victims and a few won compensation for trauma and stress.

HD

W

WAAAF, see **Women's Auxiliary Australian Air Force**

Wages boards were state tribunals to determine minimum wages and conditions as an alternative to **arbitration**. They differed chiefly in their composition and procedures: wages boards were composed of representatives of employers and employees, with an independent chair, and they could act without the formal requirement of a dispute. Unions generally preferred arbitration because it provided for official recognition and allowed for preference for union members in employment. Victoria first created wages boards in 1896; SA introduced them in 1900 and Tasmania in 1910. SA and Tasmania also had conciliation and arbitration systems, and in practice the two mechanisms converged.
SM

Wainwright, John William (1880–1948) was one of the innovative bureaucrats who steered SA's economic passage from dependence on unbalanced and unpredictable agricultural production to the broader base of mixed industry. In 1935 he advocated the development of an integrated, state-assisted industrial policy. Appointed auditor-general in 1934, he was ideally placed through his membership of powerful committees to usher his ideas into policy. In the years between the Depression and World War II he developed a twin-pronged attack on the tyranny that distance imposed on SA's inchoate manufacturing sector. First, his industrial policy offered economic inducements to industry, such as the tax-concession system that convinced General Motors–Holden to stay in Adelaide. Second, he enticed new business with infrastructure, both specially targeted, such as the reinforced-concrete and steel wharf built for ICI at Osborne, and more general projects, such as the Port Adelaide to Birkenhead Bridge. His style of management was essentially corporatist, bringing chambers of manufactures, government, and trade unions together to plan policy implementation; in 1937, he established the Industries Assistance Corporation of

SA. He strove for balanced development, and was responsible for forming Common Cause, a wartime movement directed at ending poverty and unemployment.
CAROL FORT

Wake, Nancy Grace Augusta (1912–) was known to the Germans as 'the White Mouse' during World War II when she worked with the French Resistance. Born in NZ and educated in Sydney, Wake was working as a journalist in France at the outbreak of war. She worked in the Allied Escape Route Organisation and reported on German activities until she was arrested in 1943. She escaped to England where she joined the Special Operations Executive and was dropped back into France to work with the Resistance. Her autobiography, *The White Mouse* (1985), provides a vivid account of these years. For this dangerous role she received decorations from England, France and the USA, but no Australian award. Russell Braddon's book *Nancy Wake* appeared in 1956, making her a widely known figure. After the war she moved between Britain and Australia; she joined the Liberal Party and stood unsuccessfully against H.V. **Evatt** in the 1951 election. Describing herself as 'too cosmopolitan' for the Sydney of that time, she returned to Europe but eventually settled in NSW with her second husband, John Forward. In 1994 Wake sold her war medals to the RSL.
KT

Wakefield system was a scheme for colonisation and land settlement engineered by Edward Gibbon Wakefield (1796–1862), which he outlined in *A Letter from Sydney*, published in London in 1829. Wakefield was a reformer convicted for eloping with a 15-year-old heiress, and wrote his tract on colonisation from prison. In it he proposed a theory of 'systematic colonisation', whereby the number of landowners would be regulated by setting a sufficient price for land. Revenue from land sales would then fund the immigration of free labourers, who would work for the landowners; convict labour, however, would be completely banned. Wakefield intended that the ratio of landed proprietors to labourers be such as to replicate the British class system; at the same time, the scheme would ensure a balanced proportion of men and women, and benefit England by relieving overcrowding. By industry and thrift, labourers would have the chance to buy their own land.

An area between WA and NSW was initially nominated for colonisation under Wakefield's system, but this was reduced considerably to the area contained in the colony of **South Australia**. The South Australian Act, passed by the British parliament in 1834, set out the particulars of the system. The private **South Australian Company**, formed in 1835, bought land from the commission established to manage the scheme. But Wakefield's principles of applying land revenue to migration were never fully implemented in SA or NZ, where Wakefieldian colonies were subsequently established.

HD

Walers, see **Horses**

Walkabout, and the expression 'to go walkabout', refer to the traditional periodic travelling on foot by Aborigines, either individually or in groups, over their traditional land—a practice that non-Aboriginal Australians have largely misunderstood and reproved. Managers of cattle stations in outback Australia, bemoaned the unpredictable wanderings of their Aboriginal workers, and derided the notion of a trip which, in their judgment, had no precise destination or duration. Others preferred to accept it as a condition of securing Aboriginal labour. The term *walkabout* later gained wider currency among non-Aboriginal Australians—in the bush and later more generally—and became an affectionate reference to travelling of imprecise duration and destination. *Walkabout* was the title of a monthly magazine founded in 1934 that focused on nature and the outdoors.

HD

Walker, Alan Edgar (1911–2001) was a Methodist minister at the NSW coalfield town of Cessnock. His strong social mission informed the book he wrote about the community and its needs, *Coaltown* (1945). He came to national prominence in 1952 when, as superintendent of the Waverley Methodist Mission, he led a series of evangelistic rallies around Australia under the 'Mission to the Nation' banner. He later became superintendent of the Central Methodist Mission, Sydney, and was active in the international **evangelical** movement. His commitment to peace and criticism of the **Vietnam War** brought him to the attention of the **Australian Security Intelligence Organisation**.

KT

Walker, Kath, see **Oodgeroo Noonuccal**

Walling, Edna Margaret (1895–1973) was an influential figure in Australian landscape design. Born in Yorkshire,

England, she settled in Australia in 1911 and became one of a small group of young women trained at Burnley Horticultural College in the early 1900s. In the mid-1920s she became a gardening columnist for *Woman's Home* and *Australian Home Beautiful*. Walling designed many notable private gardens in Victoria and NSW, including Cruden Farm for Elisabeth **Murdoch**. At Bickleigh Vale estate in Mooroolbark, Victoria, she designed and built several rustic bungalow cottages on large garden settings—including her own, Sonning. These cottages were harmonised in their naturalistic use of timber and stone, and in rambling gardens that blended indigenous and exotic vegetation. Walling encouraged the involvement of other landscape gardeners in her work, including the young Ellis Stones. Frequently attired in the suit and tie of her male contemporaries, Walling cut an unconventional female figure. Her published works include *Gardens in Australia* (1943), *Cottage and Garden in Australia* (1947), and *A Gardener's Log* (1948). Trisha Dixon and Jeannie Churchill consider her garden plans in *The Vision of Edna Walling* (1998).

HD

'Waltzing Matilda', the name of Australia's unofficial **national song**, is thought to have derived from the German words *auf der walz* and *mathilde*, which mean to carry one's swag from camp to camp. The song was written by poet A.B. **Paterson** in Qld in 1895 and put to music by Christina Macpherson of Dagwood Station, near Winton, Qld. Macpherson adapted the music from the traditional Scottish tune, 'Craigielea', which she heard at the Warrnambool Races in Victoria in 1894. Competing interpretations about the song's origins were documented by Sydney May in *The Story of Waltzing Matilda* (1944) and Oscar Mendelsohn in *A Waltz with Matilda: On the Trail of a Song* (1966). One theory, supported by historian and folklorist Richard Magoffin, in his works *Waltzing Matilda: Song of Australia: A Folk History* (1983) and *Waltzing Matilda: The Story Behind the Legend* (1987, 1995), is that the model for Paterson's swagman was German shearer Frenchy Hoffmeister, who was wanted by the Queensland police during the **shearers' strike**. An adapted version of 'Waltzing Matilda' used to advertise Billy Tea in the early 1900s, which made the swagman 'jolly' and the tune brighter and quicker, has since become more popular than the original. In the song's centenary year, 1995, celebrations were held at Winton and debates about the song's origins were revived.

HD

Wannan, William Fielding Fearn-Wannan 'Bill' (1915–) is a prolific chronicler of Australian folklore. He served with the Second AIF during World War II and subsequently worked mainly as a journalist. Since the mid-1950s, Wannan has published numerous works that document his particular vein of Australiana—popular legends, lore, and humorous anecdotes, particularly those dealing with the oddities and more obscure events of Australian history. Of his numerous published works, the best known include the Scottish-Australian *The Heather in the South* (1959), a work on **bushrangers**, *Tell 'Em I Died Game* (1963); an anthology of Irish-Australian folklore, *The Wearing of the Green* (1965); and the encyclopedic work, *Australian Folklore* (1970). Wannan has also written a satire on Australian local history, *Chronicles of Boobyalla* (1979).

HD

War memorials are one of the most characteristic features of the Australian townscape and express the centrality of war to Australian national identity. Despite this, there are few **monuments** that recognise the Aboriginal and European casualties of frontier warfare.

The idea of memorialising feats of war goes back to classical times, but it was not until the mid-nineteenth century in Britain that memorials were erected to ordinary soldiers rather than to individual officers and commanders. This idea spread fast, but by 1900 Australia still possessed only three war memorials—one in Hobart honouring a British regiment which left Tasmania to fight Maori in the New Zealand Wars, and two in Sydney commemorating men who had served in the **Sudan** in 1885. The **Boer War** in South Africa brought the tradition to Australian communities, more than 100 of which erected monuments. A significant number were completed even before the war had ended in 1902, and all were erected within five years of peace. In general, the designs anticipated those after the Great War (with soldiers and obelisks the most common), but there were two unusual types each constituting over 10 per cent of memorials—lamps on pedestals and drinking fountains.

World War I established the war memorial as a necessary part of almost every Australian community. Although schools, businesses, and clubs often erected honour boards, most monumental memorials were based on localities with funds raised by local donations. They were usually given prominent sites, and the Melbourne Shrine of Remembrance and Sydney memorial were designed as landmarks. This was partly because the Great War was seen as a coming-of-age of Australian nationhood, and the war memorial functioned to record this 'Anzac spirit' and to provide a location for that ceremony of nationhood on **Anzac Day**. Despite this nationalist purpose, only rarely do distinctively Australian symbols or inscriptions by Australian authors appear on memorials. The sources are normally biblical, classical, or British.

The war memorial in Australia also served as a surrogate tomb. Since the vast majority of the 60 000 Australian dead were buried in distant lands, relatives had no other focus for their grief than the local memorial. Here they could lay wreaths and contemplate a particular name carved in stone. More than one-quarter of Australia's civic memorials are obelisks or columns—traditional cemetery forms.

But Australian memorials of the Great War are distinctive internationally for the high proportion (over half) that record the names not only of the dead but also of those who served. This points to the function of the memorial in recording wartime feelings about **conscription** and service. Apart from the special cases of Ireland and India, Australia was the only belligerent state that depended upon voluntary participation, and as Ken **Inglis** has observed in 'Memorials of the Great War' (*ACH*, 1987), the memorial became a way of honouring those who volunteered and, by implication, dishonouring those whose names are absent because they shirked.

Despite folkloric belief, the stone digger is not the most common form of memorial—there are significantly fewer than both obelisks and halls. There was indeed a movement in the southern states to dissuade communities on the grounds of good taste from putting up effigies of soldiers that were available relatively cheaply from the studios of Carrara, Italy. In NSW, where a Public Monument Advisory Board was established to approve designs, the numbers of diggers were lower than elsewhere. The relatively high number of memorial halls (about one-fifth) reflects a belief in some quarters that memorials should be useful rather than monumental. Especially in comparison with England, the number of crosses is extremely low; this reflects the range of religious adherence in the community and the desire to make the memorial a centre of civic religion free of sectarian strife. Despite such aims, war memorials did frequently become centres of dispute. There were often fierce debates over the site, the design, the texts, and even the unveiling of the memorial. On occasions the Catholics refused to participate in the round of speeches and parades and ceremonies which accompanied the unveiling because it included a hymn or the Lord's Prayer. Although the small town or suburb was the archetypal setting for memorials, each of the states also put up statewide monuments—the largest being Victoria's Shrine of Remembrance.

The commemoration of **World War II** took a rather different form. 'Living memorials'—useful structures—were now regarded as preferable to stone monuments; this policy was encouraged by the federal government, which made donations for such projects tax-deductible. There were fewer dead to mourn—27 000—than after 1914–18, and the names were easily accommodated around the existing memorials. Names of those who died in **Korea**, **Malaya**, and **Vietnam** were also often added to local monuments. They were remembered too in the nation's capital on Anzac Avenue. The contrast with Washington is instructive. While the Mall is flanked by museums and monuments to presidents, Anzac Avenue is lined with war memorials, and the federal parliament building is linked spatially and visually to the **Australian War Memorial**. Like the prominence given to war memorials in local communities, Canberra honours the place of war in Australian nationalist mythology. The leading scholar of war memorials is K.S. Inglis, whose *Sacred Places* appeared in 1998.

JOCK PHILLIPS

War reporters and reporting provided news coverage of Australian military encounters from the mid-nineteenth century. They also helped to shape perceptions of national identity and, from **World War II**, contributed to knowledge about Australia's regional neighbours. Australian reporting of conflict dates from the 1860s, when Howard

Willoughby covered the Waikato War for the Melbourne *Argus*. Subsequently, the **Sydney Morning Herald** sent W.J. Lambie to the **Sudan** in 1885, and A.B. 'Banjo' **Paterson** to the **Boer War** in 1901. But the palm for Australian war reporting is invariably given to C.E.W. **Bean**, the official correspondent with the **AIF**, who won the position just ahead of fellow journalist Keith **Murdoch**. Although it was a despatch by a British correspondent, Ellis Ashmead-Bartlett, that first informed Australians about the landing of their troops at Gallipoli, Bean's determination to document the experiences of ordinary Australian soldiers played a central role in the development of an **Anzac** tradition. His dominance must be attributed to the sum of his efforts as correspondent, official historian, and founder of the **Australian War Memorial**. His name was given to a foundation established to honour Australian war correspondents.

In the same tradition, **World War II** theatres were comprehensively covered by reporters such as John Hetherington, Alan **Moorehead**, George **Johnston**, Osmar White, Guy Harriott, and Chester Wilmot, whose support for Australia's war effort always outweighed their desire to question official policies and interpretations. The interchangeability of war reporting and the writing of history also continued with the appointment of Gavin **Long**, who had covered the fall of France and the Greek and New Guinea campaigns, as official historian of Australia's role in the war. Another candidate for the position had been poet and journalist, Kenneth **Slessor**, who was the official correspondent with the Second AIF until a series of disputes over **censorship** forced his resignation in 1944. While a number of women, including Adele Shelton-Smith, Dorothy Drain, and Alice Jackson, visited various battle theatres and reported on the living conditions of troops and other non-operational activities, they were precluded from combat reporting.

Mainstream news coverage of the **Korean War**, the **Malayan Emergency** and Indonesia's Confrontation with Malaya, and **Vietnam** by reporters such as Harry Gordon, Lawson Glassop, Roy Macartney, and Denis Warner augmented, rather than reinterpreted, information supplied in official briefings and communiqués. Cold War hostilities brought some reappraisal of the reporter's role. One Australian who rejected the journalistic model of detached objectivity was Wilfred Burchett, who, having reported World War II in China and Burma from the Allied side, spent the rest of his career committed to covering communist and Third World struggles in Korea, Indo-China, and parts of Europe and Africa. The extent to which the media in Vietnam were perceived to have broken with past conventions of war reporting was reflected in the return to strict military censorship and other restrictions on journalists during the 1991 Gulf War. More recently, media coverage of the Australian-led Interfet operation in **East Timor** in 1999 attracted accusations of bias and jingoism, its hostility towards **Indonesia** linked by some commentators to the killing of five journalists in Balibo during Indonesia's invasion of East Timor in 1975.

Studies of Australian war reporting have been fragmentary and of varied literary quality. Expatriate Australian journalist Phillip Knightley's *The First Casualty*, originally published in 1975 and recently updated to include conflicts up to Kosovo, is a comprehensive international study that gives Australian reporting due consideration. *Warco* (1986) by former war correspondent Pat Burgess draws on the oral testimony of several well-known reporters, but its style is celebratory and anecdotal rather than analytical. Similarly, the collection of profiles by journalist and author Peter Sekuless, *A Handful of Hacks* (1999), aims primarily to rescue a group of well-known World War II correspondents from perceived oblivion. *From the Front* (2000), a collection of Banjo Paterson's Boer War despatches edited and annotated by Robin Droogleever, is a welcome addition to the literature. Several studies of Australian perceptions of Asia, including Alison Broinowski's *The Yellow Lady* (1992) and Gerster's *Hotel Asia* (1995), have highlighted the role of Australian war reporters in gathering and disseminating information about peoples and cultures in the Asia–Pacific region; Prue Torney-Parlicki explores this dimension at greater length in *Somewhere in Asia* (2000). A plethora of biographical and autobiographical works, including Richard Hughes, *Foreign Devil* (1972), Wilfrid Burchett, *At the Barricades* (1981), Hugh Lunn, *Vietnam: A Reporter's War* (1985), and Warner, *Wake Me If There's Trouble* (1995), have documented individuals' experiences, but the collective role of war reporting has only recently attracted historical inquiry.

PRUE TORNEY-PARLICKI

War service homes were the 'Homes fit for Heroes' which had been one of the mottoes under which Australians, as well as Britons, fought the war of 1914–18. When the war was over governments were under strong pressure to meet this moral obligation. Under the legislation establishing the Commonwealth Department of Repatriation in 1918, returned soldiers, nurses, munitions workers, soldiers' widows, and their dependants were entitled to a maximum advance of £800 at a rate of five per cent for the purpose of acquiring a dwelling. This was the first significant Commonwealth measure in support of private home-ownership, but only a fraction of those eligible were able or willing to take it up. By 1930 some 32 000 houses had been provided under the scheme. In 1945 it was extended to World War II veterans; during the following decade 225 000 applications were received and 113 000 approved. In the immediate postwar years, war service loans financed approximately 10 per cent of all new homes.

GD

Ward, John Manning (1919–90) was Challis professor of history at the University of Sydney, 1949–79, and vice-chancellor, 1980–90. Ward was educated at Fort Street and the University of Sydney, where he read both arts and law. He worked first as private secretary to the conservative premier of NSW, Sir Bertram **Stevens**. Ward intended to go to the Bar but his deafness led him to switch to academic life. While still in his twenties Ward was appointed to succeed S.H. **Roberts** as professor. Ward's stewardship of the **Sydney School of History** is treated elsewhere. His research contribution was in the field of imperial policy and administration. He developed this theme in *British Policy in the South Pacific* (1948) and *Earl Grey and the Australian Colonies* (1958); he rounded it off in *Colonial Self-Government* (1976), which argued the unfashionable line that self-government in the 1850s was the result of metropolitan, not local, pressures. His *Empire in the Antipodes* (1966) traced the imperial dimension in Australasian development, 1840–60, administering a riposte to his namesake Russel **Ward's** nationalist reading. Ward hoped to crown his career with a three-volume history of **conservatism** in NSW, the first volume of which was a biographical study of James **Macarthur** (1981), but he died tragically in a train crash before completing the project. Indications of what the other volumes would have contained appeared in his John Alexander Ferguson Memorial Lecture (1980) and in a book chapter on J.T. **Lang's** dismissal.

CARL BRIDGE

Ward, Russel Braddock (1914–95) was the author of the classic book *The Australian Legend* (1958), which avers that from the 1890s the Australian nation defined itself by the values and attitudes of the up-country bushman. Born in 1914, Ward grew up almost untouched by this bush ethos. His parents were Methodists and his childhood homes were the private schools of which his father was head. On completing his schooling at Prince Alfred College, Adelaide, Ward was, in the words of his autobiography, *A Radical Life* (1988), 'as arrant a conservative, as loyal a Briton and as nasty a snob as ever left any great public school in Australia'. All this was to change, but he remained always impeccably bourgeois in manners and appearance. The apostle of the **Australian Legend** looked like an English army officer.

He was completely typical of his class in being brought up on British history and English literature (which he loved) and learning almost nothing of the history and literature of his native land. As a radical schoolteacher in Sydney, he started to collect Australian folksongs. Until then he had never heard one. Ward's autobiography, the theme of which is the author's discovery of an Australian identity, shows how weak a hold the Australian Legend had on the respectability, whereas in *The Australian Legend* he argues the opposite, against his experience.

The book in itself is a work of mythic power for it is an account of a revelation, of a moment when a people come to know fully what was previously half-known or hidden. Ward wrote so compellingly because he was writing of his own revelation, which he displaced onto the nation and back-dated to the 1890s. Clearly he exaggerated the extent of the legend's influence, yet the book itself did much to repair this mistake. Having rediscovered the legend in the 1940s, Ward became one of the chief vehicles for spreading it among the bourgeoisie. The success of the book became the best support for its claims.

The Australian Legend was written as a PhD thesis at the Australian National University. Having been denied a post at the University of New South Wales because of his membership of the Communist Party, Ward spent the rest of his academic career at the University of New England. He wrote several general histories of Australia which depict not a nation united in its attachment to the bushman, but one of conflicting allegiances determined by class. Working-class people were nationalists; the middle class were imperial patriots. This depiction of the bourgeoisie was closer to Ward's own experience, but he drew the dichotomy too firmly, especially when he assumed that imperial patriots were careless of Australian interests. In this he took too savage a revenge on the world of the great public schools.

The general histories do not have the distinctiveness or force of *The Australian Legend*, elegant, lively, and professional though they be. Ward's claim to greatness rests on the one book. It is much more subtle than many of its critics have allowed: 'it is not so much the bushman's actual nature that matters, as the nature attributed to him by so many men of the day'. The book has survived all its critics. Historians will never destroy it; it will become a relic only when the culture-hero whom it celebrates ceases to be recognised and valued.

JOHN HIRST

Wardell, William Wilkinson (1823–99) was the leading Australian practitioner of Gothic Revival architecture. Through friendships with Augustus Pugin and John Henry Newman, Wardell was already steeped in the religious and aesthetic milieu of the Gothic Revival when he emigrated to Australia, for his health, in 1858. He was appointed clerk of works and chief architect for the government of Victoria, but retained the right to continue with private practice, even after his promotion in 1861 to inspector-general of public works. Under his leadership the major public works of Melbourne were built, including the Treasury, Customs House, and Government House. As a private architect and a devout Catholic, he designed St Patrick's Cathedral, the largest in the country, as well as several parish churches. An exhibition of his work was held in 1997 as part of the celebrations of St Patrick's centenary. **Sectarianism** and professional jealousy lay behind a series of disputes and official inquiries into Wardell's role, culminating in his dismissal on **Black Wednesday** 1878. At the invitation of Archbishop **Polding**, he moved to Sydney, where his later commissions included St Mary's Cathedral. His English, Scottish and Australian Bank, Melbourne (1883), was hailed by Robin **Boyd** as the 'most distinguished building of the whole Australian Gothic Revival era'. Ursula de Jong's *William Wilkinson Wardell* (1983) is the fullest study of his life and work.

KT

Warung, Price, see Astley, **William**

Water resources present particular problems in Australia: arid **climate**; high variability of rainfall and runoff leading to **droughts** and **floods**; topography generally unsuited to the storage of water in dams; high losses to evaporation; and poor water quality in many areas. Despite the importance of water to **Aboriginal** Australians and to the European settlers, surprisingly little has been written on the history of water resources. C.H. Munro, a major figure in Australian engineering hydrology, in *Australian Water Resources and Their Development* (1974) provided a brief history, state by state, which begins with this lament: 'It is a pity that Professors of History have not encouraged postgraduate students to carry out research on the history of water resources development in Australia.' One professor, J.M. Powell, has responded to this challenge with valuable historical studies of Victoria (*Watering the Garden State*, 1989) and Qld (*Plains of Promise, Rivers of Destiny*, 1991), and of *The Emergence of Bioregionalism in the Murray–Darling Basin* (1993).

Early beliefs about the existence of an inland sea in Central Australia and of large inland river systems crossing the continent shaped Australian approaches to water resources development by encouraging the idea that a supply of water to the dry interior would make it productive. This culturally determined notion helps to explain the extraordinary popularity of the unsubstantiated proposition put forward by J.J.C. **Bradfield** in the magazine *Walkabout* (1941), and supported by popular writers like Ion **Idriess** in *The Great Boomerang* (1941), that if water could be diverted from coastal rivers into the dry interior and stored there for **irrigation**, it would ameliorate the arid climate and increase the rainfall. An official report on his proposals by the Bureau of Meteorology and discussion of them by engineers such as J.D. Lang and W.H.R. Nimmo in *Institution of Engineers Australia Journal* (1946, 1949), clearly demonstrated that they had no scientific credibility; despite this, they retained popularity even into the 1990s, particularly among politicians such as the WA Water Resources Minister Ernie Bridge (*Mining Review*, 1991). The **Snowy Mountains Hydro–Electric Scheme** was motivated, in part, by Bradfield's ideas.

The settlement of Australia and exploitation of its resources has been inextricably linked with the provision of water supplies and modifications to the natural water cycle by individual farmers and government agencies. This has been accompanied by serious and widespread environmental degradation, as described by D.I. Smith and B.L. Finlayson in R.L. Heathcote and J.A. Mabbutt (eds), *Land, Water and People* (1988). While groundwater has not played a major part in public water supply schemes, the discovery, exploration, and exploitation of the Great Artesian Basin, mainly for the provision of water for stock, is a fascinating saga of the evolution of scientific understanding in both geology and groundwater hydrology.

Early development of the **mining** industry, particularly during the gold rushes, severely stretched local water supplies. The miners carried out many small-scale local water diversions to improve supplies; the most ambitious scheme to supply water to mining towns was the Coolgardie Pipeline, planned by C.Y. **O'Connor** and completed in 1903, which takes water 560 kilometres from the Mundaring Weir to the goldmining towns of Coolgardie and Kalgoorlie.

The bureaucratic control by government over the settlement process in Australia caused the demise of the common law system of water allocation by riparian right and the appropriation of rights to water by the government. Early privately funded attempts to develop irrigation schemes failed; Australian governments, both state and federal, have been pre-eminent in the development and management of water resources and provided the entrepreneurial drive for their development. S.D. Clark, *Australian Water Law* (1971), points out that one of the consequences of this has been the virtual absence of private legal disputes over access to water. The major responsibility for water resources following Federation remained with the state governments and this has caused tension between the eastern states over the management of the Murray–Darling Basin, where 75 per cent of all irrigation water in Australia is used. The federal government attempted to resolve these problems by establishing the River Murray Commission in 1915, which has developed into the present Murray–Darling Basin Commission.

B.R. Davidson in *Australia Wet or Dry?* (1969) showed that a significant outcome of this system in which government is the entrepreneur for development of the resource has been that major water management schemes have been built out of political considerations and were not necessarily economically justified. Environmental effects have also historically been of little concern. As degradation of the resource is becoming more serious and obvious, fundamental changes are occurring in the way in which Australian water resources are managed. The Department of Resources and Energy provided the first major overview of Australia's water resources in *Water 2000* (1983). In the south-east of Australia water resources are approaching their full development, causing a shift towards more effective management and to price-based schemes for allocating the resource.

Most of Australia's water resources are used for irrigation. However, the concentration of the population in the capital cities has made urban water supply an important issue in water resources development, beginning with the use of the Tank Stream in Sydney to supply the first settlement. Urban water has traditionally been supplied by government authorities established for the purpose (such as the Metropolitan Water Sewage and Drainage Board of Sydney and the Melbourne and Metropolitan Board of Works) with catchment areas beyond the city boundaries set aside for the provision of water. The increasing demand for water in cities has pushed these external supply systems to their limits and caused a shift to demand management and more innovative supply options, such as artificial rainmaking and harvesting water in urban areas.

Although Australia is the driest inhabited continent, it has a low population density and more abundant water supplies per capita than any other continent. It experiences much higher runoff variability than other continents (except southern Africa), which has given rise to the popular poetic description of 'droughts and flooding rains'. Despite its long-standing problems with water resources, Australia has no national water policy and, up to the present, no administrative mechanism for producing one.

BRIAN FINLAYSON

Waterloo Creek massacre, according to a massive 1992 study by writer Roger Milliss, occurred on a tributary of the Gwydir River on 26 January 1838. The Kamilaroi had been attacking stock and had killed several stockmen in the area; aggrieved squatters were demanding that government provide 'protection'. Mounted Police Commandant Major James Nunn was directed to use his 'utmost exertion to suppress' Aboriginal attacks, and in the course of this expedition his troopers and local stockmen, who had banded together, killed perhaps as many as 200–300 Kamilaroi at Waterloo Creek.

In this remote and lawless district, historian Bob Reece has concluded, there was a concerted campaign by colonists to exterminate Aborigines. It seems this resulted in a series of **massacres** between 1836 and 1838, of which **Myall Creek** was merely one. As so often on the Australian frontier, the perpetrators tried to cover up their bloody deeds, though here they were partially foiled by official investigations demanded by enraged humanitarians. Moreover, these killings became the subject of considerable rumour, which later gave rise to a rich local tradition that focuses on sites like Gravesend Mountain and Slaughterhouse Creek. Milliss's claims regarding Waterloo Creek, however, are not supported by the patchy historical record, and we might never know what happened there.

BAIN ATTWOOD

Watson, John Christian (1867–1941) became the first Labor prime minister of Australia in 1904. Watson arrived in Sydney from NZ in 1886 and was soon involved with the Labor movement. He became a member of the NSW parliament in 1894 and upon election to the first federal parliament in 1901, he became the Labor leader. After the **Deakin** government fell in 1904, Watson formed a minority government that survived for only a few months. He gave up party leadership in 1907, and resigned from parliament in 1910. He was expelled from the Labor Party in 1916 for supporting **conscription**. Al Grassby and Silvia Ordonez entitle their biography of Watson *The Man Time Forgot* (1999) and provide new evidence of his ancestry: his father was a German-Chilean, his mother a New Zealander who subsequently returned there and married a miner named Watson. Their claims for his significance are less persuasive. Watson's time in office was brief, and his influence on party policy limited. His chief achievement was to foster Labor support for the ministries of Alfred **Deakin** while consolidating the standing of his own party.

KT

Watson, John Forbes, see *Historical Records of Australia*

Wealth in Australia has been viewed in two contrasting ways. A considerable degree of equality is suggested by the image of the **workingman's paradise** and a New World society lacking a long-standing aristocracy or plutocracy. On the other hand, from early colonial times, and certainly from the **gold rush**, Australia was also known for its self-made men of wealth. Charles Dickens presents Magwitch, an Australian convict turned man of property, as Pip's benefactor in *Great Expectations* (1860–61), while **Marvellous Melbourne** was renowned for its vulgar *nouveaux riches*. Since 1980 careful historical research, too, has emphasised the **poverty** rather than the affluence of Australia's working class. This suggests a considerable degree of inequality of wealth. Reconciling the two views, and attempting to ascertain which is the more accurate, has been a considerable historical puzzle.

Our knowledge of the historical distribution of wealth in Australia (or elsewhere) is derived from a variety of sources: especially the valuation of probates left at death; estimates of the wealth of the living, derived from probate valuations but adjusted by appropriate mortality multipliers to be relevant to the population as a whole; and special surveys of Australian wealth-holding. Estimates of wealth distribution derived from the first two approaches have been offered during the past 20 years by economic historians, but are far from comprehensive. For the third type of source, Australia is fortunate in having the evidence of the remarkable Wealth Census of 1915, an official government assessment of wealth in private hands undertaken during World War I, analysed comprehensively in one of the most remarkable socioeconomic studies of Australia ever produced, G.H. Knibbs's *The Private Wealth of Australia and Its Growth as Ascertained by Various Methods, Together with a Report of the War Census of 1915* (Melbourne, 1918). Early scholars and statisticians, such as T.A. **Coghlan** in *A Statistical Account of the Seven Colonies of Australia* (8th edn, 1900), also offered statistical information on wealth distribution in Australia. During the 1980s and 1990s this subject has become one of increasing interest to scholars, with recent analyses offered by Frank L. Jones, M.P. Shanahan, W.D. Rubinstein, and G.D. Snooks. A special issue of *AEHR* devoted to this topic, entitled 'Wealth and Wellbeing in Australia', appeared in 1995.

Most recent scholarship has tentatively concluded that wealth in Australia was much less unequally distributed than in other industrial societies. This is not to say that wealth was very evenly distributed—it was not—only that it was more evenly distributed than elsewhere. For instance, Shanahan, in 'The Distribution of Personal Wealth in South Australia 1905–1915' (*AEHR*, 1995), concluded that the top one per cent of the SA population owned 30 per cent of its private wealth in 1905–15, compared with ownership rates by the top one per cent of 49 per cent of the private wealth in France, 50 per cent in Prussia, 55 per cent in the USA, and 66 per cent in England and Wales at about the same time. Among industrial societies, only in NZ does wealth distribution appear to be *less* unequal. Nevertheless, it is the extraordinary degree of wealth inequality that is most striking: not only did one per cent of the population own 30 per cent of the private wealth, but approximately one-third of the SA population owned private assets less than £100 and one-half less than £250, while nearly 10 per cent of the private wealth was owned by just 77 persons!

Given the spread of the ownership of assets since World War II, especially home ownership and the entitlement to pension rights, one might expect wealth to have remained more equally distributed than in other industrial societies. This is probably the case, although searching and accurate comparative data are difficult to obtain. Again, however, this conclusion is not inconsistent either with the growth of a small class of very wealthy persons or with long-term **unemployment** and deprivation. W*ealth* distribution, too, it should be noted, is not the same thing as *income* distribution. Wealth is, in effect, previously accumulated income which has been saved; it is strongly biased in favour of the elderly and others who have already amassed or inherited wealth. Income is certainly distributed much more evenly than wealth, especially after **taxation**; this has always been true, throughout Australian history.

If Australian wealth distribution was and is more even than elsewhere, an important factor has been the modest wealth of the very rich in Australia. The very rich have always been the subject of keen prurient interest, especially in periods of major wealth accumulation and display by the rich, particularly *nouveaux riches*. In Australia, journalistic (and serious) interest in the very rich peaked at roughly century-long intervals, in the 1880s and 1980s, coincident with the era of Marvellous Melbourne and with the boom of the 1980s. Despite the mythology of Magwitch, extremely rich men in Australia were very rare until the late nineteenth century, with the first Australian to leave £500 000 or more (Peter Tyson, a pastoralist) not deceased until 1879, and the first millionaire estate (left by David Berry, who died in 1889), a decade later. In the whole period, from the beginnings of Australian probate valuations in 1819 until 1939, only seven millionaire estates were left in NSW and nine in Victoria. This compares with 434 estates of £1 million or more left in Britain during this long period, although (unlike Australia) land was excluded from the British probate valuations until 1898. On a comparative international scale of great wealth, Australia was also in the second division: the largest single estate left in Australia in the entire period to 1939, retail merchant Samuel Hordern's £3 million in 1909, appears insignificant next to the largest British fortune, the £37 million estate of Sir John Ellerman (d. 1933), and still more when compared with the estimated £200 million fortunes of Rockefeller, Ford, and Mellon in the USA.

Only perhaps in the 1970s did the level of fortunes of Australia's richest persons begin to compare with those found elsewhere. During the 1980s and 1990s the Australian rich have been studied as never before: books like Ruth Ostrow's *The New Boy Network* (1987) document the rise of Australia's new rich, and the appearance of the annual 'Rich List' of Australia's 200 richest persons and families produced by *Business Review Weekly* has become, since 1983, a yearly media event. Perhaps the most notable feature of Australia's contemporary wealth elite is that the majority appear to be genuine 'self-made men', with one-half or more of those identified in

these 'rich lists' being either foreign-born or of minority background. Another notable feature has been the relentless increase in the scale of wealth, despite the recession of the 1990s, with several billionaire men and families headed by Kerry **Packer**. The favourable attitude of the **Australian Labor Party**, especially under Bob **Hawke**, to 'new money' also represents a historic change compared with the past. During the 1930s and 1940s, quasi-Marxist works of analysis portrayed Australia's leading bankers and industrialists of the time as reactionary malefactors of 'finance capital'. The 1980s and 1990s have seen the recent incarnations of these erstwhile malefactors hailed as national folk heroes to be placed beside star athletes in the national pantheon, an assessment which even the untimely ends of many notable careers in the early 1990s did little to diminish.

WILLIAM D. RUBINSTEIN

Weather forecasting, the prediction of future changes in temperature and rainfall, has been practised for centuries, as an art if not as a science.

Aborigines, whose yearly pattern of movement and livelihood was closely governed by the seasons, were acutely sensitive to the subtle variations in temperature, wind direction, and rainfall that signalled their approach. They also attempted, by sorcery or divination, to exercise supernatural influence over the weather, as did Europeans when, in emergency, they prayed for rain. Farmers gazed at the night sky for signs of the morrow's weather ('Red sky at night, shepherd's delight') or consulted a barometer for signs of the sudden drop of pressure that presaged a storm. More comprehensive scientific forecasting dates from the 1850s, when the colonial governments first established meteorological services under the various government astronomers to measure and record rainfall, barometric pressure, temperatures, and wind speeds and direction. The electric telegraph, which enabled the reports of scattered weather stations to be transmitted across the continent, became the foundation for a more comprehensive forecasting system. The first newspaper weather map was prepared by the NSW astronomer H.C. Russell and published in the *Sydney Morning Herald* in 1877; Victoria followed in 1881. Soon after Federation a Commonwealth Meteorological Bureau was established to run meteorological services across the nation. Once the cold and warm fronts had been plotted, and their rate of movement calculated, the forecaster could predict how and when weather might change in places that lay in their path. These techniques, enhanced by satellite imagery, radar, and weather balloons, which sample air from the upper atmosphere, remain the basis of short-term weather forecasting to the present day.

The possibility of longer-term forecasts predicting **droughts** or **floods**, or the most propitious time for sowing or reaping, has long fascinated Australians, depending, as they do, upon a fragile environment in which small variations in **climate** can have large economic consequences. Some colonial meteorologists postulated the influence of climatic cycles—Russell, for example, advanced a theory of 19-year cycles of drought, every third one being of calamitous proportions. The maverick Queensland meteorologist Inigo Jones (1872–1954) proposed that weather cycles were influenced by sunspot activity, a theory which won popular support when he successfully predicted the end of a drought in 1923. With the severe droughts of the early 1980s, Australian rainfall conditions were widely linked to El Niño atmospheric indicators. The El Niño effect, studied since the 1920s, explains the relationship between atmospheric circulation patterns and the flow of warm oceanic currents off the coast of South America.

GD

WEL, see **Women's Electoral Lobby**

Weld, Frederick Aloysius (1823–91) was a versatile and successful gentleman-colonist who achieved prominence as a pastoralist and politician in NZ, and governor in WA and Tasmania. After a Jesuit education in England and Switzerland, he emigrated to NZ in 1843, where he became a pioneer sheep farmer. Weld's political career began with his election as member for Wairu in 1853, and culminated in 1864 when he was briefly premier of the colony. Ill-health forced his resignation and return to England, but he was later appointed as governor of WA (1868–74). Weld's love of travel and practical knowledge of pioneering were assets in governing a vast frontier colony. But as a Catholic, his position on church–state questions was apt to be questioned by sectarians on both sides. His autocratic tendencies and hauteur towards the ex-convict population also brought him into conflict with his Legislative Council and sometimes with his masters in the **Colonial Office**. His term in Tasmania (1875–80) was less turbulent. His name is perhaps best known through the connection with Perth's exclusive Weld Club, of which he was the first patron.

MAREE STARKE

Welfare, social, see **Social welfare**

Welfare history is a product of the new **social history** of the 1970s concerned with negotiations between citizens and the state over **poverty** and its alleviation, **wealth distribution** and inequality, **social justice** and social reform.

In Australia **social welfare** has always been a concern of both the government and voluntary sector, bound together in an increasingly complex but always mutually dependent relationship. Earlier historians, such as T.H. Kewley, *Social Security in Australia* 1900–72 (1972), produced affirmative accounts of the transition from the nineteenth century, when **philanthropy** held sway, to the twentieth, when the triumph of an **egalitarian**, non-judgmental welfare state eliminated such regressive practices unsuited to the new nation. These optimistic records of the growth of welfare provision underestimated the degree to which private charity continued to underwrite the new system and the continuity in practices and attitudes between the old ways and the new.

Philanthropy, the new welfare historians argued, was central to social control, benefiting the philanthropists at the expense of the people they claimed to be helping, facilitating the extension of bourgeois regulation of proletarian domestic life, and thus buttressing the prevailing capitalist and patriarchal structure. 'Philanthropists', Richard Kennedy contended in *Charity Warfare* (1985), 'were a vanguard in the ruling class determination to head off revolution'. This approach reached its peak in two collections of essays, Kennedy (ed.), *Australian Welfare History* (1982), and Bob Bessant (ed.), *Mother State and Her Little Ones* (1987), both of which positioned a passive working class as victims of a dominant and self-serving bourgeoisie.

The critics of this position suggested a more complex interaction between the helpers and the helped, arguing both for a less reductionist view of philanthropic women, and for a more active negotiation on the part of those who were compelled to seek their help. Kerreen Reiger argued in *The Disenchantment of the Home* (1985) that while the women of the bourgeois charity network did wish to keep the social order intact, they were exposed to the actual conditions of working-class life and were aware that working-class women were particularly hard hit by the prevailing social conditions. It was their lot that they set out to ameliorate. Nor, indeed, were working-class women and children silent victims in this interaction. Robert Van Krieken, *Children and the State* (1991), is one of several writers who have demonstrated the way in which they courted such philanthropic intrusion into their lives, actively negotiating with those offering assistance in order to ensure the best outcome for their families.

Welfare history receives its widest circulation as survey articles included in edited collections intended for students in the social sciences. The most recent of these, Michael Wearing and Rosemary Berreen, *Welfare and Social Policy in Australia* (1994), includes five historical chapters before turning to consider contemporary debates about distribution and redistribution. More commonly the historian is confined to a single introductory chapter and expected to develop a comprehensive history of the development of social welfare in Australia.

Even historians who devote an entire volume to this subject find it difficult to encompass. The development of social security, which is essentially a federal project, is easier to discuss on a national scale. Kewley, *Social Security in Australia*, Stuart Macintyre, *Winners and Losers* (1985), and Rob Watts, *The Foundations of the National Welfare State* (1987), embody an admiration, if an increasingly guarded one, of the welfare state ideal, identifying its origins in the labour movement critique, which argued that poverty arose from structural rather than personal failings and hence that relief was a right and should not be grudgingly administered. Jill Roe in Cora Baldock and Bettina Cass (eds), *Women, Social Welfare and the State in Australia* (1983, 1988) first pointed out the gendered nature of this new welfare state, which excluded newly enfranchised women from social **citizenship** by positioning them as the mothers of the nation which their husbands and brothers would fight to defend.

Philanthropy, which allowed a far greater space to women, is more comprehensively dealt with in the two general histories of social welfare in Australia (Brian Dickey, *No Charity There*, 1980, and Stephen Garton, *Out of Luck*, 1990), although even here it tends to disappear with the triumph of the welfare state in the post-Federation era. Social security, such works argue, is the logical response to voluntary charity, discredited during the **depression** of the 1890s by its failure to cope with the extent of the need, and the harsh and unfeeling way in which it dealt with those forced to seek its aid.

Essentially organised within old colonial boundaries, philanthropy has attracted more interest in local studies like Joan Brown, *'Poverty Is Not a Crime': The Development of Social Services in Tasmania 1803–1900* (1972); Robert Cage, *Poverty Abounding Charity Aplenty: The Charity Network in Colonial Victoria* (1992); Brian Dickey, *Rations, Residences, Resources: A History of Social Welfare in South Australia Since 1836* (1986); and Anne O'Brien, *Poverty's Prison: The Poor in New South Wales 1880–1918* (1988). The emphasis of all of these studies is on the nineteenth century, despite evidence of the continuing importance of voluntary charity in filling the gaps in the social security system. The history of twentieth-century philanthropic activity in Australia is still to be written.

Specialist studies in the history of child welfare are more likely to explore the continuing relationship between the voluntary and statutory sector, although again studies tend to be restricted by state boundaries with little attempt to develop a comparative perspective. John Ramsland, *Children of the Back Lanes* (1986), and Van Krieken, *Children and the State*, address the situation in NSW; Donella Jaggs, *Neglected and Criminal* (1986), and David Maunders, *Keeping Them Off the Streets* (1984), consider Victoria, while Peggy Brock, *Outback Ghettos* (1993), and Coral Edwards and Peter Read, *The Lost Children* (1989), are but two of the growing number of books that examine the harsh impact of child welfare practices in **Aboriginal** communities.

Child welfare has also been the subject of institutionally based **commissioned history**, as have most major hospitals and other organisations which have their origins in subscriber charity. Generally the conditions of the commission deter the historian from moving outside the institutional boundaries, although two recent studies of central missions—the **Methodist Church's** response to the perceived problems of **urbanisation** and suburbanisation—have demonstrated ways in which institutional history can be developed within an **urban history** context. These are Renate Howe and Shurlee Swain, *The Challenge of the City: The Centenary History of Wesley Central Mission 1893–1993* (1993), and Donald Wright, *Mantle of Christ: A History of the Sydney Central Methodist Mission* (1984).

The influence of post-structuralism has unsettled the meta-narrative of progress which underlay the chronology of welfare history and encouraged historians to consider instead the discursive environment within which welfare systems operate. Reiger's *The Disenchantment of the Home* and Lyn Finch, *The Classing Gaze: Sexuality, Class and Surveillance*

(1993), traverse similar ground to more traditional welfare history but use the analytical categories of class, race, and gender to develop a more complex and less celebratory analysis. Post-structuralism also provides the opportunity for a diversity of voices to be heard, with users as well as providers of services becoming a subject of historical interest. Margaret Barbalet, *Far from a Low Gutter Girl* (1983), and Shurlee Swain and Renate Howe, *Single Mothers and Their Children* (1995), read across the grain of surviving records, and interrogate their gaps and silences. These new approaches suggest a way in which welfare history can have people, rather than structures, at its core.

SHURLEE SWAIN

Wentworth, William Charles (1790–1872) led moves for **responsible government** in NSW. Numerous historians have considered his life; the first biographical study was A.C.V. **Melbourne's** *William Charles Wentworth* (1934). Wentworth was born at **Norfolk Island** in August 1790, the eldest son of convict Catherine Crowley (1772–1800) and the surgeon D'Arcy Wentworth (1764–1827), who had been four times acquitted of highway robbery. The pair settled in Sydney in 1796, but never married. D'Arcy grew rich from land grants, entrepreneurial activities, and public appointments. He sent his sons to England to be educated. In 1811 William became acting provost-marshal in NSW, and two years later he accompanied Gregory **Blaxland** and William Lawson on an inland **exploration** which crossed the Blue Mountains. He then dabbled in farming and sandalwood trading before returning in 1816 to England, where he studied law, unaware of his father's questionable past until the revelations of H.G. Bennet's *Letter to Viscount Sidmouth* (1819). Wentworth's father was not a convict, as Bennet alleged, but he clearly had more in common with **emancipists** than **exclusives**. John Ritchie's *The Wentworths* (1997) examines the relationship between father and son; an expected second volume will deal with William's later career.

In 1819 Wentworth produced the first book by a native-born Australian, *A Statistical, Historical, and Political Description of the Colony of New South Wales*, in which he criticised the governor's autocratic powers and called for a nominated Legislative Council and elected Legislative Assembly. He also advocated British emigration and trial by jury. Wentworth is the 'Native Son' who dominates the second volume of Manning **Clark's** *A History of Australia* (1968). At Cambridge in 1823 he wrote the public poem 'Australasia', which predicted the rise of an antipodean 'new Britannia'. From 1824 Wentworth established a profitable legal practice in Sydney. A wild, powerful orator who was sometimes drunk in public, he defended emancipists and acquired a radical reputation as co-founder of the *Australian* newspaper. His relationship with SARAH COX (1805–80) produced a daughter in December 1825. They married in 1829 after settling at Vaucluse on Sydney Harbour. Their villa, Vaucluse House, is now a museum.

Carol Liston in *Sarah Wentworth: Mistress of Vaucluse* (1988) reveals Sarah was considered a 'fallen woman' and treated as an outcast in colonial society. Wentworth stood accused of the immorality of the convict class he defended. Jemima Eager bore a child to him in November 1830. Governor Ralph **Darling** disdained Wentworth as the 'son of a high-wayman'; Darling's disproportionate punishment of two thieving soldiers, **Sudds and Thompson**, in 1826 sparked bitter opposition from Wentworth, who tried to impeach him. Darling attempted to prosecute for libel. As a man of the people, Wentworth celebrated Darling's 1831 departure with 4000 others at Vaucluse. He became vice-president of the **Australian Patriotic Association** in 1835. In earlier days Wentworth had mixed with the **Macarthur family** and contemplated marrying a daughter, but dreams of a Wentworth–Macarthur dynasty disappeared after he quarrelled with John Macarthur over some borrowed money. Liston notes the reconciliation of September 1852, when Macarthur's sons James and Edward agreed to dine at Wentworth's table. In a sense, Wentworth came to theirs. As a Legislative Councillor from 1843 he had promoted the interests of his fellow wealthy landowners. In the early 1850s, when Wentworth chaired the committee appointed to draft a new constitution for NSW, his unsuccessful plea for an upper house based on a hereditary colonial peerage was mocked as a **bunyip aristocracy**. He denied crossing the political spectrum, declaring that he was never a democrat or republican, but 'I was a Whig, I admit, till I was ashamed of Whiggism.'

Wentworth's constitutional role is examined in J.B. Hirst, *The Strange Birth of Colonial Democracy* (1988). After seeing the revised constitution approved by British parliament in 1855, Wentworth spent his later years in England. He was buried at Vaucluse after a state funeral. Portraits are in the NSW Legislative Assembly and Mitchell Library, which holds the Wentworth Papers. His work to establish the University of Sydney is commemorated by a statue in the Great Hall. The family has a long history in public life. Wentworth's great-grandson and namesake was a prominent Liberal MHR 1949–77 and briefly a junior minister.

DAMIEN CASH

West Australian, Perth's only surviving daily **newspaper**, was first published by the Colonial Postmaster Charles Macfaull in 1833 as the *Perth Gazette and Western Australian Journal*. From the start it was a conservative journal allied to the government of the day. In 1879 the new owner, colonial-born Charles Harper, renamed it the *West Australian*. He envisaged the paper as a distinctively Western Australian publication, serving regional interests. Harper supported the landowning elite and was cautious in giving measured support to the movement for self-government.

Through the 1890s, under the editorship (and later ownership) of John Winthrop **Hackett**, the paper promoted and supported the first colonial government led by John **Forrest**. By the turn of the century the *West Australian* had consolidated its place as the colony's leading publication. In 1926, it became the major asset of a new public company, West Australian Newspapers Ltd, which also had other publishing interests. It adopted a tabloid format after World War II.

In 1969, the holding company was acquired by the Herald & Weekly Times group of Melbourne. In the 1980s, the paper fell victim to a series of takeover actions that saw it variously owned by entrepreneurs Robert Holmes à Court and Alan Bond. WA Newspapers was again floated as a public company on the Perth Stock Exchange in 1992.

LAYLA TUCAK

West, John (1809–73), Congregational minister and journalist, was the author of the most thrillingly eloquent of early Australian histories, *The History of Tasmania* (1852). West grew up in East Anglia, England, and entered the Independent ministry in 1829. In 1838 he departed for Van Diemen's Land in the service of the Colonial Missionary Society and settled in Launceston; there he helped found a city mission, a public hospital, a school, and a newspaper, the *Examiner*, which became his print pulpit. In the late 1840s he led the **anti-transportation** campaign, a cause which he prosecuted with the biblical fervour of the American abolitionists. His *History*, written at the request of a wealthy supporter, Henry Hopkins, and at the moment of the abolitionists' triumph, offered a legitimate pedigree for the new colony of Tasmania. Its virtues were not those of systematic archival research, although he drew upon the recollections of his contemporaries. He presented the colony's history as a passage from bondage to freedom, propelled by a historical dynamic that was both providential and irresistible: 'The future independence of the Australian colonies is written in the book of fate.' Yet he also recognised, and recorded with unflinching candour, the brutal mistreatment of the Aborigines. 'The laws were silent—religion and humanity were silent; and the fallen black, like the uprooted forest, was thought of as an encumbrance removed.' In 1854 he was invited by his fellow Congregationalist John **Fairfax** to become editor of the *Sydney Morning Herald*. The best account of his life and writing is A.G.L. **Shaw's** introduction to the 1971 edition of his *History*.

GD

Western Australia was not claimed for the British Crown until 1828. Britain took possession of the western third of the continent not because it valued its territory—of which all reports, save one, were unpromising—but in order to prevent the French from securing bases on its coast, which among other dangers might threaten the trade of its colonies on the further side of the continent. Before there were Australian nationalists, the British government had seen the advantages of the continent being under a single authority. To the European settlers who came to WA that has not always been self-evident. They were and are isolated from the rest of Australia by a vast desert. WA joined the Australian Federation belatedly and voted, ineffectually, to leave it in 1933. It was long a cinderella state and attributed its backwardness to the federal connection. But the great prosperity it has enjoyed since the 1960s has also encouraged the thought that it would be better off on its own. Alone of the six states, its allegiance to the Commonwealth cannot be taken for granted.

The first British settlement was at King George Sound, now Albany, an extensive natural harbour, one of only two on the whole coast. In 1826 a garrison was sent there from Sydney, from which it was supplied, in order to forestall settlement by the French. The garrison was withdrawn in 1831, by which time a settlement had been made at the **Swan River**. This was the brainchild of Captain James **Stirling** of the Royal Navy, who inspected the river in 1827 and who alone of the visitors to this coast thought he had found land suitable for settlement. Had he stepped a few more paces from the banks of the Swan he would have discovered the sandy soil which made agriculture impossible in the lands around **Perth**. On his return to Britain he lobbied for the creation of a colony, to which the government agreed, since settlement would secure possession, but warily, since it did not want to be lumbered with the expense. The settlers would have to ship themselves and their labourers at their own cost and they would be granted land in return for the amount of capital and labour they brought. Stirling himself gained the post of governor.

The settlement did not thrive. Within a few years most of the settlers had departed, and after 20 years the European population was a mere 5000. Even when they found productive uses for the soil, landowners had difficulty in obtaining and keeping labour. **Wakefield** used this failing to argue that in new colonies land should be sold, not given away, and the proceeds used to pay passages of labourers and their families. **Convicts** were explicitly forbidden from this colony at its foundation, but the landowners, desperate for a new way to prosperity, invited the transportation of male convicts, which began in 1850 and continued until 1868. Convicts gave a labour force which could not flee to the eastern colonies, and the supplying of the convict establishment gave the settlers an assured local market. The colony did better, but still grew only slowly. Farming was established to the south of Perth, in the upper Swan and over the Darling Ranges to the east, but as in the rest of Australia most of the land occupied by Europeans was devoted to **pastoralism**—to sheep on the rivers in the north-west and later to cattle in the Kimberleys.

In 1890, when the European population was 46 000, responsible government with a bicameral parliament was established, 35 years later than in the other Australian colonies. In the eastern colonies payment of members had recently been introduced for members of legislative assemblies which had long been elected by manhood suffrage, but neither of these provisions was incorporated into the WA constitution. Power was in the hands of a tightly knit group of substantial landowners and a few city merchants.

Just at this moment the sleepy hollow of the Australian colonies was transformed by a **gold rush** that was created and sustained by Australians from the east. Gold prospectors had long been moving anti-clockwise around the continent from the first fields in its south-east corner, and in the 1880s they reached the north of the colony. They found gold there and at places further south and then in the early 1890s huge deposits at Coolgardie and Kalgoorlie, 570 kilometres to the east of the capital in desolate terrain. Thousands flocked to these fields from the east, particularly from Victoria and SA which were in the depths of depression. In the 1890s the population increased almost fourfold. The easily won gold was soon exhausted and the mining passed to companies financed from the eastern colonies and London. The colony had at last found prosperity, but at the cost of being overwhelmed by outsiders, the t'othersiders as they were known in the West.

The population on the goldfields deeply resented the government in Perth, its denial of adequate parliamentary representation, its tardiness in the provision of services, and its favouring of the old farming districts, whose produce was protected by a **tariff** on imported foodstuffs. The inhabitants of the farming districts were prospering from the boom conditions, but fearful of what the rush meant socially and politically.

It fell to John **Forrest**, the first premier under responsible government, to manage this confrontation. He was a native of the colony who had married into one of the old families. The core of his policy was to borrow heavily and provide all districts of the colony with public works and to use the temporary prosperity of mining to promote the opening of the wheat belt in the interior. This secured his majority in a parliament without parties and allowed him to be what was beyond the imagining of his parliamentary following and his farming constituents, a modernising conservative. He introduced manhood suffrage and payment of members, went a long way towards giving the goldfields their due representation, and transformed the labour and employment laws to benefit working people. He set up a government bank to provide finance to farmers, which in the east was the work of radical liberals and the Labor Party. To reduce the imbalance in the population of electorates, he introduced female suffrage since women were numerous in the old farming districts and scarce on the goldfields.

Forrest supported **Federation**, but had to proceed cautiously since the old settled districts feared it. The goldminers were enthusiasts for it as a means of forcing their parochial enemies into being Australians and destroying the protective barriers which they had erected against the rest of Australia. They threatened secession if the colony did not join the Commonwealth. To bring his following to support Federation, Forrest attempted at the last minute to win better terms for WA, but when he failed, he put the constitution to referendum and campaigned for its acceptance. There was a comfortable 'yes' majority, overwhelming on the goldfields and substantial in Perth. The old farming districts voted 'no', so they were joined to the nation against their will, a coercion managed by their champion, the premier.

The t'othersiders, overwhelmingly working-class, soon came to rule WA through the Labor Party, a transition made undramatic by the statecraft of Forrest. The party, the first to operate in the West, copied its platform and discipline from the parties in the east. In 1911 it formed its first ministry and for the next 50 years was the usual party of government. Its strength was in the goldfields, the remote pastoral areas, and the working-class suburbs of Perth. It was not without support in the new wheatlands, but here its opposition to private property and its keenness to bring agricultural workers under the Arbitration Act were responsible in 1912 for the creation of its clone, the Country Party (later the **National Party**), which imitated its pre-selection ballot and strict discipline. In this wide swathe of territory, where all farmers were new settlers and struggling to survive, political mobilisation occurred rapidly. WA provided the model for the country parties in the east.

The chief business of government was the **development** of WA, which meant the development of its primary industries of **agriculture**, forestry and pastoralism. The Labor Party was ideologically committed to state ownership, but the state enterprises it created were defended as necessary for development and some of them—the sawmills, the brickworks, the shipping line—were accepted in these terms by their opponents. The enemy of development was the federal government, allegedly indifferent to the West and handicapping it by its high tariff policy on manufactured goods. The grievances were felt more intensely during the **Depression** of the 1930s, studied by Geoffrey **Bolton** in *A Fine Country to Starve In* (1972).

From the 1930s governments encouraged the development of local manufacturing industry, which remained small-scale until the early 1950s when a Liberal government by generous concessions lured heavy industry to Kwinana, just south of Perth. In the 1960s huge mineral finds, chiefly iron ore, gave the state its second mining boom and industries which did not have to be cosseted. They were run chiefly by multinational companies which were enthusiastically supported by Liberal governments (1959–71, 1974–83). The driving force was Charles **Court**, first as minister for industrial development and then as premier. Labor returned to power in the 1980s and by foolhardy and corrupt practices attempted to boost WA enterprises. After this government collapsed in ignominy, Charles Court's son Richard became premier of a Liberal government in 1993. Labor returned to power under Geoff Gallop in 2001.

With its new prosperity WA ceased to receive special financial assistance from the Commonwealth. In 1983 its population exceeded that of SA. Still the resentment against the east continues strong. Its particular focus is no longer tariffs, which have been abandoned, but Aboriginal affairs. In its huge, sparsely populated territory, a significant Aboriginal population survives. No land rights legislation has been passed and in the 1980s the state Labor government successfully pressed its national counterpart not to introduce national land rights legislation. The subsequent High Court rulings that established land rights have most relevance for WA, which has huge tracts liable to claim. The response to crime committed by young Aborigines has been the imposition of mandatory prison sentences, attracting national criticism, which has been ignored.

In 1960 Frank **Crowley** published a history of the state, *Australia's Western Third*. C.T. Stannage edited *A New History of Western Australia* (1981), which contains a revealing essay by G.C. Bolton on the writing of Western Australian history.

JOHN HIRST

Whaling emerged as a profitable enterprise in the late eighteenth century, coinciding with the beginning of British colonisation of Australia. Botany Bay was proposed as a whaling base in 1788, but the southern oceans were not officially opened for whaling until 1798. British and American whalers followed the annual migration of whales from the colder southern waters to the sheltered bays in Australia and NZ for the winter breeding season, where pregnant female whales and their offspring could easily be captured. The valuable products of whaling, including whale oil, whalebone, and spermaceti for candle-making, provided the bulk of NSW's exports during the 1830s. Engraved whale-teeth were highly prized nineteenth-century curiosities.

Hunting sperm whales in the open seas was highly dangerous, and encouraged a romanticism which has been compared to the noble, masculinist endeavours of life in the bush. By the early 1850s the promise of gold had lured sailors away from whaling; bay whaling ceased in 1851. Whaling re-emerged as an important industry 100 years later, with stations established at Albany, WA (1952), and Byron Bay, NSW (1954). Mounting opposition, however, prompted an independent inquiry in 1978. In accordance with recommendations in the subsequent Frost Report, the Whale Protection Act was passed in 1980. W.J. Dakin, *Whaleman Adventurers* (1934), and M. Colwell, *Whaling Around Australia* (1969), give the history of the industry.

HD

Wheat growing was largely unsuccessful in Australia before the 1850s. Although some progress was made in the cooler and moister Tasmania, cultivators had difficulty coming to terms with the soils and climate of NSW, which had to import grain. Edgars Dunsdorfs in *The Australian Wheat Growing Industry 1788–1948* (1956) described these years as the period of insufficient expansion. A large increase in population with the discovery of gold provided a market for wheat, and production was stimulated by the passing of **selection** legislation. These acts established the family farm as the chief productive unit for wheat growing. In the 1850s and 1860s lands north and south of Adelaide, with easy access to coastal shipping, became the premier wheat-growing area in Australia. Production was also stimulated by the invention of the **stripper**, which was ideal for harvesting in the dry conditions of SA. Southern Victoria also became a major wheat-producing district. During the last three decades of the nineteenth century the wheat frontier expanded into the Wimmera and northern plains of Victoria, the lower north and Yorke Peninsula in SA, and into the Riverina district of NSW. While production increased, yield per acre declined. The reasons for the decline, according to Dunsdorfs, were unclear. One factor was continuous cropping, while the move into less fertile regions was also important. In SA the expansion into marginal lands resulted in a retreat when rains failed in the late 1870s. The classic account of this tragedy is D.W. Meinig, *On the Margins of the Good Earth* (1962).

Between 1890 and 1920 new developments enabled the further expansion of the wheat industry. The invention of H.V. **McKay's** harvester, which winnowed as well as stripped the crop, enabled further labour-saving economies. The **stump-jump plough**, although an earlier invention, facilitated cultivation as settlers pushed into the mallee lands of Victoria and SA. The productivity of farms was improved with the development of rust-resistant grains such as William **Farrer's** 'Federation', the use of superphosphate, and fallowing practices which increased the rate of nitrate release into soils and reduced weed infestation. The decline of the profitability of wool encouraged the subdivision of pastoral estates in NSW, and by 1910 this was the premier wheat-growing state. During this period of rapid expansion, wheat farmers' incomes were increased by combining cropping with the grazing of sheep. An important long-term change in the early twentieth century was the opening up of the wheat belt in WA.

Australia's wheat farmers have always provided a relatively small part of the world trade in wheat. They have as a consequence been price-takers rather than price-setters. The rapid expansion of the Australian wheat frontier occurred during a period of worldwide growth, interrupted only by World War I, in wheat production and a subsequent decline in prices. By the late 1920s wheat farmers began to feel the squeeze of the decline in world prices, and frequently saw themselves as powerless victims of grain dealers. At the same time it became clear that the revolution in yields initiated by fallowing was based on a profound misunderstanding of soil science. Continual fallowing destroyed soil structure, and dust storms resulted in many parts of the wheat belt. The worldwide **Depression** in the 1930s added to the wheat farmers' woes. In 1930 the **Scullin** Labor government encouraged farmers to 'grow more wheat' to help with the nation's balance of payments crisis. The result was a massive increase in production and a collapse in prices.

From 1930 to 1950 the growth of the industry levelled off. However, scientific and administrative changes paved the way for growth in the 1950s. Experiments with subterranean clovers, or clover ley farming, helped to improve both soil structure and pasture. Productivity was also increased by the introduction of tractors and motorised headers. Inefficient handling of bagged wheat gave way to bulk handling, and the marketing of wheat became more organised through the formation of the Australian Wheat Board in 1939. The board guaranteed farmers' incomes, and a levy on the volume of grain delivered by farmers to the compulsory pool supported research into soils, plant breeding, wheat diseases, cereal pests, pastures, and weed control. From the mid-1950s more attention was paid to the classification of wheat to meet the requirements of international buyers and local millers and bakers. In the 1950s the average yearly planting of wheat was five million hectares. This rose to 10 million in the 1980s. During the same period the crop yield doubled. In these years WA emerged as the major wheat producer, and Qld became a minor producer. These years of growth in the wheat industry have been examined by Greg Whitwell and Diane Sydenham in *A Shared Harvest* (1991), and the best account of the environmental impact of wheat-growing is contained in Neil Barr and John Cary, *Greening a Brown Land* (1992).

In the 1980s and 1990s the wheat industry continued to be receptive to change. World competition was fierce. Agricultural subsidies in the European Union and the US Export Enhancement scheme took export markets. Wheat farmers responded to this by increasing their efficiency. New varieties of wheat were introduced and many cultivators adopted new cultivation practices—chemical weed control, minimum tillage, and direct drilling of crops. From 1989 farmers faced a deregulated market for wheat with the ending of the monopoly of the board. However, by the mid-1990s a majority of farmers still managed price risk through pooling of their wheat and averaging of incomes through marketing boards. The heart of the wheat industry remained the family farm.

CHARLES FAHEY

White Australia as a national ideal developed in the last decade of the nineteenth century, when politicians and journalists began to articulate a vision of a future Australia inhabited only by 'white' people. But the place of non-Europeans in the Australian colonies had been a subject of concern for more than half a century.

From the late 1830s some employers began to recruit labour in the Indian sub-continent, China, and Melanesia, in part as a response to the ending of convict **transportation** to NSW. Both supporters and critics assumed that Asian labourers would form a subservient class, denied economic, political, and social equality, and agreed that their entry could be decisive in the future course of colonial development. Their presence could thwart the development of an economy based on free labour and the growth of democratic political institutions open to the participation of all male adults.

The rapid increase in population as a result of the gold rushes ended the importation of indentured Asian labour to south-eastern Australia, but raised a new issue concerning the racial composition of the colonies: how to respond to the entry of large numbers of **Chinese** attracted by gold. From 1855, restrictions were progressively placed on Chinese **immigration** to the colonies, but to the 1880s such laws were seen as temporary and there was no idea of excluding all 'coloured' people.

While significant immigration of non-Europeans to south-eastern Australia ended after 1861, recruitment of Melanesian and Asian workers, for the Qld sugar industry and the less important pearling and *bêche-de-mer* fishing industries, led to a significant labour trade in the last third of the nineteenth century. Such recruitment was justified on what were ultimately racial grounds: that these industries required a strictly disciplined and cheap workforce able to perform arduous manual labour in the tropics, which was understood by employers to necessitate 'coloured' labour.

For a period it seemed as if the northern regions would develop an economy based upon indentured non-European labour, and the separation of north Qld became an important political issue in the 1880s. With Federation, however, southern opinion prevailed: the sugar industry was forced to relinquish its Melanesian workers, although its survival was guaranteed by the provision of a subsidy on sugar grown by white labour. By the end of the century, Australians had developed a clear sense of themselves as different from and superior to all non-European peoples. This outlook was nurtured by racial theories, particularly Social Darwinism, at a time of apparent global dominance of European civilisation. Racial arrogance justified and even demanded the acceptance of widespread discrimination.

In the 1890s immigration controls were extended from Chinese to all non-Europeans in NSW, Tasmania, and WA. This direct form of legislation was, however, unacceptable to the British government, which was concerned to minimise offence to Japan and India, and Australian legislators were persuaded to cloak the target of exclusion by an education test.

In 1901 the first substantive legislation passed by the Commonwealth parliament, the Immigration Restriction Act, excluded any person who 'when asked to do so by an officer fails to write out at dictation and sign in the presence of the officer a passage of 50 words in length in an European language directed by the officer'. The **dictation test**, to remain on the statute book until 1958, was administered in a language unlikely to be understood. While 52 persons passed in the period 1902–08, it seems that after 1909 no-one passed. After World War I the definition of 'white races', or of superior and inferior European racial stock, was refined and narrowed, leading to quotas on southern European and Jewish immigration.

The White Australia ideal was, however, concerned with more than the barring of immigrants. It faced inward as well as outward, directed at the non-European populations resident in the country. In addition to control of entry into Australia, it sought to control the movement of Aboriginal people within the country, and led to policies likely to bring about the numerical decline, even extinction, of those classified as of inferior racial stock, such as the forced adoption or institutionalisation of Aboriginal children—the **Stolen Generations**.

After 1901 the freedoms and rights of non-European residents contracted dramatically. Most of the Melanesians in Australia at the time of Federation were deported; Chinese were denied the right to bring their wives and children into the country after 1903; social welfare legislation specifically excluded non-Europeans and Aboriginal people; and employment opportunities were restricted, with discrimination reaching its fullest development in Qld and WA.

Australian governments did not, however, pursue the White Australia ideal to its logical culmination. A number of exceptions allowed a remnant of the Chinese communities to survive. While in theory no Chinese were to establish permanent residence after 1901, a small number did so. Thus at the 1933 Census there were more than 300 overseas-born residents of 'Chinese race' who had resided in Australia for between 20 and 29 years. In the period between the two world wars, governments gradually abandoned the idea that Aboriginal people would become extinct. In 1937 the notion of assimilation was first accepted by all states as government policy, and some improvement in facilities began.

While there were some minor indications of change before the war, the retreat from the White Australia ideal occurred after 1945. Several factors combined to produce a slow erosion of ideas of racial determinism. The revelation of the horrors of Hitler's death camps seems to have dealt a decisive blow to policies openly based on ideas of racial superiority and exclusiveness. The UN enshrined the doctrine of the equality of peoples; and in the postwar ideological battle against communism, racism came to be seen as a significant liability for the West. But the war in the Pacific had done much to further entrench white racism; wartime propaganda was often marked by crude bigotry, and the revulsion against Japanese fanaticism and disregard for human life only slowly dissipated. The postwar political leaders—Prime Minister Sir Robert **Menzies** and leader of the opposition Labor Party, Arthur **Calwell**, who held office until 1966 and 1967 respectively—never questioned the necessity for the White Australia policy, which the Liberal government sought, unsuccessfully by the 1960s, to present to the world as based not on racial but on national considerations.

Despite immigration policy, increasing numbers of non-Europeans secured de facto permanent residence after 1945: these included refugees who could not be forced to leave, primarily Chinese nationals who won asylum following the communist victory in mainland China in 1949; spouses of Australian citizens; and those admitted temporarily on economic criteria who managed to extend their period of residence. There were increasing contacts with non-Europeans in the world of business and in schools and universities as Asian students gained entry on government scholarships, and on a private basis.

Meanwhile, the policy which sought to isolate Aboriginal people from the mainstream of White Australia was abandoned. Under the lead provided by the minister for the territories, Paul **Hasluck**, the policy of assimilation was forcefully advocated and led to changes of significance by the late 1950s. The crucial shift in immigration policy occurred following the retirement of Menzies in January 1966. The way had been prepared by critics of White Australia such as the Immigration Reform Group, whose pamphlet, *Control or Colour Bar?* (1960), won converts in political and bureaucratic circles. Menzies's successor, Harold **Holt**, had for some time seen the impossibility of maintaining racial exclusion, which was almost immediately abandoned on his accession. By the early 1970s over five per cent of the intake was from the Asian region.

Until the mid-1970s research on White Australia focused mainly on immigration policy, and neglected the lives of non-Europeans and the ideas which influenced policy. The authoritative work in the first half of the century was Myra **Willard's** *History of the White Australia Policy*, first published in

1923 and reissued several times. Interest in the White Australia 'policy' was revived in the 1960s, at the time of increasing calls for reform. Important studies published in these years include A.T. Yarwood, *Asian Migration to Australia: The Background to Exclusion 1896–1913* (1964), and A.C. Palfreeman, *The Administration of the White Australia Policy* (1967). Two detailed general histories have been published: A.T. Yarwood and M.J. Knowling, *Race Relations in Australia* (1982), and Andrew Markus, *Australian Race Relations* (1994). Sean Brawley's *The White Peril: Foreign Relations and Asian Immigration to Australasia and North America 1919–78* (1995) is the most recent study of twentieth-century government policy.

ANDREW MARKUS

White, Cyril Brudenell Bingham (1876–1940) began his career as a professional soldier in 1898 with a commission into the Queensland Regiment, with which he briefly served in the **Boer War**. His appointment as aide-de-camp to the commanding officer of the Australian Military Forces enabled him to see much of the new army before he was selected to attend the British Army Staff College in 1906, the first Australian to do so. After a stint at the War Office, London, he was promoted to major and returned to Australia in 1912 to become Director of Military Operations. In this role White drew up plans to send overseas a combined NZ and Australian force of 18 000 in the event of war. These were used to organise the first contingent of troops upon the outbreak of **World War I**, when White was appointed chief of staff to William **Bridges**. Later, as brigadier-general under William **Birdwood**, White organised the successful evacuation of Gallipoli. He undertook the administration of the AIF on the Western Front. White resisted an attempt by C.E.W. **Bean** and Keith **Murdoch** to have him appointed commander of the **Anzac** Corps, rather than John **Monash**.

Upon his return to Australia in 1919 he was involved in restructuring the postwar army. He later chaired the Commonwealth Public Service Board and utilised his organisational skills in the service of **royal tours**. Claims that he was involved in right-wing **secret armies** during the 1930s remain unsubstantiated. His return to the army in 1940 as Chief of General Staff was short-lived as he was killed in a plane crash later that year. Bean, a staunch admirer of White, wrote about him in *Two Men I Knew* (1957), and he figures in David Horner (ed.), *The Commanders* (1984).

KT

White, Patrick Victor Martindale (1912–90) is generally acknowledged as Australia's pre-eminent novelist of the twentieth century. His winning of the Nobel Prize for Literature in 1973 consolidated this status, though it remains a problematic one. How far is his pre-eminence dependent on the literary qualities of his novels and their pertinence for readers, and how far on the mechanisms of the publishing industry and authorial careerism? How distinctively 'Australian' were his novels?

White's personal background was classically **Anglo-Australian**. He was born in London, but his family was of the Australian **squattocracy**. He was taken to Australia when he

was six months old, spending the next 13 years there. He then returned to England to receive his education at Cheltenham College and Cambridge. He started drafting novels when back in Australia for a few years prior to his undergraduate studies in 1932. Following graduation in 1935, he continued to base himself in England for over a decade more, with trips to the Continent, to the USA, and (as an intelligence officer with the RAF during World War II) to the Middle East. It was during this period that his first two novels were published: *Happy Valley* (1939), set in rural Australia; and *The Living and the Dead* (1941), set in London. A year after a brief return visit to Australia in 1946–47, he came back to settle near Sydney, arranging for his partner, the Alexandrian Greek, Manoly Lascaris, to join him. The couple made occasional trips to Europe over their 40 subsequent years together, and parts of White's fiction continued to explore exotic milieux; but the principal setting for nearly all his novels—including the three most commonly discussed, *The Tree of Man* (1955), *Voss* (1957), and *Riders in the Chariot* (1961)—was Australia.

Since the 1960s, White has provoked worldwide scholarly discussion. In 1991 the Sydney journalist and broadcaster David Marr published a richly detailed *Life*, fleshing out White's self-portrait of 1981, *Flaws in the Glass*. In 1994 Marr published a selection of White's *Letters*. Australian historians have attended less to White, while White once remarked that he had 'always tended to be blind to Australian history'. He did not mean the subject-matter so much as its treatment by academics or historical novelists who insisted on abiding by the documentary record. When only six years old, he had listed a 'History of Australia' among his hoped-for presents at Christmas, and at 19 he specialised in history for his Cambridge entrance examination. He found the discipline too constraining, however, and switched his undergraduate studies to modern languages.

It was not until *Voss*, with its re-creation of an expedition to the Australian desert, loosely based on the experiences of Ludwig **Leichhardt**, that White made any full-scale engagement with a historical subject. In *A Fringe of Leaves* (1976), White attempted another imaginative reconstruction of an episode in nineteenth-century Australian history: Eliza **Fraser's** capture by an Aboriginal tribe. While he strove to achieve an authentic feel for period and landscape detail, he concentrated on the mental, spiritual, and emotional state of his characters: what he called (in *Voss*) 'the country of the mind'. This approach was too mystical, too 'foreign' for the historian Ian **Turner**, reviewing *Voss* in the Melbourne periodical *Overland* (June 1958). It struck a much more responsive chord in Manning **Clark**, whose own highly charged versions of Australian history in turn impressed White.

Historians of culture and the 'creative spirit' in Australia (for example, John Rickard and Geoffrey **Serle**) have conveyed a sympathetic interest in White's work, but any concerted attempt to place it in the context of his own times has so far been left to David Marr and to the not-so-tender mercies of the 'cultural studies' analyst, Simon During (*Patrick White*, 1996).

IAN BRITAIN

Whitlam, (Edward) Gough (1916–) was federal leader of the **Australian Labor Party** 1967–77, and prime minister 1972–75. A large, commanding man of upper-middle-class origins and private-school education, he wrested control of Labor from a suspicious and defensive executive and made it into a modern social democratic party. As prime minister he embarked on an ambitious program of progressive reform, which was faltering before his government was swept from office in 1975. The circumstances of this **Dismissal** compounded the prejudices of supporters and critics. For some, he is a hero, all the more admirable in his magisterial self-regard. For others, he was a dangerous incompetent.

Whitlam entered federal parliament in 1952 as a young man after war service and legal practice in NSW. He quickly made his mark as a modernising critic of such Labor shibboleths as the **White Australia** policy and the socialist objective, but was elected deputy leader to Arthur **Calwell** in 1960. On a series of issues—advocacy of **state aid** to church schools, criticism of the party constitution, support for the US alliance, including in the **Vietnam War**—he clashed with his leader and the federal executive; he only narrowly avoided expulsion in 1966. Through augmentation of social welfare, he reworked **Chifley's** egalitarian vision of the **'light on the hill'** into his own meritocratic program of a light on every student's desk. He won the leadership of the Australian Labor Party in 1967, improved its electoral fortunes in 1969, and succeeded in reforming the constitution and rewriting the policies. Having established a personal supremacy over the Liberal prime minister, William **McMahon**, Whitlam won power at the 1972 election on the slogan 'It's time.'

In office, Whitlam began implementing his program at a breakneck pace. Federal funding of schools, free **universities**, universal health insurance, recognition of **Aboriginal land rights**, measures to improve the status of women, and national assistance to the arts were among the measures. A committed centralist in **Commonwealth–state relations**, he used tied grants to the states to expand Canberra's influence in domestic policy, while in **foreign relations** he pursued a more independent policy as Cold War polarities eased in the 1970s. Gough Whitlam and his wife Margaret, who also towered over lesser mortals, brought an urbane assurance to public life.

The government was re-elected in 1974 but lacked a majority in the Senate, and proved accident-prone. Its rapid expansion of public expenditure made it particularly vulnerable to the international recession after the oil crisis of 1973. A series of ministerial scandals set the scene for the Opposition's blockage of supply and the subsequent Dismissal. Initially defiant, Whitlam campaigned vigorously in the ensuing election and had difficulty in accepting the voters' rejection. He resigned the Labor leadership after a further defeat in 1977.

In his polemical account of the Dismissal, *The Truth of the Matter* (1979), and a subsequent justification of *The Whitlam Government* (1985), Whitlam remained preoccupied with the injustice of his fate. The new Labor government that took office in 1983 was so determined to avoid a similar outcome that it studiously marked itself off from Whitlam's grandiose politics, and packed him off to Paris as ambassador to UNESCO 1983–86. In *Whitlam Revisited* (1993), his admirers recalled the excitement of experiments in social democracy. A subsequent generation is more troubled by the lapses, especially when the liberation of **East Timor** brought further revelations of Whitlam's complicity in its conquest by Indonesia. But his stature within Labor mythology was secure, and while he occasionally delivered breathy jibes at the timidity of the **Hawke** ministry, he revelled in a growing public regard. Whitlam remains a compelling figure, consistent in his values and yet increasingly radical in his politics; the last great politician to follow his convictions, he rose and fell as the possibilities for a confident and expansive national government ended.

Leading journalists such as Paul Kelly, Clem Lloyd and Andrew Clark, Laurie Oakes, and Alan Reid have written chronicles of Whitlam's political career. His speechwriter, Graham Freudenberg, echoed the master's cadences in *A Certain Grandeur* (1977), and James Walter analysed them in a psychological study of *The Leader* (1980).

STUART MACINTYRE

Whitty, Mary Vincent (Ellen) (1819–92) was an Irish nun who established a convent for the Sisters of Mercy in Qld during the 1860s. This order was founded in Dublin in 1831 by Catherine McAuley for 'service of the poor, sick and ignorant'. Ellen Whitty trained under Mother McAuley after joining as a 19-year-old in 1839. Taking Vincent as her religious name, she was professed in 1841 and qualified as a teacher in 1842. After missionary work in Liverpool, England, she served as Mother Bursar and Mistress of Novices before being elected Reverend Mother of the Order's Dublin Headhouse in 1849 at the age of 30. During the 1840s and 1850s Mother Ursula Frayne established Mercy communities in Perth and Melbourne. At the request of Bishop James Quinn, Mother Vincent arrived in Brisbane in 1861 with five Sisters. By 1866 she had established six independent **Catholic** schools, which were open to all denominations, but the autocrat Quinn usurped her control to forge links with the government system. Rather than abandon Qld, Whitty accepted demotion when Quinn assumed direction of her community in 1865. In addition to establishing basic Catholic **education** in Qld, Mother Vincent was a pioneer of secondary education for girls and non-government care of homeless children. The Mercy Sisters also assisted unemployed young women and migrants, but Quinn rejected Mother Vincent's plan for an Aboriginal developmental centre at Maryborough in 1879. Quinn's successor, Robert Dunne, feared the hastiness and risk of her ventures and opposed schemes for a hospital and home for the aged. Mother Vincent's achievements are critically analysed in M.X. O'Donoghue's *Mother Vincent Whitty* (1972).

DC

Wik decision refers to the High Court judgment in *Wik Peoples v Queensland* (1996), which found that native title to the Wik peoples' traditional lands on Cape York Peninsula had continued to exist despite the operation of pastoral leases in the area. While the opposing view argued that the effects of pastoral leases nullified native title, the judges ruled that native title and pastoral leases could, in fact, coexist. The Liberal–National Party government, backed by pastoral interests, opposed the judgment, and legislated to limit native title. (See also **Aboriginal land rights**.)

HD

'Wild white man' was a nineteenth-century term used to describe white men who lived in the bush, usually with some degree of contact with Aborigines. The first 'wild white man' is believed to be Sammy Cox, who claimed to have deserted his uncle's ship as a child near Tamar Heads, Tasmania, in 1789 and to have lived with Aborigines until 1812. In accordance with prevailing attitudes about racial difference, these absconders, in reverting to nature, were considered 'wild', like the Aborigines with whom they lived. They were, however, redeemed somewhat in the popular imagination through association with the figure of the 'noble savage', which romanticised the role of the white man misplaced in the wild. As with American 'wild' men, the Australian type was frequently represented as strong, hardy, independent, self-sufficient, and as conquering nature. This is evident in the treatment of William **Buckley**, who survived for over 30 years without contact with white society, particularly in the portrait by W. McLeod that depicts him heroically, armed with spears and draped in the animal skins of a hunter.

The fewer documented cases of white women living among Aborigines, such as Eliza **Fraser** and the 'white woman of Gippsland' in Victoria, are framed around the gender and class assumptions of the time. A white woman did not generally choose a life in the wild of her own accord; instead, the situation befell her after being lost, stranded, abandoned, or kidnapped; and she was then kept under duress. Such women were mostly portrayed as victims—physically weak and sexually vulnerable. Newspaper reports evoked fears of their being ravished and possibly killed by Aboriginal men, although the conventional decency of the period precluded explicit mention of such horrors. For a man to choose such a life deemed him an adventurer and popular curiosity; his female equivalent, however, would have more likely been labelled mad and dangerous.

'Wild white men' in Australia fascinated nineteenth-century social chroniclers. Cases appear in early works such as **Bonwick's** account of Buckley (1856); more recent discussions about 'wild white women' appear in the work of Kay Schaffer and Kate Darian-Smith. The theme has also been treated in fiction, such as Patrick **White's** *A Fringe of Leaves* (1976), David **Malouf's** *Remembering Babylon* (1993), and Liam Davidson's *The White Woman* (1994). (See also **Captivity narratives**.)

HD

Wilderness, the name now commonly used by environmentalists to describe unspoiled or virgin **bush**, is a relatively late arrival in Australian cultural and political discourse. Colonial Australians, as the lexicographer William Ramson suggests (in D.J. **Mulvaney**, ed., *The Humanities and the Australian Environment*, 1991), used the word infrequently, and when they did so, it was to denote 'wild' or 'waste' land of low value. In the USA, perhaps because of its Puritan inheritance, 'wilderness' had also acquired some of the biblical associations of the word as a place of spiritual trial and refuge—an idea which was transmitted in turn to the first modern environmentalists, such as the transcendentalist Henry Thoreau. Since the 1920s Australians had sought to preserve native 'wildlife' and forests, but the word 'wilderness' was adopted from the USA only more recently. As Peter Read suggests in *Returning to Nothing* (1996), the spectator's sense of spiritual exaltation in the face of 'untouched' nature was directly proportional to the threat of its loss. In the early 1970s the struggle of the Tasmanian Wilderness Society to save Lake Pedder, expressed in the beautiful photographs of Olegas Truchanas, helped to fix the ideal of 'wilderness' in the popular imagination. Myles Dunphy, 'the father of Australian wilderness', defined it as somewhere 'that one may be able to travel on foot in any direction for at least a full day without meeting a road or highway'. As such, it denoted a selective human absence: the exclusion of farms, mines, dams, and logging mills, but also—more subtly—the discerning presence of the nature-loving hiker or environmentalist. The **pioneer** legend had asserted human mastery over nature; 'wilderness' asserted the moral claim of nature over humans. As Tom Griffiths argues in *Hunters and Collectors* (1996), 'wilderness' is often conceived as 'ageless', an ideal which may involve a denial of both its European and Aboriginal history.

GD

Willard, Myra (1887–?1971) became a pupil teacher in 1904 and in 1908 was awarded a scholarship to Sydney Teachers College. Allowed by the Education Department to enrol at the University of Sydney, she studied under George Arnold **Wood**, winning several prizes and graduating with first-class honours. Wood described her as 'an excellent research scholar' and supervised her postgraduate study of migration to Australia. At his instigation she wrote a prize-winning essay, which in 1923 became the first book published by Melbourne University Press. Entitled *History of the White Australia Policy to 1920*, it suffered from lack of access to departmental files, but nevertheless presented a perceptive analysis of how the policy emerged and of the system of indentured labour. For long the standard work of its subject, it was reprinted in 1967 with minor corrections by the author, and again in 1974. After completing the book, Willard returned to teaching, first at Fort Street Girls High School, then from 1928 as assistant examiner at the head office of the Education Department. Regrettably, she wrote no more history.

BRIAN FLETCHER

Williams, Richard (1890–1980), founder of the **Royal Australian Air Force**, began his flying career in 1914 when, as a young army lieutenant, he undertook three months pilot training at Point Cook, Victoria. Shortly after, Williams was appointed flight commander to the newly formed Australian Flying Corps. During his World War I service Williams was awarded the DSO and twice mentioned in despatches. He returned to Australia to help establish the Air Board, which then accepted his proposal for the formation of the Australian Air Force. The service came into being in 1920; Williams was appointed First Air Member and spent the next 18 years protecting it from attacks based on financial constraints and inter-service rivalry. It was only in 1935 that he achieved equivalent rank to the other service chiefs. The establishment of the Commonwealth Aircraft Corporation in 1936 was a triumph for Williams. Disputes with government, of which Williams gives a detailed account in his autobiography *These Are Facts* (1977), saw him moved away from control of the air force. He spent most of World War II in London and Washington as RAAF representative. Williams left the RAAF in 1946 to become director-general of civil aviation and to oversee the postwar expansion of Australian aviation.

KT

Williamson, David Keith (1942–), Australia's best-known and most popular playwright, once described his special relationship with his public as that of 'storyteller to the tribe'. He has certainly reflected contemporary Australia to itself in ways that it has recognised as true, and shown, in Hamlet's dictum, 'the very age and body of the time his form and pressure'. But Williamson's role as a maker of history goes beyond the ways in which his plays have captured the values and prejudices, insecurities and idioms of middle-class Anglo-Celtic culture.

In his screenplays for cinema and television, Williamson has often chosen overtly historical subjects. *Gallipoli* (1981) and *Phar Lap* (1983) offer relatively uncomplicated versions of the myth of the Aussie battler brought down by the devious self-interest of the Old World, and a similar dichotomy between innocence and experience underlies *The Last Bastion* (1984), a mini-series dealing with the **Curtin** government's relationship with its neo-imperialistic US allies.

His stage plays, however, have all been placed in a contemporary setting, in which the myth-making is not nearly so straightforward, and the tone characteristically hovers ambivalently between celebration and satire. Public events surround and direct his characters at every turn. *Don's Party* (1971) mythologises the tribal loyalties that intersect with political alignments in Australia in its treatment of a 1969 election night party when suddenly, for the predominantly Labor-voting guests, everything turned sour. *Jugglers Three* (1973) and its Vietnam veterans; *The Club* (1977), where economic rationalism has added another dimension to the sacred rites of football rivalry; *Sons of Cain* (1985), with its exposure of NSW government corruption; *Brilliant Lies* (1993), where gender roles become even more complicated by new legislation about sexual harassment; and *Dead White Males* (1995), where post-structuralism gives an added twist to the quest for coherent values—these, like others

among Williamson's 17 plays for the mainstream theatre, test interpersonal politics within the crucible of rapid and disruptive cultural change.

Like more conventional kinds of historians, Williamson's role has not been merely to record the age and body of the time, but to shape it. The ocker who appeared as a focus for a brash nationalist self-assertion in early plays, such as *The Coming of Stork* (1970) and *The Removalists* (1971), was as much created as observed by the playwright, and *Don's Party* has similarly entered the national vocabulary to define an event that many Australians knew, but did not know that they knew. The boundaries between invention and imitation in the role of the storyteller to the tribe are, inevitably, difficult to draw.

Peter Fitzpatrick

Williamson, James Cassius (1845–1913) was an American actor who twice toured Australia before he leased Melbourne's Theatre Royal in 1880. Two years later he formed Williamson, Garner & Musgrove—soon widely known as 'the Firm'—which went on to monopolise theatre in Australia. Its shows frequently featured famous overseas artists, including Sarah Bernhardt and the expatriate Nellie **Melba**. The firm became J.C. Williamson's Ltd in 1911, reflecting his primary role in the partnership. Ian Dicker wrote a biography, *J.C.W.* (1974).

KT

Wills, Thomas Wentworth (1835–80) played a pivotal role in the development of **Australian Rules football** in July 1858, when he wrote to *Bell's Life in Victoria*, urging that a football club be formed to help cricketers stay fit during winter. Wills co-umpired the celebrated game between Scotch College and Melbourne Grammar School on 7 August 1858, and played in early matches at Richmond Paddock. In May 1859 he joined his cousin Henry **Harrison** and others to draw up the rules of the Melbourne Football Club. By 1876 he had played over 200 games, mainly with Geelong, and was five times 'Champion of the Colony'.

Wills was born at Molonglo Plains, NSW, and spent his early youth near Ararat, Victoria. As a student at Rugby in England (1852–56), Wills excelled at rugby football and captained the cricket team. In 1857–58 he became secretary of the Melbourne Cricket Club and represented Victoria 16 times, captaining the colony on eight occasions. He is credited with introducing round-arm and overarm bowling to Victoria. In 1866–67 he coached the Aboriginal cricket team that toured England in 1868. He was a tragic figure, the privileged son of a wealthy squatter Horatio Spencer Wills, but stained by his convict grandfather, a highway robber. His father was one of 19 whites murdered by Aborigines at Cullinlaringo, Qld, in 1861. Wills escaped the **massacre** by chance and later became mentally unstable, spending time in Kew Asylum and struggling with alcoholism. On 2 May 1880 at his home in Heidelberg, Victoria, he stabbed himself to death with a pair of scissors.

DC

Wills, William John see Burke, Robert O'Hara

Wilson, William Hardy (1881–1955) was a notable student of Australian colonial **architecture** and pioneer conservationist. Born in Campbelltown, NSW, Wilson studied architecture as an articled pupil in Sydney before working and travelling in Europe and the USA between 1905 and 1910. Back in Sydney, but influenced by his American travels, he began to make drawings of early colonial buildings in NSW and Tasmania, to encourage their conservation and to emulate their simple, classical proportions in his own architecture, mainly houses in Sydney's northern suburbs. Wilson saw in the Early Colonial style an image of a social order to which an Australia, debased by modernism and moral decadence, might some day return. Travels in China convinced him of the need for a fusion of Western and Eastern spiritual traditions, a theme which he developed in the series of visionary writings which occupied his later years. In *The Dawn of a New Civilization* (1929), Wilson appears in the guise of Richard Le Measurer. His beautiful drawings perhaps did more than any other single influence to awaken public appreciation of early colonial architecture; the originals are now collected in the National Library. Cyril **Pearl's** *Hardy Wilson and his Old Colonial Architecture* (1970) is a useful introduction to a figure who deserves a major study.

GD

Windeyer, Richard (1806–47) began a long family involvement in the law when he followed the rest of his family to NSW in 1835 after being called to the Bar in London. His ability was quickly realised and he established a large practice. Obviously a passionate advocate, he was gaoled by the chief justice, Alfred **Stephen**, in 1846 for contempt of court, after almost coming to blows with the opposing counsel. Richard also took up land in the Hunter Valley where, among other agricultural activities, he made wine. He was elected to the Legislative Council in 1843, where he pursued his commitment to free trade, education, and law reform. His active membership of the Aborigines Protection Society followed on his recognition of the legal disadvantages they suffered during the trials for the **Myall Creek massacre**.

His son, William Charles (1834–97), was admitted to the Bar in 1857. He also wrote for Henry **Parkes's** *Empire*, a relationship which sparked his interest in politics. In 1860 he entered the Legislative Assembly but resigned after two years. Twice more (1899 and 1876) he was elected to the Assembly and held the offices of solicitor-general and attorney-general. Like his father, he was committed to law reform; he introduced many private bills, the most important of those carried being the Married Women's Property Act of 1879, as well as sitting on the Law Reform Commission. Also like his father, he was committed to education, and was founding chairman of the Women's College at the University of Sydney as well as its chancellor, 1895–97. In 1879 he became a judge of the Supreme Court, where he was sometimes a controversial figure, particularly for his judgment on the **Mount Rennie** rape case. His son Richard (1868–1959) was a leading barrister.

Margaret (1866–1939) was William's fifth daughter. She shared her mother Mary's interest in the suffragette movement, and was a member of the executive of the Womanhood Suffrage League and the committee to establish the Women's College in the University of Sydney. She travelled to New York in 1899 to train at the state library, and worked at a college library before returning to Sydney in 1901 and gaining an appointment at the Public Library of New South Wales. For the last 16 years of her employment there (1910–26) she was cataloguer in the Mitchell Library. To her earlier interest in the welfare of children, shown through her involvement with the Free Kindergarten Movement, she added the cause of children's libraries, and in 1909 helped found the Bush Book Club.

KT

Wise, Bernhard Ringrose (1858–1916) entered the NSW parliament in 1887 after working as a barrister for several years. He left the Free Trade Party in 1895 and became a strong supporter of Federation. He was a member of the 1897–98 Convention and later wrote the celebratory account *The Making of the Australian Commonwealth 1889–1900* (1913). Although he helped draft such important social reform legislation in his state as the Old Age Pensions Act (1900) and the Women's Franchise Act (1902), it is the NSW Industrial Arbitration Act of 1901 that is widely regarded as his greatest achievement.

KT

Woman's Christian Temperance Union was a women's organisation established in the American West in 1874 and introduced to Sydney in 1882. Branches in other cities followed, and in 1894 the organisation claimed 7400 members. Of the various organisations and movements advocating **temperance** in the 1880s and 1890s, the WCTU was the largest women's organisation and, arguably, the most effective. Bessie Harrrison **Lee** was a leading member of the Victorian branch. Its members, who were overwhelmingly middle-class and Protestant, regarded temperance as the keystone to moral reform and 'social purity'. Members campaigned against **alcohol**, which they blamed for unemployment, poverty, and lack of ambition, by marching into **pubs** with banners and placards, and demanding that men stop drinking and return home.

As the first mass organisation of women in Australia, the WCTU played an important role in women's political organisation. It was a key supporter of women's rights, particularly female suffrage, which it believed would allow women to exert a civilising effect on men. Anthea Hyslop examines the Victorian branch during the period 1887–97 in *HS* (1976).

HD

Women's Auxiliary Australian Air Force (WAAAF) was the largest of the women's auxiliary services established during World War II. Following the model of the British Women's Auxiliary Air Force, the WAAAF was formed in 1941. Earlier organisations, including the Women's Air Training Corps, the Women's Emergency Corps, and the Air League, had operated on a voluntary basis. WAAAF personnel generally worked as wireless and teleprinter operators; as war progressed they were increasingly employed as air force ground staff, but no members served outside Australia. Opposition to women joining the military forces continued during the war. As in the other women's auxiliary services, recruits were paid 60–70 per cent of the male rate.

HD

Women's Electoral Lobby is a national women's political lobby group founded in February 1972 in Carlton, Victoria. Following the example of *Ms Magazine* in a recent US election, WEL conducted a survey in order to gauge the extent to which Australian federal parliamentary candidates supported women's issues. The results demonstrated politicians' general lack of interest in feminist issues, and prompted a second, more professional survey which determined a score for each candidate. These scores, published in the Melbourne *Age*, revealed slightly stronger support for women's issues from the Australian Labor Party than from conservative candidates, and combined with the catchphrase, 'Think WEL before you vote', contributed to the **Whitlam** victory. During the state campaign in 1973, WEL continued its successful publicity through a televised forum of political leaders, each of whom was asked to answer the question 'Why should women vote for you?' Membership grew steadily, and the first national conference was held later that year. Through its regular conferences and successful lobbying, WEL raised public awareness about **feminism** in Australia. An early victory in Victoria was the removal of barriers to women in senior public service positions. It publishes a bimonthly newsletter, *Inkwel*.

HD

Women's history in Australia is largely a child of the radical politics of the late 1960s and early 1970s. Previously, the history of Australian women was composed largely of biographical sketches of women worthies and **pioneers**, especially among social and political reformers. Most often these were generated by the celebratory occasions that helped mark Australia's progression to nationhood. Like the work of some notable popular historians, such as Mary **Durack**, they sought to ensure women a place in this chronicle, even if only as helpmeets of founding fathers. Prior to the 1970s the staff of Australian history departments, as elsewhere, was largely male; and women featured little, if at all, in early works on Australian history. Margaret **Kiddle**, of the University of Melbourne History Department, was a notable exception on both counts. Though never promoted beyond senior tutor, she wrote both a biography of the nineteenth-century social reformer Caroline **Chisholm** and a social history of pastoralist families in western Victoria which acknowledged more fully the role of women.

The Social Science Research Council commissioned the first scholarly overview of women's position in Australian society, Norman MacKenzie's *Women in Australia* (1962). It was, however, the second-wave feminist movement that established the new field of women's history, and the journals of the left intelligentsia, most notably *Arena* and *Labour History*, that first provided publishing space. **Feminism**, as social theory and political practice, informed this new field, questioning both the place allotted women in the academy and the content of historical, sociological, and political research, as in the early manifesto issued by Ann Curthoys in *Arena*, 1970.

Young women students and teachers of history and politics set out in the 1970s to chart the place of women in Australian history. In 1975 four foundational texts appeared, discussed at length by Curthoys in *AHS* (1996): Anne **Summers**, *Damned Whores and God's Police*; Miriam **Dixson**, *The Real Matilda*; Beverley Kingston, *My Wife, My Daughter, and Poor Mary Ann*; Edna **Ryan** and Anne Conlon, *Gentle Invaders*. These signalled the nature of the research and writing that was to follow: always putting women at the centre of its analysis and chronicling the oppression of women by Australian culture and institutions; often provocative in tone; and sometimes inter-disciplinary in scope. Other early research appeared in a range of feminist journals born of the Australian second-wave feminist movement and feminist scholarship: *Refractory Girl*, *Mejane*, *Hecate*, *Scarlet Woman*, and *Lilith*.

The pressing need for teaching aids in the form of guides to sources and document collections produced Kay Daniels et al. (eds), *Women in Australia: An Annotated Guide to Records* (1977), and Beverley Kingston, *The World Moves Slowly: A Documentary History of Australian Women* (1977). There was also a growing stream of monographs and collections of essays in the field. Subsequently, women's history also began to find its place in major works of revision in Australian history, as in Alan Atkinson and Marian Aveling (eds), *Australians 1838* (1987). Similarly, generalist journals like *HS* and later *AHS* and the *AJPH* increasingly recognised the growth in scholarship in women's history, alongside a new women's studies journal, *AFS*.

Kay Daniels undertook one of the first major reviews of the field, in Graeme Osborne and W.F. Mandle (eds), *New History* (1982). Her analysis reiterated some of the criticisms that had followed the publication of the foundational texts already cited: the reliance on sources that reflected the perspective of male elites; the acceptance of the narrative lines set by conventional history; or, variously, the separation of women's history into an alternative, parallel strand of its own with a consequent failure fully to confront some of the major divisions among women, or to account for the gender order in Australian society. Daniels's overview signalled a growing restlessness with accounts that represented women merely as the victims of social structures and processes, to the neglect of women as historical agents. It also emphasised the need to recognise the great variety and difference among women, drawing particular attention to the notable absence of Aboriginal women in much of the recently published material.

Equally, Daniels warned against what she felt to be a conservative current emerging within the new women's history. The tensions she identified were real but sprang more from a paradox inherent to the practice of women's history. A history that seeks to find a place for women in conventional paradigms may seriously limit its own capacity to challenge those paradigms. Conversely, a history that places women at the centre of its concerns necessarily tends to the aggregation of all women *vis-à-vis* all men, and this aggregation by its very nature tends to a blurring of the variety and difference among women. At its worst, it produces that shady character, the 'average' or the 'typical' woman. Equally, a woman-centred history created quite apart from conventional history, and addressing only like minds, may soon find itself shut away in a scholars' ghetto and defined as marginal, leaving the more complacent among conventional historians to presume that women's history is none of their business. Patricia Grimshaw, writing in the early 1990s a fresh survey of the field (in K. Offen et al., eds, *Writing Women's History: International Perspectives*, 1991), concluded that the achievement of women's historians 'has dented the consciousness of the majority of academic researchers and teachers only to a superficial degree'.

By this time, however, women's history had begun simultaneously both to engage more directly with, and also to question, the paradigms of conventional history through a far sharper focus on **gender relations** and gender identity. Marilyn Lake proposed in an influential article in *HS* in 1986 that 'It is time for historians interested in gender to move beyond "women's history"—beyond the static role that lies at the heart of "contribution history"'. Jill Matthews issued a similar call in the same year in *LH*, also suggesting that such a shift would mark a distinction between '**feminist history**' and 'women's history'. Others, like Susan Magarey, expressed some reservations, suggesting that substituting 'gender' for 'women' might render the field less of a political challenge to conventional history (*AHA Bulletin*, October 1987). However, Kay Saunders and Raymond Evans (eds), *Gender Relations in Australia. Domination and Negotiation* (1992), demonstrated the fruitfulness of such a shift.

In *Creating a Nation* (1994), Patricia Grimshaw, Marilyn Lake, Ann McGrath, and Marian Quartly started from an assertion of 'the agency and creativity of women in the process of national generation', while also pursuing women's history through a focus on gender relations. In this way, *Creating a Nation* finally realised one of the initial ambitions of the new women's history, to provide a general text on white-settler Australia from a feminist perspective. Though its reception was mixed, it represents a remarkable achievement, working strictly from agendas set by women's history, while engaging head-on through the category of gender relations with that most enduring theme of Australian history—the creation of a **national identity**.

One of the most telling criticisms of this work concerns the white, Anglo-Celtic perspective at its centre, despite the clear commitment of the authors to including the **Aborigines** of Australia in their story. Writing Aboriginal women into the new women's history has proved a difficult and perplexing undertaking. White historians, however sympathetic, have been found wanting in so far as they impose the frameworks and agendas of white feminist intellectuals and theorists onto their accounts of Aboriginal women. Only in the last decade or so have Aboriginal women begun to find a place in the academy from which to speak for themselves. The first Aboriginal woman to graduate with an honours degree in history, Jackie Huggins, has repeatedly argued— for example, in *A Woman's Place in Australia* (1992)—the inadequacy of white feminist theory in the face of the oppressive relationships that have existed between white and Aboriginal women. Aboriginal women's historians are increasingly turning to different forms from the scholarly treatise in which to explore their own past. They have sought ways to express the particularities and differences among Aboriginal women, what Jennifer Sabbioni has called a 'homeland' identity, while also affirming a sense of their own Aboriginal national identity (*AHS*, 1996).

Otherwise, the practice of women's history in Australia remains one largely undertaken within institutions of higher education. As such, it is vulnerable to the shrinkage in resources which all universities have experienced in recent years, a vulnerability heightened by its standing as a relatively new field, and the insecure employment conditions of many of its practitioners. Looking back on the previous 25 years in *AHS* (1996), Jill Roe concluded that 'the prospect for women historians is at best uncertain'. More positively, there are now a handful of professors of women's history. The field is now so large and various that an entire issue of *AHS* (1996) was dedicated to reviewing its progress over the previous two decades. There, Jill Matthews celebrated the publication of almost 40 books in this area between 1990 and 1995, while also arguing that the theoretical wrangling of recent years has consumed too much energy. Finding the balance between theory and the recovery of women's stories, between focusing specifically on women and placing them in the larger social context, remains the challenge that confronts women's history.

SANDRA STANLEY HOLTON

Women's Political Association was formed in 1903 by Vida **Goldstein**, one of Australia's leading suffragettes. Its aim was to educate white Australian women to use the vote to attain economic and social reforms. It emerged from Goldstein's conviction that women should eschew party politics on the grounds that **equal pay**, the welfare of children, and equal marriage and **divorce** laws were best pursued through a separate organisation. The association was initially open to males but, following attempts by Labor men to use it for party purposes, membership was restricted to women and formal links with the Labor Party were severed. This call to avoid party politics created tensions between women, especially during World War I. The **Australian Women's National League** and the **National Council of Women** were so antagonised by the WPA's anti-war and anti-conscription stance that they refused to accept its membership of the council, which was an umbrella women's organisation. The association reached the zenith of its influence during the war, attracting those committed to peace and internationalism. It dissolved in 1919 because its founder believed that it could not meet the challenges of the new postwar order. As she moved towards spiritualism, Goldstein sought to meet these challenges in religious rather than political organisations.

JOY DAMOUSI

Women's Royal Australian Naval Service (WRANS)

had its genesis in the increasing manpower shortages experienced in the early years of World War II. Initially the **Royal Australian Navy** was reluctant to employ women: it took on only 14, most of them as telegraphists. By 1942 the navy was actively seeking female recruits, most of whom were employed in non-technical roles as drivers, typists, and cooks. By the end of the war women were working in technical fields, including intelligence and code-breaking.

When the service was disbanded at the end of the war, more than 2000 women had served with the RAN. It was re-formed in 1951, however, when the navy experienced another manpower shortage. It was eight years before the women's services became permanent, and even then they suffered greater limitations and inferior conditions. Women were banned from sea duty. This only altered in the early 1980s when women were fully integrated into the navy and the WRANS abolished. Margaret Curtis-Otter has written a history of the service (1975).

KT

Wood, George Arnold

(1865–1928) was professor of history at the University of Sydney from 1891 until his death. Educated at Owens College in Manchester and later Balliol College, Oxford, he brought to Australia a Nonconformist liberal zeal and a training in the discipline as it absorbed the new emphasis on research. Wood taught British and European history as a story of human progress and enlargement of freedom, emphasising heroic individuals and key texts. Honours students and postgraduates were directed to the close study of primary sources on aspects of British imperial history. From this emerged his own sympathetic study of the **convicts**, whose crime was to have 'championed against the rule of a selfish aristocracy those democratic and national principles which have now become generally accepted' (*PPRAHS*, 1922) and a book on *The Discovery of Australia* (1922), as well as his encouragement of the *Historical Records of Australia*. His opposition to British prosecution of the **Boer War** brought censure by the University Senate in 1902 and tempered his radicalism.

Wood fostered **school history**, and several of his undergraduates—G.C. **Henderson**, G.V. **Portus**, and R.M. **Crawford**—followed him to Balliol before returning to university posts elsewhere in Australia. He had no assistance at all until 1916, and the burden of his duties led eventually to a breakdown and suicide. His Melbourne-trained successor, Stephen **Roberts**, abandoned the high-minded humanism of the **Sydney School of History**. It was renewed at Melbourne by his former pupil, Crawford, whose biography of Wood (*'A Bit of a Rebel'*, 1975) reveals the affinity. Brian

Fletcher reassessed Wood in Stuart Macintyre and Julian Thomas (eds), *The Discovery of Australian History* (1995), and in *History and Achievement* (1999) has explored the origins and destinations of his honours students.

SM

Wool has been Australia's most significant product. It dominated exports from the 1870s until well into the twentieth century. Since 1992 coal, gold, and wheat have usually earned more, but Australia still has around 14 per cent of the world's sheep and produces nearly 30 per cent of the world's wool. The former figure is at its lowest point for well over 100 years. The latter has been fairly constant since the early 1950s, but was much higher between 1880 and 1940. Of each year's clip, never less than 97 per cent, most of it fine wool, is exported. The fine-wool market remains substantial, despite the development of synthetic fibres and growing world cotton production, and Australia's share, once around 70 per cent, is still over 20 per cent.

Economic historians, notably N.G. **Butlin**, *Investment in Australian Economic Development 1861–1900* (1964), have qualified but not challenged the claim that Australia rode to prosperity on the sheep's back. The **long boom** between 1860 and 1890, initiated by gold discoveries, was sustained by wool. Sheep numbers rose from 20 million to 102 million. NSW alone had 62 million sheep in 1892. Between 1875 and 1890, earnings from wool exceeded the combined earnings of all other exports. The extraordinary expansion, which took the industry to its geographical limits, had many ramifications. At the beginning of the period Australian wool was sold in London. By its end there was a rapidly growing Australian market attracting both Asian and European buyers, a process traced in Alan Barnard *The Australian Wool Market 1840–1900* (1958). Wool also accelerated the development of **banking**, insurance, and **transport** industries, and boosted the credit rating of colonial governments keen to undertake capital works. Butlin has stressed the part manufacturing and urban development played in the long boom, but both derived considerable stimulus from the profitability of wool. For much of the period, Australians enjoyed the highest per capita incomes in the world.

A slump in wool prices in 1891–92 gravely affected stations in the semi-arid interior, where large instalments of British capital had encouraged over-capitalisation and speculation. An eight-year **drought** began just as the financial crisis was easing. By 1902, the sheep population in NSW had fallen to 27 million. In Qld it fell from 20 million to seven million. Foreclosures increased after 1895. There were 13 000 stations in NSW in 1891, some of them bigger than many European states; by 1911 there were nearly 26 000. In the same period average flock sizes fell from 4700 to 1700. Both trends were to continue as twentieth-century governments met constant demands for closer settlement. In other states average property and flock sizes also fell considerably.

The traumas of the 1890s led to changes in the industry. Mixed farming became more common and greater attention was given to fodder crops, pasture improvement, and scientific breeding. Cross-bred flocks vied with the Merino in better-watered regions; dual-purpose sheep, of which the Corriedale and Polwarth were popular, provided both quality meat and fleeces. After a disastrous experiment with the wrinkly American Vermont in the early years of the twentieth century, the large, hardy, plain-bodied Australian Merino became the dominant strain in drier areas. The overall result of these changes was impressive. Sheep numbers passed the 1892 total in 1932, and now stand at over 200 million.

Although historians have always recognised the economic importance of wool and **pastoralism**, they chose first to write about the **Macarthurs** and others who brought the Merino to Australia and about the squatters of the 1830s and 1840s. The dramatic expansion of the industry, its maturity and relative decline, were largely ignored. A widening of interest came with the publication of Alan Barnard (ed.), *The Simple Fleece* (1962). By the 1980s there was an extensive literature on the role of wool in the **long boom** and the causes and consequences of the inflow of British capital in the 1870s and 1880s. The question of whether Australia was a victim or a beneficiary of British imperialism, for which Kosmas Tsokhas, *Markets, Money and Empire* (1990), is a good starting point, had become a central issue. More studies of the financial and marketing dimensions of the wool industry followed, with Simon Ville, *The Rural Entrepreneurs* (2000), producing a detailed account of that quintessential Australasian institution, the stock and station agent. Work on the breeding of distinctively Australian sheep culminated with Charles Massy, *The Australian Merino* (1990). There have also been attempts to count the costs of the ride on the sheep's back, irreversible environmental damage being the most obvious.

The social history of wool has not fared as well. There have been no recent accounts of pastoral settlement which reveal the breadth of understanding evident in Margaret **Kiddle's** study of western Victoria, *Men of Yesterday* (1961). Nor has much attention been given to the symbolic importance of wool in Australian rural culture. All elements of the production process, from the sheep-dog to the gun **shearer**, have generated values and myths that still shape beliefs and behaviour.

JOHN MERRITT

Work generally refers to activities that create goods or provide services, particularly when they are conducted in formal labour markets and receive financial recompense. This association of work with capitalist notions of productivity and market value emerged during the Industrial Revolution, a prolonged period of transformation which involved the rise of the factory system and subsequently the application of science and technology to enable mass production. In turn, the separation of tasks performed in the home from those in the factories was accompanied by the emergence of a male-breadwinner norm and corresponding **basic wage**. This historical and cultural construction of work produced a masculine model that had long-lasting implications for scholarship.

Initially Australian scholars treated work indirectly by concentrating on **industrial relations** between workers and employers, and negotiations between their representative institutions, over wages, hours and conditions of work, and the regulatory role played by the state in defining these aspects of employment in formal labour markets. T.A. **Coghlan**, *Labour and Industry in Australia* (4 vols, 1918), was a foundation study which provided a detailed narrative of employment patterns and wage rates in the nineteenth century. Coghlan treated labour primarily as manual labour, distinguishing the various categories of wage-earners by their levels of skill and corresponding earnings. The division between wage and salary earners was at this time, and well into the twentieth century, a fundamental one. Most work was manual and paid by piece-work or at an hourly rate. It combined intense physical effort with specific occupational skill, usually acquired on the job; earnings declined as waning health and strength took their toll. Some **business histories** provide descriptions of industrial technologies and work patterns; some **labour historians** investigated the labour process undertaken by union members; but in both, work is usually of secondary significance to the organisational aspect.

During the 1970s, this orientation was challenged by feminist historians, as well as by the critiques of the **New Left** and the new **social history**. In this context, broader questions were raised about the way sex defined work and work defined identity. In short, the need to sell human labour to provide for the necessities of life was related to **class**, **gender**, and **race relations**, as well as to ideology and consciousness. Edna Ryan and Ann Conlon, *Gentle Invaders* (1975), Ann Curthoys et al. (eds), *Women at Work* (1975), and Beverley Kingston, *My Wife, My Daughter, and Poor Mary Ann* (1975), opened up the study of women's paid and unpaid work. Ann Curthoys and Andrew Markus (eds), *Who Are Our Enemies?* (1978), dealt with the work experience of **Aboriginal** and **Pacific Island labour**, as well as the patterns of racial exclusion from the paid workforce. Jock Collins, in E.L. Wheelwright and Ken Buckley (eds), *Essays in the Political Economy of Australian Capitalism*, vol. 1 (1978), explored the labour market disadvantages of post-World War II migrants. R.W. Connell and T.H. Irving, *Class Structure in Australian History* (1980), paid particular attention to the changing forms of work and associated issues of class relations in the workplace. The range of social and cultural practices that were determined by work—relations in the workplace, the sexual division of labour, the relationship between work and leisure—also attracted attention, as did the issue of **unemployment**.

The publication of Henry Braverman's *Labor and Monopoly Capitalism* in 1974, and the debates which followed it, resulted in extensive investigations of the capitalist labour process and, as a corollary, of the organisation of work, management strategies, and conceptions of skill. Notable contributions included those of Laura Bennett (*LH*, 1986, and *Journal of Industrial Relations*, 1988); Peter Cochrane (*LH*, 1985); Greg Patmore (*Labour and Industry*, 1988, and *AHS*, 1989); Raelene Frances (*LH*, 1986, and *The Politics of Work*, 1993); and Lucy Taksa (*Journal of Industrial Relations*, 1992).

This line of research was pursued principally through industrial case studies, but generated increasingly sophisticated analyses of skill and its historical contingency.

The general picture suggested in these and other studies was of a growing subordination of labour to capital by large companies that employed many workers and introduced new technologies to increase economies of scale. Such tendencies were certainly apparent during the postwar **long boom**, but other changes were less commonly studied: the rapid growth of white-collar employment, as well as of **professional** and sub-professional occupations in the services sector and the associated importance of educational preparation for work. At the beginning of the century almost a quarter of the workforce was on farms; labourers, factory workers, and miners made up another quarter, craft workers nearly 20 per cent, while management and the professions amounted to less than 10 per cent. By 1971 one-fifth of the workforce was in management and the professions, and clerical workers made up another fifth; less than one in twelve Australians worked on the land.

With the subsequent recession in the mid-1970s, and then the protracted and uncertain restructuring of the economy, new work patterns appeared and older evils reappeared. Full-time jobs gave way to part-time ones, and centralised factory production to outsourcing and outwork. The automation of both offices and assembly lines removed the careers of office staff and bank-tellers as well as production workers. As job security disappeared, the older patterns of occupational choice collapsed. Union coverage shrank; protection of wages and work conditions declined. Work lost much of its social and cultural significance to consumption and leisure, yet came to preoccupy those who were denied employment and to dominate the curriculum in schools and universities. These changes are as yet largely unstudied by historians: the most influential account of their implications is Barry Jones, *Sleepers, Wake!* (1982). The best general survey of the history of work is Charles Fox, *Working Australia* (1991), while Fox and Marilyn Lake have edited a collection of documents on *Australians at Work* (1990).

LUCY TAKSA

Worker was a **newspaper** established by the Australian Labor Federation in Brisbane in 1890. Its founding editor was the socialist William **Lane**, and writers included Henry **Lawson** and Francis **Adams**. It began as a monthly but within two years was published weekly, and from 1892 to 1893 it also incorporated the Sydney *Worker* (Lane was briefly the editor of the Sydney paper after his return to Australia in 1899). The Brisbane *Worker* played an important role in coalescing labour opinion during the years of industrial unrest in Qld; it firmly backed the actions of shearers and waterside workers in the **strikes** of the early 1890s. Its operations were subsequently taken over by the **Australian Workers Union**, which built the weekly into the leading Sydney newspaper with a large Sydney printery. H.E. **Boote** was editor 1902–11, and during World War I the *Worker* was a leading campaigner against **conscription**. Subsequently it

became a platform for the anti-militant and shrilly nationalist views of the AWU. It ceased publication in 1974.

HD

Workers Educational Association succeeded the **mechanics institutes** as the principal form of adult education. The association was formed in Britain early in the twentieth century by Albert Mansbridge, who visited Australia in 1913. State branches were established in conjunction with the universities, which provided staff to conduct classes in a range of subjects, including history. Although the leaders of the WEA professed political neutrality, they competed with more radical forms of working-class education for influence over the labour movement. Meredith Atkinson, who directed the WEA first in NSW and later in Victoria, insisted 'the spirit of the class must be comradeship in the pursuit of truth' (R.F. Irvine, ed., *National Efficiency*, 1915), and he promoted sociology as the basis of social harmony and progress. This aspect of its work is treated by Helen Bourke (in Brian Head and James Walter, eds, *Intellectual Movements and Australian Society*, 1988) and Tim Rowse (*Australian Liberalism and National Character*, 1978). Although socialists such as Ralph Gibson, Esmonde Higgins, and Lloyd Ross conducted WEA classes during the 1920s and 1930s, the association's breach with the Left was confirmed when the Communist Party attacked it during World War II. Herbert **Heaton** and G.V. **Portus** were among the historians who worked for the WEA. Its subsequent story varies from state to state. Esmonde Higgins, who worked for the WEA after leaving the Communist Party, captures its meliorist emphasis in his 1959 biography of its NSW organiser, David Stewart, while Deborah Stephan has written a Victorian study. The fullest history is by Derek Whitelock, *The Great Tradition* (1974).

SM

Workingman's paradise was an expression which highlighted the favourable working conditions in Australia—climate, regular employment and good wages. Though in popular use in the 1850s, it was not documented until 1859 when Henry **Kingsley** used it sarcastically in his novel *The Recollections of Geoffry Hamlyn*. In 1892 it was used cynically by William **Lane** as the title of a novel, subtitled *An Australian Labour Novel*, which he published in Brisbane under the pseudonym 'J. Miller' as a means of raising funds for unionists imprisoned after the **shearers' strike**. The socialist message of the book—that greater trade unionism was necessary to bring about a true paradise for workers—was steeped in sentimentality. Lane exposed Sydney as a place of poverty and deprivation. His subsequent attempt, with members of his **New Australia** movement, to found a 'workingman's paradise'—a utopian settlement in Paraguay based on socialist ideals—was a failure. The settlement and Lane's philosophy are discussed in Gavin **Souter's** *A Peculiar People* (1968). In their 1988 publication, Ken Buckley and Ted Wheelwright used a Marxist critique to argue that Australia had been *No Paradise for Workers*, and other historians have qualified the proposition that ninteenth-century wage-earners enjoyed a high **standard of living**.

HD

World War I affected Australia more than any other event since British settlement, if only by killing or injuring over 200 000 Australians in just four years.

Australians seemed ready for war in 1914. Most were proud to be members of the British race and the British Empire. Many had been raised on tales of martial glory. Their government was building a navy and had made militia training compulsory. On 31 July 1914, with war likely, Labor leader Andrew **Fisher** declared that Australians would 'stand beside our own' and help defend Britain 'to our last man and our last shilling'. Few expected war to be so costly that the offer might have to be honoured.

On 5 August 1914 Australians learned that the Empire was at war with Germany. After passing the navy to London's control and mobilising the militia to protect the coastline, the government raised a small force to seize German New Guinea—an objective achieved by mid-September—and a larger force, the Australian Imperial Force (**AIF**), under William Throsby **Bridges**, to fight with the British army. Unlike the great continental European armies of the period, the AIF was formed from volunteers, for compulsion remained limited to soldiering inside Australia. Most volunteers came forward heeding duty's call. Others looked for excitement, a free trip to Europe, or an escape from the boredom of everyday life.

When combined with NZ troops to form the Australian and New Zealand Army Corps (ANZAC), the AIF's members were dubbed **Anzacs**. They were blooded on 25 April 1915, when they landed on the **Gallipoli** peninsula as part of an attempt to destroy the Ottoman Empire, a German ally. The landing was a shambles but the inexperienced Anzacs did not flee. War correspondents Ellis Ashmead-Bartlett and Charles **Bean** dubbed them heroes—a label which helped pride to overcome grief when Australians back home learned of the landing and its cost in lives; enlistments soared and the **Anzac Legend** was born.

Fighting on Gallipoli soon settled into a stalemate, ending in retreat after 27 000 Australian soldiers had been killed or wounded. After being vastly reinforced by more volunteers, the AIF was divided. Its light horse, led by Harry **Chauvel**, joined a small, mobile campaign of mercifully few casualties in the Sinai against an increasingly exhausted Ottoman Empire, which led to the British conquest of Palestine. The remainder of the AIF, under William **Birdwood**, joined vast British and French armies in Belgium and northern France—the war's decisive theatre, the Western Front—against a more formidable enemy, Germany.

No army commander had yet learned how to breach the great trench systems of the Western Front. Ignorance did not prevent repeated effort. By 31 December 1916, 42 000 Australians were dead or wounded, mostly in the battle of the Somme; another 76 000 were killed or wounded during 1917, mostly in the battle of Third Ypres. The surviving

diggers, as the Australian dwellers of the trenches called themselves, hung on, waiting for reinforcements, a respite from the shelling, or just for the mud to dry out.

Australians had not been prepared for a war in which vast armies were massacred without the advent of either victory or defeat. Thus the war, though it was fought far from their country, transformed their society. Tens of thousands of men were either at war or training to join it at any time. Hundreds of thousands of women and schoolchildren were making comforts or raising money for the troops. The war effort's most ardent supporters talked up recruitment and denounced shirkers, slackers, and people of German descent, along with older enemies, such as alcohol and venereal disease. Under the War Precautions Act, passed in 1914, the government assumed vast powers: it began to regulate Australia's primary production and overseas trade, to encroach on the state governments' tax and fiscal powers, and to ridicule, silence, imprison, or even deport, supposed subverters. There became little room in many lives for customary cynicism toward officialdom and indifference to world events, or even for simple privacy. So pervasive was the doctrine of ceaseless devotion to the war effort that it became impossible in some parts of the country to buy an alcoholic drink after six o'clock. (See **Temperance**.)

Even so, volunteers for the AIF were too few to replace its losses. In 1916 **conscription** for the armed forces was introduced in Britain. Though it was contrary to Labor policy, William Morris **Hughes**, Labor prime minister since October 1915, resolved that Australia should have it too. Aware of how divisive conscription would be, he asked the people to vote on it. He failed to persuade his party or most of the people, particularly unionised manual workers, who could see only the smallest reward for themselves, and many Irish Catholics, who refused to sacrifice their sons in a distant war for the Empire. In October 1916 Australians voted, narrowly, against conscription. The Labor Party expelled Hughes and his supporters, who joined the opposition Liberals to form a **National** or Win-the-War government—creating a political division which persisted into the postwar era. The people overwhelmingly returned Hughes's government in May 1917, but they were growing weary of the privation and regulation of the war. In August the biggest strike since the 1890s immobilised docks, mines, and railways throughout NSW, and in December conscription was again rejected by the electorate. Evidently most Australians supported the war, but drew short of forcing every man to risk his life fighting in it.

In April 1918 German armies broke the Allied lines on the Western Front. The threat of defeat failed to revive an increasingly exhausted Australian society. Suggestions for a compromise peace were heard, but these were overtaken by events. As the armies moved away from their trench systems, a war of movement was restored, one which the Germans, weakened by battle losses and an Allied blockade, could not win. The AIF, now under Australian general John **Monash**, joined in a great rolling-back of the enemy. Monash proved a talented commander, but the AIF, despite later claims, did not win the war for the Allies. Indeed, it was temporarily out of the front line at the moment the war ended with an armistice—rather than an unambiguous victory—on 11 November 1918.

More than 58 000 Australian soldiers, sailors, and airmen died or were killed during the war years: around one in 10 of all men aged 18 to 45. Another 156 000 were wounded, gassed, or taken prisoner. Perhaps 2000 spent the rest of their lives in hospital. The obvious gains from the fighting for Australia were the acquisition of German New Guinea; greater independence within the British Empire and a seat at the League of Nations; new markets for wheat and steel; and the Anzac legend, with its comforting affirmation of the success of the lean, resilient, and uncommunicative Australian male (see **Masculinity**). The defeat of German expansionism was less obvious, as the Allies had not fought the war for material gain, and thus the country had not been partitioned or occupied by Allied soldiers; Germany remained a great power, if a humiliated one. Sometimes even the concrete gains seemed poor compensation beside the vast casualties; the enormous cost of compensation paid to returned soldiers and their dependants for decades to come; the sense of being irrevocably cut adrift from what seemed the normality and innocence of prewar life; and, later, the failure either to destroy or to appease a resurgent Germany under Hitler.

The war's impact was so tragic and pervasive that it demanded commemoration. **Monuments** sprang up in every town and suburb. Massive **war memorials** were erected in the capital cities. Soldiers of literary bent wrote histories of their units and reminiscences of their war experience, such as Ion **Idriess's** *The Desert Column* (1932). Each year, 25 April was celebrated as **Anzac Day**—a public holiday on which thousands of returned soldiers marched down city streets, watched by thousands of people; from the 1930s, Australians gathered at dawn that day to hear 'The Last Post' and to murmur the incantation 'Lest we forget'. On the walls of thousands of homes hung reproductions of Will Longstaff's sentimental painting, *Menin Gate at Midnight* (1928), in which dead diggers rise from a field of poppies. The vast khaki army continued to exist in the minds of most Australians until the 1960s, and a grateful nation readily gave its survivors extraordinary political and social privileges. The one truly great novel on the war by an Australian, *The Middle Parts of Fortune* (1929) by Frederic Manning—who had served on the Western Front in the British army—was ignored or reviled as irrelevant or hostile to this popular national commemoration and thanksgiving.

Bean was responsible for Australia's two greatest enduring monuments to the war: the **Australian War Memorial** in Canberra and the 15-volume *Official History of Australia in the War of 1914–1918* (1921–43)—still the most comprehensive and artful treatment of the military operations in which Australians fought (see **Official histories**). Indeed, the vastness of the military volumes inhibited rather than inspired further scholarship. A civil volume in the series, Ernest **Scott's** *Australia During the War* (1936), described the

war's effects on the new nation and took as its starting-point the assumption that the war effort had united Australians.

Modern Australian scholarship on the war began in 1965–66. Ken **Inglis**, in articles such as 'The Anzac Tradition' (*Meanjin*, 1965), interpreted what the war had meant for his parents' generation, while Bill Gammage wrote an honours thesis on the AIF in France, and F.B. Smith analysed the rejection of conscription in *The Conscription Plebiscites in Australia* (1965). Several important histories followed. Lloyd **Robson's** *The First AIF* (1970) showed the exhausting effort needed to fill the AIF's ranks. Gammage's *The Broken Years* (1974) was an evocative and influential study of Australian soldiers' war experience derived for the first time from their letters and diaries. Marilyn Lake's *A Divided Society: Tasmania During World War I* (1975) and Michael McKernan's *The Australian People and the Great War* (1980) established that the war had divided more than united.

A resurgence of popular art, with the war as its theme, had a more immediate impact on ordinary Australians. The most notable works were Roger McDonald's novel *1915* (1979, reworked into a **television** series shown in 1982); Peter Weir's **film** *Gallipoli* (1981), for which Gammage was historical adviser; *The Anzacs* television series (1985); and Albert **Facey's** best-selling memoir, *A Fortunate Life* (1981, also adapted for television and shown in 1985).

The passage of time, the reduction of the British and German Empires to mere memory, the spread of pacifism, mass immigration, and participation in the disastrous **Vietnam War**, together began to extinguish the view that the Great War, however horrible, had been worth the cost. Even popular reverence toward surviving veterans declined. The first influential debunking came via a character in Alan **Seymour's** controversial play, *The One Day of the Year* (1960). By the 1990s it was a commonplace that the war had been a tragic and purposeless waste, and Australia's part in it a case of mistaken willingness by Australians to fight other people's wars. Many scholars shared these views, though not John Robertson in *Anzac and Empire* (1990), nor John Moses in *Australia and the 'Kaiser's War'* (1993).

Joan Beaumont, *Australia's War 1914–18* (1995), offers the most balanced primer on the subject at the time of writing. The best recent book on an aspect of Australia's war is Alistair Thomson, *Anzac Memories* (1994), which gently but perceptively explores the lives of three bearers of the Anzac legend.

On 11 November 1993, 75 years after the armistice, an Unknown Australian Soldier from the war was interred at the Australian War Memorial to symbolise all Australians who died in war. However Australians decide to make sense of the disaster, World War I remains the conflict against which all others are measured for effort and sacrifice.

CRAIG WILCOX

World War II was for Australia, as for almost all belligerent countries, a force for significant social, economic, and political change. Australia was involved in the war from its first day. Despite significant changes in the Dominions' constitu-

World War II

tional powers since 1914, Prime Minister R.G. **Menzies** had no hesitation in assuming that a British declaration of war in September 1939 committed Australia to war, as it had 25 years earlier. Within two months, the Australian defence forces were committed to service overseas within the strategic framework of imperial defence. This commitment was not the product of the 'expeditionary force mentality' that has supposedly characterised Australia's involvements in international conflicts, but was made with deep reservations about the growing Japanese threat in the Asia–Pacific region.

Following the model of World War I, Australia raised four volunteer infantry divisions, three of which (6th, 7th and 9th) were committed to the Middle Eastern and Mediterranean theatres. The **Royal Australian Navy** served with its British counterpart in virtually all oceans of the world, and in a remarkable display of imperial solidarity, Australia sent more than 26 000 men to serve with the Royal Air Force through the Empire/Commonwealth Air Training Scheme.

Australia was indispensable to British campaigns in the Middle East and Mediterranean, contributing to the original dramatic victories against Italian forces in the north African desert in 1941; to the catastrophic campaigns in Greece and Crete in April–May that year; to the occupation of Vichy-controlled Syria (June–July 1941); and the decisive defeat of Axis forces at El Alamein in late 1942. The controversial Greek campaign highlighted the difficulties of maintaining control of Australian forces within British command, but the potentially catastrophic implications of the commitment to the Middle East became clear only when the much-feared Japanese entry into the war eventuated in late 1941. At this time the only Australian land forces available for national defence were the 8th Division, stationed in Malaya and the islands to Australia's north, and some poorly equipped conscript militia divisions lacking combat experience. The 8th Division went into captivity when the Japanese, in a phenomenal four-month campaign, captured Malaya, Singapore (the keystone of the imperial defence strategy), Burma, and the Netherlands East Indies.

In response to this crisis the 6th and 7th Divisions were recalled from the Middle East, not (as popular memory would have it) at the behest of the recently appointed Labor prime minister, John **Curtin**, but at the suggestion of the British government. However, in a celebrated incident in February 1942 which assured Curtin his place in nationalist mythology, the Australian government resisted Winston Churchill's wish to deploy some of the returning troops to Burma, where they would have faced certain defeat.

The manifest inability of Britain to defend Australia— *The Great Betrayal*, as historian David Day (1988) and Prime Minister Paul **Keating** would have it—left Australia no option but strategic dependence on the USA. From March 1942 onwards, with the arrival of the charismatic and egocentric General Douglas MacArthur as commander of Allied forces in the South-West Pacific Area, Australian strategy was increasingly dictated by the constraints of alliance diplomacy. Australian forces played a critical role in

holding the Japanese attacks on Papua and New Guinea, but from 1943 on Australia found itself progressively consigned to the margins of the main US counter-offensive against the Philippines and Japan. After gruelling, slogging campaigns along the northern coast of New Guinea in 1943–44, Australian troops were assigned to operations in Borneo, New Britain, and New Guinea, which, at the time and in retrospect, have been criticised as 'unnecessary wars'. None made any difference to the outcome of the war, and all were unpalatable reminders of the geopolitical reality that, once the enormous industrial and military might of the USA had been mobilised, the contribution of small allies to the defeat of Japan was largely superfluous.

Despite its huge scale, World War II resulted in fewer casualties for Australia than had World War I. The total death toll (including accidents and illnesses while on active service) was 39 000 (of a population of over 7 million), in contrast with the more than 58 000 dead in 1914–18 (when the population was less than 5 million). Of these deaths over 8200 were prisoners of the Japanese, and 6500 were air crew serving in the Mediterranean and the bombing offensive against Germany.

But if the death toll was lower than in World War I, the mobilisation of the Australian population was much more extensive: 550 000 men and women, or one in twelve of the population, served in the armed forces overseas. This included conscripts who fought in Papua (an Australian territory) and the mandated New Guinea in 1942–43. After much controversy, in 1943 the Labor Party agreed that **conscription** could be extended for service in the wider South-West Pacific Area, but in the event this did not prove necessary.

The economy and society were regulated to an unprecedented degree, as the Curtin government responded to the panic of early 1942 when invasion by the Japanese appeared imminent. The Australian economy underwent major structural changes, with secondary and tertiary industries supplanting farming in gross domestic product and employment (although commodity exports remained the principal source of foreign exchange). Full employment returned for men, while women had new opportunities for employment in the auxiliary defence forces and in industries previously confined to male workers. Although the initial community response to the war was shaped by traditional notions of femininity, with women slipping easily into World War I models of patriotic fund-raising and voluntary war work, by 1941–42 the shortage of male workers in key industries made conventional inhibitions about the sexual division of labour untenable. However, the increase in the number of women in paid employment can be overestimated (in real terms there was only a five per cent increase from 1939 to 1944 in the proportion of all women working), and the hierarchical structure of the Australian workforce and the system of differential pay rates for men and women remained entrenched. Much of the redeployment of women was legitimised as being 'for the duration of the war' only, though there was a permanent shift of women out of domestic service into better-paid industrial jobs.

Changing employment patterns for women contributed to broader social tensions associated with the war: the absence of fathers; the 'neglect' of children, when married women entered the workforce unsupported by adequate childcare; the movements of population to meet the needs of the Manpower Directorate; the shortage of housing in the capital cities; and the sexual and racial anxieties generated by the presence of up to one million GIs in Australia.

Accompanying the regulation of much of social life by the state was a growth in the power of the federal government during the war. Some of this resulted from the wartime use of executive powers through national security regulations, but the federal control of income **taxation**, and national control of **banking**, became permanent. Whatever the hysteria generated by the non-Labor political parties about the threat of **socialism**, the war created a lasting consensus about the need for national regulation of economic, financial, and social welfare policies.

This extended role for government necessitated a greater professionalism in the federal **bureaucracy**, which grew threefold between 1939 and 1951. Symptomatic of the growing consciousness of a need for an educated professional elite were the Department of Post-war Reconstruction and the Department of External (Foreign) Affairs, the latter expanded to implement H.V. **Evatt's** vision of a more assertive foreign policy.

Despite its significant impact on Australia, World War II generated little mythology to match the **Anzac Legend**. Indeed, the volunteers of 1939–40 explicitly saw themselves as heirs to the tradition of 1914–18, adopting the title of the Second **AIF** and the numbering of World War I battalions. The commemoration of the war usually took the form of additions to World War I memorials, or the erecting of functional, and less visible, hospitals and recreation and sporting facilities (see **War memorials**). From the perspective of the 1990s it appears that the dominant popular memory of this war is not battles or campaign victories, but the experience of **prisoners of war**. One-third of Australians held in Japanese camps died in captivity, and names such as Changi, the Burma–Thailand railway, and Sir Edward 'Weary' **Dunlop** have an emotional resonance which even Tobruk and **Kokoda** can hardly match. POWs have come to embody anew the diggers' legendary qualities of mateship, resourcefulness, laconic humour, and survival against impossible odds.

The war has generated a considerable literature, though its coverage is uneven. The official histories (general editor, Gavin **Long**) are comprehensive, but few are as accessible to the general reader as are C.E.W. **Bean's** World War I volumes. David Horner was early into the field of strategy and high command, where he remains pre-eminent and prolific (for example, *High Command*, 1982, and *Inside the War Cabinet*, 1996). The social impact of war has been well covered with reference to Melbourne (Kate Darian-Smith, *On the Home Front*, 1990) and Qld (Kay Saunders, *War on the Homefront*, 1993), as has the impact of the American GIs (E. Daniel Potts and Annette Potts, *Yanks Down Under 1941–45*, 1985; Rose-

mary Campbell, *Heroes and Lovers*, 1989; Anthony J. Barker and Lisa Jackson, *Fleeting Attraction*, 1996). Other capital cities and the rural sector await comparable treatment. Paul **Hasluck's** two magisterial official histories (*The Government and the People*, 1952, 1970) remain the only extended study of politics and government during the war, though the **Australian Labor Party** history of Ross McMullin, *The Light on the Hill* (1991), provides a sympathetic account of what is often seen as the Golden Age of Labor. Joan Beaumont's edited *Australia's War 1939–45* (1996) provides a synthesis of all major aspects of Australia's experience of the war.

JOAN BEAUMONT

World Wide Web, see **Internet resources**

Wowser was a term which originated in Australia in the 1890s, and came to refer to a person whose values were 'puritanical' and who zealously sought to reform the morals of others. John **Norton**, the editor of *Truth*, claimed in 1910 to have coined the word in an 1899 article entitled 'Willoughby Wowsers Worried' to describe and deride killjoy reformers in a Sydney suburban council. Newspapers such as the *Bulletin* popularised the term and it was in widespread usage after World War I. Wowsers themselves claimed the term stood for 'We Only Want Social Evils Rectified'.

Wowser was a pejorative term employed by those who rejected what they saw as outmoded Victorianism and promoted a nationalism centred on the pursuit of pleasure as more truly expressive of Australian values. This included unrestricted access to many pursuits that Christians, particularly Protestants, found problematic. Some of this Christian opposition was grounded in traditional church teaching; some involved regulating rather than banning certain practices, and was allied to progressive urban reform that supported governmental intervention on a number of fronts as necessary for harmonious coexistence in a rapidly changing society. This contestation surrounded, above all, the use of alcohol, prostitution, and gambling, and leisure pursuits on Sundays, the day of worship.

Access to alcoholic drinks generated the most heated debate. **Alcohol** consumption was widespread among men in colonial Australia as modern manufacture made alcohol cheaper and more accessible. As a drug which could be addictive and lead to aggression, alcohol could have serious adverse social implications. **Temperance** associations, in which women took a strong role, moved from moral persuasion of individual users in the earlier colonial period to campaigning by the late nineteenth century for legislative controls on spaces, times, and age for the purchase and use of alcohol. Their greatest success was the introduction of six o'clock closing (See **Six o'clock swill**) during World War I, and of local licensing options, which demonstrated considerable grassroots support for 'dry' areas where no hotels were permitted. **Gambling**, embedded in male Australian culture in the form of two-up, and **prostitution** were both subjected to strong legal constraints. By the later decades of the nineteenth century legal controls on theatre, dancing, and bathing were introduced, and few public leisure activities (including commercialised sport) were permitted on the Sabbath.

During the course of the twentieth century, successive governments slowly reduced controls on many of these activities: one could well say that the wowser's view of the meaning of a good and decent society was steadily undermined, defeated even. The six o'clock swill persisted until the 1960s in Victoria and South Australia, when it was swiftly followed by increased outlets for purchase and use of alcohol. Prostitution was legalised in most states, although still subject to some regulations. From the 1930s the states in turn legalised state lotteries and off-course betting on horse races, and introduced casinos for continuous gambling. Sunday entertainments, sport, and trading have become common and well patronised.

Keith Dunstan's book *Wowsers* (1968) took a strong libertarian stand, while feminist historians, including Marilyn Lake in an article on 'The Politics of Respectability' in *HS* (1986), have pointed to some of the social disruptions arising from alcohol, gambling, and prostitution, that led female reformers to criticise these particularly male pursuits. Since the 1970s, especially with the decline of Protestantism, opposition on moral grounds is less commonly heard. Reformers nowadays are more likely to press for measures to eradicate problem gambling, to prevent drinking and driving, to educate about health problems of alcohol and prostitution, to describe the exploitation of sex workers. Smoking, by contrast, is more roundly condemned. Perhaps, except for older Australians, the term *wowser* is nearly obsolete, as the state fights to keep other addictive mind-altering drugs illegal and difficult to obtain.

PATRICIA GRIMSHAW AND PETER SHERLOCK

Wran, Neville Kenneth (1926–) served a record term as premier of NSW when he retired in 1986. He was a trade union barrister who entered the NSW Legislative Council in 1970 and moved to the Legislative Assembly in 1973 shortly before he successfully challenged for state leadership of the **Australian Labor Party**. He became premier in 1976 with a one-seat majority; by the next election in 1978 he turned this into a huge majority, and increased it even further in 1981. In 1980 'Nifty Nev', as he was known, became federal president of the Labor Party. Wran's government achieved wide-ranging reforms of the legal and electoral systems, and oversaw the establishment of the Powerhouse Museum and rebuilding of the State Library of New South Wales. His final years in office were clouded by allegations of corruption, most seriously an allegation that Wran had attempted to influence the chief stipendiary magistrate. He stood aside during the 1983 royal commission, which investigated this allegation and eventually fully exonerated him. After his retirement he chaired the **CSIRO** (1986–91), became a merchant banker, and was a founder of the Australian Republican Movement. Brian Dale's *Ascent to Power* (1985) examines Wran's relationship with the media;

Mike Steketee and Milton Cockburn produced an unauthorised biography in 1986.

KT

WRANS, see **Women's Royal Australian Naval Service**

Wren, John (1871–1953), sportsman and businessman, was born into an Irish-Australian family in Melbourne's inner suburbs and first became notorious when, in the midst of the 1890s depression, he established an illegal totalisator in Johnston Street, Collingwood. The tote made him rich and popular among the locals but incurred the wrath of police and **wowsers**. He later extended his business interests into horse-racing, professional cycling, and boxing (he owned stadiums in Sydney and Melbourne), as well as cinemas and goldmines in Qld and Fiji. He courted the powerful of both church and state—both Archbishop **Mannix** and Labor leader Frank Brennan were allegedly his friends—and pulled strings in preselection contests for the **Australian Labor Party**. But he would not have become a figure of history without the publication of Frank **Hardy's** *Power Without Glory* (1950), in which Wren appears as the evil capitalist John West, and Wren's subsequent unsuccessful prosecution of Hardy on a charge of criminal libel. Hardy's novel invited a literal reading (a list of the main characters and their aliases circulated among Hardy's supporters) but the conspiracies it suggested were largely speculative. In *John Wren, Gambler* (1971), Niall Brennan, son of Frank, sought to correct the excesses of Hardy's account by emphasising the common culture of hardship, gambling, and Irishness that Wren shared with his clients. A series of sympathetic contemporary newspaper articles by the sporting journalist Hugh Buggy was also published by the Wren family under the title *The Real John Wren* (1977). But the most searching examination of his influence is Chris McConville's 'John Wren: Machine Boss, Irish Chieftain or Meddling Millionaire?' (*LH*, 1981).

GD

Wright, Judith Arundell (1915–2000), oldest child of Philip Arundell Wright and Ethel Wright (née Bigg), was born and raised on pastoral properties held by the Wright family, early pioneers of the New England tableland region, which she was to celebrate in some of the most popular poems of her first collection, *The Moving Image* (1946). This, with its successor, *Woman to Man* (1949), established her as a major poetic presence. Readers responded enthusiastically to the richly textured symbolism of poems celebrating love, maternity, and the regional landscapes, initially of New England, then of the rainforests and coastline of Qld, where she settled in 1948 at Tamborine Mountain after her marriage to J.P. McKinney. While that relationship intensified her philosophical interest in issues of language and psychology, it was not so much this that made her distinctive among Australian poets as her increasing readiness to be a public advocate and activist on environmental and Aboriginal issues.

As anthologist (of *A Book of Australian Verse*, 1956, and *New Land, New Language*, 1957) and as essayist, Wright argued that poetry and its particular language were both instrument and indicator of any society's psychic well-being. The majority of these essays, gathered together from their various sources, can be found in *Preoccupations in Australian Poetry* (1965), *Because I Was Invited* (1975), and *Going on Talking* (1992). Such literary activities might be an acceptable aberration from a family background which had more concern for 'cattle prizes at the Show' than for poetry ('For a Pastoral Family'), but there were other concerns which gradually put her even more radically at odds with her origins than her advocacy of nuclear disarmament and her opposition to the **Vietnam War**. The contrast between her family history, *The Generations of Men* (1959), and the history of what such settlements meant for Aborigines in *The Cry for the Dead* (1981), exemplifies that shift in perception which has problematised the very concept of '**pioneers**': it requires that Australians re-evaluate their myths of nationhood, considering whether their forebears should be characterised as 'invaders' rather than 'settlers'.

Wright's poetry increasingly grew sparer and more satirical as she examined the unsettling consequences of perceiving one's self as 'born of the conquerors'. That phrase, used as the title for her 1991 collection of essays, comes from 'Two Dreamtimes'; the poem, dedicated to **Oodgeroo Noonuccal**, shows how Wright's sympathy for **Aboriginal land rights** was inextricably entwined with conservationist concerns for the land as entity rather than as the means towards pastoral production. When the two seemed to her in conflict, however, as in the 1976 policy of the Wildlife Preservation Society of Queensland, which she had co-founded in 1962, her primary allegiance went to land rights. She continued to campaign passionately on **conservation** issues, especially those relating to Qld, which had been her home since 1943—for example, her attack on pollution of the Great Barrier Reef in *The Coral Battleground* (1977). Just as commitment to conservation issues had contested commitment to her other writing in 1973–74, when she had served on the Commonwealth government's Inquiry into the National Estate and co-edited its report, so much of her attention and energy from 1979 to 1983 was spent in service on the Aboriginal Treaty Committee. The committee's document, *We Call for a Treaty*, was published in 1985, the year of publication of *Phantom Dwelling*. That book would be, she announced, her final work as poet: the pressing causes of conservation and land rights claimed the prose of the advocate. A biography by Veronica Brady appeared in 1998.

JENNIFER STRAUSS

Y

Yagan (?–1833), once classed as an outlaw, is now regarded as an **Aboriginal resistance** leader. He was born in the area south of the lower Swan River in WA, his father being a leader of the Wajuk people. Conflict with settlers over land use during 1831 and 1832 led to Yagan being declared an outlaw. When he was captured and put on trial, a local settler, Robert Lyon, defended him as a patriot who was opposing the **invasion** of his homeland. This remarkable view suggests the strong personal appeal of the man. Two early books testify to the impact he made: a diary of G.F. Moore (1884) and W.B. Kimberly's *History of Western Australia* (1897). Imprisoned on Carnac Island with Lyon attempting to 'civilise' him, Yagan soon escaped. In April 1833 he sought revenge for the shooting of his brother by leading a group of Aborigines who ambushed and killed two brothers driving a goods cart. A reward of £30 was offered for his capture 'dead or alive'. Yagan avoided capture until July, when two farm workers shot him for the reward. His back was stripped of its tribal markings and the body was decapitated. His head was sent to England for display where it was eventually buried in a communal grave. Ken Colbung was instrumental in discovering the whereabouts of the head and in having it returned to Australia in 1997. Mary **Durack** told his story in *The Courteous Savage: Yagan of Swan River* (1964).

KT

Young Men's Christian Association is a Christian youth organisation that is non-racial, non-political, and non-sectarian. The YMCA was founded in London in 1844 by an English draper, George Williams, and a branch was established in Adelaide in 1850; branches were subsequently opened in Sydney and Melbourne (1853), and in Hobart (1854). A world alliance was formed in 1855. In the nineteenth century the organisation attended to the physical and moral well-being of young men who were seen to be endangered by the perils of street life by providing recently arrived immigrants with boarding-house accommodation, and offering advice on finding employment and other lodgings. The YMCA continues to provide social, sporting, and recreational activities, as well as hostel accommodation. It promotes Christian morality and teaching, and encourages the development of leadership.

HD

Young Women's Christian Association, the female equivalent of the **Young Men's Christian Association**, was founded in London in 1855 by Emma Robarts and Mary Jane Kinnaird. The first Australian branch was founded at Sydney in 1880 and a world movement was formed in 1894. Initially the organisation was concerned with improving the lot of working-class girls through the provision of a guiding Christian ethos. Branches provided social welfare, educational and recreational activities, and hostel accommodation. The YWCA is also an influential lobby group on affairs concerning youth and women. Margaret Dunn has written a history of the movement in Australia, *The Dauntless Bunch* (1991).

HD

Yunupingu, Galarrwuy (1948–) and **Mandawuy** (1956–), brothers and Aboriginal activists, are of the Yoln(g)u people from Arnhem Land, NT. They grew up in a time of transition for their people, living partly on the Yirrkala mission and partly in the traditional manner with their clan. Galarrwuy came to public attention when he acted as court interpreter for his father, Munggurawuy, in the influential 1971 Gove land rights case. Mungguraway had a long history of struggling for **Aboriginal land rights**—in 1963 he signed the bark petition to the federal parliament initiating the land rights movement. Galarrwuy joined the National Land Council, then as chairman of the Northern Land Council (1977–79 and 1983–89), he led many successful land rights negotiations, including the Ranger Uranium agreement. Mandawuy trained and worked as a teacher, completing an arts degree. He is widely known as the lead singer of Yothu Yindi, a group which combines rock and Aboriginal styles, whose songs are powerful and poignant evocations of Aboriginal loss and that reinforce the demands for recognition of rights. Like his brother, Mandawuy advocates a treaty between Aboriginal and white Australians, and his song of that name featured on the 1991 *Tribal Voice* album. The Yothu Yindi Foundation helped establish the Garma Festival and Garma Cultural Studies Institute in north-east Arnhem Land, the aim of which is to disseminate indigenous knowledge. Both men have been named Australian of the Year—Galarrwuy in 1978 and Mandawuy in 1992.

KT

Z

Zoological gardens were preceded by small, privately run menageries, which existed in Australia from at least the early 1800s, when a collection of captive native birds and animals was kept at the Sydney Domain. A private zoo boasting exotic birds and animals opened at Botany, NSW, in 1851. Menageries also became part of public pleasure grounds, notably Cremorne Gardens (1853) in Melbourne, where faunal exhibits formed only a small part of the vast array of public curiosities and entertainments. A more scientific approach to the keeping of animals in captivity was popularised through the efforts of **acclimatisation** and zoological societies in the mid-nineteenth century. Like **botanic gardens**, zoos were designed for the collection and study of species according to scientific principles; indeed many botanic gardens introduced zoological exhibits in the late nineteenth century. A site at Royal Park, Melbourne, was set aside and laid out as a zoological gardens by the Acclimatization Society of Victoria in 1861. Other major zoos followed in Adelaide (1883) and Perth (1898). The Zoological Society of NSW, formed in 1879, managed a zoo at Moore Park, Sydney, but in 1912 work began on developing the new Taronga Zoological Park on a spectacular site overlooking Sydney Harbour. Sanctuaries for indigenous Australian animals were established at Lone Pine, Qld (1928), Healesville, Victoria (1934), and the safari-style Western Plains Zoo opened at Dubbo, NSW, in 1977. Early enclosures and aviaries, emulating those of existing British and European zoos, were small and overcrowded, and placed little or no emphasis on the habitat and characteristics of particular species. Increased criticism of this practice in the late twentieth century led to the design of larger enclosures which replicate animals' indigenous habitats.

HD

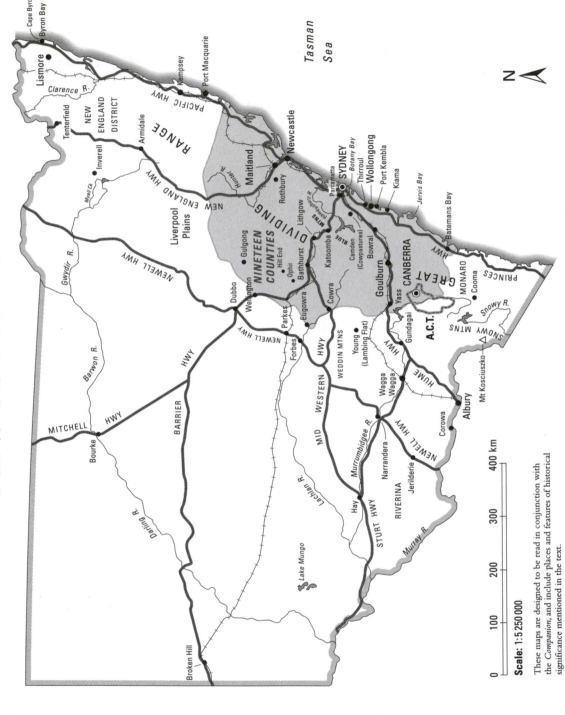

NEW SOUTH WALES

Tasman Sea

Cape Byron
Byron Bay
Lismore
Clarence R.
Kempsey
Port Macquarie
PACIFIC HWY
Tenterfield
NEW ENGLAND DISTRICT
Armidale
Inverell
Myall Ck
RANGE
NEW ENGLAND HWY
Newcastle
Maitland
Hunter R.
Rothbury
Lithgow
DIVIDING
Liverpool Plains
NEWELL HWY
Gulgong
Hill End
Ophir
Bathurst
NINETEEN COUNTIES
Eugowra
Cowra
Katoomba
BLUE MTNS
Camden (Cowpastures)
Bowral
Goulburn
Yass
SYDNEY
Parramatta
Botany Bay
Thirroul
Wollongong
Port Kembla
Kiama
Jervis Bay
Batemans Bay
Hawkesbury R.
GREAT
CANBERRA
A.C.T.
MONARO
Cooma
Snowy R.
SNOWY MTNS
Mt Kosciuszko
PRINCES HWY
HUME HWY
Gundagai
Young (Lambing Flat)
WEDDIN MTNS
Dubbo
Wellington
Parkes
Forbes
MID WESTERN HWY
Murrumbidgee R.
Wagga Wagga
Corowa
Albury
NEWELL HWY
Narrandera
Jerilderie
RIVERINA
Hay
STURT HWY
Lachlan R.
Murray R.
Lake Mungo
Darling R.
Barwon R.
Gwydir R.
MITCHELL HWY
BARRIER HWY
Bourke
Broken Hill

Scale: 1:5 250 000

0   100   200   300   400 km

These maps are designed to be read in conjunction with
the *Companion*, and include places and features of historical
significance mentioned in the text.

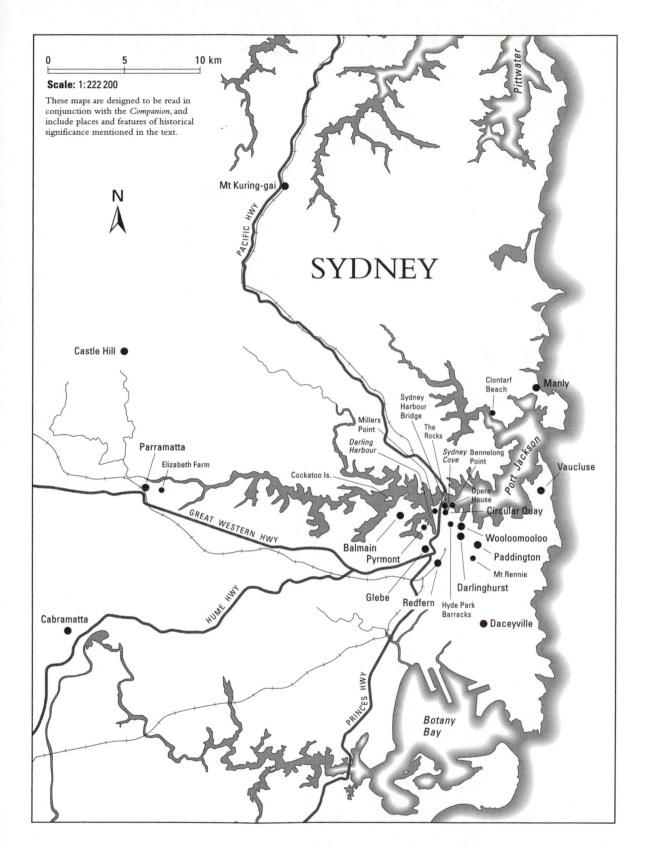

N

SYDNEY

Pittwater

PACIFIC HWY

Mt Kuring-gai

Castle Hill

Clontarf
Beach

Manly

Sydney
Harbour
Bridge

Millers
Point

The
Rocks

Darling
Harbour

Bennelong
Point

Sydney
Cove

Port Jackson

Parramatta

Elizabeth Farm

Cockatoo Is.

Vaucluse

Opera
House

GREAT WESTERN HWY

Circular Quay

Wooloomooloo

Balmain
Pyrmont

Paddington

Mt Rennie

HUME HWY

Darlinghurst

Glebe

Redfern

Cabramatta

Hyde Park
Barracks

Daceyville

PRINCES HWY

Botany
Bay

NORTHERN TERRITORY

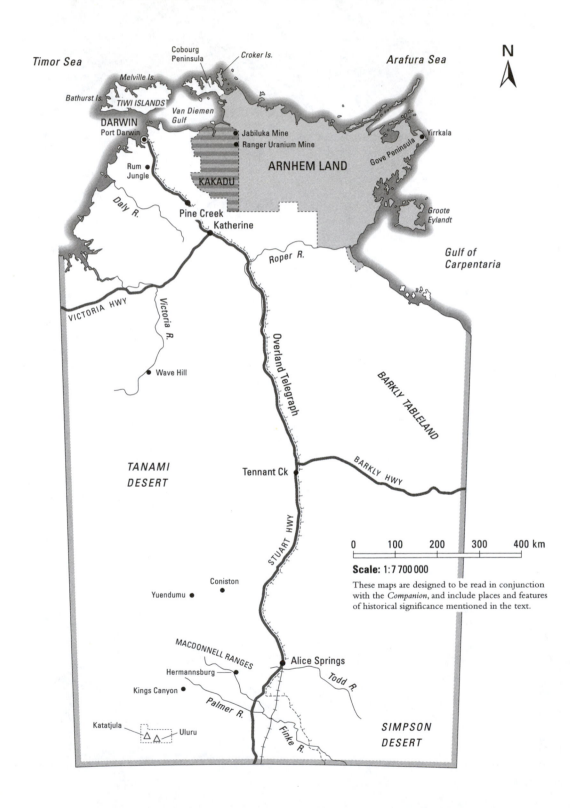

Timor Sea

Arafura Sea

N

Cobourg Peninsula

Croker Is.

Melville Is.

Bathurst Is.

TIWI ISLANDS

Van Diemen Gulf

DARWIN
Port Darwin

Yirrkala

Jabiluka Mine

Ranger Uranium Mine

ARNHEM LAND

Gove Peninsula

Rum Jungle

KAKADU

Groote Eylandt

Daly R.

Pine Creek

Katherine

Roper R.

Gulf of Carpentaria

VICTORIA HWY

Victoria R.

Overland Telegraph

BARKLY TABLELAND

Wave Hill

TANAMI DESERT

Tennant Ck

BARKLY HWY

0   100   200   300   400 km

Scale: 1:7 700 000

These maps are designed to be read in conjunction with the *Companion*, and include places and features of historical significance mentioned in the text.

Coniston

Yuendumu

STUART HWY

MACDONNELL RANGES

Alice Springs

Hermannsburg

Todd R.

Kings Canyon

Palmer R.

Katatjula   Uluru

Finke R.

SIMPSON DESERT

QUEENSLAND

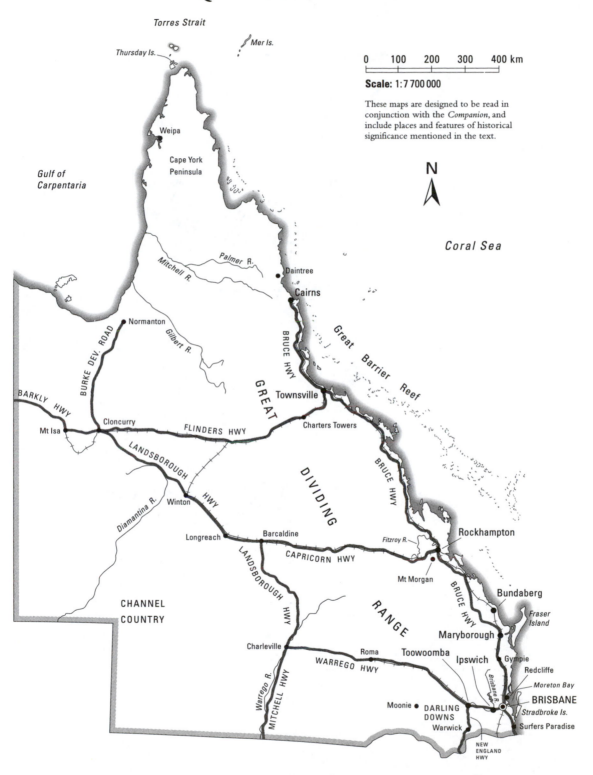

Torres Strait

Mer Is.

Thursday Is.

Weipa

Cape York
Peninsula

Gulf of
Carpentaria

| 0 | 100 | 200 | 300 | 400 km |

Scale: 1:7 700 000

These maps are designed to be read in
conjunction with the *Companion*, and
include places and features of historical
significance mentioned in the text.

N

Coral Sea

Mitchell R.

Palmer R.

Daintree

Cairns

Normanton

BURKE DEV. ROAD

Gilbert R.

BRUCE HWY

Great Barrier Reef

BARKLY HWY

GREAT

Townsville

Mt Isa

Cloncurry

FLINDERS HWY

Charters Towers

LANDSBOROUGH

DIVIDING

BRUCE HWY

Diamantina R.

HWY

Winton

Longreach

Barcaldine

CAPRICORN HWY

Fitzroy R.

Rockhampton

Mt Morgan

Bundaberg

LANDSBOROUGH

CHANNEL
COUNTRY

HWY

RANGE

BRUCE HWY

Fraser
Island

Maryborough

Charleville

Roma

Toowoomba

Ipswich

Gympie

Redcliffe

Warrego R.

WARREGO HWY

Moreton Bay

MITCHELL HWY

Moonie

DARLING
DOWNS

Brisbane R.

BRISBANE

Stradbroke Is.

Warwick

Surfers Paradise

NEW
ENGLAND
HWY

SOUTH AUSTRALIA

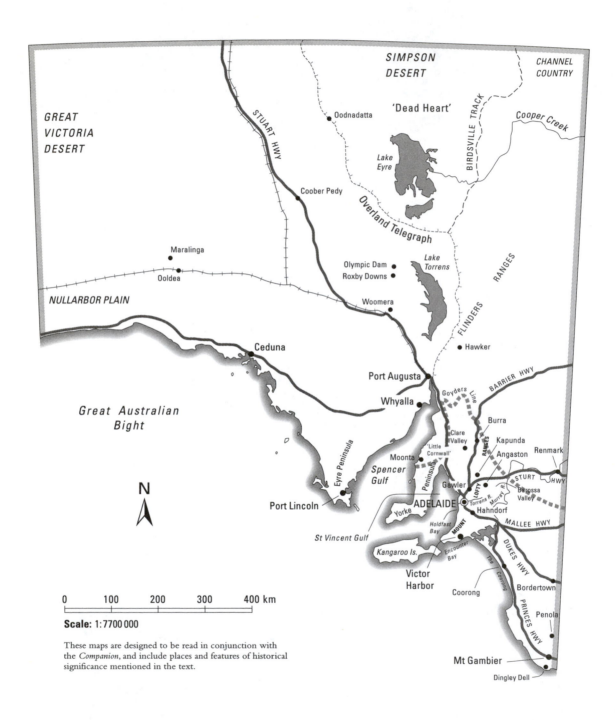

GREAT
VICTORIA
DESERT

SIMPSON
DESERT

CHANNEL
COUNTRY

'Dead Heart'

Oodnadatta

Cooper Creek

BIRDSVILLE TRACK

STUART HWY

Lake
Eyre

Coober Pedy

Overland Telegraph

Maralinga

Ooldea

Olympic Dam
Roxby Downs

Lake
Torrens

NULLARBOR PLAIN

Woomera

FLINDERS RANGES

Ceduna

Hawker

Great Australian
Bight

Port Augusta

Whyalla

Goyders Line

BARRIER HWY

Burra

Clare
Valley

Kapunda

RANGES

Angaston

Renmark

Eyre Peninsula

Moonta

'Little
Cornwall'

Spencer
Gulf

Yorke
Peninsula

Gawler

STURT HWY

LOFTY

Barossa
Valley

N

Port Lincoln

ADELAIDE

Torrens R.

Murray R.

Hahndorf

Yorke

Holdfast
Bay

St Vincent Gulf

MOUNT

MALLEE HWY

Kangaroo Is.

Encounter
Bay

DUKES HWY

Victor
Harbor

Coorong

The Coorong

Bordertown

PRINCES HWY

Penola

| 0 | 100 | 200 | 300 | 400 km |

Scale: 1 : 7 700 000

Mt Gambier

Dingley Dell

These maps are designed to be read in conjunction with
the *Companion*, and include places and features of historical
significance mentioned in the text.

TASMANIA

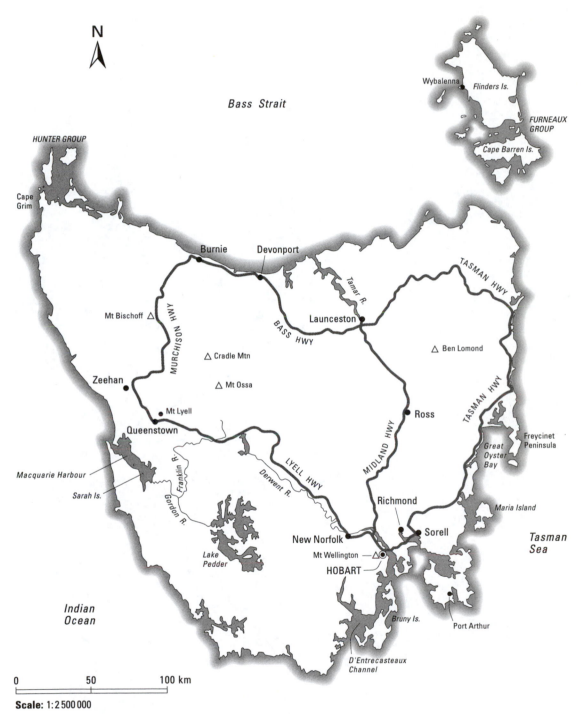

Bass Strait

N

HUNTER GROUP

Cape
Grim

*Indian
Ocean*

Burnie   Devonport

Mt Bischoff △

△ Cradle Mtn

MURCHISON HWY

△ Mt Ossa

Zeehan

● Mt Lyell

Queenstown

Macquarie Harbour

Sarah Is.

Franklin R.

Gordon R.

*Lake
Pedder*

Derwent R.

LYELL HWY

New Norfolk

Mt Wellington —△⊙

HOBART

BASS HWY

Tamar R.

Launceston ●

△ Ben Lomond

TASMAN HWY

TASMAN HWY

MIDLAND HWY

● Ross

Richmond
●

● Sorell

*Great
Oyster
Bay*

Freycinet
Peninsula

Maria Island

*Tasman
Sea*

Bruny Is.

● Port Arthur

*D'Entrecasteaux
Channel*

Wybalenna ●   *Flinders Is.*

*FURNEAUX
GROUP*

Cape Barren Is.

0   50   100 km

Scale: 1:2 500 000

These maps are designed to be read in conjunction
with the *Companion*, and include places and features
of historical significance mentioned in the text.

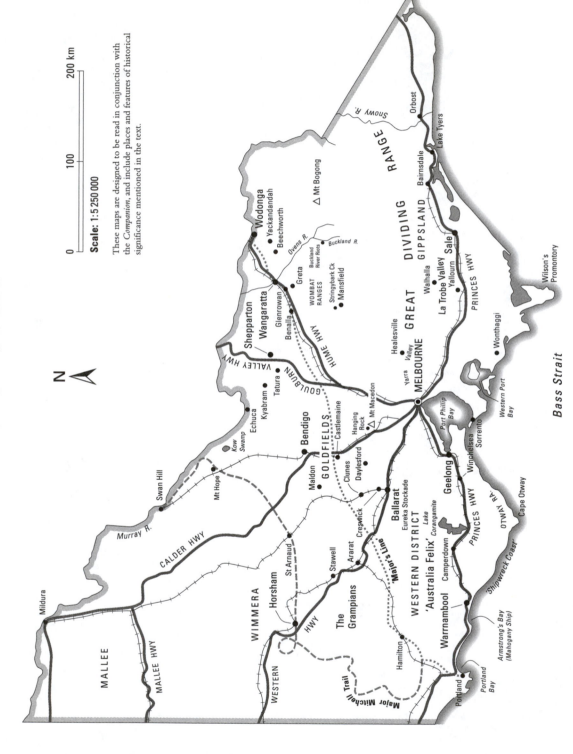

VICTORIA

N

Scale: 1:5 250 000

These maps are designed to be read in conjunction with the *Companion*, and include places and features of historical significance mentioned in the text.

0   100   200 km

Mildura

MALLEE

MALLEE HWY

Swan Hill

Murray R.

Kow Swamp

Mt Hope

Echuca

CALDER HWY

Kyabram

Tatura

Bendigo

Maldon

GOLDFIELDS

Castlemaine

Clunes

Daylesford

St Arnaud

WIMMERA

Horsham

WESTERN HWY

The Grampians

Stawell

Ararat

Creswick

Major's Line

Ballarat

Eureka Stockade

WESTERN DISTRICT

'Australia Felix'

Lake Corangamite

Camperdown

Hamilton

Major Mitchell Trail

Warrnambool

Portland

Portland Bay

Armstrong's Bay
(Mahogany Ship)

Shipwreck Coast

PRINCES HWY

OTWAY RA.

Cape Otway

Geelong

Winchelsea

Princes Hwy

Shepparton

Wangaratta

GOULBURN VALLEY HWY

Wodonga

Yackandandah

Beechworth

Greta

Glenrowan

Benalla

HUME HWY

Ovens R.

Buckland R.

Buckland River Riots

WOMBAT RANGES

Stringybark Ck

Mansfield

△ Mt Bogong

GREAT

DIVIDING

RANGE

GIPPSLAND

Walhalla

La Trobe Valley

Yallourn

Sale

PRINCES HWY

Bairnsdale

Lake Tyers

Orbost

Snowy R.

Healesville

Yarra Valley

MELBOURNE

Mt Macedon

Hanging Rock

Port Phillip Bay

Sorrento

Western Port Bay

Wonthaggi

Wilson's Promontory

Bass Strait

0   5 km

Scale: 1:140 200

These maps are designed to be read in conjunction with the *Companion*, and include places and features of historical significance mentioned in the text.

N

HUME HWY

'Heidelberg School'

Maribyrnong River

HEIDELBERG ROAD

Yarra River

Essendon

Brunswick

WESTERN HWY

Kew

Carlton

Fitzroy

Collingwood

Sunshine

Footscray

North Melbourne

Batman's Hill

Richmond

Hawthorn

Camberwell

Yarraville

Fishermen's Bend

South Melbourne

South Yarra

Port Melbourne

Toorak

Newport

Albert Park

PRINCES HWY

Hobsons Bay

St Kilda

Caulfield

Williamstown

Brighton

NEPEAN HWY

MELBOURNE

Sandringham

Port Phillip Bay

WESTERN AUSTRALIA

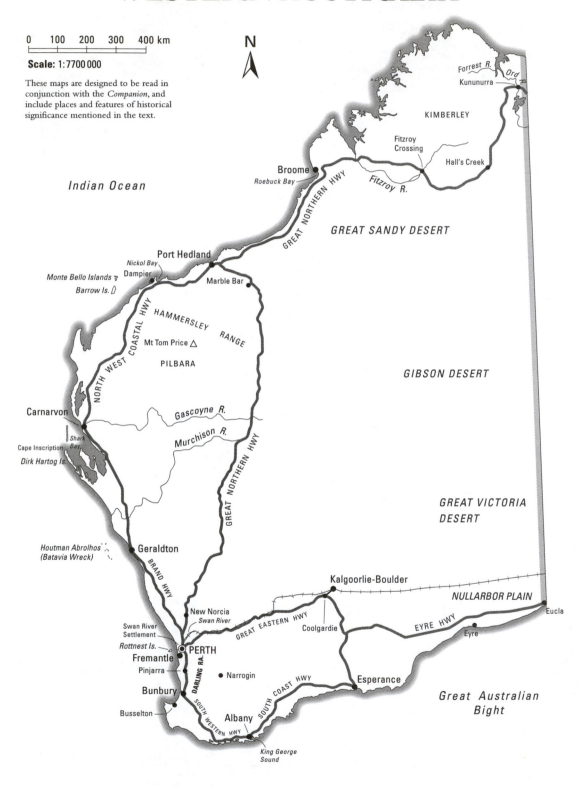

0   100   200   300   400 km

Scale: 1:7700000

These maps are designed to be read in
conjunction with the *Companion*, and
include places and features of historical
significance mentioned in the text.

N

Indian Ocean

KIMBERLEY

Forrest R.
Ord R.
Kununurra

Fitzroy
Crossing

Hall's Creek

Broome
Roebuck Bay

Fitzroy R.

GREAT NORTHERN HWY

GREAT SANDY DESERT

Port Hedland
Nickol Bay
Dampier
Marble Bar

Monte Bello Islands
Barrow Is.

NORTH WEST COASTAL HWY

HAMMERSLEY RANGE

Mt Tom Price △

PILBARA

GIBSON DESERT

Carnarvon

Gascoyne R.

Murchison R.

*Shark
Bay*
Cape Inscription
Dirk Hartog Is.

GREAT NORTHERN HWY

GREAT VICTORIA
DESERT

Houtman Abrolhos
(Batavia Wreck)

Geraldton

BRAND HWY

Kalgoorlie-Boulder

NULLARBOR PLAIN

Eucla

New Norcia
Swan River

Swan River
Settlement
Rottnest Is.
Fremantle
Pinjarra

PERTH

DARLING RA.

Narrogin

GREAT EASTERN HWY

Coolgardie

EYRE HWY

Eyre

Bunbury

Busselton

SOUTH WESTERN HWY

Albany

SOUTH COAST HWY

Esperance

*Great Australian
Bight*

*King George
Sound*

716

SUBJECT INDEX

gender relations Baines, Baynton, Chisholm, Cowan, divorce, Dixson, Dugdale, Dunkley, equal pay, family, femininity, feminism, feminist history, gay history, gender relations, Goldstein, Greer, Guerin, Heagney, Henry, *herstory*, homosexuality, Louisa Lawson, Bessie Lee, lesbian history, masculinity, mateship, Pankhurst, prostitution, Rischbieth, Edna Ryan, Rose Scott, Street, Summers, Wardley, Woman's Christian Temperance Union, women's history

government borders, bureaucracy, census, Commonwealth–state relations, constitutions, democracy, development, double dissolution, elections, Federation, inter-colonial relations, Loan Council, local government, monarchy, political parties, Premiers' Conference, prime ministers, republicanism, responsible government, secession, separation, state socialism, taxation

governors Arthur, Bligh, Bourke, Bowen, Brisbane, Collins, Darling, Davey, Denison, Eardley-Wilmot, FitzRoy, John Franklin, Gawler, Gipps, governors, Grey, Hindmarsh, Hunter, King, La Trobe, Macgregor, Macquarie, Roma Mitchell, Oliphant, Phillip, Stirling, Weld

governor-generals Richard Casey, Colonial Office, FitzRoy, governor-generals, Hasluck, Hayden, Hopetoun blunder, Isaacs, Kerr, McKell, Munro Ferguson

heritage *Batavia*, botanic gardens, Burra Charter, conservation, green bans, heritage, Historic Houses Trust of New South Wales, History Council of New South Wales, Hyde Park Barracks, monuments, Mundey, national parks, National Trusts, pioneer settlements, Port Arthur, Register of the National Estate, Rocks

historians Adam-Smith, Fred Alexander, Austin, Barnard, J.V. Barry, G.B. Barton, Bassett, Bate, Battye, Bean, Bennett, Bernays, Berndt, George Black, Blainey, David Blair, Bolton, Bonwick, Roy Bridges, Noel Butlin, S.J. Butlin, Cannon, Carboni, Casey, Charlwood, Childe, Manning Clark, Clune, Coghlan, Collingridge, Collins, Cramp, Crawford, Crowley, Cumpston, Curr, Currey, Miriam Dixson, Dutton, Ellis, Favenc, J.A. Ferguson, Finn, Fitchett, Brian Fitzpatrick, Kathleen Fitzpatrick, Freeland, Garran, Robin Gollan, Greenwood, Gullett, Keith Hancock, Harper, Alexandra Hasluck, Paul Hasluck, Hearn, Herbert Heaton, J.H. Heaton, Henderson, Hill, Horne, Robert Hughes, Idriess, Inglis, Johns, Jose, Kiddle, La Nauze, Ida Lee, Long, Lowenstein, Mackaness, Madgwick, Martin, McQueen, A.C.V. Melbourne, Melville, Mennell, Morris Miller, Mills, Moorehead, Moyal, Mulvaney, Nairn, O'Brien, O'Farrell, Palmer, Pearl, Pearson, Phillips, Pike, Portus, Price, Reeves, Reynolds, S.H. Roberts, Robson, Roe, Rolls, Rusden, Ernest Scott, Serle, Shann, Shaw, Bernard Smith, Souter, Stretton, Summers, Tench, H.G. Turner, Ian Turner, Uren, Wannan, J.M. Ward, Russel Ward, West, Willard, Wood

historic places Buckland River riots, Burra Charter, Cape Grim massacre, Castle Hill rising, Coniston massacre, Corowa Conference, Cowra breakout, Eureka Stockade, Gallipoli, Holtermann Collection, Hyde Park Barracks, Java-La-Grande, Kokoda Track, Kyabram Movement, Lake Mungo, Lambing Flat riots, Lassetter's 'Lost' Reef, Major's Line, monuments, Moreton Bay, Myall Creek massacre, New Holland, Nineteen Counties, Norfolk Island, Pilbara walkoff, Pinjarra battle, Port Arthur, Rats of Tobruk, Rocks, Rothbury incident, Sydney Harbour Bridge, Sydney Opera House, Tenterfield Oration, Uluru, Waterloo Creek massacre

historical study Aboriginal history, antiquarianism, archaeology, architectural history, archives, art history, Australian Joint Copying Project, Australian War Memorial, Australiana, autobiography, Bicentennial History Project, biographical dictionaries, biography, black-armband history, books, business history, captivity narratives, colonial history, commissioned history, constitutional history, convict history, cultural history, demographic history, diarists, directories, economic history, educational history, environmental history, ethnic history, ethnographic history, exploration history, feminist history, film, fragment thesis, gay history, genealogy, *Historical Records of Australia*, historical geography, historical journals, historical societies, historical statistics, ideas, imperial history, Internet resources, labour history, legal history, lesbian history, letters, libraries, local history, Marxist history, Melbourne School of History, military history, natural history, New Left, official histories, Old Left, oral history, painting, pastoral history, periodisation, photography, poetry, political history, post-colonialism, public history, polls, reference works, regional history, religious history, Royal Australian Historical Society, school history, science, social history, sporting history, Sydney School of History, television, urban history, welfare history, women's history

industry advertising, arbitration, aviation, banks and banking, energy, engineering, industrial relations, iron and steel, labour history, manufacturing, mining, motor car, oil and gas, Ord River Scheme, railways, river transport, shipping, shopping, Snowy Mountain Hydro-Electric Scheme, strikes and lockouts, tariff, timber, tourism, trade unions, wages boards, wheat, wool

innovations arbitration, Australian ballot, Australian Rules football, basic wage, Chaffey, eight-hour day, elections, Farrer, James Harrison, invention and improvisation, H.V. McKay, rotary hoe, shearing machines, social laboratory, *socialisme sans doctrines*, stripper, stump-jump plough, Torrens title, trugo, Vegemite

labour Accord, ACTU, arbitration, Australian Workers Union, basic wage, Boote, Darwin rebellion, domestic service, eight-hour day, employers' organisations, equal

Subject Index

wars Aboriginal resistance, AIF, Anzac Day, Anzac Legend, *Anzac,* Australian Army, Australian War Memorial, Battle of Brisbane, Bean, Birdwood, Black War, Blamey, Boer War, W.T. Bridges, Brisbane Line, Chauvel, *chocolate soldier,* CMF, conscription, Coral Sea battle, Cowra breakout, Darwin bombing, defence, *digger,* Dunlop, Elliott, *Emden,* fuzzy-wuzzy angels, Gallipoli, internment, Jacka, Kokoda Track, Korean War, Land Army, Legacy, Long, Malayan emergency, military history, Monash, Morant, Morshead, pacifism, postwar reconstruction, prisoners of war, Rats of Tobruk, repatriation, Returned and Services League, Royal Australian Air Force, Royal Australian Army Nursing Corps, Royal Australian Navy, Simpson and his donkey, Spanish Civil War, Sudan campaign, Vietnam War, Villers-Bretonneux, Wake, war memorials, war reporters and reporting, war service homes, C.B.B. White, Women's Auxiliary Australian Air Force, Women's Royal Australian Naval Service, World War I, World War II

INDIAN OCEAN

TIMOR SEA

Ashmore Reef

Scott Reef

Tiwi Islands Melville I

Bathurst I

Van Diemen Gulf

Croker

Cobourg P

Darwin

Mt
.366

Pine Creek

Katherine

Daly

East Alligato

Bigge I

Augustus I

Collier Bay

Joseph Bonaparte Gulf

KIMBERLEY

Drysdale

Durack R

Ord R

L Argyle

Victoria R

L Woods

Rowley Shoals

Derby

KING LEOPOLD RANGES

Mt Ord 937

Mt Remarkable 748

Sturt Cr

Tennant

Broome

Fitzroy

Fitzroy Crossing

TANAMI DESERT

NORTHERN

Port Hedland

De Grey R

GREAT SANDY DESERT

Dampier

Barrow I

HAMERSLEY RANGE

Fortescue R

Oakover R

L Auld

L Mackay

GIBSON DESERT

L Macdonald

L Lewis

Mt Zeil 1531

MACDON

PILBARA

Mt Meharry 1251

L Disappointment

LITTLE SANDY DESERT

Palmer R

Ashburton R

WESTERN AUSTRALIA

Kata Tjuta

L Amadeus

Uluru 867

L Macleod

Gascoyne R

Carnarvon

Wooramel R

Mt Squires 705

MUSGRAVE RANGES

Mt Woodrol 143

Shark Bay

Dirk Hartog I

L Carnegie

L Wells

Murchison R

L Austin

GREAT VICTORIA DESERT

SOUTH AUS

L Carey

L Ballard

L Barlee

L Rebecca

NULLARBOR PLAIN

L Moore

Coolgardie

Kalgoorlie–Boulder

Eucla

INDIAN OCEAN

L Cowan

Swan R

Johnston Lakes

L Dundas

GREAT AUSTRALIAN BIGHT

Perth

Fremantle

Bunbury

Blackwood R

Esperance

Albany

King George Sound

SOUTHERN OCEAN

AUSTRALIA

GENERAL REFERENCE MAP

Simple Conic Projection

0   200   400 kilometres

Metres above/below sea level.

2000 1500 1000 500 200 0 200

•	Cities and Towns		River, perennial
.1277	Spot elevation		River, non-perennial
	State boundary		Lake, perennial
	Reef		Lake, non-perennial